BIOGRAPHICAL and

Volume I

HISTORICAL

MEMOIRS OF MISSISSIPPI

EMBRACING AN

AUTHENTIC AND COMPREHENSIVE ACCOUNT OF THE
CHIEF EVENTS IN THE HISTORY OF THE STATE,
AND A RECORD OF THE LIVES OF MANY OF
THE MOST WORTHY AND ILLUSTRIOUS
FAMILIES AND INDIVIDUALS

IN TWO VOLUMES

ILLUSTRATED

THE REPRINT COMPANY, PUBLISHERS

SPARTANBURG, SOUTH CAROLINA

1978

This volume was reproduced from an 1891 edition in the
Mississippi Department of Archives and History,
Jackson, Mississippi.

Reprinted: 1978
The Reprint Company, Publishers
Spartanburg, South Carolina 29304

ISBN 0–87152–267–5 (set)
ISBN 0–87152–268–3 (v. 1)
Library of Congress Catalog Card Number: 78–2299
Manufactured in the United States of America on long-life paper.

976.2
B615
V. 1

Library of Congress Cataloging in Publication Data

Main entry under title:
Biographical and historical memoirs of Mississippi.

   Reprint of the 1891 ed. published by Goodspeed
Pub. Co., Chicago.
   1. Mississippi—History. 2. Mississippi—
Biography.
F341.B6   1978   976.2'00992   78–2299
ISBN 0–87152–267–5 (set)

79-6443

STATE CAPITOL, JACKSON.

VOL. I

Biographical and Historical Memoirs

of Mississippi

EMBRACING AN

AUTHENTIC AND COMPREHENSIVE ACCOUNT OF THE CHIEF EVENTS IN
THE HISTORY OF THE STATE, AND A RECORD OF THE
LIVES OF MANY OF THE MOST WORTHY AND
ILLUSTRIOUS FAMILIES AND INDIVIDUALS

IN TWO VOLUMES

ILLUSTRATED

Chicago
The Goodspeed Publishing Company
1891

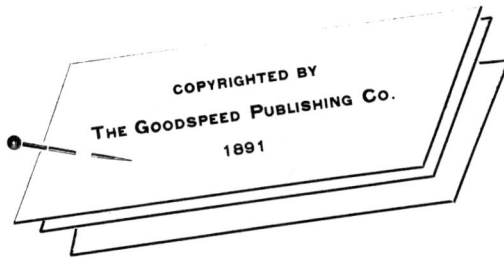
W. B. CONKEY COMPANY, BINDERS.

JOHN MORRIS COMPANY, PRINTERS, CHICAGO

PREFACE.

THE publishers, with much pleasure, present these beautiful volumes to their friends and patrons for whom they are prepared. It has cost a large sum of money and a vast amount of labor to compile the work, but the ends certainly justify the means. The volumes will be found to surpass in size and in matter the promises of our prospectus. The biographical department, always the most interesting and valuable, will be found very full and complete, and has been made, as was stated in our prospectus, the most important feature of the work. Great care was employed to prevent the representation in this department of unfit persons and families. In all cases the advice of the most respectable people of each county as to who should be thus represented was sought and, if fair, followed; and no person, no matter how humble, was excluded by reason alone of a lack of interest in our enterprise, if his occupation were honorable and his life and record pure. We thus strictly carried into effect the plan outlined in our prospectus. It is to be regretted that many deserving individuals and families of the state have failed to place their records on the pages of this standard work, though the privilege was extended to all respectable residents; and this observation is equally applicable to the department of illustrations. The omission is due either to their absence from home, their neglect to respond to our repeated requests for information, their lack of interest in our enterprise or the failure of their names to reach us, and not to any wish or intention on our part to exclude them. All honorable occupations are represented, for this is a history of the quiet lives and pursuits of the great mass of reputable people throughout the state.

The historical department proper will be found very rich in substantial matter never before in print, prepared with great care by more than a score of well-known and brilliant residents of the state—an absolute guaranty of its general interest and permanent value. Every personal sketch was submitted by mail for correction, and the proof of every special article was mailed to its contributor, for revision, before being printed. Thus every precaution was taken to insure accuracy. It is not expected, however, that no mistake has been made, for many persons neglected to revise and return the personal or other matter submitted to them for that purpose. The chapters on Counties and on Villages were not promised as a part of our work, but those subjects will be found treated at considerable length. The information therein came from such a variety of sources that we were compelled to use portions of it without verification; but nevertheless the errors, it is believed will be found few and of little consequence. The publishers will be thankful to be notified of any error which, upon examination, may be found, that they may prepare an errata sheet to be sent to every subscriber, to be pasted in the books. We will do anything reasonable to make the work absolutely correct.

The volumes are largely the product of Mississippi writers and thinkers. Over five hundred contributions were received from residents and printed in the books. It would be impossible to name all who have thus assisted us, because many of the most valuable of the short contributions were either sent anonymously or sent under the injunction of secrecy. We make general acknowledgments for special favors to all the state officials, members of the supreme bench, the press throughout the state, the clergy, the legal and medical professions, hundreds of county officials, members of secret and benevolent societies throughout the state, officers and friends of education, the state librarian, participants in the Civil war, horticultural and agricultural specialists, the levee board commissioners, manufacturers, planters, stockraisers, railway commissioners, etc., etc. Prof. Edward Mayes, of Oxford, wrote the history of the bench and bar and of education; Col. J. L. Power, of Jackson, wrote the history of secret, benevolent and fraternal societies; Bishop Charles B. Galloway and Rev. R. Abbey prepared the sketch of the Methodist Episcopal Church South and several biographies of noted persons; Col. Charles E. Hooker, of Jackson, and his son, Allan J. Hooker, of Washington, D. C., contributed the Confederate military history, and Charles E. Hooker, Jr., of Dallas, Tex., furnished the political history; Rev. Joseph B. Stratton, of Natchez, wrote the history of the Presbyterian church; Rev. M. F. Harmon, of Jackson, prepared the record of the Christian church; Rev. J. T. Christian, of Jackson, wrote the history of the Missionary Baptist church; Rev. B. G. Mitchell, of Oxford, furnished the account of the Cumberland Presbyterian church; Rev. Nowell Logan, of Vicksburg, contributed the history of the Episcopal church; S. A. Jonas, Esq., furnished the essay on literature; Maj. George W. Harper, of Raymond, wrote the history of the press; Mrs. H. B. Kells contributed the articles on the temperance movement and on the Woman's Christian Temperance Union, and there will be found rich posthumous writings, never before in print, of Col. J. F. H. Claiborne, etc., etc. In addition to this we had our own corps of experienced, efficient writers and compilers who, for many months, ransacked public and private documents and records in search of original matter and in an honest attempt to verify every line written. We are satisfied our work, in every particular, will bear the closest scrutiny and sustain our reputation for accuracy and honesty.

THE PUBLISHERS.

TABLE OF CONTENTS.

ILLUSTRATIONS.

Biographical and Historical Memoirs

OF

Mississippi.

Chapter I.

TOPOGRAPHY, NATURAL HISTORY AND PALEONTOLOGY.

MISSISSIPPI is bounded on the south by the north line of southeast Louisiana, Pearl river and the Mississippi sound of the Gulf of Mexico; on the east by the west line of Alabama, and on the northeast by the Tennessee river; on the north by the south line of Tennessee (latitude 35 degrees), and on the west by the Mississippi. It embraces also the islands in the Gulf of Mexico, within six leagues of shore, viz.: Isles Dauphin, Ronde, Corne, au Chevreul, aux Vasseau, au Chat, St. Josephs, Grand Island, and a few smaller bodies of elevated sands, or a territory extending from latitude 30 degrees, to latitude 35 degrees north, and from longitude 11 degrees 25 minutes west to 14 degrees 33 minutes west. The area in square miles, as stated in the United States census reports, is forty-six thousand eight hundred and ten, but local authorities place it as high as fifty-five thousand five hundred. The width of the state, on the line of latitude 35 degrees, is one hundred and twenty miles; on latitude 31 degrees, one hundred and eighty-six miles, and on the Gulf coast, seventy-eight miles. The length of the state, on the line of longitude 12 degrees 30 minutes, being the greater line, is three hundred and thirty miles; but the frontage on the Mississippi is continental in its proportions.

The elevations above tide water at New Orleans, on the line of the Illinois Central railroad, range from two hundred and fifty to eight hundred and fifty feet. They are a little raised above the creek or river bottoms at the towns designated, but from fifty to three hundred and fifty feet below elevated hills or plateaus in the vicinity. This is the case at Jackson, where a gradual ascent to the Capital ridge on the east and a marked ascent to the plateau on the west occur. At many of the other points on this road the difference between railroad depot locations and town locations is equally marked. The measurements begin at Grand Junction, just north of the Tennessee line, and are continued to Osyko, just north of the Louisiana line:

1

	Feet.		Feet.		Feet.		Feet.
Grand Junction	...795	Grenada	...308	Madison Station	...350	Beauregard	...450
Lamar	...645	Winona	...380	Jackson	...270	Brookhaven	...500
Holly Springs	...850	Vaiden	...355	Terry	...260	Summit	...420
Oxford	...685	Durant	...315	Crystal Springs	...455	Magnolia	...300
Water Valley	...355	Canton	...320	Hazelhurst	...430	Osyka	...250

On the Mobile and Ohio railroad, measurements were made from Corinth, just south of the Tennessee line, on the headwaters of the Tuscumbia, to state line, on the eastern boundary of the state:

	Feet.		Feet.		Feet.		Feet.
Corinth	...443	Tupelo	...280	Artesia	...244	Meridian	...336
Rienzi	...441	Verona	...307	Crawford	...316	Enterprise	...248
Boonville	...511	Okolona	...311	Brookville	...275	Quitman	...231
Booneville Summit	.513	Muldon	...304	Macon	...185	Waynesborough	...191
Baldwyn	...379	West Point	...242	Lockhart Summit	...426	State Line	...256

The data on which the engineers of this road base their elevations is the tide water in Mobile bay. This road, from its entrance above Corinth to Meridian, follows a line between the valley of the Tombigbee and the higher lands westward. South of Meridian it follows the Okatibbee and Chickasawha valleys to Buccatunna.

What may be deduced from the table of temperature and elevations? The actual existence of a land where disease is not native, and where, with ordinary care, the highest physical and mental condition may be attained. The Indians, of an age gone by forever, reached perfection here and produced warriors, high priests and orators renowned in Indian history. Beginning with Tuscaloosa, in 1539, and ending with Pushmataha, in 1824, long lines of Indian warriors and statesmen bear testimony to this fact. True, diseases exist and epidemics have fallen on the land. In the seventeenth century the yellow fever was carried hither from its home, and in the nineteenth century it was also brought here. Spanish soldiers were carried off by malaria in the sixteenth century, as French soldiers were in the eighteenth, but death under such circumstances was due almost entirely to the severe conditions of their service, the unseasonable time in which such service was carried out, and the river valleys along which they marched or were quartered. Since the country became an integral part of the United States, physical changes have been, as it were, made to meet climatic conditions, and thus a death rate of less than one and twenty-nine hundredths per centum is recorded for Mississippi, against one and eighty-six hundredths per centum for Massachusetts. As it is with the death rate, so also is it with the ordinary diseases; the proportion is about similar. Notwithstanding this happy state of affairs, the time has not yet arrived when the American Caucasian can look for health in some of the lower alluvial or extreme bottom lands. From New York to the Mississippi, along the great western trail, this species of Caucasian met with fever and ague everywhere, and only within our own time—this generation—could white men enter parts of Ohio, Indiana or Illinois, with an assurance of leaving in good health. Time and labor, improvement in manners and customs, new sanitary ideas, modern labor-saving machinery, have changed all this, and the introduction of the same improvements and practice of the same knowledge will insure health to the habitant of the low lands even as the soil will yield him wealth.

The following record was published by Affleck, in the *Southern Rural Almanac*, in 1852, from notes of Dr. Henry Tooley, of Natchez, compiled by G. L. C. Davis, for the publisher. Dr. Coleman, of Church Hill, A. H. Pegues, of Oxford, and the weather register, kept by the female students of Oakland Institute, Jackson, bring the records down to 1853, when the epidemic of that year scattered or carried off the recorders. To the foresight and industry of Geologist Wailes, in incorporating those registers in his report of 1854, their presence in this volume is due; for it is doubtful if a copy of the old almanac in which they were first published could be obtained.

Year.	Extreme of cold.	Extreme of heat.	Average temperature.	Rainfall in inches.	Late spring frosts.	Early fall frosts.
1825	Dec. 3.....27°	Aug. 10.....97°	60.5		Feb. 15....42°	Oct. 19.....44°
1826	Jan. 25....23	July 16.....92	69.2		April 11...43	Nov. 18....41
1827	Jan. 19....25	July 11.....94	68.8		Mar. 19....44	Nov. 30 ...38
1828	Nov. 23...35	July 27.....94	69.5		Mar. 17....42	Nov. 12 ...44
1829	Jan. 11....25	Aug. 6.....92	66.2		Mar. 22....32	Nov. 1 ...43
1830	Dec. 22....22	Aug. 27.....96	68.1		Feb. 14....41	Oct. 20 44
1831	Dec. 16....23	Sept. 4 91	62.9		Mar. 21....41	Oct. 28 40
1832	Jan. 26....13	July 5.....97	68.8		Mar. 18....30	Nov. 9....36
1833	Mar. 2....25	July 12.....96	67.0		Mar. 30....44	Oct. 20.....44
1834	Jan. 5.....14	Aug. 20.....98	67.0		Mar. 30....39	Oct. 20.....41
1835	Feb. 8....10	Aug. 17.....96	64.0		Mar. 23....42	Oct. 10....46
1836	Dec. 21....21	July 22.....94	65.3		Mar. 25....43	Oct. 22.....44
1837	Jan. 15....28	Aug. 3.....93	66.9		April 9.....44	Oct. 26.....42
1838	Feb. 3....18	July 6.....94	64.1		Mar. 18....43	Oct. 22.....44
1839	Nov. 26...22	Aug. 6.....95	67.8		Mar. 6.....37	Nov. 7.....42
1840	Nov. 26...26	June 30.....94	67.1	48.48	Mar. 31....41	Oct. 25.....42
1841	Jan. 18....19	July 15.....95	68.0	59.78	Mar. 18....45	Oct. 23....38
1842	Nov. 18...27	July 20.....94	67.4	43.52	Feb. 12....42	Oct. 26.....43
1843	Mar. 16 ...23	July 16.....92	66.1	78.73	April 1.....44	Oct. 28....39
1844	Dec. 17...29	July 6.....95	68.2	45.91	Mar. 31....38	Oct. 19.....41
1845	Dec. 20....21	July 23.....97	67.1	53.10	Mar. 21....42	Oct. 12.....44
1846	Jan. 10....31	Sept. 17.....95	67.7	61.84	April 14...43	Oct. 19.....44
1847	Jan. 7.....21	June 15.....93	66.7	74.72	Mar. 27....40	Nov. 19....42
1848	Jan. 10....26	....	....	17.32	Mar. 14....43	....
1849	Dec. 11....26	Aug. 16.....94	....	59.92	April 16...41	Nov. 8.....41
1850	Dec. 7.....18	Aug. 9.....95	65.6	71.27	April 7....40	Oct. 26.....36

(Rainfall column note, set vertically:) On Feb. 5, 1831, snow fell to the depth of six inches and remained ten days. Another heavy snow fell on Dec. 14 and remained until 23. The measure of rain for 1848 is only from Jan. to May, inclusive, and for 1849 from April to Dec. inclusive.

The record for the past four decades shows a lower average temperature than that for the quarter century just given. On April 12, 1857, four inches of snow fell at Jackson, and on the fifteenth of that month there was a heavy rain and hailstorm. In 1873 the coldest day experienced for thirty years here, dawned; on March 26, 1873, ice formed to a thickness of one-fourth inch; on March 28, that year, a tornado struck Canton, and on April 1 a heavy hailstorm passed over the center of the state. The great hail of April 4, 1874, penetrated tin roofs and damaged fruit and ornamental trees, and on April 10 thin ice formed on the ponds. On January 6, 1879, the thermometer at Seuter's (Jackson), fell to 7 degrees below zero. From January 8 to 13, 1886, a cold wave blew over this section. The thermometer at Eyrick's (Jackson), recorded 3 degrees below, and that at Seuter's 5 degrees below zero. On January 3 and 4, 1887, six inches of snow fell at Jackson, and a minute of this phenomenon was made by Dr. Ledbetter, who also recorded the cold day of 1879. The record of first blooms (cotton) for the eleven years ending June 24, 1850, shows: June 6, 1840; June 10, 1841; May 17, 1842; June 9, 1843; May 25, 1844; May 30, 1845; June 1, 1846; May 30, 1847; June 1, 1848; June 6, 1849, and June 24, 1850. In 1853 the cotton continued to grow and blossom until December 8, when the first killing frost fell over the state. The winter months of 1889–90 were seasonable only in name. Excepting the March frosts of 1890, there was nothing in the atmosphere to tell of winter up to the date of such frosts.

The great rivers of the state are the Mississippi, Yazoo, Big Black, and Homochitto, on the west; the Amite, Tangipahoa and Boguechitto (Big creek), in the southwest. Pearl river (Hotchiah), in the center, flowing south; the Pascagoula and Chickasawha in the southeast, and the Tombigbee, Tuscumbia and Tennessee in the northeast, with forty-one smaller rivers and two hundred and thirty-eight creeks. There are twenty-two lakes, including

Biloxi and Bay St. Louis, the large lakes in Wilkinson, Madison and Noxubee counties and in the Yazoo Delta. The Mississippi receives the waters of all territory between the bluffs and the river, the Tombigbee those of the northeastern counties, the Pearl those of the great central basin, while the Pascagoula and Amité drain their respective districts. The Tombigbee, in its whole course, drains about nineteen thousand square miles in this state and Alabama; the Pascagoula about nine thousand square miles; the Yazoo about thirteen thousand and the Pearl river about nine thousand. All those rivers have undergone changes since the days of Spanish and French exploration, but the Mississippi, more especially, was given to change. The natives, in De Soto's time, called the great river Cicuaga; the northern Indians knew it as Namesi-si-pi, or Fish river; the gulf coast Indians, Malbouchia; the Spaniards called it successively Rio Grande, Rio del Espirito Santo, Rio Esconnido, Tomiliseu, Tupata, Mico and Ri; and the French La Palisade, l'Assumption, St. Peters, St. Louis, La Conception and Mississippi.

In 1811 the earthquake, which destroyed New Madrid, Mo., made many changes along the western line of the Mississippi, and in the Mississippi river itself. Blocks of land on the bluffs were raised up bodily and cast into the river; in some places tracts of forty to three hundred acres were removed into the river. From the 15th to the 24th of December earthquake shocks occurred at short intervals, and each shock made some change in the river bottom and channel and created depressions and hillocks at random throughout the area affected. The system of levees, too, has closed up old channels, as the Yazoo pass and Old river, and controls, in a certain degree, that great channel which drains one million two hundred and thirty-eight thousand six hundred and forty-two square miles, or forty-one per centum of the whole area of the United States, extending in part or in whole, over twenty-four states, through its forty-five navigable tributaries and their feeders.

Choctaw traditions speak of the three years' drought in the early years of the eighteenth century. The Tombigbee and Noxubee rivers dried up, the animals of the forest fled beyond the Mississippi and the forest trees shriveled up and died. The droughts of modern days have been attended with some inconvenience to settlements distant from the larger rivers, and to the residents in cities. Such seasons of drought, however, occur only once in a lifetime and therefore are not considered in the natural economy of the state.

The state is not known to possess a single testimonial of the Azoic or Archian age. The deepest borings have not brought to the light of day a strata wanting in fossil remains or evidences of their existence. The same may be said of the Silurian and Devonian periods of the Paleozoic age, for geologists have not yet unearthed the simpler fossils which tell of the humble beginnings of animal and vegetable life, they have not, indeed, brought up the more complex forms of the Devonian or later life. The geologist failing, so also must the record fail. The earth of Mississippi is only new by comparison with the lands elevated above the marsh or ocean during the ages named. It is old, when compared with the great alluvial fields now forming in the far north, or with large areas of itself or Louisiana. It dates to the close of the Paleozoic time, known to scientists as the Permian period or the Carboniferous age, and comes down to man through the Mesozoic or Reptilian, and the Cenozoic or Mammalian ages. Look back from the present to the beginning of the Permian. Stand on the soil of Mississippi and go down to the depths, to the base of the carboniferous strata, and this is what will probably be found. Begin with the quaternary:

QUATERNARY.

Alluvium—Soils, sand-bars, etc.; remains of plants and animals.
Second bottom—Hommock soils; inorganic washings from higher lands.

Yellow loam—Brown and yellow brick clays.
Bluff formation—Calcareous silts.
Orange sand—Sands, pebbles, clays.

TERTIARY.

Coast Pliocene—Black fetid clays; remains of living marine shells, trees.
Grand gulf group—Light colored clays, white sandstones; remains of plants almost extinct; lignite.
Vicksburg group—Marls and limestones; remains of marine animals.
Lignitic—Black clays; remains of plants; lignite.
Jackson group—Marls and soft limestones; remains of marine animals.
Lignitic—Black clays; remains of plants; lignite.
Claiborne group—Marl, limestone, siliceous sandstone; remains of marine animals.
Northern lignitic—Black and gray clays; yellow sands; remains of plants partly extinct; lignite.

CRETACEOUS.

Ripley group—Marls and hard-white limestones; sandy loam; fossil remains well preserved outcropping.
Rotten limestone—Soft chalky limestone; clay; remains of marine animals; shark's teeth.
Tombigbee sand—Green micaceous sands; remains of ammonites and inoceramus.
Eutaw or Tuomey group—Dark colored clays; sand; remains of animals or plants rare.

CARBONIFEROUS.

Limestone—Fetid crystalline limestone; remains of marine animals.
Sandstone—Siliceous sandstone and chert; remains of marine animals.
Black slate—Hydraulic limestone.

Thus it is seen that Mississippi has escaped the changes and convulsions of no less than fourteen periods of geologic time.

The black ferruginous sandstone of the Carboniferous period is a grotesque stone in many particulars, since it is found in all kinds of shapes, sometimes appearing as slack from a rolling mill, at others as if just cast out from a modern graniteware factory. As a commercial rock it appears in regular layers, like the green sandstone of Pennsylvania or the flagstone of Lima, Ohio, and can be found in solid ledges, where it may be quarried for foundation or other rough work. This black-rock is the remnant of the ancient hill tops, and may only be found on the knolls. Near Ripley and along the sources of the Hatchie, Tallahatchie and Tombigbee this rock is found in commercial quantity and quality. Among the pine hills of Prentiss and Tippah, south of Bull Mountain in Itawamba and in the southeastern townships of Marshall and Lafayette counties, are heavy deposits, while a hill west of Water valley, one in township 12, range 2, Calhoun county, and the high ridges of East Carroll, North Attala and West Choctaw, as well as a hill near Grenada, show extensive outcrops of large, compact rock. Siliceous sandstone or whetstone presents itself in large blocks in township 4, range 1, East Tippah, and outcrops occur in Marshall, Lafayette and Pontotoc, as well as in Yallobusha; but the northern townships of Holmes and Attala form its true home, for there it is abundant. White and tinted pipe clays, potters clay, red and yellow ocher, aluminous brown iron ore and brown hematite with white glass sand are common throughout the whole orange sand region.

The limestone of the Carboniferous family is limited in Mississippi, like the family itself. The hydraulic limestone of Tishomingo is a grayish-black cretaceous rock, prominent near East Port on the Tennessee, and on the hill tops along Yellow creek. It does not claim to be as pure as common limestone, for when burned it does not slake like it and when wet partakes of the quality of Roman cement rather than lime, putty or plaster. The insoluble matter of the old rock at the old Billing's mill site is 54.201 per cent., the lime 23.247 per cent., carbonic acid 15.572 per cent., organic matter and water about 3.752 per cent., with marked traces of potash, magnesia, permanganate of iron, alumina and phosphoric acid. At Eastport the lime shows 32.603 per cent., and carbonic acid and water 27.643 per cent. On Big and Little Bear creeks outcrops of a peculiar character occur, presenting rock capable of producing excellent agricultural lime. Building stone, flagstone and grinding stone are also found in this section of the state. On Mackay's creek a commercial limestone is found, which yields from 53 to 56 per cent. of quicklime. This lime is considered pure enough for all purposes. Silica, of a whitish, pulverulent character, abounds east of Eastport. It is called chalk by the natives who confound it with the greater deposit of white pipe clay.

The cretaceous territory extends from the Tennessee line, latitude 35 degrees, longitude 12 degrees, southwest to the west line of Pontotoc, south through Chickasaw, and thence south by east to the Scooba district in Kemper county. The economic materials are marls, lime and building rock. The greater area of rotten limestone is simply an immense marl (bed) existing under this vulgar name. The cretaceous marls of the northeast are found in the greater area of Tippah, Tishomingo, Pontotoc, Itawamba, Chickasaw, Monroe, Oktibbeha, Lowndes, Noxubee and Kemper. The greensand species are found between the northeast prairies and the Flatwoods, and are said to contain about fifteen per centum carbonate of lime and a little less than one per centum of potash. The rotten limestone, because wealthy in this greensand marl, is considered valuable for fertilizing purposes. The clay marls are simply a composition of clay and rotten limestone, and show in some cases as high as thirty-five per centum carbonate of lime, but are lower in potash. The micaceous green sands of the lower rotten limestone contain very little carbonate of lime and only a trace of potash, so that in confounding them with the economic marl sands and rock the agriculturist would make a grave mistake. The marine marl extends across the state from Vicksburg to Meridian and thence into Alabama. They are very rich in carbonate of lime, sometimes yielding 90 per centum, 2 per centum of potash, 1 to 2 percentum of magnesia; while fresh water marls belong to the southern counties and particularly to the gulf group. In the absence of pure lime rock, the hard variety of the rotten limestone may be used for burning, and, when properly handled, will give 45.791 per centum of lime, as at Okalona. As a building stone it fails to stand atmospheric action; but owing to the little difficulty in cutting it into shape it is a popular building stone in sheltered corners or for inside finish.

In 1852 gold discoveries were reported on Black creek, Marion county, and a body of prospectors carried away some metallic nuggets for assay at New Orleans, where the gold theory was demolished. During the first decade of this century a bellmaker used this metal for brazing bells. It could be cut like lead, but in the furnace was minus the leaden fumes. Galena is found in the diluvium sections of the northeast as well as in Adams, Claiborne, Neshoba, Lawrence and Kemper, carried hither from Missouri with the drift. What the quantity of aluminum may be has yet to be determined.

The Tertiary conformations come next in extent to the orange sand area of the state. The territory shows heavy deposits of semi-carbonized wood coals and a collection of clayey substances of all colors. This lignite is black, as in Choctaw county, or brown, as in Lafayette, and shows its desire to become true bitumen on one side, and true bog-oak on the other. It is an uncertain commodity in every way, and, so well is this fact established, few persons avail themselves of what may be useful in it; while bituminous coal or wood is at hand for fuel, coke or charcoal. As a fuel the presence of iron pyrites destroy its usefulness;

for the sulphurous acid, in which it abounds, casts out such fumes as to render it disagreeable and dangerous. With all its faults it is always welcome in the absence of other fuels; for necessity generally suggests a means of using the gifts of nature, no matter how rough their ends may be shaped.

The ferruginous greensand and limy marls of the Tertiary formation are true fertilizers, rather than stimulants. They contain from 33 to 44 per cent. of lime, and from 30 to 35 per cent. of carbonic acid. Gypsum or plaster deposits exist in Carroll, Attala, Hinds, Madison and adjoining counties, and pure gypsum in Rankin county as well as in other sections of the state. The argillo-siliceous stone, at Fort Adams, known as the Davion rock, is an alluvio-tertiary formation. Limestone for building and burning purposes is found in quanity at Vicksburg. Burned, it will yield sixty-one pounds of lime per one hundred pounds, and, when placed flat in buildings, will last for centuries.

From 1699 to this day the commercial clays, ocher and sands of Mississippi have won attention. In the year given the French authorized Leseur to organize a geological survey party, the first in the New World, and under this authority thirteen thousand pounds of ocher were shipped to France from St. Peters' river valley. In the forties potteries existed at Natchez, at Brandon, and one in Marshall county. In 1812 two ship loads of yellow ocher were taken from the White Cliffs, below Natchez, for Boston consignees. It may be laid down that from Tishomingo to the southeast corner of Wilkinson county, and from De Soto to Pascagoula, mineral clays, as extensive as they are useful, await development. What the quantity of aluminum in the soil may be has not yet been ascertained with any degree of accuracy; but that the percentage is large, there is no doubt.

The Yellow loam region extends east from the bluff formation to the Flatwoods, embracing the eastern townships of Panola, Tate and De Soto, the northeast corner of Tallahatchie, the eastern three-fourths of Grenada, Carroll and Holmes, in all of which the bluff formation occupies nearly all the western townships. Marshall, Benton, Lafayette, Yallobusha, Calhoun, Montgomery, Webster, Choctaw, Winston, Attala, Neshoba and part of Lauderdale, form the center of the yellow loam region, while its eastern boundaries are the western townships of Tippah, Union, Pontotoc, Chickasaw, Clay, Oktibbeha, Noxubee and Kemper counties. A brown-yellow soil twenty feet in depth is found to be very productive on the uplands, but the area of such deep soils is so limited that an average of three feet is taken for the whole district. The thin soil is placed at about three inches, and through this the orange sand is so mixed or comes so near as a subsoil as to leave the land worthless for agricultural purposes. The tablelands of Marshall, Benton and Tippah are said to be the richest uplands in the state. They are marked by a six to eight-foot bed of loam resting on orange sand. The insoluble matter found in this soil measured 83.347 per cent.; peroxide of iron, 4.798 per cent.; alumina, 6.282 per cent., and water and organic matter, 4.195 per cent. In the subsoil the insoluble matter and alumina exceeded that in the loam. In Calhoun and other counties pine hills are not wanting. In Winston as in Attala the Red Hills show short-leaf pine, white, black, red and post oak, hickory, and numerous shrubs identified with good land. The ridge soils of Kemper are sandy. The bottom or valley soils of this region are similar in composition to their uplands; but on their lower waters show a mixture of native and imported soils, i. e., clay carried into the parent stream by some tributary. From this region the greater quantity of cotton is sent forth, while corn and other crops are produced here in quantities not only sufficient to supply the demands of this locality, but also those of less productive divisions of Mississippi and Alabama.

The Prairie region of Northeastern Mississippi includes the counties of Tishomingo,

Itawamba, parts of Alcorn, Prentiss, Lee and Chickasaw, all of Monroe, Clay, Lowndes and Noxubee, and parts of Oktibbeha, Winston and Kemper. In Tippah, Union and Pontotoc, extensions of the prairie merge into the Flatwoods. This is not a prairie in the sense of the word as applied in Illinois, Nebraska and other states, but the territory named embraces a large number of extensive prairie tracts, hence the name. In the eastern townships of Tishomingo the limestone and sandstone of the Carboniferous period form the principal strata, while throughout the greater area the chalky or cretaceous strata prevails, and wins for the district the name "Northeastern lime region," as applied by Hilgard in 1860.

Tishomingo and Itawamba present very few physical differences. They are rolling oak uplands, with prairie tracts and wide alluvial bottoms in the western townships, and sandy lands in the eastern ones. Even the valley of the Tennessee here fails to present an alluvial area of much agricultural value; for the hills of walnut and sycamore, the monstrosity of the region, form the river's southern bank, showing outcrops of hydraulic limestone. This harsh description must be modified in relation to the valleys of Upper Yellow creek and tributary streams, of Bear creek and other streams, which present excellent bottom lands. East Itawamba and northern Monroe present large areas of broken or hilly lands. The valley of the Tombigbee and tributary creeks are exceedingly productive, and it may be said that the plateau between the Tombigbee and Buttahatchie is capable of high production. The white lime districts of the counties named embrace the prize lands of the region north and northwest of Farmington, and round that town is an almost level tract of rich land, while between Corinth and Chawalla the land is more rolling and less productive. In the Tuscumbia bottom, southward to Parmeechee creek, and to the north line of Prentiss county, fertile lands are found. At the Chickasaw old fields in Pontotoc, the prairies proper begin. They were called "fields" by the early settlers, who conceived them to be clearings, when in fact the proximity of rotten limestone to the surface prevented the growth of trees and gave them the character of prairies. The Monroe prairie in township 14, range 6 east, there are eight inches of dark gray soil with a greenish daub subsoil, which crumbles when dry. Specks of iron ore are found in both soils. The insoluble matter is 71.539; the alumina, 13.153; peroxide of iron, 5.419; and organic matter and water, 6.992 per cent.

The prairies of Northeastern Kemper and Southeastern Noxubee are numerous and productive. The Hatchie country is one of pine hills, while, in north Tippah, a two-mile strip of excellent ridge land extends from the Flatwoods at Muddy creek to the Hatchie hill. Between the head waters of the Hatchie and Tallahatchie the pine hills begin to spread out into little plateaus, and heavy rolling lands take the place of hills capable of producing from five hundred to one thousand pounds of seed cotton per acre. The red, sandy loam, north of New Albany, between Wilhite and King's creek, is known as "The Buncombes." It is a pebbly, iron-tinged, inhospitable looking soil, but strong and productive. The Pontotoc ridge lands are highly prized, whether in that or adjoining counties, such as Chickasaw.

The Flatwoods region is a narrow strip of post-oak land, three to six miles wide, bounding the prairie region on the west. It extends from the southern bank of Tippah creek, township 4, range 2 east, through almost all of range 2, east of the Chickasaw survey, and from the southwest corner of Chickasaw county to Succarnoochee river, or about the center of Kemper county. In Oktibbeha, Noxubee and Kemper the Flatwoods are simply timbered extensions of the level lands, called prairies. Westward from the recognized

Flatwoods line, the country partakes of their character in soil and timber, but differs in its surface features, being undulating. In southwest Chickasaw, Calhoun, Webster and Choctaw counties, white oak is added to the regulation post oak, black jack and short-leaf pine of the Flatwoods proper, winning a new name for the woods here—White Oak Flatwoods. The heavy soil found in this region in Pontotoc county and at other places shows 77.854 per cent. of insoluble matter; 10.302 per cent. alumina; 5.899 per cent. peroxide of iron; and 3.689 per cent. of organic matter and water. The light Flatwoods soil, as examined in Chickasaw and other counties, shows 93.575 per cent. of insoluble matter; 1.445 per cent. peroxide of iron; 2.605 per cent. alumina, and 1.333 per cent. of organic matter and water, each soil showing a deficiency of lime and vegetable matter, as well as phosphoric acid and salts.

The Central Prairie region embraces a part of Yazoo, all of Madison and Hinds, parts of Rankin, Scott, and Leake, all of Newton, part of Simpson, all of Smith, Jasper, Clark, Wayne, and part of Jones. The name is applied owing to the number of little prairie tracts which exist between the ridge lands. The loam of Madison and Hinds counties is similar to the productive loam of Marshall. In section 2, township 4, range 3, it varies in depth from nine to twenty inches, but to insure it against drought white marl must be plentifully applied. In seasons of drought the yellow loam subsoil shrinks perceptibly, tearing brick or stone buildings apart, where provision for this shrinkage was not made, and disturbing growing crops. Nature has provided local means to combat this shrinkage, and the immense deposit of marl is not the least of such means at hand. The soils of Pearl river bottom are generally light, though true alluvial along the greater part of its course within a narrow compass. While the Hommock bottom widens out in many places to three miles northeast of Jackson, the Pearl river flats are on the east side and show a decidedly poor soil compared with the flats from Jackson to Columbia in Marion county.

The Long-leaf pine region may be said to embrace all the state south of latitude 31 degrees 40 minutes, except Wayne and part of Jones county in the northwest, and Jackson, Harrison and Hancock on the gulf coast. The surface is generally rolling, but broken along the rivers, with a sandy soil resting on a thick bed of sandy loam. In the northern tier of counties of this gulf region the short-leaf pine contests possession with the long-leaf, but the latter conquers and simply tolerates the black jack, post oak and the Spanish oaks on its southern territory. Even the husbandman has to seek on the hillside or bottom for land worth cultivation; but, when this is found, the cultivator is rewarded.

The Natchez hills region extends north from the Louisiana line, embraces two-thirds of Wilkinson, nearly all of Adams, the western half of Jefferson, all of Claiborne except about two thousand acres in the southeast corner, and all of Warren except a few townships above Vicksburg. The deposit of silt over the clay dunes and sandstone of the old tertiary measures, at some points, over seventy feet, averages about twenty-five feet. At Vicksburg silt is from forty-eight to sixty-four feet in depth south of the creek, while on the bluffs just north it ranges from ten to twenty-two feet. At Grand Gulf the deposit is fifty feet in depth; while bounding it is the Grand Gulf sandstone, covered with only a few feet of this powdery substance. A stratum of heavy brown clay generally overlays the silt to a depth of from three to ten feet on the level or rolling uplands, insuring excellent land, bearing beech, oak, hickory, elm, sweet and black gum holly, basswood, magnolia and other commercial and ornamental timber. The bottom lands here correspond with the hommocks of the interior, being second rather than first bottoms; but many fertile tracts are found between the shore of the Mississippi and the hills, owing to the transportation of silt thither from the hills—called by some the natural marling process.

The Mississippi and Yazoo river region comprises that part of De Soto extending from the Mississippi to the bluffs, all Tunica, Quitman, Coahoma, Bolivar, Sunflower, Le Flore, the western two-thirds of Tallahatchee, the western sections of Panola and Grenada, all of Washington, Issaquena and Sharkey, and the western parts of Carroll, Holmes and Yazoo counties, or about six thousand two hundred and fifty square miles. The greatest width of this famous fertile tract is sixty-eight miles, extending from Huntington, opposite Arkansas City, to the bluffs near Carrollton. From this point it narrows gradually until the bluff region strikes the river bank at Vicksburg. Of the four million acres comprised in this alluvial territory three million five hundred thousand acres are still in timber. The soil is a great cotton producer, and the Yazoo Delta is justly celebrated for its fertility.

The Gulf coast region proper embraces the three most southern counties of the state, fronting on Mississippi sound and Lake Borgne. The light, fine-grained sand, begins to show in latitude 30 degrees 52 minutes and the shallow, upland lily ponds tell the traveler that he is now in tropical lands, among the deceptive brown-water streams of the far South. Near the coast and along the Pascagoula and other rivers the long-leaf pine becomes larger, and in some places make way for pitch-pine, live oak, magnolia and Spanish oak, with an undergrowth of gallberry. The Gallberry flats, the Shell hommocks, the meadows and the marshes are peculiarly Mississippian. On the southeastern margin of Pearl river marsh are the Sea Island cotton plantations. The dark mulatto soil, resting on its thick bed of pale yellow sand, is very fertile and, where uncultivated, produces the large magnolia and other trees, and clothes the great pines and live oaks, in veils of ever living moss. The islands off the coast are accumulations of white sand, capable of cultivation at the cost of much care and labor. Cat island, however, was cultivated before the war, and, it is said, produced excellent crops. The gulf coast of Mississippi, one of the favored regions of the earth, is only sparsely settled. Within the last few years the neighborhoods of Pass Christian and Ocean Springs have been much improved and the times are full of hope for this beautiful land.

Aluminium is a constituent part of all those clays. In the sandy clays it exists in a much smaller degree than in heavy clays. The metal approximates silver in luster, is bluish white, but has never been found in a pure state. It oxidizes very little under moisture, is as tenacious as steel and malleable as gold, but requires a heat of 1,300 degrees Fahrenheit to melt. It is only about one-third as heavy as iron. It is the metal of the future.

In the Northeastern prairie region water may be obtained in the orange sand, above the freestone strata or within it, at reasonable depths. When within the cretaceous formation the water partakes of a chalybeate character, and this sometimes pertains to the numerous springs which rise from the marly or limestone strata. Between Weaver's creek and Little Sipsie, one mile west of the latter, water issuing from a bed of lignite and iron pyrites was absolutely offensive, and this conformation is so wide in the neighborhood that prior to the era of deep borings only cistern-water was available for use. At Iuka, mineral springs known as Gum spring No. 1, Gum spring No. 2, Box spring and the Peden spring are chalybeate, while south of Corinth is another heavy spring. Along the Tombigbee bluffs, round Fulton and in Bull Mountain country several medicinal springs are flowing.

In the Rotten-limestone region the people have to rely on cistern-water where deep wells have not been drilled. This is owing to the dip of the stratum (which stratum on the edge of the Flatwoods, near Houston, is one hundred feet thick) and its relation to the water-bearing sand. At Farmington, Kossuth and other places water is found from twenty to fifty feet; at Corinth water rises fifty-five feet in a well seventy feet deep; while at Boneyard deep borings are necessary. In the southern part of this region depths increase about twenty-five feet per mile; but there are exceptions to everything and in the matter of water depths particularly. Before the war an artesian well was bored, three miles north of Camargo, to a depth of two hundred feet. This produced a volume of water two hundred and two feet in hight from the base; while in the village of Camargo it rose two hundred and twenty feet in a two-hundred-and-eighty-foot well. Along the Tombigbee hommock artesian wells are numerous and the force of the water shows the reservoir or natural stand pipe to be at a much higher elevation. At Pikeville an artesian stream was struck at a depth of six hundred and fourteen feet, and at Macon seven hundred and sixty feet. In the southern part of this northeastern prairie region the currents may be tapped at from seven hundred to nine hundred feet and, in some places, as at Sparta, the drill has to make a passage of from one thousand to fifteen hundred feet to the currents.

The Flatwoods country is one of surface water. Up to 1857 cisterns and ponds were in use; but that year wells were bored in Tippah and Calhoun counties, showing good water at depths of from three hundred to four hundred feet. Ordinary wells, however, are found and when properly constructed generally insure a supply of surface water. Springs are not common.

The hard artesian and mineral waters of the country between the Mississippi bluffs and the Flatwoods, north of latitude 32 degrees 30 minutes, are varied in number and quality. Ordinary wells have to be deep to give assurance of supply in seasons of drought. The artesian waters are encountered at depths of from five hundred feet, in the lower valleys of the streams running southwest from the northeastern divide, to one thousand feet at the heads of these streams. There are artesian springs near Camden, on the road from Canton to Kosciusko, to which high medicinal qualities were attributed years before the war. The Castilian springs in Holmes county; the Chalybeate springs near Louisville, Winston county; near Pittsboro, Calhoun; at Robina, Panola; near Grenada; near Yockeney depot; Black springs in Choctaw; and the Lauderdale springs on the south line of the yellow loam region in Lauderdale county, were all held in high esteem before the war.

The Southern river region may be said to be almost totally wanting in shallow wells of good water. When the silt reposes on a bed of dense strata, above the drainage level, it is natural to expect a fairly good water; but this condition is not present very often in this region. The river and creek waters flowing from the bluff are limy to a degree. In parts of Claiborne, Copiah, Hinds, Jefferson, Adams and Wilkinson, springs of comparatively pure water are abundant.

Between latitudes 31 degrees 35 minutes and 32 degrees 35 minutes, east of the Bluff formation, natural springs exist in small numbers. Shallow wells of a magnesian character may be found anywhere in the region, but the waters are unfit for drinking until subjected to a boiling or chemical purifying process. At Canton the saline waters of such wells and at Jackson the sulphur waters necessitated the use of cistern water generally. The Sizer well here, bored before the war to a depth of one hundred feet, proved to be a true chalybeate; while a few shallow wells of freestone water were found here. The waters of the once celebrated Banston or Mississippi springs and of Cooper's wells, three miles distant, originate in the gray clays. The former are strongly impregnated with sulphuretted hydrogen or white sulphur, and contain little solids. The water of Cooper's wells, on the contrary, contain about one hundred and five grains of solid matter per gallon, and are considered strong saline chalybeates. The acid alum waters of Brandon, east of Jackson, are mineral curiosities of some medicinal value. From Jackson to Columbia, along Pearl river, mineral springs abound. Near Old Hickory in Simpson county are the great cold springs.

Stovall's springs above Columbia, like the Mississippi springs near Jackson, were favorite camping grounds of the Indians, and, from 1834 to 1860, of their white successors; so were Bradywine springs, the Lauderdale springs and Ocean springs, all celebrated resorts in early days.

The record of boring at the Penitentiary well, Jackson (kept by J. Murray up to his death in 1858 or 1859, when W. B. Blake took charge of the work), is as follows: Clay marl, twenty feet; blue sandy shell marl, eleven feet; sand with streaks of whitish or gray marl with impressions of leaves, eighty feet; wet quicksand, water-producing, seventy feet; black clays with layers of sand, leaf impressions and a catkin of willow (at four hundred feet), two hundred and sixty-eight feet; greensand with shells and streaks of gray or red clay, thirty feet; water-bearing sand, twenty feet; greensand with shells, twenty feet; ledge of gray, fossiliferous limestone, one foot; blue clay with calcareous nodules and some layers of green sand marl, twelve feet; shell marl with layers of black clay, ten feet; quicksand with mica in quantity, five feet; and white indurate clay with iron pyrites, in which the drill was working when the record closed. In July, 1860, this well produced fourteen thousand gallons per day.

Early in 1852 the wells at the college, Oxford, refused to yield their accustomed supply, and this failure was ascribed to the shocks of earthquake felt on January 23, that year. In June, 1852, the work of boring new wells was entered upon; but to the surprise of the workers, when the level of the old wells was reached—sixty-five to seventy feet—not a sign of water was given. Day after day the workers delved through the deep deposit of coarse sand until, at a depth of one hundred and forty-five feet, a stream of water signaled the completion of the work.

At the head of Well's creek in Franklin county were the great springs of pioneer days. Early in the twenties the wealth and fashion as well as the poor and invalid of the state looked to this spot as the fountain of health; but the carelessness of the proprietor and the utter want of enterprise of the capitalists of that time failed to make provision for the crowds, and the springs at Columbia, rising in popular esteem, took the position hitherto held by the Franklin springs. In 1850–51 a few buildings were erected on lot 5, section 37, township 7, range 1 east, in Franklin county, and the great natural artesian well returned into favor. In 1854 there were over thirty artesian wells drilled in Lowndes county, from one hundred and fifteen to three hundred and seventy-five feet in depth. At Bexley's, one hundred and ninety-six feet deep, a stream of one hundred and sixty gallons per minute was discharged; at Fernandez', one hundred and ninety feet deep, one hundred and fifteen gallons; while from the three hundred and seventy-one-foot well at Columbus only thirty gallons per minute were discharged. Twenty-four miles north of Columbus the Aberdeen well, five hundred and twelve feet deep, produced ten gallons of strong chalybeate water per minute. The first artesian well at Natchez was commenced in 1828 or 1829, but owing to the quicksand the project was abandoned. In 1848 deep borings were made ten miles south of Canton, and during the decade ending in 1860 many attempts to find water by deep borings were attempted and some attended with success.

The artesian system of the Bay St. Louis country is in its youth. Only a few years ago did deep borings meet with success, and since that time the great fountain of artesian water has been tapped in many places, bringing the pure waters of the Cumberland mountains to meet the waves of the gulf. The wells already in use are cased to depths varying from three hundred to nine hundred feet.

The water of the Ocean springs near Biloxi, as examined prior to 1854 by Dr. J. L.

Smith, is colorless and retains this character, so long as kept in tight vessels. When removed from the well it becomes black in a little while, owing to the presence of sulphate of iron. One gallon shows four and six-hundred-and-thirty-two-thousandths grains of carbonic acid and four-hundred-and-eighty-one-thousandths grain of sulphureted hydrogen, and of solids—traces of iodine, chloride of potassium, alumina and organic matter, with forty-seven and seventy-seven-hundredths of chloride of sodium; three and eight-hundred-and-eighty-two-thousandths chloride of calcium; four and nine-hundred-and-eighty-nine-thousandths chloride of magnesia and four and seven-hundred-and-twelve-thousandths protoxide of iron. The modern artesian waters, brought up for use within the last four or five years, are celebrated in many respects.

The analysis of the waters of Cooper's well, Hinds county, made prior to 1854 by Dr. David Stewart, shows oxygen, nitrogen and carbonic acid gas in one gallon to be nine and one-tenth cubic inches and solids one hundred and five grains—sulphate of lime being forty-two and one-hundred-and-twenty-two-thousandths, sulphate of magnesia twenty-three and twenty-eight-hundredths and sulphate of soda eleven and seven-hundred-and-five-thousandths, and other sulphates and chlorides making up the total—including six-hundred-and-eight-thousandths of sulphate of potash and three-hundred-and-eleven-thousandths crenate of lime. Modern analysis and testimonials to the efficacy of the waters of this spring, in possession of the Messrs. Spangler, the owners, prove its claims of 1854 to be well founded.

The forests of Mississippi—despised, neglected forests—are in reality mines of true wealth, waiting to reward labor and capital alike and, on the removal of their shadows, to open great tracts of fertile land to the agriculturist. It is not an exaggeration to state that over twenty billion feet of long-leaf and thirteen billion feet of short-leaf pine stand to-day in Mississippi with red gum and other commercial lumber equaling, if not exceeding, the quantity of pine. The cypress, including the red variety, long-leafed pine and the oak family make up the list of the great commercial trees of the state, with the gum tree forcing its way to the consideration it deserves. Every tree and shrub and almost every brilliant flower finds a representative here under the genial skies of the south and the great majority reach perfection here. The list of the economical forest trees is as follows: Ash (blue and white), beech, birch, barberry, bay (sweet and berry), boxelder, buckeye (dwarf), cherry, cucumber, chestnut, cottonwood, cypress, cedar, elm (red, slippery and cork-bark), elder, gum (sweet and black), hickory, maple (sugar, red, silver-leaved and swamp), oak (thirteen varieties), pine (long-leaf, short-leaf, swamp and pitch), poplar, sycamore, walnut and willow. The crabapple, cherry, haw (black and possum, huckleberry, persimmon and plum), five varieties, are also found wild, while the hazel, holly, laurel, live oak and magnolia, the myrtle and honeysuckle, cape jasmine, sassafras and a hundred other ornamental and flowering trees grow here. The orange, fig, apple, peach, grape and all berry trees flourish in the southern counties. All the beautiful runners and climbers, from the poison oak to the magnificent, but neglected, Virginia creeper, revel in the richness of land and climate, and no less than fifty-nine standard medicinal plants and ornamental shrubs reach perfection. In 1850–55 the Yazoo, Pearl and Big Black valleys were filled with the camps of the cypress lumbermen; while at Napoleon, in Hancock county, was the turpentine and camphene distillery, and throughout the pine region were hundreds of tar kilns. The sumac, as rich as that of the Mediterranean islands, is allowed to grow and wither here and, in fact, the same indictment may be returned in the case of the whole forest.

In 1739 the buffalo and bear were plenty in the Grand gulf neighborhood; La Harpe and other travelers are positive on this point. The animals of the chase, now known to be represented in this state, are the deer, black bear, raccoon, western wolf, black wolf, gray fox, panther, wolverine, otter, mink, weasel, polecat, muskrat, beaver, opossum, gray, red, black, ground and flying squirrel, prairie and woodrabbit, lank hare and wild hog. The latter is the perfected form of the imported Caucasian animal, and, though an ugly enemy to encounter in the forest, is very much preferable to the tame hog to encounter at the table. Wild turkey, partridge, woodcock, wild pigeon and water fowl, with all the smaller game birds, are found in this state, together with the birds of prey and all the feathered tribes known to ornithologists. The pigeon which once made his home here is gone, and like the white pelican and the cormorant is now only a visitor.

When Civil war was carried into Mississippi the cautious mink fled to Louisiana, and the great herds of cattle, bands of mules and horses, and droves of hogs which found peace and plenty here after coming from older fields of war in 1861-2, moved south or west in 1863-4, awe-stricken, as it were, at the sanguinary struggle between their old owners and the blue-coated adventurers from the northland. The bear, wolverine, panther, wolf and deer have left representatives in the canebrakes and forests of the state; but only the hunter can find one. The beaver is seldom or never seen, though abundant throughout the state until 1860; but some of his works remain to tell of his engineering skill and industry. Mr. Wailes tells us that the wildcat or wolverine was extraordinarily savage here as late as 1854. In Adams county, he states, this animal would enter the cabins of the negroes in quest of children. In fact workmen were attacked by one in open day, and a number of them injured. The gopher came years ago from the far north and attains his greatest size and strength here. The buffalo were here when Bienville came, and up to 1776 tracks of buffalo were reported.

The reptiles are still here, but the residents of the towns and villages see little or nothing of them, and long since they ceased to fear them. The banded and ground rattle-snake, the copperhead, the water moccasin, the highland moccasin, the cotton-mouth and the whole tribe of *Coluberidae*, embracing twenty-three families, are diminutives of the great reptiles which swarmed here during the long summer succeeding the ice age. The ground puppy or salamander, the chameleon or green lizard, the red head, striped and gray lizard, the water lizard and the spring lizard, with the toad family find a home here, as do four tribes of frogs, but the basilosauros of our age is the alligator. In the earlier years of Mississippi the *coureurs de bois* killed alligators for their hides and oil. The oil would be extracted at New Orleans, and the hides sent to France to be converted into fancy leather, an industry revived only a few years ago.

The *chelonididæ*, or turtle tribe, is well represented; four families of couta, six families of terrapin, the soft shell, the loggerhead, the snapping, the green, the hawk-bell and the mud turtle make up the list. The loggerhead sometimes measures three feet in diameter, and the emys terrapin of the couta family comes next. This latter turtle and the soft shell form the angel's food of epicures.

The finny tribe inhabiting the waters of Mississippi at present, comprise the alligator gar, the pike gar, the black gar, all sauroids; the mudfish, the cowfish, two species of salt-water catfish, two of fresh water catfish, the shovelnose and spoonbill sturgeon, the sheeps-head and pine perch, the angel fish, white perch, trout, redfish, whiting, big drum, young drum, croaker, pike, toadfish, billfish, spotted mackerel, pilotfish, pompeno, silverfish, jumping mullet, striped bass, rockfish, red snapper, snapper, yellow tail, horny-heads, goggle-eye, eel, tarpon, buffalo, sucker, gaspærgoo and a number of cyprinodonts (including the minnow), the tragon sabina or stingray, the sawfish, skate and shark. The list was prepared in 1853 by Louis Agassiz, for Professor Wailes. No less than sixty-five members of the fish tribe were reported by this learned French scientist, and this membership he distributes among twenty-four families. The sawfish sometimes enters the Mississippi, but the shark confines his travels to the waters of the gulf, leaving the gar monarch of the rivers and lakes.

The crustaceans embrace the cuttlefish, horsefoot crab, common crab, fiddler crab, small sandcrab, hermitcrab, stonecrab, seaprawn, rivershrimp, grand and petit crawfish. The oyster of the gulf coast is an excellent bivalve. Compared with the Baltimore and European oyster fisheries the oyster fields of the coast of Mississippi can scarcely be said to be half developed from an industrial standpoint, although the material is there awaiting development.

The feathered tribe is represented by eighty-nine species. The mockingbird or orpheus, thrush, oriole, hummingbird, lark and Carolina parrot are interesting residents. The raptores or carnivorous birds include the bald eagle, turkeybuzzard, crow, hawk and owl. The pelican, gannet, cormorant and loon are representative swimming birds, while the plover, duck, teal and goose, also swimmers, claim sixteen varieties. At the close of the last century the great pigeon roost, on Pigeon Roost creek, in Choctaw county, was abandoned. The tenancy of the woods by the millions of pigeon killed the trees and left the birds to seek a new home. In 1851 and 1852 they returned from Arkansas and Missouri, and reëstablished roosts in the middle counties of the states, but after their flight northward in 1853 did not return in the same numbers.

The palæontology of Mississippi is confined mainly to the remains of marine animals. It is true that on spots first elevated above sea level by the prompt volcanic action, or by the slower process of marling, or by sandbar formations, remains of great animals have been found, but nothing of the greater, the more gigantic animals, which inhabited the older lands of the continent. Bret Harte, in his inimitable verse, says:

> "I will show thee the sinuous track by the slow-moving annelid made,
> Or the trilobite, that farther back, in the old Potsdam sandstone was laid;
> Thou shalt see in his Jurassic tomb the plesiosaurus embalmed,
> In his oölitic prime and his bloom, iguanodon, safe and unharmed."

The poet would undoubtedly fail to keep his promise in Mississippi, for the remains of his animals have never yet been brought to light here. They are ancient, indeed, like Bret himself; interesting like the poet; but they never existed on or in the newer land of this state.

In 1835 a search for remains of the basilosaurus was suggested by the finding of bones in the Ouachita country of Louisiana, but not until 1843 was the search attended with success. At that time, also, part of such remains were taken from the banks of Pearl river, near Long's quarry, eight miles south of Jackson. On measuring the joints of the vertebræ they were found to be twelve inches long and eight inches in diameter. Within the city of Jackson, six miles westward on Ball's prairie, on Jones' prairie, Madison county, and in Scott and Smith counties, remains of the gigantic basilosaurus were found prior to 1854. This animal was about one hundred feet long and partook more of the character of the alligator than of the whale. He was the monster of the waters and, being amphibious, may be called the monster of the land. The name zeuglodon is sometimes given to this animal, but without any warrant beyond the desire of trans-Atlantic scientists to substitute their own pet names for American nomenclature. Remains of the mastodon have been unearthed on bayou Sarah, Wilkinson county; near the old village of Greenville, in Jefferson county; in Adams county, six miles north of Natchez, and in Warren county, near Vicksburg. Pine Ridge, township seven, range three, Adams county, appears to have been the scene of the extinction of the mastodon. From the time lands were first cultivated there, and particularly from 1810 to 1840, the bones of the mastodon have been unearthed in large quantities, and associated with them the bones of other gigantic animals, such as the megalonyx, tapir, bison, and wild horse, have been found. The discoveries suggest, indeed, a battle to the death—an army of mastodons assembled to fight the last fight for supremacy against hordes of the giants of both land and river, lake and ocean. The wild horse must have been exterminated in this fight; for when Columbus discovered the continent the Indians knew nothing of the horse. The buffalo was here when the French came. The invaders looked upon the animal as something to be preserved rather than destroyed, and under authority of Bienville, steps were taken to foster their growth. Before the close of the eighteenth century the small herds were annihilated or scattered and the last of the large animals of the state disappeared—the buffalo which La Harpe heard at Grand gulf, in 1739, live now only in history.

Near the southeastern corner of Clay county, at Plymouth bluffs, remains of marine animals were found in the forties. State geologist B. L. C. Wailes, writing on the palæontology of Mississippi, in 1854, speaks of such discoveries, and credits the micaceous shale and green sand, at the foot of the slope, with the remains of the ammonites, catillus cuveri, the nautilus, bellerophon and bacculitis faujasii, as well as exogera from the upper bluff, which had fallen to the talus and become associated with the first-named remains. Here also the pecten quinque costatus exists. In the vicinity of Aberdeen ammonites, or shells of the nautilus, are found in the form of compact calcareous rock, and other fossils are shown in the prairie rock of this section. The whole country up to Pontotoc and northwards gives evidences of being for some time the margin of the gulf, as the formation is thoroughly indicative of tide banks and, in many places, of sea bottoms. Remains of the gigantic reptile known as the mosasaurus have been found near the surface in the Macon neighborhood, and throughout the cretaceous district of the state the history of a prehistoric age is told by the silent, innocuous remnants of the mollusks and reptile habitants.

In 1848 a description of the fossils of the Vicksburg eocene beds was given by T. A. Conrad. Afterward the beds were explored from the talus of the bluff, above Vicksburg, to St. Peter's fort, on the Yazoo, better known as Hayne's bluff, and additions made to the one hundred and fifty species of tertiary fossils brought to light by Conrad. Other beds, somewhat similar, were discovered in later years on the Big Black river, on Baker's creek and on Pearl river, just below Jackson. Fish fossils are common, and the heads of different species of shark are not wanting. Indeed, on the prairie within the shadow of the state house, silicified shells of the oyster, turbinoba and flabellum were unearthed. Throughout Hinds and Rankin counties the fossils of shell and scale fish are common, and in the quarries around Jackson a thousand evidences of ancient ocean life in Mississippi present themselves to the observer.

The area of petrified wood embraces parts of Claiborne, Hinds and Copiah. Trunks of trees, petrified and asbestic, were discovered near Mississippi Springs and on the Pearl river, near Carthage. In the northern part of Hancock county, about seventeen miles north of the Bolochitto bridge, Mr. Wailes located a petrified tree in 1852, which was a true white porcelain, except at the ends, which were fragmentary and asbestic. In town seven, range one west, Adams county, at White Cliffs, on the Mississippi; on bayou Pierre, in Copiah county, and in the bed of that bayou many petrifactions were visible in 1853–4,

Jeff. Davis.

while on the Scutchaloe hills, in Claiborne, a petrified tree stood in its natural position for over a quarter of a century. The palm tree of the petrifying age appears to be very susceptible of change from wood to rock; so much so that in some instances the whole tree appears to have instantly changed, retaining all its peculiarities of fiber and color in the vegetable state. The petrifying process did not cease in 1854, for in several sections then explored additional stone logs have been discovered, such as at Cooper's springs.

The legends of the Mississippi Indians are palæontological in some respects. They speak of the Nahonlos, a race of cannibals and giants, yet pastoral in their ways, whom they met on crossing the Mississippi. These giants used the mastodon as a beast of burden until the great epidemic, which carried off the Nahonlo tribe and their mastodons simultaneously, leaving only one of the great animals to escape. This mastodon, legends naively assert, made his home on the Tombigbee for years, notwithstanding the thunderbolts of the Great Spirit. By presenting his head to each bolt sent against him he appears to have withstood the attacks of the Indian god; but they were so often repeated the giant animal fled to the Upper Chickasaw bluffs, leaped the Mississippi and turned his invulnerable head to the Rocky mountains.

CHAPTER II.

THE INDIANS, THEIR CESSIONS, FORTRESSES AND WARS.

WHEN the Spanish cavaliers, in 1540, looked in upon the wilderness, now forming the great commonwealth of Mississippi, the Indians then here were of the same race as Ponce de Leon encountered in 1512–14; as Vasquez d'Ayllon met in 1518; as defeated and drove out the wild mariner, Pamphilio de Narvaez in 1527–8. They were nations of the great Appalachian or Mobilian race, spreading its branches westward from the Atlantic to the mountains, and northward from the Gulf of Mexico to the Tennessee and beyond that river. Across the Mississippi were the Dacotahs and sundry small tribes, all moving northwardly from the southwest in the track of the pigeon—all looking toward the southwest as the cradle of their race, where the sun which they worshiped slept at night to prepare for the morrow's journey.

Who occupied the soil when the Indians came hither is a speculative subject. History speaks not of their predecessors in occupation. The careful Spanish historians avoid the subject. The keepers of the temples, the Mingos, the Great Sun himself, could not satisfy the Spanish chroniclers that a people inhabited this land before the Indians came.

The Chickasaw legends tell of a mound on which Chisca built his hut when his people settled here. The first historical mention is found in the narratives of De Soto's expedition by the Spanish writers, cited in this chapter, under date of April, 1541, when the cavaliers first saw the Mississippi, and the same instant the house of the Chisca chief located on an artificial mound. It is conceded that many of the larger Mississippi mounds were here when the Chickasaws first came; but the legends of the tribe leave testimony that the savages did

2

not know whether such mounds were natural or artificial. They were called "navels," the Indians comparing the earth to the human being, the Mississippi being the center of the world to them as the Mediterranean was to the ancients of Europe, Africa and Asia Minor.

From 1512 to 1541 the country from the Atlantic to the Mississippi was explored by men, many of them scholars, who exerted all their powers of mind and body to become masters of the aborigines, of the land and of the minerals beneath the soil. The geologist is found leading the troops toward the gold fields of the Dahlonga of modern days, and, in the far west, to the iron mountains of Missouri; the chronicler is there to give minute descriptions of the new people and the new country, and the theologian is present to discuss questions relating to faith and morals with the high priests of the pagans. Each one had his place on the expedition, and it may be stated, on written testimony, that each one filled his place acceptably; yet there is only historic mention of the mound at Chisca, and legendary mention of that in the interior.

The Natchez occupied the eastern side of the lower Mississippi valley at the beginning of the historic period. The soldiers who served in Peru were not slow to discover an affinity between the children of the southern Incas and the princes of this tribe. They were sanguinary in the extreme; their feast meant the flow of human blood, and their funerals the sacrifice of human life. All this crime found justification in their crude jurisprudence and religious belief. Their government and religion formed a refined barbarism, which required burial mounds to symbolize. Their chief was the Great Sun, who directed the orb of day, and his wife, the Great Female Sun, was the absolute despotic mistress of the nation. On the death of the Great Sun or of a prince, his cabin would be demolished and a mound raised on its location for the cabin of his successor. The Natchez inhumed their dead or placed them in tombs within or near their temples. The body was placed on a cache, and round it was drawn a covering of woven twigs. This network was covered with sticky clay or mud with an opening at the mouth, so that food might be offered to the corpse; when the flesh melted away, the bones were placed in a cane box and deposited in the temple. The dead of the plebeian Natchez were mourned for three days, the dead of royalty for a longer period, and the warrior who fell in battle was accorded a long term of demonstrative lamentation. Like the Choctaws, this tribe had general inhumations and the mounds resulted. Bertram (writing in 1791), referring to the ossuary or bone temple of the Choctaws, states, that so soon as the building is filled with the coffins of the royal chiefs and the bones of those sacrificed to attend them in the other world, a general exhumation takes place; bones, coffins, ashes of sacred fire and debris being taken to some location, piled up and a conical earth mound constructed over all. This grand funeral was generally concluded with the feast of the dead.

Thus mounds multiplied in the Natchez territory, and the fashion extended to the neighboring plebeian tribes of Chickasaws, Choctaws, Cherokees, Muscogees and other nations, not only east of the Mississippi, but also west of the river. They were the mound builders of Mississippi. Here before Columbus discovered a new world, they were also here when the pioneers of civilization traversed the land, and those mute mysterious memories of the past may still be here when a higher race than ours will wonder who we were or whence we came.

The stone fort and Caucasian remains are inexplicable phenomena—historical or rather legendary monstrosities. The stone fort discovered in Tennessee claims an age antedating Columbus, according to local writers, who state, with an air of seriousness, that, at the beginning of this century, a tree three hundred and fifty-seven years old was found growing among the ruins. History does not say who built this fort, nor is there more in history than a general reference to the Celtic and Norse exploration of this continent to warrant the supposition that a Caucasian people found a grave in the Tennessee country. Perhaps, as it is proven that bodies of Indians were washed on the European coast, the crew of a Celtic or Norse galleon may have found a refuge on the coast of America, and, fearing the stormy ocean, determined to live among the entertainers. In the history of the Choctaws reference is made to the white race they expected to find on their settlement east of the Mississippi, and to evidences of a yellow-haired people being here. The fact that remains of such a people were exhumed, and, in one instance, found in a cave in Tennessee, is well substantiated. How such remains could be so well preserved is not so incomprehensible, for the ancients had certainly a better knowledge of the embalmer's art than we have to-day. Ramphilo de Narvaez in 1528 discovered several mummies near Tampa, Fla., and eleven years after De Soto, himself, found Indians enveloped in cloaks, made from feathers or woven from the fiber of wood or bark. On March 20, 1682, De Tonti met the Great Sun of the Tensas tribe, who, as Father Zenobe describes, wore a white robe woven out of the bark of trees.

Stone forts are as rare as they are mysterious. They were built by a people who are unknown to history. The mounds in this state, on the contrary, are numerous, and belong, certainly, to the Indian age, for the Nahonlos, who were found here by the Chickasaws, were agriculturists, not given to war, fair of face, few in number, without defenses and ignorant of neighbors until the trans-Mississippians appears among them. The great ditch extending from a point below Cape Girardeau, Mo., to the headwaters of the White and St. Francis rivers, was excavated in prehistoric days, and was old when Indian legend first refers to it. Whether the object was to use this great canal for purposes of navigation or simply for drainage can never be known. The ancient inhabitants, whether Mobilians or Peruvians, may have known of the rich valley of the Nile, of the artificial ponds or lakes and canals used at one time to regulate its high waters, and resorted to the same plan here for controlling the mighty Mississippi.

Seven miles southwest of the Hatchie and fifty miles east of the Mississippi are three entrenched mounds, the ditches being from ten to thirty feet deep. The Nanewyyah, or Stooping hill, at the head of Pearl river, was a mysterious mound when the Choctaws first entered Mississippi. It is fifty feet high, twenty-five paces square on top and about sixty paces square at the talus. North of this mound may be seen the ditch and circular works. In February, 1722, when De la Harpe ascended the Yazoo, he found that the Caroas and Chocchumas had their cabins on mounds, which they found there. In 1723 De Grave, the commander of Fort St. Peter, described the mounds near the fort, nine miles from the original mouth of the Yazoo. One of the group was about thirty feet in hight. What the object of building mounds at the limestone outcrop of Haynie's bluff might be is one of the many mysteries connected with the mysterious builders. Three miles east of White Cliffs was a large mound, whereon the cabin of the White Apple chiefs had stood for generations. Near Natchez was found a piece of statuary, formed from clay and dried in the sun. The work may have been the result of an Indian artist's leisure hours, or it may have been carried thither.

In the northeastern part of Pontotoc remains of ancient works existed, and it is said that there the gallant De Soto had his fortified camp until April 1, 1541, when he set out for the trans-Mississippi country. Near by is the battlefield of Ackia, where Bienville failed to take the British post in 1736. Early that year Bienville led a force up the Tombigbee to what is now known as Cottongin port, and arrived there on April 20. Barracks were constructed and the troops were quartered there until May 25, when the white, black and red troops set out to attack the British post. During the forties a box of bullets and two petit cannon were taken from the river bed near by. The old Choctaw trail, in use when the Spaniards arrived, from Columbus northwestward to within four miles of the Chickasaw councilhouse (near the present red land known as Chickwahfalla) on Pontotoc ridge, is a reminder of those ancient days. In the old Chickasaw town Old Town, Pontotoc county, near the Boneyard, in the vicinity of Cottongin port or Tolluma-Toxa, a great quantity of human bones was discovered in the twenties, hence the name. Southeast are evidences of the earthworks erected by the troops of Bienville and Vaudreuil. About nine hundred feet back from the right bank of the Tombigbee was a mound, on which the French erected one of their works in 1736. At Chocchuma, three miles northwest of Starkville and near the waters of Trim Cane creek, in Oktibbeha county, was another ancient fortification, which the Choctaws appropriated on their coming, and around which great numbers of the tribe were cut down. Southwest of this point, in Noxubee county, the battle for possession of the great beaver ponds was fought, by the Creeks and Choctaws, in 1786. Over three hundred men, and an equal number of women and children, were killed of both tribes, and in after years another battle was fought, between the same tribes, near Brooksville. Souvenirs of those terrible days of savage warfare are unearthed from time to time.

On section twenty-five, town seven, range two east, Tippah county, a tributary of King's creek flows out of a cave between two beds of limestone. The rockbeds are connected by a natural bridge, eighteen feet long, forty-five feet beyond the mouth of the cave. Near by was the Mingo's palace, and the locality is to-day known as the King's place. Whether the clay between the limestone bodies was removed by the Indians, or gradually by the action of the stream, can never be learned.

Throughout the state galena nuggets have been brought to light at intervals from the beginnings of Caucasian settlement. Where irregular in form, geology assigns them to the drift age, having been carried down with other bodies. Where regular, as in perfect cubes, they are considered to be Indian importations, interred with their owners and holding their characteristics even after the ashes of such owners became undistinguishable from the soil.

Now look at the aborigines through the eyes of history. The introduction to them by Ponce de Leon is mild, but immediately follows war. When De Soto came we see the Creeks make war on the Uchees, and from this period to the beginning of the nineteenth century the savage was the old, old scalp-taking, sanguinary red devil that our own days point him out to be.

Indian wars in what is now the United States began with Ponce de Leon's second invasion in 1514, continued against d'Ayllon in 1515, against Narvaez in 1528, and against De Soto from May, 1539. The latter brought hither a large force of horse and foot, uniformed in gorgeous dress, armored and thoroughly equipped for war. Even the horses (Arabian steeds) were caparisoned. The great captain was a soldier in Peru, and knowing what the value of display was in South America, expected it would prove equally valuable here. On his arrival at Tampa he is certain of easy conquest. Next morning, June 1, 1539, he experienced the first shock of Indian power, and saw hordes of savages pour down upon his camp, regardless of the pomp and glitter of his army. Changing his policy, he propitiated the chief of the Hirrihiguas, and repaired in a measure the damage done by order of the cruel Narvaez in 1528. Later, he sent messengers of peace to the Muscogee chief, Acuera; but that ancient monarch received them coldly, saying: "I am king in my own land, and will never become the vassal of a mortal like myself. Vile is he who will submit to the yoke of another when he may be free. As for me and my people we choose death—yes! a hundred deaths—before the loss of our liberty and the subjugation of our country. Keep on, robbers and traitors—in Acuera and Appalachee we will treat you as you deserve. Every captive will we quarter and hang up to the highest tree along the road." (Irving's " Conquest of Florida," from Vega.) He executed this threat by instituting a system of guerrilla warfare. Many Spaniards fell, and so exasperated was their commander that he ordered a bloodhound to be let loose on the savages. The dog tore to pieces four Indians, but this had no salutary influence. On the contrary, it incited the savage mind, and Indian scouts were day and night on the lookout for Spanish scalps. Even after De Soto left the Acuera country, Vitachucco, of the Upper Creeks, sent this message to his brothers, who were captives: " Warn them not to enter my lines; for I vow that, valiant as they may be, if they dare to put a foot on my soil, they shall never go out of my land alive; the whole race will I exterminate." (Garcilaso de la Vega.) At the head of the Oconee, however, Patofa's Creek warriors joined him; not as friends, however, but to revenge themselves upon the Uchees and, at the same time, increase the enmity against the Spaniards, as they pretended to be Spanish allies. After De Soto had gone westward, this same band descended upon the Uchees and destroyed their nation at or near Silver Bluffs, S. C. On leaving Cofatchique, De Soto induced the young queen to accompany him westward; but after several days she found a means of escape and returned to her people.

Early in 1540 he is among the Achalaques, or Cherokees, in the neighborhood of the Dahlonega mines of modern times; but his scouts failed to find the rich mineral. Tuscaloosa, or the Black Warrior, was at this time a captive in De Soto's train, and was led as such into the great town of the Mobilians, then known as Mauvila, on the Alabama. This was a fortified town of eighty houses in which De Soto and his principal officers found themselves. The infantry and cavalry camped outside the entrenchments; but the Indian carriers brought the stores within the walls. At daybreak on October 18, 1540, the Indians sought revenge. De Soto escaped, losing five of his immediate attendants. For three hours the Indians kept up a shower of arrows, inflicting heavy loss on the invaders; but Moscoso, the camp master, had now arrived and an assault was ordered. The armored cavalry were dismounted and sent against the gate; they tore it down, and cutting their way through a sea of Indian humanity, made way for the infantry. The Spaniards reached the square; from the roofs of eighty houses the Indians sent showers of missiles, and to avoid this danger, the private troops fired the town. The battle had then raged for eight hours, but the god of fire was now to close it. The flames leaped around the warriors, and they were driven to close with their enemies. They fell by hundreds; none would surrender. The ruins of Mauvila, the dead bodies of twenty-five hundred Creeks, Choctaws and Chickasaws, with that of Tuscaloosa in the front, told that the first great stronghold of the tribes had fallen. De Soto lost eighty-two men and forty-two horses, including those lost in the opening three hours' engagement that morning. His supplies were also destroyed. Unfortunate De Soto! Blind to his dangers, only anxious to hold his men together, he led them farther away from the coast into the wilderness, only to meet death. At the Tombigbee crossing the Indians were assembled to oppose his progress, and a messenger sent to them was killed before the eyes of the army. Boats were built at once, and in two days the troops were west of the Tombigbee, and on December 18, 1540, entered a Chickasaw village of two hundred wigwams. It was, of course, abandoned by the owners, and, being an eligible winter position, he determined to make it a winter home. In February, 1541, the Chickasaws made a night attack on this post, fired the buildings and burned fifty horses and a large drove of swine. Within three days a new camp was established a league distant and named Chicacilla, or Little Chickasaw, and here the army remained until April 1, 1541. During this period the uniforms of the soldiers, capari-sons of horses, arms, saddles and shoes were repaired; so that when the troops came in sight of the fortified town of Alabama, they were ready for war, and carried all the defenses with the loss of fifteen men. A large number of Indians were slain. After the battle De Soto led his troops in peace to the Mississippi. Above the river, on a great artificial mound, was the house of the Chisca chief, and against it and into it the Spaniards rushed. They found only women and children, and these they held as hostages until a treaty of friendship would be entered into by their people. Determining to explore beyond the mighty river, and learning of an ancient crossing above, he traveled along the eastern bank for four days, when the army debouched on an open plateau, and there encamped for twenty days to build boats and make other provisions for pushing forward. He crossed the Mississippi above the mouth of the St. Francis river, marched northward for five days to the Casque, or Kaskas-kia, country, and unwittingly joined that people in an attack on the Quapaws. After this he moved toward the west, then returned to the Mississippi via the Arkansas river, and selected a site on the eastern bank of the Mississippi for his proposed town, among the Quiqual-tangui (supposed by some to be identical with the Natchez), a tribe of sun worshipers*. They were so hostile De Soto reconsidered his proposition to settle there, and when the Great Sun suggested to him to dry up the Mississippi as evidence of his power, if he were really the White Sun, he was convinced that life there would be intolerable. He gave orders to build two vessels for his return trip to Cuba, commissioned Moscoso chief of the army, and died.†

It is generally conceded that the Natchez were the first inhabitants of the district to which the French gave their name in 1699. They were the principals in the southern Indian confederacy at that time with the Tensas, Yazoos, Nahonlos, Coroas, Chocchumas, Tapouches, Chittemaches, Caddos, Natchitoches and smaller tribes residing in or near the lower Mississippi valley. They are not mentioned first by De Soto, owing to the fact that the Chickasaws and Choctaws, who find mention, were encountered by him first. Leaving the centuried legends of the Chickasaws and Choctaws the second place, those of the Muscogee confederacy the third place, and of the Biloxis, Pascagoulas, Tunicas, Offagoulas, Mougal-aches, Otasees, Outayhis and Alibamous the fourth place, let us, first, consider the Natchez. In 1699 they had sixty towns, claimed five thousand warriors and were governed by eight hundred princes or suns. The tribe is not noticed in history prior to the return of De Soto from the upper Arkansas country, when they are mentioned as the Quiqualtangui—a tribe of sunworshippers. On March 20, 1682, the chief of the Coroas entered into a treaty of peace with Robert Cavalier de la Salle. It appears that on March 22, 1682, Sieur de la Salle's party left the Tensas country and that night slept on an island, ten leagues down the river. On the 23d orders were given to Tonti to capture the crew of a canoe and, obeying, he was on the point of overhauling the light craft, when a hundred men appeared on the river

---

* "He attempted to overawe a tribe of Indians, near Natchez, by claiming a supernatural birth, and demanding obedience and tribute." (Bancroft, Vol. I, p. 56. Portuguese Gentleman, C. XXIX, published in 1557; Ternaux Compans, Vol. XX, p. 81.)

† "And presently he named Luys de Moscoso de Aluarado his captaine generall, and presently he was sworne by all that were present and elected for gouvenour. The next day being the 21st of May, 1542, departed out of this life the valorous, virtuous and valiant Captaine Don Fernando de Soto." (Hacluyt's translation of *Portuguese Gentleman of Elvas*, London,1609.) The burial of De Soto, in 1542, is an example of aquatic burial among the savages. His remains were placed in a wooden chest, well ballasted and lowered into the Mississippi. The Indians sometimes used basket-work in which to lower their dead, and in the case of children basket canoes. (United States reports from Spanish papers.) "At last he arrived at the province where the Ouachita, already united with the Red river, enters the Mississippi. The province was called Guachoya." (Bancroft, Vol. I, p. 55; supported by Nutall, Martin and others, denied by McCulloch and Schoolcraft, who place the site of De Soto's death at or near the mouth of the Arkansas.)

bank. La Salle called back Tonti, when the whole French command moved to a point on the opposite bank and camped. Thence Tonti was sent with a message of peace; the savages crossed to the east bank, told where their chief village was, and accompanied la Salle thither three leagues. On March 24, the head man of that tribe returned with la Salle to the French camp and went thence to the chief village of the Natchez, where the Great Sun resided, on the hillside near the river. This visit appears to have also resulted in a treaty of friendship, for Tonti, in describing the village, credits it with three hundred warriors and a people similar, in manners, customs and worship, to the Tensas and Coroas. The missionary fathers, Davion, St. Cosme, le Petit, Zenobe and other scholars of that time, as well as the officers of the expeditions of 1682 and 1669–70 have left their impressions of the fertile land of the Natchez on record and some of them, such as Pere le Petit, wrote complete descriptions of the head village. The latter believed that this was the only tribe that had a regular form of worship. Their temple was one hundred feet in circumference, built in the form of a back of a tortoise, with one small door as the only entrance and exit. Within it burned the perpetual fire. On the roof were the three wooden eagles, one red, one yellow, and one white; opposite the door was the watchhouse of the keeper of the temple and round this sacred place was the picket wall, each picket capped with the skull of an enemy who fell in battle. The interior of the temple showed shelving on which the funeral baskets, containing the bones of famous warriors and their attendants, rested; the tribal bark burned lowly but surely in the center, and there the orb of day was worshiped. All women, save the mother and sisters of the great chief, were excluded from the temple, and the rank and file of the men could only venture to the door. It was the pagan holy of holies, the home of the sacred fire and honored bones, and the forbidden place which the curious women of those days would give up life to explore. The morning sun was their God, and the Great Sun of the tribe was next in popular esteem. Like the captain of an ocean steamer, this Great Sun, with all his attendants, repaired to a mound to welcome the shining god and hold converse with him. The moment the great planet was full above the horizon his mundane namesake made his obeisance and began a crooning hymn, which was generally closed with an order to the planet to continue its westward course. In Claiborne's History of Mississippi, a quotation from Perricault's reminiscences is given to convey an idea of the Natchez queen, who died in 1703, shortly after his settlement there. "She was known as the Great Female Sun in her own right," says Perricault. Her husband, a plebeian chief, was strangled by their eldest son, so that he might be the slave of this ancient She in heaven as he was in the Natchez district. Other preparations for her funeral and journey were not overlooked. Her household goods, ornaments and dress were cast out of the cabin and placed on the high bench where the bodies of herself and husband were hitherto placed. Then the bodies of twelve children, murdered for this special occasion, were arranged on this bier and the initial ceremonies were finished. The more barbaric scenes were yet to be presented. That eldest son, now the Great Sun himself, had adequate powers within the royal constitution to sacrifice the whole tribe, were it suggested to him that his deceased mother required their services in the happy hunting grounds. On this occasion, however, her wants in this direction were limited, for fourteen scaffolds only gave notice that fourteen adults would be required to send their spirits with that of their queen. The victims offered themselves as the twelve children were offered by their parents, and the festival or dance of death was commenced in front of the temple. Four days later the grand march of death from before the temple to the queen's cabin was carried out, the parents of the strangled children, carrying their little bodies, participating therein. The adults selected for sacrifice now approached the cabin, the new Great Sun fired the building, the sacrificial party danced round the flames, the parents cast the dead bodies of their children on the ground and danced toward the temple in company with the funeral party and, when the body of the dead queen was placed in the temple, all turned their attention to the fourteen men, who were awaiting the hour of sacrifice. These were undressed, placed on the ground in a sitting posture, a noose round each neck, and relatives placed near each, on the right and left. At a signal the fourteen ropes were pulled, the dead bodies of the fourteen men were stretched upon the benches, the flesh removed from the bones, which were then dried and deposited in baskets under the body of the dead queen.

Bossu, in his natural French narrative, tells in simple language the story of Natchez sacrifice. This author has been too lightly treated by writers on southern history. His style commends him to-day, even as he won from his contemporaries a large measure of praise. In 1771 his narrative was translated, and almost a century after he wrote, his little work was made the foundation of Natchez history by Spanish, British and American writers of English. On it the following description of one of the customs of the Natchez race is based. On the death of the Great Sun his wives and many attendants were sacrificed, so that they might accompany him on the long journey to the mysterious hunting grounds. Natchez law, as already shown, provided that a warrior, not of the blood royal, who married a princess or daughter of the king, should, on her death, be her attendant in the world of the future. When Bossu was at Natchez, in 1724, the opportunity to witness the working of such peculiar laws was presented to him. Elteacteal, a commoner, married a princess, fully cognizant of the penalty. Late in the spring of that year, his wife fell sick, and Elteacteal, chivalrous Indian that he was, jumped into a pirogue and paddled to New Orleans, to seek the protection of Bienville. The latter appointed him his falconer and huntsman, and matters were prosperous for the refugee until the recall of the governor. Shortly after Bienville returned to France, and Elteacteal returned to his people as a visitor. Stung Serpent, a brother of the Great Sun and a relative of Elteacteal's wife, died at that time, and the Great Sun, knowing that Bienville was absent and the refugee in his power, had him arrested and placed in the hut with the others who were to be sacrificed. Stung Serpent's favorite woman was impatient to rush into death so that she could join her husband, saw at a glance the grief of Elteacteal, and, addressing him, said: "Art thou no warrior? Thou cryest; life is dear to thee; it is not good that thou shouldst go along with us; go with the women!" The terrorized Elteacteal acknowledged that life was dear to him, but assured the princess that, should he be spared to walk on earth until the death of the Great Sun, he would die with him. The princess then said: "It is not fit thou shouldst go with us, and that thy heart should remain behind on earth. Get away, and let me see thee no more!" The warrior looked neither to the right nor to the left, but fled. Three old women (two of whom were his relations), all tired of life, came forward to make amends for Elteacteal's cowardice. The hair of the warrior's relations was no more gray than that of women of fifty-five years of age in France, while the third was one hundred and twenty-seven years old, and had hair perfectly white— an uncommon thing; but not one of the trio was very wrinkled. The old woman was slaughtered that evening at the door of the temple, and the other two in the square before the temple. A cord was fastened round each neck with a slip knot, and eight male relatives, four pulling to the north and four pulling to the south, strangled them in an instant. Elteacteal was now absolved from all punishment for his crime of fearing death, but did not make such freedom with his brother Indians as was his wont. Instead, he studied the tricks of the French traders and soldiers, learned the Japanese and Chinese tricks of jugglery, and then returned to associate with the Natchez, and to cheat them as well as amuse them. The morning after the execution of the three old women, the favorite wife of Stung Serpent, the second favorite wife, the chancellor, the physician, his principal servant and a few old women were led from the hut of the dead Sun to the place of sacrifice. The favorite wife walked thence to the presence of the Great Sun, with whom were Frenchmen, and gave orders for all her children to assemble. The order was obeyed instantly, and, addressing them, she said:

"Children, this is the day on which I am to tear myself from your arms, and to follow your father's steps, who waits for me in the country of the spirits. If I were to yield to your tears I would injure in my love and fail in my duty. I have done enough for you by bearing you next to my heart, and by suckling you with my breasts. You that are descended of his blood and fed by my milk, ought you to shed tears? Rejoice, rather, that you are Suns and warriors; you are bound to give examples of firmness and valor to the whole nation; go, my children. I have provided for all your wants by procuring you friends; my friends and those of your father are yours, too. I leave you amidst them; they are the French; they are tenderhearted and generous. Make yourselves worthy of their esteem by not degenerating from your race. Always act openly with them, and never implore them with meanness. And you, Frenchmen; I recommend my orphan children to you. They will know no other fathers than you; you ought to protect them."

The Caucasians called the woman the "haughty lady." She was a majestic Indian matron, and never condescended to speak with others than the princes of her race, or the leading officers of the French. She was also an expert herbalist, and when army physicians failed in relieving sick soldiers or traders, the "haughty lady" always succeeded. Naturally the French regretted her determination to die, and showed this regret so unmistakably that she addressed them thus:

"I die without fear. Grief does not embitter my last hours. I recommend my children to you. Whenever you see them, noble Frenchmen, remember that you have loved their father, and that he was, till death, a true and sincere friend of your nation, whom he loved more than himself. The Disposer of Life has been pleased to call him, and I shall soon go and join him. I shall tell him that I have seen your hearts moved at the sight of his corpse. Do not be grieved; we shall be longer friends in the country of the spirits than here, because we do not die there again."

The sacrifice followed. Pills of tobacco were given the victims to make them giddy. After they were strangled, the body of the favorite wife was placed on a mat on the right, and that of the second wife on the left of the body of the late war minister, preparatory for burial. This second address brought tears to the eyes of the French. The Great Sun himself could not control his grief; for his dead brother, Stung Serpent, was his great war chief, secretary of state and field marshal. He was about killing himself, when the French officers interfered. In fact, he held the barrel of the gun to his heart, and had the heir to the throne put powder in the pan to blow himself up. The tribe trembled; but the French hid the arms of the royal armory, and put water on the powder pan and in the barrel, so that he could not harm himself. When the paroxysm of grief subsided, the would-be suicide, the Great Female Sun and all the Suns were profuse in their thanks for saving the life of the monarch, and the Great Sun promised to walk with them until death.

The Chocchumas formed at one time a part of the Natchez nation, holding the territory of the Yazoo adjoining that of the head tribe. In later years they moved to the Yalobusha country and spread out to the Tallahatchie valley. It is uncertain how many years they resided on their new grounds before venturing into the country of the Chickasaws. A spark was only required to set on fire the jealousy of the western Goths and Vandals against this division of the Natchez nation,and this spark the Chocchumas themselves supplied. They entered the Tombigbee valley without ceremony, as the men of Chicsa and Chactas did in former years, and there began the hunt, which ended in war with the immigrants of the Chickasaw and Choctaw tribes. Above Alva, on the head of Bogue creek, where their Sun, Chulohoma, the Red Fox, presided, the attack was made. The Chocchumas fell back to the ancient mounds at Lyons bluff in Oktibbeha, where they erected an entrenched camp and awaited the assault of the combined forces of Chickasaws and Choctaws. The works were circumvallated and the siege began. Day after day the Chocchumas saw their forces reduced and their leading warriors fall; but the fight still went on until the last warrior fell, and even after the Amazons of this ancient people carried on the unequal contest until death claimed them. A few noncombatant women and children escaped to tell of the destruction of the tribe. The Tensas of Louisiana were the trans-Mississippi cousins of the Chocchumas, and like them a part of the Natchez nation. Their customs were similar, and hence their written history in this particular is similar. La Salle, Tonti, Iberville, Charlevoix and Davion have written of them, and Perricault, *lui-meme*, the favorite of Frenchman and savage alike, gives a pen picture of them as seen by Iberville's party in February, 1700. On February 13, that year, the French left Natchez and proceeded up the river, in the shadow of the high banks, twelve leagues to the whirlpool, called Petit gulf, and eight leagues beyond, to Grand gulf. The object of the expedition was a visit to the Tensas, who resided four miles back from the river, and their object was attained April 16, 1700. Immediately after the arrival of the French a terrific storm sprang up; the fire-temple of the tribe was struck by electricity, and the structure, with its wealth of bones and idols, was reduced to ashes. The savage people, in a spiritual frenzy, wrung their hands, screamed, tore their hair and acted like the contortionists of old, but these active appeals to their god did not calm the elements, and human sacrifice was resorted to. Blackening their bodies and faces, parents caught up their children, and strangling the babies, cast the bodies into the flames. Seventeen children were thus sacrificed, and Perricault tells that two hundred children would have been offered up to appease the fury of the storm-god had not Iberville interposed and protected the little ones.

Following the establishment of a trading post at Natchez in 1715, by de Ursins, an employe of Crozat, the Natchez reveled in the murder of whites. In April, 1716, Bienville pushed up the river with the intention of sending information to the people of Illinois of the condition of affairs. Arriving in bayou Tunica, Father Davion informed him of the untrustworthy character of the Tunicas, who had then ceased to be allies of the Choctaws. Acting on this information, he, with his force of thirty-four infantry and fifteen marines under Richebourg, camped on an island, constructed a high *chevaux de frise*, and sent off a courier to Illinois with instructions to travel through the Natchez waters only at night. On April 24, 1716, a force of Natchez sailed toward the island, and, landing, offered the peace pipe. Bienville told them that his troops could only smoke with them, as he could only smoke with the Great Sun *lui-meme*. Some days later the Great Sun's fleet hove in sight, and as it approached, eight of the tallest warriors, standing erect, sang the hymn of peace. Immediately the Great Sun, the Little Sun and Angry Serpent, three principal chiefs, disembarked and were led within the pickets and bound. Bienville told them that all Indians guilty of the murders of the last year should be surrendered or they would have to forfeit their lives. Next day Little Sun was sent under guard toward Natchez, and in less than a week returned with the heads of two chiefs and that of the innocent brother of the guilty White Earth; but Bienville was determined to have White Earth. After him the high priest of the tribe was sent, but the wily White Earth, hearing of all this, fled to Canada. Four of the guilty chiefs were executed, and the Great Sun agreeing to get out timber and supply labor for the construction of the fort at Natchez, settled this affair, and on August 2, 1716, Bienville took possession of the fort, the event being celebrated by a dancing party of six hundred warriors and three hundred squaws.

Following the Natchez massacre of 1729, many murders were committed by that tribe, and their allies. About the last day of November, 1729, the Yazoos and Caroas arrived at Natchez and found the feast of blood still going on. The Natchez gave them a share of the stores and enjoined them to destroy Fort St. Peter on the Yazoo. On December 11 they saw Pere Souel proceeding toward his hut and shot him. On going to the hut they met with opposition from the priest's negro servant, but he too fell. On December 12 the attack on Fort St. Peter was made. Lieut. des Roches, who commanded during the absence of de Corderi at Natchez, was ignorant of the insurrection, and was the first to fall. All the men were killed, the women bearing child were torn open and young children strangled, while girls, boys and negroes were saved for servitude. This did not satiate the Indian thirst for blood. On January 1, 1730, Pere Doutreleau, of the Illinois missions, arrived at the mouth of the Yazoo, and at once made preparations for offering up the mass. Some Indians meantime approached and gave signs of friendship; but as the priest was repeating the *Kyrie Elieson* the savages fired, wounding him and killing one of his men. Thinking that his hour had come he knelt for their attack; but they stood aloof and fired again. The priest then leaped into the water and reached a boat where two of his men were, but as he looked toward the Indians he received a charge of shot in his mouth, without injury. They fled from that place, passed Natchez, where they saw the ruins smoking, and arrived safely at the Tunica post, still occupied by the French.

In 1722–5 the Natchez murdered some settlers on St. Catherine's creek, and the troops under Bienville were sent against them. He burned their villages and shot them down at sight, until their chiefs asked for peace. A condition of granting this request was the surrender of their most guilty prince. It was agreed to, the prince surrendered, was executed, and a short term of peace insured.

The great massacre of the settlers in the Natchez district, by the Natchez Indians, took place November 28, 1729. For three years this tribe viewed, with ill-concealed jealousy, the advances of the French. While fearing their superior power, the Indians often urged this jealousy to the murder point and, in too many instances, followed their bloody inclinations. In 1716 it became necessary to subject and punish them, and afterward, at short periods, salutary lessons had to be taught to them at the muzzle of the musket or point of the bayonet. The rule of the French was so genial, however, that the wise men of the tribes hesitated when measures of opposition were proposed, and often prevailed upon the great majority of their warriors to sheathe the scalping knife and cast down the tomahawk; but their human nature was ultimately driven to assert itself, notwithstanding the solemn advice given by the great Stung Serpent and his queen in 1724. One Chopart, or Chepart, was commissioned commandant at Natchez in 1727 by Perier, not on account of his ability to fill that office, but rather through the influence of friends, urged on by the aristocrat himself. His appointment was the most grave of the many errors made by the French in the science of government— it brought with it just retribution. Immediately after Chopart was installed, and contrary to all precedent in the French colonial service, he dwindled down to the condition of a drunken, lascivious brute, called the Natchez princes dogs, and claimed their fields as his. Indeed he ordered them to evacuate their principal villages and surrender their corn fields while the grain was yet young. He drove them away from their ripening crops and appropriated the grain.   This was the only act wanting to abolish the control of the princes and open the war path to the hot-headed younger men of the Natchez and their allies, including the unnatural Chickasaws.   British money, in the hands of skilled agents, was not wanting to oil the wheels of discord, and thus two hundred and fifty innocent settlers were given up to the Indian murderers, and in time the murderers themselves fell before the avengers. This damnable business destroyed the fair beginnings of industrial Mississippi, and wiped out the royal tribe of Natchez — descendants of the first human occupants of Mississippi soil.

Early in November, 1729, Chopart's tyranny brought the Indian conspirators together. To the Chickasaws and Choctaws diplomatic agents were sent to win them to the Natchez cause, and to each ambassador two quivers of twenty arrows each were given.   In case of the tribe agreeing to enter the alliance, a quiver was to be left with the great chief, minus an arrow for each day occupied by the diplomats in negotiations: the Great Sun kept a corresponding quiver in the temple at Natchez.   The morning of the 20th day, when the last arrow was taken from the quiver, the assault on all the French settlements would begin, it being understood that each warrior would be in his place.   At Natchez the high priest of the temple attended to the matutinal drawing — consigning an arrow to the fire each morning; but there was treachery within the tribe which set the caution of the high priest at naught. As has hitherto been stated, only the Great Sun and the wife and daughters of the royal house could enter the fire temple.   At this time Stelona was the senior princess.   Like the fair traitor of Michigan in Pontiac's time, she, too, had a white lover in the person of Lieut. de Mace, and to save him from the impending doom, was willing to give away the secret of her tribe, and see her father, chief White Apple, perish with her people.   She informed de Mace of the project of the Indians, and he, as in duty bound, informed the drunken Chopart.   The latter declared the information false, and ordered the lieutenant under arrest. Stelona now made an effort to save her pale-faced friends by other means, suggested by her natural cunning.   She supposed that by precipitating the onslaught, before the arrival of the allies, the French could hold the post, if not subdue the warriors, and to this end she contrived to steal two arrows from the quiver in the temple, and thus, two days before the appointed time, the high priest announced to the Great Sun that the last arrow was drawn and burned and the morning of action had arrived.   The allies were not present, but the day had come for vengeance.   Dividing into three bodies at sunrise, the right and left divisions went north and south on their murderous journey.   The center entered the post at reveille, roamed round it for three hours, appropriating ammunition, and then entered upon the slaughter.   Chopart, the direct cause of this massacre, was killed like the others, when he should have been spared for an Indian holiday.   Two hundred and fifty Caucasians were cut down.   The commander of Fort St. Peter, a visitor at the post, was among the killed. Pere du Poisson, who offered up the mass early that morning in the absence of the Capuchin rector — Father Philibert — was attending a sick person some distance away, but the next morning, while en route to administer the sacrament, had his head cut off by a chief.   After this wholesale slaughter the Great Sun presided over Thanksgiving — the heads of two hundred and fifty Frenchmen, piled at the foot of his throne, telling plainly what thanks were to be rendered for.   The ship-carpenter of the frigate " Le Marin," M. Perricault, was spared, as the savages appreciated his method of boat-building, and the tailor of the garrison, equally popular, was saved by his art.   Many women, grown children and negroes escaped the massacre through the avarice of the Indians, who looked forward to a large ransom for them; but the fate of de Mace, the effeminate lover of Stelona, is not known.   After the massacre, the Indians feasted on the stores and pillaged the supply fleet which arrived only two days before the great tragedy.

The massacre of Natchez was beneficial, in that it conveyed to the mind of Perier the insecurity of his position and the dire results of bad military and civil appointments. He dispatched Le Seur to the Choctaws to seek their aid, and sent Loubois up the river against the Natchez. On January 24, 1730, the latter sent Capt. Mesplex and five private soldiers to treat with the Natchez about their prisoners, but, as they were landing in front of the town, the savages opened fire, killing three of the little command. The others were captured, but were permitted to make known the object of their visit. Mesplex and one soldier were burned immediately, and the only survivor sent to Loubois to demand of him such little items as two hundred barrels of powder, two hundred barrels balls, two thousand flints, two hundred knives, two hundred hatchets, two hundred muskets, twenty barrels vermilion, five hogsheads brandy, twenty casks of wine, with numbers of plumed hats, laced coats and other articles of dress as well as the body of de Bronton, a former commandant at Natchez, and that of the chief of the Tunicas. The Natchez had then two new forts built, one named Fort de la Valeur and the other Fort de la Farine. They believed their position tenable, and were certain that a French force could make little impression upon their works, but the mysterious leaven of retribution was working, and a power more potent than that of France was already in their towns. On January 27, 1730, the Choctaws fell upon their principal village, rescued fifty-nine women and children, about one hundred and fifty negroes, and sent sixty warriors to the happy hunting grounds. The others fled to their works, and on February 8 saw the French fleet anchored opposite. The same day, Loubois learned of the victory of January 27, and, crossing the river, went into camp with the Choctaws on St. Catherine's creek. On February 9 the Choctaws sought a conference with the Natchez, but during the talk a Choctaw discovered a Natchez who had killed a relative, and at once killed him. This of course ended the talk, and with it the life of one Frenchman who was present. From the 14th to the 23d skirmishing was carried on. The works were assaulted on the 23d, and on the 24th the white women, children and negroes confined in Fort de la Farine were surrendered. On the 25th all the remaining whites and negroes were delivered up by arrangement with the Natchez, and by the morning of the 26th the two forts were abandoned and the last of the Natchez had fled from their country. They were next seen in what is now Catahoula parish (then part of St. Francis' ecclesiastical parish, or Natchitoches), in Louisiana, under the lead of the chief of the Fleur. Perrier tracked them to Sicily island, where the Great Sun, sixty warriors and two hundred and fifty women and children were given up by the refugees, taken to New Orleans and sold as slaves to St. Domingo planters. A number were killed, but in the night, a number of warriors fled toward Natchitoches, where they burned a Frenchwoman in sight of the post. St. Denys, enraged, made a sortie, killed many and drove the remnant to flight, and, as believed there, followed them into the wilderness. The few who fled north or east from Natchez found a home among the Chickasaws and Creeks and lost their identity, so that it may be said a great tribe, centuries old, was crushed under the weight of its crimes within two years from the date of perpetrating the capital crime at Natchez.

In February, 1730, Chevalier de Loubois erected a fort near the site of Fort Rosalie of 1716, and almost on the site of the forts erected in January, 1730, by the Natchez, named by the French Fort de la Farine and Fort de la Valeur. Loubois fort was a heavy redoubt or earthwork, springing from the bluff. This was known to the Americans as Old Fort, and was a noted point on the Mississippi until fort and bluff fell into the river.

When the French located at Natchez they found there a number of Shawanees, held as slaves. Some time before, a band of the Natchez, accompanied by bloody Yazoos and Chitachats, visited a Shawanee village and were hospitably entertained by the villagers. When the dance was at its highest the unprincipled visitors raised the war cry, and, falling on their entertainers, killed the principal chief and his children and carried off the Shawanee princess and her women to their lair at Natchez. It is said that this crime was suggested by three Englishmen, who came to purchase slaves for their Carolina plantations, and did purchase the captive Shawanees.

The Chickasaws and Choctaws, originally one people, came from the trans-Mississippi country, under the two brothers, Chicsa and Chactas. In setting out for the East a great dog and a pole were given to them, the first to be the scout of the expedition, the last to be the mute director of the march. At the close of each day's travel one of the chiefs would place this pole upright in the earth, and that point to which it was inclined by sunrise denoted the course which the tribe would follow during the day. Thus the emigrants made progress; they crossed the first large river in their path and marched far beyond it to a spot which tradition places on the head waters of the Alabama, at or near Huntsville, where the pole was unsettled for several days before it inclined to the northwest. Following this course the tribe arrived at what is to-day known as Chickasaw Old Fields, where the pole stood erect, telling them that here they should rest indefinitely. The great dog, their scout for many leagues, fell into a sinkhole in the Mississippi, whither, so long as they heard him howl, boys would be sent with scalps to feed him. Tradition further states that during the unsettled state of the pole on the Alabama sources, Chactas led his division eastward and entered into friendly relations with the Creeks, meantime holding fraternal relations with the majority of Chicsa's tribe, who moved northwest, but declining repeated invitations to reunite, until circumstances drove Chactas westward, when, with the permission of Chicsa, he selected adjoining territory and established the Chaktar or Choctaw nation, where the Spaniard and Frenchman found it.

Like the immigrants of higher latitudes in 1620, the Chickasaws are found claiming the Nahonlo country and driving out or exterminating that tribe. Within the historic period they gave battle to De Soto's troops, and afterward, down to their departure from the state, they were engaged in predatory warfare, murder, arson and rapine. Had the United States not stepped forward to circumscribe their territory and bind them to peace with their neighbors, there would scarcely be an Indian to remove westward. The massacre of the French settlers in 1720 was perpetrated by the Chickasaws and instigated by British traders. In 1722 the Choctaws burned three Chickasaw towns, and by other means avenged the uncalled-for war against the French. In 1729 they agreed to join the Natchez in that terrible crusade against the whites, and, after the destruction of the Natchez race in 1731–2, those terrible aborigines carried death into many a home and to many a traveler.

Bienville returned in 1734 as governor. He was not content with the punishment inflicted on the Natchez tribe by Perrier and St. Denys, as he conceived it to be his duty to destroy the last of that sanguinary people, who still watched along the rivers and trails for the scalps of the white travelers. To this end he dispatched a messenger to the Chickasaws, demanding the surrender of the refugees. The demand was peremptorily refused and the alternative of war was only open to Bienville. He dispatched Captain Le Blanc, by way of the Mississippi, to Fort Chartres, Ill., with instructions to Commander d'Artaguette, informing him of his plans and asking him to bring his troops down the river into the Tombigbee country by May 10. D'Artaguette, who commanded at Natchez at one time, arrived at the rendezvous on May 9, 1736, coming down Bear creek from the Tennessee.

Meantime Captain de Lusser's company was sent to secure the coöperation of the Choctaws, and having done so, to erect a fort (now Jones' bluff) on the Tombigbee and gather stores for the main army, which left New Orleans March 23, with six hundred whites, five hundred Indians and Captain Simon's negro company, and reached the neighborhood of Jones' Bluff April 20, camping at Cottongin port. On May 4 he reached a landing place within twenty-seven miles of the nearest Chickasaw town. The Illinois troops (forty-eight soldiers, exclusive of the officers and chaplain) encamped within view of the Chickasaws and English from May 9 until May 20, when his troops cried out to charge the enemy or return. He knew that Grand Pre, expected from the West, and Bienville, from New Orleans, were not yet in the field; but the voice of his men was irresistible and he ordered them forward. The first two forts and villages were captured before d'Artaguette fell. At this moment a body of five hundred Chickasaws, led by thirty English officers, attacked the little force in the rear, leaving few to tell of defeat. A boy soldier, named Voisin, led the survivors to the boats and escaped. The wounded commander, with three officers, Father Senac and fourteen private soldiers, were captured alive, and the mirage of the Custer massacre of 1876 was outlined in 1736.

As has been shown, Bienville's large force was only twenty-seven miles away when d'Artaguette's little company was defeated. There were with him twelve hundred Choctaw warriors. Had they the ears of soldiers they could have heard the sounds of battle on the 20th; but superior officers in war times suffer in their senses, the appetite alone being good. On May 24 Bienville moved southwest, and on May 26 arrived before the entrenchments of the Chickasaws. The village was well fortified, several lines of works were manned, and pickets or palisades offered obstructions everywhere. The British flag waved above the principal works, and a number of Britishers were seen moving round within. This was the town of Ackia. The foolish Choctaws urged a battle here contrary to Bienville's notions, and in the afternoon an assault was made. The besiegers could not make an impression on such works, the Choctaws were worse than useless, and after the loss of thirty-two killed and sixty-one wounded, Bienville retired to the mouth of the Yahnubbee creek, where an entrenched camp was constructed. On the 27th the Choctaws set out to take Ackia by storm, but were driven back broken in spirit. Later that day the officers urged Bienville to permit an assault, and yielding, a company from each regiment started on the forlorn hope—Contre Cœur leading. They were repulsed, and some fled. The officers then determined to enter, and forming like an iron ball cut their way through every obstacle, captured three fortified cabins, killed hundreds of Indians and held the fourth cabin until Beauchamp came up to remove the wounded. Deeds of gallantry, uncommon among the bravest, unheard of before, marked the whole assault, and reënforcements might have carried all the works, but Bienville seemed to be in a dream, and the French were defeated May 27, 1736. On the morning of the 28th they beheld the heads of their valiant comrades on the palisades, and on the 29th began the march to Cottongin port, and on June 2 arrived at their works, on Jones' bluff. The river being low, Bienville had to cast his heavy guns into the river and distribute his stores among the Choctaws. D'Artaguette lost his official friends: De Courtigny, De la Gravierre, Langlois, De Boulanger, Levieux, St. Ange and D'Essarts, on the field; himself (wounded), with Dutisme, Vincennes, Lalande, Pere Senac and fourteen soldiers were burned alive eight days later. Bienville lost De Lusser, Contre Cœur, De Juzan and many junior officers in that terrible forlorn hope; but the sergeant Regnisse, in his rescue of Grondel, won enough fame for the French arms to compensate for the defeat. Nothing but the fear of the desertion of the Choctaws held back the troops from another assault. Bienville opposed the cry of "Death or Victory."

When the British and Chickasaws learned of the defeat of Bienville, the prisoners of de Artaguette's command were led out to death. They would have been sacrificed before, had not Indian cunning held them to obtain terms from Bienville, in the event of his victory. Now they had nothing to expect from the French except annihilation, and on May 30 the priest, the officers and thirteen soldiers were pinioned to the earth, the fagots heaped round them and the feast of death inaugurated. The fires were kept low so as to insure a long feast. The Indians and their allies reveled in the terrible agonies of their victims, until one by one they became unconscious of pain and died singing the Miserere. Father Senac, eloquent in his martyrdom, gave his spirit to his countrymen and was the last to give up the soul. The one soldier reserved to tell the terrible tale to his comrades brought the news to the settlements, whence it spread throughout the civilized world.

The war of 1739 appears to have been undertaken with the object of subduing the Chickasaws rather than annihilating them. Preparations were made in 1738. In 1739 M. de. Noailles d'Aine, commanding artillery and engineers, arrived, bringing with him instructions from the minister of war to carry on operations from the Mississippi. On June 8, 1739, the ascent of the great river was commenced, and on the 14th the eleven transports arrived at New Orleans with the commands of Tremigon, Gouyon, Du Theafant, Frederre, Vileon Pepiret and Poulcurrie. On July 25 the expedition set out under Lieutenant de Vieuchatel from New Orleans in eleven transports. This haste was necessary, owing to the fact that news was brought in of the continued murder of travelers by the Chacchoumas and remnants of the Natchez, and that the heat and water at New Orleans proved a more dangerous enemy than even the Chickasaws. On August 8 nine transports under Captain de Belugard and one under Lieutenant Chaouas left the fort, and September 2, nine transports and the great canoe of De Noailles left for Fort Assumption, at the mouth of St. Francis river. On November 10 the commands were all at Fort Assumption and on the 11th one hundred and ninety French-Canadians and three hundred northern Indians, under De Longueuil, arrived from Canada, but not until November 24 was the arrival of the Illinois men reported. On that date De la Buissonniere, with forty white men and one hundred and seventeen Indians, saluted the new fort, and simultaneously came in some scouts with the scalp, ears and tongue of a Chickasaw, and live Chickasaw man and woman, and from this day to the beginning of January, 1740, Chickasaws and other Indians were brought in daily and many skirmishes reported. On January 6 De Celeron, commanding a large party of troops and Indians, left to search out the Natchez, and on March 20 returned, after Bienville declared the expedition a failure, with three Chickasaw chiefs and three Englishmen. The latter were suspected of instigating the murders and were cast into dungeons. Natchez and sundry malcontents were given up and a peculiar treaty of friendship negotiated.

The expedition of 1754 against the Chickasaws was, in its beginnings, similar to that of 1736. The same route up the Tombigbee was followed and the same forts used. Vaudreuil sent seven hundred white and twelve hundred Indian troops against the savages. He found them in strong positions, and here varied from Bienville's course by not allowing the Choctaw's to drive him into a battle where the odds were all on the enemy's side. He destroyed their unfortified towns, laid waste their fields, and then retired, leaving the Chickasaws the prospect of starvation.

When Ronan entered their country in 1771, he found them congregated in a long town divided into seven villages. Those villages were named Ashwecbooma or red grass (a fortified town), Tuckahaw (weed town), Chuckallesee (great town), Hickaha (stand still), Chickafalaya (long town), Challetan (copper town) and Meletan (the hat and feather town).

S. S. Prentiss.

The Battle creek massacre occurred in Robertson county, Tenn., some time before the surrender of Cornwallis to the Americans and as a part of the campaign plan of that British general. The Chickasaws were the terrible leaders in this affair which brought death in such hideous shape to the wives and children of revolutionary heroes.

A treaty of friendship was entered into by the Chickasaws and La Salle in 1682, where Memphis, Tenn., now stands and Fort Prud'homme was at once erected on Chickasaw bluff. The treaty of June, 1784, between Spain and the Creeks, Choctaws and Chickasaws, was made at Pensacola. Not only did the savages cede their lands but also acknowledged themselves subject to the Spanish crown, and in this cession and allegiance the Seminoles and all the tribes of the Muscogee confederacy acquiesced.

The treaty of Hopewell, concluded January 10, 1786, between the commissioners named in the Choctaw treaty of January 3, and Piomingo, head warrior and first minister of the Chickasaw nation, Mingatushka, a leading chief, and Latopoia, first beloved man of the Chickasaws, had the same provisions as that with the Choctaws—the boundaries of the great reservation being different. These boundaries extended from the ridge between the Cumberland and Tennessee rivers, at a point running northeast to strike the Tennessee river at the mouth of Duck river, thence westward on ridge to the Ohio river, down that river and the Mississippi to the Choctaw line or Natchez district, and eastwardly along that line to the lands of the Chickasaws as known in 1782. Thence the said boundary eastwardly were lands allotted to the Choctaws and Cherokees to live and hunt on, and the lands then in possession of the Creeks, except a circle five miles in diameter, at the mouth of the Ocochappo, reserved for a United States trading post.

On October 24, 1801, the Mingo and warriors of the Chickasaws agreed to the opening of a wagon road through their lands from the settlements in Mero district, Tenn., to Natchez. For this privilege they were granted $700. Samuel Mitchell was then agent, and Malcom McGee interpreter to this nation. The treaty of July 23, 1805, was agreed to by the Chickasaws, owing to the heavy debts under which they were laboring. They ceded all their country from the Ohio, at the old Indian boundary, along the left bank down to the mouth of the Tennessee, thence up the Tennessee to Duck river, along Duck river to the Columbian road from Nashville to Natchez, thence along the ridge between Duck and Buffalo rivers, eastwardly to the great ridge between the Buffalo and Tennessee rivers, thence, in a direct line, to the Great Tennessee near the Chickasaw Old Fields or eastern point of the Chickasaw claim on that river, thence northwardly to the divide between the Tennessee and Cumberland, so as to include all the waters running into Elk river, and along that ridge to the point of beginning. A tract of six hundred and forty acres was reserved for Chief O'Koy or Tishumastubbee below the mouth of Duck river on the Tennessee. The United States granted $20,000 for the payment of debts due merchants and traders, $1,000 to O'Koy and $1,000 to Colbert at the request of the national council, and $100 annually to Chinubbee Mingo, king of the nation.

In December, 1816, the Chickasaws relinquished their title to all lands north of the Tennessee, and all their claims to lands south of that river and east of a line commencing at the mouth of Caney creek, running up to its source, thence south to Gaines' road, westward on that road to Cottongin port on the Tombigbee, and down the Tombigbee to the Choctaw boundary. The consideration was a cash payment of $4,500, and $12,000 per year for ten years. Several tracts were reserved north of the Tennessee for George Colbert, Appasan Tubby and John McCleish, while two tracts of forty acres each were reserved on the south side of the Tennessee, two and one-half miles below Cottongin port on the Tombigbee, for

3

the use of Maj. Levi Colbert and heirs.   Gen. William Colbert was allowed an annuity of $100 for life, while a present of $150 cash was made to each of the following named: Chinnubby, king of the Chickasaws; Tishshominco, William McGilvery, Arpasarshtubby, Samuel Seely, James Brown, Levi Colbert, Ickaryyoucullaha, George Pettygrove, Immartarharmicko (all Chickasaw chiefs) and interpreter Malcolm McGee; and $100 each to Maj. William Glover, Col. George Colbert, Captain Rabbitt, Hoparyeahoummar, Immoukelourshsharhoparyea, Hoparyea, Houllartiv, Tushkevhopoyyea, Hoparyeahoummar Junior, James Colbert, Coweamarthlav and Iilnachouwarhopoyyea, all military leaders, in consideration of their conciliatory disposition, and as a mark of friendship by the president.

The treaty of October 19, 1818, made at Old Town, between the Chickasaws and the United States, refers to the cession of Chickasaw lands between the Tennessee, Ohio and Mississippi rivers, north of latitude thirty-five degrees, or the north line of this state.   The Chickasaw treaty of October 20, 1832, was negotiated at the council house on Pontotoc creek.   They ceded all their lands east of the Mississippi, and agreed to receive in lieu of same the net sum accruing from sales of such land by the United States.   This treaty also provided for giving their old queen, Puccaula, the sum of $50 annually during her life.   In the treaty of Franklin, Tenn., partly negotiated in August, 1830, the Chickasaws claimed all the land from the mouth of Oktibeeha creek, up that stream to a point near Walls, on the old Natchez road, thence with the Choctaw boundary and along it westwardly through the Tunica Old Fields to a point on the Mississippi river, twenty-eight miles by water below a point opposite the mouth of the St. Francis.   In 1832 the Choctaws disputed this boundary, and old men from each tribe were called in to assist the surveyors then engaged in running the survey lines.   On May 24, 1834, articles of convention and agreement point out that the Chickasaws are about abandoning their old homes.   Ishtahotapa was then king; Levi, George and Martin Colbert, Isaac Alberson, Henry Love and Benjamin Love, trusted councilors.   A number of articles in the treaty of Pontotoc creek were changed to suit the tribe, and were agreed to by the president.

Samuel Mitchell, who was the first United States agent to the Chickasaws, was unsuccessful in his suit for the heart of Peggy Allen, the daughter of James Allen, a white lawyer, and Susie, the half-breed daughter of the half-breed, General Colbert.   Mitchell, failing to win the girl's love, appealed to the squaw of General Colbert for her aid, and the old Indian woman reversed Peggy's decision, and giving the girl a number of pack horses and ten negro slaves as a marriage present, sent her to Mitchell.   She stayed two weeks with him, when one Simon Burney, of Natchez, arrived, and she went away with him.   William Mizell was an interpreter here, and a number of squawmen of Mitchell's character found a home among the savages.   Even Captain Merriweather Lewis, celebrated as the leader of the Lewis and Clarke expedition to the Rocky mountains, fell equally low, and died by his own hand in a Choctaw half-breed's house while en route from Natchez to Washington, D. C.

William Cocke was appointed agent for the Chickasaws some time after the War of 1812, and made his headquarters at Athens, Monroe county.   The half-breeds, such as the Folsoms and La Fleurs, were allies of the agents for revenue only, and had much to say in the government of Chickasaws, Choctaws, Cherokees and Creeks by agents.   Treaty after treaty was rushed through, regardless of principle, and in a few years the Chickasaws are crossing the Mississippi in bands, and ultimately in large bodies.   Samuel Dale was also an instrument in their removal, and when the red men did not move fast enough toward the horizon, such men as General Armstrong, accompanied by subsidized chiefs from beyond the river, were sent among them to represent the glories of Arkansas and win them to the new hunting grounds.

Under Jackson's administration the greater number of the Chickasaws were transferred to Arkansas and ultimately to the Indian Territory.

The Choctaws, as has been shown, came eastward with their brothers, the Chickasaws. Before leaving for the East they were impressed with the idea of meeting a white people, and warned to guard against their intrigues. Their traditions, however, only speak of the Nahonlos, a race of giants; so that what they heard of the white race must have been carried down from Algonquin sources, whose traditions point out the extermination of such a race in the uplands of the territory now known as Kentucky and Ohio. Indeed, in 1815, the remains of a female, her yellow hair and her silver wristlet, with letters after the Greek style engraved thereon, were unearthed near Carthage, Tenn., on the Cumberland river. Four years before, the remains of a man and woman were found in a cave, twenty miles from McMinnville, Tenn. The bodies were in neatly woven cane baskets, entire and dry. A dressed deer skin enclosed the body of the female, and outside this was a cloak made from strings of bark and feathers. The hair of both was perfect, that of the female being yellow and fine.

The Choctaws and Chickasaws were allies for many years, in fact until the advent of the French. They fought the Chocchumas in Oktibbeha county and annihilated that tribe, and afterward defied the power of the Muscogee confederacy, the Creeks and Cherokees. Captain Ronan, of the British forces, visited them in 1771 and found seventy villages in the two districts—the eastern district of Oypatascoola, or small district, and the western, Oscoolafaylaya. While diplomatic in their relations with the British, their hearts were with the French, and had it not been for the defection of Red Shoes and his band of marauders, it could be written that the Choctaw never raised a tomahawk to oppose the French.

The Beaver Pond war, referred to in other pages, originated in the claim of discovery put forward by the Creeks against the territorial claim of the Choctaws to the beaver meadows and dam on the Noxubee, five miles west of Cooksville. The chiefs considered the question in a friendly manner, and agreed to leave the decision to the fortunes of La Crosse. During the following few weeks the commissariats of the tribes were busy in gathering provisions for the assembly, and the chiefs of Creeks and Choctaws passed the time in the exchange of courtesies. The day for the opening of the games came at last. La Crosse as now played was not then known, but a form of it. Wickets were at each end of the grounds, and in front of each wicket the champions of each tribe stood with their bats. At a signal the contestants ran to the central point, laid the bats down in a row, and constituted the place a bettinghouse. When clothes, ponies, trinkets, daughters, sisters, sons and brothers were all put up, the game was called, the players took up their bats and retired some distance, while the ballholder pitched the ball into the air. One hundred athletes, with basket-topped bats high above their heads, rushed toward the point where it would fall and a hundred men were in earnest contest. It was the player's part to cast the ball in the direction of his own wicket, so that one of his friends could have better play-room and send it through the air in the direction of his opponents' wicket, through which it must go before the inning is lost or won. Thirteen innings constituted the game, and where the players were well matched, days might pass before the last inning was won. Umpires were not chosen from the plebeian crowd; the chiefs alone should act as such, and their decision was never questioned. On this occasion Creek and Choctaw won alternate wickets, and the last inning was called. Both sides prepared for the terrible trial of skill—the rush for the ball followed, then the wild stampede, and as the sun set, the wild cry of the Creeks proclaimed their victory. A Choctaw brave, enraged at the taunts of a young Creek, tomahawked him, and the friendly contest became a mortal combat. They fought throughout the night, and when the chiefs or mingoes gained control of their people by sunrise, one-fifth of the five thousand who were present during the play were killed or wounded. The dead were buried and a treaty of peace patched up, which was observed for some years, until a similar game was played in town sixteen, range nineteen, Noxubee, which resulted disastrously for the Choctaws.

In 1706 the Chickasaws made a descent on the Choctaw villages, carried off a number of families and sold them as slaves to the English traders, who in turn sold them to farmers in the Carolinas. This resulted in desultory warfare. It appears that at the time of the capture a large party of Chickasaw warriors were at the French post of Mobile, and before leaving heard of the attack on the Choctaws, and feared the return journey through their country. They asked the popular Bienville for an escort, and he, granting the request, detailed a squad of twenty-five Canadians, under De Boisbriant, to conduct them through the Choctaw territory. The journey up the Tombigbee was pleasant, but once in the Choctaw country the Chickasaw braves appeared ill at ease until halted by the chief of the lower village. Their stoicism now came to their relief. They were in the midst of enemies, and before a chief who considered justice first of all things. He ordered the seventy warriors to be seated, then addressed the French guards, telling them that they were ignorant of the character of the men they were protecting, and next, turning his grim eyes on the Chicka-saws, told them of the crimes of their tribe and pronounced them equally guilty. Casting down his plume, the encircling Choctaws leaped forward, and in an instant seventy toma-hawks were buried in so many Chickasaw skulls, while Boisbriant and his men, who tried to stay the massacre, were wounded. The wounded French were carried to Mobile by three hundred warriors, who waited on them day and night, and by word and deed made atone-ment. Returning, the tribe attacked the Chickasaws, and carried on war against them until 1707, while the Chickasaws, aided by the English, carried their arms sometimes into the Choc-taw country.

Vaudreuil was commissioned governor of Louisiana in 1741. Four years later the troublesome Red Shoes, chief of the Choctaws of the six towns, and a secret ally of the Chickasaws and British, led two or three Choctaw towns away from their old-time allegiance, and must be credited with the murders of that period round Mobile and New Orleans. The French encountered these guerrillas on bayou St. John, killed a great number and scattered the others. A chief of the friendly Choctaws killed his brother chief, who led the Indians against the German settlement, and Red Shoes himself was subsequently punished. It appears that the French Choctaws determined to end his treachery, and a battle ensued, in which one hundred and eighty Red Shoe warriors were placed *hors de combat*. The chief was afterward caught while en route home from Carolina with presents from the British and as chief of convoy for British traders. He was clubbed to death, but the traders' rights were respected. Their acknowledgment was ignoble in the extreme. Instead of appreciating the kindness of the French Choctaws, they distributed their goods among the two discontented Choctaw villages, had the brother of Red Shoes chosen mingo, and urged the Chickasaws to join them in a war of extermination against the French. Their methods coming to the knowledge of the French, Grand Pre, who in 1729 failed to join forces with d'Artaguette, was sent against them and cut down one hundred and thirty warriors. The remainder were granted their liberty after binding themselves to act for ever with the Choctaw tribe against the English and their Indian allies. This contract was observed until 1762, when the French ceded Louisiana to Spain.

In 1777 the Natchez district from Loftus cliffs to the mouth of the Yazoo was purchased from the Choctaws by the British for a trifling sum, supplemented by promises which were never kept. Prior to this, however, treaties of amity and trade were made between this tribe and the French, and the latter were virtually masters of the district as mentioned in the treaty of 1777 above referred to.

The treaty of Hopewell, on the Keowee, was negotiated January 3, 1786, by Benjamin Hawkins, Andrew Pickens and Joseph Martin, United States commissioners, and Yockona-homa, great medal chief of Soonacoha; Yockehoopoie, leading chief of Bugtoogoloo; Mingo-hoopoie, leading chief Hashooqua; Toboco, great medal chief of Congetoo; Pooshemastubie, gorget captain of Senayazo, and thirteen small medal chiefs of the first class and twelve medal and gorget captains, representatives of all the Choctaw nation. The signers, exclusive of the above-named, were Pooshahooma, Tuscoonoohoopie, Shinohemastuby, Yoopakooma, Stoono-koohoopoie, Tehakuhbay, Tuskahoomoch, Yoostenochla, Tootehooma, Toobenohoomock, Cshe-coopoohoomoch, Tushkoheegohba, Teshuhenochloch, Pooshonaltla, Okanconnooba, Autoona-chuba, Pangokooloch, Steabee, Tenetehenna, Tuskementahoch, Tushtalla, Cshuaangchabba and Cunnopoie. The witnesses and interpreters were William Blount, John Woods, Samuel Taylor, Robert Anderson, Benjamin Lawrence, John Pitchlynn and James Cole. This treaty provided for the restoration of white or negro prisoners to liberty, the delivering up of criminals, the punishment of citizens guilty of crimes against the Indians, the restraining of retaliation, the regulation of trade and the burial of the hatchet forever between the people of the United States and the Choctaw nation. This treaty also provided that the Choctaws should claim the lands within the following described boundaries: "Beginning at a point on latitude thirty-one degrees, where the eastern boundary of the Natchez district shall touch the same, thence east on latitude thirty-one degrees (being the southern boundary of the United States), until it shall strike the eastern boundary of the lands on which the said Indians did live and hunt in November, 1782, while they were under the protection of the king of Great Britain; thence northerly along the said eastern boundary to the northern boundary of said lands; thence west on northern boundary to the western boundary and south to place of beginning—three tracts of six square miles each being reserved for trading-posts."

On May 4, 1802, the treaty providing for a wagon road through the Choctaw lands to the lands of the Chickasaws was proclaimed. At this time, also, the old treaty line of the Choctaws and the British, running parallel with the Mississippi, was remarked, and the lands between that line and the Mississippi, from the Yazoo river south to latitude thirty-one degrees, were relinquished by the Indians. The commissioners agreed to remove all settlers, their goods and slaves, westward of this line and to demolish their cabins. The old British treaty line began on the left bank of the Chickasawhay river, ran east to the right bank of the Tombigbee, and terminated at the bluff known as Hacha Tiggeby. This was remarked in 1803, and made the new boundary between the United States and the Choctaw nation in that quarter, and the land included within that line on the north, the Chickasawhay river on the west, the Tombigbee and Mobile rivers on the east and by the United States boundary on the south, was ceded to the United States. Peter Dinsmore was then agent, Peter H. Naisalis and John Long, interpreters. In December, 1803, new boundary lines were adopted, in accord-ance with the convention of Fort Confederation. This line extended from the Spanish line at Hatchee Comesa, or Wax river, to the confluence of Chickasawhay and Buckhatannee rivers, up Buckhatannee to bayou Hooma, or Red creek, to the trail from Mobile town to the Hewanee towns and thence round by the Tombigbee and Mobile rivers to the point of beginning. Rifles, lead, powder, blankets, strouds, etc., were given for this concession.

In 1802 the Choctaw tradinghouse on the Tombigbee river was established, and the first stock of goods was carried thither on keel-boat by Louis La Fleur, via the river to Manshac, thence down the Amite river through lakes Maurepas and Pontchartrain and along the coast to the Tombigbee and up that river to the post, commanded by Lieut. P. P. Schuyler, known as Fort Stoddard. Here Joe Chambers was official trader, one G. S. Gaines, clerk, and John Pitchlyn, interpreter. They were all squawmen, as was Colonel McKee, the United States agent to the Choctaws, who resided at Mount Dexter, now known as Clinton, just west of Jackson. The boomers were then, as now, always present within or on the line of Indian territory, but the ancient boomers were more tractable and more patient, so that when the militia company, under Colonel Burnett, appeared at Rocky Springs, near Yokena, in the fall of 1802, the modest vultures fell back until the surveyors could relocate the old line between the United States district of Natchez (twenty-five hundred square miles) and the Choctaw country. This work was difficult and slow, owing to the Yazoo having deserted its old six-mile estuary for a breach made by the Mississippi, thus destroying many of the old marks made by the British surveyors.

The treaty of October 27, 1805, provided for a mail route from Knoxville, Tenn., to New Orleans, La., through the Cherokee, Creek and Choctaw nations. On June 2, 1806, the treaty by which the Creeks ceded their territory between the Oconee and Ocmulgee was proclaimed.

The Choctaws, by their treaty of November 16, 1805, ceded all their lands lying to the right of the following lines: The intersection of the branch of the Homochitto creek and Choctaw boundary, where McClarey's path from Natchez to Washington crosses that stream; thence eastwardly along this path on the east or left bank of Pearl river to a point near Broken bluff on the Chickasawhay river; thence parallel with the river to the Hiyoowannee town; thence still east four miles; thence in a direct line, nearly parallel with the river, to a line from the lower end of the Broken bluff to Faluktabunnee on the Tombigbee river, four miles from Broken bluff; thence to Faluktabunnee; thence east to the boundary between the Creek and the Choctaw nations on the divide between the Alabama and Tombigbee rivers, and thence southward on this ridge to the southern point of the Choctaw lands. A reservation of two miles square in the town of Fuketcheepoonta, and one of five thousand two hundred and twenty acres on the left bank of the Tombigbee, opposite the lower end of Hatchatigbee bluff (for the use of Alzira and Sophia, daughters of Samuel Mitchell by Molly, a Choctaw woman) were made. In lieu of this territory, the United States gave the nation $50,500, of which sum $48,000 were granted to enable the mingoes to pay their merchants and traders and claims for depredations; $2,000 to John Pitchlynn, compensation for losses. Presents and annuities to the great medal chief were also given, and fifteen hundred acres between the Tombigbee and Jackson's creek, next above Hobukentoopa, recommended to be granted to John McGrew, the claim resting on a grant made to McGrew many years before by Opiomingo, Hesnitta and others.

The treaty of October 24, 1816, made at the Choctaw trading post, ceded all the Choctaw lands lying east of the following lines: The mouth of Oktibbeha creek, the Chickasaw boundary; thence down the Tombigbee to the northern boundary of the lands ceded by the Choctaws at Mount Dexter, November 16, 1805. To those Indians were paid $10,000 on signing the treaty, and $6,000 per year thereafter for twenty years.

The treaty of Doake's stand, on the Natchez road, was entered into by the Choctaws October 18, 1820. This ceded the lands within the following described boundaries: Beginning on the Choctaw boundary east of Pearl river, south of the White Oak spring, on the Indian path; thence north to the spring, northward to a point near Doake's fence; thence to the head of Black creek, or Bouge Loosa; down that creek to a small lake; thence to the Mississippi, a point one mile below the mouth of the Arkansas river; down the Mississippi to the Choctaw line and around and along this line to the point of beginning, east of Pearl river. In consideration for this cession the United States gave the nation lands between the Arkansas, Red river and Canadian fork. (A treaty of the same date is recorded ceding these lands in Arkansas). Mushulatubby, son of the old chief of that name, was then chief of the Lower Towns, and the annual grant of $150, made to his father until death, was revived in the interest of the young chief. The treaty made complete provision against exposure of those Indians to want. Andrew Jackson and Thomas Hinds represented the United States; S. R. Overton was secretary. On September 27, 1830, in the treaty of Dancing Rabbit creek, the Choctaws agreed to cede all their lands east of the Mississippi and remove to their new territory beyond Arkansas in 1831–3. Greenwood La Fleur, Nutackatchie, or Nutucacha, and Mushulatubby were the chiefs at this time, and were present on the Dancing Rabbit creek council grounds known as Chookfahithla. In 1828 a council was called to consider this question, and the tribe was led into it by the Folsoms, La Fleurs and Pitchlyns, half-bloods, against the wishes of the full-blood chiefs, who retired. Some time after, Nutackatchie led the full-bloods toward the old councilhouse, near Folsom's cabin. The half-bloods and their friends, well armed, heard of their coming and marched south to meet them, under David Folsom, but had not gone far until Nutackatchie was seen at the head of his warriors in full war paint. Coming closer, the full-bloods halted, a maneuver followed by the less principled half-breeds. Then Nutackatchie advanced on foot to a point half way between the forces, and there stood like a pillar, looking north. Folsom advanced toward the scowling chief, the hand of friendship was offered and accepted and a battle, which promised annihilation to both sides, set aside, and the Indians were driven into a treaty by friends and enemies alike, which robbed them of their beautiful country. The treaty of Dancing Rabbit creek, carried by very questionable means, ended Choctaw power in Mississippi. Under it large numbers of the tribe went west, and later others were induced to go, but a small band remained in their native land, and their descendants are here to-day.

The American Presbyterian board of missions determined to convert the Choctaws, and in 1818 sent a number of evangelists among them. The preachers were Kingsbury, Gleason, Touse, Cushman and Hooper, who brought their families along; a single man, known as Dr. Pride, and three unmarried women, known as Misses Burnham, Foster and Thatcher. They established themselves in a small cabin in the northwestern corner of what is now Lowndes county, and gave to the location the name Mayhew. Eight years later the evangelist Cushman had charge, and moved headquarters to a place he called Hebron, a few miles northwest of the present town of Starkville. Meantime the evangelists sent out from the concern at Mayhew established one at Elliott on the Yalobusha, and appointed one Captain Smith to the chair of agriculture, under the name of Indian farmer. Smith brought his wife and daughter, who in time became evangelists and took a full part in educating the Indians up to those intellectual hights where the treaty of 1832 found them. Their newly found Christianity may have enabled them to battle with the sorrows and disappointments which followed them beyond the Mississippi, but it did not add anything to the ordinary Indian virtues of indolence and trickery, which grew up with other kindred virtues during their latter days in this state.

In 1824 Chief Pushmattaha, accompanied by his warriors, visited Washington City, and while there learned of the presence of Lafayette. Desiring to see the great Frenchman, he was led to his rooms, where through the aid of interpreters they had a long conversation.

At parting, Pushmattaha said, "We heard of you in our distant villages, we longed to see you, we have come, we have taken you by the hand. For the last time we look on the face of the great warrior whose fathers were the friends of our fathers. We go, it is the last time we shall meet, we shall both soon be in the land of shadows." The chief died a few days later and was buried with military honors in the Congressional cemetery at Washington, D. C. He was invaluable during the Creek war, wore a general's uniform and ranked as one. At Washington he sat on the President's right hand at the banquet, and when dying, Jackson called upon him to know his wishes. The hero of New Orleans had to stoop low to hear the dying warrior's last words, and he, at least, was not surprised at their import—"When I am dead, fire the big guns over me." This wish was literally carried out.

In 1706 the Chickasaws, under the lead of British officials, resorted to some strange military maneuvers to outwit the Choctaws, who were too powerful for them. Sending their women and children into the territory of a friendly pro-British Indian tribe, they deserted their country, and floating down the Mississsippi attempted to annihilate the southern allies of the Choctaw people. They appeared in force in what is now Wilkinson county, but by some means the Tunicas were apprised of their approach and fled to the Houmas nation farther down, leaving nothing for the invaders. The whole affair resulted disastrously for the inoffensive Houmas, for the Tunicas came as friends and remained as enemies. Coveting all Houmas property, as in later years the Caucasian did that of the native, they fell upon their hosts, killed more than half of their warriors and appropriated their goods, women and crops. It was the drama of Macbeth presented on a great scale. Successful for a time, natural retribution fell upon the dishonorable savages; they fled to the swamps of lake Pont-chartrain, where, with downward aspects, like beasts, their descendants may be found to-day suffering from the dishonor of their predecessors. In 1716 Father Davion was among them at bayou Tunica. On the arrival of Captain Richebourg, the priest informed him that they were a most uncertain people and advised the captain not to trust them for even a day.

The Chittemaches were, in fact, more like Chickasaws than the Mobilians. Human life was not considered by them. Pere St. Cosme, who settled at Natchez on his arrival from Canada about 1685, was killed by them at Donaldsonville on the La Fourche. Three Cana-dians who accompanied him were also murdered by them. A day of retribution came. One of the Chittemaches was carried to Mobile, where, in opposition to Bienville's wishes, the soldiers and people executed him by clubbing him to death. Shortly after Bienville proved the enormity of their crimes to the Natchez, Biloxis and Bayougoulas, who proceeded to the La Fourche and annihilated the sanguinary tribe.

The Creeks, like the Cherokees, are only connected with Mississippi through war and associations. When the Chickasaw people first came here a minority of them marched east and resided in the Creek nation for some years, and may have participated with their hosts in destroying the Yamassees of the coast, the Savannas, Oguchees and Santees. They belonged to the Southern or Muscogee confederacy up to the beginning of the Revolution, when the British purchased their friendship and used them effectually against the people they would rule or ruin. The tomahawk, bow and arrow and scalping-knife were their arms until the advent of Tecumseh in 1811, when the whole Muscogee nation assembled at Tooka-batchie to hear the prophet speak in the interest of their former British allies. At this time Tecumseh introduced the war club into the territory of the southern tribes between the Mis-sissippi and the Atlantic. In 1798 there were fifty towns in their nation, including the Appalachicola, or town of peace, and Coweta, the town of executions.

The Shawanee prophet, who was *de facto* superior of General Proctor's division of the

British army in 1813, and who was killed in the battle of the Thames, Canada (1813), when Proctor's forces were scattered by Harrison's Kentucky regiments, came south in October, 1811, to urge the tribes to enter the proposed great Indian confederacy. His address to the Chickasaws failed even as that to the Choctaws did, but he was successful with the Muscogees or Creeks, and arranged with them that so soon as they should hear of his and Proctor's successes in the North, they would fall on the Americans of the South, coerce other tribes and advance over the bodies of the whites. The Creeks, far away from Tecumseh's battle ground, did not learn of his death, and so continued to carry out the plans laid down for their guidance. The bloody massacre at Fort Mimms took place August 30, 1813, and the destruction of the Caucasian people was entered upon. The "Holy Ground," a place near Powell's ferry, on a bluff above the Alabama river in Lowndes county, Ala., was the center of Creek military power, and thither captives, old and young, would be carried to be offered up to the god of war. How many white men, women and children were burned at the stake on this "Holy Ground" can never be known. On December 23, 1813, when the Mississippians and Choctaws captured the place, they found eleven friendly half-breeds ready to be offered up. From this date to the close of the war with England, Mississippi took a full share in avenging the atrocities of the British and Indians, and at Pensacola and New Orleans destroyed the power which instigated murder and rapine.

The Cherokees are connected with Mississippi through warfare and boundary. The Tennessee river originally bore their name. In 1769 they invaded the Chickasaw country, but unsuccessfully, as the natives defeated them at Chickasaw Old Fields with great slaughter. Thirty years before this, the Cherokees opened a road from Augusta to their principal village so that travelers could ride from Savannah into all the Mississippi nations. In 1756 the English king sent Andrew Lewis to construct a stone fort at the head of Tennessee navigation (thirty miles from Knoxville), and to this the title "Fort Loudon" was given. The garrison and settlers soon began to misappropriate Cherokee property, and the Indians retaliated. A guerrilla warfare grew out of these troubles, which brought disaster to the British troops and the settlers. Ten years before the invasion of the Chickasaw nation Governor Lyttleton induced them to enter into a treaty of friendship and peace with the British, and by the same instrument bound them to kill or make prisoner every Frenchman found in their territory. The mass of the people objected to this treaty, the work of six men of their tribe, and construed it so that they could take almost any course they pleased. Early in 1760 fourteen Caucasians were killed within a mile of the fort, and in February of that year Oconostota attempted to surprise the garrison. The British had a number of Indian hostages within their inclosure, and, as a punishment for what they termed Indian treachery, put them to death without ceremony. The Cherokees then determined to carry death to every white settlement and succeeded in too many cases. The British troops sent against them were defeated everywhere, and Fort Loudon capitulated on terms—the garrison to be guarded to Fort Prince George. Oconostota and the Prince of Chota commanded this guard, but after proceeding fifteen miles bid adieu to the British and left them to the tender mercies of the Indians whom they had robbed. Next morning the camp was attacked, many soldiers killed, and several taken with the hope of ransom. This ransom, a heavy one, was ultimately offered and accepted, and the Cherokees may be said to have cast aside war and adopted the art of diplomacy. This change led to the treaties which gradually lessened their territory and closed them in between walls of rapacious Caucasians who drove them out within a few years. During the closing years of the Revolution they and their allies, the Creeks, were liberally subsidized by the British to make war upon the settlers.

The Cherokee treaty made at the Chickasaw councilhouse, and ratified at Turkey town on Coosa river, October 4, 1816, recognized the following boundaries: From Camp Coffee, south of the Tennessee river, opposite Chickasaw island, south to the top of the divide between the waters of the Tennessee and Tombigbee rivers; thence east on ridge, leaving the Black Warrior river to the right, to the west branch of Wells' creek; down the east bank of that creek to the Coosa river, and down that river. All their lands south and west of the line described were ceded by this treaty to the United States, and ratified by Path Killer, The Glass, Sour Mush, Chulioa, Dick Justice, Richard Brown, Bark, The Boot, and Chickasawlua. On July 8, 1817, the Cherokees had settled in Arkansas and ceded all their lands in their old territory of the Tennessee, provision, of course, being made for the lodges who would not move across the Mississippi. Another heavy cession was made February 27, 1819, at Washington, D. C.; but many reservations of six hundred and forty acres were made to Cherokee families who were not enrolled as emigrants. In 1839 the last of the Cherokees removed to the territory.

The Houmas, Bayougoulas and Calapissas were a united people in 1739. The Ouachas and Chaouchas, a small tribe of thirty warriors, resided near Fort les Allemands; while a remnant of the Chittemaches resided above them, and the Tunicas higher up.

In 1766 one Sir William Johnson, a squawman in the employ of the British, estimated the Choctaw nation at nine hundred warriors, and forty-five hundred non-combatants; the Natchez at one hundred warriors, and five hundred non-combatants; the Chickasaws at seven hundred and fifty warriors, and thirty-seven hundred and fifty non-combatants, and the Cherokees at five hundred warriors, and twenty-five hundred non-combatants. The Tunicas played no inconsiderable part in the drama of the early wars and treaties.

The Indians east of the Mississippi in 1825, when their removal first began, numbered one hundred and ten thousand. Of this number, there were west of the Mississippi, in 1836, five hundred and forty-nine Chickasaws, fifteen thousand Choctaws, twenty thousand four hundred and thirty-seven Creeks, seven thousand nine hundred and eleven Cherokees, and other Indians of Florida and the North, making a total of fifty-one thousand three hundred and twenty-seven. There were forty-nine thousand three hundred and sixty-five Indians east of the Mississippi, and two hundred and sixty-one thousand eight hundred and six scattered throughout the Union, or a total of three hundred and two thousand four hundred and ninety-eight.

In 1847 there were eighteen thousand Cherokees, six thousand five hundred Chickasaws, sixteen thousand Choctaws and twenty-two thousand two hundred and seven Creeks, and in 1857 the numbers were: Cherokees, twenty-one thousand seven hundred and nine; Chickasaws, five thousand eight hundred and twenty-two; Choctaws, twenty-two thousand seven hundred and seven, and Creeks, including all remains of the Muscogee confederacy, twenty-seven thousand seven hundred and fifty-seven.

The strength of the tribes in 1867 was as follows: Creeks, twelve thousand two hundred and ninety-four; Cherokees, fourteen thousand; Choctaws, twelve thousand five hundred; Chickasaws, four thousand five hundred. The Cherokee national fund was then $428,500, the school fund, $229,658.72, and the orphan fund on hand, $45,000. The amount of the Chickasaw fund then on hand, $1,052,266; of the Choctaw general fund, $454,000; school fund, $121,000. At the close of the Civil war there were three thousand freedmen (negroes) among the Choctaw and Chickasaws in the "Nation." A treaty made in 1866 provided for their adoption by the tribes, the consideration being $300,000, payable to those tribes when the treaty should be ratified. Up to 1868 the Indians protested against the adoption of the "niggers;" but the Cherokees had adopted their blacks.

In 1890 the Chickasaw tribe comprised thirty-four hundred and sixty-four Indians and thirty-seven hundred and eighteen adopted colored persons, making a total of seven thousand one hundred and eighty-two. The Choctaws numbered ninety-nine hundred and ninety-six Indians and forty-four hundred and one colored; a total of fourteen thousand three hundred and ninety-seven, all incidentally under the Indian office of the United States and self-supporting. The Indians remaining in the state of Mississippi, and taxed or taxable, comprise seven hundred and twenty-seven males and six hundred and seventy-seven females, making a total of fourteen hundred and four, living off reservations.

Chapter III.

EXPLORATION AND SETTLEMENT.

ALL that is geologically known of this state, and much of all that is historically known of her aboriginal inhabitants, have been given in the preceding chapters. In this chapter must be considered the expeditions of the Spaniards, so far as they relate to the intention of establishing colonies; the foundation of French settlements; the attempts to establish British colonies here and their liberal land grants; the failure of such attempts and the successes of the Americans. To accomplish so much, many references must again be made to the Spanish pioneers of civilization in this new world, to the Indians, and to the newer Caucasians who ultimately robbed Spain of her possessions in North Columbia.

The tendency of the Caucasian to follow the sun has been observed in all ages, from the time of the exodus of the Milesians and their settlement in Spain. To-day we see this race look toward the horizon and hear them express a wish to settle there. Only a little while ago we saw a horde of men waiting for a signal to enter Oklahoma, and at evening time to-morrow they will look after the sun, see that orb go down and wish they were where the last ray of his reflected light appears. Strange creatures! Forever they fix their settlements on the horizon—that western place where chance or means may land them.

This tendency to move westward is as natural to the Caucasian as that to move eastward is to the Mongolian. The one follows the sun, the other goes forth to meet him. The two races met on neutral ground early in the sixteenth century—the oldest people of Europe sent their adventurers to meet and conquer the descendants of the oldest people of Asia in the new world. The battle was not confined to Mexico, but extended from the Atlantic to the Pacific, and blood, both white and red, flowed freely from the shores of the Carolinas to those of Mexico.

The attempt to establish a settlement in what is now known as South Carolina was made in 1514, when Ponce de Leon, who visited Florida in 1512, returned to search for the spring which would bring youth back to the aged and make the whole world fair to look upon. The enthusiast lost his life in this wild search, and one Miruelo, a Spanish mariner, took up De Leon's ideas in a more practical form. He knew that the natives of the country of the wonderful spring had both gold and silver, and the fountain of youth failing, he would be

pleased to take the rich mineral.   A company was formed at St. Domingo, with this adventurer president, and this syndicate sent two brigs, under Miruelo's command, to occupy the
country.   The men disembarked in the Chicorean or Uchee country, at the mouth of the
Combahee river (St. Helena), made trades with the savages, and, inducing a number of them
to visit their ships, carried them off.   One vessel returned, and one was lost.   Vasquez
d'Ayllon, then the king's judge at St. Domingo, and a member of the syndicate, sailed for
Spain, received a grant of Chicorea from Charles V., about 1515, and, returning, placed
Miruelo in command of one of three ships as captain, and appointed him pilot of the fleet.
He died, however, before reaching his former anchorage, but d'Ayllon brought the fleet to it
and succeeded in beaching one of the ships at the mouth of the river.   The Indians received
him cordially; but failing to find their kinsmen returned to them, drove the visitors to the
ships and captured some of the armor and arms.   In 1516 the gulf coast was explored; in
1517 the peninsula of Yucatan was discovered by F. H. de Cordova; in 1518 Juan de Grizalba
entered the lands of the Montezumas and led the way for the greater Cortez to possess their
country in 1519–21.   Later, 1525–35, Pizarro conquered the Peruvians.   On April 13, 1528,
De Narvaez, nine months after he left Spain, arrived in Florida with four hundred infantry
and forty-two cavalry, and camped on the west shore of La Cruz or Tampa bay.   The history
of this expedition is one of adventure, hardships and disappointments.   The bones and culinary vessels discovered on Massacre island, at the mouth of Mobile bay, in 1699, by the
French, tell something of the result of the voyage, the trip of two hundred and eighty miles
across the country, the building of boats, the beginning of the return voyage to La Cruz, on
November 1, 1528, and the death of Narvaez.   Alva Cabaca de Vaca, the only surviving
officer of the proposed Florida colony, was cast on an island, west of Bay Perdido, received
by the Indians, lived with them eight years, and then returned to Spain to tell the story of
wreck and disaster.

    Hernando de Soto, already famous as a participant in the capture of Peru, now offered
to conquer and hold Florida for Spain at his own expense.   The royal permit was given, and
in 1637 he raised aloft his standard at Seville.   Before the close of that year there marched
under his command nine hundred and fifty of the bravest men in Spain, and on April 6, 1538,
his fleet of ten brigs sailed from San Lucas de Barrameda.   Twelve priests, eight deacons
and four monks accompanied the expedition.   Arriving in Cuba, a whole year was passed
there, and not until May 31, 1539, three hundred men disembarked at La Cruz (Tampa Bay)
among the abandoned campfires of the Mobilian tribes.   At dawn on the morning of June 1,
the Indians swooped down upon the camp, drove the soldiers toward the water, and would
have succeeded in crushing or drowning the refugees had not De Soto disembarked all
his forces.   A reference to the Indian chapter will point out clearly his wars with the Indians.
Here let us follow him into Mississippi, and thence to his earthly resting place beneath the
great river.   Leaving Tampa bay he crossed the Withlacooche and entered the village of the
Hirrihiguas, where he made amends for the crime of Narvaez.   There he learned of Juan
Ortez, a captive at Mucoso's town, and by diplomacy had him released.   Ortez now became
the most useful man of the expedition, being acquainted more or less with the languages or
dialects of the Appalachian race.   Again setting out, he proceeded to Cofatchique, on the
Savannah river, crossing the headwaters of the Ocmulgee and Oconee, after traveling up the
eastern valley of the Flint river.   At Cofatchique he discovered arms and armor of d'Ayllon's force.   Turning toward the northwest, he brought the queen of the Uchees along to
Xuala, not as a harlot but in regal state.   There she escaped.   He then led his troops down the
Coosa valley to the Alabama, and thence to the town of Mauvila, where the battle of October

18, 1540, was fought. His terrible victory was more disastrous than defeat, for while twenty-five hundred natives were killed, he lost eighty-two men, forty-two horses, stores, medicines and clothes. The grumblings of his officers now were heard, and to hold them together he started on that northwestern journey which led him beyond the Mississippi, and back again to the great river, leaving Moldenado (Pensacola), where he intended to build his town, far to the south. Crossing the Black Warrior above its confluence with the Tombigbee, and going northwest across the two principal heads of the Tombigbee, in Alabama, he entered what is now the state of Mississippi in latitude thirty-three degrees, fifty-eight minutes north. Continuing his course almost due west on this line to longitude thirteen degrees, three minutes, the army pushed north to latitude thirty-four degrees, fifty-one minutes, longitude thirteen degrees, two and one-half minutes, at or near where the town of Hernando now stands; thence to a point northwest, crossed the river in latitude thirty-four degrees, fifty-nine minutes, and entered the Quapaw village of the Dacotahs, where St. Francis, Ark., now stands. The trail then led south to Quiquate, just at the junction of L'Anguille and St. Francis rivers; thence along the Mississippi, on highest ground, to a point in latitude thirty-six degrees, back via St. Francis village, on a line nearer the St. Francis river to Quiquate, and thence to Coligoa at the head of the St. Francis river. From that point a southwestern course was taken, until the point now known as Fort Gibson, Ark., was reached, when the return journey to the gulf was entered upon—the Arkansas river valley route to Guaychaya, and thence down the Mississippi, being the line of march adopted. This route is clearly shown on the map drawn by Captain Eastman, United States army. The route was laid down by Schoolcraft and adopted by the bureau of Indian affairs in 1860. The historian of the Indians locates the place of De Soto's death at the mouth of the Arkansas, but other writers disagree with him on that point; while many Tennesseans vary from his ideas of the route between the Tombigbee and the Mississippi—leading the daring Spaniards to the upper Chickasaw bluff or Memphis, and driving them across the river at that point. This difference of opinion will exist to the end of time, as the original notes of the journey are akin to some modern legislative acts, and may be interpreted to suit Louisiana, Mississippi or Tennessee. A reference to the Indian history, however, will show his camps and battle grounds as well as the nations with whom he came in contact, and with the weight of authorities lead to the conclusion that the Dacotah crossing was the one used.

The authorities examined before adopting this route include Garcilaso de la Vega, who compiled his narrative from the journals of Alonzo de Carmona and Juan Colez, companions of De Soto; the Portuguese gentleman of Elvas, Alva Cabaca de Vaca (Smith's translation, 1851), Prescott's "Conquest of Florida," John G. Shea's "Life of De Soto," Pickett's "History of Alabama," Bancroft's "History of the United States," Claiborne's "History of Mississippi," Martin and Gayarre's "History of Louisiana," Nuttall, Belknap, McCulloh, Monette, and, lastly and principally, Schoolcraft's history of the tribes—the facts for which were collected and collated, regardless of cost, by order of congress, and accepted by students of Indian history throughout the civilized world. The text is based on this national record. Consider what the other authorities say :

De Soto retreated toward the north, his troops already reduced by sickness and warfare to five hundred men. A month passed away before he reached winter quarters at Chicaca, a small town in the country of the Chickasaws, in the upper part of the state of Mississippi, probably on the western bank of the Yazoo. (Bancroft Vol. I, pp. 49–50).

Historians are decidedly wrong when they report De Soto as spending the winter on the Yazoo. The Chickasas never claimed as far south as the confluence of the Yalobusha and Tallahatchie. The line between the Chickasas and Choctaws left the Tombigbee at the mouth of Tibbe, up that stream and

Trim Cane and Line creek, then due west to the Mississippi river, passing near Grenada. Before the introduction of firearms among them, their only town, or towns, was on the present route of the Mobile & Ohio railroad, commencing five or six miles north of Tupelo and extending to Red Land, on Pontotoc ridge, and was called Long Town. There was a path from Long Town to Natchez, long known as the "Old Natchez Trace." After their war with the French, the Chickasas ceased to trade at Natchez, and extended the trail to Nashville, crossing the Tennessee river at Colbert's ferry. (Claiborne Vol. I, p. 7.)

The Spaniards were guided to the Mississippi by natives, and were directed to one of the usual crossing places, probably at the lowest Chickasa bluff, not far from the thirty-fifth parallel of latitude. (Portuguese account, C. 32 and 33, taken in connection with Vega's diffuse account, I. iv. C. v; Belknap I, p. 192—"within thirty-fourth degree;" Andrew Ellicott's journal, p. 125—"thirty-four degrees and ten minutes;" Martin's "History of Louisiana," V. I, p. 12—"a little below the lowest Chickasaw bluff;" Nuttall's "Travels in Arkansas," p. 248, "the lowest Chickasaw bluff," and McCullough's "Researches," p. 526, "twenty or thirty miles below the mouth of the Arkansas."

Still shaping his course to the northwest, he struck the great river at the lower Chickasa bluff, just below old Fort Pickering in May, 1541. Any route from the Chickasa Old Fields south of the one assumed would have carried him into the impenetrable swamps of the Yalobusha and Tallahatchie. (Claiborne Vol. I, p. 8.)

Following the disastrous assault by the Chickasaw Indians upon his fortified camp, De Soto resumed his weary march in a northwesterly direction, and during the month of May, 1541, reached the Chickasaw bluff near where the prosperous and popular city of Memphis now stands. (Lowry & McCardle's "History of Mississippi," p. 13).

April 1, 1541, they marched four leagues and encamped beyond the boundaries of Chicoza. At Alibamo they fought their next battle, and then marched northward seven days through an uninhabited wilderness, and at length came in sight of Chisca, seated near a wide river, the largest they had yet discovered. Chisca is believed to have occupied the site of the present thriving city of Memphis. (Goodspeed's "History of Tennessee," pp. 109–10.)

From 1542, when the Spaniards discovered the Natchez, to 1682, when La Salle sailed down the Mississippi, there is little or nothing written of the Mississippi country. During the first decade of the seventeenth century a few Spanish settlers located on Tortuga de Mar (Tortoise of the Sea), and gave the island that title. It was also known as "Little Spain." Thirty years later, 1632 (O. S.), the islanders were alarmed at beholding a pinnace load of strange people disembarking, but were set at rest by the visitors, who stated they were French and came to seek permission to make headquarters here while hunting the wild cattle on the mainland. The permission was heartily granted, and the fifteen French adventurers from the French colony at St. Christopher made their temporary headquarters here. They soon showed their skill to the simple islanders, for standing on the shore of the island they could kill the wild bulls on the mainland in greater numbers in one day than all the Spanish hunters could in three at short range. The strangers also introduced the boucaning methods of the Caribbee cannibals, and cured large quantities of meat by jerking and salting and then drying in the sun. The industry became a great and profitable one, a greater number of French adventurers arrived, and the little colony of Spaniards saw their privileges gone. In December, 1633 (O. S.), the original settlers descended upon the intruders and drove them off, but the wild white hunters returned in a few months and destroyed every vestige of Spanish occupation. Men as rough as they were immoral, and women as bad as the men, came to the island; the beef-curing business continued to grow, and the name buccaneers was given to the inhabitants. Pierre le Gross, a sailor, was a leader among this band of cutthroats and soon organized a pirate crew to prey upon galleons and Indians alike, other ships were fitted out for that purpose, and within ten years the Spanish-Mexican commercial-marine was destroyed by the buccaneers. What villages they destroyed along the gulf coast? What hundreds of Indian lives were given up to the caprice of those desperadoes? What thousands of hopes were destroyed by those robbers? Never will the figures be given. Their days were hours of murder and rapine, their nights hours of debauchery. Few, if any, of those who fell into their hands escaped to tell of their doings; themselves kept no record, and beyond the general fact of their existence, the reported loss of galleon after galleon and their own stories of adventure, there is no record. Sir Henry Morgan, who was made a knight-baronet by Charles, king of England, for his atrocious doings on the ocean, and was appointed governor of Jamaica, cleared $3,800,000 out of his piratical feats. He was the tail of the buccaneers, but held his ill-gotten goods so closely that, in time, he was able to control the buccaneers.

In 1608 the French directed their attention to their discoveries in North America, and from Quebec expeditions were sent west and southwest. In 1632 Jean Nicollet is found treating with the Indians on the shores of lake Michigan, a little over three decades later (1669), the renowned Pere Allouez is among the savages of lake Superior, and on May 17, 1673, two heroes of the post leave Quebec to discover the great river which, they believed, would open a trans-continental waterway to China. They were none others than the illustrious Pere Jacques Marquette, S. J., and the famous explorer Joliet, after whom a town in Illinois is named. With five attendants they traversed the country to the Mississippi, and on June 17, 1673, looked upon the great river for the first time. Constructing canoes, the little party paddled down the Mississippi to the mouth of the Arkansas and up that river to Arkansas post, where the symbol of Christianity was raised above the fleur-de-lis of France. Unfavorable reports of the lower Indians, whose legends of the Spanish made the white race odious, prompted the explorers to return, and henceforth their history is connected with the country of the Illinois as far north as St. Ignace, where the bones of Marquette rest beneath the cross-capped marble column which symbolizes his strength and faith.

Robert Cavalier de La Salle and his noble lieutenant, Henri de Tonti, left Quebec in 1681, and the same year established Fort Creve Cœur on the Illinois river. The sufferings of this expedition and its disappointments were such, that at the beginning of the dreary northern winter La Salle was driven to return to Quebec for supplies. There accounts of shipwreck and defalcation by trusted clerks awaited him; but doing all that mortal could do to aid his men in distant Illinois, he again faced the wilderness, and returning via Chicago reported at Creve Cœur early in 1682. Father Zenobe and Father Hennepin accompanied him this time; but on February 6, when his headquarters moved down the Mississippi, a small party under Hennepin was detached to explore the northern country. The main party arrived at Chickasaw bluff on February 26, and at the mouth of the Arkansas four days later. Here, Pere Zenobe raised the cross, and La Salle the fleur-de-lis, as did Marquette and Joliet in 1673, and bidding farewell to the Casque Indians, entered on that journey down the river. As related in the Indian chapter, the explorers are found among the Tensas of Louisiana on March 20, at latitude 31 degrees north; on the 22d and the evening of that day they camped ten leagues down the river on an island. On April 6 they arrived at the head of the three rivers, and on the 9th camped on the shore of the Gulf of Mexico. Let Tonti, the chronicler of this historic expedition, tell the story of the building and dedication of the first claim column erected here by the French. The inscription on the column was:

Louis le Grand,

Roi de France et de Navarre, Reigne;

Le Neuvieme Avril, 1682.

The whole party chanted the *Te Deum*, the *Exaudiat*, the *Domine salvam fac Regem;* and then, after a salute of firearms, and cries of *Vive le roi*, the column was erected by M. de la Salle, who, standing near it, said with a loud voice in French: "In the name of the most high, mighty, invincible and victorious prince, Louis the Great, by the grace of God, king of France and Navarre, fourteenth of that name, this ninth day of April, one thousand six hundred and eighty-two, I, in virtue of the commission of his majesty, which I hold in my hand, and which may be seen by all whom it may concern, have taken and do now take, in the name of his majesty, and of his successors to the crown, possession of this country of Louisiana, the seas, harbors, ports, bays, adjacent straits; and all the nations, peoples, provinces, cities, towns, villages, mines, minerals, fisheries, streams and rivers, comprised in the extent of the said Louisiana, from the mouth of the great river St. Louis, on the eastern side, otherwise called Ohio, Alighin, Sipore, or Chuckagona, and this with the consent of the Chaonanons, Chikachas and other people dwelling therein, with whom we have made alliance; as also along the river Colbert or Mississippi, and rivers which discharge themselves therein, from its source beyond the country of the Kious or Nadouessious, and this with their consent, and with the consent of the Motantees, Illinois, Mesigameas, Nathes, Koroas, which are the most considerable nations dwelling therein, with whom also we have made alliance, either by ourselves or by others in our behalf; as far as its mouth at the sea, or Gulf of Mexico, about the twenty-seventh degree of the elevation of the north pole, and also to the mouth of the River of Palms; upon the assurance which we have received from all these nations, that we are the first Europeans who have descended or ascended the said river Colbert; hereby protesting against all those who may in future undertake to invade any or all of these countries, people or lands, above described, to the prejudice of the right of his majesty, acquired by the consent of the nations herein named. Of which, and of all that can be needed, I hereby take to witness those who hear me, and demand an act of the notary, required by law." To which the whole assembly responded with shouts of *Vice le roi*, and with salutes of firearms. Moreover, the Sieur de la Salle caused to be buried at the foot of the tree to which the cross was attached, a leaden plate with the arms of France, and the following Latin inscription:

LVDOVICVS MAGNVS REGNAT.

NONO APRILIS CIɔ IɔC LXXXII.

ROBERTVS CAVELIER, CVM DOMINO DE TONTY, LEGATO, RP. ZENOBIO MEMBRE, RECOLLECTO, ET VIGINTI GALLIS, PRIMVS HOC FLVMEN, INDE AB ILLINEORVM PAGO, ENAVIGAVIT, EJVSQVE OSTIVM FECIT PERVIVM, NONO APRILIS, ANNI CIɔ IɔC LXXXII.

The notary, Jaques de la Metane, signed the declaration, and, so far as a small body of explorers could lay claim to possession, Louisiana and the whole Mississippi country belonged to France, and Louis XIV., the "Grand Monarch," was certainly lord of a great domain, extending from bleak Labrador to the sunny land of Mexico, and from flowery Florida to the burning mountains of Alaska.

The party now turned their faces toward Quebec. Lieutenant Tonti was left at Fort St. Louis as commandant of a small force; Pere Zenobe was sent to France to give the details of the expedition to the king, and La Salle, *lui-meme* followed him. Certain grants were made to this great man, and on July 24, 1684, a new expedition was ready to sail and did sail from La Rochelle for the mouth of the Mississippi, via St. Domingo. De Beaujeau commanded the royal frigate, on which were the troops, while merchant ships carried the colonists, their families, officials and priests. This fleet anchored near the entrance to Matagorda bay, on the coast of Texas, New Year's day, 1685. La Salle displayed, for the first time, alarm at the situation, and the naval official, Beaujeau, sharing in this alarm, deserted the colony, taking with him the royal frigate and stores. La Salle embarked on the ship, left him and sailed east with a small crew to find the mouth of the great river. Shipwreck waited upon him, but he escaping with a few of his men, returned to Matagorda to acquaint the colonists of the situation. Without delay he set out for Fort St. Louis to seek aid from Tonti—Pere Anastase and a small company of nineteen attendants accompanying him—but before he left the valley of the Brazos, Duhant shot him down (March 19, 1687), his trusted friends and his nephew being killed just before the attack on the chief. Father Anastase gave the dead Christian burial, and shortly after Spanish troops arrested the survivors, who were condemned to the mines. The missionary fathers and the men who had no share in La Salle's death were given liberty, and after six months' travel arrived at the mouth of the Arkansas, and went thence to Fort St. Louis.

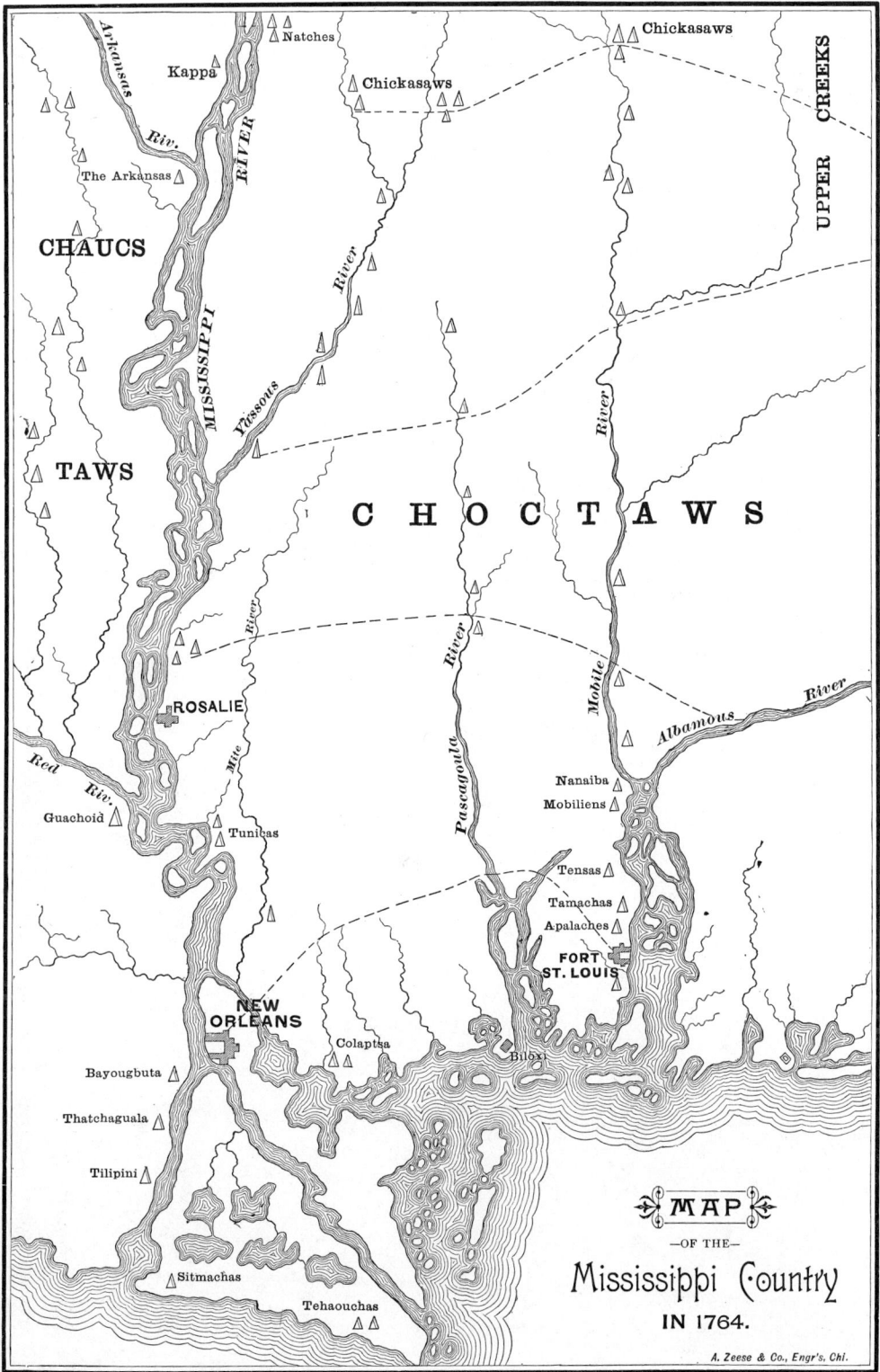

CHAUCS

TAWS

Arkansas Riv.

Kappa

Natches

The Arkansas

MISSISSIPPI RIVER

Chickasaws

Chickasaws

UPPER CREEKS

River

Yassous

C H O C T A W S

River

River

River

Mobile River

Albamous River

ROSALIE

Red Riv.

Mte

River

Pascagoula River

Guachoid

Tunicas

Nanaiba
Mobiliens

Tensas

Tamachas
Apalaches

FORT
ST. LOUIS

NEW
ORLEANS

Colaptsa

Biloxi

Bayougbuta

Thatchaguala

Tilipini

Sitmachas

Tehaouchas

MAP

—OF THE—

Mississippi Country

IN 1764.

A. Zeese & Co., Engr's, Chi.

Meantime Tonti or the Iron Hand had sailed down the Mississippi in search of La Salle, but finding the search fruitless, returned to Fort St. Louis, leaving letters for the chief with the different tribes which he met. Once at the fort, he heard the worst news that to him could be brought, and supposing that the colonists left at Matagorda bay had already found a home and friends among the Spaniards, applied himself to further the interests of his own colony and did not again venture south until 1700, when he heard of the new expeditions sent out on the track of La Salle and De Beaujeau. At Bayou Goula he met Bienville and Iberville's ships and returned with them to Natchez, where, on February 11, 1700, to the surprise of all, they found the learned Recollect St. Cosme, who, alone, had found his way to the very temple of the Natchez some months before. Tonti, the last historical character of La Salle's expedition, served France, in serving the new comers, until September, 1704, when he died in peace at Biloxi.

Before entering on the history of Bienville and Iberville's expedition and plantation a few more names may be given in connection with the prior attempts at settlement, or at civilization, along the Mississippi. Even before the Iron Hand had set out on his third trip down the river, the zealous Pere Davion had ventured among the Natchez, and for over twelve months preached to them Christian truths. He had a peculiar superstition to combat, and a task insuperable; for every morning the god whom the Natchez worshiped appeared to remind them of their centuried loyalty to him. Father Davion's words fell on rocks, so that he determined to seek the conversion of the Tunicas. Going into their country he selected the highest cliff or bluff for his home, thereon placed the cross and built an altar, where the mass was offered every morning until late in 1699, when Pere Francois J. de Montigny (written also Martigny or Montegay) arrived in search of the missionary, with instructions to take his place if Davion were sacrificed. The meeting was a happy one. The visitor brought news of the new expedition, the Indians confirmed it, and through curiosity the two Canadians set out for Biloxi to see and hear for themselves. They remained ten days among the French and then returned to their post at the cliff (La Roche a Davion, now Fort Adams), whence Montigny set out to establish a mission on the Yazoo. There is no record of them after their return to the Tunicas and Yazoos. The latter was not here when the French transports appeared in the river in 1700, and Father St. Cosme, named above, appears to have superseded them in charge. Father Davion remained for many years among the Tunicas and, it is said, won a number of warriors to the Christian faith.

The revival of colonial enterprises (1687-99) in Louisiana was as much due to the well-directed energies of M. Argoud as to the enterprise of the minister of marine—the Count de Pontchartrain. The official reports of Tonti, Zenobe, Davion, Montigny, Marquette, Joliet and others on the southland, through which they had traveled, fired the French official heart to action and urged the king to the possession of the land. The death of the chivalrous La Salle on the plains of Texas checked prompt action, and the wars of France against the wide world caused subsequent delays. The peace of Ryswick in 1697, and the success of Frontenac, Henri de Tonti and d'Iberville in the new world and on the ocean, at length insured a term of peace, so that within one year the plans of colonization were perfected. Two frigates of the line, Le Badine, of thirty guns, and Le Marin, of the same armament, were assigned for service in the Floridas and Louisiana, while sealed instructions were sent to St. Domingo to have the Le Francois, of fifty guns, in readiness to accompany the expedition westward from that island. Lemoyne d'Iberville commanded the first named frigate and her crew of two hundred marines, the Count de Surgere commanded the second, while the Marquis de Chateaumerant commanded Le Francois. Each of the war ships carried a full

4

complement of seamen and marines, while two merchantmen were assigned to carry stores and
the civil settlers.   The fleet left La Rochelle September 24, 1698, early the following year
arrived at its destination, and disembarked on the eastern point of land bounding the bay,
to which they gave the name Biloxi or Baluxi.   There huts were built to accommodate the two
hundred men, women and children—the colonists—and a fort of four bastions was commenced
May 1, 1699, for the accommodation of the troops and as a defensive work.   On this fortress
twelve large and forty-two small cannon were mounted, the name Fort Maurepas bestowed
upon it, the beginnings of settlement were made; d'Iberville appointed his brother, Antoine
Lemoyne Sauvolle, acting governor, Lemoyne Bienville, his second brother, commandant, and
sailed for France to report to the king and enlist more colonists for Louisiana.   At the close of
June, 1699, he was in the motherland, and early in July made the following report:

We took the route of Cape St. Anthony, Cuba, which we doubled on the 15th January, and on the
24th made land, near a Spanish settlement, called Apilachacola. We continued our route westwardly to
the bay of Pensacola, where we found two ships at anchor near a settlement recently made by Spaniards
from Vera Cruz. On the 30th we weighed anchor, and next day anchored, in eight fathoms water, in the
bay of Mobile. Twelve or fourteen leagues westward, we found a place, sheltered by islands and the
main land, where there is good anchorage and refuge against storms. Leaving my ships here, we set
out on the 21st for Malbouchia (the name given by the savages on this coast to the Mississippi), with two
long boats, some bark canoes and fifty-three men. We entered the river March 2, 1699. I found it
obstructed by mud banks and logs of wood, partially petrified. There were twelve feet of water. I
resolved to ascend as far as the Bayougoulas, a party of whom we had met at Biloxi. On the 7th, some
thirty-five leagues up, I met some Indians called the Mougoulaches, and on the 14th, reached their village, where we were kindly received. The chief had on a cloak of blue serge, which, he said, was presented to him by Tonti, companion of La Salle. They exhibited also axes and knives. I found no other
signs of the French having visited this river. Finding myself so far up without positive proof that this
was the Mississippi of La Salle, and that it might be said in France that I was deceived, I determined to
visit the Onamas (Houmas), among whom I knew Tonti had been; moreover, I would meet with that
branch of the river, spoken of in the narratives, which I proposed to explore. The village of the Houmas is two and a half leagues in the interior. Was well received, but obtained no additional information. The king exhibited some presents made to him by Tonti, whom they often spoke of. Retracing
my course, I arrived, on the 24th, at a small river, some five leagues above the Bayougoulas on the east
side of the river. I dispatched my chaloupes, with M. de Sauvolle, down the main river, with orders to
sound the passes, and with two canoes and four men, I determined to descend this fork or outlet. It was
very narrow and some five feet deep in low water. It was full of logs, so that in many places we were
obliged to make portages. After awhile it connects with other streams, and the navigation becomes
good. It terminates by emptying into a lake. The lake I crossed was about three leagues wide and
twenty-five long, parallel with the Mississippi, and in many places they are separated only by a narrow
strip of land. This pass, which I descended, is the most convenient route to reach the Indian villages.
There is but little current, while that of the main river is strong and rapid, and batteaux can not ascend
it without felling trees and making long detours. In descending the Mississippi M. de Sauvolle observed
a place, thirty leagues from the sea, that was not inundated. Another, some twenty leagues up, where
the high land extended back, but could not explore it owing to the dense growth of cane. There are from
eighteen to twenty fathoms in every part of this river, from the Houmas to the head of the passes. My
brother, in returning, procured from the Mougoulaches the letter which Tonti, after a fruitless search for
La Salle, had left there for him. It was dated at the village of the Quinnippesas, April 20, 1685. By
this name, it seems, he designated the Bayougoulas and Mougolouchas. I do not see for what reason he
did so, unless it was to conceal the fact from the Spaniards and other adventurers, that the Malbouchia
was the veritable Mississippi of La Salle. I reached the ships on the 31st, finding them some forty-six
leagues east-southeast from the mouth of the river. After having visited several places well adapted for
settlements, I fixed on the bay of Biloxi, four leagues north of the place where the ships were anchored.
We made choice of this point on account of the sheltered bay or roadstead where small vessels can come
and go in safety at all times. A place for permanent settlement can be selected at leisure. I erected a
wooden fort with four bastions; two are made of hewn timber, placed together, one foot and a half thick,
nine feet high; the other two of double pallisades. It is mounted with fifty-four pieces of cannon, and

has a good outfit of ammunition. I left M. de Sauvolle in command; de Bienville, king's lieutenant; Levasseur, major; de Bordenac, chaplain; Care, surgeon; two captains, two pilots, four sailors, eighteen filibusters, thirteen Canadians, ten mechanics, six masons, thirty subofficers and soldiers.

The governor returned to Biloxi December 7, 1699, with two frigates, troops, supplies and sixty Canadian colonists. Le Seur, the geologist, also arrived. The land was fair, indeed, and the climate, like that of sunny southern France, loaned a charm to the scene which pioneers could alone appreciate. They listened to the joyous melodies of the great pines, heard the song of the billows and the music of the soft Mexican breeze in the wild rice, or in the willow marsh, and the echoes of that music carried back by the reeds and canes. That Christmas of the last year of the seventeenth century was indeed one of peace and good will; for never yet were leaders or followers more true to each other, or more happy in their prospects, than were the soldiers of France, or the immigrants from Canada, who had located on that point of land between the sunlit seas of Mississippi.

During the absence of Lemoyne d'Iberville, Lemoyne Bienville led an expedition up the Mississippi, and returning encountered two ships sent down from New Jersey, by Dr. Daniel Coxe, loaded with immigrants for his claim on the river. Captain Barr was master, and, in reply to his interrogatories, was told that he was much too far east and that the river, for which he searched, paralleled this stream. Barr thanked the officer who gave this information, and turning the prows of his vessels south at English Turn, sailed in search of Coxe's claim, and ultimately returned to New Jersey with only a report of failure. Other visitors there were, such as the missionaries hitherto noticed, and the gallant Tonti. Captain De Graff, the Spanish buccaneer, was stationed there, the wonder of the Indians and French alike. He was a musician, littérateur, printer, orator, marine, soldier, athlete, bull-fighter and cannoneer. He would sight a cannon, point out the object to the curious onlookers, set the fuse and immediately the object sighted was struck. This curiosity was brought hither on the Francois and invited to stay by d'Iberville. With the equally heroic Tonti, the man of the iron hand, and the victor of death in a thousand forms, who came later, Fort Biloxi was singularly well endowed in examples of heroic men. Jean B. Lemoyne de Chateauque, another brother of d'Iberville, was here, while among the troops and officers were others famous in military and naval annals, and among the colonists, powerful foresters, who would bring a giant tree to earth with as much grace as the boys of the colony would make and light a cigarette.

Early in 1700 d'Iberville ordered the occupation of the Mississippi valley. In February the fleet was well up toward Natchez, when de Tonti was seen approaching. His fame had preceded him, and his welcome was made to correspond with his fame. On February 11, 1700, the ships anchored in the shadow of the Natchez bluffs, and a shout of welcome from Pere St. Cosme gave token that the Gaul had already possessed the land. Le Seur, the chief of the geological department, had set out in another direction with a party of twenty men, to report on the lands and minerals, while smaller bodies of explorers were sent out from Biloxi to select lands for the colonists and make report on the soil, trees and aborigines.

The main expedition, on arriving among the Natchez, halted there to build a fort. The site chosen was two thousand and ten feet back from the river, on the hights overlooking both river and interior. The timber used was large, but for some reason the construction of bastions was overlooked. Within the pentagon were the quarters for officers and men, the storehouses, and magazine, and round it was the great ditch and rough *chevaux de frise* capping the clay embankment. To this pretentious work the name Fort Rosalie was given in honor of Pontchartrain's wife, who proved an influential friend of the colonists.

The French now considered Natchez their headquarters in the interior. From this post a small party, under the lead of d'Iberville, went forth, February 13, 1700, with the object of visiting the northwestern outpost of the great Natchez confederacy—the Tensas. The scenes described in the second chapter were witnessed by the explorers; they returned heart-sick to Natchez, and thence sailed for the fort at Biloxi. Lemoyne de Bienville was dis-patched to command at Natchez, Antoine L. Sauvolle appointed acting governor, and the governor returned to France. The acting governor died of imported yellow fever, August 22, 1700, at Biloxi, and his brother, Lemoyne de Bienville, was recalled from Natchez to act. The death of a member of the Lemoyne family from disease was echoed from Biloxi to Canada, and the news carried to St. Domingo; so that when Lemoyne de Sevigny and Lemoyne de Chateauque arrived at the last-named island they heard the news and determined not to touch the plague-spot. In December, 1700, their two ships anchored at Dauphine island, and cour-iers were sent to Biloxi, ordering their brother, Lemoyne Bienville, to abandon the place and move to the bay of Mauvila (Mobile bay). This order was partly observed; for the acting governor repaired to the designated bay, leaving Colonel de Boisbriant in command of Fort Maurepas with twenty men. He found his brothers erecting a warehouse and magazine on Dauphine island, and he, after a short stay there, built Fort St. Louis de la Mobile, on the western bank of the bay, at the mouth of Dog river. Only then the true condition of affairs at Biloxi was learned—only one hundred and fifty souls, of all who were left there in health, survived the epidemic. This was the first cloud which rested over the colony. Unfortu-nately it was not to be the last. The Carolinians, urged on by the British government, won the friendship of those tribes forming the Muscogee confederacy, and then incited them to war against the French. An Alabama chief agreed to fill a boat with corn, should Bienville send one up the river. His proposition was accepted, and a pirogue, with a crew of five men, was dispatched to the Indian town. The Carolinians, learning of this friendly transaction, sent a number of young savages to intercept and kill the French, and only one of the five returned. He reported the treachery to Bienville, and the latter sent an army of Choctaws to annihilate the Alabama tribe. Prior to this, British Indians had carried their plans to the banks of the Mississippi and caused the murder of Pere Foucalt and three couriers at the mouth of the Yazoo in 1702, and of Pere St. Cosme at Donaldsonville, La. One of the red assassins in the latter case was caught and pounded to death with clubs at Mobile; while the Choctaws meted out wholesale justice to the other murderers within their villages. Such measures appeared to be wise and necessary at the time, but history shows how impolitic they were, for within a century the two white monarchies concerned in them and the confederated savages they used as tools, all lost their possessions on this continent, and had to make way for a new race—a people educated in the forests of this continent.

In 1704 d'Iberville, then in France, succeeded in urging the minister of marine to send out his brother, Jean B. L. Chateauque, with the frigate Pelican. This ship brought new troops and supplies, and with it sailed a merchantman, bringing recruits for the colony. Among the new colonists were Ettienne Buree, his large family, five agriculturists and their families; Pere la Vente, the newly appointed vicar-general, four secular priests, four sisters of charity, under Sister Jeanne Morbe, and also in her charge were twenty-three young women, whose certificates of irreproachable character were signed by Pontchartrain himself. Cather-ine de Mouthon, a female physician, was also of the party. This determination to build up the colonies on the gulf, and French interests there and in the interior, led to counter-demonstrations by the British, who induced the Indians, through skilled agents, to keep trouble alive. Chance was favorable to them, for, as shown in the previous chapter, most unlooked-for incidents sprang up, as if by magic, to increase the antipathy existing between the Mobilian tribes and the French, and ultimately to draw the Chickasaws into the ranks of their enemies. In 1706 the founder of the colony set out from France with the intention of crushing the British colonial power centered at Charleston, and then taking immediate charge of the colonies in Mississippi and Alabama; but Providence ruled it otherwise. His fleet dropped anchor at St. Domingo to embark the troops stationed there, but yellow fever, more terrible than an army, attacked his forces and brought death to one of the greatest and most noble of all the Frenchmen who gave their lives to the establishment of colonies along the gulf coast—Lemoyne d'Iberville died at St. Domingo July 9, 1706. Troubles were only beginning—sorrow after sorrow was yet in store for the colony. In 1708 a privateer, supposed to be a British war vessel, appeared before Dauphine island, and soon the storehouse there was emptied of its contents and the defenses burned. Later that year the waters swept over the place. Bienville, too slow in this, as in other things, ordered the erection of a new fort higher up the Mobile river. About the time the new buildings were completed le Chevalier de Muys set out from France with the commission of governor, but, halting at Havana in July, was stricken down by yellow fever, leaving his commissary-general d'Artaguette to proceed on his mission. This officer returned to France in 1710; but, while his report was complimentary toward Governor Bienville, it was equally denunciatory of the country and condemnatory of the young soldiers.

In 1710, two years after the character of the noble Bienville was vindicated, a grant was made to Antoine Crozat, by the French king, of all Louisiana, from the gulf to Illinois, and from the ocean to Texas. A sum of 50,000 livres was to be appropriated annually for the support of troops, and Crozat, in return, agreed to pay into the royal treasury a fourth of the product of mines, to import annually a cargo of Africans, and to settle annually two shiploads of French immigrants. After the period of nine years he also agreed to pay the officers of the territory.

In 1711 some recruits were introduced, so that in 1712 the colony contained a population of five hundred, including eighty Indian slaves. There were only fifty white women and children reported. The cost per capita to the government was 123 livres. In March, 1713, three ships arrived with fifty colonists and a battalion of infantry. In May the French frigate De la Fosse appeared off Dauphine island. On this vessel were Antoine de la Motte Cadillac, already a celebrated character in the history of Michigan, who brought his commission as governor to replace Bienville. With him were Duclos, the new commissary-general, Captain Richebourg, Le Bas, M. Diregonin and M. de Ursins, colonial directors, and a number of civil and military officials. Cadillac, jealous of the great Canadian family of Lemoyne, held aloof from Fort St. Louis, on the Mobile, and erected a fort on Dauphine island where the old buildings were burned in 1708. There he established colonial headquarters and reveled in abuse of everything he found here. It was like Cadillac. He acted similarly at Detroit, until the whole North was pleased to see him retire to lower latitudes. The directors now spread out to establish stores, and in 1715 M. de Ursins is found among the Natchez. Later Bienville was ordered to garrison that post with eighty men, but Cadillac revised the order, giving him Captain Richebourg as aide-de-camp, and reducing the number to thirty-four *chasseurs a pied*, and fifteen marines. In April, 1716, as stated in the Indian history, he is found negotiating with the Natchez, and in August of that year completed Fort Rosalie, on the plans of 1700, near the Natchez village. Leaving Major M. Palloux in command, he returned shortly after to Dauphine island, heard of the retirement of Cadillac, the appointment of l'Epinay, and the intention of Crozat to surrender his charter. In August, 1717, this intention was carried out. During the period of five years Crozat's officers ruled this district, the population was increased to seven hundred, including the troops; but the great merchant lost 20,000,000 livres. His colonists were men and women of healthy and moral constitutions, and they succeeded in founding fortunes and families which have ever since been connected with the gulf coast. Crozat surrendered his charter 1717, and the Scotch adventurer, John Law, placed his Mississippi scheme before the Duc d'Orleans.

In September of that year a charter was granted to the Western Company, or Compagnie des Indies, conceding the lands, coasts, harbors and islands of Louisiana for twenty-five years, from January 1, 1718. Law (then director of the Royal bank of France and a protege of d'Orleans); Costaignes, Duche and Manchard, of La Rochelle; Pion, of Nantes; Moreau, of St. Malo, and d'Artaguette, of Paris, the directors of the new company, agreed to locate six thousand whites, and introduce three thousand Africans in the colony. In February, 1718, their fleet left France, and early in March arrived at Dauphine island, when the commission of governor was presented to Bienville and papers recalling l'Epinay to the governor. A practical system of colonization was adopted, and liberal grants of land made to those who would settle here or bring settlers hither. As a result a number of settlements were made at Pascagoula, where M. Paris Duvernet was granted the Indian town; at Bay St. Louis, on the Yazoo; St. Catherine's bayou and in the Natchez neighborhood. On the Yazoo the leading grantees were Le Blanc, de Belleville and le Blond; near Natchez, the company of St. Malo merchants, of whom Hubert was director generale; at Pascagoula, Madame de Chaumont; at Houma, d'Ancenis, and at Bay St. Louis, Madame de Mezierres; other large grants were made in what is now the state of Louisiana. The conditions were similar to all such grants. In June, 1718, De la Houssaye and Scouvion settled on the Yazoo with eighty-two others; the former opened a plantation near Natchez. In 1719 Fort St. Peter was erected on the Yazoo by Colonel Bigart, and the following year three hundred and ninety persons located in the neighborhood. During this year, also, three hundred immigrants were landed at Natchez for settlement there; in September, Beaumanoir brought sixty settlers for the St. Catherine's country, where Bienville's large plantation was then cultivated. In 1720 thirty young women arrived and Director-General Hubert brought sixty white men to his lands. In 1721 three hundred immigrants settled on Madame de Chaumont's grant at Pascagoula. M. Colly purchased Hubert's interests on the St. Catherine, and on June 4, 1722, there were two hundred and fifty Germans, under the Chevalier d'Arembourg, added to the German colony of 1721, a number of negro workmen introduced and deVillemont's colony on Black river increased. Additions were made annually to all the settlements until the colonies at Natchez, on the Yazoo and west of the great river, became the envy of the British and the pride of the French.

Affairs on the gulf coast were not so favorable. Marbois, the historian of the period, points out the error of the effort to cover too much territory, and he was prophetic. Charlevoix, the greater historian and traveler of that time, was equally emphatic in condemning the system, pointing out that in union there is strength. During the year 1722 this great man visited all the posts from Quebec to New Orleans, and writing from New Orleans, said: "The authorities are at present engaged in seeking, to the west of the Mississippi, a place fit to make a settlement which may bring us nearer to Mexico, and they think they have found it a hundred leagues from the mouth of the river, in the bay of St. Bernard, where La Salle landed when he missed the Mississippi. There is something much more pressing and better to be done that this. I know that commerce is the soul of colonies, and that these are of no use to a country like France but for this end, and to hinder our neighbors from growing too powerful. But if they do not begin by cultivating the lands, commerce, after having enriched some few persons, will soon droop, and the colony will fail. The neighborhood of the Spaniards may have its use, but let us leave it to them to approach us as much as they will. We are not in a condition, and we have no need to extend ourselves farther." He saw that the question of locating the seat of colonial government had already bred up unfriendly feelings between men who before were friends, and that the enmity spread to the colonists. In March, 1718, Bienville determined to make New Orleans colonial headquarters, and instantly he dispatched a company of fifty men to clear the forests then occupying the tract between the streets then known as Canal and Esplanade. Another party went forth to construct a fort on the Spanish claim known as St. Joseph's bay. Lemoyne de Sevigny, commanding a frigate, arrived in 1719, and brought the first news of the war between France and Spain. He also brought instructions to make the first coast survey, and did make all those soundings which have since been adopted by the United States surveyors. Slave ships also arrived, and in July, 1720, the first cargo of the Africans was disembarked, and with them came the terrible St. Domingo yellow fever. Meantime, Bienville captured the Spanish post at Pensacola, but the Spaniards, returning, recaptured the post. The advent of three war ships, September 2, 1819, bringing a large number of colonists, enabled Bienville to assault Pensacola successfully, and thus he rewon the laurels of which Spanish soldiers tried to deprive him. (Vide military chapter.) The seat of government question was revived after this, an influential section of the directory desiring it to be located at Natchez, in opposition to Bienville's New Orleans. Director-General Hubert was, of course, interested in Natchez, and to abolish the argument of his opponents that his own pecuniary interests suggested that town, he, in 1721, sold his lands there and sailed for France. While urging the location of colonial headquarters, he died. His powerful opponents carried their point. Biloxi, meantime, was fixed upon (in June, 1722) as the capital by the directors, and to this point Bienville removed his office.

Late in 1722 the directory, acceding to Bienville's reasoning, established the capital at New Orleans and ordered the organization of nine military districts and three ecclesiastical parishes, and Pensacola was given up to the Spaniards. The military districts were Fort Toulouse, Mobile, Biloxi, New Orleans, Natchez, Yazoo, Illinois, Wabash, Natchitoches and Arkansas. To each a district judge and a commandant were appointed and plenary powers of administration given. The eastern ecclesiastical parish—Alabama, Biloxi, Mobile and Fort Toulouse—was confided to the Carmelite fathers, the Mississippi valley from New Orleans to Chicago, to the Capuchin fathers, and the Wabash and Ohio valleys to the Jesuit fathers. Mobile at this time boasted of a large brick fortress commanded by De Mandeville. At Toulon, on the Coosa, Marchmand was commandant; De Barnaval had charge at Natchez, but shortly after Maneval was placed in charge of the eighteen men holding the position; St. Denis, at Natchitoches; and La Harpe, who came to Biloxi in 1718, visited the posts in several districts prior to 1723, when he returned to France and published his reminiscences of life in Louisiana. He notices the consternation of the people and soldiers when they learned of the failure of the Royal bank of France and the escape of Law. This failure took place in May, 1720, but was not made known to the colonists until June 4, 1722, when d'Arensbourg brought the discouraging news. The tornadoes of August, 1722, and of September, 1723, the memory of the mutiny at Fort Toulon in 1721, the murders by the Indians, the mutiny of the Swiss guard in 1723, the troubles with the Chickasaws and Natchez that year, and the recall of Bienville in 1724, all contributed to check progress; yet the agricultural interests were represented by twenty-five hundred white workers, called redemptioners, and eighteen hundred

African workers. The troops then actually on service in the districts numbered eight hundred. In May, 1721–3, copper coins were sent from France to Biloxi and distributed throughout the settlements. Near the mouth of Pearl river an earthen vase of the old Indian pattern was unearthed about 1841, which contained a quantity of those coins. At New Biloxi and other places they are brought to light occasionally.

Governor Perier was commissioned August 9, 1726, and arrived at New Orleans early in 1727. The creatures who urged the recall of Bienville now ranged themselves under Perier's banner and, like some modern land speculators, instilled into his mind their own ideas of justice to the Indians. Through vicious counsels from them, Bienville had even resorted to severe measures against the savages, as already related in the former chapter, and now, unfortunately, the new governor surrendered himself to the very men who would grow rich even if all the colonists were to be sacrificed. Perier showed his hand first in the appointment of commandants and other officers—all obnoxious to the whites and Indians alike—and next in approving the tyrannical methods of his aristocratic official circle. A day of retribution was foreshadowed. It arrived, and the innocent as well as the guilty fell.

At the time of the Natchez massacre, 1729, French and Spanish planters, residents in the vicinity of the post, vied with the officials at New Orleans and Natchitoches in the elegancies of life. Along St. Catherine's bayou, from what is now known as Foster's depot, to the Mississippi, a few extensive and many large plantations existed; where Gum Ridge village now stands was a great farm; there were two on bayou Pierre, two at Walnut hills and fourteen on the Yazoo around Fort St. Peter. The population of Natchez was about five hundred whites, including the troops. All this progress was made within a decade. It was all wiped out in a day. The history of that 29th day of November, 1729, is related in the Indian chapter. The white men who escaped death or captivity at the hands of the maddened savages brought the story of death and destruction to New Orleans, and that expedition of avengers which carried almost total annihilation to the Natchez nation was organized. One noble act alone marks the conduct of the savages. The drunken debauchee, Chopart, on being found, was given over to his class among the tribe and beaten to death by them in the presence of the warriors, who would not soil their hands with such foul carrion. All the settlements on the eastern bank of the river, from the Yazoo to latitude thirty-one degrees, were wiped out by knife and tomahawk and fire. The women and children of the settlements who did not flee in time, were made captives and carried to the Natchez stronghold on the bluffs, but the men were slain and the Natchez territory was simply the wilderness of 1718.

In 1734 Bienville was again commissioned governor and Perier recalled. The former arrived in 1735, and without ceremony entered upon that campaign against the refugees of the Natchez and their allies the details of which have been already given. The five subsequent years were mainly devoted to war upon the Chickasaws east of the Mississippi and the development of what is now the state of Louisiana. In 1741 the Marquis de Vaudreuil succeeded Bienville as governor, and served until February 9, 1753, when Baron Kerlerec took his place. Vaudreuil carried fire and sword into the Chickasaw country, laying it waste, and brought with him to Canada the name of a conservative soldier, stern disciplinarian and just governor. D'Abbadie was appointed governor in 1763, and served until 1766, or four years after the secret treaty of November 3, 1762. By this treaty France ceded to Spain all of Louisiana west of the mouth of the Perdido. The treaty of Paris was ratified February 16, 1763, between Great Britain, Spain and France. The latter ceded the lands east of the Mississippi south to Iberville, thence down the Manshac to the Amité, down the Amité to lake Maurepas, and through the center of lakes Maurepas and Pontchartrain to the Gulf of Mexico, and eastward, including Mobile; while Spain ceded Florida between the Perdido and St. Mary's rivers to Great Britain, holding the island of New Orleans as a Spanish colony. In 1745 Vaudreuil caused an enumeration of inhabitants and soldiers to be made. At Natchez were eight white (soldiers) males, two African families and fifteen African slaves, while Biloxi and Pascagoula were minus inhabitants. In 1751 Vaudreuil dispatched fifty soldiers to hold the fort at Natchez.

Notwithstanding such insurance of protection, white colonists could not be won by grants of land to occupy the country, and it laid fallow until the advent of the Carolinian and Georgian pioneers. In 1763 the British extended the northern boundary of west Florida under the presumption that settlements existed along the river north of latitude thirty-one degrees. Claiborne, in his historical work (Vol. I, pp. 92, 93), referring to this extension of boundary, says:

We have no account of settlers at Natchez after the massacre. The French on the Yazoo had all been murdered. At every settlement within those limits the inhabitants had been killed or had fled, and we have no evidence of their return. Emigration from the Atlantic colonies had not commenced. We know when the Americans first came, who they were and where they settled. But the settlements that induced the extension of the line, where were these? Who were the settlers? Whence did they come? The report made, which induced the order for extension, most probably was that the district left out had been occupied and cultivated and would form an important settlement.

There is no evidence that Fort Rosalie was occupied as a French post after Perier's expedition against the Natchez in 1732, until Vaudreuil's time. He posted a small garrison there, but reports no inhabitants. We know that after the treaty of 1763, M. de Ville, commandant at Mobile, surrendered the fort there to Maj. Robert Farmer, of the British army. Captain Chabert, commandant of Fort Tombecbee, surrendered it to Capt. Thomas Ford. Chevalier Lanneau surrendered Fort Toulouse, but there is no record of Fort Rosalie, and the inference is that it and the country around had long been deserted. If this district, or any portion of it, was occupied by any but Indians after the massacre at Natchez and Yazoo, we have no means of knowing. If occupied, we have no knowledge who they were or whence they came. They could not have been sufficiently numerous for self-protection against the savages on all sides, without leaving some record. And a few scattered families would have been massacred. Besides, no claim for settlement rights or grants was ever made by these reputed settlers to either the British or Spanish authorities.

The French ministers realized in 1762 that the dream of successful colonization could not be real. The dispatch of the new governor, d'Abbadie, dissipated all doubts and prepared the French mind to receive the news that the colony which had cost the country so many gallant men and so much money was presented to Spain as a gift. D'Abbadie's dispatch was a grim truth:

If the inhabitants of Louisiana had turned their attention to anything else beyond jobbing on the king's paper and merchandise, they would have found great resources in the fertility of the land and the mildness of the climate. The facility offered by the country to live on its natural productions, has created habits of laziness. The immoderate use of taffia has stupefied the population. Three-fourths, at least, of the inhabitants are in a state of insolvency. The colony is in a state of destitution; it is a chaos of iniquities, and to reëstablish order, extreme measures must be resorted to, and officers, appointed from France, must be sent to my assistance.

From 1699 to 1741 the name of Lemoyne was connected with Louisiana, and prior to 1699 the family belongs to American history. In 1690 Capt. Charles Lemoyne was wounded at Quebec; Capt. Jacques Lemoyne de St. Helene was killed in the attack on the English settlement in Carolina; Lemoyne d'Iberville, the first governor of Louisiana (1699), died in St. Domingo, on date already recorded; Antoine L. de Sauvolle died at Biloxi in 1700, while acting governor; Lemoyne de Bienville, the second governor, died at Paris, March 7, 1767; Lemoyne de Sevigny died in 1734 while serving as governor of Rochester; Lemoyne de Chateauque, the celebrated naval officer, died while serving as governor of Cayenne; Lemoyne d'Apiguy died in St. Domingo in 1701; Jean B. Lemoyne de Chateauque was killed by the Indians on the Tombigbee river, and Paul L. de Maricour was killed by the Iroquois. They were all Canadians and all officers in the French navy or army. Lemoyne de Bienville was for forty years connected with the government of what is now Mississippi. To readers of Indian history and indeed to students of colonial policy many of his acts are incomprehensible, but when we come nearer home and read of Jackson and Harney, of Custer and Gibbons and Crooks and many other officers of the United States, we see history repeating itself, and in the fall of d'Artaguette, in Mississippi, may be seen, as in a mirror, the fall of Custer in Montana.

The land grant of October 13, 1630, was made by one Charles, the first king of that name in England, to one Sir Robert Heath. What is now the state of Mississippi, north of latitude thirty-one degrees, was included in this immense domain, and formed the portion of Heath until 1637, when one Maltravers, known in England as Lord Maltravers, became proprietor. When the French turned their attention to Louisiana, the Maltravers heirs sold or in some way disposed of their claim to Dr. Dan Coxe, in 1699, and in the same year he sent a colony hither, under Captain Barr, to claim and hold possession, but his two ships, encountering Iberville's force on the Mississippi, returned without making a landing. On March 4, 1663, Charles II. appears to have ignored the act of his predecessor, in part, if not in whole, for on that day the country between the Atlantic and Pacific and between latitude thirty-one degrees and thirty-six degrees north was granted to the Earl of Clarendon, Lord Monk, Lord Craven, Lord Ashley Cooper, Sir John Colleton, Lord John Berkeley, Sir William Berkeley and Sir George Carteret. This immense grant was extended in June, 1665, so as to embrace the states now known as North Carolina, South Carolina, Georgia, Tennessee, Alabama, Mississippi, Louisiana and Arkansas, and parts of Florida, Missouri, Texas and distant New Mexico and California. On July 25, 1729, seven of the above named had barely sense enough to take $12,500 for their claims, and in 1744 Carteret surrendered his title, but was regranted an eighth of the whole, or the territory bounded on the north by the Virginia line, east by the Atlantic, south by latitude thirty-five degrees, thirty-four minutes, and west as far as the boundaries of the original charter. The revolution "closed out" proprietorship, but the descendant of the courtier Carteret sued in the United States court for possession in 1810, was defeated there, and appealed to the supreme court, where it was pending when the war of 1812 came up to sweep away all unjust claims.

The treaty of 1763, between France, Spain and Great Britian, abolished the sovereignty of the former powers. A year after a Capt. George Johnstone arrived at Pensacola as governor, and at once sent commandants to take charge of the various posts and change their names. He also made several grants, but was not guilty of making that to the renegade Irishman, Daniel Clarke, who commanded a regiment of Pennsylvania tories in the Revolution, embracing much of the ancient Hubert plantation near Natchez, on St. Catherine's bayou. This was the deed of Gov. Montford Brown, who succeeded Johnstone in 1770. Elihu Hall Bay, however, received a large grant near Natchez, from Johnstone, and added a considerable area to it by purchase and otherwise. In 1768 Johnstone, under royal mandamus, granted twenty-five thousand acres to Capt. Amos Ogden, of New Jersey. This tract he located in what is now Adams county, but in 1772 he sold nineteen thousand acres of it to the Swayze colony for $3,800, or twenty cents per acre. In 1771 Chester, who succeeded Brown as governor, granted to the Earl of Eglington twenty thousand acres (Pine Ridge near Natchez); the Earl of Harcourt (at forks of Second and Homochitto creek), ten thousand acres; Admiral Bentinck (on Mississippi), ten thousand acres; Thomas Comyn's heirs, ten thousand acres (on Mississippi); Bay, above named, sixteen thousand three hundred and seventy-five acres (in various tracts); Admiral Rodney, five thousand acres (above Natchez); Sir William Dalling, five thousand acres (fifteen miles above Natchez); Governor Barbour, of Virginia, two thousand acres (near Grand gulf); Admiral Onslow, one thousand acres (below Natchez), and to Anthony Hutchins all the White Apple lands back of the White cliffs, and several tracts, exceeding ten thousand acres. In 1764 one Phineas Lyman, a major-general, head of the military adventurers, etc., sought a grant of twenty thousand acres, but he died before it was granted. His son, Thaddeus, went to London, England, to bring his father home, and while there he succeeded in obtaining twenty thousand acres for himself, his brother and two sisters. In December, 1773, this Thaddeus led a large colony from Stonington to New Orleans, and thence to his lands on the Big Black and bayou Pierre in 1775. In 1814 this claim was reported upon favorably in the interest of John Peck, of Boston, the legal representative.

Together with the above mentioned British grants were the following: F. A. Haldeman, three tracts near Natchez, fifteen hundred acres; John Stevenson, a few miles from Natchez, three thousand; Augustin Prevost, near Stevenson's, nine thousand; Mrs. Wegg, near Prevost's, three thousand; Alex. McCullah, thirty-seven hundred; heirs of the Pennsylvanian tory, Robert Farmer, on the Tombigbee, three thousand; Thomas Davy, claimed in 1814 by Admiral Sprye, on bayou Pierre, thirty-five hundred; William Wilton's heirs, sixteen hundred; James Amos on Mississippi, six hundred; Seth Hunt's claim on behalf of the heirs of Herbert Munster, near Natchez, two thousand; representatives of Major Francis Hutchinson, near Natchez, three thousand; John Vaughan's heirs, above Natchez, one thousand; Thomas Creik's heirs, one thousand; Capt. Thomas Boyd's heirs, near Natchez, one thousand three hundred and fifty; heirs of John Bradley, near Natchez, forty-one hundred and fifty; Maj. Thomas Gamble, near Natchez, two thousand; heirs of Maj. John Small, near Natchez, three thousand; Sylvester Fanning, Davion's Rock (Loftus hights), two thousand; heirs of John Jones, near Fanning's lands, six hundred; Admiral Ferguson, back of Natchez, three thousand; Captain Nunn, near Ferguson's lands, three thousand; Admiral McDougal, bayou Pierre, three thousand; heirs of Arthur Neil, bayou Buffalo, thirty-five hundred; heirs of William Burrows, six hundred; heirs of Phillip Affbeck, five thousand; Robert Tindall, two thousand; Samuel Fortinello, three thousand, and Louis Gordon, three thousand. Just think of it! one hundred and seventy-four thousand four hundred and sixty-five acres of the choicest lands in Mississippi given away, during the few years of British occupation, to heartless adventurers and absentees. The endorsement of such claims by the committee of public lands, led by Congressman McKee, December 21, 1814, was still a higher crime against humanity, and to lend to this endorsement an air of honesty, he denounced the citizens who bought the Yazoo lands from Georgia, calling them frauds and speculators. Congress fortunately acted in direct opposition to the report of the committee, compensated Georgia and the Yazoo claimants, and declared that the British claimants, who opposed the Revolution and then fought or aided the fight against the Union in 1812–13, could have no just claim to such lands (State papers pp. 748 to 753, Vol. II). The Spanish claims to lands previously donated by the British (1763–1781), were generally allowed. In January, 1809, Albert Gallatin reported very fully on the British grants, showing that the conditions were not carried out and suggesting that the claims be disallowed. One condition of the king's grant—"That such part of the whole tract as is not settled with foreign Protestants within ten years from date, revert to his majesty," proved the death-stroke to such claims in general. All claims by beneficiaries of the British based on grants post-dating the Declaration of Independence, were disallowed.

The treaty of 1777 between the British and the Mobile Indians defined the boundaries of the territory claimed by the French along the gulf coast, and in and around Natchez, and two years after surveyors ran the eastern line of the Natchez district. On July 11, 1772, the British issued a patent to one Campbell for a large tract, where the village of Rodney now stands. In 1840 the heirs of Campbell claimed this tract, and Chief Justice Smith, of Mississippi, was inclined to the belief that the British had a perfect right to issue patents for lands at this time and place, but American justice took another view and declared such titles invalid, save where the commissioners of 1804 confirmed them by virtue of occupation by grantees and the fulfillment of the conditions of the grant.

The British secret service reporting the progress of the storm of revolution, drove the British ministry into the liberal system of land grants. The methods however were bad, for had they subsidized their yeomanry instead of their nobility and aristocracy they could claim an army of occupation well qualified to hold the Natchez district and all the adjacent country. Their Irish policy led them astray as much as their own insular ideas. They expected that by giving away large tracts of land to their aristocrats, the latter could control immigration, as in the plantation of the confiscated lands of the Irish, but they lost sight of the distance from the center of British power and population and so missed the object sought in making the grants. An attempt was made to anglicize the south. Fort Conde (Mobile) was named Fort Charlotte; Manchac, Fort Bute; Natchez or Fort Rosalie, Fort Panmure, and so on. Even the historical Davion's rock was changed to Loftus heights. In 1764 Natchez was garrisoned and named Fort Panmure. A year later several families moved from the Roanoke valley, N. C., to a point above Baton Rouge and thence to Natchez. They claimed to be tories who could not conscientiously espouse the Revolution, but were willing to accept better lands in the Mississippi valley and the protection which the British guaranteed them there. English traders established stores at Manchac, among which was Swanson & Co.'s general trading house. They also dealt in slaves, sent up from Pensacola, then the slave depot or port of entry of the British-African slave ships, exchanging the human commodity for plantation products, such as tobacco, indigo, stave bolts, etc.

In 1774 Capt. Matthew Phelps visited the Chittaloosa or Big Black river valley, where he bought the interest of a squatter and found John Storrs, Sr., and John Storrs, Jr., recent immigrants from Virginia. Both men were in indigent circumstances, and to them Captain Phelps rendered timely aid.

In 1775 the Lyman colony arrived at Natchez. Among the principal men were: General Lyman, Thaddeus Lyman, with eight slaves; Sereno Dwight, Jonathan Dwight, Harry Dwight, with three slaves; Timothy Dwight, Moses and Isaac Sheldon, Roger Harmon, ——— Hanks, Seth Miller, Elisha and Josiah Flowers, Moses Drake, R. Winchell, Benjamin Barber, ——— Wolcott, D. and R. Magguet, Thomas Comstock, ——— Weed, Capt. Silas Crane, Robert Patrick, Ashbel Bowen, John Newcombe, James Dean, Abram Knapp, Gibs. and Nathaniel Hull, James Stoddart, Thaddeus Bradley, Ephraim Case, Hezekiah Rew, John Fisk, Elisha Hale, Timothy and David Hotchkiss, John Hyde, William Silkrag, Jonathan Lyon, William Davis, Hugh White, Thomas and James Lyman, Captain Elsworth, Ira Whitman, ——— Sage, Major Early, James Harmon, Elnathan Smith, William Hurlburt, Elijah Leonard, Benjamin Day, Joseph Leonard, John Felt, Daniel Lewis, Sr., and Jedediah Smith. The last named colonist was, for a number of years, a Congregational preacher at Greenville, Mass. He brought with him ten children, who were left fatherless immediately on their arrival at Natchez, as Mr. Smith died there. Other colonists also died, but the majority survived the change of climate and grew wealthy within a few years.

On July 30, 1776, Phelps, above named, who in 1774 returned to Connecticut to bring hither his family and friends, reported his arrival at New Orleans en route to the Black river valley. He preferred going south into the land of sunshine rather than to the Canadian land of snow. He left New Orleans August 18, 1776, accompanied by his friends from Connecticut and Massachusetts, the party comprising Captain Phelps, his wife and four children; Josiah Flowers, wife and one child; Joseph Leonard, wife and six children, and the hired boatmen. It was a fatal journey. On September 6 Flowers' wife died at Point Coupee; Leonard's wife died at Natchez; Phelps' daughter died on September 16, his son on the 23d, his wife on November 24, and on the same day his two remaining children were drowned near the mouth of the Big Black river. Seven of a colony of seventeen were lost before they reached the settlement selected for them. At that time one Philip Alston had his cabin at or near Petit gulf, and Ira Whitman and Nathaniel Hull, of the Lyman colony, had their cabins at Grand gulf. It does not appear that Leonard and Flowers met Phelps again as friends; but the latter's charity to Storrs and his son in 1774 was a verification of the Scriptural adage of casting bread upon the waters, for the indigent adventurers he then aided were now his friends, and true ones. They supplied him with food and shelter, and later, when he was able to work, gave him funds to purchase a new claim and the necessary equipment for a farm at that period.

The introduction of immigrants in large numbers during the year ending in 1776, suggested the propriety of establishing the town of Natchez according to the plans of 1775 by General Putnam, Lyman, Captain Enos and others. The site of Fort Rosalie of 1699–1718–1732 was then hidden under large forest trees, averaging twenty-four inches in diameter, and save the terrible story of the massacre of 1729, or the old iron cannon lying around, there was nothing to show of its former greatness. In the Natchez district were seventy-eight families, as many slaves and some few troops. In the village proper were ten log cabins and two frame houses, located under the bluff. The stores were kept by Hanchette & Newman; Blomart, a reduced British army officer; Thomas Barber and Captain James Willing, of Philadelphia. Willing was established there by New Orleans friends of the Revolution, notably the merchant, Pollock, and the Spanish governor, Galvez. He was the only American at Natchez, and naturally merited the contempt which his British neighbors meted out in liberal quantities to himself and his store. As a business man he did not succeed, so that in 1777 he surrendered mercantile life and sought a diplomatic mission.

As trouble waited on the French settlers of Natchez, so now it was to loom up before the British settlers. In 1777, Colonels Gibson and Linn, of the Continental army, were sent from Fort Pitt to New Orleans to procure arms, ammunition and supplies, as well as to feel the pulse of the immigrants. Oliver Pollock, then a merchant of New Orleans, a wise, liberal man, a friend of Galvez, the governor, and a pronounced American and agent of the United States, received the officers gladly. Their orders were filled—the ammunition being taken from the king's magazine—with the knowledge of the governor—and they set out for Fort Pitt, passed Natchez in safety, and arrived at their destination with good news for the army. Shortly after their return Captain Willing was sent south on a similar errand, and subsequently, through the influence of Robert Morris, Charles Carroll and John Hancock, was commissioned to win over the Natchez settlers to the Union by peaceable means if possible. Early in March, 1778, this impulsive Philadelphian, accompanied by twenty-five men, disembarked at the mouth of Big Black, published his commission and called a meeting of the settlers. Claiborne states that over a hundred men assembled. Willing, in excellent language, told them that the British were beaten, and that five or eight thousand men, under General Clark, were en route to take possession of the lower Mississippi valley. The settlers, seeking protection above all other things, took the iron-clad oath tendered by Willing, and the diplomat proceeded to Natchez, where some opposition to his scheme was manifested. Convinced of the true thought of the more influential planters there, he determined to deprive them at least of the means of yielding financial support to the enemies of the republic, and appropriated a good deal of property, made Colonel Hutchins, the prime oppositionist, prisoner, but released others on taking the oath. Pursuing his way south, he beheld an armed British merchant ship anchored at Manchac, and this also he and thirteen men appropriated. Within a month this Willing inflicted terrible damage on British interests in the South, and suggested the question: "Why not send Willing against the English regiments? He can appropriate them easily." Sir William Dunbar, a British baronet and a resident near Baton Rouge, wrote a very graphic account of Willing's expedition on May 1, 1778. It is needless to say that it differs materially from the report made by the United States agent or diplomat. The baronet himself was alarmed for many reasons, and before penning the following memoranda took care to remove his human and other chattels into Spanish territory. He says:

Upon my arrival at Mr. Method's house at Point Coupee, about a league below the fort, I there found Mr. Alexander with his negroes, having just escaped from the English side. He informed me that he had learned that the intention of the Americans was to rob and plunder every English subject who had property of any value, some few excepted, and that several obnoxious people were to meet with particular marks of their displeasure. The party was commanded by James Willing, of Philadelphia, a young man who had left this country the year before and intimately acquainted with all the gentlemen upon the river, at whose houses he had often been entertained in the most hospitable manner and had frequently indulged his natural propensity for getting drunk. * * * Several of his boats were already arrived at the fort, where they made no secret of their intentions. They had taken from the Natchez Colonel Hutchins with his negroes; they plundered Harry Stuart's house and seized the negroes and other property at Cumming's plantation; they divided the property at Castle's, taking one-half for his partner's share but leaving the other half unhurt for himself.. Presently two of the bateaux pass and land at Mr. Walker's plantation, where they shot a number of hogs and other stock. In the afternoon the rest of Willing's boats pass down and lastly, about sunset, the general himself dropped down and put ashore at Walker's, where the houses were rummaged and everything of any value secured for the commodore's use, after which the Heroic Captain ordered his men to set fire to all the houses and indigo works. The day following, this Troop of Rascals proceed downwards, a party is sent to the plains to seize Dutton, his wife and all his negroes, and at the same time burn all his staves at the river side, by which the poor man is reduced to the lowest ebb of poverty, with a family of small children. From hence they proceed to Baton Rouge, where they find no negroes on the English side but those whom, at that time, they considered as friends. There, the villains grow bold. Finding small game on the English side, they pass over the Spanish territories, and seize the negroes of Poussett and Marshall. Mine had been put at a considerable distance from the river side, by which means they could not discover them; the houses of the British gentlemen on the English side were plundered, and among the rest, mine was robbed of everything that could be carried away—all my wearing apparel, bed and table linen; not a shirt was left in the house—blankets, pieces of cloth, sugar, silverware; in short, all was fish that came in their net. They destroyed also a considerable quantity of bottled wine, though they carried away no liquor. The party which robbed my house landed at Francis', immediately below; the orders given by their head were to drive down my negroes, and if opposed by any one to shoot 'em down. They returned with information that the negroes were gone, but that much property remained in the house, which they were ordered to carry away, and accordingly made three or four trips, carrying at each time a large blanketful of the ware above mentioned. In the whole I was plundered of £200 sterling value. About this time it was discovered that Willing had left Fort Pitt with a batteau, and only twenty-five men, with orders to proceed to New Orleans and take charge of such stores as were prepared for him by Pollock, and return with the same up the Ohio, and also if he found himself able, to make capture of British property on the river, but no directions were given to disturb the peaceable inhabitants on land. Notwithstanding these orders, Captain Willing conceived the design of making his fortune at one coup upon the ruin and destruction of his old friends and intimates. His chief reason was that he had, by his folly, squandered a fortune upon the river, and 'twas there he ought to repair it. In order to effect this, his hellish purpose, he recruited and collected together on his way down all the vagabonds and rascals he met with, of which kind the river is always full, engaging them upon the alluring expectation of enriching themselves by plunder, and his numbers upon his arrival in this settlement amounted to two hundred, much more than sufficient to accomplish his design if we consider that perhaps one-half of the inhabitants were in the American interest, which circumstance being well known to the loyal part of the people, was the means of tying up their hands, and preventing their attempts to oppose the banditti, not to mention the report of their great numbers, which were at first much exaggerated. Upon learning that the party had reached Manchac, I made a trip from Point Coupee down to our settlement, and found upon my arrival a letter for me from Willing, enclosing a passport of safety for myself and negroes until further orders, the three latter words taking from it every idea of security. I placed no confidence in the words of the mighty captain, but immediately made the proper dispositions for removing my negroes to Point Coupee, where, being in the neighborhood of a Spanish post, I judged our security would be greater. This point being accomplished, I set out for New Orleans in order to see what was likely to be the end of all this plunder, and to be better able to judge what plan I ought to follow. On my way down of an evening, I met two of the American boats on their way up again for more plunder, in which they were but too fortunate. A small party of forty men had been left at Maushee by Willing, commanded by Elliot, which was attacked in the night by Mr. Chrystie. The Americans lost three or four people and the rest were dispersed and taken prisoners. Chrystie's party being small and having many prisoners, he thought it prudent to retire, by which the coast became again clear for the Willingites. The two boats under the command of Harrison and flat-nosed Elliot at length reached the settlement of Baton Rouge, and surprised Messrs. Williams, Watts and Dicas, made them prisoners with all their negroes, notwithstanding that these gentlemen had had every assurance of protection and safety, and in consequence had taken oaths of neutrality. They were all brought to town soon after my arrival, and a public vendue soon commenced of the plundered effects.

Sir William, unfortunately, overlooked the true object of the expedition. He could see at once that the killing of stock at Walker's was a necessity, for he must have known that Walker's was a cattle supply depot for Pensacola, Manchac and other British posts, and that the attachment of the other persons named to Great Britain was of such a pronounced character that the United States officer was in duty bound to render them innocuous to the point of depriving them of life. Colonel Hutchins, who was paroled at New Orleans by Willing, hearing of the determination of that official to send a company of his men to Natchez, fled from the city, and when Lieutenant Harriman and thirty-five men arrived opposite White Cliffs, there also was Colonel Hutchins commanding a body of English to oppose them. The fact of Willing's men reëntering or threatening to reënter the settlement was sufficient cause in their minds to cast aside the oath the greater number had taken, to place old Fort Rosalie, then called Fort Panmure, in a good condition and to garrison it with armed men. While making such preparations for defense, they petitioned General Campbell, commanding the Highlanders and British colonial militia at Pensacola, to send on troops at once to aid them. A force under Capt. Michael Jackson arrived in response to the petition and at once took possession of the fort, driving out the local companies under Bloomart, Lyman and McIntosh. This officer, Jackson, was so imperious, that the expelled volunteers under Colonel Hutchins (formerly captain in the Sixtieth British infantry) arrested him and placed Lyman in command. Jackson was now paroled, like Hutchins at New Orleans, but instead of flying he gathered thirty men under his flag, dashed against the fort, captured two guns and a supply of provisions, retired to the landing below, and sent thence a messenger agreeing to enter the fort and remain until a decision might be rendered by General Campbell. This proposition was accepted, and Jackson and his men were once more in possession. He expected that the Choctaws would come to his assistance, as they were then in treaty with the British, but the chief, learning from the white settlers the cause of the trouble, withdrew his force. Meantime a number of the local armed force left the fort clandestinely, and after them

Jackson sent Lieutenants Pentacoast and Holmes with a small force. On coming up with the refugees, John Felt, one of Lyman's colonists, shot and killed Pentacoast, leaving Holmes and his men free to return. Jackson was disappointed, and through some means permitted the non-military subjects of his Britannic majesty to again get control. After a little while Jackson organized a party of his men, regained control, placed Captain Lyman in prison and was virtually master of affairs until the British commandant at Manchac sent a detachment of the Sixteenth British infantry to dispossess and arrest him. The wily Jackson learned of this, and gathering his most trusted men about him, the valuable stores were collected and the party fled. Captain Foster, the new commandant, made the other men prisoners, dispatched them to Pensacola, where many of them were sentenced to death by General Campbell and his court. At that time the military posts at Pensacola, Mobile and Manchac were complete in their garrisons and equipments, and there can be little doubt that much of the supplies for the British troops and their continental and Indian auxiliaries were gathered at and distributed from those posts. On September 10, 1779, an armed vessel was in the gulf by order of congress with Capt. William Pickles in charge, and on this same date this modest ship attacked and captured the British sloop of war West Florida. It was an instance of American courage such as marked McDonough's action at the beginning of the Revolution and Perry's in 1813. For diplomatic reasons the Spanish king wished the young republic success, and for reasons of friendship for Pollock and other Americans, Governor Galvez gave this royal wish its broadest interpretation.

In May, 1779, Spain declared war against Great Britain, and on July 8 orders arrived at New Orleans outlining the part to be taken by the colony. What followed belongs to military history and is recorded therein. Enough to say that every British post before which the Spaniards appeared, from Natchez to Mobile, fell at once and Spanish troops took the places of the British regiments. The British round Natchez and American loyalists there now devised plans to aid General Campbell, who still held Pensacola, and who, though at liberty on Galvez' parole, expressed his readiness to break such parole. They put their plans in operation and, by a trick unworthy of Indians, gained* possession of the fort at Natchez, April 22, 1782, and placed the British flag aloft. The Spanish commandant and the little garrison were allowed to leave for Baton Rouge under guard of one Captain Winfree; but on their arrival at Davion's rock (now Fort Adams), they were pleased to see a large Spanish force ascending the river and made a dash for liberty. Winfree and the British guards fell back toward Natchez. The Spanish soldiers informed the commandant of the expedition of all that had occurred and he determined to disembark and pursue Winfree to his lair. The pursuer this time was an American, known in history as Major Mulligan. He came up with Winfree's men at the captain's house in the Homochitto valley, killed fourteen, wounded a greater number and made several prisoners. The news of the fall of Pensacola now reached the settlements and a general flight ensued. The settlers knew what faith they kept with both Spaniard and American, therefore expected little or no mercy and fled.

Col. Don Carlos de Grand Pre now arrived on the scene, not a moment too soon to save

---

* On page 195, Ellicott's Journal, a rare piece of local history is brought to light. It is nothing less than a sworn statement by a man who had, over and over again, denounced Captain Willing and others as great enemies of the country while himself was a paid agent of the enemy:

Maj. Anthony Hutchins maketh oath that he had not, between the 24th day of December, 1797, and the 24th day of December, 1798, any other place or employment of profit, civil or military, under his majesty, besides his military allowance as a provincial officer.

Sworn before me, the 2d day of January, in the year of our Lord 1799.

[Signed]   ISAAC JOHNSON.   ANTHONY HUTCHINS.

W.L.Sharkey

the lives of the settlers from the irritated American. He sent Capts. D. Blomart and Jacob Winfree in irons to New Orleans with Lieut. John Smith, George Rapalje, William Eason, Parker Carradine, Turney Mulkey, a Baptist preacher, George Alston and John Rowe. John Alston fled to the Chittemaches and was captured in their nation. Col. Anthony Hutchins, Capt. Thaddeus Lyman, Dr. Dwight Philip Mulkey, John Ogg, Christ. Bingaman, Philip Alston, Caleb Hansbrough, John Watkins, Thomas James, Eben. Gossett, Nathan Johnson, Thompson Lyman, John Turner, William Case and Captain Ellis sought safety in flight, and the former captain of the Sixtieth British infantry found himself safe in England. Dr. Dwight, his wife, Captain Lyman and others fled toward the British posts in the Carolinas. Butler, who in 1848 interviewed Calvin Smith on this subject, asserts that the other fugitives found refuge with a Scotchman, named Colbert, who was then living at Chickasaw Bluffs (Memphis) with an Indian family. There they organized the River brigands, who preyed upon travelers until a proclamation, permitting them to return, was published.

How did the Spaniards treat the unruly settlers? Through the influence of Alexander McIntosh many of them were pardoned immediately. Mulligan ordered one of Hutchins' negroes to be hanged; the Indians killed some members of his party while escaping; but Grand Pré's saving hand was visible. He protected the property of Mrs. Hutchins and the woman herself until she appeared before Gov. Don Pedro Piernas, who not only permitted her to hold all the property claimed by her husband, but also left her all his own personal property except twelve slaves, which he took with him to New Orleans. This gracious act on the part of Piernas was even a mystery to Grand Pre, who first suggested her protection. Later, the British grants to Hutchins were confirmed to him, and he was allowed to return. In several cases the Spanish commandant granted the confiscated lands to the innocent wives and children of the malcontents, and even appointed trusted men to guard such property for them. In September, 1782, Don Estevan Miro was appointed temporary governor-general of Louisiana and commandant at Natchez, but in November of that year was succeeded by Piernas, above named, who remained at Natchez until June, 1783, when he was ordered to make headquarters at New Orleans. Francisco Collett became commandant and served until August, 1783, when Don Philip Trevino was appointed.

In October, 1785, Don Francis Bouligny succeeded Trevino, but in March, 1786, Don Carlos de Grand Pre was sent to preside over the district, and served very acceptably until January 1, 1792, when Don Manuel Gayoso de Lemos took his place with the title of governor of Natchez. At the same time Carondelet succeeded Miro as governor-general. The census in 1785 gave a population of fifteen hundred and fifty persons, exclusive of the sixty soldiers at Fort Rosalie. In 1788 the number increased to twenty-six hundred and seventy-nine. The British soldiery and peasants were driven out or fled, but Spain was not yet secure in her possessions, for France and England had still designs on Florida, Georgia was persistent in her claim to Bourbon county, and the United States held that the treaty of San Lorenzo, made October 27, 1795, designating latitude thirty degrees north as the southern boundary should take effect. To enforce this claim Andrew Ellicott arrived at Vicksburg February 19, 1797, and at Natchez five days later. On February 27, 1797, Ellicott wrote to Governor Carondelet as follows:

NATCHEZ, February 27, 1797.

Sir: It is with pleasure that I embrace this opportunity of informing you of my arrival at this place, as commissioner on behalf of the United States, for ascertaining the boundaries between the territory of his Catholic majesty and those of the said United States.

The polite manner in which I have been received at the posts on the Mississippi, now in the possession of his Catholic majesty, demands my thanks and gratitude, and I am in hopes that similar

5

conduct will be observed on our part. I have the honor to be, with great esteem, your excellency's humble servant,   ANDREW ELLICOTT.

Two days later Ellicott hoisted the American flag, contrary to the law, but Gayoso de Lemos contented himself with an official order to fold it until the boundary question should be settled. Ellicott left it flying, however, and the governor, friendly at all times to the United States, looked upon the surveyor henceforth as something of whom the new republic wished to be rid.

A new era in the history of Mississippi was introduced on July 26, 1797. Gayoso de Lemos was commissioned governor-general, and left Natchez July 30. Major Minor was appointed temporary commandant, and served as such until November, 1797, when Grand Pre was commissioned governor of Natchez district. On March 30, 1798, the post was evacuated, and early that morning the United States troops, under Captain Guion, took possession of the works. It was well that Guion, Freeman and other United States officers came so soon after this great astronomer and surveyor; otherwise, the Spanish officers would have left the district, crediting to American officials the lowest instincts and the basest hypocrisy. See what men who knew him wrote: Maj. Thomas Freeman, sworn before court-martial at Fredericksburg, in September, 1811, charged Ellicott with being a liar, a corrupt official and a man addicted to beastly habits. General Wilkinson is very severe on this first American official in West Florida. John Walker, a son of the first district clerk at Natchez, writing from Philadelphia, June 1, 1800, says: "Mr. Ellicott and the rest of us had a very disagreeable voyage from Savannah to this city. The woman Mr. Ellicott brought to Natchez with him and had with him on the survey, became deranged on the passage, and but for Mr. Collins, Mr. Anderson and myself, would have killed herself. She is now frantic and chained in a madhouse. Mr. Ellicott must feel remorse for forcing her to remain on the line with him during the whole survey, against her own wishes and the remonstrances of her friends." On June 10, 1798, Major Freeman, in a letter to Major Guion, calls this woman "Ellicott's brazen-faced Dulcinea." Wailes, Claiborne and almost everyone who has taken up the history of his times in Mississippi, declares him to be a dangerous man, of no moral principle, filled with an idea of his own importance and willing always "to scuttle ship or cut a throat," were the remuneration in moneys or values enough and his own life secure. It was well, indeed, that the United States officers came so quickly on the scene, and by their excellent deportment, eradicated the foul stain which this Ellicott had left on American character.

On May 19, 1781, the Spanish troops defeated the British all along the line, and repossessed the posts taken from them in 1763. In the midst of their successes, they merged justice into clemency, pardoning and protecting the large number of British Americans who opposed them until Mississippi became famous for her political and religious toleration.

The action of Georgia in 1785*, establishing Bourbon county, was hypocritical to a degree. It was carried by the legislative mob, against the reasoning and desire of a small but honorable minority. Four years after its passage, Georgia sold to the South Carolina Yazoo Company five million acres, in what is now the yellow loam region of Mississippi. The price accepted was $65,000. The Virginia Yazoo Company purchased seven million acres, extending from the northeastern prairie region and including it, across the state to the Mississippi.

---

*The act of the Georgia legislature, approved February 7, 1785, established Bourbon county, with the Mississippi for its western boundary, north of latitude thirty-one degrees, and made grants of land here up to the period of cession in 1802, when Georgia transferred her territorial claims on Bourbon county to the United States. In 1803 subjects of Great Britain and Spain and citizens of France, who claimed lands here under old grants, or by virtue of occupation, were insured title by the United States, and settlers from the South Atlantic states turned their attention to the unclaimed lands on the Tombigbee and west of it to Pearl river.

The price was $93,000. Zachariah Coxe purchased three million five hundred acres in northern Alabama for $46,000, for his Tennessee Company, and actually located his lands and settled his colony there, in opposition to the United States and Spain. Opposition more stern came from another quarter, in the person of the Cherokee, Chief Glass, whose order to remove was instantly obeyed, and the Coxe block houses were destroyed by fire. Dr. James O'Fallon, connected so closely with Indian treaties in the North, essayed to take the same steps in the interest of the South Carolina Yazoo Company, and would have carried his colony into central Mississippi, had not St. Clair dispersed his forces.

Georgia now took the wheel, and on February 7, 1795, an act was passed, authorizing the sale of twenty-one million five hundred thousand acres, for $5,000,000. A number of desperate Georgians, among them Zachariah Coxe, formed into four syndicates, and purchased almost the entire state. The honor of Georgia shone forth during the session of the next legislature in the repeal of the act and the public burning of the original bill. Washington was then presiding over the destinies of the young republic, but with Georgia her own master, he could do little more than temporize. Fortunately, Spain came to the relief of the young nation, and by treaty of October 27, 1795, ceded the territory north of latitude thirty-one degrees, from the Mississippi to the Chattahoochie, down that stream to its confluence with Flint river, thence to the head of St. Mary's river and down as far as the Atlantic ocean to the United States. An arrangement between the United States and Georgia provided for the payment of $1,250,000 to the latter from the proceeds of land sales in Bourbon county and the confirmation of the title to claimants under the state's pretensions. A provision for holding five million acres to quiet the claims of such buyers from Georgia was also agreed upon, but this was ultimately settled by the payment to them of $5,000,000 for the relinquishment of their title and all moneys advanced by them to Georgia for such land grants, and thus the vicious error of Georgia, know as the "Yazoo fraud," was repaired, so far as the young republic dare venture to rectify it*.

Early in 1795 Governor Gayoso sent troops to a point near Chickasaw bluffs to begin the erection of a fort, and on May 30, that year, he moved his headquarters from Esperanza to that point and named the place Fort St. Ferdinand in honor of the saint whose fete day it was. The Chickasaws objected to the presence of the military, and interested Governor Blount, who conferred with the executive. In November, 1795, Blount wrote to Governor Gayoso, making a Colonel McKee messenger, stating that the president desired him to remove the building and troops, but McKee did not report the answer until April, 1796, Blount, meantime, intriguing with the British to take possession of Louisiana. On May 20, 1797, General Wilkinson ordered Captain Guion to take possession of the Spanish posts on the east bank of the Mississippi in accordance with the treaty hitherto ratified, and Guion proceeded down the Ohio on his mission. At New Madrid his fleet was halted by the Spanish commandant, Don Carlos Dehault le Lassus, who, however, permitted him to proceed on condition that he would not pass the lower Chickasaw bluffs until the terms of the treaty were made known to the Spanish officers. Such terms were accepted, and on July 20 Guion's force arrived at the bluffs only to find Fort St. Ferdinand abandoned and the Spanish garrison occupying Fort Esperanza (or Hopefield) on the western bank of the river under Captain Bellechase.

* In 1817 a statement made by the commissioners of the Yazoo claims, in relation to Mississippi stock certificates, showed the following amounts: Awards to the Mississippi Company, $350,000; to the Tennessee Company, $531,428.05; to the Georgia-Mississippi Company, $1,409,054.96; to the Georgia Company, $1,887,029.75, and to persons claiming under citizen's rights, $100,922.15, or a total of $4,278,434.91. Treasury certificates for $4,249,114.02 were issued in 1816, although only $431,120 was received from the sales of land up to that date. In 1817 the United States authorities placed the acreage in Mississippi territory to which the Indian title was extinguished, at five million nine hundred thousand, and the acreage then claimed by the Indians at forty-nine million one hundred thousand.

Even Esperanza was evacuated on September 1. A fort was at once erected and named Fort Adams, afterward called Fort Pickering, where a small garrison under Lieutenant Campbell was left in November, 1797, and the main body of United States troops moved down the river to Fort Nogales, commanded by Captain Beauregard, where a request for surrender would not be entertained by the commandant. With Yankee tact Guion pushed forward to Natchez, where he found Capt. Stephen Minor commanding the Spaniards, camped within a kilometer of the fort, and kept on excellent terms with the Spanish soldiers until their evacuation on March 30, 1798, under Capt. Don Jose Vidal. The United States troops took possession.

Winthrop Sargent, the governor, arrived early in August, 1798, and remained until the 8th, when he moved to Concord, and subsequently visited the venial Ellicott for inspiration. On March 29, 1798, there was only one prisoner in the district jail of Natchez; merrymaking was carried on Sunday afternoons with the same regularity that marked labor during the working days; neighbors were so in fact, and the Southern sun shed its rays on no happier people or no better people than the unofficial citizens of the United States round Natchez and in Louisiana that afternoon of March 29, 1798. The cloudy Sargent, accustomed only to criminal gayety and urged on by the unprincipled intriguer, Ellicott, looked on those health-giving amusements of the Sabbath afternoon with pretended awe, and on Monday wrote to the secretary of state a denunciation of all that was really good in the new territory, and a laudation of Ellicott and the other hypocritical ruffians who were associated with him in the defamation of a people. Sir William Dunbar, Major Thomas Freeman, Major Guion and a few other officials, protested against the outrageous lie and with effect; for a short time after the exorbitant license fees for permits to marry, to keep hotels, for passports and judicial fees—all gubernatorial perquisites—drew forth an emphatic condemnation from the planters and traders, and congress, in fact, sustained this denunciation of Sargent by condemning his system of fees and extending the principle of local government. In April, 1801, the unpopular governor left Natchez, under the pretense of visiting his home, and in July President Jefferson commissioned William C. C. Claiborne governor, having previously advised Sargent of his deposition on account of his inability to deal justly by the people. The ex-governor subsequently stated that there were no schools at Natchez, when he knew positively that two private schools, presided over by skilled Spanish pedagogues, existed before and during his short term of office. On Coles creek, where Governor Gayoso's unofficial residence stood, a school for the use of soldiers' and settlers' children was conducted up to the date of evacuation.

In 1800 Mississippi territory contained eight thousand eight hundred and fifty persons, including three thousand four hundred and eighty-nine slaves. There were nine hundred and ninety-nine white male children under ten years of age, three hundred and fifty-six between ten and sixteen, four hundred and eighty-two white male persons between sixteen and twenty-six, seven hundred and eighty between twenty-six and forty-five, and two hundred and ninety over forty-five years. The number of white females of the respective ages were nine hundred and thirty-three, three hundred and seventy-six, three hundred and fifty-two, four hundred and twenty-six and one hundred and sixty-five. Other free citizens except Indians numbered one hundred and eighty-two. In 1816 the registered tonnage of the state engaged in foreign trade was four hundred and thirty and sixty-eight-hundredths tons; of small vessels in coasting trade, one hundred and ninety-two and fifty-five-hundredths tons.

American discontent with Spain grew out of the edict closing the port of New Orleans against the United States. In January, 1803, this discontent became so marked that Governor Claiborne suggested the conquest of New Orleans with the two thousand militia of the territory, but fear of a combination of French and Spaniards prevented the acceptance of the suggestion. Eleven months later we find him on the road to New Orleans with an escort of Natchez rifles, Natchez artillery, Jefferson guards, Claiborne cavalry and Claiborne rifles. This motley crowd of semi-drilled men accompanied the governor to a point near the Louisiana line, latitude thirty degrees, leaving him in charge of the French escort from that point. On December 20, 1803, M. de Lausat, minister-plenipotentiary of the French republic, made to him and General Wilkinson formal transfer of the territory of Louisiana.

The title of the United States to public lands was obtained by five distinct methods—conquest of English colonies, treaties with France, Spain and England, cession by states under the old confederate system, contract with Georgia and treaties with Indians. The Revolution is the history of the first method; by the treaty of 1783 Great Britain surrendered everything demanded; in 1787 South Carolina, and in 1790 North Carolina, surrendered claims for lands outside their limits; by the treaty of 1802 the French republic sold Louisiana; the same year Georgia sold her claim to what are now the states of Mississippi and Alabama, and subsequently the Indians relinquished title to almost every acre of the domain. In 1780, when the success of the Revolution was known, Virginia, Massachusetts, Connecticut and New York ceded their lands in the Northwest territory to the national government, with the exception of some reservations and private claims. In the first instance the revolutionists invested their time, their military services, their moneys and lands, and many lives in the conquest of the country from the British, and borrowed about $80,000,000, also. For the purchase of Louisiana, $15,000,000 were paid; for the purchase of Florida, $5,000,000; for the Georgia claims and Yazoo lands, $6,200,000; for the Indian lands, $5,811,191; and expenses of selling such Indian and Yazoo lands up to January 19, 1830, $1,578,339, or a direct payment of $36,029,191 to France, Spain, Georgia and the Indians, apart from the incalculable sum which the Revolution cost. Such little items as a $20,000 draft sent to surveyor Jo. Dunbar, at Washington, Miss., in April, 1830, and cashed for him by the bank at Natchez, are not included in this estimate, nor are the moneys subsequently paid to the Indians considered.

The congressional act of March 3, 1803, donated one-thirty-sixth part of the lands in this state, to which the Indian title was extinguished, for the support of common schools. The area so donated was three hundred and ninety-four thousand one hundred and twenty-three and seventy-two-hundredths acres, valued at $492,654.65. On March 1, 1817, an act provided that five per cent of the net proceeds from the sale of public lands should be applied within the state to roads and canals—three-fifths of same to be expended under the direction of the state and two-fifths under direction of congress. By December 31, 1828, this fund amounted to $50,485.64.

In 1830 the trouble arising from irregular surveys was noticeable. One of the first cases was that brought forward by Green and Peter Prior, who in 1818 purchased four hundred and forty acres in section two, township fourteen, range five east, Claiborne county, from Isham Arthur. The latter bought for $880 in 1816, and sold for $1,200. The Priors made their petition in such form that, if granted, they would own one thousand one hundred and forty-five acres. It was disallowed, but a tract of four hundred and forty acres was patented to them.

The survey of that part of the state south of latitude thirty-one degrees was nearly completed at the close of 1826, and of the fourteen million one hundred and eighty-eight thousand four hundred and fifty-four acres then owned by the nation in Mississippi, eight million seven hundred and thirty-three thousand nine hundred and twenty-eight acres were surveyed and eleven million six hundred and forty-three thousand two hundred and seventy-five acres remained to be sold. On January 1, 1826, the unceded and reservation lands of the Indians of this state embraced fourteen thousand one hundred and eighty-eight and forty-five hundredths acres, equal to the total area purchased up to January 1, 1826.

The three English speaking settlements of Mississippi territory at the beginning of the Creek war in 1813 were those in the Natchez district extending up the Big Black, those in the counties now known as Jackson, Harrison, Hancock, Green and Wayne, and those in the Tennessee valley. Between each settlement were the Indians, numerous and unfriendly. South and west were the aristocratic French and Spaniards, northwest and north the wilderness, and east the Muscogees, painted for war against the Caucasian. The French settlements of 1699–1718 passed away in 1729; the British settlements of later years may be said to have died out before the close of the century or on the conquest by the Spaniards in 1781–2, and a new race of frontiersmen now had possession. The immigrants had aided in righting the wrongs which weighed them down in the old colonies; they had, as simple soldiers of the Revolution, driven tyranny off and came hither to win new triumphs. They came in time, too, for the desperate royalists of Great Britain determined to crush out the young nation, and by attacking it on all sides, destroy it. We know of the daring feats of the Mississippi dragoons in 1813–15. There is no prouder or no grander service recorded than that of Mississippians at New Orleans, where theirs and Creole valor conquered the large, well-fed, disciplined army of Great Britain on that memorable eighth of January, 1815.

With the men who had served in the Revolution others flocked in. They saw a measure of security offered in the wilderness, and the men who were not workers themselves came hither to enjoy life at the smallest possible expenditure of money and labor.

Stonie Hadje, a Creek warrior and an adopted son of the Choctaws, died in Noxubee county, in 1835. Coleman Cole, said to be the last of the Chocchumas, died near Bellefontaine about this time, and the decade ending 1840 saw many an old Indian cast aside the weeds of mortality. Years before, the noblest of the Choctaws passed away. Pushmataha was succeeded by Netakacha, even as Pushmataha succeeded the great chief Pukshanubbee. According to his own belief he had no parents; the lightning struck a great oak and out jumped Pushmataha with his paint and feathers, as a full-fledged warrior, capable of leading his tribe! He was one of the three medal chiefs of the Choctaw nation who was given the title and uniform of a general in the United States army in 1813, and in November of that year brought fifty-one warriors against the Creeks. Lieutenant Callahan directed the work of this little command of savages, but it was Pushmataha who led them. Prior to this he won renown in every raid on the trans-Mississippi towns, always returning with scalps enough to decorate the village pole. Claiborne relates many incidents in the life of this savage, which can not be overlooked. During his service against the Creeks, a soldier offered him some insult, when the chief struck him with the flat of his sword. General Claiborne told him that such a breach of discipline could not be permitted; but the stoical Indian related the character of the insult and concluded by stating: "Being only a private I struck him with the flat of my sword, but had it been you, general, I should have used the edge." On another occasion he discovered a soldier tied to a post and was told the fellow was drunk. The chief looked upon him as a martyr and, untying the prisoner, remarked, "Many great warriors get drunk." He was a polygamist of no mean character. Seeing what numbers of young warriors were annually swept away by war, he reasoned that those who were not killed should claim as many wives as possible, so that the strength of the nation may be kept up to a certain standard. His death took place immediately after his historical interview with General Lafayette, and while his old friend, Gen. Andrew Jackson, looked on the dying warrior.

Greenwood le Fleur, son of the Canadian, Louis le Fleur, by a Choctaw woman, played an important part in the drama which ended in the emigration of his tribe. He was born in 1800. His father was owner of a flatboat on the Amité and lower lakes, and through his labors transporting freight and passengers became comparatively wealthy, and when the son became chief of the Yazoo district, showed the father's money-making instincts. When the Natchez trace was opened Louis refused to permit white immigrants to settle thereon, and wisely held it for the Indians and half-breeds. Thus we see the Colberts, Folsoms and le Fleurs gathering in the shekels from travelers over this route, and growing in wealth as travel increased. Their own interests suggested that travelers should be protected, and presently "the Light-horsemen" appear to guard the trail from robbers. Greenwood was sent to school at Nashville, returned in 1817, and seven years later was elected chief. In 1828 he was reëlected, and, after the Indians were forcibly removed beyond the Mississippi, the astute Greenwood is found here at the head of a mercantile house, a plantation, an army of slaves, and a large dwellinghouse. In later years he represented Carroll county in the legislature, and in 1871 his name was given to the newly organized county, Le Flore. He aided Dale, McRay, Armstrong, and all the other friends of the Choctaws in their negotiations with the Indians, and earned from the tribe the many maledictions heaped upon him. Greenwood le Fleur was no better or no worse than the Pitchlyns, Colberts, McKees, Allens and Folsoms. They were squawmen, and, as such, were lost to all sense of morals or decency. Like le Fleur, they were children of circumstances, and the history of one is the history of all.

Jacob Young, a Methodist preacher, tells of his arrival at Colbert's ferry in 1808, and his call on Col. George Colbert. This savage was the son of a Scotchman by a Chickasaw woman. His wives were sisters—daughters of Doublehead, the Cherokee chief. Those women managed and fed the forty negro slaves and attended to their husband's tavern as well, leaving him free to mingle with the Indians and indulge in his witticisms with white travelers. On this occasion he had to speak not only with Young, but also with Richard Browning, John Travis, Jedediah McMinn, James Axley and Anthony Houston—all preachers for the new Mississippi district. Colbert was equal to the occasion. Through his influence the Natchez trace was surveyed by his cabins, so that travelers should support both his ferry and his tavern. He was certainly a prince of no estate and small power. He looked at his visitors curiously and asked, "Where are you all going?" "To Natchez." "What are you going there for?" was the next query. "To preach," was the answer. This was too seriously comic for the half-breed who, after a thorough laugh said, "Ah, Natchez people great for preach; but they be poor, lazy, thieving, bad people." Resuming his questions he asked, "Where are you from?" Young replied, "From Kentucky." Colbert did not receive the information kindly, and expressed himself thus: "Kentuckians are bad people, and white men are worse than Indians everywhere, though they have much preaching and much learning. The Indians never knew how to steal, get drunk and swear until the white men learned them. We want no preaching in our country. We are free and intend to keep it so." Colbert carried out this intention until 1818, when douceurs of divers kinds were given to him and he aided in selling the liberties of his people. To what extent he carried polygamy will never be known. He made money on the Natchez trace, received valuable considerations from the United States, and was at once sultan, grand vizier, pasha and high priest of his tribe.

The Tanner settlement of 1804 was made four miles southwest of Woodville. Robert Tanner set out from Beaufort, S. C., with a pioneer company of ninety-seven persons, arrived on the banks of the Tennessee, built rude boats there and sailed down the rivers to Fort Adams.

Harman Blennerhassett, a graduate of Trinity college, Dublin, discontented under the tyranny exercised over his country, sold his lands there and sailed for the United States in 1797. Soon after he purchased an island of one hundred and seventy acres of land in the Ohio river, two miles below Parkersburg, and had erected there a chateau, the first modern building in the state. In 1805 he was visited by Aaron Burr and led into the schemes of Mexican empire entertained by that clever rascal. Burr, *lui-meme*, was to be emperor and Blennerhassett a duke and lord-high-executioner of the empire. No wonder that the wealthy, aristocratic Irishman fell into Burr's trap and invested moneys in his enterprise. President Jefferson's proclamation and the warning of friends ultimately had some effect on the enthusiast, and, to escape arrest, he fled from his island home December 10, 1806, to seek the protection which Burr's flotilla (then at the mouth of the Cumberland) might offer. He was arrested, however, taken to Richmond, and the case against him *nolle-prossed*. Giving a period to reflection, he and another conspirator, Comfort Tyler, moved to Mississippi, where Blennerhassett purchased a plantation of one thousand acres near Port Gibson, Claiborne county. To this tract he gave the name La Cache and entered at once on its improvement. In 1813 he was a leader in the militia organization. In 1819 new trials waited on the exile. He and his eldest son, Dominic, assaulted a citizen named John Hays. He was fined $1,000, and his appeal to the Supreme court resulted only in a confirmation of the judgment. He saw real and fictitious creditors appropriate his beautiful home on the Ohio river, and even Burr's son-in-law, Governor Alston, "beat " him out of $22,500. The men who should be his friends at Natchez conspired to get hold of his property, so that it is not matter for surprise to find him seeking liberty and home in the bleak North at Montreal, again in Ireland, whence he proceeded to the Isle of Guernsey to die in 1831. His wife was the daughter of Governor Agnew of the Isle of Man. She was a poetess of some note, and, like her husband, was attached to fashion and looked for fame. Herself and husband were supported by Miss Blennerhassett from 1823 to 1831, and this maiden lady left a small estate to her widowed sister-in-law. In 1842 she returned to the United States and sought a grant from congress in lieu of the home of which lax laws robbed her; but before this grant was passed the lady died at New York and would have been buried in Potter's field had not the Sisters of Charity found a resting place for her body in the Thomas A. Emmett family burial lot. Dr. Thomas Gale became owner of La Cache plantation about 1820, and Samuel and John Coburn were proprietors in later years.

In February, 1807, when Aaron Burr was released on bail at Washington, Miss., he became the guest of Benajah Osmun, who then had his house at the foot of Hall-way hill. Near the hilltop was the cottage of the widow and her daughter Madeline. The husband sold his property in Virginia and set out for Mississippi, but was robbed and murdered by the sanguinary road agent, Joseph Thompson Hare. This daughter, Burr met and gave to her a promise of marriage which she, ignorant of his licentiousness, accepted, but the promise was never carried out, and, in later years, the lady married a Cuban merchant of Havana.

It is well to examine the title of a few early settlers. The grant to Thomas Green of land near Natchez, made September 1, 1782, was regranted February 24, 1783, to Peter Piernas, by the Spanish, and confirmed to his assignee, Robert Cochran, under the act of March 31, 1808. Thomas M. Green and William Barland testified for Green in this case. Palser Shilling testified to the arrest of T. M. Green and his slaves, the seizure of his papers and property, and the shipment of all to New Orleans. The Greens became very unruly subjects of Spain, and the course taken by the governor was the only one open to him. One Robert Cloyd came to Mississippi in July, 1796, although a grant was made to him in 1794.

He brought with him a wife and five children, made a small improvement, and died in 1796. Catura Wallis, Harrison Person, Thomas Evans and Cyrus Hamilton testified in favor of the Widow Cloyd's claim for the original grant on bayou Pierre.

Joseph Bernard's heirs claimed lands on Buffalo creek, under a grant of 1794. Benjamin Dorsey sold his lands on Homochitto river to Winfred Ryan, in January, 1797. Everard Green claimed lands on Coles creek, under a grant of 1792. Thomas Foster and family resided on Buffalo creek in 1795. Abram Taylor, wife and seven children lived in the Homochitto valley, in 1794. Job Corey and family resided on Coles creek. Alex. Montgomery built a cabin in the Homochitto valley in 1798, and in 1797 made a similar improvement on Buffalo creek, where lands were granted to him in 1789. David Carey, born in Mississippi, built a cabin in the Homochitto valley, in 1801. Prosper King resided there in 1797. James Stuart, one of Richard King's dragoons, was granted two hundred arpents by Governor Gayoso, in 1794, on bayou Pierre. Hugh Matthews had his family on the Big Black. In 1791 Henry Willis (died in 1794) bought the Sanders claim, on bayou Sara. Willis' widow married La Place, and in 1803 sold the claim to James Williams. A Mrs. Ann Savage attended to the financial affairs of Willis prior to his death. John O'Connor and Martin Carney resided on Coles creek; Henry Roach on Buffalo creek.

Justus King, a British grantee, resided on the Homochitto from 1776 to his death, in 1798; Nehemiah Carter has his cabin on Boyd's creek; William Henderson on Thompson's creek, and Charles Boardman on Fairchild's creek. In 1796 John McKay or McCoy built a cabin in the Homochitto valley. Garret Rapalje was granted ten hundred arpents at Walnut hills in 1790, and built a cabin there. He settled there with his sons, George, Isaac, Jacques and Garret. Jacques came in 1789, and died in 1797; George came in 1796; Isaac was also an early settler. Elihu Hall Bay also claimed the Rapalje lands, and brought John Givault to testify that the Watkins family had their cabin there as early as 1775. John Shackler, one of the soldiers sent to erect a fort there in 1791, remembered Governor Gayoso's statement that Rapalje had no claim, and that the cabin should not have been erected. William Vardiman claimed a homestead on Will's creek; Anthony Calvit on the Homochitto; Thomas Percy on bayou Sara; Col. John Ellis paid Thomas Green $2,000 for eight hundred arpents on Thompson's creek; Francis Jones located on Coles creek in 1788, and in ten years brought his family and slaves thither. William Thomas remembered an improvement there in 1790 or 1791. Robert Dunbar and family settled on bayou Pierre in 1781 on a British grant of 1778. Patrick Cogan and John Crunkleton were early settlers on bayou Pierre. In 1789 Adam Cloud settled on Coles creek; William Clare claimed lands there under a Spanish grant; Peter and Charles Surget resided on Feliciana creek, and Ann Brashears on bayou Pierre; Ben Foy near White Ground lick. William Irvine, Jemima Morgan, Robert Miller and Joseph Sharp are names connected with the British settlements on Coles creek. Ithmer Andrews resided on the Big Black in 1778, but, with others, was driven out by the Indians.

James Mather cultivated lands on bayou Sara in 1791. In 1788 Apple island was under water. Howard cultivated the island prior to that time for Charles Bachelot. Later one Tyler rebuilt there and purchased the land, as claimed by his heirs. Richard Trevellian and Edward Rose claimed tracts on bayou Pierre; William Vardeman, William Norris and Cahel King on the Homochitto, and Elizabeth Baker on Second creek. As early as 1776 Justus King cultivated his lands there, but was driven away by Indians in 1780. Later the tract was granted to James Kirk. William Calvet built on the Big Black in 1790; in 1779 Joshua Howard abandoned his British grant on Second creek. Richard Winn resided on bayou Pierre in 1794; Joseph Vauchreré on the Homochitto in 1788, when William Vousden surveyed for him.   William Thomas settled on bayou Pierre in 1794; Ralph Humphreys in 1789, in a cabin there purchased from Reuben White; Thomas Smith in 1795.

Early in the fall of 1795 James Cole hauled lumber to lot four, square twelve, Natchez, with the object of building, but was soon after ordered to Chickasaw bluff by his Spanish employer, and did not return until 1798.   In 1799 Thomas Fortner opened his lands on the Big Black.   William Silkrigs began the improvement of his British grant on the Mississippi in 1777.   In 1779 the Americans made him prisoner and carried him down the river.   He was afterward retaken by the British, but on returning found that the Indians had robbed his cabin and farm.   He afterwards settled in Adams county.   Patrick McDermott settled on his Spanish grant of four hundred and forty arpents on bayou Tunica in 1796, six years after he came to Mississippi.   William Hubbard (who had a wife and ten children in England) settled in his bayou Pierre cabin as early as 1774.   James Moor claimed lot one, square thirteen, Natchez, under grant of 1795, while lot one, square nineteen, to Tomasino Lord was regranted to William Dunbar.   Elijah Bunch located on Buffalo creek in 1793, and sold his claim to Peter Walker in 1797.   Hyram Swayze claimed one hundred and sixty-four arpents under Spanish grant of 1793, near Natchez, on which he had his cabin from 1782 to 1794.

The first land claim presented to the commissioners was that of February 13, 1804, by Isaac Ryan, for lands on Bassett's creek.   Francis Boykin, then a resident of Washington county for thirteen years, testified to Ryan's occupancy since 1797.   John Burney, who had a cabin on the head of House's mill creek, sold his claim in December, 1803, to James Morgan, and the former's occupancy was certified by Edward L. Wailes and J. Malone, the surveyor.   William Morgan's claim for three hundred and nineteen acres on Bassett creek branch was also presented.   Nathan Blackwell claimed a donation of six hundred and forty acres on the waters of the Tombigbee, surveyed by William Gilliam, and his occupation of the tract since 1795 was proven by Adam Hollinger and Young Gains.   Sterling Dupree claimed the lands on the Tombigbee located and built on by Emanuel Cheney in 1798, under the deed of July, 1801, from Cheney.   James Griffin claimed six hundred and eighteen acres on Smith's creek, as surveyed by Robert Ligon.   John McGrew, Sr., certified to Griffin's occupancy since 1797.   Elisha Simmons claimed four hundred and fifty-four acres on the west side of the Tombigbee, whereon he settled in February, 1801; William Rogers claimed three hundred and eighty-eight acres on the west side of the Tombigbee by virtue of his settlement thereon in February, 1800; Matthew Shaw settled the adjoining three hundred and thirty-three acres in the fall of 1802; James Caller's claim for lands on Smith creek and Tombigbee river was certified by F. Boykin, who settled thereon in 1795, abandoned it that year, when it was taken up by Jesse Bryant, who, with Henry Snelgrove, transferred the lands to Caller in 1803.   Ephraim Barker's claim for six hundred and forty acres in the Tombigbee valley sets forth that he settled thereon in 1797; Hiram Mounger claimed the lands on Sunflower creek on which Hezekiah and Solomon Wheat settled in 1795–6.   Owen Sullivan and George Brewer claimed Three River island, under the settlement rights of 1792–4, when Sullivan and William Brewer (died in 1793) located there.   Solomon Wheat's claim for lands on Bassett creek, and that of Richard Brashear, give many names connected with the early settlement of this section.

Benjamin Harrison and Thomas Goodwin were chain bearers for Surveyor William Gilliam in 1804.   Micajah Wall settled on Smith's creek in 1802.   Richard Lee settled on Jordan Morgan's claim of 1797, Wiley Barker claimed six hundred and forty acres opposite the upper end of Three Rivers island as settled by Daniel Barker in 1797.   Daniel died there in 1803; Wyche Watley claimed lands on the Sunflower, where Rebecca Kimbre settled in 1802.

She transferred her claim to Watley in October, 1802. John Brewer claimed lands on Johnson's creek under his squattership of 1797; Figures Lewis, on the west side of the Tombigbee, and on the west side of the most westerly prong of the Three Rivers, above Barker's landing, he having settled there and built a cabin in December, 1803; George Brewer, Jr., claimed the old James Watson, Alexander McGrew and Julian Castro settlement on Bassett's creek; Josiah Skinner settled on the Tombigbee in 1802; Anna Mounger in 1796; (she was the widow of Elijah Thompson, but married Sampson Mounger immediately after Thompson's death). John Jacob Abner, who settled at the mouth of the Polbyu in 1797, sold to Thomas Carson in 1803; Charles Brewer died in 1802 on Sunflower creek, and his heirs presented their claims in 1804; James Caller claimed lands two miles above Nana Hubba bluff, where Joseph Anderson settled in 1789, and Seth Dean purchased in 1803; William Hillis settled at the confluence of the Tombigbee and the Alabama in 1795, but sold to Howell Dupree in 1801; James Scott claimed the Gabriel Burrows settlement of 1797 on Bassett's creek; Thomas Bassett claimed the seven hundred and fifty acres granted to Nathaniel Bassett by the British above McIntosh bluff. On part of this claim one Stgoe Powell had his cabin. Thomas Bassett also claimed one thousand and fifty acres on Bassett's creek, granted to his father Thomas, by the British prior to 1781, and cleared before that year. There his father was murdered by British Indians in 1779 or 1780. Cornelius McCurtin claimed four hundred and eighty acres near Fort St. Stephens, as purchased by him for fifty silver dollars from Edward Lucas, July 19, 1790. Dr. John Chastang claimed four hundred and eighty acres adjoining the church at Fort St. Stephens, granted to him by the Spanish, where he resided as early as 1795. John Tally's grants of 1787 abutted on his lands as well as on those of Charles Stuart. In December, 1794, Tally sold his interests to Dr. Chastang. In April, 1799, Zadock Brashear, a settler of 1791, sold six hundred and forty acres to George Robbins. John Baptist Trenier claimed three hundred and twenty-seven acres on Grog Hall creek, near Dr. Chastang's lands; this tract was evacuated by McGillivray in 1780. In 1788 Anthony Hoggat discovered twenty unclaimed acres, which he obtained for a tobacco farm prior to 1791. Robert Walshe became owner in 1792, and continued so until 1798; Walshe was appointed Choctaw interpreter for the United States at Fort Stoddart in 1799, removed to the fort, but left his wife in possession of the land. Mrs. Walshe rented the farm to William Vardeman for an annual consideration of thirty Spanish barrels of corn. Vardeman paid the first year's rent, but refused to pay the second year, alleging that he was granted the tract by the British. Joseph House claimed six hundred and forty acres on Bassett's creek, on the fact that, in 1799, his father, Robert, agreed to take charge of Bassett's little mill, and in 1801 purchased the mill and lands. Solomon Boykin also claimed this property. Francis Stringer, who in February, 1798, settled on Stringer's mill branch of the Tombigbee, claimed six hundred and forty acres. James Frazier's claim for one thousand six hundred acres, on Toller creek, of the Tombigbee, was based on the Spanish grant of 1787. It included Farmer's tobacco farm of forty acres, which was abandoned by the Widow Farmer in 1780. Ann Lawrence, the legal representative of Moses Moore, claimed lands on the Sunflower, formerly owned by McIntosh, the interpreter and commissary to the Chickasaws during the British occupation. James Denley claimed the McGillivray lands on the Sunflower; Nicholas Perkins, Cornelius Rains (of Lawrence's creek); Lemuel Henry, of Anna Hubba bluff; Peter Malone, above Fort St. Stephens; John Baker (near the fort).

Edwin Lewis claimed six hundred and forty acres below the Hatchatigi by bluff and lake, to Sintabogue creek, conveyed to him in 1803 by Henry Nail. Wilson Carman, below Fort Stoddart; Simpson Whaley, above the fort; John McIntosh, at Turkey bluff, (granted by the British in 1775); Daniel Young, on Folsom's creek; Edward L. Wailes, near Fort St. Stephens, and a few other settlers east of Pearl river, presented their testimony to the United States commissioners of land claims, in 1804. All were then residents of Mississippi territory, and the greater number continued so until its division.

CHAPTER IV.

ORGANIZATION AND GOVERNMENTAL FORM.

TO the thoughtful there is a growth that attracts and interests far more than that development which is mere expansion. It is the growth which comes with changes to higher constitutional forms, an evolution from the crude to the more perfect. This is a development especially attractive when observed in government, where the body politic often changes its organic form as strikingly as that of the worm to the winged butterfly. We are wont to think that in our own America we have reached that form in government that corresponds to the place held by that most highly organized form of life— the human being. Indeed, the body politic is not so unlike man in many other marks. It thinks by public discussions of various kinds; it feels by public sentiment; it judges by its proper officials; its records are its memory; the laws are its will; its executive and army are its hands and arms, and its peculiar susceptibility to legal malaria or legislative yellow fever emphasizes its human characteristics, and warrants us in regarding it, at least for student purposes, not so much a collection of individuals as a social giant. With this view, our statesmen—and every voter who is not in some degree a statesman ought not to be in any degree a voter—would be able to save the social giant from many a bodily weakness or mental ailment, and insure us legal health and vigor.

Such a social giant is that people whose territory bears the old Ojibway name, Mississippi—a state of forty-six thousand three hundred and forty square miles*, with only four hundred and seventy square miles of water surface; twenty-eighth in order of size among the states and territories; about one-fifth the size of Texas; over thirty-seven times as large as Rhode Island; within a little over two thousand square miles of as large as Louisiana or New York; larger than Pennsylvania by over fifteen hundred square miles; than Virginia by over four thousand square miles, and than Tennessee by four thousand seven hundred and sixty square miles. It is a people embracing one million two hundred and eighty-nine thousand six hundred souls; twenty-first in population among the territories and states; about one-fifth the population of New York; over twenty-eight times as large as that of Nevada; within about twelve thousand of that of Minnesota, or about one hundred and thirty-seven thousand of that of Kansas; larger than that of California by over eighty thousand; than that of South Carolina by over one hundred and thirty-eight thousand, and than Louisiana by about two hundred and seventy-one thousand.

*Census of 1890.

Such a state is one of great power, and its organization and constitutional development would be interesting from that cause alone; but, aside from this, Mississippi's position, political and social antecedents, and striking, even romantic development, make her constitutional career one of the most interesting among our own or foreign states.

Covering a period of nearly two hundred years*, beginning with the Biloxi French colony, it naturally divides into two institutional, certainly, and we may say, constitutional epochs, slave and free, separated by the date, April 9, 1865, when Gen. Richard Taylor surrendered the last possible command in this state, and a new development began. This first epoch of one hundred and sixty-six years shows the territory shifted, now here now there, from old Roman law, as shown in French and Spanish control, to British, and finally to various changes under our own great republic's forms. It may be of value to let these one hundred and sixty-six years fall naturally into three periods: (1) The French period of sixty-four years, to 1763; (2) the English period of about twenty years, to 1783, when Spain had been an intruder since 1779, and continued so until 1798; and (3) the American period of eighty-two years—fifteen years as unsettled, to 1798; nineteen years as territory, to 1817; and forty-eight years as a state holding the institution of African slavery.

All of these periods have their influence in making Mississippi what it is in area, population, and government. One thing, however, was a molding power through them all, and that was the control of the great watery thoroughfare—the Mississippi river—whose controlling highland gates are in this territory. On this account there were at one time four different nations intriguing to get possession of it, not to speak of the semi savage nations who possessed the greater part. As all these nations had their representatives, resident in the territory, and who espoused the cause of their favorite power, it is not strange that accounts of character and action in those days are peculiarly conflicting, nor is it strange if each conflicting statement should seem true to those who made them; indeed each may have been true at different times, when, between capricious changes in Europe and all the uncertainties attending the gestation and birth of a new nation, men might not readily see in which direction lay the permanent good. For this reason this sketch will not speculate on the motives of the leaders of that time; the results of their actions are sufficient to prove that each tried to effect his conception of the public good. If there were different conceptions, it does not follow that the opponent must naturally have a villainous motive.

The three-cornered fight of France, England and Spain make a great part of the remarkable complications in which this territory figured, while the Indian interests and multiplicity of beliefs about the new nation of republics served to make it still more intricate and mazy. The French were holding the territory in friendly connection with the Indians, mingling with them and stamping French customs, families and names on the new country, always taking care to fortify the bluff gates at Walnut hills, and similar places along the river. They wanted the great river highway all those years from 1699 to sixty-four years later when, by their conflict with the British, whose growing colonies also wanted the river, they gave over the territory to England by treaty of February 16, 1763, and Spain also gave up the Floridas. On October 7 of that year the British king proclaimed the thirty-one degrees of north latitude as the northern boundary of the Floridas. At this point our territory is a part of the province of Georgia, excepting, of course, those coast counties below thirty-one degrees north latitude. Had England continued to possess all eastern territory, no conflict of boundary would have occurred in this state, into which British settlers now began to pour, encouraged by lavish grants of land. But meanwhile, Spain, who had

*This chapter treats 1699 as the beginning of civilization in this territory.

received all Louisiana, including the island of New Orleans, in a secret treaty with the French, November 3, 1762, began to look with longing eyes toward British territory, in which the governor of West Florida had received from the king letters patent extending its northern boundary to the latitude of the mouth of the Yazoo, and here lies the rock on which three nations continued to have trouble years afterward, namely, which was to stand, the proclamation of October 7, 1763, or these personal letters patent of June 6, 1764? Certainly when, in 1777, the British bought the Natchez district of one hundred and ten miles up to the mouth of the Yazoo the governor of West Florida controlled the grants. Meanwhile Spain saw the citizens of the British colonies rising up in independence in 1776, and although divided among themselves for and against the mother country even in the so-called West Florida, she feared their power, and well she might, for she knew she held the mouth of their great waterway. Still it was England yet, and, on the principle of dividing the enemy against itself, she aided the revolting colonies by letting Captain Milling and others furnish their river points with supplies up the Mississippi. Many circumstances led to such a division of sentiment in the southwestern colony that in May, 1781, Spain, whose eye was ever on English territory, conquered West Florida, and naturally doing as the English governor had done, considered the latitude of the Yazoo's mouth as the northern boundary.

But the United States became existent by the provisional peace of November, 1782, in which British law, falling back on its best titles—namely, the proclamation of October 7, 1763, recognized the thirty-one degree parallel as the new nation's southern boundary, and in February, 1783, next, Georgia drew her state line according to that limit. On September 3, following, the final treaty confirmed this, and an Anglo-Spanish treaty on the same day, and, of course, based upon the Anglo-American one, although not designating boundaries, ceded the Floridas entirely to Spain.

The American period was now fully begun for our territory, exclusive of the coast counties, but because the new nation was ill equipped to handle its large territory, and because Spain's hopes and fears were now focused on the great Mississippi valley, she was allowed to continue an intruder on our territory. Meanwhile in February, 1785, Georgia erected into Bourbon county that long, narrow Natchez tract based on the thirty-first parallel, and as Spain refused the freedom of the river to the fast rising upper Mississippi valley region, the Northwest set up an attitude that made Navarro, the Spanish intendant, write his government: "The powerful enemies we have to fear in this province are not the English, but the Americans, whom we must oppose by active and sufficient measures." The Northwest wants the river, and the United States government is dilatory in securing it, so Navarro urges an effort to attract the Northwestern settlers into his territory by liberal grants and thus to quiet them. This is but one phase of the efforts of the Spaniards to hold the river. Spain threatened, and commercial interests drew until about this time Bourbon county contained about ten thousand souls*; but the Northwest grew more noisy in their clamors for an open river, until in 1787 there were no less than five different popular schemes afloat for securing it. "The first was for being independent of the United States and for the formation of a new republic, unconnected with the old one, and a close alliance with Spain. Another party was willing that the county should become a part of the province of Louisiana and submit to the administration of the laws by Spain. A third desired a war with Spain and the seizure of New Orleans. A fourth plan was to prevail on congress, by a show of preparation for war, to extort from the cabinet of Madrid what it persisted in refusing. The last, as unnatural

---

*De Bow's Commercial Review, April, 1851, New Orleans.

as the second, was to solicit France to procure a retrocession of Louisiana and to extend her protection to Kentucky."*

At last, in 1788, the United States demanded the free navigation of the river—even proposing to purchase west Florida, if necessary, to secure it. To complicate matters still further, there was a four-cornered strife for the disputed territory between the United States, Georgia, the Indians and Spain. The claims of the Creeks, Choctaws, Cherokees and Chickasaws were natural, and each of the other three made conflicting treaties with them. By the treaty of June, 1784, the Indians conceded the title of Spain, and the head chief of the Muscogee confederacy acknowledged their subjection to Spain†, a fact that would influence the settlers not a little in their unprotected state. Georgia and the United States also made treaties conflicting with this and with each other, until the Spanish king so feared the influence of the American power when it once arose, that he aimed a ludicrous blow at it in 1791, consisting "in the prohibition of the introduction into Louisiana of boxes, clocks and coin, stamped with the figure of a woman dressed in white and holding a banner in her hand with this inscription, 'American Liberty.'" ‡ Although a reacknowledgment of the thirty-first parallel by a treaty with Spain was secured October 27, 1795, she still occupied the territory, because of the divided feeling of the valley population, and gave them right of deposit at New Orleans for three years. In this state of affairs it was not strange that leaders of the five parties in the valley should brand all their opponents as traitors. Even the highest officer in the valley did not escape the charge.

This same year Georgia's legislature added another element of discord, but of solution, too, when, to insist on and develop her claim, she sold about one-fourth of our present territory, about 200x82 miles, west of the Tombigbee river to the Georgia-Mississippi Company; a large portion of territory to the Georgia Company, and to the Tennessee and the Upper Mississippi Companies about two-thirds of all the territory Georgia ever claimed. This drew multitudes of settlers, but the hue and cry against the Yazoo Fraud was so great in Georgia itself, as well as the rest of the United States, that the next legislature repealed it.

Spain's delay and intrigue after the treaty of San Lorenzo, October 27, 1795, became patent to every one, but their schemes were void after the river freedom was gained with New Orleans as a port of deposit. This treaty provided that within six months after ratification commissioners of the two powers should meet at Natchez and run the boundary on the thirty-first parallel. Hon. Andrew Ellicott, the one who determined the Washington meridian, acted for the United States, and the Spanish governor, Don Gayoso, of Natchez, acted for that power. Delay did not cease after the arrival of Mr. Ellicott and his military escorts, but the continued mazes of intrigue and diplomacy did not prevent the American flag from taking permanent possession for the first time. "We encamped on the top of a hill at the upper end of the town, about one-fourth of a mile from the fort (Natchez), and on the 29th (February, 1797) hoisted the flag of the United States. In about two hours after the flag was hoisted a message was received from the governor directing it to be taken down. This request met with a positive refusal, and the flag wore out on the staff." §

The inhabitants, in order to avoid the possible cross-fire of two contending powers elected a committee to represent them, and on the 22d of June (1797), this embryonic constitution was signed:

First. The inhabitants of the district of Natchez, who, under the belief and persuasion that they

*Dr. Martin's Louisiana.
†Claiborne's Mississippi, 1879.
‡Gayarre's Louisiana.
§The Journal of Andrew Ellicott, 1803.

were citizens of the United States, agreeably to the late treaty, have assembled and embodied them-selves, are not to be persecuted or injured for their conduct on that account, but to stand exonerated and acquitted.

Secondly. The inhabitants of the government aforesaid, above the thirty-first degree of north lati-tude, are not to be embodied as militia, or called upon to aid in any military operations, except in case of Indian invasion, or for the suppression of riots during the present state of uncertainty, owing to the late treaty between his Catholic majesty and the United States not being fully carried into effect.

Thirdly. The laws of Spain in the above district shall be continued, and on all occasions be executed with mildness and moderation; nor shall any inhabitant be transported as a prisoner out of this govern-ment under any pretext whatever, and, notwithstanding the operation of the law aforesaid is hereby admitted, yet the inhabitants shall be considered to be in an actual state of neutrality during the continu-ance of their uncertainty as mentioned in the second proposition.

Fourthly. We, the committee aforesaid, do engage to recommend it to our constituents, and to the utmost in our power endeavor to observe the peace, and promote the due execution of justice.

ANTHONY HUTCHINS.	CATO WEST.
BERNARD LINTOT.	JOSEPH BERNARD.
ISAAC GAILLARD.	and
WILLIAM RATLIFF.	GABRIEL BENOIST.

Don Manuel Gayoso de Lemos, brigadier in the royal armies, governor, military and political, of the Natchez and its dependencies, etc.

Being always desirous of promoting the public good, we do join in the same sentiment with the committee, by acceding to their propositions in the manner following: By the present, I do hereby agree to accede to the four foregoing propositions established and agreed upon for the purpose of establishing the peace and tranquillity of the country, and that it may be constant and notorious, I sign the present under the seal of my arms, and countersigned by the secretary of this government at Natchez, the 22d day of June, 1797.

MANUEL GAYOSO DE LEMOS.
JOSEPH VIDAL, Secretary.

Although Mr. Ellicott and Lieutenant Pope were unanimously elected to this committee, their signatures very properly were omitted. Almost immediately this permanent committee was elected: Joseph Bernard, Peter B. Bruin, Daniel Clark, Gabriel Benoist, Philander Smith, Isaac Gaillard, Roger Dickson, William Ratliff and Frederick Kimball. Mr. Kim-ball's residence proved to be below the line.* On the 15th of July the committee held its first meeting in the house occupied by the American commissioner. Some of the old divis-ions appeared on the surface at times, but the permanent committee was strong enough to resist the appointment of a new Spanish governor, offered them in November following, and on January 10, 1798, Governor Gayoso informed Commissioner Ellicott that he was ordered to evacuate the forts at Natchez and Walnut hills. This was effected by about four o'clock in the early morning of April 1, 1798, and Captain Guion, who had superseded Lieutenant Pope in December preceding, occupied the forts, and fifteen years of uncertainty were over.

Six days later, on April 7 (1798), an act of congress was approved, by which the dis-puted territory, bounded by the Yazoo river mouth parallel and the thirty-first, and the Mississippi and Chattahoochee rivers, was to be organized as "Mississippi territory," and based on the government ordinance for the new territory northwest of the Ohio river, formed July 13, 1789, over ten years before. Two very important exceptions were made, however: (1) Georgia's claims were to be in nowise affected; (2) and slavery was allowed and limited in that "from and after the establishment of the aforesaid government, it shall not be lawful" to import slaves from without the United States. President Adams sought out for governor of the new territory Maj. Winthrop Sargent, a native of Massachusetts, and a successful secretary and acting governor of the Northwest territory. His austerity and lack of sym-

---

*Wailes' Report, 1854.

A. G. Brown

pathy with the people, however, proved a source of dissatisfaction. John Steele was chosen secretary, and Thomas Rodney, of Delaware, and Daniel Tilton, were appointed judges of the superior court. As it was a first-grade territory, other officers were of the governor's choice. They came on in August and superseded Captain Guion. The judges finally commissioned were Messrs. Bruin, Tilton and McGuire. On the 26th of August, also, Gen. James Wilkinson, commander-in-chief of the army, arrived at Natchez with United States troops, and in the following year erected Fort Adams. Under the law Governor Sargent was vested with supreme executive powers; he appointed all magistrates, inferior judges, other civil officers, and all militia officers below the rank of general. He could create counties, make laws, and enforce them. His power was no greater than that of the Spanish governors, but when, with the severe and detailed ideas peculiar to it, a Puritan mind first attempted to stamp such an order on a territory accustomed to a government so widely different in temper and conception, it was bound to come to grief. The previous condition of the territory aggravated the situation still more. On April 2, 1799, the governor divided the old Bourbon county, or Natchez district, into two counties—Adams and Pickering—the dividing line somewhat similar to the present line between Adams and Jefferson, to which latter name that of Pickering was changed.* The first presiding justice of the Adams county court was Daniel Clark, Sr. These were the first permanent counties ever organized in Mississippi, as the old Bourbon county never effected organization. Says the proclamation: "I do ordain and order by these letters made patent, that all and singular the lands lying and being within the boundaries of Mississippi territory (as described in the third section of the law of the United States, bearing date April the 7th, 1798, for establishing this government) should constitute two counties, the division of which shall be a line commencing at the mouth of Fairchild's creek, and running direct to the most southern part of Ellicottville; thence easterly along the dividing ridge of the waters of Cole's and Sandy creeks, so far as the present settlements extend, and thence by a due east line to the territorial boundary, the southern or lower division of which is named and hereafter to be called the county of Adams, and the northern or upper division the county of Pickering."

On June 4, 1800, a third stupendous county was formed by another proclamation, saying "the territorial boundaries upon the north, east and south, and the Pearl river on the west, shall constitute" the county of Washington, the part within this state being practically all east of the Pearl river and south of the railway from Jackson east.

Meanwhile dissatisfaction grew until a petition for redress was signed by "a general committee, regularly chosen by the inhabitants of the Mississippi territory:" Gerard Brandon, Hugh Davis, Samuel H. Gibson, William Erwin, Alexander Montgomery, Thomas Calvit, Thomas M. Green, Francis Smith, Moses Bonner, Cato West, Ebenezer Smith, John Foster, Joseph Calvit, John Bolls, Felix Hughes, Ebenezer Dayton, David Greenleaf, Israel Luce and Randall Gibson; and Narsworthy Hunter was made their agent to present it to congress. It was a stroke for self-government not unlike that the United States as a whole had made, and contrary to the provisions of the ordinance of 1787, and by special favor it was secured, before it had requisite population.

On May 10, 1800, congress advanced it to the second grade, with representative government composed of a council of five members appointed by the president of the United States, and an assembly composed of four representatives from Adams, four from Pickering and one from Washington counties, a ratio of one to every five hundred free white males. The election was to occur the fourth Monday of July and the day of meeting was set as the

_____
*January 11, 1802.

6

fourth Monday of September. This act began to show marks of a constitution. Natchez was the temporary capital. Little is known of the assembly, however, until after the arrival of the new governor, appointed by President Jefferson in July, 1801.

Gov. William C. C. Claiborne, a representative of Tennessee in congress when appointed, was not only an able man but one who knew and sympathized with the people of the territory to which he came. His systematic and sagacious plans soon placed the territory in the best condition it had ever experienced. He arrived at Natchez on November 22, 1801, and the legislature met on the 1st of December at Natchez, with John Ellis as president of the council and Henry Hunter speaker of the house. The seat of government was removed to Washington. Captain Narsworthy Hunter was elected delegate to the seventh congress; Claiborne county, a ribbon-like strip across the territory, was created from the north part of Jefferson;* Wilkinson county was cut out of Adams below the Homochitto river and the parallel of Richard's ferry to Pearl river; Jefferson college and the society for the diffusion of useful knowledge were incorporated and the militia were thoroughly organized and drilled, all of which showed a new order of affairs.

On April 24, 1802, Georgia's claim to any of the region covered by Mississippi was transferred to the United States on certain conditions, among which were the satisfaction of claims held by individuals, and that it should, as soon as it secured sixty thousand free inhabitants, become a state on the basis of the old Northwest ordinance of 1787. This threw all the land claims between the Indians or individual whites and the United States. The adjustment of these claims covered a long period of litigation in the national Supreme court and confirmation by acts of congress in the case of individuals. As to the Indians, for whom most of the state was a hunting reserve, except the old Natchez district, the claims of the Chickasaws in the north and the Choctaws in the most of the rest, were adjusted by treaties. At this point the Indian situation was as follows: Based upon the old British treaty of November 29, 1782, confirmed by the treaties of January 3, 1786, with the Choctaws, and January 10 with the Chickasaws, made by the United States, the Choctaws claimed all below the Yazoo mouth parallel, except what is now a large part of Warren, all of Claiborne, Jefferson, Adams, Wilkinson, and the greater part of Franklin and Amite counties—almost a triangle; the Chickasaws held all above the Yazoo mouth parallel not yet a part of the territory, as the Choctaw claim was. A treaty at Chickasaw bluffs (Memphis) on October 24, 1801, opened a road from Natchez to what is now Nashville, and one on December 17 following with the Choctaws opened a highway through their nation and relinquished all claims to the Natchez district ceded in 1786. This was made at Fort Adams by General Wilkinson. A year later, on October 17 (1802), the land in the angle of the thirty-first parallel and Chickasawha river was ceded. Of course it extended out beyond the present state line, but the purpose here is to account for the present territory of the state.

During 1803 occurred a series of events that affected the territory favorably, and forever secured the navigation of the great waterway. Even in 1801 Governor Claiborne wrote the secretary of state: "It seems to be confirmed that Spain has actually agreed to give up Louisiana to France." † This rumor, which threatened the navigation of the Mississippi, roused the whole valley even more fiercely than before, when everybody almost was ready for a conquest of Louisiana. January 3, 1803, relations had become so strained that Governor Claiborne writes again: "The Spanish authorities in Louisiana are manifesting a marked hostility to the United States. The people of this territory are agitated by the suspension of deposit (secured to us by treaty) and by a recent order prohibiting intercourse between the citizens of the United States and the subjects of Spain. There is a deep feeling of resentment in Louisiana at the prohibition, kept down for the present by Spanish bayonets. We have in the Mississippi territory about two thousand militia, well organized, and can easily take possession of New Orleans now; but reinforced by French troops, according to prevalent rumors, it may be more difficult. It is my duty to apprise you that on the river coast, and in New Orleans itself, there are many persons who would muster under our flag the moment it is displayed.'' As the year progressed, excitement rose higher, and people came into the territory ready to fight. On October 21 the United States secured Louisiana from France, and on December 20 it was transferred to Governor Claiborne and General Wilkinson, commissioners for the United States, by M. Lausat, agent for France. On February 24 following the new acquisition was consolidated with Mississippi territory, by act of congress, as Mississippi district, but on March 26 next the old status was resumed by the formation of Orleans territory, and on the next day* Mississippi territory, by act of congress, was extended to the Tennessee and Georgia lines.

Increased population led to another Choctaw cession on November 16, 1805, at Mount Dexter, including the present counties of Wayne, Jones, Covington, Lawrence, the most of Pike, a strip on the east side of Franklin and Amite, and all of Marion, Perry and Greene, above the thirty-first parallel, of course. Out of this, Amite county was organized, covering a strip, its present width, to Pearl river, on February 24, 1809. Washington was divided on December 21 of the same year, making the west part into Wayne county, and on the same day Franklin was cut off of Adams, reaching to Pearl river. On the 22d Warren was created, including all north of the Big Black to the Yazoo line. About two years later, December 9, 1811, Wayne was divided, with parts of Franklin and Amite, making Greene and Marion counties. Congress added the coast territory east of Pearl river by an act of May 14, 1812, giving the new addition a representative in the territorial assembly, and on December 14 next it was divided by a north line from Biloxi bay to the Thirty-first parallel into two counties, Jackson on the east and Hancock on the west.

Meanwhile the population had so increased that on January 9, 1808, congress gave the right of one representative. The population of 1810 was 31,306, but with about 5,000 from the new coast counties it was now about 36,000, and by resolution of congress June 17, 1812, Georgia's assent to the organization of two states out of the territory was asked, and it was especially urged on account of the Spanish intrigue among the Indians, which was more or less constant during these years, but these wars combined with that of 1812 with the British postponed the state agitation. On December 22, 1814, Lawrence was created out of Marion, continuing the custom of thus celebrating persons of noted devotion to the Union. A year later† Marion was again divided, making Pike county, and on September 20, 1816, and October 24 following, east of the Tombigbee, in the present limits of the state, was ceded by the Chickasaws and Choctaws.

The successive delegates and representatives in congress up to this time were Narsworthy Hunter, Thomas M. Green, William Lattimore, George Poindexter and Dr. Lattimore again. "Until the beginning of the year 1816,'' says Dr. Monette, "the Mississippi territory continued to include the immense regions extending from the Mississippi to the Chattahoochee river. The greater portion of this extensive territory was yet in the virtual occupancy of the Indian tribes, the white population being still contained in three separate and remote dis-

*March 27, 1804.
†December 9, 1815.

tricts. The first of these was that on the Mississippi, lying south of latitude thirty-three degrees, and extending eastward to the Pearl river. The second was comprised in the counties on the Tombigbee and Mobile rivers; the third was the isolated county of Madison, distant nearly four hundred miles from Natchez, and separated by two tribes of Indians. Between the settlements on the Mississippi and those on the Tombigby, an unsubdued wilderness of nearly three hundred miles intervened, with a few scattering settlements on the route of communication. Between these districts there was no natural or commercial connection; no community of interests or pursuits; and between the first and second, the sterile character of the lands interposed an insuperable barrier to a continuous population; the Indian nations intervening between the first and third precluded an intimate and safe intercourse. Hence the inhabitants of each of these sections were strangers to the others; but, being all within the limits prescribed for the Mississippi territory, they were included in one territorial government for temporary convenience. The great distance of Madison county and the Tombigby settlements from the seat of the territorial government gave rise to much dissatisfaction, and the plan of dividing the territory into two portions, with two separate governments, was warmly discussed during the year 1815. One of the first and most plausible plans devised by politicians was the annexation of the counties west of Pearl river, and south of latitude thirty-three degrees, to the state of Louisiana, giving that state a uniform shape, and embracing both banks of the Mississippi river. Another government, extending from the mouth of the Tombigby northward to the southern boundary of Tennessee, was desired, having its seat on the Tennessee river. Meantime, before the close of the year 1815, a memorial from the general assembly, as well as one from the people upon the Tombigby and Alabama, had been laid before congress, representing the inconveniences of the existing government and praying the division of the territory and the establishment of two separate governments. The county of Monroe, east of the Tombigby, had been organized, and formed a connecting link between the eastern settlements upon the upper and lower Tombigby, and those farther north, contiguous to Madison county."

Through Dr. Lattimore's able efforts, an act of congress was passed March 1, 1817, providing that the territory bounded by the southern line of Tennessee to the Tennessee river, "thence up the same to the mouth of Bear creek; thence by a direct line to the northwest corner of the county of Washington;* thence due north to the Gulf of Mexico; thence westwardly, including all the islands within six leagues of the shore, to the most southern junction of Pearl river with Lake Borgne; thence up said river to the thirty-first degree of north latitude; thence west along the said degree of latitude to the Mississippi river; thence up the same to the beginning," should be formed into a state. The delegates to the constitutional convention would embrace: Warren, two; Claiborne, four; Jefferson, four; Adams, eight; Franklin, two; Wilkinson, six; Amite, six; Pike, four; Lawrence, two; Marion, two; Hancock, two; Wayne, two; Greene, two; and Jackson, two, who were to be elected on the first Monday and Tuesday in June, and who were to assemble at the town of Washington on the first Monday of July following. This convention was to determine whether or not a state should be formed and form a constitution.

On July 7, 1817, the following delegates from fourteen counties organized in Washington with David Holmes, of Adams, as president; Josiah Simpson, James C. Wilkins, Christopher Rankin, Edward Turner, James Sessions and John Steele, of Adams; Cowles Mead, Hezekiah J. Balch, Joseph E. Davis and George W. King, of Jefferson; John Ford and Dougal McLaughlin, of Marion county; Noel Jourdon and Amos Bur-

*A part of it now bears this name in Alabama.

nett, of Hancock; James Patton and Clinck Gray, of Wayne; Laughlin McKay and John McRea, of Greene; John McLeod and Thomas Bilbo, of Jackson; Harmon Runnels, of Lawrence; Walter Leake, Thomas Barnes, Daniel Burnett and Josh. G. Clark, of Claiborne; Henry D. Downs and Andrew Glass, of Warren; James Knox, of Franklin; George Poindexter, Daniel Williams, Abram M. Scott, John Joor; Gerard C. Brandon and Joseph Johnson, of Wilkinson; Henry Hanna, Thomas Batchelor, John Burton, Thomas Torrence, Angus Wilkinson and William Lattimore, of Amite; David Dickson, William J. Minton and James Y. McNabb, of Pike; with Louis Winston as secretary. The constitution was decided upon and was adopted after a five weeks' session, on August 15, and on December 10, 1817, the state of Mississippi was admitted into the union.

This constitution was based upon the general conditions of the old ordinance of July 13, 1787,* and was in force until 1832. It contained the ordinance provided by the United States, and among features distinguishing it from succeeding constitutions: (1) It provided that voters should be free white males over twenty-one years of age, a member of the militia, and having paid a state or county tax; (2) a representative should own one hundred and fifty acres of land or have an interest in real estate valued at $500, and a senator three hundred acres or a $1,000 interest; (3) a minister of the gospel should not be permitted to allow the glamor of political life to entice him into the executive chairs or to membership in the legislature; (4) all civil officers, except governor, lieutenant-governor, members of the legislature, sheriffs and coroners, were to be appointed; (5) judges were to be allowed a tenure of good behavior until sixty years of age, and other officers the same tenure indefinitely; (6) state banks with state stock were made lawful, and the states credited could be voted by the legislature with nothing to interpose; (7) the judicial department embraced a supreme appellate court composed of the district judges, a superior court of law and equity for each county and held by a district judge, with power to the legislature to establish separate superior courts or courts of chancery†; a probate court in each county and with police powers, and justices of the peace. Among other provisions it contained twenty-nine items of bill of rights; gave the legislature power to suppress dueling by disqualification for office if deemed expedient; counties were thereafter not to be smaller than five hundred and seventy-six square miles; two sections were devoted to the status of slaves; until the first enumeration was made, Warren was to have one representative, Claiborne two, Jefferson two, Adams four, Franklin one, Wilkinson three, Amite three, Pike two, Lawrence one, Marion one, Hancock one, Greene one, Wayne one, Jackson one; and the senators were to embrace one for Warren and Claiborne, one for Adams, one for Jefferson, one for Wilkinson, one for Amite, one for Franklin and Pike, one for Lawrence, Marion and Hancock, and one for Greene, Wayne and Jackson.

Under this constitution the first general assembly of the state of Mississippi organized on the first Monday in October, 1817, at Washington, and continued its session until February. David Holmes was governor, D. Stewart was lieutenant-governor and president of the senate, and the speaker of the house was Thomas Barnes. Their chief attention was given to changing many of the territoral laws, providing for a system of revenue, a general militia law, and inferior and superior courts. Thomas H. Williams and Walter Leake were chosen senators to congress, although David Holmes took Mr. Leake's place in 1820, and George Poindexter was chosen representative. This was on the apportionment of December 21, 1811, of one to thirty-five thousand, when there were but seventeen states and one hun-

---

*See code of 1857.
†Hutchinson's code, 1848.

dred and eighty two representatives. This continued to be the state's share until 1832, when it received two, on a ratio of one to forty-seven thousand seven hundred population. It is probable that no one man had more to do in forming this constitution than George Poindexter.

Two more counties were formed out of this territory—Covington out of Lawrence and Wayne, on January 5, 1819, and Perry on February 3, 1820, from Greene. By this time the population had so increased that more territory was secured of the Choctaws by the treaty of Doak's stand, near the southern limit of what is Madison county now, on October 18, 1820. The commissioners of the United States were Maj.-Gen. Andrew Jackson, of Tennessee, and Gen. Thomas Hinds, of Mississippi. The Indians were given lands in Arkansas in exchange for that central region of the state not more conveniently described than by saying the present counties of Copiah, Simpson, Hinds, Rankin, most of Madison and Holmes, all of Yazoo, Sharkey, Issaquena and Washington, and small parts off of the southwest parts of Bolivar and Sunflower. Even then almost all north and east of this was reservation, which was to remain so for ten years more. In this purchase was located the new capital in 1820.

During this decade from 1820 to 1830 the state protested vigorously against a national bank in 1821 at Columbia, and the abolition movement in 1826. In 1829–30 she expressed herself, favoring the Carolina and Virginia view of the tariff and some other questions. In 1825 she extended an invitation to General Lafayette to become the guest of the state, an event which occurred at Natchez on April 18 of that year; says an eye-witness: " At daybreak, on Monday the 18th inst., a national salute announced the approach of the illustrious individual to our city. At nine o'clock, Captain Surget's troop of cavalry proceeded to Bacon's landing, where the guest of the nation was received by a committee appointed for that purpose and conducted in a splendid barouche and four, followed by his son and secretary in another carriage, to Tichenor's field, where the several uniformed corps, distinguished for beauty of appearance and discipline, were drawn up in order of review. In addition to the Natchez Fencibles under the command of Captain Quitman, the Lafayette riflemen of Captain Bobb, and the Adams guard under Captain Surget, a very fine company from Claiborne county, called the Mississippi guards, commanded by Captain Nicholas, and the volunteers of this county formed a legion and placed themselves under the command of General McComas. A review followed and addresses the state being represented by Robert H. Adams, Esq. Col. Andrew Marschalk presented a company of boys for the blessing of Lafayette, and after the event was over, a parting salute was fired at the wharf by Captain Davis.*

Counties were formed, too, during this decade; Monroe was organized out of the old Chickasaw cession east of the Tombigbee, February 9, 1821, and on the 12th of that month, the late Choctaw cession was erected into an immense county, named in honor of General Hinds. From time to time, slight changes in the old county boundaries were made. On January 21, 1823, Yazoo and Copiah were formed out of Hinds, superseding an act forming a county of Bainbridge. Simpson was formed out of Copiah, January 23, 1824, and on January 26, 1826, Jones was formed out of Covington and Wayne. Washington was formed out of Warren and Yazoo, on January 29, 1827, and on January 29, 1828, Madison was formed out of Yazoo. Rankin was next formed out of Hinds, on February 4 following, and almost two years later † Lowndes was formed out of Monroe. The

---

* Woodville *Republican,* 1825.
† January 30, 1830.

rapidity with which counties were formed toward the north during this decade showed a growth of population that demanded new territory, and which led to the removal of the mass of both the Choctaw and Chickasaw nations to the now well-known Indian territory. In 1820 the state had, exclusive of Monroe county, about seventy-five thousand, but during this decade the Hinds county purchase drew such a large immigration and the Yazoo delta cotton lands became so tempting that pressure on the Choctaws became irritating. Meanwhile, the Chickasaws had been slowly pushed out of Tennessee into north Mississippi, covering a part roughly described as all above a southeast line drawn from Helena on the Mississippi to the center of Lowndes county, aggregating about twenty counties. The pressure against both was such that the persistent advance of the white population over the lines of both led to an act passed January 19, 1830, extending Mississippi jurisdiction over the territory of both in full. It was more extensive than the act of February 4, 1829, extending legal process, as it abolished the Indian form of government, including the office of chief, validated their marriages, extended to them citizenship, and extended all laws over them. As many of them were more or less civilized and had already acquired citizenship, it was not known whether this would be successful in making citizens of them or compel them to emigrate to the West. Both resulted, and on September 28, 1830, a treaty was made with the Choctaws at Dancing Rabbit creek, by Commissioners John H. Eaton and John Coffee, providing for the removal of those of the nation who so desired, and for citizenship of others. The great mass of the nation, however, were to be removed west of the Mississippi during the autumns of 1831–2–3, by the United States. The treaty was generous and full of most interesting details *, and secured to settlement nearly twenty-seven of the present counties, approximately between the Helena-Lowndes line before mentioned, down to the line coincident with the north line of Jones, from that a line cutting the east of Simpson and Holmes counties, and another from about the center of Holmes to the mouth of the Arkansas:

About two years later, October 22, 1832, a similar treaty was effected by Gen. John Coffee, for the United States, with the entire Chickasaw nation assembled at their council house on Pontotoc creek, by which about twenty of the present counties were ceded on somewhat similar terms, except that the Chickasaws should decide when they should remove to the West. Their southern boundary had never been clearly defined, but for the purposes of this sketch it may be described as the Helena-Lowndes line, before mentioned, excepting the most of that east of the Tombigbee† river. The Chickasaws all removed by the close of 1839, and many of the Choctaws remained in the interest of their claims until 1845, when, under the direction of Colonels Anderson, Forester, Cobb and Pickens, the last of the Indians were forever removed. Their claims and counterclaims have formed no small amount of litigation in the history of the state since.

All these changes and the prospect of so many new counties, as well as some of the evils experienced by the old constitution during its fifteen years' existence, led to a demand for a revision of the constitution. On September 10, 1832, about a month before the treaty at Pontotoc creek, delegates from twenty-six counties assembled in Jackson and organized, with Gen. P. R. R. Pray, a lawyer of Hancock county, presiding. They continued in session until October 26, and, among the changes made, one of the most important was the decision that all officers, civil and military, except the High court of errors and appeals, should be elected. This was an experiment in which Mississippi led all other states. Scarcely less important was an added item in the bill of rights, abolishing the tenure of good behavior in

*Hutchinson's code, 1798–1848.
† So spelled in treaties.

office, and determining a fixed limit, and another provision restricting the pledge of the credit of the state for the redemption of debt, unless created under provisions of the constitution itself. It was in violation of this that the state became so involved in banking troubles later, by which its reputation suffered the taint of repudiation, and caused the investments of the whole South to suffer from lack of the confidence of capitalists, even if it was unjust. Property qualifications for office or suffrage were abolished, and ministers of the gospel were allowed to become legislators or grace the executive chairs, with a proper majority. The introduction of slaves as merchandise was prohibited after May 1, 1833, at a time when it was here the most valuable labor in the world.

Among the first acts under the revised form was the organization of the Choctaw cession into sixteen counties. On February 19, 1833, Holmes was taken from Yazoo, and on March 2 all the Choctaw territory was added to Holmes; but on December 23 next, the Choctaw cession was laid off into the counties of Noxubee, Kemper, Lauderdale, Clarke, Oktibbeha, Winston, Choctaw, Tallahatchie, Yalobusha, Carroll, Jasper, Neshoba, Smith, Scott, Leake and Attala.

Three years later* the Chickasaw tract was laid off into twelve counties—Tishamingo, Itawamba, Tippah, Pontotoc, Chickasaw, Marshall, Lafayette, De Soto, Panola, Tunica, Coahoma and Bolivar. The state was now thoroughly organized, and future counties would be simply parts of counties already created. Newton was formed in 1836, Harrison in 1841, Issaquena out of Washington in 1844, Sunflower out of Bolivar in 1844, and so on.

The slavery provision of the constitution caused such litigation that an amendment was introduced on February 24, 1844, giving the legislature power to regulate it as was deemed expedient.

Meanwhile the Tennessee line had been in dispute, and on February 8, 1838, its determination was decided by a commission of three from Mississippi and two from Tennessee.

In 1842 the new apportionment on the sixth census gave Mississippi four representatives on a ratio of one to every seventy thousand six hundred and eighty. On March 4, 1846, the district principle was adopted, disputing the power of congress to dictate it, as it had in 1842. It may be of interest to add that Andrew Jackson was invited to become the guest of the state in February, 1840, and that in 1848 General Taylor was also a guest of the state.

Up to 1861 there were six amendments to the constitution; the first has been mentioned; the second of 1852 and the third of 1856 provided certain changes in regard to county boards of police and circuit chancery courts respectively; two in 1856 and one in 1857 made certain time changes in elections. On November, 29, 1860, however, an act was passed pregnant with great changes for the state; this act provided for the election to convention on December 20, of delegates, who were to assemble on January 7, 1861, "to consider the then existing relations between the government of the United States and the government of the people of the state of Mississippi, and to adopt such measures for vindicating the sovereignty of this state and the protection of its institutions as shall appear to be demanded." This act with the following resolutions adopted by the legislature on the day after the passage of this act left little doubt as to the results of the convention when it should assemble. They express so well the whole temper and convictions of the situation that they are here given entire:

RESOLUTIONS OF THE LEGISLATURE OF THE STATE OF MISSISSIPPI DECLARING SECESSION TO BE THE PROPER REMEDY FOR THE SOUTHERN STATES:

Whereas, The constitutional Union was formed by the several states in their separate sovereign capacity, for the purpose of mutual advantage and protection;   .

---

*February 9, 1836.

That the several states are distinct sovereignties, whose supremacy is limited so far only, as the same has been delegated by voluntary compact to a federal government, and when it fails to accomplish the ends for which it was established, the parties to the contract have the right to resume, each state for itself, such delegated powers;

That the institution of slavery existed prior to the formation of the Federal constitution, and is recognized by its letter, and all efforts to impair its value, or lessen its duration by congress, or any of the free states, is a violation of the compact of union, and is destructive of the ends for which it is ordained, but in defiance of the principles of the union thus established, the people of the Northern states have assumed a revolutionary position toward the Southern states;

That they have set at defiance the provision of the constitution which was to secure domestic tranquillity among the states and promote their general welfare, namely: "No person held to service or labor in one state, under the laws thereof, escaping into another, shall, in consequence of any law or regulation therein, be discharged from such service or labor, but shall be delivered up on claim of the party to whom such service or labor may be due;"

That they have by voluntary associations, individual agencies, and state legislation, interfered with slavery as it prevails in the slave-holding states;

That they have enticed our slaves from us, and, by state intervention, obstructed and prevented this rendition under the fugitive slave law;

That they continue their system of agitation obviously for the purpose of encouraging other slaves to escape from service, to weaken the institution in the slave-holding states, by rendering the holding of such property insecure, and, as a consequence, its ultimate abolition certain;

That they claim the right, and demand its execution by congress, to exclude slavery from the territories, but claim the right of protection for every species of property owned by themselves;

That they declare in every manner in which public opinion is expressed, their unalterable determination to exclude from admission into the union any new state that tolerates slavery in its constitution, and thereby force congress to a condemnation of that species of property;

That they thus seek by an increase of abolition states to acquire two-thirds of both houses for the purpose of preparing an amendment to the constitution of the United States, abolishing slavery in the states, and so continue the agitation, that the proposed amendment shall be ratified by the legislatures of three-fourths of the states;

That they have, in violation of the comity of all civilized nations, and in violation of the comity established by the constitution of the United States, insulted and outraged our citizens when traveling among them for pleasure, health or business, by taking their servants and liberating the same, under the form of state laws, and subjecting their owners to degrading and ignominious punishment;

That to encourage the stealing of our property they have put at defiance the provision of the constitution which declares that fugitives from justice in another state, on demand of the executive authority of the state from which he fled, shall be delivered up;

That they have sought to create domestic discord in the Southern states by incendiary publications;

That they encourage hostile invasion of a Southern state to incite to insurrection, murder and rapine;

That they have deprived Southern citizens of their property and continue in upholding agitation of their domestic institutions, claiming for themselves perfect immunity from external interference with their domestic policy;

We of the Southern states alone made an exception to that universal quiet;

That they have elected a majority of electors for president and vice-president on the ground that there exists an irreconcilable conflict between the two sections of the Confederacy in reference to their two systems of labor and in pursuance of their hostility of us and our institutions, thus declaring to the civilized world that the powers of this government are to be used for the dishonor and overthrow of the southern section of this great confederacy, therefore,

Be it resolved by the legislature of the state of Mississippi that, in the opinion of those who now constitute the said legislature, the secession of each aggrieved state is the proper remedy for these injuries.

J. A. P. CAMPBELL,
Speaker of the House of Representatives.
JAMES DRANE,
President of the Senate.

Approved November 30, 1860.
JOHN J. PETTUS.

The convention ordered met at Jackson on January 7, 1861, and on the 9th passed the ordinance seceding from the Union. During its session up to the 26th provision was made to amend the constitution, regulate military affairs, regarding United States property, concerning postal facilities, to regulate citizenship, making a council of three for the governor, for the purchase of arms, etc., for representation in the Southern Confederacy, to borrow money to ratify the Montgomery constitution, to fix the power of these ordinances, for hospital, coat of arms and flag for the state, for the election of Confederate executives, and a few others, about half of which were passed in the January session and the rest in March. The first amendment to the constitution was on January 26, making the convention ordinances take the place of whatever they conflicted with in it, and making "Confederate States of America" replace the words "United States" wherever necessary.

With this status the state continued during the war which followed and continued in Mississippi until the surrender of Gen. Richard Taylor, on April 9, 1865, when, to all intents and purposes, the people of the seceded states were considered prisoners of war. With this ended the epoch of the institution of slavery, an epoch unique and most remarkable in the development of states anywhere; an epoch illustrating unusual growth in democratic institutions; an epoch producing able statesmen, among whom was the leader of the "lost cause;" and an epoch closing with the birth throes of a far larger career, which will be considered elsewhere in these volumes.

CHAPTER V.

—≈≋≈—

THE LEGAL AND JUDICIAL HISTORY.

DURING the occupation of Mississippi by the French, a period which extended from 1699 to 1763, there is no legal and judicial history of interest to us. The settlements at Biloxi and Natchez were military posts in effect, and the governors ruled with extraordinary powers. The claims of the British provinces of South Carolina and Georgia to proprietary rights and sovereignty in this part of the country, were fortified by no actual possession, and were fruitless until a later period.

When, by the provisions of the treaty of Paris, in 1763, the king of England became possessed of a large part of the territory of the present state, then was the first dawning of our jurisprudence. The province of West Florida was created, embracing the southern portion of the present state. Pensacola was made the seat of government. Civil magistrates were appointed. A superior court was there organized, which administered justice according to the common law of England, with jurisdiction over the whole province, and of all cases above a magistrate's usual jurisdiction. Persons charged with crimes at Natchez and other remote places, were sent thither for trial. There is, however, said to be no British record of any judicial proceedings in the Natchez district; from which fact

Claiborne draws the flattering inference of a good order which resulted from the superior character of the early immigration.

In the year 1780, the Spaniards, considering West Florida to be British territory, invaded and subjugated it. Never again was British authority exercised there. The Spanish governors, with headquarters at Natchez, were entrusted with the administration of every branch of municipal law; and they left copious memorials of the mode of their proceedings, which were deposited in the appropriate offices at New Orleans, Mobile and Natchez, until a recent period; if, indeed, they are not there now. Under their administration, property was secure. Sir William Dunbar says, in his private journal: "An Englishman may come here and recover his debts, and obtain justice as soon as in Westminster hall." Debts were collected promptly. The procedure was by a petition setting forth the amount of the demand, its consideration, and the attendant circumstances. An order was then issued to the defendant to appear on a certain day, and arbitrators designated by the commandant decided the controversy. From this period is dated the first era of our testamentary jurisprudence. In the cases of Griffing vs. Hopkins, W. 49, and Chew vs. Calvert, W. 54, the Supreme court of Mississippi decided that the Spanish or civil law prevailed during the Spanish occupation, and that it remained in force until the organization of the territorial government of Mississippi in the beginning of 1799. In a very able and earnest note to the former case, the distinguished reporter and jurist, Robert J. Walker, challenges the soundness of those decisions so far as that portion of the state north of the thirty-first parallel is concerned, basing his criticism on the authority of the Supreme court of the United States in the decisions of Fletcher vs. Peck, 6 Cranch, 87, and Henderson vs. Poindexter's Lessee, 12 Wheat., 530; but those cases, closely analyzed, only hold that the title to the soil was not vested in Spain, and that grants of lands north of the thirty-first parallel, made by her after the treaty of peace of 1782 were void— not the general, and very different proposition that Spanish law, as a rule of life and property, never existed in Mississippi. Judge Clayton, in the chapter (XXXII) contributed by him to Claiborne's history, says that "the conclusion has been generally accepted, that the Spanish law never had any intrinsic force here;" but so far as judicial ascertainment is concerned, the decisions in Walker still stand unreversed. They probably express the truth; but whether so or not, it is beyond controversy that during the period in question Spanish law was enforced, and enforced by Spanish tribunals. In the memorial of the committee of safety of 1797 laid before Governor Gayoso, the third proposition expressly admitted its operation, and stipulated for its continuance until the disturbances of the transfer to the United States should subside.

During the Spanish occupation Georgia asserted title and sovereignty over the country extending to the Mississippi. In 1783, on the 17th of February, an act was passed extending her laws and jurisdiction thither. On the 7th of February, 1785, also, Georgia created the county of Bourbon, which embraced all the lands lying between the rivers Yazoo and Mississippi, the thirty-first parallel, and the Indian country to the eastward. By that act Thomas Green, Cato West, Tacitus Galliard, Sutton Banks, Nicholas Long, William Davenport, Nathaniel Christmas, William McIntosh, Benjamin Farrar, Thomas M. Green, William Anderson, John Ellis and Adam Bingamin, were appointed justices of the peace for said county; and Abner Green, register of probates. This act was passed mainly through the influence of Colonel Thomas Green. He had been imprisoned by the Spanish governor. His wife followed him to prison, and there died. He was released, and, making a journey to Georgia, procured the passage of the act asserting the title of that state to the country. It does not appear that any of the officers appointed by it ever exercised any of the functions of their offices; but in view of the fact that subsequent judicial history has settled that the true sovereignty and ownership were in Georgia, we may well note who composed the first judicial officers, *de jure* at least, if not *de facto*, of what is now Mississippi, appointed by the authority of a free state of this Union. Claiborne says that they were "all men who, at any stage of our history, would reflect honor on the highest station."

Although Georgia, in 1788, repealed the act establishing the county of Bourbon, yet she did not abandon her claims; but, on the contrary, in the following year sold fifteen million five hundred thousand acres of land, much of which was within the controverted territory, to three syndicates; and again, in 1795, annoyed by federal interference under claim of the British title, in order to assert her right and draw population to her frontiers, she sold to four companies the greater part of the territory in dispute between herself and the United States.

These conflicting claims and the asperities arising therefrom having brought about the treaty of Madrid, October 27, 1795, by which Spain abandoned her claim to territory north of the thirty-first parallel, and agreed to remove her posts and troops therefrom, the congress of the United States passed the act of April 7, 1798, creating the Mississippi Territory.

This act defined the limits of the territory, authorized the president of the United States to establish therein a government in all respects similar to that then exercised in the territory northwest of the river Ohio (excepting that provision which excludes slavery), and by and with the advice and consent of the senate to appoint all the necessary officers therein. It also declared that "from and after the establishment of the aforesaid government, the people of the aforesaid territory shall be entitled to, and enjoy, all and singular, the rights, privileges and advantages granted to the people of the territory of the United States northwest of the river Ohio, in and by the aforesaid ordinance of the 13th day of July, in the year one thousand seven hundred and eighty-seven, in as full and ample a manner as the same are possessed and enjoyed by the people of the said last mentioned territory." Thus this act subjected the Mississippi territory to the ordinance of July 13, 1787, establishing the Northwest territory; and it is therefore necessary to understand the leading features of that ordinance. They are these: It required the appointment of a governor, a secretary, a court with common-law jurisdiction to consist of three judges, and other civil officers; it provided that the governor and the three judges, or a majority of them, should "adopt and publish in the district such laws of the original states, civil and criminal, as may be necessary and, best suited to the circumstances;" to report them to congress from time to time, the same to be in force until disapproved by congress or altered by a territorial assembly. It authorized the secretary, in case of the absence or inability of the governor, to discharge the duties of his office; it guaranteed the great religious, civil and political rights of the citizens; secured the writ of habeas corpus, trial by jury, proportionate representation in the legislature, and judicial proceedings according to the course of the common law; especially, it declared that all estates of intestates should descend to descendants according to the rule of representation, and, where there were no descendants, to collaterals of equal degree according to the same rule; that there should be no distinctions between kindred of the whole and of the half blood; that the widow's dower and her thirds should be saved to her; and that these rules should remain in force until changed by the legislature of the district. It also provided that until the governor and judges should adopt laws, estates might be devised by written or sealed wills witnessed by three; or be conveyed by lease and release, or bargain and sale, signed, sealed and delivered, and attested by two witnesses; provided, the will or deed be acknowledged or proven, and recorded within one year after proper magistrates, courts and registrars shall be appointed for that purpose.   It contained a summary of many of the propositions which subsequently found their way into the bill of rights of the state constitution and into the fundamental conditions.

Such was the short and simple code of laws under which the infant commonwealth was inaugurated.   Whether the Spanish occupation had in fact displaced the common law, as asserted by our Supreme court; or not, as maintained by Mr. Walker and Judge Clayton; certain it is that, on the organization of the territorial government, that admirable system, by the very terms of the two acts just recited, became the basis of all the jurisprudence of Mississippi.   Not so unconditionally, however, as to defeat the highest end of all law—the welfare and happiness of the people.   In numerous cases our Supreme court has decided that the common law of England is the law of this state only so far as it is adapted to our institutions and the circumstances of our people; that it may be repealed by statutes, or varied by usages which by long custom have superseded it.   Vicksburg, etc., vs. Patton, 31 Miss. 185.

Before leaving the act of organization, there is another feature which should be noticed. Section five provides that "The establishment of this government shall in no respect impair the right of the state of Georgia, . . . either to the jurisdiction or soil of said territory, but the rights and claims of said state . . . are hereby declared to be as firm and available as if this act had never been made."   A truly remarkable statute!   In one and the same breath it professes to recognize and reserve the "jurisdiction" of Georgia, and proceeds to erect a territorial government within that jurisdiction, which shall, under and by authority of the United States, administer the laws and rule the destinies of the citizens. Well might Mr. Walker, in his note to the case of Griffing vs. Hopkins, W. 54, ask "How far are the acts of the territorial government of the United States, prior to the cession by Georgia of the 24th of April, 1802, valid, it being now admitted that prior to that period this territory was a part of the state of Georgia, embraced within her legislation, and not a part of Florida, and consequently, that the organization by congress of a territorial government here prior to the cession by Georgia, was a usurpation of power?"   This utterance, let it be remembered, was that of the man who afterward declined the office of attorney-general of the United States under President Polk, was appointed secretary of the Treasury, and, having served with credit, was later made by President Lincoln the financial agent of the United States in Europe during the late Civil war.   Little wonder is it that immediately after the passage of the law Georgia entered a solemn protest against the action of congress as being subversive of her rights in the premises, and prayed for its repeal.

Right or wrong, however, so it was; and when, on the 29th of March, 1798, the Spanish forces were quietly withdrawn, Capt. Isaac Guion, at the head of a detachment of United States troops, assumed control of affairs, with the concurrence of the citizens, for the preservation of public order.   Then followed an interregnum of four months, during which there was no government other than that of Captain Guion.

Meanwhile, President Adams appointed Winthrop Sargent, of Massachusetts, governor of the territory; John Steele, secretary; and Peter Bryan Bruin, Daniel Tilton and William McGuire, judges.   Governor Sargent was serving as secretary of the Northwest territory when he received the commission as governor of Mississippi.   "He was a man," says Claiborne, "industrious, methodical and indefatigable; but his manners were repulsive and austere, and his temperament more ascetic then sociable."   Unfortunately before his arrival in Mississippi he had conceived a prejudice against the people, and he never lost it.

He seems not to have understood them, and they did not like him. His administration was one long controversy. He arrived at Natchez on the 6th of August, 1798, and entered at once upon a course which was deemed harsh, oppressive and illegal. He arrested one White for making "impudent observations;" he was strongly inclined to enforce the sedition laws by arresting Major Freeman, the American surveyor, for writing and speaking contemptuously of Commissioner Ellicott; but, says Calibrone, "his greatest stretch of authority was his appointment of a citizen (a very worthy one) with full power to administer on the estates of decedents, taking bond, security, etc., thus, by a single commission, creating an office, prescribing the laws for its administration, and appointing on officer to fill it! Truly has it been said by an astute commentator, 'Royalty could do no more.'"

Of the judges appointed, McGuire was the only lawyer. Bruin was the son of an Irish exile. He had been brought up as a merchant; had served honorably in the continental army, rising to the rank of major in the Virginia line. He afterward settled as a planter near the mouth of the bayou Pierre, and gave his name to the celebrated Bruinsburg. He served as alcalde, or magistrate, under the Spanish government; was a man of high moral character, a devoted patriot, and was greatly esteemed. Tilton was an amiable man in private life, had read law for a few months, but had never practiced.

The governor and judges did not promulgate any legislation during the year 1798. Judges Tilton and McGuire were not in the territory. McGuire seems not to have arrived until about the middle of April, 1799. Tilton arrived in January, and the first laws published by the governor and Judges Tilton and Bruin bore date the 22d of January, 1799. From that time forth, however, they enacted many laws at intervals through several months. These laws, as a code, were assailed as being incompatible with the spirit of our institutions and with the constitution of the United States, and because they were not drawn, as the ordinance required, from such laws, civil and criminal, of the other states as might be best suited to the circumstance of the district, but from Governor Sargent's notions of expediency. It seems that they were mainly copied from a code framed by Mr. Sargent, when secretary, and the judges, in the Northwestern territory, against which Governor St. Clair had protested when submitted to him, on the ground that they were original and not copied from the laws of other states, as required by the ordinance, and which the house of representatives had condemned on that ground in 1795.

Against these laws there was an indignant and emphatic protest. The objections chiefly urged were as follows: That the laws were framed by the governor himself, in violation of the ordinance of 1787, as above stated; that the crime of treason was defined, and the penalty fixed at death and the forfeiture of all property, real and personal, to the territory, while the constitution of the United States says that congress alone shall declare the punishment for treason, and by its laws no forfeiture is incurred; that the crime of arson was punishable by whipping, pillory, confinement in jail not to exceed three years, and forfeiture of all estates to the territory, while the constitution of the United States says that excessive fines and punishments shall not be imposed, and that none of these offenses shall work corruption of blood or forfeiture of estate longer than during the life of the person convicted, and that in the case of treason only; that fees of $8 were fixed on marriage licenses, of $8 on the privilege of lodging and feeding travelers, going to the governor as perquisites without any warrant of law; that every person who had occasion to leave the territory had to pay him $4 for a passport, and every one coming in had to report immediately to a magistrate; that the judges were allowed fees on judicial processes while the United States paid them for their services, etc. A congressional investigation was had, the result of which was that many of the laws and fees exacted, were condemned and annulled, the governor was tacitly acquitted of any impure or criminal intentions, and on the 10th of May, 1800, congress advanced the territory to the second grade of government, which secured for it a legislature to be elected by the people.

The judicial frame was made by act of the governor and judges, of date 28th of February, 1799. Four courts were established: First, a court of common pleas, to be held four times annually in each county, by justices commissioned for that purpose, any three of whom might preside, and with full common-law civil jurisdiction. Secondly, a court of probates, to be held four times annually in each county, by a judge of probates appointed for that purpose, with cognizance of all probate matters, except the rendering of definitive sentences and final decrees; in the latter cases the judge being required to call in two of the justices of the court of common pleas, when the court should have full probate jurisdiction. Thirdly, the general quarter sessions of the peace, to be held four times annually in each county, by justices commissioned for that purpose, any three of whom (one being a justice of the quorum) might preside, with jurisdiction over most matters of general county police, and over all crimes not punishable by life, limb, imprisonment for more than one year, or forfeiture of estate. Fourthly, a supreme appellate court, to be held by the territorial judges, once each year in each county, with appellate jurisdiction, and original jurisdiction over the graver crimes, besides all the original functions of courts of assize; of oyer and terminer, and of general jail delivery.

It is to be observed that this scheme made no provision whatever for the great branch of equitable jurisdiction. That was first arranged for in 1807, as will appear later. In the year 1799 also, another act was passed, entitled, "A law for the easy and speedy recovery of small debts," which gave a summary remedy before any justice of the common pleas or of the peace in cases not exceeding $20 (without appeal when the debt did not exceed $8), and provided that if the judgment rendered should not be satisfied the debtor should be imprisoned until the judgment and the costs were paid.

It has been shown that the judges of the supreme court were the territorial judges, McGuire, Tilton and Bruin. McGuire was probably, though not certainly, the chief justice, as is indicated by the fact that he was the only lawyer on the bench, and by the further fact that his successor, Judge Seth Lewis, was chief justice. Exactly when Judge Lewis succeeded McGuire does not appear, but it was prior to the 8th of January, 1802, since in a letter of that date to Mr. Madison, Governor Claiborne said: "The chief justice, Mr. Lewis, is a learned lawyer and a man of talents." He was a native of Sheffield, Mass., and had served in the first legislature of Tennessee as representative from Davidson county.

A letter from Governor Claiborne to Secretary Madison, of date December 20, 1801, gives a very interesting view of the estimation in which the court was held, and also the first account we have of any decision of that tribunal, which is to say, of any supreme court of Mississippi. He writes:

"The legislature is engaged on a new judiciary system. The manner in which the superior and inferior courts have heretofore been arranged is generally condemned. There is certainly room for improvement. One-half, perhaps more, of the citizens, have no confidence in the judges. The legislature participates in this feeling, and will, I fear, be inclined to legislate more against men than upon principles. It is an unpleasant state of things, and will be for me the source of much trouble. A late decision made by the superior court of this territory has occasioned much complaint, and roused the sympathies of the legislature. Subsequent to the ratification of the treaty between the United States and Spain, and shortly before this district was evacuated, the Spanish governor granted to certain of his favorites much valuable land, and to evade objections, these grants purported to have been made previous to the treaty. In some few cases these fraudulent grants were made of lands which had previously been granted in good faith. And in a case of this kind where suit had been instituted, the holder of the fraudulent grant (which falsely bore date older than the bona fide grant) obtained recovery. In the inferior court, where the suit commenced, parol testimony was admitted to invalidate the antedated grant, and the defendant had a verdict. But upon appeal to the higher court parol testimony was declared inadmissible, and the judgment below was reversed. This case is generally considered a very hard one, and the legislature, to afford a remedy, contemplated a law authorizing the admission of parol testimony; but upon my intimating that, for the present, I could not assent to such a measure, it has been dropped. A statute for the admission of parol testimony to disprove and invalidate a record would be a grave innovation upon the law of evidence. Yet I can see no other way by which these frauds can be set aside, unless indeed, as I think, a court of chancery would reach the case. And most of the lawyers here think it would not. I should be happy to have your opinion on the matter."

Pity that our first reported case should have been a blunder so gross. On the 11th of May, 1802, Mr. Madison transmitted to the governor an opinion of Atty.-Gen. Levi Lincoln to the effect that inasmuch as delivery was an essential part of every deed, and must be proven, if questioned by third parties, by evidence dehors the deed, parol testimony was competent to show delivery on a date different from that appearing in the deed itself. The work of the legislature on a new judiciary system, however, came to naught. There were no changes of moment until the year 1807.

On the 18th of November, 1803, the statutes of 13 Elizabeth, ch. 5, and 27th Elizabeth, ch. 4, in reference to fraudulent conveyances, and the fourth section of the statute of frauds (29th Charles II., ch. 3) were incorporated into our jurisprudence, with the modification of the last, that the written memorandum required need not show the consideration for the promise. The seventeenth section of the statute of frauds, in reference to contracts for the sale of goods of $50 value, seems not to have been adopted prior to the code of 1857.

Judge Tilton, in January, 1802, left the territory for Europe on a commercial expedition; and this, being regarded as an abandonment of his office, led to the appointment of David Ker, as his successor. Judge Ker was a native of Ireland. In 1794 he was a professor in the University of North Carolina. He was a Presbyterian minister; but removing to Lumberton, he became a merchant and studied law. He had served as sheriff and as clerk of Adams county. On December 21, the governor wrote to Mr. Madison that "Mr. Ker's appointment has given much satisfaction to a large majority of the citizens. He is a valuable acquisition to the bench!"

About this time, probably in 1803, Judge Lewis, finding the salary inadequate, resigned; and was succeeded by Thomas Rodney, of Delaware, an ex-officer of the continental army. In 1804, by virtue of an act of congress passed to that end, an additional judge was appointed in the territory. The appointee was Henry Toulmin.

Henry Toulmin was born at Taunton, England, in 1770. The son of a preacher, he was himself licensed to preach on attaining his majority. He emigrated to Norfolk, Va., in 1793, and there opened a seminary. Thence he was called to the presidency of Transylvania university, Ky., but resigned it in 1802, being made secretary of state. When President Jefferson appointed him one of the judges for Mississippi territory in 1804, his post of duty was out in the Washington district, where now is Washington county, Ala.

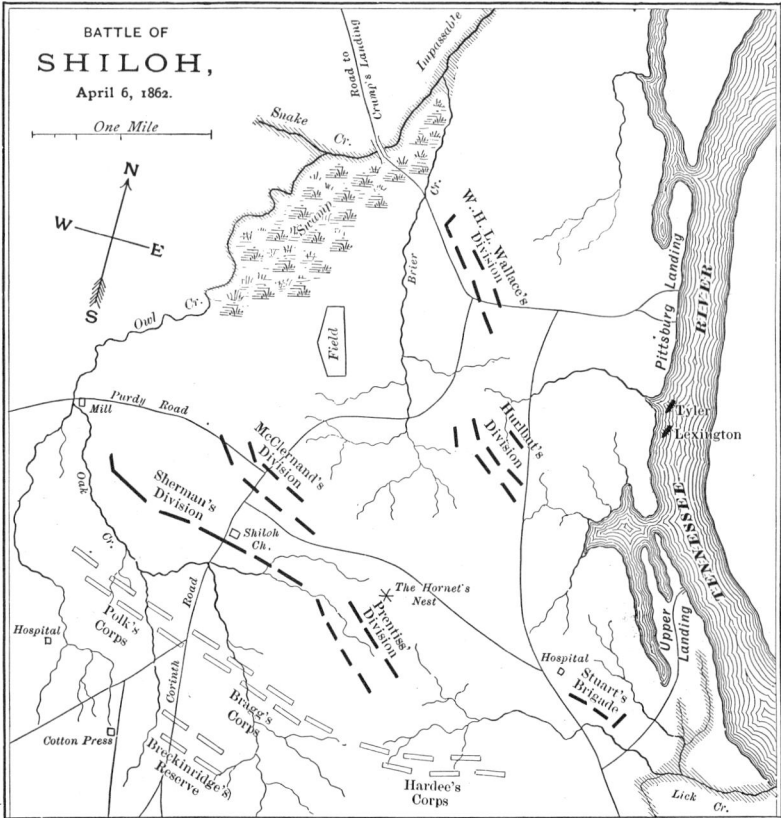

BATTLE OF

SHILOH,

April 6, 1862.

One Mile

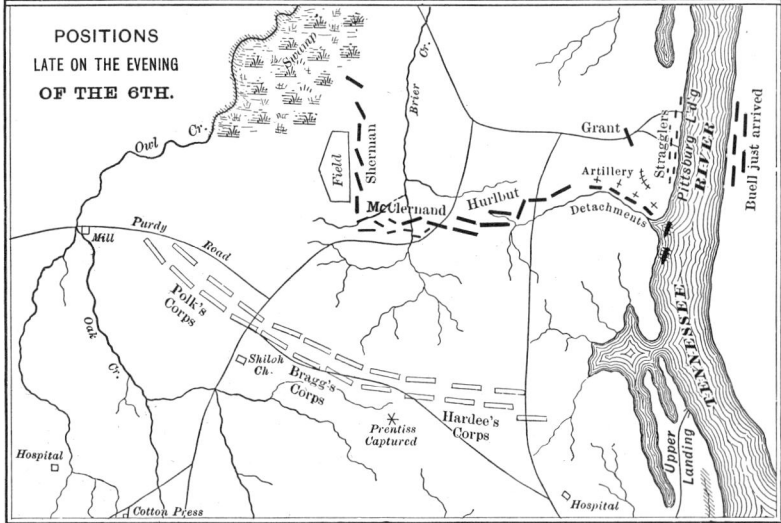

POSITIONS

LATE ON THE EVENING

OF THE 6TH.

In the spring of 1805 he, with his family, descended the Mississippi in a flat-boat to New Orleans, and thence went, via Mobile, to St. Stephens. His first court was held at Wakefield, some twenty miles below that place. He was far removed from the wealthy and cultivated portion of the territory, surrounded by a rude white population, by Creeks and Choctaws; but he was strong-minded and resolute, and gradually educated the people into obedience to the laws. He had much learning, was most generous and hospitable. His heart overflowed with tenderness; and all classes and conditions knew to whom to go for advice and succor. He often preached and officiated at funerals; and, having studied medicine, attended on the sick gratuitously. With all of those tender qualities, he was yet a man of high courage and great official firmness. A grand jury once presented him for exceeding his powers in the administration of the law. There was a congressional investigation; but so far from being condemned, he was vindicated with applause as a most efficient and deserving officer. Nor did the remoteness of his station cause his great learning and merit to be overlooked. In 1805, the year of his arrival, he was chosen by the general assembly to digest the laws of the territory. This work he performed with fidelity and skill. This first digest, or code, of Mississippi laws, is not only clear and comprehensive, but it also shows a thorough acquaint-ance of the author with the common law and an accurate conception of the needs of the territory by way of statutory modifications. It begins with the first proclamation of Gov-ernor Sargent, creating the two first counties of Adams and Pickering, and embraces all the laws in force on the 1st of March, 1808; and is especially valuable for the information it affords of the origin and progress of our jurisprudence and institutions.

The act of February 19, 1807, received the digest "as the law of the Mississippi terri-tory," and required the introduction of the acts of that session, expunging the provisions in the former that had been repealed. The fourth section declares that "the said digest and the acts of the present session shall, when printed, be entitled 'the statutes of the Missis-sippi territory, revised and digested by authority of the general assembly;' and that from and after the first day of October next (1807), all the laws of the governor and judges, and all the acts of the general assembly of the Mississippi territory, and all statutes of England and Great Britain, not contained in the said volume of statutes, shall cease to have any force or validity in this territory."

Judge Toulmin continued in office until the admission of Alabama into the Union, in 1819. His judicial functions then ceasing, he was elected to the Alabama legislature, and served in that capacity until his death, in 1824.

In February, 1807, occurred the first of the *causes celebres* of Mississippi—that of Aaron Burr. Early in January Colonel Burr, with nine boats, arrived at the mouth of the bayou Pierre, and tied up on the Louisiana shore. Secretary Mead, acting as governor, seems to have thought that his party was but the advance guard of a large force bent on hostilities. He called out the militia and sent two aides, accompanied by a colonel of the militia, to interview Burr. The result of some negotiation was that Burr surrendered to the civil authorities. Of course there was much commotion. Quite a number of arrests were made. The people were divided in opinion, and party politics was mixed with it. On the 2d of February Burr was brought before an adjourned session of the supreme court in Washington, then the territorial capital. He was attended by his counsel, William B. Shields and Lyman Harding. Judges Rodney and Bruin presided. George Poindexter was attorney-general. A grand jury was impaneled and Judge Rodney delivered to them an impressive and comprehensive charge. The attorney-general then moved the court to dis-charge the grand jury, first, because the court did not possess original jurisdiction in any

7

case; second, because the depositions previously taken before Judge Rodney and submitted to the attorney-general by the court did not furnish sufficient evidence to convict Colonel Burr of the offenses with which he was charged, so as to bring them within the Mississippi territory; third, that a warrant might issue, transmitting the accused to a court having competent jurisdiction to try and punish him, if guilty. Colonel Burr made some observations against the motion, remarking that if the attorney-general had no business for the grand jury, he had. On this motion the court divided; Judge Bruin opposing the discharge unless Mr. Burr's recognizance were immediately satisfied. Thereupon the motion was overruled, and the grand jury retired. The attorney-general left the court, being determined to prefer no indictment. In the evening, while engaged in the legislature, he was summoned by the court, and on arriving was requested to examine the presentments of the grand jury. It seems that Colonel Burr knew his crowd. Imagine the amazement of the court when this action was announced:

"The grand jury of the Mississippi territory, on a due investigation of the evidence brought before them, are of opinion that Aaron Burr has not been guilty of any crime or misdemeanor against the laws of the United States or of this their territory.

"The grand jury present as a grievance the late military expedition, unnecessarily as they conceive, fitted out against the person and property of said Aaron Burr, where no resistance had been made to the ordinary civil authority.

"The grand jury also present, as highly derogatory to the dignity of this government, the armistice (so-called) concluded between the secretary, acting as governor, and the said Aaron Burr.

"The grand jury also present, as a grievance, destructive of personal liberty, the late military arrests made without warrant and, as they conceive, without other lawful authority; and they do seriously regret that so much cause should be given to the enemies of our glorious constitution to rejoice in such measures being adopted in a neighboring territory, as, if sanctioned by the executive of our country, must sap the vitals of our political existence and crumble this glorious fabric in the dust."

The attorney-general expressed astonishment at such unwarrantable proceedings, announced that he should take no further notice of the presentments and retired. The venerable Judge Rodney then administered a severe rebuke, and the grand jury were discharged. This was a body of very respectable men, but their action was purely partisan. Quite a number of them refused to sign the presentments. Burr demanded a release from his recognizance, which the court refused. He then fled and forfeited it. It was a curious outcome, that the accused should obtain the presentment of the executive.

In the year 1807, by two statutes then passed, the judicial system was much altered. First, a county and orphans' court was established, composed of a chief and three associate justices of the quorum, any three of whom could act. It had the powers of probate (superseding the former system), and had cognizance over all matters pertaining to orphans, the registry of deeds, and the county police. Its common-law civil jurisdiction extended to all cases in which the amount involved did not exceed $200, except real actions. In Washington county, however, the limit was $1,000.

Secondly, superior or circuit courts were also established, presided over by one of the territorial judges, with general original civil and criminal jurisdiction, and appellate jurisdiction over the county courts. The judges were prohibited from charging the juries on matters of fact, but were allowed to sum up and state the testimony, and declare the law.

Thirdly, a supreme court of the Mississippi territory was organized, to be held by the territorial judges at a designated place, its jurisdiction being confined to appeals, except in chancery cases.

Fourthly, the supreme court and the circuit court of the Washington district were vested with chancery jurisdiction, being the first recognition of that jurisdiction in any of our statutes; and the territorial judges were authorized to issue all remedial writs.

The act of December 22, 1809, however, while leaving the county and orphans' court in existence, abolished the supreme and the circuit courts, and vested their jurisdiction mainly in a superior court of law and equity, to be held in each county. In December, 1810, the act of 1807 was so amended as to authorize the justices of the orphans' court to hold "intermediate courts," to be *quasi* orphans' courts, for the transaction of business appertaining thereto.

In 1809 Francois X. Martin was appointed as one of the territorial judges. This distinguished author and jurist was a native of France, born March 17, 1764. He emigrated to Martinique at eighteen; thence to Newbern, N. C.; made a printer and lawyer of himself. He wrote law books, and reported the decisions of the state. Appointed to the bench in Mississippi, he served only one year, when he was transferred to that of the territory of Orleans. He was afterward attorney-general of Louisiana, and later justice of the supreme court for thirty-two years, acquiring the distinguished title of "Father of the jurisprudence of Louisiana." He published histories of North Carolina and of Louisiana; also eighteen volumes of Louisiana reports, and a digest of the territorial and state laws, in English and French. Died December 11, 1846.

In the year 1810 Judge Bruin resigned the place which he had held on the bench since the organization of the territory, and was succeeded by Judge O. Fitz, of North Carolina, a brother-in-law of Governor Williams. Judge Martin was followed by Walter Leake, from Albemarle county, Va.; a man of sound sense and undoubted integrity, afterward United States senator and governor. In the years 1811–13, there being then nine counties in the territory, the territorial or superior court judges were four: Walter Leake, Henry Toulmin, Obadiah Jones and David Campbell. In 1813 George Poindexter succeeded Judge Campbell.

In 1814 there was another change in the judicial system. The territorial judges were required to hold, semi-annually, at the courthouse in Adams county a supreme court of errors and appeals. This was made the appellate court over the several superior courts of law and equity. If the judge below doubted as to the law or rule of decision in a case before him, he was empowered to respite the final judgment and refer the question to the supreme court. He was required, in this case, to send up a written statement of the matter or points in doubt, if not already of record, together with the other proceedings in the cause; and the supreme court granted judgment and issued execution, unless it was necessary to ascertain some fact of merit, in which case the cause was remanded to the court below for the action of a jury. The superior courts of law and equity were given jurisdiction of all suits in which the value in controversy exceeded $50, and the jurisdiction of the justices' courts was extended to that amount.

In the year 1815, Turner's Digest, made by Edward Turner, under the act of December 9, was authorized. It was, when completed, in five hundred and twenty-eight pages; is called "Statutes of the Mississippi Territory," and contains the laws in force up to 1816.

In the year 1816 the territorial judges had been increased to five in number. Josiah Simpson, of Pennsylvania, after whom Simpson county was named later, had been added; a man of vigorous intellect, and a diligent student; very methodical in his habits, with great purity of character and simplicity of manners. An impressive man, and much beloved; died in 1817 or 1818.

The first attorney-general of whom there is account was George Poindexter. He was followed in 1807 by Seth Lewis, the ex-judge. In 1814 William B. Shields, for courts west of Pearl river, and Joseph Carson for those east.

The history of Mississippi as a territory is now completed; and we are to see her embarked on her career as a sovereign state.

On the 1st of March, 1817, congress passed the "Act to enable the people of the western part of the Mississippi territory to form a constitution and state government, and for the admission of such state into the Union on an equal footing with the original states." It provided that "All free white male citizens of the United States who shall have arrived at the age of twenty-one years, and resided within the said territory at least one year previous to the time of holding the election, and shall have paid a county or territorial tax, and all persons having in other respects the legal qualifications to vote for representatives in the general assembly of the said territory be, and they are hereby authorized to choose representatives to form a convention, who shall be apportioned among the several counties," etc. The convention, when organized, was required first, to determine "Whether it be or be not expedient, at that time, to form a constitution and state government," and, if determined to be expedient, then to form one. Said constitution was required to be republican, and not repugnant to the ordinance of 1787 for the formation of the Northwest territory.

The act imposed on this privilege of admission into the sisterhood of states certain fundamental conditions. They were as follows: First, that the people agree that they forever disclaim all right or title to the waste or unappropriated lands within the territory, and that the same shall be and remain at the sole disposition of the United States; second, that every tract of land sold by congress shall be exempt from all taxation by or under authority of the state, for five years from the sale; third, that lands owned by citizens of the United States who reside without the state shall never be taxed higher than those of persons who reside within the state; fourth, that no taxes shall be imposed on lands owned by the United States, and fifth, that the river Mississippi, and the navigable waters leading into the same, or into the Gulf of Mexico, shall be common highways, and forever free, as well to the inhabitants of the state, as to other citizens of the United States, without any tax, duty, impost, or toll therefor, imposed by the state. These conditions were required to be secured by an ordinance irrevocable without the consent of the United States.

In accordance with the act of authority, the convention assembled in Washington, on the 7th of July, 1817. The following is a list of delegates:

Adams county—David Holmes, Josiah Simpson, James C. Wilkins, John Taylor, Joseph Sessions, John Steele, Christopher Rankin, and Edward Turner; Amité county—Henry Hanna, Thomas Batchelor, John Burton, Thomas Torrance, Angus Wilkinson and William Lattimore; Claiborne county—Walter Leake, Thomas Barnes, David Bennett and Joshua G. Clark; Franklin county—James Knox; Green county—Laughlin McKay and John McRae; Hancock county—Noel Jourdan and Amos Burnet; Jackson county—John McLeod and Thomas Billbo; Jefferson county—Cowles Mead, H. I. Balch, Joseph E. Davis, George W. King, Cato West and Dr. John Shaw; Lawrence county—Harmon Runnels; Marion county—John Ford and Dougal McLaughlin; Pike county—David Dickson, William I. Minton and James G. McNabb; Warren county—Henry D. Downs and Andrew Glass; Wayne county—James Patton and Clinch Gray; Wilkinson county—George Poindexter, Daniel Williams, Abram M. Scott, John Joor, Gerard C. Brandon and Joseph Johnson. Louis Winston, secretary.

The constitution was adopted on the 15th of August, without submission to the people; and Mississippi thus, on the 10th of December following, became a state with her present boundaries, Alabama being left in a territorial condition.

The most striking general features of the constitution were these: First, it provided for a lieutenant-governor; Second, it imposed a property qualification for holding the offices of governor, lieutenant-governor, or member of either house of the legislature; third, it restricted the right of suffrage to such as had paid either a state or a county tax; fourth, it required all civil officers, except governor, lieutenant-governor, members of the general assembly, sheriffs and coroners, to be appointed by joint vote of both houses of the general assembly; fifth, it allowed to judges a good behavior tenure of office until the age of sixty-five, and to other officers that tenure without any limit; except that state representatives, state senators, governors, lieutenant-governors, secretaries of state, sheriffs and coroners, had fixed terms; and the legislature was authorized to regulate the terms of militia officers and justices of the peace; sixth, it excluded ministers of the gospel from the offices of governor, lieutenant-governor, or member of the general assembly; seventh, it excluded from office any person who denied the existence of a God, or a future state of rewards and punishments; eighth, it enjoined that schools and the means of education should forever be encouraged in this state; ninth, it prohibited divorces except in cases to be provided for by law, by suit in chancery, the decree to be sanctioned by two-thirds of both branches of the general assmbly; tenth, it forbade the imprisonment of debtors after they should have delivered up their estates for the benefit of creditors, unless there should be strong presumption of fraud; eleventh, it required the general assembly to direct by law in what manner and in what courts suits might be brought against the state; and twelfth, it included the ordinance exacted by the act of congress authorizing the convention.

The provision for the judiciary was this: A supreme court was established, its jurisdiction not being defined, but left, inferentially, to the legislature; also a superior court with original jurisdiction in all matters, civil and criminal, but in civil cases only where the value in controversy exceeded $50; also justices of the peace, whose civil jurisdiction was limited to $50 or less. The legislature was empowered to establish courts of chancery, with exclusive original equity jurisdiction; and until such establishment, that jurisdiction was vested in the superior courts. The legislature was also empowered to establish in each county a court of probates, for the granting of letters testamentary and of administration, for orphans' business, for county police, and for the trial of slaves; and other inferior courts of law and equity. It was ordered that the state should be divided into convenient districts, containing each not less than three, nor more than six counties; that a judge should be appointed for each district, who should be judge of both the supreme and superior courts; provided, that in the supreme court, no judge could sit on his own decision below.

The first legislature of the new state assembled in Washington, in October 1817, and continued in session until the February following, arranging the new government. Their act of February 5 created a county court consisting of a chief and two associates (in the year following, increased to four), with the jurisdiction prescribed in the constitution. They did not, however, establish the chancery court.

In February, 1818, also, the first supreme bench was organized. William B. Shields, John Taylor, John P. Hampton and Powhatan Ellis were appointed from the first, second, third and fourth districts respectively.

Judge Shields was a native of Delaware. Says Claiborne: "He was a man of education and talent, of ardent and energetic temperament, warm in his attachments, devoted to his friends and greatly beloved by them. His personal qualities and stern integrity secured for him universal respect. He was a recognized leader of the democratic party during his whole career. As a judge he was patient, laborious, discriminating and scrupulously impartial. It was in his house that S. S. Prentiss had his first home in Mississippi." He was an influential member of the territorial legislature; was territorial attorney-general.   The bench of Mississippi did not long enjoy his presence; for in the same year of his appointment, 1818, he was transferred to the district bench of the United States.

Judge Taylor, a native of Pennsylvania, had served in the territorial legislature of 1814, and again in the constitutional convention.   He was a bachelor, of simple habits, and a student, devoid of personal ambition, yet he was the first chief justice of the state.   Unquestionably a lawyer of ability and a judge of lofty character, he commanded general confidence and respect.   He retired from the bench in 1820, and died at Natchez in 1823, while yet a young man.

Judge Hampton is thought to have been a native of South Carolina, and a member of the distinguished family in the state of that name.   He was a profound lawyer and an able judge.   His conscience was so sensitive, and his aversion to all forms of chicanery so intense, that he seems subject to the criticism of endeavoring to enforce a standard of pure morality too lofty for practical use in the ordinary affairs of life.   When Judge Taylor retired, probably, he became the chief justice, and so continued until 1826, when he retired from the bench.

Judge Ellis was a native of Virginia, said to be descended from Pocahontas.   He was a man of ordinary talents and limited literary acquirements, but of acute mind and well prepared by experience at the bar for the duties of his office.   He was a pure and upright judge.   Physically very indolent, he yet had an active mind, and wrote nearly all the opinions of the court during his membership.   He was bold and courtly in his bearing, yet cordial in manner and amiable in temper; talked little, but made others talk, and was a most admirable listener.   Altogether, a useful, honorable, patriotic man, who is said never to have had an enemy.   He was a bachelor.   In 1825 he left the bench, being appointed to fill the term in the United States senate vacated by the death of Hon. David Holmes; was returned by election in 1827; appointed United States district judge in 1832, and afterward minister to Mexico, whence he returned to Virginia and died in Richmond during the late war.

Joshua G. Clarke, who succeeded Judge Shields in 1818 from the first district, was born and reared in Pennsylvania.   He represented Claiborne county in the territorial legislature and in the constitutional convention.   In December, 1821, when the separate chancery court was organized, he was appointed first chancellor of the state, and held that office until he died at Port Gibson, July 23, 1828.   Judge Clarke was not a brilliant lawyer, but was careful, well-read and solid.   He was patient and amiable, and his opinions quite creditable.

Richard Stockton succeeded Judge Clarke.   He was a native of New Jersey, and had taken the first honors at Princeton.   An able lawyer, of remarkably modest and unassuming manners.   Resigned in 1825, and served as attorney-general for two years; afterward he removed to New Orleans, and was there killed in a duel, in the prime of life.

Joshua Child, of New England, succeeded Judge Stockton.   Well educated and with a mind naturally vigorous, his opinions are clear and forcible, resting rather upon the authority of the court itself than on an array of authorities.   Unfortunately he had a satirical and somewhat overbearing manner, and was consequently not very popular with the bar.   Foote says that he was often deeply intoxicated on the bench, and that on one occasion he rode away in a fit of ill humor, leaving the minutes of the court unsigned.   He resigned in 1831, and died not long afterward, a bachelor.

Alexander Montgomery was next in order.   Born in Adams county, he is believed to have been the first Mississippian to occupy a seat on the supreme bench.   He had only such education as the local schools could supply, but he was of vigorous and inquiring mind, with a peculiar aptitude for his profession. He became a dexterous advocate, very difficult to toll off on side issues. Of course he carried these characteristics to the bench. In addition, great moral integrity illustrated his life and career. He was, too, a kind man, of amiable and polished bearing. Retiring from the bench in 1832, he resumed the practice, and died in Warren county at a very advanced age.

When Judge Taylor, of the second district, retired in 1820, he was followed by Walter Leake, former territorial judge, and of whom account has been already given. Judge Leake retired at the end of the year 1821, having been elected governor, and was followed by Louis Winston, a native of Virginia, who was the secretary of the constitutional convention. He retired in 1824.

Edward Turner, his successor, was born in Fairfax county, Va., November 25, 1778. Educated at the Transylvania university in Lexington, Ky., he came to Mississippi in 1802, settling at Natchez. Appointed register of the land-office in 1803, and superseded in 1805, he then removed to Greenville, in Jefferson county. In 1810 he removed to Warren county, and was elected to the territorial legislature in 1811. Returned to Natchez in 1813, and represented Adams county in the territorial and state legislatures for several terms, being twice speaker. In 1815 he compiled the statutes of Mississippi territory, as already stated, and did it in a masterly manner. He represented Adams county in the constitutional convention; was attorney-general in 1820, and judge of the criminal court of Adams county in 1822. In 1824 was appointed judge of the supreme and superior courts, without solicitation, and became the third chief justice in 1829, continuing in that capacity until the year 1832. In 1834 he was elected chancellor of the state, which office he held with great credit to himself and benefit to the chancery system of the state until 1839. In 1840, again elected to the supreme bench; and in 1843, having declined reëlection, state senator for Jefferson and Franklin counties. He was of portly and commanding figure, an affectionate husband and father, a warm friend, and general favorite with the bar. His natural endowments were not extraordinary, nor were his general acquirements extensive. His long, varied, useful and successful career was rather attributable to versatility, unwearied industry, purity, impartiality, love of justice and patriotism. He died at his residence in Franklin county shortly before the late civil war.

In 1832 William L. Sharkey succeeded Judge Turner, but was on the bench only a few weeks before the court was reorganized. Of him, later.

When Judge Hampton of the third district retired in 1826, he was followed by George Winchester. This gentleman was a native of Massachusetts. Educated at Harvard college, he read law with Judge Story. An accomplished lawyer, he was so strongly attached to the common law that it used to be said jocularly that he considered any statutory change of it to be unconstitutional. He had great analytical power, a most tenacious memory, and a vast store of learning at command. His style was fluent, logical and demonstrative. His unyielding integrity, simplicity of character and charming manners made him universally beloved. He was intensely devoted to his adopted state. An ultra states-rights man, he presided over the "Southern Rights convention" at Jackson in 1849, the first organized association to resist the anti-slavery encroachments, and wrote the addresses and resolutions there adopted. In 1828 he retired from the bench, to resume the practice at Natchez, and there he died in 1851, unmarried.

Harry Cage, a Tennesseean, was his successor. His early educational advantages were limited. He was not a profound lawyer, or a man of learning, but he was, as a judge, conscientious, upright, patient, courteous, attentive, a general favorite.   He was sincere and manly in bearing, gentle and amiable, but of high courage, energetic, vivacious and genial; fond of novels, a crack shot and bold rider.   While on the supreme bench, he aided in getting up a dancing-school, and himself took lessons in it, in order to contrive money into the pockets of the great naturalist, J. J. Audubon, whom he persuaded to teach it.   He retired from the bench in 1832, was then elected to congress, and took an active part in its labors. Resigned in 1834, and retired to his plantation in Louisiana, where he died.

George W. Smyth was his successor, but he remained in office only a few weeks before the court was reconstructed by the revised constitution.   He sat during the December term, 1832.

When Judge Ellis, of the fourth district, retired in 1825, he was succeeded by Isaac Caldwell through executive appointment, for a few weeks; but John Black was elected by the next legislature.   Judge Black was a native of Massachusetts, and came to Mississippi about the time of the admission of the state.   He was an able lawyer.   His opinions are clear, succinct and logical.   In 1832 he was appointed to the United States senate, vice Senator Ellis, and in January, 1833 elected for a full term.

Eli Huston succeeded Judge Black in 1832, but was on the bench only a few months, owing to the changes of the revised constitution.

By an act passed in 1828, a fifth district was created, and in 1829 Isaac R. Nicholson appointed to it, becoming also thereby, of course, a member of the supreme bench.   Judge Nicholson was a Georgian, who had practiced law with success in northern Alabama.   He had a limited education, and no remarkable natural gifts except an inexhaustible capacity for business, and a sound judgment.   By studious accuracy he worked out success.   He was a good practitioner, and his opinions are terse and logical.   He had represented Copiah county in the legislature for many years, and was speaker in 1827.   When suspended by the operation of the revised constitution, he resumed practice at Natchez, and lived there until his death.

Livingston B. Metcalfe and William B. Griffith are stated to have been members of this court; but if this be correct, their connection with it was but transient, and left no trace. Their names are not mentioned in Walker's report, except as counsel.

The attorney-generals of the state, under the constitution of 1817, were as follows:

Lyman Harding, a native of Massachusetts, came to Mississippi while a young man. With no political ambition, he devoted all of his energies to his profession, and for many years was the acknowledged head of the bar.   In 1818 he declined physically and mentally, and died in 1820.   His successor, in 1820, was Edward Turner, already mentioned.   He, in turn, was followed in 1821, by Thomas B. Reed, from Kentucky, a man of unusual talent and learning, of haughty manners and therefore criticised, afterward United States senator. In 1825 General Reed was succeeded by Richard Stockton, already mentioned, and he, in 1827, by George Adams, who afterward was United States attorney and district judge. Richard M. Gaines succeeded Adams in 1830, and held the office until 1834.

Having now traced the personnel of the supreme court down to the period of the revised constitution, we must recur to the year 1818.

It is noteworthy that at the first term of the supreme court, that of June, 1818, a case was decided which shows that the negro could safely appeal in Mississippi to the courts for protection in his rights, even the right to his liberty.   " Harry and others vs. Decker & Hopkins, petition for freedom," was its style.   In 1784, three years before the ordinance of 1787, which prohibited slavery in the Northwest territory, one John Decker moved from

Virginia with three slaves and settled near Vincennes. He remained there until, in 1816, Indiana became a state, with a clause in its constitution prohibiting slavery. He then brought the negroes to Mississippi and sold them. Their suit for freedom was resisted on the grounds: First, that the ordinance and the constitution, if applied to such a case, would be violative of the treaty of cession from Virginia to the United States, and also of the constitution of the United States; second, that the provision against slavery, both in the ordinance and in the Indiana constitution, was prospective, and did not apply to existing slaves, since that would be to violate vested rights. But the court denied all of those claims, and declared the plaintiffs free, saying: "Slavery is condemned by reason and the laws of nature. It exists and can only exist through municipal regulations, and in matters of doubt, is it not an unquestioned rule that courts must lean in *favorem vitæ et libertatis?*" The case of the state vs. Jones was decided June, 1821. The defendant had been convicted of killing a slave, and made the point that it could not, therefore, be murder. The court said: "In this state the legislature have considered slaves as reasonable and accountable beings; and it would be a stigma upon the character of the state, and a reproach to the administration of justice, if the life of a slave could be taken with impunity, or if he could be murdered in cold blood, without subjecting the offender to the highest penalty known to the criminal jurisprudence of the country. Has the slave no rights because he is deprived of his freedom? He is still a human being, and possesses all those rights of which he is not deprived by the positive provisions of the law, but in vain shall we look for any law passed by the enlightened and philanthropic legislature of this state, giving even to the master, much less to a stranger, power over the life of a slave. Such a statue would be worthy of the age of Draco or Caligula, and would be condemned by the unanimous voice of the people of this state, where even cruelty to slaves, much less the taking away of life, meets with universal reprobation." And so it is that the first capital case reported is that of a white man sentenced finally to be hung on July 27, 1821, for killing a slave.

On the 12th of February, 1821, an act was passed, amended by one of November 27, by which George Poindexter, then governor, was authorized and requested to revise and amend the statutes of the state, arranging and consolidating all such as should be then in force. The scheme was extended by the act of June 30, 1822, in such wise as to make the new code embrace the legislation of that year.

The gentleman to whom this important work was committed, was one of the ablest and most conspicuous men ever in this state. He was a Virginian. Coming to Natchez in 1802, he was elected member of the territorial assembly in 1806, territorial attorney-general and delegate to congress in 1807, reëlected, and distinguished himself by his reply to the celebrated disunion speech of Josiah Quincy. In 1813 he became one of the territorial judges and discharged his duties with promptitude, ability and impartiality. He was a member of the constitutional convention of 1817, and the most prominent features of the constitution emanated from him. Sent again to congress, he there further distinguished himself, and before the expiration of his term, was elected governor in 1819, entering upon the duties of the office in January, 1820. Here, he was made codifier as stated above. He became a candidate for reëlection to congress, but to the surprise of every one, was defeated. He then retired to private life until he was elected to the United States senate in November, 1830, where he still increased his reputation. However, charged with changing his political affiliations, he was defeated at the expiration of his term by Robert J. Walker, and never reëntered political life. He died in Jackson, September 5, 1855.

His code was completed in May, 1822, and adopted, in one hundred and twenty-two chapters, in June.   Modeled somewhat after the Virginia code of 1819, by Benjamin Watkins Leigh, it was done with great ability.   Its adoption repealed all statutes which were of both a public and a general nature, and were not inserted in it; not, however, impairing existing rights, or preventing prosecutions for previous offenses.   Yet it was not adopted without opposition.   A portion, especially, which related to the police of slaves and their assembling, was regarded as substantially excluding them from religious worship, was vigorously assailed by the religious classes, and defeated him in his candidacy for congress.   It was repealed by the next legislature, and the obnoxious paragraphs never found their way into the code as published.

A notable feature of this code is the abolition of estates tail.   Section 24 of chapter 104, provided that all such estates should be discharged of the conditions and stand as estates in fee simple, provided that a conveyance or a will of lands might be made to a succession of grantees then living, and the heir or heirs of the body of the remainder-man, and in default thereof to the right heirs of the grantor in fee simple.   The law so remains except that, by the code of 1857, the number of donees who may be named was (and it still is) limited to two.

This code includes our anti-commercial statute, which has been introduced into every subsequent revision.   The substance of the provision is that all writings for the payment of money, or any other thing, shall be assignable, and so assignable whether the writing is drawn payable "to order" or "to assigns" or not, and that in all suits on such assigned writing, the defendant shall be allowed the benefit of any defense that he may have against the original holder, in like manner as if the suit were brought by him, provided such defense existed or was acquired before the defendant was notified of the transfer.   This statute, of course, opened the doors for such defenses as payment, fraud, failure of consideration etc., even where the paper had got into the hands of bona fide holders for value, and has very profoundly modified our commercial law.   In the case of Craig vs. Vicksburg, 31 Miss., 216, it was decided that paper made expressly payable to "bearer" does not come within the statute, and consequently is not subject to such defenses in the hands of bona fide purchasers, for the reason that the bearer, by the very language of the paper, holds in his own right and not merely as assignee.   In Harrison vs. Pike, 48 Miss., 46, a second exception to the operation of the statute was recognized, viz.: where the paper is made payable, by its terms, in another state or in a foreign country.   Then, as a general rule, the effect, by the contract itself, is to submit the rights of the parties to the laws of such other state or country, which, of course, excludes the operation of our statute.   On the other hand, in Etheridge vs. Gallagher, 55 Miss., 458, it was decided that paper made payable "to order" is subject to the statute; and so even where it has been endorsed in blank so as to be transferable by delivery.

The orphan's court was established by the act of November 26, 1821.   Presided over by a probate judge, it was to be held in each county every month.   It had full jurisdiction of all matters testamentary, and other matters pertaining to an orphan's court or court of probate.   Appeals lay to either the supreme court or the chancery court.

The county court was reorganized by the act of June 28, 1822.   It was required to be held quarterly in each county, the probate judge presiding, with two associate justices.   Its jurisdiction embraced suits for the recovery of contract debts within the amounts limited, and prosecutions of slaves for felonies.   Its civil jurisdiction was, therefore, so far as it extended, concurrent with that of justices of the peace.

In January, 1824, it was enacted that the judge of probate and the justices of the county courts, or any two of them, should hold county and probate courts in their respective counties quarterly. The judge of probate was, by the same act, required to report all his proceedings to this court for their examination and approval; and this organization continued until the year 1832.

The act of November 27, 1821, established a superior court of chancery, with exclusive jurisdiction over all matters of equity. A chancellor was provided for, to hold office during good behavior; and the state being divided into two districts, he was required to hold chancery courts twice each year, at the courthouses in Adams and Marion counties. Appeals were allowed to the supreme court in cases involving $200 of value. In 1827 the districts were increased to four, and the courts required to be held therefor at the courthouses of Adams, Lawrence, Perry and Hinds counties respectively.

Joshua G. Clarke, the first chancellor, has been already mentioned as one of the judges of the supreme court.

John Anthony Quitman was born in Rhinebeck, N. Y., September 1, 1799. Educated at the celebrated institution of Hartwick, near Cooperstown, in his twentieth year he was made a professor in Mount Airy college, near Philadelphia. He studied law, and came to Mississippi in 1821. In 1827 he was elected to represent Adams county in the legislature. Here he made much reputation, and in 1828 was appointed by the governor to the chancellorship. At the next meeting of the legislature he was unanimously elected by that body, and under the constitution of 1832, reëlected by the people, so that he held the office for six years. While chancellor he was elected to the constitutional convention of 1832, and was made chairman of the judiciary committee. In this capacity he was of great use, and one of his works was the clause prohibiting the borrowing of money or the pledging of the state's credit by the legislature. In 1834 he resigned the office of chancellor in order to devote himself to his private business, but in the next year was elected state senator. He served with distinction in the Texas war of 1836, and in our own war with Mexico he was a brigadier-general, being promoted to major-general in the regular service in 1847. His distinguished career in that service belongs to the national history. Suffice it to say that " his was the first American flag that floated over the Mexican capital, and he was the first civil and military governor of Mexico—the only American who ever ruled in the halls of the Montezumas." In 1849 he was elected governor, but having been arrested in 1851, under the direction of President Fillmore, to answer a charge in New Orleans of having violated the neutrality laws in connection with the Lopez expedition to Cuba, he resigned, because, as he stated: " The constitution has not contemplated such an event as the forcible abduction of the governor. It has not provided for the performance of his duty by another officer except in the case of a vacancy." In 1855 he was elected to congress, was reëlected in 1857, and died in service in 1858. He was remarkably strong physically, a most able lawyer, and had but few equals as a judge of equity. Mr. Walker, in a note on page 48 says of him: " The system of equity jurisprudence in this state has been greatly improved by the labors and assiduity of the present able chancellor of Mississippi, and by various statutory enactments."

While Governor Quitman was chancellor, the revised constitution of 1832 was adopted; and that fact led to some great changes in the organization of the chancery court. By the act of March 2, 1833, the circuit court was given concurrent jurisdiction of all cases in equity where the amount involved did not exceed $500, and in divorce cases; with a provision for removal into the chancery court by certiorari on affidavit of belief that a fair trial could not be had in the circuit court; also, that the court should be held in Jackson for the entire state, semi-annually; and that the chancellor should be elected by the people. In 1839, however, three districts were established, and the courts directed to be held at Jackson, Columbia and Oxford; while, in 1841, a fourth district was organized and the courts located at Jackson, Monticello, Oxford and Columbus.

Chancellor Quitman was succeeded, in 1835, by Edward Turner, already mentioned.

Robert H. Buckner, the fourth chancellor, was a Kentuckian. Elected in 1839, he retired from the bench in 1845, with impaired health and died near Jackson in 1846. He was a quiet man of studious habits. Modesty and diffidence prevented his achieving great success as an advocate; but he possessed in a notable degree the qualities of a fine chancellor. Dignified, conscientious, patient, diligent, exact, his wisdom and clear logic adorned and elevated the court.

While he was chancellor, by the act of February 26, 1842, another important change was made in the constitution of the court. A vice chancery district was organized, embracing twenty-three of the northern counties, to be presided over by a vice chancellor, elected by the electors of the district. Semi-annual terms were to be held at Columbus, Fulton, Holly Springs and Carrollton, the terms of the superior court theretofore held at Columbus and Oxford being abolished. Appeals lay from the district chancery court, as it was called, to the superior court, and, by consent of both parties, direct to the high court of errors and appeals; but writs of error lay direct to the latter court as a matter of right.

Stephen Cocke, the fifth chancellor, was a Tennesseean, who had come to Mississippi in 1818, by way of Columbus. Clerk of the Choctaw agency, afterward of the circuit court, his general education was meager. He was a state senator in 1834 and was elected chancellor in 1845. He was not a proficient lawyer nor yet a brilliant man. He was a patient and diligent investigator. His elevation was probably due to his efforts in behalf of the new Choctaw and Chickasaw counties on the question of their title to representation in the legislature of 1834.

While Chancellor Cocke was on the bench, another district chancery court was established, in 1846, composed of seventeen counties in the southern part of the state, the terms to be held at Mississippi City, Monticello and Natchez. Seven other counties were added in 1848 with a term fixed at Paulding, while at the same time, an additional seat for the district chancery court of the northern district was fixed at Hernando. In 1850, still a third district chancery court (called the middle district court) was established, embracing six counties, the court to be held in Yazoo county.

Charles Scott was the sixth and last chancellor. He was born in Knoxville, Tenn., November 12, 1811. He began to practice law in Nashville, and from thence moved to Mississippi and was elected chancellor in 1851. He was not only an ardent and thorough student of the law, but also a man of wide and classical literary culture. His duties as chancellor were discharged with great ability and fidelity. He died in Jackson during the late Civil war.

The vice chancellors of the northern district were as follows: First, Joseph W. Chalmers, a Virginian, born in 1807, who had located at Holly Springs in 1840. A profound and vigorous lawyer, he was appointed vice chancellor by the governor in 1842, discharging its duties with distinguished ability. He was afterward United States senator. Died at Holly Springs in June, 1853. Second, Henry Dickenson, of Columbus, was elected at the regular election in 1843. Third, James F. Trotter, afterward judge of the high court, elected in 1855, was the last.

The vice chancellors for the southern district were: First, James M. Smiley, born in Amite county, Miss., October 25, 1812. He graduated at Oakland college in 1833, being the first man to take a baccalaureate degree at any college in this state. Began to practice law in 1837; served two terms in the legislature for Amite county. In 1846 he was elected vice chancellor over Powhatan Ellis; was reëlected in 1850; resigned in 1852, going to New Orleans to practice law. He returned in 1859; was elected circuit judge in 1865; was appointed to the same office by Governor Alcorn in 1871; again by Governor Stone in 1876; and resigned in 1878 because of ill health. He died at Magnolia, April 8, 1879. Second, A. B. Dawson; probably appointed to succeed Smiley in 1852. Third; B. C. Buckley was the third and last. He was elected in 1853.

The first vice chancellor of the middle district was Selden S. Wright, from May, 1852, to January, 1854. He was then succeeded by George W. Doherty. In the year 1856, these chancery courts were all abolished, by an amendment to the constitution, adopted February 6, 1856, and their jurisdiction transferred to the judges of the circuit courts, by act of March 11, 1856, to be exercised after a manner to be described later. For the present, the history of this system has brought us far beyond the period of general movement, and it is necessary to recur to the year 1822.

By the supreme court act of that year it was made the duty of the court to appoint a suitable person to report its decisions and publish them. Accordingly, in 1828 Robert J. Walker was appointed reporter. His only report appeared in 1834. It contains the decisions made from the organization of the court to the December term, 1832, inclusive. Since many of the cases were decided long before his appointment, and statements of the facts, and briefs, had not been preserved; in them, only the opinions of the court could be given. The volume is, however, enriched by many learned and valuable notes by Mr. Walker.

This gentleman was born in Pennsylvania, in 1801, and came to Mississippi in 1826. Thoroughly and broadly educated, he soon achieved great eminence at the bar. In 1836 he was elected to the United States senate over Poindexter; reëlected in 1841; appointed secretary of the treasury in 1845, he was the author and most efficient advocate of the tariff of 1846. In 1857 he was appointed governor of Kansas territory; and, having taken sides with the North in the late Civil war, was appointed, by President Lincoln, financial agent of the United States in Europe. He died in Washington, November, 1869.

The decisions for the year 1833 were never reported. Robert Hughes, Esq., was appointed after Mr. Walker, and reported the decisions of 1834, but never published a report. His work was incorporated into the first volume of his successor.

Volney E. Howard, Esq., was appointed in the latter part of the year 1837, and filled the office until the close of the January term, 1843. He published seven volumes of reports; the seventh is enriched by a general index to the first six, prepared by Richard M. Corwine, of Cincinnati, but formerly a member of the Mississippi bar.

Mr. Howard was a native of Maine. He came to Mississippi in 1830. He was not only a successful lawyer, but also for a number of years the very influential editor of the *Mississippian.* In 1847 he moved to Texas.

The next reporters were William C. Smedes, and Thomas A. Marshall, of the Vicks- burg bar. They remained in office until July, 1851. They published fourteen volumes, ending with the November term, 1850. During their incumbency the legislature assumed the election of the reporter; and this step seems to have excited a good deal of bitterness in some circles. In the preface to the last volume, they say, " When the legislature stripped from the court the power, enjoyed since its organization, of electing its own reporter, and took directly upon itself, a partisan body, the election of that officer, we declined, whatever under other circumstances might have been our action, to be candidates for the station." So, also, the successor, in a preface to his last volume, says, "I was fully advised, at the commencement of my duties as reporter, being the first who ever held that station by election, that I should have much opposition to encounter;" and proceeds to complain of the assaults upon his first volume by a "partisan press." The last volume of Smedes and Marshall contains a table of cases in, and a general index to, the first thirteen volumes.

In 1844, and while Smedes and Marshall were reporters, appeared two volumes of reports of the superior court of chancery; the only special chancery reports ever issued in the state. The first was by John D. Freeman, attorney-general, and contained a series of cases decided between the December term, 1839, and the July term, 1843. In 1830 Chancellor Quitman had been authorized by the legislature to report the decisions of the chancery court, but it was not done. In February, 1842, another act was passed, making it the duty of the attorney-general to do so; and this volume was prepared accordingly.

In 1843, however, the office of reporter to the chancery court was abolished. Thereupon, the reporters to the high court, Smedes and Marshall, as a purely private enterprise, published a volume of chancery reports, covering the period from December, 1840, to December, 1843, and containing cases not reported by Freeman.

In 1847 Mr. Smedes published the first digest of Mississippi reports. It included the two chancery reports and the regular series so far as 7th S. & M.

The reporter who succeded Smedes and Marshall by election of the legislature, as stated above, was John F. Cushman, of Lafayette county. He issued seven volumes. By order of the legislature, the briefs of counsel were omitted; but in his discretion the points made by counsel, with a few leading authorities, were inserted. He also inaugurated the system of denominating the reports as "Mississippi Reports," his first volume being the twenty-third of that series.

Mr. Cushman was a native of Massachusetts. He served as representative from Lafayette county in the legislature; about 1859 he was placed on the circuit bench, but soon was appointed by President Buchanan minister to the Argentine Republic; and died in Oxford, in 1862.

His successor, in 1855, was James Z. George, of Carroll county, who held it until the outbreak of the war. He published ten volumes, being 30 to 39 Mississippi. This gentleman will be further noticed in the second volume of this work.

Three other law books of this period remain to be noticed.

In 1845 appeared "North on Probate Courts," by Ralph North, of the Natchez bar. It was a compilation of the state statutes on the subjects of the probate courts, wills, estates of decedents, infants and non-sane persons, dower, and partition; the whole methodically arranged, and illustrated with notes on the common law and American jurisprudence. To this was added an appendix of forms and precedents. This was long an exceedingly valuable book, albeit of little pretension.

In the next year appeared "Probate Court Law and Practice," by John M. Chilton, of the Vicksburg bar. It was a digest of the laws respecting wills, executors and administrators, the jurisdiction and practice in the courts of probate and equity in relation to the estates of decedents; also the law of descent, distribution, dower, and guardian and ward; including the statutes and the decisions of the high court of errors and appeals of this state, and the judicial decisions of other states of the Union on the same subject. It aspired more to the character of a treatise than did North, and it was a very creditable book for the times. Printed and bound by M. Shannon, of Vicksburg.

In 1852 Mr. Hutchinson published a manual of judicial, ministerial and civil forms; conveyances, mortgages, etc.—quite a helpful little book in its day.

The year 1825 witnessed an interesting and important struggle between the supreme court and the legislature. The court had caused a fine to be entered against a sheriff for making a false return. The officer had defended his return under a valuation law, in the nature of a stay law, passed in 1824; but the court decided that the law afforded him no protection, since the judgment had been recovered, the levy made, and all needful steps taken except the sale, before the law was passed, and that as to judgments based on pre-existing contracts the statute was unconstitutional by impairing the obligation of the contract. Thereupon the house passed a resolution requiring the sergeant-at-arms to notify the judges to appear at the bar of the house and show cause why they should not be removed from office. Judge Stockton appeared, made a written statement, and submitted the questions whether the judges had been governed by impure motives, or had decided according to established law. He cited authorities. The matter was referred to a committee, which reported that the opinion of the court as to the unconstitutionality of the law was erroneous; that the fine was illegal and unjust; that no subordinate officer should be punished for executing process which emanated from competent authority, since it is his duty to execute it, not to judge of its legality; that it knew of no power that the supreme court had to make such a declaration of the unconstitutionality of any law as to suspend its operation, and in so doing they were invading the legislative province. The committee acquitted the judges of any impure motives. The report was received and laid on the table. Judge Stockton then resigned.

The first dissenting opinion rendered in writing in the supreme court was in the year 1829, and in the case of Miller vs. Doxey, W., p. 336. It was by Judge Child. The first dissent recorded is that of Judge Turner in Bolls vs. Duncan, Dec., 1824, W., p. 161.

On the 4th of February, 1829, an act was passed extending all legal process emanating from any court, judge or justice, into and over all of the territory then within the chartered limits of the state, and occupied by the Chickasaw or Choctaw tribes of Indians; specifying the counties from which such process must go; provided, however, that such process was not to apply to any individual of either tribe. But in 1830 (January 19) a much more stringent statute was enacted. All the rights, privileges, immunities and franchises of the Indians were taken away, their chieftainships abolished, and the assumption of any of the functions thereof made criminal; the laws of the state were extended over their persons and property, their marriages validated, and the rights of citizenship given to them in so far as the state could do so. In the case of Fisher vs. Allen, 2 H., 611, December, 1837, the supreme court held that the effect of this statute was to retain in existence a tribal custom of the Chickasaws (the Choctaws had the same usage) whereby the husband acquired no right to the property of the wife held by her at the time of marriage; and, therefore, that it was not subject to his debts, although the rule was then otherwise as to the whites.

On the 15th of December, 1830, a joint resolution was passed by the legislature recommending a submission to the people of the question of holding another constitutional convention; and on the 16th of December, 1831, an act was passed pursuant to the vote, calling the convention. That body accordingly met in Jackson on the 10th of September, 1832, and Gen. P. R. R. Pray, a distinguished lawyer from Hancock county, was elected president. The new constitution was adopted, without submission to the people, on the 26th of October, 1832. It made many important changes. Chief among them were these: it provided that all officers, civil and military (except the clerk of the high court), should be elected by the people; it prohibited any legislative pledge of the credit of the state, either to borrow money or to pay debts, except under certain restrictions fully set forth in the constitution; it prohibited the introduction of slaves into the states as merchandise after May 1, 1833, and the introduction of them even by actual residents for their own use after the year 1844; it abolished property qualifications for office and suffrage, and the exclusion of ministers of the gospel from certain offices and the office of lieutenant-governor.

The provisions in respect to the judiciary were important. Not only were the judges made elective, but also their terms of office were fixed; in the case of judges of the high court and chancellors, at six years; circuit judges being given only four and probate judges two. The name of the supreme court was changed to that of the high court of errors and appeals; its jurisdiction was limited to " such as properly belongs to a court of errors and appeals;" and the bench constituted of three judges, each to be elected from a district by its electors. It was directed that the state should be divided into circuit districts, and circuit judges elected for those districts; that the circuit courts should have original jurisdiction in all matters, civil and criminal, but in civil cases only when the principal of the sum in controversy exceeds $50. The justices of the peace were continued in this small jurisdiction. The establishment of a separate superior court of chancery, with full jurisdiction in all matters of equity, was made mandatory; but the legislature was empowered to confer upon the circuit courts concurrent jurisdiction in all cases where the value in controversy did not exceed $500; also in all cases of divorce and for foreclosure of mortgages. The probate court was continued; but the county court feature was suspended, its jurisdiction being distributed between the circuit and justices' courts on the one hand, and on the other a board of county police, substantially the same as the present board of supervisors. The legislature was empowered to establish, from time to time, such inferior courts as might be deemed necessary, and to abolish the same whenever they should deem it expedient.

The adoption of this constitution and the enactment of numerous statutes designed to make it effectual rendered the revision of the code desirable. Accordingly, by act of December 25, 1833, General Pray was authorized to make one. He was empowered to alter the phraseology of existing statutes, to alter the provisions thereof so far as necessary to render the code harmonious in itself and consistent with the new constitution, and to incorporate new provisions whenever he might deem it expedient to do so. This last power wrecked the revision. General Pray, who was from Maine, was industrious and methodical and had abundant learning, but he had resided at Pearlington, near the sea coast, where lands were held mainly under old French and Spanish grants. He often attended the courts in New Orleans. Thus he had acquired a great taste for the civil law, and his code was considered to be too ambitious of originality and to smack too strongly of the Roman law. The followers of Coke did not relish it. Consequently it was never adopted. Instead, the legislature ordered a simple reprint of the public acts since 1823, and two thousand five hundred copies were published, including the statutes of the January session, 1838.

In the year 1836 an inferior court called the " criminal court " and having concurrent jurisdiction with the respective circuit courts over all crimes was established in the counties of Warren, Claiborne, Jefferson, Adams and Wilkinson. The Hon. John I. Guion was the first judge who presided over it. He held the office about a year, resigned and was followed by Hon. J. S. B. Thacher. In 1840 this court was abolished.

Howard & Hutchinson's digest of the laws was prepared in the summer and autumn of 1839 by Volney E. Howard, the state reporter, and Andrew Hutchinson, who were

appointed for that purpose. But here again was disappointment, and, although the work was adopted by the legislature, it did not meet the public expectation. Not enough time had been devoted to its preparation, and there were errors in it. Moreover, the compilers had proceeded on the assumption that Poindexter's code contained all the laws up to 1823 proper for revision, and that the reprint of 1838 included all the general enactments from 1824 to 1838 inclusive; therefore, those two books and the session laws of 1839 were taken for the material of the digest, but several important statutes had been omitted from them, and, of course, the digest was greatly defective.

On the 15th of February, 1839, two years after the decision mentioned above in regard to the Indian wives, was passed the "Act for the protection and preservation of the rights of married women." The statute provided that any married woman might become possessed of property in her own name and as her own property, and free from liability for her husband's debt, provided the same should not come from her husband after marriage; and provided that the receipt of the production of her slaves should appertain to the husband. An additional act, of February 28, 1846, secured to her the profits of her lands and the productions of her slaves. Afterward, the supreme court having decided that the terms of the statutes were not such as to secure to her the fruits of her personal labor and skill, in 1871 that was done by law. And in the last constitution, that of 1890, section 94 provides that the legislature shall never create by law any distinction between the rights of men and women to acquire, own and enjoy property of all kinds, thus placing her condition in this respect beyond even the power of the legislature to impair. A provision much like this was also in the constitution of 1869.

The act of 1839 was the first on that subject passed by any state of the Union, the basis of whose jurisprudence is the common law. The credit of this movement is usually claimed for Maine, but the statute of that state was enacted in 1841. It is said that our statute was passed mainly through the exertions and influence of a lady, Mrs. T. B. J. Hadley, who kept a popular boardinghouse in Jackson at the time. Another tradition, not to be found in the books, has it that a prominent member of the legislature who was heavily involved and was about to marry a wealthy lady had much to do with it. Probably both stories are correct.

The act of 1839, it will be observed, did not give to the married woman the power to make contracts. That was first done, to a limited extent, by the act of 1846 above mentioned. It provided that, jointly with her husband, she might make any contract for the sale or hire of her slaves, or for their necessary clothing, care, maintenance and support, and for the employment of any agent or overseer for their management; and that all contracts for supplies for either the plantation or the slaves, made by either husband or wife, should bind both, and might be enforced out of the wife's income. This statute was strictly construed in her favor. For instance, it was held that a debt for a building erected on her plantation, not being one of the items enumerated, was not enforcible against her estate. The act of 1857 further enlarged both her powers and her liabilities. She was authorized to contract for family supplies and necessaries, education of her children, carriage and horses, buildings on her lands and materials therefor, or for work and labor done for the use of her separate property; and the liability for all such contracts, as well as for those authorized by the act of 1846, was extended to the corpus of her estate, and not limited to its income as theretofore.

Neither of these statutes imposed any personal liability on the woman for even the contracts authorized, but only made her estate answerable. If a personal judgment were ren-

8

dered against her, it would be absolutely void.   By the statutes of 1871, however, the
married woman was allowed to go into trade as a femme sole; and it was provided that for her
contracts made in such trade she should be in all respects bound as if she were single.   This
meant more than trade in a commercial sense.   It meant any employment which required
time, labor and skill.

Finally, in 1880, she was emancipated from all disability to contract, and placed upon
the same footing as a man; and by the constitution of 1890, section 94, the legislature is
forbidden to remand her to the old status, or make any distinction between her and a man in
power to contract in reference to property.

The Briscoe bill was passed July 26, 1843.   In the early days of the state the common-
law rule that upon the dissolution of a corporation the debts owing by it and due to it were
extinguished, and its real estate reverted to the grantors, was recognized.   A large number
of banks, both incorporated and unincorporated, had sprung into existence.   For a short
time they produced a great inflation.   Speculation ran wild.   Debts were contracted reck-
lessly.   A factitious prosperity gilded everything and deceived almost everybody.   Of course a
revulsion came, when ruin stalked over the land; and the period from 1837 to 1840 was one
of great distress.   The banks all suspended specie payments; and continued suspension being
regarded as a cause of forfeiture, proceedings by quo warranto were instituted against nearly
every bank in the state, to have them dissolved, and thus to get rid of the debts due to them.
The banks resisted bitterly, and additional legislation was found to be needed, to facilitate the
legal remedy.   Mr. Briscoe, of Claiborne county, accordingly introduced for that purpose
the bill subsequently known by his name.   Judge Guion, of Warren, added an amendment,
which provided that the debts due to or from the bank should not be extinguished, nor its
property lost, by dissolution; but that the judge who pronounced judgment of forfeiture
should appoint trustees who should collect the assets and apply them to the payment of the
debts.   The bill, so amended, became a law, though over violent opposition.   The high
court afterward held that it effected nothing for the stockholders, and that the trustees could
not collect for their benefit, but only for creditors.   But while such was the old rule in this
state, the supreme court, in the Bank vs. Duncan, 56 Miss. 166, has repudiated the common-law doctrine, and the rule may be now regarded as settled that the creditors of dissolved
corporations will be paid out of its assets, and the stockholders get the residue.

In 1843 Mr. Hutchinson, one of the collaborators in the preparation of Howard and
Hutchinson's code, dissatisfied with the result, determined to construct a new code, of his
own motion.   He devoted to it five years of incessant labor.   It differed materially in plan
from any previously published.   It is not a revision.   Says the preface, " The laws, as passed,
are given either in text or in references.   A revision, by one person, or even by a delegated
committee, however capable and patriotic, in this age and country, must be a questionable
undertaking. . . . (It) is followed by fresh litigation, and a new train of decisions to interpret
and fix the new law.   Neither a Solon nor a Numa, nor any sole lawmaker is now wanted."
Nor is the work a digest.   " A digest purporting to include ' only the laws now in force,'
must ever be inadequate.   Nay more; such a publication has ever been and must ever be an
imposture.   Who is he who would dare assert that the laws of his own selection are all the
laws that are in force?"   Neither is it a compilation.   The publication of all the statutes
at large would have been too costly for the treasury of the state to bear, and it would have
been cumbersome to the profession.   Therefore the author took the middle course.   Such
statutes as were introduced, were in the exact terms of their enactment; such as were omitted, were noticed by brief references in notes historically arranged, in connection with the

various titles. The national and state constitutions were included, as also were the various Indian cessions, and the acts of congress ordering surveys and making donations, so far as they bore on lands in the state. The book was called an analytical compilation; and was designed to be the first of a series to be prepared from time to time, as needed. It is an invaluable compendium for reference to the statutes from 1798 to 1848. When submitted to the legislature, by act of March 2, 1848, the governor was authorized to appoint three commissioners to examine it, and on a favorable report from them as to its accuracy, to receive it and to purchase two thousand copies for the state. The commissioners were John I. Guion, C. S. Tarpley and John D. Freeman. They did report favorably, and the code was then sanctioned by the governor's proclamation; and became, under the act, evidence of the laws of the state.

Anderson Hutchinson, the compiler, was a Virginian. Before coming to Mississippi, he had practiced law in Knoxville and in Huntsville. He settled in Raymond, about 1835. In 1850 he removed to Texas, and there made such reputation that he was made one of the supreme judges. A Mexican raid into San Antonio captured him while sitting on the bench, and carried him off a prisoner. His release was finally effected by the intervention of the United States minister. He then returned to Mississippi, and engaged in the practice until his death in 1853.

No case ever tried in this state has excited so much interest and passion, or has affected its relations so profoundly as that of Hezron Johnson vs. the State, decided at the April term, 1843, and reported in 3d Cushman. It arrayed some of the finest talent, and practically involved an enormous amount of money, besides the credit of the state. The suit was brought in the superior court of chancery, on one of the bonds issued in 1838 by the state to the Union bank. Chancellor Scott rendered a decree for the complainant, and the state appealed to the high court. In that court it was represented by Atty.-Gen. Glenn and by William F. Stearns, Esq. When the court affirmed the chancellor's decision, as it did, there was a petition for a reargument, and the state was then represented by Thomas J. Wharton and Daniel Mayes, but the petition was refused, and the state finally held liable on the bond. The bondholders were represented by Messrs. Adams & Dixon. The liability of the state was denied upon two principal grounds: first, that the bonds were void because they were issued under and by the authority alone of a pretended statute which was itself void because it had not been passed in the only manner in which such a statute could be passed under section 9, article VII., of the constitution of 1832, that is by the concurrent action of two successive legislatures; secondly, that, supposing the statute to have been constitutionally passed, yet still the bonds were void because the Union bank, to which they were issued, was in law a different corporation from the one to which the issuance was authorized. As to the latter point the court held that there had been no change in the identity of the corporation. As to the former, it seems there were two statutes, an original and a supplement; the original had been passed in conformity to the constitution, and the court held that the bonds were issued under it, and not under the supplement, as was contended. This case got into politics; parties divided on it, and many a place of dignity was won and lost through it; Judge Yerger's among the latter.

By an act of the legislature approved March 1, 1854, the judges of the high court were required to appoint three commissioners to make still another revision of the laws. The judges appointed William L. Sharkey, Samuel S. Boyd and Henry T. Ellett; but Mr. Boyd resigning, his place was supplied by William L. Harris. The report of the commissioners was presented to the legislature at the regular session of 1856; but after several chapters had been passed, it was determined to postpone the residue until the first Monday of December following, and to hold a special session at that time to act upon it. This was accordingly done. The special session lasted for more than sixty days, and resulted in the promulgation of the code of 1857. It was a matter of course that with such commissioners the work should be good, and the code was a most excellent one. The criminal code has perhaps not been excelled by any in the United States. Its merit is demonstrated by the fact that the lapse of thirty-four years and the enactment of two later revisions have left it substantially unchanged. The commissioners did not follow the scheme of Mr. Hutchinson. Their code was like that of Mr. Poindexter. It was a revision, not a compilation. It not only evidenced, but it also enacted, the law. It superseded all prior statutes, of both general and public nature, which were therein revised.

In respect to the chancery courts, it required them to be held by the circuit judges at the same time and place when and where they held the circuit courts. For this reason the reports of that period commonly speak of an appeal from the chancery court of a certain county, and from the decision of a chancellor, meaning, however, an appeal from the decision of one who was circuit judge and therefore held the chancery court during, and apparently, though not technically, as a feature of the circuit court.

The high court of errors and appeals under the constitution of 1832 must next engage our attention. The first bench elected was composed of William L. Sharkey, Cotesworth P. Smith and Daniel W. Wright.

Judge Sharkey was selected as chief justice. He was born in Tennessee, in 1797. He was brought to Mississippi in 1803, settling in Warren county. Raised in poverty and laboring on the farm, he had but little opportunity to take advantage of even the limited schools of the country. With money earned by himself he attended a school at Greenville, Tenn.; afterward studying law at Lebanon, he was admitted to the Natchez bar in 1822. Removing to Vicksburg in 1825, he was sent to the legislature in 1827; and there served on the judiciary committee. Made chief justice, he served in that exalted place for eighteen years. In November, 1851, he resigned, in order to resume the practice of law in Jackson, and in that year was a member of the Nashville convention. In 1850 he declined both the consulship at Havana, and the place of secretary of war. He was one of the commissioners to frame the code of 1857. On the cessation of hostilities at the termination of the late war, he was appointed by President Johnson provisional governor, and discharged that delicate and difficult office to the satisfaction of all. He was then chosen senator from Mississippi, but the reconstruction measures of congress intervened, and he was refused his seat. He died in Jackson in 1873. Judge Sharkey was confessedly the ablest judge of this state. His sagacity was almost unerring. He could unravel the most tangled skeins, and extract the true principle from the most discordant authorities. His style was clear and strong, a little diffuse. As presiding judge, he was patient and affable.

Judge Smith was from South Carolina. He came to Mississippi before 1802, and settled in what was afterward Wilkinson county. He became a lawyer, and in 1826 represented his county in the legislature, and in 1830 in the state senate. Elected judge of the high court, his term expired in 1837, as he seems to have drawn the four-year short term. Succeeded by Judge Pray, he was, in 1840, appointed by the governor to fill the vacancy occasioned by Judge Pray's death, but was succeeded during the same year by Judge Turner, elected by the people. In 1849 he was again elected, and, in November, 1851, was made chief justice, holding the office nearly twelve years. He died November 11, 1862. The memorial bar meeting characterized him thus: "Endowed by nature with mental faculties of the highest order, with moral and physical courage which knew no fear, of humane and kindly disposition, and actuated by a conscientious rectitude and principle which nothing could swerve, Chief Justice Smith presented to the world the model character of a judge."

Judge Wright was a native of Tennessee. There he began to practice law, but in 1822-3 moved to Mississippi and settled in Monroe county. He resigned his office as judge in 1838, and not long afterward died in Pontotoc. He had a strong mind, and was a lawyer of ability, was an orator of unusual power, and especially formidable before a jury; had great personal popularity, but is said never to have delivered a written opinion. His term was filled by Judge Trotter, by appointment.

In January, 1838, P. Rutilius R. Pray succeeded Judge Smith, as already stated. Of Mr. Pray something has already been seen. He died in 1839, while on the bench.

James F. Trotter was born in Virginia, November 5, 1802. Having obtained his license he removed, in 1823-4, to Monroe county, Miss. He was several times chosen to represent the county in the state senate. In 1838 he was elected to the United States senate, vice Senator Black resigned, but before taking his seat resigned also, presumably because the bench offered more attraction. Appointed in 1838 to fill the vacancy of Judge Wright, in November, 1839, he was elected by the people for a full term; but he too resigned in 1842. He then resumed the practice at Holly Springs. Elected vice chancellor in 1855, he held that office until the court was abolished in 1857. In 1860 he was elected one of the law professors in the university, and held that chair until the suspension caused by the Civil war. On the reorganization of the courts, in 1866, he was appointed circuit judge, and occupied that bench at the time of his death in March. While on the bench he delivered many important decisions. His opinions are fluent, strong, dignified, discriminating and learned. Affable, upright, courageous, firm—his was a most attractive character.

Edward Turner was elected at a special election as successor of Judge Pray, deceased. His term expired in November, 1843, and he was not a candidate for reëlection.

Reuben Davis was appointed by the governor in April, 1842, on the resignation of Judge Trotter. He held the office until an election in August, when Alexander M. Clayton was elected. Judge Davis was a Tennesseean. He moved to Monroe county, Miss., when a young man, and engaged in the practice of medicine. Studying law, however, he became district attorney, colonel of the Second Miss. regiment in the Mexican war, member of congress. He died in 1890. He was one of the most successful criminal lawyers ever in the state.

Judge Clayton was born in Virginia, January 15, 1801. Settling in Clarksville, Tenn., he was appointed, by President Jackson, United States judge in the territory of Arkansas, but resigned and returned to Clarksville after one year. He came to Marshall county, Miss., in 1837. Elected to the high court bench, he held the seat until the end of 1851. He was appointed, by President Pierce, consul to Havana, but soon returned and engaged in the practice of law at Memphis. He was a member of the Nashville, Charleston and Baltimore conventions; and having come back to this state was in the secession convention. He was confederate judge for Mississippi. In 1866 he succeeded Judge Trotter on the circuit bench, but was removed by Governor Ames on account of his inability to take the "iron-clad oath." He was a chief promoter of the Mississippi Central railroad, and was first president of the trustees of the university. He died in Marshall county, October, 1889. Judge Clayton was a man of profound legal learning, particularly fond of constitutional law and the limitations of estates. He was patient and laborious in research, impartial and of incorruptible integrity. His opinions are most highly respected by the bar, and it has been well said of him that not one of the illustrious men who have adorned the state's judicial annals ever contributed more to the establishment of her admirable system of jurisprudence.

Joseph S. B. Thacher was elected in November, 1843, to succeed Judge Turner. He was a native of Massachusetts, and settled in Natchez about 1833. In 1837 he was elected judge of the criminal court mentioned above. His election to the high court bench was after "a spirited political canvass, entirely incompatible with the nature and dignity of the office." When his term expired in 1849, he was defeated by Judge C. P. Smith; and it is said that this result was contributed to by charges of unfair practices employed on his first election. At the same time, he was a man of pure morals, and social attractions of a high order. As a judge, he was laborious, impartial and upright.

Ephraim S. Fisher succeeded Judge Clayton in 1852. Judge Fisher was born in Kentucky, November 15, 1815. He moved to Vicksburg, Miss., in 1833; and having obtained his license to practice law, to Coffeeville in 1839. He succeeded in the profession; served a term in the legislature; and was elected to the high court bench. This office he occupied until November, 1858, when he resigned and returned to the practice. In 1869 he was appointed by Governor Alcorn to the circuit bench. In 1876 he removed to Texas, where he shortly died. He was a kind and generous man; a good lawyer, an impartial and conscientious judge, though not a profound one.

Collin S. Tarpley, was appointed in November, 1851, to succeed Judge Sharkey, resigned, but resigned himself in the following month, because of a question of the right of the governor to make the appointment. He was a native of Virginia, was raised in Tennessee, and came to Mississippi from Alabama in 1836. Settling in Hinds county, he enjoyed a lucrative practice. Died in the spring of 1860.

William Yerger was born in Tennessee, November 22, 1816. Educated at the University of Nashville, he was admitted to the bar, and moved to Jackson, Miss., in 1837. There his career was exceptionally brilliant. His magnificent ability and genial disposition compelled the recognition even of political adversaries, and he was elected to the high court bench in December, 1851, to succeed Judge Tarpley, in spite of his well-known hostility to measures popular at the time. His term of office expired in November, 1853. During the Civil war he was a member of the legislature, and in 1865 of the constitutional convention. He died at his home in Jackson, June 7, 1872. It would be difficult to exaggerate the praises of Judge Yerger. No man ever was dearer to the people of his state. A model gentleman, an exemplary Christian, a lover of his fellow-man, a devoted husband and father, sensitive yet self-controled, busy yet thoughtful of others, eminent yet modest; his personal attractions were such as to form a perfect complement to his exceptionally brilliant mental gifts. As a lawyer he was wonderfully strong, versatile and resourceful; his learning was accurate, complete and perfectly at command. His thoughts resembled intuition, and its power carried him fully to the hight of every occasion. His convictions were strong, and he had the courage to stand by them at every cost. In the great case of the Union bank bonds he laid his judicial career upon the altar of his judicial conscience.

Alexander H. Handy succeeded him. Judge Handy was born in Maryland, December 25, 1809, and came to Mississippi in 1836. He at once entered upon a most successful professional career. In 1853 he was elected to the high court bench over Judge Yerger, who was then somewhat unpopular with the majority party because of the Union-bank-bond opinion. He was reëlected at the expiration of his term without opposition. In 1864 he was appointed chief justice. In 1865 he was again elected, and in 1866 was again made chief justice. In October, 1866, he was again reëlected without opposition, but resigned October 1, 1867, because the federal government had placed the military power over the court. Removing to Baltimore, he engaged in the practice at that bar. He was soon made professsor of law in the university of Maryland, and retained the chair until he returned to Jackson, Miss., in 1871. Removed to Canton and there died in 1883. Judge Handy was a fluent speaker and polished writer. He was a most accomplished lawyer, and his opinions are characterized by great learning, independence of thought, clearness, logic and force.

William L. Harris was elected in October, 1858, to succeed Judge Fisher. His regular term began January 1, 1859, but when Judge Fisher resigned, in November, Judge Harris was appointed to fill his unexpired term. He was born in Georgia, July 6, 1807. Educated at the University of Georgia, he was admitted to practice law before his majority, and moved to Columbus, Miss., in 1837. In 1753 he was elected circuit judge; in 1856 he was appointed one of the three codifiers who gave us the code of 1857; in 1860 President Buchanan tendered him a seat upon the supreme bench of the United States, but he declined, because of the impending secession. In 1865 he was again chosen to the high court bench; and in 1867, he, too, resigned, because of the subjection of the court to military supremacy. He then engaged in the practice at Memphis, where he died, November 27, 1868. Amiable, sympathetic, chivalric, dignified and just, Judge Harris was an honorable and worthy gentleman. Learned in the law, sound of judgment, patient in investigation, he was the master of a clear and elegant style. His opinions would adorn any bench.

In October, 1863, Hon. David W. Hurst, of Amite county, was elected to the unexpired term of Judge Smith, deceased, but owing to the suspension of all business of judicial nature occasioned by the war, his occupancy of the bench was hardly more than nominal.

The attorneys-general of the state under the constitution of 1832, and prior to the Civil war, were these:

Matthew D. Patton, who succeeded R. M. Gaines in 1834; Thomas F. Collins, elected in 1837; John D. Freeman, elected in 1841, and reëlected in 1845; David C. Glenn, elected in 1849, and reëlected in 1853; and Thomas J. Wharton, elected in 1857. These elections took effect from January 1, following.

General Freeman was a native of New York, who came to Grand Gulf, Miss., when very young. Subsequently he removed to Natchez. While attorney-general he published "Freeman's Chancery reports." He was a member of the XXXIId congress, elected on the union ticket. Subsequently he resided in Jackson, engaged in the practice until his death.

David C. Glenn was born in North Carolina about 1824, but was reared in Holly Springs. Engaging actively in politics, he removed to Jackson in 1844. There he assumed a prominent position at the bar. As attorney-general he acquitted himself with marked ability. He represented the state in the great Union bank bond case. Declining to run for a third time, he removed to Harrison county, and there resided in comparative seclusion until his death, in 1868. He was, however, a member of the Charleston convention, and of the Mississippi secession convention.

Thomas J. Wharton, a native of Tennessee, came to Clinton, Miss., in 1836. He practiced his profession for a number of years, and being elected attorney-general, discharged his duties acceptably for two terms. He was circuit judge for six years, from 1882 to 1888; is a distinguished lawyer of scholarly attainments. He still lives in Jackson.

The constitution of 1832 having made the circuit bench a distinct body from that of the high court, it becomes necessary to name, at least, the circuit judges. They were as follows: Elected in 1833, Thomas A. Willis, A. M. Keegan, James F. Trotter, Alexander Montgomery and Edward C. Wilkinson; in 1834, T. B. Stribling and J. Scott; in 1835, J. Walker, Robert Hughes and G. Irish; in 1836, James M. Maury; in 1837, R. S. G. Perkins, Caswell

R. Clifton, Buckner C. Harris, David O. Shattuck, George Coalter and T. S. Stirling; in 1838, Hendley S. Bennett, Isaac R. Nicholson and J. A. Marshall; in 1840, Van Tromp Crawford, F. W. Huling and J. Battaille; in 1841, Franklin E. Plummer, G. Coalter, Charles C. Cage, Albert G. Brown, John H. Rollins, Morgan L. Fitch, Stephen Adams, H. S. Bennett, V. T. Crawford, Benjamin F. Caruthers, Henry Mounger and James M. Howry; in 1843, T. A. Willis; in 1845, Stanhope Posey, T. A. Willis, G. Coalter, Armistead B. Dawson, Robert C. Perry, Francis M. Rogers and Hugh R. Miller; about 1847, Wiley P. Harris, George Walter, George W. L. Smith and Nathaniel S. Price; about 1848, Hugh R. Miller; about 1849, John Watts and Patrick W. Tompkins; about 1851, Richard Barnett and William S. Bodley; about 1853, John E. McNair, E. G. Henry, William L. Harris, P. T. Scruggs, William M. Hancock, Joel M. Acker, William Cothran, John I. Guion and Locke E. Houston; about 1855, J. Shall Yerger; about 1858, James S. Hamm and John W. Thompson; about 1859, Hiram Cassidy and John F. Cushman; about 1861, Robert S. Hudson. The later dates are not given exactly, because the records are defective.

When the state was admitted into the Union, and the distinctive state courts were organized, of course the supreme court was no longer federal or territorial. A United States court was then organized, and a district judge appointed to preside over it The first was William B. Shields, who presided from 1818 to 1823–4; the next was Peter Randolph, until 1832–3; the next was Powhatan Ellis, until 1836–7; next George Adams, until 1838, when he resigned, and then Samuel J. Gholson until the war displaced the court itself. He resigned January 9, 1861.

Judges Shields and Ellis have already been mentioned. Judge Randolph was a citizen of Wilkinson county at the time of his appointment, having recently immigrated from Virginia. Judge Adams was a citizen of Hinds county, and was the father of Generals Wirt and Daniel W. Adams. Judge Gholson was a Kentuckian, settled in Monroe county. In 1833 he was sent to the legislature, and in 1836 to congress; major-general in the Confederate army; member of the legislature and speaker of the house. He died a few years since, full of honors, well deserved.

In the year 1838, by act of congress of June 18, the state was divided into two Federal districts, the line running about the southern borders of Attala and Carroll counties. The courts were then located at Jackson and Pontotoc.

On the 1st of February, 1860, a special criminal state court was established in Warren county, with full criminal jurisdiction. It was provided with its own judge and district attorney. This court was abolished July 19, 1870.

In January, 1861, the state seceded from the Union, and the secession convention made an amendment to the constitution of 1832 to the effect that if any part thereof conflicted with any ordinance passed by that convention such part should be, and was, abrogated. This of course was intended to effectuate the ordinance of secession.

When the war broke out, and everything was in the suspense and disorganization of that great calamity, an act was passed, on the 5th of August, 1861, suspending all actions of several enumerated characters, mainly for the collection of debts, and virtually closing the courts. After the war was over, in the case of Kaufman vs. The Bank, 40 Miss., 29, it was held that this statute was unconstitutional and void. Although that decision was not made until January, 1866, some such belief must have procured the passage of the statutes of January 29 and December 31, 1862, which suspended the running of the statutes of limitations until twelve months after the close of the war. By this means the motive to sue was taken away, and litigation practically suspended to a great extent, since no one cared to collect in Confederate or Mississippi war money a good debt which drew interets. Every one had plenty of that. So it nearly came to pass (although in a sense different from that of the original) that *"inter arma leges silent."*

CHAPTER VI.

THE EARLY WARS,

A NOTED national general of early days had occasion to write of his own "temperate course in opposition to the ardor which I discern in the executives of Louisiana and Mississippi;" and in commenting upon it in recent years, the interesting and impassioned historical writer of Mississippi, Mr. Claiborne, says: "This military 'ardor' which General Wilkinson noticed in Governors Claiborne and Mead was shared by the people, and has always been a characteristic of Mississippians and Louisianians when the country called for their services." The career of the state easily confirms this estimate, and no doubt the long and trying pioneer period of the Natchez district, with its threatening surroundings, had much to do in intensifying the tendency. The wars of ante-republic days have been touched upon in another chapter, but the period of the republic in Mississippi, covering scarcely one hundred years, furnishes a most striking array of warlike events, covering a half-dozen distinct movements, one of which was the most stupendous struggle ever witnessed on the globe, in which a son of the state was the leader of one of the two vast contending hosts, and in all of which wars and expeditions Mississippians bore a valiant part.

Of these six wars and expeditions five were national and one civil, a striking circumstance, and one which furnishes a basis for a division of the subject, the Civil war, the one fought for the states' rights, being assigned to another chapter. Of the five national wars and expeditions, the first was for protection of boundary, the second for protection of life, the third for vindication of honor, the fourth from sympathy with a fellow republic coupled with fear of invasion, and the fifth to secure a newly acquired territory. The second and third are so curiously intermingled and yet separate that they may be with equal fairness classed as two phases of one war. These national movements are: First, the Sabine expedition of 1806 to protect our Louisiana frontier from the Spaniards; second, the Muscogee war of 1812–14 against the uprising of the southern Indians in the famous Tecumseh conspiracy for extermination of the whites; third, the British war of 1812–15 in its final action at New Orleans; fourth, the Texan war of 1836; and fifth, the Mexican war of 1846–48.

The Sabine river boundary of the United States, at a time when the great trans-Mississippi region of the nation was more or less unknown, could only cause trouble when there was a highly excited popular feeling and irritation against Spanish provincial control. Many rumors were afloat of lawful and unlawful expeditions against the Spanish-Texan and Mexican region. The Spanish control of the Moble river was another source of irritation : "It is true we are few in numbers," said the grand jury of old Washington county in a petition for relief to the government in 1806; "but no two thousand souls hold a more important station in the American confederacy. We are the advance guard of civilization and republican America. If we become extinct, your influence, people of America, your influence on the southern savages is gone. The Spanish agents become possessed of an uninterrupted range of two thousand square miles." * This excited feeling was intensified along the Sabine, because of a conflicting claim of the Spanish to a more eastern boundary held ever since St. Denys of Mobile established an outpost on the site of Natchitoches in 1712. So while Governor Claiborne of New Orleans was up there organizing his frontier militia in the summer of 1806, with Major Porter of the national army, a section of the Spanish army under Captain-General Salcedo and Colonel Herrera crossed the Sabine and took post at Adaes. Governor Claiborne at once sought Governor Mead at Natchez, and both urged General Wilkinson at St. Louis to act at once, and Governor Mead proceeded to collect troops in Mississippi. The response was immediate, and on the first Sunday in October two hundred and fifty dragoons and mounted infantry under Maj. F. L. Claiborne crossed the Mississippi for Natchitoches. The other officers were: Capt. Thomas H. Williams, adjutant and quartermaster; Frederick Seip, surgeon; Heritage Howerton, quartermaster-surgeon; Joshua Knowlton, sergeant-major; and Capt. Benjamin Farrar, George Poindexter, Alexander Bisland, Basil Abram, William T. Voss, and Ralph Regan. Other later companies were a dragoon under Capt. Thomas Hinds of Jefferson, and a mounted company from Wilkinson. Amongst those from Claiborne county was Colonel White, an old gray-haired veteran of the Revolution who entered the ranks here as a private. It is proper to remind ourselves while considering any of these wars of the amount and particular location of white population. At this time it was confined to the southwestern and southeastern parts, enrolling seven thousand six hundred, six years before, and thirty one thousand three hundred and six, four years later. By the 31st of October, General Wilkinson and his army reached the left bank of the Sabine. Meanwhile, on the march, negotiations had been pending between the opposing generals, which by this time resulted in the agreement by Governor Herrera that the Spaniards should retire to Nacogdoches on the west side of the Sabine, and the American army to Natchitoches on the east to await a diplomatic settlement of the claim between the two powers.

At this point the enterprise becomes involved mysteriously, even to this day, in the notorious Aaron Burr conspiracy, for General Wilkinson receives a message from Burr, making large overtures to him to join a widespread secret movement in the Mississippi valley to capture the Spanish possessions of Mexico—a movement so far advanced that Burr was at that moment descending the Mississippi with considerable force. This determined General Wilkinson to make the settlement above mentioned, and apprise the Spanish viceroy of it, and at once concentrate his forces at Natchez and hasten to New Orleans to frustrate Burr's designs. Of course, it is a matter of national history that this theory was seriously suspicioned by many able men, not only in Mississippi, but in the nation, who charged General Wilkinson with complicity in Burr's designs very plausibly, but it was never publicly proved, and the subsequent course of events warrants the interpretation given above. The returned soldiers found all sorts of rumors rife, as they were all over the country, due to a proclamation by the president in regard to Burr on November 17. Acting Governor Mead, during

* *Mississippi Herald* and Natchez *Gazette*, June 17, 1806.

December, mobilized the militia of the territory, and General Wilkinson placed Commodore Shaw's flotilla of eight vessels, with fifty guns, in Natchez harbor*. Early in January, 1807, Burr's flotilla of nine unpretentious boats anchored opposite the mouth of bayou Pierre, on the Louisiana shore. Burr crossed over to the residence of an old friend of Revolutionary days, Judge Bruin, and learning of the military opposition prepared, wrote Governor Mead disclaiming all insinuations against him, and affirming his only purpose to be the colonization of his lands on the Ouachita river. Governor Mead secured an interview with him on the 17th, and demanded his unconditional surrender to the territorial authorities, Burr stipulating that it should be territorial and not military. Col. Benijah Osman and Lyman Harding, Esq., gave bonds of $5,000 for his appearance before Judge Rodney's court at Washington, M. T., on February 2. On that date Attorney-General Poindexter showed the case to be beyond the jurisdiction of the territory, and urged Burr's conveyance to the proper authorities. During the next night, however, he left the territory. Governor Williams had returned meanwhile, and on February 6 offered a reward of $2,000 for his capture, which was accomplished near Fort Stoddart, and he was turned over to the national authorities. It is probable that this incident had nothing more to do with the Sabine expedition than to close it prematurely and make it a bloodless campaign.

This campaign, however, had in it all the elements that were at the bottom of every uprising in that quarter, down to the close of the Mexican war, which secured the Rio Grande as our boundary, as it had been asserted to be even in Jefferson's administration. The old Natchez district, too, was closely identified with it from first to last. The Sabine-Rio Grande region seemed to be the protege of Natchez, and brave old General Quitman, who fired the Natcheans into sympathy responsive to every uprising for resistance to the hand of Mexico. The old disputed Sabine strip gathered a motley population of French, Spaniards, Mexicans, Indians, Americans and British, and proved to be a dumping-ground for all the disappointed, questionable, adventurous, outlawed, unbalanced refuse of all nations, and constant ebullition of some sort was natural. Yet in all this there were the seeds of power now showing fruit in the great state of Texas. It was in one of these ebullitions on that strip four years afterward, and extending over two years, that Col. Reuben Kemper, with Captains Ross, Perry, Luckett, Robinson, Deane and Wolforth armed themselves and hastened to the Sabine. A sort of brigand revolution sprang up on the strip, and Governor Claiborne, of New Orleans, ordered Captain Magee to suppress it. He succeeded, and resigned his commission in the national army at once, crossed the Sabine, and was chosen to head an insurrection in that province against the Spaniards; it was this that Colonel Kemper joined. The Spanish general, Salcedo, besieged them in vain, at what is now Bahia, for two months, and retreated to San Antonio. General Magee died and was succeeded by Don Bernardo, although Colonel Kemper was the active leader. They routed Salcedo nine miles from San Antonio and captured that city. Bernardo's cruelty and possibly the purpose to set up a new republic separate from the United States, led Colonels Kemper and Ross and many American ex-officers to retire, and soon after they were subdued. This was in 1813, and is mentioned as incidental to the real Sabine expedition of 1806.

This chronic disturbance in the West was by no means the chief thing that occupied the attention of about twenty-four thousand Mississippians†, who were surrounded by Indians on the east and Spaniards to the southeast. The world outside was full of fight; the British

---

* Natchez *Herald.*
† Twenty-three thousand two hundred and sixty-four free whites and seventeen thousand and eighty-eight slaves in 1812, all in south and southwest.

and Spanish empires, both among the giants of those days, played their American possessions against the young republic.   Both intrigued to gain the power of the vast Indian confederacies stretching from the Canadas to the gulf, who were smarting under the losses of years, holding a hardly-suppressed apprehension for their ultimate fate before the strides of the already great republic.   This confederacy, too, with the Spaniards of Florida, was stretched almost like an unbroken wall between the Mississippians and the great mass of the republic, leaving them in the peculiar unprotected outposts already noticed.   The Natchez and Washington (M. T.) papers bristled with exclamation points of foreign and United States news of new complications.

Among the Indians, however, were bold spirits, who discerned an opportunity to rise up among the contending whites and exterminate them all.   The required leader arose in 1811 in the person of the great Shawnee chief, Tecumseh, who fired tribe after tribe, until in October he spoke before the annual Creek assembly at Took-a-batch a.   "In defiance of the warriors of the dark and bloody ground, once our favorite hunting range," said the eloquent and powerful savage in the dialect of the Shawnees, "I have come from the great lakes of the North, and passed through their settlements like the whirlwind at night.   No war-whoop was sounded, no track was made, no fire was kindled, but see! there is blood on our warclubs!   The palefaces felt the blow but knew not whence it came.   Accursed be the race that have made women of our warriors and harlots of our women.   They have seized our country, and our fathers in their graves reproach us as slaves and cowards.   Listen!   Do you not hear their voices in the wailing winds?   The Muscogees were once a mighty people.   The palefaces trembled at your war-whoop, and the maidens of my tribe, on the distant lakes, sang the prowess of your warriors and sighed for their embraces.   And when our young men set out on the war-path the Shawnee sachems bade them 'be brave like the Muscogee!'   But now your blood has become white; your tomahawks have no edge; your bows and arrows are buried with your fathers.   You sleep while the paleface plows over their tomb and fertilizes his field with their sacred ashes.   Oh, Muscogees!   Brethren of my mother*!   Brush from your eyelids the sleep of slavery, and strike for vengeance and your country!   The red men have fallen as the leaves now fall.   I hear their voices in those aged pines.   Their tears drop from the weeping skies.   Their bones bleach on the hills of Georgia.   Will no son of those brave men strike the paleface and quiet these complaining ghosts?   Let the white race perish!   They seize your land; they corrupt your women; they trample on the bones of your dead!   Back whence they came, upon a trail of blood, must they be driven!   Back—aye, back into the great water whose accursed waves brought them to our shores!   Burn their dwellings, destroy their stock, slay their wives and children, that the very breed may perish.   War now!   War always!   War on the living!   War on the dead!   Dig their very corpses from their graves.   The red man's land must give no shelter to a white man's bones!   This is the will of the Great Spirit, spoken in the ear of my brother, the mighty prophet of the lakes.   He sends me to you.   All the tribes of the North are dancing the war dance.   Two mighty warriors across the seas will send us arms—at Detroit for us, at Pensacola for you.   I will soon return to my country, to wash my hands in the blood of the paleface.   My prophets shall tarry with you.   They will stand by your side and catch the bullets of your enemies.   When the white men approach your towns the earth shall open and swallow them up.   Soon shall you see my arm of fire stretched athwart the sky.   You will know that I am on the warpath.   I will stamp my foot and the very earth shall shake."   The keen savage made good use of the New Madrid earthquake and the predicted comet of that year.

---

* "The mother of Tecumseh was a Creek."—Claiborne's Mississippi.

The winter passed and, on congress' order of January, 1812, General Wilkinson arranged to proceed against them.

July 16, 1812, he ordered a quota drafted from each regiment of Mississippi militia, an order soon filled by volunteers from only seven companies, and placed under Brig.-Gen. F. L. Claiborne. They were unfortunately held at Baton Rouge for nearly a year, when, after Mobile had been secured in April, and the new commander, General Flournoy, had succeeded General Wilkinson, the Mississippi forces were ordered to Mount Vernon on the Alabama river on June 28, 1813. On July 18, at Camp Liberty, sixty miles southeast of Natchez, en route, the official report of " B. Blanton, adjutant pro tem," showed the force of the first M. T. volunteers, aggregating four hundred and two men; Captain Jack, thirty-four; Captain Engle, forty-two; Captain Jones, twenty-four; Captain Mead, thirty; Captain Painboeuf, fifteen; Captain Dent, fifty; Captain Scott, thirty-eight; Captain Middleton, twenty-seven; Captain Johnson, thirty-eight; Captain Foster, thirty-nine; Captain Brandon, thirty-four; and Captain Morrison, twenty-nine*. July 30 the forces reached Mount Vernon. The Louisiana troops had been placed in brigade under General Claiborne, and on August 12 the roster was as follows: Brigadier-general, F. L. Claiborne; first lieutenant, Alex. Calvit, aid; Captain Joseph P. Kennedy, brigadier-major; colonel, Joseph Carson; lieutenant-colonel, George T. Ross; major, Daniel Beasley; first lieutenant, William R. Deloach, adjutant; first lieutenant, Benjamin F. Salvage, quartermaster; John Ker, surgeon; Benjamin F. Harney, surgeon's mate; William R. Cox, surgeon's mate; captains, John Nelson, Joseph P. Kennedy, Louis Painboeuf, Phil. A. Engle, Archilaus Wells (of dragoons), Randall Jones, William Jack, Gerard C. Brandon, William C. Mead, Benjamin Dent, Hatton Middleton, Abram M. Scott, James Foster, L. V. Foelckil, Charles G. Johnson, Hans Morrison; first lieutenants, James Baily (of dragoons), Richardson Bowman, Audley L. Osborn, William Morgan, George P. Lilly, John D. Rogers (of dragoons), William Deloach, Theron Kellogg, Andrew Montgomery, John Camp, Alex. Calvit, John Allen, Robert Layson, Benjamin F. Salvage; second lieutenants, Charles Moore, Charles Barran, Spruce M. Osborn, Nicholas Lockridge, Robert C. Anderson, Benjamin Bridges (of dragoons), Kean Caldwell (of dragoons); ensigns, James M. Arthur, John Files, George Dougherty, William R. Chambliss, Thomas C. Vaughn, Robert Swan, Stephen Mays, James Luckett, George H. Gibbs, Elbert Burton, David M. Calliham, Young R. McDonald, Benjamin Blanton, Benjamin Stawell, William S. Britt, Isaac W. Davis, and John Cohn, cornet. These General Claiborne distributed, some under Captain Kennedy at Mount Vernon, some under Major Beasley at Fort Mims, a few under Lieutenant Montgomery, nine miles from the fort at Pierce's stockade, Colonel Carson at Fort Madison, and some at Fort Easely under the general himself. Major Beasley, in over-confidence, left the fort gate open, and at dinner-call on August 30, the Indians taking advantage, rushed on the fort. Captains Middleton, Jack and Baily and Lieutenant Randon were instantly with forces in place. To the gate, " Major Beasley rushed, sword in hand, and essayed in vain to shut it. The sand had washed against it and it could not be shut."† and he received a volley of bullets. The savages poured in, and the famous massacre of men, women and children began from which Dr. Holmes, Lieutenant Chambliss and scarcely a half-dozen others escaped with their lives. This terror awoke the whole Southwest to fortifying with stockades. Tennessee, as well as Mississippi, arose with General Jackson.

Governor Holmes, on September 2, called for five hundred men. Soon Captain Dough-

---

* Archives of Mississippi Historical Society. University.
† Pickett's Alabama.

erty, Captain Bullin, Captain Grafton and Captain Kempe were at Mount Vernon, and four dragoon companies, under Col. Thomas Hinds, and by December Col. George H. Nixon, who had secured the aid of the Choctaws under Chief Pushmattaha, was on the ground with militia under Capts. Robert Twilley, John Lowry, Parmenas Briscoe, Samuel Batchelor and G. Y. Glassburn. On December 23d an advance was made in three columns against the Indian prophets' fortified plan, called by them Holy Ground, near the Alabama river, made impregnable, as the prophets claimed, by the Great Spirit. The result was the rout of the savages and the laying waste of their towns. Already, in November, a paper* of the territory had said: "The cloud on our eastern border is disappearing—no more need our citizens flee to the woods and hiding places for refuge from the fell tomahawk of the savage —Jackson with his band of heroes are amongst them." Early in 1814 the terms of the Mississippi troops expired, and General Claiborne returned to Natchez. Maj. Thomas Hinds' dragoons continued under General Jackson during 1814, until the close of the Indian campaign and the capture of Pensacola, the seat of the Spaniards.

No sooner were the Indians and Spaniards secured by the occupation of Pensacola than General Jackson beheld a small squadron of British gunboats making their exit from the harbor. The papers of the territory were full of news of the movements of the United States troops and their successes against the British. The sturdy Tennessee general, with suspicions of the squadron's designs on New Orleans, proceeded to mass his troops at that point, ordering Hinds' dragoons to repair there as soon as possible. After a few days' refitting in Mississippi, Colonel Hinds marched for New Orleans, reaching there on the night of the 23d of December, two o'clock A. M. "As soon as we had camped," afterward vividly wrote M. W. Trimble, a private in Capt. Isaac Dunbar's company, "Colonel Hinds proceeded to Jackson's headquarters for orders. Before he returned, about eleven o'clock in the morning, we heard the alarm guns. In ten minutes he appeared in sight at full speed, waving his sword. We had mounted and immediately formed four abreast, and followed him in a brisk trot down Royal street. Every balcony was crowded, and the ladies were weeping and wringing their hands. Three miles or so below the city we came in view of two Louisiana rifle companies, and saw them fired upon by a large party of British concealed in an orange grove. Discovering our approach this party rapidly retreated below. Our first service was to throw down the cross-fences, from the levee to the woods, so as to open the ways for our army. We were then ordered to get as near the British lines as safety would authorize, and keep a vigilant watch over our movements. Under cover of night we rode silently down the levee, with a single file of Louisiana riflemen on foot. By the light of their fires we perceived a British outpost or guard, who were evidently making arrangements to throw out their pickets. Concealed by the darkness, we quietly passed between them and the main army and surrounded them. They seemed to be astounded, and surrendered without firing a gun—some sixty men. Resuming our march, we halted within four hundred yards of the long line of campfires indicating their position, and we could both hear and see their different detachments defiling from the swamp into the open field. About ten that night Jackson marched down from the city. The artillery formed on the levee. The Tennesseeans passed by us, and took position between us and the enemy. Two American schooners dropped down the river and anchored near by, so as to throw a flank fire on the British line. All these movements on our part were made in profound silence and under cover of the darkness, and the enemy could have no distinct conception of our presence or our numbers. A skyrocket rose from our lines and hissed through the air, and at

---

*Washington *Republican*, November 17, 1813.

the same moment a blaze of fire from our artillery, our rifles and our schooners. The atmosphere seemed to be on fire and the very earth trembled. The surprise was complete. They could not discern us or estimate our force, but these brave men, fresh from their terrible conflicts with Napoleon's veterans, coolly extinguished their fires and issued orders through their trumpets to form for action. Even amidst the roar of battle we could hear the thud of the balls mowing down their files, the cries of the wounded and the cool, clear orders given by their officers. 'Steady, men; steady!' 'Remember you are Britons!' was sounded from rank to rank. The fire on both sides was rapid and continuous. In the heat of the engagement a company of our regulars changed their position, to make room for a battery. In making this movement they encountered a company of Tennessee riflemen, and it being too dark for recognition and each company out of position, they opened fire upon each other at short distances and soon closed in a general hand-to-hand fight. The brave Colonel Lauderdale, recognizing from the familiar yell on both sides the fatal mistake, rushed in between them and commenced knocking down their guns with his sword, but lost his life in the fray—the saddest incident in this night attack. Finally the British, after having suffered severely, fell back, and we contented ourselves with the occupation of the ground. Our command was posted as sentinels, from the levee to the swamp, in front of and near to the British line. When daylight appeared their dead and wounded covered the field.

" Our first breastwork was some three miles above the British line, a ditch about six feet wide, and a bank of earth about four feet high, extending from the levee to the woods, some six hundred yards. At the extremity, next the levee, a bastion was constructed. A lot of cotton bales piled on the shore there, was used in making the bastion. Half a mile up was a second ditch and breastwork, and still another in the rear, our general evidently intending to fight, if necessary, from one to the other.

" Our dragoons were kept constantly in observation in front of the enemy, and we had frequent skirmishes with pickets and reconnoitering parties. We made no fires. Just after dark every night the British would kindle their fires, and then our riflemen would pick them off. Many of their sentinels were killed. General Pakenham sent a flag to complain of this shooting of sentinels as barbarous warfare, and that in the wars of Europe the pickets of opposing armies drank water out of the same stream. Jackson said this was a war of invasion, and he ordered his men to capture and kill every man within the range of their guns. On Christmas day my messmate, the late Lieut. C. Harris, and I were eating our ration; Colonel Hinds rode up and, pointing to some seventy or eighty horses grazing between us and the enemy's lines, ordered us to drive them in. He interpreted our look to mean that we thought it a dangerous duty, and he cried out: 'Dash on, boys! If you are killed I will recover your bodies, if it takes every man in the army to do it.' They were Tennessee horses that had got loose in the night, with their bridles and saddles on, had strayed round the army and were now nearer to the British than to us. We started and part of the way were concealed by a strip of sugarcane, but on passing out of it found ourselves in full view of the British army. It was very ticklish, and we looked back at the thicket of sugarcane, but there, where we had left him, sat our stern old colonel, with his eye upon us, looking like an equestrian statue of iron. We dashed around the horses just as the whole line of musketry opened upon us. This fire wounded several of the horses and startled the others, and shouting and yelling, with the balls whistling around us, we drove them within our lines.

"On the 30th of December the famous adventure of the ditch occurred. Colonel Hinds reported at headquarters that his pickets had detected a strong party of the British creeping up a wide and deep ditch traversing the field before us. Some doubt being expressed, he obtained permission to make an immediate reconnoissance. He formed the battalion, and said: 'Boys, you see that big ditch! It's full of redcoats. I'm going over it. Whoever wishes may follow me. Whoever chooses to stay here may stay!' And off he went at full speed, and every man close behind him. They leaped the ditch, which was crowded with soldiers, made a circuit in front of the British lines, and charged over the ditch a second time, each dragoon firing his pistol on the astounded soldiers, as they bounded over. The whole affair was phenomenal and almost supernatural, and apparently stupefied the crouching redcoats. But they recovered in time to give us a general volley, which wounded several of the troops, and tumbled over a number of horses. L. C. Harris and Charles H. Jourdan each got a bullet in the right shoulder."

About this time independent companies and individuals from every direction were flocking to the standard of General Jackson as he stood facing the British army under Gen. Edward Pakenham. More Mississippians prepared to aid him. Judge George Poindexter was on General Carroll's staff, and Capt. Samuel Dale arrived in time to join the final action. Natchez put forth her best efforts and started a company down the river under Capt. James C. Wilkins on the first day of 1815, in time to enable them to report on the field early on that famous January 8, when, with no orders to guide them, they crossed to the right levee and moved forward to aid our retreating forces under General Morgan. But let Mr. Trimble's vivid pen tell the story of that great day: "On the night of the 7th we were driven from our position in front, and compelled to fall back by an overwhelming force. There was a scattering fire during the night, and the note of preparation in the British camp could be distinctly heard. Our troops were in arms and in their proper places, at break of day. Our cannon bristled on the breastwork from the levee to the woods, and behind this was our long line of riflemen. One hundred and fifty yards in the rear sat our grim old colonel on his charger, with the whole of the cavalry. We were placed there to cover our army, in the event of its being compelled to fall back to the second position. As it turned out, we were merely silent spectators of the dreadful battle that ensued.

"About sunrise the whole British army was in motion. They advanced in solid columns, at a slow, measured step, throwing a shower of congreve rockets, and with a continuous artillery. Our batteries and the destructive fire from the schooner Louisiana, made terrible gaps in their front and flank, but these were immediately filled up. And on they came as steady as though on dress parade, until they got within range of our rifles, and then the havoc was dreadful. Three times they recoiled and were rallied again by their heroic officers, who led them up to our intrenchments. Three of these brave leaders were shot on our breastwork, while waving their swords and shouting to their men to follow. By this time the commander-in-chief and the two senior British generals had fallen; scores of officers and hundreds of men lay dead or dying on the field. The British had displayed their hereditary valor, illustrated on a thousand battlefields, and not in one more conspicuously than in this, but they now sought the cover of a canal, and the mighty conflict was over!"

This battle was fought some days after the treaty that closed the war, but it was so far from the scene of the treaty that it could not be communicated. This had nothing to do, however, with the battle's influence, for the valor of that day has given a confidence and glory to American arms that is still felt. After these weary years of war, General Jackson, as was fitting, published an address to the soldiers on January 21, and among other things he said: "The cavalry from the Mississippi territory, under their enterprising leader,

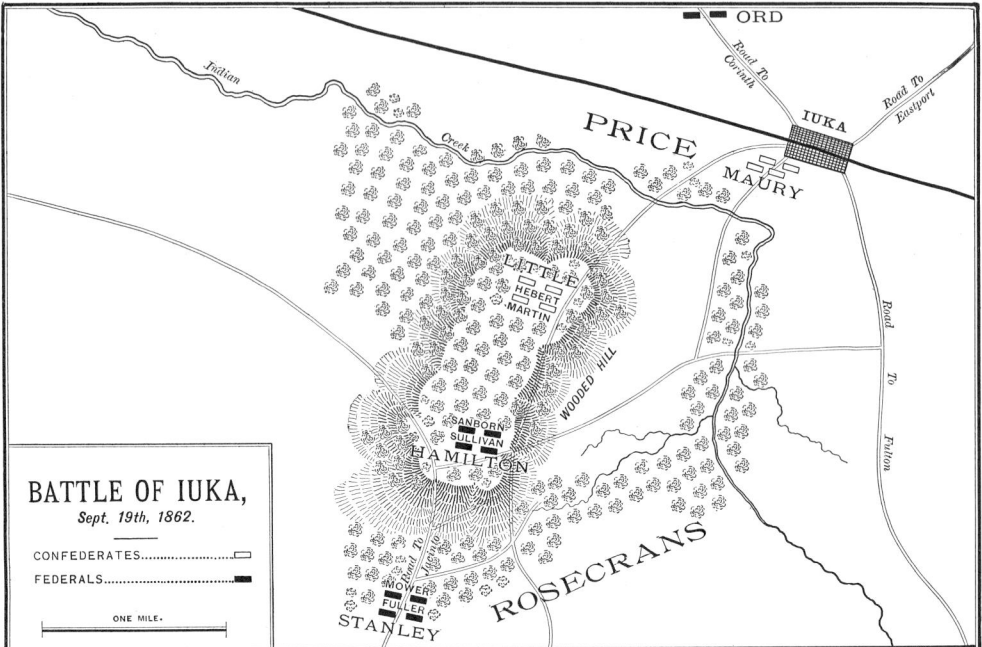

BATTLE OF IUKA,
Sept. 19th, 1862.

CONFEDERATES.......................... ▭

FEDERALS.............................. ▬

ONE MILE.

ORD

Road To Corinth

Road To Eastport

PRICE

IUKA

MAURY

Indian

Creek

LITTLE

HEBERT

MARTIN

WOODED HILL

Road To Fulton

SANBORN

SULLIVAN

HAMILTON

ROSECRANS

MOWER

FULLER

STANLEY

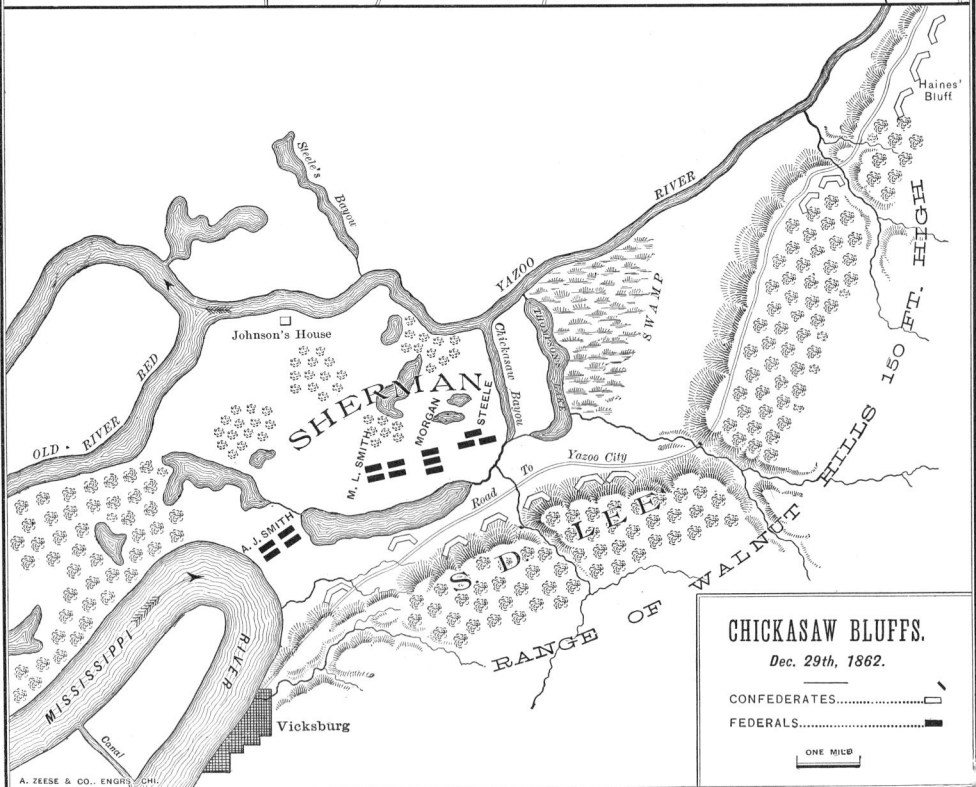

CHICKASAW BLUFFS.
Dec. 29th, 1862.

CONFEDERATES.......................... ▭

FEDERALS.............................. ▬

ONE MILE.

Haines' Bluff

150 FT. HIGH

Steele's Bayou

YAZOO

RIVER

SWAMP

Thompson

Johnson's House

OLD · RIVER

RED

SHERMAN

Chickasaw Bayou

M. L. SMITH

MORGAN

STEELE

Road To Yazoo City

S. D. LEE

A. J. SMITH

RANGE OF WALNUT HILLS

MISSISSIPPI

RIVER

Canal

Vicksburg

A. ZEESE & CO., ENGRS., CHI.

Major Hinds, was always ready to perform every service which the nature of the country enabled them to execute. The daring manner in which they reconnoitered the enemy on his lines excited the admiration of one army and the astonishment of the other. Captain Blanchard was very useful as an engineer, and merits the general's praise for the celerity and skill with which he erected the battery, which now commands the river on the right of the camp."* In his report of December 23 he speaks of Major Chotard, a Mississippian on his staff and then wounded: "Colonels Butler and Piatt, and Major Chotard, by their intrepidity saved the artillery." These brave men were joyously and appropriately received on their return to the territory. It is difficult in so scattered a series of actions as these of the war of 1812–15 to do credit to all who served. There are few instances of a population furnishing a greater proportion of its numbers for war, and under greater difficulties.

Over thirty years passed and the state had made marvelous strides, spreading her free territory to her present bounds and rising in population to nearly three hundred thousand. It was 1836. The local papers teemed with rumors of the Creek and Seminole troubles to the East, and republican affairs in Texas were culminating, and that too with many of the features of thirty years before. Texas lands were a great temptation to Americans in the Southwest; the Americans on the ground lost no opportunity to excite popular uprising against the Mexican authorities; while international law required neutrality in the United States, the old and constantly increasing sentiment that the Rio Grande, instead of the Sabine, should be our boundary, had so much power that Generals Sam and Felix Houston received aid and encouragement from high places in the revolt that finally succeeded in the fall of Alamo and the erection of the republic of Texas. Among land capitalists in Mississippi were the United States marshal William M. Gwin, James C. Wilkins, L. R. Marshall and others who then owned great tracts in Texas. The Gwins were a power in Mississippi and friends of the Houstons and of President Jackson. Add to this the fact that Gen. Felix Houston publicly recruited Mississippi troops for the Texas campaign and a plausible suspicion is aroused that elaborate plans were on foot to absorb the results of the struggle. In an April number, 1836, the Woodville *Republic* says: "The citizens of Vicksburg have contributed $3,500 in aid of Texas;" and adds that the governor states that there is not an organized company in the state. Natchez and General Quitman were vigilant, too; it is said that when "Gen. Sam Houston was retreating before Santa Anna in Texas, and that Santa Anna boasted that his march should cease only when his troops slept upon American soil and quartered in the city of New Orleans, the fiery spirit of Quitman kindled into vivid enthusiasm. He threw himself upon the highway and shouted for volunteers to the rescue. In three days he had a hundred picked men, armed and equipped at his own cost, and ready to follow him into the jaws of death for fatherland. Waiting for no orders and asking for no assistance, he hurried off with his little band and they had nearly reached Houston's command when Santa Anna was routed and his force scattered."† As late as July 22 the governor called for ten companies of cavalry—for the protection of our frontier, of course, but it became unnecessary. This may be considered as incidental to the final act of the drama that began with St. Deny's post in 1712 and only closed with the fall of the halls of the Montezumas, over one hundred and thirty-five years later.

Let us see the final act, the annexation of the young republic, and its bearing on this state's military action under Gov. A. G. Brown in 1846. Of course Mexico resisted it, and General Taylor's army had the task of conquering Mexico, and compelling recognition

---

*Washington Republican, February 1, 1815.
† "Recollections." Reuben Davis, 1890.
9

of the Rio Grande boundary.   In the president's call for troops only one regiment was wanted from Mississippi.   Volunteers by hundreds were waiting and eager for the call, and it was no sooner made than Governor Brown was embarrassed by the necessity for selecting out of so many.   Finally it was decided to accept companies from the following counties: From Hinds, two under Captains Downing and McManus; from Warren, two under Captains Crump and Willis; from Williamson, one under Captain Cooper; from Carroll, one under Captain Howard; from Lafayette, one under Captain Delay; from Marshall, one under Captain Taylor; from Yazoo, one under Captain Sharp; and from Lowndes and Monroe, one under Captain McClung.   They rendezvoused at Camp Brown, near Vicksburg, and organized, choosing one of the state's representatives in congress as colonel, a young man of West Point training and considerable experience in the United States service—Jefferson Davis—who resigned his civil office, and proceeded to secure rifles at New York.   The brilliant young captain of the Monroe-Lowndes company was chosen lieutenant-colonel, and was given command of Camp Brown and ordered to proceed to New Orleans and thence to Point Isabel, at the mouth of the Rio Grande, where Colonel Davis soon arrived with arms, and spent months in drilling them to efficiency.

The record of this regiment warrants the presentation of their roster, as enlisted in June, 1846:

List of officers, non-commissioned officers, musicians and privates of the First regiment Mississippi riflemen, in the war with Mexico (to serve twelve months).   Date of enlistment, June, 1846.*   Field and staff officers: Jefferson Davis, colonel; Alexander K. McClung, lieutenant-colonel; Alexander B. Bradford, major; Richard Griffith, adjutant; Seymour Halsey, surgeon; John Thompson, assistant surgeon; Charles T. Harlan, sergeant-major; S. Warren White, quarter-master sergeant; Stephen Dodds, principal musician; Kemp S. Holland, assistant commissary.

Company A: Captain, John M. Sharp; lieutenants, *Phillip J. Burrus, first, Thomas P. Slade, second; sergeants, †Ferdinand Bostick, first, †Albert P. Hill, second, †John A. Cason, third, †R. F. Williams, fourth; corporals, S. M. Phillips, first, †James H. Bell, second, †Edward Bowman, third, ‡William J. Miller, fourth; musicians, S. S. Caldwell, D. M. Hollingsworth; privates, John Atkins, †David F. Bailey, Winston Banks, D. H. Battin, N. Bisbee, John Bradley, ‡George Brooke, Alonzo Brown, †A. C. Capshaw, ‡W. W. Capshaw, Samuel K. Carter, Henry D. Clark, Amos B. Corwin, †Francis Cotton, ‡A. J. Cowart, †John Dillon, †Elijah Dixon, ‡Thomas J. Ellis, Robert Fisher, Elijah Floyd, †H. Floyd, ‡Daniel Forbes, †Edwin Fox, †Solomon Gardner, †W. G. Gerrald, §R. S. Gerrald, †C. R. Gordon, †R. Green, †Henderson R. Griffin, Thomas R. Griffin, ‡Caleb Grimes, †Meredith Hart, A. J. Herrod, Thomas J. Higginbotham, ‖Daniel Hughes, W. Ingraham, Albert Johnson, John Johnson, Henry R. Kenna, †J. W. Kirk, †S. D. Lavender, †Charles A. Leake, H. S. Little, †Madison M. Mason, C. J. Miller, †James M. Miller, M. R. Mobley, †William Moore, †Joseph W. Morton, J. O'Bryant, C. O'Sullivan, †Samuel O. Parker, †Peter A. Paul, ‡William H. Peaster, J. H. Penny, †W. A. Prestridge, †Emory Prewett, Milton Pyles, †Jesse Read, ‡L. D. Read, †James Richards, †Benjamin F. Ridley, R. Russell, ‡Calvin Schnebely, R. L. Shock, †John Standin, ‡Daniel Stephens, S. P. Stubblefield, W. H. Stubblefield, †Robert Swisher, A. W. Teague, †James W. Thomas, J. R. Ware, C. Wedikind, ‡H. West, W. White, †James W. Whitman, ‡Ulysses Whitman, †George Williams, ‡John Wooldridge.

Company B: Captain, Douglass H. Cooper; lieutenants, Carnot Posey, first; James

Calhoun, second; sergeants, R. McConnell, first; †Douglass West, second; E. W. Massell, third; Claiborne Farish, fourth; corporals, Francis Best, first; Charles Erambert, second; Robert Miller, third; John Y. Holt, fourth; musicians, †Westley Stewart, †Thomas H. Law; privates, †John L. Anderson, James B. Baird, Benjamin Bass, W. J. Bryant, B. M. Cage, A. G. Cage, Jr., †William L. Cage, Ido Carriger, †Douglass J. Canfield, Reuben W. Chance, †Richard P. Campitt, Thomas G. Conner, W. A. Cotton, †Nolan S. Dickson, J. W. Donnelly, †Joseph S. Fuqua, J. G. Gayden, T. H. Hampton, B. D. Harris, Samuel R. Harrison, †John Q. Herbert, James Hill, †James L. Hodge, W. J. Hodge, John S. Holt, †William G. Hope, J. R. Hutchison, John H. Jackson, J. H. Jones, Seaborn Jones, †John J. Kearsey, †J. Kyle, †A. Lanchart, †A. C. Lanchart, William A. Lawrence, James Lennex, †Hugh N. Lindsey, †Robert H. Lowry, †J. F. McClure, Daniel R. McGahey, James Martin, James M. Miller, †William H. Miller, Louis Mootry, Hiram Morgan, †Mayberry J. Morris, D. Murray, Barny Murtogh, †Robert H. Neyland, †Alexander Newman, S. Newman, †James Nichelson, †Henry F. O'Neal, William R. Rea, †George P. Richardson, S. J. Richardson, James Riddle, George Rivercomb, John Roberson, †W. S. Rotrammel, ‡Samuel Small, G. A. Smith, †Hampton H. Smith, James Z. Smith, †Peter Smith, F. M. Snyder, Walter Spurlock, †W. W. Starns, †James D. Stewart, †Calvin J. Strawn, †Clarke H. Tigner, Thomas H. Titley, Benjamin L. Turbeville, Charles Vaugel, William J. D. Way, J. M. Westrope, †Theodore W. White, Kinyon R. Whillington, W. J. Wilkinson, W. Woosely.

Company C: Captain, John Willis; lieutenants, Henry T. Cook, first; Richard Griffith, second; sergeants, Rufus K. Arthur, first; William Henry Scott, second; N. G. Watts, third; U. S. Puckett, fourth; corporals, William V. Hickey, first; †Josiah H. Goodwin, second; †John B. Markham, third; J. A. McLaughlin, fourth; musicians, †James Gwinn, †H. L. Armour; privates, †R. H. Abbott, †Robert B. Banks, †Charles Barnes, John M. Barnes, †Theodore Batts, Charles T. Bradford, †Ira O. Bradford, †William H. Bright, †Adam Brombee, †George W. Brown, F. Clark, William H. Clements, I. N. Collier, †Samuel Collins, James W. Conn, B. G. Connor, William Couch, John Craft, Edward Currie, I. M. Daughtry, †Robert H. Davis, †A. Dixon, †Philip D. Dixon, Stephen Dodds, John Dugan, George W. Dunn, Dick H. Eggleston, Charles H. Ellis, †Benjamin Folkes, †James L. Folkes, H. F. Ford, †V. I. Frier, Edward Gaffney, George H. Gray, I. M. Grey, Seymour Halsey, ‡William E. Harris, †A. Hartley, †William Henby, †Samuel Hindman, †Joseph D. Howell, James Irvine, John Jeter, James Johnson, †P. W. Johnson, †Daniel A. McKay, †Robert McKey †Wesley I. Maples, Russel M. Martin, George E. Metcalf, Joseph Miller, Howard Morris, William M. Nutter, †James D. Pack, John Preston, †Andrew L. Richards, Robert Richardson, †C. H. Russell, Benjamin M. Sims, †David Sims, Will R. Skelton, I. N. Stephenson, Jr., Levi H. Stephens, Henry Stout, †John Stout, William G. Street, F. J. Striebeck, Samuel C. Suit, G. B. Taylor, †Washington Thames, †Henry B. Thompson, †Thomas W. Tilden, †Louis Tillman, L. M. Turner, E. L. Ventriss, Samuel Wharton, †George D. Williamson, †John C. Winn, †James N. Wood, †J. Q. Woodruff.

Company D: Captain, Bainbridge D. Howard; lieutenants, Daniel R. Russell, first; L. T. Howard, second; sergeants, †Samuel A. Young, first; †Marcus C. Wellons, second; D. E. Love, third; †James M. Ramsey, fourth; corporals, E. W. Hollingsworth, first; *Thomas J. Kyle, second; †J. Durdin, third; E. Beall fourth; musicians, †Jesse S. Strickland, H. W. Jones; privates, J. G. Adair, T. M. Adair, P. G. Adkinson, Richard Applegate, H. B. Beard, †John C. Benthal, †James W. Blake, Thomas Brown, †John A. Buckholts, †James Burwell, Daniel Capshaw, †Young Carr, †Robert Clarke, Alpheus Cobb, D. P. Cocke, John Cokely, †Samuel G. Colburn, Henry Creamer, T. B. Davidson, †David R. Doyle, †W. T. S. Durham,

J. G. Elliott, A. Erving, J. Erwin, †Samuel Ferguson, †Ripley Fields, †Joel Forbes, †J. D. M. Gage, †James George, †William P. Gray, †William M. Gunter, †Harman G. Hall, †Marion Hanks, †T. Hanks, Wills C. Harill, †John R. Harper, †J. B. Heath, †Benjamin L. Hodge, †Parker F. Hood, †Alfred Hudson, †Warren Hufman, D. W. Jefferson, ‡James Johnson, O. W. Jones, R. A. Lewis, †William Lott, Neil McAllister, †John McAula, †Andrew J. McClendon, †James A. McCoy, †W. D. Martin, †S. S. Munday, ‡Oscar L. Nixon, B. F. Norman, †Hiram G. Norman, William Orr, †Franks P. Pleasants, †A. S. Powell, George W. Ramsey, ‡John Q. Reynolds, H. A. Reynolds, †Sherod Reynolds, †Benjamin B. Rhodes, †Govan A. Rowe, †H. Lindsey Russell, †John Shooke, James Somerville, B. F. Taylor, †M. Taylor, Leon Trousdale, G. W. Vance, J. D. Vance, ‡Daniel Waganon, †David Wilgus, †George Willis, R. Williams, J. N. B. Williamson, R. P. Winns, †Albert Young, †Jacob T. Young.

Company E: Captain, John L. McManus; lieutenants, Crawford Fletcher, first; James H. Hughes, second; sergeants, A. B. Patterson, first; Archibald M. Hughes, second; William W. Phillips, third; Joseph H. Langford, fourth; corporals, Francis M. Robinson, first; E. McNair, second; †William R. Langford, third; †Marcellus A. Foute, fourth; musicians, †Gad E. Upson, Calvin Hobbs; privates, John H. Bowman, Charles M. Bradford, Henry H. Bryan, A. P. Burnham, †John Campbell, Richard Clardy, Edward U. Cohea, †John W. Coleman, David Connor, Solomon M. Coulter, †Patrick Deigman, James Donald, †B. H. Edwards, William E. Estis, †George H. Farrar, Frederick Fauntleroy, †George P. Finley, Robert J. Fox, David Frazier, †Jacob Frederiks, †Hugh Gourley, †Milton F. Gourley, James T. Griffin, John Harrison, William H. Hasty, James Higdon, Henry Hipple, †John M. Hooker, John W. Hunter, Robert J. Royce, †Henry V. Keep, John Kennedy James H. Kilvey, Samuel W. Lane, George W. Laird, Isam C. Laird, Jeremiah E. Lairy, †Richard Latham, †William Lowe, James Lowry, †James B. Lyerly, Z. McNeely, †William H. Marrs, Samuel W. Marsh, William S. Martin, Silas Mechum, †James Moore, Jesse W. Moss, D. M. G. Myrick, J. M. Myrick, J. Camp Perkins, George Phillips, †Hugh W. Pierce, Henry Pomeroy, Archibald G. Price, Anthony B. Puckett, ‡James H. Rawlings, Joseph C. Reville, John Ritch, †E. W. Roberts, †D. H. Robinson, †William Schad, ‡Samuel Scruggs, William Sellers, Calvin A. Shelton, ‡James M. Shelton, Louis Siple, †Madison M. Smith, †T. T. Sorsby, William P. Spencer, †William L. Stacy, Robert I. Steele, †Perry H. Tinnin, §William Waide, James Walsh, †John Walthrope, James Ward, †John R. Williams, †James W. Williams, John N. Williams.

Company F: Captain, William Delay; lieutenants, W. N. Brown, first; J. F. Malone, second; sergeants, ‡M. D. C. Carloss, first; Thomas Swann, second; A. S. Dixon, third; ‡J. J. Tatum, fourth; corporals, James W. Blakeley, first; †J. P. Hobbs, second; J. H. Carger, third; †Charles S. Ward, fourth; musicians, —— Chester, †John Livingston; privates, H. C. Atter, J. N. Bigbee, §J. Boyd, †Thomas Z. Bragg, †D. A. Brittain, ‡William H. Broach, †A. G. Browning, J. C. Browning,† Thomas J. Buie, †A. T. Burks, D. L. Butler, ‡James N. Campbell, †M. H. Carr, ‡William Carr, Jr., †James M. Childress, W. G. Cloak, John Connar, Thomas Courtney, †Thomas D. Davis, †Warler Davis, P. J. Dunavant, †William W. Eaton, †D. M. C. Gardner, Enos Garratt, †William H. Gec, C. Goodwin, †George W. Goodwin, Benjamin Hagany, †John A. G. Hancock, †James A. Henderson, †Rufus Henry, †R. C. Higginbotham, ‡John K. Holcomb, W. Holt, ‡W. R. Humphries, †D. S. Hunter, †D. R. Jameson, Stephen Jones, ‡Thomas L. Jones, †William H. Jones, ‡Benjamin H. Joyner, ‡Absalom Knight, ‡Charles Lawson, †Charles A. Lewers, ‡A. M. Liles, M. F. Lock, †John C. Lowe, John Luckett, S. Luckett, ‡G. McKie, †Levi Maza, ‡Levi M. Meaders, C.

Moore, †James T. Morris, Joseph W. Morris, ‡J. P. Mullenax, W. H. Owens, ‡W.S. Parker, ‡D. E. Patterson, †G. Peaterson, †James L. Powell, W. W. Redding, †Arthur St. John, R. Shaw, ‡William Sheehorn, ‡T. L. Simpson, †Joseph C. Stockard, John P. Stockard, †John Strong, †William Strong, †Wilson Taylor, William Thompson, †James H. Tucker, †Joshua Turner, J. E. Turnbull, †William G. Vaughn, E. D. Wallace, ‡John Webb, F. S. Welch, †Oscar M. Zollekoffer.

Company G: Captain, Reuben N. Downing; lieutenants, Stephen A. D. Greaves, first; William H. Hampton, second; sergeants, Francis McNulty, first; Joseph M. Roberts, second; †James C. Hays, third; †Thomas A. Mellon, fourth; corporals, †Samuel D. Wooldridge, first; E. S. Charlton, second; George W. Harrison, third; Peter Sinclair, fourth; musicians, †William Lindsey, †A. M. Waddill; privates, †Thomas J. Anderson, †W. D. Ainsworth, J. M. Alexander, Asa B. Atkinson, †G. J. W. Bird, Joseph S. Bond, ‡James Boyd, Thomas Bradley, †J. S. Brown, †Charles M. Burland, Philip Burnett, V. S. Burnett, †E. P. Burney, †Sidney S. Champion, John A. Chapman, Theodore C. Chapman, E. F. Charlton, ‡Watson E. Clarke, Jeptha Conger, Louis A. Cooper, William G. Cooper, Jr., †Louis Coorpender, †William F. Coorpender, ‡Elijah Dunlap, Benjamin F. Edwards, ‡Leon F. Eilbott, Joseph Fairchild, Robert Felts, †S. R. Fondran, †W. B. Gallman, Charles H. Gibbs, James H. Graves, Job Hammond, May Hays, William F. Hutchison, Newton Ingram, †Daniel B. Johnson, †David A. Jones, ‡D. F. Kenner, †Albert M. Key, Malcom McJunis, †William Maben, †Thomas F. Mabry, J. H. Mallett, †L. J. Mapp, †Francis M. Martin, John A. Martin, †John R. Miller, John P. Moseley, Andrew J. Neely, Jesse Odoms, Richard E. Parr, †Alfred Patton, Samuel Potts, †John F. Rimes, W. L. Rimes, Hiram D. Ripley, William E. Ripley, Romulus M. Saunders, Thadeus W. Saunders, William Seay, ‡Eli Sellman, †Thomas Sellman, †R. W. Shields, †E. W. Smith, †T. C. Smith, †S. D. Sojourner, †Stephen B. Stafford, J. H. Stewart, Joshua Stone, Thomas S. Sumrall, S. B. Thomas, Joseph H. Thompson, Thomas J. Ussery, †Wilson Ware, †James M. Watson, J. J. Watts, †C. S. Williams, †James Williamson, †R. H. Wright.

Company H: Captain, *George P. Crump; lieutenants, Robert L. Moore, first; *Hugh M. Markham, second; sergeants, Horace H. Miller, first; Charles T. Harlan, second; William C. Porter, third; Albert M. Newman, fourth; corporals, Joseph Schmaling, first; John S. Clendennin, second; John J. Poindexter, third; †Robert M. Martin, fourth; musicians, Robert McNair, Theodore McMorrough; privates, Edward C. Allen, Erwin Barefield, †John Bobb, Jr., Simeon Brown, Richard S. Burney, †Stephen D. Carson, William Chaffin, Thomas Coe, §Edward Cox, †James H. Dafrien, John Dart, †Thomas J. Davidson, †James C. Davis, Daniel D. Dubose, Daniel Dunlop, †Edward Dunn, Samuel M. Edwards, †John Finch, Robert Grigg, Benjamin L. Groves, †George Hackler, †James Hackler, John A. Harris, William D. Harrison, William H. Harvey, Benjamin Hatton, Sanford H. Hill, †George W. Hise, Richard Hopkins, Isaac Johnson, Andrew Kremer, Henry H. Lanell, John J. Locke, John J. Luckin, Armstrong Lyttle, †David H. McClure, †Thomas H. McGaughey, William H. McKinney, †Moses McMurray, †Humphrey Marshall, Joseph Martin, †Frederic Mathews, †John F. Mattingly, William Moore, †William M. Moore, Philip Muldoon, Avery Noland, William Nosworthy, †Elijah A. Peyton, ‡John C. Peyton, †Henry T. Raim, Patrick Rairden, Hugh Riley, †Benjamin F. Roberts, Mitchell M. Robins, †William D. Robinson, †John Ross, Revennah Ross, Benjamin F. Sanders, †Joseph Sellers, Richard D. Shackelford, †George W. Shaifer, Joseph P. Shannon, Samuel Shaw, † Charles E. Smedes, John Smith, †James J. F. Steele, James W. Stevenson, James E. Stewart, †John Straughn, †Charles Strouse, Joseph P. Tennille, ‡John E. Vandivure, †William W. Wadsworth, †William K. Walker, Thomas White, †John M. Williams, †Rufus K. Williamson, William Winans, Augustus Wood.

Company I: Captain, James H. R. Taylor; lieutenants, Christopher H. Mott, first; Samuel H. Dill, second; sergeants, †John M Holland, first; Isaac Milum, second; †Francis A. Wolf, third; Wiley T. Byor, fourth; corporals, †Joseph Yancey, first; S. B. Yancey, second; William H. Crisham, third; †Andrew J. Forman, fourth; musicians, †Alfred Delap, E. A. Mullen; privates, †A. L. Abston, †Samuel M. Allen, Garland Anderson, John E. Bass, †Berry O. Best, John S. Branch, Joseph L. Bridges, †Leonidas Brown, †Alexander S. Burton, †Andrew J. Cole, †Samuel M. Cole, A. Collingsworth, †Charles F. Cotter, W. H. Craft, †J. H. Crawford, ‡S. H. Davis, †J. Dickinson, Perry Dorman, Joseph A. Downing, R. J. Eddings, †Charles Edmondson, William E. Epps, †Joseph Evans, †John W. Glenn, Eleana Greer, Peter D. O. Griefft, V. S. Grisham, Samuel S. Hall, Willis Hamilton, Joseph Heaton, John Hedgepeth, ‡John L. Henderson, William Hobbs, H. D. Holdeway, William Hoskins, Joseph A. Hughes, M. Jolly, †Robert Josselyn, †David H. Keeling, J. B. Kur, J. M. Kincaird, John P. Lamay, ‡James Langston, †F. G. Laniew, Patrick Lee, John Long, T. O. McClanahan, C. P. McJimsey, R. H. Malone, ‡James S. Marr, †Plummer M. Martin, ‡W. A. Martin, Nathaniel Massie, †Isaac E. Milum, †James P. Moore, L. H. Murphree, †Montgomery Naile, Jesse Oldham, †Valentine B. Orr, John Peace, †Rufus E. Phillips, John Pittman, H. J. W. Proctor, Thadeus D. Randolph, ‡J. H. C. Relnolds, †Isaac M. Shelby, ‡B. S. Shrivors, †John H. Smith, †John B. Smoot, William B. Spinks, †Spencer B. Stallions, George Taylor, Walter A. Thompson, Henry G. Trotter, William D. Tucker, James W. Vinson, T. T. Wilkerson, †Gideon Williams, †John Williams, †Trion M. Yancey.

Company K: Captain, William P. Rogers; lieutenants, William H. H. Patterson, first; William P. Townsend, second; sergeants, †William H. Bell, first; †Henry Tindall, second; James L. Covington, third; †David P. Stedman, fourth; corporals, †William P. Gillean, first; †Thomas L. Jones, second; †William R. Julian, third; J. G. Reese, fourth; musicians, †Thomas G. Ames, J. W. Hartman; privates, R. J. Allen, S. C. Astin, J. L. Bartee, Richard Bell, ‡John Brand, Edward E. Brazeale, George W. Broom, George W. Campbell, †Green B. Carey, Henry M. Cook, †John E. Cravens, †William Creight, †John W. Cummings, Benjamin F. Davis, C. F. Davis, †John E. Day, †Tolbert Dockery, John W. Dunn, †F. L. Dowsing, Moses D. Echols, †James A. Evans, Jacob Feltman, George Fisher, James Flanagan, †William Flanagan, Carman Frazee, †Edward H. Gregory, B. F. Grugett, James M. Hales, †Thomas Harrison, †Eli J. Henry, †John D. Higgason, John J. Hindsley, †H. L Howard, George Hunt, Nathaniel Johnson ‡William H. Kelley, A. A. Kerr, †Thomas L. Kewen, Andrew J. King, †Edward Kinnis, John Laughan, †Daniel B. Lewis, †Edward B. Lewis, W. D. Longstreet, †William S. McDuffie, J. E. C. McGinn, John D. McNorris, ‡William Mallett, †Charles Martin, ‡Archibald Miller, Alexander Mitchell, R. G. Mosby, William O'Rouke, Horatio P. Overton, †Joel T. Parrish, Bryant Perry, †James O. Ragsdale, H. M. Reese, ‡John Rennean, †James A. Sharman, ‡Allen Skidmore, †Platt Snedicon, †Adkinson Stewart, J. W. Stewart, James Tanner, †Richard T. Tierce, James Thompson, J. L. Thompson, R. E. Thompson, †Calvin T. Tindsley, John M. Tyree, Job Umphlott, William B. Wade, Thomas Washer, Morgan Watson, John Westbrook, Archibald H. White, †John C. Willett, †William Woodliff.

It is not the province of this sketch to recount the operations of the Mexican war, but only to indicate the well-known lines of action participated in so brilliantly by this state's regiments. In the streets of Monterey, in September, they fought with General Taylor, and here, while leading his brave assault on the Black Fort, the lieutenant-colonel, McClung, was wounded, and the colonel, Mr. Davis, was the one chosen by General Taylor to conduct the negotiations for the surrender of the city. As General Taylor moved into Mexico this regiment was under his eye on the famous field of Buena Vista, February 21, 1847, where, after three days' hard fighting, Colonel Davis, by his masterly and famous "V formation," resisted in a narrow pass the Mexican lancers under General Mignon, and saved the day to the forces of General Taylor. "The First Mississippi regiment was composed of the best-born, best educated and wealthiest young men of the state" writes Judge Reuben Davis, who himself was called to the colonelcy of another regiment of Mississippians.

Late in the fall of 1846, another regiment was sent out under Colonel Reuben Davis, but they were not destined to participate in any engagements. These were: Captains, Charles Clarke, Joel M. Acker, A. K. Blythe, A. M. Jackson, Estelle, Hymer, Liddell, McWillie, Daniel and Buckley. They organized with these officers: Colonel, Reuben Davis; lieutenant-colonel, J. H. Kilpatrick; major, Ezra R. Price; adjutant, Beverly Mathews; William Barksdale, assistant commissary sergeant; Charles M. Price, assistant quartermaster; Thomas N. Love, surgeon; and D. A. Kinchloe, assistant surgeon. They were sent on to General Taylor's command, and after some months of guard duty, the colonel and his lieutenant resigned, and returned home, whereupon Capt. Charles Clarke and Lieut. John A. Wilcox were respectively promoted to the vacant positions. It is interesting to note that in this war the brave old general, John A. Quitman, as if keeping up his early love, was one of the first on the Mexican field of war as a major-general, gave the order that placed the stars and stripes afloat over the Mexican capital, and was made the first American governor to rule there. His personal examination and maps of the ramparts of Chapultepec recall the dashing incident of Colonel Hinds at New Orleans thirty-three years before. Thus ended the final act of the drama by which these men extended our borders not only to the Rio Grande, but beyond it to the shores of the Pacific.

CHAPTER VII.

⁎⁎⋟▤⁎⁎⋟▤⋞⁎⁎

CONFEDERATE MILITARY HISTORY.

AT a called session of the legislature held in the city of Jackson, Miss., it was provided that an election be held in each county of the state on the 20th of December, to send delegates to the convention to be held at the capital on the 7th day of January, 1861, "to consider the then existing relations between the government of the United States, and the government of the people of Mississippi, and to adopt such measures for vindicating the sovereignty of the state and the protection of its institutions, as shall appear to them to be demanded."

In pursuance of the above authority the convention met at the appointed time, and organized; and the following ordinance was adopted on motion of Mr. Lamar:

An ordinance to dissolve the union between the state of Mississippi and the other states united with her under the compact entitled "the Constitution of the United States of America."

The people of the state of Mississippi in convention assembled do ordain and declare, and it is hereby ordained and declared as follows, to wit:

Section 1. That all the laws and ordinances by which the said state of Mississippi became a member of the Federal union of the United States of America be, and the same are hereby repealed, and that all obligations on the part of said states or the people thereof to observe the same be withdrawn, and that the said state doth hereby assume all the rights, functions and powers which, by any of said laws or ordinances, were conveyed to the government of the United States, and is absolved from all the obligations, restraints and duties incurred to the said Federal union, and shall from henceforth be a free, sovereign, and independent state.

Sec. 2. That so much of the first section of the seventh article of the constitution of this state as requires members of the legislature, and all officers, executive and judicial, to take an oath or affirmation to support the constitution of the United States, be and the same is hereby abrogated and annulled.

Sec. 3. That all rights acquired and vested under the constitution of the United States, or under any act of congress passed, or treaty made, in pursuance thereof, or under any law of this state, and not incompatible with this ordinance, shall remain in force, and have the same effect as if this ordinance had not been passed.

Sec. 4. That the people of the state of Mississippi hereby consent to form a federal union with such of the states as may have seceded, or may secede from the Union of the United States of America, upon the basis of the present constitution of the said United States, except such parts thereof as embrace other portions than such seceding states.

Thus ordained and declared in convention, the 9th day of January, in the year of our Lord 1861.

In testimony of the passage of which, and the determination of the members of this convention to uphold and maintain the state in the position she has assumed by said ordinance, it is signed by the president and members of this convention this, the 15th day of January, 1861.

Several amendments providing for the adjustment of the difficulties between the free and slave states of the Union were offered and lost, and also the amendment proposing to submit the ordinance to the people for ratification or rejection was voted down.

This convention also passed ordinances to regulate the military system, and to raise means for the defense of the state.

Mississippi being the second state to secede from the Union, and having resorted to a peaceable and constitutional remedy in so doing, many of her most thoughtful and conservative citizens did not think that there would be war. Mr. Davis, in his book on the Rise and Fall of the Confederate Government, says that while in the depot at Jackson waiting to take a train to Montgomery, he met Judge William L. Sharkey, who wanted to know whether in his opinion there would be war, Mr. Davis having replied that he thought there would, not that there should be war. Judge Sharkey expressed great surprise, and wanted to know how " war could result from the peaceable withdrawal of a sovereign state." Judge Sharkey, whose legal opinions are quoted as authority in this country and Europe to-day, was a whig in politics, but agreed with Mr. Davis in his opinion as to state sovereignty. Therefore there had been no preparations for war. There was not an arsenal or manufactory for arms in the state. After the passage of this ordinance, however, the state, as a prudent person, began to put her house in order. The legislature, then being in session, authorized the governor to call out the volunteer companies of the state, and arm them so far as it could be done. At the request of Governor Pettus, the governor of Louisiana furnished, for the use of the state, eight thousand muskets, one thousand rifles, six twenty-four-pound guns, with carriages, and a considerable amount of ammunition, for which courteous action on the part of Louisiana, the legislature of Mississippi, on January 21, 1861, passed a vote of thanks. About the same time, Ship island, the only federal possession in the state on the coast, was seized by the state troops. In providing the sinews of war the legislature passed an act to authorize the issuance of treasury notes as advances upon cotton. The treasury notes issued under this act were in the following form:

Receivable in payment of all dues to the state and counties, except the military tax.

On demand, after proclamation to present, the state of Mississippi will pay the bearer, the sum of   dollar(s) out of proceeds of cotton pledged for redemption of this note at the treasurer's office in Jackson, Miss. Issued   day   , 186 .

-- Auditor Public Accounts.
-- Treasurer.

The amount of these treasury notes to be issued was not to exceed $5,000,000. The act provided that any person desiring to obtain an advance should present a petition properly sworn to, to the auditor, stating the number of bales on which the money was to be advanced, average weight and character of cotton, and that the same was unincumbered, and then in actual possession and ownership. In addition to this petition, the party must give a receipt promising safely to keep and deliver the cotton at his own risk, and also execute a bond in double the amount for the advance obtained for the further security of the same. Upon presentation of petition and execution of bond and receipt the auditor was authorized to advance such party treasury notes not exceeding five cents per pound. On each bale of cotton the auditor and judge of probate court were entitled to the sum of fifty cents per bale, and for each bale over fifty received the further sum of one cent additional. These notes were redeemable in gold or silver or the treasury notes issued under this act. The governor was to make proclamation when ready for redemption and a penalty for failure to pay said advance or refusal to deliver the cotton, of imprisonment in the penitentiary and forfeiture of the bond. The legislature, also, a little later on, authorized another issuance of treasury notes to the amount of $2,500,000, for which the faith of the state was pledged, and fundable in bonds bearing eight per cent. This was to be kept as a military fund for the defense of the state. In the midst of these preparations by the legislature for the defense of the state the governor, on the 9th day of July, 1861, issued his proclamation for two regiments, to serve for and during the war, to be sent to Corinth, Miss.; also three thousand volunteers, to be received by independent companies, to go into camps of instruction. Soon thereafter he called out ten thousand volunteers to serve in defense of Kentucky, or any threatened position, for sixty days. These troops were to arm themselves with three days' rations, report at Corinth and Granada, and were to be commanded by Gen. Reuben Davis and J. L. Alcorn. The report of the adjutant and inspector-general of Mississippi, August 13, 1861, showed that the state had three artillery companies armed and equipped, six cavalry companies and eight regiments of infantry, with but few arms. The legislature made appropriations for the establishment of gunshops at Columbus and Brandon and granted charters to corporations for the manufacture of cloth in the state upon the most liberal terms.

In response to other calls from the president of the Confederacy upon the governor of the state, forty-nine regiments, with quite a number of independent companies of cavalry and artillery, were furnished by the state to the Confederate government, amounting to about eighty thousand men. The rosters of these regiments show that many of them numbered over a thousand men to the regiment. In the early part of the struggle a large number of these troops were sent to Virginia, while the remainder went to swell the Army of the West. From Corinth to Atlanta, from Manassas to Appomattox, the Mississippi troops bore themselves with such gallantry as to win the approbation of commanding generals, and the thanks of legislatures, state and Confederate. Many of them, whose terms of enlistment had expired, voluntarily reënlisted and received the thanks of the Confederate congress for so doing.

Let us see who the Mississippians were, as far as records will permit:

The following is a list of major and brigadier-generals of the state of Mississippi:

Major-generals: F. G. French, W. H. C. Whiting, William F. Martin, E. C. Walthall and Earl Van Dorn.

Brigadier-generals: Wirt Adams, William E. Baldwin, William Barkesdale, William S. Barry, Samuel Benton, William L. Brandon, W. F. Brantly, James R. Chalmers, Charles Clark, Douglas H. Cooper, Charles W. Dahlgren, Joseph R. Davis, William L. Featherston, Samuel W. Ferguson, John C. Fizer, Richard Griffith, N. H. Harris, B. G. Humphries, George D. Johnston, M. B. Lowry, Robert Lowry, John D. Martin, W. R. Miles, Carnot Posey, C. W. Sears, J. H. Sharp and F. E. Whitfield.

The following is a roster of the Mississippi regiments, with commanding officers:

I Mississippi, Wirt Adams, cavalry, Col. Wirt Adams; I Mississippi regiment, cavalry, Col. R. A. Pinson; II Mississippi regiment, cavalry, Col. James Gordon; III Mississippi regiment, cavalry, Col. ——— Smith; I Mississippi regiment, partisan rangers, Col. W. C. Falkner; II Mississippi regiment, partisan rangers, Col. J. G. Ballentine; I Mississippi regiment, artillery, Col. W. T. Withers; I Mississippi regiment, infantry, Col. J. M. Simonton; II Mississippi regiment, infantry, Col. J. M. Stone; II Mississippi regiment, infantry, Col. W. C. Falkner; III Mississippi regiment, infantry, Col. T. A. Mellon; III Mississippi regiment, infantry, Col. J. B. Deason; IV Mississippi regiment, infantry, Col. T. W. Adair; IV Mississippi regiment, infantry, Col. Jones Drake; V Mississippi regiment, infantry, Col. John Weer; V Mississippi regiment, infantry, Col. A. E. Fant; VI Mississippi regiment, infantry, Col. Robert Lowry; VI Mississippi regiment, infantry, Col. J. C. Thornton; VII Mississippi regiment, infantry, Col. W. H. Bishop; VII Mississippi regiment, infantry, Col. E. J. Goode; VIII Mississippi regiment, infantry, Col. J. C. Wilkinson; IX Mississippi regiment, infantry, Col. F. E. Whitfield; IX Mississippi regiment, infantry, Col. J. R. Chalmers; X Mississippi regiment, infantry, Col. James Barr; X Mississippi regiment, infantry, Col. R. A. Smith; XI Mississippi regiment, infantry, Col. F. M. Green; XI Mississippi regiment, infantry, Col. P. F. Liddell; XII Mississippi regiment, infantry, Col. W. H. Taylor; XII Mississippi regiment, infantry, Col. Henry Hughes; XIII Mississippi regiment, infantry, Col. J. W. Carter; XIII Mississippi regiment, infantry, Col. W. T. Barkesdale; XIV Mississippi regiment, infantry, Col. George W. Abbott; XIV Mississippi regiment, infantry, Col. —. —. Baldwin; XV Mississippi regiment, infantry, Col. F. M. Fanell; XV Mississippi regiment, infantry, Col. W. S. Statlin; XVI Mississippi regiment, infantry, Col. S. E. Baker; XVI Mississippi regiment, infantry, Col. Carnot Posey; XVII Mississippi regiment, infantry, Col. W. D. Holder; XVII Mississippi regiment, infantry, Col. W. S. Featherston; XVIII Mississippi regiment, infantry, Col. T. M. Griffin; XIX Mississippi regiment, infantry, Col. N. M. Harris; XIX Mississippi regiment, infantry, Col. Charles H. Mott; XX Mississippi regiment, infantry, Col. D. R. Russell; XXI Mississippi regiment, infantry, Col. Benjamin G. Humphries; XXII Mississippi regiment, infantry, Col. Frank Schaler; XXIII Mississippi regiment, infantry, Col. J. M. Wells; XXIV Mississippi regiment, infantry, Col. W. T. Dowd; XXV Mississippi regiment, infantry, Col. Thomas H. Mangum; XXV Mississippi regiment, infantry, Col. John D. Martin; XXVI Mississippi regiment, infantry, Col. A. E. Reynolds; XXVII Mississippi regiment, infantry, Col. J. A. Campbell; XXVIII Mississippi regiment, cavalry, Col. Thomas M. Jones; XXVIII Mississippi regiment, cavalry, Col. P. B. Starke; XXIX Mississippi regiment, infantry, Col. W. F. Brantley; XXX Mississippi regiment, infantry, Col. E. C. Walthall; XXX Mississippi regiment, infantry, Col. James J. Scales; XXXI Mississippi regiment, infantry, Col. G. F. Neill; XXXII Mississippi regiment, infantry, Col. J. A. Orr; XXXIII Mississippi regiment, infantry, Col. M. P. Lowry; XXXIII Mississippi regiment, infantry, Col. —. —. Hardcastle; XXXIV Mississippi regiment, infantry, Col. D. W. Hurst; XXXIV Mississippi regiment, infantry, Col. Sam Benton; XXXV Mississippi regiment, infantry, Col. W. S. Barry; XXXV Mississippi regiment, infantry, Col. W. W. Witherspoon; XXXVI Mississippi regiment, infantry, Col. E. J. Brown; XXXVII Mississippi regiment, infantry, Col. Orlando Holland; XXXVIII Mississippi regiment, infantry, Col. Robert McLain; XXXIX Mississippi regiment, infantry, Col. T. W. Adams; XL Mississippi regiment, infantry, Col. W. B. Shelby; XLI Mississippi regiment, infantry, Col. W. B. Colbert; XLI Mississippi regiment, infantry, Col. W. F. Tucker; XLII Mississippi regiment, infantry, Col. N. R. Miller; XLIII Mississippi regiment, infantry, Col. Richard Harrison; XLIII Mississippi regiment, infantry, Col. W. H. Moore; XLIV Mississippi regiment, infantry, Col. ————; XLV Mississippi regiment, infantry, Col. J. B. Hardcastle; XLVI Mississippi regiment, infantry, Col. C. W. Sears; XLVII Mississippi regiment, infantry, Col. James Jordan; XLVIII Mississippi regiment, infantry, James N. Jayne; XLIX Mississippi regiment, infantry, John W. Balfour; I Mississippi Jeff Davis legion, cavalry, Lieut. Col. Martin; II Mississippi Wirt Adams legion, Col. Wirt Adams; I Mississippi battalion, cavalry, Lieut. Col. A. K. Blythe; II Mississippi battalion, cavalry, Lieut.-Col. Taylor; III Mississippi battalion, cavalry, Maj. Hardcastle; IV Mississippi battalion, cavalry, Lieut.-Col. Baskeville; V Mississippi battalion, infantry, Maj. Kilpatrick; VI Mississippi battalion, infantry, ————; VII Mississippi battalion, cavalry, Lieut.-Col. Rosser.

This roster is necessarily imperfect, having been made in the early part of the war, many changes taking place before it closed. It would be impossible to note all the changes that took place in the personnel of these regiments during the war by death, accident, promotion and political influence.

To illustrate the changes that would take place—the Eighteenth, commanded by Col. W. Holder, who resigned to accept a place in the Confederate congress, to which he had been elected by the people, was succeeded by Col. W. S. Featherston, who was subsequently promoted to the rank of brigadier-general. The Nineteenth Mississippi was commanded by Col. Charles H. Mott, who died and was succeeded by Gen. N. M. Harris, who was subsequently promoted to brigadier-general. Lieutenant-Colonel Lamar was next in rank to Mott, and would have succeeded him, but after being stricken down by paralysis in battle retired from the army and served his country abroad in the capacity of diplomat. And Col. Reuben O. Renolds rose from the ranks to the command of the Eleventh Mississippi regiment, and afterward took a conspicuous part in the politics of the state.

The Thirteenth, Seventh, Eighteenth and Twenty-first Mississippi regiments were sent to Virginia and formed into a brigade, Gen. William Barkesdale commanding, who was killed at Gettysburg, and succeeded by Gen. B. G. Humphreys. The Twelfth, Sixteenth, Nineteenth and Forty-eighth were under the command of Brig.-Gen. Carnot Posey, who fell mortally wounded at Bristoe Station, Va., and was succeeded by Gen. N. H. Harris. The Second, Eleventh, Twenty-sixth and Forty-second Mississippi regiments were under command of Gen. Joseph R. Davis. The following regiments belonging to the Army of the West were brigaded as follows: The Sixth, Fourteenth, Fifteenth, Twentieth, Twenty-third and Twenty-sixth Mississippi regiments were commanded by Gen. John Adams. The Third, Twenty-second, Thirty-first, Thirty-second and First Mississippi battalion sharpshooters were under the command of General Featherston. The First Mississippi regiment cavalry, the Twenty-eighth and Ballentine's Mississippi regiment were commanded by Col. Peter B.

Starke. The Third and Fifth Mississippi regiments, with Mississippi battery, commanded by Col. W. F. Slemons. The Second Mississippi cavalry, the Fourth Woods Mississippi regiment with a Mississippi battery commanded by Capt. Cal. Roberts, were under the command of Brig.-Gen. Wirt Adams. The Twelfth Mississippi was in General Ferguson's brigade.

The First Mississippi partisan rangers, Eighteenth Mississippi battalion, Nineteenth Mississippi battalion, a Mississippi battery under command of Lieutenant Holt, belonged to Colonel McCulloch. Anderson's brigade: Seventh, Ninth, Tenth, Forty-first, Forty-fourth and battalion of sharpshooters. Walthall's brigade: Twenty-fourth, Twenty-seventh, Twenty-ninth, Thirtieth and Thirty-fourth regiments. Gen. E. C. Walthall was promoted to major-general, and was succeeded by Col. W. E. Brantley as brigadier. Anderson was promoted to major-general and succeeded by J. H. Sharp.

We will now give a few instances where these troops distinguished themselves, in brigades, regiments, companies and individuals. The Rev. J. S. Johnston, of Mobile, Ala., in his reminiscences of the battle of Sharpsburg, speaking of the part taken by Hood's division, says: "The division, nine regiments front, with no support or reserves, moved forward in splendid style. Up to that day that division had never known defeat. A part of it had made a glorious record at first Manassas; the whole of it had taken part in the 'Seven Pines;' they charged and carried the strong works at Gaines' Mill; it had made a splendid record at second Manassas; had held Fox Gap, on South Mountain, against every attempt to carry it by Burnside's division, and moved out that day, making the air ring with the well-known rebel yell. They soon met the Federals, flushed with victory, and drove them back, till they were in turn met by a fresh corps of Federals. Retreat became necessary, and the order was given to fall back. There was no rout, no frantic rushing, although the fire of musketry and cannon was terrible. When they reached the woods from which they had debouched two hours before four thousand strong, only seven hundred could be mustered. Out of nine regiments, but one field officer, besides Colonel Law, reported for duty. Colonel Liddell, of the Eleventh Mississippi, had been killed the night before in a heavy skirmish; Lieutenant-Colonel Butler and the major of the regiment were mortally wounded and left on the field; Colonel Stone, now governor of Mississippi, commanding the Second Mississippi regiment, had his upper lip shot away, and was unable to talk, yet absolutely refused to go to the rear; Lieutenant-Colonel Humphreys was severely wounded, and, unable to walk, still insisted upon remaining; Major Blair, of this same regiment, was shot in the throat while snatching the colors from the hands of the falling color-bearer. Here also fell, mortally wounded, Richard Clayton, adjutant of the regiment. Shortly after this repulse Hood was accosted by General Evans, of South Carolina, who asked, 'Where is your division?' Hood replied, 'Dead on the field!' The flags of the Eleventh and Second Mississippi regiments flying at their heads bore the names of all the battles mentioned above."

General Davis, in his report of the part taken by his brigade in the battle of Gettysburg, says: "Colonel Stone, of the Second Mississippi regiment, was wounded while gallantly leading his men in the first charge. Lieutenant-Colonel Mosely and Major Forney, of the Forty-second Mississippi, were both severely wounded. It is due to the gallantry of a few brave men to state that a few of the Second and Forty-second Mississippi, under the lead of Lieutenant Roberts, of the Second Mississippi, dashed forward, and after a hand-to-hand contest, in which the gallant Roberts was killed, succeeded in capturing the colors of the Pennsylvania regiment."

General Longstreet, in speaking of the part taken by the brigade under the command of General Humphreys, at the battle of Gettysburg, on the first day of the fight when he was struggling to take Little Round Top, one of the hights about Gettysburg, and whose importance as a *point d'appui* was not at first appreciated by the enemy, but when discerned was like magic transformed into a Gibraltar, says: "History records no parallel to the fight made by the division to which this brigade belonged. To illustrate the dauntless spirit of these men, when General Humphreys was ordered to withdraw his troops from the charge, he thought there was some mistake, and retired to a captured battery near the swale between the two ridges, where he halted, and when ordered to retire to the new line a second time, did so under protest. The men had no thought of retreat, and had broken every line they encountered."

The troops from Mississippi particularly distinguished themselves at the battle of Franklin, Tenn. Gen. S. D. Lee in his report speaking of the part borne by the brigades of Sharp and Brantly in this conflict says: "Their dead were mostly in the trenches and in the works of the enemy, where they fell in a desperate hand-to-hand fight. Sharp captured three stands of colors. Brantly was exposed to a severe enfilade fire. But these noble brigades never faltered in this terrible night struggle." At Chickamauga, Anderson's fearless Mississippians carried the breastworks in their front and drove the enemy up Crawfish Springs road and over the broken spurs beyond Missionary ridge.

Mr. Davis, in his speech to the legislature at Jackson, thus speaks of Gen. Stephen D. Lee: "And I have reason to believe that at the last great conflict on the field of Manassas he served to turn the tide of battle and consummate the victory."

In the fight at Chancellorsville seven companies of the Twenty-first Mississippi regiment were posted by General Barkesdale between Marge's house and the plank road, the two remaining regiments of the brigade being farther to the right on the hills nearer to the Howison's house. A corps of the enemy made two assaults upon Barkesdale's men which were gallantly repulsed. General Grant, in his march to Richmond, encountered the Confederates at the Wilderness, where a bloody battle was fought. Foiled in his attempt in that direction he began his flank movements, in the execution of which he was confronted by General Lee at Spottsylvania Courthouse. The line of the Confederates was formed during the night and breastworks hastily thrown up. In the construction of the line of works there was an angle formed which has since become famous as the "bloody angle." General McGowan, in his report says: "At this place our line of works made a sharp angle, pointing toward the enemy, which angle the enemy attacked in great force at the sides, having the woods and ravine in front occupied by multitudes. The right of my brigade extended some distance up the left side of the angle and rested upon nothing but the enemy. I am informed that the brigade formed in the trenches. General Harris and what remained of his brigade of gallant Mississippians made one of the most gallant and stubborn defenses recorded in history. This brigade and another remained there holding our line without reinforcement, food, water or rest, under a storm of balls which did not intermit an instant of time for eighteen hours. The trenches on the right of the 'bloody angle' ran with blood, and had to be cleared of the dead bodies more than once. To give some idea of the intensity of the fire, an oak tree twenty inches in diameter which stood just in rear of the right of the brigade was cut down by constant scaling of musket balls and fell at twelve o'clock Thursday night, injuring by its fall several soldiers of the First South Carolina regiment. The brigades mentioned (Mississippi and South Carolina) held their positions from ten o'clock Thursday morning until four o'clock Friday morning, when they were withdrawn by order to the new line established in their rear."

The most stubborn defense made by any soldiers in ancient or modern times was that of

Forts Gregg and Whitworth—gateways to Petersburg.   Spartans under Leonidas live in song and story because there were good raconteurs in those days when story-telling was one of the arts, but the muse of history will see to it that the defense of Forts Gregg and Whitworth by the little gallant band of Mississippians, occupy a niche separate and apart, not less conspicuous than that of the Spartan band.   The number of men on the two sides, two hundred and fourteen in Fort Gregg and the same in Whitworth, and five thousand advancing against them, illustrates the comparative strength of the combatants.   What lent a dramatic interest to the defense was that here was to be made the last stand for Petersburg.

The Vicksburg *Times* thus describes the part taken by Mississippians in the forts: "Fort Gregg was held by the Twelfth and Sixteenth Mississippi regiments, Harrison's brigade numbering about one hundred and fifty muskets, under the command of Lieut.-Col. James H. Duncan, of the Nineteenth Mississippi, who had been assigned by General Harris to the immediate command of that work.   The artillery in the fort was a section of the Third company of Washington artillery, under command of Lieutenant McElroy.   General Harris with two other regiments, the Nineteenth and Forty-eighth Mississippi, occupied Fort Whitworth, distant about one hundred yards, and between that work and the south side railroad."   General Harris in an official letter eloquently describes the defense: "Gregg repulsed assault after assault.   The two remnants of regiments which had won glorious honor on so many fields fought this, their last battle, with the most terrible enthusiasm, as if feeling this to be the last act in the drama for them, and the officers and men of Washington artillery, fighting their guns to the last, preserved untarnished the brilliancy of reputation acquired by their corps.   Gregg raged like the crater of a volcano emitting its flashes of deadly fires enveloped in flame and cloud, wreathing our flag as well in honor as in the smoke of death.   It was a glorious struggle, Louisiana represented by these noble artillerists, and Mississippi by her shattered band, stood them side by side together, holding the last regularly fortified line around Petersburg.   As soon as Harris heard another line had been formed he withdrew his little band, cutting his way through."

Among the heroes of that action are the following: R. R. Applewhite, captain Twelfth Mississippi regiment; E. Howard McCaleb, adjutant Twelfth Mississippi regiment; T. B. Manlove, lieutenant-colonel Forty-eighth Mississippi regiment; W. B. Thompson, private company K, Twelfth Mississippi regiment; R. H. McElwaine, private company I, Sixteenth Mississippi regiment; R. B. Thetford, private company H, Twelfth Mississippi regiment; John W. Walters, private company G, Sixteenth Mississippi regiment; Fred J. V. Lecand, sergeant company G, Twelfth Mississippi regiment; James G. Robbins, private company K, Twelfth Mississippi regiment; John A. Shields, private company G, Sixteenth Mississippi regiment; H. H. Owing, private company K, Twelfth Mississippi regiment; Harry Dey, private company G, Sixteenth Mississippi regiment; J. D. Bridger, sergeant company K, Twelfth Mississippi regiment; W. H. Dromgool, private company K, Twelfth Mississippi regiment; John W. Owen, private company D, Twelfth Mississippi regiment; L. B. Harlin, private company K, Twelfth Mississippi regiment; H. M. Colson, private company K, Twelfth Mississippi regiment; C. R. Nesmith, sergeant company K, Twelfth Mississippi regiment; G. W. H. Shaifer, private company K, Twelfth Mississippi regiment; J. H. Sims, private company K, Twelfth Mississippi regiment; J. F. Girault, private company K, Twelfth Mississippi regiment: A. M. Girault, private company G, Sixteenth Mississippi regiment; Thomas M. Rea, private company D, Twelfth Mississippi regiment; B. F. Chisholm, color guard, Sixteenth Mississippi regiment; A. K. Jones, captain company K, Sixteenth Mississippi regiment; Frank H. Foote, courier for Harris' brigade; N. S. Walker, captain company E, Forty-eighth Mississippi regiment; F. L. Mince, captain company G, Twelfth Mississippi regiment.

Fox, in his Regimental Losses, says: "There are no muster rolls of the Confederate regiments. There are partial sets of muster rolls, and monthly returns at Washington in the bureau of Confederate archives, but they are defective and incomplete. There is no way of determining accurately the mortuary loss of each Confederate regiment during its entire service." Mr. Fox states that Gen. James B. Fry makes a compilation from the muster rolls in Confederate archives, in which Mississippi's loss during the war was as follows: Killed, five thousand eight hundred and seven; wounded, two thousand six hundred and fifty-one; died of disease, six thousand eight hundred and seven; grand total, fifteen thousand two hundred and sixty-five.

The legislature of the state had not been unmindful of the care and comfort of her soldiers. It had provided hospitals for the troops in the field. At Warrenton, Va., hospitals were established and placed under the care of the Rev. C. K. Marshall, of Vicksburg, a special appropriation having been made for that purpose. Others were established at Columbus and Corinth, Miss. And for the family of the soldier provision was made. The sum of $500,000 was appropriated and special commissioners appointed to purchase provisions and clothing, and later on, when the currency provided had lost its purchasing power, the commissioners appointed were authorized to take a part of the tax collected in kind by the Confederate government to provide for the wants of the destitute families of the soldiers.

Such was in part the state's action for citizens and soldiers. But more conspicuous than any organized efforts in this behalf was the individual action of the noble women of the state. In making clothes for and nursing the sick and wounded soldiers in hospitals and elsewhere, their efforts never flagged, and there is on record to-day a resolution of the legislature thanking them for their services.

The Confederate troops having been forced to abandon Kentucky and Tennessee, took position on the line of the Memphis & Charleston railroad. The plan of the Federal government, as stated by General Halleck, was to open the Mississippi river in conjunction with General Banks in Arkansas. General Grant was to drive the Confederates into the interior as far south as possible, and destroy their railroad communications, then falling back to Memphis embark his available forces on transports, and with the assistance of the fleet of Admiral Porter reduce Vicksburg. Thus it will be seen that Corinth became a strategic point—a gateway to Vicksburg—a fact fully appreciated by both armies. So, in the spring of 1862, a large force under Grant landed at Pittsburg, on the Tennessee river, about twenty miles from Corinth. In the meantime a large force of Confederates under Gen. A. S. Johnston had assembled at Corinth, Miss., to resist their advance. General Grant moving out with his forces was met at Shiloh, Tenn., near the Mississippi line, by the forces under Gen. A. S. Johnston. A bloody battle ensued, resulting in the discomfiture of the army under Grant. He was forced back to the landing under cover of his gunboats, while the Confederates, who had lost their commanding general and quite a number of their best troops, resumed their old position at Corinth. After this repulse Grant made cautious approaches upon Corinth. The Confederate forces being greatly diminished in number in the recent battle of Shiloh, and their ranks thinned by sickness, General Beauregard, who was then in command, determined to evacuate Corinth. Before doing so, however, he sent out a force under General Van Dorn to turn the left wing of the Federal forces. General Van Dorn struck the enemy at Farmington, Miss., where a battle was fought and

Van Dorn repulsed. General Beauregard commenced to fall back with his forces on the 29th of May, and took position at Tupelo, Miss., on the line of the Mobile & Ohio railroad. Here the army was reorganized. Its roster shows that it was composed of troops from the states of Alabama, Arkansas, Louisiana, Mississippi, South Carolina, Georgia, Texas and Tennessee, the troops of the last state preponderating. The evacuation was so orderly that only a few pieces of ordnance and a quantity of damaged ammunition fell into the hands of the Federals. On June 14, 1862, General Beauregard was retired, and General Bragg assumed command of the army of the West, and soon thereafter withdrew, the larger part of the force going to Chattanooga, Tenn., leaving Price in command of the remnant of the army with orders to observe the movements of Grant's army at Corinth, with the view of opposing him in the event he should move down into Mississippi, or in case Grant should move up into Tennessee to join Buell. Then Price was to hinder that movement, and was also to move up into Tennessee, uniting his forces with those of Bragg. Van Dorn and Price were thus left independent of each other, although both were in the state of Mississippi. It would have been much better, as subsequent events demonstrated, if the command had devolved upon one alone. Van Dorn, having refitted his forces after his attack on Baton Rouge, was anxious to drive the Federal forces out of Mississippi, and proposed to Price to unite their forces in a combined attack on Corinth. Price being fettered by instructions from Bragg was unable to comply with the request. In a short time after Price had declined Van Dorn's invitation, he learned from spies in Corinth that Grant had commenced to evacuate that place and would soon be on his way to join Buell. To intercept him, or that failing, to join Bragg, Price moved to Iuka, Miss. He had in all about sixteen thousand effective men, fourteen thousand infantry and two thousand cavalry. He found the place occupied by a force of the enemy, who retreated toward Corinth, abandoning considerable stores. That was on the 19th of September, 1862. On the 21st he ordered a division to Burnsville, a station between Corinth and Iuka, on the Memphis & Charleston railroad, where the enemy was reported to be in strong force. He encountered them this side of Burnsville. The boldness of the movement created the impression that it was a strong force, but it proved to be only a reconnoissance. At this time such information as to Grant's movements was received by Price as indicated that he still occupied his old lines at Corinth without any intention of abandonment. This belief was strengthened by the arrival of a flag of truce from General Ord, at Corinth, to surrender, which Price declined to accept.

On the same day Price received another urgent request from Van Dorn to unite their forces and attack Corinth. He called a council of war, at which this request was considered. It was evident that Grant was not moving over the Tennessee river, but lay in heavy force on the left in a position to cut Price off from his base of supplies on the Mobile & Ohio railroad. He decided, under these circumstances, to march back at once and unite with Van Dorn in a combined attack on Corinth. Orders were accordingly issued to put into execution this purpose. But all the while the cavalry pickets had been sending in reports of a heavy force moving by the Jacinto road, thereby intercepting this contemplated movement. General Price sent a division under the command of General Little, composed principally of raw troops, to take position on this road so as to command the approach to Iuka. General Little had hardly formed his line when General Rosecrans with a heavy force assaulted him. The suddenness of the attack disconcerted Little's forces, and they were swept back in sight of Iuka in much disorder. Here, meeting with reënforcements, the advancing enemy was checked, and the forces under Rosecrans were driven back and beyond where the first

J. S. Yerger.

line of battle had been formed. At nightfall the Confederates reoccupied their first position. The battle (Iuka) was brief, but was one of the bloodiest and fiercest combats of the war. The loss of the Confederates was heavy, some of the regiments being almost decimated. Grant's plan was that while Rosecrans advanced by the Jacinto road south, he would attack by the Burnsville road west. As it not infrequently occurs in combined movements, it failed from a want of concert of action. General Grant deployed a large force before the troops which Price had so disposed as to guard the approach from the west by Burnsville. At sunset he had made no approach, and received intelligence from Rosecrans that his advance by the Jacinto road had met with an obstinate resistance, that he was unable to proceed any farther in that direction, but that he would occupy some hights on his right at dawn. *L'homme propose, mais Dieu' dispose,* is certainly true in war. At dawn these hights were held by Price's troops under General Maury. General Price had withdrawn the main body of his forces before Grant, leaving only enough to deceive him as to his real intentions, while they lay in the town ready to join in the attack on Rosecrans in the morning. It was with much difficulty that Price was persuaded to abandon his intention to attack Rosecrans on the following morning and follow up his original idea, to return and unite his forces with those of Van Dorn. The splendid action of his troops in driving back the forces under Rosecrans had set his heart on fire, and he confidently believed that next day victory would perch on his banners. The withdrawal of the force under Price was effected without coming into any serious collision with the enemy, Grant and Rosecrans being greatly disconcerted by his disappearance and the consequent frustration of their plans. In their eagerness to follow up Price's retreating columns they were drawn into an ambuscade and lost heavily in killed and wounded. Price joined Van Dorn at Ripley, Miss., and on the 1st of October, 1862, with their combined forces, amounting to about nineteen thousand effective men they marched to attack the enemy at Corinth. Van Dorn threw his cavalry forward so as to mask his movements while his infantry proceeded directly by the way of Davis' bridge to Corinth. On the 2d of October the troops bivouacked at Chewalla, a station on the Memphis & Charleston railroad, eight miles from Corinth. At dawn next morning the Confederates moved out to attack the enemy. The cavalry soon became engaged with the enemy's pickets, and forced them back within three miles of Corinth, where a line of battle was formed across the Memphis & Charleston railroad. The Federals occupied the defenses constructed by General Beauregard the previous spring against the army of Halleck. All the timber covering the slopes had been felled and formed an obstructing abattis, very difficult for troops to get through. The Confederates charged the line of the enemy through these obstructions under a galling fire from the artillery. They captured the battery and put the whole force of the Federals to rout. At sunset the force in front of Price's corps had been driven into Corinth. Van Dorn, fully appreciating the importance of time, was for continuing the fight, but was overruled by Price, who thought his troops unequal to further exertion on that day. The assault consequently was postponed till morning. During the night Rosecrans had not been idle, but sending his trains back to the Tennessee river he ordered up all his reserve force. It is estimated that his total effective force amounted to twenty-two thousand men. At daylight, under cover of a heavy cannonade from the batteries, Price's troops rushed to the assault. His whole corps, after terrific fighting, penetrated to the center of the town and prepared to swing and take the enemy in the left wing, but since ten A. M. Van Dorn's right had made no decided impression on the force in its front. Indeed so feeble was its assault that General Rosecrans withdrew from its front a heavy force and threw it upon Price's victorious corps. They, exhausted by incessant

10

fighting, with one-third of their men down, were unable to withstand this attack of fresh troops. They fell back, losing all the advantage gained by the conflict in the morning. Thus ended the assault on Corinth, in which Price and Van Dorn lost the flower of their army.

The day being lost, the Confederate army retired during the day to Chewalla without pursuit. Van Dorn then moved his army to Holly Springs, Miss., to await further developments. The supineness of Grant in not following up Van Dorn's forces after the battle of Corinth has been the subject of much comment by military critics. One eminent man on military affairs says that his policy throughout the war was one of "attrition," the correctness of which is borne out by his action at this time. At a snail's pace he followed the retreating Confederates from Holly Springs to Abbeville, and from Abbeville to Grenada.

It is perhaps well now to pause for a moment and glance at the condition of the army in Mississippi and the people of the state. They were an agricultural people, cultivating with slave labor. On the large plantations in the river bottoms, the rich prairie belt, which was a veritable Egypt, and on the fertile uplands, large crops of corn and cotton were raised. At the outbreak of the war more than enough could have been obtained, properly managed, to subsist an army. The citizens loyal to the state yielded cheerful and ready acquiescence to her demands, parted willingly with their substance for Confederate money, or the state's promises to pay, and submitted to the impressment of their private arms for public use. When the tocsin of war sounded, the noble young men rushed to the front at the call to arms. If they had not learned to ride exactly like Mazeppa, they were, at least, splendid horsemen all, the practice with shotgun and rifle being chief among their youthful sports. A certain manliness and individuality distinguished them. They were eager for the fray. No general of ancient or modern times ever had such material to deal with at the outset of a war. On the tented fields of Virginia, under the immortal Lee, whom they loved to idolatry and sometimes fondly called "Uncle Bob," their heroism was conspicuously shown, and under his leadership their splendid morale was preserved up to the surrender.

The history of all wars of independence, however, shows that the fires of patriotism burn more brightly at the outbreak than toward the close. This was true of the revolution of 1776. It was true of the war between the states. The paper of the government passed current at first, but was afterward rejected as worthless. The invasion of the state by the enemy, the frequent repulses and retreats of the Confederate forces, cast a deep gloom over the people of the state, shaking their confidence in the ultimate success of the Confederate cause. Their slaves were being impressed to labor on public works, removed from exposed localities, their cotton burned by the Confederate government to prevent its seizure by the enemy, and martial law was proclaimed in certain localities by General Van Dorn, raising a storm of indignation. They refused to take Confederate money for supplies, because they were forced to rely upon the Federals for traffic, and in part were afraid to furnish the Confederate authorities lest vengeance be taken on them by the enemy. So their substance was impressed. The death of Albert Sidney Johnston, and the frequent reverses sustained by the army, appear to have broken the spirit of the soldiers. Instances of desertion and straggling were manifest. To improve the morale and restore confidence, frequent changes were made in the commanding generals, but without avail. Perhaps no stronger picture of the state and the troops, and the effect of Confederate legislation and appointments at this time, could be drawn than is presented in the letter of the Hon. James Phelan, himself representative of the state of Mississippi in the Confederate senate to the president of the Confederacy:

HON. JEFF. DAVIS,

Dear Sir: I doubt not you have ascertained the unhappy condition of affairs in this state. The army, if I am correctly informed, is in a most deplorable state as to its morale and organization, bad enough before its retreat from Abbeville, where so much labor has been done and which was supposed to be so strong a position, has, I fear, put the finishing touch to its inefficiency. Pemberton has not impressed himself either upon the people or the army, while the flank movement from Friar's point by which his retreat was forced, and which it is declared might have been prevented, has dealt a staggering blow upon those who had desired to brace him with the public confidence. It seems that but a few even know that General Pemberton is at the head of the army, and his want of prominence of itself at such a crisis depresses the spirit of the people. It is yet called "Van Dorn's army," and the universal opprobrium which covers that officer, and the "lower than lowest depths" to which he has fallen in the estimation of the community of all classes, you can not be aware of. He may be but an illustration of the proverb "give a dog a bad name," etc., but so it is, and the fact, not its justice or its truth, must be confronted. He is regarded as the source of all our woes and disaster, which, it is prophesied, will attend us so long as he is connected with this army. The atmosphere is dense with horrid narratives of his negligence, whoring and drunkenness, for the truth of which I can not vouch, but it is so fastened in the public belief that an acquittal by a court martial of angels would not relieve him of the charge. I know you have confidence in him; you believe he has merit, high merit; I heard you so declare, and it may be true, but not to criticize his action with reference to the foundation of your good opinion, that opinion is not held, far from it, by those whose estimation of his character more immediately affects our common welfare. I know I hazard nothing in saying that Van Dorn's removal from the army with which he is now associated would benefit it. The army, I believe, has no respect for him, have lost confidence in themselves, and will not fight under him. A gentleman from West Point stated yesterday that the country between Houston and Oxford was full of straggling troops who openly declared that they had abandoned the army and never designed to return until they were placed under officers fit to control them.

The present alarming crisis in this state, so far from arousing the people, seems to have sunk them into listless despondency. The spirit of enlistment is thrice dead, enthusiasm has expired to a cold pile of damp ashes. Defeats, retreats, sufferings, dangers magnified by spiritless helplessness, and an unchangeable conviction that our army is in the hands of ignorant and feeble commanders are rapidly producing a sense of settled despair, from which, if not speedily dissipated by some bright event or happy change, the most disastrous consequences may be apprehended. I imagine but one event could waken from its waning sparks the enthusiastic hopes and energy of Mississippians. Plant your own foot upon our soil. Unfurl your banner at the head of the army. Tell our people that you have come to brave with them the perils of this dark hour, and appeal to every Mississippian who is not so base that he would be a bondsman to rally to your side in rolling back the insolent foe who invades our homes, and I believe a shout would welcome your presence, and a multitude respond to your appeal, that would make the invader quail before the uproar of such a popular tempest. If ever your presence was needed as a last refuge from an "Iliad of woes," this is the hour. It is not a point to be argued. It may be you would admit Pemberton to be an abler general than yourself. All such suggestions may be truth, but it does not then change the fiction, as available as fact, to the popular sentiment that you can save us, or help us save ourselves from the dread evils now so imminently pending. If those evils, so threatening now, can be averted by your presence, I need not pause to imagine and reply to objections based upon your required presence as president of the republic. That can, may, must be obviated. There is a multitude of thoughts which arise in my mind by which I could enforce the step I suggest, but they will be more than compassed by your own reflections. Give them but ample range. Its contemplation makes me feel eloquent, but I am conscious my ardor and fervency would appear but "dribbled chilliness reflected through the inky portraiture of cold white paper." "Think on these things." A vast amount of commissary stores are reported to have been destroyed at Abbeville; if so, God knows where the sustenance of the army is to be obtained. Our state is now barely able to feed itself. In fact, want is now seriously felt in certain portions. Even in this rich and usually abundant section everything is scarce. Small, lean pork is twenty cents, and but little to sell at that.

Why is it the conscript law is so inefficiently enforced? So far as I could learn in the course of my travels, conscription is a mere farce. Two months have elapsed since the enemy evacuated northern Alabama, and yet no enrolling officer has been there. Crowds of men subject to duty are everywhere on cars, boats, in the streets, stores, etc., but the subject of their conscription seems never to have entered their minds. The enrolling officers, now as important as the president, as far as I can learn, are young men, utterly unfit for that sacred and stern duty, whom nobody fears and who exercise their discretion as to exemptions with unblushing partiality and indifference. I believe the enforcement of the act in this state and Alabama to be another failure. Instead of this being, as it ought to be, a measure that saved the country, it threatens to be the cause of its subjugation. It arrested all volunteering and assumed by force the augmentation of the army, and now failing to do so, our "last end is worse than the first."

If not enforced as they ought to be with iron and unrelenting firmness, our cause is lost. You can't imagine the open, bold, unblushing attempts to evade getting in and to keep out of the army. All shame has fled, and no subterfuge is pretended, but a reckless confession of an unwillingness to go or to remain. All that gave attractive coloring to the soldier's life is now faded into cold grave shadow with nine-tenths of the army, and if permitted, in my opinion, it would dissolve to-morrow, heedless of the future. Let an iron hand be circled around it, for the pressure, take my word for it, is nearly over-whelming. There are many plausible reasons for this desire to get away which I need not detail. The vigorous enforcement of the conscription act would tend to allay this spirit of discontent. Recognize the whole system, and let popular attention be started and attracted by the prominent rich and influential men being swept into the ranks. Never did a law meet with more universal odium than the exemption of slave owners. Its injustice, gross injustice, is denounced even by those whose position enables them to take advantage of its privileges. Its influence upon the poor is most calamitous, and has awakened a spirit and elicited a discussion of which we may safely predict the unfortunate results. I believe such a provision to be unnecessary, inexpedient and unjust. I labored to defeat it, and predicted the conse-quences of its exactment. It has aroused a spirit of rebellion in some places, and bodies of men have banded together to resist, whilst in the army, it is said, it only needs some daring man to raise the stan-dard of revolt. As I opposed the provision violently, predicted the consequences, and believe they have occurred, I hope you will satisfy yourself of the truth with reference to the recommendations in your message. I shall offer a bill to repeal it the first day of the session. I am satisfied that the whole policy of admitting substitutes is wrong; the reasons I need not detail. Let me suggest one: in case of large pay, it causes a certain class of men to seek exemptions on their own account, straining to reach beyond the age, to be regarded as mechanics, etc. Again, it causes men who are liable to be ever on the search to find some man to take their place, and therefore never become imbued with the spirit of the soldier, or buckle on the harness for regular duty. A bill nearly abolishing the whole system did pass the senate, but was lost in the house by having been foolishly and unconstitutionally linked with another measure. I shall offer a bill to abolish it in toto, and wish you to give it the benefit of your recommendation.

How is it that such numbers of paroled men are traveling all over the country to their homes? Not a tithe of them will ever be heard of. Mere general orders that they should report at some place amount to nothing. If permitted to go at all, orders never reach them if published in a few smutted lines in small type in the corner of a newspaper. A reading man may read the sheet and never see the order. But not even the paper ever falls into the hands of one in a thousand for whom it was intended, and when once sheltered in the caves and mountains of the country, or lost in the general population, they are gone for-ever. A man has got but to say he is a paroled soldier and the question is settled. Paroled men ought never to be permitted to go at large, if I may use the term. Each army ought to have a camp or place where they are required to report, and no such soldier be permitted to leave without arrest except in going to such camp. I don't know exactly how the remedy is to be applied, but, I assure you, the evil is a great one. Give it your attention.

The number and character of the men scattered throughout the country and the army, and in some way connected with it, but without guns in their hands, is a subject of severe criticism and of loud com-plaint. Young men in groups and hangers-on around an officer of any rank doing nothing but exciting discontent in the working soldiery, whilst every sort of office great and small is filled with such vermin. It seems as if nine-tenths of the youngsters of the land, whose relations are conspicuous in society, wealthy or influential, obtain some safe perch where they can dodge with their heads under their wings. Partiality, favoritism, perhaps bribery and corruption sustain this acknowledged evil. It exists, at least, to an enormous extent, and should be dug up and cast out by the roots.

Again, why can not men over forty-five act as teamsters, wagon guards, and other detail, instead of taking hundreds of other soldiers from the ranks and thus weakening the line. But I am extending this too far. May God have you in his keeping.

Your friend,

JAMES PHELAN.

The inspector sent out by Mr. Davis to inquire into the cause of the evacuation of Corinth, and also why Beauregard failed to attack Halleck, in his report says that the hospitals established were inadequate and badly conducted, and that the broad hospitality and unwearying kindness of the people of Mississippi were extended to the sick soldiers with a liberality so bountiful that the thanks of the whole people are due them. In this report the inspector corroborates the statements of Mr. Phelan in every particular.

In response to the popular demand for his presence, Mr. Davis went to Jackson, arriving on the 19th of December, went to Vicksburg on the 20th, to examine its defenses, thence to Grenada, and on the 25th returned to Jackson in company with General Johnston and Pemberton. After exhorting the legislature in a fervent speech to give the governor all necessary aid in defense of the state, he returned to Richmond.

General Pemberton had been placed in command of the army of the Mississippi, and Van Dorn, smarting under his defeat at Corinth, determined by some coup d'etât or other to retrieve his lost prestige. It was known that Grant was accumulating large stores at Holly Springs in preparation for his advance on Vicksburg. To destroy these and thus force Grant to abandon his object was Van Dorn's plan. On the 15th of December all the cavalry from the enemy's front was quietly withdrawn and massed on the south side of the Yalobusha, and next morning the entire column moved out in the direction of Houston, when the column changed direction and returned to Pontotoc. Arriving at New Albany on the evening of the 18th, they crossed the Tallahatchie, and slept on the north branch. Early on the morning of the 19th the column moved in a direct line to Holly Springs. There were various opinions at the time as to the strength of the Federal garrison at Holly Springs, but the sequel proved that it consisted of a brigade of infantry, and a portion of the Seventh Illinois cavalry — a force about equal in numbers to that of Van Dorn. That night Van Dorn's forces bivouacked near Holly Springs, and at daylight moved forward to the attack. The pickets of the Federals were captured without alarming the garrison, and their whole force, completely surprised, made but a feeble resistance. The cavalry located at the fair grounds had time to form, but were not able to resist the impetuous advance of the Confederates. By noon everything was over, and Van Dorn had possession of the town, with an immense quantity of stores, and a large number of prisoners. The captured property, with the exception of a small quantity used in equipping his command, was destroyed by Van Dorn. At sunset the work of destruction was complete. The Federal prisoners were paroled, and Van Dorn moved out of town in the direction of Bolivar, Tenn., in order to make a diversion in favor of General Forrest, who was at that time operating in Middle and East Tennessee. Grant sent a heavy force of cavalry and artillery in pursuit, but Van Dorn managed to elude them and return safely to Grenada. The success of this expedition at this juncture greatly improved the morale of the army, and forced Grant to abandon, for the present, his plan of campaign, and retreat to Memphis.

On the 25th information was received that General Sherman had embarked an army at Memphis of thirty thousand men, and was descending the Mississippi river. Next day they ascended the Yazoo river, and, landing on the southern shore, attacked the lines of the Confederates under command of General Pemberton, but were repulsed. On the 29th General Sherman landed a large force at the mouth of the Yazoo, and advanced to the attack of the Confederates at Chickasaw bluffs under the command of Gen. S. D. Lee. The column of attack was led by General Blair, which came up in formidable array. The force under Lee amounted to only about two thousand five hundred men and twelve guns, while the attacking force was nearly ten to one. General Lee repulsed the attack, inflicting a heavy loss upon the enemy. Blair's losses were eleven hundred men, while those of Lee were only one hundred and fifty. On January 2, 1863, General Sherman reëmbarked his troops and reported to General Grant that he had failed in his attempts on Vicksburg. Thus, for once, was the invader driven from Mississippi's soil. General Grant dispatched General Sherman the reply that Vicksburg must be taken at all hazards. So, embarking their united forces on transports, General Grant, taking command in person, appeared near that city. Grant did not repeat the attempt by Yazoo which had proven so disastrous to Sherman, but landed on the west side of the Mississippi, and began to dig a canal through the point of land opposite the town, his object being to evade the Confederate batteries and effect a landing below. This object was abandoned by Grant in April, and marching his troops by land to a point on the west side of the Mississippi river, he ordered his gunboats and transports to run down, passing the Confederate batteries at night. The fleet passed the batteries at Vicksburg successfully, and landed at Hard Times, where the land forces were, and the next night other transports and barges followed. The fire of the batteries of the Confederates destroyed two transports and six barges. On the 29th General Grant ordered his gunboats in front of the land batteries protecting Grand Gulf, and opened a furious cannonade, which lasted for several hours. But there was little damage done on either side. In a short time the fleet appeared with transports, and successfully ran the gauntlet of the Confederate batteries. Grant then commenced to ferry over troops from Louisiana to the Mississippi shore, just below the mouth of Bayou Pierre. It appeared Grant's object was to take Grand Gulf by a combined attack from land and water, and to operate against Vicksburg from that point. Failing in this, he determined to land at Bruinsburg. General Bowen, who commanded at Grand Gulf, observing the movements of the Federal forces, sent out two brigades under Generals Tracey and Green to Port Gibson, to intercept any advance in the direction of Vicksburg. They were met by a corps of Federals advancing under General McClernand within four miles of Port Gibson. Here a sharp conflict ensued, and, although largely outnumbered, Tracey held his ground till late in the afternoon. Then Tracey began to fall back, but meeting Baldwin's brigade coming to his assistance, halted and formed in line of battle; but the Federals did not renew the engagement at that time. About daylight a more serious conflict occurred, lasting some two hours and a half. Here General Tracey was killed while gallantly leading his brigade. General Bowen, reënforcements appearing, disputed every inch of the ground, and made good their retreat across the bridge over Bayou Pierre to the post at Grand Gulf. On the 3d General Bowen, finding his position about to be turned at Grand Gulf, withdrew his forces, spiking the guns and blowing up the magazines, and moved to Hankinson's ferry, on the Big Black, where, being joined by General Loring's division, they united forces across the river, and rejoined General Pemberton.

While these events were taking place, Colonel Grierson, with three Federal regiments of mounted infantry, made a raid through the entire state. Striking the Mississippi river at Baton Rouge, his forces were taken on transports and returned to Memphis, thereby evading the Confederate cavalry sent out to intercept him. The only thing accomplished by his expedition was the capture of a few soldiers home on furlough, and the wanton destruction of the houses and unrestricted pillage of the property of defenseless women and children. The inhabitants of the country through which he passed still speak of Grierson's raid with bated breath, on account of its merciless ferocity.

The forces of General Grant, having now succeeded in forming a junction at Willow Springs, moved forward on parallel roads, one leading to Edwards' depot, and the other to Jackson. In the meantime General Gregg's brigade from Port Hudson and General

Walker from Jackson had been ordered by General Pemberton to join him, and in their efforts to obey General Gregg, on the 12th, came in contact with General McPherson's corps, and after a stubborn resistance fell back on Jackson's brigade in reserve at Mississippi Springs. Here they reported to General Joseph E. Johnston, who had just arrived to take command of the army. While Sherman's and McPherson's corps were moving on Jackson, Miss., Grant ordered McClernan's corps to Clinton. On the 14th General Johnston evacuated Jackson with his forces, retreating to Brandon. Grant immediately occupied the place with his troops. On the 15th General Pemberton's forces were reported four miles from Edwards' depot on the road to Raymond. General Johnston had ordered General Pemberton, on the 14th, to march to Clinton, where he would meet him, and with their combined forces fall upon the enemy and whip him in detail. General Pemberton, when the order was received, called a council of war, to which he submitted it, after arguing against obeying it, and finally concluded to adopt a plan submitted by the minority of his council, of which he disapproved. To quote from his dispatch to General Johnston: "My own views were expressed as unfavorable to any movement which would remove me from my base, which was and is, Vicksburg." After reaching this determination, General Pemberton began to move his forces across Baker's creek, and encamped near Champion hill on the night of the 15th. General Grant had been told in Jackson on the 14th that Pemberton had been ordered to attack his rear; therefore, he determined to unite his whole force and anticipate the movement. In execution of this plan he came up with General Pemberton's forces at Baker's creek. That commander having suddenly determined to carry out General Johnston's order of the day before, recrossed the creek. Here, General Grant having succeeded in reuniting all his forces, a bloody engagement was fought. General Pemberton had formed his three divisions in line of battle extending from Raymond to the Clinton road, where he was assaulted by General Grant with McPherson's and McClernan's corps, and a part of Sherman's corps. The attack by General Grant was steady and irresistible all along the line, and the forces under Pemberton were forced to give way. Stevenson's and Bowen's troops and the reserve artillery, well placed and gallantly served by Col. W. E. Withers, maintained the unequal contest until after four o'clock. The battle was so completely lost that about that time a retreat was ordered. The withdrawal was protected by Loring's division, and by the time the army had crossed Baker's creek he found himself so hard pressed that he was unable to cross, and after passing the enemy's left turned and led his division to Jackson, Miss. General Pemberton directed the retreat of his army across Big Black to Bovina, while he halted Bowen's troops at the railroad bridge to enable Loring's division to cross Big Black. On the 17th his forces were attacked in these lines by General Grant, and, after a feeble show of resistance, they broke and fled, leaving their artillery. They fell back to Vicksburg, and General Grant, having crossed his troops on the 19th, completely invested the place. On the 20th the forces under General Grant, under cover of a heavy artillery fire, advanced to assault Pemberton's entrenched lines before Vicksburg, but were repulsed. General Grant, convinced that the place could not be carried at that time by assault, began to make gradual approaches and to complete his investment. The sharpshooters kept up an incessant fire all the while, picking off officers and men, while the artillery did considerable damage to the works, dismounting several guns. This fire was returned by the Confederate sharpshooters, the artillery replying at intervals to the guns of the besiegers. The damage done the works was hastily repaired by the Confederates at night and the guns replaced. General Grant continued to draw in and shorten his lines about the city, and on the 10th the mortars on the opposite side of the peninsula joined in the roar kept up by the incessant fire of the artillery day and night, while the sharpshooters encircled and enfolded the works like a cloud. Every part of the city was swept by the artillery, and the citizens fled, women and children, to hastily constructed caves under the bluffs for safety. The Confederates had been in the ditches thirty-four days and nights without relief, on short rations and a limited supply of ammunition. The writer saw some of these soldiers after the surrender, near Demopolis, Ala., while bathing in the Tombigbee, and was struck with the fact that both shoulders were black and blue, simply from the frequent discharge and rebound of their guns. General Grant, in writing of the siege of Vicksburg in the *Century*, September, 1885, makes the statement that "the small arms of the enemy were far superior to ours." This is not correct. The small arms of the Confederates at Vicksburg were mostly the old flintlocks altered into percussion. If there were some good arms they were such as had been captured from the enemy.

Gen. Joseph E. Johnston was making an effort to relieve the besieged city, but with the small force under him did not think it advisable to make an assault without the coöperation of General Pemberton. Therefore on the 29th he wrote to him: "I am too weak to save Vicksburg. Can do no more than attempt to save you and your garrison. It will be impossible to extricate you unless you coöperate and we make mutually supporting movements." So closely were the lines of the besiegers drawn, however, that the means of communication was very uncertain. General Pemberton received this communication, however, from General Johnston, and on the 1st of July submitted the same to his division commanders and asked their advice as to whether he should comply therewith and attempt to cut his way out. General S. D. Lee was the only one of this council that favored making the attempt. The garrison, after having passed forty-seven days and nights exposed to burning suns and drenching rains, all the while in a murderous storm of shot and shell, without the slightest relief, was surrendered by Pemberton on the 4th day of July, 1863.

The garrison at Port Hudson under the command of General Gardner was closely invested and had repulsed several assaults upon the place, but provisions and ammunition running low, on the 9th General Gardner was forced to capitulate. Most liberal terms were allowed the soldiers of these garrisons by General Grant, and they marched out, with their personal baggage and side arms, numbering about forty thousand men. On the 28th of June, General Johnston ordered the forces under him to march to Big Black river to make an attempt to extricate General Pemberton. He spent three or four days in making reconnoissances to find the most available point of attack and to secure the coöperation of General Pemberton, and on the 3d of July dispatched a note to General Pemberton to inform him that he was about to make a diversion to enable him to cut his way out of the place, and with this object in view, he would attack the enemy on the 7th at the only point, in his judgment, which offered any hope of success. On the evening of the 4th, however, having received intelligence of the surrender, he fell back with his army to Jackson. Thus ended the memorable siege of Vicksburg. The importance of the place was fully appreciated. The most prominent citizens of Jackson, in a dispatch to Mr. Davis, urged him to send reinforcements, "that Vicksburg and the country dependent upon it should be held at every sacrifice," and Mr. Davis, fully alive to the situation, dispatched General Johnston on the 21st, "My conviction is that the most imperative necessity for action will authorize you to adopt the most desperate course the occasion may demand." It is evident that a blunder had been committed by some one high in authority, but that it was not the fault of General Johnston is abundantly shown from the proofs adduced, and from the verdict of the jury of the people which held him blameless. Gen. Richard Taylor, son of Gen. Zachary Taylor and brother-in-law of Mr. Davis, in his work "Destruction and Reconstruction," when speaking of Mississippi in this connection, says that General Johnston had been sent with a roving commission to command Bragg in Tennessee, Pemberton in Mississippi, and others in sundry places. The result was that he commanded nobody, and when Pemberton was shut up in Vicksburg, found himself helpless with a handful of troops at Jackson. On the 9th of July, General Sherman appeared before Jackson, Miss., with three corps. General Johnston had placed his troops in line of battle in anticipation of an immediate assault, but instead of attacking at once, the force under General Sherman began to intrench and construct batteries. On the 10th, however, they opened with artillery, and sent out a line of skirmishers, and in a short time the two armies were hotly engaged. Skirmishing and artillery firing was kept up with slight variation till the evacuation of the place by Johnston. There was no serious assault made, however, until the 12th, when an attack was made on the Confederate line, held by troops under General Breckinridge, which was repulsed by Slocum's and Cobb's batteries and several regiments of infantry. The Federal loss was heavy. There is a range of hills commanding and encircling the town which enabled the Federal force with artillery to reach all parts of the city, rendering it untenable. Therefore, on the night of the 19th, General Johnston being advised that the enemy had brought up heavy artillery with which to command the town, withdrew his troops to a position near Morton on the Vicksburg & Meridian railroad. The enemy followed to Brandon and then returned to Jackson, remaining only long enough to burn the town.

While this was taking place, a force of Federals was sent from Vicksburg against Yazoo city. They advanced both by land and water, and made a simultaneous attack, which was handsomely repulsed by the land batteries, which sunk an ironclad carrying thirteen guns, but the garrison made only a slight resistance, and the place was captured.

On the 7th General Polk notified General Forrest, who was in command of all the cavalry in the Mississippi, that a Federal column under Sherman was moving on Jackson, while another had taken the field from Yazoo, which he was to watch. On the 11th scouts reported to General Forrest that a large infantry and cavalry force of Federals were approaching Holly Springs by the Germantown and Byhalia roads. He immediately ordered General Chalmers to concentrate his division at Oxford, and move so as to keep on the right flank of the advancing column of the enemy, whose object was to reach the rich prairie region. Col. Jeffry Forrest, striking the path of the Federals at Aberdeen, began to skirmish with them, and was forced back to West Point. General Forrest, with McCulloch's brigade and six hundred men under Neely, and artillery, went to the support of Colonel Forrest. He had in the meanwhile ordered General Lee up with his forces, and, while awaiting his approach, disposed his troops along the Sook-a-toucha, so as to hold the bridge crossing that stream. On the 21st a force was thrown across the stream by General Forrest, which was quickly attacked by the Federals. There was a great rattle of small arms, and after several attempts to drive back the Confederates, the enemy withdrew. General Forrest, discovering the enemy was retreating, moved forward with all his force, when the enemy again took position about four miles from West Point. Here, dismounting his men, he drove the enemy about five miles, when they again halted, and securing an advantageous position behind a stout picket fence, made a stubborn resistance, but were finally dislodged. Forrest had lost, during the day, about eighty men killed and wounded, while the loss of the Federals is set down at two hundred, including prisoners. The Federals continued their retreat toward Okalona, harassed by Forrest's men, which place being reached, they drew up in line of battle on the western suburbs. Here the Confederates charged them with much vigor, and they broke and fled, abandoning seven pieces of artillery in their flight, while many of them were killed and wounded. About seven miles from Okalona they halted, and took a highly favorable position for defense. The brigades of Forrest and McCulloch coming up, General Forrest ordered a charge. Sweeping forward, they carried the first line of defense, but were met with a withering fire at the second that for a moment daunted the troops. Here Colonel Forrest, the brother of General Forrest, fell mortally wounded. The death of Colonel Forrest being communicated to General Forrest, he was overwhelmed with passionate grief, and for a while there was a pause in the battle. Quickly regaining his composure, he ordered his bugler to sound the charge, and placing himself at the head of his escort, he bore down upon the Federals with the impetus of an avalanche. They were forced back for a mile, when they again halted and confronted their adversaries drawn up in four lines of battle. This time they did not wait for the Confederates to charge, but bore down on them in fine style. The first line, being repulsed, was followed in quick succession by the others, the last line having a hand-to-hand conflict with the Confederates. Just at this time McCulloch's brigade arriving decided the fate of battle. The Federals broke and fled in all directions, their officers being unable to rally them. What was at first an orderly retreat became a rout, and but for night intervening, the entire command would have been captured. The Federals were under the command of General Smith. Their loss was reported at six hundred killed and wounded, and three hundred prisoners, while the loss of Confederates was proportionately severe.

On the 5th of June Forrest was recalled by Gen. Stephen D. Lee from Tennessee to resist the invasion of the federal forces from Memphis, the latest and most reliable information of their whereabouts being that they had left Ripley and were moving to Guntown, on the Mobile & Ohio railroad. General Lee, in command, then fell back to Okalona to form a junction with the forces of Chalmers, while Forrest was ordered to move with his command and get between the enemy and Tupelo. In motion before dawn on the 10th, Forrest struck the main body of the Federals near Brice's crossroads, and with his usual decision determined to attack at once. Brice's crossroads is about two miles from Guntown, and four from Baldwyn. The forces under Forrest amounted to about two thousand men. General Lyon, with his brigade, was ordered to feel the enemy and avoid being drawn into an engagement. Lyon, forcing back the Federal advance, found them heavily massed in front as if to attack. He ordered his men to halt and throw up temporary breastworks. Forrest, being advised of the state of affairs, ordered Lyon to move forward to the attack while he brought up the remainder of his force. The Federals made a determined and obstinate resistance, but were steadily pressed back all along the line. They now occupied the arc of a circle three-fourths of a mile in extent, the right line across the Ripley and Guntown road. They had also a heavy force of infantry as well as cavalry. The Confederates, occupying a position a little more elevated, confronted them on all sides. The offensive was now vigorously resumed by the Confederates, and the Federals, though greatly superior in numbers, were being pressed back. Their forces, constantly augmented by fresh troops, made the result extremely doubtful, whereupon Forrest repaired to the scene in person. Ordering up artillery, he directed it to be double-shotted with canister and unlimbered within sixty yards of the Federal lines, where he opened upon them, as they were just forming for an attack, with terrible execution. After two or three discharges Forrest ordered his troops to charge all along the line. The Federals were driven back, while the lines of Forrest were shortened, and consequently strengthened, as they converged upon the crossroads. The fire of Confederate artillery and small arms was rapid and desolating, and the Federals, being driven back into their artillery and wagontrains, were in inextricable confusion. Forrest, seeing their disorder, rapidly brought forward his artillery, poured into them a deadly fire, killing and wounding large numbers. The Federals were completely panic-stricken, and broke and fled in all directions. About two miles from the crossroads they rallied and made a strong resistance, driving back their pursuers upon Rice's battery, but that, opening with double charges of canister, hurled the Federals back, utterly demoralized. Here night fell, and Forrest, assembling his command, rested till the morning of the 11th, when he gave orders for immediate pursuit. He struck the Federal rear about daylight at Stubb's farm, where a slight skirmish took place, but the Federals, not having recovered from their panic of the night before, broke and fled, abandoning all artillery, wagontrains and a number of wounded. The Federal general made several attempts to rally his troops, but they were so demoralized that upon the first fire from the Confederates they broke and ran. Almost the entire expedition sent out from Memphis was captured or killed by Forrest, who also captured a large quantity of military stores, with nineteen pieces of artillery.

On the 1st of October General Lee was ordered with a detachment to interrupt the railroad communications of the Federal army from Tennessee, while the remainder of the cavalry, under General Chalmers, was to attack the Federal troops stationed along the Memphis & Charleston railroad. In the execution of this plan General Chalmers, on the 6th, attacked and drove a detachment of eight hundred Federal troops from Coldwater, Miss., and on the 12th attacked the force at Collierville with success, but on the arrival of fresh troops was forced to fall back to Byhalia, Miss., followed by eleven regiments of Federal cavalry. There, after an engagement of four hours, he was forced to fall back to Wyatt, on the Tallahatchie river, when he succeeded in repulsing his pursuers. Intelligence was received about this time from Canton that a column of Federals had crossed the Big Black and was moving toward Brownsville. They were met by General Jackson with his division, who so successfully impeded their march that they turned back seven or eight miles from Livingston and returned to Vicksburg. This ends all the important military operations that took place in the state, except such events as are hereinafter described.

On the approach of the enemy to Jackson, the archives and public records were removed from the capital to Meridian, and subsequently to Columbus. All civil law was at an end; the military was supreme. Provost guards were stationed in the principal towns, whose duty it was to protect the personal property of the citizens, enforce the conscript law and return deserters to duty. The governor and legislature in the meantime endeavored to keep the women and children from starving. The condition of affairs since '62 had been intensified by the presence of contending armies in the state. The rich and more populous part had been utterly destroyed and laid waste. The slave had run off or gone into the Federal army. There was no one left to raise a crop. The farmhouses and fencing were burned, and farming implements destroyed. The droves of fine horses and mules used to till the soil, the herds of cattle, hogs and sheep were all gone, and not even a domestic fowl remained to warn one of the approach of day. Silence and desolation brooded over the track of the armies as ominous and appalling as if smitten by the hand of pestilence. The traveler might ride days without seeing a human being or animate object. Women and children had taken refuge in secluded localities far removed from the more public thoroughfares, where, with the little remnant saved from the wreck of former fortunes, they were battling with skulking deserters and the frequent forays of Confederate troopers for a miserable existence. The people had been forbidden to traffic with the enemy, and in order to sell for the necessaries of life the little cotton which had been hidden away, were forced to avoid meeting with the troops of either army, for fear of its destruction or confiscation. J. D. Bradford, assistant inspector-general, in his report of July 7, 1864, says that he had just returned from a tour of inspection in southwest Mississippi, and the country in some places was stripped of everything that might sustain a popula tion, and in neighboring sections, where all supplies had not been destroyed, there was no surplus with which to supply those who had lost all, so there was no alternative to obtain the necessary supplies to support life but from the enemy, and recommended that the restrictions on traffic be rescinded.

In some parts of the state deserters and conscripts were banded together defying the military authorities, making raids upon government stores, terrorizing the women and children, and committing other acts of outlawry.

In a letter addressed to the secretary of war, dated March 29, 1864, Capt. W. Wirt Thompson, captain Company A, Twenty-fourth Mississippi regiment, says: "I have just returned to the army from a short leave of absence which I spent in Greene county, Miss., and therefore make my statements from a personal knowledge of their truth."

After stating that he knew there were deserters and conscripts in that part of the state, but that he did not know they were in organized bodies, he continues, "But such I found to be the case, and the whole southern and southeastern section of Mississippi is in a most deplorable condition, and unless succor is sent speedily the country is utterly ruined. Every loyal citizen will be driven from it or meet a tragic or untimely fate at the hands of those who are aiding or abetting our enemies. Several of the most prominent citizens have been driven from their own homes, and some have been slaughtered because they refuse to obey the mandates of the outlaws and abandon the country." "Every officer or soldier who enters the county, if they catch him, is forced to submit to one of the following requirements: First, desert the army and join them; second, take a parole not to molest them, or give information as to their acts or locality of rendezvous." "Government depots filled with supplies have been robbed or burned, ginhouses, dwellinghouses and barns, and the court-house of Greene county have been destroyed by fire."

In conclusion, he says, "As a Confederate officer, and a citizen of that portion of Mississippi whose friends and family are exposed to this growing evil, I have felt it my duty to lay the matter before the proper authorities." R. S. Hudson, judge of the Fifth judicial district of Mississippi, writing to President Davis, under date March 14, 1864, says: "Very many of the middle class, and a large number of the more intelligent, are drifting to the Yankees. Desertion from the army, trading with the enemy, and the removal of deserters and their families into the lines and supposed lines of the enemy is now the order of the day, and the citizen who opposes these things stands almost alone and in great personal danger. The state is now under the tacit rule of deserters, thieves, disloyal men and women. The lower and middle tiers of counties are vastly rotten. Many of our soldiers who remained in or along with the service are as destructive to property as the Yankees. They steal, destroy and appropriate without restraint. These things tend to dishearten and disaffect our best citizens, and are swelling the tide against us."

In a letter dated March 1, 1864, to Adjutant and Inspector-General Cooper, General Polk says: "The weakness and inefficiency exhibited by the bureau of conscription in this department are producing the most serious evils. Conscripts and deserters are banded together in Jones county, and others contiguous, to the number of several hundred. Have killed the officer in charge of the work of conscription and dispersed and captured his sup-porting force. They are increasing in numbers and boldness, have destroyed the houses of many loyal men by fire, plundered others and have within a few days made a raid into Paulding with wagon trains, and helped themselves largely to government and other stores."

James Hamilton, major and quartermaster of Mississippi and Louisiana, under date of March 31, 1864, writing to the assistant adjutant-general, speaking of the difficulties encoun-tered in collecting the tax in kind, quotes Capt. W. J. Bryant, his deputy, as saying that "the condition of affairs in his section of Mississippi was very bad. That the deserters had overrun and taken possession of the country, in many cases exiling the good and loyal citizens or shooting them in cold blood on their own doorsills. * * * That the deser-ters from Jones and Perry counties made a raid upon Augusta, Perry county, capturing a small part of the force there and destroying the public stores which we had collected. * * * * * * You can not realize what disservice has been done to the cause by such irregularities alienating the affections of the people and destroying the means of subsisting the army." In an amnesty proclamation dated April 16, 1864, "To all soldiers in this department absent without leave," General Polk, commanding the department, says he has "had presented to him a petition signed by the senate and house of representatives of Missis-sippi, setting forth that a large number of men now absent from their commands in this department, who in a moment of weakness were induced to abandon their duty and desert their colors, have seen reason bitterly to regret their infidelity and are anxious to return." The petitioners further said the men by reason of the lack of mail facilities had never seen the act of pardon offered by the president to return, and that they would return but for fear of punishment, and asked that another offer of pardon be tendered them.

In deference to the wishes of so large a body of influential citizens, General Polk said he would do it, although against his judgment, provided they would report to their commands by a certain time. The circular further states that the offer of pardon was not confined to the soldiers of Mississippi there. but to those of other states, who were hiding in the state. A regular campaign, with cavalry and infantry, was instituted by General Polk against these skulkers and deserters which was attended with a measurable degree of success. On the 8th of May, 1865, the army of Mississippi was surrendered by General Taylor to Colonel Canby, the armies of Lee and Johnston having previously surrendered. Thus the curtain was rung down on the last act of the military drama, and the battle-scarred veterans, returning home, having lost all save honor, were confronted with the dark picture thus feebly sketched in the foregoing pages, illuminated for a moment only by the joy and happiness of finding wife and children at least alive.

The condition of things which confronted the soldiers and returning refugee families who had been true and loyal to the state was cause enough to appall the bravest heart: to rebuild without anything — "bankstock, bonds, all personal wealth, all accumulated wealth, had disappeared. Thousands of houses, farmbuildings and animals, flocks and herds had been wantonly burned, killed or carried off. The land was filled with widows and orphans crying for aid, which the universal destitution prevented them from receiving. Humanitarians shuddered with horror or wept with grief at the imaginary woes of Africa, but their hearts were as adamant to people of their own race and color." The negroes lately, by strong hand simply set free, flocked to the towns, thereby adding to the distress and suffering, and obstinately refusing to work on the farms. Nobody had any money with which to employ negroes except those who had kept in hiding and carried on an illicit traffic with the enemy during the war. Now that the cauldron had ceased to boil this scum

rose rapidly to the surface.   Yet the true people of the state dauntlessly faced those difficulties with the same fortitude and sublime patience which had so distinguished them during
the war.   Gov. Charles Clarke, who was then the chief executive of the state of Mississippi, asked General Taylor, commanding the department, for advice in the emergency
produced by the surrender.   General Taylor, in his work on "Destruction and Reconstruction," says: "I told Governor Clark I thought his best course would be to summon his state
legislature.   The legislature would certainly provide for a convention of the people to repeal
the ordinance of secession and abolish slavery, thus smoothing the way for the restoration of
the state to the Union.   Such action would be in harmony with the theory and practice of
the American system, and clear the road of difficulties.   The North, by its government,
press, and people, had been declaring for years that the war was for the preservation of the
Union and for nothing else, and Canby and I in the innocence of our hearts believed it.   As
Canby thought well of my plan, I communicated with Governor Clarke, who acted on it."
Acting on this advice, Governor Clarke issued the following proclamation:

MERIDIAN, MISS., May 6, 1865.
To the People of Mississippi:
    General Taylor informs me that all Confederate armies east of the Mississippi river are surrendered,
with all government cotton, quartermaster, commissary and other stores.   Federal commanders will only
send such troops as may be necessary to guard public property.   All officers and persons in possession of
public stores will be held to a rigid accountability, and all embezzlers suddenly arrested.   Arrangement
will be made to issue supplies to the destitute.   I have called the legislature to meet at Jackson on Thursday, the 18th inst.   They will doubtless order a convention.   The officers of the state government will
immediately return with the archives to Jackson.   County officers will be vigilant in the preservation of
order and the protection of property.   Sheriffs have power to call out the *posse comitatus*, and the militia
will keep arms and obey orders for that purpose as in times of peace.   The civil laws must be enforced
as they now are until repealed.   If the public property be protected and peace preserved, the necessity
for Federal troops in your counties will be avoided.   You are therefore urged to combine to arrest marauders and plunderers.   The collection of taxes should be suspended, as the laws will doubtless be changed.
Masters are responsible, as heretofore, for the protection and conduct of their slaves, and they should be
kept at home as heretofore.   Let all citizens fearlessly adhere to the fortunes of the state.   Aid the
returned soldiers to obtain civil employment.   Maintain law and order.   Contemn all twelfth-hour vapor-
ers, and meet stern facts with fortitude and common sense.

CHARLES CLARKE, Governor of Mississippi.

    On the 13th of June, however, President Johnson, by proclamation, appointed Judge
W. L. Sharkey as provisional governor of the state of Mississippi, and Governor Clarke,
without authority of law, was arrested by the military authorities and imprisoned in Fort
Pulaski, the military never having left the state of Mississippi.

    Judge Sharkey issued his proclamation calling a convention, to be composed of dele-
gates who had been loyal to the Union, for the purpose of "altering or amending the constitution," so that the state might resume its place in the Union.

    The convention thus assembled ordered an election to be held for state officers, and at
the same time submitted to be voted upon by the people amendments to the constitution of
the state framed in accordance with the constitution of the United States.   Before adjournment this convention repealed the ordinances of secession, the establishment of the military
system, and all others passed by the convention of 1861.   This convention did not pretend
to deal with the question of slavery, as that matter, by the terms of the armistice between
Generals Johnston and Sherman, was to be left to the supreme court of the United States.
At the election held in pursuance of this order, state officers were elected, Benjamin G.
Humphreys being declared governor, and the liberal amendments submitted, to meet the
changed condition of affairs were adopted.   The fourteenth amendment to the constitution

of the United States was rejected by the legislature in January, 1867. Under an act of congress passed March 2, 1867, entitled "An act to provide for the more efficient government of the rebel states," Brevet Maj.-Gen. E. O. C. Ord was assigned by President Johnson to the Fourth military district, consisting of Mississippi and Arkansas, who immediately assumed command, with headquarters at Vicksburg, Miss., and proceeded to station troops and estab lish posts in the principal towns of the state. The convention called under Judge Sharkey's proclamation and the legislature had done everything they could do to restore the state to the Union; but their acts were not recognized at Washington, the state's representatives in congress being refused admission to their seats. Governor Humphreys sought to test the constitutionality of the above act before the supreme court of the United States. The motion to restrain President Johnson and Major-General Ord from the execution of this act, on hearing by the court, was denied, however.

General Ord, soon after assuming command, issued an order in pursuance of the recon struction act of congress approved March 23, 1867, for the election of delegates to a convention for the purpose of making a new constitution—to quote the act, to establish a "loyal and republican state government." To this end he proceeded to organize boards for the registration of voters, and the following test oath had to be taken before they could register:

I ———— do solemnly swear (or affirm) in the presence of Almighty God that I am a citizen of the state of Mississippi. That I have resided in said state for———months, next preceding this day, and now reside in the county of—————in said state; that I am twenty-one years of age; that I have not been disfranchised for participation in any rebellion or civil war against the United States, nor for felony committed against the laws of any state, or the United States; that I have never been a member of any state legislature nor held any executive or judicial office in any state and afterwards engaged in insurrection or rebellion against the United States, or given aid and comfort to the enemies thereof; that I have never taken an oath as a member of congress of the United States, or as an officer of the United States, or as a member of any state legislature, or as an executive or judicial officer of any state, to support the constitution of the United States, and afterwards engaged in insurrection or rebellion against the United States, or given aid or comfort to the enemies thereof; that I will faithfully support the constitution and obey the laws of the United States, and will, to the best of my ability, encourage others so to do, so help me God.

Now, the soldiers who had surrendered did so in good faith. It was an agreement between soldiers. Their conduct and acts as citizens showed a desire for restoration to the Union in obedience to law. Why, then, seek to humiliate them further by this iron-clad oath which virtually disfranchised them and placed the entire political power in the hands of ignorant and irresponsible negroes? The effect of this was to put the bottom rail on top. The life, liberty and property of the former master, now voiceless in govermental affairs, was to be passed upon by his own slave just liberated. Can a condition of things more intolerable be imagined? To increase this humiliation and assist the commanding general in carrying out these measures, a set of people known as "carpet-baggers," aliens to the state, scenting booty from afar, came and settled down like vultures to prey and fatten upon what little was left.

Orders were now issued to coöperate with the military to break up the crime of horse-stealing. In furtherance of this object, the commanding general, in a letter to George F. Mullen, J. P., Satartia, Miss., dated April 30, directed him to deliver up two horse-thieves who had been committed by the justice to jail and turn them over to the guard, who had instructions to conduct them to Vicksburg for military trial. They were afterward turned loose by the military without any investigation. So much for coöperation. Under general orders No. 25, issued September 6, 1867, General Ord authorized the removal of criminal cases from the civil courts, so that the accused might be able to show loyalty during the war. Thus any scoundrel, no matter what the charge might be against him, by reporting to the general commanding that he was loyal during the war, could have his case removed. By general order No. 12 the execution of the law in civil cases where the cause of action accrued prior to January 1, 1866, was suspended till the 30th of December, 1867. Under general order No. 15, dated June 27, 1867, he prohibited the collection of a poll tax under an act entitled, " An act to amend the vagrant laws," passed by the legislature on the 24th of November, 1865, as a violation of the civil rights bill.

Under general orders Nos. 16 and 17 he pretends to seek to secure to labor its share of the crops, and to prevent alleged frauds upon freedmen, thus interfering with the liberty of contract.

This military commander issued orders to subordinates of the Freedman's bureau to investigate all charges against landholders, and forbade the assembling of bodies of citizens under any pretext. He authorized the investigations of complaints made by citizens of persecutions by civil authority. Thus a negro, charged with theft and brought before the civil authorities was. upon complaint of persecution, turned loose by General Ord, himself the judge. He would permit no elections to be held to fill city offices, but filled them himself by appointment, requiring applicant first to take the test oath.

One has no idea of the extent of the system of espionage exercised over the white citizen at this time by virtue of these orders. A white farmer employing negroes to work on his land, upon the merest whim or caprice of the laborer, was brought before the military commission and tried, the negro being the witness against him. If the farmer chanced to have a mule or horse with the brand of U. S. A. upon him, although he could establish the fact that it was his own property which had been seized by them, he was forced to give it up, unless he could bribe the soldier making the seizure with a small sum to relinquish the alleged claim of the United States.

In consequence of this connivance, on the part of the military, with wrongdoing, and its interference with the civil authorities, the whole state was overrun with horse thieves and other malefactors. If a white man, irritated beyond endurance at the seizure of his property, should express his opinion about it in words more forcible than elegant, and that opinion thus expressed was wafted to the ears of the military, he was charged with disloyalty and arrested.

Having completed the registration in the state according to his peculiar ideas, he provides in general orders No. 31 for the holding of an election on the first Tuesday of November, 1867, to determine whether a convention shall be held, and for delegates thereto, for the purpose of establishing constitutions and civil governments for the states loyal to the Union. On November 5 the election was held, and the convention met on the 8th day of January, 1868. This convention, known in history as the "black and tan " convention—well-named, for, looking over the members composing it, a white face was rarely seen here and there—declared the ordinance of secession null and void, prohibited the existence of slavery and the payment of the war debt; declared for universal suffrage, excepting only criminals; provided for an election to ratify the constitution and the election of state officers and members of congress. This election was to be held on June 22, at which the constitution made and proposed by that convention was rejected by the people, and that, too, when the election had been held under the supervision of the commanding generals, who had stationed troops at as many as sixty places in different parts of the state. The negro himself joined with the whites in defeating this odious constitu-

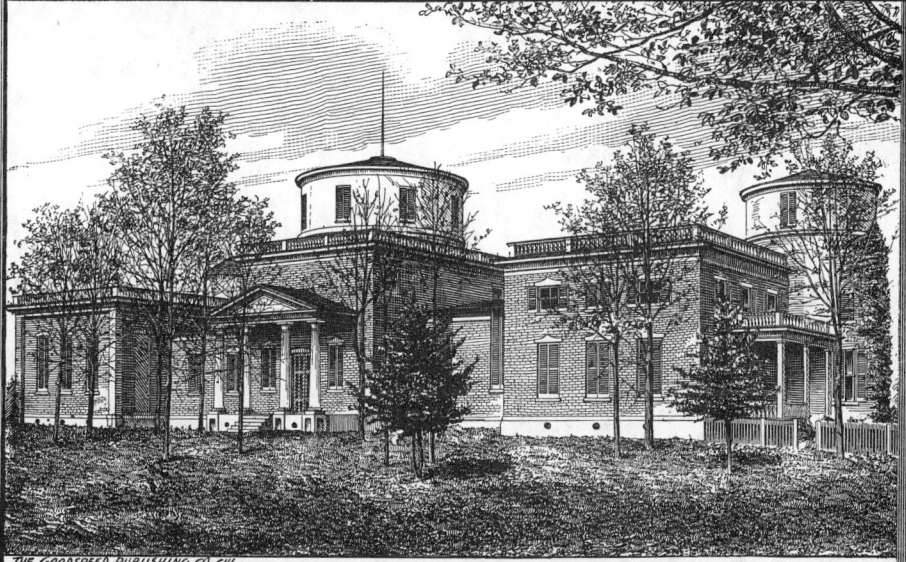

THE GOODSPEED PUBLISHING CO., CHI.

LIBRARY BUILDING.   OBSERVATORY.   LYCEUM.

THREE OF THE UNIVERSITY BUILDINGS, OXFORD.

tion. The opposition candidate was also elected. This was Gov. Benjamin G. Humphreys. On December 28, 1867, General Ord was succeeded by Major-General McDowell. In general orders No. 23, General McDowell appoints Adelbert Ames provisional governor of Mississippi, and Jasper Myers attorney-general, ordering at the same time the expulsion of Governor Humphreys and Charles E. Hooker, attorney-general. Governor Humphreys declined to vacate the office, having been regularly and constitutionally elected, and a squadron of soldiers was sent by the military commander of the post, who took forcible possession of the office and also the mansion. This wanton exercise of military authority is thus graphically described in their history of Mississippi by Messrs. McCardle & Lowry:

"Colonel Biddle, armed with an order from General Ames, called at the executive office, and demanded of the governor a surrender of it, and the archives of the state; and if refused, notified him of the hour at which he would seize them. Before the hour of seizure arrived the governor invited Dr. M. S. Craft, Marion Smith, Oliver Clifton, and William F. Fitzgerald, to be present and witness what occurred. At the appointed hour the military officer, with a file of soldiers, appeared at the executive office to carry into execution the order mentioned. On renewing his demand he was informed by the governor that his force was insufficient to take possession of his office. The officer's deportment was that of a gentleman, and he inquired what force would be necessary, and was informed that the governor would be a judge of that. Immediately thereafter the officer returned with a military company, marched them into the executive office, and instructed their commander to permit anyone who desired to pass out, but to allow no one to come in. Soon after this order and demonstration, the governor, accompanied by his private secretary, went to the attorney-general's office, and on his return, at the door of his own office, he was ordered to 'halt' at the point of two bayonets. Upon inquiry of the sergeant what that meant, he was kindly informed by the sentinel that his orders were to allow no one to enter the office, and that it was a military order from his superior officer that he was compelled to obey. The governor was thus ejected from the executive mansion."

Governor Humphreys, subsequently speaking of this event, said:

"I knew it was futile to disobey these orders, and that I must succumb, but I had the honor, the dignity, property rights, and the sovereignty of the state to guard, and I was determined to maintain those rights and yield nothing except at the point of overpowering bayonets, and that the world should know that I yielded not to civil process, but to stern, unrelenting military tyranny."

Soon after Ames' appointment as military governor, congress passed a joint resolution ordering all persons holding office in Mississippi who could not take the test oath prescribed to be removed. At the same time Provisional Governor Ames was made military commander of the Fourth military district, succeeding McDowell, who had been removed. Congress then passed an act to submit the constitution of the state proposed by the convention of 1868 to another election of the people, with a separate vote on its objectionable section. Preparations for the election were commenced by the issuance of an order by Military Governor Ames, prescribing stringent regulations relative to the registration of voters. Ames' object was to have his own henchmen sent to the legislature, so that he might be rewarded with the United States senatorship. But every white citizen who was in the war or a sympathizer therewith must be excluded from participation. In a circular letter dated November 19, 1869, addressed to commanding officers of troops stationed throughout the state, they are ordered to coöperate with inspectors of election in their several precincts in preserving the peace, said inspectors to use their own judgment as to the necessity for troops, and then apply immedi-

11

ately to the commanding officer at the nearest station, who was to furnish troops at the instance of said inspector, and if he didn't furnish them then the inspector was to apply to Ames himself. These officers were to hold their troops well in hand. In the exercise of the power of removal conferred upon him by congress, he removed civil officers without cause, substituting his own minions in their place. He interfered in civil trials and released parties accused of grave crimes. He arrested and imprisoned citizens upon the most flimsy pretext and complaint of negro politicians. And to crown his acts of infamy and military tyranny, suspended the writ of habeas corpus when there was no occasion so to do. At this election held on November 30, James L. Alcorn was elected governor, and the constitution ratified. Governor Alcorn in his inaugural said: "The military government which I have the happiness to bar this day out of the state, was no more a subject of pleasure to me than it was to any other Mississippian whose blood glows as mine does with the instinct of self-government."

The legislature which assembled on January 11, 1870, ratified the fourteenth and fifteenth amendments to the constitution of the United States, and elected James L. Alcorn and Adelbert Ames to the United States senate. Under general orders No. 28, General Gillam was appointed military commander of the Fourth military district, vice General Ames resigned.

On February 12, 1870, congress passed an act admitting to their seats the representatives from the state of Mississippi.

Thus it will be seen, and an inspection of the military acts and orders demonstrate it, that the purpose of the Federal government in substituting military for civil government in Mississippi was not for the purpose of protecting life, liberty and property of the citizen, nor to protect the lately enfranchised colored man, but simply to republicanize the state, and elect one of the military commanders, as in the case of Ames, to the United States senate. And this they called reconstruction.

In this effort of the writer to detail the principal incidents of the state as a member of the Confederacy from the cradle to the grave, and the mocking seance at which her body was made to appear, he has only endeavored to deal with facts "which you yourselves do know; show you sweet Cæsar's wounds, poor, poor dumb mouths, and bid them speak."

CHAPTER VIII.

COUNTIES OF THE OLD NATCHEZ DISTRICT.

ADAMS county is bounded on the south by the Homochitto river, on the west by the Mississippi, on the east by the Washington or Helena meridian and on the north by an irregular line beginning one mile north of township seven north, range one west of the Helena meridian, meandering in township eight, range two, to its north line, and thence to the Mississippi. Its physical characteristics vary little from those of Wilkinson county, but the proportion of cleared land to the total area is larger than that of Wilkinson, being one hundred and five thousand one hundred and sixty-four acres. The area is four hundred square miles. A few creeks rise in the county, flowing southwest, and along those streams the earliest settlements were made, except the parent settlements on the Mississippi. The population in 1800 was four thousand six hundred and sixty, and in 1812 it was ten thousand and two, made up of four thousand nine hundred and thirty-five whites, five thousand and thirty slaves and thirty-seven others. There were one hundred and sixty-six looms, six spinningmills, three hundred and forty-three spindles, two tanneries, one distillery and one tin factory in operation at that time. There were fifty-eight thousand nine hundred and ninety-four yards of cotton cloth and six thousand eight hundred and eighteen yards of woolen cloth produced. The population in 1820 was twelve thousand and seventy-six; in 1830, fourteen thousand nine hundred and thirty-seven; in 1840, nineteen thousand four hundred and thirty-four; in 1850, eighteen thousand six hundred and one; in 1860, twenty thousand one hundred and sixty-five, including thirteen thousand three hundred and eighteen slaves and five hundred and fifty-nine polls; in 1870, nineteen thousand and eighty-four; in 1880, twenty-two thousand six hundred and forty-nine, and in 1890, twenty-six thousand and thirty-one, made up of six thousand and fifty-four whites and nineteen thousand nine hundred and eighty-three negroes and other colored persons. The name was given in honor of President Adams.

The county is historical in every particular, and hence it occupies a large space in the general history of the state and in that of the city of Natchez. Within its present boundaries the warriors of the Natchez were born, and generation after generation held their territory against all comers until the Caucasian appeared.

There are many Indian mounds in Adams county, the most important of which is the Selsertown mound, in the northeastern part of the county. It is circular in form, and its base covers about five acres and is of a considerable altitude. It has been opened on many occasions, and besides human bones many articles of pottery and several implements of war and the chase were found. Other mounds are the Foster mound and a number of quite large ones in the southern part of the county.

The Natchez Indians were in possession of this territory at the time of the occupation by the whites. Their largest village was White Apple, on Second creek, but there were other settlements all over the county. In Natchez the Indians had a fort, the site of which is now occupied by the Stanton mansion.

The remains of large animals are sometimes brought to light within its boundaries. In the spring of 1890, while Captain Sargent and men were excavating a cut for the Northern Ohio & Northwestern railway in Natchez, they found the remains of a mastodon buried beneath about seventy-five feet of earth. They consist of the skull and part of both upper and lower jaw bones, also four grinders still in jaws. These teeth measure 4x12 inches on their face, and all are in a good state of preservation.

Similar remains have been frequently found in all parts of Adams county, but in a locality known as Mammoth bayou the remains have been found in such large quantities as to indicate the existence of immense herds of these monster animals in this county.

Stephen Miner was the first settler and owner of a large part of the present site of the city of Natchez. Other early settlers were Isaac Girault, Christopher Miller, John Nugent and Jacob Eiler. In the county, Sir William Dunbar, Anthony Hutchins, Philander Smith and Peter Surget settled on Second creek; Benjamin Greenfield, John W. Bryant, James Tooley, Dr. Branch and Dr. Rawlings at Washington; William Bistand, John Grafton, Samuel Ivey, Capt. Samuel Clement, Capt. John B. Nevett and William K. Brooks, at Pine Ridge; Dr. Isaac Selser, Angus MacCallum, Philetus and Arthur Andrews, and Jonathan Guice and three brothers at Selsertown.

The first printing done in Mississippi, other than that at Washington by James Ferrall, was at Walnut Hill, now Vicksburg, by Col. Andrew Marschalk, Sr., he being in command of a fort of that place. He printed a ballad, "The Galley Slave," with type and on a press brought with him.

The first newspaper in Adams county, and also in Mississippi, the *Natchez Gazette*, was issued in 1798 by Col. Andrew Marschalk. This paper, under different forms and names, such as the *Mississippi Herald* and *Natchez Gazette*, the *Washington Republic* and *Mississippi State Gazette*, was published by this father of the press in Mississippi for nearly forty years afterward. The second paper in the territory was the *Mississippi Messenger*, published by Samuel and Timothy Terrell, and was continued by Dr. John Shaw and others until 1810. Other papers published in Natchez were the *Arial, Natchez Galaxy, Natchez Courier*, the *Natchez Christian Herald*, the *Free Trader*, the *Natchez Independent*. The papers published here at the present time (1891) are the *Daily Democrat* and the *Banner*.

The *Evening Banner* was first issued as a tri-weekly on March 13, 1886, by Leon Duchesne, proprietor, and J. H. Davis, editor. In September, 1887, it was purchased by J. H. Davis, Gerard Brandon and M. C. Montgomery. In July, 1888, it was made a daily and issued in the evening. On September 1, 1888, a stock company was organized, with Abe Moses, president; Gerard Brandon, secretary; Julius Roos, treasurer, and J. H. Davis, managing editor. In March, 1889, began the issue of a weekly edition. The present officers are J. H. Davis, president; M. C. Montgomery, secretary, and Julius Roos, treasurer. The *Banner* is a stanch democrat in politics, but it was started by Mr. Duchesne as independent in political faith.

The *Democrat* was established as a tri-weekly in 1865 by Messrs. Mead & Botto, and published by that firm until July, 1866, when the firm was changed to Botto & Lambert, and continued under that management until the death of Mr. Paul A. Botto in 1879. Its first issue as a daily was December 2, 1872. The *Democrat* is now one of the best papers of the

South, its columns being filled with the associated press dispatches, all the local news, and excellently written and well-thought editorials, able essays on all current matters of public consideration. Its present proprietor, Capt. J. W. Lambert, assumed charge at the death of Mr. Botto, and has since conducted its publication. It also publishes a weekly edition, and both weekly and daily are popular and influential. It is under the editoral direction of Maj. Douglas Walworth.

Adams county has had a great many literary people, and some who have become quite distinguished. Dr. J. W. Monett, of Washington, published a history of Mississippi valley in (about) 1842; John T. Griffith, author of the "White Faun," a romance founded on tradition of Indian life, and a very popular story, about 1828; Mrs. Caroline Matilda Thayer, a poetess; Miss Eliza A. Dupuey, a story writer; Judge Joseph Shields, a life of Hon. S. S. Prentiss; Mrs. Sarah A. Dorsey (nee Ellis), several novels and a book of memoirs of Gov. Henry W. Allen. She died July 4, 1879, and gave her estate at Bonvoir and all her property to Jefferson Davis; J. F. H. Claiborne, a history of Mississippi; Mrs. Jennette Walworth, an authoress of well merited renown—her first book, "Forgiven at Last," appeared in 1869; this was soon followed by "Dead Men's Shoes;" all of her many works have been well received; she has also done much magazine writing; now resides in Natchez.

On April 2, 1799 Adams county was established out of the old Natchez district and organized with Daniel Clark, Sr., as presiding justice of the county of common pleas court. This organization took place seventy years after the massacre of the French and Spanish settlers, thirty-six years after the British took possession, twenty years after the Spaniards took possession and two years after it became a part of the United States.

The postoffices of Adams county are Arnot, population fifty-one; Hutchins, Jeanette, Kienstra, Kingston, Loch Leven, Natchez, population ten thousand one hundred and forty-nine; Stanton, Washington, population two hundred and forty, and Yeagers.

Jefferson county is one of the two first divisions of the state, established as a county under the name of Pickering. In 1799 Mississippi territory was organized into two counties, Adams and Pickering, both extending eastward to the Chattahoochie river. The territorial legislature on the 11th of January, 1802, changed the name Pickering county to Jefferson, and on the 27th of January, 1802, formed out of it another county called Claiborne. The area is four hundred and ninety square miles, extending east from the Mississippi to the Indian boundary and north from the north line of Adams and Franklin counties to the south line of Claiborne. The physical character is varied, being everything from the bluff soil on the western border to the light pine soil on the eastern border. Bermuda grass was introduced during the administration of Governor Mead. The white sandstone quarry on the Burch farm, five miles northeast of Fayette, is an index to the rock deposits.

The population in 1800 was two thousand nine hundred and forty; in 1812 it was four thousand and one, or two thousand one hundred and eighty-nine whites, and one thousand eight hundred and twelve negroes. There were one hundred and twenty-seven looms, one spinningmill, thirty spindles and two tanneries in operation. The number of yards of cotton cloth produced was thirty-three thousand seven hundred and forty-seven. The population in 1820 was six thousand eight hundred and twenty-two; in 1830, nine thousand seven hundred and fifty-five; in 1840, eleven thousand six hundred and fifty; in 1850, thirteen thousand one hundred and ninety-three; in 1860, fifteen thousand three hundred and forty-nine, including eleven thousand six hundred and sixty-six slaves and six hundred and twenty-seven polls; in 1870, thirteen thousand eight hundred and forty-eight; in 1880, seventeen thousand three hundred and fourteen; and in 1890, eighteen thousand nine hundred and forty-seven, made up of three thousand five hundred and forty-two whites and fifteen thousand four hundred and five negroes.

There were five settlements in the county, divided by recognized racial lines, in its early days. John A. Watkins of New Orleans, in his Recollections, speaks of them thus:

"(1) The northeast (Red Lick) was settled largely by the Ross, Chambliss, Cesney, Prince, Shelby and Jeffrey families. (2) The southeast, known as the Scotch settlement, where, within my recollection, Gallic was the common language, as you will readily infer from the names, was settled by the McCutchens, Camerons, McIntyres, Montgomerys, Mc-Phersons, Currys, Torrys, etc. (3) In the southwest, the Maryland settlement, with Church Hill as a common center, we find Wood, Baker, Green, Skinner, Young, Shields and many others. (4) The northwest or Rodney district, was the home of McGill, Hubbard, Hopkins, Mackey, Turnbull, Rabb, Bradshaw, Sisson, Potter, Johnson and Caleb Potter, the last three of whom were Revolutionary soldiers, for whom I drew pensions. They were in the battle of Monmouth, and when Lafayette visited Natchez in 1825, we dressed up the old fellows and sent them down. The General embraced and kissed them, and they all cried like school-boys. (5) The Cane Ridge settlement was the central district, and was bounded on the north by Claiborne county. Here settled Willis McDonald, a soldier of the Revolution, who served under Marion; Ledbetter, Watkins, Divine, Watson, Davis, Brent, Heckler, Goodrum, Bullen, Farley, Hynum, Shaw, Bolls, Gibson, Harrison and many others.

" At Union Town, Shackleford established an extensive tannery, and had branches at the old Cable place and at Mrs. Wallace's. Ellis had a public gin, as few at that day were able to run one for private use. Farley made all the hats. We killed coons and took the skins to him, and in return got a hat. Jake Warner made shoes at Union Town, Pintard was cabinet-maker, McMurchy made wagons, plows, etc., and old Getzendmar made bull-whips. Weaving was extensively carried on, but it was done by hand. Greenleaf, about 1797, established a cotton-gin factory, and that, the first gin ever used in Mississippi, was made by a negro."

The points of settlement in other words were: First, Church Hill, in the southwestern part of the county; second, Selsertown, in the southern part of the county; third, Rodney, in the western part of the county; fourth, Greenville, six miles west of Fayette, now extinct.

Greenville was laid off and established as the county seat in 1805. It was named in honor of Gen. Nathaniel Greene, of Revolutionary times. A courthouse, jail, pillory and gallows were erected, and continued in active use until 1825, when the county seat of justice was changed to Fayette.

The military organization of 1813–15, known as the dragoons, formed of companies from Jefferson, Amite, Adams and Wilkinson, and commanded by General Hinds, is worthy of special notice. It was to this command that Jackson made the short speech that has gone into history. After making a charge on a British division that was suspected to be advancing under cover of the chaparral to attack Jackson's left flank, they returned in triumph, and were met by the General, who said: "You have this day been the astonishment of one army, the admiration of the other." The company from Jefferson was reorganized as the Jefferson troop. The head of a well-known family in Mississippi was the only deserter."

A monument to Adam Rum was authorized by an act of the legislature, approved July 25, 1843. Adam Rum, a Revolutionary soldier, who participated in the battles of Brandywine, Trenton and Princeton, was a citizen of this county, and at his death left no known living relatives. His property, therefore, reverted to the state, and in his honor a marble shaft was erected in the courthouse square, surrounded by an ornamental iron fence. The monument bears this inscription: "Adam Rum was born at Frankinland, Germany, September 11, 1756, died in this county, December 1, 1822." It was erected in 1846.

Aaron Burr was arrested in this county in 1807 by a detachment of cavalry sent out by Governor Mead, at the mouth of Coles creek. His capitulation took place in the house of Thomas Calvit. He was sent next day to Washington, at that time the capital of the state, to undergo examination before the United States court, the chief justice, Judge Rodney, presiding. George Poindexter was United States attorney. Burr escaped at night, but was again captured at Mobile.

The graves of the family of Blennerhasset are pointed out near Port Gibson, on the farm of Mr. John Butler.

The notorious robber, Mason, the terror of the Southwest, and for whose head a large reward was offered, both by the governor and the people, was captured and beheaded by two treacherous members of his band. His head was taken to Washington, then the state capital, where it was recognized by many persons. His captors were also recognized as members of his band. They were arrested, taken to Greenville, in this county, tried, convicted and hanged in what is still known as the Gallows field, near the site of old Greenville. The field is now owned by Lud Churchwell. The names of the men hung were Sutton and May.

George Poindexter began his career as a lawyer in this county in 1803, was military aid to Governor Mead, representative in congress, governor of the state and United States senator. He was a man of superior ability as a lawyer and great power as a statesman. Judge Edward Turner was a member of the legislature from this county in territorial days. He married Cato West's eldest daughter, was elected attorney-general of the state, state senator, and chancellor of state under the old superior chancery court system. Andrew Jackson for a short time resided in this county, and in 1808 was married at the residence of Thomas M. Green, near Church hill, his wife having followed him to this country, then under Spanish control. Jackson had lived here twelve months, thus becoming a Spanish citizen.

Jefferson Davis in early life was a citizen of this county, and at the age of ten years received his first lessons in the elementary branches at a subscription school at old Greenville, taught by S. S. Prentiss, from the state of Maine. Davis, at that time, lived with his brother, Col. Joseph E. Davis, an attorney, at old Greenville.

The name Pickering was changed to Jefferson in December, 1801, and prior to April, 1802, Governor Claiborne appointed Cato West, Thomas Calvit, Jacob Stampley and Henry Green, justices; John Girault, clerk of county court; Daniel James, clerk of district court and Felix Hughes, master in chancery.

The sheriffs of Jefferson county in order of time are named as follows: John Brooks, Daniel Beasley, David Kerr, P. B. Harrison, Charles H. Jordon, Richard Harrison, P. O. Hughes, George Torrey, Samuel Laughman, W. B. Johnson, J. D. S. Davenport, R. F. McGinty, D. McCormick, O. S. Miles, W. E. Long, M. Howard, J. B. McCormick, F. A. Cameron, L. W. Caradine, the present incumbent. J. Remsen Holmes was appointed in 1822 by Governor Leake as the first judge of probate. He was succeeded by Phillip Dixon, Col. John L. Irwin, Hon. John M. Whitney, Robert Duncan, J. M. Ellis and G. W. Shackleford. The latter was the last probate judge, the law being then changed and a chancery court established. The chancellors are named as follows: J. B. Deason, Hiram Cassidy, T. Y. Berry, H. S. Van Eaton, Loch McLaurin and Claude Pintard, the present incumbent. A board of police was created in 1832 with Pierce Noland as its first president.

The newspapers of the county, since 1830, are the Rodney *Gazette,* a Whig paper issued in 1830; the Fayette *Watch Tower,* founded in 1839 by William B. Tebo; the Fayette *Times,* established in 1858 by J. H. King; the Jefferson *Journal,* in 1862 by A. Marschalk, Jr., and the Fayette *Chronicle,* in 1865 by W. A. Marschalk.

The first agricultural society of the county was formed in 1839 with Col. Joseph Dunbar president and Philip O. Hughes secretary.

The postoffices of Jefferson county are Cannonsburg, population thirty-one; Church hill, population twenty-seven; Fayette, population four hundred and seventy-five; Gum ridge, population twenty-nine; Harriston, Jessamine, Lee, McBride, McNair, Perth, population thirty-three; Red lick, population thirty-seven; Rodney, population seven hundred and seventy-six; Stampley, Stonington and Union church, population one hundred and twenty-six.

Claiborne county was established January 27, 1802, within the following-named boundaries, the territory being formerly a part of Jefferson or Pickering county: "Beginning on the river Mississippi at the mouth of Petty Gulph creek; thence running up the main branch of said creek four miles, or to its source, should that not exceed four miles; thence by a line drawn due east to the eastern territorial line, and all that tract of country north of the above mentioned creek, an east line south of the northern boundary of said territory, and east of the Mississippi." The name was given in honor of the governor of the territory. The total area of Claiborne is four hundred and fifty-two square miles, of which about thirty-five per cent. or one hundred and fifteen thousand acres may be called cleared land. The forks of the Bayou Pierre, their feeders and the main river, with the Big Black running along the northern boundary, render it one of the best watered counties in the state.

The population in 1812 was thirteen hundred and two, made up of fifteen hundred and fifty-two whites and fifteen hundred and fifty negroes. At that time there were ninety-eight looms, two spinning mills, sixty spindles and two tanneries representing manufacturing industry. Twenty-eight thousand three hundred and ninety-five yards of cotton cloth, one hundred and fifty yards of linen cloth and five hundred and eighty yards of woolen cloth were produced. The population in 1820 was fifty-nine hundred and sixty-three; in 1830, ninety-seven hundred and eighty-seven; in 1840, thirteen thousand and seventy-eight; in 1850, fourteen thousand nine hundred and forty-one; in 1860, fifteen thousand six hundred and seventy-nine, including eleven thousand nine hundred and sixty-four slaves and six hundred and twenty-two polls; in 1870, thirteen thousand three hundred and eighty-six; in 1880, sixteen thousand seven hundred and sixty-eight, and in 1890, fourteen thousand five hundred and sixteen, made up of three thousand four hundred and nineteen whites and eleven thousand and ninety-seven negroes.

The relation of the aborigines to this division of the state and that of the French and Spanish settlers is shown in the general history.

Sixty years ago a Mr. Parks, father of Perry and John, found near an Indian mound, where his negroes were plowing, a huge image of a bullfrog, which was cut from white limestone, and was a fine piece of sculpture, being an exact representation of a frog. It was about twelve inches from head to foot and stood about eight inches high. He at first thought it was an idol or something of that kind, but washing the dirt from it, he discovered that it was a pipe, the bowl and stem being from the top and rear, and was large enough to hold two ounces of finecut tobacco. It was taken to his house and was used as a weight to hold open the house door, which duty it has performed for over fifty years. Mr. Daniel Smith, of Port Gibson, Miss., has this ancient relic on exhibition.

It may be well to mention that the first white settlements in Claiborne county were made earlier than is generally thought. At the time of the Indian uprising against the French colony at Natchez, in 1729, there were one to two plantations on Bayou Pierre. These plantations, we must understand, do not compare with what is now termed plantations, but were merely huts in the wilderness, inhabited by the Catholic missionaries, or by adventurous hunters.

About the year 1771 Gov. Philip Barbour, of Virginia, obtained a grant of five thousand acres near Grand gulf, but it does not appear that he tried to settle any colony thereon.

Another grant of twenty thousand acres on Bayou Pierre and Big Black, extending within a short distance of where Port Gibson now stands, was granted in 1775 to Capt. Thaddeus Lyman, of Connecticut.

So far as can be discovered, the only other British grants in Claiborne county were the following: Joseph Simmons, five hundred and fifty acres, January 8, 1777; Thomas James, five hundred acres, August 15, 1777; William Vousden, two hundred acres, September 15, 1777; John Hortler, two hundred acres, May 25, 1779; William Vousden, five hundred acres, March 19, 1779.

Following is a list of the first English-speaking settlers in Claiborne county, and the grants their land was given from: P. B. Bruin, Spanish, French and Georgia; Abs. Green, Spanish; Robert Cochran, Spanish; Waterman Crone, Spanish; Samuel Cobun, Spanish; Samuel Gibson, Spanish; Tobias Broshears, Spanish; Daniel Burnet, Spanish; S. Holliday, Georgia; Robert Moore, Spanish; John McCaleb, French; Elias Barnes, Georgia; Anthony Gloss, Georgia; William Neely, Spanish; Joseph White, Georgia; James McCaleb, French; James Nailor, French; John Anderton, Georgia; Thomas White, Georgia.

A list of the six first mills recorded in Claiborne county, Miss., after its occupation by the United states, is as follows: Thomas White, February 21, 1803; George Evans, March 18, 1803; Joseph Box, June 7, 1803; Tobias Gibson, August 2, 1803; John Ross, August 18, 1803; Thomas Vanse, September 7, 1864.

The first marriages recorded after occupation are copied from the book of marriage certificates: William Jenkins and Polly Murphee, granted May 10, 1817, also James McKee and Mary McKee, granted August 15, 1816.

Early in 1802, the governor appointed the first officials for the new county of Claiborne as follows: Justices of the peace, William Downs, Daniel Burnet, James Harmon, G. W. Humphreys, Ebenezer Smith and James Stansfield; sheriff, Samuel Cobun; clerk of the county court, Matthew Conway Tierney; coroner, Samuel Gibson; militia officers, Daniel Burnet, lieutenant-colonel, and William Neely, major. On July 19, 1802, the foregoing justices organized and presided over a county court, the first court of any kind ever held in Claiborne. It is not known exactly were it was held, as no location had yet been chosen for the county seat, and the future town of Port Gibson was merely a river landing in the forest where a private ferry was kept, and with perhaps a store near the landing, that of Robert and George Cochran. (Mr. Gibson's residence was then in the upper part of the present town, about three-quarters of a mile from the bayou).

Five attorneys were admitted to practice at this first session of the county court; Drury W. Brazeale, Stephen Bullock, Edwin L. Harris, Theodore Stark, and T. E. Trask. During the session of court William Smith presented a deed containing three hundred acres of land, the first record of deed ever made in the county.

The first panel of jurors of the county were as follows, to wit: William Smith, William Lindsey, Waterman Crone, Francis Nailor, Simeon Holliday, Abram Wilkinson, Thomas White, Andrew Mundall, Richard Singleton, George W. Humphreys, William Neely, Tobias Broshears, Joseph White, John Anderton, Theodore Fortner. After the jurors received their certificates for two days' attendance, the court adjourned to meet at nine o'clock A. M., July 20, 1802.

The present courthouse was erected of brick and stone in 1839, by William H. Faulkner and George Stockdill, at a cost of $26,000, the above named gentlemen being the contractors and builders of the same.

The newspaper history of Claiborne begins in October, 1818, when the *Correspondent* was started by a Mr. W. A. A. Chisholm. The Port Gibson *Herald* was published September 1, 1842, by William F. Eisely. The first issue of the *Herald* proclaims the announcement of Hon. Henry Clay, of Kentucky, for president of the United States on the whig ticket. E. Junius Forbes, the editor and proprietor of the *Herald*, issued his valedictory June 8, 1843, and he was succeeded by W. H. Jacobs, who continued as editor and proprietor until June 6, 1851, when he was succeeded by E. Bruner, who continued the *Herald* until J. S. Mason assumed charge, and changed the title to the Port Gibson *Reveille* in 1850. This was finally named the *Southern Reveille*, on September 5, 1857, and has continued under that pseudonym down to the present time. J. S. Mason also started the first daily newspaper in Port Gibson. It was printed in Claiborne county, and was named the *Daily Southern Reveille*. It was inaugurated September 11, 1858. The date of its expiration is not obtainable, but it was possibly discontinued about 1861, at the opening of the Civil war.

The *Southern Reveille* is ably edited by Allen & Wharton. Their paper is well patronized, and the leading local topics and current news and literature of the day are well and ably treated.

Wilkinson county, named in honor of Gen. James Wilkinson, occupies the southwestern corner of the state, bounded on the west by the Mississippi, on the north by the Homochitto, on the east by parallel of longitude 14 degrees, and on the south by parallel of latitude 31 degrees, being the north line of Southeastern Louisiana. The area is five hundred and ninety-two square miles, divided into three physical districts. That district west of the east line of range two west is remarkably fertile; that forming the northeast quarter is generally poor in soil, and that forming the southeast quarter, somewhat similar to the Bayou Sara country. The population in 1812 was five thousand and sixty-eight, made up of two thousand four hundred and thirty-two whites, two thousand six hundred and thirty slaves, and six other colored inhabitants. There were one hundred and fifty-seven looms, one cardingmill, seven spinningmills, two hundred and sixteen spindles and two tanneries reported by the census enumerators. Forty-four thousand, eight hundred and sixty yards of cotton cloth were produced, with three hundred yards of linen cloth and five hundred yards of woolen cloth. The population in 1820 was nine thousand seven hundred and eighteen; in 1830, eleven thousand six hundred and eighty-six; in 1840, fourteen thousand one hundred and ninety-three; in 1850, sixteen thousand nine hundred and fourteen; in 1860, fifteen thousand nine hundred and thirty-three (slaves, thirteen thousand four hundred and fifty-six, and polls, six hundred and seventy-nine); in 1870, twelve thousand seven hundred and five; in 1880, seventeen thousand eight hundred and fifteen; in 1890, seventeen thousand five hundred and ninety-two, or three thousand eight hundred and sixty-four whites and thirteen thousand seven hundred and twenty-eight negroes.

There is near Woodville a large stone quarry of sandstone, opened up first by Judge McGehee, in 1832, when the courthouse was built, when stone could be got to supply a nation. Mastodons' skeletons are and have been found in this county in the vicinity of Pinckneyville. Major Van Eater has a fine collection of the bones, etc. Davion's Rock or Roche a Davion was the name given to Fort Adams in honor of Pere Davion, who established a mission there prior to 1716 and labored to convert the Tunicas. The ancient history of this division of the state is given in the first chapters, but subjects of interest not mentioned therein are related here.

The act of the general assembly, approved January 30, 1802, divided the county of Adams by the Homochitto river from its mouth up to Richard's Ferry; thence eastward by an imaginary line to Pearl river. That portion of the territory south of this line was called Wilkinson county.

On February 24, 1809, by an act of legislation, Wilkinson county was divided, forming Amite county on the east, but the present boundary line between Wilkinson and Amite counties was not established until June 29, 1822.

The first meeting of the county court was held at Fort Adams, but a little later the place of meeting was moved to Pinckneyville. Some years after, the seat of justice was located at Woodville, the present place, where they have a fine brick courthouse.

The first English-speaking settlers were Richard and Samuel Swayze, who entered land in 1772, and brought their families in 1773, from New Jersey; Landon Davis, with several more, settled about 1788, in what is now Wilkinson county; Hugh Davis was among the first; Joseph Dunham, Reuben Dunham, John Wall, Samuel Stockett, Gerard Brandon, settled about 1790; John Foster, William West, William Noland, Adam Lonehart, William Henderson, Daniel Clark, Isaac Johnson, Capt. Peter Smith, all about the same years, between 1788 and 1794; Col. Reuben Kemper, with his two brothers, Samuel and Nathan, who were alleged to be kidnaped, September 3, 1804 (see Monett's History of the Mississippi Valley, pages 362 and 454, Vol. II, Book V); Jacob Jones, William Ogden, John Ogden, Thomas Foster, Ruffin De Loach and John W. De Loach. The greater number of these entered land in the vicinity of Pinckneyville and Fort Adams, then known as Loftus Hights, and previously as Roche a Davion. Capt. Moses Hooke, a native of Maine and an officer in Wilkinson's army, entered land soon after coming to the fort. Col. Henry Hunter, Maj. Richard Butler, Capt. Robert Semple, Dr. John F. Carmichael, surgeon in Wilkinson's army, the others, officers, all settled in that vicinity. Nathaniel Evans, quartermaster; Col. J. F. Hamtramck, Captain Guion, all entered land before 1800.

In the state convention of 1817 the county was represented by George Poindexter, Daniel Williams, Abram M. Scott, John Joor, Gerard C. Brandon and Joseph Johnson, all of whom must be enumerated among the American pioneers of the county. Edward McGehee, W. A. Richardson, M. Liddell, William Hailey or Haile and Patrick Foley, may also be named. When the British army and navy threatened New Orleans, the pioneers and their sons rushed to arms. The late Jefferson Davis, writing to G. L. McGehee, September 16, 1888, said: "When news came of the approach of the British army to attack New Orleans, the sons of Wilkinson went in such numbers to defend the city, that the county held a draft to keep a certain proportion of the men at home for police purposes."

Pinckneyville academy, located at Pinckneyville, incorporated in 1815, and a school generally known, flourished only a few years.

Wilkinson academy, located near Woodville, and near the site of the old cotton factory, was one of the most prominent schools in the county. Here is where Jefferson Davis received his early education, and where many of the early settlers attended school.

The Wilkinson female academy, incorporated 1819, was a school conducted in a log house for many years by the Misses Ann Theodosia and Amanda Calder as teachers, in Woodville, and where the building remained until within the last few years.

Sligo academy, on the Sligo road, incorporated 1821.

The Marion academy, incorporated 1830.

Woodville classical school for boys, 1839, with a Mr. Chapman as teacher.

Woodville female academy, incorporated 1840 by the Methodist Episcopal church, was burned 1849. This school was one of the best in the county. William H. Halsey and his wife, Mary Chapman, were the teachers. They had upward of one hundred and seventy pupils and a full corps of teachers. Mr. and Mrs. Halsey were very highly educated in the North, and thoroughly accomplished. The school was founded by Judge Edward McGehee and Mr. and Mrs. Colonel Lewis.

The Brandon academy, founded in 1835 in honor of Gov. Brandon, flourished for a number of years. The building is yet standing, though in a dilapidated condition, at the intersection of the Fort Adams, Woodville and Pinckneyville roads.

The Donegal school or academy was founded 1845, at a cost of $10,500; two-story brick. Maj. P. F. Karney and H. D. Holland, trustees, and James W. Murry and daughter first teachers, etc.

The McGehee college for girls, formerly known as the Woodville female seminary, chartered May, 1861, while John J. Pettus was governor of the state by an act of the board of trustees, was changed to the McGehee college for girls. The present building was purchased by Judge McGehee, in 1862. A portion of the term during the war it was used as a hospital, but was reopened in 1864, and within the last few years the school has been put in a prosperous condition, with Rev. H. Walter Featherston as principal.

The first English-speaking printer in the old Natchez district was James Ferrall, who was appointed printer to the territorial legislature in January or February, 1802. Twenty-one years later the first newspaper in Wilkinson county was founded. The Woodville *Republican*, Vol. I, No. 1, was issued Saturday, December 2, 1823, with W. A. A. Chisholm, editor and proprietor. He was the founder of the *Correspondent* of Port Gibson in 1818. Mr. Chisholm was succeeded by Sam T. King, December 20, 1825, who continued publication until January 1, 1827, when W. A. A. Chisholm joined him. About 1828-9 King retired and was succeeded by G. D. Boyd, who continued a member of the firm, name of Chisholm & Boyd, until volume VI was completed, when Boyd retired, Voss taking his place. Chisholm & Voss published the paper until almost the close of volume VII, when Voss retired and Chisholm continued the paper alone until July 24, 1830, when G. D. Boyd became editor, and W. A. A. Chisholm, publisher. At the close of volume VII, Mr. Boyd again retired, and Chisholm conducted the paper until July 5, 1834, when Alfred Bynum was engaged as editor and served until the close of 1834, when Chisholm resumed sole control. On January 2, 1836, William Norris & Co. took charge of the paper and published it until January, 1844 (Vol. XXI), when it passed into the hands of Soule & Leatherman. In January, 1848, Mr. Soule retired, and the paper was published by J. H. Leatherman & Co., L. K. Barber forming the company. In January, 1849, Leatherman took full charge and published the paper until January, 1853, when Owen S. Kelley became publisher, and Maj. H. S. Van Eaton, editor. In 1855 Kelley was succeeded by W. C. Bonney, who published the paper until 1857, with Van Eaton. In 1857 Van Eaton was succeeded by a Major Kelley, who remained editor until 1859, when H. J. Hearsey, who is now the editor of the *Sunday States*, became editor. In 1861 the paper was discontinued. In 1865 S. McNeely and W. J. Keller purchased the paper. In 1869 W. H. Noble & Co. became the owners, and Noble edited it until 1874, when the Woodville *Sentinel*, owned by Col. J. H. Jones and J. W. Bryant, was merged into the *Republican*. Noble retiring, Jones became editor and Bryant publisher. Colonel Jones was succeeded in 1877 by J. W. Shattuck, with H. F. Simrall as his associate editor. In 1879 J. S. Lewis, the present owner, leased Noble's two-thirds interest, became the editor, purchased said interest in 1880, and in 1883 purchased Bryant's share. Bonney then became the publisher and Lewis editor and sole proprietor until the establishment of the Woodville *Courier*, since which time Mr. Lewis has had full charge, ably assisted by his son, Robert Lewis. The *Republican* has always been published as a democratic paper, except while owned by Norris & Co. in 1844, when it supported Henry Clay, and again, under the management of Noble & Co., as a republican paper. The paper has always been published here under the present name, and is one of the oldest papers in the state, being now in its sixty-sixth year.

The Wilkinson *Whig* was established about 1848 or 1849. The Woodville *Sentinel* was established by a company organized in 1871. J. H. Jones was editor, J. W. Bryant, publisher, and they continued in those positions until the *Sentinel* was merged into the *Republican* in 1874. The Centerville *Nickel*, published at Centerville, Miss., was founded in February, 1887, with J. T. Ramsey editor and H. H. Bonney, publisher. It was discontinued about eight months later. The Woodville *Courier*, Vol. I, No. 1, was issued March 30, 1888, with H. H. Bonney editor and proprietor. Fort Adams *Times* of Fort Adams was established in about 1854, soon after changed to Fort Adams *Items* and survived but a few years.

Wilkinson county boasts justly of having one of the first railroads in the United States. It was incorporated in Louisiana in 1830, and in Mississippi in 1831, with Judge Edward McGehee one of its most prominent movers and builders. It was a standard gauge road from the start. This railroad had a bank in operation in connection with it at Woodville. Also one of the first cotton factories in the state was founded by the judge, and owned and operated by him during the last years of its existence. It was burned in 1863 by the army.

The postoffices of the county are: Ashwood station, population twenty-eight; Centreville, population five hundred; Darrington, Doloroso, Fort Adams, population two hundred and forty; Pinckneyville, Primmton, Tarbert, Whitaker, Wilkinson and Woodville, population one thousand. In the chapter on the towns and cities of the state, the history of Woodville and Fort Adams is told.

Amite county, between the parallels of longitude thirteen and fourteen degrees west, and extending north from the parallel of latitude thirty-one degrees, twenty-four miles, embraces seven hundred square miles, or a total area of four hundred and sixty-two thousand eighty acres of land and water. The population in 1812 was four thousand seven hundred and fifty, made up of three thousand three hundred and twelve whites, one thousand four hundred and twenty-two slaves and sixteen others. The population by decades since 1820 is given as follows: 1820, six thousand eight hundred and fifty-three; 1830, seven thousand nine hundred and thirty-four; 1840, nine thousand five hundred and eleven; 1850, nine thousand six hundred and ninety-four; 1860, twelve thousand three hundred and thirty-six; 1870, ten thousand nine hundred and seventy-three; 1880, fourteen thousand and four, and 1890, eighteen thousand one hundred and ninety-eight, or seven thousand five hundred and nine whites and ten thousand six hundred and eighty-nine negroes. The taxable slaves, under sixty years of age, enumerated in 1860, numbered seven thousand four hundred and sixty-nine and the polls seven hundred and twenty-two. This county may be credited as the fountain-head of the Amite river, and at least five feeders of the Homochitto, as well as with feeders of other streams, such as Beaver creek, the Tickfaw and Tangipahoa. The name was given by M. d' Iberville, as a memorial of the reception given to his party by the natives in 1698. Of the total area, fourteen acres in every hundred are cultivated, but a much larger acreage, almost thirty-five per cent., is open to the husbandman, being ten per cent. more than the cultivated area in 1850–60. The pine and hardwood forests of the county show all the trees common to Southern Mississippi; fruit trees and berry bushes reach perfection, while cotton, jute, corn, rice, sorghum, sugarcane, oats, peas, sweet and Irish potatoes, pumpkins and melons yield abundantly. The meadow lands are productive, and the water power almost exhaustless. Hill and valley, with patches of prairie or level land, render Amite a territory where the immigrant from the Scheldt or the man from Maine or Vermont may select the hill or marsh or ridge or valley.

The boundary troubles of 1805–6, though quieted in the latter year, taught the people the value of organization, and for three years the question of establishing a county was discussed. The county was organized February 24, 1809, and on April 13, that year, the police jury met at the house of W. R. Richards and organized, with Micajah Davis, president. The first clerk and recorder was Thomas Batchelor, who opened the record books in 1810. In 1817 the following named were elected delegates to the convention for forming and adopting a constitution: Thomas Batchelor, Henry Hanna, John Burton, Thomas Torrence, Angus Wilkinson and Dr. William Lattimore, the latter the delegate representing the territory in congress since 1809.

Among the early English-speaking settlers were Elijah, David and James Lee, Richard Montgomery, Micajah and Charles Davis, Robert McKnight, John Bate and the persons named above. Matthew Toole, Ludwick Hall, the editor of the *Republican* in 1812, William Gardner, Zachariah Lea, Richard Hurst, John Lowry, Francis Graves; the Smileys, William Jackson and S. Weathersby were also early settlers, as well as aggressive politicians.

The town of Liberty, within seven thousand eight hundred feet of the geographical center, on Robert Montgomery's plantation, was selected as the seat of justice in 1809 and has held it down to the present time. This town was incorporated in 1828, was damaged in 1863 by the Federal troops, the college buildings destroyed and many houses burned, but it was rebuilt soon after the restoration of peace, and is now a pleasant, prosperous village. The Liberty *Advocate* was published here for about forty years by J. W. Forsyth before the *Southern Herald* was conceived. In 1871 Liberty led the towns of the State in remembering the two hundred and eighty-two soldiers who went forth a decade before to fight for their homes and died in the Confederate service. In that year a pile of Italian marble was raised. The population is placed at four hundred and twenty-six.

Gloster, a new town, was founded in 1883, in township three north, range two east of Helena meridian, about eight miles north of Centerville. It is credited with five hundred inhabitants. The postoffice villages of the county are Ariel, six miles east of Centerville, Bates' Mill, Dayton, Dickey, Echo, Gillsburg, Leaton, Merwin, Nunnery, Olio, O'Neals, Smithdale, Spurlock, Thompson and Zion Hill.

The Louisville, New Orleans & Texas railroad runs along the west line of the county, while the Illinois Central railroad runs parallel to the east line, but from five to six miles east thereof. Osyka, east of Gillsburg, on the Illinois Central railroad, 88.16 miles northwest of New Orleans, is the shipping point for the southeast quarter of the county, Summit for the northwest quarter, and Dayton, Gloster and Centerville, the shipping points for the west half.

Franklin county, erected December 21, 1809, and named after Benjamin Franklin, lies in the edge of the long-leaf pine belt, and comprises a territory of about thirty-seven miles in extent from east to west, and about eighteen miles from north to south, its total area being five hundred and fifty-six square miles. It is drained by the Homochitto river and its tributaries— Middle fork, Morgan's fork, and Wallace, Beaver and McCall's creeks. The direction of the course of the Homochitto river is from northeast to southwest. Its bottom lands are very fertile, but subject to overflow, although some portions are undulating and other portions broken and hilly. Long-leaf pine, oak of every kind, hickory, walnut, poplar, magnolia, cypress, etc., abound, and the products of the bottom lands, which are very cheap and inviting to immigration, are cotton, corn, oats, sugarcane, sorghum, fieldpeas, sweet and Irish potatoes, etc. Peaches, apples, pears, figs and other fruits do well, but are raised for home consumption only, and the same may be said of culinary vegetables. Pasturage is extensive, and the native grasses in summer, and switchcane in winter keep stock in good condition. Fine beds of marl exist on the banks of the chief river, and all that is needed to develop this region are capital and industry.

In 1812 the population comprised one thousand two hundred and sixty whites, seven hundred and thirty-five slaves, and thirteen others, making a total of two thousand and sixteen; in 1820 the total was three thousand eight hundred and twenty-one; in 1830, four thousand six hundred and twenty-two; in 1840, four thousand seven hundred and seventy-five; in 1850, five thousand nine hundred and four; in 1860 there were five hundred and eighty-two polls, with a total population of eight thousand two hundred and sixty-five, of which number four thousand six hundred and ninety-nine were slaves under sixty years of age; in 1870 the total was seven thousand four hundred and ninety-eight; in 1880, nine thousand seven hundred and twenty-nine, and in 1890, ten thousand four hundred and twenty-four, comprising five thousand four hundred and fifty-four whites, four thousand nine hundred and sixty-four colored, and six others. In 1812 the county contained sixty-eight looms, and manufactured sixteen thousand six hundred and fifty yards of cotton cloth.

In the western part of the county the Louisville, New Orleans & Texas railroad passes through from north to south, and on this line of road, near the northern boundary of the county, is located the old town of Hamburg. South of Hamburg, on the same road, are Roxie, which sprang into existence in 1885, and White Apple; Knoxville, for many years a post-office, and Garden city, of recent origin, but a great lumber and manufacturing town. The first seat of justice for the county was Franklin, situated about two and a half miles west of the present county seat, Meadville, which is as near the center of the county as may be, and was made the seat of justice about seventy years ago.

Of Masonic lodges there are two in the county, viz.: Benjamin Franklin lodge No. 11, at Meadville, and Solomon B. Stampley lodge, which latter was chartered in 1857, and held its meetings at Mount Carmel church, near Hamburg, until 1887, with Jacob Stampley as its first worshipful master. At present it holds its sessions at Roxie, and has a membership of thirty-nine.

The first newspaper published in the county was called the Franklin *Journal,* and was established July 30, 1866, by a Mr. Crawford, a deaf mute. After a life of five or six years, under the conduct of various parties, the name of this journal was changed to the Franklin *Banner,* under which appellation it survived about three years, when it expired with the death of its editor, a Mr. McGehee, son of Judge Thomas McGehee. In 1886 the Franklin *Herald* was established at Hamburg, but in 1890 the press was sold to Mr. P. C. Thompson, who conducted the *Southern Progress* at Knoxville until the latter part of 1890, when it was removed to Garden city, where it is still published, with C. F. Thompson as editor and P. C. Thompson as business manager.

Of the early church organizations in the county very little is known, although it may be surmised that the first was probably that of a Methodist society, who established what is now known as Bethesda church at Wright's campground. The Missionary Baptists established a society at Morgan's fork about 1807 and 1808, and now have additional organizations at Union, Philadelphia, Spring hill, Bethlehem, Roxie, Hamburg, New Hope, Hope hill and Mount Zion, and possibly others. The Baptists were followed by the Campbellite or Christian order, with a congregation at Knoxville. The Methodists have meetings at Beech grove, Hamburg, Singurey, Roxie, Oak grove, Meadville and Greenwood.

Franklin springs are situated about four miles north of Roxie, on the farm of T. R. Whitehead. Of these there are three large springs, surrounded by smaller ones, occupying about two acres of ground, and constituting the headquarters of Wells creek. The main spring is nearly eight feet in diameter, and is considered to be almost bottomless, as the water boils up with tremendous force, and is exceedingly clear, pure and cold, but is not thought to possess any medicinal properties, although people from abroad, who have drunk of it and bathed in it, claimed to have been benefited by its use.

About five miles south of Roxie is a bed of sandstone which forms good building material, and some years ago much of it was used for that purpose at Natchez. This stone also crops out at another point about two miles distant.

Unimproved lands in Franklin can be bought at $1 per acre, while the best improved farms can be had at $10 per acre. The soil in the uplands is of a reddish clayey nature.

Warren county extends east from the Mississippi, between the Big Black river, the southern and eastern boundary, and the Yazoo river, its northwestern boundary, to the west line of Yazoo county. Its estimated area is five hundred and ninety square miles, divided into bluff, level land and hill. Of the total area fifty per cent. is open land and much of it cultivated. All the trees, shrubs, flowers and grasses common to southern Mississippi flourish here, while the staple crops reach perfection.

The population in 1812 was eleven hundred and fourteen, made up of six hundred and fifty-eight whites, four hundred and thirty-seven slaves and nineteen colored freemen and Indians. The maufacturing industry was confined to thirty-three looms, which produced eight thousand and sixty yards of cotton cloth. The population in 1820 was twenty-six hundred and ninety-three; in 1830, seven thousand eight hundred and sixty-one; in 1840, fifteen thousand seven hundred and twenty; in 1850, eighteen thousand one hundred and twenty; in 1860, twenty thousand six hundred and ninety-six, including thirteen thousand four hundred and twenty-one slaves and ten hundred and thirty-five polls; in 1870, twenty-six thousand seven hundred and sixty-nine; in 1880, thirty-one thousand two hundred and thirty-eight, and in 1890, thirty-three thousand one hundred and sixty-four, or eight thousand six hundred and forty-three whites and twenty-four thousand five hundred and sixteen negroes, with five other colored persons. The name was given in honor of Joseph Warren, a soldier of the Revolution, who was killed by the British at Bunker Hill in 1775. The history of Warren county belongs to the general history of the state, and like that of Adams, is treated in the first chapters of this work, where the settlements of 1729 and many of the leading planters, soldiers and Indians are named. When Fort Nogales, erected in 1781–3, was handed over to the American troops, March 23, 1798, and the name changed to Fort McHenry, only sixteen white men resided in its neighborhood, Honore P. Morancy, a San Domingoan, being the leading settler. The remains of old Fort St. Peter and the Catholic mission on the Yazoo were visible where the Payne plantation of latter days is located, and the only road in the county ran along the river front, from the Big Black to the Yazoo river. The shade of the massacre of 1729 was not yet dissipated, but the names of the courageous pioneers who fell before the Indian attack were forgotten.

The county was established December 22, 1809, with the seat of justice at Warrenton, where William L. Sharkey resided since 1803. The official work of Warren was carried on there until 1836, when the offices and records were removed to Vicksburg, whither Sharkey moved eleven years before. In 1820 the first public road was opened from Vicksburg to Clinton, and in 1824 extended to Jackson, and within the decade ending in 1830 the population almost trebled, and Vicksburg assumed village proportions.

John Henderson

During the last years of the eighteenth and the first years of the nineteenth centuries the settlement of Morancy saw gathering around it a number of other settlements. The Hylands, Griffins, Sharkeys, Steels, Downs, Rapaljes and Sellers settled on the front below Vicksburg. The Scotch settlement fronting on the Yazoo swamp, above Vicksburg, embraced the Fergusons, Camerons, Throckmortons, Turnbulls and Heads, with the Jones', Jenkins', Davis' and Heads of Welsh descent, and the Gervais', of French descent. In 1805 Burwell Vick, Foster Cook and Newitt Vick settled near Vicksburg in the "Open woods." Honore P. Morancy, Dr. Emilius Morancy, the Glass family and a few others were in the county before them; but the newcomers were sharp business men rather than pastoral or professional men, and soon forged ahead in wealth and influence, for pioneership, directed by the single eye to make everything contribute to it, saw the opportunity and took advantage of it.

The postoffices of Warren county are Bovina, population eighty-two; Brierfield, Brunswick, population one hundred; Butler, Diamond, Flower Hill, Glass, Haisseyville, Haynes Bluff, Katzenmeir, Nanachewhaw, Newbell, New Town landing, population fifty-nine; Oak Ridge, population forty-three; Palmyra, population sixty; Redwood, Russellville, Vicksburg, population thirteen thousand two hundred and ninety-eight; Warrenton and Yokena, population fifty-three.

CHAPTER IX.

COUNTIES OF THE FIRST CHOCTAW CESSION AND THE COAST ADDITION.

WAYNE county was established in the first decade of the present century (1802), and received its name in compliment to Gen. Anthony Wayne. Its seat of justice is Waynesboro. It is bounded north by Jasper and Clarke, east by Alabama, south by Greene and Perry, and west by Jones. There are in the county twenty-two thousand one hundred and ninety-eight acres of cleared land, assessed at $3.29 per acre and valued in the aggregate at $119,848.

The surface of Wayne is undulating. The principal streams are Chickasawha river and Buckatunna creek, and there are numerous smaller creeks. These fine streams, running all the year, afford good water power, and there are some good sawmills which do a good business. The soil varies from rich, black prairie land to poor, sandy piny-woods land, and produces cotton, corn, wheat, oats, rye, sweet and Irish potatoes, sorghum and grasses of various kinds. All the common vegetables grow, and fruits such as apples, peaches, pears, figs, strawberries, blackberries, dewberries, etc., bear good crops for home consumption. There is good woods pasturage for cattle and sheep. More attention is being given to sheep husbandry than to any other stock, it paying over fifty per cent. on investment, sixty per cent. of the land in the woods making a fine range for stock. Some of the farmers are pur-

12

chasing improved breeds. Nearly one-half of the land in this county belongs to the United States government, and can be purchased at $1.25 an acre. These lands are well timbered, and will produce good crops, and, by using fertilizers and improved methods, can be made to yield half a bale of cotton or twenty bushels of corn per acre.

Altogether Wayne county is one of the best of its class in the state. Its pineries are extensive. Waynesboro, its county seat, does a cash business of $1,000 per day, though the town is quite small. The county, besides furnishing vast quantities of naval stores, is also specially adapted to the business of sheep husbandry. Thousands of sheep are found on its hills, and yet there is room for more. Under the touch of intelligent cultivation, the soil can be made to yield magically, and there is no good reason why this fine belt should not become one of the favored regions of the earth.

The principal towns are Waynesboro, Buckatunna, Winchester and State Line. Other villages and postoffices are named Boyce, Denham, Edney, Eucutta, Frost Bridge, Henderson, Matherville, Progression, Tokio and Whistler.

The population of this county has grown thus: 1810, one thousand two hundred and fifty-three; 1820, three thousand three hundred and twenty-three; 1830, two thousand seven hundred and eighty-one; 1840, two thousand one hundred and twenty; 1850, two thousand eight hundred and ninety-two; 1860, three thousand six hundred and ninety-one; 1870, four thousand two hundred and six; 1880, eight thousand seven hundred and twenty-one; 1890, nine thousand eight hundred and seventeen. Of this population, there were one thousand six hundred and thirty-six colored inhabitants in 1870, three thousand seven hundred and seventy in 1880 and four thousand forty-one in 1890. The county contained two hundred and sixty-two slaves in 1810. In 1860 it had two hundred and fifty-eight voters and one thousand five hundred and thirteen taxable slaves.

Settlement began about 1806, and there were sixty-two looms, and sixteen thousand six hundred and eighty-five yards of cloth were made in Wayne county in 1812, which speaks well for the rapidity with which it advanced. James, William and Joseph Patton, William Webber, Zacharia Rogers, Capt. George and John Evans were the pioneers. The first mentioned, Gen. James Patton, was later lieutenant-governor of Mississippi. Two years later came the Slays and Sumralls. William and Alexander Poe came in 1811. Somewhat later came Gen. William A., Willis and Stephen Lang, John McRae (father of Governor McRae), John H. and Collins Horn, the latter the father of Ex-Secretary of State Horn, Gen. Thomas P. Falconer, James Mayers and members of the McCarty, McLaughlin, Edwards, Chapman, Hendricks, Collins, Watts, Gray, Toole, Gordon, Cole, Grayson, Crosby, McLendon, Kelly, Warren, Jones, Brown, Howes, Horn, Falconer, Lewis, Hutts, Barber, Strickland, Keasley, Cook, Arrington, Harmon, Parker, Ivey, Hailes, Odum, Clarke, Tibby, Shepherd, Cooley, Bush, King, Wimberly, Davis and Colquohoon families. General Falconer became a member of the state senate of Mississippi, and was a delegate to the constitutional convention of 1832. James Mayers was the father of Judge A. G. Mayers and of Capt. P. K. Mayers. He served successively as justice of the peace, clerk of the court, sheriff and probate judge. Clinch Gray and James Patton were members of the constitutional convention of 1817. The earlier settlers brought their effects to the county by means of packhorses and rolling hogsheads. Among early residents of this county who were chosen to important public offices were John H. Mallory, John A. Gimbrall, James Patton, Thomas A. Willis, John H. Rollins, James A. Horn, Thomas P. Falconer, Thomas S. Sterling, Philip H. Napier, James McDugald. John J. McRae, who filled consecutively the positions of representative in the legislature, speaker, representative in congress, governor, United States senator, and later member of the Confederate congress, was reared in this county. Powhatan Ellis, who went as minister to Mexico and served as circuit judge, claimed this as his home. John Watts, who presided as judge on this circuit, also on the Hinds county circuit, was a citizen of this county, and, like Judge Mounger, always opened his court with prayer. Gen. William S. Patton was born in Wayne county.

The early settlers had no fear of the Choctaws, but built a fort at Winchester as a protection against the Creeks, the most of which is yet visible. Of this, Gen. James Patton was placed in command. Marsh Crane and Mark Cole were sent to Alabama as scouts to watch the Creeks in 1813, and brought to Winchester intelligence of the massacre of Fort Mims, the dispatches being carried in Cole's hat.

Winchester, the former county seat, was on the most direct road from the Carolinas and Georgia to Natchez, and for many years a growing place. About 1822 the courthouse at Winchester was destroyed by fire. It was rebuilt, and is now standing. The old jail also yet stands at Winchester. It was built some time in the forties, with heavy hewn pine log walls, three feet thick, by John McDonald, at a cost to the county of not more than $400 or $500. The seat of justice was about twenty years ago removed to Waynesboro, and few reminders of Winchester remain.

Wayne county's first representative in the state senate was Howell W. Runnells; its present one is A. G. Ferguson. The first representative in the house of representatives was Josiah Watts; the present one is D. M. Taylor.

Greene county was established December 9, 1811; Leakeville, named in honor of Governor Leake, is the county seat. The county was named in compliment to Gen. Nathaniel Greene, and is bounded north by Wayne, east by Alabama, south by Jackson and west by Perry county. Greene county originally extended from the Alabama line to Pearl river and from Wayne county to the Spanish possessions, and the seat of justice was located at Leaf river, near the center of what is now township two, range eight west. The Chickasawha river passes through the county from north to south, the Leaf enters the western boundary and flows southeast to its junction with the Chickasawha, the two forming the Pascagoula. The swamps of these rivers are rich alluvial bottoms, covered with a dense growth of hard woods, in almost endless variety and of inestimable value commercially. Several large creeks, tributary to the rivers, flow through the county in different directions, affording an outlet for logs, while smaller streams of the purest water are found almost everywhere and constitute a system of the finest waterpower to be found in the South.

No thorough or systematic geological survey of this county has ever been made, but no doubts exist in the minds of intelligent residents that mineral deposits occur in paying quantities, and beds of the finest marl crop out on the surface, only awaiting intelligent and systematic development to yield grand returns. Many years ago specimens of plumbago were in existence so pure that pencils cut from them were found to be as good as the best manufactured article, but the place of deposit was known to only one or two persons and their knowledge perished with them.

The Mobile & Ohio railroad touches the northeast corner of the county. Transportation is principally by wagon to railroad. Almost every resident has some cattle and sheep, and sheep husbandry is rapidly growing in favor. At State Line spirits of turpentine is manufactured. The surface of the country is generally undulating, level on river and creek bottoms. The principal timber is longleaf or yellow pine, with hickory, oak, gum, poplar, holly and magnolia on river and creek bottoms. The soil along the rivers and creeks is fertile, and the pine uplands are capable of being made to produce good crops of corn, cotton, sugarcane, rice, peanuts and sweet potatoes. All vegetables and fruits do well, especially peaches and scuppernong grapes. Pasturage is extensive and of the best quality, there being nowhere in the world a finer range for cattle and sheep. The county contains two thousand nine hundred and seventy-five acres of cleared land.

The following statistics were published in 1885: United States lands for sale, two hundred and twelve thousand acres; delinquent lands for sale by the state auditor, twenty-six thousand six hundred and forty acres; acreage in cotton in 1879, thirty-five acres; bales produced in 1879, twelve by white labor; bushels of corn produced in 1879, twenty-seven thousand two hundred and seventy-one; bushels of oats produced in 1879, five thousand seven hundred and ninety-one.

Among the many early settlers of the county the following were prominent: John Mc-Rae, John McLeod, Laughlin McCoy, John Duntzler, John Stafford, Martin Moody, Archibald McKay, Maher Lyle, John Miller, Daniel McInnis, Neil McInnis, Peter McLeod, Daniel McLeod, Wheeler Gresham, Alexander McLean, William Ball, George Williamson, William Cochran, Burrell Cochran, Edward Williamson, Neeham Cowart, Malcom Black, John Roberts, James Walley, Alexander Fairly, Charles Eubanks, K. Cooley, Walter Denny, Peter McLeod and Isaac Futch. John McRae and Laughlin McCoy were members of the constitutional convention of 1817. Alexander McLean was first sheriff. The first who represented Greene county in the state senate was Isaac R. Nicholson; Hugh McDonald was one of its first representatives in the lower house. A. G. Ferguson is the present state senator, D. W. McLeod the present legislative representative.

The villages and postoffices of this county are Adamsville, Avera, Buck creek, Kittrell, Leaf, Leakesville, State Line and Vernal. There is a church in every neighborhood, Methodists, Baptists and Presbyterians predominating.

Greene county's population was one thousand four hundred and forty-five in 1820, one thousand eight hundred and fifty-four in 1830, one thousand six hundred and thirty-six in 1840, two thousand and eighteen in 1850, two thousand two hundred and thirty-two in 1860, two thousand and thirty-eight in 1870, three thousand one hundred and ninety-four in 1880, three thousand nine hundred and six in 1890. The colored inhabitants numbered three hundred and seventy two in 1870, seven hundred and eighty-five in 1880, and nine hundred and forty-five in 1890. The taxable slaves in this county in 1860 numbered six hundred and thirty-two, the voters, two hundred and eighteen.

Marion county was established December 9, 1811. Its seat of justice is at Columbia, on the Pearl river. This county was named in honor of Gen. Francis Marion, of South Carolina, the noted "Swamp Fox" of Revolutionary days. It is bounded north by Lawrence and Covington, east by Perry, south by Pearl river, and west by Pike and Alabama. It was first represented in the state senate by David Dickson, in the lower house by Francis Le Noir. Its present state senator is Theodore B. Ford, its representative, J. M. Foxworth. This county is watered by Pearl river, Holliday's creek, Little river, Lower Little river, Abolochitto river and Black creek, which afford good water facilities and furnish fine fish of different varieties. The surface of the county on the river and creek bottoms is level; the balance is generally undulating. The soil is generally light and sandy, not notably fertile, but susceptible of being easily improved and profitably tilled. There are many reed brakes, which, when drained, are fertile under cultivation. A large portion of the bottom lands is very rich and productive, yielding large crops of corn, cotton, oats, sweet and Irish potatoes, peas, rice, peanuts, sugar cane, etc. Pasturage is extensive, the wood pastures furnishing food for stock during the summer and switchcane on the creek and river bottoms during the winter.

Some attention has been paid to stockraising with resulting profit. The timber growth consists principally of longleaf and yellow pine, and lumbermen do an extensive business along the water courses in cutting logs and rafting them to the sawmills. The New Orleans & Northwestern railroad runs through the southeastern part of the county, in the limits of which there are about twenty-one miles of railway.

Among the pioneers here may be mentioned Ebenezer and John Ford, Benjamin Rawls, D. McLaughlin, S. Foxworth, H. H. Le Noir, F. McGee, William and Sol Lott, Frank B. Le Noir, the Stovealls, John H. Webb, J. McGee, the Popes, Benjamin Hammond, Abram Ard and M. Bracy.

In 1889 there were for sale in the county four hundred and twenty-five thousand eight hundred and forty acres of government lands; the acreage in cotton was four thousand seven hundred and seventeen acres; fifteen hundred and seventy-nine bales of cotton, ninety-one thousand nine hundred and forty-one bushels of corn, twelve thousand two hundred and two bushels of oats and four hundred and thirty-seven pounds of tobacco were produced.

The people are moral, law-abiding, kind and hospitable, and receive newcomers with kindness, even genuine Southern friendliness. Religious advantages are good, and the schools are as numerous and upon as high a plane as can be expected in a county of this character. Besides Columbia, the principal points in the county are Fordsville and Spring cottage, and Wilkesburg is just beyond the line, in Covington county. Other villages and postoffices are Advance, Buford, Carley, Dale, Dexter, Ophelia, Pickwick, Piotona, Purvis, Richburg, Talawah, Waterhole and Wildwood.

The population of Marion county has been as follows at each successive census since 1820: Thirty-one hundred and ten in 1820; thirty-six hundred and ninety-one in 1830; thirty-eight hundred and thirty in 1840; forty-four hundred and ten in 1850; forty-six hundred and eighty-six in 1860; forty-two hundred and eleven in 1870; sixty-nine hundred and one in 1880; ninety-five hundred and thirty-two in 1890. Of this population there were sixteen hundred and forty-nine colored inhabitants in 1870; twenty-four hundred and fifty-one in 1880, and three thousand and fifty-four in 1890. In 1860 Marion county's taxable slaves numbered two thousand and fifty-six, and the voters three hundred and seventy-five.

Hancock county was established December 14, 1812, and its county seat is Bay St. Louis. It was named in honor of John Hancock, one of the signers of the Declaration of Independence, and is bounded north by Pearl river, east by Harrison, south by the Gulf of Mexico and west by Louisiana. It contains thirty-eight thousand three hundred and thirty-two acres of cleared land, valued at about $3 per acre. The water courses are Jordan river and part of Wolf river. The Pearl river flows along the whole western boundary of the county, affording transportation for the large quantities of lumber sawed upon its banks. The land is mostly timbered with longleaf or yellow pine, and is level or gradually undulating. The soil is sandy, producing all kinds of vegetables, prominent among which are melons, sweet and Irish potatoes, peanuts and peas; and fruits, such as oranges, pears, strawberries, blackberries, dewberries, etc., grow abundantly and find a ready market in Mobile and New Orleans. Pasturage for cattle and sheep is unexcelled. The increase of cattle is ten hundred head per annum, and about seventy-five thousand pounds of wool are clipped. At Pearlington is one of the most extensive sawmills in the South. There are six sawmills in the county, and one large and profitable woolenmill at Ullmanville near Bay St. Louis. The railroads of the county are the Louisville & Nashville, from Mobile to New Orleans, which runs along the gulf coast through the whole southern portion of the county from northeast to southwest.

The following statistics of 1888 will be of interest, especially by way of comparison:

United States lands for sale, one hundred and fifty-one thousand six hundred and forty acres; delinquent lands by the state auditor for sale, thirteen hundred and twenty acres; bushels of corn produced in 1879, four hundred and ten; bushels of oats produced in 1879, fifty-three hundred.

This is a good county to live in, and many resort to the towns along the coast for sea-bathing in summer and health in winter. All kinds of gulf salt-water fish and oysters exist in great abundance; wild turkeys, deer, wild ducks, wild geese, etc., afford fine sport for hunters.

Francis B. Le Noir, Elisha Comer, Noel Jordan, P. R. Pray, Louis Sportons, F. Netto, A. Dimetry, D. Canney, Raymond D. Creavas, Dr. C. A. Calhoun, William Frierson, Colonel Dewese, R. and H. Carr, Colonel Stuart, David Moy, F. Conly, Jourdan Smith, Joseph and William Wheat, John Orr, Captain Bordman, Charles Litchfield and Dr. Edgar were among the early settlers.

The population of this county was one thousand five hundred and ninety-four in 1820; one thousand nine hundred and sixty-two in 1830; three thousand three hundred and sixty-seven in 1840; three thousand six hundred and seventy-two in 1850; three thousand one hundred and thirty-nine in 1860; four thousand two hundred and thirty-nine in 1870; six thousand four hundred and thirty-nine in 1880; eight thousand three hundred and thirteen in 1890. The colored population was one thousand one hundred and eighty-six in 1870, one thousand seven hundred and sixty-four in 1880 and two thousand five hundred and twenty-six in 1890. In 1860 there were one thousand and sixty-seven taxable slaves and four hundred and thirty-four voters in this county.

The first state senator representing this county was Isaac R. Nicholson; the first representative, Noel Jordan. The present senator is H. Bloomfield; the present representative, Daniel B. Seal.

Besides Bay St. Louis, the principal towns are Pearlington and Gainesville. Other villages and postoffices are Anner, Gulf View, Kiln, Lacey, Logtown, Nicholson, Richardson, Stockdale and Waveland.

Jackson county, named in honor of Andrew Jackson, was established December 14, 1812. Its county seat is Scranton. Its boundaries are as follows: North, Perry and Greene counties; east, Alabama; south, the Gulf of Mexico; west, Harrison county. The first to represent this county in the state senate was Isaac R. Nicholson. Mr. McManis was the first member of the lower house. The present state senator is H. Bloomfield; representative, J. M. Pelham.

The Gulf of Mexico washes the whole southern shore of the county. The water courses are the Pascagoula river and its many tributaries and the Escatawpa river. The surface of the county is generally level along the coast and the balance is gently undulating. The timber growth consists principally of long-leaf or yellow pine, which affords a very extensive business to the lumberman and has led to the establishment of many sawmills along the coast. The lumber trade is very large, the principal output being shipped to foreign ports. The plum, peach, pomegranate, apple, fig, pear, pecan, many varieties of grape, berries, melons, etc., yield profusely and are cultivated with profit. Special features here are wine manufacture and the pecan culture, introduced by Col. W. R. Stuart.

Several canneries are in operation in this county. The grazing is good and stockraising is important, there being in the county fine Jersey cattle and splendid flocks of Spanish merino sheep. Indeed it would seem that Jackson is especially adapted to sheep husbandry. At Moss Point a window-glass factory has been established. The Mobile & New Orleans railway runs along the gulf coast through the whole width of the county.

Some of the early business centers in this county were East Pascagoula, West Pascagoula and Ocean Springs. Among the early settlers were the Krebs, H., Rene and Jean B., John Cumbest, J. W. Williams, Joseph Raby, V. Delmas, M. Qoff, J. W. Terrell, W. C. Sheldon, Thomas Rhodes, Lyman Randall, the Havenses, A. Cathcat, D. Reeves, H. Ehless, G. Helveston, Walter Denny, A. C. Steed and J. Davis. In 1878 there were in the county one hundred and fifty-one thousand one hundred and sixty acres of United States lands for sale, and thirty-five hundred acres of delinquent lands held by the state auditor. In 1879 eighteen hundred and twenty-six bushels of corn were produced and eighty bushels of oats. There are in the county two thousand seven hundred and fifty acres of cleared land

Fish and oysters are obtained in great abundance, and of the finest quality. Redfish, blackfish, red snappers, pompano, Spanish mackerel, speckled trout, sheepshead, flounders, etc., are caught for market all along the gulf coast. The county is developing rapidly, and it is probable that not many years hence it will be improved for miles along the gulf, where the beach is fine, and opened to tourists and health seekers. Not the least interesting thing in connection with Jackson county is the legend of the death song of the Pascagoula Indians, two hundred years ago, when hard pressed by their foemen, and, seeing no means of escape, the small remnant of the tribe are said to have clasped hands and drowned themselves in the Pascagoula river. There are those who maintain that the scene of this tragedy is haunted by the weird death song of those who so died. Besides Scranton, the principal towns of Jackson county are Ocean Springs, West and East Pascagoula, Moss Point, Bradford and Americus. Other villages and postoffices are Crossroads, Daisy, Escatampa, Fort Bayou, Howell, Orange Grove, Three Rivers and Vancleave.

Jackson county had a population of sixteen hundred and eighty-two in 1820, seventeen hundred and ninety-two in 1830, nineteen hundred and sixty-five in 1840, thirty-one hundred and ninety-six in 1850, forty-one hundred and twenty-two in 1860, forty-three hundred and sixty-two in 1870, seventy-six hundred and seven in 1880, eleven thousand two hundred and fifty-one in 1890. The colored element aggregated eleven hundred and ninety-four in 1870, twenty-four hundred and eighty-two in 1880 and thirty-four hundred and forty in 1890. In 1860 the number of taxable slaves in this county was ten hundred and twenty-four, the voters numbering three hundred and ninety-one.

Lawrence county was established December 22, 1814, and was named in honor of Captain James Lawrence, of Chesapeake fame. Monticello, the county seat, so established March 1, 1815, is situated on the west bank of Pearl river, and was named in honor of the residence of President Jefferson. The county is bounded north by Copiah and Simpson, east by Covington and Marion, south by Marion and Pike, west by Lincoln. During the first five years of the county's history the courts were held at Wright Mitchell's house. The first courthouse was built on the site of the present one in 1818.

That part of the county lying on rivers and creeks is level; the balance is undulating and hilly. The upland soil is sandy and not very fertile, but is easily cultivated and improved; the soil in the bottoms is quite productive. There are in the county extensive reedbrakes, such as are common to all piny-woods counties, which when drained and brought into cultivation are very rich, producing from thirty to fifty bushels of corn per acre. The products are cotton, corn, oats, rice, sugarcane, sorghum, sweet and Irish potatoes, etc., and all the various kinds of fruits and vegetables common to this part of the country grow and yield abundantly. The pasturage is good and very extensive, and stockraising and sheep husbandry can be made very profitable, the woods affording grazing during the summer and the switchcane in river and creek bottoms during the winter.

Pearl river, which flows through the county from northwest to southeast, is navigable for steamboats, affording good facilities for transportation and for floating logs to sawmills. The timber growth of the county is principally longleaf or yellow pine of fine quality. On the river and creek bottoms, red and sweet gum, hickory, various kinds of oak, poplar, sycamore, magnolia, cypress, etc., abound.

Ten years, or longer, ago there were in the county ninety-six thousand five hundred acres of government lands for sale; the acreage in cotton was seventeen thousand, eight hundred and six, and five thousand nine hundred and sixty-seven bales were produced, two hundred and seventeen thousand and forty-one bushels of corn, forty-one thousand eight hundred and nine bushels of oats, and five thousand two hundred and eighty-eight pounds of tobacco in 1879.

The towns and postoffices of Lawrence county are Bismark, Blountville, Bournham, Grange, Gwinville, Hebron, Hooker, Monticello, Oak Vale, Saulsbury, Silver Creek, Tilton, Tyrus and Whitesand.

Religious and educational advantages are generally good; the people are law-abiding and progressive and have a warm welcome for newcomers.

The population of Lawrence county was four thousand nine hundred and sixteen in 1820, five thousand two hundred and ninety-three in 1830, five thousand nine hundred and twenty in 1840, six thousand four hundred and seventy-eight in 1850, nine thousand two hundred and thirteen in 1860, six thousand seven hundred and twenty in 1870, nine thousand four hundred and twenty in 1880, twelve thousand three hundred and eighteen in 1890. The colored population was three thousand and forty-two in 1870, four thousand four hundred and seventy-three in 1880, and six thousand and eighty-two in 1890. In 1860 the taxable slaves in this county numbered three thousand five hundred and eighty-seven, the voters nine hundred and thirteen. The county contains a total area of four hundred and fourteen thousand three hundred and eighty-two acres.

The first settler in this county was Harmon Runnels, father of Gov. Hiram G. Runnels, and grandfather of Governor Runnels of Texas. Other early comers were the Mitchells, Maxwells, Buckleys, Joynes, Butlers, Hickmans, Gwins, and others equally prominent. Monticello, which was once a place of considerable importance in a business way, was also a political center, and it gave to Mississippi two of its governors, one of its secretaries of state, one of its state auditors, two of its circuit judges, three of its district attorneys, and one of its representatives in congress. The superior court was held there for some years, and the vice chancery court until 1854. S. S. Prentiss was there licensed to practice law. The legislature once voted Monticello the state capital, and upon a reconsideration, about twenty-four hours later, located it elsewhere. Howell W. Runnels first represented Lawrence county in the state senate, Harmon Runnels and Joseph Cooper in the lower house. It is now represented in the senate by Alexander Fairly and G. S. Dodds, in the lower house by Archie Fairly. The county is at this time officered as follows: D. M. Lee, sheriff; Will C. Cannon, circuit and chancery clerk; A. Sharp, treasurer; A. J. Armstrong, assessor; B. D. Bishop, county superintendent public education; Beat 1—Z. P. Jones, supervisor; T. J. Andrews, H. A. Sessions, justices of peace; J. D. Carlisle, constable. Beat 2—C. H. Moore, supervisor; James F. Newsom, C. O. Nelson, justices of peace; J. H. Newsom, constable. Beat 3—F. F. Roberts, supervisor; W. D. Boyd, J. W. Willoughby, justices of the peace; B. R. Peavey, deputy sheriff, acting constable. Beat 4—T. H. Brinson, supervisor; H. Slater, I. N. Bass, justices of the peace; G. B. Ates, constable. Beat 5—A. W. Stringer, supervisor; J. H. Polk, S. C. Stamps, justices of the peace; Z. T. Daughdrill, deputy sheriff.

Pike county was established February 9, 1815. Magnolia is the seat of justice. Its watercourses are Bogue Chitto river and its tributaries, and the Tangipahoa and its tributaries, which afford vast water power. It is bounded, north, by Lincoln and Lawrence; east, by Marion; south, by Louisiana; west, by Amite. Originally, Jacksonville, on the east side of the Bogue Chitto, was settled as the seat of justice, the commissioners who located it having been Benjamin Bagley, Peter Felder, Sr., Obed Kirkland, William Bullock and David McGraw, Sr., but after the county had grown in population, in 1816, it was taken to Holmesville, whence it was removed to Magnolia at a later date. John Felder, Laban Bascot, Felix Allen and Peter Felder were commissioners to lay out the new county-seat. This county contains seven hundred and twenty square miles, or four hundred and sixty thousand eight hundred acres of land, fully one third of which is in cultivation, the balance being fairly timbered, the predominating timber being yellow or longleaf pine, while white, red and black oak, walnut, hickory, beech, maple, cypress, and other woods are plentiful. The character of the soil is various, on the river and creek bottoms a rich loam, the hammock land not so rich, with a clayey soil which holds fertilizers and is very productive. The principal crops are corn, cotton, rye, oats, sorghum, sugarcane, rice and potatoes. The fruits are apples, pears, peaches, figs, etc. The small fruits are blackberries, dewberries, raspberries and strawberries, and they are shipped to Chicago, where they command good prices. Pasturage is good and extensive, the native woods grasses being sufficient stock food for summer and the switchcane for winter. Many have during recent years gone into stockraising with profits. Sheep do remarkably well here. There are many saw and gristmills in different parts of Pike, and a number of thrifty Northern and Western men have located here as farmers and mechanics, and most of them are doing well. The Illinois Central railroad extends through the whole length of the county north and south. Magnolia, Johnston, Summit, McComb city, Chattawa and Osyka are stations in the county on the line of this road. At McComb city are located the shops and roundhouses for the southern division of this road, and many men are there employed in building cars and locomotives. In 1879 there was for sale in this county sixty-six thousand six hundred and forty acres of government land, and the state auditor held for sale seven thousand three hundred and twenty acres of delinquent tax land. There were nineteen thousand eight hundred and forty-two acres devoted to cotton culture, and six thousand five hundred and seven bales were produced that year, while the yield of corn was two hundred and six thousand eight hundred and ten bushels; of oats, fifty-five thousand nine hundred and nine bushels; and of tobacco, four hundred pounds.

Church and school advantages are good. The postoffices of Pike county are named Chatawa, China Grove, Dinan, Dillon, Holmesville, Johnston's Station, McComb, Magnolia, Osyka, Sartinville, Smithburgh, Summit, Topisaw, Tyler Town and Walker's Bridge.

Pike county had a population of four thousand four hundred and thirty-eight in 1820; five thousand four hundred and two in 1830; six thousand one hundred and fifty-one in 1840; seven thousand three hundred and sixty in 1850; eleven thousand one hundred and thirty-five in 1860; eleven thousand three hundred and three in 1870; sixteen thousand six hundred and eighty-eight in 1880; twenty-one thousand two hundred and three in 1890. There were five thousand three hundred and twelve colored inhabitants in 1870; eight thousand one hundred and twelve in 1880; and ten thousand six hundred and seventy-two in 1890. The number of taxable slaves in this county in 1860 was four thousand six hundred and ninety-three, the number of voters one thousand one hundred and fifty-two.

A small frame courthouse early erected served as a temple of justice until 1838, when it was replaced by a brick structure, which was destroyed by fire in 1878. The first courthouse erected at Magnolia was, with the county records and other property, destroyed by a very disastrous fire August 1, 1882. Among the first county officers were Laban Bascot, sheriff; Henry Quinn, clerk. They were succeeded by Sheriff R. Sparkman and Clerk James G. McNab; they by Sheriff L. J. Quinn and Clerk T. D. Paddleford. Christian Hoover was elected first judge of the probate and orphans' court. Among the earlier of his successors were James B. Quinn and George Nicholson. The first to represent this county in the state senate was David Dickson; in the house of representatives, Vincent Garner. The present state senator is Theodore B. Ford; representatives in the lower house, Theodore McKnight and John B. Leggett.

The first settlement in this county is said to have been made by W. McNulty, in September, 1811. He came from South Carolina, and was accompanied by Michael McNulty, Sr. The pioneers entered land from the government on the principal water courses. Among the early settlers to enter land were the Carter family, who came from South Carolina, probably about 1811 or 1812, and entered a large tract of land on the Tangipahoa river. In 1812 Peter Felder, Sr., and his family, also South Carolinians, entered land on the Tangipahoa river; Green Cook entered land on the river also the same year. On the Bogue Chitto river, the early entries were made by Edward Bullock, Edmund Gatlin (there was a large family of this name), David Bullock, and the Reeves, Curtis and Wells families were also early comers. Farther down the river Robert Love made an early entry, and located thereon. A number of early entries were made on McGee's creek. John McGee came about 1811; Ralph Stovall about the same time.

Among other early settlers were David Morgan, Benjamin Bagley, James McNulty, Matthew Cox, Henry Goldman, Bedy Goldman, Thomas Heard, William Bullock, David Cleveland, Isaac Saddler, Vincent Gardner, John Brent, Jesse Harper, William Love, Edmund Andrews, Henry Raglan, James Andrews, David McGraw, Isaac Carter, Jere Smith, Richard Dillon, John Bent, William Sibley, the Prescott, Cole, Roberts, Prestige, Cooper and other families.

Covington county, named in honor of General Covington, who was killed in the war of 1812, was established January 5, 1819. Its seat of justice is Williamsburg, located near its geographical center. It is bounded thus: North by Simpson and Smith, east by Jones, south by Perry and Marion, west by Lawrence. It was first represented in the state senate by Howell W. Runnels, in the legislature by John Ship. It is now represented in the senate by A. Fairly and G. S. Dodds, in the legislature by C. M. Edmonson. There are numerous creeks, large and small, flowing through the county, which might be utilized by manufacturers, as they afford fine water power, the larger streams being Dry, Okatoma, Rogers' and Burton's creeks.

The surface of the county is undulating, along the creek bottoms level. About five-sixths of the county is finely timbered with longleaf or yellow pine, and on the creek bottoms white and water oaks, hickory, ash, beech, magnolia, etc., are found. Fish are abundant in the creeks, and deer, wild turkeys, raccoons, opossums, wild ducks, etc., are plentiful. The soil is generally thin and sandy on the uplands, but the creek bottoms are fertile. The principal products are corn, oats, sweet and Irish potatoes, sugarcane, sorghum, ground peas, field peas, all the vegetables and such fruits as peaches, apples, pears, plums, figs, pomegranates and apricots do well; while the scuppernong grape does well, and the pecan tree bears plentifully. There is good pasturage for cattle and sheep during all the year with the exception of one or two months, and stockraising could be made very profitable.

An idea of the status of this county may be obtained from the following statistics issued in 1885 by the Mississippi State Board of Immigration and Agriculture: United States lands for sale, one hundred and fifty-seven thousand two hundred and forty acres; delinquent lands held by the state auditor for sale, one thousand and twenty acres; acreage in cotton in 1879, six thousand nine hundred and sixty-eight acres; bales produced in 1879, two thousand and seventy-one; bales made by white labor, one thousand five hundred and nineteen; bales made by black labor, five hundred and fifty-two; bushels of corn produced in 1879, fifteen thousand and eighty-eight; bushels of oats produced in 1879, thirty-two thousand two hundred and fifteen; pounds of tobacco produced in 1879, four thousand seven hundred and forty-three. At this time there are thirty-one thousand three hundred and sixty acres of cleared land in the county.

Besides Williamsburg, the villages and postoffices of Covington county are Mount Carmel, Mount Olive, Okahay, Ora, Reddock, Richmond, Santee, Welch and Wilkesburg.

The population of Covington county at each successive census since 1820 is here given: 1820, two thousand two hundred and thirty; 1830, two thousand five hundred and fifty-one; 1840, two thousand seven hundred and seventeen; 1850, three thousand three hundred and thirty-eight; 1860, four thousand four hundred and eight; 1870, four thousand seven hundred and fifty-three; 1880, five thousand nine hundred and ninety-three; 1890, eight thousand two hundred and ninety-nine. Of this population, there were one thousand six hundred and forty-seven colored inhabitants in 1870, one thousand nine hundred and fifty-eight in 1880, and two thousand nine hundred and eighty-four in 1890. The county had in 1860 one thousand four hundred and ninety-three taxable slaves and four hundred and twenty-three voters.

The Ships (John and Joseph), the McAfees (Joseph and James), W. Reed and G. Harris were among the pioneer settlers in this county. Others were Hanson Alsbury, A. L. Hatton, John Colbert, F. Pope, Alex. Harper, Aaron Low, Duncan Buchanan, Archibald McCollum, Brewster and A. H. Jayne, John Bird, the Duckworth family, Dr. Hall, the Rogers family, J. Edmondson, Alexander McLeod, the Mathesons, William Esterling, the McNairs, Reuben and John Watts and the McLaurins.

Perry county was established February 3, 1820, and named in honor of Commodore Oliver Hazard Perry. Augusta is the seat of justice. It is bounded north by Covington, Jones and Wayne counties, east by Greene county, south by Jackson and Harrison counties, west by Pearl river and Marion county. The first state senator representing this county was Isaac R. Nicholson; the first members of the lower house were R. H. Gilmer and Hugh McDonald. The present state senator is A. G. Ferguson; the present representative is A. D. Draughn.

The surface of this county is generally undulating, but is level on the creek and river bottoms. The principal watercourse is Leaf river and the county is intersected by numerous smaller streams, affording fine water-power advantages in all parts. Much of the county is heavily timbered with longleaf or yellow pine; on the creeks and rivers oaks, hickory, poplar, magnolia and black and sweet gum grow. On the creek and river bottoms the soil is fertile, but is not so good remote from the streams. The principal products are corn, cotton, sugarcane, rice, peas, sweet potatoes, etc. Peaches, pears, grapes and small fruits do well, but are cultivated only for home consumption. Pasturage is very extensive for summer range, and considerable attention has been paid to stockraising, especially to sheep husbandry, but very little has been done in the way of improved breeds. The New Orleans & North-Western railroad passes through the northwestern portion of this county.

In 1870 there were in the county two hundred and ninety-three thousand and eighty acres of government lands for sale, five hundred and thirty-seven acres were planted to cotton, and one hundred and forty-six bales of cotton were produced. The production in corn amounted to thirty-eight thousand four hundred and forty-seven bushels; of oats, twenty thousand two hundred bushels. The county contains fifty-four hundred and thirty-three acres of cleared land.

Church advantages are somewhat limited, but the people are moral as a class, and give such support to religion and education as is consistent with their ability. The postoffices of Perry county are Augustaville, Batson, Griffin, Hattiesburg, McDonald's Mills, Monroe, Morristown and Stix.

This county's gradual growth in population is shown by the following figures: 1820, twenty hundred and thirty seven; 1830, twenty-three hundred; 1840, eighteen hundred and eighty-nine; 1850, twenty-four hundred and thirty-eight; 1860, twenty-six hundred and six; 1870, twenty-six hundred and ninety-four; 1880, thirty-four hundred and twenty-seven; 1890, sixty-four hundred and ninety-four. Of this population there were seven hundred and twenty-three colored inhabitants in 1870, ten hundred and seventy in 1880, and eighteen hundred and eighty-seven in 1890. In 1860 the county contained seven hundred and thirty-seven taxable slaves and two hundred and sixty-two voters.

Among the earliest settlers were the Carters (Thomas and Isaac), Samuel Coleman, Robert Little, the Deases, the Lewises, the Damerons and others. The first cattle ranch in the county was opened upon Chaney creek by Robert Chaney, in whose honor the creek was named.

Jones county was established January 24, 1826, and its seat of justice is located at Elmsville. It is bounded north by Smith and Jasper, east by Wayne, south by Perry, and west by Covington. Jones county's first state senator was Hamilton Cooper, its first representative, John C. Thomas. It is at this time represented in the upper house by A. C. Gerguson, in the lower house by A. Arrington.

The surface of the county is generally undulating, but that portion in the creek and river bottoms is level. Nearly all the land is finely timbered with longleaf or yellow pine. On the water courses there are oaks of different varieties, hickory, ash, elm, bay, beech, gum, magnolia, etc. The county is watered and drained by the Leaf and Tallahala rivers, the Bogue Homo, Tallahoma and numerous smaller creeks, which afford vast water-power facilities. Saw logs are rafted to market on the Leaf and the Tallahala. The soil is generally thin and sandy on the uplands; along the margins of the creeks and rivers it is fertile, producing cotton, corn, oats, sweet and Irish potatoes, sugarcane, sorghum, field peas, peanuts, figs, grapes, plums, apples, etc., all the small fruits doing well. The scuppernong grape is in its native element in this county, and pecans grow finely. Pasturage is extensive, summer grasses are plentiful, and the whole country lies open to grazing. Some of the citizens have introduced the breeding of cattle and sheep with much profit. In 1878 there were one hundred and eighty-two thousand and twenty acres of United States lands for sale in the county, and one hundred and sixty acres of delinquent lands held by the state auditor for sale; twenty-seven hundred and ninety-four acres were devoted to cotton in 1879, and six hundred and twenty-four bales were produced; and in the same year forty-seven thousand two hundred and sixty-nine bushels of corn, thirty thousand nine hundred and ninety-two bushels of oats, and four thousand six hundred and eighty-three pounds of tobacco were produced. There are now fifteen thousand two hundred and sixty-eight acres of cleared land within the county limits.

The people are moral and law-abiding, and church and school advantages are as good as can be expected in a sparsely settled country. The health of this section is as good as anywhere in the world.

Some of the early settlers in this county were John McCormack, John Bridges, John C. Smith, Benjamin Moss, John Strickland, Robert Crawford, Stacy Collins, John Terrall, Aaron Wilborne and James Blockwell, some of whom became prominent.

The towns and postoffices in Jones county, besides the county seat, are Amite, Curtis, Erata, Estabutchie, Gitano, Laurel, Mico, Moselle, Pinnellville, Sandersville, Soso and Wheelerville.

The population of Jones county was fourteen hundred and seventy-one in 1830, twelve hundred and fifty-eight in 1840, twenty-one hundred and sixty-four in 1850, thirty-three hundred and twenty-three in 1860, thirty-three hundred and thirteen in 1870, thirty-eight hundred and twenty-eight in 1880, eighty-three hundred and thirty-three in 1890. The colored element aggregated three hundred and eight in 1870, three hundred and fifty-nine in 1880, and twelve hundred and ninety-five in 1890. The taxable slaves in this county in 1860 numbered three hundred and eighty-three, the polls four hundred and forty-six.

Before the railroad era Jones took low rank among the counties of this state; but it has steadily advanced since the construction of the New Orleans & Northeastern railroad, which crosses it from northeast to southwest, and at this time there are twenty-six other counties in the state the value of whose cleared lands is less than that of Jones, and twenty-two others whose personal property has a lower valuation.

Harrison county is named in honor of Gen. William Henry Harrison, who was president-elect of the United States at the time of its erection. It is bounded north by Perry, east by Jackson, south by the Gulf of Mexico, and west by Hancock and Pearl river.

This county was cut off of Hancock and established February 5, 1841, and its seat of justice is Pass Christian. The soil is sandy and not very fertile, but can be made to produce good crops of fruits and vegetables by the application of oyster-shell lime, swamp muck and marls. There are several fine orange and peach orchards and vineyards in the county. The peach, apple, plum, pomegranate, pear and fig grape of many varieties, strawberries, dewberries, blackberries and melons of various kinds grow in great profusion, and yield good returns. Winemaking has made considerable progress. At Pass Christian a large plantation is devoted to the scuppernong grape, and first-class still and sparkling wines are made, which meet with a ready sale, and there are many other vineyards at other points. The land is generally undulating, and in the northern portion is covered with longleaf or yellow pine, but the trees are much smaller as the gulf is approached. Pasturage is fine for ten months during the year. Sheep husbandry is one of the most profitable industries, and many new flocks are being started.

The following statistics of 1878–9 will be found of interest, in comparison with those of a later date: United States lands for sale, two hundred and seventeen thousand two hundred acres; acreage in cotton in 1879, twenty-six acres; bales produced in 1879, eleven; bushels of corn produced in 1879, fifteen thousand one hundred and thirty; bushels of oats produced in 1879, two thousand one hundred and ten. There are now three thousand and ninety-six acres of cleared land.

W. A. Champlin was first clerk, A. W. Ramsey first state senator, and Joseph Frost and B. Bond were first representatives. The present state senator is H. Bloomfield; W. G. Evans, Jr., is representative.

The climate is salubrious at all seasons, and there is fine sea bathing all along the coast.

School and church privileges are good, there being excellent private schools, while the public free schools are maintained during four or five months each year. Pass Christian female institute is a noteworthy educational enterprise.

Besides Pass Christian, the towns and postoffices of this county are Airey, Beauvoir, Biloxi, De Lisle, Gulfport, Handsboro, Long Beach, Mississippi City, Perkinston, Ramsay, Stonewall and Wool Market. Mississippi City, Pass Christian and Biloxi are on the New Orleans & Mobile railroad, and also on the gulf. At Biloxi is an extensive tin-canning establishment, for canning shrimps, oysters, fruit of various kinds and vegetables. At Stonewall is an important manufacturing concern, which is mentioned elsewhere.

Harrison county had a population of four thousand eight hundred and seventy-five in 1850, four thousand eight hundred and nineteen in 1860, five thousand seven hundred and ninety-five in 1870, seven thousand eight hundred and ninety-five in 1880, twelve thousand four hundred and eighty-one in 1890. The colored inhabitants numbered one thousand four hundred and twenty-seven in 1870, two thousand one hundred and forty-six in 1880 and three thousand three hundred and seventy in 1890. In 1860 there were one thousand and sixty-one taxable slaves in this county, and five hundred and twenty voters.

The names of the old and earliest settlers, most of whom are now dead, are as follows: W. A. Champlin, R. Seal, John J. McCoughan, Dudley Selph, John L. Henley, W. H. Legarden, Donal McBean and William Creath.

Lincoln county was formed principally from the west part of Lawrence county and established April 7, 1870, and its county town is Brookhaven. A part of its territory came also from Jefferson, Copiah, Pike and Franklin counties. It was organized at so late a date that it contains little pioneer history not connected with Lawrence, Franklin and other counties. Among the early settlers here were Wyatt Algood, Samuel Pepper, Thomas Campbell, Reuben Bull, Givin Pepper, Hiram Case, Henry Maxwell, Jesse Maxwell and Henry Flurr, all of whom came about 1806. The inhabitants are mostly descendants of Georgian and South Carolinian ancestry.

Lincoln comprises an area of five hundred and ninety-three square miles, and is bounded north by Copiah, east by Lawrence, south by Amite and Pike, west by Franklin and Jefferson. Much of the county is well timbered yet, and a considerable portion of the balance is cleared and under cultivation. The surface is generally undulating, but is level on the river and creek bottoms. The soil is a sandy loam on ridges and a stiff productive soil predominates on the numerous river and creek bottoms. About eighty per cent. of the timber standing is longleaf or yellow pine, and on the bottoms white, red, black and pin oaks, sweet and black gum, hickory, poplar, magnolia, maple and cypress trees grow in great numbers. The crops grown are corn, cotton, sugarcane, rice, oats, peanuts, Irish and sweet potatoes, and all kinds of vegetables grow abundantly, a notable product being melons. Fruit-growing is on the increase.

The water courses of the county are the Bogue Chitto, Amite, Fair, Homochitto, East and West Bayou rivers and numerous creeks, which give fine water-power advantages. The Illinois Central railroad runs through the county from north to south, and other railroad facilities are afforded by the Meridian, Brookhaven & Natchez railroad and Wesson & Person's lumber railroad. When the railroad was finished from Osyka to Brookhaven, in May, 1857, the northeastern part of the county, except along the creek bottoms, was almost a wilderness, and its advance has since been about ten-fold. Brookhaven was the terminus of the road from April, 1862, until the general surrender of the Confederate forces. A conscripts' camp was located there from August, 1861, to November, 1864, which brought the place into notoriety, two-thirds of the state furnishing conscripts to that point.

The manufacturing interests are represented by Connerly's foundry and twenty-five or thirty sawmills and planingmills.

The population of this county in 1870 was ten thousand one hundred and eighty-one; in 1860, thirteen thousand five hundred and forty-seven; in 1890, seventeen thousand nine hundred and twelve. Of this population there were four thousand one hundred and sixty-two colored inhabitants in 1870, five thousand eight hundred and forty-two in 1880, and seven thousand six hundred and ninety-six in 1890. The county contains fifty-seven thousand and thirty-seven acres of cleared land.

In 1879 there were in the county eight thousand one hundred and sixty acres of government lands for sale, and one thousand acres of delinquent lands held for sale by the state auditor. The acreage in cotton was seventeen thousand two hundred and twenty two acres. Six thousand two hundred and eighty-six bales were produced. The production of corn and oats reached two hundred and nine thousand seven hundred and forty-seven and forty-nine thousand nine hundred and twenty-four bushels respectively, and five thousand four hundred and forty-two pounds of tobacco were prepared for market.

The following humorous story of the formation and naming of the county was contributed to this work by a prominent resident: "There was great opposition in Jefferson to having the Homochitto made the west line, as it took some of its best farms and farmers. There was quite a character in that coveted strip named Purvis Newman, a good, true man, but eccentric and bitterly opposed to the change. When the news came that the new county was formed—it was the first county established after the war—and Newman was informed that it was called Lincoln, he said: 'I know just what they named it Lincum fur. Hit was jest to aggrevate we fellers out on the Homerchitter, and as fur as I'm concerned them fellers kin take hit along to right whar old Lincum is, durn 'em?'"

There are in the county about fifty churches and about eighty free public schools, and one of the largest female colleges in the state is located at Brookhaven.

Of those who, during the period 1855–7, were prominent in the advancement of railway interests in the county, the survivors are James A. Hoskins, A. E. Maxwell, Thomas H. Lewis, E. E. Seavy and Jesse Warren. Brookhaven was the center of operations. Besides Brookhaven, the principal towns in the county are Montgomery, Bogue Chitto and Caseyville. Other postoffices are Auburn, Fair River, Redstar, Ruth and Wellman. Brookhaven is five hundred feet above the sea level. The highest point in the county is five hundred and sixty feet.

Hon. Hiram Cassidy first represented Lincoln county in the state senate. The present state senator is Theodore B. Ford. The first representative in the legislature was R. R. Applewhite; the present ones are J. A. J. Hart and R. R. Applewhite. The first county officers were appointed by the governor. John W. Moore was sheriff; F. A. Clover, clerk; John W. Stuart, circuit clerk; John M. Gartman, treasurer. The present officers are: R. W. McNair, sheriff; Felix May, chancery clerk; J. Warren, circuit clerk; Allen Smith, treasurer; E. Smith, superintendent of schools.

Pearl River county was recreated and established under an act approved February 22, 1890, from portions of Hancock and Marion counties, and derived its designation from the stream of the same name. Poplarville was made the seat of justice. It is bounded north by Marion, east by Perry and Harrison, south by Hancock and west by Louisiana.

Authority was conferred upon the governor by the act creating the county to appoint county officers, and it was provided that they should hold their respective offices until the next general election, and until their successors should qualify. A. F. Rawls, P. E. Williams,

James Smith, Joseph E. Wheat and Thomas Martin were appointed supervisors; James M. Shivers, sheriff; Rufus L. Ratliff, circuit and chancery clerk; Eli P. Stewart, assessor; Andrew Smith, treasurer; Frank B. Lenoir, enumerator.

Other historical matters, pertaining to this county's settlement, etc., are treated in connection with the counties from which it was formed. The water courses of this county are Cane creek and a prong of the Abolochitto, and Pearl river flows southwardly along its western border. The surface is level and gradually undulating. The soil, which is sandy, produces all kinds of vegetables and fruits common to this part of the country. Pasturage here is good and plentiful. Oysters and the saltwater fish of the gulf are plentiful, and there is much game, notably wild turkeys, wild ducks, wild geese, and deer, which afford fine opportunities to the sportsman.

The New Orleans & Northeastern railroad traverses the county centrally from northeast to southwest. Lumbering is carried on quite extensively, and there are several sawmills within the borders of the county. Turpentine distilling is also important. The population, as shown by the census of 1890, was whites, twenty-two hundred and ninety-eight; colored, six hundred and fifty-nine; total, twenty-nine hundred and fifty-seven. There are several churches in the county, and its educational advantages are fair, considering its newness and its small population.

This county, which was created originally in 1872 and abolished in 1879, on account of its inability to maintain itself, owing to its lack of development, has made wonderful progress since that period. When first created it had a population of only one thousand two hundred and a real estate assessment of $200,000. It is claimed that the area of six hundred and twelve square miles of Marion and Hancock counties, which go to make up the county, has a registered vote of over one thousand two hundred, a real estate assessment of $600,000, and personal assessment of $200,000. The lumber industry and turpentine distilleries have attracted Northern capital and the New Orleans & Northeastern railroad has developed these resources. It was assigned to the sixth congressional district by an ordinance of the convention of 1890. The postoffices in this county are, besides Poplarville, Chinquepin, Daviston, Hillsdale, Lumberton, McClure and Orvisburgh.

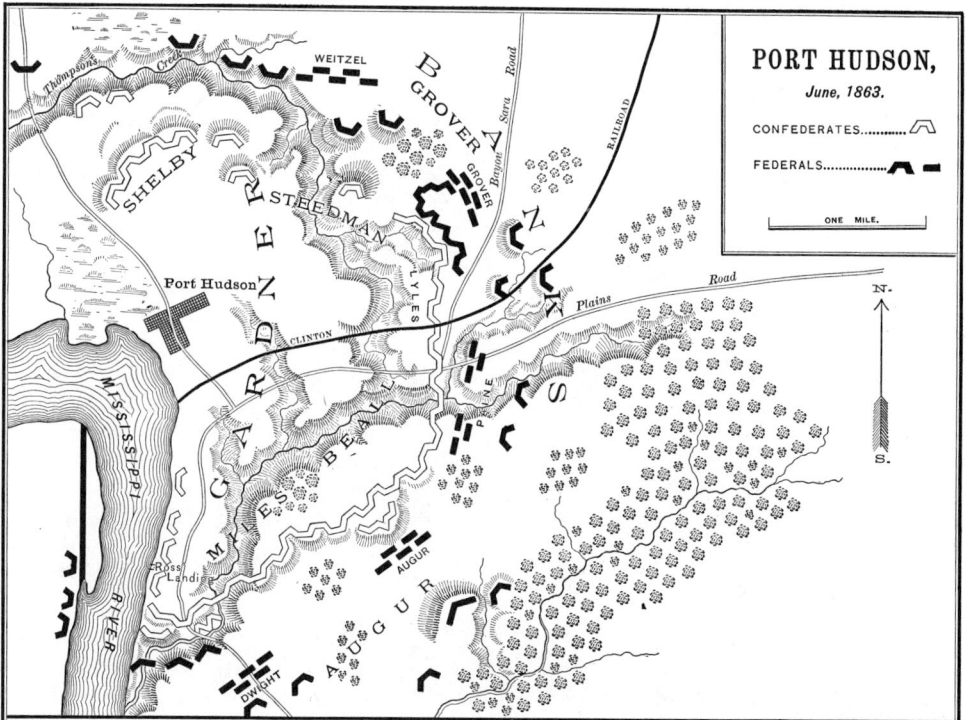

PORT HUDSON,
June, 1863.

CONFEDERATES............ ⌐⌐

FEDERALS................ ▬ ▬

ONE MILE.

WEITZEL

GROVER

SHELBY

STHEDMAN

LYLES

GROVER

Bayou Sara Road

RAILROAD

Port Hudson

CLINTON

Plains Road

PINE

MILES

BEALL

N.

S.

Ross Landing

AUGUR

AUGUR

MISSISSIPPI

RIVER

DWIGHT

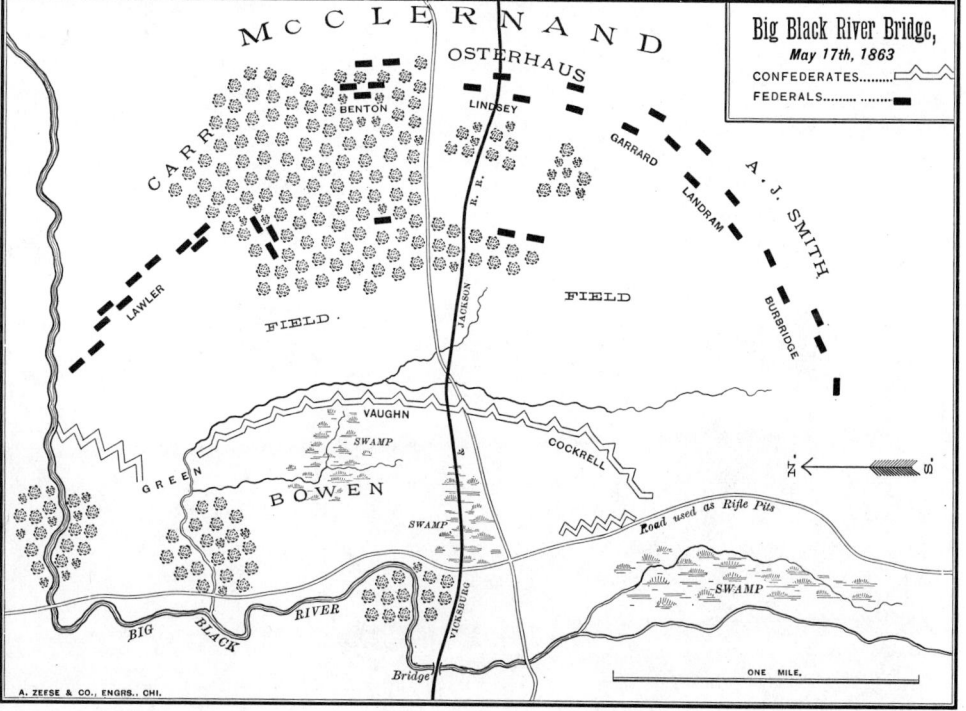

Big Black River Bridge,
May 17th, 1863.

CONFEDERATES......... ⌐⌐⌐

FEDERALS......... ▬▬

McCLERNAND

OSTERHAUS

CARR

BENTON

LINDSEY

GARRARD

A. J. SMITH

LANDRAM

LAWLER

R. R.

JACKSON

FIELD

FIELD

BURBRIDGE

VAUGHN

SWAMP

COCKRELL

N.

S.

GREEN

BOWEN

SWAMP

Road used as Rifle Pits

SWAMP

VICKSBURG

BIG   BLACK   RIVER

Bridge

ONE MILE.

A. ZEESE & CO., ENGRS., CHI.

CHAPTER X.

꧁⊛꧂

COUNTIES OF THE SECOND CHOCTAW CESSION, OR NEW PURCHASE OF 1820.

ISSAQUENA county was established January 23, 1844. Its most important towns are Mayersville, the seat of justice, and Skipwith, known as Duncansby. Other villages and postoffices are Arcadia, Shipland, Balished, Ben Lomond, Carolina, Chotard, Grace, Hay's landing, Luxembourg, Tallula and Valley Park.

The Mississippi river flows along the whole western boundary, affording cheap steamboat transportation; Deer creek flows from north to south on the eastern border. Other streams and bodies of water are Steele's bayou, Lake Lafayette, Moon lake and Five Mile lake. The county lies entirely in the Mississippi bottom. The soil is rich, alluvial loam, with buckshot back from the river. There are about fifty-five thousand acres of cleared land, the balance being much of it heavily timbered with cypress, oak, ash gum, hackberry, hickory, locust, walnut, sassafras, etc. The county produces corn, cotton and oats in great luxuriance— from one to two bales of cotton per acre and forty to eighty bushels of corn. All kinds of vegetables, fruits, etc., are raised for home consumption. The Louisville, New Orleans & Texas railroad crosses the northeastern part of the county.

The population in 1850 was four thousand four hundred and seventy-eight; in 1860, seven thousand eight hundred and thirty-one; in 1870, six thousand eight hundred and eighty-seven; in 1880, ten thousand and four; in 1890, twelve thousand three hundred and eighteen. In 1860 the number of voters was one hundred and seventy-nine; the number of taxable slaves, six thousand eight hundred and thirty-eight. The colored population in 1870 was six thousand one hundred and forty-six; in 1880, nine thousand one hundred and seventy-four; in 1890, eleven thousand six hundred and twenty-three. This county was first represented in the senate by Lelix Labauve; in the legislature, by James J. B. White. The present state senator is H. L. Foote; representative, C. J. Jones.

The county-seat was at first located at Tallula. The county, until 1876, embraced Sharkey county, now separated from it by Steele's bayou. It now has some fifty-five miles of river front, and is bounded north by Washington, east by Sharkey, south by Warren and west by Louisiana.

Col. Zenas Preston and his brother-in-law, a Mr. Atchison, were the first settlers of this county. They located at old Tallula landing. The first county court was held there. The first place opened was Ben Lomond, opposite Lake Providence. A man named Duncan was in partnership with Mr. Preston when he opened the farm. Old man McCulloch, another brother-in-law of Colonel Preston's, was also among the first settlers, coming here probably

13

about 1834, and opening a farm in the southern part of the county. Preston, Duncan and McCulloch were the owners of ten miles, extending south from Clover Hill plantation, embracing at this time the plantations of Homochitto, Carlisle, Holly Ridge, Oakley, Reserve, Duncannon, Middlesex and Elleslie, which are among the largest plantations in the county, and are each a portion of this original purchase and the property of one man, a Mr. Duncan, nephew of the original settler of this section. Of the northern portion the first settler was Ambrose Gipson, who purchased quite a large body of land. His settlement was made in the early forties. On this settlement now are the plantations known as Wadelawn, Cloverhill, besides Mayersville and a farm belonging to D. Mayer, called Mount Level. The extreme northern portion was settled by the Turnbulls and Gen. Wade Hampton's father, who owned Walnut Ridge plantation, while the Turnbulls owned Veilhood, Riverdale, Hopedale and Lakeside plantations. A Mr. Hill owned a place called Green Brier in this part of the county.

L. L. Wade was among the most prominent men in this county in his day. Coming here when the county was wholly a wilderness, he opened Wadelawn place.

Sharkey county is bounded north by Washington, east by Yazoo, south by Issaquena and west by Louisiana. The county lies entirely in the Mississippi bottom and the surface is level. The county is drained by the Sunflower river and by Deer creek, which flow through the entire length from north to south nearly paralled, and at Rolling fork Deer creek divides, the largest prong making an abrupt turn, forming almost a right angle with Deer creek, and flows nearly east for about five miles, emptying into the Sunflower river. This is known as Rolling fork, and was named by Thomas Y. Chaney on his first visit here in 1826, on account of the swiftness of the current immediately preceding its emptying into the Sunflower.

The soil of Sharkey county is of a black loam, deep and inexhaustible in every portion of the county, and bids fair to be the richest agricultural county in the state. Unimproved land can be bought for $10 per acre, and the best improved farms from $40 to $50 per acre. The products are corn, cotton, oats, potatoes and sorghum. Pasturage is very extensive and good.

The mound builders were active in this section, there being probably one hundred mounds in all in Sharkey county, the largest being one on Murphy's bayou, in the north part of the county. This one towers above the treetops. Just south of Rolling fork there is a group of five, the largest of which is about fifty feet high, almost round and very regular in form. This group is on a crescent ridge about half a mile in length. Nearly all of them in this county are found in groups and many of them are very prominent and regular in form.

The act creating Sharkey county was approved March 29, 1876, and it was formed from the counties of Issaquena, Washington and Warren. Rolling Fork is the county seat.

The following were the first officers: Hon. Leigh Clark, representative; Henry Picard, chancery and circuit clerk; J. H. Robertson, sheriff; T. C. Watson, treasurer; J. G. Davis, assessor. Col. W. T. Barnard is president board of supervisors, the other members being J. A. C. Shrader, Eugene Clark, A. P. Ferguson, D. Hunt.

The first settler in the county was Thomas Y. Chaney, who, in 1828, settled at the head of Rolling fork. The second was Benjamin F. Bookout, in 1829, on what is now known as the Helena plantation; and about three years later Mr. Bookout sold to Redding B. Heron. About the same time came Daniel Portman and John and Elish Sulsor, all of whom died of cholera in 1831. Their settlement was about half a mile below Rolling fork. Richard Armstrong came about the same time and soon after Col. William Rushing, who purchased

Mr. Armstrong's place.   John Murphy settled on Rolling fork and Thomas Beasley, an old bachelor, near the mouth of Rolling fork, where he lived a hermit life.   Calvin Belcher came from New York in 1831, a young man, and was the first settler on Sunflower river.   He was a very illiterate and very eccentric man and a great hunter, and was known as the David Crockett of Mississippi.   Judge S. S. Prentiss, who frequently hunted with him, once said of him that he was the smartest man he ever knew for an uneducated one.

There are thirty-three school districts in the county—ten white and twenty-three colored.

The first newspaper was the Deer Creek *Advance*, established in the early part of 1881 by Charles Murphy, and edited and published by him till he was killed in the summer of the same year.   In the following fall the Deer Creek *Review* was started by Charles N. Jones. This continued till some time in 1883, when it suspended, and on September 6, 1884, appeared the first issue of the Deer Creek *Pilot*, by S. W. Langford, which has since continued publication.

In 1883 the Louisville, New Orleans & Texas railroad was built through the county and the first train reached Rolling Fork October 27, 1883.

The town of Rolling Fork was incorporated with John Harsh as first mayor.   The charter was some time afterward surrendered for about two years, but was again revived, and the present mayor is J. E. Butler.

The postoffice was established in 1848, with Thomas Redwood as first postmaster, who was also the first merchant in the county.   The postoffice was named Rolling Fork, for the name of the first plantation in the county, on which it was located.   This was the plantation of Thomas Y. Chaney, the first settler in the county.

The population of Sharkey county in 1880 was sixty-three hundred and six; in 1890, eighty-three hundred and eighty-two.   The colored population is seventy-one hundred and thirty-nine.

Hinds county was established February 12, 1821, and named in compliment to Gen. Thomas Hinds.   The county seat was located at Raymond January 17, 1829.   The other principal towns are Jackson, Clinton, Edwards, Bolton, Utica, Terry, Learned, Adams, Oakley, Byram and Tougaloo.   Other villages and postoffices in the county are Bear Creek, Cayuga, Chapel Hill, Cynthia, Dry Grove, Greene Crossing, Jackson, Jonesville, McRaven, Midway, Nevada, Newman, Palestine, Pocahontas, Rayburn, Smith's Station and Thompsonville.

This county was first represented in the state senate by Samuel Calvit, in the legislature by Benjamin F. Smith.   Its present state senator is C. M. Williamson, its representatives, H. Peyton, J. F. Fitzgerald, J. A. P. Campbell, Jr., and Thomas M. Griffin.   Hinds county had a population of eighty-six hundred and forty-five in 1830, nineteen thousand and ninety-eight in 1840, twenty-five thousand three hundred and forty in 1850, thirty-one thousand three hundred and thirty-nine in 1860, thirty thousand four hundred and eighty-eight in 1870, forty-three thousand nine hundred and fifty-eight in 1880, thirty-nine thousand two hundred and seventy-nine in 1890.   In 1860 there were sixteen hundred and eighty voters and twenty-one thousand six hundred and thirty-six taxable slaves.   The colored population in 1870 was twenty-thousand six hundred and fifty-nine, in 1880, thirty-two thousand two hundred and twenty-nine; in 1890, twenty-eight five hundred and seventy-seven.

Upon Mississippi's topographical maps Hinds county is located in the central prairie region, partly, its southern portion being in the longleaf pine region; hence it lies in the south-central portion of the state, and is bounded on the north by Madison, east by Rankin, south by Copiah and west by Warren county.   Its superficial area is five hundred and fifty-one thousand one hundred and seventy-one acres, of which three hundred and sixty-two thousand two hundred and twenty-seven acres are cleared, the balance being still covered with forests of valuable timber, such as pine, all varieties of oak, hickory, poplar, elm, beech and cypress, all exceedingly valuable in the industries, readily accessible by the four lines of railway which from Jackson radiate in six different directions, and at the same time furnish the very best of tansportation facilities for every portion of the county.

Pearl river forms the eastern and Big black river the western boundary, while through-out the interior flow a large number of streams, perfectly draining and watering every local-ity, making the county a very desirable one for stockraising, an industry that is now receiv-ing marked attention at the hands of practical and progressive men generally throughout this portion of Mississippi. Generally speaking, the surface of the county is gently undu-lating, the soil being a rich, yellow loam, resting upon a subsoil of stiff clay, and often under-laid with marl and limestone. Abundant crops of corn, cotton, oats, tobacco, broomcorn, sugarcane, sorghum, Irish and sweet potatoes, red clover and native grasses, are produced annually; a total failure of crops being unknown within the memory of the oldest inhabitant. This is also one of the finest vegetable and fruit producing counties in the state, and this pur-suit is proving so lucrative that hundreds have engaged therein, particularly in the vicinity of Terry, a few miles south of Jackson, a station known as one of the most important vege-table and fruit-shipping points on the line of the Illinois Central railroad. Peaches, pears, figs, plums, strawberries and other varieties of fruits and berries grow and mature to perfec-tion there, and the interest in their culture is rapidly extending among the old settlers, while the newcomers engage therein exclusively, or combine that pursuit with stockraising, always with the most gratifying results.

Hinds is rapidly coming to the front as one of the noted stock counties in the state, much attention having of late years been paid to the introduction of fine horses and cattle, and the grading and importing of all classes of live stock. The Short-horn, Jersey, Holstein and other varieties are becoming quite numerous; in fact, the second largest herd of Jerseys in the state is owned there. The county is well adapted to this purpose, which will soon become its leading industry. Besides being well watered in every portion, its grazing is unsurpassed. The native grasses, Bermuda, crab and orchard grasses, as well as the Japan clover, grow spontaneously everywhere, affording a luxuriant pasturage the year around, and make the very best of feed when cut for hay. But little feeding or stabling is required, but better results follow when this is done, even in central Mississippi, which may be said to possess almost an ideal climate at all seasons. Domestic grasses, the clover, millet, blue grass and other standard varieties also do very well. The following figures will show this county's wealth in live stock of the different kinds:

Kind.	Number.	Value.
Cattle	9,819	$ 78,828
Horses	3,229	179,137
Mules and asses	3,930	252,607
Swine	1,047	1,686
Sheep	1,848	2,023
Total	19,873	$514,281

Yazoo county is situated about fifty miles southwestward from the geographical center of the state, and is one of the largest counties of the state, being about forty-five miles across, north and south or east and west, and having one hundred miles of river front. The face of the county is divided into two general classes, viz., the upland or hill country and the bottom, the two portions being nearly equal in geographical extent. The former is a common rolling or gently undulating region, with no high or untillable hills. The latter is a flat delta region, being a part of the great Yazoo bottom, which is itself a portion of the great Mississippi delta, extending from Cairo, Ill., to the gulf. These two regions are divided by a range of bluffs running nearly north and south, at the base of which flows the beautiful Yazoo river.

Yazoo county was organized January 21, 1823, and is bounded as follows: South by Warren, Hinds and Madison; east by Attala, Madison and Holmes; north by Washington and Holmes and west by Sharkey county. The Big Black river runs along the entire eastern and southern border, and the Yazoo passes through its center from north to south. One line of railroad, the Yazoo & Mississippi Valley branch of the Illinois Central railroad, has been built through the county, passing almost through its center, furnishing good transportation facilities for reaching every important market in this country. Several other railroads are projected in and near this county. The railroad mileage is forty-three miles, the main line of the Illinois Central railroad passing through the eastern and the Yazoo & Mississippi Valley branch through the central portions. The Yazoo is navigable all the year and is one of the best rivers of its size in the world. Silver creek, Panther creek, Tokeby bayou, lakes George and Tilby and Wolf lake afford navigation part of the time, and all connect with the Yazoo. No part of the county is remote from market.

Yazoo county embraces an area of ten hundred and sixty-eight square miles, or six hundred and twenty-five thousand acres. About two hundred and fifty-three thousand acres of the land in this famous county have been opened for cultivation and the balance is covered with forests of fine timber, of such valuable varieties as the different kinds of oak, poplar, locust, walnut, elm, beech, hickory, cypress, etc., all of great value in different industries.

The county is divided into four natural divisions, viz.: The Yazoo basin, Cane hills, Big Black basin and the Flat hills, each of which differs greatly from the other in point of fertility of soil and the ease with which it is cultivated. In the great Yazoo basin, however, are found the richest and most desirable lands in the entire valley of the Mississippi, suited especially to cotton, corn, sugarcane and jute culture. With proper care and cultivation from one to one and one-half bales of cotton are made per acre, and from fifty to seventy-five bushels of corn. In the Cane hill division is found soil of the silt formation, largely of a calcareous nature, from the great number of shells deposited as the ocean receded southward. All the products of the temperate zone are produced in the Cane hills. The Big Black basin lies along the river of that name. There the soil is of an alluvial nature, very fertile, and susceptible of a high state of cultivation. In the Flat hills division the soil is of a yellow loam nature, productive and very readily cultivated, still not so productive as other portions, but its topographical advantages have caused it to be largely utilized for general agriculture. Before the war Yazoo produced annually sixty-four thousand bales of cotton, and at this time there are handled at Yazoo city about fifty-two thousand bales per annum.

It is not probable that there is a county in the United States better supplied with all kinds of valuable timber than Yazoo. Mechanics, recently here from the North and West express surprise at the immense quantities of valuable timber they find here. In red gum, cypress, various kinds of oak, beech, hickory, etc., Yazoo has almost semi-national wealth standing in the forest. The most valuable timber is the cypress, red gum, and the various kinds of oaks. Cypress grows here in very large quantities, and equal in size to that of any other location. The red gum has but recently come into notice by lumbermen and mechanics who handle fine woodwork. It takes on a finer polish than black walnut, and for fine work has no superior on the continent. The oaks are all here in abundance.

Yazoo city, on the left bank of the Yazoo river, nearly in the center of the county, is the principal town. It contains about three thousand inhabitants, is the county-seat and the chief center of the commerce of the county. It has more commerce than almost any other town of its size. The other towns are Satartia, on the river thirty miles below; Benton, the old county-seat, ten miles back; Bentonia, Anding and Valley are new, thriving towns recently sprung up on the Yazoo & Jackson railroad; Dover, Vaughn's Station, Deasonville, Palmetto Home, Free Run, and Silver city are thriving country villages. Belle Prairie, Campbellsville, Craig, Eden, Enola, Evans, Fordyke, Hilton, Home Park, Kearney, Lake city, Mechanicsburg, Pearce, Phœnix, Redmondville, Roseneath and Zieglerville are postoffices.

The county seat was located in 1827, at a point which the act of legislature providing for the measure directed should be called Benton. Yazoo city was at that time known as Manchester, but has been known by its present name since about 1840. The present court-house was erected in 1870, at a cost of $70,000. Yazoo city was an Indian reservation, entered by Greenwood Le Fleur in 1827, under the provisions of the treaty concluded at Washington, January 20, 1825, with the Choctaw Indians. This place was known as Hanau's bluff until its incorporation as Manchester, in 1829.

The population of Yazoo county was six thousand five hundred and fifty in 1830, ten thousand four hundred and eighty in 1840, fourteen thousand four hundred and eighteen in 1850, twenty-two thousand three hundred and seventy-three in 1860, seventeen thousand two hundred and seventy-nine in 1870, thirty-three thousand eight hundred and forty-five in 1880, thirty-six thousand three hundred and ninety-four in 1890. In 1860 the number of voters was one thousand two hundred and seventy-seven; the number of taxable slaves, fifteen thousand eight hundred and ninety-six. The colored population was twelve thousand three hundred and ninety-five in 1870, twenty-five thousand three hundred and forty-two in 1880, twenty-seven thousand eight hundred and seventy-three in 1890.

The county was first represented in the state senate by Harden D. Runnels, in the legislature by Andrew E. Beaty. The present state senator is A. M. Hicks; representatives, I. M. Kelly, S. S. Hudson, C. H. Perkins, W. J. Watling.

It is said that the oldest citizens of Yazoo county now living are Dr. Abbey and F. Barksdale.

Copiah county was established January 21, 1823. Hazlehurst, the county seat, is situated on the Illinois Central railroad. The other towns are Crystal Springs, Gallatin, Beauregard and Wesson, on same railroad, and Rockport and Georgetown on Pearl river, which flows along the eastern border of the county, navigable for about six months in the year. Other postoffices are Ainsworth, Allen, Ashley, Barlow, Beech Grove, Beauregard, Bowerton, Brown's Wells, Carpenter, Gallman, Georgetown, Maharris, Martinsville, Millsaps, Miles, Rockport and Spencer. Bayou Pierre, Foster's creek, Bushy creek and numerous other creeks, afford good water power.

The Mississippi cotton and woolen mills are located at Wesson, in this county. The Illinois Central railroad runs through the county from north to south.

The surface of the county is in places level, undulating and hilly. Hazlehurst is four-hundred and thirty feet, and Crystal Springs four hundred and fifty feet above tidewater at New Orleans, La. The soil is sandy, with clay subsoil, with rich alluvial creek and river bottoms. The timber growth is pine, red, post and white oak, hickory, elm, maple, poplar, gum and cypress on river bottoms. The products of the soil are cotton, corn, oats, wheat, sugarcane, sorghum, upland rice, Irish and sweet potatoes, field peas, ground peas, and vegetables and melons of all kinds. Fruits, such as peaches, pears, grapes, figs, and all the small fruits do well and are extensively cultivated for market. At Crystal Springs there are between fifty and sixty acres in strawberries, and on the 15th of March, 1882, Mr. S. H. Stackhouse made his first shipment of strawberries to the Chicago market. Hazlehurst and other points on the railroad in this county ship large amounts of fruits and vegetables to the Western cities and New Orleans, La. Pasturage is extensive, and good for nine months in the year.

The immense pine forests east and west of Wesson will furnish lumber for sawmill men for years to come. The forests of longleaf pine will cut from ten to twenty thousand feet of lumber per acre. About ten miles northwest of Wesson are located the celebrated Brown's mineral wells, noted throughout the Southern states for their healing properties; there exist, within an area of two acres, mineral wells, highly impregnated with lime, sulphur, magnesia, iron and potash. These waters have been found very beneficial in bowel complaints, liver and kidney diseases, and have effected some cures, hardly short of miracles. A branch railroad could be extended out Bayou Pierre valley to these wells, without any considerable grading, and through one of the finest pineries in the Southern states, which can be purchased for a nominal sum. The lumber from these pineries could be sold in Wesson, and the tops of the trees could be utilized as fuel for the Mississippi mills, which consume fifty cords daily, for which they pay $2 per cord delivered.

Wesson handles twelve thousand bales of cotton yearly, worth $500,000. As the largest portion of this cotton is manufactured in the town, thereby saving all freight, insurance, storage and commission charges, our merchants are enabled to give a better price for cotton than any other town on the Illinois Central railroad. All other country produce, such as butter, eggs, milk, vegetables, wool, hides, etc., find a ready sale in our midst.

Copiah county was organized January 23, 1823, and the first probate and orphans' court was held at Coar's springs, about five miles east of the present site of Hazlehurst, with Barnabas Allen as judge. That was the principal seat of justice till Simpson county was formed from Copiah county in 1824, when Gallatin, about four miles west of where Hazlehurst is, was made the county seat. When the Illinois Central railroad was built and Gallatin left inland the town began to decline, and in 1872 Hazlehurst was made the county seat. This town was named for George H. Hazlehurst, who assisted in surveying the railroad, and has a population of about one thousand five hundred. Wesson, the largest town, is located in the extreme south part of the county, and there is located one of the largest cotton and woolen mills in the south. These mills are located about one hundred and thirty-five miles north of New Orleans and forty-five miles south of Jackson, on the Illinois Central railroad. A few years ago this was but a pine forest, worth at most $1 per acre, and now there stands here one of the most substantial towns anywhere along this line of railroad. Wesson, to-day, has a population of about four thousand and a valuation of property of over $1,500,000. The Mississippi mills alone pay taxes on nearly $1,000,000 worth of property, and they have a large investment, exempt from taxation for ten years, which will bring their property alone to nearly $1,500,000. There are three mills, all of brick, as follows: No. 1, three stories, 50x350 feet; No. 2, four stories, 50x212 feet; No. 3 (new building), five stories, 50x200 feet, two towers, six stories high, twenty feet square, with five-thousand-gallon water tanks and automatic sprinklers throughout. The tower between No. 1 and No. 2 is eight stories, with a twenty-thousand-gallon water tank, which leads through every part of the works automatic sprinklers, effectually obviating the danger of destruction by fire. A fourth building is 40x150 feet, two stories high, besides which the loom shed is one story and basement, 180x340 feet. In these buildings there are thirty thousand cotton spindles, thirty complete sets of woolen machinery and twelve hundred looms. Besides the above mentioned there is an abundance of machinery used for dyeing, finishing, etc. It requires four engines with a combined force of one thousand horse power to furnish the necessary motive power. In connection with the above buildings the mills have a large cotton warehouse, capacity ten thousand bales of cotton; which is about their requirement annually. In the basement of the loom shed they have a storage capacity of two million pounds of wool.

The system of waterworks of these mills is excellent. They have a one-hundred-and-fifteen-thousand-gallon cistern, connected with fire pumps and a six-inch water main and stand pipes at convenient points for attaching hose, which form an efficient system of waterworks, driven by two Worthington pumps capable of forcing water over the highest building. The supply is Spring creek, a mile and a half distant, and is inexhaustible. One reason for the success of these mills is the great variety of their products, of which the following is a list: Cassimeres, jeans, doeskins, tweeds, linseys, flannels, wool and cotton knitting yarn, cotton rope, cotton warp yarn, cottonades, flannelettes, gingham plaids, cheviots, checks, plaids, stripes, hickory, brown sheeting, shirting, drilling, eight-ounce osnaburgs, ticking for feathers and mattresses, sewing thread, sewing twine for bags and awnings, wrapping twine, honey comb towels, awning, balmoral skirts, etc. Very soon they will be running knitting machinery which will turn out hose and underwear of a superior quality. These goods have a reputation for excellence that is not surpassed by the product of any mills in the world, and the trade for them is drawn from almost every state and territory in the Union. These mills now employ about twelve hundred hands, but will have two thousand when all the new machinery is started up. The present monthly pay roll is from $18,000 to $25,000 which will be almost doubled when the increase of hands is required. These employes are for the most part taken from the surrounding country and adjoining counties.

The *Copian* was established at Hazlehurst some twenty-five or thirty years ago by J. F. Vance, and run by him till 1885, when it was burned, after which it was purchased by W. L. Mitchell, who was then editing the *Signal*, which was established in 1882 by Oscar Johnson. After the purchase of the *Copian* Mr. Mitchell consolidated the title and called it the *Copiah Signal*, which he has since edited.

There was a paper published at old Gallatin probably fifty years ago, and some others prior to the war, but little is known of them. At Crystal Springs was once published the *Monitor* and the Crystal Springs *Herald*, and in May, 1882, J. H. Aby began the publication of the *Meteor*, which he still publishes. At Wesson the first paper was the Wesson *Times*, and later the Wesson *Argosy* was published, and now the Wesson *Mirror*, by J. B. Adams.

In 1830 the population of Copiah county was seven thousand and one; in 1840, eight thousand nine hundred and fifty-four; in 1850, eleven thousand seven hundred and ninety-four; in 1860, fifteen thousand three hundred and ninety-eight; in 1870, twenty thousand six hundred and eight; in 1880, twenty-seven thousand five hundred and fifty-two; in 1890, thirty thousand two hundred and thirty-three. The colored population in 1870 was ten thousand three hundred and ninety; in 1880, fourteen thousand four hundred and forty-two; in 1890, fifteen thousand six hundred and thirty. In 1860 there were one thousand four hundred and sixty-two voters and eight thousand eight hundred and two taxable slaves. At this time Copiah has a larger white population than any other county in the state.

The county of Simpson, named in memory of the Hon. Josiah Simpson, was, by act of the legislature, enacted on the 23d day of January, 1824, created out of that portion of Copiah county lying east of Pearl river, and the county seat was subsequently located at Westville, named in honor of Hon. Cato West. Franklin E. Plummer, then residing there, and the only congressman who ever lived in the county, assisted in laying off the town, which was then only a crossroad place, where a grocery was kept and a store and tanyard were owned by Nathaniel O. Freeman, one of the pioneers. The first courts were held in a log cabin about twenty feet square, subsequently converted into a blacksmith shop. Soon afterward a frame courthouse was erected on the present site, which was destroyed by a fire in 1844, which was supposed to be the work of an incendiary. In 1846 a brick courthouse was built, which was also burned on the night of May 9, 1872. About a year after this the jail, a wooden building, was burned at night and a mulatto, incarcerated for murder, was burned in it. In 1874 the brick courthouse now occupied was built at a cost of about $13,000.

The early settlers, most of them, emigrated from Wayne county and the settlements on the Mississippi river, near Natchez, where they had temporarily located on their exit principally from the Carolinas and Tennessee. Among them were the Millers, Gates, Bells, Bridges, Deers, Banks, Chandlers, Briggses, Keens, Newsoms, Walkers, Berrys, Suttons, Fortenberrys, McLaurins, McNairs, Manguns, Stubbs, Kennedys, Magees, Wilkinsons, Turners, Williamsons, Womacks, Everetts, Sullivans, Touchstones, Halls, Harpers, Kellys, Goffs, Mahaffeys, Weekses, Bogans, Brewster H. Jayne, Daniel S. Farrington, Green Fenn, J. B. Mendenhall, Samuel Brown, John Dunford, the Mays, Fultons, Youngs, Bishops and Powells.

In the first settlements the more fertile lands were little sought after, as places suitable to establish stock ranches were preferable, the settlers being engaged almost exclusively in raising stock, for which the country was well adapted, having an abundant supply of running water and a luxuriant growth of grass and cane, on which the cattle kept fat the entire year without being fed. When the grass and cane began to be supplanted by a growth of bushes and game became scarce, the settlers gradually turned their attention to agricultural pursuits; the more industrious and economical of these accumulated considerable property. The means of transportation being confined exclusively to ox teams and wagons greatly retarded agricultural pursuits. The places of market being Mobile or Natchez, at least one hundred miles distant, it required a considerable time to market anything. Since other facilities for transportation have been offered, much more interest has been taken in agriculture, and lands that were once considered unproductive are now, with the aid of fertilizers, made to produce an average bale of cotton per acre, and sometimes more. Some of the lands, without fertilizing, yield fine crops of corn, peas, potatoes and oats. Considerable attention has been given to raising Louisiana cane, from which a sufficient quantity of molasses is made for home consumption. The soil is well adapted to the growth of peaches, apples, plums and some other fruits.

In the first settlements, there being no sawmills, the people had to live in log cabins, and the floors, if any, were made of hewn puncheons, but since the means of obtaining lumber is within the reach of every one, better and more comfortable houses have been built, many of which present a very neat appearance.

There are many constant clear, running streams within the county, sufficient for any ordinary water power, and no steam power seemed necessary, but within the last few years more than twenty steam sawmills have been located here, and are making lumber out of the abundance of pine timber for home use alone, as there are no means of transporting it.

Many of the early settlers were indifferent about educating their children, and there were but few schoolhouses, which were altogether built of logs, which were seldom occupied for more than three months at a time by some itinerant pedagogue, but there were a few persons who gave their children collegiate advantages. The cause of education gradually advanced, until there are now about seventy public schools, besides some others of a higher grade, and quite a number of young men and ladies annually attend the colleges in this and other states, some of whom bear off medals of honor.

The preaching among the early settlers was done mostly by local preachers, at some residence where the members would congregate at an appointed time. Soon after a few log cabins were built to be used both as schoolhouses and churches, where services were held about once a month, and churches were there organized, and by degrees a greater interest was manifested in the cause of religion, and now churches, sufficiently large to comfortably accommodate the congregations that usually attend them, have been built in almost every vicinity. The churches most numerously represented are Baptist, Methodist and Presbyterian.

For many years the legitimate sale of alcoholic drinks was permitted, and several saloons were liberally patronized, but the sentiments of the people have undergone a change, attributable mostly to church influences, and there are now no licensed liquor dealers.

The principal secret society is of the Masonic order. The chief products are cotton, corn, oats, sugarcane and rice, to which would be added as a leading industry the production of turpentine and lumber, if transportation could be had for the same.

The towns are Westville, the county seat; Jaynesville, in the southeastern part of the county; Harrisonville and Pearl, in the northwestern part, and Braxton, in the northern part. Other postoffices in the county are named Bridgeport, Caraway, Dlo, Everett, Fairdale, Glasgow, Jupiter, Magee, Mount Zion, Old Hickory, Overbey, Rials and Shivers.

The population of this county was two thousand and eighty-three in 1830, forty-six hundred and thirty-one in 1840, seventy-two hundred and twenty-seven in 1850, thirteen thousand six hundred and thirty-five in 1860, twelve thousand nine hundred and seventy-seven in 1870, sixteen thousand seven hundred and fifty-two in 1880, seventeen thousand nine hundred and twenty-two in 1890. The number of voters in 1860 was eleven hundred and seventy, and the number of taxable slaves sixty-seven hundred and twenty-four. The colored population in 1870 was twenty-one hundred and forty-nine, in 1880 three thousand and fourteen, in 1890 thirty-nine hundred and seventy-four.

The first representative of this county in the legislature was Stephen Howell, and in the state senate Charles Lynch. The present representative is Barney Smith.

Washington county, the wealthiest and one of the largest divisions of Mississippi shrievalties, lies in the west central part of the state, its western border being washed by the waters of the Mississippi river. Its area is five hundred and sixty thousand acres. About two hundred and fifteen thousand acres have been so far cleared as to be open for cultivation. These alluvial lands are of great depth, black of color, rich and productive, and their producing capacity is inexhaustible. The use of fertilizers is totally unknown, and half a century of constant cropping sees no diminution in their producing capacity. The yield of cotton ranges from one to one and one-half bales per acre, and even two have been grown. Corn yields from sixty to eighty bushels, while oats are a very fine crop. Vegetables and fruits find there a natural home, while the grasses, clover, Bermuda and other valuable varieties yield two and three tons per acre. As a desirable country for stockbreeding and feeding purposes, then, no county offers greater or better advantages. Many herds of Holstein, Jersey and short-horn cattle are found. Horses and mules are also bred. No portion of the county but has excellent railroad and marketing facilities, there being within its limits not less than one hundred and fifty miles of railroad track and twenty-two stations.

Washington is a splendidly watered county, its rivers being the Mississippi, Yazoo and

Sunflower, and Deer creek, Bogue Phalia and Black bayou. Besides there are a number of very charming lakes, which afford the most delicious varieties of the finest fish, in the greatest abundance, namely: Lake Lee, Swan lake, Lake Washington and Lake Jefferson. Some of these afford delightful resorts for fishing parties, gun clubs and excursions for pleasure, and are often taken advantage of. The rivers, creeks and lakes thus drain and water every portion of the county and supply its people with a fine food product.

Educational facilities have been provided by the establishment of eighty free schools, whose term is five months during the season. The white and colored children are equally well provided for, only their buildings are separate. Churches are also plentifully scattered about in every neighborhood, affording every one the advantages of religious consolation.

This county (not the old Washington county organized in 1800), was organized January 29, 1827, and was named in honor of the first president of the United States. Its first state senator was Henry W. Vick, its first representative William B. Prince. Its present state senator is Joseph M. Jayne; its representatives are E. N. Thomas, John T. Casey and J. F. Harris.

When Mississippi was under territorial government the boundaries of Washington county embraced all of the country from the mouth of the Yazoo river to the Tennessee line and included the territory between the Mississippi and Yazoo rivers. The county seat was Princeton, its location being on the Mississippi river about ten miles above the present boundary line between Issaquena and Washington counties. In those days of pioneer settlements Princetown was quite an important place and business center. It had in its most flourishing period a population of about six hundred. When Washington county was divided, creating the different counties now in the Yazoo delta, the county seat was moved to a point about one mile south of the present city of Greenville and given the name of Greenville (now known as old Greenville) in honor of Gen. Nathaniel Greene, one of General Washington's most trusty lieutenants. After the county seat was moved to Greenville, Princeton's importance rapidly declined. S. B. Lawson was one of the last merchants of the place, and in 1868 he sold the town site and remaining buildings to a colored man for $125.

After the late war the legislature passed an act ordering the board of supervisors of the county to locate the new county seat within three miles of the old site, old Greenville having mostly caved into the river, or been destroyed during the war. They located it on the Blantonia plantation, then the property of Mrs. H. B. Theobald, formerly widow of Col. W. W. Blanton, the original settler of Blantonia. When Colonel Blanton preëmpted this land, in 1828, there was an island, No. 83, in front of Blantonia*, consisting of about one thousand acres which has been entirely removed by the action of the river's current. The chute dividing it from the main land was then called Bacon chute by the river pilots, from the fact that a flatboat, laden with bacon from Indiana, was purchased from the owner by some outlaws, who paid him in counterfeit money. The bend of the river, extending from what is known as Carter's point to the plantation of Thomas Warfield, was, in 1832, named by Colonel Blanton's wife Bachelor's bend, from the fact that every settler in the bend at that time was a bachelor, except Col. W. W. Blanton. From 1828, when Colonel Blanton settled there, until 1835, the following prominent planters located in the bend and vicinity: Alfred Carter, William R. Campbell, Andrew Carson, of Virginia; A. W. McAllister, of Georgia; Dr. S. R. Dunn, of Philadelphia; James McCutcheon, Pinckney Montgomery, Alex. Montgomery, David Jackson, of Virginia; William Hunt, of Vermont; William Potts, Thomas Warfield, of Kentucky; Dr. Hood, of Kentucky; Howel Hinds, of Mississippi; Francis Griffin. Maj. William Hunt

*Numbered by pilots from the mouth of the Ohio down.

was the father of Capt. W. E. Hunt, formerly sheriff for sixteen years. The three earliest settlers of the county were Col. W. W. Blanton, Joseph Egg of Egg's point, and Capt. Henry John, of Lake Washington. The county rapidly filled with planters, mostly Kentuckians. Samuel Burks, E. P. Johnson, Pattison Baine, John Robb, Harvey Miller, Thomas Smith, of Longwood, and Samuel and Isaac Worthington, the Shelbys, Princes and many others came. There were, in those early times before 1830, many lawless characters, their chief being Colonel Bunch, from whom Col. Henry Johnson purchased his preëmption on Lake Washington. The lands along the river were first settled, and afterward those on Williams bayou and Deer creek. The above mentioned settlers were men of wealth and culture. Colonel W. W. Blanton, the father of Dr. O. M. Blanton, was born in Winsboro, S. C., was educated by Keene O'Hara, of Kentucky, then a noted teacher, and father of Theodore O'Hara, of poetical fame. He graduated in law, and removed with his father, Col. John Blanton, to Jefferson county, Miss. He afterward married, in Warren county, Harriet Byron McAllister, and settled in Washington county, on Blantonia plantation, the present site of the city of Greenville. The Blanton family were originally of English-Norman descent from Virginia, having settled there in the days when Virginia was a colony of Great Britain, and located in Cumberland county, on the James river. The McAllisters were from Georgia. Gen. W. McAllister, Mrs. Blanton's brother, was one of the most prominent citizens of this county, and father of the present Mrs. James E. Negus. John A. Scott was also an old settler of Washington county, and son of Governor Scott, of Mississippi territory. Wade Hampton was another.

The people near Mr. Griffin's first got their mail at Lake Port, in Arkansas, and later on at Columbia, Ark. These towns were in Chicot county, Ark. After Princeton was established that was their postoffice and place to trade.

Early settlers below Blantonia plantation, some of whom have been mentioned, were Dr. S. R. Dunn, James McCutcheon, David Jackson, Maj. William Hunt, Thomas Warfield, Major Potts, Francis Griffin, Dr. Hood. Above Blantonia was John A. Scott, William R. Campbell, Andrew Carson, Henry T. Tripes, and above on the Mississippi river was Col. John L. Martin. James Sutton, who lived on Island 83, was one of the best known of the early settlers. Dr. B. O'Bannon was from Virginia, and one of the first settlers of Deer creek.

In 1812 Washington county had two thousand and ten white and nine hundred slave population. The aggregate population was twenty-nine hundred and twenty in 1820, nineteen hundred and seventy-six in 1830, seventy-two hundred and eighty-seven in 1840, eighty-three hundred and eighty-nine in 1850, fifteen thousand six hundred and seventy-nine in 1860, fourteen thousand five hundred and sixty-nine in 1870, twenty-five thousand three hundred and sixty-seven in 1880, forty thousand four hundred and fourteen in 1890. In 1860 there were three hundred and eighty-seven voters, and thirteen thousand eight hundred and sixteen taxable slaves. In 1870 the colored population was twelve thousand four hundred and five, in 1880, twenty-one thousand eight hundred and sixty-one; and in 1890 thirty-five thousand seven hundred and three.

The subject of railroads in Washington county began to be actively considered and discussed in 1871, and in 1872 or 1873 bonds were voted in aid of a road contemplated to extend from Greenville east to the railroad system through the center of the state. The other counties along the line also voted bonds, and but for the financial crash of 1873 and a decision of the supreme court adverse to the validity of said bonds, the railroad contemplated would doubtless have been then built. A little grading only was done and the enterprise died away. In 1878, under the chief direction of Mr. Charles P. Huntington, the narrow gauge road to Deer creek was begun, Mrs. H. B. Theobold, the oldest citizen of Greenville, driving the first spike. The road was completed ten miles, to Stoneville, on Deer creek, in the spring of that year. This was the beginning of railroad building in Washington county and the Yazoo delta. In 1880 the road was completed into Sunflower county, and as far as the Sunflower river, thirty miles due east of Greenville, and down Deer creek to the Sharkey county line, thirty miles south of Greenville. In 1881 this road was sold to the Georgia Pacific railway company, by which it is now operated. It is the design of that company to extend their main line from Columbus, Miss., to the present terminus of the road, at the Sunflower river. In 1882 the charter and franchises of the Vicksburg & Memphis railroad were purchased by Mr. R. T. Wilson, a wealthy and extensive railroad builder of New York, through whom it was designed as a continuation of the Huntington system of railroads from Memphis to New Orleans. And during the past eighteen months the construction of this road has been pushed forward with remarkable rapidity, notwithstanding unusual obstacles. It is now in full operation, a link in one of the most important and far-reaching railway corporations of the nation. It enters Washington county from the south, where Deer creek enters Sharkey county. It follows along the course of this stream, on its western bank, parallel with the Georgia Pacific narrow gauge for twenty miles. It then crosses the creek and continues in a northeasterly direction to Bogue Falaya, and crosses that stream and continues to Memphis. Its general course is north and south through the entire length of the county. From Leland station, at the creek crossing, a branch diverges, which runs entirely across the northern portion of the county, into Bolivar, and terminates on the Mississippi river at a point opposite Arkansas city. From this branch, at a point five miles north of Greenville, another road is being built to Greenville, and thence south, entirely through the county, via Lakes Lee and Washington, back to the main line on Deer creek, near Rolling fork, in Sharkey county. The earthwork of these branch roads is about completed, and both are under contract to be completed and in running order by January 1. This road is known as the Louisville, New Orleans & Texas railway.

Besides Greenville, the seat of justice, the county contains the following named towns, villages and postoffices: Arcola, Belzona, Burdett, Callao, Chatham, Elizabeth, Erwin, Estill, Glen Allan, Hampton, Helm, Hallandale, James, Kenwood, Lake Washington, Leland, Leota landing, Longwood, Offutt, Percy, Pettit, Refuge, Stoneville, Swiftwater, Wayside, Wilczinski and Winterville. Greenville has a population of six thousand six hundred and fifty-five; Leland, six hundred; Leota, three hundred and fifty; Stoneville, one hundred and fifty; Arcola, three hundred and seventy-five.

Madison county was established January 29, 1828, and named in honor of President Madison. It embraced that portion of Yazoo county east of the Big Black river. The commissioners appointed to lay out and select a county seat and contract for the erection of county buildings were Jonah R. Doak, Robert Carson, Sr., Archibald McGehee, John P. Thompson and William Wilson. The first to represent this county in the state senate was Henry W. Vick; in the legislature, James R. Marsh. The present state senator is John R. Cameron; representatives, J. R. Childress and Robert Powell.

The seat of justice is Canton. Flora and Madison station are thrifty towns. Other villages and postoffices are Anderson, Baconville, Calhoun, Camden, Cameron, Cobbville, Couparle city, Kirkwood, Livingston, Lottville, Millville, Oaks, Parsonia, Prattville, Revive, Sharon, Sharpsburg, Shocoe, Sulphur Springs and Way's bluff. Runnelsville, Williamsburg and Madisonville, once flourishing towns, are now extinct.

The population of Madison county in 1830 was four thousand nine hundred and seventy-three; in 1840, fifteen thousand five hundred and thirty; in 1850, eighteen thousand one hundred and seventy-three; in 1860, twenty-three thousand three hundred and eighty-two; in 1870, twenty thousand nine hundred and forty-eight; in 1880, twenty-five thousand eight hundred and sixty-six; in 1890, twenty-seven thousand three hundred and twenty-one. The number of voters in 1860 was one thousand and one; the number of taxable slaves fifteen thousand nine hundred and thirty-four. The colored population numbered fifteen thousand one hundred and thirty-nine in 1870; in 1880, nineteen thousand nine hundred and seven; in 1890, twenty-one thousand two hundred and ninety-seven.

Madison county lies in the east-central portion of the state, and is bounded on the south by Hinds and Rankin, east by Scott and Leake, north by Attala and Holmes, and west by Yazoo county. Its superficial area is seven hundred square miles, or four hundred and sixty-eight thousand acres, not more than one-third of which has been opened. Two-thirds of the area is timbered with valuable varieties of forest trees, such as all kinds of oak, hickory, pine, gum, poplar, walnut, beech, cypress, etc., standing ready to hand for use in manufactures of different kinds, and, as yet, wholly undeveloped.

The Big Black river runs along the whole northwestern border of the country and Pearl river forms its southeastern boundary. There are numerous creeks tributary to these rivers, notably, Bogue Chitto, Persimmon, Hanging Moss, Panther, Bear, Doak's, Kentucta and others, some of which afford excellent water power for running machinery, and all of which are useful for drainage and stock-water purposes. Along these streams are found some exceedingly fertile lands, whose productive capacity is unlimited. The entire surface of the county is gently undulating, and the soil is various in character and quality, with a clay subsoil, a great deal of which is quite rich, outside of the fine alluvial in the creek and river bottoms. Limestone for building purposes of an excellent quality, as well as marls, are found in great abundance in different portions of the county.

Pasturage is quite extensive, and some of the largest and finest stock farms in the state are found there. Domestic grasses, red clover, blue grass and other varieties do well where properly cultivated, and the native grasses, Bermuda, Japan, clover, crabgrass and others grow in bountiful profusion everywhere, furnishing the very best of pasturage as well as hay for feeding or marketing purposes. It may be interesting to note here, that Madison county carried off the majority of the first premiums for its display of horses, cattle and mules at the state fair in Jackson, and, throughout the state, it is known as the banner live-stock county.

The staple product of Madison is cotton, and of this from twenty-two thousand to twenty-five thousand bales are grown annually. Besides cotton, corn, vegetables, fruits, root crops, broomcorn and sugarcane are grown with success and profit. Corn yields as high as one hundred and twenty-five bushels per acre, with proper cultivation, while early vegetables, strawberries and other fruits yield a gross income of from $300 to $600 per acre, year after year.

Immigration, the infusion of new blood, new ideas, and capital, will speedily bring about the grandest results. Nowhere is true hospitality more generally shown and the courtesies and amenities of social intercourse more scrupulously observed.

Rankin county was named in honor of Christopher Rankin. It was formerly a portion of Hinds county and was organized under an act approved January 4, 1828. The seat of justice is at Brandon, which was named in honor of Governor Brandon, and was well known early as the locality of the Brandon bank. This town is situated on the line of the Vicksburg & Meridian railroad. The other principal towns of the county are Steen's creek, Cato, Fannin, Pelahatchie and Armistead. Other postoffices are located at Chapman, Cherry, Clarksburg, Dobson, Goshen springs, King, Lucknow, Lynwood, Monterey, Pearson, Pink, Thomasville, Virgil and Whites.

The county is bounded north by Madison, east by Scott and Smith, south by Simpson, and west by Hinds. Pearl river flows along its western line and is navigable for six months during the year. Strong river has its course across the southeastern corner. These rivers and their numerous tributary creeks give the county fine water power. The Vicksburg & Meridian railroad, which runs through the center of the county from east to west, on the thirty-second parallel of latitude, is a link in the Texas Pacific railroad system. The Armistead spoke and wagon factory is an important enterprise.

The county contains about one hundred and twenty-five thousand acres of cleared land. The balance is well wooded, much of it level, a good deal of it undulating, some of it broken. There are a number of large limestone quarries and beds of rich marl in various parts of the county, and in the southern portion is a large amount of fine building stone.

The soil on the creek bottoms and much in the uplands is rich and productive. The products are corn, cotton, peas, Irish and sweet potatoes, rice, wheat, oats, barley, rye, millet and sugarcane, with vegetables of all kinds in great abundance. There are large bodies of longleaf or yellow pine, white and red oak, hickory, beech, poplar, ash, gum, walnut, cypress, etc. Apples, pears, peaches, figs, plums, apricots, pomegranates, all varieties of grapes, pecans, etc., do well and produce abundantly, as do all the small fruits.

The commissioners who located the county seat and contracted for the erection of the county buildings were William Steen, John Brown and Elijah Gentry. The first state senator who represented this county was Henry W. Vick, the first member of the lower house was Alexander Chisholm. The present state senator is Dr. J. H. Hall; representatives Pat Henry and W. A. Loflin.

The population of Rankin county in 1830 was two thousand and eighty-three; in 1840, four thousand six hundred and thirty-one; in 1850, seven thousand two hundred and twenty-seven; in 1860, thirteen thousand six hundred and thirty-five; in 1870, twelve thousand nine hundred and seventy-seven; in 1880, sixteen thousand seven hundred and fifty-two; in 1890, seventeen thousand nine hundred and twenty-two. In 1870, the colored population was seven thousand two hundred and seventy-three; in 1880, nine thousand five hundred and fifty-nine; in 1890, ten thousand four hundred and sixty seven.

Isaac B., Jesse S. and Thomas Norrell, the Steens, Simon and Henson Williams, the Webbs, John George, Archibald Laird, Thomas Bird, Joel Lewis, John Rankin, General Coffee, and others equally prominent were among the early settlers in this county.

CHAPTER XI.

~~~᠁~~~

COUNTIES OF THE THIRD (FINAL) CHOCTAW CESSION.

KEMPER county was established December 23, 1833, and named after Reuben Kemper, who led a crowd of Tombigbee men against Mobile in 1811, many of whom were killed by the Spaniards, while others never recovered from their drunken orgie at Minette. The congressional description is townships nine, ten, eleven and twelve north, in ranges fifteen, sixteen, seventeen and eighteen and fractional range nineteen —east of the Choctaw meridian. The total area is seven hundred and forty square miles, of which thirty thousand acres are cleared land. Long and shortleaf pine timbers three-fourths of the area. The county is watered by the heads of the Sucavnochee river, the Okatibbee creek and many other streams.

The population in 1840 was seven thousand six hundred and sixty-three; in 1850, twelve thousand five hundred and seventeen; in 1860, eleven thousand six hundred and eighty-two; including five thousand five hundred and sixty slaves and eight hundred and twenty polls; in 1870, twelve thousand nine hundred and twenty; in 1880, fifteen thousand seven hundred and nineteen, and in 1890, seventeen thousand nine hundred and sixty-one, made up of seven thousand eight hundred and forty-five whites, and ten thousand one hundred and sixteen negroes.

F. T. Scott was the first president of the board of police. The courthouse was destroyed by fire in 1881, with the records and documents. The great Chisholm murder case, recorded in print by James H. Duke, brought the district into notoriety even in a more marked degree than the doings of Kemper did in 1811.

The postoffices of Kemper are Binnsville, population one hundred and twenty-five; Calvert, population forty-three; De Kalb, population three hundred and four; Fort Stephens, population thirty-five; Giles, Herbert, population fourteen; Jacksonville, Kellis' store, population twenty-seven; Kemper springs, Kemperton, Moscow, Mount Nebo, population sixteen; Narkeeta, population seventy-five; Oak Grove, population seventy-four; Oktibbeha, Pea Ridge, population nineteen; Peden, population forty-three; Porterville, Preston, Prince, Prism, Rio, population one hundred and one; Scooba, population four hundred and fifty; Spinks, Sucarnochee, population ninety-two; and Wahalak, population one hundred and fifteen.

Montgomery county was named in honor of Richard Montgomery, who fell at Quebec, Canada, while leading the American troops against the British fortifications. The river and creek bottoms are level and fertile; the upland undulating and only a small portion hilly. The Big Black and its feeders water the three southern tiers of townships and the feeders of the Yalobusha the two upper tiers. The total area is three hundred and ninety-five miles,

J Alex Ventress

of which a little over a fourth is cleared and cultivated. The population in 1880 was six thousand six hundred and seventy-one whites and six thousand six hundred and seventy-nine negroes, or a total of thirteen thousand three hundred and fifty. In 1890 the total population was fourteen thousand four hundred and fifty-nine, seven thousand three hundred and seventy-two being whites and seven thousand and eighty-five negroes.

The county was established May 31, 1871, and the first meeting of supervisors was held June 26, that year, at Winona, W. B. Peery being president, Eli P. Cartlidge, Thomas C. Curry and James Thomas, all appointed by Governor Alcorn, who also appointed John C. McKenzie, sheriff; Thomas C. Blackmore, clerk of chancery court; Henry Harris, circuit clerk; T. B. Brown, assessor; F. M. Shyrock, treasurer, and W. H. Parke, superintendent of education. In 1873 a frame building was erected for courthouse purposes.

The postoffices of the county are Alva, Best, Duck Hill, population three hundred and seventy-five; Huntsville, population seventy-six; Kilmichael, Liddell, Lodi, population one hundred and twenty-five; Mayfield, Minerva, Poplar Creek, population seventy-six; Rural, Stewart, Sweatman, Thrailkill, Walker and Winona, population twenty-one hundred.

Jasper county, in townships one, two, three and four north, and township eleven south of base line in ranges ten, eleven, twelve and thirteen, east of the Choctaw meridian, was established December 3, 1833, and named after Sergt. William Jasper, a Revolutionary soldier of 1750–79. As its seat of justice, Paulding was named after John L. Paulding, who aided in the capture of the British Major Andre. The headwaters of the Pascagoula and Chickasawha rise here, and every township has its stream. In the river and creek bottoms the land is level and the soil rich, while the undulating portion of the county is generally productive. The total area is seven hundred and twenty square miles, of which about sixty eight thousand acres is cleared land. The population in 1840 was three thousand nine hundred and fifty-eight; in 1850, six thousand one hundred and eighty-four; in 1860, eleven thousand and seven, including four thousand four hundred and forty-five slaves and eight hundred and ninety-polls; in 1870, ten thousand eight hundred and eighty-four; in 1880, twelve thousand one hundred and twenty-six, and in 1890, fourteen thousand six hundred and six, made up of seven thousand three hundred and eighteen whites and seven thousand two hundred and eighty-eight negroes. The county was first settled by Joshua Terrell, James S. Terrell, Edward Terrell, D. D., Edwin S. Caraway, Francis McCormick, Elijah Hall, Reddick Rodgers, Isaac Herington, John Parker, Dr. Newman, Lewis B. Robinson, Robert Cooper, Josiah Jones, John Dean and John Cooper. David Lightsey came and settled among the Indians in 1832. The first election was held in 1834.

The first police board comprised John Lightsey, Robert Cooper, Berry Parker, William Bridges and James S. Terrell; and the first county officers were, Joshua Terrell, sheriff; Jesse G. Sims, clerk of all the courts; John C. Thomas, probate judge; William Horsey, Sr., assessor and collector; Frank McCormick, surveyor.

The postoffices of the county are Acme, Alto, Garlandville, population one hundred and twenty-five; Hamlet, Heidelberg, population two hundred and fifty-four; Jewell's Hill, Lake Como, population seventy-four; Leonia, Masengale, Missionary, Montrose, Paulding, population two hundred and twenty-nine; P. K., Rose Hill, Shady Grove, population thirty-two; Turnerville, population fifty-two; Viola, Vosburg, population one hundred and seventy-eight; and Weems.

Winston county is bounded by Noxubee on the east, Kemper and Neshoba on the south, Attala on the west and Choctaw and Oktibbeha on the north. The total area is six hundred and forty square miles, of which about fifty-one thousand two hundred and

14

fifty acres are cleared. The head streams of Pearl river find their source here, and also one or more of the head streams of the Noxubee, so that every township claims a stream. Inexhaustible quarries of lignite, silicate of alumina and some iron ore are found here.

An act to organize the county laid off a part of the territory acquired by the United States from the Choctaw tribe of Indians at the treaty of Dancing Rabbit creek, and for other purposes, was approved December 23, 1833. The territory within the following townships, viz.: Thirteen, fourteen, fifteen and sixteen, in ranges ten, eleven, twelve, thirteen and fourteen, formed the new county, which was called Winston county, in honor of Louis Winston, who was a distinguished citizen of the state.

Names of some of the first or earliest settlers of Winston county are given as follows:

Elza Anderson, Asa Allgood, Josiah Atkinson.

John H. Buckner, James Bevell, John C. Brown, Caleb Barron, Ezekiel Barron, Van S. Bell, Ephraim Butler, William B. Billingsly, Aaron G. Byram, Andrew Byerly, Joseph Bell, James Brown, Uriah Berry, Simeon Berry, Henry Barfield, R. D. Brown, M. D., David Brewer.

William C. Coleman, Jesse Crosby, Allen Crosby, Joseph P. Crosley, T. D. Connell, John Coulter, Edward Coulter, Jesse Christian, Peter Crawford, Uriah Conner.

Jesse Dodson, Uriah Davis, Daniel Doughty, H. C. Durant.

Thomas Ellington, Felix Ellis, Jonathan Ellison.

Anthony Foster, Jesse Fields, Thomas Fields, William Fox, Edward Foster, M. D., L. J. Fonville, Tobias Farr.

Alfred Gilkey, Notly Gilmore, Robert Gill, Henry Gray, LL. D., John F. George, Amze Godden, Rev. Elijah Gentry, A. G. Garrigues, Thomas Golden, A. Gillis, A. M. Grant, John F. Gray.

Joel Howell, John H. Hardy, N. G. Hudson, Benjamin Hyde, William Harwood, LL. D., Ain Hudspeth, Burr H. Head, Robert S. Hudson, LL. D., Thomas Hudson, Edward Hamilton James Hefflin, Joel Haynes, Thomas Holmes, H. L. C. Hendricks, Phelps Haynes.

Isaac Jones, Thomas Jones, Harry Jackson, Benjamin Jordan.

Levi Keese, Hamilton Kyle; Placide Krebly, Stephen Krebly, second settlers, both married Indian women.

Joshua Leach, Thomas Lovorn, Alfred Leech, Peter Lowery, Azariah Leurs, William T. Lewis, Isaac Leatherwood, H. R. Lanham.

Booth Malone, Amos C. Morris, S. R. McClanahan, Peter McClanahan, Colby McDaniel, Amzie Meek, James B. Meek, James B. McLelland, M. D., Rev. J. Marlin, Rev. John Micon, James Morrow, Reuben Mason, Swift Mullins, Stephen Miller, Sr., John McLeod, Malcolm McLeod, Samuel Murff, Sr., Reuben McKenzie, William McMillan, Sr., James McCracken, John McGowen, James Morrow, Hugh McQuien.

Allen Nabors, C. G. Nimmo, Jacob Null, D. B. Nesmith.

James Oxford, Thomas Osburn.

James R. Parks, A. W. Porter, Josiah Prestridge, Arch Porter, Samuel T. Potts, Joshua Peevy, H. W. Portwood, Hubbard Quarles, David Quarles.

Sem Robinson, Sephalin Ridgeway, Ezra Ripley (Indian), Robert H. Rogers, Daniel Roberts, James B. Rather, Peter Randolph.

D. D. Steed, L. M. Stone, LL. D., Jeptha Spruell, T. H. Smith, James M. Scott, Rev. E. R. Strickland, Aaron Stewart, Philip M. Steed, George H. Singleton, Jesse Shumaker, Noah Sherod, Col. William Shaw.

Edward Thompson, Asa Tool, Elija Tabor, Nathan Tabor.

Henry Vanlandingham.

Nath. Woodward, Thomas Wilkins, Joshua Whitehead, Josiah Woodruff, Simeon Watson, Jonas Watkins, Samuel Wregg and Thomas Young.

William T. Lewis, who settled here in 1836, was elected county surveyor in 1839 and holds that position to-day, after fifty-two years of service. To him this list of pioneers must be credited.

The representatives in state legislature were: Jesse M. Fields, Isaac Jones, John H. Buckner, William McDaniel, T. D. Connell, T. J. Hughes, T. J. Hughes, C. T. Murphy, S. W. Smyth, E. R. Huntley, John Coulters, T. C. Lynch, S. W. Godfrey, M. T. Collier, J. B. Covington, Hugh McQuien, M. A. Mills, S. W. Smyth, William Kelly, W. B. Smith, George Beaman, T. P. Miller, William Kirk, William T. Lewis, R. D. Brown, C. T. Kirk, William Capserton, Joseph S. Reed, William B. Owens, D. A. Graham, W. B. Johnson, M. A. Coleman, R. C. Jones, H. J. Gully, O. C. Watson, T. P. M. King and I. L. H. Strait, the present representative.

The county surveyors of Winston since its establishment are named as follows: George W. Thomason, Joseph Bell, T. P. Miller, William T. Lewis, William T. Lewis, Samuel C. Phagan, William T. Lewis, Allen Hudson, Joseph Hudson, John T. Sharp, A. J. Shields, William T. Lewis.

The sheriffs of Winston county were Amos C. Morris, John H. Hardy, James B. McLelland, Andrew Webb, Thomas F. Holmes, Michael A. Metts; Jared Richardson, appointed; C. C. Hudson, appointed; Thomas Houston, appointed; John L. Conner, M. A. Coleman, William B. Johnson, M. A. Coleman, George Y. Metts and H. L. W. Hathorn, the present incumbent.

The probate and chancery clerks were Benjamin Jordan, Joseph P. Crosley, E. R. Huntley, H. G. Woodruff, William G. Hudson, E. D. Hyde, J. R. Bozeman, J. M. Turnipseed; J. R. Ellis, appointed; James M. Davis, appointed; J. M. Turnipseed; William H. Hudson, expelled; John F. Sharp is the present clerk.

The circuit clerks were James Phagan, John Brown, Jesse T. White, W. B. Shumaker, J. J. McDaniel, R. M. Hight, H. L. W. Hathorn, and Bertram Webster, the present circuit clerk.

The probate judges of Winston county are named as follows James Bevill, Felix U. Ellis, William B. Smith, S. W. Smith, J. O. Woodward, J. B. McLelland, Robert Washington, E. R. Huntley, H. C. Edwards, E. D. Hyde, and James Davis, appointed, now judge of probate.

Louisville, also named after Louis Winston, was platted on a tract of twenty acres donated by Jesse Dodson. The population in 1840 was four thousand six hundred and fifty; in 1850, seven thousand nine hundred and fifty-six; in 1860, nine thousand eight hundred and eleven, including three thousand nine hundred and thirty-two slaves and nine hundred and fifty-seven polls; in 1870, eight thousand nine hundred and eighty-four; in 1880, ten thousand and eighty-seven, and in 1890, twelve thousand and eighty-nine, made up of six thousand nine hundred and seventy-seven whites and five thousand and seventy-two negroes. The towns and villages of the county are Betheden, Coopwood, population one hundred and fifty-two; Cornwell, Fearn's springs, population one hundred and fifty-nine; Hanale, population seventy-two; Hinze, Loakfoma, Louisville, population three hundred and seventy-five; Noxapater, population, twenty-six; Perkinsville, population forty-four; Perryville, population thirty-three; Plattsburg, population one hundred and fifty-seven; Pugh, Randall's bluff, population eighteen; Rome, population thirty-two; Rural hill, Singleton, population fifty; Vowell and Webster, population forty-eight.

Noxubee county is the name given to that division of the state bordering on Alabama in townships thirteen, fourteen, fifteen and sixteen north, and ranges fifteen, sixteen, seventeen, eighteen and fractional range nineteen east of the Choctaw meridian.   It is there the fountain heads of the Okanoxubee take river form.   The soil of the townships in the three eastern ranges is a black prairie resting on white or blue rotten-limestone, along the Alabama line.   Toward the west the land is rolling, and in some sections very much broken.   The name is a contraction of Oka-naka-shua or Stinking-Bullet water, a name given in Indian days by the Choctaws, who found leaden bullets in the river.   The total area is six hundred and sixty-eight square miles, of which about two hundred and fifty-three thousand acres are cleared land.   The population in 1840 was ninety-nine hundred and seventy-five; in 1850, sixteen thousand two hundred and ninety-nine; in 1860, twenty thousand six hundred and sixty-seven, including twelve thousand six hundred and seventy-nine slaves and eight hundred and thirty-eight polls; in 1870, twenty thousand nine hundred and five; in 1880, twenty-nine thousand eight hundred and seventy-four and in 1890, twenty-seven thousand three hundred and thirty-eight, or forty-six hundred and fifteen whites and twenty-two thousand seven hundred and twenty-three negroes.   Among the early settlers were William Colbert, Isham Harrison, W. C. H. Finley, George B. Augustus, Talioferro S. Howard, Joseph H. Froth, Jefferson Clements, Reuben H. Grant, H. W. Foote, Alexander B. Stevens, T. C. Billups, J. M. Cunningham and the officers named below. Noxubee county was formed December 3, 1833, out of the Choctaw purchase.   The members of the first board of police were: Isham Harrison, president; W. C. H. Finley, William Calbert, Felix Walker and Thomas Ellington, with Fleming T. Calbert, sheriff; Richard J. Swearingen, circuit clerk, and F. W. Callaway, clerk board of police.   This board organized January 18, 1834, and in July, 1834, Probate Judge Augustus held court.   Judge T. S. Sterling held the first court at Macon in the spring of 1834.   James F. Trotter was the first elective circuit judge of this, the then sixth, judicial district.   He afterward went to the supreme bench.   In 1841-2 a brick house was erected for courthouse purposes, which was replaced about 1859 by a larger house.   The present officers are: Board of supervisors—W. D. Clark, J. B. Cunningham, F. A. Denton, Jesse Blythe, J. P. Stokes; Z. T. Dorroh, sheriff; B. J. Allen, chancery clerk; John A. Tyson, circuit clerk; W. N. Haynes, assessor; D. J. Buck, surveyor; A. C. Fant, treasurer; S. M. Thomas, superintendent education; M. R. Butler, district attorney.   The Macon *Intelligencer* was the first newspaper established at Macon, in 1839, by Johnson & Horn, after several changes it was called the Macon *Beacon*.   It is now owned and edited by Philip Ferris.   The Mississippi *Sun* was established by George R. Smith about 1882.   It was removed to Shuqualak in May, 1891, by G. B. Horper, who now continues its publication.   The Noxubee *Democrat* was established in the fall of 1889, by J. E. Madison, who was killed shortly afterward.   It is now edited by Robert C. Boyle.   The postoffices of Noxubee are Alliance, Bigbee valley, population seventy-five; Brazelia, Brookville, population five hundred and seventy-five; Cliftonville, population one hundred and fifty; Cooksville, population seventy-nine, Deerbrook, Fairport, Flatwood, Gholson, population fifty-eight; Harlan, Hashuqua, population seventeen; Lynn Creek, Macedonia, Macon, population twenty-two hundred; Mashulaville, population seventy-two; Paulette, population seventy-two; Prairie Point, population fifty-two, and Shuqualak, population four hundred.

Grenada county, in townships twenty-one, twenty-two and twenty-three north, ranges two, three, four, five, six, seven and part of range eight east of the Choctaw meridian, forms part of the upper Yalobusha and Loosascoona territory, in the southern tier of counties of northern Mississippi.   The total area is four hundred and thirty square miles, of which about fifty-six thousand acres are cleared.

The Yalobusha river runs almost entirely through the center of the county, and this stream, with creeks, furnishes a large area of rich bottom land. The character of the country generally is a level tableland, soil of black sandy loam, with clay subsoil. It is very productive naturally, and responds liberally to an intensive system of farming. Highly gratifying results have been obtained by the use of fertilizers, and all that is needed to reward the husbandman is the ordinary care and industry of the prudent farmer. The chief products are cotton and corn, but the soil is well adapted to the growth of grain and grasses of all kinds. Vegetables grow so luxuriantly that this county offers advantages second to none in the country, and this industry is already under headway. Hay is now an important crop in this county, and two tons to the acre is not an unfrequent yield. Stockraising is almost general among our farmers, the people of the county having realized that it is much easier to raise stock than to buy it. The county is well supplied with an abundance of pure free-stone water, by springs, wells and living streams of clear water, some using cisterns as a matter of preference. The climate is mild and salubrious, and as nearly even as anywhere in the world. Lands can be purchased on easy terms, and range in price from $2 to $10 per acre.

The population in 1870 was ten thousand five hundred and seventy-one, made up of three thousand nine hundred and twenty-nine whites and six thousand six hundred and forty-two negroes. In 1880 the total number of inhabitants was twelve thousand and seventy-one, or three thousand two hundred and thirty-six whites and eight thousand eight hundred and thirty-five negroes, and in 1890, fourteen thousand nine hundred and seventy-four, or three thousand nine hundred and fifty whites and eleven thousand and twenty-four negroes. The revenue of the county, from all sources, for the eleven years, ending January 1, 1891, is shown in the following table, taken from the recent report of J. T. Thomas, auditor and clerk:

	1880	1881	1882	1883	1884	1885	1886	1887	1888	1889	1890
Privilege and retail	$ 6,450 00	$ 5,160 00	$ 5,285 00	$ 5,950 00	$ 5,660 00	$ 5,680 00	$ 4,630 00	$ 4,340 00	$ 4,985 00	$ 5,515 00	$ 4,988 00
Fines	773 75	1,128 75	594 50	1,338 06	1,648 00	889 54	795 57	1,201 15	493 00	778 45	1,537 86
Sundry accounts	67 00	383 00	280 35	727 38	1,291 22	462 25	446 98	162 24	2,010 52	1,645 49	922 37
County and special tax	18,756 39	12,205 28	12,891 67	23,160 78	16,727 70	36,042 13	35,162 59	26,625 70	9,256 31	8,893 10	1,074 65
School tax	1,841 17	2,515 19	2,567 79	2,659 61	2,575 27	2,550 13	2,563 40	2,618 57	2,906 68	3,490 87	4,418 86
Poll tax	1,620 00	1,492 00	1,849 00	1,843 00	1,820 00	1,930 00	1,879 00	1,912 00	2,073 00	2,026 00	1,823 00
State tax	4,017 53	4,069 51	3,399 70	3,421 33	3,151 15	3,340 02	4,734 15	5,182 75	5,902 83	7,107 73	6,406 06
Total	$33,525 84	$26,953 73	$26,867 07	$39,100 11	$32,873 34	$50,894 07	$50,211 49	$42,042 41	$27,637 34	$29,456 64	$21,170 80

This gives a total of $380,732.84 for eleven years. While the privilege and state tax are no part of the revenue of the county, yet they show the exact amount paid in taxes directly and indirectly by the taxpayers. The tax levy, five mills, made in 1891, is much lower than that of many other counties in the state, and in no county is the levy less, though there are two counties claiming a smaller levy. The assessment in 1880, including $1,717 poll tax, amounted to $1,391,147, and in 1890 to $2,279,155. In 1880 the state, county and school tax levy was twenty mills; in 1885 and 1886, thirty-two and one-half mills, and in 1890, twelve mills.

The county was formed May 9, 1870, from Yalobusha, Tallahatchie, Carroll and Choctaw, and organized with the following named members of the board of supervisors: J. D. Leflore, president; Dr. John L. Milton, secretary; F. P. Ingram, Andrew Davis and Freeland Towne.

David Green (colored) was chosen representative; J. B. Townsend, chancery and circuit clerk; L. French, sheriff; A. G. Dubard, treasurer; H. B. Heath, assessor; John S. Payne, surveyor, and W. E. Kelley, superintendent public education. The present board of supervisors comprise A. C. Leigh, president; W. W. Trussell, L. B. Yeager, W. R. Baker, E. L. Atkinson.

Dr. William McIrvine is the representative; J. T. Thomas, chancery clerk; J. C. Perry, circuit clerk; G. B. Jones, sheriff and taxcollector; R. H. Turner, treasurer; C. C. James, assessor; J. G. Gibbs, surveyor; R. T. Payne, county superintendent of education.

The first and only courthouse the county has had is a substantial two-story brick building, erected in 1884 at a cost of about $20,000, exclusive of fixtures, etc., which are valued at about $5,000.

However much the county is associated with Indian history, the French and Spanish did not risk settlement there. Prior to the advent of the American pioneers it was wholly and solely a portion of the Choctaw hunting grounds. The site of the town of Grenada was deeded to John Donly or Donnelly by the United States commissioners who signed the treaty of Dancing Rabbit creek. Some years after the American pioneers had established themselves on the Yalobusha, the villages of Pittsburg and Tullahoma were established and contested for priority until 1836, when both villages merged their names into Grenada.

The postoffices of the county are Burketon, Elliott, population fifty-three; Graysport, population eighty-seven; Grenada, population two thousand three hundred; Hardy Station, population one hundred and forty-four; Le Flore, Misterton, Peete, Providence, Tatum, Williamsville, population sixty; Yeagersville and Youngs.

Newton county was established February 23, 1836. It was settled in 1833. The following are some of the earliest: Cader Price, James Merchant, J. M. and E. S. Soper, Alex Graham, Jake Corby, Ralph Simmons, Capt. Joshua Tatum, James Ellis, Edward and Abel Chapman, William or Commodore Price, James Thames, Mint Blalock, N. L. Clarke, William and Joseph Harris, Judge Harolson, Thomas Dempsey, Jesse and Richard Pace, J. Miller; the Bonds, Joneses, Johnsons, Saffolds, McMullens, Scanlans, Kellys, Roberts, Chapmans, Walls, Wellses and Fergusons; all these have many descendants still living. There are in the county to-day about three hundred and fifty-one Choctaws, who returned from their reservation and lead a life of industry here, making fair farmers and good farm hands. The creeks forming the rivers of the southeast water the county in almost every section. The congressional description is townships five, six, seven and eight north, in ranges ten, eleven, twelve and thirteen east of the Choctaw division. The area is five hundred and seventy-six square miles, of which a tract of about sixty-seven thousand acres is cleared. The population in 1840 was two thousand five hundred and twenty-seven; in 1850, four thousand four hundred and sixty-five; in 1860, nine thousand six hundred and sixty-one, including three thousand two hundred and forty-seven slaves and one thousand and fourteen polls; in 1870, ten thousand and sixty-seven; in 1880, thirteen thousand four hundred and thirty-six. and in 1890, sixteen thousand six hundred and twenty-five, made up of ten thousand and eighty-two whites, six thousand one hundred and ninety-two negroes and three hundred and fifty-one Indians.

The postoffices are Battlefield, Chunkey's station, population fifty-two; Conehatta, population eighty-one; Decatur, population one hundred and fifty; Dormanton, Hickory, population, two hundred and ninety-four; Lawrence, population seventy-five; Lucern, Moore's Mills, population twenty-seven; Newton, population five hundred; Prospect, Rainer's, Riversville, Roscoe, Shealey, Spivey, Stamper, population twenty-seven; Union, population one hundred and twenty, and Vance.

Clarke county is in the tier of counties that adjoin the state of Alabama. It is located in the southeastern portion of the territory acquired from the Choctaws at the treaty of Dancing Rabbit creek, concluded in September, 1830. It has Lauderdale county on the north, Alabama state on the east, Greene county on the south and Jasper county on the west.

The territory of which this county was a part, was at different periods claimed and occupied by the French, who made the first settlement; by the English, who acquired it from the French by treaty; and by Spaniards, who conquered and wrested it from the English during the American Revolution. Once, also, it was a part of English West Florida, also a portion of that territory which elicited such warm political struggles in the state of Georgia at the time of the celebrated Yazoo controversy.

The Indian population of this section was scanty. They conducted a trade by means of pack horses with Mobile. On the advent of the whites a wagon trade began, which was finally displaced by the railway. According to the best information obtainable, the county was organized by a commission created in 1833, under an act of the state legislature. This commission was composed of Norman Martin, Samuel K. Lewis and John Griffin. According to authority they proceeded to hold an election and locate the county site. At that first election the following officers were chosen: David B. Thompson, sheriff; George Evans, treasurer; Henry Hailes, probate judge; William Covington, clerk of the circuit and probate courts; Norman Martin, Samuel K. Lewis, George Knight, Stephen Grice, Calvin M. Ludlow (supposed), were the members of the board of police, the equivalent of the present board of supervisors. On the organization of the board, Norman Martin was chosen to preside over its deliberations. It seems appropriate to remark just here that the present board (1891) has for one of its members Norman Martin, Jr., a son of the first presiding officer.

The county seat was first located at the geographical center of the county, but afterward, for some cause, was removed to Quitman, where it yet remains. The space necessary for the courtyard was donated to the county by John Watts, who died in the early seventies. Thomas S. Sterling was at the time judge of the district to which Clarke county was afterward attached, and then or directly afterward became a resident of the new county. The county was named in honor of the first chancellor of the state, Joshua G. Clarke, and its county seat was given the name of the second chancellor, John A. Quitman. The county, at the date of its organization, was sparsely settled. The vote at the first election was supposed to have been less than three hundred.

A difference of opinion exists as to the date of the organization of the county. Verbal statements place it in the spring of 1834, while an official map found in the clerk's office in 1876 place it on December 23, 1833. From the date of the county's organization to the year 1838 no records are extant, therefore verbal statements must be relied upon for any history of that interval. During this time Sheriff Thompson was reëlected, as perhaps, also, the other officers above named, Samuel K. Lewis excepted, who was called to represent his county in the legislature in 1835. He was the first to fill this position. Prior to its organization as a county, the inhabitants were under the jurisdiction of Wayne county.

In Besancon's "Register of Mississippi" it is found that in 1837 Larkin Evans was elected sheriff, assessor and taxcollector; George Evans, county treasurer; Henry Hailes, probate judge; Allen McLendon, representative; Samuel W. Howze, clerk of the circuit and probate courts; David Neily, John Gunn, Michael McCarthy, George Knight and Charles Long, members of the board of police. Quitman in this year had two stores, two groceries and forty inhabitants, while the white population of the county was estimated at one thousand three hundred and thirty, and the slave at five hundred and three. The cotton crop for the year 1838 was three hundred and twenty-eight bales. After the wants of the people became so numerous and varied as to demand increased facilities for exchange of products, flatboats and keelboats began to ply on the Chickasawha, going as low as the mouth of the Pascagoula. Here they received goods from New Orleans and Mobile. In 1835 the first church was established at Cedar creek by the Methodists, and to this day it retains its organization with a good membership. In 1840 the first church organized in the northern part of the county was organized at a schoolhouse near Hand's ferry, on the Chickasawha. In 1844, in the southeastern part of the county, Elmo Baptist church was established. In the half century since elapsed, these denominations and the Presbyterians, who built a church in West Enterprise in 1851, have dotted the county with houses of worship. In 1837 the first school of which there is any knowledge was opened at Hand's ferry under the supervision of Jeremiah Hennessee, an Irishman. In 1840 W. R. White opened a school at the springs near the Moore plantation. A school was taught by D. M. Heerdly, near Enterprise, in 1843. After this time the cause of education advanced steadily. George W. Sommerville, A. G. Marshall, Judge Lawson, Miss Clara Chase and others being conspicuous in this connection. The first newspaper established in the county was the Quitman *Intelligencer*, in 1851 or 1852. It was edited by A. G. Horn, though owned by J. T. Ballance.

Topographically, Clarke county is quite diversified. On the northeast extensive hills raise their heads, while in the southwest and southeast a prairie country more or less level is found. It contains fine forests of pine and a soil well adapted to agriculture and vegetable growing. The Chickasawha flows through its borders. Clarke is one of the very few counties in Mississippi possessed of mineral wealth. Vast deposits of iron ore underlie its northern border and promise much to the development of the county at no distant day.

The total area is six hundred and sixty´ square miles. Of this an area of about fifty-two thousand acres is cleared land. The population in 1840 was two thousand nine hundred and eighty-six; in 1850, five thousand four hundred and seventy-seven; in 1860, ten thousand seven hundred and seventy-one, including four thousand nine hundred and sixty-one slaves and one thousand and sixty-eight polls; in 1870, seven thousand five hundred and five; in 1880, fifteen thousand and twenty-one, and in 1890, fifteen thousand eight hundred and twenty-six, made up of seven thousand seven hundred and seventeen whites, eight thousand one hundred and six negroes and three Indians.

The postoffices of the county are Barnett, Carmichael, De Soto, two hundred and fifty-eight; Energy, Enterprise, one thousand one hundred and thirty; Pachuta, seventy-three; Quitman, four hundred and ten; Shubuta, seven hundred and eighty-four; Stonewall station and Theadville.

A cotton factory, three and a half miles south of Enterprise, making sheeting, shirting, osnaburgs, etc. It employs one hundred and eighty hands. There is a spoke factory at Shubuta, run by A. P. Hand.

The principal towns are Quitman, the county seat, Enterprise, Shubuta and De Soto, on the Mobile & Ohio railroad, and Pachuta, on the New Orleans & Northeastern railroad. There is a valuable bed of iron ore near Enterprise, and a syndicate formed to develop it, together with other industries they contemplate building up.

The citizens of Enterprise and vicinity have engaged to a small extent in truck-farming, in addition to their farms, and are making it pay handsomely. There is abundant water-power on the Chunkey and Oktibbeha rivers, and other large streams in different parts of the county. There are about one thousand four hundred bales of cotton raised in the county.

Holmes county was established February 19, 1833, and named by the board of police in honor of Governor Holmes. Extending from the Yazoo, which runs southwest and forms the western limits, to the Big Black, which also runs southwest and forms the eastern limit, it robbed old Yazoo county of coveted territory, and its establishment was so bitterly opposed that the act had to be passed over the governor's veto. At old Rankin, in the western part of Holmes county, are the site and ruins of old Fort Rankin, a United States fort that formerly stood on the line of the Choctaw nation. It is said this fort was built about 1830. It is near the present town of Tchula.

The area of the county is seven hundred and fifty square miles, and of this an area of about one hundred and seventy-three thousand acres is cleared. The soil is black and loamy in the bottom lands, and black and sandy in the uplands. The product will average a half bale of cotton or fifteen to twenty bushels of corn per acre on uplands. Cotton, corn, oats, wheat, field peas, millet, sugarcane, sorghum and the grasses do well, and remunerative crops are made. Transportation facilities on the Yazoo river on the west and the railroad on the east leave an alternative to shippers. It costs to send a bale of cotton of five hundred pounds to market by river $1.50, and by railroad $3. Forest trees are all kinds of oak, pine, walnut, poplar, ash, hickory, gum and cypress. The pasturage is extensive, the native grasses—Bermuda, Lespediza (Japan clover), and crabgrass—growing to perfection here. All the fruits—peaches, pears, early apples, figs, plums, etc., and strawberries—do well. Near Durant, and on the railroad, much attention is paid to raising small fruits, which find a ready market at Chicago. The population in 1840 was nine thousand four hundred and fifty-two; in 1850, thirteen thousand nine hundred and twenty-eight; in 1860, seventeen thousand seven hundred and ninety-one, including eleven thousand nine hundred and ninety-six slaves and one thousand one hundred and ninety-five polls; in 1870, nineteen thousand three hundred and seventy; in 1880, twenty-seven thousand one hundred and sixty-four, and in 1890, thirty thousand nine hundred and seventy, made up of six thousand nine hundred and eighty whites, twenty-three thousand nine hundred and eighty-eight negroes and two Indians.

Many of the old settlers of the county are named in the following list: Britto Smith, Burrel Scott, James Scott, Thomas Rule, John H. Truly, James M. Gwin, Wiley Davis, near Franklin, Hon. Thomas Dulaney, Charles A. Weston, Thomas Land, Samuel Barrett, L. and E. B. Noel, David Beaty, Hugh A. Fultz, Ira Mitchell, M. D., A. B. Roe, M. D., Samuel Long, Garrett Keirn, Dr. Sample, B. W. Sanders, D. J. Stall, W. Pickens, Alva Wilson, B. F. Dulaney, Samuel I. Shackelford, Samuel Haskins, Otho Belle, W. W. George, Barry Griffin, a United States surveyor, who ran the lines in Holmes county until he became a Baptist preacher; Hezekiah Harrington, A. H. Paxton and others. It is related that among the members of the first board of police, chosen in 1833, were James Scott, president; and J. J. McBride. O. W. Beall was sheriff. In 1834 Lexington was named as the seat of justice. On October 20, 1834, William E. Parker presided over the board. William Taylor and Walter Dent were members.

The postoffices of the county are Ancona, Bee Lake, twelve; Coxburg, Cruger, Dent, Durant, one thousand; Ebenezer, one hundred and twenty-two; Emory, nineteen; Eulogy, Franklin, forty-two; Goodman, four hundred and seventy-eight; Howard, Ituma, Lexington, nine hundred and seventy-five; Marcella, twelve; Marksville, Methena, Mileston, Owens, Pickens, six hundred; Pluto, Richland, thirty-two; Tchula, Thornton, seventy-six; Tolarville and West, population two hundred.

Leake county was established December 25, 1833, and named in honor of Governor Leake. It is in townships nine, ten, eleven and twelve north, and ranges six, seven, eight and nine east of the Choctaw meridian. Pearl river receives the Yockahockany, the Lobutcha, the Young Warrior and smaller streams within its boundaries and takes river form in the extreme southwest township. The total area is five hundred and sixty square miles, of which an area of about sixty thousand acres is cleared land. The population in 1844 was twenty-one hundred and sixty two; in 1850, fifty-five hundred and thirty-three; in 1860, ninety-three hundred and twenty-four, including twenty-eight hundred and thirty-five slaves and ten hundred and fifty-eight polls; in 1870, eighty-four hundred and ninety-six; in 1880, thirteen thousand one hundred and forty-six, and in 1890, fourteen thousand eight hundred and three, made up of ninety-three hundred and twenty-five whites, fifty hundred and forty-three negroes and four hundred and thirty-five Indians.

Among the white pioneers were Henry Harper, who was elected first representative; Judge John Williams, John D. Boyd (served as state senator and died while a member at Jackson of small-pox, January, 1844); Patrick Sharkey, Thomas Harris, Isom Daniel, J. E. Allen, J. M. Hooper (who built the first courthouse—built of pine poles with bark on), William Gordon, Edmond Hamilton, Elias Bennett, Uriah Babbett, Judge W. W. Arnett, Joshua Parker, Barry W. Johnson, Rev. Elijah Willbanks (of Princetown Baptist church), Benjamin F. Watkins and Abram Buford.

The first officers were elected April 10, 1834; Cullen C. Arnett was elected first sheriff, Levi J. Eastman, probate clerk; Nathan Warren, assessor and collector of taxes; John D. Boyd, president of the board of police, called the first meeting for June 19, 1834, when James Pruett, Isaac Wells, Richard H. Walker and Edward Branch, members, were present. The county seat was then called Leakeville, but on July 31, that year, the present name, Carthage, was adopted.

The regular election was held in November, 1835, when John C. Arnett was elected probate clerk; John Anderson, assessor and collector; Lewis Henning, treasurer; Benjamin Enlow, sheriff; Edwin Fox, judge of probate; John D. Boyd, president of board of police jurors.

Carthage has three churches—Methodist, Baptist and Presbyterian, all strong organizations, but no colored churches; one good school, Carthage high school; one Masonic lodge, and one lodge of the Knights and Ladies of Honor, make up the organized societies of the town.

The postoffices of the county are Carthage, population four hundred and twenty-five; Conway, Coosa, population fifty-seven; Dossville, Edinburg, population one hundred and seventy-eight; Estesmill, Freeny, Freetrade, Good Hope, population twenty-seven; High Hill, population twenty-seven; Lameta, Lena, Madden, Marydell, Ofahoma, population sixty-nine; Palona, Renfroe, St. Anne, Standing Pine, Thomastown, population fifty-four; Tuscola, Walnut Grove, population one hundred and seventy-eight; Williston and Yorka.

Oktibbeha county was established December 23, 1833. The name is a contraction of Okatibbeha or Fighting Water, the river being the line between the Choctaw and Chickasaw territories, and the scene of numerous battles between the tribes. The county is in the second tier of counties west from the eastern border and Alabama line, and in the second tier north from the center of the state. Starkville, the county seat, is situated near the center of the county and is distant, in a direct line, from New Orleans two hundred and fifty-two miles; from Mobile, Ala., one hundred and ninety-eight miles; from Memphis, Tenn., one hundred and thirty-seven miles; from Birmingham, Ala., one hundred and twenty miles; and from the Mississippi river one hundred and twenty-five miles. The average elevation of the county above the Gulf of Mexico is about six hundred feet, the drainage being southeast and northeast through numerous small creeks, into the Tombigbee and Noxubee rivers. The total area is four hundred and sixty square miles, and of this an area of about one hundred and twenty-one thousand acres is clear land. The population in 1840 was four thousand two hundred and seventy-six; in 1850, nine thousand one hundred and seventy-one; in 1860, twelve thousand nine hundred and seventy-seven, including seven thousand one hundred and eighty-six slaves, and eight hundred and seventy-three polls; in 1870, fourteen thousand eight hundred and ninety-one; in 1880, fifteen thousand nine hundred and seventy eight; and in 1890, seventeen thousand six hundred and ninety-four, made up of five thousand five hundred and eighty-five whites and twelve thousand one hundred and nine negroes.

The act creating Oktibbeha county was passed December 23, 1833, and organization completed 1834. The first court was held under a tree about three miles northwest of where Starkville is, with Gen. Reuben Davis as district attorney, and R. A. Lampkin as acting sheriff.

The county seat was located in the woods and called Starkville, in honor of General Stark of Revolutionary fame. This site was chosen on account of the presence of a spring near by known by the Choctaw Indians as Hickashebaha spring, meaning Sweet Gum grove, there being a beautiful grove of sweet gum just below the spring.

The first officials were: David Reese, probate judge; Charles Dibrell, probate clerk; Joseph Yeates, circuit clerk; J. W. Eastland, sheriff; Robert Bell, treasurer; James Wirman, ranger, and Elijah Hogan, president board of police (the same who kept the first hotel). R. A. Lampkin was first postmaster and carried the mail in his hat.

The first church society was the Presbyterian, about 1835, by Horatio Bardwell. The Baptists organized late in 1839. The Associate Reformed and Cumberland Presbyterian were established later. Beatie Tate was the first merchant.

The Starkville *Whig* was the first paper published in Oktibbeha county. It was established in 1847 by Dr. J. T. Freeman, and a few years later became the *Broad Ax*, which continued till shortly before the war. The *States' Rights Advocate* was published about the same time or for a few years prior to the war by Jesse A. Yeates. Soon after the war Lee Stillman published the *New Era* till about 1875. December, 1878, Col. J. M. Norment began the publication of the *Citizen*, which he published till his death, May, 1881, and it was continued by his widow, Mrs. M. C. Norment, till about when it came under the control of the Citizen Publication Company, and is now published by Fletcher Fondreu.

The *East Mississippi Times*, now published by William Ward, began its career December, 1869, hence is the oldest paper in the county. In 1875 Col. W. B. Montgomery founded the *Southern Live Stock Journal*, now published by the Journal Publishing Company. It is one of the most ably edited journals in the South, devoted to agriculture, horticulture, live stock, etc. The *Southern Stockman* is a recently established journal (1890), published by Edwin Montgomery.

The postoffices of Oktibbeha county are Agricultural College, Bradley, population seventy-two; Bridges, Choctaw Agency, population fifty-three; Double Springs, population one hundred and twenty-six; Hassie, Hickory Grove, Longview, Maben, Muldrow station, Oktoc, population six; Osborn, population one hundred; Sessumsville, population sixty-eight; Starkville, population two thousand; Sturgis, population four hundred, and Trimcane.

Lowndes county was established January 30, 1830. The area is five hundred and thirty-six square miles, of which an area of about two hundred thousand acres is cleared land. Its chief products are: cotton, corn, wheat, hay, oats, tobacco, fruits, vegetables, lumber, timber, horses and cattle. The leading industries are cotton mills, cotton seed oil mills, foundries, lumber mills, truck farms and dairying. The population in 1830 was thirty-one hundred and seventy-three, in 1840 fourteen thousand five hundred and thirteen, in 1850 nineteen thousand five hundred and forty-four, in 1860 twenty-three thousand six hundred and twenty-five, including fifteen thousand nine hundred and thirty-four slaves, and twelve hundred and twenty-nine polls; in 1870 thirty thousand five hundred and two, in 1880 twenty-eight thousand two hundred and forty-four, and in 1890, twenty-seven thousand and forty-seven, made up of fifty-nine hundred and forty whites, twenty-one thousand one hundred and five negroes and two Indians. Population on the east side is largely white, while on the west side it is densely black.

The county is traversed north and south by the Mobile & Ohio railroad, and east and west by the Georgia Pacific division of the Richmond & Danville railway.

The Tombigbee river, a navigable stream, divides the county north and south into nearly equal areas, the east side being sandy soil, and the west prairie.

The vital statistics show the county to be as healthful as any county in the United States, the death rate, including negroes, being about fourteen per one thousand.

The settlers in Lowndes county from 1817 to 1830 are named as follows: Richard Barry, Joseph Bryant, Jack Ames, Alex Moore, John B. Jones, Robert Jamison, N. E. Goodwin, S. S. Franklin, Henry Buchannon, John Slidel, Henry Patten, William Cook, Silas McBee, William Craven, Henry W. Hunt, Marcellus Hatch, Richard Barry, John Billington, Ovid P. Brown, Robert Haden, Kleber Kilchrist, William Moore, Jerry Leveritt, A. Duncan, Alexander Moore, Lawson Willerford, William Halbert, Zenophin Halbert, B. F. Beckwith, Jesse Bryan, O. L. Nash, Allen Brooks, Martin Brooks, E. E. Lerch, E. C. Lerch, Lawson Wilford, William Downing, Stephen Cooke, Thomas Sampson, Harry Stevens, William Nielson, George Taylor, C. H. Abut, Gideon Lincecum, Garland Lincecum, Lewis Johnson, Allen Motley, John Peachlyn, E. B. Randolph.

In August, 1819, Gideon Lincecum came with a large stock of goods and opened a store.

William Vizer had brought with him a short time before a few remnants of dry goods, overland from Alabama. On the first day of January, 1821, the first mail ever brought to Columbus was opened by G. Lincecum, the first postmaster. The first steamboat arrival was that of the Cotton Plant, Captain Chandler, in 1822. During the year 1819–20 the military road leading from New Orleans to Nashville, passing through Columbus, was opened by the United States troops.

The first county court was held at Columbus on Monday, April 12, 1830. The board consisted of Thomas Sampson, president; Macajah Brooks, and Samuel B. Morgan. The first county officials were: R. D. Haden, county clerk; Nimrod Davis, sheriff; John H. Morris, assessor and collector; O. P. Brown, county treasurer; William L. Moore, county surveyor.

The present board of supervisors are—Dr. R. McClory, president; I. H. Sanders, J. W. Gardner, A. G. Easley, and R. P. Hairston; C. L. Lincoln, sheriff; E. P. Richards, chancery clerk; J. T. Armstrong, circuit clerk; D. S. Cox, assessor; J. A. Snell, treasurer; John Sanders, surveyor.

Secret societies: Farmers' Alliance, Ancient Free and Accepted Masons, Independent Order of Odd Fellows, Knights of Honor, Knights of Pythias, Universal Benevolent Fraternity, Knights and Ladies of Honor, United Working Men and Catholic Knights of America.

The public schools of the county are seventy-nine in number, white and colored, and the State industrial institute and college for white girls. The largest county schools are: Franklin academy (at Columbus), Crawford, Caledonia, Old Zion, Cobbs Switch, Trinity and Mayhew. The educable children in the county number eight thousand eight hundred and thirty-nine, of whom there are at school fifty-two hundred and sixty-four. The amount paid for public schools in the county for the years 1889 and 1890 was $25,382.99. The industrial institute and college for white girls is paid for out of state appropriations.

The religious bodies are Methodist, Baptist, Presbyterian, Episcopal, Cumberland Presbyterian, Christian and Catholic.

Columbus, the seat of justice, was settled in 1817, one Thomas Moore erecting a log cabin that year. In 1819 a town was platted and the act of establishment provided that the sessions of court should be held there. The population of Columbus in 1890 was forty-five hundred and fifty-two. A postoffice was established there in 1821, and since that year the following named offices have been created: Artesia, two hundred and two; Caledonia, two hundred and one; Cherokee, Crawford, three hundred and fifty; Dow, Dunbar, McCown, Mayhew's station, one hundred and ninety-seven; New Hope, twenty-seven; Penn, Steenston, Swanzy and Trinity.

Carroll county was established December 23, 1833, under the act authorizing the organization of counties in the final Choctaw cession, and named after Charles Carroll, of Carrollton. The Big Black river forms the southeastern boundary of the county. The creeks are Coila, Petticocowa, Big Sand, Abattapooda, Pettacona, Pelucia, Teoctalia and Peachahala Abiacha. The total area is six hundred and fifteen square miles, and of this area about one hundred and ninety-seven thousand acres is cleared land. About one-fourth of the county is in cultivation, the balance is timbered with all kinds of oak, poplar, pine, gum, walnut, chestnut and cypress on river and creek bottoms. The soil is fertile on the creeks, on the hills not so rich, but free and easily cultivated and improved. The productions are cotton, corn, oats, wheat, field peas, peanuts, sorghum and potatoes (Irish and sweet); all kinds of vegetables and fruits. The pasturage is good and extensive, consisting of native grasses in summer and switchcane and the run of the plantation for winter. Stockraising could be made very profitable in Carroll county. Beds of green-sand marl are found near Vaiden and in other portions of the county, while lignite has been found in several localities.

The population in 1840 was ten thousand four hundred and eighty-one; in 1850, eighteen thousand four hundred and ninety-one; in 1860, twenty-two thousand and thirty five, including twelve thousand six hundred and sixteen slaves and fourteen hundred and forty-nine polls; in 1870, twenty-one thousand and forty-seven; in 1880, seventeen thousand seven hundred and ninety-five; in 1890, eighteen thousand seven hundred and seventy-three, or eight thousand and seventy-five whites and ten thousand six hundred and ninety-eight negroes.

A meeting of the first police jury of Carroll county was held March 11, 1834, at the house of George W. Green, where the town of Carrollton is located. The members present were: Daniel McEachrem, Thomas Matthews, Edmond G. Whitehead, Woodard Applewhite and John Rodgers, who took the oath prescribed by the constitution before Absalom W. Herring, one of the commissioners appointed by the legislature to organize the county. Edmond G. Whitehead was elected president of the board, and Thomas Rhodes was elected clerk. Absalom W. Herring was elected first sheriff. The clerk gave a bond for $2,000 and the sheriff one for the sum of $10,000. At the meeting of the police jurors, April 16, 1834, it was ordered that the county seat of Carroll county be located on the north half of the east half of the southwest quarter of section eighteen in township nineteen, north of range four east, and that the same be called Carrollton.

The postoffices of the county are Black Hawk, two hundred and twenty-five; Blackmonton, thirteen; Brock, Carrollton, four hundred and seventy-five, Coila, Gerenton, Hemingway, Jefferson, McCarley, Money, Smith's mills, fifteen; Teoc and Vaiden, nine hundred.

Attala county was established under authority of the act approved December 23, 1833. The Big Black river forms the western boundary of the county. The other water courses are Zilpah, Long, Apuckta, Yockanookana, Sharkey and other creeks, affording good water power. The total area is seven hundred and fifty square miles. There is about one-third of the county open lands, level on the creek and river bottoms, and the rest undulating and hilly; two-thirds well timbered with oaks of various kinds, hickory, pine, ash, gum, wild cherry, cypress in river and creek bottoms, etc. Soil on bottoms is fertile, and on uplands moderately rich, and easily worked and improved; fine beds of marl in various parts of the county. In digging a well at Thompson's sawmill, a few miles north of Kosciusko, a bed of oystershells, ten feet thick, was passed through. These marls and oystershells furnish an abundance of lime for fertilizing purposes. The products are corn, cotton, oats, wheat, potatoes, peas, peanuts, sorghum, etc.; vegetables and fruits of all kinds are abundantly grown for home consumption. The pasturage is generally good, but not much attention is paid to stockraising. Sheep husbandry could be made very profitable in this county. Several flour, saw and planingmills in the county and a large flouringmill at Kosciusko are the principal manufacturing industries.

The population in 1840 was four thousand three hundred and three; in 1850, ten thousand nine hundred and ninety-one; in 1860, fourteen thousand one hundred and sixty-nine, including four thousand nine hundred and eleven slaves and one thousand four hundred and sixty-two polls; in 1870, fourteen thousand seven hundred and seventy-six; in 1880, nineteen thousand nine hundred and eighty-eight, and in 1890, twenty-two thousand two hundred and thirteen, made up of twelve thousand six hundred and sixty-six whites, nine thousand five hundred and twenty-three negroes and twenty-four Indians.

The early settlers of Attala county, antedating its organization, were Hosea Crowder, Joseph Crowder, Ely Crowder, Levy Crowder, William S. Ross, James N. Taylor, Frank Rutherford, Presley Williams, Rolin Saggs, Bayless Oldham, John Irving, W. R. Irving, William Bell, John Short, Tom Rogers, William Dodd, Allen Dodd, Abner Armstrong, Jonathan Armstrong, John Allen, William Allen, Joseph Ivey, Chafin Sinith, Asa Day, Noah Day, Zebadiah Guess, William Cole, Isom Cole, James Cole, William Tipton, Oliver M. Simpson, William T. Irish, Dock Hughes, John Jeffries, William Calcote, Nick Fisher, the Carsons, John Biggs, William Ellington, Tom Potter, the Stapletons, Gordon D. Boyd, Bill Exum, Zack Rector, the McCarters, Jack Davis, Gray Sims, Dr. H. J. Munson, John Standard, James Fletcher, S. N. Gilliland, John Harvey, James Lilly, Charles Fuller, Alex Mabry, Daniel McMillan and Henry Musselwhite.

This county was in that region known as the Nation. The name was given in honor of an Indian maid, who committed suicide because her lover had died. Greenwood Le Flore, for whom the town of Greenwood and county of Le Flore took their names, was born in what is now Attala county.

Original settlers immigrated here from the states of Tennessee, Georgia, Alabama, Kentucky and North and South Carolinas, but mostly from Tennessee, as the soldiers en route to the battle of New Orleans were delighted with the country, and after the war returned here for permanent citizenship.

The water courses of the county are Long creek, Apookta, Seneasha, Zilpha, Coles creek, Turkey creek, Lobutcha, Yockanookany and Big Black, with their numerous tributaries, making an abundance of fertile soil in the county for agricultural pursuits.

There is only one railroad in the county, and it is known as the Aberdeen branch of the Illinois Central, running from Durant to Aberdeen, Miss., traversing about forty miles of the county, and on it are located the towns of Sallis, Kosciusko, Ethel and McCool.

The town of Sallis was located in 1874, and was named in honor of Dr. James G. Sallis, and has a population of about two hundred persons.

Kosciusko took its name from Gen. Thaddeus Kosciusko, and was located in 1834. It has a population of about fifteen hundred. It is the commercial metropolis of central Mississippi, and, owing to the culture and prominence of so many of her citizens during the history of the town, Koscuisko is now recognized as the Athens of the state of Mississippi. No town, old or young, big or little, has furnished so many distinguished men, in law, politics, science and theology as Kosciusko. A history of her illustrious men would make a book of itself.

It may be proper to mention a few of these noted gentlemen, who are known over the state: Gen. Henry Gray, Judge Robert Hudson, Judge Sam Young, Judge R. Boyd, Judge Charles H. Campbell, Judge Joseph A. P. Campbell, Judge Jason Niles, the Hons. Henry C. Niles, C. L. Anderson, George W. Cable, Bishop Charles B. Galloway and the Rev. T. A. S. Adams. These men all made their start in Kosciusko, and had their reputations before leaving it.

About twenty-two thousand bales of cotton are shipped annually from here.

Ethel was named in honor of a daughter of Capt. S. B. McConnico, and it is an attractive little village of about two hundred souls. McCool took its name from the Hon. James F McCool, of Kosciusko, and was located in 1883, and contains about four hundred inhabitants. It ships about five thousand bales of cotton annually, and does a large business. Being in a rich section, it is destined to become a large town.

W. M. Robinson was a member of the first police jury, Allen Dodd, the first clerk, William Dodd, the first representative, and William Rodgers, the first sheriff. The board held the first meeting at Redbudd springs, to which place they gave the name Paris about 1835, and in 1839 named it Kosciusko. This change of name did not immediately change the wild character of a lawless band, who made the place a rendezvous. Many years were required to root the desperadoes out, but the work was well accomplished, and for years the county has been free from highway robbers.

The postoffices are Allendale, Center, population eighty-three; Chita, Eades, Ethel, population sixty-two; Hesterville, Kosciusko, population one thousand six hundred and fifty; McCool, population two hundred and fifty; McVille, New Port, population one hundred and seven; Newtonville, Riley, Sallis, population two hundred; Shrock, Sims, Smyrna, Tolerton, Wamba, Wells, population twenty-nine; Zebulon and Zilpha.

Tallahatchie county as established December 23, 1833, embraced nine hundred square miles, since reduced to six hundred and thirty-five square miles. The first county site was Tillatoba, situated about one mile northwest of the present county site—the town of Charleston. Not a vestige of Tillatoba now remains. About two-thirds of the county are embraced in what is known as the valley and swamp, comprising a territory of great fertility, and covered over by dense forests of valuable timber, except the high lands on the Tallahatchie river and bayous, which are occupied by as rich and productive cotton plantations as can be found in the Mississippi delta, of which they form a part. The Tallahatchie river passes through the county and affords fine steamboat navigation almost through the entire year.

The population in 1840 was two thousand nine hundred and eighty-five; in 1850, four thousand six hundred and forty-three; in 1860, seven thousand eight hundred and ninety, including two thousand two hundred and forty-eight slaves and five hundred and fourteen polls; in 1870, seven thousand eight hundred and fifty-two; in 1880, ten thousand nine hundred and twenty-six, and in 1890, fourteen thousand three hundred and sixty-one, made up of four thousand nine hundred and seventy-four whites and nine thousand three hundred and eighty-seven negroes.

The first white permanent settler was Samuel Foster, who made a crop in 1832. He married a daughter of an Indian chief, Turnbull, and became a well-to-do planter. In 1833 came James Bailey, Capt. Samuel Carothers, William Sutton, Wesley Philips, Charles Bowen, John Bird and James Shaws, all from Hickman county, Tenn.

The first officers of Tallahatchie county were: B. B. Wilson, clerk of police and probate court; Green B. Goodwin, sheriff; William Sutton, assessor; William Berry, coroner; H. C. Davis, ranger. The board of police comprised William Fanning, president; A. L. Humphrey, Samuel Foster, Walter A. Mangum, Joseph Carson. The present officials are: Hon. E. D. Roe, representative; T. J. Manley, chancery clerk; L. G. Polk, circuit clerk; C. H. Fanda, sheriff; W. M. Steele, treasurer; W. H. Bell, assessor; L. R. Worley, surveyor; Rev. H. M. Morrison, Sr., superintendent of education. The members of the board of supervisors are: William S. Tatum, president; Zachariah Ray, A. B. C. Duke, Michael Hey and J. M. Evans.

Probably the first newspaper published within the present limits of Tallahatchie county was the *Tallahatchian*, from about 1856 till the war. It then suspended and resumed in 1865, and continued till about 1870, when the name was changed to the Tallahatchie *News*, and some years later merged into the Charleston *News*, after which it again became the Tallatchie *News*, now the only paper in the county and published by M. M. Kendrick. From about January, 1889, to about August, 1890, the Tallahatchie *Messenger* was published at Charleston. The *True Democrat* and the *Advocate* were also among the publications of a few years since.

The postoffices of Tallahatchie are Cascilla, population one hundred; Charleston, four hundred and seventy-five; Crevi, Graball, thirty-two; Harrison station, three hundred; Leverett, Murphreesboro, Rosebloom, Sharkey, fifty-one; Swan Lake, sixteen; Teasdale, Tulwiler and Webb. The ancient villages of Choechuma and Tuscahoma, which were built up in 1830–31, have long since disappeared, like their founders.

Le Flore county was established March 15, 1871, and named in honor of Greenwood Le Fleur, chief of the Choctaws, as its seat of justice was given his Christian name, Greenwood. The extreme length from north to south is about forty miles, and its breadth is a little over twenty. It contains six hundred and sixty square miles of area, of which less than one-sixth is under cultivation, the total cleared being sixty-one thousand acres. The population, therefore, is not very dense. Lying wholly in the region known as the Yazoo Mississippi delta, there are no hills, the general level being broken only by the abrupt descent into the deep beds of the streams. There is, however, sufficient unevenness of surface to give opportunity for ample drainage where the free flow of water is not interfered with by beaver dams, accumulations of debris and other similar obstructions. The banks of the streams are high and firm, never boggy, and, where navigable, good landings for steamboats can be made at any point. The Yazoo and Tallahatchie rivers, both navigable throughout the entire year, are deep, narrow streams, and afford, by their tortuous course and many windings, more than two hundred miles of river front within the county. The population in 1880 was ten thousand two hundred and forty-six, and in 1890 sixteen thousand eight hundred and sixty-nine, made up of twenty-four hundred and fifty whites, fourteen thousand four hundred and fourteen negroes, and five Indians. Prior to 1871 this territory was included in Sunflower and Carroll counties, and its inhabitants enumerated therewith.

The first board of supervisors assembled at Greenwood April 17, 1871, J. K. Allen president; J. M. Morris and R. B. Powell being present, with H. T. Martin, chancery clerk, and J. E. Johnson, sheriff. Both were instructed to remove records relating to Le Flore from McNutt to Greenwood.

EDWARD MᶜGEHEE

The postoffices of the county are Deovolente, Ezra, Greenwood, population one thousand; Itta Bena, McNutt, one hundred and three; Minter city, sixty two; Rising Sun, seventy-two; Roebuck; Shell Mound, one hundred and fifty; Sheppardtown, seventy-eight; Sidon, three hundred, and Sunnyside, two hundred and fifty.

The original name of Greenwood was William's landing. The town was incorporated about April, 1845, and called Greenwood. At that time there were two stores and a little hotel or tavern. The first postmaster was William Miller, and mail was received about once a month. Miller was succeeded by Jesse Woods, who was succeeded by Thomas Allen, who was succeeded by Mr. Ettinger, the postmaster during the war, who was succeeded by Mr. Upsher. Mrs. E. Strong had charge of the office until succeeded by Miss Anna Jones, who was postmistress until Mrs. Lula Stoddard was appointed. Mrs. Parish is the present postmistress.

The first church established was the Methodist Episcopal, in 1845 or 1846, followed by Presbyterian in 1848. A union church house was built in 1849.

The first paper published in Le Flore county was the *Valley Sentinel* by J. A. Williams, issued at McNutt in 1865. It was discontinued in 1870. The office was removed to Greenwood in 1873, and the name changed to the Greenwood *Times*, published by W. F. Gossom, transferred a number of times and name also changed from time to time until finally the *Delta Flag* was adopted. Bonner Richardson purchased the office and took charge of the paper in January, 1888. The Greenwood *Enterprise* was established by W. D. Cowan, in January, 1889, and he was editor and proprietor up to May, 1890, when James K. Vardeman bought and took charge of the paper. Mr. Vardeman has enlarged this sheet from a four-page seven column to an eight-page six-column journal, and has in connection a complete job office.

Sunflower county was established February 15, 1844, and named after the Big Sunflower river, which runs south through it. Prior to the establishment of Le Flore county, in 1871, Sunflower was great in area as when taken from Bolivar in 1844, extending east to the Tallahatchie and Yazoo rivers to the line of Holmes county. The total area is seven hundred and twenty square miles. One-fifth of the land is open for cultivation, and the other four-fifths heavily timbered with white and red oak, hickory, red and sweet gum, cottonwood, ash and cypress. The county, being entirely in the bottom, is level, and the soil very fertile and productive. The land produces from one to two bales of cotton per acre, or thirty to sixty bushels of corn per acre, with proper cultivation. Products are cotton, corn, peas, potatoes, sugarcane, sorghum, and all kinds of fruits and vegetables suitable to this climate.

The population in 1850 was one thousand one hundred and two; in 1860, five thousand and nineteen, including three thousand seven hundred and ninety-four slaves and two hundred and eighty-seven polls; in 1870, five thousand and fifteen; in 1880, four thousand six hundred and sixty-one, and in 1890, nine thousand three hundred and eighty-four, made up of two thousand five hundred and five whites, six thousand eight hundred and seventy-five negroes and four Indians.

The commissioners named McNutt, now in Le Flore county, as the seat of justice, but on the establishment of Le Flore, Johnsonville was selected as the county seat. The first meeting of the county board was held June 12, with William B. Smith, presiding. B. C. Bookout, E. F. Kinsey or Kinsie, Dave McLeod and Louis Cobb and the president formed the board. William S. Myers, deputy sheriff, and J. R. Baird, chancery clerk, were the officers present. At a meeting of the county board, held August 7, 1882, an election was ordered to vote on the removal of the courthouse. August 22, 1882, the members of that board were J. B. Baird, president; W. M. Duncan, John James, A. Barnett and S. L. Richardson, sheriffs, and J. Y. Walter, clerk. James Stigler, who was absent, was fined $15, but the fine was

15

remitted at the following meeting. The new seat of justice was located at Eureka by the commissioners September 8, 1882, and approved at a meeting of the board October 2, 1882. The name Eureka was afterward changed to Indianola. The contract to build a courthouse was awarded November 13, 1882, to Jesse Boyer for $2,775. This frame building was completed in 1883; the brick jail was erected subsequently, and the Faison brick block in 1888. Indianola was incorporated in 1886. Its population in June, 1890, was three hundred and seventy-five. The other postoffices of Sunflower are Baird, Faisonia, Gumwood, Heathman, Lehrton, Moorhead, Quiver, Saints Rest and Woodburn.

Choctaw county* was established on the 23d day of December, A. D. 1833, by an act of the legislature of the state of Mississippi, and then embraced the territory within the following limits, to wit: Beginning at a point on the Big Black river, at which the line between townships sixteen and seventeen crosses the same; from thence up said Big Black river to the point at which the line between ranges six and seven east crosses said river to the line between townships twenty-one and twenty-two; from thence east to the line between ranges eleven and twelve east; from thence south with said line between ranges eleven and twelve east to the line between townships sixteen and seventeen, and from thence west with said line between townships sixteen and seventeen to the Big Black river, the place of beginning, comprising an area of over six hundred square miles. The name Choctaw was given this county in memory of the Choctaw Indians, by whom the territory was inhabited and out of which the county was formed.

The area is four hundred and four square miles, of which there are about forty-nine thousand acres cleared. The population in 1840 was six thousand and ten; in 1850, eleven thousand four hundred and two; in 1860, fifteen thousand seven hundred and twenty-two, including four thousand two hundred and twelve slaves and one thousand nine hundred and twenty-four polls; in 1870, sixteen thousand nine hundred and eighty-eight; in 1880, nine thousand and thirty-six, and in 1890, ten thousand eight hundred and forty-seven, made up of eight thousand one hundred and thirty whites and two thousand seven hundred and seventeen negroes.

The postoffices are Ackerman, five hundred; Bankston, Bywy, fifty-seven; Chester, one hundred and ninety-three; Dido, fifty-three; Fentress, French Camps, two hundred and seventy-five; Fulcher, Kenaga, La Grange, thirty-nine; New Prospect, eighteen; Pinto, Reform, Spay and Weir.

The county was fully organized in 1834 by the election of William Dyse, William Rogers, Mont. Hutchins, John A. Newell and J. W. Brandon, members of the board of police, and, as members of said board, in October, 1834, they entered of the United States government at Columbus, Miss., the southwest quarter of section eight, township nineteen, range nine east, upon which a county site was located for said county, and the place called Greensboro, and remained so until January 1, 1872, at which time the records of said county were removed to a new site to be hereafter mentioned. The said board of police erected a courthouse on the lot where the Methodist church in Greensboro now stands, and in it was tried the celebrated case of the State against V. A. Stewart for stealing Judge Chanton's goods. The case was removed from Yalobusha county to this by change of venue. Garrett Neil was elected first sheriff of the county, Thomas Lindsey first probate clerk, and P. J. Campbell, first circuit clerk. The second election ever held in the county was in the fall of 1835, at which Thomas Hogg was elected probate judge; J. B. Snow, probate clerk; John Snow, circuit clerk; W. T. Legitt, sheriff, and Thomas Lindsey was

*By E. R. Seward.

elected to the legislature. In the year 1837 D. O. Shattuch was elected judge of this judicial district; J. H. Morris, probate judge; Thomas N. Davis, probate clerk; John Snow, circuit clerk; W. T. Legitt, sheriff, and William Dyse and William Rogers to the legislature from this county. In the year 1839 Drane and Graves were elected to the legislature, Edward Johnson, sheriff; A. P. Harris, probate clerk; Pinkney Barnes, circuit clerk; and J. A. Kennedy, probate judge. In this year the brick courthouse was erected in Greensboro (costing the county about $15,000), which was burned down in the year 1865, supposed by an incendiary, after robbing the county of several thousand dollars. In the year 1841 B. F. Carothers was elected circuit judge; Judge Kennedy reëlected probate judge; A. P. Harris, probate clerk; John Hendricks, circuit clerk. Bonds was elected to the senate, beating Thomas Fox about seven hundred votes. Butts and Rogers were elected to the legislature. In 1843 H. A. Snow was elected probate judge; Thomas N. Davis, probate clerk; John Nolen, circuit clerk; Edward Johnson, sheriff; Humphrey Buck, assessor and taxcollector. J. M. Hankins and Butts were elected to the legislature this year, the former of whom was a whig. In the year 1845 the celebrated race for senator took place between Edward Johnson and James Drane, in which there was great excitement, Johnson defeating Drane about thirty votes. This year C. H. Saunders was elected probate judge; Thomas N. Davis, probate clerk; James Hitt, sheriff; John Nolen, circuit clerk; H. Wood, assessor of taxes.

In the year 1847 Judge Rogers was elected circuit judge of this district, and presided as such for eight successive years; John Snow, probate judge; Thomas N. Davis, probate clerk; John Nolen, circuit clerk; S. C. Platner, sheriff. In the year 1849 Col. James Drane was elected to the senate, defeating J. B. Fox; John Snow, reëlected probate judge; Thomas N. Davis, probate clerk; John Nolen, circuit clerk; S. C. Platner, sheriff, and Dr. Dunlap and Gilbert Coffey to the legislature. In the year 1851 John Snow was reëlected judge; Thomas N. Davis, probate clerk; John Nolen, circuit clerk; Hine and Fox to the legislature on the union ticket, Drane still remaining in the senate. In the year 1853 A. W. Woodruff was elected probate judge, but shortly afterward died, and was succeeded by Judge G. H. Archer; Thomas N. Davis reëlected probate clerk; John Nolen, circuit clerk; James Hitt, sheriff. In the year 1855 the knownothing question was the great issue in the political race, and every knownothing in the county was defeated except Thomas N. Davis, who was elected probate judge; Thomas B. Thompson, probate clerk; J. J. Campbell, circuit clerk; Stone and another to the legislature; E. Parker, sheriff. The officers elected this year held their offices three years under an amended constitution, Drane still remaining in the senate. In the year 1859 Thomas N. Davis was reëlected judge; G. H. Archer, circuit clerk; Thomas B. Thompson, probate clerk, and E. Parker, sheriff, and James Edwards and Jackson Martin to the legislature. In the year 1861 G. H. Archer and Isham Trotter were elected to the legislature; J. T. Killough, probate judge; Ira McDonell, probate clerk; John Nolen, circuit, and James Drane, senator, who held their offices until the close of the war. Choctaw was, from its establishment, a democratic county, giving in most cases a majority from two to seven hundred votes. After the close of the war the state was put under military rule, and all the county officers were appointed by military authority until, in the fall of 1869, the date of the adoption and ratification of the present constitution.

In the fall of 1869 Thomas W. Castles was elected senator from this district, W. W. Hart and T. W. Conner to the legislature, but Conner died in the year 1870 and was succeeded by A. J. Hemphill. The county officers for the years 1870 and 1871 were appointed by the governor of the state. There was an election held in October, 1871, for county officers, who were installed January 1, 1872. In this election H. H. Reed was elected to the legislature and R. F. Halloway as floater; J. E. Bridges, sheriff; E. R. Seward, chancery clerk; J. G. Davis, circuit clerk; J. S. Klutts, county treasurer; John T. Middleton, assessor of taxes; John Dudley, surveyor; W. A. Dobbs, J. P. Wood, S. W. Aston, L. Thompson and J. H. Aldridge, supervisors, all of whom were democrats. There was an election held in the year 1873 with the following results: S. W. Smythes, of Winston, to the senate from this district, who died in 1874 and was succeeded by M. A. Metts; Thomas Atkins to the legislature; J. P. Thompson, floater; J. E. Bridges, sheriff; J. T. Middleton, treasurer; P. D. Gunter, assessor, who died in August, 1874, and was succeeded by H. B. Kite, by appointment; W. A. Dobbs, J. P. Wood, S. W. Aston, A. Shelton and John Snow, supervisors. In 1875 J. E. Bridges was elected to the legislature, L. Leroy Boyd, floater; D. W. Fondren, sheriff; E. R. Seward, chancery clerk; I. F. Fondren, circuit clerk; J. T. Middleton, treasurer; A. Blanton, assessor; James Huffman, D. A. Huffman, J. H. Fulcher, J. F. Bryan, and L. B. Sealey, supervisors, all of whom are the present incumbents and Simon-pure democrats. Greensboro, after its location, soon grew up to be a village of considerable business for an inland town, but was never famous for morality, but was always noted for the many murders for a town of its size committed within its limits. It was the county site for the period of thirty-eight years, and at the time of the formation of Sumner county, Greensboro, being situated in the portion of territory making Sumner (now Webster) county, became, by operation of law, the county site of said county, and is no more a part and parcel of Choctaw county.

On May 13, 1871, an act was passed by the legislature of the state of Mississippi creating a new county in this state to be called Montgomery, and in said act removed the seat of justice of Choctaw county from Greensboro to a place to be located within two miles of the geographical center of Choctaw county. G. H. Archer, S. C. Whisenant and Samuel Delooch were appointed commissioners to locate the same and they proceeded, by virtue of said appointment in the month of August, 1871, and located the site on section fourteen, township nineteen, range ten east, G. W. Gunter being the donor of forty acres of land upon which the same was located and they called the place Lagrange. Lagrange is situated on the Columbus & Greensboro road, south of Big Black river. Preparations were made at said place to receive the records of the county, and they were removed on or soon after January 1, 1872. A frame courthouse was erected at said county site costing the county about $6,500. The town built up rapidly, and for a new and inland town had a good trade with several stores, groceries, law offices and other business establishments, but on the night of January 12, 1874, the courthouse with all the records of the county were burned, supposedly by an incendiary. Of course, this was a death-knell to the thriving village as the county site, for the people of the county had never been satisfied with the changes in county boundaries, and began now to clamor for a division and a removal of the seat of justice. On April 6, 1874, the legislature of the state of Mississippi passed an act creating Sumner county, taking all the territory of Choctaw county north of Big Black river and leaving Lagrange within one mile and a half of the county line, though not removing the seat of justice. Another act was passed February 25, 1875, removing the seat of justice from Lagrange and locating a new site. Thus Lagrange ceased to be the county site and as such was of short duration. Though so shortly in existence, her inhabitants were noted for intelligence and morality, and she still remains a village with several good families within her limits whose sociability, intelligence and moral worth are an honor to any community.

The act of February 25, 1875, permanently located a seat of justice for Choctaw county, and appointed Leroy Boyd, John Kennedy and Herrod Fondren commissioners to locate a site allowing them a variance of not over two miles from the geographical center, and they by virtue of said appointment proceeded to locate the same. William Wood presented forty acres of land as a donation for said site, which was accepted by said commissioners, and the place named Chester after a town in South Carolina. Preparations were made and the county records were moved about July 15, 1875. Chester is situated within about one half mile of the geographical center of the county on the French Camp and Starkville road. French Camp is the largest town in the county, as well as the oldest, situated in the extreme southwest corner of the county and near the geographical center of the state; the location is beautiful and the water excellent. General Jackson, on his way from Nashville, Tenn., to Natchez, Miss., camped here with his army for one week in order to rest and recruit his army, and at that time a Frenchman named Louis Le Flore, who had intermarried with a descendant of the Choctaw tribe, lived there. He was the father of Greenwood Le Flore and from this circumstance it took its name. Greenwood Le Flore was afterward chief of the Indians and was commonly called the Chief of Chiefs. French Camp has grown from an Indian wigwam to be a thriving and business town, surrounded with intelligent citizens, good churches and schools. Bankston situated on McCurtain's creek in said county was once a thriving town. It was located in the year 1847 and called Bankston in memory of a man named Banks, who lived in Columbus, Ga. A manufactory of cotton and woolen goods, with John D. Nance as president, was established here and continued in operation until some time in the year 1864, when it was burned down by Federal cavalry. There was another factory on a smaller scale erected here after the war, but was soon burned down supposedly by an incendiary, and at the present time Bankston is only a postoffice. There are other villages and towns in the county, but will not be particularly spoken of in this sketch. The oldest and best known road in the county is the Natchez trace, so called from the fact that it was cut out by General Jackson and his army on their march to Natchez in this state. It runs entirely through the county in a southwesterly direction, and is said to be the straightest road for its length known.

The first newspaper published within the present limits of Choctaw county was the Choctaw *Leader*, by Messrs. Dukes & Quinn, who began its publication about 1877 at Chester, and soon after by Boyd & Mecklin, and from 1880 to 1882 by S. R. Hughston, then by Foster & Buck. It soon after became the Ackerman *Enterprise*, but was of short duration.

The *Inland Recorder* was also published at Chester about 1878.

In 1885 Charley Townsend began the publication of the *Reveille* at French Camp, and continued there till August, 1887, when he removed to Ackerman where he has since published the Choctaw *Plaindealer*. The Mississippi *Review*, at Ackerman, has been published by Miss Alice Amason since 1890.

Neshoba county was established December 23, 1833, and the name conferred on it not only on account of the number of wolves reported there, but also because a chief named Nashoba (a wolf) resided there. The present name is a contraction.

Pearl river flows through the county, which, with its tributary creeks, and the Pinnyshook, Kentawha, Beasha, Owl and Noxapater creek furnish fine water advantages. Where Philadelphia now stands was the town of Lune-bu-oosh-ah, or Burnt Frog, and in the vicinity is the mound where the Choctaws first settled in Mississippi, known as "Nanewyyah" or "Winding Hill." The surface of the county is level along the river and creek bottoms, the balance undulating and hilly.   The soil on the river and creeks is generally fertile the undulating lands good, and in the hills sandy, with a clay subsoil, easy to cultivate and readily improved.   The timber growth is pine, various kinds of oak, hickory, black walnut, beech and cypress on river bottoms.   The products are corn, cotton, oats, wheat, peas, sweet and Irish potatoes, sorghum, etc.   Vegetables of various kinds, and fruits are raised in abundance for home consumption.   Lignite, or brown coal, has been found in this county.   There are also large beds of marl in different parts of the county, and also very fertile feed brakes.   Pasturage is extensive—the native grasses for summer and switchcane and the run of the farms for winter.   The scuppernong grape grows in great luxuriance in this county and winemaking could be made very profitable.

The area is five hundred and sixty square miles, of which there are about one hundred thousand acres cleared.   The population in 1840 was two thousand four hundred and thirty-seven; in 1850, four thousand seven hundred and twenty-eight; in 1860, eight thousand three hundred and forty-three, including two thousand one hundred and fifty-two slaves and nine hundred and thirty four polls; in 1870, seven thousand four hundred and thirty-nine; in 1880, eight thousand seven hundred and forty-one, and in 1890, eleven thousand one hundred and forty-six, made up of eight thousand three hundred and twenty whites, two thousand one hundred and seventy-five negroes, and six hundred and fifty-one Indians.   A few Caucasians settled in Neshoba prior to its organization, among whom were squawmen and traders.   The postoffices are Aden, Beech Springs, forty-five; Coffadeliah, Cushtusa, Dixon, twenty-eight; Engine, Fusky, Hope, House, Java, Lake Burnside, thirty-eight; Laurel Hill, forty-eight; Milldale, twenty-two; North Bend, North Bogue Chitto, twenty-seven; Ocobla, Olney, Philadelphia, one hundred and one; Sierra, Smith, Tucker, and Watkinsville, population twenty-seven.

Quitman county has an area of four hundred square miles, of which there are about ten thousand five hundred acres cleared.   The Cold Water river flows through the center of county.   The surface land of the county is level, it lying entirely in the bottom.   The soil is alluvial bottom land of great fertility, and will produce from one to two bales of cotton or thirty to sixty bushels of corn per acre, when properly drained, cultivated and protected from overflow.   The timber growth consists of immense white oak, red and sweet gum, poplar, black walnut, hickory, and a great abundance of large and fine cypress.   The crops produced are principally cotton and corn, but oats, millet, tobacco, sorghum and wheat will do very well when planted and properly cultivated.   All kinds of vegetables and fruits adapted to the latitude are grown for home consumption.   Pasturage is very good and extensive.   All kinds of grass, such as Bermuda, orchard, herds, Johnson grass, and also red clover will grow luxuriantly.   These, together with canebrakes for winter pasture, make Quitman a fine stock county.

The population in 1880 was one thousand four hundred and seven, or five hundred and ninety-two whites and eight hundred and fifteen negroes.   In 1890 the total number of inhabitants was thirty-two hundred and eighty-six, made up of eight hundred and eighty-eight whites, twenty-three hundred and ninety-seven negroes and one Indian.

Quitman county was established February 1, 1877, from parts of Coahoma, Tunica, Tallahatchie and Panola, deriving the principal part of its population from Tunica.   Its first officials were: S. M. Crutchfield, assessor; J. A. Reid, treasurer; C. E. Standifer, clerk; J. F. Phipps, sheriff.   For a few years after organization the county was represented conjointly with Tunica county, and was first represented separately by L. Marks.   John R. Richardson, John T. Gleeson, W. D. Morgan and James Bady constituted its first board of supervisors. Some of the early settlers of the county were Thomas Dickinson, Capt. Randolph Nelson, Jacob Dubard, T. B. Smith, Thomas Hill, C. M. Phipps and the Messrs. Brown, Hatch, Mattox and Patterson.

Quitman county was named for General Quitman, who served in the Mexican war. Its first county site was old Belen, on Coldwater river, seven miles east of the present county site. In 1883 the seat of justice was moved to its present location, retaining its name. The first court met there in March, 1884. Belen derived its name from Belen gate, on which Colonel Quitman made an assault and through which he entered the city of Mexico. It was organized and incorporated in 1888, and has at present a population of four hundred. The postoffices are Belen, population one hundred and thirteen; Marks and Simpson.

Lauderdale county, named in honor of Colonel Lauderdale, who fell at New Orleans, a martyr to the cause of his country, was established December 23, 1833. The commissioners appointed to organize the county were Samuel Grayson, Asa Hartfield, William Ellis, Robert James, Henry Hale, H. W. Ward, C. Dyer, George Evans, J. Bidwell and N. Martin. The population seven years later was five thousand three hundred and fifty-eight, in 1850 it was eight thousand seven hundred and seventeen, in 1860 it was thirteen thousand three hundred and thirteen, in 1870 it was thirteen thousand four hundred and sixty-two, in 1880 it was twenty-one thousand five hundred and one, in 1890 it was twenty-nine thousand six hundred and sixty-one. In 1860 there were one thousand one hundred and forty-five voters and four thousand seven hundred and eleven taxable slaves. The colored population was six thousand four hundred and eleven in 1870, eleven thousand five hundred and thirty-eight in 1880, and fifteen thousand one hundred and thirty-four in 1890.

Bounded north by Kemper county, east by Alabama, south by Clarke county and west by Jasper county, Lauderdale has an area of six hundred and eighty square miles, of which one hundred and two thousand and twenty-nine acres are cleared land. The water power in the county is excellent on the numerous creeks and streams. There is great abundance of fine marl in the county. About one-third of the area is open land, the balance well timbered with pine, oaks of various kinds, hickory, gum, beech, chestnut, poplar, sycamore, etc. The products are cotton, corn, sugarcane, oats, peas, potatoes, etc. Vegetables of all kinds and fruits are grown in great abundance. Some few have turned their attention to fruits and vegetables for market and are doing well with them. Pasturage is extensive—Bermuda, velvet and native grasses for summer, and switchcane on the creek bottoms for winter. Considerable attention is being paid to stockraising, and this is a splendid county for sheep husbandry. Church and school advantages are good; society is excellent.

Meridian, the county seat, is an enterprising town of ten thousand eight hundred and eighty-nine inhabitants, the second largest city in the state, situated at the crossing of the Mobile & Ohio and the Vicksburg & Meridian railroads. Meridian ships about fifty thousand bales of cotton annually. The railroads of the county are the Mobile & Ohio, running north and south; the Vicksburg & Meridian, running east and west, almost through the center; the New Orleans & Northeastern; Alabama Great Southern, and Virginia, Georgia & Tennessee railroad, which make Meridian a great railroad center. The seat of justice has been at this city since 1870, at which time it was removed from Marion station, to which point it had been removed in 1866 from the original site at Marion.

Gen. Sam Dale, who has passed into history as the hero of a canoe fight with Indians on the Alabama river, was one of the first settlers. The first sheriff was Isom Pace, and the first circuit clerk was John Culbreath. Joseph A. Marshall first represented Lauderdale in the state senate, Gen. Sam Dale in the lower house. Joel P. Walker is the present state senator; representatives, H. M. Street, W. R. Denton and W. D. Witherspoon.

Besides Meridian the towns, villages, trading points and postoffices in this county are Marion station (population three hundred and forty-seven), Lockhart (population one hundred), Lauderdale station (population two hundred and seventy-five), Toomsuba (population one hundred and seventy-five), Bailey, Bunnie, Collinsville, Daleville, Hookston, Hurricane creek, Kewanee, La Place, Lizelia, Morrow, Ponta, Rushing's store, Russell, Siding, Temple, Topton, Vimville and Whynot. Before the war Lauderdale springs was a popular health resort.

Smith county is bounded north by Scott county, east by Jasper county, south by Jones and Covington counties, west by Simpson and Rankin counties, and contains an area of six hundred and thirty square miles, of which seventeen thousand and seventy-four acres are cleared land. This county was established December 23, 1833, and was named in honor of Maj. David Smith of Hinds county. Raleigh, population two hundred, the county-seat, is situated near the center of the county. The watercourses are Leaf and Strong rivers, which with their numerous tributary creeks and branches afford fine water power. That portion of the county not open to cultivation is well timbered, principally with longleaf or yellow pine. On the creek and river bottoms the surface is level, back from the creeks it is gently undulating and hilly beyond. The soil is partly red and black prairie, very fertile for corn and cotton; partly rich bottom lands and partly hill lands, free and productive, and some "reed brakes" which have been and are being drained, and when well cultivated, will make from fifty to one hundred bushels of corn per acre. On the bottoms white, red and black oak, hickory, chestnut, beech, magnolia, pecan, cypress and other varieties of timber grow.

Pasturage is extensive, wood range for summer and switchcane on the bottoms for winter. Sheep husbandry and cattle-raising could be made very profitable. Very little attention has been paid to fruit-growing; all kinds suitable to the climate do well, but are raised only for home consumption. The principal game is deer, wild turkeys, wild ducks, raccoon, opossum, partridge, etc., which afford fine sport for hunters. There are churches in every neighborhood and free or public schools for four months in each year.

Besides the county seat there are in Smith county the following-named towns, trading points and postoffices: Beger, Boykins, Brit, Bunker Hill, Burns, Currie, Daniel, Flowers' Place, Gunn, Hordville, Mize, Polkville, Royal, Standpoint, Shongelo, Sylvarena, Trenton and Taylorsville. Polkville was established about forty years ago and Trenton soon after. About 1846 Judge Lowry established a tannery and a hat factory at Raleigh.

Smith county had a population of nineteen hundred and sixty-one in 1840, four thousand and seventy-one in 1850, seven thousand six hundred and thirty-eight in 1860, seven thousand one hundred and twenty-six in 1870, eight thousand and eighty-eight in 1880, ten thousand six hundred and thirty-five in 1890. In 1860 there were seven hundred and ninety-three voters and two thousand one hundred and forty-five taxable slaves, in 1870 the colored population was seventeen hundred and eleven, in 1880 sixteen hundred and thirty-six, in 1890 seventeen hundred and forty-six.

Bolivar county was established February 9, 1836, and named in honor of the republican of South America, Simon Bolivar. The total area is eight hundred and seventy-six square miles, and of this the cleared area equals one hundred and eight thousand five hundred and fifty-three acres. This county lies entirely in the Mississippi bottom, and has a deep alluvial soil. It is very fertile, producing a bale of cotton to the acre, or fifty to eighty bushels of corn. About one-sixth of the land is in cultivation; the balance is heavily timbered with ash, sweet and red gum, hickory, white oak, pin oak, elm, walnut, cottonwood, poplar, pecan and immense cypress brakes. The population in 1840 was one thousand three hundred and fifty-six; in 1850, two thousand five hundred and seventy-seven; in 1860, ten thousand four hun-dred and seventy-one, including nine thousand two hundred and twenty-six slaves and four hundred and forty-four polls; in 1870, nine thousand seven hundred and thirty-two; in 1880, eighteen thousand six hundred and fifty-two, and in 1890, twenty-nine thousand nine hundred and eighty, made up of three thousand two hundred and thirty whites, twenty-six thousand seven hundred and thirty-four negroes and sixteen Indians.

It has had many temporary county sites, the first of which was on what is now Lake Beulah, thence it was removed to Bolivar, and after that, for a time, the courthouse and county effects had a home on a flatboat, on which court was held at various places in the river bends, until it was returned to Prentiss. In 1857 or 1858 a handsome courthouse and jail was erected at the latter place, both of which, with the town as well, were destroyed dur-ing the war. In 1865 Col. F. A. Montgomery donated land on his Beulah plantation for a county site, and he also sawed the lumber for the courthouse which was erected there at that time. In 1872 it was finally removed to Rosedale (then Floryville), when, after the original courthouse was destroyed by fire and the second one erected in its place by the insurance company, it was discarded, and the present magnificent brick building was erected in 1890. It is one of the finest county buildings in the state—an imposing structure of pressed brick, trimmed with white stone. It has dormers in the great hip roof, and is sur-mounted by a majestic cupola. The cost was over $30,000. A strong and substantial brick jail was erected in 1888, at an expense of $13,500.

Bolivar county was settled by a class of hardy pioneers and frontiersmen, some of whom were men of power and influence, and among whom were such men as Judge McGuire, Isaac Hudson, Governor Clarke, Judge Burruss, George Torrey, Miles H. McGehee, John V. Newman, Judge Kingsley, J. P. Brown, General Vick, Mr. Estell, Dr. Dodd, Colonel Fields, and many more who assisted in shaping the early destiny of the county.

Bolivar county is now traversed throughout its entire length, north and south, by two railroad lines—the Louisville, New Orleans & Texas, constructed in 1885-6, which passes along the eastern side, and the Bolivar loop of the same road, which runs along the western part, touching the river at Rosedale. Along both of these lines many towns are springing up, and immense quantities of wild land are being opened up for cultivation.

Rosedale, the county seat, is a beautiful little city, doing a rapidly increasing trade, and being built up with a most ornamental class of private residences and substantial business blocks. In the southwestern part of the county is another branch railroad, terminating at Huntington, where trains are transferred to Arkansas city, Ark. This part of the county is a magnificent cotton-growing region, in which there are many beautiful plantations. The Mound place located here, was one of the earliest settled sections of the county, and is still one of the most beautiful. At this point is the large mercantile establishment of W. E. Ringo & Co., who have also other branch stores in other parts of the county, and do the largest mercantile business therein.

The towns of Shaws, Cleveland and Shelby on the main line, and Rosedale and Gunni-son on the loop branch, are the trade centers, and rapidly growing points of the county.

The postoffices of Bolivar are Alligator, one hundred; Australia, one hundred and fifty-two; Avondale, seventy-three; Bellevue, Benoit, Beulah, twenty-five; Bolivar, two hundred and seventy-seven; Catfish Point, eighteen; Cleveland, three hundred; Concordia, Dahomy, Duncan, one hundred and twenty-four; Eutaw, Gaylesville, Gladstone, Gunnison, Huntington, two hundred; Hushpuckena, Lamont, seventy-five; Little, Lobdell, Masonton, eighty-three; Maxime, forty-two; Merigold, sixty-two; Mound Bayou, Mound Landing, seventy-four; Neblett's Landing, fifty-three; Oak Wood, Perthshire, Phalia, Renovo, Riverton, Rosedale, three hundred and fifty; Shaw, three hundered and twenty-five; Stafford, Stormville, eight; Terrene, one hundred and seventy-two, and Wright.

Scott county was established December 23, 1833. Forest, population six hundred and three, the county seat, is a thrifty town situated on the Vicksburg & Meridian railroad. The other towns, trading points and postoffices are Ilerton (population two hundred and seventy-five), Harperville, Hillsboro, Homewood, Beach, Cash, Damascus, Eley, Gilbert, Lake, Lilian, Ludlow, Pulaski, Sebastopol and Steel. The county is bounded thus: North by Leake, east by Newton, south by Smith, west by Rankin. The county is watered by several creeks and streams, tributaries to Pearl and Leaf rivers. The Vicksburg & Meridian railroad runs through the whole width of the county, affording railroad transportation. There is a large wagon factory at Lake station. The surface of the county is level on river and creek bottoms, a great deal of it undulating and some of it hilly. The timber growth consists of long and shortleaf pine, various kinds of oak, hickory, poplar, beech, red and sweet gum, etc. The soil is varied from sandy hills to stiff clay flatwoods. The most part of the county is easily cultivated and readily improved, producing good crops of corn, cotton, oats, wheat, sugarcane, rice, sorghum, sweet and Irish potatoes, and all kinds of vegetables and fruits adapted to this latitude. Pasturage is quite extensive, and some attention has been paid to stockraising, which could be made very profitable. The reedbrakes in this county are very fertile, and when well drained and cultivated, produce fifty to eighty bushels of corn per acre. Fine marl beds and limestone are found in some parts. Society is good; church and school advantages are as good as any in the state. A fine collegiate institute at Harperville affords an opportunity for a good education in the advanced studies as well as the ordinary branches. The area of the county is six hundred square miles, of which forty-two thousand two hundred and thirty-eight acres are cleared land.

John Dunn, James Russell, Wade H. Holland, Stephen Berry and Jeremiah White constituted the first board of supervisors, which organized April 7, 1834, by electing John Dunn president and Stephen Berry clerk pro tem. The commissioners who organized the county were John J. Smith, Gilbert D. Gore, James S. Jolly, Samuel Hawthorn, Morgan McAfee, F. Carr, Joe Bogan, John R. Dunn, D. W. Hopkins, Sr., John P. Smith, Robert Laird, James Bokyn and James Furlow. The first election of county officers was held April 18 and 19, 1834. John Smith was chosen sheriff; Nicholas Finley, clerk; William Ricks, probate judge.

The county seat was established at Berryville, three miles south of Forest. In 1836 it was moved to Hillsboro, and thence it was removed, thirty years later, to Forest. The first to represent the county in the state senate was Oliver C. Dease, in 1837; the first representative in the lower house was Jeremiah B. White. The present state senator is A. M. Byrd; representative, Joseph H. Beeman.

In 1840 Scott county had a population of one thousand six hundred and fifty-three; in 1850, three thousand nine hundred and sixty-one; in 1860, eight thousand one hundred and thirty-nine; in 1870, seven thousand eight hundred and forty-seven; in 1880, ten thousand eight hundred and forty five; in 1890, eleven thousand seven hundred and eighty. In 1860 there were eight hundred and fifty voters and three thousand and fifty-one taxable slaves. The colored population in 1870 was three thousand one hundred and sixty-seven; in 1880, four thousand one hundred and thirty-two; in 1890, four thousand seven hundred.

Coahoma county was established February 9, 1836, and named Coahoma or Red Tiger, owing to the number of panthers and wolverines then infesting the upper delta region.

The Mississippi river flows along the whole western border of the county. The Sunflower river runs through the center, and there are numerous lakes and bayous in the county. The Mobile & Northwestern railroad is finished and in running order from Glendale, on the Mississippi, to Clarksdale. The county lies entirely in the Mississippi bottom, with very fertile alluvial soil of two kinds—sandy and buckshot. The forest trees are various kinds of oaks, white oak predominating, cottonwood, poplar, walnut, red and sweet gum, hickory, cypress, etc. The crops grown are cotton, corn, potatoes, oats; all the grasses do well; fruits and vegetables of all kinds are grown for home use. The lands when well cultivated will produce from one to two bales of cotton per acre. Health compares favorably with the other counties in the bottom. The total area is five hundred square miles, and the area of cleared land, seventy-eight thousand five hundred acres. The population in 1840 was one thousand two hundred and ninety; in 1850, two thousand seven hundred and eighty; in 1860, six thousand six hundred and six, including five thousand two hundred and sixty-nine slaves and three hundred and seventy polls; in 1870, seven thousand one hundred and forty-four; in 1880, one hundred and thirty-one thousand five hundred and sixty-eight, and in 1890, eighteen thousand three hundred and forty-two, made up of two thousand one hundred and sixty-two whites, sixteen thousand one hundred and sixty-one negroes and nineteen Indians.

The pioneers of industry were overmastered even before the organization of the county, for the counterfeiters and road agents gained control of the section and introduced their members into the police board and offices. A committee of vigilance was organized, many of the criminals captured, and, on being found guilty, were tied, hands and feet, and drowned in the Mississippi.

The first seat of justice was Port Royal. Years ago it surrendered to Friar's Point, the present capital of Coahoma.

The postoffices are Anchorage, Bobo, Clarksdale, eight hundred; Clover Hill, Coahoma, two hundred and twenty-five; Dublin, one hundred and two; Eagle's Nest, Ernest, Friar's Point, seven hundred and seventy-six; Greengrove, Hillhouse, Jonestown, three hundred and twenty-five; Lula, Lyon, three hundred; Malone's landing, twenty-seven; Pushmataha, twelve; Rich, Sherard, Stovall and Sunflower landing, eighteen.

Clarksdale is the business center of Coahoma. John Clark has resided on the town site for the past forty-five years, the town taking its name from him, it having been platted in 1868. The advent of the Louisville, New Orleans & Texas railway in 1884 gave the place its first impetus, and since then it has steadily grown. On April 6, 1889, the entire business portion of Clarksdale was laid in ashes, entailing heavy losses and a great deal of inconvenience to the business men. Since then, however, the burned district has been rebuilt, brick and iron taking the place of the wooden structures which were destroyed, so that really the fire was of great advantage to the town in many respects. Eighteen brick business houses have been erected since the fire. A large number of residences were also erected in every part of the town.

The location is a very healthy one, no epidemics having ever occurred, while the ordinary ailments are readily controlled by the resident physicians. A board of health was organized a few years ago to look after the sanitary affairs of the town, and this is an active and efficient body. Its first membership comprised Drs. Stewart, Anderson and Bland, and Judge J. T. Butt, whose interests and those of the town are identical. Many handsome residences are seen in different portions of the town, evidencing the wealth and cultivated taste of their owners, while new ones are constantly being erected.

Clarksdale is at the head of high water navigation on the Sunflower river, and its bus- iness houses are built fronting that stream.   The river is not utilized for navigation purposes at present, although in the past it played an important part in furnishing transportation to and from the Southern markets for this section.

As before stated, the population is between eight hundred and one thousand, while new accessions are constantly being received.   The number of business houses and industries is about thirty, besides which there is a full complement of professional men of all classes. The cotton compress, the sawmills and the gristmill are important industries.

Webster county, which is bounded north by Calhoun and Chickasaw counties, east by Clay county, south by Choctaw and Montgomery counties, west by Montgomery and Grenada counties, was established April 6, 1874.   It was first called Sumner county, and in 1882 its name was changed to Webster, in honor of Daniel Webster.   The county is mostly upland, lying in the pine belt, but much of the soil is quite fertile, owing to the flowing through it of numerous streams, the larger of which are Big Black river, and Hersepen, Lindsey, Spring and Calabuta creeks.   The area is four hundred and thirty square miles, of which ninety- three thousand seven hundred and seventy-two acres are cleared land.   About one-fifth of the land is open.   It is level on creek bottoms, undulating and hilly elsewhere.   A large portion is timbered.   The principal woods are pine, several kinds of oak, hickory, poplar, beech, ash, black-jack, sweet and black gum and cypress.   The county produces corn, cotton, wheat, oats, sweet potatoes, etc.   Pasturage is extensive in the old fields and woods, but is utilized only in raising stock for home consumption.   Fruits, such as peaches, pears, apples, plums, figs and small fruits do well, but very little attention is paid to them and they are grown only for home use.   The farms are mostly small and free from incumbrance.   The best improved farms are worth from $10 to $15 per acre.   The county seat was at Greensboro, an old and flourishing town, and the former county seat of Choctaw county.   The town has now almost entirely disappeared.   In 1876 the site of the present town of Walthall (population two hundred and fifty) was made the county seat, and on May 11 of that year the records were removed to that place, where soon was built a promising town.   But when the Georgia Pacific railroad was built through the county, in 1889, it unfortunately left Walthall some five miles from its line, since when the town as declined somewhat.   Eupora, a town of importance, is on the railroad, about five miles south of Walthall.   Bellefontaine (population one hundred and seven), about four miles northwest of Walthall, is a good trading point. Another quite flourishing business place is Cumberland (population two hundred), ten miles east of Walthall.   Other postoffices are Cadaretta, Calooga, Clarkson, Crowley, Embry, Fay, Greensboro, Hohenlinden, Kirby, Lamb, Mathiston, Monte Vista, Redding, Sapa, Spring Creek, Starnes and Tomnolen.

The first officials of the county were Samuel E. Parker, representative; Dr. W. A. F. Caldwell, chancery and circuit clerk; J. W. Holland, sheriff; Aaron Hutto, treasurer; R. F. Holloway, superintendent of education.   Ira McDowell was president of the board of supervisors, of which the following were members: David Nowlin, G. W. Pollan, J. W. Starnes, Aaron Smith.

The present county officials are Hon. George W. Dudley, representative; Alexander Morrow, chancery clerk; Harry A. Gould, circuit clerk; A. P. Magness, sheriff; S. S. Waits, treasurer; W. T. Given, assessor; F. J. Sevindoll, superintendent of education; G. W. Collins, president of the board of supervisors; Elijah F. Spikes, W. F. Rowell, T. H. Middleton, J. B. White, members.   N. A. Betts was the first who represented the county in the state senate.   The present state senators representing Webster are J. R. Nolen and A. A. Montgomery.

An early newspaper, published within the present limits of Webster county, was the *Dundee*, issued at Greensboro, by William D. Roy, a Scotchman, as early as 1850. About 1854 or 1855 John McCaughey began the publication of the *Choctaw Recorder*, also at Greensboro, which he published until 1859, when he sold it to R. Walpole, who issued it until 1861, when it suspended publication until after the war, when it was revived under the name of the *Vidette*, and published until 1867. In 1877 the *Pioneer* was established at Walthall by J. B. Quinn and edited by Dr. W. E. Quin. This was afterward published by W. J. Taylor, now of the *Mississippian* at Jackson, who changed the name in 1882 to the *Warden*, which has been published by Hon. George W. Dudley since 1884. In September, 1889, the Eupora *Progress* was established at Eupora, by Joseph Marshall, but is now published by Robert Scott.

The population of Webster county in 1880 was ninety-five hundred and thirty-four; in 1890, twelve thousand and sixty. The colored population is about three thousand.

CHAPTER XII.

COUNTIES OF THE CHICKASAW CESSION.

MONROE county, named in honor of President James Monroe, was established February 9, 1821. It is bounded north by Lee and Itawamba counties, east by Alabama, south by Clay and Lowndes, and west by Clay and Chickasaw. Aberdeen, the county seat, has three thousand four hundred and forty-five inhabitants. The other towns and postoffices are Athens, Smithville, Cottongin, Central Grove, Camargo, Muldon, Prairie, Hamilton, Amory, Barttahatchie, Beeks, Bigbee, Binford, Cooper, Gattman, Gibson, Greenbrier, Grubb Springs, Quincy, Ree's store, Riggins, Splunge, Strongs and Woodson.

The watercourses of Monroe county are Tombigbee river and Town creek (navigable), with numerous small creeks and streams. The Mobile & Ohio railroad runs along the western border of the county, with a branch road from Muldon to Aberdeen. The Memphis, Selma & Brunswick and the Lexington & Aberdeen branch of the Illinois Central afford added railway facilities. Water power is abundant on the east side of the Tombigbee river. There are twenty-three watermills and twenty-six steammills in the county. About one-third of the land is in cultivation, the balance in timber and prairies. Surface of part of the county is level and the rest undulating. Limestone and rotten-limestone are abundant. Fertile prairie soil and a fine black sand soil, with clay subsoil, abound. Cotton, corn, wheat, oats, field peas and sorghum are produced. All the grasses do well, and much attention is now being paid to sheep husbandry and improved stock, with considerable success. The timber trees are white, post, red and black oaks, poplar, elm, gum, walnut, cypress, etc.

Among the early settlers were Mr. Cocke, Colonel Willis, Daniel W. Wright, the Cravens, Sandersons, Alexanders, Fords, Branches, Jacob Loughridge, Dr. Higginson, B. T. Reese, William Morse, Isaac Dyche, John Ross, Henry Hardy, the Echols, John Coulter, the Hutchinsons, Ferrisses and Martins. The population in 1830 was three thousand eight hundred and sixty-one; in 1840, nine thousand two hundred and fifty; in 1850, twenty-one thousand one hundred and seventy-two; in 1860, twenty-one thousand two hundred and eighty-three; in 1870, twenty two thousand six hundred and thirty-one; in 1880, twenty-eight thousand five hundred and fifty-three; in 1890, thirty thousand seven hundred and thirty. In 1860 the county contained one thousand five hundred and thirty-four voters and twelve thousand seven hundred and forty taxable slaves. The colored population in 1870 was fourteen thousand; in 1880, eighteen thousand and one; in 1890, eighteen thousand seven hundred and ninety-two.

The board of supervisors of this county first met at the house of Henry Greer, April 4, 1821, and was comprised as follows; Gideon Lincecum, president; Ezekiel Nash, Stephen Hannon, Wiley Harbin and Frederick Weaver.

The first officers of the county were Nathaniel Harbin, clerk of the county; Bartlett Lewis, sheriff; John G. Fulks, treasurer; Silas Brown, assessor; William L. Moore, surveyor.

The present officials are William G. Elkin, president of the board of supervisors; G. W. Parham, David Crenshaw, L. D. Booth and J. H. Roberts, supervisors; R. E. Houston, T. A. Oliphant and J. T. Dilworth, representatives; W. H. Kolb, chancery clerk; B. H. Gillespie, circuit clerk; J. A. Johnson, sheriff; John C. Wicks, treasurer; George G. Tindall, surveyor; John G. Holmes, assessor; C. C. McChandless, coroner, and E. P. Thompson superintendent of education.

Hamilton, now an old field, was the county seat in 1830, when Lowndes county was made and the county seat was removed to nearer the center of the county, and the place was called Augusta. There the seat of justice remained until about 1849, when it was removed to Aberdeen, and the present courthouse, a large brick building, was erected in 1857. Monroe is one of the wealthiest upland counties in the state.

Among the early newspapers of Aberdeen the *Democrat* and the *Sunny South* were published prior to the war, and the latter a few years after the war. The Aberdeen *Examiner* was established in 1865 by S. A. Jonas. It was a daily for about a year and a half, then a tri-weekly in 1885, since which time it has been a weekly, and one of the best in the state. It is now edited and published by Jonas & Dalton, the former being its founder. In 1877 E. P. Thompson established the *People's Weekly*, but about six months after changed the name to the Aberdeen *Weekly*, which he still publishes, with his son, Fred S. Thompson, as business manager, the youngest business manager of a newspaper in Mississippi. The *Phœnix News* was established in 1883 by Dr. J. W. Eckford, who still issues it.

Yalobusha county was established December 23, 1833. Coffeeville, population eight hundred, the county seat, is situated on the Illinois Central railroad. The other towns are Water Valley (population twenty-eight hundred and twenty-eight) and Torrence, on the same railroad, Garner (population one hundred and sixty-six), Oakland (population three hundred and twenty-eight) and Tillatoba (population one hundred and seventy-five), on the Mississippi & Tennessee railroad. The railroad machine shop, Yocona cotton factory and Shaw's foundry and agricultural implement works are located at Water Valley, a thriving town, of about four thousand inhabitants, which forms a second circuit and chancery court district.

Other postoffices are Air Mount, Hatton, Pine Valley and Velma. The surface of the land in the county is level on river and creek bottoms, the rest undulating and hilly. The

Schooner river runs through the southern portion and the Yocana through the northern part of the county, which, with their numerous branches, make it a well-watered county. Some good mill sites are here. The soil is a yellow loam, clayey and sandy, tolerably productive, producing corn, cotton oats, sorghum, sweet and Irish potatoes, wheat and rye, such fruits as peaches, pears, early apples, plums and figs. All the smaller fruits do well, but very little attention is paid to them. All the various kinds of vegetables are grown for family use. Pasturage is extensive, there being good woodland for summer range, and canebrakes on creek bottoms for winter pasture. Stockraising could be made very profitable. Lignite or brown coal has been found in the county. There are good church advantages in nearly every neighborhood, two white and two colored free schools in every township. The Illinois Central railroad runs through the county from north to south, and the Mississippi & Tennessee railroad from Grenada to Memphis, Tenn., runs through the southern corner and along the western boundary, affording ample railroad facilities. The county is bounded north by Panola and Lafayette, west by Calhoun, south by Grenada and west by Tallahatchie county, and contains an area of four hundred and seventy-two square miles, of which one hundred and twenty-six thousand nine hundred and eighty-nine acres are cleared land.

In 1840 the population of this county was twelve thousand two hundred and forty-eight; in 1850, seventeen thousand two hundred and fifty-eight; in 1860, sixteen thousand nine hundred and fifty-two; in 1870, thirteen thousand two hundred and fifty-four; in 1880, fifteen thousand six hundred and forty-nine; in 1890, sixteen thousand six hundred and twenty-nine. In 1860 there were thirteen hundred and forty-three voters, and ninety-three hundred and twenty-eight taxable slaves. The colored population in 1870 was seventy hundred and fifty-two; in 1880, eighty-one hundred and sixteen; in 1890, nine thousand and eleven. The rate of taxation is low and the county is free of debt.

March 24, 1834, Thomas C. McMackin, William Metcalf and Dempsey H. Hicks took the oath of office as commissioners of Yalobusha county. On the same date, William Winter and Robert Edsington were sworn in to complete the board. Thomas C. McMackin was made president of the board; D. M. Rayburn, clerk; James H. Barfield was the first sheriff; John Smith, coroner; Francis Clement, surveyor; John K. Mabray, assessor; Robert C. Malone, treasurer; Mathew Clinton, probate judge. The board first met at Hendersonville, and March 27, 1834, the seat of justice was located at Coffeeville, on the land of S. McCreles and D. M. Rayburn, and received its name in honor of General Coffee. The first courthouse was a small frame building, and was replaced in 1839 by a brick structure costing about $25,000, which building was again succeeded by the present beautiful brick structure costing $25,000. The following are the present county officers: Board of supervisors, James L. Eskridge, president; Thomas Badley, W. N. Frost, W. B. Scurr, William York; Charles R. Cock, sheriff; J. W. Brown, chancery clerk; James Seay, circuit clerk; Benjamin R. Winter, treasurer; R. Spearman, Jr., assessor; James D. Haile, coroner; W. T. Wynn, superintendent of schools.

Chocechuma was the first town in this county, and was the land office of the Choctaws until 1837, when it was moved to Pontotoc. Hendersonville was the second town, and flourished until the location of the county seat at Coffeeville, when it gradually declined.

The first white child born in Yalobusha county was James D. Haile, now bookkeeper for Herron & Co., at Coffeeville. S. McCreles built the first house in Coffeeville some time in 1830, and gave the place its name. E. Percy Howe published the first newspaper in the county. In the forties the Coffeeville *Times* was founded, and was succeeded by the Coffeeville *Intelligence*. After the war a Mr. Bowen reorganized the Coffeeville *Times*, which paper was continued at intervals until 1890. The Coffeeville *Academy* was founded in 1839, but its publication was soon abandoned.

Calhoun county was established March 8, 1852. Pittsboro is the county seat, situated near the center of the county. The other towns are Banner, Sarepta and Slate Spring. Trading points and postoffices in different parts of the county are Benela, Bentley, Big Creek, Cherry Hill, Cole's Creek, Hollis, Hopewell, Loyd, Matthews, Reagan, Reid and Sabougla. The Yalobusha and Schooner rivers enter the county, which, with their tributaries, give good water power. The county is bounded north by Lafayette and Pontotoc counties, east by Chickasaw county, south by Webster county, west by Yalobusha and Grenada counties, and has an area of three hundred and seventy-thousand acres, of which about sixty-eight thousand acres are cleared land. The creek and river bottoms are level, some of the surface is undulating and the balance hilly. Timber trees growing on the bottoms are gum, poplar, elm, beech, white oak and cypress; on uplands the various kinds of oak, pine, hickory, etc. The soil generally is fertile, producing corn, cotton, wheat, oats, sweet and Irish potatoes, sorghum, peanuts, field peas, etc. Fruits are grown only for home consumption; apples, pears, peaches, figs, and all the small fruits do well, and yield abundantly. Pasturage is quite extensive in the woods for summer; of native grasses, Japan clover is spreading, affording fine sheep pastures. Grist and sawmills are scattered over the county, in easy reach of nearly every neighborhood. Church and school advantages are good in nearly every portion of the county. Beds of lignite lie in various portions of the county; and coal has been found in the northeast corner, but whether in beds wide enough to work profitably is not known at present.

The population of Calhoun county in 1860 was ninety-five hundred and eighteen. The number of polls at that time was ten hundred and eighty-eight, the number of taxable slaves sixteen hundred and fifty-eight. The colored population since that time has been as follows: In 1870, two thousand; in 1880, three thousand three hundred; in 1890, three thousand five hundred. The total population in 1870 was ten thousand five hundred and sixty-one; in 1880, thirteen thousand four hundred and ninety-two; in 1890, fourteen thousand six hundred and eighty-eight.

The first board of supervisors met at Hartford, now known as Old Town, on the first Monday in May, 1852. Porter A. Davis, Lawrence Brasher, Christopher Orr, John Hunter, and James McCrory, after being duly sworn in by Ransom Murphree, justice of peace, organized by electing Christopher Orr, president and Ransom Murphree secretary. The organization of the county was completed June 8, 1852, with the following as members of board of supervisors: A. G. Hallums, Lawrence Brasher, L. P. Brantley, John Dowdy and Hiram Hall, with Lawrence Brasher as president of the board, John A. Orr, as attorney for the board. The first officers were: Alfred M. Wilson, sheriff; Alexander Armstrong, probate judge; James L. Ryan, probate clerk; John R. Brown, circuit clerk; Thomas H. Davis, assessor; Thomas Gore, county treasurer; William Hanna, county surveyor; Elom S. Grizzle, ranger; Amos Davis, coroner.

The place selected as the seat of justice was first called Orrsville, at a meeting of the board of supervisors, July 16, 1852. At the following meeting, July 26, 1852, Ebenezer Gaston gave the county a quarter section of land, and at that time the name of the county seat was changed to Pittsboro. The first meeting of the board, the record of which is dated at Pittsboro, was February 13, 1853. The present courthouse was completed in 1856, at a cost of about $10,000.

The present officers of the county are J. M. Milliams, sheriff; G. W. Miller, chancery

General Brandon

clerk; T. M. Murphree, circuit clerk; W. J. Patterson, treasurer; M. C. Hardin, assessor; C. C. Bryant, coroner and ranger; H. G. McGuire, surveyor; Joseph Griffin, representative; J. W. Lamar, senator. The board of supervisors is thus constituted: C. M. Lee, president; J. T. McCormic, M. D. L. Howell, H. S. Moore and I. N. Patterson.

The first newspaper in the county was published by O. C. Grasty. The *Democratic Banner*, now in its ninth volume, is ably edited by John C. S. Green.

Panola county has an area of six hundred and eighty square miles, of which two hundred and fifteen thousand five hundred and twenty-nine acres are cleared. It is bounded north by Tate, east by Lafayette and Yalobusha, south by Yalobusha and Tallahatchie, and west by Quitman and Tunica counties. This county was established February 9, 1835, and was named by Samuel J. Galston, who represented the county of Monroe in the legislature at the time. The name of Palona was suggested by some of his constituents, but having forgotten the pronunciation, he called the county by the name it has since borne.

The first officials were George P. Anderson, sheriff; G. B. Carter, probate clerk; B. B. Williams, court clerk; A. M. Mims, treasurer; James M. Raybum, assessor and taxcollector; Rodney Ruin, coroner, and G. H. Bayles, ranger. The present officials are William J. Miller, sheriff; William F. Carter, chancery clerk; Frank M. Johnson, circuit clerk; T. L. Needham, treasurer; Robert Ruffin, surveyor, and Benjamin Mitchell, tax assessor.

The county is intersected by the Tallahatchie river, which runs diagonally through it from near the northeast corner in a southwesterly direction. Its surface is generally level or rolling, and the soil fertile, especially in the lowlands.

The Mississippi & Tennessee railroad passes nearly centrally through the county, and situated along this line of road, which runs nearly north and south, are the towns of Sardis, Como, Batesville, Courtland and Popes, all of which are flourishing, enterprising towns. There are courthouses at Sardis and Batesville, the county having two circuit and chancery court districts. The chief productions of the county are corn, cotton, potatoes and sorghum. Many cattle, mules and horses are raised. At each of the towns above named there are flourishing schools, all of which are well attended.

Sardis, which was the county seat before the county was divided into two court districts, and which is yet one of its seats of justice, was incorporated in 1857. Its population is one thousand. The other towns and postoffices in the county are Batesville, with a population of six hundred and twenty-five, Askew's Bluff, Central Academy, Chapeltown, Como Depot, Courtland, Eureka Springs, Glenville, Havre, Kirksy, Lespideza, Longtown, Mastodon, Melrose, Parksplace, Pleasant Grove, Pope's Depot, Reynolds, Terza, The Gums and Wallace.

The population of this county in 1840 was four thousand six hundred and fifty-seven; in 1850, eleven thousand four hundred and forty-four; in 1860, thirteen thousand seven hundred and ninety-four; in 1870, twenty thousand seven hundred and fifty-four; in 1880, twenty-eight thousand three hundred and fifty-two; in 1890, twenty-six thousand nine hundred and seventy-seven. In 1860 there were one thousand two hundred and nine voters, and ten thousand and ninety-two taxable slaves. In 1860 the colored population was twelve thousand five hundred and eighty-five; in 1880, eighteen thousand eight hundred and thirty; in 1890, seventeen thousand nine hundred and thirteen.

Tunica county has a situation in the northwestern part of the state, occupying the northern portion of the famous Yazoo delta, and is bounded on the north by De Soto, on the east by De Soto, Tate, Panola and Quitman, on the south by Quitman and Coahomo counties and on the west by Arkansas. It has an area of four hundred and forty square miles, fertile, alluvial bottom, and most highly productive. Of this area there are forty-nine

16

thousand three hundred and fifty-five acres cleared.   The Mississippi river flows along the whole western boundary of the county.   The other streams are the Cold Water river, Indian creek and Flower lake, tributaries of the Yazoo river.   This county lies wholly in the bottom, and is, therefore, level.   The soil is alluvial, black sandy loam on the river front.   The black lands are chiefly stiff buckshot, and both considered very fertile.   Anything will grow well adapted to the climate—cotton, corn, oats, millet, clover, tobacco.   Much of the country is heavily timbered with white oak, red oak, red and sweet gum, walnut, cottonwood, hickory and an abundance of fine cypress.   Pasturage is very extensive, especially in the back lands, where there is cane grass, and acorns for hogs.   There are many mills and gins in the county, run by steam power.

This county was established February 9, 1836, and Dr. J. E. Nelson was the first county clerk.   The seat of justice was at various times at Peyton, Commerce and Austin, and was finally located at Tunica, where a substantial courthouse and jail were erected in 1887.   Tunica is a new town built up on the line of the Louisville New Orleans & Texas railroad.   The former county seats were all on the Mississippi river, and Austin at one time was a most important town, having a population of over two thousand, and doing a large river and inland trade.   Here was also built, in 1868, an expensive courthouse, costing some $35,000.   That building still stands in the deserted and dismantled town, and reminds the visitor of other days when the bustle and confusion of trade and traffic filled the streets.   Tunica has grown into quite an important place; it has several substantial business houses, and is surrounded by a wealthy and productive country.   The towns on the Mississippi river are Burnett, O. K., Commerce and Mhoon's.   The Louisville, New Orleans & Texas railway runs through the center of county, from Memphis to New Orleans.   Other villages and postoffices in the county are Bowdre, Busby, Clayton, Crews, Dubbs, Evansville, Glendale, Hollywood, Robinsonville and Wanamaker.   Tunica has a population of four hundred and fifty.   In 1840 Tunica county had a population of eight hundred and twenty-one; in 1850 it was one thousand three hundred and fourteen; in 1860, four thousand three hundred and sixty-six; in 1870, five thousand three hundred and fifty-eight; in 1880, eight thousand four hundred and sixty-one; in 1890, twelve thousand one hundred and fifty-eight.   In 1860 there were two hundred and forty-five voters and three thousand three hundred and fifty-two taxable slaves.   In 1870 the colored population was four thousand one hundred and twenty-seven; in 1880, seven thousand two hundred and five; in 1890, ten thousand nine hundred and thirty-six.

Itawamba county is bounded north by Prentiss and Tishomingo counties, east by Alabama, south by Monroe and west by Lee county.   It has an area of five hundred and forty square miles, of which thirty thousand seven hundred and ninety-nine acres are cleared land.   It was named in honor of an Indian named Colbert, who received the name of Itawamba under the following circumstances: The Chickasaws went out on their annual hunt, and while out a tribe from the east attempted to attack their camp and take what they had.   Young Colbert, about sixteen years of age, got the old men and boys of his tribe together, waylaid them, and killed and put to flight the whole tribe; and when the hunters returned and found out what had been done they called a grand council and made him chief.   In order to make him more conspicuous, they placed him on a bench from which fact he was called Itawamba, or bench chief.   This occurred near old Cottongin, on the Tombigbee river.

All that part of the Chickasaw bordering on the Tombigbee river was called Monroe, and February 9, 1836, Itawamba was formed out of that territory and organized into a county, embracing about half of what is now Lee county, and part of Prentiss and Tishomingo counties.

The town of Fulton, the county seat, situated on the east bank of the Tombigbee, was laid off in 1836, and Charles Warren was elected the first sheriff; Louis Gideon, probate clerk; C. H. Ritchie, probate judge; R. O. Beene, circuit clerk. The first board of supervisors met in September, 1836; J. S. Bourland was elected president. The other members were A. G. Lane, John Beene, S. S. Sperman and E. Allen.

It is probable that the first white man to visit and settle in this section was Isaac Edwards in 1827. He was soon followed by J. S. Bourland, Everett Sheffield, John and Alfred Dulaney, M. Harrison, Reuben Wizgul, H. Jamison, Holland Lindsey, Jacob Green, Dorn Patton, Charles Warren, Josiah Lindsey, E. G. Thomas, Samuel Bell, Ed. Lesley, all now dead. J. Robins and M. C. Cummings, still living, were among the first settlers in 1836. The land sales took place at Pontotoc and the county rapidly settled up.

The Tombigbee river runs through the county from north to south, and numerous creeks afford fine water power. There are several earthenware factories and some wool carding mills in the county. The river furnishes transportation during part of the year. Much of county is finely timbered. Some timber is being rafted out by the river. The principal varieties growing here are the oaks, pine, hickory, maple, beech, walnut, gum and cypress. This is a hilly county, with fertile valleys, and the chief products are corn, cotton, fruits of all kinds, oats and some wheat. The county abounds in good water from never-failing springs. Many fine streams run into the Tombigbee in this county.

Fulton, the county seat, contains about two hundred and fifty inhabitants, with good schoolhouses and churches. No railroad touches the county. Tupelo is the nearest railroad market, twenty miles west of Fulton.

In 1840 this county had a population of five thousand three hundred and seventy-five; in 1850, thirteen thousand five hundred and twenty-eight; in 1860, seventeen thousand six hundred and ninety-five; in 1870, seven thousand eight hundred and twelve; in 1880, ten thousand six hundred and sixty-three; in 1890, eleven thousand seven hundred and eight. In 1860 there were two thousand one hundred and twenty two voters, and three thousand four hundred and fifteen taxable slaves. The colored population in 1870 was nin hundred and eighty-six; in 1880, one thousand one hundred and eight; in 1890, one thousand and thirteen.

The towns and postoffices in Itawamba county are Abney, Ballardsville, Bigby Fork, Boland's, Bowen, Cardsville, Cliff, Eastman, Evergreen, Fulton (population, two hundred and seventy-nine), Ita, Jerico, Kirkville, Mantachie, Miston, Pleasant Ridge, Raburnville, Rara Avis, Ratliff, Tilden, Tremont, Tubby and Yocony.

Chickasaw county is bounded north by Pontotoc and Lee, east by Monroe, south by Clay and Webster, and west by Calhoun. It was established February 8, 1836. Houston, population six hundred and fifty, is the county seat, but courts are also held at Okolona, population one thousand nine hundred and fifty, on the Mobile & Ohio railroad. The county is well watered with creeks, running through almost every portion. In the hilly parts are numerous springs, and in the sandy lands good water can be obtained by digging from twenty to thirty feet. There are about two hundred and seventy thousand acres of land in the county, of which one hundred and twenty-nine thousand nine hundred and thirty-three acres are cleared; part level, part hilly, and the balance undulating. The timber trees are various kinds of oak, hickory, walnut, beech, ash, poplar, pine, chestnut, etc. The eastern portion of the county consists of prairies, which have a soil of great depth and fertility, of limestone formation. All the creek bottoms are very rich. The middle portion is sandy and hilly, but when fresh, very fertile. The western portion is flatwoods, and well timbered, but with a soil clayey and stiff. The products are corn, cotton, sweet and Irish potatoes, wheat, oats, all the grasses, rye, barley, etc. All kinds of vegetables do well and are grown in great abundance. Fruits, such as apples, pears, peaches, figs, grapes, apricots, etc., do well. Many are profitably turning their attention to fruit growing. Pasturage is extensive, and stockraising could be made profitable. The Mobile & Ohio railroad runs through the eastern part of the county north and south.

Besides Houston and Okolona there are the following named villages and postoffices in the county: Atlanta, Bowles, Buena Vista, Coleville, Congress, Egypt, Elise, Florence, Friendship, Houlka, McCondy, Neals, Ridge, Sonora, Sparta, Sycamore, Tabbville and Woodland.

In 1870 Chickasaw county had a population of two thousand nine hundred and fifty-five; in 1850, sixteen thousand three hundred and sixty-nine; in 1860, sixteen thousand four hundred and twenty; in 1870, nineteen thousand eight hundred and ninety-nine; in 1880, seventeen thousand nine hundred and five; 1890, nineteen thousand eight hundred and ninety-one. In 1860 the county had one thousand one hundred and sixty three voters, and eight thousand four hundred and forty-three taxable slaves. In 1870 the colored population was ten thousand and sixty-nine; in 1880, ten thousand two hundred and nine; in 1890, eleven thousand four hundred and thirty-six.

The commissioners appointed to organize the county were John Delaschmit, Richard Elliott, Thomas Ivy, Benjamin Anderson and Mr. Gates. At the first election in the county, held in April, 1836, and at every successive general election thereafter to the beginning of the war, the men named below were elected to the most important county offices: 1836—R. L. Aycock, sheriff; James K. Kyle, probate judge; Charles Graeff, probate clerk; H. M. Good, circuit clerk, who performed the duties of office through A. K. Craig, his deputy. 1837— R. L. Aycock, sheriff; Matthew Knox, probate judge; Charles Graeff, probate clerk; George W. Thornton, circuit clerk. In June, 1838, R. L. Aycock died, and J. B. Middlebrooks was elected sheriff to fill the vacancy on July 10, 1838. 1839 - J. B. Middlebrooks, sheriff; Matthew Knox, probate judge; T. N. Martin, probate clerk; G. W. Thornton, circuit clerk. 1841—J. B. Middlebrooks, sheriff; D. B. Glover, probate judge; T. N. Martin, probate clerk; G. W. Thornton, circuit clerk. 1843—Jacob Ault, sheriff; D. B. Glover, probate judge; T. N. Martin, probate clerk; G. W. Thornton, circuit clerk. 1845 Isaac Paulk, sheriff; D. B. Glover, probate judge; Jacob Ault, probate judge; T. N. Martin, probate clerk; John C. Cook, circuit clerk. 1847—William L. Baskin, sheriff; George W. Thornton, probate judge; Jacob Ault, probate clerk; William M. Moffat, circuit clerk. 1849— William L. Baskin, sheriff; G. W. Thornton, probate judge; A. E. S. Dumas, probate clerk; William M. Moffat, circuit clerk. .1851—William L. Baskin, sheriff; Jacob Ault, probate judge; A. E. S. Dumas, probate clerk; A. F. Hiller, circuit clerk. In 1852 A. E. S. Dumas died, and William B. Buchanan was elected probate clerk in May, 1852, to fill the vacancy. 1853—Anderson Bean, sheriff; J. N. Flaniken, probate judge; William B. Buchanan, probate clerk; A. F. Hiller, circuit clerk. 1855—Anderson Bean was elected sheriff; William F. Tucker, probate judge; J. S. Carothers, probate clerk; G. W. Tittle, circuit clerk. 1857—Rufus A. Bean, sheriff; William F. Tucker, probate judge; B. F. Pulliam, probate clerk; T. M. Blackwell, circuit clerk. 1859 - J. L. Flaniken, sheriff; William F. Tucker, probate judge; J. A. Loughlin, probate clerk; C. C. Thompson, circuit clerk. 1861—J. L. Flaniken, sheriff; William F. Tucker, probate judge; J. A. Loughridge, probate clerk; C. C. Thompson, circuit clerk. William F. Tucker resigned in 1861, and Allen White elected probate judge to fill vacancy. Representatives and senators and the dates of their election, in their regular consecutive order, to 1861: Benjamin Bugg (the first), repre-sentative, elected in April, 1836. Chickasaw county, having been added to an existing sen-atorial district, no senator was then elected; Henry R. Carter, representative, elected in 1837, the senator standing over; Benjamin Kilgore, representative, and James F. Walton, senator, elected in 1839; William H. Crawford, representative, elected in 1841, senator standing over; Senator Walton resigned in the early part of the year 1843, and Littlebury Gilliam was elected senator at a special election to fill the vacancy; James F. Walker, representative, and John H. Williams, senator, elected in 1843; James F. Walker, representative, elected in 1845, senator standing over; James F. Walker and R. G. Steele, representatives, and Will-iam R. Cannon, senator, elected in 1847; William K. Harrison and J. T. Griffin, representa-tives, elected in 1849, senator standing over; J. A. Orr and James McCrory, representatives, and R. G. Steele, senator, elected in 1851; James McCrory resigned in 1852, and John Ivy elected to fill vacancy; J. M. Thompson and C. B. Baldwin, representatives, elected in 1853, senator standing over; C. B. Baldwin resigned in 1854, and William F. Walker elected to fill vacancy; R. G. Steele and Uriah Porter, representatives, and J. M. Thompson, senator, elected in 1855; R. G. Steele and C. B. Baldwin, representatives, elected in 1857, senator standing over; C. B. Baldwin resigned in 1858, and J. L. S. Hill elected to fill vacancy; J. L. S. Hill and Thomas E. Bugg, representatives, and J. M. Thompson, senator, elected in 1859; J. M. Thompson resigned early in 1861; G. B. Gladney and R. M. Gunn, repre-sentatives, and J. T. Griffin, senator, to fill vacancy, elected in 1861. At the session of the legislature in 1861, a law was passed calling that convention under the first convention, to determine whether or not the state would secede from the Union, and at the convention elec-tion T. S. Evans and J. T. Griffin were elected to the convention which declared against secession.

The minutes and other records and many other papers of the circuit, chancery and pro-bate courts of the county were destroyed by fire on the 21st of April, 1863. That great mis-fortune to the county occurred in this way: The county officers and custodians of the public records and papers learned that a large body of cavalry belonging to the Federal army was on a raid approaching the town, and believing that it was the purpose of that army to devas-tate all public property, and desiring, if possible, to save the public records and papers from destruction, sought to effect their safety by removing them in a wagon to some secret place in the adjacent country. But it so happened that a squad of the soldiers took the same road, a country byway not much used, by which the officers were seeking to escape with the records. And, on overtaking the county officers, the squad of soldiers built a fire in the wagon and destroyed the wagon and its contents. In remarkable contrast with the conduct of this squad of soldiers who so destroyed the county's records—of incalculable value to the county and valueless to those who wrought the destruction—the body of the army, under the eye and command of officers, passed the town, leaving its people and property, public and private, untouched and unhurt.

An early newspaper in Okolona was the *Prairie News*, established some time in the fifties by Reuben Nason. It was published by different parties till about the beginning of the war. Soon after the war W. C. Widell began the publication of the Okolona *News*, and continued it a few years as a democratic paper, when its politics became republican, and it became known as the *Prairie News*. It was afterward purchased by A. Y. Harper, and the name was changed to the *States*, and it published several years as a democratic paper. In 1876 the *Chickasaw Messenger* was established by a stock company, and Capt. Frank Burkitt became editor. About two years afterward Captain Burkitt became proprietor, and the paper still continues under his management. Just after the war, W. J. Lacy published the *Okolonian* for about a year, and the Okolona *Monitor* was also published for a time, and later the *Lancet*, by Z. T. Trice, a short while, and from about 1888 to 1890, the Okolona *Times*, by George W. Waller and J. C. Petty.

Lafayette county was established February 9, 1836. Oxford, the county seat, is a thriving and enterprising town on the Illinois Central railroad, and has a population of two thousand. Other villages and postoffices are Abbeville, Taylor, Alesville, Bland's, Caswell, College Hill, Dallas, De Lay, Denmark, Harmontown, Holder, Kilgore, Lafayette Springs, Liberty Hill, Morganville, Noah, Orwood, Paris, Porterton, Tula, University and Walton. This county is bounded north by Tate, Marshall and Benton, west by Union and Pontotoc, south by Calhoun and Yalobusha, and west 'by Panola. It has an area of seven hundred and twenty square miles, of which one hundred and thirty-seven thousand eight hundred and ninety-three acres are cleared land. The principal streams are Tallahatchie river on the northern and Yockana river on the southern border of the county, and Yellow Leaf, Pumpkin, Hanging Kettle, Potolocomy, Cypress, Hewncane, Clear, Tobytubby, Splinter, Taylor's and Otuckolofa creeks. The soil is rich and fertile, and produces crops of corn, cotton, wheat, oats, sorghum and potatoes. Some attention is paid to wheat culture; apples, pears, peaches, figs, and the small fruits generally do well, and a few persons grow fruit for market in Chicago and St. Louis. Much of the county is well timbered, the oaks, ash, pine, poplar, walnut, beech, hickory and cypress being most common. There are in the county large beds of brown coal (lignite). There are numerous grist and sawmills. The Illinois Central railroad runs through the county from north to south, affording railroad transportation. The general topographical features of the county are rolling uplands, rising in some parts to quite abrupt hills, and many fertile valleys.

This county was early settled by a superior class of planters, who, from the natural fertility and productiveness of the soil, soon became prosperous and wealthy. Oxford, the county seat, is a beautiful city and a good business point, and is the home of many prominent and prosperous people. It was selected as the site for the state university in 1844, and has since then been a noted educational center. The city is built around court squares, in the center of which is a handsome and costly two-story brick courthouse. The government has a building here also, used for Federal court purposes and the postoffice.

Lafayette county had a population of five thousand three hundred and fifty-eight in 1840, eight thousand seven hundred and seventeen in 1850, thirteen thousand three hundred and thirteen in 1860, thirteen thousand four hundred and sixty-two in 1870, twenty-one thousand five hundred and one in 1880, twenty thousand five hundred and fifty-three in 1890. In 1860 it had fourteen hundred and fifteen polls and six thousand six hundred and fifty-seven taxable slaves. The colored population was seven thousand nine hundred and eighty-three in 1870, ten thousand two hundred and eighty-six in 1880, eight thousand nine hundred and fifty-eight in 1890.

Located on the northern border of the state, bounded by the Tennessee state line on the north, Tallahatchie river on the south, Benton county on the east and De Soto and Tate counties on the west, Marshall county is traversed from northwest to southwest by the Kansas City, Memphis & Birmingham railroad, and from north to south by the Illinois Central railroad, these two great trunk lines intersecting at Holly Springs, the county seat, which is distant forty-five miles from Memphis, two hundred miles from Birmingham, the great coal and iron center, and about three hundred and seventy-five miles from each of the cities of New Orleans, St. Louis and Louisville. The water courses of the county are Coldwater, Pigeon Roost, Chewalla, Spring creek and Tallahatchie river, on southern border of the county.

The principal products of the county are cotton, corn, small grain and every variety of vegetable that grows in this latitude. The timber growth consists of all kinds of oak, hickory, walnut, poplar, gum, beech, maple, cypress, etc. All kinds of fruits do well, such as apples, peaches, grapes, figs, plums, apricots, etc.; also the small fruits, all of which could be grown with profit for the Chicago and St. Louis markets. Apples and peaches are not a certain crop, owing to the occasional disaster of late frost; but in the absence of such frost, as is the case this year, these fruits are both superior and abundant. At the New Orleans exposition the Marshall county exhibit of apples, peaches and pears took a number of first premiums. Pears, plums, cherries, quinces, strawberries and raspberries grow readily, in the greatest quantities, of magnificent size and of delicious flavor; while blackberries flourish in every fence corner. Grapes of all known American varieties are raised with unfailing success. Pasturage is good and extensive, consisting of Bermuda grass, native grasses and switchcane. Stock farming and sheep husbandry could be made profitable.

Few places in Mississippi are so favorably situated. Holly Springs is an important station on the Illinois Central railroad. The railroad company have established here an excellent hotel. The Memphis and Birmingham branch of the Kansas City, Fort Scott & Gulf road connects the West with the Alabama and Atlantic seaboard. Thus Holly Springs is most desirably located as regards communication with the rest of the world, which fact, together with its exceptional health, makes it a comparatively good point for manufactories or industrial enterprises of any description.

Besides Holly Springs, population twenty-two hundred and thirty-two, the towns and postoffices of the county are Barton, Bethlehem, Byhalia (population five hundred), Cayce, Chulahoma, Colbert, Coleman, Cornersville, Early Grove, Hudsonville, Law's Hill, Mahon, Marianna, Mount Pleasant, Orion, Potts Camp, Red Banks, Searcy, Slayden's Crossing, Victoria, Wall Hill, Watson and Waterford. This county had a population of seventeen thousand five hundred and twenty-six in 1840, twenty-nine thousand and eighty-nine in 1850, twenty-eight thousand eight hundred and twenty-three in 1860, twenty-nine thousand four hundred and sixteen in 1870, twenty-nine thousand three hundred and thirty in 1880, twenty-six thousand and forty-three in 1890. In 1860 it had nineteen hundred and seventeen voters and fifteen thousand four hundred and forty-eight taxable slaves. The colored population in 1870 was sixteen thousand four hundred and ninety-nine; in 1880, eighteen thousand three hundred and thirty-eight; in 1890, sixteen thousand five hundred and eight.

This section suffered greatly during the war. Holly Springs, which was for a time Grant's headquarters, is famous historically as the scene of Van Dorn's raid on the Federal stores. On December 20, 1862, the dashing Southern general, with a small force, surprised the troops left behind by Grant, who was fifty miles away marching on Jackson. The Federals were all captured and paroled. Grant's immense stores, ammunition, etc., were then entirely destroyed. The medical supplies had been placed for security in a large building used as a foundry and the ammunition in a stable. The loss inflicted on Grant was enormous, amounting to millions of dollars, necessitating his return and an entire change in his plans for the campaign. Many interesting incidents of the raid are told by old residents. The old courthouse was burnt by Grant and most of the city by Van Dorn. Soon after the war the present courthouse was erected. It is a large brick building, surrounded by an unusually well-kept grass lawn, at whose edge shade trees in great and rare varieties give an additional charming effect. In the summer, when the foliage and flowers are at their best, the courthouse square is very handsome and the inhabitants have every reason to pride themselves on it.

Marshall county was established February 9, 1836, and was originally settled by a class of planters unusually intelligent, patriotic and public spirited, many of whom became prominent and well known. The merchants who founded Holly Springs were of the same class of large minded men. In ante-bellum times Marshall county was the empire county of Mississippi; its soil was very fertile, and its yield of cotton very large. Its topography is varied, being in the main slightly rolling, and well drained by many streams.

De Soto county was organized February 9, 1836, and is bounded on the north by Shelby county, Tenn., on the south by the counties of Tate and Tunica, on the east by Marshall county and on the west by the Mississippi river and Crittenden county, Ark. Hernando, population six hundred and fifty, is the seat of justice. Its surface is undulating and heavily timbered in the unimproved districts. Poplar, most kinds of oak, hickory and some walnut, are found in its forests. The county is rather thickly settled, and is a good farming district, the principal products being cotton, corn and oats. Clover is also grown to some extent, but cotton is the staple of the county. The county is traversed by the Louisville, New Orleans & Texas railroad on the west side, in the center by a branch of the Illinois Central railroad, and on the east by the main line of the Illinois Central railroad. In the aggregate there are about fifty miles of railway in the county. The area of De Soto is about six hundred square miles, of which about one hundred and eighty five thousand two hundred and ninety-two acres is cleared land. Besides the county seat, Love's station, population one hundred and fifty; Olive Branch, population one hundred and fifty, and Eudora population one hundred and fifty, are the principal villages of the county. Other trading points and postoffices are Alpika, Blythe, Bright, Cedarview, Cockrum, Cublake, Days, De Soto Front, Glover, Horn Lake, Ingram's Mill, Kelly, Lake View, Lewisburg, Miller, Mooretown, Nesbitt, Norfolk, Penton, Pleasant Hill and Plum Point.

De Soto county was named in honor of Hernando De Soto, the county seat taking his Christian name. Among the most prominent of the early settlers were B. F. Condra, Jordan Payne, B. F. Sanders, Humphrey Cobb, S. T. Cobb, William McMahan, Milton Blocker and Steven Flin. In 1840 the population was seven thousand and two; in 1850, nineteen thousand and forty-two; in 1860, twenty-three thousand three hundred and thirty-six; in 1870, thirty-two thousand and twenty-one; in 1880, twenty-two thousand nine hundred and twenty-four; in 1890, twenty-four thousand one hundred and eighty-three. In 1860 there were one thousand nine hundred and nineteen voters and thirteen thousand seven hundred and thirty-five taxable slaves. The colored population in 1870 was seventeen thousand seven hundred and forty-five; in 1880, fifteen thousand three hundred and forty-three; in 1890, seventeen thousand three hundred and nineteen.

Some of the first officials of the county were Humphrey Cobb, judge of probate court; Sam T. Cobb, clerk of probate court; Robert Atclinson, first clerk of circuit court; Hukey Brown, president of the board of supervisors. A part of the records having been lost during the war, it is impossible to give a more complete list. The commissioners to organize the county were Felix H. Walker, John D. Martin, Beverly G. Mitchell, Mr. Mosely and Mr. Cartright. The present officers are R. R. West, chancery clerk; T. R. Maxwell, circuit clerk; William H. Rollins, sheriff, and Mr. Boone, treasurer. Maj. T. M. Dockerey and L. W. Williamson represent the county in the legislature.

The handsome courthouse of De Soto county was begun in 1871 and finished in 1872 at a cost of $42,000, and is one of the best of the state.

Tishomingo county was established February 9, 1836, and contains an area of four hundred and thirty-five square miles, of which twenty-six thousand one hundred and fifty-one acres are cleared land.   Iuka, the county seat, is located on the Memphis & Charleston railroad, and contains eight hundred and forty-five inhabitants.   The other towns are Burnsville, Bay Spring, Eastport and Cartersville.   Belmont, Burnt Mills, Cripple Deer, Highland, Hillsdale, Merora, Short and Tynes are postoffices and trading points.   The county is bounded north by Tennessee, east by Alabama, south by Itawamba county and west by Alcorn and Prentiss counties.

The Tennessee river flows along the northeastern corner, and the other water courses are Bear creek, Little Bear, Cripple Deer, MacKeys, Indian and Yellow creeks, affording splendid water power.   Bay Springs cotton factory and Merchant flourmill, and several grist and sawmills are prominent manufacturing interests.

Excellent transportation facilities are afforded by the Tennessee river, and the Memphis & Charleston railroad.   About one-third of the county is open lands.   The surface is undulating, with level creek bottoms; the northeast portion broken and hilly.   The timber trees are pine, black-jack, post oak, white oak, red oak, hickory, poplar, gum, walnut, maple, cypress, etc.   The character of the soil is light, sandy, easily cultivated, and the bottom lands on creeks is rich alluvium, producing corn, cotton, oats, wheat, rye, rice, sorghum, tobacco, potatoes, etc.   Peaches, pears, plums, figs, and the small fruits do well.   This is a good county for stockraising.   Cattle and sheep find ample grazing for seven months in the year on the woods pasture.   The minerals in the county are iron, kaolin (porcelain clay), aluminous limestone for hydraulic cement, silica (seventy-nine per cent. pure), red-paint earth, fire proof brick clay, yellow ocher etc.   Iuka has seventeen mineral springs; some seasons visited by over five thousand people.   The original name of this place was Gresham's mills.   Robert Lowry's residence, four miles distant, was known as Bay Springs.

This county was first represented in the state senate by Samuel Matthews; in the legislature by Shelby Ussery.   The present state senator is C. Kendrick; representative, S. L. Rodgers.

The county of Tishomingo was named in honor of an Indian chief who died about 1836 at Iuka Springs and was buried on the site of Iuka.   The town of Iuka was named in memory of Iuka, a chief who died also while camping at the springs and was there buried.

The Iuka springs were looked upon by the Indians as the pools of new life, and to them they were carried when age overtook them to partake of their waters and to receive a renewal of youth, but to such new life could not be given.   Thus the locality of Iuka became a burial place for the Indians, and when the town was established the graves were visible all over the site.

The population of Tishomingo county in 1840 was six thousand six hundred and eighty-one; in 1850, fifteen thousand four hundred and ninety; in 1860, twenty-four thousand one hundred and forty-nine; in 1870, seven thousand three hundred and fifty; in 1880, eight thousand seven hundred and seventy-four; 1890, nine thousand three hundred and two.   In 1860 there were three thousand two hundred and sixty voters and four thousand six hundred and seventy-three taxable slaves.   The colored population in 1870 was seven hundred and forty-one; in 1880, one thousand one hundred and sixty-three; in 1890, one thousand and thirteen.

The first paper published at Iuka was established in 1850 or thereabouts.   E. P. Oden started one called the *Tishomingo Herald* in 1867, and the same year Dr. M. A. Simmon issued the Iuka *Mirror* and Dr. Davis the Iuka *Gazette.*   J. J. Chambers took the Iuka *Mirror* in 1881, and later called it the Iuka *Reporter,* by which name it is now known.

Tippah county is bounded north by Tennessee, east by Alcorn and Prentiss counties, south by Union county, west by Benton county, and has an area of four hundred and ninety square miles, of which twenty-nine thousand one hundred and eighty-four acres are cleared land. It was established February 9, 1836. Ripley, the seat of justice, has a population of seven hundred and fifty. Other towns, trading points and postoffices are Blue Mountain, which has a population of two hundred, Bulloch, Clarysville, Cotton Plant, Dumas, Falkner, Guyton, Hatchie, Heathville, Jonesboro, Leconte, Lowrey, Mitchell, Orizaba, Ridgeville, Selden, Shelby Creek, Silver Springs, Tiplersville and Walnut. The East Tennessee, Virginia & Georgia railroad (in Tennessee) runs within a few miles of the northern boundary and the entire width of the county. The Gulf & Chicago runs through the county from north to south, connecting with the Kansas City, Memphis & Birmingham railroad at New Albany. Three-fourths of the land in the county is timbered and hilly, and one-sixth bottom lands and level. The timber trees are pine, oaks, poplar, walnut, gum, hickory, ash, cypress, etc. The soil is generally productive, and produces corn, cotton, wheat, oats, rye, sorghum, millet, sweet and Irish potatoes, all kinds of vegetables and fruits. Limestone and good marls have been found in some parts of the county; also lignite (brown coal) and some traces of bituminous coal. Pasturage is generally good. Some attention is now being paid to stockraising and sheep husbandry. The watercourses of the county are the two Hatchies, the Tallahatchie and numerous small streams, making it a well-watered county. Water power is good. The various church denominations are well represented in the county, and there are good schools, one college being located at Ripley, and one at Blue Mountain.

Tippah county was established February 9, 1836. Ripley was platted in 1835 and incorporated in 1837. The population of Tippah in 1840 was nine thousand four hundred and forty-four, in 1850 it was twenty thousand seven hundred and forty-one, in 1860 it was twenty-two thousand five hundred and fifty, in 1870 it was twenty thousand seven hundred and twenty-seven, in 1880 it was twelve thousand eight hundred and sixty-seven, in 1890 it was twelve thousand nine hundred and fifty-one. In 1860 there were two thousand three hundred and seventy voters and five thousand four hundred and sixty-eight taxable slaves. The colored population in 1870 was five thousand and ninety-one; in 1880, three thousand and sixty-five; in 1890, two thousand nine hundred and seventy.

The *Southern Sentinel*, of Ripley, was established at that place May 1, 1878, by Capt. Thomas Spight. April 30, 1891, this paper published the following editorial reference to its history and success: "To-day the *Sentinel* reaches its thirteenth mile post, and we feel that it is due our readers and patrons generally, to thank them heartily for encouraging our efforts and placing the *Sentinel*, where it now stands, as one of the leading newspapers of the state. Thirteen years ago to-day the *Sentinel* was first issued with an outfit purchased at a sheriff's sale at a cost of $300; to-day the paper is issued to three thousand subscribers from a press that alone cost nearly four times the above sum. We do not mention this to brag of what we have accomplished, but to let our patrons know we realize and appreciate what they have done for us. During the past thirteen years the *Sentinel* has been through several heated campaigns, never swerving from the path of duty or democracy, always advocating measures that it conceived would redound to the welfare of the masses, and men for official positions that we deemed honest, worthy and acceptable. In this we have, perhaps, made some enemies, but the success we have achieved convinces us that our course has been endorsed by the vast majority of our people, and we are satisfied."

Pontotoc county is bounded north by Union county, east by Lee county, south by Calhoun and Chickasaw counties, and west by Lafayette and Calhoun. Pontotoc, the seat of justice, is located near the center of the county. It was incorporated in 1837, and has a population of eight hundred and fifty. The land office was formerly located there, as was also the Chickasaw Land bank, and the United States court was held there for a number of years. Other towns, villages and postoffices are: Algoma, Benbell, Brame, Cedar Grove, Cherry Creek, Chesterville, Chiwapa, Ecru, Esperanza, Furrs, Mud Creek, Plymouth, Pontocola, Prudeville, Pueblo, Randolph, Redland, Sherman, Thaxton, Toccopola and Troy.

Pontotoc county was established February 9, 1836. Its water courses are the Tallahatchie river, running along the northern boundary, and the Loosha Scoona, in the southwestern portion, with numerous creeks and branches, making it a well-watered county. The soil is a sandy yellow loam, with black and hummock land, and produces good crops of cotton, corn, wheat, oats, sorghum, potatoes, melons, field peas and all kinds of vegetables. The county has an area of five hundred and thirty square miles, of which about ninety-five thousand nine hundred and eighty-one acres are cleared land. The rest is well timbered, rather undulating, some portions level and some portions broken. The varieties of timber are oaks of all kinds, hickory, walnut, pine, poplar, ash, chestnut, cypress, etc. The school and church privileges are very good; free schools are kept four months in the year. Pasturage in the western portion of the county is very good. The hills are fifteen hundred feet above the tide water in the Gulf of Mexico; has a sober, industrious and law-abiding population. There are a number of grist and sawmills in the county. Very little attention is paid to stockraising and sheep husbandry, but many are turning their attention in that way. There are orchards in abundance to produce fruit for home consumption. Grapes do well, especially the scuppernong.

There are only twelve miles of railway in the county. The Gulf & Ship Island railroad is completed from Middleton, Tenn., to Pontotoc.

John Bell was the first who represented this county in the state senate; Willis W. Cherry was the first representative in the lower house. The present state senator is R. Wharton; the present representatives are S. H. Pitts and Jeff. D. Potter.

The Chickasaw Indians made their first settlement at the Chickasaw Old Fields, in what was afterward Pontotoc county, but in that part set off to form Lee county, at a point about fifteen miles east of the town of Pontotoc. The United States army under command of General Jackson camped on Chiwapa creek, three miles southeast of Pontotoc, on its march from Tennessee to New Orleans. Near that stream also occurred the treaty between the United States government and the Chickasaw Indians. One of the witnesses to this treaty was Stephen Daggett, an early pioneer here. Six miles south of Pontotoc was established one of the mission schools of the Chickasaw nation.

The population of Pontotoc county was four thousand four hundred and ninety-one in 1840, seventeen thousand one hundred and twelve in 1850, twenty-two thousand one hundred and thirteen in 1860, twelve thousand five hundred and twenty-five in 1870, thirteen thousand eight hundred and fifty-eight in 1880, fourteen thousand nine hundred and forty in 1890. In 1860 there were two thousand four hundred and fourteen polls and seven thousand three hundred and sixty-eight taxable slaves.

The colored population in 1870 was three thousand and twelve; in 1880, four thousand two hundred and forty-nine; in 1890, four thousand four hundred and eleven.

Lee county is bounded north by Union and Prentiss, east by Tishomingo, south by Chickasaw and Monroe, and west by Pontotoc and Union counties, and contains an area of four hundred and seventy square miles. The county varies from three hundred and eighty feet to eight hundred feet above the sea level. In all the low places artesian wells can be obtained two hundred and eighty to four hundred and fifty feet. The water is soft and pure, with very little mineral in most places. There are from thirty to forty good artesian wells in Tupelo, several in Plantersville and Nettleton, and many good ones on farms and at sawmills in the southern part of the county. The county has a remarkably variegated geology. There is every variety of soil and water. There are springs of hard and soft water not three hundred yards apart. There are black hammock and rich sandy tablelands that join each other as if put together by art. A hill of shells and sticky lime-clay is crossed, and the next one to it is sand and red clay. The principal products are cotton, corn, oats, wheat, tobacco, potatoes, etc., and all vegetables do well. Pasturage is very good nine months of the year, and this is a fine county for stockraising and sheep husbandry. The principal timbers are oak, hickory, ash, gum, poplar, beech, walnut, etc. The Mobile & Ohio railroad runs through the center of the county, from north to south, affording transportation.

It is generally said when there is no gold, silver, copper or iron in a county that it has no mineral wealth. So Lee county has no workable one, although it has many valuable mineral elements, such as tile clays, marls and mineral waters. The very best of clays for good drain tiles is abundant in many sections of the county. It is found about Birmingham, Guntown and Tupelo. It is quite abundant all along the eastern boundary of the county, and in some places the clay is fine enough to make the best of jugs and stoneware These clays have been thoroughly tested and tile made from them. When the farmers come to know that underdraining land with tile pipes is almost a necessity, these clays will be of great value, and the manufacture of tile will be a good and brisk business. Iron is a universal element, and, while not deposited, it is dispersed throughout the land and is in all mineral and vegetable matter. All the rock in the county is highly ferruginous as well as much of the hill soils. There are many springs in the county and some highly charged with the sulphate of iron and vitriol. Some of them are fully strong enough to be made places of resort for health if put in a state of improvement. There are beds of rough deposits from which phosphate of lime could be made. There are a good many deposits of marl in the county, especially in the vicinity of Baldwyn and Guntown and east of Saltillo. It has never been used to much extent. Many specimens have been tested by chemists, and some pronounced very good. There is a soft, blue limestone in the county which it is believed would make, with proper skill, hydraulic cement The shell deposits are also very numerous, both on the top and under the ground. There is a great deal of the sea deposit among them, which is a good marl and enriches the land where they are found. The shells make, when burnt like limestone rocks, the very best of quicklime.

Lee county was established by the legislature of the state of Mississippi in the year 1866, and her first officers were appointed at a meeting of the commissioners, held at Saltillo, November 12, 1866, pursuant to an act of the legislature of October 12, 1866, erecting a new county called Lee. E. G. Thomas, C. A. Marshall, Jesse Hunt, J. R. Hamill, Burrell Jackson and Jacob Bardin took the oath of office administered by J. W. Smith, justice of the peace, faithfully to discharge the duties imposed upon them, when Jesse Hunt was elected president, and E. G. Thomas secretary of the board of commissioners that proceeded to lay off said county into five districts.

At an election held December 10, 1866, the following were elected to comprise the board of supervisors: L. Temple, president of the board, from district No. 5; Josiah Lindsey, district No. 1; J. N. Hester, from district No. 2; John Files, from district No. 3; P. A. Scales, from district No. 4.

At an election held January 14, 1867, Jacob Bardin was chosen probate judge; D. P. Cypert, probate clerk; A. J. Cockran, circuit clerk; J. M. Dillard, sheriff; J. D. Parks, county treasurer; A. M. Robinson, assessor of taxes; W. A. Dozier, county surveyor; Robert Gray, coroner; W. R. Hampton, ranger; J. L. Finley, county attorney.

The county school commissioners were: G. C. Thomason, E. G. Thomas, John B. Sparks and Rev. J. D. Russell.

The grand jury for the October term of court, in the year 1867, consisted of the following named gentlemen, several of whom are now dead, and some are still citizens of the county: W. H. H. Tison, F. M. Stovall, Thomas McDonald, J. B. Hansell, Allen Walker, J. A. Brooks, G. W. Stovall, J. N. Davis, David Hoyle, S. J. High, B. Jackson, M. Pound, William Buchanan, Hugh C. Wilson, J. J. Cobb, Curtis Lowrey, James M. Armstrong, John B. Sparks, Dennis Crain and Milton Hodges. Col. John M. Simonton was in the state senate; Capt. M. Pound, Col. J. D. Wilson and Hugh K. Martin were members of the lower house of representatives.

At an election held April 15, 1867, Tupelo was elected as the seat of justice of Lee county. The first meeting of the board of police was held at Tupelo February 3, 1868. The court purchased a two-story frame building, in which they held court, until the completion of the brick courthouse in 1871, at a cost of $25,000, which was burned in February, 1873, and was replaced by its present brick building in 1875, at a cost of about $20,000. The splendid new brick jail cost $8,000. The present officers are John H. Oglesby, sheriff; Robert D. Porter, circuit clerk; Norvin Jones, chancery clerk; George M. Phillips, treasurer; F. H. Mitts, superintendent of education; R. A. Harris, tax assessor; N. C. Cherry, county surveyor; Bud Hampton, coroner and ranger. Board of supervisors: Joseph G. Williams, first district, president; Robert B. McNiel, second district; C. W. Austin, third district; John C. Partlow, fourth district; James A. Trice, fifth district.

The population of Lee county in 1870 was fifteen thousand nine hundred and fifty-five; in 1880, twenty thousand four hundred and seventy; in 1890, twenty thousand and forty. The colored population in 1870 was four thousand eight hundred and fifty-five; in 1880, seven thousand eight hundred and fourteen; in 1890, seven thousand six hundred and ninety-nine. In 1880 the personal property in the county was assessed at $703,928, of which $117,334 belonged to Verona, and $96,519 to Tupelo. Real estate was assessed at $1,197,377. The total value of real estate in 1890 was $1,557,451; of personal property, $790,000, of which $200,818 belonged to Tupelo and $56,735 to Verona.

The towns, villages and postoffices of Lee county are Tupelo (population one thousand five hundred and twenty-five), Baldwyn (population five hundred), Guntown (population three hundred), Shannon (population four hundred and fifty), Verona (population five hundred and ninety-six), Bethany, Birmingham, Coonewar, Corrona, Leighton, Longville, Mooreville, Nettleton, Plantersville, Richmondlee and Saltillo.

Volume I, No. 1, of the Lee county *Journal* was issued November, 1870, with E. C. Herndon as proprietor and G. P. Herndon as editor. Volume I, No. 1, of the Lee county *Journal and Intelligencer*, was issued May 10, 1872, with E. C. Herndon as proprietor. He was succeeded by G. M. Hubbard. As editor, G. P. Herndon was succeeded by J. M. Eckford, January 26, 1872. Mr. Eckford retiring May 3, 1872, S. M. Frierson became editor on the 24th of the same month. January 7, S. M. Frierson & Co. became publishers.

The Tupelo *Standard* was issued November 26, 1872, with James M. Norment as editor and publisher. The *Mississippi Journal*, with George P. Herndon as editor, was issued May 10, 1873. The Tupelo *Journal*, now issued by John H. Miller, editor and proprietor

264 BIOGRAPHICAL AND HISTORICAL

since September, 1879, was established in 1872 with G. P. Herndon as editor. The Tupelo *Ledger*, James L. Gillespie and J. B. Ballard, editors and proprietors, was established in 1886.

Union county is bounded north by Benton and Tippah counties, east by Prentiss and Lee counties, south by Pontotoc county, and west by Calhoun and Lafayette counties. New Albany, the county seat, has a population of eleven hundred and twenty-five. Other towns, trading points and postoffices are Ellistown, Myrtle, Rocky Ford, Alpine, Baker, Blue Springs, Darden, Etta, Fairview, Gallway, Graham, Ingomar, Keownville, Lenox, Molino Poolville, Poplar Springs and Wallerville. The population of this county in 1880 was thirteen thousand and thirty; in 1890 it was fifteen thousand six hundred and six. The colored population in 1880 was three thousand and ninety-eight; in 1890, four thousand and thirty-seven.

The area of the county is four hundred and twenty-four square miles, of which one-fourth is open, the rest being well timbered with white, red and black oak, poplar, hickory, ash, pine, gum, walnut, etc. The Tallahatchie river runs through the center of county, which, with its numerous tributary creeks, affords good water power. The soil is loamy, with a red clay subsoil, producing cotton, corn, wheat, oats, rye, sweet and Irish potatoes, sorghum and grasses of various kinds. All kinds of vegetables grow finely, and fruits, such as apples, peaches, pears, figs, strawberries, blackberries, dewberries, etc., bear good crops for home use. Pasturage is good and very extensive. Japan clover on the hills and bottoms affords fine grazing for sheep and cattle. Stockraising would be very profitable in this county. Some lignite, or brown coal, has been found, also marls and limestone in portions of the county. There are several fine grist and sawmills on the Tallahatchie river. The Chicago & Ship Island and Kansas City, Memphis & Birmingham railroads pass through portions of the county.

This county was established April 7, 1870. The first state senator who represented it was E. M. Alexander, in 1872-3. W. A. McDonald, the present state senator, was elected in 1888, and re-elected in 1890. C. O. Potter was the county's first representative in the lower house. The present representatives are Jefferson D. Potter and Robert Frasier.

Alcorn county is bounded north by Tennessee, east by Tishomingo county, south by Tippah and Prentiss counties and west by Tippah county, and was established April 15, 1870. Corinth, the county seat, is situated at the crossing of the Memphis & Charleston and Mobile & Ohio railroads, and is a flourishing and enterprising town with a population of twenty-five hundred. The Whitfield cotton factory is located here. The iron manufacturing interests are extensive, various articles of iron and steel from engines and boilers down to smaller essentials being turned out. The principal house in this line, the W. T. Adams Machine Company, does an annual business of $300,000. The Alcorn woolen mills is an important concern. The county has a number of saw and gristmills. The other towns in the county are Rienzi (population three hundred and seventy-five), Kossuth (population one hundred and thirty-two), Jacinto, Danville, Wenasoga and Glendale. Other trading points and postoffices are Burrow, Eagle, Gift, Hightown, Hinkle, Juliet, Kellum, Kendrick, Theo and Parmitchie. The Hatchie and Tuscumbia rivers, and a dozen or more creeks are in its borders, affording good water power.

The character of the soil is diversified, rich alluvial black land, river and creek bottoms, and sandy uplands, with a clay subsoil. Products are wheat, corn, oats, cotton and all kinds of vegetables. The grasses do well, clover, herds grass, orchard grass, Japan clover, and native grasses affording good hay and pasturage for stock of all kinds. Fruits, such as apples, peaches, pears, strawberries, blackberries and figs yield abundantly. Little attention is paid to stockraising or sheep husbandry, although the country is well adapted to both.

Transportation facilities are very good, two railroads named above passing through the county. About one-sixth of the county is open land, the balance well timbered with pine, poplar, white, red, post and black oak, hickory, ash, sweet and red gum and sassafras. The area is four hundred and ten square miles, of which eighty thousand three hundred and forty acres is cleared land. The church and school advantages are very good.

The following first board of supervisors met in Corinth June 13, 1870: Hon. L. M. New, president; H. Mitchell, H. C. Klyce, N. M. Aldridge, J. M. Curlee; I. N. Whiteside, sheriff; and R. J. Fleming, clerk pro tem. I N. Whiteside was soon after succeeded by E. F. Haynie as sheriff. The following are the present officers of Alcorn county: Board of supervisors—J. F. Hensley, first district; R. J. Roper, second district; L. C. Meeks, fourth district; W. A. Derryberry, fifth district; L. B. Mitchell, president; J. P. Walker, sheriff; F. P. Morrison, chancery clerk; R. P. Bomhill, circuit clerk; M. A. Powell, treasurer; R. B. Smith, tax assessor; John Butler, coroner and ranger; John D. Burge, superintendent of schools; J. J. Bell, cotton weigher; W. Y. Baker and T. J. Graves, representatives; Dr. C. Kendrick, senator.

The assessed valuation of personal property in 1890 was $460,344; of real estate, $1,028,125. The personal property valuation for 1880 was $428,136; the valuation of real estate, $848,472. The courthouse was built in 1880 at a cost of $25,000. The corner-stone was laid July 6, 1880. It was erected under the management of a board of supervisors constituted thus: S. H. Simmons, president; A. J. Stricklin, G. G. Reynolds, W. A. Parish and W. L. Burrow. The building committee comprised J. D. Bills, chairman; R. Henderson, secretary; A. J. Stricklin, W. M. Inge, D. G. Hyneman, K. M. Harrison and S. H. Simmons.

The population of this county in 1870 was ten thousand four hundred and thirty-one; in 1880, fourteen thousand two hundred and seventy-two; in 1890, one thousand three hundred and fifteen. In 1870 the colored population was two thousand seven hundred and sixty-eight; in 1880, four thousand four hundred and nine; in 1890, three thousand five hundred and seventy-one.

Prentiss county, named in honor of Sargent S. Prentiss, the distinguished lawyer, statesman and orator, was established April 15, 1870, with Booneville as the seat of justice. The following offices were appointed by Governor Alcorn, and confirmed by the senate July 19, 1870: Board of supervisors—John R. Moore, president; J. M. Moore, Alonzo Bowdry, Joseph Rodgers, M. L. Martin; Henry C. Fields, sheriff; W. H. Walton, clerk of the chancery court and of the board of supervisors. The first state senator from the county was J. M. Stone, and the first representative in the lower house was Hugh M. Street, who was elected speaker. The officers of the county at this time are: W. W. Cunningham, sheriff; W. H. Rees, chancery clerk; R. M. Hale, circuit clerk; M. L. Burns, treasurer; J. O. Whitley, tax assessor; J. B. Sanders, superintendent of education; John Bane, coroner and ranger; R. J. Moore, county surveyor; Robert Davenport, J. F. H. Carpenter, J. B. Floyd, S. T. McWhorter, J. Q. Mitton, supervisors, with J. Q. Milton as president of the board. The present state senator is C. Kendrick; representatives, E. Alexander and W. Y. Baker.

The courthouse was completed in 1872, at a cost, with some additions made soon after, of $15,000. The county contains two hundred and sixty-two thousand acres of land, about one-fourth of which is open, or cultivated, the balance being well timbered. In 1880 there were eighteen thousand one hundred and sixty acres in cotton. At this time there are twenty-five thousand acres in cotton, twenty-five thousand in corn and five thousand in oats.

The assessed valuation in 1880 of personal property was $333,161; in 1890 it was $475,000. The real estate valuation in 1880 was $750,584; in 1890 it was $871,954.

The soil of Prentiss county may be classed as good, medium and poor; on the creek bottoms, very fertile; on the undulating uplands, medium to good; on the steep hills, poor. Besides corn and cotton, the county produces oats, wheat, sorghum, peas, potatoes, etc. Vegetables of all kinds, and fruits, such as apples, pears, peaches, strawberries, blackberries, dewberries are grown and do well. Fine beds of marl have been found, and used to some extent as a fertilizer. In the cut near Booneville a large bed of oyster shells was found, in grading the railroad. Lime could be made from these oyster shells and used as a permanent fertilizer. Limestone is also found in some portions of the county. The Mobile & Ohio railroad runs through the center of the county from north to south, thus affording good railroad facilities. The numerous creeks and streams forming the headwaters of the Tombigbee river afford, in many parts of the county, fine water power. There are a number of sawmills, spokemills, canning factories and other manufacturing enterprises in the county. Booneville has three fine church buildings, Methodist, Presbyterian and Baptist, the latter in connection with a fine Masonic hall. There is a high school or college building of brick, built at a cost of $10,000. The institution is under the care of a fine corps of teachers, and affords ten months' school during the year. This county is bounded north by Alcorn and Tishomingo, east by Tishomingo, south by Lee and Itawamba, west by Union and Tippah.

The *Prentiss Recorder* was the first paper published in Booneville. J. M. Norment was editor and proprietor. He was succeeded by J. H. Miller, now of the Tupelo *Journal*. The *Pleader* was issued by Robert Summers, editor and proprietor, succeeded by Judge J. P. Pooall. The *Prentiss Plain Dealer* was founded by Thomas L. Bettersworth, editor and proprietor. Its first issue appeared November 25, 1885.

Besides Booneville, population eight hundred, the county contains the following named towns, trading points and postoffices: Altitude, Antioch, Blackland, Brown's Creek, Burton's, Dry Run, Elma, Geeville, Hazel Dell, Hickory Plains, Marietta, Millican, New Site, Old Cairo, Southland and Wheeler.

The population of Prentiss county in 1870 was nine thousand three hundred and forty-eight; in 1880, twelve thousand one hundred and fifty-eight; in 1890, thirteen thousand six hundred and seventy-nine. The colored population in 1870 was one thousand seven hundred and fifty-four; in 1880, two thousand four hundred and twenty-one; in 1890, two thousand nine hundred and twelve.

Benton county, organized July 5, 1870, from Marshall and Tippah, with Ashland as the county seat, is bounded on the north by Tennessee, on the east by Tippah, on the south by Union and Lafayette, on the west by Marshall county. The Illinois Central railroad runs through the northwest corner, while the Kansas City, Memphis & Birmingham road runs through the southern part. It is an agricultural county. The surface is level on creek and river bottoms; the other portions undulating and hilly. About one-fourth is cleared land, the balance well timbered with different kinds of oak, hickory, poplar, black walnut, beech, pine, elm, red and sweet gum, chestnut, cypress, etc. The soil on the creek and river bottoms, and also on the gently undulating lands, is very fertile; on the hills not so fertile, but easily cultivated and improved. The principal products are corn, cotton, oats, wheat, rye, barley, sweet and Irish potatoes, sorghum, etc. All kinds of garden vegetables and fruits suitable to the latitude are grown, and pasturage is quite extensive, there being an abundance of native and cultivated grasses for summer, and switchcane for winter.

R. B. W. Shepperd

Ashland, the county seat, has a population of two hundred and twenty-seven. Other towns are Lamar and Michigan city, on the Illinois Central railroad, and Hickory Flat, Maxy, Hamilton and Spring Hill; Austerlitz, Canaan, Collier, Floyd, Graves, Lonoke, Maxwell, Pegram, Pine Grove, Salem, Shawnee, Tocaleeche, Tippah and Yellow Rabbit are trading points and postoffices. The water courses are Wolf river, in the northern portion, and Tippah river, in the southern part of the county. These rivers and their tributaries give the county fine water advantages. Benton has an area of four hundred and thirty-six square miles, of which one hundred and seven thousand one hundred and forty-eight acres are cleared land.

The first representative of this county in the state senate was E. M. Alexander; in the legislature, B. T. Kimbrough. The present state senator is W. A. McDonald; representatives, B. O. Simpson, Allen Talbot. The population in 1880 was eleven thousand and twenty-three; in 1890 it was ten thousand five hundred and eighty-five. The colored population was five thousand two hundred and forty-six in 1880, and five thousand and seven in 1890.

Tate county is bounded north by De Soto, east by Marshall, south by Lafayette and Panola and west by Tunica county, and contains three hundred and ninety square miles. The annual production of cotton is about twenty thousand bales, worth about $900,000. All vegetables and fruits are largely cultivated, but no effort is made to produce them for exportation or sale beyond the border of the county. The market for the sale of cotton and the purchase of all kinds of commodities is Memphis, Tenn., which is thirty-seven miles by rail from Senatobia. But little attention has been given to fruit-growing. Apples, pears, peaches, figs, strawberries, blackberries, dewberries, etc., do well, and would be profitable if grown for market.

Fertile and easily tilled lands are in abundance yet uncultivated, and can be bought for a small part of their real value. There is a universal desire for a strong tide of white American immigrants. Good homes can be procured here for less money than in any Northern or Western state, and a warm welcome awaits all comers who bring good characters with them.

The sale of all kinds of liquor is prohibited in the entire county, and there are but few violations of the law.

The Mississippi & Tennesse railroad, now leased and run by the Illinois Central, divides the county, north and south, in halves.

On the northern and western borders the Coldwater river furnishes transportation for a large and profitable logging business. There are thousands of acres of primeval forest of the largest and finest quality, and the land can be bought with the lumber on it for much less than can be realized in clear profit from the sale of the timber.

The land embraced in this county was purchased from the Chickasaw Indians by the United States in 1832, and opened to settlers soon thereafter. Prior to that time there were a few white people here. After the opening, the influx was rapid and continuous for many years.

Among the early and more prominent settlers of the county were the following: Stephen H. Lyons, Lemuel Burford, A. L. Burford, William Flewellan, J. B. Crockett, A. M. Lea, Col. Samuel Johnson, Thomas and Stephen Williams, T. S. Tate, W. J. Veazey, J. L. Brown, J. M. Lively, Allen Elam, Wiley Fitzgerald, John Howard, Jonathan Miller, James M. Love, Thomas Downs, Charles Whitehead, Alex Reed, James Veach, John Crawford, Randolph Romel, S. W. Steel, R. E. Bailey, W. E. Patton, W. D. McFadden, Thomas Lewers, J. C. Wait, Rev. S. B. Lewers and the Wrights and Dowdys.

17

Among the prominent families of the county at present may be named the Callicotts, Browns, Veazeys, Whites, Baileys, Halls, Prichards, Burfords, Joneses, Easons, Gillilands, Andersons, Floyds, Wilbourns, Gillespies, McKinnons, Grahams, Steels, Gabberts, Moores, Hiels, Hams, Featherstones, Wilsons, Garrotts, Johnstons, Slatons, Salmons, Shands, Oglesbys, Hawkins, Allens, Crawfords, Deans, Poags, Roseboroughs.

Tate county was created April 15, 1873, and organized immediately thereafter. The new county contained about three hundred and eighty square miles, taken from the southern part of De Soto and twenty-seven square miles from the southwestern part of Marshall county. On March 6, 1876, about seven square miles were returned to De Soto, and about sixteen added from the eastern side of Tunica county. The county was named for Hon. T. S. Tate, who was a prominent citizen of the county, and who was more influential in procuring its creation than any other one man. He wished the name to be Bell county, but in this he was overruled by friends then in the legislature. He subsequently represented the county for one term in the lower house of the Mississippi legislature, and died about 1881, and is buried in the cemetery at the county site. He was a republican in politics.

The first county officers, appointed by Gov. R. C. Powers, were as follows: Josiah Daily, sheriff; O. F. West, clerk of the circuit and chancery courts; W. J. Pace, treasurer; J. R. Jackson, assessor of taxes; E. J. Litsey, superintendent of public education; J. E. Matthews, surveyor; board of supervisors—T. S. Tate, J. V. Walker, J. P. Pickle, Eli Bobo, D. T. Neighbors.

Tate county's handsome courthouse was erected in 1875, by J. H. Cocke, contractor, and cost the county, exclusive of architect's fees, $19,800. The first circuit court for the county was held on the third Monday of September, 1873, in a hired building known as Blackbourn's hall, which was used as a courthouse down to 1875.

Public free schools are taught in every neighborhood in the county, within easy reach of every child in the county. The average length of term is five months in each year. There are ninety schools in the county. The advantages to children of both races are equal. There are prosperous high schools running nine months in each year, at Senatobia, Cold Water and Arkabutla, and in many neighborhoods the free schools are supplemented by a pay-term of four months after completion of the free term.

There were in attendance upon the free schools during the last year four thousand three hundred and forty-eight whites and four thousand and ninety-one colored children, and there were seventy-two white and fifty-six colored teachers. There are no mixed schools, no white teachers of colored schools nor colored teachers of white schools.

At Senatobia is situated the Blackbourn college for white girls, a flourishing school, with an attendance of about one hundred and twenty-five girls and young ladies.

Senatobia is the county town, and is a separate school district, and by local taxation maintains Blackbourn college, and the Senatobia high school for boys, as free schools for all children of the district for nine months in each year.

Coldwater, Strayhorn, Arkabutla, Independence, Thyatira, Tyro, and Looxahoma are towns in the county. Other postoffices are Bowman, Cypress, Eckers, Independence, Irwin, Murry, Poplar and Rainey. In religion the county has Methodist, Baptist, Presbyterian and Christian churches, the first two being the more numerous, both among whites and blacks. The population is peaceable and law-abiding.

Agriculture is the chief employment of the people. There are a few manufacturing plants, which make wagons, carts, seed-planters, etc. As these employ but few workmen, there are no local labor unions and hence no strikes, nor other like disturbances.

There are but few foreign-born people here, and those are in the main industrious and thrifty citizens, and more of the same kind would find a hearty welcome.

The county was originally all covered by timber. Forest trees and oak, hickory, cypress, ash, elm, poplar, beech, mulberry, locust, gum, walnut, in fact every variety valuable for lumber except pine.

The soil is very fertile. There was no poor land originally, although some is now worn by the constant cropping. Fresh lands yield under fair culture fifty to seventy-five bushels of corn, fifteen to twenty bushels of wheat, forty to sixty bushels of oats, and one bale of cotton per acre, without fertilizers of any kind. Almost every cereal and fruit is grown successfully here.

The surface of the county is gently undulating, but there are no mountains or high hills. The climate is mild at all seasons, and for general healthfulness can not be surpassed. The diseases are mostly malarious. Lung, throat and nasal troubles are rarely found. There are but few springs. The best freestone water can be had anywhere in the county in wells from thirty to fifty feet in depth. The annual rain-fall is above fifty inches. Senatobia, the largest town, having a population of one thousand one hundred and thirty-two, was estab-lished about 1856, at the time of the construction of the Mississippi & Tennessee railroad, which connected Memphis, Tenn., and Grenada, Miss. The land on which it was founded belonged to Eli McMuller. The name is of Indian origin, and was spelled in their dialect Sen-a-ta-ho-ba, and meant black snake. The town was first incorporated about 1856, and its first mayor was William Finney, who held office down to the war in 1861. He was succeeded in regular order in the mayor's office by J. L. Medders, A. Motley, J. D. Oglesby, William Atkinson, R. L. Wait, A. A. Royall, T. E. Neely, J. C. Roseborough, J. F. Heard, J. F. Dean, W. J. East, J. B. Stamps. The incumbent at this time is J. L. Medders, who held the office more than twenty years ago.

The population of this county in 1880 was nine thousand and ninety-four white, nine thousand six hundred and twenty-seven colored. In 1890 it was eight thousand three hundred and ninety-eight white, ten thousand eight hundred and fifty-two colored.

The present officers of the county are: State senator, N. A. Taylor; representatives in legislature, W. H. Bizzell, J. R. Puryear; sheriff, P. M. B. Wait; clerk chancery court, S. J. House; clerk circuit court, W. B. Sloan; treasurer, J. M. Love; assessor, F. Lane; superintendent of education, J. F. Dean; board of supervisors, A. B. F. Crawford, S. W. Conger, J. M. Gann, T. C. House, Cain McClendon (colored).

Clay county was established May 12, 1871, from Lowndes, Monroe, Chickasaw and Oktibbeha counties. The name of the county was Colfax until April 10, 1876, when it was changed to Clay, a name more pleasing to a majority of the people. West Point, the county seat, has twenty-two hundred inhabitants, and is situated on the Mobile & Ohio rail-road. The other towns are Tibbee, Palo Alto and Siloam. Other towns and postoffices are Abbott, Barrs, Beasley, Belle, Big Springs, Cairo, Cedar Bluff, Griffith, Henryville, Mhoon Valley, Montpelier, Parker, Pheba, Pine Bluff, Robertson, Vinton and Waverly. The county is bounded north by Chickasaw and Monroe, east by Lowndes, south by Oktibbeha and west by Webster. The water courses are the Tombigbee, which runs along the eastern border, and in the county are the Tibbee, Line creek, Houlka, Chickatouchy and other streams which flow in a southeasterly direction.

The lands of this county are generally undulating or level; soil very fertile, black hum-mock, prairie and sandy; about one-third open lands and two-thirds timbered and bottom lands. It produces abundantly cotton, corn, oats, wheat, sorghum, field peas, all the grasses, fruits of all kinds suitable to the climate, and vegetables in great profusion. The open timber and bottom lands afford fine pasturage for eight months in the year, and switchcane in the creek bottoms for the winter months.   Timber trees are oaks of all kinds, hickory, ash, gum, poplar, chestnut, walnut, beech, maple, etc. Clay county is one of the best in the state. The eastern portion is largely prairie, which is very fertile. The county is well adapted to both stockraising and grain growing, and is settled by a thrifty and progressive people. It is traversed in nearly every direction by the Mobile & Ohio, Illinois Central and the Georgia Pacific railroads, all intersecting at West Point, the county seat. This city began its existence on the completion of the Mobile & Ohio railroad through this section a few years prior to the war and was incorporated November 20, 1858. The town had previously been cross roads, about half a mile west of the present town, and when the railroad was built business was removed to the present site. The location is very desirable and healthy, and the city is one of the most flourishing in northeastern Mississippi. It has an iron foundry, oil mill, compress, brick and tile factory, a wood manufacturing company and a national bank.

The first meeting of the board of supervisors was held May 17, 1872, and the board consisted of the following named persons: T. M. Abbott, who was made president; Seth P. Pool, James R. Gilfoy, George Strong and Vincent Petty.   Joseph W. Hicks was first chancery clerk; A. A. Shattuck, sheriff; Scott Sykes, circuit clerk; I. S. Rainey, treasurer; R. W. Miller, assessor; G. A. Watkins, coroner and ranger; A. P. Morrow, surveyor.   Dennis Brennan was the first representative.

Among the early settlers of this county were Hon. F. G. Barry and F. S. White, Fred Beall, J. G. Baptist, Capt. E. S. Ware, Jabez Mann, B. F. Robertson, L. F. Bradshaw and J. H. Shipman.

The population of Clay county in 1880 was thirteen thousand three hundred and sixty-seven; in 1890, eighteen thousand six hundred and seven.   The colored population in 1880 was twelve thousand one hundred and ten; in 1890, thirteen thousand and fifty-four.

The first newspaper in West Point was the *Broad Ax*, published by W. Ivie Westbrook, from about 1858 to 1860.   It was a spicy and well-edited paper. After the war, the West Point *Citizen* was published, first by J. P. Dancer, afterward by others. This paper was issued for several years. About 1877 the *Echo* was published by Thomas H. Collins, and finally, in 1881, was merged into the *Leader*, and has since been published under that name by L. T. Carlisle, who also for a short time published, in connection with the *Leader*, the *Farm and Stock Reporter*. About 1879 and 1880 George P. Herndon published the *Sunday News*.   In about 1883 the *Progress* was established by Boyd & Henderson, and after a short period, became the West Point *New Era*, and was issued by J. R. Alenan for a few years. In January, 1888, John Henderson founded the West Point *Forum*, which he still publishes, that and the *Leader*, by L. T. Carlisle, being the only papers published here now.

The present officials of Clay county are T. W. Davidson and Dr. W. B. Gunn, representatives; J. W. Brady, chancery clerk; W. L. Cromwell, sheriff; R. M. Trotter, circuit clerk; F. M. Howard, treasurer; W. T. Bryan, assessor; M. Redus, coroner and ranger; L. L. Morrow, surveyor; J. A. Stevens, superintendent of education; board of supervisors, W. H. Moore, president; N. H. Howard, George H. Burkitt, F. M. Aycock and H. T. McGee.

ADDITIONAL MILITARY RECORD*.

Field, staff and non-commissioned staff of a battalion of cavalry, commanded by Maj. Thomas Hinds, called into the service of the United States from the militia of the Mississippi territory by Maj.-Gen. Andrew Jackson, commanding the seventh military district, from the 2d of October, 1814: Thomas Hinds, major, enlisted September 14, 1814; Samuel Calvit, first lieutenant and adjutant, September 28, 1814; Peter Tiernan, first lieutenant and quartermaster, September 29, 1814; David Downing, surgeon, September 30, 1814; John T. Bowie, sergeant-major, October 1, 1814; Tactitus Calvit, quartermaster sergeant, October 1, 1814; Robert Werden, sword-master, October 15, 1814.

Roll of Capt. Samuel Gerald's company of dragoons of Thomas Hinds' battalion, Mississippi volunteer militia of the war of 1812: Samuel Gerald, captain, enlisted from October 2; 1814, to March 28, 1815; Robert G. Lowry, first lieutenant, from October 2, 1814, to March 28, 1815; Willey Jackson, second lieutenant, from October 2, 1814, to March 28, 1815; Jesse Gerald, cornet, from October 2, 1814, to March 28, 1815; John McAlpin, sergeant, from October 2, 1814, to March 28, 1815; Lewis Talbert, sergeant, from October 2, 1814, to March 28, 1815; Timothy Thames, sergeant, from October 2, 1814, to March 28, 1815; Reuben Smith, sergeant, from October 2, 1814, to March 28, 1815; William Burrows, corporal, from October 2, 1814, to March 28, 1815; George Gerald, corporal, from October 2, 1814, to March 28, 1815; John Simmons, corporal, from October 2, 1814, to March 28, 1815; Thomas Robertson, corporal, from October 2, 1814, to March 28, 1815.

Privates: John Alfred, from October 2, 1814, to March 28, 1815; Aaron Butler, from October 2, 1814, to March 28, 1815; Joseph Booth, from October 2, 1814, to March 28, 1815; Arthur Bowling, from October 8, 1814, to March 28, 1815; Thomas Baty, from October 2, 1814, to March 28, 1815; Isaiah Cain, from October 2, 1814, to March 28, 1815; John Cotton, from October 2, 1814, to March 28, 1815; Haly Cotton, from October 2, 1814, to March 28, 1815; Hugh W. Cooper, from October 2, 1814, to March 28, 1815; James Cain, from October 2, 1814, to March 28, 1815; George I. Decell, from October 2, 1814, to March 28, 1815; John Dixon, from October 2, 1814, to March 28, 1815; Thomas Edwards, from October 2, 1814, to March 28, 1815; John Erwin, from October 2, 1814, to March 28, 1815; Zeith G. Graham, from October 2, 1814, to March 28, 1815; Mitchell Griffin, from October 2, 1814, to February 13, 1815; Elisha Gates, from October 2, 1814, to March 28, 1815; Thomas L. Husbands, from October 2, 1814, to March 28, 1815; James Howell, from October 2, 1814, to March 28, 1815; Reuben Holloway, from October 2, 1814, to March 28, 1815; Robert Fleming, from October 2, 1814, to March 28, 1815; John J. Love, from October 2, 1814, to March 28, 1815; Charles Love, from October 2, 1814, to March 28, 1815; Ezekiel Moore, from October 2, 1814, to March 28, 1815; Thomas Norman, from October 2, 1814, to March 28, 1815; James Oliphant, from October 2, 1814, to March 28, 1815; Robert Pool,

* Received too late for insertion in the proper chapter.

from October 2, 1814, to March 28, 1815; Stephen Reed, from October 14, 1814, to March 28, 1815; John Silcock, from October 2, 1814, to March 28, 1815; Mathew Stoker, from October 2, 1814, to March 28, 1815; James F. Straughan, from October 2, 1814, to March 28, 1815; Samuel B. Simmons, from October 2, 1814, to March 28, 1815; Henry Stoker, from October 2, 1814, to March 28, 1815; William P. Thomas, from October 2, 1814, to March 28, 1815; John Watson, from October 2, 1814, to March 28, 1815; John Worthy, from October 2, 1814, to March 28, 1815; James Wilson, from October 14, 1814, to March 28, 1815; Nathaniel Wilson, from October 14, 1814, to March 28, 1815.

Roll of Capt. Jedediah Smith's company of dragoons of Thomas Hind's battalion, Mississippi volunteer militia of the war of 1812: Jedediah Smith, captain, enlisted from September 28, 1814, to March 24, 1815; Walter McClellen, first lieutenant, from September 28, 1814, to March 24, 1815; James Flower, second lieutenant, from September 28, 1814, to March 24, 1815; Parsons Carter, cornet, from September 28, 1814, to March 24, 1815; John F. Gilespie, sergeant, from September 28, 1814, to March 24, 1815; Benjamin Smith, sergeant, from September 28, 1814, to March 24, 1815; Thomas M. Scurlock, sergeant, from September 28, 1814, to March 24, 1815; C. G. Johnson, sergeant, from September 28, 1814, to March 24, 1815; Clark Woodruff, corporal, from September 28, 1814, to March 24, 1815; Green B. Davis, corporal, from September 28, 1814, to March 24, 1815; James Young, corporal, from September 28, 1814, to March 24, 1815; Leonard Bradford, corporal, from September 28, 1814, to March 24, 1815.

Privates: James Carpenter, from September 28, 1814, to March 24, 1815; Moses Samples, from September 28, 1814, to March 24, 1815; John Miller, from September 28, 1814, to March 24, 1815; John Boon, from September 28, 1814, to March 24, 1815; David Dortch, from September 28, 1814, to March 24, 1815; John O'Neal, from September 28, 1814, to March 24, 1815; A. Benjamin, from September 28, 1814, to March 24, 1815; William Bridges, from September 28, 1814, to March 24, 1815; Thomas McDermot, from September 28, 1814, to March 24, 1815; David Bradford, from September 28, 1814, to March 24, 1815; William Williams, from September 28, 1814, to March 24, 1815; Gideon Davis, from September 28, 1814, to March 24, 1815; David B. Stewart, from September 28, 1814, to March 24, 1815; Richard Bettis, from September 28, 1814, to March 24, 1815; Preston Brewer, from September 28, 1814, to March 24, 1815; Charles McMicken, from September 28, 1814, to March 24, 1815; Thomas Carney, from September 28, 1814, to March 24, 1815; Joseph H. Boone, from September 28, 1814, to March 24, 1815; W. Stubblefield, from September 28, 1814, to March 24, 1815; Alexander Cranford, from September 28, 1814, to March 24, 1815; Joseph L. Finley, from September 28, 1814, to March 24, 1815; N. Brashears, from November 7, 1814, to March 24, 1815; J. M. Bradford, from September 28, 1814, to March 24, 1815; Reuben Kemper, from September 28, 1814, to March 24, 1815; James Williams, from September 28, 1814, to March 24, 1815; Josephus Smith, from September 28, 1811, to March 24, 1815; Jones Shaw, from September 28, 1814, to March 24, 1815; Edmund Oneal, from September 28, 1814, to March 24, 1815; Daniel Brunson, from December 20, 1814, to March 24, 1815; Patrick Peck, from September 28, 1814, to March 24, 1815; Moses Horn, from December 24, 1814, to March 24, 1815; Richard Scott, from December 28, 1814, to March 24, 1815; Samuel Kemper, from December 28, 1814, to March 24, 1815 (died November 7, 1814); Francis Fair, from December 28, 1814, to March 24, 1815.

Roll of Capt. John G. Richardson's company of Thomas Hind's battalion, Mississippi volunteer militia of the war of 1812: John G. Richardson, captain, enlisted from September 30, 1814, to six months; Zachariah Gauldin, first lieutenant, from September 30, 1814, to six months; David Davis, second lieutenant, from September 30, 1814, to six months; James Seals, cornet, from September 30, 1814, to six months; William F. Hatfield, sergeant, from October 2, 1814, to March 28, 1815; William I. Boatner, sergeant, from December 17, 1814, to March 28, 1815; Cason Scott, sergeant, from October 2, 1814, to March 28, 1815; Henry Andrews, sergeant, from October 2, 1814, to March 28, 1815; Jared N. Richardson, corporal, from October 2, 1814, to March 28, 1815; William Reed, corporal, from October 2, 1814, to March 28, 1815; Benjamin Anderson, corporal, from October 2, 1814, to March 28, 1815; Josiah Cater, corporal, from October 2, 1814, to March 28, 1815; Joseph Whetstone, trumpeter, from October 2, 1814, to March 28, 1815.

Privates: John Anderson, from October 2, 1814, to March 28, 1815; Robert Alford, from October 2, 1814, to March 28, 1815; Ira Bowman, from October 2, 1814, to March 28, 1815; William Bryant, from December 17, 1814, to March 28, 1815; William J. Boatner, from October 2, 1814, to December 16, 1815; John Cater, from October 2, 1814, to December 16, 1815; Austin Coats, from October 2, 1814, to December 16, 1815; John Cammell, from October 2, 1814, to December 16, 1815; Benjamin T. Collin, from October 2, 1814, to December 16, 1815; John Dickson, from October 2, 1814, to December 16, 1815; Michael Dickson, from October 2, 1814, to December 16, 1815; Isaac W. Davis, from October 2, 1814, to December 16, 1815; William Evans, from January 6, 1815, to March 28, 1815; Drura Fargua, from January 6, 1815, to March 28, 1815; Edmond Ginn, from January 6, 1815, to March 28, 1815; Elisha Gower, from January 6, 1815, to March 28, 1815; Finchen Holman, from January 6, 1815, to March 28, 1815; Michael Holman, from January 6, 1815, to March 28, 1815; William Hunter, from January 6, 1815, to March 28, 1815; Samuel Harper, from October 2, 1814, to March 28, 1815; Charles Haynes, from October 2, 1814, to March 28, 1815; William Hodges, from October 2, 1814, to March 28, 1815; Charles Hester, from October 2, 1814, to March 28, 1815; James Harvey, from November 21, 1814, to March 2, 1815; John P. Hampton, from December 26, 1814, to March 28, 1815; William Irwin, from December 17, 1814, to March 28, 1815; George U. Keller, from November 21, 1814, to March 28, 1815; Jacob Keller, from October 2, 1814, to March 28, 1815; Thomas Keller, from December 17, 1814, to March 28, 1815; George Keller, Jr., from October 2, 1814, to March 28, 1815; Thomas Kelsey, from October 2, 1814, to March 28, 1815; Henry Lesenbe, from October 2, 1814, to March 28, 1815; Moses Lambert, from October 11, 1814, to March 28, 1815; Jesse McMahon, from October 11, 1814, to March 28, 1815; William Norment, from October 11, 1814, to March 28, 1815; William Noland, from December 17, 1814, to March 28, 1815; Jeremiah Noland, from December 17, 1814, to March 28, 1815; Robert Nesmith, from December 17, 1814, to February 18, 1815; Isaac Ogden, from December 17, 1814, to March 28, 1815; Peter Presler, from December 17, 1814, to March 28, 1815; William A. Richardson, from December 17, 1814, to March 28, 1815; James B. Richardson, from December 17, 1814, to March 28, 1815; Richard Richardson, from December 17, 1814, to March 28, 1815; James Reed, from December 17, 1814, to March 28, 1815; Isaac Riley, from October 2, 1814, to March 28, 1815; Thomas Scott, from December 17, 1814, to March 28, 1815; Enoch Teales, from December 17, 1814, to March 28, 1815; John Tomlinson, from December 17, 1814, to March 28, 1815; Joseph A. Smith, from December 17, 1814, to March 28, 1815.

Roll of Capt. James Kemp's company of Maj. Thomas Hinds' battalion of Mississippi territory dragoons militia of the war of 1812: James Kemp, captain, enlisted from October 2, 1814, to March 28, 1815; Alexander Murray, first lieutenant, from October 2, 1814 to October 31, 1814; Peter Bisland, first lieutenant, from October 2, 1814, to March 28, 1815; Samuel Ivey, second lieutenant, from October 2, 1814, to March 28, 1815; Charles Boardman, cornet, from October 2, 1814, to March 28, 1815; Benjamin F. Hitchin, sergeant, from October 2, 1814, to March 28, 1815; James Stout, sergeant, from October 2, 1814, to March 28, 1815; James Debett, sergeant, from October 2, 1814, to March 28, 1815; Robert Benoist, sergeant, from October 2, 1814, to March 28, 1815; Robert Dunbar, corporal, from October 2, 1814, to March 28, 1815; Joseph Semple, corporal, from October 2, 1814, to March 28, 1815; Elbert G. Head, corporal, from October 2, 1814, to March 28, 1815; George F. Wilkinson, corporal, from October 2, 1814, to March 28, 1815.

Privates: Robert Alexander, from October 2, 1814, to March 28, 1815; William Anderson, from October 2, 1814, to March 28, 1815; Peter Corbett, from October 2, 1814, to March 28, 1815; James Corbett, from October 2, 1814, to March 28, 1815; Lewis Chauncy, from October 2, 1814, to March 28, 1815; P. S. Collins, from October 2, 1814, to March 28, 1815; William Dromgoole, from October 2, 1814, to March 28, 1815; Shem Daniels, from October 15, 1814, to March 28, 1815; Samuel Davis, from October 2, 1814, to March 28, 1815; James Fletcher, from October 2, 1814, to March 28, 1815; Zadock Foster, from October 2, 1814, to March 28, 1815; Robert Green, from October 2, 1814, to March 28, 1815; James Gilbert, from December 28, 1814, to March 28, 1815; A. C. Henderson, from October 2, 1814, to March 28, 1815; Henry Hunt, from January 1, 1815, to March 28, 1815; James Hurton, from October 2, 1814, to March 28, 1815; Holland Hogg, from October 2, 1814, to March 28. 1815; Sterling Jones, from October 2, 1814, to March 28. 1815; James Jones, from October 2, 1814, to March 28, 1815; Absalom Joyce, from December 31, 1814, to March 28, 1815; Hugh Montgomery, from October 2, 1814, to March 28, 1815; Samuel Marly, from October 2, 1814, to March 28, 1815; John Martin, from October 2, 1814, to March 28, 1815; Leonard Magruder, from October 2, 1814, to March 28, 1815; Davis Montgomery, from October 2, 1814, to March 28, 1815; James Nichols. from October 2, 1814, to March 28, 1815; Charles Neiff, from October 2, 1814, to March 28, 1815; Z. B. Nettles, from October 2, 1814, to March 28, 1815; Alexander Owens, from January 8, 1814, to March 28, 1815; A. W. Pannill, from October 2, 1814, to March 28, 1815; Philip Rose, from October 2, 1814, to March 28, 1815; James Routh, from October 2, 1814, to March 28, 1815; Enoch Rose, from October 2, 1814, to March 28, 1815; William Terry, from October 2, 1814, to March 28, 1815; Thomas Willis, from October 2, 1814, to March 28, 1815; Andrew Williams, from October 2, 1814, to March 28, 1815, Robert Werden, from October 2, 1814, to March 28, 1815; Levi Whittingston, from October 2, 1814, to March 28, 1815; Alexander Owins, from January 8, 1814, to March 28, 1815; Thomas M. Green, from October 2, 1814, to March 28, 1815; Richard M. Green, from October 2, 1814, to March 28, 1815; William Ganidee, from October 2, 1814, to March 28, 1815; John R. Girault, from October 2, 1814, to March 28, 1815; Angus Ferguson, from October 2, 1814, to March 28, 1815; John Calham, from October 2, 1814, to January 28, 1815; Bryant Dougherty, from October 2, 1814, to January 28, 1815; Stephen Owins, from October 2, 1814, to January 28, 1815.

Roll of Capt. John J. W. Ross' Company of Lieut.-Col. Thomas Hinds' battalion of Mississippi volunteer militia of the war of 1812: John J. W. Ross, captain, enlisted from September 15, 1814, to March 14, 1815; Isaac Dunbar, first lieutenant, from September 15, 1814, to March 14, 1815; John L. Irwin, second lieutenant, from September 15, 1814, to December 16, 1814; H. B. Harrison, cornet, from September 15, 1814, to December 16, 1814; John H. Shanks, sergeant, from September, 15, 1814, to March 14, 1815; John Ferguson, sergeant, from September 15, 1814, to March 14, 1815; Reason W. Irwin, sergeant, from September 15, 1814, to March 14, 1815; James Truly, sergeant, from September 15, 1814, to March 14, 1815; Elam H. McDaniel, corporal, from September, 15, 1814, to March 14,

1815; Claudius Gibson, corporal, from September 15, 1814, to March 14, 1815; Michael W. Trimble, corporal, from September 15, 1814, to March 14, 1815; John F. Moore, corporal, from September 15, 1814, to March 14, 1815; Marston Clay, trumpeter, from September 15, 1814, to March 14, 1815.

Privates: Isaac Bland, from September 15, 1814, to March 14, 1815; Thomas Berry, from September 15, 1814, to March 14, 1815; Nathaniel Coleman, from September 15, 1814, to March 14, 1815; Malcolm Curry, from September 15, 1814, to March 14, 1815; Henry Carley, from September 15, 1814, to March 14, 1815; William Carson, from September 15, 1814, to March 14, 1815; Isaiah Coleman, from December 17, 1814, to March 14, 1815; James Cissna, from September 15, 1814, to March 14, 1815; Daniel Elmore, from September 15, 1814, to March 14, 1815; Elexander Findlay, from September 15, 1814 to March 14, 1815; Thomas Fake, from September 15, 1814, to March 14, 1815; Samuel Ferguson, from September 15, 1814, to March 14, 1815; John Fort, from September 15, 1814, to March 14, 1815; William Fulks, from September 19, 1814, to March 14, 1815; Abraham Foreman, from September 19, 1814, to March 14, 1815; Shadrack Foster, from September 19, 1814, to March 14, 1815; Philip Gilbert, from September 22, 1814, to March 14, 1815; George W. Given (artificer), September 15, 1814, to March 14, 1815; Samuel Guest, from September 15, 1814, to March 14, 1815; Robert Furguson, from September 15, 1814, to March 14, 1815; John G. Grady, from September 15, 1814, to March 14, 1815; Thomas Grafton, from September 15, 1814, to March 14, 1815; George Gilmore, from September 15, 1814, to March 14, 1815; Stephen Griffin, from September 15, 1814, to March 14, 1815; William Hanover, September 15, 1814, to March 14, 1815; George Handcock, from September 15, 1814, to March 14, 1815; Richard Hawkins, from September 15, 1814, to March 14, 1815; George Haynes, from September 15, 1814, to March 14, 1815; Jacob Hays, from September 19, 1814, to March 14, 1815; Richard Harrison, from December 17, 1814, to March 14, 1815; Daniel Huey, from September 15, 1814, to March 14, 1815; Levi C. Harris, from September 15, 1814, to March 14, 1815; Charles H. Jordan, from September 15, 1814, to March 14, 1815; Zachariah B. Jones, September 15, 1814, to March 14, 1815; Abraham Lainhart, from September 15, 1814, to March 14, 1815; Thomas McAlister, from September 15, 1814, to March 14, 1815; Joseph Moore, from September 15, 1814, to March 14, 1815; John Neil, from September 15, 1814, to March 14, 1815; John Odam, from September 15, 1814, to March 14, 1815; William B. Prince, from September 15, 1814, to March 14, 1815; Henry Platner, from September 15, 1814, to March 14, 1815; James Robinson, from September 15, 1814, to March 14, 1815; Eli Scurry, from September 15, 1814, to March 14, 1815; Thomas Scott, from September 15, 1814, to March 14, 1815; Dixon Stroud, from September 22, 1814, to March 14, 1815; Joel Selmon, from December 17, 1814, to March 14, 1815; Thomas Spain, from October 12, 1814, to March 14, 1815; Richard Spain, from September 22, 1814, to March 14, 1815; William Treadwell, from September 16, 1814, to March 14, 1815; John H. Truly, from September, 19, 1814, to March 14, 1815; James Terry, from December 17, 1814, to March 14, 1815; Samuel W. Watkins, from September 15, 1814, to March 14, 1815; James Whitaker; from September 17, 1814, to March 14, 1815; Jacob White, from September 15, 1814, to March, 1815; Thomas C. Vaughan, from September 15, 1814, to March 14, 1815; David Fairbanks, from September 15, 1814, to March 14, 1815; James Keith, from January 18, 1815, to March 14, 1815; Joshua Hadly, from January 18, 1815, to March 14, 1815; Thomas F. Picket, from January 18, 1815, to March 14, 1815; John Prince, from January 10, 1815, to March 14, 1815; Edward Cook, from January 8, 1815, to March, 1815.

CHAPTER XIII.

PERSONAL RECORDS, A.

THE public services of Hon. Richard F. Abbay have been characterized by a noticeable devotion to the welfare of his county, and his ability and fidelity in his present position have been seen and appreciated by all. He was born in Davidson county Tenn., June 9, 1838, the fourth of five children born to Richard and Mary (Compton) Abbay, natives of Virginia and Tennessee respectively, the former being a sagacious, practical and very successful planter. Upon his removal to Mississippi in 1838, the country was a vast wilderness, owned and inhabited by the Indians, but being favorably impressed by the appearance of the country he pluckily determined to make a location and became the owner of the plantation on which the immediate subject of this sketch resides. For a number of years he was levee commissioner for Tunica county, and in numerous other ways showed his interest in the progress and development of the county of his location, at all times aiding and supporting worthy measures. In 1883 he was called from life, having reached the advanced age of eighty-three years. His parents, Jonathan and Margaret Abbay, were members of leading families of Virginia, in which state they were born, and from which they moved in 1810, taking up their abode in the state of Kentucky, where they continued to make their home for about thirty years. They then became residents of the state of Missouri, where Mr. Abbay died in 1846, having been a useful and worthy member of society. The maternal grandparents, William and Susan Compton, were Virginians, but became early settlers of the state of Tennessee, Mr. Compton at his death in 1846 being one of the wealthiest and most influential citizens of Davidson county, of which he was one of the pioneers. The Comptons originally came from England, a member of the family coming to this country during the colonial period. with Lord Baltimore, his descendants being among the most intelligent, eminent and aristocratic citizens of the United States. Hon. Richard F. Abbay was reared and educated in the state of Tennessee, his initiatory education being received in the school at White Creek springs, where he fitted himself for entrance into the Cumberland university at Nashville, from which institution he afterward graduated in 1858. Shortly after this he began the study of law, and in the year 1867 was admitted to the Tennessee bar, after which he successfully practiced his profession for four years, being at the same time engaged in planting. During this time he made his home with his father, and upon the death of the latter he continued his planting operations, and is now the owner of two thousand acres of land, of which one thousand five hundred acres are under cultivation. In addition to looking after his planting interests he is also engaged in merchandising, and his stock of goods now amounts to about $5,000. As he has always endeavored to meet the requirements of his patrons, and has been strictly honorable in his dealings, he has built up a paying trade among the leading citizens of the section in which he resides, and has won the utmost respect and good will from all. His mental endowments are of a superior order, and he has a clear, well poised and analytical mind, and is quick of perception. His qualities admirably fit him for the profession of law, as well as for the public life he has led, and his friends have not been slow to recognize his praiseworthy qualities, and have shown their appreciation of the services he has rendered his party, and his qualities of leadership by keeping him their representative in the general assembly of the state since 1887. He possesses executive ability of a high order, and his reputation as a pure and intelligent legislator is of the very best.

Since he has been discharging the duties of this position, he has taken an active part in many of the important questions that have come up before the assembly, and especially distinguished himself is 1888, when the question of reducing the interest on certain funds donated to the state of Mississippi for the education of the children of several counties in the state, known as the Chickasaw counties, from eight to six per cent., after having agreed to pay eight per cent. for the use of the funds. Mr. Abbay was a leading spirit in the fight against the passage of this measure, and by his admirers was styled the "Chief of the Chickasaws," and was presented with a gold-headed cane in token of the immeasurable services he had rendered those counties. He was also a member of the constitutional convention in 1890, and acquitted himself with credit. The confidence which the people have in him is almost unbounded, and that he fully deserves their trust, respect and esteem can not for a moment be doubted. In 1860 he went to Cuba for his health, but returned to his native land on the last ship that entered port at New Orleans before the blockade, the Habana, which afterwards became famous as the Sumter. He immediately entered the Confederate army, but his health could not bear the hardships and exposure of a soldier's life, and after a stroke of paralysis he returned to his home and did not again enter the service. He is a stanch democrat in political views, and takes an active interest and part in every issue of the day, and for a number of years has been a political leader of his party. He has one of the most beautiful and attractive residences of which the county can boast, and the generous and true-hearted hospitality which he extends to all his friends is thoroughly enjoyed and appreciated by them.

F. M. Abbott, as a planter, possesses advanced ideas and progressive principles, and among his chief characteristics are energy, intelligence and honesty. Although born and reared in the North, he easily adapted himself to the conditions of Southern life, and has made headway and progress where many would have failed. He was born in New York state in 1843, a son of Harry Abbott, who was also born in that state in 1800. The latter was a successful merchant and farmer, but during his early manhood he was a school teacher. He was finely educated for his day, and possessed far more than ordinary attainments. His marriage occurred in his native state to Miss Louisa Bostwick of New York, and to them were born nine children, five of whom are yet living: A. F. of Marysville, Cal.; L. C. of Howard, Miss.; E. A. of Warren, Penn.; Mrs. C. L. Waters of Pennsylvania; and F. M. of this sketch. Harry Abbott was a member of a pioneer family of New York, for his father settled in the eastern portion of the state, at a time when a greater part of that state was an almost unexplored region. From the very first the members of this family have been sturdy, practical and useful settlers, some of whom have become eminent in the different callings in which they have been engaged. F. M. Abbott was educated in the Union school of Warren, Penn., and there he was married in 1870 to Miss Gertrude E. Henry. He came to Mississippi in

1865, and after one year's residence in Aberdeen, moved on his plantation in Clay county where, in 1878, he founded the present town of Abbott. Mr. Abbott was engaged in merchandising quite extensively for a number of years, but the most of his attention has been given to planting and live-stock raising, in which he has done remarkably well. He has always interested himself in political matters, and owing to his sound judgment and intelligent and practical views he was considered a fitting man to represent his district in the state senate, and filled this position with intelligence and ability from 1870 to 1874. During this time in the senate he devoted himself largely to securing legislation looking to the development and upbuilding of the state, and his immediate section in particular; among the more important acts being one creating the present county of Clay, where he resides, West Point being made the county seat, which resulted in developing that town from a way station on the Mobile & Ohio railroad into an important trade and railroad center, with an assured future second to no town in the state. He has done more than his share to build up and improve the county in which he makes his home, and has taken great interest in the proposed railroad, known as the Memphis & Atlantic, which will pass through the little town of Abbott. Much of the grading for this line in Clay county has been done by him at his own expense, and if in the near future that portion of the county should get a railroad, it will be greatly through his energy and determined efforts. He is a man of kindly and charitable disposition, is highly respected and esteemed in his county and state, and is a very pleasant and agreeable gentleman to meet. He and his wife are very hospitable and delight to welcome to their pleasant home their numerous friends. They have one daughter, Mabel H.

Dr. Richard Abbey, Yazoo City, Miss. The Rev. Richard Abbey was born in the state of New York, November 16, 1805, and was the fourth of a family of eight children. His parents, Richard and Dollie (Ellis) Abbey, were natives of Connecticut and New Hampshire, respectively. The father was a farmer by occupation, and removed from Connecticut to New York about the year 1799; there he resided until 1812, when he went to western Pennsylvania, and located near Meadville. It was not long, however, until he and his eldest son entered the army, and served through the war of 1812. The father was a commissioned officer, and was wounded in the great battle of Lundy's Lane. In 1816 he pushed on still farther west, settling in Alexander county, Ill., where he passed the remainder of his days. His death occurred in 1821. Three sons and two daughters reached mature age, only two of whom still survive—the subject of this notice and the youngest brother, M. E. Abbey. The paternal grandfather, Richard Abbey, was a native of Connecticut, and an officer in the war of the Revolution. After his father's death, Dr. Abbey lived in Illinois and Missouri for three years. At the age of fifteen years he was mail carrier, from Jackson, Mo., to Golconda, Ill. He obtained his education entirely through his own efforts, working half the year for means to keep himself in school the other half. At the age of nineteen years he came to Mississippi, and located at Natchez, where he secured a situation as clerk in a dry goods store. His services were of such value that he was soon made a partner in the business, and became the sole manager. His partner, Mr. Merrick, died in 1833, and for seven years the business was continued. In 1840 it was closed out by Mr. Abbey, and he then went to Yazoo county, where he had invested in lands. He conducted a cotton plantation thereafter. It was about this time that he was impressed with a call to the ministry, having been a Methodist from early life. For eleven years he was a local preacher in the Methodist Episcopal church South, and in 1856 he joined the Mississippi conference, and was appointed agent of the book and tract establishment of that church at Vicksburg. In

1858 he was elected by the general conference financial secretary of the Southern Methodist Episcopal Publishing house, located at Nashville, Tenn. He filled this position four years, and was the sole agent of the house until after the war. In 1867 he received an appointment as presiding elder of the Jackson district, Mississippi conference. The last four years of his stay in Nashville, during the war, he defended the property of the church against military depredation, and it was through his courage and vigilance that its confiscation or destruction by the government or the army was prevented. In 1872 he was appointed by the same house to go to Washington, D. C., to prosecute a claim against the government; a large sum of money was favorably reported by the senate committee of claims, after four years of hard work. In 1876 he returned to his former field of labor, but his failing health and strength caused him to be placed upon the supernumerary list, and he has since made his home in Yazoo city. Dr. Abbey is a hard student; he is the author of the following books and pamphlets, which are mainly of a doctrinal or scientific character: "Diuturnity," "Ecclesiastical Constitution," "Letters to Bishop Green on Apostolic Succession," "End of Apostolic Succession," "Church and Ministry," "Ecce Ecclesia," "Baptismal Demonstration," "Strictures on Church Government," "Divine Assessment," City of God," "The Priest and the Preacher," "The Preacher and the Rector," and several others. He has now in preparation a history of the Methodist Episcopal church South, during the war, a period of which there has hitherto been no published history. The Doctor was married in 1831 to Miss Julia Bathis, a native of Natchez, Miss., and an orphan girl. One child was reared from this union, Julia, wife of Dr. A. F. Magruder, deceased. Mrs. Abbey died in 1882. She was a good, kind mother, a true Christian and loving wife. Dr. Abbey has given some attention to planting since 1834, and still conducts his farming interests. In 1890 his library, a large, fine and choice collection of books, in which he took great pride, was destroyed by fire. Though a self-made man in every sense of the word, the Doctor is the peer of many a college-bred man, and is held in the highest esteem by all who have had the pleasure of any association with him. He is said to be the most extensive author in his church. A brief biographical sketch of him may be seen in Johnson's Cyclopedia. His works have, most of them, been extensively reviewed. A New York reviewer compares his style and logic to those of Butler in his great "Analogy." As a specimen of these notices, we copy the following from a "Review of Diuturnity," in the *Christian Advocate*, of Nashville: "This is one of the most remarkable books we ever read. He who begins it will scarcely set it aside till he has finished it. It makes a priori appeal to the perfections of God, the capacities of man, the phenomena of the universe, etc., to prove that our globe is destined to an 'immense' longevity. The chapters devoted to chemistry, geology, natural, mental and moral philosophy, theology, history, etc., indicate extensive reading and close observation, reminding one of the Sylva Sylvarum and the Novum Organum of the great inductive philosopher. The book is divided into five sections, respectively treating on the relation between man and his earthly residence, the physical aspects of the world, its intellectual aspects, its moral and religious aspects, the future and improved state of the world. These sections are divided into eighty-eight chapters, thus furnishing the reader a sufficient number of resting places. This arrangement, however, involves considerable repetition, which, indeed, may have been designed by the author, the more effectually to secure the comprehension and mastery of his theory by the reader. Mr. Abbey deals in bold paradoxes, and evinces no reverence for old and popular opinions. His logic has no bowels; it dispatches a venerable dogma that comes in its way with as little relenting as a city policemen dispatches a dog in the dog days. He is especially severe on the rabbinic, patristic and modern millenarian notions of the second advent of Christ and the like. He is a thorough-going 'architect of ruin.' It is not necessary to indorse the author's theory to be interested in his book, as it is original, bold, racy and suggestive. We quote a passage or two, as a specimen of his style and method of handling a subject.'' Now, near the close of his eighty-sixth year, late in 1891, the Doctor is in good health, and preaches with as much care and vigor as in former years, and with intellect as unflagging as at midlife. He holds that a man should be an industrious student to the last.

George H. Abney, whose postoffice address is Rara Avis, Itawamba county, Miss., was born in South Carolina, February 15, 1828, and is a farmer of this county. His parents were William T. and Charlotte P. Abney, both of whom were born in Edgefield district, S. C. His father died in South Carolina, soon after his return from the Indian war in Florida. His mother married Col. David Patton, of Fleming county, Ky., and he and his sisters and brothers went to Kentucky with their mother, where he received his education. In 1847, at the age of seventeen years, he enlisted in the United States army, and did gallant service in the Mexican war as a member of company L, in Colonel Butler's historic Palmetto regiment. After being stationed for a while at Lobos island, in the Gulf of Mexico, he went to Vera Cruz, where he took part in that battle; afterward in the battles fought at Contreras and Cherubusco. In the last-named fight he received a severe wound in the right leg, and was sent to the hospital at San Augustine, and afterward to Micicoca. One of the memorable incidents of his war experience was the execution by hanging of thirty deserters, of which he was a witness. He received his discharge from the United States service at Mobile in 1848, and in 1849 he married Miss Anna Griffith, a daughter of William and Mary (Abney) Griffith, both natives of South Carolina, in which state Miss Griffith was born in 1832. The subject of our sketch has devoted his life principally to farming, and is the owner of a good small farm. He is public spirited in a moderate degree and has done what he believes he should in the establishment and maintenance of schools and churches, and it may be said of him that he is ever ready to aid with his means those who call on him in need. He is a democrat politically, and he and his wife are members of no church militant. In 1862 he enlisted in the Confederate army and took part in the engagements at Shiloh and Resaca. At the time of the general surrender he was in the command of Gen. Joseph E. Johnston. He moved to Mississippi after the war, and came to be regarded as one of the solid, substantial and in every way reliable citizens of Itawamba county.

James P. Abney, a son of Robert R. and Mary A. (Roberts) Abney, was born in Jasper county, Miss., February 21, 1837. He was educated in the home subscription schools in that county, and began life at the age of twenty-one. He was married soon after (December 22, 1857) to Miss Eliza A., a daughter of Christopher C. and Catherine (Gressett) Tatum, who was born in Jasper county, Miss., March 16, 1840. In 1858 Mr. Abney purchased the farm in Jasper county on which he lived until 1860, then he bought another farm in the southern part of the county to which he removed. In May, 1861 he enlisted in company K of the Thirty-seventh Mississippi infantry, and was in the Confederate service for thirty-three months, during which time he participated in the Mississippi and Georgia campaign, and among other numerous engagements in the battle of Franklin, Tenn. After the close of his service in the war he returned home and again turned his attention to the tilling of the soil, applying himself so energetically and with so much business intelligence that he was successful beyond many others of equal opportunities. In 1869 he located on the farm on which he now resides. In connection with his planting interests he has engaged quite extensively in merchandising, and is postmaster of Montrose, Miss. He is also proprietor of a cottongin and a gristmill—two interests which are not only profitable to him, but of great convenience to the planters round about. He is the owner of thirteen hundred acres of land, five hundred of which are under cultivation. His first wife died August 23, 1890, and on the 3d day of December, 1890, he married Miss Martha J. Hinton, a daughter of James W. Hinton. By his first marriage he had eight children, who were named as follows: John W., Sarah E., James T., George V., Cora C., Oscar M., Robert L. and Paul J. Mr. and Mrs. Abney are members of the Methodist Episcopal church South. Mr. Abney ranks among the enterprising, progressive and highly respected citizens of this part of the state. Beset by all the disadvantages common to men of this section after the war, he has conducted his business with such push and intelligence that success has crowned his every effort.

W. W. Abney, of Heidelburg, Miss., was born in Jasper county, Miss., June 2, 1842, a son of Robert R. and Mary A. (Roberts) Abney. He was educated in Jasper county, Miss., and in August, 1862, he enlisted in the Boyle's battalion, known as company C, and later they were transferred to company F, of the Twelfth Mississippi cavalry, with which he served until the close of the war. In May, 1865, he returned to Jasper county, Miss., and on the 30th of the following November he married Julia A., a daughter of William and Mary E. (Ratcliff) Risher. Mrs. Abney was born in Jasper county, Miss., November 25, 1846. Soon after his marriage Mr. Abney located where he afterward resided until 1884, when he removed to Heidelburg and has since been a resident of that town. He began his business career in this county after the war, opening up eighty acres of land, surrounded by and almost covered with woods. It required a great amount of perseverance and hard work to clear it and improve it and convert it into a profitable plantation. This he accomplished, and not only this, but he added to his landed possessions until he owns now about three thousand seven hundred acres, of which he cultivates about nine hundred acres, he being one of the most extensive planters and stockraisers in the county. He is now turning his attention more to stockraising in general, and is farming more on the "extensive" plan, with the best and most modern implements and free negro labor, which is so unreliable as to require constant attention to be of much value. Mr. and Mrs. Abney are members of the Methodist Episcopal church South; and they have had ten children born to them named as follows: Samuel W., born September 15, 1866, now a merchant in Heidelburg; Catherine E., February 23, 1868, who married E. D. Travis, a merchant of Heidelburg, Miss.; Walter R., born December 22, 1869, now a medical student at Louisville, Ky.; John H., born February 12, 1872; Mary E., born January 30, 1874; Robert R., born April 5, 1876; Homer C., born October 28, 1878, who died April 2, 1879; Marvin G., born November 26, 1880; Anna E., born January 6, 1883; Carrie, born August 3, 1885. Personally speaking, Mr. Abney is a gentleman of many estimable qualities of heart and mind. He is one who wins the respect and esteem of the community in which he lives, and retains that respect. He is naturally proud of his family, and finds there his best friends and in his home the happiest place on earth.

Theodore F. Abney was born in Jasper county, Miss., September 2, 1844. He is a son of Robert R. and Mary A. (Roberts) Abney, natives of Illinois and Mississippi, respectively. They were married in Hinds county, Miss., and afterward settled in Jasper county, where they remained until 1865, when they removed to Marion county, where they made their home until their deaths. They were the parents of nine children, namely: Sarah E., Dolly C., Jessie M., James P., George P., Henry C., William W.,

Theodore F. and Robert F., all except one of whom are living. Theodore F., the subject of this notice, was educated in Jasper county. In 1863 he enlisted in company F of the Twelfth Mississippi cavalry, in which regiment he served during the entire period of the war. In 1867, at the age of twenty-three, he began business life for himself by purchasing a farm in the south part of Jasper county, on which he began operations with the determination to succeed. September 2 of that year he was married to Miss Julia M., daughter of Marcus F. and Martha (Smith) Beard. The young couple took up their residence on the plantation above mentioned and there lived until 1875, when Mr. Abney purchased land near Montrose. He owns one thousand five hundred and forty acres of land, of which about three hundred and fifty acres are under cultivation. He is also engaged in merchandising, and has a steam cottongin and gristmill, and in the management of these enterprises he supplies the recognized wants of the community and has accumulated a comfortable competency for himself. He is an enterprising, public-spirited and progressive man, highly esteemed by every one with whom he has relations, business or social. He and his wife are members of the Methodist Episcopal church South. They have become the parents of four children, named as follows: William M., who is deceased; Ida L., Edgar T., and Bessie C.

Judge Joel M. Acker, a retired ex-circuit judge, was born in the Pendleton district, now Anderson county, S. C., March 15, 1815. He is the son of Peter and Susanna (Halbert) Acker, natives respectively of Pennsylvania and Virginia. The Acker family are of German descent, and were early settlers of Pennsylvania; the Halbert family were of Welsh origin. Ancestors of both families were men who did patriotic service in the struggle of the colonies for independence. The grandparents on both sides were planters and men of much wealth, and possessed of large families. Both died in South Carolina. The father of Judge Acker was also a planter and died in the Palmetto state. He had six sons and six daughters, our subject being the fifth son in order of age, who received his primary education in his native state. He was then sent to Yale college, where he graduated with high honors in 1836. He returned to Mississippi in 1838 and began the study of law and was admitted to the bar. He practiced his profession for some time, then was elected to the legislature in 1839, and again in 1841. So well did he serve his fellow citizens that they elected him to the senate in 1845. In 1847 he organized company D of the Second Mississippi volunteers for the war, and, placing himself at its head as its captain, he went to Mexico and served with distinction through the entire Mexican war, returning to Aberdeen after peace was restored. In 1855 his countrymen again honored him with a reëlection to the state senate; he resigned this office in 1856 to accept a further mark of the appreciation the people at large had of his services—his election as judge of the ninth judicial district, which office he held till 1863, discharging its onerous duties in a highly commendable manner. When the war broke out he was appointed on the staff of General Harris, but did not leave the county. After peace was restored, in October, 1865, he was for the third time elected to the legislature, and in December, 1865, he and two other gentlemen were entrusted by General Humphreys, then governor of Mississippi, with the delicate and highly important mission of waiting upon Andrew Johnson, then president of the United States, and placing before him the acts of the legislature with reference to the status of the state in the Union, and inducing him to recognize said legislation and use his influence with congress to have it recognized and its enactments approved by congress. In this mission Mr. Acker and his associates were successful, so far as relates to the president, who, after an interview, promised his approval and influence. But the president was very soon called upon to answer articles of impeachment, and thus the object of the mission was defeated and other plans of reconstruction were adopted. This was the last public act of his life and formed a fitting finale to his public duties. Since that time he has been engaged in the practice of law, till the last few years, when he retired, leaving his mantle to descend upon his only son, James M., who is now practicing the profession his father so much honored. This son is a graduate of Oxford college, and also of the law department. He is a bright and talented young man, and gives promise of emulating his father's success in life. Judge Acker is now a large real estate owner, both in the country and city. He has always been highly successful in his life in all its phases, and it can be said of him, as it can be said of few —that after living his life in the full glare of the public light, the public returns only admiration for his deeds, and that he has come out of his political struggles with an unblemished reputation.

F. M. Acree, planter, Benoit, Miss. Mr. Acree has been a resident of Mississippi for twenty-four years, and during that time has won the reputation of being one of the most extensive and progressive planters of Bolivar county. He first located in Australia, where he pursued the arduous duties of the farm, but, in 1880, he located on his present property on Egypt ridge, where he has one thousand nine hundred acres of excellent land, with one thousand two hundred acres under cultivation. Since residing on the ridge he has made many important changes in his property, cleared land, erected buildings and made many other improvements. He is also the owner of a steam cottongin, with all the improved machinery. He was born in Alabama in 1850, and there passed his boyhood and youth, receiving his education in Montgomery. In 1888 he espoused Miss Mary B. Sellers, a native of Mississippi and the daughter of William Sellers, who was also a native of that state. Her father was an early settler of Port Gibson and was one of the most eminent lawyers of the Claiborne county bar. He came to Bolivar county in 1848, became an extensive planter, but is now retired from the active duties of life and resides with his son-in-law, F. M. Acree. He has another daughter, who resides in the Lone Star state. Mr. Acree has shown his appreciation of secret organizations by joining the Masonic fraternity when but twenty-one years of age, and is now also a member of the Knights of Pythias and Knights of Honor. He joined the former lodge at Concordia and has held the position of master. He is one of the prominent and leading citizens of his vicinity. In personal appearance he is tall and well built, his hair and beard dark, and in manners he is a gentleman in the strictest sense, living up to everything that that title implies. He was second in a family of ten children born to John E. and Mary E. (Polk) Acree, the former a native of Georgia and the latter of South Carolina. The father was a speculator and merchant. He served all through the war, enlisting in the First Alabama regiment, but soon returned to his home and recruited a company, which was attached to the Fourteenth Alabama, and was made captain of this company. He was in the engagements at Vicksburg, and was captured at Big Black river, but soon exchanged, and rejoined his company. He subsequently participated in the battle of Chickamauga, also the Georgia campaign, and was again captured in the last named state, taken to Fort Delaware and there retained until cessation of hostilities. The parents were active church members, the father of the Presbyterian and the mother of the Baptist denomination. Her death occurred in 1871 and he followed her to the grave five years later. She was of English descent.

Hon. Benjamin C. Adams is one of the most prominent and successful business men in the county, and is connected with every enterprise of importance or worthy of note. He was born in Carroll county in 1847, and is a son of Benjamin C. and Caroline (Blanks) Adams, the former a native of the Blue Grass state, born in 1815, and the latter of North

18

Carolina. The father came to Mississippi and was married in Carroll county, where he and Mrs. Adams lived for a number of years. They then moved to New Orleans, and there Mr. Adams became a member of the firm of Burbridge & Adams, commission merchants, continuing with the same until 1857. He then removed to Grenada, Miss., and there engaged in banking and resided until the breaking out of the war. After that he was occupied with his planting interests until his death in 1888. He was a man of unusual business ability, and amassed a considerable fortune, although he had but a moderate education and started with very little means. He had a brother, Christopher Adams, who died in Philadelphia prior to the war, and who was a great financier, and one of the prominent capitalists of New Orleans, of which city he was a resident at the time of his death. Their father removed from Kentucky to West Tennessee at an early date, and when his son, Benjamin C., was but a little boy, started to the West Indies for a cargo of sugar, and was never afterward heard of. Our subject's mother, who died when he was quite small, was a member of the Episcopal church and a daughter of James Blanks, who came from North Carolina to Carroll county, Miss., many years ago, and died there a well-to-do planter. His eldest son, Judge William Blanks, was the first probate judge of Carroll county, but afterward returned to Wilmington, N. C., and there died. Of the seven children born to his parents, three of whom are living, Benjamin C. Adams, Jr., was fifth in order of birth. One brother, Charles L., is a member of the firm of Winfree, Adams & Loyd, tobacconists of Lynchburg, Va., and Mary F. married Harry H. Hall, a prominent attorney of New Orleans. Benjamin C. received the rudiments of an education at Grenada, and, after his service in the war, entered the University of Mississippi at Oxford, where he took the regular course. At the age of fifteen years, or in 1863, just after the fall of Vicksburg, he joined Stanford's battery and operated in the Tennessee army in all the engagements from Chattanooga to Atlanta and back with General Hood to Franklin and Nashville. From there he went to Mobile and then back north again and surrendered near Meridian, Miss., to General Canby. He then returned home and again took up his books, entering the University of Mississippi. After reading law one summer with Justice L. Q. C. Lamar and then with Hon. W. R. Barksdale, he was admitted to the bar at Coffeeville in 1866, and has since practiced with the best success. He ranks among the prominent lawyers of Grenada county, and is well read and profound. He is a forcible and fluent speaker, and his comprehension is ready and acute. He is an active politician, is chairman of the Grenada county democratic executive committee, and a member of the democratic congressional committee. For a number of years he has been a delegate to all state conventions. He served two years as alderman, and is now serving his third term or sixth year as mayor of Grenada. He is vice president of the Grenada Creamery & Ice factory and a director in the Grenada bank. He is a prominent Mason of the Knight Templar degree, having been initiated in the William Cothran lodge. He is a member of the De Witt Clinton chapter, and is past chancellor of the Knights of Pythias, Ivanhoe lodge No. 8, and was a delegate to the Grand lodge at Columbus, Miss., where he responded to the address of welcome. He is a man of considerable journalistic ability, doing occasional editorial and corresponding work, and at the State Editorial convention, which met at Meridian, he responded in behalf of the press. He is a vestryman in the Episcopal church. He is an extensive planter and the owner of about two thousand acres in Sunflower, Carroll and Grenada counties, principally the result of his own efforts. Mr. Adams was married in 1869 to Miss Dora, daughter of William C. and Martha A. Chamberlain, natives respectively of North and South Carolina, but who came when young to Mississippi, where they were married. For a number of years this worthy couple have resided at Grenada, although Mr. Chamberlain spends considerable portion of his time at Brookhaven, where he has large lumber and sawmill interests. He is a large contractor and lumberman. Mrs. Adams was born in Yalobusha county, Miss., was educated at Jackson, Tenn., and at the female college at Columbia, Tenn., where she graduated. To Mr. and Mrs. Adams have been born four children, three now living. Mr. Adams takes a deep interest in all enterprises likely to benefit the town and county, and has a host of warm friends.

Little is known of the parentage or ancestry of Robert H. Adams, a distinguished law- yer and prominent citizen of the state, whose obscure youth and early trials left an efface- able impression upon his public career. His possession of the genius for law led him past all obstacles and gave to Mississippi one of her ablest jurists. His birthplace was in Virginia, but his education was obtained almost wholly from his contact with the hostile billows of life. While yet small he served an apprenticeship at the cooper's trade, but it does not appear that he had any inclination for that occupation. At all events, his active mind and ambition led him to the study of law, immediately after obtaining a fair knowledge of which, and after his admission to the bar, he left his Virginia home and located in East Tennessee. There he entered upon the active practice of his profession, and by his skill, audacity, adroit- ness and sheer intellectual strength, knowledge of human nature and sense of justice rose rapidly to eminence. But he became dissatisfied with his location, and, thinking to better it, moved to Natchez, which event fixes the beginning of his subsequent brilliant career at the bar. He became at once noted for his skill, logic and eloquence. Among the great lawyers of Natchez at that time he took front rank. One of his strongest powers as an advocate was his ability to melt an audience or a jury into tears. Another was his wonder- ful skill in unraveling a tangled, knotty and confused skein of evidence or law or both. He became very popular among the people, and in 1830 was elected to the United States senate to succeed Thomas B. Reed, who had died in 1829. The unfortunate death of Mr. Adams, a short time after his election, terminated ere it began what undoubtedly would have been a brilliant senatorial career.

General Wirt Adams (deceased), one of the most distinguished and respected citizens of the state of Mississippi, was born at Frankport, Ky., on the 22d of March, 1819, and was educated at Bardstown, Ky. He was private secretary to General Dunlap, secretary of war of the republic of Texas in 1839, and adjutant of Budesuist regiment in the great Indian fights of July 15 and 16, 1830, on the Neches river, where "Old Bowles," the great Chero- kee chief, was defeated and killed. After returning to the United States, he became a wealthy banker at Jackson and Vicksburg, Miss.; in 1851 and 1854 was elected to the legis- lature of Mississippi, and during this time framed the first general laws on the subject of levee protection. In the month of January, 1861, he was appointed by Governor McRea of Mississippi as commissioner to Louisiana to secure coöperation in the passage of the secession ordinance. In February of the same year, President Davis summoned him to Montgomery and offered him a seat in his cabinet as postmaster-general, which was declined on account of his banking business requiring his attention. He organized a cavalry regi- ment in September, 1861. This celebrated regiment was in drill and discipline equal to the regulars of the United States army, and it was engaged in the battles of Shiloh, Corinth, Holly Springs, Britton's lane, near Denmark, Hatchie river and Fourteen-mile creek, near Raymond. He was made brigadier-general in September, 1863, and was in command and bore a conspicuous part in the fight at Ellis Cliffs, and fought gallantly in all the battles incident to Sherman's and McPherson's raids. His command captured and destroyed the ironclad gunboat Patrol with eight Dahlgren guns and many stores. With a very inferior force he delayed and harassed Slocum in his great raid, and finally pursued him to Vicks-burg. During the pursuit, Col. Charles R. Bailey, then on General Adams' staff, performed a daring and gallant feat, many others of his command being equally brave and courageous, much of which was inspired by their gallant commander, who knew not what fear was. General Adams was engaged in nearly every eventful battle of the army of the Tennessee and made the last fight of the war east of the Mississippi, near Gainesville, Ala., capturing many prisoners, stores, etc. Here the Confederate banner was furled. All his valuable prop-erty was confiscated, and after the war he was engaged in various business pursuits. Shortly after President Cleveland took his seat, General Adams was appointed postmaster at Jackson, which office he held at the time of his death.

The W. T. Adams machine company of Corinth, Miss. The invention and manu-facture of machines and labor-saving appliances, designed to facilitate the operation of many branches of human industry, have probably exerted a greater influence in contributing to the marvelous growth and development of our country than any other cause. Notable among these great manufacturing establishments engaged in this most useful department of industry is the W. T. Adams machine company, which is engaged in the manufacture of steam-engines, boilers, sawmills, planers, re-saws, gangenders, lathmills, gristmills, cottongins and presses, mill supplies and steamfitting goods, etc. This business was established by Mr. Adams in 1879, who at that time was heavily in debt, but by indefatigable labors, per-sistent endeavor and meritorious work his establishment soon began to gain renown, and wealth began to pour in. The business was incorporated in 1887. Mr. Adams was born at Jacinto, Tishomingo county, Miss., in 1853, a son of Barnett and Lucinda A. (Sutherland) Adams, the former of whom was also born in this state, a son of Vincent Adams, who was an early immigrant to this section. Barnett and Lucinda Adams reared a family of seven chil-dren: W. T., Barnett V., Anna, Richard, Joseph (who died at the age of twenty years), Mattie P. and Robert T. Barnett Adams was a wagonmaker by trade and followed this call-ing in Jacinto for a number of years, moving to Rienzi in 1858, where he died. In connec-tion with his trade he also followed the occupation of planting. He was a member of the Baptist church and was a master Mason. His wife was a Virginian born in 1821, a daugh-ter of James M. Sutherland, who was a native of Danville, Va. He was one of the pioneers of Mississippi, and having learned the trade of wagonmaking in Virginia, he followed this calling after coming to Tishomingo county. Mrs. Adams died in 1857, at which time she was an earnest member of the Baptist church. W. T. Adams recieved a good practical education in the schools of Rienzi, and at the age of twenty-one years embarked in business for himself. After tilling the soil and clerking in a store, he became agent for the South-ern Exchange company at Rienzi, but later purchased an interest in a small foundry at that place, where he engaged in the manufacture of argicultural implements, continuing until 1879. He then came to Corinth and established a small' business, which was the foundation of the magnificent establishment of which he is now the proprietor. Since that time his business has increased so steadily and rapidly that it has grown into vast propor-tions, and now constitutes the largest business in its line throughout the entire South. The goods are standard, and are recognized as unsurpassed in materials and workmanship, and the great popularity and high reputation of the house are due, not only to the acknowledged superiority of the goods, but also to the systematic correctness of its methods, and by the spirit of fairness by which all its transactions are characterized. This establishment gives employment to about one hundred and thirty-five men, who in two days' time, can turn out a complete outfit for any ordinary mill machinery. The amount of business done at the present time amounts to at least $200,000 annually. Mr. Adams is a man of marked administrative ability, endowed with the necessary qualifications for the judicious management of this great enterprise. His energy and attention to his business is the secret of his success, and he deserves great credit for the way in which he has climbed the ladder of success. He was married in 1875 to Miss Virgie Johnston, a daughter of J. C. Johnston, of Rienzi. She is of German descent and was born in Tennessee in 1855. To their union five children have been born: Bertha, Anna O., Estelle, William T. and Winford. Mr. Adams and his wife are worthy members of the Cumberland Presbyterian church. He is a self-made man in every sense of the word, is honorable in his business methods and is a genial companion and whole-souled gentleman. He is a democrat in politics, and socially is a member of the K. of P. fraternity.

Dr. Enoch Agnew, the eldest son of Samuel and Malinda (Dodson) Agnew, was born in Abbeville county, S. C., October 30, 1808. His paternal ancestors came from the North of Ireland to Pennsylvania early in the eighteenth century—it is believed previous to 1738. There is reason to believe that the Agnews from whom he descended came from Wigtownshire, Scotland, to Ireland the latter part of the seventeenth century. James Agnew, his great-grandfather, was the first who came to America. He settled in "the manor of Maske," in what is now Adams county, Penn., in May, 1741. He was twice married. His second wife was Rebecca Scott, a daughter of Abram Scott. His eldest son by her was Samuel Agnew, who came to South Carolina possibly a little after 1770, and certainly anterior to the Revolutionary war, and married Miss Elizabeth Seawright. He is said to have been the first blacksmith who worked at that business in the present territorial limits of Abbeville county. Dr. Agnew was a grandson of this emigrant from Pennsylvania. His maternal ancestors, the Dodsons, came to South Carolina from Prince William county, Va., shortly after the Revolution. Dr. Agnew received an academical education in his native district. He read medicine under Dr. Marshall Weatherall, of Abbeville courthouse, and attended the medical college of South Carolina in Charleston two sessions, and graduated a doctor of medicine the spring of 1830, and began the practice of medicine in the neighborhood in which he was raised and soon acquired an extensive practice. He married Miss Letitia S. Todd, a daughter of Andrew Todd, of Laurens courthouse, S. C., November 22, 1832. In 1839 he removed to Due West corner (now the village of Due West), because of the establishment at that place of Clark and Erskine seminary, which ultimately developed into Erskine college. This place was but a few miles from his first residence. His field of practice was very extensive and his labors very arduous; so much so that his health failed and he was compelled to give up the practice of medicine in 1845, and then he engaged in the mercantile business in Due West, first with a brother under the firm name of E. and J. W. Agnew, and then in his own name. He was closely identified with every interest of the community in which he lived, and enjoyed the confidence and respect of his associates. He was a member of the board of trustees of Erskine college and also of the examining committee. In 1851 he purchased lands in Tippah county, Miss., and removed in 1852. After his removal to Mississippi he did not practice medicine but confined himself to agricultural pursuits. He had no ambition for political positions, though he was well qualified for such places. Although strongly solicited both in South Carolina and Mississippi to become a candidate for political offices he always declined, preferring the quietude of private life. In 1832 he joined the Associate Reformed church at Due West; after his removal to Mississippi he joined the same church at Bethany, Pontotoc (now Lee) county, Miss. In 1853 he was elected and ordained a ruling elder, which office he held until his death.   He was also the clerk of Bethany session.   For many years he was the teacher of the Bible class in the Sabbath-school, and it was to him a labor of love to explain God's holy word to the young and rising generation. From 1845 his health was far from being vigorous; for many years he suffered from an obstinate form of chronic diarrhea.   For some months previous to his death he was confined to his room, and on the morning of Thursday, March 2, 1871, he quietly and peacefully breathed his last, surrounded by his family and in the assurance of a glorious and blissful immortality.   His wife, Mrs. L. S. Agnew, departed this life February 28, 1879.   He was the father of nine children, only two of whom now survive.   Rev. T. A. Agnew of Bethany, Miss., and Mrs. M. J. Simpson, of Memphis, Tenn.   He was eminently a useful man, and his memory yet is "as ointment poured forth" in all this land.

Rev. Samuel Andrew Agnew, the eldest son of Dr. Enoch and Letitia S. (Todd) Agnew, was born near Due West, Abbeville county, S. C., November 22, 1833.   He was raised in the village of Due West, and graduated at Erskine college, South Carolina, August 11, 1852. He removed to Mississippi with his father in 1852, and entered on the study of theology in 1853, under the care of the Associate Reformed presbytery of Memphis, pursuing his studies at Erskine theological seminary, and a part of the time privately under the direction of Rev. J. L. Young.   He was licensed to preach at Troy, Tenn., April 26, 1856, and he was ordained at Shiloh church, Lafayette county, Miss., April 23, 1859.   His ministerial labors have been chiefly confined to the bounds of the state of Mississippi.   He was a stated supply of Hopewell church, now in Union county, from 1857 to 1870.   Since July 23, 1870, he has been pastor there.   He has been pastor also of Bethany church since July 31, 1868.   He has been married twice; first to Miss Nannie E. McKell, of Starkville, Miss., April 21, 1864. She died July 24, 1868, leaving two children, both of whom are dead.   He married again, January 21, 1875, Miss R. Jane Peoples, of Sardis, Panola county, Miss.   By her he has eight children, two of whom are dead.

John D. Agnew, Bethany, Lee county, Miss.   Among the representative men of Lee county, Miss., is John Dunn Agnew, a native of Abbeville district, S. C., born December 1, 1841.   His parents, James W. and Elizabeth D. (Richey) Agnew, were born and reared in South Carolina, and removed thence to Lincoln county, Tenn., in 1848.   In 1855 they came to Mississippi and settled in Prentiss county, near old Carrollville.   There the father purchased land and followed farming the remainder of his days.   He was only forty-five years of age at the time of his death.   His wife still survives, and is a resident of Guntown, Miss. They reared a family of eight children, viz.: Mrs. Hester A. Latimer, widow of B. Milton Latimer; William S.; John D., the subject of this notice; Elizabeth Iva, wife of Dr. W. G. Gamble; Rosa Lee; Sarah J., wife of W. P. Norton; James Melville and Howard.   John D. spent the greater portion of his youth in Tennessee, and received his education in the common schools.   When the Civil war broke out, he enlisted in company B, Thirty-second Mississippi regiment, and was in the service of the Confederate states army from December, 1861, until the close of the war.   He was in the battles of Perryville, Chickamauga and Atlanta, besides a number of skirmishes.   He was wounded at the battle of Chickamauga by a shell, and July 22, 1864, he was taken prisoner and sent to camp Douglas, Chicago, where he was held until June 22, 1865.   After the surrender he returned to Mississippi, and was engaged in farming in Prentiss county until 1887, when he removed to Lee county and settled in Bethany.   He embarked in the mercantile business, and, soon after coming to the place, was made postmaster of Bethany.   Mr. Agnew was married, September 5, 1865, to Miss Mattie E., a daughter of Dr. J. C. McGee, a very prominent citizen of Prentiss county, now deceased. Mrs. Agnew was born in Anderson district, S. C., but was reared in Prentiss county and educated at Ripley, Tippah county, Miss. Five children have been born to Mr. and Mrs. Agnew: Essie Q. and Sally H. still survive, and Myrtle, Lena and one infant are deceased. Essie Q. married V. H. Phillips, and to them have been born one child, Pansy F. The parents are members of the Baptist church. Mr. Phillips was born in Prentiss county, Miss., and is a son of William and Fannie (McGee) Phillips. The year of his birth was 1862. Sally H. married W. M. Burge, and they are the parents of two children, one of whom is deceased; the one living is named John Agnew Burge. Mr. Burge was reared in Prentiss county, and is a son of William Burge, deceased. His father was a prominent merchant of Baldwyn, and was highly respected. W. M. Burge was educated in Prentiss county, and enjoyed superior advantages. He was engaged in teaching school for some time. He and his wife are members of the Baptist church. Politically he is allied with the democratic party. Mr. Agnew is a member of the Associate Reformed Presbyterian church. He is a man of many excellent traits of character, and is highly esteemed throughout the community.

William Aills, M. D., is a native of Louisiana, born in 1826, but for many years past he has been one of the leading medical practitioners of the state of Mississippi. His father, Zacheus Aills, was born in Kentucky in 1800, but emigrated to Mississippi before the age of twenty. In 1825 he was married to Miss Ann Goode, a native of Mississippi, and by her became the father of thirteen children. He was an active politician, was enterprising and public spirited, and did all he could to promote the agricultural interests of the section in which he resided. He and his wife were earnest members of the Baptist church at the time of their deaths in 1869 and 1849, respectively. Both the paternal and maternal ancestors were planters, and were also members of the Baptist church, the mother's father being a Virginian by birth, who moved to South Carolina and married there at an early day. Dr. William Aills was the eldest of his parents' children and was reared in Copiah county, his education being received in a Copiah county academy, which was under the management of Prof. A. H. Frink, a very prominent educator of his day. Through his influence Dr. Aills was induced to attend the Dennison university of Ohio, from which he afterward graduated as an A. B. His medical education was obtained in Tulane university, from which he graduated in 1853, and since that time he has been practicing his profession with the highest success, his first work as a practitioner of the healing art being done at Burtonton, Copiah county, Miss. After a short time he removed to his present location in Rankin county, where he has built up a very large practice, his methods of treating the sick and afflicted that have come under his care meeting with universal satisfaction. He is skillful and talented, keeps well posted and up with the times in his profession, and being cheerful and encouraging with his patients his success has been phenomenal. In 1866 he was married to Miss Sallie D. Fariss, a native of Mississippi, by whom he has reared a family of nine children: Annie, Ella, John, Estella, Lizzie, Robert, William, Martha and Anna Beall. Ella and John died in infancy. Upon the opening of the war between the states he became a member of company A, Sixth Mississippi regiment, Confederate states army, and at the organization of the company was appointed to the position of surgeon of the same, and also to that of regimental surgeon, which position he retained throughout the war. He was a participant in the battles of Shiloh, Port Hudson, Corinth, Port Gibson, Baker's creek and in the engagements of the Georgia campaign, being with Gen. Joseph E. Johnston in one of the last battles of the war at Bentonville, N. C. Upon returning home at the close of hostilities he resumed his practice, and is now one of the oldest and most prominent physicians of the county. He has been a member of the Masonic fraternity since 1850, belonging to Evening Star lodge No. 70, of which he is worshipful master, and is also a member of the Grange, in which order he has held the position of secretary. He is the proprietor of a well-appointed drug store in the village of Steen's Creek, which brings him in a fair annual profit. Since 1857 he has been a member of the Baptist church.

William C. Albertson, of Moselle, Jones county, Miss., is the owner of one of the most extensive lumber and milling enterprises in southern Mississippi, located about half a mile south of Tuscalona station, Jones county. The proprietor of this business was born in Columbia county, Penn., August 11, 1855. He is the youngest but one of the five children of Edward R. and Almira I. (Ikeler) Albertson, named as follows: Miles, Louisa, Bartley, William C. and Eri E. William C. Albertson was educated in the home district schools in Pennsylvania, and at the Lewisburg university at Lewisburg, Penn., and when nineteen began life for himself as an employe in his brother's mill, continuing as such until 1878, then went to Hampton, Va., and entered into partnership with Lloyd Creasy in the milling business. This arrangement continued for about two years, and at the end of that time Mr. Albertson purchased his partner's interest and removed the mill to Pennsylvania, where he operated about six months and then sold it to his brother, Bartley Albertson. In company with his brother, Miles Albertson, in 1881, he purchased a mill in Braganza, Ga. In 1882 he sold his interest to his brother, and, coming to Mississippi in 1883, erected a mill at the present location. He began business on a small scale, but has increased it from year to year until he now has one of the largest mills in southern Mississippi, it having a capacity to saw sixty thousand feet of lumber daily, and an extensive planingmill attached and the necessary drying kilns. He employs to the demands of his business from one hundred to one hundred and fifty men in the various departments of lumber manufacture. He owns all of his logging stock and wagons and has a tramway provided with " T " iron rails, upon which he runs a train of four cars and a locomotive. This railway is about three and one-half miles in length and connects his mill with his large tract of timber land. Mr. Albertson was married at Bloomsburg, Penn., March 3, 1881, to Miss Mary E., daughter of Matthias M. and Margaret J. (Barber) Appleman, who has borne him two children, named Carroll O. and Malvrin M. Mr. Albertson's lumber enterprise ranks among the leading industries of southern Mississippi, and he is widely known as one of the most enterprising and successful business men in the state, his acquaintance extending throughout the lumber trade of the United States.

George R. Alcorn (deceased). The Alcorn family is a very prominent one, and is well known throughout the state of Mississippi, where many of the members have held positions of trust and honor. George R. Alcorn, who was for years a prominent feature of the county, was originally from the Blue Grass state, where his birth occurred about 1836, and was the son of Randolph Alcorn, a native also of Kentucky. The latter's father was the founder of the Alcorn family in the Southern states. Randolph Alcorn came to this county in about 1848 and engaged quite extensively in planting near the present site of Jonestown. There George R. Alcorn grew to manhood and there received a rather limited education in the common schools. When still quite young he came to Friar's Point, Coahoma county, Miss., and engaged as clerk and bookkeeper for a mercantile firm, continuing with the same until the Civil war. He then enlisted as private in Porter's company, and was promoted in order to the rank of first lieutenant of his company, filling that position until the termination of hostilities. He was in all the battles of Chalmers' command. Returning to Friar's Point after the war Mr. Alcorn reëngaged as bookkeeper for a few years, and in 1865 he was married to Miss Mary W. Cooper, a native of Tennessee, and the daughter of J. J. Cooper. In 1868 or 1869 he was elected to the office of chancery clerk, and served for several years, after which he held the office of sheriff of Coahoma county for two years. Mr. Alcorn also engaged in planting, and has made extensive improvements on many places. He was a good business man and prospered in all his enterprises. In 1877 he formed the mercantile firm of Alcorn, Wortham & Co., which position he held until his death, which occurred in October, 1878. He and wife died on the same day and of yellow fever. They left five children, all now living and residing in Friar's Point. They are named as follows: William A., Jr. (chancery clerk of Coahoma county, and probably the youngest official in that office in Mississippi), Helen (wife of J. M. Bouldin), Joseph R., George R. and Walter R., the last three attending school. Mr. and Mrs. Alcorn were members of the Baptist church, in which the former was an active worker and a liberal contributor. He was medium size and with black hair and eyes. He was a very popular official and could have held the office of chancery clerk years longer had he so desired. A vein of perseverance seems to run through members of this family, and all have been prominent in the affairs of the county and state for years. Mr. Alcorn was cousin to ex-Governor Alcorn of Eagle Nest, this county. William A. Alcorn Jr., eldest son of George R. Alcorn, was born in 1868, and was named after a relative at Clarksdale. He was educated at St. Mary's college, near Louisville, Ky., attended the law department of the university of Louisville, Ky., and in the fall of 1889 was elected chancery clerk of Coahoma county. He is now, despite his youth, serving in that office with signal ability and skill. He is slight in figure but quick and active in movement. He is guardian for the minor heirs in his father's estate. He was married on the 20th of May, 1891, to Miss Florence Pearl Yates, a very popular and accomplished young lady of Memphis, Tenn.

Ex-Governor James Lusk Alcorn, of Mississippi, comes of an old and prominent family in the history of this country, for his great-great-grandfather, who was a lastmaker by trade, came from the North of Ireland in 1721 and settled in Philadelphia, Penn. The Alcorns have been a family of mechanics, and Governor Alcorn's grandfather was a millwright, and upon moving to Kentucky, in 1810, built a mill on Dix river, which bears his name to this day. His name was William Alcorn, a native of Georgia, and was married to Miss Sarah McLean, of South Carolina. Their son, James, the father of Governor Alcorn, as well as his wife, whose maiden name was Louisa Lusk, was a South Carolinian by birth, and removed to Kentucky with his parents. He was the first sheriff of Pope county, Ill., and afterward filled the same position in Livingston county, Ky. He was a boatman by calling, and for some time was a captain on a barge, before steamboats were invented. He spent the most of his life operating trading boats of the Mississippi river, and was one of the first to ply its waters by steam. About 1846 he came to Mississippi, and for four years was a member of the board of supervisors of Coahoma county. He died in 1859, at the age of seventy-two years. He was lieutenant of a boatman's company in the war of 1812 under Captain Prior, and served until the war closed. At the battle of New Orleans he was commanding a company sent to guard a pass on Lake Ponchartrain, this move being made in order to prevent the British from flanking General Jackson. The maternal grandparents of Governor Alcorn were James and Sarah (McElwaine) Lusk, natives of Scotland, the former being in Sumter's command during the Revolutionary war, and was said to be the bravest man in the company. His wife was a daughter of General McElwaine, who was an officer of repute in the war for independence. Both the Lusks and the McElwaines were prominent and wealthy citizens of South Carolina. Ex-Governor Alcorn was born near Golconda, Ill. (when that now prosperous state was a territory), November 4, 1816, and was the eldest of eight children born to his parents. He was reared in Kentucky, and received his education in Cumberland college, at Princeton, Ky., after which he went to Jackson, Ark., and began teaching school. Upon being offered the position of deputy sheriff of Livingston county, he gave up the calling of a pedagogue, to return to Kentucky, and enter upon the duties of this position. So ably did he carry out the letter of the law, that during the latter part of the five years in which he served in this capacity, he was elected to the legislature of Kentucky, and served with credit for one term. At its close he came to Mississippi, and located at Delta, Coahoma county, then a thriving little town with a population of five hundred, but which has since caved into the river. Having read law while in office in Kentucky, and having been admitted to the bar while a member of the legislature, he, on his arrival in Mississippi, began practicing this profession in addition to operating a small plantation. His practice soon began to increase so rapidly that he devoted to it the greater part of his attention, and until being elected to the position of governor of Mississippi in 1869, he was one of the eminent, and leading practitioners of the state. Soon after his arrival in Mississippi he was elected to the legislature, and was in one of the two houses continuously for twenty years. He served as chief executive of the state two terms, then resigned this responsible position to take his seat in the United States senate, to which he had been elected. Being a man of very superior natural endowments, strengthened and enriched by the highest culture, his record as a legislator was of the highest, and weight and power accompanied his words and writing and inspired the deepest respect. At the expiration of his term he retired from politics, and returned to Mississippi to look after his large planting interests. At the secession of the Southern states, when the military board of Mississippi was appointed by the convention, there were four brigadier-generals appointed, of whom Mr. Alcorn was the third, and is now the only survivor. He went to Hopkinsville, Ky., in command of Mississippi troops, but was afterward under General Polk, at Columbus, Miss., and subsequently under General Clark. He was taken prisoner at Helena, Ark., but was there paroled in 1864. At the expiration of his parole he volunteered as a private, but was immediately appointed colonel of a detached company to execute special commission on the Mississippi river, for the purpose of preventing citizens of the South from being taken prisoners by Federal troops. Governor Alcorn has been successful in all his enterprises, and has accumulated a large fortune, being now the owner of about twelve thousand acres of land, three thousand of which are under cultivation, principally improved by himself. He erected his beautiful home in 1885, at a heavy cost, but it is one of the loveliest and most commodious in the delta. He carries a stock of general merchandise valued at about $6,000, and annually raises about one thousand two hundred bales of cotton. He was a member of the constitutional convention at Jackson in 1890, was the founder of the levee system in Mississippi, and author of all the laws relating thereto, and for three years was president of the levee board. He started in life with nothing, but obtained his education mainly by his own efforts, and was for years the support and mainstay of his father's family, and by his own exertions educated his sisters. He has ever been devoted to his family, and, being kind, generous and hospitable, he wins friends and rarely loses them. He has been a model son, brother, husband and father, and has made the happiness and comfort of his family the chief object and aim of his existence. In all matters pertaining to the welfare of the country he is still deeply interested, and his mind, as of old, is clear, concise, analytical and well poised. He proved himself eminently qualified to steer the ship of state, and, during his eventful career in public life, no duty was neglected and no work left undone. He has

J. L. Alcorn

probably done more for Mississippi than any other citizen within her borders, and in all cases proved himself wise in counsel, cool in judgment, full of resources and indomitable in action. When Mississippi seceded from the Union, although opposed to secession, he cast personal considerations aside, and, being wealthy, gave liberally of his means in support of the South, and completely fitted out the company commanded by his son, Maj. Milton Alcorn. In his younger days he was a fine specimen of physical manhood, and has ever possessed dignified and impressive manners. He was admirably proportioned, with jet black hair, and keen, black eyes that still possess their old-time fire and intelligence. In 1839 he was first married to Miss Mary C. Stewart, of Livingston county, Ky., a daughter of Milton and Narcissus (Miles) Stewart, natives of Kentucky, and of Scotch ancestry, being lineal descendants of the house of Stuart of Scotland. In 1849 Mrs. Alcorn died, leaving three children: Mary Catherine, Milton Stewart and Henry Lusk. Milton S. Alcorn was a major in the Confederate service during the war, and was a gallant soldier under Gen. Joe E. Johnston. He died in 1879. Henry was also a trustworthy and faithful soldier, but was taken prisoner and died in captivity. Governor Alcorn was married, a second time, in 1850, to Miss Amelia Walton Glover, a native of Alabama and a daughter of Williamson and Amelia T. (Walton) Glover. Her father was a planter in Alabama, and her grandparents were Allen and Sarah (Norwood) Glover, natives of South Carolina. The Glovers are of English and Scotch ancestry, and first settled on the James river, in Virginia, where they were among the first and most prominent settlers. They were a family of planters and merchants, and became very wealthy. Mrs. Alcorn's maternal grandparents were William and Justina (Gennerick) Walton, who were born in Virginia and South Carolina, respectively, the Waltons being of English ancestry, and first settled in Amherst county, Va. A member of this family was a signer of the Declaration of Independence. William Walton was a merchant and slave-trader and became very wealthy. The Gennericks were from Germany and settled in South Carolina. The maternal great-grandmother, Amelia Smith, was from Scotland, and landed in Boston the night of the Boston tea-party, during the stirring times of the Revolution. To Governor Alcorn and his second wife five children were born: Rosebud, wife of Col. E. W. Rector, speaker of the house of representatives of Arkansas; Gertrude, wife of Percy B. Russell, of Kansas; Justina, now the wife of C. J. Swift, an attorney of San Francisco, Cal.; James, who lives at home; Angeline, also at home, and Glover, who died in 1884. Mrs. Alcorn is a member of the Methodist Episcopal church.

Col. John F. H. Claiborne of Mississippi had long cherished the idea of writing the history of this state. He hoped by this means to link his name as an enduring record with the history of the state he had so long loved. So long had he thought over this subject that it had become a passion with him. The history of Mississippi was ever present in his mind. The framework had been arranged in his imagination, and as he thought over it, the passion grew stronger, and stronger; finally he took up his pen and began the work. The first volume of the history of Mississippi was completed and given to the press. Before it was given to the public the second volume was well under way. During this time the wreck and ruin of the South, as a result of secession, had been consummated. The exciting scenes of reconstruction had taken place. The terrible ordeal of reconstruction had been passed. Claiborne grasped his pen eagerly to record on the page of his history the startling events of reconstruction under the administration of Governor Alcorn. He had opposed the election of Governor Alcorn, and, in common with the people of the state, had predicted dire results of that administration, but as the administration of Governor Alcorn developed his line of policy, when his message with regard to the public schools had been published and the declaration that the whites should remain in possession of Oxford, that a university should be established for the colored people, that the schools must be kept separate, that the equality of the races should be established upon separate lines of government, each looking to the consummation and well being of the whole, Claiborne opened his eyes and saw before him the way out of the difficulties that beset us. He at once opened a correspondence with Governor Alcorn and found that functionary had a well defined policy—that lookout upon reconstruction on a practical and intelligent plan, which promised peace and prosperity to both races. Claiborne at once became a convert to the policy of reconstruction as defined by Governor Alcorn.

He discovered at once that Alcorn's policy was without selfishness, or the desire for self-aggrandizement. When he saw that Alcorn had put his foot upon every suggestion of plunder, that he had determined upon preserving the integrity of the state and the property rights of the people, he fell at once into the idea that all was not lost, if we but acted with wisdom and forbearance.

Claiborne now picked up his pen with a view of completing the second volume of Mississippi. He penned the preface to that portion of the history devoted to Alcorn's administration. This preface he submitted to Governor Alcorn, hence its preservation. It is given in full below, copied from his manuscript.

Soon after this, and when the volume had been completed and prepared for the press, Colonel Claiborne's house took fire and the manuscript mentioned was consumed in the conflagration. When, by telegram, Governor Alcorn was advised of the fact, his mortification was deep, more on Colonel Claiborne's account than his own. He remarked to his friends who were present, that the shock was more than Claiborne could bear. He knew the fact of his frail health, of his devotion to his work, and he prophesied that within a brief time Claiborne would be dead, and the history of Mississippi, so far as he was concerned, would be lost to the world. His prediction was too true. Claiborne was prostrated on his bed, and soon became a man of the past. We give here in the words that follow the voice from his tomb declaring his judgment upon Governor Alcorn and his administration. He says:

" It is no holiday task to review the career of James L. Alcorn; yet a history of Mississippi would be incomplete without it. No man has been more prominently identified with the state in critical times; no man has brought more ability, energy and self-sacrifice into its service; no man has been more misunderstood. The passions, prejudices and suspicions he encountered, to some extent, yet survive, but are gradually dissolving in the current of events, and he is now generally appreciated as a man of unquailing courage and indomitable enterprise; a patriot without stain, a statesman of extraordinary sagacity, called to the helm at the most trying period, to confront a disorganized and morbid public sentiment, to crush out old creeds, ideas and predilections, to guide by persuasion or by force a proud, intelligent, yet distrustful people into new grooves of thought and action, to conduct them from unsuccessful revolution, from the desolation of war, from the wreck of private fortunes, the overthrow of established institutions, and the iron rule of the congress, to peaceful industry, social order, and organized constitutional government.

" This was his mission. And this he accomplished under a condition of affairs without precedent in history in the presence of a new race of citizens recently rescued from hereditary bondage, superior in point of numbers, wholly uncultivated, and naturally averse to a restoration of the ancient domination and influence, deceived and misled by a venal swarm of adventurers, bummers in war and sharpers in peace, who regarded Southern property as legitimate plunder, and made the confiding colored race the instrumentality of their robberies and crimes.

"How Alcorn confronted this condition of affairs under circumstances most discouraging; how he braved the suspicions and prejudices of his former compeers and associates, placed himself in the republican ranks at the head of the emancipated voters, drove off the vultures, repressed riot and assassination, and restored civil order and prosperity will be seen and acknowledged when we look all the facts squarely in the face. He boldly entered a field wholly unexplored, which no other statesman had ever trod; opposed at every step by most of those whom he was striving to serve; with few counselors and little sympathy; deterred by no opposition; seduced from his great and patriotic object, the restoration of law and order, by no temptation of interest or ambition.

"This great object he accomplished during his official life, in the tumult and whirlwind of conflicting parties, races and antagonisms, and retired from almost dictatorial power without a stain on his character.

"It is after a study of his whole career, of his official acts and papers, in the light of events that have followed, that I have arrived at my estimate of the man and statesman.

"When he threw himself into the arena, the Southern states had been effectually subjugated. They were known only as military departments.

"The whites were to a large extent disfranchised, and what remained of civil government was virtually in the hands of negroes and a class of shrewd but unprincipled adventurers. The foremost man in the South, greater in his downfall than when at the pinnacle of power, was a prisoner at Fortress Monroe. His counselors and most illustrious generals were exiles, and the few statesmen that survived, wholly unequal to the crisis, and apparently unconscious of the revolution, were groveling in the same old ante-bellum grooves, and vainly seeking restoration upon doctrines and theories that had perished with our heroic battalions, and perished forever, under the bayonets of Grant and the sabres of Sheridan.

"Of all the public men most prominent in the councils of Mississippi, her scholars, orators and jurist consults, Alcorn was the only one who proved himself equal to the emergency.

"While many others exhibited a martyr-like devotion to their country, fidelity to long-cherished principles and convictions, and the resignation and fortitude that "lifts a mortal to the skies" and shows "the divinity within us," such men as Clarke and Humphreys and Clayton and Harrison and Watson, he, singly and alone, of all that galaxy that shone in the secession convention of 1861, seemed to realize the depth of the abyss into which we had fallen, and to know that old things had been done away with, and all things had become new. The doom was upon us, and the question was how to meet it. The solution of the problem will be found as we trace the interval of strife, of conflicting opinions, of military rule, of social demoralization, and abortive effort that intervened until Alcorn became chief magistrate and proved equal to the crisis."

William A. Alcorn, planter, Clarksdale, Miss. Mr. Alcorn, who is a descendant of one of the oldest and most prominent families of Mississippi, was the eighth of eleven children born to Randall W. and Harriet (Coffield) Alcorn, the father a native of Illinois, and the mother of South Carolina. The father was a lawyer, but followed the occupation of a planter all his life and became a very wealthy man. He was a prominent character in his native state, and equally so in the states of Kentucky and Mississippi, of which he was also a resident for some time. He filled the position of sheriff of Livingston county, Ky., for eight years, and was a member of the board of supervisors of Coahoma county, Miss., for four years. He came to the last-named state in 1851, and there his death occurred in 1859, when fifty-nine years of age. The paternal grandparents, William A. and Sarah Alcorn, were natives of the Old Dominion. William A. Alcorn, Jr., who was named for his paternal grandfather, was born in Livingston county, Ky., the 15th of August, 1841, received his education in the private schools of Mississippi, whither he had moved with his parents when ten years of age, but, owing to the breaking out of the war, his advantages for securing an education were limited. When twenty-six years of age, he started out for himself without a dollar, and he ranks as a noted illustration of that indomitable push and energy which characterize men of determination and will. His success is unusual, but due largely to his excellent judgment, strict honesty and upright dealings, and the proud position he now occupies as a representative citizen is a just tribute to his worth. He is one of the progressive planters of Coahoma county, and his fine farm, consisting of five hundred and seventy acres, with three hundred and fifty acres under cultivation, lies three miles south of Clarksdale on the west bank of the Sunflower river, and is in a high state of cultivation. He is a lover of fine dogs and thoroughbred horses. Mr. Alcorn was married in 1870 to Miss Annie Lee, a native of Mississippi and the daughter of Robert E. and Mary J. (Bullock) Lee, the father a native of Georgia and the mother of North Carolina. Of the six children born to this union all are living: Robert E., Clara L., Janye B., Benjamin A., David F. and Thomas T. Robert E. is a member of a surveying corps in California; Clara L. and Janye B. are attending the Columbia Institute at Columbia, Tenn., and the other children are with their parents in Coahoma county. Mr. Alcorn enlisted in company A, Blythe's battalion of infantry, in 1861, remained in the same for a year and then joined the Bolivar troops, company H, First Mississippi cavalry, remaining in the same until peace was declared. He participated in a great many engagements, among the most noticeable being Resaca, New Hope church, Lost Mountain, Atlanta and Jonesboro in Georgia; Franklin, Campbellsville, Pulaski, Murfreesboro and Nashville in Tennessee, and Vicksburg, Yazoo city, Champion Hills, Port Hudson, Jackson and Harrison creek in Mississippi. He was slightly wounded at the battle of Campbellsville, Tenn., but was not out of service during the war. Mr. Alcorn contributes liberally to all enterprises of a laudable nature, and is one of the county's most highly respected citizens. He has held a number of important public positions, was sheriff of Tallahatchie county, Miss., for six years, and filled the same position in Coahoma county, of that state, for two years. He was also deputy United States internal revenue collector of five counties in this state for two years. He is a brother of Judge Robert J. Alcorn, of Jackson, Miss., and cousin to ex-Governor Alcorn, of this state. In politics he affiliates with the republican party, and socially he is a member of the Masonic fraternity, the Knights of Pythias, the Knights of Honor and also the Independent Order of Odd Fellows.

L. G. Aldrich is a resident of Adams county, Miss., whose business operations have resulted satisfactorily, and who is now in the enjoyment of an income which is the result of earnest and persistent endeavor. He was born in Massachusetts in 1839, while his mother was there on a visit, and was the only child that grew to maturity that blessed the union of Lyman D. Aldrich and Sarah Davenport, both of whom were born in Worcester county, Mass. The remote progenitors of the family were Normans, who went to England with William the Conquerer, their descendants coming to America during the colonial history of this country, and are still among the prominent families of the East. The parents were married in Massachusetts, after which they went to Philadelphia, and in 1835-6 came to Natchez, Miss., where Mr. Aldrich at once engaged in merchandising, continuing that occupation and planting until his death in 1877, at the age of seventy-seven years, his wife having passed from life in 1842. Mr. Aldrich was quite active in all matters relating to the welfare of Natchez, and for some time was a member of the council. His wife had numerous connections in the East. L. G. Aldrich was educated in an educational institution of Natchez, and at the opening of the war dropped everything to enter the Confederate army, entering as a private, April 9, 1861, the Quitman light artillery. His command was sent to Pensacola, after which he was elected sergeant, then first lieutenant in August, 1861, after which he was commissioned captain in the adjutant-general's department, and was assigned to duty as adjutant-general of the army of Mobile. In August, 1863, he was ordered to Texas, and served as assistant adjutant-general of the district of Texas, New Mexico and Arizona on the staff of General McGruder until about September, 1864, when he was ordered to the frontier as adjutant-general of the frontier force of the Confederate states. He was left at Brownsville in charge of the supplies when the last battle of the war was fought and won by Col. John T. Ford, this being on the 12th and 13th of May, 1865, near the old battle-field of Palto Alto. June 23, 1865, Adjutant-General Aldrich issued the last official order of the war, after information had reached them of the surrender of the trans-Mississippi department. Adjutant-General Aldrich returned to Natchez, and after a short time devoted to merchandising he turned his attention to planting on his plantation in Washington county. In 1873 he extended his planting operations by the purchase of a sugar plantation in Assumption parish, La., and in that state is now the owner of two thousand eight hundred acres of land in two plantations, with about eight hundred and fifty acres under cultivation. He also owns a cotton plantation in Louisiana, and between six and seven thousand acres of land in Mississippi, a fair portion of which is under cultivation. The pleasant home occupied by him was erected by his father and is one of the most substantial and commodious in the city. He owns a good business block in Natchez, besides other valuable property. He was married in 1866 to Mrs. (Buckner) Wilson, a native of Virginia, and they now have two children: Lyman D., now conductor on the Natchez, Red River & Texas railroad, and Sarah Davenport, who is attending school at Columbia, Tenn. Two children died in infancy, unnamed. Adjutant-General Aldrich has always been active in the affairs of the city, and in 1885 was elected to the position of alderman, in which body he has proved himself to be one of the leading spirits. His name has ever been synonymous with industry, integrity and perseverance. His social qualities are well known and appreciated, and he has hosts of warm friends whose confidence and esteem speak volumes for his many admirable qualities. He has the happy faculty of putting all at their ease, who enter his presence. To his equals he is courteous, to his inferiors kind and considerate, and all receive that consideration due to their station. His war record was one of which any man might be proud, for he rose from the ranks to the high position of adjutant-general. He is a member of Harmony lodge No. 1, of the A. F. & A. M., and is past grand director of the K. of H. of the state of Mississippi. He is grand chancellor in the K. of P., in which order he has held all the subordinate offices.

C. R. Ales, planter, Alesville, Miss. Robert A. Ales, father of C. R. Ales, is a Virginian by birth, having been born in Charlotte of that state in 1815, and is a descendant of an old and prominent family. He removed with his parents to Henry county, Tenn., at an early date, and there resided until 1833, having married in the meantime. At that date he came to Lafayette county, settled among the Indians who were still in the northern part of the state, and was among the pioneer settlers. He became thoroughly known throughout the county and highly respected for his sterling integrity and uprightness. C. Robert Ales, who was third in order of birth of his father's family, was born in Lafayette county, Miss.,

on the old homestead, January 5, 1846. He received the education common to the early
district schools, but in the school of experience he is well versed, being to-day one of the most
progressive planters in Lafayette county. In the spring of 1862 he enlisted in company E,
Nineteenth Mississippi regiment, in which he served until the close of the war, and subsequently returned to Lafayette county, where he has been actively and successfully engaged
in agricultural pursuits since. He was with General Lee at the time of the surrender, and
although he was in most of the severe battles of Virginia, he was never wounded. Mr. Ales
was married in 1867 to Miss Sallie, daughter of L. R. Wallie, who came to Lafayette
county, Miss., at an early day. Mrs. Ales has ever been a fitting helpmate, a careful,
industrious housewife, and a kind and thoughtful mother. Both have that innate love of
home and family so much to be desired. Since early manhood Mr. Ales has been emphatically a representative citizen, and by a distinctly marked course of conduct has won and
long enjoyed the respect of his fellow-men of the county. He and Mrs. Ales are members
of the Baptist church, and are liberal patrons to all worthy enterprises which have come to
their notice. He owns a plantation of seven hundred acres, two hundred acres of which are
under a good state of cultivation, and being a liberal fertilizer, in that way secures crops
that surpass those of most planters of the county.

Charlton H. Alexander. The bar of Mississippi contains among its members many of
the brightest, most learned and most proficient lawyers of the country, and among these may
be mentioned Mr. Alexander, who, though young, has achieved a reputation that insures
for him a successful future. He was born in Kosciusko, Miss., November 12, 1858, the
second son born to Rev. J. H. and Louisa J. (Bingham) Alexander, natives of Tennessee
and Alabama respectively. The paternal grandfather, a North Carolinian by birth, was one
of the early settlers of Giles county, Tenn., where he followed the calling of a farmer
and reared a family. His son, James H. Alexander, was educated in Oglethorpe university,
Georgia, for the Presbyterian ministry, and after graduating, in 1851, he began his ministerial labors in Alabama, where he was married, but in 1855 became a resident of Mississippi,
at which time he assumed control of his present charge at Kosciusko. In 1886 he received
the honorary degree of D. D., and since that year has been a widower. The mother's parents
lived and died in Sumter county, Ala. Charlton H. Alexander was educated in the
University of Mississippi, and in 1877 was graduated with the degree of B. A., and with the
A. M. degree in the spring of the following year. He then graduated in law in 1879, receiving the highest honor in the literary as well as the law department. His first practice was
done in Starkville, in 1879, soon after graduating, his business associates being Hon. H. L.
Muldrow, member of congress (afterward first assistant secretary of the interior under
President Cleveland), and Hon. Wiley N. Nash, then district attorney of his district. They
remained associated for seven years, after which Mr. Alexander removed to Jackson, where
he practiced alone for a short time, after which he formed a partnership with Judge L.
Brame, they constituting one of the strongest firms of the city. Mr. Alexander was married
in St. Louis in 1883 to Miss Matilda A. McMillan, a native of Mississippi and a daughter
of Augustus McMillan of Monroe county, and by her is the father of three sons: Charlton
Augustus, James Addison and Julian Power. He and his wife are members of the Presbyterian church, and he has been an elder in the same for the past two years. He is one of
the directors of the Capital state bank, and in 1889 he and Judge Brame were appointed
reporters to the supreme court of Mississippi by the judges thereof, and this position they
now hold, and discharge its arduous duties in addition to their general practice.

Henry Alexander, M. D., of Hamilton, Monroe county, Miss., was born near where he

DEAF AND DUMB ASYLUM, JACKSON.

THE GOODSPEED PUBLISHING CO.
CHI.

now lives in 1835, the youngest son of Parker Alexander, a native of North Carolina, who went when a mere boy to Tennessee with his mother, and to Alabama a few years later, locating finally in Monroe county, Miss. He began his business career as a merchant and, after accumulating some means, purchased land and negroes, and was a well-known planter till his death, at which time he owned three thousand acres of land and one hundred and twenty-five negroes. He married, at the age of twenty-eight, Malvina Grigett, a native of Kentucky, then residing in Alabama. He had three children, named: Sidney A., James A. and Henry A. Mr. Alexander was a member of the Presbyterian church, and for the most of his life a member of the Masonic order. Dr. Alexander received his literary and professional education at Nashville, Tenn. He was granted a medical diploma in 1859. He had not made much progress in his profession when the war began, and at that time he offered his services to the Confederate government, and was appointed surgeon of the Eighth Confederate volunteers, composed of men from the states of Mississippi and Alabama. In 1863 he was taken prisoner and was not exchanged till eighteen months later. His service was active and exciting, and he participated in the engagements at Shiloh, Shelbyville, Murfreesboro and in other battles. Dr. Alexander lived the life of a bachelor until he was forty years of age, and in 1870 married Mary E. Roberts, of Monroe county. They are members of the Presbyterian church. The Doctor is the owner of over one thousand two hundred acres of well improved land. He lives a quiet life and is popular with his neighbors. In the days before the war he affiliated with the whig party, but since that time has been a stanch democrat.

Jacob Alexander is one of the most successful dealers in real estate in the city of Greenville, Miss. By birth he is a German, born in Prussia in the year 1834. In 1854 he came to America, and for some time was merchandising in the states of New York and Massachusetts. At the end of four years he went to Arkansas, locating on White river. From there, after the expiration of one year, he moved to Memphis, where he continued the business. In 1860 Mr. Alexander went to Paris, Tenn., and opened there a dry goods store under the firm name of Alexander & Bro. After a few years of successful dealing he returned to Memphis, where he began a jobbing business, mainly supplying the Confederate army with clothes and the necessary uniforms. In 1868 he removed to Greenville, Miss., following his mercantile pursuit up to 1872, at the end of which year he closed out his stock and began dealing in real estate. Mr. Alexander has continued in that business ever since, apparently with success. He was postmaster of Greenville for more than four years, and in 1881 was elected mayor of the city, which office he held for three successive terms. He has also been a member of the city council, and filled other offices of trust and honor with dignity and success. By dint of economy and labor Mr. Alexander has accumulated some very desirable property in Greenville. He owns several of the best business houses in the place, and his residence, located on Broadway, is one of the handsomest buildings in the city. Mr. Alexander is a married man, and the father of four interesting children. Ever since locating in Greenville he has been one of her most enterprising, progressive and substantial citizens. He is one of the leading spirits of the place, and has done a great deal to build up the city. Especially was he instrumental in securing the aid of the government to prevent further caving of the river bank. Mr. Alexander is a member of the Masonic order, the K. of P., the K. of H., the A. L. of H., the I. O. B. B., the I. O. O. F. and many other organizations. In appearance he is rather portly, has a dark complexion, and his hair is tinged with gray. He is very affable and courteous in his demeanor, and therefore has a host of warm friends in this locality. His brother, Leopold, built the first business house in Greenville.

19

W. F. Alford, Marion, Miss., was born in Greene county, Ala., October 1, 1827, and is the eldest of a family of ten children. His parents, Julius and Sarah (Sanderford) Alford, were both natives of Franklin county, N. C.; there they grew to maturity and were married. Shortly after their marriage they removed to Greene county, Ala., where they resided ten years, and thence to Lauderdale county, Miss.; this was in 1836. Mr. Alford bought land from the government and engaged in planting. He built houses, cleared the land, and soon had a good portion of it under cultivation. He was a harness and shoemaker by trade and was also a cooper; however, he devoted the greater portion of his time to planting. His wife was a member of the Baptist church, but he was a member of no church. He met with a violent death in 1860, when he was killed by a falling tree. Mrs. Alford is still living and is now in her eighty-third year. For the past five years she has been totally blind. The Alford family originated in England but were among the early emigrants to America. W. F. Alford the subject of this notice, assisted his father until he was twenty-seven years old. At the age of twenty-nine years he was married to Miss Sarah C. Crawford, of Marengo county, Ala., a daughter of Rev. Andrew J. Crawford. Mr. Crawford was a noted minister of the Methodist Episcopal church. Mr. and Mrs. Alford have had born to them nine children, six of whom are living: Anna (wife of J. S. Ross), Alice (wife of Z. Y. Craver), Lulu (wife of Romeo Glasscock), Eliza (wife of Charles Early), Joseph and William A. The mother died at her home in Lauderdale county in 1870. Mr. Alford was married a second time, in 1872, to Mary E. Parke, a daughter of Benjamin F. Parke, a prominent business man of Lauderdale county. Five daughters were born to this union: Alatha, Virginia, Frances, Ellen, and one who died in infancy. Mr. Alford owns four hundred and twenty acres of land, two hundred being under cultivation. He has lived on this plantation for the past twenty-five years. In 1858 he was elected sheriff of Lauderdale county, and served in that capacity ten years. For four years before his election he was deputy sheriff. For five years he has served as treasurer of the county, and is the present incumbent of that office. He is a candidate for reëlection in the fall of 1891. He has been constable and assessor of the county a number of times, and has been elected to public office a greater number of times than any other man in the county. He is a man of superior business qualifications, and has discharged his various duties with a fidelity that has won him the entire confidence of his constituency. He is a member of the Presbyterian church, and his wife belongs to the Methodist Episcopal church. He has been a member of the Masonic fraternity since 1850. He is a member of the Farmers' Alliance.

David J. Allen is a prosperous merchant and planter of Bolivar county, Miss., but was born in Grenada county of this state on the 14th of February, 1858, the sixth of seven children born to David A. and Elmina C. (Jones) Allen, natives of Mississippi and Tennessee respectively. David A. Allen was a merchant and planter, resided in this state for over forty years and died in Memphis, Tenn., in 1878 at the age of sixty years. He served in the Confederate army during the Civil war. The maternal grandfather, Isaac Jones, was one of the first settlers of the city of Memphis, Tenn., having removed there at a very early period. David J. Allen was educated in the schools of Memphis, his opportunities being well improved, and in 1876, at the age of eighteen years, he was better prepared than the average young man to fight the battle of life successfully. He began with no capital, received $10 a month for his labors, but wisely spent his evenings in attending night school, where he perfected himself in bookkeeping. After graduating at Robinson & Leddin's business college in Memphis, he began keeping books in 1885, which occupation he followed for five years. At the end of this time he purchased an interest in the firm of J. W. Lyman

& Co., at Australia, Miss., and at that place has been doing business ever since.   In addition to this establishment he also owns another store at Hushpuckena, Miss., the joint stock amounting to about $10,000; owns property on Poplar street in Memphis, Tenn., valued at $8,000, and has a fine plantation in this county comprising two thousand seven hundred acres, of which one thousand one hundred acres are under cultivation, but each year devotes three thousand acres to planting.   In 1880 he was married to Miss Jessie Murphy, a native of Illinois, who died December 10, 1890, having become the mother of five children: David J., Bennie K., Edwin D., Ernest and William.   Mr. Allen is a worthy and active member of the Methodist Episcopal church, socially is a member of the Knights of Honor, and in his political views is a stanch democrat, supporting the men and measures of his party at all elections.   He has been exceptionally successful in his business ventures, for although he has only been in business for himself for about eleven years, he is estimated to be worth $75,000, which fact speaks for itself as to his practical, shrewd and intelligent methods of conducting his affairs.   Although his honor has been often put to the test, it has never been found wanting, and he is regarded by his numerous friends as one of the most promising young men of the state.   He is quite distinguished in appearance, is very social in his tastes, is courteous and polished in manners and is an entertaining and fluent conversationalist.

Hon. John M. Allen, member of congress from the first district of Mississippi, was born in old Tishomingo county, Miss., July 8, 1847, and is a son of David M. and Sallie A. (Spencer) Allen, natives of Henry county, Va.   The father was a planter by occupation, and was a son of Robert Allen, also a native of Virginia.   David M. Allen was born in 1810, and died in 1875.   His wife was born in 1815, and was the eldest daughter of William and Sallie (Hill) Spencer, natives of Virginia.   She was a woman of great refinement and force of character.   Mr. Allen spent his youth in his native county, and received his elementary education in the common schools.   He chose the profession of law for his life work, and entered the University of Mississippi for the pursuit of that study.   He was graduated in 1870, and located at Tupelo.   In 1880 he was elected prosecuting attorney of the county, and in 1884 he was sent to congress, where he made a record reflecting great credit upon his constituency.   He has always been an ardent democrat, and has zealously carried out the principles of the party.   He was a gallant soldier in the service of the Confederacy, and was slightly wounded in one of the engagements.   Mr. Allen was united in marriage with Miss Georgie Taylor, of Tupelo, Miss., December 24, 1872.   She is the daughter of S. and Ann C. (Booker) Taylor, natives of Georgia.   Her parents removed to Mississippi at an early day, and were highly respected citizens.   Mr. and Mrs. Allen are the parents of three children: Annie Belle, Georgia May and Clifford.   The parents are members of the Methodist church.   In addition to his legal practice, Mr. Allen superintends the cultivation of his farm.   He makes a specialty of fine breeds of animals, and has a beautiful herd of Jersey cattle.   During the war, Mr. Allen gained the title of Private John Allen, which he still retains.   He was a gallant soldier, and is in every way a representative citizen.

J. M. Allen, farmer and merchant, Camden, Miss., is a native of the blue grass regions of Kentucky, born in Simpson county in 1833, and his parents, Silas and Elizabeth (Faizell) Allen, were natives of that state also.   The father came to Madison county, Miss., in 1836, moved his family here the following year, and followed the occupation of a mechanic, at which he was quite successful.   The mother died about 1839, and the father in 1877.   Only three of their five children grew to mature years: Caroline (deceased) was the wife of H. H. Dick; J. M. and Benjamin, who died in 1890.   J. M. Allen, the second in order of birth of the above mentioned children, passed his youthful days in Madison county, received but a limited education, and when fifteen years of age started out for himself, as a farm hand, continuing at this for two years. He then followed overseeing until the commencement of the war, when he entered the Confederate service, company A, Wither's artillery, and was assigned to the Western army. He was in the siege of Vicksburg, Jackson, Champion Hill fight and in the Chickasaw bayou fight. He served through the entire war, and surrendered at Jackson, Miss. At the close of the war he rented land, began farming in the county, and the second year bought eighty acres, to which he afterward added enough to make one hundred and sixty acres. This he sold, and embarked in ginning and milling in Attala county, which he followed for three or four years. In 1881 he bought his present farm, consisting of seven hundred and forty acres, with about five hundred acres under cultivation, and raises corn, cotton and oats. He also carries on ginning and milling and a general line of merchandise for plantation use. He has been very successful financially, and all his property is the result of his own efforts. In merchandising, his annual sales amount to about $8,000. Mr. Allen is an active democrat in politics, though he never aspires to political positions, and is a member of the Knights of Honor and the Farmers' Alliance. Mr. Allen was married in 1866 to Miss Henrietta Grafton, who bore him three children: Pauline, Ora (wife of Ed Shanno, of Alabama) and Eva. Mrs. Allen died in 1879, and in 1881 Mr. Allen wedded Mrs. Fannie (Hurst) Lytle, which union resulted in the birth of two living children: Jimmie and Willie. Mrs. Allen is a member of the Methodist church at Camden, and Mr. Allen contributes liberally to the support of schools, churches and all laudable enterprises.

Stokes H. Allen, a prominent farmer of Lincoln county, lives two miles east of Brookhaven. He is a native of Pike county, Ga., and was born June 18, 1840, a son of C. Y. and Anna J. (Brown) Allen. His father was a native of Virginia, his mother of Alabama. C. Y. Allen was born in 1795, a son of Stokes and Susana (Graves) Allen. On his father's side he was of English descent. The father of our subject was the second child, and the first son of five children: Elizabeth, C. Y., Fannie, Stephen and Thomas G., all now deceased. C. Y. Allen was educated in North Carolina, and there spent the greater part of his youth. His first marriage was to Miss Martha West in Georgia, by whom he had two children: Egbert W. and Thomas G., both now deceased. His wife died about 1836, and he was next married to Miss Anna J. Brown, and from this union there sprang eight children: Caroline, wife of G. R. Cater, living in Pike county, Miss.; Stokes H.; William B., a widower living near Brookhaven with his two children, John D. and Julia; Stephen C., who lives in Goliad, Tex., with his three children; Young D., living at Beaumont, Tex., with his two boys, Frederick and Joseph T.; Susan E., who is dead, and left one child, who is also deceased; Sarah F., wife of R. C. Breeden, living in Seattle, Wash., and who has one girl and four boys; Anna E., deceased. Stokes H. Allen came with his parents from Georgia to Alabama when he was a lad, remaining there till he was sixteen years of age, and there receiving the greater part of his education, when he came to Rankin county, Miss., and settled on a farm in the year 1855. From Rankin he moved to Simpson county, thence to Lawrence county, where the father of our subject died in 1864, the mother still living and residing with her son William. Stokes H. Allen entered the Confederate army as a volunteer in 1861, joining the Lawrence rifles, or, as it was regularly called, company C of the Twelfth Mississippi regiment, under the command of Col. Richard Griffith. He took part in the fights at Corinth and Union city, and arrived at Manassas Junction just too late to participate in the Bull Run battle. From there he went on to Richmond, and took an active part in the seven days' fight around that ill-fated city. Here he received his first wound, losing his left thumb. He was sent to the hospital in Richmond, and then went home on a furlough of thirty days. After recovering his health, he rejoined his command at Winchester, Va. Following this came the battles of the Wilderness and Fredericksburg. In 1864 he was put on the retired list, and coming back to Mississippi was there at the time of the surrender. Our subject was married, in 1866, to Miss Frances E. Smith, a daughter of Everett and Mary J. (Dunn) Smith, both the parents and daughter being natives of the state of Mississippi, the daughter being born in 1847. The mother of our subject was married first to Everett Smith, by whom she had three children: Frances E., Samuel P. and Lenora A. After the death of her first husband, she married James A. Hudnall, and had two children by this marriage: Ellison R. and Joseph A. Her second husband was killed at the battle of Corinth, and she married for her third husband Carol Bardwell. She passed away in 1887, but he still survives her, and lives in Lincoln county. To Stokes H. Allen and wife have been born ten children: Mary J., who is the wife of Wiley C. Maxwell, living in Lincoln county with her husband and two children, Hueston and Victor; Lena, who belongs to the army of school teachers; Anna, living at home, as do also Mattie W., Ethan E., Katie and Edgar I.; Emma L., Egbert C. and Flora Mc. are deceased. Mr. Allen is a democrat in principle and by example, upholding the tenets of his party on all occasions. He is also a Farmers' Alliance man, firmly believing in that union of determined men Mrs. Allen is an earnest member of the Baptist church. Mr. Allen has a strong affection for his home, having lived on it since 1868. He cleared off the land himself, and all improvements to be found on the plantation are the result of his own unaided efforts, in which he naturally takes a great deal of pride. He is a wide-awake, industrious and progressive man, and one to bring honor to his county. C. Y. Allen had one other brother named Young D. Allen, who died in New Orleans, leaving several children, named C. H., A. C., Fred, Camilla, and another who was a twin with C. H.

T. B. Alsop, M. D., residing in the town of Redmondville, is one of the successful practitioners of Yazoo county, of which he has been a resident since twenty years of age. He was born in Spottsylvania county, Va., in 1831, and is the youngest of the five sons of John and Mary (Leavell) Alsop. The parents were of English and Scotch descent. John Alsop was captain of a Virginia company in the war of 1812. He died in 1866 at the age of eighty years; the mother died in 1863. The Doctor passed his schooldays in Virginia until he was nineteen years of age. He then went to Missouri, where he remained one year, coming at the end of that time to Yazoo county, and locating on the plantation where he still lives. There were sixteen hundred acres in the place, which he cultivated until the breaking out of the Civil war. In 1863 he joined an engineering corps under Brigadier-General Ledbetter, at Mobile, Ala. When the conflict was ended he resumed his agricultural interests. Having a natural taste for the study of medicine he devoted all his leisure time to an investigation of the science, and finally possessed himself of sufficient information to enter into a practice of the profession. He has a large patronage, and has met with marked success. He is a member of the P. B. Tutt lodge No. 17, A. F. & A. M., and also of the chapter and commandry. Dr. Alsop was wedded in 1868 to Miss Nannie Day, a daughter of Robert Day, a prominent pioneer of Yazoo county. Our subject has always been conscientious in the discharge of his duties as a citizen and as a professional man. He is an ardent admirer of the South, and considers Yazoo county one of the most attractive spots in the world.

Albion Ames, farmer, Starkville, Miss. Mr. Ames' father, Judge David Ames, was a native of Canterbury, N. H., born on the 15th of May, 1788, and graduated from the Dartmouth university in 1817. He moved from Canterbury to Sparta, Tenn., practiced law for a number of years, and in 1845 came to Starkville, Miss., where his death occurred on the 25th of August, 1870. He was elected judge of probate in 1835, and held that office for thirty-one years in succession. Never in that time was his decision on any case changed by a higher court. He married Sophronia O. Fisk, of Sparta, on the 2d of January, 1827, and the children born to this union were named in the order of their births as follows: Albion, Madison F., Almira and William N., all of whom are living and have families. Judge Ames was a member of the Masonic order and in every walk of life was ever a true man. His career was marked with honor and success, and the wide circle of friends he secured he held tenaciously. He was the sixth child in order of birth born to David Ames, Sr., and Phoebe (Hoyt) Ames, the father born in Canterbury, N. H., in 1749. He died in 1812, and his wife in 1838. David, Sr.'s parents were Samuel and Hannah D. Ames, the former born in 1723. His death occurred in 1803, and his wife's in 1804. For many generations the Ames family has been noted for honesty, integrity and uprightness, and is one of the few families that have taken pains to preserve all family records. Albion Ames, the eldest child born to the marriage of Judge David Ames, owes his nativity to Sparta, Tenn., his birth occurring on the 7th of August, 1828. He was married in 1866 to Miss Margaret E. Heath, and they are the parents of the following children: Edwin M., Charles T., Almira, Mary G:, William F., Rosalie, Maggie H., Alice M. and Laura K.

J. F. Ames is a merchant of Macon, Miss., who has by earnest and persistent endeavors and by honorable business methods, built up an excellent reputation as a business man, and a large and profitable patronage. He was born in the county in which he is now residing in October, 1862, to Judge Charles B. and S. J. (Longstreet) Ames, natives of Ohio and Georgia respectively, the latter being a sister of Gen. James Longstreet. In the common schools of Noxubee county, J. F. Ames received his knowledge of the world of books, but notwithstanding his limited educational advantages, he possessed a naturally fine mind, and was wise enough to make the most of every opportunity that came in his way, and his practical views, sound judgment and financial ability have placed him among the foremost of the younger business men of the county. After his marriage, which occurred in 1882, he settled on the home plantation, and was successfully engaged in merchandising and planting for about five years, but at the death of his father, in 1888, he removed back to Macon, and in 1890 once more embarked as a merchant, which occupation now receives the most of his attention. He carries a complete and well-selected stock of general merchandise, and he may with truth be said to be one of the leading merchants of the town. His marriage was to Miss Anna Yates, a native of Mississippi, by whom he has three children: Charles F., Elliott V. and Mary. He and his wife are worthy members of the Methodist Episcopal church.

Allen E. Anderson, Jr. Among the early families to come to the state of Mississippi and carve out homes for themselves in the then almost unbroken forests, were the Andersons, who settled in Amite county, where they identified themselves with its progress and development. They were of that moral and personal integrity which go to make up the model American citizen, and were valuable acquisitions to the region in which they settled, which was then in great need of honorable, substantial and permanent residents. Squire J. C. Anderson, the grandfather of Allen E. Anderson, Jr., was one of the first to locate in Amite county, this being in the year 1821, his early home having been in the Palmetto state. He opened up a large plantation, there reared his family, and on this place was born A. E. Anderson, Sr., on the 3d of April, 1830. After reaching manhood he was married to Miss Drusilla D. Montgomery, a native of Mississippi, born in the city of Vicksburg to Rev. S.

M. Montgomery, a pioneer minister of the Presbyterian church. He belonged to one of the pioneer families of Jefferson county, and was born there to Rev. William Montgomery, also of that church, who came to this state in 1811. A. E. Anderson, Sr., was twice married, Miss Montgomery becoming his second wife. He was a planter of Amite county, and merchant for a number of years, but in 1876 became a resident of Sunflower county, and is here now residing, engaged in planting. He was a soldier in a cavalry regiment during a part of the Civil war, and was always faithful, courageous and trusty. Allen E. Anderson, Jr., was born April 13, 1863, and came with his parents to this county in 1876, and in this state and Louisiana he received some schooling, but is principally self-educated. He commenced life for himself at the age of fifteen years, a poor boy, and for some years followed the occupation of clerking, also doing work as an artist, finding it a rather difficult matter to make a comfortable living. By his persistence he soon began to conquer the difficulties that strewed his pathway, and at the age of twenty years, as he was known to be a young man of determination and undoubted courage, he was appointed to the position of deputy sheriff, in which capacity he served for about seven years. At the general election in 1889 he was elected sheriff of the county, and this position is still filling with credit to himself and to the satisfaction of the people of Sunflower county, having been reëlected in 1891 without opposition, and is now president of the sheriff association of his state. He has been conducting a plantation near Indianola for several years, and has become the owner of three thousand acres of wild land, and has about one hundred and fifty acres of land under cultivation. This property has been obtained by the accumulated earnings of years, and Mr. Anderson is now in a position to enjoy the fruits of his early labors and hardships. He is a prominent member of the Masonic fraternity, and has served as junior warden and secretary of his lodge. He also belongs to the K. of P. He was married in Hinds county, Miss., October 5, 1877, to Miss Zora Stewart, a native of this state, being reared and educated in Hinds county, of which her father, W. B. Stewart, was a resident for many years. Mr. and Mrs. Anderson have lost two children, one when an infant, and Elbert S., in September, 1879, when about seven months old.

On the 8th of March, 1820, at Knoxville, Tenn., Fulton Anderson was born to Judge William E. Anderson, a lawyer of more than local distinction. Educated at the University of Nashville, Fulton, at the age of nineteen, was licensed to practice law, which he had studied under the tutelage of his father. In 1840 he located in Hinds county, at Raymond, rose rapidly in his profession, and, having concerned himself in political affairs, was chosen, in 1847, state's attorney for the district, but the following year resigned. He then devoted himself to his profession, and soon was famous for his probity and power. He was a strong whig. In 1848 he married Miss Mary Yerger, daughter of George S. Yerger, and soon after formed a partnership with his father-in-law, which became known far and near for its strength and honor. He was elected to the Confederate legislature, and was appointed to aid in the defense of ex-President Davis—his services in the latter cause not being required. Early in 1861 he was a commissioner of Mississippi to secure the coöperation of Virginia in the secession of the Southern states, and in the convention at Richmond, having that object in view, was a powerful speaker and factor. After the war he resumed his practice, but it was found hard to rise high amid the infirmities of advancing age and the depressing gloom of the memorable days of reconstruction. He lived, honored, and loved, until December, 1874, when he passed away, leaving a memory that long will remain green in the hearts of the people of his state.

Dr. J. C. Anderson, physician and druggist, Clarksdale, Miss., owes his nativity to Alabama, his birth occurring in 1856, and was the youngest of eleven children born to Dr. Frederick H. and Catherine S. (Cole) Anderson, the parents natives of Virginia and Alabama, respectively. The father studied his profession at Jefferson medical college, Philadelphia, and in 1828 located in Alabama, securing a large practice in Franklin county of that state. He practiced there until prevented by old age, and died in 1878, at the age of seventy-five years. The mother died January 5, 1891, at the age also of seventy-five years They were members of the Presbyterian and Christian churches, respectively. The father affiliated with the whig party and was quite active in politics. He was a man of education and was a student all his life, being well informed on all subjects, but particularly versed on the lives of statesmen. He held the office of superintendent of public instruction for some time. He was well known throughout the county, and was held in the highest esteem by all. Regarding his personal appearance he was rather dark, five feet eight inches in hight, well proportioned, and weighing perhaps one hundred and sixty pounds. His son, Dr. J. C. Anderson, is a prominent druggist and physician of Clarksdale, Coahoma county. The latter passed his youthful days in Alabama and received his literary education at Florence, of that state, and Nashville, Tenn. In 1877 he took a course of lectures at Vanderbilt university, and graduated from that far-famed institution in 1880. The following year he came to Clarksdale, Coahoma county, and began practicing. In February, 1890, he started his drugstore at that place, and as he likes Clarksdale he will, in all probability, make that city his permanent home. He was married in 1881 to Miss Mary C. Allen, a native of Alabama, and to them were born two children, both deceased. Mrs. Anderson is a member of the Methodist church and a lady of culture and refinement. The Doctor is president of the board of health of Clarksdale, and was one of the organizers of and stockholder in the Clarksdale compress and warehouse company. He has been an earnest advocate of all enterprises that promise to benefit the place and is somewhat active in politics, working for the welfare of the democratic party. His store is well stocked and tastily arranged with all the goods usually found in drugstores, and his practice is steadily on the increase. He is a member of both the Knights of Honor and the Knights of Pythias. He is rather tall and well built, black hair and full black beard and dark-gray eyes. He owns town property and a neat cottage, also a tract of about seven hundred acres of valuable land in Alabama.

Among the strong lawyers of the state in early years was William E. Anderson, who had come from Tennessee about the year 1835, where he had gained a high reputation as an advocate. His qualities made him both eminent and popular. He possessed the oratorical temperament, had brilliant gifts of humor, almost intuitive perception, and an intellect at once penetrating and comprehensive. His birth occurred in Rockbridge county, Va., where he passed his youth and received the rudiments of his education. Upon reaching early manhood he began the study of law, was admitted to the bar, and soon after removed to Tennessee, in which state he attained distinction before removing to Mississippi.

William W. Anderson, merchant and planter, Anderson, Miss., is a successful merchant and planter of Madison county, Miss., and is a native resident of the same, having been born at Kirkwood, Madison county, Miss., on the 22d of December, 1850. He is the youngest son of five children born to Thomas S. and Flora (Levy) Anderson, natives of the Palmetto state. The father was a lawyer in the early part of his life, but on account of failing health he retired to the farm. He came to Mississippi in 1840, and died in Jackson, Hinds county, in 1861. The mother died in 1850. The paternal grandfather was Edward Anderson. William W. Anderson has been familiar with farming from his early youth, and received his education in his native county. At the early age of fourteen years he was thrown on his own resources, with no capital, and has made all his property by his own industry and good management. He is the owner of two thousand acres of land, with one thousand six hundred acres under cultivation, and is also engaged in merchandising, carrying a stock of goods valued at $4,000. He has a good gin and grist mill on his plantation. Mr. Anderson was married in 1876 to Miss Nannie Robinson, of Mississippi, and the daughter of Col. John and Sarah (Lowe) Robinson, also of that state. The result of this union has been the birth of seven children: William F., Nannie, John R., Thomas S., Edward, Loura, and one not christened. Mr. Anderson takes a lively interest in and assists all enterprises for the development and growth of the county and public affairs generally. He is doing all in his power to educate the poor and ignorant people of his vicinity, and a good school has been started on his plantation, which promises to be a success. He has done away with colored labor almost entirely, has white families on his plantation, and is trying to educate them. Mr. Anderson deserves great credit for the interest he takes in these families. As a citizen and neighbor he is held in the highest estimation. He and Mrs. Anderson are members of the Episcopal church, and he is a democrat in politics.

A. F. Andre, cashier of and stockholder in the Mutual bank of Crystal Springs, was born in 1835 in Sweden, where his father and forefathers, as far back as history goes, have lived as farmers and landowners. He received a good education in the language of his fatherland. At the age of seventeen, with a desire to see the world, but not with the least intention of emigrating, he left home on a sea voyage for Germany, with a friend of the family, the captain commanding the ship. For about three years he traveled over southern Europe, Asia and the West Indies, and after shipwrecks, adventures and vicissitudes of no ordinary character, he landed, in 1855, in New York. To see the great American wonder, Niagara, brought him to St. Catherines, Ontario. Here he remained for four years, employed in the office of a conveyancer and notary. A desire to see the Southern states and the "peculiar institution" that then existed, revived his roving disposition, and, in September, 1859, he arrived in Crystal Springs, Miss. After a few months' service as clerk in the railroad depot, he entered the employ of a merchant, as bookkeeper, in which situation he remained till the outbreak of the war. With the first volunteers, he joined the Sixteenth Mississippi regiment infantry, and served in Virginia, taking part in all the engagements of that command during the first year of the war. Early in 1862 he was, by order of the secretary of war, discharged from the army and ordered to report to the navy for assignment to duty. He did not accept the position offered him, but returned at once to Mississippi and joined the Thirty-sixth Mississippi regiment infantry. In this command he served as lieutenant and adjutant, and was engaged in all the battles fought in the north Mississippi campaign, under Generals Price, Van Dorn and Pemberton. During the siege of Vicksburg he received a severe wound, which placed him on detached service, but he returned to his command at Mobile in time to be present at the defense of Blakely, just at the close of the war. After the general surrender he returned to Crystal Springs and resumed his old occupation of a bookkeeper, retaining his position till 1866, when he engaged in merchandising, in which he continued for over twenty years, with marked success. He did a very large business, and was recognized as one of the leading merchants of the county, and retired only to become the cashier of the Crystal Springs bank, a position which he resigned in January, 1891, to accept that of cashier of the Mutual bank of Crystal Springs, in which he was a large stockholder, and which he helped to organize. He is one of the most progressive, thoroughgoing business men of

Copiah county, and one of its most respected citizens, being honorable and industrious in the highest degree, and possessing a thorough knowledge of the most modern and effective methods of doing business. The Mutual bank was organized with a capital of $41,000, with Hon. W. C. Wilkinson as president, and bids fair to soon become one of the most popular mercantile institutions in this part of the state. From 1875 to 1877 Mr. Andre was a member of the board of supervisors of this county, representing the Fifth district. In 1869 he married Arista, a daughter of Rev. Dr. Alexander Newton, who was a prominent Presbyterian minister of Jackson, Miss. Rev. Dr. Newton was a native of Buncombe county, N. C., and removed thence to Tennessee about sixty odd years ago. He there married a lady of Shelbyville, Tenn., and came to Hinds county, Miss., where he lived for many years, rearing a large family, and died in 1859 at Jackson, Miss. Mrs. Andre was born at Clinton, Miss., and was educated at Jackson. Mr. and Mrs. Andre are both members of the Presbyterian church, and the former is a Mason. They have one child, Mary. The career of Mr. Andre demonstrates what may be done by a foreigner of the right stamp in this country, where the avenues to business are open to all. When he located here he was without friends and without capital, except an earnestness of purpose and an indomitable will to succeed, and he now ranks among the leading and most successful business men in this part of the state. His influence is felt over a wide section, while his social, business and political standing is deservedly high and recognized by all classes.

Elisha C. Andrews, treasurer of Pike county, Miss., was born in this county in 1841, a son of Burrell Andrews, who was born in this county in 1814. James A. Andrews, the grandfather of our subject, was a native of Georgia, who settled in Mississippi in 1800, being among the pioneers. He was one of the organizers of Pike county, where he became a successful planter and business man and ended his days. Burrell A. Andrews married Mary Walker, a daughter of John Walker, a pioneer from South Carolina, and whose daughter is a native of Pike county. Mr. Andrews was a well-known planter and prominent citizen living near Holmesville, and was a soldier in the Confederate army in the war and died in the spring of 1888, his wife having died about two years before. He was a member of the Masonic order. Elisha C. Andrews is the eldest of a family of seven sons and two daughters, all of whom are living and the heads of respectable families, and all but one brother being residents of Pike county. That brother, Zeb, is living in Wesson, Miss. Our subject was reared in Pike county and received his education in the common schools. In May, 1861, he enlisted in company E of the Sixteenth Mississippi volunteers (Quitman guards), as a private, but was soon promoted to the rank of sergeant, serving as such for two years in the army of General Lee and in the division of Stonewall Jackson until the death of that lamented officer. He took part in the engagements around Richmond and Petersburg, in the Shenandoah campaign, and he also fought at Gettysburg. In August, 1864, he was taken prisoner of war at Petersburg, and confined at Point Lookout until after the surrender of the Confederate forces, after which he was paroled and discharged, and returned home after having participated in several of the bloodiest battles of the war. In 1865 he married Josephine Ellszy, a daughter of Thomas and Mary Ellszy, who died in 1866. In October, 1866, he married Miss Nancy Simmons, a daughter of John Simmons, a pioneer of this county. His wife died July 6, 1885. Mrs. Andrews was born near Osyka in this county. After his marriage Mr. Andrews located in the northeast part of the county, where he bought and improved a plantation, acquiring also considerable property in that vicinity in the shape of unimproved land, but fifteen years later he sold this property, and in 1878 bought his present plantation near Holmesville, which was in a good state of improvement. He owns about seven hundred and sixty acres of land, two hundred and fifty acres of which is tillable. He has a good residence, and has built a steam gin and sawmill and other improvements. It is ranked as one of the best plantations in this part of the county, and is known by the name of Hardscrabble. Mr. Andrews is a democrat politically, and has held several official positions of great importance, in each of which he served his fellow-citizens faithfully and well. He was a member of the board of supervisors, represented the third district in 1874, 1876 and 1877, and is now county treasurer, having been elected in 1889, with fair prospects of reëlection. He is one of the best and most careful of treasurers, and well deserves to be continued in office. He is a member of the Farmers' Alliance, the Masonic fraternity, the Knights of Pythias, Knights of Honor, and the Baptist church, in which he is a deacon. He takes an active part in the proceedings of the various lodges to which he belongs, and is a liberal and wealthy church member. By his second marriage he had seven children: Ella grew to maturity, married, and died in 1876; Laura is the wife of Lucius Holmes, of this county; Mary is a teacher in the public schools; De Witt is a popular young man; Rosa is a young lady well known in society; Ethel and Jessie are younger daughters at home. In 1886 Mr. Andrews married Miss Arvazena Quinn, daughter of L. J. Quinn, who was born, reared, and educated in Pike county. By this marriage there were two children, William and Nannie, aged five and three years respectively. Mr. Andrews is a man of high moral character, and a more sociable, hospitable man than he it would be hard to find. He is faithful in everything intrusted to his care, and is very attentive to all the details of his business, as well as to all the demands made upon him as an official.

Mrs. Ann B. Archer. This estimable and intelligent woman is the widow of Richard T. Archer, who was an extensive planter of this region, and a native of Amelia county, Va., where he was born in the year 1797, to Richard and Mary C. (Cocke) Archer, also Virginians, the former being a prominent planter on the James river. After the death of their father, which occurred during their early childhood, the two sons, Stephen C. and Richard T., resided with their mother, at the home of their grandmother, near Amelia courthouse, Va., except during their attendance at William and Mary college, Williamsburg, Va. In 1824 Richard T. Archer left home to make his own fortune, and chose the state of Mississippi as the field of his future operations, renting land in Adams county, which he cultivated for about five years. Before his lease had expired, his mother and his brother Stephen C. came overland to Wilkinson county, Miss., and after renting land near Fort Adams for several years, moved to Claiborne county, settling on the Oaken grove plantation, which is now owned by the Magruder estate. About this time Richard T. purchased a large tract of land in Holmes county, Miss., in connection with his cousin, William S Archer, of Virginia, who served several terms as senator from Virginia in congress and was very popular. In 1834 Richard was married to Miss Ann Barnes, a native of the state, born August 11, 1818, to Abram and Ann Maria (Willis) Barnes, both of whom were born in the Old North state. They became residents of Mississippi in 1802, coming hither with their parents, Col. Elias Barnes, the father of Abram, entering a large tract of land consisting of several thousand acres for himself, sons and daughters. He erected a substantial residence on an elevated piece of land which was covered by a fine grove of oak trees, and his place afterward took the name of Oaken grove plantation. His wife was a Miss Elizabeth Smith, and to them a family of ten children was born, the most of whom lived to be grown. The Colonel was a very prominent man in the affairs of this section, was very devoted to his family, and took great delight in locating his children around him in homes of their own, giving to each a large tract of land. He was a man of noble character, and was very generous and charitable in the use of his wealth, distributing it freely in various useful ways. Abram Barnes, his son, died on the 1st of November, 1830, at the age of forty-six years, having lived a very conservative, quiet and retiring life, not caring for public prominence. Like his worthy father before him, he was a successful financier, and was also liberal with his means, being ever ready to lend a helping hand to the poor and distressed. He was a director in the Port Gibson bank, and was not a member of any secret society or church organization, but always endeavored to do as he would be done by. His wife died on the 20th of May, 1827, the mother of four children, three of whom died when young. Mrs. Archer, after the death of her parents, was sent to Westchester, Penn., to attend school, where she remained two years, thence to Philadelphia, where she remained a year; while there was married to Mr. Archer, and returning with him to Mississippi he commenced planting in Claiborne county also. In 1837 they removed from the Oaken grove plantation, which was the home of Mr. and Mrs. Stephen C. Archer, to the place on which Mrs. Archer now resides, known as the Anchuca plantation. Mr. Archer modeled and constructed a very fine typical southern residence of two and a half stories, and the frescoing in these spacious rooms is very beautiful. A large double veranda extends the length of the house, which is situated on an elevation overlooking the plantation. The residence is surrounded by forest trees, and handsome drives, inclosed by cedars, lead up to this ideal home, which Mr. Archer took great delight in improving and beautifying. Mr. Archer was proverbial for his hospitality, was active in promoting the public welfare, prominent in politics and brave and fearless in his advocacy of the cause he espoused. He was an ardent patriot, and being too old to serve during the Rebellion, sought to help at home the cause in which two sons and a nephew were serving. Mr. and Mrs. Archer reared a large family, eight of whom now survive: Abram B., the eldest, served in the state troops (cavalry) during the Rebellion, and is now a planter in Holmes county, Miss.; Mary C., Jane R., Richard T., Esther B. and Branch T. reside with their mother; Ann Maria, who married Dr. C. R. Irving, a retired physician, resides on the old homestead near Amelia courthouse, Va., where her father's boyhood was passed; Lizzie B., married James Rowan Percy, of Holmes county, where they resided until the death of Dr. Percy in 1877. Stephen C. died at the age of seventeen years of typhoid fever, contracted while on picket duty. Richard T. Archer, Sr., died on October 30, 1867, having been a useful and honored member of society, and a humble Christian during the latter years of his life. His mother died at his residence in 1849, at the age of seventy-three years, having been a loving and devoted mother, and an earnest Christian. Stephen C., her eldest son, was married to Mrs. Catharine Barnes, of Mississippi, by whom he became the father of one son, Edward S. Archer, who, after the death of his parents, during his early childhood, became an inmate of "Anchuca," tenderly cared for as their own child by his devoted uncle and aunt until manhood. He resided on his plantation in Holmes county until 1861, when he enlisted in the Twenty-first regiment of Mississippi infantry, under Capt. B. G. Humphreys, Sr., who afterward became General Humphreys, and was killed in the battle of Malvern Hill, July 1, 1862. He had never possessed a very rugged constitution, and was sick in the hospital when he learned that a battle was imminent, and followed his command by slow stages, reaching them just in time to join in the fatal charge. Mrs. Archer, although in her seventy-third year, is remarkably well preserved, showing but little, either physically or mentally, the ravages of time. She manages her home place in an admirable manner, and is noted for her many charities and her kind and Christian character. She has a fine library, many of her books being very rare and costly, and she takes great pride in keeping well posted and up with the times, reading readily without glasses. She also has some very valuable oil paintings, and her home is a model of convenience, order and comfort. She possesses an intellect far beyond the ordinary, and her many worthy characteristics have won her many friends. Her great-uncle, Josiah Barnes, married a Miss Smith and settled in the Russum neighborhood in a very early day, where he reared a large family of children.

A glance at the interesting genealogy of the well-known Archer family shows that James Archer comes of very prominent people, who have become noted in the annals of American history, and who have, by their upright, straightforward course through life, kept their names unspotted and honored in the sight of God and man. The first member of the family of whom anything is known is Thomas Archer, who was a native of the Emerald Isle and who emigrated from Londonderry to the United States in 1732 and settled in Maryland. His son, Dr. John Archer, was born in 1741, and grew to years of maturity in that state, receiving his education at Princeton college, New Jersey, and graduating in the class of 1760 with Dr. Benjamin Bush, who was one of the original signers of the Declaration of Independence. Dr. Archer was a physician of far more than ordinary ability, and was the first graduate at the medical college of Philadelphia. For eight years the people of the district in which he resided kept him as their representative in congress, where he acquired an enviable reputation from 1801 to 1807 inclusive. He died in 1810. Hon. Stevenson Archer, LL. D. (from Princeton), his son, and the father of the immediate subject of this biography, was also a graduate of Princeton college, class of 1805, and in that most admirable institution of learning he acquired an education, which peculiarly fitted him for his future career. His tastes and inclinations pointed to the profession of law as his future field of labor, and as a member of this calling he became eminent and was known as a forcible, persuasive speaker. His mind was exceptionally well poised, judicial and analytical, and in both speaking and writing his style was pleasing, smooth and convincing. He represented his district in congress four terms, during which time he showed ability of a high order and was an able, incorruptible and conscientious member of that body, at all times displaying rare powers of elucidation, the most abstruse and complicated subjects being handled by him with ease and grace. He was chairman of the committee of naval affairs during President Monroe's administration. After the expiration of his second term he was appointed a judge in Mississippi territory (this being in the year 1817) by President Monroe, and was commissioned by Governor Holmes, and held his courts at St. Stephens, near Mobile, while Alabama was a part of Mississippi territory. Judge Archer came through to old Washington, Miss., from Maryland on horseback, for the purpose of discharging his duties, and his career as a jurist was marked by extreme fairness, mildness and forbearance. He returned to Maryland, and was reëlected to congress and served two terms more, eight years in all, when he was appointed chief justice of Maryland, and during the fifteen years that he filled this responsible position he displayed very superior mental endowments. Being of a quick perception, what might have cost others hours of study and research he reached at a bound, and the reasons for his convictions were always clear and well defined, as a reference to the Maryland reports will show. He occupied the front rank in his profession for many years, and, like his talented and eminent father before him, his winning manner, his power of bringing forth all that was good in others, his charity and honesty, won for him unbounded respect, confidence and esteem, and his death, which occurred in 1848, in the very zenith of his powers, was a fact deeply lamented by the citizens of his native state, to whom he had endeared himself. He and his father represented the one district in congress for sixteen years, and his son, Stevenson, eight years, twenty-four years in the three generations, which is the highest tribute that could be paid to their merit, popularity and ability. He was married in Maryland to Miss

Pamelia Barney Hays, and of the family that in time gathered about their hearthstone, three sons and five daughters grew to mature years. Of these were John G. Archer, M. D., a graduate of Princeton, settled in Louisiana and represented his parish in the state legislature, and during this time took a deep interest in the measures of that body, and was at all times ready to advance the real interests of his state; he has been dead for some years. Laura is the wife of Joseph A. Turpin, a planter of Louisiana. This aged couple lost one son, who was killed in the battle of Franklin, Tenn. They have seven children still living and twenty-three grandchildren; Mrs. Dr. Charles Chamberlain, a widow residing in Natchez, Miss.; Mrs. Elizabeth Archer, the deceased wife of Prof. Robert H. Archer, who was at the head of the Patapsco institute, a noted female college; Mrs. Dr. Lewis Williams, the deceased wife of Dr. Williams, an eminent and deceased surgeon in the United States navy. They left both children and grandchildren; Mrs. Van Bibber is the second daughter, is a widow, and although she formerly lived in Grand Gulf, Miss., and for a number of years in New Orleans, she is now a resident of Maryland.

James Archer was born in Harford county, Md., December 23, 1811, and received a very thorough education in his youth and early manhood. At the age of seventeen years he entered Yale college and graduated in the year 1830, several of the members of his class, that numbered eighty students, being noted men. Of the eighty, twenty were from the South, of whom Mr. Archer is the only survivor, and he is one of the fifteen members of the class now living. Among those who in after years became eminent was Prof. Elias Loomis, of Yale college, a poor student who worked his way through college, afterward becoming a noted author of mathematical elementary works and accumulated a large fortune, recently dead; Rev. Dr. Backus, D. D., an eminent divine of the Presbyterian church, of Baltimore; Samuel W. Dorsey, who accumulated a large fortune in Louisiana and Mississippi, willing it upon his death to his wife, who in turn willed it to Jefferson Davis, whom she greatly admired; and also a number of other men, who carved out their own career and made names for themselves. In the year 1834 James Archer came west in search of a fortune, and on Christmas day of that year arrived at Rodney, but soon after located in Port Gibson, in Claiborne county. In 1837 he settled on his present plantation, near the south line of Jefferson county, and here opened up a large plantation of one thousand acres, afterward adding to it until he had two thousand. As he was the owner of a large number of slaves before the war he put them to work under the new system of free labor and has been reasonably successful. He now has about two hundred freedmen on his plantation, which will compare with almost any others in the county. Mr. Archer has led a very quiet, uneventful life, his time and attention being given to the management of his plantation and to his other business interests. Being unobtrusive, he has never forced himself upon public notice, and being disinterested and free from selfishness he is ever ready to discommode himself to give comfort or pleasure to others. He has endeavored to keep free from politics, and has only filled public places at the earnest solicitation of friends, and for two terms served as president of the board of supervisors of Jefferson county. He was married near Rodney, Miss., on the 16th of May, 1836, to Miss Mary Ann Hunt (see sketch of Dunbar Hunt), and after a wedded life of nearly a half century, she was called from earth in March, 1885. She was a very superior lady in every respect, was kind and charitable to the poor, was a faithful friend, a loving wife, and as a mother her watchful care and tenderness only ended with her life. Her death was deeply lamented, not only by her immediate and sorrowing household, but by all who knew her. She was an active member of the Presbyterian church, of which Mr. Archer is also a member, and in which he is an elder and a Sabbath school teacher. To them a family of fourteen children were born, seven of whom died in early childhood. Rev. Stevenson Archer, the eldest living, is a minister of the Presbyterian church, and since 1859 has been pastor at Greenville, most of the time, but latterly in the vicinity of Greenville. He is married and has a family of eight children; James, the next son, is married and resides on the home plantation with his father. He was a soldier in the Confederate army during the late civil war, being a member of Capt. Put. Darden's battery, and was severely wounded at Atlanta, and for a time was disabled. Upon recovering he rejoined his command and served until the war closed; Ann, a daughter, is the wife of James C. Brandon, is the mother of three children, and has been until lately residing near Gibson's landing, La.; Alice is the wife of John P. Finlay, a druggist and insurance agent of the firm of Ferguson & Finlay, of Greenville, Miss.; Olivia Dunbar resides with her father; George F. is a prosperous merchant and planter of Greenville, Miss.; and John G., who is married and also resides at Greenville. Mr. Archer is a highly cultured and educated gentleman, and is a typical Southerner, being an hospitable, social and admirable host and a devoted friend. His friends are many, his enemies are none, we believe, and the devotion of his children proves what a kind and judicious father he has been. Mr. Archer is now in his eightieth year, "frosty but kindly." We learn that Mr. Archer has sometimes woed the muses, and we have been handed the following lines, written by him and published at the time, and spoken at the decoration of the graves of the Confederate dead at Church Hill, Jefferson county, Miss., April 26, 1876:

> Bring flowers, fresh flowers, and strew the graves,
>   Where our young heroes lie;
> 'Tis here repose our Southern braves,
>   Tread soft and noiselessly.
>
> Bring flowers, sweet flowers, ye maidens fair,
>   They died for you and me,
> Your beauteous brows to-day should wear
>   A saddened memory.
>
> Bring flowers, spring flowers, young, tender wives,
>   You owe your tribute too;
> They freely gave their precious lives,
>   A sacrifice for you.
>
> Bring full-blown flowers, ye matrons all,
>   For so you'd teach your sons
> To die at their dear country's call,
>   Like these heroic ones.
>
> Bring flowers, spring flowers, ye children now,
>   And lay them on each mound;
> The wreath that decks the conqueror's brow
>   Sheds not such glory 'round.
>
> Bring blooming flowers to grace the cause
>   For which the knightly Lee
> Drew forth that sword, whereon the laws
>   Were 'graved of chivalry.
>
> Bring wreaths of flowers and let their bloom
>   Of varied beauty tell
> Of glorious Stonewall Jackson's tomb,
>   Where his sainted ashes dwell.

Bring flowers, bright flowers, and strew them, though
  Our Southern cause seems lost;
For God, who made their colors glow,
  Knows what our conflict cost.

Fresh flowers will droop! Alas! we've paid
  For that dear cause our braves;
Like them, they'll die, but we have laid
  Them softly in their graves.

Bring spring flowers and let us show
  That love has not yet fled
From tender, sorrowing hearts that now
  Pay honors to the dead.

Bring flowers, all fresh and blooming here,
  From garden, field and wood,
And old and young, come, gather near
  And strew this sacred sod.

Bring flowers, our cause will yet revive!
  Truth crushed doth not expire;
It lives, and will forever live,
  Like some ethereal fire.

Bring flowers; the frosts of winter will
  Blight sore their lovely bloom,
But when the spring returns they still
  Afresh spring from their tomb.

Bring flowers with each advancing spring
  Throughout our Southern land,
And on green graves this offering
  Show every Southern band.

Like flowers, our cause may seem to yield
  To frost and cold defeat,
But there will be a future field,
  Where it will blossom yet.

Rev. S. Archer was the next to the eldest in a family of fourteen children born to James and Mary Ann (Hunt) Archer, the father, a native of Maryland, and the mother of Mississippi. His birth occurred in Jefferson county, Miss., in 1838, and he there passed his boyhood and youth, attending school at Oakland of that state, graduating in 1857, and later the theological school at Danville, Ky., from which he graduated in 1860. He was subsequently stationed at Greenville, Miss., and had charge of the Presbyterian church at that place for twenty-eight years, resigning in 1888. Previous to this, in 1876, he was elected to the office of superintendent of schools of Washington county, Miss., and has held that position since, being the present incumbent. During the war he was appointed chaplain of the Twenty-eighth Mississippi regiment of cavalry. He selected as his companion in life Miss Annie P. Findlay, a native of Louisiana, but who was reared in Mississippi, and their nuptials were celebrated in 1864. Her father, Dr. John P. Findlay, was a leading physician of Greenville, Miss., for many years, and her maternal grandfather, John Pelham, was of English descent and an heir to the title of duke of New Castle. Members of this family served with distinction in the war with Mexico, and also in the Civil war. The eleven children born to the union of Mr. and Mrs. Archer, eight of whom are living, were named as follows: James F., Stephenson, Alice, Helen (died in 1884, at the age of sixteen years),

A. B. Longstreet,

William H., Annie Mary, Bettie (died in 1876, in infancy), Pelham, Dunbar, Blanche and one unnamed. Mr. Archer is a Knight Templar in the Masonic fraternity, a Knight of Pythias, and a member of the Legion of Honor. As above stated he was pastor of the church at Greenville for many years and a hard worker during the yellow-fever epidemic at that place. He is now an efficient county official, and is doing much to advance the cause of education. His mother was a descendant of the Dunbar family. The great-grandmother, Jane Dunbar, was born near Natchez, Miss., in 1774, and thus the family for four generations have been residents of this state. In the Dunbar family there were five brothers, great-uncles of Rev. S. Archer, who fought shoulder to shoulder in the battle of New Orleans. The paternal great-grandfather, John Archer, was born in Maryland, and was the first one to graduate in medicine from this continent, having finished his course at Philadelphia in about 1770. He was twice a member of congress during Washington's presidency. The grandfather, Stephen Archer, was a celebrated lawyer, was judge of Mississippi territory for a number of years and subsequently chief justice of Maryland. James Archer (father of Rev. Archer), came to Mississippi in 1834, located at Port Gibson, in Claiborne county, and was an early lawyer there. After following that profession for some time, he married Miss Hunt and retired to the life of a planter in Jefferson county, Miss., where he resides at the present time. (See sketch.)

James Clum Armstrong, planter and merchant, Batesville, Miss. Among the enterprising citizens prominently identified with the growth and prosperity of Panola county, stands the name of James C. Armstrong, who is a native-born resident of the county, his birth occurring at old Panola on July 1, 1854. Owing to the breaking out of the war he received but an ordinary English education, but by observation and study he has improved this very materially since. When branching out for himself in life Mr. Armstrong selected merchandising for his chosen vocation, and, although he began with a small capital he now has a stock of goods valued at $3,000 and does an annual business of about $30,000. In connection with this business he is also quite extensively engaged in agricultural pursuits and is the owner of twenty-five hundred acres of land, of which fifteen hundred are under cultivation. He is the owner of a neat residence in Batesville, also. He was married on November 22, 1887, to Miss Emma Butts, a native of Mississippi and the daughter of David and Angeline (Hunt) Butts, natives of the Palmetto state. Mr. Armstrong is a whole-souled, big-hearted man, and bestows his means liberally on all worthy movements. Although not a church member, he is deeply interested in the morals of the community, and is upright and honorable in all his relations with the public. He takes much interest also in the development of the town and county, and does not live for self alone, but delights in assisting others. He is a man of fine business qualification. He is a member of the Knights of Honor, is active in politics and is a stanch democrat. He lost his wife on March 7, 1890. He was the third of seven children born to J. C. and S. E. (Davis) Armstrong, the father born in the Keystone state and the mother in South Carolina. The father immigrated to Mississippi about 1832, and was the first white man to settle in Panola county. He came to the state when a boy, engaged in trading with the Indians and did a great deal toward developing and building up the county. He was the first circuit clerk of the county, and filled that position in an able and efficient manner for a number of years. He was subsequently assignee of bankruptcy for Panola county for some time. He was a man of integrity and influence. His death occurred July 17, 1874.

Maj. D. B. Arnold, planter, Pope station, Miss. In tracing the lineage of the Arnold family we find that the ancestors went from Scotland to Ireland with William of Orange

20

during the conflict between the Catholics and Protestants, and during the reign of James II. of England. The major's great-grandfather, Anderson Arnold, was a native of county Antrim, Ireland, but emigrated to the United States, settled in Virginia, and there Anderson Arnold, Jr. (grandfather of subject), was born. The latter's only son, Anderson Arnold the third, was born in South Carolina and was there married to Miss Lucy B. Allen, a native also of the Palmetto state and the daughter of Liddell and Elizabeth (Downs) Allen, natives of the Old Dominion. The ancestors of the Allen family were originally from the south of Scotland, and the first emigrants from that country to America settled in Virginia. After his marriage, or in 1845, Mr. Arnold moved to Marshall county, Miss., followed planting quite extensively, and there his death occurred in 1887 at the age of seventy-five years. His wife had died in 1884. His principal occupation in life was to give his children every advantage for an education and in that he was successful. Though a thorough democrat in his political views he never aspired to office, but was happy in his domestic life on the farm. Of the eight children born to his marriage, Maj. D. B. Arnold was third in order of birth. The latter first saw the light of day in Laurens county, S. C., on the 20th of July, 1843, but was reared in Marshall county, Miss., whither his parents had moved. He graduated from the Byhalia high school in 1860, when but seventeen years of age, but the war prevented him from taking an anticipated course in Oxford. His sympathies were with the Southern states, and in 1861 he enlisted in a company known as Jeff Davis Rifles, remaining with that company until the spring of 1862, when he was mustered out of service. He then joined the First Mississippi under John M. Simonton, and continued with that company until the battle of Port Hudson, when he was severely wounded. On this account he retired from the service in June, 1863, and as soon as able to work he resumed operations on the farm which he has continued in connection with merchandising ever since. He has been an active, energetic supporter of democracy, and in 1879 was nominated for the legislature but declined to accept. In 1890 he was a member of the constitutional convention. Aside from this office he has held none except mayor of Pope station. He was married, first, in 1871, to Miss Mattie Bowen, of De Soto county, Miss., and the daughter of Maj. Charles and Elmira (Raney) Bowen, natives of Tennessee. She died in 1884, leaving two children: Lucy B. and Gussie T., both of whom are attending school at Holly Springs. In 1884 Mr. Arnold was married to Mrs. Katie Gibson, a native of Mississippi and a daughter of Thomas and Mary O'Connell from Cork, Ireland. Mr. Arnold began for himself after the war with nothing but a tract of land, and is now the owner of six hundred and forty acres of land, five hundred of which are under cultivation, and in 1884 he built a fine residence in Pope station. Mrs. Arnold is a member of the Catholic church, but Mr. Arnold, although not a member, is a strong believer in Presbyterianism. He is a Mason. He is a progressive planter and an energetic business man.

George W. Arnold, planter, Gunnison, Miss. Mr. Arnold is one of the old settlers and planters of Bolivar county, Miss. He was born at Port Gibson, Miss., on the 10th of January, 1818, and is a son of George and Mournin (Millens) Arnold, the father a native of England and the mother of Georgia. The father emigrated to the United States at an early date, landed at New Orleans, and soon after came to Mississippi, settling in Claiborne county, where he followed the trade of stonemason. The mother's people were among the earliest settlers in Claiborne county. Both were of representative families. The father died in 1831 and the mother in 1836, leaving four sons and one daughter. Of these, only Elizabeth, widow of Mr. Crowder, John Q., residing near Vicksburg, and George W., are now living. The last named was reared on his native soil and early trained to the duties of the farm. He became an overseer, and came to Bolivar county in December, 1839, to oversee and open the plantation for a Mr. Buck. He was subsequently engaged in supplying the river steamboats with wood. In 1850 he bought a part of his present plantation, now near the station of Gunnison, and although it was then a wilderness covered with canebrake, he began clearing and soon had it open for settlement. He is now the owner of six hundred acres of excellent land and five hundred acres of this under cultivation, all of which he cleared himself. His place is well improved, and he is also the owner of a good gin. Mr. Arnold was married in December, 1841, to Miss Eliza Stewart, who bore him eight children, four sons and two daughters now living, the four sons residing in this county. Mr. Arnold held the position of county assessor from 1850 to 1854. During the Civil war he served for a time in her home guards for local protection. There are only two people in the county who were residing here at the time of Mr. Arnold's settlement, and those are Dr. Rowland and Isaac Wilkinson.

Daniel Fowler Ashford, of Rose Hill plantation, is a member of the Adams county board of supervisors, district No. 2, and was born near Kingston, Miss., in 1837. His parents, James P. and Clarissa (Fowler) Ashford, were natives of the Old North state and Mississippi respectively, the father, born in 1795, and the mother near Kingston in 1811. When a young man the father came to Adams county and here married a Miss Rabb, who was born in Pennsylvania, and who was the daughter of John Rabb. The latter came to Adams county at a very early day, became a successful planter, and here his life terminated. To Mr. and Mrs. Ashford were born several children but all died young. In 1831 Mr. Ashford married, the second time, Clarissa Fowler, who still survives, and who has been a faithful member of the Presbyterian church for many years. Mr. Ashford was a mechanic and planter. He started out to fight life's battles for himself with no means, and at the time of his death, in 1847 (of yellow fever), his personal property was valued at $95,000, besides extensive real estate, mostly accumulated by his trade. He was a man of good habits, active and industrious, and was at one time one of the road commissioners of Adams county. He was of English descent. Mrs. Ashford was the daughter of Daniel Fowler, who was born on the Emerald isle in 1781, and who came to Maryland with his parents when a boy. He was left an orphan when still quite young, and he subsequently came to Adams county, Miss., where he married Miss Sarah Swayze, who was born in Adams county in 1782. Mr. Fowler became a wealthy planter and a prominent man of the county, holding the position of road commissioner, etc., for many years. He died in April, 1865, and his wife in 1845. She was the daughter of Richard Swayze. The latter, with a brother, Samuel Swayze, came from New Jersey to Adams county in 1772, and was among the first American settlers here. They were the founders of Protestantism in Mississippi, and spent the remainder of their lives in this state, leaving many descendants. Samuel Swayze was a local preacher in the Congregational church. Daniel Fowler Ashford was the second in order of birth of the following children: James P., of Huntsville, Ala.; Lucy, died in youth; Mary C. is an old maid, and lives in Texas; Elizabeth, was the wife of Y. D. Mangum, and died in Tennessee; Alfred Van Hook died in the Confederate army soon after the battle of Missionary Ridge, and Lucy Ann, who was the wife of Joseph M. Mangum, died in this county. Daniel F. was educated in the county schools until about fifteen years of age, then at Northampton, Mass., collegiate institute, then for two years at Yale college where he was taken sick, and during the winter of 1858 and 1859 attended the old medical college at New Orleans. After this he took charge of the old home place. In February, 1860, he was married to Miss Martha Thorn, a native of Kingston, Miss., and the daughter of John H. and Martha Thorn, the former born near Vincennes, Ind., and the latter near Kingston, Miss. Mr. Thorn came to Mississippi when a young man, married and spent the remainder of his days as a successful carpenter and planter of Adams county. He died in 1883, aged eighty-four, in Adams county, and his wife also died in that county. Both were members of the Methodist church. To Mr. and Mrs. Ashford have been born four children, three of whom are living. Since the war Mr. Ashford has lived on his present farm, consisting of six hundred acres, with four hundred and fifty acres cleared and producing about one hundred and fifty bales of cotton yearly. In 1875 he was elected a member of the board of supervisors, in which position he served for ten years. In 1889 he was appointed to fill an unexpired term, and reëlected the same year to serve two years. He is a member of Harmony lodge No. 1, A. F. & A. M. of Natchez, is a master Mason, and a member of Bluff City lodge No. 1145, Knights of Honor, also Natchez lodge No. 3, Knights of Pythias. He and wife and two eldest children are members of the Methodist church at Kingston. Mr. Ashford is always active in all charitable and public enterprises worthy of mention.

Clinton Atkinson was born in Marion county May 14, 1832. He is the second of nine children of James and Rhuhoma (Sea) Atkinson. His father was a native of North Carolina, and his mother of Georgia. He was reared in Mississippi and educated in the private schools of the same state. In 1850 he married Miss Eleanor S. West, daughter of James M. West, of Florida, but a native of Mississippi, who has borne him eight children: James, Floyd, Jesse, Wallace, Hugh, Emma, Hattie and Eugene. He began life for himself at the age of seventeen, and by close application to business Mr. Atkinson has accumulated quite a fortune, and is considered one of the ablest men of affairs and one of the most popular residents of this county. He combined the occupation of merchant and planter, carrying a stock of goods valued at about $15,000 and doing an annual business of about $75,000, besides owning about ten thousand acres of land, one thousand of which are under cultivation. His father was among the earliest settlers of this state, and was also a very successful business man. He led the life of a merchant and planter and became very wealthy. He died in 1849, after a career of much usefulness, respected by all who knew him. The family, which is of French and German origin, is one of the oldest and most highly respected in the state. Mr. and Mrs. Atkinson are members of the Episcopal church.

The Atkinsons of Hinds county are of Scotch ancestry. The founder of the family in this country settled in North Carolina, where he reared a large family. One family of these descendants consisted of five brothers: Henry, Benjamin, Jacob, William and John. Each left North Carolina and settled in different Southern states. William Atkinson was married in North Carolina to Elizabeth Harrison, daughter of Jethro Harrison. To this couple were given seven children, of whom Thomas was the sixth child. He was born in Nash county, N. C., February 14, 1831. In 1833 this family moved to Hinds county, Miss., where they engaged in agriculture, accumulating a fine property prior to the death of the father, in 1848. Thomas was reared on the plantation, where he thoroughly learned the details of planting and stockraising, at the same time securing from the neighborhood school a good practical education, to which he added further business qualifications, by a few years' clerkship in a large store. By careful reading and close observation, together with habits of temperance and uprightness, he has become one of those honorable and progressive citizens and planters who is considered reliable authority on all subjects pertaining to his line of business. He was married February 1, 1859, to Miss Elizabeth Hunter, daughter of Joseph Lane and Susan (Stuart) Hunter, of Noxubee county, Miss. To them have been given a number of children, of whom only three survive: Willie, Lizzie and Ethel. In 1861 Mr. Atkinson enlisted in company A, Withers' light artillery, Confederate states army. Among numerous engagements in which he participated, was the battle of Baker's creek and the siege of Vicksburg, in which he was wounded, captured and paroled. At the close of the war he returned, with his family, to a devastated home. Here, with unbounded energy, amid the most depressing surroundings, he labored to adapt himself to the new order of things and retrieve a fallen fortune. He now owns the old homestead and several thousand acres in the adjoining county. In 1889 he moved with his family to Jackson. Although residing in the city, he gives his personal attention to his business, and is regarded as one of the most enterprising and progressive planters of which Hinds county can boast. From the humblest employe to the most distinguished citizen with whom he has a business transaction, he is the soul of honor, and is held in high esteem by all who know him. From 1878 to 1880 he was a member of the board of supervisors of Hinds county; from 1882 to 1884 he was a member of the state legislature, in both of which positions his course was highly approved. He is a member of the K. of H. and the O. of G. K. His family are members of the Baptist church.

Isaac M. Applewhite, Santee, Covington county, Miss., was born in Carroll county, Miss., in 1833, and is a son of Woodard Applewhite, a native of Marion county, Miss., born about the year 1806. The father was reared in this state, and followed planting all his life. Isaac M. is one of a family of eight children, all of whom grew to maturity, but the greater number have passed away. When the Civil war broke out in 1861 he was not long in answering the call for men to support the cause of the South. In 1862 he enlisted, but after a short time he was honorably discharged; he was then employed in the commissary of the army. When hostilities ceased he engaged in mercantile pursuits, and carried on this business for ten years. In the meantime he cultivated his plantation, and now owns one of the best farms in the county. He is the largest dealer in sheep in this part of the state, and has a flock of between six and seven hundred, all of a high grade. Mr. Applewhite was united in marriage in December, 1854, to Miss Loflin, and they have had born to them one son, William W., who is still at home. Our subject is a member of the Masonic order, and he and his wife belong to the Methodist Episcopal church south. He has been prominently connected with the local politics of the county, having served as county treasurer two terms, from 1878–9 to 1880–81. He has also been justice of the peace, and has served on the board of supervisors. In the discharge of his duties as a public officer he has shown unusual executive ability, and a fidelity to details that have won the confidence of the community.

Charles J. Austin is numbered among the prominent young business men of Greenwood, Miss., and as such is deserving of mention in this connection. He was born in Cambridge, Md., October 5, 1858, and is a son of the Hon. George E. Austin, also a native of Maryland. The family is of English descent; they were among the early settlers of Maryland. George E. Austin is a man of more than ordinary ability. In his youth he received a good education, and he has since improved all of his opportunities of enlightenment. He served as a member of the last constitutional convention, and is a member of the present legislature of his state. Charles J. Austin, his son, was also given a good business education. In 1878 he came to Mississippi, and located at Grenada; soon after, however, he accepted a position with a Memphis wholesale house, as traveling man, and was thus employed for a period of six years. It was during this time that Mr. Austin established a business in Grenada, and in 1883 he placed his brother in charge there. In 1886 he abandoned the road, and came to Grenada, taking the management of the business into his own hands. Two years later he opened a mercantile house in Greenwood, and the business in Grenada was closed out in January, 1890. Two serious losses by fire have overtaken Mr. Austin, one at Grenada in 1884, and the other in Greenwood in April, 1890. Since the latter, a fine brick business block, 30x100 feet, has been erected, and here one of the most choice stock of dry goods, clothing and millinery is displayed. The success of this gentleman is more than gratifying to his friends, and reflects great credit upon himself. He began his career without a dollar, but by the exercise of natural ability and good judgment he has accumulated a competency, and ranks among the leading dry goods merchants of Greenwood. He is enterprising in all public matters, and does not confine his efforts to his own private interests. He is a member of the city council, and gives energetic support to all philanthropic measures. He is an honored member of the Knights of Pythias lodge. The Hon. George E. Austin was united in marriage to Miss Louise Lake. Mrs. Austin, the mother of Charles J., was a native of the state of Maryland, where she was reared and educated.

H. K. Austin, fruit-grower and planter of Hinds county, Miss., was born in the Green Mountain state, at Bradford, in 1831, the fifth in a family of seven children born to Benjamin and M. A. (Nutt) Austin, the former a native of New Hampshire, and the latter of Vermont, of Scotch and Irish descent, respectively. The father, who was a farmer, died in 1862, his wife's death having occurred in 1859. At the age of fourteen years H. K. Austin went to Massachusetts, in which state he worked in a book store for three years, then became an employe in the Boston locomotive works, where he learned the trade of a machinist. After remaining here for about fifteen years he was put in charge of a gang of men, but later went to New York, where he opened a shop for manufacturing steam and gas fittings, which he conducted for about five years, in the meantime making a fortune. For fear the business would not be profitable during the war he sold out and enlisted in the United State service for ninety days, the most of his service being in and around Bull Run, which battle he fought the day his enlistment expired. He was a member of the Seventy-first New York militia. At the expiration of his term of service he was engaged by the Manhattan Gold Mining company to put up their machinery, and continued in their employ for about two years. His family, at this time, was in La Fayette, N. J., and there he joined them, remaining one year, after which he moved to Mississippi and settled in Madison county. In January, 1867, he became a resident of Edwards, where he was for some time manager of Col. Withers' planting interests. Later he purchased the old Roberts place, where he now lives, being the owner of five hundred and forty acres, about four hundred of which is open land, producing annually about seventy-five bales of cotton, and from fifteen hundred to two thousand bushels of corn. He raises a good grade of horses and cattle, and keeps about forty cows, finding a profitable source of revenue in selling and shipping butter. He has some Jersey cattle, and the rest of his stock is of a good grade. He is making extensive preparations to engage in raising fruit, and at present has fifty acres in fruit trees, all of which will be in good bearing condition within two years. He has eight thousand trees in all, each one of which he expects will bring him in an annual income of $1. Five years since he began raising tomatoes, and this year (1891) he has seven acres in vines, which will probably yield him about $250 per acre. Although he had few opportunities for acquiring an education when young, he attended night school in Boston for some time while learning and working at his trade, and is now a well-posted and intelligent gentleman. He was appointed to the position of justice of the peace of Edwards district by the governor of the state, and filled this position with ability for four years. Before his regime there was no order and very little law, but he dealt out justice without partiality, was firm in his convictions, and after his term of service had expired there was very little trouble from any source of a thieving character. Mr. Austin is a member of the A. F. & A. M., the K. of P., the K. of H. and the A. L. of H. He was first married, in 1852, to Miss M. E. Richardson, of Massachusetts, who died in 1875, after having borne him five children, only one of whom is living, Harry A. Mr. Austin's second marriage took place on June 7, 1876, Miss Mary E. Champion becoming his wife, but she, as well as their two children, Lillian and Mary, is deceased, her death occurring in October, 1878. On March 10, 1881, Mrs. Coaker became the third wife of Mr. Austin, and has borne him one child, Winnie B. Mr. Austin is energetic and ambitious, and has converted his land, which was a wilderness at the time of his settlement, into finely cultivated fields. He expects soon to give up raising cotton and devote his attention to the raising of other products. He is an entertaining conversationalist, and is a whole-souled and genial gentleman.

J. S. Austin, M. D., who is located and practicing his profession at Oak Ridge, was born in Rankin county, Miss., in 1856, being a son of Leon and Martha (Morris) Austin, who were also born in this state. Leon Austin became a wealthy planter of Rankin county and at one time also owned a large number of slaves. During the war he was in the service only a short time, but during this time he was under General Hood. He and his wife became the parents of nine children: Andrew J., who was a physician of this county, died in April, 1882; Dr. J. S.; Nannie C., wife of Robert Stephenson, a planter of Warren county; Sallie E., deceased; Florence, wife of Mr. McGowan, of Hinds county; Mattie, who is a successful school teacher of Hinds county; Howell, who also resides in that county; Otho, who makes his home with his brother, Dr. J. S.; and Felix. In December, 1881, the father of these children died in Rankin county, his wife's death having occurred in 1871, both being earnest members of the Methodist Episcopal church. Maj. William J. Austin, grandfather of the subject of this sketch, was for many years a leading merchant of Jackson, Miss., and was at one time clerk of the chancery court of the state, and was a member of the committee that framed the constitution of the state when Mississippi was admitted into the Union. He also served in the capacity of state treasurer, and, being very wealthy, was a lender of money, and at the commencement of the war had about $200,000 loaned out to different parties. As his death occurred in 1863, his heirs afterward failed to collect the amount. Dr. J. S. Austin received his primary education in the common schools of his native county, and, at the age of nineteen years, he entered Mississippi college, in Hinds county, in which institution he remained for some time. In 1877-8 he attended the Louisville (Ky.) school of medicine and was graduated in June of the latter year, after which he returned home and located in Hinds county, where he practiced with success until 1882. He then located at Oak Ridge and assumed the duties of his present practice, which has reached very large proportions and spreads over a wide amount of territory. He is a close student, keeps thoroughly abreast of the times in his profession, and, accordingly, has been very successful in the treatment of his patients and is now among the rising physicians of the county. He was married in Hinds county in 1882 to Miss Virginia Birdsong, a daughter of Joseph Birdsong, of that county, and their union has resulted in the birth of three children: Leon, Everett (deceased) and Estelle. The Doctor is a member of the Alliance of this county, and he and his wife are members of the Methodist Episcopal church South.

Hon. James L. Autry (deceased) was born in Holly Springs and comes of pioneer stock, his parents being early settlers of Marshall county. He was educated in this county, studied law, and was practicing here at the breaking out of the war. He was prominently identified with the politics of the county, served several terms in the legislature and was speaker of the house while a young man. He entered the Confederate army as a private, was successfully promoted until he became colonel, and was commanding a regiment at Murfreesboro when he was shot in the head and killed. He was at first detailed at Vicksburg, subsequently became attached to the army of General Bragg, and finally became colonel. He was killed while making a daring move. He was a man of great intelligence, fine social habits, and was very popular with the Masons.

Hon. Benjamin F. Avent, a planter of Tallahatchie county, was born in Halifax county N. C., in 1829, a son of Benjamin Ward and Mary (Eley) Avent. His father was born in Nash county in 1796; his mother in Halifax county in 1800. They were married in the latter county in 1818, and had their home in North Carolina till 1848, when they came to Yalobusha county and located near Water Valley, where Mr. Avent died in 1851; his wife survived him until 1876, both having been for many years members of the Methodist Episcopal church. Mr. Avent was a successful planter who made his own way in the world unaided. His education was limited, but by self-application he became well informed, and was everywhere recognized as a good business man. While a resident of North Carolina he was for some year a magistrate, and the general confidence in him was such that he was chosen to settle the estates of a number of deceased persons. He was for many years a member of the Masonic order. His father, William A., was born on the Roanoke river in Virginia, and removed with his mother to North Carolina, marrying in Nash county and living out the balance of his life there as a planter. He served in the Revolutionary war, with rank as major. He was of French origin and a son of Benjamin Avent, a native of Sussex county, Va., and who died in that state. Sallie Ward, wife of William A., was born in the Isle of Wight county, Va., and went with her parents to Nash county, N. C., dying in Halifax county in that state. Our subject's grandfather, Edward Eley, was for many years a resident and planter of Hertford county, N. C.,where he ended his days. Benjamin F. Avent was the sixth of thirteen children—eight sons and five daughters—twelve of whom lived till maturity: William R., a planter, who was also a soldier under General Forrest in the late war and who died in 1878; John A., who was quartermaster under General George in the Mississippi department and who died in 1885, in Tennessee; Benjamin F.; Thomas E., who was in the Fifteenth Mississippi infantry, and afterward served in Mabry's cavalry until the close of the war, receiving a wound at Shiloh; Joseph L., who was also a member of the Fifteenth Mississippi regiment, and was wounded at Shiloh, and was later transferred to a cavalry regiment in which he served till the war was ended, and who now lives in Texas; Charles B., who was a private in General Chalmers' command, and was wounded at Holly Springs, but served till the close of the war and is now living at Water Valley; and others who became respected citizens and were reasonably successful in life, among whom may be mentioned the only surviving sister of Mr. Avent, Mrs. Martha Lewis, of Water Valley, who married Dr. Theodore Lewis, now deceased. Our subject was educated in the common schools and at the academy in North Carolina. He came with his parents to Mississippi, and in 1854 was married to Mrs. Georgiana Merriweather, daughter of Colonel Stern and Louisa Simmons, natives of Lincoln county, Ga. Mrs. Simmons died in her native state, whence Colonel Simmons came to Mississippi in 1834, locating in Yalobusha county and dying near Vicksburg, where he was on a visit about 1848. He was a well-to-do planter and a man of influence and good social standing. Mrs. Avent was born in Lincoln county, Ga., and had one child by her first husband, Mr. T. P. Merriweather, and has had six by her present husband, four of whom are now living. Since his marriage Mr. Avent has lived continuously in Tallahatchie county, and on his present farm since 1871. This plantation comprises about eight hundred acres, which he has secured by his own efforts and upon which he has placed the most of the improvements. He is a member of the Farmers' Alliance, and has been quite active in political and public affairs and was elected to the legislature in 1868. Since 1850 he has been a member of the Methodist Episcopal church, and his wife has been connected with the Baptist church since childhood. The children born to Mr. and Mrs. Avent were named as follows in the order of their birth: Mary L., the wife of Prof. R. T. Payne, superintendent of education in Grenada; Benjamin W., who died in April, 1889; Octavia Simmons; Georgiana, wife of Albert T. McElrath; Robert Cromwell, who died at the age of three years, and Lena B. Florida M. is the daughter of Mrs. Avent by her first husband. Mr. Avent was a member of Merrin's battery in Mississippi. He was at Baker's creek, Corinth, Jackson and elsewhere. He was in service constantly from 1862 till the close of the war with rank of sergeant of artillery. He is a thrifty, progressive man; beloved by his family; respected by his fellow-men and helpful to the extent of his means to all public enterprises.

ᏨHAPTEᏒ XᏉI.

PERSONAL NOTICES, B.

A SUCCESSFUL merchant and planter of Fort Adams, Wilkinson county, is Darling Babers, who was born in Barnwell district, S. C., in 1840, and at nine years of age was brought by his parents to Bienville parish, La., where they engaged in planting. The father was John Babers, a native of South Carolina, born in 1800, and reared an orphan. His parents were from Virginia. John, the father of Darling, attained his majority in South Carolina, where he engaged in planting. He was a strong democrat, and belonged to the militia of South Carolina. His second marriage was with Alpha Lard, a native of South Carolina, born in 1808, and died in 1857, aged forty-nine years. To this union were born six children, all of whom lived to be grown, but four of whom are now deceased. Those living are Darling, and Alpha, the widow of Joel Glass; she has four children, all of whom were reared in this county. Those deceased are Julia, who died in Wilkinson county in 1857; James P., a planter and merchant of Fort Adams, who died in 1867 and was succeeded in his business by his brother, Darling; Ferman, who died soon after the first battle of Manassas, Va., while in camp at Manassas, aged nineteen years; Elizabeth, who died in 1865, was the wife of John Snelling and lived in Louisiana. The father was first married to a young lady, by whom were born ten children, all of whom lived to maturity but one. Joseph, one of the sons, served in the late war in the Confederate army, and died in camp on Cisley Island, La. Daniel died in Florida, William in Louisiana, and John in Texas. Henry and Andrew live in Louisiana. Mary married Mr. Williams, and died in 1859. Martha married Joseph Hadwin, and lives in Louisiana. Leve L. died in Wilkinson county Miss.; Charles died in childhood; Louis C. died of yellow fever in

1855, in Williamson county, Miss. The father of these children died in 1864, in Louisiana, on the place he had settled on Saline river. He was a member of the Baptist church, in which he took much interest and was active, serving as deacon and in other capacities. He possessed a high sense of honor, was popular and passed a useful life. Mr. Lard, the maternal grandfather of Darling, lived to the extraordinary age of one hundred and seven years, and died in the year 1846. He was a soldier in the Revolutionary war, as were also his six brothers. The maternal grandmother died at ninety-three years of age. They had a large family, all of whom are now deceased. The parents were Baptists. The father died in South Carolina and the mother in Alabama. Darling Babers in youth attended the Saline institute, and in November, 1860, went to the Red river country, where he secured a clerkship, and in April, 1861, when the war broke out, joined the Ninth Louisiana regiment in the company then called the Brush valley guards. He participated in the following engagements: Winchester in 1862; Cross Keys, 1862; seven days' fight around Richmond; Malvern Hill, 1862, where he was wounded by a minie-ball through the right shoulder; Gettysburg; the wilderness; was wounded and taken prisoner at the battle of Spottsylvania courthouse, shot through the left hand, was in front of the tree twenty-two inches in diameter that was cut down by minie balls, and was in General Hill's corps. He was through all the engagements of the valley campaign of Stonewall Jackson. When taken prisoner he was conveyed to to Washington city, where he was kept for sixty days and was then transported to Fort Delaware, where he was confined until the close of the war. In June, 1865, he was released and came home to Fort Adams, where he clerked a short time. He then engaged in planting, and upon the death of his brother succeeded him in the mercantile business at Fort Adams in 1867. Here he has since continued the business and is now the leading merchant of the place. He is also engaged in planting to some extent. He was married first to Fannie Kline, a native of Fort Adams, and daughter of Seth Kline, one of the early settlers of this place, who followed the occupation of shipping merchant. This marriage took place in 1868, but in 1875 his wife died at the age of thirty-one years. She was a member of the Catholic church. By this union were born four daughters. She was well educated at Mrs. Reed's school at Baton Rouge, and was a woman of noble character and purposes. Isabell, the first child, died an infant; Jennie Darling, the second, graduated from the Visitation convent of Mobile, Ala., in July, 1890; Lucy Lee and Fannie Sheppard were both at St. Mary's convent in New Orleans. Mr. Babers was married the second time, in 1876, to Miss Eliza S. Row, daughter of Benjamin Row, an old and respected settler of this county, and by this union were born seven children, two of whom are deceased: Evelyn McNulty, John E. (who died at six months), Bertram, Ferman, Edith Alpha, Lenore La Barron, George Darling (who died at six months) and Sarah Elise. Mr. Babers has a private tutor for his children, and when they are old enough will send them away to fine schools. Mrs. Babers and her children are members of the Catholic church. Mr. Babers in politics is democratic, and takes some active interest in political matters. He has served on the board of county supervisors, and is a man well liked and respected. He is one of the most sensible and substantial citizens of this county.

James E. Backstrom, Water Valley, Miss., the subject of this biography, is one of the leading druggists of Yalobusha county, and for twenty years has been identified with the growth of Water Valley. He was born in Neshoba county, Miss., December 17, 1847, and is a son of James L. and Elvira (Rogers) Backstrom, natives of South Carolina and Georgia respectively. James L. Backstrom was born about the year 1812, and was the son of Jonas Backstrom, a native of South Carolina. About the year 1836 or 1837 the

latter came to Mississippi and settled near Philadelphia, Neshoba county. There he followed farming, and was considered well to do at that time, as he was one of the most
extensive planters in the county. Politically he affiliated with the whig party, and was
well posted on the leading issues of the day. He reared one child; two other boys were
born, but died in youth. James L. Backstrom, the second in order of nativity, was educated at Columbia college, S. C., and was graduated from the Charleston medical college. He came to Mississippi a short time after his father, and settled in Philadelphia,
where he engaged in the practice of his profession. He was a very skillful physician,
and soon became the leading practitioner of the county, being called in all important cases
of consultation. Politically he wielded a strong influence, controlling the elections to a
great extent. He was elected a member of the legislature, and held that office at the time
of the breaking out of the Civil war; in his early life he was a member of the whig party.
He was a man of unusual force of character, and every movement to which he lent his aid
was sure of success. He was a devoted admirer of Jefferson Davis and Ethel Barksdale.
His family removed to Yalobusha county in 1866, and settled near Water Valley, where he
spent the remainder of his days, retiring during the last years of his life from the active
practice of his profession. During the war he served as lieutenant of the sixty-day men
under Alcorn, but soon after the war he returned to his practice, having lost heavily by the
ravages of the conflict. During the latter years of his life he became a member of the
Methodist Episcopal church, and gave to that body the same earnest effort which had
always characterized all his actions. He died in 1882, honored and lamented by a host
of citizens. He was deeply mourned by his widow and son, James E. Two other sons,
Theodore B. and Edgar, died in youth. The mother of these children was a woman of
refinement, and a devoted Christian. She died in the year 1888, in this county.

John L. Backstrom, uncle of James E., lived and died in South Carolina. He had
three sons, who served in the late war, two of whom lost their lives in battle. Thomas, the
third son, was supposed to be mortally wounded, but survived, and is yet living in Chester
district, S. C., near the old home place. David M. Backstrom came to Mississippi with his
father, Jonas Backstrom, and was a member of the convention that carried the state out of
the Union. He was a states' rights whig, and and a prominent, wealthy citizen of Neshoba
county. James E. Backstrom was reared in Neshoba county, and received his education in
the common schools of the county and the University of Oxford, Miss. He was united in
marriage to Saida J. Mauldin, a native of Neshoba county and a daughter of R. L. Mauldin,
of South Carolina. Mr. Mauldin came to Mississippi when a young man, and married
Sarah J. Sitton, and settled in Neshoba county, where he lived until after the war; he then
moved to a place near Water Valley, where Mrs. Backstrom was reared. She is one of a
family of seven—four sons and three daughters. Mr. and Mrs. Backstrom are the parents
of eight children: Theodore E., a student at Emery college, James L., Fannie E., Pearl
Rivers, Alice, Lillian, Ella and Thad. The father and mother are members of the Methodist Episcopal church, and are highly respected citizens. Mr. Backstrom enlisted during the
late war in the Fourth Mississippi cavalry, company K, and served until the surrender.
Politically he affiliates with the democratic party, and takes a great interest in the action of
that body. He is a member of the firm of Backstrom & Rogers, one of the oldest drug
firms in the city; they are faithful and reliable druggists, and fully understand the business
of compounding drugs. In addition to his commercial interests Mr. Backstrom is engaged
in planting to a large extent. He is a member of the Masonic order and also of the Independent Order of Odd Fellows.

N. T. Baggett is the present efficient incumbent of the office of chancery and circuit court clerk of Sharkey county, Miss., and has discharged the duties of this position with credit and honor since 1885. He was born in Tuscaloosa county, Ala., in 1857, being the seventh of ten children, three sons and one daughter now living, born to William E. and Lucinda (Robertson) Baggett, the former born in Tennessee and the latter in North Carolina. To Tuscaloosa county, Ala., Mrs. Baggett was taken when a girl by her parents, and there Mr. Baggett also removed when young, their union taking place there. In 1874 they came to what is now Sharkey county, where Mr. Baggett died in 1877 and his widow in 1884, both having been earnest members of the Methodist Episcopal church. Mr. Baggett was an industrious and substantial citizen, and became a fairly successful planter. Isaac Robertson, the maternal grandfather, was reared in North Carolina, and from there he removed to Alabama where he was called from earth in 1886 at the advanced age of eighty-eight years, he having also lived the life of an agriculturist. He was a soldier in the war of 1812. The living brothers and sisters of the immediate subject of this sketch, are as follows: John R., G. M., and Anna G., who is the wife of William Wagoner of Vicksburg. N. T. Baggett was brought up on a plantation and was given the advantages of the country schools near his home. At the age of twenty-three years he began life for himself as deputy sheriff of Sharkey county, in which capacity he continued for four years, then spent one year as a merchant, and in 1885 was elected for a special term as chancery and circuit clerk, and has held the office ever since without opposition. He is an energetic, enterprising and promising young man, and through his economy and good management has acquired a good property. He is a member of the firm of Baggett Bros., general supply merchants, and besides his interest in this business, he also owns an interest in one thousand eight hundred acres of land, six hundred of which is under cultivation, producing about four hundred bales of cotton per annum. All this property has been acquired by his own efforts since the year 1880, for at that time he began an independent career with no capital, save a goodly supply of pluck, energy and push. He is senior warden of Deer creek lodge 356 of the A. F. & A. M.

John Bagwell, farmer, Ackerman, Miss. Mr. Bagwell was originally from Alabama, born on the 3d of January, 1833, and is of English descent, his grandfather Bagwell being a native of England. His parents, Frederick and Margaret Ann (Crawford) Bagwell, were natives of the Palmetto state, the father born in 1799. The latter followed the occupation of a farmer all his life and removed from South Carolina to Alabama in 1817. In 1836 he removed to Mississippi, located in Choctaw county, near the present residence of his son John, and took up land to which he afterward added until at the time of his death, in 1864, he was the owner of three hundred and eighty acres. His widow survived him ten years, dying in 1874. Both were members of the Methodist church, he a steward in the same for a number of years. He was the father of thirteen children, twelve of whom lived to be grown and ten now living. Mr. Bagwell being poor and in debt, could not give his children the educational advantages he desired, but allowed them one year's schooling, which all obtained but our subject, who never attended school more than a few days. He remained and assisted his father in paying off his indebtedness until he was twenty-five years of age, carrying mail, his father having taken the contract. In 1858 he was united in marriage to Miss Sarah Frances Turner, a native of Oktibbeha county, born in 1842, and the daughter of Frank Turner, one of the early settlers of Mississippi. After marriage Mr. Bagwell began farming on land he had previously bought, first purchasing one hundred and sixty acres, to which he added from time to time until he now has over eight hundred acres, of which he cultivates two hundred. His principal productions are corn and cotton. He also raises cattle and horses for market. Mr. Bagwell deserves much credit for his enterprise, thrift and good management, and is one of the county's best citizens. To his marriage were born fifteen children, thirteen of whom are now living: Mrs. Lora A. Graves, Martin Fred and William Frank (twins), Henry H., John P., Joe Lee, Anna L., Lena, Jane, May, Robert, Effie May and Marcus. When the war cloud, which had so long hovered over our land, burst, Mr. Bagwell showed his willingness to aid the Southern cause, and in May, 1862, enlisted in company I, Fifteenth infantry (Choctaw guards), and was in the battles of Peach Tree creek and Franklin. He was captured at Nashville and taken to Camp Douglas, where he remained six months, or until the close of the war. Returning home he again engaged in farming, beginning anew. He and Mrs. Bagwell are church members, he of the Methodist and she of the Baptist church. Mr. Bagwell is a strong advocate of the principles of the Farmers' Alliance.

Col. James S. Bailey, a prominent attorney and highly esteemed citizen, was born in Hickman county, Tenn., in 1819, a son of James and Isabella Bailey, cousins, and natives of Fayette county, Ky., who removed with their parents to Logan county, Ky., where they were married. About 1810 they removed to Hickman county, Tenn., and came with a number of other Hickman county families to Tallahatchie county, Miss. At that time there was but one white family—that of Samuel Foster—living in the county. Mr. Bailey settled on Tillatoba creek, a few miles north of Charleston, where he improved a farm and died in November, 1864, his wife having died in 1850. The latter was a member of the Presbyterian church. Mr. Bailey was a man of limited education, but had good business abilities and was success-ful in life. His father and one of his uncles removed from Augusta, Ga., soon after the Rev-olutionary war, to the site of Lexington, Ky., where they built a fort in which our subject was born. They afterward removed to Logan county, where they spent the balance of their lives. They were of Irish parentage, and both did gallant service in the Revolutionary war for the struggling colonies. They left a great number of descendants and relatives of their name in Georgia. Colonel Bailey, as he is familiarly known, is the youngest of three sons and three daughters, and the only one now living. Jane married Donnell Lacy and removed to Texas many years ago, where she and her husband both died; Margaret married William Lane, who died in Tennessee, and afterward she became the wife of Smiley Caruthers, who died here before the war, she surviving him until some time after the war; Emeline married P. H. Thornton, and both of them died in this county; Thomas was killed at the age of twen-ty-one, while on a bear hunt, by the accidental discharge of a gun; our subject was the next in order of birth; John M. became a merchant and planter, was a soldier in the Confederate army, and died at Oxford. Colonel Bailey remained at home until about the age of seven-teen, receiving there his preparatory education. From the age of seventeen to twenty-two he was a student at Hopkinsville, Ky., in the meantime studying law. He was admitted to the bar in 1842, and has practiced at Charleston ever since with much success, being the old-est member of the Tallahatchie county bar. In 1843 he was elected to represent his district in the lower house of the legislature. He was reëlected in 1845, and was again elected in 1875, and reëlected in 1877 and 1879. During the last few sessions he served as chairman of the judiciary committee. He was married in 1846, while in the legislature, to Sarah S., daughter of Hon. Pryor Lea, of Jacksonville. Mr. Lea was born in Knoxville, Tenn., where he married, removing from there to Mississippi, locating in Jackson, where he was for some years a prominent attorney, then removing to Texas, where he died in 1886. He was a mem-ber of congress from East Tennessee during Jackson's administration, and was one of the founders and original trustees of the State university of Mississippi. Mrs. Bailey, who was a native of Kentucky, died in February, 1869, after having been long identified with the Presbyterian church. To her husband she bore eight children: Pryor Lea, who became a planter and died in 1844; James, also a planter, who died in 1882; Spencer, a lawyer, who died in 1887; John, the only surviving son, was educated at Oxford and graduated in law at the Cumberland university at Lebanon, Tenn., and is now practicing his profession with his father; he was elected to represent his district in 1879; Lavinia is the wife of J. S. Brown, of northwest Mississippi; the next in order of birth is Belle; Sarah is the wife of William Bryan, of Birmingham, Ala.; Ellen is the youngest of the family. The oldest sons of Mr. and Mrs. Bailey were all educated at the State university in Mississippi, and the daughters at the female college at Oxford. Colonel Bailey is now one of the oldest inhabitants of the county. He has seen its gradual development from a vast wilderness to its present condition, and has done his part manfully toward effecting this change. He has never been an enthusiast in public matters, but he has had the interest of the county at heart, and done his share in creating a healthy public atmosphere. Politically he was a whig, but since the war he has been a democrat, and he has been a member of the Masonic order for many years.

Joseph W. Bailey, a planter of Copiah county, Miss., was born in New York city in 1835, a son of Joseph and Jane (Weldon) Bailey, both of whom were born in Ireland in 1808. Joseph Bailey came to America in 1831 and was married not long afterward. He was a stonecutter by trade, and in 1837 located in Philadelphia, where he lived for half a century, dying in 1887. When he was about eleven years of age Joseph W. Bailey came to Natchez, Miss., to live with his three uncles: George, Thomas and William Weldon. George Weldon married, but his wife died in a short time. Neither of the others ever married. At one time these men were the wealthiest and most extensive contractors and builders in the state of Mississippi. George and Thomas Weldon were born in Ireland, and William is a native of Canada, where his parents had located after the birth of his older brothers. The three settled at Natchez about 1835. During the war Thomas Weldon was chief of the secret service of the state of Mississippi, a responsible position, the delicate duties of which he performed with much ability. He equipped a company known as the Tom Weldon's rebels of Mississippi at his own expense, and supported all of the needy families of his company while their husbands and fathers were doing battle for their country. Two years after coming to Natchez, and while attending school, our subject ran away from home and went to sea. Not long after he found himself upon the broad Pacific ocean, and for five years gained a livelihood by working in the vessels that plied along the coasts of North and South America, and during a portion of this adventuresome time he was a member of the army of Chili. In 1858 he married Harriet Dees, a daughter of Hamilton F. and Martha Dees, and to him and his estimable wife were born eight children, five of whom are living: Pearl M., at home; Joseph W., living in Texas and now representing the fifth congressional district of that state in the congress of the United States (he is not only the youngest congressman in office, but proving himself possessed of special abilities to cope with legislators of twice or thrice his years); Imogene is the wife of Dr. J. R. Brucker of Texas; Aileen, the wife of H. P. Fox of Copiah county, and lastly Miss Ethel W., who is yet at home with her parents. In 1862 Mr. Bailey entered the Confederate service by taking charge of the naval ship St. Philip, thus devoting to the service of his state and country that knowledge which he had gained during that period of his life when, as a runaway boy, he became a sailor on the Pacific. He then entered the navy yards at Yazoo city, but after this city was captured he enlisted in company F, of the Fourth Mississippi regiment, but was soon chosen to act in the secret service department, in which he served ably and effectively. The most important battle in which he participated was that at Jackson, Miss. While he was absent in the war, his wife had removed with her family to Crystal Springs, and there he went after peace had been declared, and, having previously served as apprentice to the carpenter's trade, he now turned his attention to contracting and building, and for a number of years he was a prosperous merchant at Crystal Springs. He was connected with the Masonic lodge of Crystal Springs and of lodge No. 21, Knights of Pythias of Crystal Springs, of which he was a charter member. He and his entire family are members of the Baptist church. He is a man who stands high in the community, and is heartily liked and respected by the people at large, not only on account of his fine old family, of which he is justly proud, but also upon his own merits as a man and citizen.

Col. S. M. Bailey, Bailey, Miss., was born in Cleveland county, N. C., December 8, 1829, and is a son of John and Ruth (Linton) Bailey, natives of North Carolina. The parents were reared and married in their native state, and lived there until they had eight children. In 1853 they removed to Forsyth county, Ga., where they purchased a plantation. The father died there in 1864. He and his wife were members of the Baptist church. They had nine children born to them, seven of whom are living. Colonel Bailey is the only one residing in Mississippi. He came to Lauderdale county in 1858, and located on the farm where he is now living. He was but nineteen years old when he began life for himself, choosing the occupation of farming. In 1850 he was married to Terrissa J. Anglin, of Gwinnette county, Ga. Two years after his marriage he was caught in the mighty tide of emigration that swept to the Pacific coast, upon the discovery of gold in California, and remained there until 1856. When he had saved $5,000 in gold he returned to Georgia, and for one year tilled the soil of his native state. He then removed to Mississippi. Colonel and Mrs. Bailey have had born to them four children: John A., James P., Anna L. and Ruth E. The two daughters are deceased. The mother died July 29, 1887. She was a worthy member of the Baptist church. Colonel Bailey was married, a second time, to Mrs. Irene Walker, widow of William Walker, in February, 1890. She had one son by her first marriage, David J., a promising young man of eighteen years. Mrs. Bailey's maiden name was Jemison, and she was born and reared in Alabama. In 1862 Colonel Bailey enlisted in company C, Forty-first Mississippi infantry, and took a part in many of the most noted engagements of the conflict. At Chickamauga he was struck on the left hip by a shell, and was disabled two months; during this time he was in the hospital at Atlanta, Ga. At the siege of Atlanta he was shot with a minie-ball in the foot, and had a ninety days' fourlough in consequence of this wound. He was paroled at Montgomery, Ala., after which he returned to his home, and resumed his agricultural occupations. He has also been interested in the milling business. He has been on the plantation where he now lives for thirty years. He is well and favorably known throughout the county, and is highly esteemed for his many excellent traits of character. He is a member of the Baptist church, while his wife belongs to the Methodist Episcopal church. He is a member of the Masonic fraternity, and has been associated with that body for the past thirty years. He has never aspired to any political notoriety, but has discharged his duties as a private citizen with fidelity to his convictions of right and wrong. John A. Bailey, the elder son of Colonel Bailey, was born in Gwinnette county, Ga., April 15, 1858, and was brought by his parents to Mississippi at the age of six months. He has, therefore, lived all his life in Lauderdale county. He was graduated from Cooper institute in 1878, and the same year he was united in marriage to Miss Walterine McClung, of Louisiana. Seven children have been born of this union: Daisy, Monroe, Anna, Leon, Claude, Celeste, and an infant not yet named.   Mr. Bailey has made farming his occupation through life, although at one time he contemplated the study of law, and read under the direction of Capt. John W. Smith, of Meridian, for several months.   He abandoned the idea, and has made a marked success of his farming operations.   He owns eight hundred acres of land, and has about half of it under excellent cultivation.   His principal crops are cotton and fruit; he has a large orchard of apple and pear trees, and a fine variety of peaches; he also raises small fruits in abundance.   Mr. Bailey is a member of the Baptist church, while his wife belongs to the Episcopal church.   He is a member of the Masonic fraternity, and affiliates with the Democratic party.   He was a member of the constitutional convention of 1890.   He is a member of the Farmers' Alliance, and is lecturer of Lauderdale county.   He is in every way worthy of the esteem in which he is held by the people of the county.   James P. Bailey, the second son of the Colonel, is a practicing physician at the town of Bailey.   He was graduated from the medical college at Louisville, Ky., in 1882, and has since built up a fine practice at Bailey, and in the surrounding neighborhood.   Colonel Bailey owns one thousand acres of good land, six hundred of which he has well improved and in a good state of cultivation. Before the war he was in good circumstances, and owned a number of slaves.

Samuel C. Bains, Vaiden, Miss., is a native of Alabama, born in Tuscaloosa county, January 15, 1821.   The Rev. James Bains, his father, was born, reared and educated in South Carolina; he became a minister in the Baptist church, and in 1827 he removed to Mississippi, and settled in what was then the Choctaw nation, where he did the work of a pioneer preacher for two years, being called at the end of that time to his eternal home; his wife survived him until 1848; she was married, a second time, to a Mr. Stigler.   The family of Mr. Bains consisted of three sons and one daughter, Samuel C. being the youngest and only surviving member.   He grew to manhood in Holmes county, where he received his education.   He remained with his mother until he had attained his majority, and then started out in life upon his own responsibility.   In 1849 he embarked in the mercantile trade at Franklin, Holmes county, where he sold goods for a period of ten years, the three years following that being passed in Choctaw county.   In 1861, when there was a call for men to go to the defense of the country, he abandoned his private interests and raised a company of one hundred and forty men, known as the Vaiden artillery; he was made captain of this company, and did valiant service throughout the entire war.   In the battles of Corinth and Shiloh he made a very gallant stand, and he was also in the siege of Vicksburg, where he was taken prisoner.   He was afterward exchanged and rejoined his army, and participated in the siege of Mobile.   After the war he again took up business pursuits, and until 1888 was in the mercantile trade.   He began life at the bottom of the ladder, but by good management and naturally fine qualifications he has attained a position of which any man might be proud.   In Carroll county he has been called to many offices of trust and responsibility, and has exhibited an executive ability far above the average.   He was first married in Holmes county in 1849, his wife dying at the end of one year.   In 1852 he was united to Miss Henrietta Sample, a daughter of Washington Sample.   She died in 1872, having had born to her seven sons: Lee holds a government position in Washington, D. C.; George is a druggist in Birmingham, Ala.; four sons are engaged in commercial pursuits at Bessemer, Ala., and the youngest is a student at home.   Mr. Bains married his present wife at Greenwood, in 1874—Mrs. Florence Peebles, widow of the late Dr. J. H. Peebles, of Greenwood, and daughter of Dr. E. R. McLean, who was a prominent physician at Greenwood for many years, and a pioneer of the place.   He was an active member of the Presbyterian church, and one of its liberal supporters.   He was a most excellent man in every respect, and one of

Yours truly, in His name —
Mary E. Erwin

whom any community may well be proud. He died at the residence of his daughter in Vaiden, July 3, 1883. Mrs. Bains was reared, educated and married in Mississippi. By her first marriage she has one son, J. H. Peebles, a leading druggist at Winona, Miss. By the last marriage two children have been born: James McLean Bains and Frank E. Bains. Mr. Bains is a member of the Masonic order, belonging both to the blue lodge and chapter. He is a live, progressive member of the Methodist Episcopal church, while Mrs. Bains belongs to the Presbyterian church.

Among the leading professional men of Lafayette county is W. H. Baird, M. D., of Oxford, who is an ornament to his calling, and a citizen whom any community would be proud to claim. He was born in Noxubee county, Miss., in 1844, and is the fourth of a family of eight children born to J. M. and Eliza T. (Rupert) Baird; the father was born in Asheville, N. C., in 1809, and the mother was a native of Georgia, born in 1814; the paternal ancestors were of Scotch-Irish extraction, and the maternal lineage was German. The father was reared to the occupation of a farmer, but chose the profession of medicine for his life work. He was a student at the University of Lexington, and did not come to Mississippi until 1837, when he began the practice of medicine. He soon met and married his wife, who came to Kemper county, Miss., with her parents, about the year 1830; after his marriage he removed to Noxubee county, Miss., and thence to Lowndes county, where he resided twenty years. He retired from professional work and became an extensive planter. In 1865 he went back to Asheville, N. C., where he died in 1878; his wife survived him until 1887. They were highly respected members of the Christian church. Dr. Baird, the father of our subject, was a student all his life long, both in a professional and literary direction; he made a special study of the New Testament in the Greek, and was a man of broad learning and culture; politically he adhered strictly to the principles of the whig party. Dr. W. H. Baird passed his youth amid the scenes of agricultural life, and in 1866 bade adieu to the home of his childhood, and went to Charleston, S. C., where he entered upon the study of medicine; he was graduated in New Orleans in 1869, and at once began practice at Indianola, Sunflower county, Miss.; there he resided until 1888, when he came to Oxford, and began to give some attention to planting. Dr. Baird was married in 1871 to Miss Addie McLemore, a native of Mississippi and a daughter of Col. John D. McLemore; her father was an early settler of Carroll county, and for a time before the war was the largest taxpayer in the state; he was a stanch democrat, and an earnest worker in the ranks of his party. The Doctor and his wife are the parents of seven children: Sallie, McLemore, Mary, Madison, William, Geren and Susie. Dr. Baird is one of the pioneer projectors of the Georgia Pacific railroad, giving time, money and influence to aid in its completion; it is largely due to his zeal in the matter that it has been completed; it has demonstrated the possibility of railroad construction in the bottom lands, and has opened up much of Sunflower and other counties to the outside world. The Doctor did a large and successful practice in the county, where he was for many years the leading physician. He is a member of the Masonic fraternity, and of the Knights of Honor and the Knights of Pythias. Mrs. Baird is an active member of the Methodist Episcopal church. Doctor Baird and two brothers, John R. and Joe B. Baird, were soldiers of the Confederate army, and with a feeling of pride remember their services as locally patriotic. They were prompt to respond to all duties, and though history records their cause a vain and unsuccessful one, they still have the consciousness of believing they did the part of good citizens with the lights then before them.

A well-known attorney of Indianola, Sunflower county, Miss., Hon. Thomas R. Baird, is possessed of a reputation in professional as well as social life of which any man might feel

21

proud. He early received distinction as a lawyer, for he showed himself to be a man of superior intelligence, and as he was ever close and attentive to business, succeeded in making for himself a good practice. Being of a modest and retiring nature his greatest difficulty for a long time was in appearing before the public and in making speeches. He was born in Lowndes county, Miss., December 11, 1850, to Dr. James M. and Elizabeth (Rupert) Baird, who were born in North Carolina in 1809 and Milledgeville, Ga., and died in Asheville, N. C., in March, 1877, and in 1884, respectively. Dr. Baird was given an excellent literary education in Transylvania university, of Lexington, Ky., and also graduated in the medical department of that institution, after which he removed to Mississippi and located in Noxubee county. After practicing there for a few years he went to Lowndes county, and up to 1860 was one of the leading medical practitioners of that section. Sunflower county then became his home, after which his attention was given to looking after the interests of his plantation, which was located on the Sunflower river. In 1866 he returned to his native state of North Carolina, and until his death followed the occupation of merchandising at Asheville. Mrs. Baird was a daughter of John Rupert, of Milledgeville, Ga. Thomas R. Baird was one of a family of five sons and three daughters that grew to mature years; but one sister, M. J., wife of Thomas J. Lee, is now deceased. Hon. John R. Baird is an extensive planter and trader of Sunflower county, and served as a delegate to the last constitutional convention at Jackson, Miss. Dr. W. H. Baird is a practicing physician of Oxford, Miss., and J. B. Baird is a planter of this county. These three brothers served the Confederacy in the Rebellion, the Doctor holding a captain's commission. The youngest brother, Robert W., is a planter and merchant of this county, and the surviving sisters are: A. C., wife of John H. Richards, a planter of Lowndes county, and Miss Victoria, who is a resident of Asheville, N. C. Thomas R. Baird has been a resident of this county since his twelfth year, but in 1866 accompanied his parents to North Carolina, and in the town of Asheville he received the advantages of a superior school. This he supplemented in later years with a few terms in the University of Kentucky, in which institution he also read law. He continued his legal studies with Judge Bailey in Asheville, and was admitted to the bar by the supreme court of that state in the month of January, 1871. The same year Mr. Baird returned to Mississippi, and was admitted to the bar of this county by the first court held here by Judge Fisher, in 1871. Mr. Baird first opened an office at Johnsonville, but upon the removal of the county seat in 1882 he came to Indianola, where he has since made his home. Here, in the midst of able and experienced competition, he built up an enviable reputation for himself and is now enjoying the reward of his former diligence and attention to every detail of his profession. He has distinguished himself by winning some very difficult cases, and throughout Sunflower, as well as the surrounding counties, he has made a reputation for ability, earnestness and zeal. He has always identified himself with the democratic party, and by his numerous friends was elected in 1890 to represent this county in the state legislature, where his actions were in accordance with the best interests of the state and county. He served on several important committees, and was strongly opposed to the division of the counties and the forming of a new county to be called Jeff Davis county. He made a strong fight against this measure and contributed largely to its defeat. He was married in this county in January, 1890, to Miss Anna, daughter of S. L. Montgomery, of Indianola. Mrs. Baird was born and reared in Mississippi and was educated at Canton. This couple are very social and hospitable, and in their pleasant and comfortable home display qualities which are essential to a successful host and hostess. They are favorites in social circles, and are esteemed and respected by all. James Beden Baird, the grandfather, was a North Carolinian, and was one of the first settlers west of the Blue Ridge mountains. He inherited Scotch and Irish blood of his ancestors, who were among the pioneers of the Old North state.

The occupation which Thomas F. Baker still continues to follow has received his attention the greater part of his life, and it is but the truth to say that he is thoroughly posted and well informed, and his labors in this direction have contributed very materially to the reputation Jefferson county, Miss., enjoys as a rich planting region. He was born on the plantation which he is at present tilling on the 21st of September, 1824, but his father, Thomas Baker was born in New Jersey, and as a child came with an elder brother to Jefferson county, Miss., and attained to years of manhood in this and Adams county. As a means of obtaining a livelihood he first began merchandising at old Greenville, a calling he followed with fair results for a number of years. Being of a very patriotic disposition and bitterly opposed to tyranny, he immediately enlisted as a soldier in the war of 1812, and went with his regiment to New Orleans, but arrived there too late to participate in that battle. He was married in Jefferson county, Miss., to Miss Eliza Green, whose people were very prominent and among the earliest settlers of this region. Her father, Everard Green, was born in Jefferson county, the youngest son of Col. Thomas Green, a native Virginian who settled on a plantation adjoining the one on which Mr. Baker is now living, this being in the year 1772. He had obtained a Spanish grant and was the owner of several thousand acres of land. The old Gayoso fort is located on this place, and the Spanish Governor Gayoso first resided here, tradition having it that Mr. Green also lived at the fort. Col. Thomas Green, who was the only magistrate in this part of the state at that time, performed the marriage ceremony for General Jackson and Mrs. Roberts, at which time the latter was residing in Mr. Green's family. Colonel Green had a family of several sons and one daughter; Thomas M. was elected and served as the second congressman for the territory of Mississippi; Everard reared a family of one son and three daughters, the eldest of the latter being the mother of Thomas F. Baker. Everard Green became one of the most influential men of Jefferson county, Miss., and during a lifetime of hard, earnest endeavor, became a wealthy planter. He died in the prime of life, having been a methodical, honest and efficient business man. After his marriage Thomas Baker settled on the plantation on which his son, Thomas F. Baker, is now residing, where he built a house and opened up a large plantation, on which he resided until his death, which occurred in the year 1832, his most estimable and worthy wife surviving him a few years, dying in 1837. The career of Mr. Baker is but another evidence of the possibilities that young men have for advancement in the world when supported by a strong resolution to rise. He commenced life for himself in a very humble way, and by native ability, tact and indomitable perseverance he in time found himself in affluent circumstances, and at his death left the heritage of an untarnished name to his children and an example of a noble, upright career to all young men. Thomas F. Baker is the elder of two sons, the other member being Everard Green Baker, a planter at Hazelhurst, who was twice married and at his death, in 1890, left a number of children by each wife. Thomas F. spent the happy, healthy life of a country boy, and while learning to manage and look after his father's plantation his studies were not neglected, and at the time of his entering St. Joseph college at Bardstown, Ky., he was as well advanced as any youth of his years. He finished his studies in the above mentioned institution about the year 1843, then returned to the state of his birth, and for a calling began following in his father's footsteps, and his career as an agriculturist has been marked by substantial returns. In 1854 he purchased the old home place, which at that time was very much run down and depreciated in every way, but he immediately repaired the residence, graded the lawn, set out shade trees and began the fertilizing and cultivation of his land, and by other means also greatly improved it. Here he has since made his home, and here, with true Southern hospitality, he delights to gather about him his numerous friends, his duties as a host being discharged with grace, cordiality and tact. His plantation of seven hundred and fifty acres near Church Hill is a valuable one, and this with his home plantation makes some of the most desirable property in the county. Although he has never been prominently identified with political affairs and has never been an office seeker, his numerous friends and admirers elected him a member of the board of supervisors and he took his seat as a member of that body in 1880. Here his desire for the progress and welfare of the county was made manifest, and his sound views on all matters, his pleasant and convincing manner of expressing his views, soon brought him into prominence, and during the ten consecutive years that he served as a supervisor, four terms were spent in the capacity of president. He made a beau ideal public servant, efficient, punctual, industrious, honest and uniformly courteous to all with whom he came in contact. He was married at Church Hill on the 31st of May, 1849, to Miss Martha Y. Payne, her father, James Payne, being one of the early and successful planters of Jefferson county, and the state. He was a very prosperous merchant for a number of years also, becoming widely known as an efficient, trustworthy and successful man of business. Mrs. Baker was born and reared at Church Hill, but received her education in an excellent institution in Natchez. After a married life of about nineteen years Mrs. Baker was called from life, leaving, besides her husband, a family of ten children—six sons and four daughters—the eldest of whom was fifteen years of age and the youngest about one year old. From that time forward Mr. Baker was both father and mother to his children and successfully reared all to mature years. Their names are as follows: Thomas, who died in 1882, leaving a widow and one child; Frank; Jane; J. Holmes, a rising young lawyer of Indianola; Ida M.; Edgar W., a merchant of Greenville, Miss.; Everard G., who died in 1885; Robert, a planter of Louisiana; Cora, wife of James Lee of Sunflower county, Miss., and Alice. Mrs. Baker was an earnest member of the Episcopal church, Mr. Baker also adhering to that faith. His home is a most comfortable and cheery one and he is devoted to his children, entering into all their schemes and plans with heartiness, encouragement and good will. His single daughters keep house for him, and their home is considered a most hospitable one.

J. Holmes Baker. As a leading citizen of Indianola, in its professional, business and social life, lending eminent strength to her bar, tone to her finance and grace to her society, Mr. Baker commands attention from the historian who would wish to do this city justice. He is one of the ablest of attorneys, and has few peers in his comprehensive knowledge of state and international law, and has conducted many cases to a successful issue. He was born at Church Hill, Jefferson county, Miss., October 4, 1855, his father, Thomas F. Baker, whose sketch appears in this volume, being born in Jefferson county also. J. Holmes Baker was given better advantages than the average boy, and besides attending a private school at Church Hill, supplemented this with a few terms in Jefferson college, where he was an exemplary and painstaking student. After completing his studies, he engaged in teaching school, and for some six years successfully followed this calling in Church Hill, where he built up an excellent reputation as an instructor and disciplinarian. While teaching school, he commenced the study of law, under the able instruction of Judge Shields and Judge Thomas Reid, and in the town of Fayette was admitted to the bar, by Judge Chrissman, in the month of May, 1879. Soon after this he came to Sunflower county, and opened an office at Johnsonville, which was then the county seat, being associated with Thomas H. Torrey, a former resident of Fayette, Jefferson county, Miss. When the county seat was changed from

Johnsonville to Indianola, Mr. Baker also came here to reside, his partner, Mr. Torrey, having died in 1881. The present firm of Orrick & Baker was established in 1890, and is now considered one of the leading and successful firms of the city. Mr. Baker has taken quite an active part in local politics, and has held several official positions of honor and trust. In 1879 he was appointed superintendent of public instruction, and served in that capacity until he resigned the office in 1886. He was then elected to the office of county treasurer, and discharged the duties of this responsible position for two terms in a most efficient and satisfactory manner. His office was a model of order, and in every department the most perfect arrangement was manifested, showing the workings of a well-directed mind. He has served as a delegate to county, congressional and state conventions, and has at all times been true and loyal to public trusts, and has recently received the nomination of his party as state senator of his district. He has achieved an enviable reputation, and has fully gained the confidence of the people. He was married in Madison county, in October, 1882, to a most estimable lady, and has an interesting family of three daughters, the eldest of whom is eight years old. Mr. and Mrs. Baker are members of the Episcopal church, and the former is a Royal Arch Mason. He is one of the public-spirited men of the county, is a man of exemplary habits and sterling character, and is a social and agreeable gentleman to meet.

W. J. Baker is a Madison county Mississipian, born on the 20th of January, 1845, the third of nine children of S. S. and Eliza (Austin) Baker, the former a native of Tennessee and the latter of Mississippi. S. S. Baker became a resident of Mississippi in 1838, settling in Madison county, where he became the owner of considerable land. Although he studied medicine at one time he never practiced, preferring to devote his attention to planting, for which he seemed to have a natural aptitude. His great-grandfather was a native of Ireland, and his wife's people were early settlers of South Carolina. W. J. Baker's opportunities for acquiring an education were not of the best in his youth, but he succeeded in obtaining a fair education by applying himself to his books at home. At the age of sixteen years he became a member of a company in the Twelfth Mississippi militia, but afterward enlisted in Ward's artillery, and saw service in Virginia, taking part in the battles of Broad Run, Spottsylvania courthouse, Wilderness, Cold Harbor and the engagements in and around Richmond. Immediately after the surrender he returned to his home and the same year raised a crop. In 1871 he went to Texas, but after farming there with his brother for one year he returned to his home in Mississippi. He is now the owner of one thousand three hundred acres of land, about eight hundred acres of which are open land and three hundred acres in pasture. Mr. Baker raises cattle for the market, also a few Jerseys and keeps about seventy-five head of common stock. He raises about a dozen horses and mule colts each year and finds it very profitable. He has also found sheepraising profitable, but has not been engaged in it extensively. He has three hundred and fifty acres of fine timber land, and on the cultivated portion of his land he annually raises about one hundred bales of cotton and seven thousand bushels of corn. He is a hard worker, and although he practices economy he is not at all niggardly. He was married in 1872 to Miss Almyra Adkins, a native of Mississippi, by whom he has eight children, seven of whom are living: Inez, Eleanor, Willie, Joseph, Anna, Thomas and an infant. Mr. Baker and his wife are members of the Methodist Episcopal church, and socially he is a member of the A. F. & A. M. and the K. of H.

W. R. Baker, Clifton Baker and E. R. Baker, comprising the firm of Baker Brothers, prominent planters and stockbreeders of Grenada county, Miss., are the sons of Jesse R. Baker, who was born in Georgia in 1810. The father was an early settler of what is now Grenada county, coming to his present location in 1835, and becoming not only a wealthy and influential planter but an esteemed and highly respected citizen. He opened up a large tract of land, and added to this, as he could, until at one time he was the owner of four thousand acres in this and adjoining counties, with two thousand five hundred in the home place where the Baker Brothers are engaged in stockfarming. Although a democrat, and well posted on the current topics of public interest, Mr. Baker took no active part in politics, but pursued the even tenor of his way, preferring to look after the interests of his mammoth estate. He was a member of the Primitive Baptist church, and took considerable interest in the progress and development of the same. He moved to Montgomery county in 1876, and there his death occurred in May, 1886. He was single when he first came to Mississippi, and was married to Miss Martha Talbert in 1839, a native of one of the Carolinas, who came with her parents to Tennessee when a child, but moved to Mississippi soon after. She was the eldest daughter of Pinckney Talbert, who was at one time a prominent and well-to-do planter of Yalobusha county. To Mr. and Mrs. Baker were born fourteen children, seven of whom are living, and named in the order of their births as follows: Andrew Jackson, resides in Tom Green county, Tex., and is there engaged in the hardware business. He is the present legislative representative from the county where he resides. He was educated at Oxford, Miss., but while attending that institution the war broke out and he entered the Confederate army in the company known as the University Grays, with whom he served until the close. He was made captain of the regiment, but was taken prisoner and held at Fort Delaware until after the surrender. He was also wounded while in service. Returning from the war to Montgomery county, Miss., he embarked in merchandising, which he carried on very successfully for a number of years. In 1876 he was elected to represent that county in the legislature, and after this took up the study of law, being admitted to the Mississippi bar. From there he went to Lafayette county, practiced law at Oxford, and in 1882 was elected representative of that county. Two years later he removed to the Lone Star state where he now resides. He is a very prominent man in politics, and is one of the leading citizens where he resides. The next child in order of birth is Mrs. A. H. Gatis, who is now a resident of Memphis, Tenn. W. R. Baker, senior member of the firm, was schooled in Oxford, also, and afterward settled on the home place, where he still resides. He was first married to Miss Idella McElrath in 1880, daughter of Frank McElrath, a prominent planter of what is now Grenada county. One child, Virgil T., was born to this union. After the death of his wife Mr. Baker married Miss Fannie L. Calhoun, of Tallahatchie county, Miss., in 1890, and daughter of William Calhoun, who was a successful planter and ex-sheriff of the county. Mr. Baker is a prominent man of the county, and at present is a member of the board of supervisors. Clifton Baker, also a member of the firm, graduated in the literary department of the university of Mississippi at Oxford in 1881, and was admitted to the practice of law in 1883. For a year he was engaged in merchandising at Cleveland, Miss., and resides there now, but is actively engaged in the practice of his profession. He was appointed mayor of Cleveland by Governor Stone in 1891, to fill an unexpired term, and was elected April 1 to the same office. Jefferson D. Baker resides at Duck Hill, Miss., and there follows the occupation of a planter. He received his schooling at Lexington, Ky., taking a commercial course, and was married to Miss Mabel Allen, of Holmes county, in 1888. Fannie L. Baker resides at Duck Hill with her brother, and is a highly accomplished young lady, graduating from the female college of Oxford, Miss., in the literary and classical course in 1882. Eppie R., the youngest member of the firm of Baker Brothers, secured a good literary education at Oxford, and resided in Montgomery county with his parents until in December, 1890, when he came to the old place. He was married to Miss Lula Holman, of Carroll county, 1889, and daughter of A. J. Holman (who died in January, 1891, at the age of fifty years, and who was a substantial and successful planter). She was one of a family of four children, and was educated at Winona, Duck Hill and Carrollton. To Mr. and Mrs. Baker has been born one child, Gertrude. Mrs. Baker is a member of the Baptist church, and Mr. Baker is a member of Grenada lodge, Knights of Honor, No. 983. The Baker Brothers are all democrats in politics, and W. R. is a member of the Knights of Pythias, Ivanhoe lodge No. 8, Grenada, Miss. The brothers are extensively engaged in planting and stockraising, and are progressive and thoroughgoing business men. The mother of these children is still living in Montgomery county, and is sixty-seven years of age.

John A. Ballard, farmer and merchant of Ballardsville, Itawamba county, Miss., was born in South Carolina April 14, 1827, a son of Thomas C. and Rebecca (Grimes) Ballard, both of whom were natives of Virginia. The mother was a member of the Baptist church, and the father in every way favored and supported it. They had five children born to them: Andrew J., Thomas C., William, Susan, and John A., above mentioned, who is the only one in the family now living, and who was the second in order of birth. He came to Mississippi when young, and located in Itawamba county. His education was begun in South Carolina, and was finished here in the common schools. January 3, 1849, he married Jane E. Sandlin, who was born April 7, 1827, in South Carolina, a daughter of James and Elizabeth (Gregory) Sandlin, and the third in their family of ten children: Mary, Alfred, Jackson, Jessie (deceased), Green (deceased), Thomas (deceased), Sarah (deceased), John R. (deceased), Sisley (deceased) and Jane E. To Mr. and Mrs. Ballard were born fourteen children: Thomas C. married Sallie E. Cooper; Andrew J. married Anna Cason; William D. married Ida Bowlin; James M. married Addie Jones; David S. married Trannie Keyes; George W. married Ada Francis; Finis E. married Della Lanford; Joseph B.; Elijah F.; Rebecca became the wife of W. F. Watson; Mary married W. A. Williams; Marcia V. married J. H. Pearce; Eva J.; John A., Jr. (deceased), married Maggie Francis. Mr. Ballard enlisted, in 1862, in Captain Boulden's company, and served in a Mississippi regiment under General Goulston for a time, later serving under Major Ham in the campaign through northern Mississippi. Late in 1863 he hired a substitute and returned home. Afterward, when the law was passed prohibiting the employment of substitutes, he again took the field in the fall of 1864, and served under General Goulston in General Forrest's command until the close of the war. He and his wife are members of the Missionary Baptist church, and his children are either members or attendants of the same. Politically he is a democrat. He has lived on his present plantation since 1850, and may be fairly regarded as one of the pioneers of the county. He began merchandising in 1871, and carries a large stock of goods adapted to the needs of the community, having the only store at Ballardsville. He is the owner of about twenty-five hundred acres of land, and has on his place a steam cottongin and sawmill. These statements may be taken as some indication of the fact that he ranks among the wealthy men of the county, and it may be also added to his credit that he has been the architect of his own fortunes, his large possessions having been gained through his own unaided efforts. While he has been accumulating for himself, he has not been unmindful of the needs of others, and has ever been liberal in his contributions to all causes tending to the general good. He is a master Mason.

John E. Barbee is a most honorable and upright gentleman, and the fine plantation and cozy home of which he is now the owner has been earned by his own endeavors. He was born in Marshall county, Miss., February 5, 1849, the eldest of three children born to Thomas N. and Susan (Morgan) Barbee, natives of Alabama. When still a youth the father came to

Mississippi and began planting in Marshall county, but about 1850 settled in Coahoma county, where he spent the rest of his days. In 1862 he enlisted in the Confederate army, serving until 1864, when he was assassinated by two men. His parents were Elijah and Menika (Poe) Barbee, natives of Alabama, the former a minister of the Baptist church. The maternal grandparents were William and Margaret (Nelson) Morgan, of Alabama. John E. Barbee was reared in Coahoma county, and owing to the early death of his father and from the fact that he was compelled to care for his mother and sisters, he acquired very little early education, his knowledge of matters and things being acquired from practical experience. He began life for himself with eighty acres of land, but is now the owner of five hundred and twenty-six acres, four hundred acres of which he has put under cultivation and improved since 1876. He is a plain, but substantial and useful citizen, and, although disinclined to make a show or display, gives generously of his means in the support of worthy enterprises, so far as his means will allow. He has always been very energetic and industrious, and although his literary education has been neglected, his practical views and excellent natural judgment and sense have won the respect of all who know him. He is spoken of in the highest terms by his neighbors and friends, and fully merits the approval of all. He was first married in 1874 to Miss Fannie Franklin, a native of Georgia and a daughter of Edmund and Lucinda (Spear) Franklin, also natives of Georgia. He was left a widower, in 1877, with one child to care for, Thomas N. In 1879 he married Miss Mary Barbee, of this state, daughter of Joseph and Mary (Moore) Barbee, who were also born in this state. This wife died in 1884, having borne him three children: John C., Letha C. and Robert. He married his present wife, who was formerly Miss Viola Stovall, in 1884. She was born in Alabama, of which state her parents, Robert and Josephine (Coopwood) Stovall, were also natives, and has borne her husband two children: Fannie O. and Walter E. Mr. Barbee erected him a comfortable and pleasant home in 1877, and being an earnest and devoted member of the Christian church he is very much interested in the religious as well as literary training of his children, and is admirably aided by a faithful Christian wife, who is a true helpmate to him.

J. H. Barber, fourth child in a family of seven, was born in Twiggs county, Ga., August 29, 1823. He is the son of J. H. Barber, Sr., and Mary Ann Barber, nee Collins, natives of North Carolina, born respectively in 1785 and 1787. The father, one of the pioneers of Mississippi, settled first in Wayne county and later in Clarke county. He died April 27, 1857, his wife following him in 1859. Mr. Barber is of French and English extraction. His brothers and sisters respectively, were: Cassie, John C., Isaac and Seaborne, Jr., the last named living in Texas. Mr. Barber's early advantages for receiving an education were meager, but his natural disposition to advance manifested itself, and spurred him on in the acquisition of much useful knowledge. In 1844 he began work on his own account, having nothing to start with but his indomitable energy. He was married in 1844 to Miss Ann Boykin, of Simpson county, Miss., but a resident of Clarke county. She was a daughter of James Boykin, a farmer of Clarke county. They have had twelve children: William B., Caroline, Mary A., James, Thomas, Sarah E., Isaac Newton, Josephine, Abel, John W., Samuel E. and Henry W. All survive except Caroline and James. William B. married a Miss Martha McCleod; Thomas, a Miss Nannie Moon; Sarah married a Mr. R. U. Lyon; Josephine, a Mr. B. A. Weeks; Abel, a Miss Fannie Ryan; John married a Miss Mattie Harris; while Samuel is a commercial traveler representing a St. Louis house. He is now preparing himself for the practice of medicine; Henry W. is preparing himself for the profession of dentistry, and Thomas is a physican, residing in Meridian, Miss. John and Abel are both merchants, the former in Ruston, La., the latter in Durant, Miss. Mr. Barber is a mechanic, and did much beneficial service for his country during the late war. He owns seven hundred and twenty acres of land, valued at several thousand dollars, four and one-half miles northwest of Shubuta, which is heavily timbered with oak, pine and hickory. He grows great quantities of corn, cotton, potatoes, etc. He uses home compost, as he is not partial to commercial fertilizers. He has held many minor positions of importance; is a member of the Masonic order, and a stanch democrat. He is a Methodist of over forty years' standing, as is also his wife, while almost all of his children have embraced the same faith.

A planter and mill owner of Clarke county, William B. Barber, was born in this county in 1845, a son of J. H. Barber. Such education as he had was acquired in the public schools while he was yet quite young. He enlisted in company F, of Parren's regiment of Mississippi cavalry, and served through the Georgia campaign. He was in action in the battles at Atlanta, Kingston and numerous other points. About 1867 he engaged in farming where he now lives, on Shubuta creek, about one mile north of Shubuta. His mill business was established in 1879. He has been successful as a planter, and owns about one thousand acres of land. His mill has a capacity for cutting about ten thousand feet of lumber and ginning about seven bales of cotton per day. He has about two hundred acres of land under cultivation. A portion of his land is well timbered with a fine variety of hard woods. In 1867 he married Miss Martha J. McCleod, a daughter of R. J. McCleod, of De Soto, Clarke county, who was born in 1847. Mr. and Mrs. Barber have had born to them the following children: Frank, Edna, Mary, Henry, Dora and John. Of these none are living. He has reared the following: Ira W., William E., Thomas, Edwin, Mattie and Clara B. Mr. Barber is a Mason. He is a life-long democrat, and is a supporter of the means and measures of that party. He is interested in schools and churches, and he is a contributor toward all worthy objects calculated to benefit the public. He and his family are members of the Methodist Episcopal church.

John D. Barefield, Spinks, Kemper county, Miss. John D. Barefield, a planter of Kemper county, Miss., was born in the county in which he resides in 1858, and is a son of James and Nancy J. (Terry) Barefield. The father was a son of David and Eliza (Barnes) Barefield, natives of Georgia, and during his childhood came with his parents from Georgia, which was also his native state. David Barefield was a son of James Barefield, who was an early settler of Noxubee county, Miss. Both the grandfather and the great-grandfather died in Mississippi, and they reared large families who were universally respected. The grandmother of our subject died in Texas at the age of eighty-four years. James Barefield spent his early life in this county, and was married in 1856. His wife was a daughter of Gideon and Celia A. (Pretly) Terry. They reared a family of three children: James G., Eliza, and John D., the subject of this sketch. The father died in the Civil war, in which he served three years. He was a prosperous planter, and a man who was esteemed by all who knew him. Mrs. Barefield was married a second time, being united to W. C. Brack. Three children were born of this union: William C., Ella and Benjamin F. The mother still survives and resides in this county. She and her first husband were members of the Baptist church. James T. Barefield, a brother of John D., is also a resident of Kemper county. He married Miss Maggie Daws, and to them were born five children: Lulu, James W., Minnie, Rosa, and an infant not yet named. He is a planter by occupation and in good circumstances. John D. was reared to the life of a planter, and was educated in his native county. At the age of nineteen years he started out to meet the responsibilities of life on his own account. In the fall of 1882 he was married to Miss Bettie Edwards, a daughter of Zeno and Bettie

(Spinks) Edwards. Mrs. Barefield was born in Clarke county, but was brought to Kemper county at the age of two years; her mother had died when she was but five months of age. Three children have been born to Mr. Barefield and wife: Terry E., Lela and Janie. The mother is a member of the Missionary Baptist church. Mr. Barefield affiliates with the democratic party, and is actively interested in all the efforts that are being made in behalf of the new South. He belongs to the Masonic fraternity. He has been prosperous in business, and owns two hundred and eighty acres of land, a greater portion of which is under cultivation.

One of the most prominent planters of Grenada county, and one of its very early settlers, is Col. H. H. Barksdale, who was born in Lauderdale county, near Florence, Ala., in 1852, and was the son of Alexander Barksdale, who was born in Halifax county, Va., in 1798. The father was reared in that county, and in August, 1823, he was married in Lauderdale county, Ala., to Miss Mary S. Scruggs, who was also a native of the Old Dominion, born in Cumberland county in 1794. She was reared in Tennessee, and came by wagon to Mississippi with her husband, where they resided the remainder of their days, the father dying in what was then Yalobusha county, on the 2d of October, 1850, and the mother in April, 1881. Their property, near the present residence of their son, Col. H. H. Barksdale, is still owned by that gentleman. He was the second in order of birth of the children born to his parents, and was reared in Mississippi, attending the neighborhood schools, where he secured a good practical education. After the death of his father he assumed charge of the home place. In 1862 he served for a time in a company of state troops and then formed a regiment in the vicinity of the home place (Third Mississippi cavalry), of which he was made colonel, succeeding James Barksdale, who was for a time lieutenant-colonel of the regiment, but afterward was made colonel of a Georgia regiment. Colonel Barksdale participated in the following battles: Collierville, Jackson, Harrisburg, Atlanta, and was in the fight from Pollard to Pensacola, Ala., where his regiment put the Union soldiers to flight. He was also in the battles of Jonesboro, Peach Tree creek, where he lost nearly all his men, and was in a number of severe skirmishes. After the war Colonel Barksdale returned to his planting interests and soon became very wealthy. He owns seven thousand acres in the home tract, and is one of the most extensive planters in the county. With care and perseverance he has attended to his adopted vocation, and with energy and thoroughness his successful results have been reaped until now he is in possession of a competency fully sufficient to warrant him in passing the remainder of his days in peace and plenty. In 1853 he was married to Miss Sallie Aldridge, and, in the house where he is now living, she was born in 1833. Her parents, Lewis and Louisa (Collins) Aldridge, were natives of Alabama, born in 1800 and 1805 respectively, and in that state they were reared and married. Mr. Aldridge and wife moved to Mississippi in 1835, located in Choctaw county, where they continued to reside until 1845, and then moved to the present property of Colonel Barksdale, which was then unbroken and unimproved. Here they reared their family and cleared a large tract of land. Both were very highly respected. The father was a member of the Baptist church, and in 1846 was elected and ordained a deacon of the same. He always stood on the higher plane of Christian life, and exhibited, in a large degree, in his intercourse with others, the spirit of Christ, exerting an influence in all the circles in which he moved that commended to all the religion of the gospel. His death occurred in 1863, and when the time came he quietly laid down his armor and went to receive the reward of a well-spent life. His name still lives among the people, and the recollection of his many virtues will always form a potent stimulus in the pursuit of things pure and holy. His wife was also a very active member in that church, and was an earnest Christian in the truest sense of the term. Her death occurred in 1874. To their marriage were born ten children, nine of whom lived to be grown, and four daughters are yet living, Mrs. Mary Corley, now in Texas, Mrs. Barksdale, Mrs. Margaret O'Neil, of Texas, and Mrs. Susan Collins, also of the Lone Star state. Those deceased were: F. M. Aldridge, a prominent attorney of Coffeeville, who was killed in the battle of Shiloh, and at the time of his death was lieutenant-colonel of a regiment. He left a wife and three children: George W. died in 1864, leaving a wife and three children in Grenada. William H. was a soldier in the civil war, and afterward followed planting in Grenada county until his death in 1881. He left four children: Mrs. Martha Minter died in Grenada; Lewis was killed in the battle of Salem, Miss., in 1862. Mrs. Colonel Barksdale was educated in Grenada, also in the Judson institute at Marion, Ala., and is a highly accomplished lady. She is a member of the Baptist church, and is prominent in every good word and work, both she and the Colonel being liberal supporters of the church. The latter adheres strictly to the democratic party in his political principles. He is a very extensive planter, and besides the seven thousand acres of the home place, which is under cultivation, he is the owner of considerable more land.

Dr. Warren F. Barksdale, physician, merchant and planter at Hardy station, Miss., was originally from Alabama, born December 31, 1829, and his parents, Alexander and Mary S. (Scruggs) Barksdale, were natives of the Old Dominion, the father born in Halifax county in 1802. After growing up, the latter went to Tennessee, was there married and soon after moved to Alabama, where he located near Florence, Lauderdale county. He there followed agricultural pursuits until 1835, when he moved with his family by wagon to Mississippi and settled in Yalobusha county. He purchased land within a few miles of Grenada, and, although he started with limited means, he was thoroughgoing, industrious and persevering, and at the time of his death, in 1850, was worth about $25,000 in land and slaves. He was a stanch democrat, and although he took considerable interest in politics he never aspired to office. Both he and Mrs. Barksdale were honored members of the Methodist church and he was a class leader and one of its most liberal supporters. Socially he was a member of the Masonic fraternity. Mrs. Barksdale was a very earnest and devoted Christian, and was known far and wide for her hospitality and generosity. She was ever ready to assist those in trouble. She was born in 1796 and died in 1886. Of the eight children born to the above-mentioned union only one besides the subject of this sketch is now living, Col. H. H. Barksdale. Those deceased were: Alexander H., in the Confederate service and killed at the battle of Murfreesboro; William R., a graduate of Oxford university, both from the literary and law department, and a prominent lawyer of Grenada, (he served as district attorney for several years and was a member of the legislature at the time of his death in 1875. He left a widow and two children. He was a sharp, shrewd and very brilliant lawyer. His widow is now the wife of a Mr. George, of Meridian, Miss.; Narcissa married Rev. J. N. Temple, of Kentucky, and died in Columbia, Tenn., in 1866, leaving a husband and four daughters to mourn her death; John A. was born in the Choctaw country of Mississippi and was called "Choc" for short (he was in the Confederate army, was adjutant in B. T. Humphrey's brigade and was killed at Spottsylvania courthouse, Va;) Finch was the second child in order of birth and died in Yalobusha county in 1845, at the age of eighteen years. Dr. Warren F. Barksdale was reared in Mississippi, having arrived in that state with his parents when but five years of age, and was educated in Mississippi and Kentucky. He attended school at Georgetown, Ky., and then entered the medical department of Louisville university, from which he graduated in 1855. After this he commenced practicing at the old home place and in 1860 came to Hardy station, where he has continued his profession since. In connection with this he is also engaged quite extensively in planting and also runs a general supply store. Dr. Barksdale is a prominent physician and has a large and paying practice. He possesses a mind clear, penetrating and comprehensive, is thoroughly posted in his profession and is a practitioner of decided talent. He was married, first to Miss Mellie D. Crowder, a native of Mississippi and the daughter of R. D. Crowder, who was one of the very wealthy planters of the vicinity of Grenada. Mrs. Barksdale died in 1868 at the age of thirty years, leaving four children, all now living: Stella, a graduate of the school at Memphis, Tenn., is regarded as one of the foremost young ladies of the state (she is first assistant of the Coffeeville institute, Mississippi); Mary, now Mrs. Conway, was also a graduate of the school at Memphis, Tenn., and now makes her home at Paris, Tenn.; John N. is a leading attorney at Grenada, and is a member of the law firm of Longstreet & Barksdale; Annie Z. graduated from the school in Grenada, and is the wife of F. P. Collins, merchant of Hardy station. The mother of these children was a member of the Baptist church. Dr. Barksdale's second marriage was to Miss Jennie McLaughlin, of Grenada county, and the daughter of Laughlin McLaughlin, a native of Scotland. One child, Minnie, is the result of this union. She is at home at present and is a graduate of the Grenada school. She also attended school at Nashville. Her mother died in 1869 at the age of twenty-five years. The Doctor's third marriage was to his present wife, Miss Nannie Gattis, of Yalobusha county, and daughter of Allen Gattis, a successful planter of the county. To this union have been born six children, three of whom are living at the present time: Jennie Warren, now attending the Memphis school; J. Fountain and Lulu G. Those deceased were: Maggie, who died at the age of two years; William R. died also at the age of five years, and Ethel at the age of two years. The Doctor takes no very active part in politics more than to vote and keep himself posted on all the leading topics of the day. He is the owner of four or five thousand acres of land, with about one-fourth under cultivation, and handles about four hundred bales of cotton yearly. He was one of the first settlers of Hardy station. The Doctor was reared in the Methodist faith, and, although not a member, believes in the Christian religion. Mrs. Barksdale is a member of the Baptist church.

George Washington Barlow, a planter, whose postoffice address is Crystal Springs, Copiah county, Miss., was born in Rankin county, in 1848, a son of Green and Mary Barlow. His father, who was a native of Mississippi, was a life-long planter, and married Mary Byrd, a daughter of George and Susan Byrd, who were both born in South Carolina, but removed at an early date to Mississippi. While living in Simpson county, Green Barlow served on the police board. He bought land in Copiah county, and took up his residence there in 1866. These worthy people had nine children, the following of whom are living, six in all: Susan, wife of Thomas Gatling, of Rankin county; John, of Simpson county; Rachel, wife of Hezekiah Moran, of Copiah county (deceased); Willey G., Copiah county, and Francis of the same county. At the age of nineteen years Mr. Barlow began life for himself on the plantation on which he now resides. During the Civil war he was for ten months in the Confederate service, but took part in no general engagements. He is a member of the Farmers' Alliance and one of the model farmers of the state, having taken premiums as the best farmer in the county. It is no uncommon thing for him to produce fifty bushels of corn per acre on land which a few years ago did not produce more than fifteen bushels per acre. In 1867 he married Sarah Murray, a daughter of Jefferson and Margaret Murray, of Simpson county, who has borne him four children: Maggie, wife of William Burt, of Copiah county; Hattie, who lives at home; Dora, wife of John Slay, of Copiah county, and Luther, who lives at home also. Mr. and Mrs. Barlow are members of the Baptist church. Mr. Barlow is short and heavy set, with closely cut beard and dark hair and eyes. He is a whole-souled and genial man, and is well known to the best citizens of this and adjoining counties. His plantation is one of the most productive and best appointed in this part of the state.

The humanizing influences of Christianity are shown in thousands of directions, but in none to a more marked degree than that of medical and surgical science. Sharkey county, Miss., has many accomplished physicians, and among these is Dr. William H. Barnard, who, besides devoting his attention to healing the sick, is also engaged in planting and fruit-growing. He was born and reared on the place on which he is now residing, his parents, Joseph L. and Mary (Robb) Barnard, having been born in Adams county, Miss., the former in 1823. He afterward settled in Sharkey county, coming to the Deer creek valley with Colonel Barnard about the year 1846, and became the owner of a fine plantation, on which he died, in 1853. His wife, whose birth occurred in 1825 or 1826, was the daughter of George F. Robb, merchant and planter of Adams county at the time of her birth, later moving to Kentucky, where he followed the same business and resided until his death. He was the father of four sons and one daughter, of which family three sons are still living, and are residents of Kentucky. The daughter, Mrs. Barnard, was reared and educated in Adams county, Miss., and died in 1870. She was an earnest Christian, and for many years was a worthy member of the Methodist church, in which faith she died. She bore Mr. Barnard two sons and one daughter: Dr. William H.; Mary, who died at the age of thirteen years; Joseph L., who died in 1889, at the age of thirty-seven years, leaving a widow, one son and three daughters to mourn his loss, the names of his children being: Joseph, Tock, Ida H. and Annie. The mother of these children was Miss Ellen Watson, and she now resides near Rolling Fork. After the death of Joseph L. Barnard, his widow married again, her second husband being N. B. Brown, and her third husband William Dupree. Dr. William H. Barnard attained manhood on the place on which his father settled on coming to this county, and obtained his education in Oakland college, of Claiborne county. He afterward entered the Hospital medical college, of Louisville, Ky., from which institution he was graduated as an M. D. in 1878, upon which he returned to Anguilla, and entered upon the practice of his profession, his efforts as a practitioner of the healing art meeting with good success. He is the owner of a good plantation of seven hundred and twenty acres, of which about five hundred acres are under cultivation. On this admirable plantation he has at least six thousand bearing fruit trees, and everything about his plantation shows that a man of intelligence, energy and thrift is at the helm. He was married to Miss Ida C. Creath, a daughter of D. Creath, but was called upon to mourn her death in 1881, she being at that time only twenty years of age. The Doctor is a member of Rolling Fork lodge No. 356, of the A. F. & A. M., and by his numerous friends is considered a genial, whole-souled gentleman, and strictly straightforward and upright in all his business transactions. He is very fond of field sports, and is considered one of the best shots in the county. He owns a fine dog, a pointer, called Don, white and tan in color, of whom the *Commercial Herald*, of Vicksburg, speaks in the following language: "The other illustrious dog that adorns the world with his living presence is a pointer in Sharkey county, that brings in all the fuel for his mistress' kitchen, and when the stock is being fed, will take corn, ear by ear, and put it in the mangers."

Col. William T. Barnard. The pioneer settler of the Barnard family in America was Joseph Barnard, who was born, reared and married in England, and at a very early day came to the territory of Mississippi, in company with the Lippincotts, Elliotts and Dunbars and made a home for himself and family in the wilds of what is now Adams county. He became prominently identified with the progress and development of the section which he had chosen for his home, and proved that he was a man eminently fitted for the life of a pioneer, for he was hardy, courageous, energetic, enterprising and honest. He was president of the board of managers of his district for a number of years, and unfortunately, when just in the prime of life, was called from earth. His widow afterward married again, but bore her second husband no family, only surviving Mr. Barnard a few years. Their family consisted of three sons and one daughter: Lucy, who became the wife of William Ship, settled in Adams county and lived to be extremely old; Joseph died in Adams county in 1830, having been a soldier in the War of 1812; Thomas settled in Adams county, where he died about 1845, and William, the father of the immediate subject of this sketch, all of whom married and reared families. The birth of the latter occurred in Adams county about 1784–5, and after the death of his father, Joseph Dunbar was made guardian of himself, his brothers and sister. Upon reaching manhood he was married to Miss Barbara, daughter of Thomas Foster, one of the very early settlers of Adams county, he and his wife being natives of Virginia and very wealthy. Two of his brothers also became large real estate holders around Natchez, but another brother, John, became a wealthy citizen of Texas. Mrs. Barnard was born in Adams county in October, 1800, her birth occurring on St. Catherine creek, within three miles of where her husband was born. She was reared and educated near Natchez, being one of a family of twelve or thirteen children, that lived to be grown and became the heads of families. At the time of her death she was eighty-five years of age. Her union with Mr. Barnard resulted in the birth of seven children, three of whom—one son and two daughters— died in early childhood: Louisa dying when a young lady just after leaving college, and Joseph L. and Henry C., who died in early manhood, leaving families. William T. is the only one of the family now living. The father of these children became colonel of a volunteer regiment in Adams county during the war of 1812, and was held in reserve for the battle of New Orleans. His life in Mississippi was devoted to the cultivation of the indigo plant, and, like his father before him, the materials for the clothing worn by himself and family were raised and manufactured on his own plantation. His widow was married to William R. Brooks, a native of Tennessee, by whom she became the mother of two children: George and Mary, both of whom are now deceased. Col. William T. Barnard was born in Adams county, Miss., September 10, 1821, and was reared on the home plantation in Adams county. At the age of eleven years he was sent to Oakland college in Claiborne county, and while in that institution was a classmate of Abijah Hunt, Joseph Noland, Finley Freeland and others. Upon leaving Oakland college he entered Jefferson college, and from this institution entered Yale college, but before matriculating was induced to return to his former alma mater, but left his sister Louisa in the female department, from which she afterward graduated. He reëntered Jefferson college, taking an irregular course, and upon leaving that institution was an exceptionally well-informed young man. At the age of nineteen years he was married and settled on the home place in Adams county, where he resided until 1846, when he came to his present location. He purchased a fine tract of land here at a cost of $10 per acre, but added to it from time to time until he became, prior to the war, the owner of twenty-two hundred and fifty acres of some of the finest and most fertile land along Deer creek. His first marriage was to Miss Sarah Chaney, who was born and reared in West Feliciana parish, La., near Bayou Sara, a daughter of James Chaney, an early settler of that state. She was educated at Jackson, La., but in 1849, soon after her marriage, died in this county, leaving a family of four children, three of whom lived to be grown and one dying in infancy: Sarah

Louisa is the wife of Dr. J. C. Hall; Mary J. is the deceased wife of Dr. Isaac Chaney, and William B. resides near his father. Mr. Barnard married his present wife in July, 1856, she being Mrs. T. C. Likens, nee Eudora J. Creath, who was born and reared in Vicksburg and educated in Jackson, Miss., and Columbia, Tenn. Mrs. Barnard's parents died when she was a girl, her father having been a lawyer of considerable prominence and a large land owner on Silver creek and near Haines bluff on Yazoo river. She was reared an Episcopalian, but she and Mr. Barnard are at the present time members of the Methodist Episcopal church of Anguilla. Mr. Barnard has been a prominent man in the municipal affairs of this section, and in 1850 represented Issaquena county in the state legislature, being reëlected the following term. He has since been connected with the board of supervisors of this county several years, being the first president of the board from the fourth district. Since that time he has been retired from politics, although he was at one time strongly urged to accept the nomination of senator from this district, but firmly refused to allow his name to go before the convention. He was a member of the first levee board of the Mississippi valley of which Governor Alcorn was president, representing Issaquena county. He was elected on the whig ticket to the state legislature, and during the war was a strong Union man and was very much opposed to secession, but owing to his popularity and long residence in the county he was not persecuted during the turbulent times of war, notwithstanding the fact that he honestly expressed his views. He is one of the oldest residents of the county, and has been a valuable acquisition to this section. In social life he is highly esteemed for his conversational powers and his kind and agreeable manners, and as he is free from selfishness, is ever ready to discommode himself to give comfort and pleasure to others, and is kind, generous and hospitable; he wins many friends and rarely looses them.

William B. Barnard is a prosperous planter of Sharkey county, Miss., and on the plantation of four hundred and eighty acres which he owns he raises annually one hundred and sixty-five bales of cotton. He was born in Adams county, Miss., in 1846, being the only son of Col. William T. Barnard, whose sketch appears in this work. His sisters are Sarah Louisa, wife of Dr. J. C. Hall, and Mary Jane, the deceased wife of Dr. William I. Chaney. William B. Barnard attended the schools near his home until the opening of the war, then the unsettled condition of affairs prevented him from attending longer, and in 1863 he joined the Confederate army, becoming a member of company D, Twenty-eighth Mississippi cavalry, which operated with the army of Tennessee, Armstrong's brigade and Forrest's corps. He was also with Johnston's army for a time and went with him to Atlanta, then went back to Tennessee with Hood and participated in the battles of Franklin and Nashville. He was then in Alabama for some time, and at the close of the war surrendered at Gainesville and returned home to finish his education at Pass Christian. On the 18th of December, 1868, he was married to Miss Lizzie, daughter of H. R. and Virginia O. West, natives of Kentucky and Tennessee respectively, who, after their marriage, purchased land in Vicksburg, on which they both spent the remainder of their days, the former's death occurring before the war and the latter's in 1871. Mr. West was a planter and reared a large family of children, but only two of his ten children grew to maturity: Winston, a planter of Washington county, and Mrs. Barnard. The latter was born in Vicksburg and has borne her husband three children, two of whom are living, William B., Jr., dying while attending school at Baton Rouge, in his fourteenth year. The two living are: West and Virginia Lou. These children were left motherless on the 15th of July, 1874, she having been an earnest and worthy member of the Methodist church. Since 1868 Mr. Barnard has resided on a part of the old homestead, "Mount Alvarez," at Aquilla, and is in excellent circumstances financially. His second marriage took place in April, 1877, Miss Henrie G., a daughter of Henry H. G. and Lizzie R. Stevens, natives of Warren county, becoming his wife. Mr. Barnard has always taken quite an interest in politics, and in 1883 was elected to the position of sheriff of Sharkey county, the duties of which position he discharged for two years with credit to himself and to the satisfaction of all concerned. Although he has been retired from active political life for some time, he has still the county's interests at heart, and not only by precept but by example endeavors to set a good example to the rising generation. He is progressive, industrious and of temperate habits, and his honesty and morality have never been questioned, for he has at all times endeavored to follow the teachings of the golden rule, and that he has succeeded is fully attested by the numerous and warm friends who gather about him. He and his estimable wife are earnest members of the Methodist church, and socially he is a member of Rolling Fork lodge No. 356, of the A. F. & A. M., in which order he was at one time junior warden.

Mrs. Amelia Barr is a Canadian by birth, born December 3, 1826, the seventh child born to Abel Bigelow and Amelia Tilton, the former being a native of Massachusetts, and the latter of New Hampshire, their ancestors being also New Englanders. The father was a merchant, and, after residing in Canada for some time, returned to the states in 1834 and settled in New York, where he engaged in farming until his death in 1867. The mother's people were also agriculturists. Her father was a soldier in the war of 1812, holding the rank of colonel. In 1851 Mrs. Barr left home in New York, and came to reside with her eldest brother in Vicksburg, Miss., in which city she remained until 1861, when she moved to Bovina. She was married, July 24, 1865, to Dr. William Barr, a native of Paisley, Scotland, whose father was a naval surgeon in the British army. He was very finely educated, and was a graduate of the University of Scotland at Glasgow, his career in this institution being an exceptionally distinguished one. He was honored with several prizes for proficiency in languages and medical sciences, and received his diploma in 1839. Dr. Barr came to Warren county, Miss., where his uncle, who was a physician, resided, and immediately entered upon the practice of his profession, and during the war did considerable service as a surgeon in the Confederate army, but was not in the regular service, his practice during this time being gratuitous. During a yellow fever epidemic his practice became so arduous that his vital forces were impaired, and there was laid the foundation of a disease which resulted, five years later, in an apoplectic stroke. From that time until his death in 1890, five years later, he was a helpless invalid. In religious views he was at one time a strict Presbyterian, but he afterward embraced the Episcopal faith, and was confirmed. Her union was without issue, and she now lives with a family servant in Bovina. Her brother, David Tilton Bigelow, did a good work in the fifties, distributing books and publications throughout the state, and particularly in Warren county. He was at one time a reporter for and manager of the Vicksburg *Whig*, with which paper he was connected for five years. In 1853, when yellow fever raged in Vicksburg, he rendered valuable aid to the sick and afflicted, and his noble and untiring efforts were warmly appreciated by all. He died in 1858 from the effects of an injury which he received on board the steamer Eclipse, caused by the boiler's pipe bursting.

Prominent among the members of the legal profession of Lafayette county is Col. Hugh A. Barr, Oxford, Miss., the subject of this brief biographical notice. He was born in Abbeville, S. C., and is a son of William H. Barr, D. D.; his father was a minister in the Presbyterian church, spending his whole life in charge of one congregation; this pastorate covered a period of forty years, which was terminated by his death in 1843. Hugh A. Barr passed an uneventful youth. In 1842 he went to Mississippi, and located in Oxford, where he had a brother James, who was a lawyer; he had settled there in 1840. Mr. Barr began the study

J. W. Vick

of law with his brother, and in 1843 he was admitted to the bar; in 1845 he formed a partnership with his brother, which existed until the death of the latter in 1849. In 1851, December 9, he was united in marriage to Miss Mary E. Hodge, a native of Mississippi; she lived until 1876, when she passed to the other life, leaving one daughter, Emma, wife of R. N. Miller. His second marriage was in 1879, when he was united to Mrs. A. J. Black, nee Bowen. They are both members in high standing in the Presbyterian church. Mr. Barr affiliated in early days with the whig party, and is now a stanch adherent to the principles of the democratic party. He was a member of the constitutional convention in 1865, and takes an active interest in the topics of national importance. He has been the attorney of the Illinois Central railroad, and the lines which were formerly under another management, since the year 1865. He is careful and painstaking in his business, and has justly earned the reputation of being a safe and reliable counselor. He is devoted to his professional work, is a close student, and is one of the most successful lawyers in the state.

Albert K. Barrier, M. D., Phœnix, Miss., physician and surgeon, a leading practitioner of Yazoo county, was born in Neshoba county, Miss., December 7, 1859, and is the eldest of seven children of Forister and Frances E. (Kelly) Barrier, natives of Mississippi. The father is a planter in Yazoo county, and is a highly respected citizen. The paternal grandparents were John and Nancy Barrier, and the maternal grandfather was Albert Kelly, of Tennessee. Dr. Barrier attended the private schools of the neighborhood until he was twelve years of age, and then entered the Cooper institute of Lauderdale county, Miss., where he was a student four years. He began his medical studies at the Louisville medical college in 1882. He was there two years, but was not graduated until 1885. He then began practice in Yazoo county, and has built up a paying business. He is the leading physician of his neighborhood and has met with uniform success; he is ambitious to keep up with the discoveries of the science, and devotes a considerable time to reading in professional lines. He finds some time to give to agriculture and superintends the cultivation of eighty acres of land; he owns in all two hundred and twenty-seven acres. The Doctor was united in marriage in 1882 to Miss Maggie Z. Warren, of Mississippi, a daughter of L. B. and Fanny Z. (Mobley) Warren, also of Mississippi. They have had born to them four children: Leonidas F., Victor W., Maggie R. and Fanny M. The parents are members of the Methodist Episcopal church South. Dr. Barrier belongs to the Knights of Honor and is allied with the democratic party. He has the general welfare of the county very near at heart, and may be depended upon to use his best efforts for its growth and advancement. Although he was twenty-one years old when he first faced the responsibilities of life, and had no capital, he has won a permanent place in the county's first ranks of citizens.

William J. Barron, physician, Sturges, Oktibbeha county, Miss. Joseph and Hannah (McClanahan) Barron emigrated to Choctaw county, Miss., about 1830, from the Palmetto state, and bought land from an Indian named James Terreill. As one of the first emigrants he selected one of the finest places in his section, paying Terreill $600 for his claim and possessions here. Joseph Barron had several occupations. While living he made use of the rude utensils used by the aborigines, in constructing Terreill's remarkable and beaver-like log cabin, still standing, September, 1891. As one of the evidences of its substantial construction, about the year 1884 a cyclone swept over the premises, laying waste to all the buildings and timber, stripping from the house every shingle (or board), leaving each rafter and log as perfect as at the hour of its completion. The hewing with the common pole ax on this remarkable structure would be hard to excel in this day with the improved broad ax. Among other relics, such as stone hatchets and arrowheads, was a peculiar climbing or step ladder

22

made of poplar, one step above another, so one could climb to the housetop or run up a tree. Here, on Bogue Foliah, Joseph Barron built the first watermill among the Indians in Choctaw county. He also established a cottongin there, and packed the first bales of cotton with a crowbar; he also erected a blacksmith shop and manufactured extra fine rifle gun barrels, and made bells for his large herds of horses and cattle and the wild deer, which had also been domesticated and roamed over his fields and woodlands, covered with fine grass and cane, where the wild wolves howled their midnight revels after visiting the sheep pastures. He worked his farm at first with Indian and slave labor combined. Among the Indians thus hired were Yambee and We Yambee, who soon became insulted at the slaves, and no compromise could satisfy the Indian laborers here. Mr. Barron became quite wealthy, consisting of land, fine herds of cattle, horses and slaves or negroes. His house was headquarters for all emigrants from the East. Among the first settlers were the McClanahans, the Fondreus, the Mimses, the Snows and Childerses. The first teachers or educators were George McDuffey and James Rossey. To this union of Joseph and Hannah (McClanahan) Barron were born twelve children: John, James, Ezekiel, Mary, Nancy, Elizabeth, Solomon, Marshall, Thomas, Caleb, W. J. and R. P. Barron. Joseph Barron died in 1850 of pneumonia, his widow survived him about six years; were of Baptist faith religiously, and were of Scotch and Irish descent. James Barron married Elizabeth Childers, was a farmer and merchant, with perhaps one of the first country stores established. He died, leaving seven children. Ezekiel married Julie Griffith, raised six sons, all living. He was a soldier in the Mexican war along with the illustrious Jefferson Davis. He was afterward a merchant and farmer. His carbine breech-loading gun carried in the battles in the Mexican war is still well cared for and preserved as a relic in the family. Solomon is one of the three now living, and is in Roby, Tex., a very successful stockman, and an early emigrant to the Lone Star state. Marshall was killed by lightning while riding in company with a deputy sheriff of Madison county, near Canton and Sharon, his umbrella directing the electric current with great force through his body, while the sheriff escaped, although nearest the tree struck. Thomas R. Barron married Mary Childers. He was born a natural philosopher and mechanic, always prospered in life, died in 1857, leaving his wife and two daughters, Alice and Cornelia. Caleb and Elizabeth fell victims to that terrible scourge of dysentery which prevailed in 1852. Caleb died on his feet walking toward the door in the Indian log cabin built by James Terreill. Mary married Terry Crawford, and they also died of dysentery in 1852. John and Robert died quite young. Nancy married D. C. Snow, emigrated to Western Texas, is still living, a widow, with her only son, John Snow. Dr. William J. Barron, physician at Sturges, Miss., owes his nativity to Choctaw county, Miss. He is one of the twelve. He was also born in 1834, had very limited educational advantages, and after his parents' death he went through on horseback to Lebanon, Tenn., where he remained fifteen months at school before returning home. From there he went to New Orleans, studied medicine in the University of Louisiana, graduating in 1859. Returning to Mississippi he at once began practicing near Sturges, where he has since continued, and where he has met with great success. He is a man of strong and vigorous mind, a deep thinker, and a very entertaining conversationalist. He is the owner of several tracts of land in Choctaw and Oktibbeha counties, also in Holmes, with fine water-power and mills in Oktibbeha. However, his entire time is given to his profession and drug store at Sturges, Miss. His estimable wife, who was formerly Miss Elizabeth Edwards, is a native of Choctaw county and the daughter of James H. and Parthenia (Crawford) Edwards. Dr. and Mrs. Barron were married in 1858, and six children resulted from this union: James, W., the oldest son, was the youngest state senator in Mississippi in 1886 and 1888, and is a lawyer by profession and local attorney of the Illinois Central railroad; William Y. is a farmer in Choctaw county; O. L. is an M. D., practicing with his father at Sturges, and local surgeon for the Illinois Central railroad; Thomas E. is a farmer near Roby, Tex.; Nannie L. is the wife of Dr. D. H. Thomas, and they live on the place bought by her grandfather of James Terreill, the Indian; Mary P. lives in Sturges with her parents; Dr. W. J. Barron espoused the cause of the Confederacy in the late war between the North and South in 1861. He enlisted in company I, Fifteenth Mississippi infantry, is a member of the Masonic fraternity, lodge No. 119, of Choctaw county, lives within two miles of where he was born in 1834, and his name is a household word even among the oldest citizens. Col. William Humphries, of Columbus, Miss.; Robert McClanahan, of Cold Springs; Dr. McClanahan, of Galveston, and Dr. McClanahan of Gatesville, Tex., are all first cousins of his, and born in Mississippi among the earliest settlers.

David N. Barrows, a prominent citizen of Jackson, Miss., was born in Wareham, Plymouth county, Mass., in 1816, the second in a family of four children born to William and Lucy (Nye) Barrows, who were also natives of the Bay state, where their ancestors settled during its very earliest history. The father became one of the thrifty farmers of New England, and succeeded in acquiring a comfortable competency. He was major commanding the militia at the time of the invasion of Wareham by the British, in 1814, proving a faithful and trusty officer. The maternal grandfather, David Nye, commanded a company of minutemen at the time of the invasion of Fairhaven by the British, in the spring of 1778, and did effective service in that capacity. At the first town meeting held in Wareham concerning British oppression, in 1773, he was appointed chairman of an important committee, and in the militia company that responded to a call April 19, 1775, his name appears as a private. March 8, 1779, he was appointed by the town on another important committee, and later was the first representative sent by Wareham to the general court (legislature). The maternal great-grandfather of the subject of this sketch, Rev. Rowland Thatcher, was the first minister of Wareham. Rowland Thatcher, his son, was born in Wareham, March 13, 1745, and was married January 28, 1773, to Elizabeth Nye. He was a member of Capt. David Nye's company, that marched to Fairhaven. Lot Thatcher, of the same family, also served during the Revolutionary war, being a private in Capt. John Gibb's company, with whom he went to Rhode Island. David N. Barrows was educated in the common schools of his native town, and began life for himself at the age of fifteen years as a clerk in a store. In the winter of 1834 he had a violent attack of pneumonia, then called lung fever, and being confined to the house all winter, was earnestly recommended by his three physicians to seek a warmer climate and never attempt to spend another winter in that rigorous country. Accordingly he left home the 1st of October, 1835, to seek health and fortune in a strange land. Having met friends amongst strangers, he was induced to come to Mississippi, and arrived at Vicksburg the latter part of October. He mentioned his purpose to his landlord, who that evening introduced him to the owner of a large shipping and commercial house, located where the ferry crossed Big Black river, and where there was a small village called Bridgeport. He reached there by stage about 12 o'clock next day and immediately commenced business, where he continued to improve in health. In the spring Mr. I. M. White, his cousin, moved from North Carolina and went into business in Jackson, and so strongly did he urge Mr. Barrows to come there and engage in his store in charge of his books that the latter decided to do so, and reached that city on the 1st of May, 1836. He remained as bookkeeper a short time, then purchased the interest of Colonel Stone in the firm of Hall & Stone, large dry goods merchants, and changed the firm name to D. N. Barrows & Co. This business continued about two years, but, not proving profitable, it was then closed out. Mr. Barrows then had a proposition made him by an old commission house in Natchez, and in June, 1839, he left Jackson to accept the position, where he remained as bookkeeper and cashier five years. The business was then brought to a termination, and Mr. Barrows returned to Jackson, where he has since continuously resided. In 1844 he engaged in the insurance business, and is now the oldest agent in the state of Mississippi. He represents some of the best insurance companies of the world, some of which are: London & Liverpool & Globe; Home, of New York; the Phœnix, of Brooklyn; the Underwriters' Agency, of New York; the Western Assurance Company, of Toronto; the Crescent, of New Orleans; the Phœnix, of Hartford, Conn.; the Equitable Life Assurance Society, of New York, and others, making twenty-two in all. He has been very prominent in the Masonic and I. O. O. F. fraternities, having joined both orders as soon as he became of sufficient age. He was zealous and active and held many of the prominent offices in both orders. He was worshipful master of Silas Brown lodge of the A. F. & A. M. for about ten years, and was grand secretary of the grand chapter some time, but finally had to decline office on account of failing health. He was grand master of the grand lodge of the I. O. O. F. in 1847–8, and was grand representative in the grand lodge of the United States twelve years, when he declined further nomination, not having physical strength to attend the lodge meetings. In 1862 he was elected mayor of Jackson, in which capacity he served until 1868, when he was deposed by military authority for refusing to take the iron-clad oath. He was deputy Confederate treasurer of Mississippi during the war, which position he held until hostilities ceased. Since then he has been devoting his time and attention to his private pursuits. He was first married in 1845 to Miss Eleanor Langley, a native of North Carolina, who died in 1849, and in 1854 his second marriage was consummated, Miss Carrie E. Moseley, a native of Georgia, becoming his wife. To them two children have been born: Charles C., who graduated from the medical department of the University of Virginia in 1879, afterward, in 1880, graduating from the University of New York city, was house physician in Bellevue hospital in 1880–2, and is now obstetrician in the same and a large practitioner in the city, and Mary M., wife of Dr. Wirt Johnston, of Jackson, Miss., a sketch of whom appears in this work. Mr. Barrows and his family are members of the Presbyterian church, and he is one of the trustees in that church. Mr. Barrows is a fine looking and well preserved gentleman, and his kind and benevolent expression is a correct index of his character. He is one of the oldest and ablest business men of Mississippi.

Maj. A. P. Barry was born in South Carolina in 1814. There he passed his boyhood days and received his primary education. When he was about fourteen years old his father, Charles M. Barry, moved to Greene county, Ala. The latter was born in South Carolina, January 4, 1777, and was a son of Andrew Barry, who was a native of Virginia. The Barrys, who were of Scotch descent, emigrated to Virginia and settled at what is now known as Barry's bridge. Capt. Andrew Barry, the grandfather of our subject, was one of the organizers of Nazareth church, and was one of its first elders. This church was the first one in the district, and was erected in 1765. The Captain was an officer during the war of the Revolution. His son, Charles M., learned the trade of a saddlemaker, but later became a farmer. He was married October 12, 1813, to Miss Jane Davitt, a native of South Carolina, who was born October 29, 1792. They had six children, of whom Maj. A. P. Barry was the eldest and only son. The daughters were named Mary Ann, Margaret R., Elizabeth J., Martha Lucinda and Catherine. The latter and our subject are the only ones now living. She became the wife of John A. Walker and now resides in Columbia, Tenn. In 1830 Charles M. Barry removed with his family to Alabama, where he engaged in farming. He and his wife were lifelong members of the Presbyterian church. He died February 19, 1845, and his widow survived him until August 31, 1856. Maj. A. P. Barry began the study of medicine, but his health became impaired and he secured an engagement as a clerk in a store, in which he continued until he reached the age of twenty-one years. He then engaged in merchandising on his own account at Clinton, Ala., trading with more or less success for five or six years. Retiring from the mercantile life, he was in 1838 elected justice of the peace. The duties of this office, collecting and settling up estates, his farming operations, all engaged his attention for the next four years. After this he engaged in the cotton commission business in Mobile, though he retained his residence in Greene county. This enterprise he continued for about twelve years so successfully that he amassed a snug little fortune. Thinking he was ready to retire from business and desiring a healthy location for his future residence, in 1858 he purchased a fine plantation in Copiah county, Miss., consisting of one thousand eight hundred and sixty acres, for which he paid $18,000, and he stocked it well and placed upon it about seventy negroes. For all of this property he paid cash, and he had just begun to think himself fairly well established when the war broke out. In 1860 he canvassed the county in behalf of the Bell and Everett ticket. He was opposed to secession, and in 1861, after South Carolina had seceded, a proposition was made in Mississippi to take a similar action, and a mass meeting was called of all parties, at Gallatin, to take such action as was thought best for the state. During the deliberations a resolution was offered, instructing the delegates of the state convention to vote for the immediate withdrawal of the state from the Union, regardless of the action of any other state. This was to Mr. Barry as if a bombshell had exploded in the assembly. He drew up and attempted to introduce a resolution, instructing the delegates to consult with and await the action of the sister slave states, but this resolution was tabled before its reading could be completed, and Mr. Barry withdrew from the convention with about one hundred and fifty followers. He was tendered the nomination of delegate, which, after declining, he decided to accept, knowing that he could not be elected, but desiring to oppose the plans of the Secessionists as much as possible. His action in opposing the secession movement excited great indignation in the county against him, and his life was in danger. After the state had seceded and war had begun, his interests being vested here, he directed his energies entirely to the defense of his country. His son, Charles, enlisted in the first company sent from Copiah county. He was wounded at the battle of Seven Pines, and, although unfit for duty, afterward returned to the service and was killed in the last fight at Richmond. Mr. Barry enlisted in 1863 in the army of Ten Thousand. He was sent to Columbus, Ky., to join the forces which there resisted Pope's advance into that state, after which he returned home. When General Grant landed at Port Gibson, and the foragers, or, more properly speaking, plunderers, were harassing the country, he organized an independent company of old men and boys of twelve or fifteen years of age, and drove the marauders back to the river. Realizing his position as a commander of an independent company of volunteers subjected him to death if captured, he applied to Johnson and received a captain's commission. Desiring to enter the regular service, he was tendered the office of colonel by the captains of seven companies, forming a regiment, but his wife at that time lay at the point of death and he felt that he could not leave her. While in the regular service in Kentucky he was captain of company A, in Percy's regiment, under Gen. Alcorn. During the whole period of the war he was engaged in business for the Confederate government, though he did not participate in active military service except as mentioned above. After the war he found himself obliged to begin life practically anew. He was elected to the state legislature, serv-

ing in that body in 1865–6, where he introduced a number of important bills, the most notable of which was the agricultural lien law (not the one now in existence), which provided for
the mortgaging of growing crops or crops to be grown.   He was married in 1840 to Miss Dru-
sella Harness, who was born in Alabama in 1824, and was a daughter of John S. Harness, of
York district, S. C., but for many years a resident of Clinton, Ala.   Mrs. Barry died in 1863,
leaving five children: Amanda Imogene, Charles H., Andrew Porter, William J. and Richard
E.   Of these William and Andrew are now living.   Major A. P. Barry's second marriage
took place February 15, 1866, to Miss Kate C. May, who was born in May, 1844, in
New Orleans, La.   To this union three children were born, named as follows: Mary
May, Fanny Harris and Robert Rea, the last-mentioned of whom, died August 14,
1886.   Mary and Fanny are unmarried, and are still members of their parents' household.
Of the first children, Andrew Porter is at Houston, Tex., and is a civil engineer in the employ
of the city; William J., who has a natural taste for mechanics, pursues his employment in
the railway shops at Harrison, Miss.; Amanda Imogene, married Hugh A. Kincannon, who is
now cashier in a bank in Tupelo, Miss., to whom she bore one daughter, named Imogene,
the Major's only grandchild, who is now a teacher in the Tupelo high school.   In December,
1888, Major Barry and his wife adopted Miss Florence Jones, an orphan of Natchez, who is
now about fifteen years of age.   Major Barry was made a master Mason in 1847 in the
George Washington lodge No. 24, at Clinton, Greene county, Ala.   He took the Royal Arch
degree in 1848, and the Council degree in 1850.   James B. Cherry was initiated into Washington lodge in 1846.   Thomas I. Gathright was initiated a year or two after the Major's
identification with the lodge.   Cherry became a Presbyterian preacher, and Gathright became
the founder of a school; they and our subject, a prosperous planter, then came to Mississippi.   At the semi-centennial of the grand lodge of Mississippi, Major Barry was reëlected
grand treasurer, Cherry was elected grand chaplain, and Gathright was elected grand master, thus three of the most important offices in the Grand lodge were filled by members who
were made Masons in the George Washington lodge No. 24, a comparatively insignificant
lodge, that, in its most prosperous and palmy days, could never boast of more than thirty
members.   Major Barry was first elected treasurer of the Grand lodge, A. F. & A. M., of
Mississippi, in 1866, which office he has held ever since, with the exception of a portion of
one year.   In March, 1866, he was elected treasurer of the grand chapter, a responsible
position, which he has filled to the present time.   About the same time he was elected
treasurer of the grand council, continuing in that office until the grand council was merged
into the grand chapter.   In 1889, when the council was again made a distinct organization,
he was again made grand treasurer of the grand council.   During the existence of the Home
Masonic Insurance order, Major Barry was its treasurer also.   He is now a member of the
Hazlehurst lodge No. 25, A. F. & A. M., Summit chapter, and Tupelo council.   He was for a
number of years a member of the State grange, and was the organizer of the first grange in
Copiah county.   For three years he was one of the trustees of the lunatic asylum; just prior
to Governor Ames' incumbency was appointed by Governor Hill United States commissioner.
Major Barry and all his family, except one, Andrew Porter, who is a Baptist, are members
of the Christian church.   For many years Major Barry has been trying to induce the grand
bodies to take up the subject of an orphans' home.   He has, within the past two or three years,
succeeded in awakening an interest in the matter with a considerable promise of its ultimate
success, a fund having been created which is now rapidly accumulating, and this is to be
devoted to that purpose.   Always a man of strong convictions, of quick and accurate conceptions, and of good judgment, the Major has, on many occasions through life, met with

strong opposition, but has lived to see most of his opponents defeated, and the principles he advocated triumphant. His career has always been marked by disinterestedness and public spirit. He has ever been a supporter of principles rather than of men. In person he is rather tall, and has a large frame which is slightly bowed by age, but in spite of his seventy-seven years, which have made his full flowing beard white as snow, his step is light and elastic. His eyesight is so good that he reads without glasses, and his memory being unimpaired, his knowledge of past anecdotes and current events is extensive. He is a very entertaining conversationalist, and his wide acquaintance with the leading men of the South, and his long and prominent career in the Masonic fraternity, have given him a fund of anecdotes and reminiscences that seems exhaustless.

In the village of Columbus, on December 10, 1821, William S. Barry was born. His preparatory education was academical, after which he was sent to Yale college, graduating with distinction about the year 1845. Returning to Mississippi, he became a student of law in the office of Harrison & Harris, and by the strength of his mind, energy and his application, soon attracted the attention of all with whom he came in contact. He was courteous, polished in language, eloquent and logical, and in the local debating associations, even while yet a boy, created marked attention. Upon his admission to the bar he became a partner of Judge J. S. Bennett, and soon rose to the top of his profession. For some reason, not altogether clear to the historian, he retired from practice and became a planter in Oktibbeha county, where his talents soon made him conspicuous in local politics. In 1849 he was elected to the lower house of the legislature, and two years later was reëlected. His legislative record is without reproach. In all measures leading to the advancement of the state and the promotion of the public welfare he took a conspicuous and honorable part. In 1852 he removed to Sunflower county, locating in that portion which was afterward set apart as Le Flore county. In 1853 he was elected to the lower house of congress where he became prominent for his alertness, skill and readiness and eloquence in debate. He took a strong partisan position, and in his opposition to the know-nothings secured by his marvelous speeches a national reputation. He declined a reëlection to congress and resumed the practice of law in Columbus, in partnership with Thomas Christian, which firm was noted for its strong probity and commanding influence. But he did not confine himself wholly to law; politics had a fascination he could not resist. His aptitude for the " give and take " of partisan politics, made him a leader of the democratic party in that portion of the state. He was again elected to the legislature and was made speaker of the house, in which responsible position he showed great fairness and skill. In 1861, in the secession convention, he served as a delegate from the county of Lowndes, and was president of that historic body. Previous to this, he had also been a member of the Charleston convention of 1860, from which body, with others from the Southern states, he had seceded. He served as one of the seven delegates from Mississippi to the convention of the Southern states held at Montgomery, and later became a member of the provisional congress. No sooner had the war begun than he obtained from President Davis authority to raise a regiment for the Confederate cause, whereupon he resigned his seat in congress, and in the spring of 1862 organized and mustered into service the Thirty-fifth regiment of Mississippi volunteers. As an officer and a soldier Col. Barry showed great bravery and was regarded as one of the ablest of the Confederate commanders in the army to which he belonged. It encountered General Grant in many engagements, leading up to the siege of Vicksburg, and when the latter capitulated, was surrendered with the army of General Pemberton. Later he shared the hardships and pitched battles of the Georgia campaign and the fierce struggles around Atlanta, and at Altoona he was severely wounded and did not rejoin his regiment until it had reached Mobile. Here with his command he was captured, April 9, 1865. Thus ended his splendid military career. He returned to the practice of law, and continued the same until his death, at Columbus, January 29, 1868. His wife, to whom he was married in 1851, was Miss Sallie Fearn, daughter of Dr. Thomas Fearn, of Huntsville, Ala.

Near the little postoffice of Shell Mound, Le Flore county, Miss., resides Hon. William S. Barry, the subject of this brief biographical notice, in whom are embodied all the faculties which go to make up a successful merchant, planter and attorney. Mr. Barry was born in Columbus, Miss., November 27, 1857, and is a son of the Hon. William S. Barry, also a native of Mississippi. He received his literary education in Virginia, and at the university of Oxford, Miss. He then took up the study of law, and for this purpose he entered the law department of the university of Virginia; he was graduated from this institution, and took a post-graduate course; in 1884 he was admitted to the bar of Carroll county, but located in Le Flore county before he took up the practice of law. In the spring of 1888 he came to Greenwood, and formed a partnership with Colonel Coleman, which continued until his removal to Shell Mound; there he owns a plantation store, a plantation and some other real estate. In his political opinions Mr. Barry is identified with the Democratic party. In 1887 he was elected to represent his county in the state legislature by the democratic party, and discharged the duties of this office to the entire satisfaction of his constituency, and with great credit to himself. In addition to all his other business interests Mr. Barry is president of the Oil Mill company, and has been, since the organization of that body. He is one of the most capable business men in the county, and is so esteemed by all with whom he comes in contact. He was married in Huntsville, Ala., May 25, 1882, to Miss Bernice S. Steele, a daughter of Colonel Matthew W. Steele, a native of North Carolina. Mrs. Barry was born, reared and educated at Huntsville, Ala. This worthy couple are members of the Presbyterian church, of which Mr. Barry is an elder. He belongs to the Masonic fraternity, being a master mason.

On the 26th of April, 1834, William R. Barksdale, subject of this sketch, was born in Lauderdale county, Ala. In October of the same year he was taken by his parents to Yalobusha in Mississippi. His parents were natives of Tennessee, and were influential and exemplary citizens, conspicuous for their social worth and distinguished virtues. In 1851 William R. Barksdale, after having received the advantages of the best schools of his county, was sent to the State university at Oxford, where he graduated with honor in 1855. While in college he was noted for his studious habits, ambition, and the ability with which he mastered all studies he pursued. Immediately after his graduation, so favorably had he impressed his instructors at the university, and so high a character had he borne while there, that for two years he was employed in the university in the capacity of a professor. In 1857 he entered the law department of the university, and two years later graduated as a bachelor of law. Succeeding this, he returned to Yalobusha county, and opened a law office at Grenada, and entered upon a most brilliant career as a practitioner. So strong was his mind, and versatile his genius, and eloquent his oratory, that in a short time he had attained a state reputation. At the age of twenty-six, so popular had he become, and at the same time influential, that he was selected as a delegate to the memorable convention of January 9, 1861, which passed the ordinance of secession of Mississippi. When the war broke out, he immediately enlisted in the Confederate cause, and in 1862, after passing through various ranks, was promoted to the position of adjutant-general on the staff of Gen. W. S. Featherston, with the rank of a major, in which capacity he served gallantly until 1864, when he was transferred to the staff of General Walthall. In all of these positions he served faithfully, and was a gallant officer and soldier. At the close of the war he resumed the practice of his profession in his old county, accepting with resignation the changed condition of the Southern states. He was soon elected to the position of district attorney, in which capacity he served for several years. In 1875 he was elected to the lower house of the legislature, and took a prominent position as one of the debaters in that body. His speeches are noted for their dignity, eloquence, logic and fervid fancy. Unfortunately he died at Grenada January 10, 1877. His name is held in high esteem throughout the entire state.

Among the ablest and most prominent lawyers of ante-bellum times was Roger Barton, who was born near Knoxville, Tenn., 1802. His father was Dr. Hugh Barton, a man of more than usual ability; a skillful practitioner of medicine and a Virginian. After Roger Barton had received a fair education in one of the colleges of East Tennessee, he began, in 1824, the study of law at Knoxville, under William E. Anderson, and after his admission to the bar, and after having practiced at Knoxville for several years, he located at the town of Bolivar, and took as a partner V. D. Barry, with whom he remained associated for some time. In his practice he showed from the start unusual ability, and in a short time was sent to the Tennessee legislature, and was later chosen attorney-general of the state. Here he made his name famous as one of the ablest criminal lawyers of the Southwest. His power before a jury was said to have been almost irresistible. In 1836 he removed from Tennessee and located at Holly Springs, Miss., where he became associated in the practice of law with Joseph W. Chalmers. Here he soon secured an enormous practice and great popularity. In 1838 he was sent to the legislature of Mississippi, and the following year was reëlected. From this time forward he took a conspicuous part in the political affairs of his adopted state. For twenty years he continued to be the leader of his party in northern Mississippi. Any office he chose to secure was within his grasp, but he was not an office-seeker; he preferred to let the office seek him, and in the many responsible and trying positions he held, served his constituents honorably. In the great political contests of 1840 and 1844 he obtained prominence by his eloquence and logic as a partisan debater. He was both versatile and witty, humorous, broad-minded and brilliant, but at the same time showed high consideration for his adversaries, and never descended beneath due dignity. In 1837 he served as a member of the commission to settle the claims of the Choctaw Indians, and in 1849 was nominated by his party for congress, but immediately entered the convention and declined the honor. He was appointed by President Pierce United States consul to Cuba, which honor he also declined. He continued to practice his profession and to serve his fellow-citizens until 1855, when he passed away.

In reviewing the history and early settlement of Smith county, Tenn., we find, prominent among the pioneers, the name of William Baskett, who located there about the year 1825. The Baskett family were among the oldest settlers of North Carolina and of Scotch descent. William Baskett removed from Tennessee to Mississippi in 1831, and located in Hinds county on Society ridge, near Jackson. In 1836 he moved to Carroll county, settling in that section now embraced in Montgomery county. He resided there until 1845, when he took up his abode in Black Hawk, Carroll county. A few years later we find him in Copiah county, near Hazelhurst, where he remained until death; he passed from this life in 1867. He had been successful in his business, and had accumulated some property, but lost heavily by the late war. He was married in North Carolina to Mary Whitehouse, a native of that state, and by which union five sons and five daughters were born. She died in 1851, and he was married a second time, by which union three sons and two daughters were born.

Captain Baskett, and two brothers are the only surviving members of the family.   B. F. Baskett is a merchant in Bessemer, Ala., and G. W. Baskett is a practicing physician at Vanalstine, Tex.; Walton Baskett was a soldier in the Civil war, and died in the service of the Confederate army.   Capt. L. T. Baskett was born in Smith county, Tenn., February 9, 1830, and was an infant when his parents removed to the state of Mississippi; he attended the common schools during his boyhood, and received an education that fitted him for the duties of commercial life.   When a young man he began clerking in Carroll county, and followed this calling for a number of years.   He acquired a thorough, practical knowledge of the business, and the foundation of his future success was laid at this time.   In 1858 he secured a situation as a clerk on a steamboat on the Yazoo river, and was afterward captain of a boat which ran on the Red and Yazoo rivers.   In 1861, when there was a call for troops to go to the aid of the country, he left the river, surrendering his private interests to the demand of the government.   He enlisted in the Twenty-first Mississippi volunteer infantry as a private, was promoted to a lieutenancy, and served through the war in that capacity.   He participated in many important engagements, was wounded in four different battles: Malvern Hill, the Wilderness, Gettysburg and Petersburg, being entirely disabled from service in the last named.   When this life of toil, privation and danger was ended by the declaration of peace, the Captain returned to Carroll county, and the three years following he was again captain and clerk of a steamboat.   He then took up agricultural pursuits, and for two years was occupied with planting.   In February, 1870, he removed to Greenwood, and embarked in the mercantile trade, and since that time has been identified with the progressive commercial men of the place.   In his political opinions he has ever held to the principles of the democratic party.   He has held several official positions of trust and honor, has been mayor of Greenwood, and was a member of the board of supervisors.   In 1886 he was elected sheriff of Le Flore county, and at the expiration of his term he was reelected to the office.   Upon the organization of the bank of Greenwood he was elected president in 1890.   He is also president of the Greenwood Building & Loan Association, and vice president of the Le Flore Ice & Coal company.   Captain Baskett has been twice married; first he was united to Miss Martha McLean, of Middleton, Carroll county, Miss., in 1864; two years later she died. The second marriage occurred in Vicksburg, Miss., in November, 1870, when he was joined to Miss Claudine L. Gibson.   Mrs. Baskett is a daughter of Gibeon Gibson, one of the well known planters of Mississippi and first cousin of Senator Gibson of Louisiana.   She was born in Jefferson county, Miss., but was educated in Lexington, Ky.   One child was born of the last marriage, Tullian L. Baskett, who died at the age of six months.   Captain Baskett is one of the most conspicuous figures among the business men of Le Flore county.   He gives great support to all measures tending to advance the interests of the community, and is a citizen honored and respected by all with whom he comes in contact.

John H. Bass, Shubuta, Clarke county, Miss.   John Bass, father of John H. Bass, of Shubuta, Clarke county, Miss., was born in Marlborough district, S. C., in 1783, and was a United States soldier in the war of 1812.   He was married to Miss Mary Harris, of South Carolina, and they had nine children: Elizabeth, James S., J. W., Sarah A., M. A., M. J., Anna Moselle, D. Catherine and John, all of whom, except two, survive, and all of whom, except one, are residents of Mississippi.   Mr. Bass died in 1872; Mrs. Bass about 1838.   He was a successful planter and a charitable citizen, benevolent to a fault, and in every way a model man.   John H. Bass, our subject, was born June 5, 1831, in Marion district, S. C., spent his early life on the farm, and had limited educational advantages.   In 1861 he enlisted at Columbus, Miss., in the regiment commanded by Colonel Barry.   Owing to ill health, though always ready to go, he was compelled to remain out of active service. However, he was honored with the position of lieutenant of a home company. Mr. Bass began life for himself September 5, 1865, the date of his marriage, and located in Clarke county, Miss., three and one-half miles from Shubuta. When he came out of the war he had in money only $1.25. He purchased land in 1871, and by constant accretion he now owns over two thousand acres of the average land of Clarke county, and grows cotton, corn, oats, etc., employing about forty men and two hundred and ten mules in its culture. His annual yield of cotton is about one hundred and twenty-five bales. His plantation is self-sustaining. He uses some commercial fertilizer, and farms intensively. On his plantation is found some longleaf pine and some fine hardwoods. He is a member of the Masonic fraternity, is a democrat, though once a whig, and is a Methodist, his family also belonging to that church. He was married to Miss M. V. Sherin, of North Carolina, though at the time of their marriage a resident of Lowndes county, Miss. She is a daughter of E. E. Sherin. The Sherins are one of the first families of North Carolina. By this marriage Mr. Bass had three children: Joseph A., Miss M. E. and an infant who died unnamed. Joseph A. died in April, 1885, at Shubuta. Mrs. Bass died in 1885, and Mr. Bass later married Mrs. Anna (Morrison) McCloud, of Clarke county, Miss., a daughter of Benjamin J. Morrison, who is a merchant of De Soto, and who was a lieutenant in the Confederate service in the late war. Mr. Bass is interested in schools, churches, etc., and has ever been a liberal contributor to all worthy interests.

George M. Batchelor is one of Warren county's progressive planters, and although the history of this section is filled with the deeds and doings of self-made men, no one in Warren county is more deserving the appellation than Mr. Batchelor, for he marked out his own career in youth, and has steadily followed it up to the present, his prosperity being attributable to his earnest and persistent endeavor and to the fact that he has always consistently tried to follow the teachings of the Golden Rule. He was born in Amite county, Miss., December 2, 1839, the second child born to Napoleon and Ellen D. (Noland) Batchelor, the former being a native of Mississippi. His father was the owner of a large plantation in Madison parish, La., and another in Warren county, Miss., and spent his last days in Warren county. His grandfather, Thomas Batchelor, was a delegate to the first constitutional convention of Mississippi in 1817, and also held at one time the position of chancery clerk of Amite county. He came from South Carolina, where his ancestors, who were of French Huguenot extraction, settled on coming to America, about the time of the French Revolution. The Nolands originally came from Ireland, and became residents of Georgia. The early life of George M. Batchelor was spent on his father's plantation and in attending the common schools, but he afterward, in 1858, graduated from Oakland college, Miss., and in 1860 from the Lebanon (Tenn.) law school. Before he could enter to any great extent upon the practice of his profession, the war came up, and he entered company H, Twenty-first Mississippi volunteers, Confederate states army, and became a part of the army of Northern Virginia, stationed at Manassas. He was in the Peninsular campaign, and took part in the battles of Savage station, Malvern Hill, Fredericksburg, Antietam, Harper's ferry, and in 1864 was transferred to the cavalry department of Mississippi, Wert Adams' brigade, after which he was in several small battles before Lee's surrender. His command surrendered to General Canby. Upon his return home, Mr. Batchelor began farming, and is still successfully following that calling. In 1886 he was elected by his democratic friends to the position of state senator, and served from 1886 to 1888, during which time he voted for the calling of a constitutional convention, which resulted in a new constitution being framed. He introduced a bill for the reforming of the jury system, for the opening up of Big Black river to navigation and for an improved system of working the public roads of the state. He was also in favor of a liberal state policy toward railroads, and introduced a bill giving certain parties charter rights to build electric railroads in Vicksburg, and approved of the measures organizing the state militia as suggested by the general government. In fact, during his legislative career, he at all times showed himself true to the interests of his state, and was an able, intelligent and incorruptible legislator. He has been regarded as an able, active and indefatigable leader of his party in Warren county, and his eminent services to his party, his sound judgment and practical ability have been recognized by his numerous friends. He is the owner of twelve hundred acres of land, and has four hundred acres under cultivation. He was married in 1875 to Miss Jennie R. Aldridge, a daughter of Dr. W. O. Aldridge, of Kentucky, and the children born to their union are as follows: Edith May, Alfred Gordon, Roswell Booth, Helen Douglas, Mary Noland (deceased) and Emma Warren.

J. M. Batchelor, planter, was born in Amite county, Miss., August 3, 1842, and was the third child born to Thomas and Margaret (Stuart) Batchelor, the former of whom was born in this state, his father and grandfather being natives of South Carolina. They were all wealthy planters, and the paternal grandfather of the subject of this sketch was at one time clerk of the court of Amite county at an early day, and was one of the framers of the first court of the state. Thomas Batchelor was a planter, and before the war moved to Louisiana. His wife was a member of the Stuart family, near Woodville, Miss., the male members of her family being planters. J. M. Batchelor spent some time in the field schools, but at the age of sixteen years entered Oakland college, Mississippi, the two subsequent years being spent in a military institute of Kentucky. After leaving this institution he joined a cavalry company in Louisiana, as a lieutenant, but afterward enlisted as a private in an infantry company, and before being captured was promoted. He was in the Peninsular campaign and took part in the engagements at Winchester, Chancellorsville, Wilderness, Fredericksburg, Antietam, Harper's ferry, and was captured at Spottsylvania courthouse. He was sent to Belle Plain, thence to Fort Delaware, where he was kept a prisoner until the close of the war. He returned home at the cessation of hostilities, and soon after went to Texas, but after remaining in that state for eight months he returned to his home in Louisiana, where he was engaged in planting for about seven years. In 1872 he located about fifteen miles southeast of Vicksburg, and there speculated in stock and did general merchandising for six years. He has been prominent in local politics, is a democrat politically and is an exemplary citizen. He was married in 1875 to Miss Victoria Batchelor, his cousin and daughter of Napoleon and Ellen (Noland) Batchelor. His wife has had excellent educational advantages, and for some time attended school in Burlington, N. J. They have five children: Charles J., Bertha, Thomas V., Albert A., Jr., and Noland Stewart. Mr. Batchelor is the owner of seven hundred and seventy acres of land and has two hundred and fifty acres under cultivation. He and his wife are Episcopalians, and he belongs to the K. of H. and is a member of the American Legion of Honor.

One of the oldest, best known and most highly esteemed families of Amite county, Miss., was founded here about the year 1802 by John Bates, who was born in the land of oatmeal and thistles, and came to the new world with his father, Richard Bates, at a very early day, being among the first residents of South Carolina. He inherited many of the sterling principles of his Scotch ancestors, among which may be mentioned unswerving honesty, industry and frugality, and with the end in view of bettering his financial condition he came to the state of Mississippi at the above mentioned date, and time proved the wisdom of his change of abode, for he became well to do. Richard Bates, father of Marshall P. Bates, subject of this sketch, opened up a large farm about eight miles from Liberty, Miss., and here he reared his family and resided until his death, which occurred about the year 1867. He was born in Barnwell district, S. C., October 15, 1796, and when a small lad was brought to Amite county, and grew to manhood on the old homestead. He was married here to Miss Eliza Jane Smith, a native of the county and a daughter of Ambrose Smith, one of the pioneers of this region from Virginia, who settled here about 1806 and opened up a farm near the town of Liberty. He was the youngest of a family of five children, and after his marriage he settled near the old homestead, and, being a man of excellent financial ability, he became wealthy. Besides owning several valuable plantations, he had slaves to the number of two hundred, and much valuable personal property. All this he lost during the Rebellion, including several hundred bales of cotton, but by his superior business capabilities he afterward retrieved his broken fortunes in a measure, and at the time of his death, in 1867, was in comfortable circumstances. He was married three times, his first wife dying in 1834. He gave liberally of his means in support of the Baptist church, of which he had long been a member, and at all times manifested a charitable spirit, for he was keenly alive to the sufferings and misfortunes of others, and no one appealed to him in vain for consolation or succor. Marshal P. Bates has been a resident of Amite county, Miss., since his birth, which occurred near Liberty, July 15, 1828, and his youth was spent on his father's plantation and in attending the common schools, where he acquired a good practical education. In November, 1846, he left the shelter of the parental roof to take up the hardships and privations of a soldier's life, and became a member of Colonel Anderson's regiment and General Scott's division, and for eight months, or until the close of the war, was on duty in Mexico. After returning home and farming one year, he, in 1849, was appointed deputy chancery clerk, and served in that capacity until his election to the office of chancery clerk in 1852, and at the close of his first term was reëlected, continuing to hold the position through eight consecutive years. At the end of this time he retired from public life and returned to his plantation, eight miles east of Liberty, bearing with him the consciousness of having performed every duty faithfully and well and to the entire satisfaction of his numerous friends. After following planting for a number of years, he moved to Liberty in 1883, and is there still residing, although he is still the owner of the old home farm, which consists of thirteen hundred and forty acres. He also owns a small farm adjoining Liberty. He was married in this county, May 4, 1858, to Miss Cornelia Carroll, a native of Amite county and a daughter of Dr. Edward Carroll, one of the pioneer physicians of the county. Mr. and Mrs. Bates have three children that are living: Charles C., a merchant of Centerville, Miss.; Dr. M. P., Jr., a practicing physician of Liberty, and Emma C., wife of Jeff. Causey, a merchant of Gloster, Miss. Mr. and Mrs. Bates are members of the Liberty Presbyterian church, and socially he is a royal arch Mason.

The most efficient clerk of the chancery court of Amite county, Miss., is Henry M. Bates, and as a painstaking, zealous and efficient official has not his superior in this section of the country. He has always resided in this county, for here he was born on the 15th of December, 1836, and the people have had every opportunity to judge of his character and qualifications, and that he is held in the highest esteem is a sufficient testimonial. He is one of five sons and one daughter that grew to mature years, two brothers dying before the Rebellion. The sister grew up, was married, but is now deceased. Henry M., M. P., and Hon. James E. are the only surviving members of the family. The latter served as a member of the state legislature, his work, while a member of that body, being very efficient and praiseworthy. The parents of these children were Richard and Eliza Jane (Smith) Bates. The youth of

Henry M. Bates was spent as a farmer's boy, and, notwithstanding the fact that he had plenty to do his schooling was not neglected, and he succeeded in acquiring a very practical education in the common schools and in Mississippi college. After completing his studies he returned home, and until the opening of the Rebellion his time was employed on his father's plantation. After the firing on Fort Sumter he was one of the first to respond to his country's call for troops, for he was very enthusiastic in his espousal of the Confederate cause, and in the early part of 1861 became a member of company C, Seventh Mississippi infantry, with which he served until the month of July, 1864, when he was discharged on account of a wound he had received. He entered the service as a private, but for gallant conduct was promoted to the rank of first lieutenant, and participated in all the engagéments of his regiment, following the varying fortunes of a soldier with fortitude and courage up to the time of receiving his discharge. He was with the army of Tennessee the greater part of the time, and at the battle of Atlanta lost his left leg, this being on the 28th of July, 1864. After the war he returned to Liberty, Miss., and for several years successfully conducted a plantation. He was called upon to discharge the duties of his present office in the year 1876, and at each succeeding election has been reëlected, for he has proved himself to be the right man in the right place, and every department of his work is given the most minute and careful attention. He has made a beau ideal public officer, and that his services are appreciated is shown by his long continuance in office. Among his many worthy traits of character may be mentioned efficiency, punctuality, industry, honesty and courtesy to all. He has ever been very appreciative of a kind action done him, and it may be truly said of him that he never violated a friendship. To his credit be it said that his life has been illustrated with many kind deeds, and his acts of charity, though seldom made public, have been numerous and extensive. He was married in 1858 to Miss Harriet A. McKnight, a native of the county and a daughter of Thomas McKnight. His second and present wife he married in March, 1861, she being Miss Louisa P. McKinney, also of this county, a daughter of T. S. McKinney. To his first union one daughter was born; Harriet A., who is now the wife of Harris Brashear, and his second union resulted in the birth of seven children; Etta, wife of R. D. Moore; Lula, wife of F. F. Faust of Amite county; Henry M., married; Dora, Bessie, Elliott and Leslie. Mr. Bates is ever found at the post of duty, and to those who call upon him he is courtesy itself, and a very pleasant and agreeable gentleman to meet. No man in the entire county is more highly respected and esteemed, and that he fully deserves this popularity goes without saying.

Judge William S. Bates was born in Franklin county, Ala., in 1830, a son of H. W. and E. E. (Bourland) Bates, the former of whom was born in Franklin county, Tenn., and the latter in Hickman, Ky. They became acquainted in Franklin county, Tenn., and were there married about 1829. Robert P. Bates, the paternal grandfather, came to the United States from Ireland when a boy, and first located in White county, Tenn., at Sparta, where he was married to Miss Hannah Hill. Ebenezer Bourland, the maternal grandfather, was a native of Kentucky. Judge William S. Bates is one of a large family, of whom he was the eldest. His brothers and sisters are as follows: Maj. Robert P., of Corsicana; Mary C., widow of Thomas Dutton; Maggie, wife of V. B. McFadden, of Memphis, Tenn.; Thomas, a resident of New Mexico; E. H., an extensive cotton planter of Bremond, Tex.; Lizzie, wife of J. M. Casey, of Greentown, Miss.; Abigail, wife of Dr. J. M. Bourland, of Curtis, Ark.; Finis L., an attorney of Memphis, Tenn.; Alice, wife of J. M. Gusta, a banker of Corsicana, Tex.; Jeffie, wife of Mr. Lockard, of Winona, Miss.; and Knox, a resident of Western Texas. Judge William S. Bates spent his boyhood in the county of his birth, but at the age of twelve years removed to Itawamba county, Miss., where he spent his youth. He labored hard on a farm, and after the crops were laid by found some time to attend school. At about the age of eighteen years he began attending college in Tennessee, where he remained for about two years. After leaving this institution he was sent by his father to open a country store at what is now Guntown, and there remained for about two years. On the 4th of July, 1854, he went to Pontotoc to read law with the firm of Fountain & Bradford, with whom he remained for two years, being admitted to the bar in 1856. He immediately entered upon his practice in Pontotoc, where he was successfully employed until December, 1862. He was married in 1858 to Miss Susan Martin, a daughter of Judge Martin, and the same year of his marriage was elected probate judge of Pontotoc county, and in his official capacity showed much discrimination and judgment. In 1860 he was temporary editor of the Pontotoc *Examiner*, where he remained until the expiration of his term of office in 1862. He then immediately removed to Houston, but soon after entered service in the Confederate army as a private in the Twenty-fourth Mississippi infantry. He was immediately placed in the quartermaster's department, but was afterward transferred to the brigade ordnance department, in which he remained until the war closed, when he was paroled at Gainesville, Ala. Upon returning to his home in Houston, Miss., he resumed the practice of his profession with Judge Martin, with whom he had entered into partnership in 1858. Their practice has been from the first successful and extensive in Chickasaw and adjoining counties, principally in civil cases. Judge Bates has never aspired to criminal practice. He is a conservative democrat, and favored reconstruction. He is a conspicuous leader in his profession, is skillful in planning his cases, is wise in counsel, is cool in judgment and full of resourses. He is a public-spirited citizen, and as such has contributed of his time, influence and means to the benefit of the public. His union has resulted in the birth of twin daughters: Scottie, wife of W. W. Tabb, of Houston; and May, wife of W. A. White, a hardware merchant of West Point, Miss.

Dr. A. S. Baugh, of Polkville, Smith county, Miss., was born in Marion county, Miss., in 1832. His father, Bartholomew Baugh, was a native of Virginia, and his mother, who was Miss Nancy Carney, was a native of Tennessee. The former, who was born in 1787, left his native state when but a child, and located with his parents in Salem, N. C. He was educated in the city schools, and when he became of sufficient age he engaged in planting. Removing to Shelby county, Tenn., he there married and came on to Mississippi, some time during the twenties. He was a son of Josiah Baugh, also a native of Virginia, and a veteran of the Revolutionary war, who served under General Morgan, and at the battle of the Cowpens received a bullet in his thigh, which he would never allow to be removed, although it was near the surface, preferring to carry it as a memento of the days that "tried men's souls." He was a son of English parents, who came to America in early life. On his mother's side he was a descendant of the ancient Waldenses. Dr. Baugh often speaks of that stream of blood in his veins. The subject of this notice grew to maturity in Copiah and Simpson counties, and removed with his parents to Smith county in 1849, and having been reared on a plantation, he engaged in planting until 1853. At that time he began teaching school, and followed that occupation until he entered Mississippi college at Clinton, Hinds county, in 1854. After he left the college he taught school two years, at the same time taking up the study of medicine in the office of Dr. Finch; and in 1858 he removed to Moscow, Tex., and there engaged in the practice of medicine with Dr. R. T. Walker, of that place. Living there one year he returned to Mississippi and located in Polkville, where he has since resided. When secession was proposed by many of his fellow-citizens he strenuously opposed the idea, and it was some time before he could bring himself to take up arms against the old flag, which his grandfather had shed his blood to establish. But in 1864 he entered the Confederate service as a druggist, and at Oxford, Miss., was appointed assistant surgeon, in which capacity he served until the close of the war. Returning home in the fall of 1865, he entered the medical college at New Orleans, La., from which he was graduated in the spring of 1866, with the degree of M. D. Returning to Polkville he was married to Miss Ella Croft, a daughter of Reuben Croft, a pioneer settler of Smith county. Dr. Baugh has been engaged in the practice of medicine thirty-three years at Polkville, except one year, during which he was in the army. No man has done more for the poor according to his means than he. His annual contributions to the poor and to the churches amount to between three and four hundred dollars. Dr. Gambrel, editor of the *Baptist Record*, in speaking of him, says: "He is an institution in that part of the country." The poor often say that "there never will be another Dr. Baugh in this part of the country." He has a most interesting family, consisting of two daughters and one son. His articles for the press are noted for scientific value, deep thought and simplicity of style. Dr. Baugh is the owner of a plantation of about three hundred acres of productive land. He is a member of the Masonic fraternity, presiding many years as worshipful master of his lodge. He is an active member of the Missionary Baptist church, and is a useful and highly respected citizen, who would be an ornament to any community in which his lot might be cast.

A well-known planter and miller of Columbia, Marion county, is George Baylis, who was born in Jones county, Miss., in 1825, and remained in his native place until he was twenty-six years of age, receiving his education in the common schools. In his twenty-third year he was married to Miss Lucretia Rawls, a daughter of Benjamin Rawls, a native of South Carolina. Of this union were born five children: Mary F., who married E. J. Wall; Alice, wife of Hugh McInnis; John R.; Robert S., and Zulieka, wife of W. F. Simmons. The mother of these children died in May, 1864, and Mr. Baylis was married again, to Caroline Fenn, and four children were born of this marriage: Lucretia, who married Edward W. Lampton; Ella E., wife of Jabez Rawls; George F. and W. Lamar. Mr. Baylis settled on the plantation he now occupies in 1852. Soon after locating there he was elected a member of the board of police, and held that office until after the war. He has been actively interested in all political questions and matters of public importance, but has declined to accept public office. He favors liberal education, and is a liberal contributor to all charitable and philanthropic institutions. He is a member of the Methodist Episcopal church South, as are all the members of his family. His father, George Baylis, Sr., was born in Charleston, S. C., and was reared in Orangeburg district, where he resided until he had attained his majority. He then came to Mississippi. He was married to Miss Mary Elzer, a daughter of Evan Elzer, and they have had born to them eight children: Elizabeth, wife of J. D. Knight; George, the subject of this notice; William; John M., M. D.; Robert, deceased; Wyatt, who was killed in the siege of Vicksburg; Jane, wife of Dr. John Gillis, and Mary, who died just as she was coming into womanhood. The grandparents of our subject, William and Elizabeth Baylis, were natives of England, and emigrated to America soon after their marriage. They passed the remainder of their days on this continent. Mr. Baylis was a fine mechanic, and his son, George Baylis, Sr., was also a mechanic, although he gave much attention to farming; he was a local preacher in the Methodist Episcopal church South, and devoted the latter part of his life to this work. George Baylis, Jr., is one of the most enterprising men of Marion county. He owns a gin, saw and gristmill, and does a large and extended business. During the war he was detailed to look after the families of Confederate

Tho Rigby

soldiers, and performed the duties of this office with the greatest consideration and kindness. He is a man who has the entire respect and confidence of the community.

Like many other of the representative citizens of Calhoun county, Capt. T. L. Beadler, planter, trader, etc., Big creek, was born in Tennessee, his nativity having occurred in Weakley county, immediately on the Kentucky line, in 1837. He is the second of five children—three sons and two daughters. His parents were of Virginia stock. His father, F. G. Beadler, settled in West Tennessee in an early day, and married Susan Clemmons. Captain Beadler has two brothers and one sister residing in Moscow, Hickman county, Ky., all of the family now living. Captain Beadler clerked and taught school until near the age of twenty years, when he came to Mississippi, attended a select school for young men a year, then engaged in mercantile business at what is now known as old Big creek. He did a profitable business until the breaking out of the war between the states, when he closed out his business and enlisted in company F, Twenty-ninth Mississippi infantry, commanded by Col. E. C. Walthall, afterward major-general. He participated in all the battles in which his command was engaged, viz.: Mumfordsville, Perryville, Murfreesboro, etc., until the battle of Chickamauga, when, after three days' hard fighting, he was captured and taken to Camp Douglas, Chicago, where he remained in prison until June 13, 1865. On July 1, 1865, he returned to his home in Mississippi. Captain Beadler was in command of his company on several important occasions. During his imprisonment at Camp Douglas he was in charge of the commissary department to receive and distribute such articles as were sent to the prisoners by the Confederate government or by their friends within the Federal lines. After the loss of four years in the service of his country, in the prime of life, Mr. Beadler returned home broken in fortune but not in energy and sagacity, and turned his attention to farming and trading in stock. We find him now one of the progressive, thoroughgoing and best business men of the county, and by his close, shrewd business tact has accumulated enough of the world's goods to rear and educate his family, and those that he has turned loose upon the world will rank with the best in their profession. We find Mr. Beadler honored and respected by all his neighbors. On several occasions he has been a candidate for legislative honors; takes an active interest in the political events of the day; is well read and posted in all the events of the government. He is a strict adherent to the democratic party; takes an active interest and supports with his influence and means all enterprises looking to the advancement of the moral, educational and religious interests of his community. Mr. and Mrs. Beadler are members of the Methodist Episcopal church South, and he is a member of Chapel Hill lodge No. 227, A. F. & A. M., and was master of said lodge for several years. Mr. Beadler is strictly temperate in all things, and may be termed a prohibitionist. Captain Beadler, in 1861, a few months prior to his entering the Confederate army, was married to Miss Mary S. Petree, of Big creek, Miss., a daughter of R. D. Petree, Esq., a native of South Carolina, and one of the early settlers of Calhoun county. Mr. Petree was a blacksmith by trade, and came to Mississippi with rather limited means, but by industry and perseverance acquired a fortune of nearly $75,000 in about twenty years, dying in 1863, in the prime of manhood. We find Mr. and Mrs. Beadler happily and comfortably situated with a nice residence upon a fine fertile farm, surrounded by intelligent, moral and religious people. They have a family of eight children—five sons and three daughters: Eugene S., physician at Water valley, Miss., graduated from the Louisville (Ky.) medical school, also Bellevue hospital medical college, New York, before he was twenty-one years old, and is now one of the leading physicians of Water Valley; Clarence V. is a merchant of Coffeeville, Miss., a graduate of the Bowling Green (Ky.) Southern normal school; Effie is attending Centenary female college, Cleveland, Tenn.;

23

Clyde, Ernest, Adrian, Mabel and Roy; all the last five at home, with the exception of the baby and Roy, who are attending the home school. Mr. and Mrs. Beadler are both small in stature, but their children are fine specimens of humanity, especially those who have developed into manhood. Mr. and Mrs. Beadler seem to believe and practice the idea that each succeeding generation should be an improvement upon the former mentally and physically if possible.

A prominent lawyer of West Point, Clay county, Miss., is Capt. Fred Beall, who was born July 10, 1837, in Campbell county, Ga. His father, Noble P. Beall, was born in 1799, and was a son of Gen. Frederick Beall, for many years a leader in the military and public affairs of Georgia. Gen. Frederick Beall was a native of Virginia, but came with his parents at an early day to South Carolina, and thence he moved to Georgia, and after an active and successful life of sixty years or more died in Campbell county, respected and loved by all who knew him, for he had been the friend of all, the poor and oppressed as well as the rich and high-born. The mother of Capt. Fred Beall was Justianna D., daughter of Capt. Matthew Hooper. She was born in 1801 in Anderson district, S. C. Her father was an intelligent merchant, of broad and extensive culture. He was a fine classical scholar, and in his old age found great pleasure in reading Virgil and Horace and other like authors. Noble P. Beall and Justianna D. Hooper were married when they were respectively nineteen and seventeen years of age, and lived happily together for sixty years, each attaining the advanced age of seventy-nine. Noble P. Beall was twice completely broken up, and all his property swept from him on account of security debts, incurred by him for the benefit of relatives, but with that indomitable energy which he possessed, he never surrendered to misfortune, but renewed his efforts at every adversity, and with the help and encouragement whichhis noble wife ever gave him, he bravely encountered, and successfully overcame every obstacle and difficulty in life. In 1839 he, with his brother-in-law, Col. James D. Wood, moved with their families to Tishomingo county, Miss., and bought large bodies of land near Eastport, on the Tennessee river. This was then a wild and unsettled part of the state; there was not even a cornmill in the county; they ground their corn on handmills, like the old-fashioned coffeemill. In this new and untried land Noble P. Beall began life anew. He opened up a fine plantation, which he successfully operated until he was again broken up by the devastations of the Federal army, which invaded that part of the state in 1862, and carried off all his slaves, horses, mules and cattle and destroyed everything else he had except his lands. Having lost all he had by the war, and all his children having married and scattered through Mississippi, Alabama, Tennessee and Georgia, he and wife moved back to Georgia in 1872, and settled in Cartersville, Bartow county, where they had three daughters then living. Noble P. Beall was never a politician or office seeker, but always took an active interest in public affairs, and was all his life a consistent democrat, and never cast other than a democratic vote. He and his wife were active members of the Baptist church, and were always found on the moral side of every question. They were the friends and strong supporters of the cause of education, and at great expense educated their children far beyond what other parents in that part of the state usually did. Capt. Fred Beall when in his seventeenth year was sent to Union university, at Murfreesboro, Tenn., and in two and one-half years completed the full A. M. course of that excellent institution, and at once, as a stepping-stone to his chosen profession, the law, began to teach school. At the age of nineteen he was elected principal of a male and female academy upon a salary of $1,200 per year. Two years later he was elected the successor of president W. S. Webb, principal of the Starkville female institute, at Starkville, Miss. While teaching he devoted all his spare time to the study of history and law. When the war between the states broke out, he gave up his school and enlisted as a private soldier in the cavalry service, and continued actively in the Confederate army until its close. Though in an extremely low state of health when he went into the army, so much so that his physicians advised him not to enlist, and warned him that he could not stand the service, and that to attempt to do so would be his early death, yet he never had a furlough on account of sickness, nor was he ever sent to a hospital. He was never absent from duty, and no man was ever truer or more faithful to the Southern cause than he. His first promotion was made on the battlefield, from the position of a private to that of orderly-sergeant. At the battle of Iuka he rendered a very valuable service to General Price, and saved from capture a part of his forces that had been cut off, and were about to be surrendered. Through a perfect hailstorm of bullets, he sped his horse a full mile to where the forces were fighting, and under his direction they were led safely out, for which service he was complimented by General Price. Capt. Beall was a great favorite of General Forrest, under whom he served about one year. The command to which he was attached at the close of the war was under General Wheeler.

When the war closed Capt. Beall located at West Point, and for a few months taught school again, until he could get another start in life. In 1859 he had married Miss Emma G. Brame, a daughter of Mrs. N. F. Brame, of the vicinity of West Point, and a young lady of rare beauty and grace and of superior culture, and when he returned to his young wife and two little children on the 17th of May, 1865, there was no sadder heart in all the South than his. The cause for which he with his countrymen had fought, and for the success of which many of the noblest, truest and bravest of his friends had freely and voluntarily given their lives, had gone down forever before the overwhelming and victorious armies of the Northern states. He who had faced death on many a hard-fought battlefield now wept like a child. While his command had formally surrendered at Washington, Ga., he, in keeping with a resolution he had made when he went into the army, that he never would be made a prisoner alive, refused to surrender, and with a young friend started to join Gen. Dick Taylor, then in command near Mobile, but when they reached the Coosa river, they met some of General Taylor's command who informed them that he had surrendered and also that the Trans-Mississippi army had surrendered. Nothing was then left them but to go on home, which they did, and neither he nor his young friend ever surrendered.

Reared in the school of state rights democracy, the overthrow of the Southern Confederacy was to Captain Beall the overthrow of a great and fundamental principle, upon which the Federal union had been established. However, he did not, at this juncture, have time to stop and mourn over the downfall of the Confederacy; the result must be accepted, and, as far as possible, something must be done for the support of wife and children. He not only had absolutely nothing, but owed about $1,000 in debts incurred in 1861 and 1862, which he was not permitted to pay in Confederate money as they became due. For a few months he taught school, and in the meantime revived his law studies, and in 1866 he began the practice of law, and at once went into a very lucrative practice, which he has retained ever since. At the time he was admitted to the bar West Point was a way station on the Mobile & Ohio railroad in the western part of Lowndes county, and eighteen miles from Columbus, the county seat. He at once began to agitate the question of the formation of a new county, with West Point as the county seat, which was accomplished in 1870, though the county was not organized until 1872. To the efforts of Captain Beall, in this behalf, more than any one else, is due the formation of Clay county. He has always taken an active interest in the cause of education, and was very largely instrumental in the building of the fine public school building, in which is now conducted one of the best graded schools in the state. He has for many years been the chairman of the board of trustees of the city schools. He is an active working member of the state bar association, and has served several years as chairman on the committee of legal education and admission to the bar. He is now, and has been for many years, president of the West Point law and library association. No one in Clay county is more familiar with its general affairs, and no one has done more toward its general improvement and advancement than he. He has always taken an active interest in politics, and to the full extent of his ability and means he contributed to the overthrow of carpet-bag rule in Mississippi in 1875, and to the maintenance of democratic rule in the state since. Unyielding and uncompromising in his devotion to the principles of democracy, he always refused to go into any kind of fusion of parties, and when, in 1873, the democracy of the state met in convention at Meridian, and the majority resolved to disband the party, and unite with what was known then as the conservative republicans, headed by Senator J. L. Alcorn, and try to overthrow the bitter enders, at that time led by General, then Governor, Ames, Captain Beall, with others who were in the minority, refused to be disbanded, but then and there proceeded to organize another convention, which appointed a new state executive committee, to perpetuate the organization of the democratic party. Captain Beall was made a member of that committee, and aided in the preparation of a stirring address to the true democracy of the state, urging them to stand by the time-honored principles of the party, and to never give up the fight. In 1875 the party was reunited, and made that memorable fight for liberty and home rule, which no Mississippian can ever forget. As soon as radicalism was overthrown in the state, Captain Beall took the position that Mississippi should have a new constitution in place of the one made by negroes and carpet-baggers, and he never ceased to work for this until it was accomplished in 1890, though he stood almost solitary and alone in his position on this question for many years. Though always taking an active interest in politics, Captain Beall has persistently refused political office. He has been a man of fixed principles and determined resolutions, and realizing that political office-holding is a delusion and a snare, he, at an early age, resolved never to be a candidate for any political office, and right well has he kept that resolution, though often urged by his fellow-citizens to accept office. An uncompromising democrat, yet Captain Beall has always been popular with all classes, and possibly no lawyer in his part of the state has had a more liberal share of the best practice from members of the republican party. He has ever been an ardent advocate of the absolute equality of all persons before the law, and would have the theory that all classes are equal before the law made practically so. Though it is now more than a quarter of a century since the war between the states closed, yet Captain Beall's devotion to the cause, to which he gave four of the best years of his young manhood, is unabated, and he takes a deep interest in gathering up the history of those bloody years, and in looking after the poor old Confederate soldiers of his county. His professional services are always given freely, without money and without price, to the widow and orphans of his old comrades. Through him the Clay county camp of Confederate veterans was organized, numbering now about two hundred and fifty old Confederate soldiers. The camp showed their appreciation of the Captain by unanimously electing him their commander, which position he now holds. Captain Beall had the misfortune to lose his first wife after there had been born unto them three children: Fred M., Emma and Willie. Fred M. is now practicing law at West Point, Miss.; Emma is unmarried; Willie married W. P. Pope, of Columbus, Miss., who has since been admitted to the bar, and is practicing with his father-in-law. Captain Beall married, a second time, in 1874, his present wife having been Miss Chattie A. McEachin, daughter of Peter and Mariah McEachin, formerly of North Carolina. The present Mrs. Beall is a lady of the highest culture, an earnest Christian worker, beloved by all who know her. The fruit of the last marriage is one daughter, Zoe, yet a little schoolgirl, in disposition and character much like her mother. Captain, Beall, wife and all his chidren, are members of the West Point Baptist church, except his daughter, Willie, who went with her husband to the Presbyterian church. He is also a member of the board of directors of the Young Men's Christian association of West Point, and of the state executive committee of that organization.

Middleton Beasley, a prominent planter of Copiah county, Miss., was born in Dollington district, S. C., in 1818. He was the son of Daniel and Catherine Beasley. His father was born in South Carolina in 1790, and devoted his life exclusively to farming. He was married at about the age of twenty to Catherine McClelon, a daughter of Dennis and Delilah Mc-Clelon, of South Carolina. He came with his parents to Mississippi in 1813, locating first in Lawrence county, and after one year coming to Simpson county, where he remained till his death, which occurred in 1863. Mr. and Mrs. Beasley had thirteen children: Fairby, who became the wife of Evan Shivers, of Simpson county; Rebecca, who married L. Holifield, of Simpson county; Middleton; Irene, who married William L. Lane; Willis Walker; Duncan O., of Simpson county; Louisa J., who was married to Lafayette Swilly, of Louisiana; Caroline, who became the wife of Archibald Smith; Jefferson M., of Lawrence county; Delilah, who married Daniel Dampier, of Simpson county; Levina, who was joined in wedlock to Henry Smith, of Lawrence county, and Thompson, who lives in Copiah county. Daniel Beasley was the son of John and Millie (Smith) Beasley. John Beasley was a soldier in the Revolutionary war. Middleton Beasley began life for himself at about the age of eighteen years, upon a plantation in Simpson county, where he remained for five years. At the end of that time he came directly to Copiah county, where he has since lived. In 1837 he married for his first wife Elizabeth Cammack, a daughter of Thomas and Jemima Cammack, who bore him nine children, the following five of whom are yet living: Delilah, wife of Henry Harrison; Thompson, of Copiah county; Matilda, the wife of E. H. Little, of Copiah county; Catherine, wife of T. J. Norman; Jasper, who lives in Copiah county. After the death of his first wife Mr. Beasley married, in 1885, Mrs. Hattie (Harvey) Smith, who was the daughter of Elijah and Elizabeth (Watts) Harvey. He has had two children by this second marriage: Lillie P. and Middleton, both living at home. Mrs. Smith had nine children by her first marriage, five of whom are yet living: Kirby D., Amelia, Francis M., Ora and Belle. Mr. Beasley is a member of the Masonic order, and connected both with the Blue lodge of Quitman and the Royal Arch chapter No. 18, of Hazelhurst. He and his wife are members of the Methodist Episcopal church. He was connected with the state militia during the war, but was not in active service. Two of his sons gave their young lives to the Confederate cause. Mr. Beasley is one of the wealthiest farmers in the county; a careful, progressive and conservative business man, who has made his own way in the world, and has acquired his possessions by honest work and good management. It is a satisfaction to say that such a man must needs stand high socially and in a business way.

A most prosperous and enterprising citizen, R. F. Beck, was born in the state of New York in 1841, but in 1865 came to Vicksburg, since which time he has been one of the leading and most substantial citizens of the place. He is extensively engaged in contracting and building, which calling he has successfully followed since his first residence here. He is the eldest son born to William and Mary (O'Brien) Beck, who were born in the Emerald Isle, the former crossing the ocean to America about the year 1838 and settling in Troy, N. Y., where he began work as a stonecutter, being awarded the contracts for the canal, lock and bridge work. At a later period he formed a partnership with his brother and established a business at Albany, being engaged in furnishing stone to builders. About the year 1859 he removed to Poughkeepsie, N. Y., where he was in the grocery business for many years and where he spent his declining days, dying in September, 1890, his wife having passed from life in 1887, both members of the Catholic church. R. F. Beck received but a common-school education, but the active business career he has since led has been an education in itself, and he is now an intelligent and well-informed gentlemen. He first started out in life for himself in the city of St. Louis, Mo., whither he went in 1865, but a few months later came to Vicksburg, and here has since been engaged in contracting and building. In a very short time he became the most extensive builder of the city, and soon after started a brick-yard and began the manufacture of his own brick, his yards being now among the largest in the state. In addition to supplying his own needs he sends large quantities of his product up the delta and to Louisiana. About 1880 he began planting and is now the owner of three fine plantations: One, at Timber lake, in Bolivar county, is one of the most fertile in the state, comprising two thousand four hundred acres, of which about one thousand two hundred acres are under cultivation; another is in Arkansas and Louisiana, and he is also the owner of several thousand acres of land in the vicinity of Vicksburg that produce about one thousand bales of cotton annually. Mr. Beck is identified with the building up of Vicksburg, and is interested in a number of enterprises, being president of the Vicksburg building association, director of the First National bank, an organizer and now a director in the Home insurance company, director in the Yazoo & Tallahatchie steamboat line, secretary and treasurer of the Vicksburg & Delta transportation company, the Vicksburg compress company, the Wharf & Land company, and the Wharf & Elevator company. In 1875 he erected an elegant home on South street, which is one of the finest private residences in Vicksburg. This ideal home is elegantly and artistically furnished and contains many and valuable works of art and bric-a-brac collected by Mrs. Beck. He was elected an alderman from the first ward, and after serving one term moved to the fourth ward, and in 1878 acted as mayor, in which capacity he served for a short time, being then elected to the position. His popularity is attested by his having been elected sheriff of Warren county three different terms, serving in all six years, and is now serving his third term as mayor. Under his progressive administration Vicksburg has improved very materially, many works of a public character having been completed and many private enterprises started, the policy of the city being such as to encourage enterprise of all kinds. In 1880 he was a delegate from this district to the republican convention at Chicago, and four years later was a delegate to Chicago, during which convention he favored the nomination of Chester A. Arthur for the presidency. He is a member of and attends the state national conventions, and has always interested himself in the political affairs of his section. In 1876 he was married to Miss Mary Ella Rigby, a daughter of Col. Thomas Rigby, and their union has resulted in the birth of three children, two of whom, Thomas Rigby and Mary, are living, both of them handsome and promising. Mr. Beck is a self-made man, very active and energetic, and during his business career he has erected a large number of the finest buildings of Vicksburg. He is of medium stature, has brown hair and mustache and has a fine forehead, showing that he is a man of superior mental endowments. His wife is a talented and beautiful woman, of the pure blonde type, is a fine conversationalist and has fascinating manners. She possesses artistic ability of a high order and her taste and judgment in this matter has enabled her to place many beautiful works of art in her home. She has two beautiful and rare pieces of Goeblin tapestry, many handsome pieces of bronze, and almost innumerable articles of virtu, collected at her order from various parts of the world, the whole making one of the most costly and beautiful private collections in the South.

Richard Capel Beckett is a distinguished attorney of West Point, and during the twenty-three years that he has practiced his profession has shown himself to be endowed with superior ability, his comprehensive knowledge of the law and the soundness of his judgment securing him almost immediate recognition at the bar. He was born in Pickens county, Ala., about one and a half miles south of Pickensville, on August 24, 1845, to Dr. James McKinney and Willie E. Beckett, the former of whom was born in Columbia, S. C., on March 14, 1805, and the latter in Marengo county, Ala., on June 28, 1821. Dr. Beckett received a fine education in his youth, and graduated from the university of South Carolina, at Columbia, in 1821, and afterward gained quite a reputation by publicly opposing the retention of Dr. Cooper as president of the university, on account of his views on religion. Dr. Beckett studied medicine, and for a number of years during his early life was quite prominent in his profession. On January 3, 1832, he married Juliet Margaret Johnston, who died in 1835, leaving one son, Newton Johnston Beckett, born September 9, 1834. In 1836 or 1837 Dr. Beckett moved to Pickens county, Ala., where, on June 24, 1840, he married Mrs. Willie E. Carleton, the young widow of Warren Carleton, and in 1853 he moved to Monroe county, Miss., and located near Aberdeen. In 1857 he purchased the Gullett gin factory at Aberdeen, and, in 1859, took Dr. J. L. Tindall into partnership. The factory turned out three hundred gins annually and was enlarged to include corn and flour mills, a wool-carding machine, a lumber kiln, a planingmill and a foundry. From the fall of 1860 to the fall of 1861 R. C. Beckett was superintendent of the corn and flourmills and wool-carding machine, and during the winter of 1861 was bookkeeper for the factory. In the fall of 1861 the Confederate government offered $100,000 in gold for the factory, which was refused, but Drs. Beckett and Tindall converted it into a rifle and cannon factory and sawed off, bored out and restocked all the old sporting rifles throughout the country for the use of the army and the state troops. In the early part of 1862, when they were about prepared to turn out regular arms and cannon, two strangers applied for work, claiming to be experts in gunmaking, and were employed without sufficient investigation, for, in a short time, the factory was burned down one night, after the second attempt, and these two men disappeared the same night. Dr. Beckett then moved out on his farm, where his wife died on August 22, 1865. In December, 1871, he moved to West Point, where he died on January 8, 1873, an earnest member of the Presbyterian church, as was his wife. Dr. Beckett was a fine scholar, and in his early life was quite an active politician, serving in the senate of Alabama from 1847 to 1851. He was an able and intelligent legislator, and during the time from 1840 to 1853 that he was a member of the board of trustees of the University of Alabama, displayed much discrimination and judgment. In 1848 he was a Lewis Cass elector from the fourth congressional district of Alabama. He was the youngest but two of fourteen children born to Margaret Beckett, who was born in county Antrim, Ireland, on May 12, 1763, and on July 10, 1782, was married to James Beckett Sr., who, in the latter part of the last century, came to the United States and, with his wife, settled in South Carolina. He died in 1812, and his wife died in Columbia, S. C., on August 16, 1851, almost a lifelong member of the Presbyterian church. The maternal grandfather of the subject of this sketch, Britton Capel, came from Baltimore, Md., and settled near Montgomery, Ala. He married Sarah Terrell, was a well-known Methodist minister and became a wealthy planter. They had two sons and two daughters: Jabez, Louisa Ann, Willie E. and Frank. Jabez was a soldier in the Mexican war, where he was severely wounded in the head. He settled in Texas, where he died several years ago, having held several state offices. Louisa Ann married B. F. Tarver in 1827, and died March 25, 1859, near Montgomery, leaving five sons and four daughters.

Willie E. married Warren Carleton, who died soon after, on September 25, 1836, and she afterward married Dr. Beckett, and by him had five children: James, Richard Capel, Frank, Jessie and Britton. Newton J. Beckett died at Shelbyville, Tenn., on January 14, 1863, at which time he was captain of company I, Forty-first Mississippi infantry. He had been a popular and talented lawyer at Aberdeen, and, on September 16, 1856, went to Kansas as captain of a military company, during the exciting times of that period, while just twenty-two years of age. In 1858 he was elected a justice of the peace in Aberdeen, and in 1860 was elected probate judge of Monroe county. He and Dr. Beckett were both Masons. He received the lodge degrees at Aberdeen in 1856, was junior warden of the lodge in 1857, worshipful master in 1859, 1860 and 1861, and junior warden of the grand lodge in 1860. He was also a law partner of Judge Francis M. Rogers, who was killed in the storming of Fort Donelson. His widow, Mrs. Olivia C. Beckett, resides with her sister and brother-in-law, Mrs. and Capt. W. G. Weatherford, in Memphis, Tenn. James served in the Forty-first Mississippi infantry, was afterward a teacher by profession, and died in Monroe county in April, 1871, and Britton died there in October, 1871. They, with Newton J. and their father and mother, are all buried at Aberdeen, in the new cemetery, in lot or square 306. Frank, who is a lawyer at Vernon, Tex., was a boy during the war, but served a short time in the Mississippi state troops. Jessie is the widow of R. N. Dominick, who died at West Point on May 10, 1891.

R. C. Beckett received his education in the high school of Aberdeen, where he was always awarded the highest medals for scholarship until he was barred from competing, and at the southern university of Greensboro, Ala., being a collegemate of Governor Seay. Upon the burning of the factory at Aberdeen, he joined company I, Forty-first Mississippi infantry, and served until December, 1862, under General Bragg, from the fight at Farmington near Corinth till after the close of the Kentucky campaign, when he was discharged for disability. He then went to the Southern university until June, 1863, and in July, 1863, joined a company which afterward became company B of the Sixteenth Confederate cavalry, and served as orderly-sergeant till the close of the war, first under Generals Pillow and Wheeler in northern Georgia in the cavalry engagements at Lafayette and Rome, then back toward Tennessee to cover Hood's movement, when he with his command was sent to protect Mobile, Ala., under General Liddell. They were in the engagement at Pollard or Pine Barren near Pensacola, and in the siege and storming of Fort Blakely, but escaped to Mobile, and finally surrendered to General Canby at State Line, Miss., in May, 1865, and were paroled at Gainesville, Ala., about the middle of the month. He was wounded at Rome, Ga. After the war he began clerking in a store at Aberdeen, but at the end of one year commenced teaching school while he studied law, and in February, 1868, was admitted to the bar at Aberdeen. He then formed a partnership with Hon. R. E. Houston in the practice of his profession, which continued for one year, when he went into co-partnership with Col. C. R. Barteau, and toward the close of the year 1869 became associated in the law practice with F. G. Barry. In August, 1871, he moved to West Point, and in 1876 again became associated with Mr. Barry, who had in the meantime also moved to West Point, they constituting one of the strongest law firms in northeast Mississippi, and Mr. Barry having served in congress from March 4, 1885 to March 4, 1889. The style of the firm is Barry & Beckett and they practice in all the state and Federal courts, and are well known as able and talented lawyers. On September 23, 1874, R. C. Beckett was married to Miss Blanche, daughter of W. C. Tucker, a Tennesseean, who removed to Columbus, Miss., where he and his wife died. Mrs. Blanche Beckett was born in Columbus on November 5, 1853, and died in West Point on

March 1, 1889, leaving two daughters: Willie Capel and Blanche Mabel, and three sons: Clarence Tucker, Bergie Barry and Richard Capel. She was a member of the Baptist church. On August 14, 1890, R. C. Beckett was married, a second time, to Mary C., daughter of Rev. A. A. and Catherine E. Bell. Mr. Bell was born in Franklin county, Tenn., and from there removed to Alabama, and in 1869 came to West Point, where he died in 1882, at the age of sixty, being still survived by his widow, who was born in Clarke county, Ky., in 1832. He was a minister of the Cumberland Presbyterian church. Mrs. Mary Beckett was born in Fayetteville, Tenn., was educated principally at the Columbus female institute of Columbus, Miss., and is a member of the Cumberland Presbyterian church. Mr. Beckett is a member of the Knights of Honor. In politics he is a democrat, but has never sought office, and has confined himself strictly to the practice of his profession. In June, 1891, the highest medal for excellence in scholarship was awarded to his daughter Willie in the public graded school of West Point, having over four hundred pupils. The name was originally Becket, but was Americanized by Dr. Beckett in accordance with a custom prevailing at the time of doubling the final consonant in proper names.

Among the most prosperous young planters of De Soto county, Miss., is Whyte Bedford, of Blythe, Miss., a brief biographical sketch of whom will be found in the following lines. He is a native of Panola county, Miss., born September 18, 1854, and is the oldest of a family of nine children. His father, Benjamin W. Bedford, a native of Tennessee, married Sallie McGehn, a Mississippian. He was a planter in his native state, and came to Mississippi in 1832; he died in 1866. His father, Benjamin W. Bedford, Sr., married Nancy Whyte. He died in 1883, at the age of eighty-nine years; he was also a resident of Mississippi from 1832. Whyte Bedford grew to manhood amid the scenes and surroundings of his birth. He received a liberal education, being a student at the university of the South in 1871, at Oxford in 1872–3, and at the East Tennessee university, Knoxville, Tenn., from 1873 to 1876. After leaving school he engaged in the mercantile trade at Lynchburg, Miss., and has since retained his interest in the commercial world. He carries a stock of goods valued at $3,500. He is also a planter, owning sixteen hundred acres of land, seven hundred and fifty of which are under cultivation. He owns real estate in Memphis, Tenn., and has some property in Nashville, Tenn., and Florida. Although he began with small capital he has amassed a considerable fortune. He was married in 1879 to Miss Katie H. Hart of Kentucky, a daughter of Capt. Ed. R. and Helen Hart. He has given liberally of his means to support public enterprises of merit, and has been one of the live factors in the growth of the county. He affiliates with the democratic party, but takes no active part in the movements of that body. He is a man of wide influence, and by his fair dealings has won many stanch friends and admirers in the business world. Socially he is affable, courteous and kind, and ranks among the leading men of the county.

F. M. Beeks of Monroe county, Miss., was born May 27, 1830, in Laurens county, S. C. He was the eldest son of Samuel Beeks, who was born in Newbury, S. C., about 1807, and received his education in the common schools of that state. He was a hard student, and at the age when most young men are still in school he was induced to accept employment as a teacher. When he was twenty-two years of age, he married Belinda E. Andrews. After his marriage he engaged in farming, in which he continued until his death. Although not a politician in the ordinary sense of the word, he was deeply interested in all that pertained to the good of the community, which he served as a justice of the peace for a number of years. He was a member of the Odd Fellow's lodge of Aberdeen, in which he was elevated to the highest official station. He came to Mississippi from South Carolina in 1849, locating two miles from Athens, in Monroe county.   He was the father of ten children, who were all born while he yet lived in South Carolina.   F. M. Beeks received his education in the common schools of South Carolina and Mississippi, fitting himself for teaching, a profession which he followed until 1866.   In that year he married Miss M. J. Daniel, who bore him five children: James William, Mary Jane, Nettie Lou, Luther Clarence, and Francis M.   In the second year of the war, Mr. Beeks enlisted in company C, Forty-third Mississippi regiment, and participated in the last battle at Corinth, where he was taken prisoner.   He was soon exchanged and did not reënter the service.   He is a member of the Knights of Honor lodge of Aberdeen, and is connected with the Methodist Episcopal church of Friendship.   He is one of the honest, industrious, self-made men of this county, held in the highest esteem by all with whom he has business or social relations.

A prominent merchant and spoke manufacturer, near Cortland, Miss., is C. T. Bell, who is one of the wideawake, enterprising young business men of the county, and has fully demonstrated his business qualities in the short time he has been in business.   Although he has only been engaged in merchandising since 1888, when he started with a small capital, he is now doing an annual business of $20,000, which speaks for itself.   Aside from this, he runs a steam sawmill and cottongin, to which he has now added a Defiance, Ohio, spoke lathe No. 1, which has a capacity of turning out twenty-five hundred spokes per day.   As the forests all around this place abound in unexcelled spoke timber, within easy access to railroad transportation, Mr. Bell has shown his good judgment in investing his money in this enterprise, which he is prepared to run to the full capacity of his machinery, and do an all-year-round business, having turned out ten thousand or more in the rough daily.   Mr. Bell is the fifth son living born to the union of J. M. D. and L. M. (McCracken) Bell, the father a native Kentuckian, born in Logan county, and the mother of Maury county, Tenn.   J. M. D. Bell is a very extensive and successful farmer of Panola county, and is the owner of sixteen hundred or more acres of land, with about one-half under cultivation.   He is also quite a prominent stockraiser.   He is active in politics, and a strong Alliance man.   His children, six in number, were named in the order of their births as follows: William T., a farmer of the county; C. T.; Sarah O., wife of J. C. Fowler, Jr.; Mary T., wife of W. D. Walker; L. M. and J. M. M., the last two at home.

Elijah J. Bell, Hernando, Miss., has been closely identified with the commercial history of De Soto county since 1869, at which time his residence here began.   He was born in Chatham county, N. C., and is a son of Thomas and Rebecca Bell, also natives of North Carolina.   Fourteen children were born to them, of whom he is the youngest.   His father was a planter by occupation, and passed his life in North Carolina.   He died there in 1861, at the age of seventy-four years, respected by the entire community.   He was more than ordinarily successful, and accumulated a large property.   His father, Enoch Bell, was also a planter in North Carolina.   The family was one of agriculturists, having no aspirations for political honors.   Elijah J. received his education at Trinity college, North Carolina.   In 1864 he enlisted in the Confederate service, in company B, Fifth North Carolina regiment.   He participated in the battles around Petersburg, and was constantly on duty from the time of his enlistment to his surrender.   After the war was over, Mr. Bell returned to his home, and reëntered school at Trinity.   He continued his studies there for one year, and then went to Baltimore, Md., where he entered a commercial school; he was graduated in 1867.   For one year he was engaged in planting, and then made some investments in mercantile business.   He has been prosperous in all his undertakings, and is an example of what energy, thrift and perseverance can accomplish.   He owns twenty-five hundred acres of land, a greater portion of which is under cultivation. He is proprietor of Belle Meade Jersey farm, and a member of American Jersey cattle club. In this branch of farming he takes much interest, and is justly proud of his herd, numbering about one hundred. He is a member of the firm of Payne & Bell, owning one-half the business; they handle about $60,000 annually. This is one of the largest firms in Hernando, and one of the most reliable. (See sketch of Colonel Payne.) Mr. Bell was married in 1871 to Miss Mina B. White, a native of Mississippi, and a daughter of Col. T. W. and Mina B. (Meriwether) White, natives of Georgia. (See sketch of Colonel White.) Mrs. Bell died in 1878, leaving two children: Mildred and Mina, both of whom are living. Mr. Bell was married, a second time, in 1886, to Miss Lu Lee Bowdre, a Mississippian, and a daughter of Maj. A. R. and Lucy (Meriwether) Bowdre, natives of Georgia. Three children have been born of this union: Rebecca, Lu Lee, and an infant, deceased. The parents are members of the Baptist church, and Mr. Bell belongs to the Knights of Honor. He is a most estimable gentleman, of rare good judgment, of well-defined purposes and opinions and excellent business qualifications.

One of the pioneer educators of the state of Mississippi, entitled to a space in this volume, is Prof. J. C. Bell, Baldwyn, Miss., a planter of Prentiss county, Miss. He was born in Laurens district, S. C., May 11, 1830, and is a son of William Bell of Abbeville district, S. C. His father was born in 1798, and was a son of William Bell, a native of Ireland, who fought in the war of the Revolution. He immigrated to this country and was married to a Miss Waters, and they reared a family of five children: Thomas, Peter, William (the father of our subject) David and Mrs. Vandever. William Bell was reared in South Carolina, and removed to Alabama in 1845, settling in Pickens county. There he followed farming until his death, which occurred in 1833. He was married to Miss Mary Crues, who was born in Abbeville district, S. C., in 1808, a daughter of Jonathan Crues. Her mother's maiden name was Elizabeth Greene, a niece of General Greene. Her father was a soldier in the Revolutionary war. The mother was married, a second time, to a Mr. Lomax. The mother of Professor Bell died in Pickens county, Ala., in May, 1863. She and her husband reared a family of nine children, all of whom lived to be grown: James died in the war; Mary is the wife of P. G. Martin; J. C. is the third born, Thomas also died in the war; Martha, wife of Jeffra Henry, is deceased; Joseph Newton is a resident of Pickens county, Ala.; Francis M. is a planter of Lowndes county, Miss.; Benjamin F. lives in Pickens county, Miss.; Dorothea married Mr. Gann and resides in Scott county, Miss. Professor Bell lived until he was fifteen years of age in his native state, when he removed to Alabama; he returned to South Carolina and was graduated from one of her foremost educational institutions in 1860; there were twenty-four in the class of which he took the honors. He came back to Pickens county, Ala., and engaged in teaching at Liberty academy, continuing there nine years. At the end of that time he went to Carrollton, the county seat of Pickens county, and was engaged in teaching there for five years; thence he went to Deerbrook, Noxubee county, Miss., where he taught for five years; his next scene of action was West Point, Miss., where he remained but one year. He then came to Baldwyn and for two years continued his labors as a teacher. He then abandoned the profession and settled on a farm known as the Richardson plantation, two and a half miles west of Baldwyn, in Lee county; there he owns three hundred and sixty acres, besides five hundred and forty acres in Tupelo county. The war swept all his property accumulated previous to that time away, and since then he has been obliged to keep closely to his profession in order to retrieve his fortunes in any measure. Professor Bell was married near Pulaski, Tenn., to Mary Barmore, a native of Pickens county, Ala., who was left an orphan and reared and educated by an aunt, Miss Morris. Nine children were born to Professor Bell and wife: William D., a farmer of Noxubee county, Miss.; Eliza, wife of J. W. Carr; Alice, a highly accomplished teacher; Lewis, a farmer in Texas; Zana, wife of T. R. Stubbs; Fannie I.; Maggie M., Daisy and Susan Rebecca. All of the children have been given an excellent education. He and his wife are members of the Presbyterian church. Politically he affiliates with the democratic party. In 1862 he enlisted in the Confederate service, joining the Seventh Alabama infantry. He was elected first lieutenant and afterward was made captain. He was in some important engagements and several skirmishes, doing valiant service. He is a member of the Baldwyn lodge, A. F. & A. M., and of the I. O. O. F.

The family of James R. Bell, of Bentonia Miss., is of Irish and German origin. The earliest emigrants to this country came in pioneer days, facing all the trials and privations incident to the settlement of a new country. Our subject was born in Holmes county, Miss., December 5, 1831, and is the son of William J. andLouisa (Hoover) Bell, natives of Georgia and Mississippi, respectively. They were the parents of four children, of whom James R. is the second. The father removed to Mississippi in 1824, and located in Holmes county, where he passed the balance of his days, his death occurring in 1837. His parents, Eleazer and Mary (Causey) Bell, were from Virginia and South Carolina, respectively. The maternal grandparents of Mr. Bell were Joseph and Elizabeth (Zeigler) Hoover, of South Carolina. He spent his youth in Mississippi and attended the private schools of the neighborhood. He was trained to the occupation of planting, which he has always followed. He owns seven hundred and sixty acres of fine land, and has placed three hundred acres under cultivation. He has been twice married; he was first united to Miss Celeste Dunn, of Mississippi, a daughter of James L. and Mary (Tucker) Dunn, natives of South Carolina. Seven children were born of this marriage, only two of whom are living: Robert J. and Martin A.; the latter was a Methodist Episcopal minister, and an able and eloquent speaker; he won several different medals at college for his superior oratory. At the age of twenty-eight years he passed from this life, deeply mourned by a wide circle of friends. Mr. Bell's second marriage was in 1862 to Miss Susan M. Williams, of Mississippi, a daughter of Anthony Williams, a native of the state of New York. The subject of this notice was a member of the Confederate army, enlisting as a member of company B, Twelfth Mississippi regiment volunteer infantry. He went out as first lieutenant and received several promotions. At the close of the war he was lieutenant-colonel of his regiment. He participated in the following battles: Seven Pines, Petersburg, Cold Harbor, Wilderness, Chancellorsville, Spottsylvania courthouse, Gettysburg, Antietam and Williamsburg. He was seriously wounded in the battle of Seven Pines, and in 1864 he was taken prisoner and carried to Fort Donelson, where he was held until the close of the war. He and his wife are worthy members of the Methodist Episcopal church. He belongs to the Masonic and I. O. O. F. fraternities, and is the county lecturer for the Farmers' Alliance, having taken an active interest in that body since its organization. Politically he affiliates with the democratic party. He is a man of public spirit, and has liberally sustained all public enterprises.

One of the leading attorneys of Mississippi is Judge Thomas P. Bell, of De Kalb, who has been a resident of Kemper county since 1844, when his parents removed to this state from North Carolina. His father, Dr. Samuel Bell, was born in Ireland, and was educated in the city of Dublin. He was a son of Henry Bell, and the year of his birth was 1798. He immigrated to the United States in 1820, and during the remainder of his life was engaged in the practice of his profession. In 1844 he removed to Kemper county, and in addition to his professional work he opened about two thousand acres of land, which were well improved under his supervision. He was a man of pronounced political views, but had the interests of his adopted country at heart. His wife was born in Ireland in 1800. She was a daughter of Thomas and Bessie (Duke) Parke. They reared a family of eight children: Henry, Eliza, Mary A., Fannie, Eleanor, Thomas P., Margaret J. and Hettie. The father died in 1857, and the mother survived him until 1865. Judge Bell, the subject of this notice, was born in North Carolina in 1835, and was but nine years of age at the time his parents removed to Kemper county, Miss. He was educated in this county and at Tuscaloosa, Ala. He began the practice of law in 1856, in this county, and he was elected probate judge when he was twenty-one years of age. In 1876 he was elected a member of the state legislature from Kemper county, when he reflected much credit upon his constituency. In 1861 he enlisted in the Confederate service, being elected lieutenant of company C, Thirteenth Mississippi volunteer infantry. He was in the engagements at Manassas, Fredericksburg, Gettysburg and Sharpsburg, and when General Barksdale was promoted Judge Bell was taken on his staff. He was serving as his aid-de-camp when the General was killed at Gettysburg. After the war he settled on his plantation, where he lived until he was elected a member of the legislature. He was a member of the constitutional convention of 1890. In 1865 Judge Bell was united in marriage to Miss Amelia Eiland, a daughter of Dr. O. G. and Mary (Hatcher) Eiland, natives of Alabama. Mrs. Bell was born at Marion, Ala., in 1841. Her father was a prominent physician there, and was one of the founders of the female college in that place. Four children have been born to the Judge and his wife: Samuel and Canning are living, and James and Mary are deceased. Mrs. Bell died in October, 1889. She was a worthy member of the Baptist church. The Judge belongs to the Methodist Episcopal church. He is a member of the Masonic order, and is a man of generous impulses who believes in home and home protection. He is a stanch patriot, and is as loyal to his friends as to his country. He owns some real estate, having about four hundred acres south of De Kalb which he has improved.

William Bell, a planter and merchant of Hinds county, Miss., and a native of Rankin county, was born on the 12th of August, 1838, the elder of two children born to Edwin and Eliza (Eley) Bell, both of whom were born in the Old North state. The Bells came to America prior to the Revolutionary war, from the Emerald isle, and the grandfather of William Bell was a soldier in the war of 1812. The mother's people were of Scotch-Irish descent. Edwin Bell removed to Mississippi in the year 1833 and settled on a plantation of considerable extent in Hinds county. William Bell was an attendant of the common schools up to the age of fifteen years, then entered Mississippi college at Clinton, which institution he attended for two years, at the end of which time he entered the drug establishment of Banks & Horn, at Clinton, as a salesman, and during the five years that he remained with them he won the entire confidence of his employers and was considered by them a valuable assistant. Upon leaving them he went to North Carolina on a visit, and while there enlisted in the Twenty-fourth North Carolina regiment of infantry, the most of his service being in the state of Virginia, under Ransom, and was a participant in the battles of Antietam, Plymouth, siege of Petersburg, the seven days' fight around Richmond, and the battle of Five Forks. At the close of the war he returned to Mississippi and turned his attention to planting, and that same year (1865) raised quite a crop of cotton. All his accumulations had been swept away during the struggle for supremacy between the North and South, and for some time after the cessation of hostilities he farmed on shares. His first purchase of land was made in 1869, since which time additions have been made at different times until he now has one thousand eight hundred and ninety-five acres, which he considers worth at least

$10 per acre. He has about one thousand acres under cultivation, on which he raises annually two hundred and fifty bales of cotton and two thousand bushels of corn. He has a steam cottongin and gristmill, and is also interested in the raising of horses, cattle, sheep and hogs, which enterprise he has found to be quite profitable. His land is in a fine state of cultivation, and under his watchful care it is not allowed to run down, but is kept in excellent farming condition, and the buildings and fences in good repair. In connection with his plantation he conducts a good general mercantile establishment, and is doing a prosperous furnishing business. He has always been ambitious, and does not consider it beneath him to earn his bread by the sweat of his brow, and as a natural result he has been successful in his business enterprises. He has always been interested in local politics, and in 1882 was elected to the position of magistrate for four years, and in 1886 to the position of supervisor, during which time he was president of the board for four years, and with the appropriation made by this board he commenced the bridge over the Pearl river. He also had the school terms lengthened and taxes lessened. Socially he is a member of the Knights of Honor and the Knights of Pythias. He was married in February, 1866, to Miss E. A. Beeman, a native of North Carolina, and by her has the following family: Janadius B., Willie Ellen, Maggie E., Edwin B., Annie L., Wes. H., S. D. C. and Lucille. Two children are deceased. Mr. Bell has taken a deep interest in the education of his children, and has given them good advantages. Willie and Maggie have completed courses in the Central female institute at Clinton, and Annie L. will finish her course in 1892. He and his family worship in the Baptist church, of which himself and wife are earnest members. They are leading citizens of the section in which they reside, and move in the highest social circles.

William G. Benbrook, mayor of Natchez, was born in that city in 1837, and is the son of Dr. Daniel G. and Margaret (Boyer) Benbrook. His father graduated from the Ohio state medical college at Cincinnati at an early day, and while he was still a young man (perhaps about 1828), he came to Natchez, where he engaged in the practice of his profession, in which he was very successful. Here he resided until 1846, when he moved to New Orleans, and there his death occurred in 1850. Mrs. Benbrook died in Natchez in 1861. Mayor Benbrook was reared in Natchez, secured a liberal education in the public schools of that place, and has made that city his home all his life. In 1858 he selected as his life companion Miss Hannah Parsons, a native also of Natchez, and the daughter of Alexander H. and Matilda Parsons, who were early settlers of Natchez, where they spent their entire days. To Mr. and Mrs. Benbrook were born ten children, four of whom are living. Mr. Benbrook followed clerking in his native town until the breaking out of the war, and he then joined the Natchez light infantry for sixty days, serving as first lieutenant. At the expiration of service he came home, and soon joined the Breckinridge guards as orderly sergeant and served about two years. He was then discharged on account of disability, and did not again return to service. Since the war Mr. Benbrook has been very active in all enterprise pertaining to the welfare of the city and county, and is an indefatigable worker for the democratic party, having served for many years as a member of the democratic county executive committee. He also served for a number of years as city treasurer, then as assessor of Adams county, and in 1888 he was elected mayor of Natchez, being reëlected to that office in 1890. He has known the people of Natchez and Adams county from infancy, and they have had every opportunity to judge of his character and qualifications, and their confidence in him has been intelligently placed. He is also a very prominent Mason, being a member of Andrew Jackson lodge No. 2, Natchez, in which he has held all the principal offices, being at the present time past grand commander of the Knight Templars of Mississippi.

He was a delegate to the Masonic conclave held at Chicago in 1880. He has also held all the offices of Natchez lodge No. 3 of the Knights of Pythias, and is president of the Endowment rank of Bluff City lodge No. 1145 of the Knights of Honor. He and Mrs. Benbrook are members of the Presbyterian church.

Calvin Smith Bennett, a planter of Adams county, Miss., where he was born on the 20th of December, 1848, is the son of Edwin R. and Mary Louisa (Smith) Bennett, the father born in New Castle, Del., in 1811, and the mother in Adams county, Miss., in the same year. When a young man the elder Bennett came with his brother, Henry L. Bennett, to Adams county, Miss., married here, and here passed the remainder of his life, dying in 1876. In early life he was a merchant in Natchez, but afterward became a prominent planter. His wife died in 1877; both were members of the Presbyterian church. He was the son of ex-Gov. Caleb B. Bennett, who fought with De Kalb in the Revolutionary war and part of the time was major on General Washington's staff. For participating in the war he was suspended from the Quaker church of which he was a member. He was governor of Delaware two terms, and was a member of the Order of Cincinnati. He died in 1830 at the age of seventy-eight years, and is buried at Wilmington, Del., his native state. He was of Scotch-Irish origin. His wife was born in 1757 and died in 1838. His parents were Joseph and Bettie Bennett, who were married in 1755, and who died in 1792 and 1808, respectively. Calvin Smith, the maternal grandfather of our subject, was born in Massachusetts on the 25th of December, 1768, and came to Adams county, Miss., with his father, Rev. Jedediah Smith, in a very early day. Here he married his wife, Priscilla, and settled in the wilderness, with no neighbors within miles of them, building a rude hut for their first house on the place where Calvin S. Bennett now lives, known as Retirement. Mr. Smith worked as a carpenter in Natchez for some time in his early married life, while his wife, unaided and unprotected, attended to clearing and planting the farm until they had accumulated sufficient means to enable them to purchase their first negro, for whom they paid $100. They were very industrious and accumulated a large fortune. They passed the remaining years of their life on the Retirement plantation, ten miles southeast of Natchez, he dying in 1840, and she six years later. They were the parents of twelve children, ten of whom grew to manhood and womanhood, to whom they left handsome fortunes. Two of the daughters married Gillespies, two more married Bennetts, two married Feridays, and one a Mr. Ralston. Their sons were: Luther (died in infancy), Calvin Stephen, Benijah O. and Robert L. The last three married; Stephen and Benijah reared families, Robert died childless. Calvin Smith Bennett was the fifth of six children—four sons and two daughters—viz.: Katharine Priscilla, Edwin R. (deceased) and Henry L. (deceased), both of whom died in the service soon after the Shiloh battle (but were at home), aged eighteen and sixteen years, respectively, and both belonged to the Tenth Mississippi infantry; Mary Louisa (the wife of James M. Ogden), Calvin S. and Caleb (who died in infancy). Calvin S. was educated at home, at Kingston, at Oakland college and at Tours in France. He is a member of the Knights of Honor, Bluff City lodge, Natchez, No. 1145, and of the American Legion of Honor. The following, relative to the Smith family, is copied from the original manuscript, which was written in 1829:

"*The late Rev. Jerediah Smith and his wife, Sarah Cook, of Granville, Mass.*—He had lived eighteen or twenty years previous to the year 1776 in the town of Granville, and officiated as the pastor of the Presbyterian church of that town. At the commencement of the Revolutionary war, not being favorably inclined to that measure, he was disposed to abandon a country that threatened the horrors of civil war. He was, therefore, easily prevailed upon by Thaddeus Lyman, who held a large tract of land by some title from the

British government in the new state of Mississippi, to emigrate to this country with a number of families, with a view of settling the lands belonging to Lyman, with promises of the most flattering kind. Another strong motive with Mr. Smith was, that he had a brother, Elnathan Smith, who had been in the Mississippi country one or two years, having left his wife, Hannah Bates (sister of the late Nathanial Bates, of Granville, and Jacob Bates, of Northupton) and his two daughters with their friends at Granville, and had written to them to join him, giving the most glowing accounts of this new country—a place where they would all become prosperous and happy. Under these flattering views the Rev. Mr. J. Smith, his wife and family of eleven children—nine sons and two daughters—left Granville for the country of the Mississippi in April of 1776. The children are named as follows: Ebenezer, William, Sarah, Josephus, Philetus, Israil, Philander, Philoniela, Calvin, Luther and Courtland. The eldest son, Jedediah Smith, late of Bradford, was married at the time and chose to remain in New England. Thus making a family of twelve children. The emigrating party was detained some time at Middletown, in consequence of some suspicions that British officers, who were prisoners, were secreted in the vessel which the emigrants were to go in. A Mr. Whitmore, half-owner of the vessel, was also going out on her. Lyman and Whitmore were both arrested. After some time Lyman was discharged, but Whitmore was tried and condemned to suffer death. He was supposed to have been executed, but from information obtained in Middletown in the year 1827, it was stated that he was reprieved and living at that time. The vessel finally left Middletown about the middle of May, and after many chases by British armed vessels and a most boisterous passage of two months, arrived at the mouth of the Mississippi river. In ten or twelve days they ascended to the city of New Orleans, but were prevented from landing by the Spanish authorities, and had to undergo a kind of quarantine, owing to the prevalence of smallpox. In this situation the two families remained until the middle of August, when a small craft was procured to ascend the river to Natchez. The boat had gone but a few miles when a squall arose and came near sinking it, but they finally landed at the house of an Englishman by the name of War. Finding the boat was too heavily laden, they left part of their furniture, wearing apparel and library and a large portion of the bedding and farming utensils with this gentleman. At that time the country was settled but a short distance above New Orleans, and this only at long intervals. At Baton Rouge, Point Coupee and Natchez only could accommodations be had. The greater part of the way was a perfect wilderness; however, much hospitality was shown the strangers except where Roman Catholic bigotry prevailed. In such cases the idea of a minister of the gospel or a priest being openly married and having a family of children was abhorrent, and they viewed the party as horrible heretics. The weather was extremely warm, with showers two or three times a day, rendering the situation of the two families very uncomfortable, being exposed to alternate rain and hot sun. After fifteen days of such exposure they arrived at a place called Fort Adams, about forty-five miles below Natchez. At Fort Adams the Rev. Mr. Smith heard of the death of his brother, Elnathan, which caused great sorrow and gloom to the whole party. Shortly after this the Rev. Mr. Smith was taken with a violent fever. The weather continued very hot with constant rain, and the situation of so large a family in an open boat aggravated the fatal disease, that was soon to deprive him of his life. He became delirious and in his frenzy jumped into the river, but was fortunately rescued from a watery grave, but it hightened his fever; he became ill and died the seventh day, two days after their arrival at Natchez, September 2, 1776. His body was buried on a high bluff about two hundred feet above the level of the river in the common burial ground which has since all caved into the river. The heads of the two families being dead, distress and sickness, misfortunes and privations of every kind awaited the strangers. The savage tomahawk was also a great terror to them, and they had to keep in companies for mutual protection against the Indians. To add to the distress of the families, the property left with the English gentleman near New Orleans was all confiscated by the Spanish authorities, being included in his property as an alien and enemy, England then being at war with Spain. Suffice it to say, that at the present day, 1829, these two families that suffered so much are among the most numerous, wealthy and respected families in the states of Mississippi and Louisiana."

A representative citizen of Bolivar county, A. W. Benoit, was born at Columbus, Miss., in 1857, and there received a liberal education. When sixteen years of age he engaged as clerk in St. Louis, Mo., continued there one year, and then followed the same business at Columbus for three years. In 1877 he came to Greenville, clerked until 1880, and then engaged in planting for two years. In 1883 he was engaged as manager for James T. Richardson in the mercantile business, and has the supervision of four large stores. He has accumulated considerable property, and is among the most enterprising citizens of the locality. Benoit, which was named in honor of him, is a most thriving and growing village, and Mr. Benoit is the spirit of its progress. Mr. Richardson has erected a large brick business block, several stores, and there are other business houses. Mr. Benoit has the exclusive management of four stores that do an annual business aggregating over $200,000, and is also in partial charge of the large estate of James Richardson, the largest cotton planter in the world. Mr. Benoit is a shrewd and intelligent business man, and has had experience in this line from youth. He is a member of the Knights of Pythias and Knights of Honor orders. He is rather active in politics, and in July, 1890, he was appointed cotton taxcollector of Mississippi levee district. Mr. Benoit was married in 1879 to Miss Ida Blanton, daughter of William C. Blanton, and the fruits of this union have been five children: Ruth, Blanton, Luellen, Celeste and Adelle.

Charles G. Bentley, farmer, Bentley, Miss. Samuel Bentley, grandfather of Charles G. Bentley, was a native of the Old Dominion, born near Culpeper courthouse, and was a representative of an old and honored family of that state. After marriage to a Miss Staples, also a native of Virginia, he moved to Georgia, and there resided until his death. He held the office of magistrate for a great many years, and held other local positions. He was a soldier in the Revolutionary war. His son, Jesse H. Bentley, was born in Georgia in 1809, and was married in that state to Miss Barbara Moon, who was born there in 1815. Of the eleven children born to this union only three are now living, and of these Charles G. Bentley is the youngest. The other two are Mrs. Tabitha J. Reaves, of Bentley, and Mrs. Malita McGarity, also of Bentley. After marriage Jesse Bentley and wife emigrated to Alabama, but after residing there for a short time removed to Mississippi, settling in what is now known as Bentley in 1844. There the father entered and purchased the land upon which his family now reside. He was a millwright by trade, and in 1849 or 1850 he erected a mill on Buck river, this being the only one in the country for many years. This was a combined mill, grinding corn and wheat and sawing timber. Mr. Bentley was a strong advocate of education, and took a decided interest in all matters relating to the same. In politics he was a democrat. His death occurred in 1884, and a short time before that he became a member of the church. He was a man universally respected and esteemed for his many good qualities. Of the large family of children of which he was a member, only one, Jerry, is now living. The latter resides in Forsyth county, Ga. Mrs. Jesse Bentley is yet living, and is a member of the Methodist Episcopal church, which she joined at an early age. She is now enjoying excel-

24

lent health for one of her years, and resides on the old place. She was the third of a good-sized family, only one other now living, Charles G. Moon, who resides in Georgia and is engaged in planting. As above stated eleven children were born to Mr. and Mrs. Bentley, and those deceased are: John D., died in Alabama when a child; Jesse S., died at the age of twenty-four years; Elizabeth J. was the wife of S. S. Shook, and died, leaving her husband and four children; Sarah, died in infancy; Susan, died after growing up; Jeremiah F., died, leaving a wife and four children at Eupora; S. D. A., the youngest child, died in 1890 at the home place. Charles G. Bentley was born in Elbert, Ga., in 1839, and remained with his parents until the breaking out of the war, when he entered the Second Mississippi regiment, but soon after was discharged. He then entered the Forty-second Mississippi regiment, company G, and served with the same until just before the surrender. He was in the following battles: Gettysburg, Wilderness, and with Lee's army in all the engagements around Petersburg and Richmond. He was first captured near Williamsport, while on the retreat from Gettysburg, and while on the way to Hagerstown he made his escape, rejoining his company at Williamsport soon after. While out on duty Mr. Bentley was captured the second time by two scouts, but later made his escape and captured the two men who had taken him prisoner. Their names were Brown and Mooney, of Pennsylvania. Mr. Bentley was shot through the hand south of Petersburg, but was only disabled for a few weeks, and did not leave his company. He was made orderly sergeant in the spring of 1863, and was sergeant-major of Camp Lee, Richmond, Va., on detached service, for six months. In February, 1865, he went to Washington, D. C., and later to Indianapolis, Ind., thence to Illinois, and there remained from March until September of that year, when he again returned to the old home place in Mississippi. There he has since resided, engaged in farming. He first embarked in merchandising at Hopewell for a few years, followed the same occupation at Bentley for a short time, and since then has carried on his farming interest. Mr. Bentley was first married to Miss Sarah Hardin, of Calhoun county, Miss., and the daughter of E. H. Hardin, one of the pioneer settlers of that county, who received his final summons there. The latter was the father of eleven children, Mrs. Bentley being third in order of birth, and five of whom are now living: John J. and Bailey reside on the old home place, William resides near Bentley, Mrs. Virginia Hodge also lives near the old home place, and Carroll resides in the Lone Star state. The mother of these children is also deceased. Mrs. Bentley died in 1874, at the age of twenty-three years, leaving two children, Robert Lee and Jesse H., both young men, the former living with his grandmother and the latter with his uncle, Reeves. Mrs. Bentley was a member of the Baptist church. Mr. Bentley's second marriage was to Miss S. C. Reeves, a native of Alabama, and the fruits of this union have been three children: William, at home; Charles J., also at home, and Sarah Allie. Mrs. Bentley is a worthy member of the Baptist church, and although Mr. Bentley is not a member of any church he is a believer in the Christian religion, and is a straightforward, upright citizen. In politics he is a conservative democrat. He is president of the Alliance, and has held the office of justice of the peace of his precinct for many years.

A prominent lawyer of Holly Springs, and a nephew of Thomas Hart Benton, the senator from Missouri, was Hon. Samuel Benton, who passed his life in Mississippi, mainly at Holly Springs. During the late unpleasantness between the North and South his sympathies were with the Confederacy, and in 1861 he entered the army as captain of a company raised in Marshall county. He was wounded in a battle in Georgia, and died from the effects in a hospital in that state. He was a thorough student, a man of strong and vigorous intellect, a concise and logical reasoner, and a politician of considerable prominence, having been a member of the lower house of the legislature for some time. As a lawyer he had an established reputation. He was married to a Miss Knox, and she and one child, a son, survive him.

S. H. Berg, of Aberdeen, Monroe county, Miss., was born in Norway, near Christiana, in 1844, the son of Hanse and Martha Berg. His father was a contractor and builder in Norway, and died in his native country, leaving a family of five children. The subject of our sketch received a limited education, but, becoming restive under his father's restraining hand, he left home during his parents' temporary absence, when only eleven years of age. He walked seven hundred and fifty miles to Troneum, where he worked for several years. He then began contracting and building for himself, carrying this work on in northern Norway. One of his contracts was to tear down a stone castle that was built, according to the records, in 900. At this time, fearing that he would be drafted into the military service, he sailed for America in 1867, landing at Quebec. From there he went to Chicago, thence to Rock county, Wis., and from there he went to New Orleans, La., where he worked at his trade all up and down the river. He then went up the river to Memphis, and in 1870 came to Aberdeen, Miss., where he has since been engaged in business. In 1876 he bought the mill he now owns and runs. Previous to this time he was a successful contractor and builder, as the Aberdeen college and the operahouse, which are monuments of his skill, will prove. His attention is now divided between his mill and his brickyard. He carries on an immense business, as he has from forty to one hundred and sixty men in his mill (according to the building season); keeps logging camps, and carries a stock of from four hundred thousand to five hundred thousand brick always on hand in his brickyard, said to be the finest yard in the state. He is a member of the Masonic order, is a Knight Templar, and also a member of the Knights of Honor. He is a man whom his fellow-men like to honor, both in the town and county, as they have proven by electing him a member of the board of selectmen six consecutive times, which necessitated a service on his part of twelve years. He is a man who deserves his high rank, for he is an upright, honest and energetic man. There is not a more public-spirited man in the city of Aberdeen than he, nor is there a more liberal contributor to any public enterprise than is Mr. Berg to this land of his adoption. He has been a man of many adventures on land and sea, and a man who, in his own words, "has seen many hard times, and many ups and downs," but the high degree of success he has attained proves the metal that was in him.

Among the noble men of Claiborne county, Miss., who fulfilled their destiny and are now no more, may be mentioned Samuel Bernheimer, whose walk through life was characterized by the most honorable business methods, by the keenness of his commercial instincts, by his devotion to his family, and by the interest he took in the welfare of his fellow-men. He was born in Hohenems, Austria, September 12, 1812, being of a noble and wealthy family. His parents, Simon and Bella Bernheimer, lived to ripe old age, having had born to them a numerous offspring, of whom five sons and four daughters lived to mature ages and raised worthy families. At an early age Samuel Bernheimer was put in a good school, but at the age of twelve years, in connection with the continuance of his studies, he followed the calling of a clerk, during which time he laid the foundations for his future successful mercantile career. Upon attaining manhood he determined to seek his fortune in America, and after an ocean voyage of six weeks he landed at New York city, in which place he almost immediately engaged in merchandising on Grand street. A short time afterward he removed to Charlestown, S. C., in which city he followed the same calling until the yellow-fever scourge visited that region, when he departed to seek a more healthful clime, going first via New Orleans to Woodville, Miss., and then to Liberty, Amite county, Miss., where he once more embarked upon a mercantile career. After some time, while on a visit to New Orleans, he met and was united in marriage to Miss Henrietta Cahn, a native of Westerspach, Prussia, with whom he returned to Liberty, where he continued to pursue his calling, and in 1847 their eldest son, Marcus, was born at that place. Mr. Bernheimer next decided to locate at Port Gibson, Miss., and, although he had but little capital to start with, he began merchandising there on a small scale, and being an able financier, possessing much pluck and perseverance, his labors were soon rewarded, and he gradually acquired some wealth. As soon as his means would allow he began dealing very extensively in the finer line of goods, such as are usually imported from Italy, Austria, Switzerland and England, and in a short time he controlled the largest trade among the leading families, not only of Port Gibson, but of the surrounding country. In 1851 and 1852 he associated with him in business his two brothers, first Jacob and then Adolph, the firm taking the name of S. Bernheimer & Brothers, and thus established the business grew to a still more solid and substantial basis, for both brothers were shrewd and practical business men, but shortly after this connection was formed, Jacob Bernheimer died of yellow fever, say in 1853, and was buried at Grand Gulf, Miss. Shortly afterward William Cahn, a brother of Mrs. Samuel Bernheimer, was admitted to the firm, having been for some years previous an attache, and a few years later withdrew and established himself in business separately. Adolph, the other brother, continued a member of the firm until 1865, when he withdrew and established himself in business at Mobile, Ala., forming a partnership with Jacob Pollock, his nephew, the firm becoming J. Pollock & Co. They dealt extensively in the wholesale of dry goods, and soon became known as the largest and most successful dealers throughout that section of the South, but in 1874 Mr. Adolph Bernheimer, owing to ill health, retired from active participation in the business, about which time Mr. Leopold Lowenstein joined the firm. S. Bernheimer & Brothers lost heavily during the late Civil war, and at the close of hostilities they found that all their hard-earned wealth had been swept away, and that they were very deeply in debt. Always practical, Samuel, being left in sole charge of the assets at Port Gibson, immediately set about to adapt himself to the altered conditions of Southern life, and, adjusting his business habits and methods to meet the requirements of the new regime, at once made a move to retrieve his fallen fortunes, and toward paying the firm's indebtedness, and although a heavy load had been laid upon his shoulders, his former experience and methodical habits tided him safely over this trying time. He soon found himself out of deep water and floating on a prosperous tide, and in bringing about this desirable result, his son Marcus lent him valuable aid, and assisted him in liquidating his debts and repairing the losses sustained during the war. Some years before his death he resigned the active management of his business and placed it in the competent hands of his sons, Sidney and Jacob, but still continued to be a silent counselor and was ever ready to lend valuable aid in time of need. He was an accomplished and polished gentleman, both by instinct and training, and in personal appearance was decidedly prepossessing. He possessed generous, true-hearted and hospitable instincts, and being kind and social in disposition he won numerous friends, and rarely lost them. He was very liberal with his means in contributing to enterprises of worth, and being a man of intellect, who kept himself thoroughly posted on all the current topics of the day, his wealth was used to a good advantage. After a long life of success and usefulness, he was called from the scene of his earthly labors on the 23d of October, 1888, and was laid to rest in the Hebrew cemetery, Rev. Dr. Leucht, of New Orleans, officiating. A large concourse of people followed him to the grave, the business houses of the town were closed, and business was generally suspended as a mark

Samuel Bernheimer

of respect to the memory of a worthy and noble man. Joseph Bernheimer, the youngest one of his brothers, came from the old country and visited him on several occasions, at one time living with him a number of years. He, too, was of a kind disposition, an intelligent and worthy gentleman, and soon became known to the numerous friends he made throughout this section as Uncle Joe, and finally, returning to Austria, died there several years since at the age of sixty-two, leaving but his widow with no children.

Mrs. Henrietta Bernheimer, relict of Samuel Bernheimer, now resides at the old home place in Port Gibson, Miss., is a highly cultured lady, and a most faithful and devoted mother, and while feeling heavily the loss of dear ones, husband, son and daughter, yet presides at her home, which her yet active care ever preserves and renders bright and comfortable, and there affection and kindness reign supreme. She bore her husband six children, all of whom lived to be grown: Marcus, the eldest, was educated in the schools of Port Gibson, also at Baton Rouge, La., and at the military institute, Marietta, Ga. While at the latter place and a mere boy, the third year of the Civil war caught him with the enthusiasm of youth, and he entered the Confederate service, first into the Georgia cadets, afterward in the quartermaster's department under Maj. L. O. Bridewell, where he remained until hostilities had ceased. After the war, in 1867, he entered Soule college of New Orleans, where he took a hurried commercial course, graduating in commercial law and bookkeeping, then returned to Port Gibson to resume his duties behind the counter and assist his father, with whom he labored earnestly and faithfully to build up the old-time trade, and to meet the heavy losses which the former company of S. Bernheimer & Bros. had sustained. At the age of twenty years he went to New York city and arranged all the former indebtedness of the old firm. After his return home, he and his father, together with Mr. Adolph Bernheimer, of Mobile, continued to meet the obligations as fast as their business would admit, and soon paid off the ante-bellum indebtedness of the old firm, and continued to be the leading merchants of the county. In 1873 Marcus made a trip to Europe, visiting the childhood's home of his parents, and soon after his return to Port Gibson removed, in 1875, to St. Louis, where he formed a partnership with Nicholas Scharff, of Vicksburg, in the grocery business in the city of St. Louis, the firm being known first as Scharff & Bernheimer, wholesale grocers and dealers in flour, provisions, grain and farming implements, etc., and as Scharff, Bernheimer & Co., later. He was married January 8, to Miss Ella Heyman, who was born at Wheeling, W. Va., but reared and educated in Philadelphia—a refined and accomplished lady—and by her is the father of four children. He is now president of the Merchant's exchange of St. Louis, the most prominent commercial body in the West, and is one of its most prominent and active members. Being alive to the interests of his city, and possessing business ability of a high order, he is one of the most prominent figures in the commercial circles of St. Louis. Louis Bernheimer, son of Samuel Bernheimer (deceased), was born November 11, 1848, in Port Gibson, Miss., his education being received at this place and at Columbus, Ohio, after which he entered into business with his father and brother, proving himself a useful partner. In 1881 he went to St. Louis, Mo., forming the firm of Bernheimer & Co., with Max M. Bodenheimer, a former employe of Scharff & Bernheimer, and they did a very successful business in sugar, coffee, etc. In January, 1884, he became a member of the firm of Scharff, Bernheimer & Co., and was largely instrumental in extending the business of the firm throughout the West and Southwest. He was married May 1, 1884, to Miss Blanche Trounstine, a daughter of Joseph Trounstine, of Cincinnati, Ohio, a young lady noted for her accomplishments. At the untimely age of thirty six years Louis Bernheimer was called from life, and during his severe and lingering illness, even up to his last moments, it was his greatest desire to be remembered as an honorable, truthful man, and of him it was truly said, " His whole life since his boyhood years, in every walk, whether social, political, or in his business pursuits, was but an exemplification of the noble character istics, honor, truth and civility." He was one of the most promising business men, and was an enthusiast in any cause in which he interested himself, and promised to have been one of the leading business men of St. Louis. In disposition he was kind and affectionate, and was devotion itself to his immediate family and relatives. The next child born to Samuel Bern heimer, was a daughter, Carrie, who was born, reared and educated in Port Gibson. She is the wife of Nicholas Scharff, of the firm of Scharff, Bernheimer & Co., of St. Louis, Mo., and by her husband is the mother of seven children. Clara, another daughter, became the wife of Leopold Lowenstein in 1874, and on November 19, 1889, her death occurred, she having become the mother of four children: Aaron and Maurice, two bright little boys, who now temporarily live with the Bernheimers at Port Gibson, and the other two children, Josie and Sidney, being with their father in Mobile, Ala., where he is a member of the firm of J. Pol lock & Co. Sidney Bernheimer was the fifth child born to his parents, and first saw the light of day in Port Gibson, Miss., May 30, 1858, at which place his education was also received, being supplemented by a course in Springhill college, Alabama, in which institu tion he was a thorough and faithful student and at the head of his classes. After his return to his native town he began assisting his father, became prominent in the counsels of the firm until July 1, of this year; was at the head of the firm of S. Bernheimer & Sons, being its chief business manager. He is one of the most brilliant business men of the state, is thoroughly practical in his views, and his commercial instincts are always keen and far-see ing. His marriage, which occurred January 8, 1888, was to Miss Fannie R. Goetter, a most estimable young lady, who was educated in New York city, becoming there thoroughly accomplished in literature, art, music, etc., to whom has just been born a daughter. Jacob Bernheimer is the youngest of his parents' children, his birth occurring in Port Gibson, on October 8, 1863. He obtained his initiatory schooling in his native town, but completed his education at Mobile, Ala. In 1881 he became a member of the firm of S. Brenheimer & Sons and is one of its most energetic and useful members. He possesses much business tact, and is an affable, thorough, gentleman, and in personal appearance resembles his father, many of whose traits he has also inherited. The withdrawal of his brother Sidney from the firm in July of this year (1891) leaves Jacob in sole charge of the business and the estate, which heavy load he assumes as the line of succession, which he is eminently worthy of tak ing up, and for which it is bespoken of him that he will succeed, as he possesses every attri bute for success, and being surely deserving of such. The old homestead is thus narrowed in its habitues to the two—mother and youngest unmarried son—but the memory and example of its former head and guide still sheds luster, serving to encourage those left behind in the performance of their mission of duty to all, and the good name of the Bernheimers is not only a cherished heritage to those bearing it, but all Port Gibson is proud of claiming them as of their own.

S. B. Bigham, who was born in Middle Tennessee, March 22, 1822, is a son of H. B. Bigham, a native of North Carolina, who first saw the light in 1798. William Bigham, the grandfather of S. B. Bigham, was born in Pennsylvania in 1755, and served in the Revolu tionary war, in which he was wounded. The mother of our subject was Miss E. Ramsey, who was born in North Carolina in 1800. She and H. B. Bigham were married in 1821. Five sons and one daughter were the fruits of this marriage, of whom S. B. Bigham was the first born. After the death of his wife, H. B. Bigham was married to Miss Catherine Gurner, by whom were born to him nine sons and two daughters. He was engaged in farming and as surveyor in Tennessee until 1839, when he and his family removed to Pontotoc county, Miss. He and his wife were members of the Methodist church. He died in 1862, and his second wife died in 1887. Seven of his children are now living. S. B. Bigham married Miss R. J. Phifer in 1844, who was also born in middle Tennessee in 1828. They have had six children, their eldest son being a minister of the Baptist church. S. B. Bigham enlisted in 1862, in the Confederate army, under Gen. S. J. Gholson, and rose to the rank of first lieutenant, participating in several engagements, among which were those at Jackson and Tupelo, Miss. Receiving his discharge in 1865, he returned home, and engaged in planting, with such success that he is now the owner of about eight hundred acres of land. During the same year he was elected county surveyor, and served in that capacity for two years. In 1876 he was elected county treasurer, in which responsible position he served for eight years. Mr. and Mrs. Bigham are members of the Methodist church, to which they have always been most liberal contributors. He is a useful and influential man, highly respected by all of his fellow-citizens, without regard to political affiliations.

Among the most prominent residents of Lowndes county, Miss., will be found Maj. J. M. Billups, president of the Insurance banking company at Columbus, who was born at Lexington, Oglethorpe county, Ga., in the month of January, 1824, a son of Thomas C. and Sarah A. (Moore) Billups, who were also Georgians by birth and of Welsh extraction. In 1835 the family removed to Mississippi, and the father became a very extensive planter of Noxubee county. He was prominent in everything pertaining to the interests of his section, which he represented several terms in the state legislature, being an old Henry Clay whig. Upon the death of his wife, in 1845, he married again, his second union resulting in the birth of one child, J. S. To his first marriage the following family of children were born: Maj. J. M.; Joseph P., who died in September, 1887; Susan J. (Sherrod), a widow; Thomas C.; J. S.; Sarah A., deceased; Amanda J., deceased, and William H., who is also dead. Thomas C. Billups was a member of the union convention, and at his death, in 1866, he was one of the foremost men of his county. In the University of Georgia, at Athens, Maj. J. M. Billups was educated, graduating in 1844, after which he returned to his home in Noxubee county, Miss., and engaged in planting, but becoming dissatisfied with his location and business, he removed to Athens, Ga., in 1851, where he embarked in merchandising and the banking business, and made his home for six years. In January, 1857, he returned to Mississippi, and up to 1862 was interested in merchandising and planting. He then cast aside all personal considerations to take up arms in defense of the land of his birth and the country he loved, and was instrumental in raising company B of the Forty-third Mississippi regiment, being elected its captain. After remaining in the service, he was promoted to brigadier-quartermaster with the rank of major, under Gen. John Adams, and in July, 1864, by order of Gen. Jo E. Johnston, was sent to Okalona as supply quartermaster for the army of the West, where he remained until the close of the war. He then returned to Columbus, and, after a short time, to Mobile, Ala., where he was a successful cotton factor and commission merchant, under the firm name of Whitfield & Billups, for a period of five years, after which he returned to Columbus, Miss., and began business under the firm name of Billups & Banks, which connection has continued up to the present time. In March, 1873, Mr. Billups was elected president of the Columbus Insurance banking company, which position he has held uninterruptedly ever since. He was a director of the Mobile & Ohio railroad, and was president of the board of trustees of the Columbus female institute for fourteen years. He is a stockholder in nearly every important enterprise in the county, and is an extensive landholder and an enterprising citizen. The amount of land which he has under cultivation amounts to about eleven hundred acres, and is principally devoted to the raising of cotton, although other Southern products are cultivated. He was first married, in 1846, to Miss Sarah M. Phinizy, of Athens, Ga., by whom he had the following children: Anna M.; Horace; Jacob P., married to Miss Tarlton, of Mobile, Ala.; Susan A., wife of R. F. Hudson; Sallie P.; John M., Jr., and Margie P. His second marriage, which occurred in 1867, and was to Mrs. Sarah Mott, the widow of General Mott, resulted in the birth of three children, Joseph P., Mary J. and Bettie G. Mr. Billups has been a member of the Methodist Episcopal church for many years, and for the past twenty years he has been one of its officers, and is president of the board of stewards.

T. C. Billups is the owner of a fine tract of prairie land, comprising about four thousand acres, on which is raised cotton, corn, oats, clover, etc., considerable attention being also given to propagation of a good grade of stock. He was born in the county in which he is now residing, January 26, 1839, a son of Col. Thomas C. Billups, a sketch of whom appears elsewhere in this volume, and here has spent the greater part of his life. He was attending the University of Georgia, at Athens, when the war broke out, and he did not stay to complete his studies, but in April, 1861, enlisted in the Confederate service, and two years were spent in the infantry and two in the cavalry. He was a lieutenant during the latter part of the war, and surrendered at Gainesville, Ala., after which he returned to Columbus and engaged in planting, a calling he has since successfully followed. In connection with this he conducted a mercantile establishment for several years. He is a stockholder in the Columbus Insurance banking company, and socially is a member of the Independent Order of Odd Fellows, in which he has filled all the chairs, and was deputy grand master for some time. He is also a member of the Knights of Honor, the American Legion of Honor and the United States Benevolent association. In 1875 he was united in marriage to Miss Ida J. Sykes, a daughter of Col. James W. Sykes, by whom he has four children: Marcella S., Elizabeth J., James S. and Thomas C. Mr. Billups and his family are members of the Methodist Episcopal church, and move in the best social circles of Columbus. They have a beautiful and comfortable home in the town, and are well known for their kind hospitality.

Gen. J. S. Billups, a planter residing at Columbus, Miss., was born in November, 1849, a son of Col. Thomas C. Billups and brother of Maj. J. M. Billups, a sketch of whom appears in the history of this state. Gen. Billups was educated in the University of Mississippi, but upon nearing the time of graduating he left school, and was united in marriage in 1868, after which he settled down to make a home for himself and bride in Columbus. After several years devoted to the drug business he turned his attention to planting, and is now the owner of three thousand acres of fine land, on which his principal crops are cotton and corn. In addition to this valuable plantation he has a fine stock and dairy farm consisting of eight hundred and eighty acres, all in pasture, over which roam several hundred head of fine stock. He has over one hundred fine milch cows, and is extensively engaged in the dairy business, his enterprise being attended with good success. A visit to his plantation or stock farm will convince any one of his practical and intelligent views and his thorough knowledge of planting and dairying. In 1870 he joined the riflemen of Columbus, and in 1873 was elected ensign, afterward second lieutenant, then first lieutenant, which position he continued to hold until 1883, when he resigned, being afterward elected an honorary member. In 1889 he was persuaded to once more join his old command, and was elected lieutenant-colonel of the Second Mississippi regiment, and a few months later brigadier-general of the first brigade of Mississippi national guards, commanding the northern division. It is a title of which he may well feel proud, for he has served long and faithfully. His men are well drilled, and comprise two regiments of infantry of twenty companies, a battalion of cavalry of six companies, and four companies of artillery, they constituting the first brigade of the northern division, of which he is in command. General Billups is a member of the Masonic fraternity, in which he is a Knight Templar. He was married November 5, 1868, to Miss Wildie Sykes, a very estimable lady of Columbus. Their union has resulted in the birth of three children: Misses Wildie, Fannie and Ida. He is greatly admired and respected wherever he is known, and his home in the city of Columbus is far-famed for its beauty and elegance.

A member of the well-known legal firm of Birchett & Shelton of Vicksburg, Miss., is George Keith Birchett, who, since 1866, has been a law practitioner, being first associated in the practice of his profession with R. J. Miller, who was killed in 1874, and four years later forming a partnership with John D. Gilland which lasted up to 1890, when he and Mr. Shelton formed their present firm. Mr. Birchett was born in Warren county, Miss., in 1840, to Dr. George K. and Ann D. (Skinker) Birchett, natives of Petersburg and Orange county, Va., respectively, of which state their ancestors had been residents for many years. An uncle, Robert Birchett, was a prominent newspaper man of Petersburg, and another uncle, George Keith Taylor, was a leader of the Federal party for many years, and was a representative in the legislature from Prince George county, Va. Dr. George K. Shelton graduated in medicine from the University of Pennsylvania, and his first practice was done in his native state. About 1836 he came to Mississippi and settled in Warren county, but in 1849 took up his residence in Vicksburg, and up to the time of his death, in 1866, ranked among the leading physicians of this section. He was an earnest and close student throughout life, and for years acted as hospital physician. He was a man of very high moral character and was universally respected and esteemed. In personal appearance he was prepossessing, was five feet nine inches in hight, was rather spare, and had dark hair and large blue eyes. His wife died in 1863, an earnest member of the Episcopal church. George Keith Birchett was educated in the University of Virginia, and has seven diplomas from that college. He entered the Confederate army in the spring of 1861, in the Twenty-first Mississippi regiment, Barksdale's brigade, and assisted in the capture of Maryland hights, the battles of Antietam, Fredericksburg, Chancellorsville and Gettysburg, and after that battle he was made acting adjutant of the regiment, and was so acting at the battle of Chickamauga, where he was wounded, and was disabled until the spring of 1864, when he was made assistant commissioner for the exchange of prisoners for the trans-Mississippi department, and acted as such, with headquarters at Shreveport, until the close of the war. In 1866 he was elected clerk of the circuit and chancery court of Warren county, serving until the death of Judge Yerger in 1868, when he resigned. He immediately began the practice of law, having been licensed by Jacob S. Yerger before his death, and formed his first partnership with R. J. Miller, as mentioned above. In 1880 he was chosen as a suitable person to fill an unexpired term in the state legislature, in which capacity he showed that he was able and trustworthy. He is a courteous and polished gentleman, and is at the head of one of the brightest legal firms of Vicksburg. He is the owner of two fine plantations in Warren county, comprising three thousand three hundred acres, with one thousand acres cleared, and also owns a good store in Vicksburg. He was married in June, 1885, to Miss Hattie W. Payne, a daughter of M. R. Payne, who was among the early citizens of Warren county, and to their union two children have been born: Virginia and Edward. Mrs. Birchett is a member of the Episcopal church, and Mr.

Birchett is a member of the Knights of Honor and of the Knights of Pythias, and was for a time grand master of the I. O. O. F., and grand representative of the grand lodge.

One of the pioneer planters of Hinds county, Miss., is the well-known and highly esteemed J. J. Birdsong, who was born in Sussex county, Va., on the 9th of November, 1810, the fifth of eight children born to Thomas and Rebecca (Jarred) Birdsong, they being also natives of the Old Dominion, the former of whom was a planter and died in his native state in 1820. J. J. Birdsong attended the common schools until he attained his fifteenth year, at which time he began managing a plantation, which occupation he continued for about one-half year, using the money thus obtained for school purposes the remaining half of the year. He came to Mississippi the spring before he was twenty-one years of age, on an inspecting tour, and liking the appearance of the country very much he moved here the following year and opened a general mercantile establishment with his brother, which venture proved quite profitable. For the two succeeding years, or until the fall of 1835, he dealt in negroes, and found this a very remunerative occupation. He then turned his attention to planting, and in 1837 moved to his present plantation, which now contains one thousand six hundred acres, having given each of his children a section of land when they came of age. He greatly prospered as a planter, and prior to the war had accumulated a great deal of worldly wealth, being the second largest taxpayer in the county. From 1861 to 1865 he lost it all, with the exception of his land. He has now nine hundred acres of land under cultivation, annually raises about one hundred bales of cotton and a large amount of corn. He was married on the 28th of March, 1838, to Miss Brown, of South Carolina, by whom he became the father of eight children, four of whom are living: Mrs. Harriet J. Birdsong, Mrs. Jennie Lee Pond, Samuel B. and Rebecca J. Cassey. The family are members of the Methodist Episcopal church, and he is a member of the A. F. & A. M., and was master of his lodge for many years. He is now a Knight Templar. He has held the position of magistrate four years, and has been a member of the board of supervisors fifteen years.

Thomas A. Birkhead, Vaughan, Yazoo county, Miss., was born in Randolph county, N. C., in 1829, and is the son of Lingurn and Margaret (Cotton) Birkhead, natives of North Carolina, and of English ancestry. The first members of the family who immigrated to America settled in Maryland, and removed thence to North Carolina. Both the paternal and maternal grandfathers were soldiers in the Revolutionary war. The father died in 1875, at the advanced age of over ninety years. The mother passed away in 1836. There were nine children in the family, all of whom grew to maturity, and six of whom are now living. Mr. Birkhead received his education in the common schools of North Carolina and at Normal college (now Trinity college), North Carolina, where he was a student for two years. He came to Mississippi in the year 1851, and was engaged in teaching school in Yazoo and Holmes counties for ten years. December 22, 1859, he was united in marriage to Miss Mary J. Wardlaw, a daughter of Zachariah Wardlaw, of Hinds county. Six children were born of this union: E. Carrie was born June 24, 1862, and died September 4, 1862; L. Walter was born September 26, 1863, and died in Boerne, Tex., November 19, 1890. Hattie, the wife of W. P. Harris, died in Hot Springs, Ark., July 25, 1890, to which place they had gone to regain their health. Their remains were brought back to Yazoo county and interred in the family graveyard. After his marriage Mr. Birkhead engaged in agriculture, and in 1870 he settled on his present farm, where he is still living with his three remaining daughters, Jessie, Kate and Emma. His farm consists of five hundred acres and is well cultivated, and he superintends the cultivation of it himself. During the war he was in Major Montgomery's command of state troops. He has always been actively interested in local politics and all affairs pertaining to the welfare of the community in which he lives. He has witnessed many changes in Yazoo county, and takes much satisfaction in the fact that he has done his share in its growth and development. Mrs. Birkhead died in July, 1888, and is deeply mourned by her family and a wide circle of friends.

The mercantile interests of Simpson county, Miss., find a fit representative in the well-known merchant James I. Bishop, of Westville. Mr. Bishop's parents, David and Hephzibah (Powell) Bishop, were both natives of Mississippi, and the father followed the occupation of a planter all his life. James I. was born near Westville, Miss., on the 25th of October, 1843, and received a limited education in the common schools. In February, 1862, he enlisted in company A, Fourth Mississippi cavalry, and was later attached to General Forrest's division, and participated in many of the most notable engagements. He was wounded at one time, but not so severely as to disable him from service. He was mustered out at Gainsville, Ala., on the 17th of May, 1865, after which he attended school for a brief period. Subsequently he was engaged for a few months as clerk in a store at Westville, and in December, 1867, he embarked in merchandising on his own account at that place with two partners. This business flourished, and for the past ten years he has been individual manager and owner. A gentleman of high character, his business ability and integrity are well known, and full confidence is accorded him. He is public spirited and takes an active and prominent part in all matters of moment. In 1871 he was elected treasurer of Simpson county, served two years, and since that time has not held office. He was married on the 19th of June, 1873, to Miss Josephine Rayland, formerly of Rankin county, and to them have been born two daughters: Lilian May and Mary Theodocea, both of whom are having all the advantages necessary for a good education. Mr. Bishop is a member of Westville Masonic lodge No. 78.

Dr. B. D. Bishop, physician and surgeon, and superintendent of the public schools of Lawrence county, Miss., was born in Simpson county, Miss., in 1852, a son of David and Hephzibah (Powell) Bishop. He was born in 1810 and died in 1877. He was an active politician of the democratic party, served for many years as justice of the peace, fought in the Confederate cause during the Civil war as a member of a military organization and was a consistent member of the Baptist church. The mother of our subject lives in Westville, Miss., in Simpson county. She was born in 1818, a daughter of Elder James Powell, a Baptist minister of considerable note in Mississippi and Georgia, who was born in the last named state. He died in 1850 and had one son, who also became a minister; this is the well-known Vincent T. Powell, of Rankin county, Miss., whose son, Elder T. S. Powell, became the leading minister of the state, and is now residing in the state of Indiana. He graduated from the Mississippi university, at Clinton, Miss., and from the theological seminary at Louisville, Ky. He is the author of an entertaining book entitled Five Years in Mississippi. The parents of Dr. Bishop had eight children, all of whom are now living: Mrs. Martha A. Whitfield, of Simpson county, Miss.; J. U. Bishop, of Westfield, Miss.; J. C. Bishop, of Simpson county; Albert G., of Copiah county; Dr. B. D. Bishop; Mrs. A. M. H. Patterson, living in Simpson county; Mrs. Candace Williams, of Simpson county, and Mrs. Theodosia Weatherby, also of Simpson county. Dr. Bishop was reared in Simpson county, Miss., where he attended the common schools, afterward going to Oxford, Miss., in 1873. In 1875 he went to Clarksville, Tenn., where he remained for two years, going thence to the Nashville medical college. He took up the practice of his profession in 1879 in Lawrence county, Miss., and has been a medical practitioner there ever since, except during three years while he was a resident of Pike county, and was for a short time engaged in the drug

trade at Brookhaven, Miss.   He was married in 1881 to Miss Jennie Larkin, a daughter of
F. J. and Mary (Keagin) Larkin, natives of Mississippi.   Mrs. Bishop was reared in Brookhaven, Miss., and graduated from Whitworth college.   She has had two children, one of
whom, Maude Marrable, is now living, and the other, Mary Larkin, is deceased.   In politics
the Doctor is a democrat, and takes an active and helpful interest in everything tending to
the good of his county and state.   In 1889 he was appointed superintendent of the public
schools of Lawrence county, to fill a vacancy made in November, and in February, 1890, he
was elected to the same office, which he still holds and the duties of which he discharges to
the satisfaction of all interested in educational affairs.   He has won high rank professionally,
and is a very successful planter.   He is a member of the Baptist church, while his wife is
identified with the Methodist Episcopal church South.   Mr. Bishop is a great lover of the
beauties of nature, and takes great pride in beautifying his grounds, cultivating the flowers
himself with much care and patience.

The state of Massachusetts gave to Mississippi the eminent lawyer and jurist, Judge
John Black.   He came here about the time Mississippi was admitted to the Union, and
in 1826 he became so prominent that he was appointed one of the judges of the supreme
court, which position he filled with credit until 1832, when he was appointed to succeed Senator Ellis in the senate of the United States, and in the following year was elected under the
new constitution for a full term.   He was a lawyer of commanding ability, full of fiery eloquence, patriotism and a high sense of justice, and few lawyers have left a more honorable
record.   As a judge, he possessed the faculty of going to the bottom of any question submitted to his judgment.   He was unquestionably one of the great lawyers who gave to the
Mississippi courts their high character among all states of the Union.   While in congress,
his opposition to President Jackson in regard to the bank of the United States led later to
the passage in the Mississippi legislature of resolutions censuring him for what was claimed
to be his failure to properly represent the people of this state.   The resolutions declared
that, owing to this proposition, it was his duty to resign his position from the senate of the
United States, and he was accordingly invited to do so.   It does not appear that he paid any
attention to this request, for he continued to serve two years afterward, when he then
resigned, and resumed the practice of law, and continued the same until his death.

Mrs. Mary S. Blake is the widow of Col. Benson Blake, who was one of the most successful and extensive planters on the Yazoo river.   Colonel Blake was born in Maryland, in
1811, a son of Joseph Blake, who was descended from the noted Blake family, of England,
and was a nephew of Commodore Blake, of English fame.   After coming to America, all the
male members of the Blake family followed the calling of planters.   Col. Benson Blake
received excellent educational advantages in his youth and was a graduate of three different
colleges, Amherst and Union, before he was twenty-one years of age, and shortly after attaining his majority he graduated from another.   He removed from his native state to Mississippi
in 1832, and settled in Warren county, where he engaged in planting, but, not meeting with
much success, he entered upon the practice of law in 1836, having previously graduated from
a law school of Baltimore.   From 1836 to 1840 he was a successful practitioner of his profession, but after his marriage he settled on the plantation now owned and occupied by his
widow, which is one of the largest on the river, comprising about six thousand acres in all,
with about one thousand five hundred acres improved and in a fine state of cultivation.
When the war opened in 1861 he attached himself to the staffs of Generals Breckinridge and
Smith, and was afterward appointed by General Van Dorn provost-marshal of Vicksburg,
in which capacity he acted prior to and during the siege of that city.   After its fall he car-

ried his slaves to Georgia, where he placed them on a plantation, after which he attached himself to the chief of the Confederacy, and was frequently called upon by Mr. Davis to do government business of a private nature. At the close of the war he returned home and brought one hundred and twenty-five negroes back with him from Georgia, in spite of the fact that they were free. Only three of all this number are living at the present time—one man and two women—who still remain with Mrs. Blake. To Colonel and Mrs. Blake six children were born: Anna F., wife of Eugene Martin, a cotton broker of Vicksburg; Minnie G., Henry L., Vernon B., Caroline F. and Daniel W. In 1873, when in his sixty-third year, Mr. Blake was called from life, since which time Mrs. Blake, with the assistance of her sons, has admirably conducted her plantation. Mrs. Blake is a daughter of Henry Legrand Connor, and traces her ancestry back four generations to Peter Girard, who was born on the Rhone river in France, and in 1758 came to America and settled in South Carolina. Henry Legrand Connor married Susan Baker, a sister of the military governor of Louisiana. Mrs. Blake's father was a graduate of West Point, being in the same class with Hunter and Horenzo Thomas, adjutant-generals of the United States. He filled a number of important political positions in Mississippi, and when only forty-six years of age his death occurred. He died near the city of Natchez, on a tract of land granted his father in 1775 by the Natchez Indians, and which is still in possession of the family. The residence on this place was burned by an incendiary in 1875. Mrs. Blake has in her possession some of the oldest papers in the state of Mississippi—the colonel and lieutenant colonel's commissions to her maternal grandfather, granted by George III. of England in 1758 and 1766. She lives on her beautiful plantation on the Yazoo river, and her residence is a handsome and imposing one, beautifully and tastefully furnished. It stands on an eminence two hundred yards from the main road and is surrounded by magnificent forest and ornamental trees. During the Rebellion she was on good terms with many of the leading officers of the Union army, and General Sherman frequently visited at her house. Colonel Blake was first married to a Mrs. Ferguson in 1839, and through her secured the Blakely plantation. She was a Miss Downs, a sister of Col. Alfred Downs.

A prominent merchant and planter, Gunnison, Miss., is S. C. Blanchard, whose father, Nelson Blanchard, was a native of the Blue Grass state, and followed the occupation of a planter all his life. He left his native state and emigrated to Hinds county, Miss., as early as 1817, but in 1845 settled in Bolivar county. He located near Concordia, secured a large landed estate and became a most extensive planter, clearing about five hundred acres near Concordia, and as much more at other places. He was married in 1847 to Miss Mary A. Marshall, a daughter of William Marshall, one of the early settlers of Hinds county. Mr. Blanchard was a true Christian and was a liberal contributor and supporter of the Methodist Episcopal church, which he had joined at the age of nineteen years, and in which he held the position of steward from the age of twenty until his death in 1870. He built the first Methodist church in Bolivar county in 1848, and secured a missionary from Louisville as first pastor. At that time there were many people in the county and across the river in Arkansas who had never attended church and this was of great benefit to them. Mrs. Blanchard is still living. Their family consisted of eight children, of whom S. C. Blanchard is the eldest in order of birth. The latter was educated at Shelbyville, Ky., and after the war started out for himself as a planter. This occupation he continued until 1879, when he opened a store at Concordia, and there remained until the fall of 1890, when he moved his stock of goods to the new town of Gunnison, on the railroad. As he expects to make this town his permanent home he will erect a handsome residence in the near future. Mr. Blanchard has two other stores, one at Shelbyville, which he started in June, 1890, and the other at Rosedale, which he started in November of the same year. The business at the last-named place is in a handsome building, well fitted up, and the goods are tastily arranged. He carries a stock of goods valued at $15,000, and is doing a good business at both places. His planting interests consists of six hundred acres of land, under cultivation, and located at two places, on the river and near Shelbyville. Mr. Blanchard cleared the most of this and also has three hundred and forty acres of wild land. He was married in 1869 to Miss Eva McCoy, of Montgomery, Ala., and daughter of David McCoy, a lawyer. Only one child has been born to this union, Nelson C. The family worship at the Methodist Episcopal church. Mr. Blanchard joined that church at the age of sixteen years, and has been steward since seventeen years of age. He has also been secretary of the quarterly conference of the Concordia church for twenty years. He is a member of the Masonic, Knights of Honor and Knights of Pythias organizations, and has been secretary of the Masonic lodge and financial reporter of the Knights of Honor for several years. In politics, though openly and vigorously advocating the best man for office, he is not otherwise pronounced or active. He is a shrewd and successful merchant and a man who has the entire confidence of the people.

Price Blanchard, of Gunnison, Bolivar county, Miss., is a native-born resident of this county, his birth occuring in 1862, and is the son of Nelson and Mary (Marshall) Blanchard, natives of Kentucky and Mississippi respectively, and both representatives of old and honored families. At an early day the father came to the Bayou state and located in Hinds county, where he resided for some time, and then moved to Bolivar county. He was among the pioneers there, and went actively to work to improve and cultivate a large plantation he had entered, becoming a very extensive planter at Concordia. His death occurred in 1872. He was a member of the Methodist Episcopal church, in which his widow, who is yet living, still holds membership. Price Blanchard was reared in Concordia, received his education in the common schools, and then clerked for some time in his brother's (S. C. Blanchard) store. In 1882 he was married to Miss Kate Waggoner, a native of Bolivar county, Miss., and the daughter of R. M. Waggoner, a physician and early settler of Australia, Miss. In 1889 he opened a store at Gunnison, was the first merchant of that place, and sold out in 1891. His marriage has been blessed by the birth of two interesting children— Reuben Marshall and Eddie Price. Mr. Blanchard has just completed a fine residence, a two-story frame, and everything is convenient and comfortable about his place. He owns a good plantation near Concordia, and has it well improved and well cultivated. He has been very successful in his several occupations.

No name in the memorial department of this work on Mississippi is more worthy of mention than that of Hon. Joseph Blankinship. This gentleman was born in Wilcox county, Ala., September 27, 1840. He is a son of Edmond and Jane (Boggan) Blankinship, natives of Virginia and North Carolina, respectively. Edmond Blankinship was the son of John Blankinship, a native of Virginia, who emigrated from there to Butler county, Ala., at an early day. John Blankinship became the father of twelve children, of whom Edmond was the eldest. The latter's first wife was Jane Boggan, and they were married in Butler county, Ala., and shortly after located in Wilcox county of the same state, where Mrs. Blankinship died in 1849. He subsequently married Mrs. Elizabeth Taylor, and died in 1862. He was the father of nine children, all of whom were by his first wife. Hon. Joseph Blankinship was educated in Alabama, and in 1861 enlisted in the battery known as the Jefferson Davis artillery, with which he served as a private until the battle of Seven Pines (Fair Oak), when he was promoted to a corporal, in which rank he served until the close of the war. He participated in a number of hard-fought engagements, of which the following are a few of the most worthy of mention: Seven Pines (Fair Oak), Mechanicsville, Cold Harbor, South Mountain (Boonsboro), Sharpsburg (Antietam), Fredericksburg, Chancellorsville, Gettysburg, Middletown, Petersburg and a number of skirmishes and minor engagements. His command surrendered at Appomattox courthouse, April 9, 1865. He soon after returned to Alabama, and from there, in June, 1865, came to Jasper county, Miss., where he was married, October 22, 1865, to Miss Patience, the daughter of William and Emily (Rogers) Thigpen. Mrs. Blankinship was born in Wilcox county, Ala., September 8, 1846, and removed with her parents to Jasper county, Miss., in 1858. In 1881 Mr. Blankinship was elected to the legislature and served one term. He and his wife are members of the Baptist church. They are the parents of ten children, namely: Emily J., Rebecca D., Eula, William E. (deceased), Roberta, Susannah D. (deceased), Zenobia, Joseph S. (deceased), Clyde, and the eldest of the family, who died unnamed in infancy. Mr. Blankinship is the owner of eleven hundred acres of land, and is also interested as a partner in the Blankinship & Massey sawmill at Bay Springs. He resides at Lake Como, Miss., where he has a typical Southern home. In connection with his other interests, he is quite largely and very successfully engaged in general merchandise business. In Mr. Blankinship, the community has a faithful and unswerving friend, ever alert to serve its best interest, and generous in his contributions toward every movement tending to the general advancement.

In Hurricane Creek, Lauderdale county, Miss., resides James L. Blanks. James W. Blanks, father of James L. Blanks, was born in Georgia in 1806, spent his early life on the farm, and took up his permanent residence in Mississippi in 1851. He was married to Sarah Adear, of South Carolina, in 1826. He died about 1886, his wife about 1876. J. L. Blanks, the subject of this sketch, was born in 1835 in Gwinnett county, Ga., and came to Mississippi with his parents and settled in Lauderdale county. His opportunities for acquiring an education were not good. He was married in 1854 to Miss Eliza A. Williams, of Lauderdale county, Miss., and has had ten children—five sons and five daughters: Callie, Irving, Joseph J., Sarah, Elizabeth, Charles F., John H., Laura May, Ida Gray and Edward A., and seven of these survive. He engaged in planting, and continued in that business till 1861, when he enlisted in the Sixth Mississippi battalion, Colonel Sears commanding. Owing to continued bad health, Mr. Blanks was discharged in the autumn of 1863. Returning home, he resumed planting. He had entered land from the United States government in 1855, the homestead where he now resides. By additional purchases he increased his landed interest of one thousand two hundred to one thousand four hundred acres, which ranks as average land of the county. Mr. Blanks has some exceedingly fine soil, one hundred and twenty bushels of corn, two bales of cotton and one hundred and fifteen bushels of oats per acre having been raised upon it. Mr. Blanks is one of the best farmers of Lauderdale county, having, perhaps, taken more premiums for heavy yields than any other of its citizens. His average yield of cotton is one bale per acre. He is a strong advocate of the use of commercial fertilizers, fertilizing heavily all crops grown. Mr. Blanks is a strong friend of education. His son, John H. Blanks, is a graduate of Howard college, Birmingham, Ala., and also of Nashville medical college. He is now engaged in the hospital of the college, having won the position because of merit. Mr. Blanks and his wife are members of the Primitive Baptist church, of twenty-five years' standing. A daughter of Mr. Blanks, Callie, is married to Dr. M. V. B. Miller, of Meridian, Miss. He has a nephew who is professor in the Nashville medical college. He is one of the state's best citizens, and has a host of friends.

Orville Martin Blanton, M. D., was born on Blantonia plantation, in Washington county, Miss., July 22, 1828, the year in which his father, William Whittaker Blanton, located in Washington county. The latter was a skillful surveyor, and surveyed most of the land in the vicinity of Greenville. He was born in Winsboro, S. C., May 3, 1798, a son of Col. John Blanton. The latter was born in Cumberland county, Va., and when a young man went to South Carolina, and thence removed, later, to Shelby county, Ky., where he engaged in raising thoroughbred horses and cattle until his removal to Jefferson county, Miss., where he was one of the earliest settlers, locating near Rodney. William Whittaker Blanton had a fine literary education, and was a graduate in law, but devoted his time to land speculation after he came to Mississippi, having been trained in this line by his father. He was in every way a most worthy man. Orville Martin Blanton was reared at Blantonia plantation. He attended a military institute near Frankfort, Ky., and later graduated in medicine at the University of Maryland. He was married to Martha R., daughter of Dr. George Smith, of Live Oak plantation, Warren county, Miss. She was born in Greensville county, Va., but when a child came with her parents to Warren county, Miss. Of this union three daughters were born: Lola, now Mrs. John B. Dabney, of Botetourt county, Va.; Belle Orville, now dead, who became the wife of Dr. J. S. Walker, and Georgia, twin sister of the latter, now Mrs. Samuel D. Finlay. Dr. Blanton served during the war as surgeon of two companies of the First Louisiana heavy artillery, stationed at Vicksburg, and commanded by Maj. Harry Clinch, when Vicksburg was attacked by Admiral Farragut, and part of his fleet passed the city on the 28th of June. The Doctor was honorably noticed in general orders by Gen. Martin L. Smith for his devotion to the wounded under such heavy fire. He is a prominent Mason. Mrs. Harriet Byron Theobald, so well known and well beloved, who died at her residence in Greenville, Miss., January 23, 1888, in the ninetieth year of her age, was the wife of William Whittaker Blanton, and the mother of the immediate subject of this memoir. She was born at Greensboro, Ga., April 17, 1798. Her father, Capt. John McAllister, was a distinguished officer of the British army during the war of Independence. In 1810 she moved with her parents to the old town of Washington, near Natchez, Miss. One morning, while journeying thither, floating down the Tennessee river, when they had reached a point near the present site of Chattanooga, then in the midst of a vast wilderness, they saw an Indian approaching their boat in a canoe. At once her father became satisfied that he was a spy sent to ascertain the strength of the party and their ability to resist an attack, and notified all hands to be on the alert and ready for instant defense, if an attack should be made, and arming himself and servants, he made ready for the expected encounter. Here young Harriet exhibited that firmness and courage which distinguished her after life, by arming herself with a butcher knife and taking her place among the boat's defenders. The spy evidently made an unfavorable report, as they were allowed to pass on without molestation, and made a safe journey to their destination. Eight years later, on March 26, 1818, she was married to Col. W. W. Blanton, on the Walnut hills, near Vicksburg, Miss., with whom, in 1828, she moved to Blantonia plantation, where the city of Greenville now stands. The plantation consisted of about five thousand acres of splendid land. Here, in March, 1838, she suffered a heavy loss in the death of her husband, who was a model husband and father and honored man of business. Continuing to live on at Blantonia, and ever taking the warmest personal interest in the opening out of what was then a very thinly settled country, Mrs. Blanton, in June, 1841, became Mrs. Theobald, her second husband being Dr. Samuel Theobald, of Lexington, Ky., who died at Greenville in 1867.

When the present city of Greenville was founded after the war, Mrs. Theobald, whose plantation was selected as the most eligible site in Washington county, donated all the streets, those splendid thoroughfares that are the pride of the town and the admiration of visitors. She also gave the ground for the old public school, for the public library, the courthouse, and all the churches in the town except the Baptist, toward which she afterward liberally contributed. To the churches she was always a benefactress, and especially to that of the Methodists, of which denomination she was an earnest and steadfast member. She was converted in her tenth year, and was an upright and consistent member of the church for about eighty years, always contributing liberally toward the support and spread of the Gospel. Nor were her charities confined to home interests. Worthy objects, educational and otherwise, in adjoining states, appealed not in vain to her generous heart. Only a few months before her death she presented to the Methodist female college at Grenada, Miss., the sum of $1,000. She gave free right of way to the Georgia Pacific railway company. To the Louisville, New Orleans & Texas railroad company she gave five acres of land for depot purposes at Greenville, together with right of way; and her donations to private individuals comprise more than fifty valuable lots. She was one of the largest subscribers to the river front revetment fund, taking bonds to the amount of $1,100. Such is a brief outline of the life of the mother of Greenville, an outline, however, that can give but a faint idea of the vitality, the integrity of purpose, and the true womanhood of its subject. For more than half a century she had been the foremost inhabitant of these parts. The first fire engine in Greenville was called after her, Harriet B. Theobald. It was her hand that drove the first spike in the Greenville, Birmingham & Columbus railroad, now the Georgia Pacific, the earliest road to reach Greenville, and in which she was largely interested. When the First National bank received its first issue of bills, it was to Mrs. Theobald, as was most fitting, that the first bills were sent. Throughout a life entered into with zest, courage and Christian fortitude, the deceased lady was called upon to bear much sorrow. Twice a widow, she was also deprived of seeing all of her children grow up to maturity. Of twelve of these, but one survived to solace her latter years, Orville Martin Blanton, a loving and devoted son, a highly respected citizen, and a member of the city council. She left four grandchildren and eleven great-grandchildren. Mention has been made of Mrs. Theobald's attachment to the Methodist church. To the pastors in charge at Greenville she was indeed a mother. Three of these stood at her bedside: Rev. Standifer, for four years her religious adviser, and, as he eloquently expressed it on that sad morning, almost her son; the Rev. Honnell, presiding elder of the Yazoo Delta district, and the Rev. J. A. Bowen, then in charge of the Methodist church. With these at hand, and surrounded by the members of her family, who loved her so dearly, her gentle spirit glided into everlasting rest. Though of an advanced age, Mrs. Theobald possessed a remarkably fine constitution and great strength of mind, and was able to fight the battle of life for a far longer period than is accorded to the most of the human kind. Few have lived a better or more consistent life than this Christian lady, whose loss the rich section of which she was one of the pioneer settlers, and the city of Greenville, which she founded, so deeply mourn. During a residence of sixty years in Washington county she endeared herself to all its people, and was closely identified with its progress and development. Full of honors and of years, she has gone to a better world, and her life, so historical, so exemplary, and so beneficial to all around her, is now a memory of the past. One who knew her well and loved her as a mother said at the time of her death: "God bless her memory. Surely the world is better for her having lived in it. Can as much be said of us when we go?" William Campbell Blanton, son of Mrs. Theobald, and brother of Orville Martin Blanton, was born at

25

Blantonia, now Greenville, September 20, 1830, and died at Fredericksburg, Va., April 19, 1869, leaving a widow and two children. He was an extensive planter of cotton, and served during the late war in company D, Twenty-eighth Mississippi cavalry, and toward its close was detailed into Colonel Henderson's scouts, who operated along the Mississippi river. He married Miss Georgiana Smith, a daughter of Dr. George Smith, of Live Oak plantation, in Warren county, Miss. His son, W. W. Blanton, who lives on his plantation three miles from Greenville, married Miss Florence Alexander, of Hinds county, and has one son and one daughter. The daughter of William C. Blanton, Ida Blanton, married Augustus W. Benoit, of Greenville, the present collector of the levee tax, and general agent for Col. James Richardson's extensive cotton plantations, and has one son and three daughters.

John N. Blasingame was brought up to the life of a planter by his father, Joseph Blasingame, and, like the majority of boys, he has followed in his ancestor's footsteps, and is now one of the leading agriculturists of his section. He was born in Pulaski county, Ala., September 21, 1828, but his parents were born in the Palmetto state, after their marriage moving to Alabama, where the father died in 1840, and the mother, whose maiden name was Mary McAfferty, in 1849. To them a family of ten children were born: Adaline, Lovell E., Lizzie and Thomas, deceased; and Mitchell, Sarah Jane, Phœbe Ann, John Newton, Joseph and William. John N. Blasingame attended school until he was eighteen years of age, and during this time applied himself diligently to his work and acquired a good business education. He was about fifteen years of age when he commenced to make his own way in the world, and after spending two years at work on a plantation, he commenced overseeing for Colonel Shepp, with whom he remained for four years. The following nine years were spent in a like capacity with a Mrs. Jones, but in November, 1864, he left her employ to enlist in the Confederate army, becoming a member of company I, Fourteenth Mississippi volunteers, with which he served until detailed to raise provisions. He was at Dadeville, Ala., at the time of the surrender, after which he returned home, and was married on January 6, 1866, to Miss Phœbe Ann, daughter of Lewis and Lucy B. Irrion, natives of Georgia. Soon after his marriage he moved to the state of Mississippi, and here has since been successfully engaged in planting, owning altogether about three hundred and thirty-six acres of land, which are well tilled, and which yield a larger profit than many much larger plantations. His union has resulted in the birth of a daughter, Lucy B., who was born in 1870, and is now the wife of Henry Lee Banlin, a native of Tennessee. Mr. and Mrs. Blasingame are among the useful and upright citizens of the section in which they reside, and are generous and hospitable. They are worthy members of the Methodist Episcopal church, and he is a stanch member of the democrat party.

An honorable and progressive young planter, John M. Bleecker, is one of the best known residents of Franklin county, Miss., for here he has resided all his life, his birth occurring in 1855. His father, Ebenezer Bleecker, was born in England, but when about eleven years of age he and a brother ran away from home and came to the United States, their first year in this country being spent in New York city. At the end of this time young Ebenezer came to Franklin county, Miss., and has never since heard from his brother. In 1849 he was taken with the gold fever, and as he was absolutely fearless and possessed the pluck and perseverance for which the Englishman has become famous the world over, he determined to seek his fortunes in the gold mines of California, and in that state spent two or three years in mining. Fortune favored his endeavors, and he returned to Franklin county with a heavy bank account, the result of his determined and persistent efforts. In 1852 he was married here to Miss Johnson, and after making several changes of residence, he finally settled in Meadville, where he engaged in merchandising, a calling that received his attention up to 1876, when he removed to three miles southwest of the town, where he took up his abode on a fine plantation of which he was the owner, and here passed from life in September, 1888, at the age of seventy years. He was a worthy member of the A. F. & A. M. lodge at Meadville. Upon the opening of the Rebellion he joined the Confederate forces, and for two years, or until disabled, he was faithful to the cause of the South. His widow was born in Franklin county in 1833, and is still living. Her parents, James and Helen (Spain) Johnson, were born in Maine and Jefferson county, Miss., respectively, the former coming to this region when a young man, and taking up a permanent residence here after his marriage. After successfully devoting life to planting, he died, about 1843, an earnest member of the A. F. & A. M. His widow survived him until 1885, when she, too, passed away, having been an earnest member of the Methodist church. She was a daughter of James and Nancy Spain, who were among the first residents of this county, the father dying here, and his wife passing from life in Yazoo county. James M. Bleecker was the second of seven children, he and a sister being the only surviving members of the family. Those deceased are Bernice, William, Mollie, Stephen and Charley. Sallie, the sister, is the wife of L. E. Davis, of Roxie. James M. was educated in Cooper institute, in Lauderdale county, and while in that institution made a good record for himself as a studious and conscientious pupil. In 1875 he was married to Clara, daughter of Philip and Amanda (Tillman) Whitley, the former of whom was born and reared in Franklin county, but was married in Louisiana, where he lived for some years. He and his wife, who was born in Louisiana, now reside in McComb city. Mrs. Bleecker was born in Point Coupee parish, La., and has borne her husband six children, four of whom are living. Since his marriage Mr. Bleecker has resided on the old home plantation, which contains six hundred acres, of which he is the owner. He is also the owner of a fine tract of land in Middle Fork. He was justice of the peace three years, and his wife is a member of the Methodist church.

The well-known firm of Bloodworth, Walton & Co., merchants, Beulah, Miss., was established in business in April, 1888, and now carry a stock of goods valued at $12,000, and do an annual business of $50,000. The members of this firm are live business men and have been very successful. They carry a large and well-assorted stock of dry goods, groceries, hats and caps, boots and shoes, notions and sundries, and they are tastefully arranged in a showy room. The building is comparatively new, and has been repaired and refitted by the firm. Beulah bids fair to become one of the most thriving towns in Bolivar county, and the firm of Bloodworth, Walton & Co. may be counted to keep thoroughly apace with it. N. B. Bloodworth, senior member of the firm, was born in Tippah county, Miss., in 1849, and of the eight children born to his parents, Joseph and Hester (Bridges) Bloodworth, he was the youngest. The parents were natives of Tennessee, and the father followed the occupation of a planter the principal part of his life. He died in the fifties, and the family afterward moved to Tallahatchie county, Miss., where N. B. grew to manhood. His scholastic advantages were limited, and at the age of twenty-one years he engaged as a merchant at Ross' Mills, where he remained four years. In 1880 he moved to Rosedale, and engaged in merchandising under the firm name of Bloodworth & McGuire. In 1884 he came to Beulah, and four years later founded his present business. He is a man of enterprise, and has excellent business qualifications. In 1876 he espoused Miss Mary H. Ellis, a native of Mississippi, who bore him two children, Ida (died at the age of four years) and Vera. Mr. Bloodworth is a member of the Masonic, Knights of Pythias and the Knights of Honor orders. He is not very active in politics, but his vote is cast with the democratic party. Mr. Walton, another member of the firm, has been a resident of Bolivar county for many years, and has a large and fine plantation near Beulah.

Coahoma county, Miss., is the birthplace of Mrs. Lou E. Bobo, her birth having occurred August 31, 1848, she being the elder of two children born to James and Eudora (Killebrew) Bobo, natives of the Palmetto state and Tennessee, respectively. The father came to Mississippi about 1845, and located in Coahoma county, where he became a successful and esteemed planter and resided until his death in 1850. His widow, in 1855, married G. W. Armstead, a planter, of Alabama, by whom she has five children. The paternal grandparents, Spencer and Louisa (Sims) Bobo, were South Carolinians, but the family originally came from France. The maternal grandparents were James and Ellen (Barry) Killebrew, of Scotch-Irish descent, and natives of Tennessee. In the state of Mississippi Mrs. Lou E. Bobo was reared, the greater part of her education being received at home. In 1866 she was married to A. K. Bobo, a son of Dr. William and Margaret (Boyce) Bobo, of South Carolina. Dr. Bobo became a resident of Mississippi in 1855, and located in Panola county, where, having retired from the practice of his profession, he engaged in planting, which calling he continued to follow until his death. A. K. Bobo was reared and educated in Mississippi, and in 1863 enlisted in the Confederate army, and was on active duty, under Captain Floyd, of Panola county, until he was wounded and disabled. At the close of the war he returned to his plantation in Panola county, but shortly after came to Coahoma county. Mr. Bobo was an able financier, but in the midst of his usefulness, and while in the prime of life, his career was closed, his death occurring in 1887. He and his wife became the parents of eleven children, five of whom are living, viz.: Barham F., Hettie, Barry, Charles and Mattie. Mrs. Bobo has erected a beautiful home, at a cost of $6,000, and is a stockholder in the Compress Company at Clarksdale. She is a zealous member of the Baptist church, and gives liberally of her means to various charities. She carries a general mercantile stock, valued at $10,000, but the business is managed by her eldest son, B. F. Bobo, who is now twenty-one years of age. He was educated in Bowling Green, Ky., and Memphis, Tenn., and is an intelligent young man, possessing excellent business qualifications. Hettie, the eldest daughter, was educated in Bowling Green also, and has developed considerable artistic talent. To her children Mrs. Bobo has proved a devoted and affectionate mother, their physical, moral and intellectual welfare being the chief object and aim of her existence. She is admirably fitted to be a friend and companion to them, for she possesses strong social instincts, is cultured and refined and is warmly interested in their well being.

The subject of this biographical notice, A. R. Bogard, Abbeville, Miss., was born in Lafayette county, Miss., in July, 1853, and is the son of E. H. and Catherine (McEachin) Bogard, natives of Mississippi and North Carolina respectively. The grandparents removed to Maury county, Tenn., and resided there until 1843, at which time they returned to Mississippi; since then E. H. Bogard has been a resident of Lafayette county. In 1862, when there was a call for men to go to the defense of the country, he enlisted in the army of the Mississippi, and in the following years experienced all the varied fortunes of war. He was wounded by a spent shell at Atlanta, receiving injuries which confined him to the hospital for several months; after his recovery he rejoined his command, and served until the surrender. He then returned to his home in Lafayette county, Miss., only to find that everything but the land had been swept away by the fearful ravages of war. With the aid of his sons he went to work to repair, as far as possible, the damage that had been done. The family had not suffered alone in the loss of property, but the war, coming as it did, deprived the children of any superior educational advantages, and the opportunities they had in the common schools were very limited. The family consisted of eight children, two of whom were born of the first wife, whose maiden name was Wilson. Mr. Bogard was married a second time in 1852, to Miss Catherine McEachin. Our subject is the oldest child of the second marriage. He remained under the parental roof until he reached man's estate, and then engaged in agricultural pursuits; he also gave some attention to the carpenter's trade, and in the fall of 1876 he went to work in a general store at Abbeville. In 1877 he began work as an employe of Jacobs & Hexter, with whom he continued six years; from this firm he went to Houston & Son, and at the end of two years he opened a store for himself at Abbeville; he has conducted this establishment up to the present time; he carries a stock worth $2,000, and does an annual business of $20,000; he ships an average of four hundred bales of cotton; he owns his residence property in Abbeville, and is in a position of financial independence. Mr. Bogard was married in 1883 to Miss Joe S. Logan, a daughter of Capt. John W. Logan. Two sons and two daughters have been born of this union: the first daughter died in infancy, unnamed; Kittie Hudson, the second daughter, is now five years old; John Logan was born February 28, 1888; Edward Hexter is nearly a year old. Mr. Bogard and wife are members of the Methodist Episcopal church, and he belongs to the Knights of Pythias. He has always been a liberal contributor to educational and religious movements. The Bogard family, being early settlers in the county, are widely and favorably known throughout the country; they are high-minded and honorable citizens, and move in the best circles of society.

Marion M. Boland, merchant, Big Creek, Miss., is a native of Edgefield district, S. C., but was partly reared in Calhoun county, Miss, where he received a common-school education. During the Civil war he enlisted in the Ninth Mississippi battalion of cavalry, and this was afterward attached to the Twenty-eighth Mississippi regiment of cavalry. He participated in the battle of Fort Pillow with General Forrest's command, and was on skirmish duty a considerable portion of the time. He surrendered at Gainesville, Ala., on the 8th of May, 1865, and afterward returned to his home in Mississippi. In December, 1868, he began merchandising at old Big creek, and in January, 1871, he came to Big creek, Calhoun county, Miss., where he has been actively and successfully engaged in mercantile pursuits ever since. He does an annual business of from $12,000 to $20,000. Mr. Boland was first married to Miss Amanda Denley, a native of Calhoun county, Miss. She was the daughter of M. W. S. Denley, a farmer and prominent citizen of Calhoun, who is now deceased. Mrs. Boland died in 1878, leaving two children—a daughter and son : Emma D. and Mannie. Mr. Boland's second marriage was to Miss Alice E. Smith, who was born in Georgia and partly reared in Calhoun county, the daughter of Jesse Smith, who was killed while a prisoner by Federal troops at Nashville, Tenn., during the war. To Mr. and Mrs. Boland were born five children, three now living: Emerson, Eugene and Carl. Those deceased were named Walter and Clyde. Mr. Boland is a member of the Methodist Episcopal and his wife a member of the Presbyterian church. He is active in politics and adheres strongly to the democratic party. He is the son of E. W. Boland, a native of Lexington district, S. C., born in 1824, the grandson of Abraham Boland, who was born and reared in Lexington district also, and the great-grandson of John Boland, who came to the United States during the Revolutionary war. The great-grandfather served in this war and afterward settled in Lexington district, S. C., where the family became one of the prominent ones of that state. He was a farmer and had learned the tailor's trade, but did not work at that after coming to America. He reared a large family of children and Abraham was the only one by his first wife. The grandfather of M. M. Boland, Abraham Boland, followed farming principally, but had learned the blacksmith's trade, which he followed a part of the time. He was married to Miss Christina Seas, also a native of Lexington district, S. C., and the result of this marriage was the birth of nine sons and one daughter, all of whom lived to mature years. They were named as follows: William resides at Big creek, where he has made his home since 1850, and is married but has no children (he is a prominent member of the Methodist church and one of the old and highly esteemed citizens of the county, being now in his eighty-second year); Joseph and Frederick are twins; the former resides in South Carolina and the latter is deceased; John Adams (deceased); Levi (deceased); John Mark resides in South Carolina; Catherine married George Shealy and died in South Carolina; E. W., father of M. M., resides at Big creek, Miss.; John Middleton resides in South Carolina, and Ozro is deceased. E. W. Boland, the father of Marion M. Boland, came to Mississippi in 1853 and settled on the place where he now lives, being one of the leading planters and merchants of Big creek. He was married in South Carolina to Miss Susan Bowers, a native of the Palmetto state, born in 1822, and the daughter of Jacob Bowers, who was also a native of that state but who was of German lineage. Mrs. Boland was reared in her native state and is yet living in the enjoyment of comparatively good health. They had nine children, five besides our subject now living: William, farmer and miller, near Slate springs; Jacob B., at Big creek, engaged in farming and milling; Mrs. Amanda England, wife of W. J. England, now resides in Big creek; Jefferson D., farmer, of Calhoun county, and C. E., merchant, at Big creek. Those deceased were: Mrs. Catherine Carter, wife of J. T. Carter, died leaving her husband and two children; Laura Ann, died in South Carolina when a child, and Cromwell, died in Calhoun county when quite young. The parents of these children are yet living. Mr. Boland served as a soldier in the Civil war, first in the Twenty-ninth Mississippi regiment of volunteer infantry, and after the surrender of Vicksburg he joined the army at Mobile; he was in the artillery department. He was home on a furlough at the time of the surrender. Since then he has continued his farming operations. He is a Mason, a member of Chapel Hill lodge No. 227, and he and Mrs. Boland are members of the Methodist church, to which they contribute very liberally.

One of the enterprising men of Durant is Richard A. Bolling, who was born in Sumter county, Ala., February 5, 1852. He came with his parents to Holmes county, Miss., in 1854; received a fair literary education at Clinton, Miss., and a good business education at the St. Louis commercial college. After completing his business course at the last named place, Mr. Bolling came to Durant, and was engaged as bookkeeper for eight years. In 1880 he bought a tract of land adjoining Durant, and put a few acres in strawberry plants as an experiment. This succeeded so admirably that he has increased his average from year to year, and now has about thirty acres in strawberries alone. He is making a great success of this industry, the net returns for berries averaging from $3,500 to $6,300 annually. During the berry season Mr. Bolling pays out for help weekly from $300 to $700. He is also in the vegetable and dairy business. He commenced the latter business in 1880, and now has a fine herd of Jersey cows, his milk and butter product amounting to $100 per month. In the vegetable line, as one item, Mr. Bolling raises about six hundred bushels of sweet potatoes annually. He is a most thorough business man, has excellent judgment, and is a fine manager. He was married in Durant, in 1880, to Miss Ida May Drane, who was born in Kentucky and educated at Anchorage of that state. Her father, Dr. W. H. Drane, is now deceased. Mr. and Mrs. Bolling have three children living: Alma, Eva and Richard A., and two deceased. Cecil died at the age of five years, and Mary at the age of four years. Mr. Bolling takes an active part in church matters, is deacon in the Presbyterian church, and has been an official member for a number of years. He is a Master Mason. He is the third in order of birth of four sons born to Maj. John H. and Mary C. (Hatch) Bolling, the former a native of Virginia, born near Petersburg in 1811, and the latter born near the city of New Berne, N. C. The father went to Alabama when a young man, was married there, and was engaged in planting and merchandising in that state until 1854, when he moved to Mississippi, locating in Holmes county. He followed planting there until his death, in 1855. His wife survived him until 1879. Mr. Bolling held a number of local positions while a resident of Alabama, and filled them in an able and satisfactory manner.

The family of James M. Bonney, of Satartia, Yazoo county, Miss., is of Scotch-Irish origin, and was identified with the earliest settlement of the state of Mississippi. In fact, they located there before it was a state, and long prior to the time that the Indians left this section. Dr. C. B. and Catherine Bonney were natives of Virginia and Tennessee, respectively. The Doctor located at Natchez, Miss., in 1827, and engaged in the practice of his profession for three years, at the end of that period he came to Yazoo county, where he became one of the leading physicians. He was also a prominent figure in politics, and represented the county in the state legislature for one term. James M. is the fourth of a family of twelve children of Dr. and Mrs. Bonney. He was born in Yazoo county, April 1, 1841, and was educated in the Kentucky Military institute at Frankfort and at Shelbyville. He was graduated at Frankfort in 1860. His father met his death on the steamer Carter, which was blown up in 1866. His maternal grandfather was John B. Hall, a native of Tennessee. Mr. Bonney has been engaged in planting since he left school; he owns a plantation of eight hundred acres, two hundred and fifty of which he has under cultivation. He was married in 1866 to Miss Matilda Wildy, a native of Mississippi, and a daughter of W. W. Wildy, of Virginia. They have had one child born to them, Caleb W. Our subject did his country service in the late war, being a member of General Morgan's company, of Kentucky, and of company H, Twenty-ninth Mississippi volunteer infantry. He was in the engagements at Farmington, Murfreesboro, Perryville, Mumfordsville, Chickamauga and Lookout Mountain. At the last-named place he was captured and carried to Johnson's island, where he was held until the surrender; he received a wound in this battle which disabled him for some time. He is a member of the I. O. O. F., and is a strong Alliance man. Politically he affiliates with the democratic party, and enters heartily into all philanthrophic and benevolent enterprises. It is to such men that the present advanced position of the county is due.

Judge B. B. Boone, Booneville, Miss., was born in Lincoln county, Tenn., April 6, 1831, and is a son of Reuben H. and Fineta (Reece) Boone, natives of South Carolina and Virginia respectively. They removed to the Chickasaw nation in 1835, where they purchased land and passed the remainder of their days. Reuben Boone was a man of ability and a recognized leader among the democrats of his state. When a boy he read law and practiced the profession to a small extent after coming to Mississippi. He was a member of the legislature for many years, and was in the senate for eight years. His father, Benjamin Boone, was a descendant of a brother of Daniel Boone, and was a native of North Carolina. He was a noted preacher in the Baptist church. He married Mary Wilson, and they reared a family of five children. The mother died when the children were young, and he married a second time, but no children were born of this marriage. The father of our subject died in 1857, and the mother died in 1855. They had seven children born to them: Mrs. Mary Williams, William H. H., Francis M., John D., Jordan, Benjamin F., J. M., and B. B., the subject of this notice and the youngest born. B. B. Boone was reared in Mississippi in the vicinity of Rienzi. He chose the profession of law for his life work, and in 1857 was admitted to the bar; he began his practice in Tishomingo county, and was a member of the firm of Reynolds, Boone & Reynolds. They did an extensive business and had a wide reputation as men of superior ability. The Judge was elected a member of the legislature in 1857. In 1859 he organized a military company, which was known as the Tishomingo rifles, and when the Civil war broke out in 1861, he went with this company to the battlefield. His health soon failed, and he was obliged to abandon the cause in which he had enlisted. He was then appointed clerk of the circuit and chancery courts of Tishomingo county, a position he held until the close of the war. In 1865 he was again sent to the legislature, and in the following year he was appointed judge of the Ninth district. He discharged the duties of this responsible office six years. In 1890 he was a member of the constitutional convention. He has always taken a deep interest in the political movements of the country, but of late years he has devoted his time to the cultivation of fruits. In 1870 he removed to Booneville, Prentiss county; he has a plantation within one-half mile of the village, which he has well under cultivation. The Judge was united in marriage to Miss Lou Petty, a daughter of John T. and Maria (Neal) Petty, natives of North Carolina, now deceased. Mrs. Boone was born in North Carolina, and died in Mississippi in May, 1861. Two children were born of this union: James, a resident of Texas, and Bessie H., who died at the age of thirteen years. Judge Boone was married a second time to Miss Margaret C. Petty, a sister to his first wife. To them were born Lou M., Reuben W., John M., Frank T., and Fannie F. Mrs. Boone is a member of the Methodist Episcopal church. Judge Boone is one of the most prominent characters of Prentiss county, either in social, political or agricultural circles, and enjoys the highest respect of the community.

Hon. James B. Boothe, attorney, Sardis, Miss. Mr. Boothe was born in Gates county, N. C., on the 1st of March, 1844, to the union of William R. and Margaret A. (Ballard) Boothe, both natives of the Old North state also. The father came to Mississippi in 1846, located in Yalobusha county, and there followed agricultural pursuits. He in 1855 removed to Tallahatchie county, continued his occupation as a farmer, and also engaged in merchandising. He was a member of the board of supervisors for twelve years and was president of the same the principal part of that time. Although perhaps the oldest man in the county, now in his eightieth year, he can still do a good day's work, and is engaged in carrying on a small plantation at the present time. He is a member of the Methodist church. James B. Boothe, the second of seven children born to the above-mentioned union, was reared in Yalobusha and Tallahatchie counties and received his literary training in the schools of the same. When about seventeen years of age the war broke out and he left school to enter the Confederate service (1861), enlisting in company F, Twenty-first Mississippi regiment, with which he remained until the battle of the Wilderness, where he lost his right arm. He was in the seven days' fighting in and around Richmond, and in both the Maryland campaigns. He also participated in the battles of Antietam, Maryland Heights, Gettysburg, Fredericksburg, Chickamauga and Knoxville. In 1864, after the battle of the Wilderness, on account of being crippled, he returned home and taught school for about a year, after which, in 1865, he was elected clerk of the circuit and chancery courts of Tallahatchie county. He remained in that office until 1869, when he was removed by Military Governor Ames because he refused to take what was known as the test oath, a refusal to do which disqualified any official then in office. While an incumbent of that position, Mr. Boothe read law under Col. W. H. Fitzgerald of the Twenty-first Mississippi regiment, and was admitted to the bar at the last term of court held while he was clerk (1868), but did not begin practicing until out of office. On retiring he imme-

diately formed a partnership in the profession with Col. J. S. Bailey at Charleston, Tallahatchie county, which continued until in 1874, when Mr. Boothe came to Sardis. He there
formed a partnership for the practice of law with J. G. Hall, with whom, in 1870, he had
been associated in publishing and editing a paper called the Tallahatchie *News*, devoted to
the interests of home rule, as opposed to carpetbag rule. The courts were suspended during
the military regime, but as soon as the regular courts were again held, they sold their paper
and resumed the practice of law. The law partnership with J. G. Hall continued until
1882, when Mr. Hall was appointed chancellor. In 1885 Mr. Boothe was elected to represent the sixth senatorial district in the state senate, and acquitted himself with honor and
credit at the sessions of 1886 and 1888. In 1890 he was a member of the constitutional
convention from the second congressional district as a delegate from the state at large. Mr.
Boothe is a talented man, a shrewd practitioner, a forcible and eloquent speaker and one
whose public career is above reproach. While holding the different offices and positions of
trust with which he has been honored, Mr. Boothe has jealously guarded the interests of his
people, and faithfully discharged his duty in whatever capacity they have seen fit to place
him. He has been United States commissioner for fifteen years. Mr. Boothe was married
in 1868 to Miss Annie E. Hill, a native of Panola county, and a daughter of William C. of
the Palmetto state. Mr. and Mrs. Boothe's marriage was blessed by the birth of three
children: William E., Estell and Lillian, all students of Oxford university. The son is taking a law course. Mr. Boothe has been attorney for the Mississippi & Texas railroad company, and now the Memphis division of the Illinois Central railroad company, for about sixteen years. Socially he is a member of the Knights and Ladies of Honor, the American
Legion of Honor, and the Independent Order of Odd Fellows. He has represented the
last named order in the grand lodge of Mississippi, and was district deputy grand master of
the same for some time.

One of the most enterprising and successful planters of Lee county, Miss., is Dr.
John F. Booth, of Guntown, who was born in Granville county, N. C., in 1818, and
is a son of Harper Booth. His father was born in Mecklenburg county, Va., September 13, 1775, and was a son of Mr. Thomas Booth, whose ancestors emigrated from
England to America, and settled in Virginia. Thomas Booth was a soldier in the Revolutionary war. Harper Booth was the eldest of a large family. He lived in Virginia until
his marriage, when he removed to North Carolina and engaged in planting. He was a
zealous democrat, and took an active part in political matters. He was magistrate for
some years in North Carolina, but was not an aspirant to public office. He was a Union
man, and a very patriotic one. His death occurred in 1859, at the home of Dr. Booth
whom he was visiting. About 1854 he removed to Mississippi to make his home with his
children. His wife, whose maiden name was Nancy H. Jones, was a native of North Carolina and a daughter of Vinkler Jones, a wealthy planter. They were members of the
Methodist Episcopal church, and were among the very earnest and able workers of that
body. They had born to them eleven children, nine of whom were reared to mature years:
George W., Mrs. Harriet Byron Sledge, Mrs. Ann Howard Allen, William Armistead,
Thomas Harper, Martha, Alexander Grandison, James Madison and Dr. John F. Dr.
Booth spent his early life in North Carolina, and was deprived of the benefits of thorough
mental discipline in his youth. As soon as he was able to do for himself, he took advantage of every opportunity that presented itself to him for acquiring knowledge, and
devoted his leisure time to literary studies until 1843. He then began the study of medicine in Alabama, where he had resided since 1838. He pursued a line of reading under the

direction of his brother, Dr. G. W. Booth, a graduate of the medical department of the University of Pennsylvania. He then attended lectures at Louisville, Ky., and was graduated in 1848. He began practicing the same year in Tishomingo county, at a place called Carrollville, which is now extinct. It was pioneer work, and the journeys he made to see his patients were long and tedious, as his practice extended over a territory of twenty miles square. He had but little to start with, but by economy and wise management he succeeded in getting a hold in the world, and has since accumulated a competency. He was first married in 1849 to Miss Nancy J. Smith, a daughter of Stephen Smith, of Maury county, Tenn. She died in 1858, leaving one child, George Washington, a merchant in Guntown, Miss. Mrs. Booth was a member of the Methodist Episcopal church, a devoted Christian, a good mother and a faithful wife. Dr. Booth was married again in 1868 to Mrs. Emily D. Birge, a daughter of Larkin Gambrell. By her first marriage she had one daughter, who died at the age of three years. By her second union five children were born: Jennie, wife of Robert Epting, Hattie Harper, John Fletcher, Bernard Hess and Emily Alice. During the war Dr. Booth organized a company and saw some active service. Owing to disability he was discharged, and was surgeon to the home guards. Since the war he has given his attention to the mercantile trade, until of late years he has let the responsibility rest upon the younger shoulders of his son, George W. He owns about twenty-five hundred acres of land in Lee county, and has one thousand acres under cultivation. Politically he affiliates with the democratic party, although he takes little action in its movements. He is a member of the Masonic order, and he and his wife belong to the Methodist Episcopal church, of which he was steward for a number of years.

R. M. Bordeaux, sheriff of Lauderdale county, Miss., was born in this county in 1850, a son of T. D. Bordeaux, who was a native of North Carolina, of French Huguenot descent. His great-grandfather was born in France, and, coming to America, was a soldier in the Revolutionary war, afterward settling and dying in North Carolina. A. D. Bordeaux, paternal grandfather of Sheriff Bordeaux, was a planter in North Carolina, and a lifelong resident of that state. The father of our subject came to Mississippi about 1834, and located in Lauderdale county, where he died in 1885, having been all of his life a planter. He had five sons and two daughters, four of whom are living. A. D. Bordeaux, Jr., was killed at the battle of Knoxville; R. H. Bordeaux died in Texas, in 1875; T. D. Bordeaux died February, 1891; two other sons are named R. M. and C. O. Bordeaux. Two of the daughters became, respectively, Mrs. M. E. Walker and Mrs. H. E. Walker. Sheriff Bordeaux was reared in this county, and was prepared for college in the common schools and by a private tutor. He was on the point of entering the university when the war began and prevented the completion of his studies, though he was not old enough to enter the service of his country. He was engaged quite successfully in planting up to the time of his first election to the office of sheriff, which occurred in 1883, and he has been reëlected at each successive election since (four times) and is now a candidate for his fifth term, having given entire satisfaction to the people of the county regardless of their political affiliations. He was married, in 1871, to Miss Callie Walker, by whom he has nine children, all living. He is a Knight of Pythias and a Mason, and he and his family are members of and attendants upon the services of the Methodist Episcopal church. He owns a small planting interest, and is recognized not only as an efficient and trustworthy officer, but as a prominent and useful citizen.

Dr. John Mallory Borders (deceased) was a native of Georgia, as was also his father, John H. Borders, whose birth occurred in 1797. The elder Borders married a Miss Gray, and in 1833 emigrated to Lowndes county, where he purchased land at $3 per acre. He still survives and is ninety-four years of age. John Mallory Borders was but three years, of age when he came with his father to Mississippi. He graduated at Louisville medical college when twenty-four years of age, practiced in Brooksville for twenty-five years, and was also a planter of marked success. He was married to Miss Mary E. Beck, of Noxubee county, and their union resulted in the birth of two interesting children, Isaac Daugherty and John Mallory. Since the death of her husband Mrs. Borders has displayed excellent ability in the management of her affairs, and is a woman of good judgment and business acumen. She is cultured and refined and stands very high in the social scale. Dr. Borders was long identified with all that promoted the best interests or his community, and was loved and respected by all classes. His passing away was a common calamity. The record he has left as a citizen, a professional man, and an aider of the race, should, and will, inspire his noble little sons to an imitation of his many virtues and a following in his footsteps.

Charles Boster is the proprietor of the Cottage by the Sea hotel, at Pascagoula, Miss., which was opened in 1886 and will accommodate about sixty guests, and is the most completely furnished and equipped hotel on the coast of the Mississippi sound. It is situated on the beach where there is always delightful bathing. There is a fine wharf, and bathhouses have been erected for the convenience of the guests of the cottage. The hotel is lighted throughout with gas, and the culinary department is unsurpassed. The rates are very moderate. Mr. Boster is a native of Hamburg, Germany, born in 1828. He was educated in Germany, and at the age of seventeen came to the United States, and enlisted in the navy and served on board the frigate Cumberland during the war with Mexico. After the close of the war he went to New York, and sailed from that port on a voyage around the world. He was on a whaling vessel and was absent three years in the Arctic regions. He met with many adventures and not a few hardships, when at sea, but gained that rich experience which comes only from seeing many lands and nations. On his return to the United States he took up his residence in New Orleans, where he engaged in the mercantile and steamboat bus'ness. He has resided in this city and along the gulf coast for forty years, and few men are better known along the Gulf of Mexico than he.

In 1886 he opened this hotel at Pascagoula, and it is needless to say that it has been managed with marked success. Mr. Boster has held different public positions of honor and trust, and has been for years, and is at present, a member of the board of health of Pascagoula, and is prominently identified with all the progressive movements of the place. Since 1854 he has been a member of the Masonic fraternity. He is a man of genial disposition, and has that kind consideration for the rights and comforts of other people which fit him peculiarly for the business he so successfully conducts.

Another citizen of Natchez, of foreign birth, who has become prominent in business circles, is Louis Botto, who was born in Genoa, Italy, in 1838, and his parents, John and Giacinta Botto, were also natives of that city. The parents remained there until 1846, and then sailed for the United States, locating in Mississippi at Vicksburg, where they remained a short time, and then came to Natchez. The family had but small means at that time, and after accumulating a small amount, the father embarked in the grocery business, and by his industry and close attention to business became quite well off. There he passed the closing scenes of his life as an honest, well-respected citizen, his death occurring in 1879. His wife died in 1848. Louis Botto came with his parents to Mississippi, received his education in the public schools of Natchez, and early in life engaged in the grocery and liquor business with his father. This he has continued with marked success up to the present time, and is now one of the oldest business men in Natchez, as well as one of its wealthiest citizens. He owns about fifteen hundred acres of land, several good business blocks and residences in Natchez, and other valuable property, all the result of his own effort. He is a liberal supporter of all public enterprises, and is officially connected with many of the leading business interests of the city. He is one of the founders and has since been vice president of the First national bank of Natchez; is vice president of the Banner publishing, printing and paper company; and is president of the Rosalie cottonmills and the Natchez compress and warehouse company. The latter was organized in 1886, and has a capital stock of $70,000. It has a ninety inch "Morse" press, and presses from forty thousand to fifty thousand bales per annum. It employs five white and thirty-five or forty colored employes, with a pay roll of $1,500 per month. The plant covers an area of four acres, and draws its supply from several of the southwest counties in Mississippi, besides portions of Louisiana. Mr. Botto is a man of good business experience, progressive in his ideas, and is respected in both commercial and social circles. He was married in 1883 to Miss Fannie Quegles, a native of Natchez and the daughter of John B. Quegles, one of the wealthy citizens of Natchez. Mr. Botto and family are members of the Catholic church. Mr. Botto has one sister, Kate, who is the widow of John Hill. His only brother was the late Paul A. Botto, who was born in Genoa, Italy, in 1840, and who came with his parents to Natchez, Miss. There the latter was educated, but at an early age left a comfortable home and spent a number of years in seeing something of the world. During this time he learnt the art of printing in St. Paul, Minn., and afterward was in charge of a newspaper in Alexandria, La., until 1859. He then left that city and returned to Natchez, where he engaged with his brother in merchandising until the breaking out of the war. He then joined the Natchez fencibles as orderly sergeant, and remained in the service until he was captured near Petersburg, in 1864. He was then sent to Point Lookout prison. His services as a soldier and an officer were meritorious, and met with the general approbation of his comrades and superior officers. After the war he returned to Natchez, and at once began a life of energy and prosperity. In October, 1865, he established the Natchez *Democrat* as a triweekly paper, and continued in the editorial chair until his death, on October 31, 1879. As an editor he was calm, conservative and deliberate, and devoted to the interests of the people with whom he lived. On the 17th of April, 1873, he married Mary Quegles, a sister of his brother's wife.

J. R. Bounds was born in Pickens county, Ala., in 1830, and is a son of William and Martha (Tier) Bounds. His father was a native of North Carolina, and a son of George Bounds. He removed from his native state to Alabama and thence, in 1834, to Kemper county, Miss. Politically he affiliated with the democratic praty. He was not a politician and was not an office-seeker, but his superior judgment and stern sense of justice so eminently fitted him for the office that his fellow-citizens induced him to become justice of the peace, and as such he served for a number of years, and was very faithful and efficient in the discharge of his duties. He was a planter by occupation, and met with more than ordinary success in all of his undertakings. He died in 1849, and was buried at West Kemper church. His wife was a native of North Carolina. She passed from this life in 1840, and rests beside her husband in the old burial ground above mentioned, having been a faithful member of the Baptist church for many years. They reared a family of nine children: Elizabeth, Dollie, Mary, William, Jessie, George, Martha, Susan and James R., the subject of this sketch. James R. Bounds was four years old when his parents moved to Kemper county. Here he has passed his childhood, youth and manhood. He was educated in the local schools, and in 1855 married Miss Martha A. Swearingen, who was born in Clarke county,

Ala., a daughter of M. M. and Emma (Wilson) Swearingen. Eleven children have been born of this union: Mary (deceased), George W. (deceased), William M., James R., Jr., Emma, Jessie L., Annie D., Susan B., Helen L., Eugene and Phenie. Their daughter Emma married Mr. W. H. Wilkerson, and has three children. Annie Donie is Mrs. W. H. Cole, and has a daughter named Annie. Susan B. is Mrs. W. H. Ross, and has had two daughters, S. E. and Callie, the first mentioned of whom died May, 1890. William M. married Lizzie Ross, and has five children (R. R., George W., Anna, Dahla and Joseph E.). James R, Jr., married Amanda Chandler, and they had two children, Annie, who died in June, 1882, and Chandler, and the mother dying in 1887, the father married Miss Callie Ross, who bore him one child in 1887 (Jessie B.). Jessie L. married W. J. Adams, who died September 4, 1890. J. L. Bounds was married June 23, 1891, to Florence Rea. Mrs. J. R. Bounds died January 9, 1883. She was an affectionate wife, a tender mother and a faithful member of the Baptist church. During recent years Mr. Bounds has given his entire attention to agriculture. He owns a tract of seven hundred acres, and has a large portion of it in an advanced state of cultivation. In 1862, when there was a call for men to leave their homes and go out to battle for the Southern cause, he enlisted as a private in company K, of the Forty-third Mississippi regiment, and participated in many important engagements. He was in the siege of Vicksburg, where he was taken prisoner, and was in the battles at Franklin and Nashville, Tenn. His record as a soldier is one of which he may well be proud, and in future years it will be referred to by his descendants as showing his true Southern spirit at a time when every man who was not for the South was against it. For eighteen years from 1871 Mr. Bounds as a dealer in general merchandise was identified with the commercial interests of Kemper county, and did much to elevate its standing in the mercantile world. Politically he affiliates with the democratic party, as did his father before him. He is a man of generous impulses, and has given liberally to the support of educational enterprises and for the establishment and maintenance of churches. Mr. Bounds is an enterprising and progressive man, who, as a citizen, has done his full share toward the development and improvement of his town and county.

Dr. E. C. Bourland, physician, merchant and farmer of Cardsville, Itawamba county, Miss., was born August 22, 1827, a son of James S. and Mary (Hudspeth) Bourland. His father was a native of South Carolina, and his mother was born in North Carolina. They were both members of the Primitive Baptist church. To them were born seven sons and seven daughters, and of this family Dr. Bourland was the sixth child in order of birth. He received his education in Mississippi, and began life for himself at a comparatively early age. He was married November 28, 1849, to Miss Matilda J. Atkins, a native of Alabama, and a daughter of Alfred and Anna (Shaw) Atkins. Mrs. Bourland's father was born in South Carolina, and her mother in North Carolina. Dr. and Mrs. Bourland have had ten children, of whom eight were sons: John V. (deceased), James A., William B., Madison A., Wesley E. S., Walter L., Benjamin C., Neal A., Flora J. and Mary A. M. August 18, 1862, Dr. Bourland enlisted in the Confederate army and became a member of the command of General Berry, at Van Buren, Miss., with which he went to Panola, thence to Grenada, thence back to Panola, thence to Abbeville, and thence to Greenwood, and was engaged in the fight at that point. There he was transferred to the command of General George, and was given authority to raise a company of cavalry, which was known as company K of the regiment to which it was attached, and of which he was elected captain. This company was placed under the command of Major Ham, and was put on line of defense at Tuscumbia river, near Corinth, and was there stationed for eight months. Dr. Bourland was in engagements at Rowin, Twenty-mile creek, Brison's cross roads, Campbelltown, Baldwin, and in a number of skirmishes of less importance. In April, 1864, he was transferred to General Bell's division, later to General Buford's division, and still later to General Chalmers' division, with which he went to Columbus. His regiment was there detached and ordered to Jackson, Miss., and he was in the battle of Seven Miles, near Jackson, and fought at Harrisburg, and later took part in the battle of Atlanta, Ga. From that place he returned to Cotton Gin, Miss. He came home February 26, 1865, on account of ill health, intending to return to service, but before he was able to do so the war had closed. The Doctor may be said to be a life-long democrat, and he cast his first presidential vote for Lewis Cass, of Michigan, and he has voted the straight democratic ticket since. He enjoys in a remarkable degree the esteem of his fellow-citizens, and as a physician has the confidence of a large number of familes. He is a well-wisher and an advocate and helper of every movement having for its object the advancement of public interests.

An eminent practitioner and planter of Ashland, Benton county, is P. M. Bowden, M. D., who was born in Richmond county, N. C., in March, 1839, the fifth in a family of thirteen children, born to James and Jane (Green) Bowden, both of whom were born and reared in that county, where they were married and lived until 1846, when they removed to Benton county, Miss., where Mr. Bowden bought land and engaged in planting. He was a planter pure and simple. He took an active part in politics, although he did not seek political preferment, but such was the public confidence in him that, after the war, he was appointed member of the board of registration. He was widely known in the community, and was a consistent member of the Presbyterian church, and helpful to all measures tending to the public good. His wife, the mother of the subject of our sketch, died in 1855, having lived an exemplary Christian life as a member of the Methodist Episcopal church. For his second wife Mr. Bowden married Miss Mary A. Wells. They had born to them two children. Mr. Bowden died in 1873, and Mrs. Bowden in 1891, there being at this time only eight of the family living. At the age of twenty-one Dr. Bowden began practicing at Baldwin, Miss., having attended the New Orleans medical school and also the Jefferson college at Philadelphia, from which he graduated in the spring of 1861. In the same year he enlisted in company K, of Col. Kit Mott's infantry regiment, which was attached to the army of Virginia, and to which he was for some time attached as regimental surgeon. He was disabled in the fight at Harrisburg, Miss., a minie-ball plowing his right arm, producing a flesh wound, on account of which he was sent home on a furlough, returning to his command as soon as it was healed, and serving until the close of the war, when he was paroled at Gainesville, Ala. He did not resume the practice of medicine immediately after the close of the war, but passed some time as a schoolteacher. In 1873 he again hung out his professional shingle in Benton county, but in the following year he retired from the profession and engaged in planting, in which he has since been very successful. He was married in 1862 to Louisa Ward, a daughter of Turner and Margaret Ward, and they have had born to them four children: James R., Margaret (deceased), George W. and Mary A. Mrs. Bowden died of cancer in 1869, and in 1873 Dr. Bowden married Miss Sarah S. Hasher, by whom he has had seven children: William H., Marshall W., Lulu M., Julia A., Benjamin A. H., Viola (deceased) and Maybel. The Doctor owns six hundred and forty acres of land, three hundred and seventy-five acres of which are now in a state of high cultivation. He has never aspired to any official position, but has been content to live the life of a plain, successful tiller of the soil, and is regarded by his fellow-townsmen as a high-minded, enterprising citizen, a firm and unswerving friend, and a benevolent neighbor. He has probably done as much in support of schools, churches and other public interests generally as any other man of equal means in his part of the state. The social standing of his family is high, and his home is one of the most hospitable in the county. Mrs. Bowden is a member of the Baptist church.

An attorney at law, well known throughout Hancock county and the state of Mississippi, is E. J. Bowers, Bay Saint Louis, a native of the state, born at Canton in June, 1865. His father, E. J. Bowers, Sr., was also an attorney, and for several years was mayor of Canton. He died there in 1881, and his wife died in 1878. The parents were both natives of North Carolina, although Mr. Bowers was taken to Tennessee in his infancy. He was reared in Hardeman county, Tenn., and was admitted to the bar at Holly Springs, Miss., but practiced many years at Canton. Our subject is the only son of his parents; he received his literary education at the Mississippi military institute, leaving the schoolroom when fifteen years of age. For two years he kept books, and then began the study of law, being admitted to the bar in March, 1883, when he was yet in his eighteenth year. The following year he removed to Bay Saint Louis, and for three years was in partnership with Benjamin Lane Posey. This relationship was dissolved in 1887, and since that time he has had two partners. At the present time, however, he is alone in business. He has built up a fine and extensive practice, and is considered one of the leading lawyers of his section. He possesses unusual talent, has a keen, clear intellect, and a quick and decisive judgment. He is city attorney for the Bay, and when but twenty-two years of age he was elector on the democratic ticket for the sixth congressional district of his state. He was the youngest man who has ever had that honor conferred upon him in the United States. From the years 1885 to 1888, in addition to his law practice, Mr. Bowers was engaged in journalism as the editor of the Bay Saint Louis *Progress*, and in 1888 was elected orator of the Mississippi Press association. He takes great interest in educational affairs, and at present occupies a prominent position on the school board of his city. In September, 1888, he was united in marriage to Miss Lulu Posey of Bay Saint Louis. One child has been born of this union, E. J., Jr. The parents are members of the Methodist Episcopal church. Mr. Bowers is a man of strong social instincts, and is a member of several different fraternities. He is genial and courteous in manner, and has a host of friends among his clients and acquaintances.

The Bowie family. This noted family is of Scotch descent, the early members of which came from the land of "thistles and oatmeal" and founded a home for themselves in Maryland during colonial times. Members of this family became very distinguished, two becoming governors of that state, also holding other offices of trust. Dr. Allen T. Bowie was born in Maryland on the 24th of August, 1813, and received his medical education in an institution of Baltimore; later, after leaving, at Kenyon college, Ohio. He became a resident of Natchez in 1837, and the next year was married here to Miss Matilda J. Routh, a daughter of John Routh and a native of Mississippi. After his marriage Dr. Bowie began planting in the Pelican state, and followed that calling exclusively and profitably until the outbreak of the war. He erected a beautiful home in Tensas parish, on Lake St. Joseph, in 1859, at great cost, but this magnificent structure was burned to the ground by the Federals during the Rebellion. During the latter part of the war he came to Natchez and resumed planting on his old place, and he passed from life on the 12th of September, 1872, at Natchez, Miss., his widow surviving him until March 7, 1882, when she, too, was called to her long home. They were members of the Episcopal church, and to them a family of three sons and one daughter was born: John Routh, Allen T., Thomas C., and Ann Smith, who died of yellow fever October 10, 1871. John Routh was a graduate of Chapel Hill college, and in 1861 entered the Confederate army, and at the close of hostilities was paroled as sergeant of the signal service, having served almost entirely in Mississippi. He was married, and at his death, which occurred on the home plantation September 25, 1878, he left a widow and eight children. Thomas C. was educated at Chapel Hill, but left this school to enter the Confederate army with his brother, at the close of the war receiving his parole on the staff of General Majors. He died on the 2d of April, 1880, leaving a wife and three children. Allen Thomas Bowie is the only surviving member of this family, and, like his brothers, was educated at Chapel Hill, N. C. He left the graduating class to enter the Confederate army, and went out with the Tensas cavalry, being paroled as captain at the surrender in 1865. He was in the battles of Shiloh, siege of Vicksburg, Champion Hill, and the engagements around Jackson. His marriage, which occurred on the 21st of November, 1867, was to Miss Ann Matilda Routh, after which he followed planting and merchandising at Natchez, then began railroad work as conductor. In 1882 his train met with an accident, whereby he lost his right leg, and was compelled to retire from the road. During Cleveland's administration he was in the postoffice in Natchez. His family consists of the following children: Allen Thomas, Jr., and Matilda Routh. He and his estimable wife are members of the Episcopal church. John Routh, the maternal grandfather of A. T. Bowie, was born in Natchez in 1791, of which place his parents were early pioneers from Wales. He became an immensely wealthy planter, and all his life was very active and enterprising. He was in the battle of New Orleans in 1815, going to that city with the Wilkinson rifles on a flatboat from Natchez. He was a member of the Louisiana legislature for some time, and died in that state in 1867, an old landmark. A Miss Bowie, sister of Dr. Allen T. Bowie, became the wife of Reverdy Johnson, of Maryland.

Richard S. Bowman, Benton, Yazoo county, Miss., was born in Yazoo county, Miss., in 1854, and is the only son of Claiborne and Elizabeth (Stephens) Bowman. His father was a native of Pike county, Miss., born in the year 1819; he was the second of a family of eleven children born to Richardson and Nancy (Riley) Bowman. Richardson Bowman immigrated from Ireland to America when a boy and settled in Covington, La. All his life he was engaged in agricultural and mercantile pursuits. He was a soldier in the war of 1812, holding the commission of first lieutenant under General Claiborne; he was in the battle of New Orleans. Soon after the close of this war he removed to Pike county, Miss., where he resided until about 1828; he then came to Yazoo county, settling with his family near Benton; he improved a large tract of land, and was one of the leading pioneers of the county. He accumulated a handsome fortune and reared a large family of children, who have occupied a high place in the social and political circles of the state of Mississippi. He died in 1835. Richard Bowman, grandson of the above-named gentleman, is now living on the old homestead. It is one of the best improved plantations in the county, and consists of between eight hundred and a thousand acres. Mr. Bowman is a young man of enterprise and ambition, and is certain to make his mark in the history of the new South. In 1878 he was united in marriage to Miss Lettie Swayze, a daughter of B. and Octavia (King) Swayze. Mrs. Bowman's parents were connected with the early settlement of the county and saw many of the privations and hardships of pioneer life. Five children have been born to Mr. and Mrs. Bowman: Octavia, Henry Y., Lizzie, Annie and Carrie. The parents are members of Bowman's chapel of the Methodist Episcopal church. Mr. Bowman belongs to Benton lodge, Knights of Honor, of which he is ex-director. He was a representative of this body to the Grand lodge of 1890. Although never aspiring to public office, he takes an active part in local politics. He contributes liberally to all public enterprises and those movements having for their object the elevation of morality and the advance of Christianity.

A Chickasaw county planter, Isaac Box, was born on the 11th of September, 1823, a son of James and Jane (McRoy) Box, of South Carolina and Franklin county, Tenn., respectively, their marriage taking place in 1822 and resulting in the birth of nine children: Isaac, Sarah (Howset) deceased, Elizabeth A. (Gibson), William (deceased), Robert, Permelia A., Louisa P. (deceased wife of a Mr. Miller), Mary S. (the deceased wife of a Mr. Parker) and Virginia (Harrington). The father of these children was a planter all his life, and was successfully following his calling at the time of his death, in 1879, which occurred in Chickasaw county, whither he had moved in 1851. His widow survived him until 1890, when she passed away at the age of eighty-two years. While a resident of Tennessee James Box held several county offices and was a wideawake, pushing and prosperous man of business and a useful and influential citizen. Isaac Box was born in the state of Tennessee, and at the early age of ten years began to make his own way in the world, being far more capable than the majority of boys to fight the battle of life for himself. After a time he began handling horses, and subsequently spent about thirty-seven years as an overseer. In 1837 he came to Monroe county, Miss., and in 1858 to Chickasaw county, where he has since followed the calling of a planter and has accumulated a comfortable competency. His plantation, which is a very beautiful one, comprising fourteen hundred acres, is in excellent agricultural condition and is conducted in a manner that shows Mr. Box to be a man of progressive views and thoroughly apace with the times. Everything about the place indicates an untiring thrift and industry, and as the place is naturally a very attractive one, all the time, energy and money expended upon it are repaid fourfold. Mr. Box was first married to Miss Elizabeth Lackey, who died in 1851, leaving him with a son, James H., who is a merchant of Mississippi. In 1857 he took for his second wife Miss Mary E. Waferd, of Tennessee, by whom he became the father of six children: Bessie (Maberry), deceased; Isaac, deceased; Emma (Williams); Charley B.; Rufus O., and one that died in infancy. Mr. Box was called upon to mourn the death of his second wife in 1879, since which time he has remained a widower, making his home with some of his children. He is a member of the Methodist Episcopal church of Buena Vista, and is an earnest contributor to the same. During the Civil war he served in Duff's regiment of cavalry, enlisting in company F, in 1862.

The sheriff of Pike county, Miss., Alfred A. Boyd, was born in Texas, August 10, 1842, a son of Andrew G. and Ann (Whitehead) Boyd, his father a native of Wilmington, Del., and his mother of English birth. The latter came to this country in infancy. They were married in Delaware and in 1839 emigrated to Texas, making the journey by water. After his arrival Mr. Boyd engaged in the drug business, but died at about the age of forty-five years in Memphis, Tenn., January 1, 1852. His widow lives at Summit, aged about seventy-five, exceedingly active and healthy for one of her years. Sheriff Boyd is the third child in a family of two sons and four daughters, of whom the sons and one daughter are living. When he was but four years of age his parents left Texas, locating finally in Memphis, Tenn., where the father was appointed inspector of ports, in which position he served until his death. In 1852 Mr. Boyd removed with his widowed mother to Petersburg, Va., where he grew to maturity, receiving the advantages of a thorough training in the public schools. He came to Mississippi in 1859, locating near Summit, in Pike county, where agricultural pursuits occupied his attention until the outbreak of the war when he early entered the Confederate service as a member of company E, Forty-fifth regiment of Mississippi volunteers, and served during the war in the commands of General Braxton Bragg, Joseph E. and Albert Sidney Johnston. He participated in the battles of Shiloh, Perryville, Murfreesboro and in the Chickamauga and Atlanta campaigns, and was wounded at Shiloh and Murfreesboro.

26

While acting as color bearer of his company at Shiloh, on the morning of the first day's fight, he was struck in the breast by a rifle bullet and his life was saved by the interposition of a small account book which he carried in his pocket. Immediately following the battle of Shiloh he was commissioned lieutenant, and after the battle of Chickamauga he was promoted to the captaincy of his company. He was taken prisoner at Marietta, Ga., in 1864, and was confined on Johnson's island near Sandusky, Ohio, until the close of the war. Returning to Summit he was a prominent resident there for a number of years, during which period he served the city as a member of the board of aldermen and as mayor. He was elected sheriff of Pike county in 1883 and has been reëlected in every subsequent election. No more unequivocal evidence can be desired of the efficiency with which he has filled the office and the high place he holds in public esteem. He married Miss Jennie Wicker, a native of Amite county, Miss., in 1864, and she died ten years later, leaving a daughter named Annie W. In 1876 Mr. Boyd was a second time married to Miss Fanny Lamkin, a daughter of Hon. John T. Lamkin, who represented this district in the Confederate congress, and a native of Holmesville, Pike county, becoming his wife. Mrs. Boyd died in 1884, leaving two children: Oliver W. and John T. Mr. Boyd is a man of commanding presence, being six feet two and one-half inches in hight, splendidly proportioned and straight as an arrow. He is genial, courteous and of exceedingly pleasing address, straightforward in his dealings, fearless in the discharge of his duties and of exemplary habits; he has the respect and esteem of all who know him. An ardent prohibitionist, he has done more toward the modification of the liquor traffic in his county than the majority of its citizens. He is a member of Summit lodge No. 231, and of Royal Arch chapter No. 90, of the A. F. & A. M., of Summit lodge No. 93, of the I. O. O. F., and of De Leon lodge No. 40, of the K. of P. of Summit.

James H. Boyd (deceased) was born in Mason county, Ky., and being there reared on a plantation, he had but limited opportunities for obtaining an education. However, his remarkable powers of observation and his naturally fine mind remedied this in a great degree and he became one of the most intelligent and well-posted men of his section. At the age of eighteen years he came to Mississippi to join his brother, Gordon, and first located at Woodville, in Wilkinson county, and for a time assisted his brother in conducting a newspaper at this place, which training was of great benefit to him. After a short time he went to Bayou Sara, La., at which point he and his brother conducted a drug establishment quite successfully for some time. He came to Jackson, Miss., about 1832 or 1833 and made a permanent settlement, and for quite a long period his attention was given to various occupations, mainly merchandising. He soon became a prominent citizen and was elected to the position of alderman, then mayor, and held the latter position for three terms. During the fifties he was engaged in steamboating, and built and ran two boats on the Pearl river named the Pearl Plant and Bloomer. He also followed this calling on Red river, and during this time attained the rank of captain and lost a boat. In 1843 he was married to Miss Eliza Ellis, a daughter of James E. and Sarah (Morehead) Ellis, both natives of Kentucky, their ancestors having been Virginians. In the Morehead family there have been three governors, two of Kentucky and one of North Carolina. Mrs. Boyd came to Mississippi in 1840 with her brother, Turner M. Ellis, who had settled in this state a few years before and afterward successfully followed the calling of a merchant for thirty years. During the war Mr. Boyd was a member of the state militia, after which he engaged in the commission and auction business, afterward opening a furniture establishment which, for a long time, was the only one in Jackson, and at which he did fairly well. He always took an interest in educational matters and for years before and after the war was a member of the city school board. He joined the Presbyterian church about 1844, and from that time was an earnest and active worker for the cause of Christianity, being an elder of that church for over thirty years. He was prepossessing in personal appearance, being five feet ten inches in hight, and had dark hair and expressive dark brown eyes. He died July 4, 1877, being still survived by his widow, who resides in the handsome home erected by her husband. She is an earnest member of the Presbyterian church, and has endeavored to rear her children in the fear of the Lord. Her union with Mr. Boyd resulted in the birth of six children— three sons and three daughters: Newton Halsey is in the railroad business at Fort Worth, Tex., is married and is the father of four children; Sallie E. is the wife of Lyman C. Gunn, now of Sedalia, Mo.; Mary Eliza is the wife of R. F. McGill (see sketch); James A. is a merchant at Wesson, Miss.; Susan M. became the wife of Benjamin G. Harris, of Fort Worth, Tex., and died in 1881, leaving one child; and John Hargrove, now a minister of the Presbyterian church in Memphis, Tenn., where he has a very thriving church which he has been the means of building up. He took a full literery course at Clarksville, Tenn., grad-uating in 1883, then entered the theological department at Princeton and graduated in 1886. He took charge of the churches at Winona and Durant, Miss., and in March, 1889, located in Memphis, Tenn., and the following November married Miss Ella Henry, a member of a prominent family of Clarksville of that state.

William A. Boyd, the subject of this memoir, was born in Abbeville district, S. C., on the 27th of October, 1833, near what was known as Wardlaw's bridge, on Little river. His parents, Capt. John L. Boyd and Sarah A. (Gray) Boyd, were both natives of Abbeville dis-trict, and were married on the 25th of December, 1832. This happy marital relation was of short duration, as the latter died on the 12th of July, 1835, when the subject of this sketch was not yet two years old. For the next five years, during which time his father remained a widower, little William was the object of tenderest care by doting grandparents, who lived hard by, and supplied, as far as possible, the place of a Christian mother. On the 30th of July, 1840, Captain Boyd took for his second wife Mrs. Ruth R. Huey, a most excellent Christian lady, by whom he became the father of five children: John Allen (deceased), Joseph Lyman (who was killed in the battle of Seven Pines), Rosaline S. (deceased), Alice Josephine (deceased), and Sarah A. (deceased). Capt. John L. Boyd was a prominent planter, a public-spirited citizen, who contributed freely and liberally to public institutions and enterprises. To him, and to men of his enlarged views, is the district (now county) of Abbeville indebted for that refinement and advanced civilization so manifestly characteristic of her people. He and his family were old school Presbyterians and worshiped at Lebanon church, some four miles south of Abbeville village. For fifteen years, under the old militia system of South Carolina, he was captain of the Warrenton militia company, and prided in fostering and encouraging the martial spirit of his state. After a short illness he died at his home in Abbeville district, on the 21st of August, 1856, and in the forty-fifth year of his age. His widow afterward removed to Tippah county, Miss., where she died in the year 1862. In the year 1847 William A. Boyd, then about fourteen years old, was sent to Tippah county, Miss., for the purpose of attending a school, known as Bamboo academy, located one mile southeast of Ripley, the first session of which was then being taught by his maternal uncle, the Rev. W. A. Gray, a Presbyterian minister, who for forty years was pastor of the Ripley Presbyterian church. Though a plain log structure, Bamboo was in all respects a classic school of high order, and under such teachers as Rev. W. A. Gray, Prof. Bethay, Henry M. Warner and C. A. Brougher, paved the road to much future

usefulness in the community and to the state. Here W. A. Boyd entered upon and completed the course of study necessary to admit him to the sophomore class in the University
of Mississippi, where he matriculated in the month of September, 1851, and remained three
years, graduating in the year 1854. Connected with this class from first to last were eighty-
three young men, thirty-six of whom finished the prescribed course and received diplomas on
the 13th of July, 1854. Of these many became renowned in the learned professions, and
quite a number filled high positions of honor and trust both in the state and in the nation.
On the 12th of March, 1855, Mr. Boyd was happily matched in marriage to Miss Sarah J.
Smith, daughter of James S. Smith, a prominent citizen of Tippah county, Miss.
She still lives to cheer in prosperity and console in adversity the companion of her life. A
few days after marriage Mr. Boyd took charge of the Cherry Creek high school, in Pontotoc
county, where he remained until the close of the year. In the year 1856 College Hill
academy, a preparatory school of high order, located five miles from the State university,
engaged Mr. Boyd to become its principal, and here he expected to remain, but the death of
his father, in South Carolina, compelled him to give up the school before the close of the
year. In the year 1857, having so arranged his father's business as to enable him to return
to Mississippi, and the citizens of Ripley, in the meantime, having erected a splendid school
building, he was induced to take charge of it for one year. During these three years as
educator his efforts were successful, financially and otherwise. Many young men, under his
training, became honored and useful citizens. Notwithstanding his fixed purpose to make
teaching the prime business of life, failing health, superinduced by sedentary work, determined him to quit the schoolroom, and in the latter part of 1857 he bought and settled the
farm five miles east of Ripley, upon which, for the third of a century, he has continuously
resided—an humble but a pleasant home. The freedom of farm life had, and still has, for
him a fascinating charm, and the health-giving influence of an active existence stilll preserves to him the flush of a vigorous manhood. On account of physical disability, resulting
from an injury received in early boyhood, Mr. Boyd was exempt from military service during
the late war, yet his sympathies were heartily with the Confederacy, and more than once
was he subjected to the vengeance of Union soldiers because of his devotion to the Southern
cause—twice incarcerated, his property destroyed, and himself and family for more than a
year exiled from home. Nothing daunted, his convictions strengthened under the influence of
misfortunes, and in the home sphere his services were scarcely less valuable than they might
have been in the tented field. Mr. Boyd has always taken an active interest in the political
affairs of the country. He is and has ever been in hearty accord with the national democratic
party, and for many years has taken an active part in state and national campaigns.

    In 1861 Mr. Boyd was, by the nearly unanimous vote of his county, elected to represent it
in the state legislature. At this time the chief business of the legislature was to aid the Confederacy by furnishing men and means to prosecute the war, to provide for indigent
families of Mississippi soldiers, and generally to promote the Southern cause. In this service Mr. Boyd, though at that time the youngest member of the body, discharged his duty
with honor to himself and to the entire satisfaction of his constituents. His next public service was rendered the state in the annual sessions of the legislature of 1872-3. This was
indeed, a most, if not the most, gloomy period of Mississippi's eventful history. 'Twas the
dark penumbra of the reconstruction period, remembered with feelings of horror by all true
Mississippians, when carpetbaggers and negroes, like barnacles, had fastened on to Mississippi, and as so many "mournful facts," were driving the ploughshare of destruction through
the best interests of society. In this critical juncture Mr. Boyd's people again summoned

him to the councils of the state, where, as in all the past, he proved equal to the emergency, and together with a little handful of true Mississippians, he stood as a breakwater against the angry tide intended for the ruin of his people. To this day that noble little band of patriots is remembered as the old guard of Mississippi, and, certainly, to their determined courage in opposing the wily schemes of the carpetbagger is to be traced the state's comparative freedom from financial embarrassment. In 1884 Mr. Boyd was again called from the retirement of rural life, and elected for four years to serve his senatorial district in the senate of the state. Union, Benton and Tippah counties composed the senatorial district. Here, as elsewhere, he ranked with the leaders of the senate. But the crowning service of his public life was rendered his state in the year 1890. The state had long groaned under the evils of the state constitution, which had, under carpetbag regime, during the reconstruction period, been foisted upon a helpless people. After much discussion and deliberation, the legislature of 1890 issued a call for a state constitutional convention, to be assembled in Jackson on the 12th of August, 1890. Here was opened up a wide field for the best intellect of the state. The conditions were peculiar. Political problems such as had never before claimed the prudent deliberations of patriot statesmen awaited solution. The race problem, in its relation to intelligent state government, loomed into view as the question of the hour. The best and purest men in the state were sought out and elected to constitute the convention. The wisest of the delegates contemplated the delicate work before them, and approached the perplexed questions to be grappled with feelings akin to fear. Mr. Boyd represented Tippah county in that convention, and it can be truthfully said that in the handling of the most intricate questions there were few men more conspicuous than he. A firm believer in the virtue of the people, a sturdy defender of yeomanry, he was ever foremost in advocacy of such fundamental reforms as would strengthen the weak and protect them against the power of the strong. To him are the people of Mississippi indebted for many wholesome features incorporated into their new organic law. In private life it has fallen to the lot of but few men to enjoy more fully the unbroken confidence of his neighbors. Plain and unpretending, his familiar-like bearing toward all is to him a sure guarantee for the good-will of all with whom he is socially related. His wife's native geniality and suavity of manners insure domestic happiness, and strengthen the bond of friendship with all around her. Mr. Boyd and his wife are and since early life have been, members of the Presbyterian church, and have all the while held their membership in the church at Ripley, Miss. For twenty years Mr. Boyd has been a ruling elder in this church, and is now its senior officer. He is broadly liberal in his feelings toward Christians of other denominations, and has often been heard to express contempt for narrow-minded denominational bigotry. He at an early day became a member of that broadly benevolent order, the Knights of Honor, and in his zeal for its success has delivered many addresses in advocacy of its principles. His membership in the Knights of Honor is with Ripley lodge No. 2242, at Ripley, Miss. From what has already been said of Mr. Boyd's advocacy of organized benevolence, the reader has doubtless anticipated the fact, now here stated, that he is an active member of the farmers' movement, known as the Farmers' Alliance and Industrial Union. His anxious solicitude for the welfare of the agricultural classes led him early to espouse a cause which seemed to promise some relief from the ills of which they complain. He has, however, no sympathy with any effort to give to the organization a partisan political drift, but has, from the beginning, favored the policy of contending for political and legislative reforms within the lines of existing political party organizations. Beyond this he thinks the alliance can not safely go. To the national democratic party he looks with confidence for all that is valuable to the country in the shape

of relief or reform. The life which we have but imperfectly sketched is that of an humble, unostentatious farmer, indeed, a farm laborer, who, when visited by our reporter,
was found between the plowhandles, and the facts on which this sketch is based were given
in the open field, while the plow stood waiting in the unfinished furrow. Such a life is full
to overflowing of unrecorded incidents of interest not here given. But enough has been
stated to emphasize the golden truth that "there can be no excellence without labor;" that
true worth is developed by sincerity of purpose, and can come alone from honesty of effort.

Since locating in Bolivar county, Miss., W. C. Boyd, planter of Gunnison, has
enjoyed the reputation of being not only a substantial and progressive planter but an
intelligent and highly esteemed citizen. He was originally from Vermont, born in 1834,
and was the youngest of three children born to Robert and Hannah (Colton) Boyd, the parents natives of the North of Ireland. The father and mother came to the United States in
early life, and the former followed the occupation of a planter until his death, in 1835. The
mother died in Canada about 1885, at an extreme age. W. C. Boyd attended school until
thirteen years of age, and then, after working on the farm in Vermont for four years, emigrated to Desha county, Ark., where he resided one year. In 1852 or 1853 he came to Bolivar county, Miss., made Concordia his home, and there worked at the carpenter's trade. He
followed this until the outbreak of the war, and, in the spring of 1861, assisted in recruiting
a company. He was elected third lieutenant of the McGehee rifles, joined this company
late in the fall and served with it during the entire war. He was in many battles and, on
account of a wound received at Kenesaw mountain, was absent from his command for ninety
days. Later he joined his company in front of Atlanta. He was at Macon, Ga., and subsequently was acting adjutant of the post of Atlanta until cessation of hostilities. He then
returned to Bolivar county and followed carpentering until 1870, when he began tilling the
soil. He now has a beautiful plantation of about two thousand two hundred acres, six hundred of which are under cultivation, and he has cleared most of the land and made all the
improvements. In 1890 he erected a good barn at a cost of $2,500 and has good houses for
manager and tenants. He was married in 1870 to Miss Sallie E. Deane, who was born in
this county, and whose father, Dr. Deane, was an early settler and a leading physician for
many years. He died in 1858. To Mr. and Mrs. Boyd were born nine children, seven of
whom died in infancy. Those living are Robert Oliver and Mary Laudie. The family are
members of the Methodist church. Mr. Boyd is a chapter Mason and a member of the
Knights of Honor and the Knights of Pythias organizations. He is deeply interested in
educational matters. He is now a member of the board of supervisors and has done a large
amount of bridge-building for the county. The contracts for the county during the past
twenty years have been as much as $75,000. Mr. Boyd has taken contracts for levee con-
struction for several years past, and these amount to from $15,000 to $35,000 each year.
Although quite active in politics, Mr. Boyd is no officeseeker, and his election to the office of
supervisor was the will and act of the people, not his desire or choice. In his official duties
he is conscientious and scrupulously exact.

About the year 1830, Samuel S. Boyd, a native of Maine, located in Mississippi for the
practice of law. He formed a partnership with Alexander Montgomery, and rose at once to
the front rank of his profession. He was one of the most scholarly lawyers of the bar in
that early day. He possessed a powerful intellect, great energy, and was brilliant and magnetic in debate. He possessed all the artifices necessary to make one conspicuous in law.
His weaknesses were few. The consequence was that few lawyers in the state could cope
with him in the management of deep law questions. In 1837 he was selected one of the

special judges in the case of Vick et al. vs. the mayor and aldermen of Vicksburg, and was selected to deliver the final opinion of the court. This opinion is yet famous for the wonderful penetration and fresh, bright views of this great case. New precedents were established by him on important questions of law, and the reasons leading up to such precedents were set forth in an irresistible train of logic. He continued to practice for many years with great success, and secured more than a state reputation for learning, probity and eloquence. Unfortunately for the state, he passed away in the prime of life.

Among the most substantial and reliable farmers of Yalobusha county is John P. Boydstun, Water Valley, Miss., the subject of this brief biographical sketch. He was born in Hardeman county, Tenn., in 1828, and is a son of Benjamin and Elizabeth (Jacobs) Boydstun, natives of Tennessee and South Carolina respectively. The father was born in 1804, and the mother just five months later. They were married in 1825 in Tennessee, to which state her parents had to come to engage in agriculture. Walter Jacobs, the grandfather of our subject, on the maternal side, lived to be an elderly man, rearing a family of nine children. Mrs. Boydstun was the eldest daughter; she was the mother of ten children, and died in the year 1843. Six of the children lived to maturity, and two of them are now living: the subject of this notice, and R. W. Boydstun of Water Valley; William P. died in Mississippi leaving a wife and four children, Martin V. died at Macon, Ga., he was a member of the Fifteenth Mississippi volunteer infantry, company F, and just before the war, was graduated from the medical college of Nashville, Tenn.; Amanda was the wife of G. W. Robinson; America married William Snelling. The father of Mr. Boydstun was a farmer by occupation, and after the death of his wife he came to Mississippi in 1845, and settled in Yalobusha county; there he purchased land which he had partially improved at the time of his death, which occurred three years later in 1848. He was married a second time, to Susana Walker, of Yalobusha county. He was a member of the Baptist church, in which he took an active interest. John P. Boydstun was reared from his sixteenth year in Mississippi, but received the greater part of his education in Tennessee. On the death of his father, he began farming on his own account in the neighborhood of his old home, and has since resided there. In 1852 he was married to Miss Martha Ann Carr, a native of Georgia, but for many years a resident of Yalobusha county; her father, Hawkins B. Carr, was one of the earliest settlers of that county. Of this union, eight children were born: Theodore; Sarah, the wife of John Johnsy; Findly D.; Dora Lee, the wife of W. E. Edger.; Emma C.; Beulah Ann; William H., and John P. The last named enlisted in the Fifteenth Mississippi volunteer infantry, company F, and served as a private. He was in the battle of Corinth, the siege of Atlanta, and other important engagements; he was under both Hood and Johnston, and did gallant work in the cause. He was paroled at Greensboro, N. C., when he was under Johnston. After the surrender he returned to his home and resumed his farming. To him, as to many others, the war brought heavy losses; he had just sold his farm, and receiving his pay in Confederate money, he found himself at the close of the war $370 in debt, so he had to begin life over again. He first rented a place for three years, and in 1868 he purchased his present place. The plantation contains several hundred acres, all of which is under good cultivation. A general farming business is carried on in the most systematic manner. Mr. Boydstun and his wife are members of the Baptist church at Big Springs. The membership of this society numbers about forty, and they own a church building erected at a cost of $600. Politically, our subject affiliates with the democratic party.

In Warren county, John R. Brabston, M. D., of the allopathic school, is one of the foremost physicians, although he has only practiced his profession since 1882. He was born in the county in which he is now residing September 2, 1853, being a son of James M. and Roche (Robinson) Brabston, both of whom were born in Mississippi, the former being a prosperous planter, who, in 1852, took up his abode in Warren county, where he became a well-to-do agriculturist. He was a well-educated man, being a graduate of the military college of Washington, Miss. His father, Thomas Brabston, emigrated from his native state of North Carolina to Kentucky with Daniel Boone, but soon after, with his brother, floated down the Mississippi river and found employment on a Mississippi plantation. At this time he was quite young and an orphan, but his honesty and energy soon won him many friends and especially ingratiated him in the good opinion of his employer, Mrs. Greenfield, with whom he remained until he had amassed considerable property, when, about 1810, he married Miss Anna Aldridge and made a home for himself, eventually becoming the largest cotton planter of Mississippi. Dr. John R. Brabston received his early education under the instructions of a private tutor, his rudimentary knowledge of medicine being acquired in the office of Dr. Hunt, of Vicksburg. He then spent one session in Tulane university, of New Orleans, and one session in the Memphis medical college, from which institution he was graduated. At the age of twenty-nine years he began practicing his profession at Snyder's bluff, on the Yazoo river, but one year later located on the home plantation. During his collegiate career he spent considerable time in the hospital, so that upon engaging in general practice he was eminently fitted for a successful career, and he has fully fulfilled the promise he at that time gave. He is the owner of a plantation of over one thousand acres in Warren county, one-third of which is under cultivation. As a practitioner of the healing art Dr. Brabston has met with the best of success, and the health of many of the citizens of the section in which he resides is due to his skill and talent. He is located at Palmyra, in Davis bend, and is doing remarkably well. He is unmarried. His mother's people, the Robinsons, came originally from England and settled at Baltimore, Md., but gradually members drifted to South Carolina, then to Georgia, and then some of the family reached Mississippi in the year 1803.

Samuel L. Braden, Enola, Yazoo county, Miss., was born in Williamson county, Tenn., November 23, 1823, and is the eldest of a family of ten children. His parents were James and Jane A. (Cisine) Braden, natives of Tennessee. The father was engaged in agriculture, and followed this vocation all his life. He died in 1872, and his wife passed away the same year. James Braden was a son of Samuel Braden. The subject of this notice was reared on a plantation in his native state, and was trained to habits of industry and thrift. He acquired an ordinary education in the common schools, and in 1842 he removed to Mississippi. He located in Holmes county, where he resided for eleven years, at which time he came to Yazoo county. He owns four hundred acres of land, one hundred and forty of which he cultivates with the greatest care and skill. He considers agriculture a science, and works upon that basis. Although his acreage is comparatively small, he harvests abundant crops, and is always surrounded with plenty. He was married in 1868 to Miss Maria McSarley, a Kentuckian by birth. When there was a demand for men to take up arms in defense of their country he was not slow to realize his duty, and enlisted in 1861 in company I, Twelfth Mississippi volunteer infantry. He served in this regiment for one year, when he was thrown from his horse and disabled. He then came home and remained one year, joining Adam's cavalry at the end of that period. He was in the service until the surrender, and although he was not in any noted engagements, he saw a great deal of fighting. He was twenty years of age when he went out to seek the fortune which might be in store for him. His capital was pluck, energy and thrifty habits, and these have been his faithful servants. He is noted for his honesty and integrity of character, and is honored where his name is known. He has a beautiful residence on the banks of the Yazoo river, where that generous hospitality, characteristic of the Southerner, is dispensed to all who cross the threshold.

Judge W. D. Bradford (deceased), came to Pontotoc county at an early day. He became deputy marshal under his brother, Gen. Alexander Bradford, who was one of the first marshals of Mississippi. He began the study of law when quite young, and was admitted to the bar of Pontotoc county at the time he attained his majority. He soon became known as one of the most brilliant young lawyers of this part of the state. He was noted for his success in criminal cases, being an able advocate and unusually well informed concerning the intricacies and minutæ of the law practice. He became associated in the practice of his profession with Charles D. Fontaine, about 1848, a partnership which continued until just before the beginning of the late war. As commander of the famous Bradford battery, he covered himself and his men with glory. After the war he was elected circuit judge, and served as such from 1872 to 1878. He was married in 1847 to Miss Rosalie, the daughter of Col. Nathaniel W. Dandridge, of Henry county, Va. Unto this union have been born five children, only two of whom are now living.

The Brandon family. Gov. Gerard C. Brandon's father was a native of Ireland and was engaged in an insurrection against England in defense of the liberty of his country. This failed and he was forced to flee to America. He landed at Charleston, S. C., and was there a short time prior to the Revolution, in which he served as colonel under General Marion and led the cavalry charge at King's mountain. After the war he married a Miss Nugent and removed to Adams county, Miss., when that state was a territory. He settled Selma plantation, near Natchez, and here Gerard C. Brandon, the future governor, was born in 1788. He was prepared for college by Rev. Dr. McDowell and entered Princeton college, but being dissatisfied there he was sent to William's and Mary's college, in Virginia. There he graduated, dividing first honors with William C. Rives, afterward minister to France. He began the practice of law at Washington, Miss., and served for a short time as a soldier in the war of 1812. In 1816 he married Miss Margaret Chambers, of Kentucky, and afterward abandoned law for planting, residing for a time in Wilkinson county, near Fort Adams. His first wife having died, he married Miss Elizabeth Stanton, of Natchez, in 1824. He was a member of the first constitutional convention and at the next session of the legislature he was speaker of the house. He was lieutenant-governor under both Leake and Holmes. He was elected governor in 1827 by a large majority and served two years. His administration was marked by firmness, independence and decision. In a message he strongly urged the impolicy of allowing negro slaves to be brought from other states into Mississippi, and during his term this dictum was followed. He granted few pardons and none except from well-proved innocence. So popular was Governor Brandon that at the end of his second term, in 1832, he was offered the United States senatorship, but declined the honor and retired from active public service. After this he lived for a time in Wilkinson county and did much for its improvement, being especially active in the cause of education. His last appearance in public life was as a delegate to the state constitutional convention in 1837. He opposed the clause which made the judiciary elective and advocated the present method of appointment. In private life he was kind, affable and the soul of honor. His keen sense of humor and fine conversational powers made him the central figure in all social gatherings. He was very fond of field sports. His death occurred on the 28th of March, 1850, when sixty-two years of age. His younger brother, Gen. William L. Brandon, was born in Wilkinson county in 1800, and spent all his life there as a wealthy planter. His death occurred in 1890. He received a fine collegiate education and led a life of industry and usefulness. He was a general in the Confederate army, serving in Virginia, and lost a foot at Malvern hill. He also had three sons who served in the Confederate army: William, Robert and Lane. Governor Brandon also had three sons in the Confederate army: William, who was killed at Chancellorsville; Aaron, killed at Fredericksburg, and George. He had three other sons: Dr. James (deceased), Dr. Spencer, of Wilkinson county and Girard.

Gen. William L. Brandon was born in 1802, near old Washington, Adams county, and settled in Wilkinson county in 1824, near Pinckneyville, on the tract of land entered by his father, Gerard Brandon, in 1790. Here he reclaimed, from the primeval forest the Arcole plantation, on which he resided to the day of his death, on Friday, October 8, 1890, at two P. M. General Brandon, always a prominent member of the community in which he lived, was by profession a planter. General Brandon, his father, was a native of Ireland, and came to America during the Irish insurrection, and entered the continental army, in which he served with some distinction. He was in the famous battles of King's mountain, and at the taking of Ferguson, and held a commission. Soon after the declaration of independence he had come to a place called Galveztown, in the British possessions, near the present Lake Pontchartrain, where he settled, but when Galvez captured it from the English he moved to Attakapas, and from there to the Natchez district, about the time Don Stephen Minor was governor of the Spanish possessions. He then took up land near the old seat of Washington, soon after 1780, and numerous other large tracts in what is now Adams and Wilkinson counties, among them the one upon which his grandson, Capt. Robert L. Brandon, now resides, in all comprising about three thousand arpents. His family consisted of four sons and three daughters, of whom William L. was the youngest. Gerard C. Brandon, the eldest, was governor of the state in 1827 and 1830. Matthew N. and Robert Emmet, the next two, grew to manhood and were married, but some years after their marriage died; each had claims near the present residence of Robert L. The daughters were Elisabeth (who married William Staunton of Natchez), and Margaret (who married Captain Smith of the United States army, then stationed at or near Washington, in the Natchez district). William L. was educated in Virginia and at Princeton, N. J., and then returned to the home place and soon afterward came to Arcole plantation, where he passed the remainder of his days. He soon became quite prominently connected with the politics of the county and state, and was a member of the legislature about the year 1835. He also took great interest in military tactics, had a taste for military affairs, and was elected major-general of the district militia in which he took an active part and so distinguished himself, that during the war with Mexico he was candidate for the colonelcy of a regiment but was defeated by Gen. Reuben Davis. During the late war, though three score years of age, he promptly raised a company of volunteers of which he was made captain, and left for the scene of war in Virginia, where the company was mustered into the service of the Confederacy, at Richmond, April 28, 1861, to serve during the period of the war. This company soon afterward became company D, Twenty-first regiment Mississippi volunteers, Longstreet's corps, army of Northern Virginia. Upon the organization of the regiment he was chosen lieutenant-colonel, and commanded this regiment at the bloody battle of Malvern Hill with such conspicuous skill and daring as to win high and honorable mention from his superior officer. Though sixty years of age then, he left a leg on that stricken field. After the battle he was removed to Richmond, Va., where his leg was amputated and where he remained in the hospital several months, pluckily and steadily recovering. While there he was visited by Hon. H. S. Van Eaton and found to be in most excellent spirits, full of animation, expressing himself thus: "I am doing first rate; I'll soon be out of this; my wound is doing well, healing by first intention, and in less than a month I'll be back with my regiment." His splendid grit and confidence surprised Mr. Van Eaton, who said to him, "I'm afraid, Colonel, your fighting days are over." To which he replied, "Not a bit of it; I'll live to give 'em fits yet." Mr. Van Eaton afterward said of his visit, "I was never more astonished. I had expected to find a much suffering, perhaps a dying, man, and here he was, cheerful as of old, making light of the loss of a leg, thinking only of how soon he could return to his command and resume active duty in the field." As soon as he was able, he started home, where, by the kindness of Dr. Redhead, he was fitted out with a wooden leg, and started back to join the army then in Georgia, where he exchanged his wooden leg for a better one. After the battle of Chickamauga, owing to his great age and crippled condition, together with the feeling that he was in the way of the promotion of younger and more active officers, he resigned his commission, but was subsequently assigned department duties with the rank of brigadier-general with headquarters at Enterprise, Miss., which position he held until the close of the war. A gallant officer, a gentleman of the old school, whose heart was as tender as a woman's, the words sans peur et sans reproche express a fitting tribute to his character as a man and a soldier. Returning to his home, he resumed his labors to replace the losses sustained by the war, which amounted to many thousand dollars. The General was a man of unusual intellectual power, and greatly devoted to his books and papers. He owned many valuable works, and was well informed on a great variety of subjects. He was a man of commanding appearance, fine looking, with large head and broad brow, and stood six feet one inch high, and weighed from two hundred and five to two hundred and twenty pounds. His hair was dark, his eyes blue, and his face indicated great will-power and self-control. He was devoted to his family and friends, was often referred to in settling difficulties of the surrounding country, and during the day of dueling was often chosen as a second, not from choice on his part, but by the earnest desire of his friends, who knew that he would have fair play. He would not accept the position unless the parties concerned would give him full charge, as he was opposed to dueling if the matter could be honorably settled without bloodshed. He took great delight in his home, and enjoyed hunting so much that he always kept a pack of hounds, and was the president of a club called the High Kelter, a hunting club formed in the neighborhood, and spent many a day at his favorite sport. He was always fond of a practical joke, and could take a joke as well as crack one. The General in earlier life made a study of medicine, and was often consulted professionally by his people and by the families on his plantations. He was first married in 1825 to a Miss Ann Davis, a descendant of the Wade Hampton family. By her union with Mr. Brandon were born two children. The mother and her children soon died, and the General was married in 1833 to Ann Eliza Ratliff, a native of Louisiana, who was born in 1815 and died in 1840. Her parents were from North Carolina, and came to Louisiana, where they were quite prominently connected with the early history of that state. To this union were born four sons, three of whom lived to be grown: Eugene, who died at the age of two years, was the youngest; William R., who lives in Louisiana, served in the late war. He was severely wounded in the hip at Gettysburg. He was a graduate of Union college, New York, and of the medical college of New Orleans. Robert L., now living on the old home place, is a graduate of Yale college, in the class of 1856, which comprised ninety-six members. He was a classmate of Chauncey M. Depew, Henry B. Brown, David J. Brewer, W. D. Magruder and others, all of whom are among the most eminent men of the country. He was in the late war with Adams' brigade, and was made adjutant at the close of the war; Lane W. was a graduate of Harvard college and served in the late war, going out in 1861 and remaining all through the struggle. He was wounded at Malvern Hill and at the battle of Chickamauga. In this battle he was captain and in command of the company, and was wounded while charging the enemy's line and was at first thought to be mortally injured, but survived, and was finally, just before the surrender of Appomattox, captured and taken to Johnson's island, where he was kept until the final release. He is now living in Louisiana engaged in planting, and is clerk of the courts at Bayou Sara; Robert L. is now living on the old homestead of his parents, engaged in planting, and is one of the county's leading citizens. He is married to Miss Fannie P. Towles, the daughter of John T. Towles, a native of Louisiana, and one of the representative planters, who is now deceased. To Mr. and Mrs. Brandon are born three children, all of whom are living: Lane W., Robert E. and Belle. Mr. Brandon was first married to a sister of his present wife, Belle Towles, who was born in Louisiana in 1838, and died in 1876, having been a member of the Episcopal church. To that union were born five children, three of whom are living: John W., Gerard C., Anne R., Elizabeth Ratliff (who died at the age of three years), and Fannie Peyton (who died at the age of two years). Anne R. took the Peabody medal at Natchitoches, La.

A prominent planter and retired physician of Adams county, Miss., Dr. A H. Brenham, resides on his estate at Elsyon Fields, four miles from Natchez. He was born in Frankfort, Ky., in 1828, being the second child of John Herndon and Ann Eliza (James) Brenham, who were native Kentuckians, and whose ancestors, of English and Irish descent, respectively, came to America during colonial times, taking part in the Revolutionary war. John Herndon Brenham had seven brothers who fought in the war of 1812 along the Canadian frontier, six of whom were killed. Mr. Brenham died before the birth of the subject of this sketch. The latter received his literary education in the University of Kentucky, graduating in 1845. He came to Mississippi in 1847, mainly on account of his health, and while here concluded to study medicine, and began carrying out this decision with Gov. L. P. Blackburn, after which he entered the medical department of the Louisville university, graduating in 1849, taking a post graduate course the following year. He then began practicing in Natchez in partnership with his former preceptor, Dr. Blackburn, which partnership continued until 1853, when Dr. Blackburn withdrew, and Dr. Brenham continued with a younger brother, Edward M. Blackburn. In 1854 he removed to Vidalia, where he was actively engaged in practicing until 1863, having, without doubt, the largest practice of any physician in the county. September 13, 1863, his fine residence in Vidalia was destroyed by fire by the Federals, and all his library and valuable surgical instruments were destroyed. He was married, in 1853, to Miss Bell Marsh, a daughter of Cyrus and Isabella Marsh, a native of Natchez. She died of yellow fever the same year of their marriage, leaving one child which did not long survive her, its death occurring in infancy. His second marriage was to Miss Victoria Ford, and was consummated in 1859. She was the daughter of Thomas J. and Elizabeth Ford, natives of this county. The family reside in Natchez, but since retiring from practice the Doctor has given his attention to looking after his extensive and valuable real estate. He has been somewhat active in politics, and in 1879 was elected state senator, a position he held for eight years in succession. While in Louisiana he was nominated by his party as a candidate for state senator, but by reason of his extensive medical practice, had to decline when nomination was eqivalent to an election. The Doctor lost his excellent wife on March 17, 1890, she having borne him two children: Anna Ford, who died in infancy, and Luke Blackburn, who is now living with his father and is interested with him in valuable planting property. He was educated in Pass Christian, Miss., and is an intelligent and promising young man. The Doctor possesses decided literary tastes, and has always been a close and conscientious student. Although he is now sixty three years of age, he is actively alive to the issues of the day, and is deeply interested in all matters pertaining to local improvement. He is of the stuff of which noble men are made, and he is conceded by all to rank among the highest civilians.

H. H. Brewster, planter, of Lauderdale county, Miss., is well and favorably known to the majority of the residents of this section, for he has been connected with the planting interests of this section for over thirty years. He was born in Florida in 1824, but at the age of five years was taken to Alabama, and there he was brought up, receiving his education in the old fieldschools of that period. He was married to Miss Sarah Edwards, of Alabama, in 1852, and to their union a family of eight children have been born: Joseph F., Jackson L., Louisa L., Mary, Martha, Alice, Hiram W. and Margaret, all but one of whom are married. Hiram W. is a graduate of the Nashville medical college and a successful practitioner of Lauderdale county. In 1861 H. H. Brewster enlisted in Mayberry's brigade of state troops, but at the siege of Vicksburg was captured and paroled. After being exchanged, he joined Forrest's command, and was afterward at Harrisburg, Miss. When the war was over he returned home, and began farming on the old Brewster homestead, ten miles east of Meridian. At various times he has owned land to the amount of one thousand acres, although he now owns only about four hundred acres. He is now considered one of the leading planters of his section, and deservedly so, for from the soil he has obtained a handsome competency. He has a host of friends, due to his kindly disposition, uniform steadiness of character and honesty of purpose. His father, James Brewster, was born in Georgia in 1794, of Irish parents, and about 1819 was married to Miss Mary Smith.

A prominent planter and stockraiser of Cascilla, Miss., is Armour L. Bridgers. His parents, T. J. N. and Susan Hicks (Estes) Bridgers, were natives of Tennessee, and in that state were reared and married. The father followed merchandising in Memphis for a number of years under the firm title of Armour, Lake & Bridgers, and he then moved to Huntingdon, Tenn., and some time in the thirties, prior to 1835, he came to Yalobusha county, Miss., and embarked in merchandising at Coffeeville. Some time in the fifties he came to his plantation in Tallahatchie county, and there made his home until about 1859, when he returned to Coffeeville. When the war broke out he again removed to his plantation, and there died, in 1874, at the age of sixty years, after an active and successful business career. He was a self-made man in every respect, was well known and very popular. He was once a member of the Mississippi legislature from Tallahatchie county, was a whig, and was ever active in political as well as public affairs. He was a prominent Mason. His first wife died in Coffeeville in 1845. This union was blessed by the birth of six children, only one besides Armour L. now living, Mrs. Hattie A. Hale, wife of J. D. Hale, of Coffeeville. The paternal grandfather, Sampson Bridgers, was born in Nash county, N. C., and there grew to manhood. When a young man he went to Tennessee, resided there for many years, but spent the closing scenes of his life in Mississippi, his death occurring in Charleston about 1856. He was a planter by occupation, and of Welsh descent. His wife, who was formerly Miss Elizabeth Nicholson, died in Coffeeville about 1846. Her mother was a Drake, a lineal descendant of Sir Francis Drake. Armour L. Bridgers was born near Coffeeville, Yalobusha county, Miss., in 1846, received his education at Coffeeville, and was attending Mountain Home academy, Alabama, when the war broke out. About 1863 he joined General Forrest's cavalry, and served with him in Mississippi and Tennessee until cessation of hostilities. In 1867 he was married to Miss Sallie Fisher, a native of Tallahatchie county, Miss., and the daughter of Judge E. S. and Martha Fisher, natives of Kentucky and Virginia respectively. When a young man, Judge Fisher came to Mississippi, located in Tallahatchie county, and there practiced law for some time. He then removed to Jackson, and was on the supreme bench for a number of years, after which, in about 1858, he returned to his plantation in Tallahatchie county. To Mr. and Mrs. Bridgers were born three children. Mr. Bridgers resided on the farm until about 1873, and then removed to Grenada, where he embarked in merchandising, continuing this until 1877, when he again returned to the farm. He was president of the board of supervisors in 1875 and 1876, and he has shown his appreciation of secret societies by joining the Masonic fraternity, Cascilla lodge No. 411, and is a member of the Independent Order of Odd Fellows, Cascilla lodge No. 110, and of the Farmers' Alliance. He assisted in organizing the first two mentioned lodges. He belongs to one of the earliest families in the county. Mrs. Bridgers, who is an exemplary member of the Episcopal church, is an excellent lady and one held high in the estimation of all.

A leading merchant at Bogue Chitto, B. E. Brister, and one of the leading lumber manufacturers of Lincoln county, is a native of Lawrence county and was born in 1853, a son of Benjamin Brister and his wife Cynthia (Jones) Brister, natives of Mississippi. His father, Benjamin Brister, was the son of Benjamin Brister, who was a native of South Carolina, and came to Mississippi, locating in Lawrence county, where he became a planter and reared a family, living to an advanced age. He was a leading member of the Methodist Episcopal church and took an active and helpful part in extending all of its various interests. He was an exhorter of ability and often filled the pulpit very effectively. Near his home place a church was built, named in his honor, the Brister church, many years ago. He had five sons and several daughters who lived to maturity, married and have had families. Benjamin Brister, Sr., was one of the younger members of the family; he was reared in Mississippi, where he became a planter and died in 1868, at the age of fifty-two years, his wife dying in 1870 at the same age. She was a daughter of Bessey Jones, and was born in Mississippi, where her father was an early settler and reared a large family, all of whom grew to maturity. Mrs. Brister was the third of her father's children, and passed her early life in Lawrence county. There are three of them still living: Mrs. Patsey Dailey, the wife of Rev. Mr. Dailey of Lincoln county; Mrs. Elizabeth Tyler and Mrs. Margaret Greer, who is living in this county also. On his father's side our subject has one uncle living, Bird Brister, of this county. The other members of the family are deceased. To Benjamin Brister, Jr., and wife were born six children—three sons and three daughters—one of whom, Vincent Brister, died in 1886 at the age of forty-eight, at Bogue Chitto, leaving a wife and seven children; Mrs. Savilla Williamson lives in Lincoln county; Mrs. Ivry Sistrunk lives in Lawrence county; Iravascus lives in Lincoln county, and is engaged in milling; Mrs. Dollie Williams lives in Lincoln county on the old homestead; while our subject forms the sixth. He was the youngest child and was born and reared in what is now Lincoln county, procuring such an education as was obtainable to him in the common schools. His parents having died when he was quite young, he was obliged to make his own way in the world at an age when most young boys would have been acquiring an education. The most of his time was spent in the cotton fields, and he was able to devote only a few months at most to his schooling. For two years after the death of his father he remained with his mother, having the family to look after and to help to support. In the fall of 1870 he came to Bogue Chitto, with the intention of attending school, but after a few weeks the school was discontinued and he entered the employ of his older brother, with whom he remained until 1872, when the establishment of the latter was burned out. He had charge of the business, and thus was afforded an opportunity to show his qualities of mind, and in fact he did become known as an enterprising, successful young business man. In 1876 he obtained control of a small portable sawmill and engaged in the manufacture of lumber. A few years later he and his associates built a mill at Magnolia, now worth $100,000, the principal part of the machinery having been put in in 1885. In connection with this business he carries on an extensive mercantile trade. The mills connect with the timber tracts by a tramway eight miles long, which intersects with the Illinois Central railroad. Mr. Brister married Florence Eugenia Bonds, a native of Amite county, Miss., and a daughter of Pascal Bonds, who died when she was but little more than a child. Her mother was Miss Amanda Crane, who still survives, and since 1872 has made her home in the family of Mr. Brister. She had but two children, a son and a daughter. W. P. Bonds lives at McComb city, Miss., where he holds the position of train-dispatcher for the Illinois Central railroad. Previous to her coming to Bogue Chitto, the mother lived in Summit, Miss., for a time, and was a member of the Methodist Episcopal church. Mr. and Mrs. Brister have had four children, one of whom is deceased: Willis Bessey, Bennie B., Hugh Ernest and Louis. The family are members of the Methodist Episcopal church South. Mr. Brister is a democrat and a member of the Masonic order, Knights of Pythias, Knights of Honor and Knights and Ladies of Honor, and to the last named order Mrs. Brister also belongs, as a member in good and regular standing. Beginning life with no capital, Mr. Brister has been very successful, and is now accounted one of the wealthiest men of the county. His business abilities are first-class, and few men in this section have taken better advantage of such opportunities as have been afforded him. While his own interests have engrossed his attention to a great extent, he has never lost sight of the public welfare, and there are few of his fellow-citizens who have been more helpful to the general good of his community than has Mr. B. E. Brister.

Thompson M. Brister, Deasonville, Miss., was born in the section that is now known as Lincoln county, Miss., June 29, 1824, and is the youngest of a family of nine children. His parents, Thompson and Susan (Mitchel) Brister, were natives of Virginia, and emigrated overland to Mississippi at a very early day. They resided in Lawrence county until 1832, and then came to Yazoo county and settled on the plantation now occupied by our subject; there are four hundred and eighty acres in the place, and it is under excellent cultivation. The father died in 1853, at the age of eighty-three years. The mother died in 1847. The children all grew to mature years, but only Rhoda Brusarde, of Louisiana, and Thompson M. still survive. Mr. Brister spent his early days in Yazoo county, and assisted in the support of the family until he was twenty-one years of age. He then engaged in agricultural pursuits, which he followed until the war broke out; during that time he was in the state service under Captain Powell. He was married in 1845 to Miss Elizabeth Ellison, a daughter of Moses and Mary Ellison. Mr. and Mrs. Ellison were among the pioneers of Yazoo county. Nine children were born to Mr. and Mrs. Thompson: William F., a farmer in Colorado; Thompson M., Jr., a farmer in this county; Susan, wife of Dr. V. Berry of Georgia; Mary, wife of R. G. Berry, who is engaged in planting in Yazoo county; Mattie, wife of E. S. Harris, a merchant of Deasonville, with his brother, D. B. Harris; E. W., who resides with his father; Elizabeth, wife of D. B. Harris, a merchant of Deasonville; Major M., a merchant at Vaughn's station and Deasonville; and Benjamin S., a farmer. Mr. Brister has added to the original plantation of his father and has six hundred and fifty-five acres, all well improved and well fenced. He makes about eighty bales of cotton annually, and does a general farming business. The family are members of the Methodist Episcopal church. Mr. Brister has always contributed to the support of worthy enterprises having for their object the advancement of the interests of the community, and is convinced that morally, socially and financially the county has never seen better days than the present.

W. T. Brister, Deasonville, Miss., has been a resident of Yazoo county since his birth in 1831. He is the second of a family of seven children born to John and Elizabeth (Brister) Brister, natives of Virginia. The father removed to this county from Lawrence county about the year 1830 and entered several tracts of government land, which he sold after improving them. In this way he made a considerable amount of money, and although he came to the county a poor man, at the time of his death he owned twenty-three hundred acres of fine farm land, and before the war he had fifty slaves. He died April 24, 1880, at the age of seventy-seven years. His wife is also deceased. Their seven children all grew to maturity, but only one of them is now living, the subject of this sketch, who has lived his entire life within the borders of Yazoo county, and is now the owner of the entire family estate, which consists of twenty-one hundred acres. He was married in 1853 to Miss Mary Moore, a daughter of John Moore of Madison county, Miss. Eight children were born to them, six of whom are living and well settled in life, and residents of Yazoo county. Mrs. Brister died in 1864. In 1873 Mr. Brister was married a second time, being then united to Miss Emily Campbell, a daughter of Gus. Campbell of Yazoo county. They became the parents of seven children, four of whom are living. The change and growth of Yazoo county have been watched with deep interest by our subject. When he first began planting, Yazoo city, twenty-five miles away, was the nearest market place, and a railroad was then unknown. Game of all kinds was plentiful, and the entire country lay very near to nature's heart. Mr. Brister has been a forceful factor in this development, and to him much credit is due. He is a member of the Masonic order, belonging both to the blue lodge and chapter. Mr. and Mrs. Brister are members of the Methodist Episcopal church of Deasonville.

A gentleman worthy in every way of being classed with the successful merchants of Sharkey county, is William Britton, for by his own industry he has become a half owner of an excellent and paying mercantile establishment on the Helena plantation. Mr. Britton was born in Madison county, Miss., in 1853, son of William J. and Fannie (Johnston) Britton, who were born, reared and married in Bertie county, N. C., and about 1845 came to Madison county, Miss., where Mr. Britton was engaged in planting for a number of years. He then removed to New Orleans, where he opened a mercantile establishment, and conducted the same until after the war, when he removed to Pass Christian, where he owned some land, and for some time was also United States internal revenue collector with headquarters at Hazelhurst. He afterward returned to Madison county, where he died in 1871, having been a worthy member of the Episcopal church. He was a man of good business capacity and noted for his worthy business principles, and the high reputation which he won was fully merited. He inherited a fine property from his father, as did his wife from her father, and their united wealth was handled with skill by Mr. Britton, so that it materially increased during his lifetime. His father, William Britton, was a Virginian, but at an early day removed to North Carolina, where he spent the rest of his life as a merchant and planter. Mrs. Fannie (Johnston) Britton is still living in Madison county, Miss., and is now about sixty-five years of age. Her father was John T. Johnston, who was born in North Carolina about 1802. He and his brother, Samuel G., came to Mississippi and purchased land in Madison county and Issaquena (now Sharkey county), became very wealthy, and here died before the immediate subject of this sketch was born. William Britton is the third of four children born to his parents: Margaret, widow of Charles

R, A, Hill

C. Parson, of Memphis; Fannie, wife of Prof. L. W. Sewell, an Englishman and president of the Sewell school, of Memphis; William, and John (deceased). William Britton was educated in Bellevue high school, near Lynchburg, Va., and in the University of the South at Sewanee, Tenn., after which he clerked for a few years in New Orleans. He then assumed charge of his mother's plantation at Rolling Fork, which consists of two thousand acres, of which fifteen hundred acres are under cultivation, producing about eight hundred bales of cotton each year. Since 1886 he has done an annual mercantile business of $40,000, which fact speaks for itself in regard to his qualifications as a business man. He inherits many of the sterling qualities of his father, being public spirited, enterprising and energetic. He gives every promise of becoming one of the wealthiest and foremost citizens of Sharkey county, and at the present time commands the respect and esteem of all who know him. He has been married twice, first in 1878 to Miss Mary, daughter of William G. Poindexter, of the same family as ex-Governor Poindexter. She was born in Yazoo county and died in 1882, leaving one son, William. In 1888 Mr. Britton took for his second wife Laura, daughter of Maj. Samuel T. and Meta Nicholson, natives of North Carolina, who came with their parents to Mississippi and were married here. Mrs. Nicholson died about 1883, but her husband survives her and is a prosperous planter of Livingston, Miss. During the Rebellion he was a major in the Confederate army. Mrs. Britton was born in Livingston, Miss., and has borne her husband one son. Mr. Britton is a member of Deer Creek lodge No. 356 of the A. F. & A. M. at Rolling Fork and also belongs to Rolling Fork lodge No. 3175, of the K. of H. He and his wife are prominent members of the Episcopal church and are highly esteemed in the social circles in which they move.

The third child in a family of five, W. E. Britton, Shubuta, Clarke county, Miss., was born in Wayne county, Miss., May 22, 1832. His father was born in South Carolina and immigrated to Mississippi and settled in Wayne county. He was married to Miss Phœbe Conklin, of New York. His occupation was that of farming, and he was successful in it. He died in 1866, and was preceded many years by his lamented wife. W. E. Britton had only ordinary opportunities for educational advancement, but he attended the common schools of the time and availed himself of such opportunities as they afforded. He began work for himself at the age of eighteen years, in 1850. In 1858 he was married to Miss Marion B. McRae, of Wayne county, Miss., a daughter of Daniel E. McRae, a successful farmer of Wayne, who bore him ten children: Catherine E., Phebe J., Mary Ellen, Belzora Arbell, Emmarillus, Isodoro Ann, William Thomas, Margaret Missoria, Daniel John and Lafayette Hand. The third, fifth, eighth and tenth mentioned of these are dead. Mr. Britton enlisted early in the war in the Thirty-sixth Alabama regiment, under the command of Col. Woodruff. He saw his first active service at Chickamauga, and was in the battles of Resaca and New Hope church; later he was at Kenesaw mountain, then at Marietta, where, owing to sickness, he went to the hospital at Montgomery, Ala. Having returned home he did not reënter the service. After the war he engaged in farming, purchasing land early in the seventies, and now controlling about two hundred and fifty acres of land of average value. He grows corn, cotton, potatoes, oats, etc., though cotton and corn constitute his principal crops. He uses commercial fertilizer in his farming, and considers it a good investment. Mr. Britton has four daughters married: Catherine E., married to T. R. Brock; Phebe J., is married to A. H. Stallings; Belzora Arbell, married G. M. McRae; Isodoro Ann, is married to R. H. Meeks, all of Clarke county, and farmers and mechanics. Mr. Britton has been a member of the Masonic body, meeting at Shubuta, whose charter was lost, and is

27

a member of the Farmers' Alliance and president of his local organization, No. 978. Politically he is a democrat. He is a Methodist, and his family are also members of that church.

In the state of Virginia, December 25, 1813, Walker Brooke was born, and there he passed his early years. He secured in youth a good education, and was graduated from the university of the state at the age of twenty-one, at which time he showed unusual intellectual qualifications. Succeeding this, he studied law under the celebrated Judge Tucker, whose learning, refinement and high sense of justice were firmly implanted in the student's mind. Soon after this he went to Kentucky, where he taught school, and two years later he came to Mississippi and located at Lexington, in Holmes county, where he began the practice of his profession. His fine talents were soon appreciated, and he was sent to the legislature of the state, where he was one of the most eminent and active members. In 1851 he was appointed to the United States senate, to fill the unexpired term of Senator Foote, who had been elected governor of the state. In 1861 he was a member of the convention which adopted the ordinance of secession, and was one of the committee of fifteen to draft that ordinance. Succeeding this, he was selected one of the delegates to the provisional congress at Montgomery. He was in politics an uncompromising whig, but when the South seceded, he joined himself to its cause. As a lawyer, Mr. Brooke was one of the most learned in his profession. He enjoyed literature, and cultivated himself accordingly. He was a great student and a wide reader of books, and having a keen perception, became a great judge of men, and hence possessed a judicial mind. He never resorted to cunning or deceit, but was free, outspoken in manner and eloquent. Perhaps his most distinguishing characteristic as a lawyer was his remarkable penetration, and the force and skill with which he handled his logic. It can be justly said of him that he was one of the most eminent lawyers of the state. He died in 1869, at Vicksburg.

Josiah C. Brooks, M. D., is what might be termed a self-made man, for at the early age of thirteen years he began an independent career, not only poor in purse but also in his knowledge of books and of the world. He was born in Huntsville, Ala., January 4, 1856, the second of four children born to John and Margaretta (Barnard) Brooks, natives of Illinois and Alabama, respectively. In 1864 John Brooks enlisted in the Confederate army, being at that time seventy years of age, but died a very short time after entering the service. In 1868 Josiah C. Brooks began to make his own way in the world, and although he had to undergo numerous hardships and meet with numerous disappointments in his early career, he possessed sufficient pluck and determination to keep him steadily at work, and in verification of the old adage that "everything comes to those who wait," he is now in excellent circumstances. He owns a half interest in the mercantile firm of J. C. Brooks & Co., at Deeson, who carry a stock of goods valued at $5,000. Dr. Brooks also owns a half interest in the firm of Brooks & Connell, at Shelby station, and a one-half interest in eighty acres of land lying three miles east of that place, his property being now valued at about $8,000. He came to this county in 1881 and began working under adverse circumstances, and by his own exertions has acquired his present property. He is an earnest student, has a thorough knowledge of the medical profession and, as his ability is thoroughly known, he has a lucrative practice. He was married in 1889 to Miss Annie D. Walworth, by whom he has one child, Douglas W. His wife is a daughter of Douglas Walworth, editor of the Natchez *Democrat*, he being one of the oldest editors of the state of Mississippi and a stanch democrat in his political views. He is a very able and talented journalist, but has never taken an active part in politics. Dr. Brooks is a member in good standing of the Methodist Episcopal church, and socially is a member of the A. F. & A. M. and the K. of H. He is one of the leading physicians of the county, is respected and honored by all who know him, is a true gentleman in every sense of the word and his future career is bright with promise.

The tenth governor of the state of Mississippi, Albert G. Brown, was born in Chester district, S. C., May 31, 1813, and was the second son of Joseph Brown, a respectable planter of that state. In 1823 Joseph Brown, desiring to locate in a larger and more lucrative field in which to carry on his agricultural pursuits, and where he could rear his children to a higher fortune than his own, immigrated to the West and established a home in what is now Copiah county, in the state of Mississippi. The white man had not yet taken possession of the "new purchase," and the fire in the wigwam of the red man had scarcely died out, so recent had been his departure. To this wilderness Mr. Brown came with his family and with his two young sons, Edwin and Albert, and a hired man, erected his buildings and began the improvement of his land. At first tents were set up in the unbroken forests, for it will be remembered that the ax of the pioneer had not found its way into this section of the state, and then "patches" were cleared for crops. Young Albert was utilized, for there were to be no idle hands in the work of building up a new home. He minded the stock, worked on the farm, went to the gristmill and attended school when occasion would permit. In this manner his early days in Mississippi were spent. The future at first did not appear very bright, but after a few years of hard work, good management, and the practice of the most rigid economy, fortune began to smile on the family, and well-stored granaries, herds of cattle, fat hogs and fine horses could be seen about the plantation. Poverty had disappeared and thrift sat smiling at the door. About this time Albert, whose inclination for books had been strongly marked, was given more time for study. He was kept pretty closely to such schools as the neighborhood afforded, and the most of his leisure time at home was also given to his books. In 1829, having attained much proficiency in the rudiments of an English education, and having given evidence of intellectual power, he was sent to the Mississippi college, then under the management of Dr. D. Comfort. He remained there three years, endearing himself to a large circle of schoolmates, and especially to his venerable preceptor, who took great interest in the progress of his pupil. From that school he was transferred, in the winter of 1832, to Jefferson college. Here, after remaining six months, he became dissatisfied with the institution and returned home, under a partial promise of his father of a regular collegiate course at Princeton or Yale. But his father, after considering the cost of such a course, and having the care of a numerous family of sons and daughters, was constrained to forego the pleasure of gratifying his son's desires. Thus closed the schooldays of Albert G. Brown. With an education unfinished, and disappointed in his long-cherished hope of finishing his studies at one of the old schools, he was, at the age of nineteen, left to determine his future course in life. This was a critical period for him, but he was equal to the emergency, and few young men disappointed in like manner and thrown back upon their own resources would have acted wiser. He went to Gallatin and had an interview with E. G. Peyton, a prominent lawyer of that day, and made arrangements with him to enter his office as a law student. The next day he began the study of the law. Within a year from that date he was examined before the supreme court of Mississippi and was licensed to practice. Though closely attending to his studies, he found time during his hours of recreation to give some attention to social matters and so cultivate those whose acquaintance was desirable. It was thus that he, by his courteous deportment and genial manners, laid the foundation for that singularly personal popularity which in after years ever followed him. While at Jefferson college he took a course of military training, and when this was made known to the people of his county they elected him colonel of militia.

This was at the age of nineteen years, and was the first office ever held by him. The following year he was promoted to the rank of brigadier-general of militia. He was less than twenty years of age when he was admitted to the bar, and he suffered no little at the time lest the question should be asked: "Are you twenty-one?" This was the only question that he could not have responded to satisfactorily, but, fortunately for him, it was not asked. He began the practice of his profession in the autumn of 1833, and was successful from the first. He rose rapidly in his profession and soon took rank with the oldest and most distinguished members of the bar where he practiced. General Brown (by this title he was then known) had taken an active interest in politics from the time he began his law studies, and in 1835 his political career was opened.

In November of that year he was elected to the state legislature to fill the first vacancy occurring after he was twenty-one years old. It was an interesting period in the legislation of Mississippi, and there was great competition for seats. His county (Copiah) was entitled to three representatives, and with himself there were nine candidates, nearly all democrats, or, as they were called, Jackson men. It was the plan among aspiring and ambitious politicians to defeat young Brown that he might not be in their way in the future. It was maintained by some that he was too young, but the principal charge was that he was of unsound political faith, and this was based upon the ground that his father was a whig, or that he was not ashamed to call himself a Federalist of the old school. After a hot contest General Brown was elected, leading his next highest competitor by about seventy-five votes. He discharged his duties as a representative with marked ability and to the entire satisfaction of his constituents, who, at the next election, returned him. He took a prominent part in all the debates, and before the expiration of his second term, the speaker's seat having become vacant by reason of the sickness of the presiding officer, he was by acclamation chosen speaker pro tem. This period was an exciting one in the legislative history, and if the debates at that time had been preserved they would have exhibited to an admirable degree the political forecasts of Mr. Brown. Though with one exception the youngest member of the house, he advised his more aged compeers in many an earnest appeal against that system of banking which in subsequent years rendered the financial policy of Mississippi noted throughout the country. General Brown took his seat in the legislature for his second term in January, 1838. The banking system had already given way and was tottering to its fall, when Governor Lynch, the first and last whig governor of Mississippi, recommended the legislature to express its opinion of the subject of a national bank, and made an elaborate argument in favor of that institution. His message was referred to a committee of which Mr. Brown was made chairman. In his report he strongly opposed the establishment of the bank on the ground of inexpediency and unconstitutionality. For want of space his report can not be given. The position taken was, that the government of the United States had no constitutional right to charter a national bank, and that it was inexpedient and improper to charter such an institution at that time, even had the congress a right to do so. The report elicited the warmest applause from the anti-bank party, and the reverse from those who were in favor of it. In the fall of 1838, while Mr. Brown was absent, the bank party took advantage of a general panic in the public mind, and the financial embarrassments in the state, to have drawn up written instructions requiring Mr. Brown to support for the United States senate a man in favor of the bank, or resign. He chose the latter. Although during the excitement of the panic seven hundred and fifty out of the nine thousand voters in his district had signed these instructions, he did not hesitate to announce himself as a candidate to fill the vacancy occasioned by his own resignation. He made an able and thorough canvass of his county, and was returned in triumph to the legislature by a majority of one hundred and fifty votes over his bank competitor. The opposition was naturally confounded, and his supporters and anti-bank friends throughout the state were greatly elated at his signal success. The democratic state convention assembled soon after, and although General Brown was not yet twenty-five years of age he was unanimously nominated for congress. The whigs had swept the state in the previous election, and the bank interests of Mississippi were in the zenith of their power, so that the chances for his success were anything but flattering. However, undismayed by the unfavorable outlook, he entered at once upon an active and vigorous canvass of the whole state. His addresses were able and convincing, and the result was that he and his colleague, Jacob Thompson, were elected by a large majority, he leading his ticket by several hundred votes. The state was redeemed and the bank thraldom ended. This success took General Brown from a lucrative practice which he had built up by his legal ability, and placed him in the halls of congress. He took his seat in the United States house of representatives in December, 1839, being then something over twenty-five years of age. He was equal to his new position and filled it with honor to himself and satisfaction to his constituents. After the adjournment of congress in 1840 Mr. Brown returned home and entered into the presidential canvass for Van Buren. His speeches were brilliant and remarkable specimens of stump oratory, and though they failed to carry the state for Van Buren yet they placed General Brown in the front rank as an orator and political debater. At the close of his term in 1841 he was nominated for the second time, but from pecuniary considerations he was constrained to decline the honor. He consented to stand for the judgeship of the circuit court, and, as an evidence of his great popularity, he was supported by men of every shade of political and religious opinion. He was elected over his distinguished opponent, Judge Willis, by a vote of twenty-three to one, though he was barely eligible to the office on account of his youth. He held this position until 1844, when he resigned to accept the governorship of the state, to which he had been elected by the democrat party after a very exciting contest. The main issue in this contest was as to whether the state was or was not liable for the bonds issued in her name and known as the Union bank bonds. Judge Brown maintained that the issue of these bonds was in violation of the state constitution, and that in consequence the people were under no obligation to pay them by taxation. In this issue he encountered great opposition, but was finally sustained by the people at the polls. The administration of Governor Brown will long be remembered as one of the most fortunate which the state of Mississippi ever had. With this election terminated the Union bank bond controversy, and he was left free to look after the financial and other interests of the state. He proved to be a man of great financial and executive ability. He found the treasury bankrupt and the officers of the state paid in a paper known as auditor's warrants, then at a depreciation of fifty cents on the dollar. He gave his earnest attention to reviving the credit of the state, and had the satisfaction at the end of two years of seeing the auditor's warrants at par with gold, and at the close of his second term to have a surplus of several hundred thousand dollars in the treasury. He was an earnest advocate of education and did much to advance the common schools, and by his energetic labors the State university was established. One marked feature of his second term was its fidelity to the payment of the Planter's bank bonds. In this regard he said that "wherever there exists a debt against the state, contracted in good faith and with proper regard to the constitution, it must be discharged to the last mill. Of this character do I regard the bonds issued on account of the Planter's bank, and come what may, the state can never shrink from the payment of them."

Before the expiration of his second term he accepted the nomination, which was made

unanimous, of the fourth congressional district, and although it was known that his gubernatorial term did not end until January, 1849, and he could not take his seat until two
months after the session had opened, yet he was elected without opposition. He took his
seat pending the heated debate growing out of the Mexican war, and made an able and eloquent speech in its defense. In this address he said: "Other gentlemen may do as they
please, for me and my people, we go for our country. We write on our banner: 'Millions for
defense, but not one cent for tribute.' Tax our property, tax our supplies, aye, tax us millions on
millions for the defense of our country's flag and our country's honor and we will pay it, but if
you ask us to pay one cent of tribute to your lordly manufacturers we rise up in rebellion against
you. Take our property for the defense of our national honor, but do not plunder us to
make the rich man more rich." At all times and under all circumstances Governor Brown
was the steadfast friend of the toiling millions, and advocated every measure that tended to
advance them financially and intellectually. He was in favor of disposing of the public
lands freely, and giving a home to every man who had none. He had no objection to the
government selling her lands to those who were able to pay for them. He was reëlected to the
thirty-second congress, during which the exciting question came up for the admission of California as a state, and the fugitive slave bill. He was opposed to the admission of California,
and was in favor of the fugitive slave bill. Although Governor Brown wished very much to
retire to private life at the close of the thirty-second congress, yet the people insisted on his
serving another term. He was reëlected, and was the only one of the delegation that was
returned. He warmly espoused the cause of the states' rights democracy, and the others
were what were then known as Union men. At the end of this term he retired to private life,
to resume his law practice, but he was again called by the people to serve them. He was
elected by the Mississippi legislature to the United States senate to fill a vacancy caused by
the failure of the previous legislature to elect a successor to Walker Brooke, whose term had
expired. He took his seat in the senate January 26, 1854. His course while a member of
this body was marked by the same ability that he displayed in the house. He became one of
its leading members, taking rank with its ablest business men as well as its most eloquent
debators. He was reëlected, which took him into the war period, when his state withdrew
from the Union. It might in truth be said that his public life ended at this time. He
returned home and was active in his support of the Confederacy. At the very beginning he
enlisted in the service, and raised a company that was known as the Brown Rebels, of which
he was elected captain. It was mustered into the Eighteenth Mississippi as company H. He
participated in the battle of Manassas, also some other engagements when he was elected to
the Confederate congress as senator from Mississippi. In this capacity he had but very little
to do, as the Confederacy did not attain a position requiring much legislation. In October,
1835, Governor Brown was united in marriage to Elizabeth Frances Taliaferro, a Virginian
lady of rare accomplishments, great personal worth and of excellent family. She survived
this marriage only about five months. He married his second wife, Roberta E., the youngest
daughter of Gen. Robert Young, of Alexandria, Va., January 12, 1840. This marriage
resulted in the birth of two sons: Robert Y. and Joseph Albert. Governor Brown had a fine
plantation in Hinds county, where he lived from 1860, except when in the army and in the
Confederate congress, until his death, June, 1880. The great secret of his public success was that
he was able, that he was honest and that he was true to his convictions and true to the people. When asked by a friend how it was that success had always attended him, he replied:
"I never forgot that I was one of the people." This was the key note to his political life.
After the close of the war he retired to his plantation and took no further part in public

matters. He accepted, honestly, the results of the war and advised the people to do the same. He took the position that the rights of the negro should be recognized and maintained as they are expressed in the thirteenth and fourteenth amendments to the constitution, and he said if that was not done more decisive measures would be adopted by the Federal government. When the fifteenth amendment became a part of the constitution his position was that the negro should be treated exactly the same as the white man, though he regarded this amendment as a mistake, and was not an advocate of the other two amendments. He had great faith in the people, and believed all his life that when once a political measure was argued before them properly they would invariably vote right. He was a man of wonderful sagacity, thoroughly understood the masses and what they were likely to do. When the war opened he said that it would be a long, bloody and exhausting one, and his only fear was that the patriotism of the people would not hold out. He was a great admirer of Stephen A. Douglas, and regarded him as a truly great man, and sided with his views more than with any of the other leading politicians of that period. Though successful to a remarkable degree in public life, and honored by the highest positions within the gift of the people of his state, yet he always regretted entering public life, and about the last advice he gave his son Joseph was to eschew it. He told him that if he had his life to live over he would never seek a public position and would never accept one.

Col. Robert Y. Brown. The history of this brilliant young man, who, for a few short years, was so bright a star in the galaxy of Mississippi's most talented and promising young men, will be of more than passing interest to the many readers of this volume. He was the eldest scion of his father's house, being a son of Gov. Albert G. and Roberta Y. Brown, his birth occurring in Copiah county, Miss., October 8, 1841, and his death at New Orleans, October 15, 1866, after a very short illness. For seven years he was an only son, and his boyhood days were passed while his father was in public life, as a member of congress, judge of the circuit court, governor of his state and United States senator. Governor Brown always kept his family with him, and, owing to his brightness and pleasant ways, young Robert was made much of by his father's numerous friends and visitors, and it is to be attributed to the unceasing and watchful care of his mother, who was a highly accomplished lady and a leader in Washington society, that he grew up to man's estate with the purity of his character unsullied by almost constant contact with the world. His early education was not forced, but his mind was gradually nurtured and cultivated, until at length application to his studies became not only easy to him but also a pleasure. A love of truth was early planted in his heart, and it is believed that he was never guilty, in the whole course of his life, of the slightest deception or insincerity. He was also singularly unselfish and habitually industrious, never neglectful of his parents' wishes, never unkind or dishonest in his intercourse with his companions, never uttering an unclean or profane word, and always using his influence with those about him to be just and to do right. At the age of fifteen years he was sent to Georgetown college, D. C., and after having passed his preliminary examination the faculty expressed the opinion that he might, as he was a bright youth, graduate in four years. He entered upon his collegiate course with great vigor, and in a little over three years he took the second honor in a class that was large and contained many students who were his seniors in years as well as college life. Though educated in the faith of the Episcopal church, in which he was baptized, and adhered to through life, he was always warm in his praise of his Jesuit teachers, and vindicated them from every charge of attempting to control or influence the religion of their pupils. Almost immediately after his graduation from Georgetown college he entered the University of Virginia as a law student, where he applied himself with great energy to his books, and made rapid progress. An eminent member of the faculty declared that he had one of the best legal minds that had ever come under his observation. He had been at the university scarcely a year when the war clouds began to gather over the state. Robert at once wrote to his father for permission to leave the university and join the army. This permission was granted and he went directly home, feeling that his first duty was to the state of his birth. The very day of his arrival home he stepped into line as a private soldier in his father's command, which was known as the Brown Rebels. He entered upon his military life, as he had that of a student, with all his might, giving his whole strength to the cause he had so earnestly espoused. At the end of six months, having participated in the battles of Manassas and Leesburg, where he distinguished himself for his bravery, he was elected by his comrades as first lieutenant of his father's company. Soon after he was raised, almost by acclamation, to the captaincy of his company, and participated in nearly all the battles fought in Virginia during the first three years of the war, commencing with Manassas and ending with Cold Harbor. He was in the seven days' fight before Richmond, at Fredericksburg, Sharpsburg and Gettysburg, and later at Spottsylvania and the Wilderness. He was an active participant in seventeen bat- tles, and was also in numerous hot skirmishes. During the whole of the engagement of Antietam he was in the midst of the fight, cheering and encouraging his men by his indom- itable spirit and courage. When Major Campbell was wounded and carried from the field he took command of the regiment and handled it with the coolness and skill of a veteran. He was twice wounded and twice taken prisoner while serving with the army of Virginia. At Gettysburg his brigade was repulsed while leading a desperate charge under General Barksdale, and, being left wounded on the field of battle, he was picked up by the enemy and sent to Johnson's island, where he remained a prisoner for eight months. It is cred- itable to him as a soldier, and affords another instance of his candor, that he had no com- plaints to make of his captors, but praised them for the uniformity of kindness and respect extended to him.

Soon after his last liberation he was promoted by the president and took rank as major in the Sixth Mississippi cavalry. The colonel of his regiment being killed in battle, he was promoted to the rank of lieutenant-colonel, and when the order was made for the consolida- tion of the Sixth and Eighth Mississippi regiments, Lieutenant-Colonel Brown passed the required examination before a board of officers, and was placed in command with the rank of colonel. In this capacity he served until the final surrender, when, along with Gen. Dick Taylor's army, he received his parole and returned home. By his gallant and soldierly con- duct he had raised himself from a private to the rank of colonel, and this before he was twenty-three years of age. On the day after his return, Colonel Brown entered his father's office and resumed the study of law. He felt that there was no time for regrets or inaction, and immediately put his shoulder to the wheel, a trait of his that had been conspicuous from boyhood. He still had his country to restore and build up, and he applied himself to his studies with undiminished ardor until the fall of 1865, when, having resolved to cast his fortunes in New Orleans, he went to that city and applied himself to the mastery of the peculiar jurisprudence of Louisiana. In less than four months he was admitted to the bar, but finding that a twelve months' residence, or a license from another state, was necessary to his practice there, he returned to Mississippi, was examined by the supreme court, and receiving his license from that tribunal to practice his profession, he went back to New Orleans and entered at once upon his legal career, under the most auspicious circumstances. In the summer of 1866 he joined his parents for a little recreation in the country, but returned to

New Orleans the last of September, full of life and hope, and apparently in the most vigorous health. He was taken ill about the middle of October, and as before stated died very suddenly. Thus amid the high hopes and promises of youth, at the dawn of a career, whose setting bade fair to be most brilliant, he was called before the bar of God, and let it be hoped into a brighter and happier life. By all who know him,

> " His name will live
> Through long succeeding years,
> Embalmed by all their hearts can give,
> Their praises and their tears."

Joseph Albert Brown, attorney at law, at Jackson, Miss., was born at Washington, D. C., February 12, 1849, and is the second son of that distinguished statesman of Mississippi, Albert G. Brown. (See biography of Governor Brown in another part of this work.) The early years of Mr. Brown were spent in Washington and in Copiah county, alternating between the two places as the attendance of his father upon the sessions of congress would require. During the war period he was in Hinds county and in Virginia, a part of the time with his brother, Col. R. Y. Brown, and a part of the time with his father. After the war, he was sent to the Summerville institute, in Noxubee county, Miss., where he pursued his studies for two years, preparing for college. He then entered the university at Oxford, Miss., where he was graduated in 1868, standing second in his class. He continued his studies, and was graduated from the law department of the university in 1870, at the head of his class, and delivered the valedictory address, for which he received the highest compliments. It was regarded as among the best that had been delivered before that institution. He was admitted to the bar and removed to Jackson, where he entered upon the practice of his profession, which he has continued up to the present time. Born to a liberal competence, the pursuit of any vocation was to him a matter of choice rather than a necessity, but possessed of a strong constitution, a good education and an active vigorous mind, a life of idleness was not to his taste, so his life has been gauged between that of a professional man and a gentlemen of leisure and culture. While engaged in his professional duties, he has spent much time in travel, both in this country and abroad, storing his mind with useful knowledge. He possesses many characteristics of his distinguished father, and would easily succeed in the public walks of life, but remembering his father's dying injunctions, he has avoided all avenues that would lead to political preferment. He has made several trips to the state of Washington, where he has made some large and profitable investments, and speaks of that state and its future in very enthusiastic terms. Mr. Brown is a man of good personal appearance, genial and attractive in his manner, and of a kind disposition. He is well informed upon public and private topics, and is an interesting conversationalist. He is a devoted husband, an affectionate father, and his beautiful home, adjoining the capitol building, is his world. He has surrounded his family with all that his refined and cultivated taste could dictate, supported by ample means. December 15, 1880, at Jackson, he wedded Lizzie, the daughter of George W. and Annie (Virden) Sullivan, of St. Louis, Mo., and by her is the father of two children: Alberta and Joseph, both bright, interesting and promising.

Andrew Brown. Willis Brown, the father of Andrew Brown, of Whynot, Lauderdale county, Miss., was born in Hancock county, Ga., in 1801, and emigrated to Conecuh county, Ala., in 1818. He was a lifelong agriculturist, and was married to Miss Fanny Dewberry, of Alabama, about 1826. He died in 1868, Mrs. Brown having passed away in 1834. Mr. Brown's grandfather, on his father's side was John Brown, of Georgia, probably of Scotch-Irish descent. His grandfather on his mother's side was James Dewberry. Andrew Brown, the subject of this sketch, was born in Conecuh county, Ala., in 1828. He received instruction in the common schools, and resided, and when old enough labored, on a farm. At the age of sixteen, he removed to Choctaw county, Ala., and settled in the western portion, where he remained until he returned, in 1850, to Conecuh county. He was married in October, 1850, to Miss Tabitha Kelly, of Alabama, by whom he had three children: John Willis, Thomas Josiah and Frances. The first mentioned son was married to Miss Tucker, of Alabama; the second to Miss Booker, of Alabama, and Frances to Mr. Booker of Alabama. After planting successfully for a time, Mr. Brown enlisted in the Confederate army, in 1861, with General Forrest's cavalry and was connected with the commissary department nearly all the time, until in 1862 he was discharged, and later he enlisted in the Second Alabama regiment, Colonel Carpenter commanding, and served with it until the close of the war. After the war he again engaged in farming in the southeastern portion of Lauderdale county, Miss., where he purchased land, and by constant accretion owned and controlled about one thousand acres. He now owns five hundred acres as good as the average land of the county and grows cotton, corn, oats, potatoes, etc. Making his farm self-supporting, he uses commercial fertilizer to some extent and thinks it profitable. A portion of his land is covered with heavy pine timber. In connection with his planting interests he is engaged quite extensively in milling and ginning. Mr. Brown held the office of justice of the peace, and is at present a member of the board of supervisors of Lauderdale county, Miss., a most responsible position which he fills with eminent ability. Mrs. Brown died in 1866. She was a member of the Baptist church (Missionary). Mr. Brown was married in November, 1867, to Mrs. Nancy P. Brown, of Lauderdale county. By her former marriage, Mrs. Brown has five sons and one daughter: J. P., G. D., C. B., R. C., J. F., and Frances Eugenia. Mrs. Brown is a member of the Missionary Baptist church. Her daughter, Frances Eugenia, is married to Mr. Brock; J. P. married a Miss Bryan; G. D. married a Miss Brock; and C. B. married a Miss Pippin. Mr. Brown is strictly honest and punctual to every obligation, a friend to education; benevolent, always willing to aid those who need his assistance; in his family relations, perfectly congenial. All of his success is due to his own efforts, for his devotion to business has been great and his energy unflagging. As an official he has given the highest satisfaction.

The mercantile establishment of which Mr. E. P. Brown is one of the proprietors, is a representative and popular one, and has secured a prominent place in popular approval. Mr. Brown was born in Lauderdale county in June, 1861, to R. F. and Elizabeth (Perkins) Brown, the former of whom was born in this county, and the latter in Mobile, Ala. The mother came to Mississippi with her parents when a small girl; grew up in Lauderdale county, and here married Mr. Brown, by whom she became the mother of three sons and two daughters: B. R., E. P., Lanie (deceased), Lena, and Floyd (deceased). The father was a planter and merchant, his store being located at Lockhart, where he met with flattering success. He was well respected and esteemed by all who knew him, but never aspired to official position, although a number were offered him. Although not a member of any church, he was a liberal contributor to the cause of religion, and, in fact, aided largely with his means all worthy enterprises. He enlisted in the Confederate service in 1861, serving throughout the entire war, after which he returned to his home and followed planting until his death in 1885, at Lockhart. He was an active member of the A. F. & A. M. His wife, who died in 1871, was a worthy member of the Methodist Episcopal church. In 1862 E. P. Brown began the life of a merchant in Lockhart, where he conducted business alone until 1890, when his elder brother, B. R. Brown, became the partner of E. P. Brown in 1890, and the firm is now known as E. P. & B. R. Brown. They carry a stock of general merchandise valued at about $6,000, and do an annual business of $4,000. The merits of their stock, combined with the superior inducements which judicious buying and an intelligent appreciation of the wants of customers enable the house to offer, have secured for the house a deservedly large patronage. Both members of the firm are married. E. P. Brown was married in 1887 to Miss Lillian O'Hara, which union has not resulted in the birth of any children. B. R. Brown was married in 1885 to Miss Sadie Ware, by whom he has one son: Ernest. E. P. Brown is the owner of four hundred acres of good land, of which one hundred acres are under cultivation. B. R. Brown is the owner of two hundred and fifty acres, and they, in partnership, own two hundred and fifty acres. Both are live and energetic men of business, well liked by all who know them, and are doing well in the enterprise in which they are engaged. The immediate subject of this sketch is a member of the Methodist Episcopal church, as is also his wife, but his brother is not a member of any church. They carry on planting in connection with their mercantile operations and are wideawake and progressive young business men.

The sheriff and collector of Copiah county, Capt. Edward W. Brown, was born in Hinds county, Miss., in 1840, a son of Drury and Sarah F. (Wells) Brown, natives respectively of North Carolina and South Carolina, who came when quite young to Hinds county, where they married, and where Mrs. Brown died in 1853, having been for many years a consistent member of the Baptist church. Mr. Brown married Elizabeth Grant, by whom he had one child. In 1855 he removed to Copiah county, where he died in 1857. In early life he was a merchant at Brown's Mills in Hinds county, Miss., and for some years he was deputy sheriff and later was for twelve years sheriff of Hinds county. After his removal to Copiah county, he practiced law, in which he was quite successful. He was a man of fair education and broad and liberal views, a good thinker and possessed of fine business qualifications, and had it not been for his unbounded generosity, he might have been wealthy, though he was well to do as it was. He was deeply interested in the Masonic order, in which he took the highest degree conferred in Mississippi. In the early part of the war he was colonel of the Eighth Mississippi infantry, and served for a few months in Northern Mississippi, but the pressure upon him of his large planting interests, and the settlement of estates for others, induced him to resign and return home, though he was afterward chaplain of the Thirty-sixth Mississippi infantry in the army of Tennessee until the close of the war. After the war ended, he resumed his law practice. His sister, who became the wife of John Chandler of Kentucky, and died at Hazlehurst, was the only other member of the family who came to Mississippi. His father was Alfred Brown, who died in North Carolina. Nothing is known of our subject's maternal grandfather. Capt. E. W. Brown is the oldest of three children living, of eight who were born to his parents; the second is Abbie D., widow of Anderson Bradley Cates, of Brownsville, Miss.; the third is William W. Brown, of Oklahoma city, Oklahoma. Our subject was reared in Raymond and educated at Mississippi college at Clinton. In 1861 he joined company A, of the Tenth Mississippi infantry, and served about one year at Warrenton on the gulf coast, then reënlisted in company K, of the Thirty sixth Mississippi infantry, and soon after was made sergeant-major of the regiment, and about two months later, adjutant, which position he held till the close of the war, serving with the Southern army, taking part in the fighting at Vicksburg and other hard-fought engagements. Afterward his regiment joined Johnston's army at Selma, Ala., and participated in the Atlanta campaign. While on the way back to Tennessee under Hood, Captain Brown was wounded at Altoona, Ga., and captured and held prisoner of war about thirty days. For some time thereafter, he was in their hospital and did not rejoin his command until it fell back to

Blakely, near Mobile, where it was disbanded and he came home. During the few years immediately succeeding the war, he taught school in Claiborne and Copiah counties. Later he was principally engaged in farming until 1875, when he was elected circuit clerk of Copiah county, which office he filled with great satisfaction for twelve years, until 1887, when he was elected sheriff, to which position he was reëlected in 1889. He is a genial gentleman, popular socially, and is influential. He has large planting interests, owning about one thousand acres, the most of which he acquired by inheritance. He is an ardent democrat, and is very active politically, and has frequently been delegate to district and state conventions. He stands high in several social orders; he is past master Mason of Hazlehurst lodge No. 5, which is represented in the grand lodge; is past dictator of Copiah lodge No. 1422, Knights of Honor, which is also represented in the grand lodge; he has been C. C. of Copiah lodge, No. 60, Knights of Pythias; he is also a member of the American Legion of Honor, of the Knights and Ladies of Honor, and is a member of good standing in the Baptist church. He was married March 24, 1864, to Miss Bettie P., a daughter of Maj. Benjamin F. Nelson, one of Copiah county's most worthy citizens, a sketch of whom appears elsewhere in this work. Mrs. Brown was born in Copiah county, and is a most excellent Christian lady, and is a member of the Baptist church. She bore her husband eight children: Lena May, Ida Belle (wife of Frank M. Redding, of Vicksburg), Sallie E., (wife of R. F. Hargrave), Willie A., Edward W., Reid, Otis, and Bettie P., (better known as Q. T., a cute little girl).

A prominent planter of Lee county, Miss., George Brown, of Saltillo, is the subject of the following biographical sketch. He is a native of Kemper county, Miss., born in the year 1841, and a son of Robert and Dorcas Brown. His father was born in the year 1800, and was a son of Samuel and Elvira Brown, natives of Ireland. Robert and Dorcas Brown became the parents of and reared a family of seven children: Margaret, Samuel, Narcissa, Harriet, James, Mary and George. The father died in May, 1858, in Monroe county, Miss. The mother was a daughter of James and Mary Strait; she died in 1862. The parents were both members of the old school Presbyterian church, and the father was a democrat. George Brown passed an uneventful youth until the breaking out of the Civil war, when he enlisted in company C, Second Mississippi regiment, under Colonel Falkner. He was in some very notable engagements, among them Corinth, Vicksburg and the Georgia campaign. After the cessation of hostilities he returned to his home and engaged in the more peaceful pursuit of planting. He was married in 1867 to Miss Emily Sisk, a daughter of A. T. and Mildred (Galloway) Sisk. She was born in Itawamba county, Miss., in 1848. Mr. and Mrs. Brown are the parents of twelve children, seven of whom are living: Robert A., William D., Leroy G., Lemon G., Mildred D., Mary C. and an infant. Mr. Brown removed from Monroe county to Lee county in 1874, and six years ago he came to his present plantation. He has one thousand acres of excellent land, one-half of which he has brought to a high state of cultivation. He has accumulated his property through his own efforts, and has won a place in the front rank of Lee county's most successful planters. He and his wife are members of the Old School Presbyterian church. He is a democrat in his political views, a member of the Masonic order and a Knight of Honor.

A general merchant, planter and the postmaster at Cascilla, John H. Brown, was born in Carroll county in 1857, the son of Enoch B., who died when our subject was in his eighth year. The boy was adopted by his uncle, his mother's brother, James Key, but when he was old enough he determined to take his fortune in his own hands, so, bidding good-bye to his uncle, he found employment for the first year as a laborer on a plantation; afterward he attended school for a few months at Hardy's station, Miss., later working in a sawmill for his board and clothes. From this work he turned again to farming, in which he continued for two years at fair wages. Being of a speculative turn of mind, the young man next directed his efforts to buying cotton seed on his own account, a business which he relinquished to open a confectionery store at Ross' mills. This establishment, though quite insignificant at the outset, developed in 1878 into a general merchandise store. This enterprise Mr. Brown continued for eighteen months, spending thereafter a year in the river bottoms of Bolivar county, Miss., as a farmer and planter. Later he farmed for one year in the hills in Tallahatchie county, whence he returned to the bottoms, and made another crop there. He now relinquished farming for a time, and again engaged in the confectionery business at Jones' bayou, in which he continued for a short time only, when he returned to Tallahatchie county. He was married, in January, 1881, to Ione, a daughter of Lindrey Whitten, who died in what is now Grenada county, when Mrs. Brown was a little girl, she having been born in that county, one of his three children. After his marriage, Mr. Brown lived at Ross' mills, where he was a planter and merchant, the firm being, for a time, Whitten, Brown & Co.; later it was Brown & Ross for two years, when it was changed to Brown & Ellet. The concern was removed to Cascilla in 1884, and since 1885 Mr. Brown has been the sole proprietor, doing a business of about $35,000 per year, and handling about five hundred bales of cotton yearly. He owns about fourteen hundred acres of land, raising about eighty-five bales of cotton annually. Mrs. Brown's mother is now Mrs. Martha L. Ross, wife of David L. Ross, a prominent planter of Tallahatchie county. She was a daughter of George Reid, of Tennessee, but was born in De Soto county, Miss. She lived in several different counties in Mississippi, and is now living in Tallahatchie county. Her father was a native of Tennessee, and while young came to Mississippi. He was married in Grenada county, and died in 1865, his wife, who was a native of that county, dying in 1862. He was a mechanic of much ability, and at the time of the Civil war showed his patriotism by enlisting as a soldier in the Confederate army. Mr. and Mrs. Brown were parents of several children, some of whom died when quite young. One of the children (Walter) died in 1856; a daughter (Patty), who became Mrs. Latham, died in Tennessee about 1871; another son (Benjamin L.) went to Montana about twenty years ago, where he is now a prominent stockdealer, in which business he has been wonderfully successful. Mr. Brown is a member of Cascilla lodge No. 411, A. F. & A. M., in which he was once junior warden. He was a charter member, and has served as vice grand of Cascilla lodge No. 110, I. O. O. F. Starting in life with nothing, Mr. Brown has had such success that he is now recognized as a leading merchant in Tallahatchie county. He is full of push and energy, and to these qualities, in conjunction with his well-known integrity and mercantile honor, he owes his present enviable business position.

It is doubtless owing entirely to the industrious and persevering manner with which John T. Brown, of Waterford, Miss., has adhered to the pursuits of agriculture that he has risen to such a substantial position in farm affairs in his county. Born in Haywood county, Tenn., he is the son of Samuel and Nancy (Musgrave) Brown, both natives of Greene county, N. C. The parents attained their growth in their native county, were married there, and immediately afterward removed to Haywood county, Tenn. They were among the very earliest settlers of that county and first put up a tent on the land they had previously entered. Mr. Brown and an old colored man that he had brought with him from North Carolina went to work to build a house. The colored man, whose name was Lewis, and his wife, whose name was Irene, who also came with Mr. and Mrs. Brown, remained with that gentleman all their lives, both dying before the war. To Mr. Brown's marriage were born six children, John T. being the only son. The daughters were: Elizabeth, wife of Dr. James Hudson; Anna, wife of John Dickerson; Mary, wife of Charles Henry; Percy, wife of William Emerson, and Nancy J., wife of A. A. Emerson. Anna and Percy are now deceased. The father followed the uneventful life of a farmer and was a quiet, unassuming man. He was a devoted and consistent member of the Baptist church up to the time of his unfortunate death, which occurred in 1852, in Haywood county, Tenn. Mrs. Brown received her final summons in 1862 at the same place. She was also a worthy member of the same church. John T. Brown came to Marshall county, Miss., in 1856, and was married the same year to Mrs. Sallie J. Martin, daughter of Malcom McNeill, of Marshall county. Mr. Brown bought his present farm the same year he came to this county and has resided on the same ever since. He and his wife have reared two children: William Oscar, and Theodosia E., wife of Thomas McNeill, of Paris, Tex. Mr. McNeill engaged in the brokerage business. William Oscar was educated in the Southwestern Baptist university, Tennessee, and is traveling for the Peters factory of the American Biscuit company, Memphis. John T. Brown is the owner of one thousand two hundred and eighty-six acres of land, has five hundred acres under cultivation and raises corn and cotton. He is also quite deeply interested in stockraising, has some fine blooded animals, best probably in the county, and raises a great many horses and mules every year. Mr. Brown was elected a member of the board of supervisors in 1872, served two terms (four years), and during that time was president of the board. He also held the office of magistrate for four years. In 1890 he was elected to the legislature, and is the present incumbent of that office. He is a member of the Masonic fraternity, Waterford lodge No. 141, and has been junior and senior warden, also worshipful master. He is also a member of the Farmers' Alliance. During the war, or in 1862, Mr. Brown enlisted in company G, Seventh Mississippi cavalry, under Colonel Balentine, Armstrong's brigade, Jackson's division in the Western department, and was in the battle of Lookout mountain, Vicksburg, Resaca, Jonesboro; siege of Atlanta, and various others of minor importance. He was captured at Selma, April 2, 1865, and was a prisoner at the time of the surrender, being paroled in Alabama. Returning to Marshall county, Miss., Mr. Brown has followed farming up to the present time. He held an enviable position among the prominent and successful men in Marshall county. During the war he served his state in a very serviceable manner, but has rendered it even more valuable service not only as a reliable public official but as an industrious farmer and law-abiding citizen. He is a member of the Baptist and his wife a member of the Methodist church.

Yalobusha county has never known a more efficient and capable chancery clerk than John W. Brown, who by his honorable, efficient and upright career as a public servant, has won a place in the annals of the state of Mississippi. He was born in Yalobusha county, Miss., January 15, 1846, and is a son of James M. and Sophia A. (Lester) Brown, who were natives of Alabama and South Carolina, respectively. The father was born in 1822, and was a son of John Brown, also a native of Alabama, and a farmer by occupation. About the year 1834 he came with his family to Yalobusha county, and settled near Oakland, where he reared his children. There were William, James, John, Alfred, Samuel, Perkins, Doc, Jane, Elizabeth, Nancy, Mary Ellen, Julia Ann, and Alfred; Samuel and Mary Ellen are the only surviving members. James M., the father of John W., was the second child, and passed his youth in Yalobusha county. He received his education in the common schools, and when he had reached man's estate he engaged in farming on his own responsibility. He followed this occupation through life in the vicinity of Oakland. He died in 1849, a man highly respected by all. Three of his children lived to be grown: Benjamin R., Nancy Jane and John W. The mother died in 1870. She was an earnest Christian woman, devoted to her home and children. She was fifty years of age at the time of her death. Her father, James D. Lester, married a Miss Lindsey, a native of South Carolina. (See sketch of Captain Lester.) John W. Brown passed his youth in the same employments as usually fall to a farmer's son, and received his education in the common schools and Spring Hill academy, and after the war he was a student at West Union, Tenn., where he took a special course. In 1867 he engaged in farming near Oakland, and devoted his time and attention to these interests until 1873. In that year he was elected tax assessor of Tallahatchie county, holding that office for two years. He then returned to Yalobusha county, and resumed his agricultural pursuits until 1876, when he was elected tax assessor of Yalobusha county. Later he held the position of deputy sheriff, under L. R. Wilson, for a period of two years. Until 1886 he was engaged in trading, and in that year he was again made deputy sheriff, under Charles R. Cock. In the fall of 1887 he was elected chancery clerk, and has discharged the duties of that office faithfully and with marked ability. In September, 1863, he enlisted in the First Mississippi cavalry, Captain Lester's company, serving until November 11, 1864, when he lost his left arm at Shoal creek, Ala. He was cared for in the hospital at Florence, Ala., and afterward was taken to Tuscumbia, where he remained but a short time. He came home, making most of the journey on foot, consuming about twenty days. He participated in the battles of Jonesboro, Peach Tree creek and Dallas, Ga., and all the battles of the Georgia campaign. After the surrender, he spent one year in school in Tennessee, as above stated. He was married in 1867 to Miss Roxie Ann Tatum, who was born and reared in Yalobusha county, Miss., and a daughter of John S. Tatum, a native of North Carolina, and one of the early settlers of this county. He reared a family of nine children, eight of whom still survive. Mr. and Mrs. Brown are the parents of two children: James S., who is in the employ of the Louisiana, New Orleans & Texas railroad, and Lela B. They are members of the Baptist church of Coffeeville, and are active and liberal supporters of the same. Politically, Mr. Brown affiliates with the democratic party.

A planter, residing two miles north of Enterprise, Miss., is L. B. Brown, Jr., who was born in Wayne county, Miss., in 1834. He is a son of L. B. Brown, Sr., who was born in Georgia in 1800, and emigrated with his father John Brown to Wayne county in 1818. John Brown was a very prominent citizen of Wayne, and amassed a handsome fortune in stockraising. L. B. Brown, Sr., was a progressive and successful farmer, having accumulated a large fortune early in life. He married Martha R. Booth, only sister of Capt. Joseph Booth, of Monroe county, Ala. She was born at Cheraw hill, S. C. The father of our subject possessed many excellent qualities, and was highly esteemed by his neighbors. In politics he was a Jeffersonian democrat, and took an active part in all public matters. He and Mrs. Brown were members of the Presbyterian church, in which the former was a ruling elder. He died at Enterprise in 1850. Mrs. M. R. Brown survived her husband for many years, residing at Enterprise, where she died in 1879 at an advanced age. The early life of L. B. Brown, Jr., was spent in Lauderdale county, Miss. He received the principal part of his education at the Presbyterian college at Clinton, Miss. Upon the death of his father he removed with his mother to Enterprise, where he has since resided. In 1854 he married Miss Annie Alston, daughter of Col. William W. Alston, of Clarke county, Ala. She was born in Rapides parish, La., in 1833. Their son Alfred Alston Brown was born in Clarke county, Ala., in 1855, and married Miss Adine Baldwin, daughter of Rev. John B. Baldwin, of Meridian, Miss. They have only one child—a daughter—Aimee Clifton Brown. Alfred A. Brown is a planter, and resides near Enterprise, where he is well and favorable known. Mr. L. B. Brown, Jr., and Mrs. Brown are members of the Presbyterian church at Enterprise, in which he is a ruling elder. In politics he is a democrat and has represented Clarke county in the lower branch of the state legislature, and the district composed of Clarke and Lauderdale in the senate. Always active in public matters, he took a prominent part in the establishment of the Agricultural and Mechanical college of Mississippi, located at Starkville. Upon the passage the law creating that institution, he was appointed by Governor Stone a member of the board of trustees, in which position he served for twelve years, assisting in perfecting and placing it upon a prosperous and successful basis. He held the position of deputy internal revenue collector for southeast Mississippi during the administration of Mr. Cleveland, and was removed from office when Mr. Harrison was elected. In 1861 he enlisted as a private in company B, Thirty-seventh Mississippi regiment, commanded by Col. Robert McLain, but on account of physical reasons he secured a discharge, and joined a cavalry company under Capt. W. P. Curlee, which formed part of the command of Gen. N. B. Forrest. He acted as orderly sergeant of his company until the reorganization of Forrest's command at Columbus, Miss., when he received a lieutenant's commission from that officer, and was assigned to duty in company C, Ashcroft's regiment. He was in several engagements and was, near the close of the war, captured at Selma, Ala., by General Wilson's command, where he remained a prisoner only a few days, having made his escape. At the conclusion of peace he resumed his chosen vocation and has continued a planter ever since. On the reorganization of his county after the war had ceased, he was elected a member of the board of supervisors from the Enterprise district, and devoted two years of faithful service in the interest of his people. Mrs. Annie Brown is descended from a prominent and widely-known family of South Carolina. Her grandfather (Lemuel J. Alston) was a very popular and wealthy citizen of Greenville, S. C., and was twice elected to congress from that state. Her mother was Mary Burgess, of Halifax, N. C., who was also highly connected, and enjoyed a most favored social position at her native home.

L. P. Brown, merchant of Meridian, Miss., was born in Jackson, Miss., in November, 1849, the fourth in a family of ten children born to William J. and Sarah W. C. (Lincoln) Brown, the former of whom was a Georgian, and the latter a native of Boston, Mass. William J. Brown, after attaining manhood in his native state, came to Mississippi and located in Jackson, where he followed the calling of a merchant, and was among the very first business men of the city. Although seventy-eight years of age, he still takes an active interest in mercantile life, his mind and body showing but little the ravages of time. He met his wife in Philadelphia, Penn., where she had just finished her education. She is a distant relative of Abraham Lincoln, and is also still living, both being worthy and still active members of the Methodist Episcopal church. Throughout his long life Mr. Brown has never aspired to office, his mercantile business receiving his chief time and attention. He is an honorable, high-minded Christian gentleman, and has been a very successful financier. He is a member of the A. F. & A. M. fraternity, and he and his family have always moved in the highest circles of society. L. P. Brown was educated in the common and private schools of the country, and, after obtaining a fair education, began life for himself at the age of twenty years. After he had read law for a short time he gave it up on account of his health, and began clerking in a mercantile establishment in Meridian, which calling he followed for several years. In the year 1885 he embarked in business for himself as a general merchant and cotton buyer, and this business he has followed up to the present day. The superior quality of his goods and his honorable methods of conducting business have met with substantial results, and he is now wealthy, being the owner of a handsome residence, business block and a number of tenement houses in Meridian. He is an energetic, enterprising and public-

N. H. Whitfield, M. D.

spirited citizen, and is now president of the board of trustees of East Mississippi female college, is president of the board of directors of the Y. M. C. A., is a member of the state executive committee of the Y. M. C. A., and is secretary of the state prohibition executive committee. He has been an official in the Methodist Episcopal church for twenty-one years, holding various responsible positions, and is regarded by all who know him as a worthy Christian. He has never been a participant in the political affairs of the county, but has devoted his best energies to the moral and religious elevation of mankind, and has been liberal in his contributions to churches and schools. He was first married in New Orleans, in 1878, to Miss Mollie Harmon, who died in 1881, leaving him with two children to care for: Mary Clara and Frank Harmon, the latter dying in infancy. In 1884 Mr. Brown took for his second wife, Miss Wilhelme Streator, of Carroll county, Miss., who has borne him two children, Lincoln P. and Hadie (a daughter). Mrs. Brown is an earnest worker in the Methodist Episcopal church.

The editor and proprietor of the *Progress*, Water Valley, Miss., is Capt. S. B. Brown, one of the representative citizens of Yalobusha county, and it is fitting that a brief sketch of his career should find place in this record. He was born in Buckingham county, Va., and is a son of Garland and Martha (Brandsford) Brown, natives of Virginia and descendants of a French Huguenot family. Mr. and Mrs. Brown were reared, educated and married in their native state, the former being a planter by occupation. He was a captain in the war with England in 1812, and in one of the encounters of that war he had a leg broken. His father was a soldier in the Revolutionary war, and was present at the surrender of Cornwallis, being in command of a company as a commissioned officer. He and his wife reared a family of four sons and two daughters. He was a man of large means and was highly respected as a citizen. Garland Brown, with his younger children, removed to Mississippi in the year 1845, the mother having died in 1843, at the age of sixty-seven years. She was an earnest Christian and a zealous worker in the Methodist Episcopal church, of which she was a member. She had born to her thirteen children, eleven of whom grew to maturity, and two of whom are now living, our subject and John G., a resident of the state of Texas. The latter has been a member of the state senate, and is well and favorably known throughout the state, having lived there since 1850. The other children were: George; Maria, the wife of a Mr. Brown, who has one child surviving her; Mrs. Mary Haines, who had a large family, highly educated and filling positions of honor and distinction in the state of Virginia; Mrs. Sarah Taylor, wife of Dr. Taylor, and the mother of two sons; Benjamin, a minister in the Methodist Episcopal church; Mrs. Martha Ford, and Capt. R. M. Brown, who served in the late war as a faithful, gallant soldier. He was editor of the *Mississippi Central*, a paper published in Water Valley, and for several years was a member of the state legislature. The father of these children, on coming to Mississippi, settled in Marshall county, where he died in 1855, aged seventy-eight years. He was a worthy member of the Methodist Episcopal church, and a citizen whom any community might be proud to claim. Capt. S. B. Brown was reared and educated in Mississippi. He received his elementary education in the common schools, and had the further advantage of a collegiate training. At the age of nineteen years he began teaching in Marshall county, and was very successful in this profession. In 1859 he was united in marriage to Mary Y. Derden. In the fall of 1860 he was elected principal of a male academy in Panola county, Miss. When the Civil war broke out he joined a company of infantry volunteers that was raised in the neighborhood of Eureka, Miss., where he was teaching, and was made orderly sergeant at the organization of the regiment at Grenada, Miss. This company became company I of the Thirty-third regiment Mississippi volunteers,

28

of which he was elected lieutenant. Lieutenant Brown participated in the following battles, fought in Mississippi: Corinth, Davis' mills, Champion Hill and Jackson; Baton Rouge and Port Hudson, La. He was with Gen. Joseph E. Johnston in the Georgia campaign, and participated in all the battles of that celebrated campaign from Dalton to Jonesboro, including the siege of Atlanta. He was promoted to be captain of his company at Atlanta, Ga. He was with Hood in his Tennessee campaign, and had his right arm broken at the battle of Franklin, Tenn, November 30, 1864. He retreated from Tennessee with the Confederate army; was granted a leave of absence, on account of his severe wound, from which he did not fully recover for several years. At the close of the war he resumed teaching. In 1869 he was elected superintendent of schools of Yalobusha county, Miss., serving for eight years. In 1871 he was made principal of the schools of Water Valley, Miss. In his political opinions Captain Brown affiliates with the democrats, and is one of the ablest men in his party in the county. He has been a member of every democratic convention, state and county, since 1871, and served as a member of the democratic state, county and district executive committees for several years. He was appointed by the governor of the state to represent his senatorial district in the inter-state immigration convention held at Asheville, N. C., December 20, 1890. He is an enthusiastic member of the Masonic fraternity, having been master of five different lodges, and high priest of his chapter. He is also a Knight Templar and eminent commander of St. Cyr commandery of the Knights Templars at Water Valley. He is a member of the Methodist Episcopal church, of which he is also a trustee. An active and influential member of the Mississippi press association, he has been its president and has in other ways advanced its interests. Interested in all public movements that will advance the community, he is a ready supporter of every worthy enterprise. Mrs. Brown was born and reared near Coffeeville, Miss., and was a daughter of John Berden, who was an old settler of Yalobusha county, coming from Alabama to that county in 1835. His wife was a Miss Porter, who had born to her eight children, only two of whom are now living. Mrs. Brown is next to the youngest, and Mrs. Elizabeth Campbell, wife of Dr. Campbell, a prominent physician of the county, and who is now deceased, is the other surviving member. Mr. and Mrs. Brown have had born to them four children, two of whom are living: Garland D. is the assistant editor of the *Progress*, and is also a real estate dealer and insurance agent; he was educated in his native county and was then graduated from a commercial college in St. Louis, Mo.; he is also an enthusiastic and bright young Mason; is master of Valley City lodge No. 402; has taken all of the degrees in Masonry from entered apprentice to knight templar inclusive. Mary Lynn, the other child, is now a student at the Female college at Huntsville, Ala. She was graduated from the high school of Water Valley in the class of 1889, taking the highest honors in a class of twenty-two, and a prize medal valued at $25. The Water Valley (Miss.) *Progress*, of which Capt. S. B. Brown is editor and proprietor, assisted by his son, Garland D., was established in 1882 under its present management. It is an eight-column folio, all home print, democratic in politics, and devoted to the educational, moral and material interests of the community in which it has a large circulation. It is issued weekly, and is the organ of the democratic party of Yalobusha county, as well as one of the leading papers in Northern Mississippi.

J. E. Browning, whose postoffice address is Ecru, Pontotoc county, Miss., was born in Greenville district, S. C., in 1832. Rev. Elijah Browning, his father, was also a native of that district. His mother, who was Miss Mary Crawford, was born in Virginia in 1803. They had twelve children, of whom seven are yet living. Mr. Browning was a clergyman of the Baptist church and preached the gospel for twenty years. He was county treasurer of

Pontotoc county about the close of the war. The family came from South Carolina in 1845. The subject of our sketch began life for himself in 1857. He married Miss Susan Smith, daughter of J. L. Smith, a well-known planter, and eleven children were born to them: Mary J., wife of James Hattox; Lottie E., the wife of Will Spain; James E., who is married to Joanna Bigham; Rebecca S., the wife of J. J. Bigham; John M., who never married; J. E. and J. H., who are deceased; Maude S., M. E., Nannie E. and L. C. Mr. Browning enlisted in 1862 under Captain Smith, of Colonel Moore's regiment of Mississippi volunteers. He was wounded at the battle of Corinth and returned home October, 1862. As soon as he recovered his health he turned his attention to planting. Mr. and Mrs. Browning are members of the Baptist church, and have always been most liberal in their contributions to educational and religious enterprises generally. Mr. Browning is the owner of about four hundred and thirty-five acres of land, about one hundred acres of which are under cultivation. He and his sons are the owners of a sawmill which has a capacity of five thousand feet of lumber per day. Mr. Browning ranks among the self-made, independent, highly respected citizens of that county.

Dr. L. S. Brownlee, of Pachuta, Clarke county, Miss., is of Scotch-Irish descent and is a son of James Brownlee, who was born in South Carolina about 1810 and came to Lowndes county, Miss., in 1821. This pioneer was a mechanic and farmer. He was married to Miss Prudence Taggart, of Pickens county, Ala., about 1829. He died in 1853; Mrs. Brownlee in 1882. Dr. S. L. Brownlee was born May 29, 1842, in Lowndes county, Miss., and spent his early life on the farm and received his first instruction in the common schools. At sixteen years of age he began work on his own account. At nineteen he entered the medical department of the University of Nashville, and in 1870 reëntered the same school and graduated therefrom in 1871. He enlisted in the Fourteenth Mississippi regiment, Colonel Baldwyn commanding, and saw his first battle service at Fort Donelson, where he was captured. He was carried a prisoner to Camp Douglas and remained there nine months, when he was paroled and exchanged in 1863. He reëntered the service and later was transferred to Forrest's cavalry. He was in the battle of Harrisburg and surrendered in 1865. Dr. Brownlee was married in 1863 to Miss Eliza Snell, of Lowndes county, Miss. He has had three children: Enninna, Charles R. and Lona E. The two last mentioned are living. Lona E. is married to Mr. E. S. Berry, of Jasper county, Miss. Dr. Brownlee resides in Pachuta, a flourishing town on the New Orleans & Northeastern railroad, ten miles southwest of Enterprise, where he is practicing his profession with success. His standing is shown in the fact that he is medical examiner for two New York insurance companies. The Doctor is a member of the Missionary Baptist church. Mrs. Brownlee is a Presbyterian. The Doctor has some agricultural interests and has been engaged in merchandising for some years.

A physician whose skill has won him a large practice is Dr. John Brownrigg, who stands high in the estimation of his fellow-citizens, for, in addition to being a leading medical practitioner, he is a true gentleman in every particular, and is a very liberal contributor to worthy enterprises. He was born at Wingfield, on the Chowan river, in North Carolina, December 6, 1829, a son of Richard T. and Mary W. (Hoskins) Brownrigg, of that state, the former of whom studied medicine in his early manhood, but never practiced the profession. Although of a retiring and modest disposition, he possessed a vast fund of knowledge, which his friends were not slow to recognize, and while a citizen of the Old North state he was elected a member of the state legislature, serving in that body with ability and distinction. He removed to Columbus, Lowndes county, Miss., in 1837, where he became a wealthy planter and died in 1847. His grandfather, Richard Brownrigg, of Wingfield, N. C., was the first to establish a fishery, worked by horse power, for herring and shad, on Albemarle sound. The family is of English-Irish descent. To Gen. Richard T. Brownrigg and wife three sons were born: John, Richard T. and Thomas, and two daughters, Elizabeth B. and Sarah. Dr. John Brownrigg was a resident of North Carolina until he attained his sixth year, when he was brought to Columbus, Miss., by his parents, and here received his literary education in the academies and private schools, and at his father's plantation home, under private tutors who were thorough and practical educators, one of whom was a graduate of Yale college, and the other of Maynooth college, Ireland. At an early age he began the study of medicine and for some time was a student in the University of New York city, and, in 1851, graduated from the Jefferson Medical college of Philadelphia, Penn. He began practicing in the country eight miles west of Columbus, but, in 1861, gave up his practice to enter the Confederate army, becoming a private in the Tombigbee rangers of the army of Mississippi. He was soon elected surgeon of his regiment, commissioned by Governor Harris, of Tennessee, his company having volunteered to aid that state before she seceded, and was subsequently transferred to the regular Confederate service and became surgeon of Blythe's Mississippi regiment. After the battle of Shiloh he was sent to Columbus, Miss., to establish a hospital for the wounded, and afterward became post surgeon there, where there were several hospitals. He was then made chief surgeon of the third military district, department of Mississippi and east Louisiana. After the sieges of Vicksburg and Jackson, Miss., he was sent back to take charge of the general hospital for the wounded, at Jackson, Miss., to which were transferred the wounded from the battle of Baker's creek, also. He then became surgeon of the Twentieth Mississippi regiment, from which he was assigned to the hospital for Loring's division, at Canton, Miss. He next became chief surgeon of cavalry west of Alabama, on the staff of Gen. S. D. Lee, which command embraced Lee's and Bedford Forrest's divisions and several detached commands and several hospitals. He served in Virginia, reaching Harper's ferry before Virginia seceded, and was there when Colonel Jackson, afterward known as Stonewall Jackson, turned over the command to Gen. Joseph E. Johnston. He served, also, in Tennessee, Kentucky, Missouri and Mississippi. After the close of the war he entered upon the practice of medicine and surgery at Columbus, Miss., and has continued the same up to the present time, his career being marked by eminent success. He has devoted much time to obstetrics and gynæcology, and, although he has delivered about one thousand women, he has never lost one in labor. He is a member of the Lowndes county medical society, the Mississippi state medical association and the Southern surgical and gynæcological association. He is also president of the board of health of Columbus, Miss., and local surgeon of the Georgia & Pacific railway. He is a member of the I. O. O. F., the K. of H. and the Protestant Episcopal church. He was married in 1864 to Miss Elizabeth Yerger, of Jackson, Miss., a daughter of Hon. William Yerger, formerly of the supreme bench. They have one son, Richard T., who is practicing law in Dallas, Tex. The Doctor is the only son of his father's family now living, his brother, Richard T., having been killed at the battle of Lake Bisland, La. He was a major on Gen. Sibley's staff.

Mrs. A. V. (Moore) Broyles, widow of Dr. Erasmus Broyles, is the tenth in order of birth of the thirteen children of James Moore, a native of Kentucky, who moved to Alabama at the age of twenty-one, shortly after his marriage to Abigail Woods, and lived there until 1845, when he came to Monroe county, Miss., where he died in 1865. He was a successful planter, and for many years a consistent member of the Baptist church. Mrs. Broyles received her education at the Aberdeen high school, and was married in 1849 to Dr. Erasmus Broyles, a native of East Tennessee, who then and afterward resided in Monroe county, Miss. He received his literary education in South Carolina, and afterward fitted himself for his profession in a leading medical college. She is a well-educated, intelligent lady, an earnest Christian woman, who has devoted herself zealously to rearing and training her children, all of whom have given, or promise to give, such success in life as will insure them the respect and consideration of all with whom they may come in contact.

A successful planter and merchant of Quincy, Monroe county, is Dr. Ira G. Broyles, who was born in Lincoln county, Tenn., in 1816, the son of Isaac and Mary (Whittenberg) Broyles, the former a farmer, who was a volunteer soldier and fought with General Jackson in the Seminole war. Dr. Broyles received his education in Tennessee, and was later a clerk in a dry goods store in that state. At the date mentioned he went to Mount Hope, Ala., and there read medicine with a distinguished resident physician. He moved to Monroe county, Miss., in 1849, and through the remainder of his active life was engaged in the practice of his profession. In the late war the Doctor took a very useful part by assisting the families of many who had gone to the front. Dr. Broyles was never married, and knows the full value of that much-vaunted single blessedness—the life of a bachelor. He is the owner of about one thousand four hundred acres of well-improved land. Politically he is a democrat, though he has never taken any active part in politics, and has never been prevailed upon to take an office. He is a helpful and consistent member of the Methodist Episcopal church. His sister, Mrs. Ann White, was born in 1825. His brother, Jacob, was born in 1802, and is residing in Armory, Miss. Isaac, another brother, born in 1818, is living in Texas. While his father and mother were residents of Tennessee, living a pioneer life in a little old log cabin, one day a huge rattlesnake came into the house, drove his mother out and held possession until killed by a large dog, ever afterward a great favorite with the family. The Doctor is one of the wealthiest men in the county, widely known and very popular.

One of the wealthiest and best known citizens of the state of Mississippi is Dr. Alexander A. Bryant, a resident of Coffeeville, Yalobusha county. He was born in Richmond county, Va., in 1829. His parents, Thomas and Susan (Pope) Bryant, were natives of Virginia. In 1840 they removed to Mississippi, settling in Marshall county, where Mr. Thomas Bryant purchased a tract of land near Holly Springs. He was fortunate in business and acquired considerable property. He was a soldier in the war of 1812, volunteering as a substitute for an old gentleman who had been drafted. He died in De Soto county, Miss., in 1854, having removed to that county in 1852; he was fifty-seven years of age. His wife was born in 1797 and died in 1846; she was the daughter of Ezekiel Pope, who was one of the early settlers of Westmoreland county, Va. His ancestors came from England. He married Rachel Packett, a Virginian by birth, and to them were born three sons and three daughters. Alexander Bryant, the grandfather of our subject, was of Scotch ancestry, his forefathers having immigrated to this country as early as 1720. The land on which they settled on the Rappahannock river, in Virginia, has never passed out of the family, and is now owned by Alexander Bryant. The grandfather served in the Revolutionary war, as did also Ezekiel Pope. He married Susan Lyles, and to them were born several children. The parents of Alexander A. reared a family of two sons and four daughters, all of whom are living except one daughter; their names are as follows: Mrs. E. C. Still, John W. Bryant, Mrs. Fowler, Mrs. Weber. The subject of this sketch was reared in Mississippi and received his education at Holly Springs. In 1851–2 he was a student in the medical college of Louisville. He began the practice of his profession in 1853 in Lafayette county, Miss., and remained there until 1866; in that year

he came to Coffeeville, Miss.   He decided to abandon his profession and embark in the mercantile trade.   He formed a partnership with S. B. Herron, the firm name being Bryant &
Herron; this relationship continued until 1878, when Mr. Bryant retired, devoting his whole
time to his landed interests, which are very large.   He owns about seven thousand acres of
land in Mississippi, five thousand five hundred of which are in Yalobusha county; he also
owns vast tracts in other states.   The Doctor was united in marriage in 1860 to Miss Margaret Steen, a daughter of W. H. Steen, of South Carolina.   She was born in Mississippi in
1844, and all the relatives bearing that name, except J. B. Steen, her father's brother, are now
deceased; they were early settlers in Rankin county, Miss.   Mrs. Bryant was an only child.
Her mother's maiden name was Elizabeth Lusk; she died at the residence of her daughter in
1889, aged eighty-two years.   Mrs. Bryant was educated in Pontotoc county, Miss., and was
a woman of rare attainments and unusual force of character.   She died in December, 1884,
leaving three sons and one daughter: Edgar, an attorney of Arkansas, was elected judge
of the Fort Smith district in 1890; William C. is one of the proprietors of the Birmingham
Wholesale Dry Goods company; Clyde, who takes her name from the river Clyde, Scotland,
is a highly accomplished young woman, and was educated in Nashville, Tenn.; Alexander,
the youngest, is named for his father.   In his early life Dr. Bryant became connected with
the Masonic fraternity.   In his political opinions he affiliates with the democratic party, and
he is an enthusiastic supporter of the principles of that body.   He has a most comfortable
home, where he is surrounded with all the luxuries of modern life.   He is a man fully abreast
of the times, of broad, liberal views, generous in his support of public measures, and withal
a citizen of whom any state may well be proud.   The original home place, that was settled
by his ancestors in 1720, is a tract of twelve hundred acres; the name of Alexander is a family
name, and with one exception it has never been held by one of any other name; Alexander
Bryant is the present owner of this place.   The father of the Doctor was a musician of no
little note.   He delighted in singing the beautiful Scotch ballads, and, in fact, was pleased
with anything pertaining to the native land of his ancestors.

One of the oldest and most highly respected citizens of Lee county, who has been prominently connected with its history for many years, is Samuel Bryson, of Bethany.   He
is a native of South Carolina, born August 15, 1809, in Laurens district, the son of James
and Elizabeth Ann (Blakely) Bryson, also natives of South Carolina.   James Bryson was a
son of William Bryson, a native of Ireland, who emigrated to America with his parents,
and settled in South Carolina.   There he grew to maturity, and was a conspicuous figure
during Revolutionary times.   He was twice married, but his children were born by
the first union.   James Bryson, father of our subject, was born, lived, and died in
Laurens, S. C.   He died in 1831, aged sixty years.   He was a soldier in the war of 1812.
His wife, Elizabeth Ann Blakely, was the daughter of Thomas and Margaret (McGaffick)
Blakely, natives of Pennsylvania and Ireland respectively.   They reared a family of eight
children, of whom Elizabeth Ann was the oldest.   She lived to be eighty-six years of age,
and died September 27, 1874.   Our subject is one of a family of thirteen children: William,
Thomas, Samuel, James, Hampton, Margaret (wife of Alfred O. Sheills), Polly, Eliza, Henry,
Porter, Emily, Presley and John.   Eliza married William Caldwell, and Emily is the wife
of Matthew Bryson.   The family emigrated to Mississippi in 1851, making the journey from
South Carolina by wagons.   Samuel Bryson settled on the place where he now resides.   He
was married December 5, 1833, to Miss Jane Milam, a native of South Carolina.   She died
August 1, 1857.   They had born to them twelve children, three of whom are yet living:
William D., Thaddeus M., and Mary E., wife of Robert Gambrel; the names of the other

children were, Alvinus, Wilson, Elizabeth, Margaret (the wife of T. W. Houston), Nancy, Samuel, Martha, Jane, Eliza G. and Milton. Four of the children and the mother died at the same time of flux. Mr. Bryson was married a second time, October 25, 1860, to Margaret A. Crockett, widow of Eli Crockett. Her maiden name was McCullough. Seven children were born of Mrs. Bryson's first marriage, one of whom survives, Thomas J. Those deceased were Anna E., John M., David E., Benjamin F., Ruth E. and Priscilla. Three children were born to Mr. and Mrs. Bryson by their second union: Calvin L., Ludie P., and Argile, deceased. They are now bringing up a little girl, Abby Adelia, daughter of W. D. Bryson. Dr. Bryson and wife are members of Bethany church. Politically he adheres to the principles of the democratic party. He is a man of superior business qualifications, and accumulated a large amount of property. He has been able to assist his children in making a start in life, giving to each of them at one time $2,000. Thaddeus M. Bryson, a son of Samuel Bryson, was born December 12, 1845, and was but six years of age when his parents removed to Mississippi. He was educated in the common schools, but owing to the late Civil war his advantages were extremely limited. He left the schoolroom for the battlefield, and enlisted in the Thirty-second Mississippi regiment. He saw a great deal of active service, and was seriously wounded at Chickamauga. He had a furlough of seventy days and rejoined his regiment at Tunnel hill, Ga. He was wounded again at Jonesboro, in the right hand, and before that, by a spent shell. After the surrender he made his way home, and found that everything there had been laid waste. He went to work with a will to assist his father, and by their joint management, soon recovered a portion of their property. The son operated a saw and ginmill in connection with the planing, and for several years led a very busy life. He was married December 20, 1866, to Miss Louisa E. Young, a daughter of Francis and Elvira (Caldwell) Young, natives of South Carolina. Mrs. Bryson was born in October, 1847. Nine children having been born of this union: Mary J., James Y., M. Ella, Samuel F., Anna E., Effie E., Essie E., John M. and Zilphia. The Brysons are of excellent lineage, and stand second to no family in the community.

James M. Buchanan was born in Lawrence county, Tenn., in 1837. He is the son of Hon. Franklin Buchanan, who was born in Giles county, Tenn., in 1812, and whose early life, from the age of fifteen years to the year 1831, was passed as an employe in the office of the clerk of his county. In the year just mentioned he was married to Adelaide Simonton, and after that event he became a farmer. He was elected three times to represent his district in the Tennessee legislature, and was speaker of the house in 1846. Mr. Buchanan was a very public-spirited man, and took deep interest in the political affairs of his state. He was the father of ten children, the following named of whom are still living: James; Mrs. Adelaide McIntosh, of Nashville, Tenn.; Mrs. Isabella Fowlkes, of Buena Vista, Miss.; John M., of Texas. Mr. Buchanan was a member of the Baptist church. He came to Monroe county in 1850, and died in March, 1851. James M. Buchanan received his education at that famous Tennessee college, Jackson. His chief occupation has been that of a planter. About ten years ago he established a store on his plantation, and does an extensive local mercantile trade. January 4, 1859, he married Sarah A. McGaughy, of Lee county, Miss., and they have had six children, named as follows: William F., Evalina, Sallie, James, Mary and John. Mr. Buchanan is a member of the Knights of Honor, and he and his wife are members of the Cumberland Presbyterian church, the house of worship being near his plantation. In 1862 he enlisted in company B, of the Fortyfifth Mississippi regiment, commanded by Captain Martin. He did service at Perryville, Resaca, Jonesboro, Chickamauga and Franklin, and in other engagements. He was paroled in 1865. Mr. Buchanan is a well-to-do farmer and a successful merchant, possessed of good business qualifications, and enjoys the respect of the community in which he lives.

The superintendent of the East Mississippi insane asylum at Meridian, Miss., is Dr. J. M. Buchanan, an experienced and intelligent physician, well fitted by years of practical experience and study for the responsible position he is now filling. He was born in Chickasaw county, Miss., October 5, 1855, a son of Thomas J. and Sophia (Martin) Buchanan, natives of the Old North state, who came to Mississippi in the thirties, settling in Chickasaw county, where they still reside. The father is now a retired planter. Three of the five sons born to him served in the Confederate army during the Civil war: William M., Joseph W. (captain of the Buena Vista Hornets of the Twenty-fourth regiment) and Thomas J. Jr. The other two members are H. C. and Dr. J. M. The latter was the youngest of the sons and was reared in Chickasaw county, receiving his literary education in the University of Mississippi, from which he graduated in 1878. He then entered upon his medical studies, and in 1879 graduated from the medical department of the University of Virginia. He, however, continued his studies two years longer, taking a post-graduate course at the city of New York also, thereafter spending eighteen months in the different schools of Europe, principally in Vienna and London, where he perfected himself in his profession. He then returned to his native land, and after spending one year in Chickasaw county, Miss., he removed to Little Rock, Ark., where he remained for two years, fifteen months of this time being spent as first assistant physician of the Arkansas state lunatic asylum. He then resigned that position to accept a similar one in the East Mississippi insane asylum in 1884. Two years later he resigned this position to engage in private practice at Meridian, which he continued for three years, receiving his appointment to his present position in March, 1890. The Doctor now has full charge of the asylum, which has about two hundred and fifty inmates, one hundred and twenty-six being males and one hundred and twenty-four females, forty-five of the women and forty-three of the men being negroes. The asylum has six wards, three for each sex, and a visit through this institution gives plain and satisfactory evidence that everything is kept in perfect order, and is admirably managed. Dr. Buchanan is eminently qualified to successfully fill this position, for besides being well-posted in that branch of the science which treats of aberration of the mind, he is an excellent manager, possesses sound good sense and very practical views. He is a member of the A. F. & A. M., and the K. of P., in which he is grand prelate of the grand lodge. He was married in November, 1885, to Miss Sallie M. White, a native of Memphis, Tenn., and a worthy member of the Presbyterian church. The Doctor is a member of the State medical association, Lauderdale county association and the association of medical superintendents of American institutions for the insane. There is a farm attached to the asylum, consisting of six hundred acres, of which about one hundred and twenty are under cultivation, devoted to the raising of vegetables, supplies, etc., for the inmates. The Doctor has the general management of this also, but it is under the immediate charge of the steward, R. E. Moody. Dr. W. O. Porter is the assistant physician. He is a graduate of the Louisville hospital medical college, and has held his present position since 1890.

Probably the most popular physician of Calhoun county is the subject of this sketch. Dr. S. T. Buchanan's parents, Alfred and Mary (Smith) Buchanan, were natives of North Carolina, and his paternal grandfather, Joseph Buchanan, was a native of Scotland, but came to America at an early day, settling in North Carolina. The Doctor's maternal grandfather, Sipon Smith, was a native of England, but emigrated to North Carolina and was a leading minister in the Methodist Episcopal church. He was quite a prominent man and lived to be quite aged. He was the father of four children all of whom lived to be grown. One of them, Rev. Thomas Smith, moved to Tuscaloosa, Ala., embarked in merchandising, and was also engaged in ministerial work for some time. He then went to San Antonio, Tex., and there died in 1888, when quite an old man. He was very highly respected. Another son, William Smith, was also a prominent leader in the Methodist Episcopal church and was an active Sunday-school worker. He was also quite aged at the time of his death. A daughter, Mrs. Nancy Crowdered, resided in North Carolina, and there died, leaving a family of young children. Mrs. Buchanan, the mother of Dr. Buchanan, was the youngest member of this family. She was born in Wake county, N. C., but received her final summons in Chatham county of that state in 1882 at the age of eighty years. She was a very active woman, hale and hearty, and enjoyed good health up to the time of her death. She was the mother of eleven children by her union with Mr. Buchanan, reared her large family, and saw them married and with children of their own before her death. She had nearly two hundred grandchildren and great-grandchildren. She was a member of the Methodist church from early girlhood, was a very active worker in the same, and reared all her children to be honest, upright members of that church. Alfred Buchanan, father of the Doctor, was reared in his native state, and was one of a large family of children, most of whom lived to be grown. He died about 1848. Politically he was a stanch democrat, and socially he was a member of the Masonic fraternity. Of the eleven children born to his marriage nine are yet living: Karion, widow of Thompson Lawrence; Wesley (now deceased) was a physician of North Carolina, where he practiced his profession for many years; Ethelbert followed farming, and died in North Carolina; Samantha resides in North Carolina and is the wife of C. Maddox; Mrs. G. A. Utley, widow of Jacob Utley, who died during the war; Nancy resides in North Carolina and is the widow of Elias Cox; Hilliard S. resides in North Carolina; Mary Louisa, wife of Mr. Mansfield; Flora Jane resides at Slate Springs, Miss., and is the wife of M. C. Palmer. Dr. S. T. Buchanan was born in Chatham county, N. C., in 1824, and attained his growth and received his education in the common schools of his native state. He read medicine at home under his brother, and took lectures at the old University of Philadelphia, Penn., from which he graduated in 1848 or 1849. He then practiced with his brother for a few years, and in January, 1853, came to Mississippi, located at Benela, where he continued to practice until within the last few years. He is one of the representative men of Calhoun county, as well as one of its very early settlers, and is a physician of acknowledged ability and prominence. He had a large and extensive practice, and rode for many miles to see his patients. His marriage occurred in November, 1853, to Miss Sarah A. Gaston, a native of Alabama, and the daughter of Judge Hugh Gaston. Her father was judge of Calhoun county, of which he was an early settler, and his death occurred there in 1868. His brother, Ebenezer Gaston, was an old bachelor and a very wealthy man. The Judge was the father of five children, one besides Mrs. Buchanan now living, J. E. Gaston. Those deceased were: James M. and Hugh William, both killed in the war; Harriet E., died when fourteen years of age. To Dr. and Mrs. Buchanan were born six children, three now living: Mary A., wife of Dr. Lawrence; James W., at Eupora, Miss., and Clara Anna, at home. Those deceased were named Wesley G., died when less than a year old; Ella J., married A. J. Underwood, and died one year later leaving her husband and an infant, both of whom are now in Texas, and Willie had just finished his literary course at Oxford, Miss., and was in the second year of his law course when he was taken with malaria hematura and died. He was a very promising young man, was moral and upright, and his untimely death was deeply regretted. Dr. Buchanan entered the service during the Civil war, but was so strongly urged to return that he was made one of the supervisors of the county, where he was kept for his practice, etc. In connection with his practice the Doctor has also been engaged in farming, and he was the founder of the Benela mill, which was incorporated in 1878 as the S. T. Buchanan Mill and Manufacturing company. He is the owner of about two thousand acres of land and has four hundred acres under cultivation. He has a mercantile establishment at Eupora, and this is conducted by his son. The Doctor and wife are members of the Methodist church, and he is among the most liberal contributors to the same. He had a partial stroke of paralysis in 1888, and this has disabled him very materially from business.

Dr. Charles E. Buck (deceased). There is in the development of every successful life a principle which is a lesson to every man following in its footsteps, a lesson leading to higher and more honorable position than the ordinary. Let a man be industriously ambitious, and honorable in his ambitions, and he will rise whether having the prestige of family or the obscurity of poverty. These reflections are called forth by the study of the life of Dr. Charles E. Buck who, during life proved himself eminently worthy the confidence reposed in him by all classes, and that as an honorable, upright citizen his reputation was not merely local but extended over a wide stretch of country. He was a native of Claiborne county, his birth occurring April 4, 1836, being the youngest of four children born to his parents, the other members of the family being as follows: Miriam is the wife of James W. Watson, a graduate of Princeton college and now an extensive planter; William is a planter of note of Louisiana, is a graduate of Princeton college and is married to Mrs. Catherine Servis, and Caroline resides on the Magnolia plantation home, the battle site of Port Gibson, Miss., which was fought in May, 1863. She is a graduate of Port Gibson college, and is a lady of decided culture and refinement. She is still a close student, and makes a point of keeping thoroughly posted on all the literary and current topics of the day. She is a devoted member of the St. James Episcopal church, of Port Gibson, Miss., and her many acts of benevolence are the cardinal points of her noble Christian character. The father of these children, William Richardson Buck, was born in Strasburg, Va., in 1790, and set an example which his sons afterward followed by graduating from Princeton college. He was a typical Southern gentleman, chivalrous, courteous and kindly, and by his superior business qualifications amassed a large fortune. He volunteered to serve in the war of 1812, and while in the service was appointed as midshipman on the American Peacock, and the gallant fight between this noted vessel and the English Epewier took place on the Mediterranean sea was participated in by Mr. Buck, who so distinguished himself that he was awarded a beautiful sword, set with costly jewels, as a testimonial of his bravery, by the United States congress. In 1822 he was united in marriage to Mrs. Maria Flower, a native of Louisiana. She was a daughter of Dr. Flower, one of the early pioneers of this country under the Spanish rule. Her family is a noted one, and is prominent in the history of Louisiana. Mrs. Buck was an accomplished lady, a noble and wise mother, and a true Christian in precept and example. The early training of Charles E. Buck was received in the old field schools, from which he entered the once famous Oakland college, of Mississippi, in which he graduatd in the classical course. He next entered Princeton college, New Jersey, and in the year 1856 graduated with honors. After his graduation from this institution, he entered the University of Virginia, at Charlottesville, as a medical student, in the fall of 1857, and also graduated from the Medical college of New Orleans, making in all four diplomas which he has received. He was a close and faithful student at all times, and after leaving college, although he was compelled to abandon his practice for some time, and devote his attention to his landed interests, he kept himself well posted in medical lore, as well as the current topics of the day. On November 22, 1864, he was married to Miss Sarah Letitia Jefferies, a member of the noted Jefferies family, a full and correct account of which family is given in the memoirs on another page. Their marriage was solemnized by Rev. J. B. Walker, of Port Gibson. Mrs. Buck was born March 29, 1845, and has borne her husband three sons and one daughter: Edward Jefferies, a graduate of the state university, at Oxford, Miss, completed the law course in that institution in 1888. He is a young gentleman of excellent business qualifications, and being ambitious and energetic, will undoubtedly make a success of his career. He is now filling the important position of claim agent on the Missouri Pacific railroad, his headquarters being in St. Louis. William Henry, the next son, graduated from the Naval academy, at Indianapolis, Md., as number eleven in a class of forty-three. He is now on a two years' cruise on the flagship Philadelphia. Nathaniel Jefferies is in attendance at the University of Mississippi, at Oxford, in which he is taking a full classical course, and will graduate in 1891. He possesses scholastic attainments far beyond the average, and is especially gifted in modern languages and Greek and Latin. He is now taking a post-graduate course, after which he will enter the law department. The only daughter of her father's house is Katharine Watson, who graduated from the Port Gibson female college in 1890, and is now taking a post-graduate course in French, Latin and vocal and instrumental music, and will enter the Peabody conservatory at Baltimore in the fall of 1891. At the opening of the Rebellion, Dr. Buck was a volunteer in the first regiment from Claiborne county, which went by the appellation of the Claiborne guards, or the Twelfth Mississippi infantry volunteers. After two years spent in Virginia, the principal battlefield of the Civil war, he was elected captain of his company, and was called home to raise a company of cavalry, which he accomplished, and was soon joined to the army of Mississippi and Tennessee. Dr. Buck went through the entire service without receiving a wound or being captured, and no braver soldier ever trod the crimson turf of a Virginia battlefield. His men, like him, were brave soldiers, and were conspicuous for their adherence to duty. Returning home, he commenced to rebuild his fallen fortunes, devoting his attention to his landed interests, and in the accumulation of property was successful, becoming well and comfortably off. He adhered to the principles of the democratic party, and on this ticket was elected to the office of sheriff of Claiborne county, Miss., in 1876, being unanimously reëlected to the position. His reputation as a pure and intelligent official was the very best, and he became beloved and popular for his many worthy traits, and for his simplicity and gentleness of manner. He died on the 29th of November, 1878, mourned not only by his loving wife and children, but by the many who knew and loved him and whom he had aided. He was, while in life, a devoted member of the Methodist Episcopal church, as is his estimable widow, and they became well known throughout the county for their many charities. The following article was written in memory of the departed:

IN MEMORIAM.

DIED.—In Port Gibson, Miss., November 29, 1878, Charles E. Buck.

The committee appointed to draft resolutions of respect to the memory of brother C. E. Buck reported the following:

Whereas, it has pleased God, in His inscrutable providence, to remove by death our dearly beloved and most worthy brother, Charles E. Buck, while in the discharge of his duty as sheriff of Claiborne county, Miss.,

Resolved, that we, his brothers and sisters, bowing in humble and tearful submission to the chastening hand which has been laid so heavily upon us, sympathizing with our beloved sister in the great sorrow which has come upon her and her fatherless little ones, and in recognition of the worth of our deceased brother as a member of our order, as a husband, father, Christian citizen and officer, do testify our sorrow at his death by wearing the Patron's badge of mourning for thirty days, and having these resolutions spread upon the minutes of this meeting.

Resolved, that the secretary be instructed to transmit a copy of these resolutions to the widow of our deceased brother, and one to the *Southern Reveille* for publication.

G. W. H. SHAIFER,
WILLIAM H. KERR.
W. McD. SIMS,

Flower Hill Grange, 1879.   Committee.

The funeral of Dr. Buck was a splendid tribute to his work, and a solemn demonstration of public grief. The church was densely packed, and as the choir, with tremulous voices, opened the services with "The Sweet By and By," every head bowed in reverence, and tears flowed from the eyes of many. The discourse by Rev. E. H. Mounger was the theme of universal praise, and the whole service was a fitting testimonial to the worth and public services of the departed. The business houses at Port Gibson were closed, through respect and admiration for this excellent man. He possessed a most admirable character, and was able, scholarly and executive, and possessed a reputation which was without a blot. He was an ideal public officer, the soul of honor, punctual, painstaking and faithful, and his word was considered as good as his bond. As a citizen he was all that could be desired, and as a husband and father was faithful, true and kind. His manly, upright life is a living example to all who knew him, and the county of Claiborne, as well as the state of Mississippi, took proper measures to bring to justice the cowardly assassin who shot him down while in the faithful discharge of his duties. His memory will long be cherished by all who knew him, and his kindly, Christian life will be a lasting monument to his memory.

Madison Webster Buckley, son of Joseph E. and Mary I. (Rogers) Buckley, was born at Buckley's store, Jasper county, Miss., October, 1852. His father was born in Georgia September, 1820, the son of Elijah and Nancie Buckley, and removed to Perry county, Ala., when a young man, and in 1843 to what is now known as Buckley's store, Jasper county, Miss., where he operated a mercantile business and a plantation with considerable success, dying January, 1888. He was married in 1840, while yet a resident of Alabama, and has had five sons and three daughters: Elizabeth is now Mrs. Dear, who is a widow and lives in Lauderdale county, and has borne her now deceased husband, Hardy C. Dear, five sons, namely: Willie, Joseph, Hardy, Robert and Mosley. Angie, now Mrs. Perry, wife of Sim Perry, is a resident of Newton, Newton county. Reuben M. married Rennie Barnett, and is now living in Enterprise, and connected with J. E. Buckley & Son in the mercantile business. He has now three children, namely: Joseph Charles, Mary Inez and R. M. William F. married, first, Mattie Hamrick, and they had two children, namely: Angie and Eugenia. He married, secondly, a Mrs. Sidney Henges, and they have two girl children. Mary J. married, first, John Dear, and had born unto them John F. Dear. She is now married to John Mc-Mellan, of Jasper county, Miss. John L. Buckley, the fourth son of Joseph and Mary I. Buckley, was born September, 1863, at Buckley's store, Jasper county, Miss. He was educated in the common schools of Jasper and Clarke counties, and graduated at the University of Mississippi (Oxford) June, 1885. In 1887 he graduated in law at Cumberland university, Lebanon, Tenn., and began the practice of law in January, 1888, at Enterprise, Miss., where he is still located. He married Lida Brannan, an orphan daughter of James and Lida (Wainwright) Brannan, who was born at Escatawpa, Washington county, Ala., but was raised and educated by her uncle, Thomas L. Wainwright, superintendent of the Stonewall cotton mills, at Stonewall station, Clarke county, Miss. John L. and his wife have born unto them one daughter, Gertrude. He is a member of the Knights of Honor of Enterprise, and politically, a democrat. Joseph E. J., the fifth son, remains unmarried, and resides with his mother on the old Buckley homestead in Jasper county, seven miles west of Enterprise. The mother of Madison Webster Buckley, and the other seven children, was a daughter of Reuben and Elizabeth (Waters) Rogers, and was born in Alabama in 1825. Their grandmother Rogers is still living in Perry county, Ala., at the advanced age of ninety years. Their father was a member of the Masonic fraternity, and both parents were connected with the Baptist church. Their father, Joseph E. Buckley, was among the early settlers of Jasper county, and became quite widely known as a successful planter and merchant. He started business in a small way, but by industry, perseverance and prudence he amassed a competency, and was favorably known as a citizen and business man throughout Jasper and surrounding counties. He was in the highest degree public-spirited, and was everywhere relied upon as a willing contributor to every worthy enterprise. Madison Webster, the first son of Joseph E. and Mary I. Buckley, was educated at the public schools of Jasper county and graduated at Summerville institute. He began life for himself in 1874, was a member of the mercantile firm of Joseph E. Buckley & Son, at Enterprise, proprietors of a successful business, which is still continued under the same firm name. He was married in November, 1878, to Helen Harvy, a daughter of Jones and Mary Harvy. This lady was born in Mississippi in 1855, one of a family of seven children. Madison Wabster Buckley and his wife have reared eight children, seven of whom are boys, and who are named: Walter, Wade, Webb, Wilson, Emmit, Mary Helen, Samuel Ray and John. Both of the parents are members of the Baptist church, and devout Christians. M. W. Buckley is identified with the Knights of Pythias and Knights of Honor of Meridian and Enterprise respectively. He was for ten years a member of the city council, and is now president of the board of trustees of the Enterprise high school. In business he is very prudent, consequently successful, planting extensively in connection with his mercantile operations at Enterprise, Newton and Meridian, owning several good farms of one hundred acres each in Jasper and Clarke counties. He is active and energetic and awake to all public interests. Politically he is a democrat.

The widow of the ex-chancellor of the state of Mississippi is Mrs. Sarah F. Buckner, who was born on the 5th of December, 1813, in Claiborne county, being also reared there. She is a daughter of Thomas and Emily (Willis) Freeland, who were natives of Maryland and North Carolina. Mr. Freeland was born June 6, 1787, and died in January, 1855. His father, Frisby Freeland, was also born in Maryland, and, with his children (his wife having died some time before) emigrated to Mississippi and located on a tract of land, containing two thousand two hundred acres, a short distance above Bruinsburg, in Claiborne county. On this land are a number of large mounds, which are supposed to be the work of the moundbuilders. Mr. Freeland was a man of more than ordinary scholastic attainments, and upon coming to the Mississippi territory he engaged at once in the culture of cotton, and made a signal success of the venture. He was a large slave-owner, and was noted for his magnanimity, his generosity and kindly spirit. He was a member of the body that framed the constitution for the state and represented his county in the senate and house of representatives. Although he was not a man who sought office, his brilliant intellect at once marked him as a leader of men, and the people of Mississippi were not slow to recognize that he would make them a worthy representative. He was an active and earnest worker for all worthy causes, and was particularly earnest in his labors in the Presbyterian church. His mother was a Miss Rolle, a native of Maryland. Her parents were natives of England, who settled on a large tract of land near Baltimore, which land is still owned by the heirs of the Rolle family. Mr. and Mrs. Freeland became the parents of eight children, all of whom lived to be grown, four dying in Kentucky while en route to Mississippi, their deaths resulting from measles. Those who survived were Mrs. William Chew, Mrs. Sarah Johnson, Thomas and Augustin. Mr. Freeland gave each of his daughters large tracts of land near Washington and Rodney, to his sons the home place, and to each of his four children, large numbers of slaves. He was a stanch Union man, a whig in politics, and died in the seventy-second year of his age in 1816 or 1817. He was a man who believed in the education of the young, and gave each of his children excellent educational advantages. His son Thomas (father of Mrs. Buckner) was reared in Maryland, where he was also educated, and upon coming to Mississippi read law with Lyman Harding, of Natchez, one of the leading lawyers of the state. Being born of wealthy parents, it was not necessary for him to practice his profession, and he accordingly retired to his plantation and gave himself up to its cultivation. Although he was for some time a member of the state legislature, he never took much interest in politics, the honors of a public life having no fascination for him. He died in the Presbyterian faith when sixty-eight years of age. His wife was born in 1792 and died when only twenty-two years of age, leaving a daughter, who is now Mrs. Buckner. The latter received her first instruction in the paths of learning from a private tutor, but at the age of ten years she was put to school in the Elizabeth academy, near Washington, the principal of which school was Mrs. Caroline McThayer, a daughter of the noted General Warren, who fell in the battle of Bunker Hill. On the 9th of November, 1830, the marriage of Robert H. Buckner and Miss Sarah F. Freeland took place, Mr. Buckner being a native of Virginia, his birth occurring on the 18th of June, 1802. When but a small boy he removed to Kentucky with his parents, and there attained his majority. He graduated from Bardstown college and read law under Judge Richard A. Buckner and Benjamin Harding, and after obtaining a license to practice in Kentucky he came to Mississippi, where he was granted license by the court over which Judge Childs presided at Monticello, after which he located at Monticello and began the practice of his profession. While at this place he formed a copartnership with Robert H. Adams, and one year later they moved to Natchez, where Adams was elected to congress some time after. Mr. Buckner then associated himself with John T. McMurran, which connection continued amicably until 1833, when Mr. Buckner removed to Jackson, Miss., where he continued to practice until his death, which occurred on the 11th of September, 1845. He possessed a clear, analytical, concise and well-poised mind, and both in speaking and writing was logical and ornate, his arguments at all times being forcible, smooth and convincing. He occupied the front rank in his profession for a number of years, and his success at the bar and the eminent reputation he attained as chancellor of the state of Mississippi were secured rather by the force of native talent and culture than by tact. He was laborious in research, was always thoroughly prepared in his cases, and never permitted the interests of his clients to suffer. In the high position of state chancellor, to which he was elected, he displayed executive ability of the highest order, and showed himself to be a man of strong and resolute will, great firmness, practical sagacity, and possessed a keen insight into the motives and methods of men, which characteristics eminently fitted him for the honorable and responsible position of chancellor. He accumulated a comfortable fortune, and at his death left his family free from care and want. Although not a member of any church, he was a believer in the Christian religion, and socially was a Knight Templar in the A. F. & A. M. He was first buried in Jackson, Miss., but later his body was moved to the home place of his wife in Claiborne county, where it now peacefully reposes. To their union six children were born—two sons and four daughters—only three of whom lived to be grown, two being now alive: Mrs. John M. Parker, of New Orleans, and Mrs. Nellie Anderson, wife of Dr. Anderson, one of the leading physicians of Port Gibson. Mrs. Emma Evans was the other daughter. She became the wife of Louis D. Evans, and at the time of her death left a family of five children. Mrs. Buckner is now residing with her daughter in Port Gibson, has for many years been an earnest worker in the Presbyterian church, and is a true and earnest Christian, the love and esteem of her family and friends testifying in an eloquent manner to her noble qualities of heart and head.

Another representative citizen of Lafayette county who owes his nativity to North Carolina is Edwin T. Buffaloe, planter, Oxford, Miss., who was born in Raleigh in 1837, and who was the fourth in a large family of children, eight of whom are still living, born to Bryant Bell and Annie A. (Cherry) Buffaloe, both natives also of the Old North state. Bryant B. Buffaloe was born in 1804, is still living, and makes his home with his son, Edwin T. Although eighty-seven years of age, he is still active, and his mind is as clear as ever. He was an agriculturist, and the only one of all his children who followed in this calling is Edwin T. The paternal grandfather, William Buffaloe, was born in North Carolina, and served in the Revolutionary war. Edwin T. Buffaloe came to Mississippi with his parents when a child, and, with them, located at Holly Springs, Marshall county, in 1848. There he remained until the outbreak of the war, when he enlisted in 1862, with Captain Lysles, and served in the following memorable battles: Perryville, Ky., Murfreesboro, Tenn., Chattanooga, Chickamauga and others. He was at Lookout mountain, Missionary ridge, and was before General Sherman in his famous march to the sea. He was also in the fight at Jonesboro, Nashville and Franklin, Tenn. Mr. Buffaloe was married in January, 1862, to Mrs. Taylor, of Summerville, Tenn., and the fruits of this union were four children—two sons and two daughters. He has a fine farm of seven hundred acres, and two hundred acres of this are under cultivation. He and family are members of the Methodist Episcopal church South.

Lafayette county can not boast of a more patriotic and useful citizen than H. Aubrey Buford, planter, College Hill, Miss. Mr. Buford is of English descent, his great-grandfather having left that country to come to this at an early date. His grandfather, Philemon Buford, was a native of the Old Dominion. Born in Lunenburgh county in October, 1765, he moved to York or Abbeville district, S. C., where his oldest son, Goodloe Warren Buford, was born, in September, 1794. Then he moved to Greene county, Ala., resided on and owned the land where now stands the city of Eutaw, Ala. Goodloe W. Buford was married to Selina Grace Stephenson, January 2, 1823. She was the daughter of Thomas Stephenson, who had located in that county (Greene) with a colony from South Carolina. From there they all went in a colony to Maury county, Tenn., and settled in what is known as Frierson settlement, and established or located Zion church (Presbyterian), with Dr. Stephenson as their first pastor. In the year 1834 Goodloe W. Buford moved to Yalobusha county, Miss.; the next year to Lafayette county, Miss., where he reared his family and resided until his death, July 6, 1887. He located a large tract of land between the Toby Tubby and Hurricane creeks, and donated a one-fourth section of land to school and church purposes, the same on which College church now stands, and where his body rests. He was influential in locating around him his father and brothers, and in drawing to that locality many Presbyterian families. He served as deacon and elder in the church until his death. His brother, R. Harper Buford, represented Lafayette county many years in the legislature, also later on, his younger brother, A. J. Buford. While the father of our subject was not much of a politician, he was a whig, and a strong supporter of Henry Clay, as a statesman. H. Aubrey Buford, our subject, was born in Maury county, Tenn., in 1828, and was third in a family of children—four sons and four daughters - born to the above mentioned union. He was reared where he now lives, and his early educational advantages were not of the best. He was married in 1851 to Miss Sarah Gill, a native of Lancaster district, S. C., and the daughter of Lewis Gill, who was the son of Col. George Gill, of Revolutionary fame. Mr. and Mrs. Buford have had seven children, four of whom are still living. In 1863 Mr. Buford enlisted in the Confederate army, and was in the following engagements: Murfreesboro, Chickamauga, Lookout mountain, and was with General Bragg in his campaign through Kentucky. He was captured at the battle of Lookout mountain, and was taken to Rock Island, Ill., where he remained until the close of the war. He then returned to his home, and engaged once more in planting, which occupation he has followed with signal success since, being the present owner of over a thousand acres. He has a beautiful home, five miles northwest of Oxford. He and family are members of the Presbyterian church, and he is an elder of the same at College Hill.

Paul C. Buford, planter, was born on the place on which he is now residing September 7, 1847, and was the fourth in a family of eight children born to Thomas N. and Jane C. (Tankersley) Buford, who were born in the state of Alabama, and were there reared, educated and married. A short time after the celebration of their nuptials they removed to Lafayette county, Miss., and purchased land near College Hill, the deeds for which (two) were signed by Martin Van Buren and (one) by James K. Polk, who were then presidents of the United States. Mr. Buford was one of the pioneers of the country and settled here among the Indians and wild animals, and for a long time endured the hardships and privations of pioneer life that he might make a home for his family. He was quite successful as a planter, and being a shrewd and far-seeing business man he engaged in the commission business in Mobile, Ala., for some time prior to coming to Mississippi. He never aspired to any official position in the county, much preferring to follow the peaceful and quiet life of the planter, and at the time of his death was the owner of nine hundred and sixty acres of land, which his widow, who is now aged seventy-three years, still owns. Mr. Buford was well and favorably known throughout the county as a high-minded Christian gentleman, and at the time of his death in 1875, at the age of sixty-six years, he was a consistent member of the Presbyterian church. He was liberal in the use of his means to enterprises deserving his patronage, and as an honorable and useful citizen had not a superior. Paul C. Buford began life for himself at the age of twenty-two years as a clerk in a store at College hill, but at the end of one year he returned to the home plantation, and has since been engaged in planting, and is now the owner of about one thousand three hundred acres, of which five hundred are under cultivation. His principal crop is cotton, but he also gives considerable attention to other southern products, and is a thoroughgoing and practical planter. He was married in 1878 to Miss Louise S. Barry, a daughter of W. A. Barry. To them two sons and two daughters have been born: Annie L. (deceased), Pauline (deceased), Harry and Ernest. Mr. and Mrs. Buford are members of the Presbyterian church, and doubtless no man in Lafayette county is more universally respected than he. To know him is to have a high admiration for him, for he is possessed of those sterling characteristics which make a true man, and being genial and hospitable in his intercourse with those around him, he has a host of warm friends.

J. C. Bull, Benton, Miss., was born in Jasper county, Ga., January 16, 1811, and is a son of James H. and Lovey (Campbell) Bull. The parents were born, reared and married in North Carolina, and removed from that state to Georgia; thence they came to Mississippi, and settled in Lawrence county in 1817. They resided there fourteen years, during which time the father was magistrate; he also represented Lawrence county in the legislature of Mississippi. The family removed to Yazoo county in 1834, and settled on a plantation which J. C. Bull had been cultivating for one year. The father died in 1840 at the age of sixty years; the mother survived him ten years. They reared a family of six children, all of whom grew to maturity and married. The subject of this sketch is the only one living. He spent his school days in Lawrence county, and was married there at the age of twenty-two years to Miss Lydia King, a daughter of David King. He then came to this county and began to open up his plantation; at that time it comprised two thousand acres, and at the beginning of the Civil war he owned three thousand acres. Mr. Bull has two children who were born of his first marriage: David King and James H., both farmers in Yazoo county. To them he has given a generous portion of his land. The mother of these children died in 1850, and Mr. Bull was married, in 1859, to Mrs. Mercy Ogden, who died in 1861. Mr. Bull has been a member of the Baptist church for fifty years, and has faithfully discharged his duties. As a citizen he has been enterprising and progressive, and although he was at one time possessed of a considerable amount of property, it has been consumed in the payment of security debts. He is a man having a keen sense of justice, and is highly respected by the entire community.

Mrs. Mary E. Bullen is a most estimable, intelligent and charitable lady residing in Jefferson county, Miss., and here, where the progressive, industrious and successful planter is the rule and not the exception, Mrs. Bullen ranks among the foremost in this calling, for she is shrewd, far-seeing, and an excellent manager, and every part of her plantation, which comprises about one thousand two hundred acres, is properly attended to. This land is situated about eight miles west of Fayette, and from it Mrs. Bullen derives a paying annual income. She is the daughter of Abraham Mayberry, a native of Virginia, who was born May 25, 1790, and in early life removed to Tennessee, from which state he came to Jefferson county, Miss., his marriage occurring here in the month of May, 1825, to Miss Lucretia Boles, a daughter of James and Elizabeth (Scott) Boles. To Mr. Boles and his wife two sons and three daughters were born, Lucretia's birth occurring on the 19th of May, 1802. Abraham Mayberry was an extensive planter in the early days of Jefferson county, and upon his death April 9, 1836, left his wife and five children well provided for. His daughter, Mary E., was married to Benjamin A. Bullen on the 5th of May, 1842, the birth of the latter having taken place on the 27th of February, 1821. He is a son of Samuel Dudley and Lydia M. (Marble) Bullen, the former a native of Vermont, born September 8, 1788, near Bellows Falls, in Windham county, on the Connecticut river. He was the youngest of nine children, and the son of Rev. Joseph Bullen, who came to Mississippi as a missionary to the Chickasaw Indians in the year 1799. His son, Samuel Dudley, father of Benjamin A., came to this county in 1800. Samuel Dudley Bullen was a great temperance worker and was an excellent Bible student. While serving in the war of 1812, at the battle of New Orleans he held the rank of captain. He was the father of eleven children. His wife, Lydia (Marble) Bullen, was born in Jefferson county, Miss., May 5, 1800. Mrs. Bullen, the immediate subject of this sketch, became the mother of four children, three daughters, of whom two are living at the present time, the only son dying in infancy. All are members of the Methodist Episcopal church of Greenville, in which Mr. Bullen was class leader for a number of years. He was a man of most exemplary habits, was kind and faithful to his family, was an excellent neighbor and friend, was law-abiding, and was progressive and enterprising in all his views. He was one of the charter members of the A. F. & A. M., and for many years acted as its secretary. Mrs. Bullen is a lady in every sense of the term, and is one whose refined presence

29

and noble qualities of mind and heart have endeared her to a large circle of friends. She has reared her daughters to honorable womanhood, and can look back with pride at her success.

The Hon. Docton Bunch, Benton, Miss., was born in Bertie county, N. C., in 1825, and is the seventh of a family of eleven children. His parents, Elijah and Elizabeth (Brown) Bunch, were also natives of North Carolina, where they spent their entire lives. The father died in 1855, and the mother in 1842. All but one of the children grew to maturity, and four are still living. Mr. Bunch spent his boyhood and youth in his native state, but at the age of twenty-one he came to Mississippi, leaving home and friends to go out into the world and seek his fortune, and it has not been a fruitless quest, as his efforts have been crowned with success and he is now one of the well-to-do men of Yazoo county. When he first came to the county of Yazoo he was employed as overseer by Col. John M. Sharp. He enlisted in the Confederate cause, and for one year was in the state service; he was then detailed for salt-making in Clarke and Baldwin counties, Ala. After the surrender he returned to the Sharp farm, and finally rented it until 1872 or 1873. He then invested his means in land, purchasing nine hundred and thirty-four acres in one tract. As his means have increased he has made additional purchases of real estate, until he now owns four thousand five hundred acres. For the past ten years he has been an important member of the commercial circles of Yazoo county, owning a store in Benton in which he carries a stock of goods valued at $6,000; he handles from seven hundred to nine hundred bales of cotton annually, and does a thriving business. He has been a conspicuous figure in the political history of the county; in 1878, he was a member of the state legislature, and in 1890 he was a member of the constitutional convention; for a number of years he was a member of the board of supervisors of the county, and in all these varied capacities he discharged his duties with a zeal and fidelity that won for him the gratitude of his constituency. Mr. Bunch was united in marriage in 1848 to Miss Marthenia McNeal. There were born of this union three children, who are still living: W. J., D. S., and Maggie, the wife of C. C. Pepper, deceased. Mrs. Bunch died in 1866. Mr. Bunch was married a second time in 1867, to Miss Addie Owen; four children were born of this marriage: Callie A., wife of W. W. Wilburn, of Holmes county; John H., a student at Oxford university; Rebecca and Mollie, students at Brookhaven. Mr. Bunch is a member of the P. B. Tutt lodge No. 17, A. F. & A. M.; he has been master of this lodge, and is the present treasurer. He and his wife are both members of the Methodist Episcopal church, of which he is steward.

Though past the allotted age of man, three-score years and ten, Mr. Nathan Bunckley is still acknowledged to be a leader in the affairs of Franklin county, and as he has resided here from his birth, which occurred in 1817, he has taken a deep interest in her progress and welfare. The property on which he is now residing has been in possession of the family since about the year 1807, at which time the paternal grandparents, although natives of Georgia, came thither from the state of Tennessee. This land the grandfather, John Bunckley, improved in an admirable manner, but died before Nathan had any recollection of him. He was of Irish descent. His wife was a Miss Tinsley, and also died in this state and county. Ransom Bunckley was reared principally in the wilds of Franklin county, receiving a backwoods education. He was married here and remained on the old home farm until 1856, when he removed to Morehouse parish, La., where he became the owner of a large plantation, on which he breathed his last in 1872, leaving a fine property to be divided among his descendants. During the war of 1812 he volunteered his services, but was not mustered into the service. He was a member of the board of supervisors of Franklin county in an early day, and was a member of the A. F. & A. M., being a member of Ben Franklin lodge No. 11, at old Franklin, and the Royal Arch degree, at Natchez. He was married three times, his second wife being Mrs. Mary Ann Pendergrass, who was a native of Mississippi and died in 1853. His last wife was Minerva Richmond, who is still living. His first union was to Miss Catherine Pickett, a native of South Carolina, whose mother died when she was young, her father afterward marrying again. He died while emigrating to Mississippi, and his daughter Catherine was reared by an uncle, Nathan King, in Franklin county. She bore Mr. Bunckley five children—four sons and one daughter: Nathan, Ransom (deceased), Susan, wife of F. P. Jones, of Jackson parish, La.; Marion, who died when young, and Douglas, who died about 1861. The father of these children is supposed to have been born in Georgia in 1796 or 1797, but was reared in Franklin county. Nathan Bunckley was educated in the country schools near his home, but was afterward given the advantages of St. Mary's college, near Lebanon, Ky., the year of 1838 being spent in that institution. In 1840 he was married to Elizabeth Ann, daughter of Henry and Sarah Richardson, Mr. Richardson's death occurring in Pike county when Mrs. Bunckley was a young girl. He was a merchant, and was in all probability a native of New York. His wife died at the home of Mr. Bunckley in 1841, having been born in South Carolina. She came to Mississippi with her parents. Mrs. Bunckley was born in Amite county and died in 1865, leaving five children: William, a planter of Louisiana; Stephen, a planter of Amite county; Albert, at home; Cynthia, wife of R. F. Butler, and a little daughter that died in infancy. Mr. Bunckley has spent all his life on the place on which he is now residing, which consists of three thousand five hundred acres. Besides this he has nine hundred acres in different tracts in Amite county and Louisiana, and the yield from the cultivated portion of this land is from one hundred to two hundred bales of cotton each year. He was a member of the board of supervisors for some years and for a considerable time was a member of the school board after the war. He was a stanch Union man during the Rebellion and put forth every effort in opposition to secession, and throughout that long and bloody struggle never wavered in his allegiance to the stars and stripes. He was so universally esteemed and highly respected that he was molested but little by the Confederates during the war, although his sentiments were well known. He is a member of Ben Franklin lodge No. 11, at Meadville (A. F. & A. M.), and is a member of Natchez chapter. Some years before the war the postoffice of Bunckley was established at his house and there has since remained, he being its efficient and trustworthy postmaster. His father acquired a large property but lost $23,000 by a New Orleans firm, soon after the war, speculating too heavily in cotton.

George C. Buntin was a well-known planter in Tallahatchie county. He was born in Halifax county, Va., in 1824. His parents were William amd Frances (Cardwell) Buntin, of Halifax county, where his father was born in 1783 and his mother in 1792, and where they lived until 1833, when they came with other families to Mississippi, and settled near the present site of Coffeeville. There Mr. Buntin improved a good farm, upon which he lived until his death in 1855. His wife, who was a member of the Cumberland Presbyterian church, died in 1860. Mr. Buntin was known as an honest, industrious citizen, and came to be a well-to-do planter. William Cardwell, the father of Frances Cardwell, a Virginian, came with Mr. Buntin to Mississippi, where he died in 1836, and was buried at Coffeeville. He was born in 1765, and married in Virginia, his wife dying previous to his removal to Mississippi. George C. Buntin is the fifth of nine children who were born to his parents, and the only one of the number now living. Christopher died and was buried in Tallahatchie county in June, 1881; William died in Coffeeville in 1843 in his twenty-fourth year; Alexander died and was buried in Tallahatchie county in 1879; Elizabeth became the wife of

Robert F. Hubert, and died and was buried at Coffeeville in 1876; John died in Virginia at the age of two years; Robson died at the age of nine years, in 1840; Harriet became the wife of D. M. Rayburn, died in January, 1841, and was buried at Coffeeville. George C. passed his boyhood on a farm, and at home and in the public schools at Coffeeville acquired a fair English education. He was married in 1847, in the house in which he now lives, to Sarah E., daughter of Col. Robert and Anna H. Robson. The father was born in Charlotte, Va., in 1804, the mother in Union district in South Carolina in 1808. Mr. and Mrs. Robson were married in Hardeman county, Tenn., and came to Mississippi in 1833, and there spent the balance of their lives. Mr. Robson offered his services to the Confederate government at the time of the war, became captain of a company, and died at Murfreesboro. His wife died in 1864. She was a worthy wife and mother, and a consistent Christian woman, and for many years previous to her death was a member of the Cumberland Presbyterian church. Mr. and Mrs. Robson were among the original settlers of Tallahatchie county, and deserving of a place in the pioneer history of this section. The former became a merchant and planter, and had business relations with the leading people throughout this part of the state. Early in his life he was in a militia company in Tennessee, of which state Mrs. Robson was a native. They had eight children, four of whom died in infancy. Mary Ellen became the wife of W. O. Mabry, a farmer, and has four sons; Anna E. is the widow of Robert J. Gunthrie; Rev. William H. Robson, D. D., of the Cumberland Presbyterian church, now located at Macon, was a graduate of the State university at Oxford, and is a theological graduate of Princeton college, Princeton, N. J. He is one of the best scholars in the South, and was ordained a minister in 1882. Robert R., who will probably be elected in the fall of 1891 to represent the county in the legislature, is also well educated, having graduated from the university at Oxford. He practiced law for some years with considerable success, and is said to be an able orator. He is a member, and has been for several years ruling elder in the Cumberland Presbyterian church, but is now managing the home plantation, and devoting much attention to the breeding of fine saddle horses. Mr. Buntin's daughters were graduated from Union female college, Oxford. Mr. Buntin lived in Yalobusha county until 1860, in which year he removed to his present farm, where he has since resided, with the exception of the period of 1872 to 1875 inclusive, when he was a resident of Coffeeville. He owns thirteen hundred acres of land, and is regarded as one of the most thorough farmers in this section of the county. He and his wife are members of the Cumberland Presbyterian church, with which he has been connected for nearly fifty years, and of which he has been ruling elder thirty-four years. Mr. Buntin has been severely handicapped through life by delicate health, which interfered materially not only with his schooling during his youth, but with his subsequent business career. A few years after the settlement of the family in Mississippi, his health became so poor that he concluded to try some of the health resorts of Tennessee. He made the journey on horseback, and after staying several months at different springs in that state without satisfactory results, he went to Virginia, where he so fully recovered his health that he returned to his home in such fine physical condition that his mother did not recognize him. His chief aim has been to properly educate his children. Owing to the lack of public schools of merit, with the aid of a neighbor, Mrs. Sherman, he built for them a school on his farm, and employed teachers to instruct them, and afterward, as has been stated, gave them good academic and collegiate educations. Prof. Robert Guthrie, whom Mr. Buntin's daughter Anna E. married in 1873, at that time filled the chair of mathematics in the university at Oxford. He was later elected president of Union female college, Oxford, which position he held two years. Afterward he practiced law successfully for a time. He died of consumption, in southwestern Texas, in December, 1882.

At an early day the Burch family, now so well known, sought a home for themselves in the (then) wilds of Mississippi, Buckner Burch moving with his wife and children from Virginia to this region and settling on Coles creek in Jefferson county about the year 1776. The country was in its primeval condition at that time, but with the fortitude and determination characteristic of the early pioneer, Mr. Burch made his family as comfortable as the rude facilities of that day afforded, and immediately began felling the sturdy oak and otherwise clearing his land, preparatory to raising the products of the South. He did not live to see the fulfillment of his desires, for in the prime of life he was foully murdered by a negro, who was afterward hung for his crime at Pensacola by Spanish authority. Washington Burch, son of Buckner, was born among the Alleghany mountains while his parents were en route to Mississippi, and in this state he attained manhood. Although the schools of that day were very primitive, he, by self-application, became well informed, and as he was of a mechanical turn of mind he devoted his attention to this work and is said to have built the first cotton gin to run by waterpower in this part of the state, it being erected on one of the tributaries of Cole's creek. Washington S. Burch, son of Washington Burch, and father of the subject of this sketch, was born and reared in this county and was here united in the bonds of matrimony to Miss Adaline Dunbar, whose father was Col. Isaac Dunbar, who served under General Jackson in the war of 1812, being wounded at the battle of New Orleans. Washington S. Burch, after living a well-spent life, was called from the scene of his earthly labors about the year 1843. His widow afterward married H. W. Dangerfield, and until her death, which occurred in 1864, was a resident of Fayette. Out of a family of thirteen children that were born to Mr. and Mrs. Burch, only three grew to mature years: Nannie B., the deceased wife of R. W. Campbell, of Fayette, her death occurring in 1858; Eliza, who was married twice, her first husband being James Miller and her last James B. Wigginton, of Ocean Springs, Miss.; and Isaac W. Burch, our immediate subject, who was born in this county on July 4, 1834. On November 19, 1850, at the age of sixteen years, he was married to Miss Lizzie B., daughter of David McCaleb, one of the pioneers of Mississippi. Mrs. Burch was born and reared in this county and after her marriage located with her husband on the farm near Fayette, there remaining two years. In 1854 Mr. Burch removed to Claiborne county, but in the month of December, 1856, returned to Jefferson county and has since been a resident of the plantation on which he is now residing. This place has been in possession of some member of the Burch family, by gift or purchase, since 1794, it being a part of an extensive Spanish grant. Mr. Burch is the owner of about six hundred acres of valuable land, and on this property is a fine bed or quarry of kaolin, which is supposed to be the finest in the state. Mr. Burch has some samples of building rock and some pressed brick manufactured from this quarry, both of which are said to be equal to anything of the kind in Mississippi. He contemplates building a factory and engaging in the manufacture of pressed brick and building rock, but at the present time is, in connection with farming operations, devoting considerable attention to merchandising, a calling he has followed since 1886. He has been postmaster of Stonington since 1883, and in the discharge of his official duties, as well as a merchant and planter, is intelligent and faithful. He and his wife have no children of their own but have an adopted daughter, who is the widow of William Whitney. She has one child, Earl Frost Whitney, whom Mr. and Mrs. Burch have also adopted and are rearing.

William M. Burdett, a well-known and highly-respected citizen of Washington county, Miss., was born in Greenville, Miss., in 1867, being the third of five children born to Richard M., and Minerva (Heard) Burdett, the former of whom was born in Virginia, and while a young man came to Mississippi, locating at Natchez. Here he remained for a while, but afterward took up his abode in Greenville, where he engaged in planting and merchandising at Deer creek, continuing until his death, which occurred in 1884. He enlisted in the Confederate army at the opening of the Rebellion, under Colonel Blackburn, and served in his cavalry company until the war closed, making a brave and faithful soldier. His wife was born in Mississippi, and was a daughter of N. A. Heard, a native and planter of Georgia. William M. Burdett was reared in the state of Mississippi, and in his early youth was given the advantages of the schools of Jackson, and is now a well informed young man. In 1889, with hopefulness and pluck, he set energetically to work to make his own way in the world, and his independent career was commenced as a planter and merchant at Burdett station on the Louisville New Orleans & Texas railroad. He owns a third interest in sixteen hundred and thirty acres of land, one thousand being under cultivation, the most of which he himself cleared. The mercantile firm of which he is a member, and in which he owns a one-third interest, has a stock valued at $3,500, and he and his partners own the house in which they do business. He has put about $15,000 worth of improvements on his plantation, and for so young a man is exceedingly well to do, and has a bright future before him; for he possesses excellent business qualifications and has sufficient energy to carry out his views. He, his mother and his brother-in-law, J. B. Hebron, own large planting interests, their property being very valuable.

For many years Gen. Henry L. Burkitt has enjoyed the reputation of being a practical and successful man, not only as a substantial and progressive planter, but as one intelligent and thoroughly posted on all public matters. He was elected, and served four years in the senate of Mississippi, from 1883 to 1887. He was born in Halifax county, N. C., October 28, 1818, but the year following his parents removed to Giles county, Tenn., where he was reared and where he lived until 1836. His parents then removed to Lawrence county, Tenn., where they are buried and where he resided for about seventeen years. While in that state, in 1839, he was elected major of the Lawrenceburg militia, and was promoted in 1852, when he was elected and commissioned by the governor of Tennessee to the position of brigadier-general. This position he held eight years, commanding the militia of the counties of Lawrence, Wayne, Hardin and Hickman. While in that state he practiced law fifteen or twenty years, and was quite an extensive contributor to the newspapers and journals of the day, and his articles, which were on popular subjects, met with the approval of critics as well as the public generally. In 1850 he published a second edition of the Kehokee Baptist association which had been originally published by his grandfather, Lemuel Burkitt, and Jesse Read, in 1803, and sold several thousand copies in the United States. In 1882 he published a popular work entitled "Burkitt's Maxims and Guide to Youth." In 1885 he published a small work against prohibition, which circulated very extensively. In 1889 he published a second edition of his Maxims much improved. In 1854 General Burkitt removed to Waynesboro, Tenn., but in 1864, while he was in the Confederate army, his family were refugees from the battlefields to North Alabama, and remained near Mount Hope until the close of the war. Then he removed his family to Palo Alto, Miss., near which place he has since mainly devoted his time and attention to planting and with the best results. During the war he spent one year in the Confederate army, serving as clerk of the Ninth Tennessee cavalry. He is in the accepted sense of the word a self-made man, having quarried his success from the gloomiest realities of life. He obtained his education through his own efforts after he was grown. In his energy, industry and economy he sets an example worthy of imitation by humble youth. It has been said of him by a man of note that he was a man who was never still. By the aid of his good wife he obtained a comfortable estate before the war, but lost it in that terrible struggle. The property he now owns, amounting to a competency, has been obtained since the war through his own indomitable perseverance and continuous efforts and those of an industrious and economical wife. May 23, 1841, he married Miss Louisa Howell, of Alabama, and by her became the father of five children: Hon. Frank Burkitt, of Okolona, Miss.; Burges L., deceased; James, of Amory, Miss.; Mary E., deceased wife of T. J. Fisher, of Tennessee, and Exile, of Jackson, Tenn. The mother of these children (a model housewife) died September 29, 1889, and September 2, 1890, Mr. Burkitt married her sister, who was then a widow, Mrs. M. J. Walker, of Corinth, Miss. General Burkitt became a member of the Masonic fraternity at Waynesboro, Tenn., and was a member of the lodge at Palo Alto until its charter was surrendered to the grand lodge, since which time he has not connected himself with any lodge. General Burkitt claims that he is a descendant from William Burkitt, a distinguished divine and writer of England, who was born in 1650 and died in 1703, the author of Burkitt's notes on the New Testament, an able and popular work; but he has no certain evidence of his ancestry beyond Thomas and Mary Burkitt, who settled near Edenton, N. C., in the early part of the eighteenth century. They were from England and were the parents of Lemuel Burkitt, who was born in that state in 1750 and was a resident of Northampton county. He was married to Miss Hannah Bell, of Virginia, and died about 1807 at his home in North Carolina. He was a distinguished preacher of the Baptist faith, and was a man of noble impulses. He and his wife became the parents of five sons and three daughters: Thomas and Henry died when young; Lemuel, Jr., was a resident of North Carolina, where he died after raising a family; William reared a family in Tennessee, but afterward removed to Illinois, where he died, and Burges, the youngest son, was the father of Gen. Henry L. Burkitt, the subject of this sketch. In the month of August, 1814, Burges Burkitt married Miss Mary Hardin, of North Carolina. They were born in that state March 28, 1791, and March 4, 1788, respectively. Burges Burkitt was a carriagemaker by trade, at which he served an apprenticeship in Virginia, but the greater part of his life was spent on the farm. He moved to Giles county, Tenn., in 1819, but prior to this had been a soldier in the war of 1812, being a sergeant in his company, which was stationed at Norfolk. He was a minister of the Baptist church, and died in Tennessee February 15, 1844, his widow surviving him until March 4, 1862, when she, too, passed from life at the age of seventy-four years. He and his wife became the parents of six children: Lucy C., wife of Thomas A. Richardson, of Lawrenceburg, Tenn.; Henry L.; James B.; Mary H., a widow now residing in Texas; Joseph B., a soldier in the Mexican war, who died at Monterey, September 22, 1846, from a wound received by a cannon shot the previous day, and John B., a resident near Palo Alto, Miss. General Burkitt claims to have been a practical man and a success in life. He often expresses his gratitude to a liberal public who reached out a helping hand to him in the hour of need. Providence has smiled upon his labors, showered blessings upon his pathway, and crowned his industry with success. While a member of the state senate of Mississippi he received many compliments from editors and reporters. We give the following from the *State Ledger* as a sample: "Gen. Burkitt does not speak often in the senate, but when he does speak he has always something sensible to say."

N. E. Burnham is a native of Camden county, N. C., and was born March 16, 1835. His father was born in the same place in 1810, and his mother April 15, 1815. They were married in 1831, Mrs. Burnham having been a Miss Martha Spence. Mr. Burnham was a successful planter in North Carolina, but removed to Scott county, Miss., in 1837. Both he and his wife were members of the Methodist Episcopal church, and he was a liberal contributor, not only to churches of his own denomination, but to all those that had worthy objects to present for support. He died in 1883, his wife having preceded him in 1880. Our subject was the second oldest of thirteen children born to his parents. He came to Mississippi with them, and, after receiving such an education as was obtainable in the common schools, began active business life for himself, in 1868, as a planter, and has continued successfully in it ever since. Previous to 1868, however, in May, 1861, he enlisted in the Tenth Mississippi regiment, commanded by Col. W. T. Burt. Among other engagements, he took part in the first battle of Bull Run, in the fight at Leesburg, seven days' battle of the Wilderness, Cold Harbor, Malvern Hill, Chambersburg, Chancellorsville, Spottsylvania courthouse, Fredericksburg and Petersburg, returning home in April, 1865. He is the owner of seven hundred and sixty acres of land, about three hundred acres of which are improved. He has also been in the general merchandise business in Fannin, Forest and Brandon, and is interested at the present time in a store in Harperville, Miss. In 1884–5 Mr. Burnham was a member of the board of supervisors of Scott county. He and wife are members of the Baptist church, and he is connected with the Masonic lodge, No. 217, at Harpersville, Miss. Mr. Burnham married Miss Sarah McCabe, a daughter of J. W. McCabe, a well-known planter and mill owner of this state. They have had twelve children, and ten of them are living: Millie Belle, Charles E., Florence J. (deceased), Hattie May, Henry M., Blanch L., George H., Kirk W., Katie, Sallie (deceased), N. Edgar and John Raymond. Millie Belle and Charles E. are graduates of Huddleston college, at Harpersville, Miss., of the class of 1890. None of this large family are married.

Patrick Burns is one of the prosperous general merchants of Natchez, Miss., and by his superior management and rare business ability and efficiency has done not a little to advance the reputation the town enjoys as a commercial center. He was born in the Emerald Isle in 1836, a son of James Burns. At the age of twenty-one years he determined to seek his fortune in America, and in 1857 landed in New Orleans, soon after which he came to Natchez. He immediately identified himself with the interests of this section, and upon the opening of the war in 1861, he enlisted in company B, of a Louisiana regiment, and was in the battles of Grand Gulf and Port Hudson. At the fall of the latter place he was captured, and kept a prisoner on Johnson's Island and other places for twenty-two months, and was paroled at Richmond shortly before the surrender, and at the time of the general surrender was in a hospital at Macon, Ga. He entered the army as a sergeant, and at the time of his capture wore the epaulets of a lieutenant. After the war was over he returned to Natchez, and engaged in hard labor, for he was utterly without means, but his many sterling qualities and honesty soon became well known, and in 1873 he borrowed sufficient money to start a bakery on a small scale. He was very successful in this enterprise, soon extended his business, and shortly after bought out a store on Commerce street. Three years later he established himself at his present stand, in the angle of Pine and St. Catherine streets, where he put in a full and choice stock of general merchandise, which is now valued at about $10,000, his annual sales being very large. He started a shoe trade on three dozen shoes, but now has the largest stock of boots and shoes in the city of Natchez. His store is commodious, and as he has at all times dealt very fairly with his patrons, his trade is very large. He has a fine cotton storehouse and two warehouses, for he is very extensively engaged in speculating in cotton. He has shown himself to be an excellent financier, for he commenced with absolutely no capital, and by his own push, enterprise and perseverance, has become wealthy. Besides the above-mentioned property, he is the owner of a good plantation in the country and other valuable town property. By his honorable conduct through life he has won many friends, who respect and esteem him for the many worthy traits of character he has shown. The family are members of the Catholic church.

J. H. Burrow, Saltillo, Lee county, Miss., who has been identified with the mercantile interests of Lee county since 1867, is the subject of the following biography. He was born in Lauderdale county, Ala., in 1838, and is a son of William and Susan (York) Burrow, natives of Alabama. William Burrow is a son of Durab Burrow, who in early life removed to Alabama from Virginia. His wife was Rebecca Burrow, and they had three sons and three daughters. William was the youngest son, and was reared in Alabama. In 1845 he removed to Mississippi, and settled two miles below Richmond in Itawanba county. There he followed agricultural pursuits for a time, and then went to Richmond, where he embarked in the mercantile trade. For some years he carried on the business successfully, and removed thence to Mooreville, Lee county, where he was engaged in the same business until his death, which occurred in 1863, in his fifty-fifth year. He was a member of the Masonic order, and politically was a stanch whig. His wife died at Mooreville in 1857, at the age of forty-five years. She was a worthy member of the Cumberland Presbyterian church. They had nine children born to them, five of whom are now living: Joseph B., James, Mrs. Montgomery, Mrs. Ackers, and J. H., the subject of this notice. J. H. was the second child and grew to manhood in Mississippi. He had very meager educational advantages, and at the age of eighteen years he started out in life for himself. He embarked in the mercantile trade at Mooreville, which he carried on until the breaking out of the Civil war. He then abandoned private interests, and enlisted in Company H, Forty-third Mississippi regiment, and participated in many of the most noted engagements of the conflict. He was paroled at Verona, Miss., in 1865, after which he came back to Mooreville, and resumed his place in the commerce of the town. At the end of two years he came to Saltillo, and has since conducted a thriving business. He was married to Miss Evelyn Mitchener, a daughter of M. B. Mitchener, an early settler in the county, now deceased. Mr. and Mrs. Burrow are the parents of five children: Nora, wife of C. B. Davis; Sadie, wife of J. R. Dabb; Barlow, Charlie, a daughter, and Tabbs. Mr. Burrow is a member of the I. O. O. F., of the Masonic order, and of the Knights of Honor. Politically he adheres to the principles of the democratic party, but takes no special interest in that body further than exercising his right of suffrage.

John C. Burrus (deceased), who was an esteemed and highly respected citizen of Bolivar county for many years, was born in Limestone, Ala., in 1814, and was the son of Charles Burrus, a native of Virginia. The elder Burrus came to Alabama at a very early day, and became an extensive planter and merchant. He was very successful and remained in that state until his death in 1820. Carolus Burrus, the father of Charles Burrus, was an officer in the American army in the Revolutionary war. The family is of English origin. On the maternal side the Colemans were a distinguished literary family. John C. Burrus was educated in the University of Virginia as B. A., studied law, and was admitted to the bar at Huntsville, Ala. His guardian had brought his property to Mississippi, and as soon as Mr. Burrus was educated he also came to Mississippi to attend to his interests. In 1836 he first rented a place in the northern part of Bolivar county, and the next year bought a large tract of land on the river, now Neblet's landing, where he cleared about four hundred acres. There he resided until 1847. In 1839 he married Miss Louisa McGehee, a native of Wilkinson county, Miss., and the daughter of Archie McGehee, who was born in Georgia, and who was a pioneer settler of Wilkinson county. Mr. McGehee was a soldier in the war of 1812, and moved to Madison county, Miss., before it was organized, thus being a pioneer of both counties. He died in Hinds county of that state in 1850, after having lived for some time in Huntsville, Ala., to educate his children. In 1848 Mr. Burrus located at Riverton, and in 1850 settled permanently at Egypt ridge, where he secured fourteen hundred acres, seven hundred acres of which he soon had under cultivation. In 1860 he erected his fine mansion, now occupied by his widow and children, and there his death occurred in 1879. He took a deep interest in all things for the welfare of this county, and especially in educational matters was he interested. He held the office of probate judge for some time, and was a fluent speaker and a deep reasoner, his thoughts being always expressed with force and logic. He was a member of the Methodist Episcopal church, and was noted far and wide as a most liberal, kind-hearted man. He was quite a sportsman and was very fond of hunting, etc. In personal appearance he was about five feet ten inches in hight, slender, but strong and with a fair complexion. His marriage resulted in the birth of eleven children: Charles, died in 1881; Elizabeth, died in 1865; John, was married in 1870 to Miss Barritt, of Kentucky, who died in 1885, leaving two daughters; Margaret L. is unmarried; Archie Clement served sixteen months in the Confederate army, enlisting but when sixteen years of age and serving in Ross' Texas brigade, on detached service as scout. He was captured in Bolivar county in 1865; was sent to Alton prison, where he remained three months, and was paroled just at the close of the war. He attended college for one year at Nashville, but is otherwise self-educated. He studied law with his father, but never practiced. He is at present a member of the board of supervisors of the fourth district. He is vice president of the Farmers' Alliance of Bolivar county, and a member of the democratic executive committee, and was tendered the endorsement of the alliance for state senator from that county, which he refused. He resides with his mother and unmarried sister on the old homestead, Hollywood, which was cleared and settled by his father. He is an energetic, active and progressive citizen. The other children are Florence, Kate, and Ethel (who became the wife of Dr. Sutherland), and Percy (who married Miss Wade, of Mississippi, who died in 1879, leaving one little girl). This gentleman is an energetic farmer and a man whose sterling qualities make him respected by all. Mrs. Burrus, after a long life in Bolivar county, is now perhaps the second oldest living resident of that county. She has seen many changes and recalls incidents of the past in a very pleasing and interesting manner. She possesses a clear, bright intellect, and is one whose womanly graces and virtues are well known. The years seem to sit lightly on her pleasant brow, and but few traces of silver are seen amid the black hair combed smoothly from her forehead. The family own one thousand acres of good tillable land, and have six hundred acres under cultivation. This old homestead, Hollywood, was named by Mr. Burrus, Sr., and is a very fine old place.

I. H. Burt, retired, Alesville, Miss. The parents of Mr. Burt were among the first who settled in Lafayette, Miss., having located here as early as 1836, and at a time when it was inhabited by the Indians. The father, Hardy Burt, was born near Raleigh, N. C., about 1784, and was a planter by occupation. After his marriage to Miss Martha Lane, he located near Decatur, Ala., and there resided until 1836, his children all having been born there. At that date, learning that northern Mississippi had been opened for settlement by the whites, he emigrated to that state and located in Lafayette county, where he passed the closing scenes of his life. His father, John Burt, was also a native of North Carolina, and was a Revolutionary soldier. The mother of I. H. Burt was the daughter of Joseph Lane, who served with distinction in the Revolutionary war. I. H. Burt was born near Decatur, Ala., on the 21st of June, 1822, and was married in 1845 to Miss Sarah M. Caruthers, daughter of Samuel Caruthers, who was also among the pioneer settlers of Lafayette county, locating a few miles west of Oxford, where he passed his last days. He was an extensive planter, and successful in farming. To Mr. and Mrs. Burt were born six children, three of whom are still living: One son is in Bowie, Tex., and the two daughters reside near where they were born and reared. Mr. Burt is gifted with that social disposition, with that happy frame of mind, which always looks on the bright side of life. Among his neighbors he is recognized as a man of unimpeachable character, and one who has the good will of all who know him. In his religious preferences he is attached to the Baptist denomination, having been identified with that church since 1848, at which time his wife also professed her faith. Shunning politics and desiring no office, Mr. Burt devoted himself to farming, in which he was eminently successful. After the death of his wife, which occurred in August, 1887, he resided on the old homestead until recently, since which time he has made his home with his daughter, Mrs. S. R. Whitton. Before the war Mr. Burt had amassed a considerable amount of property in slaves, and although he lost heavily during that stirring period, he has since retrieved an independence.

William H. Busby was born in Pike county, Miss., October 1, 1861. He is the eldest of seven children born to his parents, Ezekiel and Clarinda (Hodges) Busby, who are both natives of Mississippi. The father is a planter of Pike county and has lived there all his life. His paternal grandparents bore the names of Ezekiel and Sallie Busby; his maternal grandparents were Edmund and Martha Hodges, who were natives of South Carolina. The subject of this sketch was brought up on his father's plantation and was educated in the public schools of the place, receiving private tutoring as well, and a commercial course. Since attaining his majority he has followed the life of a planter, owning four hundred acres of land, of which he has improved and has under cultivation about seventy acres. In the year 1885 he was married to Miss Florence O. Huffman, a daughter of George W. Huffman, a native of Mississippi, of which state Miss Huffman also claimed nativity. To Mr. and Mrs. Busby have been born three children, named: Fred G., Maggie V., and Lee H. Both Mr. and Mrs. Busby are members of the Missionary Baptist church. Mr. Busby began life for himself at the age of twenty-one with no capital except his earnestness of purpose and a determination to succeed, aided by his industrious habits and ability, and that he has succeeded in his aim the thriving state of his plantation suffices to prove. It would be well for the county to possess many more as thrifty, energetic and determined young men as Mr. Busby, who can proudly claim that his possessions are entirely the result of his own efforts. He is a man deserving of success and the respect in which he is held by all who know him, as he is also a man liberal in his gifts to all laudable enterprises, according to his means.

Henry Anderson Busick is a member of the well-known mercantile firm of Busick & Stevens, of Brandon, Miss. He was born in Alamance county, N. C., in 1837, a son of G. L. Busick, a prosperous planter of that state and county. After attending the common schools of his locality, he attended the preparatory schools at Monticello, Barnesville and Hillsboro, receiving a good practical education. In 1861 he removed to Jackson, Miss., where he followed the calling of a clerk until 1864, when he left Mississippi to take up his abode in the Lone Star state. In partnership with Major Stevens, of Huntsville, Ala., he, in 1865, opened a general dry goods establishment in Port Sullivan, Tex., later removed to Evergreen, and in 1867 closed out the business and returned to Jackson, where for a year he was in the employ of Robinson & Stevens. For a year following this he was engaged in business in Brandon, then began merchandising at Morton, as a member of the firm of H. A. Busick & Co., remaining thus engaged for four years. In 1874 he returned to Brandon, and in partnership with his brother, D. W., and Mr. Stevens, a brother of Major Stevens, once more opened an establishment here, the style of the firm being Busick, Stevens & Co., and then Stevens & Busick. The business of which they are now the proprietors was established in 1844 by William Richardson & Co., but the style of the firm was changed as follows: Richardson, Lowry & Co., in 1854; Robinson, Reynolds & Co., in 1855; Robinson, Stevens & Co., in 1861; Stevens, Willis & Co., in 1866; Stevens, Busick & Co., in 1867; Busick, Stevens & Co., in 1874, and in 1885 the present firm of Busick & Stevens was organized. During the war, the large frame building then occupied was destroyed by fire, though the books were saved. The present firm occupy a large building, one hundred and sixty feet deep, three stories high in the rear and two in front, with commodious warehouses, etc., attached. It is perhaps safe to state that since the organization of the present firm the annual business transacted has reached the sum of $100,000. No firm connected with the business has ever failed or suspended, so far as known, or called for an extension of paper. Messrs. Busick & Stevens are business men of rare ability and strict integrity, and are practical, experienced and energetic. Besides their admirably conducted mercantile business at Brandon, they are largely interested in the Jackson Fertilizer company, of Jackson, Miss., of which Mr. Busick is a director, and the Jackson Grocery company. They also hold stock on the First National bank of Jackson. Mr. Busick is an extensive landholder in Rankin county, and is also the owner of considerable property in Reidsville, N. C., valued at about $10,000, and in a valuable zinc mine of Missouri. He feels a just pride in his business career, for the property of which he is now the owner has been accumulated through his own efforts, and he has the satisfaction of knowing that he has never claimed a penny that was not justly his. On coming to this state, he was compelled to borrow $100, with which to make the journey, but owing to the economy which he was never ashamed to practice, and to his energy, push and honesty, he was soon in comfortable circumstances. These principles he has endeavored to instill into the minds of his sons as sure stepping-stones to a successful business career. Every step of his financial and commercial career has been illustrated with acts of liberality, and his excellent business ability and keen foresight have made his one of the leading mercantile establishments of the county, and has earned for him a handsome fortune. His success has been remarkable, and the confidence which the people repose in him, in all respects, is rarely equaled at the present day. He was married in Reidsville, N. C., in 1875, to Miss Anna E. Glass, of Coswell county, a niece of Colonel Richardson, president of the World's exposition at New Orleans, which union has resulted in the birth of three sons and four daughters. At the same time, Col. A. J. Boyd and Miss Belle Richardson were married, in the same church. Immediately after this memorable double wedding, Mr. Busick and Colonel Boyd and their brides set out upon an extended tour of the North, and visited every point of interest in the Middle states and many in Canada.

George W. Butler has followed the calling of a planter the greater part of his life, and as an independent tiller of the soil his career has been a successful one. He was born in Lauderdale county, Ala., December 23, 1839, being the fifth of six children born to Thomas F. and Mary E. (Ingram) Butler, natives of Tennessee and Alabama respectively. The father was a very extensive and successful physician, in connection with which he followed planting. He came to Mississippi in 1840 and located near Sardis in Panola county, where he became an eminent medical practitioner, and resided until his death in 1851. His paternal ancestors came from England and first settled in Virginia, but gradually became scattered throughout the South and West. George W. Butler has been a resident of Mississippi from the time he was one year old, and was given the advantages of the schools of Sardis. He began making his own way in the world at the age of eighteen years, and upon the opening of the Rebellion, in 1861, he enlisted in company E, Twelfth Mississippi regiment, Sardis Blues, and took an active part in the battles of Richmond, Seven Pines, second Manassas, Sharpsburg, Gettysburg, Fredericksburg and many others. He was captured just before the close of the war at Selma, Ala., but managed to make his escape and returned home, where he was at the final surrender. Soon after the close of the war he came to Coahoma county and became manager for D. L. Childress, continuing with him for about six years, after which he began opening up his present plantation. Although he began the battle of life with no capital he has done well for himself and family, and is now the owner of eight hundred acres of land, three hundred of which are under cultivation, the most of which he has opened and improved himself. He is quiet and unobtrusive in manners, and has aspired to no higher honor than to be a good citizen, to follow the teachings of the golden rule and to rear his children to useful citizenship. He has not only been a model citizen but he has also been an exemplary Christian and a faithful and kind husband and father. He was married in 1869 to Miss Sallie A. Brown, a native of Mississippi and a daughter of J. D. and Sarah (Hastings) Brown of Louisiana, by whom he has eight children: Mary B., Benjamin B., Robert H., George W., Sarah F., Martha A., Dixie and Thomas D., all of whom are living and make their home with their parents. Mr. Butler, his wife and two sons are members of the Methodist Episcopal church, and he is a Mason, a member of the Knights of Honor and Knights of Pythias. Four of his brothers served in the Confederate army during the Rebellion, his brother Robert being a flag-bearer in his company. His father was a soldier during the Mexican war.

Dr. Hansford D. Butler has long been a prosperous and successful medical practitioner of Washington county, Miss., but with a view to locating a drug store in Cleveland, has lately moved to this place. He was born in Lawrence county, of this state, May 29, 1852, the eldest of seven children born to Charles C. and Sydnia A. (Longino) Butler, also Mississippians by birth. The father devoted his life to planting, and spent his days on Mississippi soil, and at the time of his death, in 1884, left his family in comfortable circumstances, and his children with good and practical educations with which to commence the battle of life. His wife survives him, and has made her home with the subject of this sketch, in Washington county, on Deer creek, since 1886. She is now sixty-four years of age. The paternal grandparents, Luke and Patience (Coor) Butler, were of Scotch descent, and were born in North Carolina and South Carolina, respectively. The maternal grandparents, John T. and Anna P. (Ramsey) Longino, were of Irish descent, and were South Carolinians by birth, but Mr. Longino afterward became a very prominent man in the affairs of Lawrence county, Miss., of which he was one of the pioneer residents, and in which he held positions of honor and trust. Dr. Hansford D. Butler was reared in the county of his birth, but in his youth was given excellent educational advantages, and in the University of Mississippi he acquired his literary education. In 1882 he began reading medicine, and graduated in that profession from Tulane university, of New Orleans, La., in 1886, passing his examination in a very satisfactory manner. After completing his course he returned to Greenville, Miss., and being a faithful and conscientious student, and a skillful practitioner, he soon built up a remunerative patronage, his name becoming a familiar household word throughout Washington county. Dr. Butler is a man of great determination, and in his vocabulary there is no such word as fail. He enters heart and soul into his work, and he is usually successful in his business enterprises as well as in his practice. Although his practice in Washington county was large and remunerative, Cleveland presented to him a more inviting and promising field, and here he expects to engage in the drug business, a calling for which he is admirably fitted, for besides possessing a thorough knowledge of drugs, he is accurate, methodical and painstaking. By his own efforts he has become the owner of five hundred and twenty acres of land, and on the two hundred acres that are under cultivation, he has two comfortable residences. Upon making the purchase the land was heavily wooded, and all the improvements have been made since he became the owner. Although he is unmarried, he is taking care of a widowed sister with three children, his mother also making her home with him, and to them he is deeply attached. His habits are excellent, his principles as a man of business are clean and pure, and he is conscientious in every relation and duty of life. He is an active, worthy and earnest member of the Baptist church, of which he is a liberal supporter, and that he has endeavored to follow the teachings of the golden rule is amply attested by the numerous friends that he has gathered about him. He keeps fully apace with the progress made in his profession, and being a worthy member of the Knights and Ladies of Honor, he was medical examiner of that order for two years. In personal appearance he is prepossessing, is above medium hight, his complexion being fair and his eyes blue. Hon. A. H. Longino, who was once chancery clerk of Lawrence county, being afterward state senator and United States district attorney, is an uncle of Dr. Butler.

James P. Butler, an extensive planter of Laurel Hill plantation, also Ellis or White Cliffs, and Ormonde plantations, consisting of about five thousand five hundred acres in all, and situated about twelve miles below Natchez, is a son of Pierce and Mary Louisa (Stirling) Butler, the father born in Natchez, Miss., in 1817, and the mother in West Feliciana parish, La., in 1820. They were married in the last-named place in 1840, and there Mrs. Butler died in 1845. Mr. Butler was an extensive sugar planter, and was a man of prominence and ability, devoting his time and attention exclusively to his private interests. He was educated at Philadelphia and at West Point, although he was obliged to quit the latter place on account of ill health. He then assumed charge of his father's immense estate in Louisiana. His death occurred in West Feliciana parish, La., in 1889. His father, Judge Thomas Butler, was a native of Carlisle, Penn., and was a man of talent and education. He prepared for the law, and in early life went to Adams county, where he practiced his profession, and was married in the same house in which his grandson, James P., now lives, to Miss Ann Ellis, a native of Adams county. Judge Butler practiced law in Natchez with success for a number of years and then removed to West Feliciana parish, La., where he owned large planting interests and where his death occurred in 1847. At that time he was judge of the district court, which position he had filled with distinction and honor for many years, and he was also a member of the United States congress from Louisiana at one time. As a lawyer his argumentative powers were clear, vigorous and incisive, his comprehension ready and acute, and the succession of his thoughts closely logical. He reared a family of four sons and four daughters, one son and two daughters now living. He was a son of Thomas Butler, who was a native of the Keystone state, where he spent all his life. He and four brothers were officers in the Revolutionary war, serving with distinction, and being frequently honored by Gen. George Washington for their valor, ability and fearless conduct. They were the sons of Irish parents, and the first generation born in America. Grandfather Henry Stirling was also a native of West Feliciana parish, La., where he spent his entire life as a wealthy and prominent planter. He was well educated and a man of ability and understanding. He died about 1842. His wife, whose maiden name was Mary Bowman, was born in Pennsylvania, at Brownsville, and came to Louisiana after her marriage with Mr. Stirling. She died in that state about 1852. She was an Episcopalian in her religious views. Alexander Stirling, the father of Henry, was a native Scotchman, and came direct to Louisiana at an early period of that state's history. He became quite wealthy as a planter. James P. Butler was born in West Feliciana parish, La., in 1842, and was the second of three children—two sons and a daughter—the latter, Anna L., becoming the wife of Henry C. Minor, a planter of Terre Bonne parish, La. The son, Captain Thomas, a planter and lawyer of West Feliciana parish, was educated at Oxford, practiced law successfully for a number of years, and was district judge one term. He was captain of a company in the First Louisiana regiment, serving with General Bragg. He was captured at Blakely near the close of the war and paroled, after which he served on General Liddell's staff. James P. Butler was educated at Oxford, Miss., until the breaking out of the war, when he espoused the cause of the Confederacy and joined the First Louisiana artillery as lieutenant of Company I. The last two years of the war he served as adjutant of his regiment. He operated at Fort Pike, La., Vicksburg, Mobile, etc., and surrendered in north Mississippi at the close of the war. Afterward he was engaged in business in New Orleans until 1875, when he removed to his present home. In the meantime (1871) he was married to Miss Mary Louisa, daughter of Jilson P. and Sidney Ann Harrison. Mr. Harrison was born in Mount Sterling, Ky., in 1806, and when a young man came to Vicksburg, where he practiced law until 1840. Previous to this, in 1834, he was married in Natchez, and in 1840 he removed to New Orleans, where he engaged in the cotton factorage business, with J. U. Payne, under the firm name of Payne & Harrison, until his death in 1874. He was once mayor of Vicksburg. Mrs. Harrison was born at Washington, Adams county, Miss., and is still living at the age of seventy-eight years. She is the daughter of Prof. Charles M. Norton, who was born at Winchester, Va., and who married a Miss Terrell, of North Carolina. They were early settlers of Adams county, and Professor Norton was for a number of years president of Jefferson college, holding that position at his death. His father, George F. Norton, was born at Winchester, Va., and when five years of age was taken to England and educated at Cambridge. When he and his mother started to return to the United States the vessel was captured, and they were taken to the island of Madeira, where the mother died. After about eighteen months on that island, Mr. Norton proceeded to Virginia, where he married a Miss Thurston, and where he passed the remainder of his days. Mrs. Butler was born in New Orleans. She is the mother of two sons: Pierce and James P. Mr. Butler descended from a most worthy and intellectual family, and the same may be said of Mrs. Butler's parents and grandparents. The original owners of Laurel Hill and Ellis Cliffs plantations was Richard Ellis, a native of Virginia, and one of the first Americans who settled in Adams county. He died about 1770. The property then descended to Dr. W. N. Mercer, a grandson-in-law of Richard Ellis, he (the Doctor) having married (1823) Miss Ann E. Farrar, a daughter of Benjamin Farrar, who married Mary Ellis, the daughter of Richard Ellis. Dr. Mercer was a native of Maryland, and was a surgeon in the United States navy. He continued to reside on the plantation until 1840, when he removed to New Orleans, and there his death occurred in 1874, at the age of eighty-three years. He always spent a portion of his time in the latter part of his life on the plantation, and kept it in good condition. After his death the property fell to Pierce Butler, the father of its present owner.

Robert S. Butler is the popular sheriff and collector of Franklin county, Miss., and as a public official he has not his superior, for besides being faithful, efficient and painstaking, he is very trustworthy and possesses undoubted courage and determination, qualities that are very essential to the successful conduct of the office. He was born in Amite county, Miss., in 1853, to Robert P. and Emma K. (Dobyus) Butler, who were born in 1812 and 1832 respectively, and with the exception of about one year that they lived in Arkansas, they have spent all their lives in that county. For many years they have been members of the Baptist church, and Mr. Butler is an honest, upright citizen, and is a planter in moderate circumstances. He was reared in the wilds of Amite county, with very meager advantages for acquiring an education, but possessing a naturally active mind, he became an exceptionally well-informed man and became one of the progressive citizens of that county. He was a member of the state militia during the war, and for a long time was a Mason. His father, Aaron Butler, was born and reared in Georgia, and was married there to Mary Day, removing about the year 1802 to what is now Amite county, settling in the woods, thirteen miles north of where Liberty now is. On an excellent plantation that he improved there he spent the rest of his life, dying at the age of ninety-three years. He was one of the very earliest of the settlers of this region and built one of the first cottongins in the county. During the war of 1812 he served for six months and was a participant in the battle of New Orleans. Two of his brothers, Jabez and George, came with him to Amite county, where they became industrious planters and spent the rest of their lives. The maternal grandfather, William Edward Dobyus, came, a young man, to Amite county, where he was united in marriage to Miss Mary Hicks, whose native birthplace was Pike county. They spent the greater part of their lives in Liberty, there passing from life in 1838 and 1837, respectively, the former being a member of the A. F. & A. M. Robert S. Butler was the second in a family of five sons and three daughters, four sons and two daughters now living, all being residents of Amite county but himself. He was given the advantages of the common schools, and as he improved these opportunities to the utmost he was enabled, at the age of seventeen years, to begin teaching school. At the end of one year he began working as a farm hand, continuing until 1873, when he was married to Miss Cynthia Bunckley, a daughter of Nathan Bunckley, whose sketch appears in this volume. Mrs. Butler was born in Franklin county and has borne her husband three children. Mr. Butler was engaged in planting on the Homochitto river until 1884, since which time he has discharged the duties of sheriff and collector, to which position he has been elected four times. From 1880 until he was made sheriff he was president of the board of supervisors of Franklin county. He is now worthy master of Ben Franklin lodge No. 11 of the A. F. & A. M. at Meadville, and is a worthy member of the Methodist Episcopal church. He has always interested himself in politics, is a good campaign worker, and in 1890 was a delegate to the congressional convention. His eleven years of official life have been meritorious and upright and he has won for himself popularity and esteem. He is affable and courteous in his demeanor, and meets with favor everywhere.

Rev. W. R. Butler was born in Rankin county, Miss., in 1828. His father, L. C. Butler, was a native of Kentucky, born April 14, 1800, and his mother, who was Elizabeth Burns, was born in North Carolina in 1806. They were married in Wayne county, Miss., in 1822, and had nine children, of whom W. R. Butler was the third in order of birth. Mr. Butler was a planter who located in Rankin county in 1828, and moved thence to Scott county in 1831, remaining there until 1856, when he removed to Texas. Our subject came with him and grew to maturity in Scott county. The father died in Texas, March 24, 1871, and the mother passed away in Scott county in 1854. Rev. Mr. Butler received a common-school education, then read theology and became a preacher of the Baptist church in 1849. He taught school for some years in Scott county, Miss., and for seven years he held the position of county superintendent of the public schools, resigning in 1882. He was married in August, 1854, to Miss Julia E. Long, of Hinds county, Miss., who has borne him twelve children: Eugene H., married; Laura E., wife of W. E. McGee; Edward J., married, and Hiram J., Mary E., William L., George L., Lucy E., Anderson S., Alice M., Eula B. and Julia, all unmarried. George L., Eugene H. and Hiram J. received a good high-school education, principally at Harpersville college. Mr. Butler has done long and effective work

Jas. Scott.

in the ministry, and has been quite successful as a planter, owning three hundred and sixty acres, of which about sixty-five acres are now under cultivation. He is a member of the Masonic order, and is, in every sense of the word, a useful and progressive citizen, and one who is highly respected by all who know him. He has for sixteen years been moderator of one of the largest Baptist associations in the state, and is now the oldest citizen in Scott county in point of citizenship, having lived in said county nearly sixty years.

Rev. Zebulon Butler, D. D., of Port Gibson, Miss., is the founder of the Presbyterian church at this place, and for thirty-three years was its pastor. He was born in Wyoming valley, Penn., September 27, 1803, his father being in the Revolutionary war under Washington, the maiden name of the latter's wife being Lord. Chester Butler, brother of Zebulon, was a member of the United States senate from Pennsylvania. This family were Episcopalians in faith and were very intelligent, refined and wealthy. Dr. Butler was educated at Princeton college, graduating in 1822, and while in that institution he was regarded a fine scholar, very amiable and of great popularity among the students. In the early part of his collegiate course he gave little thought and attention to religious subjects, was full of humor and always ready for amusement, mingling freely with the gay and wild students in all their sports. In his senior year a religious revival prevailed in the college; he experienced religion and changed the whole current of his life. After graduating he took charge of an academy in his native town, and in pursuance of a long-cherished plan, commenced the study of medicine. On reflection he found that his public profession of religion involved a surrender of his plans and of himself to the Lord Jesus Christ, and left him no liberty to follow the promptings of worldy interests or human ambition. He looked about him and saw that the fields of grain were ready for the reapers, but the laborers were few, and this thought deeply impressed him and led him to select a course of action differing from the wishes of his friends and the former purposes of his life. After an earnest inquiry as to what the Lord would have him to do, all doubts were removed from his mind, and he submissively surrendered himself to the ministry. Under the force of this conviction he abandoned the study of medicine, and in the fall of 1823 entered the theological seminary at Princeton. During his senior year Dr. Alexander placed in his hand a letter written by some citizens of Vicksburg, Miss., in which was described the spiritual destitution of that place, and an earnest request was added that some young man from the seminary should be sent to preach the gospel to that new and growing city. This letter deeply affected Mr. Butler, and he promptly agreed to go. He was soon after licensed by the presbytery, and mounting his horse made his way overland to Vicksburg, meeting with many adventures on the way. He reached his destination in the fall of 1826, at which time he was only twenty-three years of age and exceedingly youthful in appearance. He found that there was not a single house of worship in the place, and only a feeble band of Methodists had been called together under the ministry of Rev. John Lane. The only place suitable for holding worship was the upper room of a building, the lower floor being occupied by a saloon. Mr. Butler and Mr. Lane cordially fraternized, and made common cause against impiety, immorality and lawlessness. Mr. Butler soon established a stated appointment at Clinton, a flourishing town before the location of the state capital at Jackson, and his way to that place was through the town of Port Gibson, the only mode of traveling being on horseback. As he was riding through the streets of the town, some one hailed him and placed a letter in his hand. It contained an invitation from the citizens to preach the gospel to them. There was but one place of worship in the town, for the Methodists had a small church organization, and a few months after accepting the invitation he organized a Presbyterian church in the courthouse, consisting of twelve mem-

30

bers, Mr. Alexander Armstrong being chosen ruling elder.   He then, for some time, preached alternately at Fayette, the new seat of government of Jefferson county, but the interest which the citizens of Port Gibson took in the cause of Christianity soon demanded all his attention.   Many influential ladies united with the church, but there were scoffers in those days who were unwilling to tolerate a mere boy in breaking up their gay amusements and changing the whole order of things.   Still he persevered, and many a night burned the midnight oil in poring over his books and sermons.   He imparted singular pathos and animation to his delivery, and his eloquence and earnestness often melted his hearers to tears, and was instrumental in bringing many to the feet of Christ.

Although singularly youthful in appearance he was handsome and magnetic, and his earnestness and zeal in laboring for the Divine Master was, in time, followed by excellent results.   After holding mother meetings, establishing Bible classes and Sabbath-schools, and going from house to house to impress upon his hearers the divine truths of Christianity, an extensive revival of religion followed, the converts numbering persons of all classes.   Among them were ladies who had been the leaders of fashion, lawyers, merchants, physicians, the old and the young, many of whom had been former scoffers.   Very speedily a handsome brick church was erected, of which he was chosen pastor, and soon he was sent for by other churches over a wide extent of country, his name becoming a familiar household word.   For many long years he was regarded with unbounded confidence and affection.   The leading and primary object of the founders of Oakland college was to raise up in the Southwest a native ministry.   An unknown donor contributed $25,000 to endow a theological professorship, and in 1837 the presbytery of Mississippi, which at that time controlled the college, elected Mr. Butler temporary professor until a permanent arrangement could be made.   In a short time the Rev. S. Beach Jones, of New Jersey, was elected professor.   While this professorship continued many young men, not merely of the Presbyterian, but also of other churches, entered the ministry.   In the mean time numerous calls from other churches were sent Mr. Butler, but he refused with such promptitude that it soon became understood that he intended to make his permanent home in Port Gibson.   To the end of his life his ministerial brothers regarded him as the beloved disciple.   He always conceded, in all Presbyterian arrangements, a conspicuous place to his brethren; and in all appointments of presbytery he was always the most zealous and active in laboring in poor and desolate congregations.   In 1860 the old church in which he had preached so long and so successfully was torn down and supplemented by a more elegant, spacious and costly edifice, the erection of which reached to $40,000.   Into the new house he was never permitted to enter, for he was called before the bar of God before the building was completed.   On one morning he rode around the church in a carriage, and with anxious eye surveyed its exterior, but was too weak to enter, and rode sadly away.   He never left his room again.   He was aware that the sands of his life were ebbing fast, but death found him with his lamp trimmed and burning.   He spoke exultingly of his full assurance of faith and immediate entrance into heaven, his last words being, "Glory to God, glory to God!"   He died on the 23d of December, 1860.   In 1829 he was married to Miss Mary Ann Murdock, a lady eminently qualified to be a helpmeet to this noble man; she entered heart and soul with him in his good works, much of her husband's success in the ministry being attributed to her influence.   She was born in Ireland in 1811, but in her infancy was brought to Fort Gibson, where she grew to maturity.   She was married at her mother's residence in Lexington, Ky.   She died October 5, 1863, having borne her husband eleven children, two sons of whom are living: L. John Butler, of Port Gibson, and Clarence Y. Butler, of Colorado, the latter a civil engineer.   L. John Butler is a cotton planter and civil engineer in Mississippi, a citizen of good standing and known integrity; he married Miss Kate Humphreys in November, 1868, and has a son named John H. Butler, and three daughters, named Ruth Conyngham, Sarah Humphreys and Mary Kate Butler.

J. T. Butt, attorney, Clarksdale, Miss. The father of J. T. Butt, Samuel A. Butt, was a native of Kentucky, and was a minister in the Christian church, traveling for many years through Central Kentucky, where he became most extensively known. He also traveled through the interior of Mississippi, and is still living, at the age of eighty-four years. He was married to Miss Permelia Hite, a native of the Old Dominion, whose death occurred in August, 1859. The paternal grandfather, Ambrose Butt, was born on the Emerald isle, came to the United States in early life and settled in Virginia, where he married Miss Sophia Randall, a relation of Samuel Randall. Ambrose Butt was a brother of Isaac Butt, of Ireland, who was the first mover of home rule for Ireland in the house of commons, and who was also the grandfather of Charles Stewart Parnell. Ambrose Butt and family moved to Kentucky soon after Boone located in what is now Lincoln county, and with a few others, were actually the first settlers in that beautiful country. He was a Methodist minister, and was also a successful agriculturist. He became well known, and died about 1880, when in his one hundredth year. The maternal grandfather, Patrick Hite, was also a native of Ireland, and came to the United States when but a boy, settling in Virginia, where he married Miss Elizabeth Jones. He soon after moved to Kentucky, and located in Lincoln county, near the residence of Ambrose Butt. He followed the occupation of a farmer, and was also quite a mechanic, making spinning wheels for the early settlers through that section. He died in 1855, when quite aged. He was selected as judge, and held the first criminal court of (then) Lincoln county. He was not a lawyer, but was chosen for his general fitness and ability. J. T. Butt was born in Lincoln county, Ky., in 1832, and was the second of five children born to his parents. He remained and assisted his father on the farm until sixteen years of age, after which he went to a preparatory school, and in 1852 entered Bacon college at Harrodsburg, from which institution he graduated in 1854. He then immediately began the study of law, and soon after entered Transylvania college, Lexington, from which he graduated in June, 1857. After this, for a year, he was engaged in private study with Chief Justice Robinson, and was admitted in March, 1858. The following November he came to Mississippi, and located at Canton, in Madison county, where he practiced until the outbreak of the war. In 1861 he organized the second company for the Confederate army in Madison county, and was elected captain, but was taken sick, and could not go out with his company. He therefore resigned. In September he went to Virginia and joined company B, Eighteenth Mississippi infantry, as private. In 1863 he was taken prisoner, while temporarily in command of Fredericktown, Md., and after being detained for a few months, was exchanged. He was then appointed colonel on General Lawton's staff, and served in that capacity until the close of the war. He then returned to Attala county, Miss., where his family was then staying, and later located at Kosciusko, where he began the practice of law and where he continued until 1888. He was quite active in politics, but no officeseeker. He had the leading practice there for years. His marriage occurred in 1860, to Miss Belinda Swayzee, daughter of Richard Swayzee, one of the early settlers of Yazoo county from Adams county, and one of the wealthy planters. In 1888 Mr. Butt and family came to Clarksdale, Coahoma county, Miss., where they have since resided. They are members of the Christian church, and Mr. Butt is a member of the Masonic fraternity, also the Knights of Honor. To Mr. and Mrs. Butt were born four children: John S. studied law at Lebanon, Tenn., graduated, and was admitted in February, 1884, when just twenty-one years of age. He received his literary education at Kosciusko.

In 1891 he was married to Miss Hattie Hammond, of Kosciusko. When admitted to the bar, he formed a partnership with his father, under the title of Butt & Butt. His wife is a member of the Presbyterian church. He has bought property, and built a neat home in Clarksdale. He is secretary, treasurer and attorney of South Home Building & Loan association, of Atlanta, and is a bright and studious as well as a rising young lawyer. He is tall, and has a light complexion. Another son, Cary, is a dentist at Clarksdale. The two other children are Emily and Lamar. J. T. Butt is a man of ripe knowledge and studious habits, and has had great experience as a lawyer. The firm now practice in Coahoma and adjoining counties, and do a very profitable and extensive business. Mr. Butt is a rather large man, has a light complexion, a short gray beard, and is pleasant and agreeable in his manners. He is well pleased with the future prospects of Clarksdale and Coahoma county. He owns a summer residence at Kosciusko, where his family spend a part of their time.

Maj. G. W. Bynum, farmer, Corinth, Miss. Like many of the prominent and successful agriculturists of Alcorn county, Miss., Major Bynum is a native North Carolinian, born in Chatham county in 1839. He is the son of Joseph Bynum, the grandson of Mark Bynum, and the great-grandson of Luke Bynum, who was a native of England, and of Scotch-Irish descent. The latter came to America at a period antedating the Revolution, and with two brothers, Tapley and Green, served in that war. Afterward they settled in Virginia, and became industrious and successful planters of that state. Luke married and became the father of eleven children, of whom Mark Bynum (grandfather of subject) was second in order of birth. He was a native Virginian, and of the large family of which he was a member, all lived to be grown with the exception of one, Green, who was drowned in Haw river, North Carolina, at the age of ten years. Another child, Millie, married Greene Poe, and settled in Forsyth county, Miss., where they reared a large family. She died in Mississippi when over eighty years of age. Carney Bynum, still another child, died at an advanced age. He was manager of the Bynum Manufacturing company's mills on Haw river. Mark Bynum moved to North Carolina, and settled in Chatham county at an early date. He became a very successful farmer, and there resided until his death in 1842, over seventy years of age. Joseph Bynum, father of subject, was reared in North Carolina, his native state, and was there married to Miss Sarah Ward, also a native of the Old North state. He moved to Mississippi in 1852, settled in Old Tishomingo county, near Hatchie turnpike on Hatchie river, and, like his ancestors before him, became a prominent farmer. He owned a large number of slaves, and became quite wealthy. His death occurred on his farm when seventy-six years of age. He was an old line whig in politics, and, although he never took a very active part in politics, he was strongly opposed to separating the Union. He was a well-informed man, and kept thoroughly posted on the current events of the day. He was a member of the Methodist church. His wife was born in 1804 and died in 1885, an earnest and devout member of the same church. She was the daughter of William Ward, a native of Virginia, whose father was a native of Scotland. Mrs. Bynum was the eldest of a large family of children, and was reared in her native state. Only one of these children is now living, Prudence Greene, who resides in North Carolina, and is now quite aged. Two brothers, William and Joseph Ward, served in the Mexican war. To the Major's parents were born eleven children—eight sons and three daughters: Thomas (has been a resident of Smith and Kaufman counties, Tex., for thirty-five years; has a family), Miss Anna (enjoys single blessedness on the old homestead in Mississippi), James (died when young in Mississippi), William L. (is farming in Mississippi), Dr. Mark (in Texas), Miss Sarah (at the old home place in Mississippi with her sister Anna), G. W. (subject), Turner (single, on the old home place; represented Prentiss county in the legislature several times), Joseph (near Rienzi, Miss.), N. M. (at Kossuth, engaged in farming and merchandising) and Minnie (wife of J. A. Kimmons, resides at Kossuth, Miss.). Of the six sons, all served in the army of north Virginia, and in the same company and regiment, company A, Second Mississippi regiment, Col. J. M. Stone, who is now governor of the state. All received wounds except Turner, who was captured at the battle of Gettysburg, Penn., and taken to Fort Delaware, Md., where he was retained until the close of the war. William and Joseph both received wounds in their hands; Dr. Bynum was slightly wounded in the side; Thomas received but a slight wound. Major and Turner Bynum entered the army in 1861, before the first battle of Manassas. Major G. W. was first wounded in the thigh at Sharpsburg, Md., then at the battle of Gettysburg he received a wound in the calf of the leg, and at Powder Springs, Ga., he was shot through the neck, the ball going in on the left side and coming out on the right, just behind the spinal column. He was paralyzed for a time. He was in command of his regiment when he received the last wound. He participated in the following engagements: First battle of Manassas, Seven Pines, Fair Oaks, seven days' fight around Richmond, Suffolk, Va., Fredericksburg, Antietam, Gettysburg, South mountain, and after being transferred to Mississippi he was in the battles of Jackson, Miss., Brice's cross roads and Atlanta, where he was dismounted. Afterward he was at Jonesboro and at Selma, Ala., where he lost his horse on the 2d of April, 1865. He went out as a private, but was promoted to adjutant, then captain, afterward major of his regiment, and then was commissioned lieutenant-colonel. After the war he returned to his home in Alcorn county, and there he has since resided. He was educated in the common schools, and graduated from the Wesleyan university of Alabama previous to enlisting in the war in 1861. After the war he followed farming and also taught school for several years. During Cleveland's administration he was appointed postmaster at Corinth. He is a democrat in politics. He was married to Miss Fannie Dilworth, who was the eldest of three children born to the marriage of Col. A. B. Dilworth, a very prominent and highly respected citizen of Mississippi. Colonel Dilworth was in the legislature several sessions, and was secretary of state and auditor of public accounts for a number of years. He entered in the quartermaster's department the fore part of the war, but, owing to the loss of an eye, was not asked to serve. He was born in Rockingham county, N. C., in 1814, and came to Mississippi in 1836, settling in Old Tishomingo county, near Rienzi, where he led a life of usefulness. He was a stanch democrat, was a very progressive man, and was well known all over the state. He is now living near Memphis, Tenn., with his daughter, Mrs. C. F. Robison. His wife, who was formerly Miss Sarah Taylor, is a sister of Drs. Taylor, of Booneville and Corinth. She died in 1881. Mrs. Bynum was educated at Huntsville, Ala., and Jackson, Miss., graduating at Huntsville's Female academy. To Major and Mrs. Bynum have been born nine children, five of whom are living: George, John T., Andrew, Mark and Joseph. Andrew and Joseph are at home, George and Mark are engaged in merchandising in Alabama, and John T. is a physician in Texas. Those deceased were infants. Major Bynum is a member of the Masonic order, chapter and Blue lodge, and he and wife, and all the sons, hold membership in the Methodist church. The Major is engaged in farming adjoining Corinth, and stands among the first-class farmers of the county.

Dr. Joseph M. Bynum, Rienzi, Miss. For a period of over thirty years, he whose name heads this sketch has been a resident of Alcorn county, Miss., and during that time he has been one of its most prominent men. His long residence here and his intimate association with its various material and official affairs have gained for him an extensive and popular acquaintance throughout the state. He is a native of the Old North state, born in Chatham county in 1835, and his parents, Turner and Julia (Ward) Bynum, were natives also of that county and state, the father born in 1808, and the mother in 1814, both of Welsh descent. His great-grandfather, William Bynum, who was a planter by occupation, served in the Revolutionary war and was in the battles of Guilford courthouse and Cowpens. His grand-father, Mark Bynum, also followed the occupation of a farmer, and lived in North Carolina. He was a leading member of the Baptist church, and died in 1840 at the age of seventy years. He was the father of eight children, and Turner Bynum was next to the youngest in order of birth. The latter passed his boyhood days in his native state, became quite an extensive planter, and, like his father before him, was a leading member of the church, but in his case, the Methodist church was the one of his choice. He was also quite a politician of the whig order, and was a member of the legislature for many years, succeeding himself. He was also chairman of the county courts for a long time, and in every public capacity he displayed rare adaptability and fidelity to the trusts reposed in him. He died in 1863, on his home place in North Carolina, where he had passed all his life. His wife, formerly Miss Julia Ward, was the youngest daughter of a large family of children born to William and Elizabeth (Riddle) Ward, natives of North Carolina, in which state they passed their entire lives. Mrs. Bynum died in 1870. She was a member of the Methodist church, a true Christian, and a devoted wife and mother. Dr. Bynum is the eldest of the twelve children born to his parents, seven of whom are still living. Three died in infancy, and those who grew to manhood and womanhood are: Dr. Bynum, Mrs. Elizabeth Lambeth, Taylor, Alvis, Mrs. Sallie Whitfield, Mrs. Minnie Stone, Mrs. Mattie Hawkins, James and Rufus. Dr. Joseph M. Bynum attained his majority in North Carolina, and graduated from the medical department of the University of Pennsylvania in 1858, serving one year as resident surgeon in St. Joseph's hospital, Philadelphia. He then came to Rienzi, Miss., and there practiced his profession until the war. In March, 1862, a company known as the Zollicoffer Avengers (named after General Zollicoffer, who was killed in one of the first battles of Kentucky), was organized in his village, and this constituted company A of the Thirty-second Mississippi regiment, commanded by Gen. M. P. Lowery, who afterward became brigadier-general. Dr. Bynum was commissioned first lieutenant of the company, but acted as surgeon of his regiment. He had charge of one of the hospitals at Murfreesboro during the engagement at Stone river, also had charge of the sick at Chattanooga, but on account of failing health he resigned, and was employed in the revenue department of North Carolina until cessation of hostilities. After the war he returned to Mississippi and engaged in merchandising and farming, doing an extensive business until the fall of 1890, when his entire stock of goods was consumed by fire. The Doctor took a very active part in the reconstruction of the state, after the war, and was in favor of returning into the Union. He has always been a man of political aspirations, and in a different state, or with different political views and convictions, these aspirations would have been satisfied. In 1881 he made a canvass of Mississippi for state treasurer, with Hemingway, but the democratic ticket was declared elected. He was candidate for congress with J. M. Allen in 1888, but on account of his politics he was again unsuccessful. He was a delegate to the national convention when Blaine and Logan were nominated, and was republican elector for the first district of Mississippi. He has taken a very active part in national, state and county politics, and is a leading republican of the state. He is strongly in favor of a protective tariff, and greatly in favor of supporting home institutions, etc. Dr. Bynum was nominated as a commissioner to the World's Fair in 1890, and commissioned by the president for eight years. He is on the agricultural committee of the World's Fair. He was appointed supervisor of the census of the first district of Mississippi by President Hayes.   Dr. Bynum is one of the most progressive and influential men of his day.   Straightforward, clear-headed, well balanced and conservative, he would ably represent the people in any capacity.   In 1860 he was married to Miss Annie Rees, a native of Mississippi, and the daughter of John Rees (see sketch of W. H. Rees, of Booneville). This union has resulted in the birth of five children: Lizzie (died in 1887, was the wife of Dr. Stanley), John T., Mary, Annie and Joseph.   Mrs. Bynum and all the children are members of the Methodist church.   Socially, the Doctor is an Odd Fellow.   He is one of the leading farmers and stockgrowers of the county, and in everything connected with the farm he displays excellent judgment and thoroughness.

Capt. A. M. Byrd, lawyer, Philadelphia, Miss., was born in Sumter county, Ala., and to the union of John and Elizabeth (Tann) Byrd, natives of Georgia and Alabama, respectively.   The father died at Clinton, La., during the war, and the mother, in 1868, came with a family of six children to Neshoba county, and located in the northeastern part of the same. There the children grew up and attended the common schools of the county.   At the age of twenty-one Captain Byrd attended college in Tennessee, and subsequently spent two years in the Cooper institute in Lauderdale county, Miss.   He graduated in the law school at Lebanon, Tenn., in 1884, and was admitted to the bar at Philadelphia immediately after his return to that city.   Since then he has been located there.   He held the office of county superintendent of public institutions from 1886 to 1890, at which time he gave up the office, having been elected to the senate in the fall of 1889.   He filled that office in such a satisfactory manner, and so fully testified as to the wisdom of the people's choice, that he will return to that position, there being no one in opposition to his election.   He assumed the duties of editing the Neshoba *Democrat*, which has had an extensive circulation since 1880, and he is also proprietor of the same.   Socially Captain Byrd affiliates with the Masonic fraternity.   He is a liberal, genial gentleman, and one who has a host of warm personal friends. He was married, in 1887, to Miss Maggie, a daughter of Capt. J. A. Simmons, formerly a resident of Neshoba county, but now of Decatur, Tex.   Captain Simmons served as sheriff of Neshoba county from 1872 to 1886, at which date he went to Texas.

C. R. Byrnes, Jr., is one of the prominent and successful handlers of real estate in the city of Natchez, Miss., and as he is a practical business man in every sense of the word, a shrewd calculator, possessed of untiring energy, and is one of the men who has helped to make the city what it is, he is, without doubt, very popular.   He was born in Claiborne county, Miss., in 1851, being the eldest of fourteen children born to C. R. and Catherine (Smith) Byrnes, the latter being a granddaughter of Calvin Smith, one of the earliest residents of Natchez, coming hither from New England in 1776.   His son was married to Miss Eliza Forman, a member of an old and prominent family of Jefferson county, and thus two of the oldest families of Adams and Jefferson counties were united.   Many of their descendants live along the Mississippi river, from Natchez to New Orleans, and are among the most substantial and prosperous citizens of the state.   The paternal grandfather was born in New York city, and in colonial times was interested in shipping, being part owner of a line of ships plying between that city and Liverpool, England.   The paternal great-grandfather of the subject of this sketch, Robert Ralston, was a lawyer, and after coming South followed this occupation at Pointe Coupee, La., where he died in early life, leaving two children. C. R. Byrnes, Sr., was reared by his maternal grandmother in Claiborne county, and all his life his attention has been given to planting, at which he has been successful.   He and his wife are worthy residents of the section in which they reside, and are members of the Episcopal church.   They reared a large family of children, seven of whom are living.   C. R. Byrnes,

Jr., was educated first at home and afterward in Vicksburg, but after attaining his eighteenth year he began looking after his father's real estate interests, which occupied his attention for about six years. During this time he acquired a practical knowledge of real estate values, and now his judgment is acknowledged to be second to none. He was married, in 1881, to Miss Helen Metcalfe, a daughter of Dr. Orrick Metcalfe, and very soon thereafter located on the plantation he had purchased in Claiborne county, and there remained and tilled the soil for five years. At the end of this time he came to Natchez, and at once engaged in the real estate business, at which he has done remarkably well, the utmost confidence being reposed in him by all who know him. He pays every attention to the interests of nonresidents, is prudent and far-seeing, and as he is noted for leniency, fair dealing and honest integrity, his friends are numerous. He is unerring in his estimate of land values, and besides being enterprising and pushing, he is careful as well. He has made several of the largest sales ever made in the South, and recently, in connection with a Boston syndicate, perfected a sale of one hundred and forty-four thousand acres in Concordia parish, La. This land was the property of the Mississippi & Red River Delta Land company, of which Mr. Byrnes was the efficient secretary, and through his influence the transaction was brought to a successful issue. He is now secretary and manager of the Arlington land company, which is capitalized at $56,000, and this comprises a tract of suburban property purchased by a syndicate, and which is being steadily improved. A bridge has been erected over the bayou at State street, and the entire addition has been graded. Where one year ago were growing thrifty fields of cotton are now standing many elegant city residences. Mr. Byrnes has just completed a handsome residence, which is a fine specimen of the old Southern country home, the rooms being large and the halls spacious. A veranda completely encircles the building, and is finished in good taste and modern style, the entire cost of this comfortable and pleasing home being $5,000. His real estate operations have been very extensive in this state and Louisiana, and he is at present the correspondent for the Corbin banking company of New York, and has made many loans; also local agent of the Mutual life insurance company of New York. He is the owner of a good plantation in Concordia parish, La., comprising sixteen hundred acres, three hundred acres of which are under cultivation, well improved with buildings and an excellent cotton gin. Although this land has been in his possession but a short time, he has, with his usual enterprise and energy, brought it to its present admirable state of cultivation. He also owns an excellent estate of three hundred acres in Claiborne county, and a small place near Natchez. He is a member and secretary of the Natchez & Adams county immigration society, and is strongly in favor of encouraging both immigration and capital from the North and East, and fully understands that if that plan succeeds it will bring great prosperity to the South. He has become one of the most extensive operators in land sales in Mississippi, and within a few years has, by push, enterprise and indomitable perseverance, built up a very large trade. He is keen and shrewd, though strictly honorable, in his business transactions, and being thoroughly practical and unerring in his estimate of land values, he is considered a leader in his calling. He is in correspondence with other agents in almost every city in the Union, and has in many ways shown the advantages of Natchez and Adams county, thus materially benefiting both; for through his influence many substantial, enterprising and honorable families have been induced to settle here permanently. He recently sold the fine old estate, the former home of Governor Gayoso, Concord, which was for years the home of the minors, to a New York man. He is at all times wide awake to the interests of this section, and as manager of the Arlington land company he has given abundant proof of his admirable business qualifications, for the stock has been advanced over three hundred per cent. since its organization, a fact that stands to his credit without doubt. A worthy history of Adams county, Miss., could not be written without mention of Mr. Byrnes, for since locating here he has been one of the most enterprising and desirable of residents, and has been largely instrumental in making the city the thriving and prosperous place it now is. He is above medium hight, well proportioned, has a fair complexion, and is decidedly prepossessing in appearance. He has the easy carriage and perfection of manners that mark the true Southern gentleman, and is a most courteous and obliging business man, being on the most friendly terms with all with whom he has relations. He and his intelligent and accomplished wife are members of the Episcopal church, and are the parents of three children, Charles Metcalfe, Helen and Katharine.

Robert Lee Byrnes, pharmacist, of Natchez. Among the more recent acquisitions to the business interests of Natchez, the establishment of which Mr. Byrnes is the proprietor has obtained a substantial footing which might well belong to an older house. Mr. Byrnes is descended from an ancient English family, noted for their loyalty to the crown, a member of which came to New Jersey in 1640, settling at Monmouth courthouse, where some of the family still reside. The historical records of that state mention them as prominent in the Revolution and also as filling many positions of confidence and trust years afterward. His maternal ancestors are also English, but are from South Carolina, where the name of McCaleb has always been held in great esteem. They came to Mississippi early in the present century, settling in Claiborne county, near the birthplace of the subject of our sketch. His grandfather, Robert Ralston Byrnes, married into this family. His father, Isaac Byrnes, was associated with Mr. Mintum, his brother-in-law, in the shipping business in New York, and was the first to establish the Red Star line, now plying between New York and England. Mention of this line was in Harper's *Monthly* in 1870, or thereabouts. It was afterward owned by Grinnell & Co. Robert Lee Byrnes was born in Claiborne county, in 1865, being the tenth of fourteen children of Charles R. and Catherine P. (Smith) Byrnes, a short history of whom is given in the sketch of C. R. Byrnes, Jr. R. Lee Byrnes was partially educated in the schools of Adams county, at Natchez, and graduated from the Jefferson college of Washington, Miss., in 1881. He connected himself with the drug business in Fayette immediately after leaving school, continuing there until he engaged in business for himself, in October, 1889, at the corner of Main and Commerce streets, Natchez, Miss. He carries a stock of goods only to be found in a well-kept, reliable store, and has that thorough knowledge of the business, and those natural qualifications for its management so essential to success, and there his future career is bright with promise. His personal popularity is also the cause of considerable patronage, and the people have had every opportunity of discovering that he can be thoroughly relied upon at all times. Although a young man, he is rapidly and surely making his way among the energetic business men of Natchez, and, attending strictly to each minor detail of his business, he cannot fail to succeed. He has a large business at his branch store, at 506 Franklin street, which was established in July, 1890, with a fine stock of goods. He commands a large prescription trade at both stores. He was married in September, 1889, to Miss Helen C. Feniday, daughter of Hon. J. C. Feniday, president of the police jury, and an extensive planter of Concordia parish, La. Charles Feniday Byrnes, their little son, was born in 1890.

CHAPTER XV.

INDIVIDUAL MEMOIRS, C.

ANOTHER successful planter of Mississippi is Henry M. Caffey, of Duck Hill, who owes his nativity to the Old North state, his birth occurring in Guilford county on the 5th of August, 1823. His father, Henry Caffey, was also a native of the same county, and was reared to mature years there. He was married in that state to Vina Thompson, a native of the same state and county, and the daughter of Robert Thompson, who was of an old and prominent Maryland family. Mr. Caffey followed farming in North Carolina after his marriage until 1844, when he moved to Mississippi, settling in Choctaw county, where he followed planting until his death about 1859. His wife had died several years previously. The paternal grandfather, Thomas Caffey, was a native of Maryland, of a prominent family of that state, and was of Scotch descent. He was a soldier in the Revolution. Henry M. Caffey, subject of this memoir, was reared and received a common-school education in his native county. He went with his father to Mississippi in 1844, settled in Choctaw county and there followed farming for a number of years. He then moved from there to Montgomery county, of that state, and located in Duck Hill in 1881, buying residence property there but at the same time continuing his planting. He commenced life for himself empty-handed, and has, by his own industry and excellent business management, accumulated a handsome fortune, and now leads a quiet and peaceable life in one of the most beautiful homes in his quiet little town. Wherever H. M. Caffey is known, his word is as good as his bond, and he uses his hard-earned money for the benefit of his family and friends, and is ever ready to help a good cause and to build up the waste places in his county. He has built and now owns several nice brick stores in Duck Hill, which will stand as a monument to his enterprise and public spirit. On the 3d of April, 1849, his nuptials with Miss Mary Tindell were celebrated. Mrs. Caffey was born in North Carolina, and her father, James Tindell, was also from that state originally. Mr. and Mrs. Caffey have one child, a son, William, who is at home. Mr. Caffey is a member of the Presbyterian and his wife a member of the Baptist church.

It is a pleasure of the historian to note that Thomas Yancey Caffey, of Hernando, De Soto county, has been a resident of De Soto county for more than fifty years, and is certainly entitled to a space in this record of Mississippi's most worthy citizens. He was born in North Carolina September 26, 1815, and is a son of Robert and Jane (Flack) Caffey, natives of North Carolina. They were the parents of six children, of whom he was the third. His father passed all his life in the state in which he was born, passing to his eternal rest in 1854. The Caffey family is of Irish lineage, and those who first emigrated to America settled in

Maryland. The maternal grandfather, Andrew Flack, was of German descent. The subject of this notice was brought up in his native county and had reached man's estate before he bade farewell to the scenes of his childhood. He removed to Mississippi in 1837 and located at Holly Springs, where he staid about two years; he then came to Hernando, and has since made it his home. The first work he did was carpentering; the people of the community, recognizing his ability and integrity, called him to offices of trust, which he filled for eight years. In 1852 he entered the mercantile trade and has been in this line of business ever since. By energy and thrift and the exercise of good judgment he has accumulated a comfortable fortune; he owns twelve hundred acres of land, one-half of which is cultivated to a high degree, and has $30,000 which he loans. He was married in 1842 to Miss Louisa J. Hanks, of Tennessee, a daughter of George W. and Catherine (Doty) Hanks, also of Tennessee. One child was born of this union, Emma Louisa, the wife of Charles H. Robertson, a biography of whom will be found elsewhere in this work. Mr. Caffey is the master of his own fortunes, as he began with no capital and a limited education. He would be considered a success under any circumstances, but in view of the odds against which he has worked, too much can not be said in his praise. For fifteen years he was treasurer of the county of De Soto, and discharged his duties ably and satisfactorily. He is a member of the Masonic order. The following fact is related in evidence of Mr. Caffey's energy and thrift: At the age of fifty years he, with one boy, raised $1,700 worth of cotton, at an outlay of $29.50, and three hundred and seventy-five bushels of corn, walking a distance of a mile and a half daily to and from his work, making three miles in all. He is still in vigorous health, an honored and respected citizen.

About the time of the formation of the state government of Mississippi, Harry Cage, a native of Tennessee, located here and commenced the practice of law. His early education had been limited, but he succeeded in time in acquiring a state reputation as a practitioner, although he could not be characterized as a profound lawyer or a man of great learning. In 1829 he was chosen a member of the supreme bench of the state, and continued occupying that position until the courts were reorganized under the constitution of 1832. He was then elected to congress, and in the eventful canvass which occurred at that time showed exceptional fitness for the arena of politics. His professional qualities were vivacity and congeniality and a readiness to adapt himself to changed circumstances. His social qualities were preponderant. He was quick at repartee, witty, often fanciful and brilliant, and through all of his speeches ran a pathos of great power. Though not the most eminent lawyer in the state, he could properly be classed as one of those, having by his natural gifts and application secured a state reputation. In 1834 he resigned his seat in congress and located on a plantation, where he passed away.

No review of Port Gibson would be complete in the business and commercial arena without a biographical sketch of William Cahn, one of the enterprising merchants of this pretty little city. He carries on an extensive and important wholesale and retail general mercantile business, occupying two distinct stores in order to accommodate his large and well selected stock, which embraces everything used by the people of Claiborne county. He is a gentleman of known and tried integrity and honesty and his establishment is well and favorably known throughout this, as well as many of the adjoining counties, as the headquarters for first-class goods and reasonable prices, as well as for courteous treatment and fair dealing. The best classes afford Mr. Cahn a liberal patronage, and no man stands higher in commercial circles. He is amply supplied with capital, purchases in the leading markets, and none but the best of goods, and transacts one of the most flourishing businesses in Port

Gibson.   He is the leading cotton-buyer and handler of this product, and is fully identified
with the best interests of his town and county.   His establishment was open to the public
in 1867, and he has kept fully apace with the times ever since.   For a term of years he has
been connected with the town council as alderman and trustee of the public schools, and as
he has ever been a patron of education he has been much interested in the school system of
Claiborne county.   He has ever advocated public interests in the way of railroads, mills,
etc., and any measure which would develop and improve the town found in him a liberal
patron, both in purse and influence.   He was born near Frankfort-on-the-Main in Germany
in 1831, but since becoming a subject of Uncle Sam he has been one of his most stanch
and reliable German-American citizens.   His parents, Meyer Cahn and wife, were also native
Germans, and were honest, industrious and God-fearing people.   William Cahn was married
in Port Gibson, Miss., in 1866, to Miss Minnie Kiefer, who was born in Port Gibson in 1848.
Their union resulted in the birth of seven children—five sons and two daughters: Cora Lee,
a graduate of the Locquet-Leroy institute of New Orleans, finishing the scientific course in
1886, also taking a full course in music and French, married in 1891 to Mr. Thomas Jefferson Feibleman of New Orleans; Maurice G., a graduate of Chamberlain Hunt academy,
of Port Gibson, is in the mercantile business with his father; Julia D. is taking the scientific
course in the same institution from which her sister Cora graduated; Edwin I. is attending
the Chamberlain Hunt academy; and Bernard R., aged eleven years, Milton Loris, aged six
years, and Louis Kiefer, aged three, are at home.   Mrs. Cahn's father, Louis Kiefer, was
born in Alsace, France, in 1812, where he followed merchandising prior to coming to the
United States in 1835.   He located at Port Gibson, Miss., where he became well known
for his success as a business man and for his honor and integrity in all his dealings.   He
died in 1886 and is now sleeping his last sleep in the cemetery at Port Gibson.   His
wife, Marie Roser, was also born in Alsace, in 1814, and died in 1882, in Port Gibson.
Their family consisted of five children: Julia (deceased); Emanuel, a merchant of this
town; Mrs. Cahn; Rebecca, the wife of Isadore Newman, a wealthy banker of New Orleans;
Fannie, wife of Charles Newman, a wealthy cotton factor of that city, and Alice, wife of
Samuel E. Worms, a rich merchant of New Orleans.   Mrs. Cahn, as well as her brothers
and sisters, received an excellent education.   Mr. Cahn was a soldier in the Sixteenth Mississippi infantry volunteers, C. S. A., for two years, and as he possessed a splendid constitution, he bore the hardships and privations of a soldier's life well.   He has always supported
the principles of democracy, and socially is a member of the Masonic fraternity, the K. of
P. and the K. of H.   He and his family are devout devotees of the Jewish church and
are members of a society in Port Gibson known as Gemilas Chesed.

Distinguished among the new school of lawyers that have made their advent since the
war, and who is worthy to wear the mantle of such illustrious disciples of Themis as Poindexter, Sharkey, Prentiss, Quitman, Holt, Yerger and their compeers, is Solomon Saladin
Calhoon, of Jackson, Miss.   In juridical scholarship and forensic power he is without a
superior in the state, and the tiara of the most brilliant of these great lawyers can be grace-
fully worn by him.   Judge Calhoon was born near Brandenburg, Ky., January 2, 1838, and
is the eldest son of George and Louisiana (Brandenburg) Calhoon.   The Calhoons were an
old and prominent family of Virginia, of Irish-Scotch ancestry, their tribal name being Cal-
quhoun.   Samuel, the father of George Calhoon, was born in Fauquier county, Va., and
was a man of note.   He was among the first settlers of Kentucky, where George, the father
of Judge Calhoon, was born.   Louisiana Brandenburg's father, Solomon, was a Virginian
by birth.   His father, Matthias, and his uncle, Jonathan, were political refugees from

Prussia. Louisiana Brandenburg was born in Kentucky in 1818. George Calhoon was a lawyer by profession and a man of prominence in the politics of Kentucky. He was a member of the legislature of that state contemporaneously with Thomas A. Marshall. In 1836 he moved to Mississippi and located at Canton, to which place he was followed by his family in the fall of 1838. By his marriage with Miss Brandenburg he became the father of six children, named, respectively: Solomon S., John, George, Charles, Hoche, William McWillie and Walter C. John has been a member of the legislature of Mississippi, and is at the present time mayor of Holly Springs. Mr. Calhoon died at Canton in 1853, and his widow in 1873. Judge Calhoon's education was attained at the old fieldschools and at the Cumberland university of Tennessee. After leaving the university he taught school, and at the same time read law. He entered no law office, but beneath the broad canopy of heaven, selecting some friendly tree for a temporary shade, pursued his studies. At the early age of nineteen he was admitted to the bar, securing his license to practice from C. P. Smith, then chief justice of the state. His means were limited, and, to defray expenses until he could get into a lucrative practice, he took the editorship of the Yazoo City *Democrat*, at the same time forming a copartnership with Col. S. M. Phillips. While editing the *Democrat* he was elected secretary of the state senate. Early in 1859 he was invited to take charge of the *State Rights Democrat*, at Helena, Ark., which he accepted. This was pending the important controversy in that state between Robert W. Johnson, United States senator, and Thomas C. Hindman, member of the lower house of congress. He remained there about one year in charge of the paper, having also a law office with William R. Barksdale, who was subsequently killed at Shiloh. In the early part of 1860 he returned to Canton and formed a copartnership with Franklin Smith. His law practice was suspended at the commencement of the Civil war. He cast aside his briefs and enlisted for the struggle, championing the cause of the Confederacy. He was mustered into the Mississippi Rifles as a private, which subsequently became a part of the Tenth Mississippi regiment. He went through all the grades of promotion up to lieutenant-colonel, which position he held at the surrender of his command at Greensboro, N. C., under Gen. Joseph E. Johnston. He was in all the leading battles fought by the army of Tennessee under Generals Johnston, Bragg and Hood. He was wounded twice at Shiloh. At Chickasaw Bluffs he commanded the artillery during the engagement with the gunboats Lexington and Conastoga, which retired after two hours and a half of hard fighting. He was in the battle of Murfreesboro, where he was again wounded. Judge Calhoon's war record is a very creditable one. As a soldier he was distinguished by his devotion to duty, for his promptness in enforcing discipline and his readiness in obeying orders. He was always prudent, collected and brave. No officer was more solicitous of the welfare of his men, which won for him their confidence and affection. Colonel Calhoon returned home and resumed the practice of his profession. In common with all the good and true men of the South who had enlisted in her cause, the war had brought much trouble and sorrow to him. He had suffered heavily financially, but by far the greatest loss to him was the fall of those brave and noble friends who responded to the call to arms and faithfully and gallantly served in the cause of the South, had passed from the dread carnage of war to the peaceful home beyond. He sought not to forget the past or drown his disappointment in Lethean waves of dissipation, but, with the nobler aim of righting up the wreck and obliterating, as far as possible, the dissastrous effects of the great conflict, he addressed himself with greater energy than ever before to the duties of his profession. He also sought to have the results of the war accepted, and to have the people put forth their vast powers of recuperation, that the new commonwealth might be greater and more prosperous than the old.

In the fall of 1865 he was elected district attorney of what was then the fifth judicial district, composing the counties of Yazoo, Madison, Holmes, Leake and Attala. This election was for an unexpired term, and in 1866 he was selected for the full term of four years. In 1868, in common with nearly all the civil officers of Mississippi, he was deposed by the Federal General Gillem, because of his inability to take the test oath. He continued the practice of this profession, forming a copartnership with Judge J. A. P. Campbell, who had for the same cause been deposed from the circuit judgeship. He rose rapidly in his profession and became distinguished for legal ability, and was a prominent factor in the political affairs of the state. This partnership continued until Mississippi again resumed her habiliments of statehood (1876), when he was appointed circuit judge for the then fifth district, composing the counties of Yazoo, Madison, Hinds and Copiah. His partner, Judge Campbell, was elevated to the supreme bench. Judge Calhoun was reappointed at the end of the term (six years). He retired from the bench in the fall of 1882 to resume his practice and secure a more remunerative field for his legal labors. He removed to Jackson and formed a copartnership with Marcellus Green, a bright, rising young lawyer of that city. This partnership, which still exists, was to the advantage of both. One has the calm, accurate judgment acquired by age and experience in the practice, while the other has the activity, energy and aggressiveness of youth. Though not desiring political office, Judge Calhoon has always taken an active interest in politics. He was a delegate at large to the Baltimore convention which nominated Greeley. He was also a delegate to the democratic national convention at St. Louis which nominated Cleveland. He prepared the democratic platform for the state convention in 1889, and drafted the address of the state executive committee at that time. He has been three times a member of the state democratic executive committee, and was nominated to the state constitutional convention of 1890 with instructions, which he declined, not desiring to serve in that body so hampered. He was then nominated without instructions and accepted. Upon the organization of the convention he was elected president, and discharged the delicate and responsible duties of this position with great credit to himself and general satisfaction to all. Judge Calhoon was united in marriage June 5, 1859, at Canton, Miss., to Augusta, daughter of Joseph M. Roberts. This union was a short one, for Mrs. Calhoon died in April, 1862. His second marriage was to Maggie, youngest daughter of Governor McWillie, and was consummated on the 21st of December, 1865, in time resulting in the birth of one child, that died in infancy. Judge Calhoon is a man of fine presence. He is five feet ten inches in hight, and of good proportions. His bearing is dignified, at the same time cordial and winning. His hair is light-brown, and he wears a beard and mustache; this, with a fair complexion, blue eyes and a kind, intellectual countenance, makes a prepossessing whole. His mind is acute, analytical, strong and vigorous. In matters of law his judgment is accurate, with intuitive conceptions of legal principles, sustained by a retentive memory. As a debater he is clear, sagacious and convincing; a man emphatically of argumentation. He has few equals when dealing with questions of fact, and his powers of separation and condensation of facts and their application are remarkable. In debate his manner is courteous, earnest and attractive, and respectful to those who differ from him. As a judge he was popular, and his decisions upon questions of law were regarded as final. He has a kind heart and a sympathetic nature, and is broad in his charities, "never letting his right hand know what his left hand doeth." He is simple in his tastes and liberal in his hospitalities, making his house the home of his friends, where his kind, genial nature is a source of pleasure to all. Add to the above a devoted husband and an unfaltering friend, and a fair presentation is made of one of the most popular members of the Mississippi bar.

A practicing physician and surgeon of Tallahatchie county and son of Thomas J. and Margaret (Meek) Calhoun and relative of Hon. John C. Calhoun, one of the most prominent figures in our national history, is Dr. James M. Calhoun, who was born in Abbeville district, S. C., 1832. His father was born in the same place about 1807, his mother was born in York district about 1812. They were married in Abbeville district about 1830. In 1837 they came to Tallahatchie county and settled on an improvement on Tillatoba creek, southeast of Charleston, moving about two years later to Preston, in Yalobusha county, to avail themselves of educational advantages there afforded. They lived in Preston about two years and then returned to their farm, where Mr. Calhoun died October, 1843, aged about thirty-six. He has a place in local history as one of the original settlers of Tallahatchie county and as a successful planter and progressive man. He was a son of William Calhoun, and elder brother of the distinguished statesman, J. C. Calhoun, who was born in Abbeville district, S. C., where he spent his life as a planter and reared a large family. His father, Patrick Calhoun, was a native of Ireland, who came to America prior to the Revolutionary war, and had the pioneer experiences and endured the pioneer hardships common at that time. He became a planter and died in Abbeville district. William Calhoun married Miss Catherine De Graffeinreid, of Swiss descent. The mother of our subject died in 1869, aged fifty-seven years. She was a daughter of James Meek, a native of York district, who came to Tallahatchie county about 1840, became a planter there and died in 1844. He was of Irish descent, and his wife was Miss McCaw, also a native of York district, who died at Preston, Yalobusha county, Miss., about 1842. They were both members of the Presbyterian church. They had born to them four sons and three daughters, of whom Dr. J. M. Calhoun was the second. William M. received an academic education in Mississippi and became a well-known planter and for four years served Tallahatchie county as sheriff. Henry T. received an academic education and was a member of the Tillatoba grays, a cavalry organization with which he served in the Confederate army during the Civil war. John C., a planter, was also a member of the same company. Ione C. is the widow of Henry Harper, who was killed at Murfreesboro December 31, 1862. He served as captain of company B, Twenty-ninth Mississippi infantry, having formerly been a successful lawyer at Charleston. Elizabeth C. became the wife of Dr. Robert W. Harper, a physician of Le Flore county and a brother of M. Henry Harper. Margaret T. was educated at Pontotoc and died in 1881. Dr. James M. Calhoun received his early education at the Preston academy and graduated from the State university of Mississippi in July, 1853. He consumed the interval from then till 1858 in teaching a school and reading medicine, and in 1860 he graduated from the medical department of the University of Tennessee, at Nashville. He practiced his profession at Preston until the beginning of the war, when he joined the Pontotoc dragoons, commanded by Capt. John H. Miller, a Presbyterian minister, which organization was attached to a regiment forming a part of the army of Tennessee. He entered the service as a private, and was afterward made assistant surgeon of the Second Mississippi cavalry, in which position he served until the close of the war. He participated in the Atlanta and Georgia campaigns and in the fighting on the way back to Tennessee and surrender at Artesia, Miss.; returned to Preston, whence he removed a few years later to the Cascilla neighborhood, where he has been for the last twenty-three years in the active practice of his profession, being everywhere recognized as one of the oldest and most successful physicians in Tallahatchie county. Dr. Calhoun is a true type of the old-fashioned Southern gentleman, friendly, hospitable, of more than the average natural ability and education and an interesting conversationalist. He has been fairly successful in life, and is the owner of about one thousand two hundred acres of land, some of which is productive and profitable. He is well informed on the issues of the day, but has never taken a specially active part in politics, preferring to devote his time to his profession.

George W. Calvert, Calvert, Miss., a well-known planter and merchant of Kemper county, Miss., of which he is a native, was born January 28, 1852, and is a son of Adam and Leah A. (Windham) Calvert. The father was born in Ireland in 1824. His parents, William and Esther (Greenlea) Calvert, emigrated to America when he was yet a child, and settled in Alabama. In 1833 they came to Kemper county, and the father engaged in planting and also embarked in the mercantile trade. He and his wife both spent the balance of their days there. Adam Calvert and Leah A. Windham were united in marriage in 1840, and reared a family of children, nine of whom are living: Mary, now Mrs. Vance; Elizabeth, now Mrs. Roberts; George W., the subject of this biography; James M.; Jeff. D.; Anna, now Mrs. Dr. Cochran; Mattie, now Mrs. Mulholland; Willie, Emmet and Virgie. The father died in 1880. He was a member of the Cumberland Presbyterian church, and of Center Ridge lodge, A. F. & A. M. For a number of years, also, he was justice of the peace. Politically he affiliates with the democratic party, and takes an active interest in all matters of importance to the public. The mother of our subject was born in Mississippi in 1828, and was a daughter of B. B. Windham, a planter and mechanic by occupation, and one of the early settlers of the state; he died in Alabama in 1885. Mrs. Calvert is still living and resides in Kemper county; she is a consistent member of the Cumberland Presbyterian church. George W. spent his early life on a farm in Kemper county, where he was trained to all the details of agriculture. He was educated in this county, and at the age of twenty-one years he engaged in farming on his own account. He was married in 1874 to Miss Lou Mulholland, a daughter of Joseph and Fannie Mulholland, both of Irish lineage. The Mulholland family was one of the earliest to settle in Mississippi. Mr. and Mrs. Calvert are the parents of five children: Stella, Preston, Jessie, Ivan and Essie. Mr. Calvert has been very prosperous in his planting, and owns about twelve hundred acres, the greater portion of which lies within the borders of Kemper county. In 1886 he entered the commercial circles of Kemper county, and in this branch of business he has also met with success. Politically he affiliates with the democratic party, and is connected with all matters of public importance. He and his wife are members of the Cumberland Presbyterian church, in which they are faithful workers. Mr. Calvert's father and brother William were both soldiers in the Civil war; William died in the army, and the father served almost the entire period.

Charles Brantley Calvit is the fortunate possessor of the plantation known as Liberty Hall, which makes one of the finest homes in Franklin county. He was born on this place in 1827 to William and Elizabeth (Spires) Calvit, the former of whom was born on the Potomac river, probably in Maryland, in 1783. In his early boyhood he was brought by his parents to Franklin county, and was reared in the neighborhood of where his son, Charles Brantley Calvit is now residing. After his marriage, he settled in the woods on what is now the Liberty Hall plantation, and this place he greatly improved, by his own earnest and unfaltering efforts, becoming a wealthy man. For the industry, enterprise and public spirit that he at all times manifested, and for the kindness of heart and generosity that at all times showed itself, he commanded the admiration, respect and affection of all who knew him. He was an active worker for the democrat party, and for the general welfare of the public, but was never an office seeker, the allurements of public life, or the temptation to the exercise of political power (other than as a private citizen), being insufficient to entice him from the

Henry. L. Burkitt

retirement of home life and pursuits. He assisted in the capture of Aaron Burr, was a believer in law and order, and was a man of worthy principles. He died in 1853, and his widow about the close of the war, she being a member of the Baptist church. Mr. Calvit was one of four sons who lived to be grown, their father being John Calvit, who was born in Maryland, in which state he was married to Miss Brantley. At a very early day he removed to Franklin county, Miss., but afterward located in Yazoo county, where he died when the subject of this sketch was a small lad. He was very fond of pioneer and back-wood's life, and as he was a good shot, a great hunter and Indian fighter, he was better cal-culated than the most, for that life. He had several brothers: Sandy, Anthony and Mum-ford, who came to southwest Mississippi in early times and became wealthy planters, the last named being at one time sheriff of Adams county. John Spires, the maternal grand-father, was a Kentuckian, and when a boy, was captured by the Indians, with whom he spent his youth, becoming very familiar with their customs and language. After his release, he made his way to Mississippi, and was married in Franklin county to Miss Hester Ford, who was born and reared in Natchez. Mr. Spires became successful as a planter, and both he and his wife have now been dead for many years. Charles Brantley Calvit is the eighth of a family of fourteen children born to his parents, and of this large family only he and his brother, Theodore G., of Louisiana, are now living. He received his education in the neigh-boring schools and at Oakland college, after which he spent one year in Louisiana. In 1855 he was married in Wilkinson county, and after residing there one year, returned to the place of his birth, where he has since made his home. He, at one time, was very wealthy, and although he lost heavily during the war, he has since retrieved his losses in a great measure, and is now the owner of two thousand two hundred acres of land. He served for some time in the Confederate army on detached duty, under Colonel Wirt Adams, but since that time has given his undivided attention to the peaceful pursuit of farming. He is a member of Solomon B. Stampley lodge No. 222, of Roxie, and is a public spirited and enterprising gentleman. He is very popular throughout this section, and is exceptionally well posted on local affairs. His first wife was Mrs. Elizabeth Landers, a daughter of Daniel Wilson, of Kentucky, but an early settler of Amite county, where he died, after having fol-lowed the life of a planter. Mrs. Calvit was born in Amite county, September 3, 1862. In 1865, Mr. Calvit married Miss Sarah E., daughter of Willis Freelove Carter. Mrs. Calvit was born in Adams county, and by Mr. Calvit is the mother of four sons.

John M. Cameron, county treasurer of Warren county and a member of the firm of Peatross, Cameron & Co., coal merchants, was born in Warren county in 1849, the eldest in a family of six children born to Dougald A. and Catherine (Mann) Cameron, both of whom were born in Mississippi. The father was a successful planter and a prominent man of his day in his community, but while in the prime of life, in 1858, was called from earth. His widow died in 1889, a member of the Methodist Episcopal church. The paternal grandfather, Daniel Cameron, was a Scotchman, and came to America at the end of the last century, settling in Franklin county, Miss., where he followed the life of a farmer and spent the rest of his days. He left four sons and two daughters, all of whom grew to maturity and left families. John M. Cameron received few advantages in his boyhood, owing to the opening of the war, but as he was too young to enlist in the service, he began managing his mother's plantation, continuing until 1867, when he engaged as a clerk at Grand Gulf, and from that time until 1869 followed the calling, in the meantime learning bookkeeping. In the last-named year he went to Rocky Springs, where he filled the duties of manager of a mercantile establishment for four years, then came to Vicksburg and became

31

bookkeeper for the firm of Mattingly, Flowerree & Co., coal merchants, and their successors, Mattingly, Son & Co., remaining as their trusted employe seventeen years, at the end of which time with his present partner he succeeded to the business. The firm has a large river and city wholesale and retail trade, owning tug-boats, coal barges and wharves essential to their river trade. Mr. Cameron has been quite active in politics, and in 1885, by his numerous friends, was elected to the office of county treasurer, being reëlected in 1887 and again in 1889, and is now ably discharging his duties. He is practically a self-made man, as the property which had been accumulated by his father was mostly swept away by the war. His education has also been mainly secured by his own efforts and he is now a well-informed gentleman and a representative business man as well as an ideal public officer. He has made business his study from youth up, and has put to a practical use the knowledge gained in the school of experience. He has, perhaps, one of the most complete agricultural libraries in Mississippi, and has made fruit culture a study and experiment. He is social, courteous and very popular, and his numerous worthy traits of character have won him many warm friends. He is of medium stature, strong and robust, has black hair and eyes, and is decidedly fine looking. He was married in 1877 to Miss Kate McLean, a native of Claiborne county, and a daughter of Edward McLean, an old settler from Kentucky. To their union seven children have been born, only three of whom are now living: Edward R., Irene E., and Stanley M. Mr. Cameron belongs to the A. F. & A. M., and the K. of H. His wife is an active and earnest member of the Methodist church.

Hon. John Ruthven Cameron, planter, Canton, Miss., is a descendant of sturdy Scotch ancestors, his paternal grandfather, Daniel Cameron, having emigrated from that country to this with five brothers, and settled in Franklin county, Miss., in 1809. The latter's son, Malcolm Cameron, was born on the 4th of February, 1817, and in addition to the common-school education obtained in his native country, he attended Oakland college, Mississippi. He was a planter, spending all his life engaged in that occupation in Mississippi, and was never a candidate for any political office. He was married in 1841 to Miss Tennessee Penquite, a native of Mississippi and the daughter of Dr. Abraham Penquite, who was born in Virginia. The latter was an eminent physician in his day, and was a very successful business man, owning a large fortune at the time of his death. In 1841 Mr. Cameron removed to Madison county, Miss., and located on the property now owned by our subject. He was a very extensive planter, was a prominent whig in his political views, and died in 1873. His marriage with Miss Penquite resulted in the birth of two children, both of whom died in childhood. Mrs. Cameron died on the 24th of January, 1844, and the following year Mr. Cameron took for his second wife Miss Mary Matilda Montgomery, a native of Mississippi and the daughter of Eli T. and Mary (Crockett) Montgomery. The Montgomery family is one of the oldest and most prominent ones of the state of Mississippi. John Ruthven Cameron was born on the site of his present home in Madison county, Miss., on the 3d of July, 1846, and was the only child born to Malcolm Cameron's second marriage. He inherits Scotch-Irish blood from the Montgomery side of the family, and his great-grandfather Montgomery reared a large family of sons who not only became fine business men and amassed large fortunes, but who were eminent and distinguished men in Mississippi. John R. Cameron grew to manhood in his native county, and although his educational advantages were limited, he is a man well posted on all subjects and is educated in all the practical affairs of life. He is a self-made man, principally, and owes his prosperity to his industry and good management. In 1863 Miss Virginia Chick, a native of Mississippi and the daughter of Richard A. and Jane (Davis) Chick, became his wife. Her parents were natives, respectively, of Virginia and Mississippi. Mr. Cameron's union resulted in the birth of four children: Lillian, who married Dr. Staples, of Kentucky, removed to Texas and there died in 1888; Malcolm, now has charge of his father's business on Deer creek, Sharkey county, Miss., and is a successful young business man; Virgie and Abraham Penquite are at home. Both of Mr. Cameron's daughters were educated in Bardstown, Ky. Soon after his marriage Mr. Cameron raised a cavalry company in Madison and adjoining counties and commanded the same until the close of the war. He surrendered at Jackson. After the war he began improving land on Deer creek, Miss., and, although he inherited a large landed estate at his father's death, he has largely increased it, and now has about ten thousand five hundred acres. In 1877 he was elected to represent Madison county in the legislature and received every vote polled. He served his term out, was not again a candidate until 1887, when he was elected to the state senate and is the present incumbent. Intellectually, Mr. Cameron is the peer of any in the honorable body of which he is a distinguished member, and in all offices of public trust he has served with credit and distinction. In 1889 he was a candidate for governor of Mississippi before the democratic party and made a strong and creditable race. Though defeated, no man, perhaps, in the state, stands higher in public esteem than John R. Cameron. He is a patriot and statesman of whom the people may well feel proud; the people's interests are his, and he has fostered them as jealously as a mother watches her child. He and family are members of the Presbyterian church and he is a Knight Templar in the Masonic fraternity. He is essentially a Mississippian, is proud to own the South as his birthplace, and nothing affects the state of Mississippi that does not affect him. He lives where he was born and is bound by the strongest ties to his state, county and people. His highest hope is to retain the ante-bellum type of civilization and the customs of his father and contemporaries. His greatest desire is to have a typical Southern home, and he takes great pleasure in beautifying his place. Many of his father's slaves are still with him and are devoted to him. Unlike many people of the South, Mr. Cameron does not make a trip east during the summer months, but his doors are thrown open at that time and his house filled with guests for weeks. As a host he is unexcelled, and in the full sense of the term he is a Southern gentleman. His home is provided with all kinds of amusements, billiard tables, bowling alleys, etc., and he spares no pains to make his guests enjoy their stay at his home. He is one of the noblest men of the South, is kind and generous to all, and instead of magnifying faults in others he finds excuses and overlooks them.

Robert M. Cameron, a prominent planter of Clarke county, Miss., was born in that county in 1853. He was the second of five children of Daniel and Sarah (Bass). His father settled in this county in 1850. He was born in North Carolina in about 1824, the son of Norman Cameron who was a native of Scotland. He is still living, engaged in planting. He is a Mason and a member of the Methodist Episcopal church South, and a Democrat. The mother of our subject was born in South Carolina in 1820, the daughter of John Bass. Mr. and Mrs. Cameron were married in Alabama, when they moved to Mississippi. The children are: Mary C., Robert M., Sarah N., Lou C. and Joseph D. In his early life Robert M. Cameron lived in Clarke county, where he was educated, and at the age of twenty-one he married Nora Peel, daughter of David B. Peel, also of this county, but who was born in Alabama in 1854. Mr. and Mrs. Cameron have seven children, named as follows: James A., Lillie V., Robert A., Bella L., Thomas F., David P. and Dewitt D., all of whom are living with their parents, both of whom are members of the Methodist church (Episcopal) South, the children also being attendants upon the service of the same religious denomination. Mr. Cameron is a man of much public spirit, taking a helpful interest in all things pertaining to the public good. He is liberal in all his support of education and religion, and has given according to his means to benevolent institutions of different kinds. He has been for many years engaged in planting, and about a year ago started in the milling business, doing most of the grinding and ginning for his section of the county. In a business way he has been success-ful, all that he possesses having been acquired through his own efforts. He is not a man who devotes much of his time to politics, preferring rather to attend strictly to his home interests. His father served in the Confederate army during the war, enlisting in 1863 in Miller's cavalry company.

James D. Cammack, a planter of Copiah county, Miss., was born in Sumner county, Tenn., in 1812. He is the oldest living child of Thomas and Isabella Cammack, both of whom were born in Ireland, the former in 1784, and the latter in 1786. Thomas Cammack came to America with his mother, his father being dead, when he was thirteen years old. They located in South Carolina. His wife came to America with her parents at the age of three years, and they also settled in South Carolina. Thomas Cammack was bound out to learn the jeweler's trade when a boy, but his employer failing to send him to school, accord-ing to contract, he ran away, and found employment on a farm, thus beginning a career which he followed till the end of his days. He married Isabella Neally about the year 1800, and to them were born four children, of whom are living, James D. (our subject) and Jane, the wife of Julius Alford, of Copiah county. After the death of his first wife, Mr. Cammack married Jemima McLemore, and to them were born ten children, all of whom are deceased except two. Thomas Cammack spent his early life in South Carolina, and removed when comparatively young to Tennessee, and in 1815 he moved to Wayne county, Miss., where he lived two years, after which he moved to Perry county, and in 1826 he moved to Copiah county, where he lived until his death. He was a member of the Masonic order, and also a member of the Methodist church. At the age of twenty-two years, James D. Cammack married Lucretia A. Corley, daughter of Seth and Temperance (Watkins) Corley, of Copiah county. They have had born to them twelve children, nine of whom are living: Martha J., wife of Archibald Steele (deceased), of Copiah county; Rankin, of Crystal Springs; Thomas J., of Texas; Lucretia, wife of William T. Gray, of Copiah county; James M., of Copiah county; Francis A., the wife of Thomas Matheney, of Crystal Springs; Sarah A., wife of D. H. Tillman, of Copiah county; Mary the wife of Samuel McQuean, and John F., of Crystal Springs. Our subject has been a farmer all of his life. He is a member of the Masonic order, and has reached the highest degree in the Blue lodge. He has also taken the chapter and counsel degrees. He has been a member of the Methodist Episcopal church for sixty-five years, and with that organization his wife and family are all identified. The success which has been attained by Mr. Cammack is but the just reward of legitimate endeavors, he having been all his life an honest, industrious and persevering man, rendering unto his fellowmen that which was their due, and sparing no effort to make such progress as to assure to him-self and his children respectable positions in society.

Charles H. Campbell, cashier of the bank of Winona, is a native of Mississippi, born in Carroll (now Montgomery) county on the 13th of February, 1841, and is a son of Capt. Charles P. Campbell, who was born in Halifax county, N. C., in 1808. The father was married in his native state to Miss Rebecca Webb, also a native of that county and state, and he and family emigrated west to Mississippi in 1836. They settled in Carroll county, in the part now embraced in Montgomery county, and there Mr. Campbell followed planting and reared his family. During the Mexican war he was captain of a company from 1846 to 1849 and took his company to the front, but was not in time to participate in the war. He was a member of the Methodist church and died in 1865, his widow following him to the grave a few months later. Their family consisted of eight children—three sons and five daughters. Two of the sons grew to maturity, and another son, James M , was a soldier in the Confederate army. He served in the Fifteenth Mississippi infantry, was wounded, and afterward, in 1862, died of fever at Duck Hill. The daughters are all married and have families. Charles H. Campbell was reared to mature years in his native county, and educated in the private schools of the same. In April, 1861, he joined the Fifteenth Mississippi infantry, Confederate army, with his older brother, and served as lieutenant until the close of the war. He participated in the battles of Fishing creek, under Zollicoffer, was in the battles of Shiloh, Corinth, Vicksburg, Baton Rouge, Baker's creek, the engagements from Dalton to Atlanta, and around that city in the numerous every-day engagements. He was also at Decatur, Ala., and at Franklin, Tenn., where his leg was broken by a shot, and he was permanently disabled. He was paroled at Franklin, Tenn., and afterward returned home. Mr. Campbell was the first agent of the Illinois Central railroad at Winona appointed on the road, and, in 1866, he was again appointed agent at that place, serving in that capacity until the latter part of 1867, when he resigned. Mr. Campbell was married in Franklin, Tenn., November 19, 1867, to Miss Fannie E. Morton, who was born, reared and educated in that city. She is the daughter of Jacob H. and Susie P. Morton. After his marriage Mr. Campbell located at Union city, Tenn., where he was engaged in merchandising for two years. In 1870 he returned with his family to his native state and county and there followed planting for one year. Mr. Campbell was elected circuit clerk of Montgomery county, and located in Winona, serving two years in that capacity. He was then elected sheriff and taxcollector, and at the expiration of his term was reëlected, holding that responsible position for three terms, fully testifying as to the wisdom of the people's choice. In 1880 he engaged in the banking business at Winona, and five years later the bank of Winona was organized with a capital stock of $50,000. Mr. Campbell was elected cashier, and has filled that position up to the present date. He is one of the representative business men of this county, and is energetic, enterprising and public-spirited. Mr. and Mrs. Campbell's union resulted in the birth of five interesting children: Minnie, Maude, Bessie, Morton and Charles. Maude, the pride and hope of the family, died June 20, 1870, at the age of sixteen years and six months. She was one of the noblest and most perfect types of young womanhood that the country has produced, kind, intelligent and useful. She was cut off in the springtime of her promising life. This was the first great affliction that her family were called on to suffer. Mr. Campbell and wife are members of the Methodist church and he is a Knight Templar in the Masonic fraternity. He represented the Winona commandery at two different times in the grand lodge. He is also a member of the I. O. O. F. and the Knights of Honor.

A man who by strength of character and mental powers rises to eminence in a learned profession is a monument to the intellectual grandeur of his race. Such a man is Judge Josiah A. P. Campbell, of Jackson, at present chief justice of the supreme court of the state of Mississippi. He is a descendant of an old and prominent South Carolina family, where he was born March 2, 1830, to Robert B. and Mary (Patterson) Campbell, both of whom were also born in that state, the former December 6, 1796, and the latter January 24, 1797, they being of Scotch and Irish descent, respectively. The former received his primary education at the Willington and Liberty academies, the latter being known at the present time as the Washington and Lee college. Subsequently he entered Princeton university, where he remained three years studying theology. After leaving the university he was admitted into the ministry of the Presbyterian church, in which capacity he labored until his death, which took place at Canton, Miss., in 1870. His widow survived him one year, departing this life in 1871. They were the parents of six children: Robert B., Josiah A. P., James A., Mary L., Charles H. and Jane E. Robert was a member of the Fortieth Mississippi regiment. He was promoted to the rank of major, was a brave and intrepid soldier, and was killed at Vicksburg, Miss., during its siege. James A. was colonel of the Twenty-seventh Mississippi; was taken prisoner at the battle of Lookout mountain, and was sent to Johnson's island, where he died and was buried. Charles H. was a captain in the Thirteenth Mississippi, and served through the entire war, losing an eye. He is at present circuit judge of the fifth judicial district, and resides at Kosciusko, Miss. Mary is the wife of Dr. Scarborough, a leading physician at Kosciusko. Jane is the wife of James M. Grafton, a prominent planter in Madison county. Judge Campbell received the rudiments of his education at home, and in the common schools, but also attended school for a time in Lawrenceville, Ga., afterward entering Davidson college, North Carolina, where he completed his course. From there he went to Madison county, Miss., where his father located in 1845, and began the study of law with Samuel Ford. He was admitted to the bar at Kosciusko, June 12, 1847, being then only seventeen years of age. He opened his law office at the same place and rose rapidly in his profession, soon building up a large practice. He remained there, except during the war period, until 1865, when he was elected circuit judge to fill an unexpired term. He was first elected to the legislature in 1851, on the democratic ticket. This was the first election at which he could vote. He then retired and once more began devoting his exclusive attention to the practice of law, which was much more congenial to his tastes. In 1859 he was again brought out by the people for the legislature, was elected and became speaker of the house. When the state seceded in 1861, Judge Campbell was chosen as a delegate to the constitutional convention at Montgomery, Ala., at which place two sessions were held, being then moved to Richmond, where it became, after the formation of the Confederate constitution, the provisional congress. After the expiration of his term, March, 1862, Judge Campbell became a member of the Confederate army, and was elected captain of company K, Fortieth Mississippi. At the organization of the regiment at Meridian, he was chosen lieutenant-colonel, and his regiment was assigned to General Herbert's brigade and General Little's division, under General Price. His first engagement was at Iuka, September 19, 1862, where they fought against General Sherman's forces. Colonel Campbell is of the opinion that this was one of the sharpest infantry fights of the war, which opinion is sustained by General Sherman's memoirs. It was at this battle that General Little was killed. During this battle, toward its close, Colonel Campbell commanded his regiment, continued in command, and led the regiment at Corinth October 4, 1862, where he was wounded. He was able to rejoin his regiment at Grenada, where the Confederate troops were confronting Grant. Subsequently the troops moved to Vicksburg, and while there Judge Campbell received notice from the secretary of war that he had been appointed by President Davis, and confirmed by the senate, to the rank of colonel of cavalry and assigned to duty as a member of the military court of General Polk's corps. He reported to that officer and held the assignment until the surrender of the Confederate army at Appomattox. This court had jurisdiction to try any military offender from the lowest rank to the highest, and the position was one of great responsibility. After the surrender elections were ordered by the governor of Mississippi to fill vacancies, and Colonel Campbell became a candidate for the circuit judgeship of the fifth judicial district, composed of the counties of Attala, Leake, Madison, Yazoo and Holmes. He was elected, and at the expiration of his term was reëlected in the fall of 1866 for a full term. During his second term the test oath which the Federal government had adopted and which all officials were required to take, was presented to him. Being unable to take this oath, he resigned his office and retired to private life. He immediately opened a law office at Canton, to which place he had removed in January, 1869, and soon after formed a copartnership with Judge S. S. Calhoon, which continued advantageously to both for seven years. In 1876, when the democratic party again resumed control of the political destinies of the state, he was appointed judge of the supreme court for a term of nine years by Governor Stone, which was confirmed by the senate. This was without solicitation by him. He was reappointed by Governor Lowry in the same way, and is at present serving out his second term. Judge Campbell has been the recipient of many honors. In 1870 he was elected professor of law of the University of Mississippi, but this position he declined. Subsequently he was appointed by Governor Alcorn one of the commissioners to codify the laws of the state, which resulted in the code of 1871. In 1878 he was invited by the legislature to prepare and submit a code of laws, and this difficult and responsible task he accepted. He prepared and submitted a code, which was adoped by the legislature, and became the code of 1880, and, as few alterations were made, this may be considered a high compliment to his legal ability and learning. In 1883 the honorary degree of LL. D. was conferred upon him by the University of Mississippi.

In 1890 he was invited by the legislature of the state of Mississippi to deliver an address at the statehouse on the occasion of memorial services on the life and character of Jefferson Davis. This was a pleasing task, and Judge Campbell delivered an eloquent address which was pronounced one of the finest eulogies ever given a man. So eloquent was this address, so full of sublime and appropriate thought, that it is difficult to quote from any part of it. It should be taken in its entirety to be fully appreciated, but one passage is here given: " Whether our people acted wisely or unwisely, and were culpable for loving the Union so well, and clinging to it so long, must remain unanswerable forever. Looking back, it is not surprising that the North should have been unwilling to part with the South. It was natural that the citizens of each section should adhere to it. I have never blamed a Northern man for supporting his country in the contest which followed; and before the bar of justice and fairness, I demand the same recognition for myself and countrymen in supporting ours. We are all, to a large extent, creatures of education and victims of circumstances. This is our native earth, and rights to which we were born were in jeopardy. Men love their land, ' because it is their own, and scorn to give aught other reason why.'" This address might be spoken of as did Queen Katherine of the eulogy paid by Griffith to Cardinal Wolsey:

> "After my death I wish no other herald,
> No other speaker of my living affections,
> To keep mine honor from corruption
> But such an honest chronicler as Griffith."

Judge Campbell was united in marriage at Kosciusko, May 23, 1850, to Eugenia E., daughter of Rev. W. W. and Nancy (Dotson) Nash. They have seven children, all of whom are living: Charles C., Robert B., Josiah A. P., Jr., Minnie C. (now Mrs. R. M. Damerson), Newton N., Nannie B. (now Mrs. Edward Yerger) and Willie N. Robert has served in the legislature and was a member of the constitutional convention. Josiah is at present a member of the legislature from Hinds county. Judge Campbell is a man of imposing presence, of dignified and courtly bearing, and would attract attention in the most thronged streets or public gatherings. He is fully six feet two inches in hight, perfectly upright in carriage and extremely well proportioned. His countenance is marked by vivid intelligence, his eyes are blue and his pleasant face is unshaven. He is a fond husband and a devoted father; in all his social relations he is considerate, kind and the soul of courtesy. His home is the world in which he lives, and he makes it the center of his life and happiness. To his professional attainments are added that peculiar refinement which comes of high culture and a generous nature. The biography of this soldier, statesman and jurist might properly be closed here, for his works will perpetuate his name to history, and will be his own monument, yet a few more words will not be inappropriate in closing. Though not educated or trained for a military life, yet when in arms he took front rank, and was a brave, efficient and gallant officer. As a statesman and legislator he has proved himself to be farsighted, wise and profound. It is, however, as a jurist that he is most widely known. This is his special field of labor, and in it he stands exalted. He is a forcible, eloquent and convincing advocate, discussing the most intricate questions of law with clearness and eminent ability. As a judge he is upright and pure, and his decisions are only given after careful thought. He has great power of dispatching business, and his careful and analytical mind enables him to readily master the legal points of a cause, while he conscientiously watches with a jealous eye the scales of justice that they may be equally poised. Thus he is held by the people of his state, for whose welfare and advancement he has ever labored at the bar, on the battle-field, in the legislative halls, and in the forum as one of their leaders. The utmost vigor of his mind he gave to discharging his duties as a jurist, and in this field his counsel was sought by the people. As the Mussulman turns to Mecca for his spiritual light, so do the people of Mississippi turn to their distinguished jurist, Judge Josiah A. P. Campbell, for their law.

One of the able lawyers of Greenville, Miss., is Hon. Robert Bond Campbell, a native of this state, his birth occurring in Kosciusko, Attala county, on the 20th of September, 1853. He was second in order of birth of eight children born to Josiah A. P. and Elizabeth (Nash) Campbell, the father a native of South Carolina and the mother of Alabama. At the age of seventeen, or in 1847, the father began practicing law, and in 1876 he was appointed a member of the supreme court, in which capacity he is still serving (see sketch). Robert B. Campbell was educated at Roanoke college, Va., and in the University of Mississippi at Oxford. After reading law with his father he was admitted to the bar on the 29th of September, 1874, after which he immediately began practicing at Canton, Miss. In 1880 he came to Greenville, and on the 8th of March, 1887, he formed the present partnership of Campbell & Starling. Though never an aspirant for political acknowledgement he was a member of the state legislature in 1888, and was a delegate to the state constitutional convention in 1890. He was appointed by the governor under the recent constitution as one of three commissioners to codify the laws of Mississippi, and his father had codified the laws of Mississippi twice previously. He was elected to the above-mentioned positions without solicitation, and filled the same with credit to himself and his constituents. He is a rising young attorney, and has had a thorough preparatory training, both literary and professional. Mr. Campbell was married on the 1st of May, 1876, to Miss Lucy Dancy of Canton, daughter of William E. Dancy, and to this union were born five children: Eugenia Maggie (deceased), Edwin, Patterson, Lucy (died in 1886), and Robert B. (died in 1886). The family are members of the Baptist church.

William R. Campbell (deceased), who was one of the representative citizens of Bolivar county, was born at Argyle plantation, Washington county, Miss., in September, 1842, and his father, William R. Campbell, Sr., was a native of the blue grass regions of Kentucky. The elder Campbell came to Mississippi when there were very few settlers, engaged in merchandising at Vicksburg, was married there, and there resided until 1842, when he moved to Washington county, the same state. He located on a large tract of land, made many improvements and became prominently identified with the interests of the county. He was of Scotch extraction. Our subject's maternal grandmother, Rebecca Horner, was a native of Denmark. William R. Campbell, Jr., attained his twenty-first birthday in Washington county, received his education at Emmettsburg and other towns in Virginia and finished by taking a course in a commercial college at St. Louis. One year later he entered the Confederate army, in Captain Clark's company, was second lieutenant of a cavalry company and before the close of the war was promoted to the rank of captain. He was aide-de-camp to a commander at Chickamauga and was in that corps for some time. After the war he followed planting for two years on his mother's plantation, and in 1867 was married to Miss Sophia Johnson, of Lexington, Ky. In 1868 he came to Bolivar county, located on the plantation where his widow now resides, and here made many and vast improvements, clearing about two hundred acres. He soon became quite prominent in politics, and after taking charge of the sheriff's office for the man elected to that position, was himself elected to that position in 1877, serving faithfully and efficiently until his death in April, 1878. He left five children, who are named as follows: William R., Stella, Louise, Sallie and Charles. Mr. Campbell was a member of the Christian church, and his widow and children hold membership in that church at the present time. Mrs. Campbell has a fine plantation, five hundred acres, with four hundred acres under cultivation, and this plantation, Woodlands, is situated two miles from Lamont and is kept in excellent condition.

E. S. Candler, Sr., is a leading lawyer of Iuka, Tishomingo county, Miss., and a prominent man in that part of the state. He is a son of Hon. Samuel C. and Martha (Beall) Candler. He is of an old and prominent family of Georgia, which, for a number of generations, has been intimately connected with the various interests of the state. Samuel C. Candler was born December 6, 1809, near Milledgeville, the former capital of Georgia. He was a son of Daniel Candler, of Columbia county, Ga., who was born in 1781, and whose father was a soldier in the Revolutionary war, and also a native Georgian. His wife was Sarah Butler Slaughter, whose father was also a rebel. Daniel Candler was a planter, and died at the early age of thirty-three years. His son, Samuel C. Candler, the father of our subject, was thus left an orphan of tender age, and was reared by his mother on the plantation, but at the age of eighteen years he moved into Cherokee county, Ga., then inhabited by the Indians, and there engaged in the mercantile business. He was elected sheriff of this county when he was barely twenty-one years old, and then was elected to the legislature, and before his term of office expired. In 1830 he removed to Carroll county, Ga., and died there in 1873, at sixty-four years of age. During this time he was a member of the legislature several times. In 1860 he was a Douglas democrat, and was a member of the national democratic convention which met that year at Charleston, S. C., and in the memorable contest in which Mr. Lincoln was elected president he was an elector on the Douglas ticket. He opposed secession with all his power and influence, but after Georgia withdrew from the Union he believed it his duty to go with the state, and gave the Southern Confederacy his sincere and cordial support. He was married, December 8, 1833, to Martha Beall, daughter of Noble P. Beall, who was born December 6, 1819, and who is still living. Noble P. Beall was born in Franklin county, Ga., in 1798, and married Justiana Hooper, who was born in 1800. Both of these were of Revolutionary ancestry. The mother of E. S. Candler, Sr., was one of twelve children. The subject of this sketch is one of eleven children: Hon. Milton A. Candler (who was a member of the XLVth and also the XLVIth congress), Ezekiel S., Noble D. (who died in 1887), Julia Florence, Jessie, William B., Lizzie F., Asa G., Samuel C., Warren A. and John S. Warren A. is now president of Emory college, at Oxford, Ga., and John S. is solicitor general of one of the judicial circuits of Georgia. Samuel C. Candler and his wife were members of the Methodist Episcopal church. Their children are all church members, being distributed among the Baptist, Methodist and Presbyterian churches. The early life of E. S. Candler, Sr., was spent on the farm and at school. He received a classical education, graduating from Cherokee Baptist college in 1859, taking the highest honors of his class. He read law and was admitted to the bar, and began the practice of his profession in 1860 in Carroll county, Ga. He was born December 6, 1838, in Campbell county, Ga., about twenty miles from the city of Atlanta. He came to Iuka, Miss., in 1870, and from then till January, 1875, was principal of the Iuka male academy, and had a large and prosperous school. In 1875 he resumed the practice of law at Iuka, which he has continued successfully until the present time. In August, 1860, he married Julia Bevill, of Bellville, Hamilton county, Fla., whose parents, Granville and Sarah Bevill, were of French descent, but natives of Georgia. The wife of E. S. Candler, Sr., was born February 27, 1842, and was the youngest of seven children. He and his wife are members of the Baptist church. Mr. and Mrs. Candler have only three children, all sons: Ezekiel S., Jr., Daniel Bevill and Milton A., the first of whom is a lawyer at Corinth, Miss., and one of the brightest and most promising of the young lawyers of the state. He was one of the electors, and as such cast a vote for Mr. Cleveland for president in 1888. He married Nannie Hazlewood, of Lawrence county, Ala., who was a daughter of Thomas B. Hazlewood. The other two, Daniel B. and Milton A., are members of their father's family, the first engaged in farming and the latter still in school. Mr. Candler is a member of the Knights of Honor and Knights and Ladies of Honor, and a democrat of the strict construction school. His interest and confidence in the improvement and development of Mississippi is unbounded. He is a strong friend to, and an active promoter of, all educational enterprises, and is a member and president of the board of trustees of the Iuka normal institute, one of the most flourishing and noted institutions of the state. He is the owner of the largest acreage of lands in his county, most of which is covered with the finest of timber, and is also fine farming land; and it being in an exceedingly healthy country abounding in fine streams of water, Mr. Candler is enthusiastic in his description of its many beauties and excellencies.

Julius O. Canfield was born on the plantation on which he is now residing July 1, 1841, a son of Orlando C. Canfield, who was born in South Breton, Conn., on the 4th of April, 1791. He was of English descent and a lawyer by profession, and a graduate of Yale college, and after his removal to Greene county, N. C., in 1822, he continued to practice law, in which capacity he became well known. While at that place he was united in marriage to Miss Mary D. Roach in 1828, by whom he became the father of the following children: Mary, Augustus R., Julia O., and Julius O., living, and Charles B., Sarah T. and Henry C., deceased. In 1837 Orlando C. Canfield removed with his family to Lowndes county, Miss., and settled on the plantation that is now owned by Julius O. The latter received a practical education in the common schools, and at the time of the opening of the Civil war he was deep in his studies. He at once cast aside his books to enlist in the Confederate army and became a private in company C, Thirty-fifth Mississippi infantry. The first active engagement in which he participated was at Iuka, but later he was in the engagements at Corinth and Vicksburg. In the siege of the last-named place he was taken prisoner, but was soon afterward released and returned to his home, where he commenced devoting his attention to planting, a calling that has occupied his attention up to the present time. He was married November 19, 1869, to Miss Charity, daughter of Nevett and Mary (McKinnie) Edwards, and as they have no children of their own they are rearing a child of a deceased brother of Mr. Canfield, James Burton Canfield. Mr. Canfield is a member of the A. F. & A. M., is a democrat politically, and has long been a member of the Methodist Episcopal church.

Will C. Cannon, circuit and chancery clerk of Lawrence county, is one of the most prominent and worthy citizens of that county. He was born in Lawrence county in 1856, where he was reared and educated. He was the youngest of a family of seven children, born to Jesse D. and Adeline L. (Oatis) Cannon, who were natives of Georgia and Mississippi, respectively. Jesse D. Cannon was born in 1815, and was the son of Jesse D. Cannon, Sr., a native of Georgia. The grandmother of our subject, Frances Hardesty, was also a native of Georgia, who lived and died in that state, leaving her husband with nine daughters and three sons to mourn her loss. Mr. Cannon, with his children, most of whom were grown and married, came to Mississippi when Jesse D., Jr., was a small boy, and settled in Lawrence county on Silver creek. Their son was educated in the common schools. He married Adeline Oatis in 1835. He removed soon after to a point on Dry creek, near the home of his bride. The father of our subject was a mechanic, and worked at his trade in connection with planting. He was very successful in life, and accumulated considerable property, dying in 1859. He was a well respected citizen, who took no active part in politics, while having the welfare of the public at heart. He was a member of the Baptist church at Silver creek, and was its clerk some years before his death. Matthew Cannon, one of his brothers, was for a number of years judge of the probate court. He reared a family of three children, all of whom are deceased. Judge Cannon was a man of good mind, whose opinion was sought in all matters of importance. He was a prominent member of the Baptist church. Joseph Cannon, another brother, died while a very young man. Of his sisters, two remained in Georgia, two quite late in life removed to Texas, and five of them came to Mississippi. Mrs. Nancy Robertson is yet living in Covington county, Miss., with one of her grandchildren. She was the wife of Elder Norval Robertson, who was for forty years the pastor of the Bethany church of this county, and who was one of the leading ministers in the state. He was quite well known as an author, having published a treatise on theology. He died June 1, 1878, aged eighty-one years, leaving his wife, one son and four daughters, his son and one of his daughters having since died. Mrs. Robertson was born in Georgia in 1812. Those of her children who are yet living are: Miss Sallie Robertson, Mrs. Laura Beal and Mrs. Lou Hemeter. Mrs. Cannon was born in Lawrence county, Miss., in 1819, being a daughter of John H. and Mary H. (Buckley) Oatis, natives respectively of Georgia and South Carolina. Mr. Oatis came to Hancock county, Miss., when a young man and there married, removing about two years later to Lawrence county, where he located on Pearl river. Still later, he took up his residence at a point on Silver creek, removing thence to a place on Dry creek, where he followed planting until his death in 1863, at the age of seventy-two years. He was a soldier in one of the early wars, and was promoted to the rank of colonel. He was quite active in politics, and was at one time United States marshal of Mississippi. In his earlier life he was a whig, but during the troublesome times preceding the war, and during the period after, he was a democrat. He was a man of good attainments, well posted on general topics, and especially conversant with the history of our country. He was a member of Bethany church, of which he was one of the most liberal supporters. He was for many years a Mason. At the time of the beginning of the war he was quite wealthy, owning considerable land and quite a number of slaves. His wife died in 1887, lacking at that time but thirteen days of being ninety-three years old. She was born in South Carolina, and came with her parents to Mississippi, locating in Hancock county. A short time afterward they removed to a point on Pearl river in this county. She was the second child and eldest daughter of a family of five sons and six daughters born to Edward and Narcissus (Castello) Buckley, natives of South Carolina, her father having been of English descent, and her mother of Scotch descent. Her grandfather, Edmund Buckley, or Berkley, was kidnaped when a child, and brought from England to South Carolina, where he was bound out to service until his twenty-first birthday, not being permitted to learn even so much as the alphabet. After he became his own master, he began planting for himself. He married and had a family of eight children.

The father of John Oatis was Jeremiah Oatis, a native of Georgia, and of Irish descent, who came to Hancock county, Miss., where he died in middle life. His wife, Jane (Sinkfield) Oatis, was a native of Georgia, whose forefathers were Germans. Mrs. Oatis survived her husband many years and married a second time. By her marriage with Mr. Oatis she had four children, of whom three were sons; the father of Mrs. Cannon was the second in order of birth. William died of paralysis while quite young. Jacob, who became a wealthy planter near Vicksburg, died at the age of seventy-two years. The daughter, Mrs. Mary Colvert, died in Hinds county. It may be regarded as somewhat singular that the above four children and Mr. Oatis himself, all died of paralysis. To the parents of the subject of this sketch were born the following children: Mary, who died unmarried, in 1885; John, who was killed at Chattanooga, Tenn., during the late war; Blanche is unmarried and makes her home with her mother in Monticello, Miss.; Edward died in Monticello, of a fever; David Judson was married and lives in Claiborne county, where he is engaged in planting; he also has twice served his native county, Lawrence, as sheriff; Frank, who lives on the homestead in Lawrence county; and Will C. Cannon, who was educated mostly at his home and at the private schools, and became a teacher before he attained his majority. After teaching for some time in Lawrence county, he was made deputy sheriff, in which capacity he served for three years. He was then made deputy county clerk. Three years later, 1887, he was elected circuit and chancery clerk, which office he has since held with honor to himself and to the satisfaction of his fellow-citizens. He pays the most devoted attention to the duties involving upon him, and he is one of the most popular officials in the county, being recognized, at the same time, as one of the most able business men. A democrat in politics, he is fully alive to the interests of his party. He was married December 28, 1887, to Miss Mary L. Huffman, a native of Summit, Miss., and a daughter of Dr. John and Mary (Graves) Huffman. Her mother was born in Vermont and reared in New York, and her father in Pike county, Miss. Five children were born to them, two of whom are deceased; John, Mary L. and Farrar are living. Mary L. was reared and educated in Summit, graduating from Lea female college. To Mr. and Mrs. Cannon has been born one daughter, Hazel Louise. Mr. and Mrs. Cannon are members of the Baptist church, of which Mr. Cannon is the clerk. Mrs. Cannon was formerly connected with the Presbyterian church. They have one of the most pleasant homes in Monticello, where they dispense the most liberal hospitality. They are well known and highly respected by all who have the honor of their acquaintance.

William R. Cannon, a distinguished and truly great and good man, was the eldest son of Rashae Cannon and Sallie Vinson. He was born in Darlington district, S. C., April 9, 1804. His father was of English descent, and was truly a politician of the Jackson school. He was firm and decided in his character, and was possessed in an eminent degree of wisdom and high honor, which fitted him to train and educate his children. He was for thirty years in succession a member of the senate of South Carolina, showing conclusively how he was esteemed by the people of his state. The mother, Sallie Vinson, was born in Newport, R. I., and was quite young when she came to Charleston, S. C., and assumed the duties of a wife and mother. She was intellectual, gentle, refined and religious, espousing the faith of the Congregational church. Her pious training left its impress upon her son, William, who was her fond and constant companion. Thus, his character was well formed when but a child. It was during this period of his life that he determined never to taste spirituous liquors, smoke or chew tobacco, which he faithfuly kept during his entire life. He had the misfortune to lose his mother in early youth, thus depriving him of his best earthly friend, but the moral and religious tone of her instruction to him gilded his future life with culture and refinement. He received a common-school and academic education in Darlington village. About the year 1821 his father sent him to the fostered institution of the state, the South Carolina college, located at Columbia. He was placed under the tutorship and guardian care of its able president, the celebrated Dr. Cooper (whose name is a household word to every South Carolinian). His course while at college was classical and complete. After graduating with honor in a class composed of some of the most gifted young men of that day, he pursued the study of law at the same institution, often excelling the other members of the class. After a thorough course his name was enrolled at Columbia on the list of attorneys, as stated by O'Neal's "Bench and Bar of South Carolina." Being endowed with a fortune, he made the law more a pastime and pleasure rather than a profession. Soon after his return from Columbia to Darlington village, he married Miss Jane C. Witherspoon, of Georgetown, S. C. Her early death left to his fond care two little daughters. During his life in South Carolina he made annual tours to New York by steamer from the port of Charleston. Upon one of these occasions, a terrific storm dashed the billows with more than ordinary fierceness against the vessel. The entire crew and passengers despaired of life, each one praying for deliverance. It was then that Mr. Cannon was brought face to face with death. He then made his mother's God his God, surrendering himself entirely to his Savior. From that moment his faith never swerved, and after reaching his home he united with the Methodist Episcopal church, and ever afterward lived a consistent Christian life. In 1830 began the exciting time of nullification, which severed the best of friends. This dreadful time of turmoil and anxiety caused many sons of South Carolina to leave their native homes and seek asylums in the far West. Noted among this number was Rashae Cannon and his two sons, William and Thomas. They felt a pang of deep sorrow to abandon the soil of South Carolina for a home among strangers. But they claimed allegiance to the principles of Andrew Jackson, so in the year of 1835 they moved with intrepid steps to Mississippi, bringing with them their families, their negroes, flocks and herds, and settled twelve miles northwest of the Tombigbee river. Lowndes county at that early date was but sparsely populated. The town of Columbus was in its infant state. Very soon a prosperous tide of emigration came pouring in, which caused its rapid development. There was no family more influential, wealthy, or intelligent than the Cannon family, so comfortably domiciled in their new home. The brothers and sisters were each in their turn sent off to the best colleges in the Southland, and obtained finished educations which secured for them a permanent influence with their new friends and acquaintances. William R. Cannon married the second time, in the spring of 1836, his distant cousin, Miss Eliza J. Cannon, at Darlington, S. C. She was the daughter of the late William Henry Cannon, so complimentarily mentioned by the historian, W. Gilmore Simms. When the young, fair and intellectual bride reached her Western home, she began with energy to embellish it, and very soon it was like an oasis in contrast with the log huts and uncultivated gardens of most of the inhabitants. This rural but artistic home was soon sought out by the politicians of that early period of Mississippi. Mr. William R. Cannon's influence and support were considered a passport to success, for he had been truly portrayed as one in whose character was blended modesty, integrity, gentleness, wisdom and firmness, consequently those who were so fortunate as to gain his friendship felt repaid for days of fatigue and travel. It was about the year 1836 that S. S. Prentiss and Samuel I. Gholson made their celebrated canvass for congress. Each of these gentlemen had warm friends and adherents. While Mr. Cannon listened spellbound to the eloquence of the gifted Prentiss, and personally loved him and admired his genius and ability, still, when the test came he cast his vote for his faithful party friend, Gholson. In the year 1842 Colonel Cannon was nominated and elected to represent Oktibbeha county in the lower house of the legislature (into which county he had moved about this date). His able course and his devotion to duty made his career distinguished for peculiar usefulness. At the close of his term he was elected senator from the counties of Chickasaw, Choctaw and Oktibbeha, by a very large majority. His services were brilliant and very conspicuous for ferreting out frauds in the treasury of the state, as he was put upon the financial committee. He was made president of the senate, over which body he presided with ease and judgment, and was called upon a number of times to act as governor in the absence of that high official.

In 1850 Colonel Cannon was elected president of the state democratic convention which met in Jackson, and presided with dignity and grace. This same year the contest for governor between Jefferson Davis and Henry S. Foote was violently bitter. While Colonel Cannon was a personal and true friend to Foote, he warmly supported Mr. Davis. They both were adherents to the state rights wing of the democratic party, and personally were to each other as Jonathan and David. This family at Columbus have still in their possession many confidential letters of Mr. Davis to Colonel Cannon. Mr. Davis was frequently a guest at the home of Colonel Cannon, and upon the death of the latter he remarked to a friend, "I have lost my best friend. Cannon was the purest, truest, noblest and best man I ever knew." Such a compliment from such a source would attest the greatness of any man. Colonel Cannon left his palatial home in Oktibbeha county, which had been the garden-spot of Mayhew prairie, where Quitman, Davis, Brown, Sharkey, Foote, Yearger and McRae, and a host of the great men had been entertained in such profuse elegance and hospitality, and moved to Columbus for its educational advantages. Colonel Cannon was one of the most zealous and distinguished members of the Masonic fraternity in the state, having filled the highest positions. In 1854 he was elected grand master of the grand Masonic lodge of the state, and after his time had expired was strongly solicited to accept the grand mastership the second time, as his administration had met with universal commendation on account of its smooth and able rule, but he firmly declined a reëlection. He was at one time also grand high priest of the grand chapter of the state. Cannon lodge, in Chickasaw county, is named in honor of him. At the time of his demise, Colonel Cannon was master of Columbus lodge No. 5 in the city of Columbus. In 1856 Colonel Cannon was one of the delegates for the state at large to the democratic national convention, which met at Cincinnati, June of that year, which nominated James Buchanan and John C. Breckinridge as the democratic standard bearers for president and vice president of the United States. In the year 1857 he was in attendance upon the University of Oxford, where he was selected to award the medals to the graduates. His speech was so replete with eloquence and good taste as to electrify the entire audience. This same year he was called upon by the whole state to make the gubernatorial race. His almost indifference to respond to the call, and his strict regard for principle, made him positively refuse to make the canvass. However, when the convention met at Jackson, his name was put in nomination, as was also Colonel McWillie's. An entire day of voting, even until twelve o'clock at night, kept Colonel Cannon ahead. But Maj. Ben Bradford, a delegate from Monroe county, who personally felt friendship for Cannon, but as he wanted a certain railroad measure carried, and was aware of the fact that Cannon was opposed to it, and would veto the same if elected governor, he (Bradford) made a motion that no proxy vote should be cast, knowing that the other two delegates, Columbus Sykes and Tom Davis, were necessarily absent and had sent down their proxy by him. The members not knowing the motive that actuated Major Bradford, voted for the motion to be carried. Consequently, the next day, McWillie was nominated by one vote. So soon as it was called out, Colonel Cannon, with grace and dignity, arose and conducted Colonel McWillie to the stand, and in the most laudatory terms introduced him. Each member felt the power of such intoxicating eloquence and true magnanimity. Many of the members exclaimed aloud, "If we had only heard Cannon speak before the ballot was cast, he would have been nominated by acclamation." Colonels McWillie and Cannon had been friends in South Carolina before they emigrated to Mississippi, so they loved each other now. And instead of going to his home in Madison county, he (Colonel McWillie) accompanied Colonel Cannon to his home in Columbus, where he was received in confidence by every member of the household, who waited upon him in the most hospitable and luxuriant manner. Many friends were invited to meet him, and after a week's delightful sojourn he returned home. Their friendship was cemented even closer than before, and continued until death separated them. In the close of the year 1857 Colonel Cannon, in company with his wife, and a dear friend, attended conference of the Methodist Episcopal church at Selma, Ala. This meeting with the bishop and ministers gave him great happiness. His love for his church was intense. He was one of the ruling spirits and pillars of the Methodist Episcopal church at Columbus. Consequently, when it was read out that Edwin Baldwin was sent to that station, his joy was complete. Alas! could he have lifted the vail and seen that in three months this same sweet, sainted minister, would pronounce his funeral sermon. But would it have alarmed him? No, he was not afraid to die. As soon as he returned to his home he had a call to go to the grand lodge at Jackson. The exposure to cold while making these two trips, developed rapidly into typhoid fever which lasted over two months. During his illness his two able physicians untiringly attended upon him, alternately sitting up night after night, until the day came when his heart-broken family had to tell him good-bye. He expressed not a single fear, but with strong faith pointed his family and hosts of friends (who gathered to see him die) to that heavenly mansion that was prepared for him. He had a sweet word for each of his children and for his wife, and on the 15th of April, 1858, he breathed out his wellspent life in the arms of Jesus. He had been a benefactor to the poor, giving his hundred dollars where others had only given cents. His death made a void in church and state, and above all in his home, that never can be filled. His life was an example of Christian purity and love. As the slow hearse bore his remains to the city of the dead, closed stores and bank draped in crape, and the longest procession ever seen in Columbus, attested the fact of his popularity, and the sad hearts who mourned for his loss.

His wife (who is now the relict of the late A. B. Meek, poet, orator and statesman) and two daughters survive him. His daughter, Mrs. Foote, nee Hurger Cox, died a number of years ago, after a beautiful life well spent. Two of his sons, both noted for intellectual endowments, also passed away in their early manhood. Mrs. Judge Price, one of his daughters, resides in New Orleans; she is the mother of seven pretty, accomplished daughters, Nona, the third one, gifted in music. Mrs. Samuel M. Meek still lives with her gifted mother, in the old homestead at Columbus. The eldest son, William C. Meek, who received the medal in his class at the University of Alabama, for oratory, is associated with his father, S. M. Meek, in the practice of law. Alex Beauford, the second one, is one of the most reliable and skillful business young men in the South. He is true, courteous, brave, and a great favorite with all who know him. Samuel M., the youngest son, is a wise, noble boy, and is in high favor with one of the best literary papers of the South. Her two older daughters, Alice and Susie, are both cultivated and refined, having received the most thorough and finished education in literature and classics. Carrie, who bore the sobriquet of Little Wonder by the press of the state, when only nine years of age, for elocution, is a splendid vocal and instrumental musician. She completed a full literary course in her sixteenth year, having read, besides two French works, also Cæsar, Virgil and Horace in Latin, and is, withal, an artist. Julia, who is still a child, is modest, graceful, and possesses rare ability as a scholar, has a fine voice and has read several books in the French language. She is thoroughly practical and is bright and intellectual. All of these grandchildren feel proud of their gentle ancestry, dating back on the Meek-line to James II. of England's reign, their illustrious progenitor; on the maternal side, to Robin Adair, a rich nobleman of Scotland. The Cannon-Meek family have in their possession the hickory stick of their great-great-great-grand-father, William Henry Cannon, with which he defended himself from an assault of a squad of Tories. All of his sons had enlisted in the war, and he was left alone, being over seventy years old. One day while in the public road, a squad of these vile torymen made an attack upon him; he so bravely and gallantly defended himself, that General Tarleton, who happened to ride up about that time, gave them orders to desist. Although a foe he had the instinct to discern courage and patriotism. The stick is covered all over with the saber hacks, though it has lasted far beyond a century. In endeavoring to give a sketch of Colonel Cannon's life, we have failed to portray his distinguished acts and noble deeds in a manner commensurate with its intrinsic greatness, but space forbids. So we leave the rest to those who knew him best and loved him most.

Col. Thomas E. Cannon, Verona, Lee county, Miss. Col. Thomas E. Cannon has been a representative citizen of Mississippi since the 9th of February, 1835, and is certainly entitled to a space in this record. He is a native of Darlington district, S. C., born April 24, 1811, and is a son of Rasha and Sarah (Vinson) Cannon. His father was a native of the same place, born September 20, 1771, a member of one of the oldest families of the state. He was left an orphan in his youth and was thrown upon his own resources. On December 5, 1801, he was married and reared two children: William R., who became well known in the political circles of Mississippi, and a Mason of high rank; and Col. Thomas E. Cannon. The mother of these two sons was a native of Newport, R. I., and her death occurred September 28, 1816. The father was married to Parmelia Gee, and two children were born to them. Later he was united to Mary A. McIver, and they had ten children. He was a man of great force of character, and wide influence, was a member of the state senate of South Carolina for a number of years, and was opposed to nullification. He was a planter and merchant before he came to Mississippi. He was a man of temperate habits, and was never known to be sick but a few days until about two weeks before his death. He was a member of the Baptist church and a Mason, and died in Lowndes county, Miss., June 17, 1850. Colonel Cannon spent his early life in attending school, and in 1831 he was graduated from the university of South Carolina, then presided over by Dr. Thomas Cooper. After leaving college he became a clerk in his father's store, and in 1834 he was overseer on his plantation. The same year he determined to seek a new field of labor, and February 9, 1835, he located in Mississippi in the prairie fifteen miles west of Columbus. After coming to Mississippi he was married August 23, 1838, to Penelope M., a daughter of Hon. Gen. Jesse Speight, who afterward went as senator from Mississippi to the United States senate. Five children were born of the union: William R. and Louisa J. are both dead; Sallie V. married O. F. Bledsoe, of Grenada, Miss.; Mary S. married N. M. Hay; and Penelope M. married W. E. Turner, and are both living at Verona. The mother of this family died May 9, 1848. The Colonel then married Mary S. Du Bose, daughter of Samuel L. and Mary A. Du Bose, of Darlington district, S. C., on February 21, 1850. Three children were born to them: Anna M., wife of Z. T. Trice, of Okolona, Miss.; Melville D. and Adella V., who died at the age of one and a half years, in Columbus, Miss. Their mother died January 2, 1862, in Columbus, Miss. Colonel Cannon was married again, in 1868, to Maggie E. James, a native of Courtland, Ala., and a daughter of W. W. James. Our worthy subject removed to his present home from Columbus, Miss., in December, 1869, since which time he has been engaged in farming, etc. He has been a member of the board of supervisors of Lee county, Miss, for twelve years, and eight years of that time as president. Before leaving South Carolina he made a profession and joined the Baptist church in 1833, but after coming to Mississippi he joined the Methodist Episcopal church South and takes an active interest in all branches of religious work. He has been a member of the Masonic order since July 5, 1845, and a Knight Templar since March 9, 1853. He is a man well-known throughout the state, and is highly respected for his many sterling traits of character.

Dr. John C. Caraway, physician, Philadelphia, Miss., was born at Hickory, Newton county, Miss., and of the ten children born to the union of James E. and B. E. (Wall) Caraway, he was third in order of birth. The elder Caraway came to Mississippi with his parents when a child, and located with them in Jasper county. There they remained for some time. After growing up Mr. Caraway removed to Newton county of that state, married, and there passed the remainder of his days as a successful planter. During the late unpleasantness between the North and South he was in the Confederate army, but on account of ill health he did but little active service. He was an honest, upright citizen, and a man held in high estimation by all. His son, Dr. John C. Caraway, passed his boyhood and youth in assisting his father on the farm, and secured a good practical education in the common schools. He subsequently began the study of medicine and attended medical lectures from 1879 until the spring of 1882, at Mobile and at the Louisville medical college, graduating from the latter institution in the last-mentioned year. In the spring of 1883 he established himself at Philadelphia, Miss., and has since become one of the most extensive and successful practitioners in Neshoba county. Socially the Doctor affiliates with the Masonic fraternity, and the Knights of Honor.

David Carder, a planter of Tallahatchie county, was born in Tennessee in 1841. He was a son of David and Nancy Elizabeth (Sutherland) Carder. His father is thought to have been a native of Alabama. He removed to Tennessee, where his wife died when David was two years old. She was a Christian woman, a member of the Baptist church. Mr. Carder's second marriage was to Susan Calbert, who died in Tennessee, also, having borne her hus-

32

band five children, all of whom are deceased. Mr. Carder spent one year, soon after the war, with his son David, in Tallahatchie county, returning to Tennessee, where he died in 1869. Our subject was the youngest of two sons and six daughters. He is the only one of the family living in Mississippi, and, so far as he knows, his brothers and sisters are all dead. Moses joined the Confederate army in Arkansas during the war, and has never been heard from since. The others were named Mary, Susan, Lottie, Sallie, Fannie and David. David Carder never had an opportunity to acquire an education. He attended school but very little, being obliged to begin life for himself at about the age of thirteen years as a farm hand, in which capacity he worked until after the war. In 1855 he came to Tallahatchie county and found employment upon the farm on which he now lives. In 1861 he joined the Tallahatchie rifles, of the Second Mississippi infantry, and served through the war in the army of Virginia, participating in engagements at Fredericksburg, Antietam, Malvern hill, in the Wilderness, Manassas junction and other battles and skirmishes. He was transferred to the ordnance department, and the last year of the war was wagonmaster; he surrendered with General Lee, and returned to Mississippi. He was married in 1866 to Lucy Elizabeth, daughter of Willis and Jane Shaw, then and until the end of their lives residents of Talla-hatchie county. Mr. Shaw was a planter of moderate means. Mrs. Carder was born in Tallahatchie county. She has borne her husband eleven children, seven of whom are liv-ing: Dr. Thomas A., a practicing physician of Coahoma county and a graduate of the Memphis medical college; Napoleon, a telegraph operator, also living in Coahoma county; Nancy Jane, wife of Alexander Williams; Louanna; Frances Rebecca; Lydia Elizabeth and Virginia are those who survived. With the exception of about one year, 1873, passed in Arkansas and in Boone and Jackson counties, Mr. Carder has lived in Tallahatchie county since 1855, and on his present farm since his return from Arkansas. He is the owner of four hundred and eighty acres of land, two hundred and forty of which lie in the river bottom. This he has acquired from his own unaided efforts, and on his home farm has put the improvements which mark it as one of the finest in this county. He has cleared about one hundred and fifty acres of the bottom land, which was originally covered with timber. Mr. Carder is a hard-working, industrious farmer, honest and upright in his dealings and a good citizen in every sense of the term. Though deprived of such educational advantages as he could have desired, he has still always been a steadfast supporter of the schools, and his elder children have, at considerable pains and expense, fitted themselves educationally to be good and useful citizens.

Eugene Carleton, Decatur, Miss., a son of Montgomery and Martha S. (Dickinson) Carleton, was born in the state of Alabama, in the year 1840. At the age of fourteen years he came with his parents to Newton county, Miss. They located within one mile of Decatur, and there he has since lived; he was educated in the common schools, and was trained to agricultural pursuits. In 1862 he abandoned the pursuit of husbandry, and enlisted in the cause of the South, becoming a member of the Thirty-ninth Mississippi volunteer infantry under Colonel Shelby, and serving until the close of the conflict. He was in the battles of Corinth and Port Hudson; from the latter place he went to Georgia, and remained in that state until the close of the war. At Altoona he was wounded, and also at Franklin; he was twice taken prisoner, but was paroled both times. When peace was declared he returned to his home, and for some time gave his attention to teaching school. He has for several years been prominently connected with the public offices of the county, and has made a faithful and efficient servant. He was in the chancery and probate courts previous to 1869, and in 1871 he was elected chancery clerk; for sixteen years he held this office, his return for so many successive terms being a high tribute to his integrity and ability. In 1887 he was elected county superintendent of schools, and has since filled this responsible position. Mr. Carleton was united in marriage, in 1867, to Miss Mary Keith, a daughter of M. M. Keith; she bore three children, and was called from this life in 1872. Mr. Carleton was afterward married to Miss Cornelia, daughter of M. P. Williams, of Newton county, Miss. Four children were born of this union. In December, 1890, our subject had additional honor paid him by being appointed postmaster of Decatur; his former connection with public offices has especially fitted him for this position, which he is filling to the entire satisfaction of the public. He is the owner of a fine farm of four hundred acres, adjoining the town site of Decatur; he superintends the cultivation of this, and is a planter. He belongs to the Masonic order; and also the Knights of Honor.

Among the self-reliant and truly self made men of Lauderdale county, Miss., may be mentioned Mr. D. H. Carlisle, who was born in 1850, in Choctaw county, Ala., where he grew to manhood on a plantation, and was married to Miss Cynthia Carlisle, a native Alabamian, also born in Choctaw county. Their union was blessed in the birth of the following children: Valentine, Monroe, Minnie, Mattie and Luther, living. Two children are deceased. Mr. Carlisle was educated in the common schools and was reared on a plantation, learning the details of that most noble and independent of callings, agriculture. The same year of his marriage he removed to Lauderdale county, Miss., settling in the eastern portion, where he engaged in farming and mechanical work. In 1866 he purchased land from a railroad company, to which he has since been constantly adding, until he now owns and controls five hundred and twenty acres of as fair land as there is in the county. A considerable portion of his land is covered with heavy timber of the most valuable kind. He cultivates about one hundred acres and raises on an average ten bales of cotton each year. In connection with his planting interests he is the owner of a good sawmill, which is fitted up with $1,000 worth of valuable machinery, the capacity of which is one-half million feet of pine yearly. He has considerable land which will yield forty thousand feet of lumber to the acre. His land is well watered, is in an excellent neighborhood, and being very fertile, is valuable accordingly. This property is the result of indefatigable industry and persistent endeavor, and Mr. Carlisle is a man of whom his section may well feel proud, for he is the soul of honor, is industrious, enterprising and public spirited. He is a member of the Methodist Episcopal church and of the Farmers' Alliance. He is a son of John S. Carlisle, who was born in the Old North state about 1805. He came to Alabama when a boy and was married in that state about 1826 to Miss Amelia Witty. He died about 1889, his wife's death occurring in 1881. His mother, Nancy Carlisle, lived to the remarkable age of one hundred and two years. She died in 1871.

G. W. Carlisle, the efficient commissioner of immigration and agriculture of Mississippi and a successful real estate agent of the city of Jackson, was born in Lawrence county, near Monticello, in 1855, the sixth of seven children born to Edmond J. and Dullie B. (Maxwell) Carlisle, both of whom were born in this state. The paternal grandfather was a Georgian by birth and came to Mississippi in 1812, settling in Lawrence county, where he followed the occupation of a planter and resided until his death. He had several sons in the Mexican war, one of whom died while in the service. The maternal grandfather, Henry Maxwell, came to Mississippi from the state of his birth about 1817, became a very successful planter and merchant of Lawrence county, and socially and mentally was among the most prominent citizens of the section in which he resided. He died in 1876, at the age of eighty-nine years, leaving an unblemished reputation as a heritage to his children. Edmond

J, Carlisle was reared in Lawrence county, and although he received limited advantages of a literary nature, he became a well-informed gentleman. He began life for himself as a planter and was successfully following this calling at the time of the opening of the Civil war, at which time he dropped his farming implements to join the Confederate army, and was a brave and faithful soldier. Upon his return to his home he resumed planting, which calling he followed with merited success until his death, in 1871. His widow survives him, and is a member of the Baptist church. G. W. Carlisle obtained a limited education in the common schools of the country, and from ten until eighteen years of age he labored on a plantation. He then became a clerk in a store at Monticello, and some time after was selected deputy clerk of the chancery court, the duties of which position he ably discharged for two years. In 1879 he was appointed chief land clerk by Auditor of the State Gwin, and during the seven years that he held this position he acquired a full knowledge of the land system of the state. He resigned this position in 1886 and was elected commissioner of agriculture and immigration of the state by the state legislature without opposition, and still fills this position, being unanimously reëlected in 1890. He is a real estate agent of considerable note, and deals largely in timber lands throughout the entire state, farming land to a great extent, and also in city property in Jackson. In all his transactions he is reliable and accurate, and enjoys the confidence of the public at large. He is considered an authority upon all real estate matters, and his business is steadily increasing from month to month. He owns about six thousand acres of land, mainly in the Yazoo delta, some of which is under cultivation, and the balance has located on it some of the most valuable timber in Mississippi. He owns two residences and one valuable storehouse, and some unimproved land in Jackson, all of which is valuable property and the result of Mr. Carlisle's own determination, energy and push. Mr. Carlisle was married, in 1882, to Miss Virginia Fearn, a native of Mississippi, born at Canton, and a daughter of Judge George R. Fearn, of Dallas, Tex., formerly of Alabama, a prominent lawyer. To this union two children have been born: George Fearn and Willie. Mr. and Mrs. Carlisle are prominent members of the Methodist Episcopal church South, and he is of a social and agreeable disposition, and in business circles is looked upon as one of the most reliable and efficient of financiers.

Henry Carlisle, a general merchant and planter of Prairie station, was born in the county of Antrim, Ireland, in 1834, a son of Daniel and Nancy Carlisle, both natives of Ireland, and life-long residents there. Mr. Carlisle was the fourth of five sons and one daughter born of these parents: John, a planter of Clay county, served in latter part of the war under General Gohlson; William, died in Clay county three years ago (he was a well-known planter, and did service in the late war); Mary A.; James, resident of Scotland; Adam, planter, residing in Egypt, Chickasaw county; and Henry, who was educated in the public schools until about the age of eighteen, when, leaving Ireland, he came with his brother William to Mississippi, and for about two years was employed by E. L. Willey & Co., wholesale grocers at Aberdeen; later he was with Strong, Williams & Co., for one year, and for the succeeding year in the warehouse, storage and commission business at Aberdeen, after which he went to Egypt, where he was railroad agent from 1859 to 1861. Early in the latter year he joined the Buena Vista rifles, part of the Seventeenth regiment, which was commanded by Colonel Featherstone. Early in his military career he was sergeant of company A. After the battle of Manassas — the second Bull run fight — he was made first lieutenant. Subsequently he was in the battle of Ball's bluff, but in 1862 he resigned and came home, joining Tomeler's battalion of General Van Dorn's command, in which he held the rank of lieutenant. He was stationed at Jonesboro, Ark., and was in the Georgia and Atlanta campaigns. He was afterward at Charlotte, S. C. He did more than four years' hard fighting. In January, 1866, he became railroad agent at Prairie station, a position which he held until 1871, when he began merchandising, in which he has continued until the present time. In connection with his store he is the owner of about three thousand acres of land in this and adjoining counties, which produce about four hundred bales of cotton annually. His success in life has been gained entirely by his own unaided efforts. He is active in politics, and takes a deep interest in all public matters, especially those relative to the public welfare. He is a man highly successful in all his undertakings, and is looked upon by his neighbors with great respect and regard, and by the community at large is considered to be an upright, well-disposed man worthy of all good that may come to him.

John F. Carlock has successfully followed the calling of a merchant in Tate county, Miss., since 1887, and being a genial and whole-souled man he has won numerous friends throughout the section in which he makes his home. He began life in Marshall county, Miss., March 21, 1848, the eldest and only surviving child of John and Fannie (Carlock) Carlock, who were born in North Carolina and Alabama, respectively. Mr. Carlock, Sr., removed to Alabama in early life, in which state he received his education, but he transferred his residence to Marshall county, Miss., after his marriage, which occurred when he was about thirty-five years old. After a residence of a few years in this county, he located in Tate county, where he passed the remainder of his life, dying in 1873. His widow survived him until 1886, when she, too, passed away. John F. Carlock, their son, passed his early years and received his rudimentary education in Marshall and Oxford counties. He made rapid progress in his studies, for he possessed a naturally fine mind, and was well qualified to battle with the world upon starting out in life for himself. Upon attaining his majority he turned his attention to planting, at which he has been very successful, being the owner of a large estate amounting to twenty-four hundred acres. In 1887 he purchased a one-third interest in the mercantile business of J. V. Patton, thus forming the well-known firm of Carlock & Patton. The small capital with which he began has been judiciously invested in business, and has increased to the handsome proportions which it has now attained. Mr. Carlock may well feel proud of his success, as it fittingly marks his ability and constant attention to business. His military career was short, for he enlisted in the service the last year of the war, and was in but one engagement, a sharp skirmish at Coldwater, Miss. Mr. Carlock is said to be a confirmed bachelor, though still in the prime of life.

Edward W. Carmack (deceased) was born in Franklin county, Ala., in 1825, one of the four children of Cornelius and Agnes (Smith) Carmack. At an early day his father, who was a native of Virginia, removed to Alabama, and there became a public man, representing Franklin county in the legislature. After coming to Tishomingo county, he was a member of the Mississippi legislature, and was elected speaker of the house. He located here in 1845, and was in every respect a man of public spirit and enterprise. In politics he was of the old Jacksonian democratic faith. Edward W. Carmack came with his father to this county, and his boyhood days were spent amid the scenes of a plantation life. He received a good literary education, having graduated from the old Franklin college. At the age of twenty he became a school teacher in this county, and continued in that profession for about eight years. During this time he was for some years principal of the Euclid academy. He was elected probate clerk of old Tishomingo county, and held that position for fourteen years. After the division of the county, he acquired control of the old county buildings, and established a school in the old Tishomingo courthouse, which he continued with much success until his death, which occurred in 1882. He was married, in 1850, to Elizabeth, one of the seven children of William and Nancy Turner, natives of Tennessee. Her parents moved to this county about 1846. Their children were Louise, Susan, Nancy, William, Elizabeth, Tennessee and Miranda. Mr. and Mrs. Carmack had eight children: Mary, now Mrs. Reynolds, of Jacinto, Miss.; Frank T., of Iuka; Nancy, who became Mrs. Cunningham, and resides at Booneville, Miss.; John C., who lives at Jacinto; Susan P., now Mrs. Miller, of Farmersville, Tex.; Edward W., Mattie R. and Elizabeth. Mr. Carmack was an energetic and very prominent man, well educated, and in every respect highly esteemed. He was a man of very decided opinions. His school was one of the first of Mississippi in this part of the state. The influence of Professor Carmack was such over his students that they, out of respect for his memory, placed a handsome monument to his grave. Mrs. Carmack, though quiet and retiring, was an active spirit in the life of her husband and the home of her children. Dr. Frank T. Carmack, of Iuka, Miss., is a son of Edward W. Carmack, above mentioned, and was born in Tishomingo county November, 1854. He received his primary education at Jacinto, and in 1880 was graduated from Vanderbilt medical college, at Nashville, Tenn. He began the practice of his profession at Iuka, Miss., in 1884, and has continued it with growing success until the present time. At this time he is health officer of Tishomingo county. He was married, in 1884, in Alcorn county, to Miss Willa Bynum, daughter of William and Emily (Gibson) Bynum, who was born in that county in 1861. Dr. and Mrs. Carmack have had three children: Dora, Ruth and Frank, the last mentioned of whom is deceased. Doctor is a Knight of Honor, and a member of the Methodist Episcopal church. He is an ardent supporter of the cause of public education, and is devoted heart and soul to the improvement and development of the county, and to the advancement of all its important interests. He is a democrat, and takes a helpful but quiet part in the local and state politics.

Samuel W. Carothers, a planter of Clay county, Miss., was born in Giles county, Tenn., in 1850, a son of Hugh, Jr., and Jane (Wells) Carothers, who were born in Tennessee and Virginia in 1809 and 1815, respectively, their marriage taking place in Tennessee in 1831, to which state the mother moved with her parents when but six years of age. Hugh, Jr., has always devoted his attention to planting, and now resides on a fine farm near Louisburg, Tenn. He is the son of Hugh, Sr., and Martha (Irving) Carothers, North Carolinians by birth, the former of whom was also an honest tiller of the soil and a son of Robert and Martha (White) Carothers. Robert Carothers was a native of Ireland and came to America about the middle of the eighteenth century, settling in the Old North state. In 1794 he went to Tennessee and in that territory settled among the Indians. He died soon after and left a large family to fight the battle of life as best they might. Hugh Carothers, Jr., although eighty-two years of age, has a splendid memory and can recount with much interest the hardships and privations of his boyhood days. He was one of nine children, the other members of the family being as follows: Margaret (Goodman), Robert A., Eliza (Wilson), Jane (Goodman), Sarah (Reed), Edward, Martha (Cathy) and William, all of whom are deceased with the exception of Hugh, Jr., who was the fifth of the family, and Martha. To Hugh Carothers and his wife, Jane, a family of fourteen children were born, the following of whom are living: Martha L., wife of Thomas Murray, of Tennessee; John E., of West Point; Dean, of Tennessee; Molly, wife of James Murray, of Tennessee; Samuel W., the subject of this biography; Thomas, of Giles county, Tenn., and Wilts, of Louisville, Ky. Samuel W. Carothers received his education at Mar's Hill, Ala., and first started out in life for himself as a farmer of Tennessee, this being at about the time he attained his majority, remained in that state four years, at the end of which time he came to West Point, Miss., and for some time, in connection with planting, he was also in the livery and stock business. In 1889 he withdrew from the livery business and moved to his plantation near Abbott, Clay county, and is now engaged in planting, his landed estate amounting to one thousand three hundred and sixty-eight acres in Clay and Monroe counties, a large portion of which is finely improved. He uses all the latest improved machinery in his planting operations, and, owing to this fact and to the fact that Mr. Carothers' ideas are shrewd and practical, this business is proving highly remunerative. He takes much interest in the raising of fine stock, his cattle being of the Holstein and Jersey breeds, and his swine Poland-China, and of this, as well as of his planting operations, he is making a decided success. He was married in 1883 to Miss Fannie Watson, of Monroe county, Miss., a daughter of Rufus and Fannie Watson, both of whom are deceased. To Mr. Carothers and his wife three children have been born: Rufus, Inez and Fannie.

N. L. Carpenter is one of the oldest inhabitants of Natchez, Miss., but is a Virginian by birth, born in 1805. He was the second child born to Joseph and Sarah (Buell) Carpenter, both of whom were born in the Nutmeg state, and lived for a time in Virginia, after which, in 1809, they moved to a point near Buffalo, N. Y., where the father bought a large amount of property in what is now that city. There he resided until his death in 1834, his widow passing from life in 1845, both being worthy members of the Presbyterian church. Mr. Carpenter was a very busy, active and enterprising man, and at the town of Lancaster, N. Y., near Buffalo, he erected two sawmills, a flourmill, a tannery and other buildings. In the town of Lancaster N. L. Carpenter was reared and educated, and about 1828 or 1830 was engaged in the stage and hotel business. In 1833 he came to Natchez and began building and carpentering, but after following that for one winter he went to St. Louis, and the next winter went to New Orleans, in which city he was engaged in trading for some time. He then came to Natchez and made a permanent settlement, and here became an extensive builder for many years. In 1850 he erected a planingmill to get out lumber for his own use and to sell, but during the war turned his business to cottonginning, and is still the owner of a large public gin in the city of Natchez. In 1871 he started in the cottonseed oil business, of which he was an extensive manufacturer for some time, but also purchased cotton and was in the commission business as well, and was the owner of a line of steamers. About 1876, in connection with his sons, he was one of the promoters of the Natchez cotton factory, and of that mill has been a director ever since. He is also interested in the Rosalie cottonmill, the ice company and the city gas company; in fact, has aided materially every enterprise tending to promote the interests of this section. He was married at Buffalo in 1837 to Miss Julia Ann Luce, who died in 1865, having borne four children: Helen E., Allen D., Joseph N. and Frances (deceased). Mr. Carpenter has been an extensive traveler and has visited nearly all the countries of Europe and all the principal cities. He made two trips to the old world, has traveled all over this country and has also visited the principal islands of the Pacific ocean. He is the owner of a plantation near Natchez known as Dunleith, and on it is one of the finest homes in the state. Here he makes his home with his son Joseph N. He has seen many changes in this section since locating here, and, like the majority of men, he has had his ups and downs of success. In the tornado of 1840 he lost about $10,000, but this he afterward far more than retrieved. Nearly every public enterprise for the past fifty years has received his support, and Natchez has no citizen who has identified himself more thoroughly with her success than has he. His sons were soldiers in the Confederate army and are now active business men of this city; worthy citizens and progressive men. Although Mr. Carpenter is now eighty-five years of age he is yet vigorous and hearty and oversees his large business interests the same as in his younger days. He is hale and hearty to a remarkable degree, his mind still less than his body showing the ravages of time. He is a member of the I. O. O. F.

D. S. Carr, the father of John W. Carr, was born in North Carolina in 1800, and was married to Miss Margaret Duffy of that state about 1821, removing to Georgia about nine years after his marriage. In 1848 he removed to Clarke county, Miss., and there devoted himself to planting, but died in Newton county of this state about 1883, his wife having passed from life some time in the forties. He was a member of the Primitive Baptist church but his wife was a Presbyterian. John W. Carr was one of seventeen children and was born in Henry county, Ga., January 21, 1833. From his native state he removed to Mississippi with his father, and being reared on a farm received what education he could obtain at intervals. In 1857 he went to Georgia, where he remained in school one year, after which he returned home. He enlisted in the Confederate service in 1861, going out with Colonel Holland for sixty days. He then returned home and reenlisted in the Seventh Mississippi battalion, becoming a member of company E, which was under command of Captain Pierson, who was later killed at Vicksburg. His command was in the battle of Corinth, but Mr. Carr was sick in the hospital at Saltillo at that time. From Corinth his command marched to Holly Springs, Mr. Carr joining it at Waterford, and was afterward transferred to Vaiden and then to Yazoo city. They went by boat to Snyder's bluff, twelve miles above Vicksburg, and forty-seven days after their entrance into Vicksburg they were compelled to surrender to General Grant on the 4th of July, 1863. After eight days' time Mr. Carr was paroled, and went into parole camp at Enterprise. He returned home on the 20th of July, 1863, and was married to Miss E. A. McNeill of Clarke county, Miss., July 30, 1863. In the following February he was exchanged and returned to service, and after some time spent at Mobile he went to Pollard, Ala., thence to Montgomery and Selma. He returned home on furlough of forty days but afterward rejoined the Confederate army and was in the engagement at New Hope church and in the defense of Atlanta. He was also with Hood in his disastrous Tennessee campaign, being in the engagement at Altoona and Franklin, receiving a slight wound in the latter engagement, after which he was in the hospital some time with his brother Samuel F., the latter dying while there. Upon recovering he reported for duty at Meridian and took transportation to Mobile, but was afterward captured at Blakely on the 9th of April, 1865, being taken as a prisoner to Ship island, thence to New Orleans and later to Vicksburg. He was discharged at Meridian on the 10th of May, 1865. To Mr. and Mrs. Carr the following children have been born: Mary Victoria, Samuel Alexander, Ida Lee, John L., D. W. and Henry L. The eldest daughter is the widow of J. W. Smith, who died in 1889. She has two children—Rennie Elois and Josiah Curtis. During the war Mr. Carr purchased one hundred and sixty acres of land, which constituted his worldly possessions at the close of hostilities. By energy and perseverance he has become the owner of three hundred and twenty acres, which will produce one-half bale of cotton to the acre, and twenty bushels of corn. He uses some commercial fertilizer on his plantation and home compost. His wife is a member of the Missionary Baptist church and is a worthy and upright lady. Their son, Prof. Samuel A. Carr, is a rising young educator of the county, with a bright future before him.

In endeavoring to trace the genealogy of the Carradine family, we find that they were early residents of the Old North state and of Spanish origin. The paternal grandfather of Leonard W. Carradine, Fayette, Miss., Parker Carradine, came from Georgia, direct to the locality now known as Jefferson county, Miss., about the year 1772. He married Miss Penelope Hill, of Georgia, a family which has since become famous for its distinguished sons. She died in Madison county, Miss., about the year 1835. His brother, David, married her sister, and was the grandfather of Dr. James S. Carradine, of New York city, and Rev. Beverly Carradine, of St. Louis. On account of a leading part taken by himself in a revolt against the Spanish authorities in favor of the United States in 1781, Parker Carradine, together with several others, was seized by the Spaniards and carried to New Orleans in irons. At the end of six months they were released, owing to the clemency of the Spanish governor. During the territorial period he held the office of United States commissioner. He served as sole inspector for Villa Gayoso and Cole's creek of the first election ever held in Mississippi for a representative allowed to the American settlers to congress. He died about 1820 on his plantation near Old Greenville, Jefferson county, where he had passed through so many stirring events. His youngest son, William Rapalie, was born in 1819, was educated at Translyvania university, Ky., practiced law at Shreveport, La., and died in Natchez at the age of twenty-five. He married, in 1837, Miss Rebecca Chew Wilkinson, and they had but one child, Leonard Wilkinson. She was married in 1843 to John Hunter, a young Marylander, who was at the time deputy marshal of the state of Mississippi under Marshal William Guinn, and afterward became a successful merchant. He was collector of the port and mayor of Natchez for many years and was holding the latter office at the time of his death. He also held the office of general disbursing agent of the Confederate government for Louisiana and Mississippi. His death occurred at Natchez in 1863. He was popular with all classes, a devoted husband and the kindest of fathers to his stepson, having no children of his own. The Wilkinsons were an old Maryland family who came to the colony with Cecil Calvert (Lord Baltimore) and intermarried with that family, the latest instance having been the marriage of Frances Chew (great grandmother of subject) to Mumberd Calvert, one of the earliest sheriffs of Mississippi. On February 21, 1774, Ann Herbert Dent, daughter of John Dent, married William Wilkinson. She was a direct descendant of a younger son of the house of Herbert, who had also come over with Cecil Calvert as was a custom of younger sons of noble houses at that period. A brother of hers went West and was one of the ancestors of Mrs. General Grant. A sister went to Georgia and was the grandmother of the Longstreets. In 1798 Mrs. Ann H. (Dent) Wilkinson, her husband having died, moved to Washington, Miss., induced to do so by her kinsman, Gen. James Wilkinson, who was in command of the newly purchased region and who was engaged in the work of organizing a territorial government. Her family consisted of George (grandfather of L. W. Carradine) and six daughters. At the battle of New Orleans George Wilkinson was on the staff of General Wilkinson and was commissioned by General Jackson to report news of the victory to the territorial seat of government at Washington, Miss. Isaac Dunbar married Mary and afterward Elizabeth; Sandy Calvert, for whom the city of Calvert, Tex., was named, married Barbara; Thomas Miller married Ann Herbert; Sarah, the eldest, married Dr. Briscoe, of Washington city, and lived to the age of ninety-three years; Jane, the youngest, was the wife of Gen. James Long, who was commander of the Americans in Texas during their first struggle with the Mexicans in 1819. Mrs. Long was one of America's greatest heroines, if not one of the greatest of any land or age. Mirabeau Lamar in his history of Texas, and Foote in his history of Texas and the Texans, do full justice to her career. In 1820 she left Jefferson county, Miss., to join her husband in Texas. One year later she was with a detachment in a fort on Galveston island while General Long was with the main body at Goliad. The detachment was ordered to join the main body by forced marches. It was imperatively necessary to leave her behind with a three

weeks' old infant and a female negro servant. For a number of days she, with the assistance of her servant, loaded and fired the morning and evening guns, kept lighted the watch
fires and beat the reveille and tattoo, thus deluding the Mexicans under Santa Anna, who was
then a young man, until the Americans had succeeded in their object. Santa Anna's
admiration for her heroism was such that he offered to grant any wish that she might
make. She only desired to be sent to her husband, who in the meantime had been defeated
and sent as a prisoner to the City of Mexico. He then gave her a safe conduct to that place,
which she succeeded in reaching only to find that her husband had been assassinated, or so
represented, the day previous. To the day of her death she refused to believe the story and
remained unmarried. Her death occurred in 1881 at the age of eighty-three.

In opening the state fair at Bryan, Tex., in 1879, Jefferson Davis appeared with her
before the thousands present, and introduced her as the mother of Texas. She was revered
by all Texas, and enriched by both the republic and state of Texas. The maternal grandfather of our subject was Eliza Green Freeland, whose mother was Frances Chew. She
moved in 1806 to the vicinity of Washington, Miss., in company with several other
families of her near relatives from Calvert county, and Sarah, a sister of Frances Chew, was
the wife of Beverly S. Grayson, who was noted in the early history of Mississippi. Sarah
was also the mother, by previous marriage, of Governor Fielding Bowie, of Maryland.
Claiborne, in his history of Mississippi, mentions the above named families as: "the emigration from Maryland, consisting for the most part of educated and wealthy planters: the
Covingtons, Graysons, Chews, Calvits, Wilkinsons, Freelands, Wailes, Bowies and Magru-
ders," from Calvert and Prince George's counties. Leonard Wilkinson Carradine was
born at Roakly, the old family residence near Washington, Miss., on the 22d of January,
1838. He passed a part of his boyhood in Jefferson county, then moved with his parents to
Natchez in 1848, and received his education at Yale college and the university of Virginia.
He left the latter institution to enter the Confederate army in 1861. Having become permanently incapacitated for further active service from the effects of camp fever after the
Kentucky campaign of 1862, he continued to serve the Southern cause as a deputy disbursing agent, also in the secret service until the close of the war. After this, he planted in
Louisiana and Mississippi for five years with varying success. In 1871 he moved with his
family to southeastern Texas, where he invested in some real estate and engaged in business, but before he could make a success of this, circumstances beyond his control forced
him to return to Mississippi. Since 1874 he has been a farmer in Jefferson county, the
locality with which his ancestors were so long identified. In 1883 he received the appointment of county superintendent of education, and the following year was elected sheriff, having served his county in the latter office nearly four terms. Although the county has long
been well and justly noted for the faithfulness, superior capability and sterling honor of her
officials, Mr. Carradine has fully sustained this reputation. He is most admirably fitted to
perform the functions of his office, for he is not only courteous and kind in his demeanor,
but is very courageous and firm. Everything about his office moves with clockwork precision, and that an intelligent and painstaking official is at the helm is seen at a glance.
Since 1885 he has been a resident of the town of Fayette, but still gives some attention to
farming. Personally and in every private relation and duty of life, too much can not be
said in his praise. He married Miss Emma Rivers on the 2d of November, 1863, second
daughter of Col. Douglas L. Rivers, whose residence was in Natchez, and planting interests
in Louisiana. Colonel Rivers was born and reared in Virginia, and came from one of its
oldest and best families. His mother was a Miss Rives and cousin to Alexander and John

C. Rives. He was educated a lawyer, was state senator for several years, and filled the position of provost-marshal of Concordia parish, under the Confederate regime. He was a noble specimen of manhood, physically; genial, brave and chivalrous in character, and the several scars upon his person bore witness to many encounters in the defense of principle or the fair fame of woman. He died October 10, 1873. Mr. and Mrs. Carradine were the parents of seven children, of whom three survive: John Hunter, the eldest, a young physician at Fayette, graduated at Mount St. Josephs, Maryland, and at Tulane medical school, New Orleans; he also attended one term at the medical department of Vanderbilt university, Nashville; Rebekah Wilkinson, and Emma Herbert, who inherited her mother's musical talent, and is taking a course at the Cincinnati conservatory of music. Mrs. Carradine's mother is yet living and well preserved, abounding in reminiscences of the past, and delighting to relate the incidents and history of early and eventful times, as she received them from the lips of the actors themselves who have long ago passed away. But few families have been longer or more completely identified with the early history of either Maryland or Mississippi.

Vicksburg, the metropolis of Mississippi, famed in war and in peace, is noted for the number of her citizens who have achieved distinction in the various callings of life. Her soldiers have illustrated the highest types of valor and manhood upon the most celebrated battlefields of our country. Her statesmen have been among the foremost in controlling the policy, and shaping the destiny of the nation. Her lawyers have stood in the front ranks of their profession. Among her divines and physicians are many men of mark and brilliant reputation. And yet to her merchants, her business men, Vicksburg is also largely indebted for the proud position which she now occupies. It was their skill, industry, pluck and confidence that materially aided her in repairing the waste of the devastating civil conflict, in constructing the foundations of an enduring prosperity, and in extending the sphere of her influence. Among those who have thus contributed to the advancement of Vicksburg no one has acquired greater popularity, or accomplished more, than Edward C. Carroll. At the institution of every new enterprise he is with those who lead; when the interests of his adopted city are assailed, he is there to defend; no occasion finds him lacking, no call of duty is by him unheeded. These hastily sketched outlines of his career only faintly suggest the fullness, completeness and strength of his active manly life. He was born in Maryland in 1838, and is, therefore, still in the prime of life, and although he has done much and well, it is the universal wish of all who know him (and who in Vicksburg and the Mississippi delta does not?) that many years may elapse before his daily record of good deeds is closed. His father, Charles C., and mother, Ann (Smith) Carroll, were also natives of Maryland. His father, however, removed to the city of St. Louis in 1839, and resided there until his death, June 16, 1882, at the ripe age of seventy-one years. He was an accomplished lawyer, and at one time occupied the position of city attorney. His talents were recognized and appreciated even before his departure from his native state, for he was elected to the legislature from Somerset county before he had attained his majority. His son, Edward C. was the fifth of eight children and was reared and educated in St. Louis. His sturdy independence and native energy were early manifested, for at the age of fourteen years he began to earn a livelihood as a clerk in that city. The great river which gives prominence to both St. Louis and Vicksburg, and upon which they must mainly rely for the maintenance of their prestige, probably at that immature age directed and influenced young Carroll and finally determined the choice of his vocation. From 1859 to 1867 he officiated as clerk upon a number of the steamboats plying the Missouri and Mississippi rivers, and in the latter year he located at Vicksburg, where he accepted employment as the cashier of W. M. Williams & Co., then owning the wharfboats at that port, afterward succeeding that firm in the wharfboat business under the firm name of Carroll, Green & Co. From that time until the present he has been closely identified with the steamboat interests of the Mississippi river and tributary streams. His promotion to places of responsibility and power was rapid. In 1873 he became superintendent of the P. line operating steamboats in the Yazoo river (in its day one of the most successful corporations in Mississippi) and finally became the largest owner, and president, of said company and its successor. In 1876 he was appointed to the responsible position of agent for the famous Anchor line steamers at Vicksburg, and has held that office continuously ever since. Captain Carroll's duties were not confined to the organization or management of river transportation lines. His occupations are most varied, and he is actively connected with the leading financial institutions which have proved factors in the promotion of the trade of Vicksburg. In fact, it seems almost incredible for one man to discharge so faithfully and successfully the onerous tasks with which he is burdened by reason of the diverse interests he represents. This is made clear by a brief recital of the numerous organizations demanding his care and attention. In addition to his superintendency of the Anchor line steamers at Vicksburg, he is now a director of the Yazoo & Tallahatchie transportation company, whose boats navigate the Yazoo, Tallahatchie and Sunflower rivers. He was one of the promoters, and is now a director, of the Merchants' national bank; he is president of the Vicksburg Hotel company, president of the Yazoo-Mississippi delta timber company, a director of the Vicksburg cotton press association, vice president of the Hill city oil mills, vice president of the D. W. Flowerree ice company, director of the Mississippi Home insurance company, director in the Vicksburg gas light company, superintendent of the Mississippi river elevator company, chairman of the Vicksburg harbor committee since its organization in 1883, a member of the Meteorological board of the United States signal service of Vicksburg. He was chairman of the committee to secure the location of the Louisville, New Orleans & Texas railroad shops at Vicksburg, which have been recently built at a cost of $150,000. He is also an active member of several fraternal and social organizations, being a member of the order of Knights Templar of Magnolia commandery No. 2, a member of the order of Red Cross, the American Legion of Honor, the Knights of Honor, the Progressive Order of Elks and of the Nogales social club of Vicksburg. He is a vestryman of the Holy Trinity Episcopal church of Vicksburg. He was married in 1875 to Miss Nellie T. Wilson, the daughter of Victor F. Wilson now deceased, who was the originator of the Ice & Coal company, and one of the most influential citizens, of the city of Vicksburg. He has two sons and three daughters, namely: Edward C., Jr., Nellie W., Jr., Wilson F., Katie T. and Eliza T. We deem it needless to say in conclusion that Captain Carroll is a true type of the generous, courteous, refined and hospitable gentleman.

James Carroll, M. D., of Yazoo city, Miss., was born in the beautiful Emerald isle, county Leitrim, January 10, 1833, and is a son of Peter and Kate (Smith) Carroll, natives of the same county. The father was a farmer by occupation. The Doctor passed his childhood and early youth in his native land; he was educated in Bottomstown, county Limerick, Ireland, and when he was nineteen years of age he emigrated to the new world to seek the fortune there might be in store for him. He landed in the city of New York and soon after went to the state of Georgia, where he taught school for a period of two years. During this time he employed his leisure moments in the study of medicine, and in 1855-6 he attended medical lectures in New York city. He was graduated in 1857 from the University of Louisiana, and located in Yazoo county, at Belle Prairie, where he began practice. In 1872 he was united in marriage to Miss Mary Schmidt, a native of Germany and a daughter of Joseph Schmidt. Eight children have been born to the Doctor and wife, six of whom are living: Peter J., Miles, Kate, James, Jr., Louis T. and Mary L. In 1873 Dr. Carroll removed to Memphis, Tenn., but the following year he came back to Yazoo county and settled in Yazoo city. He has established a prosperous drug business, which he manages in connection with his professional work; he carries a complete line of goods of the first quality; he owns two dwelling houses, owns his business house, which is one of the best in the place, and a section of land in Washington county, Miss. For two years he was city physician of Yazoo city, discharging his duties with entire satisfaction to the public. He and his family are devout members of the Roman Catholic church, and are highly respected members of the community.

In early colonial days the Carsons were among the French Huguenots who, on account of religious persecution, formed an asylum in Ireland, and then came to America, and located in Pennsylvania and Virginia. Most individuals of that name now residing in the United States are descendants of those pioneers, from whom have sprung some of the best men and women of this or any other country. Andrew Carson, father of Andrew B. Carson, planter, of Greenville, Miss., left his home when a young man, and started out to seek his fortune in the great and then almost unknown and half-civilized portion of the country known as the Mississippi valley. This was about the year 1818. He then located in Chicot county, Ark., but a few years later settled on a tract of land three miles above the present site of Greenville, Miss., where he cleared a plantation, and there made a permanent home. Soon after locating on his Mississippi possessions, he was united in marriage to Miss Elizabeth J. Ross, a native of Tennessee. The Rosses were pioneer settlers of Middle Tennessee from South Carolina, and her parents were among the early settlers of Warren county, Miss. To Mr. and Mrs. Carson were born the following children: Samuel B., Andrew B., Mary L. and Eliza J., and of these Andrew B. is the only one now living. The parents were both members of the church, and noted for their hospitality, kindness of heart and noble and generous acts and thoughts. Mr. Carson was an old line whig, and an active partisan during the palmy days of that well-known political party. Andrew B. Carson was born March 1, 1836, in Washington, county, Miss., and his life was comparatively uneventful until the Civil war. He received instruction from private tutors at home, and subsequently attended educational institutions in his native state and Kentucky. In 1856 he graduated from a business college at Cincinnati, Ohio, and soon after this returned home, where he was appointed deputy sheriff of Washington county. Miss., on August 3, 1857, holding this position for three years. At the end of that time, his superior capability, his sterling honor and his courage and firmness as an officer became so apparent, that he was elected sheriff over six opponents, with a large majority of all votes cast, and although the bond required for that office at that time was little short of half a million dollars, it was given without the least trouble, he being popular, and his constituents having full confidence in his ability and integrity. He filled that position, in all, about eight years, until he was forcibly ejected from office by military rule in 1868, and during the war, when the county seat was destroyed by the Federals, he carried away and preserved the sheriff records. When the war closed, he carried the records to the Federal commander at Vicksburg, wishing to turn them over, make settlement, and have his bondsmen released. The officer in command, Gen. Morgan Smith, United States army, when he found the records had been preserved during the war by the careful foresight of Mr. Carson, refused to accept them, saying tersely, but firmly: " You took good care of them during the trying times of the last four years of war, and you are the best custodian for them." In this, as in other duties, he never betrayed a trust reposed in him, and no man in Washington county stands higher in the estimation of the people for integrity and honor than does Mr. Carson. During the war he acted as scout, and did his duty as a private soldier in the service of the Confederacy. Mr. Carson was married to Mrs. Mary Bell (Johnson) Blackburn, daughter of Capt. Henry Johnson, who was the youngest brother of the noted Col. Dick Johnson, slayer of Tecumseh, and vice president of the United States. Her father was one of the earliest settlers on Lake Washington, Miss. Mrs. Carson had three daughters by her first marriage: Julia, Lou and Prue, and one son, Henry Johnson Blackburn, all of whom are living. By her marriage to Mr. Carson there was one son, Matthew F. (deceased). Mrs. Carson's first husband, Capt. George T. Blackburn, was a near relative of Joe and Luke Blackburn, of Kentucky, and a native of that state. Mr. Carson is a large cotton planter in the Mississippi delta, cultivating annually about two thousand acres, and he has been a true and life-long democrat. He and wife are cultured, refined, courteous and hospitable, occupying a high position in society and in the hearts and affections of all who know them.

A. T. Carson, father of Robert B. Carson, M. D., Durant, Miss., was born in Georgia, and came to Mississippi in 1834, when a single man. He first settled in Tallahatchie county, but subsequently went to Yazoo county, where he met and married Miss Laura Edgar, a native of that county and the daughter of M. Edgar. He became one of the foremost planters of Yazoo county, reared his family there, and there received his final summons in 1890. His widow still survives him. Dr. Robert B. Carson was born in Yazoo county, Miss., on September 12, 1846, to the above mentioned union, and there spent his youth and received his primary education. He subsequently continued his studies at the State university at Oxford, Miss., and then began the study of medicine, taking his first course of lectures in 1868–9, and graduating in the class of 1870. He began practicing medicine at Benton and continued there for five years. In 1875 the Doctor located at Durant, has continued there ever since, and has established an excellent practice. In January, 1864, he enlisted in the Confederate army, Colonel Wood's cavalry, and served until the close of the war, participating in a number of small engagements and skirmishes. Dr. Carson is a republican in politics, but has never made himself obnoxious by intruding his views. He is esteemed and respected by his political opponents, and has many friends among them. He has held several local offices, and has discharged the duties of the same in a very creditable manner. He was appointed postmaster, first, under President Hayes and served four years. During the present administration (Harrison's) he was again appointed to that position, and is now serving his second term in that capacity. The Doctor was first married in Yazoo county to Miss Bettie Luce, who is now deceased. There were six children born to this marriage, and two daughters, young ladies, attend to the postoffice business. Dr. Carson married his present wife in Durant, Miss Mary Ramsey, a native of Mississippi, who was reared and educated in this town. She is a member of the Methodist and the Doctor a member of the Presbyterian church. He is a Royal Arch Mason, a member of the Knights of Honor and the Knights and Ladies of Honor, and is medical examiner of both the last-named organizations. He is a member of the state medical society, and was a delegate to the national medical convention at Chicago. He is health officer of Holmes county, and devotes his entire time to his large practice.

Samuel S. Carter is the president of the First national bank of Jackson, Miss., and its prosperous condition is largely due to Dr. Carter, who possesses experience, sound judgment and efficiency. He was born in Holmes county, Miss., the younger of two children born to

Richard and Louise (Sample) Carter, both of whom were born, reared and married in South Carolina and came to Mississippi about 1838. The father was a merchant and died soon after settlement in this state. His widow afterward married Rev. William Harris, a Presbyterian minister, who conducted a large school and was an experienced and successful educator. The mother died in 1855, and Mr. Harris later in the same year. Samuel S. Carter attended his stepfather's school until he was fifteen years of age and then entered the State university at Oxford, from which he graduated in 1859. Immediately succeeding this he entered the New Orleans medical college, from which he graduated in 1861. He soon afterward entered the Confederate army, becoming a member of company K (Burt Rifles), of the Eighteenth Mississippi regiment, soon after which he was made assistant surgeon, and remained a member of Humphries' brigade until the close of the war. Immediately after reaching his old home he was married to Miss America P. Sample, of Holmes county, and settled on a plantation which he continued to till for about five years. Following this he turned his attention to merchandising, and was successfully engaged in this business until January, 1885, when he sold out. He has been quite active in politics, and in 1875 was elected to the legislature from Holmes county, and, with the rest of the ticket, was the first democrat to be elected from that county. He was again honored by an election in 1877, and upon being once more renominated declined to serve. In May, 1885, he came to Jackson and organized the First national bank of this city, and after serving six months as vice president, he was made president, although the sole management of the bank was in his charge from the start. The first nine months after the organization of the bank, it was run on a capital of $50,000, which was at the end of this time increased to $100,000, the surplus and undivided profits reaching the amount of $175,000. This bank is recognized as a sound and substantial financial institution, its methods being safe and conservative, and its credit of the highest character. Dr. Carter is one of the directors of the Light, Heat and Water company, is a stockholder in the Jackson grocery company, and is secretary and treasurer of the Capital fertilizer company, and stockholder and director of the Compress and Warehouse company, the most of which institutions he assisted in organizing. Dr. Carter is finely educated, and is especially well-posted in literary and medical topics, although he is well up with the times on all subjects. He has not practiced his profession since the war, much preferring to devote his time and attention to planting and business, in both of which he made a success. He is one of the far-seeing, shrewd and practical business men of the state, and since the management of the First national bank has been in his hands it has reached a financial status highly satisfactory. He has one daughter, Hallie. His wife is a member of the Presbyterian church, is a worthy Christian lady and is a faithful wife and mother. They have a beautiful and comfortable home in Jackson and move in the highest social circles of the city.

Hon. R. A. Carter, merchant and postmaster at Rees' store, was born in Aberdeen, Miss., in 1847, the fifth child of Mr. and Mrs. D. G. Carter. His father was born at Snow hill, N. C., and came with his parents at the age of three to Monroe county in 1819. The family located on a farm near Columbus, in what is now Lowndes county. Mr. Carter received his education at the La Grange university. He prepared to enter the law department, but, not liking his teacher, relinquished the idea of engaging in the legal profession, and became a merchant, first at Hamilton, then at Aberdeen, where he was postmaster for four years, during the administration of President Buchanan. He was married to Lucy C. Hutchinson, of Monroe county, in 1837. His wife was the eighth child born to Capt. Richard Hutchinson, a veteran of the war of 1812. Mr. Carter turned his attention to farming in 1859. He was appointed and held the office of assessor for several years, and during the late war served for a short time in a militia organization.   His wife died in 1870 and after that event he became one of the family of his son, R. A. Carter, at whose house he died in 1875. Politically, he was an old Andrew Jackson democrat.   He was a man of the highest morality and intelligence, popular among his friends and neighbors.   His wife's father, the grandfather of the subject of this sketch, was born in Georgia in 1775.   He was a man of considerable wealth and prominence, who entered a large tract of land in this county, which he purchased through the influence of General Price, at twenty-five cents an acre.   He died in Monroe county, October 27, 1859.   R. A. Carter received his education in the common schools of this county and later attended some of the Aberdeen schools.   Although very young at the outbreak of the Civil war, he became a soldier in 1864, at sixteen years of age, and was in active duty about twelve months, remaining with his company until the close of the struggle, and returning home in May, 1865.   He served in company A of the Second Mississippi regiment, under Colonel Morphis.   After the war he was engaged in farming till 1869, when he embarked in the mercantile business at Rees' store, which he has since continued in connection with his agricultural operations.   He has served one term as justice of the peace, and in 1880 and 1881 represented his county in the Mississippi legislature. This latter honor was conferred upon him by the voluntary act of the people at large, for he was never an officeseeker, as was proven by the fact that he declined a second nomination. In 1870 he married Miss Martha L. Golightly of Monroe county, who was born in Alabama. They have had five children: Frank D., Mary A., Katie L., Lena, and one who died in infancy.   The eldest, Frank D., is in Memphis, Tenn., finishing his education, and all are bright and intelligent young people, who promise in time to take a high position in social and business circles.   Mary A. is especially noted as a fine musician, who, if she lives, will graduate in music before the close of the present year.   Mr. Carter is a member of the Masonic order, having for some years been connected with the Masonic lodge at Caledonia. He and his wife are members of the Methodist Episcopal church.

A little over half a century ago Dr. W. D. Carter, father of Dr. Nat. G. Carter, physician and druggist, Ripley, Miss , cast his lot with the people of Tippah county, Miss., and from the first he rose rapidly in his profession to a prominent position in the first rank of physicians of the state.   He was born in Wilson county, Tenn., about 1818, and there passed his youthful days, assisting on the farm and attending the country schools, in which he received a good common education.   He came to Ripley about 1840, and like many other young men who afterward distinguished themselves in public and professional life, commenced teaching school, and at the same time studied medicine.   He attended the Medical university at Louisville, Ky., graduated from that well-known and far-famed institution, and subsequently began his successful career as a practitioner.   This he continued until his death on the 24th of May, 1888.   In 1845 he married Miss Fannie Green, daughter of Judge C. A. Green, formerly of Ripley, and to them were born six children—three sons and three daughters.   Of these, two, the eldest and youngest, are deceased, the last being Charlie, who was murdered in the discharge of his duties while assisting to arrest some outlaws in Arkansas a few years ago.   Two sons and one daughter survive.   One son, Dr. N. G., is the subject of this sketch, and the other, Hardy, who is known to every man in Tippah county, is a distinguished lawyer and district attorney in Arkansas.   The mother of these children died in 1857, and in 1884 Dr. Carter married Miss Hermie E. Winkler, a daughter of Rev. Dr. Winkler, of Alabama, one of the most eminent ministers of the Baptist church in the South.   By the last marriage there were two little children—a daughter and son, the latter born during the last illness of his father.   Dr. Carter was a man of strong

KATE TUCKER INSTITUTE, BYHALIA.

The Goodspeed Publishing Co. Chicago

and vigorous mind, of great originality and unconquerable will. These qualities added to his handsome appearance, his high sense of honor, his kindness of heart and his great knowledge of human nature, made him a leader of men, and few in his time exerted a greater influence over those with whom he was associated. The giant mind, the willing heart and hand that so often ministered to others in the alleviation of suffering and the prolonging of life, were powerless before the reaper Death—the physician could not heal himself. He will not soon be forgotten, for his self-erected monument in the hearts of the people is crowned with beautiful flowers of affection. As an evidence of the stronghold he had upon the affections of the people, on the day of the burial every house in town was closed, all business was suspended and the entire population turned out to pay the last tribute of respect to the grand old man, and every neighborhood in the country for miles around was represented. His son, Dr. Nat. G. Carter, was born in Ripley in December, 1850, and was there reared and liberally educated. He read medicine with his father and attended the Louisville medical college, from which he graduated in 1872. He immediately began practicing in Ripley, and in connection with this engaged in the drug business, being quite successful in this dual occupation. In 1874 he selected as his companion in life Miss Willie Falkner, daughter of W. C. Falkner, and they have two interesting children—both daughters. Dr. and Mrs. Carter are members of the Baptist church, and he is an uncompromising democrat in his political views.

The Caruthers family trace their origin to Scotland, from which country two brothers of that name emigrated to the United States and settled in the Old Dominion. One branch drifted through Kentucky into Missouri; the other into South Carolina and Tennessee. Dr. C. K. Caruthers, planter, Como, Miss., comes of the latter branch, his birth occurring in Tipton county, Tenn., on the 22d of January, 1837. He was the fourth of seven children born to T. N. and E. M. (Gaither) Caruthers, natives of South and North Carolina respectively. About 1824 the father removed to Tennessee, was one of the pioneers of Madison county and a successful and progressive planter of the same. He had accumulated considerable property before his death, which occurred in 1867, at the age of sixty years. Dr. C. K. Caruthers was educated in his native state, graduated in medicine from the University of Virginia in 1858, and from Jefferson medical college, Philadelphia, the following year. After this he located in Panola county, Miss., and devoted his time and attention to his profession for one year, starting out with a large practice from the first. In 1861 he enlisted in the Confederate army as a private in company I, Second cavalry regiment, under Colonel Martin, and was soon after promoted to a lieutenancy, in which capacity he served faithfully until the battle of Shiloh. He then succeeded Captain Davis in the captaincy of his company. Afterward, by seniority, he commanded the First Mississippi battalion of sharpshooters until after the battle of Corinth. When his command reached Grenada he resigned his commission and was appointed to the position of surgeon, being assigned duty in the Seventh Tennessee regiment of cavalry. He afterward served as senior surgeon of the first brigade of Forrest's cavalry until the close of the war, and was paroled at Gainesville, Ala. Returning home he resumed the practice of medicine, and had a large, successful and lucrative practice until 1876, when, on account of failing health, he abandoned it to engage in merchandising and planting. He has continued the latter occupation very successfully since, and is a wideawake, enterprising man. He was a member of the board of supervisors for six years, and part of the time was president of the same. In 1887 he was elected to the legislature and acquitted himself with credit in that body. In 1889 he was elected to represent the sixth senatorial district in the state senate and is the present incumbent. In

33

this office, as in all others, Dr. Caruthers has ever guarded the best interests of his people, and is an able representative. In 1867 he was married to Miss Pattie Ellis, a native of Bailey Springs, Ala., and the daughter of Maj. A. G. and Mary (Hewlet) Ellis, the father a native of Virginia and the mother of Tennessee. This union has resulted in the birth of six children: Pattie, Ida, C. K., Kate, Ellis and Genie. The two eldest are attending school at Columbus, Miss. C. K., Jr., is in the military academy at Huntsville, Ala. Dr. and Mrs. Caruthers are members of the Presbyterian church, but their three daughters hold membership in the Methodist church. The Doctor is a member of the Masonic fraternity, the Knights of Honor and the Ancient Legion of Honor.

One of the largest manufacturing establishments of Jackson county is the sawmill of Hunter, Benn & Co., which was erected according to the plans and specifications of John F. Casey, of Scranton, Miss. It was begun in March, 1889, and was completed in July of the same year. It is 40x241 feet, and has a capacity of seventy thousand feet per day. There are three dry kilns, and the mill is thoroughly equipped throughout with all the modern improvements and conveniences. It fronts on the east bank of the Pascagoula river, and the Louisville & Nashville railroad runs a switch into the yards. About sixty-five men are employed besides the timber crews. The originator of this concern is Charles Casey, a native of New Brunswick, born in 1844. He was educated in his native country at College Hill. His father being a lumber merchant, he was naturally trained to the business. At the age of eighteen years he bade farewell to the parental roof, and started out into the world, dependent upon his own resources. He first went to Pennsylvania, and erected the first circular sawmill at Williamsport that was built in that part of the country. He did an immense business there until 1870, and then went to Brunswick, Ga., where he operated a mill for one year. He then went to Port Hudson, and formed a partnership with Dr. Hill in the milling business. He sold his interest, and removed to Clinton, La., where he owned and operated two mills for eight years. While residing here he was married to Miss Mary E. Pipes, a daughter of David Pipes, the present state treasurer of Louisiana. His next place of residence was New Orleans, where he erected the Clipper sawmill, the firm being Clarey & Casey. This partnership existed two and a half years, when Mr. Casey sold out, and engaged in the machinery business, selling all kinds of saw and wood machinery. For four years he was thus employed, and at the end of that period he came to Scranton, Miss., where he has had the management of Hunter, Benn & Co.'s business. His wide experience has fitted him for this position, and he has been very successful in his conduct of the business. Mr. Casey has reared a family of six children: William H., Eudora P., Maude A., John F., Jr., Alsena, Edward G. The father is a member of the Knights of Pythias, and is also a Knight of Honor.

Hon. John T. Casey comes of English stock, for his ancestors, at a remote period, came to America from that country and settled in North Carolina, where some of their descendants are still residing, being a practical, thrifty and substantial people. The father, Graham Casey, was born in the Old North state, but when a young man went to Virginia, and followed merchandising in Norfolk until his death in 1855. His wife, Charlotte C. Cook, was also born in North Carolina, her father, Dr. David T. W. Cook, being a South Carolinian, and a soldier in the war of 1812, holding the rank of captain of his company, and participating in the battle of New Orleans. He was of Irish lineage. The paternal grandfather, Dempsey Casey, was a Baptist minister, a native of North Carolina, while his wife, who was a Miss Crafts, was a native of Portsmouth, Va. Hon. John T. Casey was born in North Carolina, in 1832, but was reared in Virginia, receiving his initiatory education in the schools of that state, completing his education in Mississippi college, at Clinton. In 1856 he became a salesman in a general mercantile store at Clinton, but about 1859 decided to devote his life to planting, which calling he has since followed. He is now the owner of two hundred and fifty acres of land, and a part of the two hundred acres which he has under cultivation he himself opened. He has given his attention to the political improvement of the country rather than to the acquirement of wealth, but has a comfortable home and a fair income. He has wielded the widespread influence as a politician, and his labors for the success of the democrat party, of which he has always been a member, have been thoroughly appreciated by his numerous friends, who have elected him, a number of times, to official positions of honor and trust. He was a member of the board of supervisors of this county for about two years, and at the present time belongs to the board of Mississippi levee commissioners, and since 1888 has held the position of state representative, and has discharged his duties in a manner that has reflected great credit upon himself and supporters. In 1858 Mrs. Hattie E. Catlett became his wife, she being a native of Louisiana and a daughter of Robert L. Dunn, a merchant of Mississippi. To them three children have been born: Charles G., Robert L. and Jack H., all of whom reside near their parents and are thrifty, industrious and estimable citizens and members of society. Being a warm Southerner by birth and education, he enlisted in the Confederate army when the war opened, becoming a member of company A, First Mississippi artillery. Although he entered as a private he was soon promoted to the rank of sergeant, and was in the battles of Vicksburg and Chickasaw bayou. During his entire service he was not wounded and at the close of the war was paroled by General Canby, U. S. A., being at Jackson at the time of Lee's surrender. He is one of the following children: Caroline, who died when young; Lydia, who is unmarried and resides in Virginia; Eliza, unmarried, resides in Sharkey county, Miss.; Jane, married Judson Pettus, of Virginia; Dempsey, Virginia and Charles died when young; Almedia, married William Jarvis of Virginia, and lives in Norfolk; John T. (subject), and David C., who is a planter in Sharkey county. This and Issaquena county he represented in the state senate in 1886–8, and is now a prominent member of the alliance. Hon. John T. Casey has been a resident of Mississippi since 1854. He is a prominent member of the Masonic fraternity, belongs to the I. O. O. F., and he and his wife are worthy members of the Baptist church.

Hon. D. C. Casey is a prosperous planter of Rolling Fork, Miss., and was born in Norfolk, Va., in the year 1845, to Graham and Caroline (Cook) Casey, they being natives of the Old North state. Soon after their marriage they removed to Norfolk, Va., where Mr. Casey died of yellow fever in 1855, having followed the life of a merchant. His father was of English descent, and was a Baptist minister in North Carolina. Mrs. Casey, the mother of the immediate subject of this sketch, came to Mississippi about 1870, and died here in 1881, a worthy member of the Baptist church. She was a daughter of John Cook. The subject of this sketch is the youngest of four sons and five daughters, and until the opening of the war was an attendant of the public schools near his home. In 1861 he joined company I, Seventh North Carolina infantry, and for about ten months served on Oregon inlet and Roanoke island, after which he joined the navy, serving on board the Fannie after it was captured off Albemarle sound, in 1862. He was next on board the Nansemond, after which he served on the Harriet Lane, until turned over to the state of Texas, in 1863. He next went to Shreveport, La., and served on the ram Missouri, his next move being to Richmond, Va., where he remained until 1865. At one time, while serving on picket duty on the James river, he was wounded, but not seriously. After the war had ended he came to Mississippi, and until

1868 was a resident of Hines county, after which he settled in the county in which he is now residing, where he was married, the same year, to Mrs. C. E. Thomas, daughter of Dr. D. O. Williams, a native of Tennessee. The latter came to Mississippi when a young man, and for many years was a resident of Hinds county, but after the death of his wife he married again, and removed to Arkansas, where his death occurred in the year 1856. Mrs. Casey was born in Hinds county, Miss., and her union with Mr. Casey has resulted in the birth of two children, who are now deceased. Although Mr. Casey has given the most of his attention to planting, he was also, from 1874 to 1879, and in 1885, engaged in merchandising. He is the sole owner of one thousand acres of land, and also owns a one-half interest in nine hundred acres, this property being acquired by his own persistent labors. In 1879 he was appointed taxcollector of Sharkey county, and in 1885 was elected for four years a member of the state senate, from what was then the twenty-sixth, but is now the twentieth district. During the first session he was on the committees on penitentiary, registration, election and levees. During his second session he was chairman of the committee on levees, and a member of the committee on county and county boundaries, etc. He took an active part in endeavoring to defeat the constitutional convention bill, and it was mainly through his efforts that the veto by Governor Lowry was sustained. He is a member of Deer Creek lodge No. 356, of the A. F. & A. M. (in which he has held a number of minor offices), Rolling Fork lodge No. 3175 of the K. of H., and Rolling Fork lodge No. 1097, of the A. L. of H. He is a member of the democratic state and congressional executive committee and the state alliance executive committee. He has been one of the most prominent men of Starkey county in public matters, and is of a very decided character.

With the development and advancement of any great commonwealth are indissolubly connected the names and careers of certain men who, uniting their efforts, and with the love of their country at heart, have sought the advancement of their respective callings, and thus reflected credit not only upon themselves, but upon their professions and their state. Thus it is that Mississippi has within her borders many men toward whom she may justly point the finger of pride, and whose names are synonymous with her advancement morally, intellectually and financially. If in any one line her advancement has been greater than in other directions, that one is in the administration of justice, for among the members of her bar have been enrolled the familiar names of eminent jurists, conscientious judges and talented lawyers. Standing preëminent among his fellows, and enjoying an honored distinction as one of her greatest criminal lawyers, is Judge Hiram Cassedy, of Brookhaven, and his career is a remarkable example of the success that comes to him who strives, for his success in life has not been the result of chance, but of his individual and continuous efforts.

Few possessions are more valued and wished for than strength, but it is not generally considered that only through long, patient and continuous effort can it be attained. It is thought of rather as a happy accident or a native gift to be passively grateful for, than as a natural and certain result of toil and striving. In bodily strength, for example, the infant gains it through constant motion, the boy through active play, the man through tug and toil and burden. This is equally manifest in moral and mental strength. The strong mind is one which has accumulated power through hard mental activity. Much earnest study, much effort of thought, have combined to give it that vigorous force and elasticity which, to its possessor, is so valuable a boon. We look with pleasure upon the man thus favored. We admire his clear thought, his sound judgment, his keen discrimination; we envy the ease with which he detects the point of an argument, or solves an intricate question or applies a principle, but we do not see and seldom even imagine what toil and patience may have been the source of his admired strength. The one whom all men honor for his virtue and integrity, to whom wrongdoing offers no attraction, and who performs each duty as it arises apparently without effort, has not gained this power by treading flower-beds of ease. The obstacles overcome, the trials which have been so hard to bear, have called forth the fortitude and heroism which are parts of every noble nature. It has come to him through effort and sacrifice, and the more it has cost the greater the reward.

Born of Scotch-Irish ancestry, Judge Cassedy inherited the fundamental principles of industry, integrity and determination of purpose which have become the attributes of his whole after-life. His father, Hiram Cassedy, a native of Pennsylvania, came to Mississippi when a lad, and there alone, without money or friends, a cripple from boyhood, he bravely took up the burdens of life and was afterward permitted to look back upon those early struggles from a position of prominence, for he became one of the leading jurists of the South and had few equals and no superior at the Mississippi bar. (See personal sketch elsewhere.) He married Mary Proby, of Franklin county, Miss., and to them were born six children, of whom there are but two survivors, Judge William Proby Cassedy, of Summit, and our present subject. He was born upon his father's plantation in Franklin county, Miss., July 4, 1846, and after becoming of sufficient age attended the little district school of his neighborhood for a few months during the winter period. This afforded but meager advantages, however, and his earlier education was the especial care of his mother, a talented lady of more than ordinary attainments for her time, and a graduate of Washington college, of Adams county, Miss., and her careful training and moral teachings made a lasting impression upon his after-life. He was just approaching manhood when the war cloud, whose muttering had been heard upon our horizon, suddenly burst, deluging our country in fraternal blood. He was loyal to his section, and in 1863, at the age of seventeen, he entered the Confederate service, offering his life, if needs be, in defense of his state. He enlisted in company I, of the Fourth Mississippi cavalry, under command of Col. T. R. Stockdale, now a member of congress from the sixth district of Mississippi and was attached to General Forrest's army, following his regiment through all the varying vicissitudes of war, and participating in all its campaigns and engagements until 1865. The Federal General Wilson was at this time making his famous cavalry raid through Alabama, and when near Selma a portion of his command came suddenly upon a Confederate scouting party, taking a number of them prisoners, among whom was our subject. He was taken to Columbus, Ga., and there paroled, and returned to his home, where he had been but a short time when the surrender at Appomattox put an end to the conflict and dropped the curtain of war upon the altar of sacrifices upon which were piled the mangled and bleeding bodies of so many of America's bravest and best.

The excitement of the war having subsided, he began, with the aid of a private tutor, to fit himself for college, and in 1865 was among the first to become a student of the University of Mississippi, at Oxford, where for two sessions he applied himself with diligence to his studies. He then began the study of his profession in the law department of that university, and in 1868 became the proud possessor of its diploma, and at once entered upon the practice of the law at Meadville. During this time the state, already suffering from the burdens of war, was endeavoring to rebuild its shattered fortunes under the oppressive and never-to-be-forgotten reconstruction period. The government was being administered by a horde of political tricksters, assisted by a motley assemblage of ignorant negroes. This form of government was highly objectionable to all of the better class of people, and, repudiating the same, Mr. Cassedy was chosen as representative from Franklin county, but, as the legislature did not convene, he was not called upon to act. While pursuing his studies at Oxford he met Miss Bettie R., the talented daughter of Col. Robert W. Durfey. She was at that time a student at the Union female college, at Oxford, from which she afterward graduated. The acquaintance of the young people soon ripened to mutual affection and, in November, 1868, they were united in marriage and together faced the responsibilities of life. In March, 1869, they removed to Brookhaven, which has since been their place of residence and where Mrs. Cassedy presides over their happy home with stately and becoming grace, enjoying, with her husband, the universal esteem of their wide circle of friends and acquaintances. Three sons and three daughters have come to them to bless their home and cast the golden gleam of the sunshine of happiness into their lives. Of this family the eldest, Hiram, Jr., is private secretary to Governor Stone, Robert D. is a stenographer, Mary is a student at the Industrial Institute and College of Mississippi, while Bessie, Carrie and William P. are at home, members of their father's household. Immediately after coming to Brookhaven Judge Cassedy resumed the practice of his profession, and has rapidly mounted to the topmost round of the ladder of success, becoming at once a conspicuous figure in legal circles. In 1871 he was the democratic nominee to represent the counties of Lincoln, Lawrence and Pike in the state senate, and in the election following defeated by a majority of three hundred his opponent, who was the incumbent at that time, and who, in the previous election, had carried the district by a majority of seven hundred. Taking his seat in 1872, he was the youngest man in the senate, being then but twenty-five years of age. There was represented the talent of the state, men of learning and of prominence, but he filled his difficult position in a most exemplary and creditable manner, and never had a constituency a more earnest, conscientious and painstaking representative. He served in the senate until 1874, during one session of which he was chairman of the judiciary committee, a most fitting compliment and recognition of his ability bestowed upon him by his fellow-associates. During his service in the senate he was indefatigable in his efforts for the public good and welfare of his state. He vigorously opposed all bills exempting the property of corporations from taxation, holding that such was benefiting the few at the expense of the many, and to his earnest efforts is due, in no little measure, the defeat of a bill for the consolidation of the Mississippi Central and the New Orleans, Jackson & Great Northern railroads, whereby they would become the recipients of valuable privileges without proper compensation to the people of the state. Upon his retirement from the senate in 1874 he was appointed chancellor of the judicial district composed of the counties of Lincoln, Pike, Franklin, Jefferson and Claiborne, but the following year he resigned this position, having been elected district attorney for the tenth judicial district, then composed of Lincoln, Pike, Amite, Wilkinson, Adams and Jefferson counties. The dockets of all the courts in this district were at that time crowded with criminal cases, to the almost complete exclusion of civil cases. He at once entered upon his duties, and soon demonstrated his ability as a prosecutor, dealing out evenhanded justice to all, and sparing no guilty one, that the dignity of the law might be upheld and the moral standing of the state sustained, and in that capacity won a reputation for himself second to none.

In 1879 he was reëlected by a large majority and continued in that capacity until 1884. During that time he represented the state in some of her most important cases, among which were the Long case, and the Hawley murder trial—cases attracting much attention and widely reported in the reports of Mississippi. Since his retirement from the district attorneyship, he has devoted his attention principally to criminal cases, acting for the defense, and his success has shown his great ability as a criminal lawyer. As a defender, he has achieved some of the greatest legal victories known in the history of the South, the Hamilton-Gambrell case and the Rising Sun tragedy being widely quoted in the press of the United States. Judge Cassedy, as a lawyer, is a striking example of the diversity of talents. Whether his powers of persuasion are more fully put in requisition in vindicating the innocent, or in bringing offenders to justice, it will be difficult to decide. Not only has he demonstrated his ability in criminal cases, but is, as well, an able exponent of civil law. He is a careful student and deep thinker, his fertile mind readily grasping the points involved. When in court, he becomes engrossed in his case and appears the model lawyer, and his piercing eyes fairly blaze in their sockets under the excitement. He is a man of commanding presence, and, as a speaker, is forcible and eloquent, his deep resonant voice thrilling all who come within its range. So great is his power of argument, so clear his exposition of evidence that these, coupled with his earnest and impressive manner, seldom fail to convince his hearers. To his colleagues and opponents, he is ever considerate, treating them with deference and respect. As a citizen, he is amiable and courteous, is an interesting conversationalist, possessing an inexhaustible fund of humor and anecdote. He is public spirited and generous to a fault, giving liberally of his means to all charitable enterprises without ostentation, and every movement tending toward the advancement of his town, educationally, morally and otherwise, finds in him an earnest and ardent advocate. Socially, he has attained to the Blue lodge in Masonry, and is a member of Hilzeim lodge No. 1447, Knights of Honor. He is an active and conspicuous figure in the political affairs of his state, and has represented his district in congressional and district conventions, and was an alternate delegate to the democrat national convention in 1888. The Judge is a kind and indulgent father, and when for a time he can lay aside the cares of a professional life, he seeks the enjoyment of his home, and there, surrounded by his loved ones, gives himself over to the enjoyment of domestic happiness. The passing years have dealt leniently with him, and though time has tinged his hair with gray, he is still in the prime of life, and it is to be hoped that fate has yet in store for him many years of usefulness. Looking back over the past, he can trace his progress in such tokens as awaken admiration and esteem, and enjoy that satisfaction which is the just reward of him who, surmounting all obstacles, presses bravely forward and endures to the end.

Hon. William P. Cassedy, judge of the sixth circuit court of Mississippi, comprising the counties of Pike, Amite, Wilkinson, Franklin, Jefferson and Adams, was born in Franklin county, Miss., October 29, 1849, a descendant of the first Cassedy who settled in this state, Hiram Cassedy, who was born in Chambersburg, Penn., September 7, 1820, and came to Mississippi in 1840. This pioneer, who was a cripple from boyhood, embarked on a steamer and made his way to Natchez, Miss. There alone, without money or friends, the brave boy started out in life in his adopted state. He was offered a position as copyist, and being unable to write, he, with indomitable courage, began to acquire a knowledge of writing, and with the aid of a private tutor soon fitted himself to fill the position offered him. Having begun his education thus, he continued his studies, devoting his spare moments to his books, and soon accepted a position as teacher in the schools of Franklin county. He afterward related, as an amusing incident, how he would study at night and keep one day ahead of his pupils. In this manner, deterred by no difficulties and pressing bravely forward, he overcame all obstacles, and was afterward enabled to look back upon the struggles of his boyhood from a position of eminence. He later became deputy probate clerk of Franklin

county, and began the study of law.   In this he was assisted by Judge Kinney, the author
of Kinney's Blackstone, and by Col. Richard Webber, at that time a prominent attorney of
Mississippi, who formed a friendship for Mr. Cassedy, and took him into his office, rendering
him every aid in his power.   Mr. Cassedy became a prominent factor in social and political
circles of his county.   In 1850 he was elected to represent Franklin county in the state legislature, in which he was a member continuously until 1858.   In 1856 he was elected speaker
of the house, and officiated in that capacity until his retirement in 1858, when he was elected
circuit judge of his district, and served until after the late war, at which time he retired from
the bench.   He continued the practice of his profession, however, and was universally
regarded as one of Mississippi's leading jurists and lawyers.   His death occurred in Pike
county March 26, 1881, in his sixty-first year.   He had removed to that county in 1872.
He held so high a place in the estimation of the people that after his death the citizens of
Pike and Franklin counties each secured by popular subscription an elegant oil portrait of
him as he appeared upon the bench.   These paintings were hung in the courthouses of the
counties, but unfortunately the one in Pike county was destroyed in the courthouse fire of
1882.   About 1844 Mr. Cassedy had married Miss Mary Proby, a native of Franklin county
and a daughter of Hon. William Proby, many years a probate judge of Franklin county, a
Virginian, who came to Mississippi prior to the formation of Franklin county, and after that
event donated a portion of his plantation as a county seat, which land is occupied by the
courthouse at the present time.   To this union three sons and three daughters were born,
two of whom died in infancy, and of whom there are but two survivors: Hon. Hiram Cassedy, of Brookhaven, and the subject of this sketch.   Mr. Cassedy, aside from being a prominent lawyer in ordinary cases, was distinguished as a criminal lawyer.   He always acted for
the defense, and for years he was connected with every case of prominence in this region, and
so great was his success that he came to be looked upon as almost invincible.   Hon. William
P. Cassedy was the fourth child in his family, and his boyhood days were spent in his native
county.   During the war he was attending the public schools and managing the plantation
at home, and after the war he was a student in the University of Mississippi at Oxford.   In
January, 1870, he began the study of law under the preceptorship of his father, and in June
of that year received license to practice in the courts of that state.   It is a fact worthy of
note that he had not at this time attained his majority, but the Mississippi legislature
removed his disability as a minor, thus making possible the granting of his license.   In
December, 1872, he was married to Miss Julia M. Herring, a native of Franklin county and
a daughter of John W. Herring, an extensive planter.   From that time until 1881 he devoted
his attention to the occupation of agriculture and to some extent to the practice of his profession.   In the spring of the year last mentioned he removed to Summit and formed a partnership with his father, which terminated afterward by the death of the latter.   In December, 1890, he was appointed judge of the sixth circuit court of Mississippi, succeeding Judge
Ralph North, of Natchez, who had resigned.   To Mr. and Mrs. Cassedy have been born two
sons and two daughters: Annie J., James, Burt and Mary H.   Although not a member of
any church the Judge and his family are regular attendants upon the services, and liberal
supporters, with the material interests, of the Methodist church.   Politically he is like his
father, a stanch democrat, and socially is a member of the I. O. O. F. and the Freemasons.
He is one of the most respected citizens of Summit.

    Mrs. Martha Catching, whose postoffice address is Georgetown, Copiah county, Miss., is the
widow of Dr. Joseph B. Catching.   Dr. Catching was born in Pike county, Miss., in 1828,
and is one of seven children of Philip and Matilda Catching.   Philip Catching was one of

three brothers who came from Georgia about 1820, and settled in Mississippi, the others being Jonathan and Joseph Catching. These three brothers are the originators of this name in the state, and their descendants are different families of Catchings through all parts of the state, some of the members of which have held various positions of trust in state and national offices. Philip Catching represented his fellow-citizens in both branches of the legislature, and was a member of the first constitutional convention of the state at the time of secession. The Doctor received his medical education at New Orleans and Louisville, Ky., and began practicing in 1846. To him and his wife were born thirteen children, named as follows: Dr. Philip Catching, of Copiah county; Franklin B., of Copiah county; Margaret, wife of I. C. Enochs, of Jackson, Miss.; Walter S., of Copiah county; Dr. Joseph M., of Hazlehurst; Lucy, who is a member of her mother's household; Nina R., wife of C. O. McKinnell, of Copiah county; Mattie, who died in 1883; Charles S., who died when about fourteen months old; M. Pallie, wife of A. A. Lilly, of McComb city, Miss.; Richard O.; Courtney Q. and Lulu B. Dr. Catching was a thoroughgoing, honorable, progressive, self-made man, a well-informed and distinguished gentleman of the old school, who had a wide acquaintance of the men of the state who lived during the time, and was held in high respect by all classes. Three of his sons, residents of this county, are well and widely known in this section, and a brief sketch of each is given in this connection. Mrs. Catching is a highly intelligent lady, and a descendant of one of the good old families of this state; a model wife and mother, she has nobly performed her duty in rearing her family, fitting them for honorable positions in society. Dr. Philip Catching was born in 1848, in Copiah county. He received his medical education at New Orleans, and graduated with the degree of M. D. in 1871, since which time he has been engaged in the practice of his profession, devoting a portion of his time to planting, and being connected with his brother, Frank B., in the mercantile business. He was married in 1873 to Miss Harriet A. Allen, the daughter of Elbert H. and Martha (Love) Allen. She has borne him seven children, five of whom are living: Hugh L., Walter W., Philip M., Elbert H. and Kattie. The Doctor is a member of the Hazlehurst lodge, Knights of Pythias, and he and his wife are identified with the Methodist church. He has a large and growing practice, extending in the distant parts of Simpson and Copiah counties. Frank B. Catching was born in Copiah county in 1850. He is the son of Dr. Joseph and Martha Catching. At the age of about twenty-four he embarked in business life for himself, as a planter, in which he has continued until the present time, though during the past nine years he has been a leading merchant at Georgetown. He was married in 1876 to Mary L. Steele, daughter of Archibald and Martha Steele, a sketch of of whom appears in these pages. Mr. and Mrs. Catching have had born to them five children, all of whom are members of their household. Their names are Myra P., Frank B., Archibald Steele, Joseph B. and Mary. Walter S. Catching, another son of Joseph and Martha Catching, was born in 1855. He received his education at Centenary college at Jackson, La., and at Emory and Henry college in Virginia, graduating from the last-named institution in 1877. He studied law for two years, and soon after was admitted to the bar, and for three years practiced, but in 1883 he located upon his present plantation, to which he has devoted his entire attention since. When he came to this beautiful farm, it was a portion of an almost unbroken wilderness, but to-day comprises about three hundred acres of improved and highly productive land. In 1884 he was married to Miss Ida Sanders, daughter of William J. and Martha (Simmons) Sanders, of Madison county. She has borne him three children: Martha L., Walter W. and Greenville. Mr. Catching is a member of the Knights of Honor and Copiah lodge No. 60, Knights of Pythias, of Hazlehurst.

Hon. Thomas C. Catchings of Vicksburg, was born in Hinds county, Miss., January 11, 1847; entered the University of Mississippi in September, 1859, and, after passing through the freshman and part of the sophomore years, left to enter Oakland college, Miss., where he passed into the junior class in the spring of 1861; entered the Confederate army early in 1861, and served throughout the war; commenced the study of law in 1865 after the termination of the war; was admitted to the bar in May, 1866, and has since practiced law in Vicksburg; was elected to the state senate of Mississippi in 1875 for a term of four years, but resigned on being nominated in 1877 for attorney-general; was elected attorney-general of Mississippi in November, 1877, for a term of four years, was renominated by acclamation in August, 1881, and elected in the following November, resigning February 16, 1885; was elected to the XLIXth and Lth congresses, and was reëlected to the LIst congress as a democrat, receiving eleven thousand six hundred and twenty-four votes, against four thousand six hundred and fourteen votes for James Hill, republican.

In enumerating the enterprising and progressive citizens of Alcorn county, Miss., Robert C. Cates, merchant and farmer, Kossuth, must not be overlooked, for he is acknowledged by all to be one of the foremost men in his capacity as a progressive merchant. He first opened his eyes to the scenes of this world in Mississippi in 1841, and is the son of Pleasant and Hattie (Anderson) Cates, both natives of Tennessee, where they were married. Their children, four in number, were named in the order of their births as follows: Robert C., Luke (resides in Tupelo, is married and has one child, Mary A.), Mary (is the wife of S. R. Stribbling and resides at Tupelo—she is the mother of four children: Oscar, Minnie, Anna and William), and Elizabeth (is the wife of J. P. Baldridge and resides at Fulton, Miss.—she is the mother of six children). The parents of the above-mentioned children moved to Mississippi in 1866, settled at Fulton, and there they reside at the present time, the father engaged in farming. Robert C. Cates received a good, practical education in McNairy county, Tenn., and he selected as his companion in life Miss Elizabeth Huggens, a native of Tennessee, born in 1845, and the daughter of J. M. and Elizabeth (Robinson) Huggens. Mr. and Mrs. Huggens were the parents of fourteen children, and Mrs. Cates was the youngest of this family. Her mother died in Tennessee in 1875, but the father is still living and makes his home in Tennessee. Mr. Cates' union was blessed by the birth of seven children, only three now living: Hettie, Joseph R. and Minnie, all at home. Those deceased were: Luke, Lorane, Leon and Emma. Mr. Cates came with his family to Mississippi in 1865, commenced merchandising at Kossuth and has continued there ever since. At the breaking out of hostilities between the two sections in 1861, he enlisted in the Confederate army and served in a Tennessee regiment under Col. Preston G. Smith, and was first in the battle of Belmont, then Shiloh, and after that was in the cavalry with General Forrest. He was in the battle of Harrisburg, Bryson's cross roads, Athens, and a number of severe skirmishes. He was paroled in 1865 and came home, where he followed farming for one year. After that he engaged in merchandising and is well known and respected for his qualities as a business man, citizen and member of society. In his political views he affiliates with the democratic party, and his first presidential vote was for G. B. McClellan. Socially he is a member of the Masonic fraternity, a master Mason. Both he and wife hold membership in the Missionary Baptist church, and are strong supporters and liberal contributors to all educational and religious enterprises.

Robert Catlett, planter, Canton, Miss., is one of the class of men singled out by nature to show what a man can accomplish by push and energy. He is a self-made man, and what he has won in the way of this world's goods is wholly due to his own good fighting qualities.

He was the sixth of twelve children born to William and Annie (Mallory) Catlett, natives of the Old Dominion. The father was a planter in his native state and died in 1855. The mother received her final summons in 1850. Robert Catlett was born in Fauquier county, Va., on the 19th of March, 1826, and attained his growth and received his education in his native state. His father having a large family to support, Robert remained at home and assisted on the farm for five years after attaining his majority. In 1852 he came to Mississippi with no capital, and by his own industry and perseverance has accumulated a fortune. Planting has been his principal occupation, and he is now the owner of one thousand six hundred acres of land, three hundred of which are under cultivation. He has been unusually successful in this pursuit, and the secret of his success has been that he raises almost everything needed to carry on a prosperous business, cattle, horses, etc. He gives liberally to all worthy enterprises and he and family are members of the Baptist church. He is a member of the Masonic fraternity and in politics affiliates with the democratic party. Mr. Catlett was married on the 13th of March, 1863, to Miss Maggie Burton, a native of Mississippi and daughter of David and Eliza Burton, of Alabama. To this union have been born sixteen children: Annie E., William J., Robert B., Penn T., Mary L. (deceased), Walter C., Anora, Mallory, Maggie, Helen, Lillian, Lucy, Gertrude, David F. and Ashby. The other child was not named. Mr. Catlett was in the late war, enlisting in 1862 in company I, Twenty-eighth Mississippi regiment cavalry, and was in the same until close of war. He participated in the following battles: Vicksburg, Jackson, Atlanta, Selma, Lost mountain, Bethel church, New Hope church, Twin mountain, Peach Tree creek, Cassville, Jonesboro and Selma, Ala.

To the person who applies himself to any one occupation which he has chosen as his calling in life there can be only one result—that of success, and a high place in the esteem of those with whom he has come in contact. Edwin Cato is no exception to this rule, for by strict attention to his calling and the exercise of his mental faculties, which are far above the average, he has acquired a good competency. The Cato family was among the early and most prominent families to settle in the eastern part of Jefferson county, Burrel Cato taking up his abode there about the year 1820, moving thither from Wayne county, where he had resided for a few years while en route to this section from North Carolina. He opened up a large farm here, here reared his family and here also made his home until his death. Of three sons born to him, Sterling C., the father of the immediate subject of this biography, was the youngest. He was born in Wayne county August 12, 1816, but attained man's estate in Jefferson county, whither he came with his father. He was married here to Mrs. Rebecca McLaurin, a daughter of Norman Gillis. Mrs. Cato was born in Mississippi, and after her marriage with Mr. Cato they located on the old homestead which had belonged to the Cato family, and here Mr. Cato successfully followed the occupation of planting. He was a man of exemplary habits, gave his time and attention to his business and farming interests for many years, and at the time of his death, which occurred December 6, 1878, he was a member of the Presbyterian church. His widow survives him and resides on the home place, aged seventy-five years, having borne a family of two sons and four daughters that grew to years of maturity: Cora (deceased) was the wife of W. B. Scott; Georgia is the wife of J. B. Mullins, of Franklin county; Gertrude is the widow of Lewis Cato; Laconia is the wife of N. B. Gillis; W. L. Cato is a planter of Franklin county; and Edwin, who has spent his life in this county. In his youth he was given the advantages of the Union Church high school, after which he went on the farm with his father, with whom he remained until the latter's death. He was married February 19, 1879, to Mrs. Martha

E. Cato, daughter of Maxwell Newman, of Franklin county, in which county Mrs. Cato was born, reared and educated. After their marriage they settled on the old Cato homestead, but at the end of a few years he opened a general mercantile establishment at Union Church, purchasing a half interest in an established business at this point in January, 1885, since which time he has conducted it very successfully. He also owns an interest in a general mercantile house at McNair, and also in a like establishment at Russum, Claiborne county. He carries an excellent and complete stock of goods, and by strictly fair dealing with all, as well as by his courteous and pleasant manners, he has built up a good patronage. The old home farm is still in his possession, and in addition to his duties as a merchant, he successfully manages this farm. He is a shrewd financier, and socially as well as in a business way he is a very pleasant gentleman to meet. He and his wife have no children of their own, but are rearing three orphans, two boys and one girl, the children of Mrs. Cato's sister, who is deceased. Mr. Cato and his wife are Presbyterians, and are hospitable, charitable and upright citizens, and by their many worthy characteristics have many warm friends.

Rev. Levi J. Caughman, of Burns, Smith county, Miss., was born in Edgefield district, S. C., in August, 1849, the eldest in a family of five children born to James D. and Mary E. (Wise) Caughman. Both of the parents were natives of the same district. The father moved with his family to Smith county in 1858 and engaged in planting. In 1861 he enlisted in the Confederate army and served gallantly until he was killed at Atlanta. Our subject grew to manhood in this county and received such an education as was afforded by the common schools. In 1866 he married Miss Elizabeth Jamison, a daughter of John Jamison. In 1867 he engaged in planting which he has followed successfully until the present time. In 1871 he became a member of the Missionary Baptist church, and in 1878 he began preparing for the ministry. He was ordained in 1880, and since that time has been in charge of several churches of this denomination. In 1883 he was elected county treasurer of Smith county, and filled that office with such satisfaction from January, 1884, to January, 1886, that he was again elected to the same office in 1887 and served from January, 1888, to January, 1890. Early in the history of that body he became an active member of the Farmers' Alliance, in which he has held offices ever since. In 1888 he acquired an interest in a coöperative store at Burns and has been actively identified with that enterprise. He owns about five hundred acres of land, which, with other property, has been accumulated by his own unaided efforts, having relied solely on his own business ability and perseverance to make his way in the world. He is a member of the Masonic order. Mr. and Mrs. Caughman are the parents of nine children.

John B. Cauthen, merchant and planter, Kirkwood, Miss., the third in order of birth of nine children born to Milton and Sarah (Barrow) Cauthen, owes his nativity to Kershaw district, S. C., his birth occurring in 1831. The parents were natives also of the Palmetto state, but came to this county in 1838, and here the father died in 1868. The mother is still a resident of the county. All their children grew to maturity and seven are now residing in Madison county. When about twenty-three years of age John B. Cauthen began life for himself as a planter, and continued this occupation until the opening of the conflict between the two sections. He then entered the Confederate army, company A, Captain Ward's battery, Heath's division, Hill's corps of northern Virginia, and served through the entire war. He was in all the engagements in which his battalion participated, including seven days' fight at Richmond, battles of the Wilderness, Cold Harbor, Mine Run, Gettysburg, besides numerous minor engagements. He escaped being wounded or taken prisoner, and was paroled at Appomattox courthouse. Returning to Madison county, he engaged in farming and settled on his present farm, then consisting of seventeen hundred acres of land, in 1876. Since then he has reduced his farm to eleven hundred and forty acres, one-half of which he cultivates to corn and cotton. He also has a steam gin and cornmill, and in connection is also engaged in merchandising, carrying a stock of goods valued at about $2,500, and doing an average business of $10,000 annually. Mr. Cauthen was married in 1859 to Miss Clementine Harris, daughter of Matthew and Eliza (Allen) Harris, and the fruits of this union are six living children: Malvina, widow of R. M. McCool, now living with her father; Robert, at home; Anna; Nannie, wife of Henry Evans of Camden; Burdette, at home, and Campbell C. Mr. and Mrs. Cauthen are members of the Presbyterian church, at Greenwood, and he is an elder in the same.

Joseph F. Cazeneuve, Bay Saint Louis, Miss., sheriff of Hancock county, was born in Bay Saint Louis November 28, 1855, and is a son of John B. and Harriet (Bontemps) Cazeneuve. The father was a native of France, and the mother was born in Bay Saint Louis. The maternal grandfather was born in France, and the maternal grandmother was a Spaniard. John B. Cazeneuve emigrated to America and located in Mississippi about the year 1851. He was married in New Orleans and came to Bay Saint Louis, where he engaged in contracting and building. He followed this vocation for many years. His death occurred March 12, 1874, but his wife survived until 1883. They were the parents of but one child, Joseph F., the subject of this notice. He received his education in his native place, and took a commercial course at St. Stanislaus college. Here he had a thorough training in bookkeeping, and secured a position as bookkeeper, which he held for nine years. He was then appointed deputy sheriff, and at the end of four years he was elected to the office of sheriff. He has held the office four consecutive terms, and is a candidate for reëlection without opposition. His long years of service as bookkeeper were a strong testimonial of his fidelity, and since his connection with the office of sheriff the business has been transacted with the greatest accuracy and dispatch. Mr. Cazeneuve was united in marriage July 23, 1878, to Miss Martha Longren, of Bay Saint Louis. Six children have been born to them: Jessie H. R., Mabel V., Martha C., Louis F., Louisa G. and Mary I. Our subject is a member of the Catholic Knights of America, and is secretary of the local branch. He is president of the St. Joseph Benevolent association, and holds the same position in the local building and loan association of Bay Saint Louis. Politically he affiliates with the democratic party, and is a member of the Bay St. Louis democratic club, of which he is vice president. He belongs to the Farmers' Alliance, and is secretary of the local assembly. He is a member of the Roman Catholic church. He is a man of fine social qualities, is very popular in his town and county, and is numbered among the most progressive and enterprising citizens.

Hon. Joseph W. Chalmers (deceased) was a native of that grand old state, Virginia, and was a descendant of one of the prominent families of the same. He was well educated there, and at an early period emigrated to Mississippi, settling in Holly Springs. He became a partner in the law practice with Robert Barton, was vice chancellor of this district, and was United States senator for a time. He was a man of strong mental caliber, a profound thinker and reasoner, and was one of the most prominent men of the state. He died in Holly Springs prior to the war, leaving three sons, two of whom, Gen. James R. and Judge H. H., became quite distinguished. The former was educated in South Carolina, studied law and practiced his profession in Holly Springs before the war. He raised a company, entered the Confederate army as captain, and was afterward made brigadier-general. He was a true and tried soldier. After cessation of hostilities he returned to Holly Springs and resumed the practice of law.   Later he was elected to congress, and so great was his popularity that he filled that honorary position two terms.

Judge H. H. Chalmers (deceased) was born in Tennessee, and was the second in order of birth of three children born to the marriage of Hon. Joseph W. Chalmers, a prominent lawyer of Mississippi.   Judge Chalmers came to Marshall county when a small boy, and was prepared for college by Dr. Whitehorn, of Holly Springs.   He graduated at Oxford, and afterward began practicing law.   After the war, in which he served faithfully in the Confederate army, he located at Hernando, and, in partnership with Colonel White, carried on a very successful law practice.   He was appointed to the supreme bench from that place, and later removed to Jackson, where his death occurred quite suddenly, while still in vigorous manhood.   He had the full confidence of both bench and bar, and was possessed of noble qualities of both mind and heart.   He was one of the ablest men of the state.   He left a widow and one daughter.

Hon. J. W. Chamberlain, a member of the firm of Chamberlain & Brandon, cotton commission merchants and lumber dealers of Natchez, Miss., was born in the Keystone state, Erie county, in 1836, and was the third in order of birth of five children—two sons and three daughters—born to Reverend Pierce and Christina B. (Whitehill) Chamberlain.   The father was a native of New Castle county, Del., and was married to Miss Whitehill, who was born in Lancaster county, Penn.   Shortly after marriage they removed to Erie county, Penn., from there to Newark, Del., in 1845, and there Mr. Chamberlain received his final summons in 1852.   His widow died in Columbia, Penn., in 1882.   Both were devout members of the Presbyterian church.   Mr. Chamberlain was a talented man and an able Presbyterian divine, receiving theological training at Princeton (New Jersey) college, and afterward followed the ministry until a few years prior to his death, when he was compelled to abandon it on account of bronchial trouble.   He was of English Quaker parentage.   Of their children, all are living, Hon. J. W. Chamberlain now residing in Mississippi.   The latter was educated in the high school and then at the college at Newark, Del., and when but nineteen years of age (1855) came South as a civil engineer.   He spent a few years in Jefferson and Holmes counties, Miss., and then went to St. Joseph, La., where he prosecuted his labors as an engineer until the war.   He then joined company G, Sixteenth Mississippi infantry, and served in the Virginia army, beginning with the second Manassas, and participating in nearly all the leading engagements of that campaign until the battle of the Wilderness, when he was shot through the abdomen.   He lay on the battlefield one week before he was taken to the hospital and received surgical aid.   He remained on his back, scarcely able to move, for six months, and with very little or no hopes of recovery.   After sufficiently recovering he was assigned to the topographical engineering corps and remained in that until the close of the war, when he returned to St. Joseph, La.   There he was married in 1866 to Miss Matilda Heddeman, who was born in New Jersey, and who, when quite small, went with her parents to Richmond, Va., thence to South Carolina and later to Mississippi.   Mrs. Chamberlain's father, Professor Heddeman, afterward returned to the East and died in New York city.   He was a school teacher and a German.   His wife died in St. Joseph, La. To Mr. and Mrs. Chamberlain were born four children, three of whom are now living. After the war Mr. Chamberlain engaged in merchandising at St. Joseph, La., remained there until 1875, and then located in Adams county, Miss., nine miles from Natchez, where he owns a fine plantation of six hundred and fifty acres.   He has followed this occupation ever since, but in 1887 he engaged in the cotton commission business, and later added building material to the trade.   This he has since carried on and is now a resident of the city of Natchez.

Prior to the war he served a number of years as surveyor of Tensas parish, La., and in 1878 he was elected to represent Adams county in the Mississippi legislature, and reëlected in 1880, serving four years in that capacity. He is a prominent Mason, a member of Harmony lodge No. 1, and is also a member of the Knights of Honor, Bluff City lodge No. 1145. He and wife hold membership in the Episcopal church.

Lewis H. Champlin, Pass Christian, Miss., member of the bar of Harrison county, is the subject of the following biographical sketch, and is well worthy of mention in this record of the leading men of Mississippi. He was born in Mississippi city, Miss., and is a son of William A. and Margaret (Smith) Champlin, natives of Connecticut and Liverpool, England, respectively. The parents were married in New Orleans by the Rev. Theodore Clapp. The father was born in the year 1809, and at the age of thirteen years he left the parental care and went out to meet the world, relying upon his own resources. He secured a position on an ocean vessel and followed the sea for several years. He became captain of a vessel which plied between New Orleans and Liverpool, but he finally left the water and became a merchant in New Orleans. He carried on this business until 1839 and then came to the territory which is now Harrison county, Miss., locating at Mississippi city. He soon won a reputation for excellent judgment and executive ability, and was elected the first clerk of Harrison county. He studied law and was admitted to the bar in 1842 or 1843, following the legal profession up to the time of his death, which occurred in 1885. He craved no political honors, but was often urged to accept nominations for public office. In 1874 he allowed his name to be used as a candidate for the legislature of the state, and he was elected. This and one other occasion were the only times he held public office. He was a self-made man in every respect, and a man of much more than ordinary attainments. He could read both French and Latin, having picked up these two languages without assistance. He reared a family of eight children: William, Dr. A. P., Lewis H. (the subject of this notice), Edward T., C. C., Z. T., George W. and Margaret E. (wife of P. B. Hand). The sons were all soldiers in the Confederate service, and, with the exception of Edward T., are all living. Lewis H. was reared in Harrison county and received his education in the common schools. The war came on just as he was ready to enter the university, so his advantages were comparatively limited. He volunteered in company E, Twentieth Mississippi regiment, and served until the surrender. He was captured at Fort Donelson and was held at Camp Douglas seven months. He was in all the battles of his regiment and saw some severe service. After the close of the struggle he returned to his home and taught school and studied law until 1869. In that year he was admitted to the bar and engaged in the practice of his profession. Since 1885 he has given his entire time and attention to legal work and to the real estate business. He controls a large amount of property and is doing a large and important business. Like his father, he has no political aspirations. He was chairman of the democratic county executive committee and has frequently been a delegate to the conventions of his party. He was married in 1866 to Mrs. Sarah (George) Poindexter, and three children were born to them: W. E., clerk of the Mexican Gulf hotel and county assessor; M. E., wife of W. B. Beard, of Cypress, Ark., and Georgia. The family belong to the Episcopal church. Mr. Champlin is a member of the Masonic fraternity. He owns some valuable property, is a man loyal to home interests and is a representative citizen of Harrison county.

J. T. Chandler, M. D., Oxford, Miss., a leading physician and prosperous druggist of Lafayette county, was born in South Carolina in 1831, and is the eldest child of T. W. and

Julia (Wiley) Chandler, natives of North Carolina. The paternal grandfather, Josiah Chandler, removed from Virginia to North Carolina; he was of English descent, and the maternal ancestors were of Scotch extraction. Dr. Chandler was educated in the University of Oxford, and in 1859 he entered the medical department of the University of Pennsylvania at Philadelphia; he was graduated in the class of 1861, and came at once to Lafayette county. There he entered the Confederate army in company B, First Mississippi cavalry as lieutenant; he assisted in recruiting the company, and the second year was made captain; he served in this position one year, and was then wounded. He was disabled six months, during which time he resigned. In March, 1863, he entered the hospital at Port Hudson as surgeon, and had been there but a short time until the surrender of that point. He went to New Orleans with the sick, returning in October. He was then made medical inspector of the staff of Gen. Stephen Lee, a position he filled for six months. At the end of that time he was appointed surgeon of the Eighteenth Mississippi cavalry, and was filling this position at the close of the war. After the surrender he came to Oxford and engaged in professional work; he has won a large and enthusiastic patronage. In 1876 he opened a drug store, where he carries a full stock of drugs, paints, oils and toilet articles. Dr. Chandler was united in marriage in December, 1868, to Miss Lulie N. Thompson, daughter of William Thompson. Seven children have been born to this union: Julia, L. M., Annie J., Lulie May, Wiley, T. W. (who died at the age of nineteen years in April, 1889), and an infant unnamed. The Doctor is a member of the Masonic order, a Knight of Honor, and belongs to the A. O. U. W. He owns five hundred acres of land, one hundred and fifty of which are in a high state of cultivation. The place is well improved, and the remaining portion of the land is of best quality. He also owns his residence.

During a professional career of over thirty years Dr. William I. Chaney has become noted as a practitioner of the healing art throughout his section, and justly deserves the eulogiums bestowed upon him by his professional brethren. He was born at Port Hudson, La., January 28, 1828, being the eldest of two sons and one daughter born to the marriage of Thomas Y. and Emily M. (Johnson) Chaney, who were born in East Feliciana parish, La., in 1805, and Thibodeaux, La., in 1813, respectively, their marriage taking place in their native state in 1826. They afterward removed to what is now Sharkey county, where Mr. Chaney had become possessed of a tract of land where Rolling Fork now is, while on a surveying expedition with Stephen Howard, the celebrated government engineer and surveyor, in 1826. He was the first white settler to locate in what is now Sharkey county, and here became possessed of a very valuable plantation, which he named Rolling Fork, from the stream which he had named while on his first visit here. On this place he spent the rest of his days, dying in 1835. He was a man of excellent habits and character, and was also very generous and courageous. He settled in a dense wilderness of canebrake, miles from any other settler, and during his lifetime Vicksburg was his nearest trading point. His father, George Chaney, was born, reared and married in South Carolina, and about 1800 removed to East Feliciana parish, La., where he passed from life. He was a son of Bailey Chaney, a native of England who, just before the Revolutionary war, came to America and lived near Annapolis, serving in the war against his mother country. He afterward removed to South Carolina, where he died. The maternal grandfather, Col. Isaac Johnson, Jr., uncle of Gov. Isaac Johnson, of Louisiana, was born and married in New Orleans, and in the state of Louisiana spent his entire life, being an able lawyer and a wealthy planter. He held many prominent official positions, such as district judge, etc., and in whatever calling he labored he displayed marked ability and fidelity to the duties of the positions he filled. He was a

colonel in the war of 1812 and was at the battle of New Orleans. His father, Isaac Johnson, Sr., was born in England, and there married a French lady but became a resident of
America while this country was still under English rule. He was also a lawyer and planter,
and died at Thibodeaux. The children born to Thomas and Emily (Johnson) Chaney are:
Sarah, the first white child that was born in what is now Sharkey county, was educated at
Patapsco institute, near Baltimore, Md., and is now the widow of L. P. Franklin, a prominent lawyer of Baltimore and a very classical gentleman and able politician; Thomas Y.,
Jr., died in 1861. He received a fine classical education in the University of Virginia and
graduated in medicine from the University of Pennsylvania in 1856, and also at New Orleans
in 1857, and practiced medicine at Rolling Fork until his death. Dr. William I. Chaney
was also given a fine classical education, being an attendant of that noble institution of
learning, Princeton college, New Jersey, of which he is now A.M., being of the class of
1852, and graduated in medicine from the University of Pennsylvania in 1854 and from the
University of New York the following year. The following four years were spent as a surgeon on shipboard between New York and Liverpool, but since that time he has been a medical practitioner of Rolling Fork, and during the war he served as a surgeon in the Confederate army. On Wednesday morning, March 24, 1863, Crockett Carter, an overseer on what
is now the Good Intent plantation, on Little Deer creek, brought the news to Rolling Fork
that a fleet of Federal gunboats was on its way up Deer creek toward Rolling Fork, upon
hearing which Dr. Chaney and his friend, James Leach, mounted one of his finest race-
horses and proceeded down the creek to learn if the report was true. Upon learning that it
was, they hastened back to Rolling Fork, and the Doctor at once dispatched Crockett Carter in
one of his own fine raceboats with two of his best oarsmen (slaves) with a message to General Hebert, who was in command of the Confederate post at Snyder's bluff, eighty miles
distant on Yazoo river. The message was safely delivered about sunup of the next day, and
at sundown of the same day Gen. W. S. Featherston and Gen. Stephen D. Lee landed at the
mouth of Rolling fork with about two thousand eight hundred troops, where they were met
by Dr. Chaney, who piloted them overland to Rolling Fork. In the meantime the Federals
had reached the place with eight gunboats, seven transports and about six hundred
marines under Commodore Porter, and had quartered themselves in the residence and
grounds belonging to Dr. Chaney. At daybreak on the 26th, while the Federals were lying
about the lawn sleeping, about thirty Confederate sharpshooters were picketed by Dr.
Chaney, and as soon as it was light enough opened fire on the Federals, who were sleeping on the grounds, taking them completely by surprise. They at once fled to their gunboats, and a running fire of three days was kept up. In the meantime, a few miles below
Rolling Fork, on the 27th, the Federals were reinforced by General Sherman with about
six thousand troops, but being doubtless deceived as to the numbers of the Confederates,
they continued to retreat, and were driven as far as the Yazoo river, which place they
reached Sunday evening. This spirited little encounter doubtless delayed the surrender of
Vicksburg for several months, the object of the expedition being a flank movement on Snyder's bluff. Dr. Chaney was married in 1862 to Miss Mary J., daughter of Col. William
T. Barnard, of Sharkey county. She was born in Natchez in 1842 and died November 10,
1867, an earnest member of the Baptist church. The Doctor is exceedingly well read in
his profession, and, possessing an exceptionally retentive memory, is a very intelligent and
interesting conversationalist. He is the oldest inhabitant, in point of residence, in the
county, and is more familiar with its early and later history than probably any other person;
in fact, it can truly be said that nothing has transpired in the county with which he is not

34

familiar, for many of the transactions of early times were related to him by his mother. These incidents possess great interest to those who are interested in the struggles, privations and hardships which the early pioneer settlers were compelled to undergo, and would fill a volume in themselves. Many of the names of the settlers who followed his parents to this region are yet perfectly familiar to him, and he can tell with precision the location of each family. He commands the universal esteem of the community in which he resides, and as his ability as a physician has never been questioned, he has a very extensive practice. He has never desired publicity or notoriety, and has never held nor sought to hold public office. He is now the owner of nine hundred acres of land and is otherwise well fixed financially. His mother was a lady of true Christian character, was cultured and refined and was always found ready to do any act of kindness for the needy. She died June 11, 1869, in the fifty-seventh year of her age, and her remains now rest in the old family cemetery in the town of Rolling Fork, beside those of Thomas Y. Chaney, pioneer of Sharkey county.

David T. Chapman, Newton, Miss., one of the leading planters of Newton county, was born in Garlandville, Jasper county, Miss., in 1839, and in the same year his parents removed to Newton county, where he grew to maturity with a large family of brothers and sisters. He was reared to the occupation of a planter, and received his education in the common schools. He was married in the year 1861, and soon after enlisted in the Southern cause, becoming a member of the Thirty-seventh Mississippi regiment, under Captain Loper. He was in the siege of Vicksburg and other important engagements. At the close of the struggle he returned to his home, and with a brave heart and willing hands he went to work to retrieve his fortunes, which had been so broken by the ravages of war. His efforts have met with a generous response, and to-day he is one of the most independent planters in the county. In 1878 the people called him to fill the office of a member of the board of supervisors, and he served in this capacity four years. In November, 1881, he was elected to represent his county in the state legislature during the sessions of 1882 and 1883. He was reëlected to this same position in 1885, and served during the sessions of 1886 and 1887. He is a stanch democrat, and as such has been honored by the people of his county. He has shown excellent qualifications for the transaction of public business, and is highly esteemed by his constituency. Mr. Chapman's parents were Edward E. and Talitha (Tool) Chapman, the father being a native of South Carolina. He came to Mississippi in the pioneer days of that state, and saw the development of wild, uncultivated lands into the most fertile plantations. He was a devout Christian, a consistent member of the Baptist church, and his life was filled with good works. David T. Chapman and wife are members of the Missionary Baptist church. They are the parents of eleven children, all of whom are living. Mr. Chapman affiliates with the A. F. & A. M. fraternity, and is a Mason, both by precept and example.

The estate which T. P. Chapman is engaged in cultivating embraces three hundred and twenty acres of land, well adapted to the purposes of general farming, and in his business operations he displays those sterling principles characteristic of those of Mississippi birth, of which industry and wise and judicious management are among the chief. He was born in Rankin county, in 1839, being one of eleven children born to A. F. and Eliza (Ship) Chapman, the former of whom was born in Georgia in 1810, and the latter in Louisiana in 1815. The father was brought to Mississippi by his parents in 1813, and was reared to a knowledge of farm life in Wayne county, receiving fair educational advantages in his youth. He was a stanch whig in politics but was never an aspirant for office, being content to earn his competency by tilling the soil. His father was a Virginian by birth but the mother's father was a native of Georgia. T. P. Chapman was given the advantages of a fair education in his youth, and he made the most of his opportunities and is now a well-informed and intelligent man. In 1859 he was married to Miss Rachel Myers, who was born in Rankin county, Miss., and who has borne him twelve children. Mr. Chapman has taken an active interest in local political matters and is the present coroner of Rankin county, and a candidate for reëlection. He is the present efficient postmaster of Chapman, and has been deputy sheriff of the county for some time. He is also a skilled machinest and has done some work for railroad companies, in the way of framing bridges, that reflects much credit upon his ability. Upon the opening of the war in 1861, he immediately enlisted in the Confederate army, becoming a member of company A, Eighteenth Mississippi regiment, and was in the engagements at Malvin Hill, Seven Pines, Fair Oaks, the siege of Yorktown, and many others. He was captured at Cedar Run, Va., in 1864, and was imprisoned at Point Lookout. He is a member of the Farmers' Alliance.

Among the natives of New England who located in Mississippi for the practice of law was Judge Joshua Child. He came here about the time the state was organized and established himself in the city of Natchez. He was well educated, and possessed a mind of great breadth and great vigor, and in a short time was well known to the legal profession throughout the state. In 1825 he became a member of the supreme bench, and as a judge was among the ablest of those who occupied that responsible position. He resigned his seat in 1831. He never married, and died soon after his resignation. He possessed great courage, and one one occasion was engaged in a duel with General Joor, in which encounter both parties were badly wounded.

Henry Chiles, of Lauderdale, Miss., was born in Mobile, Ala., in July, 1844, the fifth of eight children born to Henry and Elizabeth (Fluker) Chiles, natives, respectively, of South Carolina and Alabama. When a young man, Henry Chiles, Sr., removed to Alabama, where he met and married Miss Fluker, their union being consummated in Sumter county, in 1823. After residing at Linden for a number of years, where Mr. Chiles was engaged in merchandising, they removed to Mobile, in which city Mr. Chiles devoted his attention to the banking business. About 1846 they took up their abode near Lauderdale Springs, Mr. Chile's attention being given to planting, until the Missouri & Ohio railroad was built. He was then appointed agent. After the Missouri & Ohio railroad had been established, he became ticket and freight agent at Lauderdale, being the first agent the company had at that place. After successfully filling this position for a number of years, and giving perfect satisfaction to all, he resigned and left this company's employ and turned his attention to other pursuits. He was an upright and respected gentleman, and his death, which occurred at his home in Lauderdale in 1879, was deeply regretted by all. His wife, who died in April, 1866, was a member of the Baptist church, and although he did not belong to any religious denomination, he believed in the Christian religion. Only three of their children are now living: Nathaniel H., Isabella, wife of J. C. Ulick of New Orleans, and Henry. The latter started out for himself at the age of twenty-one years as agent for the Missouri & Ohio railroad at Lauderdale, and was the company's efficient representative at that point for eight years. At the end of that time he resigned to embark in merchandising in Lauderdale, in partnership with a Mr. Simmons, the firm name being Chiles, Simmons & Co., later Chiles & Walker, and so continued up to the time that the East Tennessee & Virginia & Georgia railroad was built. Mr. Chiles then sold out his interest in the store and took the agency for that railroad at Lauderdale, this being in 1878, and is still serving them in that capacity. He has proved a capable and courteous official, and has given perfect satisfaction to his employers. He has been successful in managing his affairs, and is the owner of five hundred acres of good land near Lauderdale, and since 1881 has been engaged in the hotel business in the city, the hotel building being located on a portion of this land near the depot. This property is very valuable, and as the hotel is nicely furnished and well managed, it is netting Mr. Chiles a satisfactory income. In 1878 he was married to Mrs Tartt, widow of E. Tartt, by whom she became the mother of two children: Sallie B. and Elnathan. Her union with Mr. Chiles has resulted in the birth of seven children: Anna, Henry, John W. (deceased), Ada, Joel P., Agnes W. (deceased), and Cebelle A. Mr. Chiles is not a member of any church, but socially is a member of the A. F. & A. M. He is whole-souled and generous, is a capable and generous business man, and has numerous warm friends.

The first member of the illustrious and well-known Chotard family to seek a home in the new world was John Marie Chotard, a native of Brittany, France, who was an officer under the governor of the island of St. Domingo, and on that island was married to Miss Henrietta Lofont, a daughter of the governor. He sent his children to France to be educated, but during the insurrection on the island he also returned to his native land, and came soon after to America, making a permanent settlement in Adams county, Miss., about the year 1805. His wife had died while on the voyage from St. Domingo to France, and after coming to this country he was married in Georgia to a Mrs. (Williams) Willis, and made a settlement on a plantation on the Liberty road in this county on which he made his home until his death, August 8, 1810. His first marriage resulted in the birth of two children : Henry E. and Amenaide. The latter was married in France, and there made her home throughout life, but the son, Henry, came hither in 1808 and at once entered the army as lieutenant, and took an active part in the Creek war. Later he became a soldier in the war of 1812, and while serving on General Jackson's staff on the battlefield of New Orleans was, for gallant conduct, promoted to the rank of major. At that time was serving as adjutant-general, and while stationed at Baton Rouge, was married, in 1819, to Miss Frances Minor, a daughter of Maj. Stephen Minor. In 1821 he resigned from the army and settled permanently at Natchez and purchased a tract of land comprising several thousand acres, which became the magnificent Southern homestead, Somerset, which has been in possession of the family ever since. Every enterprise to which he turned his attention prospered far beyond his expectations, and in addition to his plantation in this county, he owned much valuable property in other parts of the state and in Louisiana. He became a noted man throughout this section, for he was a man of strong will power, great energy and large fortune, and his ample means was used liberally for the good of his fellow-men and for the upbuilding of the county and state in which he had so long made his home. He was a man among men and was considered by all to be among the highest civilians. He was called from earth in 1870, having been left a widower in 1864. His union was blessed in the birth of nine children, all of whom, with the exception of one, grew to maturity: Amenaide (widow of E. K. Chaplain of Maryland, by whom she has four children); Fannie; Henrietta; Maria, wife of Capt. F. B. Conner; Catherine, deceased wife of Horatio Eustis; Richard, deceased; John Charles, deceased; Henry, of Louisiana, and William, who died in infancy. All these children that are living are residing on the old homestead in Adams county, with the exception of Henry, who, with his son Henry, is living on their plantation in Concordia parish, La., having lost his wife three years since. His wife was a granddaughter of Maj. Stephen Minor, therefore his first cousin.

The most important science bearing upon man's happiness, comfort and welfare, is that of medicine, and Henry Christmas, A. B., M. D., of Tchula, is a credit to the profession, being classed among the prominent practitioners of Mississippi. He is a native Mississippian, born in Madison county on the 20th of February, 1842, and was educated in Tennessee, at Washington institute and Lebanon, graduating with the degree of A. B. in the class of 1860. He subsequently studied medicine at Clinton, Miss., under Dr. Stokes, and then took his first course of medical lectures at New Orleans in the class of 1860 and 1861. He reached home just in time to join the Confederate army in the spring of the last-mentioned year, and enlisted as a private in the Eighteenth Mississippi infantry. He was promoted to the rank of captain and was on detached duty as commissary of his regiment. He served in that department until after the battle of Manassas, when he resigned and was promoted to the position of assistant surgeon, in which capacity he remained until the close of the war. He was the youngest assistant surgeon of the army of Northern Virginia. After the war Dr. Christmas returned to Holmes county, remained there a short time, and then went to New Orleans, where he completed his course of lectures, graduating in the spring of 1866. He then began practicing in Holmes county, and there he has remained ever since, actively engaged in his chosen calling. The Doctor has ever taken an active part in politics, and has rendered valuable service for the democratic party of Holmes county. He represented that county in the legislature of 1880, was one of the foremost advocates in establishing the state board of health in 1880, and his speech before the house on that bill was eloquent and forcible, placing him among the first orators of that honored body. He has since retained his reputation as an orator, and is noted for his readiness to respond with a speech on nearly all occasions. He is in request as a speaker on nearly all public gatherings. The Doctor was reëlected to the legislature in the fall of 1883, served another term in the lower house, and was one of the most active members in the legislature of 1884, on the principles of railroad supervision. As a member of the railroad committee the Doctor worked for the best interests of Holmes county and saved her a large amount of money by helping her out of the levee district. He was also a strong advocate in that body for the A. and M. college and I. I. and C. female college. Dr. Christmas still takes a great deal of interest in local politics but is not an aspirant for office. He now devotes his time almost exclusively to his profession and is one of the leading and successful physicians in Holmes and adjoining counties. He was married in Holmes county on the 29th of December, 1863, to Miss Lucy R. West, a native of Mississippi, where she was reared and educated, and the daughter of James R. West. Her grandfather was Gov. Cato West. To this marital relation were born three children: Mary, wife of Henry Waterer of Yazoo city; Sallie P., a young lady, and James R. W., a young man of seventeen. Socially the Doctor is a Royal Arch Mason, is master of his lodge, and he is also a member of the Knights of Honor and the Farmers' Alliance. He was formerly a member of the grange, and was lecturer of the county grange for twelve years. He is a fluent and ready speaker, stands very high both morally and socially, and these qualities added to his handsome appearance, his kindness of heart and that subtle, undefined power called personal magnetism, exert a great influence over those with whom he comes in contact. He and Mrs. Christmas are members of the Methodist church. The Doctor's father, Harry Christmas, was a native of Carolina, his birth occurring in Warrenton, where he spent his youth. He came to Mississippi when a young man, located in Madison county, but subsequently removed to Bolivar county, where he became a very wealthy and prominent planter, owning about two hundred slaves. He was killed in a steamboat explosion in 1850, when only about forty years of age. He was married in Jefferson county, Miss., to Miss Anna Dixon, daughter of Rodger Dixon, who was born in Mississippi, but who was of English parentage. Grandfather Dixon was a soldier in the English army and was knighted for gallantry and deeds of daring on the field of battle. His family have the coat of arms presented him in honor of his services. Of the six children born to Mr. and Mrs. Christmas, three sons and three daughters all grew to mature years, but Dr. Henry and one brother are the only survivors.

Judge J. B. Chrisman was born in Christian county, Ky., but removed with his father to Brandon, Miss., in 1836. He was apprenticed to the printing business with S. N. Adams, editor of the Eastern *Clarion*, of Paulding, Jasper county, Miss., and in that city grew to manhood. In 1850 he became editor of the Southern *Journal*, at Monticello, studied law, and in 1852 was elected to the lower branch of the state legislature from Lawrence county. He was subsequently elected clerk of the circuit court of that county, and in 1860, to the state senate from Lawrence and Pike counties. At the beginning of the war he entered the army as a private in Captain Prestidge's company, and immediately thereafter was appointed by Jefferson Davis as commissary with the rank of captain and with orders to report to the commissary general. He served from the beginning until the close of the war under orders from that department, being near the close of the war assigned to a district composed of south Mississippi and east Louisiana, with officers and men under his direction. He commenced the active practice of law in 1865, and in 1878, his ability and knowledge of his profession were recognized, and he was appointed to the position of judge by Governor Stone. In 1884 he was once more appointed to this position by Governor Lowry, and in 1890 was again appointed by Governor Stone, the same year being a member of the constitutional convention. Judge Chrisman is one of Mississippi's noblest sons, and one of whom she may justly feel proud. During the years in which he has served in the capacity of judge, he has dealt out justice with an even hand, and his leading characteristics have been extreme frankness, honesty of purpose, indomitable will and energy. He possesses fine powers of elucidation, and weight and power accompany his words and writing and inspire respect and conviction. His ability as a jurist was known and recognized all over the state, and he was acknowledged to be a man of deep convictions and unquestioned integrity, and a conscientious and exemplary Christian. He is at all times the advocate of justice and right, and presided with ability over the largest and most important district of the state. He was married in 1854 to Miss Caroline Fox, a daughter of General Fox, a native of North Carolina who served in the senate of Mississippi several terms, and for some time an officer in the war of 1812, and to their union four children have been born. In the domestic circle he is a model husband and father, and in social life he is highly esteemed for his fine conversational powers and for his agreeable, courtly and kindly manners. He and his family worship in the Baptist church. Two brothers besides himself served in the Confederate army during the late war, and Capt. Thomas Chrisman was killed in the battle of Vicksburg. His mother was Miss Clara A. Bledsoe, a daughter of Joseph Bledsoe, of Christian county, Ky. The Chrismans are of German descent, the first representatives of the family in this country being three brothers who settled in Virginia, one of whom was the great-grandfather of Judge J. B. Chrisman. Miss Annie Clara Chrisman, who had started for Brazil as a missionary and lost her life in the great Johnstown flood, was the Judge's niece.

In the year 1809, in the town of Natchez, in Mississippi territory, J. F. H. Claiborne was born. When fourteen years of age he was sent to Virginia to be educated, and at the age of eighteen entered the office of B. W. Leigh, a distinguished lawyer of Richmond, where he began the study of law. While here he seems to have contracted a lung disorder which troubled him more or less all the remainder of his life. He was forced to return to

Mississippi before the completion of his studies under Mr. Leigh, but later he resumed the same at Natchez, in the office of Griffith & Quitman. Here again, he was compelled to stop and go to sea, upon the advice of physicians, for his health. He spent the winter on the island of Cuba, and seems to have recovered, in a measure, his former strength. At the expiration of six months, he returned to Virginia and entered the law school of Alexander Smith, and within a year thereafter was admitted to the bar. He returned to Natchez in the midst of an animated political contest, and was induced to take charge of the editorial columns of one of the principal papers of the state, but this task, as might have been expected, proved too severe for his physical condition, and in a short time he was compelled to sever his connection with the paper. He had in the meantime formed a great liking for politics and showed remarkable fitness for its requirements. Before he had attained his majority he was sent to the legislature, and was twice reëlected by increasing majorities. In his twenty-fourth year, having previously removed to Madison county, he received the democratic nomination for congress from the state at large. During this contest, Mr. Claiborne supported Van Buren for the presidency. He took the stump, and from the start became a power in the state. It is said he delivered addresses in every county in the state, and often at every precinct in the county. The result of the contest was that Mr. Van Buren received a small majority in the state and Mr. Claiborne was elected by a large majority to congress. In congress, Mr. Claiborne took a conspicuous and animated part in the debates, and stood high as a party leader. The congressional records reveal many interesting passages between Mr. Claiborne and his party opponents in congress. On one occasion, had it not been for the interposition of Mr. Calhoun, undoubtedly Henry A. Wise, of Virginia, would have challenged Mr. Claiborne to mortal combat, and on still another occasion, he narrowly escaped a challenge from Mr. Peyton, of Tennessee. Mr. Claiborne was very prominently connected with the state bank question, which caused so many dissentions and so much bitterness in early years. When the time for reëlection occurred, Mr. Claiborne was triumphantly elected. The bank party, as it was then called, claimed that this election, which had occurred in July upon a proclamation of the governor, was for the coming special session of congress only. This was done, as a matter of course, to defeat the long term of Mr. Claiborne, who opposed the bank party. Accordingly that view seems to have prevailed, for in November following, a second election was held and Mr. Claiborne was defeated. He had not been, however, a candidate, but received over six thousand votes, entirely complimentary, a gratuitous testimonial of his popularity with the people. Under the election of July, Mr. Claiborne claimed to have a full right to his seat in congress for the entire term. This was opposed by the bank party and by Mr. Prentiss, who had been elected in his place. It was in the contest over this seat in congress that Mr. Prentiss made his famous speech, and it was during this contest also, that Mr. Claiborne suffered a violent hemorrhage of the lungs (from which he never afterward fully recovered), occasioned, no doubt, by the excitement and anxiety. The house, apparently, was unable to decide the contest otherwise than by sending the representatives back to the people of Mississippi, who were left to decide the matter in another election. Mr. Claiborne was so debilitated that upon the advice of physicians he went to Cuba to recuperate, and in his absence the election occurred and he was defeated by a small majority. He never afterward sought or would accept office. He connected himself with the press, the duties of which he loved, and continued to uphold the fundamental principles of democracy, and the welfare of his state. However, in 1842, he was appointed one of the commissioners to settle the claims of the Choctaws under their last treaty with the United States, and he was chosen president of this board of commissioners,

Owing to the fact that many of these claims had been purchased by a company of speculators, and owing to their determination to get wealthy out of their speculations, a bitter fight was waged before the board in support of the rival claims.   Mr. Claiborne promptly exposed the entire scheme of the speculators, and laid a pamphlet containing such exposition on the desk of every member of congress.   Finally the plan recommended by Mr. Claiborne to allow the Indians the value of their claim, to remove them West, to fund the money and pay them an annual interest was adopted.   Few public affairs in Mississippi have occasioned more bitterness than this.   In 1844 Mr. Claiborne took charge of the *Jeffersonian*, at New Orleans, which was published in both French and English, and at the same time, of the *Statesman*, published in English and German, and devoted twelve hours daily to these papers. In 1853 he became the editor of the *Louisiana Courier*, and advocated the nomination of Franklin Pierce for the presidency.   About this time his health became so poor that he was obliged to give up active business pursuits and seek the seacoast to recuperate.   There he remained until the war broke out.   He was the author of several interesting biographical works, and was also the author of the history of Mississippi, only one volume of which was issued; the second volume while in an advanced state of preparation was unfortunately destroyed by fire.   He is known as the historian of Mississippi.   The University of the state conferred upon him the degree of LL. D., and various other societies honored him with membership.   He was a man of unusual purity and dignity of character, and his memory is revered by the people of the entire state.

A. J. M. T. O'Dyer Clanton is a descendant of Col. Robert Clanton, deceased, who was one of the very first settlers of the great county of Panola, Miss., and one of the noblest, bravest and best of Christians.   The latter was born in Sussex county, Va., May 28, 1787, and was of Scotch and Irish or English blood and of a giant family.   He was an expert with tools, firearms and the sword.   His father, John Clanton, served in the war of 1776.   He had a large family and much property, and his two elder sons were Drury and Henry Clanton, who immigrated to Missouri and Texas respectively.   Robert was the youngest and smallest, though over six feet in hight, and sinewy and very active.   He married Miss Deborah Murphy, an Irish girl, April 15, 1815, and had one son born of her, but both soon died. He married Mrs. Sallie Wilson, October 14, 1818, who was formerly Miss Sarah Smith, a native of Halifax county, N. C., but who was raised in Portsmouth, Va., by her uncles Tom and John Brooks, who were the principal citizens of the town of Portsmouth.   She was an orphan who was born September 15, 1796.   Her former husband, Capt. James Wilson, was lost on his first voyage out from Norfolk after their marriage.   She is believed to have been of English and German blood.   About twelve or eighteen months after his death she moved to Murfreesboro, N. C., and engaged in the millinery business through the kindness of friends, for she was still poor, with one baby girl she called Eliza, who lived and married Matthew Clanton, and bore him a large family of children.   About 1819 Robert Clanton was a well-to-do citizen of Murfreesboro, N. C., having built near there a fine watermill, and being the owner of a very rich farm.   But sickness forced him away from the rich cotton land, and, emigrating West, the family first stopped at Murfreesboro, Tenn., in 1822, then settled in Madison county, Tenn., Col. Clanton owning a farm now midway between Jackson and Denmark, where he had a store.   He named his place Mount Olivet, and there most of his children were born.   In Tennessee he was called a good farmer, and he made money, for he was very energetic, industrious and economical.   In 1836 he bought a large keelboat and loaded it with provisions, etc., at Jackson, Tenn., and with great difficulty and at great expense he brought it up to Burlingham, Miss., on the Tallahatchie river, making the river navigable.   Col. Robert Clanton opened a provision store in his boat and one in 1837 on his farm, about two miles and a half north of Burlingham.   This was then called the Indian Nation, and his principal customers were the Chickasaw Indians, and his son Timothy, his clerk, gained the love of the Indians, who said, "Timmy no cheat Indian."   His keelboat was sunk at Burlingham.   In 1837 or 1838 he moved to Belmont, Miss., and he built the first grist and sawmill on Clanton's creek ever erected in Panola county, and planted the first orchard in the county, and was the principal stockholder in the company that built the first bridge across the Tallahatchie at Belmont, and became the sole owner.   The bridge was built of heart cypress and was six hundred yards long.   Its first cost was $3,000 and his son Alfonson was the first tollkeeper.   He assisted in organizing Panola county, being of the Belmont party, and was one of the delegates to locate the county seat, and his party elected a majority of the delegates, but influences were brought to bear which resulted in the location of the county seat at Panola town.   In 1836 he began the improvement of a large tract of land about ten miles east of Belmont, on the hills, on which he raised one or two crops, but which, owing to an unexpected law of congress, as it would seem, as well as to the purchase of Mr. M. McGehee, he had to abandon, unremunerated for his many improvements. Having his choice of sections by favor, in 1836, he purchased for $2,500 section ten, township seven, range seven west, of Walker, Williams and Williams, which is a very level section.   He cleared large fields, built a fine residence and ginhouse and planted a large orchard.   But having purchased many town lots in Belmont, and Belmont having failed to secure the seat of justice, his loss was almost ruinous, and his troubles were augmented by a great drift, which compelled him to ply a ferry-boat in crossing the Tallahatchie river.

In 1840 he moved upon the section mentioned, where has since been the home of his heirs.   The locality has since come to be known as Clanton city.   Colonel Clanton lived a Christian democrat in word and deed, and, after a long illness, his death occurred on the 19th of May, 1856.   He was a strong, well-learned, Jackson democrat, having in his younger days lived with General Jackson in Tennessee and imbibed and assimilated some of his noble patriotism; a volunteer in the cavalry of the war of 1812–14 and postmaster for many years at Rees' crossroads.   He was an early member of the Christian church and always a zealous Bible reader, and having studied the Scriptures for five years almost without intermission, a great light seemed suddenly to burst upon him, which he could see but which he was never able to explain, though he often tried to do so.   He reared a large family, to all of whom he gave a thorough education, or, at least, the best he could afford them, requiring them to be truthful and honest and Christians and patriots, for his grandfather, McGlemery was a Baptist preacher from Scotland and he an early Baptist.   His widow survived him until August 26, 1872, and died as she had lived, a devoted Christian, for Mrs. Sarah Clanton was one of the noblest Christian women that ever lived.   In 1833 she was immersed "in the name of the Father, Son and Holy Ghost," after studying the New Testament diligently.   She tried to live up to its commandments, and was an example of excellency in her Christian duties, both as a mother and as a wise teacher of their children, and they were a joyous, pious, thoughtful and industrious family, with every hope, apparently, of great future glory and renown in their beloved United States.   But death stops often the pride of us all, and thus were they made to mourn their losses; but Col. Robert Clanton was second to no one, nor was his family second to any other.   But thus the "Lord giveth and the Lord taketh away, and blessed be the name of the Lord."   Mr. and Mrs. Clanton reared a family of eight children.   The eldest, Dr. and Rev. Timothy Robert Clanton, was a good man and a learned doctor and preacher of the Baptist church.   The Lone Star state gave him a wife late in life, of whom he wrote, saying, "She is sixteen and a wife indeed." Lieut.-Col. Theodore Clanton, who died at the early age of twenty-one, was elected lieutenant-colonel of militia when only nineteen or twenty years of age. He was one of the most talented of young lawyers and bravest of men, and his death seemed the fall of the glory of his father's house. He died January 28, 1840. Adeline Lydia, widow of Joseph M. Clark (formerly a merchant of Belmont, Miss., a pure and good man who was reared in Washington, D. C., died in 1850), has lived a Christian widow more than forty-one years, and is now the owner of the old homestead. Alfonson J. M. T. O'Dyer Clanton, in 1849 and 1850 was a student at Bethany college, Va. He was immersed in 1850 by Rev. A. Campbell, and thinks that the mantle of the latter has fallen upon him. He is the author of small books entitled "The Science of Government and Law," "Six Lectures on Revelation," "Yellow Fever Manual," a "Greek Grammar" and other small volumes, and has burned about five thousand pages of his early manuscripts. He is also the inventor of two improved firearms, a corn planter, a mosquito net, a new sweet cream process and numerous other useful articles and processes. Sarah Victoria Clanton (deceased) was, it is said, a great beauty, and at her early death was pronounced one of the noblest women that ever lived. She was the wife of Dr. P. H. Armistead, and left three little girl children: Ellen, Sally and Adie. Miss Ellen died a sweet maiden; Sally is the wife of Capt. S. L. Windham, treasurer of Panola county; Adie is Mrs. D. R. Perry, and the mother of a large family. Capt. Joseph William Clanton (deceased) graduated from Bethany college, Va., with second honors, and united with the Christian church in 1850. In 1853 he taught school in Middletown, Miss.; he studied law under J. W. A. Watson, of Holly Springs, Miss., and practiced law at Panola, Miss. He married Miss Gillion and left one little daughter, now Mrs. Willie Outtin, of Hampton, Va. He was beloved and honored by his democratic friends. This party was ever in the minority in Panola county before the Civil war, but he never deserted it or its principles, and was two or three times its nominee for the office of probate judge. He was the first lieutenant of the first volunteer company of infantry organized in Panola county and which served at Pensacola, Fla. He was said to have been the finest looking officer in the Confederate army and to have been shot at the head of his regiment in a daring and most dangerous position, near Marietta, Ga., May 28, 1865, a ball having entered his forehead while he was leading the troopers (of whom he was in command) in a gallant charge. He died captain of company F of the Twenty-eighth Mississippi cavalry. His remains were brought home after the war and interred in the family graveyard by the kindness of his widow's father, John Gillion. Thus have cruel hardships, merciless and unchristian wars taken many noble men, and thus did those flowers of Col. Robert Clanton's family pass away; for 'tis said that "Death loves a shining mark," which seems to have been exemplified in this household. Yet still "a remnant few remaineth," a few pretty grand and great-grandchildren and three only of the original children, who reside on and own the old homestead and land, yet all three single and childless, excepting as it may be said as of Jesus or Paul or Washington or Jackson, "they lead many to glory eternal, calling them their children." Benjamin Jackson Clanton was one of the first graduates from the law school at the university at Oxford, Miss., and he bore off high honors. He was a volunteer of the late Civil war, and during the war was immersed by James E. Matthews, a Christian preacher. Now he is a land owner and lives on the old homestead of the family. "The last shall be first" is Scriptural utterance, and it was exemplified in this family in the death, before that of any other member, of Celestia B. Clanton, the last born of the Clantons, who died at the age of nine months, truly mourned for many long years by this bereaved family. It has been said of her "she could say 'chickie' at the age of six months, and walk and talk at the age of nine months,'' and "her poor remains do still lie in the old dear Belmont hills, whereon she was born in 1837." All of the family except Theodore and the babe just referred to, both of whom died very young, were immersed "in the name of the Father, Son and Holy Ghost."

Like many other successful and prominent citizens of Madison county, Miss., Dr. William Clanton, of Camden, owes his nativity to the Old North state, his birth occurring in Warren county in 1832. His parents, William C. and Martha (Kearney) Clanton, were natives also of that state, and both were of Scotch-Irish descent. They spent their entire lives in North Carolina, the father engaged in planting and merchandising. He was quite a prominent man, politically and socially, and held the office of sheriff of Warren county for fifteen years. He died in 1862. He was noted for his benevolence to the poor, and was honored and respected by all. The mother died in 1837. He was a member of the Methodist, and she of the Baptist church. Of the seven children born to this union all grew to maturity, and four are now living: James D. (deceased), Landen T. (deceased), Robert K. (residing in North Carolina), Sarah A. (wife of Dr. William H. Joyner, deceased, of Madison county), Isabella F. (wife of William Thornton, deceased, of this county), Angeline A., (deceased wife of Dr. William A. Church). Dr. William Clanton passed his youthful days in Warrentown academy and in the University of North Carolina, from which he graduated. In 1855 he attended medical lectures in Philadelphia, and came to Madison county, Miss., the following year, settling near Camden. He there began the practice of medicine, and was married in 1858 to Miss Sallie Purviance, of Madison county, the daughter of A. and Elizabeth (Shrock) Purviance. Mr. Purviance was a native of North Carolina, and a descendant of the old French Huguenots. The same year of his marriage Dr. Clanton went to Louisiana to look after his large planting interests there, and in 1863 he refugeed to Texas, where he remained until the surrender. He then returned to Louisiana. In 1868 he moved to Camden, Miss., and there he has made his home ever since. For about twenty-seven years he has had a good practice in Madison county, and, although he has a good farm in that county, he attends strictly to his profession. He takes a deep interest in politics, though he does not aspire to any office, and socially is a member of the Masonic fraternity and the Knights of Honor, having taken seven degrees in the former organization. The Doctor and wife are members of the Methodist church, and he is steward in the same. He takes a great interest in all church work and in everything pertaining to the welfare of the county His marriage resulted in the birth of two children, Paul and Bessie, both at home.

Charles Clark was for many years among the most prominent of those whose lives are a part of the history of Mississippi, which record would be incomplete without a mention, however brief, of his life and character, and his great services to the state. Incidentally, mention is briefly made of these in another sketch. The family of which he is a member came over with Lord Baltimore when he first colonized the new state of Maryland, and many of the descendants of this family now live in Washington city. An uncle, John D. Clark, recently died here, having reached his ninety-fifth year. His grandfather was a Revolutionary soldier, and lived with his father in the state of Ohio, to which state he had removed while the great city of Cincinnati was a mere village. In this city he was born about the year 1810, and received a collegiate education. Before he was of age, about the year 1831, he came to Mississippi, in which state he was destined to take no second place, settled in Jefferson county, and began at once to teach school and to read law. It was not long till he attracted the attention and won the regard, among others, of Gen. Thomas Hinds, one of the heroes of the battle of New Orleans, and then the most conspicuous character in South Mississippi, and who remained his unswerving friend as long as he lived. Soon mastering the intricate science of the law, much more difficult then than now, as then studied in the old English law books, he got his license, and from that time on his course was upward and onward. In politics he was a whig, and as such he was elected once or twice to the legislature from that county. In the great excitement which followed the compromise measure under which California was admitted to the Union, he took sides with the great leader of the whig party, Henry Clay, and was elected after an exciting contest with Captain Johnson, an honored citizen of Jefferson county, who still lives, to the convention which was called in 1851 to take into consideration the relations of the state of Mississippi to the Federal Union. The Union sentiment largely prevailed among the people of the state and the delegates, and after its organization the convention passed resolutions in accordance with the prevailing public sentiment, and adjourned without further action. Not long after this he moved his residence to a plantation he had bought some years before in Bolivar county, and upon which he continued to reside until the close of his long, honored and useful life, in December, 1877. After General Clark removed to Bolivar county, the sectional feeling, both in the North and the South, continued to grow until after the defeat of Mr. Fillmore for president, whom he supported. In 1856 he became a convert to the secession sentiment, fast becoming the prevailing sentiment, and cast in his fortunes with the democratic party. He was, however, elected once as a whig to the legislature of the state from Bolivar county, but was afterward a member of the democratic state convention of 1860, and one of the delegates to the national convention which met in Charleston, S. C., in which he supported Breckinridge for the nomination for president. When the convention adjourned without making a nomination, to meet again in the city of Baltimore, he again attended, and when the convention divided, one party nominating Douglas and the other Breckinridge, he returned to his home prepared to accept the election of Mr. Lincoln as evidence that the North no longer desired a union with the slaveholding states on equal terms, and ready to test the last extreme in resisting what he believed would result in the overthrow of the independence of the Southern states. The legislature, immediately after the election of Mr. Lincoln, called a convention to meet in January, 1861, and General Clark was a candidate for delegate to this, but was defeated by Miles H. McGehee, the sole issue being, not as to the right of the state to secede, but whether the state should act independently, or wait for the coöperation of other Southern states. General Clark was in favor of the separate action of the state, and Mr. McGehee was in favor of acting in concert with the Southern states in whatever should be deemed to be best for their mutual protection. When the convention met, so overwhelming was the sentiment in favor of separate action, that Mr. McGehee himself gave way to it and voted for the immediate secession of the state. General Clark, at an early age, had a great fondness for a military life, and devoted time and study to military tactics. The earliest recollection which the writer has of him is, when a boy, he attended a great military drill in Jefferson county, now numbered among the things that were, and saw him mounted and reviewing the militia, dressed in gorgeous uniform, with nodding plume and shining epaulettes. He was the observed of all observers, and, indeed, except the general and his aides, there were no uniforms on the ground.

The first real opportunity he had to engage in military life was the Mexican war, for which he organized a cavalry company, but no cavalry being asked from Mississippi and the First regiment of Mississippi volunteers then fully organized, he did not succeed then in getting into service. When the second regiment was formed he at once organized a company, of which he was the captain, and joined the regiment which organized by electing Reuben

Davis its colonel. The regiment had not long been in Mexico before Colonel Davis resigned and Captain Clark was at once and without opposition elected colonel. The regiment was never engaged in action, for it was in the western part of Mexico, and after the battle of Buena Vista the seat of war had been transferred to the front of General Scott's advancing army. He remained, however, with his regiment until the close of the war and returned home with the reputation of a thorough soldier. Hence when the convention decided that the state was free and independent and proceeded to the formation of an army, he was elected third brigadier-general of the four who were chosen. Mr. Jefferson Davis was elected major-general, Earl Van Dorn first, C. H. Mott second, Charles Clark third and J. L. Alcorn fourth brigadier-general; of these General Alcorn alone survives. By the call of Mr. Davis to the presidency of the Confederacy and the appointment of General Van Dorn and General Mott to be brigadier-generals in the Confederate army, General Clark became major-general of the state troops. But when in a few weeks they were turned over to the Confederacy, General Clark was appointed brigadier-general in the Confederate army. He served first at Corinth, where he was engaged in organizing into regiments and brigades the troops which were being rapidly raised in Mississippi, but he was soon afterward ordered to Virginia. There he did not remain long, but was transferred to the army of Gen. Albert Sidney Johnston, and in the battle of Shiloh or Pittsburg Landing he commanded a division. In that battle he was severely wounded in the shoulder, and carried the ball with him to his grave. He did not permit this wound to keep him from the army long, but when the army under General Bragg was ordered into Tennessee, General Clark remained in Mississippi, serving under General Van Dorn, who commanded that department. He commanded a division under General Breckinridge in the disastrous attack upon Baton Rouge, where he received a ball which shattered his right hip. He was left on the field of battle, it being impossible for the Confederates to remove him when they retreated, and he was carried into the city. Realizing as he did the grave nature of his wound, he asked that he might be carried into New Orleans to his old friend, that eminent surgeon, Dr. Warren Stone. His request was kindly granted, and he remained in New Orleans until he was exchanged, his wife having been permitted to come to him and nurse him. Unable to again take the field, he was elected in 1862, practically without opposition, governor of the state, and was reëlected in 1864. Though still suffering from his wounds, which indeed never healed, and unable to walk without crutches, he devoted all his energies and ability to the sustaining of the waning fortunes of the Confederacy. When the end came he immediately convened the legislature, and in a manly and patriotic message, while regretting that the fortune of war was against us, he advised complete and ready acquiescence and obedience to the Federal law. In a short time the Federal authorities at Jackson demanded of him the surrender of the gubernatorial office and the records and archives of the state. This he at once, but politely, firmly refused to do, adding that he had received his trust from the people of the state and that to them alone would he surrender it. Resistance was unavailing, but not until he was arrested by an armed force did he leave his office, and even then protesting against what he deemed to be an unnecessary act of usurpation upon the part of the Federal authorities. Judge T. J. Wharton, of Jackson, Miss., who was then attorney-general of the state, has but recently described this closing scene in the part which Mississippi took in the great drama of the war to the writer, and told in thrilling tones and with an emotion which the lapse of time has not wholly subdued, how he stood with his tall form resting upon his crutches, his arm raised in indignant protest at the insult heaped upon the state in his person; the Federal soldiers silent, but stern, ready to obey any command, as worthy to rank among the pictures which preserve to succeeding generations the heroism of their fathers. From Jackson he was soon taken to Fort Pulaski, where for some time he remained confined, but by the exertions of his wife and his numerous friends in the state, among whom was his old friend and adjutant-general while in the service, Maj. W. H. McCardle, his release was at length secured and he returned to his home in Bolivar county. Here he resumed the practice of the law, and at once found his true place at the head of his profession until 1876, when he accepted the office of chancellor, which office he held at the time of his death. He took an active part in the redemption of the state in 1875 from the carpetbag misrule, and he was one of the trusted leaders of the people in that great and triumphant struggle, and he had the happiness of seeing before he died the state he loved so well and for which he had done so much fully redeemed. Soon after he obtained his license to practice law he was united in marriage with Miss Ann Eliza Darden, of one of the oldest and most prominent families in Jefferson county. She preceded him to the tomb, not quite two years. They had several children, of whom four survive: Fred Clark, his only son, a leading lawyer of Bolivar county and superintendent of education for the county; Mrs. Mary Adelia Montgomery, of Natchez, Miss.; Mrs. Emma Cooper, of Bolivar county; and Mrs. Ann Eliza Jacobs, living in Columbia, Mo. General Clark was also prominently connected with the educational interests of the state, having been from the first one of the trustees of the State university at Oxford, Miss., which office he held at the time of his death. To that institution he gave his untiring care, and aided it to rise from small beginnings to its present grand proportions. He was a great man; he was equal to every occasion, and no place he ever filled found him unprepared. This tribute to his memory is by one who for many years was honored with his friendship and who knew and loved him well.

Fred Clark, lawyer, Rosedale, Miss., was born in Bolivar county in December, 1852, youngest of the four children of Governor Charles and Ann E. (Darden) Clark, who were natives of Ohio and Mississippi respectively. He received his literary education at Oxford, Miss., studied law at the University of Virginia, and graduated from that institution in 1874. In the fall of that year he commenced practicing in Bolivar county, and with the exception of three years, between 1882 and 1885, he has been a resident of his native county. He is a rising lawyer, and in the town which has known him from boyhood he has built up a creditable practice. He is a moving spirit in both political and educational matters, and is county superintendent of education and chairman of the democratic executive committee. Mr. Clark was married in 1876 to Miss Margaret Winchester, of Natchez, daughter of Josiah Winchester, an old lawyer of that city. Eight interesting children have been born to this union: Frances S., Ann E., Margaret G., Charlotte M., Louisa, Charles, Frederick and J. Winchester. Mrs. Clark is a worthy member of the Presbyterian church. Mr. Clark is the owner of considerable town property, and also owns a plantation of one thousand acres, with four hundred acres under cultivation.

Elijah T. Clark, of Yazoo city, one of the largest planters of Yazoo county, has resided in the state of Mississippi from childhood. He was born in Charlotte county, Va., July 25, 1834, and is the fifth of a family of seven children. He is a son of Henry and Catherine (Brooks) Clark, of Virginia. The family removed to Mississippi in 1842, but the father only lived until the following year; the mother survived until 1846. Elijah T. was sent to the private schools of the neighborhood, and acquired an education sufficient for all practical needs. He is both a merchant and planter; he owns thirty-five hundred acres of rich farm land, seventeen hundred acres of which he has brought to a high state of cultivation. He is one of the first merchants of the county, carrying a stock of $5,000, and transacting a large business annually. He remained at home with his family until he was twenty-one years of age, and then started out in life to seek his fortune. He has been more than ordinarily successful, and his prosperity is due solely to his own exertions. He was united in marriage, in 1876, to Miss Sarah A. Johnson, a Mississippian by birth, and a daughter of R. G. Johnson, Esq. Of this union eight children have been born: William Thomas, Richard Dunn, Henry Lafayette, Annie Laurie, Addie E., Edna Gray, Andrew Relton, and Reason Grief. Mr. Clark was a soldier in the late war, enlisting in 1862 in company I, first Mississippi light artillery, and serving until the declaration of peace. He participated in the engagements at Chickasaw bayou, Vicksburg, Atlanta, Blakely, and Harrisburg, where he was taken prisoner and sent to Ship island; there he was held until the close of the war. He was slightly wounded in the last named battle. Politically he affiliates with the democratic party. He has been one of the potent factors in the building up of the county, and like a true, loyal citizen that he is, has given liberally of his means for the carrying out of worthy enterprises.

John Clark, planter, Clarksdale, Miss., the oldest living settler and founder, and sponsor of the town of Clarksdale, was the fourth in a family of ten children born to Hawkins and Elizabeth H. (Jennings) Clark, both natives of England. The parents left their native country, immigrated to British America, but after a few years came to the United States, located in Philadelphia about 1832, and here the father followed his profession—that of an architect. In November, 1837, he, with his son, John Clark, made a visit to New Orleans, and there the father died of yellow fever in the summer of 1839. The mother and the remainder of the children continued to reside in the city of Brotherly Love until the former's death, which occurred in 1880, at the venerable age of eighty-four years. She was a worthy and consistent member of the Episcopal church. John Clark was born at Ashton, England, in March, 1823, and after remaining in New Orleans for two years he came up the Mississippi river to Port Royal, at that time the county seat of Coahoma county. He was of an adventurous disposition and soon penetrated into the interior, shortly after engaging in the timber business with Thomas Flint Porter as a partner. Soon afterward Mr. Porter was killed and Mr. Clark formed a partnership with a brother of his late partner, Edward Drake Porter, the same continuing about two years. Mr. Clark had been very prosperous, and about that time he bought nearly a hundred and two acres of land on which the town of Clarksdale now stands. He gradually bought much more of the fine land in that vicinity, until at the outbreak of the war he owned about three hundred and sixty acres, with one hundred and fifty under cultivation, all cleared by himself. He was in the army a short time and was then appointed taxcollector of his district. When the war closed, he was left with little but his land. He continued planting, and in 1869, started the town of Clarksdale, opened a store and sold a number of lots, but naturally the town did not grow very rapidly until the advent of the Louisville, New Orleans & Texas railroad. A postoffice was established about 1875, and on the arrival of the railroad in 1883–4, the property became very valuable, Mr. Clark selling off many lots on which are now erected fine business blocks. He bought land from time to time, and soon became one of the largest planters in the county. He is now the owner of five thousand acres of land, most of it in the vicinity of Clarksdale, and has two thousand acres under cultivation. In 1860 and 1861 he erected his fine home, has since made many improvements and now has a handsome and tasty residence. He has two steam gins with the latest improved machinery and a sawmill which has sawed millions of feet of lumber for the town and railroad, but now saws only for private use. His place is well supplied with tenant houses, of which he has just completed about twenty new ones.

He has been continually engaged in mercantile pursuits since 1869, and now carries a full line of plantation supplies. He has not been active in politics but votes for the best man. He was married in 1854 to Miss Eliza Alcorn, a native of Kentucky and the daughter of James Alcorn, who came to this place in 1844. Mr. Alcorn was one of the pioneers of the county, and his death occurred in 1859. His son, James L. Alcorn, was senator and ex-governor of Mississippi (see sketch). To Mr. and Mrs. Clark have been born the following children—eight sons and one daughter: Hawkins (manager of the store), John (in Texas), Walter (conducting his father's plantation), Eugene Lusk (died in 1885, at the age of twenty-two years), Guy Peace and Paul (now at school in Massachusetts), Charles (died at the age of two and a half years), Charles W., and Blanch M. (wife of Hon. John W. Cutrer, senator for this district and a successful lawyer). Mr. and Mrs. Clark are members of the Methodist church. Mr. Clark was one of the organizers of the Clarksdale Bank and Trust company, and is president of the same at the present time. He is a director and stockholder in the Clarksdale Brick and Manufacturing company, and a stockholder in the Compress company. In these and all other enterprises Mr. Clark has given his cordial support, and has done much to attract trade and capital to the beautiful little city of Clarksdale so appropriately named after him. The Clark family is an old and representative one, the members of which have been noted for their clear, well-balanced, active intelligence. Mr. Clark is a perfect specimen of the hospitable Southern gentleman, and his luxurious home is a haven of hospitality. He is of medium size, has bright, blue eyes, and gray hair and beard. Mrs. Clark is pleasant and amiable and a lady of culture and refinement.

Col. Richard C. Clark, one of the oldest citizens of Lee county, Miss., was born in Brunswick county, Va., January 30, 1814, a son of John Clark, also a Virginian, who was a prominent planter. His father died when he was a lad of twelve years. When he was fourteen years old he left his mother, and, in care of an uncle, started for Clarke county, Ala., under whose teaching he was reared, and to whom he is indebted for his business experience, which proved so useful to him in after life. In 1832 he returned to his mother in Virginia, when the care of the family of three fell to his lot, the older brother being somewhat dissipated and careless of the responsibilities which were rightly his. He did his duty faithfully until his mother passed from this life. In 1850 he embarked in the mercantile business, at a small town on the west prong of the Bigbee river, Monroe county, Miss. The building of the Mobile & Ohio railroad absorbed the little town, moving it to the new road. Then the subject of this notice moved to Verona, Miss., where he entered mercantile life on a larger scale. Later he entered into business with his three eldest sons: John, at Tupelo, Miss.; Robert, at Shannon, Miss., and B. T. Clark who remained with him at Verona. His mother was quite an enterprising woman, leaving Virginia with but a small estate, left her by her husband, and moved to North Alabama, where she remained a few years, then to Monroe county, Miss., where she died, leaving an estate valued at $75,000. She was a devoted member of the Methodist Episcopal church. She reared five children to mature years, and gave them a good education for that day. Our subject was married to Miss Susan Hodges, of Smith county, Tenn., in 1835. She was born in 1822, a daughter of Robert Hodges, a well-known minister of North Mississippi, where he had removed. Eleven children were born to this union: John, the eldest, is at the head of the old and well-known firm of Clark, Hood & Co., Tupelo, Miss.; Robert B. is the head of the firm at Shannon, Miss., and also with his father, carrying on a large planting interest in Monroe county, Miss.; B. T. is at the head of the firm of B. T. Clark & Co., Nettleton Miss. The eldest was captain of artillery in the late war, and was assigned as chief of ordnance on Gen. Henry Little's staff, Price's division; Thomas is assistant

S. C. Gholson Jr, M.D.

cashier in the bank of Tupelo; David H. lives at Verona, and is in the drug business at Tupelo; Joseph M. is a planter of Lee county; Mattie is the wife of H. A. Kencommon, the present cashier of the bank of Tupelo, sketch of whom will be found elsewhere in this volume; Susan (wife of J. W. Keys) and her husband reside with their parents at Verona, she being the youngest daughter. Those deceased are Mary, former wife of W. S. Harris, of Louisville, Ky.; Josephine and Richard C. died in infancy. In 1878 Colonel Clark, with his old friend and former partner, A. H. Haymond, founded the Lee county bank at Verona. In 1887 this was merged into the bank of Tupelo. He has been president of the concern since its organization. Before the war he was worth some $200,000, which was nearly all swept away, and after the declaration of peace, he had to begin at the beginning and tread the same toilsome road of his earlier years. One of the industries to which Colonel Clark used to give much attention was cotton growing. He had constantly used tobacco for forty years, but in 1885 he became convinced of the injuriousness of the habit, and abandoned it at once. It is needless to add that a man who was not master of himself could not have performed this feat of will. Politically, he is a stanch supporter of the democratic party. His first presidential vote was cast for James K. Polk. He has been a member of the Methodist Episcopal church since 1833, and has served the church in every capacity excepting that of minister. His wife is also a devoted member of the same church. He is a Mason, served as master of Blue lodge eight years, and high priest of the chapter two years. In early years he was well skilled in Masonry. He has never aspired to political fame, has been nominated repeatedly, but would never accept. He is a man of liberality, and the poor seldom apply to him in vain. Although he is seventy years old, he is erect of form and well preserved, both in body and mind, a man of great sobriety and regular habits.

Joshua G. Clarke was a native of Pennsylvania, where he was educated. Before the formation of the state government he came to Mississippi territory, and soon made himself prominent in political affairs. He became a member of the territorial legislature from Claiborne county, and also in 1817 was a member of the convention convened to form the state government. He was one of the most conspicuous and active members of that body. In 1820 he became a member of the supreme bench, and the following year, upon the foundation of the special chancery system, was appointed the first chancellor of the state, which position he held with great credit until 1827. He was a lawyer of commanding ability, broad-minded, upright, skillful, and possessed the utmost confidence of his associates and the people of the state. His temper was always under control, yet was sufficiently strong to give zest and earnestness to everything he said. He possessed great learning, which he continued to improve until the time of his death, which occurred at Port Gibson in 1828. The high character of Mississippi judicial decisions is in a large measure due to Judge Clarke.

Dr. N. L. Clarke, a physician and surgeon of Meridian, Miss., was born near Decatur, Newton county, Miss., August 23, 1857, a son of Nathan L. Clarke, for more than fifty years a minister of the Baptist church, and now the editor of the *Mississippi Baptist* at Newton, Miss. This well-known clergyman was a native of North Carolina, and came to Mississippi about 1830, and has lived most of his life since then in Newton county, being now in his eightieth year. He married Miss Evaline Powell, also a native of North Carolina, who bore him five sons and five daughters, and eight of these are now living: G. P., of Decatur; Mary, the widow of Richard L. Williams; Mrs. P. T. Williams, of Texas; J. B., of Decatur; C. P., of Texas; Mrs. Susan Gallaspy, of Decatur; Dr. N. L., mentioned above; Mrs. Evaline Parks, of Texas. By his second marriage Rev. Clarke had one son, Dr. Lee M. Clarke, of Newton. Dr. N. L. Clarke, who is the immediate subject of this notice, was educated in the

35

common schools and in the high school of Decatur. He took up the study of medicine at the age of twenty-one years, and graduated from the Louisville medical college in 1883. He began the practice of his profession in Newton county, Miss., and there resided until January, 1885, when he removed to Meridian, where he has built up a large and successful practice. He is president of the Lauderdale county medical association, and is a member and vice president of the Mississippi state medical association. He is editor of the *Mississippi Medical Monthly*, published at Meridian, Miss. During the past few years he has made a great study of, and made a specialty of, the diseases of children, in the treatment of which he has acquired a lucrative patronage. He is a member of the Knights of Honor. March 25, 1883, he married Miss Carrie Melton, of Meridian, and he and his wife are members of the Baptist church. The Doctor stands high not only professionally but in social and commercial circles, and is recognized as a man of great public spirit.

Judge Alexander M. Clayton (deceased) was born in Campbell county, Va., January 15, 1801, the first month of the first year of the century. He did not receive a collegiate education, but was well and thoroughly educated in the best academies of the county in which he lived. At that time, the beginning of the present century, Virginia presented to the world a larger number of great statesmen, able lawyers, grand orators and profound jurists than any state in the Union; he was therefore fortunate in being born at such an hour, when he had the inspiration caught from the example of such an array of prominent men. Upon attaining his majority he read law in Lynchburg, Va., and was admitted to the bar in 1823, after which he immediately located at Louisa courthouse, and practiced there for three years with as much success as a young and inexperienced lawyer could reasonably expect. Upon being admitted to the bar Judge Clayton did not lay aside his classics, with which he became familiar during his scholastic career, but, by frequently consulting them, retained his knowledge of them to the end of his life. He was a man of literary taste and culture, and of vast and varied information on every subject of importance outside of his profession. In 1826 he married Miss Mary Walker Thomas, of the same state, a well-educated, refined, intellectual, Christian lady. Dissatisfied with the prospects Virginia then held out to the young lawyer, he moved to and located in Clarksville, Tenn., where he found a strong bar, many of whose members ranked as the first lawyers of the state. But by close attention to his business, hard study, manly deportment and unflinching courage, the young Virginian rose rapidly in public favor, and soon enjoyed a large and lucrative practice. While at Clarksville he was sorely afflicted by the death of his wife in 1832. To his sensitive nature this affliction was crushing in its effects. In 1836, while still at Clarksville, he was appointed Federal judge of the territory of Arkansas, by Andrew Jackson, then president of the United States. Judge Clayton accepted the appointment, but owing to his bad health resigned the office at the end of the first year of his term, and returned to Clarksville. In 1837 he moved to Mississippi, purchased a large tract of land in what was then Marshall county, near the town of Lamar, converted this into a large plantation, and there passed the remainder of his days. On coming to this state he engaged at once in the practice of law at Holly Springs, where he found an able and powerful bar. Judge Clayton immediately took rank with the first lawyers of the state, and as an astute, painstaking, well-read, correct reasoner, full of legal lore, he was the peer of any man in the state. In 1839 Judge Clayton was married a second time, to Miss Barbara A. Barker, of Clarksville, Tenn., but this happy union was broken in 1879 by the death of Mrs. Clayton. In 1842 a vacancy occurred in the supreme court bench of the state, and Judge Clayton was elected to fill that vacancy. In 1844 he was elected by the people of this state to the same office, for a full term of six years.

His opinions while in this office were terse, clear, forcible, accurate, and well supported by authority. He was a candidate for reëlection to the supreme bench in 1851, but was defeated by Hon. E. S. Fisher. In his defeat in that year Judge Clayton shared the fate of his whole party. He was a delegate from Mississippi to the world-renowned Nashville convention in 1849, and was a prominent member thereof. In 1860 he was elected a delegate from Marshall county to the state convention which passed the ordinance of secession in January, 1861, and during the struggle between the North and South he was an able and fearless defender of Southern rights. During the administration of President Pierce, he received the appointment of consul to Havana, but after a few months' service he found his health giving way, and resigned the office and came home. In 1866 he became a candidate for circuit judge of this district, was elected, and served until he was removed under the resolution of congress, passed in 1868, declaring every civil office in the state vacant. After his removal from the circuit bench in 1868, he was engaged in the management of the large estate of which he was the owner, and in the practice of his profession, frequently employed in important suits involving large amounts, and presenting intricate questions of law. At the time of his death he was attorney for the Illinois Central railroad company for the county of Benton, in which he lived, and was also a trustee of the State university. His death occurred on September 30, 1889, at the age of eighty-nine years, and he had been a member of the bar for sixty-six years. He was a firm believer in the Christian religion, a member of the Episcopal church, and a regular attendant upon its services. His last moments were calm and peaceful, and his entrance into the world of disembodied spirits was taken in complete composure.

On the 6th of October, 1808, George R. Clayton was born in Athens, Ga. His parents were Hon. Augustine S. and Julia (Carnes) Clayton. In 1827, after a brilliant collegiate career, George R. graduated with honor at the University of Georgia, and immediately thereafter began the study of law in the office of his father, who was one of the ablest jurists of the state. Upon his admission to the bar, George R. began the practice of his profession in his native town, and he soon became prominent. In 1834 he became a member of the legislature of Georgia, where he distinguished himself in the general legislation. About this time he was united in marriage to Miss Ann R. Harris, daughter of Gen. Jephtha V. Harris, and in 1836 removed to Mississippi, where he took up the practice of law, and soon acquired a wide reputation as a conscientious member of the profession. His tastes and the qualities of his mind led him into politics, in which he showed exceptional fitness. In 1843 he took an active part in supporting the candidacy of Albert G. Brown for governor. One of the principal questions before the people of the state at that time was the question of repudiation of the payment, on the part of the state, of the bonds of the Union bank. Mr. Clayton, in common with Albert G. Brown, favored the policy of repudiation. This policy prevailed, as it was sustained by the people of the state, and Mr. Brown was triumphantly elected. Mr. Clayton played no inconsiderable part in this memorable political contest. In January, 1837, by an act of the legislature of the state, the Mississippi Union bank was incorporated with a capital of $15,500,000, which large sum was to be raised by a loan, under the management of a board appointed by the legislature, and composed of three individuals from each county, who were authorized to open books for subscriptions of stock in their respective counties. It was upon the bonds thus issued that the contest spoken of occurred. Those who subsequently favored the repudiation of these bonds, did so upon the general proposition that one generation has no right to place upon a future generation a binding obligation of that character, and was sustained by no less an authority than Thomas Jefferson. Other important considerations induced the people of the state generally to favor repudiation, and this policy, as stated, eventually prevailed. When the question of secession arose, Mr. Clayton announced himself in favor of state rights, and favored the separation of the Southern states in order to maintain that policy. He was a member of the secession convention, in the proceedings of which he took an active and prominent part. As a practitioner of law, Mr. Clayton was one of the most distinguished in the state. He died in Athens, Ga., in 1867.

George W. Clayton, planter, merchant and postmaster, at Alto, Jasper county, Miss., was born in this county December 5, 1841. He is a son of Isham H. and Mary E. (Boulton) Clayton, natives of South Carolina, who emigrated to Mississippi at an early day, locating first in Perry county, and later in Jasper county, where they lived out the balance of their lives. They were the parents of seven children, as follows: Thomas, William H., Ann B., Rufus K. (who was a captain in company A of the Fortieth Mississippi regiment, and at the battle of Iuka, Miss., had his right arm shot off, thus receiving a terrible wound, from the effects of which he died), Susan C., George W. and James P. George W. Clayton was educated in the schools of Lauderdale and Jasper counties. In 1862 he enlisted in company A of the Fortieth Mississippi regiment, and served but a short time, when he was taken sick and was discharged on account of disability. Returning home, he joined the state militia, of which he was a member for about one year. Coming again to Jasper county, he was married, April 15, 1863, to Miss Mary S., daughter of John H. and Elizabeth E. (Harper) Cook. Mrs. Clayton was born in Jasper county February 1, 1845. After their marriage they made their home for a time with Mr. Clayton's parents on the old home plantation. In 1867 they located on the place where they now live, and have lived there continuously ever since that time. Mr. and Mrs. Clayton are the parents of seven children, as follows: Rufus P., born April 27, 1866; Mary E., born December 20, 1867; Lelia C., born October 27, 1869; Ellen P., born September 19, 1871; Isham P., born December 31, 1873; George W., born June 3, 1881, and John W., born February 8, 1884. Mary E. married, August 28, 1889, Prof. Stone Deavours, the principal of the Pleasant Hill schools. They have had born to them one child, Adaline, June 8, 1890. Mr. Clayton is a member of the Masonic fraternity, and is in all respects a moral, helpful and respected citizen. He was elected a member of the county board of supervisors in 1877, and served two years. He takes little active interest in politics, but has pronounced views on all subjects of public interest, believing it better befits the average citizen to cast his ballot quietly and intelligently, than to join noisily in public discussions, which can be of little personal benefit to him, and neglect his own private affairs.

Isham H. and Mary Elizabeth (Boulton) Clayton came to Mississippi from South Carolina at an early day; they settled in Greene county, where they lived until what is now Jasper county was purchased from the Indians; they then removed to Jasper county. They had seven children: William H., Thomas A., Mary Ann Bethia, Rufus K., Susan C., George W. and James Pinkney Clayton. Thomas A. Clayton died in infancy, William H. and Isham H. Clayton (the father) died of yellow fever in Mobile, Ala., in the year 1847. Mary Ann Bethia was married to Joseph Cook and is the mother of a large and respected family. Rufus K. Clayton, the pride of the family, the comfort and stay of his widowed mother and the protector of his young brothers and sisters, was killed at the battle of Iuka, while leading his command in a gallant charge. Susan C. Clayton is the wife of H. M. Hartfield. George W. Clayton, youngest and only living brother of J. P. Clayton, is a respected gentleman. This brings us to our subject: James Pinkney Clayton, familiarly called Pink, was born August 12, 1844. His early days were spent in school in Pleasant Hill. When sixteen years old he entered school at the Summerville institute, but was there only a short time when he returned home to answer his country's call for volunteers. He enlisted with Capt. R. K. Clayton in Hardcastle's battalion, which was soon disbanded at Vicksburg. Most of the company reorganized under Capt. R. K. Clayton and became company A, Fortieth Mississippi regiment, with which they served until the close of the war. J. P. Clayton was in a number of hard-fought battles; he endured the privations and hardships incident to a soldier's life and was never known to shirk duty. After the surrender in 1865 he returned home and devoted his attention to planting. November 6, 1867, he married Rebecca Celia, a daughter of George D. and Sallie (Millsaps) McCormick. They went immediately after the marriage to live as he had always done, with his mother, and have never changed their residence. He owns about twenty-five hundred acres of land and plants quite extensively. He is energetic, industrious, a thoroughly practical and thoroughly reliable man, planter and citizen, who commands the highest respect from all. His home is noted for generous hospitality. In 1878 he was elected to the office of county treasurer, which he held for one term with great credit to himself and to the entire satisfaction of the people of the county. His mother, Mary Elisabeth Clayton, died November 7, 1881, aged eighty-one years. Mrs. Clayton's father (George D. McCormick) was a native of the Colleton district, S. C., her mother a Mississippian and daughter of Judge Uriah Millsaps.

The calling of the physician, when properly conducted, is one of the noblest to which a man devotes his life, and to say that Dr. E. C. Clements has made a proper use of the powers given him would be stating the facts of the case very mildly indeed. To his skill and talent the gratitude of hundreds is due, but he is now living retired from the active duties of a professional life. He was born in Tuscaloosa county, Ala., in 1828, being a son of Hardy and Susan (Hargrove) Clements, both of whom were born in Edgefield district, S. C., about 1780. The father received a common-school education, and when, becoming grown, left home in search of a fortune, his capital consisting of a small pony, which he rode, and $100 in cash. He first went to Georgia, thence to Tennessee, and in the town of Fayetteville spent some time as a schoolteacher. He next went to Tuscaloosa county, Ala., where he was married twice and spent the rest of his life, dying in 1867. He became a wealthy planter, for he owned before the war over one thousand slaves, and at the time of his death twenty thousand acres of land, and for some years he was engaged in the manufacture of cotton and woolen goods for the use of himself and family. He was much interested in public affairs, and for some years held the office of county commissioner, during which time much was done to improve and develop Tuscaloosa county. Socially he was a member of the A. F. & A. M. His first wife died when the subject of this sketch was about eighteen months old, and he afterward married Miss Mariah Pegues, his first wife bearing him three children, and his last wife five. Mr. Clements was of Scotch descent, and came of a long-lived race, for his mother lived to be nearly one hundred years of age, and her eight children all lived to be over sixty. Dr. E. C. Clements is the youngest of three sons, two of whom became physicians. Rufus H., the elder one, was a planter and lawyer, and died in Tuscaloosa county, Ala., in 1868. He graduated from a law college of Cambridge, Mass., but did not practice much. He was a man who interested himself in public affairs, and was a member of both houses of the Alabama legislature. Dr. Luther M. Clements, the other brother, graduated from Jefferson medical college of Philadelphia, Penn., and was all through the Confederate army, a part of the time acting as surgeon, and at other times as captain. Dr. E. C. Clements was educated in the University of Alabama at Tuscaloosa, and in 1852 graduated from the Jefferson medical college of Philadelphia, after which he practiced in his native county until 1857. He then came to Noxubee county, Miss., and farmed until the war closed, but since 1867 has been a resident of what is now Sharkey county, and was engaged in practicing here for some years. He is now the owner of about six hundred acres of land, and with the exception of a few years spent at Iuka and Tuscaloosa, Ala., his home has been at Rolling Fork. When the war opened he became a member of company A, First Mississippi cavalry, "Noxubee cavalry," and operated in Mississippi, Kentucky, Tennessee, Alabama and Missouri, taking part in the battles of Shiloh, Corinth, and many others. In the summer of 1863 he was transferred to a Tennessee regiment, and until captured, in August, 1864, was stationed at Fort Morgan, Ala. He was taken to New Orleans, then to Governor's island, New York, where he remained until the 5th of December. While being taken to Elmira, N. Y., and on the first night's journey, he made his escape from the train about one hundred miles from New York city, and made his way to Philadelphia, where he had friends, and where he obtained some money to enable him to continue his journey home. He went to St. Louis, thence to Memphis, Tenn., arriving home in the month of January, 1865. He was soon after called to the service again, and was in Mobile until that city was taken by the Federals, whereupon he went northward, and was in Meridian, Miss., at the close of the war. He was first married in Montgomery, Ala., to Miss Julia, daughter of Judge Frank and Lavinia Bugbee, the former being a prominent lawyer and noted jurist of Alabama. Mrs. Clements was born in Montgomery, and died in 1858, leaving one daughter, who is now the wife of D. F. Robertson, a prosperous merchant and planter of Columbus, Miss. Dr. Clements' second marriage took place on the 31st of December, 1863, Anna, daughter of Judge H. W. and Frances Foote, becoming his wife. Judge Foote was born in South Carolina, and when a young man came on horseback to Mississippi, in which state he is now living with his fourth wife. He was a member of both houses of the legislature, and also ably filled the position of circuit judge. He was captain of a company of Mississippi cavalry in the Confederate army at the beginning of the war. He is an able lawyer of East Mississippi, is wealthy, and is an earnest member of the Methodist church, being superintendent of the Sunday-school for about forty years. He has served several times as a delegate to the general conference of that church, and was for some years one of the trustees of Vanderbilt university. Mrs. Clements was born in Macon, Miss., and has borne the Doctor six children, four of whom are living: Anna P., Fannie F., William H. and Sybil May. The Doctor has been a member of the A. F. & A. M. since 1854, and is now a demitted member of Deer Creek lodge. He and his wife are both very active workers in the church, and are very popular with all classes, having done much to promote the growth of Christianity in Rolling Fork. Some of the Doctor's near relatives have become eminent, a half brother being for some time a member of congress from Alabama, and an uncle, Gen. Benjamin Clements, being a very prominent citizen of Nashville, Tenn.

Among the professional men of Mississippi who have deservedly attained eminence, may be mentioned Thomas J. Cochran, M. D., who was born in the county in which he is now residing on the 18th of January, 1849, to John H. and Helen (Hightower) Cochran. They removed to Lauderdale county, Miss., some fifty or more years ago, and since that time Mr. Cochran has devoted his attention to planting, for which he has seemed to have a natural aptitude. He has never aspired to political preferment, being content to obtain his living from the rich farming lands of Mississippi. His wife died in 1886, at her home at Daleville, Lauderdale county, Miss., at which time she was an earnest and worthy member of the Methodist Episcopal church. Mr. Cochran is also a member of this church, and socially belongs to the A. F. & A. M. His father was a settler of this region before the Indians vacated the country, when but little of the land had been cleared or was under cultivation, and when the woods were infested by wild animals of many kinds. The Cochran family is one of the oldest and best known in the country, every member of which is noted for honorable, upright conduct, as well as for his charity, generosity and hospitality. John H. Cochran is still living and has now reached his sixty-second year. Dr. Thomas J. Cochran was educated in the Cooper institute in Lauderdale county, and began the study of medicine in 1873 in the office of Dr. Rhodes of Daleville, attending the Charity Hospital Medical college at New Orleans in 1874–6, graduating as an M. D. in the spring of the latter year. He began practicing his profession at Fort Stevens, in Kemper county, Miss., the same year of his graduation, and remained there until 1889, when he removed to Daleville, his old home, and is there now located. Through undoubted merit and strict attention to his business he has built up a lucrative practice, and professionally as well as socially, he has entered the majority of the homes of the section in which he resides. In connection with his practice the Doctor has been carrying on farming, and although he is the owner of a good two-hundred-acre plantation, of which about one hundred acres are improved and under cultivation, he has devoted the principal part of his attention to his practice. In 1879 his union with Miss Anna Calvert was celebrated, she being the daughter of Adam Calvert, of Kemper county. To their union a son and daughter have been born: William R. and Mabel G. The Doctor and his wife are members of the Methodist Episcopal church, and like his father before him, he is generous, charitable and hospitable.

C. W. Cochran, a merchant of Daleville, Miss., was born in Lauderdale county, Miss., May 9, 1852, the son of J. H. and H. G. (Hightower) Cochran. He began life for himself at the age of twenty-one years, and for some time acquired his sustenance from the soil. He was educated in the Cooper normal college of Daleville, and in 1879 attended the Southern business college at Louisville, Ky. Upon his return home he purchased a stock of general merchandise, which he opened to the public at Daleville, and this establishment he has successfully conducted in connection with planting ever since. He is the owner of one thousand acres of land, about six hundred of which is improved and under cultivation, and on this land he raises about two hundred and fifty bales of cotton each year, besides doing an annual business of about $18,000 with his stock of goods, which is valued at nearly $5,000. He has proven himself a successful financier, and as he has always been the soul of honor in his business transactions, and is possessed of a laudable ambition to make the most of his life, he is eminently deserving of success. In September, 1882, he was united in marriage to Miss Lizzie, daughter of D. B. Sanford, of Ouachita Parish, La., but their union, as yet, has not been blessed in the birth of children. He and his wife are members of the Methodist Episcopal church, and by their many kindly characteristics have won a host of warm friends. The Cochrans are one of the best known families in Lauderdale county, and are highly esteemed by all who have the honor of their acquaintance. Mr. Cochran has never aspired to any official position, but has devoted his energies of mind and body to his business interests, and his efforts have resulted in success. He is generous, liberal and high-minded, and has numerous friends.

Charles R. Cock, the present sheriff of Yalobusha county, Miss., was born within one-half mile of where he now lives, in the year 1847. His father, Charles William Cock, was born in Tennessee, and in his childhood was brought to Mississippi by his parents, Charles and Mary (Walker) Cock, who were among the earliest settlers of Yalobusha county. Charles Cock was a farmer by occupation, and adhered to the principles of the Whig party. The house in which he dwelt was erected by him, and is still standing. He died in 1845, and was past sixty years of age. His wife lived to be nearly ninety years of age. They were the parents of seven children who lived to be grown, three of whom are still living: Mrs. Melissa Morrison, Mrs. Mary Wilkie, and Charles W. Cock, the father of the subject of this notice. He was reared and educated in Yalobusha county, and was married to Frances A. Robinson, a native of this county and a daughter of R. Robinson. Mr. Robinson was a native of Virginia, and removed to Water Valley about the year 1840; he owned a farm where the machine shops now stand; there were six children in the Robinson family, two of whom are now living: G. W. and W. E. Robinson. Mrs. Cock was the youngest of the children; she had born to her two children: Virginia, who married W. M. Palmer, and Charles R. She died in 1861, at the age of thirty years; she was greatly beloved by all who knew her and deeply mourned by her family. The father of Charles R. served in the late war as a lieutenant of his company; he removed to Texas in 1859, and was married there a second time to a Mrs. Wommack; by this union two children have been born: William M. and Ollie. Mr. Cock is a member of the Masonic order, is democratic in his political opinions, and is a member of the board of supervisors. Charles R. Cock passed his youth on the old home place in Yalobusha county, Miss.; he acquired his education in the common schools, and then learned the trade of a molder in the foundry of Water Valley, which he followed for several years; he then turned his attention to farming, in which he has been engaged until his election to the office of sheriff of Yalobusha county in 1885; his opponent was R. V. Pearson, who had held the office for ten years. In addition to his official duties he finds time to attend to some private investments; he is interested in a livery, feed and sale stable in partnership with Z. R. Stevenson; they keep the finest and best turnouts obtainable, and by their strict attention to business have won a large and substantial patronage. Mr. Cock was married to Miss Lucy A. Talliaferro, a native of Marshall county, Miss., and a daughter of William and Eliza (Allen) Talliaferro; the parents were married in Alabama and came to Mississippi, where they were pioneers in Marshall county; the mother is yet living, but the father is deceased; there were eleven children in the family—three sons and eight daughters; the sons are all deceased. Mrs. Cock is one of the youngest members of the family, and was educated at Holly Springs, Miss. Mr. and Mrs. Cock have had born to them eight children: Bettie, who is in Tennessee at school; Eva, William, Pearl, Bulah, Jessie, Edward, and George deceased. During the war Mr. Cock served in the state militia, being stationed at Grenada. He is a member of the Masonic order, belonging both to the Blue lodge and chapter; he also belongs to the Methodist Episcopal church.

Charles H. Cocke, ex-president of the Industrial institute and college of the state of Mississippi at Columbus, was born in Powhatan county, Va., March 12, 1851, a son of Gen. Philip St. George Cocke, who became prominent in the history of the Old Dominion. He was a graduate of the West Point military academy, and for two years was a soldier in the United States army, holding the position of second lieutenant of artillery. He raised a cavalry company in Virginia known as the Powhatan troop, which he armed at his own expense at the opening of the Rebellion. As soon as he reported for duty to the military authorities of his state he was made colonel of his regiment and put in charge of a brigade. After the battle of Manassas he was made brigadier-general and served as such until his death, which unfortunately occurred in the latter part of 1861. He had been a planter by occupation for many years, and built one of the handsomest country residences in Virginia, which was known by the name of Belmead. He was president of the Virginia agricultural society for many years, and in 1857 took the first action of any one in the United States, and perhaps in the world, to endow the chair of agriculture in collegiate institutions, to which he was a liberal contributor. He gave $20,000 for this purpose to the Virginia military institute, Lexington. He was widely and prominently known, and was a man of sterling principles, brilliant intellect and generous disposition. He was married to Miss Courtney Bowdoin, by whom he became the father of four sons and six daughters, all of whom reached their majority, and seven of whom are now living: Louisiana B. (Kennon), S. B. (Wilson), Lucy C. (Bridges), Philip St. George, Courtney (Barraud), Mary A. and Charles H. The paternal grandfather, Gen. John H. Cocke, of Bremo Bluff, Va., was a soldier in the war of 1812. The property of which he was the owner at Bremo Bluff, Va., and which is still in possession of the family, was granted to the Cocke family during the reign of George II. of England, and having never been sold, it has been handed down in the family from generation to generation, and Gen. John H. Cocke was the first to build a house of any pretensions thereon. Charles H. Cocke was educated in the University of Virginia, taking a thorough and extensive literary and scientific course, completing his term there in 1874 with certificates and diplomas in six schools. The same year he moved to Columbus, where he taught school in 1874–5. He then followed the calling of a planter until 1883, when he had temporary charge of Franklin academy. In 1888 he was elected president of the state Industrial institute and college, but resigned in 1890, since which period he has devoted his time to his own private interests. He owns a large area of land in Lowndes county, most of which is under cultivation, and the principal crops are cotton and corn. He is a director of the Columbus Insurance and Banking company, of the Columbus Compress company, and is a stockholder in the Tombigbee cotton mills. He was married in 1876 to Miss Rowena L. Hudson, a native of Georgia, by whom he has three children: Fontaine A., Charles H., Jr., and Rowena L., all members of the Episcopal church.

In 1816, when Stephen Cocke was yet a boy, his parents moved to Columbus, Miss., where the father had been sent as an agent of the government to the Choctaw Indians, and here, later, Stephen Cocke served in the capacity of a clerk under the agency of his father. His education was necessarily limited, but upon arriving at manhood, he was elected clerk of the circuit court of his county, and while thus engaged began the study of law. In 1834 he became a member of the legislature, and distinguished himself for his advocacy of the formation of the new counties out of the Choctaw and Chickasaw sessions. In 1845 he was elected chancellor of the state, which position he held for a term of six years. He possessed no particular distinction as a lawyer or as a judge, but is remembered particularly in his efforts in behalf of the admission of the new counties spoken of.

In 1795, in South Carolina, Benjamin Cockrell, of Noxubee county, Miss., was born. He was the son of William Cockrell, who was a patriot of the Revolution, and was captured at Bunker Hill. He was carried a prisoner to the East Indies, where he married a Miss Brown. Benjamin Cockrell was married to Miss Eliza Robinson, who was born in 1800. They emigrated to Noxubee county, Miss., in 1833, and settled near Deerbrook, and thence moved to Alabama for a time, and, during the Civil war, returned to Noxubee county, Miss. John R. Cockrell, the subject of this sketch, and a son of the last named, was born in 1827, in South Carolina, and came to Noxubee county, Miss., in 1833, where he has since resided. He owns three thousand acres of the choice land of Noxubee county, Miss. His farm is largely sown to red and white clover, Lespedeza and Bermuda grass. Mr. Cockrell is one of the most extensive stockraisers in the country. On his farm may be found over forty registered Jersey cattle of the finest strain, and more than a hundred Ayrshire and Durhams, some of them registered. Mr. Cockrell is also largely engaged in breeding Southdown and Shropshiredown sheep of imported stock. His farm is supplied with beautiful horse stock, some imported; also jennets and jacks. The choicest poultry is also raised on his farm. Mr. Cockrell's farm is most emphatically one of the best in the state in all its departments. Elegant buildings adorn the landscape, and the water supply is all that one could wish. Mr. Cockrell plants on an extensive scale, his average cotton crop being four hundred bales, in the production of which forty mules are employed. He is also engaged in merchandising and milling. His elegant property is the product entirely of Mr. Cockrell's energy and management, as exercised since the war, which left the South in a state of devastation, untillable and almost uninhabitable. He was married to Miss Mary A. Wells, who was born in Noxubee county, Miss., in the year 1841.

C. C. Coffee, Meridian, Miss., is one of the representative business men of Meridian, Miss., and the following space will be devoted to a brief sketch of his career. He was born in the state of Georgia in the territory now included in Dodge county, in July, 1849, and is the seventh of a family of twelve children. His parents, Peter H. and Susan Ann (Rogers) Coffee, were born and reared, married and died, in Georgia. The mother passed away in 1862, and the father was married, a second time, to Miss Martha Ann Sheldon; they have three children. Peter H. Coffee was a plain, practical farmer, with firm convictions of right and wrong, and deep integrity of character. He was a member of the Methodist Episcopal church and belonged to the Masonic fraternity. He died in 1885. C. C. Coffee began life for himself at the age of eighteen years, and embarked in the mercantile business at Hawkinsville, Ga. He remained there three years, and then sold out, engaging in the wholesale manufacture of pumps at Memphis, Tenn. The concern was known as the Kenesaw Manufacturing company, and he was vice president of the corporation; the company failed and he bought all the stock, and conducted the business alone until 1888, when he came to Meridian; he then purchased the carriage and buggy works factory at that place, which he operated until 1889. In that year he closed out the business, and at the present time is devoting his time to the real estate business. He owns stock in the dummy line and Bernette Park company, and is one of the most progressive, pushing men of the place. He has made many friends, and by his fair, honorable dealing has established a reputation that would be a credit to any man. In 1884 he was married to Miss Ella C. Ragsdale, and they have one daughter, Anna C., aged six years. Mrs. Coffee is a consistent member of the Presbyterian church.

Charles C. Coffey is the present efficient and trustworthy circuit court clerk of Jefferson county, Miss., and during his residence within the borders of this county, which has extended over his entire life, he has proven himself a gentleman of irreproachable morals, and of a charitable, kindly and honorable disposition. He was born on the 27th of January, 1853, and was fortunate enough to receive his education in the University of Mississippi, which institution he attended during the years of 1867–9, and during this time acquired the reputation of a conscientious and painstaking student. He entered public life at an early age, and although he was appointed to the position of deputy assessor at the age of nineteen years, he proved himself eminently trustworthy and capable of filling the position, and following this was employed as deputy sheriff, filling these positions during a period of twelve years. While discharging the duties of these offices he looked after his mother's plantation also, and although his attention was fully occupied, he neglected no part of his work, and his services received the approval of all interested. In January, 1884, he was elected to the position of circuit clerk, and in this capacity has shown himself a man of sterling honesty and superior capability. Every thing about his office shows that neatness and order hold full sway, and the most perfect arrangement is manifested in every department, showing the workings of a well-balanced and intelligent mind. He has filled the position up to the present time, and has proved himself a most efficient public servant, being punctual, honest and uniformly courteous to all. He has a farm of three hundred acres lying near the thriving town of Harrison, but as the duties of his office occupy his entire time, he leases his land, but as the soil is exceptionally productive and fertile, he derives from it a fair annual income. He is a man of strong temperance principles, as will be acknowledged when the fact is known that while a young man he preferred to give up a lucrative position as clerk in a general store rather than sell liquor at the bar which had been erected by his employer. This incident, however, was no detriment to his subsequent career, and his fidelity to his principles was soon rewarded, for his services were soon sought by a stronger and better firm, which valued the principles shown and was willing to give him employment at an increased salary. He took an active part in politics during the days of reconstruction, and since that time has given his attention to the affairs of state and public policy. The utmost confidence of the people has been given him and has not been bestowed in vain, and he is always ready to aid any enterprise tending to redound to the general good of the county. His reputation as an honest man has remained untarnished, and he has at all times borne himself in an upright manner. He was married on the 29th of February, 1880, to Miss Olive S. Bullen, a daughter of James Bullen, of this county, she having been left an orphan when about five years of age. To them four interesting little children have been born: Charles Lamar, Coralie A., Anna O. and Erma L. Chesley S. Coffey, the father of Charles C., was a native of Maury county, Tenn., but when about fifteen years of age came to the state of Mississippi and apprenticed himself to the trade of shoemaking, becoming so thoroughly familiar with the work that in a few years he bought out his employer and successfully conducted the establishment until about the breaking out of the Mexican war, when he sold his shop and purchased a plantation near Fayette, containing sixteen hundred acres. He then joined the Second Mississippi regiment with the rank of lieutenant, but was afterward promoted to captain. He remained in Mexico for two years, at the end of which time he returned to Fayette and erected a tannery and shoe factory on his place, which he continued to operate for many years in addition to his planting interests. He was the owner of a large number of negroes, and was considered one of the wealthiest men of this section. When the Civil war became an assured fact, he was among the first to respond to what he considered the call of duty, and was captain of company D, Nineteenth Mississippi regiment, the first regiment mustered into the service of the Confederate states for and during the war. The regiment was raised by Brigadier-General Mott, of the Mississippi army, assisted by Hon. L. Q. C. Lamar. The regiment numbered eight hundred men, and the company of which Mr. Coffey was a member was known as the Thomas Hinds guards of Fayette, Miss., and composed of the sons of the best families in the community. The names of the officers are as follows: Commissioned officers—Captain, C. S. Coffey; first lieutenant, Robert Duncan; second lieutenant, P. H. Burch; third lieutenant, T. J. Key; non-commissioned officers—orderly-sergeant, W. F. Schwing; second sergeant, C. J. Liddell; third sergeant, T. G. Manifold; fourth sergeant, W. H. Terry; fifth sergeant, James McClure; corporals—first corporal, D. P. Wyatt; second corporal, J. C. Stampley; third corporal, R. C. McPhail; fourth corporal, W. L. Stephen. At the time of being mustered into service the company was composed of thirteen officers and fifty-three privates, rank and file sixty-six. Recruits were subsequently added to the number of twenty-two, making a total of eighty-eight. Of this company but nine members, three officers and six privates, returned home at the close of the war. Captain Coffey was severly wounded at Williamsburg, Va., May 5, 1862, and the following February he resigned his position and returned home, after which he was appointed as a member of the board of conscript, which position he filled until the close of the war. During the early history of the county he served on the board of police of Jefferson county, and was otherwise interested in preserving law and order in this section of the country, and aided largely in its progress and development. He was a member of the I. O. O. F., was a charter member of Thomas Hines lodge No. 58 of the A. F. & A. M., of which lodge all his sons are members. He was a consistent member of the Methodist Episcopal church, in which he held the office of steward for many years. His marriage, which occurred in 1849, was to Miss Missisippi S. Davis, the daughter of a resident of Yazoo county, Miss. To them seven children were born, four sons and one daughter of whom are living at the present time. Mr. Coffey was called from life in the month of February, 1869, his wife dying in November, 1884, both being buried at Fayette.

Solomon Cohen, merchant, Gunnison, Miss., a member of the large mercantile firm of Frank, Cohen & Co., was born in London, England, in 1856, and was the fourth child born to Samuel and Sarah Cohen. He attended school in his native country until 1872 and then sailed to the United States, where he expected to make his start in life. He first started out as a clerk and followed this occupation in Greenville, Miss., for three months. He then came to Concordia, Bolivar county, engaged with Toben & Co. for five years, and was then with Frank & Co. for some time. In 1882 he was admitted as a member of the last mentioned firm and the title was changed to Frank, Cohen & Co. in 1888. Two years later, on the completion of the railroad, they removed to the new town of Gunnison, erected a large store and filled it with a choice stock of goods, valued at $20,000. Their annual sales amount to $250-000, and they control about six thousand bales of cotton and one hundred thousand sacks of cottonseed. They ship their cotton to Fater, Frank & Co., of Memphis, Tenn. In the year 1888 Mr. Cohen was married to Miss Hannah Sellers, of Memphis, Tenn., and to them was born one child, who died unnamed. Mr. and Mrs. Cohen are members of the Congregational church at Memphis. He is a member of the Knights of Honor and the I. O. B. Although he started a poor boy, at the foot of the ladder, Mr. Cohen has always made his services so valuable to his employers, by studying and thoroughly posting himself on all points of their business, that they found it hard to get along without him. In every case he made their interests a duty to which he gave his whole attention and undivided care. For this he received his reward, and was promoted by Toben & Co., but, thinking there were brighter prospects for the future in an offer made by Frank & Co., he joined with them, and is now the prosperous partner of a wealthy firm. Their business extends far and wide, and this firm is well known throughout the delta. Thus, step by step, can be traced the progress of one of Bolivar county's influential merchants and self-made men.

A wideawake, industrious farmer, who by his own exertions and industry has accumulated a handsome property, is William J. Coke, of Gift, Miss., a native of Middle Tennessee, and a son of Spillsberry and Myra (Bard) Coke, both also natives of Tennessee. The paternal grandparents were Richard and Elizabeth (Tribble) Coke. Spillsberry and his wife left their native state and moved to Arkansas, where both received their final summons. They were the parents of twelve children, who are named in the order of their births, as follows: Susan (widow of Mr. Justin, is the mother of two children, William and Fredonia, and makes her home with the former), Sarah (widow of Mr. Boyers, resides with her children in Arkansas), John M. (married a Miss Harris, and now resides in Arkasans; he is the father of seven children), Richard F. (married Miss Anna Burrow, and is the father of four children: John, Thomas, Amanda and Myra; he is a resident of Alcorn county, Miss.). The children deceased are: Daniel, Martha, Mary, Elizabeth, Thomas, Eliza and Hardy. William J. Coke, the fourth child in order of birth of the above-named children, and the second son, was born on the 10th of May, 1833, and passed his youthful days in his native state, receiving his education in the common schools. He came to Mississippi in September, 1855, settled on a farm in Alcorn (then Tishomingo) county, and began farming on rented land. He was married on the 10th of July of the following year to Miss Naomia Brooks, a native of Mississippi, and the daughter of Thompson and Rachel (Blackwood) Brooks, both natives of Alabama. Mr. Brooks was a tailor by trade, but later in years became an extensive stockraiser. He and wife were the parents of three children: California, William and Naomia. Mr. Coke's marriage resulted in the birth of eight children: Richard F. (married Miss Fidelia Stephenson, and is the father of four children, viz.: Clyster, Della, Marquess and Rufus; his wife died in April, 1885, and his second marriage was to Miss Virginia Jones, who bore him three children: Obediah, Edward and Susan; he lives near his father), William T. (married Miss Deanna Turner, and is the father of three children; Ernest, Vester and Hubert), Mollie (deceased, was the wife of Thomas Jones, and left one child, Minnie), James H. (home with his parents), John N. (deceased, married Miss Hannah Hendricks, and left his wife and one child, Herman), Thompson (with his parents), Walter J. (with parents) and Luther N. (also with parents). Mr. Coke espoused the cause of the Confederacy, and in 1862 enlisted in Beauregard's scouts in Baxter's battalion. He was in the battle of Corinth, Boneyard, and a great many skirmishes throughout Mississippi, Alabama and Tennessee, and held the rank of lieutenant in Colonel Lowerie's regiment. He was paroled in the spring of 1865. Mr. Coke is a democrat, and both he and wife, as well as the children, are members of the Mississippi Missionary Baptist church. In connection with his fine farm, Mr. Coke is the owner of a good country store at Gift, and is doing a good business.

George E. Colbert is one of the enterprising and substantial merchants of Attala county, Miss., and is a native of the state in which he resides, his birth having occurred in Noxubee county September 17, 1848. His father, H. H. Colbert, was born in Georgia, and when a young man came to Mississippi and was married in Noxubee county to Miss Martha Beeman, a native of North Carolina. He was a planter throughout life, at which he was reasonably successful, and was following this calling at the time of his death in 1854. After the death of her husband Mrs. Colbert moved with her family to Leake county, and her eldest son, who afterward became a colonel in the Confederate army, assumed the management of her plantation and business and took charge of the family. He had been well educated, and for a young man possessed exceptionally sound judgment and practical views, and accordingly was successful in everything he undertook. He was a delegate to the convention that framed the ordinance of secession, and afterward raised the first company from Leake county. He was elected colonel of the Twenty-seventh Mississippi regiment of infantry, the first regiment of the Confederate army. He was later made colonel of the Fortieth Mississippi infantry, which regiment he commanded until the close of the war, when not in command of a brigade. After the battle of Franklin, Tenn., notwithstanding the fact that he had a furlough in his pocket, he resolved to stand by the Confederacy to the last, and started across the country to North Carolina and joined Johnston's army. He was put in command of Loring's division, and was leading that army when killed in March, 1865. George E. Colbert was left an orphan at the age of fifteen years, and when the war closed between the states his property, consisting of slaves, being freed, he was left entirely destitute. He was then compelled to take upon himself the burden of life. By his own exertions he educated himself in Professor Gathwright's school, and afterward engaged in clerking at Carthage, where he received thorough and practical business training, which admirably fitted him for a successful career. In 1880 he embarked in the mercantile business for himself at Carthage, and during the five years that he remained at that place he built up an excellent reputation for honorable business methods and for courtesy and attention to the wants of his patrons. He has been a resident of McCool since 1885, and has a large and lucrative trade throughout this section. His store building is commodious; his stock of general merchandise is large and complete, and he does an annual business of about $80,000. He handles about two thousand bales of cotton throughout the year, a considerable portion of which is raised on his own land. He owns several thousand acres of land, a considerable portion of which is in good farming condition. He is one of the most prosperous business men of the county, and attributes much of his success to the hard school in which he received his early training. He was married in Rankin county, Miss., in 1869, to Miss Ella Vogt, a native of Mississippi and an orphan. To them a family of seven children have been born: Mattie, Musette (both of whom are attractive young ladies and graduates of Huntsville female college, of Huntsville, Ala.), Willie (who is attending Central female college), Bruce, George E., Jr., Ella and Vogt C. Mr. Colbert and a brother, William H., a wealthy merchant of Hinds county, are the survivors of their family. Mr. Colbert is a large man, six feet tall, heavily built, and his brother is a little larger than himself, the two together weighing five hundred and sixty pounds. George E. Colbert is of a very genial nature, and has the happy faculty of making those around him feel at once at their ease. He is domestic in his tastes, is deeply attached to his family, and has provided for them a beautiful home at McCool, to which he delights in welcoming his numerous friends. He is full of generosity and charity, and, being free from selfishness, he is ever ready to discommode himself to give comfort or pleasure to others.

Jacob A. Cole, of Summit, Pike county, Miss., was born in this state in Smith county, April 17, 1843. He is the sixth of the eleven children born to Mark and Martha (Curtis) Cole, both of whom were natives of Mississippi. The father was a planter until his death, which occurred in 1878. Our subject was reared in his native state and educated in the private schools of the county. He began life on his own account at the age of twenty-one years, with no capital. He is now a well-to-do planter owning two hundred and seventy-five acres of land, one hundred and fifty acres of which are well cultivated. In 1868 he married Miss Mary A. Reeves, a native of this state and a daughter of J. J. Reeves, also a native of Mississippi. To this union there have been born twelve children, as follows: Benjamin F., Annie L., John W., Wiley J., Mary O., Jacob M., Pattie, and others who are not yet christened. In 1861 our subject enlisted in the Confederate service in company A, Fourteenth regiment, cavalry, which was composed of men from Mississippi and Louisiana. He was in this company but a short time, being discharged because of poor health. He was out of the service for six months and then reënlisted in the same company, with which he remained until the close of the war. He was in the battles of Baker's creek and Clinton. As he was in the cavalry service he of course was in a great many fights, but not in regular engagements. He is a member of the Farmers' Alliance, and is a liberal contributor to all laudable public enterprises, and to all interests that pertain to the good of the community.

William A. Cole, of Garlandsville, Jasper county, Miss., was born in Lowndes county, Ala., in 1830. He was the youngest of a family of eight children, five of whom are yet living. His parents were William and Martha (Alford) Cole, and were natives of Georgia. The former was born in 1789, was one of a large family and came to Garlandsville in 1868. He came of old Virginia stock, and his forefathers served the cause of the colonies in the Revolutionary war. Our subject grew to maturity on his father's plantation in Alabama and removed to Jasper county in 1860. He received his education at the common schools of his county. In 1861 he enlisted in Captain Loper's company, with which his active service was brief, however, as he was discharged on account of disability. Returning home, he went out a little later in a cavalry company with which he served until the close of the war, taking part in most of the battles of the Georgia campaign. Since the war he has been engaged in planting, and has gradually added to his possessions until he now has a plantation of more than a thousand acres, well stocked and well equipped, and he owns a general merchandise store in which he carries a line of goods suitable to the needs of the community. He was married in 1872 to Miss Emma, the daughter of James A. Jones, formerly from north Mississippi, but then a resident of Garlandsville. To Mr. and Mrs. Cole have been born five children, all of whom are living. Mr. Cole has been a member of the Masonic fraternity since 1851. He and his family are communicants of the Methodist Episcopal church South, and he gives liberally of his means toward the support of all worthy enterprises which are presented to him for his aid.

Edward P. Coleman, planter, Melrose, Miss., was born in Panola county, Miss., on the 4th of February, 1852, and there grew to manhood, receiving his education in the private schools of the same. When seventeen years of age he was thrown on his own resources, with no capital, but by dint of hard work and close attention to business he has accumulated considerable property. He is the owner of a plantation of two thousand acres and one thousand acres of this is under cultivation. His farm is well cultivated, is very productive, and Mr. Coleman is considered one of the substantial men of the county. He is possessed of those advanced ideas and principles regarding agricultural life which seem to be among the chief characteristics of Mississippians. He is a stanch democrat, is a prominent man of the county, and was elected a member of the board of supervisors in 1889, which position he filled in a highly creditable manner. He was married in 1886 to Miss Lyde Carruthers, of Mississippi, and the daughter of Dr. S. P. and F. L. Carruthers, also natives of the Bayou state. The result of this union was the birth of one child, Ruth. Mr. Coleman and family are members of the Methodist Episcopal church, and he is a member of the Knights of Honor. He assists with his means and influence all worthy enterprises to improve or develop the county. He is considered one of the first planters of the county and has been successful in everything he has ever undertaken. His beautiful residence, situated six miles south of Como, is in one of the most productive portions of the county and has every convenience that money can purchase. Mr. Coleman is the third of six children born to Edward and Amanda M. (Pope) Coleman, natives of Kentucky and Tennessee, respectively. The father was an extensive planter of Mississippi and the owner of a great many slaves before the war. The paternal grandparents, William H. and Ann Coleman, were natives, respectively, of Virginia and Kentucky, while the maternal grandparents, Dred and Eliza Pope, were natives of North Carolina.

Elias A. Coleman, planter, Canton, Miss., was born in Madison county, Miss., on the 18th of November, 1855, and comes of one of the oldest and wealthiest families of that county. His parents, Christopher C. Coleman and Sallie (Mosby) Coleman, were natives, respectively, of Mississippi and Tennessee. The father was a very extensive planter and was very wealthy, owning a great deal of property before the war. During that eventful period he lost his slaves, and, like many other prominent men of the South, retrograded instead of advancing afterward. He lived a life of usefulness and was honored and respected by all. Our subject's maternal grandmother, Nancy Mosby, was a native of Tennessee. Elias A. Coleman, the younger of two children born to the above mentioned union, passed his boyhood days in assisting on the farm and in attending the private schools of Mississippi. He then engaged in planting, and this has continued to be his chosen occupation. He is now the owner of a fine estate, consisting of one thousand six hundred acres, with eight hundred acres under cultivation, and has been moderately successful in this pursuit. He is a man of excellent judgment, sound practical sense, and is well thought of in the community. He is the only male member of the family now residing in the county. He contributes liberally to all enterprises that have for their object the welfare of the county. In politics he adheres strongly to the democratic party. He has been married twice; first, in 1881, to Miss Lou Smith, a native of Mississippi and the daughter of John and Sarah Smith. To this marriage have been born three children: Mittie, Lou A. and one not named. He was married the second time, in 1887, to Mrs. Gus. (Smith) Reid, a sister of his first wife. Mr. and Mrs. Coleman are members of the Presbyterian church.

Moses W. Coleman is a progressive planter of Bolivar county, Miss., and is a practical, shrewd and intelligent man of business. His birth occurred in Lowndes county, of this state, March 3, 1846, the seventh of eleven children born to Franklin J. and Lucinda E. (Adams) Coleman, who were born in South Carolina. Franklin J. Coleman came to this state in 1835 and here made his home until his death, which occurred in 1869. Although exempt from service he served in the Confederate army during the Rebellion, and after eight months of hard service his health failed and he returned to his home, this being in 1862. His parents were Jesse and Elizabeth (Jordan) Coleman, South Carolinians, who removed to Alabama, where they spent their last days. Hon. A. J. Coleman, who was a member of the Alabama legislature for twelve years, was an uncle of Moses W. Coleman. The maternal grandparents were William and Matilza (Lindsey) Adams, of South Carolina, the former of whom came to Mississippi in his old age. He was of English descent, as were also the Lindseys, the Colemans being of English and Welsh ancestry. Moses W. Coleman was principally reared in Bolivar county, where he is acknowledged to be a prosperous and practical planter, and although his early educational advantages were not of the best, only three months of his life being spent in school, he has acquired an excellent knowledge of matters and things by contact with the world and the business affairs of life. Since he attained his majority he has been working for himself, and believing that it is not so much the dew of heaven as earnest labor that fertilizes the soil, he manfully put his shoulder to the wheel and has become the owner of eighteen hundred acres of land, of which fourteen hundred acres are under cultivation, and have been improved from canebrake. He erected a neat residence on his plantation in 1869 and another in Cleveland in 1889, in which place his real and personal property amounts to some $18,000. Being one of the first settlers of the eastern part of the county and progressive in his views, he had done more for this section and the town of Cleveland than any one of its residents, and was the first man to sell goods in the eastern part of the county, his stock of merchandise in Cleveland now amounting to about $2,000. In 1872 Miss Kate C. Taylor became his wife, she being a native of Madison county, Miss., and a daughter of Leonard L. and Sudie (Shearer) Taylor, natives of Alabama. To Mr. and Mrs. Coleman the following children have been born: John M., James B., Susie M., Moses, Franklin, Wiley A., Corrie, Ethel, Annie Hester and Amon L. Five of this family are living and reside with their parents. Mr. Coleman, his wife and one daughter are members of the Methodist Episcopal church, and socially he belongs to the A. F. & A. M., and the K. of H. Mr. Coleman deserves much credit for the admirable way in which he has surmounted the many difficulties that have strewn his pathway, for besides starting out in life after he had attained his majority with little or no means, his education was very limited also, owing to the fact that his father settled in a new country where schools were very few, and of an inferior description, and was not able financially to send his children away to school. Mr. Coleman's present knowledge of affairs has been acquired through hard experience, and as he has endeavored at all times to live a life of Christianity, and has been liberal in helping the needy and aiding his fellowmen, no man stands higher in the love and esteem of his fellows. Indeed, it is said by those who know him that he and perhaps two or three other men have made the county what it now is. He has never speculated but has followed the quiet life of the farmer, and has been rewarded with abundance, his property real and personal being richly worth $80,000, most of his property consisting of as fine bodies of land as are to be found in the Yazoo delta.

Among the pioneer families of Madison county, Miss., was that of Isaiah Coleman, who settled there at an early day. For a few years he resided in Jefferson county, Miss., where E. H. Coleman, the father of the subject of this sketch, was born, who passed his boyhood and youth in Madison county, however, and acquired an education at Oakland college. He was married in Jefferson county, Miss., to Miss Mary Gilchrist, daughter of the Hon. Malcomb Gilchrist, one of the pioneers of Jefferson county, and one of the earliest representatives in the legislature. The Gilchrist family was from North Carolina. After his marriage, E. H. Coleman located in Madison county, on land entered from the government by his father. He had been engaged in planting but a few years when he was cut off in the early prime of manhood, about 1854, being twenty-eight years of age. His widow survives him at this writing. She is the mother of four children, two of whom are living: Anna, the wife of Chancellor Peyton, deceased; Mrs. Peyton is the founder of the Industrial institute of Columbus, Miss.; the other child is Samuel R. Coleman, in whose name this short biography is written. He was born in Madison county, Miss., October 19, 1847. He received more than an ordinary literary education at Hillsboro, N. C., during the war, and the University of Mississippi after the war. In 1864, although only seventeen years of age, he ran away from Hillsboro and entered the Confederate army, joining the battalion of Bradford's scouts, which operated between Natchez, Vicksburg and Port Hudson. He served until the close of the war, and then entered the University of Mississippi, for the purpose of continuing his studies. After he had finished the course laid down by that institution, he returned to his home, and took charge of the home place, where he carried on planting for several years. Abandoning agriculture, he went to southern Mississippi, and taught school in Copiah, Lincoln and Jefferson counties for several years, in fact until 1877. He had read law in 1867, under the personal direction of Col. L. Q. C. Lamar, now associate justice of the United States supreme court, and afterward, in leisure hours, when teaching school, being admitted to the bar in 1875. As before stated, he continued to teach until 1877. In January, of that year, he came to Greenwood, and entered upon the practice of law. Since that time he has devoted his energies and time to making for himself a place in the foremost ranks of the attorneys of Mississippi. Politically, he affiliates with the democratic party, and zealously supports all party measures. He has served as a delegate to numerous county and state conventions. He was married in Greenwood, February 13, 1879, to Miss Lucy Wadlington, who was born and reared in that part of Carroll now Le Flore county, being a daughter of one of the pioneer families in Madison county, that finally settled in Carroll county. Mr. and Mrs. Coleman have two children living: Lizzie May and Samuel E. Believing in the benefits growing from close association with his fellow-men, Mr. Coleman is an active member of the Knights of Pythias. He is a progressive citizen, a man of earnest, honest thought,

36

and one of whom his professional brothers may be proud. Though often solicited by his fellow-countrymen to represent them in the legislature of the state, he has invariably declined, preferring the quiet of home to the turmoil of political life, yet holding no duty too arduous when called upon by his clients to render professional services. The weak and oppressed, the widow and the orphan, always gain a ready sympathy and command of his services.

Dr. T. P. Coleman, Oxford, Miss., has been identified with the professional history of Lafayette county since 1878, since which time he has been one 'of the leading physicians and surgeons. He was born in North Carolina in 1836, and is the eldest child of James and Mary Ann (Smith) Coleman, also natives of North Carolina. The paternal grandfather, Phillip Coleman, was born in Strasburg, Germany, and emigrated to the United States in his youth, settling in Pennsylvania; later he removed to North Carolina, where he passed the remainder of his life. The maternal grandfather was of Scotch-Irish extraction, and was a native of North Carolina. James Coleman grew to manhood in the state in which he was born, and followed farming as an occupation; he died in 1848, and his wife is still living. T. P. Coleman, son of the above, was educated at Davidson college, North Carolina, graduating in the class of 1855; the following year he began the study of medicine in that world-renowned institute, the University of Pennsylvania, and was graduated from the medical department in 1859; he returned to North Carolina, and was deeply engrossed in the practice of medicine when the great Civil war burst upon the country. He did not shirk his duty for private interests, but at once enlisted in a company and was afterward assistant surgeon of the Fifth North Carolina cavalry. He served in this capacity until the close of the war, and then settled at Gold Hill, N. C., resuming the practice of his profession. He resided there until 1868, and then removed to Mississippi, locating in Panola county. In 1878, as before stated, he came to Oxford, and has since been engaged in professional work, in addition to which he is also interested, to a considerable extent, in farming and stockraising. The Doctor was first married, in 1869, to Miss Willie L., daughter of W. S. Jones, of Panola county. She died in 1875, leaving three children: Daniel G., Annie M., and Willie Jones. The second marriage was in 1881, when Dr. Coleman was united to Mrs. S. F. Thompson, a daughter of George Fox, an early settler of Panola county and an extensive planter; she was first married to a son of Jacob Thompson. The family are all members of the Episcopal church, and the Doctor is a member of the Masonic fraternity; he is a member of the State Medical association, and is well posted on all topics of professional interest. He was one of the active promoters of the public school building of Oxford, and was a member of the building committee. This is an excellent structure and reflects credit upon those who managed its erection. Dr. Coleman has been a member of the board of aldermen of Oxford for four years, doing good service to the town in that capacity. He is one of the firm of R. R. Chilton & Co., dealers in drugs; they carry a full line of drugs and have conducted a successful business since 1880.

Jonathan N. Collier has been a resident of the state of Mississippi almost from the time of his birth, which occurred in Worcester county, Md., in 1824, coming to Warren county, Miss., with his father, Robert Collier, in 1829. The latter was a mechanic and followed his occupation until his death in 1830. By his wife, formerly Miss Margaret Nichols, of Maryland, he became the father of seven children, to wit: Jane A., who died in 1877, at about the age of seventy years, was married three times, first, to Felix Thompson, second, to John W. Miller, and lastly to William B. Sims; James M. was a planter and died in 1878, at the age of sixty-four years; Robert J. died at the age of fifteen years; George W., a planter, died in Hinds county, Miss., in 1877; Joshua A., a planter, died in Sharkey county, Miss., in

1873; Levin H., died in 1880 at Arcola, Miss.; and Jonathan N. The Colliers came from England in the early days of American settlement and became residents of the state of Maryland, of which state the Nicholses were also residents, coming thither from England. Mrs. Collier had two brothers: James, who lived and died in Maryland, and Thomas, who was in the war of 1812 and died while in the service at Baltimore. Jonathan N. Collier was educated in the public schools of Warren county, but it must be said that his advantages were very meager. He acquired the most of his knowledge of books by his own efforts after he had left school. After the war, to obtain bread, he began practicing law in Deer Creek, a calling he continued to follow for two years, and for six years was justice of the peace in the same place. He began life for himself by planting at the early age of sixteen years, and although he left home without a cent and was bankrupted by the war, he now has an excellent little plantation of one hundred and fifty acres, one hundred and twenty of which are under cultivation, all of which was cleared and improved by himself, and on which is erected a comfortable and substantial residence. He was first married in 1851 to Mrs. Savilla C. Knox, a daughter of Simon Robinson. She was born in South Carolina, and by Mr. Collier became the mother of four children: Patton K., who died at the age of twenty-one; James M., who is in Fresno, Cal.; Giles M., who died in 1870, and Lucretia, who died in infancy. After the death of this wife, Mr. Collier married, in 1859, Miss Mary Ann Robertson, who has borne him two sons, to wit: George, who resides near Arcola managing a plantation, and Garvin, who is still at home. The mother of these children is a granddaughter of the celebrated Horseshoe Robertson, of Revolutionary fame, and was born in Horseshoe Bend, S. C. Mr. Collier, in 1846, enlisted in company C, First Mississippi Rifles, and while in Mexico, was in the battles of Monterey and Buena Vista, receiving his discharge in 1847. During the Rebellion he entered as orderly sergeant in company G, Fortieth Alabama regiment, this being in 1862; was promoted to second lieutenant and then to first lieutenant. He was in the siege of Vicksburg, the battle of Missionary ridge, and was on the retreat through Georgia, being wounded at Noonday creek in 1864, his left arm being disabled. Prior to the war he had accumulated a fortune valued at from $20,000 to $25,000, mostly in negroes, but of course lost them all by the emancipation proclamation. His present property, which amounts to about $10,000, was accumulated in about fifteen years. Since the war closed he has lived a quiet, uneventful life, continuing to steadily pursue the even tenor of his way, and is now in the enjoyment of a hale and hearty old age. He is a Mason, a democrat, and has served as a member of the board of supervisors. During the forty years that he has resided in Washington county he has proved himself to be one of the most substantial, upright and worthy citizens, and liberal aid and support have been given by him to all laudable enterprises. He is a pleasant, agreeable and intelligent conversationalist and one is at once impressed with his remarkable memory and his knowledge of state affairs. Although a self-made man, and made under the most discouraging circumstances, he possesses rare qualifications as a citizen.

There is probably no man more widely known in De Soto county, Miss., than DeWitt C. Collins, M. D., Pleasant Hill, where he has been actively engaged in the practice of medicine for the past thirty-seven years. He was born in Halifax county, Va., November 1, 1829, and is the fourth of a family of ten children. His parents, Jones W. and Margarette (Tunes) Collins, were also natives of Virginia. The father was a primitive Baptist minister; he came to Mississippi in 1837, and died in 1851; he was among the first settlers of De Soto county, and faced many trials and privations in those days of frontier life. The paternal grandfather of the Doctor was John W. Collins, of Virginia, and the maternal grandfather was John T. Tunes, also a Virginian by birth.   Dr. Collins was reared in Mississippi and was educated in the private schools of the community.   In 1852 he went to Memphis, and entered the Botanico Medical college, from which he was graduated in 1854.   He at once began practice, locating near Pleasant Hill, De Soto county.   At the age of twenty-one years he began to face the world on his own account, and without any capital acquired his professional training, and established himself in business.   He is the owner of one hundred and forty-five acres, one hundred of which he has placed under good cultivation.   He was united in marriage in 1855 to Miss Elizabeth J. Dunn, a native of Georgia.   They have had born to them six children: Charles S., Mary E., Ida J., Annie C., Alice B., and Lelia D.   They are all members of the Methodist Episcopal church South.   Dr. Collins is a member of the I. O. O. F. fraternity.   He has always been a liberal contributor to laudable public enterprises, and has assisted materially in the upbuilding of the county.   In addition to his plantation he owns a valuable piece of real estate in Memphis.   Politically he affiliates with the democratic party, but takes no active part in the movements of that body.   He is a lover of law and order, and believes in the election of honest, upright men.   Although sixty-two years of age he has lost none of his youthful vigor, and his strong, muscular frame is still erect.   He is a fine type of manhood, courteous in his manner, social of disposition, and well worthy of the high esteem in which he is held.

Every community has among its citizens a few men of recognized influence and ability, who, by their systematic and careful, thorough manner of work, attain to a success which is justly deserved.   Among this class is Elisha P. Collins, so well known in Pope, Miss., as a prominent planter and a successful merchant of Panola county.   He was born in Henderson county, Tenn., May 13, 1845, and was the fourth of ten children born to James D. and Louisa (McKenzie) Collins, natives of Tennessee.   The elder Collins moved to Marshall county, Miss., in 1847, and there followed the occupation to which he had been reared, that of a mechanic.   He reared five of his ten children to maturity, all of whom became highly respected and a credit to their parents.   The paternal grandfather, Peter Collins, was a native of Scotland.   Elisha P. Collins was reared in Marshall and Lafayette counties, Miss., and on account of his father not being able to send him off to school, he obtained very little education save what a good native ability has enabled him to gather in his career through life.   Entering the Confederate army when but sixteen years of age, in company B, First Mississippi cavalry, he participated in the battle of Spring Hill, the Johnson campaign through Georgia, and Hood's campaign through Tennessee.   He surrendered at Selma, Ala., and then returned home, resuming his occupation as a farmer.   He started after the war penniless, but he has kept steadily to work, and is now in very comfortable circumstances indeed.   He is a hard-working, cautious business man, is upright and honest, and what he has accumulated in the way of this world's goods has been the result of his own good fighting qualities.   For four years after the war he followed farming, then attended school a year, and subsequently became salesman in the store of C. F. Chapman, in Pope, continuing in that capacity for seven years.   After this he returned to his farm, operated it for six years, and then returned to Pope, where he purchased one-third interest in the business of F. C. Simms & Co.   In 1887 he bought out his partners and became sole proprietor of the business, his annual sales amounting to $20,000.   He is also the owner of about two hundred acres of land.   Mr. Collins was married in 1874 to Miss Lou T. Sims, a native of Mississippi and a daughter of Thomas M. and Unica (Rogers) Sims, natives of Virginia and Mississippi respectively.   The fruits of this union have been four children: Lilly S., Minnie Lee, Katie Lou, and Daisy Weston, all at home but the eldest, who is attending school at Blue Mountain college. Mr. and Mrs. Collins are members of the Baptist church, and Mr. Collins is deacon in the same. In politics he is an outspoken democrat, strongly opposed to what is known as the subtreasury scheme.

Frank Pierce Collins, merchant of Hardy station, and a successful planter of the county, comes of an old and honored family of Mississippi. He was born in Yalobusha county (now Grenada county), near Hardy station, in 1854, and is the son of Joseph and Elizabeth (Johnson) Collins, the father a native of North Carolina and the mother of Virginia. Joseph Collins was born on the 31st of March, 1779, and was first married on the 12th of April, 1804, to a Miss Williams, who bore him these children: Louisa (born in 1805, is the mother of Mrs. Col. Barksdale; see sketch of Col. H. H. Barksdale), Moses (died at middle age, leaving a family), and one that died when a child. Mr. Collins came to Mississippi in 1835, and on the 17th of November, 1847, he married Miss Elizabeth Johnson, who was a native of the Old Dominion, and the daughter of Dock Johnson, of that state. The children born to this union are named, in the order of their births, as follows: Joseph (born August 15, 1849, and died January 27, 1865, while attending school), Moses B. (is a planter of Coahoma county, Miss.), Franklin Pierce, Lizzie (wife of George W. Jones, a leading merchant of Grenada; see sketch), and Susanah (wife of William C. McLean, a prominent attorney at Grenada; see sketch). Of the above mentioned children Joseph and Lizzie were twins. Mr. Collins was one of the most influential and prosperous men of the county, and was the owner of considerable wealth at the time of his death, which occurred on the 30th of November, 1858; was the owner of large tracts of land in Coahoma and Yalobusha counties, and the owner also of considerable real estate in Grenada. He was a leading member of the Baptist church, and was one of the builders and founders of Antioch church, which is the oldest organization in Yalobusha county. He was one of its most earnest and faithful workers and liberal supporters. He took no part in politics except to vote, but was a great admirer of Franklin Pierce, and named his son after that illustrious man. After the death of Mr. Collins, his widow married Charles Lindsay, of Virginia, born in 1827, and one daughter, Fannie, was the result of this union. She is the wife of R. E. Winberley, and resides in Coffeeville, Miss., where she is proprietress of the Newberger hotel, one of the best equipped in that city. Franklin Pierce Collins was reared in his native county, and supplemented a common-school education by a two years' course at Thomas Gathright's school in Noxubee county, Miss. He then returned to the home place, and there remained until coming to Hardy station. He commenced merchandising at the last named place in 1882, and in connection carried on planting and stock farming with great success. He is the owner of about twelve hundred acres of land, and makes about one hundred and fifty bales of cotton yearly. He has also been quite successful as a merchant, his annual sales yielding him about $20,000 per year. He wedded Miss Annie Z. Barksdale, an accomplished and attractive young lady, and a graduate from the school at Jackson, where she excelled in art and elocution. She is the daughter of Dr. Barksdale, of Grenada. Mr. and Mrs. Collins are the parents of one child, Lizzie. They are members of the Methodist church at Grenada, and are very highly respected, socially and otherwise. He votes with the democratic party.

Will E. Collins, planter, Mayersville, Miss., the second child and eldest son of T. Jeff and Martha (Spurlock) Collins, was born in Carroll parish, La., in 1844. His father, who was a native Kentuckian, went to Louisiana in 1830 with his two brothers, William and George, both older than himself, and with them located in Carroll parish, where they were among the first settlers. They were extensively engaged in planting and merchandising, accumulated considerable property in slaves and real estate, and became prominent men of the parish.

The father was a lieutenant in the Mexican war and was in the battle of Buena Vista. He was with General Taylor, and served with distinction during the entire war. His death occurred in 1862. He followed planting his entire life, and was one of the most successful planters of the parish. He was a member of both the I. O. O. F. and the A. F. & A. M. lodges. By his marriage to Miss Spurlock, a native of Louisiana, he became the father of eight children: Mary E. (of Sharkey county, Miss.), Hattie (now Mrs. J. W. Harrington, of Atlanta, whose husband served as colonel in the Federal army under General Banks), Martha (now Mrs. J. T. Grambling, of Sharkey county), Janie (wife of E. V. Miller, who is brother of the attorney-general of the state), Ann (wife of John Stephen, a planter of Issaquena county), Daniel B. (deceased) and Thomas G. (deceased). Will E. Collins received his literary education at La Grange military academy, and graduated from that institution in 1862. After leaving school he served his county as drillmaster for a short time, and then entered the Confederate army, company A, Eighteenth Louisiana infantry, Mouton's division. While in the army he participated in the battles of Mansfield, Texarkana and Shiloh, and in the last-named engagement his regiment was badly slaughtered. It was afterward reorganized and consolidated with the Crescent regiment, and then participated in the battles of Texarkana, Mansfield and others. He was paroled in Shreveport, La., and then returned home, where he engaged in steamboating on the Mississippi river and tributaries. In 1867 he came to Issaquena county, and the following year embarked in merchandising, which he followed until 1873, after which he was deputy sheriff for four years. The two years following this he was cotton taxcollector for the second Mississippi levee district, and in 1879 he was elected a member of the board of supervisors, serving in that capacity for two years. The same year he began planting, and this has continued ever since. He was appointed justice of the peace of the Fourth district by Governor Stone, and has held other local positions. He is essentially a modern man, full of energy, enterprise and push, and is well posted on all subjects of interest, especially on the early settlement of the county. He has one of the finest libraries of selected books said to be in the county, and is a regular correspondent for various agricultural papers, chiefly the *Home and Farm*, of Louisville, and the *Southern Farm*, published at Atlanta, Ga. He is a member of the Odd Fellow lodge, and Deer Creek lodge No. 156, A. F. & A. M. Mr. Collins was married, in 1877, to Miss Mary E. Smith, sister of R. M. Smith (see sketch), and to them have been born four children: Willie, Mamie, Robert and Jefferson.

W. H. Collins, merchant, Booneville, Prentiss county, Miss., was originally from North Carolina, born in Anson county, of that state, September, 1828. He is a descendant of Zacheus Collins, who came to this country during the war between the colonies and Great Britain, and took part in that struggle. After the Declaration of Independence and peace was declared, he settled in North Carolina, where he married Miss Anna Head and became the father of two sons and a number of daughters. William, the elder moved to the state of Illinois, in its early settlement, and from the meagerness of the postal service in those days, was lost to the balance of the family. Zacheus, the younger son, remained in his native state, where he married Miss Elizabeth Sharp, and was the father of seven sons and two daughters. Surviving his first wife, he married the second, a widow lady, Mrs. Walden, who lived only a few years after this event, leaving one son as the fruit of this marriage. The father of these children was by occupation a farmer, and like his mother, who died at the advanced age of one hundred and four years, lived to a ripe old age. William, the third son by the first wife, and the father of the subject of this sketch, was born November 3, 1803, and was married to Miss Mary Faulk, second daughter of Nicholas and Rhoda Faulk, in 1824. They reared a family of eight children, five of whom are now living: William H.,

Jordan W., Moses L., Ephraim and Mary J. The father followed the pursuit of his ancestors and was a farmer. In politics he affiliated with the democratic party. Both parents were consistent members of the Baptist church to the end of life. The father was also an official member of his church for a number of years. Mrs. Collins died in April, 1854, and Mr. Collins followed her to the grave in May, 1878, and rest together in the family graveyard. W. H. Collins was the second son of this marriage, and like the average country boy, in his early life became familiar with the duties of the farm, and received a practical education in the common schools. He left school in 1854, and followed the business of teaching in North Carolina for two years, when he was elected surveyor of Union county, which office he filled for eight years. In 1858 he was a candidate for the office of sheriff in his county and was defeated by a plurality of sixty-seven votes. He was also a justice of the peace in his county for a number of years, and resigned the office when he left the Old North state. He was married in 1861 to Miss Parmelia Doster, a native of his state, as were also her parents, James M. and Nancy (Hargett) Doster. Mrs. Collins was born in Mecklenburg county, in 1840, about the time of the formation of Union from subdivisions of Anson and Mecklenburg counties. She was the eldest of the following children: Robert, John R., Amanda, Leah, Alice, Fletcher G., Mary J. and Minor J. Mr. and Mrs. Doster, with their family, moved from North Carolina in 1866, and settled in Marshall county, Miss., where they prospered in farming for six years, and then moved to Alcorn county in the same state, where they were alike successful till 1887, and again they moved, this time to the Lone Star state, settling in McLennon county, Tex., where Mr. Doster died in a few months, and Mrs. Doster survived him only about two years. The balance of the family moved from there to Hardeman county, northwest Texas, where they are reported to be in prosperous condition. Mr. Collins, after marriage, settled in his native state, and in 1862 enlisted as a private under Capt. L. A. Johnston, company A, Fourth regiment North Carolina cavalry, under command of Col. D. D. Ferrebee, and served in the Southern army alternately as private, regimental commissary and bugler till the surrender of Gen. R. E. Lee's army at Appomattox courthouse, Va. Among the principal engagements in which he participated were those about Franklin, Va., Middleburg, Upperville, Gettysburg, Brandy station, Manassas junction and about Petersburg and Richmond, connected with some important sallies, one of which was led by General Hampton in rear of General Grant's army at Petersburg, capturing a good number of prisoners, two thousand and four hundred head of beef cattle, and destroying immense quantities of provisions and other stores. After the surrender Mr. Collins returned to his home in North Carolina, arriving there the 17th of April, 1865, where he found everything in a state of dilapidation—fences rotting down and fields grown up in bushes and briars. But gathering up as best he could he planted a crop and succeeded in making enough to carry him over to the next year. In 1867 he moved, with his family, to the state of Mississippi, and settled in De Soto county, where he was profitably engaged in the pursuit of farming for five years.

In 1873 he came to Prentiss county and located in Booneville, where he has resided ever since. Here he embarked in the grocery business, following it with success, and is now classed among the foremost business men of the place. He owns a handsome residence, with everything seemingly pleasant and convenient about the premises. His marriage resulted in the birth of six children, four of whom are living: Rufus H., Winnie D., Albert L. and Howard B. Mr. and Mrs. Collins are both members of the church, and though united hand and heart in all other affairs of life, yet they have suffered themselves to be divided in church life, he being of the Baptist persuasion and she of the Methodist, though she has the honor of carrying the balance of the family with her in religious faith. Rufus H., the eldest son, quit school in 1882, and has followed the railroad business continuously since that time, and is now operator in telegraphy. Minnie D., the only daughter, graduated in English literature and music at Huntsville female college, 1883, and was married to Rev. E. L. Spragins, a Methodist minister, in 1884. They are at present stationed at Plano, Collin county, Tex., and have the care of two charming little daughters, E. Louise and Lyda May. In character Mr. Collins seems to be one of those unassuming gentlemen whose chief aspiration is an honest living, without that morbid ambition which sometimes leads to the wreck of fortune and character in pursuit of political fame or distinction, which at best may last but for a season. He has held some minor positions in his adopted home. For a short while he was county surveyor of Prentiss and alderman in his town. He is also a master Mason and a Knight of Honor, and has occasionally held office in both these orders and at present holds office in both his lodges. He is a man of public spirit, however, and deeply interested in educational and religious enterprises and, in fact, anything which inures to public good, and, like his father, is a stanch democrat and alive to the interests of his party; but without accepting it as perfect or believing it the only field in which a good man can be found, however, he believes it is one in whose hands our national interests are safe and one of the best political parties in the world.

W. H. Collins, Dover, Miss., has been a life-long resident of Yazoo county, and is one of her most loyal and patriotic citizens. He was born December 15, 1833, and is a son of Saebary and Mary (May) Collins, natives of Georgia. His father came with his parents to Pike county, Miss., at the age of ten years. When sixteen years old he enlisted as a soldier in the war of 1812, and at the age of nineteen years he was married. In 1821 he came to Yazoo county; there were then but few white people in the county; deer roamed the forests at will, and there were bears, panthers, and wild-cats in great numbers. He first entered eight hundred and eighty acres of land, nearly all of which he improved. At one time he owned nineteen hundred and forty acres, the whole of which he lost on a security debt. He was a stanch believer in the principles of the democratic party, with which he voted all his life. He died in 1868, and his wife died in 1871, both being seventy-three years of age at the time of death. W. H. Collins passed his boyhood days in the county of Yazoo, and was early trained to the occupation of planting. At the age of twenty-one years he began life for himself, and was engaged in agriculture until the breaking out of the Civil war. He entered the Confederate service in 1861, enlisting in infantry. He was mustered out of the infantry in three months to aid in forming General Withers' light artillery. He and two brothers were in the siege of Vicksburg, and at Port Hudson, where they lay in the ditches forty-nine days; they were captured, and were paroled at Natchez and afterward exchanged. He then joined Colonel Woods' cavalry, in which he fought until the end of the war; he was in several close skirmishes, and saw some active service. When peace was declared he resumed his agricultural interests, and also made some investments in mercantile trade at Dover, Yazoo county. He has about one hundred and fifty acres under cultivation, and at present owns but three hundred acres, having sold off the greater portion. Mr. Collins was united in marriage in 1864 to Miss Leila High, a daughter of John and Mary (Long) High, natives of the old Keystone state. By this union a son and daughter have been born: Annie, wife of F. F. Holmes, of Bentonia and C. Dudley. Mrs. Collins died May 25, 1888. Our subject is a member of the Masonic fraternity and belongs both to the Blue lodge and chapter; he has served as master of the former, and as high priest of the latter. He belongs to the Knights of Honor and to the Knights of Pythias. He has always given public questions much serious attention, and has aided liberally in the carrying out of all movements which have tended to the growth and progress of the community.

John J. Coman, a well-known general merchant of Iuka, Tishomingo county, Miss., is one of eight children born to James M. and Elizabeth J. (Mason) Coman. His father was born February 9, 1808, at Wadesboro, N. C., and was the son of Robert and Jane W. (Prout) Coman. He removed to Athens, Ala., with his parents when young, and was educated at that place and at Huntsville, Ala., and began business for himself in 1825 at the age of about seventeen years, and became a merchant and planter. He was married in Alabama about 1832 and moved to the eastern part of Tishomingo county, Miss., in 1844, where he engaged in farming and merchandising. His prominence here may be inferred from the fact that he was the first chancery clerk of Tishomingo county after its division. He had a family of seven children, of whom six are living: Mary, who is the wife of Governor Stone; Sarah; Margaret, who married Judge Alexander; James W.; Rebecca and John J. Robert died in 1861. Mr. Coman came to Iuka in 1860, and afterward, until his death, in 1886, took an active and helpful interest in the progress of the town, serving his fellow-citizens at one time as a member of the common council. Politically, he was an adherent of the democratic party. At the beginning of the war he was too old for military service, but served the Confederate cause at all times in any way within his power. He was long a member of the Masonic fraternity. He was an active, public-spirited, successful business man and enjoyed the respect of all who knew him. The mother of our subject was born in Virginia in 1813, a daughter of Robert and Mary Mason. Her father was prominent in Virginia, but moved to Alabama soon after 1820. He and his wife were both members of the Methodist Episcopal church and they died at Athens, Ala., where they had long made their home. Mrs. Coman was a cousin of John Mason, who was secretary of war during President Buchanan's administration and also represented the United States at the court of St. James. She died in Iuka, Miss., in 1876. The early life of John J. Coman was spent in the mercantile business, with which he became connected at the age of sixteen. He passed ten years at Athens, Ala., and then went to Texas. After two years' residence there he came to Iuka, Miss., and succeeded to his father's business. He has carried this on interruptedly to the present time. In 1884 he married Miss Anna Greasbeck, daughter of William and Maria (Fuller) Greasbeck. Her father was born in New York city in 1818, a son of Abraham and Elizabeth (Alexander) Greasbeck, his mother having been a daughter of Rev. Carlos Alexander, of Onondaga county, N. Y., and his wife, who was a daughter of Asa Fuller, of Little Falls, N. Y. Mrs. Coman was born in the state of New York, February 27, 1855, one of four children of her parents, named as follows: Maria E., Mary E., Laura and Anna. Her mother died in Little Falls, N. Y., in 1864, and her father married Harriet G. Philips, a daughter of John Philips, and she had four children: Elizabeth, Celia, Harriet and Frederick. Mr. and Mrs. Coman have two children living and have lost two by death: James G., Celia R., Mary (deceased) and Margaret (deceased). Mr. Coman has, besides his large store, a plantation of four hundred acres, located three miles east of Iuka. He raises cotton, corn and other products common to this section, and is somewhat interested in live stock, making a specialty of goats and sheep. Both as a merchant and as a planter he has been very successful. He is a member of the Presbyterian church, in which he holds the office of elder, and of the Knights of Honor. For the past five years he has held the office of secretary and treasurer of the city council of Iuka. In his youth he had only common-school advantages, but since that time he has informed himself by general reading and observation to such an extent that he is one of the most intelligent men in the town. The lack of educational advantages in his boyhood impressed upon his mind the need of better school facilities at this day, and he is one of the most ardent friends of education in the county. He has also contributed liberally to the support of schools, churches, charities and other good objects, and is recognized as a public-spirited and useful citizen. Politically, he is a democrat, and his local influence is not inconsiderable, as is evidenced by the fact that he has served as chairman of the democratic county committee.

B. J. Conner is a planter of Attala county, Miss., but is a Georgian by birth, his father, Uriah Conner, a native of Newberry district, S. C., having moved to Georgia in 1816, settling in Franklin county, where he became a successful planter. He was also an active politician, and filled with credit a number of local positions of honor and trust. While a resident of the state of Georgia he was married in 1813 to Miss Rebecca Chaplear, and to their union ten children were born: Harriet, Eliza, Mary, B. J., Francis T., Elizabeth, Uriah M., John L., Julia C. and Gabriel. Only three of the family are now living. Uriah Conner was a soldier in the war of 1812, from its commencement to its close, and was discharged at Mobile, Ala. He died in Mississippi in 1849, his widow passing from life in Attala county, Miss., in 1887, on the old homestead. The paternal grandparents were natives of South Carolina, while the mother's people were Georgians. B. J. Conner was reared principally in Mississippi and in this state was married in 1844 to Miss Ann L. Porter, an Alabamian by birth. She was born in 1822 and has borne her husband the following children: Isabel, Susan, Beryl T., Uriah B., Rebecca, John H., William, Mary (deceased), Mattie F. (deceased), Lucian, a physician now in Texas; Lucy, Julia, Charles (deceased), Henrietta and T. O. Conner, present chancery clerk of this county. Mr. Conner is one of the oldest planters of Attala county, and has a very desirable and fertile plantation in the northern part of the county, on which he raises an abundance of the principal products of the South. He is known far and near for his generosity and hospitality, and so friendly are his relations with all who know him that he is familiarly known as Uncle Boley Conner.

Capt. Farar B. Conner. The first member of this well-known family to come to Adams county, Miss., was William Conner, a native of South Carolina, who, as early as 1790, settled at Natchez, where he followed the occupation of a lawyer. He was married to Miss Mary Savage, and afterward turned his attention to planting, in which occupation he succeeded in a remarkable manner, and became wealthy. They had several children, among whom was William Conner, born in Adams county in 1797. He was married to Miss Jane Elizabeth Boyd Gustine, a native of Carlisle, Penn., their union taking place in 1824 and resulting in the birth of ten children, six of whom are living at the present time: Lemuel P.; Farar B., the subject of this biography; Richard E.; Margaret, wife of General Martin, of Natchez; Annie E., wife of Dr. Bisland, also of Natchez, and Mary D., wife of T. C. Witherspoon, of St. Louis, Mo. Capt. Farar B. Conner first saw the light of day in Adams county, Miss., in the year 1834, and after obtaining a better schooling than is usually secured, he finished his education in the famous college of Yale at New Haven, Conn. Upon commencing to make his own way in the world he began following the occupation of a planter, and this has received the greater part of his attention up to the present time. In 1856 Miss Mary E., the daughter of John T. McMurran, became his wife, but after a wedded life of seven years he was called upon to mourn the death of his worthy and estimable wife, she leaving him with two children to care for, another child having previously died. Mary Louisa and John McMurran died in childhood, and Benjamin Farar is living. When the war became an assured fact Mr. Conner espoused the Confederate cause, joining a company of cavalry from Adams county, his being the first to leave Natchez. He was a private in the army of Virginia until the fall of 1862, when he was promoted, and in 1863 became a member of Bragg's army, being on the staff of General Martin. He was wounded and captured at the battle of Shelbyville, and was in the military prison at Johnson's island for thirteen months. At the end of this time he started for home, with the intention of again entering the Confederate army, but before he could reach the Confederate lines the war had closed. He then spent five years as a planter in the Lone Star state, at the end of which time he returned to Natchez, which place he has since made his home. He is a kind, generous and hospitable gentleman, and in the domestic circle is a model husband and father. His sympathies are keen, and to alleviate the sufferings and misfortunes of others he has been liberal in his charities. His manners are polished and courtly, and to the numerous friends that have gathered around him he is faithful and true. December 10, 1889, he was married to Miss Maria Chotard, and he and his wife are now residing on the old Chotard homestead.

Andrew Conner, father of W. McD. Conner, of Macon, Noxubee county, Miss., was born in North Carolina about 1798, and married Rosanna McDavid, and died in Noxubee county, Miss., in 1853. He purchased land here in 1836, and removed here in 1847, and was a successful planter. His widow yet survives him, and is a resident of the northeast part of the county. This lady now owns one thousand two hundred acres of land, and is an extensive planter. She is now ninety-one years of age, and is the oldest inhabitant in the county. She was the mother of eleven children. W. McD. Conner was born in Alabama in 1822, and at the age of twenty-one years settled in Noxubee county and engaged in planting. He has been a member of the board of supervisors, and has held the office two or three terms. He was married to Miss Sarah Jane Conner in 1847, and has had twelve children, named: Jedediah, Edwin, Mary, George, Taylor, Andrew, Samuel, Richard, Kate, Sallie, Annie, and Ross, five of whom are yet living. He owns one thousand six hundred acres of the choice land of Noxubee county, and his average crop of cotton is two hundred and fifty bales. Mr. Conner is one of the best known and respected citizens of Noxubee county, a man of the finest honor and the broadest hospitality. From all points of reckoning he comes up to the full standard of a man.

Lemuel Parker Connor is one of the sincerest and most honorable of men now engaged in the legal practice in the state of Louisiana, and, being exceptionally talented, he has achieved a high reputation for legal ability at the bar of Vidalia. He was born in Adams county, Miss., October 30, 1827, to William C. Connor and wife, the former's ancestors coming hither from South Carolina. Lemuel Parker Connor was wisely put to school as soon as he had attained a suitable age, and was afterward entered at that noble and noted institution of learning, Yale college, where he received an education which has fitted him in an admirable manner for the duties of life. After leaving college he commenced the study of law in the office of that eminent lawyer, Mr. McMurran, of Natchez, but although becoming eminently fitted, did not practice his profession during his early manhood. He was married January 6, 1848, to Miss Elizabeth Frances, daughter of Judge Turner, and for some time thereafter was engaged in planting in Mississippi and Louisiana, a calling he was following at the opening of the Rebellion. He then entered the Confederate service, and held the rank of colonel on General Bragg's staff. He resumed planting after the war was over and he had returned from the field of battle, and this he continued to follow up to 1884, when he began his law practice. His union with Miss Turner resulted in the birth of ten children: Fannie Eliza (deceased), Jane G., wife of Lidale Randall, Mary M. (deceased), Eliza (deceased), Rebecca, now the wife of John H. Gay, of Colorado, a son of Hon. Ed. J. Gay; William A. (deceased), Theodocia, Edward T. and Lemuel P., Jr. The latter was educated at Baton Rouge, but studied law in New Orleans, and was admitted to practice by the supreme court in January, 1884. After a short time spent in Louisiana he came to Natchez in 1888 and was here married to Miss Mary McCreary Britton, a daughter of Audley C. Britton. To their union one child was born, whom they named Audley Britton, in honor of Mrs. Connor's father. The last child born to Lemuel Parker Connor and his wife was Fannie Eliza.

William W. Coody, Phœnix, Miss., is one of the leading citizens of Yazoo county, and is entitled to representation in this record of the prominent men of the state of Mississippi. He was born in Warren county, Miss., September 23, 1853, and is a son of Warren R. and Sallie C. (Rundle) Coody, natives of Mississippi. The father was a planter by occupation, and was engaged in that calling at the time of his death, which was in 1855. The paternal grandparents were Archibald and Eliza Coody, of Georgia and Mississippi, respectively. Archibald Coody was prominently identified with the early settlement of the state of Mississippi, to which he removed in 1827. Until William W. reached his majority he remained at home, assisting in the cultivation of his grandfather's plantation. At the age of twenty-one he started out in life for himself; he had attended the private schools of the neighborhood, and afterward studied law. He was admitted to the bar in 1878, and has been occupied with professional duties since that time. In 1881 he made some investments in the mercantile trade; he established a store at Phœnix, where he carries a stock of $2,000, and transacts a large business. He also owns eight hundred acres of land, a large portion of which is under cultivation. In 1874 Mr. Coody was married to Miss Victoria A. Pitchford, of Lexington, Miss., a daughter of Lawrence and Sarah J. Pitchford, also of Mississippi. They had born to them two children: Minnie A. and Sarah V., deceased. The parents and child are members of the Baptist church. In his political opinions Mr. Coody adheres to democratic principles; he was a member of the democratic executive committee for two years, 1888 and 1889. In all philanthropic movements he has been earnestly interested, and has figured extensively in the temperance work of the county, and has given liberally of his means for the carrying on of this work, than which he considers none more important. He is honored and respected by the entire community.

A. H. Cook is one of Warren county's progressive citizens, and here he was born, September 24, 1849, and has spent his life. His parents, Jared R., and Minerva (Hinds) Cook, were well-known residents of this section for many years, the former's birth occurring here. Upon attaining manhood, he went to Raymond, where he clerked for two years, then returned to Warren county and began farming, which calling he continued to follow until his death, of yellow fever, in 1878. His father was a graduate of the college at Bardstown, Ky., and became a man of considerable prominence in this county. During the war, a squad of colored soldiers attacked his house, wounding him and killing his wife. The Federal army took active measures, and captured and executed nine of the murderers. The maternal grandfather, John Hinds, was a native of Ireland, and became a resident of Vicksburg, Miss., when it contained only one or two stores. He clerked for a short time, then purchased land, cleared it, and began planting, which calling he was following at the time of his death in 1861. A. H. Cook received private instruction up to the age of thirteen years, and after attaining his seventeenth year, he entered the college at St. Louis, in which establishment he remained one year. He then returned home, and began merchandising near Vicksburg, continuing two years. He then followed planting in Warren county for about ten years, then moved to New Haven, Tenn., where he remained three years, but has since been planting near Bovina, Miss. His plantation aggregates about two thousand acres, a large amount of which is under cultivation, and in addition to the usual plantation products, he is quite extensively engaged in the raising of horses, cattle, sheep and hogs. For the past four years he has been in the service of the Equitable Mortgage company, as inspector. He has taken quite an active interest in local politics, and is a member of Bovina lodge No. 112, of the A. F. & A. M., in which he holds the position of junior warden, and also belongs to the American Legion of Honor. He was first married to Miss Ada Bryan, a daughter of Dr. E. H. and L. E. (Newman) Bryan, of Warren county, by whom he became the father of a son, whom they named Jared Bryan. His wife's death occurred in 1873, and his second marriage was consummated November 19, 1881, to Mrs. Jennie Baldwin, a daughter of William Hogan, a planter of North Carolina. He and his wife are members of the Episcopal church.

Col. Edwin Gray Cook, the oldest living resident of Vicksburg, Miss., was born in Virginia, while his parents were on a visit to that state, November 29, 1809. He was the eldest son born to Foster and Martha W. (Sills) Cook, both of whom were born in Virginia, the paternal ancestors being of Irish descent and the maternal ancestors of Welsh descent. Foster Cook began life for himself as a schoolteacher, but at an early day removed to Mississippi with Newit Vick (the founder of Vicksburg), and for a short time was a resident of Jefferson county. He afterward went to the Open Woods settlement of Warren county, of which he was the first settler, and located all the eight sections of land in the open woods for the four members of the Cook, and four members of the Vick family, who resided on their homesteads. When dead, they were buried in their gardens. After many years, their graveyards are of considerable size, still to be seen. He became the second merchant of Vicksburg, beginning business about 1824, and in partnership with George Wyche, did a large mercantile business in Warren and several adjoining counties. He improved a large tract of land and erected thereon a very handsome residence, a typical Southern home, which continued to be the home of his family and descendants for many years. He was a nephew of the wife of Newit Vick, and died in 1827. After his death his widow married Judge Bland, by whom she became the mother of several children. She and Mr. Cook were worthy members of the Methodist Episcopal church. The Cooks, Fosters and others, established an excellent school, which they called the Open Woods academy, which, at that time, was the second in importance in the state. Edwin G. Cook was reared on his father's fine estate and was educated in Open Woods academy and in Transylvania college, but upon the death of his father he left school, returned home and entered the county clerk's office as deputy clerk, and upon attaining his majority he was appointed to the position of clerk, the duties of which position he discharged with faithfulness and efficiency until the formation of the new constitution, about 1833, when he retired. He then assumed the management of the old homestead but was not long allowed to remain in retirement, for in 1836 he was elected a member of the board of police, which body elected him their president, and held this position for some time. In 1852 he was elected to the position of county treasurer, and so ably did he discharge his duties that he held the position continuously up to 1863, when he was ousted by General Grant on the 4th of July. He soon after removed to Hazlehurst, where he purchased a fine plantation and has since resided. He was collector of internal revenue for the first district of Mississippi during the presidency of Andrew Johnson. He has since been an active member of the board of supervisors of Copiah county. He was first married in 1835, on the 15th of July, to Miss Henrietta V. Harris, a daughter of Dr. Hartwell Harris, a prominent man of this county, and by her became the father of five children: Mary V., now the widow of Dr. James M. Hunt, being the only living child of this union. Dr. Hunt, who was a very superior physician, is now deceased. He left two children: Edwin Cook, now a practicing physician of Vicksburg, graduated from the Tulane medical college of New Orleans, and Bessie F., who was educated in a college for young ladies at Nashville, Tenn. She is Colonel Cook's only granddaughter and is very beautiful, as well as highly accomplished and refined. She is often spoken of as being as good as beautiful, and in the land of lovely women she holds her place with grace and dignity. Colonel Cook's wife died in 1853, of yellow fever, and in December, 1856, the Colonel took for his second wife Olive M. Curtiss, a daughter of Rev. William M. Curtiss, a native of New York. Her mother was a daughter of Levin Wales, appointed by President Jefferson suveyor-general of all United States lands south of Tennessee. His descendants are numerous in Mississippi and Louisiana. His mother was Sarah Howard, of Maryland, whose grandfather was the celebrated Duke of Norfolk. His union resulted in the birth of four children, two living: Edwin M., a merchant at Hazlehurst, and Olive Wyche, who also resides there. Colonel Cook has for years been an active worker in the Methodist Episcopal church and has been a local preacher for many years, working often in the commodious brick church held by white Methodist trustees for the colored mission in Vicksburg, of the Methodist Episcopal conference, Methodist Episcopal church South. He is a fine old gentleman, highly accomplished, is in the enjoyment of good health and is honored by all who know him. It is a singular fact that Mr. Cook was elected to office nearly every two years from 1830 to 1860, when he differed from the strongest party of the county; and in these days when official dishonor is so often heard of, it may be stated not to Mr. Cook's discredit that he is still comparatively poor, after having handled county money by the thousands and United States funds running into the millions.

Francis I. Cook, whose postoffice address is Alto, Jasper county, Miss., was born in Abbeville district, S. C., December 12, 1841, a son of Frederick and Sarah (Cox) Cook, both of whom were also natives of Abbeville district, S. C. His father was born in 1810 and his mother in 1808, and they were married in their native district, where the father died in March, 1886, and the mother is still living on the old homestead. They were the parents of nine children: Mary, Rebecca, Sarah F., Ann E., Francis I., Agnes M., Isabelle S., Toliver, and Eliza M. Francis I. enlisted June 1, 1861, in company C of the Seventh South Carolina regiment, with which he served until the close of the war. Returning home, he was married December 12, 1865, to Mary E., a daughter of Abiah and Nancy A. (Thornton) Robertson. In 1866 Mr. and Mr. Cook removed to Mississippi and located in Jasper county, where Mr. Cook has since been a successful planter. At this time he owns nine hundred and twenty acres of land, of which about one hundred and twenty-five acres are in a good state of cultivation. They have had born to them eleven children, named as follows: Frederick, Frank I. (deceased), Minnie L., Sallie M., Carlos A. (deceased), Jabez P. (deceased), Harvey E., Frank D., Mary A., Fannie I. and Carrie E. Mr. and Mrs. Cook are members of the Baptist church. Mr. Cook is, in the truest sense of the word, a self-made man, having made his own way in the world and attained to such success as has not been vouchsafed to a majority of his fellow-citizens. He has always been too busy a man to take an active part in politics, but there is no question of public interest that does not engross his attention, and no man can be more conscientious than he in his exercise of his privileges as a voter. He has always given special attention to the causes of religion and education, and his aid to these interests has been frequent and generous.

J. H. Cook, Sr., is, on his father's side, of German descent and on his mother's side of Irish descent. He is an extensive landowner, whose postoffice address is Paulding, Jasper county, Miss. He was born in Abbeville, S. C., December 20, 1816, a son of Philip and

Mary (Irwin) Cook, both of whom were natives of that state. They were married in their native county and the mother died there in 1828, the father marrying twice subsequently and removing to Lauderdale and thence to Jasper county, Miss., where he died at the home of J. H. Cook, Sr., in the year 1844. He was the father of fifteen children, of whom the subject of this sketch, the fourth in order of birth, began life for himself at the age of nineteen years. In 1837 he came to Mississippi and located first in Newton county, whence he removed to Lauderdale county, where he was married in October, 1839, to Elizabeth O., daughter of Edward and Mary (Carroll) Harper, who was born in Jasper county, Miss., in 1822. He was a resident of Lauderdale county until 1841, when he removed to Jasper county, Miss., where he has since made his home. In 1858 he removed to his present plantation. Mr. and Mrs. Cook have had born to them eight children: Philip C., who died in the war; Francis L., Samantha, Frederick M. B. (deceased), Sarah S. (deceased), Napoleon B., Eleanor O. and John H. Frederick M. B. Cook was a man of considerable importance and was a candidate on the republican ticket for the membership of the state constitutional convention. He was waylaid and assassinated by unknown parties, who concealed themselves in an old house and fired upon him as he passed. J. H. Cook is a member of the Masonic order, and he and his wife are members of the Methodist Episcopal church South. Mr. Cook is the owner of two thousand four hundred acres of land, of which about three hundred acres are cultivated. In addition to this he was formerly the owner of and has given over to his children more than one thousand acres. He is industrious, energetic and highly enterprising as a man and citizen, helpful to everything tending to benefit the public, and he commands a high degree of respect from all who know him.

James Valentine Cook, planter, Belen, Miss., son of Silas and Lydia (Clemens) Cook, was born in Tuscaloosa county, Ala., August 27, 1833. and no doubt inherited his taste for agricultural pursuits from his father, who was a very successful planter. The Cook family was originally from England and the first emigrant to America located in Virginia and the Carolinas. Silas Cook was born in South Carolina and came to Mississippi with his parents, Daniel and Mary (King) Cook, natives of North and South Carolina respectively, in 1815, when but a child, and located near Columbus, Miss. After growing up he went to Alabama, and was there married in 1832 to Miss Clemens, a native of Tennessee. After remaining in Alabama one year, Mr. Cook and his family returned to Mississippi, and there he continued planting until his death in 1869. He was very prosperous in that capacity and was a man universally respected. Mrs. Cook's parents, Jacob and Frances (Simms) Clemens, were natives also of North and South Carolina, respectively. James Valentine Cook was reared in Lowndes county, Miss., and received his literary training in Columbus, Miss. In 1860 he graduated from the medical department of the University of Louisiana at New Orleans and practiced in that state until the breaking out of the war, when he volunteered his services to the Confederacy, entered a Louisiana company and was immediately made second lieutenant. This company went to Richmond, Va., where Mr. Cook received an appointment as senior assistant surgeon in a Louisiana hospital in Richmond, remaining there until March, 1864, when he was assigned duty on General Mahone's brigade as assistant surgeon. There he remained until August of the same year. He was in the battle of Gettysburg, Anderson's division, and was afterward appointed surgeon in the Confederate navy, being assigned duty on the gunboat Spray on the coast of Florida. There he remained until the close of the war, after which he returned to Mississippi, where he resumed his practice and in connection carried on planting. He moved to Coahoma in 1876, remained there until 1880, and then retired from practice, settling on his plantation in Quitman county, where he now resides. He has been successful in accumulating considerable property and is now the owner of seven hundred and twenty acres of land with four hundred acres under cultivation, all of which he has improved from the forest. Dr. Cook is one of Quitman county's most substantial and enterprising citizens, and has been identified with its best interests from the time of its organization. He is an energetic, thoroughgoing man, is a liberal contributor to all benevolent and religious enterprises, and though not a member of any church is a firm friend to Christianity. He is a man of steady habits, of firm convictions, and acts fearlessly in whatever he thinks to be right, regardless of other men. He is a stanch democrat in politics, and a stanch patriot for the state of Mississippi.

John. S. Cook is a planter of Clay county, who was born in Lowndes county, Miss., in 1844, a son of Silas and Elidia (Clements) Cook, the former of whom was born in South Carolina in 1809. He was a worthy tiller of the soil, and when about twenty years of age came to Mississippi and located in Lowndes county, where he was married, about 1828, to the daughter of Hardy Clements, and by her became the father of nine children, the following of whom are living: James V., Fannie (Mrs. Davis, of Aberdeen), John S. and Kate (Trull), of Alabama state. The parents of these children died in 1871, the mother's death occurring about twenty days before the father's. John S. Cook received his rudimentary education in Springfield, Ala., and in 1866 moved to what is now Clay county, Miss., and here has since resided. Prior to this, however, in 1861, he entered the Confederate army as a private, in which capacity he served in company A, First Mississippi battalion, which was under command of J. O. Banks, and took an active part in the following engagments: Pensacola, Corinth, Chickamauga, Peach Tree creek, Atlanta and Nashville. He was wounded twice during his service, at Corinth and at Nashville. He was taken prisoner at Corinth, and after being in captivity for a few days was exchanged, and was captured a second time at Vicksburg, this time being held a prisoner of war for four months. In 1873 he was married to Miss Ivy Townsend, who died three years after their marriage, leaving him a daughter, Floy, who is now being educated at Canaan, Ala. Mr. Cook is a man of more than ordinary intelligence, is very social and gracious in his manners, and is thoroughly honorable in all his dealings. He is well to do, and has an excellent and valuable farm.

Among the many prominent attorneys of Clarksdale is Hon. Samuel C. Cook, who was born at Oxford, Miss., in 1855, and who is the third son of M. J. and Martha (Bumpass) Cook, natives, respectively, of North Carolina and Tennessee. The father was reared in his native state, and came to Mississippi in 1845, settling at Oxford, where he was extensively engaged in merchandising. He and wife are still residing there, and are esteemed members of the Cumberland Presbyterian church. The mother's people were residents of Jackson, Tenn. Both were prominent families. Hon. Samuel C. Cook was reared at Oxford, began the study of law at the University of Mississippi at that place, and graduated from that institution in the class of 1878. He entered upon the practice of his profession at Durant, Holmes county, the same year, and after continuing there for two years removed to Batesville, Panola county, where he remained until 1888. The same year he came to Clarksdale, where he secured a good practice and became identified with the interests and advancement of that place and Coahoma county. He represented Panola county in the legislature in 1886, and was in the legislature from Coahoma county in 1890. He was on the judiciary committee both terms, chairman of the committee of levees, and introducer of the resolution to investigate the Hemingway deficit. He is the Clarksdale correspondent of the *Appeal Avalanche*, is a candidate for district attorney, and would make an able and efficient officer. In 1882 Mr. Cook was married to Miss Lizzie Murphy, a native of New Orleans, but reared in Durant, Holmes county, Miss., and the daughter of Dr. Charles T. Murphy. The

last-named gentleman was for many years a prominent physician of Holmes county, and was a Mason of high degree, being at one time grand master of the grand lodge of the state. He was also a member of the state legislature for several terms. His death occurred in 1889. To the union of Mr. and Mrs. Cook were born two children: Charles died at the age of two years, and Edward Mayes, whose death occurred when four years of age. The family are members of the Methodist Episcopal church. Mr. Cook was one of the organizers and is the secretary and attorney of the Yazoo Delta Investment company, also a stockholder in a number of other corporations of the city, to all of which he lent a helping hand at the time of organization. He is about the average size, and has light hair and blue eyes.

Alexander J. Cooke, a prominent merchant of Cumberland, Miss., is the fourth of nine children born to the union of William P. and Sarah E. (Moore) Cooke, the father born in South Carolina in 1813 and the mother in Jefferson county, Ala., a year or two later. The parents were married in Jefferson county, Ala., and subsequently removed to Sinclair county, where Mr. Cooke died in 1872. His wife had died in 1860. Both were members of the Missionary Baptist church. Mr. Cooke was a successful planter, stockraiser and merchant and an industrious, honest, upright citizen. He was a stanch democrat all his life and was a quiet, unassuming man. He was one of a large family of children born to Elias G. Cooke, who was of Scotch descent. The elder Cooke was a planter and mechanic, served in the war of 1812, also the Creek war, and died in St. Clair county, Ala. He was quite a prominent Baptist and had many warm friends. The maternal grandfather, Jack Moore, was born in Ireland and when a boy came with his parents to America. He resided many years in Alabama and afterward removed to Tishomingo county, Miss., where he died. He was a planter and a member of the Baptist church. The nine children born to William P. and Sarah E. (Moore) Cooke are named in the order of their births as follows: J. E., now of Walker county, Ala., was for some time engaged in merchandising at Cumberland; Dr. Osborne B. was a physician and merchant for some time at Cumberland, but now of Maben, Miss.; La Fayette, a merchant and miller in his native county; Martha J.; America E., wife of C. C. Clines; Huldah C., wife of William Dunlap; Mary D., wife of George Clines; and two deceased. The daughters all reside near the old home. Alexander J. Cooke was born in St. Clair county, Ala., in 1844, reared on a farm, and his educational advantages were not of the best. When but sixteen years of age, or in 1861, he joined company E, Fifty-first Alabama mounted infantry, and served as sergeant for some time. After this he was a scout, principally in the Tennessee army under Generals Wheeler and Morgan. He fought at Stone river, Tenn., Missionary Ridge, Beech Grove and was in the Georgia-Atlanta campaign. He then went to Tennessee and was in Northern Alabama at the time of the surrender. He was never captured or wounded, but had many hairbreadth escapes while scouting, his work being very hazardous and laborious. After the war he attended school a short time, and then followed farming and merchandising in Alabama until 1877, when he married Miss Sarah Elizabeth Cain, a native of Tuscaloosa, Ala., born in 1848, and the daughter of Robert and Sarah Cain, both natives of the Palmetto state. The parents moved from their native state to Alabama and there the mother died. The father is living in Birmingham of that state. Mr. and Mrs. Cooke's union was blessed by the birth of three children, viz.: Gussie, born March 8, 1878; Osce, born December 18, 1879; and Ola, born October 28, 1881. The same year of his marriage Mr. Cooke came to Cumberland, Webster county, Miss., where he has since been engaged in merchandising. He is also the owner of a steam sawmill and large amounts of land, being one among the largest landowners in the county, and owns a large tannery also. He has accumulated all his property by his own exertions and excellent busi-

37

ness ability.   He enjoys the fullest confidence of the people, is honest and upright, and is a
most desirable citizen.   About 1889 he had his progress very much impeded by a severe accident, in which he came very near losing his life.   He and four of his neighbors went to
Memphis to buy goods and on their return home were obliged to lay over one night at Winona
to change cars.   While sleeping in the upper story of a boardinghouse they were awakened
by an alarm of fire.   Mr. Cooke quickly arose, dressed himself, and undertook to go down
stairs, not knowing that the fire was in that building.   On opening the door the flames and
smoke burst in, cutting off all hopes of escape in that quarter.   Mr. Alford broke out one of
the windows, Mr. Cooke took his companion by the hand and let him drop to the ground, a
distance of about eighteen feet.   He then jumped out himself, but sustained severe injuries
from which he will never recover.   The four companions were not awakened and were burned
to death, their charred remains being found among the debris.   One of them was James
Thomas, already referred to, and another H. L. Lawley, who was a first cousin of Mr. Cooke.
Mr. Cooke is treasurer of El Dorado lodge, Masonic fraternity, No. 184, at Cumberland, and
he, wife and daughter are members of the Missionary Baptist church.

The Cooper family is of English origin, and descended from three brothers who came to
this country in colonial times.   One settled in New York, one in New Jersey and one in Virginia.   The paternal grandfather of Dr. John A. Cooper, physician, Friar's Point, Miss.—
William Cooper—was a native of the last named state, and emigrated from there to Fayette,
Miss., at an early period, being among the pioneers of that region.   This is one of the representative families of the state.   The Doctor owes his nativity to Kentucky, where his birth
occurred in 1846, and is the second child born to William and Isabella (Atchison) Cooper,
both natives also of the Blue Grass state.   The father was a successful planter, which occupation he followed the principal part of his life.   In politics he was an old line whig.   His
death occurred in 1871.   The mother died in 1849.   Her ancestors, the Atchisons, were of
Irish descent, and settled in South Carolina at an early date.   Her father was one of the pioneers in the vicinity of Lexington.   Dr. Cooper was reared in his native state, educated at
Wabash college, Indiana, and began the study of medicine at Jefferson college, Philadelphia,
in 1857, graduating from the same in 1860.   In the fall of that year he came to Coahoma
county, Miss., and in the spring of 1861 he enlisted in the Confederate army, company A, of
Morgan's squadrons.   In 1862 he was advanced to the rank of captain of company L, in
Duke's regiment, was captured at Cynthiana June 27, 1864, and sent to Johnson's island,
where he remained until May 20, 1865, when he was exchanged.   He was then attached to
the trans-Mississippi department, but did not reach the field as the surrender occurred about
this time.   He was in the Indiana and Ohio raid, was in all the battles of Morgan's campaign,
was at Chickamauga and Missionary Ridge.   Dr. Cooper's prospects for promotion were very
flattering at the time of his imprisonment, and had it not been for this unfortunate terminus
to his advancement he would in all probability have held the rank of lieutenant-colonel.
Returning to Coahoma county, Miss., after the war, Dr. Cooper settled at Friar's Point,
where he began the practice of medicine, and is to-day one of the oldest practicing physicians
of that county.   He has had many surgical cases, most of them particular ones, and has been
very successful.   In 1876 he engaged in the drug business, in partnership with Dr. Simmons,
under the firm title of J. L. Simmons & Co., and this continued until 1883, when Dr.
Cooper assumed charge.   Aside from this he has planting interests, being the owner of three
hundred and fifty acres, all well cultivated and improved, and one thousand acres additional,
well timbered, and which he is engaged in improving at the present time.   In 1879 he erected
his residence in Friar's Point.   He was married January 18, 1871, to Miss Sallie Warren, a

native of Mississippi, whose parents were from the blue grass regions of Kentucky. She died in 1876, leaving two children: Anna Warren (who has considerable musical talent and at the present time is attending the Conservatory of Music at Boston; she graduated at the high school at Memphis when sixteen years of age) and Sallie (who died at the age of seven months). Dr. Cooper took for his second wife Miss Lelia Maynard, their marriage occurring in January, 1880, and this union resulted in the birth of three children: Ethel Maynard, John A., Jr., and Lelia. Mrs. Cooper was born in Friar's Point, Miss., and is the daughter of D. B. Maynard. Socially the Doctor is a member of the Masonic fraternity, was charter member of Coahoma Lodge No. 104, and was past worshipful master for fifteen years. He is now high priest of Friar's Point, chapter No. 112. He is also a member of the Knights of Pythias and the Knights of Honor. In politics he is somewhat active, but although a worker for the democratic party he is no officeseeker. He has been chairman of the democratic executive committee for several years. In his personal appearance the Doctor is tall, rather heavy set, dark hair and full beard and blue eyes. He is a pleasant, social gentleman. The family are members of the Methodist Episcopal church.

The great-grandfather, on his father's side, of Hon. John Addison Cooper, merchant and planter, Belen, Miss., was born in England, and emigrated to the United States, locating in Georgia in its pioneer days. His son, John Cooper, was born in that state and married Miss Delilah Gibson, a native of South Carolina. John served in the Florida war and was made major of a battalion, but resigned and took a private's place in his company from preference. His son, William S. Cooper, was born in Tennessee, and was there married to Miss Caroline P. A. Eochs, who was also a native of that state. William S. came to Mississippi in 1844, was one of the first settlers of Chickasaw county and one of its most esteemed citizens, living the quiet and uneventful life of a tiller of the soil until during the Civil war. He enlisted in the Confederate army in the beginning of the year 1863, and served as a faithful soldier until killed at the battle of Franklin, Tenn., in November, 1864. To his marriage were born eleven children: John Addison Cooper being second in order of birth. The latter was but fourteen years of age at the time of his father's enlistment, having been born in Chickasaw county, Miss., November 14, 1849. At this age he was left by his father in the full management of his business. Since that time he has not only taken care of himself, but a part of the time of his mother. He left home and began for himself in 1871, located in the neighborhood of his present place, then in Tunica, but now Quitman county, and although he started out for himself with nothing but a horse and saddle, purchased on credit, his clothing and ten cents in money, he has, by his industry and excellent management, accumulated a comfortable competency. He is not a man to accumulate great wealth, being too generous and open-hearted, but prefers rather to assist with his time and means all worthy enterprises and to advance the interests of Quitman county. Since locating in this county he has been one of the leading and substantial citizens; was elected chancery clerk of the county in 1885 and in that capacity was a faithful officer for four years. He has been mayor of Belen, and is at the present time representative in the state legislature, of Quitman county. He has held various county offices and other positions of trust at the hands of the people of his county, and has discharged the duties of the same with great credit to himself and the perfect satisfaction of his constituents. As a representative of his county he has studied the best interests of his people, and this has ever been uppermost in his mind and heart. He is a successful planter, being the owner of five hundred acres with one hundred and sixty acres under cultivation, most of which has been opened and improved under his direction and management. He is also actively engaged in merchandising in the town of Belen, carrying a stock of goods equal to the trade demand of his place of business. Mr. Cooper was married in 1876 to Miss Mary E. Lawler, a native of Coahoma county, Miss., and daughter of J. N. and Martha (Ridley) Lawler, both natives of Alabama. Mr. and Mrs. Cooper are the parents of three interesting children: Virgil V., Martha C. and Alcorn Preston. Mr. Cooper is a member and liberal supporter of the Methodist church.

Tim Ervin Cooper, of Jackson, Miss., associate justice of the supreme court, was born July 5, 1843, in Copiah county, Miss., on a plantation, and is the son of William A. and Mary E. (Ford) Cooper, the former of whom was a lawyer, combined with which occupation he followed the calling of a planter. He was a native of the state, having been born in Lawrence county, in 1818. His father, Joseph, was a native of North Carolina, from which state he immigrated to Mississippi in the early part of the present century. Joseph's father was a Baptist minister, and came to Mississippi in the latter part of the eighteenth century. He was of English-Irish ancestry. Mary Ford's father was a lawyer by profession, and at one time was on the circuit bench of Louisiana. Judge Cooper's maternal grandfather, Ervin, was a colonel in the Revolutionary war. The Ervins were also of Scotch-Irish descent. William A. Cooper died in 1851, his widow still surviving him. They were the parents of five children: Walter N., Joseph F., Mary (wife of Scott), Tim E. and William B., all of whom are living but the latter, who died in New York in 1886. After the death of the father the family removed to Jackson, and there resided until 1858, when the widow removed to Georgetown, Ky., remaining there until 1860, when Judge Cooper entered the University of North Carolina at Chapel Hill. The war interrupted his studies and he left college to return home for the purpose of enlisting on behalf of the seceded states. He became a member of company K, Eighth Mississippi regiment, Burt Rifles, which had been organized at Corinth in April, 1861, and his first engagement was at Manassas, where his regiment fought in D. R. Jones' brigade. His next battle was at Ball's bluff. His regiment was in nearly all the engagements in northern Virginia and the Peninsular campaign. He also fought at Savage station, Malvern hill and at Sharpsburg, where he was taken prisoner with his brother, who was wounded. He was released in time to join his command at Fredericksburg, and participated in that battle, where his regiment was captured. He succeeded in making his escape, and, going to Baltimore, quietly remained with friends until his regiment was exchanged. When he heard of this he went to the Federal officer and surrendered. He rejoined his regiment at Fortress Monroe, soon after which his command joined Lee in his march into Maryland. This led him to the field at Gettysburg, where he participated in the second day's fight, being under General Longstreet. After that battle he was promoted to sergeant-major and acted as adjutant of the regiment until the close of the war. From the field of Gettysburg his regiment was ordered to the Western army, and under Bragg was in the battle of Chickamauga, and then at Knoxville against Burnside. After the latter engagement, the regiment was ordered back to Virginia, and he participated in the battles of the Wilderness, Spottsylvania, Cold Harbor and all the engagements of that terrible campaign. He was then in the siege at Richmond. Pending this siege he received a furlough home, arriving there in February, 1865. Before he was ready to return to the scene of action, the enemy had cut off his communications and he was unable to rejoin the army before the surrender. Though only seventeen years of age at the time of his enlistment, he made a fine record as a soldier, being always ready for active duty, and discharged his duties with credit to himself and to the cause. After the war Mr. Cooper read law in the office of William Yerger for a time and was then with King & Mayes, at Gallatin. He was admitted to practice at the latter place in 1866, and from there went to Monticello, where he began practicing his profession, remaining there some five months. He then removed to Crystal Springs, Miss., where he practiced with success until 1872, at which time he opened an office at Hazlehurst, Copiah county. He was not only successful there at the bar, but he established himself as a lawyer of unusual ability, and attracted the attention of the people of the state. In February, 1881, he was called from his private practice to accept the position of associate justice of the supreme court to succeed Judge James Z. George, who had been elected for the United States senate. He was reappointed in 1888, and is now serving his second term. Judge Cooper was married in Adams county, Miss., November 1, 1866, to Mary E., daughter of John B. and Ella (Grafton) Dicks, and to them were born nine children: Barber D., Mary, Rufin T., Tim E., Ella M., Mayes, Bartlett, John and Joseph, all of whom are living. He is a member of the I. O. O. F., and the K. of P. He had three brothers in the Confederate army. Walter was a member of the Eighteenth Mississippi, and served chiefly in the northern army of Virginia, and Joseph and William were in the cavalry service. Judge Cooper is a man about five feet, eight inches high, with a finely chiseled, intellectual face, well proportioned figure, rather inclined to corpulency but not to an extent to impair the lightness and activity of his motions. His eyes are blue and full, his hair light brown, his forehead expansive and marked with thought, his bearing is easy, yet dignified, and his whole manner indicative of a man possessed of intellectual power. He is a man of noble instincts and liberal in his views, kind and generous in his disposition, with simple, unaffected and true manners. He took his post where nature and education placed him—in the very front rank of the profession. He has maintained his ground with lawyers that are classed among the most gifted in the country, while he is still at that period of life where ambition points to, and mental activity assures, a higher fame. As an advocate Judge Cooper is forcible and convincing; his command of language is good and his delivery attractive. He makes himself master of all the facts and law points of the case, and then he presents them with great force and effectiveness. His knowledge of the law, his love of justice, his high sense of honor, his poise of mind, qualify him in an eminent degree for the bench, where he has the confidence of the bar and the people.

Daniel K. Coor, a retired planter of Copiah county, Miss., was born in what is now Lawrence county in 1817. He is the son of John and Anna Coor. His father was born in North Carolina in 1785, and his mother was born in Tennessee. John Coor came to Mississippi in 1814 and located in what is now Lawrence county, and lived there till 1820, when he moved to what is now Copiah county, and at that time he bought a large tract of land of the Indians. He was married in 1816 to Anna Kethly, and to them were born nine children, only two of whom are living: Daniel K., the eldest, and Ann J., the wife of Dempsey P. Welch, of Texas, who was next in order of birth. Mr. Coor was a veteran in the war of 1812. He was the first sheriff of Copiah county, and died at his home in 1838. His wife survived him until 1872. Daniel K. Coor had a limited education, owing to the fact that he had to work very hard to help support the family in this then new country. In 1847 he was married to Miss Susan Allen, of Copiah county, and began life for himself. He removed at once to a farm upon which he lived till a few years ago, when he removed to Hazlehurst. During the war, although his health was very poor, he served his state in the commissary department. In 1842 he joined the Gallatin lodge No. 25, A. F. & A. M. He was a member of Chapter 17 and Council No. 6. In 1862 he joined R. B. Mayes lodge of I. O. O. F. He is also a member of the Knights of Pythias lodge at Hazlehurst. Mr. and Mrs. Coor have had four children, named as follows: Dicy A., deceased; John A. and Laura E., who were twins, the former being dead, and the latter now the wife of John S. Stackhouse, of Crystal Springs, Copiah county, and Susan L., who lives at home. Mr. Coor was one of the pioneers of the county and has witnessed its development from a county in the pioneer state to its present proud agricultural and commercial status. Quiet and retiring in his manners, he never sought public preferment and such official positions as he has occupied have been accepted only at the earnest solicitation of his fellow-citizens. As a business man, he has been successful in an eminent degree, and in every relation of life he enjoys the respect and esteem of all who have the honor of his acquaintance.

H. St. L. Coppee is an able and experienced civil engineer, who has charge of the improvements of the harbor of Vicksburg, Miss. He was born at West Point, N. Y., in 1853, the second of six children born to Henry and Julia (DeWitt) Coppee, the former of whom was born in Georgia and the latter in New York. Henry Coppee was born at Savannah, October 13, 1821, of French West Indian parentage. His early education was obtained in Chatham academy, then one of the finest educational institutions of the South. He entered the sophomore class of Yale college in the summer of 1836, where he remained one year. He then turned his attention to the study of engineering, and later was employed on the Georgia Central railroad from Savannah to Macon. In 1841 an appointment to West Point was given him, and four years later he graduated from that famous military academy in the artillery. In 1846, when the Mexican war broke out, he was sent to the front, although not attached to any regiment, procured his dispatch to the seat of war, and was in the service throughout the entire struggle—two and one-half years. Besides participating in a number of minor actions, he was engaged in the siege of Vera Cruz in February and March, 1847; the battle of Cerro Gordo on April 17 and 18, 1847; the battles of Contreras and Cherubusco, both of which were fought on August 20; at the storming of the castle of Chapultepec on September 13, and in the capture of the City of Mexico on the following day. For gallant and meritorious conduct on the battlefield of Cherubusco he was breveted captain, and received a vote of thanks from the legislature of the state of Georgia. From the close of the war until 1855 he was stationed at West Point, at the end of which time he resigned his position in the army to accept the position of professor of English literature and history in the University of Pennsylvania. After filling this position with great ability until 1866, he resigned to accept the presidency of the newly established Lehigh university, which he organized, but this position he also resigned in 1874, although he once more filled the position a year later. Since that time he has been the professor of English literature and history and international and constitutional law, in the same institution. He was a member and secretary of the board of visitors to West Point in 1868, and in 1870 made a tour of Europe. In 1870 Dr. Coppee was appointed regent of the Smithsonian Institute for a term of six years, and has twice been reëlected by congress, first in 1880 and later in 1886, and has also been a United States commissioner of government assay of coin in 1874 and 1877. He was deputy to the general convention of the Protestant Episcopal church in 1874–77–80– 83–86, and is president of the Aztec club, an association of officers who fought in the Mexican war, a position held at various times by Generals Grant, Hancock, and other famous American soldiers. He is an honorary member of the Pennsylvania Historical society, of the American Philosophical society, and is corresponding member of the Delaware Historical society. In 1848 he received the degree of A. M. from the University of Georgia, and in 1866 the degree of Doctor of Laws from both Union college and the University of Pennsylvania. Some of the most important of the works of Dr. Coppee are as follows: "Elements of Logic," issued in 1857; "Gallery of Famous Poets," in 1858; "Elements of Rhetoric," in 1859; "Gallery of Distinguished Poetesses," in 1860; "Select Academic Speaker," in

1861; "Manual of Battalion Drill," in 1862; "Evolutions of the Line," in 1862; edited the "Translations of Marmot's Spirit of Military Institutions," in 1862; "Manual of Court Martial," in 1863; "Songs of Praise in Christian Centuries," in 1864; "Life and Services of General Grant," in 1866; edited the United States Service Magazine from 1864 to 1866; "Manual of English Literature," in 1872; was editor of the "Translations of Comte de Paris' Civil War," in 1877; "Conquest of Spain by the Arab Moors," in 1881, besides many occasional and fugitive pieces in the various leading magazines of the country. Dr. Coppee was married on July 9, 1849, to Miss Julia De Witt, a daughter of John De Witt, Esq., of one of the early families of Holland which came across the water to the new colony of New Amsterdam. Their union was blessed in the birth of six children, the second of whom, H. St. L. Coppee, is now in charge of the government works on the Mississippi river at Vicksburg. As a child he was educated in Philadelphia, but was a student at Lehigh university from 1869 to 1872, from which institution he was graduated as a civil engineer. He was first employed by the Texas Pacific Railway company from 1872 to 1874, during which time he made surveys in California and Arizona, and was resident engineer at San Diego, Cal. After the panic he returned to the East via the Isthmus of Panama, and in 1875 and a part of 1876 he was employed on the Pennsylvania railroad, and was on special engineering duty at the Centennial exhibition at Philadelphia in 1876. In this year he was also inspector of the Bethlehem Iron company, of Bethlehem, Penn., at which place his father resides. In October, 1878, he went to Memphis, Tenn., and was there employed in making surveys of rivers and harbors, and obtaining data pertaining to the general nature of sediment-bearing streams of Arkansas, Tennessee, Louisiana, and Mississippi, under the direction of Maj. W. H. H. Beauregard, corps of engineers U. S. A. In 1882 he took local charge of the improvement of Vicksburg harbor, and is now in charge of that work, which is being rapidly advanced under his direction. At various times he has had charge of the levee and other public works, and as he has had much experience in this line, as well as in river work, no more competent or worthy man for the position could be found. He is a keen business man, and as he is energetic and pushing he has thus far made a success of his life. In July, 1884, he was married to Miss Mary Bell Marshall, a daughter of Judge Thomas A. Marshall, and to their union three children have been born, two of whom, Ellen Marion and Eugenia, are living. He is a member of the Aztec club, of the American Society of Civil Engineers, and of the L. of H., and he and his wife belong to the Episcopal church. He has been a permanent resident of Vicksburg since 1882.

Ira A. Cortright is a prosperous general merchant of Sharkey county, but is also engaged in planting, and is the efficient postmaster of Rolling Fork. He was born in Wayne county, N. Y., in 1849, to Isaac and Permelia (Wright) Cortright, both of whom were born in New York, where they spent their lives. Mr. Cortright was an industrious farmer, and died in 1890, his wife passing from life in 1863. The paternal grandfather, Saphrine Cortright, was also born in New York, and there was called from earth before the subject of this sketch was born. He was a farmer, and of German descent. Ira A. Cortright is one of three brothers now living of a family of eleven children, consisting of six boys and five girls, his brother, James H., coming to what is now Sharkey county in 1869, of which he is a prominent planter. They were both reared on a farm, receiving the advantages of the common schools, but at about the age of sixteen years Ira A. began the battle of life for himself, as a clerk in a store, which calling he continued to follow in his native state for about five years. In 1871 he became a resident of Sharkey county, Miss., and opened a mercantile establishment near Rolling Fork, afterward moving to the town, where he has continued in the business ever since, meeting with marked success. He also owns and operates a good steam sawmill and cottongin at Rolling Fork, and by his own shrewd management, he has become the owner of twelve hundred acres of land, of which two hundred acres are under cultivation, and a one-half interest in eight hundred acres, his brother owning the other half, and on their land they raise about three hundred bales of cotton each year. Mr. Cortright was married in 1881 to Miss Sarah Greenfield, an intelligent and accomplished lady, and a native of York state. Mr. Cortright holds membership in the Masonic lodge in New York, and belongs to lodge No. 3175, of the K. of H. of Rolling Fork. He is a thoroughgoing and live business man, full of enterprise, push and zeal in whatever he undertakes. He has the interest and welfare of his adopted country at heart, and thoroughly identifies himself with every interest of this section. He commands universal respect and esteem, and fully deserves the good opinion in which he is held by all.

In sketching the life of Edward W. Cossitt, merchant, it is but just to say that his name as a business man and citizen is above reproach, and that he has won the confidence and esteem of all who know him. He was born in Hardeman county, Tenn., to Lewis C. and Matilda (Harris) Cossitt. His father was born in New York in 1793, and was a Mason. His mother was born in 1832. Lewis C. Cossitt removed to Tippah county, Miss., for the purpose of teaching school, but from 1845 until his death, which occurred August 1, 1847, he followed the calling of a planter. His death left his widow with four children to care for: Lewis Pearl, who was born October 23, 1833, is now a Baptist minister and resides at Blue mountain, Miss.; Frederick G. was born July 6, 1839, and died in 1885; Henry Clay was born November 23, 1843, and in 1861 enlisted in the Federal army, in the Eleventh Illinois cavalry, under Captain Johnson, and died in 1863; and Edward William, the subject of this sketch, who was born in 1847. Two children of Lewis C. and Matilda (Harris) Cossitt died in childhood: Edward A., who was born in June, 1837, and died May 7, 1838, and William C., who was born May 19, 1841, and died in 1842. The father of these children was a member of the A. F. & A. M., and was a liberal contributor to worthy enterprises. He was a man of sound principles and instilled into the hearts of his older children lessons of honesty, which have remained with them to the present day. Edward W. Cossitt commenced life for himself as a planter in Tippah county in 1866, but prior to this, during the war, he served in the Federal army as a teamster in the Eleventh Illinois cavalry, receiving his discharge in 1865. He then returned to planting, continuing to 1888, since which time the most of his attention has been given to merchandising, his stock of goods being valued at $3,000. He owns about five hundred acres of land and has one hundred acres under cultivation. He is a member of the Knights of Honor. He was first married in 1867 to Miss Sarah E. Butler, to whom were born two children: Lelia B., wife of John Duncan; and S. M. Mr. Cossitt took for his second wife Miss N. E. Rich, a daughter of a planter of Tippah county, and their union resulted in the birth of three children: W. L. (deceased), Alda L. and Charles E.

Albert P. Cottrell, a liveryman and stockbreeder at West Point, Miss., was born near Waverly, Lowndes (now Clay) county in 1841, a son of David and Elsie (Hooks) Cottrell, who were born near Norfolk, Va., in 1801, and in Wilson county, Tenn., in 1809, respectively. David Cottrell was left an orphan at the age of ten months, and was taken to rear by an uncle, with whom he remained until fourteen years of age. He then left for the (then) wilds of Tennessee to make a fortune for himself, and in that state he married and lived until 1836, when he removed from Giles county, Tenn., to Mississippi, and settled in the woods bordering the Tombigbee river, where Waverly now is. He was one of the pioneers of what was then Lowndes county, for Columbus at that time was a mere village and the country a vast wilderness. He opened the first plantation in the community in which he settled, but the latter part of his life was spent in West Point, where he died in 1883, after a useful and well spent career. He was well respected and lived an honorable and upright life. His wife died in 1872, a member of the Methodist church. The maternal grandfather, Mr. Hooks, died in Middle Tennessee, a planter. Albert P. Cottrell was one of two surviving members of a family of eight children, the other member being M. J., wife of John V. Stacy, a planter of Clay county. Three sons served in the Confederate army: John, who died in 1865, was a member of Perrin's regiment of Mississippi troops from 1862; James, a member of Fourteenth Mississippi volunteers died at Camp Douglas, Ill., having been captured at Fort Donelson. Albert P. was educated at and in the vicinity of West Point, and by his father was brought up to a knowledge of planting. In 1861 he joined company C, Fourteenth Mississippi infantry, but one year later joined the cavalry under General Wheeler, and fought at Shiloh, the Kentucky campaign, Murfreesboro, Chickamauga, Missionary Ridge and the Atlanta campaign. He was then with Wheeler on his raid through east Tennessee and to Florence, Ala., but was with General Forrest at Selma, Ala. Soon after this he came home, where he was at the time of the general surrender. After the war he farmed one year, the succeeding year being devoted to merchandising, but he has since been engaged in the livery business, and for some seven years has given much attention to the breeding of Jersey cattle, his herd of forty head being one of the finest in the state. For ten years he was the efficient marshal of West Point, and is now discharging the duties of alderman, and is captain of the West Point camp of Confederate veterans. His life has been spent in the vicinity of where he now lives, and he has ever manifested a deep interest in the progress and development of this section, being enterprising, public spirited and progressive. He is straightforward in business, shows excellent judgment in the management of his affairs and has accumulated a fair fortune. He is very popular with all classes, is genial in disposition and has a wide acquaintance and many warm friends. He was married in 1873 to Miss Sophia A., daughter of Granville and Eveline Wilsford, who came from Tennessee to what is now Clay county about 1862 and afterward removed to Arkansas, where he died about 1881, having served in the Confederate army throughout the Rebellion. His widow is now residing at West Point. Mrs. Cottrell was born in Tennessee, and her union with Mr. Cottrell has resulted in the birth of six children. She is a member of the Methodist church, and Mr. Cottrell is a member of the Masonic fraternity and the K. of H.

W. Samuel Coulter, Williamsburg, Miss., a son of William Coulter, was born in Williamsburg, Covington county, Miss., and there grew to man's estate. He is the eldest of a family of four children, three of whom are living. The father was born and reared in Covington county, and was a son of Jesse Coulter, a pioneer of the county. Jesse Coulter married Nancy Williamson, and they reared a family of six children—two sons and four daughters. The subject of this notice was reared to the life of a farmer and received his elementary education in the common schools. His advantages in this direction, however, were very limited, and it was mainly through his own efforts that he fitted himself for teaching, a profession which he followed two years. Upon his first examination he received a first-grade certificate and was a successful educator. In the fall of 1889 he was elected sheriff of the county, to fill an unexpired term, and in the autumn of 1890 he was reëlected to the position. The duties of this office he discharged with rare fidelity and a firmness and courage of his convictions that at once won for him the reputation of a most excellent official. In January, 1891, Mr. Coulter was married to Miss Nanny Mathison, a daughter of William Mathison. He is an active member of the Methodist Episcopal church South, and belongs to the Masonic fraternity. He is a gentleman of genial disposition, courteous in his manner and possessing a host of friends throughout the county.

Capt. George S. Covert, furniture manufacturer and builder, of Meridian, Miss., was born in Glynn county, Ga., in 1835, a son of Isaac and Amelia Covert, both of whom are now deceased. He was educated in Detroit, Mich., where he was principally reared, in which city he engaged in building after he had obtained a sufficient knowledge of the calling. He later spent several years in St. Louis, but in 1855 came to Mississippi, and until the opening of the war was engaged in contracting and building in Madison county. Upon the opening of hostilities he enlisted in company C, of the Eighteenth Mississippi regiment, with which he served until Lee's surrender at Appomattox courthouse. He enlisted as a private, but at the close of the war, by meritorious conduct, he had attained the rank of captain. He was wounded at the battles of Fredericksburg, Gettysburg and the battle of the Wilderness by gunshots and shells, the last wound being quite serious and compelling him to remain under hospital treatment at Richmond for five weeks. He was in all the principal battles in Virginia, and in every emergency proved himself a faithful soldier and a gallant officer. After the war he was a resident of Madison county for one year, but since 1867 has been a resident of Lauderdale county, his home being in the town of Meridian. Upon first coming here he started a bucket factory and sawmill, but this establishment was unfortunately lost by fire in 1868 without insurance. He immediately rebuilt his sawmill, which he successfully conducted for four years. He then erected a cotton factory, the first and only one in the town, but this was burned a year later, but was not insured. He next engaged in the manufacture of sash, doors and blinds in 1870, continuing its management until 1888, at which time he sold out, and since that time has successfully managed a furniture factory, which is still in successful operation. He manufactures cheap and second grade furniture and store and office fixtures. All this time he has carried on contracting and building, and has put up a great many of the finest residences of Meridian. He is the contractor for the Southern hotel, which is a six-story building, containing about two hundred rooms, the building to be completed by the 1st of October. This is one of the handsomest hotels in the state, and under Captain Covert's able management will be substantially built. The captain is one of the leading citizens of the town and is wideawake, public spirited and well liked.

Capt. J. J. Cowan was born in the year 1830, in Warren county, Miss., and was one of a family of twelve children. He was first sent to Mississippi college, at Clinton, and afterward completed his education in Cumberland university, of Lebanon, Tenn., which at that time was a leading institution of learning in that section of the Union. He was married at the early age of twenty years to Miss M. L. Craig, and at once embarked in business in Vicksburg, which was carried on for many years under the well-known firm name of Cowan & Chapin. Commencing with a small capital, he pursued his business so earnestly, so ably and so successfully that upon the outbreak of the war he had accumulated a comfortable fortune. The call for arms met from him a prompt and ready response, and with the enthusiasm, sturdy devotion and disinterested patriotism that inspired Southern hearts, he left his large business interests and raised and equipped a battery of artillery, well known throughout the bloody conflict which followed as Cowan's battery. Attached at first to Colonel Wither's regiment, the only regiment of artillery ever organized in the Confederate service, he was stationed at Haine's bluff to defend Yazoo river. He successfully performed this duty, repulsing the attack of General Sherman's troops, and next took part in the defense of Vicksburg against the Federal fleet. Assigned to General Loring's division, he was in the disastrous battle of Baker's creek, was cut off from that general in the retreat that followed, and entered Vicksburg with the scattered remains of General Pemberton's army. Captain Cowan, with his faithful command, occupied an important position in the line of defense during the ever memorable siege of forty-seven days, and surrendered with the besieged army. The history of the privations that came after the place was invested, the nights of sleepless peril, the days of anxious care, the insufficient, unwholesome food, the life in shelterless trenches, exposed to prolonged cannonading or sudden assault, can never be written. The surrender of Vicksburg found Captain Cowan shattered in health, but as soon as his parole expired he reported for duty to Gen. Joseph E. Johnston, and his battery shared in all the glorious conflicts and hard-fought battles of the immortal retreat to Atlanta. With unfaltering courage he next followed the intrepid Hood in his ill-fated Tennessee campaign; was in the bloody battles of Franklin and Nashville, and the subsequent terrible retreat. He was transferred to General Maury's command at Blakely for the defense of Mobile, and there his battery fought stubbornly until the retreat of the infantry left them surrounded by the enemy. This was the last engagement of the war, and, so far as known, Captain Cowan fired the last guns. Enduring all the horrors of prison life on Ship island, a dangerous spell of illness, brought on by anxiety of mind and privations of body, proved nearly fatal, when the end of the conflict secured his release. Broken in health, his fortune swept away, Captain Cowan commenced anew the struggle for a competency, and although he met with varied fortunes and had many ups and downs, he continued to persevere, and is now one of the leading and successful business men of Vicksburg. Notwithstanding the hardships he had to endure during the war, he is now in good health, and weighs about two hundred pounds. He is a fine-looking gentleman, his hair and beard being quite gray; is five feet ten inches in hight, and still, in his upright and dignified carriage, shows evidences of his early military life.

Of that sturdy and independent class, the planters of Mississippi, none are possessed of more genuine merit or stronger character than Tarlton B. Cowan. He was born in Sevier county, Tenn., July 20, 1826, being the fourth of eight children born to David and Nancy (Haney) Cowan, both of whom were Tennesseeans, but came to Mississippi in 1830, locating in Warren county, where the father was engaged in planting. Mr. Cowan died in this county in 1863, surviving his wife by nine years. After the death of his father, Tarlton B. Cowan enlisted in Company G of the Vicksburg battery, J. J. Cowan, a cousin, being in command of the company of which he was a member, his elder brother, L. B. Cowan, being lieutenant of the same. He was in the engagements of Resaca, Tenn., and at Atlanta, Ga., and was constantly engaged, from the time he entered the service, until he was wounded at Atlanta, August 4, 1864, which unfitted him for further service. During the siege of Vicksburg Union soldiers made a hospital in his yard. He received only fair educational advantages in his youth, and at the age of sixteen years began to make his own way in the world, and as he and his brothers clung together and worked in unison, they soon accumulated considerable property as planters. In 1872 Mr. Cowan removed to Issaquena county and purchased eighteen hundred acres of land, of which sixteen hundred and seventy-five acres are under cultivation, since which time he has opened up six hundred acres of wild land, and has added by purchase three hundred and nineteen acres, being now the owner of about twenty-two hundred acres. He has stock to the amount of $20,500, and is a director in the First National bank of Greenville; has a $5,000 stock in the Bank of Port Gibson, and carries a stock of general merchandise worth $3,000, for the purpose of furnishing supplies to his hands. He has always been a stanch democrat, but has never desired political honors, although he has, on various occasions, been solicited to accept various positions. He has been a very successful business man, and although he has never ventured as far in speculation as some men, he has steadily added to his possessions, and is now wealthy. Being very public spirited he is liberal in contributing his means to worthy enterprises, and in social, as well as business, circles, he is much admired and highly esteemed. He is a member of the A. F. & A. M. He has remained unmarried throughout life, and only three of his immediate family are now living. His paternal great-grandfather, David Cowan, came from Ireland and settled on the French Broad river in Tennessee. His maternal great-grandfather, Richard Haney, was an Englishman, who settled in Virginia, afterward drifting to Tennessee, following the calling of a planter, which has been the chief occupation of his descendants.

William B. Cowan, Oxford, Miss., a most substantial and worthy citizen of Lafayette county, Miss., was born in Holly Springs, Marshall county, Miss., in 1840. He is the second of a family of three children of William H. and Elizabeth (Woods) Cowan. The parents were natives of North Carolina, where they were reared and married. In 1836 they removed to Mississippi and settled in Holly Springs, the father was a blacksmith by trade, and among the first buildings erected in the town was his shop. In 1844 he moved to Tallusa, and thence to the western edge of the county, where he located on a farm, there he passed the remainder of his days, his death occurring in 1871; his wife died in 1841. He was a self-made man in every sense of the word. Beginning in life a poor man, he accumulated a considerable amount of property by his own effort, and at the outbreak of the Civil war he was possessed of a comfortable fortune. He was a progressive citizen, a supporter of all worthy enterprises, a good neighbor and a true, stanch friend. He was a member of the Episcopal church, and in his political opinions adhered to the principles of the democratic party. William B. Cowan, son of the above, passed his youth in the quiet and retirement of farm life; he was given the opportunities of a good education of which he took advantage. In 1863 he was united in marriage to Miss Sue Parsons, a native of Mississippi; she died in 1869, having had born to her one son, James Gray, who died in 1865, at the age of two years. In 1866 Mr. Cowan began farming, and has continued in this occupation ever since, his efforts being rewarded with more than ordinary success. In 1880 he turned his attention to the profession of teaching, and for four years he taught the Wall Hill school. He was also mayor of this place for a period of seven years during which time he discharged his duties with strict fidelity. In 1871 he was married to Miss Ellen Parker, a daughter of W. B. Parker, a pioneer farmer of the county. Four children have been born of this union: Minnie was graduated in 1890 with the degree of A. M. at Whitworth college, being the only student to take this degree; she received her preparatory education at Jackson, and finished the course at Whitworth college in three years. In 1889 she secured the E. D. Miller medal for Latin scholarship; this medal was awarded by T. Marshall Miller. In 1890 she entered the State university to pursue the Latin, French and English languages. William Buford and John Kuhl are students at the State university, and Elizabeth Ellen, the fourth child, is at home. The family are members of the Methodist Episcopal church. Mr. Cowan is a member of the Masonic order.

James H. Cox, a well-known planter of Monroe county, was born near Cotton Gin in 1856, the son of John B. and Augusta Cox. His father was born in Alabama in 1807, and was educated at Franklin college. He came, with other members of his family, to Monroe county in 1843. He was a planter all of his subsequent life. He was a member of the Masonic order and of the Christian church. He entered the Confederate service in 1862, and was in the battle at Fort Pillow. Later, while at home on a furlough, he was taken to Memphis, but secured his pardon by the payment to a speculative Northerner of $500 in gold, a horse and five bales of cotton, valued at $1,250. He died April 8, 1879. His wife, formerly

Miss Augusta J. Hunt, was the daughter of James and Harriet Hunt, both of whom were natives of Abbeville, S. C., and came to Mississippi in 1840. The father was a clerk in a store during his earlier life, and in later life was a farmer. He, at one time, served as justice of the peace. He died in 1864; his wife in 1879, at the age of eighty-six years. To Mr. and Mrs. John B. Cox were born three children: Mary E. (now Mrs. Prowell); James H. and Walter L. Mrs. Cox survives him, living on the old homestead. John B. Cox was a son of John Cox, born in 1794, in Giles county, Tenn., who followed the life of a planter. He married Mrs. (Jennings) Billps, of Alabama, who bore him three children, viz.: John B., Mary J. (Adams) and Lucy A. (Wicks.) Upon coming to Monroe county in 1843, this pioneer bought six thousand acres of land from the Indians. Grandfather Hunt was a strong Unionist, and always opposed to the war. During the war a party of Yankees hung him, in order to make him give up his money, and after his wife gave them $100, they cut him down, while life yet remained to him. Grandmother Hunt was a cousin of Hon. A. P. Butler, of South Carolina, a lady of much education and culture. J. H. Cox was educated in the Aberdeen schools, after which he turned his attention to planting, and now owns one of the most extensive plantations in Monroe county. In 1887 he married Miss Mary A. Mitchell, of this county, and they have three children. Mrs. Cox is the daughter of James and Sarah (Rogers) Mitchell, the former a native of South Carolina and the latter of Monroe county.

John C. Cox, planter, is a Perry county Mississippian, his birth having occurred there on the 11th of August, 1819. His parents, John C. and Mary L. (Hurgor) Cox, having been born in South Carolina. They became residents of Perry county, Miss., in 1818, but in 1832 located in Lowndes county, settling on a good plantation eight miles west of where the town of Columbus now is. His family and Prowells' were the first white settlers of the county, and in early times experienced many hardships and privations in order to obtain a competency for themselves and their families. John C. Cox was called from life in the month of October, 1855, his wife's death having occurred in 1868. From his early youth up to the year of 1846, John C. Cox resided on the plantation on which his father settled on first coming to this section, then purchased the property on which he is now residing, which is near the town of Columbus, where he has a beautiful and comfortable home. His plantation indicates that he is thrifty, persevering and energetic, for it is thoroughly and carefully tilled, and is a model of neatness. Mr. Cox is a well informed and intelligent man, notwithstanding the fact that he only received a common-school education in his youth. He was married on the 21st of July, 1846, to Miss Sarah, daughter of William M. and Louisa Ervin, South Carolinians by birth. Mr. Cox served as a private in company H, Perrien's cavalry, Mississippi regiment, in 1863, and was at the battle of Atlanta, New Hope church, and in many smaller engagements, in all of which he acquitted himself creditably. His union resulted in the birth of three children, only one of whom is living, James Ervin. John C. and Catherine are deceased. Mr. Cox is a wideawake and public-spirited citizen, and politically is a democrat.

One of the leading and most successful physicians of Alcorn county, Miss., is Dr. E. A. Cox, of Baldwyn, who has acquired a flattering reputation and does credit to his profession. He was originally from Franklin county, Ga., born in January, 1834, and his parents, Michael and Mary (Thornton) Cox, were natives of the same state, the father born in Franklin and the mother in Jackson county. The paternal grandfather, Arris Cox, was a native Virginian and his father was a native of Scotland, coming to America prior to the Revolution, in which he served as a common soldier. Arris Cox and family moved to Georgia, settled in Franklin county, followed farming and were among the very first settlers. He lived to be one hundred and four years of age. His wife, Ruth Cox, lived, also, to a good old age. They had three sons and two daughters, all of whom grew up and had families. One daughter, Mary, married a Mr. Bowen and died in Georgia; Mrs. Rhoda Anderson died when very old in Georgia; Reuben came to Mississippi in 1834 or 1835, settled in Pontotoc, then Yalobusha county, and there followed farming near Coffeeville. He was born in 1803 and died in 1889, leaving a large family of children and grandchildren; Michael, father of our subject; and Matthew, who served in the Indian wars of Alabama and Georgia and died near where he was born in Georgia. Michael Cox was born in 1808 and was reared in his native county. At the outbreak of the Indian wars he volunteered as a soldier under Colonel Morris, and was a captain in Colonel Turk's regiment in the wars of 1835 and 1836. He and family came to Mississippi in 1839, overland, and were about twenty-four days in making the trip. They settled in Tippah county, near Ripley, and the father purchased a small tract of land, to which he afterward added more, until he became one of the leading farmers of the settlement. There he passed his last days. During the Civil war he enlisted in the sixty days' troops and served as captain. He passed a very active life and was honored and respected by all. He was a prominent democrat and was magistrate for a number of years. He was a member of the Baptist church, of which he was deacon, and was one of the leading members of the same. He took a leading part in every enterprise of importance and was a man of good judgment and sound, practical sense. He was a master Mason, having joined that fraternity when about forty-eight years of age. His death occurred in 1885. His wife was born about 1813 or 1814 and was also reared in Georgia. Her death occurred in 1850. She also held membership in the Baptist church. Their union resulted in the birth of eight children—six sons and two daughters—four sons and two daughters living at the present time, viz.: Dr. E. A., our subject; Dr. J. M.; Michael, died in 1877; R. Y., residing in Texas; W. J., also in Texas; Mrs. J. Young, of Tippah county, Miss., and Mrs. Ruth Hill, also in the Lone Star state. The father of these children was married to Mrs. Stovall, by whom he had one daughter, Mrs. Mary Stewart. His third marriage was to a Mrs. Webb, who bore him two children, Miss Johanna and N. L., both living on the old home place. His fourth marriage was to Miss Hamilton, who is yet living on the old home place. Dr. E. A. Cox was reared in Tippah county and his educational advantages were very limited, never having attended school after he was ten years of age. However, he has ever been a student, and is a man well posted on all subjects of moment. He began the study of medicine in 1852 with Dr. J. B. Ellis, a leading physician, and, in 1856 and 1857, attended lectures at Jefferson Medical college, Philadelphia. He graduated from what is now known as Tulane Medical college, Louisiana, in 1868. During the war he served as surgeon in the Seventh Mississippi cavalry, commanded by Lieut. L. B. Hovis, until about the time of the surrender, when he was made lieutenant-colonel of the Second regiment of Mississippi reserve troops. He was in the following engagements: Collierville, Moscow, Salem and Coldwater, and at the battle of West Point, Miss., he was under the command of Chalmers. After cessation of hostilities he returned to his profession and later graduated as above stated. He practiced at Ripley, Miss., until 1868, when he located at Baldwyn, where he has become one of the most popular and successful physicians. In connection with his practice he is engaged in farming and fruit-growing. Miss N. T. Henderson, who became his wife, was born in Tippah county on the 6th of January, 1838, and died in 1880, leaving one child, William M. Cox, who graduated from the University of Virginia in 1882, and also took a literary course at Clarksville, Tenn., graduating as B. A. and M. A. He is now one of the leading attorneys of Baldwyn. He married Miss Forrest Allen, the youngest daughter of David M. Allen, and sister of John M. Allen. He is an elder in the Presbyterian church and his wife is a member of the Christian church. They have one child, a son, E. A. Cox. Dr. Cox took for his second wife Mrs. E. J. Pearson, of Prentiss county, and a member of the Presbyterian church, in which the Doctor has been an elder ever since its organization. Dr. Cox's brother, Dr. J. M. Cox, is another very prominent and popular physician of Prentiss county. The latter was born in Mississippi on the 6th of June, 1842, and attended medical lectures at Louisville, Ky., completing his course in 1877. He then commenced practicing at Orizaba, Miss., but soon went to Falkner, thence to Baldwyn, where he has resided ever since. His skill as a physician immediately gave him a large practice, and by his pleasant, genial manner he has won a host of warm friends. He is one of the leading physicians of the town of Baldwyn. During the Civil war he enlisted in April, 1861, in company B, Second Mississippi regiment volunteers, under Capt. J. H. Buchanan and Col. W. C. Falkner, infantry. This company was organized at Harper's ferry, and Dr. Cox was in the first battle of Manassas; afterward he was in the medical department of the field, and continued in that capacity through all the campaigns of North Virginia. He was paroled on the 13th of April, 1865, and was married on the 12th of June of the following year to Miss Martha S. Chambers, a native of Mississippi, born 1843, and the daughter of John M. Chambers, a Baptist minister, and Mary E. (Seal) Chambers. She was the second in order of birth of nine children. To Dr. and Mrs. Cox were born four interesting children, three now living: Ella, Nancy G. and Charles C. The one deceased was James M. In his political views the Doctor affiliates with the democratic party. He and Mrs. Cox are members of the Baptist church, as are also Nancy and Charles C. Ella is also a Baptist in belief. Dr. Cox contributes liberally and gives his hearty support to all educational or religious enterprises.

Among the prosperous, enterprising business men of La Flore county is Andrew M. Craig, of Greenwood, Miss. He is a native of Alamance county, N. C., born August 24, 1846, and is a son of John W. and Melinda (Miner) Craig, also natives of North Carolina. The father was a planter of Alamance county, N. C., and there reared his family; he died there about the year 1889. Andrew M. Craig grew to manhood in his native county; he received his elementary education in a private school in Alamance county, and then entered Chapel Hill college. In 1864 he forsook the schoolroom, bade farewell to his hopes and plans, and enlisted in the Confederate army. He participated in the battle of Belfield, Va., Fort Fisher and in several lesser engagements. He was paroled at Greensboro, N. C., and after the close of the war he returned to school at Chapel hill, continuing his studies there for one year. In 1868 he came to Mississippi and in 1871 located at Greenwood. He secured a position as clerk and for a number of years was thus employed. Finally, in 1880, he embarked in mercantile trade on his own responsibility; it was only in a small way, as his means were limited, but he added to his capital little by little and increased his stock gradually; he attended strictly to business, and by wise management and the exercise of his unusual qualifications, he has built up a large and prosperous business. In addition to this business he carries on two plantations, having under cultivation about four hundred acres of land. He adds yearly to the cleared land, as he owns about one thousand acres in Le Flore county. In his mercantile business he handles about one thousand bales of cotton annually. Mr. Craig was married in Greenwood, February 18, 1885, to Miss Cappie H. Henry, niece of Dr. Henry, a history of whom appears on another page of this volume. Mrs. Craig was born in North Carolina, and was educated in her native state and in Virginia. Two children have been born to Mr. and Mrs. Craig: Joseph D. and William L. The mother is a member of the Methodist Episcopal church, while Mr. Craig belongs to the Presbyterian church.

Waterman Crane (deceased), an honorable and upright gentleman, who was one of the very earliest settlers of Claiborne county, Miss., is well remembered by the people of the county, for many of the old landmarks of this section are indelibly associated with his memory. When a young man he came to this region from Halifax, Nova Scotia, and near the town of Bruinsburg he entered land on which he spent the remainder of his days, his career as a planter being highly satisfactory. Like the majority of the early settlers he was compelled to undergo many hardships and privations, wore homespun clothing and attended religious services in private houses, or in "God's first temples, the groves." Wild game of various kinds roamed the woods at will, and Mr. Crane became quite a noted hunter. He was united in marriage to Miss Catherine Brashear, a noble woman, who made him an ideal wife, and his children an affectionate and faithful mother. She was born in 1764, and died November 15, 1830, having been an earnest Christian throughout life. On her tombstone are inscribed the following words: "Blessed are they that die in the Lord." Also the following poetry:

> " Friend after friend departs;
>   Who has not lost a friend?
>   There is no union of hearts,
>   That finds not here an end."

She bore her husband the following children: Elijah (who died March 20, 1810, aged twenty years), Eden (born October 15, 1799, and died January 17, 1819), Silas B. (born June 3, 1792, and died January 7, 1820), Robert (born September 15, 1804, and died February 14, 1824), and Clarissa (who was born in the latter part of 1798, in Claiborne county, being here married to William Christie at the age of seventeen years. She bore her husband one daughter, who became the wife of Rev. S. R. Bertron, for a history of whom see sketch of William Hughes. After the death of Mr. Christie his widow married William Young, who was born in Stephenson, Ayrshire, Scotland, April 16, 1786, and died March 10, 1863. Mrs. Young lived a life of great usefulness, and was loved devotedly by her daughter and those that knew her intimately, for her character was gracious and lovely. She was deeply devoted to her family, and endeavored, by every means in her power, to make her home an ideal one, surrounding all those who came within her influence with a watchfulness and care that only ended with her life. She departed this life February 5, 1877). Two of Mr. Crane's sons were killed by the Indians. He was a member of the first board of supervisors of the county, and was noted for his hospitality over a wide extent of territory. He departed this life in February, 1826, and on his tombstone are found the words: "He was much esteemed for unwavering integrity and strict honesty in all his relations with his fellow-men. Being an early settler in this new country, the calls on his hospitality were numerous, and never was the friendless and stranger turned away from his door." The old settlers speak very highly of Waterman Crane, many of whom spent their first night in his house on coming to the territory of Mississippi. He is closely related to many of the first families of the county by the marriage of his sons and daughters. He was a member of Bethel Presbyterian church, in which he took a deep and abiding interest, and was one of its most liberal supporters, and a man whose nobility of character will be treasured, remembered and emulated by his descendants for many years to come.

J. L. Crawford was born in Benton county, Miss., September 20, 1848, the third in a family of seven children, born to John L. and Mary (Nunnally) Crawford, natives of Alabama

Fraternally Yours
Robert Patt,

and Virginia respectively, who came with their parents to Mississippi about the time they attained to manhood and womanhood. They were married in that portion of Tippah county which has since been cut off to form Benton county. His father was a farmer by occupation and an influential man in this community. He and his wife were members of the Baptist church. He was a successful farmer and owned considerable land and slaves before the war. Our subject's mother died in 1869, his father in 1875. J. L. Crawford began life for himself at the age of seventeen as a private in the Confederate army in 1864, and served under General Armstrong in the state service, receiving his discharge in the spring of 1865 after the general surrender of the Confederate forces. Returning home he engaged in planting, and in 1867 he married Miss Mary Craig, a daughter of James T. Craig, of Benton county. They had six children: Mary F., Hal and Willie A. (deceased); James A., Walter and Effie. Mr. Crawford is the owner of one thousand acres of land, about ten per cent. of which is under cultivation. He also owns a planingmill valued at about $5,000, and a stock of general merchandise worth about $2,000, in Hickory flats. He is one of the most substantial business men of the town, and his occupations amount to about $15,000 annually. His family affairs and his family have engrossed his attention almost to the exclusion of everything else, and, though he has taken a deep interest in all public affairs, he has never had any political aspirations for any political or official position. Since early manhood he has been an earnest advocate for schools, colleges and churches, and a liberal supporter of them, and has never failed to contribute fully as much toward futherance of such institutions as any other man of his means in the county.

N. B. Crawford is a South Carolinian but of Scotch descent, born in Edgefield district in 1835, a son of Robert H. and Mary (Jennings) Crawford, the former of whom was born in South Carolina in 1795 and the latter in Edgefield district of that state in 1800. The paternal grandfather, David Crawford, was a Virginian, but after removing to South Carolina represented Edgefield district in the state legislature a number of times, in which capacity he was serving at the time of his death. He was a successful financier and became a well-to-do planter. He reared a family of five sons and two daughters, as follows: Robert H.; James; William H. (who removed to Mississippi about 1836, afterward represented Chickasaw county in the state legislature and later removed to Texas, where he died in 1891); Benjamin Franklin, a resident of Holmes county, Miss.; John A., who died at Belton, Tex., in 1864 or 1865; Frances, the deceased wife of Cyrus Sharp, and Caroline (deceased), all of whom received practical English educations. The boyhood of Robert H. Crawford was spent on his father's plantation, and at the early age of seventeen years he enlisted in the war of 1812, in which he served as a private. In 1816 he was married to Miss Jennings, a daughter of William and Tabitha Jennings, the former of whom was a planter and merchant in Edgefield district, where he made his home until his death after which his widow came to Mississippi where she passed from life. After his marriage Robert H. Crawford continued planting in South Carolina until 1839, when he came to Mississippi and settled in the vicinity of Atlanta, in Chickasaw county. He purchased a half section of fine bottom land, which he successfully tilled and in time accumulated a competency for himself and family. He became very popular, and for about twelve years held the office of county assessor, and was at one time a candidate for sheriff, being beaten by the opposing candidate by only four votes. He was a democrat, and adhered strictly to the principles of his party. He reared a family of thirteen children—seven sons and six daughters—all of whom lived to mature years, those living at the present time being as follows: James D., a planter of Grenada county, Miss.; Robert A., a planter of Chickasaw county, Miss.; Bennett O., a planter near Attala, Chickasaw county, Miss.; Eliza, wife of Joel Ellisa, also residing near Atlanta; Nathan Barrett, the immediate subject of this sketch; Samuel S., a planter and trader of this county and William H., a planter of this county. Those deceased are: Tabitha, the deceased wife of Ezra Carpenter, of Texas; Mary, the deceased wife of C. C. Bingham, of Texas; Sarah, the deceased wife of W. T. Hamilton, of Mississippi; Priscilla, the deceased wife of Sterling Carpenter, of Mississippi; and Nancy, the deceased wife of W. G. Crough, of Calhoun county, Miss. Robert H. Crawford was a member of the Baptist church, in which faith he died in 1864. His widow survived him until 1874, when she too passed away, a member of the Missionary Baptist church.

The early educational advantages of N. B. Crawford were exceedingly limited, the only education of service to him being that which he acquired after he had set out to make his own way in the world. His boyhood was spent on the home plantation, which was one of the first to be cleared up in the county. Upon starting to make his own way in the world, at the age of twenty-two years, he began clerking in a general store in Atlanta, continuing one year, when he engaged in planting, which calling he followed up to 1862. He was married on the 12th of July, 1857, to Miss Cyrena Jane Harley, of German descent, a native of Tennessee, born near Humboldt, in 1841, her parents being Moses J. J. and Cyrena (Jackson) Harley, Tennesseeans by birth. To Mr. and Mrs. Crawford nine children were born: Van E., wife of Dr. J. W. Abernathy, of Atlanta; Yancey, wife of J. E. Logan, a merchant of Webster county, Miss.; Jennie, wife of A. C. Maron, a merchant of Atlanta; Ama, clerk in the pension office at Washington, D. C.; Joseph W., in school at Houston; Ella May, also at school there, and Lou, Rena and Harley at home. In 1862 Mr. Crawford dropped his farming implements to enlist in the Confederate army, and in March, 1862, he became a private in company H, Thirty-first Mississippi infantry. In September of the same year he was chosen lieutenant, being afterward promoted to first lieutenant, in which capacity he served until three days before the close of the war, taking part in the battles of Baton Rouge, Vicksburg, Peach Tree creek, Resaca, the engagements around Atlanta and the battle of Franklin, where he was twice wounded, being disabled for service for sixty days. He was a participant in every battle in which his regiment took part save one, which occurred while he was laid up from his wound. At the reorganization of his company he was offered a commission as captain, but being determined to enter the cavalry service he resigned his commission. Three days later the Confederate army surrendered. Mr. Crawford then returned to his planting operations in Mississippi, but in 1867 opened a general mercantile establishment, the firm taking the name of Crawford & Harley. Although at the close of the war Mr. Crawford only possessed $7.50 in money he owned a fertile plantation of two hundred and sixty acres. This, however, did not aid him materially for some time, for he had no stock or farming implements with which to till it. After hiring out for two years he, by good management and economy, managed to lay by $800, which he invested in a stock of merchandise. He has been constantly engaged in the business ever since, in which he has been very successful, and has a large and paying patronage. At first a large part of their stock of goods, which amounted to $3,700, was purchased on credit, but this indebtedness was soon paid off and additions were made to their stock, of which Mr. Crawford became sole proprietor in 1872, his partner's interest amounting to $5,500. After conducting affairs alone until 1885 he associated himself with his brother-in-law, A. M. Harley, since which time the firm has been N. B. Crawford & Co. Mr. Crawford is the owner of three thousand three hundred acres of land, of which he cultivates between eight hundred and one thousand acres. This land is in nine different tracts in Chickasaw county and one tract of nine hundred and sixty acres in

Kansas, which is devoted to the raising of wheat, the land in this section being given to cotton and corn. He is interested to some extent in stockraising, and makes a specialty of Durham cattle and Berkshire and Poland China hogs. Besides raising sufficient stock to run his plantation, what he derives from his sales amounts to quite a comfortable sum annually. He has his own sawmill, cottongin and cornmill, and besides doing his own work he does sawing, ginning and grinding for his neighbors. Mr. Crawford has been interested in the political affairs of his section, and when only twenty-three years of age was elected to the position of justice of the peace, serving two years. In 1881 he was elected to the state legislature by his numerous friends, and so ably and efficiently did he fill this office that in 1883 he was reëlected, serving two years longer. He has been tendered the nomination for state senator several times, but has always declined to make the race. He is a member of Atlanta lodge No. 362 of the A. F. & A. M., and has held the office of junior and senior warden, but declined to serve as worshipful master, not having the time to devote to the work. His granduncle, William H. Crawford, was at one time a candidate for president of the United States. He was called upon to mourn the death of his wife in February, 1885, she being an earnest and worthy member of the Missionary Baptist church at the time of her death. She was a noble wife, and was in every sense of the word a true helpmeet to her husband. In November, 1885, Mr. Crawford was united in marriage to Miss Sudie C. Frazee, of French descent, who was born in Illinois November 12, 1860, a daughter of Joseph and Anna (Stone) Frazee, both of whom were born in Kentucky and removed to Indiana, thence to Illinois, in the legislature of which state Mr. Frazee's brother was a representative. By his present wife Mr. Crawford has two children: Annie Bert and Josie. He and his wife are members of the Baptist church.

R. L. Crook, of Bolton, Miss., was born in December, 1850, in Smith county, Miss., the youngest of four children born to L. E. and Mary (Carr) Crook, the former of whom was born in South Carolina and the latter in Mississippi. In 1832 R. L. Crook came to Mississippi and for one term before the war acted as sheriff of Smith county. He died in 1885. R. L. Crook attended the common schools up to about the age of sixteen years, then began farming on his father's place, continuing this occupation three years. He then opened a mercantile establishment in Morton, Scott county, Miss., and during the six years that he remained there he was very successful, and did a yearly business of about $50,000. He next engaged in the same business in Bolton with Messrs. Geddes and McLauren, and here has since met with phenomenal success. Besides the annual business of about $200,000, he owns land to the amount of three thousand five hundred acres, of which about one-half is under cultivation, which he manages in connection with looking after the interests of his store. His chief crops are cotton and corn, the former amounting to about four hundred bales yearly. He also raises a few horses of a good grade each year. He is the efficient and trustworthy cashier of the Hinds county bank, which was established in 1890 with John Geddes as president, and with a capital of $25,000. They are doing a good general banking business. Mr. Crook is a member of Bolton lodge No. 326, of the A. F. & A. M., of which he was master for six years, and is a member of lodge No. 1361 of the Knights of Honor, of which he became dictator at the time it was organized. He has also filled the chair of honor in the Knights of Pythias, of which he is a worthy and active member; in fact, he has always taken considerable interest in secret society work. He was married in 1874 to Miss Bettie Geddes, a native of Scott county, Miss., and by her has the following children: Robbie Bell, Charley E., John Geddes, Allie and Pauline. The family are members of the Methodist Episcopal church, in which Mr. Crook holds the position of steward.

Mr. Crook is a gentleman possessing fine business qualifications, is well posted and up with the times, and he and his family move in the highest social circles of the town and section in which they reside.

De Soto county can name no man whose successes in life are more thoroughly of his own making than William A. Crossett, of Hernando, Miss. He is a native of the county in which he now resides, born August 12, 1850, and is the youngest of a family of seven children. His parents, Andrew and Delilah (Cupp) Crossett, came from South Carolina and Alabama, respectively. The father settled in De Soto county about the year 1830, and engaged in planting near Hernando; he was a cautious, modest man, making no large ventures, nor going into debt. He was of a retiring disposition, and had no aspirations for public office or political honors. He died in 1881, at the age of eighty years; his wife still survives at the age of eighty-one years. The paternal grandfather emigrated to America from Ireland, and settled in South Carolina. The maternal grandfather was John Cupp; he lived to be ninety years old. The ancestors, both maternal and paternal, were agriculturists. The Cupps were of German lineage, and were early settlers of Alabama. William A. Crossett was reared in De Soto county, and acquired a practical education in the common schools. The breaking out of the war prevented his pursuing his studies to any advanced extent, but the training he had, supplemented by a broad experience, has developed a keen judgment and excellent business qualifications. At the age of eighteen years he began life for himself, and through his own efforts he has accumulated all his present possessions, viz.: twenty-five hundred acres of land, twelve hundred and fifty of which he has placed under cultivation; one-half interest in the business of W. A. Crossett & Co., and a store on his plantation near Lake Cormorant. W. A. Crossett & Co. do an annual business of $30,000, and the plantation store a business of about $6,000 annually. Mr. Crossett has been treasurer of De Soto county four years. He was married in 1872 to Sallie E. Scott, a native of De Soto county, Miss., and a daughter of Joseph and Elizabeth (Mays) Scott. Of this union six children have been born: Mary La Eula, Donnie A., William Walter, Lila Maud, Joseph Andrew and Sallie Girtrude. The parents and two older children are members of the Cumberland Presbyterian church. Mr. Crossett is a Mason and also a member of the Knights of Honor. He is self-made in every sense of the word, and his accomplishments are such of which any man might well feel proud. As a citizen he is honored and respected by all.

Rev. William A. Crum was born in Tipton county, Tenn., in 1837, the youngest of the two children of Eli and Rachael (Ayers) Crum. His father was a native of North Carolina; his mother of Tennessee. His grandfather on his father's side moved from North Carolina to Alabama in 1812, and lived out the balance of his life in that state. The father of our subject was reared in Alabama, and from there went to Tennessee while yet a young man. There he met Miss Ayers, whom he afterward married, in 1829. He removed from Tennessee to what was then Tippah county, Miss., in 1837, before the Chickasaw Indians had left the country, and he may be properly termed one of the oldest settlers of the state. For a number of years he was a member of the Tippah county board of supervisors. He was well and favorably known throughout the state as a high-minded, Christian gentleman, and was an elder in the Cumberland Presbyterian church for many years. The mother of our subject died in 1858, his father in 1860, at their old home in Tippah county. William A. Crum was educated in the common schools, and during his entire life he has been engaged in planting. In 1855, at the age of eighteen, he married Miss Mary M. Smith, a daughter of John Smith, of Tippah county. They had nine children, named as follows: Emma, wife of John P. Smith; Rachel, now Mrs. J. T. Armor; William E.; Mallie O., deceased; C. Lee; Sarah E.

wife of W. H. Cox, Jr.; Mary L., wife of J. T. Wall; Benjamin, deceased; and Martha C. Mr. Crum enlisted in company G, of the Seventeenth Mississippi infantry, under W. S. Featherstone, of Holly springs, in 1861, and was in the battle of Bull Run, the seven days' fight at Richmond, and other engagements in Virginia. At Gettysburg he received two severe gunshot wounds—one in the leg and the other in the body—and was captured and taken to the hospital at Baltimore, Md., where he was shortly afterward paroled. As soon as he was able he returned to his home, too badly disabled to rejoin his command, and having to walk with the aid of a crutch for about four years. After he became able to work he resumed his farming occupation, and has tilled the soil with considerable success ever since. He was a delegate to the state constitutional convention to conform the constitution of the state to the reconstruction policy of the government in 1865, and in 1875 he was elected a member of the legislature from Benton county. He is a very prominent man in the community, and has been active in the political affairs of his town and county, as well as in those of his state. He and his wife are members of the Christian church, in which denomination he has been a well-known and efficient minister for the past twenty-six years. He owns six hundred acres of land, one hundred and sixty of which are under cultivation, and on the old homestead where his parents lived and died he may be said to have lived all his life, having been only three months old when his parents located thereon. For the past ten years he has been postmaster at Hickory flats, where he has taken a deep interest in all local affairs, and where his family are in high esteem among a large circle of acquaintances. Mr. Crum is the only living representative of his family. He is everywhere looked upon as a progressive citizen, and an honorable, straightforward business man. In the former period of his life he read law, was admitted to the bar and practiced for eleven years—four at Ripley and seven at Hickory flats. In all the various pursuits to which he has devoted himself, he has been successful always, and as planter, preacher, lawyer and public official he has won for himself the respect of all with whom he has had dealings.

Hon. Jonathan Culpepper is a prominent Mississippian, and is universally regarded as one of the successful men of his time. Although his advantages for acquiring an education while growing up were quite poor, he possessed a naturally fine intellect, and made the most of every opportunity which presented itself, not only in his youth, but throughout his entire career. After proving himself a true and tried soldier of the Confederate army throughout the Civil war, he returned home, after peace had been declared, with the sum of $10 in his pocket, which constituted his worldly possessions, and although he deeply regretted the outcome of the war, he did not fold his hands and uselessly repine, but at once bent all his energies toward rebuilding his fortunes. He is now in independent circumstances, is regarded as the soul of honor, and his name commands unlimited credit. He was chosen by his numerous friends to represent Lauderdale county in the state legislature, and it is a remarkable fact that he did not seek the office, nor did he attend more than one precinct canvass, yet he distanced all competitors. A man of solid worth, he is one of the few strong men of the county, in spite of every adverse circumstance. He was first married to a Miss Hunter, who left him a widower, after which, in 1878, he was married to Miss Susan Preston, by whom he has three children: Blanche, Nell, and Louise.

Hon. M. C. Cummings, a prominent farmer and citizen of Itawamba county, Miss., was a son of Levy and Naoma (Keas) Cummings. He is the sixth of their family of eleven children, and was born in Limestone county, Ala., October 17, 1810. His father was born in Virginia about 1780, and was a member of one of the old families of that state who participated in the war of 1812. He was married in Virginia, and later removed to Kentucky, and thence to Limestone county, Ala., where he died in 1845. When he removed to Alabama the country was new and peopled with Indians, who were at one time so troublesome that he was obliged to leave the state, but returned a year or two later. He and his wife were members of the Primitive Baptist church. The latter died when Mr. Cummings, our subject, was about five years of age. She was a native of Virginia. The children were named Mason, Nancy, Jordan, Isaac, Catherine, David, M. C., Malachi, Levy, Rial, Betsey and Washington. Of these only M. C., Levy and Rial are now living. The subject of this notice was reared upon his father's plantation, and began to do for himself at the age of eighteen years. He emigrated to Western Tennessee and settled near Perdy, where he engaged in planting. He lived there several years, and in February, 1833, came to Columbus, Miss., where he married Miss Sarah, daughter of Hugh and Jennie (Thompson) Rogers, who were natives of South Carolina. Their five children were named as follows: John, William, Hugh, Jennie and Joseph. Mrs. Cummings was born in South Carolina, in 1815. She has borne her husband no children, but they have reared twenty-seven orphan children. The family removed from Columbus to this county in 1836, and located on the present site of the Fulton hotel. Mr. Cummings was the first settler in Fulton, and came at a time when the country was practically uninhabited except by Indians, who were not hostile, however, but showing good dispositions toward the settlers and who lived by hunting and fishing, some of them raising small patches of corn. He was the owner of a tract of land embracing the site of the present town of Fulton, and there is a place near there where he cleared the timber off in 1836, and upon which a good crop has been raised every successive season since. He built the Fulton hotel, which was the first public house in the county, and of which he was for some time the proprietor, though he has made planting his principal occupation. He is the owner now of about ten thousand acres of land in this county, about twenty-five per cent. of which is under cultivation. He has occupied his present residence, about one mile north of Fulton, since 1854, and he was influential in the organization of his county, which took place some twenty years prior to that date. In 1839 he was elected probate judge, and in 1841, he represented the county in the state legislature. He was a member of the state convention of 1860, to decide upon some action in view of the political troubles of that time, and strongly opposed secession, but when secession was an accomplished fact, he did all in his power to aid the Confederate cause. He equipped a company which was commanded and organized by Captain Turner, and was known as the Cummings Grays, expending some $1,500. In 1861 he represented his district as state senator, and filled that office with distinction during the entire war period. After the war he found that his property had been damaged to the extent of at least $100,000, but he at once set about the work of rehabilitation, resuming planting and gradually engaging more and more extensively in the cotton trade. He has been for forty-five years a member of the Methodist church, of which his wife is also a member. Although he has been an earnest member of the democratic party, he has, since the war, practically retired from politics. His operations in a business way have been very extensive, and he was the builder of most of the houses and of the Methodist church of the town of Fulton, and is the largest land owner in Itawamba county.

William Curphey, sawmill owner and lumber merchant of Vicksburg, Miss., was born on the Isle of Man in 1844 and was there educated. At the age of twenty-five years he came to America and settled in Cleveland, Ohio, where he followed the trade of a carpenter. He came to Vicksburg in 1870, and engaged in contracting under the firm name of Curphey & Bro., which he continued until 1882. He then turned his attention to his present business, which he conducted with success alone until 1890, when he entered into partnership with another gentleman, and the firm is now known as the Ouellette, Curphey Lumber company. The capacity of their mill is about twenty-five thousand feet per day, but they have in process of erection a mill which will have a capacity of fifty thousand feet per day, and when completed will be one of the largest establishments of the kind in this portion of the state. The timber which they use is mostly ash and oak, and is sold mostly in the Eastern markets, but a great deal of cypress is used for home consumption. They are also placing a planer in operation, and as the house is already erected, it will be soon in operation. The engine will be of one hundred and fifty horsepower, and it as well as all other necessary machinery has already been purchased. The sales will amount to about five million feet annually at the present time, but when their new engine gets in good running operation they fully expect to raise the amount to eight million feet. At present they have some seven million feet of unsawed timber, and Mr. Curphey is the owner of about one thousand acres of fine timber land, which will be also excellent for agricultural purposes when improved. This land is situated on Deer creek, in Washington county, and lies along Louisville, New Orleans & Texas railroad. Mr. Curphey is one of the leaders of his calling in the state, and does the largest business of the kind of any firm in Vicksburg. He was married in this city in 1879 to Miss Ellen Caley, by whom he has five children: Elizabeth, Charles, Eleanor, Esther and Sarah. Mr. and Mrs. Curphey are members of the Episcopal church, and he is a member of Vicksburg lodge No. 26 of the A. F. & A. M., in which order he has filled various chairs; is also a member of the K. of P., George Washington lodge, in which he is prelate; the K. of H., the American Legion of Honor and the Elks, in which orders he has taken a prominent part. Mr. Curphey is a thoroughgoing and practical man of business, and fully merits his present success.

James H. Currie, De Kalb, Miss., a prominent attorney of Kemper county, was born in the county November 8, 1854, and is a son of Archibald C. and Isabelle (McNeill) Currie. The father was born in Robinson county, N. C., in 1806, and was a son of Angus Currie. He was educated for a teacher, and followed the profession for a number of years. At the age of twenty-five years he was married, and removed from North Carolina to Alabama, where he remained one year. In 1838 he came to Kemper county, Miss., and settled in the neighborhood of Kemper springs, where he opened a plantation of one thousand acres. He was from this time devoted to agricultural pursuits, and passed the rest of his life on his plantation. In his political opinions he affiliated with the democratic party. He was a member of the board of police, of which he was president for some time. He was a man of broad public spirit, and high scholarly attainments. He belonged to the Presbyterian church. At the breaking out of the Civil war he did not go into the service, but five of his sons went out in defense of the Southern cause: Daniel M., Angus F., Archibald A., William C. and John R. Angus and John were both killed in battle, and the others went through the entire struggle. Daniel and Archibald were both wounded. The father died in 1869, in Kemper county. The mother was born in Richmond county, N. C., in 1811, and died in 1880. She was a daughter of Daniel McNeill, and a woman of rare attainments. She was well educated, a wide reader, and above all, was possessed of that deep integrity of character which won the love and admiration of all with whom she came in contact. She was the mother of ten children: Daniel, Flora A., Angus, Archibald A., William, John, Elizabeth, Margaret, Albert C. and James H. All are living but three, the two who died in the war and Archibald A., who died of yellow fever at Meridian, Miss., in 1878. He was treasurer of Lauderdale county, and was a man highly esteemed by the entire community. James H. Currie, the youngest of the children, received his education in the common schools of his native county and at Cooper Normal college. He began the practice of law in De Kalb in 1884, under

Major Evans, who died in December, 1887. Mr. Currie had just entered practice the year previous to the death of Major Evans, so he was able to take up the greater portion of the Major's business. In addition to his professional interests, he owns about three thousand acres of land, which he cultivates with much success. He was married in 1887 to Miss Frances Neville, a daughter of Andrew L. Neville. (See sketch of James Neville.) Mrs. Currie was born at Mobile, Ala., in 1868, and received her education there and in St. Louis. Mo. Mr. and Mrs. Currie are the parents of two children: James H., Jr., and Francis N. Mr. Currie is a member of the Knights of Honor, and Masons. Politically, he affiliates with the democratic party. He has represented his county in the state legislature, displaying an ability for the conduct of the affairs of government that won the admiration of all his colaborers. He has been superintendent of education for four years. He is deeply interested in the progress and growth of the South, and is ardently loyal to home industries. He and his wife are members of the Presbyterian church.

J. T. Currie, retired planter, Greenville, Miss., was the sixth in order of birth of seven children born to Angus and Mary (Campbell) Currie, natives of North Carolina, whose ancestors were among the prominent families of Scotland. The father followed the occupation of a planter, and after residing in his native state for many years moved to Alabama, where he died soon after. The mother died in 1863, during the Civil war. J. T. Currie was born in North Carolina in 1830, but was reared in Alabama, where he secured a good practical education. In 1862 he enlisted as a private in company K, Second Alabama cavalry, and was advanced to a position on the wagon trains. After cessation of hostilities he returned to his home in Alabama, and there continued to reside until 1868, when he came to Mississippi. When starting out for himself it was but natural, perhaps, that he should choose planting as his occupation in life, as he had been trained to it from early boyhood, his father before him having followed that pursuit. When coming to Mississippi he first located in Coahoma, remained there two years, and then, in 1869, came to Washington county, where he has since made his home. He bought a plantation on Deer creek, and in a few years was the owner of thirteen hundred acres of land, with five hundred acres under cultivation, all the result of his own good management. He also bought and improved another place of seven hundred acres. In 1889 he sold his fine plantation for $50,000 and is now residing in Greenville, engaged as a capitalist. Mr. Currie's success is a fair example of what can be accomplished by perseverance and close attention to business, even in planting in this county. He made a fortune in less than twenty years. His methods were to treat his colored labor well and honestly, and to manage reasonably close himself. He has a comfortable and pleasant home and can now enjoy the fruits of his labor.

Hon. Malcolm M. Currie is a worthy and representative agriculturist of Franklin county, Miss., and acquired his knowledge of the calling from his father, Malcolm Currie, who was also a tiller of the soil, and the knowledge thus acquired has been put to practical experience. He was born in Jefferson county, Miss., in 1829, being the youngest in a family of four sons and six daughters born to Malcolm and Rhoda (Farrar) Currie, the former of whom was born in Scotland, in 1780. In his boyhood he was brought to America and after residing in North Carolina until he was a young man, he removed to Jefferson county, Miss., his parents dying here. He was married in Adams county, but located in Jefferson county, and afterward lived for some years on the Pearl river. After his return to Jefferson county he died at the home of the subject of this sketch in 1863, having been a successful planter. He served in the War of 1812, and in religious faith was a Presbyterian. His wife was probably born in Adams county, and died when young, a daughter of Alex. Farrar, who was one of the first residents of Adams county. Hon. Malcolm M. Currie is the only one of his parents' family that is now living. He was educated in Jefferson county, and after attaining a suitable age, he engaged in teaching, and some years later in planting. In 1857 he was married to Miss Amelia Ione, daughter of John and Cynthia Higdon, who spent their lives in Franklin county, Mr. Higdon being a planter. Mrs. Currie was born in this county and has borne her husband eight children, two of whom are living. In 1876 Mr. Currie was elected to the state senate to fill the unexpired term of Henry McClure, and the duties of this position he discharged with ability and honor and to the entire satisfaction of all who had elected him to the position. He is a man of unquestioned honor and integrity, and throughout his life has been a substantial, law-abiding and honorable citizen. He is the owner of about twelve hundred acres of land, the most of which has been acquired by his own efforts, and in connection with attending to his plantation he is also engaged in teaching school. His brother Edward, who is deceased, was a member of the First Mississippi (Jefferson Davis' regiment) in the Mexican war.

CHAPTER XVI.

SPECIAL SKETCHES, D.

AMONG the prominent lawyers of the state is Austin Mortimer Dahlgren, who was born in Natchez, Adams county, Miss., October 3, 1856, and is a son of Gen. Charles G. Dahlgren, a native of Philadelphia. The General was a son of Bernard Dahlgren, who came from Stockholm, Sweden, as the first Swedish consul to America; and who was a direct descendant from Gustavus Adolphus, king of Sweden. General Dahlgren received his education in Philadelphia, and was private secretary to Nicholas Biddle, the famous Philadelphia banker, and president of the old bank of the United States. In about 1826 he was sent to New Orleans to establish a branch bank of the United States, and was soon afterward sent to Natchez, Miss., where he was also connected with a banking establishment. He was so much pleased with this place that he determined to settle there, and accordingly embarked in the commission and banking business at that point, and afterward became one of the largest cotton planters in that section. He carried out his undertaking very successfully, and became one of the prominent men of Mississippi. When the Civil war broke out, he organized and equipped at his own expense the Dahlgren guards, Third Mississippi regiment, and when the conflict ended he had won the title of brigadier-general. He was appointed one of General Polk's staff a few days before the Bishop was killed. After the cessation of hostilities, he found his plantation ruined and his wealth swept away. All industries being crippled in the South, and having a large family, he removed to New York city, and engaged in the practice of law, and as many wealthy and prominent men had known him in his wealth and prominence, he was very successful in this venture, and was enabled to support himself and family in comfort. He died in 1889. He was twice married, first in 1840, to Mrs. Mary M. Ellis, nee Mary M. Routh, the daughter of Job Routh, who came from Wales, and was the largest cottonplanter and slaveowner in the South, having some twelve cotton plantations in Mississippi and Louisiana, and owning several hundred slaves. General Dahlgren was married, after the death of his first wife, to Miss Mary E. Vannoy, of Nashville, Tenn., in 1860. He has ten sons and two daughters living. The subject of this notice is the fourth son by his first wife. He passed a portion of his youth in Natchez, and was graduated from the Shenandoah Valley academy, at Winchester, Va. He then came to Beauvoir, to live with his sister, Mrs. Sarah A. Dorsey, after the death of her husband, Judge Samuel Dorsey. Mrs. Dorsey was a noted linguist and novelist and an enthusiastic Southerner, and at her death bequeathed Beauvoir and a large amount of her other property to ex-President Jefferson Davis, on account of the services he had rendered the South. Mr. A. M. Dahlgren, while at Beauvoir, studied law under ex-President Jefferson Davis and his nephew, Gen. Joseph R. Davis, and was admitted to the bar in 1878, and at once entered upon a good practice. He and General Davis established and edited the *Seashore Gazette* at Pass Christian, Miss. Mr. Dahlgren now lives at Beauvoir, and has offices both at Mississippi city and Biloxi, and has won a wide reputation for his ability, excellent judgment and honorable bearing. He has taken a deep interest in the politics of the state and has held several minor offices in the county, and was elected on September 5, 1891, by a handsome majority over strong opponents, to the state legislature, to represent Harrison county for four years, from January, 1892. He is a master Mason and belongs to the Legion of Honor, and is an honorary member of the Commercial Travelers' association, and the United States Mutual Accident association, and a commissioner of deeds for Alabama and Louisiana. He is a man who will always have a host of friends. One of his uncles was Admiral John A. Dahlgren, of the United States navy, who invented the cannon that bears his name, the Dahlgren gun. One other uncle was the celebrated Count De Rohan, who fought in every European war for the past forty years, and received the highest honors and titles from several crowned heads. Mr. Dahlgren was married in 1881, to Miss Frances Mildred Smith, of Rochester, N. Y. They are both worthy members of the Presbyterian church. He is a lineal descendant from Gustavus Adolphus, king of Sweden, and the Scotch-Irish Earls of Mortimer.

James H. Dalton, deceased, of New Albany, Union county, Miss., was born in Pontotoc county, Miss., in 1842. When he was a child his parents removed to Palestine, Tex., where he remained till he was seventeen years of age, when he returned to New Albany, Miss., and became a student in the Young Men's seminary at Cotton Plant, Tippah county, Miss. At the beginning of the war he enlisted in the Second Mississippi regiment, under Col. W. C. Falkner, of Ripley. Soon, however, he became the private secretary of Gen. Joe Davis, in which capacity he served until the close of the war. He was present at all the battles about Richmond, the battles at Manassas junction, Antietam, Chickahominy, Gettysburg, Fredericksburg, Chancellorsville and Cold harbor. He was also present in the engagements around Petersburg, and surrendered with Lee's army at Appomattox courthouse. At Gettysburg he was severely wounded, and there he was made prisoner of war, but escaped within a few minutes after his capture. After the war he devoted his attention to planting, which he followed with considerable success until 1872, when he became sheriff under J. A. McBride. This was his first official work, but he attended to all of its details so thoroughly that he soon became the natural leader of the democratic party in Union county, having gained the confidence of the adherents of that party. He did effective service in delivering that part of the state from republican misrule. He began the practice of law in 1877, and became known almost at the outset as an able, straightforward advocate and attorney. In 1879 he was placed on the democratic ticket as a nominee for the state senate against W. A. Boyd of Tippah county, but a democratic nomination at that time was not equivalent to an election. Many members of the party inclined to join the greenback movement, which was then strong in this section. He met in debate such men as Gen. A. M. West, of Holly springs, and Hon. W. A. Crum, of Benton county, and others, and was elected by a handsome majority. He ably advocated the election of Col. James M. Stone for governor in 1881, when the latter was defeated by Hon. Robert Lowry by but three votes. Had Governor Stone been elected, there can be but little doubt that Mr. Dalton would have been made chancellor. He continued his legal practice with uninterrupted success, having been retained in some of the most noted criminal cases in this part of the state for the past few years. At the time of his death he was attorney in Union county for the Kansas City, Memphis & Birmingham railroad company. He was a Mason in high standing, and popular in business, social and political circles. It is said of him that he had no personal enemies and that his liberality amounted to prodigality almost. He left a wife and four children, all sons. Of these, L. W. Dalton of New Albany, Miss., is a prominent young lawyer in legal partnership with Z. M. Stephens. He studied law under his father's directions and was admitted to the bar in 1877. He was married in 1888 to Miss M. T. Mitchell.

Charles B. Danforth is a typical Mississippi planter, substantial, enterprising and progressive, and such a man as wields no small influence in the community where he makes his home. He was born in De Soto county, Miss., August 31, 1854, the fourth of seven children born to Thomas B. and Lucretia (Morgan) Danforth, the former of whom was born in the Green Mountain state and the latter in Tennessee. Thomas B. Danforth came to this state when about thirty-five years of age, and until his death, which occurred in 1877, at the age of eighty-five years, he was a resident of De Soto county, where he labored as a bookkeeper and held several offices of trust. His widow survived him until 1889, at which time she passed from life, being in her seventy-third year. She and her husband were members of the Baptist church. The maternal grandparents were Theophilus and Nancy Morgan, natives of Virginia. They were all planters and prominent citizens of the state in which they lived, and were honored and respected. Charles B. Danforth was reared in De Soto county, in the public schools of which he received his education, also studying at home to some extent. The most practical part of his education, however, has been acquired in the school of experience, for since the age of eighteen years he has fought the battle of life for himself, and has just cause to be proud of his record. He is almost wholly a self-made man. He came to Coahoma county, Miss., in 1879, and became manager for Stewart Brothers, in which capacity he remained until 1889, when he purchased a plantation for $25,000, and is now the owner of one thousand seven hundred and fifty acres of fine land, seven hundred of which are under cultivation. In addition to the usual plantation products he is raising cattle to some extent, and the enterprise promises to be a successful one. Mr. Danforth has met with good fortune in his ventures, for, besides being industrious and economical, he is enterprising, and the soul of honor in his transactions. Although he is public spirited he does not care for public honors, preferring greatly to pursue the even tenor of his way as a planter. He possesses pleasant and agreeable manners, and stands well in the estimation of those who know him.

Capt. Walter H. Daniel, Binnsville, Miss., who is prominently identified with the agricultural interests of Kemper county, Miss., was born in Wilcox county Ala., on March 7,

1834, and is a son of Dr. J. W. and Sarah (Robinson) Daniel. His father was born in Edgefield district, S. C., in 1810, and was a son of Jesse and Martha (Bond) Daniel. The maternal grandfather was Major Bond of the Revolutionary war. The father of our subject was married in his native state, and removed, in 1832, to Wilcox county, Ala., where he was engaged in agriculture and the practice of medicine. He died in Butler county, Ala., in 1881. He was a member of the Methodist Episcopal church. Politically he was allied to the democratic party, and was a conspicuous character in the political history of Wilcox county. He was a sheriff of the county, and represented the people of the state in the legislature of the state. His wife was also a native of Edgefield district, S. C., and a daughter of Dr. Allen and Sarah (Hill) Robinson. They removed to Alabama in 1819, one year after her birth, and settled in Monroe county, when the Indians still had possession of that territory. Later they went to Wilcox county, and there the parents of our subject were married. They reared eight children of whom Capt. Daniel is the eldest; the others are: Sumter L. James A., Jessie, John, Ludovick, Mary and Thomas. Their father died in May, 1881, and the mother died in the same month in 1888. She was a consistent member of the Methodist Episcopal church. Captain Daniel spent his early life in Wilcox county, where he received his education. In 1861 he enlisted in Dallas county, Ala., joining company I, Second Alabama cavalry. He went out as a private and was made lieutenant, and then captain, in which capacity he served until the close of the war. He was in many important engagements and was in some of the hardest fought battles, Resaca and the siege of Atlanta being the most noted. After the surrender he came to Kemper county, taking up agriculture and embarking in a mercantile trade. He also has milling interests in the county. He owns about four hundred acres of land, and has it all well improved. Captain Daniel was married in Wilcox county, Ala., in 1865, to Mary Stewart, a daughter of M. and Elizabeth (Colley) Stewart. One child was born of this union, but is deceased. The mother also died in 1869. Captain Daniel was married a second time, in 1871, to Miss Ida F. Williams, a daughter of Richard and Sallie (Barlow) Williams, natives of South Carolina and Alabama, respectively. The father was born in 1810, and is still living; the mother was born in 1814, and died in 1884. They were both members of the Methodist Episcopal church. Mrs. Daniel was born in Wilcox county, Ala., in 1855. She is the mother of four children: Sallie, Lora, Lula and Walter. She is a member of the Methodist Episcopal church. The Captain and his family are highly respected in the community in which they live, and are well worthy of the esteem in which they are held.

The L. N. Dantzler Lumber company was established in 1887, and is one of the wealthiest corporations in Southern Mississippi, having a capital stock of $200,000. L. N. Dantzler, of Moss Point, is president; L. N. Dantzler, Jr., is vice president, and J. L. Dantzler, is secretary. They employ about two hundred men, and ship to all points of the globe. They own three lumber schooners, and operate two sawmills, one of which has a capacity of one hundred thousand feet per day, and the other, thirty thousand feet per day. They have an interest in three tugboats, Leo being one of the finest on the gulf. L. N. Dantzler, the senior member of the firm, was born in Greene county, Miss., December 31, 1833, and is a son of John L. Dantzler, a native of South Carolina. His father came to Mississippi at an early day, and was one of the pioneers of Greene county. He was a farmer by occupation, and reared a family of six sons, our subject being the youngest. He received a good education, being graduated at Centenary college, Louisiana, in 1851. He then engaged in the mercantile trade at Mobile, Ala., where he resided for a few years. Afterward he became interested in the cotton commission business, which he followed until the breaking out of the

Civil war. He then enlisted in the Woodruff rifles, Twenty-first Alabama regiment, and served three years. He received a gunshot wound in the hand at the battle of Shiloh, after which he was honorably discharged, and put in the secret service, in which he remained until the surrender. He came to Moss Point, Jackson county, Miss., after the war, and purchased an interest in the business of W. Griffin & Co., extensive lumber dealers and merchants. This relationship existed ten years, and was then dissolved by mutual consent, Mr. Dantzler taking one of the mills, and continuing business alone until the present corporation was effected, when his two sons took stock. They own fifteen thousand acres of fine pine timber land, and are doing a very large and prosperous business. These gentlemen are all well fitted for business life, both by education and natural endowment, and Jackson county may take a just pride in a corporation representing so much wealth and talent. Mr. Dantzler was united in marriage in 1856 to Miss Evan Griffin, and eleven children have been born to them, seven of whom are living: J. L., L. N., Jr., A. F., G. B., Mary E., Emma D. and Anna L. The parents are members of the Methodist Episcopal church, and Mr. Dantzler belongs to the Knights of Honor.

Jesse H. Darden is one of the most extensive planters, and one of the largest land owners in the county of Jefferson, Miss., and as he was born here on March 14, 1811, and has resided in the neighborhood of where he now lives all his life, he has an extensive acquaintance throughout this section, and is noted for his exemplary Christian life and for his quiet and unobtrusive demeanor. His maternal grandfather was a Virginian, was a soldier in the Revolutionary war, and at an early day emigrated to the state of Georgia with his family, where he spent the rest of his days, passing from life in the year 1811. His paternal grandfather was also a Virginian. Buckner Darden, father of Jesse H., was born in Georgia in the year 1774, and, on his father's extensive plantation, in that state, he attained the age of twenty-four years, at which time he left his native roof tree, for the purpose of seeking his fortune, and finally drifted to Jefferson county, Miss., taking up his abode near Fayette. In April, 1800, two years after his arrival here, he was united in marriage to Miss Maria, daughter of Jesse and Maria (Jones) Harper, after which they soon settled on the plantation on which the subject of this sketch was born and now resides. To Buckner Darden and his wife a family of fifteen children was born, eleven of whom arrived at years of maturity, three brothers and two sisters living at the present time: Samuel W., a planter, who resides in this county; Jesse, the second son; Andrew J., residing on the old homestead, and two sisters, one living in Tennessee and the other in Texas. While Buckner Darden was not a politician, he was intimately connected with the early history of Jefferson county, and had the reputation of being a good and highly respected citizen, and a leader of society. It is related of him that he assisted in the capture of Aaron Burr, which took place in the vicinity of his home. Jesse H. Darden is a man of excellent education, for in his youth he was given the advantages of Centre college, of Danville, Ky., and while in that institution improved his opportunities to the utmost, and has since kept fully abreast of the times. His early life was spent on his father's plantation, and prior to his father's death, which occurred June 30, 1831, he bequeathed to him a small farm, to which he has added from time to time, until he now owns a tract containing fifteen hundred acres. In July, 1832, he was married to Miss Susan Sillers, daughter of Walter Sillers, of North Carolina. Mrs. Darden was a woman of superior intelligence and education, having graduated from the Washington female college in her girlhood. She departed this life, February 25, 1880, having become the mother of ten children, seven of whom arrived at mature years: Mrs. Martha Wade, Mrs. Laura Short, Mrs. Irene West, Jesse B. and George Y., the latter two being successful planters, and are residing near their father. Mr. and Mrs. Darden united with the Presbyterian church in early life, and in this church he has filled the office of elder for more than fifty years. He is a strict temperance man, the temperance organization being the only secret order of which he has ever been a member. He is a kind, courteous and obliging gentleman, and as his devotion to progress and welfare of the county is well known, he is given a leading place among the worthy citizens of this section. Although he did not serve in the Rebellion, he was called upon to furnish men to assist in erecting fortifications, and cheerfully did so.

> "The boast of heraldry, the pomp of power,
> And all that beauty, all that wealth e'er gave,
> Await alike the inevitable hour;
> The paths of glory lead but to the grave."—*Gray.*

Capt. Put Darden (deceased) was a leader of the people, and was especially warm in his advocacy of the rights of the husbandman, his brilliant mind, his eloquence as a speaker and his sound judgment being all brought to bear in their interests. He was ushered into this world on the 10th of March, 1836, in Jefferson county, Miss., and after being thoroughly drilled into the common branches in his native county, he entered the State university of Mississippi, where he was a faithful, earnest and painstaking student, and as a reward was graduated at the early age of twenty years. He immediately began devoting his attention to agriculture, a calling to which he had been brought up, and continued to follow this calling until the opening of the Rebellion, when his patriotism of and love for the South caused him to be one of the first to respond to the call of the Confederacy for troops. He enlisted as a lieutenant of artillery under Albert Sidney Johnston, and was with him in the memorable battles of Bowling Green and Shiloh. On account of the excellent judgment he at all times manifested and for his bravery, he was promoted to the rank of captain, and took command of what was known as Darden's battery, with which he did most valiant and effective service. He followed the varying fortunes of war under Generals Beauregard, Bragg, Hardy, Joe E. Johnston and Hood until the close, serving with distinction in all the great engagements fought by these distinguished commanders. After the final close of the war, Captain Darden returned to his home and farm and began the hard struggle to retrieve his fortunes, and by devoting all his interests and bending all his energies to this object, he managed to gather around him a comfortable competency. Early in the history of the Patrons of Husbandry, Mr. Darden allied himself with that order, as he was deeply impressed with its principles, and by the benefit to be derived by a thorough promulgation of the principles of this order, Captain Darden soon became the most zealous worker in this organization, his ability, energy and enthusiasm in advancing and building up this order, soon bringing him into prominence. He was promoted to master of the State grange, in which position he served for thirteen consecutive years, and each year made the circuit of the state, visiting each county and lecturing in the different towns. Being an eloquent, forcible and logical speaker, his words carried conviction with them, and he did untold good in making the workings of the order better known and appreciated. His fidelity to the order was rewarded and he was elected master of the Patrons of Husbandry of the United States, and at the conclusion of his first term he was reëlected at the meeting of the order at Lansing, Mich., and held the position with fidelity and ability until his death in July 17, 1888. His leading characteristics were extreme frankness, honesty of purpose, indomitable will and energy, and these worthy traits inspired respect and confidence in him. His death was felt as a great loss to the order and the various lodges throughout the states, and the national order passed resolutions in his honor. He was ever a stanch democrat, and in the memorable struggle of 1875 he was the acknowledged leader of the people of Jefferson county, and did valuable service for the party and the people in restoring their rights. He was a strong advocate of the purity of the ballot and was unswerving in his advocacy of the sovereignty of the people. He was married first soon after arriving at his majority, but unfortunately lost his wife soon after. After the war he married Miss Ellen Griffing, and his third wife was Miss Mary Lou Harper, a daughter of Captain Harper, a sketch of whom appears in this history. Mr. Darden married his fourth wife in Claiborne county, Miss., November 5, 1885, she being Miss Kate Aby, daughter of T. J. Aby. Mrs. Darden was born and reared in Claiborne county, and is a lady of superior mental qualities and was a fitting wife for such a man as Captain Darden. To Captain Darden's first marriage one son was born: John P., who is now a resident of Texas. His third wife bore him four children: Harper, Evelyn, Mary Lou and Put. His fourth marriage resulted in the birth of three children: Helen A., Tom, Aby and Charles Put. Captain Darden was a very active member of the Christian church and gave most liberally of his means for church and benevolent purposes. He had long been superintendent of the Sunday-school and socially was a member of the Knights of Honor. His widow, who is an active church worker, has managed his affairs with superior business ability, and is endeavoring to rear her children to honorable maturity.

A lifetime spent in pursuing one calling will result in substantial success, especially if energy and perseverance are applied, and such is found to be the case with Hon. Thomas L. Darden, who, from boyhood, has given the occupation of agriculture the principal part of his time and attention. His father, John P. Darden, followed this calling before him, and both were born in Jefferson county, Miss., the former January 20, 1842, and the latter August 7, 1808. John P., upon arriving at man's estate, was married to Miss Margaret Fleming, of Adams county, and soon after removed to near Vicksburg, on the Mississippi river, and there followed planting for a few years. He then returned to his native county, locating in the northeastern part, but at the end of a few years he settled on the plantation of which his son, Thomas L., now has control. The plantation which he opened here was very large and valuable, and was admirably managed by Mr. Darden, who thoroughly understood every detail of agricultural life, and put his knowledge into practice. He was a man of superior business capacity and tact, and devoted his time and energies to the proper conduct of his affairs, and at the time of his death, September 4, 1865, was in excellent financial circumstances. His widow died on the 9th of July, 1869, having borne him a family of two sons and three daughters: Mrs. C. F. Whitney (of Fayette), Hon. Put. Darden (deceased), Mrs. Josephine Whitney, Mrs. Sue Armstead (of Hopkinsville, Ky.), and T. L. Darden. The paternal grandfather of the subject of this sketch, David Darden, was one of the pioneers of Jefferson county, Miss., from the state of Georgia. Hon. T. L. Darden was brought to the farm where he now resides when an infant, and here grew to manhood, receiving the advantages of the common schools. He had also made some progress in Latin and Greek, and the higher mathematics, when the opening of the war put an end to his studies, and he enlisted in the Fourth Mississippi cavalry, company H, and served the Confederate cause until the final surrender, laying down his arms with his commander, Forrest, at Gainesville, Ala. The most important engagement in which he took part was Harrisburg, Miss., an all-day's fight June 14, 1863, and the fights from Port Hudson to the Tennessee line. After the surrender he returned home with the consciousness of having served the Southern cause with fidelity and ability, and once more took up the duties of everyday life, taking charge of the home place and business. He has taken an active part in politics since the war, and on the democrat ticket, the principles of which he has always espoused, he was elected to represent his county in the legislature during the session of 1889–90, during which he served on the committees of agriculture and education, also on the joint committee to examine the books of the public officers. He was one of the first to associate himself with the Grange movement upon its organization in Mississippi, and has taken an active part in both local and state granges, being elected overseer of the latter, and was reëlected at the last annual meeting. He is also a member of the Farmers' Alliance, having joined the order in 1886, and is now serving as treasurer of the state alliance, and as president of the county alliance, since its organization in Jefferson county. Mr. Darden is a strong and faithful worker in both the grange and alliance, and at all times endeavors to promote the interests of the producer. He was married in Adams county, November 29, 1872, to Miss Sophia McCaleb, daughter of Dunbar McCaleb, a prominent planter of Adams county, Miss. Mrs. Darden was born, reared and educated in her native county, and has borne her husband nine children: William McC., Maggie Mae, Thomas L., Jr., Josephine W., Sue A., Hellen K., J. Dunbar and Hattie P. (twins), and Julius Put. Mr. Darden is well known to the majority of the residents of Jefferson county, and of that sturdy and independent class, the planters of the state, none are possessed of more genuine merit or a stronger character than he. He has always had the county's interests warmly at heart, and his career is an example of what energy, industry and perseverance, when intelligently applied, will accomplish. His extensive acquaintance and long connection with the affairs of this vicinity have rendered him well and popularly known, and he and his accomplished and amiable wife have many warm friends.

William P. Darden is one of the best known citizens of Jefferson county, Miss., and although he was born in Claiborne county on May 30, 1850, and has only been a resident of Jefferson county since the year 1883, he has interested himself in every worthy enterprise, and as a substantial citizen has become universally known. His father, George Darden, was born in this county, and was a brother of Jesse Darden, a sketch of whom appears in this work. For his companion through life George Darden took Miss Martha Bolls, of this county, a daughter of Alexander Bolls, one of the pioneer planters of the county. After his marriage Mr. Darden settled in Claiborne county, and on a good plantation of which he became the owner he reared his family and resided until his death, which occurred in the month of May, 1882. He was a man of decided worth, possessed intelligent views on all matters, and was a public-spirited and law-abiding citizen. Being an enthusiastic Southerner in principle, he espoused the cause of the Confederacy, and for three years was in the Confederate army. Mr. Darden was an active member of the Presbyterian church, and at the present time his widow survives him. W. P. Darden is the second in order of birth in a family of four sons and four daughters, all of whom have attained mature years, W. P. Darden and a sister being married. The former was brought up in Claiborne county, and in his youth received far better educational advantages than the average, for he completed his knowledge of books in Oakland college. After farming with his father up to the latter's death, he began working independently, and the year following came to Jefferson county, and near the town of Red Lick he followed merchandising for two years. In 1885 he moved to the town, and of this place has been one of the wideawake and enterprising business men up to the present. He carries an excellent line of general merchandise, and by excellent and upright business methods he commands a paying trade. His interest in the welfare of this section is well known, and he is now serving his second term as magistrate, having made an impartial and strictly

honorable official. He was married in this county January 2, 1887, his wife being Miss Kate Scott of this county, and a daughter of Mr. and Mrs. C. E. Scott, all being natives of Jefferson county. Mr. Darden and his family have an interesting family of three children, Elaine, Katesie and Willie, all daughters. Mrs. Darden has been connected with the Baptist church for some time, and as a charitable and amiable lady has not her superior in this section of the country. Socially Mr. Darden is a member of the Knights of Honor and the Knights and Ladies of Honor.

Mills C. Daughtrey, planter, Canton, Miss., a native Virginian, born on the 7th of January, 1835, is of English origin and a descendant of the old Quakers of Virginia. He was reared in his native state, received his education in the private schools of the same, and in 1863 emigrated to Mississippi, where he has since followed planting. When he first started out for himself he followed merchandising at St. Louis from 1857 to 1861, when he abandoned his business to enter the Confederate army as captain of a company he had raised himself, known as the Camp Jackson Avengers, by the boys, but never having a name until united with Wise's legion. Mr. Daughtrey was detached and united with the war department, which position he held until cessation of hostilities. He was in the following battles: Seven Pines, and all the engagements around Richmond, Va. Mr. Daughtrey then returned to his home and has been engaged in planting ever since. He is the owner of twelve hundred acres of land, and has three hundred acres under a good state of cultivation. He was married in 1863 to Miss Annie C. Hart, a native of Virginia, and the daughter of John D. and Sofa E. (Smith) Hart, also of Virginia. The fruits of this union have been three children: Charles H., Paul C. (deceased) and Baron C. He and family are members of the Episcopal church. In his political views Mr. Daughtrey is strictly democratic, and socially he is a member of the Masonic fraternity, Knights of Honor, Knights and Ladies of Honor and Knights of Pythias. He is an earnest advocate of all principles to advance the interests of the county and contributes liberally to all. He has a beautiful residence on his farm six miles southwest of Canton, and is an honored and respected citizen of the county. He is the second of four children born to Mills C. and Mary A. (Wickham) Daughtrey, natives also of the Old Dominion. The father followed merchandising in his native state until his death in 1857.

Robert Davenport, planter, Booneville, Miss., better known as Bob Davenport, was born in Greene county, Ga., in 1811, and is a son of Henry and Elizabeth (Easley) Davenport. The father was a native Virginian, born in Halifax county in 1777, and was one of three children reared by Henry Davenport and wife, the latter being also a Davenport and a distant relative of her husband. Henry Davenport, grandfather of our subject, and his father, whose name was also Henry Davenport, came from England at an early day and settled in the Old Dominion. Both were Revolutionary soldiers. Henry is an old name in the Davenport family, and has been handed down from generation to generation. Henry Davenport, father of our subject, was reared on a farm in Virginia and after his marriage moved to Georgia, where he followed the occupation to which he had been reared, farming. He was married about 1800 to Miss Elizabeth Easley, a native, also, of Virginia, and a daughter of Robert Easley, of Halifax county, that state. Of the ten children born to this union, seven reached mature years: Amanda F., now Mrs. Watts; Thomas, died in 1880; Henry, died in Sumter county, Ga.; Robert, our subject; Smith, died in 1889; Elizabeth Mattox, deceased; William, deceased, and three died in infancy. The mother of these children died in Greene county, Ga., in 1822, and the father received his final summons at Salem, the same state, in 1857. Both were members of the Missionary Baptist church. The father followed

39

farming all his life, was also largely engaged in stockraising and was quite successful in all his enterprises. He was a democrat in politics and, socially, was a member of the Masonic fraternity. Robert Davenport was reared to farm life, and it was but natural, perhaps, that when starting out for himself he should select farming as his chosen occupation. He received a fair education in the common schools, and when twenty-one years of age started out for himself. He was married in his native state in 1833 to Miss Martha Hester, born on the 14th of February, 1819, and the daughter of Stephen and Elizabeth (Smith) Hester. Mr. and Mrs. Hester were the parents of eight children, of whom Mrs. Davenport was the youngest. Her mother died in Georgia and her father in Louisiana. To Mr. and Mrs. Davenport were born ten children, of whom the following lived to be grown: Sallie A., now Mrs. Green, of Booneville; Fannie Easley, now Mrs. Davenport and a widow, of Texas; Robert B., in Texas; Stephen, who was major of a battalion and was killed in 1863. He was married and left a wife and one child, William Henry. His widow, now Mrs. P. W. Nash, resides at Booneville; Henry was killed at the battle of Gettysburg, and was captain of a company in the Forty-second Mississippi, and Elizabeth. A son, Joseph H., died at the age of eleven years. Mr. Davenport moved from Clark county, Ga., to Tishomingo county, Miss., in 1839, settled near the present site of Booneville, and entered land at fifty cents an acre. He followed farming up to 1849, and in that year was elected to the office of county sheriff, serving in that capacity for six years. He was then out one term and afterward was elected two more years. He was sheriff of Prentiss county from 1878 until 1880, filling out the term of John Hodges. Mr. Davenport has been a lifelong planter, but in 1857 he engaged in the lumber business, which he continued for some time after the war. He is a member of the board of supervisors, and, socially, is a member of the Masonic fraternity, having taken the royal arch degree. He and Mrs. Davenport are members of the Methodist church. He was an old line whig before the war. Mr. Davenport takes a deep interest in school and church affairs, and in fact all that tends to the improvement and development of the county. He has been a resident of Prentiss county for fifty-two years, and is highly spoken of by all.

G. M. C. Davis, lawyer, Carthage, Miss., was originally from Alabama, born in Benton county on the 7th of May, 1842, and his father, Colonel Martin Davis, and his grandfather, George Davis, were both natives of Georgia. Colonel Davis grew to manhood in his native state and was married to Miss Mimy Barnett, a native also of Georgia, and the daughter of Uriah Barnett, also of that state. After his marriage Mr. Davis settled in Alabama, but in 1847 moved to Mississippi, first settling in Winston county, where he remained until 1854, and then located in Attala county, where he was engaged in trading, speculating and merchandising. He became quite wealthy, and traded in slaves and stock in all the adjoining counties. He was colonel of the militia in Alabama. He died in 1878, and his wife had died a few months previous. G. M. C. Davis was one of a family of seven sons and five daughters, all of whom grew to mature years, married, and became heads of families. Two brothers and a sister are now deceased. One brother, Rev. J. J. Davis, is a minister in the Baptist church. He was a member of the Texas legislature. The others are planters and merchants. G. M. C. Davis was reared in Attala county, Miss., and was principally self-educated. When the tocsin of war sounded in 1861 he enlisted in the Confederate army, Twentieth Mississippi, but was afterward transferred to the Thirtieth Mississippi, and served as lieutenant until the final surrender. He was in the army of Tennessee and participated in the battles of Perryville, Ky., Murfreesboro, fights around Atlanta, Chickamauga, Franklin and Nashville. After the war he returned to Attala county, embarked in merchandising at Center, and sold goods for several years. He then studied law and was admitted to the bar at Kosciusko in 1873, locating at Carthage the following year. He has worked up a good practice and has had some most important murder and civil cases. He takes an active part in politics during campaigns and was elected and served several years as county treasurer. He is a zealous democrat, but since then he has declined all political positions, preferring to devote his time and talents to his business. Mr. Davis was married in Attala county in 1859, when eighteen years of age, to Miss Nannie I. Dodson, a native of Tennessee, but who was reared and educated in Attala county. She is the daughter of Dr. W. R. Dodson, one of the pioneers of the county. To Mr. and Mrs. Davis have been born seven daughters and one son: Della, wife of R. L. Jordan, a merchant; Jessie was educated at Columbus college and is a school teacher; Kittie; Dora, wife of R. M. Millsaps, a merchant; Luella-Willie (a daughter); Alice and George Lowry. Mr. Davis is senior warden of Pearl River lodge, A. F. & A. M., and protector in the lodge of Knights and Ladies of Honor at Carthage. Mr. Davis is one of the leading attorneys of Leake county, and is devoted to his practice.

Hon. George W. Davis, Ocean springs, Miss., was born in Jackson county, Miss., April 17, 1842, and is a son of Samuel and Alvira A. (Ward) Davis, natives of Georgia and Mississippi, respectively. The father removed to Mississippi in 1823, and settled on the Pascagoula river at Plum bluff, Jackson county, afterward removing to Ocean springs. He was a planter by occupation. He died in 1879, but his wife is yet living. They reared a family of eleven children, nine of whom survive: Harriet, George W., Sarah, Abraham J., Henry S., Nora, Sherwood E., Elias S. and Belle. George W. was reared to farm life, and was educated in the common schools. In 1861 he enlisted in company G, Third Mississippi volunteer infantry, and was in the service three years. He left the command at Meridian, Miss., on the retreat from Jackson, and went to his home for a supply of clothing, as he was almost destitute. While there he received word from the commanding officer not to return for duty. He went to New Orleans and remained in the enemy's lines until the surrender. He had been promoted to the position of second lieutenant. He was a loyal soldier, true to his principles and convictions. After the surrender he returned to his home and resumed his agricultural enterprises. Later on he invested in a mercantile business in Bluff creek, which he conducted nine years; thence he removed to Ocean springs and has been engaged in the same business. He carries a nice, well-selected stock of general dry goods, and is doing an extensive business. He also deals in real estate. He was treasurer of the county one term, and was also a member of the board of supervisors one term. He has not been an aspirant for political honors, but through the urging of his friends he has allowed his name to be used as a candidate for the state legislature. He was elected in 1891, and will doubtless reflect credit upon his enthusiastic constituency. He is a popular man, and has the entire confidence of the community. He was married, in 1869, to Miss Margaret Bradford. Five daughters have been born to them: Cinnie, Madie, Sadie, Mamie and Georgia. Mr. Davis is a member of the Knights of Pythias, and he and his wife belong to the Missionary Baptist church.

Ira E. Davis has been long and worthily identified with the interests of Hinds county and the town of Bolton, Miss., and no history of this immediate vicinity would be complete which failed to make mention of the services he has rendered. He was born in Dinwiddie county, Va., July 7, 1832, the ninth child born to Joseph E. and E. P. (Manlove) Davis, the latter being a second cousin of Thomas Jefferson. The father was a Virginian, but his ancestors came originally from Scotland about the year 1788. He became a resident of

Mississippi about 1837, and settled at Mount Albon in Warren county, but about twelve months later moved to Vicksburg and from there to his plantation, where he died in 1847. His wife's people were from England. Ira E. Davis attended the common schools and did farm work until he arrived at the age of eighteen years, at which time he went to La Grange, Ky., entering college, where he remained two years. At the age of twenty years he began teaching school, a calling he followed about seven years, during which time he read medicine, and, although he never took a course of lectures, he is well posted and has mostly done his own family practice. He went into the probate and chancery clerk's office as deputy, at Raymond and Jackson, Miss., where he remained until 1871, when he moved to Bolton, where he was appointed to several public positions by governors then acting, but declined. He was elected magistrate of his district for eight years, and during this time had several cases of prominence come up before him: W. C. Wells vs. Cal. Johns and wife, which case went to the supreme court and Mr. Davis' decision sustained; the criminal prosecution of the State vs. Mort Lorance et al., the parties being convicted of grand larceny and sent to prison and penitentiary; and the case of Mrs. Robinson vs. Withers & Black (suit to recover damages), which was sustained by the higher court, and a number of other noted cases. Mr. Davis is the owner of valuable property in the town of Bolton, and about twenty-three hundred acres of land, a large portion of which is adjoining the town of Bolton, about five hundred acres being under cultivation, and four hundred acres in valuable timber land. About 1888 Mr. Davis began raising horses and cattle of a good grade, is gradually increasing this business and expects, in time, to make this his chief occupation. After the war he began business in Hinds county without means or influence, but has been very successful in his ventures and is now wealthy. He is deservedly proud of his career, for his success is due to his own intelligence, forethought and diligence, and to the fact that he has given his own personal supervision to the different enterprises in which he has engaged. His home in Bolton is a very beautiful one, and everything about it indicates refinement and taste. Mr. Davis takes much interest in beautifying his place, and has collected and set out on his lawn many beautiful native flowering plants. He was married in the month of September, 1856, to Miss Bradley, daughter of N. H. and Sarah Bradley, of White county, a native of Tennessee, by whom he has five children, four of whom are living: J. H., Thomas B., S. A. and Percy D. The mother of these children died in 1883, after which Mr. Davis married Mrs. Dr. Baker (nee Miss Bounds), of Putnam county, Tenn., their happy union occurring in 1889.

On the 10th of December, 1784, Joseph Emory Davis was born in Georgia, near Augusta. His father, Samuel Davis, had been a soldier in the Revolutionary war, and served in the cavalry of Georgia, his native state, from his seventeenth year to the termination of that war. When Joseph was twelve years old, his father moved to Christian county, Ky., and here Joseph grew to manhood. He received a common school education and at an early age was placed in a mercantile establishment, and soon afterward began the study of law in the office of Judge Wallace, of Russellville, Ky. In 1811, in company with his father's family, he moved to Wilkinson county, Miss., and there continued the study of law under Joseph Johnson. The following year he was admitted to the bar, and opened an office at Pinckneyville of that county. He soon removed to Greenville, where he remained until 1820, and occupied a very prominent position as a member of his profession. In 1817 he was elected a delegate to the convention which organized the state government. In 1820 he removed to Natchez and formed a partnership with Thomas B. Reed, who at that time was a leader of the state bar. Mr. Davis was a lawyer of fine ability, having an intellect of great vigor and a character above reproach. He was quick to observe the weak points in cases of an adversary, and possessed a readiness to take advantage of all omissions or errors promptly as they appeared. In 1827, for some reason not altogether clear, he retired from the practice of law and became a planter. From this time until the beginning of the war, in 1861, he lived quietly upon his plantation, honored and respected by all, and during that long period amassed a large fortune, which was swept away by the war. He was the eldest child of a family of ten, of whom the youngest was Jefferson Davis. He died at Vicksburg, September 18, 1870, in the eighty-sixth year of his age.

James H. Davis, merchant, French Camp, Miss., is a member of the well-known firm of Davis & Carter, general merchants of French Camp, Choctaw county, Miss., who established their business in 1872, and have an annual sale of about $35,000. The firm of Davis, Carter & Co. established a store at Weir in 1883, and are doing an annual business of about $45,000, being about the strongest mercantile firm in the county. Mr. Davis was born in Sumter county, Ga., in 1846, and is a son of James M. and Hattie (Hughes) Davis, the father born in Wilmington, N. C., in 1813, and the mother in Edgefield district, S. C., in 1815. The parents were married in Sumter county, Ga., and in 1849 came to Attala county, Miss., where they remained until about 1856. They then went to West Feliciana parish, La., thence to St. Helena parish, and there Mrs. Davis died in 1874. Mr. Davis is now living in Florida, and is engaged in fruitgrowing. He is a member of the Baptist church, as was also his wife. He was of French Huguenot stock, and was left an orphan at an early age. He was in the militia a short time during the war. He is a member of the Masonic fraternity. Grandfather Hughes died when Mr. Davis was an infant. Of the three children born to his parents James H. Davis is the eldest in order of birth. The others are: Louisa, wife of Rev. R. J. Steward, a Baptist minister of Liberty, Miss., and Joseph, who died in 1876, was a planter of St. Helena parish, La. James H. Davis was reared on the farm, equipped with a common-school education. After the war he attended school, then clerked, etc., and in 1870 he engaged in merchandising at French Camp, continuing alone until the present firm was established. He is prominent in business and social circles, and no man stands higher in the estimation of the people than he. He held the office of mayor of French Camp at one time, and was formerly a member of the I. O. O. F. at that place, but the lodge is not now in existence. He is a member of the French Camp lodge Knights and Ladies of Honor, No. 1312; Kosciusko lodge Knights of Honor No. 1387, and of the Knights of Pythias at Kosciusko. He was married in 1873 to Miss Lucy Carter, a native of Attala county, Miss., and daughter of Moses T. Carter, a member of the above mentioned firm. Two children were born to this union. Moses T. Carter, father of Mrs. Davis, was born in Chester district, S. C., in 1824, and was a son of John T. and Hannah (Smith) Carter, and the grandson of Blake Carter, who was also a native of Chester district, S. C. His maternal grandfather, Charley Smith, was a native of Ireland, but died in South Carolina. Moses T. Carter, the second of eleven children, was married in 1844 to Miss Mary Ann Fair, daughter of John and Catherine Fair, natives of Ireland. In 1868 he engaged in merchandising in connection with farming, at French Camp, and the firm is now known as Davis & Carter. They also have a store at Weir, and are live business men. Mr. and Mrs. Carter have been members of the Baptist church for nearly forty years.

J. C. Davis, a planter of Copiah county, was born near the place where he now lives, in this county in 1846. He is a son of Volley and Louisa Davis, the first mentioned of whom was born in South Carolina in 1809, and led the life of a farmer. He came to Mississippi in 1821 with his parents, Zius and Isabella Davis. He married Louisa Allred, of Copiah county, and to them were born seven children, four of whom are yet living, their names being Martha E., the wife of B. H. Sojouner, of Copiah county; J. C., our subject; Cornelius J., of Copiah county, and Lavoy H., of Pike county. Volley Davis was a member of the Masonic lodge, and he and his wife were members of the Baptist church. The career of our subject as a planter began when he was but sixteen years old, and continues to the present time, but during the past few years he has connected milling operations with his other business interests. He is recognized by all who know him as a man of more than ordinary enterprise. His plantation is well improved, and presents a neat and substantial appearance, and it is worthy of note that he is the owner of the only reaper and binder that is to be found anywhere in this section of the state, an indication that he has honored the more progressive principles of his Northern agricultural brethren. In 1863 Mr. Davis enlisted in company E of the Fourth Mississippi cavalry, and although he was in the service till after the surrender, he was in but one general engagement, that at Harrisburg. He is a member of the County Farmers' Alliance, and he and his wife are identified with the Baptist church. In 1874 Mr. Davis married Mary Douglas, the daughter of George W. and Virginia Douglas, of Copiah county. To them have been born six children, four of whom are living: Carl, Pearl, Earl and J. C., Jr.

J. H. Davis is the president of the Banner Publishing company, and is the able and talented editor of the Natchez *Evening Banner*, one of the breeziest, most popular and best journals of this section. Mr. Davis is a native of Lawrence county, Mo., where he was born in the year 1853, to William R. and Christina A. (Hickman) Davis, the former of whom is still a farmer of that county. J. H. Davis, although occupied with the monotonous duties of farm life in his youth, early evinced a desire for learning, and with the view of supplementing the primary education which he had received in the vicinity of his home with a more thorough knowledge, such as could be obtained in advanced institutions of learning, he left the parental homestead and entered the State university at Columbia, Mo., and from this institution was graduated in 1878. Quite soon thereafter he entered the government employ in the engineering service, under the Mississippi river commission, in which capacity he labored for five years. In 1883 he came to Natchez, Miss., and with his wife opened a female school, which is now known as the Natchez female college, and is still under the control of Mrs. Davis. This is considered a fine educational institution, and is well patronized. Since 1886 Mr. Davis has been editor of the *Banner*, which has, under his able editorship, become a very popular paper. His marriage, which occurred September 15, 1881, was to Miss Lizzie McD. Field, a native of Boone county, Mo., who was a classmate and a graduate of the same class in the University of Missouri. To their union one child has been born, William Provines. Mr. and Mrs. Davis are members of the Presbyterian church, and have by example, as well as precept, endeavored to live worthy Christian lives. Mr. Davis is a member of the Phi Delta Theta society, and at the time of his graduation was valedictorian of his class.

The family of Samuel F. Davis comes of good old English stock, but he was born in New Bedford, Mass., in the latter part of the last century, and as early as 1811 became a resident of Natchez, Miss. He became a prominent merchant of this place, and after a few years was united in marriage to Miss Maria Vidal, a daughter of Don Jose Vidal, Spanish commander of Louisiana after 1798, one of the most distinguished officers in the Spanish service. He became possessed of a grant of land, and on this land the town of Vidalia was laid and named in his honor. A large portion of this property is still in possession of the family. The marriage of Samuel Davis and Miss Vidal resulted in the birth of a number of children, only four of whom grew to mature years, Samuel Manuel, Celestine A., Alfred Vidal and Pauline. Samuel married Miss Charlotte Duncan, daughter of Dr. Stephen Duncan, and died in 1878, leaving two children, who are now residing in Europe. Celestine married Dr. William Byrd Page, of Philadelphia, and died in 1888, leaving also two children, S. Davis and Margaret. Alfred married Miss Surget, and after her death took for his second wife Miss Dunbar of Natchez, and is now living in Pass Christian. Pauline was married in 1858 to Dr. Robert Carter, of Virginia, and they also have two children, Robert S. and Pauline. Dr. Robert Carter was born in Virginia in 1827, and was the eldest of four children born to Thomas and Juliet Muse (Gaines) Carter, they being also Virginians. The Carters are of ancient origin, and have become wealthy and prominent citizens in whatever locality they have resided. The Doctor was educated at home by private tutors, and in a college of his native county, but supplemented these advantages by an attendance in Princeton college, New Jersey, and the high school of Virginia, where he distinguished himself as a faithful and painstaking student. He began his medical studies in the University of Virginia, but finished them in Philadelphia, after which, in 1849, he entered the United States navy as surgeon, and during this time traveled in nearly every habitable part of the world. While coasting along the Pacific coast, in 1850, he stopped in San Francisco, when the business portion of that now famous and prosperous city consisted of but two blocks. He was on the Page exploring expedition, on the Rio de la Plata river and its tributaries, which lasted about four years, after which he was stationed at Annapolis, Md., as surgeon until he resigned in 1858. After his marriage to Miss Davis, in June of that year, he came to Natchez, and here engaged in planting on the old Vidal estate in Louisiana, the property of his wife. They now own sixteen hundred acres of land, with one thousand under cultivation, and as Dr. Carter gives this plantation his personal supervision, it is kept in admirable farming condition. After residing here six months they removed to Philadelphia, but in 1861 came back to their estate, and for three years during the war their home was in the city of Natchez. After the termination of hostilities they again resided in Philadelphia for some time, but from there went to Newport, R. I., where they lived for three years. In 1869 they went to Europe, and for eight years were traveling over the continent, and since that time he and his family have been living alternately in the North and South. Mrs. Carter is now in Philadelphia, and her daughter, Mrs. Walter L. Biddle, a widow, resides in Europe. The son, Robert Shirley Carter, is a resident of the old plantation in Louisiana. Dr. Carter has seen much of the world, and as he is a man of much erudition, he has thoroughly appreciated all he has seen. He keeps well posted and informed on all subjects, and is now principally engaged in managing his plantation and selling lots in Vidalia, while he makes his home in Natchez.

John E. Davis is the proprietor and operator of the West Point grain mill and gin, and is one of the city's representative citizens. His birth occurred in Pickens county, Ala., in 1840, but his parents, Abraham S. and Margaret (Henry) Davis, were born in Fairfield district, South Carolina, and North Carolina, respectively. When young, they came to Pickens county, Ala., where they were married and resided until the death of Mrs. Davis in 1853, while at a health resort in Calhoun county, Miss. Mr. Davis married again and moved to Oktibbeha county, Miss., where he died in 1860, a member of the Methodist Episcopal church. He was a successful and well-to-do planter and was a man of no little prominence and influence in the different sections in which he resided. He had three brothers and three sisters: John, William, Amos, Ella, Mary and Clara, all of whom are deceased. Mrs. Davis was a daughter of Robert Henry, an early settler of Pickens county, Ala., who was a planter by occupation and died when the subject of this sketch was a small lad.   John E. Davis was the second of four sons: Robert P., who was a member of an Alabama regiment, army of Virginia, died while in the service; William A. died in Clay county about 1882, and James O., who left home in 1865 for California, stopped for a short time in Salt Lake city, and was never afterward heard from.   There was also a half brother, Leroy T., who had been educated for the ministry and died in Clay county about 1880.   John E. Davis received his rudimentary education in his native county and then spent a few years in South Carolina until the war broke out, when he joined company E, Fourteenth Mississippi infantry, and served in the western army until the first day's fight at Fort Donelson, when he lost his left arm and was removed before the fall of the fort.   Being unfitted for further military duty he began to look about him for something to do.   After the war he clerked at Prairie station until 1868, when he came to West Point and engaged in merchandising and milling, the firm being Mann, Henly & Davis for about three years.   The mercantile firm of White & Davis was then formed, and about two years later was changed to White, Heard & Davis.   After continuing thus for about two years Mr. Heard retired, and the firm continued as White & Davis.   A few years later Mr. Davis retired and again engaged in the milling business, and in 1885 erected his present mill, which is a handsome brick structure, 48x95 feet, two stories in hight, and well equipped to do a profitable business.   It is considered the finest mill in the state, and the product turned out is of excellent quality and is in great demand.   Mr. Davis owns other valuable property in the city and a fine farm of four hundred and eighty acres, well improved.   Mr. Davis' success is due to the economy he has practiced and to the fact that his energy was unbounded and his views on all matters sound and enlightened. He has always given personal supervision to his affairs and has never neglected one department of his work to attend to another.   He stands high as a citizen, is active in the upbuilding of the city, and possesses a jovial and genial temperament.   He is straightforward in all his business transactions, and fully deserves the success that has attended his efforts.   He is charitable in his views and liberal in the use of his means.   He is a member of the A. F. & A. M., and is unmarried.

Gen. Joseph R. Davis is one of the most distinguished attorneys of the city of Biloxi, Miss., and is a logical reasoner, decisive in statement, and is possessed of sufficient eloquence to render his declamation vigorous and of the most convincing order.   He was born in Wilkinson county, Miss., January 12, 1825, a son of Isaac and Susan (Gartley) Davis, who were of Welsh and Irish origin, respectively.   The father settled in Mississippi in 1810, during the primitive days of this state, and experienced the hardships and privations which seem incident to the life of the pioneer.   He was an officer in Andrew Jackson's command during the War of 1812, and became well known throughout the state of Mississippi.   He was an elder brother of Jefferson Davis.   His grandfather, Samuel Davis, was an early settler of Mississippi.   The boyhood days of Gen. Joseph R. Davis were spent in Madison county, Miss., but he was given the advantages of some of the best schools of Nashville, Tenn., and afterward graduated from the Miami university of Oxford, Ohio.   He seemed to have a natural aptitude for the profession of law, and, after thoroughly fitting himself, entered upon the practice of this science in 1857, which he continued until the opening of the Civil war, when he enthusiastically enlisted in the service of the Confederacy and was soon elected lieutenant-colonel.   He was with the Tenth Mississippi regiment, stationed at Pensacola, Fla., but prior to this, however, he was captain of a Madison county (Miss.,) company.   He afterward became a colonel on the staff of President Jefferson Davis, his uncle, but later became brigadier-general in the command of Gen. Robert E. Lee, with whom he remained until the war terminated. Since the war he has been a resident of Harrison county, Miss., his home, the most of this time being at Biloxi. Prior to the war, in 1860, he was elected to the state senate, but when the war opened he decided that he could render better service to the Confederacy in the field and resigned his position willingly, after due deliberation. In law, as well as in war, he has been, and always will be, the recipient of the highest honors of his comrades and fellow-citizens. He was married in 1848 to Miss Peyton, and secondly, in 1879, to Miss Margaret Green. He has two daughters.

A few years ago there was delivered an address before the alumni of one of the most con-servative colleges in the valley of the Mississippi, entitled, "The Three Black Graces." The speaker developed the idea that these "Graces" were the ministry, medicine and law; his comparison of them ran, black, blacker, blackest. Being himself a physician, he probably located medicine in the middle position as occupying the golden mean. However this may be, we do know that few callings in life furnish so broad an opportunity for charity as that of a physician, and we very much doubt if any professional men do as much work from pure kindness of heart. M. G. Davis, M. D., was born in Guilford county, N. C., April 13, 832, and is a son of John H. Davis, a native of the same state. His grandfather, Gen. Hamilton Davis, was a general in the war of the Revolution, and the sword that he carried through that con flict is still in the possession of the family. John H. Davis was reared and educated in North Carolina, and there married Hettie E. Geren, born in the same state. Mr. Davis removed to Mississippi about the year 1834 and located in Choctaw county, removing thence to Carroll county in 1844. He was a prominent planter, controlled large tracts of land and made a success of his business. He was an honored member of the Methodist Episcopal church. His death occurred in 1874, and his widow lived until 1877, her decease taking place at Greenwood. Dr. M. G. Davis is one of a family of nine children who grew to mature years. One brother, Joe L. Davis, was killed in the siege of Richmond, Va. The Doctor passed his boyhood in Carroll county, receiving a fair education at the Milton academy. Having chosen the profession of medicine for his life work, he entered upon its study in Carroll county, in 1850. He took his first course of lectures in Jefferson Medical college, Philadelphia, in 1852, and continued his studies until 1854, being graduated in the spring of that year. He then returned to Carroll county, and thence removed to Yazoo county, Miss., where he entered upon the practice of his profession, in which he was actively engaged at the time the Civil war broke upon this country, and men abandoned their professions, trades and arts, and went to the aid of their country. Dr. Davis enlisted in 1861 in the First Mississippi volunteer cavalry as assistant surgeon, and was transferred to the Fifth Mississippi cavalry. He had charge of the hospital at Winona for about four months, and after the close of the war he remained in practice in this place until the year 1870. He was also in the drug business in Winona, and met with a severe loss by fire there. In September, 1870, he located at Greenwood and has devoted his time and energies to the profession of medicine. He has some investments in mercantile business that bring him a fair income. The drug store of Drs. Davis & Henderson is well stocked with a fine line of drugs and medicines, and has a large patronage. Dr. Davis is a member of the state and county medical associations, and for many years has served on the county board of health. March 8, 1855, he was united in marriage to Miss Lizzie Taylor, a daughter of John Taylor, formerly of North Carolina. Mrs. Davis was born in Alabama, but grew to womanhood in Carroll county. She was a consistent member of the Baptist church. The Doctor belongs to the Masonic order, and also to the Knights of Pythias.

Dr. M. M. Davis, Nettleton, Miss., has been a member of the medical profession since

1858, when he graduated from the medical school of New Orleans. He is a native of the state of Alabama, born January 15, 1836, and is a son of James W. and Jane Davis, natives of Georgia. The father was born in 1790 and was a son of Moses Davis, also a native of Georgia. James W. Davis removed to Monroe county, Miss., in 1836, and engaged in planting. At that time there were few white settlers, but many Indians still inhabited this territory. Mr. Davis' residence was the home of many distinguished candidates while canvassing for office, among whom were John A. Wilcox and Henry S. Foote. He was a soldier in the war of 1812 and participated in many battles. He and his wife reared a family of ten children. He died in 1851, December 25. He was a man highly respected and honored, but received no more merit than is due the pioneers of any country. His wife, Jane Davis, was born in Alabama in the year 1800, a daughter of David Robinson, who died in Arkansas in 1848. They were married in 1818. She was a consistent member of the Christian church. Her death occurred in Pontotoc county July 4, 1889, at the age of ninety years. The names of their children are as follows: Amanda, widow of Charles Payne; Jasper N., of Pontotoc county; Emily E., wife of Smith Shaw, of Chickasaw county, Mississippi; Mary J., wife of J. C. Fitzgerald, of Chickasaw county; William P., of Blue springs, Union county; Melvina W., wife of J. T. Williams, a resident of Troy, Miss.; Louisiana, wife of Elisha Springer, is now deceased, leaving three children: James J., a member of the Forty-third Mississippi regiment, was killed at Corinth; Lindsey L., a member of the Second Mississippi regiment, was killed at Sharpsburg, Penn., and M M., the subject of this notice. The Doctor came to Mississippi with his father while he was still a youth, and he has since lived in Monroe and adjoining counties. He received his education in the common schools of the country and in 1855 began the study of medicine with Drs. Young and Armstrong. After finishing a course of reading with these physicians, he entered the medical school of New Orleans, and, as before stated, was graduated in 1858. In the same year he began practicing at Planterville, but removed to Richmond, and thence to Eureka, where he resided twenty-one years. In the year 1860, January 5, the Doctor was united in marriage to Cornelia U. Barnes, a daughter of William and Mary Barnes. Her father died in 1863, but the mother survived until 1875. Dr. and Mrs. Davis are the parents of ten children: Claude B., La Chapelle L. (wife of J. M. Hicks, is the mother of three children), William L. (married Willie Rhoades, and is engaged with his father in the mercantile business in Nettleton), Keith B., Ozelle, Fannie R., Nellia C., Clifford M., Bertha C. and Lindsey. In 1862 Dr. Davis entered the service as a surgeon, enlisting in the Thirty-fifth Mississippi regiment, and afterward being transferred to the Thirty-seventh Alabama regiment. After the war he engaged in mercantile pursuits to some extent, and now has established both at Saltillo and Nettleton a good, substantial business. He carries at the two places a stock of goods worth $11,000. He has partially abandoned his professional labors, and only occasionally makes a visit to a patient. He affiliates with the democratic party, and was a member of the democratic executive committee for fifteen years. He has been very influential in church and charitable work, and has contributed liberally of his means in the building up of the county. His professional career was one of success, and as a merchant he occupies a place in the county. Claude B. Davis, a son of the Doctor, was born January 5, 1861, in Lee county, Miss. He received his earlier education in the common schools, and later he went to Mars hill, at Florence, where he was graduated in 1878. In 1879 he engaged in the mercantile business in Saltillo, and has since established a prosperous trade, aggregating between $25,000 and $30,000 annually. He handles the bulk of the cotton marketed at that point. He was married to Nora Burrow, a daughter of Capt.

J. H. and Eva (Mitchener) Burrow (see sketch of Captain Burrow). Of this union one child has been born, Maude. The parents are members of the Christian church. Mr. Davis is a member of Lodge No. 355, Knights of Honor. Politically he is identified with the democratic party. He is a man of public spirit, and has always been interested in the growth and prosperity of his county.

Phil. W. Davis, the subject of this sketch, was born in Kemper county, Miss., July 11, 1842, and is a son of William A. and Harriet J. (Wilkinson) Davis. His father was born in Cumberland county, N. C., in 1817, and was a son of Thomas Davis. He was a merchant and a miller by trade. In 1832 he came with his father to Lauderdale county, Miss., where they engaged in building the first mills erected in the county. The father afterward moved to Texas, where he died in 1855. William A. Davis came to Kemper county in 1838, and engaged in milling, farming and merchandising. In the same year he was married. Eight children were born of the union, three of whom survive, viz.: J. E. (the eldest), Phil. W. (the subject of this sketch) and Harriet E. (the youngest). The father died in the Confederate army December 1, 1862; the mother lived until 1871. Phil. W. Davis enlisted in 1861 in company G, Eighth Mississippi volunteer infantry, and participated in all the battles of the western army from Perryville, Ky., in 1862, to the battle of Franklin, Tenn., November 30, 1864, in which he was severely wounded in the left hip, from which wound he never sufficiently recovered to do manual labor until two years thereafter. He was married December 11, 1867, to Miss Martha J. Tinsley, a daughter of John J. Tinsley, one of the earliest pioneers of the state of Mississippi. Mr. and Mrs. Davis have eight living children, viz.: Virginia A., Hattie C., William A., Mattie J., John, Lilla A., Eva P. and Phil. W., Jr. Mr. Davis is a member of the Longstreet lodge No. 268, A. F. & A. M., and in his political opinions affiliates with the democratic party. He has been justice of the peace, and for four years has been postmaster of Oktibbeha. He has a large body of land well improved, and is merchandising, milling and farming. He has accumulated his property through his own efforts. He has given liberally of his means for the support of all laudable enterprises, and is a citizen loyal to all the interests of home.

Mississippi has the distinction of having given to the Southern Confederacy its president, though he was born in Christian county, Ky., June 3, 1808, and that state disputes Mississippi's claim; but the fact remains that Jefferson Davis was almost a life-long resident of Mississippi, a lover of her soil and institutions, long the most distinguished conservator of her interests, and in many respects the ablest exponent of her patriotism. In national politics he was the confrere and successor of John C. Calhoun, his public career having lapped on and completed Calhoun's and involved the whole extreme Southern view of the relation of the Federal government to slavery in the territories. In the senate he was the peer of the most brilliant of the statesmen of the ante-bellum days, ranking with Calhoun, Webster and Clay, and the people of Mississippi know that he bore himself absolutely without fear and without reproach. Mr. Davis was the youngest of ten children of Samuel Davis, who served in the mounted troops of Georgia, his native state, during the entire period of the American Revolution, and about 1806 located in Christian (afterward Todd) county, Ky., whence he removed to Wilkinson county, Miss., in 1811. Two of Mr. Davis' uncles were also patriot soldiers in the war for independence, and it is not remarkable that as a youth he should have felt within him a martial spirit and the desire to be a soldier. He was graduated in 1828 at the United States military academy, at West Point, and served in warfare against the Indians until 1835. During this period he participated in the Black Hawk war, and saw much arduous service.

Resigning his commission, he returned to Mississippi, where he married a daughter of Gen. Zachary Taylor, who did not live long, however. During the period 1835–43 he was engaged in cottonplanting, but at the same time was active, politically, as a democrat, and in 1844 interested himself in the election of James K. Polk to the presidency. In 1845 he was elected to represent his district in congress, in which body he distinguished himself by participation in debates on military affairs, the Oregon question and the preparations for the Mexican war, but resigned his seat to take command of the First Mississippi rifle regiment, at the head of which he joined the army of General Taylor on the Rio Grande. He participated in the storming of Monterey and in the battte of Buena Vista. At the latter battle, he, no doubt, saved the army of General Taylor from serious disaster, by promptly and gallantly throwing his regiment into the breach caused by the precipitate and cowardly retreat of an Indiana regiment. At the close of the war he was offered but refused to accept the rank of brigadier-general of volunteers. He was appointed United States senator from Mississippi in 1847, to supply the vacancy left by the death of Senator Speight, and became celebrated as a zealous defender of slavery and an advocate of the doctrine of state's rights. He was elected in 1850 for the term beginning March 4, 1851, but in the fall of that year resigned his seat to enter upon a canvass for the election of Franklin Peirce to the presidency and to become a candidate for governor of Mississippi against Henry S. Foote, who was elected. In acknowledgment of his services, President Pierce, in 1853, appointed Mr. Davis secretary of war. His administration of the affairs of the department was signally able, and won for him the praise of distinguished men of all parties. As late as the administration of Mr. Hayes, after the Civil war had brought its asperities and sectional resentments, Hon. George W. McCrary, then secretary of war, pronounced Mr. Davis the ablest head the department had ever had. He again took his seat in the senate for the full term of six years, in December, 1857, but the triumph of the anti-slavery cause in the presidential election of 1860, the secession of the Southern states and dependent events led to his resignation and his retirement from the service of the United States. February 22, 1861, he was chosen provisional president of the Southern Confederacy; and at an election in November following, he was elected president for six years. After the fall of Richmond and the collapse of the Southern Confederacy, Mr. Davis was captured at Irwinsville, Ga., May 10, 1865, and was for nearly two years a prisoner in Fortress Monroe, awaiting trial for treason. He was liberated on bail, his chief bondsmen having been Gerritt Smith and Horace Greeley, of New York, and all proceedings against him were discontinued. During and for a time after the war, it was the custom of the Federal extremists to refer to Mr. Davis as a traitor. The question as to whether or not he was a traitor has been thus strongly put by Dr. Brownson: "Treason is the highest crime and deserves exemplary punishment, but not where there has been no treasonable intent; where they who committed it did not believe it was treason, and on the principles held by a majority of their countrymen, and by the party that had generally held the government, there was no treason. Concede state sovereignty, and Jefferson Davis was no traitor in the war he made on the United States, for he made none until his state seceded. He could not then be arraigned for his acts after secession, and at most only for conspiracy, if at all, before secession." It was the consciousness of its own shortcomings before the Civil war that influenced the government to refrain from treason trials after the South was defeated. The withdrawal or attempt to withdraw of the Southern states from the national union was only an abnormal development of the particular side of American politics brought to a culmination by the sectional differences caused by negro slavery. The idea that the Union was a league and a voluntary association of states for mutual benefit was extremely common everywhere until after the War of 1812, though the right of secession was either unthought of or kept in the background, except in such isolated instances as the Virginia and Kentucky resolutions of 1798, from which it may perhaps be drawn by argument, and Tucker's edition of Blackstone's Commentaries in 1803, in which it is completely formulated. There was very little national feeling at any time, and it is perhaps not too much to say that the national government owed its continual existence during this period to its control of the great western territory in which states and individuals had a common interest.

After 1815 the national idea grew rapidly and increasingly in those states in which slavery had ceased to exist, because of the growth of manufactures, commerce and banking interests which ignored or were embarrassed by state lines; because of the rapid internal transfer of population to new states without historical associations, and because of great influx of foreigners who thought of the United States, not of any particular state. All of their influences, with the possible exception of the second, tended to shield slavery and strengthen the South in its adherence to the principle of state sovereignty; and by a reactionary movement it had become stronger in 1860 than it had been in 1787-8, and community of interest had imparted to it a formidable character of sectional sovereignty. While the United States extended only to the Mississippi, the Ohio formed a safe boundary between the new slaveholding and the non-slaveholding states. When settlement passed the Mississippi, the dividing line was lost. When Louisiana was acquired in 1803, she was a slaveholding territory by French and Spanish law, and congress did not attempt to prohibit slavery within her borders. Consequently slavery spread across Arkansas into Missouri, which was admitted as a slave state in 1821; with its admission was coupled a proviso prohibiting slavery for the future in the remainder of the Louisiana purchase north of latitude 36 degrees 30 minutes, and the whole was known as the Missouri compromise. When California, Utah (including Nevada) and New Mexico (including Arizona) were acquired from Mexico in 1848, a conflict between the two sections, so much stronger in wealth and population, was a more serious matter than in 1821. As perfected after 1833 the Calhoun theory may be thus summarized: The constitution was a compact formed by states only; the states entered and came out of the convention which framed the constitution, in 1787, as sovereign states; new territory acquired was not national territory, but the common property of all the states, not to be governed absolutely by congress but in such a way as to maintain the rights of all the states in it; congress had no right to legislate against the admission of either free state or slave-state settlers to such territory; the Wilmot proviso or similar legislation was therefore unconstitutional. It is not intended to give in detail here a history of the slavery question, its agitation and the war in which the animosities thus engendered culminated in 1861. Suffice it to state that Mr. Davis fully voiced the opinion of Calhoun, and until the end of his life maintained the righteousness of the doctrine of state's rights. He thus stated his unalterable position in round terms in January, 1850: "We maintain that it is the right of the people of the South to carry this species of property to any portion of the territories of the United States; that it rests, under the constitution, upon the same basis as other property." After Dred Scott had obtained a verdict in Missouri for assault and battery against those who had whipped him after his return to that state; after the state supreme court had reversed it on appeal; after he had brought suit in the Federal court as a resident of New York, and the case had been taken thence by writ of error to the supreme court, in March, 1857, that court fully sustained the original Calhoun theory that negroes were "no part of the political people of the United States in the view of the framers of the constitution; that they were property, not persons, with no more rights than the white race chose to allow them; that a territory being a part of the United States, the government, and the citizens both, enter it under the authority of the constitution, with their respective rights defined and marked out; and that the Federal government can exercise no power over the citizen's person or property beyond what that instrument confers, nor lawfully deny any right which it has reserved." On this decision the Southern leaders took firm hold. Before the close of Buchanan's term the ultimatum which Mr. Davis had presented in 1850, which included a proposition to extend the Missouri compromise line to the Pacific along the parallel 36 degrees 30 minutes north, was offered again by him in seven resolutions which were passed by the senate May 24 and 25, 1860. They were much like Calhoun's of 1837 and 1847, except that the fifth provided for protection to constitutional rights in the territories through congress should the territorial governments prove inadequate, and the whole made up the new Southern program that neither congress nor a territorial legislature could prohibit slavery in a territory; that both were bound to protect slavery; that the rights of the people of the territory to prohibit slavery accrued only when they came to form a state constitution; and that congress was then bound to admit the state with or without slavery, as its people should elect. This was the platform upon which the cotton-state delegates insisted at the Charleston convention; and the refusal of the convention to adopt it led to their withdrawal and the breaking up of the convention. Mr. Davis' resolutions were introduced, March 1, 1860, as much as an ultimatum to the convention of the following month as to the country at large. The event which crystallized the theory of secession into practice was the election of President Lincoln in 1860. After his liberation from Fortress Monroe Mr. Davis went to Europe. On his return he became president of a life insurance company of Memphis, Tenn. In 1881 he published "The Rise and Fall of the Southern Confederacy," in two volumes. He died at New Orleans December 6, 1889, and was buried under the monument to the army of northern Virginia. At the time of his death he was engaged in the preparation of a series of sketches of war time.

Gen. Reuben Davis was born in Tennessee near Winchester, the youngest of a family of twelve children. When he was five years old his parents moved to Alabama, where the land had recently been purchased from the Indians, many of whom still roamed through the dense forests. Here the future general soon grew to be on friendly terms with the dusky inhabitants, and was taught by them to use the bow and arrow, and with them he had many wild experiences. With the help of his father and five brothers he cleared up a farm, his father having purchased a section at the public sale. He remained here till he was sixteen years of age, attending school about three months in the year. In this way he learned to read and write and also the rudiments of arithmetic, and a smattering of Latin. He was naturally an ambitious boy, and longed with all the force of his nature to be out in the strife of life, and to have a share in the rewards which are held out to those who are successful in its struggle. His first great sorrow was the death of his mother, whom he loved most passionately and who was a lady of great sweetness and tenderness of character. His strong desire was to become a lawyer, but his father persuaded him to take up the study of medicine, which he did under the tutelage of his brother-in-law, Dr. George Higgason, of Hamilton, Monroe county, Miss., thus becoming a citizen of that locality over sixty years ago. He located in Russellville, after studying for two years, and had distinguished success there and at other points in the state where he practiced, but the remuneration not being satisfactory and his heart still clinging to the old idea of studying law, he turned his attention to it in spare moments and soon obtained a license from Judge Lipacomb. He determined to go to

Monroe county again, so, in January, 1832, with $3 in his pocket and no immediate prospect of getting any more, he started forth and finally located at Athens. His first fee was $25, in lieu of which he took a small building, and, tearing it down, he rebuilt it for a dwelling to cover the heads of his delicate wife and himself. In the spring of 1835 he became a candidate for district attorney, and was triumphantly elected, which was an important step toward his future success. At this time he devoted himself steadily to the study of criminal law and with such success that at the end of four years he had put by a surplus of $20,000, and had more business than he could attend to. He practiced his profession diligently till the outbreak of the Mexican war, when he became colonel of a regiment that served bravely in that sanguinary conflict. In 1857 he was elected to congress, where he remained till his duty called him to the front in the Civil war, and through which he served as a brave, noble and efficient officer. His sudden death, while absent from home, was a shock to his many friends. The bar of Mississippi on his demise drafted a lengthy set of resolutions, which they published in the leading newspapers, and a copy of which they presented to his widow. The following are the eloquent remarks made by Judge Acker on this mournful occasion:

Mr. President—I rise for the purpose of contributing my testimony to the virtues and worth of our lamented fellow-citizen, Gen. Reuben Davis, and to pay tribute to his memory. Reuben Davis was no ordinary man, but a genius of the highest order, and would have been distinguished in any community in which his lot might have been cast. His first appearance in public life was as a prosecuting attorney for the then ninth judicial district of Mississippi, in 1836–7, immediately after the organization of the Chickasaw cession into counties. In 1842 he was, by executive appointment, made justice of the high court of errors and appeals. In January, 1847, he was elected colonel of the Second Mississippi volunteers, in the war with Mexico, which commission he resigned in June, 1847, and returned home, owing to his failing health. Soon after, he was elected to the state legislature. He was twice elected to represent this district in congress, and at the period of the state's secession resigned his seat and returned to participate in the dreadful conflict then pending between the states. He was influenced in this course by the same noble impulses that prompted Lee and other illustrious Southrons, who held that their first allegiance was due to the states of their nativity or adoption. In 1861 he was appointed by Governor Pettus, major-general of state troops, at the time when the Federals were endeavoring to obtain possession of the Cumberland and Tennessee rivers, and his last public trust was as a member of the Confederate congress. In all of these varied positions he acquitted himself with honor and distinction and signal benefit to his country. But, while General Davis stood forth a prominent figure as soldier and statesman, his highest distinction was as lawyer and advocate; indeed, as a criminal lawyer, he had no equal in Mississippi or superior in this country. As a private citizen he was public-spirited, progressive and liberal; as a friend he was faithful and true; as a husband and father, kind and considerate. He was always ready to fly to the relief of the poor, the persecuted and the unfortunate, and softly susceptible to

> "The sympathetic tear that flows
> Down virtue's manly cheek for others' woes."

He was a brave man: "As full of valor as of kindness, and princely in both." It will be many years before Mississippi will see another Reuben Davis. She may, and doubtless will, have orators eloquent and statesmen learned, wise and profound; she may and will have soldiers brave, chivalrous and fearless, who will rise up to defend her in the emergencies that must in the future arise, but as a wise and patriotic statesman, a profound lawyer and eloquent advocate, she will "rarely look upon his like again."

Richard Davis, planter and merchant, Tchula, Miss., has been a resident of Mississippi for considerably over half a century, coming with his mother from Louisiana, his native state, when but three years of age. His father, who was a native Virginian, born in 1780, was one of the very first settlers of Wilkinson county, Miss. He was married twice, and by his first wife had eleven children, all of whom are deceased. His second wife, who was a native of Tennessee and an early settler of Holmes county, Miss., bore him six children of whom the subject of this sketch is next to the youngest. The mother died in Holmes county in 1853, the father in 1833 in West Feliciana, La. Both were members of the Methodist church and took a great deal of interest in religion. The paternal grandfather, Micajah Davis, was born in the Old Dominion and was a Quaker in his religious views. The great-grandfather, Micajah Davis, was also a native of that state. Our subject's maternal grandfather originally came from Tennessee but nothing farther is known of him. Like his father before him, Richard Davis has followed planting and merchandising all his life, and has been fairly successful in both pursuits. He is the owner of twenty-eight hundred acres of excellent land, six hundred acres under cultivation, and his principal productions are corn, peas and cotton. He was married in 1869 to Miss Marcella O. Reilly, a native of northern Alabama. When a child Mrs. Davis went with her mother to Yazoo city. The latter was a native of Virginia and Mrs. Davis' father was born in Ireland. Mrs. Davis was the next youngest of six children born to her parents, three of whom are now living. Mrs. Davis' parents were Catholics, of which church she is a member. After his marriage Mr. Davis continued on the old homestead, where he has resided ever since, never having moved since early childhood. He is a strong temperance man, and has never been addicted to the use of alcoholic drinks or tobacco in any form. Formerly Mr. Davis was a whig, but he now affiliates with the democratic party, and for a number of years was president of a democratic club at Tchula. During the war his sympathies were with the South, but on account of ill health he was never mustered into the service. However, although not a soldier, he did all in his power to promote the interests of the Confederate states. Few persons have resided as long in Holmes county as Mr. Davis or know as much of the early settlement as he, who came on the first steamboat that ever ascended Tchula lake.

Robert J. Davis, a resident of Vaiden, Carroll county, Miss., was born in Wilkinson county, Miss., August 29, 1833, and is a son of Hugh W. Davis, a native of Louisiana. The father was a man of superior education, having received his training in a school of high grade in Louisiana. He was married there to Margaret A. Scott, a daughter of James Scott, and also a native of Louisiana, where she was reared and educated. Mr. Davis removed to Mississippi and settled in Wilkinson county, where he was engaged in planting for a few years. In 1834 he went to Holmes county, and in 1842 he came to Carroll county. He was prosperous in his business relations, and had accumulated a considerable property. He died in 1861, and Mrs. Davis passed away four years later, in 1865. Robert J. is one of a family of five sons and two daughters, who grew to mature years. The eldest brother, Hugh, was a soldier in the Confederate army. He died soon after joining the regiment in 1861; he was at Knoxville, Tenn., and his father went there to attend to him in his illness, and he, too, was stricken down and died there. Lewis also joined the army, and served through the war. His death occurred soon after the surrender. Joseph P. died just as he had reached man's estate, and the youngest brother, Jefferson, died in Carrollton in 1878. Robert J. grew to maturity at Old Middleton, where his father had settled in early days.

He was educated there in a private school, and at the age of eighteen years he left the parental roof and went to Greenwood, Miss., where he engaged in clerking. It was during this time, in 1853, that the yellow-fever epidemic struck that place. At the end of two years Mr. Davis returned to Carrollton, where he clerked for a number of years. He was united in marriage October 3, 1855, to Mary A. Jenkins, a daughter of John Jenkins, of Memphis, Tenn. Mrs. Davis was born in the state of Tennessee, but was educated at Franklin college, Holly Springs, Miss. Mr. Davis was appointed deputy clerk of the circuit court of Carroll county in 1857, and in 1862 enlisted in the Confederate states army. He returned to Carrollton, and was again made deputy clerk. He held this position until 1875, when he was elected to the office of clerk of the circuit court. He acted in this capacity until 1881, when he resigned and began farming. During the years of his public life he had acquired the drink habit. Realizing that this enemy was about to overcome him, he left the town, and in the quiet and solitude of agricultural life he combated this foe to its death. He is a radical temperance man, and in this mastery of appetite gives us an example of what the will of man can accomplish. In 1887 Mr. Davis was again elected clerk of the circuit court. In December of that year he moved to Vaiden, and took charge of the chancery and circuit clerk business. He has now been connected with the circuit and chancery clerks' office for about twenty-five years, and there are no details of the transaction of the business that escape him. He is a most efficient officer, and a most willing servant of the public. Mr. and Mrs. Davis are the parents of five children. Margaret E. is the wife of James B. Thompson, a planter in Tallahatchie county, and is the mother of three children. The other daughter is Mary F., and the three sons died in infancy. They have one adopted child, Eva May Brady. The family are active members of the Presbyterian church, and Mr. Davis is a deacon of that body. He is a member of the Independent Order of Odd Fellows, having joined that fraternity in 1855, and has served in all the official capacities of the subordinate lodge. He also belongs to the Masonic order. He is a man of social, genial disposition, and has those traits of character that go to make a loyal citizen and a stanch, true friend.

Judge Thomas N. Davis, the most conspicuous and popular citizen of Webster county, is now a resident of Greensboro, where he located as early as 1836. He was born in Lewis county, Ky., in 1808 and is a son of Capt. George N. and Harriet (Bragg) Davis, natives respectively of Maryland and South Carolina. Both went with their parents to Kentucky at an early day, were married in that state, and there passed the remainder of their days. Mr. Davis was a wealthy planter and salt manufacturer for a number of years. He was captain of a company of soldiers and fought with General Harrison at the battle of Tippecanoe. He was the youngest in order of birth of a large family of children born to Nicholas Davis, who was a native of Maryland, but who was a pioneer of Kentucky, where his death occurred. He was of Welsh origin. Of the eight children born to his parents Judge Davis was second in order of birth, and is the only one residing in the county. He was reared on a farm, secured a common-school education, and in 1831 was married to Mrs. Susan Larkins (nee Strode), whose daughter by her former marriage became the mother of Dr. J. R. Nolen (see sketch). Mrs. Larkins was the daughter of Colonel Jeremiah Strode, a native of the Old Dominion, who went with his father to Kentucky, and his settlement is still known as Strode's station. After the death of his wife Colonel Strode went to the Lone Star state and there passed the closing scenes of his life. He was colonel of the regiment in which Captain Davis was captain during the battle of Tippecanoe. Mrs. Davis was born in Kentucky and died in 1847. By her marriage to Judge Davis she became the mother of

40

six children, viz.: George, died in 1863, leaving a family; Harriet Amanda, died when young; Susan, died in infancy; William A., a planter of Webster county, served in the Fifteenth Mississippi infantry as a private until after the battle of Franklin, Tenn.; Nancy, wife of Richard S. Cramer, and Lucy, widow of Arnold J. Brantley, who afterward married Henry C. Diggs, with whom she is now living in Winona, Miss. Judge Davis' second marriage was to Miss Martha Cunningham, a native of Georgia, and a daughter of James Cunningham, who came to Choctaw county, Miss., at an early day, followed planting, and there received his final summons. In 1836 Judge Davis came to Greensboro from Kentucky, and the next year, 1837, was elected probate clerk on the whig ticket, but was defeated in 1839. Again, in 1843, he was elected to the same office and served twelve consecutive years, when he was elected probate judge, which position he held without interruption until 1869, when he was removed by the radicals. From 1878 to 1880 he was president of the board of supervisors of what was then Sumner county (now Webster county), and then followed a term in the legislature. Throughout his entire public career he has retained the undivided confidence and esteem of the people. A few years ago he retired from active life and removed from Greensboro to his farm two miles southeast of Greensboro, where he has a very pleasant home. He is the owner of four hundred and twenty acres, with about one hundred and fifty acres under cultivation. He has been a member of Greensboro lodge No. 49, A. F. & A. M. since 1845, and has been past master in the same. He has been a member of the Methodist church for over thirty years. The Judge served twelve months in the Confederate war against the Federal government, and was for about three months of that time provost-marshal of Grenada, Miss.

Alexander Deale, father of Balus E. Deale, Macon, Noxubee county, Miss., was born in South Carolina in 1782, emigrated to Alabama in 1818, and thence removed to Noxubee county, Miss., in 1832. His wife, Margaret Lawrence, was born in 1787, in South Carolina, and died in 1869. Alexander Deale died in 1844. By occupation he was a planter. Balus E. Deale, one of a family of eight children, was born in Alabama in 1828, and, at four years of age, removed to Noxubee county, Miss. He was married to Miss Baker, in Virginia, in 1851, later to Miss Addie Windham, and, in 1874, to Miss Margaret Skinner, who graduated from the Pickensville female institution in the year 1860. By his first marriage he had three boys: Willie Earle, George Baker and Harry Gaines. By his second marriage he had one child—a daughter—Maggie Lee. Mr. Deale is a useful citizen and stands very high in every way, and has only delicate health to cause him trouble. He lives in a palatial home and signs of prosperity surround him.

Prof. H. A. Dean, principal and founder of the Iuka Normal institute, was born near Shelbyville, Bedford county, Tenn., in March, 1844, a son of Daniel and Amanda F. (Heard) Dean, who were born and grew to maturity in Tennessee, and there married. His father was a resident of Hickman county, Tenn., for a number of years, and at the time of his death was treasurer of that county. His widow ended her days there also. They had nine children, all of whom, except Professor Dean, are living in Tennessee. The latter was reared on the farm and had the advantages farmer boys usually had, attending school in winter and laboring on the farm in summer. At seventeen he heard and answered the call of his state for volunteers. He was mustered into the Confederate service as a member of the First regiment of Tennessee cavalry. A private he went into the army, a private he was mustered out by General Sherman when Joe E. Johnston surrendered the army of North Carolina, having served under the great cavalry leaders, Forrest, Van Dorn and Wheeler. He still has a vivid recollection of Shiloh, Holly Springs, Chickamauga, Mission ridge and the many battles fought on the retreat from Dalton to Atlanta and Nashville. In June, 1865, he returned to his father's, in Tennessee, and found what the most of the Confederate soldiers found, parents, younger brothers, and sisters with scant supplies of provisions, farming implements and stock, and no means or prospect of any to aid in starting in business or procuring an education. The future seemed dark, yet the ex-soldier determined to have a university education. Without means he entered upon his self-imposed task, expecting to get his degree in ten years. He entered school in 1866, and since that time has been engaged in going to school and teaching, four years excepted. In 1869 he received his first diploma, from the Union seminary, at Newbern, Tenn. While teaching, to obtain money to pay the expense of his education, he displayed such aptness in teaching and managing that some of the best schools in West Tennessee were constantly demanding his services. New life and an increased enrollment of boarding and local students attested his fitness for the positions filled by him in these schools. The university idea was still in his mind though, and in 1880 he entered the National Normal university at Lebanon, Ohio. After two years' work in and for the university, he received the degree of master of arts. He determined now to put in operation a scheme held in mind for ten years, that is, establish a school of his own somewhere in the South. He had resuscitated schools for others; his work now was to make one for himself. He found Iuka, Miss., well adapted to his purposes. It is a town of about one thousand inhabitants, located in the northeastern part of Mississippi, on the Memphis & Charleston railroad, and eight miles from the Tennessee river. The people are social and peaceable, the soil is productive, the timber is excellent, the scenery round about is picturesque and beautiful, and the country is one of the most healthful in the South. Here the earth abounds in minerals for the mineralogist and with the relics of past ages for the geologist. The wild woods and groves blossom in beauty for the botanist and teem with living wonders for the zoologist. The springs that gush forth from hillsides and valleys possess various medicinal and healing properties. Here the debilitated finds his tonic, the dyspeptic his antidote, the bilious his relief and the weak his strength. Here are the fountains of youth of the red man as he roamed the unpeopled wilds in his search for the spirit fountains which are yet known in traditional history. But now the white man seeks them for the cure of disease to which modern flesh is heir. Most of these springs have not been retouched by the hand of art, but are as the red man left them, hence their more refreshing charm and romance. Hence there are special inducements for the student who seeks both the Pierian spring for intellectual power and the fountain of youth for new strength to his body. Satisfactory arrangements were made, and in September, 1882, he opened the first successful independent normal school in the South. The buildings known as Iuka male academy and Iuka female institute were leased for a period of ten years for the purpose of building up a permanent normal school. The two schools conducted in the above named buildings were consolidated with Humboldt (Tenn.) normal institute, a school of influence and reputation. Since the organization of the Iuka normal institute the school has rapidly grown in public notice and favor and is in a fair way to become the normal school of the South and thus realize the whole aim of its principal and teachers. The success of its students and graduates, with their energy, vim and enthusiasm, in the various fields of enterprise, and the constant demand for trained teachers from this school, are sufficient indications that the normal is one of the leading institutions of the South. The patronage was almost local in 1882. The school has now over two hundred pupils enrolled in daily attendance. About one hundred of these are boarding pupils. The indications now are that the annual enrollment this year will reach four hundred and fifty.

The normal has been popular from the first in Iuka. There is perfect harmony, all are working for the school with a zeal and determination that will be sure to crown the principal's plan with the highest success. The board of trustees of this institution embraces several of the prominent men in this section. It is constituted as follows: Col. E. S. Chandler, Sr., president; J. W. Jourdan, secretary; George P. Hammerly, W. H. Lockwood, John B. McKinney and Hon. J. M. Stone, of Iuka; Hon. J. A. Blair, of Tupelo; Hon. Fred Beall, of West Point; Col. Newnan Case, of Fulton; Col. John W. T. Falkner, of Oxford; Hon J. A. Green, of Corinth; Hon. J. J. Gage, of Grenada; Dr. W. L. Lipscomb, of Columbus; Col. J. L. Power, of Jackson, and B. F. McRae, of Iuka. The departments are as follows: Primary, training, classic, commercial, intermediate, scientific, fine arts, preparatory and penmanship, and all are in charge of competent instructors. Professor Dean was married in October, 1872, to Sarah E., daughter of Guy Douglass, of Newbern, Tenn., and they have two children: Anna N. and Guy D. Politically, he affiliates with the democratic party, but he is too closely devoted to his business to mingle in public life, and has no taste for politics, as it is usually manifested. He and his wife are members of the Methodist church South.

As a planter and miller John M. Dean has attained an enviable reputation, for in conducting his operations he has brought his sound good sense and his practical views to bear, and as a result has accumulated a fair share of this world's goods. He was born in Lancaster district, S. C., the fourth in a family of seven sons born to the union of T. W. and Martha (Latham) Dean, the former of whom was born in Virginia, and the latter in South Carolina. They were married in the mother's native state, but at an early day removed from there to Tennessee, and five years later to Mississippi (in 1836). The father died here in 1879 at the age of ninety years, and the mother one year and one month later in her eightieth year. They were upright and worthy citizens, and had, for many years, been members of the Cumberland Presbyterian church. Their seven sons grew to maturity, but James A., Isaac D., A. J. and William L. are deceased, the latter being killed at the battle of Chickamauga, Tenn., while a member of the Ninth Mississippi infantry. Those living are Charles L., a planter of this county; John M. and David L., a furniture dealer of Senatobia. John M. Dean spent his youthful days in Yalobusha and De Soto (later Tate) county, Miss., and his early playfellows were the little Chickasaw Indians. At the early age of seventeen years he opened a grocery supply store at what was then called Buck Snort, but is now Independence, but finally added dry goods to his stock, and successfully conducted this business for ten or twelve years. At the end of this time he purchased a section of land in the neighborhood of where he now resides, and erected thereon a large flour and sawmill which he operated by water power, having two Leffel turbine water wheels, one forty-six and the other thirty-horse power. His flour mill was one of the largest and best ever run in the South, and for many years he turned out twenty thousand barrels of fine flour yearly, besides large quantities of corn meal. Owing to great falling off of the wheat raised in Mississippi his large mill has long since ceased to run, but he operates in its stead a corn and sawmill and a cottongin. Mr. Dean has been in the milling business for over thirty-five years, and no man more thoroughly understands every detail of this work than he. Of his plantation, which comprises one thousand four hundred acres, he has seven hundred acres under cultivation, and besides this he has between eight and nine hundred acres of Mississippi river bottom land in Bolivar county. On his home plantation, which is situated about seven miles from Senatobia, and the same distance from Coldwater, he has an elegant modern residence, of fine architectural design without, and conveniently and tastefully arranged within. He had the misfortune to have a residence equally as good burned to the ground some ten years since. After the close of the war he followed merchandising in Senatobia for some six years, during which time he was reasonably successful. He was married on the 14th of February, 1855, to Miss Martha E. Crawford, a daughter of John and Mary J. (Sullivan) Crawford, who were born in North Carolina, and were among the earliest and most worthy families of this state. The father died on the 21st of October, 1889, but his widow survives him at the age of eighty years. Mr. Dean and his wife became the parents of eleven children: William A., who died November 5, 1882; Charles C., who is in business in Leland, Miss.; Robert, who died in 1868; J. F., a lawyer of Senatobia, also county superintendent of public instruction of Tate county; Tobia, in business at Leland; Cora L., wife of Otho McGee of Leland; Lula C., at home; Isaac W., who died in infancy; Oscar, Edna May and Homer. Mr. and Mrs. Dean are members of the Missionary Baptist church, of which he has been a deacon ever since the organization of the Hickory Grove Baptist church. He is a member of Ebenezer lodge No. 76 of the A. F. & A. M. of Senatobia. In the use of his means he has always been liberal, and has assisted in the building up of worthy enterprises. The early life of his brother Charles L. was very similar to that of his own. He was born on the 19th of February, 1829, and at the age of twenty-five years he left home and began doing for himself. February 25, 1853, he united in marriage to Miss Mary C. Hudson, a daughter of Edmond G. and Catherine (Garrett) Hudson, all of whom were born in the Old Dominion. After his marriage Charles L. clerked with his brother John for some time, after which he served an apprenticeship in his brother's mill, a calling he followed for between fifteen and twenty years, during which time he won the reputation of being one of the best millers in the state. He is the owner of an admirably-kept plantation of one hundred and forty acres, on which is a pleasant and comfortable home. In addition to the management of this land he does burr dressing and gin sharpening, at which he is an expert. His marriage has resulted in the birth of six children: Martha C.; Mary A., wife of Nicholas Compton; Medella P., wife of Fayette Dean; Nettie J., wife of A. J. Wallace; Allie Dixie, wife of J. L. Walker, and Lydia V., wife of W. B. Crenshaw; all of whom reside near their father. Mr. and Mrs. Dean and their two eldest daughters are members of the Presbyterian church, of which he is an elder. He is a member of Ebenezer lodge No. 76 of the A. F. & A. M. of Senatobia, and in his support of laudable enterprises he has always been very liberal.

Samuel M. Dean, general merchant of Iuka, Miss., was born October 27, 1826. He was the son of Aaron and Mekey (Day) Dean. His father was born in South Carolina in 1799, and was the son of Samuel Dean and Guiney (James) Dean. His early life was spent in that state, where he was reared a practical planter. In 1839 he removed to Mississippi and located four miles west of Iuka, on land bought from the government, which he improved and then engaged in planting. He was married while still a resident of South Carolina, and his wife bore him twelve children, two of whom died when young. The others came with him to Mississippi. They were: Mary C., Ballard B., Samuel M., Hephsibah L., John J., Whitner W., who died young; Whitner W., who is still living; Joseph, now deceased; Robert M., Hortensia V. and Anna. The father of this family was an early and prominent settler here, and he and his wife were members of the Missionary Baptist church. The latter was born in South Carolina in 1804, and was a daughter of Ballard and Sylvia (Mayfield) Day. Mr. Dean died in 1849 and his wife died in 1889, at the age of eighty-four. Both died in this county. The early life of our subject was spent on his father's plantation, and he acquired a good common school education. In 1850 he embarked in business life as a general merchant, continuing in that occupation for seven years. In 1862 he enlisted in company A, commanded by Captain Dixon, which formed a part of Moreland's regiment, Roddy's division, Forrest's command, Confederate army. He served through the war as commissary and quartermaster. He was paroled in 1865, and, returning home, again engaged in merchandising and farming in which he has continued with much success until the present time. He is the owner of one thousand eight hundred and forty acres of land, located two miles northwest of Iuka. He was married in 1856, in Tishomingo county, to Miss Millie Biggs, daughter of Jessie and Sally (Ashcraft) Biggs. Her father was born in North Carolina and her mother in Tennessee. Mrs. Dean was born in 1839 and was one of six children in her father's family: William, Henry, Millie, James, Thomas and Jefferson W. Her father was an early settler here, and was a farmer and miller who was well known throughout the county. He died in 1877, his wife having preceded him in 1862. Mr. and Mrs. Dean have had born to them eleven children, named as follows: Sallie V., Anna B., Ardelia D., Jodella, Laura E., Samuel S., (who died in 1887), Whitner W., Lawrence L., Clarence C., Orion O. and Gertrude. Of these, Sallie married Robert Carter, and is living in Iuka; Ardelia, now Mrs. Jefferson Leatherwood, is living at Pecan Point; Laura married Anderson Patterson and is living in Iuka. Mr. and Mrs. Dean are members of the Methodist Episcopal church and of the Knights and Ladies of Honor. He is also a member of the Knights of Honor and a Free Mason. In politics he is a democrat, and has been for several years a member of the city council of Iuka. He is deeply interested in everything that has a tendency to the development of the county or state, or improvements for the general interests, and the demands upon him by schools, churches and various charitable interests which appeal to the benevolence of the ordinary American, are almost invariably met with cheerful alacrity and generosity, which mark him as one of the most liberal-minded of men, and one of the most helpful of citizens.

Capt. James M. Dearing, planter, is an example of what may be accomplished when the spirit of determination is exercised in connection with the everyday affairs of life. His planting operations have resulted satisfactorily, and he is now in a position to enjoy all the conveniences and many of the luxuries of life. He was born in Rowan county, N. C., June 12, 1831, to Alexander B. and Ruth (Rogers) Dearing, who were of Scotch descent, and natives of North Carolina. They became residents of Lowndes county, Miss., in 1833, purchasing land on which they remanied until 1840, when they took up their abode in Alabama, where the father died in 1862 and the mother in 1859. Of seven children born to them, four are living: James M., Mollie, Myra and Alice. Mary, George and Philip are deceased. His early educational advantages were good, for, besides graduating from the State university of Alabama, his initiatory training was received in first-class educational institutions. As he was brought up to a farm experience and thoroughly understood every detail of this vocation, he determined to make it his life occupation, and has since been intimately and prominently identified with the agricultural interests of this section. He began for himself at the age of twenty-four years, in Clarke county, Miss., where he remained until the breaking out of the war in 1861, at which time he joined company D, as a private, being soon after promoted to the position of captain of his company. In 1862 he was called from the scene of conflict to his home on account of the death of his father. A short time later he moved to Lowndes county, purchasing the plantation where he now resides, on which is a pleasant and comfortable residence. He was married in September, 1856, to Miss Mary C. Eddes, a native of North Carolina, and of eight children born to them three are living: Alexander, James M. and Clarence. Mr. Dearing was called upon to mourn the death of his estimable wife on the 1st of August, 1878, since which time he has remained a widower. He is a member of the Methodist Episcopal church, and politically is a democrat.

Among the enterprising merchants who have largely contributed toward building up the mercantile fame of the town of Enterprise, and whose establishment affords an apt illustration of the progress and development of the place, may be mentioned that of F. H. Deas, who founded his mercantile establishment about 1876. The stock carried by him is of large size and extensive variety and contains everything pertaining to a general line of goods. Although his patronage is large it is constantly on the increase, and Mr. Deas has shown himself to be a man of exceptionally fine businesss qualifications and sound judgment. He was brought up to a knowledge of mercantile life by his father, in the city of Mobile, Ala., where he also obtained his literary education, learning during his youthful days the calling of a civil engineer. In his native city (Mobile, Ala.,) he followed civil engineering for some time and assisted in surveying the Mobile & Ohio railroad through the state of Mississippi. After locating in Enterprise he met the lady who afterward became his wife. He has since identified himself with the interests of Clarke county, and has shown himself to be one of the most public spirited, enterprising and useful citizens.

O. J. Deavours is a Texan by birth, born in Weatherford, April 24, 1865, the third of five children born to John and Adaline C. (Moore) Deavours, natives of Alabama, the father being a merchant and planter by occupation. He came to Mississippi in 1867 and located in Tishomingo county, where he remained until his death in 1876, serving fourteen years in the capacity of clerk of the circuit court. He served throughout the Rebellion under Gen. Kirby Smith, and was a true and tried soldier to the cause he espoused. The paternal grandfather was a member of the Mississippi legislature for several terms, and his father was a soldier in the Revolutionary war and was a participant in the battle in which Sergeant Jasper distinguished himself. The mother's people were of Scotch-Irish descent, and like the Deavours were very prominent in war, politics and in commercial circles. J. B. Moore, an uncle of O. J. Deavours, is a member of the state senate of Alabama. Mr. Deavours was reared in Mississippi and educated at Iuka. Upon leaving school, at the age of twenty-one years, he immediately began merchandising in Clarksdale, and here has been very successful as a business man, fulfilling the promise he gave while a student. He started out with quite a small capital, but his present possessions show that he is a talented and shrewd business man. In addition to a fine plantation of seven hundred and fifty acres, all of which are under cultivation, he is a member of the firm of Broaddus, Deavours & Co., their stock of general merchandise being worth about $15,000, their annual sales amounting to $60,000. In this lucrative business Mr. Deavours owns a one-third interest. He inherited some property at his father's death, but in strong contrast to the majority of young men, he has managed it prudently, and has largely increased it, although, he has been in business only a short time. He is industrious, is the soul of honor, is courteous and agreeable in his manners, and these attributes are, without doubt, the secret of his success. He is of attractive presence, is of medium stature and has light hair and intelligent gray eyes. While in school he was a close and faithful student. He is now engaged to marry a very beautiful and wealthy heiress, one of Mississippi's fairest daughters.

Col. E. G. De Lap is the senior member of the well-known firm of E. G. De Lap & Co., insurance agents, of Natchez, Miss. This gentleman was born in a log house near Monroe, Wis., in the year 1838, and was the youngest of twelve children born to Rev. Robert and Elizabeth (Kinny) De Lap, both parents being natives of the state of New York. They were early residents of the state of Illinois, and about 1837 removed to Wisconsin, where they resided until their respective deaths, the father having been a minister of the Methodist Episcopal church for over fifty years, preaching the gospel in Kentucky,

Illinois, New York and Wisconsin. E. G. De Lap was given the advantages of a common-school education, and at the early age of fifteen years began the battle of life for himself, and by contact with the world and by close observation he became a well-informed man. He was married in 1857, and has a family of four children. In 1862 he enlisted in company B, Twenty-third volunteer infantry, United States army, and was with Sherman in his march to the sea. He was also at Vicksburg and was on detached service. He received his discharge in Natchez, Miss., March 21 or 23, 1864, by order of the secretary of war, which enabled him to accept a position in the United States treasury department as local special agent of the United States treasury at Natchez, and in this capacity served one year. After the war he engaged in business in the town, and here has since resided. Since 1880 he has been in the insurance business. His partner was John A. Dicks, a pushing and enterprising man of business, but in 1884 they dissolved partnership, since which time Mr. De Lap has been associated with a Mr. Guice, a shrewd and honorable business man. They now represent twelve of the best insurance companies of the world, and do a fire, life, accident and tornado insurance. The Colonel, as he is familiarly called, is an honorable and excellent gentleman, and as a business man is considered by one and all to be one of the best of which Natchez can boast. After the war he chose to remain in Natchez, where fortune had drifted him, for he was pleased with the place and the people, but he was not classed among the carpetbaggers of those times, for he identified himself with every interest of the South and of the people among whom he had decided to cast his lot. His second marriage took place in 1874, and was to Miss Laura L. Cozzens, a daughter of Brown Cozzens, the father of the latter being an officer in one of the early Indian wars. Mr. De Lap now lives on the old estate, Bellevue, the old home of Don Girrault, a Spaniard, around which place clusters much historic interest. This is a fine old place, and comprises about fifty acres in Natchez. To Colonel De Lap's last marriage one child has been born: Laura Louisa. The family attend the Methodist Episcopal church, and the Colonel is an active worker in the Sabbath-school. He was made a Mason in Natchez in 1865, becoming a member of Harmony lodge No. 1. He has taken all the degrees in Masonry, has held high office in each degree, and since 1868 has been a member of the grand lodge, since which time he has attended every meeting of this lodge. He was elected grand warden in the grand lodge in 1885 by one vote for all; in 1886 he was elected senior grand warden by one vote for all, and in 1887 was elected grand master in the same way. He is enthusiastic in his praise of Masonry, and at all times endeavors to further the interests of this order.

George W. Delbridge was born in Brunswick county, Va., January 10, 1840, the eldest of six children of James D. and Martha J. (Collier) Delbridge, three of whom were born in Virginia, the other three in Mississippi. In 1847 they removed to Lafayette county, Miss., and after purchasing and planting until 1856 they moved with their family to Oxford, where Mr. Delbridge entered the employ of the railroad company as station agent, a position he held with credit until the opening of the war. In 1862 he joined the Confederate service, and after the war closed he renewed his connection with the railroad company at Oxford, acting in the capacity of agent up to 1868. He then opened a mercantile establishment in Oxford, but after following this business for about one year he sold his stock of goods and engaged in the hotel business, and in 1871 purchased a farm near Oxford. He soon after returned to his former occupation of planting, and at about this period acted in the capacity of county treasurer to fill out the unexpired term of Mr. Dennis. Being among the early settlers of the county he was well known, and for two years he filled the position of magistrate. At the time of his death, which occurred at his home near Oxford, July 7, 1890, at the age of seventy-one years, he was an earnest member of the Methodist Episcopal church, and had for many years been a member of the Masonic fraternity. He was liberal and public spirited. His widow is now in her sixty-eighth year, and is rather feeble. When eighteen years of age George W. Delbridge began to make his own way in the world as a clerk in a store in Oxford, and followed that occupation until the Civil war, when he enlisted in the Confederate army, was assigned to the army of Virginia, and went directly to the front. He was in the engagements of Gettysburg, Seven Pines, Petersburg, and various other engagements of minor importance. He was wounded in the leg by a gun shot at Seven Pines, and was kept in the hospital at Richmond until once more fitted for duty, which was at the end of four months. He was again wounded in the fight near Petersburg by a minie-ball just above the right ear, but as the ball had been spent before reaching him it did not penetrate only under the skin. It was, however, a serious wound, and he was sent home on furlough, where he remained for about three months. At the end of this time he rejoined his command at Petersburg, and was there captured on April 2, 1865, and taken to Point Lookout, Md., where he was kept until June, when he was paroled and returned home, where he engaged in his former occupation of clerking. His early education was obtained in Oxford, and in 1868 he succeeded his father as station agent at that place, in which capacity he served until the latter part of 1870, when he was appointed by Governor Alcorn as circuit court clerk, and was elected to the same position at the election of 1871 for four years, being supported by both political parties without opposition. In 1875 he was married, and the following year he removed to the plantation, upon which he is now residing. He owns one thousand and eighty acres of land, and has about five hundred acres improved. He is a practical planter, is well and favorably known throughout the county, and has always been regarded as an honorable, upright gentleman. His wife was formerly Miss Lucretia Lewis, a daughter of Abner Lewis. They have one son and two daughters: Georgia, Abner J. and Lucretia Lewis. Mr. Delbridge is a member of the Methodist Episcopal church, and his wife is a Presbyterian. He is a member of the A. F. & A. M., and he and his family move in the highest circles of society.

Thomas J. Denman, a planter and merchant of Tallahatchie county, was born in Carroll county in 1858. He was the son of Richard and Mary E. (Sullivan) Denman. His father, who was a native of Georgia, came to Mississippi during the pioneer period. Settling in Monroe county, he removed after a time to Choctaw county, and from there to Carroll county; here he married and lived until 1866; during that year he came to Tallahatchie county. Here he lived until January, 1889, when he removed to Sardis, Panola county, where he has since lived. He has been a life-long planter, beginning with no capital except honesty and determination to succeed, until he has acquired a competency. He served four years in the Confederate army, part of the time in a cavalry company during the Civil war, but he was for a considerable time in the infantry, being captured at Fort Donelson and imprisoned at Indianapolis, Ind., for six months and one day. After that he rejoined his command, serving in a cavalry organization until the close of the war. He surrendered with General Forrest at Selma, Ala. Returning home, he resumed planting. He is a member of the Sardis lodge and Royal Arch chapter of the Masonic order. He was four times married, the first time to the mother of our subject, who died August 12, 1876. Mr. Denman's paternal grandfather was John Denman, who was born and married to Martha Hooper in Franklin county, Ga., where he lived until the removal of the Indians west of the Mississippi, in which he assisted. He then settled in Monroe county, whence he removed to Yalobusha county, where he lived for ten years, and thence removed to Choctaw county, where he died in 1863, at the age of eighty-five years. In early life he was a planter, and before then was a keelboatman on the Tombigbee river.   He was twice married.   The grandmother of our subject was his first wife.   She reared a large family of sons and daughters and died in Yalobusha county.   His great-grandfather, John Denman, was a native of Ireland, who early came to America, where he passed the rest of his life.   Thomas J. Denman is the sixth of eleven children, of whom four daughters and two sons are living.   He was reared on a farm, becoming familiar with all the details of farm life and work and having only such education as was afforded by the common schools of the time and locality.   In 1881 he married Miss Ada E., daughter of William and Mary Crenshaw, natives respectively of Itawamba and Yazoo counties, who were married in the latter county.   Both are now residents of Tallahatchie county, where Mr. Crenshaw is a planter.   He was a soldier in the Confederate army during the late war.   Both he and his wife are members of the Methodist church.   Mrs. Denman was born in Tallahatchie county, and has become the mother of five children, of whom four are living.   She is a large, noble-looking lady, beloved in her home and popular in society.   Nearly all of Mr. Denman's life has been devoted to the planting interest, but for some years past he has also been engaged in the mercantile trade, having a store on his farm, which is owned and managed by the firm of T. J. & I. C. Denman.   He has lived on his present plantation, eight miles south of Charleston, for eight years, and is the owner of three hundred and twenty acres, mostly good bottom land, much of which he inherited from his father.   He is a prominent Mason, and in 1885 and 1887 was worshipful master of George Washington lodge No. 157, A. F. & A. M., at Charleston.   In 1889 he assisted in the organization of the Cascilla lodge No. 411, A. F. & A. M., of which he was made worshipful master, which position he now fills.   He is one of the county's sturdiest planters, with a good reputation for honesty, and is favorably known in the country round about.

Iredell C. Denman is a cousin of T. J. Denman, and lives four miles south of Charleston, in Tallahatchie county, Miss.   Like his cousin, he is a prosperous planter, while at the same time he is engaged in commercial pursuits, being a member of the firm of T. J. &. I. C. Denman; also president of Mead Landing Commercial association.   He was born in Choctaw county, Miss., in February, 1848, the son of John H. Denman, who was an elder brother of Richard Denman (see sketch of T. J. Denman).   The father, John H. Denman, was also born in Franklin county, Ga., coming with his father, when a mere lad, to Mississippi, at the time of the removal of the Indians of that state.   He received a very limited education, as one can easily judge when the primitive days of Mississippi are remembered. At the age of twenty-five he married a widow lady, whose maiden name was Eliza Graves, a native of North Carolina, who died in Choctaw county in March, 1850.   She was the mother of six children, three by each husband, all of whom survived her.   The father lived a widower three years, when he married Miss Julia A. Sullivan, who presented him with four children, three of whom are living in the neighborhood of their mother at Prescott, Ark., where the father spent his last years on his prosperous plantation, where he passed away, in 1886, at the age of sixty-six years.   Our subject was reared on a farm, receiving such an education as could be obtained in country schools, up to the age of fifteen, when the peaceful tenor of his schoolday was interrupted by the war drum, and fired with the patriotism which swept so fiercely over the South, he joined the army of Tennessee in 1863, though he was a mere lad, serving in company A of a Mississippi battalion till the close of that long and bloody struggle.   He was married January 31, 1870, to Sarah E., a daughter of George F. Taylor, who was born in Alabama, where he lived till 1865, when he came to Carroll county, Miss., and was killed in 1870 by a log rolling over him.   The wife of the subject of this sketch was also born in Monroe county, Ala., in 1850.   She has presented Mr. Denman with nine children, four only of them now living. They live in a beautiful home four miles south of Charleston, Miss., which consists of two hundred and eighty acres of valley land, two hundred of which are under the plow, and which he has accomplished by his own efforts. He and his wife are members of the Baptist church, and Mr. Denman is a prominent Mason, being the worshipful master of George Washington lodge No. 157, at Charleston, for three successive years; he is also a member of Charleston lodge No. 108, I. O. O. F., of which he was at one time the secretary; he is also a member of Macon Leigh lodge, Knights of Honor, No. 3233, at Charleston. Mr. Denman is justly proud of his family. They all stand high in the community, while the head of the house is looked up to as an honorable, upright business man, and one who is worth all the respect that is given him by his large circle of friends, who admire him for the success he has honestly earned.

Walter Denny, Moss Point, Miss., the oldest lumber manufacturer of Jackson county, Miss., was born in Jackson county, Miss., April 24, 1816, and may be considered a pioneer of the state. He was a son of Walter Denny, Sr., a native of Pennsylvania, who emigrated to Mississippi about the year 1800, and located in the territory which is now the northern portion of Jackson county. The Indians were then numerous, and civilization had made little impress upon the country. He followed agriculture for some years, and in 1828 removed to Greene county, Miss., where he was engaged in planting until his death, which occurred in 1848. He was justice of the peace for a great many years, and took a lively interest in local politics. He was an intimate friend of Judge Sharkey and General Claiborne. He reared a family of two sons and eight daughters, only one son and one daughter surviving. Our subject removed with his parents to Greene county, Miss., when a lad of twelve years. His opportunities for acquiring an education were extremely meager, but he made the most of the advantages which came in his way, and in early life became a conspicuous figure in the history of Greene county. He was sheriff of the county for ten years, and the year he removed to Jackson county, the people of Greene county nominated him in convention as a candidate for the legislature. This honor, however, he declined to accept. In 1853 he came to Jackson county, and located at Moss Point, where he purchased a sawmill and began the manufacture of lumber. He has been engaged in the business continuously since that time. He had a partner for a short time, but he is now deceased, the widow retaining an interest in the firm. Mr. Denny was a member of the legislature during the war, and voted for secession. He was enrolling officer and taxcollector during the latter part of the war. Since that time he has given his attention to private interests. The present firm was incorporated in 1890, with Walter Denny president; A. S. Denny, vice president; and A. P. Denny, secretary and treasurer. They own two shipping vessels and a locomotive, and are transacting an immense business. Mr. Denny was married in 1850 to Miss Nancy McKennon, and there were born to them four sons: A. S., A. P., Samuel and Walter M., a sketch of whom appears on another page of this history. Mr. Denny was married a second time, at the close of the war, to Mrs. Harwell, of Kemper county, Miss. Four children were the result of this union: Horace K., Emma, Mamie and Alexander. Mr. Denny is a member of the Masonic fraternity and of the Presbyterian church. He is one of the most widely known men of Jackson county, and has a host of friends throughout the surrounding country. He is personally acquainted with the large dealers along the coast, and transacts business with firms in Europe and Cuba.

Walter M. Denny, Scranton, Miss., the present circuit and chancery clerk of the courts of Jackson county, Miss., was born in this county, at Moss Point, October 28, 1853, and is a son of Walter Denny. He received his elementary education in the common schools and at Roanoke college, Virginia, and was graduated from the law department of Oxford university, Mississippi, in 1874. After completing his legal studies, he abandoned the idea of practicing the profession, and embarked in the lumber trade, as an employe of his father. He also invested in the mercantile business, and was thus occupied until 1883, when he was elected to the office of circuit and chancery clerk. He is an efficient and reliable officer, and has discharged his duties with such satisfaction to the public that he has held the position continuously since his election in 1883. He is in the prime of life, is naturally possessed of good business qualifications, and is in every way well fitted for official service. He was a delegate to the constitutional convention from Jackson county in 1890. He is a conspicuous figure in political circles, and has a host of friends who are pleased to keep him where his abilities are of such value to the general welfare of the community. Mr. Denny was married in 1875 to Miss Huldah Randall, of Moss Point, and they are the parents of eight children: Walter M., Jr., Catherine, Huldah and Celeste (twins), Lyman R., Nancy, Grace and Irene. Mr. Denny is a member of the Masonic fraternity and of the I. O. O. F., and takes a deep interest in the action of these societies. He is a Presbyterian in his religious faith.

E. H. Dial, attorney at law, of Meridian, Miss., was born in Sumter county, near Gainesville, Ala., May 7, 1853, a son of Joseph R. and Emily (Woodard) Dial. The father was a native of South Carolina and his mother of North Carolina. Down to the time of the war the former was a planter, but since the close of the war, until his retirement, he was engaged in the lumber business. Of his children who grew to maturity only two are now living. These are the subject of this sketch and a sister, younger than himself—Mrs. Idelette Watkins, the wife of Hon. E. Watkins, a well-known citizen of Chattanooga, Tenn. The former was reared in Sumter county, Ala., and in Meridian, Miss., to which place he removed when he was twelve years old. He attended the schools of Meridian until 1872, and later entered the University of Mississippi and graduated with the centennial class of 1876. For about a year thereafter he divided his time between employment in the Capital state bank at Jackson, Miss., and the study of law. He was admitted to the bar in 1877 and for eighteen months thereafter practiced his profession in Kemper county, Miss., at the expiration of that time removing to Meridian, Miss., where he has since lived and continued his professional career. In 1881 he was a candidate for secretary of state before the democratic convention, and, though he had several opponents, he was defeated by only thirty votes by Henry C. Meyers, the incumbent of the office, and then only on the eleventh ballot. He has twice been a candidate for mayor of Meridian, his opponent, Thomas H. Griffin, defeating him the first time by a small majority and again in 1890 by only forty-six votes out of one thousand four hundred cast. He was the first editor-in-chief of the Meridian *News*, which was established in 1886. He has natural talents for newspaper work, and is regarded as one of the ablest journalists in the state, and in other departments of literature he has evidenced an ability of no mean order. Among his other productions is a play called "Queen of the East," which has been produced successfully several times in Meridian, Miss., and which he wrote in aid of the Confederate monument fund. He is now president of the Meridian Confederate Monument association and honorary member of Walthall camp No. 1 of Confederate veterans. He owns considerable real estate in Meridian, and has done much to advance the material interest of the town. His professional career has been a success, and he is regarded as one of the leading attorneys of that part of the state. Possessing fine natural powers of oratory, which he has cultivated very highly, he is regarded as one of the most pleasing, forcible and effective speakers in the state. He has been frequently called upon on important occasions and has been of great service to the democratic party in his city and county during their campaigns. In 1881 he was elected a member of the democratic state executive committee, in which capacity he served four years. He was married December 9, 1879, to Miss Annie Thompson, of Oxford, Miss., and they have three children living: Emily, William T. and an infant. He is a member of the Presbyterian church, in which he holds the office of deacon.

James N. Dickerson, planter, Sardis, Miss., is numbered among the first settlers of Panola county, and has resided on the same place for over half a century. He is a planter, the owner of six hundred acres, with one hundred and fifty acres under cultivation, and has also followed the milling business for forty-one years. His birth occurred in Shelby county, Tenn., on June 28, 1836, and he was the third of eight children born to David N. and Betsy (Bantly) Dickerson, natives of Tennessee. The father was a tanner, and followed that trade until too old to continue, when he embarked in the milling business, becoming the owner of a combined steamsaw, gin and gristmill, which he operated until his death in 1879. The paternal grandfather, Benjamin Dickerson, was a native Virginian, and was a soldier in the Revolutionary war. James N. Dickerson came to Mississippi with his father in 1838, and received his education in the private schools of that state. At the age of twenty-one years he began for himself with no capital, and by industry and good management he accumulated a handsome property and is now classed among the wealthy citizens of the county. He was married in 1869 to Miss Mary J. Baker, a native of North Carolina and the daughter of John Baker, also of the Old North state. They had three children, all of whom died at birth with the exception of one, Madora. In 1861 Mr. Dickerson enlisted in the Confederate army, company G, Nineteenth Mississippi regiment of infantry, and served until about three months before the war ended. He then received a furlough and went home, never afterward entering the service. He participated in the following battles: Second Bull Run (Md)., Manassas (Md.), Chantersville (Md.), Yorktown, Williamsburg, Seven Pines, seven days' fight, Malvern hill, Winchester, Fredericksburg, United States ford, Appomattox courthouse, Harper's Ferry, Sharpsburg, Gettysburg and others. He extends a helping hand to all public enterprises that tend to the development and growth of the country, and is very social, friendly and accommodating. He is a stanch democrat in politics.

William H. Dickerson, planter and merchant, Friar's Point, Miss., was born in Warren county, Miss., on the 6th of January, 1854, and was the youngest of three children born to Peter and Mary A. T. (Hope) Dickerson. The father was a native of Maryland, and was a very wealthy farmer and merchant. He was the son of Henry and Nancy (Barves) Dickerson. Mrs. Dickerson was originally from Tennessee, and her parents, William and Narcissa M. (Sampson) Hope, were natives of Tennessee and Pennsylvania respectively. William H. Dickerson passed his boyhood and youth in Mississippi, and received his education at St. Mary's college, Kentucky, also at Woodland college, Tennessee. In 1870, or when sixteen years of age, he started out for himself, and with the capital furnished him invested it in such a manner as to bring good returns, and he is now one of the wealthiest planters in Coahoma county. He is the owner of about eight thousand acres of land, and has four thousand acres under cultivation. He is also the owner of a good store, and carries a stock of goods valued at about $8,000. The same systematic condition of affairs about his farm is apparent in his course as a man; thorough in all that he does, he allows no worthy movement to drag for want of support, and contributes liberally to all public enterprises. Mr. Dickerson was married in 1889 to Miss Lula H. Howard, of Indiana, and the daughter of John M. and Jennie C. (Cotton) Howard, the father a native of Kentucky and the mother of Indiana. Mr. Dickerson is thoroughgoing and progressive in his views, and is considered by all as one of the best business men of the county. He is very courteous and agreeable in manner and a true Southern gentleman, being hospitable and gracious to all who enter the doors of his fine dwelling, which is built in the old castle style. He is one of the largest stockholders in the Friar's Point box and woodwork factory, also the Friar's Point oil mill and manufacturing company, and jointly with H. W. Session (who is secretary of the company) owns about one-half the stock in the land, loan and improvement company of Friar's Point. He also owns the Riverside hotel building and a block known as Dickerson's block in Friar's Point, amounting altogether to from $50,000 to $60,000, and pays $4,000 taxes. Mr. Dickerson is about the average in hight, and with his blue eyes and fair complexion has dark hair.

P. M. Diggs, planter and merchant, Acona, Miss., is one of the successful planters of the county, and in connection with that industry is also engaged in merchandising at Acona, where he has established a fair business. He is the owner of eight hundred acres of choice land, has about four hundred acres under cultivation, and like most of the planters of the county, his principal crops are cotton and corn. In 1855 Mr. Diggs was wedded to Miss Martin, and of the seven children born to this union only one is deceased: W. H., Elizabeth (died in infancy), M. R., C. M., J. M., K. H. and D. M. Mrs. Diggs was born in Mississippi, and her parents were natives of Georgia and Mississippi, respectively. During the Civil war Mr. Diggs enlisted in Stark's regiment. Subsequently he was appointed cotton agent, and entered the swamps to guard cotton that the government had bought. After the war he returned to his home, and has since been quite actively engaged in the above occupations. He was born in Henry county, Tenn., in 1832, and was the fourth in order of birth of six children born to Harris and Mary (McRae) Diggs, the father a native of North Carolina. The parents were married in 1824, came to Mississippi in 1836, and settled in Marshall county. Their children were named in the order of their births as follows: Caroline (deceased), Emeline, Harvey (deceased), P. M., Mary C. and Elizabeth (deceased). The father was a planter all his life, and he and his wife were worthy members of the Methodist church. They both died in Marshall county, Miss., he in 1842, at the age of forty-two years. Our subject's paternal grandfather was a native of the Old North state, and died in 1840.

The parents of Hon. George G. Dillard, attorney, Macon, Miss.—Thomas W. and Sarah B. (Dunpree) Dillard—were married in 1829 and in 1836 emigrated to Oktibbeha county, Miss., where the mother died during the Civil war. The father was a native of Tennessee, born in 1808, and now resides with his son, Senator George G. Dillard, who was the eldest son of eleven children, and was born in Oktibbeha county. He spent his early life on the farm and at intervals attended the common schools. In 1857 he entered the University of Mississippi and graduated from that institution in 1861. On the opening of hostilities he enlisted in the Fourteenth Mississippi regiment, Colonel Baldwin commanding, and was in the battle of Fort Donelson, escaping after its surrender. He next joined the Thirty-fifth Mississippi regiment, and later was made adjutant of the regiment. He was captured in the surrender of Vicksburg and paroled. Then with the Thirty-fifth Mississippi regiment, after having been exchanged, he joined General Johnston's army at Centerville, Ga., and took part in the campaign before Atlanta. He followed Hood to Tennessee and was at Franklin and Nashville. He was captured with his regiment at the latter place, and was carried a prisoner to Camp Douglas. When peace was declared he was paroled and came home. Later he located in Macon, Noxubee county, and engaged in mercantile pursuits. In 1871 he began practicing law, met with fair success, and in 1872 he was chosen mayor of Macon, which office he held for seven years. In 1883 he was elected to represent his district, the county of Noxubee, in the state senate, and in 1887 he was reëlected to that office, being the present incumbent.

He was one of three delegates chosen to represent his county in the constitutional convention of 1890 and took a prominent part in its deliberations. He is one of the three commissioners appointed by the governor to conform the statutes of the state to the new constitution, as provided by that instrument. He has been again elected state senator for four years from January, 1892. He succeeded R. C. Patty, deceased, as a member of the board of trustees for the industrial institute and college, a state institution located at Columbus for the education of white girls. Senator Dillard is unmarried. He is a member of the I. O. O. F., the A. F. & A. M., the Knights of Honor and Knights of Pythias, and is a consistent member of the Episcopal church. He is a fearless champion of the right, and because of his devotion to his state's best interests, his name is respected and honored throughout her borders. There are few men in the state who have a stronger hold on its people than Senator Dillard. Of him an admiring friend has said: "He is a politician with no greed for office, but when in office he has a pride and an ambition to serve not circumscribed by local lines or party bearings, but comprehensive as the interest of the people whom he serves. He has proven himself a bold champion of honesty, and has won from Mississippians the distinguished title of the 'watchdog of the treasury.' "

Among the prominent business men of Winona who are natives of this state and county is Alfred C. Dimond, merchant, Winona, Miss., who was born March 15, 1853. He is a son of E. P. Dimond, and grandson of Stewart Dimond, who was a native of the Old North state, but who moved to Williamson county, Tenn., at an early day. The father, E. P. Dimond, was also born in North Carolina in 1817, and moved with his parents to Tennessee, where he received a fair education. In his early manhood he taught school, and in about 1842 settled in what now constitutes Montgomery county, where he engaged in planting. He was married there to Miss S. A. Townsend, also a native of North Carolina, but reared in Mississippi, and the daughter of Daniel Townsend, one of the pioneer settlers. Mr. Dimond was a planter in this county for a number of years, but he is now retired and resides in Winona. His son, Alfred C. Dimond, divided his time in early youth in attending the schools of Winona and in assisting his father on the plantation. He remained under the parental roof until twenty-one years of age, and then engaged in the sawmill business, manufacturing lumber for about two years. He then clerked for about six months, after which he bought a half interest in the store with Mr. E. G. Whitehead, and was engaged in general merchandising with him until his death in 1887. After that Mr. Dimond continued the business by himself for one year, and in 1888 the firm of Dimond & Hawkins was formed. They carry a large stock of general merchandise, and do a large furnishing business. They have a patronage established that indicates appreciation of their reliable goods and fair dealing methods, and their goods are second to none in the town. On the organization of the Citizens' bank Mr. Dimond was one of the first to take hold of this enterprise, and he is at present a stockholder and one of the directors of that institution. Mr. Dimond selected as his companion in life Miss E. G. Whitehead, and their nuptials were celebrated in October, 1883. She was a sister of E. G. Whitehead, his former business partner, and was born in Carroll county, but was reared and educated in Winona. Their union has been blessed by the birth of three children: Jennett W., Eddie W. and Mary Ray. Mr. and Mrs. Dimond are members of the Baptist church.

Andrew McD. Dinsmore, of Noxubee county, Miss., is a son of James Dinsmore, who was born in Ireland, of Scotch parentage about 1764, and emigrated to America about 1794 and settled in Buncombe county, N. C. From there he removed to east Tennessee in the latter part of the century. He was a Revolutionary patriot and was in the battle of Bunker Hill. He received a pension for his services in that war, which was continued to his widow after his death in 1837, she having survived him for more than a score of years. Andrew McDonald Dinsmore was born in Rhea county, Tenn., in 1808, and removed to Madison county with his parents when an infant. There he lived until fourteen years of age, then removed to Morgan county, Ala., where he remained until 1840, when he came to Noxubee county, Miss., where he now resides one mile east of Macon. He was married to Minerva B. Beauchamp, in 1837, and had seven children—five daughters and two sons. The sons only are living. One of these, John R. Dinsmore, is an eminent attorney at the Macon bar; the other, James A., is an extensive farmer, living seven miles north of Macon. Mr. Dinsmore has been a farmer and planter for sixty years. As a planter he has been uniformly successful, never owing any man a cent he could not pay. Mr. Dinsmore has been a Presbyterian for more than fifty-five years, and has occupied the important position of elder of his church for more than forty years. He owns three hundred and eighty-five acres of good, average land, and grows cotton and corn principally. He ranks with the leading men of his county, and his course through life has been such that he is held in the highest esteem by his fellow-citizens of all classes.

Of the many prominent names which make up the strength of the Mississippi bar, that of John R. Dinsmore takes a foremost place, and his experience in Noxubee county as a legal practitioner dates back to 1876, in which year he opened an office in Macon. Mr. Dinsmore was born one mile east of Macon in 1855, a son of Andrew M. and M. B. (Beauchamp) Dinsmore, the latter being a sister of Judge John J. Beauchamp, a very prominent lawyer of Macon and an upright and useful citizen. John R. Dinsmore was educated in Cumberland university of Lebanon, Tenn., and in 1876 graduated from the law department. During the year of 1875 he was orator of his class, and debated for a medal which was awarded him May 24, 1876. He was reared on a plantation, and after making some money at this calling he spent it in perfecting himself for his profession, and upon locating in Macon, unlike the majority of young barristers who wait in vain for a client, he soon stepped into popular favor and rapidly gained a lucrative practice, which he has since held and greatly increased. From 1878 to 1879 he held the office of deputy sheriff, and in the fall of the latter year was elected to the position of justice of the peace, and in 1880 to the position of mayor of Macon, in which capacity he served with credit six or seven terms. He is a deacon in the Presbyterian church, and socially is a member of the I. O. O. F., in which order he has passed all the chairs and been a representative to the grand lodge. For a period of five months after graduating in law Mr. Dinsmore taught in a free school, which had greatly deteriorated in merit, and did much to build up the school and make it a credit to himself and the section in which he resided. Much credit is due him for the interest he has taken in educational pursuits and for the assistance and encouragement he has given all worthy enterprises. In July, 1891, Mr. Dinsmore received the nomination by the democratic party of Noxubee county as a member of the legislature, and his friends feel satisfied he will make a good representative. Although there were seven others before the people for this place, and Noxubee county is only entitled to three representatives, yet Mr. Dinsmore (the youngest man among the candidates) received the nomination in the first primary, leading his ticket, not only for that office, but for all offices. His vote will be appreciated when it is known that one of his competitors was the speaker of the house of representatives of the state and three others had served in the legislature and were very popular men. Indeed, all his competitors were strong, good men, and his nomination is regarded as a decided compliment by every one in his county. In this county the nomination from the democratic party is equal to an election, hence there is no doubt about his election. In December, 1884, Mr. Dinsmore married Miss Quintilla Dent (daughter of William Dent, deceased), by whom he has two daughters: Mary W. and Alma E. Dinsmore.

Robert Doak, manufacturer of superior tinware, and wholesale and retail dealer in general hardware, crockery, paints, oil, sash, doors, blinds, wagons, roofing, etc., was formerly a member of the firm of Doak & Laurence, and is one of the leading merchants of northern Mississippi. He is a native of Grenada county (then Yalobusha county), Miss., born in 1838, and is a son of Boyd Doak, of Tennessee, who came to Mississippi when a young man. The elder Doak settled near Canton, now in Madison county, and there entered large tracts of land. His place of residence is still known as Doak's stand, in the eastern part of Madison county, where, on the 20th of October, 1820, the chief head men and warriors of the Choctaw nation were assembled and signed a treaty, relinquishing five and a half million acres of land. The Federal government was represented by Major-General Jackson, of Tennessee, and Maj.-Gen. Thomas Hinds, of Mississippi. Mr. Doak took part in moving the Indians to the West, and in about 1830 he settled on Yalobusha river, where he engaged in planting. He was married in Mississippi to Miss   , a native of that state. He was an active and worthy member of the Presbyterian church, and a liberal contributor to the same. During the Mexican war he served under Sims, and, being a good judge of stock, was retained as government contractor to supply the Mexican army with mules, wagons and supplies, etc., until after the war. He died with yellow fever in 1878, at the age of seventy years. His wife died in 1844 or 1845, leaving four children. Of these Robert Doak was third in order of birth. When but a boy he went to Holly Springs, and after remaining there for some time moved to Aberdeen, Miss., where, when sixteen years of age, he began learning the tinner's trade. In 1861 he entered the Confederate army, Eleventh Mississippi regiment, commanded by Moore, and was taken prisoner at the battle of Gettysburg, Penn., in July, 1863. He was taken to Fort Delaware, and was there confined until after General Lee's surrender in 1865, when he was paroled and came to Grenada, Miss., in July of the same year. He began working at his trade in that city, and in May, 1866, opened up a tinshop, gradually increasing his business until he is now the sixth largest hardware merchant in the state. In 1884 he erected a large double two-story brick building, and his annual sales yield him about $50,000. Aside from this he has a general stock of hardware at Eupora, Miss., on the Georgia & Pacific railroad, where he has erected two two-story buildings. In 1880 Mr. Doak formed a partnership with Samuel Laurance, with whom he continued until the latter's death in 1887. Mr. Doak is the president of the Grenada ice factory, established in 1890 at a cost of $22,000, and with a creamery attached. He is also one of the directors of the Merchants' bank, has been alderman of Grenada for a number of years, is connected with the school board, etc., and is one of the directors of the Central Fair and Live Stock association. Mr. Doak was married to Miss Pauline Gerard, of French descent and a native of Natchez, where she was reared. To this union were born five interesting children: Robbie, Gerard, Juliette, Estelle and John. Mr. and Mrs. Doak and one daughter are members of the Episcopal church. Mr. Doak is a self-made man, having commenced with nothing after the war; he is one of the ablest men of the county. He is principal owner of the creamery and ice factory. In politics he adheres to the democratic party.

Sol Dobson, sheriff, is one of the most efficient and popular officials of Rankin county, Miss., for in the discharge of his numerous duties he has shown himself to be shrewd, practical and possessed of undoubted courage. He was born in Covington, La., in 1840, a son of Joseph J. and Nancy J. (Mangum) Dobson, natives of Georgia and Louisiana, respect-

41

ively. While in his early manhood the father removed to Louisiana, where he became a well-to-do planter and merchant and was married. In 1842, having fallen sole heir to his father's estate in Georgia, he returned thither overland by private conveyance and made a settlement. While returning to Louisiana in the same manner he was murdered by highwaymen and robbed of all the money he had about him. Sol Dobson is one of the two children born to his union, and in 1841 was taken by his mother to Rankin county, Miss., where she afterward married a second time. In the schools of this county he received his early education, and upon reaching a suitable age started out to make his own way in the world as a planter, a calling he followed with good results until the opening of the Rebellion, when he enlisted in the Eighteenth Mississippi regiment, army of Virginia, and served throughout the entire war, participating in many of the fiercest battles of the war. He was wounded in the right shoulder at the battle of Ball's bluff in October, 1861, and was rendered unfit for service until the following spring. He was wounded on three other occasions, but not severely. He was captured near Beaver Dam station, Va., and was kept a prisoner at Washington, D. C., for about sixty days. At the battle of the Wilderness he was promoted to a position on Longstreet's staff, with the rank of first lieutenant, and filled this position until the war closed. Shortly after returning home Mr. Dobson pursued a two years' private medical course, but deeming the mercantile pursuit more conducive to the making of money, he engaged in that business, which he continued with success until 1877. He lived a retired life for the following six years, at the end of which time, at the earnest solicitation of his numerous friends, who fully appreciated the services he had rendered his party, he consented to become a candidate for the position of county sheriff, and was ultimately elected to this office. He has been thrice reëlected, for the efficient manner in which he has discharged the duties of this position has ingratiated him in the good will of the entire public; he is an exceptionally popular official. He has made an ideal public officer, for besides being most trustworthy, efficient and conscientious, he is energetic, punctual and strictly honorable. He is a Royal Arch Mason of high standing, and is a member of the Baptist church. He was married in 1858 to Miss N. F. Laird, of Biloxi, Miss.

William A. Dockery is considered by all, and justly so, to be one of the most reliable business men in Bolivar county, Miss. He was born in De Soto county of this state, November 10, 1865, being the second of six children born to Maj. T. C. and Mary F. (Atkins) Dockery, whose birthplace was the Old North state. The former was quite prominent in the political circles of his county, and at two different times was its representative in the general assembly of the state. He also held the office of sheriff for ten years, and upon the opening of the Rebellion organized a company for the Confederate service and was at once made its captain. It became a part of the Twenty-second Mississippi regiment, in which Mr. Dockery was afterward promoted to the rank of colonel. He served with distinction until the battle of Corinth, when he was wounded and disabled from further service. He was an extensive and successful planter until the opening of the war, but since that time the most of his attention has been given to the raising of stock, a business for which he has a taste and for which he seems peculiarly adapted. He is a well-known politician of this section, and being a man of intelligence and honest in his convictions, he wields considerable influence among his acquaintances. His father was Gen. Alfred Dockery, of North Carolina, the maternal grandfather being Dr. William S. Atkins, a very prominent man in his profession, and well-known throughout the state of North Carolina. William A. Dockery inherits Scotch blood of his paternal ancestors, and to him have descended many of the sterling qualities for which the Scottish people are noted. He was reared in De Soto county, Miss., and received an excellent education in Oxford college, where he obtained a most thorough and practical education. At the age of twenty-one years he became a bookkeeper in an establishment belonging to his uncle, James Dockery, but in 1888 gave up this position to come to Bolivar county, where he has been successfully engaged in the occupation of planting and has accumulated the following property: A one-half interest in two thousand acres of land, of which two hundred acres are under cultivation, which land has been put in its present admirable state of cultivation by him and his partner, J. M. Dockery. Altogether, they cultivate about one thousand six hundred acres of land, of which about one thousand four hundred acres are rented, besides which William A. Dockery owns a one-half interest in the mercantile establishment of William Dockery & Co., their stock of goods being valued at $8,000. Mr. Dockery also owns $3,000 worth of real estate in Cleveland, and, for so young a man, is exceedingly well fixed financially. That he deserves his good fortune is acknowledged by all, for he is not only charitable and free in the use of his means but he is also industrious, plucky and pushing, and has accumulated his property by his own earnest and persistent endeavors since he attained his majority, as prior to that his time was given to his father. He comes of one of the finest families of the state, is of very steady habits and is devoted to business, being considered safe and reliable by all who know him.

Hon. Samuel L. Dodd is a leading resident of Kosciusko, in Attala county, Miss., and near here his birth occurred July 19, 1848. His father, Allen Dodd, was born in Mercer county, Ky., January 14, 1808, while his grandfather, George Dodd, was born in Fauquier county, Va., in 1778. During the early history of the Blue Grass state George Dodd removed thither, and settled in Mercer county, Ky., and in that state he reared a large family of children. There Allen Dodd was reared and educated, and married Miss M. C. McKee, a daughter of James McKee, of Lancaster, Ky. He became a very extensive stockdealer and trader, and annually shipped large numbers of horses and cattle South. About 1833 he came to Mississippi and located on a plantation near Kosciusko, Miss., where he reared his family and resided until his death, October 22, 1890. His widow still survives him. Hon. Samuel L. Dodd is one of a family of eight sons and five daughters that grew to mature years, six of the members of this family being now deceased. James M. graduated at Westminster college, Mo., and upon the opening of the Civil war he returned home and joined the Twentieth Mississippi, Confederate states army. He served the Confederate cause faithfully until the battle of Donelson, when he was severely wounded, and while being conveyed to his home died on the way. W. O. Dodd was also an attorney, having graduated from the University of Mississippi in 1869, and until his death, of consumption, which he contracted in the army, he was a successful lawyer of Louisville, Ky. He died December 13, 1886. Hon. Samuel L. Dodd is next in order of birth, then comes John L. and Joseph C., both of whom were educated in law and literary institutions, and practiced their professions at Louisville. Robert is a merchant in Wilmore, Ky. George A. and Edgar are planters in Attala county. One sister is living, Mrs. Mattie Saffold, of Durant, Miss. Hon. Samuel L. Dodd is a graduate of Westminster college, Mo., in the class of 1869, after which he took a law course at Lebanon, Tenn., graduating in June, 1873. He immediately began practicing at Kosciusko, and he has strictly devoted his attention to his profession, and as he has shown a thorough knowledge of the law, and never allows the interests of his clients to suffer, he has built up a very extensive practice. He has served as chairman of the democratic executive committee for a number of years, and was a delegate to the national convention that nominated General Hancock for the presidency. He has also served as a delegate to numerous state conventions, but is not an aspirant for office, much preferring to devote his time and talents to his profession. He was married in October, 1875, to Mrs. Eva Webb, a daughter of R. B. Webb, who was for years circuit court clerk and county treasurer. Mrs. Dodd was born and reared in Attala county, and received her education in the University of Mississippi. She has borne her husband five children: Lottie, Walter, Mary, Harvey and Ruth. Mr. Dodd is a prominent member of and elder in the Presbyterian church, in which church his father was an elder for fifty years. He is a member of the K. of P., and is a very social and pleasant gentleman to meet. He is a man of exemplary habits, strong moral character, and in his tastes is very domestic. He is a fine looking gentleman, is tall and slender, and of light complexion. He is vice president of the Merchants' & Farmers' bank in Kosciusko, Miss., and manifests much interest in every enterprise that aims to build up the resources and the material interests of his people.

William E. Dodds was born in Copiah county, Miss., in 1848. His parents were Samuel D. and Dicy (Miller) Dodds, the former a native of Tennessee and the latter a native of Mississippi. (See sketch of George Dodds.) He was born and reared near Hazlehurst, and received his education in the common schools of the county. The beginning of the war curtailed his educational advantages to a considerable extent, and on account of the failing health of his father, at the age of about eighteen years he was called to assume charge of the home plantation. In 1874 he married Miss Temperance Corley, a native of Copiah county, who was born in 1850. After his marriage he remained on his mother's place, having charge of the conduct of her business affairs until 1885, when he purchased Lucky Hit plantation, which was settled by Capt. H. G. D. Brown, a brother of Governor Brown, " of whom no one spoke evil." The plantation consists of seventeen hundred acres, of which about six hundred acres are under cultivation. The residence is beautifully located near the eastern side of the plantation, and a handsome park surrounds the house, which is approached by an avenue of majestic oaks. It is the most beautiful situation in the county, and the home is one of the most hospitable. Up to the time of the purchase of the Lucky Hit plantation Mr. Dodds had given almost his entire attention to raising corn and cotton. Since then he has gone quite largely into stockraising, breeding principally horses and mules. He bought the plantation with the intention of making it a stock farm, and is working to that end as rapidly as possible. When he came to this plantation it was considerably run down and presented a somewhat dilapidated appearance, but he has now everything about it in good repair, and secures a good yield from the land he cultivates. He is a thoroughgoing, practical man, energetic and enterprising, and a hard worker himself. He is training his sons in the same manner, meaning to make them first practical farmers, and then when they are of suitable age to send them to some good institution of learning. At the age of twenty-one he was elected road overseer, and has been reëlected at every election since, for he takes the greatest interest in the construction of good roads, and keeping them in first-class repair. Although no politician nor an office-seeker he is a stanch democrat, and takes a deep interest in all political affairs, giving his influence and most practical aid to the party of his choice. He is a member of the Legion of Honor of Hazlehurst, and also of the Knights of Honor. He and wife are members of the Damascus Baptist church, one of the oldest religious organizations in the county. To Mr. and Mrs. Dodds five children have been born: Samuel De Kalb, James Conley, William Hooker, Myra Eddicce and George Sturgis. Mr. Dodds is a man of medium hight and is strongly built, with hair and mustache slightly tinged with grey. As a citizen he is highly respected; as a neighbor he enjoys the esteem of the whole community, and he has the friendship of most of the prominent men in the county, while he is ranked as a power in local politics.

Hon. George S. Dodds, of the firm of Dodds & Mayes, prominent attorneys at law of Hazlehurst, and who is also a representative of the thirty-eighth senatorial district in the senate of the state of Mississippi, was born in Copiah county in 1855, a son of Samuel D. and Dicy (Miller) Dodds. His father, a native of North Carolina, was born in 1812, and his mother in Copiah county in 1823. Mr. Dodds was reared on a farm in North Carolina, and received a good common-school education there. When young, he removed with his parents to Tennessee, and from Tennessee he and six brothers came to Mississippi, three of them stopping in the northern part of the state, and four locating in Copiah county. All of them are now dead. There were three daughters, two of whom are now living. Mr. Dodds was married about 1844, and passed the balance of his life here, becoming a successful planter, and dying in 1872. He was a member of the Masonic order, and for a long time before his death had been a member of the Baptist church. He was active in all public matters, but not an aspirant for any official position. He was industrious, honest, had good business abilities and was a useful and prosperous citizen. During the late war he served the Confederacy a short time as a member of the state militia. His brother, Dr. W. P. Dodds, a prominent physician, was a member of both branches of the legislature from Franklin county, and is now a representative from the same. His father, John D., was born in North Carolina, and removed thence to Tennessee, where he and his wife both died. He was a planter, and served in the war of 1812, under General Jackson, taking part in the battle of New Orleans. He was born of Irish parents, and his wife was of Welsh nativity. Mr. Dodd's maternal grandfather, Aaron Miller, was a Tennesseean by birth, but one of the first settlers in Mississippi between Jackson and Natchez. He is well remembered as a landlord, as he ran a public house three miles south of the present Hazlehurst, having died in 1868, after a long residence there. Mrs. Dodds, though known by the name of Miller, was only an adopted daughter of this old pioneer, who never had any children of his own. George S. Dodds is the sixth of eight sons and four daughters, nine of whom are living: Dr. A. M. Dodds, the eldest, is a prominent physician of Franklin county, and was in the cavalry service of the late war; William E., a prominent planter of Copiah county; James O., a planter and miller of this county; George S.; John M., a planter and liveryman of Hazlehurst; Mary, wife of P. Moody, of Crystal Springs; Clara, wife of W. C. Haley; Anna, and lastly, Emma, wife of Henry Price, of Crystal Springs. Our subject received his primary education at Hazlehurst, and in 1876 graduated from the Mississippi college at Clinton. He taught school for a time, and then read law with Judge M. E. Cooper, now one of the judges of the supreme court of the state of Mississippi. He was admitted to the bar in 1878, and formed a partnership with Judge H. C. Conn, and afterward with the late J. B. Harris, the present firm of Dodds & Mayes being a later organization. In 1878 he was elected mayor of Hazlehurst, and during the session of 1880 and 1881 was reading clerk of the state legislature. In 1882 he was elected a member of that body, and served as chairman of the committee on appropriation; in 1884 he was honored by the position of presidential messenger from Mississippi; in 1885 was elected to the state senate for four years, and served as chairman on the committee on corporations; was reëlected in 1889, and was made chairman of a very important committee on the judiciary. In 1889 Mr. Dodds lacked but one vote of defeating the distinguished Colonel Hooker for congress. His political career has been one of success and honor, and such is the confidence reposed in him by the public that he bids fair to attain to still higher preferments in the future. He is a prominent member of the Knights of Honor, being identified with the Copiah lodge No. 1422. He has been dictator, and is now grand assistant dictator of the Knights of Honor for this state. He is also a member of the Copiah lodge

No. 60, of the Knights of Pythias.   January 1, 1880, he married Miss Shelley, a daughter of Dr. W. S. and Maggie J. Webb.   Her father, who is president of Mississippi college, and a member of a very prominent family, was born in New York, and educated in some of the celebrated educational institutions in this country.   He came to Mississippi prior to the war, and previous to his coming here had been twice married.   Mrs. Dodds was born at West Point, Miss., and has but one child—a daughter.   They are members of the Baptist church, and are liberal supporters of all its interests.   In Senator Dodds we have an example of a self-made man of this country, beginning life at the age of sixteen, with nothing in the world but his brains, who has become self-educated as well as self-made, and has been in every way remarkably successful.   He stands high as a citizen, as a business man and as a representative of the interests of his fellowmen, and is an example in every way worthy for them to emulate.

John M. Dodds, a liveryman and planter, was born in 1857, in Copiah county, where he now lives, a son of Samuel D. and Dicy (Miller) Dodds, some account of whom appears above in this work, in the sketch of his eldest brother, George S. Dodds.   Mr. Dodds was educated at Clinton and at the Mississippi university at Oxford.   At the age of twenty-two he began life for himself as a planter, in which business he has been interested continuously until the present time, though in January, 1891, he moved his family to Hazlehurst, where he is engaged in the liveryman business.   In 1888 he married Myrtle Steigler, a daughter of Frank and Marian Steigler, of Holmes county, very old settlers in that part of the state.   They have had one child, Marian L.   Mr. Dodds is a member in good standing of lodge No. 60, Knights of Pythias, of Hazlehurst, and he and his wife are devout and helpful members of the Baptist church.   Our subject is one of the most prominent and promising young men of the town; he is of middle hight, dark hair and beard; his manner is pleasant and friendly, and he is rapidly gaining a wide acquaintance, not only with the leading men of this section, but with many throughout the state.   He is energetic and ambitious in a business way, and it can not be doubted that the future holds for him much success which will place him among the leading men in this part of the state.

G. L. Donald is the present sheriff of Clarke county, Miss.   He was born in Sumter county, Ala., in 1840, a son of Simon and Ann (Dotson) Donald.   His father was born and married in South Carolina and settled in Sumter county, where he died in 1841.   He reared a family of six children: Franklin, Matilda, Isabella, Margaret, Sidney and G. L.   Our subject is the son of John Donald, of South Carolina, who was of Scottish parentage.   His ancestor, Alexander Donald, emigrated to North America from Scotland about the year 1700, and settled with his wife in the colony of Virginia.   The entire family moved to the state of South Carolina afterward.   The mother of G. L. Donald was born in Georgia and died in this county in 1862.   The father was a member of the Methodist Episcopal church, the mother of the Baptist church.   The former was a planter, a successful business man, and a large slaveholder.   He was a democrat in politics.   Mr. Donald spent the earlier years of his life in Clarke county, attending school at Quitman.   In 1856 he entered Oxford college, from which he graduated in 1859.   In 1861 he enlisted in company G of the Thirteenth Mississippi regiment.   At the outset he was first lieutenant, but in 1862 he was made captain of the company.   In the early part of 1863 he was elected major of the regiment, which he commanded till the close of the war, near the end of which he was in command of Barksdale's brigade.   He did much gallant and oftentimes hazardous service, but was never wounded or taken prisoner of war.   He participated in the fights at Manassas junction, Leesburg, Chancellorsville, Appomattox, Cold Harbor, the seven days' fight at Richmond,

Fredericksburg, Harper's Ferry, Antietam, Cedar Run, Gettysburg, Knoxville and Chickamauguа. After the war he returned to Clarke county and engaged in planting. In 1867 he married Mary E. Hicks, a daughter of Thomas F. and Eliza (Everett) Hicks of that county, who has borne him nine children: George L., who is living in Meridian, Miss.; Benjamin H., now the deputy sheriff of the county; Sidney and Franklin, twins; Anna, Maggie, Walter, Mary and Laura. Mrs. Donald was a native of Clarke county, though her family came from North Carolina and settled at an early day in Mississippi, where her father became a planter. In 1870 Mr. Donald was elected to represent his county in the legislature, and served during the sessions of 1870 and 1871. In 1886 he was elected county sheriff, and has held this office, greatly to the satisfaction of the people at large, up to the present time. He was a member of the constitutional convention of 1890. For fifteen years prior to 1886 he served as land agent for the Mobile & Ohio railroad company. He was superintendent of the state penitentiary in 1876 and 1877. He has always been active in the interests of the democratic party, and as a public man, as well as in business relations, has met all obligations fairly and squarely. He is interested in schools, churches and other worthy institutions to such an extent as to make him a useful, helpful citizen. He is a member of the Knights of Honor of Shebutah, and he and his family are members of the Baptist church. He owns a fine residence and farm about two miles west of Shebutah, and is the proprietor of about one thousand acres of land altogether, which lies within the borders of this county.

R. W. Donnell is one of the thrifty and successful planters of Tunica county, Miss., and is now cultivating some six hundred acres of land, the most of which is devoted to cotton, but of his home plantation, which he purchased in 1871, he has only two hundred and fifty acres under cultivation. All the improvements on this place have been made by himself, and besides the excellent cottongin which he erected, his buildings are all comely, substantial and commodious. He has a fine, thrifty and promising orchard of five hundred pear trees, the largest in the delta, and his place is neat, orderly and handsome, showing that a man of thrift, good taste and judgment has the management of affairs. He is shrewd, active and enterprising, and his practical views on agriculture are in a great measure owing to the fact that he was reared to a farm life by his father and in his youth learned lessons of industry, perseverance and prudence which were the stepping-stones to his present success. When the Rebellion broke out he was attending school, and although he had been an earnest disciple of Minerva he became as earnest a follower of Mars and his books were cast aside for a sword and gun. He enlisted in company D, Twentieth Tennessee regiment of infantry of the Confederate states army, and afterward took part in the battle of Fort Donelson and many minor engagements. After hostilities had ceased he went to Illinois, in which state he was in business for two years, at the end of which time he went to New Allensville, Ky., at which place he was also in business. Since 1871 he has been a resident of Tunica county, Miss., and it can with truth be said that he is one of its leading and progressive citizens. He was married in 1868 to Miss M. P. Donnell, a native of Florida, and by her he is the father of the following children: Mary D., Jennie P., Claude H. and John H., all of whom are intelligent, well educated and refined. The family are worthy members of the Presbyterian church, and are liberal in their contributions to the same. Mr. Donnell was born in Tennessee in 1846, being the fourth child born to R. W. and L. A. (Green) Donnell, who were born in North Carolina and Tennessee, respectively. Mr. Donnell is an excellent and substantial citizen, is prepossessing in personal appearance, being above medium hight, and is a hospitable and generous gentleman.

G. L. Doolittle, Newton, Miss., was born in Newton county, Miss., in 1851, and is a son of R. W. and Amelia (Blalack) Doolittle. The father was born in Edgefield district, S. C., in 1809, and the mother, in the same state in 1807. They were married in their native state, and thirteen children were born to them. The parents removed from South Carolina to Alabama in early days, and thence in 1842, to Mississippi. They located in Newton county, where the father engaged in farming. The mother died in 1857, and in 1861 Mr. Doolittle was married a second time, to Mrs. Virginia Duff, and of this marriage four children were born. Mr. Doolittle saw no service during the war, but was a member of the state militia for thirty days. In his agricultural pursuits he was quite successful. He was a member of the Baptist church. and a generous supporter of the society. He died in 1889, at the advanced age of eighty years. G. L. Doolittle is the ninth child of the first marriage of his father. In 1870 he started out in life for himself, choosing agriculture for his occupation. In the same year he was married to Miss Mary O. Atkinson, a daughter of Lewis Atkinson, of Georgia; she was born in 1851, and at the age of nine years was brought to Newton county, Miss. Mr. and Mrs. Doolittle have no children, except by adoption; they have taken into their care and protection two children, whom they will rear and educate. Mr. Doolittle is a member of the Knights of Pythias, the Knights of Honor, the Farmers' Alliance, and the Farmers' grange. He is the owner of five hundred and sixty acres of good land, and has placed two hundred and fifty acres under cultivation. He raises annually fifty bales of cotton, and carries on general farming. He has just erected a comfortable residence, and all his surroundings bespeak the thrift and prosperity of the proprietor. In all affairs pertaining to the public welfare our subject lends a helping hand, and readily takes rank among the most enterprising citizens of Newton county. The family belong to the Cumberland Presbyterian church, taking a deep interest in all the movements of the society.

Among the representative, thoroughgoing and efficient officials of Noxubee county, Miss., there is probably no one more deserving of mention than Z. T. Dorroh, county sheriff, for his residence within its borders has extended over his entire life, his birth having occurred here on the 28th of May, 1847. His parents, William and Jane (Beard) Dorroh, were born in South Carolina and Georgia respectively, but in 1832 the former came to Mississippi and located in Noxubee county, being present at the treaty with the Indians. He purchased land from the government and followed planting until his death, which occurred in February, 1870, his wife's death having occurred in 1859. To their union eight children were born, three of whom are living: Sarah (Atkinson), James and Z. T. After the death of his wife Mr. Dorroh married again, his second union resulting in the birth of four children: Chastain, Ella, Orlando and Eliza. Z. T. Dorroh was reared in Noxubee county, received a high-school education and was brought up on a plantation, learning, thus, the details of a calling which he followed until the latter part of 1863, when he enlisted in Captain Doss' company, and for nine months was a member of the Confederate army, at which time he was a mere youth. After the war was over he resumed farming, and until he was made bookkeeper in the sheriff's office in January, 1886, this occupation received his attention. He held this position until he was elected to the sheriff's office in 1889, and so ably did he discharge his responsible duties and so satisfactory were his endeavors to the people, that he is a candidate for reëlection without opposition. He is the owner of an excellent plantation of four hundred and twenty acres, which he has successfully conducted in addition to his other duties. In 1873 he was united in marriage to Miss Laura McDonald, by whom he has five children: Nellie G., Ivy L., Lillie E., Lallie and Ethel H. Mr. Dorroh is a member of the A. F. & A. M., the I. O. O. F. and the Knights of Pythias, and he and his wife are members in good standing of the Baptist church.

William Francis Dowd was a native of South Carolina, born in the district of Darlington, December 31, 1820. His ancestors, who were of Irish origin, were valiant soldiers in the Revolutionary war, and his father was a captain in the War of 1812, and afterward a distinguished clergyman of the Baptist persuasion. In 1832 William F. Dowd was taken by his parents to Tennessee, where a farm was secured near the town of Jackson, and here he was reared to manhood. In 1841 the family removed to Monroe county, Miss., locating at the village of Smithville, and while here William F. laid the foundation of his legal career. He was admitted to the bar in 1846, and the following April appeared in court for the first time. Soon after his admission he became a member of the firm of Coopwood, Herbert & Dowd, of Aberdeen, one of the strongest legal firms of that time in the state. From the very start Mr. Dowd was recognized as a lawyer of more than usual promise. He was a brilliant speaker, adroit in debate, and soon took an active part in politics, and about this time became the editor of a newspaper at Aberdeen, published in the interests of the Whig party. In 1854 he was united in marriage to Miss Ann W. Brown, daughter of Col. James Brown, of Lafayette county. At this time the practice of Mr. Dowd was enormous. It is said that his income from his profession, during the year of his marriage, amounted to the sum of $20,000, which in that day was equivalent to five times as much as at present. In common with Jefferson Davis, Mr. Dowd maintained the right of secession of the sovereign states. This he had done openly for a number of years prior to the war, and when the struggle was at last precipitated upon the country he promptly offered his services to the Confederate cause. He was commissioned to raise a regiment, and accordingly mustered the Twenty-fourth Mississippi infantry, and was elected its colonel. He participated in the battles of Corinth, Perryville, Lookout mountain, Missionary ridge and elsewhere, in all cases showing exceptional bravery and ability as a military leader. During the latter part of the war his health became so enfeebled that he was compelled to retire from the service in the field and was appointed one of the judges of the military court for Northern Alabama, and thus continued to the close of the war. Upon the conclusion of peace he formed a partnership with Messrs. Sale & Phelan, and a little later with Sale alone, which was maintained until 1876, when it was dissolved. After that Colonel Dowd continued the practice alone. He was a hard student, not only of law, but of everything else which he undertook to master, and, as a result, greatly injured his health, and during his later years was thus compelled to forego active work in his profession. Few lawyers in the state showed greater capacity for the profession of law than Colonel Dowd. He possessed great penetration, and took special delight in what has been called hair-splitting, and in this particular probably he had no superior in Mississippi. He possessed, to begin with, a splendid constitution, but the energy with which he applied himself ended in the permanent impairment of his health. His death occurred at Aberdeen, November 28, 1878.

James M. Doyle, a planter, was born at Old Preston, Yalobusha county, Miss., August 18, 1843, a son of William T. and Elizabeth Anne (Holt) Doyle, natives of Virginia, both having been born about 1807, in Prince Edward county. About 1834 he came to Yalobusha county, making the journey with teams, and settled in the woods on Middle Tillabeta creek, near the present site of Garner station. From there they removed to near Coffeeville and thence to Preston. From Preston they removed to a point three miles east of Garner station, and there Mrs. Doyle died in 1856 and Mr. Doyle in 1869. Mr. Doyle was a self-made man who accumulated a good property, mostly in slaves, which he lost at the time of the war. His education was somewhat limited, but his business capacity was good, and he was energetic and public-spirited. He was the only child of his parents and was left an orphan at a very early age, and was reared by his aunt. His father, a Scotchman by birth, was a soldier in the Revolutionary war and died in Virginia. Both Mr. and Mrs. Doyle were members of the Missionary Baptist church for many years. Mr. Doyle's grandfather and grandmother both died in Prince Edward county, Va., where the former was a planter. He was also, as was his father-in-law, Mr. Flippam, a soldier in the Revolutionary war. Our subject was the fourth of eight children, and the only one now living of the number; John and Robert died in 1861, the former at home, the latter at Corinth, both belonging to the Fifteenth Mississippi infantry; Elizabeth became the wife of E. C. Cartledge, of Montgomery county, and died in 1887; Mary died when quite young; Ann Jane became the wife of A. K. Duke (deceased) and died in 1881; Adelaide, who was the first wife of A. K. Duke, died in 1868; Amanda became the wife of F. M. Duke and died in 1881. James M. Doyle was educated in the common schools of this county, and in 1861 joined the army, enlisting in company E of the Twenty-ninth Mississippi infantry. His first engagement was at Corinth; he afterward fought at Murfreesboro, Chickamauga, Missionary ridge, Resaca and in all the engagements through the Georgia and Atlanta campaigns. Returning with Hood, he was wounded at Franklin, Tenn., and after spending six weeks in the hospital, joined the army of General Johnston, with which he surrendered at Jonesboro, N. C., as orderly sergeant. He was wounded also at Murfreesboro, Missionary ridge and Atlanta. After his return home he resumed the life of a planter. In 1868 he married Sallie, a daughter of George and Sallie Swaringen, natives of Alabama and Tennessee, respectively, both of whom came with their parents to Yalobusha county, where they married and lived the remainder of their lives. Mrs. Swaringen dying in 1858, and Mr. Swaringen in 1889; the latter in Arkansas, where he had been a planter since 1884. Both were members of the Missionary Baptist church. John S., father of George, was one of the pioneers of this county, where he died a well-to-do planter. Mrs. Doyle's maternal grandfather, Wilson Frost, was also an early settler here. He came from Tennessee, was a well-known planter and died previous to the war. Mrs. Doyle was born on the farm upon which she and her husband are now living. She has had nine children, seven of whom are now living. Mr. Doyle lived near Garner for two years and then removed to his present plantation, five miles southeast of Oakland. This estate consists of nine hundred acres of land, five hundred of which are cleared, producing from sixty to one hundred bales of cotton annually. He is a member of Oakland lodge No. 82, A. F. & A. M., in which he has been senior warden, and held other offices; he is also a member of Oakland lodge No. 97, I. O. O. F. Mrs. Doyle is a member of the Missionary Baptist church, with which her husband was originally connected. Our subject is a man of push and enterprise, and fine business qualifications, who has made his way unaided in the world and honestly won such success as he has attained. He is a well-to-do planter, and an enterprising citizen, honored and repected by all.

As an example of the usefulness and prominence to which men of character and determination may attain, it is but necessary to chronicle the life of Hon. Elijah Steele Drake, one of the sagacious, practical and skillful attorneys of the state of Mississippi. He comes of a highly cultured and intellectual family, all the members of which possessed superior intelligence and became distinguished in the different callings in which they engaged. He was born in Jefferson county, Miss., on the 14th of October, 1841, being the eighth of twelve children—eight sons and four daughters—of which large family only two members survive, the subject of this sketch and Rev. J. P. Drake, who is an eminent divine and an able and talented writer. The members of the family who are deceased are: H. W., who was one of the foremost attorneys of Tensas parish, La., which he represented in the legislature of that state; A. F., who was also one of the well-known lawyers of that parish; Rev. W. W., who was one of the most eminent divines the Methodist Episcopal Church South ever had. He was twenty-seven years of age at the time of his death, at which time he held the position of presiding elder. His congregation has since erected a memorial tablet to his memory in the church at Greenville. Magruder died in the Rebellion, and the remainder of the family died when young. The father, Dr. Benjamin Michael Drake, D. D., was one of the most worthy and eminent men in Southern Mississippi, and was a man who held intelligent and refined views on all matters of public interest. He held the important position of president of Elizabeth female college at Washington, Miss., in 1828, the first incorporated institute in the state, and also, in connection with Judge McGee, was the founder of Centenary college, at Jackson, La. It was he who erected the first Protestant church in New Orleans, this being as early as 1823. He was born in Robeson county, N. C., September 11, 1800, and at the age of seven years was taken by his father, who had been an officer in the Revolutionary war, to Kentucky. Rev. Drake became a man of great prominence in the state of Mississippi, and the record of this amiable and cultured gentleman is one of which any man might be proud. His well-known qualities of heart and head won for him innumerable friends, and his eloquence as a divine and his truly Christian character will keep his memory green in the hearts of those of his day and generation, as well as for many coming years. He passed from life in 1860. His wife, whose maiden name was Susan H. P. Magruder, was born in Jefferson county, Miss., April 2, 1811, and is still living at the advanced age of eighty years. She is a graduate of Elizabeth college, Mississippi, one of the most famous institutions of its kind in the state, and for many years she was a worthy contributor to many religious papers, and, notwithstanding her advanced age, still occasionally contributes an article. She makes her home with her son, Hon. E. S. Drake, with whom she expects to spend the rest of her days. Mr. Drake acquired his early knowledge of books at his home, and, after becoming sufficiently fitted, entered the grammar school in Jefferson county, later becoming a student in Centenary college, which institution he attended from 1858 to 1860, graduating with the honors of his class of nineteen in 1860. Upon finishing his course and after the war had become an assured fact, he became a member of Jefferson's artillery, Confederate states army, which was afterward known as Darden's battery, and was assigned to the front under Gen. Albert Sidney Johnston and took part in the engagements at Shiloh, Perryville, Murfreesboro, Chickamauga and the engagements of the Georgia campaign, being also at Nashville and Franklin. Mr. Drake was wounded at Decatur, Tenn., in which engagement his battery lost forty men and many horses. His wound, which was in the neck, confined him to the hospital for one month. His battery was surrendered by Gen. Dick Taylor, May 4, 1865, and he, with four brothers who were in the service, returned home, another brother having died while in the army. Mr. Drake found himself, at the close of the war, with no means whatsoever, so in order to obtain the necessary funds, he at once opened a private school and devoted his leisure moments to the study of law. Subsequently he and Capt. W. S. Schwing organized a high school at Fayette, Miss., under the name of the Phœnix academy, which they continued to conduct, during which time Mr. Drake was admitted to the Mississippi bar. Soon after this event he removed to Port Gibson, August, 1867, opened a law office at this place, and has been one of the public-spirited citizens, and one of its foremost and eminent lawyers. He is a man of very superior natural endowments, strengthened and enriched by the highest culture. His mind is clear, concise, analytical and well poised, and he impresses one at once as a man of great strength, depth and grasp of mind. The most abstruse and complicated subjects are handled with ease and grace and made perceptible and plain to the most ordinary understanding. Weight and power accompany all his words and writings, and inspire respect and conviction, and the ripe scholarship and logical judgment which he possesses would insure anyone marked success. His wife, who was formerly Miss Ellen D. Turpin, was born in Jefferson county, Miss., is an accomplished and amiable lady. Their marriage was consummated September 21, 1869, and has resulted in the birth of six children: Joseph T., is a graduate of Washington and Lee university, of Lexington, Va. He has chosen law as his profession, and is now associated in the practice of that profession with his father, and gives every promise of becoming eminent. Before he could be admitted to the bar, he was emancipated by the chancery court, as he was under age. Ruth is a graduate of Port Gibson female college, and took a two years' post-graduate course in music, art, Latin and French. Katie A. also graduated from the above-mentioned college in June, 1890. Nellie D. is attending the same and is very bright and promising. Henry Winbourne has attained the age of thirteen years and is attending the Chamberlain Hunt academy, is also a bright student, and Laura S., the youngest of the family, is also attending the female college at Port Gibson.

Mrs. Drake's father, Joseph A. Turpin, was a native and solid planter of Adams county, Miss. He was born in 1815, was educated in the University of Virginia, and although he has attained the advanced age of seventy-five years, he is in the enjoyment of comparatively good health and is a resident of Point Coupee parish, La. His wife, who was formerly Laura Archer, was born in Harford county, Md., was a graduate of Mrs. Willard's famous female college of Troy, N. Y., and is now in her seventy-fourth year. Mr. Drake was reared a whig but espoused democratic principles, and although not strictly an ultra partisan, is true to his party. In his official career he has performed his part with brilliancy and in a manner highly satisfactory to all. He was elected to the legislature from his county for 1876-7 and that term has been noted in history as one of the most positive, able and executive legislatures which had assembled in the legislative halls of the state. While in session that body passed some of the most important measures that had ever come up before the legislative assembly: The radical reduction of taxes from fourteen mills to six mills state tax, and thorough revision of the official body; the impeachment of the governor, the lieutenant-governor, the superintendent of public instruction; in fact, the entire judicial system was reorganized, and the judges relieved of their positions, which had been filled very unsatisfactorily. The action of the legislature during the entire term was memorable and was productive of intrinsic and inestimable good. Mr. Drake is a trustee of the Port Gibson female college, which position he has held for the past twenty years, and he is also the college's attorney and fills the same position for the Chamberlain Hunt academy. He is one of the attorneys for the Port Gibson bank, is one of its directors, and for the past twenty-three years has been superintendent of the Methodist Episcopal Sunday-school. Notwithstanding the fact that he has been a very active business man he has never neglected his religious duties, and is a worthy Christian gentleman, striving at all times to do as he would be done by. He is a strict supporter of temperance and morality, practicing what he preaches in all things, is devoted to his family, and in his beautiful and comfortable home dispenses that generous hospitality for which he has always been noted.

B. B. Drane, M. D., Torrance, Miss., a leading physician and planter, of Yalobusha county, Miss., was born in Columbia county, Ga., December 5, 1830, and is a son of Benjamin and Sarah (Germany) Drane, natives of the same county and state as the son. The father was born in 1803, and is a son of William and Casandria (Magruder) Drane. Mrs. Drane was a cousin of General Magruder. They were married in Maryland, and with a cart and one horse they journeyed to the state of Georgia, where they settled and reared a family. By energy and industry they amassed a fortune. William Drane died at the age of sixty years, while his wife lived to be ninety years old. They reared a family of five sons and two daughters, all of whom lived to maturity, and one of whom is yet living, the father of our subject. He grew to manhood in Georgia, and was married there; in 1838 he removed with his family to Mississippi and settled in Choctaw county, where he still lives on the place which he first made his home. He is engaged in farming, and has followed that occupation for many years. Mrs. Drane, wife of Benjamin Drane, died in 1859; she was born in 1808, and he is now eighty-eight years of age. To them were born twelve children—seven sons and five daughters: James G., died in 1890; B. B. is the subject of this biography; William T., died in Choctaw county; Robert A., died in 1885; Mrs. Mary E. Stewart, died in 1890; George W. C. is a wealthy resident of South America; John H., chancery clerk of Montgomery county, Miss.; Edgar S., a farmer of Choctaw county; Mrs. Sarah V. Orr, Mrs. Georgia A. Drane and Mrs. Elizabeth C. Tabor; the last two named are widows and live on the home farm. Dr. Drane first attended school in Choctaw county, and then went to Winston county, Miss., where he was a student for some years. There he began the study of medicine with Dr. B. N. Ward, a prominent physician of the county, and in 1852 he took a course of lectures in Augusta, Ga. Thence he went to New York city, and entered the University of New York, and graduated from the medical department in 1854. He then returned to Mississippi, and practiced in Choctaw county for a short time; then he went to Waverly, Miss., but remained there only one year; next he located in Grenada, and for fifteen years was engaged in the practice of his profession. At the end of that period he came to his present home near Torrence, where he has given much attention to agriculture in addition to his professional work. He was first united in marriage to Harriet Guy, a daughter of Maj. C. H. Guy, of Grenada, a full sketch of whom appears on another page of this work. Mrs. Drane died in 1864, leaving one son, Guy Drane, who is now living in Texas, engaged in railroad work. Mr. Drane was married a second time, to Miss Margaret A. E. Land, in 1870. She was a Miss Gage, a daughter of the Rev. James B. Gage. He was a citizen of Torrance, and an early settler of Mississippi; he was born in Georgia in 1804, and is a minister in the Baptist church; he was married to Miss Sanders, May 15, 1823, and came to Mississippi in 1839; he died in 1873, January 2, honored and respected by a host of acquaintances. Mrs. Gage died in 1871, aged sixty-three years. To them were born four sons and five daughters: Mary J. E. (deceased), was the wife of Major Wiley; Dr. John J.; Margaret E. A.; Missouri K., deceased; Dr. Mathew W., deceased; Dr. James B.; Mrs. Anna P. Cundiff; Mrs. Sarah B. Raddick; Dr. Benjamin C. Mrs. Drane was first married to Benjamin Land, a native of North Carolina; he died in 1868. Mr. Drane entered the Confederate service in 1861 as a surgeon; he went from Grenada to Gainsboro, Tenn. He was operating surgeon in the hospital, and a member of the examining board until the close of the war. He takes no active interest in politics beyond the exercise of his right of suffrage. Mrs. Drane is a member of the Baptist church, in which she is an active worker.

Col. James W. Drane, planter, French Camp, Miss., owes his nativity to Georgia, his birth occurring in Columbia county on the 14th of April, 1833, and he comes of distinguished ancestors from both sides. His parents, Hon. James and Matilda B. (Shaw) Drane, were natives also of Columbia county, Ga., the father born in 1808 and the mother in 1829. The parents came to Choctaw county, Miss., in 1836, settled in the woods in the southern part of the county and there the father followed the occupation of a planter until his death on the 8th of March, 1869. He was a great hunter all his life, was a champion marksman and killed one hundred and ten deer the first year of his residence in Choctaw county. He was a very popular and prominent man, serving with distinction in the lower house of the Mississippi legislature from 1837 to 1843, and in 1845 he was the regular nominee of the democratic party for state senator, but was defeated through fraud. Again in 1849 he was the candidate of his party for that position and served continuously until 1866, being president of that body for several of the later terms. In 1858 he was a prominent candidate for governor until the day of the convention, when, on account of the ill health of his wife, which would prevent him from canvassing the state in his behalf, he sent his son, James W., then quite a young man, to the convention at Jackson to withdraw his name. It was not without considerable effort that the withdrawal was accepted, and without doubt had his name remained before the convention he would have been nominated and elected. He was offered a brigadier-general's commission by President Davis but was prevailed upon by his family to refuse it. His father, William Drane, was born in Prince George county, Md., in 1765, and died in Columbia county, Ga., on the 7th of February, 1847. He was a successful planter and the youngest son of James Drane, who was an Englishman and who came to Prince George county, Md., where he reared seven sons: James, Anthony, Steven, Thomas, Benjamin, Walter and William. Colonel Drane's maternal great-grandfather, Ninian B. McGruder, descended from the rebellious Scottish McGregor who, tradition says, was banished and the name changed on account of adherence to Sir William Wallace and other rebel chiefs. Mr. McGruder was a native of Maryland and probably died in Columbia county, Ga. Col. James W. Drane was the second in order of birth of the following children: Mary C., widow of Maj. William C. Staples; Virgil C., a planter of Choctaw county, enlisted in the Confederate army, company I, Fifteenth Mississippi infantry and exchanged to company I, Thirty-first Mississippi, in the Tennessee army, and served all through the war (he was wounded in the head at Franklin, and surrendered with Johnston's army in 1865); and Matilda C., wife of Hobert D. Shaw, died in 1864. Colonel Drane became inured to the duties of farm life at an early age, and supplemented a common-school education by attending the Methodist college at Sharon and later the State university for two years. In 1854 he married Miss Fannie Hemphill, a native of Rome, Ga., and the daughter of Gen. James Hemphill (see sketch of Dr. A. J. Hemphill). Mrs. Drane was a worthy member of the Presbyterian church and died on the 20th of September, 1884. This union resulted in the birth of nine children, viz.: Hon. James, died in 1889; (he was educated at French Camp, Stonewall college, Tennessee, and at the State university. He became a promising lawyer at Chester, and was one term in the legislature. He was a young man of fine literary attainments and a bright future was opening before him, but he was powerless before the pale reaper. Such a man at any age is no trifling loss to any community, and how much more serious the blow which strikes down one in the very vigor of life, with the prospect of many years of usefulness and honor before him); Butler, died in 1860; Dr. William, is a graduate of the medical department of the University of Tennessee, at Nashville, and is now a practicing physician of Choctaw county, Miss.; Francis, Jefferson Davis, Anna M. B., Mary, Hugh M. and Lillian. Dr. Jefferson Davis Drane graduated at the medical department of the University of Tennessee in February, 1886, in a class of sixty-one students, and took the third medal when he was only twenty years of age, and is now a practitioner of medicine at French Camp, Miss. The Colonel's second marriage occurred in 1885, to Mrs. Sallie G. Whitfield, a daughter of Rev. Horatio J. Bardwell, and a native of Oktibbeha county, Miss. Colonel Drane followed farming and merchandising until 1862, and then joined the Thirty-first Mississippi infantry as captain of company I, which he commanded until the fall of

1862, when he was made major and later lieutenant-colonel at Meridian, Miss., for his gallantry at Peach Tree creek. It is said he was commissioned colonel, but he did not receive the commission. He fought at Baker's creek and all around Vicksburg. He belonged to Johnston's army all the time after Baker's creek fight. From there he went to Jackson, Miss., where he joined General Johnston's army at New Hope church. He fought all the way to Peach Tree creek and was shot nearly to pieces, receiving a severe wound in the head, another in the left shoulder, one in the left arm, rendering it almost useless, one in the side and in each leg. For twelve months after the close of the war he was unable to rise from his bed. Every field officer and every line officer, with the exception of one in his command, was killed or wounded in the Peach Tree creek fight. At the time of entering service Colonel Drane was Confederate tax collector, but turned that office over to his father and entered the Confederate army. After the war he engaged in merchandising, shipping mules, etc., for a number of years, but more recently has devoted his entire attention to farming. He has lived for fifty-five years almost in the same neighborhood, and since 1869 on his present farm, two miles north of French Camp, where he has a fine home of about one thousand acres. He and Mrs. Drane and all but one of the children are members of the Presbyterian church. Colonel Drane is doubtless the most conspicuous character in Choctaw county at the present time, especially never to have been in public life. He is a large man, but is badly crippled from his war service. He stands very high in the estimation of every one as a strictly honest, moral and upright citizen. The Colonel has an uncle, Benjamin Drane, now living in Choctaw county, Miss., who is eighty-eight years of age.

Judge J. R. M. Du Berry, an old and representative citizen of Pittsboro, and one of the first settlers of Calhoun county, Miss., was originally from Warren county, N. C., born in 1816, and was the son of John Du Berry. He was left an orphan at an early age, and when ten years old he went with an uncle to Middle Tennessee, where he remained for some time. He then went to Summerville of that state, but in 1834 went from there to Madison county, Miss. He soon returned, however, to Tennessee, and there attended school, but in 1836 enlisted in the Florida war. The following year he returned to Tennessee, and again entered the schoolroom. In 1839 he returned to Mississippi, and in this state he has made his home ever since. He first settled at Grenada, was engaged in keelboating on the Yalobusha river, but subsequently went to Greenwood, where he managed a mercantile establishment for a firm in Grenada for two years. In 1846 he returned to the last-named town, and soon after came to Big creek, where he purchased the stock of J. J. Ramsey, and conducted the business for six years. After this he was engaged in business in Pittsboro for three years. In 1855 he was elected probate judge, and held that position until 1861, when he raised a company known as "Yaller jackets." After the war Mr. Du Berry returned to Pittsboro, where he has since resided, esteemed and respected by all. He has held many positions of trust in the county, was deputy clerk for some time, deputy revenue collector for Calhoun county soon after the war, and he took the census of that county in 1880. Mr. Du Berry was married to Miss M. A. Gibbs, of Grenada, and of the eight children born to this union, five are now living: Mrs. Elizabeth Enochs and Mrs. Alice Payne Shaw, both of whom are widows; John R., of Coffeeville, Miss.; Miss Fannie, at home, and William C., at Coffeeville. Those deceased were Miranda, died when an infant, Mattie A. and James R. M. The mother of these children was a worthy member of the Methodist Episcopal church, and died in August, 1890, at the age of sixty-two years. Judge Du Berry is a prominent member of the Methodist Episcopal church also. In politics he affiliates with the democratic party. He was a member of the I. O. O. F. lodge in 1842, the sixth lodge in the state, and was also a member of the Masonic lodge at Grenada, No. 31. At the present time (1891), he is a member of Pittsboro lodge No. 155, and mayor of Pittsboro.

Beauregard Du Bose, of Ellisville, Jones county, Miss., was born in Choctaw county, Ala., January 9, 1860, a son of William J. and Lucinda A. (Bell) Du Bose, both natives of Georgia, where they were married, and whence they removed to Alabama, where they lived till 1866, when they located in Wayne county, Miss., in which place they still reside. They are the parents of seven children: Louisiana, Theodore, Delaware, Beauregard, Magnolia, Ada and Effie. Beauregard, the immediate subject of this notice, has been a resident of this state since 1866, when he came with his parents. In 1876 he found employment as a clerk in the store of Turner & Taylor, at Waynesboro, Miss., with whom he remained till September, 1880, when he formed a partnership with S. T. Taylor, of the firm of Turner & Taylor, and engaged in merchandising at Old Ellisville, Miss., in charge of a store of which he and Mr. Taylor were joint owners, Mr. Taylor remaining at Waynesboro. In 1884 they sold their stock of goods to Theodore Du Bose, and on account of ill health our subject retired from business until September, 1889, when he formed a partnership with Herrington & Hill, under the firm name of Herrington, Du Bose & Hill, and entered upon a business career which has placed their house at the head of the mercantile interests in this town. Mr. Du Bose was married in Perry county, Miss., March 15, 1883, to Miss Celia G., daughter of Daniel and Mary (Granberry) Carter, who was born in that county September 4, 1858. In 1887 Mr. Du Bose was elected a member of the board of supervisors of Jones county, and as such was one of those in charge of the erection of the new courthouse. Though not an active politician, he is a strict adherent to the principles of his party, and takes a deep interest in all questions of public import, and he is especially solicitous for the growth and advancement of Ellisville, and for the various interests affecting the weal of Jones county. He has been quite successful in life, and is one of the many sterling citizens of this part of the state, who have been not alone the architects of their own fortunes, but creators and conservators of the public welfare. He is a member of the Masonic fraternity, and also of the Methodist Episcopal church South, while Mrs. Du Bose is a communicant of the Baptist church. They have had one child, Annie Eloise, who is now deceased.

C. W. Dudley's ancestors were among the distinguished families of Kentucky, and his paternal grandfather, Dr. Benjamin Winslow Dudley, was a physician of note. The latter stands at the head of his profession as a lithotomist, even to the present day, performing more successful operations of that disease than any previous or subsequent physician. He practiced at Lexington, Ky., and was principal of the surgical department of Transylvania college, Lexington, the greater part of his days. He wrote quite extensively on scientific matters relating to his profession, and is now known among physicians as one of the brightest practitioners of the past. His son and the father of our subject, Dr. C. Wilkins Dudley, was also a native of Kentucky. He studied medicine and practiced until 1853, when he was married to Mrs. Margaret (Erwin) Johnson, who was also born in Kentucky. They afterward moved to Mississippi and made Washington county their permanent home, the mother dying there in 1862, and the father in 1881. In 1860 the father erected a fine brick mansion, which in its day was one of the stateliest in the county. This handsome dwelling, noble in proportions and artistic in design, stands in a large park facing Lake Washington, and commands a view of unsurpassed loveliness. The only child born to their union was C. W. Dudley, whose birth occurred on his father's plantation, Mount Holly, in Washington county, Miss., in 1850. He was educated in Kentucky, and when a stripling of sixteen came to Mississippi, where he engaged as clerk for Messrs. C. P. & M. Williams at Longwood. In 1876 he embarked

Frank Hawkins

in business for himself at a place known as Burn, near the head of Lake Washington, and there carried on business for three years. After this he began merchandising at Stella landing, on the Mississippi river, remained there for two years, and in June, 1882 he was elected cotton tax collector for the Mississippi levee district, comprising Bolivar, Washington, Issaquena and Sharkey counties. As a man of superior intelligence and capability he was most admirably fitted to perform the duties of this position, and held the same until July, 1890. He bought his present plantation, the old estate of his parents, from J. W. Erwin (his half brother) in 1880, and of the eleven hundred and eighty-five acres in this tract he has ten hundred and fifty-six acres cleared and under a high state of cultivation, two hundred and fifty acres of which he cleared himself. He has advanced and progressive ideas in the management of his plantation, and all his improvements are of a first-class order. His house is handsomely furnished, has all the modern improvements, gas, hot and cold water, closets up and down stairs, and many other conveniences. In June, 1890, he opened a store on his place, is doing a good business and carries a stock of goods valued at about $5,000. In the last four years he has put in about $20,000 worth of improvements on his place. He has been quite active in politics since 1875, but is at home only in the winter, as he travels during the summer months. During the summer of 1890 he was in Europe. He is a Knight Templar in the Masonic fraternity, is an Elk and a member of the Knights of Pythias.

Maj. P. B. Dugan, president of the First National bank of West Point, Miss., is a gentleman of varied talents, wide experience, excellent business capacity, and being genial in disposition and straightforward in his business methods, he stands high in the estimation of the public. He was born in Newberry, S. C., in 1837, to William H. and Mary (Dugan) Dugan (distant relatives), who were also natives of Newberry district, in which they lived until about 1845, when they emigrated to Noxubee county, Miss., where the remainder of their days was spent, the father's death occurring in 1866, and the mother's in 1857, she being an earnest and worthy member of the Cumberland Presbyterian church at the time of her demise. Mr. Dugan was a planter and miller by occupation, and, although his early educational advantages were somewhat limited, he was naturally intelligent, possessed a sound and practical mind, and became well to do. Owing to the early death of his father, he was compelled to fight the battle of life alone, and was, in every sense of the term, a self-made man. P. B. Dugan was the eldest of seven children, and is the only one of the family that is now living. A brother, Burr Dugan, was killed in the battle of Nashville in 1865, having enlisted as a private in the Confederate army when quite young, becoming a member of the Fourteenth Mississippi infantry. Another brother, Reese, was also in the Confederate service the last year or two of the war, and, although almost a boy in years, he rendered valuable aid to the Confederate cause. P. B. Dugan received his initiatory training in the country schools of Noxubee county, which he attended until about sixteen years of age, after which he finished his literary education at Summerville institute, in that county. In 1856 he began the study of medicine with Dr. J. S. Smythe, of Summerville, and continued under Dr. Warren Stone, of New Orleans, in the years 1857–9, and in the University of Louisiana, at New Orleans. He began practicing his profession in Winston county after leaving New Orleans, but was soon interrupted by the outbreak of the Civil war, when he abandoned his practice to become a votary of Mars, enlisting in company F, of the Fourteenth Mississippi infantry, in which he served a short time as lieutenant, and was then made captain of the company. Captain Dugan was first engaged in actual battle in the engagements which took place around Fort Donelson in February, 1862, and was captured at the fall of that place. He was first imprisoned at Camp Chase, then on Johnson's island until

42

September, when he was exchanged and rejoined his command in Mississippi. He operated in that state for some time, and at the battle of Jackson was wounded in the left leg. He was afterward in the Georgia and the Atlanta campaigns, and in one of the engagements about Atlanta, receiving another wound, which disabled him for some time. He rejoined his command at Florence, Ala., and although not able to take part in the engagement at Franklin, he was in the battle of Nashville, where he commanded his regiment with gallantry and courage, having previously been promoted from the rank of captain to that of major. From Nashville his command fell back to Tupelo, where he was taken sick and was unable to again enter service. He was a distinguished officer, conspicuous for his bravery and soldierly bearing, and upon the cessation of hostilities he returned to his home with the consciousness of having performed every duty faithfully and well. In 1866 he located at West Point, where he has since made his home. He practiced medicine with marked success until September, 1873, when his partner, J. L. Moseley, died, and he afterward devoted his attention to the drug business until 1878. He then disposed of his stock of drugs in order to give his entire attention to the cotton commission business, in which he had been engaged for two years previously.

In 1880 he became a partner in the Stockard, Bonner & Co. banking firm, and so continued until the organization of its successor, the First National bank, in 1882, since which time he has been its president. It is one of the most prosperous institutions of the kind in this section of the state, has a capital of $75,000 and a surplus of $30,000. It has added largely to the banking capital and financial interests of West Point, and the facilities for the expeditious transaction of business are of the best. The management of the company is perfect in system, and its directors are gentleman of well-known stability, including a number of the leading business men of the city. Major Dugan was married in 1869 to Miss Martha A., daughter of Lemuel and Mary Westbrook, natives of North Carolina, who came to Mississippi at an early day, and died near West Point a number of years ago. Mrs. Dugan was born near this place, and of the three children she has borne her husband only one is living, a daughter. She is a member of the Cumberland Presbyterian church, a true Christian in every respect, and an affectionate and faithful wife and mother. Major Dugan has been a member of the A. F. & A. M. lodge at Summerville for many years, but has never united with the lodge at West Point, although he is a member of West Point lodge No 157 of the K. of H. From 1871 to 1873 he was connected with the West Point *Citizen*, which journal was published under his supervision until the plant was destroyed by fire in the last mentioned year. In every respect he is one of the leading citizens of West Point, and is liberal in the use of his means for the benefit of the public. He has been quite an extensive traveler, and the summer of 1883 he made a tour of Europe, visiting places of interest in Scotland, England, France, Italy, Switzerland, Germany, Belgium and Holland.

James H. Duke, a wealthy planter and merchant of Scooba, Miss., was born at Gainesville, Sumter county, Ala., March 10, 1846, and is a son of Horace M. and Sarah J. (Harwood) Duke. His father was a native of Albemarle county, Va., a son of James Duke and Nancy (Biggers) Duke, and emigrated thence to Alabama in the early settlement of that state. There he was married and reared a family of six children, three of whom survive: James H., the subject of this biographical sketch; Robertine E., now Mrs. Carr, and Horace M. He was a merchant by occupation, and was generous of the means he had accumulated. In 1861 he enlisted in the Confederate cause, for which he raised a cavalry company. He was captured on the James river at Richmond, and was sent to Johnson's island, where he contracted typhoid fever, from which he never recovered. He was buried near the foot of the

Blue Ridge mountains in Albemarle county, Va. Politically he was allied to the democratic party, and at one time was deputy sheriff of Sumter county, Ala. He was connected with the Baptist church, and was a man of excellent traits of character. His death occurred in 1865. His wife was born near Richmond, Va. She was the daughter of S. B. M. and Elizabeth (Ellison) Harwood. She passed her last days in Greene county, Ala., the year of her death being 1857. James H. was reared to the mercantile trade, and received his education in Gainesville, Ala. In 1860, July 5, he came to Scooba, where he was employed as clerk until 1863. In that year he enlisted in the Confederate cause, and was made an officer in R. O. Perrin's regiment of cavalry. He was in the service about two years, surrendering in 1865. He was in the Mississippi campaign and through the siege of Atlanta and Savannah, Ga. After the war was over he engaged in mercantile business on his own account. His capital was very small, and it is through wise management and the exercise of rare, good judgment that he has accumulated the property he now owns. The firm name was J. H. Duke & Co., until 1870, when he purchased the entire business. As his means increased he invested in land, and now owns about twenty thousand acres, all of which is in the state of Mississippi, except five hundred acres in Alabama. Mr. Duke was married in 1870 to Miss Elizabeth G. Horrell, a daughter of Dr. E. W. and M. J. (Phillips) Horrell, of New Madrid, Mo. She was born in 1849, and is an only child. Her parents are both deceased; the father died in 1881, and the mother about 1856. Mr. and Mrs. Duke have a family of five children: John G., Rachel G., Pearson H., Sarah E. and Elizabeth H. The father and mother are members of the Presbyterian church. Mr. Duke is a Mason and member of the finance committee of the grand lodge of Mississippi, and has been master of the lodge at Scooba three terms. He is also a Knight of Honor, of which order he has been dictator several times, and chairman of the grand trustees of the grand lodge of Mississippi of the same society. Politically he affiliates with the democratic party. In 1885 he was a candidate for treasurer of the state, and was defeated by a very few votes. He was an alternate delegate to the national convention from Mississippi at large, when Gen. Hancock was nominated for president of the United States, and alternate delegate from his congressional district when Grover Cleveland was nominated. In all the proceedings of his party he has taken an active interest. His opinions and counsel are always sought in matters of importance, and he has proven a most reliable guide. He has been a member of the state executive committee of the democratic party several different times since the war between the states. The Duke family is of English origin, and is traced back to Henry Duke, a grandson of Cleverious Duke.

Dr. J. W. Dulaney, physician, Rosedale, Miss., was born in Madison county, Miss., in 1848, and comes of a family of physicians, his father and several uncles having successfully followed that profession. He is the only child living born to the union of William Johnson and Mary (Gassaway) Dulaney, the father a native of the Old Dominion and the mother of Tennessee. The former was a graduate of the Philadelphia medical college, and at an early date came to Mississippi, settling in Madison county, of that state, in 1831. He came to this state to make his fortune, and accomplished his object, for everything that he undertook prospered, and he became very wealthy. He was ambitious to excel in every thing he attempted, and in his profession, planting, fortune and in good deeds he was indeed among the foremost. He was one of the leading members of the Christian church, was noted far and wide for his benevolent and generous disposition, and spent his money freely in alleviating the distress of the needy and afflicted. He educated several orphan girls, aided and assisted many widows, and his life was full of good and noble deeds. His death, which occurred in 1880, was the occasion of universal sorrow, for all felt the loss which would be sustained by the departure of such a man. Although one of the most prominent men in the county, and one who took a deep interest in political affairs, he never aspired for office. He was married four times. His fortune was all swept away by the war, but he afterward, in a measure, retrieved it and died in very comfortable circumstances. His wife's people were from Tennessee. His father was a native of Virginia, of an old and prominent family of that state, and was a large millowner. Dr. J. W. Dulaney passed his youthful days in attending school in his native county, and in 1862 he entered the Confederate army, Adams' regiment, and was with Harvey's scouts at the siege of Vicksburg. When sixteen years of age he was regularly mustered, and was paroled at Jackson, Miss. After this he engaged in teaming from Jackson and Vicksburg until he had earned sufficient means to send him to school for a year or two, and then followed farming on his father's plantation for five years, studying medicine in the latter's office during that time. While planting for his father he had saved about $1,200, and in the winter of 1871–2 he attended the University of Louisiana, graduating in 1873. After this he practiced at home for three years, and in May, 1876, came to Rosedale, where he has since built up a large practice. He came to this county to make his fortune, and although on arriving he only had a horse and buggy and $20 in money, he has been unusually successful, owning both town and country property. He was engaged in merchandising for some time, started a good drug store in 1888, and has also carried on planting. He was health officer of the county for eight years, and is at present a member of the state and tri-state medical associations. He has been quite active in politics, and was appointed mayor by Governor Lowry in 1890, and was elected in 1891 to the same position he is holding at the present time. Dr. Dulaney is greatly interested in the advancement of the city, and accepted the office only in the hopes of benefiting the place. On the 15th of November, 1877, he espoused Miss Hattie Montgomery, daughter of Col. F. A. Montgomery (see sketch), and they have three children living and one deceased: Mary, Hattie, Frank (died at the age of seven months) and John W. The Doctor is a member of the Christian and Mrs. Dulaney a member of the Methodist Episcopal church. In the year 1890 the Doctor erected a new residence in town, a two-story frame, one of the handsomest buildings in the place. He is one of the directors of the Rosedale & Mississippi valley railroad, and socially is a member of the Masonic fraternity, of which he is master, the Knights of Honor and the Knights of Pythias, having held office in both the last-named organizations also. In 1882, during the overflow of the Mississippi river, Dr. Dulaney went to the break in the levee at Riverton, and, with the assistance of an Indian, rescued seventy-five people. It took him all day, and was a thrilling and dangerous experience. He has passed through two yellow fever epidemics, and while health officer of the county he attended over two hundred cases of smallpox at the pest house. He stood manfully at his post all through this, and fought the dread diseases with all the skill and knowledge of the medical science.

Dr. Octavus Dulaney, of Copiah county, Miss., was born September 15, 1846, in Hinds county, Miss. He was a son of Addison and Ann Maria Dulaney. His father was born in Culpepper county, Va., November 12, 1808. He was a member of the Masonic order, and both he and his wife were communicants of the Baptist church. His mother, Ann Maria Sinclair, was born in Fauquier county, Va., March 16, 1804. They emigrated to Mississippi in 1833 or 1834, locating at Raymond, in Hinds county. They had seven children, four of whom are now living: Alpens, at Gallman, Miss.; Bell, wife of J. M. Hand, of Texas; Octavus, of Copiah county; Addison, of Hinds county, Miss. Dr. Octavus Dulaney received his professional education at New Orleans medical college, graduating in 1870. In 1871 he married Susan C. Rogers, a daughter of James T. and Caroline Rogers, of Simpson county, Miss. Mrs. Dulaney bore him six children, four of whom are living: Lilla Bell, Ina Gertrude, Octavus, Jr., and Stella May. After the death of his first wife he married Esther Johnson, November 30, 1884, a daughter of Robert and Elizabeth Johnson, of South Carolina, by whom he had two children—Dalton and Annie Dula. The Doctor has a large practice, which extends over a good portion of Copiah and Simpson counties. In connection with his practice he devotes much of his time to the interests of his fine plantation, and is regarded not only as a skillful physician but also as a very successful planter. In 1862 he enlisted in company C of Robert's battalion, in which he served the Confederate cause zealously until the close of the war. He is a member of and has been for many years the secretary of, the Charles Scott lodge No. 136, A. F. & A. M. He is also identified with the Farmers' Alliance, and he and his estimable wife are devout worshipers of the Baptist church.

James M. Duncan, a leading planter and one of the oldest and most respected citizens of the county, was born in Greene county, Tenn., on the 28th of October, 1813, and inherits Scotch blood from his paternal grandfather, who was a native of Scotland. The latter and a brother came to the United States prior to the Revolution, and the brother was killed by the British near Norfolk, Va. The grandfather settled in Botetourt county, Va., and there reared his family, consisting of George, Jerry, Amos, Benjamin, David and two daughters. The fourth child in order of birth, Benjamin, grew to manhood in Virginia, and when a young man went to East Tennessee, where he was married in 1812 to Miss Nancy Ross, also a native of the Old Dominion, and a daughter of William Ross, who served in the Revolutionary war, and was present at the surrender of Cornwallis. Mr. Ross has several sons, who served in the Creek Indian wars. Mr. and Mrs. Duncan continued to reside in Greene county, Tenn., until November, 1822, when they moved to Limestone county, Ala., and from there to Shelby county, Tenn., in 1834. The father followed merchandising from the close of the Indian wars, in which he served as a lieutenant in Captain Waterhouse's company, until about 1850, when he carried on planting in connection with that occupation. He was a stanch whig, and although he took an active part in politics, he would never hold office. He was a Mason of rank and was one of the leading business men and prominent citizens of Shelby county. He died June 1, 1860, honored and respected by all. His wife died in the same county in 1836, leaving six children—three sons and three daughters, two of whom are yet living: James M. Duncan, the subject of this sketch, and the eldest child; and Mrs. Ann Reembert, of Shelby county, Tenn. After his wife's death Mr. Duncan was married the second time and became the father of two children by this union, a son and daughter, both now deceased. James M. Duncan passed his boyhood and youth in Limestone county, Ala., and there received his education. In 1836 he started out in life for himself as a merchant at Mooresville, Ala., Limestone county, and there continued until the spring of 1840. He first came to Mississippi in 1838, to administer upon the estate of George Dillard, and being pleased with the state he moved there in the fall of 1840. The following year he commenced farming upon the estate he now owns, and there he has continued to reside up to the present time. On a part of the place now owned by Mr. Duncan a fight took place between the Choctaw and Choechumas Indians, in which the last named tribe was almost exterminated. Two members of the tribe, girls, were picking berries and thus escaped death. They were adopted by the Choctaw tribe, and it is from them that the traditions of the tribe are handed down. The town of Choechumas was laid off after the Choctaw treaty, and it was at one time the largest town in northern Mississippi. When he first came to Mississipp Mr. Duncan had very little to start with, being the owner of three full-grown negroes, a half-interest in another one, and an infant slave. The latter is still on the old home place with Mr. Duncan, and is getting quite gray. Before the war Mr. Duncan became the owner of ninety-three slaves and three thousand acres of land, all the result of his energy and good management, but during that memorable struggle he lost almost everything. He is yet the owner of twenty-three hundred acres of excellent land, and is not only one of the county's most successful and prominent planters, but is honored and esteemed as a citizen. He was first married while living in Alabama to Miss Mary H. Gamble, who was born and reared in that state. She died on the 21st of June, 1840, leaving two children: Benjamin G. and Mary, both of whom are deceased. The former served as a soldier in the Civil war, and was a member of Captain Stanford's battery, and was wounded at the battle of Murfreesboro. His death occurred on the 6th of April, 1880, in Grenada. The other child died in Alabama when young.

Mr. Duncan's second marriage was to Mrs. Susan Augusta (Girault) Sykes, widow of Dr. J. B. Sykes, whom she had married in 1847. Her parents, James A. and Susan (Dunbar) Girault, were early settlers of Mississippi. James A. Girault was born near Natchez, Miss., in 1793, and died at Jackson, Miss., March 24, 1851. His father, Col. John Girault, who was the son of John Girault, was born in the city of London, England, February 24, 1755, and died at the Bay of St. John, near the city of New Orleans, May 28, 1813. He was a colonel in the Revolutionary war under Gen. George Rodgers Clark; was in all the early campaigns against the Indians; was secretary for Governor Gayoso, and when the War of 1812 broke out his sword was again taken from its scabbard and not returned until Col. John Girault was one of the heroes of the battle of New Orleans. He was one of the bravest of the brave. He was married in 1788 to Miss Mary Spain, who was born in Virginia in 1766, and to them were born twelve children, James A. Girault being the fourth in order of birth. Col. John Girault's parents were Huguenots, and were obliged to flee from France on account of religious persecution. The Girault family settled the "Retreat plantation," near Natchez, some time after John Girault's marriage, for his eldest child was born there in 1789. James A. Girault was married on the 30th of November, 1825, to Miss Susan Dunbar, who was born on the 18th of February, 1810, and who died at the age of eighty-two years. She was a member of the Episcopal church for forty years, but later in life united with the Methodist church. She was a conscientious Christian and was loved by all. Three of their children are now living, Mrs. Duncan being the fourth child in order of birth. She was born at Bellevue, near Natchez, on the 19th of October, 1832, and was educated at Grenada. Following is a copy of a commission issued to James A. Girault by David Holmes, governor of Mississippi territory in 1814:

"DAVID HOLMES, GOVERNOR OF THE MISSISSIPPI TERRITORY,

To all who shall see these presents, greeting: Know ye that, reposing special trust and confidence in the integrity and abilities of James A. Girault, I do appoint him clerk of the supreme court of errors and appeals, and do authorize and empower him to execute and fulfill the duties of that office according to law; and to have and to hold the said office with all the powers, privileges and emoluments to the same of right appertaining, from the day of the date hereof, unless the governor of the territory aforesaid, for the time being, should think proper to revoke and determine this commission. In testimony whereof I have caused these letters to be patent, and the seal of the territory to be hereunto affixed. Given under my hand at the town of Washington the 7th day of December, in the year of our Lord, 1814, and the independence of the United States of America the thirty-ninth. (Signed.)   DAVID HOLMES."

James A. Girault came to Tallahatchie county, Miss., at an early date, settled at old Elliott, which was an Indian mission school at that time, and later moved to the place now owned by D. L. Holcomb, known as the Bellevue place. Mrs. Girault's father, who was known as Major Dunbar, died near Natchez, Miss. To Mr. and Mrs. Duncan were born nine children, five of whom are now living: Robert D., engaged in merchandising at Greenwood, Miss.; James M., resides at Vicksburg and is teller in the Delta bank; Annie E., married R. S. Turnage and lives in Memphis, Tenn.; Blanton C., is a merchant of Grenada, Miss.; and Katie A., who is single and a highly accomplished lady. Those deceased are: Mary, died in 1852; Nancy Ross, died in 1859; John G., died in 1866; and Susan H., who was the wife of Thomas P. Lampkin, died in 1883, leaving two beautiful young daughters, Helen and Elouise. Mrs. Duncan is a member of the Methodist church. Mr. Duncan is a democrat in politics and is the only one of the older members of the family who voted with that party, they being whigs.

Gen. John Anthony Quitman (deceased), ex-governor of Mississippi, was born September 1, 1799, at Rhinebeck, Dutchess county, N. Y., but in early manhood he removed to the southern part of the state of Mississippi and died on the banks of the great river that bears that name, where he had made his home for nearly forty years. So true was he to the people of his adopted state, and so revered was he by them, that none ever reproached him with his Northern birth, nor suspected his fidelity to the interests and institutions of the country where he had chosen to make his home and rear his children. Owing to his father's express desire, he began to study for the ministry, and under the able instructions of the former, Dr. Frederick Henry Quitman, he was thoroughly drilled in the languages. Dr. Quitman was a missionary from Prussia to Cuzacoxa, and later was called to the Lutheran church at Rhinebeck, in which his morning services were conducted in German, and the evening services in English. After some time Gen. John A. Quitman decided that the study of law had more charms for him than the life of a minister offered, and in his twentieth year became a graduate of the same. He was educated in that noted institution of learning, Hartwick college, New York, and afterward pursued the study of law in Philadelphia, Penn. He then started West to make his own way in the world, and as the facilities for traveling at that day were poor and his means were limited he walked across the Alleghany mountains in Pennsylvania and settled in Chillicothe, Ohio, where he practiced his profession for a short time. He then came to Mississippi and settled at Natchez, and here the former student of divinity became an able, talented and influential lawyer; an upright and eminent judge; an energetic and wealthy planter; a daring soldier and skillful general; an illustrious governor of his adopted state, and finally died an honored member of the United States congress. At the time of his settlement in Natchez (1822) the country was in an undeveloped condition, but here the energy of his character, his brilliant intellect and his indomitable push and enterprise soon made him a man of mark. "It was," said his successor in congress, "as a professional man and jurist that he made for himself his first and most enviable character. At the bar, always true to the honor of his profession, he was strictly faithful to his client and to the court; to his associate as well as opposing council, he was kind, courteous and obliging; toward all the members of the profession, pleasant and agreeable in all his relations; and such was his known sense of right and honor, that his advocacy of a cause gave it the merit of justice, which usually carried with it success." In 1827 he was elected to the State legislature; the following year was made chancellor, and presided in the court of equity for three years. In 1839 he was again invested with the ermine for a time, being elected judge of the high court of errors and appeals, and during this time made an enviable record for himself for sound judgment, fairness and legal knowledge. As a member of the state constitutional convention in 1833, he fully understood the requirements of his state, and as his mind was clear and concise, his style of speaking logical, ornate and convincing, he did valuable service while a member of that body.   In 1835 he was elected to the state senate, and being chosen its president became, by virtue of his office, the governor of the state of Mississippi, and so continued for some months.   In his message as governor in 1836 he advocated a liberal system of education for the people, as well as other notable and worthy measures, and as his reasons for his convictions were always clear and well defined, they carried due weight.   In 1836, when Texas was struggling to achieve her independence, he repaired thither to offer his services and although he saw but little fighting he had many thrilling adventures, which served as a good schooling for his subsequent illustrious military career.   Doing everything well that he undertook, he, in his early career, gave promise of the martial spirit and aptitude for military affairs for which he afterward became so distinguished.   Although prevented by circumstances from being with the column which fought the battle of San Jacinto (that ended the war), he rendered valuable aid to the cause of the Texans.   He returned to Mississippi and again addressed himself to the varied tasks of civil life, but in 1846 the war with Mexico came up and he immediately raised a company and started for the field of action.   He commanded this company as captain for a short time, then was appointed brigadier-general of volunteers and was afterward promoted to the rank of major-general, being in command of the Palmetto regiment.   He was first under Taylor and then under Scott, and in many memorable battles he shared the glories of those noted generals.   He was under one in the battle of Monterey and marched with the victorious eagles of the other from Vera Cruz to the city of Mexico, during which campaign he was in many daring exploits.   On the morning of September 13, 1847, his division assaulted the castle of Chapultepec.   Dashing across the plain they carried the batteries that they found on their route, forced their way up the side of the steep hill on which that ancient fortress stood, in the face of a destructive fire, and having gained the summit, united in a grand assault upon the castle.   It was carried and with it was secured the key to the city of Mexico.   In the afternoon of that day Gen. Quitman led his division in an attack on the Belen gate, which they carried at the point of the bayonet in the face of a most destructive fire, and his troops were the first within the city walls.   A red silk handkerchief was raised on his sword and was the first American flag to float in that city.   He received the surrender of the citadel and was appointed by Gen. Scott governor of the city.   For his distinguished services the congress of his country voted him a sword, and never was testimonial more richly merited by man.

At the close of this war General Quitman laid down his arms forever, and returned to Mississippi, where, as a mark of love and respect, he was elected in November, 1849, governor of the state, his majority being very large.   He was installed in office in January, 1850.   Five years later he was elected to the lower house of congress, where he was placed at the head of the committee on military affairs, and while discharging the duties of this position was called from life.   He had carried out the trusts laid upon his shoulders by the public with ability and fidelity, and he was ever found firm, inflexible and fearless in the performance of whatever he believed to be his duty, and to many of the great designs that were projected during his time he lent valuable aid.   He took a prominent part in many measures that promoted his country's welfare, and in the performance of his duty added new luster to his country's flag and vigorously maintained her honor.   He stamped his impress deeply upon the institutions of his state, was in every respect the poor man's friend, the defender of the oppressed, and it may with truth be said that he had not lived in vain.   In the year 1820, while a resident of Ohio, he was made a Mason, and after his removal to Natchez he joined Harmon lodge No. 1, being elected three years later grand marshal of the grand lodge, and in 1824, master of Harmony lodge, attaining to the degree of royal arch.   Assiduous in every department of

Masonry, he was a member of Natchez council No. 1., of the royal and select masters, and upon his return from Mexico in 1848 he received the Thirty-third degree of Masonry in Charleston, S. C. At the same time he became an inspector-general, he was made an honorary member of the grand lodge of South Carolina and the same honor was paid him by the grand lodge of New York. He wielded a widespread influence in everything to which he devoted his attention, and this influence was used for the good of his state, country, and for the different towns which had been named in his honor. In 1824 he was married to Miss Eliza Turner, a native of this county and a daughter of Henry Turner, who was born in Fairfax county, Va.; was an extensive planter and when quite young died on his estate. Mrs. Quitman was a most beautiful and accomplished lady, fitted to shine in any society, and to her belonged the distinction of being chosen as the partner of General La Fayette at a ball given in honor of the latter at Natchez, on the occasion of his visit to that place. To the General and Mrs. Quitman were born eleven children, three of whom are now living: Mrs. Duncan, Mrs. Lovell and Mrs. Ogden. Mrs. Lovell's husband, W. S. Lovell, was a naval officer and was a member of the expedition that went in search of Dr. Kane in the Arctic regions, afterward making another expedition to that region. Rosalie (Mrs. Duncan) lives on the old estate adjoining Natchez, was married in 1861 to W. P. Duncan, who was born in Pennsylvania and died in 1862. In 1825 General Quitman purchased the magnificent property near Natchez, and here erected a stately home. The park and grounds contain seventy-five acres, and bear many marks of his taste and habits. During his lifetime it was the resort of statesmen, scholars and all notable people who visited Natchez, and in this abode of refinement and good taste he dispensed hospitality with true Southern gallantry, and with the courtly manners of a gentleman of the old school. This fine old typical Southern mansion is still the home of Mrs. Duncan, his daughter. During the Civil war the Federal soldiers were quartered on the place and the officers were stationed in the house. In personal appearance the General was five feet ten inches in hight, his complexion was florid, his eyes a keen clear gray, and although rather slender, he was well knit and strong. In character he was generous, free and frank, and as he was keenly alive to the sufferings and misfortunes of others, no one ever appealed to him in vain for aid or consolation. He was always the friend and adviser of young men, and many men who are living at the present time owe their prosperity and start in life to his encouragement and the fatherly interest he took in their welfare. His mother was Elizabeth Hueck, daughter of the governor of the island of Cuzacoxa, and a native of Holland. She and her husband died in Rhinebeck, after having become the parents of seven children, of whom General Quitman was the fourth.

J. S. Duncan, whose postoffice address is Pontotoc, Miss., was born in Pontotoc county in 1840. He is a son of John F. Duncan, a native of Franklin county, Ala., who was born in 1812. He first married a Miss Brotherton, in 1830. To them were born four children. Sarah F. Cole, who married John F. Duncan, was born in Tuscola, Ala., in 1820, and was his second wife. They were married in Pontotoc county in 1836, and Mr. Duncan engaged in planting, and in the grocery trade at Bridgeport, Miss. He was a man of considerable political influence. He served Pontotoc county as a member of the board of supervisors, for four years, and was also state magistrate. As far back as 1850 he was elected to represent Itawamba county in the state legislature. Mr. and Mrs. Duncan had nine children, of whom three are yet living. In 1860 he married, for his third wife, Miss Carrie Souter, who bore him eight children, all of whom are living. He was a member of the Baptist church, and always a liberal contributor to churches, schools and all public institutions. He was successful, as a business man, during the period before and after the war. He died in 1880. J. S.

Duncan began life for himself in 1861, enlisting in the Confederate service under Capt. John H. Miller, as a private in the First Mississippi volunteers. He was present in engagements at Belmont, Shiloh and Corinth, and was with Van Dorn's command at the capture of Holly Springs, Miss., January, 1862. He was wounded at the battle of Powder Springs, and after his recovery was at the fight at Dallas, and in the engagements about Atlanta, and in another sharp fight at Brice's Crossroads. He was captured at Powder Springs, Ga., in 1863, and was taken to Camp Chase, Ohio. After his release he went to Richmond, Va., and reëngaged in active service. He took part in the battle of Selma, and in 1864 he returned home. He was married in 1866 to Miss K. S. Wells, who was born in South Carolina in 1852. Her father, J. S. Wells, was a prominent farmer. Mr. and Mrs. Duncan have three children: Vallie L., Effie T. and Edward F. Mr. Duncan has been election commissioner for Pontotoc county for eight years. He is the owner of about four hundred acres of land, about eighty acres of which are improved. He is a member of the Pontotoc lodge No. 81, A. F. & A. M., and he and his wife are members of the Baptist church. He is a progressive, enterprising planter, and man of business, and has done his full share toward the furthering of all objects tending to the public good.

Dr. Stephen Duncan (deceased) was a native of the Keystone state, born in Carlisle March 4, 1787, and was educated at Dickinson college, in his native city, from which he graduated in medicine in 1805. Three years later he came to Natchez, and practiced his profession there with marked success for a number of years. He subsequently became very extensively engaged in cotton planting, and was one of the largest planters in the South. He was one of the most successful and thorough business men in the Union, and from a small capital amassed a great fortune, being one of the leading capitalists of the South. He was president of the State bank at Natchez during the most prosperous days of Adams county, and was a man of strong and vigorous mind, rare sagacity, wonderful ability, great enterprise, and was noted for the interest he took in public afairs. He was not alone noted for his acumen as a business man. He was a litterateur of more than average attainments, and he arose to a prominent position in the first rank of physicians. He was twice married, first, to Miss Margaret Ellis, a descendant of one of the prominent pioneer families of Adams county, and after her death, or in 1819, he was married to Miss Catherine Bingaman, a very intelligent and refined lady, who was born at Natchez in February, 1801, and who died October 1, 1868. She was a sister of the lamented and distinguished Col. Adam L. Bingaman, who graduated with high honors in belles-lettres from Harvard college, and who became one of the wealthiest planters of Adams county. He was born in 1793, and died about 1867. His wife was a Miss Julia Murray, the daughter of a celebrated Unitarian clergyman of Boston. Colonel Bingaman was the acknowledged leader of the democratic party for many years, and was a member of the legislature with Hon. S. S. Prentiss, who was perhaps his only superior in the state as a debater and politician. Mr. Bingaman was a man of rare qualifications for a popular leader, being gifted by nature in mind and personal appearance (which was most dignified and commanding), with a polished education and fascinating manners; he was a natural orator. Dr. Duncan continued to reside at Natchez until 1863, when he removed to New York, and there his death occurred January 29, 1867.

The history of the medical profession of Yazoo county would be incomplete without a sketch of R. L. Dunn, M. D., of Yazoo city, Miss., who has been a leader among his brethren in the science for more than thirty years. In reviewing his life from the beginning, it is found that he was born in Adams county, Miss., October 7, 1835, and is the eldest of a family of nine children. His parents were David and Lavinia G. (Glassburn) Dunn, natives of Mis-

sissippi. The father was born in the year 1800, and was reared to the occupation of planting, which he followed all his life. He was a man of moderate means, and devoted his life
to his family and to the education of his children. He died in 1863, his wife surviving him
until 1881. She was sixty-three years old at the time of her death. The paternal grandfather of the Doctor was Richard L. Dunn, a native of Ireland, and one of the earliest settlers of Adams county, Miss. Dr. Dunn was educated at Centenary college, being graduated
in 1856. After leaving his literary studies, he began his professional work, and was graduated from the medical department of the University of Louisiana in 1859. He located at
the head of Honey island, in Holmes county, Miss., where he entered at once into practice.
His health failing him, he left that point, and came to Yazoo county. When there was a
call for the brave and fearless men to go out in defense of their country, he enlisted in 1861,
in the Eighteenth Mississippi regiment, of the Confederate army, but was not permitted to
go into the service, on account of his failing strength. Not to be defeated in his patriotic
impulse, he waited until 1862, and then applied to Capt. John M. Clark, who was raising a
company in Yazoo county at Yazoo city, and was accepted. The company was attached to
the Forty-sixth Mississippi regiment, and he was appointed assistant surgeon, which office he
filled until the close of the war. He was with Johnston on his retreat from Chattanooga to
Atlanta, and was also in the siege of Vicksburg. He started with Hood on his campaign
through Tennessee, but was left in charge of the wounded on the battlefield of Altoona, Ga.,
where he was still staying at the time of the surrender. In 1865 he returned to his home,
broken in health and fortune. But with the zeal and courage of the true Southerner, he
went to work, and to-day the ravages of war are no longer visible in his path. In March,
1866, he was united in marriage to Miss Stella W. Gibson, a daughter of Tobias Gibson, one
of the most favorably known citizens of Natchez, Miss. Mrs. Dunn is the mother of two
children: Stella, and Claude G., who is in school at Clarkville, Tenn. In November, of the
year he was married, Dr. Dunn resumed his medical practice in Yazoo city, where he has
done a large and successful business. He is a close student, a wide reader, and fully alive
to the demands of the times. He believes there is no excellence without great labor, and the
proficiency which he has attained is due to this conviction. In the midst of his busy life he
finds time to direct the cultivation of a large plantation, and also owns a handsome residence
in Yazoo city. He and his wife are members of the Methodist Episcopal church. He
belongs to Yazoo lodge No. 42, A. F. & A. M., and to Magnolia commandery No. 2, K. T.,
Vicksburg, Miss., being past high priest of Royal Arch chapter No. 8, of Yazoo city. In 1889
he was grand representative of his lodge to the grand lodge of Mississippi, and for many
years was worshipful master of his lodge. He is a member of the I. O. O. F., and has arisen
to the position of noble grand and chief patriarch of the encampment. He is past chancellor
of Yazoo city lodge No. 23, and is medical examiner of section 441, K. of P. He is past
dictator and medical examiner of Yazoo city lodge No. 1936, K. of H. He was a charter
member, and elected first chief officer of both the Knights of Pythias and the Knights of
Honor.

David J. Dunn, Yazoo city, Miss., was born September 22, 1844, in Yazoo county, Miss.,
where he has passed the greater portion of his life. He is a son of David Dunn, whose history appears in the sketch of Dr. R. L. Dunn. He received his education in his native
county, but his opportunities in this direction were cut short by the late Civil war, and he
abandoned the schoolroom for the battlefield. He enlisted in 1861 in company C, Forty-sixth
Mississippi volunteer infantry, tasting all the experiences of military life. He was in the
engagement at Vicksburg, where he was captured; he soon afterward rejoined his command

at Enterprise, Miss., and was in the retreat through Georgia. In 1863 he was paroled to the naval department of Mobile bay, and remained there until the surrender. He then returned to his home and engaged in agriculture. In 1866 he began his career as a hardware merchant, and has met with marked success. He carries a stock of $3,000, and does a good, profitable business. He owns a handsome residence in Yazoo city, and some other valuable real estate there. He was married in 1873 to Miss Anna Gibson, a daughter of L. Z. Gibson. Mrs. Dunn was born in Mississippi, as was also her father. Mr. Dunn and wife have had born to them three children: Richard L., David G. and Charles M. The parents are worthy members of the Methodist Episcopal church. Mr. Dunn has represented the people of Yazoo in the office of city treasurer, and as a member of the city council, where he has been a faithful servant. He is a member of the Masonic fraternity. He is a man of quiet and retiring manners, attends strictly to his own affairs, and is thoroughly unostentatious.

Dr. S. R. Dunn, one of the oldest practitioners of Greenville, Washington county, Miss., is a native of that county, his birth occurring near Greenville on the 24th of August, 1842. He first attended the school of J. Caughey, later other schools in the county, and in 1859 he entered Emery and Henry college, Virginia, where he remained until the outbreak of the war. In 1861 he returned home, enlisted in the Confederate army, Byrne's battery from Greenville, Miss., as a private. Byrne's battery after the battle of Shiloh having disbanded, he served in R. Cobb's Kentucky battery until September 1863, when he was transferred to the trans-Mississippi department and was appointed lieutenant of cavalry in Captain Broaddus company, Wright's regiment. He participated in the battles of Shiloh, Farmington, bombardment of Vicksburg, battle of Baton Rouge, Hartsville, Murfreesboro, Beach Grove and Jackson, Miss. He was captured at Greenville in November, 1863, taken to Camp Morton, Ind., thence to Camp Chase, Ohio, and from there to Fort Delaware where he was detained twelve months. He was then taken to James river, exchanged, and arrived at Richmond on the 10th of March, 1865. He was not again on duty. While at Fort Delaware he studied medicine under Maj. W. G. Owen, of Morgan's command, and after coming home in the fall of 1865 he went to Philadelphia, where he entered the Jefferson medical college, graduating on the 10th of March 1867. The same year he went to Memphis, Tenn., began practicing, and was there during the cholera and yellow fever plagues of that year. In December of the following year he returned to Greenville and has been in constant practice here since, having built up a patronage highly complimentary to his skill and ability as a physician. He is considered one of the best surgeons in the delta. His marriage to Miss Amanda Rucks, a native of Mississippi, occurred on the 9th of October, 1873, and the result of this union has been the birth of four children: Marion Rucks, Samuel R. (died in 1884 at the age of over four years), Harriet Theobald (died in 1884 at the age of one year), and Lucile. Mrs. Dunn was the daughter of Arthur and Mary Margaret Rucks and the granddaughter of Judge James Rucks, an early settler from Tennessee. Mrs. Rucks was a daughter of John K. Yeager, whose brothers were prominent men in the history of the state. Dr. Dunn is a member of the I. O. O. F. and his estimable wife holds membership in the Catholic church. He is a member of Greenville medical association, Washington county medical association, state medical association, of which he was vice president, and the tri-state medical association of Mississippi, Arkansas and Tennessee, of which he has been president. He is also a member of the American medical association and the American public health association of the United States and Canada. The Doctor is tall, measuring six feet three and three-quarters inches in hight, is well proportioned, and a fine-looking man. He was third in a family of fifteen children born to Dr. S. R. and Bettie Ann (McAlister) Dunn, but only two besides our subject now living: Thomas K., an attorney in Nevada county, Ark., and Sallie, wife of Mr. Pond of Meyersville. The parents were natives of Pennsylvania and Louisiana respectively. The mother was the daughter of Thomas McAlister, Sr., who resided at Water Proof, Tensas parish, La., and who was a brother of Mrs. Harriet B. Blanton, subsequently Mrs. Theobald. The paternal grandfather, Rev. Thomas K. Dunn, was a prominent physician of Philadelphia, where he resided for many years but later in life came to Mississippi and resided at Greenville with his son (father of Dr. S. R. Dunn, Jr.) until his death in 1853. He was a close student of medicine, and on his arrival here he continued to practice his profession, but at the same time did not neglect his ministerial duties. The maternal great-grandfather, Captain McAlister, was in the British army and was captured at the battle of Bunker hill by the colonial forces. After the war he located in Georgia. Dr. S. R. Dunn, Sr., graduated at Jefferson medical college about the same time with Prof. S. D. Gross and afterward went to Cincinnati, where he practiced in the hospitals during an epidemic of cholera. Some time after this he went to Kentucky, remained there a short time and then went by flatboat to the present site of Greenville, where he was induced to locate. He was thus perhaps the first physician in Washington county. He bought land that later became the site of old Greenville. In 1838 he was married to Miss Bettie Ann McAlister, who was of an extensive and prominent family. He remained in Washington county until his death in 1860, which was caused by a septic wound received while holding a post-mortem examination on a woman who had died from puerperal fever. He was partial to the Episcopal church. He was a member of the Masonic order, affiliated with the whig party, and had been a member of the state legislature. He also had the nomination for congress but made no effort for the office. He was a member of the levee commissioners and an active promoter of the first levees of this county. He was a member of the A. F. & A. M. Mrs. Dunn received her final summons in 1861, about a year after the death of her husband. She was a devoted member of the Episcopal church.

Dr. H. T. T. Dupree is a physician of much merit, and in the interests of humanity he is a diligent worker and faithful in the discharge of every duty. He was born in Virginia on the 11th of March, 1822, the seventh of nine children born to Henry and Rebecca (Francis, Dupree, the former a native of Greenville county and the latter of Southampton county, Va. The Duprees were French Huguenots, and came to the United States during the early settlement of the colonies. Henry Dupree was a soldier of the War of 1812, but in addition to being a planter by occupation, he was also engaged in railroad building and helped to build the first railroad in Virginia from Wilmington to Petersburg, and from Garysburg to Norfolk. He was an expert bridge builder, and whenever an important piece of work was to be done the contract was usually awarded him. He also erected the first ginhouse in Virginia and operated the first ginstand, purchasing all the cotton brought to his stand, at which he made a great deal of money. He died in West Tennessee in 1860. Dr. H. T. T. Dupree attended the common schools of Virginia, North Carolina and West Tennessee, up to the age of nineteen years, then began studying medicine with an elder brother, to which his father was very much opposed, afterward attending lectures in the Botanic Medical college of Memphis, Tenn., from which he graduated, the time spent in preparing for the practice of medicine occupying three years. The two succeeding years were spent in practicing, after which he entered the University of Louisville, Ky., where he took one course of lectures. Upon first coming to Mississippi he settled at Vernon in Madison county, but soon after removed to Raymond, where he remained continuously until the close of the war. Immediately succeeding the war he turned his attention to planting, after which he only practiced his profession occasionally. He also opened a mercantile establishment in Raymond, in 1866, which he successfully conducted until the 1st of January, 1878, at the same time operating his plantation, which comprised ten hundred and forty acres until 1877, when it was increased by four hundred and thirty acres. Three-fourths of his land is open, producing on an average, three hundred bales of cotton and four thousand bushels of corn yearly. He has a steam cottongin and sawmill for his own use, and is quite extensively engaged in raising horses and hogs. He began contracting for county convict labor in 1886, pays the costs and gets the use of the prisoner for his term of sentence and fines. He has one of the best improved places in the county, and has a beautiful residence and fine and substantial outbuildings. He was in the sixty days' service during the war, at the end of which time he returned home and volunteered in the militia. He was afterward released, from some unknown source, to go home and practice medicine in the absence of other physicians. He has taken no active part in politics since 1875. He was married in 1859 to Miss Lizzie Fairchild, a native of Hinds county, by whom he has two children: John and Emma. The mother of these children died in 1863, the Doctor's second marriage taking place the following year, Miss Maggie Herring, a native of Hinds county, becoming his wife, who died in 1878, after having borne him three children: Samuel F., Thomas H. and Willie; the last died in 1878. On the 8th of March, 1881, he was married to Miss P. C. Yellerly, of Madison county, but the two children which were borne to their union are deceased. Four members of the family are members of the Methodist Episcopal church. The Doctor is a member of the A. F. & A. M.

The father of Dr. William W. Durden, planter, Lexington, Miss., John A. Durden, was born in Warren county, Miss., about 1825, and his grandfather, Anthony Durden, was a native of Tennessee. The latter came to Mississippi at an early day, and although he started out a poor boy, he became quite wealthy as a merchant and planter. He was well educated, and became one of the prominent men of Warren county. His son, John A. Durden, was born in Warren county, and there grew to manhood, and was there married to Miss M. C. Selser, daughter of George Selser, a prominent planter of that county. Mr. Durden moved to Holmes county in 1855, engaged in planting in the western part of Holmes county, and there reared his family. He held many prominent positions of trust in the county. His death occurred in Lexington on the 24th of December, 1889. His wife was an active worker in her church, and was a woman of earnest, Christian character. Their family consisted of three sons and seven daughters, all of whom grew to mature years. Dr. William W. Durden, one of the above mentioned children, was born in Warren county, Miss., on the 28th of March, 1845, but was principally reared and educated in Holmes county. In 1862 he joined the Confederate army — Thirty-eight Mississippi infantry, company A—as a private, when but a lad of seventeen, and served until the close of the war. He was in the battle of Harrisburg, siege of Vicksburg, and was taken prisoner at the last-named place, but was shortly afterward paroled. He then joined Forrest's cavalry, and served with that until cessation of hostilities. He afterward returned to Lexington, studied medicine with Dr. Gadberry, and took his first course of lectures at the University of Philadelphia, in 1867 and 1868. He then took private instruction and completed his course the following year, graduating in the spring of 1869. Returning to Holmes county he practiced there for some time, and in 1872 took a course of lectures in the College of Physicians and Surgeons, New York city, graduating in that year. After this he was in active practice in Lexington for ten years, was very successful, but gave it up in 1882. He has been engaged in planting since 1874, and for ten years has been one of the largest planters of the county. He owns about fifteen thousand acres in LeFlore, Tallahatchie and Carroll counties, and has about three thousand four hundred acres under cultivation. He is one of the largest tax-payers in LeFlore county. He owns some real estate on Lookout mountain, and has a residence there. Dr. Durden is an active politician, has served as chairman of the democratic central committee, and has held local positions in the county. He was married at Sidon, LeFlore county, on the 22d of September, 1872, to Miss Sallie S. Robinson, daughter of Col. J. S. Robinson, formerly of Claiborne county, Miss. Colonel Robinson was a very prominent planter and was a great friend of Governor Humphreys. He died in 1879 and left a large estate. Mrs. Durden was an only daughter. She was born and reared in LeFlore county, and was a graduate of Nazareth academy, Kentucky. Dr. and Mrs. Durden are the parents of four living children: Adele, a graduate of Nazareth academy; Marie and Mamie attending school at that academy and Eula, a miss of six years. They lost their only son, Willie R., on the 1st of January, 1891, when four years of age. The Doctor and family are members of the Catholic church. Dr. Durden spends the summer months with his family at his residence on Lookout mountain.

R. W. Durfey, one of the leading liverymen in the city of Jackson, Miss., is a native of Washington county, of this state, where he was born in 1858, the fourth child born to R. W. and Eliza (Askew) Durfey, both of whom were born in the Old Dominion, and came to Mississippi when young, the former settling in Washington county, where he engaged in planting. In 1858 he moved to Yazoo county, and in 1862 became a resident of Madison county, where he resided until his death in 1878, his wife having previously passed from life in 1867. R. W. Durfey was reared in Yazoo and Madison counties, and upon first starting out to make his own way in the world he acted as clerk in a railroad office, after which he was on the road in different capacities, and finally became conductor on the Illinois Central railroad from 1875 to 1882. He then successfully conducted a livery stable at Canton until 1889, when he came to Jackson and erected his large stable, which is 50x220 feet, the largest in the state of Mississippi and fully stocked. It is finely equipped with carriages, buggies, etc., and his horses, of which he has about fifty, are kept in excellent condition, and are always ready for use. He has land to the amount of about one thousand acres, one plantation being in Hinds county and the other in Madison county, and on the former he raises large numbers of horses and mules annually, and also makes a specialty of raising Shetland ponies. His stable in Jackson is a fine brick structure, substantially erected, and is under the management of a man who is capable, intelligent and honorable, attributes which are essential to a good repu-tation as a business man. He is a stockholder in the Jackson bank, and socially is a member of the A. F. & A. M. and the K. of H. In 1877 Mr. Durfey was married to Miss Johnson, daughter of Captain Johnson, of Holmes county, and by her is the father of one son and four daughters: Lena, Nannie, Bettie, Minnie Bell and James Caldwell. Mr. Durfey and his wife are attendants and members of the Methodist Episcopal church.

Col. Samuel M. Dyer, a leading merchant of Benton, Miss., was born in Albemarle county, Va., in 1839, and is the fourth of a family of seven children born to Francis B. and Sallie (Gassaway) Dyer. The father was a native of Albemarle county, Va., and the mother came from Maryland. The paternal grandfather was an Englishman, who settled in Albe-marle county in his eighteenth year, and died on the place where he had settled in his eighty-fifth year. The father was an attorney at law, and stood high in his profession. He was also a Mason of high rank; he died in 1840, and the mother passed away at Richmond, Va., in 1883, in her eighty-third year. They were the parents of seven children, five of whom lived to maturity, but only two of whom survive: Celia A. is the wife of W. T. Staples, a commission merchant of Richmond, Va.; and Samuel M., the subject of this biographical sketch. Col. Dyer spent his early life in Virginia; he was educated at the Episcopal high school near Alexandria, Va., and at the age of fifteen years he began merchandising at Scottsville, Va., where he remained six years. From this point he went to Richmond, and in 1855 came to Benton, Yazoo county, Miss. He was first employed as a clerk, and occupied the same position until the breaking out of the war; he then enlisted in company D, Third Mississippi volunteer infantry, which company he raised, and of which he was elected captain by acclamation. He was in General Loring's division of the Army of Tennessee, and served through the entire war. He took part in the engagements at Vicksburg, Barker's creek, Jackson, and in all the battles around Atlanta, and the engagement at Peach Tree creek. He was with Johnston on his expedition from Dalton, Ga., and was under Hood. During a gallant charge at the battle of Franklin, Tenn., he was shot in the ankle, which necessitated the amputation of his right foot. He was taken prisoner and sent to Camp Chase, Ohio, where he was held until June 16, 1865. Upon the reorganization of the army in 1862 he was elected major of his regiment, and was promoted by degrees to the office of colonel. When peace was declared he returned to Yazoo county, and for four years immediately after the war he was sheriff; he was removed from office by Governor Ames. He then began the mercantile business in Benton, which he has carried on with such marked success since that time. He has a line of dry goods and plantation supplies, all of which are well selected. He owns about one thousand acres of land in different tracts, six hundred acres being under cultivation. He has always taken an active part in the politics of the county, and is frequently a delegate to political conventions. Colonel Dyer was married in 1866 to Miss Mary R. Grayson, a daughter of William S. and Latitia E. (Reed) Grayson. Mrs. Grayson's father, Thomas B. Reed, was United States senator from Mississippi. William J. Grayson, the father of Mr. Dyer, was a profound and scholarly man, and was the author of works theological and philosophical. Miss Mary R. Grayson was renowned for her beauty and her rare intellectual attainments, and was universally beloved. Colonel and Mrs. Dyer are the parents of three children: Mary wife of John E. Cooper, a hardware merchant of Greenville. Tex.; William Grayson and Latitia E., a student at college in Port Gibson. Our worthy subject and his wife are members of the Methodist Episcopal church. Colonel Dyer takes an active interest in church work, and is superintendent of the Sabbath-school. He has given generously to the support of public enterprises, and is a citizen highly esteemed for all his sterling traits of character.

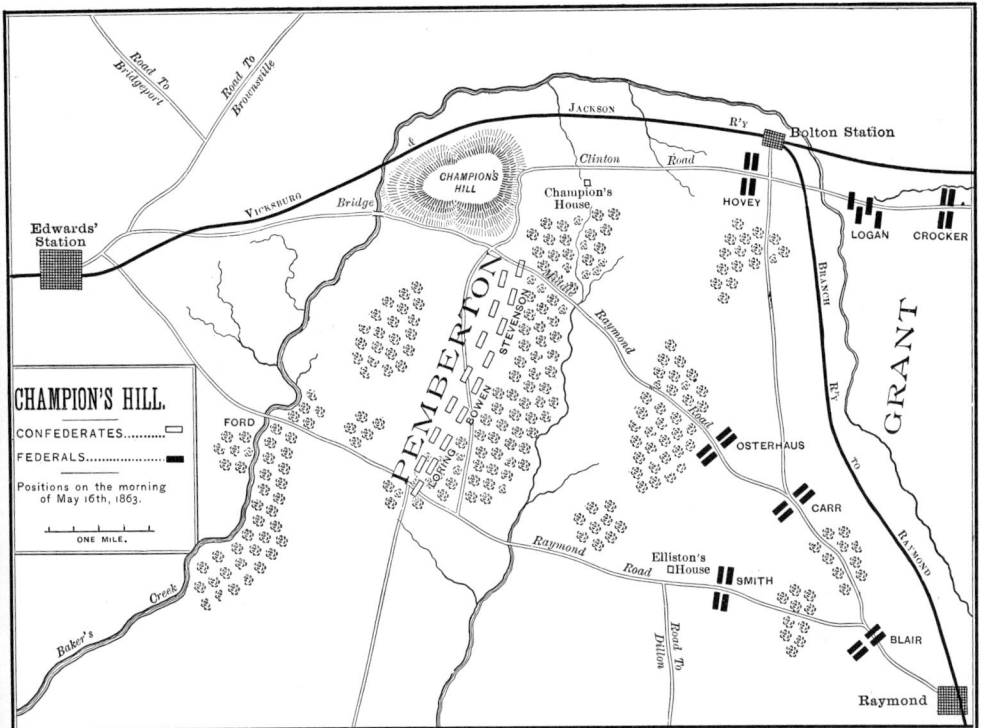

ROAD TO BRIDGEPORT
ROAD TO BROWNSVILLE
JACKSON
CLINTON Road
R'y — Bolton Station
CHAMPIONS HILL
Champion's House
HOVEY
LOGAN
CROCKER
VICKSBURG
Bridge
Edwards' Station

CHAMPION'S HILL.

CONFEDERATES..........□
FEDERALS......................■

Positions on the morning of May 16th, 1863.

ONE MILE.

FORD
PEMBERTON
STEVENSON
BOWEN
LORING
Raymond Road
GRANT
OSTERHAUS
CARR
Raymond Road
Elliston's House
SMITH
Dillon Road To
Baker's Creek
BLAIR
Raymond

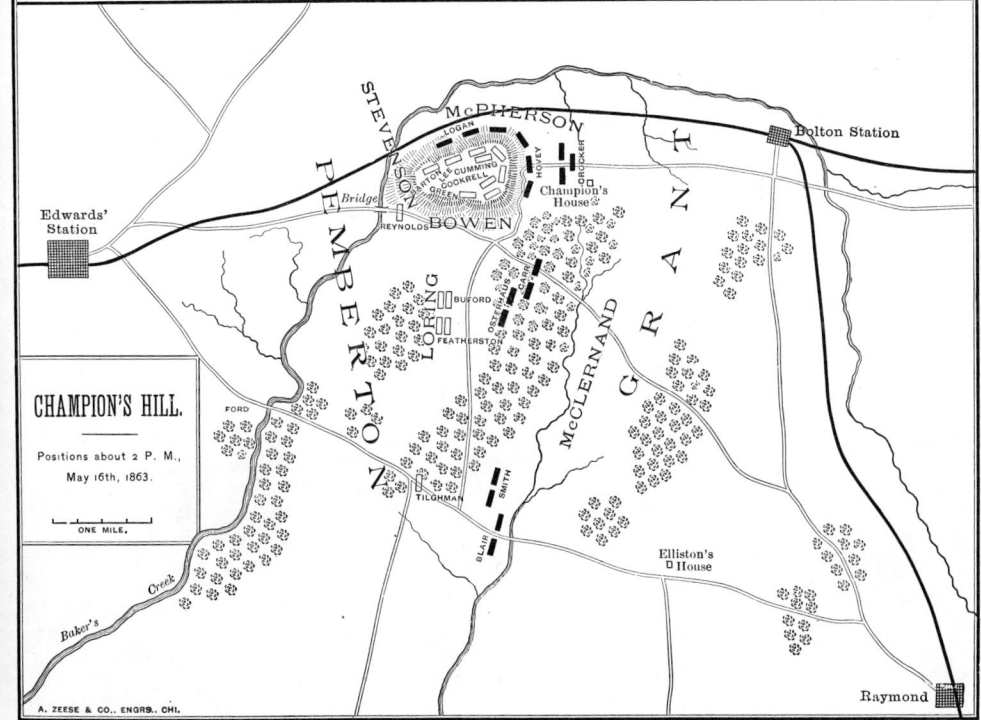

STEVENSON
McPHERSON
PEMBERTON
Logan
Bolton Station
BARTON & CUMMING
GREEN COCKRELL
Hovey
CROCKER
Bridge
Champion's House
Edwards' Station
Reynolds
BOWEN
GRANT
LORING
BUFORD
McCLERNAND
OSTERHAUS
FEATHERSTON

CHAMPION'S HILL.

Positions about 2 P. M., May 16th, 1863.

ONE MILE.

FORD
PEMBERTON
TILGHMAN
BLAIR SMITH
Baker's Creek
Elliston's House
Raymond

A. ZEESE & CO., ENGRS., CHI.

GHAPTER XVII.

PROMINENT FAMILIES, E.

ONE of the prominent men of Leake county, and among those who have resided in the county for the long period of nearly half a century, is Col. Joseph D. Eads, attorney, who first made a settlement at Carthage, this county, in 1843. Previous to this he had read law and had been admitted to the bar, in Indiana, in 1840. After locating here Colonel Eads began practicing his profession, and with marked success, until within the last few years, when he practically retired, although he still keeps his office. He has never taken an active part in politics, but he has, however, held several local offices of trust and honor, and is the present mayor of Carthage. He is a prominent member of the Masonic order, and is master of Pearl river lodge No. 105, having served in that capacity for a number of years. He is also a member of the chapter and council, and has served as high priest of the former. He has represented his lodge in the grand lodge of the state a number of times. Colonel Eads was married in Leake county, in 1846, to Miss Callie Harper, daughter of Logan Harper, one of the early settlers of this county. Mrs. Eads was born in Tennessee, but was reared in Leake county, Miss. One child has been born to this union, Callie, who is the wife of W. H. Colbert, one of the wealthy merchants of Mississippi, now residing at Utica, Hinds county. In 1850 Colonel Eads was married to his second wife, Miss Margaret J., daughter of James Treadwell. Mrs. Eads was born in Walton county, Ga., but was reared in Calhoun county, Ala. Her death occurred in 1889. She was a most estimable lady, a true and faithful wife for nearly forty years, and died as she had lived, respected and esteemed by everyone. There were three children born to this union: Josie, wife of S. D. McGaughy, a merchant of Whitewright, Grayson county, Tex.; Ellen, wife of F. M. Triplett, a merchant of Canton, Miss., and Maggie, wife of O. A. Luckett, a prominent lawyer of Carthage. Colonel Eads is a native of West Virginia, born in Monroe county on the 23d of March, 1817, and at this writing is in his seventy-fifth year, a hale, hearty, active man. His father, William L. Eads, was also a native of Virginia, where he married Miss Elizabeth Douglass, mother of subject. The father followed farming in his native state, reared his family there, and there received his final summons, dying full of years and honors in 1871, at the age of ninety years. He was an active and prominent member of the Methodist church. The Colonel's paternal grandfather, Samuel Eads, was born on the eastern shore of Maryland, February 22, 1732, but was of English parentage. He and the maternal grandfather, Henry Douglass, served in the Revolutionary war. Colonel Eads has been a member of the Methodist church since about the age of twenty-one, and has always been active in church work. He is strictly temperate in his habits and attributes his good health principally to that. He never drinks

43

liquor of any kind and is even prejudiced against tea and coffee. He is a powerfully built man, and although his hair and beard, which are quite white, give him a venerable appearance, he is still strong and vigorous.

Thomas W. East, merchant, miller and farmer, is the senior member of the firm of Thomas W. East & Sons of Red Star, Miss., and resides nine miles northwest of Brookhaven, Miss. He was born in Lincoln county (then Copiah county) April 13, 1834, a son of Joel and Catherine (Lofton) East. His father was a native of Kentucky and son of Talton East, a native of South Carolina, and his wife, who was Miss Zilpha Walker. His mother was born in Mississippi and they were married in Franklin county in 1833. Talton East emigrated from Kentucky, by way of the Mississippi river, to Natchez, and thence to six miles north of Clinton, La., in the spring of 1809. Joel East was the sixth in a family of seven children, and his wife was the sixth in a family of eight children. The latter is deceased, and her remains lie in Friendship cemetery in Lincoln county. After her death, Mr. East married Mrs. Zilla Pitman, who is also dead. Although a prominent planter of Copiah county, he lived on what is known as the Jackson and Liberty road, seventeen and one-half miles south of Gallatin, where for many years prior to his death he kept a public house for the entertainment of horse and mule drivers from Kentucky and Tennessee, en route to and from different portions of Louisiana, and the general through travel to the capital and various sections of the North and South before the construction of the South Carolina railroad. The subject of our sketch received his education in the common schools near his home, and was the eldest in a family of thirteen children. In 1856 he married Miss Kizziah East, who was born in Copiah county, Miss., in August, 1833, the sixth in the family of seven children of Isaac and Margaret (Smith) East. Mr. and Mrs. Thomas W. East have had four children born to them. Marion B. died in infancy, and is buried on the home place. William T. was born May 23, 1866, and is a partner in the firm of Thomas W. East & Sons, and postmaster at Red Star. In politics he is a democrat, having cast his first presidential vote for President Cleveland. He was married April, 1890, to Miss Jessie M. King, who was born in 1873. James W. was born October 4, 1867, and is a member of the firm above mentioned, and holds the office of assistant postmaster. He is a democrat and also cast his first presidential vote for Cleveland. Albert E. died at the age of eleven years, and is buried in the home burying-ground. The subject of our sketch was a whig from the age of twenty-one to the presidential election of 1856, and as the Whig party put forward no candidate at that time, he voted for Millard Fillmore. At the election of 1860 he voted for Bell and Everett. He voted against secession in 1861. In 1876 he cast his vote for Samuel J. Tilden, and in 1884 for Grover Cleveland and again for Cleveland in 1888. He was strongly opposed to the secession of the states, but when he saw that war was inevitable, he naturally decided to cast his lot with his neighbors, friends and relatives of the South. He volunteered in the Confederate army in 1862. He was first stationed at Camp Moore, and went thence to Port Gibson, where he remained about two months, going from there to Port Hudson, where he was taken sick and removed to a hospital at Clinton, La. There he remained until October 12, 1862, when he was discharged and came home. In February, 1863, he was elected to fill the unexpired term of W. D. Brown, who had died, as justice of the peace. In the following November he was elected to the same office for a full term. He did not reënlist in the Confederate army, but served the Southern cause as a traveling agent for the hospital at Brookhaven, gathering supplies for the sick and wounded soldiers, at the same time acting as assistant agent for caring for the soldiers' widows and children in Copiah county. After the war he resumed planting, and in 1871, built a watermill with the operation of which he combined the business of corn production and cotton-ginning, and since that time has done an extensive business in the last named department (cotton-ginning). On account of the scarcity of water in 1885, he replaced his waterpower by steampower, which has enabled him greatly to increase his ginning capacity. He began merchandising in 1884 and has met with continued success. Red Star was then known as East's mills precinct. The postoffice was established in 1888 under its present name, with William T. East as postmaster, and his brother James was assistant postmaster. Mrs. East died October 7, 1887, and was buried on the home place. She had long been a devout Methodist, to which church her husband also belongs. Mr. East and his sons are strong prohibitionists and fired the first cannon that opened the local option campaign in Lincoln county, in 1886. He is a man of great public spirit, and has the welfare of his town, county and state at heart. His support of churches, schools, and charitable and beneficial interests generally has been liberal in the extreme. His business qualifications are of the highest order, and he is recognized as one of the leading merchants and business men of this part of the state, and it may be said that his sons inherit in a marked degree his talent for commercial management. Though in no ordinary sense of the term a politician, he takes a deep interest in, and is exceedingly well informed upon, all questions of public moment, and his influence is felt none the less because it is exerted quietly, nor is it the less beneficial because he is a helpful, earnest citizen, and not a professional place hunter.

The man who is the subject of this sketch, Col. Hiram Eastland, was born in Lincoln county, Tenn., in 1829, and moved to Hinds county, Miss., in 1836 with his parents, where he remained one year. In 1837 he located in Hillsboro, where he grew to maturity. Colonel Eastland's father, Capt. Alfred Eastland, was a native of Spartanburg, S. C., and was born in 1806. He removed to Madison county, Ala., where he married Miss Eliza Petty. About 1828, he located in Middle Tennessee, from there removed to Scott county, Miss., and died in Waco, Tex., where he was visiting a son in the year 1870. Col. Hiram Eastland was married in Scott county, to Miss Bettie Smith, a daughter of John J. Smith, who was a native of North Carolina, and one of Scott county's pioneer settlers, being one of the very first to clear out a place for a home in the wilderness, and becoming one of its prominent men. He took a keen interest in the general welfare of the county. He was the first sheriff of Scott county, and took an active part in the removal of the Indians from that part of the state of Mississippi. After the close of the war, the Colonel removed his business from Hillsboro, Scott county, to Forest of the same county, and engaged in the mercantile business in partnership with M. D. Graham, and he has been very successful in his venture up to the present time. He and his family are members of the Missionary Baptist church. His family consists of six living children—three boys and three girls. One son is in business at Meridian, Miss., and the other two sons are in Forest, the one a druggist and the other a practicing physician. Socially, Colonel Eastland is a Mason of long standing. He is also a member of the Knights of Honor. He is a man who ranks high in his county and there are none to whom more honor is due.

Mrs. Lucy M. Eaton, widow of the late James A. Eaton, whose residence is at Eatonville, Perry county, Miss., was born at Monticello, Lawrence county, Miss., January 1, 1853. James A. Eaton was born in South Carolina October 3, 1832, and died at his home in Mississippi October 12, 1888. He came with his parents to Mississippi when quite young, and his early life was devoted to planting. At the age of about thirty-five years he began merchandising at Monroe, Perry county, Miss. He afterward located at what is now known as Eatonville, and in his honor the town took its name. He was married January 11, 1852, to Susan Hathorn, who bore him four children: Eliza A. (deceased), Susan F. (deceased), James A.

(deceased) and Samuel C. Mrs. Eaton died November 19, 1860, and March 28, 1867, Mr. Eaton married Fannie H. Barnes, who bore him five children: Van B., Maggie S., William E. (deceased), Walter S. and Robert E. Lee. Mr. Eaton's second wife died June 30, 1875. May 23, 1877, he married Miss Lucy N. Gouvenaux, the subject of this sketch, who is the daughter of Charles and Margaret F. (Collins) Gouvenaux. Her father, who was a native of France, came many years ago to New Orleans, La., and afterward located near Monticello, Miss., in Lawrence county, where he became a newspaper publisher and resided till his death. He was a soldier in the Mexican war, and served with great bravery and distinction with a rank as first lieutenant. He was the father of two children: Annie C. (deceased) and the lady whose name appears above. After his death his widow married John Hutchins, by whom she had four children: George W. (deceased), John J., Jessie B. and Maggie (deceased). Mr. and Mrs. Eaton had three children: Mary G., Annie G. and an infant who died unnamed. Mr. Eaton was a member of the Masonic order, and a communicant of the Baptist church. He was an energetic business man, and his social qualities were such as to endear him to all who knew him. He was honest, industrious and liberal-minded and a public-spirited man, and did his full share in the development and improvement of his town and county.

Col. William H. Edmonson was born in Mecklenburg county, Va., in 1817, the eldest son of a family of five children raised by Richard H. and Angelina (Ogburn) Edmonson. His father was a native of Virginia, dying in that state in 1828. He was a farmer, and the names of his children were William H., Charles, James, Edwin and Angelina. Mr. Edmonson's mother was a daughter of Rev. Charles Ogburn, for fifty years a clergyman, and she claimed Virginia as her native state. His brothers, Charles and James, were merchants in Virginia, and Edwin was killed during the war. After the death of her first husband Mrs. Edmonson married a Mr. Simmons, and died in 1873. The early life of our subject was passed in Virginia, and he came to Mississippi in 1837, settling at De Kalb, Miss., and in April, 1838, came to Jasper county. There he was a merchant and hotel-keeper, and was married in 1840 to Malinda Street, a daughter of Solomon Street, who bore him a large family of children, of whom they reared eight sons and two daughters: James, Charles, Edwin, Solomon, Samuel O., Richard T., William H., Foot L., Angelina, Ora, all of whom are dead except four of the sons: Samuel O., who is proprietor of the Gaston house, of Enterprise; Foot L., who is a liveryman in the same town; Richard T. and William H., who are living in Texas. Colonel Edmonson came to this county in 1859, locating in Enterprise. He held the office of sheriff in Jasper county, was mayor of Paulding, was for many years justice of the peace, and for six years was county sheriff. In connection with his other enterprises he ran a blacksmith shop and a stage route. Since coming to Clarke county, where he is a well-known hotel-keeper and merchant, he has held a number of offices, having been mayor of Enterprise, one of the justices of peace, and one of the county supervisors, president of the board. He was in service in the late war, ranking as major at the camp of instruction at Enterprise. He lost three sons in the late war, named James H., Edwin and Charles. Before the war he was a whig, but since that time he has been identified with the democratic party. He has been connected with business and public interests in this section since his settlement, and is numbered among the pioneers of this part of the state. Although in his seventy-fifth year, he is one of the county board of supervisors now. He is a royal arch Mason, and has been a member of the Methodist Episcopal church for forty-five years.

One of the most reliable planters and merchants of Kemper county is E. Edwards, of Kellis' Store, Miss., a short biographical sketch of whom will follow. He was born in Greene county, Ala., in 1826, and is a son of Isaac and Ludia (Nail) Edwards. His father was born in Virginia, but spent his early life in South Carolina; thence he removed to Greene county, Ala., and there married and reared a family of three children: Madison, Julia A., and E., the subject of this notice. Isaac Edwards was twice married, the second union being to Lydia Nail. She died in 1881 at the advanced age of eighty-nine years. Her native state was Georgia. The father of our subject was born in 1790, and he lived until 1845; he died in Mississippi, to which state he had removed two years before his death. He was a Mason, a member of the Baptist church and a whig in his politics. He was a good business man and accumulated some property. E. Edwards received his education in the common schools, and in 1849, when he was twenty-three years of age, he engaged in farming on his own account. The same year he was united in marriage to Miss Jane Neely, a daughter of David and Mary Neely, of Kemper county, Miss. Eight children were born of this union: James M., Thomas C., Robert L., Mary E., Alice, Augusta, Willie and Maud. The mother died in October, 1879; she was a native of Mississippi, born in 1832; she belonged to the Baptist church, in which she was an earnest worker. Mr. Edwards was married again December 15, 1886, to Miss Avie Beasley, a daughter of William and Addie (Lumpkin) Beasley. Mr. and Mrs. Edwards are members of the Baptist church. He is an ardent democrat, and belongs both to the Blue lodge and the chapter of the Masonic order. As a planter he has been very successful, and now owns fifteen hundred acres of land. He has a large saw, grist and cotton mill which he manages most efficiently. In addition to these industries, he oversees a large store at Kellis' Store, where he transacts a profitable business. Having been a resident of Kemper county since 1849, he has witnessed a wonderful change and a gratifying growth in every direction. He has been a potent factor in all developments and has lent both his aid and influence to all enterprises calculated to be of benefit to the public. Mr. Edwards' family are scattered and are living in various places. Mary E., married George Hanes, and resides in Meridian; Alice married Jesse Gully, and lives at Fearn's Springs; Augusta is Mrs. Guy Jack, and is a resident of Scooba, Miss.; Willie married C. B. Dorroh; Maud is at home; James M. and Thomas C. are married; Robert L. is single.

J. M. Edwards, merchant and farmer, Shuqualak, Miss., who is related to some of the best old families of Mississippi, is a man whose enterprise, energy and business sagacity place him among the state's most progressive citizens, destined to be long felt as a factor in all that constitutes the solid development of her grand possibilities. He was born near De Kalb, Kemper county, Miss., in 1850, and was the son of Elisha and Ann Jane (Neeley) Edwards, the former born in Alabama, in 1826, and the latter in Clarke county, Miss., in 1829. Mrs. Edwards died in 1879, but her husband yet survives. J. M. Edwards became familiar with the duties of the farm at an early age, and received his primary education in the common schools. He subsequently attended the Summerville school, taught by Gathright, a distinguished educator, who came there first in the sixties, and later graduated from Eastman's commercial college at Poughkeepsie. After this he embarked in business on his own account, and in 1872 the firm of Edwards, Nethery & Co. was established at Shuqualak, Noxubee county. After three years the firm was dissolved, and he continued the business alone until 1886, when he associated with himself his brother, T. C. Edwards, who withdrew from the firm in 1888. For three years after this Mr. Edwards continued an undivided business, and then admitted a brother, R. L. Edwards, and C. B. Dorroh, a brother-in-law, to the firm, which now does an extensive general merchandising business. Mr. Edwards embarked in the stock business in 1883. He is identified with the substantial development of his county, owning some of the finest pure-blood Devon cattle in the South, besides many Devon and Jersey grades. On the famous Ballard place, five miles east of Shuqualak, may be seen scores of horses and mules, which, together with the adaptation of this magnificent property indicate the future promise of the great South as a stock country. Through this splendid plantation flows the beautiful Noxubee river. Six miles of wire fence, and as many miles of river environ it. This elegant property, as the record shows, was sold since the Civil war for the handsome sum of $40,000. Mr. Edwards also owns and controls four thousand additional acres, or a total of seven thousand five hundred acres of the average land in Noxubee county. His annual production of cotton is about two hundred and fifty bales. Mr. Edwards was married in 1881 to Miss Mamie C. Beasley, of Noxubee county, and they have had four children: Mary Alice, Bessie Bland, Henry Beasley and Annie Ethel. The three eldest survive. Socially Mr. Edwards is one of the most affable, easy and agreeable gentlemen one could wish to meet. Being truly companionable, he is not a character to be easily forgotten.

A successful physician of Oktibbeha county and a planter of considerable experience is Dr. J. W. Edwards, of Sturges, Miss., who owes his nativity to Choctaw county, Miss., where his birth occurred in 1845. His parents, James H. and Parthenia (Crawford) Edwards, were natives of Alabama, the former born in 1820 and the latter in 1824. The elder Edwards was reared on the farm, received a limited education, and when old enough to choose his occupation in life, very naturally selected that with which he was the most familiar. He removed to Mississippi when about twenty years of age and was married in Winston county in 1842 to Miss Crawford. He and wife then moved to Choctaw county, resided there until 1871, and then came to Oktibbeha county, where his death occurred in January, 1885. His widow is still living and resides in Sturges. Of the six children born to this union two, Catherine and Peter, died in infancy. The others are as follows: Elizabeth (wife of Dr. William J. Barron; see sketch), Nancy (deceased), James W. (subject), and Mary Jane (wife of Dr. William Edwards, of Sturges). James H. Edward was a prominent man in his county, was a delegate to the convention when the state seceded, and afterward represented the county in the legislature (1862-3). During the war he served in the state militia. He was a member of the Masonic fraternity. Dr. J. W. Edwards passed his boyhood and youth in Choctaw county and had good educational advantages up to the breaking out of the war. In May, 1861, he entered the Confederate army, company I, Fifteenth Mississippi regiment infantry, known as Choctaw guards, as a private and served until the close of the war. He was in the battle of Fishing creek, Ky., where he was shot through the hip and disabled for about two months, and then joined his regiment just in time for the desperate battle of Shiloh. He was in the battles of Baton Rouge, Port Hudson, Baker's creek, siege of Jackson, and through the Georgia campaign to Atlanta, where he was captured on the 3d of August, 1864. He was taken to Camp Chase, Ohio, retained there eight months and then taken to Richmond, where he was exchanged. He was then given a sixty days' furlough and by the time that expired the war had closed. After this he began the study of medicine under Dr. William J. Barron and entered the University of Louisiana (now Tulane university), from which he graduated in 1871. He began practicing in Oktibbeha county at Whitefield, now Sturges, and in connection with his practice is now engaged in farming. He is the owner of about eighteen hundred acres in this, Choctaw, Winston and Holmes counties, and cultivates about two hundred acres of this. He is also engaged in raising horses and mules. Miss Lizzie Edwards, who became his wife in 1868, was born in Alabama, the daughter of Dr. William Edwards.

Her death occurred about a year after her marriage. In 1882 Dr. Edwards married Miss Jennie Shropshire, a native of Alabama, born in 1856, and the daughter of Felix and Amanda Shropshire, both natives also of that state. Mr. Shropshire moved to Mississippi in 1865. Dr. Edwards' marriage was blessed by the birth of three children—two sons and a daughter: Melborne (born September, 1883), James Felix (born July, 1886) and Leland Lewis (the daughter, born January, 1889). Dr. Edwards entered upon a political career in 1870, was nominated for the legislature in 1887, and in 1890 he was elected to the constitutional convention. He is a member of Whitefield lodge No. 365, A. F. & A. M., and is a chapter member at Starkville. He is also a member of the Knights and Ladies of Honor at Sturges.

Thedore A. Eggleston is a native of Lowndes county, where he is now residing, his birth occurring here on June 29, 1841, a son of Edward C. Eggleston, who was born in Hanover county, Va. The father came to Mississippi in 1837, and became a wealthy planter and merchant of Lowndes county. He was of a kind and generous disposition, was a man of more than ordinary intelligence, and for eleven years he was the efficient and trustworthy sheriff of this county, serving from 1857 until the opening of the war, and from the close of hostilities until his death, January 5, 1873. In connection with planting and merchandising he successfully conducted a hotel and livery stable in Columbus, following these callings for about five years. His first purchase of land was eighty acres, about five miles from Columbus, but he in time became the owner of eight thousand acres. He was married to Miss Matilda B. Lea, who died in the year 1863, and by her became the father of seven children: John W., Martha J., Sarah, Lemuel R., Theodore, Thomas L. and Leon M. Theodore A. was attending Wesley university, at Florence, Ala., at the opening of the war, but in the early part of 1861 he enlisted in the Florence guards of the Seventh Alabama, in which regiment he served for twelve months, when he was discharged, and enlisted in the Second Forest guards, taking part in the engagements at Harrisburg, Prairie Mound, Athens, Franklin and Nashville. His regiment was disbanded at Nashville, after which he returned to Columbus, where he has ever since resided, with the exception of 1882, when he was in Abeline, in the hotel business. At the end of this time, upon becoming a resident of Columbus, he was chief of police for four years, in which capacity he served with credit to himself and to the satisfaction of all concerned. He was married, April 22, 1862, to Miss Sarah M. Peoples, a daughter of James and Amanda (Bailey) Dudley. To Mr. Eggleston and wife the following children have been born: Mary J. (deceased), Lillian (deceased), Theodore, Godwin (deceased), Sarah M., William (deceased) and Bishop (deceased). Mr. Eggleston is the owner of a good plantation comprising three hundred and twenty-four acres, and is a worthy and upright citizen. He is a member of the Methodist Episcopal church, the A. F. & A. M. and the democrat party. His brother, Thomas L., was born in this county May 29, 1847, and was here given the advantages of the common schools. During the war, as he was too young to enter the army, he conducted his father's business, and is now the owner of one hundred acres of land. He was married, February 12, 1873, to Miss Peoples, by whom he became the father of five children: Ernest and Claude, deceased, and Daisy, Maud and Thomas E., living.

The parents of George W. Elliott, planter, Gunnison, Miss., Joseph Warner and Mary E. (Bennett) Elliott, were natives of the Empire state, and came to Mississippi about 1830, settling on Concordia island, where Mr. Elliott cleared a very handsome place. This is now nearly all washed away. He was an active politician, was one of the early probate judges of the county, and also held the position of justice of the peace for many years. He had quite a fair complexion, was over six feet in hight, and was finely proportioned. His wife died in

1879, and he followed her to the grave in 1880. George W. Elliott was born on his father's plantation on Concordia island April 26, 1842, and was the youngest of a family of seven children. He grew to manhood there, and remained under the parental roof until the breaking out of the war, when he enlisted in the Confederate army, company E, Twenty-eighth Mississippi cavalry, under Captain Mason. He was in all the engagements around Vicksburg, was also in Tennessee, and participated in the battle of Franklin as well as numerous skirmishes. He was with a company in Bolivar county at the time of the surrender. After the war Mr. Elliott engaged in farming for himself on Concordia island, and in 1871 came to his present property, one and a half miles from the village of Gunnison, and there cleared a tract of eighty acres. He has a pleasant little home, and everything is kept in the best of order. He also owns one hundred and twenty acres on Bogue Phalia, which he is now engaged in clearing, and another tract of eighty acres near Marigold, half improved. He has business stands on his place and on the Bogue. Mr. Elliott has been twice married, first to Miss Ann Arnold, daughter of William Arnold, who was one of the old settlers of Claiborne county. She died in 1875, leaving two children, both of whom have since died. His second marriage was to Miss Mary E. McGehee, daughter of James McGehee, a native of Tennessee. She came to Mississippi with other members of her family in 1872, and four years later was married to Mr. Elliott. Four children have been born to this union, only one now living, Charles A. Mrs. Elliott is a member of the Methodist church.

James Wesley Elliott, of the firm of Williams & Elliott, of Magnolia, was a Mississippian by nativity, and was born in Pike county, July 17, 1854. The Elliott family was among the earliest settlers of that county, where they removed from South Carolina in 1812. Wiley Elliott, the father of our subject, was born in Pike county, February 20, 1819, and married Miss Eleanor C. Barr, a native of Lawrence county, Miss., who was born April 13, 1822. Mr. Elliott served in the Confederate cause during the war as a member of the Third regiment of Mississippi volunteers. Mrs. Elliott died August 5, 1879, having borne her husband six sons and six daughters, of whom James W. Elliott is the sixth in order of birth. He attended the district schools of his neighborhood, and afterward entered the business department of the Soule's college at New Orleans, from which institution he graduated after completing the course. In the spring of 1886 he became associated in business with his brother-in-law, Mr. S. B. Williams, a sketch of whom appears elsewhere. Prior to that time he had been in the employ of Mr. Williams as a clerk. He is a charter member of the Jefferson Davis lodge No. 68, Knights of Pythias at Magnolia, and is a Master Mason. Mr. Elliott is an active, thorough-going business man, interested in all public movements for the advancement and improvement of his town, and although he is comparatively young, his success has been such as to mark him as a man of more than ordinary ability.

One of the rising young professional men of Yazoo county is John W. Elliott, physician and surgeon, Lake City, Miss. He was born in Leake county, Miss., October 26, 1861, and is the seventh of a family of eight children. His parents are Dr. J. C. and Sarah (Crosby) Elliott. Dr. Elliott, Sr., removed to Mississippi from Tennessee in 1849, and began the practice of medicine, which he has continued ever since. He is one of the oldest practitioners in the county, and has a wide patronage. Dr. John W. Elliott grew to manhood in Mississippi. He was a student in both the public and private schools, and when he had finished his literary education, at the age of nineteen years, he entered the medical department of the University of Louisville, Ky. He was graduated from this institution in 1883, and returned to his home, where he has since been practicing. In addition to his professional duties, he finds time to superintend the cultivation of one hundred and twenty-five acres of land. His plantation consists of two hundred and eighty acres. In 1890 he was united in marriage to Miss Maggie Wise, a native of Mississippi. He is a member of the Knights of Pythias, taking great interest in the organization. In his politics he is democratic, always a stanch supporter of its principles. He is public-spirited, generous in his giving, and a man of whom any community might well be proud. He is a success in his profession, and with the strength, ambition and ability with which he is possessed is sure to make his way to the very front.

Dr. Robert Elliott is a wideawake and progressive citizen, and is thoroughly posted and up with the times. He was born in the county in which he is now residing, in the month of January, 1858, the eldest son of R. T. Elliott, the latter's father having at one time been surveyor and chancery clerk of Hinds county. The Doctor's father was a native of Mississippi, but his ancestors were from Loudoun county, Va. He was a planter. His mother's maiden name was Ritchie. The Doctor spent about two years in the Sisters' school of Vicksburg, from which place he entered college at Cape Girardeau, Mo., where he remained for about five years. He did not finish his course there, but returned home and began working on the home plantation with his father, to whom he rendered valuable assistance in many ways for about four years. In 1880 he went to New York city and entered Bellevue medical college, from which institution he graduated. Immediately upon his arrival home he opened an office in Edwards and entered upon the practice of his profession, but as he did not particularly care for his calling he, at the end of four months, chose the more independent and less laborious occupation of a planter. He is the owner of five hundred acres of land, which he is personally superintending, and under his able management this land produces two hundred bales of cotton each year and a sufficient amount of corn and hay for home use. The Doctor is decidedly progressive in his views and is thoroughly imbued with the spirit of progress. He has traveled extensively in the North and East, visiting all the prominent resorts and cities of those sections, and being interested in the education of the rising generation, he very much regrets that more of the sons and daughters of the South are not educated for teachers, instead of importing educators from the North. The Doctor was married in 1886 to Miss Minnie Dromgoole, of Hinds county, Miss., and to their union two children have been born—L-Mar and an infant. Mrs. Elliott is an earnest and worthy member of the Methodist Episcopal church.

The cashier of the Merchants & Planters' bank of Hazlehurst, Isaac Newton Ellis, was born in Copiah county, Miss., in 1849, a son of Hon. Latt Warren and Anna (Roberts) Ellis. His father was born in Georgia in 1799, and his mother first saw the light in Tennessee about the year 1809. These two young people went with their parents to Louisiana, where they afterward married. In 1823 this couple came to Mississippi, choosing Copiah county for their location, and settled in the western part of the county in the midst of the primeval forests, and near Pine Bluff, on the Bayou Pierre creek. Here they took up land, improved it, and spent the rest of their lives together very happily, till the death of Mr. Ellis, in 1857, whom his wife followed after a mourning period of six years, passing away in 1863. Both of these pioneers were devout Baptists. Mr. and Mrs. Ellis were some of the very first settlers in the wilderness of Mississippi, which teemed with wild animals and wilder Indians. The husband was a hard-working, industrious man, such as the exigencies of the time demanded, and became a successful farmer; the wife was a brave, loving mother and helpmate in the truest sense of the word. As might be expected, when the conditions of the times are recollected, only an ordinary education could be obtained by Mr. Ellis, so that we may in truth call him a self-made man. He was active in all public affairs, and a most ardent democrat, serving his county several terms as a member of the legislature. He was well known and as well respected for his sturdy honesty and integrity. He was one of a large family born to George Ellis, who moved from Georgia to Louisiana, locating in Washington parish, where he died. Mrs. Ellis' parents also probably died in this same parish, as the two families came there together. Our subject is one of thirteen children born to Mr. and Mrs. Ellis, in the early Mississippi days, and of this large family only four are living: John, a merchant of Hazlehurst, was in the Twelfth Mississippi regiment, army of Virginia; Mrs. John R. Robinson; Mrs. Thomas Holliday and our subject, all live at Hazlehurst. Four of the thirteen children laid down their young lives in the Confederate cause, during the late bitter struggle, namely: Capt. George W., who was a captain in the Western army for a time, but whose brave spirit was not content with such inactive service, and resigning his captaincy, he joined the army of Virginia and was killed at the battle of Spottsylvania courthouse, May 12, 1864; Thomas B., who was killed near Petersburg, Va., in 1863; Benjamin F., who died at home during the war while a member of Roberts' artillery, and William C., also, when quite young, went into the war in the cavalry service. He died at home toward the latter part of the war. Our subject was brought up on his father's plantation and went to school till he was sixteen years of age, when he served in the militia during the last year of the war. When peace came, he attended the Cumberland university at Lebanon, Tenn. After this he clerked and became a bookkeeper for some time, and in 1872 was elected to the office of chancery clerk, of Copiah county, which position he filled in a creditable manner for four years. He then engaged in merchandising at Hazlehurst, Miss., till 1882, when he and Maj. R. W. Millsaps organized the Merchants & Planters' bank, of which they are the sole proprietors and of which the latter is president, while Mr. Ellis is the cashier. The capital stock of this institution is $50,000, and it is in a most prosperous condition. Mr. Ellis was married in 1872 to Georgia, a daughter of John D. and Caroline Stapleton, who are both natives of Georgia, where they lived till about 1870, when they came to Copiah county, and where they both died. The father was a farmer and a good man. Mrs. Ellis was a native of Georgia. Mr. and Mrs. Ellis are both members of the Baptist church in good and regular standing. Mr. Ellis was bereft of his parents too young to have much personal knowledge of them, but he is justly proud of those hardy pioneers who bravely took their lives in their hands and, going to a wilderness where white men's feet seldom trod, there made a home and reared a family. Too much respect and admirmiration can not be paid characters like theirs, and it is from men and women like them that the bone and sinew of this country were made. Personally, Mr. Ellis is a man who stands high in the community upon his own merits; he is a most excellent financier and one of the foremost business men in the county. The wealth he possesses is solely the result of his own industry, economy, ability and integrity.

Judge Powhatan Ellis came to Mississippi before the state was admitted to the Union, and entered upon the practice of law. He was a native of Virginia and had been well educated, not only in his profession, but in general literature as well. He at once rose to prominence and popularity in the territory, and in 1818 became a member of the supreme bench and one of its ablest members. He continued to fill this position with much credit until 1825, when he was appointed to a seat in the senate of the United States, rendered vacant by the death of David Holmes, and two years later, was elected for a full term to the same high position, which he held until 1832. He was then appointed a Federal district judge, and a little later, United States minister to Mexico. He was principally distinguished for his great energy and patriotism, and thus became one of the best judges of the state. It is said that he delivered more opinions while upon the bench than any other judge who ever occupied that position.   As a senator of the United States he was equally alert and ready upon all questions of public importance.   He died in the city of Richmond, Va.

W. C. Ellis is a prosperous general merchant of Rankin county, and by his superior intelligence and rare business ability and efficiency he has done not a little to advance the reputation the county enjoys as a commercial center.   He is a native of Mississippi, his birth occurring in 1857, but his father, Gray Ellis, was born in North Carolina in 1812, and throughout life followed the calling of a farmer.   He was educated in the common schools of his native state, and became an intelligent, well-posted and influential citizen of the community in which he resided.   He was an active member of the Masonic fraternity and was public-spirited and enterprising.   He was married to Miss Evalina B. Ward, and of five children born to them only four are living at the present time.   Mr. Ellis died in 1864, but his widow survives him, being a resident of the village of Steen's Creek in Rankin county, Miss.   W. C. Ellis spent his early days in Rankin county, in attending the common schools, but he finished his literary education in the University of Kentucky, during which time he was a faithful and conscientious student.   Upon the completion of his collegiate course he returned to Rankin county, Miss., and engaged in merchandising, and although he commenced in a modest way, his business continued to steadily increase, for his earnest wish was to please his patrons and to conduct his business in an honorable manner, and his place of business became popular accordingly.   Since commencing business in 1877, it has grown to large proportions, and his establishment is now one of the best known in the county.   The calling to which he devotes his attention suits him admirably, and his efforts are being crowned with success.   He is the owner of two excellent steammills, and his real estate amounts to two thousand one hundred and forty acres, on the cultivated portion of which large crops of cotton and corn are raised.   He has accumulated all this property by his own exertions, and he well deserves the respect and esteem with which he is regarded by his numerous friends. He is interested in the political affairs of the county, and socially has been a member of the A. F. & A. M. since 1878, being a member of Evening Star lodge No. 70.   He is an earnest member of the Baptist church, and in every relation and duty of life endeavors to do as he would be done by.   He was married in 1881 to Miss Florence Norrell, a daughter of Hon. Thomas N. Norrell.   She was born in Mississippi and has borne her husband four children.

A retired planter of Yazoo county, Thomas P. Ellison, Deasonville, Miss., is one of the earliest settlers of this community, and has experienced to the fullest extent what it means to be a pioneer.   He was born in the state of Tennessee in 1809, and is the fourth of a family of fourteen children.   His parents, Johnson and Susan (Poor) Ellison, were natives of South Carolina and Georgia respectively.   They removed to Yazoo county in the fall of 1827, when Benton had one log house, and Manchester one store.   The surrounding country was thinly settled, and neighbors were very few.   When death visited the family and claimed for his own one of the brothers, Thomas P. himself dug the grave, and the father made the coffin that was to receive the remains of one of his own children.   The mother died the following year from the exposure that must always be encountered in a new settlement.   The father lived until 1844.   Seven of the children grew up, and all are now deceased except Thomas P. and one sister, Mrs. Mary Gold, of Georgia.   Mr. Ellison was married in 1832 to Miss Mary Moore, a daughter of Gibson and Elizabeth Moore.   Mr. Moore was an early settler of Big Black river in Madison county.   For twelve years Mr. and Mrs. Ellison lived on Mr. Moore's plantation, but in 1850 they removed to their own plantation.   It consists of six hundred acres of land, which they have improved by the cultivation of the soil and the erection of substantial buildings. They have reared a large family: Linda, the wife of Robert Martin, of Arkansas; Susan, wife of King Bull; Mary J., wife of James Shelling; Caroline, wife of Frank Brister, of Louisiana; Mattie, deceased wife of Mr. King; William, who was lieutenant of the Eighteenth Mississippi regiment, and fell at the battle of Gettysburg; Thomas, a member of the same regiment, who was killed at Richmond; Moses, a planter in Florida, Mr. and Mr. Ellison are members of the New Hope Methodist Episcopal church, and have always taken an active interest in the affairs of the church. Politically he has also been a conspicuous character in the county, and in every direction he has been a citizen who is honored and respected.

Ex-sheriff and representative of Calhoun county, Miss., and one of the representative men residing in the same, is Capt. Edgar R. Enochs, the son of Thompson and Sarah (Steen) Enochs, natives respectively of North and South Carolina, the father born in 1790 and the mother in 1791. The parents were married in 1811, and to them were born twelve children—seven sons and five daughters—all of whom lived to be grown and four are living at the present time: Isaac S. resides in West Tennessee, near the old home place; Mrs. Amanda Craven resides in Tate county, Miss., and Mrs. Caroline Williams resides in Clay county, Ark. Those deceased were: Washington C., Miles W., Francis A., Cynthia, Mrs. Mary Ann Treywick, William T., Gabriel V. and Mrs. Jane Reed. The father of these children followed the occupation of a planter during life and received his final summons in Tennessee in 1876. He was a democrat in politics. He was a member of the Methodist Episcopal church and was an earnest worker in the same. He was one of a large family of children born to the marriage of Enoch Enochs, who was a native of North Carolina, and a second cousin of Andrew Jackson. Two of Enoch Enochs' sons entered the ministry and the others followed agricultural pursuits. He with several of his sons served with General Jackson in the war of 1812. Capt. Edgar R. Enochs was born in Lincoln county, Tenn., in 1821, attained his growth and received a limited education in that state. He came to Mississippi in 1847, settled on the land purchased near where he now lives in Calhoun county, and here he has since resided, respected and esteemed by all. He was first married in June, 1857, to Miss Julia B. Campbell, of Carroll county, Tenn., who came with her parents, John L. and Jane B. (Cole) Campbell, to Mississippi in 1840. They were natives of North Carolina. Mrs. Enochs was reared principally in Mississippi, where her death occurred in November, 1880, at the age of forty-two years. She was the mother of eleven children, five of whom are still living: James E., Sarah J. Bryant, Mrs. Mary L. Murfree, Thompson L. and Georgia I. Those deceased all died in infancy except Mrs. Cordelia Moxey. Captain Enochs' second marriage was to Miss Annice S. Swoffer, a native of Jackson county, Ala., who was reared in Mississippi. She was the daughter of Saunders Swoffer, a native of Alabama, who came to Mississippi in 1845. To the Captain's second union were born two children: Enoch J. and Mary Ena. The Captain is an old soldier, having served faithfully in both the Mexican and the Civil wars. He was with Colonel Haskell in the Second Tennessee regiment of volunteers during the former war and was in the battles of Monterey, Vera Cruz and Cerro Gordo. In 1861 he joined company F, Fourth Mississippi, and was with Colonel Drake, serving until the close of the war. He was paroled at Jackson, Miss. He was wounded just before the siege of Vicksburg, had his shoulder blade broken and was taken at Fort Donelson, thence to Johnson island, Ohio, where he was retained for seven months. After his release he entered the army at Jackson, Miss., and was again captured at Vicksburg, where he surrendered in July, 1863. He was in the battle of Fort Henry and Fort Donelson, Tenn., Resaca, Ga., and was also in the Georgia campaign. He was made captain of company F, Fourth Mississippi, in 1862, at

Jackson, of that state, and served in that capacity until the close. In the fall of 1865 Mr. Enochs was elected sheriff and held that position in a creditable manner for two terms. In November, 1887, he was elected to represent Calhoun county in the legislature and held that position for one term. In his political views he is a democrat and is also a most earnest supporter of that party. He was engaged in merchandising from 1853 to 1861, at Pittsboro, and since then he has followed the occupation of a planter. He is well and favorably known all over Calhoun county. He and Mrs. Enochs are members of the Methodist Episcopal church.

Capt. Thomas T. Enochs, the son of Stokley H. Enochs, and the grandson of Enoch Enochs, is a native of Carroll county, Tenn., his birth occurring on the 18th of December, 1822. The grandfather was a representative of one of the most highly respected families of North Carolina, in which state he was born on the 11th of December, 1796. He moved from there to Bedford county, Tenn., at an early date; thence to Carroll county of that state, and in 1839 to Union county, Miss., where he settled near old Albany. There his death occurred in 1840. He was a soldier in the Creek and Indian war. Of the nine children born to his marriage, seven sons and two daughters, all lived to be grown. Stokley H. Enochs, the fourth in order of birth of these children, was born in Bedford county, middle Tennessee, on the 16th of February, 1796, and there continued to reside until his death, which occurred on the 18th of November, 1826. He followed the occupation of a farmer, and served with his father in the Creek war. He was wedded to Miss Jane McChristian, a native of Tennessee, born near Shelbyville, and the fruits of this union were four children, who are named in the order of their births as follows: Jason A., born April 4, 1824, resides near Austin, Tex., and is engaged in farming. He is a minister in the Baptist church. Capt. Thomas T. Enochs, subject; Miles, died, leaving a family in Arkansas; and Margie A., who was born on the 4th of March, 1826, and who died leaving a husband and two children. After the death of her husband Mrs. Enochs was married to Andy Hopkins, by whom she had eight children, three of whom now reside in Texas. Her death occurred in Texas in 1850. Capt. Thomas T. Enochs was reared in his native state by his grandfather, Enoch Enochs, and remained there until grown. The grandmother, Lydia Enochs, was born in North Carolina on the 30th day of July, 1773, and died in New Albany, Miss., in 1845. She was a member of the Methodist church. The grandparents were highly respected and esteemed in the community in which they lived, and the grandfather held the office of justice of the peace there for over twenty years. Captain Enochs was educated both in his native state and in Mississippi, and in 1844 he started out in business for himself at New Albany. Four years later he came to Benela, Miss., and here he has since made his home. He is one of the old landmarks and is a man held in the highest estimation as a citizen and neighbor. On first coming here he engaged in merchandising, erected the first building in what is now Benela, and continued business there until 1881, with the exception of two years during the war. He was married on the 30th of August, 1845, at New Albany, to Miss Sarah J. Collins, a native of Alabama, born in Tuscaloosa county in 1828, and the daughter of Jesse and Elizabeth Collins. Mr. Collins was born in Georgia and moved from Alabama to Mississippi in 1834, locating in what is now Union county, and there he continued to reside for a number of years. Subsequently he moved to a place near Pittsboro, and there his death occurred His wife died at Houston, Chickasaw county, Miss. They were the parents of eleven children, seven of whom lived to be grown, and six are living at the present time: Martha, resides in Texas; Sarah J., wife of subject; Mrs. Mary Payne, resides in Arkansas; John L., formerly resided in Coffeeville, Miss., but is now in California (he was appointed by President Cleveland as agent in the internal revenue department); Emily, wife of F. J. Kelley, now of Memphis; and B. F., resides in Houston, Miss., engaged in merchandising. To Captain and Mrs. Enochs were born eleven children, seven of whom are living: William B., engaged in merchandising at Eupora, Miss.; Mary E., wife of T. W. Scott, resides at Houston, where her husband is engaged in merchandising; Thomas B., resides at Water Valley; James B., engaged in merchandising at Eupora, Miss.; Alice, resides at Houston, Miss., and is the wife of Daniel H. Shell; Bodie, at home; and Emma, also at home. Those deceased were: Isaac, died in 1849, at the age of nearly three years; Margie Ann, died in 1851, at the age of five months and eight days; Sarah A., died in 1854, at the age of four years and nine days; and John B., died in 1872, at the age of nearly ten years. In 1863 Captain Enochs enlisted in company B, Nineteenth Mississippi cavalry, was in Forrest's brigade, and participated in the following battles: Moscow, Fort Pillow, Brice's crossroads and at Harrisburg, Miss. He was also in the battle of Selma, Ala., but did no fighting. Before entering the service he was taken prisoner at Corinth, Miss., but was soon released. He organized the company of which he was made first lieutenant and afterward captain, and was in charge of the same until after the battle of Selma. While making a charge with his regiment at Fort Pillow, the Captain was shot twice through his clothes, and had a ball pass just above his ear, touching his hair and whiskers. After the war he returned to his home and resumed merchandising and farming. In politics he has always been a stanch democrat. He has been a member of the board of supervisors, and has held other responsible positions. He took an active part in the organization of the Masonic lodge at Benela, was one of the charter members, and held positions in the same from the beginning until it went down. In 1871 the Captain represented Benela lodge No. 140 in the grand lodge, which was held that year at Holly Springs. Captain and Mrs. Enochs are members of the Methodist Episcopal church, and are active workers in the same. He was made postmaster at Benela in 1850, has held that office the principal part of the time since, and is the present incumbent.

The Woman's Christian Temperance Union of Mississippi would not have a history were it not that Mary E. Ervin served it as president, well-beloved, from December, 1884, to May, 1888. Heredity was as conspicuously operative in working out the character the world knows as Mollie Ervin, as it was in producing a Frances Willard. Her father, B. D. Anderson, in the early days of Mississippi a lawyer and land agent of Pontotoc, was a Virginian by birth, closely related to the Gilmers, Minons and Dabneys, so well known in the history of that state. In 1838 Colonel Anderson represented his county in the legislature. He was known as a character—a man of strong prejudices, but which were based on an intense conviction of right or wrong. He abhorred position secured chiefly by the distinction of wealth, and trained his children to recognize a lord in the humblest man. Though never a professing Christian, he held religion in profoundest respect. The night after his wife's death he handed her Bible to his son William, a boy of fifteen years, and the eldest of six children, saying: "I have not professed to be a Christian, not even a believer, but your mother believed this book, and she is the only person I ever knew who lived a perfectly consistent Christian life. As long as this is a home I desire this Bible to be read aloud to us, together, every night, because your mother loved it"—and it was so read. At this time he sent his little daughter, Mollie, then thirteen years old, with an uncle, into every store in town to be introduced to the merchants as the responsible head of his house. From that time till her marriage, eleven years later, she was her father's constant companion and friend. Close as is the tie of mother and child there is, perhaps, no holier, sweeter bond than that between the great-souled father who leads an adoring daughter into all things high and rare, and molds her after the large pattern of his own thought. The tone in which some such women say "my father" almost brings a hearer on his knees. Mary Ervin's mother was the daughter of Rev. Jacob Lindley, a Presbyterian clergyman, who was for twenty years the president of the Athens, Ohio, college. While he was pastor of a church near Cincinnati the Cumberland Presbyterians held a camp-meeting in the neighborhood, in which Mr. Lindley assisted and affiliated. Being arraigned by his presbytery for so doing, he handed in his credentials and joined the Cumberland church, his whole congregation going with him, as recorded in Mc-Donald's history of the Cumberland church. The eldest brother, Rev. Daniel Lindley, was for forty years a missionary in Africa, for the Old School Presbyterians, under the American board of missions. When his daughter was seventeen years of age Rev. Jacob Lindley moved to Pontotoc, and established there the first female school in North Mississippi, on the site of which there has never yet ceased to be an educational institute. His daughter assisted in the school till her marriage in 1839. Mrs. Anderson was a constant teacher in the Sunday-school, nursed the sick, comforted the sorrowing and filled the place of Lady Beautiful and Bountiful in the lives of her neighbors. At the age of thirty-one the vision of this world faded to her dying eyes. Calling her little daughter to her bedside, before the heavenly vision filled her rapt gaze, she said: "Mary, bring your father and the children to heaven with you."

It is not wonderful that such marked individuality on both sides should have found a resultant in a character like Mollie Ervin's, that has followed conviction rather than convention, with whom, from her childhood, "the tradition of the elders," has weighed light against the inward voice, that whispers the direct command of the Master. There was a time when every morning the celebrated duellist, Colonel McClung, carried her off in his arms to hear her sing, the sweet voice of the child having strange power to tame the fierce, imperious spirit, to whom blood was the only reparation for injury, under the rude education of wild pioneer life in the Southwest. The solemn charge of a dying mother intensified the religious tendency of her nature, and from that hour this child-mother lived a life set apart. No young man was ever in her presence a half hour without her finding out if he were a Christian; yet, with all this realization of the unseen realities on which life and character must be builded, Mary Ervin possessed a buoyancy and joyousness of spirit, a warmth and tenderness of nature, that carried fun and sunny hope everywhere. Those about her depended upon her, and in her youth she began to carry the glad tidings of the evangelist to the perishing. Work for souls has been her joy, and many there are "for her hire;" who say, "Mrs. Ervin pointed out our Lord and I followed Him." The gift of the Spirit which has seemed especially poured upon her, has been that of faith. The will to ask is given to the multitude, but the power to hear the word of command, and literally to walk hour by hour by it, is the gift only of the few who know the secret of the Lord. In her W. C. T. U. work, Mrs. Ervin set out without purse and without scrip. There was no organization, no treasury behind her. She had heard the "Go, daughter!" and without money even to buy a ticket has been known to be seated on a train, in the firm conviction that the Lord who had started her out would see the paying of her way; "And He did, He did" she joyfully says as she recounts how it came to pass. As president of the organization she traveled over much of the state, organizing many unions and inspiring men and women to rouse up to a sense of personal responsibility toward the liquor traffic. Miss Willard was called of God to national leadership. As firmly is it believed that Mrs. Ervin was called to the pioneer work for prohibition and to rally the white ribbon in Mississippi. She stepped out into the void as no one else in the state could have done, and the wonderful way in which she was carried from point to point, in which the Almighty hand was spread out beneath her trusting feet, and the spiritual life which everywhere followed the uplifting of the W. C. T. U. standard "For God and Home and Native Land," convinced many of the divine sanction of this work, and has probably given Mississippi the prohibition leadership in the South. It is a rare treat to be invited to the old Ervin homestead, five miles from Columbus, interesting in those things which time alone can supply. One looks first at Dr. Frank Ervin, the noble Christian gentleman, who said when the call came to his wife to walk the trying ways of W. C. T. U. development, "You must go; if I hold you back God may require one of our sons as the sacrifice to my selfishness." This kind of heroism one unconsciously matches by the recollection that when Mrs. Ervin was married, she was by education and membership a Presbyterian; but after awhile she said quaintly, "I see if the doctor is saved it has to be in the Methodist church," and without delay she left her own church for her husband's spiritual interests. There are two heads in council in that Christian home; one or the other leads in family prayer, asks the blessing at table; parents and children know each the others' hearts; the music and the fellowship make a visitor in this house feel it is good to be here. Six sons and daughters vividly reflect ancestral individualities. During the mother's "progress" for the W. C. T. U. the eldest daughter, Sarah, held the helm in the family ship with a steady judgment and grace that revealed a character equal to the rare beauty of her face. Set aside for three years from action by sickness, Mrs. Ervin yet retains a place in the executive committee of the W. C. T. U., and is again resuming work in her chosen field of the evangelistic and social purity departments for which she is remarkably equipped. Probably no other woman is so widely known in the state among all ranks of persons, or so much loved or sharply criticised for the singularity of her faith and the boldness of her action against the liquor traffic. A liquor drummer was once trying to sell a saloon-keeper a bill of goods on the streets of Columbus. "Oh," he said, "no use to buy no more liquor here. We got vun vooman vat is te verry deevil. She not let no whisky pe sold." Just then Mrs. Ervin came into sight in her open buggy, driving her old horse, Prohibition. "There she, there she now!" cried the saloonman excitedly. The drummer looked at the plodding turnout, at the old gray shawl surmounted by a Methodist bonnet with a sweet, rather jolly face under it. "That woman," he said, after a leisure survey, "why, there's nothing in her!" "You not know her," said the other contemptuously, "there's hell in her!" The saloon element in the legislature has not loved her any better or dreaded her any less as day after day she has sat in the representative hall, gauging its moral tide on whose ebbs and flows legal suasion for the drunkard-maker depended. Mrs. Ervin has been a large part of whatever has been done in the state for prohibition, and when the victory comes no one will have earned a better right to hurrah; for the burden and heat of the day, the darkness of the night, the fire of the evening, and harder still the misjudgment of friends, the hot rage of battle for the home and God have been bravely and gently borne, and one day this people shall rise up and call her blessed for her faithful and unremunerated work to help win Mississippi, in all its borders, to Christ.

Among the genial citizens of Coffeeville, Yalobusha county, Miss., Capt. J. L. Eskridge takes a leading place, and is fully entitled to the space accorded him in this history of the prominent men of the state. He was born in Sumter county, Ala., in 1829, and is the son of Taliaferro and Sophia (Bonham) Eskridge, natives of South Carolina; the father was born in 1800, and died in 1862, and the mother was born in 1805, and passed away at the home of Captain Eskridge in 1857; they were united in marriage about the year 1824, and removed to Alabama a short time afterward; their residence here was of short duration, however; they next went to Mississippi and settled near Grenada, engaging in farming on a small scale.

Lock. E. Houston

Richard Eskridge, the grandfather of the captain, came to Mississippi soon after the son, and was present at the sale of the Choctaw lands, and purchased a large tract on Bogue creek in what is now Carroll county; he settled on this land, where he passed the remainder of his days; he was eighty-five at the time of his death. He was the father of five children: Thomas, Samuel, Mary Ann, Rebecca and Taliaferro. The last-named was a farmer by occupation, and in his political opinions adhered to the democratic party. He reared a family of eight children: Elizabeth, wife of Joseph Swain; Nancy, wife of Judge J. W. Tackett; Mary, wife of D. D. Wilkins; Samuel B. and J. L. Those deceased are, Burdette R., Pierce B. and Sophia. Captain Eskridge has passed the greater part of his life in Yalobusha county, and is one of the hardy pioneers to whom the county is indebted to-day for her standing. He acquired more than an ordinary education in the common schools, and made the most of all his opportunities for bettering his condition in life. He was married in 1856 to Mrs. Metcalfe, a daughter of Curtis Terry, a man who stood high in his county; he reared a family of five sons and three daughters, two children dying in infancy. Mr. Terry bought land at the Choctaw sale, and came to Mississippi to live; he was a man of a gentle, religious nature, and was an ardent worker in the Methodist Episcopal church; he died at the age of seventy-five years, and his wife died in 1849, just ten years before his death. The children who lived to be grown were Willis, James, Sally, Lovina (widow of John Beene), John, Granderson, Emeline (the wife of our subject, was first married to William M. Metcalfe, who died in 1854, leaving no children). Mary was burned to death at the age of four years. Captain Eskridge enlisted in 1861 in the Twenty-eighth Mississippi cavalry, company B, and served to the end of the conflict; he participated in the engagements at Franklin, Tenn., and at Atlanta, Ga. He was under Gen. Joseph E. Johnston, of whom he was an earnest admirer. At the breaking out of the gold fever he started for California, but did not pursue the long and dangerous journey to the end. He has been very successful in all his business undertakings and has accumulated considerable property. January 1, 1883, he was elected by the people of the county to the office of supervisor, and has held the office for four consecutive terms; during his second term he was made president of the board, and he has made a most faithful and efficient officer. He has held other positions of trust and honor within the gift of the people. Before the war he was a member of the Whig party, but since that time he has belonged to the democratic party. He has a delightful home overlooking Coffeeville, and is surrounded with many of the luxuries of life; he has several acres of land adjacent to the home place, which he has set to a fine variety of fruit. He and wife are highly esteemed in the community in which they live, and are deserving of their popularity.

E. S. Estes, son of William and Susan H. Estes (nee Shelton), was born in Rankin county, Miss., August 25th, 1840. His father, Wm. Estes, M. D., and his mother were natives of Virginia. The former emigrated to Tennessee in 1821, and in 1836 came to Mississippi. He resided in Rankin county till the close of the war, when he removed to Clarke county, Miss. He practiced his profession for forty years with success. He was descended from Scotch-Irish parents and from the founders of the house of Brunswick, and bore relation to Lord Bacon. Dr. Estes died in April, 1871, Mrs. Estes in 1886. E. S. Estes, subject of this sketch, spent his early life on a farm and attended the common schools, and began business on his own account at nineteen years of age. He was employed for several years by a mercantile firm at Enterprise, Miss. In 1862 he enlisted in the Twenty-eight Mississippi cavalry, Col. Peter B. Stark commanding, and for eighteen months he was engaged in detached service. He was in a slight engagement at Coldwater, Miss. Going to Tennessee and joining VanDorn's army, he was in an engagement at Thompson's station. He passed

44

into Georgia, and there, owing to ill-health, was discharged. Returning to Enterprise, Miss., he engaged in mercantile pursuits. In 1864 he married Miss Mattie F. Meyerhoff, of Clarke county, a native of Alabama, and has had six children: Sue M., Mary C., William M., Anna Maria, Charles E. and Elisha S., all of whom, except the fourth named, survive. Mr. Estes was in the mercantile business until 1875, when he returned to farming, and now owns some of the best land in Clarke county and is one of the most enterprising farmers. He plants cotton, corn, etc., and is quite extensively engaged in vegetable culture. He is a Methodist, an Odd Fellow, a member of the Masonic body, a Knight of Honor, and is a member of the Farmers' Alliance. He is secretary of the Clarke county fair association. Mrs. Estes and their three oldest children are Methodists also. Mr. Estes is a claimant for $140,000 of merchandise seized by the French in 1810, and carried to Copenhagen and confiscated. On settlement in 1831, the United States assumed all of the indebtedness of France to citizens of the United States. This claim is perfectly just, and the claimants, it is hoped, may soon receive their deserts. The original claim was due to Francis Meyerhoff, a native of Germany, who was duly naturalized here. His son, Charles F., was the next claimant, and later, his children, one of whom Mr. Estes married. Mr. Estes is a believer in education, and both of his daughters are graduates of the East Mississippi female college. His son, William M., is a student at the Southern University at Greensboro, Ala. Mr. Estes' father was a soldier of the War of 1812, and held the rank of captain. His brother, William E., was a member of Jefferson Davis' regiment in the Mexican war. Two other brothers filled the positions of captains in the Thirty-second Texas regiment. Mr. Estes, who is a cousin of Chancellor Estes and of Judge Estes, both of Memphis, is one of the very best citizens of his county, and a man of more than ordinary force of character.

W. G. Evans, Jr., Mississippi City, Miss., attorney at law, is a leader of the bar of Harrison county, and the following space will be devoted to a brief outline of his career. He is a native of the county, born January 28, 1843, a son of Rev. W. G. Evans, also a native of Harrison county. The paternal grandfather, Thomas Evans, came from South Carolina, and was among the first settlers of Mississippi. He located in Harrison county, twenty miles north of Mississippi City, where he engaged in farming and stockraising. The father of our subject was a member of the legislature in 1864, representing Jackson county. He was a minister in the Methodist Episcopal church, and for more than forty-five years was a prominent preacher, organizing and building many churches. He had three sons and three daughters. W. G. Evans, Jr., is the only child of the first marriage. He was educated in Harrison county in the private schools and Seashore seminary, which was under the care of the Rev. C. H. Bell, and located in the town of Handsboro. The war coming on, this school was closed, and Mr. Evans enlisted in the Confederate army as sergeant, and served through the entire war. After the surrender he was connected in various capacities with the timber and milling business, which he followed until 1877. He did not abandon it wholly then, but in connection with his duties took up the study of law. He was admitted to the bar of Hancock county in November, 1881, and for a short time was located at Stonewall, Miss. In 1883 he removed to Mississippi City, and has since devoted his entire time and attention to the law. He has risen to a high rank in his profession, and has won a reputation far beyond his own county. In 1890 he represented Harrison county in the legislature of the state, giving entire satisfaction to his constituency. His first marriage was to Miss L. A. P. Waldon, of New Orleans, and six children were born of the union, five of whom are living. He was married a second time to Miss Alice Waldon, in 1883. They have had five children, one of whom is living, Charlie, a bright little fellow of six years, the pet and almost the idol of his father. Mr. Evans owns about four thousand acres of land and some valuable property along the coast, and is regarded as one of the leading men of the gulf coast of Mississippi.

A well known merchant of Lee county is C. B. Evans, Shannon, Miss., a native of Louisiana, born February 14, 1848. He is a son of Isaac and Charlotte Evans, natives of Pennsylvania and Louisiana, respectively. The father was born October 7, 1807. He was a mechanic, and for a number of years was judge of a court, and was also collector of internal revenue. At the age of sixteen years he made the journey from Harrisburg, Penn., to Pittsburgh, Penn., on foot, and drifted thence to Cincinnati, Ohio, and then to Louisiana. His parents were both natives of the Keystone state, and followed him to Cincinnati, where he remained seven years; they both lived to be ninety-three years of age. The subject of this notice received his education in New Orleans, and in the year 1870 he left that city to go to Cincinnati, where he expected to have some assistance from an uncle in securing a situation. The different views they held upon political questions separated them, and he was thrown upon his own resources. He finally succeeded in getting employment with Lewis & Neblet, as commercial traveler. In 1876 he had a flattering offer from J. P. Smith, Sons & Co., which he accepted. After a few years he was made a partner in the business, but at the end of eight or nine years his wife induced him to leave the road, and to go into business for himself. He was married September 30, 1873, to Miss M. A. Bright, a daughter of Robert W. and Mary J. Bright, natives of Illinois and Alabama, respectively. Mr. and Mrs. Evans have had born to them two children, one of whom is deceased. Politically he is a dyed in the wool democrat, casting his first presidential vote for Horace Greeley. He has never aspired to public office, but all questions of public interest have had his careful consideration. On January 15, 1864, he enlisted in the Confederate service under Captain Duff. He was in several skirmishes, and was mustered out in 1865 at Morganza. Mr. Evans is a member of the Masonic fraternity, and has belonged to the Christian church for fifteen years. The mercantile business which he conducts at Shannon is of considerable importance. He carries a stock of $7,000, and has established a fine patronage. He is a man of the highest honor and integrity, and has the confidence of the entire community.

John H. Evans, county surveyor of Clarke county, Miss., and a prominent resident of De Soto, was born in Wayne county, Miss., November 15, 1824, the second in a family of ten children belonging to Jehu Evans and Sarah P. (Hicks) Evans. A short sketch of the life of Jehu and Sarah P. (Hicks) Evans will be found in the following obituary: " Died, June 24, 1877, at his residence in Shubuta, Clarke county, Miss., Jehu Evans, at the advanced age of eighty-one years, eight months and sixteen days. Mr. Evans was born October 8, 1795, in Edgefield district, S. C. In the year of 1810 he emigrated to the Louisiana territory, and settled in what is now Wayne county, a few miles above old Winchester. About 1821 he was united in marriage with Miss Sarah Peques Hicks, who still survives. Ten children were the fruit of this marriage, five of whom still survive. Mr. Evans was a volunteer in the war of 1812, and was mustered into service at Myrtle Springs, in Wayne county, Miss., and was subsequently elected captain of his company. The company marched to Pensacola, Fla.; a regiment was there formed, to which Mr. Evans' company was attached, and Wade Hampton, Sr., of South Carolina, given command of the regiment as colonel. Colonel Hampton was soon ordered to New Orleans to take part in the memorable battle of the 8th of January. On its way thither the regiment had some heavy skirmishes with some hostile Indians along the coast, and finally arrived in New Orleans the day after the battle of New Orleans, and in time to assist in burying the dead and in ministering to the wounded and dying. At the expiration of his term of service, Mr. Evans returned to the bosom of his family and friends, and engaged in surveying with Mr. Hicks, a government surveyor, about Pensacola, Fla., and Mobile, Ala. In the year 1832 he removed to Clarke county, Miss., and engaged in agriculture, and remained there till about five years ago, until by age and infirmity he could no longer perform the active duties of farm life, when he went to Shubuta and resided with his daughter, Mrs. Martha I. Yates, where he died. Mr. Evans was successful in his engagements, and hundreds of friends remember the pleasant moments spent at his old home. For twenty-two years he was county surveyor of Clarke county. He was a man of great decision of character, a good citizen, a benevolent neighbor, a confiding friend, a loving father and husband. For more than a quarter of a century he was a member of the Baptist church, and died, it is believed, in hope of a blessed immortality. Thus has lived and passed away one of the pioneer citizens of this county. He was interred at the family burying-ground, at his old residence, in the exact place he selected many years ago, followed by weeping wife, children and neighbors." Obituary: "Mrs. Sarah P. Evans died at the residence of her daughter, Mrs. M. I. Yates, in Shubuta, Miss., on the 4th of December, 1885. She was born in North Carolina, in January, 1801, came to Mississippi in 1815, lived in east Mississippi about seventy years, and was eighty-four years and eleven months old. She was the widow of the late Jehu Evans, one of the first settlers of this county, memory of whom will be recalled with deep respect, and the mother of John H. Evans, Dr. I. S. Evans, B. F. Evans, Mrs. M. I. Yates and Mrs. Dr. McIntosh, and a sister of Thomas F. Hicks, Esq. Mrs. Evans was a very intelligent, hospitable and sympathetic lady, always ready to obey the voice of her generous heart. She was amiable in every social relation and observed a liberal charity in the truest ways. She was a member of the Baptist church, and illustrated in her days of strength the meekness and righteousness of one to whom was revealed the truth and the faith delivered. Dead and gone at last, after much patient suffering, she has found the diadem and the glorious beauty of the brighter life."

The early days of John H. Evans were passed in this county, where he received his education, and where he was married in 1845 to Sarah A. Phillips, a daughter of Thompson and Lydia (Seale) Phillips, who was born in Marion county, in the state of Mississippi. Her father, Thompson Phillips, was born in South Carolina, in January, 1795. Her mother, Lydia Seale, was born in North Carolina in October, 1800. Her father died in 1835. Her mother died in 1874. Thus have passed away the fathers and mothers of John H. and his wife, Sarah A. (Phillips) Evans. Mr. and Mrs. Evans have had born to them nine children—six sons and three daughters—named as follows: Sarah (deceased); Alfred T., a physician, residing in Richland parish, La.; Mary L. (deceased); John A., a farmer and clerk in a store of general merchandise in Shubuta; Virginia A. (deceased); Thomas H. (deceased); James B., now circuit clerk in Clarke county; Newton I., a farmer; William P., a commercial traveler. Mr. Evans began farming in 1846, and has continued that occupation until the present time. He has been quite successful in a business way, and is the owner of about nine hundred acres of land in Clarke county. He is an agent of the Alabama Land and Development company, whose headquarters are at Mobile, Ala. During the late war, Mr. Evans served in the capacity of recruiting officer for some time, and was for a time a member of the Thirteenth Mississippi infantry. During the later years of the war he was engaged in manufacturing salt, at the government salt works, to benefit destitute families of the state. His first public office was that of captain of militia in the county of Clarke in the year 1844. After this he was elected major of militia. Subsequent to this he served as member of the county board of supervisors and justice of the peace, and for the past eighteen years has been the county surveyor for the county of Clarke. He has been a member of the Masonic order since 1848. In politics he is a democrat. Mr. Evans, in his early boyhood days, was raised among the Choctaw Indians, in the territory of east Mississippi. He learned to undergo hardships in the early settlement of his father in the territory of Clarke county. He can, at his present age, almost walk down any man in the woods. He was at one time in his younger days one of the best hunters and horseback riders in the country. He has been known to run a deer down on horseback and catch it, then mount his horse and take the deer up before him. On the way home the horse ran away for half a mile or more along the road, until a party was met, who saw the situation, and caught the horse by the bridle and stopped him, without injury to rider, horse or deer. On one occasion he killed at one shot with a rifle two large bucks. A number of times with a double barreled shotgun he has killed three deer, killing two with one barrel and one with the remaining load as they ran off. Mr. Evans, in 1867, went to Brazil, South America. While there, in traveling through the country on horseback, he espied an ostrich, and having a gun, he put spurs to his horse. After a chase of some two miles or more, he overtook the immense bird, stopped his horse, and shot it dead before it reached a distance of forty paces. He is in the ordinary sense of the term a live and a self-made man, having been the architect of his own fortunes, depending solely upon himself for what he has accomplished, and enjoying the respect of his neighbors therefor.

John Henry Evans has been a resident of Washington county, Miss., since the year 1853, and his example of industry and earnest and sincere endeavor to succeed in life is well worthy of imitation. He was born in Virginia on the 7th of July, 1827, being the youngest of seven children born to Robert and Lucy (Gatewood) Evans, they being also natives of the Old Dominion. In 1848 Robert Evans left the state of his birth and settled in the Blue Grass regions of Kentucky, he and his wife being called from life there when quite advanced in years. The Evans family first came from England and settled near Port Royal, Va., one member of the family being the richest man to settle in that country. Robert Evans served throughout the war of 1812, holding the rank of sergeant. Both the paternal and maternal grandfathers of the subject of this sketch were in the Revolutionary war. The Gatewoods were from Scotland, being also among the first residents of Virginia. John Henry Evans was reared in Virginia, but at the age of twenty-one years he went to Franklin county, Ky., where he became manager of a large plantation belonging to W. S. Waller, with whom he remained four years, then removing to Shelbyville, Tenn., at which place he made his home for two years. Leaving Tennessee he came to this county and at first became overseer on the plantation belonging to Gen. A. W. McAllister, in whose employ he remained for four years. He followed the same calling for different planters until 1865, when he began planting in copartnership with W. L. Nugent, who was administrator on the estate of Dr. S. R. Dunn. In 1869 he purchased the plantation of eight hundred and fifty-eight acres which he owned up to 1882, when, desiring a change of business, he sold his farming interests and moved to Greenville, where he has since been engaged in loaning money on real estate. He is now opening up a plantation on the Louisville, New Orleans & Texas railroad, northeast of Greenville. He is the owner of a small amount of residence property in the town of Greenville, and has the most of his means in mortgages on property in this county. He has a comfortable home on the corner of Poplar and Nelson streets, and here is now living in the enjoyment of a comfortable income. When he came to this county he was a total stranger and had but $200 in money, but he soon won many friends and by close economy amassed sufficient property to keep him in luxury for years. Not having disciplined himself to such a life and being of a naturally active disposition he continued in business, and is now successfully following the above mentioned calling. His superior business tact is appreciated by his friends and for the past four years he has been a member of the city council, being chosen by the democratic party, of which he has long been a member. He is now in his sixty-fourth year, but is yet hale and hearty, and as he has always been a man of great determination, whatever enterprise he has undertaken throughout life he has made a success of, and has endeavored to keep clear of debt and to keep his good name untarnished.

John Joseph Evans, of Aberdeen, treasurer of the state of Mississippi, is a native of Georgia, his birth occurring at Madison, Morgan county, on August 8, 1842. His parents were William J. and Adeline E. (Hurd) Evans, also Georgians, the former being born in Wilkes county, May 16, 1810. They removed to Mississippi in 1845, locating in the prairie of Monroe county on March 18 of the same year. From there they went to Aberdeen in 1851, where the father engaged in planting, a calling he followed up to the time of his death, March 5, 1885. His wife's death had preceded his by many years, her death occurring on September 5, 1851. Eight children were born to them: Mary, Faulkner H., Thomas R., Andrew J., Martha L., Julia A., John J. and Eliza W. Mary and Andrew died young, and Faulkner, who was a physician, died in 1884. The paternal grandfather of John Joseph Evans was of Welsh extraction, and his maternal grandfather of Irish lineage. His early life was that common to the planters' sons before the war, they being always generous in their expenditures upon their families. In February, 1858, he was sent to the Georgia Military institute, where he remained until December, 1859, when he entered the Western Military institute at Nashville, Tenn. He left the institute when the war opened, returned home, and in April, 1861, joined the Eleventh Mississippi regiment, company I, as a private. The regiment was organized at Corinth by the election of William H. Moore as colonel. From Corinth they moved to Lynchburg, Va., where they remained two weeks, when they were mustered into the Confederate service by Gen. Kirby Smith. From there they were ordered to Harper's Ferry, and were brigaded with the Second, Eleventh, Fourth and Sixth North Carolina regiments, composing the Third brigade, with Gen. B. E. Bee commanding. They remained at Harper's Ferry about three weeks, when they were ordered to Winchester, from which place they marched to the field of Manassas. Mr. Evans' company did not participate in the fight, but companies A and F of the Eleventh were there in time for it. The other companies were delayed by a railroad accident. After this fight they moved to Acquia creek, where they went into winter quarters. In the spring of 1862 his command moved to Yorktown, remaining there a few weeks, then moving on to the Chickahominy, near Richmond. There they were engaged in the battle of Seven Pines, under Joseph E. Johnston. After this hard-fought battle Mr. Evans' command was detached from Lee's army and sent to Staunton, Va., to reinforce Stonewall Jackson. After this service they returned and were engaged in the seven days' fight around Richmond. At the conclusion of this fight he was promoted to sergeant-major of his regiment. After recruiting for a month the command moved out to engage in the second battle of Manassas, in Hood's division, which, like the first Manassas, was in favor of the Confederates. The great battle at Sharpsburg followed, in which T. C. Holliday, adjutant of the Eleventh Mississippi, was wounded, and Sergeant Evans was detailed to take his place. Their next engagement was at Culpeper courthouse, where all of the field officers were killed. From Culpeper the command moved to Goldsboro, N. C., where they spent the winter protecting railroads and doing garrison duty. In the spring of 1863 the command first moved to Suffolk, and from there to Fredericksburg. While at Culpeper, by an order from the war department, the Eleventh Mississippi was brigaded with the Second Mississippi, the Twenty-sixth, Forty-second and Fifty-fifth North Carolina and the First Confederate battery, with Joseph R. Davis in command. This was subsequently known as Davis' brigade. These troops arrived at Fredericksburg too late to participate in that battle. Later they were ordered to join the main army, then moving northward through Maryland. Lee's movement north was checked, and the two great armies, the Federal and the Confederate, came together on the hills and valleys of Gettysburg to struggle in deadly combat for supremacy. A part of Davis' brigade arrived in time for the first day's fight. The Eleventh Mississippi was behind, and only arrived in time for the third day, when they also took part in the engagement. The Eleventh was in Heath's division and A. P. Hill's corps.

It was in the charge through the wheat field for Round Top at Pickett's left that Mr. Evans' company I made a charge, and came out with thirty-six men killed and wounded. The adjutant-general was killed, and Adjutant Holliday was promoted to his place, Captain Evans being made adjutant. From the disastrous field of Gettysburg the command returned to Virginia, engaging on the way in the fight at Falling Water, where Captain Evans commanded the Eleventh regiment. Arriving at Culpeper courthouse the command went into winter quarters. When activities commenced in the spring of 1864, the Eleventh was ready for action, and its first battle, the Wilderness, was one of the hottest in which it had engaged during the war. The brigade (Davis) fought all day, and at night became separated from the division. The following day it was commanded by Col. John M. Stone of the Second Mississippi. During the day T. C. Holliday was killed, and Captain Davis was appointed adjutant-general. From the Wilderness the command moved on to Spottsylvania, and took part in that battle. From that field they moved on to Petersburg, and on the way had a fight at Davis' farm on the Weldon railroad. Proceeding, they moved in around Petersburg and took position within the fortifications. October 14 they were ordered out to the extreme right of the army at Hatchie's run, to reinforce a troop of cavalry. They defeated the enemy and then went into winter quarters. In December, the enemy, having cut the Weldon railroad, they were taken from their quarters and sent down to recapture it. This accomplished they returned to their quarters. About the middle of December they were ordered out and moved against the Federals on the left, the latter having made a feint on Petersburg. In the spring of 1865 came the series of fights around Petersburg, in which the Eleventh Mississippi participated. After the surrender of that place the command moved on to Appomattox, where the army of Lee surrendered. In the storming of the works around Petersburg, Davis' brigade, occupying the extreme right, was left to protect the retreat of Hill's troops, and in that action the greater portion of the men were captured, including Captain Evans. While a prisoner he made his escape by swimming across a dam at Hatchie's run. He overtook his command about five miles distant, and was with it at the time of the surrender April 9. After being paroled Captain Evans returned to his home at Aberdeen, making the trip overland on his charger, a pleasure he was permitted to indulge in through the magnanimity of General Grant. For several years he gave his attention to planting, and in 1883 was elected chancery clerk of Monroe county for a term of four years, being reëlected in 1887. In 1889 he was nominated by the democratic party for state treasurer, and was duly elected. January 6, 1890, he was installed into office. By the terms of the new constitution his term is extended two years, or to 1896. Mr. Evans was married in Monroe county, April 9, 1867, to Julia M., daughter of John and Lucy (Traylor) Tompkins, of Albany, Ga. They have had five children born to them: Mary H., William G., John J., Juliann T. and Carrie E., all of whom are in the enjoyment of good health. He is a member of the Knights of Honor and the Knights of Pythias. Captain Evans' army record is one of which he may well feel proud, for be it remembered that he was only in his nineteenth year when he enlisted—a mere boy—and his success and rise was remarkable. He was a natural born soldier, brave and fearless in action, and always ready for duty, and is now one of the most popular men of his state. He has a splendid physique, stands six feet two inches in hight, and is well proportioned. His head is covered with brown hair, and he wears a moustache. His eyes are blue, and, unless his mind is disturbed, are always kindly beaming. Nature has endowed him with fine social qualities, which he has improved by cultivation, responding ever to his large, warm heart, and whether as host or guest, or whether from casual meetings in the daily walks of life, the sunshine of his nature makes all those happier on whom it falls.

Marion McKay Evans, Moss Point, Jackson county, Miss., was born in Handsboro, Harrison county, Miss., July 5, 1850, and is a son of William J. and Louisa McKay, also Mississippians by birth; their immediate ancestors, however, were from South and North Carolina, respectively, the Evans family being prominent citizens of the Marion district of South Carolina. Marion M. Evans received his education mainly at Salem high school in Greene county, Miss., and at the age of sixteen years he entered the mercantile business. He was employed as a clerk, and followed this calling steadily until 1876, when he established himself in business at Moss Point in partnership with Lyman Randall, the firm name being Randall & Evans. He was afterward associated with J. W. Griffin and L. N. Dantzler successively in business at Moss Point. Mr. Evans has always been identified with the political movements of his county, and in Freemasonry he has been a conspicuous figure. He arose rapidly in the order, and was appointed district deputy grand master in 1880 and 1881, and deputy grand master in 1885. He was elected junior grand and senior grand warden successively, and in 1889, was made grand master of the Masons. His administration as grand master of Masons in Mississippi was marked by the agitation of the saloon question in Masonry. This created considerable excitement for a time, but the majesty of the law was not only maintained, but harmony was restored completely. In 1885 Mr. Evans became a candidate for secretary of state, having as his opponents Col. D. P. Porter, Hon. W. A. Roane and Hon. George M. Govan, all gentlemen of the highest character and unusual popularity. Mr. Evans, although the youngest and the least known in the state, soon won a large following, and in the convention led in the ballot eleven consecutive times; on the twelfth ballot Govan led, and was nominated on the thirteenth. In consideration of the worthiness of their foe, the friends of Mr. Evans felt that they had made a gallant fight, and were highly gratified that their antagonist had been so hard to overcome. In 1889 Mr. Evans was a candidate for lieutenant-governor, with several able opponents. When the convention was met, he was nominated by acclamation before the close of the first ballot, and was elected to the office the following November. In 1875 he was married to Miss Emma K. Airey, of Natchitoches, La., a lady of refinement and culture, and a member of an old and highly influential family of that section. Four sons and one daughter have been born to Mr. and Mrs. Evans. Our subject has always lived on the seacoast of Mississippi, the first twenty-four years of his life being spent in his native town, and the remainder at Moss Point. He is a Methodist in his religious convictions, and is a prohibitionist, but not of the third party. He is an ardent democrat. He is a man of strong convictions, and is possessed of the courage to maintain any position he may take.

Thomas R. Evans is a planter who has been identified with the interests of Lowndes county from his twenty-sixth year, at which time he came thither from Morgan county, Ga., where he was born, September 23, 1833. His childhood days were spent near the town of Madison, Ga., and there received his initiatory training, finishing his literary education in Pennfield (Mercer) university. He removed to Monroe county, Miss., in the year 1846, and from there enlisted, in April, 1862, as a private in company F, Forty-third Mississippi volunteers, afterward taking part in the engagements at Iuka, Corinth, Vicksburg and others. He was promoted to the commandership of the post at West Point, Miss., but this position he resigned in 1864, and moved to his plantation near West Point, where he remained until 1865, since which time he has been a resident of his present plantation. He was married on December 16, 1856, to Miss Sallie L., daughter of John and Matilda Morton, both of whom were born in Georgia, and their union has resulted in the birth of six children: Addie M., Mattie (deceased), William G., John M. (deceased), Charles W. and Sallie L. Mr. Evans is a member of the Methodist Episcopal church, is a democrat politically, and is a member of the Farmers' Alliance. His parents, William G. and Adeline (Heard) Evans, were Georgians by birth, but in the year 1845 removed to Monroe county, Miss., where the father was called from life in 1889, the mother having died in 1851. They became the parents of children named as follows: Faulkner Heard, Thomas R., William A. (a physician); Martha L. (deceased), John J. (state treasurer of Mississippi), and Jesse M., Eliza W., Julia A. and Mary.

One of the most reliable druggists of Hancock county, Miss., Thomas L. Evans, Bay Saint Louis, Miss., was born in New Orleans, La., in 1855, and is a son of Thomas L. Evans, Sr., a native of Philadelphia. His father was a wealthy capitalist, and removed from his native city to New Orleans is 1855; there he died three years later. He had two sons, our subject being the only surviving one. He was reared in New Orleans, and received his education in the schools of that place. He was graduated in pharmacy from the Tulane university March 17, 1881, and immediately opened a drug business in New Orleans, which he carried on until 1890. In that year he came to Bay Saint Louis, Miss., and established himself in the same business. He carries a fine line of drugs and toilet articles, and is fast winning that patronage which excellent goods handled intelligently are sure to attract. There is no druggist in the county better fitted for the responsible position of prescription clerk than he. He is ambitious to excel, and keeps himself well posted by a wide reading of druggists' periodicals. Mr. Evans was married, in 1886, to Miss Mamie Ryan, of New Orleans. One child has been born to this union, Lelia C. The family are devout members of the Roman Catholic church.

W. A. Evans, the subject of this sketch, is a member of a family that, in its various ramifications, has added much to the solid worth of the citizenry of this and other Southern states. Two divisions of this family are located in northeast Mississippi; the descendants of a third are in western Mississippi. The descendants of James Evans are located chiefly in the western portion of Monroe county. They are of large influence. William G. Evans, one of the largest planters of east Mississippi, was the father of the subject of this sketch. He was a gentleman of the old school, a pleasing host, a man of positive convictions and good judgment. No one was more of a balance-wheel for his community than William G. Evans. Dr. Evans' mother was Miss Adeline E. Heard, a woman cultivated and refined, and of a family highly esteemed in many Southern communities. She reared seven children. A daughter, Mrs. Columbus Love, has recently died, leaving a daughter. Mrs. J. W. Bozeman is the wife of Dr. J. W. Bozeman, a leading Baptist minister, living in Meridian. Mrs. T. W. Moore is the wife of one of Aberdeen's most enterprising business men. The four sons fought through the Civil war as valiantly as became them. Dr. Falkner Evans died several years ago, leaving no children. Capt. T. R. Evans is one of the largest planters in Lowndes county. Capt. J. J. Evans is now treasurer of the state of Mississippi, and is perhaps the most popular man in the state. Dr. William A. Evans was born in Madison, Ga., December 5, 1836. When but nine years old his father moved with his family to his planting interests in Mississippi, being one of the earliest settlers on its prairies.   Dr. Evans' literary education was obtained at the University of Mississippi.   He studied medicine in Jefferson medical college, of Philadelphia, the College of Physicians and Surgeons, of New York, and in the medical department of the University of the city of New York, from the last of which he received his degree.   He served in the army of Northern Virginia from May, 1861, to November, 1862, when he was transferred to the army of Mississippi.   In May, 1863, he organized the hospitals at Marion, Ala., and remained there as surgeon in charge until February, 1864.   At this time he reported to Lieutenant-General Polk as assistant medical director.   After General Polk's death he served as assistant medical director under Lieutenant-General S. D. Lee, until the end of the war.   In May, 1864, he was married to Miss Josephine Wyatt, in Marion, Ala.   They have had seven children: Walter and Lovelace died in childhood; Miss Addie Evans, the only daughter, is an artist of reputation; Herbert is the youngest boy and the only one at home; Gus, Wyatt and Tindale are assuming positions in the communities in which they live.   In March, 1869, Dr. Evans located in Aberdeen, Miss., the home of his youth, and since that date he has practiced his profession in that community. Being strictly attentive to business, possessed of good mind and good educational basis, it is needless to say that his practice has always been large.   There is no class of men whose lives become so interwoven with the lives of a community as those of physicians, and this, true of the class, is eminently true of Dr. Evans.   No part of his life has been given to public affairs; his clientele has claimed it all.   There is no truth more forcibly taught by the breadth of this century than the necessity of a division of labor.   Dr. Evans' consistent devotion to his department of a community's life work has borne fruit in the esteem in which he is held by this community.   He is now vigorous and strong, with many years of usefulness before him.

One of the most prosperous planters, as well as one of the largest landowners in the county of Itawamba, is William M. Evans, who was born in Georgia in the year 1818.   He is a son of William and Sela (Dunn) Evans, who were members of old families of Georgia, his ancestry having settled there about the beginning of the present century.   He was reared on a plantation and given the advantages of a common-school education in his native state.   He began to do for himself at an early age, and has been so successful that he is regarded as one of the self-made, wealthy men of the county.   In 1844 he married Sarah A. Pierce, a daughter of John and Betsey (Skinner) Pierce, and she was a native of Georgia.   Her parents were also natives of Georgia and members of well-known families there.   To Mr. and Mrs. Evans seven children have been born—two sons and five daughters—of whom two died young. Those living are Martha A., Elizabeth, John T., Susan F. and William D.   Mrs. Evans died in 1862.   She was a model wife and mother, and for long years a member of the Methodist Episcopal church.   In 1863 Mr. Evans enlisted in Col. John M. Simonton's regiment, but was soon sent home on account of disability and detailed to provost duty, which he continued till the close of the war.   Politically he is a democrat, standing high in the estimation of his party and fellow-citizens generally, which is attested by the fact that he has been five times elected a member of the board of supervisors of Itawamba county.   He is a member of the Methodist Episcopal church South, and is liberal in his contributions to schools, churches and to all worthy objects.   He is the oldest settler in his part of the county, and has lived on his present plantation since 1865.   He is the owner of four thousand six hundred acres of land, the largest amount owned by any one man in the southern part of the county of Itawamba.

K. W. Exum, Vaughan, Yazoo county, Miss., was born in Yazoo county, Miss., April 30, 1848, and is the eldest of a family of three sons.   His father, Edward Exum, was a native of South Carolina, and settled in Yazoo county about the year 1832. He was a farmer by occupation, and was very successful. His death occurred in 1858. His wife, whose maiden name was Mary A. Day, was a native of Amite county, Miss., and a daughter of Robert Day, one of the pioneer settlers of Yazoo county. Mrs. Exum is still living on her plantation, where she has resided since her marriage in 1847. Their children are K. W., the subject of this notice, R. D., who lives with his mother, and E. W., of Utah territory. K. W. Exum was reared on a farm in Yazoo county, and received a limited education. With the exception of one year at school in Kentucky, he attended the primitive schools of pioneer days. On account of the death of his father he remained with his mother until he was twenty-seven years of age. Her estate was much involved at the close of the Civil war, but with the aid of her sons she managed to regain the most of her possessions. Mr. Exum began farming on his present plantation in 1878. The place then consisted of one hundred and sixty acres, to which he has added two hundred acres. He has made numerous improvements on this place. There is a large, comfortable dwelling and convenient barns for the storing of crops. In addition to this plantation he owns four hundred and eighty acres of land adjoining Vaughan, and two hundred and forty acres in another tract. It is all choice land, and about one-half is under excellent cultivation. He has been successful in all branches of agriculture, and his estate is the result of his own industry and wise management. He was married in 1875 to Miss Susan V. Ledbetter, a daughter of Richard and Martha A. (Hendricks) Ledbetter, who were prominent pioneer settlers of Yazoo county. Seven children have been born to Mr. and Mrs. Exum: Mary E., twin sister, Annie L., Nannie D., Richard L., Sue V. and Hallie. Mr. Exum is a member of the Knights of Honor of Deasonville, being the assistant presiding officer. From his early manhood he has felt a deep interest in the political questions of the day, and has taken an active part in local politics. He is now candidate for sheriff of Yazoo county. He is in the prime of life, is energetic and progressive, and thoroughly loyal to the interests of Yazoo county.

CHAPTER XVIII.

⇁·⊛·⇀

NOTABLE PERSONS, F.

PROMINENT among the citizens of Clarke county is Jack Fairchild, of Roy, a son of Robert Fairchild, a planter, who was born in South Carolina about 1760; married Miss Nancy Taylor, of Newberry, S. C., about 1783; removed to Mississippi about 1812, using packhorses, and died about 1853, Mrs. Fairchild having died about 1849. Jack Fairchild was born in 1821 in Perry county, Miss., and removed, when young, to Jones county, later to Lauderdale county, and thence to Clarke county, Miss., where he now resides, eleven miles east of Enterprise, on the Enterprise and Energy road. He was married in 1840 in Lauderdale county, Miss., to Miss Eliza Jolly, a daughter of Bradley Jolly, of Lauderdale county, Miss. They have had ten children: Elizabeth, R. E., William B., Martha J., Melissa Ann, Lofton M., James M., Jack, Monroe, Nathan M. and Eliza Virginia. Seven of these survive and are married. Prior to the war Mr. Fairchild was engaged in planting, which he resumed after the return of peace. He owned, formerly, some two hundred acres of land, which, by additions, now amounts to one thousand four hundred acres of as good land as the average soil of Clarke county, Miss. Much of it is heavily timbered with longleaf pine, and he has also about two hundred acres open to cultivation. He is largely engaged in sheep husbandry, having about four hundred or five hundred head of the Merino, Cotswold and Southdown breeds. He sells principally to the local trade. From two brothers from Wales the present American Fairchilds are supposed to have sprung. From the one of the two who settled at Charleston, S. C., those of the Fairchild family residing in the South are probably descended.

Few, if any, industrial or professional pursuits have within the last few years made such rapid strides as that of the profession of medicine, and among the leading physicians of Hinds county, Miss., who have availed themselves of all new ideas and put them into practice, may be mentioned Dr. Peter Fairly. He first saw the light of day in Greene county, Miss., April 17, 1841, being the eighth of eleven children born to Alexander and Margaret (Thompson) Fairly, natives of the Old North state. The father was born in 1797, was reared in his native state and there graduated from Floral college. He is of a literary turn of mind, and for some fifteen years was engaged in teaching school, during which time he won an enviable reputation as an educator and disciplinarian. He is an extensive reader, and is well-posted in all the general topics of the day, and although he has attained the advanced age of ninety-four years, he is in good health, and his mind shows but little the ravages of time. He came to Mississippi in 1823, locating in Greene county, where he was engaged in planting and stockraising, making a decided success of both callings. He accumulated a large and valuable property, and is now in the enjoyment of a handsome competency. Although he has never been a politician, he has represented his county in the legislature of Mississippi, during which time he made a faithful and intelligent legislator. He is now residing in Covington county with his wife, an estimable, intelligent and motherly old lady, who is now in her eighty-seventh year. They have seen sixty-eight anniversaries of their marriage, and all their children grew to maturity, married and became parents. Nine are now living, and three of the sons have held some of the most responsible positions of their county. The Fairlys are of Scotch descent, the paternal grandfather of the subject of this sketch being a native of Scotland. Dr. Peter Fairly was reared in Greene county and was educated at Salem high school, obtaining a good English and classical education. In 1868 he graduated from Tulane university of New Orleans, having previously gone through the war, being lieutenant of company I, Seventh Mississippi regiment throughout the entire conflict. He was in all the battles of the West from Shiloh to Atlanta, and at the battle of Peach Tree creek he was severely wounded. He surrendered at Greensboro, N. C., after which he returned home, taught school and studied medicine as above stated. His first practice was done in Covington county, where he remained for eleven years, when he was called (in 1879) to Brandon to settle the affairs of the Rankin county saving institution, and here he continued to make his home for ten years, during which time he was actively engaged in the practice of his profession. In 1889 he came to Jackson, where he has built up a large and lucrative practice. He is an able representative of the medical fraternity and one of whom the profession may well be proud. He is superintendent of the State institution for the blind, succeeding Miss Maggie Langley, she succeeding her father, Dr. W. S. Langley, and in this capacity has shown himself an able and successful manager. By his undeviating efforts and faithfulness to his profession he has accumulated considerable property and in addition to his profession is now farming, extensively in Rankin county. He is a gentleman in every sense of the word, as well as being an exemplary Christian. In 1880 he was married to Miss Leila Langley, a native of Mississippi and a daughter of Dr. W. S. Langley. To the Doctor and his wife the following children have been born: Albert L., Peter A., Sophia L. and Maggie M. The Doctor and his wife are members of the Presbyterian church, in which he is ruling elder, and socially, he is a member of the A. F. & A.M., the K. of H. and the A. O. U. W.

It is an undeniable truth that the life of any man is of great benefit to the community in which he resides, when all his efforts are directed toward advancing its interests, and who lives according to the highest principles of what he conceives to be right, helping others and caring for those who are unable to do for themselves. Such a man is Mr. George W. Faison, who has been one of the highly successful and enterprising merchants of this section for many years. His name has become a familiar one to the people of Sunflower, as well as the surrounding counties, and his genial and sincere nature, no less than the business in which he is engaged, has tended to bring about this result. He was born in Southampton county, Va., August 7, 1830, in which state his father and grandfather before him were born, the birth of the former occurring in Sussex county in 1810. Squire Faison, the grandfather, inherited French blood of his ancestors, who were early residents of Virginia, in the history of which state they became well known. Capt. Hiram Faison, father of George W., grew to maturity in the county of his birth, and was there married to Miss Sarah West, a daughter of William West, who belonged to a pioneer family of Virginia, and was a soldier in the Revolutionary war. After his marriage Capt. Faison settled in Southampton county, where he was engaged in planting until his death, about the year 1842, becoming prominent in the affairs of that county. He served in the capacity of captain of militia, and held local positions of honor and trust, and for many years was a prominent member of the Baptist church. His widow survived him about two years, dying in 1844. George W. Faison is the eldest of a family of three sons and two daughters that grew to mature years, and in the county of his birth he attained to man's estate. In 1851 he determined to seek a home for himself in a new locality, and took up his abode in Fayette county, Tenn., where he was engaged in farming for a number of years. In 1858 he moved to Mississippi and located in Issaquena county, where he followed merchandising and planting for about four years. Since that time he has been one of the foremost residents of Sunflower county, his residence being at Faisonia. He first engaged in planting at this point, but in 1866 also embarked in merchandising, and since locating here has had several branch stores. His first store was established at Indianola, where he did business for about one year, and in 1870 another establishment was started in Johnsonville, which was successfully conducted for about six years. He sold out this establishment in 1878, and in 1881 opened a store at Greenville, conducting affairs there in a highly successful manner for about two years. In 1888 he built a fine business block of three storerooms in Indianola, where he has conducted affairs under the firm name of Faison & Son. They now have three complete stores, one at Faisonia, one at Shaws and the other in Indianola. They carry a very large stock of general merchandise and do an annual business of about $250,000. Mr. Faison is one of the largest planters of Sunflower county. He has under cultivation about three thousand five hundred acres of land in this county in several plantations, in addition to which he has some two thousand acres of wild land. Mr. Faison commenced business in this county after the war almost empty handed, but his own industry and superior business capacity and management have accumulated a large estate, and he is now one of the most substantial business men in this section of the country. He was married in Tennessee in 1854 to Miss Ellen R. Fields, a native of North Carolina, but reared in Mississippi, a daughter of Jesse Fields, one of the early residents of Issaquena county. Mrs. Faison was called from life in this state in 1863, having borne one son, George W., Jr., a sketch of whom immediately follows this. Mr. Faison married his present wife in this county in 1869, she being Mrs. Anna M. Waites, a daughter of Judge Smith, a former circuit judge and a member of the Mississippi legislature. Mrs. Faison was born and reared in Hinds county, Miss., and has borne her husband the following children: Walter B., William M., Addie E., James P. and Edmond H. Mr. Faison's career thus far in life has been one of which he has every reason to be proud, and owing to his many sterling characteristics he possesses many warm friends throughout this section. He has long been prominently connected with the Methodist Episcopal church, and all things of a public nature which point to the material benefit of the county receive his support.

Among the shrewd, successful and far-seeing young business men of this section is Mr. George W. Faison, Jr., who, like his father, possesses business ability of a high order. He was born in Issaquena county, Miss, February 23, 1861, and in 1863 was brought by his parents to Sunflower county, his early youth being spent in Faisonia. He was given the advantages of the schools of this county, and his education was completed at Washington and Lee college, Virginia. Upon his return from college he began clerking in his father's store in Faisonia, continuing with him for five years. During this time he received a most thorough business training and laid the foundation for a successful career in later years. In 1885 he engaged in merchandising at Shaws, and for about three years successfully conducted affairs at that point. In 1888 the present partnership of G. W. Faison & Son was formed, with a store at Faisonia, Shaws, and a double store at Indianola, their annual sales being very satisfactory. Mr. Faison is a young man of sterling qualities of character, and as a business manager has not his superior among the young men of this section. His habits are unexceptionable, and he is highly esteemed and respected in social as well as business circles.

Richard B. Faison. This successful, pushing and energetic planter, was born in Southampton county, Va., October 4, 1838, to Capt. Hiram Faison, and in the state and county of his birth he grew to manhood, receiving a fair English education in a private school. At the age of twenty-one years, or in 1859, he came west to Mississippi and for some time was engaged in clerking in a store belonging to his brother, George W. Faison, in Issaquena county. In 1863 he became a resident of Sunflower county, and for some time thereafter was engaged in farming on the Sunflower river, which occupation he discontinued in 1866 to once more follow the calling of a clerk in his brother's store. In 1873 he located on a plantation, and is now the owner of three hundred and twenty acres of land, of which about one hundred and forty acres are under cultivation. His land is well improved and his residence is a very commodious, substantial and pleasant one. He has also a good cottongin and other buildings. Since 1888 he has conducted a plantation and neighborhood store on his place, which is bringing him in fair returns, but he has for some time past lived in Indianola in one of the largest and handsomest residences in the place. He was married in this county in July, 1875, to Miss Sarah Carter, a native of Louisiana, born and reared in Morehouse parish, a daughter of John Carter. Their union has resulted in the birth of six children: Annie, John H., Ella Clara and Ethelin, and two children now deceased: Robert Lee, who died in infancy in 1888, and Richard B., an interesting lad, who was called from life in 1891 at the age of thirteen years. Richard B. Faison, like his brother George W., began life a poor boy, but has by his own industry and good management accumulated a competency. In agricultural matters he is practically informed and well posted and his example is one well worthy of imitation. He lost his left arm in childhood, yet by his indomitable pluck has reared his family in comfort and has accumulated a fair share of this world's goods. His reputation has remained unblemished throughout a long business career, and for his Christian character and for the enterprising and public spirit that he has always manifested, he is highly esteemed by all who know him. Of the property that he has acquired by the sweat of his brow, he gives liberally in the support of worthy institutions and may well be considered an acquisition to the community in which he resides.

The following space will be devoted to the memory of the deceased lawyer and author whose brilliant career was cut off by the hand of the assassin at the highest tide of his prosperity. Col. William C. Falkner, Ripley Miss., was born in the state of Missouri in 1833, and was a son of Joseph Falkner. The father was a native of Tennessee, and married Miss Caroline Word, a native of the same state; they removed to Missouri and settled at St. Genevieve. There our subject was reared until he was fourteen years of age, when he went to Ripley, Miss., to live with an uncle. He was employed by the sheriff of the county, and worked at the jail and attended school until he was eighteen years of age. It was about this time that he assisted in the capture of a murderer by the name of McCannon. The guilty man confessed his crime; the confession was written up by Colonel Falkner and published, its sale bringing him the first money he had earned in his life. At the outbreak of the Mexican war he volunteered in Capt. Alex. Jackson's company as a private; he was soon made first lieutenant, but soon received a wound which disabled him; before he was again fit for duty the war had closed. He was married in 1847 to Miss Holland Pearce, of Knoxville, Tenn. He then began the study of law and was admitted to the bar at Ripley, and was successfully engaged in the practice of his profession at the time the Civil war broke upon this country. For a time he was a leader of the Know-nothing party of Tippah county, and edited a paper known as the *Uncle Sam*, which was the organ of the party, and kept it together. He entered with spirit upon the Civil war, raised a company which bore his name and of which he was captain. In 1861 he was elected colonel of the Second Mississippi regiment, and took them to Virginia, where they were mustered into the Confederate service at Harper's Ferry. He led them in the first battle of Manassas and Bull Run. At the end of twelve months he returned and secured a large number of recruits, which he took to Virginia and organized into a regiment. On account of ill health he came home, and soon afterward received a commission from President Davis to raise a regiment of cavalry. He raised the Seventh Mississippi cavalry, and served with them during the war. After the surrender he resumed the practice of law, which he continued until about 1868, when he conceived the idea of building the railroad from Middleton, Tenn., to Ripley, Miss., and through his efforts this was completed in 1872. He was a Tilden elector in 1876 for the second congressional district; he made a hard canvass of the district, and lead the ticket. In 1887 he began the extension of the railroad south, and in 1888 he completed it to Pontotoc, where it is now terminated, there being in operation sixty-four miles. Colonel Falkner was manager, controller and president of the road, and it owes its existence to his efforts. In the midst of all these pressing commercial duties, Colonel Falkner still found time for the culture of the intellectual side of his nature, and from 1865 to 1886, he wrote three books, two novels and one book of travels. "The White Rose of Memphis," which has had a large circulation, was published about 1880; in 1882, "The Little Brick Church" was published, a novel of much literary merit. In 1883 the Colonel made a trip to Europe, and the next year he published an account of this jaunt called "Rapid Ramblings in Europe." In 1869 John W. T. Falkner, son of Colonel Falkner, was admitted to the bar, and he retired in favor of his son. In 1889, while in New York, he was nominated to the legislature of Mississippi, and on November 5, of the same year, he was elected to the office, and at five o'clock of the same day he was assassinated while standing in the street of Ripley by R. J. Thurmond. The Grenada *Sentinel* characterized the trial which acquitted this man as a mockery of justice, and such it would seem in view of all the evidence. But, as the *Sentinel* further adds: "It is a happy reflection to know that money and corruption have no sway in the world to come." John W. T. Falkner is the only child of the first marriage. He was educated in the University of Oxford, studied law, and was graduated in 1869; he was at once admitted to the bar, and has been engaged in practice since that time. In 1886 he was appointed assistant United States district attorney, and served until 1888. He was married in 1869 to Miss Sallie A. Murry, a native of Mississippi. Of this union five children have been born, two of whom are deceased. The parents are members of the Methodist Episcopal church. Mr. Falkner is a member of the I. O. O. F. and the Knights of Pythias. He is a devoted student of his profession and a lawyer of much more than ordinary ability. Colonel Falkner was a high degree Mason, and was buried by that body. He was a man of many talents, a writer of clear, pure literary style, a business man of the finest qualifications, and a lawyer of high rank; he was the leading spirit in every enterprise leading to the elevation of Oxford, and was a liberal supporter of religious and educational institutions. He was a man of fine appearance, and the heart that sent the pulses of life through his manly form was as tender as a woman's. Colonel Falkner's first wife having died, he married a second time in 1850, and has three daughters living, the fruits of this union. Two of them married, one to a prominent physician residing at Ripley, Miss., Dr. N. G. Carter, the other to Mr. Edward F. Campbell, of Memphis, Tenn.

The Goodspeed Pub. Co., Chicago

O. W. Blanton.

C. H. Fant, Friar's Point, Miss., a prominent planter of Coahoma county and secretary and treasurer of the Friar's Point oil mill, was born near Huntsville, Ala., in 1837, and was the youngest of eight children born to John B. and Jane (Barber) Fant, both of whom are descendants of prominent Virginia families. The father moved to Alabama about 1835, and in the winter of 1837 from there to Holly Springs, Marshall county, Miss., where he was among the pioneers. He was a very prominent citizen and president of the board of supervisors for many years. He bought property in Coahoma county and followed agricultural pursuits there for some time. His death occurred near Holly Springs in 1883, at the age of eighty-three years. His wife had received her final summons in 1863. Both were worthy members of the Methodist Episcopal church South, and he was a liberal contributor and supporter of the same up to the time of his death. During the Civil war he lost heavily, but repaired his fortune later. C. H. Fant was reared in Marshall county, Miss., attended the school there, and graduated at a college at Florence, Ala. In 1858, or when twenty-one years of age, he began manufacturing at Florence (Ala.) woolen mill, and during a portion of the time was manufacturing the Confederate gray for uniforms. He was burnt out by the Federals in 1864. The year previous to this Mr. Fant enlisted in company F, Fourth Alabama cavalry, as private, was with General Forrest in his Tennessee raid and was in the Mississippi campaign. In 1864 he was made lieutenant of his company and served in that capacity until peace was declared, being discharged at Selma, Ala. During the last year of this memorable struggle Mr. Fant was in almost constant skirmishes and engagements. He afterward farmed one year in Alabama, and in 1867 came to his present place in Coahoma county, ten miles south of Friar's Point, on property that was once owned by his father, six hundred acres, with four hundred and fifty acres under cultivation. He cleared about one-half and made all improvements. In 1878 he moved to Friar's Point, where he has a fine place and about one hundred acres of land. He was one of the promoters and organizers of the oil mill at Friar's Point, and this establishment is, perhaps, the best equipped in Mississippi. They have the best improved machinery and excellent buildings. Mr. Fant was married the first time, in 1857, to Miss Lula Foster, of Florence, Ala., who died in 1875, leaving four children: Annie, Edward, Foster and Ellington, all now living. Several children died in infancy. In 1878 Mr. Fant took for his second wife Miss Addie Maynard, a native of Mississippi, and the daughter of Decatur Maynard (see sketch of George F. Maynard). One child, Henry Wallace, is the result of this union. The family are members of the Methodist Episcopal church South. Mr. Fant is now one of the active managers of the oil mill, which enterprise is very prosperous for its recent establishment. He is also a stockholder in the Friar's Point Loan and Improvement company. Mr. Fant is tall, large-framed, rugged and hearty, and genial and courteous. He has dark hair tinged with gray, and dark eyes. He is one of the leading, enterprising and prosperous men of Coahoma county.

Dr. Joshua C. Fant was born in South Carolina in 1832, and moved with his parents to Noxubee county, Miss., when quite a small boy. He graduated in medicine in Charleston, S. C., in 1857, and located in Macon, Miss., where he lived until removed by death, October 25, 1889, at fifty-seven years of age. Dr. Fant was a true Christian, faithful, useful and honored citizen, and a popular and successful physician. By his genial and cheerful disposition and ability as a medical man he enjoyed a large circle of friends and patrons, by whom he was much admired and esteemed. He served with distinction as surgeon during the late war, but owing to a lack of data we are unable to give any particular action. He died as he had lived, with full confidence in the redeeming blood of Christ.

45

George Porterfield Farley (deceased) was a man whose career was honorable in the sight of God and man, and as a law-abiding, public-spirited and enterprising citizen he had not his superior in his section of the country. He was born on the 4th of July, 1811, on what is now known as the Wattsland plantation, and on this place his family now resides. He owned at one time one thousand nine hundred acres of land, which, after his death, which occurred October 9, 1879, was divided among his heirs. On the 10th of September, 1837, he was united in marriage to Mrs. Mills, of this county, and by her became the father of eight children—three sons and five daughters. The sons died in infancy, and one daughter, Buena Vista, in her sixteenth year. The other four daughters still survive, their names being: Chestina P., wife of A. J. Melton (see sketch); Charlotte P., widow of Dr. Hayes; George P., widow of L. J. Slay; and Thetis M., wife of W. A. Killingsworth. After the death of her husband Mrs. Farley took up her permanent abode on the homestead, and in her own right is the owner of seven hundred and forty-two acres of land, all of which she leases. She is quite extensively engaged in stockraising, and her cotton crop usually averages about thirty bales annually. Mr. Farley was a strong Union man during the Rebellion, and was chosen as a member of the reconstruction convention at Jackson, and also otherwise took a prominent part in the current issues of the day. He was a leader in whatever he undertook, and for his intelligent views on all matters, and for his charity and liberality, he was looked up to and respected by all who came within his influence. His father, Robert Farley, was twice married—first to Miss Mary E. Watts, a descendant of the Lee family, she being a relative of Gen. Robert E. Lee. The result of this union was two sons and four daughters. George Porterfield was a son of this union. After the death of his wife he was married to a widow by the name of Jordan, who bore him one son and two daughters. Of his entire family one son and six daughters attained mature years, and settled in Jefferson county, Miss., where they spent their entire lives, all being now deceased, except one daughter by the last union. Robert Farley was a Virginian by birth, and first saw the light of day in the year 1779. He came to Jefferson county, Miss., in the year 1793 in search of a fortune, and in this was successful, for he obtained a Spanish grant of land near where the family now reside, and here gathered around him a considerable amount of worldly goods. The Farley family are well known in this section and are considered among its most substantial citizens. They move in the highest social circles and are well known for their intelligence, kind hospitality and charity.

Among the rising young men of Yazoo county is John M. Farish, of Valley, a brief outline of whose career will occupy the following space. He was born in Yazoo county May 15, 1866, and is the elder of two children of William T. and Mary (Jackson) Farish, natives of Alabama. The father removed to Mississippi at an early day, and settled in Yazoo county, where he engaged in planting. He followed this occupation until his death, in 1890. He was a son of George Farish, who was a Virginian by birth. The maternal grandparents of John M. were John M. and Cynthia Jackson, of Alabama. He was reared in his native county, attending the public and private schools until he was nineteen years of age. Having finished the junior year at Harperville college and chosen the profession of medicine for his life work, he entered the medical college at Louisville, Ky., where he pursued his studies for two years. He was graduated with the class of 1888, and returned to Yazoo county, entering at once into practice, and was admitted to membership in the Mississippi state medical association. Although young in years and experience, he has won a profitable practice, and his skill, energy and ambition will soon place him in the front ranks of the profession in his county. In addition to his professional duties he superintends the cultivation of his plantation. He owns five hundred acres, one hundred of which are under excellent cultivation. He was located at Sartatia until the death of his father, when he returned to the parental roof, and together with his brother, George W., has been carrying on the business left by his father. The farm lies principally in the Yazoo river valley, and is one of the most fertile and productive in the whole county. The mother of our subject, and he also, belong to the Missionary Baptist church. Mr. Farish is an active member of the Farmers' Alliance. Politically he affiliates with the democratic party.

Capt. William S. Farish, lawyer, and the present prosecuting attorney for the district in which he lives, owes his nativity to Woodville, Wilkinson county, Miss., where his birth occurred on the 5th of March, 1843. His parents, Hazelwood M. and Jane L. (Davis) Farish, were natives of Virginia and Mississippi respectively, and his maternal grandmother, who was the youngest sister of President Jefferson Davis, was also a native of Mississippi. At the age of fourteen years the grandmother married Robert Davis, who was an officer and served with distinction in the War of 1812. Her death occurred at the age of eighteen years. She left two children, Jane L. and Ellen M., the latter now the wife of Thomas S. Anderson, who was the brother-in-law of Governor McWillie, of this state. Hazelwood M. Farish was one of the leading and distinguished attorneys of Mississippi, to which state he had moved at an early day, and was contemporary with Judge Simrall, of Warren county, and other noted lawyers of his day. His argumentative powers were clear, vigorous and incisive, and his knowledge of the law profound. He died in 1849, when in the hight of his success. Capt. William S. Farish, the eldest of three children, the others being Dr. R. D., of Mayersville (see sketch) and Fannie A., widow of W. J. Stout, received the rudiments of an education in the schools of the county in which he was born, and at the age of seventeen years entered the University of Mississippi. Previous to graduating, hostilities began between the North and South, and Captain Farish left school and joined the Eighteenth Mississippi regiment, serving with this regiment in the first battle of Manassas (which occurred three days after his joining). Shortly after this engagement he was discharged on account of sickness, and three months later, with restored health, he went to Richmond, where he spent a month at the presidential mansion. He was then promoted to a cadetship in the regular army of the Confederacy, and rejoined his old regiment at Yorktown, Va., without reënlisting. After the battle of Williamsburg he went to Richmond and there found orders to report to Gen. Kirby Smith, then in east Tennessee. He served for a few months on General Smith's personal staff and was then assigned by him as aid-de-camp to Col. Thomas Taylor, who was commanding a brigade under General Smith. Captain Farish was with the last-named General in Bragg's campaign through Kentucky, but this brigade was not engaged either at Richmond or Perryville of that state. During the retreat he was for awhile with the rear guard and was in some severe skirmishes. Afterward, Stephen's division, to which Taylor's brigade belonged, was ordered to Vicksburg under General Pemberton, Taylor in the meantime being promoted to the rank of brigadier-general. Previous to the siege of Vicksburg by General Grant, Taylor was relieved of the command of his brigade, the Confederate senate having refused to confirm his appointment. Captain Farish then reported to General Pemberton and was sent by him as special bearer of dispatches to Richmond, Va. He took the last train that left the city of Vicksburg, and when ready to return there from Richmond, found the city invested with Grant's army, and he could not report to General Pemberton. He was then ordered to report to Gen. Joseph E. Johnston, at Jackson, and was by him assigned to duty in his ordnance department, of which Captain Evans was in command, and there remained until the exchange of Gen. Stephen D. Lee, who was captured in the fall of Vicksburg. Shortly after the exchange mentioned, Captain Farish was assigned to duty on General Lee's personal staff, where he remained until the latter surrendered with General Johnston's army at Greensboro, N. C., in April, 1865.   Captain Farish served under General Lee in the cavalry fights at Moscow and Harrisburg, Miss., and in numerous minor engagements.

Not long after his assignment to the staff of General Lee, Captain Farish attained his majority, and was examined for promotion in the regular army of the Confederacy.   He was first made lieutenant in the regular service, and shortly afterward captain in the provisional service.   Lee, after being promoted to the rank of lieutenant-general, was assigned to the command of Hood's corps in General Johnson's army in front of Atlanta, and Captain Farish went with him to that command.   He participated in the heavy fighting in and around Atlanta and in the battle of Jonesboro.   He was with General Lee's command in Hood's Tennessee campaign, and took part in the battles of Franklin and Nashville.   General Lee was wounded in the foot during the retreat from Nashville, and left his command for a season.   Maj.-Gen. D. H. Hill was assigned the command of General Lee's corps, and not long afterward this corps was ordered to Goldsboro, N. C., to coöperate with troops in that section, to oppose Sherman's advance from the coast toward Richmond.   Captain Farish served as aid-de-camp to General Hill during the movements of the armies through North and South Carolina, and participated in the battles fought with General Sherman's advance.   At the battle of Kingston the Captain was slightly wounded in the left knee, the only wound received during his entire service of four years.   Shortly before the surrender of General Johnson, General Lee had sufficiently recovered from his wound to rejoin the army and resume command of his corps, and with him Captain Farish surrendered his sword in the little town of Greensboro, as before mentioned.   Captain Farish then returned to his home, but found his property destroyed, and the inheritance that should have been his scattered in every direction.   He immediately commenced planting, but this was not at all to his taste, the labor and the season being both against a successful termination of his hopes. In 1867 he attended the University of Virginia, took the degree of B. L., and early in the year 1869 began the practice of law in Vicksburg, where he remained over a year.   In 1871 he moved to Mayersville, Issaquena county, and there he has had a very successful practice, and is considered one of the most talented attorneys of the fourth district.   He is a clear, comprehensive thinker, an excellent reasoner, and the succession of his thoughts is closely logical.   In personal appearance the Captain is about five feet ten inches in hight, slender build, piercing brown eyes, a long, pointed mustache, and is a man who would attract attention in any assembly by his distinguished appearance.   In 1878 Captain Farish was elected to the state senate, served one session, and then resigned, in order to run for the office of district attorney, to which office he had been nominated by the democratic party.   In this race he was beaten by the republican nominee, C. W. Clark, who resigned in 1880, and Captain Farish was then elected by a handsome majority.   He has been twice reëlected to this office by handsome majorities, for terms of four years each, and is the present incumbent. He was a delegate from the county of Issaquena to the constitutional convention of 1890. The Captain was married in May, 1880, to Miss Kate M. Power, of Natchez, Miss., a daughter of Stephen F. Power.   Captain and Mrs. Farish are the parents of four interesting children: W. R., Rosalie, Stephen D. and F. P.

Dr. R. D. Farish, physician, Mayersville, Miss., who is a descendant of old and honored families on both the father's and mother's side, was born in Wilkinson county, Miss., in the year 1845, and is now one of the leading physicians of Issaquena county.   His father, Hazelwood Farish, was a native of the Old Dominion, and his mother, Jane L. (Davis)

Farish, was born in Mississippi. After his marriage Hazelwood Farish settled in Wilkinson county, Miss., and was considered one of the ablest and most distinguished lawyers in the state. He died in 1849. He and wife were the parents of three children, who were named in the order of their births as follows: Hon. W. S., an attorney; Dr. Robert D. and Fannie, widow of W. Stout, formerly of Arkansas. The grandfather served with distinction as an officer in the Revolutionary war, and Wilkinson county now has charge of his side arms. The maternal grandmother was a sister of the late Jefferson Davis of the Confederacy. Dr. R. D. Farish was in attendance at school when the war broke out, but in 1862 he abandoned his books and enlisted as a private in company I, Thirty-ninth Mississippi infantry, attached to the armies under Generals Price, Johnston and Pemberton. For nearly two years he served as private, and was afterward made ordnance sergeant in the regular army by commission from the secretary of war, and stationed at Demopolis, Ala. After the evacuation of Mobile, Ala., he was placed in charge of a steamer to transfer ordnance to Columbus, where he was stationed when notified of General Lee's surrender. He then turned over the supplies in his charge to the government officials at Macon, Miss., and went to Meridian, of that state, where he was paroled by General Canby. After the war the Doctor entered the University of Virginia, and later entered the medical department of the University of Louisiana, from which he received his diploma in 1869. He first commenced practicing in Wilkinson county, remained there three years, and then moved to Issaquena county, where he has practiced ever since. He is sanitary physician and health officer of the county, and mayor of the village of Mayersville. He is also chairman of the democratic executive committee of the county. He was married in 1876 to Miss C. H. Power, of Natchez, daughter of Stephen F. Power, and niece of Gen. N. H. Harris of Confederate fame. The father, a Mexican veteran, was formerly from New Orleans, but moved to Natchez, where he became one of the prominent men of the city. To the Doctor's marriage there were born five children, four of whom are living: Robertson Davis, Hazelwood P., Caroline, Robert W. (deceased), and Jefferson Davis. Mrs. Farish is a member of the Episcopal church, a graduate of St. Simeon's academy, New Orleans, and an accomplished scholar and musician. Although he takes considerable interest in politics, Dr. Farish is by no means an officeseeker. He has shown his appreciation of secret societies by becoming a member of the Masonic fraternity, W. H. Stephen's lodge No. 121, of Vicksburg, the Knights of Pythias, Lee lodge and the American Legion of Honor. Unlike his brother, Captain Farish, the Doctor is of medium hight, fair complexion, and is inclined to corpulency. He is a leading physician of the county, and has won an enviable reputation as a practitioner of the healing art throughout the Yazoo delta.

Dr. Caleb F. Farrar, physician and surgeon, Kingston, Miss. Grandfather Alexander Farrar was a native Virginian, but when a boy was taken by his parents across the mountains into Tennessee, and from there they floated down the Tennessee, Ohio and Mississippi river to a point just above Natchez, where they were surprised by the Indians, and all killed except two sons and a daughter. One of the sons died soon after, and the daughter married, but had no issue. The other son, Alexander, was left to struggle for a livelihood as best he could, and he became a wealthy planter, settling on Cole's creek on what is known as Moss Grove plantation. He married and there spent the balance of his days. His son, Daniel Farrar, was born in Adams county, Miss., and was there married to Miss Eliza King. They both died in that county, Daniel in 1845 and his wife in 1864, she being a member of the Methodist church. He had followed planting all his life. To their union were born seven children—three sons and four daughters, viz.: Hon. Alexander K. (deceased) was an extensive planter and prominent man of the county, having held various county offices. He was also a member of the legislature for a number of years, was in the state senate, and was a member of the board of supervisors, etc. He married Ann M. Daugherty, and by her became the father of four sons. His second wife was a Mrs. Leslie, now Mrs. A. N. Ratcliff. Thornton died while young; Mary Jane became the wife of G. W. Baynard, of Natchez; Dr. Caleb F. (subject); Ann Eliza was the wife of C. N. Vaughn, who died, leaving two children, a son and a daughter; Henry B. is deceased; Sarah Sophronia (deceased) was the wife of B. F. Swayze; Daniel S., who married a Miss Campbell, of Jefferson county, Miss., both living, and have four sons. Dr. Caleb F. Farrar was born in Kingston settlement in 1824, was educated at Centenary college and by a private tutor at home, and in 1846 he graduated from the medical department of the University of Pennsylvania. Since that time he has practiced in the vicinity of his birth, and is a conspicuous figure in what is known as Jersey settlement, or Kingston vicinity. He is a physician of marked ability, of numerous resources, and is one who keeps thoroughly apace with the times. He is upright and moral, and is an extremely interesting conversationalist. He is more familiar with the early history of the Jersey colonists than any other man now living. The Doctor was first married in 1848 to Miss Rachel E. Fowles, daughter of William B. and Matilda Fowles, the former born in New York city in 1800. William B. was left an orphan when four years of age, and he and a sister were taken by their uncle, Capt. John Ogden, to the headwaters of the Ohio, and from there they came down the river on a flatboat to Natchez. Mr. Fowles remained with his uncle for many years, and was married, in 1824, to Miss Matilda Luce, with whom he settled on the Mandamus grant, opened up a fine farm, and, with the exception of a few years' merchandising at Kingston, spent the rest of his life as a planter on that plantation. His death occurred in 1877. He was a man of great industry, and of excellent business ability, and accumulated a handsome property. He was magistrate for many years, and at one time was a member of the lower house of the legislature. His wife was born May 17, 1808, and died February 22, 1855. They reared a large family. Mrs. Farrar was born here, and died in 1860. The Doctor was married the second time to Mrs. M. J. Boyd, daughter of Daniel and Jane Smith, both natives of Adams county, where they spent their entire lives, Mrs. Smith being a sister of Dr. Farrar's father. Mr. Smith was a planter and a public-spirited man. The Doctor is a member of Harmony lodge No. 1, and has taken the Knight Templar degree. He and wife have held membership in the Methodist church for many years. Their residence at Kingston, consisting of ninety acres of land, is a part of Mandamus grant. Mrs. Farrar is an interesting and cultured lady. The Doctor's maternal grandfather, Caleb King, was born in New Jersey, where he was reared and married. In 1772 he came with the Swayzes and the New Jersey colonists to Adams county, and there passed the remainder of his days. He was an extensive planter and a prominent citizen. He reared two daughters, one becoming Mrs. Farrar, and the other the wife of Thomas Eaton, who was born in Pennsylvania, but who came to Adams county when a young man. Here he was married, and soon after returned to Kentucky, thence to Illinois, where he died. His wife had previously died in Kentucky.

John S. Featherston, M. D., is thoroughly fitted by study and experience for his profession, and as a physician and surgeon has built up a reputation for skill and ability that is not merely local, but extends over a large extent of territory. He was born in York county, S. C., January 1, 1845, to R. W. and R. J. (Smith) Featherston, who were born, reared and married in South Carolina and emigrated to Mississippi in 1845, locating near Macon, in

Noxubee county, where Mr. Featherston followed the calling of a planter and carpenter until the opening of the war in 1861, when he enlisted as a lieutenant in company H, Fifth Mississippi infantry. He was made captain of his company shortly afterward, but after the battle of Shiloh his health began to fail him, and on account of disability he was discharged from the service and came home, where he died in the fall of 1862. His widow and three children survive him, the names of the latter being Letitia, wife of D. Bell; Dr. J. S. and W. L., a merchant of Macon. Two children are deceased. Dr. John S. Featherston was reared in Noxubee county, being but an infant when brought thither by his parents, and his literary education was obtained in the common schools of his adopted county. He remained on his father's plantation until the Rebellion, and in 1861, although but sixteen years of age he enlisted in company H, Fifth Mississippi regiment, and the first year served as a corporal. He was next promoted to lieutenant and was subsequently made captain of his company, being then but eighteen years of age. He made a gallant and faithful officer and notwithstanding his youth he commanded the utmost respect from the members of his company, who not only respected but also esteemed him. At the battle of Chickamauga he was wounded by a gunshot, also receiving a wound in the battle of Atlanta, July 22, 1864, both of which were quite serious and kept him in the hospital for some time. He was at Murfreesboro, the bombardment of Fort Pickens and in Bragg's Kentucky and Tennessee campaigns, Shiloh, Peach Tree creek and was in the engagements from Chattanooga to Atlanta. After the final surrender, Dr. Featherston returned home, and after pursuing a medical course in the University of Louisville, Ky., he graduated in the spring of 1869, and has been an active practitioner ever since. He is a member of the county and state association and the Southern Medical and Gynæcological society. He is a member of the A. F. & A. M., the I. O. O. F. and the K. of H. He is now associated in the practice of his profession with Dr. H. A. Miner, of Macon, they constituting one of the strongest firms in their section of the state. The Doctor was first married in 1874 to Miss Emma Dismukes, who lived only a few months. In 1877 he was married to Mrs. Fannie Eckford. She, as well as himself, is a member of the Methodist Episcopal church South. The Doctor owns a handsome home and has a plantation in the country.

Gen. Winfield Scott Featherston was born in Rutherford county, Tenn., on the 8th day of August, 1820. His father, Charles Featherston, was a native of Chesterfield county, and his mother, Lucy Pitts, was a native of Essex county, Va. They were married in Essex county, Va., on the 29th day of January, 1795. Charles Featherston moved from Virginia with his family to Tennessee in 1815, locating first in Sumner county, but settled in Rutherford county in 1818. Gen. W. S. Featherston, the youngest of seven children—three sons and four daughters—was born and reared on a farm; his father being a poor man, he participated in his early boyhood in the labor incident to farm life, thereby acquiring habits of industry and economy, and a good constitution. He was educated in the best academies of the country, but was deprived of a collegiate or university course through lack of means. In 1836, while he was at a high school in Columbus, Ga., hostilities broke out between the Creek Indians and Georgians. He joined a volunteer company and served as a soldier until the Indians were subdued. During this war, upon one occasion, when it was specially dangerous to stand guard, the Indians having picked off several sentinels from a certain post, the commander called for volunteers for that post, and upon W. S. Featherston offering he was assigned to that station. In 1837 he returned to his native county, and went to school to that distinguished educator, Samuel P. Black. Although without the advantage of a collegiate course, General Featherston acquired a better education than many who pass through college or university, possessing as he did a thorough knowledge of the English, Latin and Greek languages. Having completed his studies, thinking he would like a mercantile life, he entered his brother's store in Memphis, but at the expiration of nine months, having discovered his mistake and fully determined upon the law as his profession, he pursued the study with such earnestness, and acquired a knowledge of it so rapidly, that at the end of three months he was admitted to the bar in Houston, Chickasaw county, Miss., in 1840, before he was twenty-one years of age. He rose speedily in his profession and soon acquired a lucrative practice as well as a high stand in his profession as an able lawyer. A hard student, correct reasoner and profound thinker, he always discovered the fundamental principle involved and rested his cause upon it. From his early boyhood he was never an indifferent spectator as to what was transpiring in the political world, and from his majority took an active part in nearly every campaign by his speeches on the rostrum and arguments to the individual citizen. In 1847, seven years after his admission to the bar, he was nominated by the democratic party of his district as its candidate for congress over very strong competitors in his own party, men of experience and ability. He was scarcely eligible to the seat on account of his youth, without experience and had never been a candidate for any office. His opponent, the nominee of the whig party in the canvass, was the celebrated duelist, Col. A. K. McClung. McClung was a much older man than Featherston, a man of experience, of talents and an able debater, and had just returned from the battlefields of Mexico, where he had distinguished himself for gallantry and knightly courage. He entered the campaign upon his crutches, compelled to do so by two bleeding wounds he bore upon his person as evidences of his bravery at the battle of Buena Vista. Under the circumstances it was generally believed at the opening of the campaign that McClung's election was inevitable. But after a canvass of unusual interest and great excitement, in which the two candidates met each other in joint discussion in every county in the district, General Featherston was triumphantly elected. This would have been a great achievement and brilliant victory for any man, young or old. Military glory, which Colonel McClung had so justly earned and gallantly won, was at that time not only at par, but commanded a heavy premium. Renominated for congress in 1849, General Featherston was opposed by Judge William L. Harris, of Columbus, as the whig candidate. Judge Harris was a man of talents, culture and fine attainments, a fluent speaker and an able lawyer, a formidable opponent in a political campaign, but after a thorough canvass of the district General Featherston was elected by the usual party majority. Renominated in 1851, he was opposed by John A. Wilcox, of Aberdeen, the union candidate. In this canvass General Featherston was defeated along with the entire states' rights party, to which he belonged. Jefferson Davis, the candidate of the states' rights party for governor, was defeated by H. S. Foote, the union candidate for that office. General Featherston resumed the practice of law, but served on the Pierce electoral ticket in 1852. As a member of congress he introduced one of the first measures to levee the Mississippi river. The nomination for congress was again tendered him by his party in 1853, but he declined and remained within the quiet walks of his profession from 1852 until the beginning of the Civil war. He moved from Chickasaw county to Holly Springs, Marshall county, Miss., in 1857. In December, 1860, he was sent by his state as a commissioner to the state of Kentucky to confer with her authorities on the subject of her withdrawal from the Federal union with her sister Southern states. Mississippi having seceded, Gen. W. S. Featherston was among the first to respond to the call for volunteers, and raised a volunteer company which was mustered into the Seventeenth Mississippi regiment at Corinth, he being elected colonel of that regiment. His regiment was ordered to Virginia, and served in the Virginia army during 1861 and 1862. He was promoted to brigadier-general on the 4th of March, 1862, for skill and gallantry in the battle of Leesburg or Ball's bluff. In the Virginia army he was in the first and second battles of Manassas, the battle of Leesburg, the seven days' battles around Richmond, was with General Lee on his first campaign into Maryland, and took part in the capture of Harper's Ferry; was in the first battle of Fredricksburg, in December, 1862. He was wounded on the fifth day of the battles around Richmond, at Frazier's farm. In January, 1863, he was transferred from the Virginia army to the army at Vicksburg. General Johnston having asked President Davis to send him a skilled brigadier-general, General Featherston and his brigade had petitioned to be transferred when the enemy first reached Mississippi, and so the transfer was offered General Featherston. The following letter from President Davis to General Featherston, in which the president quotes General Lee's reply to himself in regard to the transfer of the Mississippi brigade and its officers, shows for itself the deservedly high esteem they placed upon General Featherston and his command.

RICHMOND, VA., November 7, 1862.

GEN. W. S. FEATHERSTON, *Sir*: The communication signed by you and many of the officers of your brigade, submitted to the president by Capt. W. R. Barksdale, was referred to the perusal of Gen. R. E. Lee, who says:

"This brigade has done excellent service and has earned deserved reputation in every battle. The advantages presented by a transfer of services to Mississippi, viz.: the facility of recruiting its thinned ranks, and the comforts it would secure to the men are apparent. But the same reasons would withdraw every regiment from the army except those from Virginia, to their own state and divide us up into thirteen detachments, the very thing our enemy desires. I do not anticipate an idle winter for the army of north Virginia, and think it will require every support. I can not, therefore, recommend the transfer of so gallant a brigade as the Mississippi brigade."

The president assures you of his sympathy with the feeling expressed in connection with the defense of Mississippi, but desires me to remind you that the object may be best effected by attacking and defeating the enemy's best army wherever found.

I have the honor, sir, to present you the compliments and best wishes of the president.

Very respectfully,

BURTON N. HARRISON,
Private secretary.

The following communication from the Twelfth Mississippi regiment speaks for itself of the esteem and appreciation of the soldiers for their commander:

CAMP TWELFTH MISSISSIPPI REGIMENT, }
January 19, 1863. }

To BRIG.-GEN. W. S. FEATHERSTON, *Sir*: We, the undersigned first sergeants of the Twelfth Mississippi regiment, representing the sentiment and opinion of the enlisted men of our respective companies, do hereby earnestly solicit your attention to the following communication:

We have been informed that you expect to surrender the command of this brigade and go to the army of the West or to the army of northern Mississippi. If you have not fully determined to bid us a last farewell, we would respectfully insist on your remaining with us, but if you have, then we can but petition that you exert yourself to obtain permission from the proper authorities to get us transferred to your command, wherever it may be. Knowing and appreciating full well the gallant manner in which you conducted the Mississippi brigade on every bloodstained field of glory, we can but lament your departure. From the time you took command of the illustrious trio of Mississippi regiments, prior to the ever-memorable battles before Richmond, we have watched with pride, commingled with exultation, the increasing reputation of this brigade and her gallant leader upon every subsequent field.

Never can we forget the matchless generalship you displayed upon the crimsoned plains of Ellison's mills, Gaines' farm, Frazier's farm and Manassas, and, by your wise orders, obtained for us the laurel wreath of victory, and praise from the ardent admirers of our country's defenders.

Sincerely hoping your fame may never decrease, we remain, dear sir,

Most respectfully yours,

ROBERT HUNTER, company A,
ROBERT G. FRASER, company B.
J. A. CALTHARPE, company C,
F. R. LLOYD, company D,
D. G. CARABINE, company E,
M. A. MYERS, company F,
PAUL A. BOTTO, company G,
E. P. DOUGLAS, company H,
JAMES A. WEST, company I,
R. A. OWEN, company K.

Soon after General Featherston's arrival at Vicksburg he commanded the expedition sent from Vicksburg to meet Commodore Porter's fleet of gunboats ascending Deer creek. During this expedition he had continuous fighting with the enemy for four or five days. A fleet of seven gunboats and a division of infantry were turned from the expedition and driven back to their line of defense by one brigade, one battalion, one company of cavalry, and two small batteries without other support within a hundred miles. He, with his command, participated in the battle of Baker's creek, or Champion hill, and all the engagements around Jackson, Miss. After the battle of Baker's creek, when Pemberton retreated into Vicksburg, General Featherston, with his and General Lee's brigade, was ordered to hold the enemy in check until the army could cross Baker's creek and Big Black river. General Lee, with his brigade, was withdrawn, however, just after taking position. General Featherston held his position until the enemy flanked him on both sides, when he retreated in good order to a line farther back, which he held until the enemy succeeded in forcing a way between his command and the main army, taking possession of the bridges over Baker's creek, thereby surrounding him. However, he cut his way out with his entire command, and passed down the creek, thinking to be able to cross at a ford, but finding the enemy in possession of the ford in overwhelming numbers, and himself completely cut off from Vicksburg and Pemberton's army, he retreated to Jackson, Miss., and joined Gen. Joseph E. Johnston. He was with Johnston in his campaign from Resaca to Atlanta and commanded Lovering's division a large part of the time. He was with Hood on his campaign into Tennessee. He was in the battle of Franklin, in which he led seven charges; also the battles of Columbia and Nashville. General Featherston was selected on General Hood's retreat from Nashville to command a division of eight brigades of infantry, constituting a rear guard to coöperate with the cavalry in holding the enemy in check until Hood's army could reach and cross the Tennessee river. He was paroled at Greensboro, N. C., with Johnston's army, in 1865. As an evidence of the high regard in which his comrades in arms held him at the time of his death, he was grand commander of the United Confederate Veterans of Mississippi, and the following resolution was passed at their reunion in Jackson, Miss., on the 2d of June, 1891:

Whereas, official notification of the death at his home, in Holly springs, Miss., at 9 P. M., on the 28th ultimo, of General Featherston, grand commander of the grand camp of Confederate Veterans of Mississippi, has been communicated to this reunion: therefore, be it resolved, that, recognizing the eminent military and civic services of our late comrade, and recalling his devoted loyalty to and sympathy for the memory of the cause we have organized to commemorate, and in which he bore a conspicuous part—first as an officer under Generals Johnston and Lee in Virginia, and later under Generals Johnston and Hood in the west, the United Confederate Veterans in reunion assembled, do hereby express their deep sorrow at his death, acknowledge their irreparable loss in being denied his continued valuable services in a cause so near his and the hearts of us all, and their inexpressible regrets at the inscrutible decrees of an allwise Providence have deprived them of the fond privilege of his courtly presence and wise councils at this, a reunion to which he had so devotedly contemplated and looked forward to with the renewed enthusiasm of youthful vigor ; second, that we tender to his bereaved family our sincerest condolence, and the Grand Camp of Confederate Veterans of Mississippi our deepest sympathy.

After the surrender in 1865 he returned to his home in Holly Springs, Miss., where he resumed the practice of law. He was prevailed upon to accept a seat in the legislature of 1875, and in that legislature led the attack upon Ames' republican administration, and before the end of the session had the satisfaction of seeing the republican party driven from power, the corrupt carpetbag governor, Ames, from the state and a democratic administration inaugurated. In 1880 he was again reluctantly persuaded to accept a seat in the legislature, and was chairman of the judicial committee which formed a new code of laws for the state. He served for six years upon the circuit bench of the state with great dignity and ability, and refused a reappointment. Retiring from the bench, he resumed his practice at Holly Springs, Miss. He was a member of the constitutional convention of 1890, and although past his three-score years and ten, he was one of the most tireless workers on the floor, always commanding the profoundest respect and attention from his colleagues. The distinguished United States senator J. Z. George, a member of the convention, when asked if he would speak on a certain day on the suffrage question promptly replied, "No, I give way to Gen. Featherston, he is the man we need to hear." The following resolution, which was unanimously adopted by a rising vote, by the democratic state convention at its meeting July 15, 1891, is an evidence of the esteem he was held in by his people.

The democracy of the state of Mississippi, since it last assembled in convention, has been sadly bereft by the loss of one of its most distinguished leaders, Gen. W. S. Featherston.

General Featherston was a man of incorruptible integrity, and his long and useful life was without spot or blemish. He filled many official positions, and each of them always in such a manner as to reflect credit upon himself and honor upon the state. As a citizen he discharged the full measure of his duty to his fellow-men; as a judge he was fair, conscientious and learned; as a democrat, one of the party's ablest advocates and most valued advisors; as a soldier, he never wavered in his devotion to the Southern cause, and he evinced this by heroic and gallant conduct on the battlefield in defense of the South; as a father and husband he was tender, loving and true; therefore, be it resolved, " That we extend to his bereaved family our heartfelt sympathy, and assure them of the high esteem in which he was held by the people of Mississippi." General Featherston was married in 1848 to Miss Mary Holt Harris, of Columbus, Miss., a daughter of the Hon. Thomas W. Harris. She lived only a few months. He married a second time in June, 1858, Miss Lizzie McEwen, a daughter of Col. A. C. McEwen, of Holly Springs, Miss. He lost his second wife in the epidemic of 1878. The fruits of this second union were eight children, two of whom died in infancy, Charles and Lucius, and two, Joseph Winfield and Georgia L., fell victims to the yellow-fever epidemic of 1878, along with their mother. The remaining four are living in Holly Springs. Dudley M. engaged in the practice of law, and his three sisters, Elise Pitts, Lilia Cloyd and Lucy Elose living with him. In 1889 General Featherston was urged to become a candidate for governor, by leading men from different parts of the state, and reluctantly yielded to their solicitations, but although one of the leading democrats of the South, he failed of the nomination by the democratic party, of which he was a lifelong member. He was characterized by an independence which prevented him from being popular with the politicians, and those who is this day and time shape political affairs. Too honest to stoop to the tricks of the ordinary managers, he was defeated for the nomination of governor, but was all the more honored and beloved by the people on that account. General Featherston has filled every trust to which he has been called with marked ability and fidelity, both in peace and in war. He never sought office, and only accepted when tendered him. His integrity was never questioned. No charge of corruption, either private or public, was ever made or insinuated. He lived and died an honest man that no money or position could buy, or flattery seduce from the path of duty and rectitude. He departed this life on the 28th of May, 1891, at his home in Holly springs, Miss., surrounded by his weeping family and sorrowing friends.

Radford J. Fedric, a planter of Tallahatchie county, was born in Person county, N. C., in 1819, and died May 16, 1891. He was the son of John and Lucy (Vaughn) Fedric, both natives of the same county, who spent all of their lives there, his father dying there in 1821. The latter was a planter and a son of John Fedric, a native of France, who came to America as a soldier with General Lafayette, and served under him until the close of the struggle, when he returned to France and brought his family to North Carolina, where he became a planter and lived there the balance of his life. But few of his descendants are left in that state. He was a man of fine education and exceptional abilities. Mr. Fedric's grandfather, Granville Vaughn, lived and died in North Carolina, where he was a planter. Our subject was the third of four children—three sons and a daughter—born to his parents: Ransom M. became a mechanic, and lived and died in Person county, N. C.; Ellen married, and lived in Guilford county, N. C.; our subject was the next in order of birth; James M. enlisted in the Confederate army in Virginia, and served bravely through the war. Radford J. Fedric was apprenticed at the age of seven years, and never had an opportunity to attend school, except during about six weeks. He learned the carpenter's trade, which he followed until he removed to Mississippi, where he remained a few years, removing to Alabama in 1839. In 1846 he was married in Pickens county to Emma, daughter of Daniel and Margaret Turnipseed, natives of Richland district, S. C., who moved from there to Alabama, where they died in 1856 and 1859, respectively. He was a more than well-to-do planter, leaving at his death an estate valued at about $300,000, which he acquired by his own unaided efforts. He had eight children—three sons and five daughters. Mrs. Fedric was born in South Carolina, and died in Tallahatchie county in 1884, having been a Methodist for many years. She bore ten children, the following of whom are living: Samuel, a carpenter of Tallahatchie county; David and John, who are both planters; Margaret, wife of S. S. Cross, a planter of Tallahatchie county. Mr. Fedric was married the second time, in 1885, to N. M., daughter of James Albert and Jane Murphree, who were born in Alabama and Mississippi, respectively. Mr. Murphree came to Mississippi when a young man, and was married in Yalobusha county, where he still lives, a well-to-do planter. He was for several years justice of the peace, and he and his wife have been members of the Baptist church from childhood. The present Mrs. Fedric was born in Yalobusha county, and has a son, Radford J., Jr. In 1847 Mr. Fedric came to Lowndes county, Miss., and in 1860 removed to Choctaw (now Montgomery county), and in 1872 to Tallahatchie county, locating on the spot where he resided until his death, which was then in the midst of a dense forest. He was the owner of six hundred acres of land, one hundred and fifty of which are under cultivation. This fine property he secured by his own industry, perseverance and business ability. In 1861 he became a soldier in a company of Texan rangers, and served under General Forrest during the entire period of the war, first as a private, later as a lieutenant, and toward the close of the struggle as assistant quartermaster, traveling over most of the state for supplies. He was in nearly every engagement in which his command took part. The first company with which he was connected comprised an organization of one hundred and ten men, and he was one of only two who survived at the end of the war. He was exceedingly fortunate in his military experience, never having been either wounded or made prisoner. He was relieved at Columbus in February, 1865, and returned to his family and home interests. From 1874 to 1878 he was a member of the board of supervisors of Tallahatchie county, representing district 3. He was a strictly temperate man, and as a matter of considerable pride he frequently stated in his closing years that he had never been under the influence of liquor and had never wagered a dollar in his life. In politics he was quite active, taking much interest in local affairs as well as in all important state and all national affairs. He was a member of the Masonic fraternity, and was dimitted from the Columbus lodge, A. F. & A. M. He was long a professing Christian and a communicant of the Baptist church.

Maj. G. D. Fee (deceased) was originally from Chester district, S. C., his birth occurring on the 12th of October 1822, and his death on the night of March 3, 1869, at Oxford, Miss. He remained in his native state until twenty-one years of age, at which time he located in Memphis, Tenn., where he became interested in business as a cotton broker, and was very successful in that industry. He afterward located at Holly Springs, Miss., and there engaged in merchandising in partnership with Judge Fant. In 1857 he located at Oxford, Miss., and during the year 1859 was married to Miss Bettie Reynolds, daughter of Benjamin H. Reynolds, of Columbus, Ga. Mr. Reynolds moved to Mississippi, located in Lafayette county, and became a very extensive planter. His death occurred in the spring of 1859. Maj. G. D. Fee was characterized for his energy in business. He was regarded as a man of great forethought as a merchant and was also, at all times, thoroughly posted on those questions pertaining to the general welfare of the country, being ever ready to engage in any scheme calculated to promote the interests of the town and county in which he lived. It was universally conceded that he was the leading spirit in charitable and other works and that he was a well-informed man with a good fund of common sense from which to draw. The merchants and planters and citizens generally awarded to him the position of leader in all public enterprises. As a member of the Masonic fraternity, he manifested the same zeal and energy that characterized his business life. He was punctual in the discharge of all his duties, and had won the distinction of master of the lodge, high priest of the Royal Arch chapter and the illustrious grand master of the council of royal and select masters, all these positions held in the town where he lived. At the grand convocation of the grand chapter of the state in January, 1869, he was promoted to the office of grand high priest for the current year. He was a Mason in its truest sense. He was charitable and benevolent, and his hand was ever open when relief was sought by the poor and needy. He was elected to the legislature in 1868 by an overwhelming majority, as he had acquired the esteem and confidence of the entire community. During the Civil war he was a firm supporter of the Southern cause, and filled the important position of commissary at home, having had three discharges on account of poor health. At his death he left a wife and three children—two sons and a daughter: C. H. and George D. are engaged in merchandising in Texas, and are very successful in this line. Mrs. Fee had four brothers: William R., Edward W., Charles H., and Mitchell A., who served in the late war, the first three being members of Captain Stanford's battery, the latter being an uncle of Mrs. Fee's. The youngest went out with Captain Lowery, who afterward became governor of the state. Mitchell died from an attack of typhoid fever soon after the battle of Manassas.

William O. Feemster, physician and surgeon, Nettleton, occupies a leading place in the professional ranks of Lee county.   He is a native Mississippian, born February 7, 1842, and is a son of M. B. and M. M. (King) Feemster, natives of York district, S. C.   The father was born February 9, 1804, and removed to Tennessee in 1818.   He was graduated with the class of 1822, from the Washington college, east Tennessee, and was a minister of the Cumberland Presbyterian church for sixty-one years.   He was united in marriage on January 8, 1824, to Miss M. M. King, a native of South Carolina, and to them were born nine children, seven of whom lived to be grown.   The mother died at Little Rock, Ark., at the residence of her daughter, in November, 1887.   The father died January 8, 1884.   Their eldest child, A. W. Feemster, was born in 1827.   He is now a widower, his wife and three children being deceased; Elizabeth E., deceased, left a family of six children; Mary A., widow of Thomas Gibson, is the mother of five children, she resides in Texas; Samuel K. is a minister of the Cumberland Presbyterian church in Arkansas; M. Jeannie is the wife of G. W. Terry, of Prescott, Ark.; Annis C. married S. H. Buchanan, D. D., and is a resident of Clarksville, Ark.; John Calvin, the fourth child, died when four years old; Margaret E., the third child, died at the age of eleven years.   Dr. Feemster attended the common schools of Mississippi and Arkansas until he had acquired a good foundation for a professional education.   He then chose the science of medicine for his life study, and entered the Nashville medical college to take his first course of lectures.   He was graduated from this institution in 1872, and has since been engaged in the active practice of the profession.   He is a man of marked ability and has a decided gift for this vocation.   He has won a large practice in Nettleton and the surrounding country, and numbers his friends by the host.   He was married October 30, 1871, to M. A. Foster, a native of South Carolina, and a daughter of Joshua and L. M. Foster. They are the parents of ten children, all of whom are living: L. C., Mattie L., William B., Minos B., Mary A., Ida J., Margaret E., Laura B., Clara and Lucile.   On January 10, 1861, Dr. Feemster enlisted in the Confederate service at Boonsboro, Ark., under P. Buchanan in the state volunteers.   In the September following he reënlisted under Capt. George Robards in the Confederate volunteer service for three years or during the war.   He was seriously wounded at the battle of Corinth, in September, 1862, and again at the battle of Baker's creek, in May, 1863, and received a slight wound at the battle of Saline, Ark.   He was promoted to the office of color sergeant at Baldwyn, Miss., in October, 1862, and later to the rank of junior second lieutenant.   He was mustered out of the service April 16, 1865, at Arkadelphia, Ark.   He adheres to the principles of the democratic party, but has never been an aspirant to public office.   He belongs to the Knights of Honor, and is a worthy member of the Cumberland Presbyterian church.   His wife is also a member of the latter organization.   Dr. Feemster is noted for his liberal contributions to all charitable and philanthropic movements, and is a citizen of much credit to his community.   He is possessed of those sterling traits of character which make the most loyal patriots and the stanchest of friends.

A. D. Felder, M. D., is one of the leading physicians of Pike county, and was born in Amite county, July 27, 1861.   His father, Dr. Charles F. Felder, was born in Amite county, and was a physician there for many years.   Not only was he conspicuous in his profession, but he was a prominent factor in politics, having represented Amite county in the state legislature and his district in the state senate.   He later removed to Texas, where he died in the spring of 1875, at the age of sixty-one years.   He married Jane Lea, who bore him one child, Dr. A. D. Felder, who grew to maturity at the home of his parents, and at the age of seventeen years became a student at the Mississippi college.   Soon after he became a student of medicine at the Louisville medical college, at Louisville, Ky., from which he graduated in the spring of 1885.   Immediately after he began the practice of his profession in Amite county.

In January, 1890, he located in Magnolia, where he has built up a large and lucrative practice. In November, 1886, he married Miss Ada Lenore. The Doctor is a charter member of the Jefferson Davis lodge No. 68, Knights of Pythias, and Mrs. Felder is a prominent member of the Methodist Episcopal church.

Ira L. Felder, whose postoffice address is Summit, Pike county, Miss., was born in that county February 17, 1847. He was the second of five children of G. N. and Frances (Hodges) Felder, both of whom were natives and life-long residents of Pike county. His grandfather, John Felder, was among the pioneers of this part of the state. He was a native of South Carolina. His maternal grandfather was Edmund Hodges. Mr. Felder was reared and educated in the private schools of this part of the county. He took up the battle of life at the age of fourteen, with no capital except an earnest desire to succeed, and by close application to business has accumulated a considerable property, owning now five hundred and thirty acres of land, one hundred acres of which are under cultivation. He was married in 1866 to Miss Mary S. Rollins, a native of Mississippi, and daughter of Thomas and Elvira (Huffman) Rollins, both also natives of that state. They had two children: Francis E. and Mary C. In 1870 he was again married, this time to Miss Virginia Kirk. She was a daughter of George Kirk, of Tennessee, and also a native of that state. She has borne Mr. Felder eight children: John I., now deceased; George L.; Nannie D.; Gabriel S., also deceased; Samuel L.; Louis L.; Peter O. and Vernon Y. Mr. Felder served in the late war, enlisting in 1864, in company C, of the Fourteenth Confederate regiment of volunteers, as a substitute for his father. Mr. Felder and his family are members of the Methodist Episcopal church, and he is a member of the Farmers' Alliance. He is an honorable, highly respected citizen, and has contributed very liberally to all things tending to the upbuilding of the county and to the benefit of its inhabitants.

Lovick V. Feltus, a planter, of Natchez, who was named after his maternal grandfather, Lovick Ventress, owes his nativity to Wilkinson county, Miss., born in 1831, and is the son of Abram M. and Eliza Ann (Ventress) Feltus. The father was born in New York state, about 1796, and when about eighteen years of age he came on horseback to Natchez. From there he went to Wilkinson county, and was the first to embark in merchandising in Woodville, erecting his store in the woods. He followed this business for ten or twelve years and was then made cashier of the Planters' bank at that place, until it suspended business. After this he followed planting successfully until his death in 1861. He was a self-made man, started in business with no capital, and soon became one of the wealthy and influential citizens. He was prominent in all matters relating to the growth and prosperity of his town, and was one of the founders of Woodville lodge, A. F. & A. M., and of St. Paul's Episcopal church at that place. His father (Rev. Henry J. Feltus) was born in Ireland, married in Dublin, and soon after, about 1797, he came to the United States, locating in Brooklyn, N. Y., where he spent the remainder of his days as an Episcopal minister. His wife, whose maiden name was Ryan, also died in Brooklyn. The mother of our subject, Eliza Ann (Ventress) Feltus, was born in Wilkinson county in 1805, and spent her entire life there, dying in 1889. Her father, Lovick Ventress, came from Tennessee in a flatboat to Wilkinson county at a very early period and became a wealthy planter. He and wife died there, leaving two sons and one daughter: Hon. James A., who died soon after the war (he was a wealthy planter of Wilkinson county, and was once a member of the Mississippi legislature); Mrs. Feltus; and William C. S., who died at Louisiana. He was a wealthy sugar planter. Lovick V. Feltus was one of the following children born to his parents. William J., who was educated at the University of Virginia, became a prominent attorney at Woodville, who died in 1861; Henry J., of Baton Rouge; Lovick V.; Col. Abram M., was a graduate of Pennsylvania university, studied law at Woodville, and at the breaking out of hostilities between the two sections he enlisted in the Sixteenth Mississippi infantry, Confederate army, served with the rank of colonel, and was killed at Spottsylvania courthouse; Peter G. died in Wilkinson county about 1886 (he was a well-to-do planter, and served in the Confederate army as lieutenant of company K, Sixteenth Mississippi); James A. V., a planter, of Leland, Washington county, Miss., and a member of the board of supervisors, also served in company K, Sixteenth Mississippi, during the Civil war; Edward R., of Natchez; Martha R.; Eliza A., now Mrs. Fraley, and Charlotta G., now Mrs. St. Clair, of Leland, Miss. Lovick V. Feltus graduated with honer from the University of Pennsylvania, in 1857, and then clerked in New Orleans until 1861. He then joined the same company in which three of his brothers served, and operated in the Virginia army as lieutenant, but part of the time he was detailed as captain on General Featherston's staff. The company to which he belonged participated in the following engagements: Port Royal, Winchester, Cross Keys, Cold Harbor, Malvern hill, second Manassas, Harper's Ferry, Sharpsburg, Fredericksburg, Gettysburg, Wilderness, Spottsylvania courthouse, Darbytown road, Weldon railroad, Deep Bottom, Reame's station, Five Forks, Drewry's bluff, Crater at Petersburg, Hatchie's run and Fort Gregg. He was never captured or wounded and was always ready at roll call. After the war he returned to Woodville, followed planting for one year, and then embarked in sugar planting for eight years, in Iberville parish, La. In 1882 he came to his present plantation, four miles east of Natchez, consisting of two hundred acres, and where he has a pleasant home. He has been engaged in planting the greater part of his life. He was married in February, 1861, to Miss Ella E. Randolph, a native of Wilkinson county, Miss., and the daughter of John H. and Emily J. Randolph natives respectively of Nottoway county, Va., and Wilkinson county, Miss. Mr. Randolph came with his parents to Wilkinson county when a boy, was married there, but afterward removed to Iberville parish, La., where he spent the remainder of his days as an extensive sugar planter. He was quite a prominent citizen. He died about 1885. His widow is now living in New Orleans. She is the daughter of Moses Lidell, who in early life came to Natchez, where he clerked for a number of years. He then went to Wilkinson county, where he was among the pioneers, but afterward removed to Catahoula parish, La., where he received his final summons. Judge Peter Randoph, the father of John H., was one of the first settlers of Wilkinson county, where he became a wealthy planter, and where he passed the closing scenes of his life. He served as judge in Virginia, and was one of the celebrated Randolphs of that state. To Mr. and Mrs. Feltus were born five children: Abram M., a merchant of Iberville parish, La.; John H. R., clerking for his brother; William J., now a clerk in Simmons' hardware company, of St. Louis; Emily J. and and Ella E. Mrs. Feltus is a member of the Episcopal church. Mr. and Mrs. Feltus are descended on both their fathers' and mothers' sides of distinguished families.

J. A. V. Feltus has been a resident of the state in which he is now residing all his life, for here he first saw the light of day, in the year 1839. His father, A. M. Feltus, was born in New York state, in 1796, but in 1816 came to Natchez, Miss., then moved to Woodville, where he became president of the Planters' bank of Mississippi, continuing as such for a number of years. He afterward turned his attention to planting and merchandising, following the former occupation until his death, which occurred at Woodville, June 20, 1861. His wife was Miss Eliza A. Ventress, a sketch of whose family occurs in that preceeding this. The paternal grandfather, Henry J. Feltus, was a native of Ireland,

and from the time of his arrival in this country until his death was the pastor of an Episcopal church in New York city. J. A. V. Feltus was reared in Wilkinson county, Miss., but received his education in Oxford. In 1865 he began making his own way in the world, and his time has been given to the occupation of planting, a calling for which he seems admirably adapted, for he is now wealthy. He is a half-owner of the plantation Deerpark, which contains twenty-five hundred acres, and his home place, known as Three Oaks, contains seven hundred and fifty acres, five hundred being under cultivation. On this plantation the town of Leland is built. Upon the opening of the Rebellion Mr. Feltus volunteered his services to the Confederate cause, and throughout the war served in company K, Sixteenth Mississippi regiment. He was in every battle of the Virginia campaign, with the exception of the first battle of Manassas, and saw some hard service. He has a handsome residence, which he erected in 1876, at a cost of $4,500, and as he has always remained a bachelor, his sister, Miss Martha R. Feltus, keeps house for him. She is a lady of culture and intelligence, and, being of a kind, charitable and modest disposition, she is admired and esteemed by all who know her. The town of Leland, which has a population of five hundred, was laid off by Mr. Feltus, who has done a great deal to make the town a prosperous and thriving one. Since the place was organized he has been a member of the town council, and the enterprise and prosperity of the place is a monument to the push and enterprise of Mr. Feltus. He has always affiliated with the democratic party, but has no desire for political honors, notwithstanding the fact that he is now one of the town council. The town was platted in 1884, was incorporated in 1885, with a population of two hundred, and now has two excellent hotels, about twenty business houses, one church for the whites, two churches for the colored people, two building and loan associations, a public school building for both races, and a school for white children, which is in operation ten months out of the year. This thriving little town is on the Louisiana, New Orleans & Texas railroad, a branch of which runs from Leland to Greenville and from Leland to Arkansas city. Mrs Feltus' parents were Episcopalians, and became the parents of the following children: William J., who died in Wilkinson county in 1865 (had been a lawyer in New Orleans, but at the time of his death was engaged in planting); J. H. was formerly a sugar planter, but is now retired from business, and is residing in Baton Rouge; L. V. is engaged in planting, three miles from Natchez; A. M. was killed in the battle of Spottsylvania courthouse in 1864, being lieutenant-colonel of the Sixteenth Mississippi regiment, to which he was promoted from the rank of lieutenant, which office he held upon entering the army; P. G. died in Wilkinson county in 1883, having followed the life of a planter, serving throughout the Rebellion, was lieutenant-colonel of company K, Sixteenth Mississippi regiment, taking part in all the engagements in the state of Virginia; Martha R.; Eliza A., wife of J. B. Faley, a native of Pennsylvania, now a resident of New Mexico; Charlotte J. is the wife of A. M. St. Clair, and resides in Leland, Miss.; Edward R. is a retired planter, of Natchez, and J. A. V., the subject of this biography.

Norman Ferguson is an enterprising, highly-esteemed citizen of Tuscalona station, Moselle postoffice, Jones county, Miss., and is a manufacturer of spirits of turpentine and resin, being also a proprietor of a cottongin and gristmill. This gentleman is a native of Moore county, N. C., and was born November 18, 1855. His parents were Fergus and Catherine (McDonald) Ferguson, also natives of North Carolina. They were the parents of seven children, namely: Sarah C., Mary A., Donald L., William, Elizabeth J., John and Norman, our subject, who was the eldest member of the family. His connection with the turpentine business began in North Carolina in 1872, and he has followed it without inter-

46

mission to the present time. In 1884 he came to Mississippi and settled at the present location, where, in connection with his father, he purchased a large tract of land and established a turpentine plant, which the two have carried on very successfully ever since. Mr. Ferguson was married in North Carolina, October 28, 1880, to Miss Isabelle, the daughter of D. M. and Mary J. (Campbell) St. Clair, who has borne him five children: Walter P., Sarah C., Julius T., Frederick D. and Henry F. Mr. Ferguson ranks among the most enterprising and prosperous business men of the county, possessing all those personal characteristics to make a man not only successful in commercial enterprises, but popular in social circles as well.

Gen. S. W. Ferguson, secretary and treasurer of the board of Mississippi levee commissioners, at Greenville, Miss., was the eldest in a family of eleven children born to James and Abby Ann (Barker) Ferguson, the parents, natives of South Carolina. Though educated for the bar the father followed the occupation of a planter the principal part of his life, and during the War of 1812 was commissioned a lieutenant of the Eighth infantry of the regular army, serving as aid-de-camp to General Pinckney, in Georgia, Florida and South Carolina. Returning to his plantation after cessation of hostilities, he continued to reside there until his death, at the age of ninety years. He was married in 1831. He was one of the representative men of South Carolina, and was a member of the legislature of that state for twenty years in succession. Both parents were members of the Episcopal church. The paternal grandfather, Thomas Ferguson, was born in the year 1726, and was a most extensive planter. During the Revolutionary war he was one of the council of safety who refused to sign the articles for the surrender of the city of Charleston, and for this he and all his family were taken prisoners and banished from that locality. The great-grandfather, James Ferguson, came to America with Oglethorpe. On the mother's side the Barkers were from Rhode Island. The grandfather, Joseph Barker, was an early settler of South Carolina, and a merchant at Charleston. Gen. S. W. Ferguson was born in Charleston, S. C., in 1834, passed his youthful days there, and attended the private school of Christopher Coates, until the age of sixteen years. In 1852 he entered West Point and graduated from that institution in 1857. He was brevetted second lieutenant under A. S. Johnston in the expedition against the Mormons, and was sent to the Pacific coast, being stationed at Walla Walla. In March, 1861, he returned to New York, resigned, but was at once commissioned captain in the regular infantry of South Carolina, being aid-de-camp to General Beauregard and serving on his staff until after the battle of Shiloh. In April, 1861, he received the keys at the surrender of Fort Sumter. He participated in the first battle of Manassas, also in many skirmishes in the Old Dominion, and about the time of the battle of Shiloh he was appointed lieutenant-colonel of the Twenty-eighth regiment of Mississippi cavalry, serving about Vicksburg and on the river. In the summer of 1863 he was made brigadier-general of cavalry, and operated in Mississippi, Alabama, Tennessee and Georgia. He was on almost constant skirmish duty and took a prominent part in many of the principal engagements. He was a most efficient military man, cool and far-seeing, and one whose courage and intrepidity could be relied upon at all times. He was with President Davis at the last council of war held at Abbeville, S. C., early in May, 1865, and his brigade was disbanded in May of that year. After peace was declared, General Ferguson came to Greenville, Miss., studied law and was admitted in November, 1866, practicing at this bar for many years. In 1885 he was appointed a member of the Mississippi river commission by President Arthur, to fill the position of Captain Eads who had resigned, and served in that capacity until April, 1890. Previous to this, in 1876, he was made president of the board of Mississippi levee commissioners, continued in this position until 1882, and two years later was appointed secretary and treasurer, which position he is holding at the present time. On the 28th of August, 1862, he was united in marriage to Miss Kate Lee, daughter of William Henry and Ellen (Ware) Lee, a native of Kentucky, born in 1842. She was educated in her native state, and after her marriage to General Ferguson she accompanied him on all his campaigns. She was an excellent horse-woman and while riding from the Mississippi river to the Atlantic ocean took copious notes of her adventures during that interesting period. These she has since written out, and they form a pleasing narrative of many camp-fire episodes and military incidents. Mrs. Ferguson is of a literary family, her mother being quite a poetess, and her aunt, Catherine A. Ware, the author of nine books, of which "The Household of Bouviere" is her best work. Her father, William Henry Lee, was a native of Virginia and a descendant of Richard Henry Lee, who came to America during the reign of Charles I. William Henry Lee was educated at Norfolk, Va., after which he resided in New Orleans for some time and then came to Mississippi, making a permanent settlement at Vicksburg about 1840. He was considered one of the best planters in the South, being very extensively engaged in this occupation, and after residing near Vicksburg for some time he moved to an estate on Deer creek, and made that place, Ditchley, his home until his death in 1874. He was a cousin of Gen. Robert E. Lee. In personal appearance Mr. Lee was strikingly handsome. He was over six feet in hight, well proportioned, a cavalier of "ye olden times," and was familiarly called Gay Harry Lee. He was a member of the Episcopal church, and a member of the Masonic fraternity. He was married about 1841 to Mrs. Eleanor Percy (Ware) Ellis, a native of Mississippi and the daughter of Nathaniel and Sarah (Percy) Ware. She had previously married a Mr. Ellis, by whom she had one child, Mrs. Sarah (Ellis) Dorsey, who was also an authoress and who left an estate to Jefferson Davis.

The Wares were natives of South Carolina. Nathaniel Ware was a self-educated man, having worked his own way in life, and after studying law was admitted to the bar in Washington, D. C. He became very wealthy and left a large estate in Texas. He was an extensive traveler, had gone over a considerable portion of Africa and had written a book on his journey in that country. He had been a student all his life and was of a distinctive literary turn. To General and Mrs. Ferguson were born five children, four of whom are now living: James Du Gue (planter), Nathalie, Harry Lee and Percy. The one deceased was named Eleanor Percy. The family are members of the Episcopal church. General Ferguson is a Knight Templar in the Masonic fraternity, Greenville lodge No. 206, and has held official positions in Hillyer chapter and Delta commandery. He has been chancellor commander of the Knights of Pythias, Stonewall lodge, and is a member of the Knights of Honor and the Legion of Honor. The General and Mrs. Ferguson have a very pleasant home, and their children are studious and literary in their tastes. Mrs. Ferguson began writing in her youth, took prizes at school for compositions and has written many stories. In 1889 she published "Cliquot," a work received with considerable favor, and she has in manuscript another work that will soon be produced. She is a lady of pleasing manners, and has the personal characteristics of not only the Percys but other ancestors noted for their beauty, grace and literary traits. Her mother was considered very handsome and had a remarkably fine figure. While on a visit to Europe and at a court ball, given by King Louis Philippe of France, he called her the Fannie Elssler of America. She was dressed in black velvet and pearls and was looking very lovely.

William J. Ferguson is a progressive and useful citizen of Hinds county, Miss., but was born in Attala county of this state on the 25th of April, 1849, the eldest of a family of six children born to Daniel E. and Caroline (Denman) Ferguson, also natives of this state. Daniel E. Ferguson spent twenty years of his life in Franklin county, and during the Civil war served in the quartermaster's department with General Forrest. He was a son of William and Patsey (McDonald) Ferguson, and a grandson of a Scotchman who came from the land of thistles and oatmeal to seek a home in the new world, settling in North Carolina. The McDonalds are also Scotch. William J. Ferguson was reared in Choctaw and Hinds county and received his knowledge of books in the common schools, thus obtaining a fair, practical education. At the age of eighteen years he began life for himself as a clerk, which calling he continued for about two years, when he opened a fancy grocery store at Auburn, Hinds county, Miss., which business soon grew to a general mercantile establishment. From 1870 to 1880 he conducted business two miles east from Adams, at the same time managing a plantation, and both these enterprises were crowned with success. Since 1881 he has been the proprietor of a fine mercantile establishment in Adams, which brings him in an annual sum of $15,000. He is also interested in a like establishment at Pickens, the firm name of which is Blair & Ferguson, the annual sales of which are about $40,000. Mr. Ferguson owns about one thousand acres of land, seven hundred being under cultivation, on which is a nice residence, and some valuable real estate in Adams, all of which is the result of his own efforts, for upon starting out in life for himself he had no means. He is a whole-souled, large-hearted man, full of kindness and generosity, and greatly enjoys helping others who are not so fortunate as himself. In every transaction in life he has been strictly honorable, and is a high-toned and upright gentleman. He was married in 1874 to Miss Sallie C. Noble, a native of South Carolina, and a daughter of William A. and Fannie (Brady) Noble, also natives of the Palmetto state. Mrs. Ferguson is related to John C. Calhoun and Governor Noble. She is also a lineal descendant of the Houstons, one of the most noted families of South Carolina. The Nobles were also leading citizens of that state and were of Scotch stock. They resided principally in Abbeville district. To Mr. and Mrs. Ferguson the following children have been born: Emma E., Carrie C., Annie Belle, Lalla Rookh and Mamie. Mr. Ferguson and his wife are members of the Baptist church, and he is a Mason of high rank and also belongs to the K. of H. and the K. of P.

Frank Ferrell, M. D., was born in Maury county, Tenn., in 1831, the eldest son in a family of eight children, belonging to John M. and Harriet (Saunders) Ferrell. The father was a native of North Carolina, the mother of Virginia. Mr. and Mrs. Ferrell were married in Tennessee, and lived there for about ten years, moving in 1839 to Marshall county, Miss., where Mr. Ferrell bought land and engaged in planting, and is a plain, practical farmer, never aspiring to any official position, but satisfied to attain success as a farmer. He lived and moved in the best circles of society, was a helpful, public-spirited man, giving liberally to schools, churches, and all other institutions tending to the good of his county. He was well and favorable known, and was a high-minded Christian gentleman. Mrs. Ferrell died in 1853 at her home in Marshall county, the death of Mr. Ferrell occurring in 1864 at the old family homestead. The subject of our sketch was educated at Holly Springs at the St. Thomas Hall Episcopal school. He entered the New Orleans school of medicine in 1858, graduating two years later, and began practicing his profession near Ashland in 1860, but in 1861 he enlisted in the Confederate service, and was detailed for hospital duty at Corinth, Miss. In 1862 he enlisted in the Thirty-fourth Mississippi regiment of infantry, under the command of Col. Sam Benton. He was appointed assistant surgeon in this regiment, in which capacity he served nearly three years, until commissioned regimental surgeon in 1864, the duties of which office he performed until the close of the war. When Johnston's army, to which the regiment was attached, surrendered at Greensboro, N. C., in April, 1865, at which time the Doctor was paroled, he returned home and resumed the practice of his profession at Salem, Miss. In 1867 he married Mary Frank Ayres, a daughter of Dr. A. M. Ayres, who has borne him four sons: Frank (a student at Oxford), Augustus S. (at Cecilian college in Kentucky), Carl and Choppin. Mrs. Ferrell died in 1883, and Dr. Ferrell married for his second wife her sister, Sallie J. Ayres, who has two sons and one daughter: Chaille, Seth and Lucile. The Doctor lived at Old Salem till 1871, when he moved to Ashland, the seat of justice of Benton county. He owns one hundred acres of land in the suburbs of the town, and combines the practice of his profession with that of a planter. He is well and favorably known throughout Marshall and Benton counties, and is a high-minded, honorable citizen, and one of the ablest physicians in his part of the state. He has always been very liberal to all educational, religious and all other promising public enterprises.

C. C. Ferrill, clerk of the chancery court of Clarke county, and a prominent resident of Quitman, is the eldest son of George W. and Mary (McDonald) Ferrill. His father was a native of Georgia, born in 1804. He was married in Perry county, Miss., in 1831, having come to this state in 1814 with his father, Bryant Ferrill, locating in Jackson county, Miss., and he may be regarded as having been one of the earliest pioneers of this part of the state. He was reared to a farm life, and as soon as he became old enough he engaged in planting on his own account. He was quite successful, and in time came to be a large slaveholder. He became the father of four sons and two daughters, of whom C. C. Ferrill was the eldest; Sarah is the wife of R. D. Weens, of De Soto; Susan, who was Mrs. B. J. Morrison, of Kentucky, and is now dead; George W., of Thomasville, Ga.; Benjamin F., of Ellisville, Miss.; Richard, now living in Laurel, Miss. The father was one of ten children born to his parents, and was for many years a member of the Methodist Episcopal church and long identified with the Masonic fraternity. He was a public-spirited man, and before the war an old-line whig. After the war he affiliated with the democratic party, dying in 1881. The mother of our subject was born in South Carolina in 1814, a daughter of Neil McDonald, who moved to Mississippi about 1820. She was reared in this state, and still living at Quitman, Clarke county, Miss. She is an active and prominent member of the Methodist Episcopal church. The early life of C. C. Ferrill was passed in Alabama and Mississippi. He was educated at Montrose, Jasper county, Miss. When a young man he engaged in the mercantile business, which he has followed until the present time. He lived in Mobile from 1850 to 1855. In 1862 he raised a company, afterward company F, of the Thirty-seventh Mississippi regiment, and of which he was captain. He was in action at Iuka, Corinth, Vicksburg, and all the battles of Johnston's and Hood's campaigns in Tennessee. He was made prisoner of war in 1864, at Nashville, Tenn., and confined at Johnson's island, in Ohio, until after the surrender of the Confederate forces. After the war he came to Clarke county, where he has been a merchant ever since, excepting during 1872 and 1873, when he was sheriff of the county. He was elected to his present office— the clerk of the chancery court of Clarke county—in 1887. He has been quite active in politics ever since the war. He is a member of the Masonic order, and also of the Knights of Honor. He was married in 1860 to Anna B. McCaskill, of Moss Point, Miss., a daughter of Alex. McCaskill. She was born in 1839, and has six children: John, of Shubuta, Miss.; Charles A., of Paperville, Miss.; Ollie S., a commercial salesman; Emma, who resides with her parents; Cicero C. and George F. He and his wife and their entire family are members of or attendants upon the services of the Methodist Episcopal church.

John W. Fewell,* attorney at law, Meridian, Miss., is a son of Thomas T. and Sarah A. (Leachman) Fewell, and was born in Fairfax county, Va., October 18, 1844. His parents were of English ancestry, but were born in Virginia. The father, who was a farmer and merchant and lived and died in Virginia, had two sons and four daughters, only three of whom are living: John W., Robert A. and Laura R., all residents of Meridian, Miss. Mr. Fewell was reared in Virginia and accustomed to all the details of farm life. He received the basis of his education in the country schools and later attended the Fairview seminary in Culpeper county, Va., and the Piedmont academy in Fauquier county. In his seventeenth year he enlisted in the Prince William county cavalry troop, which afterward became company A, of the Fourth regiment of Virginia cavalry, for a time under Gen. J. E. B. Stuart and later under Gen. Fitzhugh Lee, in Wickham's and Mumford's brigade. He served in the seven days' battles around Richmond on the staff of Gen. Roger A. Prior, and afterward in the Gettysburg campaign as a courier under Gen. "Jeb" Stuart. He was captured during the Gettysburg campaign and taken to Fort Delaware, from which he escaped in September, 1863, and he rejoined his regiment and served with it until within eight days of the surrender at Appomattox, his service having been brought to a close by the loss of a leg at the battle of Five Forks, April 1, 1865. In 1866 he began the study of law in the office of Hon. John Randolph Tucker, in Middleburg, Loudoun county, Va. In October of that year he entered the law class in the University of Virginia, where he remained two years, graduating in June, 1868, with the degree of bachelor of laws. He removed to Meridian in January, 1869, where he has since been engaged in the practice of his profession, also taking an active part in the political affairs of the state. On the restoration to rule of the democratic party in Mississippi, he was, with singular unanimity, elected to the state senate. In this body he was a leading member, and bore a distinguished part in the great work wrought out by that legislative assemblage of the real people of the state. In 1886 he was a candidate for a seat in congress, and during the balloting of two days in the nominating convention he steadily held the foremost place, his selection being prevented finally only by what is known as a dead-lock. He has served his party as chairman of its executive committee in the city of Meridian and county of Lauderdale, and he is at present a member of its state executive committee. In his own city and throughout the state he has long been known as a leader of the democracy, and on the hustings and through the press he has always been ready to oppose, in and out of his party, all who sought to impair its organization or authority. Naturally, then, when in 1890 the state convention of the democrats cast about for its truest and strongest and wisest representatives, all eyes turned to Mr. Fewell as a proper delegate from the state at large to the convention to frame a new constitution for the state, and he enjoyed the rare honor of having a nomination without the show of opposition from any quarter. In that convention—the ablest convention ever assembled in the state—he bore himself with a loftiness, a courage and an unselfish devotion to the best interests of his people equaled by few and surpassed by none. An active and earnest member of the chief committees, it was his good fortune to more than meet the high expectations of a generous public in his labors in the work of constitution making. He is the exceptional man, possessing a great head united to a great heart. He is a strong thinker, an acute reasoner, an eloquent speaker. He is a sincere, direct, positive man—a true man in the best and highest sense. Neither friend nor enemy ever doubted his attitude, or misconceived his purpose. He is a man strongly loved and blindly trusted by a great host of friends, and his enemies know him to be honest and open and above all indiscretion, and

*Written by a distinguished member of the Mississippi bar.

their respect at least he enjoys. Almost from the day of his appearance in the courts of his adopted state, he was recognized not by the bar only, but by the public as well, as a man who was to make his mark in his profession. This he proceeded speedily to do, and for nearly a quarter of a century he has commanded such a practice as few lawyers in the state ever enjoyed. His success at the bar was phenomenal, for the young and unknown advocate demonstrated on every occasion his title to rank with the oldest and best of the leaders of the bar, and, for many years past, he has been confessedly without a superior in the courts before which he appears. Though preëminently successful at the bar, Mr. Fewell has been always free from arrogance or any affectation of superiority, or suspicion of any artfulness. His nobility of character shines undimmed in the turmoil and conflict of professional life. In connection with his legal practice he is general attorney of the Queen & Crescent railway system in Mississippi. Ever since his residence in Meridian he has taken a deep interest in its progress and prosperity, and has led in nearly every enterprise tending to its development. He is the chief owner and the president of the Meridian Gas Light company and of the Meridian Electric Light company. He was married in 1870 to Miss Olivia Gaines, by whom he has six children, three of whom are sons. He is a member of the Presbyterian church and is liberal in his aid, not only to that but to other churches, as well as schools and general beneficial interests. His standing at the bar is deservedly high, and his acquaintance extends throughout the entire South.

H. J. Fields is possessed of those advanced ideas and progressive principles regarding the business affairs of life, which seem to be among the chief characteristics of the average North Carolinian. He is now engaged in merchandising and planting, and in both occupations is doing entirely well. He was born in Northampton county, N. C., in 1842, to Jesse R. and Lucy Fields, but at the early age of two years was left motherless. The father, with his family of five children, then came to Mississippi, and the first two years of their stay in this state were spent in Madison county, at the end of which time Sharkey county became their home, Mr. Fields obtaining employment as overseer for J. T. Johnson on the Helena plantation. At the end of a few years he removed to Washington county, where he spent the rest of his days, dying in 1855, at the age of forty-four years. He was married four times, but only his second wife bore him children, their names being as follows: Martha, who married C. Belcher; Ellen, who became the wife of G. W. Faison, of Faisonia, Miss.; Henry, who died at Clinton, Miss., while serving in the Confederate army, and Elizabeth, who is the wife of J. W. Browder. H. J. Fields, the youngest member of the family, was reared in Mississippi, and upon the opening of the Rebellion, like the majority of Southern youths, enlisted in the Confederate army, becoming a member of Wirt Adams' regiment of cavalry, afterward participating in the battle of Shiloh and numerous skirmishes. He was paroled near Greenville, Ala., and returned to his home, where, in 1867, he commenced planting on a part of the plantation of which he is now the owner and where he laid the foundations of his present success, by hard work, close attention to business and by denying himself many of the conveniences and luxuries which the young men of the present day think indispensable to their welfare and happiness. As a reward for his early industry he has now a comfortable fortune, and is engaged in tilling upward of fifteen hundred acres of land on which he has an excellent general supply store, also conducting a branch store at Anguilla. He is now one of the largest planters of Sharkey county and is what may be termed a self-made man. He is a member of the board of supervisors of the county and is one of its most enterprising citizens. He was married to Miss Martha K. Sullivan, a native of Issaquena county, Miss., a daughter of John Sullivan, of Tennessee. To their union the following children have been born: Laura K., Jesse H., Jr., Margie, Thomas, Grover Cleveland, and Lillie, an infant.   Mrs. Field is an estimable lady, and is an earnest and worthy member of the Methodist Episcopal church.

Capt. James L. Finley, Tupelo, Lee county, Miss., was born in Hawkins county, Tenn., September 8, 1836, and is a son of Samuel and Lucy (Etter) Finley.   His father was a native of Maryland and was a son of William and Mary Finley, natives of Maryland and Virginia, respectively.   Samuel Finley was a son of William Finley, who was a native of Ireland and emigrated to America soon after the surrender of Cornwallis.   The father of our subject removed to Mississippi in 1849 and settled at Richmond, which is now in Lee county; two years later he removed to Campbelltown and resided there until his death, in 1862.   He was seventy-one years of age.   Politically, he was identified with the whig party.   His wife died in 1878 at the age of eighty-two years.   Captain Finley was the youngest of a family of four children.   He was educated at Irvin college, Tennessee.   He studied law at the Fulton institution and was admitted to the bar of Mississippi in 1860.   He began his legal practice at Fulton, Miss., and his first case was in the justice's court. He won the case, received five silver dollars as a fee, and spent the whole at Van Amburg's show.   He continued the practice of his profession until the breaking out of the Civil war. He enlisted in March, 1861, as a member of company B, Tenth Mississippi regiment; he was made first lieutenant at once and was afterward promoted to the captaincy.   To follow his career in detail would only be a repetition of the experience of the many brave sons of the South who abandoned home and family to defend a cause which they deemed a just one.   He was in many of the most noted of the battles, served with all the bravery and courage which characterized the Southern army.   After the war he returned to Mississippi and located at Guntown, removing thence to Tupelo, Miss., in 1877.   He was married to Miss Kate M. Thomas, a daughter of E. G. Thomas, deceased.   Her mother's maiden name was McFadden, and she is also deceased.   Captain and Mrs. Finley are the parents of five children: Edwin C., a civil engineer who graduated from the University of Mississippi in 1889, Robert Smith, Mamie, Howery and James A.   Captain Finley was elected attorney of the district, which is composed of Tishomingo, Alcorn, Prentiss, Itawamba, Lee, Chickasaw and Monroe counties.   He filled this office eight years, and during that time three noted murder cases were tried – the Simmons, Shaw and Smith cases.   He is the local attorney of the Kansas City, Memphis & Birmingham railroad.   He was one of the prime movers of the Helena, Tupelo & Decatur railroad.   Politically, he is identified with the democratic party.   He is a Mason, having attained to the degree of Knight Templar.   He is also a Knight of Honor and a Knight of Pythias.   The Captain owns a fine tract of land in the county and has about two hundred acres under cultivation.   Mrs. Finley and daughters are members of the Methodist Episcopal church.

John P. Finlay is the son of Dr. John L. Finlay, a native of the Nutmeg state, and grandson of John Finlay, who was a Scotchman by birth.   The latter was educated for the Presbyterian ministry under the Rev. Dr. Chalmers, but after completing his studies came to the United States, located at Baltimore where he espoused the cause of the Baptists, and took a congregation there (First Baptist church, known as the Round Top church).   He afterward went to Lebanon, Ohio, and from there to Memphis, Tenn.   He was a ripe scholar and a devout Christian.   His death occurred at his son's residence in Old Greenville at an advanced age.   Dr. John L. Finlay was a graduate of three different medical colleges, and had olso obtained a good literary education.   He left his native state, went to Louisiana and located near Lake Providence, where he practiced his profession for a few years.   He then came to Greenville, practiced here for some time, and after a few years started a drug store, which was the first in Greenville or in Washington county. He continued this business, and at the same time practiced medicine until his death in 1862. He acted as treasurer of Washington county for a number of years, and was a successful business man and physician. In 1844 he was united in marriage with Miss Ann B. Pelham, a native of the Old Dominion and of English descent. This marriage occurred in Mississippi, and the fruits of this union were nine children—three sons and six daughters—one son and one daughter deceased. The remainder of the children reside in Greenville, as does the mother. She is a member of the Methodist church South. John P. Finlay was born November 12, 1848, in Washington county, Miss., and was there reared and principally educated. After attending two years at Oxford, Miss., he spent two years at the Philadelphia school of pharmacy, and has since been engaged in the drug business at Greenville. From the time he was fourteen years of age much of the duties of a father have devolved upon him. The family was thought to be in good circumstances when the father died, but this was a mistake, and what little was left was used or destroyed by the armies during the war. In 1865 Mr. Finlay started the business he is now engaged in at Greenville, and it has since grown to its mammoth proportions, being one of the largest and most complete retail drug stocks in Mississippi. Mr. Finlay was married to Miss Alice Archer, a native of Jefferson county, Miss., born in 1848, and daughter of James Archer, who was one of the oldest, prominent and most worthy citizens of Jefferson county and the state. The nuptials were celebrated on December 12, 1872, and have resulted in the birth of nine children, four of whom died in childhood. Those living are John L., Mary P., William H., Thomas P. and Stevenson A. Mr. and Mrs. Finlay are members of the Presbyterian church. Mr. Finlay was county treasurer for twelve years, and a member of the city council about the same length of time. As a councilman he was chairman of the finance committee, and also chairman of other committees. During the yellow-fever epidemic of 1878 he was the only druggist who remained at his post of duty during the whole time, and did much during that dreadfully trying period to alleviate suffering and care for the dead. He is a public-spirited citizen, and has ever been in favor of all things that had a tendency to build up the country or benefit his fellowmen. He and Gen. S. W. Ferguson have been engaged in the fire insurance business for a number of years, and represent fifteen of the leading companies. They do a lucrative business. Mr. Finlay is a Knight Templar in the Masonic fraternity, and has been presiding officer of the Blue lodge. His father was also master of the first and only Masonic lodge ever in old Greenville. Mr. Finlay is a member of the Knights of Pythias, Knights of Honor, and the American Legion of Honor. He is an elder in the Presbyterian church, and he is at the head of almost all the creditable enterprises in the town and county.

Another prominent citizen of Mississippi was Ephraim S. Fisher, who was born near Danville, Ky., November 15, 1815. He was educated in that state, and early exhibited unusual worth and ability. He became a great student, and was for a time given employment as an assistant in the school where he was educated. In 1833 he went to Vicksburg, where he studied law under Joseph Holt. In 1838 he was licensed, and immediately began the practice. He went, almost at a bound, to the top of his profession. In 1839 he located in Coffeeville, Miss., and while here entered the arena of politics. He went to the legislature, but refused to be reëlected, and continued the practice of law. In 1851 he was elected a judge of the high court of errors and appeals, and served with honor until about 1859, when he resigned and resumed his practice. He at first opposed secession, but finally went with his state, and during the war was a colonel of home guards. In

1865 he was nominated for governor.   In 1869 he was appointed circuit judge.   He died in
1876 in Texas, whither he had removed.   He was one of the ablest and most upright
of the public men of Mississippi.   He helped make the history of the great state.

L. T. Fitzhugh, A. M., president of Whitworth female college, Brookhaven, Miss.,
is a native of Brandon, Rankin county, Miss., and was born July 8, 1841.   His parents were
Drew and Martha R. (Batte) Fitzhugh, natives of Virginia.   President Fitzhugh received his
collegiate education at Centenary college, Louisiana.   March 14, 1861, he married Miss
Juliet Deloney, a native of Clinton, La., and a daughter of Hon. Edward Deloney, M. D.,
a very prominent physician of that place.   After the war he engaged in teaching at Sylvarena,
Miss.   Four years later he became principal of the Rankin Masonic institute, in Rankin
county, Miss., in which capacity he served until the fall of 1875, when he was elected principal
of the University high school, University, Miss., in which capacity he served until 1886, when
he was elected to the presidency of Whitworth female college.   He found the institution in
a prosperous condition, and has advanced all its interests since that time.   Being a natural
educator, he is well fitted in every way for the control of an institution of this kind, and he
brought to bear upon his work here long experience and a trained judgment, which
have crowned his every effort with success.   Rev. W. B. Murrah, D. D., vice president of
Whitworth female college, Brookhaven, Miss., was born in Pickensville, Ala., in 1854, a
son of Rev. William Murrah, who was a native of Georgia, and his wife, Mary Cureton Murrah, a native of South Carolina.   Mr. Murrah died at the age of eighty-one in 1887 at
his home in Columbus, Miss.   His widow is still living in Lowndes county, Miss., with her
daughter, Mrs. Dr. Harrington.   Rev. W. B. Murrah was reared in Summerfield, Ala.,
where he received his primary education.   His preparatory education was received at Columbus, Miss.   He afterward entered college at Greensboro, Ala., where he graduated in 1874,
and the degree of D. D. was afterward conferred upon him by Centenary college, Louisiana, in the year 1888.   He began preaching in the year 1874, his first work having been
done on the Vinton circuit in northern Mississippi.   Later he preached at Oxford, Winona
and Aberdeen, and in 1886 was appointed vice president of Whitworth female college, and
has held that position until the present time, performing his duties with credit to himself,
and to the entire satisfaction of every one concerned.   He was married while living at
Oxford, Miss., in 1881, to a daughter of President Fitzhugh, of this college.   Mrs. Murrah
is a woman of rare accomplishments, and possesses remarkable personal attractions.   Dr.
Murrah was honored by his church with a seat in the general conference which met in St.
Louis in 1890, and was appointed by the bishops of his church a member of the ecumenical
conference which met in Washington city in 1891.

Col. Robert W. Flourney, a son of Robert Flourney, was born in Montgomery county,
Ga., March 5, 1811, and completed his education at the University of Virginia in 1832, and
afterward practiced law at his home in Georgia for more than twenty years.   In 1856 he
removed to Mississippi, locating on his plantation near Albany, then of Pontotoc county, now
of Union.   Before the war, he was one of the most extensive slaveowners in northern Mississippi.   When the war seemed imminent, he was a pronounced Union man, and in 1860 and
the early part of 1861 did all in his power to keep the state of Mississippi in the Union, but,
as history has proven, his efforts and those of other noble men in this direction were unavailing.   When the state seceded, he cast his lot with his people, and organized a military company, of which he was captain, and went with it to Richmond, Va.   Upon mature reflection,
he could not bring himself to bear arms against the United States government, and a few
days after his arrival at Richmond he resigned his commission, and returned home, remain-

ing there during the entire war period, a strong advocate of the union of the states, which required more moral courage than would have been demanded of him at the front. Colonel Flourney is a stanch republican, and as such has been placed in nomination to represent his district in the state legislature, but owing to the democratic supremacy, he was defeated by the opposing nominee, Mr. Lamar. Colonel Flourney is a man of undaunted courage and unquestioned bravery. In every relation of life he has proven himself strictly upright and honest. He is a respected citizen, of benefit to the community in which he lives, and is a member of the Methodist Episcopal church, and is also a member of the Masonic fraternity.

E. P. Flowers is a planter and merchant of Hinds county, Miss., and throughout his life he has been honorable and upright in his methods of conducting his affairs, and as a reward has become well to do and has numerous friends. He was born in Warren county, Miss., April 3, 1855, the fourth child born to Ignatius and Sarah (Brooks) Flowers, they also being native Mississippians. The father was a planter by calling and died in 1863, while fol-. lowing this occupation. His people were from the Old North state. E. P. Flowers was edu-cated in early life by a private tutor, but later attended the common schools until he was twenty years of age, at which time he left the halls of learning to take upon himself the duties of life as manager of his mother's plantation. After its division he and his brother each operated one-half of it, and he still conducts five hundred acres, of which he is the owner, also renting a considerable amount of land. He raises large crops of cotton and corn and has shown himself to be an intelligent and practical planter. A considerable amount of his land is covered with a fine growth of valuable timber. In 1889 he opened up a general mercantile establishment on his plantation, and does a large furnishing business. His stock of goods is valued at about $3,000. He is unmarried.

Col. U. G. Flowers is a planter of Warren county, Miss., who was born at Mount Carmel, Covington county, Miss., April 17, 1820, the youngest child of Uriah and Elizabeth (Watson) Flowers, being the only one of their nine children who is now living. His parents were North Carolinians, who came to this state in 1819, and after about four years' residence in Covington county came to Warren county and settled on the Oakland plantation, which is now the old homestead. Ignatius Flowers, the grandfather, was a native of Maryland, while the Watsons are descended from an old English family, who settled on the James river, in Virginia, and were engaged in planting. Both families were slaveholders from the time they landed in America up to the time of the emancipation proclamation and were prominent people in the different sections in which they resided. Col. U. G. Flowers had the advantage of a primary schooling for only about two years, but at the age of fifteen years he entered an engineers' school at Georgetown, Ky., in which he remained one year. In 1839 he was for a short time in the law department of Harvard university, after which he returned to his father's planta-tion, where he remained until 1857, when he went to Europe for the purpose of sightseeing and traveling for his health. He traveled over England, Scotland and a part of Ireland on foot, visiting London, Liverpool and many historic places in that country and Ireland, about six weeks being also spent in Paris. In the latter part of the year he returned home, and during the war traveled quite extensively throughout the United States and visited many of the leading cities of the North, some time being spent in the vicinity of Chicago. Owing to the fact that he contracted physical disability when a young man, with which he is still troubled, he was unable to serve in either army during the Rebellion. Upon the fall of the Confederacy the Colonel returned to his plantation in the South and adopted vigorous measures to rebuild the fortune which the war had laid waste. He engaged actively in planting, was successful, and even now, notwithstanding the low price of cotton, is doing a prosperous business. He is the owner of the old homestead and has in all about one thousand seven hundred and eighty acres, of which five hundred are under cultivation, and a considerable portion of the remainder covered with valuable cypress timber. He raises cattle and horses for the market and has found this industry to be a profitable one. He is of a decidedly literary turn of mind and has written a number of excellent articles for publication, which have appeared in well-known journals, but has always used a *nom de plume*. He has also composed a few poems, but as he did not consider them sufficiently meritorious they have never been given to the public. In personal appearance he is tall and spare, his hair and beard being very white. In social life he is highly esteemed for his rare conversational powers and courtly manners, and although he has seen fit to remain unmarried he is very social in his tastes and has a host of warm friends throughout this section of Mississippi.

J. M. Floyd, the proprietor of the Floyd hotel at Shubuta, Clarke county, Miss., was born in Horry county, S. C., in 1817. He was the second child of a family of four children born to Cornelius and Mary (Rawls) Floyd. His father was a native of South Carolina and a son of Maj. Samuel Floyd and a planter, who was married in North Carolina and settled and reared his family in South Carolina and who died, when quite a young man, in 1826. The mother of our subject was born in North Carolina and was a daughter of John Rawls. After the death of her first husband she married Joseph Hays. She had four children whose names are Mary, Dennis, William and Martha A. Her children by her first marriage were Anna S., J. M., Samuel H. and William C. She moved to Mississippi in 1832, locating in Covington county and was interested in planting, and she died there in 1856. His mother's family moved to Smith county about 1836. Both of Mr. Floyd's grandfathers did gallant service in the Revolutionary war. His parents were both members of the Methodist Episcopal church. His father dying when he was quite young, his recollection of him is limited. Mr. Floyd passed his early years in South Carolina. He began life for himself at the age of seventeen at farming, and later he beame a clerk in a store, a position which he retained until 1839, when he removed to Texas where he remained, however, but a short time. In 1841 he married Anna J. Smith, the daughter of Augustus and Sarah (Enzor) Smith, her father being a native of Connecticut and her mother a native of South Carolina. Mrs. Floyd was born in 1825. Her children are: Sarah C., now Mrs. John McCormick, of Meridian; John C., a resident of Clarke county; Maria L., who married T. B. Hudson, a resident of Shubuta; Samuel H., one of the prominent merchants of Shubuta; Susan E. and George A., who are both at home. Wilson A. Floyd, another and the oldest son of this worthy couple, was wounded during the Civil war, at Murfreesboro, Tenn., and died at home in 1862. He was connected with the Eighth Mississippi regiment and was acting as adjutant-general. Up to the time of the war Mr. Floyd was a planter and merchant. At the time the war began, his business was well established here, but it was broken up during those troublous times, but was revived after peace was declared. In the ante-bellum days he had been very successful in his business undertakings, having considerable landed property and thirty-two slaves. Since then he has been quite successful as a planter and has carried on a good mercantile business. During the last twelve years he has also been in the hotel business. In 1852 he was elected probate judge in Smith county, an office which he held for twelve years. Formerly an old-line whig, he is now a stanch democrat, actively interested in his party, its principles and its measures. He is a master Mason, and with his family has long been identified with the Methodist Episcopal church. He is regarded as an upright, energetic citizen, who takes a deep interest in everything pertaining to the public good.

S. H. Floyd, of the firm of Weems & Floyd, of Shubuta, Clarke county, Miss., was born in Smith county in 1858. He is a son of John H. Floyd. (For some mention of his parents and family history see sketch of J. M. Floyd.) He was educated in Clarke county, and left school at the age of fifteen years to become a clerk in a general merchandise store at Shubuta. In 1883, in company with Mr. W. L. Weems, he opened a general mercantile business, which now amounts to about $150,000 annually, the largest of its kind in the county. The firm started on a modest scale, for the means were limited, but by honesty and prudent management they have advanced in the mercantile world until their business is one of the largest on the M. & O. railroad between Meridian and Mobile. Their cotton trade is exceedingly heavy, and during the season just closed they handled two thousand three hundred bales. Their trade requires the assistance of five persons in their store. They have a turpentine distillery in Wayne county, Miss., with a capacity of about six hundred barrels per year, and they own a tract of land of about two thousand five hundred acres, most of which is connected with their turpentine distillery. September 19, 1882, Mr. Floyd was married to Miss Mittie Hall, the daughter of Dr. I. B. and Anna (Hand) Hall. Her parents were for a few years residents of Kemper county, but were natives of Georgia, Dr. Hall of Rome, and Mrs. Hall of Columbus. Mr. and Mrs. Floyd have four children living, and have lost one by death. Their names are: Samuel H., Earl N., John Milton, Mittie and Gladys, the latter dying in infancy. Mr. Floyd is a member and a trustee of the Methodist Episcopal church. His wife is connected with the Baptist church. In politics he is a democrat, and takes an active interest in all public measures, being regarded as a valuable citizen in all of his relations. He is exceedingly helpful in the support of schools and churches, and is a member of the city council of Shubuta.

Maj. William J. Floyd, the subject of this sketch, was born September 30, 1829, in Gibson county, Tenn., and is a farmer by profession and has followed the occupation of a planter all his life, as did his father before him, and is the owner of sixteen hundred acres of land with one thousand acres under cultivation. During the trouble between the two sections in 1861 Mr. Floyd espoused the cause of the Confederacy, and enlisted in the Hudson company, commanded by Capt. Alfred Hudson, serving until the battle of Shiloh, when he was promoted to the rank of lieutenant. In 1862 he was made first lieutenant of the Mississippi troops, the company known as Peach creek rangers, and was with the same until 1863, when he was elected captain of company H, Eighteenth Mississippi regiment of cavalry. In 1864 he was promoted to major of the same regiment and held that position until the war ended. He was slightly wounded twice and was in the following engagements: Shiloh, Fort Pillow, Memphis, Guntown, Harrisburg, Holly Springs, Selma and others. He was a brave and trustworthy officer and served the Confederacy faithfully and well. He was married on the 8th of March, 1864, to Miss Susan C. Maxwell, who was born in Mississippi and who was the daughter of Hon. W. C. Maxwell, of Alabama, who was quite a prominent man in his county in his day. He represented Panola county in the legislature one term. To Mr. and Mrs. Floyd have been born six children: Ida A. (deceased), William M., Pattie L., Bedford F., Robert F. (deceased), and the other not named. Mr. Floyd and family are members of the Missionary Baptist church. He is a member of the Masonic fraternity. He gives his hearty support to all worthy public enterprises, is regarded as a most desirable citizen, and is interested in the welfare of the county. He was elected sheriff of Panola county in 1866 and was a trustworthy and efficient officer. He was the fifth of ten children born to John and Martha (Jackson) Floyd, natives of the Palmetto state. The father was a planter. He came to Mississippi in 1840, was among the first settlers of the county of De Soto, and was a prominent citizen. He was justice of the peace for a number of years. His death occurred in 1858. The paternal grandparents were David and Mary Floyd. This family is of Scotch descent.

The bar of Yalobusha county, Miss., is given much force and brilliancy by the member-ship of Judge Anderson B. Fly, of Water Valley, one of the leading attorneys of the state of Mississippi. He was born in Maury county, Tenn., November 11, 1825, and is a son of Joshua and Sarah Fly, natives of Tennessee; the father was born in the year 1800, and the mother 1802; they were married in 1819, and removed to Mississippi in 1834, settling in Yalobusha county near the spot where Water Valley stands. Mr. Fly entered land on which he passed the remainder of his days. He was a man of much refinement, and was an earnest worker in the Methodist Episcopal church. He died in September, 1875, honored and respected by all. A few years before his death he was obliged to give up active ministerial work, on account of ill health. His wife died in 1862; she was a member of the same church as her husband, and was a thorough Christian. The impression she made upon the minds of her children has ever been a guide in the right direction, and her memory is revered by each of them. The family consisted of thirteen children, ten of whom lived to maturity, and six of whom are now living. Anderson B. is the eldest; he received his education at Jackson, Tenn., and at the early age of eighteen years was licensed to preach by the Methodist Episcopal conference; for a number of years he was engaged in this labor, and in connection with it gave much attention to the study of law. In 1853 he was admitted to the bar, and plead his first case in Calhoun county. He located at Coffeeville where he practiced his profession until the breaking out of the late war. In 1867 he returned to Yalobusha county and again took up legal work. In 1873 he came to Water Valley where he has since resided, devoting his time and energies to his profession. Before the war he affiliated with the whig party, but since that time he has been a stanch democrat. He was elected chancery judge in 1876, and served until 1884. He was married to Miss Margaret J. Giles, of Lafayette county, Miss., a daughter of William and Lucinda Giles. The parents were natives of North Carolina, and emigrated to Mississippi in 1839, settling in Lafayette county, to whom were born six children, one of whom is yet living—Mrs. Sarah Spears. Mrs. Fly died in 1879, aged fifty-three years; she was a zealous member of the Free Methodist church. Six children were born to her: Joshua H. died in 1878 of the yellow fever; William C. is a druggist in Gal-veston, Tex.; A. W. is a practicing physician of the same place; Anderson B. Jr., lives in Water Valley; David R. is also a druggist and is with his brothers in Texas; Albert S. is a traveler, Central America being the scene of much of his journeying. Judge Fly was mar-ried a second time, to Laura Claunch, who was born and reared in Texas, a woman of unusual force and refinement. Five children were born of this union: Charles T., George W., Sarah Eloise, Matthew De Witt, and Nigil Edwin, who at the age of two years and four months weighed forty-five pounds. Mrs. Fly is a member of the Free church. This church was organized by the Judge in 1878, and has a membership of one thousand souls. There are now two conferences, and small organizations in different parts of the South. Judge Fly was chaplain of the Second Mississippi regiment, and after the proclamation of Davis com-manded a company of scouts. Judge Fly has now associated with him in the legal business R. F. Kimmons, an energetic, young lawyer, who has made a success of the profession and who would be an ornament to any bar. The Judge is an able attorney, a wise counselor, and a man who has won the respect of all with whom he has come in contact.

James M. Fly, a retired school teacher and the present nominee for county superintend-ent of education of Wilkinson county, Miss., was born in Panola county, Miss., in 1835, the third of eight children born to Rev. A. T. M. and Eliza (Jones) Fly, both of whom were born in Maury county, Tenn. The paternal grandfather, William Fly, was born in Tennessee, where he was a very successful planter. He was a soldier in the Seminole war, a stanch

Jacksonian democrat, and was a popular and influential citizen. The great-grandfather was a Virginian, and was among the earliest pioneers of Tennessee, a settler of Maury county, where he reared a large family, which is now scattered, several of them coming to the state of Mississippi, where their descendants are still living. The family is of English descent, several brothers coming to the new world and settling at Norfolk, Va., during the colonial times. One brother is known to have settled in Pennsylvania, another in Georgia, while the progenitor of that branch of the family now in Mississippi settled in Virginia. The maternal grandfather, Willis Jones, was born in Maury county, Tenn., and there he passed from life on the plantation which he had successfully managed for many years. He was of Welsh descent. Rev. A. T. M. Fly was educated in the state of his birth, and while still a young man became a minister of the Methodist Episcopal church. In 1830, at the age of nineteen years, he was married, after which he preached in the northern part of the state until 1850, when he was sent to Wilkinson county, Miss., having in charge a large circuit in several counties. In 1855 he was sent to Natchez, and died in that city of yellow fever on the 1st of October of the same year. He was of a mild and kind disposition, and owing to his noble qualities of heart and head, and his love of his fellowman, he drew around him numerous warm friends wherever he resided. He was very prepossessing in personal appearance, having dark hair, blue eyes and fine complexion; was five feet ten inches in stature and weighed one hundred and sixty pounds. His first wife died in 1846, after which he married Miss Ellen Rabb, of Madison county, by whom he has two children, H. W. Fly and John N. Fly, now living. After his death his widow married again, and is now residing in Wilkinson county. James M. Fly was brought up in northern Mississippi, being an attendant of Centenary college of Jackson, La., from 1853 to 1856, graduating in the latter year. He began teaching school that fall in Point Coupee parish, La., but a few months later began teaching in the public schools of Natchez, where he remained until 1860. In the fall of 1861 he commenced teaching at another point, continuing until April, 1862, when he closed his school and entered the Confederate army, becoming a member of the Conner battery, which was attached to the First regiment Mississippi artillery. He was afterward transferred to the trans-Mississippi department, and was in the battles of the lower Red river in Louisiana. He remained in this state until the close of the war, the most of the time being in the commissary and quartermaster's departments. When hostilities had terminated, he went to Texas, where he conducted private schools and followed the life of a pedagogue until 1871. His health then failing him he returned to Natchez, and in Adams county again resumed teaching in 1878. In 1881 he opened a female college at the Concord place, in the old Gayoso home, and here he built up an excellent school and conducted it successfully until 1884, when he moved to the city and taught the following year. In September, 1885, he moved to Centerville, and for a number of years immediately following this he was a teacher in both the public and private schools. He has been quite active in politics, and in 1876 and 1877 he was secretary of the democratic executive committee of Adams county, Miss., and is now the nominee of the democratic party for county superintendent of schools of Wilkinson county. He was married in 1857 to Miss Mary E. Anthony, a native of Holmes county, Miss., who was brought to Natchez in early childhood by her mother, her father having died soon after birth, and to her union with Mr. Fly six children were born, three of whom are living. Ella died at the age of five years; Ida, who married J. R. Kirkpatrick, of Natchez, and became the mother of two children, died December 25, 1889; Nora, wife of W. C. Jelks, resides in this county; Anthony is married and a druggist of Centerville; Susie died in infancy, and James is the youngest member of the family.   Mr. Fly and his family worship in the Methodist Episcopal church. In 1886 he erected him a very beautiful residence in Centerville, the finest in the place. He has a fine young fruit orchard and is much interested in fruit culture.   He is considered one of the most thorough and successful educators of the state, and is a very fine disciplinarian.   Should he be elected to the position of county superintendent, he will without doubt fill the position admirably and greatly improve the public schools of the county.

Dr. M. R. Fontaine.   John de la Fontaine was born in the year 1500, and was martyred in 1563.   His son was Abraham Fontaine, and Madame Brousseaux was a member of the family of the next generation.   Of the next, Rev. Peter Fontaine was born in 1633, and of the next, another Rev. Peter Fontaine was born in England, at Taunton, in 1691, and emigrated to America in 1716, locating in Virginia, and becoming the rector of Westover parish. He died in 1757.   Succeeding him was Peter Fontaine, who was born in 1720.   He married Miss E. Winston.   His son, John Fontaine, was born in 1750, and married Miss Martha, daughter of Patrick Henry, of Revolutionary fame.   Unto them were born the following children: Patrick Henry, who married Nancy Midler; Charles D., who married Miss Carrington; Martha H., who married N. W. Dandridge; and John J., who married Mary Redd. Unto Patrick Henry Fontaine and his wife were born Edward, Charles D., Martha, Nancy, Elizabeth and Mary B.   J. D. Fontaine, of Pontotoc, Miss., is a son of Charles D., while Madison R. Fontaine descended from John J. and Mary Redd.   John D. Fontaine was born in Pontotoc in 1841, and received a good common-school education.   At the outbreak of the Civil war he enlisted in the Confederate service, serving four years as a private in the army of Tennessee.   At the close of the war he immediately returned home and began the study of law, under the direction of his father.   He was licensed to practice law in April, 1867, and immediately began active duties in his profession, in partnership with his father, in which relation he continued until the latter's death in 1871.   Soon after he formed a partnership with C. B. Mitchell, under the firm name of Fontaine & Mitchell, which was continued until 1888, when the firm dissolved by mutual consent.   Mr. Fontaine has been connected with some of the most noted criminal cases of northern Mississippi.   Charles D. Fontaine, Mr. Fontaine's father, was born in Virginia and reared in the same state.   When a young man he went to Mobile, Ala., but afterward, in 1837, he came to Pontotoc.   His father, Patrick Henry Fontaine, came at the same time from Henry county, Va., to assume the duties in a responsible position in a land office, which was then located here.   The younger Fontaine soon took up the study of law, and soon was admitted to practice at the bar.   Shortly after being licensed he was elected to the legislature, and was twice elected to the same office.   In 1840 he married Miss Sallie A. Dandridge, a daughter of Thomas B. Dandridge, a native of Henry county, Va., who located in Pontotoc prior to this time.   In 1853 he was a candidate for circuit judge, and in 1855 he was candidate for governor of the state.   His first partner in the practice of his profession was —— Freeman.   Later he formed a partnership with Judge W. D. Bradford, and that firm continued until near 1860.   After the war he and his son, John D. Fontaine, became partners as above stated.   He was one of the most finished and accomplished orators, and the best general lawyer in the state.   Of elegant address and charming conversational powers, genial and friendly, he is one of the greatest social favorites in the state.   Patrick Henry Fontaine became a planter of prominence before the war, owning much land and a number of slaves.   Dr. Madison R. Fontaine was born in Henry county, Va., and was educated in Emery and Henry college in Washington county, Va.   Soon after his graduation he began the study of medicine.   He was granted

J. E. Noble M. D.

a diploma, with the degree of M. D., at the Jefferson medical college at Philadelphia in 1846, and at once began the practice of medicine in Virginia, and in 1850 came to Pontotoc. Since that time he has ranked among the leading physicians of northern Mississippi, and is known as one of the best and most skilled surgeons in the state. When the Civil war broke out, in 1861, he was at once commissioned as a surgeon in the Confederate army, and was placed in charge of the principal hospitals at Vicksburg during the siege. On account of his superior ability he was chosen from at least one hundred surgeons to take charge of all the wounded of the different hospitals, and bring them by way of New Orleans and the gulf, to the hospitals at Mobile. This was an undertaking of no small difficulty, and one requiring great dilligence and exceeding care. When he arrived at Mobile with his charges, he turned them over to the various hospitals, and was assigned the duty at Meridian, and soon thereafter was appointed inspector of the hospitals for the cavalry corps of General Johnston's army in Mississippi, a position which he filled with great satisfaction until his appointment as senior surgeon of Ferguson's cavalry corps, which he held until the close of the war. Returning to Pontotoc, he again resumed the practice of his profession, in which he has continued with increasing success until the present time. In 1870 he married Mrs. Elizabeth Gates (nee Gillespie), whose father was an Alabamian, and who has borne him three children. Dr. Fontaine's father, John J. Fontaine, was born in Henry county, Va., in 1788. He was a planter by occupation, and about 1811 he began the study of medicine under the famous William T. Banks. He was remarkable for his close application to business and gave his entire attention to the study of his chosen calling until the War of 1812 broke out, when he gave up everything for his love of country. He went to Washington and offered his services to the government. His assistance not being required, he returned home and soon became engaged in recruiting troops for the United States service. He afterward became famous as Lieutenant Fontaine, and he knew not the meaning of fear or danger. He distinguished himself at Lundy's Lane and Fort Erie, and was highly complimented by the commanding officers. After the war, he resumed the study of medicine and became a physician of much prominence. He gained a splendid education, and was deeply read in many sciences. He was a polished gentleman of the old school, the soul of honor, and was admired by a large circle of acquaintances, including many of the most prominent men and women of his time.

September 20, 1800, in Farquier county, Va., Henry Stewart Foote was born. He received a finished education at Washington college, Virginia, graduating in 1819, and two years later was admitted to the bar, and in 1824 removed to Tuscumbia, Ala., where, for a time, he was connected with a democratic newspaper. In 1826 he became associated in the practice of law at Jackson, Miss., with Anderson Hutchinson. He became prominent and popular, and was soon an active participant in politics. In 1847 he was elected to the United States senate, and took a conspicuous part in the proceedings of the compromise measures of 1850, and was chairman of the committee on foreign relations. In 1851 he was elected governor of Mississippi, defeating Jefferson Davis. In 1854 he went to California, but in 1858 returned and resumed the practice of law at Vicksburg. He was strongly opposed to secession, and continued the opposition in the Confederate congress and in open hostility to President Davis. He opposed a continuance of the war, and favored the terms of capitulation offered by President Lincoln in 1863–4. After the war he was appointed superintendent of the United States mint at New Orleans, and while holding this office died at Nashville in 1880. He was one of the strongest lawyers and politicians of the state. He was the author of the "Bench and Bar of the Southwest," "Texas and Texans" and "Sylla and Charyldis." As an orator he had scarcely a superior in the state.

47

Judge H. W. Foote, jurist, soldier and planter, is a resident of east Mississippi, and in this section, which has long been the seat of wealth, culture and refinement, he has resided since early manhood. Although born and reared in Chester county, S. C., he was early attracted to this section by the fertility of its virgin soil, and having imbibed those principles of probity, honor and candor so characteristic of natives of the Carolinas, he was eminently fitted to occupy a leading position in whatever section he might settle, and especially so in a new country. Being pushing and enterprising in spirit, and possessing an inexhaustible fund of courage, he removed westward before he arrived at the age of manhood, and in the favored region of Macon, Noxubee county, Miss., he cast his fortunes. Prior to leaving the state of his birth he had begun the study and prosecution of law under the direction of that distinguished attorney and jurist, Col. Z. P. Herndon, but, being under age, he was not admitted to the bar until after he came to Mississippi. Soon after reaching his majority he became a candidate for clerk of the circuit court, and so honestly, faithfully and capably did he discharge the trust that for eight years he was elected to this position by his admiring constituents. During the extended period that he filled this position it became a very lucrative one, worth from $5,000 to $6,000 per year, the flush times in Mississippi being then at their fullest flow. About this time a hot contest between Hugh L. White and Martin Van Buren was at its hight, and Mr. Foote espoused the cause of the former with the warmth and fervor of a true Carolinian. He remained an unswerving adherent of the old whig party until it was succeeded by the union party in 1851. He vigorously opposed the repudiation course of Mississippi, and acted with the bond-paying party and supported successively Williams, Shattuck, Fontaine, Rogers and Clayton for governor, upon this issue. Believing that the rights of the Southern states could be preserved in the Union, and that secession would but result in disaster, Mr. Foote opposed secession with all the fervor of his mature manhood, and probably made the last speech in opposition to it that was made in Noxubee county before the convention met that adopted the ordinance of secession. When the war became an assured fact, he was true to the principles he had imbibed in his youth, for, recurring to that period, it is found that when a mere lad of seventeen he was a volunteer in his native state under the Jeffersonian and Calhoun banner of nullification, and now has the commission which was granted him by Robert Y. Hayne, governor of South Carolina, as first lieutenant of a volunteer company. When Mississippi seceded he was found ready to do battle for home, property and liberty, and, as it was apprehended that there would be trouble with the negroes, Mr. Foote raised a company for home defense, composed of many of the best citizens of Noxubee, of which he was chosen captain. After the battles of Manassas, Bull Run and others, the Southern hearts were fired, and the Home company changed their name to the Noxubee cavalry, and marched to Tennessee to support General Cheatham, became an active part of his brigade, and participated in the bloody struggles at Belmont, Shiloh, etc. At the reorganization of the army in north Mississippi, Captain Foote was called home—where he had left his children without the protection of a mother even—by Gov. Charles Clarke to take charge of and organize the militia in that part of the state, and after this had been done efficiently a large regiment of cavalry, consisting of thirteen companies and over one thousand three hundred men, were ordered to elect their field officers. Mr. Foote was soon after informed that he had been unanimously elected colonel, and although his services were needed by his family, he could not resist what he considered his country's call, and how well he performed his duties let the survivors of that splendid legion answer for him. In 1865, at the earnest solicitation of his numerous friends, he became a candidate for circuit judge, and although his opponent was one of the ablest and most popular judges of the state, he was elected, and for four years in this trying and responsible position he administered justice with an even hand, and so satisfactory was his work that he was triumphantly reëlected over the same able and accomplished competitor. During his second term the reconstruction acts were passed by the Federal congress, and during the pursuance of these measures Federal legislation became so inimical to Southerners who had participated as to render it unsafe for them to remain in state offices, and Judge Foote determined to resign his judgeship, and held his last term at Columbus, retiring from the bench two years before the expiration of his second term. The frequent affirmance of his decisions by the supreme court attested his profound knowledge and astute judgment of the noble science of law, and his career on the bench brought into play the versatility and superiority of his genius. He returned to his home in Macon and resumed the practice of law, devoting his matured energies to this work and to the supervision of his planting interests during the dark days up to 1875, but as this period of misrule became too heavy to bear, and the chains too galling to be longer tolerated or worn by men who dared to call themselves men, the leading citizens of east Mississippi led the whites to victory in the revolution of 1875, and Judge Foote was one of the foremost of this band.

While a member of the state senate from the district composed of Noxubee, Kemper and Neshoba counties, he was fearless and frank in the expression of his views, and that he was an able legislator is attested in looking over the journals of the senate. He is a stanch member of the democratic party, and is much more interested in local than in national politics. Although he commenced the battle of life at Macon with limited financial resources, by attention to business principles, and a successful law practice, he was the owner of one hundred slaves at the opening of the war in 1861, and cultivated one thousand acres of land. He also has a considerable amount of money at interest, making in all a comfortable fortune. The result of the war left him destitute, with the exception of his land and stock, and in the unsettled condition of affairs, even these were of little profit, as many a fortune was lost in planting operations under the new regime. Besides his Noxubee plantations, Judge Foote's wife owned a magnificent body of land of about three thousand acres in Issaquena county, but it was left in ruins at the close of the war. Under his efficient management this magnificent property has been restored, and now over one thousand acres are in a fine state of cultivation, and make one of the best improved plantations on Deer creek. The Louisville, New Orleans & Texas railroad runs through this plantation, at the lower part of which is a flag station, which makes it one of the most accessible and desirable of properties. Judge Foote also owns another splendid plantation on the same stream in Washington county, which has about five hundred acres under cultivation, and in connection with his son, Mr. Hoger L. Foote, owns a delightful settlement on Steele's bayou, containing five hundred acres. A prairie farm of five hundred acres, nine miles east of Macon, is also his property, but his special pride is his stock farm, containing one thousand acres, situated on the west bank of the Noxubee river, two miles south of Macon. Judge Foote recognized the fact that to raise cotton profitably it was necessary to raise needful home supplies, and he determined to devote one farm exclusively to stock, to supply meat and mules to his other plantations. Six hundred acres of this farm are devoted to pasture, and are finely adapted to the purpose for which they are intended. An artesian well affords pure and abundant water, the pasture abounds in native grasses and there is a considerable area in blue grass, orchard grass and also an abundance of lespedeza or Japanese clover. On this farm the Judge has demonstrated satisfactorily that stockraising pays. All necessary supplies for keeping the stock in good condition during the winter months are raised on the farm, and every facility is used for bringing about good results, and as a result Judge Foote is one of the leading stockmen of the South. In the domestic circle he is a model husband and father, is devoted to his family and makes their happiness and comfort his chief object and aim in life. While filling the active and important duties of clerk of the circuit court, he courted and won for his wife Miss L. F. Dade, a daughter of Col. H. C. Dade and Catharine (Lewis) Dade, a niece of General Washington. To their union a family of four sons and three daughters were born, all of whom are living with the exception of the eldest son, who died, leaving a wife and four children, living at the present time in Birmingham, Ala. The eldest daughter became the wife of Dr. E. C. Clements, son of Hardy Clements, late of Tuscaloosa county, Ala. She, with her family, and the youngest son of Judge Foote, now state senator, reside on Deer creek, in Sharkey county, Miss. The other daughters married brothers, T. J. Patty and Henry Patty, the former a merchant, stockraiser and planter, and the latter a promising young lawyer, of Atlanta, Ga. The other sons live in Lowndes and Noxubee counties, Capt. H. D. Foote, a planter of the former and Thomas Foote, a lawyer of Macon. Mrs. Foote died in 1855 and two years later the Judge contracted a second marriage, his union being to Miss Mary Foote, a cousin of his first wife and a supposed distant relative of his own. One daughter was born to them, Mollie Frances, who is also directly descendant from the Washington family, the mothers of the two wives being sisters. While in Macon in 1863 he met and married Mrs. Sybilla A. Messinger, relict of G. W. B. Messinger, and their union was consummated in December of that year and existed harmoniously for twenty years, or until the death of Mrs. Foote. She left one child, Miss Georgie, who is a handsome and accomplished young lady. The above statements are taken from a sketch of Judge Foote in the *Planters' Journal*, of August, 1884, and may have changed in some respects. His daughter, Miss Georgie, is now the wife of Dr. W. M. Paine, of Aberdeen, son of the late Bishop Paine, of Mississippi. His last union was to Miss Eleanor W., daughter of Rev. Curtiss. For thirty years he was actively engaged in the practice of his profession, with the exception of the time he was in the army and on the bench, but for some years has been retired from the practice of his profession and devotes his time to looking after his varied and engrossing interests, in visiting his children in their various homes, and in church and Sunday-school work. He has long been a member of the Methodist Episcopal church, and his counsels are constantly required by the church in her work. Although somewhat advanced in years he shows but little the ravages of time, either mentally or physically, and has before him many years of usefulness to his fellowmen and pleasure to himself. He has a beautiful home, elegantly appointed and favorably situated, and here he dispenses hospitality with a generous and gracious hand. He is a member of the board of trustees of Vanderbilt university and is president of the Farmers and Merchants' bank, of Macon, Miss.

Hon. H. L. Foote is a gentleman who has attained prominence, not only as a planter but also as a merchant, and in the capacity of state senator from the twentieth district, he is proving himself a man of far more than average intelligence. He was born in Macon, Miss., in 1855, to Judge Henry W. and Mary (Dade) Foote, both of whom were born in South Carolina, where they were reared and married, coming in an early day to Macon, Miss., where their home has been for about fifty years. Judge Foote is now living with his fourth wife. He has been one of the foremost lawyers of the state for many years and is a man whose brilliant intellect has fitted him for any position within the gift of the people of his state, for the many prominent positions which he has held have been admirably filled, and in a manner betokening a man of sound views and progressive and original ideas. He is well known and highly respected by the highest class of society and the most distinguished men of the state. He was for some time chancery clerk of Noxubee county, was district judge for some years and has served with ability in both house of the state legislature. He was a colonel in the Civil war, made a brave, faithful and intrepid soldier, and did much to further the cause of the Confederacy. Although he started in life with a limited education, through his own untiring efforts he became a finely educated man, and has been a most useful and eminently successful citizen. He is an active worker in, and a member of, the Methodist church, and is strictly temperate in all his habits. The gentleman whose name heads this sketch was the youngest of nine children born to his father's first marriage, the names of the other members of the family being as follows: Fannie (deceased); Maggie (deceased); Ann, wife of Dr. E. C. Clements; Catherine, who afterward became Mrs. Patty, is deceased; William, who was a planter, and a lieutenant in the Confederate army, died in 1875; Henry D., of Columbus, Miss., who was also in the Confederate army, holding the rank of captain, and was imprisoned at Camp Douglas, Ill.; Thomas is a lawyer and is associated with his father, and was once mayor of Macon, and Emily is the wife of Henry Patty, a lawyer of Atlanta, Ga. Hon. H. L. Foote received his initiatory training in the schools of Macon, and in 1872 graduated from Bryant & Stratton's Commercial college of Cincinnati, Ohio, three years later graduating from Eastman college of Poughkeepsie, N. Y. For two years following his graduation he was engaged in merchandising at Macon, and followed the same occupation at Haney Grove, Tex., and since 1877 on his present plantation—Council Bend and Egremont, which places comprise thirty-five hundred acres, about fifteen hundred acres being under cultivation, yielding about six and seven hundred bales of cotton each year. The most of this property he has earned by his own efforts since 1877, at which time he became a merchant at Egremont. In 1885 he was elected sheriff of Sharkey county, was reëlected in 1887 and in 1889 was nominated by acclamation, with no solicitation on his part, to the state senate from the twentieth district, and served on the committees on levees and finance. On March 1, 1878, he was married to Miss Mattie Cavett, daughter of J. R. Cavett. She was born near Macon and died in December, 1878. Mr. Foote's second marriage occurred in 1882, to Miss Eva P., daughter of George Cooper, of Yazoo county, Miss., a planter and Methodist minister. Mrs. Foote was born at Lake Washington, Washington county, and has borne her husband one son. Mr. Foote is a member of Rolling Fork lodge No. 3175 of the K. of H. and Deer Creek lodge No. 356 of the A. F. & A. M., at Rolling Fork. Mr. Foote is progressive in his views and owns one of the finest plantations in the Yazoo delta. His wife is a member of the Episcopal church.

On Downing creek in the state of North Carolina, within a few feet of the South Carolina line, were born four brothers, all of whom removed to Marion county, Miss., and among whose descendants there have been many men and women of great force of character, some of whom have arisen into prominence in Mississippi and Louisiana. The brothers were John, Joseph, Stephen and Ebenezer Ford. They came to Marion county among the very earliest settlers, when the switch cane and the wild peavine made the pine forests a paradise for the stockmen. John Ford left a family of seven, viz.: Joseph Ford, a distinguished lawyer of Shreveport, La.; Rev. Thomas Ford, a Methodist minister, who went to Hinds county; David Ford, who went to Texas; Rev. Madison Ford, who became a celebrated preacher and died in Madison county, Miss.; Mrs. Womack, of Rankin county; Elias Ford, the father of Mrs. Catherine Rain, and Mrs. William B. Holloway, of Williamsburg, in Covington county, and Samuel Ford, who became a citizen of Louisiana. Among the children of Joseph and Samuel are many who are prominent in politics and society, such as Chauncey Ford, of New Orleans, an able lawyer, Mrs. Judge Randall Hunt, of the same city, and others of prominence who live in Shreveport. Stephen Ford lived and died in Marion county. His children all removed to the counties of Hinds and Copiah; they were Rowan, Joseph, Rebecca Ford, Priscilla Foster and Elizabeth Browning.   Joseph Ford moved with his three brothers, John, Stephen and Ebenezer, from North Carolina to Mississippi in the year 1809. His wife was Sarah Rawls, and to them were born five children: Ebenezer, James, Solomon, Caroline and Sarah; Caroline married Jacob Funches, of Hinds county, Miss., and Sarah Edmond Funches, of the same county.   James and Solomon Ford lived and died in Marion county, each leaving a large family.   They married cousins, of the same name, one the daughter of Jacob, the other of Sampson Pope.   Judge Ebenezer Ford, the son of Joseph Ford and Sarah Rawls, first married Mary A., the widow of John Morgan and daughter of Jacob Pope; eight children were born of this union: Sarah, the wife of James M. Carr; Harriett, the wife of the Rev. Alfred Farr; Elizabeth, the wife of William Patten; Sophronia L., the wife of Calvin Ford; Eugenia,wife of the Hon. W. D. Carmichael, of Hinds county; Mary Janet, the wife of Calvin Ford; Joseph M. Ford and James E. Ford, Eugene and Monet Ford, of Gloster, Miss., and Harry and Jerome Ford, of Magnolia, Miss., who are successful business men, are the sons of Mary J. Ford and grandsons of Judge Ebenezer Ford.   J. Ira Ford, the promising young lawyer of Jackson county, the son of J. M. Ford, is a grandson of Judge Ebenezer Ford and of his first wife Mary A. Ford.   Mrs. Ford died in 1843, and Judge Ford, afterward married Juliet A. Swift, who on her father's side was of a numerous and prominent family in Vermont, claiming consanguinity with the famous Dean Swift.   Her mother was a Bulkley, of Weathersfield, Conn., and she cherished to the end of her life the diary of her grandfather, Captain Bulkley, who served with distinction in the Revolutionary war, and through whom she received a historical curiosity in the shape of a document for the exchange of prisoners, signed by George Washington and Sir Henry Clinton.   Her brother, Theodore Swift, was an eminent lawyer who lived for a long time at Monticello, and who was noted for his great wit, and for his accurate knowledge of the law.

The Weathersfield family of Bulkleys were related to the Sedgwicks, to which family General Sedgwick belonged.   While at he brother's house in Monticello, Juliet A. Swift met and married Judge Ebenezer Ford, of Spring college, who was a planter and a man of large wealth.   Judge Ford, though not a practicing lawyer, had pursued the study of the law as a recreation, and was actually well versed in the elementary principles of the profession, so that he filled for many years, with great credit to himself, the office of probate judge of Marion county.   In the days when Wiley P. Harris was on the bench, and the lawyers rode the circuit, Judge Ford's home was the stopping place between Gainesville and Columbia for the Judge and lawyers and the wits who followed the courts, and who found a welcome and a pleasant entertainment for the spare days intervening between the terms at Columbia and at Gainesville.   At Spring cottage were born Thomas Swift Ford, Theodore Bulkley Ford and Emma J. Ford.   Judge Ford died in 1858, and his widow took her three children to Manchester, Vt., in the spring of 1859, the eldest being then eleven years of age.   At that place there were superior advantages for acquiring an education.   There the boys pursued their studies at Burr and Burton seminary, and the elder finally went to Middlebury college, where he was graduated in 1866.   He was the youngest member of the class.   The family then returned to Columbia, Marion county, where the elder son studied law and the younger medicine.   Thomas S. Ford was elected to the legislature in 1869, when just of age, was again elected in 1871, and served two years in the lower house.   He was elected district attorney in 1875, and held the office eight years.   In 1885 he was appointed attorney-general by Governor Lowry to fill the unexpired term of T. C. Catchings.   He was elected delegate to the constitutional convention in 1890 from the state at large, receiving the highest vote cast for any one of the fourteen candidates. Dr. Theodore B. Ford graduated in medicine from the University of Louisiana, and settled at Columbia. He developed extraordinary aptitude for his profession. His skill in the treatment of disease, his kindly bearing to all, made him many friends, who brought him to the front in politics on several occasions. He served in the legislature of the state in 1876, 1878 and 1882 in the lower house, and one term in the senate, beginning with the year 1888. The names of the descendants of Ebenezer, the brother of Joseph, John and Stephen, will be found elsewhere in this work.

Rufus R. Ford, a resident of Washington and civil engineer and surveyor, is, like many other prominent citizens of the county, a native of Mississippi, born in Franklin county on the 31st of January, 1836. He was educated in Franklin and Jefferson counties, and took a thorough course in civil engineering with a Mr. Graham, a relative. He followed that occupation for several years, and at the breaking out of hostilities between the North and South he was appointed to operate on the coast as a surveyor. This position he declined and volunteered as a private in the Confederate army, company A, Seventh Mississippi infantry, with which he served about a year. He was then made a civil engineer and operated with General Bragg and General Johnston in the Tennessee army. He was wounded and captured at Mumfordsville, Ky., but was soon afterward paroled. In July, 1861, he was married to Miss Emma A., daughter of Stephen and Lucina Kennedy, natives of South Carolina and Louisiana respectively. Her parents were married in Adams county, Miss., and there the father died in 1854, and the mother, Lucina, in 1882. He was born in Edgefield district, S. C., September 2, 1774, and was a planter by occupation. Mrs. Ford was born in Adams county December 4, 1841. To Mr. and Mrs. Ford were born seven sons and two daughters, all of whom have had good educational advantages. With the exception of about ten years in Franklin county, Mr. Ford has resided in Adams county ever since the war, and has followed surveying nearly all his life, in Louisiana and Mississippi. He is also the owner of three thousand acres of land, all the result of his own industry. He was for four years county surveyor of Franklin county, and was once elected to that office in Adams county but declined to take the oath then required. He is an industrious, energetic man, and is ready and willing to aid with his time and means any enterprise for the advancement of the county. Mrs. Ford has been a member in good standing in the Christian church for thirty years. Mr. Ford was the eldest and the only one now living of three children—two sons and a daughter: Rufus R., born January 31, 1836; Percival F., born in 1837, and Mary Jane, born about 1839, of Absolom and Mary J. (Holloway) Ford, natives of South Carolina and Clinton, La., respectively. His mother was Jane, daughter of Robert Holloway. Her first marriage was to Archibald Graham, by whom she had two sons. Mr. Graham, who was a United States surveyor, died about the time his younger son was born. The elder son, DeWitt Clinton Graham, was a man of talent, an able surveyor and lawyer, became judge of the probate court in Franklin county, Miss., and was for several terms a member of the Mississippi legislature, and was noted as a mathematician of the state. When a boy, Absolom Ford came with his parents to Jefferson county, Miss., was married in Franklin county, and there his death occurred about 1840. Mr. Ford was a planter, was a soldier in the War of 1812, and participated in the battle of New Orleans. He had a brother, John Ford, and his father was also John Ford. The latter was born in South Carolina, and at an early age (1805) came to what is now Franklin county, where he settled a Spanish claim. He became quite well off and died there. He was of Irish descent. After the death of Absolom Ford his widow married Joseph Lord, an Irishman, who was educated for the priesthood. He died in Franklin county, and she in the same county in 1872. She was a member of the Methodist church. Mary J., sister of our subject, became the wife of George P. Butler, of Franklin county, and died. His brother, Percival, deceased, was a soldier in the Confederate army. Our subject's maternal grandfather, Robert Holloway, was probably born in the Palmetto state, but when a young man went to Louisiana where he was married. From there he came in an early day to Franklin county, where he and his wife both died. He was a farmer.

Thomas F. Ford is well and favorably known to a host of acquaintances and friends throughout this section, and is a fair example of what can be accomplished by industry and perseverance. He has become one of the influential men and prosperous planters of Amite county, and as he was left an orphan in early boyhood and has made his own way in life, is deserving of much credit. His father, Bartlett Ford, was born in Franklin county, Miss., in 1829, and in the county of his birth attained manhood. He was married in Amite county, to Miss Rebecca Cain, a daughter of Elijah Cain, of Georgia, but their married life was of short duration, for he was called from life in 1858, his widow following him to the grave in 1860. The paternal grandfather, Freeman Ford, was a Georgian, and at an early day moved with his family to Mississippi, taking up his abode on a plantation on Homochitto river, in Franklin county, where he reared his family. Thomas F. Ford was brought to Amite county when a child of eleven years, his birth having occurred in Franklin county November 6, 1849, and after the death of his parents he made his home with an uncle. In 1863, when a strippling of fourteen years, he joined the Seventh and Eleventh Arkansas cavalry, which was commanded by Colonel Griffin, and although but a boy did valiant service until the close of the war, his service being in north Mississippi and Louisiana. He was paroled at Jackson, Miss., after Lee's surrender, and returned to Amite county. On the 18th of January, 1866, at the early age of seventeen years, he was united in marriage to Miss Josephine E. Gordon, a daughter of Ephriam Gordon, who died when Mrs. Ford was a small child. She was reared and educated in Amite county, and at the time of her marriage was also seventeen years of age. Mr. Ford commenced to make a home for himself and wife without money or influence, and although he rented land for a number of years, and was compelled to deprive himself of many luxuries and conveniences, he managed to save some means, with which he purchased some land. He has since purchased, owned and traded several plantations, but on his present place has resided since 1884. He is now the owner of a plantation containing six hundred and eighty acres, of which about three hundred acres are open land. Everything about his place indicates that a man of thrift and energy has control of affairs, and as all this property has been obtained by his own efforts, and cost him many hours of hard labor, he thoroughly understands how to take care of it, and render it more valuable. His management has always been excellent, and as a financier he has proved himself able and successful. He is reasonably careful in his expenditures, but not in the least niggardly so, and when aid and support is needed for any worthy enterprise, he is one of the first to give his assistance, both in regard to influence and money. To himself and wife a family of nine children have been born: Mary Jane, Bartlett (a clerk in Gloster), Hiram K., Alma I., Charles C., Morris, Carrie R., Lovel and Leo. Mr. Ford, his wife and four of their children are members of the Baptist church, and socially he is a member of the Masonic fraternity and Knights of Honor.

Thomas W. Ford, retired merchant and planter, Empora, Miss. Mr. Ford's grandfather, Wyett Ford, was a native Virginian and a man of superior ability. When a young man he went to Georgia, and married in that state and there passed the remainder of his days, dying in Milledgeville while clerk of the supreme court. He was the father of three sons and one daughter: Thomas B.; Abraham, who died in Texas; Dr. Andrew J. and Mrs. Mary McCroy, who is now a resident of Bellefontaine, Miss. After her husband's death the mother of these children married a Mr. Goar and then moved to Bellefontaine where her death occurred One of the sons, Dr. Andrew J. Ford, was a very prominent surgeon and also quite a literary genius. He was born on the 6th of November, 1825, graduated in physic at Philadelphia, afterward served as surgeon in the Mexican war and then filled the same position on the frontier under Gen. Albert Sidney Johnston until the breaking out of the Civil war. He then resigned and obtained services under the Confederate government, but was afterward made chief surgeon in General Johnston's corps. After the war he was professor of anatomy in a medical college in Baltimore, which position he was holding at the time of his death which occurred in Charleston, S. C., in March, 1868. The eldest son of the above mentioned children, Thomas B. Ford, was born in Milledgeville, Ga., on the 2d of October, 1821, and being left fatherless at quite an early age was partly reared by an uncle, Abram Ford, with but little schooling. In 1846 he came to Bellefontaine, where he soon afterward married Mrs. Elmira (Hicks) Hog and followed the occupation of a planter and merchant until the opening of the Civil war. He then raised a company of volunteers, company K, and served in the Fifteenth Mississippi infantry as captain until the battle of Shiloh, when he organized another company which he commanded in the cavalry until cessation of hostilities. He surrendered near Selma, Ala. He was captured five times, but soon after always managed to make his escape. Once while at home at Bellefontaine he was captured and while under guard the first night, when about ten miles west of Bellefontaine, he watched his chance while the guard was dozing and was soon a free man. He operated all through the Georgia and Atlanta campaign. After the war he farmed for a few years near Bellefontaine and then removed to northwest Mississippi, his death occurring at Cold Water in 1883. He was a charter member of Adelphian lodge, A. F. & A. M. No. 174, of which he was worthy master a number of years. He was a self-made man in every respect, and became a very useful and wealthy citizen. Mrs. Ford is still living at Bellefontaine. She came with her parents to what is now Webster county in 1835, and there she first married Judge Thomas Hog. He came from Alabama to Mississippi with a load of goods, and in 1834 settled at Bellefontaine, where he at once engaged in merchandising. He was the first settler there, and followed merchandising until his death, about 1842. He was one of the first representatives of Choctaw county in the state legislature and was probate judge at one time. He was an uncle of the present governor of Texas. Grandfather Hicks came to what is now Webster county in 1835, and died near Bellefontaine many years age. He had a son, the late Rev. A. B. Hicks, who was a distinguished Baptist minister. To Thomas B. and Elmira (Hicks) Ford were born three children—a son and two daughters: Thomas W. (subject), Lou (wife of R. Lamb, of Texas) and Zuby F. (wife of E. Wright, of Euporia). Thomas W. Ford was educated at Bellefontaine, and when twenty-one years of age started out for himself as a farmer, and afterward continued tilling the soil until 1875, when he was elected circuit clerk of Webster county. He filled the position for eight years in a very efficient manner, and fully testified to the wisdom of the people's choice. He subsequently engaged in merchandising at Walthall, and when the railroad was built he removed to Eupora, where he continued merchandising until recently, when he sold his stock. He was the second merchant at Eupora. He built and still owns a fine two-story double brick block, the best one in that town. He also owns about eight hundred acres in different tracts, all the fruits of his own labors, and is not only one of the moneyed men of the county, but one of its best business men.   He is a member of Adelphian lodge, A. F. & A. M.   Mr. Ford was married in 1876 to Miss Lenora Roberts, a native of what is now Webster county, and the daughter of Frank and Mary Roberts, natives, respectively, of Georgia and Mississippi.   Mr. and Mrs. Roberts were married in what is now Webster county, and there the father died in December, 1883.   He was a successful planter.   He was in the late war, and was a member of the Baptist church.   Mrs. Roberts is still living and is a member of the same church.   To Mr. and Mrs. Ford have been born two children.   Mr. Ford is a member of the Methodist and his wife a member of the Baptist church.

It is a fact recorded in history that the first English emigrants to America were a superior race, with most progressive views of government, liberty and laws, and who sought out homes in the New World in obedience to impulse, prompted by lofty ambition and an earnest desire to benefit the race.   From these ancestors sprung men who subsequently became eminent in the different localities in which they located.   Richard H. Forman is a descendant of one of the earliest and most illustrious families of the state of Mississippi, and is deserving of especial mention in a work of this kind, for he, as well as his most worthy progenitors, has done much to bring the county and state to its present state of civilization and cultivation.   The family is of English origin, the members of which trace their ancestry back to the illustrious family of Gordons, that was related to Lord George Gordon Byron. The first of the Forman family to come to America was in the year 1675, their residence at first being in the state of New Jersey, but in the year 1790 some members of the family drifted into Mississippi territory, which was then under the control of the Spanish govern- ment, and settled at Natchez.   Since that time the Forman family have been identified with the history of Mississippi, and the name has been prominently before the people on numerous occasions.   Joseph and Elizabeth Forman, the great-great-grandparents of Rich- ard H. Forman, were married in England about the year 1732, their union resulting in the birth of four sons and one daughter: Joseph, Ezekiel, Elizabeth, Stephen and David. Joseph, the eldest son, was born October 27, 1743, was married to Miss Amelia Gale, April 24, 1765, and by her became the father of five children: Elizabeth, Stephen, William Gordon, Joseph and Matthias.   Stephen, the eldest son, was the grandfather of Richard H., and his son, Stephen, was the father of the latter.   Stephen Forman was born in New Jersey, and when still but a youth came to Mississippi, and was married here in the year 1825 to Miss Keziah B. Howell, a cousin of Mrs. Jefferson Davis, and unto them a family of three sons and two daughters were born, the following of whom are living: Mary Jane, the eldest, is the wife of Maj. Thomas Reed, an eminent attorney at Natchez; Stephen S., also living in Natchez, and Richard H., whose name heads this sketch.   Charles H. and Martha are deceased, the latter having been the wife of the late Hon. Thomas C. West, of this county. Richard H. Forman was born February 19, 1833, in Jefferson county, and was educated at Oakland college, one of the earliest institutions of learning in this part of the state.   Decem- ber 6, 1860, he was married to Miss Emily A. Batchelor, who made him an exemplary wife and a faithful and devoted mother to his children, and died May 31, 1883, leaving her husband with four children to mourn her loss—one son and three daughters: George D., Lura, Evelyn and Saidie L., all of whom have received the advantages of a good education, Lura being a graduate of Fairmount female college.   Evelyn was educated in the Fayette academy and in the Natchez literary institute, Saidie, the youngest daughter, having also attended the Fayette academy.   A short sketch of the son, George D., immediately follows this.

In the fall of 1852 Mr. Forman went to New Orleans with the view of making that city his permanent home, accepting a position in a cotton factorage and commission house, remaining there during the winter and summer of 1853, through the yellow-fever epidemic, when that disease was more fatal than it ever had been before or since, the mortality reaching three hundred per day. In the fall of 1853 his health failed, and he was compelled to abandon his position and return to his native home, Rodney. After sufficiently recovering his health, he engaged with one of the principal business houses in the town, and then three years later engaged in the general mercantile business on his own account, and was doing a paying business at the outbreak of the war, which forced him to close, as it did many other Southern merchants. In 1858 or 1859 he was elected a member of the board of aldermen of Rodney, and served more than one term. In 1861 he was appointed commissioner to look after and provide for the destitute families of Confederate soldiers, which position he held until the close of the war, feeling anxious to do all he could for the Confederate cause, and being physically unable to go into active camp life. In 1862 he was elected a member of the board of trustees of the public school in Rodney, and served during the war. In the same year he was elected justice of the peace, and in 1864 was reëlected. After the close of the war he was removed from office, as were other county and state officers. In 1865 he came in possession of some valuable lands and turned his attention to farming, and, being a young farmer without old fogy notions in his head that older farmers had, he at once adapted himself to the new order of things. Recognizing the freedom of the colored man, and respecting his rights, he went on with his farming operations more successfully than many of lifetime farmers. In 1869 the people of Jefferson county met, organized and incorporated the Jefferson County Planters', Mechanics' and Manufacturer's association, which had annual meetings and exhibitions. In 1871 he was elected a member of the board of directors, and served until 1877, when he was elected president. He declined a reëlection to the presidency, but continued on the board of directors until 1884, when he was again elected president, and served until the association was disorganized, about four years ago. Some ten years ago the farmers organized the Jefferson County Stock Breeders' association, and Mr. Forman was honored with the presidency. The object of the association was to encourage the raising and improving of all kinds of stock.

In 1874 or 1875 there were in this county seven subordinate granges, from which was organized a county grange. Mr. Forman was a member of one of the subordinate granges and of the county grange, acting as secretary of one and treasurer of the other. This organization has gone down in Mississippi, and there is now but one grange (the Phœnix) in this county.

In 1878 Mr. Forman was made one of the trustees of the Fayette female academy, and served in that capacity several years, having several children of his own to educate, and feeling much interest on the subject of education.

In 1884 he was appointed by Gov. Lowry a commissioner of the state of Mississippi to the World's Industrial and Cotton Centennial exposition at New Orleans, beginning on the first Monday in December. In 1887 he was appointed by the Governor a delegate to the interstate convention of farmers, held in Atlanta, Ga., on the 16th of August. In 1888 the farmers of this county organized the Jefferson County Horticultural association, and he was honored with the presidency. This association was intended to encourage the raising of all kinds of fruit and vegetables for shipment to Northern and Western markets. During the political excitement in Mississippi, along in the seventies, for a number of years he was a member of the county democratic executive committee, and for several years chairman of the committee until he asked to be relieved. He also served several years on the congressional executive committee. Away back in the sixties there was a local emigration association, and he was elected a member of the board of directors and served several years. In 1862 he was appointed a commissioner to ascertain the names of all volunteers from this county who had been mustered into the service of the state or of the Confederate states for at least six months with the names of the companies to which they belonged. Also the names of all volunteers who had enlisted as recruits or attached themselves to companies formed without the limits of their county or state. In 1864 he was appointed a commissioner to ascertain the names of all soldiers who had been mustered in the service of the Confederate states or of the state of Mississippi from Jefferson county, and also the number of persons dependent upon each of said soldiers who needed assistance, whether such dependent persons were the wives or children, or near relatives of said soldiers who had been heretofore assisted or supported by them, and report the same, together with the names of any disabled or indigent soldiers. Since 1870 he has attended as a delegate numerous democratic nominating conventions, both county and state. Mr. Forman has been prominent in the political field for many years and is now a member of the county board of supervisors. He has for many years held the position of trustee in the Presbyterian church, of which church some of his children are also members. He is at present residing on a fine and well-improved plantation, his residence being two and a half miles west of Fayette, and here he dispenses hospitality with a liberal hand, being noted for his courtly and polished manners. Socially he is a member of the Knights of Pythias and the Knights of Honor. January 18, 1888, he was united in matrimony to Miss Lydia Dockery, the handsome and accomplished daughter of Gen. Thomas P. Dockery, of New York. George D. Forman, son of the above mentioned subject, was born at Rodney, Miss., December 29, 1861, and in the year 1879 was graduated from the University of Mississippi at Oxford. He soon after returned to Rodney and became a bookkeeper for William J. Martin, which position he filled in a very faithful and conscientious manner for several years. In October, 1884, he entered general mercantile business at Fayette, and by his faithful attention to every detail of the work and his methodical business habits, he is doing a paying business. He deals extensively in cotton and planters' supplies, and although he was alone in business until March, 1890, he has since been associated with Capt. H. M. Peden. Mr. Forman has a bright future before him. Soon after entering business at Fayette he was married, December 4, 1884, to Miss Effie Torrey, a daughter of Hon. George Torrey, of this county. Mrs. Forman was born in July, 1861, and was given the advantages of the Fayette female academy, and left that institution a bright and accomplished young lady. She is a professor of Christianity, and is an earnest and consistent member of the Presbyterian church. Her union with Mr. Forman has resulted in the birth of four children: Richard T., Maggie M., George D. and Effie. The entire family occupy a most enviable position in the social circles of the county, for they have ever been fond of society, and in their pleasant and attractive homes, where an air of refinement and good taste pervades, the generous and true hearted, yet unostentatious, hospitality displayed is the delight of the many friends who gather beneath their roof tree.

The Foster family. In the seventeenth century three brothers named Foster were banished from England for supporting Cromwell, and they came to America. One settled in New Hampshire, another in Virginia, and the third in South Carolina. From the last-named branch sprang James Foster, who was probably born in that state, and who was probably the eldest of his father's family. During the Revolutionary war he and several of his brothers came to Adams county, Miss., where James soon after purchased a large tract of land from the Spanish authorities, a part of which has since been known as Foster Mound plantation, and which has ever since been in the possession of the Foster family. On this plantation, seven miles northeast of Natchez, there is an Indian mound, and on the top of this mound, soon after his removal here, Mr. Foster erected a double log house of round logs for a tobacco house, but this was soon afterward occupied as a dwelling, and has been so used ever since. It has been very much improved and enlarged, and is now stuccoed inside and out, and at the present time is occupied by his grandson, Erastus Bridgers Foster. Prior to the war this was one of the most attractive places in Adams county. Here Mr. Foster died on November 14, 1835, and as he was born on August 2, 1752, he was over eighty-three years of age. He was married twice, his first wife being Charlotte Foster, and his second Elizabeth Smith. The latter was born in 1762, and died October 13, 1837. Mr. Foster was an extensive and successful planter, was a Revolutionary soldier, fought at Fort Moultrie, and retained his gun, which was given, by his grandson, E. B. Foster, to the Confederate government during the late war. Among the children born to James Foster, while a resident of Foster Mound, was William J. Foster, whose birth occurred in 1798. There he was reared and educated, and succeeded his father in the planting industry. He was married in 1825 to Miss Mary Maury, who was born in Canada in 1811, and who came with her uncle, James Carson, to Natchez in 1821.

After the war Mr. Foster removed to near Baton Rouge, La., to improve some wild land which he owned there. There his death occurred in 1870, and his wife followed him to the grave in November, 1883, her death occurring on Foster Mound, Adams county. Her father was an officer in the British army and was stationed in Canada, where he died when she was a little girl. Her mother died in Adams county, Miss. To Mr and Mrs. William Foster were born seven children: Ezilda Rosezille, died near Baton Rouge ; James A. J., served for a short time in the Confederate army, and died in Louisiana in 1879 ; Mary E., the widow of Rev. William Brown, who was a Methodist minister and who died of yellow fever in New Orleans ; Virginia, died while young ; Francis A., deceased; William P. S., deceased, and Erastus Bridgers. The last named is the owner of the old Forest Mound plantation, and he was born in 1842 in the same room that his father was. He was educated in the common schools, and supplemented this by a course in Jefferson college. In 1861 he joined the sixty-day troops and served at Bowling Green, Ky. In June, 1862, he joined Darden's battery of Jefferson's artillery, and operated in the army of Tennessee, all through the Georgia and Atlanta campaigns, and back with Hood to Franklin and Nashville, thence south, and surrendered at Natchez at the close of the war. In 1865 he married Miss Josephine B. Rogillio, a native of Yazoo county, Miss., and a cousin of her husband. She is the daughter of Sidney and Eliza Rogillio, the father born in East Feliciana parish, La., and died in Yazoo county, Miss., and the mother born in the Foster Mound house and died in Claiborne county, Miss. The father was a planter. To Mr. and Mrs. Foster have been born two children: William J. and Minnie, both of whom were born in the same room as their father and grandfather. Mr. Foster is the owner of six hundred acres of land and is a thrifty and progressive planter. Mrs. Foster is a member of the Methodist church. Mr. Foster has in his possession numerous papers and documents formerly belonging to his grandfather. Among them is the original deed for the old Foster Mound place, which bears the date of 1783, and is signed by Don Stephen Minor.* He also has a bill of sale bearing date of 1790, for a negro named Cæsar, with which there is connected a peculiar incident, as follows: A Dr. Cox, while cruising on the coast of Africa, was captured by a negro chief, and

* This may be Miro instead of Minor.

while in captivity the Doctor taught his captor to read and write, after which he was liberated and returned to his family, afterward living in Adams county. Some time afterward the negro chief was captured, brought to Natchez, and sold to James Foster. The negro one day met Dr. Cox and at once recognized him, gave him a cordial embrace. The Doctor was surprised, and even alarmed, until the negro made himself known. So great was the feeling that the Doctor took steps for the negro's emancipation and Mr. Foster was paid $350 for him.

Foster & Foster, attorneys, Hernando, Miss. H. R. C. and A. A. Foster were born February 19, 1861, and March 22, 1869, respectively. They are the third and seventh of a family of nine children born to John U. and Harriet Wayne (Fleming) Foster. The mother was born in Alabama, and the father came from Georgia to Mississippi in 1859; he located in De Soto county, where he engaged in planting; he was a lawyer by profession, but the breaking out of the Civil war soon after he came to De Soto county determined a different course for him. In 1861 he raised a company for the Confederacy, and entered the ranks of the Horn lake volunteers as captain; at the end of one year he resigned his commission to become the captain of a company of scouts; he retained this position to the close of the war. He was once taken prisoner, but on account of his high rank as a Mason he was released. When volunteers were called to storm Santa Rosa his company was one of the first to offer its service. He was a brave soldier, and was possessed of unusual powers of commanding. While he was not a close student he was a fine scholar, and a man of superior intelligence and discernment. He was well versed in military tactics. After the war he lived on his plantation in De Soto county until his death which occurred in 1877. The paternal grandparents of the subjects of this notice were William and A. E. (Brown) Foster. The grandfather of the paternal ancestry was a colonel in the Creek war; he was a planter and lived a quiet life. The great grandfather on the mother's side, J. U. Brown, was also a soldier in the Creek and Mexican wars, serving as a major. The great-great-grandfather, William Foster, lived to be one hundred and ten years of age. His father, William Foster, with three brothers, Harrison, Henry and Thomas, came from Middlesex county, England, about the year 1650, and settled in Massachusetts; thence they removed to Fairfax county, Va., and from them the family is sprung. They were Puritans in their religious faith. The maternal grandparents were William H. and Harriet C. (Spencer) Fleming, natives of South Carolina. The grandfather Fleming was a physician and a planter. He retired from active business life at the age of forty-five years, and died in 1861, his wife and four children surviving him. The great-grandmother on the mother's side was a niece of Gen. Anthony Wayne. The Fleming family in America is descended from William Fleming and Bishop Ross, of the Episcopal church, both of whom emigrated to America about the year 1660 from Scotland. The Foster brothers are of the sixth generation from these two ancestors. They have been reared in De Soto county, Miss. H. R. C. Foster received his literary education at home under the direction of his gifted mother, a woman of great culture and refinement. She was educated in Mobile, Ala., and Philadelphia; she has always been a reader, and is one of the best posted women of the county. The eldest son of the family, of the firm of Foster & Foster, read law for two years under the direction of Judges Powell and Buchanan, and was admitted to the bar in 1886. He has been very successful in his professional work, and gives promise of occupying a place in the foremost lines of the lawyers of the state. A. A. Foster attended the schools of De Soto county and finished his course at Lebanon, Ohio. He then read law in his brother's office for two years, and at the end of that time was admitted to the bar in 1890. He is young in the work, but possesses all the traits that promise success. H. R. C. Foster is a member of the Baptist church, while the mother belongs to the Presbyterian church. He is also a member of the Knights of Honor. Mrs. Foster owns six hundred and forty acres of land, four hundred acres being under cultivation; she has a pleasant residence in Hernando, Miss. She is a woman of the typical Scotch character, and has reared her children to paths of rectitude and honor. Her brother, A. Wayne Fleming, was a very brilliant young physician, being graduated with the highest honors at Oglethorpe, Ga., and later from the University of Pennsylvania. He distinguished himself during the war for his great daring and courage. He entered as second lieutenant, and was promoted to a captaincy, at one time commanding five hundred sharpshooters.

Robert E. Foster, planter, Hays' Landing, Miss. Mr. Foster's father, Milton H. Foster, was a successful druggist in his younger days, but later engaged in planting, and now resides on the farm that he has owned for forty years. He was a native of Tennessee, and moved with his parents to Mississippi at a very early day, the Foster family being considered among the most prominent during ante-bellum days. His uncle, Dr. Grant, was marshal of Mississippi during that time, and Mr. Foster served as deputy under him. This was before General Jackson was noted in the state. Milton Foster was married to Miss Eliza H. Greenlee, a native of Mississippi, and they reared a family of four children, who are named in order of their births, as follows: Sarah (wife of C. H. Pearce), Robert E., Milton D. and Maryetta (wife of W. G. Herrington, of Claiborne county). Mr. Foster served three or four years in the late unpleasantness between the North and South, and during that time held various offices in his company, filling them with honor to himself and to the satisfaction of his comrades. After cessation of hostilities he returned home and again turned his attention to planting. He and Mrs. Foster are worthy members of the Methodist church. Robert E. Foster was born in Copiah county, Miss., in 1851, and after receiving his early education in the common schools attended Summerville institute (near the Tennessee line) for some time. After finishing his education he returned home, bought a farm of four hundred acres, with one hundred and forty under cultivation, in Issaquena county, and in 1882 settled upon this. He has added to the original tract two hundred and forty acres, and now has about three hundred and fifty acres well cultivated. He raises annually two hundred and twenty bales of cotton and plenty of corn, and he also raises an excellent grade of stock. He has a fine young peach orchard, the fruit being large and of an excellent flavor, and his farm in the way of improvements is the admiration of all beholders. He has good houses and outbuildings for his tenants, and this year he has added about eight or ten new tenant and box houses to his farm. He has lately put under cultivation about one hundred acres of new land, and this makes his property still more desirable. He is the only man in the county who raised any oats of importance this year, and his crop yielded forty bushels to the acre. He stands among the best men of his state as a successful planter, and, although he is now only in the prime of life, he has made a financial success, so far, in his chosen occupation. Mr. Foster served as a member of the board of supervisors for six years, and is a member of the same at the present time as president. He is a member of the Knights of Pythias, Hays' Landing lodge No. 16, has filled various offices in the same, and is also a member of the American legion of Honor and is a prelate of this order. Mr. Foster was married in January, 1877, to Miss Nannie E. Heath, daughter of John Heath (see sketch), and the fruits of this union have been three children. Annie E., Robert H. and Mary L. Both Mr. and Mrs. Foster are members of the Baptist church.

Carroll county boasts no citizen more worthy of mention in this connection than G. Summerfield Fox, of Carrollton, and the following space will be devoted to a brief account

of his career.   He was born in the state of Alabama, May 22, 1830, and is a son of John
Fox, a native of Virginia.   His father married, in Halifax county, N. C., Miss Elizabeth
Mason Campbell, a native of North Carolina and a member of an old family of that state.
Mr. Fox removed from Virginia to Alabama at an early day, and settled in Limestone county,
where he engaged in farming.   He died there in 1833, when our subject was a child of
three years.   The mother survived him many years, her death not occurring until January
31, 1874.   G. S. is next to the youngest of a family of eleven children, all of whom grew
to maturity.   One brother, Dr. F. A. Fox, was a graduate of law and medicine, and practiced the latter profession in Yalobusha county and Fort Worth, Tex., for a number of years.
He died in April, 1866.   John A. Fox, the eldest, died in Yalobusha county, Miss., and
Mary A., the youngest, died in Jefferson county, Ark., both the same day, February 5,
1874.   Up to his sixteenth year Mr. Fox lived in Alabama; he then came to Mississippi
with his mother and settled in Yalobusha county on a farm; there he remained until 1854,
taking charge of the plantation and the other business of the family.   In 1857 he came to
Carroll county and made a permanent location on the plantation where he now lives.   His
dwellinghouse is said to be the first hewn-log house that was built in Carroll county.   The
plantation is situated about one mile from Carrollton, and consists of seven hundred acres,
in a high state of cultivation.   Mr. Fox is one of the most successful planters of the county.
Before the war he had acquired a fine estate, but it was all swept away, excepting the bare
land.   He has, in the last quarter of a century, somewhat retrieved his shattered fortunes,
but the efforts devoted to regaining what was so needlessly destroyed might much better
have been applied to the acquisition of new fortunes.   Mr. Fox was married in Carroll
county, Miss., December 18, 1851, to Martha J. Compton, a daughter of Richard Compton,
and a half sister of the Hon. H. D. Money, of Washington city.   She died in August, 1855,
leaving two sons, John S. and Richard C.   Both are grown and married, and in business;
the latter is one of the largest and most successful merchants of Montgomery county.   Mr.
Fox was married a second time, July 16, 1857, to Miss Ellen D. Butt, a daughter of Dr.
John W. Butt, of Carroll county.   Mrs. Fox is a Mississippian by birth and education.   She
is the mother of six sons: Falls N., who died at the age of seventeen years; Albert Sidney
J., who grew to manhood and died at the age of twenty-two; Lee, a planter and merchant;
Thomas Stonewall Jackson, a merchant of Carrollton; Ed. Walthall Fox, a successful
planter of Carroll county; and Falls, a lad of fifteen years.   Mr. Fox has always been a
strong advocate and supporter of democratic principles.   He has held several local offices of
trust and honor; he served as a member of the county board of supervisors, and was chosen
president of that honorable body for two terms.   He is a prominent member of the Masonic
order; he has been master of the Blue lodge for five terms, and has been high priest of his
chapter.   He is a member of the Methodist Episcopal church, and has been steward of that
society.   While he is upward of sixty years of age, he is active and strong, and few days
pass without his driving or walking from his plantation to town.   He is a man highly
respected by all for his deep integrity of character, and as a loyal, patriotic citizen he is
without a superior in the whole county.

The great-grandfather of Dr. Jackson A. Fox, merchant and physician, Louisville,
Miss., Henry Fox, was a native of Germany, and when a young man came to America,
locating in South Carolina.   After residing there for some time he moved to western Tennessee, and there passed the remainder of his days.   His wife was an English lady.   Their
son, William Fox (grandfather of subject), was a native of South Carolina, where he was
reared and married, but later moved to Greene county, Ala.   In 1835 he came to Wins-

ton county, Miss., settled in the woods three miles southwest of Louisville, and there improved a good farm. He was one of the first settlers of the county and was a very successful farmer. He was industrious and influential, and one of the best men in the county. He died in March, 1867, at the age of eighty-three. He was an active worker in the Cumberland Presbyterian church. One of his two sons that lived to be grown, Rev. N. J. Fox, was a prominent Cumberland Presbyterian minister and was educated in Cumberland University, Lebanon, Tenn. He ministered to the spiritual wants of the fellowman for many years and died at his home in Louisville, July 14, 1891, age, seventy-six years. The other son, William H. (father of subject), was born in Greene county, Ala., in 1820, and received a liberal education. He moved with his parents to Winston county, Miss., and there met and married Miss Nancy Dumas, a native of Winston county, Ala., born in 1822. In 1860 he and wife removed to Attala county, Miss., resided there seven years, and then located in Winston county, where Mr. Fox died on the 2d of February, 1891. Mrs. Fox is still living Both were members of the Cumberland Presbyterian church, and he was an elder in the same for thirty-five years. He was a successful farmer for many years. He was a member of the police board of Attala county, and had been a member of both the Masonic and Odd Fellow orders. He was industrious and generous to a marked degree, was forward in all charitable enterprises and was active in all church matters. To his marriage were born five children—two sons and three daughters—who are named in the order of their births as follows: Mary E., wife of J. M. Edwards, of Union city, Tenn.; Georgiana, died in 1867; Dr. Jackson A., William M., and Caroline R., wife of Hon. R. C. Jones, who is an attorney at Louisville, and the son of Dr. Gilford Jones, a celebrated divine of Tennessee. Dr. Jackson A. Fox was born in Louisville, Winston county, Miss., in 1849, and received his education in that city and vicinity. He then commenced reading medicine, and in 1876 graduated from Louisville medical college in a class of about eighty. After this he practiced for one year in Neshoba county, then in Webster county, and for twelve years has been at Louisville, near his old home. In January, 1880, he engaged in a general merchandising and has retired from active practice. He is one of the best merchants of the county and is doing an annual business of about $50,000. In 1890–91 he handled about one thousand bales of cotton. He started in life without any means, has educated himself, and is now one of the county's substantial citizens. He is a member of the A. F. & A. M., Louisville lodge No. 75, and chapter No. 36. He was married in May, 1878, to Miss Mattie Wragg, a native of Louisville, Miss., and the daughter of David and Nancy Wragg. Her parents were married in Noxubee county, Miss., but many years ago came to Winston county, where Mr. Wragg died, on the 1st of January, 1865. His wife is still living. Mr. Wragg was a successful merchant and a prominent citizen. Dr. Fox's marriage resulted in the birth of two children. He and Mrs. Fox are members of the Cumberland Presbyterian church. The Doctor is progressive and takes an active interest in all public matters of a laudable nature. He is not a politician, but works for his party, and was a delegate to the state convention that nominated Governor Lowry. He is a gentleman of experience, judgment and energy, is very popular, and excels as a business man.

Dr. Thomas J. Fox, druggist and physician, Slate Springs, Miss. The father of Dr. Fox, Thomas Fox, was a native of South Carolina, born in 1795, and when a young man moved with his parents to Tennessee, where he was married to Mrs. Elizabeth Brent. She was born in 1790 and was of Irish descent, her mother having been born in the Emerald isle. She was a number of years her husband's senior. Their marriage resulted in the birth of eight children, who are named, in the order of their birth, as follows: Unity

48

(deceased), John (farmer at Slate Springs), Henry (at West Point), Mrs. Sarah Lay (deceased), Joseph (merchant, married, and resides at Slate Springs), Jesse H. (died in Texas), Dr. Thomas J. (subject), and David D. (deceased). After his marriage Thomas Fox moved to Alabama, remained there about fifteen years, and then located on a place near Slate Springs, in Choctaw county, Miss. He was among the first settlers, and there his death occurred at the age of eighty-two years. He followed agricultural pursuits all his life and was a man highly respected. He was elected to represent that county in the convention one term, and was nominated for senator, but was defeated by three votes. When Calhoun county was formed he served that county in the legislature two terms. He was a self-made man, and was very indulgent to his slaves. He was an earnest worker in the Baptist church. He was appointed to write the history of Zion association of Choctaw county. His father, Henry Fox, was a native of South Carolina and a descendant of a representative family of that state. Late in life the latter moved to Mississippi, settled near Slate Springs, and there died at the age of eighty-four years. He was a member of the Baptist church, to which he was a liberal contributor, and in politics was a stanch whig. His family consisted of eight children, most of whom lived to be grown, married and have families. Dr. Thomas J. Fox was reared at Slate Springs, where he has since resided, and in 1852 he started out for himself as an agriculturist. After this, in 1856, he began the study of medicine under Dr. S. W. Land, and afterward attended lectures at Memphis, Tenn., graduating in 1858. He then began practicing at Slate Springs, and later moved to Banner, of that county, where he remained but a short time. He then returned to Slate Springs, and here he has since made his home. Miss Mary S. Burns became his wife in 1859, and to them were born ten children: Bettie (wife of T. J. Ligon, of Webster county, Miss., who has had two daughters, now deceased), T. S. (farmer of Slate Springs), Fannie (wife of Henry Tharpe, of Eupora, Miss.), Grandville L. (graduated at the medical college at Louisville, Ky., now practices medicine at Slate Springs, and is associated with his father in the drug business), Louella (a teacher), Lillian (wife of Lee Mallory, of Slate Springs), Blondie (at home), Melvinia, alias Dot (at home), and LaMar (also at home). Dr. and Mrs. Fox are members of the Missionary Baptist church. In politics he is a Democrat. The Doctor is one of the leading druggists and physicians of Slate Springs, and is also interested in agricultural pursuits. He belongs to the Masonic fraternity. Mrs. Fox's parents, Judge Smith and Martha Ann (Embrey) Burns, were born in North Carolina and Georgia respectively, the father's birth occurring in 1814. He was the son of Benjamin and Susan (Smith) Burns and received his name from his mother's family. His parents were natives of England and North Carolina respectively, and when he was but a child they moved to St. Clair county, Ala., where they located and remained until he was about seventeen years of age. They then moved to the Creek Purchase, what is now known as Calhoun county, and from there to Talledago county, Ala., where they received their final summons, the father at the age of seventy and the mother a few years later. The father served in the War of 1812. Their family consisted of nine children, three besides the Judge now living: Benjamin F. (resided in Alabama, and is dead), Theodore R. (also in Alabama), and Therrell M. (who resides in Slate Springs). Those deceased are: Albert N. (died in Grenada county, Miss., in 1891), Mrs. Melinda McCain, Mrs. Harriett Dobbins, Mrs. Adeline Vance, and Melissa. Judge Smith Burns remained with his parents until twenty-two years of age, had limited educational advantages while growing up, and what learning he has since acquired has been the result of his own exertions. He worked at blacksmithing with an uncle for a short time, after which he opened a shop in a town in Alabama and there remained until 1843. He then came to Mississippi, settled near what is now Hopewell postoffice, and there remained until coming to Slate Springs. Since coming to this state he has been engaged in merchandising, farming, and blacksmithing. The judge was first married in Alabama to Miss Martha Ann Embrey, who died in 1844 at the age of thirty years. She was the daughter of Joseph Embrey, a native of Georgia and a planter by occupation. To Judge Burns and wife were born three children, one besides Mrs. Dr. T. J. Fox now living: Joseph Thomas Burns, who resides near Slate Springs. The Judge's second marriage occurred in 1846 to Miss Louisa M. Young, a native of Williamson county, Tenn., born in 1825, and the daughter of Henry Young, of North Carolina. He and Mrs. Burns are members of the Baptist church, and he is a member of the Masonic fraternity. He is now retired from active business. He was a member of the board of police both before and after the war.

Stephen M. Foxworth, deceased, was born in Marion district, S. C., in 1782, and there grew to man's estate. He was married to Miss Elizabeth Graham, and they removed to Marion county, Miss., either in 1810 or 1811, and located on the plantation which is now occupied by S. E. Foxworth. There they passed the remainder of their lives. Mr. Foxworth's ancesters were of English extraction. By his first marriage he had three children; Samuel G., John, and Mary, who married Alexander Graham, both being deceased. The mother died in 1824, and Mr. Foxworth was married a second time, to Mrs. Elizabeth Funches, a daughter of Jacob Rumph. Three children were born of this union: Stephen E., Harriet P. (wife of Walter A. Lemon) and Julia A. (who married Dr. J. O Magee.) John Foxworth, a son of the first marriage, was born in 1812, in Marion county, Miss., where he received his education. In 1851 he was united in marriage to Miss Elizabeth Rowles, and they became the parents of three children: Mary E., wife of Jesse W. Fortenberry, Eugene E., and Charles R. John Foxworth had accumulated a handsome property before the war, owning at that time one hundred and three slaves. He applied himself very closely to business, and became one of the wealthiest men of the county. At the close of the war he began dealing in live stock, his market being Mobile, Ala. Through this industry he retrieved his fortunes, and is now the largest resident land owner in the state. Eugene E. Foxworth, planter and stockraiser, was born at the old home place, about eight miles south of Columbia, Marion county, Miss., in 1856. There he was reared to the life of a planter, and received his education in the common schools. He was married in 1881 to Miss Ella, a daughter of Joe M. Ford, of Columbia. Of this union have been born three sons and three daughters. Mr. Foxworth is a man of superior business qualifications, and has made a marked success of all his undertakings. He is largely interested in the raising of live stock, and owns a part of a stock ranch in Montana.

Franklin W. Foxworth, Columbia, Miss., a son of Samuel G. Foxworth, was born in 1839, on the old homestead, three miles south of Columbia, Marion county, Miss., and is the fourth of a family of eight sons: John P.; Stephen A.; George W., who died in the war in 1862; Franklin W., the subject of this notice; Job M.; Alexander E., and Jerome S.; one died in infancy. The father was born in South Carolina about the year 1808, and the mother, whose maiden name was Nancy S. Pope, a daughter of John Pope, was a native of North Carolina, born in 1810. Franklin W. Foxworth passed an uneventful youth amid the scenes of his birth, and received his education at Centenary college, Jackson, La. When the Civil war broke out he quickly responded to the call for men, and went into the service for one year. In 1862 he returned to his home, and was married to Miss Missouri Atkinson, a daughter of James and Ruhema (See) Atkinson. Nine children have been born to them, six of whom are still living: Henry C., Charles, Oscar J., William, Mattie and Bessie.

Henry C. married Miss Celia, daughter of Benjamin B. Lewis, in 1889; he is engaged in the mercantile trade in Columbia, Miss., and bids fair to rise to a high rank in commercial circles.   Mrs. Foxworth, wife of our subject, is the daughter of pioneer parents; her father removed from North Carolina to Marion county, Miss., where he was among the first settlers. He was a prominent planter in the county and was noted for his thrift and energy.   He was extensively engaged in both mercantile and agricultural pursuits, and was a citizen honored and respected by all who knew him.   Mr. Foxworth is a planter by occupation, and owns sixteen hundred acres of land on the Pearl river.   His undertakings have been attended with prosperity, and good fortune has been his guardian.   The family adhere to the doctrines of the Methodist Episcopal church South.

Lawrence Fragiacomo, proprietor and owner of the Lawrence house, one of the finest and best conducted hostelries in the South, came to the United States in 1855, and after a short residence in New York city sailed for Havana, shortly after landing in New Orleans.   One month later he removed to Mobile, where he remained two years, and after another two years spent in New Orleans he came to Jackson, in which city he landed in 1859.   After a brief stay here he went to Vicksburg, thence to New Orleans, but in 1867 once more returned to Jackson, which has been his permanent abode ever since.   He began keeping a restaurant soon after, which he conducted until 1878, when he embarked in the hotel business solely.   He had previously opened his establishment in West Jackson in June, 1877, which consisted of two rooms and was the germ of the present fine hotel of which he is the proprietor.   In January, 1889, he completed his hotel, a fine three-story brick building, containing seventy-five rooms, all of which are handsomely and neatly furnished for the accommodation of the numerous patrons of the house.   Mr. Fragiacomo makes an ideal host, for he is ever solicitous of the comfort and welfare of his guests, and is courteous, agreeable and kind hearted.   The excellence of the cuisine of the Lawrence house has made it widely known, and is largely patronized by the traveling public, which fact speaks warmly in its favor.   Mr. Fragiacomo is the owner of some valuable city property and has a fine small farm of twenty-five acres near Jackson, which is highly improved and which, under his direction, has become a remarkably beautiful place.   He was for a long time a member of the Jackson Fire company, at first of Company No. 1, then Gem No. 2, and is now an honorary member of West Jackson No. 1. During the Civil war he became a member of company A, Tenth Mississippi regiment of the Mississippi rifles, and while in the western army was a participant in the battles of Shiloh, Chickamauga, Murfreesboro, Resaca, the engagements of the Georgia campaign, being in eight general battles in all and seventeen skirmishes without receiving a wound.   He was married May 26, 1868, to Miss Ellen Blake and to their union four daughters have been born, Mary, Anna, Nellie and Josie.   Mr. Fragiacomo and his family worship in the Catholic church.   He is a practical and successful business man.

Meshach Franklin, one of the prominent farmers of Early Grove, Marshall county, was born in Surry county, N. C., and is the eldest son in a family of six children born to Hardin P. and Martha E. (Franklin) Franklin, who were born, reared and married in the same county and state.   While residing in their native state the parents had born to their union four children: Meshach; Anna E., wife of John A. Wilson, of Boliver, Tenn.; Jesse H., also residing near Boliver, Tenn, and James H., who is now residing in Santa Barbara county, Cal.   The parents removed to Marshall county, Miss., in 1849, located on the farm now owned by Meshach, one mile east of Early Grove, and two children were born in this state: Mildred E., and Hardina P., wife of J. W. Kelsey, of Marshall county, Miss.   Hardin P. Franklin, father of subject, studied medicine in his early days and graduated at Philadelphia, Penn. He practiced medicine a few years in North Carolina, but preferred farming, so he gave up the medical profession and devoted his time exclusively to his large estate, a section of land in Marshall county. He was one of the early settlers and most prosperous farmers. He was a plain, practical tiller of the soil, a good citizen and neighbor, and a man universally esteemed and respected. He died in 1853. After his death Mrs. Franklin continued to operate the farm, reared her children in the best society and gave them fair educations. Her death occurred in February, 1874, a consistent member of the Methodist Episcopal church South. Meshach Franklin attended the University of Mississippi at Oxford for three years and graduated in June, 1860. He enlisted in the Confederate army in May, 1861, in the University Grays of Oxford, company A, Eleventh Mississippi infantry, commanded by Colonel Moore, and went direct to Harper's Ferry. His first engagement was the first battle of Manassas, and soon after that he was detailed as assistant commissary sergeant, serving in that capacity until the close of the war. In January, 1865, he obtained a furlough and came home. He was at Grenada, Miss., on his way back when the surrender came, and went from there to Memphis, where he was paroled in June, 1865. He then returned to his home and the following year went to Hardeman county, Tenn., where he taught school for a year. Returning to Marshall county again he resumed the occupation of farming, and in May, 1866, was married to Miss Julia P. Wilburn, of Fayette county, Tenn. Their marriage has been blessed by the birth of five children: Wilburn B., James H., Mattie E., Julia A. and Meshach. Mr. Franklin owns one thousand three hundred acres of land, a nice two-story frame residence situated one mile east of Early Grove, and about eight hundred acres under cultivation, the greater portion of it operated by tenants. The principal crops are corn and cotton, and of the latter his farm yielded one hundred and fifty bales in 1890. He has a steam gin on his place, and the number of bales ginned annually are about three hundred. Mr. Franklin is a member of the Masonic fraternity, Knights of Honor and the Farmers' Alliance. He was magistrate for four years, was a member of the board of supervisors for the same length of time, and is well and favorably known all over the county. He and Mrs. Franklin are members of the Methodist church South, and move in the best circles of society.

Robert L. Franklin was brought up to the life of a planter by his father, John A. Franklin, and, like the majority of boys, has followed in his ancestor's footsteps, and is now one of the leading agriculturists of Clay county. He was born in Pickens county, Ala., in 1841, a son of John A. and Seleta C. Franklin, the former of whom was born in North Carolina about 1814. When about twenty-three years of age he was married to Seleta Stell, a daughter of George and Elizabeth Stell, of Alabama. To Mr. Franklin and his wife eleven children were born: Elmyra (Mrs. McDougald, of Arkansas); Tempy, the widow of Mr. Carpenter, of Colorado; George W., of Arkansas; James R. and John W., also of that state; Robert L., Oliver, and Mattie (Mrs. Green), of Arkansas. John A. Franklin came with his family to Mississippi in 1843, and settled at Ripley, in Tippah county, but afterward moved to Itawamba, and finally to Noxubee county, where he died in 1859. His widow survives him, and resides at Hamburg, Ark., in her seventieth year. The father was a member of the Masonic fraternity, which he joined in Itawamba county, and upon his death in Noxubee county, was buried by that order. He was, as is his widow, a member of the Baptist church. Robert L. Franklin received a common-school education, and at about the age of twenty-five years began to make his own way in the world. In 1865 he was married to Miss Anna Goldson, of Oxford county, Miss., a daughter of William D. and Permelia A. Goldson, and their union has resulted in the birth of ten children: Minnie A. (Mrs. Milton), Mary E., Edith C.

(Mrs. Jones), Willie L., John B., Charley A., Julia S. and Mattie L. being the only ones now living. Upon the opening of the war in 1861 he became a member of company H, Fifth Alabama regiment, under Jackson, and fought at the battles of Seven Pines, Yorktown, the seven days' engagement at Richmond, Chancellorsville, Bull's Run, the first and second Manassas, Sharpsburg, Petersburg and Fredericksburg. He was wounded at Malvern Hill, and lay ten days in the hospital at Richmond, and at the battle of Chancellorsville he lost his left arm from a rifle shot. After remaining in the hospital for some time, he was honorably discharged from the service and returned to his home, where he has since devoted his attention to planting, and has done well. His plantation is a fertile and admirably conducted one and is situated on a beautiful prairie, and he has the consciousness that it was obtained through his own endeavors, and not from inheritance. He is an enterprising and industrious planter, and has proven himself a good business manager.

Capt. Alex. Fraser, farmer and stockraiser, Elliott, Miss., the youngest of seven children—three sons and four daughters—born to Angus and Catherine Fraser, owes his nativity to Canada, his birth occurring on the 14th of April, 1832. His parents, when children, left their native country, Scotland, and came to Canada, where they grew to maturity and were married. There they passed the remainder of their days, the father engaged in farming. He and his wife were members of the Presbyterian church. His father died in Scotland, but the maternal grandparents of our subject lived in Canada.. Capt. Alex. Fraser is the only one of the above mentioned family now residing in Mississippi. He early became familiar with the duties on the farm and secured a fair education in the common schools of his native county. When about seventeen years of age he went to Michigan and was contractor on a railroad from Detroit north for about a year and a half. About 1850 he went to British Columbia, and was agent for the Hudson Bay Fur company for three or four years among the Indians of that rigid climate. After this he spent about five years in St. Charles county, Mo., engaged in farming, and in 1859 he came to Memphis, Tenn., where he was engaged in the slave trade in that state and Arkansas until 1860. From there he came to Mississippi, and was engaged as a timber contractor for the Mississippi Central, now the Illinois Central railroad, for about ten years, except three years during the war when he ran a blockade between Greenville and St. Louis, part of the time for himself and part of the time for the government. He was married in September 1869, to Miss Margaret Crowder, a native of Grenada county, and the daughter of Mr. Green and Mary Crowder, natives of Tennessee and South Carolina respectively. When but children her parents came to Grenada county, grew to mature years and were married. The Doctor was one of the wealthiest planters of the county, being worth nearly $400,000 at the breaking out of the war, owning nearly all of Grenada. He came to Mississippi about 1833 and entered the best land in the country. The Indians were still there, and with their assistance he selected some very valuable tracts of land, owning about eleven thousand acres in all. He was one of the most enterprising, progressive citizens of his time. He had two brothers in this county and they owned very extensive tracts of land also and became well known in financial circles. The Doctor died in 1867 and his wife in 1888. Both were members of the Baptist church and he was a prominent Mason. To Mr. and Mrs. Fraser were born two daughters. Since 1872 Mr. Fraser has lived on his present farm at Elliott station, and of the one thousand seven hundred acres that he owns he has one thousand two hundred under cultivation, producing about three hundred and fifty bales of cotton yearly. He also raises enough corn and hay to supply the place. He is a prominent planter and a representative citizen of the county. Although not a soldier during the Civil war his whole heart was enlisted in the cause of the South, and he at one time gave his check for $3,000 for the benefit of the Confederate prisoners in Memphis. He is a member of the I. O. O. F. organization at Grenada, lodge No. 6, and has taken the highest degree in that body; also of the encampment. He is a charter member of Bouford lodge, Knights of Honor, at Duck Hill. He is a member of the Presbyterian and his wife a member of the Baptist church.

John D. Frasier inherits Scotch blood of his father, John D. Frasier, who was reared and educated in his native land and came to the United States in 1845 and located in what is now Lincoln county, Miss. He opened a mercantile establishment, first at old Rock-haven and later at Bogue Chitto, Lincoln county, where he continued in business for a num-ber of years. He was married in Lawrence county to Miss Julia Brown, who was born and reared in Lawrence county, Miss., she being a daughter of William Brown, a pioneer planter of Lawrence county. Mr. Frasier died in 1857, and his wife in 1860, they having become the parents of two sons and three daughters that grew to mature years, John D. being the third child in order of birth. Up to eighteen years of age he spent his youth in Lawrence and Copiah counties, and after one year spent in Hinds county in 1870 he came to Jefferson county, locating on a large plantation in the west part of the county, where he has made his home for the past twenty years. All his operations have been carried on according to the most advanced and progressive ideas, and have resulted to his own good and to the benefit of those with whom he has come in contact. He has long since gained the reputation of being among the very foremost tillers of the soil in this portion of the county, and has been a leader in the use of labor-saving machinery and keeping his place in a high state of culti-vation. He raises on an average four hundred bales of cotton annually, gives much atten-tion to other crops also and raises a good grade of stock. Although he had very limited school advantages in his boyhood he naturally possessed a fine mind and has acquired a good business education by self application since coming to years of maturity. He is very prac-tical, yet exceptionally shrewd in his views, and at all times displays keen foresight and excellent business acumen. By the proper use of these faculties, with which nature has endowed him, he has acquired a comfortable fortune since settling in this county and is far better fitted than the average to enjoy his good fortune. He is not in the least niggardly, in fact is exceptionally liberal with his means and the dollars which he has earned by the sweat of his brow often find their way into the pockets of the poor. He has served two terms as a member of the board of supervisors, and as he has always taken an active interest in local politics he has served as a delegate to county, state and congressional conventions. His marriage was celebrated in Jefferson county on February 16, 1886, Miss Blanche B. Dent, a native of this county, becoming his wife. Although she was reared here her edu-cation was obtained in Ireland, where she was thoroughly fitted to shine in any society. She was an only daughter, but has borne her husband three children: Julia, J. Donald and Alma. Mrs. Frasier is a member of the Catholic church, and socially Mr. Frasier belongs to the K. of H.

Thomas Freeland, who died January 5, 1855, aged sixty-nine, came to Mississippi about the year 1800. He is the son of Frisby Freeland, and grandson, on his mother's side, of Sir Francis Rolle, who married the daughter of Sir Thomas Foote, lord mayor of London. Rev. Thomas Moore, in his book called " Devonshire," in which there are handsome engrav-ings of the Rolle seats "Stevenstone house" and "Bicton," states that "the vast accumu-lation of property enjoyed by Lord John Rolle is solely at his disposal, there being no heirs bearing the name of Rolle in England." At his death, his wife, Lady Rolle, through her personal influence at court and powerful friends in parliament and adherents among the high dignitaries of the Church of England, on the plea that her nephew, Mark Trefusis, was descended from Bridget Rolle, and also by asserting that the heirs at law in America of Lord Rolle had not answered the advertisement in the London *Times* of May, 1845, nor put forward their claims, succeeded in having Mark Trefusis assume, by royal license, the name of Rolle. He then took possession of the acres, millions, country seats, town house in Upper Grosvenor street, London, and all the rich collections of ancestral treasures, family portraits and jewels. But there was a limitation in the letter's patent of Queen Victoria, granting Mark Trefusis the right of proprietorship, which limited the succession to his male heirs, or failing that, to his younger brother, Col. Walter Trefusis, who died without leaving a son, December 3, 1885. At Mark Rolle's death, he being now (1891) nearly seventy, the Free-lands of Mississippi and the Rolles of Maryland will be the rightful heirs of one of the greatest estates is England. Thomas Freeland was a wealthy planter and resided near Rodney, Miss. He was a man of the highest character in every sense. A member of the Presbyterian church, and one of the founders of Oakland college church, which he helped liberally to endow. In July, 1852, he was sent as a delegate to the Baltimore national convention, which nominated for the presidency Gen. Winfield Scott. He married Sarah Greenfield Skinner, of Maryland. The only surviving child of that marriage was Frisby Augustin Freeland, who married Virginia Perkins, daughter of Mary Fontaine and Jesse Perkins. Of this marriage two children were born: Thomas and Mary Fontaine. Mr. Freeland died at the age of thirty-four years, having been an honest, upright and useful member of society. He was educated at Oakland college, Mississippi, after which he studied law, but never practiced that profession, preferring to give his attention to planting. Some years after his death his widow married Maj. A. D. Banks of Virginia. Mrs. Banks is a highly accomplished woman, and in her youth was thoroughly educated in a select school, where she showed great proficiency as a Latin and French scholar, and also in music, becoming a brilliant performer on the piano. She and her daughter, Miss Mary Freeland, have traveled extensively, and their literary tastes, their fine conversational powers as well as their gracious manners, gathered about them and won for them the friendship and admiration of eminent people in this country and abroad. Many of their winters have been spent in Washington, D. C., where they move in the highest social circles. They reside on a fine cotton plantation near Vicksburg, Miss. Their family mansion is a commodious and imposing structure, and an air of refinement and good taste pervades all its surroundings. In this ideal Southern home a generous and true-hearted hospitality is displayed that is the delight of the many that enter its portals.

Prominent among the medical profession of Carroll county, Miss., is Dr. Thomas W. Fullilove, Vaiden, Miss., whose history will occupy the following space. He was born in Carroll county, Miss., July 31, 1851, and is a son of Thomas J. Fullilove, a native of Oglethorpe county, Ga., born August 20, 1807. The father of Thomas J., was named John. His grandfather was a native of England, and was the only member of his family who emigrated to the United States. Thomas J. Fullilove removed to Antanga county, Ala., when he was still a young man, and there married Mary Adaline Taylor, who was born, reared and educated in that state. After a few years he removed to Noxubee county, Miss., and at the end of two years, about the year 1843, he moved to Carroll county; he settled on a plantation on which he lived until death; he passed out of this life in October, 1888; his wife had died in 1856. He was a worthy member of the Methodist Episcopal church, and was a Royal Arch Mason. He was a man of great integrity of character, had excellent business qualifications, and no one of the community stood higher than he.

He lost heavily in personal property by the war, but was enabled to retrieve his fortunes. His family consisted of three sons and two daughters: J. H. Fullilove is at present a farmer in Texas; A. B. Fullilove resides on the old home farm in Carroll county; Mrs. S. T. Hairston, wife of Dr. S. J. Hairston, resides in Ozark, Ark.; Mrs. M. A. Weems is the wife of Dr. H. Weems, of Van Buren, Ark.; Thomas W. received his education in the University of Mississippi, and in Emory and Henry college, Virginia, graduating from the latter institution in 1871 with the first honor of his class. He then began his medical studies, taking his first course of lectures in the medical department of the University of Virginia in the session of 1873–74. In the fall of 1874 he entered Bellevue Hospital Medical college, New York city, and was graduated in the spring of 1875. He then received an appointment on the staff of Charity hospital, New York, where he practiced and for one year received instruction from the leading physicians of New York city. In 1876 he returned to Carroll county, and in July of that year he located in Vaiden and began the practice of his profession. He has built up a large practice and has met with more than ordinary success. His honesty and integrity has won for him the respect and confidence of all. He takes an active interest in the proceedings of his profession, and is a member of the State Medical association, also the American Medical association. In addition to his professional duties he finds time to direct a fine plantation which is located near Vaiden. In the spring of 1890 the Doctor spent three months in New York, taking a supplementary course of lectures. He has left nothing undone in his power to fit himself for the duties of his profession, and well deserves the reputation he has won. Dr. Fullilove was united in marriage in Memphis, March 13, 1879, to Miss Annie Rivers Knott, a daughter of the Rev. J. W. Knott, of the Methodist Episcopal church. She was born and reared in Memphis, and educated at the State female college. She is a fine musician and highly accomplished in art. The Doctor and his wife have an adopted daughter, Annie Rivers, a bright little girl of nine years. They are both worthy members of the Methodist Episcopal church. Dr. Fullilove belongs to the Knights of Honor.

James M. Futch is one of Hinds county's (Mississippi) progressive planters, and in this calling, which has been his lifework, he has displayed much practical knowledge, discrimination and judgment. He was born in Bull county, Ga., January 8, 1811, the sixth of eight children born to Thomas and Elizabeth (Cook) Futch, natives of North Carolina and Georgia respectively. In 1812 Thomas Futch came to Mississippi, locating in Marion county, during its very early history, which place continued to be his home until 1824, at which time he became a resident of Hinds county, where he passed the uneventful but useful life of a farmer until his death, in 1842. He was of a retiring disposition and never aspired to public honors. His father was a native of Germany. James M. Futch was reared to manhood in Mississippi, and although he received but little early education, he has since stored his mind with a great deal of useful information, and is a well-informed and intelligent man. Upon attaining his majority he started out to make his own way in the world without influence or capital, except in the way of his own stout heart, willing hands and determination to bend the force of circumstances to his will, and as a planter, to which calling he was reared, he has been quite successful and is the owner of about one thousand five hundred acres of good farming land, of which eight hundred acres are under cultivation. The most of his life has been spent on his plantation three miles from Raymond, but in 1875 he erected him a very cosy and pleasant house in town, where he has since made his home. His quiet life has suited his taste and inclinations and, like his father, he has never sought for public office. He is of a retiring and unpretentious disposition, but thoroughly enjoys the comforts and luxuries which his early toil has enabled him to obtain.   He was married in 1855 to Miss Olivia Bedwell, a native of Mississippi and a daughter of James W. and Mary (Nicholson) Bedwell, the former a native of South Carolina and the latter of Alabama.   To Mr. Futch and his wife nine children have been born, six of whom are living at the present time: Edward D., Forrest D., Katie E., Anna O., Harriet L. and James L., all of whom still reside with their parents.   Mr. Futch is a member of the A. F. & A. M., and he and his wife are worthy members of the Baptist church.

Although the original members of the Futrell family in America were successful agriculturists, the present generation has departed from that pursuit somewhat, and there can now be found lawyers, doctors, ministers and commercial men among them.   William E. Futrell, merchant, Byhalia, Miss., was born in Fayette county, Tenn., in 1844, and his parents, Etheldred and Edna (Fitzgerald) Futrell, were natives of the Old North state.   The elder Futrell was born in 1793, and was a planter by occupation, as was also his father, who was a native of England, and who probably located in the Old Dominion after reaching this country.   William E. Futrell came with his parents to De Soto county, Miss., in 1844, when but an infant, and there grew to manhood and received his education.   When sixteen years of age he enlisted in company E, Twenty-eighth Mississippi cavalry, General Armstrong's brigade, General Jackson's division, and was in all the sieges of Vicksburg.   He was also in Tennessee and Alabama, and was captain of his company when mustered out of service. At the close of the war he engaged in merchandising at Byhalia, and there he has continued to reside up to the present time.   He is a thoroughgoing, enterprising business man, and has built up a lucrative trade, doing an annual business of about $75,000.   He is the only merchant in the town who began with its earliest history.   Aside from his business here, Mr. Futrell is engaged in different enterprises in Memphis, etc.   In 1869 he was married to Miss Vallora Johnson, daughter of Col. V. M. Johnson, of Benton county, Miss., who was a prominent citizen.   Mr. Futrell has two children by his marriage, a daughter and a son.   He is a good business man, and by close attention to his calling and by his social, pleasing manners has accumulated considerable wealth.   He is public spirited, takes a deep interest in all worthy movements and is liberal to a fault.   The family hold membership in the Episcopal church.

GHAPTER XIX.

PRIVATE MEMORANDA, G.

harles Betts Galloway was born in Kosciusko, Miss., September 1, 1849. He was reared at Canton, Miss., his father having removed thither during his early childhood. He united with the church in 1866, under the pastorate of Dr. C. G. Andrews. Soon afterward he felt moved by the Holy Spirit to consecrate his life to the work of the ministry. Accordingly, having graduated from the State university in the summer of 1868, he was a few weeks afterward granted license to preach. In December of the same year he joined the Mississippi conference, being only a little over nineteen years of age. He was married September 1, 1869, to Miss Hattie E. Willis, a daughter of Capt. E. B. Willis, of Vicksburg. In this choice of a life companion, the Bishop has been most fortunate, his wife being of the highest type of true Christian womanhood, whose faith, constancy and wise counsels have been his strength and inspiration through his eventful life. He was a brilliant preacher from the start, and rose rapidly in the ministry. Within six years from the time he entered the conference as a probationer, he was stationed at Jackson, the capital of the state. He was a member of the general conference of 1882, and was perhaps the youngest member of that body. At the close of that conference he was elected editor of the New Orleans *Christian Advocate*, the place having been made vacant by the election of Dr. Linus Parker to the bishopric. During the same year the title of doctor of divinity was conferred upon him by his alma mater, the University of Mississippi. Four years later, when in the thirty-seventh year of his age, he was elected to the episcopacy. In this church no other man has ever been called to this high office at so early an age. Bishop Galloway is a typical Southerner. He is of uncommonly fine physique, a model of physical conformation and expression. He possesses great dignity without ostentation. He is humble without affectation. He is a man with strong convictions and marked individuality, and would sooner surrender his life than his principles. He would have made a distinguished jurist, a grand political leader, or a military chieftain worthy of knightly spurs, had not God wanted him for the work of the ministry. He reads men and things as he reads books; and his decision as to policies and methods are prompt and certain. The horizon of his survey is broad, and his conclusions are reached with a promptitude and definiteness in perfect accord with the vigor of his intellect and the enterprise of his progressive manhood. The Bishop is a man of very great versatility. While his preaching ability is of a high order, he is not a preacher only. He can do many other things besides preach, and do them well. He is a fine writer. His style is limpid, smooth, easy, graceful and sufficiently ornate. His four years of editorial life sufficed to show that he possesses the journalistic instinct in its fullness. As an editor he not only knew how to write, but what to write about. No fine-spun metaphysical theories, no dry-as-dust theological essays weighted down his columns. His themes were such as touch the hearts and homes of men. He knew just how and when to touch those social movements that affect the thought and life of the church. His editorials were widely copied, and left their impress upon the church. Naturally pacific in his temperament, he never initiated a controversy with sister churches; nevertheless, when controversy was forced upon him, his tactics proclaimed him a master of the art. More than one ecclesiastical bigot was made to bite the dust in bitter agony. He is a decided success on the rostrum. There is a generous vein of humor in his composition. This quality he represses in the pulpit. On the rostrum, however, he sometimes gives it vent in such a way that if you were behind the door you might imagine that John B. McFerrin was again on mundane shores and at his old occupation or taking a collection. His gifts in this respect, however, are always made subservient to the cause of truth and righteousness. While he has lectured on many subjects, he is perhaps nowhere stronger than on the temperance platform. For years he has been recognized as a champion of the temperance cause. Before his connection with the New Orleans *Advocate*, he was for a time editor of the *Temperance Banner*. For a number of years previous to his election to the episcopacy he was chairman of the Mississippi State Prohibition executive committee, a non-partisan organization which, besides other good results, secured the enactment of the present local-option law, a measure by means of which about half the area of the state has been redeemed from the curse of the saloon. In all parts of the state his voice has been heard crying out in thunder tones against the iniquities of the liquor traffic. During these years of agitation he often received anonymous letters threatening his life. The only effect of such missives was to intensify his zeal and multiply his labors in the good cause.

What has been said is sufficient to show the Bishop is a prodigious worker. More, however, needs to be said on this subject, and there is no better way of saying it than by quoting from his friend, Prof. R. S. Ricketts, of Whitworth college. As introductory to this quotation, let it be stated that during his editorship of the New Orleans *Advocate*, he was also pastor of the church at Brookhaven, the seat of Whitworth college. During the four years of his dual work as pastor and editor, an account of his weekly work and travel would read almost like a story of romance. It began with two sermons on Sunday, in addition to regular attendance upon Sunday-school in the morning, and occasional preaching at a mission appointment in the afternoon. Monday morning early found him at his desk in the *Advocate* office (one hundred and thirty miles away), where two laborious days were spent in getting out the paper, and Wednesday evening he was again in Brookhaven in time to conduct the prayer meeting. Between Wednesday and Sunday time was usually found for pastoral visiting at home, and for a lecture fifty or a hundred miles away in aid of some enterprise of the church. The "Prohibition Handbook" and the "Life of Bishop Parker" were written during the intervals of these manifold labors. Add to this the leadership of the prohibition movement in the state, and we have the record of a very busy life. Concerning his social qualities, the same facile pen has this to say : "It might be supposed that one so continually occupied would have little time for social pleasure. On the contrary, however, he is 'given to hospitality,' and has a pleasant word of greeting, even for those trying callers who have never learned the art of timely departure. At his home the brethern, ministers and laymen, are cordially received and delightfully entertained, for the Bishop is not only a good talker, but a most inspiring listener as well. He looks at you when you speak to him, and while you can not sometimes escape the thought that he is looking through you also, yet persons generally go away from an interview with a sense of having said, as well as heard, a gratifying number of good things. And what enhances his charm as a listener is the feeling that the interest he manifests is in no degree affected, but real. Like all born leaders of men, he charges himself with whatever is potential in the thought or experience of those he meets, and is thus better prepared to exert that magnetic power which attracts attention and commands a following. He is what the pine woods people call 'a friendly man.' He remembers names and faces. He enjoys a laugh, and laughs all over; he likes a good story (it must be clean and without malice), and tells one with relish even if it be at his own expense. To this genial disposition he owes in some measure his large acquaintance with public men, an acquaintance which he uses to good effect in the interest of moral reform. The Bishop has a distinctive home life, and has impressed himself more upon his family than many who have not undertaken half so much in the interest of the public. He is one of his family, not unmindful of domestic concerns, and keenly alive to the plans and pleasures even of the little ones; enters heartily into the ambitions and success of school life, and enjoys the last new song, in which, if of the spiritual kind, and not over difficult of execution, he joins with a great voice." Episcopal robes have not in the least diminished his appetite for multifarious work. He is almost constantly on the wing. Besides his routine duties of presiding in district and annual conferences, he is now here, now there; first in this state, then in that; lecturing on missions, church extension, education, and similar themes. On the question of education he is enthusiastic for a forward movement on the part of the church. In this interest he not only delivers able and telling addresses, he also engages in what is usually thought to be the more arduous work of raising money. To him, however, there is no arduousness in it. If he had to choose between taking a collection and sitting down to a luxurious dinner, he would doubtless make sure of the collection and risk his chances for dinner. It is not strange, therefore, that he is preëminently successful as a money-getter. If there is any man who can get "the last nickel" out of an audience, he is the man. This talent, superadded to his oratorical gifts, makes him immensely serviceable in the work of building and endowing colleges. Some of his most fruitful work has been in this field. It would take much space and a great deal of time to tell of his long-continued and successful labors in behalf of Millsap's college and Galloway college, to say nothing of various other institutions. As a bishop he has now been before the church long enough to vindicate the wisdom of his election. In the pulpit, in the conference room, and in the cabinet, he measures up to the high standard which the church has set for her chief shepherds. Should Providence favor him with long life, he will grow in favor with the church with each revolving year.

Dr. William G. Gamble is a planter of Saltillo, Lee county, and resides on his plantation, four and one-half miles west of Saltillo. He is a native of Wilcox county. Ala., born in 1834, and is a son of Samuel S. and Martha (Gaston) Gamble, of Fairfield district, S. C., and Chester district, S. C., respectively. The parents were reared and educated in their native state, but were married in Wilcox county, Ala. Samuel S. Gamble was a son of James Gamble, a native of Pennsylvania; and he died in Alabama in 1840, at the age of sixty years. He was a successful farmer, and politically was allied to the democratic party. Martha Gaston was a daughter of Hugh Gaston of South Carolina, a saddler by trade. He died in 1837, in the eighty-fourth year of his age. Dr. Gamble is the fifth of a family of six children: Martha, Sarah, wife of Dr. J. M. Boyd, Mary, wife of Dr. G. L. Hutchinson, James, William G., and Ann; all are deceased excepting Mary and our subject. The Doctor was reared amidst the scenes of his birth, and received a good literary education, which laid the foundation of the professional training he afterward received. He was graduated from the college at Tuscaloosa, Ala., in 1855, and the following year began the study of medicine under the preceptorship of Dr. A. C. Mathison, of Camden, Ala. He afterward entered the University of Louisiana and was graduated from the medical department. This event occurred in 1859, and he began practicing at once. He served during the war as assistant surgeon in different hospitals of the western army. He had first enlisted as a private in the Forty-second Alabama regiment, company C. When the war was over he returned to his home, and practiced his profession there until 1869. His health failing at that time he abandoned his practice, and in 1871 he came to Mississippi, purchased land, and has since made it his home. Dr. Gamble was united in marriage to Miss E. I. Agnew, a daughter of Wilson and E. D. Agnew, natives of South Carolina. She was also a South Carolinian by birth, but was reared in Tennessee until her twelfth year. Her parents then removed to Mississippi. She was born in 1849, and died in 1885. Seven children had been born to the Doctor and his wife: Mary, Gertrude (deceased), Hugh, Samuel (deceased), Wilson (deceased), Lois and Paul. Dr. Gamble takes an especial interest in the education of his children, and is fitting them for any duties that are likely to befall them. Politically he is not an enthusiast, but discharges his duties as a citizen by exercising his rights of suffrage faithfully and conscientiously. He is a loyal citizen, devoted to home industries, and the advancement and growth of home enterprises.

Among the household words of Mississippi homes, none are perhaps more prominently identified than the name of Dr. J. B. Gambrel. He is of French extraction. His great-grandfather, John Gambrel, was a patriot, under Marion, the hero of the Pedee. His early ancestors were of an agricultural turn, and were fairly successful as farmers. It was a family possessed of strong characteristics. Abhorring the holding of office, they possessed almost a passion for the military. His grandfather was Daniel Gambrel, and his father Joel Bruton Gambrel, who was born in South Carolina in 1809, and married to Miss Elvira Williams, of South Carolina, who was some five years his junior. In 1842 he immigrated to Tippah county, Miss. (now Union), where he died in 1875. Mrs. Gambrel yet survives. Dr. Gambrel, the fourth son of Joel Bruton Gambrel, was born in Anderson county, S. C., in 1841. His early life was passed upon the farm, and the old fieldschools were attended as chance afforded. In 1860 and 1861 he attended the Cherry Creek academy, Pontotoc county, Miss. The war coming on, he enlisted in company I, second Mississippi regiment, Colonel Falkner commanding at first, later Col. John M. Stone; the former, lately a writer of some reputation, the latter, governor of Mississippi. Being assigned to duty in Virginia, he took part in the first battle of Manassas, saw service in the Maryland campaign, and was in the seven days' battle about Richmond. In 1862 he was put in command of scouts, and in this capacity was connected with various armies. With the military daring of his ancestors, he went out, on one occasion, with his little scouting party of four, and in ninety days captured sixty-three prisoners. While engaged as a scout he became acquainted with Miss Mary T. Corbell, of Nansemond county, Va., whom he married within the Federal lines on January 13, 1864. Turning from the altar to the field, he particularly distinguished himself at the battle of Falling Water. After the main body of the troops had crossed on the pontoon bridge, it was discovered that a brigade of North Carolina troops had been left behind. He immediately returned and rescued six hundred of them, but himself was forced to swim for his life. For this daring act he was promoted to a first lieutenancy, and granted authority to raise a company and become its captain. This was the special recognition of President Davis. The company which he raised saw service in western Tennessee and northern Mississippi, under special instruction from President Davis to keep the Federals whipped in—whipped back to their lines. Among the members of this company who have since become famous, was Private John Allen, for years, and now, the representative of the first congressional district of Mississippi. It is also worthy of mention that Dr. Gambrel and his men drove in the pickets and opened the battle of Malvern Hill. He also was on the field of Gettysburg on the memorable first day of July. Among his most daring feats may be mentioned his escape from capture at Memphis, when, with twenty-nine men, he cut his way through a force of three hundred Federals, after a loss of two horses, and himself wounded. After the war he entered the Baptist ministry. About 1867 and 1868 he taught school at Wallerville, Union county, Miss., where he also served the church as pastor. In 1869 he accepted the pastorate of the church at West Point, which he retained for two years, and then became pastor at Oxford, where he remained for five years. During this time he became a student in the university for special work. Under his ministry, from a membership of a dozen, his church increased to one hundred members. In 1876 he assumed charge of the church at Clinton, and became editor of the *Baptist Record*, the new paper established by the state convention. He continued in the capacity of editor for nine years, and, on being elected secretary of the mission board, he removed to Jackson. During the next two years he organized the present system of benevolent agencies in the church of the state. In 1889 he engaged to raise $50,000 for the endowment of Mississippi college, at Clinton, which task it was thought would require five years. In two and one-third years it was accomplished. Dr. Gambrel is an active worker for prohibition. He is chairman of the State Executive Prohibition committee, and is connected with the national prohibition movement. He also holds the important position of president of the Law and Order League of the city of Meridian. He takes an active interest in favor of moral reform in politics. In 1890 he delivered an address to the American Baptist Educational society, the only one printed in full. As fraternal messenger to a meeting in Cincinnati, he delivered an address which was most widely copied. Dr. Gambrel, as a speaker, is fluent and easy, but not demonstrative. There is a vein of humor about his remarks, at once pleasing and expressive. As a writer, he is strong and vigorous, rarely assuming a position that is not impregnable. In person he is tall and erect, graceful and commanding. He is individual in the highest degree, and, taken all in all, is one of the strongest characters in the personnel of the state. It will be remembered that he is the father of the martyred Roderick Dhu Gambrel, who, young as he was, has left a lasting name in the annals of the great, the noble, and the good. The Doctor is the possessor of eight other interesting children, some of whom even now are not unknown to the world of letters.

W. Perkins Gardner belongs to an old and prominent family that originally came from Georgia and settled in Amite county, Miss., about the year 1817, this family being headed by Hon. William Gardner. He was a man well fitted for pioneer life, for he was courageous, did not dread privations, was industrious and enterprising. He opened a large plantation here, soon became known as a rising man and in time became wealthy, his property being the result of his untiring endeavors. He at all times gave much attention to political matters, and besides representing Amite county in the state legislature, where he had an excellent opportunity of advancing his sound and practical views, he filled numerous other offices of trust and honor in the county. His son, Sylvester Gardner, was born in Georgia in February, 1813, and when a child of four years was brought by his parents to this state and county, where, notwithstanding the primitive condition of the country and the scarcity of schools, he succeeded in obtaining a practical education eminently sufficient to fit him for the practical duties of life. After reaching manhood he taught school in Arkansas and Louisiana for some time, but in this county was married to Miss Amelia B. Johnson, daughter of William Perkins Johnson, who came to this state from South Carolina in 1818. Mrs. Gardner was born in the Palmetto state, but was reared in this county. After his marriage Mr. Gardner located on the plantation on which the subject of this sketch is now residing, and, although he commenced life a poor man, became by industry and superior management well to do in worldly goods. He was a shrewd and successful financier, inherited many of his father's sound and practical views and in time received his reward in the shape of a more than ordinary degree of prosperity. He was a prominent member of the New Providence Baptist church and was one of its strongest supporters, giving liberally to the support of the gospel and to all charitable and worthy enterprises. He was a most consistent Christian and was beloved and honored by a large circle of friends and acquaintances. In 1876 he moved to Magnolia, Pike county, Miss., where he was called from life in the month of February, 1881, having for some time been an earnest member of the Masonic fraternity. His wife preceded him to the grave four months, having borne him two children: W. Perkins and a daughter, now the wife of Rev. J. A. Hacket, a minister of the Baptist church and editor of the *Southern Baptist Record*, published at Meridian, Miss. W. Perkins Gardner was given the advantages of the schools of Amite county, and in assisting his father on the plantation attained to an admirable degree of physical vigor. Here he was married, on the 20th of April, 1871, to Miss Mary E., daughter of G. B. McLain, and after his marriage he took charge of the home farm and has since devoted his attention to planting, raising corn, cotton, etc. His plantation comprises twelve hundred acres, of which six hundred acres are open land, and the annual amount of cotton he raises amounts to about one hundred and fifty bales. Like his father before him, he is much interested in church work and has served his church, the Baptist, as a delegate to several associations, and at the present time is treasurer of the Mississippi Baptist association and is serving his church as deacon. He has been a professor of Christianity since his youth, is known for his many Christian acts of charity and kindness and for the prominent part he takes in all good works. To himself and wife a family of six sons and two daughters have been born: Sylvester C., who is attending college at Starkville, Miss.; Berry, also attending the same institution; Lena E., who is attending a female college of Blue Mountain, Miss.; Velma, Clifton, Perkins, Lee R. and Charles, the last named being an infant. The old homestead on which Mr. Gardner is residing is situated about midway between Liberty and Gloster and is an exceedingly healthful location, for in thirty-three years Mr. Sylvester Gardner did not pay out over $100 to doctors, and W. Perkins Gardner has not exceeded that sum in the past nineteen years. Mr. Gardner is a very earnest Christian and lets nothing interfere with his religious privileges and duties. He is very liberal with his means and, as he is hospitable, generous and kindly, he has many warm personal friends.

In preparing this brief outline of the life of Jesse W. Garth (planter), facts appear which are greatly to his credit. His intelligence, enterprise and integrity, as well as many other estimable qualities, have gathered about him numerous friends and have won for him a well-deserved popularity. He was born in Morgan county, Ala., March 9, 1830, a son of Jesse W. and Unity (Dandridge) Garth, of English descent, and natives of Hanover county, Va. The father was a lawyer and politician of considerable note, and became one of the wealthiest planters of the South prior to the war, his landed interests being enormous and his slaves numbering twelve hundred. He died in 1870, and his wife in 1833, their union having been blessed in the birth of five children, four of whom are living at the present time: Elizabeth, Sallie, Mary and Jesse W.; William was the other member of the family. During the early days of the subject of this sketch he learned the details of planting, and for many years he has had the reputation of being an agriculturist of decided merit. This could

hardly be otherwise, for his father was very thorough and practical in his views, and he imbibed those principles of energy, enterprise and probity that have since been of material benefit to him. He owns five thousand acres of land in one body, which lie about eighteen miles southwest of Columbus, and on this land, since 1888, he has given considerable attention to the raising of stock, having in his possession a large and very fine thoroughbred horse, and cattle of an excellent grade. His land is well adapted for the purpose of stock-raising, and promises in time to become one of the best and largest in the state. Mr. Garth was fortunate enough to obtain a collegiate education, his alma mater being an institution at La Grange, Ala., having previously been an attendant of Henry college. Upon finishing his literary education, he began studying law in the Cumberland university, of Lebanon, Tenn., from which institution he afterward graduated. In 1851 he was elected to the state legislature and, after finishing his term satisfactorily, he returned to planting, which has since been his calling. In the winter of 1862 he removed to Mississippi, where he has since made his home. In March, 1874, he was married to Miss Phelix, daughter of Dr. and Sarah (Millwater) Manning, natives of Alabama. They have two children: Mary and Willie.

Charles H. Gates is a man of superior business qualifications and throughout his career he has displayed traits of character which are greatly to his credit. His intelligence, enterprise and integrity have acquired for him a popularity not derived from any factitious circumstances, but a spontaneous tribute to his merit. He has held a number of local positions of trust, the duties of which positions he always discharged with the same care and fidelity which characterized his career in business circles. He was born in Franklin county, Miss., June 27, 1852, and after obtaining an ordinary common-school education, entered his father's mercantile store and may be said to have been reared to mercantile business. After remaining with his father for several years he began an independent career, and in 1879 came to Jefferson county, taking up his abode in Harriston in 1883. He was one of the very first to erect a storehouse in the town, and although he commenced his mercantile career in a very humble way, his establishment slowly but surely gained in favor, and from time to time he was enabled to enlarge his building and increase his stock of goods. He now carries the most extensive and select stock of general merchandise in Harriston, and in connection with the successful conduct of this establishment he owns and conducts a first-class hostelry, which is largely patronized by the traveling public. As a business man he is wideawake and pushing, is thoroughly honest and upright, and any one having business transactions with him will find him strictly honrable. Since the town was incorporated he has been a member of the town board and has used his influence toward advancing the interests of this flourishing little place. On the 15th of March, 1876, he was united in marriage to Miss S. C. Dangerfield, who was born and reared in Jefferson county, but was educated in Richmond, Va., she being a daughter of Lewis Dangerfield. Mr. and Mrs. Gates have two bright and promising little children; Howell and Berenice. Mrs. Gates is an earnest member of the Methodist Episcopal church, and socially Mr. Gates is a prominent and active member of the A. F. & A. M. and the I. O. O. F. of Fayette, being also a member of the K. of H., the K. of P. and the American Legion of Honor. His father, C. F. Gates, was born in Mississippi, in the city of Natchez, and in this state grew to manhood. He was married in the city of his birth to Miss S. J. Seal, who was also born in this state, and of a family of four sons and two daughters, born to them, all grew to mature years, but two sons are now deceased; the youngest son, Rev. E. C. Gates, who was a prominent minister of the Baptist church and J. S. Gates who was a merchant of Natchez and died in that city. G. W. Gates, another son, is a farmer of Franklin county, and is well to do. The father of these children is still living,

49

and is a worthy agriculturist of Franklin county, where he has resided for the past forty years.

Like many of the prominent men of Panola county, Miss., James P. Gates, planter and merchant, of Park place, started out to fight life's battles for himself with little or no means, and what he has accumulated in the way of this world's goods is the result of his own hard work and indomitable energy. He was the fourth of fourteen children born to John and Mary A. (Benge) Gates, the parents natives of Tennessee. The father came to Mississippi in 1848, and followed planting in that state until his death in 1870. He served as a soldier in the Mexican war. The maternal grandfather, Richard Benge, was also a native of Tennessee. James P. Gates was born in Shelby county, Tenn., on December 25, 1846, and two years later was taken by his parents to Mississippi. He there passed his boyhood and youth, and received his education in the private schools of Panola county. At the age of twenty years he started out for himself as a merchant and planter, and has been moderately successful in each occupation. He is the owner of two hundred and forty acres of land, one hundred and seventy acres under cultivation, and carries a stock of goods valued at $2,500. He selected as his companion in life Mrs. Lou C. (Carter) Hudson, and their nuptials were celebrated on May 26, 1871. She was a native of Mississippi, the widow of J. C. Hudson, and the daughter of William M. and Martha E. (Hall) Carter, natives of Tennessee. To Mr. and Mrs. Gates were born two children, Pattie C. and Jennie L. During the Civil war, or in 1865, Mr. Gates enlisted in the Hudson battery, and remained in the same until cessation of hostilities. He and family are members of the Methodist church, and Mr. Gates is also a member of the Masonic order. He is a democrat in politics, has held the office of bailiff, but although elected justice of the peace, would not serve. He is a worthy citizen, and gives his aid and countenance to all enterprises for the public weal.

Prof. T. L. Gates, B. S., president of Pleasant Ridge normal institute of Itawamba county, Miss., was born in Alabama on November 4, 1863, a son of P. H. and Nancy C. (Nelson) Gates, the former a native of Alabama, the latter of South Carolina, both of whom were lifelong and zealous members of the Methodist Episcopal church. They had six children. Of these, Mary C. is the wife of W. F. Nabors, of Itawamba county, and has borne him four children; Charles V. married Miss Mollie Nabors, has four children and is also a native resident of Itawamba county; Prof. P. A. Gates is a well-known educator; Rebecca L. and Hattie C. are unmarried. Prof. T. L. Gates is the fourth in order of birth. After attending the public schools of Mississippi, he went to Iuka, where he was a student for two years. He was then engaged for a time in teaching school, but finally graduated at Iuka, Miss., with the degree of B. S., in 1889, and immediately afterward, in company with his brother, Prof. P. A. Gates, he founded Pleasant Ridge normal institute, which they still control. This educational institution is situated in the northeast portion of Itawamba county, at Pleasant Ridge, a beautiful location surrounded by natural timber. The main building is a frame structure, two stories high, with a seating capacity of five hundred. It was built by the Professors Gates just prior to the opening of the school in 1889. The faculty of this institution is constituted as follows: Prof. T. L. Gates, president; Prof. P. A. Gates, co-principal; W. P. Stewart, assistant principal. December, 28, 1890, Prof. T. L. Gates married Miss Mary Stewart, who was born in Mississippi, December 25, 1864, and received her education in the public schools of that state. They live in a cozy cottage, located near the school building. Both are members of the Methodist Episcopal church South, and politically Professor Gates is a democrat. Prof. P. A. Gates was born in Alabama, February 17, 1866, the third son and fifth child of his father's family. After attending the public schools in Mississippi he graduated at Iuka, Miss., with the degree of A. B., in 1889, but previous to this, in 1887, he had begun teaching in the public schools. He is a democrat, a master Mason and a Methodist. The value of such institutions as the Pleasant Ridge normal institution can rarely be estimated, and this is one of the best of its kind. The brothers Gates are educators by natural inclination as well as by study and experience, and educators of a high order of ability, and their work is gaining in favor as it becomes known. This promises in time to develop into one of the leading educational institutions of this part of the state.

Sampson Gathings, a well-known planter of Monroe county, was born in Anson county, N. C., in 1823. His parents were James and Jane (Jackson) Gathings, both natives of Virginia, but who were married in North Carolina, to which state they removed with their parents, and where Mr. Gathings died in 1844. His wife survived him till 1883, and died in Anson county, N. C. His father was a farmer and trader, and a member of the Baptist church. He was of German and his wife of English descent. The subject of this sketch was the fourth of seven children, named as follows: James (a planter, who died in Texas), Philip (a planter, who now resides in Texas), Susan (widow of the late D. A. Covington of Monroe, N. C.), Sampson, George W. (planter of Monroe county now deceased), Jackson M. (planter, residing in Monroe county), Mary (widow of Sidney Randall of Clay county). Mr. Gathings received such education as was available to him in the common schools, and at Lake Forest institute in North Carolina. In 1843 he married Martha, daughter of Wilson and Jemima Chambers, natives and lifelong residents of North Carolina. Mrs. Gathings was born in Anson county, N. C., and died about 1854, having borne him two children: Jennie V., who is the wife of Thomas Randall of Bessemer, Ala., and Sampson Jr., deceased. For his second wife, Mr. Gathings married, in 1861, Susan, daughter of John J. and Eliza Williamson, natives of North Carolina, but later living in Tennessee, where Mr. Williamson died, his widow surviving him. The present Mrs. Gathings was born in Maury county, Tenn. They have three children: James C., practicing physician at Nashville and later at Memphis, Tenn.; Clinton, railroad agent at Oakland, Tenn., and Melville W. Mr. Gathings came to Monroe county in 1843, locating on a small improvement, and has since lived in different parts of the county, and for twenty years on his present farm near Prairie station. Altogether he owns about one thousand acres of land in different tracts. This produces every year from two hundred and fifty to three hundred bales of cotton. He is recognized as one of the most successful, well-to-do planters of Monroe county, and it is a source of much gratification to him to know that his success is due solely to his own enterprise, industry and perserverance. He possesses an enviable business reputation, and his plantation is one of the finest in the county, and his home is one of the most hospitable. For a short time during the war he did service under General Forrest, and is justly proud of his war record, although it does not cover a lengthy period. He is one of the pioneers of this county, having been one of the first to begin opening up the prairie which, until that time, had remained untouched by the plow, the timber land having been settled long before. He is one of the most practical farmers in the county, and also one of its leading citizens—a man of genial disposition and one who has a large number of friends among all classes. He and his wife are members of the Methodist Episcopal church South, and formerly he was a member of the Independent Order of Odd Fellows.

F. Gautier & Sons, West Pascagoula, Miss., are among the largest lumber manufacturers of Jackson county, having been established there for more than twenty years. They started in business with a small capital, erecting a mill with a capacity of ten thousand feet per day. When their trade demanded it they increased their capacity to thirty thousand feet per day. They employ twenty-two men in the mill, and find a ready market for all the lumber they manufacture. The firm consists of Fernando, the father, and Henry and Walter, the sons. The father was born at sea, near the island of Juan Fernando, in 1823, his parents at the time being on a voyage to South America. He was reared and educated in New Orleans, and, after leaving school was employed as a clerk in a cottonhouse. For several years he followed this occupation, when he removed to Mississippi. He erected a small sawmill near Biloxi, which he operated until after the war. After the conflict was ended and peace declared, he sold out and removed to West Pascagoula, where he has since resided. He was united in marriage to Miss Theresa Fayard. They have had eleven children born to them, nine of whom are living: Henry; Ada, wife of R. Thompson; Walter; Eve, wife of Hon. John M. Pelham; Mina, wife of John O'Donohoe; Emma, wife of Charles G. Johnson; Julia, wife of W. M. Canty; and Eugene and Adam. The children were all born in Mississippi. Henry was reared and educated in Harrison county, near Biloxi. He was trained to the lumber business, and has always followed milling. The last year of the Civil war he served in company C, Twenty-fourth Mississippi battalion, and since the war ended has been in business with his father. He was married in 1875 to Miss A. Hull, of Mobile, Ala. They have two children: Louise and Aline.

J. D. Gay was born in Alabama, January 6, 1819, the fourth son of James Gay, a native of North Carolina, who moved to South Carolina, where he married Martha Bates. In 1818 Mr. and Mrs. Gay moved to Alabama, and about four years later came to Monroe county, Miss., when the subject of our sketch was about three years of age. Mr. Gay was a cabinet maker by trade, but engaged in farming after his marriage with Miss Bates, in which he continued to the end of his life. His father, and the father of his wife, both did patriotic service in the Revolutionary war. J. D. Gay received his education in a Catholic school in Kentucky, and was later a clerk for a firm engaged extensively at Mobile. During the few years immediately preceding his marriage, he was not engaged in any active business, but lived a life of leisure, devoting his time mostly to hunting and fishing. His first wife was Miss Anna Franks, by whom he had nine children, and, after her death, he married her sister, Mrs. Lauretta Swepston, who also bore him nine children. Of his family of eighteen children, only six are now living. At the time of the war Mr. Gay was too much advanced in life for military service, but he took an active part in furnishing supplies to the army—at one time giving sufficient money to purchase sixty pairs of shoes, for use in a certain regiment, for which he also furnished provisions for ten days. He has always been very charitable, and it is probable that he has given more to the needy in this community than any one else. In politics he is a democrat of the old school, but he has never been an active politician, and never accepted any office, though he has often been urged to do so.

When it became necessary for Capt. William L. Gay, Greenville, Miss., to choose some occupation in life, it was but natural perhaps that he should choose agricultural pursuits, for he was early taught the duties of farm life, and his father and grandfather before him had been successful planters. He is a native-born resident of Washington county, Miss., his birth occurring here on the 10th of November, 1839, and is the only child born to the union of William H. and Caroline A. (Parker) Gay, the father a native of Kentucky and the mother of Virginia. The former came to Washington county, Miss., in 1836, engaged in planting, and two years later was married to Miss Parker. He became one of the successful planters of the county and continued this pursuit until his death in 1848. The mother died in 1888, a worthy member of the Methodist church. The paternal grandfather came to this county about 1838, followed planting, but soon died. William L. Gay was reared on his father's estate, received his education in Tennessee and Kentucky and finished his literary course at the University of Mississippi. He then entered the military college at Nashville and graduated from that institution in 1860. At the breaking out of war he entered the Confederate army, company I, Twenty-second Mississippi regiment as lieutenant, and was in all the battles of the West from Shiloh and Corinth to the Georgia campaign, with Generals Hood and Johnston, being with the latter general at the surrender. After the first year he was captain of the company, being promoted to that position before the battle of Baton Rouge on the 4th of August, 1862. He was wounded in the battle of Shiloh and also at Peach Tree creek. Returning to Washington county, Miss., after the war, Mr. Gay engaged in planting, and this he has followed exclusively and successfully ever since. He has fine property on Deer creek with six hundred and fifty acres under cultivation, and other portions which he is engaged in clearing at the present time. In 1890 he erected a fine residence in the suburbs of Greenville, and there he now resides, surrounded by all the comforts of life. By his marriage, which occurred in 1869 to Miss Kate Shelby Blackburn, a native of Washington county, but who was reared in Louisiana, there was born one child, Mary. The family hold membership in the Episcopal church. Mrs. Gay's father, Dr. Blackburn, was an early settler in Washington county, and she is connected with the Shelbys, an old family of this county.

In sketching the business circles of Carrollton, no man will be found more worthy of consideration than Maj. Joseph J. Gee, Carrollton, Miss. He is a native of Virginia, born near Petersburg, September 11, 1834. His father, Peter Gee, was also a native of Virginia, and was born in the year 1803. He married Mary A. Moore, a Virginian by birth, and a sister of Col. O. J. Moore, of Winona. Mr. Gee removed to the west, as Tennessee was then considered, in 1836, and settled near Memphis, and thence, in 1841, he came to Carroll county. He engaged in planting and merchandising in the eastern part of the county, where he remained a number of years. He then removed to Carrollton, and resided there until his death, which occurred in 1883. His wife survived him but a few months, dying in the same year. Major Gee is one of a family of two children. His sister, Mrs. Bingham, is a resident of Carrollton. He grew up in this county, receiving a country-school education. At the age of seventeen years he left the parental roof, and began the battle of life at Old Middleton, and sold goods there for a number of years; in fact, he continued at this point for five years, then he removed to Carrollton, carrying on the same business. In 1861, when there was a call for men to go to the aid of the country, he enlisted in the Fourth Mississippi volunteer infantry, company H, and was elected second lieutenant. He was soon made captain and then major, in which office he served until the close of the war. He participated in a number of engagements, the most important being Fort Henry, Fort Donelson, Vicksburg, and Port Gibson. He was twice taken prisoner, and the last time was held on Johnson's Island, being exchanged from that place and paroled at the close of the war. He then returned to Carrollton, and again took up the more peaceful pursuit of mercantile life. He is one of the most successful business men in the county. By wise management and economy he has amassed one of the best estates in the county, and is one of its heaviest taxpayers. In consideration of the fact that this property has been accumulated by his own efforts, through honorable, upright dealing, Major Gee quickly ranks among the most capable men of the community. He was married in the county of Carroll, Miss., December 3, 1868, to Miss C. A. Kimbrough, a native of this county, and a daughter of O. L. Kimbrough, one of the early pioneers. The Major and his wife have had born to them three sons and three daughters: C. J. (the eldest son), Mary C., O. K. (the second son), Florence A., Clinton L., and Stella R. Major Gee is a man well posted on all the leading questions of the day, both political and financial. He is of a social, genial disposition, of excellent habits, and has a large share of those traits of character that go to make up a popular citizen.

Hon. James Z. George, of Carrollton, was born in Monroe county, Ga., October 20, 1826. His father having died in his infancy, he removed, when eight years of age, with his mother to Noxubee county, Miss., where he resided two years, then moved to Carroll county, where he was educated in the common schools. He volunteered as a private in the First regiment of Mississippi volunteers in the Mexican war, commanded by Col. Jefferson Davis, and was at the battle of Monterey. On his return he studied law and was admitted to the bar in Carroll county. In 1854 he was elected reporter of the high court of errors and appeals, and reëlected in 1860, and prepared and published ten volumes of the reports of the decisions of that court, and afterward prepared and published a digest of all the decisions of the supreme court and high court of errors and appeals of that state, from the admission of the state into the Union to and including the year 1870. A member of the convention· in Mississippi in 1861 which passed the ordinance of secession, he voted for and signed that instrument. He was a captain in the Twentieth regiment of Mississippi volunteers in the Confederate states army, later a brigadier-general of state troops, and afterward colonel of the Fifth regiment of Mississippi cavalry in the Confederate states army. He was chairman of the democratic state executive committee of Mississippi in 1875 and '76. In 1879 he was appointed one of the judges of the supreme court of Mississippi, and elected chief justice. In February, 1881, he resigned his seat on the supreme bench to take his seat in the senate on the 4th of March of that year, and was reëlected in 1886. His term of service will expire March 3, 1893. As a constitutional lawyer, Mr. George ranks with the best in America. His work against the force bill brought him into wider prominence than he had before enjoyed, and demonstrated the fact that he is not only profoundly learned in the constitution of the United States, but is thoroughly conversant with the constitutions of the various states forming the Federal union. He is a Southern man, and a Mississippian in all that the term implies, and none of the statesmen who have become known as the stanch friends of the Southern people are nearer their hearts than he.

Capt. W. W. George, vice-president of the First National Bank of Meridian, Miss., was born in Versailles, Ky., in the year 1842. He is a son of W. W. George, Sr., who was also a native of Kentucky. His honored father was judge of the probate court of Woodford county, Kentucky, for a number of years, and died while an incumbent of that office in 1884. He had a family of six sons, five of whom are now living, our subject being the second eldest. He was educated at Versailles seminary, Versailles, Ky., from which place he went to Louisville, Ky., graduating at a commercial college there in the year 1861. After his graduation he found employment in a bank, where he laid the foundation of that knowledge which served him in good stead in after years. He returned to Versailles and soon became a member of the firm of George & Wilson, bankers. After a successful business course of several years, he sold out his interest in this concern and organized a bank at Bairdstown, Ky., under the firm name of W. W. George & Co. At the end of seven years' time he again sold out to his partners and removed to Meridian, Miss., in the year 1873, going there as cashier of the People's bank, holding that position until Frederick Wolf was made president of the bank, when Mr. George was elected vice-president. He continued this office till 1855, when the People's bank was merged into the First National bank, and he was made vice-president of this new concern. Having gone into the banking business before he was twenty-one years of age, Captain George has naturally a wide experience as a banker and can proudly point to the fact that during all of these years he has never been connected with a bank that ever failed or that did not make money every year he was attached to its corps of officers.   Captain George is a member of the Knights of Honor, is a stockholder and president of the Meridian water works, president of the Bonita Park dummy railroad line, a director in the Mississippi Land & Mining Company, in fact, he is identified with every public enterprise of Meridian at the present time and has been an active member of many others in the past, among which may be mentioned the presidency of the board of directors of East Mississippi insane asylum, which position he occupied for many years.   Capt. W. W. George became a Benedict in the year 1862, taking unto himself a wife in the person of Miss Agnes Thornton, of Versailles, Ky.   This union has been blessed with four sons: Abner H., Ernest T., Stanley E. and Alex. L.   The Captain and his entire family are members of the Presbyterian church.   Mrs. George's grandfather, Dr. John Blackburn, was a Presbyterian minister, and Gideon Blackburn, her great-grandfather, was also a Presbyterian divine as well as president of Center college, of Danville, Ky.   The Captain is a man most highly esteemed, as can be inferred from the public offices he has held in Meridian, while socially no one is his superior.

Robert Germany (deceased), a successful merchant and planter of old Centerville, Amite county, Miss., well known to the people of this portion of the state, stood high as a representative business man and citizen.   He was a native of Georgia, born in 1799, and was the second child of a family of six sons and one daughter born to James Germany, a native of the same state.   The latter was one of the old settlers of this district, and followed the occupation of farming.   With his family he came on horseback and on foot from Georgia, and settled in the vicinity of old Centerville, where he reared and educated his children.   He engaged in planting, and was a man of peculiar habits and a member of the Baptist church.   He was strictly honest in all his dealings, and led a life of activity and usefulness.   He was democratic in politics, though he took no active part more than to regularly poll his vote for the democratic candidates.   About the year 1815 or 1816 he held the government contract for carrying the mail from Natchez to Covington, La., on Lake Pontchartrain, the mail being carried by his son, Robert, the subject of this memoir.   He died at an advanced age in Kemper county, Miss., where he had gone to live with his son, William.   His children were: John, Robert, William, Benjamin, James, Henry and Elizabeth.   The latter first married Nathan Land, one of the early and prominent planters of this section.   Nathan Land made for himself a competency, having come here a poor man, and by his energy and hard work laid the foundation of his success.   At middle age he met with a misfortune of getting one of his legs broken, which resulted in the amputation of the limb below the knee.   He was a man of excellent habits, strictly honest, and upright, pure-minded, stout-hearted, a credit to his family and his race. He died in 1849, aged eighty-seven years.   He had one son (John) who died in 1864.   After his death his widow married Thomas R. Craft; she died about 1854.   All of his family are now deceased but Henry, who lives in Louisiana, where he is quite extensively engaged in planting.   Robert, the subject of this memoir, attained his majority in the vicinity of Centerville.   His sole schooling was received at the hands of "Yankee" Smith, who followed teaching on coming to Mississippi, being a native of Vermont.   This teacher later was the leading merchant of Centerville; his sales at one time reached $100,000 for one year.   He purchased the home place of James Germany.   Robert at the age of sixteen years carried the mail for his father on horseback from Natchez to Covington, through almost a wilderness, infested with Mason's band of robbers and cutthroats.   Later he engaged in work in the store of Mr. Smith for many years, and succeeded him as a merchant and continued the business until about 1843, and also engaged in planting, and in time owned the greater portion of the land where Centerville is now located.   As a merchant he did a large credit business without much loss.   In 1837 he suffered severe losses in the financial crash of that date.   It took him several years to build up his former stock and trade.   Retiring from merchandising, he led a quiet life until his death in 1869.   He was a member of the Methodist Episcopal church, of which he was a liberal supporter.   He was a stanch whig and a Union man, but when the war broke out he took sides with the Confederacy and was loyal to his state.   He was postmaster of old Centerville for many years.   He was married first in about 1827, to Louisa Cosby, a native of Georgia, who was reared in Mississippi.   She was a cousin of Judge McGehee's first wife.   She came here with her parents and was reared and educated at the old seat of Washington, Miss.   She was the daughter of James Cosby, a respected planter of Wilkinson county, a native of Georgia, whose wife was Margaret McCall, a native also of Georgia.   To this union were born two sons and three daughters, all of whom lived to be grown, but none of whom are now living.   Louisa died at middle age, and was a member of the Methodist Episcopal church.   She was devoted to her family, a loving mother and a good woman, and bore her husband six children: Margaret (now the widow of William Dickson), Albert (now living in Louisiana, where he follows teaching.   He served in the Confederate army in the Civil war, and was a member of Col. J. N. Jones' regiment.   He was taken prisoner at Vicksburg, where he was paroled); Robert H. (who was born and reared in Amite county, and served in the late war in the Forty-Fourth Mississippi regiment [Confederate], first known as ' Blair's battalion," and was in the battle of Shiloh, where Colonel Blair was killed.   Robert H. was wounded through the thigh by a gun-shot, was taken prisoner, but soon after made his escape by assistance of the Confederate wagon-master.   He was recaptured at Brookhaven and soon after paroled.   He surrendered at the close of the war at Macon, Ga.   He then returned to Amite county, where he resided until within the past few years, and then became a resident of Wilkinson county).   Charles C. was born and reared in Amite county, and in 1855 began clerking for H. S. & T. W. White, of Woodville, but at the breaking out of the war enlisted in the Ninth Louisiana battalion as a private.   He afterward joined the First Louisiana regiment and was in a number of skirmishes, and was paroled at Clinton, La., in 1865.   He then returned to the home place and engaged in farming in Amite county until 1873.   He then engaged in merchandising in old Centerville, and came to his present place in 1884, where he has since conducted the business.   He was commissioned postmaster of old Centerville in 1859, and recontinued during the war by the Confederacy.   He was married to Miss Mary E. Robinson, a native of Franklin county, Miss., who died November, 1857, by whom he had three children: Robert G., Louisa C. and James H.   The latter is yet living, now in Amite county, but the other two died in infancy.   The second marriage of Charles C. was to Sarah E. Anderson, the daughter of J. W. Anderson, of Amite county.   She was born and raised in Amite county, and is a niece of Judge Smiley, as was also his first wife.   They are leading members of the Presbyterian church, in which he is a deacon and one of the liberal supporters.   He is a member of the A. F. and A. M., Centerville lodge No. 351.   In politics he is a democrat.   He devotes his time and attention to his store.   Mrs. Germany is a very estimable and accomplished lady, a pure and devoted Christian.   Cornelia, the next child of the subject of this memoir, was married to R. J. Bownan, a prominent lawyer of Louisiana.   For a time she lived at Clinton, but afterward moved to Alexandria, La., where she died, leaving one son, Ira, who is now a physician of Texas, a graduate of the Philadelphia medical college.   Harriet C., the next child, died in 1887 near Port Hudson, La.   The subject's second wife was a Mrs. Norwood, of Clinton, La., by which union were born four children, one of whom died aged seven years; the others are yet living.   Mary is the wife of John R. Carter, of old Centerville. James N. lives on the old home place, and William M. is at old Centerville and has charge of the old home of his father, and is a successful farmer. This family is one of the most highly respected in this portion of the state.

On May 19, 1808, Samuel J. Gholson was born in Madison county, Ky. In 1817 he was taken to Alabama, where he grew to manhood, receiving a meager education. Later he studied law under Peter Martin, of Russellville, Ala., and in 1819 was admitted to the bar, and continued to practice until 1830, when he removed to Athens, Miss. Three years later he was sent to the legislature, and was continued there until 1836, when he was elected to congress for a special term, and in 1837 was regularly reëlected. As a congressman he was active, able and aggressive. In 1838 he was constituted a judge of the United States district court, which position he occupied with unusual vigor until the Civil war broke out, when he resigned his position, and soon after became a member of the state secession convention. He promptly enlisted as a private, was soon elected captain, and saw active service. He fought at Fort Donelson, where he was wounded, and upon his recovery raised another company and joined General Price at Iuka and Corinth, receiving another severe wound at the latter battle. In 1863 he was appointed major-general of state troops with instructions to guard the railroad property of the state. He was in many small engagements, and was wounded at Denver and at Egypt, losing his arm at the last-named engagement. After the war he resumed his practice, but in 1866 was elected to the legislature. He continued his practice, but in 1878 was sent to the legislature again, and was chosen speaker of the house.

Dr. Samuel Creed Gholson, Sr., Holly Springs, Miss., who has retired from the active duties of his profession, is a thorough student, a deep reasoner and thinker, and, being ardently attached to his profession, he still visits in consultation his former patrons when desired to do so, and continues his membership of the State Medical association. He was born in Cumberland couty, Va., on the 23d of September, 1828, and is the elder of two children of Judge William Y. Gholson and Ann Jane (Taylor) Gholson, also natives of the Old Dominion. His father graduated at Princeton, N. J., studied law with Chancellor Creed Taylor in Virginia, was admitted to the bar, married, and at once began practicing his profession. In 1834, having lost his wife at the birth of a daughter, now Mrs. Ann Jane (Gholson) Glasgow, and residing at this date in Richmond, Va., he left his native state and finally located at Pontotoc, Miss., where he secured a large practice. He was one of the organizers and one of the earliest trustees of the university of Mississippi. He married in second marriage Miss Elvira Wright, a daughter of Judge Wright, of Pontotoc, Miss. This union also resulted in the birth of two children, a daughter, now deceased, who married Hon. E. W. Kittridge, a prominent lawyer, of Cincinnati, O., and a son, William Y. Gholson, Jr., who graduated just before the civil war, at Harvard university, Mass., entered the union army as adjutant of an Ohio regiment and was killed in battle. In 1844 he removed to Cincinnati, O.; practiced his profession successfully there; was elected judge of the superior court of that city, and finally was appointed to the bench of the supreme court of Ohio. He retired from the bench with the highest encomiums of press and public. His father, Hon. Thomas Gholson, was a member of congress from Virginia, and died at the age of thirty-three years from the effects of a wound received while acting as volunteer aid on the staff of General Porter, in the war of 1812. His mother, Ann Yates, was a daughter of William Yates, a colonel in the revolutionary war and granddaughter of the Rev. William Yates, president of William and Mary college in 1764. She married, in second marriage, the Rt. Rev. George W. Freeman, bishop of Arkansas and Texas. Dr. Gholson's maternal grandfather, Samuel Taylor, was born in Kentucky, his father having been one of the earliest settlers of that state from Virginia. He removed to

Virginia, read law with his uncle, Chancellor Taylor, and, after beginning the practice, located finally in Richmond, Va., where he attained great success and prominence in his profession. The doctor was reared in Virginia and received his academic education in the schools of Richmond and Cincinnati. After several years of office study, he attended lectures and graduated at Richmond in 1851. He then crossed the ocean to France, studied at Paris for two years, returned to the United States and opened an office in Cincinnati, O. In September, 1854, being threatened with pulmonary disease, he removed south to Holly Springs, Miss., where he resumed practice and has since resided. In March, 1861, he was appointed by President Davis surgeon of the Ninth Mississippi regiment, stationed at Pensacola, Fla., where, in October, 1861, he was captured while in pursuit of his official duties, after the night battle on Santa Rosa island; liberated in a short time, but paroled to leave Florida. Returning home, he was given charge of St. Thomas general hospital, a military hospital at Holly Springs, Miss. In the fall of 1862, having transferred the effects of the hospital to Jackson, Miss., he was assigned to duty as brigade-surgeon with General Chalmers' cavalry command; but, his health being already impaired by hospital duty, he was unable to bear the exposure incident to cavalry service, and he resigned and returned home. He was married in 1855 to Miss Mary H. Caruthers, daughter of Dr. S. O. Caruthers, who was born in Virginia, but was reared and educated at Holly Springs, Miss. Eight children born of this union are now living: William Yates, druggist; Samuel C., Jr., practicing physician; Edwin, practicing lawyer, of Cincinnati, O.; Arthur and Cary F., in business in Holly Springs; and Anna J., Norman G. and Mary Virginia, minors.

The Hon. W. D. Gibbs, of Bentonia, is a native of Yazoo county, Miss., born in August, 1839, and the eldest of a family of eight children. His parents were Judge Q. D, and Sarah A. (Dorsey) Gibbs, natives of Tennessee and Kentucky respectively. The father came to Mississippi in 1837, and settled in Yazoo City, where he entered upon the practice of his profession; he became one of the most prominent lawyers of the place. When the Civil war broke out he went out as captain of a company, which office he held until his death, which occurred July 1, 1862. He was probate judge in the early part of his life, and at the time of his death was a member of the state legislature from Yazoo county. His father, Gen. G. W. Gibbs, was a noted lawyer of Nashville, Tenn., where he practiced for thirty years. The maternal grandfather was Charles Dorsey, one of the pioneers of Kentucky. Our subject received his literary training at the University of Nashville, Tenn., and the University of Virginia, and in 1859 he received a diploma from the Lebanon Law school, of Tennessee. He was married in January, 1860, to Miss Louisa Johnson, of Yazoo county, a daughter of John Johnson. Five children have been born of this union: Lula, Quesney D., Washington D., Lee, and John. Mrs. Gibbs' father was a Mississippian, and a wealthy planter. Mr. Gibbs was captured during the war, in 1863, and was carried to Camp Morton, Ind., where he was held for thirteen months. He is a democrat in his political opinions, and has taken an active interest in the movements of the party. He was elected state senator in 1877, but refused to be a candidate for re-nomination in 1881. He was elected to represent Yazoo and Holmes counties in 1885, and served his constituents with fidelity and marked ability. Mr. Gibbs was a soldier in the late war, enlisting in company K, Col. Wirt Adams' regiment of cavalry, and serving until the close of the conflict. He has been successful in his business operations, and is now the owner of twenty-six hundred acres of land. He is a conspicuous figure in the work of the Farmers' Alliance, and has made several able speeches and written some very scholarly articles upon this subject. In fact, there has been no movement of importance in the county which has had for its object the uplifting of the people, in which Mr.

Gibbs has not taken a deep interest. He is one of the men who have made many efforts to promote the welfare of the community, and without whom civilization would, indeed, be of slow growth.

Charles W. Gibson, of Aberdeen, Monroe county, Miss., is a native of Oktibbeha county, Miss., and was born August 31, 1855. He is the son of William W. and Mary K. (Rogers) Gibson, natives of Vermont and Tennessee. The father was a schoolteacher in his early days, and afterward a merchant, coming to Mississippi in the thirties, where the greater part of his life was spent, and where he held some county offices. He died in Philadelphia in 1876, but the mother is still living. She has six living children: O. A., Charles W., J. A., S. W. Gibson, Mrs. F. E. Stevens and Mrs. L. G. Joiner. The subject of our sketch was reared in his native county, attending school and working on a farm until he was fifteen years of age, when he removed to West Point, Clay county, Miss., where he clerked in a store, and later was employed by the Mobile and Ohio railroad as a night watchman, but was soon promoted to the position of assistant agent and telegraph operator, which he held for two years, and was then made agent at Shuqualak, Miss., and held this position until 1881, when he was promoted to a similar position for the same road, at Aberdeen, Miss., in which capacity he served them for four years, when he entered upon a mercantile life in a copartnership with Mr. T. S. Cunningham, under the firm name of Cunningham & Gibson, who are still doing a profitable business. Subsequently he accepted the position of general Southern agent for the Evansville & Terre Haute railroad, which he held for two years, and was then offered, and accepted, the position of general cotton agent by the Mobile & Ohio railroad, with headquarters at Aberdeen, his jurisdiction extending over the entire cotton traffic of this company. He still holds this responsible position. In February, 1890, he organized the Gibson-Moore Manufacturing company, and is the secretary and treasurer of it. This thriving company manufactures spokes and farm wagons, and employ fifty men. Mr. Gibson is entirely a self-made man, and is recognized as a live, energetic business man, worthy of the high success he has attained. He is a member of the Masonic order and Knights of Honor. He was married in 1879 to Miss Alice H. Beasly, a native of Macon, Miss., and at the time a resident of Shuqualak, Miss., by whom he has three children: Walter B., Annie M. and Charles R. Mr. Gibson and wife are both zealous members of the Missionary Baptist church, in which he is a deacon.

J. G. W. Gibson, of Benton county, Miss., whose postoffice address is Potts Camp, Marshall county, Miss., was born in Monroe county, Miss., in 1836, the eldest of four children born to William W. and Anna (Burdine) Gibson. His father is thought to be a native of Alabama; his mother was born in South Carolina, dying in Mississippi in 1886. Mr. Gibson was reared principally in Tennessee, and began life for himself at the age of seventeen. He was a mill hand working for ordinary day wages, in which he continued for about fifteen years. In 1855 he went to Texas and worked there in the milling business for one and one-half years, returning to Tennessee in 1857, and doing the same kind of work for two years more, when he removed to Tishomingo county, Miss., where he was employed still in mill work until the outbreak of the war. In 1861 he enlisted in company I, One Hundred and Fifty-fourth Tennessee infantry, attached to the army of Tennessee, and participated in the battles of Belmont, Shiloh, Richmond, Prairieville, Murfreesboro, Missionary ridge, Chickamauga, and was on the campaign from Dalton to Atlanta, Ga. He was wounded three times—at Atlanta, Shiloh and Murfreesboro. In the engagement last mentioned he was shot through the neck; at Atlanta he was shot through the nose, the ball passing downward through the mouth and jaw, piercing his tongue and destroying several of his

teeth. He was in the hospital at Macon, Ga., about three months. At Murfreesboro he
was captured and kept prisoner for several months at Nashville, until he was finally exchanged
at City Point, Va., and returned to his command, with which he served until the close of the
war. At the time of the surrender of the large company of one hundred and four with
which he started out at the beginning of the hostilities only three men—B. A. McGaughey,
J. P. Horton and himself—remained. After the war he returned to Mississippi and
resumed the milling and lumber business in Tishomingo county. He was married in 1867 to
Mary J. Milford, and had two sons—John F. and William T. (deceased). His wife died in
1882, and in 1887 he married Louisa J. Dean, who died in Benton county, January 30, 1888.
While a resident of Tishomingo county, Mr. Gibson owned one-half interest in a large sawmill in which an extensive lumber business was carried on. In 1887 he bought his partner's
interest in this concern, and moved the machinery to Benton county, where he now has a mill
with a capacity of ten thousand feet of lumber per day. He sells annually one million five
hundred thousand feet of lumber. In connection with his sawmill he owns and operates a
planingmill. The machinery of both of these mills is valued at about $3,000. He employs
twenty men regularly, and keeps forty head of cattle, which he uses in his log and lumber
business. He is the owner of eight hundred and fifty acres of land, mostly heavily timbered,
and has a fine residence and eleven tenement houses and a large commissary building on his
mill property. He buys his supplies at wholesale and sells them to his hands, thus affording
them a convenient means of obtaining the necessities of life without going to a distance to
procure them. He is a life-long lumberman, and what he possesses was acquired by industry, economy and thrift, as he started in the world with nothing and toiled under discouraging circumstances, with a perseverance and a brave spirit that has won for him the success he
has attained. He has always been too busy to dabble in politics, and never had any political
aspirations, though his interest in the public welfare is deep and abiding. He is a member
of the Methodist Episcopal church South, and has been a liberal contributor to all public
enterprises, as well as to the establishment of schools and churches.

Hon. J. M. Gibson is a well-known and eminent lawyer of this section and is prosecuting attorney of the Eleventh district. He was born in the county in which he is now residing, July 26, 1856, being the second child born to J. M. and Eliza C. (Stevens) Gibson, the
former a native of Mississippi and the latter of South Carolina. The paternal ancestors
were among the first settlers about Natchez, coming from North Carolina in 1776. The
paternal grandfather, David D. Gibson, was born in Adams county, Mississippi, and was
twice a member of the state legislature from that county, but afterwards removed to Warren
county, first settling in the southern part and dying soon after. His son, James M. Gibson,
father of the subject of this sketch, was an active and prosperous planter, and in his political views was a democrat. He was married three times and was the father of twelve children, seven of whom are now living. Three of his sons were soldiers in the Confederate
army, enlisting as soon as they were sixteen years of age. They all served throughout the
war, but David, who served in Harris' brigade, died in Texas in 1887. The father died in
1889 after a long residence in Warren county, his wife passing from life in 1874, a member
of the Baptist church, her husband having been a member of the Methodist Episcopal
church. In the common schools of Warren county J. M. Gibson, whose name heads this
sketch, was educated, acquiring a good practical knowledge of the world of books. In
1878 he began the study of law in the city of St. Louis, but the following year he returned
to Vicksburg, and on the 7th of February, 1879, he was admitted to the bar and at once
entered upon his practice. In the fall of that year he was elected to the state legislature

from Warren county and served with distinction and to the satisfaction of all concerned for two terms, leaving behind him a record of faithfulness, ability and carefully performed duty. After the close of his legislative career he formed a law partnership with Judge A. W. Brien, which was one of the ablest law firms of the county, until the death of Mr. Brien in 1885. In 1889 Mr. Gibson became associated in the practice of his profession with Joe D. Bien, they now constituting a very strong legal firm. In 1887 Mr. Gibson was elected to the office of prosecuting attorney and has proved the right man in the right place. He is a conscientious student and is earnest and painstaking in the preparation of his cases, his clients' interests never being neglected. He is decidedly literary in his tastes and has contributed both prose and poetry of much merit to the popular journals and magazines of the day. As a lawyer he has made a fine record for himself, and his section will undoubtedly have further use for him in future days. He is very social in his tastes and is at all times a courteous and polished gentleman in his business relations as well as in society and by his own fireside. He is a member of the A. F. & A. M., the K. of P. and the Elks. He was married in 1884 to Mrs. M. E. (Mower) Spears, a native of the state of Mississippi.

Dr. J. W. Gilbert, physician and surgeon, Verona, Miss., has been identified with the medical profession of Lee county since 1878, and is entitled to mention in this record of the leading men of the state of Mississippi. He was born in Lauderdale county, Ala., in 1845, and is a son of W. A. and Sarah E. (Oliver) Gilbert. The father was a native of South Carolina, born in 1814, and was a member of one of the leading families of the state. He was a merchant by occupation, and politically affiliated with the whig party, but was opposed to the Civil war; however, he espoused the Southern cause. He was a son of John Gilbert. He was a member of the Baptist church, and a member of both the Blue lodge and chapter of the Masonic fraternity. His wife was born in Alabama in 1824, and was a daughter of William Oliver; she died of yellow fever in 1878. They reared a family of six sons: Albert A., Adoniram J., Joseph E.; twins, Henry C. and Daniel W.; and J. W., who is the subject of this notice. Dr. Gilbert's early life was spent in Lawrence county, Ala., where he attended the common schools and acquired his elementary education. In 1862, at the age of sixteen years, he enlisted in company G, Fourth Alabama cavalry, and saw much active service, being engaged a large part of the time as a scout in the enemy's rear. At Selma, just before the close of the war, most of his command were captured, but he succeeded in escaping. When hostilities ceased, and he turned his attention to the pursuits of civilization, he took up the study of medicine under Calvin A. Crow, an old practitioner of Moulton, Ala., and ex-vice-president of the State association. In 1868 he attended lectures at Louisville, Ky., and in 1870 he was graduated from Bellevue Medical college, New York city. He then located at Tuscumbia, Ala., where he practiced some years. He was secretary of the North Alabama Medical association for four years, and served as president of the same body for one year. In January, 1878, he removed to Verona, Miss., and soon established himself in a fine practice. He is personally well suited to the profession he has chosen, and he has given himself the benefit of all the opportunities available in this country. He is a very popular man, both in his profession and out of it, and has a host of friends and admirers. He is a member of the Knights of Honor, and of the Masonic order. He has been a member of the Baptist church since 1859, and in his political opinions he is a democrat. The doctor was married in 1866 to Miss Laura Harris, a daughter of William and Nancy (Stovall) Harris; she died within a few months after her marriage. He was married again in 1870, to Naomi Harris, a sister to his first wife. Three children were born of this union: Minnie, Edward and Thomas. Minnie married H. B. Cobb, and Edward married a Miss McPherson. Dr. Gilbert lost the mother of these children January 1, 1880, and his third union was to Miss Ella Anthony, a daughter of Dr. J. A. Anthony, of Terrell, Texas. She is a native of Tennessee, and was educated in Nashville, Tenn., by Dr. Fanning, her mother dying during her childhood. Two children have been born of this marriage: Cecile and James A. The subject of this notice is president of the Lee County Medical society and a member of the Mississippi State Medical association.

Judge J. D. Gilland, judge of the ninth circuit court district of Mississippi, was born in South Carolina in 1849, the fourth in a family of six children born to Rev. J. R. and Mary C. (Gibbes) Gilland, the former a Presbyterian minister and a teacher by calling, being a professor of mathematics in Davidson college, North Carolina, having also taught in many other places. In 1871 he came to Mississippi, and for several years preached the gospel in Hinds county, but died in South Carolina in 1877, his widow still surviving him. The paternal grandfather, Thomas Gilland, was born in Ireland, but came to the United States and settled near Chambersburg, Pa., where the rest of his days were spent, and where his son, Rev. J. R. Gilland, was born and reared, his education being received in Jefferson college. The mother's people were descended from Robert Gibbes, a colonial governor of South Carolina, and the maternal grandfather, Wilmot S. Gibbes, was a physician of considerable note in Chester district, South Carolina. Mrs. Mary C. (Gibbes) Gilland was a granddaughter of Chancellor De Saussure, of the Palmetto state. Judge J. D. Gilland was educated by his father in his youth, and began life for himself as a teacher. He went to Arkansas in 1868, and followed this calling in Mount Holly, Camden and College Hill, after which he went to Missouri, and read law at Palmyra. In September, 1871, he came to Mississippi, and settled at Raymond, where he continued the study of law, and was admitted to the bar in May, 1872, and began practicing his calling at that place. He soon moved to Vicksburg, however, and was located here in constant practice until he was appointed to the bench in February, 1890. He has been very successful in adjusting the differences of the people of this district, is an eminent and able jurist, and is deservedly popular. He is a self-made man, and for a time was one of the leading members of the Vicksburg bar, but is now one of the most popular judges of the state. He was one of the incorporators of the People's Savings bank, of Vicksburg, of the Hills City Oil mills, is a stockholder in the Vicksburg Compress association, and is the owner of a fine home on Cherry street. He is a member of the Knights of Honor, and is an elder in the Presbyterian church, in which he and his family are members. He was married in 1872 to Mrs. Emily J. (Lundie) Sherard.

That substantial and highly respected citizen, William A. Gillespie, Greenwood, Miss., is a native of Pennsylvania, born in Mercer county, December 25, 1832. His father, John Gillespie, was also a native of the Keystone state, born in Washington county about the year 1800. Samuel Gillespie, the father of John, removed with his family to Mercer county at an early day, and was prominently identified with the settlement and development of that county. For thirty years he was a magistrate, and was a man honored by all who knew him. The Gillespies are of Scotch-Irish descent, and were among the earliest settlers of the state of Pennsylvania. John Gillespie passed his youth in Mercer county, Penn., and was there married to Sarah Clark, a native of New Jersey, and a daughter of Samuel Clark, one of the pioneers of Mercer county. Mr. Gillespie was a trader and speculator, and for a number of years was engaged in boating and trading on the Mississippi, Ohio, and Yazoo rivers; he owned and operated a trading boat for a long time. He owned a store at Black Hawk, Miss., where he carried on an extensive trade. His death occurred in 1846; his widow lived until 1880. William A Gillespie is the third born of a family of seven children who grew to mature years: One brother, John W. G., is in the tobacco trade in Philadelphia, Penn.; J. J. C. Gillespie is in the railroad business in Chicago (these two gentlemen were in the Federal army during the Civil war); the fourth son is engaged in the mercantile trade in Pennsylvania. William A. passed his youth in acquiring an education and in learning the carpenter's trade. In 1852 he came South, being then only twenty years of age, and located at Greenwood. He at once engaged in the business of building and contracting, and continued this work for a period covering several years. In 1861 he enlisted in the Confederate army, joining the twentieth Mississippi volunteer infantry as a private; he was made sergeant, and his regiment joined the Army of Virginia, but was soon transferred to the Western army. He was afterward put on detached duty at Mobile, Ala., and there he worked in the shipyards, assisting in the building of the ram Tennessee. He participated in the engagement at Fort Donelson, was taken prisoner and sent to Chicago, where he was held at Camp Douglas for several months; he was paroled, returned to Mobile, and remained there until the close of the war. After the declaration of peace he came back to Greenwood, where he again took up the duties of life. He has built up a business second to none in the community. He has erected a great many residences and business houses in this and adjoining counties, and by his faithful and conscientious dealing he has won for himself a a reputation which would credit any calling in life. He is conservative in his political opinions, but acts with the democratic party. He has represented the people in several local offices, has been a member of the town board, and of the board of supervisors, being president of the latter body. In the discharge of all public duties he has shown that same fidelity which has characterized all his transactions in life. He was married in De Soto county, Miss., November 14, 1855, to Miss Rachel Emma Hudson, a native of Tennessee, but reared in the north of Mississippi. Her father, John C. Hudson, was prominently identified with the early settlement of Marshall county, Miss., and was in the battle of New Orleans with General Jackson. Four children have been born to Mr. and Mrs. Gillespie: Charles C. is assessor of Le Flore county and a merchant of Greenwood; Carrie E., a graduate of the State university of Oxford, Miss., is also engaged in the mercantile trade at Greenwood, where she carries a full line of books, stationery and notions (she is doing a good business, and furnishes yet another example of woman's ability to enter the arena of trade with man); William D. is a law student in Texas, and Sallie E. is a student at the college at Columbus, Miss. Six children of Mr. and Mrs. Gillespie died either in infancy or early childhood. The family are members of the Methodist Episcopal church, where they are active, consistent workers. Fraternally Mr. Gillespie is identified with the Masonic order, being a member of the blue lodge and chapter; he has represented his lodge at the grand lodge of Mississippi for thirty years, and is well and favorably known in Masonic circles throughout the state. He is one of the leading citizens of Greenwood, and a man whose genial manners and upright dealings have won a host of friends.

Z. T. Gilmer, farmer, Hazel Dell, Miss., enjoys the reputation of being a substantial and progressive farmer and an intelligent and thoroughly posted man in all public affairs. His father, Robert Gilmer, was a native Virginian, and when a young man started with his parents to Texas. He stopped, however, in Chickasaw county, Miss., but the parents moved on to the Lone Star state, and the father died on the road. The mother located in Texas, and there her death occurred in 1878, at the advanced age of one hundred and one years. The father of our subject was married in Chickasaw county, Miss., to Miss Sallie Griffin, a native of Mississippi, and their union resulted in the birth of eleven children, Z. T. Gilmer being seventh in order of birth. The father removed to Alcorn county, Miss., bought land, and engaged in farming, but in connection also carried on the carpenter trade. He was an honest, practical farmer, and never cared for official honors. His wife died at home, near Rienzi, in 1862, and the father was married the second time, in 1865, to Mrs. Amelia Slaughter, a widow with three children. This marriage resulted in the birth of three children. Z. T. Gilmer was born in Rienzi, Alcorn county, Miss., on the 11th of October, 1853, and was but a small boy when his father married his second wife. Thinking his stepmother unkind to him, Z. T. did not live at home, but, with his three sisters, went to live with an elder brother, who was married. He remained with his brother until eighteen years of age, and in the meantime moved with him to Alabama, where, when but eighteen years of age, he was married to Miss Sarah C. McDonald, a native of Georgia. Her parents moved from Georgia to Alabama when she was small, and her father was a railroad man. Mr. Gilmer remained in Alabama until 1890, and then bought his present farm in Prentiss county, Miss. This consists of six hundred and forty acres of excellent land, with about one hundred acres under cultivation, and it is one of the best improved and most beautiful farms in the county. Mr. Gilmer is progressive and enterprising, and a very successful farmer. During the three years he was a resident of Birmingham, Ala., he worked at the carpenter trade and followed bridge building for the Louisville & Nashville railroad for ten years. He and Mrs. Gilmer are members of the Baptist church, and, although but comparatively new residents in the county, they have already won a host of warm friends. They have no children, but Mr. Gilmer is a liberal contributor to schools, churches, etc.

Col. Isaac N. Gilruth, Yazoo City, Miss., has been prominently identified with the fortunes of Yazoo City and Yazoo county since 1865, at which time he located there. He was born in Scioto county, Ohio, May 24, 1841, and is the seventh of the eight children born to William and Rebecca (Austin) Gilruth, natives of Virginia. His father was reared in Ohio, and was engaged in agricultural pursuits. He was a man of fine business qualifications, and became one of the wealthy men of the Scioto valley. He lived a quiet life devoted to his family. All of his children lived to mature age, and each one had a liberal education. He died in 1878, at the age of eighty-four years. His parents were Thomas and Mary (Ingles) Gilruth, natives of Perthshire, Scotland. Thomas Gilruth was one of the pioneers of Ohio, and was one of the early settlers on the French grant in the Scioto valley. Isaac N. was reared in the Buckeye state and received his education in the common schools of his native county. The breaking out of the late Civil war prevented his pursuing a college course. In 1861 he enlisted in company F, Twenty-seventh Ohio volunteer infantry, as lieutenant, and was promoted to the rank of colonel and brevet brigadier-general, holding all the offices from that of lieutenant to the last named. He participated in the battles of Corinth, Resaca, around Atlanta, and was with Sherman on his famous march to the sea; he was in the fight at Bentonville, the last of the war. He was mustered out at Louisville, Ky., after which he returned to his home. In the same year, 1865, he came to Yazoo county, as before stated. He has since been very extensively engaged in planting and merchandizing, and has one of the largest plantation supply stores in Yazoo City and doing an annual business of $150,000. He owns a private cotton warehouse having a capacity of twelve hundred bales, and is one of the largest cotton dealers in the place. He is also a director of the Bank of Yazoo City, as well as of the Yazoo City Oil Works company. He is the largest taxpayer in the county, and furnishes an excellent example of what a Northern man may accomplish in the South. Colonel Gilruth was married in 1872 to Miss Julia M. Devlin, a native of Mississippi and a daughter of Col. J. M. Devlin, of Winona, Miss., a large cotton factor of that place. Six

F. A. Montgomery

children have been born of this union: Pauline, Georgiana, Willie, Isaac N., Jr., Lockie and Thomas K. Mrs. Gilruth is a worthy member of the Presbyterian church. Although Colonel Gilruth was a soldier in the Union army, he is deeply interested in the South and its prosperity, and is highly esteemed by his fellowcitizens.

Max Ginsburger, merchant, of the well known firm of Ginsburger & Wile, leading business men of Grenada, is a self-made man in every sense of the term and deserves the encomiums of all for his pluck and energy. His life affords an example that well might be imitated by the young men of to-day, for at an early age he was thrown on his own resources and had to fight his own way in life. He was born in Jeffersonville, Ind., in 1852, and was the son of Morris and Theresa (Wile) Ginsburger, natives of Bavaria, Germany, where they resided until 1848, when they crossed the ocean to America. They then followed peddling until the death of the father in 1854. The mother, who is now sixty-nine years of age, resides in Grenada with her son Max. There were only two children born to this marriage, our subject, who is the elder, and Mollie, who also resides in Grenada. The latter's birth occurred about two months after the death of the father. Max Ginsburger commenced life in Louisville, Ky., as a bootblack and newsboy, and in 1865 came to Mississippi, where he engaged as salesman in the store of Mr. Wile. He continued in that position until 1875, when he became a partner, forming the above firm. Success is the best test of merit in this life, and Mr. Ginsburger is in every way a successful man. The firm does an annual business of $100,000 and handles about three thousand bales of cotton yearly. Mr. Ginsburger is president of the Compress company, is one of the directors of the Merchants' bank and is also engaged in planting in this and adjoining counties. He was a member of Gov. Lowry's staff in 1887 and 1890, and was commissioned major while serving as aid-de-camp. He was chairman of the democratic executive committee of this county for four years and also chairman of the district democratic executive committee for the same length of time. He was a member of the congressional committee for four years and has been a member of the board of aldermen of Grenada. He is a stanch democrat and takes a decided interest in all political affairs as well as everything else pertaining to the welfare of the county or state. He is a member of Grenada lodge No. 6, I. O. O. F., and of the Knights of Pythias, lodge No. 8. He is a very popular man in the county, and no one has a larger speaking acquaintance than he. The compress was bought in 1881 at a cost of $17,000 by Nichols & Wilder, succeeded by Mr. Ginsburger. This has a capacity of four hundred and fifty bales of cotton per day.

Robert Gordon, planter, was born in Davidson county, Tenn., in 1844, son of Robert Bell and Sarah A. Gordon. His father was born in 1817, in Davidson county. He was a graduate of a well-known educational institute at Nashville, Tenn., and for several years, after completing his education, was salesman in different stores in Mississippi and Tennessee. In 1840 he married Sarah A. Ogborn, of Tennessee, who bore him seven children, all of whom are dead, with the exception of Robert Gordon, the subject of our sketch. Robert Gordon was the son of James and Margaret (Bell) Gordon, the former born in Scotland, in 1779, and emigrating to America in 1800, locating in Nashville, Tenn. He was three times married— first, to Miss Bell; second, to Miss Huesdon; third, to Miss Isabella McNeir. He was a man of considerable wealth, owning several steamboats, one of which was the Brandywine. Besides these interests, he was also a merchant and successful farmer. He died in 1858. James Gordon's brother, uncle to the late Robert B. Gordon, was also a native of Scotland, who came to America in 1810, settling in Mississippi in 1835. Before the war he was known as one of the wealthiest men in the South, if not in the Union. At one time he paid taxes on more than $1,000,000 worth of assessable property. He was the owner of five hundred slaves, and owned the site and laid out the city of Aberdeen, Miss., besides being the proprietor of the greater part of the land adjoining the town on the west. Robert Gordon received his education at the Kirkwood school, at Nashville, Tenn., and during all of his active career he led the life of a planter. He was married, in 1877, to Thrace Easley, and has two children, named Anna and Robert Easley. Mr. and Mrs. Gordon are devout members and helpful supporters of the Methodist Episcopal church, and Mr. Gordon is a member of the Knights of Honor, and is also identified with the Farmers' Alliance. For eight consecutive years he held the office of commissioner of elections, and has always taken an active part in the local political affairs. He was especially active in the political revolution of 1875, when the state was wrenched from the power of the carpet-baggers and redeemed to the democratic party. Soon after the outbreak of the war, Mr. Gordon enlisted in company C of the First Tennessee regiment, but closed his career as a cavalry scout. He took part in the battles of Missionary ridge, Cheat mountain, Chickamauga, Balte, and in the Georgia campaign. Thrace Easley, now Mrs. Gordon, was the daughter of Robert W. and Jane A. Easley. Her father was a planter early in life, but later read law, and engaged in the practice of that profession. Robert W. Easley, her brother, is practicing law in Florida.

Dr. Thomas Hill Gordon, a practicing physician and surgeon of Oakland, Yalobusha county, was born in Grenada in 1847. Grenada was then in Yalobusha county. Now it is in Grenada county. He was a son of Hilliard J. and Hannah Wright Gordon. His father was born in Anson county, N. C., in 1811. His mother, also a native of North Carolina, was born in 1824. In 1846, Mr. Gordon, then unmarried, removed to Carroll county, and Mrs. Gordon came with her parents to the same county soon after. They were married in Carroll county in 1846 and settled in Grenada, and have lived in that county ever since. Mr. Gordon was a carpenter, and then he became a planter, in which latter occupation he was fairly successful. He served in the militia during the Civil war. He was a member of the Masonic lodge at Grenada. Both he and his wife have been active workers in the church interests. Prof. James Gordon, grandfather of our subject, was of Scotch descent, but is thought to have been born in North Carolina, where he spent his life and became a prominent educator. He was for many years a magistrate and represented Anson county in the state legislature. Taken all in all, he was a prominent man in his part of the state. He reared a family of four sons and five daughters, of whom Hilliard J. was the only one who came to Mississippi. He was a man noted for great firmness of character, for successful teaching, an able conservator of such public interests as were entrusted to him. His grandfather on his mother's side was Thomas H. Wright, also a native of North Carolina, who lived in his native state until about 1827, when he removed to Carroll county, Miss., where he and his wife, who was Miss Pricilla Kinneair, both died, one about 1866, and the other 1886. He was a well-to-do planter, and he served his town as magistrate for many years. Our subject was the eldest of nine children, all but one of whom are living. Their names are as follows in the order of their nativity: Thomas Hill; Buckner, now a resident of North Carolina; William; Hilliard J.; Sallie, wife of Jacob Dubard of Grenada county; Susan, now Mrs. Willey Beard, also of Grenada county; Eliza, wife of W. B. Barnes, of the firm of Cuff & Barnes, merchants of Grenada county; Ellen, who died at the age of sixteen. The Doctor received his education principally at Grenada. From 1866 to 1870 he was successfully engaged in teaching school and in the prosecution of his medical studies. He read for his profession with the late Dr. W. W. Hall, of Grenada. In 1872 and 1873 he attended the Louisville Medical college. In 1875 he graduated from the medical college of Alabama at Mobile, and began the practice of his profession in Carroll county. Two years later, he moved to Grenada county, where he remained for one year, going thence to Tillatoba, where he made his home for four years, when he removed to Oakland, where he has built up a good practice and ranks among the best physicians of this section. He is a fellow of the Mississippi state medical association. In March, 1880, he married Miss Lizzie R., daughter of John and Mary A. E. Tatum, both natives of Georgia, in which state they were married in 1844, coming immediately after to Tallahatchie county, where they settled upon a small improvement, which they cultivated and so managed that it came to be known as one of the best farms thereabout. Upon this place they lived until 1882, since which time they have been residents of Oakland. Mr. Tatum is a man of good natural abilities and was fairly well educated. He began life with next to nothing, and has acquired a valuable property. He is of quiet disposition, industrious, friendly and universally esteemed for his fairness and honesty. He is now about seventy-two years old and with his wife is a member and attendant upon the services of the Methodist Episcopal church. They became the parents of eight children but one of whom lived: Mrs Gordon, who was born in Tallahatchie county. The Doctor is a member of the Masonic fraternity and has long been identified with the Oakland lodge No. 82, A. F. & A. M. He is also a member of the Grenada lodge of Knights of Pythias and of the Farmers' Alliance. He and his wife are also members and liberal supporters of the Methodist Episcopal church. Doctor and Mrs. Gordon, with Mr. and Mrs. Tatum—the latter's parents—are living as one family in Oakland and own together about three thousand acres of land, most of which is well cultivated, and they also own a valuable steam saw and gristmill. Like his father-in-law, the former started in life poor, but he has been persevering and energetic and has succeeded beyond his expectations. Upon their large plantation they produce about two hundred bales of cotton annually, besides a sufficient quantity of hay, corn and other farm products to supply the plantation. Mr. Tatum, who has passed his threescore years and ten, is personally supervising the plantation to a considerable extent. The Doctor stands high both in private and professional life, and has been more than ordinarily successful in his profession and financially. His wife is a graduate of the State female college, Memphis, Tenn., and a lady of education and refinement. Their sunny, Southern home is one of the pleasantest and most hospitable imaginable.

George Morgan Govan, secretary of state for the state of Mississippi, was born in the county of Marshall, now a part of Benton county, Miss., October 30, 1840, being a son of Andrew R. and Mary P. (Jones) Govan, the former of whom was a native of South Carolina, of which he was a prominent resident. He was educated at Columbia college, and became by occupation a planter, which calling he followed extensively. In 1826 he was elected to the United States congress from the Orangeburg district, where he was born and reared, and was contemporaneous with Clay, Webster and Calhoun. He retired from congress and active politics to give his whole time to his large agricultural interests, and after living for some time in Tennessee, emigrated to Holly Springs, Miss., where he had previously purchased a large tract of land. He remained there engaged in planting up to the time of his death, which occurred in June, 1841. His father, Andrew, was a native of Scotland. Mary P. Jones was born in New Berne, N. C., and was there reared by her uncle, Eaton Pugh, a prominent man of that state. Her father was a ship merchant, of English ancestry. She died in 1888 at the advanced age of eighty-eight years. There were born to this couple eight children: Eaton P., Daniel C., John J., William H., Andrew R., George M., Sally G. and Bettie C. Sally G. was married to Christopher H. Mott, who was the second brigadier-general appointed from Mississippi to serve the Confederacy. It was General Mott who raised the first war regiment in Mississippi for the entire war—the Nineteenth Mississippi—of which he was made colonel, with L. Q. C. Lamar, his law partner, as lieutenant-colonel. He was made brigadier-general in 1862, and was killed at Williamsburg on the retreat from Yorktown. His body was temporarily buried at Richmond, but was subsequently brought to Holly Springs, where it is now reposing. He was a soldier in the Mexican war with Jefferson Davis in the First Mississippi. Eaton P. died in 1880, and Andrew R. was killed at the battle of Chickamauga in 1863, holding the rank, at the time of his death, of lieutenant-colonel of the Seventeenth Mississippi, in Humphrey's brigade. George M. Govan's early life was like that of most planters' sons. He attended the old fieldschools when they were in session, and otherwise occupied his time in social and sportive amusements. At the age of fifteen he was sent to St. Thomas hall at Holly Springs, which was founded by the celebrated Dr. Francis L. Hawks, and this school he attended until the war came on, when he enlisted in the service March 27, 1861. He was mustered into company B, Ninth Mississippi, at Holly Springs, and sent to Florida, where the regiment was organized, and remained at that point until February, 1862, when the regiment was ordered to Cumberland Gap. The men had enlisted for twelve months and at the expiration of that time they were mustered out of service, this being on the 12th of March. Mr. Govan returned home, raised a company of new men, and was elected first lieutenant. It was mustered into company I, Ninth Mississippi, at Corinth, which regiment formed a part of General Chalmer's brigade. He was subsequently raised to the rank of captain. When E. C. Walthall was made brigadier-general, Captain Govan was appointed inspector-general on his staff. Upon General Walthall's promotion to major-general, he was made inspector-general of Walthall's division, in which position he served until the reorganization of the army—a month before the close of the war—when he was made major of the Twenty-fourth Mississippi regiment, which was formed by the consolidation of the Twenty-fourth, Twenty-seventh, Twenty-ninth, Thirtieth and Twenty-fourth, the regiments originally composing General Walthall's brigade; Major Govan served in this capacity until the surrender of General Johnston's army at Greensboro, N. C., when he returned home. His first engagement after he left Pensacola was at Mumfordsville, Ky., in September, 1862. In this fight his company lost heavily, all the officers but himself being wounded, also many of the men. Following this was the Kentucky campaign under General Bragg. His command missed the fight at Perryville, having been sent to head off Gen. Jefferson C. Davis of the Federal army, who was moving to form a junction with General Buell. The next engagement he was in was at Murfreesboro, in December, 1863, in which fight his regiment held the extreme right the first day and suffered severely. They fell back to Shelbyville, where Major Govan, having been placed on the staff of General Walthall, reported to that officer for duty. As a staff officer he participated in the battles of Chickamauga, Lookout mountain and Missionary ridge. Then followed the Atlanta campaign, in which he took part in the battles of Resaca, Cassville, Kenesaw mountain, New Hope church, Peach Tree creek, and the fight on the 21st and 22d around Atlanta and Jonesboro. From there his regiment joined Hood in his march back to Tennessee, and in their movements their troops used the same breastworks that had protected the Federal army but a few days before in their march to Atlanta. They crossed the Tennessee river at Florence, where followed the battle of Franklin, and the first and second days' fights around Nashville, which forced the retreat of Hood, the recrossing of the Tennessee into Mississippi to Tupelo, where his army rested until ordered to North Carolina, where General Johnston again took command. The battle of Bentonville soon followed, which ended the military career of Major Govan. He then returned home to more agreeable pursuits, feeling that though the cause for which he had offered his life, and had given four years of valuable time, had been defeated, yet he had discharged his duty faithfully and to the best of his ability. He was conspicuous in action for his coolness and bravery, and was beloved by his men.

After his return home he engaged in farming and took an active part in politics against the radical party, and when the democrats came into power in 1876 he was elected clerk of the house of representatives, being reëlected in 1877–8. At the expiration of his term he retired to private life, and once more began giving his attention to his farming interests. In 1880 he was appointed secretary and treasurer of the Mississippi Valley company, a corporation owned by the Illinois Central railroad company, and moved to Macomb City, Pike county, Miss., where he and his family still reside, to assume the duties of the office. In 1884 he was elected to the legislature from the counties of Pike and Amite. In 1885 he was nominated by the democratic convention held at Jackson as secretary of state, and was elected and installed into office in January, 1886. In 1889 he was renominated for the same position, which was a handsome compliment paid to his worth as a citizen and his popularity as a public official. Major Govan is possessed of a good physique, is about six feet in hight and is well formed, a model of a soldier. His eyes, which are hazel, beam with kindness. He wears a beard and mustache which are tinged with gray. He is a man of genial, social tastes; as a friend he is warm and true; as a neighbor, charitable and kind; and as a citizen, worthy. He was married at Elyton, Ala., February 26, 1865, to Jane B., daughter of Cotsby and Eliza Edmonson, of Holly Springs. To them three children have been born: Andrew R., Eliza, and Jane H. Major Govan is a member of the Masonic order, the A. O. U. W., and the Knights of Pythias.

The life and character of John Grady, of Adams county, Mississippi, will bear a much more detailed history and analysis than is here given, for he has wielded a wide influence, and the manner in which he reached his present financial standing denotes him to be an individual above the ordinary. He was born in Ireland in 1840, being the fifth child born to Daniel and Mary (Higgins) Grady, who came to America in 1850 or 1853 and settled in Ohio. They afterward located in Illinois, where the father followed farming until his death, which occurred in 1888, his widow still surviving him, making her home in Chicago with her eldest child, a daughter. John Grady came to the United States with his mother in 1853 and received his education in his native land, in Ohio and Illinois. In 1866 he came to Natchez and here at once engaged in merchandising, but the following year returned to Chicago and remained a short time. He was then in business in Louisiana for a short time, but in 1872 embarked in business at his present stand. He erected his present business block in 1886, it being a two-story frame at the corner of Madison and Cemetery streets, and carries a full line of general merchandise, valued at several thousand dollars. Besides this he owns seven residences in the town. In 1872 he was united in marriage to Miss Mary Minogue, of Chicago, and by her has two children: Margaret Mary and John. Mr. Grady was made a citizen of the United States in 1874, and since that time has taken an active interest in the affairs of this country, and being a man of intelligence has kept thoroughly posted up with the times. In 1884 he was elected an alderman from the first ward and has been reëlected to that position at each succeeding election, being chosen by the democratic party, of which he has been a member ever since his naturalization. He has been a member of the St. Joseph T. A. B. society since its organization, and its interests he advances in every way in his power. For five years he has been chairman of the hospital committee, and in that body is one of its most active workers. He is essentially a self-made man, is prepossessing in appearance, and in his business transactions with the public he has ever been the soul of honor.

Hon. F. M. Glass was born in Holmes county, Miss., in 1834, a son of D. S. and Sarah (Tubb) Glass, the former of whom was born in Alabama in 1810, and removed to Mississippi in 1823, first making a short stay in Pike county. He then removed to Holmes county, where he married, his union resulting in the birth of the following children: F. M., the subject of this sketch; Winston, who was born in 1836 and died in 1838; Malinda, born in 1838; Nannie, born 1840; Mary, born in 1842; H. C., born 1844; and D. S., born in 1848. Another child died in infancy in Texas in 1843. D. S. Glass and his family resided in Texas for about ten years, then returned to Mississippi. in which state the mother spent the rest of her days. Some time after their return, Mr. Glass went to Canada, where he spent one year, and upon his return to his home in Mississippi was taken sick in Ohio, and there died, July 3, 1854. His father was one of the first residents of this state, and was here massacred by Indians. The maternal grandfather, Samuel Tubb, died about 1838, his widow's death occurring some eight years later. D. S. Glass was an active politician, and served as deputy sheriff of Holmes county, Miss., a number of times. He was an active member of the A. F. & A. M., and assisted in the organization of many lodges throughout this state and also in Texas. He assisted in organizing Rusk lodge, in Cherokee county, Tex., besides many others. F. M. Glass has spent his life in the state of his birth, and was here united in marriage to Miss Minnie A. Wade in 1855, she being also a native of this state, and their union has resulted in the birth of the following children: D. E., born in December, 1856, was educated in Oxford university, and is now a successful merchant in Florida; Lavesta A. was born in 1859, died in 1860; J. W. was born in 1861; Fred, born in 1864, died in infancy; Sallie Kate, born in 1867, died in February, 1889; Lennie A. and Josephine, born in 1870, Josephine died in 1871; Winnie C. was born in 1873; Henry Clay, born in 1876; Annie May, born in 1879; and Clyde was born in 1881. Mr. Glass has always been a planter, and his principal crop has been cotton. He has a comfortable and pleasant home in Sallis, and is surrounded by numerous warm personal friends, who admire and respect him for his many estimable qualities of both mind and heart. He has taken an active interest in the politics of his state, and has represented Attala county in the state legislature two different terms, was a member of the last constitutional convention, and is now a popular candidate for chancery clerk. His career as a legislator was marked by earnest, conscientious and intelligent labor, and he took an active interest and a leading part in the discussions that came before that body. He has been a member of the Masonic fraternity since 1858, is a Knight Templar, and is a member of Bluff Springs lodge No. 196. He has been a member of the I. O. O. F. since 1867, and was at one time a member of the Grange. When the Civil war came up he dropped his farming implements and took up arms in defense of the Confederate cause, becoming a member of company A, Fifteenth Mississippi regiment, with which he served throughout the Atlanta campaign, taking part in many important engagements in Tennessee and North Carolina.

In North Carolina in 1824 David C. Glenn was born. His father died when he was very young. At an early age he began the study of law with J. W. Chalmers at Holly Springs, and in 1842 was admitted to practice, and soon afterward entered actively in the uncertainties of politics. In 1844 he went to Jackson, where he soon attracted wide attention for his eloquence and brilliance. So rapidly grew his fame that in 1849 he was chosen attorney-general of the state. He became a member of the Charleston convention and of the Mississippi secession convention. He favored secession and impressed his individuality upon the convention. After the war he resumed the practice, and in 1869 passed away, leaving a memory that is yet fresh and green.

Calvin E. Glidewell is an extensive, successful and well-known cotton planter of Chickasaw county, Miss., but is a native of Pickens county, Alabama, where he was born in 1840. His parents, William and Salina (Warren) Glidewell, were born in Virginia and Tennessee in 1807 and 1813, respectively, their marriage being consummated in 1829. With his youthful bride Mr. Glidewell removed to Alabama in 1830, in which state they became the parents of nine children, only three of whom are living at the present time: Martha (Burlison), Calvin E. and Thomas, the latter a planter in the Lone Star state. After the death of the husband and father in 1847 his widow and surviving children removed to Chickasaw county, Miss., in 1849, and in their adopted state they began a new life. Calvin E. Glidewell, like a dutiful son, remained faithfully by his mother, with the exception of the time he spent in the war, until her death in 1888 at the age of seventy-five years. He was married in 1869 to Miss Anna McQuarta, by whom he has an interesting family of nine children: James, Irwin, Maggie, Mattie, Henry, Lula, Callie, Milton and Stella. Mr. Glidewell, although he received a somewhat limited education in his youth, knows the value of a good education and is giving his children excellent advantages, the four eldest being attendants of the school of Okolona. He and his worthy wife are members of the Methodist Episcopal church. While engaged in planting in 1861 the clash of arms caused him to throw down his agricultural implements and take up arms in defense of the land he loved, and in the early part of 1861 he became a member of company A, Thirty-first Mississippi regiment, and took part in the battles of Shiloh, Vicksburg, Baton Rouge, Peach Tree creek, Atlanta and others, and at all times acquitted himself creditably and as becoming a soldier. He was paroled at Greensboro, N. C., in 1865 after the surrender of General Lee and returned to his home near Okolona, Miss. He has in his possession a Confederate half-dollar which was given to him a few days before the final surrender by Jefferson Davis.

Dr. Locke C. Glover, planter and retired physician of Grenada county, Miss., was originally from Tennessee, his birth occurring in Bedford county January 18, 1819. His parents, Lancaster and Elizabeth (Locke) Glover, were natives af the Old Dominion, the father being born in Sussex county. His mother, with her parents, moved to Tennessee and settled in Rutherford county in 1806, her marriage to Lancaster Glover being celebrated on Christmas day of the following year. They settled in Bedford county, and there resided until 1822, when Madison county, West Tennessee, became their home, and continued to be such until December, 1836, during which time they tented at Big Black camp ground on six different occasions. They then came to Marshall county, Miss., but returned to Tennessee in 1843, and were residents of Shelby county until their respective deaths in 1858 and 1853, the father being eighty-three years of age. Both were very active members of the Methodist church for upward of forty years, and the father was class-leader in the same for twenty-five or thirty years. In early life he was a machinist and millwright, but in later years, or in 1822, he became a moderate planter. His parents died in Virginia when he was but a boy. His grandfather was an English sailor, who settled in Virginia at an early day and became provisional governor at one time. He reared nine sons, who settled in different states. One of the nine sons was the grandfather of the subject of this sketch. The maternal grandfather, Charles Locke, was a native of Virginia, where he married Mary Batts, and about 1806 removed to Rutherford county, Tenn., where he spent his life up to 1837, and the remainder of his days in Shelby county, Tenn., his death occurring about 1845. He was of English descent, and followed the occupation of a planter all his life. Dr. Locke C. Glover was the sixth, and is now the only surviving member in a family of thirteen children, ten of whom (six boys and four girls) lived to be grown. All of them became members of the Methodist church, and the father and all his sons were members of the Masonic fraternity. Three of the sons lived to be over seventy-three years old, and out of the six three became physicians, one (C. C. Glover) a minister and two merchants. All were sober and competent business men, and none were ever tried by the church or state for a breach of the law so far as Dr. Glover has ever learned. Dr. Locke C. Glover received a classical education in Tennessee and Mississippi, and in 1845-6 he attended medical school at Wetumpka, Ala., graduating from the Botanical School of Medicine at Memphis, Tenn., in 1847. He subsequently practiced in De Soto county, Miss., for about three years, and then removed to Monroe county, thence one year later to Columbus, but only resided there two years, when he returned to Aberdeen and vended Glover's bayberry syrup and liver medicine, and sold drugs. In 1858 he moved to Memphis, and practiced there, and also sold Glover's bayberry syrup and liver medicine until 1862. He then practiced in different parts of Mississippi until the cessation of hostilities. After this he was engaged in merchandising at West Point, of this state, but since 1872 he has been following the occupation of a planter. His landed estate is eight hundred and fifty acres at home, with above two hundred acres cleared, and he also has two hundred and sixty acres in Tallahatchie bottom. He was married in 1865 to Miss Caroline Lafayette Majet, who was born about 1837 on the farm where the Doctor now lives, and who was the daughter of Nicholas Majet [see sketch]. She died in February, 1880, having borne two children, one now living, Charles Locke Lancaster, who was born August 6, 1874, in the house in which the Doctor now lives. He is a brilliant young man with a bright future before him. Dr. Glover was a member of the Masonic fraternity in Hernando in 1847, and is now demitted from the lodge at Columbus. He was elected to take the chapter degrees at Grenada, Miss., in 1864 or 1865, but want of jurisdiction prevented their being conferred on him. He is also a member of the Farmers' Alliance. Mr. Glover has been a member of the Methodist church for about forty years, and has ever been a liberal contributor to its upbuilding and support. He has never been under arrest or charged before any court, the church or his lodge with any crime or misdemeanor, and he has never been drunk, and does not know that either of his brothers has ever been.

Dr. William L. Godbold is a practicing physician and surgeon and a successful planter of Knoxville, his birth occurring near Meadville in 1837. He is a son of James R. and Virginia B. (Sessions) Godbold, the birth of the former occurring in Fairfield district, S. C., in 1818. When about ten years of age he was brought by his parents to Franklin county, Miss., and here he received a common school education. About 1835 he was married and settled near Meadville, and about 1851 located at Knoxville, where he died in 1870, a well-to-do planter. He was practically a self-made man, and by his industry, economy and close adherence to business he accumulated a handsome fortune. While growing up he learned lessons of industry, frugality and economy, which he never forgot and which stood him in good stead during subsequent periods. His honor was above question, and throughout the greater part of a well-spent life he was an earnest member of the Methodist Episcopal church, of which his wife, who was born in Franklin county, Miss., and died in 1851, was also a member. After her death Mr. Godbold married again, his second wife being Miss Missouri A. Weathersby, who was born in Amite county and was a daughter of Loderick Weathersby. Levi Godbold, the grandfather of Dr. William L., was a South Carolinian, and about 1828 came to Franklin county, where he spent the rest of his life engaged in planting. He and his wife both died within a few hours of each other in 1869, on the day of their sixty-second wedding anniversary. Both had been professed Christians and members of the Methodist church for many years. They reared two sons and three daughters to maturity. Jesse Sessions, the maternal grandfather, was born in the Old North state, whence he came at a very early day to Franklin county, Miss., where he became a wealthy planter and spent the rest of his life. Dr. William L. Godbold is the eldest in a family of two sons and one daughter, born to his father's first marriage: Thomas J., who died in 1863 while at home from the war on furlough (he was a lieutenant in the Seventh Mississippi infantry); Sarah L. died at the age of nine years, and only the Doctor is left. He received his early education in the country schools near his home, after which he entered Centenary college at Jackson, La., after which he began the study of medicine with Dr. Stephen Van Allen, a celebrated physician of Franklin county, Miss. From that time until the opening of the war he attended the University of Louisiana, at which time he joined company K, Seventh Mississippi infantry, and for a time operated on the coast of Mississippi and afterward in Tennessee. He was at Shiloh and Farmington, but the most of the time until the close of 1863 he was on detached duty, when his military career ended. After the war he resumed his medical studies and in 1868 graduated from the University of Louisiana, and has since practiced in and about Knoxville, being one of the leading physicians of the county. He is exceptionally well known in his professional capacity, for his efforts have been well repaid, and throughout this section his name is almost a household word. He served with credit in the legislature in the session of 1886 and again in 1888 and was the author of several local bills that became effective. As a legislator he was noted for his intelligence and faithfulness to his principles, characteristics for which he has always been well known. In the session of 1886 he was a member of the committee on railroads, public health and quarantine and in the next session filled the same position with the exception of being on the committee for penitentiaries. For some years after the war he was quite active in local politics and through the long struggle made by the democracy of Mississippi to throw off the incubus of Republican misrule, he was ever found at the front, inspired by no other motive than a love of country and a patriotic desire to see the government of his state restored to the hands of her people. He is a member of the Solomon B. Stampley lodge No. 222 of the A. F. & A. M. at Roxie, of which order he is a warm supporter. He was married in 1863 to Miss Cornelia, daughter of James and Emily Dunckley, the father's birth occurring in South Carolina. When a young man he became a resident of Wilkinson county, Miss., where he was married and spent the rest of his life, following the occupation of planting. He died in 1876 and his wife in 1872. Mrs. Godbold was born in Wilkinson county and is a cultured, refined and intelligent lady, admirably qualified to move in the best society circles. She is an earnest member of the Christian church. The Doctor is the owner of about one thousand acres of land near Knoxville, the most of which he has acquired by inheritance. All measures of morality, temperance, education and others of like nature find in him a strong advocate, and it may with truth be said he is found among the foremost patrons in any reliable, uplifting movement.

S. Goldsmith, merchant, Greenville, Miss., is in every sense of the word a selfmade man. Beginning business with $140, he has grown up with and materially advanced the interests of Greenville as well as his own, until now he is one of the brightest and most prosperous merchants of the Yazoo delta. His trade extends to Arkansas and Louisiana as well as the length and breadth of Mississippi. Mr. Goldsmith is of foreign nativity, his birth occurring in Germany in 1845, and is the second in a family of seven children born to Emanuel and Henrietta (Goetz) Goldsmith, natives also of the old country. S. Goldsmith was educated in Germany and came to the United States in 1864, going immediately to Iowa, where he clerked in a store at Davenport for two years. From there he went to New Orleans, thence to Jackson, Miss., and there clerked until September, 1868, after which he returned to New Orleans.   In December, 1868, he came to Greenville and engaged as clerk for Alexander & Marshall, with whom he continued until 1870, after which he was with Wilczinski & Co. for one year.   In the year 1871 he embarked in the grocery and restaurant business for himself, in partnership with M. Sievers, under the firm name of Goldsmith & Sievers. The same year Mr. Goldsmith bought his partner out and thus laid the foundation for his present prosperous calling.   He began the wholesale grocery and provision business in 1876, and in 1890 separated the retail and wholesale business which is now carried on separately.   The retail store carries a stock of goods valued at $5,000 and the wholesale stock is valued at $25,000.   His annual sales equal $250,000.   He has fine large stores, has an excellent stock of goods and is a popular and successful business man.   In 1889 he erected his wholesale business block, its dimensions being 50x173 feet, at the corner of Poplar and Washington avenues, and the second floor of this fine brick building is devoted to his large cotton salesroom and offices and the ground floor, besides his own store, is occupied by the Bank of Greenville.   Mr. Goldsmith has also erected other business houses, which he has sold, and in 1885 he erected a fine residence on Washington avenue.   He also owns a fine plantation of three thousand acres, with one thousand acres under cultivation, and has cleared and improved the most of it himself. _ Besides this he owns land in Bolivar and Sunflower counties, warehouses on the river front, is a stockholder in the Bank of Green-ville, also the Electric Light company, the Delta Insurance company and the Valley Land company.   In 1871 he wedded Miss Eugenia Newman, a native of Germany, and to them have been born eleven children: Emanuel, Archie, Lulu, Leopold, Ralph and Max (twins), Gertrude, Hazel, Godfrey (deceased), Grover Cleveland (deceased) and Gabriel (deceased). Mr. Goldsmith is a member of the Masonic fraternity, American Legion of Honor, the Knights of Honor, the Knights of Pythias and Buaibrith Kashershel Bazel.   His parents are both deceased, the father dying in 1870 and the mother in 1882.   The former was a mer-chant in Langenselbold, near Frankfort-on-the-Main.

Nathan Goldstein, a member of the well-known firm of Weiss & Goldstein, Greenville, Miss., was born in Europe in 1848, and when eight years of age went with his parents to England.   He subsequently came to the United States, located at New Orleans, and there, after completing his education in that city, he eventually embarked in business for himself. Thinking that perhaps he could further his interests he came to Greenville, Miss., in 1869, and four years later became a partner with Mr. Weiss under the firm name of Weiss & Goldstein, which enterprise has become one of the most prosperous ones in Yazoo delta.   Since the death of Mr. Weiss the business has been conducted by Mr. Goldstein, but the firm name has not been changed, the former partner's interests being still retained by Mrs. Weiss. This firm does a large plantation supply business, carries a general stock of merchandise and also does a wholesale trade.   Since his arrival in Greenville Mr. Goldstein has been most active in town development, and if he can prevent it no worthy movement is allowed to fail for want of support.   He was for many years an active member of the town council and in 1881 he was elected a member of the board of supervisors.   He was at once made president and has been the presiding officer of the board since.   He has been a promoter and an officer in nearly all the commercial enterprises of Greenville; is a stock holder in all the banks and a director and officer in most of them; is one of the official board of the Cotton Compress works; is president of the Delta Liquor & Tobacco company; vice president of the Delta Insurance company and president of the Cotton exchange.   He is a moving spirit in all commercial enterprises of the town and most of them owe much to his encouragement and activity. Ten years ago he organized a Hebrew congregation and has been its president for the past five years. He also assisted in organizing the Hebrew Benevolent society, and has been a liberal contributor to it since. In society matters Mr. Goldstein has, in the past, been one of the most active members and an organizer and a charter member of most of them. He is a member of the Masonic, the Knights of Pythias, the Elks, Legion of Honor and several Hebrew societies, in all of which he has held office and been their representative in the grand lodge many times. He is a gentleman of experience, judgment and energy, is thoroughly known all over the city, and is everywhere popular. Since his marriage to Miss Weiss, in 1876, he has been mainly occupied with his home, which is one of the pleasantest in Greenville, and in the active prosecution of his many business interests. Mr. and Mrs. Goldstein's union has been blessed by the birth of three children, a son and two daughters. In personal appearance Mr. Goldstein is of medium hight, has a fair complexion and is a fine looking gentleman.

Col. James Gordon was born in Monroe county, Miss., December 6, 1833. He is the only son born to Robert and Mary E. (Walton) Gordon. He had a sister who died in childhood. His father was a native of Scotland and his mother a native of Amelia county, Va. The former came to Mississippi directly from Scotland and located in Monroe county, during the old territorial days, when this section was under the control of the Chickasaw tribe of Indians, whose king was Ish-taho-topa, and his queen was Puc-caun-la. Colonel Gordon's parents were married in Monroe county, but moved to Pontotoc county in 1834 and purchased the farm which is now occupied by Colonel Gordon. Robert Gordon was a large landowner and slaveowner before the war. One of the pioneers of this section, and practically a successful planter, he became well and favorably known throughout the country. He was an honorable and highminded Christian gentleman. He never aspired to any official position. He and his wife were members of the Methodist Episcopal church. He was one of the witnesses of the treaty made with the Chickasaws, and he gave his signature as such. He was a great personal friend of the chief, Levi Colbert, whose Indian name was Itawamba. Mr. Gordon died in March, 1866, and his wife died in February, 1869, on the farm where Colonel Gordon now lives. James Gordon, being the only heir, the old homestead descended to him. His father purchased a section of land, which included the home place, from the Indians, the owner of this part being named Mollie Gunn, and she deeded it to our subject. The father of Mollie Gunn was a native of Virginia, and was a tory during the revolutionary days. After coming to Mississippi he maintained his loyalty to the British government until he died. Always celebrating the birthday of King George III., he refused to let his people celebrate the Fourth of July. Colonel Gordon was educated at the University of Oxford, graduating in 1855, and remained on the old homestead, pursuing the uneventful life of a planter until the outbreak of the Civil war. During this period, in 1856, he represented his county in the state legislature. He made several trips to Europe, where he has relatives. In February, 1856, he married Miss C. Virginia Wiley, a daughter of Yancey Wiley, of Oxford, Miss. They had two children: Annie, born December, 1856, who is now the wife of J. T. Barrow, of Okolona, Miss., and who was educated at the Chickasaw female college, of Pontotoc; and Robert J., who was born July, 1877. Mrs. Gordon is a member of the Presbyterian church. Colonel Gordon had been so prosperous that, when the war began, he was the owner of considerable landed property and of five hundred slaves. An enthusiast for the cause of the South, he raised the first company of cavalry that went from north Mississippi, arming and equipping it out of his own private means. Of this organization he was captain. He went with his men directly to Richmond, and the company was attached to the Jeff Davis legion under General Stewart. In 1862, after the battle of Seven Pines, he came home and recruited a regiment of cavalry, of which he was made colonel. This organization was known as the Second Mississippi regiment of cavalry, of Armstrong's brigade. At Corinth Colonel Gordon led the advance at the beginning of the battle, and covered Van Dorn's retreat to Holly Springs. He was also in the engagements at Iuka, Franklin, and in numerous other important and minor engagements, from first to last, taking part in thirty-three battles and skirmishes. In 1864, at the request of the Selma naval company, he was sent to England by President Davis to purchase a privateer for use in the Confederate service. He was successful in the contracting for the building of this vessel, and when en route for home, he took the yellow fever at Nassau and came very near dying, but arrived safely at Wilmington, N. C., January, 1865, on the day that Fort Fisher fell. He had not set foot in town, however, before he was captured by the United States troops, and was confined in a prison ship at Old Point Comfort. He succeeded in making his escape February, 1865, and went to New York; where he concealed himself until the fourth of March, when he managed to get to Canada, where he reported to Jacob Thompson, who was an uncle of Mrs. Gordon, and who was a representative of the Confederacy there, with headquarters at Montreal. While there he formed the acquaintance of J. Wilkes Booth, and from that fact he was suspected by the United States government authorities of implication in the assassination of President Lincoln. Securing a pass from General Dix, under the provision of which he was permitted to go to New York, he had no great difficulty in satisfying the authorities that he was innocent of any participation in the great crime mentioned. After taking the oath of allegiance, which was administered by General Dix in person, he returned to his home in Pontotoc in July, 1865, and resumed planting on the old family homestead. In 1877 he was elected to represent the county in the legislature, and he was again elected member of the same house in 1885. Prior to the war Colonel Gordon was assessed upon property valued at $1,600,000. He is now the owner of three thousand acres of land, one thousand of which are under cultivation. His residence, which is located two miles south of Pontotoc, is one of the most stately and elegant in the northern part of Mississippi. He is one of the most extensive planters in this part of the state. He has on his plantation a herd of thoroughbred Jersey cattle, in which he takes great pride. He is widely known as an honorable, highminded gentleman, of no little social and political influence. He has distinguished himself also in the field of literature, having during the past twenty years been a frequent contributor to the various Northern journals and periodicals, under the nom de plume of Pious Jeems. Among the more prominent magazines for which he writes are the *Century Magazine, Turf, Field & Farm*, of New York, and the *American Field*, of Chicago. His works have also appeared in the London *Field* and in many other high-class periodicals, his contributions being much sought. His importance as a resident of Pontotoc is enhanced by the fact that he is the oldest citizen known to other men in this town and county. He is a member of the democrat state committee, and has been in attendance at almost all of the democratic state conventions for many years, taking an active part in the political affairs of Mississippi and being acknowledged as a political leader in this community. He has been for many years a member of the Masonic fraternity and is a Knight Templar. All his life the Colonel has been a diligent student, not only of books, but of human nature and the works of God spread about him on all sides. His library is one of the finest in this part of the state. While a member of the legislature he secured the benefit of the convict labor in the building of the narrow gauge railroad from Middleton, Tenn., to Pontotoc. The people of this part of the state give him full credit for the legislation in which the construction of this road was made possible. His services in this direction having been recognized by the management of the railway, they gave to him a life pass over the line. There is no man in this section who has the general interest nearer at heart than Colonel Gordon. In the work which he has accomplished for his fellow men there has been so much good that he has been everywhere known to be a humanitarian. His interest in churches, schools and all other laudable public enterprises has been great, and his contributions have been willing and liberal, and he is of so genial and friendly a nature that he is well liked by all who have the honor of his acquaintance.

James B. Gordon, of Jacksonville, a highly successful planter of Kemper county, Miss., was born October 30, 1856, and is a son of James J. and Catherine (Reardon) Gordon. The father was born in Sumter county, S. C., October 16, 1829, and was a son of John Gordon. He was reared to the life of a farmer, but was at one time interested in the mercantile trade in South Carolina. In 1856 he removed to Kemper county, Miss., and engaged in agriculture. At the time of his death he owned one hundred and sixty acres of land. He was married in South Carolina, and nine children were born of the union: Virginia G., Susan E., James B., John S., Mary C., Samuel C., William R., Linnie F., and J. J. The father died in Kemper county in 1873, May 23. He was a member of the Presbyterian church and belonged to the I. O. O. F., being an officer of the lodge. He spent four years in the service of the South, enlisting in the Thirteenth Mississippi regiment. He took a deep interest in his fellow men, and was always ready to help any cause that would be of general benefit. His wife is a daughter of William and Susan Reardon. Mrs. Gordon is a member of the Presbyterian church, and a resident of Kemper county. James B. passed his childhood in this county, as he was but two months old at the time his parents removed to the county. He was united in marriage October 26, 1882, to Bettie Clark, and three children have been born to them: Alline, Mary and Jessie. Mr. Gordon is a member of the Presbyterian church, and his wife belongs to the Baptist society. Politically he adheres to the principles of the democratic party. He owns five hundred acres of good farming land, and has been very successful in all the branches of husbandry which he has taken up. He is a man of honor and integrity, and has the confidence and respect of all who know him.

Rev. Cornelius W. Grafton is a worthy Christian gentleman and throughout the forty-five years of his life, whatever his hand, heart or mind has found to do he has done it with all his might. He has devoted his time to the spiritual and mental wants of his fellow mortals and has done far more than the ordinary man to raise the standard of morality in the different localities in which his lot has been cast. He is a man of fine presence and in his bosom there beats a heart that is warm enough to sympathize with the sufferings of all humanity, and not one of the human family was ever turned from his door hungry, or cold from nakedness. He is always ready to lend a listening hand to the woes of the afflicted and needy, and his purse is ever open to the wants of the poor. It can be truly said of him that " he is one of nature's noblemen." The Grafton family was among the early settlers of Adams county, Miss., for there Thomas Grafton the paternal grandfather of Rev. Cornelius Grafton settled about the year 1800. He was very patriotic and at the opening of the war of 1812 enlisted under General Jackson and participated in the noted battle of New Orleans, being one of the "cotton bale sharpshooters." From Adams he removed to Jefferson county, but a few years later removed to Madison county, where he reared his family of five sons and three daughters, all of whom grew to mature years, married and became the heads of families. Of that family three sons and two daughters survive. George Grafton, one of the members of this family and the father of the subject of this sketch, was born in Jefferson county in 1822, but after his removal to Madison county he was married there to Miss Rebecca Patrick, a native of Adams county, and a daughter of Captain Patrick of that county. After his marriage, Mr. Grafton began devoting his time to the noble pursuit of farming but dropped all personal considerations when the war came up to aid the Southern cause, being in an escort company until near the close of hostilities. He returned home to find his plantation laid in waste, but without stopping to brood over the results of the war he immediately put his shoulder to the wheel, resumed planting and in time partially retrieved his shattered fortunes. He died in November 1887, his wife having passed from life in 1875, their union having been blessed in the birth of three sons and two daughters. Rev. Cornelius Grafton, one of these children, was born in Madison county, December 21, 1846, and his youth up to sixteen years of age was spent in his native county. In 1864, imbued with the spirit of the times, he entered the Confederate army, serving first for a short time in Cowan's battery of light artillery, after which he joined his father in Loring's escort and afterward served in Morgan's cavalry brigade, following the varying fortunes of this brilliant cavalry leader until near the close of the war, when he was transferred to Wirt Adams' command, receiving his parole at Gainesville, Ala. Soon after his return home he entered a preparatory school in Rankin county, and from this institution entered the University of Mississippi at Oxford, where he took a most thorough course, graduating in 1868 with the highest honors of his class. He at once engaged in teaching school at Sardis, Miss., where he taught for five sessions, entering in 1871 the theological seminary at Columbia, S. C., and graduating in 1873 after having taken a two years' course. He was licensed to preach in 1872 by the presbytery of Central Mississippi and after completing his theological studies he was ordained by the presbytery of Mississippi and was given charge of the Presbyterian church at Union Church, of which he has had charge ever since. In 1884 Mr. Grafton was elected principal of the Union Church high school, a position he has held ever since although the school has been converted into an academy, and under his able management has become one of the best institutions of the kind in the state. Mr. Grafton has had several additional buildings erected, to accommodate the increasing number of his pupils, and for the instruction of the one hundred and fifty pupils of which the institution can boast he has a competent corps of five teachers. He is deserving of much credit for the progress the institution has made under his charge, for it has been built up from the foundation and has been of much benefit to the surrounding country, and a very superior class of people now reside in that locality. Mr. Grafton was married in North Mississippi, May 14, 1873, to Miss Sue Doak, a daughter of Rev. D. G. Doak, a Presbyterian minister. Mrs. Grafton was born in Tennessee, but was reared near Oxford, and was a lady of very superior mental endowments. She was called from life in the month of June, 1885, leaving her sorrowing husband with five small children to care for, the youngest being but an infant. Nobly has he fulfilled the duties that have fallen upon him and has reared his children unaided, being all in all to them. He is a kind, tender and affectionate father, and looks after their welfare with the utmost devotion. Their names are, Henry Doak, Nellie, Mary, Thomas Buie and Susie. Rev. Grafton is held in the highest esteem by all, and is fondly loved by his children, relatives and friends. He is one of the most conscientious of workers, and the institution he has founded has done untold good in Jefferson and adjacent counties.

J. M. Grafton, planter, Sharpsburg, Mississippi. The Grafton family is of Scotch-Irish descent and a very old and prominent one. The paternal grandfather, Thomas G. Grafton, was one of a family of four brothers who emigrated from Yorkville district, South Carolina, and settled in Jefferson county, Mississippi. In 1836 he moved to Madison county of that state, purchased two hundred and forty acres of land for $10,000 and entered several thousand acres at twelve and one-half cents per acre. Of the six sons born to his marriage G. W. Grafton was the eldest in order of birth. The latter grew to manhood in Madison county and was there married to Miss Rebecca Patrick, a native of Mississippi, who bore him the following children: J. M. (subject); C. W., who, after serving for four years in the Confederate service, graduated with first honors at Oxford university. He also took a thorough theological course at Columbia Theological seminary, South Carolina, and is now president of a large school at Union Church, Jefferson county, Miss., which was the first church in Mississippi and was founded by Mr. Grafton's great-grandfather; A. M., a farmer and educator of Madison county; Laura, wife of J. A. Cook of this county; and Margaret, wife of W. H. Brown, also of Madison county. The mother of these children died about 1880, and the father followed her to the grave in 1888 when seventy years of age. Both were sincere Christians and active members of the Presbyterian church, of which Mr. Grafton's ancestors had been members for a number of generations. J. M. Grafton was born in Madison county, Miss., in 1844, and was reared to the arduous duties of the farm. At the breaking out of the war, or in 1861, he enlisted in company E, Twenty-fourth Mississippi infantry, when but sixteen years of age and served through the entire war, participating in all the engagements in which his command took part, including Perryville, Murfreesboro, Chickamauga and Missionary ridge. He was wounded twice in Kentucky and was captured at Missionary ridge. After returning home he engaged in farming and school teaching, but is now exclusively engaged in the former occupation, farming on a large scale and raising about one hundred and fifty bales of cotton yearly. He raises his own corn and forage and is engaged in raising stock to some extent, principally mules. He is active in politics and is a democrat. He is a member of Pickens lodge, Knights of Pythias, and is a charter member of the Camden lodge, Knights of Honor. He is also an Odd Fellow and Mason. He was married in 1868 to Miss Betty Campbell, daughter of Rev. R. B. and Mary (Patterson) Campbell, a very prominent family of South Carolina, who settled here at an early day. To Mr. and Mrs. Grafton have been born two daughters: Thalia, at home, and Lilly, at the female institute at French Camp. Mr. and Mrs. Grafton and daughters are members of the Presbyterian church.

Thomas Grafton, one of the highly esteemed old residents of the city of Natchez, Miss., was born here in 1821, being the third son born to Allen and Elizabeth (Willey) Grafton, who were born in South Carolina and Kentucky respectively. The paternal grandfather, John Grafton, was born in the north of Ireland, and in 1790 came to America, settling at first in South Carolina, and in 1800 in the town of Natchez. Here he purchased land and engaged in planting, at which he was reasonably successful. He was a Presbyterian in religious belief, and was one of the founders of the Pine Ridge church, which was one of the first churches of that denomination to be erected in the Southwest. He died in 1819. The maternal grandfather, James Willey, was also born in Ireland, and prior to the Revolutionary war came to America, taking up his abode in Pennsylvania. He held a commission in the continental army during that war, and at that time removed with his family to the, then, wilds of Kentucky, after which he was in the campaign in Illinois with General Clarke. In 1787 he came to Natchez, purchased land near this city and in Louisiana, and until his death, which occurred soon after, he was engaged in planting. The parents of Thomas Grafton were married in this state, and his father became a large landholder, and made an excellent home for his family six miles north of Natchez, at which he died in 1856, his wife's death occurring three years earlier of yellow fever. They were members of the Presbyterian church. Thomas Grafton was reared on his father's plantation and had the advantages of the common schools, and began business by managing his father's estate before he had attained his majority, continuing until about the age of thirty years. He was married in 1852 to Miss Catherine Collins, a native of Hinds county, and a daughter of Reuben Collins, one of the early settlers of this state from South Carolina. Mr. Grafton, by his honorable, upright life, soon won many warm friends, who showed their appreciation of his merits by electing him to the house of representatives, in which body he served during the session of 1852–3, proving himself an able, faithful and incorruptible legislator. In 1865 he was elected to the position of county treasurer, an office he held for six consecutive years, and it may with truth be said that he made a beau ideal public official, for he was painstaking, zealous, honorable and efficient. About 1865 he also began the life of a journalist by establishing the Natchez *Post*, which paper he conducted for one year, after which he was on the Natchez *Democrat*, as assistant editor, a short time after becoming editor-in-chief, in which capacity he continued for thirteen years. He was also editor of the *Banner* for a year or two. He has written much of a historic character of this section, and as he has lived here all his life and his memory is remarkably clear, he may be said to be an authority on the past. To himself and wife ten children were born, six of whom are living at the present time: Elizabeth, wife of President Raymond of Jefferson college; W. Kirby, a merchant of Natchez; Mollie, Janie, Hattie, Seaton. Those deceased are: Collins W., John Lally, Thomas and Mattie. The family are members of the Presbyterian church, and Mr. Grafton has long been a member of Harmony lodge No. 1. of the A. F. & A. M.

M. D. Graham, the subject of this biographical sketch, was born in Autauga county, Ala., in the year 1829. He lived here only a short time, when he removed with his parents to Sumter county, where he remained with them till 1846, at which time the family located permanently in Scott county. From that day M. D. Graham has made Scott county his home. He was reared on a farm, and at the age of twenty-one had the unusual honor conferred upon him of being elected to the office of circuit clerk, which he held for one term, and was then elected sheriff of the county and served in that capacity for five years. At the end of that time he formed a partnership with Mr. Eastland, and has been very successful in his undertaking up to the present time. In 1855 he married Miss Eliza Eastland of this county, who is still living. Their union was consecrated by the birth of two children. The father of Mr. Graham, Daniel Graham, was a native of North Carolina, born in 1803, and in 1827 was married in the state of Alabama to Miss Neill Smith. He followed the vocation of planting and died in 1836 while he was still in the prime of manhood. A brother of M. D. Graham, Judge Thomas B. Graham, was born in 1833 and came to Scott county in 1846 with his mother. He graduated at the University of North Carolina, Chapel Hill, and afterward practiced the profession of law, which he has followed all his life. He served four years in the Confederate army, and organized the first company that was raised in the beginning of hostilities; he was elected captain of this company, became colonel, and was in command of the Twentieth Mississippi regiment at the time of the surrender. He has been a man whom his fellowmen have delighted to honor, as is evidenced by the offices conferred upon him. He was a member of the state senate at the time Governor Ames was impeached; he was appointed chancellor by Governor Stone during his first term, and has been reappointed every time since. Both the Judge and M. D. Graham have always been very active, politically speaking, and have at all times affiliated thoroughly with the democratic party, of which they are natural leaders in their section of the state. They are also both of them most worthy and respected citizens and good men, whom their fellowmen honor with their trust and confidence.

J. A. Orr

Narcissus D. Graham was born in Fairfield district, S. C., in 1827, and was the fourth in a family of ten children, five of whom are still living: Mary, now Mrs. William West, of Choctaw county, Ala.; Margaret, now Mrs. John W. Davis, also of Choctaw county; Narcissus D., the subject of this sketch; T. W., who is a resident of Florida; Lottie, now Mrs. Edward Jones, of Jones county, Miss. Mr. Graham's parents were natives of South Carolina. They left that state in 1834, locating in Sumter county, Ala., where they spent the balance of their lives. Narcissus D. Graham grew to maturity in that county, and came afterward to Mississippi, locating where he now resides. He was married in 1858 to Miss Martha Jones. During the war one of his brothers died while serving for the Confederate cause. John, who was in General Harvey's command, was killed in battle. Mr. Graham is the owner of a plantation of about three thousand acres, all in one body of land, and most of which is fine prairie land. He is a member of the Masonic fraternity and is a worthy and consistent member of the Methodist church. He is an enterprising, progressive, well-to-do planter, who is respected by the community at large. He is one of those solid, substantial citizens who honor the community in which their lots may be cast.

Absalom Grant (deceased) was for thirty-two years a worthy resident of Mississippi, and was a man who possessed an original and thoughtful mind, whose advanced ideas and progressive principles resulted in his own good and the good of those around him. He was born in North Carolina, and upon coming to Mississippi, in 1846, he settled on a plantation in the neighborhood of where Oak Ridge now is, which is still in possession of the Grant family. He brought with him a number of slaves from his native state, and being an excellent manager he made planting a success, and at the commencement of the war was prospering. He was extremely public-spirited, was a popular and leading man in the section in which he resided, and for many years was an earnest and devoted member of the Methodist Episcopal church South. His death, which resulted from yellow fever in 1878, was deeply regretted by a large circle of friends and acquaintances, and his place in business and social circles was found hard to fill. His widow, who still survives him, was formerly Miss Martha R. Jones, and is now in her seventieth year. She is a member of the same church to which her husband belonged, and has always endeavored to live the life of a true Christian. She has children named as follows: H. T., S. E. (widow of A. M. Cameron), Richard C. (merchant and planter at Oak Ridge), S. P., Robert C., B. W. and Mattie R. (wife of J. T. Stephenson.)

H. T. Grant has made his way to the front ranks among the energetic planters of Warren county, Miss., and owing to the attention he has always paid to each minor detail he has accumulated a fair share of this world's goods. He was born in the Old North state in 1838 and is a son of Absolom and Rebecca (Jones) Grant, for a history of whom see sketch of Absolom Grant. H. T. Grant came to Mississippi with his father in 1846 and was here educated in the common schools, commencing life for himself at the age of eighteen years, as overseer on the plantation of his uncle, T. C. Jones, with whom he was at the opening of the Rebellion. In 1861 he enlisted in company H, of the Warren volunteers of the Twenty-first Mississippi and was in the battles of Seven Pines, Savage station and Malvern Hill, where he was wounded in the thigh, from the effects of which he was confined in the hospital for two weeks, at the end of which time he was again ready for service. He rejoined his command, which was close to Richmond, after which he took part in the engagement at Harper's Ferry, Fredericksburg, Chancellorville, where he was taken prisoner and sent to Fort Delaware. One month later he was exchanged and joined his command in the Virginia valley. He was then a participant in the battles of Chickamauga, Knoxville, Bean station,

51

Wilderness, Spottsylvania courthouse, Cold Harbor, Berryville, Cedar creek and various skirmishes. He surrendered at Appomattox courthouse, was paroled and made his way home mostly on foot. He engaged at once in planting on a small scale, for although he had plenty of improved land he had no stock. After tilling the soil with his father for three years, then began working alone. After his marriage he moved to his own plantation, on Big Black river, and now has one hundred and fifty acres under cultivation, the most of which is in the Big Black bottom. He has a fine cottongin and general mercantile store on his plantation, the latter business being established in 1885. He has been quite successful as a merchant and in this enterprise has made money. His wife was formerly Mrs. Virginia (Young) Hill, daughter of J. J. Young of this county, and to their union three daughters have been born (Rebecca, Virginia and Margie) and three sons now deceased. Mrs. Grant was the mother of two children by her first husband but both are now deceased. She is a member of the Methodist Episcopal church and is an estimable and refined lady. Mr. Grant has prospered in all his enterprises and has a beautiful and comfortable home.

Clinch Gray, the father of Hon. Henry Gray, was a son of Thomas Gray, of East Tennessee, a lawyer and minister there for sixty-four years, and was born in North Carolina in 1775, and emigrated to Tennessee, and later to Wayne county, Miss. His education was good, and he was appointed to the position of surveyor by the United States government, and surveyed township five across the entire state. This township includes the northern part of Greene county. He made some crops during the time, however. He was married in 1810 to Miss Margaret Evans, of South Carolina, a daughter of John Evans, a successful planter. They had six children: Thomas, Mary, John, Henry, Chelly, and Clinch. Of these Henry and John survive. The father died in 1822, his widow in 1858 or 1859, having been for many years a Baptist. Henry Gray, the subject of this notice, was born October 8, 1818, in Wayne county, Miss. His advantages for education were limited. He began life on his own account at the age of twenty-four years, and during the year in which he reached that age he was elected sheriff of Wayne county. Before that time, however, he had attended two sittings of the court at Winchester, then the county seat of Wayne. It is very likely that Mr. Gray is the only man ever elected to so responsible an office at so youthful an age. He filled the position for six years, and then returned to his farm. In 1850 he was connected with the taking of the national census. In 1864 and 1865 he was a member of the Mississippi legislature. Mr. Gray was married in 1847 to Miss Mary Haraldson, a daughter of Abner Haraldson, a planter of Newton county, Miss., who bore him five children: C. M. Gray, John L. Gray, W. G. Gray, T. J. Gray, and Sallie Gray. C. M. Gray married Miss Melissa DuBose; John L. Gray married Miss Mary Dougherty; William G. Gray married Miss Annie DuBose. All are residents of Wayne county, Miss. Mr. Gray has been a Mason. Politically he is a democrat. He is a member of the Missionary Baptist church of Waynesboro, of which Mrs. Gray is also a member. Three of these children are Baptists and one is a Methodist. Mr. Gray purchased land in 1846, and by additional purchases now owns more than four hundred acres, though he at one time owned one thousand two hundred acres, a distribution having been made between the children. His chief crops are corn and cotton. On the arrival of Mr. Gray's parents the country was a wilderness, and the travel was by packhorses, which fact is sufficient to give his family place among the pioneers.

E. H. Green is a farmer and merchant of Hinds county, Miss., but was born in Madison county, of this state, February 22, 1848, the second in a family of three children born to the marriage of T. K. Green and Roena York, the latter a native of Tennessee, whose ancestors were of English descent. The Greens were from Scotland. T. K. Green was a farmer by occupation, and at one time had accumulated a large amount of property, but financial trouble overtook him and he became considerably embarrassed. He at one time held the position of postmaster of Meridian Springs, an old, abandoned office of Hinds county, and he was at one time justice of the peace of Madison county before the war. He died in 1856. E. H. Green had poor opportunities for an education in his youth, but he attended the common schools occasionally up to the age of eighteen years, with the exception of the time spent in the army. At the age of sixteen years he entered Wither's light artillery, company A, and saw considerable service in Mississippi, being at Jackson when that city surrendered. He then returned home and farmed with his mother until he became of age, at which time he commenced operations on his own account, making his first purchase of land in 1869, which consisted of four hundred acres of fertile land in Madison county. To this purchase he has since added as his means permitted, and he now has a plantation of two thousand two hundred acres, which is considered one of the finest in the county. One thousand acres are under cultivation, and yield two hundred and fifty bales of cotton and two thousand bushels of corn annually. He raises cattle for the market and a few horses (roadsters). In 1881 he embarked in general merchandise, and in 1887 considerably enlarged his venture. He is quite active in local politics, and was elected a member of the board of supervisors of Hinds county in 1879, serving two terms. He is a member of the K. of H. and the A. O. U. W. and K. of P. In 1874 he was married to Miss Cornelia Ball, a native of Hinds county, by whom he became the father of five children, four of whom are living: Joseph W., Cornelia, Bertha and Alma. His wife died in 1883, and two years later Mr. Green took for his second wife Miss Annie L. Ball, by whom he has four children: Myrtle, Roena, Annie and Edward. Mr. Green and his family worship in the Baptist church. He is a very enterprising gentleman, and the property of which he is now the owner has been obtained through his own exertions. He has a large steam cottongin on his plantation, and expects soon to put up another. He is of a very kind and hospitable disposition, and is generous in contributing of his wealth to worthy enterprises. He is worth about $50,000.

The entire life of Hon. T. K. Green has been passed in ceaseless activity, and has not been without substantial evidences of success, as will be seen at a glance at his present possessions. He was born in Hinds county, Miss., in 1850, and was the younger of two children born to Thomas K. and Roena (York) Green,* both of whom were born in North Carolina, the town of Greensboro taking its name from this family, who were among the oldest settlers of the section and of English descent. Thomas K. Green came with his family to Mississippi at an early day, and followed planting in Hinds county until his death, which occurred in 1853, his widow surviving him until 1874, when she, too, passed away. In Hinds county the subject of this sketch was reared to manhood, and began life behind a plow, a calling he continued to follow for several years after commencing life for himself. In this manner he laid the foundation for his present fortune. His estates in Louisiana now consist of over six thousand acres of land, it being in the best cotton regions of that state and would on an average yield from twelve hundred to fifteen hundred bales of cotton each year. His first purchase of land in that state was in Concordia parish and consisted of four thousand acres. He later purchased two other plantations of twelve hundred and thirteen hundred acres each, and has some eighteen hundred acres under cultivation. On his estate in Louisiana he has erected good dwellinghouses, a cottongin on each place and employs over three hundred and fifty adults. He has been a resident of the city of Natchez since 1886, and there has a

---

* There are several important discrepancies between the data furnished by the two brothers. See sketch of E. H. Green.

pretty and comfortable home, though down to the present year he retained his citizenship of Louisiana. He was married in 1880 to Miss Ellen H., daughter of Bourbon Shotwell, an old resident of Mississippi. To Mr. and Mrs. Green four children have been born: Annie, Edna, Thomas K., Jr., and Laura, the eldest members of whom are attending school. Mr. Green has always been an active politician, and while residing in Louisiana was a member of the state legislature, and in 1880 was elected a member of the police jury. He was elected to the position of sheriff of Concordia parish, La., in 1886 and to the state legislature of Louisiana in 1888. He is a man of superior intelligence, and as a public official was faithful to his trusts, conscientious in the discharge of his duties, was the soul of honesty and universally courteous. He made an intelligent legislator and was keenly alive to the interests of the state and to the people. He is prepossessing in personal appearance and is just in the prime of life, being now forty-one years of age. He is a model American citizen, for he possesses that moral and personal integrity and clear, well-balanced, active intelligence which adorn the private station and make and keep the public service pure.

Among the substantial planters of Sunflower county, Miss., is Henry H. Green, who has made it his object and aim in life to promote the agricultural interests of this section. Although a native of Alabama, born in Green county on December 10, 1840, when an infant less than one year old he was brought to Mississippi by his parents, who for a time resided in Itawamba county, and came in 1853 to Sunflower county, locating on a plantation on Sunflower river. Henry H. Green grew to manhood in this county, being the youngest of four sons and three daughters that arrived at mature years, all of whom are now deceased with the exception of Henry H., who remained under the shelter of the parental roof until he attained his majority. In 1861 he joined the Confederate army, becoming a member of the Third Mississippi regiment, in which he served until the final surrender, participating in a number of important engagements, among which may be mentioned Peach Tree creek and the engagement of the siege and surrender of Atlanta. In the last-named engagement Mr. Green received a flesh wound in the leg and was disabled for further duty. While at home on furlough the news of the final surrender reached him, and, after recovering from his wound, as a means of livelihood he engaged in carpentering and the manufacture of lumber for a few years in this and adjoining counties. In 1868 he began planting on rented land and by good management was enabled, in 1870, to purchase a small place, to which he has since added until he now owns two good plantations on Porter's bayou and two places on Indian bayou, making in all about one thousand acres of land. His home place is about three miles from Indianola and is well improved, his residence being pleasant and comfortable. All this property has been acquired since the war, for at that time he had not a dollar that he could call his own. By his own untiring diligence and persistent effort he has accumulated an excellent competence, and now enjoys his good fortune as he fully deserves to do. He was married in Lee county in 1870 to Miss Io Anna Palmer, who was born, reared and educated there, a daughter of R. W. Palmer of that county, but a former resident of South Carolina. To Mr. and Mrs. Green a family of four children have been born: Dora Lee, Warren Hudson, Edwin Walter and Palmer. One son, William Wiley, died in May, 1889, at the age of twelve years. Mr. and Mrs. Green have long been members of the Methodist Episcopal church South, of Faisonia, and for some time past have resided in Carrollton, Miss., so that their children could have the advantages of the excellent schools of that place and have rented their plantations. Wiley Green, the father of Henry H., was born in Johnson county, N. C., in 1799 being of Scotch descent. He grew up and was married in his native state to Miss Penny O'Neil, a native of the same state and county, but of Irish descent. They first moved from the Old North state in 1832 and farmed in Alabama up to 1840, at which time they came to Mississippi as mentioned above. He died on his plantation in this county in 1867, his wife having passed from life in 1854. He was an active member of the Primitive Baptist church.

The name of Joshua Green represents one of the earliest settlers of Jackson, Miss., who did as much, if not more, than any other one man towards advancing and developing her commercial interests. Mr. Green was born at Havre de Grace, Md., in April, 1811, being a son of Joshua Green and Elizabeth Myers, who were of Dutch and Scotch ancestry. The family first located in Pennsylvania, and from there removed to Maryland, where the elder Joshua Green was interested in shipping, and also operated an extensive fishing plant on the Chesapeake, near where the town of Havre de Grace stands. He and his wife died at the old homestead in the above-named town. Te subject of this sketch left home at the age of fourteen, and going to Baltimore, entered the wholesale drug house of Whittington & Co., where he remained until 1835. In 1833 he took charge of their credits and shipping department in the South, and rode across the country, through Virginia, Tennessee and Mississippi, making collections, and, generally, looking after the interests of his firm. In 1835 he left the firm and opened a drug house in Jackson for himself. He married, in 1837, Elizabeth, daughter of Joseph Jarvis, a merchant of Baltimore, and to this marriage ten children were born: Joshua J., Orlando, William H. H., Joshua J. (the second), Clara, Marcellus, Albert A., Thomas M., Ada Belle, and Orlando (the second). Those now dead are Joshua J., the elder; the two Orlandos and Clara, the latter being the wife of W. H. Barnett, of Vicksburg, her death occurring in 1869. Of the children of the marriage Joshua Green Barnett alone is living. The first Orlando died in infancy and the other at the age of twenty-five years. Joshua J., the elder, died when about eleven years of age. Mr. Green continued the drug business until 1858, when he sold out. Previously, in 1854, he went into the banking business, the bank being known as Green's Exchange bank, but subsequently as J. and T. Green's bank, he and his brother Thomas being partners in it. This bank was in operation in 1863, but in May of that year the Federal troops, when Jackson was captured, took possession of the same, and took all its transportable assets. Mr. Green was a strong Union man before the war, and used all his influence to prevent secession. In politics he was a whig. He was opposed to slavery, upon principle, only keeping such slaves as were necessary for his household. He had been extremely successful in his business operations and amassed a large fortune, consisting of manufacturing and mercantile interests. In 1858, desiring to advance the manufacturing interests of the state, he erected a large cotton factory at Jackson, which was one of the pioneer cotton factories of that section of the country, giving employment to from five hundred to one thousand hands. When the Federal troops came into Jackson this factory was burned by order of General Sherman, notwithstanding Mr. Green had had a conference with the General to try to induce him not to destroy his property. General Sherman took the matter under consideration, and in the meantime sent a guard to protect the property. Subsequently he wrote Mr. Green that, as a military necessity, he would have to destroy it, but promised it should be paid for, and it was laid in ashes. Though application was made with General Sherman's written evidence to congress, the property was not paid for. Mr. Green's bank, with the rest of his property, met with the same fate, the valuables in the bank being taken out by Federal officers. After the city was destroyed by fire and the site became an objective point between the contending armies; there was organized, for the protection of life, and what little property that remained, a police of home guards, of which Mr. Green was made captain. After the war, with his fortune gone, Mr. Green again opened a banking house on a small scale, and by his energy and remarkable financial ability his establishment became a decided success. He again prospered, and in 1867, having obtained a charter, he organized the First National bank of Jackson, and became its president, with his brother Thomas as cashier. This management continued until 1872, when the charter was surrendered, and he again established a private bank, under the name and style of J. & T. Green. In 1877 they organized under a state charter as Green's bank, and thus Mr. Joshua Green continued his banking business until 1884, when, having undertaken to finance the contract for the construction of the Memphis, Selma & Brunswick railroad, from Memphis to Selma, and having made large advances to the backers of that railroad, and they having become insolvent and unable to pay, the bank became a heavy loser and was obliged to suspend. This was in July, 1884, and at the instance of Mr. Green the bank was placed in the hands of a receiver. Subsequently, the assets of the bank were turned over to him by unanimous consent of creditors, with an extension of time granted to meet its liabilities. He immediately opened a bank in his own name, under the style of J. Green's bank, and was operating it with success, when, in January, 1887, he was taken with pneumonia, and, on the 20th of that month, he suddenly died. He had progressed very successfully toward the liquidation of his affairs, and when he died he left a large amount of assets, which were replaced in the hands of the receiver for administration. Thus passed away one of Jackson's most worthy citizens. Mr. Green took an active interest in all public affairs, and was in deep sympathy with every enterprise tending to promote the prosperity of the country, but he never aspired to public office. Along in the thirties, while he was living at Baltimore, he volunteered, with others, to aid the authorities in putting down the riots there. Mr. Green was a man of robust constitution, standing six feet two inches in hight, weighing two hundred and twelve pounds. He had never had a serious spell of sickness in his life prior to that which caused his death, and gave every promise of living to a ripe old age. He was a man of great activity in business, possessing a clear, sound judgment regarding commercial enterprises, and was a remarkably skillful financier. All his business transactions were marked by the most signal integrity, which won for him the implicit confidence of all who knew him. He was liberal in his charities and generous in his hospitality. He was strong in his convictions and brave and unfaltering in the maintenance of what he believed was right. His mind was of inventive turn, and many labor-saving devices in his factory were the offspring of his genius. At the time of his death he was working on a model of armored cruisers to prevent, by construction, the danger of penetration and enable them to be made comparatively light. It is difficult to estimate the value of such a man to a community or state. He has passed away, yet his memory remains green in the hearts of those whom he left behind, and who had learned to love and honor him.

The subject of this sketch, Marcellus Green, is the son of Joshua Green, whose memoir appears in this work. He was born August 12th, 1851, at Jackson, Miss., and has resided there continually. Desiring to follow the mercantile career, in 1868 he attended Soule's commercial college in New Orleans and there graduated. After pursuing a commercial course for a short while he peceived what an obstacle a deficient education was and he determined to acquire a collegiate education, which by reason of the Civil war had been neglected. His resolution changed his whole career. He went to the University of Virginia in 1869, and remained there, graduating in various schools, until 1872, when he returned to Jackson and began the study of law with Harris & George. He was admitted to the bar in 1874, and in 1875 he formed a partnership with Judge George L. Potter, one of the most eminent lawyers of the state. Judge Potter died suddenly in 1877, and, though young, Mr. Green successfully managed the practice of the firm, and thenceforth has had a large and lucrative patronage. In 1882 he formed a partnership with Judge S. S. Calhoon, who then resigned from the bench, and this firm still continues. In 1886 he was admitted to practice in the supreme court of the United States. When quite a young man he became a member of the Episcopal church, and he has been quite active in church work, holding at various times different official positions both in the parish and diocese. On April 24th, 1879, he married Lulah Edelen Garner, daughter of the late Col. George G. Garner and Ann Elizabeth Wynn. Colnel Garner was the son of Capt. Hezekiah Garner, U. S. A., and Lucy Edelen, of well-known Virginia and Maryland families. Her mother was of the Lewis family of Georgia. Upon his marriage Colonel Garner resigned his commission as lieutenant in the United States army, and afterward in the Civil war became adjutant-general on Gen. Braxton Braggs' staff. Mr. Green's family consists of five children, named Garner Wynn, Lulah Edelen, Gertrude Elizabeth, Elise Langdon, and Marcellus. Though devoted to his profession he is prominent and active in the encouragement and support of both public and private enterprises in his city and state. He was one of the founders of the waterworks at Jackson, an enterprise which reflects credit on the city, and is its secretary and treasurer. He was one of the organizers of the Mississippi Compress & Ware House company, and of the Jackson Fertilizer company, of both of which he is a director. He is also interested in the First National bank of Jackson, and in the Jackson bank, and in the Morris Ice company. His zeal is enlisted in the public service as well as private business. He has been trustee of the Institute for the Blind, a state charity, and is now trustee for the state lunatic asylum. In 1890 a commission was created to erect an asylum for the colored insane, of which he is president. He was state commissioner at the celebration of the centennial of the promulgation of the constitution of the United States in 1887. He has genial manners and an affectionate, charitable disposition. By nature and cultivation his talents are adapted to his profession. He is a close student, a deep thinker, a logical reasoner and a fluent, forcible speaker. His success is the merited reward of his ability and industry.

A. A. Green is the general manager of the Jackson Fertilizer company, and as a business man he has shown himself to be competent, reliable and successful. He is a native of the city of Jackson, where he was born in 1853, the fifth of seven children born to Joshua and Elizabeth J. (Jarvis) Green, whose sketch appears above. He was educated in Virginia, and was a member of the class of 1878 at Princeton college, New Jersey. He began the study of law in Jackson, and in 1878 was admitted to the bar, but having injured his health by close application to his books he did not adopt his profession, but became exchange clerk in Green's bank of Jackson. In 1881 he started a fertilizer factory, which was the first of the kind to be established in Mississippi, and called it Green's Fertilizer factory, and, although his plant was rather limited, it was a success from the start and was soon doing a prosperous business. In 1887 he incorporated it as the Jackson Fertilizer company, and the officers which were then elected have remained unchanged up to the present time, and all of them are among the leading and successful business men of the city. This plant is located in South Jackson, on the Pearl river, and the annual increase in business has been on an average of from fifteen to twenty per cent. There was sold in 1889 about five thousand tons, mainly in Mississippi. R. L. Saunders is president of this company, E. Virden is vice-president, R. W. Millsaps is secretary and treasurer, and A. A. Green is general manager. The affairs of the company are judiciously and efficiently managed by Mr. Green, who is a business man of enterprise and accurate methods. The trade extends to every part of the state, and the "Royal C" brand, which was originated by Mr. Green, has now become very popular. He is a director of the Capital State bank, a director and secretary of the Morris Ice company, and is a stockholder in the Jackson Grocery company. In 1886 Mr. Green was married to Miss Frank Turner, of Winona, a daughter of Dr. Turner and granddaughter of Col. O. J. Moore, who is a member of an old family and on his plantation the town of Winona is now standing. Mr. Green is an Episcopalian in his religious belief, but his wife is a Methodist.

George F. Greene, planter, Natchez, Miss., was born in Warwick, R. I., and is the son of Hon. Simon Henry and Caroline C. (Aborn) Greene, both natives of Rhode Island. They passed their entire lives in that state. The father became a very wealthy man, all the result of his own efforts, and was a manufacturer. He was a representative and state senator for many years and also held various town offices. He was one of the founders of the public school system throughout New England. Mr. Greene's great grandfather, Christopher Greene, was born in Rhode Island, and was a cousin of Nathaniel Greene of revolutionary fame. Christopher Greene raised and commanded a regiment in the Revolutionary war and was killed at the battle of Red Bank, in Delaware, refusing to be captured. George F. Greene is a lineal descendant of Roger Williams on both his paternal and maternal side, and is of the eighth generation. He was the youngest but one of eight sons, and received his education at Warwick, R. I. In 1858 he went to St. Louis and engaged in business until 1866, when he removed to New Orleans, where he was engaged as a cotton factor until 1875. He then came to Adams county, Miss., and the same year was married to Miss Julia Dunbar, who was born on the "Forest plantation," where they now live, and which consists of eleven hundred acres of land. She is the daughter of William and Mary (Field) Dunbar, the father born on Forest plantation, Adams county, Miss., in 1793, and the mother in New Jersey on the 27th of January, 1801. Her parents were married in Princeton, N. J., in 1827, but settled on the plantation of Mr. Dunbar. Mr. Dunbar was educated at Princeton, graduated in medicine at Philadelphia, Penn., but instead of practicing he managed the estate of his father. He died on the plantation in December, 1847, and his wife died in 1875. William Dunbar's father (also named William Dunbar) was a native of Scotland, was educated in Glasgow, and while a young man came to New Orleans, thence soon after to Baton Rouge, where he married. While a resident of that city he was engaged in the culture of indigo and continued at this until 1792, when he moved to Adams county, Miss. There he entered large tracts of land from the Spanish government and served that government as civil engineer and surveyor a number of years. He died in 1810, and his wife, who was formerly Dinah Clark, an English lady, died there also. Mr. Dunbar's first settlement was the Forest plantation on which, after his death, his widow erected a magnificent mansion. It was destroyed by fire in 1852. Mrs. Greene's maternal grandfather, Richard Stockton, was one of the signers of the Declaration of Independence. The Dunbar family was one of the honored and representative ones of Adams county and held a high position socially.

Among the people of Webster county the name of Dr. John R. Greer, physician and surgeon, Cumberland, Miss., is a familiar one, for he is not only a successful practitioner, but as a citizen and neighbor is highly esteemed. He was born in this county in 1842 and his parents, Dr. Thomas J. and Harriet A. (Redditt) Greer, were natives of Tennessee, the father born in 1810 and the mother about 1817. When but children, Mr. and Mrs. Greer went with their parents to Grenada, Miss., were married there, and then removed to what is now Webster county, where Mrs. Greer died in 1880. The doctor died at Winona very suddenly in 1884, while en route for Tennessee. He received his medical education at

Transylvania university, Lexington, Ky., and practiced his profession for fifty years. He was a member of the Masonic fraternity. He was one of three sons and several daughters, his two brothers being able lawyers of Tennessee. The doctor was a man universally esteemed and respected. He was one of the pioneers of Webster county, settling there when the country was a vast wilderness, and there reared a family of three sons and four daughters, viz.: Mary, wife of F. M. Roberts; Dr. John R; Susan (deceased) was the wife of Dr. W. L. Dottery; David died when a boy; Thomas (deceased); Willie, wife of Rev. J. C. Finnelle, a Baptist minister; and Sarah E., wife of J. W. Martin. Dr. John R. Greer received a good English education at the home school and became a fair Latin scholar. In April, 1861, he joined company B, Eighth Tennessee, for twelve months, and served as lieutenant. The first four months he was in the Virginia army, after which he was in the Tennessee army, being in many of the leading engagements of that campaign. At the end of twelve months he resigned and joined company E, Fifteenth Mississippi, serving in that command until peace was declared. He was all through the Georgia and Atlanta campaign and was with Johnston until his surrender on May 3, 1865. He was in active service over four years; but was never wounded nor captured. Returning home after the war he followed farming for two years and then spent two years as a bookkeeper in a hotel in Havana, Cuba. He subsequently returned to Mississippi, studied medicine at Grenada, and in 1874 graduated from the Louisville medical college. He then began practicing at Spring Valley, Webster county, continued there three years and afterward removed to Walthall, where he practiced one year. He then returned to his farm, where in connection with his practice he cultivated the soil for a few years. For the last five years he has resided at Cumberland and is one of the leading physicians of the county. He has spent nearly all his life in his native county and is well and favorably known, standing high in the estimation of all as a successful practitioner and a useful citizen. He owns a good farm of two hundred and thirty-four acres on Spring creek. In 1876 he married Miss Julia L. Barmore, a native of Winston county, Miss., and the daughter of Reuben P. and Fannie Barmore, who came from Alabama to Mississippi at an early day and lived for a number of years in Winston county. They afterward moved to Choctaw county and there both died. To Dr. and Mrs. Greer were born six children: Thomas, Elise, John (deceased), Joseph, James, and Mamie. The Doctor is a member of the Farmers' Alliance, and he and wife are members of the Christian church.

D. Greif is the leading dry goods merchant and clothier in West Point, Miss., and since his business was established, in 1885, has been doing an annual business of $30,000. He is energetic, active and experienced, and endeavors at all times to please and accommodate his patrons and to keep a choice stock of goods on hand, and as a result his trade is large and constantly on the increase. Mr. Greif was born in Germany in 1861, a son of A. Greif, who died in his native land of Germany a few years ago, having been a cattle dealer by occupation. His widow, who survives him, is still a resident of Germany, but is soon to remove to Mississippi to make her home with her sons. D. Greif attended the public schools of his native land from the time he was six until fourteen years of age, the two following years being spent as a clerk in a mercantile establishment, during which time he obtained a clear insight into the workings of that business. He then left home and native land to try his fortunes in America, and after clerking in a store in Baltimore until 1881, he went to Nashville, Tenn., in which city he clerked three years longer. While there he was married to Miss Tillie Cohen, a native of New York city, who was taken by her parents, when two years old, to Nashville, in which city she was reared and educated. After his marriage Mr.

Greif came to West Point, Miss., and during 1884 was the manager of his father-in-law's business, but the following year engaged in business for himself. About two years later his entire stock was destroyed by fire, but was fortunately covered by insurance, so he was enabled to once more embark in business. In 1888 he erected the two-story brick building which he now occupies, and where his business has steadily and rapidly increased, and besides this, is the owner of a fine residence, which property is not the result of luck or speculation, but of indomitable will, untiring energy and strict economy. He is one of the most progressive and enterprising of the citizens of the city, and spares no pains nor effort to further enterprises of merit, and has been exceptionally prominent in the establishment of manufactories, etc. He is a director in the Building and Loan association, and a stockholder in the First National bank. Socially, he is a member of Cannon lodge No. 159, of the A. F. & A. M., Prairie lodge No. 42, of the K. of P., and West Point lodge No. 527, of the K. of H.; being also a member of the Jewish order of Benai Brith, and last year was elected as one of the city aldermanity of which he now holds a position. He occupies a high social position, is an admirable citizen, and as a business man has not his superior in this section. He realizes that West Point is a very desirable and favored locality, and that all that is needed to make it a leading Southern city is more enterprise and push among the business men. He has a brother, Moses Greif, who is a merchant at Greenwood, Miss. He is expecting to make a trip to Europe in June, 1891, and upon his return, which will not be before September, he will bring his mother with him.

The mercantile trade has long constituted one of the leading features in the commercial pursuits of the country, and in this line is to be found in Booneville a thoroughly representative house controlled by W. G. C. Gresham, who is regarded as an upright and energetic man of business and respected in commercial and social circles. Mr. Gresham was the second child born to the union of James F. and Keziah (Lacy) Gresham, the father born in Alabama in 1820. The paternal grandparents, George and Margaret (Files) Gresham, were natives of Alabama, and came to Mississippi as early as 1838. They settled at what is now known as Bay Spring factory, then known as Gresham mills, and in connection with the milling business Mr. Gresham carried on farming. He took very little interest in politics, but was quite domestic in his tastes. He died some time in the fifties. He was the father of five sons and four daughters, James F. being the eldest in order of birth. The latter received a common school education, and when a young man engaged in manufacturing cotton goods at Bay Spring factory, of which he was the founder and builder in 1851. He was engaged in this business for many years, but in connection also engaged in merchandising and farming until the breaking out of the war. He was an active business man and accumulated a large fortune. He was married in the neighborhood of Gresham mills to Miss Keziah Lacy, and two children were the fruits of this union: Margaret, now Mrs. Brown, residing in Texas, and William G. C. (subject). Mrs. Gresham died in September, 1845, when our subject was but seven days old. Mr. Gresham took for his second wife Miss Sevilla Tipton and reared two children: F., now Mrs. Ledbetter, and Andrew J. Mrs. Gresham received her final summons in 1876, and Mr. Gresham's third marriage was to Miss Eliza Carter. Mr. Gresham was a member of the Masonic fraternity, a Royal Arch Mason, and was quite prominent in politics, holding the office of sheriff and other responsible positions. In 1861 he enlisted in a company called the Cape Horn grays, which was attached to the Second Mississippi regiment under Col. A. E. Rennols, and he subsequently was appointed to the quartermaster department. He was in a number of important engagements, was at Baker creek and was captured and paroled at Vicksburg. After the war he returned home and immediately set to work to retrieve his fallen fortunes. His death occurred on the 27th of February, 1891. William G. C. Gresham was born at Bay Springs, Tishomingo county, Miss., on the 1st of September, 1845, and was reared to a business life by an industrious father. He received a common school education, but on account of the breaking out of the war his school days were shortened. In 1863 he enlisted in the Sixth Mississippi cavalry under Captain Brown, Colonel Harris' regiment, and on the 14th of July, 1864, at the battle of Harrisburg, he was wounded in the right leg, below the knee. He was captured, taken to Tupelo, and after being released, returned home, where he entered the store December, 1866. He was married in 1868 to Miss Laura Elder, who died at the end of about a year, without issue. In 1870 he wedded Miss Amanda Price, daughter of Richard Price, and the fruits of this union were five children: James M., Alma, Goldie, William G. and M. Bayard. In 1874 Mr. Gresham started out in business for himself as a merchant in partnership with Mr. Lacy, under the firm title of Lacy & Gresham. This was changed to James F. Gresham & Co., and in 1878 it was changed again to W. G. C. Gresham & Co. Mr. Gresham is a member of the Knights of Honor, and he and family are members of the Methodist church South. He is a democrat in his political views and a hearty sup-porter of all worthy enterprises, contributing liberally to all churches, schools, etc. He has been steward of the Methodist church and superintendent of the Sunday-school for about twenty years. He is a self-made man and a very successful one. His views on the temper-ance question have always been pronounced and outspoken. He was the first man to circu-late a petition against saloons in his county, which has now, and for a number of years has had, local option.

Hon. Henry C. Griffin, a prominent citizen and postmaster of Natchez, Miss., is the son of Alonzo M. and Maria L. (Cordery) Griffin, the father a native of Pittsburg, Pa., born in 1811, and the mother of Baltimore, Md., born in 1818. Alonzo M. Griffin, when but a boy, left his home and came to Natchez, living a number of years with an uncle, Peter Little, who had emigrated to that city in the latter part of the last century. Mr. Little brought the first steam engine that was ever in that vicinity, and with it operated a sawmill for a number of years. He afterward engaged in planting, and became one of the wealthiest men in Adams county. His death occurred in 1857. Alonzo M Griffin remained in Natchez until grown, and then returned to the East, where he married Miss Cordery, of Baltimore, returning to Natchez in 1836, where they made their future home. He was postmaster of Natchez under President Taylor, and died in 1872. Mrs. Griffin was killed by a falling house in 1886. Her father, James Cordery, was a native of Baltimore, and built the first dockyard and the first vessel in Chesapeake bay. Hon. Henry C. Griffin was born in Natchez in 1844, received his education in the public schools of that city, and is the fourth of ten children, all living. When but seventeen years of age, Henry C. joined the Natchez Fencibles, company G, Twelfth Mississippi, and served as corporal, fighting at Seven Pines and all the principal engagements of the Virginia campaign, until the battle of Frazier's farm in Aug-ust, 1862, when he was severely wounded in the foot, which disabled him from further service. In 1872 he was elected mayor of Natchez, and in 1875 was elected as state senator from the Natchez district. In July, 1884, he was appointed special agent of the general land office for the United States government, with headquarters at Jackson, and this position he held with credit during the democratic administration, principally through popularity and through the influence of many friends among his political opponents. He continued in that office until 1890, and was then made postmaster of Natchez. While serving as mayor, he was, for about two years, editor of the Natchez *Sun*, an independent paper. In 1890 he was the republican candidate for congress in the sixth district, and made a very creditable showing at the polls. He received many complimentary notices through the press during the campaign, as a shrewd politician and a man whose character was unassailable. In August, 1887, he was united in marriage to Miss Harriet E. Beard, a native of Natchez, and the daughter of William and Clara A. (Stockbridge) Beard, the father a native of Pennsylvania and the mother of Texas. When a young man, William Beard came South and was married at New Orleans, but was an early settler at Natchez, where he died in 1862. Mrs. Beard is still a resident of Natchez, and is a member of the Methodist church. To Mr. and Mrs. Griffin have been born four children, all sons: William T., Henry B., Marion C. and Charles C. Mr. and Mrs. Griffin hold membership in the Episcopal church.

John Griffin was born on the 15th of September, 1826, near Warrenton, Mississippi, on the Magnolia plantation, where his grandfather, Jonah Griffin, settled in 1795. The grandfather was a native of South Carolina and came to Mississippi via Tennessee and Mississippi rivers, bringing with him his large family, slaves and stock. He died on his place in Mississippi at a ripe old age. His son Francis was reared upon this plantation in Warren county, and received his education at Transylvania university at Lexington, Kentucky, traveling from his Mississippi home to that place on horseback. While there the second war with England occurred and he enlisted in a Kentucky regiment under Governor Shelby and served under General Harrison, participating in the battle of the Thames. Returning to Mississippi after the war he was there married to Miss Downs, who died in a short time. His second marriage was to Leanora Scarlett, a cousin to his former wife and a native of Warren county, Mississippi. Her parents were early settlers of that county and worthy people. By the second marriage there were five children, the subject of this sketch being the eldest. In 1828 Francis Griffin moved to Washington county, Mississippi, located at the foot of Island No. 84, and opened up a plantation which he named Refuge. He came up to this his future place of residence in keel-boats, and in his new home saw much of the hardship of pioneer life, as most of his possessions had been swept away a short time before in a mercantile venture. He was a member of the Mississippi legislature and judge of the county court. He was considered a man of great force of character and was said to be the largest cotton planter in the world. He died in 1865 at Refuge plantation, in his seventy-third year. His wife died in 1837. John Griffin, son of the above union, passed most of his boyhood at Refuge. In 1836 he entered school at Holly Springs, Miss., where he remained but a few months when he was called home by the death of his mother. After this he did not return but later entered a school in Sumner county, Tennessee, where he remained for about two years. He then attended a school at Shelbyville, Ky., for six years; after which he studied at the University of Virginia for some time and later entered the law department of the University of Louisville, from which he graduated in 1857. After this he returned to his home in Mississippi and for a time was variously employed, for the most part assisting his father in his business. He was married on the 22d of March, 1852, at Shelbyville, Ky., to Miss Sarah Lane, daughter of John Lane, then marshal of Kentucky. To this marriage were born ten children. Mr. Griffin was formerly an old line whig and was opposed to secession, but since the war has affiliated with the democratic party, although very broad and conservative in his views, especially on questions of a national character. He has devoted much time to hybridizing and improving cotton and has been quite successful. He crossed the sea-island cotton with the common variety and vice versa, thus improving the length and character of the fiber without sacrificing the yield per acre. This has only been accomplished by repeated crossing, selecting and experimenting in many directions, which may still reach better results. Mrs. Griffin is a member of the Episcopal church. Their son, John L , is the present sheriff of Washington county.

J. Wyatt Griffin, a member of the Moss Point Lumber company, is the subject of the following notice. He was born in Perry county, Miss., in 1849, and is a son of William C. and Elvira (Patson) Griffin, who are also natives of Perry county, Miss. The Griffin family were among the early pioneers of the state of Mississippi. The father of our subject has spent the greater part of his life in agricultural pursuits, giving special attention to the raising of livestock. He is well and favorably known throughout Perry county, where he still resides. He was twice married. J. Wyatt and William are the children of the first marriage; nine children were born of the second union, eight sons and one daughter. J. Wyatt is the eldest of the family and was reared in Perry county, Miss., and trained to agriculture. When he was old enough to go out into the world, he embarked in the lumber business; he got out timber from Black creek in Perry county, making the start in business which has proven so successful. In 1880 he removed to Moss Point, and was connected with L. N. Dantzler in the sawmill business for some time. He then formed a partnership with Mr. Houze, the firm name being Houze & Griffin. The relationship existed four years, and in January, 1891, they incorporated with a good capital, and the name was changed to the Moss Point Lumber company. They ship lumber to distant points and do an extensive and profitable business. Mr. Griffin is vice-president of the company. He is a man of excellent business qualifications and has a complete knowledge of the business in which he is engaged. He was married in December, 1876, to Mary C. McCallum, and two children were born of the union: Laura D. and Anna. Mr. Griffin is an honored member of the Knights of Honor and of the Methodist Episcopal church, South.

William Griffin, Moss Point, a highly respected citizen, has for many years been identified with the history of Jackson county, and is well worthy of mention in this record of Mississippi men. He was born in the year 1800, in Burke county, Ga., a son of William and Mary (Stewart) Griffin, natives of Georgia, and is now ninety-one years of age. His parents, about the year 1801, settled in Washington county, Ala., where they saw many hardships and privations. The father died in Greene county, Miss., at the age of fifty-three years. He had but one child, the subject of this notice. The mother was married a second time to a Mr. Clarke. She died in February, 1854. William Griffin, Jr., was reared in Perry county, Miss., which was then a territory, the Indian population of which far exceeded the white. He was reared to agricultural pursuits, but turned to any vocation that would afford an honest living. He represented the people of Perry county in the state legislature. He was faithful to the duty that presented itself, and became a prominent citizen. In 1853 he came to Moss Point, and embarked in the lumber business, being one of the first to erect a sawmill there. After the war he was a member of the Sharkey convention. He used every effort and all his influence to prevent secession, and was a Henry Clay whig. He was married in 1823, March 20th, to Mary Carter, and nine children were born of the union; five of them are living : William C., Dr. E. F., Mrs. L. N. Dantzler, Mrs. J. F. Moore, and Mary. The mother died in 1889. Mr. Griffin is now ninety-one years of age. He has been a successful business man, and has accumulated a competency. He still has some investments in the lumber business in Moss Point.

W. H. Griffin, as a merchant, is progressive, enterprising, and industrious, and by his upright methods of conducting his affairs he has gained sufficient patronage to bring him in a handsome sum annually. He was born in Tuscaloosa county, Ala., in 1844, to J. T. and E. S. (McConnell) Griffin, the former of whom was born near Mammoth cave, Ky., in 1816, of which cave his father, Spencer Griffin, was at one time owner. The latter was of Irish descent, but a native of Virginia, in which state he was married to a Miss Day, afterward removing to Kentucky, from which state he moved to South Carolina with his family. In this state the boyhood days of J. T. Griffin were spent, but his advantages were limited, as a three-month term of school was the longest he ever attended. He was very desirous of becoming an intelligent and well-informed man, and as a means to this end many of his nights were spent in studying by the light of pine knots. At the age of twenty years he was sufficiently fitted to engage in teaching school, and this occupation he followed with success for three years. At this time he was united in marriage to Miss E. S. McConnell, of Tuscaloosa county, Ala,, but who was born in Jackson county, Ga., in 1820, a daughter of John McConnell, of Scotch-Irish descent. The latter became a well-to-do planter, and was the owner of a large number of negroes, to whom he gave large patches of land, which they cultivated at night. What they obtained from this land they were allowed to keep, and many of them accumulated considerable means, and, after the war, were enabled to start in life for themselves. Mr. McConnell kept a postoffice in his own house, which was known by his name, and in addition to his fine plantation and the large number of slaves of which he was the owner, he was an extensive dealer and raiser of cattle. Soon after his marriage J. T. Griffin engaged in keeping a hotel, and in connection with his brother bought horses and mules in Kentucky, selling them in Mississippi. About this time he was brigadier-general of the state troops of Alabama, and drilled his troops at a point about ten miles north of Carrollton, Pickens county, Ala., at which place was located the drillground. Prior to his marriage he was a soldier in the Florida war, being at that time only nineteen years of age. In 1846 he removed from Alabama to Chickasaw county, Miss., and here in time became so thoroughly and favorably known that he represented Chickasaw county in the house of representatives at intervals for thirty-five years. He was formerly a whig in politics, but at the organization of the Greenback party he became a candidate for congress on that ticket. He was a member of the Masonic fraternity, in which he attained to the chapter, and near the close of his life he became a member of the Christian church. He died on January 25, 1889. His widow, who still survives him, united with the Methodist church when a girl. W. H. Griffin is one of thirteen children, ten of whom lived to maturity: Mary C., wife of H. L. Pratt, of Hohenlinden, Webster county, Miss.; James M., of Houston, and Lucretia (twins), the latter being the wife of J. M. Harley, of Tishomingo; J. T.; William H.; Martha A., wife of J. M. Harris, of Prudeville, Pontotoc county, Miss.; Malinda Ellen, wife of J. E. Hobson, of Houlka, Miss.; Joseph, a surveyor of Houston; Laura M., wife of J. E. Jamison, of Houston, and Leonora S. Jack, Jr., is deceased. W. H. Griffin spent his youth on his father's plantation north of Houston, and while not attending school his services were required on the home plantation. He attended school for about four months throughout the year until he was fifteen years of age, at which time he was sent for one year to the boarding-school of Captain Fitzpatrick. During this time volunteers were called for service in the Confederate army, and Mr. Griffin, with the enthusiasm of youth, left school at the age of sixteen years, and enlisted in company H, Eleventh Mississippi infantry, in which he served until August 29, 1862, when he was severely wounded in the side by a ball, which caused considerable injury to one of the bones. He was also wounded in the wrist in the same battle by a ball which broke the bone. In October, 1863, he was discharged for disability, and although his wound had not yet healed, he joined the cavalry the following April, serving in the Eighth Mississippi until the war closed, being paroled at Gainesville, Ala. He was in the battles of Chickahominy, Cedar mountain, the second battle of Manassas, Harrisburg—where he was twice injured by spent balls, being disabled for three weeks—at Brice's crossroads, at Selma, and Gainesville, Ala. Upon his return home he acted as bookkeeper and collector for his father during the remainder of 1865, and the following year engaged in planting, but sold out his interest in his crop to take upon himself the duties of deputy chancery clerk with his brother, with whom he remained six months. From the sale of some stock and other property which he owned he raised about $300, with which he took a course in Bryant & Stratton's business college in St. Louis, Mo., finishing his course in four months. Upon leaving that institution he found himself in debt to the extent of $100, but he managed in a short time to repay the loan, and on a crop which he raised on his father's land that same year he realized $250. After holding a clerkship in Okolona during 1868, he in 1870 went to Louisville, Ky., where he was in the sewing-machine business for some time, after which he took the agency for the Wheeler & Wilson sewing machines in Florida and Georgia. In 1872 he began putting down cement paving, in partnership with a Mr. Lancaster, but this calling did not prove as remunerative as his former callings had done and he discontinued it. From August, 1872, until the following spring he made his home with his father, at which time he undertook the management of his father's plantation, and by July 4 sold his interest in the crop for $125. He then purchased the stock of goods belonging to W. J. Harrill, which amounted to $4,400, but a few months later sold out and in June, 1880, went to Redland, five miles north of Houlka, where he remained six years, at which time he purchased a house and store building in Houlka, and in that town has resided ever since. He is the owner of about two thousand acres of land in eight tracts in Chickasaw and Pontotoc counties, in addition to the management of which he is extensively engaged in dealing in livestock, and to a small extent in stock-breeding. He is essentially a self-made man, and the greater portion of his property has been acquired by his own efforts. He was a candidate for the office of supervisor of Pontotoc county after a residence there of only two years, but was beaten by the opposing candidate by only one vote. He is a member of John S. Kane lodge No. 259, of the A. F. & A. M. of Houlka, Miss., and has long been a member of the Christian church, in which he is one of the teachers in the Sunday-school and has a class numbering twenty-nine. On October 25, 1877, he was united in marriage to Miss Missouri A. Baskin, who was born in Chickasaw county, Miss., in 1852, a daughter of William P. and Sarah J. (Holliday) Baskin, who now reside in Houlka. To Mr. and Mrs. Griffin one child was born, which died in infancy.

John W. Griffis, merchant and president of the Grenada bank, is a native of Yalobusha county, Miss., born in what is now Grenada county in 1847, and is the son of Jesse Griffis, and the grandson of Nicholas Griffis, who reared a family of ten children, one of whom is yet living, Mrs. Hardy of Hardy station (see sketch). A native of the Palmetto state, born in the famous old Edgefield district, Jesse Griffis showed in his character the sterling qualities which have made the best type of Carolinians famous for their worth, intelligence, and honor the world over, and which have made their names synonyms for courage, truth and honesty. He came to Mississippi in 1837, settled in Yalobusha county, and there resided until his death, on December 5, 1889, at the age of eighty-four years. He was married while in South Carolina to Miss Jane S. White, also a native of Edgefield district, born in 1820, and who died at the age of forty years, a faithful member of the Baptist church, having joined the same at the early age of fifteen years. To this union were born seven children. Jesse Griffis was a quiet, unobtrusive gentleman, who believed in doing his best to discharge the full measure of his duty to his fellowmen, his country and his God, and whose hand and voice were ever ready to calls of charity, friendship and patriotism. He was a man of decided piety. More than two-thirds of his long life were spent in earnest Christian toil, and for forty-four years he filled, with credit to himself, the office of deacon of Mount Paran church. He was noted among men for his integrity and honesty, and for all those noble traits that mark a man of purity of character. No one ever thought of doubting his word or impugning his motives. At a ripe old age he passed to the rest and the reward he had so richly deserved by a long life of usefulness, probity and unblemished integrity, leaving surviving him four daughters, one son and a large number of grandchildren and other relatives who had in his untarnished life and honorable career a proud heritage of goodness and virtue. Three only of these children are now living, and all reside in Mississippi. John W. Griffis, the fifth in order of birth of the above mentioned family, was reared on a farm in Yalobusha county and his early scholastic advantages were received in the common schools, preparatory to entering college. When fully ready and about the right age to enter, the war broke out and he flung aside his books to enlist in company K, Third Mississippi regiment of cavalry. After the battle of Salem, Miss., he was appointed third lieutenant. He was wounded in the breast at Atlanta, Ga., and was confined to the hospital at Eufaula, Ala., for a number of months, but finally rejoined his command at Milledgeville, Ga. He participated in the following battles: Salem, Miss.—the Atlanta campaign—Wyatt and Clinton, Miss., Jonesboro, Ala., and was paroled at Livingston, Ala., in 1865. Returning to the home place he engaged in planting for one year and then went to Hardy station where he embarked in merchandising, continuing there until 1872. He then came to Grenada and was employed as salesman for Robert Mullin two years and Lake Bros. for four years. He established his present business in 1879 and is doing a general merchandising business of upward of $140,000 per annum, being one of the largest dealers in the county. Mr. Griffis is a self made man, having commenced with little else than a pair of willing hands and the determination to succeed. He was chosen president of the Grenada bank in September, 1890, and is one of its heaviest stockholders. His marriage to Miss Cora Mullin of Grenada, Miss., daughter of Robert and Mary Mullin, natives of Belfast, Ireland and Tennessee respectively, occurred in 1876. Mrs. Griffis is a member of the Methodist Episcopal church and is one of its very liberal supporters. Mr. Griffis is one of Grenada's best citizens and most prominent men. He is a democrat, but takes no especial interest in political affairs. Aside from his mercantile and banking interests he deals in real estate and is one of the directors of the Central Fair and Livestock association.

B. W. Griffith has been connected with the Capital State bank since 1878, the first five years serving in the capacity of bookkeeper, since which time he has filled the position of cashier in a very capable and satisfactory manner. Mr. Griffith is a banker of experience and sound judgment, to whose efficiency is largely due the prosperous condition of the bank, much of his financial ability being inherited from his worthy and honored father. He was born in Jackson in 1853, the second of a family of four children born to Richard and Sallie (Whitfield) Griffith, the former of whom was born in the Keystone state in 1815, and the latter in Mississippi. Richard Griffith, after the death of his father, which occurred when he was a lad, removed to Ohio with his mother, and in the university of that state he graduated with first honors. He soon after came to Vicksburg, Miss., and began life as a schoolteacher, but on the outbreak of the Mexican war he enlisted in the service and was made adjutant of the First Mississippi volunteers, commanded by Col. Jefferson Davis, in whose regiment he was during the entire war. Upon his return to his home he was elected to the position of state treasurer, at the end of which term he was reëlected. While Buchanan was president he was appointed marshal of the southern district of Mississippi, and was holding that position at the outbreak of the Civil war. He at once volunteered in the

W. S. Featherston.

Confederate service, was immediately elected colonel of the Twelfth Mississippi regiment of infantry, and was attached to the Army of Virginia. He was soon made brigadier-general, commanding the Seventh Mississippi brigade, and on the 29th of June, 1862, was killed in one of the seven days' fights before Richmond. He was a warm friend of Jefferson Davis, and had every reason to believe that he could be made a major-general, but declined the position, fearing that it was offered him merely from friendship. He was a fine student of military tactics, and was a brave, faithful and efficient officer, conspicuous for his faithfulness to the Confederate cause, as well as for his strict adherence to duty. After his term as state treasurer had expired he located permanently in Jackson, where he engaged in the banking business, which calling continued to be his chief occupation until the war opened, the business being conducted during his absence by his partner, J. D. Stewart. He was married three times, his first wife, a Miss Carpenter formerly, bearing him a son, R. C., who served as a lieutenant in the Civil war. His second wife, a Miss Hatch, of Vicksburg, lived but a few months after their marriage. His third union was to Miss Sallie Whitfield, and occurred at the home of her father, Rev. Benjamin Whitfield, in Hinds county, Miss. The latter was an able minister of the Baptist church, and became well known throughout the western portion of the state, whither he moved from North Carolina. He was the chief factor in the organization of Mississippi college, at Clinton, and was an active worker up to the day of his death, in 1872. To Mr. Griffith's last union four children were born: Jefferson Davis, B. W., Lucy A., wife of Henry F. Baily, of Jackson, Miss., and Richard. B. W. Griffith was educated in Mississippi college, at Clinton, and graduated at the close of 1872 with first honors of his class. He was then engaged by the board of trustees of that institution as professor of mathematics, but before entering upon his duties he entered Eastman's business college at Poughkeepsie, N. Y., and being perfect in every examination was graduated at the end of eight weeks, which was the first and only time this ever happened in the history of the institution. He began his duties as teacher in the college in the fall of 1872, which he discharged in a manner to merit the highest commendation from all, and during the two years that he was the occupant of this position he justly held rank among the prominent and distinguished instructors of youth of the country. In 1874 he began studying law, was admitted to the bar two years later, and practiced his profession until 1878, when he began filling the duties of his present responsible position. He was married in 1879 to Miss Cora Griffing, of Claiborne county, a daughter of David C. Griffing, a member of an old and prominent family of this state. To Mr. Griffith and his wife the following children have been born: Richard, David C., Benjamin W., Cora and Sallie. Mr. Griffith is treasurer of the state Y. M. C. A., the Mississippi college, the Baptist state convention board, was a founder and is a director of the Building and Loan association, and is a director of the Jackson Fertilizer company. His brother, Jefferson Davis, is now a leading physician in Kansas City. He graduated from Bellevue hospital, of New York city, and is now president of the Medical college at Kansas City, where he located in 1873. After graduating in 1871, he spent two years as an instructor in the hospital. He is becoming eminent as a surgeon, for he makes that branch of his profession a specialty, and seems to have a natural aptitude for the same. He was married to Miss Sallie Comingo, a daughter of Hon. A. Comingo, of that place, by whom he has two children.

Richard Griffith, general manager of the Mississippi Compress and Warehouse company, at Jackson, is thoroughgoing, practical and intelligent, and is eminently fitted for this position. He is a native of the city of Jackson, where he was born in 1860, the youngest child of Richard and Sallie (Whitfield) Griffith; for a further history of whom see sketch of B. W. Griffith.

52

Richard Griffith, Jr., was educated at the Mississippi college, but left school in 1881 and began clerking in a warehouse of this city.   One year later he purchased the warehouse and conducted the business of cotton weighing and storing until 1889, when he sold out to the Compress company, which consolidated and became the Mississippi Compress and Warehouse company.   Mr. Griffith became its general manager, and since the business has been in his hands the company is becoming prosperous and its stock is increasing.   Its compress is the Morse compress, which was exhibited by S. B. Steers & Co. at the cotton exposition at New Orleans, and is supposed to be the best ever erected, it having a record of loading one hundred and one bales of cotton in one car.   The storage capacity of this company is ten thousand bales of cotton, which shows the spacious dimensions of its plant.   Mr. Griffith is one of the organizers and is now a director of the Jackson bank, one of Jackson's solid and successful business organizations.   He owns a beautiful and commodious residence in Jackson, which he and his family enjoy to the utmost.   He was married in 1885 to Miss Mary Jo. Cooper, a daughter of Joseph W. Cooper, of Jackson.   Her father, who was a native of Mississippi, was a member of one of the old families of the state, was a well known planter of Holmes county and died in 1873.   He owned plantation interests in Holmes county to the amount of two thousand six hundred acres, of which one thousand two hundred acres are under cultivation.   This land is situated in the Yazoo delta, is extremely fertile and is one of the finest plantations in that section.   Mr. Griffith and his wife are members of the Baptist church and the Methodist Episcopal church, respectively, and he is a member of the I. O. O. F., the K. of P. and the American Legion of Honor.   His reputation as a man of business is deservedly high, and his efficient management of the Mississippi Compress and Warehouse company, of Jackson, has given it a wide reputation, and his knowledge of every detail of the business, and his prompt and satisfactory methods of dealing, have caused this enterprise to prosper from its inception to the present time.

J. L. Griggs is one of the foremost merchants of Macon, Miss., and is a progressive, useful and enterprising citizen in every respect.   He was born in Kemper county of the state in which he resides in 1841, a son of Anderson C. and Eliza A. (Scudday) Griggs, who were born in Georgia and South Carolina respectively, but were principally reared in Alabama.   The father was educated in the University of Alabama, and about 1835 removed to Kemper county, Miss., and in 1845 located in Noxubee county, where he followed the calling of a planter until his death in 1849.   His widow still survives him, and resides in Macon.   Their union was blessed in the birth of six children, all of whom are deceased with the exception of the subject of this sketch, who is the eldest of the family.   He received his early schooling in Noxubee county, but in 1861 graduated from the Cumberland university of Lebanon, Tenn., the same year enlisting as a soldier in the Confederate army, becoming a member of company F, Eleventh Mississippi infantry, in which he served two years, when he was transferred to Colonel Armstead's regiment of cavalry.   He was made lieutenant of company K of this command, the duties of which position he discharged with ability until the final surrender, participating in many hotly contested engagements.   After the war was over he returned to Macon, Miss., where he followed the calling of a planter for about ten years.   He then removed to the town of Macon, where he has since been engaged in merchandising, and has, owing to the honorable business methods he has practiced, built up a large and lucrative trade throughout the surrounding country.   He deals largely in general merchandise, buys and sells cotton, has a large furniture and undertaking establishment, and is the proprietor af the Magnolia livery and sale stables.   He is a fine financier and the owner of much valuable real estate, is vice president of the Merchants and

Farmers' bank, and is interested in nearly all the leading and worthy enterprises in and around Macon, being considered by his fellow-citizens a representative man. He is a member of the Masonic fraternity, the K. of P., and the K. of H., in all of which orders he is a leading and active member. In 1863 he was married to Miss Lucy K. Winston, a native of Tennessee, by whom he has five children—Minnie, wife of V. C. Cavett, of Jackson, Tenn.; Lulu J., Martha E., Mary W., and Joe Len. Mrs. Griggs is a member of the Presbyterian church.

E. J. Guice is one of the conscientious men engaged in business in the city of Natchez, and by his honorable business methods he is now enjoying a safe and constantly increasing custom. He was born in Franklin county, Miss., in 1825, being the seventh of eight children born to Jacob and Susanna (Grantham) Guice, who were born in Tennessee and South Carolina respectively, the former coming to this state with his parents in 1789. His grandfather, Jonathan Guice, located at Fort Rosalie, but some time thereafter removed with his three brothers to Franklin county, where he became the owner of a valuable plantation, on which he erected the first cottongin in the county, and on which he died after having spent a long and useful life. He was a Pennsylvanian by birth. Jacob Guice inherited German blood of his father and many of the characteristics of that people, among which may be mentioned thrift, industry and honesty. He was a captain in the war of 1812, held the office of justice of the peace, was the postmaster at Portersville, and on the plantation of which he was the owner he resided until his death, which occurred in Jefferson county in 1851. He had long been a member and was an active worker in the Methodist Episcopal church. E. J. Guice was reared on his father's plantation, and at the age of twenty-two years was married and began farming in Tensas parish, La., on his own responsibility. After a short time he removed to Louisiana, and after becoming the owner of a plantation there he resided on it for nearly ten years. From that time until 1872 he resided in Franklin county, but has since been one of the prominent settlers of Natchez. Here he first began merchandising in wholesale and retail dry goods house, but for some time past had been in the insurance business, being with the firm of E. G. De Lap & Co. He has taken an active part in the affairs of this city since his residence here and was one of the incorporators of the Natchez cotton mill, and for some time was one of its directors. The maiden name of his wife was Lucilla Coleman, a daughter of Isaiah Coleman, a member of an old Jefferson county, Miss., family. To them one child was born, Charles Isaiah, who died at the age of two and a half years. Mr. and Mrs. Guice are members of the Methodist Episcopal church and he is a Knight Templar in the Masonic fraternity. He is a most estimable citizen, is a member of a prominent firm of insurance agents, has been very active in his time, and is now enjoying the fruits of a well spent life.

Among the people of Adams, as well as the surrounding counties, the name of Dr. N. L. Guice is by no means an unfamiliar one, for he has been actively and successfully engaged in the practice of his chosen profession since 1858; He was born in Franklin county, Miss, in 1838, the second in a family of nine children born to A. J. and Clarissa (Higdon) Guice, both of whom were born in this state. The paternal grandfather, Daniel Guice, was one of the early pioneers of the state, first taking up his abode in Adams and afterward in Franklin county, his time and attention throughout his life being given to planting. He was prominent in the Methodist Episcopal church for years, was magistrate of Franklin county, and died on his farm in that county in 1850. A. J. Guice also followed the occupation of planting, was justice of the peace for years, and in his early days was captain of a military company. He died on his farm in 1886, at the age of seventy-four years, his first wife having passed from life in 1856. He afterward married again and he and his family were members of the Methodist Episcopal church. Dr. N. L. Guice remained on the home plantation until he attained his twentieth year, and in the meantime obtained a good practical education, including Latin and Greek, in the common schools. About 1856 he began the study of medicine, and two years later graduated from the University of Louisiana, after which he at once began practicing in Jefferson county, Miss. Here he remained, building up an enviable reputation and a fine practice, until 1886, since which time he has been a resident of Natchez. He is a member of the State medical association, of which he was president in 1887–8, and is also a prominent member of the American medical association, and has written numerous valuable articles for different medical journals throughout the country. He is literary in his tastes, and his articles for different scientific journals have been highly commended. He has a fine library, but it is far from consisting entirely of medical works. He is amiable, social and friendly in disposition, and as his success as a practitioner has been pronounced, he has a large practice and is deservedly very popular. He speaks highly of Natchez as a healthful location, and pronounces malarial diseases very scarce in that city. Socially, he is a member of the Masonic fraternity, the K. of H. and the K. of P. He has always taken an active part in the political affairs of his country, and was a leader of the democratic party in Jefferson county, being especially active in the campaigns from 1875 to 1885. He was married in 1881 to Miss Florence Pugh, a native of West Virginia, her father and mother being Virginians, but in the month of January, eighteen months after their marriage, she died leaving one son, Charles Pugh. His second marriage took place at Parkersburg, W. Va., April 29, 1890, his wife being Miss Annie Neal, a member of an old family of that state. She is a finely educated lady, and is a worthy member of the Episcopal church.

John I. Guion was a native of Adams county, Miss., and was educated in Tennessee, finishing with law at Lebanon of the same state. He returned to Mississippi and formed a partnership for the practice with W. L. Sharkey and located at Vicksburg. This partnership was dissolved in 1832 by the appointment of Mr. Sharkey to the circuit judgeship, whereupon Mr. Guion formed a partnership for the practice of law with the great lawyer and orator, S. S. Prentiss. In 1836 Mr. Guion was appointed to the criminal court bench, but a year later resigned and formed a partnership with W. C. Smedes. He was sent to the legislature and in 1851, was president of the state senate, and the same year was acting governor in the place of Governor Qitman, who had resigned. Succeeding this he was elected judge of the circuit court, and thus continued to serve until his death, in 1855. He was a skillful lawyer, an eloquent speaker, and a profound judge.

Dr. H. S. Gully, of Meridian, Miss., was born in Kemper county, Miss., February 15, 1860, a son of H. J. and Anna J. (Lamper) Gully, natives of Alabama and South Carolina. The Gully family were early settlers in Kemper county, and the grandfather was one of the first sheriffs elected after its organization. He was a prominent man, well known there until his death. The family took a high position in the county. His father, Hon. H. J. Gully, a planter by occupation, is living in Winston. He represented Kemper and Winston counties in the senate and Winston in the legislature. He was a captain of a company in the late war, and received a wound at the battle of Franklin. He had three sons, and one daughter, of whom Dr. H. S. Gully is the second. He remained in Kemper county until he was thirteen years old, and received his literary education at the Cooper institute in Lauderdale county, and graduated from the Louisville (Ky.) medical college February 25, 1885, with second honors in a class of eighty. He was for four months a physician in the Louisville hospital, and later practiced a year at Shuqualak, Noxubee county, Miss. In 1888 he was appointed assistant superintendent of the Eastern Mississippi insane asylum, a position which he filled creditably for two years, since then having been engaged in private practice at Meridian. He is a member of the State medical association and of the Lauderdale County medical association, and ranks high as a physician and surgeon. He is a member of the Independent Order of Odd Fellows and of the Knights of Pythias. He is also examining surgeon for his lodge in the latter order. He is a gentleman who has won the esteem of the community and county in which he lives, both as a man and as a physician and surgeon, and is one who well deserves such admiration.

A prominent planter of Bolivar county, after whom the town of Gunnison was named, is Arvin N. Gunnison, planter, a native of Georgia, and of the five children born to his parents, Arvin and Sarah (Putnam) Gunnison, he was third in order of birth. The parents were natives of New Hampshire, in which state their nuptials were celebrated, and about 1859 they moved South, locating at New Orleans, where the father, who was a machinist, engaged in business under the firm name of Gunnison & Chapman. He was engaged in manufacturing arms for the Confederate government, and on the capture of that city and the destruction of so much valuable property, he moved to Macon, Ga. He there continued business and converted a cottongin shop into a factory for that purpose. After the war he came to Washington county, Miss., engaged in planting, and in 1869 came to Bolivar county, where he purchased five hundred and twenty-eight acres, about one-half of which was cleared. This property was then three miles from Concordia, and is now the present site of Gunnison. Mr. Gunnison made quite extensive improvements, and became well known throughout the county. His death occurred in February, 1882. During the flood of that year great damage was done to this property. In personal appearance Mr. Gunnison was rather above the average hight, was rather slender and had dark hair and eyes. His widow and two sons are now residing in New Hampshire. Arvin N. Gunnison was born in the year 1865, was reared in Mississippi, and what education he has received is mainly the result of his own application. After the death of his father, and when but seventeen years of age, he assumed charge of the plantation, cleared more land, and now has five hundred acres under cultivation, the whole property being thoroughly improved. He has fifteen good tenant houses on the estate, and is the owner of a superior steamgin. He is now about to erect a new residence, which promises to be a model of neatness and convenience. The railroad was built in 1889, and a station established on Mr. Gunnison's property was named for him. Mr. Gunnison at once began selling lots, and soon quite a little village was established. Although not yet two years old, this is one of the busiest stations on the line of road, and in it are some of the largest and best stores in the county. A postoffice was established in 1889, and Mr. Gunnison was appointed postmaster. He has had a store on his place since 1886, and carries a stock of goods valued at $2,000, while his annual business yields him about $16,000. This is mainly to supply his own tenants. The town of Gunnison is surrounded by a magnificent country, very productive and thickly settled, and the back country is rapidly being opened, thus promising a prosperous future for the town. Around it are already scattered a number of beautiful homes, and many more will soon be erected in the town, for it is a desirable and attractive place of settlement. Mr. Gunnison, though a very young man, has exhibited great business capacity and an unusual faculty for management. His active interests are naturally more centered in and around the town that bears his name and he may be depended upon to generously contribute, toward its advancement. In personal appearance he resembles his father to some extent.

The fine plantation of Curtis H. Guy, planter, Grenada, Miss., consisting of one thousand six hundred acres, is situated eleven miles west of the city of Grenada, and is one of the most productive and fertile tracts of land in the county. It is kept in the best of condition by Mr. Guy, who is one of the foremost planters, and who handles annually one hundred and fifty bales of cotton. He was born in Grenada county in 1843, on what is yet known as the Old Guy place, settled by his father in 1834. The paternal grandparents, Dr. Joseph and Esther (Sharp) Guy, were natives respectively of North and South Carolina, and the former was of Irish extraction. He moved from his native state to Tuscumbia, Franklin county, Ala., in 1825, or '26, and there his wife died in 1845. He was a physician of considerable prominence, had a good practice, and was the only one in Elbert or Franklin county for many years. He was a stanch democrat in his political views and he and wife were worthy and exemplary members of the Presbyterian church. Their union was blessed by the birth of ten children, three daughters and seven sons, all of whom lived to be grown. The youngest one, Albert, is yet living in Colbert county, Ala., where he has made his home since 1825. Another son, the father of our subject, Curtis Haywood Guy, familiarly known as Major Guy, was born near Raleigh, N. C., in 1799, and was second in order of birth of the above mentioned children. He was reared in his native state and there married his first wife, Miss Harriet Alexander, a native also of the Old North state, who died about 1826, leaving one child, Julius A., who still survives and is a citizen of Grenada county, Miss. The father was then married in Tipton, West Tenn., to Mrs. Harper, whose maiden name was Miss Eliza Scurlock. She had three brothers, Miles, William and Timothy. The first was killed in the Mexican war, the second, serving also in that war, was captured by General Santa Anna, but succeeded in making his escape. He died near Houston, Tex., at an advanced age, leaving a large family of children. Timothy settled in Jackson, Tenn., practiced law, and there died, leaving three daughters and two sons, all of whom are living. Major Guy moved from Tennessee to Yalobusha county, Miss., in 1834, and there resided until his death on the 5th of December, 1870. He was one of the leading men of Yalobusha county (afterward Grenada county), a prominent politician, and always took an active part in the canvass before election, attending all public meetings and conventions held in the county. He held the position of representative of Yalobusha county for eight terms, and then refused to serve any longer. He was a well read man and kept thoroughly apace with the times. Although not a member of any church he was one of the county's best and noblest citizens, and was kind, hospitable and charitable and a liberal contributor to all enterprises worthy of support. He was very popular, had many warm friends, and few, if any, enemies. He had been very successful in all enterprises undertaken, and was a substantial and wealthy citizen. His last wife died in 1865 at the age of sixty years. She was a grand, good woman and much respected. Previous to her marriage to Mr. Guy she had married a Mr. Harper, by whom she had three children, two daughters and a son, all of whom lived to be grown but are now deceased. Camelia married Capt. T. H. Mumford, who was the first man to run a steamboat up the Yalobusha river to Grenada; Martha married George Golladay, a prominent attorney at Grenada, and now has a son engaged in merchandising in that place, and Richard H. Harper, who died in Holmes county in 1881, leaving a wife and child. To Mr. and Mrs. Guy were born the following children: Leander belonged to Ballentine's regiment, Armstrong's brigade, and was killed at Atlanta. He left a wife and one son, the former since married and the latter deceased. Harriet married Dr. Benjamin Drane, of Grenada, and died in October, 1865, at the age of thirty years, leaving one son. Joseph was a soldier in the Fifteenth Mississippi regiment during the war, and died at the old home place at Grenada on the 25th of November, 1870, at the age of thirty years. Curtis H. Guy, the youngest child, remained on the old home place, near Grenada, until 1870, and then came to his present property. He was educated in Grenada and selected his wife in the person of Miss Ione Thomas, daughter of Archie Thomas, of Grenada. She was born in Tallahatchie county, Miss., on the 11th of April, 1851, and died on the 31st of August, 1875, leaving two children : Archibald Trimble and Curtis Scurlock, both named after their grandparents. Archibald died in September, 1880. Mr. Guy took for his second wife Miss Mary Trimble, daughter of Dr. Trimble (see sketch), and a native of Spring Hill, Tallahatchie county, Miss. When but six weeks old she was taken by her parents to a place near where our subject now resides, and there she grew to womanhood. She was well educated in the common schools and at St. Agnes school, Memphis, Tenn. By this last union Mr. Guy became the father of eight children, six of whom are yet living: Shelly, Clare, Lynn Trimble, Marie, Eliza Rebecca, Edith (deceased), Greene Trimble and an infant, older than Rebecca, that died unnamed. In 1861 Mr. Guy entered the Confederate service in the Fifteenth Mississippi cavalry, and served until the close of the war, being paroled at Grenada. He fought in the battles of Corinth, Vicksburg, Harrisburg and was with General Forrest in his raid to Memphis. He was one of nine men who entered Gayoso hotel and captured forty-four Union officers. Afterward he was ordered to Selma, Ala., but the fight was over before he arrived there. Mr. Guy was one of the South's bravest and most valiant soldiers. He had his horse shot from under him during a skirmish at Grenada on the 1st of January, 1865. Like his father, Mr. Guy takes an active and prominent part in politics and his vote is ever cast with the democratic party. He was a delegate to the convention at Grenada when Barry was elected to congress, was at Winona when Mr. Lewis was nominated to congress, and was at the state convention that nominated Governor Stone. Mr. Guy has been a delegate to conventions ever since he was old enough. He is a member of the Knights of Honor at Grenada, and Mrs. Guy is a member of the Presbyterian church. Both are highly respected and this is one of the leading families of the county.

Hon. Albert B. Guynes, of Copiah county, Miss., where he is now engaged in planting, was born in above county in 1848, a son of Henry H. Guynes, a native of Tennessee. His father devoted his entire life to agricultural interests, and came to Mississippi with his parents when quite young, and married Mary B. Finley, a daughter of John and ——— Finley, of Copiah county. His father, the grandfather of our subject, was the son of John and Matilda Guynes, both natives of Tennessee. To Henry Guynes and wife were born eleven children, three of whom are now living: William P., of Grant parish, La. ; Felix R., of Calvert, Tex., and Albert B., our subject. The father served his county as a member of the board of supervisors for a number of years. At the time of the Civil war he was too old for military service, but his family was represented by five sons, three of whom died or were killed. He was a member of the Masonic fraternity, and he and his wife were communicants of the Baptist church. Albert B. Guynes received a good common school education. He prepared himself for teaching, which profession he entered upon at the age of seventeen and followed for about ten years. After that he turned his attention to farming, and during a short period had a store upon his plantation. Wishing to give his children as good an education as the advantages of the place afforded in that part of the state he moved his family in the fall of 1890 to Gallman, where he now resides. In 1870 he married Emma J. Ramsey, a daughter of T. J. Ramsey, whose sketch appears in this work. To Mr. and Mrs. Guynes have been born five children, four of whom are living: Charles O., Jasper F., Eula R., and Andy M. His eldest son entered Mississippi college in 1891. Mr. Guynes is a member of the Baptist church, of Charles Scott lodge No. 136, A. F. & A. M., of the Knights of Honor, also of the Knights of Pythias, and the American Legion of Honor. His social, political and commercial standing is high. He was chosen to represent his county in the constitutional convention of 1890. He was also a member of the house of representatives in 1882 and reëlected 1884. He was an advocate of state supervision of railroads, and in the house journal for 1882, in a report in which he dissented from the recommendation of the majority, are set forth his views, which, though failing at that time, have been since enacted into law. In 1891 he preferred to retire from public life and so spoke and wrote, but his services were again demanded and he was again elected by the democratic party, of which he has always been a member, to a seat in the state legislature by a large majority. The Crystal Springs *Meteor*, a paper published in Copiah county, has this to say on his election in 1891: "Hon. A. B. Guynes. This name is a household word in Copiah county. It seems that every opportunity is seized by our people to honor anew a man who has been so conspicuously faithful to the many trusts confided to his keeping. To merit such confidence and trust and to have it acknowledged by an admiring public is certainly the brightest jewel in the crown of a public man. Mr. Guynes will reflect great credit upon the county, and this paper has the utmost confidence in his integrity and ability." He has been for two years president of Copiah County alliance and is a strong advocate of its principles and demands.

In connection with his planting operations Capt. J. J. Guyton, Guyton, Miss., has also been engaged in general merchandising since 1873, and has met with substantial results in both occupations. He is one of the most successful farmers and business men in Tippah county, owning at the present time about two thousand three hundred acres of land, with five hundred acres under cultivation, and a stock of general merchandise worth about $8,000. In 1889 Mr. Guyton shipped eleven hundred sixty-one bales of cotton and nine hundred bales in 1891. He is engaged in buying and shipping and does an annual business of $30,000. He was born in Union district, S. C., January 11th, 1840, and was the eldest in a family of seven children, born to Abraham J. and Luvicy (Warlick) Guyton, natives of South Carolina and North Carolina, respectively. The maternal grandfather was a blacksmith by trade and a great axmaker in early times, people coming for miles to have him make axes for them. Capt. J. J. Guyton came to Mississippi from South Carolina with his parents in 1851. They located in Tippah county, and there the father bought land and engaged in planting. He was a plain, practical farmer and never aspired to any official position. Previous to the war he was a large land and slave owner, and was well and favorably known all over Tippah county. He was a true Christian, an excellent citizen and the best of neighbors, Both he and wife were members of the Baptist church. Mrs. Guyton died in 1866 and Mr. Guyton in 1881. There are now six of their children living, four sons and two daughters. Captain Guyton was educated in the common schools of the country, and at the age of sixteen years went to Ripley, where he studied medicine with Dr. Carter Stone. He remained with that gentleman until twenty-one years of age, clerking in his drug store, and in 1861 enlisted in company D, of O'Conner's guards, commanded by Capt. J. H. Buchanan, and this was organized into the Second Mississippi regiment at Corinth, Miss. He was under Colonel Faulkner, and was appointed by him as quartermaster-sergeant of the regiment. Still later he was appointed by him to the position of first lieutenant and adjutant of the regiment, and in 1862 he was appointed captain and A. C. S., serving in that position until cessation of hostilities. He was in General Stark's brigade, General Chalmers' division and General Forrest's cavalry corps. He served through the entire war and surrendered at Gainesville, Ala. Returning to his home in Tippah county he engaged in farming, and was married in February, 1867, to Miss Mary E. Graham, who bore him three children, one son and two daughters, Hattie L. (wife of J. I. Swain of Love Station, Miss.), Sallie M. and Leeoty H. (deceased). Mrs. Guyton died November 1, 1875, at her home in Tippah county. She was a consistent member of the Baptist church. Mr. Guyton was next married in October, 1877, to Callie D. Hoyle, of Lee county, Miss., and they have three sons and two daughters: David E., John F., William F., Pearl V., and Callie D. Mr. Guyton educated his two eldest daughters at the female college at Blue Mountain, Miss. Mr. Guyton is favorably known all over Tippah county, has always been a liberal contributor to schools, churches and all other enterprises of a laudable nature, and is called the "poor man's" friend, never having been known to turn any one from his doors hungry. He is a member of the Baptist and Mrs. Guyton is a member of the Methodist church. Mr. Guyton's plantation is located on the Narrow Gauge railroad, ten miles south of Ripley, and the station is called Guyton. The postoffice is also named for him and he has filled the position of postmaster since 1880.

Hon. John E. Gwin, attorney, Lexington, one of the brightest of the legal talent in Holmes county, Miss., was born in that county in December, 1844. His father, James M. Gwin, was born in Carroll county, Tenn., about 1808, and was one of the old settlers of that state. He was reared there, and about 1828 came to Mississippi, locating at Natchez, where he was deputy United States marshal for some time. He was associated with Dr. William M. Gwin (a cousin), also from Tennessee, and made his home in Natchez for a number of years. About 1836 he removed to Holmes county, of that state, located on a farm west of Lexington, and there made his home until quite aged. He was married in Wilkinson county, Miss., to Miss Susan V. Davis, a daughter of Hezekiah Davis, and of an old and prominent family of Mississippi. She was born in Wilkinson county. When well advanced in years, Mr. Gwin moved to Lexington, and resided with his son until his death in 1887. He was a prominent farmer, and accumulated a large estate. His wife died in 1878. He was a prominent Mason. Hon. John E. Gwin, the second in order of birth of the three sons born to this union, was educated by private tutors at home, and then entered the Lexington schools In 1862 he enlisted in the Confederate army, Thirty-eighth Mississippi infantry, company A, as private, and served until the close of the war. They were mounted in the fall of 1863. He participated in the Deer Creek campaign, where there was some heavy fighting, was in a great many skirmishes, and was in Colonel Greerson's raid through Georgia. During that raid he was shot through the head, the ball entering just below the temple and coming out at the nostril. And although not badly hurt, he was disabled for two months. During that time he went home, but, after recovering, returned to his regiment. During the siege of Vicksburg he was on detailed duty, and his company and regiment were captured by the enemy. Mr. Gwin participated in a great many skirmishes and small engagements, and in the summer of 1865 he was paroled at Gainesville, Ala. In 1865 he commenced reading law with Judge J. W. Dyer, and took a course of law in the University of Louisiana in 1866 and '67, graduating in the latter year. Mr. Gwin then located in Lexington, and has had an extensive practice here since. He takes an active part in all political campaigns, but does not aspire for office. In November, 1885, he was elected to the legislature, and served one term in the lower house, being chairman of several committees, while a member of that body. Besides his practice, Mr. Gwin has been engaged in planting since 1885, and is the owner of several large tracts of land, in Le Flore and Carroll counties. As a lawyer Mr. Gwin ranks among the prominent ones of his part of the state, and is a deep reasoner and a clear and forcible speaker. He has been on several very important cases, viz.: the defense of Capt.

S. H. Whitworth, J. K. Harkins and Mr. McClean for the killing of Mr. Ivy and Mr. Aston in Le Flore county in 1888. The case was taken to Greenville, and resulted in acquittal, after a tedious two weeks' trial. Mr. Gwin was also in the celebrated case of Cox vs. Redmond for defendant ; also the case of Eugene Story vs. Mississippi. Mr. Gwin was married first in Lexington in June, 1869, to L. R. Gage, a native of Texas, and the daughter of James E. Gage, of Macon, Miss. She was reared in the last named state, received her education there, and there her death occurred in July, 1878. They became the parents of two children : Susie, a young lady, and Julia Alice, who is attending Nazareth academy. Mr. Gwin was married the second time in 1881, in Grenada, to Miss Bella Hughs, a native of Grenada, Miss., and the daughter of Dr. Hughs, of the last named place. The three children born to this union are named as follows : Sallie Hughs, Joe Willie and Bella Hughs, all daughters. Mr. Gwin is a member of the Knights of Honor and the Knights of Pythias. He and Mrs. Gwin are members of the Episcopal church.

Lewis T. Gwin, a prosperous and progressive merchant of Cleveland, Bolivar county, Mississippi, was born in De Soto county, this state, on the 19th of August, 1858, the eldest of six children born to the marriage of William B. Gwin and Mary K. Tinsley, natives of Kentucky and Tennessee respectively. Although born on Blue Grass soil William B. Gwin spent most of his life in Mississippi and died in De Soto county in 1878. Before the Rebellion his attention was given to planting, but after the war had closed and his slaves had been emancipated he devoted his time to his trade, that of a mechanic. His father, Tarlor Gwin, was a North Carolinian who moved to Kentucky after his marriage, coming soon after to Mississippi and locating at Warrenton, this being before the town of Vicksburg was platted. He was of Scotch-Irish descent and was a man of intelligent and progressive views. The maternal grandparents were Coleman and Margaret (Henderson) Tinsley, natives of Tennessee. Lewis T. Gwin was reared in De Soto county, Mississippi, and although his advantages for acquiring an education were somewhat poor, he managed to attend the public schools for some time. While he has never received the literary training only to be obtained in schools or colleges, he has been trained under the rigid but unerring teacher of experience, and as he commenced to make his own way in the world when a mere lad he has profited by his early trials and is now an independent and original thinker. His father was an invalid the latter part of his life and on Lewis' youthful shoulders fell the care of supporting his mother and five children, until the latter could earn their own livelihood. He devoted his time to following the carpenter's trade and farming, by which means he was able to care for the family in a very satisfactory manner until 1884, at which time he began doing for himself. The following year he went to Texas, but a few months later returned to the home of his childhood and opened a mercantile establishment, which business he continued with success up to the present time. In this business he is associated with a Mr. Bashee and their stock of goods is valued at about $6,000, besides which they own some valuable real estate property in the town. Their mercantile establishment is the best in the town and by their honorable business methods and courtesy and attention to their customers they have built up a payable trade. Mr. Gwin is an enterprising, but cautious, business man, is possessed of unbounded energy and deserves much credit for the excellent use he has made of his life. He has discharged every duty that has been laid upon his shoulders willingly and faithfully, and his record as a son, brother, business man and citizen is alike honorable and worthy of respect. He is unmarried.

ᏩHAPᏖᎬᏒ XX.

FAMILIES OF PROMINENCE, H.

A NATIVE Georgian is C. B. Hagans, whose birth occurred in 1826; since 1858 he has been a resident of Warren county, Miss. He is now next to the eldest of five surviving members of a family of twelve children, born to Edward and Hartie (Porch) Hagans, who were also born in Georgia, the former moving to Talladega county, Ala., at an early day, at which place he engaged in planting. He died, in 1866, at the age of eighty-two years. C. B. Hagans spent his early life in Talladega county, and at the age of twenty-five years engaged in planting, a calling he has followed, with good results, up to the present time. Upon first coming to Warren county, he followed the calling of an overseer for some time, but, upon the opening of the war, turned his attention to other pursuits. He rented land planted until 1872, when he purchased his present property of two hundred and fifty acres, of which two hundred acres are under cultivation. He is a successful and experienced planter, and although his plantation is not as large as many others, it is tilled in such an admirable manner that it yields a larger profit than many much larger places. His property has been acquired through his own efforts, and it is acknowledged by all his acquaintances that his honesty and fair dealing is above question. He was married, in 1855, to Miss Louisa Ware, a native of Alabama, by whom he is the father of six children: J. D., R. W. (deceased), E. H., a resident of Louisiana; G. W., also a resident of that state; C. A., of Warren county, Miss., and M. F., also of this county. Mrs. Hagans died on the 6th of February, 1891, at the age of sixty years, having been an earnest and constant member of the Methodist Episcopal church South, for many years. Mr. Hagans also belongs to that church, is a member of Bovinia lodge No. 112, of the A. F. & A. M., and is an active and public-spirited citizen. His brother Sherrod resides in Alabama; D. C. is unmarried and makes his home with his brother, C. B. Hagans; Sarah, a sister, is the wife of Perry Bullard, of Mississippi, and Amortah is the wife of W. Deacon, and resides in Alabama.

Dayton Hale comes of an old and honored family of the Bay State, but was himself born in the town of Columbus, Miss., of which he is the efficient and trustworthy postmaster, March 10, 1849. His parents, Harrison and Anna M. (Dayton) Hale, were born in Winchendon, Mass., and Basking Ridge, N. J., respectively, both being of good old Puritan stock. William L. Dayton, the maternal great-uncle of the subject of this sketch, was a very prominent man of his day; and during President Lincoln's first administration was minister to France, and in 1856 was a presidential candidate on the ticket of Fremont and Dayton. The Hales are of English origin. Harrison Hale moved first to New

York from his native state, but is 1835 became a resident of Mississippi, at which time he located in Columbus, Lowndes county, where he was among the first settlers. After clerking for eight years for Dr. Sidney S. Franklin, he formed a partnership with Abraham Murdock in the mercantile business, but was also engaged in the manufacture of leather, wool hats and iron. Their factory, which was located about sixty miles from Columbus, was a very extensive one for that day, but was destroyed by fire during the war. Their business relations lasted for over thirty years, and were not only harmonious but were profitable as well. Moses Hale, the grandfather of Dayton, was examined for a certificate to teach school by James Murdock in Massachusetts, but, strange to say, their sons were totally unacquainted, and had never even heard of each other until they met in Columbus, Miss. Harrison Hale was captain of a militia company which was organized in this county. He was a charter member of the Columbus riflemen, organized in 1837, and was an active and honorary member until his death, in 1868. He was a whig politically, was a leading member of the I. O. O. F., and for them purchased and laid out what is now known as Friendship cemetery, and, in fact, was a leader in many public enterprises. One of his ancestors, Artemas Hale, was a member of congress from Massachusetts, and was also a member of the state senate. He lived to be ninety-eight years of age, and two other members of the family lived to be over ninety-seven years of age. To Harrison Hale and his wife five sons and three daughters were born, three sons and one daughter now living: Dayton, Moses A., William C., and Anna Dayton. Dayton Hale was educated in the town of Columbus, and at the age of sixteen years began working for himself as a clerk for his father, after which he began manufacturing saddle blankets, continuing until his establishment burned down in 1873. As soon as possible he rebuilt and continued to conduct his manufactory until 1880, at which time he engaged in sawmilling, which occupied his time and attention up to 1885. In February of that year he was appointed to the position of postmaster of Columbus, Miss., a position he has capably filled up to the present time, being reappointed by President Cleveland, and recommissioned by President Harrison. He has discharged the duties of this position very efficiently and to the entire satisfaction of the public. He was first married to Miss Ophelia Tillman, by whom he has one child, Dayton, and his second union was to Mrs. Olive (Kirkland) Marion, who had one child by her former husband, Robert F. Marion. Mr. Hale is a member of the I. O. O. F., and he and his wife are members of the Presbyterian church, in which he has served as deacon for four years and elder for fifteen years.

R. W. Haley, a prominent planter, whose postoffice address is Okolona, Miss., was born in that place in 1849. His father was Dr. Samuel Haley, and his mother's maiden name was Legrove. Dr. Haley was born in 1811 in Tuscaloosa county, Ala., and was a planter and merchant, as well as a physician. In the latter capacity he was known in Alabama, Tennessee and Mississippi. He joined the Masonic order in North Fork, Ala., and was a member of more than ordinary prominence. He and his wife were communicants of the Baptist church. He had five children, all of whom are living: Fannie A., Peregrine, R. Weston, Alice and Emma. Dr. Haley died in Mississippi in 1881. R. Weston Haley received his education in the schools of Memphis, and married Beulah Greeenwood, of Monroe county, who bore him six children, five of whom are living: Charles, Greenwood D., Thomas A., Sarah C. and Durwood S. Mr. Haley is a member in good standing of the Chickasaw lodge No. 720, Knights of Honor, and he and his wife are members of the Methodist Episcopal church. Mrs. Haley was a daughter of D. C. and Sarah (Dale) Greenwood. The latter was born in Marion county, Ala., was reared in Sumter county, of the same state, and received her education at Demopolis, Utah and Livingston. Her parents were Hugh and Catherine Dale, the former a life-long planter, a man of good education and great nobility of character, and who was elevated to a high rank in the Masonic order. The old Dale plantation in Alabama, though it has changed hands, is still in good repair, and is a landmark in that part of the state. Mr. Dale was born in Ireland, and emigrated to America at the age of eighteen. He was a member of the Presbyterian church and his wife of the Methodist Episcopal church. Five of their children are yet living: John C. (planter and miller, of Tipton county, Tenn.); Baliva E. (a planter of the same place); Sarah D. (now Mrs. Greenwood); Martha H. (Mrs. Sampson), the two last named living in Monroe county, Miss., and Kate (Mrs. Hadily), a prominent teacher in Louisiana. D. C. Greenwood was born in Quincy, Monroe county, Miss., in 1826, the son of Thomas and Lydia Greenwood. He was a Mason and Knight of Honor, having joined the first named order in Aberdeen in 1851, and the last mentioned at a later date in Okolona. In early life he graduated from the law department of a Virginian institution, but was never a legal practitioner. He was of a literary turn of mind and inclined towards a journalistic career, finally becoming editor of the Aberdeen *Independent* and Chickasaw *Messenger*. He served in the Civil war as first lieutenant in Ferguson's command. Mr. and Mrs. Greenwood had twelve children, eight of whom died while young: Edward E. died at the age of nineteen, just as he had completed preparations to enter college; Thomas D. died at the age of twenty-five years, an Oakford graduate, who carried off the honors of his class, and made the best record of any student in the college up to that time. Mrs. R. W. Haley is a graduate of the school of Verona, and received her diploma with high honors.

The name of Dr. Andrew J. Hall is one of the most influential in Natchez, and one of the most respected in Adams county. He is modest but earnest in the practice of his profession, a skilled physician devoting his entire time to the service of humanity. He was born in South Carolina, March 12, 1839, and was the sixth in a family of twelve children born to Fenton and Ruth (Clark) Hall, who were born in South Carolina and Georgia respectively, and died near Corinth, Miss., the former in 1884 and the latter in 1885, having reared a respectable family of high social standing. The Doctor removed with his father's family from South Carolina to Mississippi in 1848, and after receiving a good English education he became familiar with agriculture on his father's farm till later he became interested in the mercantile pursuit and located in that business at Madison, Ark., in 1860. War being declared between the North and South, he returned to Mississippi in 1862 and enlisted as a private in company D, Thirty-second Mississippi regiment under Col. M. P. Lowrey (who afterward became brigadier-general). After participating in the battle of Chickamauga, he was promoted to General Lowrey's staff as aid-de-camp and was afterward assigned to duty as assistant adjutant-general, in which capacity he served till the close of the war. After Chickamauga he was engaged in the battles of Missionary ridge, Ringgold gap and all the battles of the Georgia campaign including the siege of Atlanta, and returning with Hood into Tennessee, was engaged in the battles of Spring Hill, Franklin and Nashville. His next move was with Hood's command into North Carolina, but on reaching South Carolina, received orders from the war department transferring him to General Taylor's command at Mobile, Ala., but before reaching that point received notice of the surrender of the Confederate forces. His war record was a most excellent one, his name being sent to the department at Richmond for a medal for gallant conduct on the field at Chickamauga, but he says he was not entitled to it more than thousands of other soldiers whose names were not mentioned. Although he fought for a losing cause, he had no cause to regret or be ashamed of his military career, having so carried himself as to win the admiration of his comrades and official

promotion on the part of his superior officers.   He was a member of the famous division commanded by General Pat Cleburne, who was known by the sobriquet of the Stonewall of the
West.   After the war he lost no time in repining over the results of the war, but immediately
located in the town of Pontotoc and engaged in merchandising, to which calling his attention
was given until 1869, after which he embarked in the insurance business.   About this time
he formed a desire for the study and practice of medicine, and with this end in view entered
the Louisville medical college and later the Bellevue hospital medical college of New York
city, from which he graduated in March, 1879.   At the end of this time he returned to Mississippi and soon built up a lucrative practice at the town of Pontotoc.   In 1886 he removed
to the city of Natchez, where he has secured a substantial practice among the very best
families of the city.   His reputation with the medical fraternity is by no means local.   He
has made an enviable name for himself through his high professional attainments.   He was
married in 1867 to Miss Valeria R. Huntington, a native of the town of Pontotoc, her parents
being John and Salina Huntington, the former a dentist.   To Dr. Hall and his wife were born
two children: Frank H. and Deseret R.   The Doctor has always taken much interest in public
enterprises, in the educational, religious and moral interests of the community and country
at large.   He is a man of broad sympathies and of liberal views; a consistent member of
the Baptist church, he combines his religion with his professional life.   He is a member of
A. F. & A. M. and the Knights of Honor.   In personal appearance he is prepossessing and
his manners are courteous, pleasant and affable.   He is a man of well rounded character.

The present efficient circuit and chancery clerk of Covington county, Miss., Evans Hall,
of Williamsburg, was born within the county's borders, at Mount Carmel, in 1845.   Here he
was reared and educated in the common schools.   He is the eldest of a family of nine children, born to Dr. A. H. and Mary A. (Evans) Hall, natives of North Carolina and Louisiana,
respectively.   Dr. Hall was born in 1814, and came to the county when a youth.   He attended
a medical school in Willmington, N. C., and after leaving his studies, was appointed receiver
of the land office at Augusta, Miss.   When he was ready to begin his professional work he
located at Mount Carmel, and formed a partnership with Dr. Gartman.   The life of a pioneer
physician is not an easy one, and the Doctor's was no exception to the rule; his patients were
scattered over the territory between Pearl and Leaf rivers, a distance of forty miles, and the
newness of the country rendered travel excessively laborious.   Evans Hall, son of the Doctor,
served as a soldier in the Civil war, from 1863 to the cessation of hostilities.   He was a member of the Fourth Mississippi cavalry, and saw some active service.   When the war was ended he
returned to his home, and in 1866 was united in marriage to Miss Effie McDonald, a daughter of Alexander McDonald, and a niece of Judge J. E. McNair.   In 1874 Mr. Hall took
charge of the circuit court and chancery court work by appointment, and since that time he
has succeeded himself by election.   He is well fitted for the duties of this position, and has
discharged them with a promptness and intelligence that have left no room for complaint.
At the present time he also has some commercial interests, which are conducted under the
firm name of Hall & Harper.   In his religious faith he is connected with the Presbyterian
church, of which he has been an active ruling elder for many years.   He is a member of the
Masonic order.   He is a man of decided convictions, and with courage to carry them out in
spite of popular opinion.   He has a wide acquaintance throughout the county, and has the
honor and respect of the entire community.

G. Q. Hall is a descendant of a distinguished Tennessee family.   His grandfather,
John Hall, of Lebanon, was a lawyer of great learning, in whose office and under whose
guidance the distinguished Mississippi jurist, William L. Sharkey, read law, and there, it

is said by Judge Sharkey's biographer, the foundation was laid for the eminence subsequently attained by him as a lawyer and jurist. His great-uncle, Gen. William Hall, was prominent in the legislative and political affairs of that state, and was elevated to the gubernatorial chair. The father of the subject of this sketch moved to Mississippi in the thirties and founded the town of Hopahka, in Leake county, which was the favorite rendezvous of such celebrities as Guion, Prentiss, Hicks, Forester and others. He was associated with Colonel Forester in removing the Choctaws to the Indian territory. Mr. Hall was born in Leake county in 1851, and though too young to be in the army, was intrusted, at the age of thirteen, with the management of his father's plantation while his father and elder brother were in the Confederate army, the one as captain of company C, Sixth Mississippi infantry and the other as high private in Barksdale's brigade, and afterward as captain of a cavalry company. In 1869 he entered the freshman class at New Middleton, Tenn., under the tutorship of those superior educators, J. P. Hamilton and N. J. Finney, and completed the four years' course of collegiate study in thirty-six months and was elected by his class as the valedictorian. Returning home with his "sheepskin" and without a dollar, he farmed and taught school, occupying every spare moment in the study of law, and was admitted to the bar and located in Carthage, Leake county, in September, 1875, where he soon built up a lucrative practice. Mr. Hall was never a candidate for office, but was appointed superintendent of public instruction for Leake county, in January, 1876, and held that place continuously for about seven years. Under his administration, school warrants enhanced in value from forty cents to par in two years. Mr. Hall was, with one exception, chairman of every political convention and executive committee in Leake county from 1875 to the date of his removal to Meridian, Miss. In October, 1884, he removed to Meridian, and formed a law partnership with that distinguished Mississippian, the Hon. Joel P. Walker, under the firm name of Walker & Hall, which firm is enjoying a large and lucrative practice. He is trustee of the graded schools of Meridian, Miss., and is a director of the Meridian National bank, of which institution he is an ex-vice-president. He was married in Madison station, Miss., in the year 1875, to Miss Kate Montgomery, an accomplished lady and one of the oldest and most respected families in Mississippi.

Judge James G. Hall (deceased), was born in Grenada, Miss., on the 19th of August, 1847, and was tenth in order of birth of eleven children born to Rev. James G. and Elizabeth (Woods) Hall, natives of North Carolina. The parents removed from their native state to Mississippi in 1837, and there made their home until 1878, when the father, mother and several members of the family fell victims to the yellow fever epidemic. The father was a minister in the Baptist church for more than fifty years. He had been married twice and was the father of a large family, only one of whom is now living. Judge James G. Hall passed his youthful days in the county of his birth and received an academic education there. The war put an end to his hopes of a regular collegiate education, but he continued his studies after the war, teaching school at the same time. In 1867 he began the study of law under the late Judge E. S. Fisher, was admitted to the bar in August, 1868, and immediately began practicing with Col. W. H. Fitzgerald, in Charleston, Tallahatchie county. In 1869 he was appointed county attorney, but was removed, with other civil officers, in the same year, by the military governor, Ames. In 1871 he removed to Sardis, Panola county, Miss., and soon entered into partnership with Hon. L. P. Cooper, which continued until the removal of the latter to Memphis, Tenn., when he formed a partnership with Hon. J. B. Boothe, and this continued until his appointment as chancellor of the district in 1882. Previous to this, in 1875, the good people of Panola county sent him to the legislature, and though one of the

youngest members of the session of 1876 and 1877, he was among the most useful and influential. Industrious, painstaking, vigilant, conservative, he was well fitted to assist in reclaim-
ing the state from the confusion resulting from the misrule and corruption of the so-called
reconstruction era. To the high and honorable office of chancellor he was reappointed at the
expiration of his first term, and, had he lived, would have continued until September, 1890,
the expiration of his term, at which it was his previously announced intention to retire from
the bench and resume the practice of law. It was universally conceded that he was an able
and conscientious chancellor, and his decisions gave general satisfaction. Even where parties
and their counsel had been disappointed, they gave him credit for being actuated alone by a
just conception of the law and a good conscience. Judge Hall was not only a good lawyer, a
faithful legislator and an able counsellor, but he was, above all, a noble Christian gentleman,
and was so recognized by all who knew him. He never passed over an error to gain popularity, but had the courage of his convictions, and dared to do and to say what he believed to
be right in the face of all opposition, no matter how powerful. He was a strong advocate of
the cause of temperance, and struck many a blow which will tell in later years even more
potently than it did when given. To his church, the Baptist, although a comparatively
young man, he was a pillar that could withstand every storm, and amid all his secular work
he was never known to neglect a church duty, but, as superintendent of the Sabbath-school,
and leader in the choir, he was always at his post. As adviser and counsellor of his pastor,
or in any church work, we doubt if he had a superior in any church or denomination. In
speaking of him his pastor said: "No pastor of any church ever had a better or more earnest
and unselfish helper than I have had in Judge Hall." His death occurred on the 21st of
January, 1890, and was the occasion of universal sorrow, for all felt what it was to lose such
a man. He lived a life that has left a tender memory behind, and that was an exemplification of the purest and most exalted principles. Although dead, he still lives, for his peerless
example remains to be of far more value and benefit than gold, and more enduring than life
itself. Judge Hall was married in 1872 to Miss Belle Thornton, an excellent and accomplished daughter of one of the most prominent families of Tallahatchie county, Miss. She is
a native Mississippian, and the eldest of four children born to P. H. and E. A. (Bailey)
Thornton. She was reared in her native state and received her education at Oxford. This
marriage resulted in the birth of three children: Lizzie L., Annie B. and Charles P., all at
home. Mr. Thornton was a native of Tennessee, as was also his father, P. H. Thornton, and
was of English origin. The Baileys were of Irish extraction.

S. H. Hall is a planter and sawmiller of Senatobia, Miss. He was born in Chickasaw
county of this state in October, 1845, the second in a family of seven children born to Hiram and
Martha (Hollifield) Hall, both of whom were born in Rutherford county, Tenn., where they grew
up and were married. They removed to Chickasaw county in 1846, and here the father died
in 1888 at the age of sixty-seven, his wife's death having occurred in 1859. Six of their seven
children grew to maturity: John C., who died in prison at Rock Island, Ill., in 1862, having
been a member of Middleton's company of Mississippi infantry; S. H., the subject of this
sketch; James W., a farmer of White county, Ark.; Sarah S., wife of J. A. Morgan, a farmer
of this county; Hiram E. (deceased) was a postmaster of Senatobia; and Senath Asile, the
deceased wife of John Wynn, of Crawford county, Ark. Hiram Hall, the father, was very
active in politics, and was a member and president of the county board of Calhoun county
for twelve or fifteen years, and in 1872 and 1873 represented this county in the state legislature, being elected to that office by the republican party. He has also been a member of
the county board of Tate county, in which he acted as president. He was a member of

Ebenezer lodge No. 76 of the A. F. & A. M. of Senatobia, and was a member of the Grange from the time of its organization in 1872 until it became extinct. He was of a generous disposition, and schools and churches, as well as other worthy enterprises, found in him a hearty and substantial supporter. The school days of S. H. Hall were spent in Chickasaw county, and there he was married in November, 1867, to Miss Frances V. Davis, a daughter of Dr. R. H. and Martha (Ellis) Davis, the former a native of Alabama, the latter of Georgia. Mrs. Hall was born in Mississippi, and her union with Mr. Hall resulted in the birth of twelve children, the following of whom are living: William B.; Lela E., wife of William Williams, of Senatobia; Henry H., Hubert G., Effie M., Clyde, Payne and Marie. Mr. Hall lost his estimable wife on the 31st of December, 1888, her death being deeply lamented, not only by her immediate sorrowing family, but by all who knew her. In July, 1863, Mr. Hall enlisted in the Confederate service, becoming a member of company B, Nineteenth Mississippi cavalry, and served in Forrest's brigade until July 14, 1864, when he was wounded at Harrisburg, Miss., and disabled for further service. Prior to this he was in the engagements at Moscow, Tenn., Brice's crossroads, West Point and Pontotoc. He was second sergeant of his company. In December, 1869, he became a resident of Tate county, Miss., and soon after his arrival purchased one hundred and sixty acres of land, which, by industry, good management and shrewd business tactics, he has increased to fifteen hundred and thirty acres. At the same time of his purchase he put up a good sawmill, which he has since operated, about 1881 adding a cottongin, crusher and thresher, E. C. Townsend being his partner. He cultivates between six and eight hundred acres of land, which he devotes to the raising of cotton and corn. He is interested in all matters pertaining to agriculture, and has taken great pains to improve his plantation by fertilizing. He conducts a good supply store and blacksmith shop, both of which have proven paying enterprises. He has been president of the Tate County Alliance since its organization, and holds the same position in his subordinate lodge. He is vice president of the Tate County Stock Breeders' association, is a member of the Memphis Building & Loan association, and is a steward in the Methodist Episcopal church at Chestnut Ridge. Socially he is a member of lodge No. 1568 of the K. of H. of Senatobia. He has a beautiful and pleasant home, and he is deservedly proud of his admirably kept plantation, and of his career as a man of business.

S. T. Hall is a druggist and planter of Houston, Miss., but was born in Tuscaloosa county, Ala., in 1830, a son of S. T. and Nancy (Fawcett) Hall, both of whom were born in Union district, S. C., the former's birth occurring in 1792 and the latter's in 1795. They were reared and married in their native state and about 1825 removed to Alabama, where they made their homes until their respective deaths, the father's demise occurring in 1856 and the mother's in 1882, the latter being an earnest and worthy member of the Baptist church at the time of her death. S. T. Hall, Sr., was a soldier in the War of 1812, and for some time served as bailiff in Tuscaloosa, Ala. To this union four sons and five daughters were born, the following of whom are living: Richard, who resides near Greensboro, Ala.; Samuel T.; Thomas J., who resides in Tuscaloosa county, Ala.; Nancy, wife of Jefferson Naugher, of the same county; Elizabeth, widow of Martin Springer, of Chickasaw county; W. R., Sarah, Loudusky and Catherine (deceased). S. T. Hall, the subject of this sketch, spent his youth in the neighborhood of his birth, but received only meager advantages for obtaining an education. At the age of twenty he left Alabama and came to Chickasaw county, Miss., where the most of his literary education was obtained at night by his own efforts. For some time after arriving here he followed planting and overseeing, both of which occupations he followed until 1862. He was married in 1855 to Miss Huldah A. Lip-

53

sey, who was born in South Carolina in September, 1833, a daughter of Arthur and Margaret (Laulk) Lipsey, to which union were born two sons and four daughters: John Thomas, who resides in Arkansas; Samuel Marion, at home; Mary Ann (deceased), Margaret N. (deceased), Minnie J., at home, and Nettie Ellen, wife of Oscar Knox, of Pontotoc. In 1862 Mr. Hall enlisted in the Twenty-fourth Mississippi infantry as a private and served until the close of the war, proving himself a true and trusty soldier to the cause he espoused. He took part in the engagements at Murfreesboro, Dalton, Resaca, Marietta, Kenesaw mountain, Franklin, Nashville, Atlanta, Jonesboro and a great many minor engagements and skirmishes. He was slightly wounded at Resaca and Jonesboro, but did not leave the field. After being paroled at Gainesboro, N. C., April 26, 1865, he returned to his home to once more take upon himself the duties of planting, walking the entire distance of over one thousand two hundred miles, there being eight whites and two negroes in the party. When they had reached Russellville, Miss., they were met by a party of outlaws who attempted to rob them of what valuables they possessed, but were met by stubborn resistance, and Mr. Hall and his friends managed to get safely away. At that time Mr. Hall owned a half section of land seven miles east of Houston, to which he has added until he now owns eight hundred acres in one tract and four hundred in another, all in Chickasaw county. This entire property has been acquired by his own efforts, for which he deserves much credit. In 1875 he removed to Houston, where he engaged in the livery business and two years later opened a drug store, which he still conducts in connection with his livery establishment. In 1879 he opened, in connection with his nephew, E. J. Hall, a general mercantile store, in which he was interested until the 1st of September, 1887. Mr. Hall is a member of the Christian church, but his wife, who died in September, 1887, was a member of the Methodist Episcopal church. On the 29th of March, 1891, he took for his second wife Mrs. Ann Gamblin, a native of Chickasaw county, daughter of Isaac and Mary Paulk and widow of Frank Gamblin. Mr. Hall is a member of Pikeville lodge of the A. F. & A. M., of Buena Vista, and is a Royal Arch Mason, of Houston chapter.

William G. Hall is one of those successful planters of the South who deserves more than ordinary credit for the successful manner in which he has made his way through life, for, by his own energy, perseverance and good management he has become the owner of two hundred and ninety acres of fine farming land, the most of which is fine river bottom land. This land is situated about three miles (by rail) northeast of Meridian, and is devoted principally to the raising of cotton, corn and potatoes. Mr. Hall is a native of Mississippi, where he was born in 1847 in Lauderdale county, and upon attaining a suitable age he was sent to the common schools, where he obtained sufficient education to fit him for the practical duties of life. He was brought up to the life of a planter, and upon starting out in life for himself it is not to be wondered at that he determined to make planting his chief calling. He was married in 1875 to Miss Annie White, a native of the same county as himself, and by her he is the father of three children: Sidney, Mary and Margaret. Although he began to make his own way in the world under adverse circumstances, he has done well and now constitutes a living illustration of the fact, that industry, perseverance and honesty are the stepping stones to success and independence. He is of a rather retiring disposition, but is very benevolent and has heart large enough to take in all mankind. He is a friend of education, is a Methodist in his religious views, and socially is a member of the K. of P. and the Farmers' Alliance. In addition to planting he has given considerable attention to stock-raising, the most of his cattle being good graded Jerseys. His father, who also bore the name of William G. Hall, was born in South Carolina in 1810, and was married to Miss Mary Odum, of Alabama.

William Hamel, Yazoo City, Miss., was born in the kingdom of Hesse, Germany, December 4, 1843, and is the seventh of a family of ten children, His father's name was Henry Hamel. At the age of sixteen years he bade farewell to the fatherland, and sailed from the city of Bremen, to seek his fortune in the new world. He landed in Baltimore, Md., in 1860, and in the autumn of that year, came to Yazoo county, Miss. He was energetic and willing to do anything that presented itself, so the first work he did was to carry lumber from the yard of Frank Gieman. In a short time he secured a position with the Yazoo Icehouse company, and remained there until 1862, when he enlisted in company I, First Mississippi light artillery, Bowman's battery, with which he served until the close of the war. He was in the siege of Vicksburg, and other less important engagements. At Blakely, he was taken a prisoner and carried to Ship Island, where he was held until the surrender. In 1865 he returned to Yazoo City, and for a year and a half he was engaged in draying. He then formed a partnership with Paul Rogers in the sawmill business, which continued five or six years. He was associated with William Brown, to whom Mr. Rogers sold his interest, and about the year 1887 he bought Mr. Brown's share in the business, which he has since conducted by himself. In 1878 he became a stockholder in the Yazoo oil works, and is the present efficient president of that corporation. He is also a stockholder in the bank of Yazoo City, and has some agricultural interests; he is a member of the hardware firm of Crain Bros. & Co., who do a large business. Mr. Hamel was married in 1869 to Miss Mary Nearman, a Mississippian, and a daughter of F. H. Nearman. Of this union seven children have been born: Frank H., Nettie, Blanche, George, Katie, Alice and Joseph. The family are members of the Roman Catholic church, and highly respected members of the community. Mr. Hamel's career is one to inspire every young man who has an honest desire to succeed in life. He began at the very bottom of the ladder; was a foreigner, surrounded by a strange people, speaking an unknown tongue, and yet in the face of all these apparently adverse circumstances he has succeeded, and succeeded well, showing that "pluck" will win, where "luck" often fails.

Mary Elizabeth Hamer, the subject of this sketch, is the eldest daughter of the late learned and beloved Dr. Charles J. Mitchell and his gentle, cultured wife, Mary L. Davis, who died when her daughter was only four years old. Dr. Mitchell was, after much persuasion, induced to give his children to their grandparents, and although he afterward married Miss Lucy Bradford, Mr. Davis' niece, to whom the children were much attached, their grandparents would not give them up. Lise, as she was familiarly called, had become the fondest object of her grandfather's affections. She accompanied him in his daily rides about the plantation, inspecting crops, the pastures, where large flocks of sheep and herds of Durham cattle were kept, visiting in early morning the milking pens, where a hundred cows contributed their milk to landlord and slave. Thus she grew up with a taste for plantation life and accustomed to the supervision of many things. Her early youth was spent under the care of private teachers in the winter, and in traveling in the summer months, and these long trips were her greatest grievance, as she thought it a hard fate to be taken from home, when it was a very paradise of fruit and flowers (for Hurricane was famous then for its beautiful gardens), to travel through hot cities and visit stupid watering-places. She did not realize then, as she did later, that it was anxiety about her more than any other consideration which induced her grandparents to leave a home as much beloved by them as by herself. To strengthen a rather weak constitution, she was encouraged in all kinds of outdoor sports. She was taught to ride on horseback almost as soon as she could walk. When quite a young girl she could swim very well, and could shoot birds and ducks on the wing. When she was about seven years of age her grandfather, wishing to show his brother, Hon. Jefferson Davis, some fine colts, permitted her and two of the little boys of the family to accompany them to a field where there were about forty mares and colts grazing. She was riding a pretty, willful little mare, called by one of her own pet names, Lizzie Dumps, and the little boys rode a gentle Indian pony. For some cause the mares and colts began to race across the fields. The children's horses at once took fright, and the little boys soon tumbled off; but the mare, with her light burden, went at full speed, heading for the high orchard fence. Mr. Jefferson Davis, a few years before his death, in relating the incident, said: "My brother was riding a large, awkward horse, but mine was very swift, and, after a moment's pause, fearing to frighten the mare still more by pursuit, I determined to take the smaller risk, and, urging my horse to the utmost, I overtook the little rider, seized the horse by the bridle and turned its head within a few feet of the fence." After soothing her by praises of her good riding, she was permitted to ride home in triumph, between her grandfather and uncle, while the little boys had to walk back in disgrace. Mrs. Hamer said even in childhood she often wondered why her grandfather, who was so devoted to her, would allow her to take such risks. She frequently rode horses that were so wild it would take two stout negro men to help her mount; and his look of surprise if told she was afraid to kill a large snake would cause her to chase the next one, even into the weeds. She understood afterward it was to correct the natural timidity of her nature. There was nothing she would not risk or try to accomplish to win a word or look of approval from her idolized grandfather. During the high water of 1859 a crevasse very unexpectedly occurred in the levee on the adjoining plantation, and Hurricane, much to the dismay of Mr. Davis and family, was overflowed. He was just convalescent from a severe spell of illness, and Mrs. Davis, so greatly depressed by the wholesale destruction of her beautiful gardens, they determined on spending some months in Europe. Their grandson, who was at the commercial college in New Orleans, and their granddaughter, who was then at Nazareth academy, Kentucky, accompanied them in their tour through Great Britain and the continent. They were in Paris when Napoleon III. and his army returned from Italy. The 15th of August had been selected for the grand entry, and for two or more weeks preparations were being made for the occasion, while the army was encamped at the Champ de Mars. The procession through the city was the greatest pageant they had ever witnessed, and they were singularly fortunate in the location of their windows, which overlooked the intersection of Rue de la Paix and the Boulevard des Italiens, which large space was so densely packed with people that even the long line of mounted police could scarcely withstand the pressure. Some detention occurring in the rear of the procession, a halt was made just as Napoleon, with his staff and bodyguard, on their superb white horses, was passing their windows, and they were included in the gracious smiles and bows he and his generals gave the enthusiastic multitude. A few days later Mr. Davis left Paris for Switzerland, to place his grandson, J. D. Mitchell, at college, where he remained until the beginning of hostilities at home, when he ran the blockade and joined the Confederate army, in which he served until the end of the war. On their return from Switzerland, three weeks later, they were surprised to find that all traces of the great celebration had disappeared—triumphal arches, statues and columns, some so grand and substantial they had supposed they were intended to be permanent—all were gone, and Paris had assumed its wonted appearance.

In November the family left for home. Mr. Davis engaged an accomplished Swiss lady as governess for his granddaughter; but, as Hurricane was one of the most hospitable of Southern homes, she was much discouraged by the frequent interruptions to her lessons in the arrival of company; the excursions, hunting parties, horseback rides and other irresistible distractions to students in the country—distractions which have so many pleasant reminiscences for old age. But these happy days were not to continue, for already the dark clouds of war were gathering—Abraham Lincoln being elected president, the South indignant and defiant, states seceding, Mr. Davis elected president of the Confederacy, and her grandfather heart and soul with the cause. After the seat of government was removed from Montgomery to Richmond, Miss Mitchell accompanied her grandparents in a visit to the president and family. She spent several weeks with them, at the Spottswood hotel, and afterward at their residence, where Miss Mitchell enjoyed the charming society of Richmond, and met many distinguished persons since become historical. Mr. Davis again returned to Hurricane, but on the surrender of New Orleans, fearing the arrival of gunboats, he removed his family, slaves and stock to a plantation twenty miles back of Vicksburg, where their security was but temporary. After Grant's army surrounded Vicksburg, marauding parties of the enemy frequently visited the place, carrying off stock and other property, and inducing the more able-bodied negroes to run away. Mrs. Davis' health was very delicate, and, as the prospects at Vicksburg became more desperate, Mr. Davis sent her and other ladies of the family to the neighborhood of Jackson. But Miss Mitchell refused to leave him, and for three weeks they remained in the place, in a constant state of suspense and excitement, expecting visits from the numerous squads of Federal cavalry which made nightly depredations upon that and neighboring plantations; listening day and night to the bombardment at Vicksburg; alarmed when the cannonading ceased; cheered again by the sound of the guns, which they hailed as signals that the gallant little city still held its own against such overwhelming odds. On the night of the 3d of July Miss Mitchell, hearing voices outside, seized her revolver, which she always kept under her pillow; but, in going to the door, recognized the voice of one of the servants, who told her a courier from General Johnston had dispatches for his master. Ever on the alert for any danger threatening her grandfather, she still felt suspicious of the stranger; but Mr. Davis at once admitted him, and found he bore a letter from Gen. J. E. Johnston, urging him to leave at once, as Vicksburg would be surrendered next day. Mr. Davis fearing this sad termination to Vicksburg's gallant struggle, had patched up old wagons, which had been left by the enemy, and with such oxen as had escaped capture succeeded in getting conveyances enough to carry off the sixty-five women and children, and a few men who had remained faithful to him, with such of their baggage as could be packed in. There was only room in the wagons for one small trunk apiece for Mr. Davis and Miss Mitchell; for all of the slaves must have their clothes and bedding too. On leaving Hurricane, the house had been left fully furnished, as if the family were only going on a summer tour; though they had taken many trunks, books, pictures, etc., to adorn their new home. Now they could select only such things as would be most necessary to their comfort. There was no room in the wagons for even the pretty guitar, or little writing desk; all must remain and share the fate of the household treasures left at Hurricane—to be carried off by the soldiers, or burnt with the dwelling. At sunrise Miss Mitchell was awakened by an unusual noise and bustle in the house, and, on leaving her room, she found the yard invaded with soldiers, the house full of Confederate officers, and her grandfather in private consultation with General Johnston. The servants having prepared breakfast for as many as could be served, the soldiers quietly and sadly continued their march. In the rear of the army, amid clouds of dust, and in the heat of a July sun, the procession of wagons slowly followed Mr. Davis' carriage. At Jackson they were joined by Mrs. Davis, other members of the family and friends. As skirmishing had already begun, they had to hasten on.   Henceforth they were refugees, starting out on that long exile from home, the misery and discomfort of which they could not yet imagine.   Taking long and weary journeys through Mississippi and Alabama, they were subjected to many hardships and great anxiety. In one of the temporary stopping places Miss Mitchell's dear grandmother died, surrounded by relatives and friends, who by their loving ministrations, tried to compensate for the lack of home comforts and the luxuries to which she had been accustomed.   President Davis, hearing of her extreme illness, went to Lauderdale to see her, but could only remain a few hours.   Her life had been spent in ministering to the comfort and happiness of others, and her memory is kept sacred in the hearts of all who knew her best, urging them to imitate her noble example.   After this sad event Miss Mitchell became, if possible, more devoted than ever to her grandfather, doing his writing, reading aloud, and exerting her utmost ingenuity, to obtain for him the necessities his delicate health required, to give him pleasure and comfort.   Those years of privation were a school where lessons of fortitude, patience and wisdom were learned, preparing her for the long and bitter struggle which the loss of the cause brought upon them.

Once more, after the death of Mrs. Davis, Mr. Davis made an effort to reach a place of safety, this time directing his course toward Georgia, but hearing that Sherman was rapidly approaching, he changed his route and went to Tuscaloosa, Ala.   There he built cabins for the negroes, and told them they must help support themselves until he could take them back to Mississippi.   For some time Tuscaloosa proved a safe retreat, but near the close of the war it was invaded by the enemy.   Mr. Davis, on hearing of the approach of the Federal troops, took his granddaughter a few miles into the country, where they were hospitably entertained by an old farmer and his wife.   The Federal troops burned the public buildings and the bridge across the Warrior river, and in this last act some of their cavalry was cut off. In trying to reach their command they passed around by the farm where Mr. Davis was staying.   He had driven over to a neighbor's, and when the alarm was given that a company of cavalry was rapidly approaching Miss Mitchell, remembering that in her grandfather's trunk were packages of papers, addressed in his name, became alarmed lest, seeing them, they would pursue and capture him, she hastily gathered them up and threw them into the fire.   The troops were in such haste to rejoin their command, however, that they halted for a few moments only.   On Mr. Davis' return she told him what she had done.   "Why, my daughter!" he exclaimed, "those were very valuable papers; but I do not so much mind their loss as that you should have become panic-stricken."   "Oh," she said, "I was not frightened for myself.   Why, old Mrs. C. and I were planning how, with the help of the negro woman, we could capture them, but her husband said we were fools, so we had to abandon the idea." Mr. Davis laughed heartily, and never again reproached her with the loss of the papers, which in all probability would have shared a worse fate, for a few days later another company robbed his trunk, took the mules which had just been harnessed to his carriage, and carried off Miss Mitchell's riding horse, the last of the many fine horses brought from Hurricane. After Lee's surrender Mr. Davis spent the summer in Tuscaloosa, but early in the fall started on his return to Mississippi, with pretty much the same conveyances, filled with ex-slaves, who had never left him.   Poor things!   They had intensely longed for their old home, and they thought and talked of nothing but Hurricane.   On arriving at Vicksburg Mr. Davis sent the negroes on to the plantation, but, as it was still in possession of the Freedmen's bureau (for it had been, during the war, a depot for fugitive slaves), he and his granddaughter remained in Vicksburg.   Here they were afterward joined by Dr. Mitchell and family in their return from Texas, which state they had chosen as a place of refuge during the war.

In Vicksburg Miss Mitchell made many friends, among whom she was the ideal Southern gentlewoman, beloved and honored by all. Her beautiful devotion to her grandfather, and her repeated refusals to marry, so long as he lived, seemed to place her above others. Through her efforts the choir of the Catholic church became famous. She sang like a prima donna, and collected a number of fine vocalists, with a master professor to lead them, and the music of St. Paul's became the attraction of the city. No place of its size had so fine a choir, with so many splendid voices so admirably directed. After her grandfather's death Miss Mitchell surprised society by announcing her engagement to Mr. W. D. Hamer, of Alabama, who had first addressed her during the war, but was not then accepted, because of her self-imposed filial duty. After her marriage they determined to reside upon the plantation, and to rebuild and restore it to its former beauty; but, through inexperience in managing free labor, harassing lawsuits, two overflows, and, on two occasions, the desertion of her tenants en masse, a heavy debt fell upon them, which, at the death of her husband, she conscientiously assumed, though legally she could have avoided doing so. This was a task which many experienced men would have shrunk from undertaking, but Mrs. Hamer devoted herself to its accomplishment with mind and heart. She soon became convinced that labor-saving machines must supply the want of efficient laborers necessary to make planting remunerative, and constant thought evolved the invention of an implement which was pronounced most excellent by competent judges, and its merits were acknowledged by a certificate from the agricultural department of the great cotton exposition of 1885. The following notice of Mrs. Hamer's invention is taken from the *Planters' Journal*:

"HURRICANE, Miss., Sept. 15, 1885.

"The undersigned, a committee designated by the authority of the National Cotton Planters' association to examine a new agricultural implement invented by Mrs. M. E. Hamer, of Warren county, Miss., and called a 'cotton chopper,' did, on the 15th inst., visit her plantation for that purpose. Mrs. Hamer had seeded two or three acres in cotton, very late, which were found in condition to practically test the implement. The ground was rather wet for the work, but the test to which the chopper was put satisfied each of us that it was constructed on a sound principle, and if manufactured by a competent mechanic it would be exceedingly valuable and labor-saving in chopping out the crop. We think it would efficiently go over eight acres per day, leaving the cotton in small bunches. The chopper cultivates nearly the entire area of ground over which it passes, removing the grass and weeds, so that the plants could be at once reduced to a stand with the hoe, at a great saving of time and expense.

(Signed.)

H. F. SIMRALL.
T. C. BEDFORD.
J. B. O'KELLEY."

Mrs. Hamer has also been ever full of zeal for the moral improvement of her tenants, making every effort to induce them to marry. Her gifts of bridal dresses and wedding cake have aided greatly her teachings on the dignity of matrimony. In her ministrations to the sick and needy she is a true sister of charity. With material comforts she offers them the spiritual help of the word of God, consoling and saving many a soul, reaping a rich harvest for the King of Kings. In studying the welfare of her children she thinks not of her own feelings, but heroically endures the separation from both of them, that they may enjoy every advantage of education. She lives a quiet but very busy life, with her bachelor brother, seeking contentment in the faithful performance of every duty, and in the hope of making Hurricane as happy and beautiful a home for her children as it was for her in her own happy childhood's days. When life's pilgrimage is ended she hopes to rest in the little graveyard, where sleep so many of her loved and honored dead—from her youngest babe to her great-grandfather, Samuel Davis.

Joseph L. Hamer was born in Anson county, N. C., in 1832, the fifth in a family of ten children, six of whom were sons, born to Thomas and Sarah (Cheairs) Hamer, natives of North Carolina and South Carolina respectively. His paternal grandfather was of Scotch descent, and his mother's parents were of Irish descent. Thomas Hamer, the father of our subject, grew to manhood in South Carolina, whence he removed to North Carolina, where he married and lived for many years. He emigrated to Mississippi in 1840 and located in what was then Tippah county, now Benton county, near old Salem, where he bought land and engaged in farming so successfully that at the time of the war he had accumulated considerable property, including eighty-five slaves. He was among the early settlers in this part of the country, and was a plain, practical farmer, not at all ambitious politically, hospitable, benevolent and highly regarded by all who knew him as a highminded Christian gentleman. He and his wife were members of the Methodist Episcopal church. The latter died in 1856, he surviving her till 1874, when he passed away at their old homestead near old Salem. Our subject began life for himself at the age of twenty-two years as a planter. In 1855 he married Mary O. Wilcox, a daughter of Charles G. Wilcox, of Benton county, but his first wife dying in 1859 he later married Eugenia E. Spencer, who died in 1875. Still later, and for the third time, he married Mrs. Bettie Strickland, a daughter of ex-Governor Matthews, of Mississippi. He has had thirteen children in all—three sons and ten daughters: Ophelia J. (wife of J. G. Threadgill), Ann E. (wife of H. W. Hardaway), Thomas S., Robert C., Nancy (wife of C. W. Brinkley), Sallie and Rosebud, still being alive, while the others died in infancy. Mr. Hamer owns one thousand two hundred and fifty acres of land, nine hundred being under cultivation. In the fall of 1862 he enlisted in company H, of the Fifth Mississippi cavalry under Colonel McGirk, which regiment was attached to the army of Tennessee. He participated in the engagements at Jonesboro, Ga., and Harrisburg, Miss., and various others of minor importance, serving until the close of the war, when in April, 1865, he was paroled at Gainesville, Ala. Returning to his home in Benton county he again engaged in planting and farming, in which he has been quite successful ever since, his course being such as to win for him the respect of the people throughout the country. He is a Mason and his wife is a member of the Episcopalian church, upon the services of which his family are also attendants. He has always been a liberal contributor to the support of schools, churches and helpful public interests.

Dr. S. D. Hamilton, a successful physician of Waterford, was originally from South Carolina, his birth occurring on the 13th of February, 1849, and his father, William K. Hamilton, was also a native of that state. The latter was married to Miss Mary McGowen, a native of Ireland who came to America when but fifteen years of age, and to this union were born four sons, who are named in the order of their births, as follows: William McGowen, John D., Robert W. and S. D. The eldest, William M., was killed in the first battle of Manassas. The father of these children was a farmer, and passed his entire life in his native state, dying in 1882. The mother died four years later, in York county, S. C. Both held membership in the Presbyterian church. Dr. S. D. Hamilton left his native state and came to Marshall county, Miss., in 1871, having, previous to leaving South Carolina, studied medicine for two years. He resumed his studies in Mississippi under Dr. Warren, at Waterford, and after remaining with him one year entered the Louisiana university at New Orleans, and graduated from that institution in 1874. He then returned to Waterford and began the practice of his profession the same year. There he has remained ever since, and is one of the foremost physicians of the county. The Doctor was married, in 1881, to Miss Maggie Tatten, the only daughter of Ben Tatten, who was a planter in Marshall county, Miss. They have born to this union four children: William, Ben, Mary (deceased), Lillie and Samuel D. The Doctor owns good residence property in Waterford, an undivided interest in one thousand acres of land with J. C. Tatten in Marshall county, and he also has an undivided interest in his father's estate in South Carolina. He and wife are members of the Presbyterian church. The Doctor is a Knight Templar in the Masonic fraternity, is a Knight of Honor, an Odd Fellow and a member of the A. O. U. W. The Doctor is a young man of acknowledged ability in the medical profession, and as an auxiliary to that he has carried on the drug business in Waterford for ten years.

Dr. S. W. Hamilton was born at Paris, Ky., in the month of December, 1816, the fifth child in a family of seven children born to William and Rebecca (Ward) Hamilton, the former of whom inherited a large estate from his father, who removed to the state of Kentucky about the time of Daniel Boone, and became a successful planter. William Hamilton became a resident of Mississippi about 1836, and after becoming a resident of Clinton, filled the positions of mayor, justice of the peace, notary public and postmaster. His wife was a native of Petersburg, Va. Dr. S. W. Hamilton was an attendant of the common schools up to the age of twelve years, when he entered an educational institution of Marion, Mo., where he remained for about two years. About this time his father became a resident of Tennessee, and S. W. left the school which he had been attending in Missouri and entered college at Memphis, Tenn., and during the two years that he remained there made rapid progress in his studies. He then came to Mississippi and joined his elder brother, James Hamilton, who was in charge of a Presbyterian church; then spent the two and a half succeeding years with Mr. Comfort at school. He then entered the mercantile establishment of Scott & Avery, remaining with them two years, when he became an employe of Spires & Charlescroft, and a year later of Parham & Gibson, in whose employ he remained four years. The two succeeding years he spent in traveling over the South. In 1841 he went to Richmond, Madison parish, La., but about a year and a half later came to Clinton, Miss., and was engaged in the collection of claims for merchants until 1842, when he began the study of law with Gen. Henry S. Foote, abandoning it at the end of one and one-half years to take up the study of medicine with Dr. J. B. Morgan, of Clinton, in two years' time fitting himself to enter college. He took two courses of lectures at Louisville, Ky., receiving his diploma. In May, 1846, he removed to Louisiana, where he followed the practice of his profession until 1848, after which time, until the opening of the war, he was a successful medical practitioner of Madison parish. In 1861 he became first lieutenant of company A, Fourth Louisiana battalion, with which he served until 1863, the most of his service being in West Virginia, under General Floyd. On account of ill health he returned home in 1863, but later was assigned to the surgical department. Upon his return to Louisiana he resumed the practice of his profession, and was a leading medical practitioner of that state until 1863. During the yellow fever scourge of 1878 he was at Delta, La., from which place he came to Mississippi. For the past two years Dr. Hamilton has not practiced his profession, only as his most intimate friends desire. He was first married in 1850 to a Miss Pegram, of Petersburg, Va., by whom he has four children: Mrs. Mattie Whitfield, Mrs. Winfield (whose husband is the general ticket agent of the Cotton Belt railway), Belle (who married Charles Webb, who is an employe of the Texas Pacific railroad at Texarkana). The mother of these children died in 1859, and in 1863 the Doctor's second marriage was celebrated, Miss Sallie Goodwin becoming his wife and the mother of two children: Mrs. Judge Byrne (of Texarkana, whose husband is a leading lawyer of Arkansas), and G. W. Hamilton (who is an employe of the Louisville, New Orleans & Texas railroad). Dr. Hamilton is a Mason, a member of the I. O. O. F., and his wife is a member of the Presbyterian church.

William Stewart Hamilton. In any worthy history of Washington county, Miss., the name that heads this sketch should be given an enviable place among the leading citizens and its selfmade, reliable and wealthy business men. His experience in life has been a varied one, but at the same time one that reflects only credit upon him as a man. He was born in Wilkinson county, Miss., December 1, 1857, being the first child born to Jones S. and Caroline A. (Stewart) Hamilton, who were also native Mississippians. The former was educated in the Centenary college, Louisiana., and soon after engaged with Scott, Cage & Co. as a commission merchant of New Orleans, and at the close of this engagement became deputy auditor of the state of Mississippi, which office he held four years. Before the war he was for several years sheriff of Wilkinson county, and after serving one term in that office was elected for a second term, but resigned this position to enter the Confederate army, enlisting at the beginning and serving until the close of the war. He was for some time colonel of his company and made a faithful and intrepid soldier, serving the Confederate cause with a faithfulness and earnestness of purpose highly commendable. Since the war he has represented Hinds county in the state legislature and has been one of the leaders of the democratic party in Mississippi. William Stewart Hamilton was reared in Jackson, Miss., but received the principal part of his literary education in the Collegiate academy of Baton Rouge, La. At the age of sixteen years he entered the employ of the gas company of Jackson, Miss., as a clerk, where he continued to render efficient service for five years, learning, in the meantime, sterling business habits which were of material benefit to him in his subsequent career. At the end of the five years he was made secretary of the company, and ably discharged the duties of this position for six years. In 1888 he came to Greenville and became an employe in the Merchants & Planters' bank, where he remained until elected cashier of the Citizens' bank of Greenville, which position he now holds. In the fall of 1890 he was appointed by President Harrison to the position of postmaster of Greenville and is still discharging the duties of this position in a manner that is highly satisfactory to all. He was for two years city collector of Jackson, and in every official capacity in which he has served he has endeavored to do his duty, and his efforts have been attended with success. He stands well in this part of the state as a reliable and successful man of business, and as he has not drifted from one thing to another, but has endeavored to faithfully perform the duties that have been laid upon his shoulders, he has been richly rewarded, not only with worldly goods, but in the confidence, respect and esteem of his fellowmen. In 1884 he was married to Miss Julia Y. Sullivan, a native of Missouri, and a daughter of George W. and Anna (Virden) Sullivan, the latter being a sister of E. & S. Virden, the most extensive merchants of Jackson, Miss., and to their union four children have been born: George S., William S., Jr., Fannie and Emma. Mr. Hamilton and his wife are members of the Episcopal church, and socially he is a member of the A. F. & A. M., in which order he has attained to the knight templar degree, and is a member of the board of custodians of the state of Mississippi, which position he has held for six years.

Dr. W. W. Hamilton, physician and surgeon, Brooksville, Miss. Dr. J. P. Hamilton, the father of the subject of this sketch, was born in the state of Georgia in 1821, and about 1830 emigrated to Alabama, settling in Pickens county, and afterward removed to Mississippi. He was married about 1846 to Miss Harriet A. Perry, of Pickens county, Ala., who died in Tallahatchie county, Miss., in June, 1883. He was a soldier in the Confederate army, but came home to practice his profession, as his services were indispensable there; he being excused by an unanimous vote of his company. Aside from his practice, the Doctor is a planter of moderate proportions, giving some attention to stockraising. His son, Dr. W. W.

Hamilton, was one of a family of nine children, and was born in Carroll county, Miss., in 1856. He moved from there to Tallahatchie county in 1865, and thence to Noxubee county in 1880, locating at Brooksville, Miss. He attended the hospital college of medicine at Louisville, Ky., and graduated from that institution in March, 1879, with second honor faculty medal. In 1888 he took a postgraduate's course in the New York polyclinic hospital. Dr. Hamilton is of quite a scientific turn of mind, and is destined at some time in the near future to win peculiar distinction in his chosen profession. Applying the old criterion that ' a workman is known by his tools," Dr. Hamilton must be ranked very high. He gives much attention to gynæcology and general surgery, and has also devoted much attention for the last two years to microscopy, bacteriology and general pathology. The Doctor has built up an extensive practice, which is not confined to his county, but one which extends into adjacent counties. He possesses many valuable instruments, consisting of electrical batteries, a microscope, amputation cases, etc. Dr. Hamilton stands very high socially, and is a citizen of whom his county and state may well feel proud. The predictions are that his name will some day occupy a very elevated position in the temple of fame. In addition to his practice the Doctor is proprietor of a handsome drug store, which presents the appearance of being not only neat and well kept, but rather extensive and well assorted for so small a town.

Among the lawyers and judges who have graced the bar and bench of Mississippi few, in the last quarter of a century, are more deserving of notice than Hon. James S. Hamm. For the last thirty years, Judge Hamm has occupied a prominent position among the leading lawyers of the state, and it is a source of regret that the limits of this work will not permit a more thorough analysis of his character as a lawyer and judge, and of the many prominent characteristicts which adorn and beautify his life. Judge Hamm is a native of the Old Dominion. After having graduated at the university of his native state, he devoted himself to the study of law, and upon his admission to the bar, turned his face westward and stopped for a brief period at Gainesville, Sumter county, Ala., where he remained only a short time and then settled, in 1850, at De Kalb, the county seat of Kemper county, Miss. The sixth judicial district, in which the young lawyer decided to strike for fame and fortune, was one of the best and wealthiest in the state, and many able and eminent lawyers graced the bar of each county seat, and practiced throughout the entire circuit. Thus surrounded, the young lawyer saw the difficulties in his path, but with a zeal, earnestness and perseverance rarely equaled, he applied himself to the intricate labors of his profession, and soon bacame its recognized head in his own county, and ranked among the ablest lawyers in the district. At that period circuit judges were chosen by the people, and in the summer of 1858, Mr. Hamm announced himself as a candidate for judge of the sixth judicial district, canvassed the district, addressing the people in public assemblages in every county, and though he was opposed by an old, able and popular lawyer, he was elected by a large majority. At the expiration of his four years' term of office, Judge Hamm was reëlected, his term of office extending during the period of the war between the states. At the close of the war, Judge Hamm resumed the practice of his profession in the sixth judicial district, and in 1868 he removed to Meridian, the county seat of Lauderale county, and there continued in the laborious and successful practice of the law until 1876, when he was appointed by the governor to the circuit judgeship, which office he held until 1882, when he resumed the practice of law, in which he is still engaged at Meridian. It will be observed that since his admission to the bar, a great portion of the life of this gentleman has been spent in wearing the judicial ermine. He not only acted as judge, but he was a judge, in every true acceptation of the term, firm, dignified and courteous to the members of the bar; polite, impartial and just to litigants. The writer, who is

himself a lawyer of large experience, ventures nothing in saying thất no circuit judge in
Mississippi ever commanded more respect, or filled the office with more distinguished ability.
His decisions of legal questions, always commanded the highest respect, and his charges to
grand and petit juries showed that he was a master of the science of law, and his clear, strong
intellect, and perfect command of the purest English, enabled him to make the simplest
understand the principles enunciated.   When off the bench, in the capacity of practitioner,
Judge Hamm was eminently successful.   Fluent, easy, and strongly argumentative, his
speeches to courts and juries rarely failed to carry conviction.   As a man of literary culture
Judge Hamm has few superiors.   In his intercourse with the world, its men and women, he
combines the *suaviter in modo* with the *fortiter in re*, and is a great talker, rather than a great
conversationalist.   One never tires in his company, and never fails to be interested and
instructed.   In politics Judge Hamm has never belonged to the strictest sect of states' rights
democracy.   In religion he is a Methodist.   Judge Hamm has been happily married twice.
His first wife was a daughter of Mr. Hampton, a leading farmer and merchant of Kemper
county, Miss.   His second wife was the daughter of Rev. Jefferson Koger, a distinguished
Methodist minister of Noxubee county, Miss., who lost his life for the cause of his native land
at the battle of Perryville.   It is to be regretted that lack of space forbids a more complete
and perfect sketch of this eminent man, who is an ornament to the bench and bar of Mississippi, whose sky is studded with so many luminous names.

George P. Hammerly, general merchant, of Iuka, Tishomingo county, Miss., was born
in Limestone county, Ala., in 1829, was one of eleven children born of John and Sarah
(nee Price) Hammerly.   His father was born in Berkeley county, Va., in 1799, and who was
a saddler by trade.   He early removed to northern Alabama, and there married, in 1825,
Sarah, daughter of William and Nancy (nee Reed) Price, who was born in Tennessee in the
year 1800.   Her father was a native of North Carolina, who came to Tennessee early in life,
and the family moved thence to Alabama about 1820, locating in Limestone county, where
Mr. Price engaged in planting, and where he and his wife both died.   Mr. Hammerly's
father was a mechanic, who devoted his entire attention to his home interests, and took no
part in public life.   He was a member of the Methodist Episcopal church; prominent in the
Masonic order; an old line whig, and died in 1882, at his home in Athens, Ala.   He raised
six children, of whom George P. Hammerly is the eldest.   The others were Lydia M.,
Nancy R., Eliza A., John H. and William G., the last mentioned of whom died in Alabama
in 1860.   Their mother, who was also a member of the Methodist Episcopal church, died in
Athens, Ala., in 1883, and the entire family, with the exception of the subject of this sketch
are living in that town and in its vicinity.   Nancy R. married William Hendricks and Eliza
became the wife of Robert Ragsdale.   George P. Hammerly's earlier years were passed in
his father's shop and in attending the common schools at Athens, Ala.   At the age of twenty-
one he became a clerk in a store, though he had previously learned the saddler's trade with
his father.   Upon coming to Mississippi, in 1851, he found employment in a store at Eastport,
where he remained six years and thence came to Iuka in 1857.   Here he was also employed
as a clerk for two years, and in 1859 he opened a store on his own account in the block in
which he is now doing business.   In 1863 he enlisted in company D of Colonel Johnson's
regiment, Alabama cavalry, in which he held the position of lieutenant.   He served about
two years and participated under General Forrest in the engagements of Day's Gap, Iuka,
Moulton, Brice's Crossroads, Harrisburg, Athens and Selma.   He was in a large number of
skirmishes in addition to the engagements mentioned, but was so fortunate that he was never
wounded nor taken prisoner, though he had a number of narrow escapes.   He was paroled

at Iuka, May 20, 1865. After the war he was reëngaged in the mercantile business, which he has continued to the present time; during the many panics having never failed. He was married in 1858 to Mary A., daughter of Dr. A. M. and Mary A. (nee Richardson) Scruggs. Dr. Scruggs was a native of Tennessee and was born about 1810. He was reared in Alabama and became a prominent physician there. His home at this time is near Memphis, Tenn., though he was a resident of this county from 1844 to 1852. His wife was born in northern Alabama about 1816, and Mrs. Hammerly was her only child. She was a member of the Methodist Episcopal church, and her death occurred in Alabama in 1838. In 1840 Dr. Scruggs married Miss Sarah Sutton, who bore him six children. After her death, he married Miss P. A. Walton, by whom he had five children. Mr. and Mrs. Hammerly have had borne to them eleven children, of whom Mary B. (now Mrs. Wells, of Grand Junction, Tenn.); Edwin T., (who is employed in his father's store); Lelia and Laura are living. The following are deceased: Finch, John A., William G., George P., Martin R., Job and Sallie L. Mr. Hammerly has for many years been connected with the Methodist Episcopal church, in which he has served as recording steward for the past quarter of a century, and during the same period he has been superintendent of the Sunday-school connected with his congregation, and his wife is also a member of the same church. He has been for twenty-five years a trustee of the Iuka female institute, and is the president of the board, and he is also a member of the board of directors of the Iuka normal institute and bank of Iuka. He is a member of the Masonic order and politically he is a democrat. He was a member of the city council for a long time and for several years served as its secretary and treasurer. In connection with his merchandising interests, he has long carried on the lumber business in a successful manner; he is the owner of about twelve hundred acres of land. He takes a great interest in public affairs and has contributed his full share toward the improvement and development of his town and county.

Rev. James M. Hampton owes his nativity to Tennessee, his birth occurring in Lincoln county on March 9, 1817, and is a son of Samuel Hampton, a native of North Carolina. The elder Hampton emigrated to Tennessee soon after his marriage with Miss Elizabeth Barnett, a native also of North Carolina, settled in Lincoln county and there followed farming until about 1845. He then moved to Mississippi and settled in Itawamba county, where he continued to reside until his death in 1876, when about eighty-four years of age. He was a soldier in the War of 1812, and in politics affiliated with the whig party. He held membership in the Methodist Episcopal church, and was a man respected and esteemed by all. To his marriage were born thirteen children, most of whom lived to be grown and seven of whom are now living. The mother of these children died on April 2, 1871, at the age of seventy-five years. Mr. Hampton was married the second time when eighty-two years of age. Both parents were members of the Methodist Episcopal church South, joining before the division of that church. The children now living are Mrs. Bethema C. Blackburn, Mrs. Frances Hughey, Mrs. Elizabeth Hughey, Mrs. Martha Harrell, Samuel F. and Lafayette, the last two residing in Arkansas. Rev. James M. Hampton, the third in order of birth of these children, was reared in Tennessee and secured a fair education in the common schools. In 1846 he moved to Mississippi, located where he now lives, and since then has been actively engaged in agricultural pursuits in connection with his ministerial duties. In 1837 Miss Christian E. Guinn became his wife, and since then has been a true companion and helpmate to him through the varying scenes of life. She was born in Stokes county, N. C., in 1814, and was the daughter of Thornton P. Guinn, a native of Virginia. Her grandfather, Duke Atwater Guinn, was a native of Ireland, and came to America at an early date, settling in the Old Dominion.

Later he moved to North Carolina and there carried on agricultural pursuits. Mrs. Hampton's father died in North Carolina, and her mother afterward came to Mississippi, where she received her final summons. They were the parents of twenty-one children, eleven of whom grew to mature years and had families. Mrs. Hampton, the only one now living, passed her girlhood and received her education in her native state. Her brother, A. B. Guinn, was one of the first settlers of Calhoun county, and he located on the land which Mr. Hampton now owns, and there resided for some time. The place at that time had few improvements, but after Mr. Hampton located on it he cleared and made many changes. He is the owner of three hundred and fifty acres of land with one hundred and fifty acres under cultivation, and is an agriculturist of advanced ideas. Mr. Hampton served for a short time during the war as captain of company F, Twenty-ninth Mississippi regiment, which was under the command of Gen. E. C. Walthal, but owing to sickness he was honorably discharged, after which he returned to his home, where he has since resided. He became a member of the Methodist Episcopal church when thirteen years of age, and in 1844 he was licensed to preach in Fayette county, Tenn. After coming to Mississippi he continued his ministerial duties as a local preacher. In 1847 he was admitted into the Memphis conference and his first circuit was that of Aberdeen, in Mississippi, where he continued until within the past few years. He is now a superannuated member of the North Mississippi conference, and devotes a portion of his time to the ministry in the surrounding neighborhood. Mr. Hampton has ridden on horseback many thousands of miles to fill appointments. To his marriage were born four children, only one now living: Mrs. Mary Elizabeth Provine married John W. Provine, who was killed at the battle of the Wilderness (see sketch of R. N. Provine), and who left a wife and two children: Texana Elizabeth (resides in Florida and is the wife of S. L. Bitting), and Mrs. Clara Willie (wife of J. W. Forrest, resides in Montgomery county, Miss). The mother of these children has always made her home with her parents; Samuel T. died when about eight years of age; Ann Caroline died at the age of about six years; and Monoah Hardin was drowned in Yalobusha river when in his twentieth year. Mrs. Hampton and daughter are members of the Methodist Episcopal church South. Mr. Hampton was a whig in his political views previous to the war, and since then he has adhered to the democratic party. He was a member of Chapel Hill lodge No. 227, A. F. & A. M., but is now a member of Pittsboro lodge No. 155.

Mrs. Elizabeth Gwynn Hancock is successfully engaged in conducting a fine plantation of one thousand two hundred acres near Clarksdale, and comes of a very old and prominent family of Kentucky, her ancestors having come from Virginia and Maryland. She was born in Louisville, Ky., the eldest of six children born to Nicholas and Elizabeth (Greathouse) Gwynn, both of whom were born on the blue grass soil. The father was a cotton dealer of New York, but the most of his life was spent in Louisville as a banker, being president of one of the leading banks of that city, and a leader in its business circles. He has become very wealthy and is the owner of a beautiful home and one of the finest plantations in Coahoma county, Miss., which his daughter, Mrs. Hancock is now cultivating and managing. His father, Fielder Gwynn, was a tiller of the soil and inherited English blood of his father, who came from England with Lord Baltimore and settled on Gwynn's Island near Baltimore, Md. The maternal grandparents were Isaac and Elizabeth (Ridgeley) Greathouse, natives of Virginia and Maryland respectively, after their marriage being classed among the "F. F. V's." In 1875 Elizabeth, the daughter of Nicholas and Elizabeth Gwynn, was married to Russell Hancock, a native of Missouri and a son of Gen. W. S. and Elmira (Russell) Hancock, the former a native of Pennsylvania and major-general of the United

States army, and the latter of Missouri, the Hancocks being very prominent and wealthy. Russell Hancock came to Mississippi in 1871 and became a prosperous planter of Coahoma county, also taking an active and prominent part in public affairs. He was very public spirited and moved in the highest social circles of this section, and his death which occurred in Mississippi at the untimely age of thirty years was lamented by a large circle of friends. Mrs. Hancock is a highly accomplished and intelligent lady, is gracious in manner, and her beauty and kindness of heart have won her numerous admirers and friends.

J. E. Hand, a son of E. E. Hand and E. W. Hand (nee Eliza W. Gibbs), was born in Jasper county, Miss., November 2, 1859. His father was a native of North Carolina, born in 1823. His mother was born in South Carolina, and is now sixty-one years of age and a resident of Waynesboro, Miss. Mr. Hand is of Scotch-Irish descent. Since his father's death, which occurred in 1875, he has had charge of the family affairs. Until he was fifteen years of age he attended the schools of Waynesboro, and then entered into contract with a mercantile firm of that town, where he was employed for fourteen years. In 1888 he came to Pachuta, Clarke county, Miss., where he embarked in merchandising on his own account, associated with Mr. J. S. Turner, of Vosburg. His firm (J. E. Hand & Co.) also own and operate a turpentine distillery, producing annually about twenty-five thousand gallons of spirits of turpentine and three thousand barrels of resin, valued at about $12,000. The purchasers of these articles are from all parts of the United States. The company has its own cooperage establishment. Pachuta is eleven miles west of Quitman, the county seat of Clarke county, and is surrounded by immense pine forests, affording good facilities for a perpetual output along this line. Mr. Hand does some farming. His mercantile interest amounts to perhaps $15,000 annually. He is regarded as one of the foremost business men of the county, and has ever done his part toward the promotion of all worthy public interests.

P. B. Hand, lumber manufacturer, Handsboro, Harrison county, Miss., was born in Onondaga county, N. Y., May 19, 1834, and is a son of Miles B. and Helen (Dowd) Hand, who were also natives of the Empire state. The father was a mechanic by trade. In 1847 he removed to Mississippi, taking with him the machinery and furnishings for three saw-mills, and located on the present site of Handsboro. The land was then heavily timbered, and civilization had not yet made a strong impress. Mr. Hand put up the first foundry, and operated his sawmill in connection for several years. He erected all the mills that were built from this point to Biloxi before the Civil war. He was widely known in lumber circles, and a citizen of much enterprise. He died in 1890, in Harrison county, in his eighty-fifth year. He had three sons, L. M., P. B. and George G. P. B. Hand was reared from his twelfth year in Harrison county. He received the most of his education in New York, and was trained in all the details of the lumber business, including the trade of a machinist. At the age of twenty years he left his father's home, and went out to seek his fortune in the world. For twenty-five years he was absent from Handsboro. During that time he built twelve different sawmills, but in 1886 he came back and purchased the old homestead. It is beautifully situated on Bayou Bernard, directly opposite the sawmill plant, and is one of the most luxurious and ideal homes. There is an orchard containing two thousand trees, bearing pears, and a pecan grove of four hundred trees, and all the surroundings are indicative of comfort and plenty. Mr. Hand has made a success of the lumber industry, his shipments being made to New Orleans principally. He was married to Miss Margaret Champlin.

Hon. Thomas L. Hannah, planter, Reform, Miss. Mr. Hannah's grandfather, John Hannah, was a native of the Emerald isle, but it is not known whether he came to the

United States previous to the Revolutionary war or after. He first settled in North Carolina, but at an early day removed to east Tennessee, and thence to Alabama, where his death
occurred near the site of Birmingham, before the subject of this sketch was born. His son,
Cullinas Hannah, was probably born in North Carolina, but if so he went, when very small,
with his parents to Tennessee, Blount county. There he was married to Miss Mary Lowe,
and removed to Jefferson county, Ala., about seventy-five years ago. A number of years
later he removed to Pickens couuty of that state, and there his death occurred in October,
1858, when about sixty years of age. Mrs. Hannah was born in Tennessee, and died in that
county also in 1880. Both were active members of the Methodist church, and he was class
leader for many years. He followed the occupation of a planter and became quite wealthy.
He was with General Jackson in the Seminole war, was a self-made man and one of considerable influence. He was a lifelong and ardent democrat, but not a politician. The maternal
grandfather, ——— Lowe, was a planter, and died in Bibb county, Ala. To Cullinas and
Mary (Lowe) Hannah were born seventeen children—ten sons and seven daughters—all but one of
whom lived to be grown, but only four now living. Seven served in the Civil war, viz.: John
L., who was too old for the regular service, was in the militia as lieutenant. He died since
in Calhoun county, where he once served as probate judge; James was captured at Corinth
and died at Camp Douglas; William was in an Arkansas company in the Confederate army,
and died at Saline county, Ark.; Samuel died in Tennessee, while serving in the Nineteenth
Alabama; Henry, a planter of Pickens county, Ala., was in the Thirty-fifth Mississippi all
through the war in the Tennessee army, and Cullinas was in the Forty-first Alabama, and
died at Chattanooga. Hon. Thomas L. Hannah, the sixteenth in order of birth of the above
mentioned children, was reared to the arduous duties of the farm, and when seventeen years
of age he left home, equipped with a common school education, and began for himself as a
farm hand, thus continuing until the breaking out of the Civil war. His sympathies were
with the Southern cause, and in September, 1861, he joined company A, Twenty-seventh
Mississippi infantry, serving first as orderly sergeant, and the last two years as lieutenant.
He fought at Murfreesboro, Chickamauga, Lookout Mountain, and was captured at the last-
named place on November 23, 1863, and imprisoned at Johnson's island, Ohio, until June 13,
1865. After being released he returned at once to Oktibbeha county, Miss., where he had
made his home since 1857, and was married, August 13 of that year, in Pickens county, Ala.,
to Miss Sarah E. Elrod, a native of Anderson district, S. C., and the daughter of Elijah and
Thersa Elrod, both born in the Palmetto state, where they were married. From there her
parents removed from Pickens county, Ala., in 1855, and there the father died in 1866. The
mother died in 1890. Both were Methodists, and he was a local minister of that denomination for many years. To Mr. and Mrs. Hannah were born ten children, three sons and
four daughters now living: Lulu (wife of H. T. Worthy), James S., John J., Nora, Tessa,
Birt Sims and Neva. Mr. Hannah resided in Oktibbeha county until 1867, and then came
to Choctaw county, where he rented land for three years. In 1870 he purchased his present
property of one hundred and sixty with eighty acres cleared, and he also has eighty acres in
Webster county. He has commanded some influence in politics, having served with distinction one term in the legislature, where he enjoyed the confidence of his contemporaries
and the respect of his opponents. No man stands higher in the opinion of the people of
Choctaw county than he. While a member of the legislature he served on the committee on
claims, and in 1890 he was a member of the constitutional convention. He is a member of
the Masonic fraternity, La Grange lodge No. 363, is also a member of the Farmers' Alliance,
and is president of the county alliance and the county subordinate alliance. He is not a

member, but is in sympathy with the Methodist church. He is active in politics, and was a delegate to the state convention in 1889. He is one of the most prominent public men in the county. He is postmaster of Reform postoffice at his home.

W. C. Harbour, merchant, was born in Perry county, Ala., October 10, 1835, the second child born to the union of William Harbour and Tempie Redford, both Alabamians, who were reared, educated and married in their native state, there also rearing their children. The father was a plain and practical planter, an honorable and upright citizen, and in his business operations was fairly successful. After the death of his first wife in Perry county, Ala., in 1840, he took for his second wife Miss Lucretia Nalley, by whom he became the father of four sons and four daughters, six members of which family are now living. W. C. Harbour, one sister and a half-brother reside in Mississippi, the sister being the wife of J. M. Fuller, of Kemper county. Mr. Harbour came to Mississippi about 1855, was married the same year, and immediately thereafter returned to his old home in Perry county, Ala. Before that year had passed he once more returned to Mississippi, and for some time thereafter devoted his attention to planting and merchandising in Kemper county. In 1887 he removed from Kemper to Lauderdale county that he might educate his children in Cooper institute of that place, and since that time has been in the mercantile business in Daleville, being at the head of the firm of W. C. Harbour & Sons. Their stock of general merchandise is valued at about $7,000, their annual sales amounting to $15,000. Besides this Mr. Harbour is the owner of six hundred and forty acres of land in Kemper county, one hundred and forty acres at Daleville, on which he has erected a nice two-story frame residence. He has never aspired to any official position, his entire attention being devoted to planting, stockraising and merchandising, and as his business ventures have resulted satisfactorily and he is prudent, though not in the least niggardly in the use of his means, he has become quite wealthy. His wife, Caroline, was the daughter of David Jones, and by her he became the father of five sons and five daughters: John B., William D.; Tallulu (wife of John Davis, of Kemper county), Anna (wife of W. T. Riley, is now deceased); Daniel E., George L., Robert L. and Haney. Mr. Harbour is a gentleman whose friends are numerous and his enemies few. He has endeavored to follow the teachings of the golden rule, and that he is an earnest Christian is undoubted. He and his worthy wife are members of the Methodist Episcopal church, and socially he belongs to the A. F. & A. M.

A popular young business man of Ackerman, Leake county, Miss., William H. Hardage, was born in this county in 1860, and is a son of Martin S. and Elizabeth (Brantley) Hardage, both natives of Georgia. The elder Hardage was left an orphan at an early age, and being thrown upon his own resources, as might be expected his educational facilities were not of the best. However, he made up for this by self-application in later years, and became a well-informed man. During his youth and early manhood he followed farming, and when twenty-four years of age he was married, selecting for his wife Miss Elizabeth Brantley, daughter of Jones Brantley, a planter in his native county. Immediately after his marriage Mr. Hardage emigrated to Mississippi, located in Leake county, and began making a home for himself and family. He purchased land, engaged in tilling the soil, and this continued up to the breaking out of the war, when he flung aside the implements of peace to take up the weapons of warfare. He entered the infantry, and during the four years of service in the Confederate army, although in many battles he received but one wound, and was not disabled. Returning to Leake county after the war, he resumed his occupation of farming, and this he still continues, although he has at times been engaged in merchandising. He resides at Madden, Leake county, Miss. To his marriage were born nine children, one of whom

54

died in infancy, viz.: Sallie, wife of John M. Thomas, a farmer of Leake county, Miss.; Dona, wife of John A. Thomas, also a farmer of the same county; William H. (subject); Mattie, wife of M. S. Sanders, a farmer and merchant of Leake county; Verine L., Pat C., Tommy and Jimmy. William H. Hardage secured a good practical education in the common schools of his native county, and when seventeen years of age he attended the university at Oxford a year. He subsequently taught school about the same length of time. He preferred merchandising to farming, and engaged as clerk in a general store at Madden, Miss., serving in that capacity three years. He then engaged in business for himself, in partnership with his father, at Ackerman, Miss., and there he has since continued, handling exclusively hardware and furniture. He is wideawake and enterprising, and has among his patrons the best class of citizens. He was married in 1883 to Miss Alice L. Austin, a native of Raymond, Miss., born in 1865, and the daughter of Samuel B. Austin, a prominent planter, now retired, residing in Ackerman. To Mr. and Mrs. Hardage have been born four children, the elder two and youngest being daughters and the other a son. They are named: Addie, Stella, Laurin and Willie. Mr. and Mrs. Hardage are both church members, but of different denominations, he a deacon in the Missionary Baptist and she a consistent member of the Methodist church. Mr. Hardage is one of the charter members and holds the office of vice-president in Ackerman lodge, Knights of Honor. He also holds the office of financial secretary of Ackerman lodge No. 1290, Knights and Ladies of Honor.

H. W. Hardaway was born in Benton county, Miss., September 30, 1851. He was the youngest son in a family of eight children that gladdened the home of John P. and Alice (Wyatt) Hardaway. These parents were both natives of Greensville county, Va., which was the county of their birth, marriage, and where they lived till the year 1847, when they moved to Benton county, Miss. The father was a doctor and planter, although he never practiced medicine after he left the state of his boyhood. He left an enviable reputation behind him when he left the historic state of Virginia, as he had practiced medicine there for twenty years. When he located in Benton county, Miss., he gave his entire attention to planting, in which he was quite successful, accumulating considerable property in land and slaves, one hundred and twenty-six of whom called him master when the war came. Like all Southerners, he was liberal in a broad sense of the word, was a good citizen, a beloved neighbor and a public-spirited man. He embraced the Episcopalian faith, dying in April, 1861, his wife following him in 1872. Only three of their eight children were left to mourn their death: the subject, a brother; John W., and Susan E., wife of A. T. Mason. Our subject began life for himself at the age of fifteen; as the war came at the time, he would have been attending to his studies under different circumstances, the consequence being that he attended only the common schools of his native county in the early years of his life. He took up planting, which he followed till 1873, when he engaged in the mercantile business at Lamar, Miss. In 1880 he removed to Michigan City and opened up a store of general merchandise, continuing this business in connection with farming till the present time. He owns four hundred acres of land, three hundred of them being under the plow, and his stock of general merchandise is worth $5,000, while he does an annual business of about $50,000. He was married in 1885 to Anna E. Hamer, a daughter of J. L. and Eugenia (Spencer) Hamer, and they have had five children, four of whom, three sons, died in infancy, and Eugenia, a daughter, is still living. Mr. Hardaway is a member of the Knights of Honor and Knights and Ladies of Honor. Mrs. Hardaway is a member of the Methodist Episcopal church, while the subject was raised an Episcopalian. Mr. Hardaway is a man whom his fellowmen have delighted to honor wherever he has been, as is proved by the offices of trust they have conferred upon him. Among these may be mentioned his election to the office of chancery clerk of Benton county in 1887, and of which he is the present incumbent; was the mayor of Michigan City for four years, and has been an alderman of the same city for a number of years. It is needless to say that he is well and favorably known or that he and his family move in the best circles of society. He is a man who likes to use the wealth at his command for the furtherance of the public good, and as soon as he becomes convinced that an institution is a laudable one, he gives most generously to its support.

Richard H. Hardy, one of the old and highly respected pioneers of Hardy Station, Miss., was born in Edgefield district, S. C., in 1814, and in 1836 was married to Miss Lucy Griffis. The latter was born in 1810, and is the only one of a family of ten children born to Nicholas and Judith (Hardy) Griffis, who is now living, although all of them lived until well along in years. In 1844 Mr. and Mrs. Hardy emigrated to Mississippi, and went overland, being a month on the road. In 1850 they settled at what was afterward called Hardy Station, Mr. Hardy being the founder and first resident of the place. This station was founded in 1861, incorporated in 1872, and Mr. Hardy was the first postmaster. To Mr. and Mrs. Hardy were born two children: Jesse J. and Barbara Ann, the latter now living in Grenada county. Jesse J., the only son, died of measles on the 21st of May, 1862, at the age of twenty-four years, ten months and seven days. He was born in Edgefield district, S. C., but the principal part of his life was passed within the borders of Grenada county, where his many virtues were known and where he was held in the highest estimation. He had been an exemplary member of the Mount Paran church for a number of years prior to his death, professed peace with God, and his last moments seemed to indicate a bright foretaste of heaven. He left a widow and two children: Jesse, Jr., who is now with J. W. Griffis, a merchant of Grenada; and Lucy Frances, who is at Okadrickama, Yalobusha county. He was a soldier during the Civil war, enlisting in company E., Twenty-ninth Mississippi regiment, and in his death the Confederacy lost a noble soldier, his bereaved wife and children a devoted husband and father, and society one of its brightest ornaments.

> " There is no death! The stars go down,
> To rise upon some fairer shore;
> And bright in heaven's jeweled crown
> They shine forevermore.

> " And ever near us, though unseen,
> The dear immortal spirits tread;
> For all the boundless universe
> Is life—there are no dead."

Mr. and Mrs. Hardy are earnest and faithful members of the Mount Paran church, which was founded in 1840, and of which they are the oldest members. Mr. Hardy is a democrat in politics, and he and family are highly esteemed in the community.

Capt. William Harris Hardy, Meridian, Miss., was born near Colirene, Lowndes county, Ala., February 12, 1837, and is the elder of two surviving sons. His parents were natives of South Carolina. His father, Robert W. Hardy, was born in Edgefield district, and his mother, Temperance L. Hardy (nee Toney), was born in Greenville district, and both were descended from Revolutionary stock who fought under Greene and Marion in the war for independence. They emigrated with their parents in 1818 to Alabama and settled, the Hardys on Town creek, in Dallas county, and the Toneys in Butler county, near where the present town of Greenville is located. Subsequently the Toneys moved to Lowndes county and settled on Panther creek, near the present village Colirene, where, in 1830, Robert W. Hardy and Temperance L. Toney were married. There were born to them one daughter and four sons, viz.: Margaret Elizabeth (afterward the wife of H. W. Evans, but who died at Paulding, Miss., September 16, 1877), Hance Dunklin (who died at Sylviarena, July 4, 1858), William Harris (who resides in the city of Meridian, Miss.), Thomas Judson (a lawyer and ex-state senator, who resides at Ellisville, Miss.), and Miles Boardman (who died at four years of age in Lowndes county, Ala., in 1844. Robert W., the father of our subject, was a planter and achieved fair success in his vocation, and was esteemed in the circle in which he moved as an amiable, honorable and upright man. He and his wife were honored members of the Baptist church, and were esteemed for their piety and liberality. They had only such limited education as could be acquired in the rude or primitive country schools of those early days, which usually opened when the crops were laid by in June, and closed when the cotton picking began in September. His mother, Temperance L., was a woman of great energy and force of character, strong native intellectual powers and esteemed for her noble qualities of head and heart. This noble Christian woman died at her residence in Paulding on the 16th day of September, 1877, preceding her only daughter to that better land only a few hours. Her husband two years after married Miss Carrie Chapman, of Paulding, a good woman of kind heart but delicate health. Of this marriage two sons were born, Marian and Miles, now ten and eight years of age respectively. Their mother died at Paulding in June, 1888, and the two little boys with their aged father moved to Ellisville, Miss., and entered the family of T. J. Hardy, when, in February, 1889, Robert W. Hardy died at the ripe age of seventy-nine years. He was interred in the family plat in the cemetery at Paulding, leaving to his children the noble heritage of a life and character without a stain of dishonor upon it. Captain Hardy attended the country schools taught in the neighborhood of Town Creek, Ala., until he was sixteen years old, when he was sent to Cumberland university, at Lebanon, Tenn. Owing to an attack of pneumonia in the winter of 1855 he left the university before completing the course, and in the latter part of that year he went to Mississippi and took a country school at Montrose, in Jasper county, where he taught during the year 1856. Then he was employed to teach at Flowers' place, in Smith county, during the year 1857. Here he established a male and female academy and named it Sylviarena, which name it bears still, and the academy is in a flourishing condition, and a little village by that name has sprung up around the school. Whilst teaching he read law and spent a part of the year 1858 in the law office of Shannon & Street, at Paulding, and in September of that year was admitted to the bar, and located at Raleigh, the county seat of Smith county. His previous preparation in his chosen profession and his studious habits speedily secured for him a good practice, and he soon developed those forensic powers which in later years distinguished him as one of the best orators in the state. A few of his published speeches compare favorably with the finest productions of the great men of the South who have made that section of our great country famous for its orators. Among these published addresses may be mentioned his address delivered at Paulding in 1867, before a lodge of sorrow held in honor of the Masons who were killed in the war, his address before the literary societies of Mississippi college in 1873, his defense of C. H. Williams in the great arson case at Meridian in 1875, his eulogy on Jefferson Davis in New York city, December, 1889, and his address of welcome at a reunion of Confederate veterans at Meridian in October, 1890. Many of his best efforts were made in capital cases in the courts but never published. Captain Hardy was first married with Miss Sallie Johnson at Brandon, Miss., on the 10th of October, 1860. She was a native of Gallatin, Tenn., and was descended from Virginia stock, her mother, Ellen Weaver, having been born near Weaverville, Fauquier county, Va., and her father, Thomas H. Johnson, near Farmville, Va. She was noted as well for her exquisite beauty of face and form as for her sweet disposition and gentle manners. She was universally beloved and admired by all who knew her. She died of typho-malarial fever at Paulding, Miss., the 16th day of September, 1872, leaving six children: Mattie (now Mrs. W. S. Lott), Mary Willie (now Mrs. A. S. Barnes), Ellen T., Thomas R., Lizzie C. and Jefferson D., all of whom still survive her. After Captain Hardy's marriage, as stated above, he continued the practice of his profession at Raleigh until the spring of 1861, when the stirring events of that year occurred, resulting in the war between the states. He raised a company in Smith county upon the first call made by the governor for troops, known as the Defenders, and was elected captain and mustered into service on the 27th of April, 1861. On the 29th of June he was ordered to report at the camp of rendezvous and instruction at Corinth, Miss., where his company became a part of the Sixteenth Mississippi infantry regiment, company H. In the latter part of July his regiment was ordered to Manassas, Va., where it formed a part of Crittenden's brigade, composed of one regiment from each of the states of Mississippi, Alabama, Georgia and North Carolina. This afterward became Trimble's brigade of Ewell's division and participated in all the battles of the valley campaign under Stonewall Jackson, and also in the seven days' battle around Richmond in which McClellan's grand army was routed. The valley campaign of Stonewall Jackson is one of the most memorable in the annals of warfare. Within thirty-five days he marched nearly two hundred miles and defeated four armies, either one of which was larger than his army, viz.: Milroy's, Banks', Fremont's and Shields'. After the battles around Richmond the Confederate government adopted the policy of brigading state troops together, and under this policy the Sixteenth Mississippi regiment, with three other regiments, formed what was known as Featherston's brigade and afterward as Pasey's, and lastly, Harris' brigade, and its last battle was fought in bloody Fort Gregg, just before Lee's surrender, that being the last battle of the gallant remnant of that army which will live in history forever. Captain Hardy participated in all the battles of his command up to and including Sharpsburg, or Antietam, as called by the Federals. He was in bad health, and upon the recommendation of his brigade surgeon, accompanied with the written statement that he could not recover in camp or the hospital, he resigned from the army, knowing that he would in a few days be promoted to lieutenant-colonel of his regiment by the promotion of the colonel to be brigadier-general, and the resignation of the lieutenant-colonel, Captain Hardy being the senior captain in the regiment, but his health would not admit of his remaining.

Upon his resignation his company held a meeting and unanimously adopted a series of resolutions attesting his high soldierly character and conduct and expressing their deep regret at losing their brave, true and tried commander. He went home, and by careful nursing sufficiently recovered his health by June, 1863, to reënter the service. He was offered and accepted the position of aid-de-camp on the staff of Brig.-Gen. James Argyle Smith, of the army of Tennessee, and shortly after joined the command then confronting Sherman on his advance from Dalton to Atlanta. He participated in all the battles of his command in that memorable campaign back to Atlanta and with Hood's campaign to Nashville. After Cleburne's death, at the battle of Franklin, General Smith took command of the division composed of his (Smith's) Georgia brigade, Govan's Arkansas, Granberry's Texas and M. P. Lowery's Mississippi brigades. Smith commanded this division up to the surrender of the army at Greensboro, the 26th of April, 1865. During this period Captain Hardy was the acting assistant adjutant-general of the division and surrendered with the command on the date above mentioned, near High Point, N. C. On his return from the army he removed from Raleigh to Paulding, in November, 1865, and resumed the practice of law, in which he was very successful, being employed on one side of nearly every important cause arising in the courts of east Mississippi. Whilst residing at Paulding in 1868 he projected a railroad to run from Meridian to New Orleans. The scheme was incorporated in 1870 as the New Orleans & Northeastern railroad company. In 1871–2 he had the preliminary surveys made, S. D. Browne, of Mobile, being chief engineer. Captain Hardy was made general counsel of the company in 1872, and in 1873, by his advice and with his assistance, a contract of purchase was made with Governor Lindsay, of Alabama, for what is now the Alabama Great Southern railway. The state of Alabama was in the possession of the road under a purchase at bankrupt sale, she having indorsed the bonds issued by the road and bought the road to protect her interests. It was necessary that the contract of sale so made by Governor Lindsay to the New Orleans & Northeastern railroad company should be ratified by the legislature. When that body met, through the influence of certain bondholders of the company, the sale was not ratified. Pending this effort to acquire the Alabama Great Southern railroad, Captain Hardy removed, in April, 1873, to Meridian, the better to push his railroad scheme and to enlarge the sphere of his practice, but within one month after his removal to Meridian came "Black Friday" in New York, the beginning of the greatest financial panic which this country ever experienced in its history. It paralyzed all business enterprises, prostrated every industry and spread gloom and dismay to every part of this country. During this year, 1873, on the 1st day of December, Captain Hardy was united in marriage with his present wife, Miss Hattie Lott, daughter of Hon. E. B. Lott, of Mobile, Ala. She is a woman of splendid physique and fine attainments, holding a commanding position in the highest social and intellectual circles of the city in which she lives. To them have been born three sons and one daughter, viz.: Harris Hawthorne, Lamar, Toney Arnold and Lena May; the eldest of these died when he was eleven months old. He pursued his profession assiduously till 1880, when, prosperity having returned to the country, he took up again his project of building a railroad from Meridian to New Orleans. The old organization had become extinct and the road almost forgotten by all others, but after months of patient toil he succeeded in getting up the old outstanding stock and bonds of the company and reorganizing it, and in the reorganization he was elected vice president with the active management of construction. The scheme was ridiculed by many as visionary and impracticable, as Lake Ponchartrain had to be bridged; but in November, 1884, the first train ran through from Meridian to New Orleans, crossing the lake on the then longest bridge in the world, it being twenty-one miles long, built on creosoted pile trestles, sixteen miles of which, however, covered the approaches. Thus, fifteen years after its conception, this great enterprise was completed, and Captain Hardy proved to be wiser than his critics. The construction of this railroad was one of the greatest works of public improvement ever constructed in the state, as it developed that vast area of territory known as the piney woods region of the state, famous for its magnificent longleaf pine forests, its beautiful streams and health-giving climate, but which was practically valueless for lack of lines of transportation. The building of this railroad brought millions of acres of land into market; towns and villages, schools, churches, newspapers, telegraph and telephone lines sprung up as by magic, and millions of dollars' worth of property put upon the tax rolls where before there were only hundreds. This railroad will stand as a monument to the wisdom and foresight, as well as the indomitable will, untiring energy and perseverance of Captain Hardy. He has a state-wide reputation for his liberality in all works of benevolence. He was a trustee of the Confederate soldiers' orphan asylum, located at Lauderdale, Miss., and upon the resignation of Hon. Thomas S. Gathright, president of that institution, he was chosen as his successor and served three years. There were over eight hundred orphans of Confederate soldiers raised and educated at this home, and when there were no more Confederate soldiers' orphans to raise and educate the home was closed and the property sold. He was grand master of the Grand lodge of A. F. & A. M. of Mississippi for one term, 1872, and declined reëlection; was for ten years a trustee of Mississippi college, six years president of the Mississippi Baptist state convention, and one year a vice president of the Southern Baptist convention. In religious faith he is a Baptist, having joined that church in his boyhood, and his benefactions to that denomination have been numerous and liberal for one of his means. In politics he is democratic, but never aspired to political preferment. He was a presidential elector on the Tilden and Hendricks ticket in 1876, has declined repeated calls to run for congress, and in 1874, when the democratic party was disbanded by the Meridian convention, over thirty counties withdrew from the convention and, determined to preserve the democratic organization, by these he was tendered the nomination for governor, but whilst he opposed the policy of disbanding the party he was opposed to nominating a ticket, and his counsel prevailed. He is known throughout the state as a progressive, public-spirited man, who is full abreast of the times in all matters of public interest that tend to develop the resources of the state and improve the condition of the masses. In 1872 he organized the Meridian Gas Light company and served as its president for two years. In 1884 he organized the Meridian national bank and served as its president one year. He was instrumental in having the railroad shops of the Queen & Crescent railroad system located at Meridian. In all these enterprises a spirit of unselfishness and liberality characterized his conduct so conspicuously as to mark him as a man of noble aims, free from avarice and greed—a real benefactor.

In 1886 he was elected president of the Gulf & Ship Island railroad company, and he accepted the position and entered upon its duties and responsibilities with his usual zeal and energy. This road was projected before Captain Hardy was born. It was intended to run from some point on Mississippi sound opposite Ship Island harbor in Harrison county northward to Brandon or Jackson. He procured an amendment to the charter, by which it is run as near centrally through the state as practicable to the Tennessee line. The object is to develop and utilize the splendid harbor at Ship Island, by connecting it with the shore and with the interior by a trunk line of railway. When he took charge of the enterprise it had no money and no credit, only a charter. He soon enlisted capital, and bought some five thousand acres of land with one mile front on the beach, three miles west of Mississippi city, and laid out a city and named it Gulfport. From this point he began the construction of the road northward, and at this time has twenty miles in operation north from Gulfport, and the road graded to its intersection with the New Orleans & Northeastern railroad at Hattiesburg, which latter town, by the way, was laid out by him in 1881 and named in honor of his wife, Mrs. Hattie Hardy. Captain Hardy's ambition is to lay the foundation of a great commercial city at Gulfport that shall rival Mobile and New Orleans. He maintains that the true lines of commerce are with the parallels of longitude and not latitude, because commerce is exchange, and peoples who live on the same parallels of latitude have nothing to exchange, since their products are the same. Hence our commercial relations with the fifty millions of people south of us ought to be conducted through some port on the gulf of Mexico; that Ship Island harbor is far the best natural deep water harbor on the Gulf; that the construction of the Nicaragua canal, or any trans-isthmian way, will revolutionize the commerce of the world; that the ships of India, China, Japan, Australia and Central and South America would then come through the Gulf of Mexico, and make it the Mediterranean of the new world. Hence his scheme for building a railroad from Ship Island harbor centrally through the state to Jackson, Tenn., to connect with the system of roads there leading to Chicago, St. Louis and the great Northwest, as well as the great cities of the East. The project in its conception is a grand one, and, if successful, will mark its projector as one among the wisest and greatest benefactors of this great country. Socially he is rather reserved and dignified, but those who know him best esteem him highest. He is fond of music and children, and also of literature, and possesses one of the best selected private libraries in the state. As a neighbor and friend he is kind, generous and true to a fault. In stature he is six feet two inches high, weighs about two hundred pounds, and is in the full vigor of physical and intellectual manhood, and it is hoped he may live to complete his great undertaking, by which the commercial independence of his state is to be wrought out and established, and numberless thousands of the human race blessed. Such men always make the world better by having lived in it.

Jefferson Hardwick, a successful planter of Yazoo City, Yazoo county, was born in Holmes county, Miss., September 8, 1838, and is the third of four children. His parents were Josiah C. and Lydia A. (Tabor) Hardwick, natives of Virginia and Alabama respectively. The father was one of the pioneer settlers of Mississippi, locating there in 1821. He was one of the conspicuous characters of the county and lived to be eighty years old, his death occurring in 1886. His father was William A. Hardwick, a native of Virginia. The maternal grandfather of our subject was William Tabor of South Carolina. Jefferson Hardwick grew to maturity in the state in which he was born, and acquired his education there. The advantages were indeed meager, but by making the most of his opportunities and the cultivation of a naturally keen judgment he has been able to fulfill all the duties that have come to his lot. He is a planter by occupation, and owns sixteen hundred acres of land; three hundred and fifty acres are in an advanced state of cultivation and yield abundant harvests. Mr. Hardwick was united in marriage in 1866 to Miss Ellen Johns, of Mississippi, a daughter of William Johns, Esq., of Virginia. One child was born of this union, Lula O. He was married a second time in 1872 to Miss Fanny A. Donelson, who was born in Mississippi, a daughter of William Donelson, Esq., of Tennessee. Mr. Hardwick saw service in the late war. He enlisted in company D, Eighteenth Mississippi volunteer infantry in 1861. He remained in this company ten months, when he was discharged on account of ill health. He was out but a short time when he joined company I, First Mississippi artillery, serving until the surrender. He was in the engagements of Chickasaw bayou, Vicksburg, Harrisburg, Atlanta, and Blakely. He was twice taken prisoner; first, in 1863, at Vicksburg, where he was held but seven days, and second, at Blakely in 1865; he was carried to Ship Island and held there until the close of the struggle. Politically he affiliates with the democratic party. He has been a potent factor in the upbuilding of the county and is highly respected by the whole community. He owns a beautiful residence situate four and one-half miles south of Yazoo City, which is one of the most thrifty and enterprising towns in the state of Mississippi.

Prof. H. E. Harlan, who has attained considerable prominence in his chosen profession, teaching, was born in Noxubee county, Miss., in 1862, and is one of eight children, five now living, born to W. S. and Mary A. (Hunter) Harlan, the parents natives of Maury county, Tenn., and the father born in 1818. W. S. Harlan and family emigrated to Noxubee county, Miss., about 1837, and there the father received his final summons in 1865. He was followed by his wife in 1886. Prof. H. E. Harlan was reared near Macon, and his early days were spent on the farm. At the age of fourteen years he entered the school of Webb

Brothers at Culleoka, Tenn., where he was prepared for college. In 1879 he entered the sophomore class of the University of Mississippi, and the next year entered Vanderbilt university, from which he was graduated in 1882. When at Culleoka he stood at the head of his class; at Oxford, was second-honor man, and at Vanderbilt, to the scholarship of $100 in the department of modern languages. He was a member of the Beta Theta Pi fraternity at the last two named institutions. After graduating he accepted a position in Hardin college, Savannah, Tenn., remained there one season, and then, taking the advice of his physician, gave this up and devoted himself to a more active life, engaging in merchandising and milling. In 1889 he resumed teaching at Boligee, Ala., and later, at Brooksville, Miss., where he is now engaged. Professor Harlan's future as an educator is quite encouraging, and his friends may look to see him attain great prominence in his profession. He has recently become one of the proprietors of the Fairview male and female college, located at Binnsville, Kemper county, Miss., a school of more than local reputation, having a large patronage from Mississippi and beyond her borders. Professor Harlan married Miss Nettie Hunter, of Maury county, Tenn., in 1881, and she died in 1890, leaving three children: Eugene, Morse and Anna M. In 1890 he married Miss Mollie McLeod, of Noxubee county, Miss., who is now engaged with him in teaching at Brooksville.

Among the respected physicians of Lauderdale county, Miss., may be mentioned Dr. S. B. Harmon, who has devoted the greater part of his life to healing the sick, and for his many kindly deeds has received a portion of his reward in this world, for he has the confidence, respect and love of his fellowmen and the consciousness that he has driven sorrow and despair from many homes by his skill and talent as a physician. He was born in Alabama in 1850, attended the common schools in his youth, and grew up on a farm. In 1877 he entered the Alabama medical college at Mobile, and for four years practiced his profession in that state and Lauderdale county, Miss., but in 1881, in order to more thoroughly fit himself for that calling, he entered the medical department of the University of Kentucky at Louisville, from which he took the degree of M. D., and has since been one of the first-class practitioners of this county. He owns between seven and eight hundred acres of fine farming land, on a considerable portion of which is heavy timber (the longleaf pine) which he is engaged in milling. This is located twelve miles east of Meridian, on the Meridian and Butler road, and is considered exceptionally valuable land. In 1882 he took for his wife Miss Cora M. Pigford, of Lauderdale county, Miss., and their union has been blessed in the birth of four children: Stephen M., Thomas C., Charles H. and Miriam Kate. Mr. and Mrs. Harmon are members of the Methodist church, and in his political views he is a democrat, taking an active interest in politics. He is a model citizen in every respect, is kind of heart and liberal in the use of his means. His father, John N. Harmon, was born in the Palmetto state about 1816, and in 1843 was married to Mrs. Wallace (formerly Miss M. B. Nelson, of North Carolina), whose birth occurred in 1829. He died in 1886, but Mrs. Harmon still survives him, being a resident of Marion, Miss.

A history of Covington county would not be complete without mention of Alexander S. Harper, Santee, Covington county, Miss., who was born in Wilkinson county, Miss., in 1807, In 1817 he removed with his parents to Marion county, Miss., and there resided until he was twenty-five years of age. He then came to Covington county, and has since made it his home. His father, Samuel Harper, was a native of Georgia, and was a soldier in the war of 1812. He was a son of Alexander Harper who was brought by his parents during his infancy from Ireland to South Carolina. Alexander S. Harper was educated in the common schools of Marion county. Soon after coming to Covington county he was elected a member of the board of police, and served four years.   He was afterward elected probate judge, and served in this capacity for eight years.   He has since been identified with the political record of Covington county, and has held almost every office within the gift of her people.   He has been a faithful official, a loyal citizen, a true and tried friend.   He was married in 1835 to Miss Martha Hathorn, and to them were born six children, five of whom grew to maturity. Both his sons, Alexander and Samuel, were soldiers in the Civil war, and Alexander was killed at the battle of Atlanta.

George W. Harper was born at Alexandria, Va., on January 8, 1824, being the eldest son of Samuel D. and Sarah Keys Harper.   When only a few years old, young Harper's parents moved to Wheeling, now in West Virginia, then a town with a population of from three thousand to four thousand inhabitants.   At thirteen years of age, in compliance with an irrepressible inclination, George W. Harper began learning the newspaper business, under S. H. Davis, in the office of the Wheeling *Daily Gazette*, who had himself been a pupil of Gales & Seaton, of the renowned *National Intelligencer*.   In Wheeling young Harper frequently saw and heard Henry Clay, on his trips to and from Washington, and of course learned to regard him as the beau ideal of statesman and patriot.   When little over seventeen, Harper was made foreman of the office, and often editor pro tem.   He warmly went in for " Tippecanoe and Tyler too," in the memorable " coonskin, hard cider, log cabin and red paper " canvass of 1840, and in his enthusiasm crossed the river to New Lisbon, in Ohio, and established the *Western Palladium*, which he continued until the following year.   He then returned to Wheeling, and with a partner, purchased the *Daily Gazette*, but not succeeding to his expectations, he came South in 1844, and located at Raymond, in Hinds county, Miss. He found employment on the *Southwestern Farmer*, then conducted by his uncle, N. Green North, an eminent Presbyterian divine, and D. M. W. Phillips, who afterward attained distinction as an agricultural writer and educator.   The *Southwestern Farmer* was conducted with marked ability, but in the summer of 1844 was discontinued.   Soon after Samuel T. King and George W. Harper established the *Hinds County Gazette*, a success from the very start. It was decidedly whig in politics, maintained all the issues of the party, struck hard blows for it, but in all other matters guarded vigilantly the public interests, and was universally regarded as an honest and able journal.   Mr. Harper was soon elected mayor of his town, and likewise major of the county militia.   He was elected delegate to the convention of 1848, that nominated old Zack for the presidency.   Strongly pressed by his old friends in Ohio to go there and conduct a campaign paper, he yielded to their importunities, and the Steubenville *Journal,* a campaign paper of extraordinary cogency and efficiency, was the result. The ensuing winter he returned to Raymond, Miss., and to the *Gazette*, and in 1860 became its sole proprietor, as he had from the first, with the few months' exception noted, been its sole editor.   In the great contest of 1850-51, on the compromise measure, Major Harper, through the *Gazette* and on the stump, took a strong conservative position, concentrating around it what was then styled the union party.   In 1851, in the largest convention ever assembled in the county, he was nominated and elected as one of the union members of the legislature.   He was made chairman of the committee on penitentiary, and inaugurated the manufacture of cotton goods in that institution.   He was reëlected to the legislature in 1853, by a commanding majority.   In the memorable contest of 1860 he supported Bell, of Tennessee, for president, and continued his strenuous efforts to avert disunion, but when, in a paroxysm of desperation, the state seceeded, Major Harper, though deeply regretting and deprecating her precipitation, and knowing the tremendous odds she must encounter, nevertheless determined to share her destiny.   When the war and all its fury burst upon the

South, Major Harper entered the Confederate service, and was actively engaged in the commissary department until the close of the struggle, an affection of the eyes, from which he had suffered since a child, forbidding his becoming a fighter in the ranks. At the close of the war he returned to the *Gazette*, and alligned himself with the democratic party, which had virtually absorbed the old whig organization, and throughout the period of reconstruction advocated conciliatory measures and a peaceful acceptance of the terms of the surrender. In 1875, at the time of the great political upheaval in Mississippi politics, George W. Harper was again elected to the legislature, and served with great distinction. He was on the impeachment committee, and took a leading part in the events that brought about the abdication of Gov. Adelbert Ames. After that time, and until 1884, he devoted himself to the newspaper profession, and will leave behind, when death finally comes to claim its own, a record of faithful performance of duty and of consistent actions, that can not but be a pride to all who bear his name. The *Gazette* is still published at Raymond, his son, Sam D. Harper, being the editor and proprietor. George W. Harper, in 1852, was married to Anna L. Sims, a niece of the eminent statesman, Gen. Cowles Meade, so distinguished in our territorial history. She still lives, as do also ten sons and daughters, fruits of the marriage. George W. Harper is now mayor at Raymond, and also justice of the peace of the fourth supervisor district, which position he has held for many years.

Maj. James Nairne Harper, a planter and prominent citizen of Tallahatchie county, was born in Lincoln county, Ga., April 19, 1805, the son of Robert and Lucy (Cross) Harper, natives of Maryland and Orange county, N. C., respectively. They married and settled in Halifax county, Va., and at a comparatively early date removed to eastern Georgia, and afterward to Lincoln county, Ga., where Mr. Harper died in 1826. Mrs. Harper died at Tallahatchie county, Miss. Both have been members of the Baptist church, though Mr. Harper was formerly a Scotch Presbyterian. He was a successful planter, who began with no capital and prospered so well that, at his death, he left a fine estate. At one time he held the office of tobacco inspector in Georgia. Perhaps his best claim to historical notice is the fact that at the age of sixteen he enlisted as a private, and served the cause of the colonies in the Revolutionary war until the close of the struggle. He was a man of good natural abilities, and had a fair English education. His father, Banister Harper, was one of three brothers, Englishmen, who came to America at an early date and located in Maryland, removing afterward to Georgia, where he died. His wife was Margaret Nairne. Shepard Gross, grandfather of our subject, was born in North Carolina, and died in Georgia. His daughter, who became the mother of James Nairne Harper, was a well-educated lady. Mr. and Mrs. Harper had eight children, of whom Major Harper was the youngest, except one, being the only one now living. He received his preparatory education at different academies in Georgia and South Carolina, finishing at Franklin college, Athens, Ga. In 1828 he married Mary Susanna Jones, daughter of Col. William Jones, a noted Virginian by birth, who became a prominent citizen of Lincoln county, Georgia, but died in Warren county of the same state, where he had been for some time in active business as a planter and banker. He saw active service in the War of 1812, and was during the larger part of his life a prominent man. Mrs. Harper was born in Augusta, Georgia, and died July 14, 1860. This Christian woman was for many years, prior to her death, a member of the Presbyterian church. She bore her husband twelve children, namely: Dr. Robert W. Harper, a planter and physician, who received a fine collegiate education and graduated in medicine at Augusta, Ga. (became a surgeon in the Confederate army in General Walthall's command); Correli M. became the wife of Col. William T. Wynn, deceased, the father of

Judge J. H. Wynn, a prominent attorney of Greenville; James N. graduated from the University of Mississippi, and died before the war, while preparing for the ministry; Henry J., also a graduate of the University of Mississippi, became a captain in the Confederate service, and was killed in the battle of Murfreesboro; Lucius S. also graduated from the state university, and was killed in the battle of Medon, Tenn.; Charles E. received a good English education, and had prepared for college at the time of the outbreak of the war, went into the war at the age of seventeen, and was killed in the fight at New Hope, Ga., after having just captured a piece of artillery; Mary A. became the wife of Joseph A. Thompson, a planter of Tallahatchie county; Chalmers was killed by being thrown from a horse in 1864; Jerry M. and Mary S. died in infancy, and two others died unnamed. Henry J. Harper was a man of fine talent and an able lawyer. The beginning of the war found him engaged in the practice of his profession at Charleston, in partnership with Col. James S. Bailey. He joined the Tallahatchie rifles, but was not mustered into the service with that organization, but in July, 1861, he became a member of the First Mississippi cavalry, entering the service as a private, receiving his discharge the following December on account of ill health. Returning home, he soon after organized a company which soon became a part of the Twenty-ninth Mississippi infantry, and was known as company B, of which he was lieutenant, and of which he became captain about five months later, continuing in command until his death, December 21, 1862. His remains lie in the Confederate cemetery at Murfreesboro. For his second wife Major Harper married Eusebia Fisher, July 21, 1861. She was born in Kentucky, and was a sister of the late Judge E. S. Fisher, a distinguished lawyer and physician of Mississippi. She died in 1870. She was a lady of fine talent and education, a devoted wife and mother, and had been for some time a member of the Christian church. He was married again in 1874 to Mrs. Margaret R. Cox, daughter of John Fox. She was born near Huntsville, Ala., and came with her parents to Mississippi. This excellent lady was in her early years a Methodist and later a Presbyterian. She died in 1890.

In 1834 Major Harper came to Tallahatchie county, and purchased a tract of land upon which he now lives, and in the winter of 1835-6 he brought his family here, where he has since made his home. He has cleared about thirteen hundred acres of land, and is the owner altogether of about two thousand acres. He obtained his title of Major through his rank in the militia of Georgia, in his early manhood. About 1837 he founded Preston academy, in Yalobusha county, which was a very popular institution of learning in the pioneer days of Mississippi, and at which many of the prominent men of the state received their early education. Mr. Harper has always been active in politics and all affairs of public moment, and in many ways has been the most conspicuous figure in this county. He is a charter member of George Washington lodge No. 157, A. F. & A. M., at Charleston, of which he was once worshipful master. He has taken the Royal Arch degree, and was formerly prominent in Masonry, but, owing to advancing age, has not been active for some years past. He has been an elder in the Presbyterian church for more than half a century, and all of his children, and all of his grandchildren save one, have been baptized in the same faith. Major Harper's chief aim in life has been to educate his children, and, with their interest and the general interest in view, he was led to the establishment of Preston academy previously mentioned. The fact of his having lost four gallant and promising sons in the Confederate service during the war, another meeting a sad and sudden death at home during the same period, has cast a shadow over the happiness of the family, through which the sun has never since shone as brightly as before. In his old age he was an intelligent, exceedingly bright and affable man, fond of a joke, and widely known as a story teller. During his later years in Georgia he was personally familiar with nearly every man in the state who had a state or national reputation, and is yet very much attached to that grand old state. His acquaintance in Mississippi has not been quite as extensive, yet he is personally acquainted with most of its distinguished citizens, and thoroughly familiar with its history. He has always been active in politics, and zealous in every movement looking for the advancement of the country. He has never permitted himself to become a public officer.

John H. Harper, a prominent planter of Clarke county, Miss., is located eight miles from Quitman. He was born in Jasper county in 1840, and is the second of a family of nine children born to George and Edna B. (Huff) Harper, six of whom are living. His father was born in South Carolina in 1804, and moved to Mississippi in 1832. He was married while still a resident of South Carolina. His children who are living are William F., John H., Americus T., Sarah E., Winfield S., Mary M., Thomas M. and Susan M. The worthy father died in May, 1890, his wife having died in 1864. They were members of the Baptist church. Mr. Harper was a practical planter during the latter part of his life. His early years were passed in teaching school. He was successful in whatever he undertook, and was everywhere recognized as a helpful citizen. His early life was spent in Jasper county; there he was educated, and in 1865 married Sarah H. Johnston, daughter of John Johnston. Previous to this, in 1861, he enlisted in company F, of the Sixteenth Mississippi regiment, for service in the Confederate cause. He was in engagements at and about Richmond, Fredericksburg, and in all the battles in which the Virginia army took part. At the battle of Petersburg he was wounded in the arm and thigh, and at the battle of Fort Gregg he received another wound in the head. He was taken prisoner of war, and carried to Hart's Island, New York harbor. During his term of service he gained a commission as corporal. After the war he returned to Jasper county, and engaged in farming. Mr. and Mrs. Harper have eleven children: William A., John W., Thomas J., Leon R., Sarah O., Charles C., Daniel L., Edward O., Stella M., Annie B. and another daughter, Sarah E., who died. The family moved to this county in 1870, where Mr. Harper has become a well-known planter and quite an extensive breeder. He is a member of the Masonic lodge and the Farmers' Alliance. Politically, he is a democrat, taking a deep interest in all political questions of the day. In 1891, through the kindness of his friends, he was elected to the state legislature of Mississippi. He and his wife are both members of the Baptist church.

A glance at the lives of representative men whose names appear in this volume will reveal many sketches of honored and influential citizens who have resided many years in the county, but among them none are more worthy or deserving of mention than Hon. William L. Harper, who is a true type of the Southern gentleman. In his veins flows some of the best blood of which America can boast, and of which he is justly proud. He has always been a man of unquestioned honor and has kept the name he bears, which has descended to him from a long line of illustrious and honored ancestry, pure in the sight of God and man. His parents, William and Louisa (Lewis) Harper, were born in Virginia and Mississippi, respectively, the former being the youngest in a family of seven sons and seven daughters born to his parents. He was made familiar with the duties of plantation life in his youth, but this did not occupy his entire attention, for much of his time was devoted to acquiring an education. About the year 1807, or when he was twenty-five years of age, he decided that the territory of Mississippi offered a better field for a young man to make a name and fame for himself than the state of his birth, and accordingly came to Jefferson county, and in time became the owner of about three thousand acres of land. Soon after his arrival in the state of his adoption the war between the United States and Great Britain known as the

War of 1812, broke out, but in this Mr. Harper did not take part, preferring to employ a substitute and devote his attention to his plantation. In 1818 he was married to Miss Louisa, the second of three daughters of Mrs. Martha Lewis, a widow and a native of Jefferson county. Mr. Harper and his wife began housekeeping on the place near where Hon. William L. Harper now resides, and there the latter was born on the 21st of November, 1822, this being within two miles of where he now lives. His advantages for obtaining an education were very good, and in 1842 he was graduated from Oakland college, soon after which he was married to Miss Ann T. Sanders, of Georgetown, Ky., she being a young lady of exceptional intelligence and refinement and a graduate of a college in her native town. In regard to her private life, she endeavored to live up to the teachings of the golden rule, and that she succeeded in living the life of a true Christian was fully attested by the love and respect that was accorded her, not only by her husband and children, but by all who knew her. After a happy married life of eighteen years she was called from earth, her death being earnestly mourned by her husband, four sons and five daughters. Six of these children still survive her: William, a farmer of Texas; Emma H., wife of B. B. Paddock, of Fort Worth, Tex.; Walker S., a planter of Washington county, Miss.; Matthew C., a teacher of Jefferson college, near Natchez; Ann T. and Betty E., both residents of Texas. Mary Louisa, the widow of Captain Darden, died June 10, 1884; Victor F., the captain of the schooner Hebe, was lost in the Carribean sea by the capsizing of his boat in the year 1874, and the other member of the family died in early childhood. In 1864 Mr. Harper married again, his second wife being Miss Annie E. Coulson, daughter of John S. Coulson, a prominent clothing merchant of Natchez. Mrs. Harper was educated in the Spingler institute of New York city, this institution being under Gorham Abbott, a brother of the famous historian, John S. C. Abbott. She left this school an accomplished intellectual and refined young lady, eminently fitted to shine in any society, and her subsequent career has fully carried out the promise she gave in early womanhood. She is a leader in all matters of a public nature where members of her sex are called upon to participate, and her example of earnest Christian endeavor is well worthy of emulation. She has three sisters, all of whom are women of brilliant mind. One sister, Mrs. Kells, has devoted the greater part of her life to educational work and for some time was principal of Fairmount college, later becoming principal of the Episcopal school at Pass Christian. She then filled the chair of physiology, hygeine and natural history at the Industrial institute at Columbus, Miss., but resigned this position to enter the journalistic field, becoming editress of the *White Ribbon*, the leading W. C. T. U. paper in the state. Mrs. Harper also has four brothers: Joseph, the eldest, is a merchant in Dallas, Tex.: Samuel is a planter and merchant in Louisiana; William is a planter living in Mississippi, and Benjamin is a commercial traveler. Mr. Harper and his wife are the parents of four sons and one daughter: Grantley B., the eldest son, is a conductor of the Natchez, Jackson & Columbus railroad, is married and resides in Natchez; Somers is in the railroad shops at Harriston; James C. lives in Alabama; Bartlett is a telegraph operator, and Lurline. the daughter, is at home with her parents. She has received many advantages, and it may with truth be said that her opportunities have not been thrown away, for she is a cultured and accomplished young lady. When the Civil war broke out, in 1861, Mr. Harper espoused the cause of the Confederacy with the enthusiasm of a native Southerner, and was given charge of a battery. At the battle of Shiloh he received a severe wound, for the ball nearly severed the tendon of Achilles, just above the left foot. At the end of one year's service he returned to his home near Fayette and there has since resided, the most of his attention being given to the peaceful pursuit of farming. He has been much interested in the current issues of the day and has been prominently before the public in different capacities on various occasions. In 1854 he was a member of the state legislature and served in the same capacity during 1882 and 1884. He and his family are worthy members of the Presbyterian church, in which he holds the office of trustee, and both he and his wife are noted for their labors in behalf of Christianity and morality, as well as for their liberal, progressive and charitable views. Their many talents place them among the leaders of society in Jefferson county, and their home is an attractive and most hospitable one. They have reared their children to honorable manhood and womanhood, and in the autumn of their lives are content to quietly enjoy the numerous blessings with which they are surrounded. Mrs. Harper's paternal ancestors were Huguenots, and her records trace her family in unbroken line back to the time of Louis XIV. Her family were of the Le Comptes, and, on coming to America, settled in Maryland, the bay of Le Compte deriving its name from the Le Compte family.

Hon. Jobe Harral, Eudora, Miss., is one of the oldest citizens of De Soto county, and for many years he has been prominently connected with its political and religious history. He was born in Smith county, Tenn., on the 8th day of November, 1820, and is the third child of Whitfield and Judith (Bird) Harral, natives of South Carolina and Georgia respectively. They reared a family of eight children: John, Whitfield, Jobe, Sarah, Martha, Lorinzo, William and Parmenio, six sons and two daughters; all of whom are now dead except Whitfield, now living in Houston, Texas, and Jobe, the subject of this sketch. The father was early imbued with the principles of John C. Calhoun, firmly believing that a state had the right to judge of an infraction of the Federal constitution, and peaceably to withdraw from the Union if she deemed such withdrawal necessary to secure her safety, and he lived and died in the democratic faith. He was a planter by occupation, and lived a life of great usefulness, dying at the ripe age of sixty years, honored, respected, and loved by all who knew him. The paternal grandfather, Henry Harral, was of English descent, but was born in Sumter district, S. C., and continued there to his death. The maternal grandfather was Jobe Bird, a Virginian, who left the state of his nativity and settled near Eatonton, in Putnam county, Ga., where Mr. Harral met his wife, Judith Bird, and where they were married. When Jobe Harral was about one year old, his father returned to Georgia, and after remaining there about three years, he moved to Russellville, in Franklin county, Ala., where Jobe Harral was reared and educated. He enjoyed superior advantages in school, and made the most of his opportunities. At the age of about twenty-three years he came to Mississippi, and located in De Soto county, where he has continuously resided. He has been a conspicuous figure in the politics of the county, and has ever been keenly alive to the public good. In 1860 he made a speech in the courthouse in Hernando, in which he warned his fellow-citizens against secession, arguing with all the earnestness of a patriot about to be sacrificed for the country, persuading them that if they did secede the Southern states would be conquered, and their slaves would be emancipated. After events proved the soundness of his judgment, and his almost prophetic forecast. It was through his agency that a convention was called, and a Douglas electoral ticket was put in the field in Mississippi in 1860. He has been mayor of Hernando, and is now mayor of Eudora, and is regarded and known as an honest, efficient and faithful officer. In 1882 he was elected to the state legislature, and made a splendid record for great discrimination, and marked judgment of measures and men. It was while he was a member of the legislature that he inaugurated a war on whisky that has now made more than half of the state prohibitory, and will soon plant prohibition in the other half. At the period of his advent into the legislature, Mississippi paid an annual tax to the whisky fiend of about $10,000,000.   It is only in the light of such facts, that his great services can be properly estimated.   At this time, August, 1891, he is making a canvass for the state senate, and such is his masterly handling of facts, his power of logic in arranging and presenting them, and the fiery eloquence with which he moves the heart, that hundreds flock to hear him every day, and many come from long distances.   He is a Baptist minister of renown, has written much and ably in support of Baptist faith and practice, and is an able, efficient and zealous worker.   He has been moderator of the Coldwater Baptist association a number of times, and fills that position now.   For thirty years he has been preaching in De Soto county, and much of that time in other parts of the state, and during his career, no tongue of slander has been lifted, and no word of fault has been uttered against him.   He has nobly kept himself unspotted from all men.   He owns five hundred and seventy acres of land, three hundred of which he has placed in a good state of cultivation.   In addition to his agricultural pursuits he finds time to superintend a stock of merchandise, valued at about $1,200 and a postoffice of considerable business.   Mr. Harral has been married to three wives, two of whom are dead.   In 1840 he was united to Miss Ann Prilliman, of Virginia, a daughter of Jacob and Elizabeth (Grayson) Prilliman.   Three children were born to them: Chester A., Lou J. and Telemachus, the first and last being deceased.   In 1852 he was married a second time to Miss Sophronia Paslay, a native of South Carolina, and a daughter of Austin and Gillie (Green) Paslay, who were also South Carolinians by birth.   Seven children were born of this marriage: Fanny Fern, Jane, Evelina Graves, Carrie, Montrose, Vannie Gilley and Arthur.   Jane, Montrose and Vannie are the only surviving ones.   His second wife dying in the early spring of 1864, he was, on the 9th day of April, 1865, married to Miss Susan Taylor, a native of England, and a daughter of Samuel and Margaret (Anderson) Taylor, also English.   Mrs. Susan Harral is widely known for her highly cultivated intelligence, and her intellectual and social qualities, as well as for her glowing hospitality.   Mr. Harral is a member of the Masonic order, and is a strong advocate of its principles.   As a merchant he has been successful, as a politician he is above reproach, and as a minister of the gospel, he is able, zealous and fearless in his presentation of its truths, as it appears to him.   He is a close powerful reasoner, and is listened to with the greatest interest by the multitudes who flock to hear him.

Capt. Cornelius Lee Harris was born in Marshall county, Miss., in the year 1841, the eldest of a family of six children born unto John O. and Oney A. (Allen) Harris, the former a native of middle Tennessee and the latter of the state of Alabama.   His father was one of a numerous connection by the name, living in Marshall, Holmes and Lowndes counties, Miss., many of whom have attained eminence and distinction in the service of state and the various vocations of life, but as a marked feature of the family have kept intact its principal characteristics, to wit, individuality of mind, independence of thought, conservatism in action, and in the main they are good managers and prosperous livers.   The subject of this sketch came with his parents to Tippah county, Miss., when quite young, and here grew to maturity. Losing his father at the age of twelve he had early to become the manager of the farm, which prevented his obtaining more than the limited education which the high schools of the county could give.   In 1859, before his nineteenth birthday, he was married to Miss Frances Lee Craig, a most excellent lady, the daughter of an esteemed citizen and extensive planter in those ante-bellum times.   This good lady, whose positive worth, intrinsic merit, and striking good sense, whose kindness, liberality and charity have been the admiration of all who knew her, still survives.   In 1861 Captain Harris, not yet at his majority, enlisted as a private in company D of the Second Mississippi volunteers under Col. W. C. Falkner.

He was soon appointed orderly sergeant, and after the battle of Manassas he was elected second lieutenant, and in a few months was promoted to the office of first lieutenant, and was offered the captaincy at the reorganization of the regiment, but declined. After a little over a year's service, a difference originating between him and an officer of the same company, he resigned his commission, went home, and was not actively engaged in the army service during the remainder of the war. At the close of the war, which left him as it left most others, with nothing of this world's goods, he was engaged in teaching school. Soon after forming a copartnership with Chesley Hines, his brother-in-law, a mechanical engineer by trade, they engaged in the business of sawmilling. The special adaptation of this firm to the business with Captain Harris as business manager, accounts for the phenomenal success which crowned their efforts from the beginning. This firm did the largest saw and grist-mill business that was ever done in Tippah county, doing also a mercantile business in the same connection, and at the end of ten or twelve years they had each accumulated a small fortune. In 1877 the firm purchased from Capt. R. J. Thurmond a one-third interest in the Ship Island, Ripley & Kentucky railroad. Captain Thurmond also sold to Col. W. C. Falkner another third interest at the same time. Captain Harris was elected business manager and superintendent of the road, which position he has held for fourteen years, and still retains. Though the road had lost money up to the time of his taking charge, his official reports show he paid a dividend of seven per cent. on the invested capital the first year of his management, and has made as high as twenty-seven per cent. in one year. As a business man, always sound, active and energetic, he has the reputation of having made a success of everything he has undertaken, and in a lifelong association with his associates in business not a jostle or unpleasant difference has occurred. For twenty-five years the trusted agent, handling the fortunes of others, his integrity has never been questioned, his word is his bond to those who know him, and his known love for honesty, fair-dealing and justice mark the distinguishing elements of his character. Positive in his convictions, firm in his purposes, though conservative and compromising in matters of uncertainty and doubt, he is kind and generous to all, liberal in his aid of charities, and a free dispenser of private hospitalities, with a home that is ever open to his many friends. Though fickle fortune has smiled for him more than for some others, he makes no parade or outward show of wealth, preferring to remain the plain private citizen. Though often solicited he has never run for a public office nor held one, except county superintendent of public education, to which he was appointed. He is a Free Mason of high degree, a democrat in politics, in religion a Universalist.

John M. Harris, merchant and planter of Cascilla, Tallahatchie county, Miss., was a native of Tallapoosa county, Ala., and was born in 1830, a son of Major and Jane (Baker) Harris, natives of Georgia, who were married in Alabama, and lived in that state until 1842, when they came to Yalobusha county, moving thence to Tallahatchie county, and settling in the valley west of Cascilla, where Mrs. Harris died in 1844, Mr. Harris surviving until 1862, when he died at the age of about sixty-four years. Mrs. Harris, during most of her lifetime, was a consistent member of the Primitive Baptist church. Mr. Harris was a soldier in the United States army during the War of 1812, and later, as a democrat, was quite prominent in political affairs. Both Mr. and Mrs. Harris removed with their parents when quite young to Alabama. Francis Baker, the maternal grandfather of our subject, was a native of Georgia when he removed to Alabama, removing in 1836 from Alabama to Yalobusha county, where he was successful in life, becoming a well-to-do planter, and died in 1844. Always deeply concerned in religious matters, he made a study of theology, and during a portion of

55

his life was a minister of the Primitive Baptist church. Major Harris was twice married, his second wife having been Mrs. Mary Potts, by whom he had three children. John M. Harris was the fifth in his father's family of three sons and three daughters, named as follows: Sallie, who became the wife of James Ellis, and is deceased; Mary, who is the widow of Edward Talbert; Martha, who married Lewis Miller, who is deceased; Henry, now deceased, served during the late war as a member of a Texan company; Joseph, who was also a member of a Texan company, in the Confederate service, is deceased. John M. Harris was educated principally in Tallahatchie county, his advantages being confined to those afforded by the home schools. He took up the active affairs of life at the age of twenty-one, becoming a planter. He was married in 1852 to Fannie, daughter of George and Debora Reed, natives of Tennessee, who came to Yalobusha county at an early day, and died at Tallahatchie county, the former, about 1864, and the latter, about 1858. Mr. Reed was a successful planter. Mrs. Harris, who was a native of Tennessee, has borne her husband four children: Walter, who is engaged in planting; Fosdaner, now Mrs. George W. Trusty; Jennie, wife of J. W. Burt, a merchant of Cascilla; Joseph R., a merchant and planter at Cascilla. Since 1852 Mr. Harris has lived in Tallahatchie county, in the same neighborhood where he now resides. Until 1882 he gave his attention exclusively to planting, but in the year mentioned he erected a storehouse where Cascilla now stands, and opened up a general mercantile trade. Here has sprung up one of the most thriving villages in the country, of which Mr. Harris was the first merchant. Since 1889 he has had a partner, Mr. G. W. Trusty, in the business, which is carried on under the firm name of J. M. Harris & Co., and aggregate about $5,000 annually. Mr. Harris has for some years been a member of the Masonic fraternity, and he was treasurer of Cascilla lodge No. 411, A. F. & A. M., being also a member of Cascilla lodge No. 410, I. O. O. F. He was one of the founders of, and is a stockholder in the Cascilla male and female high school, a recently established and flourishing institution. He has always had the interest of his town and county at heart, and has probably contributed as generously as any one man for the progress and prosperity of Cascilla, of which village he is known everywhere as the founder. For many years Mr. and Mrs. Harris have been members of the Missionary Baptist church.

L. F. Harris, although at the present a planter of Hinds county, Miss., is a Georgian, his birth having occurred in Talbott county of that state, April 10, 1855, being the second of six children born to M. T. and C. A. (Mason) Harris, they being also natives of Georgia. The father, who was a practical and extensive farmer, was a private in both the Mexican and Civil wars, and died July 18, 1869. L. F. Harris attended a private school until he was about sixteen years of age, then began looking after the interests of the home plantation, in Georgia, for his mother, continuing in this capacity until he attained his majority. In 1871 he came to Mississippi, and the first labor done by him in this state was as a planter in Rankin county, where he remained seven years. Since then he has been a resident of Hinds county, and here, in 1890, became the owner of his present plantation, which comprises eleven hundred and twenty acres, and is known as the Wilson place. Eight hundred acres of this land is under cultivation, and two hundred and fifty acres are in pasture. The annual yield of cotton is about seventy-five bales, and corn is raised to the extent of three thousand five hundred bushels. He has steam cottongin and gristmill on his place, the former turning out four hundred and twenty-five bales yearly. Mr. Harris was married on the 16th of December, 1884, to Miss Mary Wilson, a native Alabamian, and by her is the father of four interesting little children: Hendon, Mason, Hernando and Sam Houston, the latter being an infant. Mr. Harris is a skillful and experienced planter, and in the conduct of his valuable plantation he is practical and thorough, and keeps thoroughly apace with the times. He and his estimable wife are worthy members of the Baptist church.

Matthew J. Harris is a worthy and representative planter of Warren county, Miss., and acquired his knowledge of the calling from his father, Matthew J. Harris, Sr., who was also a planter, and who put his knowledge to a practical use. The father, as well as his wife, whose maiden name was Rebecca A. Perkins, was a native of Virginia, and in 1861 came to Mississippi, and located on the plantation on which the subject of this sketch now resides. This land was purchased in 1848, but was not resided upon by the family until the opening of the war, as they owned a fertile and extensive plantation in Virginia, and left the property in Mississippi in the hands of an overseer. Mr. Harris, besides his extensive landed possessions, had accumulated considerable property in the way of slaves, and upon the opening of the war, in 1861, had in his possession about forty. He died in 1868, but his widow still survives him, makes her home with her son, Matthew J., and is now in her sixty-second year, and an earnest member of the Methodist Episcopal church South. They reared a family of three children: Aurelia F. (deceased) was the wife of Asa Minter, of Madison county; Matthew J., and Harley F., who reside on the home plantation with their mother. Matthew J. Harris was born in 1854, and was educated in the county in which he now resides. At the close of the war he entered Sharon college, in Madison county, and when only nineteen years of age he took charge of the home plantation, and has since controlled the same. He was married in December, 1886, to Miss Fanny K. Edwards, a daughter of Benjamin Edwards, of this county, which family originally came from Virginia. To Mr. and Mrs. Harris two children have been born: Natalie, and B. Edwards, who died at the age of two years and three months. Mr. Harris is about six feet three inches in hight, and is of fair complexion.

R. W. Harris, the immediate progenitor of J. M. Harris, was a Virginian, born January 16, 1819, a son of Robert and Rebecca (Rice) Harris, who were also born in the Old Dominion. The father, Robert Harris, was a planter and a soldier in the War of 1812, and his wife was a sister of Colonel Rice of Virginia, who distinguished himself in the War of 1812, and was a member of one of the "F. F. V's." She and her husband reared a family of four children: Margaret A. E., married Joseph Wyche of Virginia; R. W., Matthew J., deceased, and Catherine S., who married Dr. Matthew H. Wall, of Kentucky. R. W. Harris married M. Perkins, of Dinwiddie county, Va., daughter of Joel and Lucy Perkins, October 1, 1839. In 1848 he came to the state of Mississippi, and the following year settled on the place on which he is now living. He came hither in a private conveyance, the journey from Virginia taking about two months, and during this time he suffered many inconveniences and hardships. The land on which Mr. Harris settled was somewhat improved, there being some two hundred acres under cultivation, but the buildings were only of logs. Of this property Mr. Harris has since improved a large amount, and has erected a magnificent, old-fashioned Southern residence, the surroundings of which are very beautiful and attractive. He made a handsome fortune prior to the war, but during that period the greater part of it was swept away. However, he is now in good circumstances, and has everything for the comfort and happiness of his declining years. To himself and wife a family of thirteen children were born, seven of whom lived to be grown: R. B. P., who was a surgeon in the Confederate army, and died in 1878; Margaret E., wife of Charles Harris; Rebecca R., wife of William Robb; James M.; Thomas B., now deceased; William T., also deceased, and Martha W., wife of J. R. Baker of this place. Of his plantation Mr. Harris has about one hundred and fifty acres under cultivation, it being now under the control and management of his son

James, and his son-in-law, J. R. Baker. His wife, who died April 27, 1886, in the sixty-third year of her age, was a member of the Methodist Episcopal church South; Mr. Harris is a Baptist. He is a man of much intelligence, and tells many interesting anecdotes of the privations and hardships of early times. Upon his settlement in the county there were only two or three families within a radius of many miles and the country was but very little improved. As late as 1857 he and Major Harris killed as many as nine bear in one season. He is tall, of dark complexion, and wears a full beard, which is now snow white. He is prepossessing in personal appearance, and is a pleasant and agreeable conversationalist.

J. M. Harris is a planter and merchant of Warren county, Miss., and was born in the county in which he now resides October 28, 1853, being a son of Robert W. and Mary (Perkins) Harris, who were born in Virginia, the former removing to this state in 1844, settling in the neighborhood in which his son is now living, and engaged in planting. The country being new, his operations were conducted on a rather limited scale compared with the present day, but he owned quite a number of slaves. J. M. Harris was, from the time he was two years of age, reared by Maj. R. P. Harris, whose residence in Mississippi dated from 1830. He settled on the plantation on which J. M. now resides, and although he was a successful planter he did not own many slaves. The country, upon his arrival here, was in a wild state, abounding in all kinds of game, but here he determined to make his home, notwithstanding the fact that canebrake covered the hills as well as the bottom lands. Owing to the fact that the country was infested by Indians whose treachery the whites feared, companies of militia were formed, in one of which he held the rank of major. He was a man of profound learning, was a fine Greek and Latin scholar, and at the age of twelve years had read Virgil, Homer, and the life of Cæsar in the original. He was of an adventurous disposition and at an early age sought a home in what was then called the wild West, and this section was improved by the good he accomplished. Although a leader in whatever he undertook, he always refused to accept any position of honor or trust although warmly urged to do so by his numerous friends. In his political views he was a strong whig, differing decidedly from his kinsmen in this section in that respect. He was married in 1842 to Miss Mary Rice, of Virginia, but their union was without issue. Upon the opening of the war Major Harris opposed secession with all the strength of his steadfast nature, and consequently did not take an active part in the Civil war, although he lost heavily during the war, some seventy negroes being freed. He accumulated the property on which J. M. Harris is now residing, from 1830 to 1860. He was an upright and noble man in every respect, and his death was felt as a great loss to the community, notwithstanding the fact that he was a non-combatant. He was foully murdered by a negro in 1864 who, at the same time, tried to kill J. M. Harris, then a lad of eleven years, while he was with the Major looking for stock on the plantation. The widow of Major Harris still survives him, and although seventy-eight years of age, shows but little the ravages of time, either mentally or physically; her tales of early life in Mississippi being both interesting and instructive. J. M. Harris has been married twice, first in 1879 to Miss Mary Lindsey, of Vicksburg, a daughter of Judge L. Lindsey, but her death occurred in April of the following year, she being a worthy member of the Christian church. They became the parents of one child, who was born at the death of his mother, and whom they named Robert L. In 1887 Mr. Harris took for his second wife Miss Lucy Browne, of Yazoo county, daughter of Miles T. Browne, of Norfolk, Va., who is at the present time an extensive planter in Yazoo county. Mr. Harris has served in the capacity of justice of the peace, and in connection with planting was for some ten years engaged in merchandising, but for about two years past has devoted his attention to the former calling. He is a substantial citizen, and is much looked up to and respected by those who know him. His wife is a member of the Methodist Episcopal church South.

T. D. Harris, of Brandon, Miss., was born in Maury county, Tenn., in 1833, a son of Richard and Mary (Davis) Harris, the former of whom was a Virginian, but removed to Tennessee in 1828, where he followed the occupation of planting until his death. T. D. Harris received his education in the common schools of his native state, but in 1852 left home to seek his fortune in Mississippi, and for two years, after locating in Brandon, he worked in a livery stable for nothing save his board and clothes. The following year he was given a good salary, at the end of which time his salary was raised to $75 per month. In 1855 he was elected to the position of city marshal and was appointed deputy sheriff. The succeeding year he purchased a half interest in a livery barn and also opened a retail grocery store, and as he gave his personal supervision to these callings he was very success-ful. In August, 1861, he went out as second lieutenant of company B, Sixth Mississippi regiment, and after the battle of Shiloh he was appointed commissary captain of cavalry. In 1863 he was elected to the position of sheriff of Rankin county, but was not permitted to leave his position in the army until the office of regimental commissary was abolished, when he returned home to take upon himself the duties of sheriff, in which capacity he served until 1869, when he was removed on account of disability. In 1870 he was appointed treasurer, but resigned the same year to again accept the sheriff's office made vacant by the death of the former incumbent. In 1874 he was again appointed sheriff to fill a vacancy, and in 1877 was elected to the regular term of two years. Since that time he has given his almost exclusive attention to handling real estate, having invested all his surplus capital in land. He has sold a large amount of real estate to negroes in the last few years, amounting to about $12,000 worth, and still has thirty-six thousand acres for sale. He also owns some valuable property in Jackson. He was married in 1859 to Miss Kate Watts, of Covington county, Miss., a daughter of John Watts, who represented Covington, Lawrence, Perry and Marion counties in the state senate in 1834-5. To Mr. and Mrs. Harris one child has been born, Mollie, wife of W. B. Collier, of Brandon. Mr. Harris is a Royal Arch Mason and belongs to the Knights of Honor. He is a fine business man, and by his own perseverance and push has become wealthy.

Thomas W. Harris (deceased) was born in Georgia and came with his parents to Mis-sissippi in youth. They settled at Columbus, and there he was reared and partly educated. He studied law, and after a few years' practice came to Holly Springs, where he spent the active years of his life. He married a Miss Mason, and after her death a Miss Watson. He became a leading lawyer of north Mississippi, and for many years was one of the prominent legal lights of the Holly Springs bar. During the Civil war he raised a com-pany at Holly Springs, was elected captain, and served in that capacity until peace was declared. After this he was at Fort Worth for eighteen months, was for a short time in Memphis and then came to Holly Springs, where his death occurred in 1890, leaving a widow and three children. He was a member of the Presbyterian church. He was genial and entertaining, literary in his taste, and well posted on all subjects. He was a leading crim-inal lawyer and always for the defense.

Judge Wiley P. Harris. This distinguished jurist is a native of Mississippi, his birth occurring in Pike county, on the 9th of November, 1818. He is a son of Early and Mary (Harrison) Harris, the former of whom was a Virginian by birth, and a son of Buckner Harris of that state. The paternal grandmother was Nancy Early, of old Virginia stock, who removed to Georgia at an early day. The Harrises were from South Carolina. Early Harris was a farmer by occupation and emigrated to Mississippi when it was a territory, dying there when the subject of this sketch was about six years of age. Judge Harris was assisted in his education by an uncle, and then by an elder brother, who was a prosperous business man. His preliminary education was obtained in the common schools of the country, after which he was sent to the University of Virginia, where he was graduated. He then prepared for the bar by a two-year course of study at the law school of Lexington, Ky., but in 1840 he returned to Mississippi, and in that state was admitted to the bar, opening his law office there. He rose rapidly in his profession, and became noted for his success at the bar, and in the year 1846 he was elevated to the bench, from which he retired to resume his regular practice. In 1850 he was a member of the state convention, called to consider Federal relations, and in 1855 was nominated and elected to congress by the democratic party, to represent the district. After serving one term he retired from political life and went back to his profession, which was more congenial to his taste and his mental culture. Subsequently he removed to Jackson, Miss., where he could have a larger field for his practice. He was elected to the secession convention in 1861, and then to the convention at Montgomery, which established the Southern Confederacy. He served through the provisional congress, after which he retired to official life to devote himself to his law practice, which he continued uninterrupted by any call to public life until he was sent to the constitutional convention of 1890. Judge Harris was married in 1851 to Fannie, a daughter of Judge Daniel Mayes, by whom he had seven children. His wife died in 1882, Mr. Harris and their children surviving her. In his social relations, Judge Harris is sympathetic and hospitable, strong in his affections and genial in his manners. He is a man of prepossessing personal appearance, tall, straight and of courtly bearing. He is light complexioned, for his hair is light and his eyes gray. His countenance of a Grecian cast, and this with a smoothly shaven face makes up the personal appearance of the Nestor of the Mississippi bar. Judge Harris possesses a brilliant mind, naturally gifted in the analysis of legal subjects, which culture and training has greatly enhanced. His penetration is quick, his perception intuitive and his judgment accurate. Certainty followed him in his professional career, and he arose step by step in rapid succession until he reached the top round of legal fame. He has studied deeply every phase of jurisprudence and so familiar is he with all its branches that the great principles of law have become ingrafted in his own individuality. In the argument of a cause his powers of reasoning and perception are equally praised. He pays no attention to oratorical display or declamation, but presents in a clear, logical form, his arguments. With the keenness of a Damascus blade he cuts away all sophistry and false coloring of an adversary and subjects every grain of fact and every principle of law to his rigid analysis. He is conscientious in giving his opinions on law points, never attempting to mislead the bar or the bench. As a judge he possessed the unbounded confidence of the bar, and as a lawyer he is held by the courts in highest esteem. By common consent, Judge Harris stands at the head of the Mississippi bar; a bar that is not excelled in forensic eloquence or legal learning by any in the United States.

J. R. Harris, a native of Copiah county and a son of Dr. Wiley P. Harris and Mary V. (Ragsdale) Harris; his wife was born in 1833. Dr. Wiley P. Harris was born in Georgia in 1801 and became a practicing physician, attaining eminence in his profession. He was a private soldier in the Seminole war, in Florida, and shortly after its close he emigrated to Mississippi. He was married, either in Mississippi or Tennessee, to Mary V. Ragsdale, a native of the last mentioned state, by whom he had nine children, six of whom are now living: Amantha L., deceased wife of S. J. Morehead, of Brown's Mills; L. B., a lawyer of Hazlehurst; James Raglan; Sarah A., widow of Douglas Neat; Robert W., of Texas, and Eliza, who is unmarried. In the latter part of his life Dr. Harris conducted a plantation, to which he gave such time as he could spare from his professional duties. He was prominent in political affairs, and was the candidate at one time for governor. He was a member of the Masonic fraternity. His death occurred in 1845, his wife's one year earlier. After the death of his father our subject was taken in charge by his eldest sister, with whom he resided till he attained his majority. He was given the advantages of a first-class old field-school, and acquired a good English education. After leaving school he entered the law department of the Transylvania university, at Lexington, Ky., graduating in 1854 at the age of twenty-one. In the same year he began the practice of his profession at Gallatin, where he remained till 1857, when, on account of failing health, brought about by too close confinement to his profession, he was obliged to seek active outdoor employment. He removed to the farm of his father-in-law, where he engaged in planting. In a couple of years he purchased land of his own, to which he removed, and upon which he placed many improvements. After the death of Mr. Rice he purchased his old homestead, where he now resides. His farm consists of one thousand three hundred and fifty acres, about three hundred of which he plants to cotton. In 1887 he opened a store on his plantation, and in 1889 a post-office, named Maharris, was reëstablished at his store, and Mrs. Harris was appointed postmistress. In 1856 he married Mary A. Rice, a daughter of C. B. N. Rice, first cousin of ex-Governor Brown. He has six children living: Hezekiah Brown, James R., Mamie M., Mattie Caither, Robert Rice and George Wiley. In the winter of 1861 Mr. Harris enlisted in the sixty-day infantry, which was then being recruited. Upon the expiration of the term of his enlistment he enlisted again, in company E, of the Fourth Mississippi cavalry. He was mustered into the Confederate service as a private, and was promoted to the rank of orderly sergeant. He took part in the battle of Harrisburg and was in many smaller engagements. He was paroled at Gainesville, Ala. Mr. Harris comes of a good family of more than ordinary ability. All of his male kinsfolk have been professional men. He himself is a man of well-balanced mind, and his standing is high, socially and politically. Though he is strong in the democratic faith, his attention has been too closely engrossed with his own business to allow him to take any conspicuous part in politics, and although he has often been urged by his friends and admirers to allow his name to be used as a candidate for various offices, he has always steadfastly refused to do so.

Hon. James T. Harrison, Jr., counselor at law at Columbus, Miss., has been a leading attorney of Lowndes county for many years. This branch of human endeavor has brought into play the most brilliant talents, of which he is capable, and he is admirably adapted to honorably prosecute this most exalted of professions. He was born in the city in which he now resides May 21, 1848, and is a son of J. T. Harrison, Sr., who acquired a state reputation, and whose sketch appears in this volume. James T. Harrison, Jr., who was so fortunate as to receive his education at Princeton, N. J., and in 1869 graduated from Washington and Lee college. Prior to this, however, in 1863, when only fifteen years of age, he enlisted in a company of state militia, under Capt. T. B. Shockley, and served as an escort company with General Withers, General Pillow, General S. D. Lee, General D. W. Adams, General Forrest and General Dick Taylor. He received but one slight wound during his service. After graduating in the above mentioned college he became associated with his father, and is still engaged in the practice of his profession under the firm name of Harrison & Laurdam, which firm shines as a star of the first magnitude in the firmament of Mississippi law. They are men of broad intelligence, and are sufficiently learned and sufficiently traveled to recognize that all are equal before man's, as before God's tribunal. Mr. Harrison's knowledge of law, and his popularity with all classes led to his election to the state legislature, during which time he was chairman on the committee of colleges and universities, and the passage of the bill for the establishment of the industrial institute for female whites (at which time it was the only institution of the kind in the United States) was in part due to his wisdom and labor. He was appointed chairman of the board of trustees of this institution, and to him the credit is due of having it located at Columbus. He was an ardent worker for this college and having accomplished his point, he has ever evinced a deep interest in the same. In 1886 he was reëlected to the legislature, and by the speaker of the house was given his choice of chairmanships of the different committees. He became chairman of the committee on appropriations, and for one year was chairman of colleges and universities. After serving his term he retired from politics, and has since devoted himself to his profession, but owing to the urgent request of his friends he is the present popular candidate for state senator. There has never been an enterprise started in Columbus with which he has not identified himself, and the different railroads which have been established have found in him a hearty supporter, he being a director in several. He has been a deacon of the Baptist church for some time, and socially he is a member of the A. F. & A. M., in which he is a Knight Templar, and also belongs to the I. O. O. F. His kind, courtly and agreeable manners, and his generosity and upright conduct in all his business affairs have made him very popular in his native county, where he has been known and respected from boyhood. During the war, while in the service, he was male a sergeant on the battlefield, and although subsequently offered two staff positions for gallantry, they were refused. In 1884 his marriage with Miss Fannie S., daughter of Capt. R. C. Moore, was celebrated, and by her he is the father of two children: J. T., Jr. and Nellie.

Dr. Luther D. Harrison, Clarksdale, Miss., is a native of Virginia, his birth occurring in that state in 1853, and is a son of L. D. and Martha A. (Johnson) Harrison, descendants of old Virginia families. The parents were born in Alexandria, Va., and are residents of that state at the present time. The father was a merchant by occupation, but is now retired. He was a member of the city council, and was one of the prominent and leading men of that city. Dr. Luther D. Harrison attained his growth and secured a thorough education at Alexandria, Va., graduating in the literary course at St. John's college in 1869. He then began studying medicine, attended Washington university at Baltimore, in 1869-70, and then studied with Dr. Warner, at Guilford, Va., until 1874. After this he took a course of lectures at Cincinnati Ohio medical college, and graduated from that institution in 1875. He subsequently came to Mississippi, located in Franklin county, and took the practice of his uncle, Dr. M. C. Johnson, who had settled at Turners, Franklin county, in 1853, and who had been the leading physician of the county for years. After relinquishing his practice to his nephew, Dr. Johnson retired to his plantation, where he resided until his death in 1888, when quite old. Dr Harrison remained in Franklin until 1889, and then came to Clarksdale, Coahoma county, Miss., and here he has secured a most encouraging practice. He has bought property in the town and is permanently located. Miss India B. Stringer, who became his wife in 1889, was born in St. Joseph, La., and is the representative of an old family. To the Doctor and wife have been born one son, Marmaduke J. The Doctor is a member of the Knights of Pythias order. In personal appearance he is about the average size, has dark brown hair and eyes, dark side whiskers and mustache and is a good looking man.

William H. Harrison, LL.D., M. D., was the youngest of three children born to Luther

D. and Martha A. (Johnson) Harrison, both natives of Virginia. The father followed merchandising at Alexandria, Va., for many years, and during the Civil war held an official position. The paternal grandparents, John D. and Betsey C. Harrison, were natives of the Old Dominion, and the grandfather was a prominent man in the state, holding the position of clerk of the court for a number of years. The maternal grandparents, Edward M. and Mary Johnson, were natives of Virginia also, and previous to the war Mr. Johnson was a very wealthy man, owning a great number of slaves. William H. Harrison was born in Alexandria, Va., on the 3d of February, 1857, and was reared in that state. He was born of a sturdy line of ancestors, and inherited that vim and determination of purpose and untiring energy which have characterized his afterlife. He attended school at St. Timothy's academy, Herndon, Va., also the Potomac academy, Alexandria, Va., from which he graduated, and carried off the highest honors at each place. He took the first honor (gold medal) at Louisville medical college in 1885 and 1886. In the last named year he attended the summer course at Kentucky school of medicine, and graduated at Louisville medical college with gold medal in 1886 and 1887. Previous to this he had attended lectures at the medical department of Georgetown university, and on the 24th of June, 1880, he graduated from the law department of that institution. Dr. Harrison is a descendant of one of the best families of Virginia. He is a brilliant conversationalist, is social and courteous to all, and is one of the most prominent physicians in the county. He was married on the 11th of April, 1888, to Miss Alice Adams, a native of South Carolina, and they are the parents of two children: Kate A., and Luther, both living. Mrs. Harrison comes of quite a noted family. She is the daughter of John R. and Kate (Henderson) Adams, natives of South Carolina, and the granddaughter of James H. and Jane M. Adams, also natives of South Carolina. The grandfather, James H. Adams, was governor of South Carolina from 1854 to 1856, and was a representative man of the country at that time. He figured quite prominently in the first settlement of South Carolina. Her maternal grandparents were John and Martha Henderson. Dr. Harrison is a member of the Masonic fraternity, and in his political views affiliates with the democratic party. He is surgeon for the Tallahatchie and River Side division of the Louisville, New Orleans & Texas railroad, and has several appointments as examiner for life insurance companies. He contributes liberally to all worthy enterprises. In personal appearance he is a little above the average in hight, has dark hair, a fair complexion and fine blue eyes.

Dr. M. K. Harrison, physician, Deer Brook, Noxubee county, Miss. Isham Harrison was born in Greenville, S. C., in 1788, and married Miss Harriet Kelly, also a native of that state. They subsequently emigrated to Alabama, and in 1832 moved to Noxubee county. He was one of the first settlers of the county, and helped to lay off the town of Macon. His family comprised thirteen children—seven boys and six girls. Five of his boys fought in the Confederate ranks during the late war; the other two died some years before. James E. and Thomas attained the rank of brigadier-generals, Isham and Richard were colonels, and the subject of this sketch served as a surgeon. M. K. Harrison was born in Alabama in the year 1829, but was reared in Mississippi. Adopting the practice of medicine for his chosen profession, he took a thorough course in the medical department of the University of Louisville, Ky., and graduated in 1855. In the year 1859 he married Mary Bradford, of Aberdeen, Miss., the daughter of Gen. B. M. Bradford, one of the wealthiest and most prominent men of the state. They have five children: Benjamin B., Julia K., Isham, Nina C. and Robert. He has practiced his profession almost continuously since 1855, and his reputation as a popular and successful physician is firmly established. In connection with his practice he has at times been engaged in agriculture. During the struggle between the two sections he served under General Forrest, and surrendered at Gainesville, Ala. The Doctor was present when the first flag was unfurled, and was at the post of duty when the last shot was fired. He is a cousin of Wiley P. Harris, also of James T. Harrison, and is related to Wade Hampton and Gen. S. D. Lee.

Lyman Harding, first attorney-general of Mississippi, was born in Massachusetts. There he was given a good education. Emigrating to Maryland he became a schoolteacher and soon began to study law. Receiving a license to practice his profession he emigrated to Louisville and there opened an office, but met with no success, and was obliged to work his way to Natchez, and arrived there soon after the territorial government was established, and not long afterward had worked himself into a good practice, which developed speedily into the most remunerative one in the territory. On the organization of the state he was elected attorney-general. He died in 1820.

Hon. William Littleton Harris was born in Elbert county, Ga., July 6, 1807. His father was Gen. Jephtha V. Harris, his maternal grandfather Maj. Richardson Hunt. He graduated from the University of Georgia at Athens in 1825, and was admitted to the bar in 1827, when he was less than twenty-one years old, by special legislative favor, and began to practice his profession in Washington, Wilkes county, and soon attained to considerable eminence. In 1837 he removed to Mississippi; in 1853 was elected judge of the circuit court of the sixth judicial district; in 1856 was appointed by the legislature to assist in the codification of the laws of Mississippi. He was reëlected to the circuit bench in 1857, and was elevated to the bench of the high court of errors and appeals in 1858. In 1860 President Buchanan offered to seat him on the bench of the supreme court of the United States, but he declined the honor because of the approaching disruption of the union. In 1861 he was again chosen a judge of the high court of errors and appeals of Mississippi, but resigned in 1868 on account of political troubles, and removed to Memphis, Tenn., where he died in November, 1868.

Hon. Alexander H. Handy, of Canton, Madison county, was born in Somerset county December 28, 1809. He was educated and admitted to the bar, and in 1836 removed to Mississippi. He was admitted to practice in the high court of errors and appeals in January, 1837, and entered upon a successful career. He was chosen to a seat upon the bench of the high court in 1853, and in 1860 was reëlected without opposition. He was again elected a judge of the high court in 1865, and in January, 1866, was appointed chief justice of Mississippi. In November following he was reëlected without opposition, but resigned October 1, 1867, by the courts being made subordinate to the Federal military power, and removed to Baltimore and there engaged in the practice of his profession, but was soon made professor of law in the University of Maryland, and as such served until 1871, when he resumed practice at Jackson. In October, 1877, he was admitted to practice in the United States supreme court. Always a firm believer in the states' rights doctrine, he favored secession, and was prominent in Maryland as an advocate of that measure. In 1862 he published a pamphlet entitled "Secession Considered as a Right in the States Composing the Late American Union of States, and as to the Grounds of Justification in Exercising the Right." He is a profound lawyer and is a polished writer and fluent speaker.

Hon. James T. Harrison was born near Pendleton, S. C., November 30, 1811. His father, Thomas Harrison, was a distinguished lawyer, an officer in the War of 1812, and afterward comptroller-general of the state. His mother was a daughter of John Bayliss Earle. At eighteen he graduated with distinction from the University of South Carolina, then studied law under James L. Pettigru, of Charleston. In 1834 he established himself in practice at Macon, Noxubee county, and became a partner of John Ruff. Two years later he removed to Columbus, where he made his permanent address and achieved great success. He was a delegate to the convention of the Southern states at Montgomery, and was in the Confederate congress during the entire period of its existence. On the reorganization of Mississippi, under the Johnson administration, he was elected to the Federal congress, but was refused admittance with the balance of the Mississippi delegation. He was chosen to represent the bar of Mississippi on the occasion of the anticipated trial of Jefferson Davis, and expressed an opinion, which facts verified, that the trial would never come off. He was a learned geologist. His death occurred in Columbus, May 22, 1879.

Nathaniel H. Harrison is accounted a prosperous planter of Noxubee county, Miss., and, like the majority of native Mississippians, he is progressive in his views, and of an energetic temperament. Mr. Harrison was born in the county in which he now resides, November 11, 1858, a son of Nathaniel H., Sr., and Celeste (Bush) Harrison, the former a native of Virginia and the latter of Georgia. The paternal grandfather, William A. Harrison, was also a Virginian by birth, and some time in the twenties removed to Mississippi and located in what is now Noxubee county, where he purchased land from the government and followed planting for a calling. His was one of the first families of this section, and at that day Indians still roamed the forests in large numbers, and wild animals were very numerous. He died near Macon, Miss., having been a useful and sturdy pioneer of the early days of this state. His son, Nathaniel H., followed in his footsteps, and also became a planter, becoming the owner of a large plantation and numerous slaves. He died at the close of the war a comparatively young man, being only about thirty-five years of age at the time of his death. The mother died in 1858, when the subject of this sketch was but eleven days old. He was left an orphan by the death of his father, at the age of seven years, and he was cared for by his relatives, who gave him good educational advantages. After attending the schools of Macon and the Washington university of St. Louis, Mo., he entered the University of Virginia, and in 1880 was graduated from that institution. Immediately after finishing his collegiate course he engaged in the mercantile business in Macon, and there successfully continued for about six years. Since then he has devoted his attention to planting and the stock business, and is quite an extensive dealer in standard-bred horses and Holstein and Jersey cattle. He raises some very fine animals, both in horses and cattle, and his successful career as a Southern stockman has demonstrated the fact that this is a profitable industry in the South. He buys and sells stock in large numbers annually, and the farm which he devoted to the raising of his herds comprises one thousand eight hundred acres beautifully located and well watered. He raises red clover, Lespedeza and Bermuda grasses, and now has on hand about thirty head of fine horses and twenty-five head of blooded cattle. Much attention is given to the care of his stock during the months of winter, and that this is a wise and necessary precaution is shown by the fact that his stock always commands fancy prices. He is very proud of this valuable and beautiful farm, and is deservedly so, for everything about indicates that constant care and supervision is given it. He has a beautiful home in Macon, and is surrounded by all that goes to make life enjoyable—domestic happiness and prosperity, a clean conscience and abundant means. He is full of energy, pluck and ambition, and is devoted to his occupation, and the success that has attended his efforts shows that he is admirably fitted for the life. He is the owner of about three thousand acres of land in Noxubee county, on the cultivated portion of which he raises large crops of cotton annually, besides a considerable amount of corn and other Southern products. He was married in 1881 to Miss Fannie Holman, a native of Macon, by whom he has two children.

John Hart, Pickens, Miss. Daniel Hart, deceased, was born in Pike county, Miss., in 1815, on the 24th day of December, and was a son of John and Martha (Meredith) Hart. He was the fourth of a family of six sons and two daughters. The sons all settled in Yazoo county, and all reared families. Four of them entered the Confederate service, but the other two, including Daniel Hart, were cripples and unable to serve. James Hart died a prisoner of war, and two were killed in battle. Daniel Hart first settled on a small piece of land, not more than one hundred acres; to this he later on added sixty acres and placed the whole under good cultivation. He was married in Pike county, January 2, 1845, to Miss Eliza Armstrong, whose parents were from Tennessee and Georgia. Eleven children were born of this union. Nine of them grew to maturity, and five are now living in Yazoo county and doing well. One son, Daniel, Jr., carries on the home farm; he has one of the finest fruit orchards in the county. Daniel Hart, Sr., was a devout Christian, and an elder of the Cumberland Presbyterian church for twenty-five years; the mother and several of the children were members of the Cumberland Presbyterian church, and sincere in their devotion. John Hart, grandson of Daniel Hart, was born in Yazoo county in 1845, and is the seventh of eleven children. His parents, James and Jane (Smith) Hart, were natives of Mississippi. He grew to manhood in his native county, and has been engaged in planting for several years. He is a member of the Masonic order, and of Live Oak lodge, Knights of Pythias, Pickens. James Hart, his father, was a native of Pike county, Miss., where he passed his youth; he was married there, and in 1842, with four of his brothers, removed to Yazoo county. He died at Camp Morton, Ill., a prisoner of war; two of his brothers died in the service and one was killed in the battle of Shiloh. James Hart settled on four hundred acres of timber land, which he improved during his lifetime. His wife still lives at the age of seventy-five years. Ten of their eleven children lived beyond infancy, and one died at the age of ten years; the others were named as follows: Mrs. Mattie Bell, of Jackson, Miss.; Mrs. L. F. Davis, of Yazoo county; Mrs. A. J. Nance, of Yazoo City; Mrs. W. R. Hudson, deceased; Mrs. C. A. Pope, of Texas; Mrs. Emma Stebins, of Madison county, Miss.; John, James and William. The three brothers are prosperous farmers, raising between three and four hundred bales of cotton annually. They are men of unquestionable integrity of character, and are numbered among the leading citizens of the community.

J. J. Harry, physician and surgeon, Handsborough, Harrison county, Miss., was born in Jasper county, Miss., in 1855, and is a son of J. F. Harry, a native of Alabama. His father removed to Mississippi a few years before the war, and first located in Scott county; thence he moved to Jasper county, where he died in December, 1880. He was a farmer by occupation. Dr. Harry received his literary education in the University of Mississippi at Oxford, and in the Washington and Lee university, Virginia. He began the study of medicine at an early age, and was graduated from the medical department of the Tulane university of New Orleans in 1878. He then located at Ocean Springs, and devoted his whole time to the service of the victims of the terrible epidemic of yellow fever that swept the country that year. In 1879 he went to Handsborough, Miss., where he has since resided. He has won a large and appreciative patronage, and by his skill and success has gained an enviable reputation in the fraternity. He was president of the board of health of the county for a number of years. He is a member of the American Legion of Honor, of which he is secretary and medical examiner. Dr. Harry was united in marriage to Miss Mollie Lienhard, and they have had two children born to them: Henriette L. and John L. Mrs. Harry is a consistent member of the Presbyterian church.

Dr. Samuel Hart, chancery clerk, Carrollton, Carroll county, Miss., a native-born citizen of Carroll county, Miss., first saw the light of day January 9, 1855; his father, Hon. Samuel Hart, Sr., was born in the state of Indiana in 1813, and during his youth came with his father's family to Columbia county, Tenn., where he was reared and educated; there he married Amanda Ayers, a daughter of Isaac Ayers, the head of another pioneer family. Mr. Hart removed to Mississippi in 1836, and located in Carrollton, where he was one of the early settlers. He became prominently identified with the history of the county. He held several positions of trust and honor, and was a member of the constitutional convention of 1851. In 1846 he had been elected probate clerk, and served in that capacity for eight consecutive years. At the end of his term of office he engaged in merchandising. He was a heavy loser by the war, but succeeded in regaining his property to a certain degree. He was a conspicuous member of the Masonic order, being a Royal Arch Mason, and a high priest of his chapter. He was a leading member of the Presbyterian church, and served as an elder of the same for twenty-five years. He died in Carroll county in the fall of 1887, aged seventy-six years. Mrs. Hart survived him three years, passing away in April, 1890. Dr. Samuel Hart, son of the above, is one of a family of four sons and three daughters who lived to maturity: Harry, the eldest, was a soldier in the Confederate army; he died of yellow fever at Grenada, in 1878; he was a commercial traveler for a number of years, and at the time of his death was a merchant of Grenada; Charles H. died in Texas, and the youngest brother resides in Carrollton; the three sisters all married and reared families. Dr. Hart passed his boyhood and youth in Carrollton, receiving a fair English education. He then studied medicine under Dr. Vasser, a skilled physician of Carrollton; he took his first course of lectures at the Louisville medical college, and was graduated from that institution in February, 1877. He then engaged in the practice of his profession for a period of two years, abandoning it at the end of that time to accept the position of deputy chancery clerk; in his earlier years he had discharged the duties of this office at the same time he was pursuing the study of medicine. He served continuously as deputy until elected to the office in 1887, and in January, 1888, he took charge of the business pertaining thereto. He had no opponent at the primary or general election, and of the whole number of votes cast he received all excepting nine. He makes one of the best and most satisfactory officials the county has ever known. He is affable and courteous in his manners, and is ever ready to give assistance to those looking up matters of record. He is a candidate for reëlection, and his popularity will probably win him the race. Dr. Hart was married in Carrollton, December 31, 1879, to Miss Hattie M. Miller, daughter of Jacob Miller, deceased. Mrs. Hart was born near Little Rock, Ark. Her father was a Confederate soldier, and was killed at Chancellorsville. Dr. and Mrs. Hart have had born to them two children: William Harry and Minnie A. The Doctor is a worthy member of the Presbyterian church, of which he is an elder.

L. L. Harwell, Lee county, Miss., was born in Giles county, Tenn., December 7, 1832, and is the eldest of a family of twelve children. His parents, G. G. and Eveline (Pullen) Harwell, were natives of Virginia and Tennessee respectively. The paternal grandfather removed from Virginia to Tennessee at an early day, and settled near Pulaski. There the father of our subject was married and resided seventeen years. In 1845 he removed to Lee county, Miss., and purchased land, which he cultivated during his lifetime. He was a successful planter, a loyal citizen and a loving father. He was a faithful member of the Methodist Episcopal church. His death occurred in 1848, his wife and six children surviving him. The mother was married a second time, to Samuel Rowan, but they had no children. She died September, 1872. Three of the family are now living: Sarah E., wife of W. F. Rowan; Irene, wife of A. R. Stevenson, and L. L., the subject of this sketch. He and two brothers were soldiers in the late war. The brothers were both slain in battle. He enlisted in company H, Second Mississippi cavalry, and was in several important engagements. He was paroled at Gainesville, Ala., in 1865, and returned to his home, taking up the pursuit of agriculture. He was married in 1858 to Miss Nannie Humphreys, daughter of Maj. John T. and Jane (Vernor) Humphreys, natives of South Carolina. In 1839 Mrs. Harwell's parents removed from their home to Pontotoc county, Miss. Mr. and Mrs. Harwell have four children, all living at this time: William H., Sarah J., Anna V. and John T. Sarah J. married L. H. Dabbs, William H. married Miss Minnie Grace, daughter of John L. and Mary Grace, and Anna is the wife of A. E. Estes, of Henderson, Tenn. The children have all received a liberal education. Mr. Harwell owns a good farm, which is under good cultivation. He and his wife are members of the Presbyterian church. He has never aspired to any political office, but is known as a plain, practical farmer, stanch in his principles, and true to his convictions.

T. M. Harwood (deceased) was a man whose sterling worth of character was recognized by all, and although he was called from the scene of his earthly labors while in the prime of life, and when many others were just entering upon a career of usefulness, he had already become a man of note throughout this section, and his death was deeply deplored by a large circle of friends and acquaintances, as well as by his own immediate and sorrowing household. He was born in the town of Grand Gulf, Miss., October 21, 1850, being a son of the late Dr. Benjamin and Eleanor Harwood, of which once large and happy family only one member is now living. As a business man Mr. Harwood possessed qualities of a high order, and as he was energetic and thorough in everything he undertook, he was correspondingly successful financially. He held the office of deputy sheriff under the administration of Dr. Charles E. Buck, who was killed, and for years prior to his death was actively engaged in official work of Claiborne county. Having resided in the county from the time of his birth, he was thoroughly known, but during the whole course of his life naught was ever said derogatory to his character or honor. At his death, which occurred on Sunday, March 27, 1887, he left a young wife and one child to mourn his loss, besides innumerable friends and acquaintances. The beautiful burial service of the Episcopal church was read over him, and he was laid in his last resting place in Port Gibson, which was the home of his infancy, boyhood and manhood. Mrs. Harwood is a daughter of Charles A. Pearson (deceased), who was a well-known and prominent resident of this region.

The father of W. H. Harvey, farmer, Starkville, Miss., Theophilus Harvey, was born in northern Alabama, and in connection with merchandising, at which he was very successful, he also followed planting. He was married in Philadelphia (whither he had gone to buy goods) to Miss Rebecca Hutchison, whose father was a Kentucky merchant. They met by appointment in Philadelphia, and their marriage resulted in the birth of eight children, six of whom are living and named in the order of their births as follows: William H. (subject); Dr. H. P., of the United States navy; Thomas B., an attorney at St. Louis; Emma B., wife of Terrel B. Joiner, of Sherman, Tex.; W. A., a merchant of Sherman, Tex., and Ada Lee. William H. Harvey, the eldest child, was born in Oktibbeha county, Miss., in April, 1848, and after receiving his primary education in Crawford, Lowndes county, Miss., he entered Gathwright school in Summerville, Noxubee county, where he remained until the close of the war. He then engaged in merchandising in partnership with his father, continued this for five years, and then turned his attention to farming. In 1872 Miss Ella A. Outlaw, a native of Oktibbeha county, Miss., born in 1855, and the daughter of Dorsey A. and Clara E. (Harris) Outlaw, became his wife. Her parents were both natives of North Carolina and came to Oktibbeha county early in the thirties, probably about 1831 or 1832, as squatters, took up government land and became wealthy. They built one of the first houses in the county, and the first one with glass windows. At the time of his death Mr. Outlaw was the owner of four large plantations, on one of which (the old homestead) our subject now resides. These plantations averaged about sixteen hundred acres each, and besides this Mr. Outlaw was the owner of tracts in the Mississippi bottoms and in Clay county. He was a very pious man, a member of the Baptist church, and was instrumental in building Salem church. He was a shrewd, practical planter and a man respected and esteemed by all. He died in March, 1870, and his widow made her home with her son-in-law, Willian H. Harvey, until her death in 1884. To Mr. and Mrs. Harvey were born three children, viz.: William Henry, who is attending A. & M. college at Starkville; Clara, who is attending the State industrial institute and college, and Thomas L., who was thrown from his horse in June, 1890, and killed. Mrs. Harvey died in June, 1885. She was a member of the Baptist church and Mr. Harvey is a member of this church also. Mr. Harvey is a member of the Farmers' Alliance, and contributed the charter for a sub-alliance. He is a member of the Oktibbeha Rangers and is second sergeant of the same. Mr. Harvey was the first farmer in this county to use self-feeding cottongins, barbed wire for fencing, wheeled cultivator plows for cotton and corn and other modern implements for the farm, especially the purchase and use of the mowing machine; and at the time the mowing machine was introduced his neighbors for miles around came to see the machine at work. It was a show to them.

John E. Hauff, a well-known resident of Washington county, Miss., was born in South Carolina, April 25, 1845, being the second of five children born to James E. and Mary (Barwick) Hauff, the former a Virginian and the latter a native of South Carolina. James E. Hauff came to Madison county, Miss., in 1852, dying at Sharon in this state in 1861, having followed the calling of a mechanic throughout life. The Hauffs were originally from Germany, and upon coming to this country settled in Virginia. The Barwicks are Scotch and are descended from the McKinzie family of South Carolina. None of the ancestors of John E. Hauff ever held office as far back as he knows but lived quiet and uneventful lives, following honorable pursuits. John E. Hauff was reared on Mississippi soil and although the war opened when he was only fifteen years of age, he volunteered and was mustered into Company G, Eighteenth Mississippi regiment, but was discharged the following year on account of his youth. Being a warm sympathizer of the cause of the Confederacy he enlisted again, the same year, having only remained at home a few weeks. This time he joined Luckett's company of Wirt Adams' cavalry and was a faithful soldier of the Confederacy until peace was declared. He served as a scout the greater portion of the time, having been in the battle of Manassas, Leesburg and Malvern Hill and on the retreat through Georgia. When the news of Lee's surrender reached him he was at Gainesville, Ala., from which place he returned home. In 1865 he began life for himself without a penny, and with only a very ordinary education, and with a widowed mother, three sisters and one brother depending on him for a livelihood. Although he had been true to the South and had gallantly defended her rights, the true battle of life now began, and he returned home only to find that chaos and poverty reigned and that a very dark outlook for the future awaited him. With the same intrepidity that had characterized his career as a soldier, he began to rebuild what the war had laid waste, and for some time acted as a plantation manager for others. About five years since he became the owner of his present plantation, which comprises eight hundred acres of land, of which six hundred acres are under cultivation, and has a modest, but very tasty, neat and commodious residence in Glen Allen.   In 1870 he was married to Miss Laura Tillman, a native of Mississippi, who died five years later, leaving two children: Edward and Annie, the latter of whom is now deceased.   In 1887 he was again married, his wife being Miss Nannie B. Dicken, a native of Mississippi, and a daughter of Henry L., and Sally (Beaman) Dicken of Mississippi.   His present wife has borne him two children: George Victor and Mabel.   Mr. Hauff has been a hard working man all his life, and while he has not amassed a very large fortune, he has placed his family beyond the reach of want, and has the satisfaction of knowing that his property has been obtained by his own industry. He is perfectly contented with his lot and his happiest hours are spent with his wife and children, to whom he is a kind and thoughtful husband and father.   Socially he is a member of the Masonic fraternity.

Emil Hauptmann, a well-to-do merchant of Leland, Miss., was born in Poland, Russia, 1856, and possesses that independent spirit, that enterprise, push and industry, necessary for a successful business career.   His parents, Sigmund and Anna (Grams) Hauptmann, were also born in Poland, the former being a teacher in the public schools of that country, and for the past thirty years has held the position of government cashier.   Emil Hauptmann was educated in the schools of his native land, but came to the conclusion that America offered a good field for a young man of enterprise, and in 1873 became a resident of "the land of the free."   His first work here was done in the state of Pennsylvania, where he was engaged in the manufacture of iron for some time, after which he removed to Louisiana, and for six years, from 1876 to 1882, was engaged as a salesman in a mercantile establishment in Water Proof.   At the end of this time he opened an establishment of his own, but at the end of two years made a trip to Europe, visiting Germany, England, France, Poland and Russia, returning to this country the same year.   He then came to Leland, Miss., and at this point is the popular proprietor of an excellent mercantile establishment, his stock of goods being valued at about $4,000.   Besides this he owns his store building and residence, valued at $3,000.   He was married in 1888 to Miss Laura Toler, who was born in this state, and by her is the father of three children: Anna, and Freddie and Edwin (twins).   Since 1885 he has held the position of mayor of Leland, and has been devoted to the welfare of the town. While he has not resided here a great while, he is an honored and esteemed citizen, and although he is modest and retiring in disposition, his numerous good qualities are well known and thoroughly appreciated.   Although he is not wealthy, he has a good and constantly increasing business and a comfortable and pleasant home.   He is pleasant and courteous at all times, and is thoroughly public spirited, identifying himself with every worthy enterprise.   He and his wife are worthy members of the Baptist church, and socially he belongs to the Knights and Ladies of Honor.

Among the wealthy and retired citizens of Montgomery county, Miss., stands the name of Hon. Frank Hawkins, retired planter, Winona, Miss., who was originally from Franklin county, N. C., born September 10, 1815.   His father, Col. John D. Hawkins, was a native of the same state, born in Warren county in 1781, and his mother, whose maiden name was Jane A. Boyd, was born in Virginia in 1784.   The maternal grandfather, Alexander Boyd, a native of Mecklenburg county, Va., was one of the pioneers of that county, and Boydstown was named in honor of him.   He reared a large family, and all became prominent planters and merchants.   Col. John D. Hawkins graduated in law, but subsequently located on a plantation in Franklin county, N. C., where he engaged in planting and where he amassed a large fortune.   He took an active part in politics, and represented his county

Yours truly,
Wiley N. Nash,

in both branches of the legislature. He died on his plantation in Franklin county, N. C. He was the son of Philemon the third, who lived and died at Pleasant Hill, Warren county, N. C., born in 1752 and died in 1833, and who married Miss Lucy Davis, also a native of Warren county, born in 1775 and died in 1809. Philemon the third was the son of Philemon Hawkins the second, who was born in Gloucester county, Va., in 1717, and who died in Warren county, N. C., in 1801. The latter married Miss Delia Martin, of Brunswick county, Va., born in 1743, and who died in 1797. Philemon the second moved from the Old Dominion to Warren county, N. C. He was the son of Philemon the first, who was born in England in 1695, and who arrived in Virginia in 1715. While a resident of his native country he had married Miss Anna Howard, and after coming to Virginia he located in Gloucester county, where he had relatives who had preceded him. He was a descendant of Sir John Hawkins, admiral. Hon. Frank Hawkins was one of a family of six sons and four daughters that grew to mature years and became heads of families. Five of the brothers and one sister are now living, and all are over sixty years of age. One brother, the eldest, Col. James B. Hawkins, is a resident and planter of Matagorda county, Tex. Another brother, Dr. William J. Hawkins, graduated in medicine, is now retired and resides at Raleigh, N. C. He is president of a bank. Capt. J. D. Hawkins, the third brother, is a large planter and cotton factor. A. D. Hawkins, over sixty years old, is a banker at Tallahope, Fla. Col. P. B. Hawkins, now deceased, was a colonel in the Confederate army. The sister, Miss Jane Hawkins, resides at Raleigh. Hon. Frank Hawkins passed his boyhood and youth in his native county, and he and three brothers were educated at Chapel Hill, N. C. Another brother was educated at the College of William and Mary. Frank was married in February, 1836, to Miss Ann C. Read, who was born in Halifax county, N. C., in 1821, and who was reared and educated in that county. She is a granddaughter of Colonel Southerland, of Revolutionary fame. After his marriage Mr. Hawkins settled in Granville, N. C., where he carried on planting for a number of years, and in 1845 removed to Mississippi, settling in Carroll county, where he was successfully engaged in planting, which occupation he has followed all his life. He has ever taken an active part in political matters, and has served three terms in the lower house of the legislature. He moved to Winona in 1873, and has since lived retired. His family consisted of three sons and one daughter. One son, John D., was a soldier in the Confederate army, and died in 1866. He left a wife and two children, a son and daughter, the latter marrying George McLeanan, attorney at Winona. R. R. Hawkins, banker and merchant of Vaiden, Carroll county, Miss.; and Frank Hawkins, Jr., the third son, is the cashier of the Citizens' bank at Winona, both have families. The daughter married James C. Purnell (see sketch). Mr. Hawkins and family are members of the Episcopal church, in which he has acted as vestryman and senior warden for a number of years. Mr. and Mrs. Hawkins are descendants of prominent families, and are highly esteemed in the community in which they live.

G. R. Hawkins was born in Warren county, Miss., April 28, 1846, and in the county of his birth he has resided up to the present time, owning an interest in twelve hundred acres of land, four hundred of which are under cultivation, devoted to the culture of cotton, corn and other products of the South. He is the sixth child born to George W. and Eliza Anne (Wilson) Hawkins, the former of whom was born in Missouri about 1815. He came to Mississippi in his youth and located above Vicksburg, but soon after bought a tract of land at Mount Albon, which he successfully operated, being also engaged for some time in building ginhouses and presses throughout the country. His father was of Irish birth, but in the latter part of the eighteenth century immigrated to America and settled in Missouri, becoming

56

a tiller of the soil. The mother's father came from Scotland to America about the same time as the Hawkinses, and after residing for some time in Kentucky came to Mississippi about 1825, and near the town of Bovina, in Warren county, kept what was known as Wilson's tavern. In his early youth G. R. Hawkins attended the private school kept by M. Arnold Hannam, but in 1868 began taking charge of his father's farm, and was afterward married to Miss Agnes Adams, a daughter of Thomas Adams, of Jefferson county, Miss. Their children are Sallie M., Henry Downs, William Mercer, George Marshall, Herbert Harold and Agnes Courtney. The mother of these children died of swamp fever in 1883, and Mr. Hawkins' second marriage was consummated April 15, 1885, the maiden name of his wife being Lottie C. Child, of Natchez, her father, H. Y. Child, being a prosperous china merchant of that city. To his second union one child has been born: Evangeline H. Mr. Hawkins was elected one of the supervisors of Warren county in 1879, but after serving one year resigned to remove from the county. In 1887 he was elected to the position of magistrate, and is still ably discharging the duties of this position. He has also been a member of the school board of his district for six years. In 1880 he removed to Issaquena county, where he had the management of Mount Level plantation for four years, after which he made several changes of residence before moving to his present place. He is a progressive planter, and one who is making money by superintending his own work, making his own repairs and attending strictly to every detail of his calling. He was again elected a member of the board of supervisors in 1891 to serve four years.

W. C. Hawkins, a son of Gabriel Hawkins and Martha E. Hawkins (nee Lawrence), was born in Pickens county, Ala., in 1868. He spent his early life in Alabama, where he attended the common school and laid the foundations for his education. After this preparatory course he attended the Commercial college at Lexington, Ky., in the spring of 1886 and then the Southern university at Greensboro, Ala. After this he served as clerk in mercantile establishments at Enterprise, Miss., and Hattiesburg, Miss., until 1891, when he embarked in business for himself, becoming manager of the firm of Hawkins & Thompson at Pachuta, Clarke county, Miss., where he does a general mercantile business, and has enjoyed a good trade. He has a landed interest of two hundred acres or more, besides his store. The paternal grandfather of the subject, Herbert Hawkins, in the forties moved with a large family from Spartanburg district, S. C., to north Alabama. The father of the subject, Gabriel Hawkins, was well known in Alabama as a Methodist minister, but was at the time of his death in 1885, at Rose Hill, Jasper county, Miss., a member in active service of the Mississippi conference of traveling preachers; the wife is yet living and resides in Enterprise, Miss. They had eleven children, of whom four sons and three daughters are living, W. C. Hawkins being the sixth son by birth, the third living. The first, G. L. Hawkins, is manager of the corporation, Hawkins & Co., well known at Hattiesburg, Miss.; the second, Rev. H. G. Hawkins, is superintendent of public instruction of Clarke county, Miss., though when his term of office expires in 1892, his whole attention will be given to the ministry. The remaining son, I. F. Hawkins, youngest brother of W. C. Hawkins, has also entered the ministry. The subject was married in August, 1890, to Miss Lillie Capers, of New Orleans, La. The place of her nativity is Ocean Springs, Jackson county, Miss.

In January, 1867, J. C. Head, merchant, Greenville, Miss., came from Georgia to Greenville, Washington county, Miss., and there engaged in agricultural pursuits. In 1876 he purchased a farm to which he has since added until he now has under cultivation thirteen hundred acres in various tracts in Mississippi and Arkansas, all mainly improved by himself. In 1882 he began business in Greenville and now, under the firm name of Head & Co., has a large wholesale and retail grocery. He is also an extensive dealer in carriages and wagons under the firm name of J. C. Head & Co., and under the firm name of Head & Hunt is conducting a large livery and sales stable, all of which are prosperous and doing a good business. Mr. Head was born in Georgia on the 1st of May, 1846, and received but a limited education in his native state. In 1863 he entered the Confederate service, company I, Thirteenth Georgia infantry, served in Virginia, was in the battle of the Wilderness and all the engagements of that campaign. He was in the siege of Petersburg and surrendered at Spottsylvania courthouse where he was slightly wounded. After recovering he followed farming in his native state until 1867, when, as above stated, he came to Mississippi. In March, 1877, he was married to Miss Mary A. Buckner, a native of Bolivar county, Miss., and daughter of John W. Buckner, of Kentucky, and P. M. Buckner, of Mississippi. The following children were born to this union: Mamie Buckner, John Columbus, Olive Clyde, Clara Lee, Jessie Emile (who died in infancy) and Guy Stanhope. The family are members of the Methodist Episcopal church and Mr. Head is a member of the Knights of Honor. Aside from his many mercantile enterprises Mr. Head has been quite extensively engaged in farming and in this, too, has been very successful. He is a selfmade man and merits the esteem of all for his perseverance and determination. He was the fifth child born to Richard C. and Clara A. (Champion) Head, both natives of Georgia. The father died in that state in 1886 and the mother the year previous. Both were worthy members of the Methodist church. The father was a successful tiller of the soil and followed that occupation nearly all his life. The paternal ancestors were among the prominent families of South Carolina and the maternal ancestors were from Georgia.

S. L. Hearn, a general merchant at West Point, is also connected with the West Point foundry and machine shops, a leading stockholder in and president of the West Point manufacturing company, vice president of the First National bank and one of Clay county's best and wealthiest citizens. He was born in Chickasaw county in 1849, but was reared in Attala county by his parents, Asa and Mary (Crocker) Hearn, the former of whom was born in Georgia, but at an early day removed with his father to Monroe county, Miss. He was married in Monroe county, and from there removed to Chickasaw county, thence to Attala county, where he made his home for the remainder of his days, dying near Jackson, Miss., in 1863, while in the service of his country. He was a well-to-do planter and teacher, and was an honorable and useful citizen and member of society. He belonged to the A. F. & A. M. and the Baptist church. He was the only child of Jacob Hearn, who removed from Georgia to Mississippi, but afterward returned to the former state, and died in Walker county at quite an advanced age. He was a well-to-do planter prior to the war. He had been married three times. The maternal grandfather died in South Carolina when Mrs. Hearn was a small child. She is still living and resides at West Point. Of a family of three sons and six daughters born to her union, six are now living. S. L. Hearn was brought up as a farmer's boy, with a common-school education, and at an early age began the battle of life for himself as a planter, a calling he continued with fair results until 1878, when he came to West Point and engaged in merchandising, which has since been his occupation. He is now one of the leading merchants of the place, and is one of its most enterprising and prominent citizens. He started in life a poor boy, and by his untiring energy and good business management he has accumulated a handsome competency which he has in real estate in West Point, and also in other valuable investments. He is one of the most popular citizens of the city, and is a leader in financial and business circles. He possesses a wonderful capacity for business, and is a genial and courteous gentleman, upright in all his

894 BIOGRAPHICAL AND HISTORICAL

methods of conducting his affairs. He has a magnificent home in West Point, and is deservedly proud of his record as a financier. He was married in 1871 to Miss Hattie, daughter of Rev. Dr. James A. Ware, a South Carolinian by birth, who came to Pontotoc county, Miss., at an early day, where he became a prominent physician and Baptist minister and one of the county's best citizens. He and his wife both died there. Mrs. Hearn was born in Pontotoc county, and has borne Mr. Hearn two children. They are members of the Baptist church, and Mr. Hearn is a member of the Knights of Honor.

Hon. Joel A. Hearne, planter, Ripley, Miss. Mr. Hearne's paternal great-grandfather came from St. Christopher's Island, in the West Indies, but he was probably born in Ireland. He was a blanket merchant. His son, Jesse Hearne, grandfather of our subject, was a native of Maryland, born about 1758, and served as a soldier in the Revolutionary war. Thomas Hearne, father of subject, was born in North Carolina in February, 1793, and was one in a family of four sons: George W., Jesse L. and William Spencer, all of whom were reared to manhood in North Carolina. In 1814, being twenty-one years (born 1793), Thomas started out to fight life's battles for himself, and when grown was married to Miss Diana Hearne, also a native of the Old North state. In 1822 they located in Wilson county, Tenn., remained there one year, and then located in Carroll county. In 1844 he came to Tippah county and there his death occurred in 1855. Joel A. Hearne, one of eight children born to the above mentioned union, owes his nativity to Tennessee, his birth occurring in Wilson county in 1823. He passed his boyhood and youth in Carroll county of that state and when twenty-one years of age cast his first vote for Henry Clay, for president, in 1844, in 1845 located in what is now Union county where he resided until 1880. He was the first mayor of New Albany, which was organized in 1850, and held that position until the breaking out of hostilities between the North and South. In 1848 he engaged in merchandising and continued this business until 1873, when he established the New Albany Union, which he ran until 1876. After this he followed planting until 1880. He was married in 1858 to Miss Dansby who died in 1878 and in 1880 he was wedded to Mrs. W. T. Fleming. In 1865 he was elected to the legislature from Pontotoc county and served until 1867. Mr. Hearne was appointed by Governor Alcorn, when Union county was formed out of Pontotoc and Tippah county, with Joe J. Nutt, S. H. Hall, S. H. Ferguson and Charles Williams, to constitute the board of supervisors to organize Union county. This county was organized on the 19th of July, 1870, with George W. Wiley as probate clerk, Judge Levi Jarvis, as circuit clerk; Hartwell F. Wells, sheriff; J. A. Hickman, treasurer and S. H. Norvell, assessor. Socially Mr. Hearne is a member of the Masonic fraternity. He and Mrs. Hearne are members of the Methodist church. Mrs. Hearne is the owner of about sixteen hundred acres, in Tippah county, on which is a beautiful and convenient residence.

It is perhaps only natural that when starting out to fight life's battles for himself Col. John Heath, Sr., should select planting as his chosen occupation, for he had been trained to the duties of the farm from early boyhood, and was perfectly familiar with all its details. He first began as agent for a planter in Claiborne county, and continued in this business for various men for twenty-six years. In 1859 he came to Issaquena county, Miss., was manager of H. P. Duncan's plantation until 1864, and the following year was manager for Mr. Bullett, at Egg point, Washington county. In 1866, on account of failing health, he went to Claiborne county for recuperation, and the two years following was agent for Christopher Hampton (brother of Gen. Wade Hampton), on Lake Washington. During the years 1869-71 Mr. Heath leased Homochitto plantation from H. P. Duncan, and worked that for himself very successfully until 1872. He then purchased two places, both together, consisting of two thousand four hundred acres withal, with one thousand five hundred acres under cultivation, and he is now residing on one of them—Shiloh plantation. Since purchasing, he has made a great many improvements on both, has erected good tenant houses and a fine residence for himself and family. He has never taken a prominent part in politics, but attends strictly to his planting interests, in which he has been unusually successful. He has been a member of the board of supervisors for four years, and also served as justice of the peace for some time. He has been twice married, first in 18ᵒ2 to Miss May M. Stewart, of Copiah county, Miss., and the daughter of Thomas Stewart, a planter of that county. To that union were born seven children, four of whom survive: John W., a planter; Thomas A., a physician and planter; James P., a planter, and Nannie E., wife of R. E. Foster, who is also a planter. These children are all residents of Issaquena county. Mrs. Heath, who was a consistent member of the Methodist church, died in 1864. In 1868 Mr. Heath was married to Miss Louisa Taylor, of Washington county, who died in 1874, leaving one daughter, Maggie L. (deceased), who became the wife of Rev. A. L. Johnson, minister of the Baptist church. Mrs. Heath was a member of the Methodist church. Colonel Heath has always enjoyed good health, is a well-preserved man, and although sixty-nine years of age, looks hardly a day over fifty. He has ever been industrious and enterprising, and has made all his property since the war. The Colonel was born in Jefferson county, Miss., in 1822, and is the son of Adolph and Júlia (Mayers) Heath, both natives of the Keystone state. The parents moved to Natchez, Miss., in 1803, and settled in that city when there were but three houses. They made the trip on a flatboat, with only the assistance of two or three young men. Mr. Heath remained in Natchez but a short time, and then moved to Jefferson county, which was then an almost unbroken wilderness. Indians roamed at will, bears, panthers and other wild animals abounded, and the few settlers, who were mostly planters and the owners of slaves, experienced all the hardships of pioneer days. When he first settled in the county, Mr. Heath did not own any slaves, but after moving to Claiborne county he purchased a plantation and soon became quite wealthy. His death occurred there in 1853, and his wife died three days later, both of yellow fever, which swept the state that year. Both were members of the Baptist church from the time they were quite young. Of their large family of children eight lived to be grown: Elizabeth (of Claiborne county, is the widow of Joel Perkins), Louisiana (of Claiborne county, is the widow of Thomas Clark), Mary A. (also of that county, is the widow of James Marlar; Sarah A., is the wife of Joseph McVoy, of Louisiana), Samuel M. (died, leaving a family in Colorado), Abram (died, leaving a family in Hazlehurst, Copiah county, Miss.), John, and Adolph (who died, leaving a family in Yazoo City). Mr. Heath never took an active part in politics, but attended strictly to business (planting). He was a soldier in the War of 1812.

Dr. T. A. Heath, the second child born to the union of John and Mary (Stewart) Heath of Issaquena county, received his literary education in Clinton, Miss., and in 1878 he entered the Hospital college of medicine at Louisville, where he graduated in the spring of 1881. Returning to his home immediately after graduating, he located first in Washington county, close to the city of Greenville, and there practiced his profession for two years. After this he practiced at Mayersville for two years, but on account of failing health moved to Issaquena county, near his father, and there he has resided since, carrying on planting in connection with his practice. He is largely interested in farming and has a fine place of eight hundred and fifty acres with two hundred and sixty-five acres finely improved. He has good tenant houses, one for every fifteen acres, and all are kept in good condition. His own handsome residence is not on this farm but is on seventy-five acres adjoining his father's estate, and this is one of the prettiest locations in the county. His fine farm yields him one hundred and fifty-five bales of cotton annually and plenty of corn to run his farm. He has also a very lucrative practice and is a very successful physician. The Doctor was married in 1887 to Miss Nona Hull, of Claiborne county, youngest daughter of Capt. P. C. Hull, a planter of that county, who was formerly from Virginia. He was one of the leading men of Claiborne county and was captain in the war with Mexico, where he was honorably mentioned in the war department. He served with considerable ability throughout that war. His wife, Caroline Bethea, was born in Mississippi. They reared five children, who are named in the order of their births as follows: Kate, wife of J. F. McCalef, of Claiborne county; Lucy (deceased) was the wife of Mr. Patterson; Mary, wife of A. H. Davis, of Bolivar; Anna and Nona. The last named was left an orphan when quite young. She is a member of the Methodist and Dr. Heath is a member of the Baptist church. He is a Mason, a member of Lake Washington lodge No. 328, also a member of the Knights of Pythias, Hays' Landing lodge No. 314, and is medical examiner of the last-named organization. He is also a member of the American Legion of Honor at Vicksburg. Dr. Heath has served as a member of the board of supervisors of Issaquena county, but has never taken any great interest in political matters. He takes a great interest in blooded horses, of which he has several, and is the owner of a fine colt from a celebrated trotting horse.

James P. Heath, Hays' Landing, Miss., has been a successful planter since 1885, when he left the parental roof and commenced planting on his own responsibility. He now is the owner of a fine place ten miles south of Mayersville, and he has four hundred and fifty acres under cultivation. He is not only one of the most successful planters of the county, but is an influential citizen, and, although young in years, has held a number of the local offices of trust. In 1883–4 he was a member of the board of supervisors, and he has shown his appreciation of secret societies by joining the Knights of Pythias organization and Hays' Landing lodge No. 116. He has held all the different chairs of this order, and is the present past chancellor. He was born in 1858, and is the son of John and Mary Heath (see sketch). He received his early education in Clinton, Hines county, Miss., and in 1890 he selected as his companion in life Miss Lurena Smith, sister of Robert Smith, and daughter of R. M. and Margaret Smith (see sketch). In personal appearance Mr. Heath is about five feet eight inches in hight, weighs about one hundred and ninety pounds, has a fair complexion, and wears a fine blonde mustach.

J. B. Hebron enjoys the reputation of being a progressive citizen, and, although quite young in years, he is well posted on all the general topics of the day. His birth occurred in Warren county, Miss., in 1860, being one of a family of fourteen children born to John L. and Adaline L. (Cameron) Hebron, the former a Virginian, and the latter a native of Florida. The former removed to the state of Mississippi about the year 1820, and in the county of Warren followed the life of a planter and nurseryman, dying there about 1862, having served throughout the War of 1812 as a colonel. He was of Irish descent, and his wife was a Scotch lady. After receiving a fair education in the schools of Warren county, Miss., and having learned the intricacies of farm life of his father, J. B. Hebron, in 1874 began planting, and has continued this calling up to the present time. He is now with the firm of Hebron, Burdett & Co., and owns a one-third interest in their store and land, the latter amounting to one thousand six hundred and thirty acres, of which one thousand acres are in a good state of cultivation, and have been improved to the amount of $15,000, the stock of general merchandise being valued at $3,500. This property he has succeeded in accumulating by his own unaided efforts. He was married in 1888 to Miss Nannie Burdett, a native of Mississippi, and a daughter of Richard M. and Minerva (Heard) Burdett, the former a Virginian and the latter a native of Mississippi. Mr. Hebron has filled the position of marshal of Leland, and is now a member of the board of supervisors of Washington county, being elected on the democrat ticket, of which he has long been a member.

John L. Hebron, Jr., is a gentleman well known in Washington county, and his entire career has been such as to win him the respect and esteem of all who are favored with his acquaintance. He was born in Vicksburg, Miss., in 1864, but his father, John L. Hebron, Sr., was born in the Old Dominion. The latter was brought to Mississippi in early childhood, and was reared within its borders. In 1858, after studying two years, he graduated in medicine at the New Orleans medical college, and practiced continuously until 1876, serving as a surgeon during the Civil war. In 1876 he was elected to the state legislature from Warren county, where he had been making his home, and made an intelligent and trustworthy legislator. At the end of his term he left the political field and leased the state penitentiary for five years, but at the end of two years sold his lease to Mr. Jones S. Hamilton. In 1880 he began planting in Washington county, continuing this calling until 1887, when he once more resumed the practice of medicine. In 1860 he was married to Miss Elington, she being a lady with a very strong and active mind. She received an excellent education in her youth, and turned her attention to literature in maturer years, being the authoress of two books, entitled "Songs from the South" and "Faith or Earthly Paradise." She has contributed to the various papers of Mississippi for the past thirty years, and is an honorary member of the Press association. She is a most estimable lady, and is one of the foremost workers of the W. C. T. U. of the state. The paternal grandfather was born in Virginia, also his grandmother, the latter's name prior to her marriage being Miss Julia Sills. The subject of this sketch was educated at Clinton and Oxford, Miss., graduating at the head of his law class. He made a brilliant record while in the University of Mississippi, for his motto was "Stay at the top." Having been chosen by the society of which he was a member to represent it in an oratorical contest, he carried off the honors on this occasion also. He was sent by the Phi chapter of the Delta Psi fraternity to the national meeting of the fraternity in New York city, and was there unanimously chosen annual orator. In 1887 he began the practice of law, in connection with which he followed planting; but in 1890 dropped his books to devote his whole attention to the latter calling, and although his career as an attorney was short it was very successful. His agricultural operations have been abundantly prosperous, and he is now the possessor of one thousand three hundred acres of land, of which one thousand one hundred acres are in a good state of cultivation. His land is very valuable, for it is at all times kept in the best of order, and everything about it shows that a man of thrift, push and enterprise is at the helm. His home is called Cunningham, and he is now enjoying the tranquility which this retreat affords. He has been prominent in the political affairs of the county, and is now a popular candidate for state senator, for the successful filling of which position his many talents admirably fit him. He was married in 1888 to Miss Nettie Porter, of Florence, Ala., and she, as well as himself, is a worthy member of the Presbyterian church. In personal appearance Mr. Hebron is rather heavy but well built, and has dark brown hair and mustach. He is fine looking, and is very courteous and gentlemanly in his manners, ease and confidence being inspired in his presence. He is eminently capable of filling any position with credit to himself and his constituents, and in the general assembly of the state would add prestige to the county which he would represent.

George Heckler is one of those wideawake, thoroughgoing gentlemen who are bound to make their way in the world with little help from outsiders. He possesses the perseverance, energy, thrift and honesty of his German ancestors, and every enterprise to which he has devoted his time has resulted satisfactorily, a fact that speaks louder than words can do as to his many excellent business qualities. He was born near where he now resides on November 16, 1842, but both his parents, George and Mary (Betz) Heckler, were native Germans, and in the land of their birth received their education and rearing. The father immigrated to the United States in 1838, and soon after engaged in merchandising in Rodney, where he continued to follow an active business life until his death in 1855, falling a victim to yellow fever. His marriage, which was celebrated in Vicksburg, Miss., resulted in the birth of four sons and four daughters who grew to mature years, of which family George and the daughters are the survivors. The former grew up in Rodney, his youth being spent at school and in clerking in his father's store. Being a native of the South he warmly sympathized with the Confederate cause during the Civil war, and fully demonstrated this fact by enlisting in the Twenty-second Mississippi infantry in 1861, and being a faithful supporter of the cause he espoused until the final surrender. He took part in the battles of Franklin, Nashville, Corinth, the three engagements at Peach Tree Creek, Atlanta, Champion Hills, and a great number of smaller engagements and skirmishes. He received a slight flesh wound at Marietta, Ga., but was not disabled. After the termination of the war Mr. Heckler returned to Rodney, since which time he has been one of the leading merchants of the place. In addition to this he has given considerable attention to planting, and raises annually about three hundred bales of cotton, utilizing the seed in his oilmill, which he erected in Rodney in 1884. The business that he does in this respect is a flourishing one. Since devoting his attention to planting, a calling which he has followed with success since 1874, he has done remarkably well and is classed among the leaders of this calling in the county. Full of life and spirit, he is also a thoughtful man, and closely applies himself to whatever he has in hand. He is the possessor of much personal popularity, and is highly esteemed by all who know him, for his prominent characteristics are an acute sense of justice and right, singular fairness and liberality, a mind just and liberal and a kind and generous heart. He has served in numerous local offices of trust and honor, and almost continuously since the war has held the position of town treasurer, having also been a member of the council. He is a member of the Masonic fraternity, being worshipful master of his lodge, and is also a member of the K. of H., the K. & L. of H., and the A. L. of H. He was married in the year 1868 to Miss J. C. Schuster, a native of New Orleans but of German parentage. Their union has been blessed in the birth of five sons and two daughters: George V., who is in the store with his father; Mary Lou, a young lady; Edward Lee, John S., Fred, Mike and Herbert. Mr. and Mrs. Heckler are members of the Presbyterian church, in which he has been an elder for some time. Mrs. Heckler's father, a German by birth, is the foreman of the Rodney oilmill, and is an enterprising and industrious gentleman, living near Rodney.

Washington Irving Heidelberg, of the firm of W. I. & T. M. Heidelberg, general merchants, of Heidelberg, Jasper county, Miss., was born in this county October 31, 1840. He is a son of Samuel C. and Martha (Granberry) Heidelberg, natives of Georgia, who emigrated to Mississippi in the pioneer days of this section, and afterward settled in Jasper county, where the mother died, and the father still lives, at the advanced age of eighty-two years. They were the parents of fifteen children, named as follows: Adilade J., George C., Washington Irving, William W., Samuel C., Martin L., Elizabeth, Nancy J., Isabella F., Mary, Amelia J., Alletha, John, Daniel W. and Thomas M. Washington Irving Heidelberg was the third of the above-named family in order of birth. After having atttended for some years, and with good results, the home subscription schools of Jasper county, he enlisted as a Confederate soldier in September, 1861, in company H, known as the Jasper Blues, of the Twenty-seventh Mississippi regiment, of Walthall's brigade, and commanded by Captain Nixon. With this organization he served until the close of the war, participating in a number of hard-fought engagements, of which the following were the most important: The bombardment of Pensacola, Fla.; the battle of Perryville, Ky., where he received a slight wound in the thigh; the battle of Murfreesboro, Tenn., where he received another wound in the thigh; the battle of Missionary Ridge and Lookout Mountain, the engagement at Resacca, Ga., and in others throughout the Georgia campaign until he reached Atlanta, Ga., where, on August 3, 1864, he was shot through the wrist, and was disabled from duty for ninety days. After his recovery from this injury, he joined Doyle's battalion, in which he served until the close of the war. He then returned to Jasper county, Miss., where he has since made his home. He was married March 7, 1867, to Miss Matilda E., daughter of James and Ann (McDonald) Foley. Soon after he settled on land near where the town of Heidelberg now stands, which he had previously purchased. In 1882 he laid out on a portion of his landed property the town of Heidelberg, which was named in his honor. It now contains six general mercantile stores, a drug store, two hotels, a livery stable, two cottongins and gristmills, three churches for whites and one for colored people, two schools, one of them for the colored children, and the usual variety of mechanic shops and small business places. In 1887, in partnership with Thomas M. Heidelberg, he opened a general mercantile store, and the firm has since done an extensive business. Mr. Heidelberg is also largely interested in planting, owning about one thousand acres of land, all of which is well improved, and the finest residence in Jasper county, located three-quarters of a mile east of the business center of the town of Heidelberg. He and his wife are members of the Methodist Episcopal church South, and he is everywhere known as a strictly honest and very enterprising business man, success having crowned his efforts in a remarkable degree. Mr. and Mrs. Heidelberg have eight surviving children, named as follows: Mattie A., who graduated at Martin college, Pulaski, Tenn., June 4, 1891; Seth L., Irving M., Samuel C., James E., Albert Lee, Lurlein E., and an infant daughter, who is not yet named.

Thomas Erskine Helm is a native of Woodford county, Ky., where he was born on the 3d of December, 1813, the tenth of eleven children born to Thomas and Elizabeth (Buck) Helm, natives of the Old Dominion, where the father was born in 1768 and the mother in 1773. The most of the father's life was spent as a farmer of Woodford county, Ky., and prior to his death, which occurred in 1849, he succeeded in acquiring a handsome property. His ancestors were from England, and were among the early settlers of Virginia. His wife survived him until 1851, when she was called to her long home. Thomas Erskine Helm was reared in the state of his birth, and was educated in Transylvania college, of Lexington, Ky., but left school before completing his couse and came to Mississippi in 1833, stopping for a short time in Natchez. From that time until the opening of the war he was engaged in planting, and although he accumulated a fine property prior to this time, the principal part of it was swept away. He then sold what property he had and engaged in banking, and from 1873 until 1885 he owned and operated the Capital State bank, at the end of which time he sold out to a Mr. Barnett, but is still a stockholder in this bank and its vice president. He has been a successful business man, and besides his property in Jackson he owns a one-half interest in five thousand acres of land in Louisiana, all of which is the result of his own earnest and prudent endeavors. In 1835 he was married to Miss Mary Biggs, a native of Mississippi, who died in 1875, having borne him six children:

William Newton, who died while serving in the Confederate army; Joseph L., also died a martyr to the lost cause; Erskine (deceased); Elizabeth, deceased wife of William B. Richardson; Thomas, a property owner of Jackson, and Anna M., wife of John H. Odeneal. Mr. Helm is deeply attached to his children, and has ever proven a wise, kind and indulgent father. His children and grandchildren say he has lived and labored for them, and that a kinder, more affectionate and generous father and grandfather never lived. He is a member of the Presbyterian church, is one of the prominent old citizens of Jackson, and although he is several years past the allotted age of three-score years and ten, his mind is clear and active as of yore, and he still possesses sound business judgment.

No man has been more justly entitled to an enviable place in the history of Washington county, Miss., than Maj. George M. Helms, for he has been usefully and honorably identified with the interests of this county, and with its advancement in every worthy particular. The many years that he has spent in earnest and sincere endeavor have contributed very materially to the success that has fallen to his career. He was born in Christian county, Ky., October 4, 1839, and from his parents, Presley M. and Ann E. (Blakemore) Helms, he inherits Welsh, French and English blood respectively. Both parents were born in the Old Dominion, and in 1834 removed to Kentucky, where they spent two years in farming; then they moved to Montgomery county, Tenn., where he continued the same occupation until the war freed all his slaves. At its close he removed to Texas, settling near Waco, where he remained an esteemed citizen until his death, in 1886, having attained the advanced age of eighty-six years. He never aspired to any political position, but lived a quiet, retired and truly Christian life. Maj. George M. Helms removed to Tennessee with his parents, when a child, and in that state attained manhood and was educated, being a student in the Masonic college of Clarksville, Tenn., until within a short time of graduating, when he received the appointment of civil engineer on the Mississippi & Tennessee railroad, which position he discharged with ability for three years. In 1860 he became a resident of Washington county, Miss., and was assistant engineer on the levees at Greenville until the opening of the late war, when the clash of arms caused him to cast aside personal considerations to take up arms in defense of what he considered to be right—the Confederate cause. He became a member of Byrnes' battery, and belonged to a company that was raised and equipped in Washington county, and with which he went to Camp Boone, where he was detailed to solicit horses for the company, and succeeded in securing about one-half enough for the battery. When his company reached Green river he was detailed for engineering duty under Engineer Major Gilmore of Nashville, Tenn., and was assigned to the obstruction of the Cumberland river, and to the locating of a battery at Gowans' Island, twelve miles below Nashville. Just as the obstruction was within seventy feet of completion Fort Donelson fell, and he was ordered to abandon his works, and was assigned to the staff of General Hardee as engineer. After the evacuation of Nashville he was ordered to destroy all bridges in the rear of the company, then retreating to Huntsville, Ala., and thence to Corinth. Major Helms was in every battle of the army of Tennessee, the most prominent of which were Shiloh, Murfreesboro, Perryville, Chickamauga, Lookout Mountain, Missionary Ridge, Ringgold Gap, Dalton, Resaca, Kenesaw Mountain, and Marietta, and was constantly engaged from the 5th of April at Dalton until the 28th of July at Atlanta. At Corinth, Miss., he was granted a furlough, and made a three days' visit to his home in Washington county, at the end of which time he rejoined the army at Charlotte, N. C., and there met Major Gilmore, chief engineer, who ordered him to report on his march southward and westward, the purpose of President Davis being to cross the Mississippi river at Gaines Landing, Ark. He reported to General

Breckinridge, who was acting as the president's chief of staff at Washington, Ga., and the latter remarked, casually, to Major Helms that the stay at Washington had given Mr. Davis three days' start, but the Federals must be kept under the impression that he was still at Washington.

After they had started their march westward and were five miles out from Washington, they were met by a company of Federal cavalry, who demanded their surrender under the cartel as agreed upon by Grant and Lee. General Breckinridge with Col. Theodore Harrow (author of "Bivouac of the Dead"), Maj. Wilson Cabel and Cliff Breckinridge, all of whom were members of his staff, left after having advised Col. Robert Breckinridge, who commanded the forces and Major Helms, to tell the men to surrender at the first post and to go quietly to their homes. Major Helms, who was loath to "give up the ship," asked General Breckinridge if there was no hope beyond the Mississippi river and received the intelligence that there was none, and that Gen. Kirby Smith would have to yield under the first pressure. He surrendered at Athens with three companies of Morgan's command, commanded by one of the captains. Major Helms held the positions from lieutenant to major of engineers during his service, with staff of corps commanded by Hardee, then Polk, then Breckinridge, and Hinman until Hood recovered from a wound received in Virginia, and was with the latter until he was promoted to succeed General Johnston. Stephen D. Lee succeeded Hood, and Major Helms served with him until meeting President Davis at Charlotte, N. C. After his return to Greenville Major Helms was appointed assistant engineer on the levees, and in the year 1868 he was promoted to chief engineer, serving the most of the time in that capacity until 1878. In 1875 he was solicited to take forcible charge of the sheriff's office, and this he did, holding the office until the regular election. Since 1880 he has given his undivided attention to planting and is now the owner of seven thousand acres of fine land, two thousand acres of which he has put in a good state of cultivation since 1880. He was married in 1888 to Miss Anna Belle Eakin, a daughter of Judge Eakin, of Washington, Ark., the latter being judge of the supreme court of Arkansas at the time of his death. Major Helms was called upon to mourn the death of his wife in 1888, her death occurring on the 8th of June. She left one child that soon followed her to the grave. Major Helms is one of the leading spirits of Washington county, and in every calling in which he has been engaged through life he has shown himself to be far sighted, shrewd, intelligent and practical. He possesses no ordinary intellect and his mind has been enlarged and broadened by the highest culture and by contact with the business affairs of life. He is generous and kind in disposition, and to the sufferings and misfortunes of those less fortunate than himself he is keenly alive, and those who apply to him for aid are never sent away empty handed, if deserving. In appearance he is prepossessing for he possesses a fine physique and very black hair and eyes, the former being now slightly tinged with gray.

William M. Hemeter, of Hattiesburg, Miss., one of the leading merchants of Perry county, Miss., was born in Covington county, Miss., in 1853, and is the son of George and Martha J. (Schogins) Hemeter, natives of Alabama and North Carolina respectively. They reared a family of eight children, named as follows: Joseph, William M. (the subject of this biographical notice), Marcus, David K., George, Nettie (wife of Warren Lowry, of Perry county), Florence (who married Thomas M. Thames, of Covington county) and James. The father was born about the year 1828, and emigrated to Mississippi at an early date. William M., passed his youth on a farm, attending the common schools during the winter season. In 1874 he was sent away from home to school, and did not return for two years. In 1877 he embarked in the mercantile trade at Williamsburg, Covington county, Miss., and remained there until 1885. He then located at Eatonville, where he conducted a general store, under the firm name of Hemeter & Eaton. He has been very successful in all his undertakings, and occupies a place among the most enterprising merchants of the county. He was married in November, 1876, to Miss Mary Eaton, daughter of W. J. Eaton, of Covington county. One child was born of this union, and in 1882, Mrs. Hemeter died. In 1884 Mr. Hemeter was married a second time, being united to Miss Lou Robinson, a daughter of N. L. Robinson, deceased. He and his wife are worthy members of the Baptist church. Mr. Hemeter is a man of great integrity of character, firm in his convictions of right and wrong, and a steadfast, loyal citizen.

Dr. Andrew J. Hemphill, physician and druggist, lives where he settled after the close of the war, twenty-five years ago, at French Camp, Choctaw county, Miss, a beautiful and thrifty little village, eight miles from the railroad, located on fertile and productive soil, at the confluence of several small streams, and surrounded by a section of country densely populated by small planters. Here the Central Mississippi presbytery has recently located the Central Mississippi institute, and the French Camp Male academy, schools of high grade for the education of boys and girls. Dr. Hemphill, a son of Gen. James and Anne (Boyle) Hemphill, was born in Jackson county, Ga., October 24, 1832. General Hemphill, the only child of his father, was born in Chester district, S. C., in 1800. His father died while he was an infant. His mother married Mr. Sanders and moved to Florida, and he was left to the care of an aunt. She moved with him to Jackson county, Ga., where he received a fair English education, and was married to Anne Boyle, youngest daughter of Peter Boyle. From there he moved while Dr. Andrew J. was an infant, and settled in Van's Valley, in the Choctaw nation, northwest Georgia. He was a commissioned officer in removing the Indians from that section to west of the Mississippi river; served as a private in the Creek war, and was afterward elected brigadier-general of Georgia militia. He was one of the commissioners who located Rome, the county seat of Floyd county, Ga., and afterward served with credit in both houses of the Georgia legislature from that county. He was a successful planter and merchant, and accumulated large property, but being of a generous and liberal nature lost the larger portion of it by indorsing for friends. In 1848 he sold his property in the valley to his brother-in-law, William Montgomery, and removed and settled in Choctaw county, Miss., near the present town of Weir, and there his death occurred about 1868. His wife followed him to the grave about five years afterward, and now they together rest in Lebanon cemetery. Grandfather Hemphill was a native of north Ireland. He crossed the ocean and settled in Chester district, S. C., where he died while his only son was an infant. Grandfather Peter Boyle was a Scotch Irishman who, having just finished his education in 1775, crossed the ocean to America, prospecting. While he was lingering in this country, independence was declared, and he volunteered and joined the American army, and served through the entire Revolutionary war. At the close of the war he was married to Miss Hannah Todd, in Virginia, and moved with her to Jackson county, Ga., and engaged in farming. To them were born three sons: John, Robert and Peter. John and Peter, with their families, went to Texas. Robert settled near Alpena, Chattooga county, Ga. They also had three daughters: Katherine, Rebecca and Anne. Katherine, the eldest, married William Montgomery, and they died in Van's Valley. Rebecca, the second daughter, married Charles Hemphill. Anne, the youngest, married Gen. James Hemphill. To Anne and Gen. James Hemphill were born three sons and seven daughters. The eldest, Col. John B. Hemphill, received a liberal education, studied law and was admitted to the bar at Rome, Ga. He was elected colonel in the Georgia militia. In 1849 he moved to Mississippi and located in Kosciusko, Attala county. Several times he represented that county in the legislature, was twice elected district attorney in the fifth judicial district, one term during the war. He was a good lawyer, but physically weak. For this reason he never entered the Confederate service. After the war he settled near Avalon, Ellis county, Tex., where he engaged in planting. He died in 1880.

The second son, James R. Hemphill, received a collegiate education, graduating in Knoxville, Tenn., in 1848, studied law and entered into practice in partnership with his brother at Kosciusko. During the war he volunteered, and served in the Confederate army as first lieutenant in the Cooper guards, Twentieth Mississippi infantry. He was captured at Fort Donelson and held as prisoner about one year on Johnson's Island, Ohio; was exchanged and rejoined his command in Virginia, and was with the remnant of Lee's army at the final surrender. He had previously represented Attala county in the state legislature. After the surrender he turned his attention to teaching, and became a popular educator. He died December, 1889, at his father's old home, near Weir. He was a scholar, a true friend, an affectionate husband and father, a Christian gentleman, and that he was a brave soldier was proven on Virginia's blood-stained battlefields. The oldest daughter married Dr. Madison Montgomery, of Chattooga county, Ga. He was a man of fine intellect and a prominent physician and a leader among his people. He represented that county in both branches of the Georgia legislature. He moved to Mississippi in 1858; both he and his wife died about 1880. Another daughter married Col. James M. Drane, of Choctaw county, Miss., who entered the Confederate service as captain and was promoted to the colonelcy of the Thirty-first Mississippi infantry. She died in 1885. Another daughter married Col. William H. Coleman, who went into the Confederate service from Texas. After this he was settled at Mineral Wells, Palo Pinto county, Tex. He died in 1890. Besides the aunt, who reared him, Gen. James Hemphill knew of only three other relatives of his name, cousins: Charles, Nancy and Philip Hemphill. Charles and Philip Hemphill lived in Van's Valley. Nancy married Col. James Ladelle, who lived in Rome. These three families moved to Mississippi. Charles Hemphill, who was also his brother-in-law (having married Rebecca Boyle), settled at French Camp, where they both died. They have now one living son, Dr. J. W. Hemphill, a practicing physician and an elder, who lives near Rocky Springs, Warren county, Miss. Philip Hemphill and Col. James Ladelle settled in Carrollton, Miss., died there, leaving large and influential families, lawyers, physicians and planters in that section. Dr. Andrew J. Hemphill, the seventh child and third son, received an academic education, studied medicine, attended the New Orleans school of medicine during the sessions of 1856–7, and graduated in 1858 from the University of the city of New York; the same year he located and entered upon the practice of his profession with Dr. Ozias Lewis, at Kosciusko, Miss. Two years afterward he moved to Vaiden, Miss. At the commencement of the war between the states he volunteered as a private and joined the Vaiden artillery, but was assigned to the duty of surgery of the battery in the Tennessee army. He rendered important service on the battlefield of Shiloh and elsewhere, was always faithful and constant in the performance of his duties, sympathizing with and contributing to the comfort of the sick and wounded. After the war, his county devastated and his fortune swept away, with a profession alone to fall back upon, he located at French Camp and resumed practice, also establishing a small drug business. In 1870–71 he represented his county in the legislature and served on engrossed and enrolled bills and railroad committees. He married first, in 1864, Mrs. Mary T. Vaughan, daughter-in-law of Maj. Henry Vaughan, of Yazoo county, and the youngest daughter of Gen. William Clarke, of Jackson, Miss. Gen. William Clarke was a native of North Carolina and a minister of the Christian church, and twice treasurer of Mississippi about the time of Governor Foote's administration. Mrs. Hemphill was also a member of the Christian church. She died in 1870, leaving the Doctor three daughters, two of whom are engaged in teaching in the public schools in Ellis county, Tex. One finished her education at the I. I. & C., Columbus, Miss. The other graduating at the C. M. I., French Camp, Miss.

Dr. Hemphill's second wife, Miss Eugenia Meek Hughes, he married in 1872. She was a native of Louisville, Miss., and a daughter of Dr. J. C. Hughes and Caroline Meek Hughes. Mrs. C. M. Hughes was reared near Grenada, and died in Louisville, Miss., about 1851. Dr. J. C. Hughes is a native of Pickens county, Ala., has a liberal education, and received his medical education from the Charleston and Jefferson medical college, Philadelphia, from the latter of which he graduated. He has again married and engaged in the practice of his profession at McCool, Miss. He is an elder and all his ancestors are Presbyterians. Grandfather Hemphill and Peter Boyle, and all their descendants were members of the Presbyterian church, and politically democratic, and in the late civil strife voted for secession, believing in the correctness of the states' rights doctrine, and the construction of the constitution as rendered by Stephens and Jefferson Davis. To Dr. and Mrs. Hemphill were born nine children, six of whom are living, two sons and four daughters, and they are sparing no pains to educate them, being fortunate in having excellent schools located conveniently near. Dr. Hemphill was made a master Mason in De Witt Clinton lodge, Vaiden, Miss., in 1860, and there being no lodge convenient he has never renewed his connection with the order. The Doctor is a gentleman of culture and an excellent physician, enjoying the unbounded confidence of his patients. As a correct business man of high standing he has been successful in nearly all his undertakings. He owns about one thousand acres of land, subdivided into small farms, and nearly all under cultivation. He is modest and unassuming, loving to spend his idle moments in his sequestered home amid the prattling of the babes.

The medical profession of Yazoo county, Miss., is well represented by Dr. C. R. Henderson, who resides at Deasonville. He is a native of Yazoo county, born in 1838, the eldest son of a family of five children. His parents, D. C. and Mary A. (Ogden) Henderson, were natives of North Carolina and Mississippi respectively. About the year 1835 they settled on a plantation in Yazoo county, where they spent the remainder of their days. The father was prominently identified with the early political history of the county; he died in the year 1853, and the mother passed away a few months later in the same year. They reared a family of five children: Lucie, deceased, was the wife of K. Exum, of this county; Mrs. Bettie Baskin, of Madison county, Miss.; Daniel T., a member of company F, Mississippi volunteer infantry, who fell at Gettysburg, having been promoted to the office of first lieutenant; Joseph D., a farmer of this county. The Doctor received his education at Mississippi college, Clinton, Miss., being graduated from this institution in 1858. For the purpose of pursuing his medical studies he went to Philadelphia, and entered Jefferson medical college. After two years of diligent work he was graduated with the class of 1860, and was just beginning his practice when the Civil war broke out. In May, 1861, he entered the Confederate service as second lieutenant of company F, Eighteenth Mississippi volunteer infantry. He served in this position one year, and was then appointed surgeon, in which capacity he served successfully until the surrender, at that time he was at Gainesville, Ala., attached to Forrest's command. He participated in the engagement at Manassas the first time, and was at Leesburg. At the close of the war he returned to Yazoo county and resumed the practice of his profession. In addition to this work he finds time to superintend his plantation of four hundred acres, one half of which is under cultivation.

He is a member of the Masonic order, belonging both to the Blue lodge and chapter, and is a Knight of Honor. Dr. Henderson was united in marriage in Hinds county, Miss., to Miss Hattie Sexton, of Warren county, Miss., a daughter of David and Rebecca (Gibson) Sexton who were natives of Pennsylvania and Mississippi respectively. Two children have been born to the Doctor and his wife: James S., of Dumas, Ark., and Mary R. The parents are worthy members of Bethel Baptist church, and have been liberal contributors to its support. They have witnessed many changes in Yazoo county, but they have been in the right direction, and are of a character to reflect credit upon the influential citizens among whom the Doctor's family takes first rank.

Chester W. Henderson, a prominent planter of Wilkinson county, was born here October 5, 1847, and was the third child of a family of five born to Joseph A. and Amy Ann (Lanehart) Henderson, both of whom were natives of this county. Joseph was born October 1, 1815, and was the son of Joseph Henderson, Sr., a native of South Carolina who came to Mississippi territory about 1812 and settled near Woodville. He came here with his family, consisting of a wife and four children, and afterward five were born in this county. Joseph, the father of these children, died at an advanced age, honored and respected, having lived a useful life. His wife, the mother of these children, survived him for some years. Of the children born none are supposed to be yet living, unless it is the youngest son, Robert, whose whereabouts are unknown. The father of Chester W. was reared and educated in this county, and commenced for himself when a young man, and married and settled north of Woodville, where he remained about eighteen years engaged in farming. He went out in the Confederate militia, but owing to ill health returned to his home place. In 1867 he purchased a place on Bayou Sara creek, where he resided until his death, August 21, 1885. He was a member of the Christian church, with which he had united later in life, and was an elder and one of the most active members and liberal supporters. He was strongly opposed to secession, and was a Union man, but the pressure of circumstances compelled him to adopt the course he did. He took no part in political matters, but kept himself posted on public affairs. He was married August 16, 1842. His wife was an earnest worker of the Christian church from girlhood, and was a most dutiful and loving mother, always ready to administer to the wants of her children. She died June 26, 1883, aged fifty-nine years and eight months. The eldest of these children was Mary, who died October 14, 1845, aged two years, one month and fifteen days. The next child was Amanda A., born April 2, 1845, and is now Mrs. C. H. Wood, and lives on the old home place and has a large family of children. Chester W. was the third child. Adam C., the fourth, was born December 31, 1849, and is now living in Louisiana, where he is engaged in planting. He is married and has five children. Cornelia E. was born March 16, 1852, and is the wife of Elijah McDonald, and lives on Bayou Sara creek, near Woodville, and has a large family. Chester W. was educated in Wilkinson county, and upon attaining manhood started in business for himself, engaging in planting. He was married to Florida M. Woodruff, who was born in this county January 26, 1855, and died November 24, 1877, leaving one child four months old, James A., born July 12, 1877. This child has been an invalid since its birth. The mother was the daughter of Allen D. Woodruff, a native of Tennessee, and Elizabeth L. Johns, a native of this county, where she was born and reared, and is yet living on the home place of her birth. By this union were born three children, who lived to be grown. The eldest married Chester W. Henderson. David, another, is now living in Louisiana engaged in planting. The third, Mary L., is the present wife of Chester W. She was born and reared in this county. They were married December 2,

1879, and by this union were born five children: Florida, born March 24, 1881; Walter, April 21, 1883; Kate, June 20, 1886; Lillie, July 5, 1888, and an infant girl unnamed. Mr. Henderson settled on his present place in January after his marriage, where he has since resided engaged in planting, and is now engaged also in stockraising. He is one of the most intelligent and progressive planters in the county, and stands high in society and citizenship. He is an earnest democrat, but takes no active part in public affairs. He is a member of the Independent Order of Odd Fellows, Wilkinson lodge No. 10, of which he is at present noble grand, and is also a member of the Legion of Honor.

In Greenock, Scotland, in 1755, John Henderson was born, and was descended from a very strict family of Covenanters. He was educated in Sterling, Scotland, in which place his father was a practicing physician, the name of the latter being William, who was named in honor of his father, William Saughy Henderson. Dr. William Henderson was married to Miss Isabel Allen, a daughter of William Allen, who suffered much persecution on account of his religious belief, in the time of Ebenezer Erskine. At an early date John Henderson came to America, and in 1787 settled at Natchez, Miss., while this section was still under Spanish rule, and made his home in Natchez until his death in 1845, at the advanced age of eighty-five years. While Spain still had control of this region, he lived a quiet, unobtrusive life, but when the territory of Mississippi came under control of the United States government, he sprang at once into prominence, not only as a business man, but also as a leader of Protestantism and Protestant enterprise. He was the leading spirit in founding the First Presbyterian church in Mississippi, at Pine Ridge, in Adams county, and was one of its first elders. Subsequently he, with others, organized the First Presbyterian church at Natchez, which was in the year 1817, and was also one of its first elders. He was a man of considerable literary attainments and a vigorous intellect. Thomas Henderson was his second son, and throughout his life deeply interested in church matters, education and colonization. He was for many years an elder in the Presbyterian church at Natchez, and a vice president of the American colonization society. He was also a member of the board of directors of Oakland college, Mississippi, and at one time was a member of the board of directors of the public schools of Natchez. By careful attention to business he acquired a large fortune, and dispensed his wealth with remarkable freeness, his donations to charities and worthy enterprises being at all times liberal. He was married in 1829 to Miss Bathsheba Putnam, a great-granddaughter of Gen. Israel Putnam, of Revolutionary fame. She was born at Belpre, Ohio, and died in 1841. Mr. Henderson's death occurring in 1863, at the age of sixty-five years. To their union two sons and one daughter were born. The latter, Julia P., who was born in 1830 and died in 1870, was a lady of some literary attainments. Two of her books: "Anna Balfour" and "Mary and her Scholars," were published by the Presbyterian board South and used as Sunday-school literature. She also contributed articles of merit to religious papers and other journals. John W. Henderson, eldest son of Thomas Henderson and Bathsheba Putnam, was born in 1832, graduated at Oakland college, Mississippi, in 1853, and was engaged in planting at the opening of the war. He went from Natchez in 1862, as first lieutenant of Breckinridge guard cavalry; was in most of the engagements in which the Western army participated, and was paroled at Greensboro, in N. C. Subsequently he engaged in merchandising, and in 1882 was appointed superintendent of public schools of Natchez, and Adams county, a position he is filling at the present time. He was married in 1857 to Miss Ellen Newman, a native of Natchez, and to their union six children have been born: Ellen, Corinne, Waldo Putnam, Florence, Anna and Thomas Newman. For years he was an elder in the Presbyterian church, as were his grandfather and grandmother before him. Mr.

ILLINOIS CENTRAL RAILROAD DEPOT AND HOTEL, HOLLY SPRINGS.

Henderson also is superintendent of the Sunday-school. His brother Mr. Thomas A. Henderson, second son of Thomas Henderson, is now bookkeeper in the Britton & Koontz bank. He was educated in Oakland college, and was a soldier in the Confederate army, serving in the cavalry throughout the entire war. He was captured and in prison at the time of the surrender. After his return, he was for a time, professor of mathematics in Oakland college, and later in the Huntsville (Texas) college..

John Henderson, deceased, was born in Bridgeton, Cumberland county, N. J., February 28, 1795, and was a son of a native Scotchman. At an early age he was left an orphan, but through his own efforts he acquired a good elementary education. The first business in which he engaged was trading, or flatboating, on the Mississippi river, and his leisure time on these voyages was occupied in reading Blackstone. He was finally enabled to enter the law school of Cincinnati, Ohio, and at an early day came to Natchez, Miss., where he was joined by S. S. Boyd and S. S. Prentiss on landing, thus beginning a friendship that continued without intermission during the continuance of their lives. Boyd & Prentiss remained in Natchez, but he proceeded thence to Woodville, Wilkinson county, Miss., where he at once assumed a leading position in the legal profession. He soon became famous as a pleader and orator, and won a state and national reputation. It was while here that he was married a second time to Mrs. Louisa A. Post, nee Fourniquet, in 1830, his first wife having died before he came to Mississippi. About the year 1837 he moved to Bay St. Louis on the gulf coast of Mississippi, and two years later located at Pass Christian. He aided very materially in the development and growth of this place, and much of its present prosperity is due to his foresight and generous efforts. In 1840 he was elected United States senator, and served six years, after which he resumed his practice and stood second to no member of the Southern bar. Daniel Webster said of him that he was the greatest land lawyer in the United States. In the official report of the resolutions of the bar of the supreme court of Mississippi upon his death, is found the following tribute to him: "In the legal and political career of their brother, the bar have presented a striking instance of the honors and rewards which, in a free government, await every individual who brings to the discharge of his duties earnest and persevering industry, high moral courage, and a faithful adherence to the principles of honor and integrity in his dealing with mankind. Thirty years ago the deceased came to Mississippi a stranger and unknown, without wealth, without influential friends and without the advantages which early mental training and discipline confer upon every one in the race of life; but by patient industry, unwearied application, punctilious honor and the faithful performance of his obligations to society, both as a lawyer and a man, he attained eminent rank among the members of the bar and a prominent and distinguished position as a politician in the state. The members of the bar of this court point with pride to his career as a happy illustration of the influence of American institutions upon the life and character of the citizens; and in the decease of their brother have lost one of the most eminent and distinguished among them." Mr. Henderson died at Pass Christian on the 15th of September, 1857. He had two sons who survived him: John Henderson, Jr., who died in 1866, leaving two sons, John L. Henderson, a real-estate agent and abstractor of land titles, and Louis F. Henderson, an eminent botanist, both residing in Olympia, state of Washington. Elliot Henderson, a son by the second marriage, is the only son now living. The early struggles of Mr. Henderson made him tender and considerate to the poor and oppressed. It was this feeling that prompted him to espouse the cause of the young republic of Texas, and it was mainly through his unceasing efforts in behalf of this struggling young nation that it

57

was finally annexed to the United States, and its freedom assured. And again, when Gen. Narcisso Lopez made an appeal in behalf of the oppressed people of Cuba to Mr. Henderson, he found a sympathetic listener and an open purse. Together, they inaugurated the first expedition to Cuba against Spain, under the command of Lopez, Mr. Henderson nearly bankrupting his private fortune in the undertaking. For this act he was indicted, arrested and tried at New Orleans. He was prosecuted by the United States district attorney, Thomas A. Hunton, assisted by the brilliant Judah P. Benjamin, afterward attorney-general of the Confederate states, and subsequently queen's counsel in England. Mr. Henderson defended himself, and the jury, standing eleven to one for acquittal, the government dropped the case. Elliot Henderson, his only surviving son, was born in Woodville, Wilkinson county, Miss., January 9, 1833. He received his early education in Pennsylvania and Massachusetts. While opposed to secession, he espoused the Confederate cause as soon as Mississippi severed her connection with the government of the United States, and he at once enlisted in company A, Hampton's cavalry, and served faithfully on active duty till the termination of the war. He then took up the study of law, and was admitted to the bar in 1868, since which time he has been actively engaged in practice. He was state senator for the seacoast district for the sessions of 1882 and 1884, and was a member of the constitutional convention of 1890. He has been mayor of Pass Christian, where he resides, for five years, and has used his best efforts in building up home interests. He was married in 1875 to Miss Fanny G. Hewes, a daughter of William G. Hewes, of New Orleans, who established the Bank of America in said city, and who was one of the first presidents of the Morgan railroad, and was a well-known and successful merchant of that place.

Hon. William Gaston Henderson, Handsborough, Harrison county, Miss., collector of customs, Pearl River district, Miss., was born in Milton, Caswell county, N. C., August 3, 1828, and is a son of Alexander and Mary (Wallace) Henderson. He is a lineal descendant of a long line of eminent lawyers and judges in North Carolina, and seems to be a natural judge. He is fine looking and genial, and dignified in his manners and extensively popular with all parties. His parents were natives of New Berne, N. C., and emigrated to Mobile, Ala., in 1838, where the mother died the following year. The father was a farmer by occupation, but for several years was engaged in the commission business. His planting interests were extensive, and he owned some bank stock in North Carolina, and was cashier and president of the Milton bank. He died in 1843, near Kingston, Tenn., while on a journey from North Carolina to Mobile. There were twelve children in the family, two of whom are living: Mrs. L. H. Glenn, of Memphis, Tenn., and William Gaston Henderson. He is the youngest son, and at the death of his mother, in 1839, he went to Holly Springs, Miss., to live with his brother-in-law, Judge Joseph W. Chalmers. He remained there until 1843, and then returned to North Carolina, making his home with his brother-in-law, Rawley Galloway. He attended school until he was sixteen years of age, and then began teaching. He followed this vocation for about one year, and at the end of that time took up the study of law under Judge R. M. Pearson, chief justice of the supreme court of North Carolina. For two years he was tutor to the Judge's children, giving this service for his board and tuition fee. He obtained a license from the supreme court of North Carolina to practice in the county and superior courts, and in 1851 he removed to Aberdeen, Miss., where he formed a partnership with Col. R. O. Reynolds. He continued there until 1858, when he went to Okolona, Miss., practicing his profession there until 1869. When the Civil war broke out he enlisted in the Chickasaw Rangers' cavalry company, and served as first lieutenant for one year. Upon the reconstruction of the army of Virginia in 1862 he was elected captain of company B, Jeff

Davis legion, and served under J. B. Stewart and Wade Hampton. He served as captain until June 21, 1863, when he received a gunshot wound which proved a very serious thing; he was obliged to go upon crutches two years. For gallantry on the field he was promoted by the Confederate congress to the rank of major. In 1864 he was transferred from the Virginia army to Forrest's cavalry as major and lieutenant-colonel of the Fifth Mississippi cavalry. About the close of the war he was put on the board of examiners for the promotion of officers. At Columbus, Miss., under an act of the Confederate congress of 1862 he was awarded a medal and placed on the roll of honor in acknowledgment of his gallantry in the field. There were but two Mississippi regiments in the Gettysburg campaign receiving this reward. After the cessation of hostilities he resumed his practice in Okolona, Miss., and resided there until 1869. In that year he went to Mississippi City, and formed a partnership with Judge George Wood. In 1870 he was appointed chancellor of the first chancery court district of Mississippi, by Governor Alcorn, serving four years. This was done through his friends and not by his own solicitation. In 1875 he was reappointed by Governor Ames, but was thrown out under the reconstruction of 1876. After serving two years and leaving a splendid record for sound legal judgment, having only been reversed by the supreme court in six years three times, he again took up his professional work at Mississippi City, and in 1878 was appointed collector of customs of Pearl River district, by President Hayes. He was reappointed by President Arthur, and in 1885 he was thrown out by President Cleveland. Returning to the bar, he was engaged in practice until 1889. June 26th of that year, he was appointed by President Harrison to the office he now so ably fills. He has been very successful in his profession, and has discharged the duties of the various offices he held with ability, fidelity and excellent judgment. In 1855 he was married to Miss Dona, daughter of Major David Hubbard, a prominent politician of northern Alabama. Four children of this union are living: Mrs. Laura Fowler, Dona, wife of Willian Liddle; Mary W. and William G., Jr., having lost their eldest son, David Hubbard, in 1875. Mr. Henderson was nominated by the republicans of the sixth congressional district of Mississippi, to represent them in congress, but he declined to make the race on account of ill health.

George E. Herndon was born in Elbert county, Ga., on the 25th of June, 1819, a son of Michael Herndon, a native of the Old Dominion, in which state he successfully tilled the soil until his death, in 1857. He was united in marriage to Miss Sarah J. Seale, who died in 1838 or 1839. Soon after the death of his mother George E. Herndon left the parental roof to seek his own fortune, and, although he had received a limited early education, he was naturally bright and intelligent, and being also energetic he was well calculated to fight the battle of life successfully. He came to Lowndes county, Miss., in the fall of 1839, and here began overseeing on a plantation, a calling he followed for five years. He then purchased a plantation of his own, on which he lived for about four years, then followed the calling of an overseer until 1865. He then once more returned to his plantation, the tilling of which occupied his attention up to 1891, since which time he has resided on his present plantation, which comprises four hundred and eighty acres. He is energetic and practical in his methods of doing business, and is the soul of honesty and truth in all his transactions. He was married in 1844 to Miss Louisa Copeland, who died in 1855, having borne three children: Charley Scott who died in 1867, Sarah Elizabeth, and Joseph A. Mr. Herndon's second union was to Miss Ann E. Wolfington, and was consummated in December, 1856. Her parents were David Wolfington and Miss Annie McIntyre, of Scotch descent. During the Civil war Mr. Herndon was first in the state service, and after participating in the siege of Vicksburg, he was detailed to obtain provisions, which he did. He then returned to his old home, but was again detailed to raise supplies for the Southern troops. He has been a resident of Lowndes county for over half a century, and is deeply attached to the home of his adoption, and has identified himself with every worthy interest of this section. He is a member of the Methodist Episcopal church, is a democrat in politics, and in 1868-9 served as supervisor of the county, in which capacity he was faithful to the interests of his county.

Hon. Joseph P. Henry, M. D., holds first rank among the professional men of Greenwood, Le Flore county, Miss., and is entitled to a space in this volume. He was born in Colerain, N. C., November 19, 1824. His grandfather, the Rev. Robert Henry, was a native of Colerain, Ireland, and was educated in that country. He emigrated at an early day to the United States, and settled in Virginia. Thence he removed to North Carolina, and settled in Bertie county, where he reared his family. Robert Henry, Jr., the father of Joseph P., grew to manhood in Bertie county, and there married Miss Sarah Thomas, a native of North Carolina, and a daughter of a well-known family in that community. He was a large planter and held a position of much prominence in his county. He died in 1834, his wife surviving him until 1852. There was a family of eleven children, but two of whom survive: Dr. P. T. Henry, of Kittrell, Vance county, and Dr. Joseph P. Henry. The latter passed the first eighteen years of his life in his native county, and was then sent to college by his guardian. He became a student at Water Forest, a Baptist college of North Carolina, and acquired a thorough literary education. He then went to Raleigh, N. C., where he studied medicine under the preceptorship of Dr. Charles E. Johnson, a physician of note in that city. In October, 1847, he went to New York city, and there began a course of medical studies, under the direction of Dr. Whittaker, who afterward became a professor and lectured in one of the medical colleges. Dr. Henry remained with Dr. Whittaker in study and practice until 1850, when he removed to Mississippi, and made a permanent location at Greenwood. In the practice of his profession he has won not only a reputation as a skilled practitioner, but has proven himself one of the most humane and generous beings. During the yellow-fever epidemic of 1853, and again in 1855, he stood by the sufferers, nursed the sick and buried the dead. Again, during the late Civil war, he remained stanch, firm and true, giving his professional service and ready sympathy to the people of Greenwood and the surrounding country. Let it not be supposed that this heroism has been forgotten, as many yet living hold the Doctor in grateful remembrance for the aid he rendered in their hour of trial and affliction. In addition to his professional interests, the Doctor has a large landed estate. He has over one thousand acres under cultivation, and about thirty two hundred acres in a wild state. This land is in one body and lies within the borders of Le Flore county. Although he came empty-handed to his new Southern home, by his wide practice and excellent business management he is now the owner of a fortune. December 24, 1857, Dr. Henry was united in marriage to Mrs. L. H. Jackson, a daughter of Joseph Dittoe. Mrs. Henry was born in Amite county, Miss., was reared and educated in Grenada, Miss. The Doctor has taken quite an extensive interest in local politics. He was a leading member of the whig party before the war, but since that time he has been identified with the democratic party. He was elected representative from Le Flore county in 1886, serving one term in the state legislature. He has ever striven earnestly and diligently for the welfare of his county, has been liberal with his means in supporting public measures, and is looked upon as one of the most progressive citizens. He and his estimable wife have reared two orphan children, one of whom is now the wife of A. M. Craig, a leading merchant of Greenwood, a full sketch of whom is published in this history; the other child, the daughter of a deceased brother, is now being educated at Salem, N. C.

Robert Hiram Henry. One of the most potent powers of modern civilization is the press. It enters every town and hamlet, and opens broad its pages of knowledge. No place is so remote, where civilization dwells, that it does not find an entrance. It is the great educator of the masses, and to it they turn for instruction and amusement. A journal conducted by an intelligent, honest, conscientious and liberal editor, is far reaching in its influence for good. It is one of the noblest of callings, and one in which there is an extensive field of usefulness. So thought Robert H. Henry, when he determined to be a journalist and have a newspaper of his own. Mr. Henry, of Jackson, Miss., journalist, manager, and one of the proprietors of the *Clarion-Ledger*, was born May 15, 1851, near Hillsboro, Scott county, Miss., to Patrick and Mary A. (Chambers) Henry, the latter being natives of Alabama, and emigrated to Mississippi at an early day. Mr. Henry settled in Monroe county, and Miss Chambers in Scott county. They subsequently met, a mutual attachment was formed, and they were married in 1850. The Henry family were from Virginia, and were connected with the distinguished Patrick Henry, of Revolutionary fame. Mr. Henry was a farmer and contractor, and by his wife became the father of six children: Robert H., Catherine, Thomas M., William A., Mary V. and Anna L. Mary (who was married to Albert Robertson) and Catherine are dead. Anna married Jefferson Montgomery. The second marriage of Patrick Henry was to Miss Callie Story, who bore him two children: Pattie and Honoure. When of sufficient age, Robert H. was sent to the village school at Hillsboro, but at the age of fifteen, upon his parents' removal to Forest, he entered school at that place, which he attended for about a year and a half. At the end of this time he entered the office of the Forest *Register*, to learn the art of printing and to study for the journalistic profession. He remained with the *Register* for one year, when he went to Brandon, and engaged with the *Republican*, on which paper he served for three years. In 1871 he left the *Republican*, and going to Newton, Miss., commenced his career as journalist by establishing the Newton *Ledger*. This paper was issued every Thursday, and in politics was democratic. After continuing the *Ledger* at Newton for four years, he, in 1875, removed to Brookhaven, where he purchased the *Citizen*, and conducted it with his paper under the name of the Brookhaven *Ledger*. He continued the publication of this paper for eight years, with eminent success. In 1883 he removed to Jackson, and purchased the *Comet*, which he merged into the *State Ledger*, continuing its publication with fair success.

In 1886 Mr. Henry became a candidate for state printer, and was elected after a very hard and exciting contest. With the aid of this office, the financial condition of the *Ledger* was much improved, and its success largely increased. In 1888 the *State Ledger* was consolidated with the *Clarion*, owned by Col. J. L. Power, and is now published under the name of the *Clarion-Ledger*. During this year Mr. Henry was reëlected to the office of state printer, and in 1890 was the third time honored with this office, defeating the most powerful combination ever organized in the state, a great compliment to the efficient and honest manner in which he had discharged his duties. This was one of the most stubborn contests ever held in Mississippi for any position, and attracted attention from every part of the state.

In January, 1890, Mr. Henry made the venture with a daily paper, which, like all his newspaper enterprises, proved a success. In truth, Mr. Henry is justly regarded as the most successful newspaper man in Mississippi.

In 1884 he was a delegate to the national convention at Chicago which nominated Cleveland, and was the author of the resolutions passed by that convention, in honor of Tilden and Hendricks. Mr. Vilas, who was chairman, appointed a committee of one member from each state, designating Mr. Henry as chairman, to present the resolutions in person to Mr.

Tilden. In the discharge of this honorable commission, he proceeded, with the committee, September 3, 1884, to New York, where he was met by Mr. W. M. Whitney and escorted aboard Mr. Tilden's private yacht, the Viking, in which, with the committee, he sailed up the historic Hudson to Yonkers, to the sage of Grayston's private residence. Mr. Tilden, at this time, was quite feeble, and only the chairman of the committee was presented to him. Mr. Henry had a very pleasant interview with Mr. Tilden, and presented the resolutions and a carefully prepared and appropriate address, which Mr. Tilden responded to in suitable terms. After Mr. Cleveland was inaugurated, Mr. Henry received the appointment of national bank examiner for Texas, New Mexico and Arizona, which position he held until he was elected state printer, when he resigned the former office. He was a delegate to the national convention which nominated Hancock, in 1880, and was one of the reading clerks at the last democratic national convention at St. Louis, in 1888.

The *Clarion*, which was consolidated with the *Ledger*, in 1888, was estsblished in 1837, and is the oldest continuous newspaper in the state. The *Clarion-Ledger*, as now published, is the product of Mr. Henry's perseverence, energy, experience, knowledge of journalism and the art of printing. It is the official journal of the democratic party, has a larger circulation than any Mississippi paper, and is one of the most complete newspaper plants of the country. It is an ably conducted paper, clean, bright, and instructive in its pages, prompt in furnishing the news of the day, broad and liberal in its discussion of the topics of the time, and devoted to the interests of the state, the party it represents, and its numerous patrons.

Mr. Henry is truly a self-made man. His parents being poor, were unable to give him a classical education or furnish him with the means to begin business. Thus thrown upon his own resources at an early age, he owes his success in life to his untiring energy, perseverance and ambition. While carrying out, unaided, his ambitious projects, he was not selfish, but generously assisted his brothers and sisters in their education, his mother dying the first year of his marriage. He was married November 22, 1871, at Brandon, to Ida W., daughter of Thomas H. Johnson, of that place. There has been born to them seven children: Robert H., Jr., Thomas P., Mary W., Annie L., Miller C., Ida V. and Houston H., all of whom are living, with the exception of Annie and Houston.

William H. Hendrick, of the firm of Hendrick & Wilds, liverymen and mule dealers of Natchez, was born in Jessamine county, Ky., in 1822, and although but a recent arrival in the beautiful town of Natchez he has won the confidence and esteem of all by his courteous manners, fair dealing and general integrity. He and family stand very high socially. Mr. Hendrick's father, Joseph W., was born and reared in Hanover county, Va., and soon after the war he went to southern Kentucky, thence to Jessamine county, Ky., where his death occurred. He was a self-made man, was quite wealthy, and was moral, honest and industrious. He married Miss Mary Tillman, who also died in Jessamine county. Their family consisted of four sons and four daughters, two of whom are now able Presbyterian ministers in Kentucky: James P. and John T., both of whom were educated at Danville, Ky.; another son, the subject of this sketch, William H., was educated in the common schools of Kentucky, and until his removal to Natchez, Adams county, in 1882, he followed farming and stockraising with marked success. He has made a specialty of buying and selling mules all his life, and few are better judges of that animal than he. He still continues that business quite extensively, and makes the livery business a secondary matter. He owns two of the best livery barns in Natchez besides a fine residence property. Like his father, Mr. Hendrick has made all his property by his own exertions, and is one of the shrewd, experienced business men of the place. He is a genial and pleasant gentleman to meet, and is a devout

Christian. He has been married three times, first to Miss Elizabeth Howe, a native of the blue grass regions of Kentucky, who died in that state, leaving six children, four now living: one in Kansas City, one in Chicago and two in Kentucky. Mr. Hendrick's second marriage occurred in 1861 to Miss Susan Stockwell, of Natchez. She died while on a visit to New Orleans after the war, and his third marriage was with Mrs. Fannie (Bradley) Boutura, a native of Henry county, Ky., who came to Natchez with her parents when a girl, and was there married to Mr. Boutura. Mr. Hendrick resided in his native county until about twenty-one years of age, and then went to Fleming county, Ky., and there resided until his removal to Natchez, Adams county, Miss., in 1882. He has been a member of the I. O. O. F. since attaining his majority, also a Mason for many years, and is now a member of Andrew Jackson lodge of Natchez. He and wife are prominent members of the Presbyterian church in that city.

W. F. Herrin, manager of the Pascagoula Lumber company of Moss Point, is a native of the state of Alabama, and was reared in the section which was then Macon county. Until he was eighteen years of age he was employed on a farm. Not being desirous of following agricultural pursuits all his life, he went to Florida and investigated the lumber resources of that state. In 1874 he came to Moss Point, Miss., as a lumber inspector, a position which he filled for different firms until 1886. The Pascagoula Lumber company, recognizing his ability acquired from years of experience, made him manager of their establishment. They have a capital stock of $100,000, and own two mills; they employ about two hundred men, and do an immense business, their annual output being twenty-five million feet of lumber, which they ship to all parts of the world. They own ten barges, and keep the mills open all the year. They own several thousand acres of pine timber lands, and have been very prosperous and successful. Mr. Herrin is a gentleman who is thoroughly acquainted with the minutest details of the business, and has served his employers with a fidelity and loyalty to their interests that have won for him their entire confidence. In 1876 he was married to Miss Sarah Baird, of Mobile, Ala., and they have had seven children. Mr. Herrin is a member of the Masonic order, the I. O. O. F., and Knights of Honor.

S. L. Herring was born in Hinds county, Miss., in October, 1839, the youngest of six children born to Samuel and Harriet (Fairchild) Herring, the former a native of South Carolina and the latter of Georgia. Samuel Herring was a carpenter by trade, but farmed the greater part of his life, this calling being his occupation at the time of his death in 1843. He inherited English blood of his ancestors, who settled in South Carolina at a very early period. S. L. Herring attended the common schools until about the age of eighteen years, then took charge of his mother's plantation, and made his home with her until her death in 1878, at which time he inherited one hundred and sixty acres of her estate. At different times he has added to this land, and of two thousand acres, of which he is now the owner, he has about one thousand five hundred acres under cultivation. He raises about three hundred and twenty bales of cotton each year, seven thousand bushels of corn, and runs two cottongins for his own and neighborhood use. He has stock in the Merchants' National bank of Vicksburg, and, with the notes and mortgages which he holds, he has about $20,000 on deposit. In the first part of the war he enlisted in company C, Third Mississippi, Johnston's army, and took part in all the battles in and around Vicksburg. He was captured at Jackson and sent to Camp Morton, Indianapolis, Ind., where he remained until the close of the war. During this time he lost all the property he had, with the exception of his land, and upon his return home after the war was over he had to commence anew. He made hard work and close economy his watchwords, and his untiring efforts have resulted in the accumulation of a handsome competency. He was first married in 1868 to Miss Maggie Ragan, but a few months after their marriage his wife died. His second marriage took place in 1870 to Miss Sallie Yellowley, a native of Madison county, Miss., by whom he had four children: Willie, Edna, Robert and Maud. Mr. Herring has taken much interest in educating his children, and is giving them good advantages to become intelligent and useful citizens. He and his family are members of the Baptist church, and he belongs to the Knights of Honor.

Jefferson T. Herrington, of the firm of Herrington, Dubose & Hill, dealers in general merchandise, cotton, wool and country produce at Ellisville, Miss., was born in Jones county, Miss., May 9, 1852, a son of Darling and Martha A. (Walters) Herrington. The father was a native of South Carolina and was born in 1812. At an early age he emigrated to Jones county, Miss., where he resided until his death which occurred September 17, 1887. The mother was born in Jones county, Miss., December 2, 1821. They were married in Jones county, and afterward settled near Ellisville, where Mr. Herrington died, Mrs. Herrington surviving him and making her home with her children. They were the parents of sixteen sons and daughters: Mary E., Jesse, Rebecca, Jackson, Joel and Joseph (twins), Jasper, Sallie, Julia A., Jefferson T., Jordon A., Lovina, Morgan H., Martin B., Dicey and Darling J. Jefferson T., the immediate subject of this sketch, was educated at the home schools and at the Rawls' Springs school, and about 1875 began teaching, which profession he followed during the next five years. While thus engaged, he was married December 27, 1876, to Miss Celetta M., a daughter of Benjamin and Margaret (Collins) Bynum, who bore him six children: Nora V., Floyd, Beulah P. (deceased), Maud, Thomas J. (deceased), and Bessie. Mrs. Herrington was born in Jones county, Miss., in October, 1853. In March, 1878, Mr. Herrington purchased land ten miles north of Ellisville, upon which he settled, and was engaged in planting until 1883, when he took up his residence in Ellisville, engaging in business here as a member of his present firm, in October, 1889. It is due in no small measure to Mr. Herrington's business capacity and devotion to the interests of the concern that it has taken such a high rank among the leading mercantile establishments in this part of the state. He is a public-spirited man, who, since his residence here, has availed himself of every opportunity to assist movements having for their object the building up of the local business interests and the good of the community at large. He is a member of the Masonic order and of the Knights of Pythias, and he and his wife are members of the Baptist church.

James R. Herrington, Rio, Kemper county, Miss., was born in Kemper county, Miss., May 15, 1839, and is a son of John and Phœbe (Bates) Herrington. The father was born in Georgia, and was a son of Harvey Herrington. He was reared amid the scenes of his birth, and when he left home went to Alabama, where he was married. He then removed to Florida, and in 1833 he came to Kemper county, Miss., and entered government land. He reared a family of eight children: Elizabeth, Sarah, William H., John A., Hampton J., James R., George R. and Joseph A. The father died in Neshoba county in 1874. He was an acceptable minister of the Baptist church, and a man of broad, public spirit. The mother of our subject was born in South Carolina, and died in Kemper county, Miss., in 1886; she was a worthy member of the Baptist church. James R. was reared to the occupation of a planter, and received his education in this state. In 1862 he enlisted in company D, Thirty-sixth Mississippi volunteer infantry, and participated in some of the most noted of the battles of the Civil war. He was wounded at Iuka by a gunshot in the face, the marks of which he carries to this day. He was with the army from Resaca to the end of the Georgia campaign; he was also in the sieges of Atlanta and Vicksburg; was with Hood in Tennessee, and was at

Blakely at the time of the surrender. He was in the service about four years, and was twice taken prisoner. Shortly after the close of the war he settled in Kemper county, which he has since made his home. He owns fourteen hundred acres of land, of which he cultivates two hundred successfully, the balance being timbered land. He also owns a steam-saw, gristmill and cottongin. He was married in 1861 to Miss Harriet A. Emmons, a daughter of Daniel and Eliza (Weather) Emmons, natives of Virginia. Mrs. Herrington is a native of Kemper county, Miss., where her parents settled at an early day. Mr. and Mrs. Herrington have had born to them twelve children, seven of whom are living: James J., Hampton J., Emma D., Thomas J., Samuel E., John A. and Iva C. Those deceased are George R., Eliza, Wiley R., Sallie and Catherine. George R. married and had one child, Iona. James J. married Elizabeth Bankston, and has three children: Robert L., J. J. and Lettie Lee. Hampton J. married Martha Hendon, and they have one child, Lillie. Emma D. married J. E. Ward, and they have one child, Ivan. Mr. Herrington is a member of Longstreet lodge No. 268, A. F. & A. M., and also belongs to the chapter and council. He is identified with the Farmers' Alliance and votes the democratic ticket. His wife is a member of the Baptist church, and he has always been a liberal supporter of movements of both the church and state which have for their object the elevation of humanity.

John T. Hester was born in Copiah county, April 11, 1857. His father, Ephriam Hester, was a son of Thomas and Martha Hester, both of whom lived and died in North Carolina, and he was born in that state August 15, 1813, and was left an orphan at an early age and his education in consequence was somewhat limited. He removed with his mother to Rankin county about 1841, and in 1844 removed to Copiah county, where he met and married Miss Mary A. Price, a native of Copiah county and who was born in 1827. She was a daughter of Charles and Isabel (Bufkin) Price. Her parents were natives of South Carolina, who removed to Mississippi about 1820. Ephriam Hester reared four children, named Martha A., the wife of L. Q. Wright, of Copiah county; John T., our subject; Isabel, educated at Hillman college, the wife of Robert O'Quinn, of Copiah county, and Sallie E., educated at Hillman college, who is unmarried and lives at home. The father was a lifelong planter, and he and his wife were members of the Baptist church. He died February 4, 1875, and his widow still survives him, living on the old homestead. John T. Hester was educated at the common schools in vogue in his youth, near his boyhood home. At the death of his father, which occurred before he should have left school, he was compelled to assume control of his father's estate, of which he has been in charge to the present time. In 1880 he purchased three hundred and twenty acres of land adjoining the old homestead on the north, and two years later he purchased two hundred and forty acres more, which is principally woodland. He has now about one hundred and seventy acres of that land under cultivation, growing principally corn and cotton. He gives considerable attention to the raising of horses, cattle, hogs and sheep. He is also interested in fruit-growing, and has about five thousand trees set out, many of which are of a bearing age, including peach, pear, plum and apple trees. He does not make cotton his principal crop, but grows corn, oats, potatoes, grasses, peas and other things. In 1884 Mr. Hester married Miss Mollie Strahan, a daughter of Dr. William and Martha Strahan, and a native of Copiah county. They have three children, named William E., Mary A. and John S. Our subject is of modest bearing, genial, whole-souled and hospitable, one of those quiet, unassuming men, who takes great interest in the affairs of the community, but makes no boasts of what he has accomplished. His farm is in a good state of cultivation and is well improved and provided with modern conveniences which is worthy of note in view of the fact that when he located here it may be truly said he settled in the woods. He is a member of the Hazlehurst lodge of Knights of Honor, and is a charter member of the Copiah lodge No. 60, Knights of Pythias.

F. S. Hewes, circuit and chancery clerk, Harrison county, Miss., was born in New Orleans, La., May 25, 1830, and is a son of William G. Hewes. His father emigrated from Massachusetts, his native state, to Louisiana in 1818, and settled in New Orleans. He was a merchant and was president of two banks, the Commercial bank and the Bank of America, and of the New Orleans & Opelousas railroad. He died in 1861. The mother of our subject was a native of England, and her maiden name was Maria Kentlearle. F. S. Hewes was brought up in New Orleans, and spent part of his school days there, and a part in Mississippi, he went to California in 1849, overland, and remained there about five years. He was associated with his father in business for several years, and became familiar with the exact methods which had insured his father's success. In 1861 he enlisted in company H, Third Mississippi volunteer infantry, and served until the surrender. When the war was ended he went to Pass Christian and embarked in the lumber business, running a sawmill in connection with it. In 1875 he was elected to the office of chancery and circuit clerk, and has held it continuously since, having been elected for five terms, four times without opposition. He has discharged the duties of the office with fidelity and ability that have won the confidence of the entire community. He was married in 1856 to Miss Cora S. Newton, and eleven children were born of the union, all of whom are living. His second marriage was to Mrs. Fannie Laun, daughter of Gen. Wirt Adams, and they have four children. Mr. Hewes is a member of the Masonic fraternity and is deeply interested in that body. He is a citizen thoroughly loyal to home enterprise, and has always contributed to those movements which had for their object the elevation of society.

Hon. Samuel Hickman, a prominent farmer, miller, and one of the best citizens of Lawrence county, is a resident of Monticello. He was born in Pike county, Miss., in 1827. He is a son of Aaron and Eleanor (Sandifer) Hickman, natives of South Carolina. His father came to Mississippi when a young man, with his mother and other members of the family, about 1810, and were among the earliest settlers of this state. They located on Topisaw creek, now in Pike county, where he grew to maturity, married and engaged in farming. His mother died some time between 1838 and 1840; she was a daughter of Faraday Tyler, a native of South Carolina. Her husband died in that state previous to the removal to Mississippi. They had eight children, four of whom were sons, all of whom lived to maturity, and all of whom are now dead. The father of our subject was the youngest of these children; they all came to Mississippi at the same time, and some of the sons, having been previously married, brought their families with them. William Hickman was the eldest, and he and his brothers Daniel and Aaron were married. They all located on Topisaw creek, and here they lived the remainder of their lives. William served in the War of 1812, under Jackson at New Orleans. All were members of the Baptist church. William N. Sandifer, the father of the mother of Samuel Hickman, was born in Barnwell district, S. C., in 1802, and came to Mississippi with her parents. Her father was a native of South Carolina, who came to this county soon after the Hickmans, locating also on Topisaw creek, where he became a planter, and where he died in 1850, at a very advanced age. He had a family of four sons and two daughters, all of whom lived to maturity. He was in his time a prominent democrat of the old school. The mother of our subject was the next to the youngest in her father's family in the order of birth, and, in common with others of her generation in this locality, had but limited educational advantages. Her parents, who were tillers of the soil, removed in 1846 to a place on Pearl river, where they lived until their deaths. The father died in 1876, aged eighty-six years; the mother died in 1862. Both were members of the Baptist church, and the former was in politics a democrat. They had a large family of children, seven of whom were sons and all of whom lived to maturity; four of them are living at the present time: Mrs. Faraday Jones is the widow of A. V. Jones; Samuel Hickman; Joshua Hickman served during the early period of the late war in the Confederate army; Allie is the wife of Monroe Sills and lives in this county; Charles died of typhoid fever; William A. died during the war; Jesse, who enlisted in the late war in the army from South Carolina, for service during the Civil war, and died at New Orleans of smallpox; Willis died at home; George W. was captured during the late war and has never been heard of since; Rebecca became the wife of Bird Brister, who survives her; Elizabeth H. was the wife of G. W. Reeves, and she and her husband are both deceased; Martha died unmarried. The boyhood of our subject was passed in Lawrence county. His educational advantages were limited, but he attended the Piney woods school about three months. Being naturally a lover of books, he has supplemented his limited education by general reading, in which he has persisted during most of his life. He began business life for himself soon after he became of age. In 1851 he was married and settled on a river below Monticello, Miss., removing to his present place in 1863, where he has since resided and engaged successfully in planting, milling, etc. During the year of his arrival here he built a sawmill, cottongin and gristmill, which he has operated since and which have been not only a source of profit to him, but of great convenience to the surrounding planters. Starting out with no capital, but being possessed of great energy and having confined himself closely to business enterprises, he has steadily gained financially until he is regarded as one of the well-to-do men of the county. His wife was Miss Amanda J. Smith, a native of Lincoln county, Miss., and a daughter of Isaac Smith. Her father was born in South Carolina and became a leading planter of Lincoln county, where he died in 1855. His wife, who was Miss Sallie Dickerson, was also a native of Mississippi and died some years before her husband. To this union five children were born—two sons and three daughters — of whom Mrs. Hickman was the youngest and is the only one now living. The others were: Tabitha (the wife of Judge Louis Maxwell, both of whom are now dead), Martin, Derrell, Dennon are all deceased. Her father married for his second wife Miss Lewis, by whom he had three sons and four daughters who are living and one child who is dead. Mrs. Hickman was reared and educated in what is now Lincoln county, making her home with John Dickerson until her marriage with Mr. Hickman. To Mr. and Mrs. Hickman have been born five children, one of whom is deceased. Of these Isaac A. is a merchant in Monticello and a leading planter of this county, who is married and has three children; Jesse W. lives near Vicksburg, where he is engaged in planting; Sallie A., one of the brightest, most beautiful and accomplished young ladies of Lawrence county, was recently married to Dr. T. H. Butler, a prominent physician and son of H. D. and R. J. (Longino) Butler; William C. is living in Texas, and Samuel D., who died in infancy. Mr. and Mrs. Hickman have one of the pleasantest homes in the county, and are noted for their hospitality and their charity, and are held in the highest regard by all who know them. During all his life Mr. Hickman has not only devoted his personal attention to his business interests, but with willing hands has himself taken hold to assist in whatever work was to be done. This fact, taken in connection with his ability and business management and the high reputation and unlimited credit which his well-known honor and integrity have given him, accounts for his great success in life. In politics he is a democrat. In 1861 he was elected a member of the police board. In 1882 he was elected to represent his county in the legislature. He is exceptionally well posted on the political history of our country, and is conversant with the leading topics of the day. He is a member of Eastern Star lodge No. 76, A. F. & A. M, of Monticello, and he and his wife are members of the Baptist church.

Allen M. Hicks, Myrleville, Miss., one of the most popular officials Yazoo county has ever known, was born in Maury county, Tenn., June 5, 1835, and is a son of George and Julia A. (Gantt) Hicks, natives of Virginia and Maryland, respectively. The father was a merchant by occupation, and did some ministerial work in the Methodist Episcopal church. From 1843 to 1847 he represented Neshoba, Attala and Leake counties in the senate of Mississippi, and he also represented Leake county in the legislature. He removed to Yazoo county in 1847, and died the following year. The mother died of yellow fever, in 1853. They reared a family of ten children, of whom the subject of this notice is the only surviving member. Mr. Hicks spent his school days at Oxford university, but he was compelled to give up his college course in the junior year, on account of poor health. In his nineteenth year he began farming on the plantation where he has since resided. During the late Civil war, he was for two years in the commissary department, as his health would not permit of his going into more active service. Politically, he is identified with the democratic party, whose policy he has always zealously supported. He was elected to the state legislature in 1875, and was reëlected in 1877 and 1879. In 1881 he was appointed county superintendent of education, which office he held until 1889, when he resigned, having been elected to the state senate, a position which he still holds. During the time he was superintendent of education he gave universal satisfaction, both to teachers and patrons, and is held in kindest remembrance by all with whom he came in contact. In 1859 he joined the Masonic order, in which he has risen to a high degree and attained considerable prominence. He has been junior grand warden of the grand lodge of Mississippi, and deputy grand master; for the past ten years he has held the office of D. D. G. M. He was master of the county grange during the palmy days of that organization, and for one year was overseer of the state grange. He is a member of the Farmers' Alliance, and is one of the directors of the alliance manufacturers. In all these various positions he has shown marked executive ability, and a fitness for public business, which the people of Yazoo county have not been slow to recognize. Mr. Hicks was united in marriage, in Yazoo county, Miss., in 1861, to Miss Martha Bostick, a daughter of Capt. Ferd Bostick, one of Mississippi's most gallant soldiers, who fell at Malvern, near Richmond, Va. Mr. and Mrs. Hicks have had born to them four children: Addie J., wife of W. A. Crouch, deceased; Lillie B., wife of H. D. Wiley; Mattie D., wife of Dr. C. B. Holmes, and Allen G. Mr. Hicks has been one of the important factors in the growth of Yazoo county, and to him is due much credit for the phenomenal progress made since the days of the war.

Joseph G. Hicks, M. D., of Warren county, Miss., was born in Vicksburg in 1841, and comes of excellent stock. His parents Joseph T. and Mary M. (Cowen) Hicks, were born in North Carolina and Mississippi respectively, the former inheriting English blood of his ancestors and the latter English and Irish blood. The paternal great-grandfather brought with him to this country his coat of arms, having belonged to a very aristocratic family of his native land, and after reaching America settled in Rhode Island, where he resided until his death. His son, the grandfather of Dr. Hicks, removed to North Carolina, where he turned his attention to planting and reared his family. He was quite successful in his operations, acquired considerable property and died prior to the war with Mexico. The father of Dr. Hicks was educated in Virginia and became a leading resident of his state. He moved to Vicksburg about 1838, and until his death, in 1841, was a prosperous planter. His widow survived him until 1887, when she, too, passed away. Dr. Joseph G. Hicks was their only child. He received his rudimentary education in the schools of Vicksburg and at the age of fourteen years entered St. James' college of Washington county, Md., in which institution he remained one term. He then completed his junior term in Hampton-Sidney college of Virginia and when eighteen years of age began attending a commercial college of New Orleans, from which institution he graduated in 1860. Upon the opening of the Civil war he joined company A, Twenty-first Mississippi infantry, but was put upon the retired list on account of ill health and afterwards joined Cowan's battery and was made sergeant of company G, First regiment, Mississippi artillery. He participated in the following battles: Baker's creek, Jackson, Miss., Dalton, Resaca, besides numerous engagements of less note. Just after the battle of New Hope church he was wounded in the right hand by a sharpshooter, was placed on the retired list and was left at Jackson, Miss. At the close of war he returned home broken in health, and a financial bankrupt with the exception of his plantation, which had been laid waste. He set to work at once to repair the damage done and until 1869 was engaged in planting. He then entered the medical department of Tulane university of New Orleans, in which he remained during the sessions of 1869–70, and 1870–71 attended the Louisville medical college, where he graduated. He then returned to his home and upon the old homestead entered upon the practice of his profession. It has for many years been extensive and lucrative, but of late years he has almost wholly devoted his attention to planting, being the owner of four hundred and eighty acres of land, with about three hundred acres under cultivation, on which is raised annually from seventy-five to one hundred bales of cotton. He is a member of Bovina lodge No. 112, of the A. F. & A. M., in which order he is an active member. He is fine looking, is a talented and intellectual gentleman and is perfectly honorable in all his business transactions. He is unmarried.

Robert H. Hicks, chancery and circuit clerk of Greenwood, Le Flore county, Miss., was born in Lauderdale county, Ala., May 26, 1838. Dr. John C. Hicks, his father, was a native of Virginia; he was a man of superior ability, and acquired a fine education in his profession. When a young man he went to Tennessee, and was married in Nashville, to Anna N. Waters, a native of Maryland; however, she had been reared and educated in Nashville. Dr. Hicks settled in northern Alabama at an early day, and was engaged in the practice of his profession there for a number of years. In 1837 he removed to Mississippi, and located in what is now Carroll county; here he resumed his professional work, and also gave some attention to planting up to the time of his death, which occurred in August, 1865. He had long been identified with the history of Carroll county, having settled there when it was a part of Sunflower county; he was the first probate clerk of the latter county, and was highly esteemed throughout the community. He was a soldier in the War of 1812, and was a member of General Jackson's staff. Mrs. Hicks survived her husband several years; she passed away about the year 1875. She was a sister-in-law of Dr. Robinson, of Nashville, who was said to be the first white male child born in that city. Robert H. Hicks, son of the above, is one of a family of four sons and three daughters, who grew to mature years. The eldest brother, Dr. Bernard Hicks, is deceased; John W. is a merchant in Greenwood; D. W. is a planter in northern Alabama. Robert H. spent his youth in Carroll county; he attended the Wesleyan university at Florence, Ala., and there received a good education. After finishing his studies he clerked for a time, and also was interested in planting. In April, 1861, he entered the Confederate army, enlisting in the Eleventh Mississippi infantry; he served until the close of the war; he participated in the battle of Seven Pines, the seven days' fight around Richmond, was at Gettysburg and Sharpsburg, and the principal engagements in northern Virginia; he was paroled at Appomattox, Va., and after the close of the war he returned to Carroll county.

Soon after he came to what is Le Flore county, and for a number of years was clerking at Sheppardtown. In April, 1885, he was elected chancery and circuit clerk to fill an unexpired term. At the general election in 1887 he was reëlected to this office, discharging his duties with decided ability, and a quick sense of the demands of the position. He is a candidate for reëlection, and will doubtless win in the race in the fall of 1891. He is also the treasurer of Greenwood, and takes an active interest in the welfare of the city. Mr. Hicks was married in Carroll county, Miss., August 18, 1868, to Miss Phie Merrell, daughter of the Hon. J. W. S. Merrell. Mrs. Hicks was born, reared, and educated in Carroll county. She is the mother of seven children: Robert H., Jr., Mary Belle, Bernard, Waters, Lucy, Alice, and Rosa Lee. The parents are members of the Methodist Episcopal church, and are active workers in all movements for the advancement of the public interests. Mr. Hicks is a member of the Masonic fraternity, and also belongs to the Knights of Pythias and the Knights of Honor.

Dr. J. A. Hill, Craigs, Yazoo county, Miss., was born in York county, S. C., in 1816, and is a son of Solomon and Nancy (Cabeen) Hill. Col. William Hill, his grandfather, was a soldier in the war of the Revolution. His father spent his life in South Carolina, and died there in 1826. The mother survived until 1852, passing away in Yazoo county, Miss. There were eight children in the family, of whom the Doctor was the fourth and is the only surviving member: W. Randolph Hill, a man well-known in Yazoo county, died in 1868; Thomas died in 1844; Judge A. P. Hill died in Canton, Miss., in 1868; Gen. D. H. Hill died in Charlotte, N. C., in 1890; he was a general in the Confederate army. Dr. Hill was educated in his native state, but in 1842 he removed to Yazoo county, Miss., and engaged in planting. Here he studied medicine, and was graduated from the Louisville Medical college, Ky. He practiced two years on Silver creek, and in 1849 when the gold fever swept the country he went to California, where he remained until 1862; he was engaged in mining, merchandising and irrigation, and also did some medical practice. When he came back to Mississippi he settled again on Silver creek, where he has since been carrying on the plantation in the interest of his brothers' heirs. He is a member of the Masonic lodge, has always taken an active interest in political questions, and has been one of the leading men of the community. He is the last representative of one of the prominent families of antebellum days.

Col. James L. S. Hill, a retired planter, has been a resident of Mississippi since 1855, but was born in Chester county, S. C., in 1818, a son of Moses B. and Mary (Glenn) Hill, the former of whom was also born in Fairfield county, S. C. During his early life he received a good education, and fitted himself for a teacher, which profession he followed the remainder of his days, winning an enviable reputation for thoroughness and discipline. In connection with this occupation he followed the calling of a civil engineer, the most of his vacations being devoted to surveying. To himself and wife a family of four children were born: Moses, Mary (deceased), Sarah S. (Gregory), and James L. S. Mr. Hill inherited Irish and Scotch blood of his ancestors. His maternal grandfather was a soldier in the Revolutionary war, as was also his wife's paternal great-grandfather, both of whom fought bravely and well for the cause of the colonists, the former being in the command of General Washington. The early life of James L. S. Hill was spent as a clerk in his uncle's store, in Union county, S. C., after which he went into the mercantile business for himself, but devoted the greater part of his attention to planting, to which calling he had been reared, and of which he had a thorough, practical knowledge. He has been successful as a financier, and as age began to creep upon him he found his means sufficiently ample to permit his retirement from the active duties of life, and is now in the enjoyment of a comfortable income. He has a beautiful and comfortable residence in Okolona, and here he and his worthy wife dispense a generous hospitality. His fine mental qualities fitted him in an eminent degree for a successful public career, and during the four terms that he was a member of the Mississippi legislature he demeaned himself as a legislator of ability, honor, and activity, and was always faithful in the discharge of every duty. He also served efficiently in the capacity of sheriff of Chickasaw county for one term. In 1846 he was married to Miss Mary Sartor, who died after having borne him three children, all of whom are deceased. His second union was to Miss Margaret A. Beaty, of South Carolina, a daughter of Robert and Mary (McKey) Beaty, who were of Scotch-Irish descent, and whose fathers were in the Revolutionary war. Mr. Hill and his wife are worthy members and liberal supporters of the Methodist Episcopal church South, and, in fact, give liberally of their means to enterprises of a worthy nature. He has been a member of the Masonic fraternity for about thirty years. He entered the Confederate army as captain of company C, Thirty-first regiment, Mississippi volunteers. After about two years of service he returned to his home, and later served on post duty in the state troops, holding the office of colonel. His career throughout life has been one of usefulness and activity, and he has, and fully deserves, the respect of all who know him.

Nathan C. Hill, of Ellisville, Jones county, Miss., was born in Smith county, in this state, July 26, 1857, and is one of the most prominent men in the town above mentioned. His parents were Israel and Mary (Martin) Hill, both natives of Jasper county, Ga., where the former was born in 1806, the latter in 1812, and where they were married. Subsequently they removed to Alabama, and thence at an early day to Smith county, Miss., where the father died in June, 1881, the mother, who still survives him, living in Smith county. They became the parents of ten children: Sarah, Caroline, Susan, Mary, Amanda, Elijah, William T., Joseph M., Fannie C., and Nathan C.—the subject of this sketch, and the youngest of the family. Mr. Hill was educated in the subscription schools of Smith county, and at Neophogen college, at Gallatin, Tenn. In January, 1878, he began reading law with Judge E. Currie, of Raleigh, Miss., and on October 18 of the same year was admitted to the bar, having been examined by the following board: Gen. Robert Lowery, Maj. Samuel H. Terrall, and Judge E. Currie. Immediately after his admittance to the bar Mr. Hill went to Paulding, Miss., and began the practice of law, which he continued at that place until November, 1880, when he went to Yazoo City, Miss., and there practiced his profession until December, 1881. From that time until February, 1883, he was again a resident and a legal practitioner at Paulding, and at the date last mentioned came to Ellisville, where he has since successfully pursued his professional career. He occupies the first law office built for that purpose in Jones county—a beautiful wooden structure divided into three commodious compartments. His large library is unsurpassed for value and completeness by any legal library in southern Mississippi. It may be said of Mr. Hill that he has rapidly won his way to a high standing in his profession, having acquired an extensive and quite lucrative practice, and has gained the highest approbation from his brother practitioners. In connection with his law practice he devotes a portion of his time to the business of the firm of Herrington, Dubose & Hill, dealers in general merchandise, cotton, wool, etc., of which he is a member. Mr. Hill was married at Raleigh, Miss., January 6, 1879, to Lou Mangum, a daughter of James A. Mangum, who has been for thirteen successive years sheriff of Smith county. This estimable lady died July 2, 1883, after bearing him two children: Horace and Fannie, both of whom are deceased. October 9, 1884, Mr. Hill married Hattie D. Gatlin, a daughter of Edward Gatlin, who was born at Shubuta, Clarke county, Miss., January 18, 1865. Mr. and Mrs. Hill have four children: Claude E., Ethel, Nathan C., Jr., and Hattie. Mr. Hill is a member of the Masonic order, and he and his wife are communicants of the

Baptist church.   Mr. Hill has established his reputation for public enterprise and spirit, unsurpassed by that of any of his fellow-citizens, and since his residence here, Ellisville has had in him a stanch and trusty friend.

Phelix J. Hill, Blackland, one of the most enterprising farmers of the county, was born in Alabama in 1847, and was next to the youngest of twelve children, five sons and seven daughters, born to G. B. and Nancy N. (Hicks) Hill, both native Virginians.   The father was a farmer by occupation.   He moved from the Old Dominion to Tennessee, thence to Alabama and settled on a farm in Lauderdale county, where he continued to cultivate the soil until his death in 1852.   The mother is still living and makes her home with her son Phelix J.   She is a worthy member of the Methodist church.   Their children were named in the order of their births as follows: Thomas J. (resides in Arkansas and has a wife and three children), Andrew I. (resides in Prentiss county, Miss., is married and has nine children: Josephine, Henrietta, Luther, Fannie, Letha, Wess, Luda, Lelia and Richard), Ellen (widow of William English, resides in Texas with her two children: Cordelia G. and Mary A.), Mary (wife of Alex. Neley, is the widow of Thomas Bradshaw, by whom she had three children: Minnie, Fannie and Ellen), Misniar (wife of B. F. Windham, resides in Arkansas and is the mother of twelve children), Nancy A. (wife of William Glover, resides in Prentiss county and is the mother of one child, Oscar), Henry (was killed at the first battle of Manassas, and was buried on the battlefield), William J. (died and left a wife and three children: William, James and Polira), Sarah (was the wife of Neal Rodgers and died leaving one child, Henry), Saludy (was the wife of Robert Johnson and died leaving five children: Willie, Phelix, Henry, Cordelia and Ida), and Artimissa (died when young).   Phelix J. Hill came to Mississippi with his mother when a boy, received his education in the common school of that state, and started out to fight life's battles for himself as a farmer.   He located on his present property and in 1867 was married to Miss Margaret P. Windham, a native of Mississippi, born in 1848 and the daughter of Sim and Eleanor (James) Windham, whose nine children were named in the order of their birth as follows: Simon, Benjamin, Jack, Susan, Anna, Harriet, William (deceased), Wess (deceased), and Margaret P. (deceased).   To Mr. and Mrs. Hill were born four children: Dr. J., William T., Francis A. and Arthur T., all with or near their father. After the death of his first wife, or in 1877, Mr. Hill was married to Miss Amanda E. Garner, who was born in Mississippi in 1856, and who was one of eleven children born to Garner and Phœbe E. (Blaylock) Garner.   The children were named in the order of their births as follows: Mattie, Thomas, Samuel, John, Alonzo, Amanda, Starling, Phœbe, William C., Anna L. and Andrew (deceased).   By his second marriage Mr. Hill became the father of five children: Jennie, Pink, Horace, Lillie and Milton E., all at home with their parents.   Socially Mr. Hill is a member of the Knights of Honor.   In politics he is a stanch democrat, cast his first presidential vote for Horace Greeley, and has voted that ticket ever since.   He is a supporter of all worthy enterprises, and is one of the representative citizens of the county. He owns a large farm, nicely located and well improved.   He is a Methodist in his belief and his wife is a member of the Baptist church.

Robert Andrews Hill was born in Iredell county, N. C., on the 25th day of March, 1811.   His paternal grandfather, Robert Hill, and maternal grandfather, James Andrews, as well as his grandmothers, were Scotch-Irish, and emigrated from Ireland to Pennsylvania, and from there moved to Iredell and Rowan counties, N. C., at an early day. His father, David Hill, and his mother, Rhoda Andrews, were married in 1804, and continued to reside in Iredell county until September, 1816, when they removed, first to Giles county and thence to Williamson county, Tennessee, where their son Robert was brought up,

E. A. Rowan

and remained until December, 1844. His father was a man of strong intellect, and more than ordinary culture for a private and unpretending citizen in his day and time. His mother was a woman of fine intellect, well read, and of more than ordinary thrift and energy. They had but the one son and four daughters, two older and two younger than the son. His father settled on a tract of land, heavily timbered, and in clearing it in 1821 broke down his constitution, from which he never recovered, although he lived until September, 1843, when he died at his home on the farm he was opening. The only property owned by him at the time his health gave way was the little farm, and the usual amount of personal property then owned by small farmers. Then the support of the family, consisting of the father, mother, and seven children, fell on the mother and children, Robert being only ten years old, and at that age he commenced plowing, and did all other labor of which he was capable. The following year he did all the plowing save three days done by a hired man, which produced a sufficiency of corn to support the family, and he so continued to work until 1831, when he cultivated a small field on Saturday and taught school the balance of the week, having rented out the balance of the farm. The only opportunity he had for attending school was a few weeks after laying by the crops before fodder pulling, and a few weeks before gathering the crops, and a few weeks in the winter, but seldom a whole week at a time, as he had all the wood to cut and haul, and to cut for the fires, and all the milling to do. The schools attended were the most ordinary old fieldschools of that day, with the exception of three months spent with a good teacher, which time he devoted to the more advanced English studies, and five months to the same teacher in 1832. The balance of the education he acquired was at home, aided by his father. No time was spared from his books when not at work or attending to other business. He taught school a part of the years 1833 and 1834. In 1833 he married Miss Mary Andrews, with whom he has lived until the present time, nearly fifty-eight years. In October, 1834, he was elected constable of his district, and served until March, 1836, when he was elected justice of the peace, which office he held until December, 1844, when he resigned to enter the practice of the law, for which he had no other preparation than that acquired as justice of the peace, which constituted him one member of the county court. During the nearly nine years he acted as justice of the peace he tried many litigated causes, but only one appeal was taken and that was affirmed. He settled in Waynesboro, Wayne county, Tenn., where he formed a partnership in his profession with Mr. Elijah Walker, an able lawyer, and afterward for many years circuit judge of the district. The firm did a good business until the fall of 1847, when Mr. Hill was by the legislature elected attorney-general for the circuit, and two years afterward Mr. Walker was elected judge. Mr. Hill was reëlected by the legislature in 1853. The mode of electing all judicial officers was transferred from the legislature to the people, which took effect in 1854. Mr. Hill, being a whig and the district overwhelmingly democratic, was defeated by a majority of one hundred and twelve votes. In 1855 he moved to Jacinto, Tishomingo county, Miss., and engaged in the practice of his profession in partnership with the Hon. John F. Arnold, who was then and had been for a number of years probate judge of the county, which partnership continued until Mr. Hill was appointed judge of the united courts of Mississippi, the 1st of May, 1866.

In 1858, Judge Arnold having declined to serve as probate judge any longer, Mr. Hill was elected probate judge, and continued to serve as such up to the war, and during the war, by the consent of both sides, the duties having nothing to do with the war, and being restricted to such judicial acts as were proper had no war existed. After the war closed Judge Hill was appointed chancellor for his district by Provisional Governor Sharkey, which office he held until appointed to the Federal bench. Though he has never been what is properly termed a politician, and never sought political position, he has decided opinions on all public questions, and is strongly attached to our system of national government, so far as it relates to questions in which two or more states are interested, and holds that those questions and subjects in which the people of one state alone are interested pertain alone to the state; that each government in its own sphere is supreme; that the power of each emanates from the people, by the people and for the people. Hence, it was natural for him to be opposed to the attempted withdrawal of his state from the Union, which he opposed as best he could until the war was commenced, after which he took no part on either side, but addressed all his time and efforts to the relief of the distresses produced by the war, irrespective of the side to which the parties belonged, being by request a mediator between the military forces on both sides and the people until the close of the war. The appreciation of the people of his county was manifested by his receiving as a delegate to the constitutional convention called by Governor Clarke all the votes of his county save two, which convention, however, did not meet, and by his receiving out of a vote of about two thousand all the votes but about eighty to the constitutional convention called by Governor Sharkey in 1865, which met and acted, but the acts of which congress did not approve. He was not a candidate in either election. Judge Hill was nominated to the Federal judgeship by President Johnson, who knew him personally, and by the earnest request of friends who knew him in Tennessee and Mississippi, and especially the request of the Federal officers, with whom he had transacted much business on behalf of the citizens of the county in which he lived during the war, irrespective of their relations in regard to the war, in the release of prisoners, reclamation of property, and other matters, and especially in obtaining permission to procure and distribute funds and provisions for the families and widows of Confederate soldiers, and in protecting these supplies when obtained. The Federal army occupied the county for two years, or nearly that long. It was mainly through the influence of these officers that the Judge's confirmation was obtained, and especially that of Generals Thomas, Rosecrans, Jeff C. Davis, Dodge and Hatch, who gave as a reason why it should be done that he would enforce the laws of the United States, but with as little oppression and hardship as the circumstances and the nature of the case would permit; and that he would do justice by and give reasonable satisfaction to the people. Such was the advice given to the Judge by General Thomas after the appointment was made, the General being at the time the military commander of the state. The same advice was given at the same time by Chief Justice Chase, which was a great relief to the Judge in his new and delicate position. Justice Wayne, of Georgia, was at the time assigned to the fifth judicial circuit, of which Mississippi is a part, but he soon afterward died, when Justice Chase was temporarily assigned to the circuit; but neither ever visited the state or performed any judicial act with regard to it, so that Judge Hill was practically without any aid until after the appointment of Judge Woods as circuit judge in 1869, who only visited the southern district for the purpose of hearing appeals once in two or three years, and on a few occasions to sit with Judge Hill, at his request, in important cases in which the United States was a party. Justice Bradley, who was assigned to the circuit for a number of years, only visited the state once, and then only to hear appeals, and their successors have done no more. The state is divided into two districts, the northern and the southern. Judge Hill was district judge, with the powers of a circuit judge, in the northern district, in which no other judge had any jurisdiction until the 1st of May, 1889, when a circuit court was established, but practically it is as before. It is believed that no one judge has passed through such troublous times and met with so many difficult problems, with so little aid in their solution, as has Judge Hill, which will be more fully stated hereafter. The thirteenth amendment to the constitution of the United States, and the constitutions of the states which had passed emancipation ordinances, declared the former slaves free, but conferred on them no other civil rights, leaving those questions to congress and to state legislatures. The colored population in this state thus made free outnumbered the white population. The first legislature that convened, unable to foresee, and dreading the worst results growing out of the new relations, before then being masters on the one side and slaves on the other, passed a number of acts which, if they had been enforced, would have placed the colored man in almost as helpless a condition as he was in when a slave, being without the care and protection of his former master, whether that care was the result of humanity or self-interest. But, fortunately, before any Federal interference, it was ascertained that public opinion and humane feeling rendered most of these enactments a dead letter. But on the 9th day of April, 1866, congress passed over the president's veto what is known as the civil rights act of congress, in effect declaring these acts void and giving to the colored population the same civil rights and privileges as those enjoyed by the white population, and imposing severe penalties upon those who should attempt to enforce these objectable acts of the legislature. Judge Hill brought with him from Washington a copy of this act of congress, and went immediately to the legislature and informed the judiciary committee that he believed this act to be constitutional, and that he would feel it his duty to enforce it—the jurisdiction to do so being conferred by the act of congress upon the Federal courts; but that, as its enforcement would intensify the ill feeling between the races, then much too bitter, there was an easy way out of the difficulty, and that was for the legislature at once to repeal all these laws, when there would be nothing for the act of congress to act upon. This the legislature did at once, and there has been but one indictment under the law, and in that case upon the proof on the trial the defendant was acquitted; so that this first difficulty which met the Judge was happily overcome. On the 2d of March, 1867, congress passed the bankrupt law, which remained in force for eleven years and gave the court an immense amount of business, and in which the Judge had not only to construe the act itself, but many of the laws of the state not before then construed by the supreme court of the state. In 1867 the reconstruction act of congress was passed, which placed the state virtually under military control, and prohibited the state judges from issuing the writ of habeas corpus, or otherwise interfering with the military commander in causing the arrest of citizens and in the disposition of them. The Federal judge was the only power in the state with jurisdiction to interfere with the military power for the relief of the imprisoned citizen, which it frequently did and set the prisoner free. Whilst the court declined to hold the act unconstitutional under the existing conditions, yet he held that the act of congress was not intended to deprive the citizen of the right to a fair and speedy public trial, to be informed of the accusation against him, to be confronted with the witnesses against him, to have compulsory process for obtaining witnesses in his favor, and to have the assistance of counsel in his defense, and in case of conviction that he should not be subject to any cruel and unusual punishment. Under this act of congress no citizen was made subject to answer for any act not made criminal by the common law or the statutes of the state in force in the state at the time the state attempted to withdraw from the Union, on the 9th day of January, 1861, and no punishment could be inflicted under this act except that provided by the laws in force annexed as a penalty for their violation. In other words, it was not intended by congress to interfere with the constitutional rights of the citizen, only that in a certain class of offenses a different forum was provided, composed of military officers of the government, who were supposed to be free from local or other prejudices then existing growing out of the changed condition of the races. This construction of the act has never been reversed by the supreme court of the United States, and can never now be brought in question, as it is in the past.

Prior to May the 31st, 1870, there existed in a number of the Southern states, and especially in portions of the state of Mississippi, a secret organization known as the Kuklux Klan, which was oathbound, with the penalty of death against any of its members who should refuse to obey its orders, or who should make known its secrets. These bands so disguised themselves and their horses that they could not be distinguished. They met in secret conclave and planned their operations, determined who should be their victim, and without notice of the charge against them, whipped or killed their victims, black or white, and drove others from their homes. They became so powerful that those who disapproved their acts were afraid to make it known lest they would fall victims to their lawless pleasure. The colored people were most usually their victims. Congress, to arrest this evil, passed what is usually called the Kuklux act, more properly the Civil Rights act of 1870, subsequently amended by authorizing the president to suspend the habeas corpus in certain cases, and to proclaim the military laws in force. As a matter of self-protection, the colored people in certain portions of the state were preparing to organize themselves for defense, which, if it had been persisted in, would have resulted in a war of races, in which slaughter and destruction would have reigned for a time so appalling as to be beyond contemplation. A large number of persons were arrested charged with belonging to the klan, and with murders and other outrages. The United States military forces were employed in making these arrests, which could not have been made otherwise. Indictments were found by the United States grand jury. Motions were made to quash the indictments and discharge the prisoners on the ground that the act of congress was repugnant to the constitution of the United States. The questions arising upon the motions were argued at great length and with great ability by able counsel on both sides, and duly considered by the Judge, who was satisfied from the information he had obtained that one of three events must take place, and that within a very short time, which were: that he must for the time take the jurisdiction, and through the court try to stop the lawlessness, or the president would suspend the writ of habeas corpus and declare the state to be under military rule, as in the state of South Carolina, or there would be a war of races; and believing that with the court he could manage it better than the president with his military force, and that either would be better than a war of the races, although entertaining serious doubts with reference to the power of congress, under the constitution, to confer jurisdiction upon the court to try and punish these offenders, he for the time maintained the jurisdiction, and overruled motions to quash; but as a way out of the difficulty, proposed to those charged that if they would agree to an entry on the record of a verdict of guilty by the jury (not a plea of guilty, as that would stop the defendant), that a nominal fine would be entered upon the defendant's entering into recognizance, with good security, under a penalty of $1,000, that he would keep the peace toward all the citizens of the United States for the period of two years. This was done, the defendants were discharged, the klans dissolved, and the matter ended. It is not believed that any fines were paid, and thus ended this trouble. But there were still others growing out of the civil rights act of 1870, and the amendments to it, which were not unconstitutional, and mainly growing out of the fifteenth amendment to the constitution of the United States, and the election of representatives to the congress of the United States, and which have given rise to numerous and perplexing questions which have had to be met and disposed of, most of which have been settled by the supreme court of the United States in accordance with the decisions made by Judge Hill, who had to act upon them before any of them were decided by the supreme court. But no appeals were taken from the judgments had in Mississippi. These laws are still in force. Whether they will so remain or be supplanted by others is still in the future. The internal revenue laws of the United States have been a source of much litigation in this state, and for a time no waymark could be found to guide the court. Some of these laws have been repealed, but others remain in force. Also the laws for the protection of the timber on the public land, about which judges differ, besides many other questions unknown in the state until after the war, and some not until in recent years—all, with a few exceptions, have been heard and decided by Judge Hill sitting alone. He has been entitled to retire upon his full salary since the 25th of March, 1881; but being in good health, and thinking that it would be getting something for nothing, and being urged by the citizens of the state and by the members of the bar of both parties not to retire, he has devoted his time and attention, at his own expense, to his judicial duties, seldom adjourning his court without having disposed of everything on the docket ready for trial. The most remarkable circumstance in Judge Hill's forty-seven years of official connection with the different courts, as stated, is that he never failed during that time to attend a court from sickness of himself or family, and in all only three times from other causes. In addition to almost constant judicial labor performed by Judge Hill, he has for many years been a trustee of the State University of Mississippi, located at Oxford, as well as of other educational institutions, in all of which he has taken a deep interest, for some of which he has freely opened his hand financially. He has in this way intimately identified himself with the young men, many of whom have taken prominent positions in different states and are his warm friends. Although never a member of the legislature or of congress, and but once of a constitutional convention, he, on a number of occasions, took an active part in procuring legislation by both, and in framing the constitution of the state in 1868, but he was not a member of this convention. In compliance with a request of the citizens of the state he visited Washington at the commencement of the congress of 1865, and by request of the senators and representatives who had been elected by the people of Mississippi, remained in Washington to represent as best he could the interests of the people of the state, both before the departments and in procuring such legislation as could be had by congress, all of which was at his own expense, without any pecuniary compensation from anyone. The bitter contest then existing between congress and the president greatly embarrassed his efforts, and postponed a part of the legislation until after he was compelled to leave and enter upon his judicial duties. The most important relief obtained was procuring the suspension of the direct land tax on the lands in this state, which were then being collected, amounting to about $484,000, but a small portion of which had then been collected. Judge Hill, feeling that to force the collection of that tax at that time would have the effect of transferring to merciless speculators a large portion of the lands of the state, and especially that belonging to widows and orphans who had no means of payment, prepared and had presented to congress a petition, and with it a bill suspending the further collection of these taxes until otherwise ordered by congress, which bill and petition were referred to the proper committee and pressed for immediate action. The committee decided to report it to congress and advise its immediate passage.

Representatives from other states in which only a portion of this tax had been paid, requested that the suspension should embrace all this uncollected tax. The act was passed in a short time after the Judge left Washington. This tax remains unpaid until this day, and by an act passed by the last congress is not only remitted, but that already paid has been refunded. Judge Hill, from a long experience as a practicing lawyer and judge, both in

Tennessee and in Mississippi, was impressed with a number of radical changes in the judicial system of this state, rendered the more necessary by the changed condition resulting from the war. Some time prior to the meeting of the convention in 1868, was prepared the article constituting the judicial system of the state, by which the judges and chancellors are appointed by the governor and confirmed by the senate, in the same manner in which Federal judges are nominated by the president and confirmed by the senate, instead of being elected by the people as before. Another important change was the establishment of separate common law and equity courts, and giving to the latter jurisdiction over testamentary matters, before that time vested in the probate courts. This system worked so satisfactorily that it is continued in all its force in the constitution of 1890. The most valuable service rendered by Judge Hill in his mediatorial capacity during the war was that immediately after General Hood's retreat from Nashville. His army, on crossing the Tennessee river, spread broadcast over the country, and especially over Tishomingo county, and being in a suffering condition, both man and beast, his soldiers took, consumed and wasted almost everything in the way of food upon which they could lay their hands, so much so that there was not corn enough left to feed the people, let alone the little livestock left, for six weeks. The women and old men came in numbers to the Judge to know what could be done to prevent starvation. The Judge, being assured by General Chalmers, in command of the Confederate cavalry, promised that if the railroad, then intact, should remain so, they would send back from the prairies, where there was a great abundance of corn, sufficient to replace that taken by the cavalry forces. Gen. George H. Thomas with a large Federal force had just crossed the Tennessee river at Eastport. Judge Hill went to that place and presented to General Thomas the true condition of the people of the county and of the surrounding country—that starvation was at the door, that there were no wagons or teams with which to bring corn from places where it could be obtained, and not sufficient to take the people to it. He requested that the railroad might be left intact, with the privilege of running a train under a flag of truce, and in that way furnish the people with bread; and when it was obtained, that it would not be taken by his army. To this request General Thomas gave a ready assent, and directed the Judge to return and say to the people that in addition to what corn could be obtained by the railroad, he would supply the remainder needed, which was done under his orders, to the amount of $100,000 worth, giving full army rations to each member of every family making application, without any inquiry as to whether anyone had or had not been in the Confederate army. At the same time, upon request, General Thomas made other orders for the benefit of the people, which generosity was, as it should have been, greatly appreciated by an afflicted people. Judge Hill having long advocated the establishment of an intermediate court of appeals so that each individual might have a rehearing before another court of every case decided against him, was anxious to see such a court established before retiring from the bench. This court was provided for by the act of the Fifty-first congress, and the Judge, as a member of that court for the Fifth judicial circuit, aided in its organization in June, 1891. He also desired to see the court building in the city of Vicksburg completed, and to dedicate that elegant building by holding in it the first court, which he did in July, 1891. Having passed his four-score years, with a quarter of a century on the Federal bench, and witnessed the establishment, as well as taking part in the organization of the circuit court of appeals, with one of his former clerks as clerk of that court, and having seen the completion of the Federal building at Vicksburg, with its beautiful court accommodations, and a court organized in the same, he retired from the active duties of his judicial position on the 1st day of August, 1891, to spend the remainder of his days in quiet and rest with his family and his friends;

and though eighty years of age he still retains the active use of all his mental powers, so that no one can say that he remained upon the bench beyond the years of his usefulness. On the contrary, his retirement, though richly deserved, falls like a personal bereavement upon the bar and the people of the state. The young and the old have found in Judge Hill a faithful friend, and nearly all the members now at the bar of the state, having grown up under him, regard him with feelings of veneration for him as a judge, admiration for him as a man, and love for him as a friend, for friend he has indeed been to every good man and every good cause. Long in the public service and always interested in men and their affairs, their progress, their homes, their marriage, their wives and their children, it is safe to say that he knows more people by name and has more intimate friends than any other man in the state. He is honored by the aged, reverenced by the young, admired by the rich and the poor, trusted by the lawyer and the client, and loved by all. So that it is not strange that he said in his valedictory to the bar, "If I have an enemy in the state I am glad that I do not know it," for such a man can have no real enemies. There may be some whose interests have been crossed by the opinions of the court, who have doubted the wisdom of those opinions, but it would be hard to believe that even these or any of them ever thought of imputing anything but the purest motives in the Judge. And he has so woven the law of kindness into the laws of the government that those whom he has sentenced were often drawn to him rather than repulsed by the sentence, going to and returning from their punishment as friends rather than enemies to the law and the court. Everywhere and always, and no less in his age than in his manhood years, Judge Hill's mind has been characterized by a strong, vigorous common sense which amounted almost to genius. To this has been added a good memory, and an accurate sense of what is right between man and man. He would do no man an intentional wrong. He has freely condemned the actions of parties and of men when, in his opinion, they were wrong in themselves or against public policy, but in public speech and in private conversation, where he could not say well of a man personally, he would not say ill. And in him the United States has had a wise judge, the state a good citizen, the bar an able expounder of the law, society an affable, courteous Christian gentleman, the church a faithful member, and every man a friend. But this article would not be complete without one more remark regarding one who has been such a lover of men, for he could not be unmindful of his own home, and if anything were needed to round out the character of Judge Hill in its simplicity, beauty and purity, it might be found in him as a husband, father and grandfather in his home at Oxford. Here he lives with his wife, Mary Andrews Hill, in her seventy-eighth year, who has been a true and courageous helpmeet during every day of the nearly sixty years of their married life. With them are their daughter, Mrs. Marietta Hill, a woman of fine culture and rare talents, and her husband, Mr. George R. Hill, who has for many years been clerk of the United States courts for the northern district of Mississippi, and with them their two children, Robert A. Hill, Jr., and Mary Myrtle, respectively fourteen and twelve years of age. Thus the three generations, the grandparents, parents and children, make a home which no one can visit but to remember for the sunshine and beauty that it contains. Here it is that the evening of Judge Hill's life will be spent, surrounded by those who love him best and whom he best loves, and visited by his many friends. May the vigor of his body and the clearness of his mind contradict the borrowed time on which he now lives, for many years yet to come, is the wish of all who have met him in the different walks of life.

Samuel Van Dyke Hill, M. D. (deceased), was a Tennesseean, who was born in Nashville on the 25th of July, 1835, and inherited the gracious nature of both his parents: the catholic and capacious intellect of the father, and the quick perception and charming colloquial powers of his cultured mother. In his eighth year he was removed by his parents from Tennessee to Chickasaw county, Miss., and though the hand of misfortune had scattered the fruit of his father's toil, yet he found ample guidance in his mental growth under the tutelage of his accomplished mother and scholarly father, both of whom saw and nurtured with pride their son's genius. During this time the schools in the vicinity in which he lived and the Columbus high school yielded him a fair knowledge of the classics and mathematics. In his eighteenth year he procured employment in a drug store in Aberdeen, Miss., in order to study pharmacy and lay the foundation for a medical career, and soon after, by dint of his earnings and his father's aid, he was enabled to enter the university of Louisville, Ky., and sat under the sound of the great Cross's voice, at a period when the faculty of that institution embraced a galaxy of medical stars. He next entered the department of medicine in the university of New York, from which he received his diploma in March, 1857, and while a member of these well-known medical colleges, although he was a diligent student in clinics, surgery became his chief delight, in the difficult and delicate mysteries of which he became famous in his subsequent career. He entered upon the practice of his profession at Palo Alto, Miss., in connection with his father, but soon after came secession and war. He at once offered himself as a private in the ranks, for he loved his birthland and was willing to uphold its honor on the battlefield; but even at that early age his brilliant reputation in his chosen art was such that he was called to exercise the arduous duties of a surgeon in the Confederate army, receiving his appointment in January, 1861, as assistant surgeon, and in 1863 as surgeon. His efficiency, skill and signal success in hospital, camp and on the battlefield in Virginia and the West are well known, and from October, 1862, to the end of the war he was in charge of the Quintard general hospital. Just at the opening of the war he obtained in marriage the heart and hand of Miss Jenny Calvert, near Palo Alto, Miss., and although she was almost a child in years, and reared to a life of luxury, she forthwith forsook a home of wealth and ease and went with her husband to his post along the lines of Lee and Johnston in Virginia. Returning to Macon, Miss., at the close of the war, Doctor Hill immediately entered into a large and lucrative practice, and for twenty-four years, until his fatal malady compelled a truce to his labors, he never knew rest or relaxation. He was a member of the state medical association from its organization after the war until his death, and was elected and served as its president in 1871. He was also a member of the American medical association, having several times been elected a delegate from the state medical association. He was elected a delegate to represent the state association in the International medical congress that convened at Washington, and while he gratefully appreciated these honors, they were never sought by him. He would have as readily accepted a call to the bedside of the lowliest sufferer, and there are legions of grateful hearts that would bear witness to this, whose only treasury was gratitude out of which to pay him. The excellent quarantine laws of Mississippi are in a measure the product of his wisdom and labor, and at the organization of the state board of health in 1877 he was appointed one of its members, in which capacity he served continuously by reëlection up to the time of his death, at which time he was filling the position of president. These are the salient points, briefly sketched, in Doctor Hill's career, and the highest honors within the gift of his professional brethren in the state had been conferred upon him and came to him entirely unsought, for he was worthy of them. No man in the state more thoroughly represented the profession in its higher and more beautiful aspect than he, and he was what Lord Bacon has termed a "full, ready and correct man." He was not only thoroughly learned in his profession, but by an extensive course of study he had reaped in nearly every field of literature and art, and was equally ready with tongue or pen to give proof of encyclopedic knowledge. He rarely missed a meeting of the state medical association, took an active part in the discussions of medical topics, and his graceful, yet modest' encounters with members during their deliberations, the admirable and lucid style in which he expressed himself, his gentleness and deference toward his associates, are well remembered by the profession, each one of whom honored and loved him, and will bear witness to his high regard for medical ethics, his admiration for the successful and his sympathy for those struggling for success. No matter how obtuse or unusual the subject to be discussed, he was ready to illustrate either from the stores of his reading or the field of his experience, and possessed a remarkable faculty of extemporaneous discourse. So simple, so admirable and so apt was his pure English in logical sequence, that it excited the admiration of every listener and inspired in him the same spirit of zealous pursuit of knowledge. He was a frequent contributor to the volumes of transactions of the association, and his articles were characterized by strength and simplicity of style, a thorough treatment of the topic under discussion, and a familiar acquaintance with authorities, ancient and modern. He participated actively in the medical reforms instituted by the state medical association, and contributed largely to the stability and success of the state board of health. For thirty years or more, from the first flush of his manhood, he was day and night absorbed in the duties of a profession perhaps the most trying on brain and body of any in the field of science, and as he possessed a very nervous organization and a powerful mentality, the loving eyes of his family and friends saw, or thought they saw, the failure of the body to uphold the burden which the brain imposed upon it. At last Bright's disease set in, and the end soon followed. He placed himself under the treatment of Drs. Love and Bryson, of St. Louis—the latter his former pupil and a distinguished specialist in that disease—but professional skill was of no avail, and his eyes were closed in death at the home of his brother, Ewing Hill, of St. Louis, whither he had gone with his devoted wife on the 14th of October, 1889, while in the zenith of his manhood and the summit of success. The endless appeals of the suffering overcame, in his noble breast, the first and highest law, self-preservation, and his sternest vows for rest and recuperation always vanished under the touch of pity. His death was a calamity to the community and the state, both professionally and as a wise and patriotic citizen, and it may with truth be said that one of the brightest and highest stars in the firmament faded and went out. He left behind him a devoted wife and two daughters: Miss Maggie and Mrs. Vick (Hill) Jones, whose love and pride in him knew no bounds.

William H. Hill, M. D., of Sylvarena, Smith county, Miss., was born in Noxubee county, Miss., in September, 1840, one of a family of six children of Sherrod and Mary (Smith) Hill. His mother was a daughter of Elam Smith, a native of North Carolina, who located in Greene county, Ala., at an early day. His father died in 1843, leaving four of a family of six children, named: Thomas Y., Elam, William H. and Mary, all of whom grew to maturity; and Robert and Manassas, who died very young. Their mother married for her second husband James H. Woods, who died in 1867. Doctor Hill received a common-school education and had little time to decide upon a career when the war began. He enlisted in company A, of the Eighteenth Mississippi regiment, and was transferred to the medical department after the battle of Ball's bluff. During the winter of 1863–4 he attended medical lectures at Richmond, Va. After the war he returned to Raleigh, Smith county, Miss., and engaged in the practice of medicine, meanwhile attending lectures at Tulane university, at New Orleans, from which he graduated in the spring of 1869, with the degree of M. D. He was married in 1865 to Miss Edna McAlpine, of Greene county, Ala., who bore him one child, a daughter, named Sarah. In 1879 the Doctor located in Sylvarena, where he has since been very successfully engaged in the practice of his profession, having a greater demand for his services than any other physician who ever lived in the county. In the fall of 1888 he was elected to represent his district in the state senate, in which body he served with much distinction. He is a helpful supporter of all educational institutions, believing firmly that to be useful the people must be enlightened. He was instrumental in the establishing of the Sylvarena high-school, in which he was for some years a trustee. In 1890 he was appointed by Governor Stone as a delegate to the Southern emigration convention, which met at Asheville, N. C., in the fall of that year. He was also appointed medical health officer of his county by the governor in 1890. This position he still holds. Doctor Hill is very unassuming and a most conscientious, Christian gentleman, who believes in doing all the good he can at all times, and there are very few in this community who have been instrumental in benefiting it more than he.

The parents of McKinney W. Hilliard, planter, Dublin, Miss., John and Maria (Pickard) Hilliard, were natives of North Carolina, and the father followed the occupation of a planter. He came to Tennessee at an early day, and died in that state on February 29, 1889, at the age of eighty-two years, his death occurring on the anniversary of his birth. The paternal grandfather, Epps Hilliard, was also a native of North Carolina, the family being an old and representative one of that state. He was in the Revolutionary war, and figured quite prominently in the same. McKinney W. Hilliard was born in Maury county, Tenn., on March 20, 1837, and was the seventh child born to his parents. He attained his growth and received his education in his native state, attending Jackson college, Columbia. In 1857 he started out for himself as an overseer of slaves, and continued at this until the breaking out of the war. He then enlisted in the Confederate army, company B, Seventh Tennessee regiment of cavalry, and remained in the same until cessation of hostilities, being promoted to the rank of sergeant in the meantime. He participated in the battles of Union City, Yazoo City, Harrisburg, Brice's crossroads, West Point, Ripley, Holly Springs, Corinth, Jackson and most of the battles in Mississippi. He was captured at the battle of Centerville, Ala., carried to Selma, of that state, and placed in the barracks with about twenty-five hundred other prisoners. After remaining there for seven days, he was removed to Montgomery, and subsequently to the Georgia and Alabama line, where he was paroled. Mr. Hilliard was married November 30, 1864, to Miss Louetta W. Tucknis, a native of Tennessee, and a daughter of Thomas J. and Sallie E. (Hilliard) Tucknis. Of the three children born to this union, Florence M., Mirna and McKinney, only Florence M. is now living. Mr. Hilliard is an extensive planter, and cultivates about sixteen hundred acres of land. In politics he was formerly a whig, but since the war he has affiliated with the democratic party. He contributes generously to all worthy public enterprises, and is one of the representative citizens of Coahoma county.

Rev. Walter Hillman, LL. D. This skillful educator and honorable gentleman was born on the island of Martha's Vineyard, Mass., January 9, 1829, the second child born to Walter and Adaline (Norton) Hillman, the paternal ancestors having been of Welsh descent. The Doctor's immediate ancestor, several times removed, was kidnaped from the coast of Wales when a very small boy, with another lad of about the same age, and was taken to Martha's Vineyard, where they were apprenticed to a man until they should become twenty-one years of age. At that time young Hillman married and settled on the island; but his companion, returning to his old home in England, was lost at sea. Dr. Hillman's father was a ship captain for twenty years, being in the whaling business, then became a merchant on the island, and in this, as well as in his other enterprises, was successful. He was a member of the legislature of Massachusetts one term, and was prominent in the section in which he resided. He died in 1877. Dr. Walter Hillman attended the common schools until about fourteen years of age; then he entered Dukes county academy, where he remained two winters; after which he attended an educational institution at Yarmouth Port one session, and was at Fair Haven, Mass., a short time. He then entered the Connecticut Literary institute at Suffield, where he remained eighteen months, and then entered Worcester academy, at Worcester, Mass., from which he graduated. He then entered Brown university at Providence, R. I., from which he also graduated in 1854. After remaining in this institution two years he secured the position of subprincipal of the Worcester academy, and five months later accepted the position as classical instructor in Pearce academy in Middleboro, Mass., remaining here also five months. At the end of this time he returned to Brown university, from which he graduated at the above-mentioned date with the degree of A. M. under Dr. Francis Wayland. On commencement night he met Dr. Urner, president of Mississippi college, to whom he had been previously recommended as a suitable person to fill the chair of mathematics and natural sciences in Mississippi college. He arrived at Clinton, Miss., October 1, and assumed his duties. After remaining in this institution two years he resigned to become president of the Central Female institute, which position he now holds, in the thirty-fifth year of his incumbency. Previous to the war he was ordained a minister of the gospel, and preached some as an evangelist, having no regular charge except during the war, when he was chosen pastor of the Baptist church of Clinton. After the war and while still president of the Female institute he was chosen president of Mississippi college, the object being for him to resuscitate it, and although he found it in its buildings in a destitute condition, minus doors, windows, roofs, etc., and the grounds laid waste and unfenced, he set energetically to work to restore it to its old-time prosperity. It was without pupils and almost totally destitute of resources, but Dr. Hillman borrowed money of Northern friends with which to pay off the debt of $10,000, and thus released the college from the judgment hanging over it. In the winter of 1866 and 1867 he started with nine pupils in the preparatory department and two in the collegiate, there being one member of the faculty besides the Doctor. During his presidency of six years the debt of the college was paid off, the buildings put in order, the number of pupils had increased to one hundred and ninety and the faculty to eight professors and teachers. As he was acting in the capacity of president of two institutions, with a large corps of teachers and two sets of students, he found his duties far too arduous, and was compelled to resign the presidency of Mississippi college, but in doing so left it out of debt and with money in the treasury, and an endowment as then supposed to be worth about $40,000. Since then his attention has been devoted almost entirely to the Female institute (recently named in honor of him Hillman college), which has greatly prospered under his able rule. Since the close of the war he has been closely connected with the public schools of the state, having served many years as chairman of the executive committee of the state teachers' association, being also president of the same for one year. Through his advocacy of common-school work, and especially by a plea he presented to the legislature at one of its sessions, the appropriation made for common schools was nearly doubled. As he has taken a great interest in the work of common schools, Dr. Hillman has every reason to congratulate himself that he has done much to mold public sentiment and to cause the public school to enter more fully into popular favor. The Doctor is also a planter, being the owner of thirty-five hundred acres of land, of which about one-half is under cultivation, devoted to the raising of cotton, corn, grass, etc. He was the second in his section to introduce the mowing machine in making hay, and the first to use the tedder. The property of the Hillman college belongs to the Doctor. When he took charge of it it was in charge of a board of trustees, who were building the largest building for school purposes for young ladies west of Richmond, Va., but the war bankrupted the board, and they gave the property into Mr. Hillman's hands to pay off the debt and own the property. Within the past year a new school edifice, which has been named after the Doctor's wife Adelia hall, has been built. The Doctor still keeps his summer home at Martha's Vineyard. He was married in Providence, R. I., September 18, 1855, to Miss Adelia M. Thompson, but their union has never been blessed by children. Mrs. Hillman is a graduate of Warren Ladies' seminary, of Warren, R. I., and has at various times taken special studies from masters in French and German and art. She was principal of one of the public schools at Providence, R. I., for some time, and was head lady teacher of a young ladies' seminary at Maysville, Ky. On two different occasions she has been tendered the position of president of the W. C. T. U. She retired from the active duties of teaching in 1876, having been both pupil and teacher for forty years, and is now president of the central committee of the women's mission society of the Baptist denomination of Mississippi, which has over four hundred branch societies, and with her general supervision of Hillman college matters thus finds her time fully employed. A cultured and refined Christian lady, she is admirably fitted to be the wife and helpmate of such a man as Dr. Hillman.

Among the people of Amite county, Miss., the name of Dr. John H. Hines is a familiar one, for during the years that he has devoted to the healing art in this section he has won an enviable reputation, not only as a practitioner, but also as a citizen and friend. The family originally came from England, and John Hines, the first member of the family to come to America, settled in Virginia, this being in the latter part of the last century. He was very independent in his views and in the struggle of the colonists with the mother country he espoused the cause of the former and was a faithful soldier to the cause during the Revolution. J. H. Hines, his son, was born in Albemarle county, Va., but being of an adventurous disposition, fearless and bold, he determined to seek a home for himself in what was then the wilds of Mississippi. After a residence here of several years he again pushed westward and spent the rest of his days in Louisiana. He was a local elder of the Methodist Episcopal church South. His son, William B. Hines, the father of Dr. John H., was born where the town of Huntsville, Ala., now stands, in the year 1819 and in the month of January, but in Mississippi was reared to manhood. Being of a deep, religious nature he determined to become a minister of the gospel, and in the year 1846 he joined the Mississippi conference, since which time he has been one of the leading and eminent divines of the Methodist Episcopal church South, and has served in nearly all the districts of the Conference of Mississippi. He is now located in Waynesboro and although he is now in the "sear and yellow leaf," his mind is still as keen as of yore and physically his health is unimpaired. He is still serving constantly and faithfully in the interest of Christianity and in the year of 1890 did not miss an appointment, which is more than can be said of many more youthful ministers. His wife, was formerly Miss Jane F. Coppedge, a native of North Carolina and a daughter of Charles Coppedge. Mrs. Hines was reared and educated in her native state but was married is this state. Their son, Dr. John H. Hines, was given a good education at Jackson, La., and in Tennessee, and as he was bright and intelligent beyond his years, he made the most of every opportunity and became an exceptionally intelligent young man. In November, 1861, he entered the Confederate army, first becoming a member of Blythe's battalion, which afterward became a part of the Forty-fourth Mississippi infantry until the latter part of the war, when he was placed on detached service by General Bragg, followed the varied life and fortunes of his regiment with fortitude and courage, proving himself a valiant soldier. Among the principal engagements in which he took part may be mentioned Shiloh, Murfreesboro and Chickamauga; in the first of which he commanded his company, being at the time orderly sergeant. At the close of the war he was paroled at Jackson, Miss. He soon after began the study of medicine in Wilkinson county, and took his first course of lectures in the medical department of the Louisiana university in the winter of 1865–6, completing his course in the winter of 1867, graduating in the month of March. Soon after this he located in Amite county, and here has built up as large a practice as he can well attend to. He was engaged in the drug business in Gloster, being a member of the firm of Hines & Harrell, which was established in 1883, being the first of the kind to be opened in the town, but the style of the firm was afterward changed to Hines & Lamkin, and so continued for one year. The Doctor opened a drug store on his plantation in 1885, and has conducted this in connection with the practice of his profession up to the present time. The Merwin postoffice was established at this point in 1880, of which Dr. Hines has been the only postmaster. He was married in this county in 1868, to Mrs. Amanda L. Rogers, daughter of Thomas Toler. Mrs. Hines was born and reared in Amite county, and by her first husband, Dennis H. Rogers, she became the mother of one son, Thomas H., who is grown and married. To her union with Dr. Hines the following children have been born: Bennett M., John H., R. Edward, Sarah Annabel, Martha J. and Mary T., a bright little miss of five years. Mrs. Hines is a member of the Baptist church, while the Doctor and his two eldest children belong to the Methodist Episcopal church. The Doctor also belongs to the Masonic fraternity and is a stanch supporter of democratic principles, taking quite an active part in local politics. He has served as a delegate to both county and district conventions, and from 1876 to 1879 he was assessor of Amite county. As a physician of merit, his reputation has become widespread, notwithstanding the fact that he is modest and unassuming in his demeanor. He is a true gentleman in every respect and his cheerful countenance, encouraging words and judicious treatment are instrumental in insuring the convalescence of his patients.

L. D. Hines, a popular young business man of Ripley, is a native of Tippah county, Miss., born in 1860. He grew to maturity in this county, and when a young man embarked in business for himself. By giving it his undivided attention he soon began to realize on his enterprises and was soon enabled to branch out. By close application to business and attention to all its little details he is to-day the leading merchant in Tippah county, and ranks foremost among the best in northern Mississippi. He is courteous and pleasant in his treatment of all, and is eminently fitted for the business in which he is engaged. His first venture was in the livery business, which brought him in big returns, and in 1887 he embarked in the mercantile business, which from the start was almost phenomenal in its success. Mr. Hines is also interested in the Hines & Harris Manufacturing company, of Ripley, and the Gulf & Chicago railroad, which runs from Pontotoc, Miss., to Middleton, Tenn. In 1883 he still further showed his good judgment and sense by selecting for his life companion Miss Ella Thompson, an estimable young lady of Middleton, Tenn., and daughter of Judge D. C. Thompson, of the same place. To this union have been born three bright children: Lottie, Mayree and Douglas. Socially Mr. Hines is a member of the Knights of Honor organization at Ripley. His father, Chesley Hines, was born in Hardeman county, Tenn., where he resided with his parents until eleven years of age. He then went to Missouri, made his home there until about the age of eighteen years, when he came to Tippah county, which was then a new country, and brought with him an inexhaustible amount of latent energy. Although he had never attended school a day in his life until twenty-one years of age, a few years later he was possessed of a good practical education and was well posted on all subjects. He entered a common country school at the above age, and in the remarkably short space of three months was as far advanced as any pupil in the school. He possessed the much desired faculty of centering his whole mind on the subject in hand, and this probably accounts for his rapid progress. He was an expert mathematician and a natural born mechanic, both of which he put into practical use. He also gave bookkeeping some attention, and was a practical accountant. His first venture was in the sawmill business in 1859, but he did not make a success of this. In 1860 he began farming and continued at this until in 1861, when he enlisted in the Confederate army, company G, under Captain Huddleston. At Perryville, Ky., his right leg was shattered between the knee and ankle, and when he recovered he was a cripple for life, as that limb was much shorter than the other. In 1865, in partnership with Capt. C. L. Harris, he again embarked in the steam sawmill business, and from this time his success was assured. He and Captain Harris were eminently fitted to work together, and this they did in various successful enterprises until the time of Mr. Hines' sad death. In 1877 they became interested in the Gulf & Chicago railroad, Mr. Harris becoming superintendent and Mr. Hines taking charge of the motive power. In 1879, while running an engine, Mr. Hines lost his life in an unfortunate wreck. He was a kind husband, an indulgent father, and a man held in high estimation by all. His widow, whose maiden name was Elizabeth Harris, still survives him, and is surrounded by her children.

Maj. John H. Hobbs' career has been one of usefulness in the community in which he resides, and he is regarded as an intelligent and thoroughly posted man in all public affairs. He was born in Hardin county, Ill., March 7, 1846, the fifth of seven children born to Ezekiel and Melissa (Gibbs) Hobbs, the former of whom was born in Illinois and the latter in Virginia. Mr. Hobbs was an extensive planter in his native state and after a well-spent and useful career he was called from life in 1850. John H. Hobbs was reared in Desha county, Ark., and his earliest recollections are those of spending his time upon a farm, and in attending the public schools of Arkansas. He has been a resident of Bolivar county, Mississippi, for about one year, and is the owner of an excellent little plantation of one hundred and twenty acres, of which twenty-five acres are under cultivation. His career as a soldier is one of which he is deservedly proud, for no braver or more faithful soldier or officer ever trod the crimson turf of a battlefield than he. He enlisted as a private in 1862 in company A, of Maj. Ned. Saunders' battalion, under Van Dorn, and with this company remained until 1863, when he was changed to Price's army, and was with that famous general in his raid through Missouri and Arkansas, serving until the close of the war. In 1863 he was promoted to the rank of sergeant-major of his company and after serving in this capacity, very efficiently, for some time his command was consolidated with a regiment under Col. Arch. Dobbin, known as Dobbin's regiment. He took an active part in the following engagements: Coffeeville, Miss., Holly Springs, Miss., Thompson's station, Tenn., where he received a slight wound, and as he was with Price on his raid he took part in nearly all the engagements of that campaign, fighting almost constantly. He belonged to a skirmishing party and consequently participated in many engagements and skirmishes not chronicled in history. He has every reason to be proud of his career as a soldier, for he not only possessed undoubted courage but he was strict in his adherence to duty, and possessing an excellent physique and indomitable will power he bore the privations and hardships of war well. In 1869 Miss Susie H. Key, a native of Tennessee, and a daughter of Landon P. and Mary E.

(Easley) Key, became his wife and their union has resulted in the birth of the following children: Claude, Milton G., Mary, Melissa G. (deceased), Frank R., Gibbs, Beulah (deceased), Horace E. (deceased), and Emma B. So far as his means will allow, Mr. Hobbs has been liberal in his contributions to laudable public enterprises tending to build up and improve the country, churches and schools finding special favor in his sight.

M. Hodgdon, retired planter, was born near Portsmouth, New Hampshire, May 23, 1818, the seventh in a family of ten children born to Ephraim and Abigail (Thomas) Hodgdon, they being also natives of that state, the father a farmer. Mr. Hodgdon had the advantages of the free schools only up to the age of fourteen years, and at the age of fifteen went into a hotel at Portsmouth, of which he had charge during the greater part of his stay of five years. He then came South, and in February, 1840, found himself in Vicksburg, Miss., a perfect stranger. He immediately went to the swamps as a woodman, and for four years kept a woodyard on the banks of the Yazoo river, during which time he accumulated a snug little sum of money. He then concluded to go to St. Louis, Mo., but there lost his hard-earned money and was back in Mississippi in ten months' time. He once more engaged in the wood business, continuing until 1862, when he could have realized $40,000 on his worldly possessions. He purchased his present plantation in 1863, which comprises four hundred and five acres, and on this place he moved immediately after making his purchase. A considerable portion of his land is in pasture and he raises a few stock cattle, but the cultivated portion of his land he rents out. He owns valuable property in Edwards, and possesses ample means upon which to retire from the active duties of life. Although not in the service during the war he acted as taxcollector for about two years during that period. He was also elected magistrate during this time. He was first married in 1843 to Mrs. Frances Skofield, a native of North Carolina, but was called upon to mourn the death of his wife in 1855. The following year he married Mrs. Sarah H. Hewse, who died in 1876 just after returning from the Centennial exhibition at Philadelphia, Penn. Mr. Hodgdon's third marriage was celebrated in 1877, Mrs. Susan P. Street becoming his wife. His unions have not been blessed in the birth of children.

Robert S. Hodges, M. D., was born in Smith county, Tenn., in July, 1830. He is the youngest of a family of four children, of Robert and Elizabeth (Turner) Hodges. His parents were natives of North Carolina, and moved to Tennessee with their fathers' families when they were small children, and were there reared and married. The father was previously married to Susanah Turner, sister of his second wife, by whom he had two children: Berryman, deceased, and Susanah, the wife of Col. R. C. Clark, of Verona, Miss., and who died in Smith county, February, 1822. It was in the latter part of the same year that Mr. Hodges married Miss Elizabeth Turner. In December, 1838, he removed from Tennessee to Tishomingo county, Miss., having his stock with him. On the road the family camped near Franklin one evening, and during the night the notorious outlaw and horse thief, John A. Murrell, and his band, stole from him six head of horses, leaving him only two horses with which to continue his journey. He finally arrived safely with his family and their personal effects, but was obliged to return to Tennessee for horses with which to make a crop the following year, and it is worthy of note that that crop was the first crop made in that county. Mr. Hodges was one of the pioneers here, and was obliged to go fifteen miles for men to help raise his house. He purchased two sections of land, and soon opened up quite a plantation. He was a practical, energetic business man, and accumulated considerable property, just previous to the war owning, besides the land, about thirty slaves. During the latter part of his life he was a local Methodist preacher, and did ministerial work in different parts of the county.

In the early part of the war he was arrested by the Federal troops and taken to Alton prison, where he died on the 1st day of November, 1862. His wife died in 1864, at her home in Tishomingo county, and now only three members of the family are living: Robert S.; Mrs. Clark, his half-sister, of Verona, Miss., and Nancy W., the wife of Nathaniel Allen, formerly of Alabama, but now living near Verona. Doctor Hodges was educated at La Grange, Ala., graduating in 1852. He remained in the college, as rector of the grammar school, for twelve months, and in 1853 began the study of medicine in the office of his uncle, Dr. B. D. Hodges, near the old homestead in Tishomingo county, with whom he remained about two years. He graduated from the Louisville university in 1855, and during the same year began the practice of his profession, at his old home, where he has continued it from that date to the present, having been for thirty-six years the doctor of this community. There is no resident of this county who has been here longer than he has, and he is favorably known, throughout its length and breadth, as an honorable, high-minded citizen, a good and charitable neighbor, and a skillful and successful physician. He was married in 1853 to Miss Louisa A. Southall, of Allsboro, Ala. They have a family of three sons and one daughter: Walter A., who is a practicing physician in Iuka, Miss.; Paul, who is a law partner with J. B. Reynolds, of Florence, Ala.; Blanche, the wife of Harvey Hughes, who lives in Meridian, Tex., and Robert S., Jr. The Doctor has always been quite extensively interested in planting, to which he has devoted such time as has not been consumed in the practice of his profession, and he is the owner of fourteen hundred acres of land, about two hundred acres of which are improved. He is a member of the Methodist Episcopal church South, and has been a member of the Masonic fraternity since 1876. The Cartersville postoffice is in the Doctor's office, and he was appointed postmaster in 1867, and has held the position continuously ever since, during changing administrations. He is a public-spirited man, with broad and liberal views, and his aid to the community in which he lives has been neither stinted nor infrequent.

E. H. Hoffman, circuit and chancery clerk of Hancock county, Miss., was born in New Orleans, La., October 2, 1849, and is a son of Conrad and Agnes (Weisberger) Hoffman, natives of Baden, Germany. The father emigrated to the United States, and located in New Orleans in 1847; there he was married. In 1849 he came to Bay St. Louis, and for many years carried on the trade of a shoemaker. He died in 1883. He reared a family of two sons and five daughters. E. H. Hoffman is the eldest of the children. He was brought up in Bay St. Louis, and was educated at St. Stanislaus college, where he received the mental training that has so well fitted him for the duties of his present position. For a short time he was deputy clerk, and in 1879 he was elected to the office of clerk of Hancock county, which he has held continuously ever since. He has made a most efficient officer and has carried on the business of the office with a zeal and ability that have inspired the greatest confidence in his constituency. He owns a nice residence in the Bay, and is surrounded with peace and plenty. He was married in 1881 to Miss Catherine Riensech, and five children have been born to them: Catherine A., E. H., Jr., Alvina R., George W. and an infant. The family belong to the Roman Catholic church. In his political opinions Mr. Hoffman has affiliated with the democratic party. He has taken a deep interest in the movements of that body, and is well posted on all the leading issues of the day. He is a man true to his principles, true to his friends, and true to himself; a citizen of whom any community would be proud.

David L. Holcomb, who is following the occupation of a planter in Grenada county, Miss., was originally from North Carolina, his birth occurring in that state in 1844. He is the son of David and Eliza (Crump) Holcomb, natives also of the Old North state, and the

Fraternally Yours,
J. L. Power
Grand Secretary.

grandson of Philip Holcomb, who lived to a very old age. The latter was the father of seven children, all of whom lived to be grown, but only one now living: Rachel, who resides in North Carolina and is the wife of Daniel Long. David Holcomb, father of subject, was born in 1807 and was reared in his native state. After his marriage, or in 1859, he moved over-land to Texas and settled in the southern part of the state, Gonzales county, where he resided until his death in 1872. He was elected sheriff of Surry county, N. C., at the age of twenty-one, and held that position for one term. He was a democrat in his political views and was well read and well posted on all political matters. He was a very successful planter and before the war owned a great deal of property in the Lone Star state. He was a moral, upright and much esteemed citizen. His wife, who was born in 1814, was a very active member of the Baptist church. She died in Texas in 1883. They were the parents of ten children, all of whom lived to be grown, but only one besides our subject living at the present time: William F. Holcomb, who resides in Texas and is engaged in the hardware business at Luling, Caldwell county. Those deceased are: James P., who died at Los Angeles, Cal.; Sally A., the wife of W. R. Johnson, died in Texas; Sophronia was the wife of Quinn Van, and died in the Lone Star state; Carolina, wife of A. J. Boldin, died in Texas also; Marga-ret, wife of A. J. Aulford; Columbus A., Daniel E. and George all died in Texas. David L. Holcomb was reared in Texas and early initiated into the duties of farm life. On the 24th of November, 1862, he entered Captain King's company, Hardeman's regiment, and partici-pated in all the fights of the trans-Mississippi department. He was in Harrison's brigade, Texas volunteer infantry, of the trans-Mississippi department of the Confederate states army, and served until discharged at Richmond, Tex., on the 24th of May, 1865, remaining true to the colors to the last. He remained in Texas until 1867, and then came to Mississippi, settling near Bellevue Place, which he purchased in 1885. Mr. Holcomb now has about seventeen hundred acres and has eight hundred acres under cultivation, all the result of a determined spirit, for he had but fifty cents after returning from the war. He was first married in 1868 to Miss Molly Turner, daughter of Robert Turner (see sketch of R. H. Turner), and to them were born two children, Lida and Paschal, the latter in Memphis, Tenn., with Lowenstein & Co. The mother of these children died in 1878, and Mr. Holcomb was afterward married to Miss Georgia Williams, daughter of Dr. J. M. Williams, now living in Grenada and a planter by occupation. Four children have been born to this union: Clyde, May, Edwin and Hortense. Mr. and Mrs. Holcomb are members of the Methodist Episcopal church and active workers in the same. Both the elder children were educated at Grenada college, but Paschal supplemented this by a course at Buena Vista, Miss. Mr. Holcomb takes some interest in politics and affiliates with the democratic party. He has been a member of the county con-vention and has filled many other positions. He is one of the leading planters of the county, has his large estate under good management, and on this has one of the finest residences in the county.

John Holder, grandfather of Col. W. D. Holder, of Jackson, Miss., removed from his native state, Virginia, and joined Daniel Boone and party on their journey to the state of Kentucky, and assisted in building a stockade fort on the Kentucky river at a place known as Boonesboro, in 1775. The Indians infested the country round about and made frequent attacks upon the fort, which was always successfully defended. Of the party in the fort were the daughter of Daniel Boone, Jemima, also Betsey and Fanny Calloway, sisters of Flanders Calloway, one of the young adventurers; there was also a young Henderson; all of these except Holder had gone with Boone from the Yadkin river, N. C. When the eglantine, hydrangea and other wild flowers were drooping their beautiful heads over the pellucid waters

59

of the Kentucky river, the three young girls mentioned set out in a light canoe, intent upon an evening row, to gather wild flowers for their young lovers, and decorate their rugged habitation. They had not proceeded far when a party of six Indians, who had stealthily concealed themselves along the caney banks, rushed out and captured the boat and party. The screams of the affrighted girls soon brought the heroic little garrison to arms, and a rescuing party, consisting of Boone, Calloway, Holder, Henderson and one other, was organized and started in pursuit. Boone, knowing the habits and usages of the Indian so well, found no difficulty in taking their track, which was marked by broken twigs, fragments of torn garments and such other marks as could from time to time be left by the thoughtful girls, who were confident that a rescuing party would be on the trail. On the evening of the second day, the Indians, feeling that they had evaded pursuit, and being successful in killing a buffalo had kindled their camp fire, and while five of the number were engaged in skinning the buffalo the sixth was left to guard the captives. Boone at once took in the situation, and so disposed and instructed his gallant band, that each with his unerring rifle was to single out his Indian and at a given signal were to fire simultaneously, himself selecting the Indian who stood guard over the girls. At the report of the guns the five red men bit the dust, and the sixth fleeing in wild fright, the overjoyed girls rushed in wild delight, and were soon in the arms of friends and lovers. In winding their way back to the fort, the story goes—Calloway told his tale of love to Jemima Boone, Henderson to Betsey Calloway and Holder to Fanny Calloway, resulting at an early day thereafter in the marriage of the respective pairs as named. This small band was reinforced from year to year, until Kentucky, the " dark and bloody ground," was peopled with a brave and enterprising race, and the red man driven into the western wilds. Boone and Calloway removed with their families and many friends and followers to the Missouri river and in the counties of Boone and Calloway many of their descendants still live. Holder remained in Kentucky and his family drifted South and settled in Tennessee. Richard Calloway Holder, the father of Colonel Holder, was born in Madison county, Ky., near the old fort. He was a captain in the War of 1812, going as a volunteer from Kentucky, and operating in the northwest and in Canada. After the war he was elected clerk of the court, after which he engaged in raising and dealing in horses, building up quite a trade in Georgia and South Carolina. He was married to Miss Dunbar in Georgia, after which he removed to Tennessee and settled in Franklin county. Two daughters—Sarah J., Fanny L—and one son, William Dunbar, were the issue. The mother died when the son was only a few weeks old. Her mother surviving and being a member of the family, took charge of and reared the infant. In 1839 the family, consisting of grandmother, father and three children, removed to Mississippi; the grandmother dying in 1844 and the father previously in 1842. Meanwhile the sisters had married; the son settled temporarily in 1841 with his father near Houston, Miss. His father dying there, the son soon thereafter moved to Pontotoc, Miss., and was appointed deputy United States district clerk and subsequently deputy United States marshal; in 1853 was elected to the Mississippi legislature, serving one term, not asking for a reëlection. In June, 1854, he was married near Oxford, Miss., to Miss Bowles; ten children, eight boys and two girls, being the result, six boys and one girl surviving. Their mother died in Jackson, Miss., in 1887. In April, 1861, W. D. Holder organized a company of infantry, and in May following was mustered into the Confederate service, joining the Seventeenth Mississippi regiment, then at Corinth, Miss. W. S. Featherston, col.; John McGuirk, lieutenant-col.;—Lyle, major. His command was ordered to Virginia and took part in the battle of Manassas or Bull run, next in the battle of Leesburg or Balls bluff, next in the seven days' fight on the Chickahominy. Meanwhile Featherston had been promoted to brigadier-general and the regiment reorganized by electing Holder colonel. Holder, while in command of his regiment, was wounded at Malvern hill, the last battle of the seven days, having the left thigh broken near the body. Partially recovering from this wound, he resumed command of his company and took part in the battle of Chancellorsville. He next moved with the army of northern Virginia into Pennsylvania and took part in the battle of Gettysburg, where he received a wound in the abdomen, resulting in permanent disability. The ball was cut out four years after the war. He resigned his command in the army and was elected to the Confederate congress to succeed Gen. Reuben Davis from the Northeast district of Mississippi, 1863. He served until the end of the war. Afterward he engaged in farming in Mississippi and was appointed deputy auditor in 1886 and is now holding that position.

S. F. Holditch, whose postoffice address is Ecru, Pontotoc county, Miss., was born in Lawrence district, S. C., in 1825. There his father, who was George Holditch, was born February 14, 1789; and his mother, Jennie Finley, was born in the same place in 1799. They were married in 1817. His father, who was a carpenter by trade, was, during much of his life, a planter in Mississippi, where he removed in 1846. He was the father of nine children: William H., who is deceased; John F.; Margaret C., the wife of W. D. Sloan; S. F., who is married; Mary E., is deceased; J. N. Collins, deceased; Emma, who married J. Pruett; Laura F., the wife of J. Wilkins; Dorothy, the wife of Doctor Cullens. Mr. Holditch died in 1862, and his wife died in 1889. They were members of the Baptist church, and he was a contributor to all local interests, religious, educational, or otherwise. Personally, he was very popular and made many warm friends among all classes. While yet a mere youth, in 1815, he was in service in an Indian war in Florida. S. F. Holditch began life for himself in 1850, engaging in the mercantile business at New Albany, Miss. One year later, although he had been successful, not liking the business he disposed of it and removed to Pontotoc county, Miss., and engaged in planting near Wallerville, Miss. In 1852 he married Miss Frances Smith, daughter of Elijah Smith, a farmer. To this union were born six children: Roenna J., the wife of George Stephens; Jefferson D., who married; Lewis B., deceased; Sidney M., Jennie E. and George W. The last three are unmarried. In 1861 Mr. Holditch enlisted in the Confederate service, under Colonel Falkner, in the Second regiment, in General Whiting's brigade, of Joe Johnston's division. Later he served under Colonel Falkner, in the Fourth Mississippi cavalry. He was in the battle of Bull Run, and in 1862 he was promoted to a lieutenantcy of a company in the Fourth regiment, under General Chalmers. Returning home, in 1865, he has since been engaged in planting. He is the owner of about four hundred acres of land, about one-half of which is under cultivation. He is a member of the Farmers' Alliance, and is regarded as an honest, upright, and, in every way, an estimable citizen.

Prof. G. A. Holley, B. S. & M. Acct., and Prof. J. T. Holley, B. S., Oakland Normal institute, Yale, Itawamba county, Miss. Prof. G. A. Holley, B. S. & M. Acct., the senior principal of the Oakland Normal institute, was born in Alabama, November 27, 1859. He is a son of R. C. and Emiline J. (Jackson) Holley. His mother was a relative of Gen. Andrew Jackson, and has borne her husband seven children: Martha L., the wife of A. J. Raper; R. A. married Miss Maggie Wreich; Susan is the wife of Monroe Wreich; Charles D. is a teacher; F. M. is a planter. Prof. G. A. Holley is the second of the family. After attending the free schools of Alabama, he came with his father to Mississippi, at the age of nineteen, and located on a plantation in Itawamba county. He soon became a student in the Highland Home school, at Rara Avis, where he remained for a year and a half, going thence to the Iuka Normal institute, having previously attended the National Normal university, at

Lebanon, O. He finished his education at Iuka, graduating with the degrees of B. S. & M. Acct., in 1886. After teaching for a year at the Cooper Normal college, he, in partnership with his brother, Professor J. T. Holley, founded Oakland Normal institute in 1887, a more extensive notice of which appears below. He was married December 26, 1886, to Miss Cordelia P. Hale, who was born in Mississippi, March 14, 1868. She is a daughter of Nathaniel Hale, who was a native of Tennessee, and her mother of Alabama, both of whom are members of the Missionary Baptist church. They had two children: James N. and Cordelia P. To Mr. and Mrs. Holley have been born two children, one of whom is living: Zena Hester. Politically, Mr. Holley is a democrat, and he cast his first presidential vote for Grover Cleveland. He is a master mason, and a member of the Missionary Baptist church. He is a strong advocate of temperance reform, and a friend of any measure tending to the elevation and ennobling of mankind. Prof. J. T. Holley, B. S., junior principal of the Oakland Normal institute, a younger brother of Prof. G. A. Holley, was born in Alabama, April 24, 1862. After attending the public schools of Alabama and Mississippi, he entered Iuka college, and went thence to Cooper college. The degree of B. S. was conferred upon him in 1887, at the Cooper Normal college. He was the third child and second son of his parents, and came with them to Itawamba county when young. In 1889 he was married to Miss Mackie M. Senter, who was born in Mississippi in 1869, a daughter of R. T. and Malinda (Priddy) Senter, and the second of their eight children. To Mr. and Mrs. Holley has been born one son: Chester Orville. Professor Holley is a democrat, and, like his brother, cast his first presidential vote for Grover Cleveland. He and his wife are communicants at the Missionary Baptist church. He is no less an advocate of the temperance reform than his brother, and as an educator has attained a high rank. Oakland Normal institute is situated in the eastern part of Itawamba county, about twelve miles east of Fulton, in a beautiful oak grove, from which it takes its name. The main building is 40x50 feet, and two stories high, and has a seating capacity of about seven hundred. The school property cost about $4,300, and the building was erected by Prof. G. A. Holley. The institution was chartered in 1891, and is still under the control of the Professors Holley. It is the only educational institution in the county that confers degrees. Its faculty is constituted as follows: G. A. and J. T. Holley, principals; G. A. Holley, professor of the natural sciences, school government and methods of teaching, and bookkeeping; J. T. Holley, professor of mathematics, grammar and English literature; E. C. Reel, B. A., professor of Latin, Greek, logic, criticism, mental philosophy, political economy, law and government; Miss Marie Underhill, B. E., teacher of elocution and rhetoric; A. J. Hodges, teacher of history and geography; W. J. Clark, teacher of penmanship; Miss Eva Boydstun, teacher of instrumental music; Mrs. C. P. Holley, B. S., teacher of drawing and painting; Mrs. M. M. Holley, D. B., teacher of the primary department; Miss Winona Boydstun, M. E. L., typewriter, stenography teacher; Miss Eva Boydstun, teacher in vocal culture; J. T. Holley, vocal music; A. J. Hodges, general correspondent. Beginning life without capital, these gentlemen have made the best of every opportunity that has been presented, and in the Oakland institute they have built up an educational institution that would do credit to older founders and a much older section of the country, which is becoming more and more popular as its merits become known.

Benjamin P. Holliday, a farmer of Monroe county, was born two miles west of Prairie station on the farm on which he still resides, in 1846. He is the son of Col. John and Maria (Speight) Holliday, who were born in North Carolina in 1803 and 1817, respectively. Mr. Holliday came to Mississippi in 1837 and married there, settling where our subject now lives. In 1852 they moved to Aberdeen, where Mr. Holliday died in 1881, and where Mrs. Holliday still lives. Mr. Holliday never gave his attention to any other vocation than that of planting. He served as colonel of militia in North Carolina; was an A. F. & A. M., standing high in that order; was a very successful planter, as was proven by the fact that he accumulated a handsome property. He was the son of William Holliday, a native of North Carolina, where he was a merchant and planter. His grandfather was Hon. Jesse Speight, a native of North Carolina, where he served several years in congress. In 1836 he came to near where West Point now is. He was a noted lawyer and politician, and represented Mississippi in the United States senate at the time of his death, and was succeeded by Jefferson Davis. Our subject was the fifth of ten children, of whom four are living: Mary A. (wife of Judge Baxter McFarland); Mariah S. (wife of William G. Elkin, president of the Bank of Aberdeen); Walter R. (a planter), and our subject. A son, Capt. T. C. Holliday, was killed at the battle of the Wilderness, having served from the beginning of the war on General Davis' staff. Benjamin P. Holliday was educated in the common schools of Monroe county. In 1863 he joined company C, of the Sixteenth Confederate volunteers. He fought at Lafayette, Resaca, at Atlanta and at Mobile. He was paroled at Gainesville, Ala., May 6, 1865. After his return home he clerked for some time and was engaged in the mercantile business for a year or two in Okolona, Miss. Since that time he has lived on the old home place. He and his brother Walter are the owners of over three thousand acres of land—one of the best farms in the county or state, and which raises about five hundred bales of cotton annually. It is out a way on the prairie, and people often drive out to see this model farm. The brothers inherited a portion of it from their father, but have added greatly to it by their own efforts, and it is a place of which they may well be proud. Mr. Holliday is a member of the A. F. & A. M., of Aberdeen lodge. He is a tall, fine looking man, and is noted for his genial ways and the hospitality which always keeps the latchstring out in this plantation of the sunny South. He comes of a family of which any man might well boast, and is naturally proud of that fact, and the life of Benjamin P. Holliday proves that he intends to add luster to the name he bears.

I. N. Holliday, farmer, Sharon, Miss., came originally from Georgia, his birth occurring in Wilkes county, December 20, 1824, and his parents, Richard I. and Mary E. (Evans) Holliday, were natives respectively of Maryland and Georgia. They came to Madison county in 1844, and there the father followed the uneventful life of a farmer until his death, in July, 1857. He was very active in politics. The mother died in 1852. Of the seven children born to this union, all grew to mature years, married, but only two besides our subject are now living: Thomas L., a farmer of this county, and Emily, wife of Frank Cetchings, of Copiah county. I. N. Holliday, the fifth in order of birth of the above mentioned children, started out for himself at the age of twenty-one years without any capital, and in fourteen years had made $25,000. Miss E. A. Tisdale, who became his wife in 1846, was the daughter of William and Frances (Finney) Tisdale, natives of Virginia. The fruits of this union were ten children, seven of whom are living. In 1861 Mr. Holliday entered the Confederate service, company E, Eighteenth Mississippi cavalry, and served as courier for General Loring. He was in all the battles of his command from Resaca to Atlanta and back to Nashville and Franklin. At the close of the war he had three hundred and twenty acres of land, but he now has twenty-three hundred acres and raises about one hundred and fifty bales of cotton per annum, besides raising all his own corn and forage. He is also quite extensively engaged in stockraising—Shorthorn and Holstein cattle and Southdown sheep. For thirty-five years he has been a member of the Masonic lodge, and has been treasurer of Sharon lodge for years. He is also a charter member of the Knights of Honor. He has always taken a deep interest in politics, and was very active in 1875 and 1876 in helping to establish a better form of home government. He has been industrious and thoroughgoing all his life, and has amassed a fortune by his own efforts. He and Mrs. Holliday are members of the Methodist church. Their children are named in the order of their birth, as follows: William T., a farmer of Madison county; Joseph E., of Sharon; Louisa, wife of J. M. Holley; Annie, wife of George Galloway; Martha, wife of H. C. Turner; Sallie, wife of J. M. Pace; and John. All the children live in Madison county. Mr. and Mrs. Holliday have about thirty-three grandchildren.

Thomas A. Holloman, Phœnix, Yazoo county, Miss., is the eighth of a family of eleven children. He was born the 9th day of December, 1852, to John B. and Nancy (Bruffey) Holloman, natives of Missouri. The father emigrated to Mississippi in 1852, where he engaged in mercantile pursuits and agriculture. He was very successful in his business and when he had accumulated a considerable estate he retired from active business circles. His father was Edmond Holloman of North Carolina. Thomas A. grew to manhood in Mississippi, Yazoo county, amidst the surroundings of his birthplace. He enjoyed more than ordinary educational advantages. He attended the private schools of the neighborhood until he was eighteen years of age and then entered the Southern university, Greensboro, Ala., where he was a student for four years. He was graduated with the class of 1876 with the master's degree, when he returned to his home and entered a mercantile business life. He owns one hundred and sixty acres of land, thirty acres being under cultivation. He carries a stock of goods valued at $3,000 and transacts a large business annually. He has been twice married. First in 1879, he was united to Miss Julia White, a native of Alabama, but reared in Louisiana and a daughter of the Rev. Benjamin F. White of the Louisiana conference of the Methodist Episcopal Church South. One child was born—Thomas W. Mrs. Holloman died August 25, 1882. Mr. Holloman was married a second time, February 25, 1885, to Miss Laura S. Warren of Yazoo City, Miss., a daughter of L. B. Warren, Esq., who was for many years cashier of the bank of Yazoo City. This union resulted in the birth of four children; Julia R., deceased, Elbert A. deceased, Ellen S. and Melville G. The father and mother are members of the Methodist Episcopal Church South. Mr. Holloman is also a member of the Knights of Honor. He was elected a member of the board of supervisors of Yazoo county in 1882–4. He is a prominent character in the political ranks of his county, and takes a deep interest in all public matters. In the work of his church he is also very faithful and efficient. He has been a lay member of the Mississippi annual conference of the Methodist Episcopal Church South for ten years, and has served on many important boards. He is the present treasurer of the board of church extension of said conference. He was a member of the general conference of his church held at Richmond, Va., in 1886, and at St. Louis, Mo., in 1890. He has shown himself worthy of these positions, and has the universal esteem of the community.

Among the prominent planters of the state who have become noted for their success in this pursuit may be found Col. Ira G. Holloway, planter, Oxford, Miss., who is in every way worthy of the reputation he bears. He was born in Tuscaloosa county, Ala., in 1832, and came with his parents to Monroe county, Miss., in 1842. They located on a plantation, and there the Colonel passed his boyhood days. His early scholastic advantages were good, and at the age of twenty-two he completed his education in the university of Mississippi. After this he took up the study of medicine, but the death of his father prevented his going on with that profession, as he had to look after the business the latter had left. Since that time he has devoted his time to agricultural pursuits. When the war broke out in 1861 he went out with the third company from Monroe county, but was soon taken sick and obliged to return home, where he remained until 1864. He then again enlisted and served until the close. He had two brothers in the Confederate army, Z. N. and J. L. The former was slain at the bloody battle of Shiloh, and the latter is now a planter of Crittenden county, Ark. Colonel Holloway owns an extensive plantation in the Mississippi bottoms, twenty-four miles south of Memphis. He is an active member of the Baptist church, and a liberal contributor to all worthy undertakings. He is generous, public-spirited, and finds his greatest pleasure in the happiness of his friends and in the gratification of every wish of his family. His first marriage was to Miss Bettie Love, of Aberdeen, Miss., who bore him nine children. After her death he married Mrs. Shotwell, formerly a Miss Brown, daughter of Col. James Brown. Colonel Holloway was elected to the legislature by the democratic party in 1871 and served until 1875, at which time he retired from politics, and has devoted his attention to his plantation since. He became a Mason in 1860, and since then he has been active in the various branches of that lodge. In order to give his children better educational advantages, he moved to Oxford in 1886, and there he resides at the present time. His father-in-law, Col. James Brown, was born in Maury county, Tenn., on the 25th of October, 1796, and died near Victoria, Tex., on the 16th of January, 1880. He was of Irish descent, his grandfather, James Brown, having emigrated from the Emerald Isle to Virginia when a youth. The latter removed to Guilford county, N. C., where Joseph Brown (the father of the Colonel) was born in 1772. In 1778 Grandfather Brown attempted to migrate from Guilford to the Cumberland country, a task not only very tedious but very hazardous, as the intervening country was full of Indians. He attempted to reach Nashville by descending the Tennessee river and ascending the Ohio and Cumberland rivers in a boat. The party passed the Chickamauga towns safely, but the Indians sent runners across the mountains to intercept them at Running Water town and Nickajack, where they were all captured and killed except the father of the Colonel, his mother and two little sisters. They were prisoners for many months, but were finally released. The Indians hesitated for some time before releasing Joseph Brown, for they feared he would return and revenge himself by destroying them. They were right in their surmises, for he did return with a company raised for that purpose, and entirely broke up the band. Col. Joseph Brown settled in Maury county, Tenn., and at his house the first court ever held in the county convened. The first trial involved but $16.50, in which Thomas H. Benton, the noted United States senator of Missouri was a participant. In this house Col. James Brown was born, and there grew to manhood. His early educational advantages were limited, as school facilites were not very good at that early date, and in his early school days he was a classmate of James K. Polk. He became one of a company and was engaged in surveying Chickasaw lands. He was also one of a party that ran the Winchester survey between Tennessee and Mississippi, and engaged in land speculations, which proved eminently successful. Colonel Brown returned to Maury county in 1825 and was married there to Miss Annie Williamson, sister of Col. McCord Williamson, secretary of state under Governor Reynolds of Mississippi, and Mrs. William S. Burney. He then located in Jackson, Tenn., and after the death of Mrs. Brown in 1833, he removed to Mississippi, locating permanently in Lafayette county, in 1836. There he surveyed the Chickasaw lands, this being ordered by the government. In this way he familiarized himself with the value of lands, and when they were put into market he purchased largely, thus becoming very wealthy. Colonel Brown distinguished himself in everything he undertook, and everything seemed to prosper in his hands. He owns extensive plantations in Lafayette, Panola, Tunica, Coahoma, and Bolivar counties. In 1840 he married Miss Mary Strong, a highly cultivated and intelligent lady, and to them were born three daughters, all of whom live consistent Christian lives. The Colonel took great interest in educational enterprises and established Mount Sylvan, eleven miles west of Oxford, and tendered it to the Oxford presbytery, for the Cumberland Presbyterian church. It was successfully conducted by Dr. Robert Morris and by S. G. Burney, D. D. Colonel Brown also educated several young men for the ministry. He became a member of the board of trustees and was one of its most useful adjuncts. While he was not a classical scholar, he was one of the best trustees the university ever had. Any cause he espoused was sure of success, for he never abandoned it until the desired end was obtained. He represented his county as senator, twice in the legislature. When the Mississippi Central railroad scheme was first inaugurated he early became enlisted in the project. He was made a director and was also a stockholder when it was incorporated, and gave his time and means for its support. Through his instrumentality it runs where it now does, as a few miles west was selected by the engineers. He was ever a friend of his state, his county and his town. In 1818 he served with General Jackson against the Seminole Indians, and all honor is due him for his deeds and his worth. His father was a minister of the gospel for more than forty-eight years, but his history is too well known to try to add to it.

Capt. John C. Holmes, farmer and merchant, Fearn's Springs, Miss., is one of the pioneer settlers of the county and an agriculturist of advanced ideas and principles. He was originally from Buncombe county, North Carolina, born 1817, and was the son of Thomas and Margaret (Craig) Holmes, both natives of Virginia, the father born in 1786 and the mother in 1798. The parents were wedded in Buncombe county, North Carolina, and when the captain was an infant they removed to near the town of Birmingham, Ala. About 1822 they removed to Pickens county, were among the pioneer settlers, and in 1834 they located in Winston county, on Hashuqua creek, where the father began at once to improve a farm. The same year he built a grist and saw mill, the second in Winston county, and this he operated for many years. He was an early settler of this county also. The father had received but an ordinary education, but he was a man of excellent judgment, natural ability and broad intellect. He was justice of the peace and a member of the board of police for a number of years, and was an old school democrat in politics. He died in 1874, in full communion with the Methodist church. His wife died in Alabama in 1833, and he was married twice afterward. He had one child by each of the last marriages, but both are deceased, one dying during the war. Mr. and Mrs. Holmes were both left orphans at an early age, and being cousins were reared by an uncle. Their eight children were named in the order of their births as follows: Jesse, died in Texas; John C., Thomas F., died on the old farm in Winston county in 1890; Amanda J., widow of Asbury Fleetwood; Julius M., of Texas, was in the late war; Payton G., was also in the late war and died in the Lone Star state; Stokely M., of Texas, also, was in the war and held the rank of major of a Texas regiment, and Rufus F., of Winston county, was also in the war between the two sections. While the Confederates were making the charge at Peach Tree creek he was wounded in the knee and left in the rear. While there he noticed a Federal soldier some distance away and beckoned him to approach. This the latter did, and when he got near enough Rufus drew a large knife and ordered the soldier to carry him to the Confederate camp, which was done by the latter without any hesitancy. Capt. John C. Holmes passed his boyhood days on the farm, received a common education and has added to this by observation and study until he is fitted to conduct almost any kind of business. He was married in 1837 to Miss Martha A. Reed, a native of Jefferson county, Mississippi, born in 1818, and the daughter of William and Jemima (Stampley) Reed, both natives of Mississippi, where they spent all their lives, the father dying in Madison county. To Captain and Mrs. Holmes were born four children: Margaret (deceased), was the wife of E. B. Suttles; Callie, is the wife of James P. McGraw; Robert (deceased), was sergeant in the Fifth Mississippi under Captain Reed, and died near Pensacola in December, 1861; Mary is the wife of Timothy Anderson. Since his marriage the Captain has resided on his present farm, and is one of the leading landowners in the county, owning about two thousand acres and about one-fifth of Hashuqua factory, nearly all the fruits of his own labor. He was engaged in merchandising about twenty years before the war and has continued the same most of the time since. In 1868 he and others erected a cotton factory in the neighborhood and it was known as "Hashuqua factory." This Captain Holmes operated with fair success for fifteen years and since then it has been leased to different individuals. For fifteen years prior to the war Captain Holmes was postmaster at Fearn's Springs; was also justice of the peace, and was once a member of the board of police. In 1851 he was elected as a Unionist to the States' Rights convention that met at Jackson. He was a member of the militia a short time during the war. He is a member of Winstonville lodge No. 277, which was organized about 1863 with the Captain as worshipful master. Mrs. Holmes was a member of the Baptist church and died in 1890. She was an excellent woman.

James J. Holt was born in Yazoo county, Miss., June 21, 1863, and is one of the most enterprising young planters of the community. He is the youngest of a family of eight children born to Robert S. and Ann C. (Masily) Holt, natives of Kentucky and Tennessee, respectively. His father came to Mississippi in the pioneer days, and settled in Yazoo City, where he engaged in the practice of law. He followed this profession, successfully, until his death, which occurred in 1867. Joseph Holt, a brother of Robert S., also located in Yazoo City, and, while they were not partners in business, they often worked in the same suits. Joseph Holt was judge advocate-general during President Johnson's administration, and was a very conspicuous figure in the early political history of the county. James J. passed an uneventful youth, receiving his education in the public schools. He acquired a practical knowledge of bookkeeping, and has devoted some time to that work. At present, however, he is giving his entire time and attention to agricultural pursuits. He owns three hundred acres of land in the Yazoo valley, and two hundred acres have been developed into as fine farming land as lies within the borders of Yazoo county. He has made many modern improvements and surrounded himself with all the comforts of life. The growth of the country and the upbuilding of the county have been matters of the greatest importance to Mr. Holt, and he has not been slow to assist in these affairs, and to give zealous support to all worthy enterprises. Politically, he adheres to the principles of the democratic party. The Holt family is of English origin, and was one of the earliest to settle in America.

Hon. Joseph Holt was born in Breckinridge county, Ky., in 1807, was educated at Danville and thoroughly trained for the law. Admitted to the bar at Elizabethtown, in 1828, he became district attorney there, and later removed to Mississippi, in 1837, locating first at Jackson, then at Vicksburg. With the prestige of the prominent part he had previously taken in the race of Richard M. Johnson for the vice-presidency, and his wonderful speech in the national democratic convention of 1836, his reception in this state was flattering, and he was speedily recognized as one of the brightest lights of the bar of Mississippi. Ten years later he removed to Louisville, Ky. In 1857 he was appointed commissioner of patents; in 1859 he became postmaster-general; in 1860 he was made secretary of war; in 1862 he was appointed judge advocate-general. After the trial of the assassination conspirators and the execution of Harrold, Payne, Atzeroth and Mrs. Surratt he retired from view and lived in obscurity.

Capt. Charles B. Hood, a member of the firm of Clark, Hood & Co., Tupelo, Miss., was born in St. Clair county, Ala., in December, 1828, and is a son of William and Cecelia (Quinn) Hood, natives of Georgia. The father was born in 1796, and died in Monroe county, Miss., in 1885. He was a minister of the Missionary Baptist church, and preached the gospel for twenty-three years. In 1846 he removed to Mississippi from Alabama, and gave some attention to agriculture, although he devoted his best efforts to the ministry. His wife died in 1885 at the age of eighty-two years. She was a member of the Baptist church, and a worthy Christian woman. She was a daughter of John Quinn, a native of South Carolina, but her grandfather was born in Ireland. Captain Hood is the fifth of a family of nine children: Hiram; Narcissa, widow of S. Rogers; Calvin D.; Almeda, deceased, was the wife of E. Merritt; Charles B., Sidney, deceased; Franklin D., deceased; John D., deceased; and Elizabeth, now Mrs. Williams. The Captain grew to manhood in Monroe county, Miss., and received but a limited education. At the age of twenty-one years he left the paternal roof and engaged in farming on his own account. The following year he came to Mississippi, where he engaged as a clerk; thence he went to Pontotoc, Miss., where he remained until the Civil war. There he was employed by Martin & Duke, with the exception of one year. After the war he went back and clerked for the new firm of Duke & Martin. In 1872 he came to Tupelo and formed a partnership with the gentlemen with whom he is now associated. The firm of Clark, Hood & Co. do an immense wholesale and retail business, employing a capital of $100,000. The different departments of the business are superintended by competent men. They have two stores besides the one at Tupelo; one is at Shannon and the other one is at Nettleton. Capain Hood was married to Miss Martha L. Wiley, a native of Alabama and a daughter of Joseph Wiley, a planter of Pontotoc county, Miss. Six children were born of this union, two of whom are deceased: Mabel, Joseph F., Edwin D., and Hattie Lee. Maggie and May were twins; they were beautiful girls, but death claimed them at the age of four years. Capt. Hood enlisted in the Confederate service from Pontotoc county. He was made second lieutenant, and was promoted to the first lieutenancy. When his regiment was reorganized the second time at Greensboro, N. C., he was made captain of one of the three companies into which the regiment was divided, being appointed by President Davis. Soon after this the company surrendered at High Point, N. C. Captain Hood participated in many of the most important engagements of the conflict, and had many narrow escapes from death and captivity. Politically he is an ardent democrat. He has held the position of alderman of Tupelo, and there is not a citizen of the place who has devoted more honest effort to her interests. He and his wife are members of the Presbyterian church, of which he is an elder. He belongs to the Masonic order, having reached the degree of Knight Templar. He is also a member of the I. O. O. F. He has filled some of the highest offices of both lodges, and is highly regarded not only by the fraternities but by the entire community. He has made his way in the business world solely by his own efforts, and the high position which he has attained in the commercial circles of Mississippi is a reward of which he is in every way worthy.

Rev. William Hoover was born in Pike county, Miss., at Oak Grove, the home of his father, Judge Christian Hoover, one mile from Myrtle Place, his present residence, January 25, 1832. His father, Christian Hoover, son of Christian Hoover and Mary Zeigler, was born in Orangeburg district, S. C., November 24, 1796. He came to Mississippi when it was a territory and a wild country, inhabited principally by Indians and wild beasts. He was a soldier in the war of 1812; was at the battle of New Orleans. He married Mrs. Mary Neyland Nailer, April 8, 1823. She was a sweet-spirited Christian woman, of remarkable beauty of person and soul, and to him was as the flower-garden of the Lord. He was one of the earliest settlers of the state, and subsequently became a prominent figure in Mississippi, being active in local and state politics. His first official position was that of justice of peace. Later he was a member of the board of supervisors and was probate judge for twenty years. He represented Pike county in the state legislature, and was a representative of his district in the state senate. He proved true to the trust reposed in him, and was honored and respected even by his political opponents. He was a successful farmer, and amassed a large fortune. He was a devout Christian, and avoided even the appearance of evil; was generous and kind to the poor, and helped many to independence who would otherwise have eked out a miserable existence. He was a man of prayer, and did not dare to sin. He had over one hundred negroes on his plantation. The circuit preacher, who preached in his home also preached to the negroes, and many of them were taught the way of life, and bless the memory of this sainted man for the happy homes they had there, and refer with pride to his care of them in sickness or trouble. His beloved wife died February 3, 1858. By her he had fourteen children; only eight survived the mother. He was a true democrat; was a well-read man; had a splendid library. His children were well educated in the best schools. He married a second wife, Mrs. S. S. Equeen, of New Orleans, La., May, 1859. By her he had two sons. On July 27, 1868, he gathered up his feet in death, and joyfully went home to God. Truly he deserved the eulogy pronounced by Solomon on old age: A hoary head is a crown of glory, if it be found in the ways of righteousness, and a good name is rather to be chosen than great riches, and loving favor more than choice gold. William, the sixth son of Christian and Mary Hoover, was reared on the farm, attending school near his home until he was sixteen years of age. After that time he entered Centenary college, at Jackson, La., where he was a student for four years, when his health became impaired and he was compelled to relinquish his studies, and was thus prevented from graduating. In 1852 he was married to Miss Martha L. J. Thompson, a native of Mississippi, who was reared near Greensburg, La. She was the daughter of Alexander Thompson, of Georgia, and Dorothy Prior Womack, of St. Helena parish, La. She was educated at Readville seminary, Baton Rouge, La. In a quiet, humble way she was a leader in church and temperance work, and her best energies have been spent in the service of God. She is gifted in prayer, and it has been said that her prayers contain more theology than some preachers' sermons. To Mr. and Mrs. Wm. Hoover have been born nine children: Christian R., Thomas Y., William J., Robert M., Mattie A., John S., Diotician A., Virginia D. and Wheat A. Mr. Hoover is a successful planter, owning six hundred acres of fine land, about a third of which is tillable. After the war he had a church built for the negroes to worship in, and also largely assisted in building a chapel near his home, called St. Mary, in memory of his mother. During the Civil war he was chaplain in the Thirty-third Mississippi infantry, but owing to his position he, of course, was not a participant in the battles. He has been a local preacher in the Methodist Episcopal Church South for thirty-five years. Until the last five years he has been employed by the Mississippi conference on mission and circuit work. His family, which is of German origin, was one of the oldest in this part of the South. Mr. Hoover is a well-rounded character in every relation of life, is liberal-minded, progressive, and has contributed his full share toward the establishment and maintenance of beneficial institutions, and aided everything that has a tendency to further the interests of his county and his people.

William N. Hood, a prominent citizen of Washington county, Miss, is descended from one of the oldest and best-known families of the state of Kentucky, members of which took a

prominent part in its early history. He was born in Lexington, Ky., in 1832, to Dr. William
S. Hood, of Clark county, of that state, who for some years practiced medicine, but afterwards
abandoned it, when comparatively young, to take up the calling of a planter, continuing this
occupation until his death, which occurred on the Ohio river near Shawneetown, Ill., by the
explosion of the steamboat James Jackson. He was very successful in all his business enterprises, and at his death left his family well provided for. His widow, who was formerly Miss
Mary A. Smith, was born in Scott county, Ky., to Capt. Nelson Smith, whose native birthplace was Louisa county, Va. The paternal grandparents were Lucas and Frances (Wills)
Hood, the birth of the former occurring in what is now Clark county, Ky. (then Virginia),
the latter being also a native of the Old Dominion. James Hood, the great-grandfather,
was a major in the Revolutionary war, throughout which he served, being under Gen. Anthony
Wayne. He also took part in some of the early Indian wars of Kentucky. The maternal
great-grandfather, William Smith, was born in Louisa county, Va., was a planter and lived
the greater part of his life in Fayette county, Ky., where he reared a large family of children, Col. D. Howard Smith being his grandson, holding the position of auditor of Kentucky
for twelve years. Gen. G. W. Smith was his great-grandson. His wife was a Miss Rodes, a
native of Virginia. William N. Hood was the eldest in a family of three children, the other
two members of the family being Elizabeth Waller, wife of William R. Fleming, who died in
Lexington, Ky., in 1864, and Thomas Howard, who resides in Cynthiana, Ky. Although he
was a practitioner of medicine at one time, the most of his life has been devoted to the
drug business. Col. William Dudley married a great aunt of Mr. Hood's. The latter was
reared on Blue Glass soil and was educated in Georgetown of his native state. In 1858 he
began business on his own account, at which time he purchased his father's property in
Washington county, Miss., and began planting, which has been his chief occupation ever since.
In 1856 his marriage to Miss Clara Hickman, a native of Paris, Ky., was celebrated, she being
a daughter of William Hickman, of that state, her mother being a Miss Trueman, of Maysville, Ky. To Mr. Hood's marriage the following children were born: William Hickman,
a merchant of Magenta; Mary S., who resides at home; Clifton Rodes, also at home; Thomas
Howard, a merchant of Greenville; Elizabeth, at home, and Dabney H., who is attending
school at Versailles, Ky. Mr. Hood has always been a democrat in politics and in the progress and development of the county he has taken a deep interest and has done much toward
bringing it to its present admirable state of cultivation and civilization. He has a beautiful
and comfortable home on Deer creek, and with his family about him he is prepared to spend
the rest of his days in ease and comfort. His wife is an earnest worker in and a member of
the Baptist church.

 Thomas H. Hood, a member of a firm who deal in gents' furnishing goods, boots and
shoes, etc., was originally from the Blue Grass state, born in 1865, and is fourth in order of
birth of seven children born to William N. and Clara (Hickman) Hood, the parents, natives
also of that state, Scott and Bourbon counties respectively. The paternal grandfather, Dr.
William S. Hood, was a native also of Kentucky, and came to Mississippi at an early day,
acquiring property in Washington county. He had most extensive planting interests here
and was one of the county's prominent citizens. He was killed in a steamboat explosion.
After his death his son, William N. (father of the subject), assumed charge and came to
Greenville, where he made his home before the war, and where he has since resided. He,
with his uncle, L. R. Smith, has one of the finest plantations in Washington county. This
is called Magenta, and is on Deer creek. There are 1,300 acres under cultivation. Of
the seven children born to his marriage six are now living: W. H., Mary S., Clinton R., David

Hickman (died at the age of seventeen years), Thomas H., Elizabeth and Howard. Thomas H. Hood was educated in Washington county, and in 1883 began buying cottonseed for the Greenville oilworks. In 1884 he went to Bolivar county and clerked for W. E. Ringo & Co., for sixteen months after which he became manager in the mercantile business of E. F. Miller at Chickory Landing. There he remained two years and then embarked in business with Green, Clay & E. F. Miller at Kentucky Landing, under the firm name of T. H. Hood & Co. At the end of one year Mr. Hood sold out and came to Greenville, where he engaged in his present business. This firm carries a stock of goods valued at about $10,000 and have a rapidly increasing trade. Mr. Hood is thoroughly experienced in business matters and is a rising young business man. He has one of the best stores in Greenville.

There is a no more popular or useful man in Mississippi than the eminent lawyer, orator, soldier and statesman, Hon. Charles E. Hooker, of Jackson, who was born in Union district, S. C. He graduated from the Cambridge law school, and removed to Jackson, Miss., and entered upon the practice of his profession. He was elected district attorney of the River district in 1850, and was elected to the Mississippi legislature in 1859, but resigned his seat to enter the Confederate army, and was wounded during the siege of Vicksburg. Later he was promoted to the rank of colonel of cavalry, and assigned to duty on the military court attached to General Polk's command. He was elected attorney-general of the state of Mississippi in 1865, and reëlected in 1868, and, in common with the other civil officers of the state, was removed by the military authorities. He was elected to the XLIVth, XLVth, XLVIth, XLVIIth and Lth congresses, and was reëlected to the LIst congress as a democrat, receiving eleven thousand nine hundred and seventy-seven votes against three thousand eight hundred and eighty-seven votes for Kernaghan, republican. Mr. Hooker is a Mississippian in all that the term implies except by nativity, and when he adopted the state as his he gave to her all there was of his manhood, his talent and his patriotism. She has not an interest that is not near to his heart, not a cause for sorrow or for rejoicing that he does not make his own. There is no measure looking to the welfare of Mississippi and Mississippians that he does not aid if necessary with pen and tongue and purse. As a representative of the state in the national congress and before the country at large, he is the living embodiment of her spirit and her chivalry, and the clearest-headed and clearest-voiced advocate of her development and her advancement. For all that he is and for all that he has done for them he is loved by the people of Mississippi, and his fame as a statesman of the broadest views and most unselfish purposes, and as the "silver-tongued orator of the South," has extended to the remotest parts of the Union. He has sons on whom the mantle of his sturdy manhood will fall, and who promise to live after him something like the useful life which he has given to the state. These are Charles E. Hooker, Jr., a brilliant young lawyer of Dallas, Tex., and Allan J. Hooker, who occupies an honorable position at the national capital.

John Hopkinson, Wesson, Miss. Every man in the United States, by birth or its equivalent, shares or is a shareowner in the glorious privileges of our government to forge through the ranks of the many and become one of the few. A man who possesses the ability to do this—who by years of patient toil and unswerving loyalty to truth and integrity forces his way through the multitudes of others equally as ambitious and determined and wrests from the world a meed of victory, does not need a piece of academic parchment, learnedly inscribed, to make his life valuable to the community in which he lives, for by his sterling methods and his high moral purpose he has become a leading factor in the conservatism of the good government of his community and a valuable example to those whose efforts in human progress have just begun. Such a man Mr. John Hopkinson, the subject of this sketch. Mr.

Hopkinson was born in Lancashire, near Manchester, Eng., in the year 1840. His early education consisted of the regular scholastic studies of the common schools, and continued only until he was twelve years of age, at which time he was obliged to begin caring for himself. It is a tender age for a boy to start out in life's efforts, for he can scarcely be expected to understand what the full meaning of the world suggests; but many of the most respected and best-informed men of the day are those who began early in life to learn the lessons of labor and self-support. Mr. Hopkinson is one of such men. Endowed by nature with more than the common allotment of perception and force of character, his progress has been onward from the start. He made many changes in his early life, but always for the purpose of improving his mind and advancing his earnings. At the age of twelve he began work in a cottonmill near Manchester, and continued in that position until he was twenty years old. He then devoted four years to learning the manufacture of woolen fabrics in a large mill at Manchester, and he is to-day regarded as one of the most expert designers and finished calculators in the manufacture of cotton and woolen goods in America. He is an inventor of no small note, and has planned and executed some of the best methods of advanced manufacture in use to-day. In 1866 he came to America and began his career in the land of liberty at Philadelphia, where he entered the employ of Charles Spencer & Sons at Germantown. From those mills he went to the great mills of Aaron Jones at Germantown, and from there he soon went to Chambersburg, Penn. Believing, as he says, in the advice of Horace Greeley, he soon went farther west and settled at Johnstown, Penn., and worked in the woolenmills at that place, which at that time had five thousand operatives. Here Mr. Hopkinson remained until he had saved up considerable money, when he removed to Ohio, and in company with a friend rented a mill and started out on his own hook as a manufacturer of woolens. The adventure was not a success, and in a short time Mr. Hopkinson removed to Eminence, Ky., where he met Miss Delilah Cooley, of Langford, and married her. After his marriage he removed with his young wife to Grayhampton, Ky., and began work in the Anderson cotton factory. He remained at this point in the employ of the mills until 1873, when he came to Wesson and immediately entered the service of the great Mississippi mills, just then ro-organized and put into solid shape by Col. Edmund Richardson. Mr. Hopkinson entered the Mississippi mills as a foreman in one of the important departments, and in a short time was advanced to a more important place of trust and executive responsibility, and continued to advance until in a short time he was made general superintendent of the whole vast concern. In this position he has continued ever since and is looked upon as the practical father of the mills; knowing every detail in and out, every stop and start, he conducts the vast institution with a degree of exactness and profit to the owners and contentment to the employes only equaled by the magnitude of the mills themselves. Colonel Richardson reposed the utmost confidence in his superintendent, and it was never misplaced or abused. Colonel Richardson's eldest son, Mr. James S. Richardson, in a recent note to the writer, in connection with the history of his eminent father, further attests Mr. Hopkinson's virtues and truly remarkable executive ability by saying, " The great success of the mills is in a great part attributable to Mr. Hopkinson, the superintendent, who has been with the mills since they started, and to whom the government of its employes is entirely entrusted." To the mind familiar with the government of a mill employing two thousand people, these words speak volumes. They tell of the watchful and tireless care and kindly consideration that are absolutely necessary to successfully treat so vast a subject. Mr. Hopkinson has accumulated a comfortable fortune by strict economy and sobriety. He owns a handsome house in easy reach of the great mills, and while seated in this well-earned place of rest and comfort, surrounded by his good wife and children, the latter being two boys and two girls, his contentment is complete. In person Mr. Hopkinson bears a little resemblance to the typical Englishman. He stands about five feet eight inches in hight, and is compactly built. He has a penetrating yet kindly eye and a mild speech. He is pleasant in conversation and when talking of Colonel Richardson or his late employer and associate in the mill management, Captain Oliver, he is eloquent and intense. "I loved them both," said he to the writer, "but of course, I knew Captain Oliver more intimately, and there never lived a more manly man, a better friend or more just employer than he."

Hugh A. Hopper, general merchant and planter, of De Kalb, Kemper county, Miss., was born in Alabama in 1837, and is a son of John and Drucilla Hopper. When he was seventeen years of age his parents removed to Mississippi and settled on a farm, where he was trained to all the details of agriculture. He received his education in the common schools. He was married, at eighteen years of age, in Kemper county to Miss Catharine McRae, a daughter of James and Sarah (McArn) McRae. They had six children born to them: Emma, who is now Mrs. Cotton, a resident of West Virginia; James A.; Mary, now Mrs. Rosenbaum, of Kemper county; Thaddeus A., Ella and Effie, who died in childhood. The parents are members of the Presbyterian church. Mrs. Hopper died in 1882, and her remains were buried at De Kalb. Mr. Hopper enlisted, in 1861, in company H, of the Thirty-sixth Mississippi volunteer infantry, and served until the close of the struggle. After the war he was appointed sheriff of Kemper county, and was afterward elected treasurer. In the discharge of the duties pertaining to these offices he was faithful and efficient, and gave entire satisfaction to the people of the county. Since retiring from public office he has devoted himself to agriculture, in which he has been equally successful. He owns fifteen hundred acres of land and carries on a general farming business. He has a half interest in a mercantile business which is managed by his son, James A. He was one of the early settlers of the county and has been one of the potent factors in its development and progress. James A. Hopper was born in Kemper county, Miss., in 1864, and received his education in the common schools and at Oxford university. In 1883, after leaving school, he engaged in mercantile trade, his father owning the other half interest in the business. He has displayed good judgment and more than ordinary ability, and bids fair to take his place in the front rank of Kemper county merchants. He was married in 1890 to Miss Sarah Delchamps, of Mobile, Ala., a daughter of J. J. and Sarah Delchamps. Mrs. Hopper was born in Mobile, Ala., in 1864. She is a devoted member of the Episcopal church. Mr. Hopper belongs to the Masonic order. In his political opinions he adheres to the principles of the democratic party. In addition to the mercantile interests he owns some real estate in Kemper county.

Joshua Beaumont Hopson is one of the intelligent and deserving young planters of Coahoma county, and as he is industrious and enterprising, he gives promise of becoming one of the leading men of this section. He was born in this county on the 18th of November, 1870, the second of three children born to William H. and Mary R. (Porter) Hopson, both of whom were native Mississippians. The father was a very successful planter of this county, and during the late war served throughout the entire struggle in the Confederate army. He died in 1873, leaving behind him a record of honesty and industry which might well be followed by the rising generation. His parents, William H. and E. Tennessee (Badget) Hopson, were born in Kentucky, in which state they were members of prominent and respected families. The maternal grandfather was a Confederate soldier, and commanded his company. The Porters were from Missouri, where they were well known and prominent. Joshua B. Hopson was reared in the county of his birth, and was educated in the agricultural college and at Oxford. On account of failing health he left school in 1889 and took charge of a plantation, and although he has been familiar with planting all his life, he has succeeded admirably for so young a man, and is now the owner of ten hundred acres of some of the richest land in Coahoma county, six hundred of which are in a good state of cultivation, a large portion of which he has opened and improved himself. He devotes his entire time to his planting interests, and is a thoroughly practical and competent business man. He possesses excellent morals, is modest and quiet in demeanor and is strictly temperate. Being agreeable and very social in his tastes, he has won a wide circle of friends. He has a good business education, is a practical civil engineer and is a great reader and close student.

Mrs. L. M. Hopson owes her nativity to Robertson county, Tenn., and is the daughter of Benjamin and Mary (Williams) Mallory, the father a native of Virginia and the mother of North Carolina, descendants of representative families of those states. Mrs. Hopson was married in Tennessee to Dr. Howel H. Hopson, who was also a native of Tennessee, and the son of Joseph and Mary (Harrison) Hopson, and the fruits of this union were four children, two sons and two daughters. The eldest child died in infancy and the remainder are named as follows: Joseph J., Howel J. and Lillian. Dr. Hopson removed from Tennessee to Coahoma county, Miss., in 1867, located on the plantation formerly owned by his father, three miles south of Clarksdale, and there resided until the time of his death, which occurred on the 31st of December, 1879. Mrs. Hopson and two sons now survive him. They reside on the old plantation, consisting of eighteen hundred acres of land with nine hundred and forty acres under cultivation in the fertile bottoms of Sunflower river, and are successfully engaged in cultivating the soil. In the year 1890 five hundred bales of cotton were raised on the place, and this is doubtless owing entirely to the good management and industrious and persevering manner in which Mrs. Hopson superintends everything. She has a nice two-story frame house, good outbuildings, and quite a number of tenant houses. She is a member of the Methodist church South, and is a lady of culture and refinement. Her husband, Howel H. Hopson, studied medicine and practiced his profession for three years prior to the war. After that eventful period he devoted his time and attention to agricultural pursuits. He was a member of the Masonic fraternity.

Capt. James A. Hoskins is one of the leading citizens of Lincoln county, Miss., and was a native of Christian county, Ky., being born in 1832. He is a son of George C. and Nancy (Harned) Hoskins. His father was a native of Mead county, Ky., and was born in 1806. His mother was born in Meade county, Ky., in 1808. They were married near Brandenburg, and soon after moved to Hopkinsville, Christian county. In 1846 they came to Mississippi, where Mr. Hoskins engaged in planting and other business operations, being a mechanic of considerable ability and a man of more than ordinary enterprise. He erected a gristmill which, when it was completed, was the only one within a radius of thirty miles. Here the family lived for some years. The father died in Livingston, Ala., in his forty-seventh year. He was the youngest of sixteen sons and one daughter, all of whom lived to maturity, married and had families, and all of whom, except himself, lived to an advanced age. The death of Mr. Hoskins was caused by the formation of an abscess on his face, in consequence of having a tooth extracted. Of this large family most of them passed their lives in Jefferson, Meade and Hardin counties, Ky., and are buried near there. The eldest son of Mr. Ventrees, who married the only daughter of this family, was a musician of great ability and a master of the violin, as was also the eldest son of the family of Hoskins. It is a remarkable fact that there was not one ne'er-to-do-well among these sixteen sons, and that

H. W. Foote.

every one of them became well to do or wealthy. The original Hoskins family came from West Virginia. Col. John Hoskins, the first cousin of the subject, a colonel of infantry on the Federal side, was killed at Hoskins Crossroads, Ky., during the late war. After the death of Mr. Hoskins, Mrs. Hoskins remained a widow until 1873, when she died at the house of her son, James A. She had been for many years a member of the Baptist church, with which she united at Brandenburg, Ky. In 1841, upon the occasion of her baptism and that of eighty others, it was necessary to cut the ice, which was three feet thick, in order that the subjects for baptism might be immersed by Elder Fisher, a leading Baptist minister of that state. To Mr. and Mrs. Hoskins were born a large family, all of whom are living: Elizabeth, became the wife of Edward Rothrock, who died in Texas in 1889, leaving five sons and one daughter; the others are William S., James A., George W., Ellen, who married Alfred McClendon and lives in Brookhaven; Zachary T., Thomas D., who lives at Los Angeles, Cal. All of these, except the last mentioned, are living in Brookhaven. Our subject was reared in Kentucky and learned the trade of a machinist with Gaty, McCune & Co., of St. Louis. In 1849 he assisted in the removal of the Indians from Scott county, Miss. He built one of the first mills in Neshoba county, Miss., on the Pearl river, in which the lumber was cut with a circular saw. Since that time he has planned and built more than sixty sawmills in different parts of Mississippi. He came to Brookhaven in 1853, and there put up the first circular sawmill in this part of the state, where he has since been engaged in the manufacture of lumber. In connection with several other parties he bought seven miles of land along the line of the Jackson (now the Illinois Central) railroad. He was one of the lessees of the state penitentiary for ten years, and one of the builders, with convict help, of seventy-eight miles of the Gulf & Ship Island railroad to the gulf. He also built the railroad from Memphis to Holly Springs, working some eight hundred hands, employing six hundred hands alone in the grading operations. He was also the constructor of the Hoskins branch from Brookhaven, of which road he was general manager. He married Miss Lizzie A. Whitworth, of Brookhaven, a daughter of the founder of the Whitworth college. She was born in the last-named place in 1839, and has borne her husband twelve children: James M., Isaac W.; Jennie Davis, the wife of Charles Chrisman, son of Judge J. B. Chrisman, judge of the district in which they now live; George C., W. Warren, Samuel W., Bessie M., Julia, Launa Jones, Hamilton, Thomas, and Mattie. Mr. Hoskins served during the late war as the captain of the organization known as Hoskins' battery, which he recruited and equipped, and which entered service May 11, 1861, and was paroled after the war, May 11, 1865. He was on duty at Grand Gulf, Port Gibson, Port Hudson, Raymond, Yazoo City, Chickamauga, Jackson, Meridian and Rome and on the one hundred days' campaign never missed a fight. He was within sixty feet of General Polk when that officer was killed, and was between General Eckles and Captain Ward, of Huntsville, Ala., when the former had his left leg shot off and the other received a mortal wound in the hip, from which he died the following day. He saw service also in the Tennessee campaign, and at Mobile, Ala., where he was sent to a place on the Tombigbee river to mount heavy guns; thence he went to Demopolis, thence to Meridian, where he was paroled. He was never wounded seriously enough to disable him. Politically Mr. Hoskins is a republican from principle, and has generally acted with the republican party since the war. He has never been an aspirant for office; the demands upon him in his business were too numerous for him to accept offices when urged upon him. He was a member of the Masonic lodge, was master of Brookhaven lodge for sixteen years, and is also a member of the Knights of Honor. Mrs. Hoskins died in November, 1890, a devoted Christian woman. Mr. Hoskins is well known through the county as a liberal supporter of all enterprises tending to the good of the public.

Dr. J. W. Hough is one of the leading homeopathic physicians of the state of Mississippi. He came to this state from Ohio, having received his literary education there, and fitted himself for the practice of medicine in the Ohio Medical college of Cincinnati. After reaching Mississippi he decided to locate in Jackson and here he has been a regular and exceptionally successful practitioner ever since. In his treatment of diseases of children he has been singularly and uniformly successful. He is a close and careful student of pathology, as he finds it in his practice, and is a leader in the use of new and rational remedies as introduced by his school of medicine. During the yellow fever epidemic of 1878 he contracted the fever after having successfully attended to many cases, and for his school of medicine in his adopted state he predicts a brilliant future, for wherever it has been practiced by physicians of education, it has always proven most satisfactory, and particularly so in cases of yellow fever. He is now the only practicing physician of Jackson that was here before the war. Although he studied at and graduated from an allopathic school, he soon perceived the superiority of the homeopathic practice, and though for a time he practiced both, he gradually discarded the former and has, for many years, been a successful practitioner and an enthusiastic advocate of the latter. The Doctor has never been an active politician, but was formerly an old line whig. Although he has been identified with the interests of Jackson he has never been an owner of real estate in that city until 1891, when he purchased a fine and valuable piece of property. He has ever remained unmarried. His father, Washington Hough, was a Virginian.

Sam J. House, clerk of the chancery court of Tate county, Miss., is one who well merits the high esteem in which he is held by his fellow-citizens, being active and energetic in all public enterprises and of that genial, generous temperament which is so characteristic of Southern gentlemen. He was born in Madison county, Ala., April 7, 1841, being the sixth child of Samuel J. and Louisa (Chambless) House. With the ardor of youth he entered the Confederate army at the age of twenty years, enlisting in the "Old Ninth" infantry of Mississippi on the 27th day of March, 1861, this being the first regiment to leave the state. His first service was at Pensacola, Fla., under General Bragg, where he was stationed for nearly a year, concluding his first year of service at Cumberland Gap. He was mustered out of service April 3, 1862, at Grand Junction, Miss. Not satisfied with this experience, he reënlisted in the Second Mississippi cavalry as first sergeant of company D, which position he held until the end of the war. He was no "carpet" soldier, but was an active participant in several hotly contested engagements, among which may be mentioned the bombardment of Pensacola, September, 1861; Cumberland Gap, March, 1862, and later, while in the cavalry, his regiment served as an escort for Brig.-Gen. F. C. Armstrong in an engagement at Thompson's Station, Tenn., where he was twice wounded, a musket shot passing through his thigh and a ball hitting his foot, passing entirely through. These slight injuries did not diminish his courage, however, for he was soon back in his place, and served until the close of the war, being finally paroled at Columbus, Miss., in May, 1865. During this time he was in the last fight at Corinth, under Gen. Earl Van Dorn; the engagement at Selma, Ala.; at Iuka, under Gen. Sterling Price; in the Georgia campaign, under Gen. Joseph E. Johnston, from Adairsville to Atlanta, he was in numerous engagements. At the close of the war he returned to Tate county, where he followed farming and milling until he met with an accident which deprived him of the use of his left hand, it being disabled in a cottongin in 1877. Since then he has held several offices of trust to which he was called by the people of his county, among them being those of deputy taxcollector, deputy sheriff, and later he was elected by the democratic party to the office of chancery clerk, which position he now holds for the second term. He now is, and always has been, a stanch democrat of the old school. Mr. House is happy in his family relations, marrying in 1884 Miss Nellie Dean, daughter of D. L. and Annie (Walker) Dean. They have an interesting family of three children, having lost one. Mr. House belongs to a fine old Southern family, his father, Samuel J., being a native of Bertie county, N. C., removing in early life to Madison county, Ala. He was the father of nine boys and two girls, eight of whom are still living. The family removed to Mississippi in December, 1858, where both parents were residing at the time of their death, that of the mother occurring in 1872, and the father's four years later. In religious belief Mr. House favors the Primitive Baptist faith. Mrs. House is a Presbyterian. Both enjoy the respect of the community in which they live, and are greatly sought in its social life. Mr. House is a prominent member of the Masonic fraternity, in which he has attained to the Royal Arch degree. He also belongs to the Knights of Honor.

George Houston, planter and miller of Calvert, Kemper county, Miss., was born in the north of Ireland in 1840, and is a son of James and Margaret J. (Evans) Houston. The father was also a native of the Emerald isle, and died there in 1886. He reared a family of seven children, four of whom emigrated to the United States; three of them settled in Mississippi (George, John and James), and one in Pennsylvania. The mother died in her native land in the same year that her husband passed away. James Houston was a son of John J. Houston, and the mother of our subject was a daughter of George Evans. George Houston passed his early youth in the north of Ireland, but at the age of seventeen years he bade farewell to the scenes of his childhood, and sailed away to America, in search of the fortune that might be in store for him. After landing he came at once to Mississippi, and settled in Kemper county, where he secured work on a plantation. In 1862 he enlisted in the cause of his newly adopted home, joining company A, Fortieth Mississippi volunteer infantry. He was in the engagements at Iuka, Corinth, Vicksburg, Atlanta, the Georgia campaign, and at Nashville and Franklin. He was taken prisoner at Vicksburg, and again at Nashville, when he was sent to Camp Douglas, Chicago, and held until the close of the war. He went to farming after the declaration of peace, and by industry and good management he saved some means which he invested in land; he was very successful in his agricultural enterprises, and is now the owner of twelve hundred acres which are well improved. He is a prominent member of Longstreet lodge, A. F. & A. M., and belongs to the Farmers' Alliance. Mr. Houston was united in marriage in 1861 to Martha E. McKee, a daughter of Thomas McKee. Two children were born of this union: Jane, who married J. W. Chisan, and is the mother of two children, Ellie R., and Rufus R., and Martha E., who married Calvin C. May; they have one child, Mary J. Both of these families are residents of this county. The mother of these children died in 1866; she was a consistent member of the Missionary Baptist church. Mr. Houston was married a second time in 1866 to Miss Mary C. Clay, a daughter of H. P. and Katharine (Milligan) Clay. H. F. Clay was a native of South Carolina, born in 1812, and a son of Simon Clay; he came to Lauderdale county, Miss., in 1842, and resided there until 1851, when he removed to Kemper county; there he passed the remainder of his days, dying in 1879. He was a planter by occupation, and accumulated some property. Mr. Houston's mother was born in South Carolina in 1815, and was a daughter of William McKee. She died in Texas in 1887. Mrs. Houston is a native of Alabama. Three children were born of the second marriage: John C., Nannie N., and Minnie L. Nannie N. is married to J. F. Talbert, and is the mother of one child, George. The parents are members of the Baptist church. Mr. Houston adheres to the principles of the democratic party. He is a man who is self made in every sense of that term, and is an honor to his community.

The firm of Houston & Woods, attorneys at Meridian, Miss., is composed of W. T. Houston and William R. Woods. W. T. Houston was born in Newbern, Ala., May 4, 1849, a son of S. M. Houston, a native of Tennessee, who was a merchant of that place, and who came to Alabama as a journeyman printer. Locating at Eutaw, Ala., he established the Eutaw *Whig and Observer*, a newspaper devoted to the interests of the whigs, and the publication of which he continued for several years. Meantime he met and married Miss Mary E. Hendon, daughter of Dr. William T. Hendon, a retired physician and planter. Soon after the birth of the subject of this sketch, Mr. Houston sold his interest in the newspaper and removed to Newbern, where, as above stated, he was a merchant. In 1857, in search of more lucrative mercantile opportunities he removed to Uniontown, Ala., with his family, where he resided until 1867, with the exception of three years during the war, when they refugeed to Bibb county, Ala. Removing later to St. Louis, Mo., Mr. Houston there continued the mercantile business for some years, finally reëngaging in the printing business, and dying in that city in 1891, leaving a widow, two sons and three daughters. Of this family, W. T. Houston was the eldest. He attended school at Newbern, Ala., Uniontown, Columbiana, Montevali and Green Springs, and for a summer term in Marion, Ala.; at Green Springs he was under the instruction of Henry Tutwiler, the greatest educator in the South. After the removal of the family to St. Louis, he was for some time his father's clerk and bookkeeper, but later became private tutor for the son of Judge Logan Hunton, and during that engagement began the study of law under Judge Hunton. In 1869 he entered the law department of the Washington university of St. Louis, and was admitted to practice in the summer of 1870, but finding, as many another young lawyer had done, that his practice was not sufficiently extensive to suffer much from his absence from the office, he returned to the law school in the fall of 1870, and graduated in the summer of 1871, with the degree of bachelor of laws. In the spring of 1872, as a result of having had to support himself by teaching at night while waiting in the office for clients during the day, his health gave way and he went to Greensboro, Ala., with the hope of there recuperating, and at the same time acquiring some little practice. The time from March to the middle of October was employed in overseeing a plantation. Finding no litigation in the courts of that section of Alabama and no promise for the future, in November, 1872, he went to Aberdeen, Miss., to visit and consult his uncle, Judge L. E. Houston, then in the active practice of his profession and a member of the legal firm of Houston & Reynolds. Through the instrumentality of Colonel Reynolds he was admitted into partnership with the gifted Col. J. R. McIntosh, then doing the largest practice at Okolona. May 27, 1874, he married Miss Mary Fooshee, the orphan daughter of Francis M. Fooshe, a planter, who came to Mississippi in 1857, and bought land four miles east of Okolona, and who married a sister of Chancellor LaFayette Haughton, late of Aberdeen, Miss., whose father was likewise a planter. In the summer of 1876 the partnership between Mr. Houston and Colonel McIntosh was dissolved by mutual consent and the former retired from his profession to assume the presidency of Okolona savings institution, then the Bank of Okolona, after associating himself with J. W. Buchanan, the partnership continuing until the appointment of the latter to the bench of the circuit court. His next partner was a young man named Kimbrough, now of Texas, who was succeeded by R. P. Williams, now of Meridian, and he by James H. Barr, now of Chattanooga, Tenn. In the fall of 1887, his uncle, Judge Houston, having been elevated to the circuit bench, and Colonel Reynolds having died, our subject was invited by Judge Houston and the widow of Colonel Reynolds to take charge of the office and docket of Houston & Reynolds and wind up the litigation in which that firm had been concerned as counsel. This he did, removing in the fall of 1887 to Aberdeen, forming a partnership with D. W. Houston and R. O. Reynolds, sons of L. E. Houston and R. O. Reynolds, of the late firm of Houston & Reynolds, and who are now, as Houston & Reynolds, the leading law firm of Aberdeen, his family following in the spring of 1888. In the fall of 1889, after Judge Woods' appointment to the supreme bench, Mr. Houston was invited to come to Meridian and take charge of his docket and practice in conjunction with his partner and son, W. R. Woods, which proposition he accepted, removing to Meridian in November, 1889, where he has since lived. He was elected to the state senate from the tenth district, composed of Chickasaw and Pontotoc counties, in the fall of 1885 for a term of four years, beginning at the opening of the session on the first Tuesday after the first Monday in January, 1886. He declined to become a candidate for reëlection. He is a member of the Masonic fraternity and of the Knights of Pythias. He and his wife are communicants of the Protestant Episcopal church. They have four children: Samuel Marion, Mary G., Bettie W. and Viva B., the youngest in her eight year. William R. Woods, of the above firm, is a son of Judge Thomas H. Woods, now on the supreme bench, and was born December 12, 1867, in Kemper county, Miss. He moved to Meridian with his parents at an early age. He began the study of law in his father's office and was graduated in law from the University of Mississippi, in 1887, when but twenty years of age. He began practice as a member of the firm of Woods & Williams; and upon the dissolution of this firm, he was associated with his father until the latter's elevation to the bench, when the present firm of Houston & Woods was formed. Mr. Woods is a member of the city board and is the youngest alderman ever elected in Meridian. He is a member of the Masonic fraternity, and holds the office of junior grand deacon in the grand lodge of that order, and is a Knight Templar. He was married in January, 1889, to Miss Annie K. Whitfield, daughter of Dr. Richard H. Whitfield. He was the youngest railway postal clerk ever in the United States service, and held his appointment under President Cleveland.

Lock E. Houston is of Scotch ancestry, though they came to this country from the north of Ireland. His great-great-grandfather and great-grandmother, with their family, came directly to this country in 1735. They located in Pennsylvania, where they remained for a number of years until the children were grown, and many of them married, then removed to that portion of Virginia now Rockbridge county, near the Natural bridge. Here his great-great-grandfather and his family and their descendants remained, and Robert Houston, the father of the subject of this sketch, was born in the year 1760, and grew up and married. Judge Houston's mother's maiden name was Martha Blackburn, and she was the daughter of Captain Blackburn, who fell gallantly fighting in the battle of King's Mountain, and the niece of Rev. Gideon Blackburn, a distinguished Presbyterian divine, well-known in the early days of Tennessee, and sometimes jestingly called "General Jackson's fighting preacher" because, although a Presbyterian minister, he was possessed of a martial spirit. Judge Houston's father, Robert Houston, removed from Rockbridge county, Va., to Tennessee while comparatively a young man, though a man of a family by his first wife, and settled in Blount county, but owing to the Indian hostilities he removed with his family to Knox county early in 1800. He purchased lands here and become a somewhat prosperous farmer. He was a soldier in the War of 1812, and returned home at its close and remained quietly on his farm until death claimed him in 1836. He was twice married and had eight children by his first wife, all of whom are dead. By his second wife he had but five children: George Blackburn, Joseph E., Judge Lock E., Samuel M. and Elizabeth; of the five two only are dead: George B. and Samuel M. Houston, the first of whom died in Iowa; the latter in St.

Louis, Mo. Our subject was raised in his native county, and was educated at the Knoxville university, where he graduated in 1840. After his graduation he spent some time as a teacher in Alabama, and during that time spent such time as in justice to his patrons he could, in studying law under the advice and instruction of the distinguished firm of Murphy & Jones, then occupying a leading position in the courts of Alabama. In the early part of 1843, after examination in the presence of the Hon. Peter Martin, then presiding judge of the Tuscaloosa district of Alabama, Mr. Houston's license to practice law was granted, and in a very short time he located in Aberdeen, Miss., and commenced the practice of his profession. Business was not extensive in the law at that time, but was gradually improving. Soon thereafter, the then judge (Adams) resigned for the purpose of going into the practice of law, and tendered Mr. Houston a place in his firm, which was accepted, and business increased in the country, from the volume of which the influence of Judge Adams' name soon drew a good practice. In the fall of that year Judge Adams was elected to congress, which turned over his business and influence to his young partner, giving him as much business as he could well handle. In the year 1847 our subject was elected to the legislature for two years. In 1853 he was appointed, by the then governor of the state, Henry S. Foote, to fill a vacancy caused by the resignation of the Hon. Francis M. Rogers. After the close of his term of appointment Judge Houston returned to his practice. But in 1855 he was nominated, by what was denominated the know-nothing or American party for congress against the regularly nominated candidate of the democratic party, Judge Bennett, in a district of seventeen counties; in four of which Judge Houston had never set foot, and did not during the canvass enter those counties, with which the democratic candidate was well acquainted and made a thorough canvass, and yet Judge Houston was beaten by only a little over two hundred votes in a voting population of something over twenty thousand; and in which, two years thereafter, General Davis was elected over General Clark, the know-nothing nominee, by over three thousand votes. In 1863 Judge Houston was elected to the legislature, and elected speaker of the house of representatives. He served all through those trying and eventful times until the war closed; at the end of which time he was elected a member of the constitutional convention, by the people of his county, to help in the reconstruction of the state. This convention nominated candidates for congress, and it is needless to say that Judge Houston was their first choice, but he declined to accept the honor. He went back to his profession and has won an enviable reputation as a brilliant and successful lawyer, and one who stands in the front ranks in his profession in the state of Mississippi. He formed many partnerships, among them one with Gen. Reuben Davis, which continued until the General took his seat in congress in 1858. In 1887 he was appointed to the circuit bench, and he has been on the bench ever since, where he has given entire satisfaction by the able and just decisions he has rendered. Judge Houston was married in 1857 to Miss Susan Maury Parrish, who was a native of Nashville, Tenn., and who died in Aberdeen, Miss., in 1874. Her father was David Winston Parrish, of Nashville, the schoolmate and cousin of Commodore Maury, and both of whom were in their boyhood pupils at Harpeth college, not far from Nashville, Tenn., of General Jackson's "fighting preacher," Rev. Gideon Blackburn. Judge Houston has seven living children—four sons and three daughters: The eldest son is Robert Parrish; the second son is Lock E.; the third son is David Winston; the fourth son is Joseph S. The eldest daughter is Mrs. Mary H. Gillespie; the second daughter is Mrs. Lizzie H. Johnston, and the third daughter is Miss Sue Maury Houston. As above stated the Judge has always been a successful man, the only defeat he has ever had to acknowledge being that of his contest with Judge Bennett, way back in 1855, when he ran against the Judge as congressional candidate on the know-nothing ticket and was defeated by a small majority.

Volney E. Howard early prepared himself for the practice of law. He settled in Mississippi about 1830. In 1837 he was chosen reporter of the decisions of the high court of errors and appeals. He also took a prominent part in politics, and was for several years editor of the *Mississippian*, the leading democratic organ of the state, at Jackson. In 1847 he removed to Texas and in 1850 was a member of the Texan legislature. Later he was sent by the president of the United States on a mission to California, where he located and achieved additional fame as a lawyer.

B. F. Howard, planter, West Station, Miss. Planting has formed the chief occupation of this gentleman, and the wideawake manner in which he has taken advantage of every method and idea tending to the enhanced value of his property has had considerable to do with his success in life. Born in Copiah county, Miss., in March, 1832, he was one of twelve children and has had ten brothers and one sister, four of whom are living. Their parents were James and Ann (McCullin) Howard, both natives of the Old North state. The father moved to Mississippi about 1817, and first settled in the wilds of Copiah county and there remained until 1844, when he moved to Attala county. He was a successful planter, and reared his family in Copiah and Attala counties. His wife died about 1858, and he followed her to the grave in 1866. B. F. Howard was married in 1859 to Miss Margaret Stuckey, daughter of William Stuckey, a large planter and slave owner, of Attala county. She died in 1879, leaving six children. Joseph married Millie Dean, and is a well-to-do planter in Attala county; Madison married Cora Mayfield, and is a planter in the same county; Dora is the wife of W. G. Conner; Mollie is the wife of Thomas Land; William is a druggist in West Station; John is attending school; B. F. Howard was educated in Hinds and Attala counties, and in 1862 enlisted in the Confederate army as a private, in company A, of the Fortieth regiment Mississippi infantry. He served in the Tennessee army until the close of the war and participated in the battles of Corinth, Big Black, Old Town Creek, Franklin, Nashville, and others too numerous to mention. He was slightly wounded at the battle of Corinth. Returning to Attala county after the war he engaged in farming. Mr. Howard was married the second time in Holmes county, in June, 1879, to Miss Sue Myra McAfee, born in 1845, a daughter of Hon. James Taliaferro McAfee, who was born and raised in Georgia, moved to Mississippi in 1843 and died in 1853—an energetic planter, who served in the legislature two terms from Attala county. He married Rebecca Dickerson, a native of North Carolina, and to them were born thirteen children, six sons and seven daughters. Five of their sons served in the Confederate army; one son, Col. John Miller McAfee, who was killed at the battle of Seven Pines, commanded the Second Mississippi battalion. Mr. Howard's second union was blessed by the birth of two children, one son and a daughter: Leslie Carl, born in 1885; Maggie Sue, born in 1888. Mr. Howard is a member of the Methodist church. Mr. Howard has been engaged in planting in Attala county since 1875, and has resided near West Station, in that county, and is the owner of several places there. In the winter of 1890 he moved to town. Although not active in politics, Mr. Howard affiliates with the democratic party, but does not aspire to office. He is a master mason.

John M. Howard, merchant, Howard, Miss., was born in Holmes county, Miss., March 3, 1862, and is a son of Isaiah Howard and the grandson of James Howard. The latter was born in North Carolina, and was one of the pioneers of Copiah county, Miss., where he became a successful planter and where he reared his family. Isaiah Howard was born in Copiah county, August 25, 1824, received a moderate education there, and about 1845, when a young man, came to Holmes county, where he opened a plantation. He was a soldier in the late war, Forrest's command, and served in the quartermaster's department until cessation of hostilities. He is now retired from the active duties of life and is residing at Durant. He was married in Holmes county to Miss Martha Stanfield, a native of Holmes county, where she was reared and educated, and the daughter of Washington Stanfield, of this county. John M. Howard was one of three children born to this union who grew to mature years, and is the only one now living. He received a good business education at Durant, but is mainly self-educated since attaining his majority. In 1876 he commenced clerking, followed this for several years at Durant, and thus became thoroughly familiar with merchandising. He was married in Alabama, March 17, 1885, to Miss Leila Moore, who was born, reared and educated in that state, and who was the daughter of Dr. Joseph Moore (deceased), who was a successful physician of Marengo county, Ala. Mr. Howard came to his present location in 1886, and in partnership with Mr. Abbott, engaged in general merchandising, the partnership continuing for three years, when Mr. Abbott retired. Since then Mr. Howard has continued the business alone. He has three store buildings, dry-goods, groceries, etc., and does an annual business of $60,000. He is also the owner of a large steam ginhouse, a good residence, and in connection with his other enterprises is engaged in planting, raising annually two hundred bales of cotton. Mr. Howard is a shrewd, practical business man, one of the best in the county, and is a social, pleasant gentleman to meet. He has made a great many improvements in Howard station, and is active in all enterprises for the good of the county, and a leading democrat of this state.

J. W. Howard, breeder of Holstein cattle in Aberdeen, was born in Gallatin, Tenn., 1844, the son of B. R. and Mary M. (Baker) Howard. His father was a native of Kentucky, his mother of Tennessee; the one born in 1810, the other in 1813. They were reared in Gallatin, and lived there till 1855, when they came to Aberdeen, where Mr. Howard died in 1857, his wife in 1888. They were for many years members of the Presbyterian church, of which Mr. Howard was an elder. Mr. Howard was a man of average literary attainments, but of uncommon business qualifications, who passed the most of his active career as a merchant and cattle buyer. Captain Howard's maternal grandfather was a planter, and died at Gallatin, Tenn. The Captain is the third of four sons and two daughters born to his parents: Daniel F., who was a member of the Twenty-fifth Mississippi infantry, and was killed at Fort Donelson; Isaac B., merchant at Salem, Ala., who was a member of the same regiment, and served through the war, taking part in the Georgia and Atlanta campaign, and also participating in the engagements under Hood and Johnston, in Tennessee and elsewhere, and surrendered with the latter's command; J. W., the subject of our sketch; William E., boot and shoe merchant at Aberdeen; Mary A., who married J. A. Gillespie, and died in 1864, her husband afterward marrying her sister, Mary E. Howard, who is a widow and now lives in Aberdeen. Our subject received his education at Aberdeen, but left school in 1863 to join company C of Saunder's cavalry battalion, with which he fought from Rome, Ga., to Atlanta; also serving under Johnston in North Carolina, and receiving a wound at Statesville, N. C., which necessitated his returning home. He surrendered with the troops at Meridian, Miss. During his last year of military service, he was the captain of a company engaged in scouting. After the war he was engaged for two years in the horse and mule trade, with which he combined planting, which he continued after relinquishing the business mentioned. In 1875 he was elected sheriff of his county, the first democratic sheriff since the war, and he was reëlected in 1877, thus serving with credit for four years, altogether. After retiring from office, he again engaged in the horse and mule trade, and soon after embarked in the breeding of Holstein cattle, beginning with a herd of seven and operating so successfully that he now has a magnificent herd of a hundred and fifty, nearly all thoroughbreds, and widely and truthfully known as the finest and largest herd in the state, if not in the South. He has been awarded the premiums in three states: Meridian, Miss.; Birmingham, Ala., and Baton Rouge, La., for sweepstakes, best herd and milk and butter, respectively. He has a fine stock farm of three hundred acres, located seven miles southwest of Aberdeen, on the line of the Muldon and Aberdeen branch of the Mississippi & Ohio railroad, all under fence; also four hundred acres in fine clover. He raises sufficient corn and hay for home consumption, and some for the market. His stock ranch is one of the finest in the state. Besides the property mentioned he has a magnificent home in the suburbs of Aberdeen, consisting of fifty-three acres. He also owns considerable business property. He was married, in 1868, to Minnie K., a daughter of Keith and Mary Bowen, natives respectively of Union, S. C., and Knoxville, Tenn. After his marriage in Tennessee he moved to South Carolina and lived for some years at Waterloo, returning later to Tennessee, whence he came in 1855 to Chickasaw county, and in 1863 to Aberdeen, where he died in 1881, his widow surviving him. He was a planter and stockdealer of considerable note, who served the Confederacy during a portion of its struggle. Mrs. Howard is the third of nine children born to her parents, seven of whom are living. She was educated in Aberdeen, at Thrace Miller school, and at Cincinnati, Ohio. She was born in Waterloo, S. C., and is the mother of three sons and one daughter, all of whom are being well educated. Mr. and Mrs. Howard are members of the Presbyterian church. Our subject is a thoroughgoing business man, and has been almost uniformly successful in the enterprises to which he has devoted his attention. Mrs. Howard is a lady of fine attainments and elegant manners, a favorite in society, and beloved in the family circle for her many domestic virtues.

Judge James Moorman Howry, deceased, was born in Botetourt county, Va., August 4, 1804. His ancestors came from Europe in colonial times and settled in Virginia and Pennsylvania. His father removed to Tennessee in December, 1811, and located near Rogersville; there he received a solid elementary education in the fieldschools of the country, which was steadily and continuously supplemented by studious habits. He was an industrious and energetic boy, and at an early age was placed in the mercantile house of Francis Dalzell, in Rogersville, where he developed that capacity for business which has characterized his life as one of great usefulness and activity. He was afterward employed in the office of the chancery clerk, acquiring there a taste for the legal profession, which he followed through life. He had not at this time saved sufficient means to enable him to pursue the study of law, so for several years he conducted a mercantile house for Col. George Hale. During the latter part of this time he employed his leisure hours in the study of law, and when he abandoned mercantile life entirely, entered the office of Gen. Peter Parsons, of Rogersville. For two years he applied himself diligently to the study of law, and was admitted to the bar, and practiced one year at Rogersville. At the end of the time he removed to middle Tennessee, where he arose so rapidly in the profession that at the ensuing convention he lacked but one vote of being nominated attorney general for the Twelfth Tennessee district; he was afterward appointed to this office by Governor Carroll. For several years he was clerk of the house and senate of the Tennessee legislature. He soon obtained a large lucrative practice at the bar, and was one of the most successsful lawyers of that period. In 1836 he removed to Mississippi and entered upon a splendid career of professional practice and social prominence. In 1840 he became a candidate for circuit judge, but was defeated by Judge Huling; this election was held to fill a vacancy, and at the regular election, in 1841, Colonel Howry was elected to the circuit bench for the full term. Judge Huling was of the opinion that his term had not expired, and when Judge Howry went to Holly Springs to assume the duties of his office he found the bench occupied by Judge Huling. After considerable altercation, of a kind which is peculiarly characteristic of the legal profession, Judge Howry won the day, and Judge Huling was obliged to abdicate. He refused to hold court at one time for some lawyers, for the reason that one of them had assaulted him for a ruling he had made and the others stood by without offering him any defense from the attack of the irate Solon. On the establishment of the University of Mississippi, in 1844, Judge Howry was appointed one of the trustees of that institution. His services on that board was acknowledged by his colleagues to have been of the greatest worth, and their records are filled with resolutions of respect and tributes to his memory. His zeal and earnestness in behalf of the university earned for him the title of its father, and it was with natural and pardonable pride that he saw one of his sons enter the present board. His own connection with it was severed when the institution fell under the control of a republican administration in 1870. In 1857 he was elected state senator, and filled this office two terms, distinguishing himself as an earnest advocate of the interests of the university. He was a man full of the most generous impulses, and was a patron of every meritorious enterprise. His knowledge of the law reached to the depths which can be attained only by the joint exercise of diligence, temperance and talent, and these qualities, united with kindness of heart and geniality of manners, disclose a character worthy of all admiration. Judge Howry reared a family of eleven children, eight of whom are now living. He died at Oxford in 1884; his wife had passed away in 1870. No biography of Judge Howry would be complete without a reference to his fame as a Mason and Masonic writer. Becoming a member of that order at the age of twenty-one, he became known throughout the United States for his zeal and intelligent knowledge of Masonry. His contributions to Masonic literature are valuable, and he ranked in that noble order with Albert Pike and Robert Morris, with whom he was on terms of intimate friendship. He was grand master of Masonry, grand high priest of Royal Arch Masons, and thrice illustrious grand master of Cryptic Masonry. Judge Howry was equally conspicuous in the councils of the Cumberland Presbyterian church, of which he was a member for over forty years. Warm in his temperament, ardent in his nature and firm in his convictions, he was a marked man in any crowd and a force in any community. Of him it was truly said by another, himself a distinguished citizen of Mississippi, that in all the various relations of judge, legislator, trustee of the state university, churchman, citizen, friend and neighbor, Judge Howry was one of the few men whose connection with the fraternity conferred honor upon it.

Charles Bowen Howry, one of the most progressive and successful attorneys of the state of Mississippi, was born in Lafayette county, in the town of Oxford, in 1845, and is a son of Judge James Moorman Howry (see sketch). He was educated in the University of Mississippi, and at the age of sixteen years he offered his services to the Confederate government; these, however, were declined on account of his delicate health. He returned home from Virginia, and in March, 1862, he joined the Twenty-ninth Mississippi regiment, then being organized by Colonel (afterward General) Walthall, with whom he served until the close of the war, attaining the rank of captain. He was in the battles of Chickamauga, Lookout Mountain, Missionary Ridge, Resaca, Atlanta, Jonesboro, and several others of importance; he was wounded in the storming of the Federal works of Franklin, Tenn., and was with General Johnston's army when he surrendered in North Carolina. He returned to his home, and began the study of law under Prof. L. Q. C. Lamar; he afterward became a student in the University of Mississippi, and was graduated in 1867. He was admitted to the bar, and practiced with such immediate success and ability that in 1870 he was appointed state's attorney for one of the largest districts in the state by Governor Alcorn; but this lucrative position he declined. In 1874 he removed to St. Louis, where he was succeeding admirably in professional work when his health gave way, and he was obliged to return to Mississippi in 1878. He was elected to the legislature of the state of Mississippi in 1880, and reëlected in 1882, serving on the judiciary committee and as chairman of the committee on state universities. By his activity, industry and clear judgment he won a reputation as a leading legislator. After returning to private life, he resumed the practice of his profession. In 1882 he was appointed trustee of the University of Mississippi; upon the expiration of his term he was reappointed for a term of six years by Governor Lowry. In 1885 he was appointed by President Cleveland United States attorney for the northern district of Mississippi, retiring upon the incoming of President Harrison's administration in 1889; he had discharged the duties and responsibilities of this office with great credit to himself, and to the entire satisfaction of the public. He has seen frequent service in the state conventions of his party, and has served for some years for the state at large as a member of the state executive committee. Mr. Howry has not been an office-seeker, never but once having offered himself voluntarily as a candidate. In 1890 he was a candidate on the democratic ticket for congress, but was defeated for a party nomination. He was elected to represent Mississippi on the national democratic committee in 1890. He is an ardent democrat, but conservative and tolerant of the opinions of others, both in political and other matters. He is a frequent contributor to the press, and has much literary taste and acquirements, but devotes his greatest energies to his profession, of which he is sincerely fond, especially in the courts of chancery. He has been an active and prominent member of the Mississippi Bar association and of the American Bar association from their organization. Mr. Howry was married, in 1869, to Miss Edmonia Carter, a daughter of Dr. Carter, of this county, formerly from Virginia; she died in 1879, leaving two children: Lucien and Willard. The second marriage was in 1881, when he was united to Miss Hallie Harris, a daughter of Dr. Samuel Harris, of Lowndes county. Two children have been born of this union who are living, and one is deceased: Charles B., Jr., Bessie, and Hallie, who died in 1888. Mrs. Howry is a member of the Presbyterian church, and Mr. Howry is in sympathy with the same church. Mr. Howry has given some attention to agriculture in addition to his legal duties, and has a plantation of one thousand acres well improved, and has great faith in the future of his state and section. As a lawyer Mr. Howry is noted for his intellectual energy, and so mastering the principles of law applicable to his cases that he becomes a formidable competitor at any bar. He is possessed of great dignity of character, and enjoys the reputation of being unwavering in fidelity to his clients and friends.

Samuel M. Howry, who is the present postmaster of Oxford, was born in that place in 1848, and is a son of Judge James M. and Narcissa (Bowen) Howry (see sketch of James M. Howry). He received his education in the common schools of Oxford, and was also a student of the state university. In 1866 he entered the employ of his father as clerk in a dry goods store, and continued in this line of work for four years. He then embarked in the mercantile trade upon his own account, and conducted the business for three years, discontinuing it at the end of that time. In 1879 he was appointed United States marshal, but after a few months he entered the service of the government as an internal revenue officer. In one year he was reappointed to the marshal's office, which he filled most acceptably until

1884. He was made foreman of construction of the Federal building which was being erected at that time, discharging his duties with rare good judgment and ability. In April, 1889, he was appointed postmaster of Oxford, and in this position his best business qualifications have full exercise; no detail of the office is overlooked by him, and the business is conducted on the most systematic plan, giving entire satisfaction to the public. Mr. Howry was united in marriage in November, 1873, to Miss Donna McCord, of Corinth, Miss. Six children have been born to this union: Frank M., Percy McCord, Mabel Clare, Samuel M., Jr., Wilford Hall, and Marcus Taylor. The family are members of the Cumberland Presbyterian church. Mr. Howry is a member of the Masonic fraternity, and also of the Knights of Honor. He is a man of broad public spirit, and to him Oxford is indebted for many of her most worthy enterprises. He was one of the main projectors of the public school building, which is an ornament and credit to the town. He has always been interested in educational affairs, and for three years he was a trustee of the school.

Mrs. Elizabeth C. Howze, Hernando, De Soto county, Miss., was born in the state of Alabama, and is the fifth of a family of seven children born to Sewell and Sarah (Young) Newsom. The mother was a native of Tennessee, but the father was born in Alabama. He came to Mississippi in 1858, and settled in Marshall county, and engaged in planting; later he removed to De Soto county, and there he was elected to fill the office of treasurer of the county. He has always been prominently identified with the public measures of the community in which he lives; he is now seventy-six years of age. Mrs. Howze was reared and educated in Mississippi and Tennessee, and had superior advantages for the times in which she grew to womanhood. In 1866 she was united in the holy bonds of marriage to William D. Howze, now deceased. He was born in Tennessee, and was a son of Isom and E. W. (Wilson) Howze, natives of North Carolina and Virginia respectively. He made a very bright record during his college days at La Grange, Tenn. When there was a call for men to go to the defense of this country he responded at once, enlisting in 1861 in the First Mississippi volunteer infantry. He participated in the battles of Fort Donelson, Port Hudson, Harrisburg and Atlanta; at Fort Donelson he was taken prisoner, and was held captive at Johnson's island for two years. After the close of the war he took up teaching, and from 1865 to 1872 he was in the schoolroom. In 1872 he was elected clerk of the circuit court, holding this office until 1876, when he was made treasurer; this office he filled four years, and in 1880 he was elected a member of the board of supervisors. Thus it will be seen the confidence that was reposed in him by all the people of the county. In 1885 he became deeply impressed with the idea that it was his duty to preach the gospel; he accordingly entered the Baptist ministry, confining his labors to De Soto county. He died in 1890, having lived a life of great usefulness to his fellowmen. His widow and five children mourn his loss. The names of the children are James A.; Bourdoun, wife of E. B. Wilson; Eva B.; William Duke and Isom W. Mrs. Howze owns four hundred and eighty acres of land, two hundred and fifty of which are under cultivation; she also has a very nice residence in Hernando. She is rich in the possession of a family of dutiful children, who are an honor to the mother who bore them. One of the daughters is unusually talented, and has done some painting that betrays this fact beyond question. Mr. Howze was independent in his political opinions, and had the courage of his convictions to the extent of doing the thing he considered right in the face of any opposition that might be brought to bear upon him. He thus gained the confidence and highest respect of all high-minded people.

G. H. Howze, Moss Point, Miss. The Moss Point Lumber company, one of the most flourishing corporations of Jackson county, was chartered in February, 1891. Originally the firm was Howze & Griffin, and was established in 1887. The firm now consists of G. H. Howze, president; J. W. Griffin, vice president; H. C. Herring, secretary; E. Bloomfield, treasurer. The mill is located two miles above Moss Point on Dog river, and gives employment to forty-five men. The best improved machinery is used, and the output materially increases the aggregate of industries of Jackson county. G. H. Howze, the president of this concern, was born in Clarke county, Miss., in 1848, and is a son of Thomas T. and Amelia (Grandbury) Howze. The father was a native of Mississippi, and in his youth saw much of the privations and trials of pioneer life. He is now a resident of Moss Point, Miss. Our subject was reared in his native county, and received a limited education there. The breaking out of the Civil war demoralized schools as well as other institutions, so that he with many another youth was defrauded of the right which is every child's—a good education. He worked on a farm until he came to Jackson county in the latter part of the year 1865, when he became interested in the lumber industry. With the exception of a few years devoted to the tug-boat business, Mr. Howze has been one of the leading lumber dealers in Jackson county since 1865. He has had a wide experience in the business, and no man is better fitted for the duties of president of this corporation than is he. He was united in marriage, in 1872, to Iola Bradford. They have had born to them three children: Cora, Albert and Bessie. Mr. Howze is a member of the Masonic order and of the Knights of Honor.

M. J. L. Hoye, deceased, was born in Monroe county, Ga., in 1842, and passed from this life at Decatur, Miss., in the month of August, 1890. He removed from his native state to Mississippi in 1856 and located in Newton county. During the late Civil war he served with great bravery as first lieutenant of the Thirty-ninth Mississippi; he was captured at Port Hudson, and was held a prisoner at Johnson's island, Ohio, until the close of the war. Upon the declaration of peace he returned to his old home a penniless boy. Having a good education he secured a country school, which he taught with great success. This he followed for three years; then he married Miss Bettie, the daughter of Alexander Russell, a native of North Carolina, and a pioneer settler of Newton county, Miss., and soon opened a mercantile establishment at Decatur, Miss., where by close application and honest dealing he built up a good business. As soon as his capital had increased sufficiently he began business at Newton, Miss., which soon became the strongest house in the county. Both houses are now in a flourishing condition. He was a man of extraordinary intelligence and would have stood foremost in whatever business or profession he might have chosen, says one of Mississippi's greatest sons. He was very conscientious in his dealings with his fellowmen, and in his death not only his family and intimate friends mourn his loss, but hundreds that are wholly dependent on the sunshine and rain for their daily bread. He was a member of the Baptist church, having made confession and been immersed when a prisoner at Johnson's island. Mr. and Mrs. Hoye had born to them nine children, seven of whom still survive. He was an honored member of the Masonic order, of the Knights of Honor and of the Knights of Pythias.

The Hoyle family, very highly respected and well known throughout Lee county, Miss., is descended from German ancestors, who emigrated from Wiesbaden before the Revolutionary war. The great-grandfather of our subject served as a soldier in the Revolutionary war, and was given land warrants in North Carolina, where he settled after the struggle for liberty was ended. He was the father of John Hoyle, a planter by occupation and a minister of the Methodist Episcopal church. He was the father of D. L. Hoyle, a native of North Carolina, who married Catherine Ligon, a native of South Carolina. They removed to Gwinnett county, Ga., and there our subject, Dr. J. M. Hoyle, was born December 18, 1836. His father was a member of the Masonic order and was identified with the democratic party. He was a prominent member of the Methodist Episcopal church, of which he was steward for many years. The Doctor's mother died in 1843, at the age of twenty-four years, leaving four children: J. M., John W., David and Catherine. The father was married a second time to Mrs. C. Johnson, a daughter of Benjamin Cleveland, of Georgia. Two children were born of this union: Callie D., wife of Joseph Guyton, and Benjamin C. Mr. Hoyle was married a third time to Ellen McCord, but there were no children. Mrs. Hoyle is living on her husband's old homestead. She is a member of the Methodist Episcopal church. Dr. Hoyle grew to manhood in his native state and received an excellent elementary education. At the age of eighteen years he began the study of medicine under the preceptorship of Dr. M. Wilson, of New Albany, Miss. He afterward attended lectures at the University of Tennessee, and in 1857 was graduated from the Berkshire medical college, Pittsfield, Mass. He began his practice in Pontotoc county, where he remained until the breaking out of the Civil war, when he enlisted in the Confederate army, was appointed assistant surgeon and was assigned to the Eighth Georgia regiment. He was in many noted engagements and saw much hard service, but it was an excellent training-school and he had a rare experience for a young physician, being three years surgeon in charge of some of our largest hospitals in Mississippi and Alabama. After the war he returned to Pontotoc, and the following year he came to Chesterville and thence to Tupelo. He has been interested both in mercantile and agricultural pursuits, and studied law, so that he was admitted to the bar in 1876; but he did not follow this profession to any extent. In 1878 he was elected a member of the legislature, and was reëlected in 1884 and 1886. Dr. Hoyle was married to Miss Amanda C. Johnson, a daughter of Harvey Johnson. She was born in 1838, and was reared in Georgia by her grandfather, her mother and father dying in her childhood. Dr. Hoyle and his wife have had born to them two children that are still living: John W. was born in 1860, and is a lumber manufacturer of Tupelo; Minnie May is thirteen years of age. The parents are both members of the Methodist Episcopal church. The Doctor is a member of the State medical association and was president of the Lee county association of physicians in 1890. He has been ambitious to succeed in his profession, and long ago attained a rank among the first practitioners of the county. He is a member of the Masonic order and belongs both to the Blue lodge and chapter. He is also a Knight of Honor. As a citizen he has the respect and confidence of the entire community.

Rev. L. J. Hubbard, a clergyman and prominent planter of Iuka, Tishomingo county, Miss., was born in South Carolina in 1818. He is a son of David Hubbard and his wife, Martha (West) Hubbard; was born in North Carolina. His father came to Mississippi and located in this county in 1844. He was a successful planter and had a family of six children, named John, David, Isaac, James, L. J. and Lucinda. His parents, both of whom were members of the Methodist Protestant church, died in this county, his father in 1876. Our subject was reared to farm life and at the age of twenty he married Miss Susan Simpson, who has borne him eleven children: Martha, who married M. C. Chenault, who died in 1888; Barbara married William A. Lemmons, Mollie died in 1885, Sallie married W. W. Harvey, Addie married M. D. Adams, Callie is married to Prof. W. F. Hundley, Fannie is married to Mead Farless, Permelia is married to G. H. Pruitt, Janey died in 1853, Thomas L. married Mollie Adams, and William C. is the youngest. Of these Barbara, Addie, Callie, Fannie, Permelia, Thomas, Sallie and William C. are residents of this county. Mr. Hubbard, who has resided on the plantation, which is about four miles south of Iuka, owns about three hundred and twenty acres of good land. He formerly owned a tract of land which was very large, beside a small one, which includes the present site of the town of Iuka. He came to the county in 1846 and located within a few yards of Iuka Springs, which he owned at the time. When he sold these springs he had it stipulated in the deed by which they were transferred to other ownership, that all the schools and citizens of Iuka should have the free use of their waters at all times. He is a public-spirited man, who takes great interest in education and his interest in churches may be inferred when it is stated that he has been a local preacher for forty years while he has lived there. During the Civil war he served the Confederacy for two weeks, being too old for the regular service. He was once elected and served in the county for one term as county treasurer. Both as a soldier and as an official he discharged every duty devolving upon him with the utmost fidelity. W. C. Hubbard, the youngest son of Rev. L. J. Hubbard, is an enterprising druggist of Iuka. He was born in 1860 and was reared to farm life and began business for himself at the age of twenty, engaging first in the drug trade as a clerk in 1882, later obtaining a store of his own. He is registered in the school of pharmacy of Mississippi. He is regarded as one of the most public-spirited young men of the county, and everything tending to the advancement and improvement of his town and state has his unqualified support.

W. J. Hubbard is an example of what can be accomplished by energy and business tact under the most adverse circumstances. From a poor boy, laboring for $7 per month, he has become one of the very best citizens of the state, and one who is aiding in the development of the economic problem of cotton manufacture in the South. To say the least, he is emphatically a success. He was born in Georgia in 1846, and in 1870 was married to Miss Margaret Finch, of Noxubee county. To this union were born six children: Lelia M., John H., Lillie M., Pearl E., Prince D. and Lexie J. He espoused the cause of the Confederacy, and in 1861, when but fifteen years of age, he enlisted under Col. W. S. Barry, in the Thirty-fifth Mississippi. He participated in the battles of Corinth and Iuka, and was captured at Vicksburg and paroled. He was a soldier with Johnston in the Georgia campaign. He went with General Hood to Tennessee, and was in the battles of Murfreesboro and Nashville. He was captured at the last-named place and carried to Camp Douglas, where he remained until the final surrender. On being finally paroled he returned to his old home in Noxubee county, Miss., was employed as a laborer on the farm for two years, at $10 per month, and at the close of his time he engaged with a company of local manufacturers of cotton goods at the above rate per month for two years, and was then engaged in lumber milling for the same length of time. Having five shares of stock transferred him, he became eligible to the office of secretary and treasurer. He was elected to that office in 1872, on a salary of $600 annually, and served in that capacity for three years. Then, with an associate, he rented the property belonging to the company and continued this for six years, after which he purchased his partner's interest and carried on the business alone. At this factory are consumed annually four hundred and fifty bales of cotton, which is converted into osnaburgs, carpet warp, knitting cotton and cotton yarn. The factory is located sixteen miles west of Shuqualak, Noxubee county, Miss., and Mr. Hubbard has connected his factory with his office in Shuqualak by telegraph. In connection with his factory he has a general store. He is also engaged in merchandising at Shuqualak and is a general cotton buyer. He owns about two thousand acres of average land in Noxubee county. Mr. Hubbard's manufactured goods are shipped to St. Louis and Chicago. His business is increasing to such an extent that he contemplates increasing the capacity of his factory by the addition of improved machinery, etc. He has also a fine local trade in certain grades of goods, and this is increasing. Mr. Hubbard is a member of the Baptist church, and socially he is a Mason. His parents, E. J. and Mary (Mangum) Hubbard, were married in 1841, and emigrated to Winston county, Miss., in 1855. The father was born in Georgia about 1815, and after coming with his family to Winston county, followed teaching for some time. His death occurred in 1857, and the mother followed him to the grave in Noxubee county in 1868. They were the parents of three children.

William Hudspeth (deceased), was originally from Alabama, his birth having occurred in Jackson county, in the year 1828, and was a son of William Hudspeth. The father was a native of either Georgia or Alabama, but emigrated to Mississippi as early as 1843 or 1844, and located in the northern part of the state when the country was practically new. William Hudspeth was about fifteen years of age when he came with his parents to Mississippi, and in that state were passed his youthful days. In the fall of 1875, he was elected chancery clerk of Benton county, and so well did he fill this position and so great was his popularity that he continued to hold that position until his death in 1887. He was energetic, well informed, and was noted for his purity of thought and unselfish principles. He was a member of the Methodist Episcopal church, took a leading part in all religious matters, and was a conscientious Christian. His life was full of good deeds. He was public-spirited and was a man who at all times had the interests of the county and state at heart. He not only left a wife and family to mourn his departure, but many warm friends who felt the loss which would be sustained by the death of such a man. His son, George W., taught school two years when he was quite youthful; since which time he has served as deputy chancery clerk, under his father and H. W. Hardaway, and has, by his straightforward course, won many friends, as is shown by his unanimous nomination for the office of chancery clerk at the recent democratic primary election.

Dr. C. S. Hudson, physician and surgeon, Yazoo City, Miss., has been identified with the medical profession of Yazoo county since 1876, and has made a reputation during his career for skill and reliability. He is a native of Winston county, Miss., born February 20, 1851, and the third of a family of eight children. He is the son of Robert S. and N. E. (Gray) Hudson, of South Carolina. The father was an attorney who distinguished himself as one of the ablest members of the bar of the state. He served as circuit judge during and after the war, and held the office of district attorney. As a member of the legislature of Mississippi he wielded no inconsiderable influence, and was widely known as a conscientious, faithful representative. He came to the state in his boyhood with his father, who settled in Noxubee county. He died in 1889 in his sixty-sixth year. His wife survives him, and is a resident of Yazoo City. The paternal grandmother of our subject was a descendant of the house of Spencer, and the maternal grandfather was descended from the Von Grays, natives of Prussia; he, himself, was a first cousin to Frederick the Great. He emigrated to America, and settled on a Dutch grant in South Carolina. Dr. Hudson grew to manhood in Yazoo county. He received his literary education at Oxford, and was graduated in medicine from Tulane university, New Orleans, La., in 1876. Immediately after he began the practice of his profession in his native county, locating upon the Yazoo river above Yazoo City. There he remained until 1884, when he came to Yazoo City, and soon after he opened his office won a paying patronage. He has been a faithful student of the science of medicine, and has met with marked success in his practice. In 1882 he was united in marriage to Miss Katie Love, of Mississippi, a daughter of DeWitt C. Love, whose biography appears upon another page of this history. Mrs. Hudson died in 1886, leaving no children. She was a consistent member of the Presbyterian church. The Doctor is an elder in the same church, and is a member

L, 2, C, Lamar

of the Knights of Pythias. He owns a comfortable residence which he had erected after coming to Yazoo city.

John C. Hudson, planter, Pine Valley, Miss., was originally from Yalobusha county, Miss., his birth occurring in 1848 within a short distance of where he now lives, and is a son of Arthur and Minerva (Hancock) Hudson, the former a native of North Carolina and the latter of South Carolina. The paternal grandfather, John Hudson, moved from North Carolina to Yalobusha county, Miss., in 1834, and settled where his grandson and namesake now lives. He entered six hundred and thirteen acres of land, and there cultivated the soil until his death in 1845. When he first located in Yalobusha county the country was wild and unbroken, and settlers were few and far between. He was a leading member of the Methodist Episcopal church, as was also his wife, whose maiden name was Sarah Mangram. She was a native of North Carolina, and died in 1870 at the age of eighty-two years. They were the parents of six children, all of whom lived to be grown, and one is now living, Mrs. E. E. Coleman, who now resides in Williamson county, Tex. The other children were named as follows: Arthur, father of subject; John was in the employ of the railroad and died in the hospital at St. Louis, Mo.; Mrs. Nancy Rushing died in Texas; Mrs. Sarah Boyd died in Alabama, and Mrs. Mary Ray died in the Lone Star state. Arthur Hudson, one of the elder children of this family, was born in 1811. He emigrated to Mississippi at an early date, settled in Kemper county, and in 1837 moved to Yalobusha county, where he located on the tract of land entered by his father. There he remained until his death, in April, 1871. During the Civil war he was in the militia for home protection. Like his father, Mr. Hudson was a worthy member of the Methodist church, and was class leader in the same for many years, and was steward of said church at the time of his death. In politics he was identified with the democratic party. He was married in South Carolina to Miss Minerva Hancock, who received her final summons in 1858. She was a member of the same church. Their family consisted of ten children, five of whom are still living: William resides in Yalobusha county, and is engaged in farming and preaching, being a minister in the Missionary Baptist church; James resides in Grenada county, Miss., is a farmer and owns thirteen hundred acres of land; Thomas L. and Mrs. Sarah F. Wilson of Yalobusha county. Those deceased were: Tabitha, who died in 1858, at she age of seventeen; Josephine died when young; Jane, who married John Stearns, died in 1870, her husband having died in the late war at Chattanooga, Tenn.; she had five children; Jacob died in 1858 at the age of four years, and an infant died unnamed. The father was married the second time to Miss Caroline Hall, by whom he had four children, all living: Missouri Ann, wife of H. C. Newman; Henry J., Ambrose P., and Annie E., wife of Andrew J. Cost. The mother of these children is yet living, and makes her home on the old farm place in Yalobusha county. She holds membership in the Baptist church. J. C. Hudson left home at an early age, and although he could neither read nor write, he improved all his spare moments, and in 1874 began teaching in the public schools, continuing there until in 1880. Previous to this, however, and after leaving home, he was in the farming business for eight years, and saved enough money to purchase land in Calhoun county, where he resided for six years. In 1882 he moved to the home place, where he has an excellent tract of land, and where he has continued to reside up to the present. He is one of the leading farmers of the county. The residence erected by grandfather Hudson in 1834, where J. C. Hudson now resides, was taken down only a few years ago. Mr. Hudson was married, in 1876, to Miss Mary T. Cobb, of Calhoun county, and to them have been born two children, Gertrude and Ethel, the last named dying at the age of seven months. Mrs. Hudson was a native of Calhoun county,

Miss., and was the daughter of Peter M. Cobb, of North Carolina, who was one of the early settlers of Calhoun county. Mrs. Hudson is a member of the Missionary Baptist church, and Mr. Hudson leans toward the Primitive Baptist church. He is a democrat in politics.

Judge R. S. Hudson (deceased) was one of the most prominent members of the bar of Mississippi, and made for himself a career that is worthy of record. He was born in Edgefield district, S. C., August 17, 1820, and was the youngest child of James Hudson, also a native of South Carolina. He was educated in Tennessee by his own means. He lived with Robert Spencer after the death of his father, which occurred when he was about fifteen years of age, but was not sent to school by him. He did not complete his college course on account of the failure of his eyesight. He devoted his leisure time to the reading of law in his uncle's office, and after his death he entered the office of Henry Gray, Esq., an eminent attorney and member of the bar of New Orleans for some years. He was admitted to the bar in 1844, and began practice in and near Louisville, Miss. Afterward he practiced in the higher courts of the state. In 1856 he was elected to the office of district attorney, when he removed to Yazoo county on account of its being the center of his work; he owned a large plantation in this county, on which he resided. In 1862 he was appointed to the office of circuit judge to finish an unexpired term of Judge Henry, deceased. At the end of the term he was elected to succeed himself, and held this office until the close of the war. He then returned to his practice, which he preferred to political honors and position. His public services had given such universal satisfaction that in 1875 he was prevailed to become a candidate for the legislature; he was elected to the office, but at the end of the term respectfully but positively declined all offers of public office. He again settled to the duties of his profession, which he carried on to the time of his death, which was in 1889. Judge Hudson was united in marriage in 1844 to Miss Elvira Gray, a native of South Carolina and a daughter of Frederick and S. (Atkin) Gray. They had born to them eight children; they all grew to maturity, and all received a liberal education; three of the sons are professional men and have bright prospects of future success and prosperity. Mrs. Hudson is still living, an honored Christian woman and a mother deeply beloved. Of the Judge's career as a lawyer too much can not be said in praise. While his education was chiefly that of an advocate, he was successful in every department of the profession, for whether before a jury or a court of equity he always proved himself equal to caring for his side, however able his opponent might be. In his death the state lost a good citizen and wise counselor, the profession an old landmark, his friends a kind and considerate neighbor, and his family a father and husband whose memory will always be revered.

William Hughes is one of the county's most worthy citizens as well as one of its oldest settlers and representative planters. His parents, Benjamin and Nancy (Brashear) Hughes, were born on blue grass soil, in Bullitt county, from which place they came in 1824 to Mississippi territory, the first night of their stay in Claiborne county being under the roof of Waterman Crane. The following day they went to Port Gibson, and after renting a plantation and raising one crop near that place they moved to the town, where Mr. Hughes opened a mercantile establishment. During the many years that he remained in business at this point he became very wealthy, but owing to his desire to aid and benefit his friends and to his kindness of heart and liberality in going their security, he was brought to the verge of bankruptcy and was compelled to suspend business. He then went to New Orleans, where he was a commission merchant until his death, July 7, 1842, at the age of fifty-four years, which occurred at Grand Gulf, Claiborne county, Miss., and he was buried at Port Gibson. He possessed a naturally fine intellect, which was strengthened and broadened by an education which far exceeded that usually given the youth of his day, and this peculiarly fitted him for an active business career. He was at one time president of the Grand Gulf bank, and in his politics was a stanch supporter of the whig party. He was a soldier in the War of 1812, holding the rank of captain of his company, and received his commission from William Henry Harrison, as follows:

SENECATOWN, Headquarters, August 13, 1813.

CAPT. BENJAMIN HUGHES, Assistant Quartermaster-General, Franklinton.

Sir:—Agreeable to the power vested in me by the secretary of war, you are appointed assistant deputy quartermaster-general of the army of the United States, to take rank from the date thereof.

WILLIAM HENRY HARRISON.

Captain Hughes was a man of commanding presence, was five feet ten inches in hight, was finely formed and had dark hair and brown eyes. His figure was finely proportioned and his manners were easy, cordial and pleasing. As an extemporaneous speaker he was fluent and eloquent, and being very public-spirited and deeply interested in all the current issues of the day he used his gift on many occasions to an excellent advantage. His opinions carried weight with them and his friends both near and far often consulted him when in any difficulty or in doubt as to what course to pursue. He extended aid, both in money and sound advice, to many an enterprising young gentleman who was ambitious to win fame and fortune for himself, and as the foundations of their success was in a great measure owing to him, his kindness and generosity will not readily be forgotten. As a business man he followed a course of strictest integrity and this, together with his many other virtues, wielded a wide influence in commercial circles and tended to enhance and promote honorable business methods in those who had previously simply looked to their own interests, forgetting the divine law. His death was a heavy blow to his immediate family, relatives and friends, for among them he was a sort of patriarch, looked up to and confided in by all as a friend, counsellor and protector. Uncle Ben was a name often heard in the various homes of the community, and never was it uttered but with the deepest veneration and regard. Although not a member of any church he was a believer in the Christian religion and was a generous supporter of its institutions. His memory will long be kept green in the hearts of the many who knew and trusted him in life. His wife was born on the 7th of January, 1777, was finely educated and was married in Kentucky. She was a member of the Presbyterian church, was a faithful Christian, and a devoted and loving wife and mother, her care for her family throughout her entire life being most earnest and watchful. She bore her husband a family of twelve children, four of whom attained maturity, the subject of this sketch being the only one who is living at the present time: Mary Ann was first married to Dr. B. W. Morehead and afterward to Dr. R. W. Harper; William comes next in order of birth; a sketch of Henry, another son, appears in this work, and Maria J. became the wife of Hon. W. T. Magruder (see sketch). The other children died in infancy.

William Hughes, whose name appears at the head of this biography, was born on the 12th of January, 1825, was reared in and around Port Gibson, and in the common and high schools of this section and in Oakland college he acquired an excellent education. Before he had graduated from Oakland college his father died, and he immediately returned home to assist the family and look after their interests. At the age of eighteen years he commenced to make his own way in the world as a clerk, and afterward as a merchant for several years, but sold out his stock of goods in 1852. He then resumed clerking, continuing until 1857, when he came to his present location and took upon himself the duties of a planter. In 1856 he was married to Miss Mary Bertron, a native of the county, born, reared and married in the house in which she is now residing. Her birth occurred in 1837, her parents being Rev. Samuel R. and Caroline (Christie) Bertron, and she was the younger of their two daughters, the other daughter being Clara, now the wife of Charles T. Purnell, and a resident of Wattsboro, Va. She is a woman of culture and refinement, her early education being received at home under a private tutor in the Port Gibson academy and in Miss Dinah Posthwaite's school in Natchez. In 1851–2 she attended Mrs. Willard's female seminary in New York, from which institution she graduated with high honors in literature and music, being also a highly gifted Latin and French scholar. Mrs. Hughes also attended the above-named institutions, in which she was a very creditable pupil, and is now a lady of considerable literary attainments and an accomplished musician. Rev. S. R. Bertron was a man whose ability placed him among the highest civilians. He was born in Philadelphia, Penn., in which city he was also educated and married. He graduated from Princeton college in the class of 1828, and subsequently the theological seminary of the same place, and as he possessed an active and vigorous mind, coupled with a remarkable memory, he attained an enviable place in the literary world. In early youth he chose the South as the field of his labors, and by his marriage he became connected with some of the most influential and worthy families of Claiborne county, Miss., and for some fifty years thereafter he figured conspicuously in the social and ecclesiastical history of this section. The first few years of his life he devoted to the ministry exclusively, and as a minister of the Presbyterian faith he showed himself to be a man of broad intellect and profound erudition. He first ministered to a congregation in Philadelphia, but after removing South his labors were gratuitously bestowed upon public churches, and although he at length abandoned active service as a minister on account of bronchial affection, which disabled him from public work, yet his interest in the cause of Christ never knew diminution or loss of enthusiasm. He was a faithful attendant of the church of Port Gibson, and was one of its most liberal contributors. As a husband and father he was devoted to his family, and entered with zeal into all the plans and schemes of his children. He was married three times, his second union being to Mrs. Catherine M. Barnes, a daughter of James Crane and granddaughter of Waterman Crane, by whom he became the father of a son, James C., who died at Port Gibson, leaving a widow and three children. His third marriage was to Miss Otille Mueler, a sketch of whom appears in this work. To this union a son and two daughters were born. Rev. Samuel R. Bertron died of yellow fever at Greenwood plantation October 7, 1878, in the seventy-third year of his age. His grandson, Bertron Purnell, died of the same disease on the afternoon of the same day, and they were lowered into their graves at the same moment, with one ceremony. Rev. Bertron was of highly respectable parentage, his father being a successful practicing physician of the city of Philadelphia, and his mother a granddaughter of Governor Reading, whose name is found in the first pages of New Jersey history. His union to his first wife (Caroline Christie) took place on the 5th of August, 1834, in the city of Philadelphia, Rev. James Patterson officiating. She was an amiable and intelligent woman, and was a daughter of William and Mrs. Clarissa (Crane) Young Christie, and a granddaughter of Waterman Crane. Mrs. Caroline Bertron was born on the 25th of March, 1818, and died April 13, 1839, being the only daughter born to her parents. She was ardent in her affections, gentle in her demeanor, benevolent in disposition, upright in principle, exemplary in every religious duty, and from all with whom she came in contact she won an abiding affection and respect. William Christie, her father, was also born in this county, and died on the 14th of February, 1819, at the age of thirty-one years. His widow was married to William Young in 1821, a native of Scotland, a man of genial disposition, beloved by all who knew him and very prominent in his day as a member of the Bethel church and a trustee of Oakland college. He died in 1863, his widow surviving him until February 5, 1877, when she, too, passed away at the age of seventy-nine years and one month. She was an exemplary woman in every respect, a devoted member of the Presbyterian church, and her home was always open to the friendless and needy, she being known far and near for her hospitality. To William and Mary (Bertron) Hughes nine children were born, six of whom are now living: William Y. is a bookkeeper for William J. Martin, one of the leading merchants at Rodney; Caroline C., wife of T. F. Daniel; Clarissa Y., Mary B., Emily M. and Louisa T. Those deceased are: Nannie, wife of Smith C. Daniel, her death occurring on the 30th of September, 1887, at Greenwood, at the age of nineteen years. Her character was very amiable and lovely, and she was beautiful and accomplished. She left two little children: Smith C. and Mary. The other two children that are dead are Henry and James C. Mr. and Mrs. Hughes have a family of which they have every reason to be proud for they are all prepossessing in appearance, are highly gifted and possess excellent principles. During the late war Mr. Hughes became a member of Captain Magruder's company of Hughes' battalion, which afterward became a part of the Fourth Mississippi cavalry. Soon after his enlistment he was detailed to act as quartermaster-sergeant, afterward becoming ordnance sergeant of the Fourth Mississippi cavalry. He was captured by Banks' army at Springfield Landing, La., below Port Hudson, just before the battle of Port Gibson, but made his escape and returned to his command and served until the close of the war, when he was paroled at Gainesville, Ala., and returned home to resume planting. In early life he was a whig in politics but now is a conservative democrat, but takes little interest in politics. He is a stanch supporter of schools, is an earnest worker for the cause of temperance and supports all good works. He and his wife enjoy a comfortable and pleasant home on their plantation in the Bethel neighborhood. They own about two thousand acres of land, of which about seven hundred are under cultivation. Mrs. Hughes is a devoted member of the Presbyterian church, as are all her family, but although Mr. Hughes is not a member of any church he is a believer in the Christian religion.

Col. Henry Hughes, the subject of this sketch, was one of the noblest of men and a brilliant writer and an accomplished scholar and thinker. Intellectually Henry Hughes was a most remarkable man. Entering college at a very early age he fulfilled all the promises of his precocious childhood, and in a class all of whom were his seniors in years he early took the place of honor and held it undisputed to the end. An unusual combination of gifts met in him and so equally that it was difficult to say what was his special endowment. If he essayed the mathematics, you would have said that in this department of human science he was fitted especially to excel; if the languages, you were equally surprised at the ease, accuracy and elegance of his exercises; if philosophy, you were astonished at the clever, original and comprehensive grasp with which he seized its grandest generalization and measured its profoundest depths; and to him was given the crowning endowment of an exalted nature, a keen and passionate sense of all that is beautiful in nature and art. If we are not mistaken the two faculties of his nature which predominated, taking an old classification as our guide, were the reason and the imagination. He was a born philosopher and a poet. It was not possible for him to consider any fact or phenomenon as single and isolated—analysis was only valuable to him as it led to a grander synthesis, and every step of induction was prized only as it gained him a higher point from which to sweep a wider horizon. Nor did any man ever enter into the spirit of Solomon's declaration, "God hath made all things beautiful in his time," more fervently than he. His love of the beautiful was a passion, and if sometimes his imagination ran riot and broke the bounds of his own chastened and cultivated tastes such offenses were rare and abundantly atoned for by exquisitely beautiful passages, which may be read and reread with unalloyed delight. The tendency which finally mastered and subordinated all others was to abstract thinking; and the topic upon which he exercised his intellect during his whole life was that fruitful one to which so many of the profoundest thinkers and the most ardent philanthropists have consecrated the flower of their years and the fullness of their powers—namely, human society; its defects, its crimes and sorrows, its perfectibility and the best means by which it may be changed from a battle of cruel and selfish antagonisms, or an armed neutrality, into a harmonious and wholesome order. The public mind at the period of his graduation was deeply agitated, as indeed it was during the lifetime of that generation, on the subject of slavery, which would of necessity bring before a scholar and thinker all the social problems suggested by that topic; problems not by any means peculiar to Southern society and as yet unsolved by any. Disposed by his earlier studies and reflections to judge the institution of slavery vigorously and even unfavorably, he gradually, as his mind matured and his studies widened and deepened, became satisfied that society in the South had more nearly realized the objects of human society than any other upon earth, and that it contained within itself the simplest means by which to actualize an ideal and perfect social organization. Before leaving college he had methodized his thoughts, and in some measure prepared himself for their public vindication in a treatise entitled, "Sociology." Its publication was postponed until after his visit to Paris. In that city he became acquainted with the leading writers of his time on social questions, made himself more familiar with the language and literature of France, revised and completed the work just mentioned and published it shortly after his return. In this book he disclosed the peculiar opinions and the peculiar object to whose propagation and attainment he devoted the remainder of his life. It is the key to that life. No man ever pursued a life purpose more clearly designed and firmly fixed, with more conscientiousness, diligence and loyalty to a great idea than he. The subject of this sketch was a life-long student; not in any particular profession, for though a lawyer and transacting ably and faithfully the business intrusted to him, he cared little for its drudgery or emoluments. He sought neither office nor power nor wealth, but he sought and almost worshiped as an ideal, culture; the culture of his whole nature, to be a perfect man, was almost his morality, intellect and religion. His whole ambition was to be remembered as a benefactor to man, to contribute, by just thought, to the sum of human wisdom and thereby to the sum of human happiness. He was a politician, but he sought no office; a statesman, but he sought no power; a thinker and a writer, but he sought no honors. He was a true patriot, living, thinking, writing, toiling, suffering, battling and dying for the common weal. Closely akin to his intellectual and consistent with it was his moral character. He was the most unselfish and generous of men. In the long and frightful march from Manassas to Gordonsville, thence to the Peninsula, from which he returned to Mississippi before the evacuation, he was seen ordinarily trudging on foot at the head of his men whilst some sick or worn-out soldier was mounted on his horse. Hundreds of dollars from his own scanty pay and means were expended for the comfort of his men, with not simply no hope, but no desire or care for its return. In the campaign in Virginia he had weekly prayer meeting in his tent, and suffered nothing but official duty to interrupt it. Among the papers scanned by the eyes of the mother, whom he almost worshiped, is found one dated and signed by himself and which reads thus: "I pray Almighty God to make me one of the wisest and best of men." To an affectionate sister, whose anxieties had prompted some intimation of the necessity of preparation for death, he said: "Why, I was converted when I was a child." To a pious lady, who sent him, on his deathbed, a message begging him to pray, he replied: "I have prayed all my life," and it was his habit to pray regularly three times a day. What judgment can we form from such facts but that God's spirit had been purifying this soul and preparing it for more exalted honor and more extended usefulness in worlds whose holy desire is met by heavenly satisfaction, and holy hope and faith by an unclouded vision and an eternal fruition. Fifteen months before his death, on the breaking out of hostilities between the Northern and Southern states of the old Union, he entered the service as a private in the Port Gibson riflemen, of which he had been a member for years. He was shortly elected to the captaincy of the Claiborne guards, and subsequently to the colonelcy of the immortal Twelfth Mississippi regiment. In this position he was soon recognized as a man of signal ability and resources, for he had long been preparing for such a position, for he thoroughly posted himself on the art of war, and procured every book of any value within his reach on every branch of the service. When he entered the army few men in it surpassed him in the knowledge of the science of war. Designated by the commander of his division to construct some fortifications in front of Bull Run, he discharged that duty in so scientific and thorough a way as to elicit the warm commendation of the most distinguished officers of the army, and it is a singular coincidence that victorious Confederate soldiers possesssed and employed with deadly effect these very works in the second battle of Manassas. From Manassas to Gordonsville, thence to the Peninsula, he marched at the head of his regiment, encouraging the timid, supporting the weak, comforting the sick, in all things showing himself a skillful, daring and humane commander. Many who shared with him the toil and danger of these memorable marches live to bear testimony to his cheerfulness, his courage and above all his tenderness and care of his exhausted and half-starved soldiers. In these dreary toils was laid the foundation of disease which carried him to his grave. He returned from Virginia with authority from the war department to raise a regiment of Partizan rangers for the defense of this and adjoining counties on the Mississippi river. He engaged in this duty with the energy and zeal which characterized him, and brought to the organization and equipment of this new command all his former skill and knowledge, tested and perfected by the experience of a long and arduous campaign in Virginia. In spite of the drafts made on the population by the conscript law he was rapidly accomplishing his object, when it pleased God to arrest his career of honorable usefulness and lay him upon the bed of anguish and death. His disease, inflammatory rheumatism, left him scarcely free from suffering and entailed complications distressing to heart and sense, yet he persisted in rising from his bed and prosecuting his work. When his partially formed regiment was ordered to Port Hudson he was carried on his bed to Fayette to report to his commanding officer and to superintend its departure, and then turned homeward to die, yet still hoping and believing that he would live. To the last he clung to life; he desired to live, yet was willing to die if he must. To a friend who stood by his bedside he faintly whispered something, only partially understood, and seeing that he was not comprehended spelled one of the words, and repeated "*nos sumos purificate.*" A few moments after he was indeed purified forever from earthly sins and sorrows. He fell a martyr to the cause for which the nation was struggling, as truly as though amid the roar and tumult of the battlefield he had yielded up his life to his country, on Friday, the 3d day of October, 1862. Thus ended the life of one of this country's noblest men.

Capt. M. W. Hughes was born in County Tyrone, Ireland, in August, 1841, his parents, Peter and Bridget (Canavan) Hughes, being also born there. Captain Hughes is a brother of Col. Felix Hughes, who was a prominent levee commissioner and contractor, and was killed at Baton Rouge during the Civil war. The Captain's ancestors, on both sides, were farmers. At the age of nine years he was brought to America, and his first permanent home in this country was at Vicksburg, Miss., where he was employed by his brother during the winter on levee work, and in summer attended the common schools of the county until he was sixteen, when his brother sent him to St. Joseph's college at Bardstown, Ky., for the purpose of securing a commercial education, as well as to take a course in civil engineering. His inclinations were toward mathematics, and during the four years that he remained in this institution he made an enviable record for himself. After graduating on the 3d of June, 1861, he returned home, and as his brother Felix was raising a company, he enlisted and was commissioned lieutenant, and took part in the engagements at Belmont, Shiloh, Baton Rouge, Corinth, Champion's Hill, siege of Jackson, Dalton, Resaca, Kenesaw Mountain, and was severely wounded at Peach Tree Creek, being shot through the breast, the bullet lodging near his spine, where he carries it to this day. He was afterward wounded by a fragment of shell, which injured his vocal organs to such an extent that for twelve months he was deprived of the power of speech. Soon after the battle of Shiloh he was promoted to a captaincy, and after his partial recovery from the shell wound he rejoined his regiment at Atlanta, but could not command on account of his lack of voice and was placed on the retired list for sixty days. He was afterward put in command of the railroad at Jackson, being general inspector at the same time, and there he received a commission from the Confederate secretary of war to organize a company, but only a portion of it was raised, and these men were detailed as scouts and kept General Johnston informed of the movements of the Federals after the fall of Vicksburg. He was at Jackson when the war closed. His company was first organized as the Sarsfield Southrons, afterward company C, Twenty-second Mississippi, and during his service he was wounded thirteen times. When peace was declared he secured state contracts for levee work in Louisiana and Mississippi, and built levees south of the Arkansas line to Tensas parish, La., among which may be mentioned the Ashton levee. At one time he had the contract for all the Mississippi levees, and but for the interference of Governor Ames, just as he was in a position to make money, he would have soon been in independent circumstances. That governor recognized the levee board and revoked all outstanding contracts, Hughes & Searles having the contracts for all levees in Bolivar, Washington and Issaquena counties. About 1887 Mr. Hughes retired from levee work and has since been devoting the greater part of his attention to his plantation in Sharkey county, which consists of four hundred acres, one hundred and fifty being under cultivation, but is also the owner of one hundred acres within one-half mile of Vicksburg, which is destined to make him a fortune soon, as the city is growing rapidly in his direction. His residence is situated on a hill, covered with beautiful shade and ornamental trees, and everything about the place indicates that it is a model Southern home. He has always taken quite an interest in local politics, is supervisor of his district, and socially is an officer in the Knights of St. John society. On the 27th of June, 1887, he was married to Miss Minnie Henry, a daughter of W. P. Henry, of Vicksburg, and a native of Ireland. He came to Vicksburg before the war, and for several years was engaged in merchandising. Captain and Mrs. Hughes have one child, a beautiful little daughter, Alberta May. The family are devout members of the Catholic church. Captain Hughes is a nephew of Thomas Canavan, one of the first settlers of Vicksburg. He is quite proud of his brother's war record, and has a large oil painting of him hanging in his parlor, in which he is dressed in the uniform of a Confederate colonel.

William Hall (deceased) was born July 19, 1825, in Spottsvylania county, Va. He was the ninth in a family of ten children born to Brodie and Elizabeth (Herndon) Hull. Brodie

Hull's family were of Welsh descent, and his father was a nephew of the celebrated Commodore Hull. This distinguished naval officer was born at Derby, Conn., March 9, 1775· In 1798 he became lieutenant in the new navy created by congress during the difficulties with France. He served with credit in the West Indies and Mediterranean, and on the outbreak of the War of 1812 was captain of the frigate Constitution. By skillful seamanship he escaped the close pursuit of five British vessels, and on August 10 he captured the British frigate Guerriere off Newfoundland, after a conflict in which the Guerriere was so severely cut up that Hull was forced to burn her. A gold medal was given to him by congress. He died at Philadelphia, February 13, 1843. Brodie Hull, the father of the subject of this sketch, was a prominent man in Virginia, a farmer and planter by occupation. He died in 1827, and four years later his widow removed to Marshall county, Miss., with her family and bought the plantation upon which the widow of William Hull now resides. She was an exemplary woman, who reared her family to become respectable members of society, and died in 1844, having been for many years a consistent member of the Baptist church. There is not a member of the family of Brodie Hull now living. Upon the death of his mother, William Hull inherited the old homestead, upon which he lived from the time of his birth till he died in 1890. He was educated at Washington college, at Lexington, Va., graduating in the class of 1844. Upon his return home he engaged in farming, and though he never had any political aspirations, he became quite prominent in the public affairs of the state, and was an active party worker, having been several times a delegate to state conventions, and represented his district as a delegate to the national convention at St. Louis when Grover Cleveland was renominated for the presidency. He was married in 1846 to Miss Mary Clayton, a daughter of Judge A. M. and Mary W. (Thomas) Clayton. (See biographical sketch of Judge Clayton, appearing elsewhere in this work.) They have had born to them eight children—five sons and three daughters—three of whom are living: Mary W., wife of John D. Martin, a well-known lawyer of Memphis; Elizabeth, wife of Rice Fant, of Holly Springs; and Authur W., the only son, who was educated at Oxford university. At the time of his death Mr. Hull was the owner of three thousand two hundred acres of land, most of it under cultivation. He was one of the most successful planters in northern Mississippi before the war, and was the owner of one hundred slaves. His family has always and justly been regarded as one of the first in this part of the state or country. Mr. Hull was liberal in his support of all enterprises and movements having in view the enhancement of the public weal. Since his death his widow and her children have lived on the beautiful homestead where he lived and died, and one of the sons has met with marked success in her management of the plantation.

G. Wilson Humphreys is one of the oldest and most successful planters, as well as one of the oldest settlers of Claiborne county. He was born on the plantation on which he is now residing (known as Oakland) September 16, 1819, being a son of David G. Humphreys, who was born May 17, 1794, and died January 11, 1871, and grandson of G. W. Humphreys, who was born in South Carolina, March 23, 1771, and died December 15, 1843. The father of the latter was Colonel Ralph Humphreys, who was also a South Carolinian, and served as a colonel in the Revolutionary war, afterward receiving the pension of a colonel, the last money he received being spent in the purchase of a clock which is now in possession of the subject of this sketch. The first of the family to come to America were three brothers who came from England in 1632 (for a further history of whom see sketch of Governor Humphreys). Soon after the close of the Revolutionary war Ralph Humphreys went with his regiment to Michilimackinac, where a fort had been established, where he remained several years, leaving his wife in South

Carolina. She sold their plantation there, took her negroes and emigrated to east Tennessee, sailing down the Tennessee, Ohio and Mississippi rivers landing at the famous Grindstone Ford landing of the north fork of the Bayou Pierre river. The country was under the Spanish governor, Gayoso at that time, and from him Mrs. Humphreys secured a large tract of land. Soon after this her husband obtained a furlough, and the long and toilsome journey to be with his family for a short time was made on horseback, during which time, no doubt, he suffered many privations and hardships. A few months after reaching his family he sickened and died, being buried at Grindstone Ford. He was of a brave and fearless disposition, and possessed much resolution and firmness. His widow, who was much younger than himself was rich and beautiful, was left with one son, George Wilson, the grandfather of the subject of this sketch. She afterward married Col. Daniel Burnett, a Spanish officer, and one of the most distinguished men of the territory at that time. He was a member of the territorial legislature until his death, and was strongly talked of for governor. He was a man of ability and took an active part in political matters, holding all the offices from magistrate to president of the senate, being widely known throughout the entire state. While serving in the War of 1812 he was at the battle of New Orleans, making a brave and faithful soldier. He died and is buried at Grindstone Ford. He and his wife lived to a ripe old age, she surviving him several years, and now sleeps by his side. George Wilson Humphreys grew to manhood on the plantation that is still owned by G. Wilson Humphreys. He was given excellent educational advantages, owned a fine library and took great pride in keeping himself well posted and up with the times. Although he was not an active politician he served in the state legislature for some time, and was an earnest member of the A. F. & A. M., he and one other member, being the only ones of the family that ever united with that order. Although not a member of any church, he believed in the doctrine of the Campbellites, and was very charitable and liberal with his means, and a leading projector of one of the first academies of this county. He organized a company, of which he was made captain, and was a participant in the battle of New Orleans. His financial enterprises were prosperous and he became a wealthy planter. He was married to Sarah, daughter of Capt. David Smith, who came from her native state of Tennessee to Mississippi in her girlhood, settling near Clinton. Her marriage with Mr. Humphreys was consummated January 17, 1792, a sister of hers marrying Hiram J. Reynold, fourth governor of the state of Mississippi.

To Captain Humphreys and his wife a large family of children were born, three sons and three daughters living to maturity and marrying, the rest dying in childhood. Mrs. Humphreys was born on the 19th of January, 1776, and died December 20, 1817, having been an earnest member of the Methodist Episcopal church, as were most of the Humphreys. She was an ideal wife, mother and friend and for her many noble and Christian traits of character she was loved by all. David G. Humphreys, her son, started in life at the bottom of the ladder, but by hard work and careful industry he amassed a fortune, being at one time the owner of forty thousand acres of land. He devoted his time strictly to his planting operations and as a reward for his faithfulness to duty accumulated ample means for his declining years. He held no public office, but at one time were a director of the Grand Gulf Railroad Banking company. He was also a patron of education and was one of the founders of the Port Gibson female college, which was first called the Port Gibson academy, it being afterward sold at sheriff's sale, he with the board purchasing it and giving it to the Methodist Episcopal conference. Later it was again sold by the sheriff, when he purchased it himself and gave it to the Methodist Episcopal conference of Mississippi. He was an active worker in the Methodist Episcopal church, being one of the heaviest contributors toward building up the Methodist Episcopal church of Port Gibson; was very charitable, and as he always endeavored to follow the teachings of the golden rule, he won the respect, good will and love of all who knew him. He was married to Miss Mary Cobun, a native of this county, a descendant of an early settler of this region, Samuel Cobun, Sr. She was born July 31, 1794, and died July 19, 1874, an earnest Christian and a noble and charitable lady. She bore her husband five sons and two daughters, all of whom grew to maturity, with the exception of the eldest son and daughter who died when young. G. Wilson Humphreys, the immediate subject of this sketch, was next to the eldest of his parents' family, and in this county was reared and educated, his first knowledge of books being obtained at home. After attending Oakland college one year he entered Augusta college of Kentucky, from which institution he graduated in August, 1839, after which he returned home and looked after his father's business for a number of years. He then began studying law in Transylvania university of Lexington, Ky., and while in this institution was a classmate of General Blair, James Clay and Chief Justice Divine, who died in Texas in 1889. He graduated in 1843, after which he returned home and was soon after married to Miss Catherine B. Prince, a native of this county, born August 24, 1825, and a graduate of Port Gibson female college. She was a most faithful wife and mother, and was very conscientious in the discharge of every duty. She united with the Methodist Episcopal church at the same time as her husband (soon after their marriage), and was a faithful worker in the same until her death, which occurred November 24, 1870. During the war she was president of the ladies' aid society, and the clothing which was prepared for the soldiers was made on the plantation on which Mr. Humphreys is now living and was contributed by his father. To Mr. and Mrs. Humphreys seven children were born, all but one of whom living to be grown: Benjamin, who died October 7, 1878, of yellow fever, at the age of twenty years, eight months and twenty days, was a student in the Kentucky military institute at Frankfort, and was a very brilliant and promising young man. William P. was born on the 9th of November, 1845, and was educated in the Port Gibson academy. He was a member of Captain Buck's company, Colonel Mayburn's cavalry regiment, and was accidentally shot while on the march to attack Natchez, under Gen. Wirt Adams, and died from the effects of the wound November 6, 1863. Catherine B. was born December 29, 1863, and died September 16, 1870, having been educated in Port Gibson female academy and the Nazareth school of Kentucky. She was married to F. F. Myles, son of Dr. Myles, of Port Gibson, and bore him one daughter, who is now at Mrs. Blake's school in New Orleans. Mary Cobun was born August 7, 1860, and died September 13, 1863. Those that are living are David George who was born February 18, 1847, and was educated at Port Gibson academy, Greenboro, Ala., and in the University of Mississippi, at Oxford. He was with General Forrest in Tennessee during the Civil war; Samuel C., who received the same advantages as his brother, was born March 4, 1849; Bayless E. was born November 23, 1851. The sons of Mr. Humphreys live on adjoining plantations, David on the Hermitage place, Bayless on the Oaklawn plantation, and Samuel C., who is on the Ashland farm, all well-to-do and industrious and substantial citizens. Mr. Humphreys has one of the finest libraries in the county, consisting of many rare volumes of great value, and was the owner of Audubon's works, now out of print. Many of his happiest hours are spent in his library, but he is also very fond of field sports, and is considered a good shot. He is a fluent and intelligent conversationalist and is considered by all to be that noblest work of God—an honest man.

Benjamin Humphreys is a native-born resident of Claiborne county, Miss., and as such is looked upon with esteem and respect by those who know who and what he is. He has been

an important factor in the growth and prosperity of this section ever since he attained manhood, and is a true type of the progressive and enterprising Southern gentleman. He was
born in the month of February, 1827, being the fourth in a family of nine children—seven
sons and three daughters—three of the family now living, born to David George and Mary
(Cobun) Humphreys, a full account of whom is given in the sketch of G. Wilson Humphreys.
The parents were married in 1820, and were accounted among the wealthiest citizens of the
county, their home, which was beautiful and attractive, being the delight of the many friends
who gathered about them. They are now deceased and their remains are resting in the
Hermitage, in Claiborne county. Benjamin Humphreys obtained his scholastic education
in Centenary college, a Methodist institution, and being an apt pupil he made rapid progress
in his studies. Later he fitted himself for the medical profession but as he had inherited
wealth, he found that his time was fully occupied in properly caring for his estates, and he
accordingly relinquished a professional life. He was married on the 6th of November,
1850, to Miss Mary Scott Jefferies, at Scrogy the old family homestead of the latter,
and in time their union was blessed in the birth of nine children—one son and eight
daughters: Catherine Flynn (deceased), was the wife of Joseph Brown, a nephew of
Gov. Albert Brown, of Mississippi; Mary Cobun is the wife of Samuel Briscoe, nephew
of General Briscoe, of Vicksburg, Miss.; Priscilla Shelby, was educated in Port Gibson college and resides with her parents; Bliss Prince received her education in Brookhaven
female college, and is an excellent musician; and David George, who makes his home with his
parents, has a good practical education, and is devoting his attention to planting. Mrs.
Humphreys is a lady of very superior mental endowments, and in social life she is highly
esteemed for her rare conversational powers and winning and agreeable manner. She is
devoted to her family, enters into all the plans and schemes of her children, and has a decided
taste for music and the fine arts. She was born June 30, 1830, and in her early girlhood
received her education under an English tutor, taking the same heavy studies, such as Latin,
Greek and mathematics, as her brother, and as her mind was clear and well poised she became
a finished scholar. Her benevolent principles are well known, and by her generosity and
hospitality she wins many friends and rarely loses them. Warmly espousing the cause of
the South in the Civil war, Mr. Humphreys enlisted as a volunteer in the Confederate army
in 1861, and was chosen second lieutenant of the Sixteenth Mississippi infantry volunteers,
from which rank, by gallant conduct, he was afterward promoted to captain of company B,
of his regiment, for those around him recognized in him the genius to command, and as a
faithful and efficient officer he was unsurpassed. He was in Stonewall Jackson's brigade,
but was transferred to Hughes' battalion as major, being neither wounded nor captured. In
politics he has been an active and efficient member of the democratic party, but exercises his
right of franchise for the best interests of his country. As a business man he has been successful and prosperous. Always practical, he adapted himself readily to the altered conditions
of Southern life produced by the war and the abolition of slavery; and adjusting his business
habits and methods to meet the requirements of the new regime, he has made headway and
progress where so many who were successful planters under the old regime have failed. He
and his family spend a part of their summers at the seaside each year, but the most of their
days are spent at their pleasant home, and among their numerous friends in Port Gibson.
Mrs. Humphreys' old homestead, Vaucluse, located four miles from Port Gibson, comprises
a fine tract of land. This is one of the typical Southern homes, so well known in song and
story, and was one of the gayest resorts for the young generation in the palmy days of the
South.

Gov. Benjamin G. Humphreys (deceased) is well known in English history. The progenitors of the name in the United States came to the colonies long before the Revolutionary war, and here its members have multiplied and scattered throughout the land. Unquestionably, inasmuch as the name is a peculiar one, all those possessing it have a common origin. From an examination of heraldry among the English people it is learned that the family was early divided into six branches, each one of which had a special coat of arms, all of which may be seen in the Herald office at London, where they have been since 1340. All these coats of arms, which differ in minor details, show a general similarity and a common origin, and unquestionably originated during the crusades, because all are surmounted by a cross, in fact, the family name has been traced directly back to the time of Peter the Hermit, in the eleventh century. From that time down to the present, hundreds of the best citizens of this and other lands have held this honorable name. Among the pioneers who settled in Claiborne county was Col. Ralph Humphreys, who moved from Hampshire county, Va., in a flatboat in the spring of 1788 down the Monongahela, Ohio and Mississippi rivers to Natchez. On the 10th day of September of that year he located in what is now Claiborne county, on Bayou Pierre at Grindstone Ford. He had two sons: George Wilson and Ralph, the latter of whom was killed accidentally when a lad of fourteen years. The other son, George Wilson Humphreys, in due time married Miss Sarah Smith, daughter of Maj. David Smith, who afterward distinguished himself in the Creek (Indian) war at Talladega and at New Orleans during the War of 1812, and for his conspicuous services was honored by the legislature of Mississippi by having one of the counties of the state named for him. Major Smith was a native of South Carolina and of German Huguenot extraction. Governor Humphreys was of Celtic origin and belonged to the special branch now known as Welch. His ancestors, during the early invasions of England, were driven from Wales and forced to settle in the north of Ireland. Here one of his ancestors married a Scotch lady named Montgomery, and by her reared a family who distinguished themselves in opposing the English "orders in council." This led to strong restrictive measures against them by the officers of the crown, and they were forced to immigrate to the colony of Virginia, where in 1776, in common with the colonists, they took up arms against the mother country to secure their honor and independence. From this particular branch of the Humphreys family have descended three distinct lines of pioneers, who have penetrated all parts of the West and Southwest. Alexander and David Humphreys settled in Kentucky, Perry W. Humphreys in Tennessee, Ralph Humphreys in Mississippi, John and Alexander Humphreys in Louisiana. None of these arose to any great eminence, but all were sober, industrious, sturdy and honest pioneers. Some have adorned the bench in their localities, some have graced legislative halls, and some have expounded the gospel of Christ from the pulpit. Ralph Humphreys, the great-great-grandfather of Governor Humphreys, married a Miss Walker, a near relative of Gen. Felix Walker and Judge Samuel Walker, of New Orleans. Ralph Humphreys, the grandfather of Governor Humphreys, attained the rank of colonel in the Revolutionary war. He married Miss Agnes Wilson, a niece of James Wilson, of Pennsylvania, a member of the convention which framed the constitution for the United States. In 1793 George Wilson Humphreys removed from Grindstone Ford onto a piece of land on the north side of Bayou Pierre, known as the Hermitage, which particular tract of land had been obtained by Mrs. Humphreys from the Spanish government.

Gov. B. G. Humphreys was born August 26, 1808, at the Hermitage, but in 1811 was taken by his parents to the bank of the Mississippi, just below Milliken's Bend; but two years later the family returned to the Hermitage, where the mother died December 20, 1817. Our subject, then a lad of nine years, was soon afterward sent to his grandfather Smith's, in Kentucky, where he attended school at Russellville and vicinity. He continued in school there and in Mississippi until 1821, when he was sent to Morristown, N. J., by water on the Gulf and Atlantic, and and after twenty-four days landed at Staten Island, and soon after went to Morristown. He was placed in the family of William F. King, of that city, where he remained three years, spending his vacations in New York city with his guardian, Dr. Hunt. He took a preparatory course, expecting to enter the college in the fall of 1825, but was sent for by his father in 1824, and thus ended his school life in New Jersey. Instead of returning home by water he went by stage across the country via Cincinnati, Ohio. Upon reaching Mississippi his father placed him in a store at Port Gibson, where he worked as a clerk, and during the succeeding winter secured the appointment as cadet of West Point through the assistance of Hon. Thomas N. Williams, then United States senator from Mississippi. In April, 1825, in company with Dr. Joe Moore, he went up the river to Wheeling, Va., and crossed the Allegheny mountains to Washington city, thence to Wilmington, Del., where he entered school to prepare himself for the examination of entry at West Point. He reviewed his studies under W. John Bullock in six weeks, and then started for West Point, where he arrived in June, 1825, and creditably passed the examination. He was admitted to the class of Joseph E. Johnston, Robert E. Lee and a number of others who afterward distinguished themselves on both sides during the great Civil war. He was a diligent student, and greatly enjoyed the routine and discipline of that famous institution. However, he became involved in a Christmas frolic, which ended in a riot, for which breach of discipline he, with thirty-eight others, was expelled from the institution. This unfortunate event the Governor always afterward regretted. In May, 1827, he returned to Mississippi, where he entered upon the duties of an overseer on his father's plantation, relieving him of all care. This he continued for several years, in the meantime taking great interest in books and athletic sports. He made a particular study of law, in which his active intellect took the greatest delight. On March 15, 1832, he married Miss Mary McLaughlin, eldest daughter of Hon. Dugald McLaughlin, of Marion county, and immediately thereafter settled on Big Black river in Claiborne county, and entered upon the labors of a planter. His wife died March 17, 1835, leaving two children: Thomas McLaughlin, who died at the age of four years, and Mary Douglass, who grew to womanhood and married Isaac Stamps, a nephew of Jefferson Davis. Mr. Stamps entered the Confederate army during the late war, arose to the rank of major, and was killed at Gettysburg while gallantly leading his command into action. His widow resides in New Orleans, where she is a prominent teacher in the public schools of that city. After the death of his wife Governor Humphreys returned to the Hermitage, and for a time lived with his father. In 1837 he was prevailed upon to become an independent candidate for the legislature from his county, and after an exciting canvass was triumphantly elected, and took his seat in 1838. In 1839 he became the whig candidate for the state senate, and was elected by the narrow margin of two votes. At the expiration of his term he returned to his plantation and, as he thought, from public life. He was a strong advocate and member of the old whig party, as were so many of the best minds in the South during that early period. December 3, 1839, he married Miss Mildred Hickman Maury, eldest daughter of Hon. James Harvey Maury, of Port Gibson. Judge Maury was a native of Kentucky and a descendant of the famous De La Fontaine family of France.

In the fall of 1840 Mr. Humphreys returned with his family to his plantation on the Big Black river. Six years later he bought a tract of land in the Yazoo valley on Roebuck lake, in Sunflower county, and for a time was engaged in fitting it up for habitation. He here passed a happy life with his family, in reading and in following his hounds, of which he kept a fine pack, and took the greatest interest in the sport. When the late war broke out he entered the service early in 1861, and joined a company formed in Sunflower county and was elected captain. He was ordered to Virginia, and soon after, in September, was promoted to colonel of the Twenty-first Mississippi regiment, and was assigned to the army of Virginia under Gen. Joseph E. Johnston. He continued to command this regiment until the battle of Gettysburg, where he was promoted on the field for gallantry in action to a brigadier-general-ship. Thus he served until he was wounded at Berryville, Va., September 1, 1864, by a gun-shot wound in the breast, which disabled him for a considerable period. He returned to Mississippi late in the fall of 1864, and on February, 1865, received orders to take charge of a military district in southern Mississippi, which he did, and while thus engaged the war ended. Mr. Humphreys was the first governor elected after the war, and was inaugurated in October, 1865, succeeding Gov. W. L. Sharkey, and held the office until the fall of 1868, when he was ousted by Generals McDowell and Ames, the latter of whom was appointed military governor. He remained in Jackson for some time, doing an insurance business for several years. In 1869 he removed to Vicksburg and continued the same business until 1877, when he went to his plantation in Le Flore county, a new county recently formed of part of Sunflower and Carroll counties, where he died, December 20, 1882, at the age of seventy-four years. He had been an earnest Christian for many years, and loved the house of God, loved the friendship of good people and loved all good things. As a legislator and ruler, his people's praise is his monument. As a patriot and soldier his fame will stand immortal on the page of history. As a Christian he rests from his labors and his works do follow him. His last union resulted in the birth of ten children: James Maury, who died September 3, 1851; Benjamin George, who died July 25, 1852; Sarah Smith, who died at Port Gibson September 25, 1845; Julian M., died July 12, 1849; Lucinda S., who died of yellow fever at Warrenton, September 2, 1855; and a son who died when quite young, and three sons who are still living: John Barnes Humphreys, who is a resident of Carrollton. He was married in Holmes county, Miss., in 1878, to Miss Ella Hoskins, a daughter of Capt. John S. Hoskins, and a native of Holmes county, where she was also reared and educated; they have four children: Benjamin George, Sallie Barnes, James Maury, Mildred Maury and a son, John Barnes, who died in November, 1890, at the age of seven years. Next came a daughter, Elizabeth Fontaine, who married James C. Bertron, in 1878, and died the same year. The next son of Governor Humphreys is Dr. David Smith Humphreys, who resides in Leoto, Washington county, Miss. He was married to Miss Sallie Hoskins, daughter of Capt. John S. Hoskins, and a sister of his brother's wife, and by her is the father of two daughters: Sallie Walton and Mary Stamps. The last son of Governor Humphreys is Benjamin George Humphreys, who married Miss Louisa Yerger, a daughter of William Yerger, of Greenville, Miss. She was born in Jackson, Miss., but was reared and educated in Greenville. They have one son, William Yerger. The widow of Governor Humphreys and their surviving children are earnest members of the Presbyterian church, of which she has been a member for many years, although the Governor was one of the pillars of the Methodist Episcopal church for an equally long period.

Dr. D. S. Humphreys, physician, Leota Landing, Miss. Dr. Humphreys' great-grandmother and her two sons, Ralph and George Wilson Humphreys, came down the Ohio and Mississippi rivers in 1786, and settled on Bayou Pierre (now in Claiborne county), Miss. Her husband, Ralph Humphreys, was a colonel in the Revolutionary war, and afterward came to Mississippi, where he joined his family. He died the following year, and his son, Ralph, died about the same time. The other son, George Wilson Humphreys, named after his mother's family, married a Miss Smith, and located at Grindstone Ford, Claiborne county. Afterward he settled and cleared the Hermitage plantation, which is still owned by his descendants. His wife died about 1819. By his marriage he became the father of a large family of children, Benjamin G., the father of subject, being the seventh in order of birth. He was born at Hermitage plantation August 26, 1808. He was but eleven years of age at the time of his mother's death, and he then went to Georgetown, Ky., to attend school, riding a pony all the way. He subsequently attended school at Morristown, N. J., and still later entered West Point, where he graduated. He was twice married, first to Miss McLaughlin, who died, leaving two children: Thomas and Mary, and afterward to Miss Mildred H. Maury, who was originally from Tennessee. When but four years of age, or in 1826, she came with her father, Judge Maury, to Port Gibson, Miss. After his marriage, Mr. Humphreys was actively engaged in planting, and this occupation carried on until his death. He served several times in both branches of the state legislature prior to the war, and at the breaking out of that memorable struggle he was strongly Union in his sentiments. Notwithstanding this, when Mississippi seceded, he went with her and organized the Sunflower guards of Sunflower county, where he owned an estate. He entered the army as captain, and afterward was made colonel of the Twenty-first Mississippi regiment, and later brigadier-general of the brigade. He was wounded at the battle of Perryville in the army of northern Virginia, and was not in active service afterward. In 1865 he was elected governor, and reëlected in 1867, but was dispossessed from office by Federal military authority the same year. He subsequently lived a life of retirement on his plantation, Itta Bena, until his death, on December 23, 1882. He was a member of the Methodist church, and a Christian in every sense of the term. He left a widow and four children: Mary (widow of Capt. Isaac Davis Stamp, who commanded company I, Twenty-first Mississippi regiment, was killed at the battle of Gettysburg, and he was a nephew of Jefferson Davis), J. B. (married Miss Ella Hoskins, a native of Mississippi, and is now engaged in planting in Le Flore county), Dr. David S. (subject), and Benjamin G. (married Miss Louise Yerger, daughter of William Yerger, of Greenville, Miss., a place settled by his father in 1848, and which still belongs to his heirs). Dr. David S. Humphreys was born in Claiborne county, Miss., in 1860, and received his literary education in the University of Mississippi. In 1880 he began the study of medicine, and graduated at Tulane university, La., in 1883. After this he began practicing at Itta Bena, Le Flore county, but moved to Leota in February, 1888, and has continued practicing his profession since. He is progressive in his ideas, and has met with flattering success. He was married, in 1886, to Miss Lallie Hoskins, of Lexington, Miss., and daughter of Capt. J. S. Hoskins, one of the old settlers of Holmes county. The fruits of this union are three children: Sallie Walton, Mary Stamps and D. S., Jr. Dr. and Mrs. Humphreys are members of the Presbyterian church, and the Doctor is a member of the Masonic fraternity and the Knights of Honor.

Col. John Cobun Humphreys was born in Claiborne county, Miss., on his father's Hermitage plantation, June 8, 1821. His father cleared the primeval forest and canebrake from the land, and his early days were cast amid a hardy race of pioneers. Essentially agricultural through a long line of ancestry, his boyhood fell amid the struggles of his father with poverty and the environment of an early settler, in laying the foundation of an after princely fortune. Early taught the principles of economy and industry, by the hardy training of early life, he ripened into a manhood rich with manly virtues. He lived at a period that was the border line between the stern, stalwart virtues of the pioneer and the after opu-

Jas. S. Madison

lent ease of a country grown wealthy. He illustrated the nobility of the one, while able to enjoy the leisure and elegance of the other. Bred of a people whose latchstring hung on the outside of the door, his name became a synonym for generosity and hospitality. Far and near, those who knew John Cobun Humphreys, knew that his heart was in his hand. He was educated in Kentucky and graduated with distinction at a time when an honor at college was no idle term. He afterward took a course of law at the University of Virginia, passing the course with ease to his diploma. Returned from college shades to the sterner walks of life, he spent a few years with horn and hound and gun, being a superb sportsman, and then married Sarah Stuart, of Jefferson county, daughter of James Stuart. The fruit of this union was six children: David George, Kate Cobun, Moreau Stuart, John Cobun, James Leon and Blount Stuart. Of these three are living: David George, Kate Cobun (now Mrs. L. J. Butler) and Moreau Stuart. Although a graduate of law, the inherited instinct for agriculture prevailed, and he launched his ardent nature with tireless energy and enthusiasm into the business of a cotton planter. Here his success was commensurate with an exceptionally broad and active brain, and at the breaking out of the war he was master of a large fortune in cotton, land and slaves. Let it be said to his memory that the genial heart that beat with so much kindness and gentleness to mankind at large was especially considerate and forbearing toward these wards of his authority, these humble charges upon his time and care. No master was ever kinder to his slaves, no slave had a more genial master. In politics he was originally a whig, but afterward yielded allegiance to the democratic party, and was to the last a stanch democrat. On sectional questions an ultra Southern man—for the union under the constitution—but otherwise a strong advocate of secession. In support of these principles, when the war came, as a logical sequence, he placed all he had at the disposal of his country, and a Confederate soldier he looked upon as one of his family. He organized a regiment of state troops, but owing to the invalid condition of his wife was not able to engage in active service. At the battle of Port Gibson he was taken prisoner, and from that time until the close of the war he was confined on Johnson's Island, Ohio. Here in this prison family, in the long weary days of confinement, amid the bravest and best the Confederacy had, with high and low alike, his name was never mentioned save with affection; and those who had the privilege to know him best, learned to love him most, and it is probable that few left this prison more generally known and more cordially loved than this big, broad and generous heart. What was his was always his fellow-prisoner's, and the open-handed generosity, big-hearted sympathy and kindness that had made him a universal favorite at home, won the undying love of these brave and gallant Confederate hearts, in the long, weary prison " days that try men's souls." Such was the universal testimony of every prison-mate who learned to know him at Johnson's Island. After the war he devoted himself to cotton planting in the endeavor to rebuild the wreck war had made of his fortune. Deprived of fortune, his buoyant nature bore him up amid trial and difficulties, amid all the exasperating environments of the reconstruction era. He lived to see his family grown and educated—the great ambition of his life. What was his was theirs, and all was made to contribute to their happiness, for he never thought or cared for self. Self-sacrifice and self-abnegation were his great and chief and most ennobling characteristics; and never a man lived more absolutely for his family. With an exceptionally vivacious temperament and brilliant power to entertain, his conversation was the charm of every company and accompanied by an exhaustless flow of genial *bon hommie* spirits, and his society was at once the attraction and delight of every circle. He died while attending a Mississippi valley and river convention in St. Louis, Mo., December 5, 1875, and there then ceased to beat a heart filled with a generosity, a charity and a human-

62

ity as broad and as cöextensive as his fellowmen. He was buried at his old home, and amid the blessings and affectionate remembrance of all his family, sleeps forever. Sarah Stuart was born February 27, 1825, and was married to John C. Humphreys February 21, 1844. Mrs. Sarah Humphreys died February 4, 1863. She was the daughter of James Stuart, of Jefferson county, and was born at the old Stuart homestead, near Fayette. She was the mother of six children. She was a woman of superior intelligence, well educated and a great reader. Her life was devoted to her family, and with tireless and ceaseless effort she clung to the lifework of rearing her children. In every relation of life she was loyal and faithful—wife, mother and friend. She rests beside her husband at Glen Sade. D. George Humphreys, the eldest child, was born in Jefferson county, Miss., at the old Stuart homestead, his mother's childhood home, December 13, 1844. His childhood was passed at his father's old home, Glen Sade, near Port Gibson, and his early education was received there. He was afterward a student at Prof. W. H. N. Magruder's collegiate academy at Baton Rouge, and was at school at the fall of New Orleans. He at once returned home and joined the army at seventeen. His first service was as a scout for Hoskins' battery, stationed at Grand Gulf to fire upon passing transports of the enemy.

After one of the attacks on some passing boats, the Federal fleet steamed up and landed a battalion of troops and burned Grand Gulf, and this force, under Lieutenant De Kay of General Williams' staff, marched out into the adjacent country. A short distance out the scouts met them. Humphreys was in advance, and first to see the enemy. With his father's old deer gun, at five paces he delivered his fire, and Lieutenant De Kay fell, mortally wounded by a full charge of buckshot. His last words, as he saw the scout, were "Forward! Come up men!" He was a brave Federal officer. This force then returned to their boats. As Lieutenant De Kay's cortege was passing along the streets of New Orleans, a lady of the city, Mrs. Phillips, happened to laugh, whereupon she was arrested by order of General Butler and imprisoned on Ships Island. Lieutenant De Kay's chief, General Williams, was shot from his horse at the battle of Baton Rouge, by a Confederate soldier, who cut his silk scarf in two, and sent half of it to the scout who killed De Kay. In general orders for gallantry on the field, Humphreys was appointed by Col. Henry Hughes sergeant-major of his regiment, known as Hughes' legion. This command was ordered to Port Hudson, and under Powers and Logan operated there outside of the fort until its surrender. Afterward it was assigned to Forrest, and remained with him until the close of the war as the Fourth Mississippi cavalry, following that doughty trooper to the end. At the close of the war Humphreys attended college at Greensboro, Ala., and afterward graduated in law at Oxford, Miss., under L. Q. C. Lamar. He returned home and adopted and is now engaged in the pursuits of his ancestors—cotton planting. His life has been devoted to the effort to save the remnant of his father's estate left by the war, which effort, that this estate remains still intact amid the wreck and ruin of so many around it, may be said to have been rewarded with more than ordinary success. Kate Cobun Humphreys (now Mrs. L. J. Butler) was the only daughter. She was born August 26, 1846, at her father's old home, Glen Sade, near Port Gibson. She was educated in Port Gibson, her closing days at school being spent amid exciting scenes of hostilities, that at and near her home were of the nature of border warfare on neutral territory—a section occupied by Confederates then by Federals—and held by neither. After the battle of Port Gibson, when a Yankee attempted to take her carriage horses, she pluckily held to them and saved them. She married L. John Butler, a son of Rev. Zebulon Butler, of Port Gibson, and has four children: John Humphreys, Ruth, Sadie and Mary Kate Butler. Her life has been one of loyal devotion to family, as will be cheerfully attested by brothers, husband and children. No Confederate soldier ever came within her presence, who did not recognize her allegeance to the cause and her devotion to all who wore the gray. The bonnie blue flag was the ensign under which her earnest and most ardent affections were enlisted—a true "daughter of the Confederacy." Moreau Stuart Humphreys was born at Glen Sade, December 17, 1849. Too young to join the army, his school days were cast amid the wild checkered scenes of neutral-ground warfare, where friend and foe held alternate sway. After the war he attended college at Greensboro, Ala., and later at Oxford, Miss. Returning home, he became a cotton planter, and is now living on his plantation in Louisiana. He inherited from his father a strong taste for field sports, and became, like him, a superb shot and an ardent and successful sportsman. His pointer, Tyler, is entitled to be joined with his master in this history, as he had on many a field and at many field trials given the names of both to song and story. John Cobun Humphreys, Jr., was born June 5, 1850; died May 3, 1866. Named for his father, possessed of his heart and head, the promise of a bright manhood was unfulfilled from his early death. James Leon Humphreys was born April 19, 1852, at Glen Sade, and died December 8, 1888, at San Antonio, Tex. Stop for a moment, passerby, and reflect upon the memory of a perfect man. If such there be, such was this blameless life. Monuments of stone or brass reaching the skies could tell no more. He was a model child, a ripe scholar, a learned lawyer, a Christian gentleman. He graduated at the Kentucky military institute, where he was lieutenant of his company, and in law at Ann Arbor, Mich. He began his practice at St. Louis, Mo. When there but a short time he was elected first lieutenant in a company commanded by a son of John C. Breckinridge, and in this capacity assisted at the head of his company to quell the riots of 1876. On account of his failing health he moved to San Antonio and lived there until the tomb enfolded the form of this most noble and perfect Christian gentleman. "None knew him but to love him. None named him—but to praise." Blount Stuart Humphreys was born November 5, 1855, at Glen Sade, and died at Louisville, Ky., April 5, 1891, while attending medical lectures. He was the youngest child; his a brilliant brain, a generous heart, a tempestuous bosom, a sad, tempest-tossed life.

> " O death, where is thy sting?
> O grave, where is thy victory?."

George F. Hunt (deceased). Nature seems to have intended Mr. Hunt for a long and more than ordinarily useful life, but, alas for human hopes and expectations, while just in the meridian of life his career was closed forever. If industry, hard work and ceaseless activity could accomplish anything, then Mr. Hunt was bound to make a success of his life, for in him were found all the characteristics mentioned, and he deserved more than ordinary credit for the handsome home he secured for himself and family. He was born in Jefferson county, Miss., October 2, 1827, his father, David Hunt, being one of the pioneers and most prominent men of the county (see sketch of Dunbar Hunt). George F. Hunt was given superior advantages in his boyhood, and after graduating from Oakland college, he, on October 10, 1848, was married to Miss Anna Watson, the ceremony being performed by the president of Oakland college. Mrs. Hunt is a daughter of James Watson and a sister of Maj. A. C. Watson, a sketch of whom appears in this volume. She was born in the county in which she is now residing, but received her education in Adams and Claiborne counties, being a graduate of Mar City institute of Natchez, Miss. After their marriage Mr. Hunt located on his plantation seven miles from Fayette, his beautiful, commodious and comfortable home being known as Huntley, and here he and his wife dispensed hospitality with a liberal hand to their numerous friends. Mr. Hunt was one of the wealthiest and most successful planters and business men of the county, and besides his home estate owned another large plantation and was the owner of a number of slaves. As a manager he was exceptionally shrewd and far seeing, and all his energies were devoted to improving his place and making those about him comfortable and happy. Although he was the owner of slaves he was a strong Union man during the Civil war; was bitterly opposed to secession, firmly believing that the Confederacy could not long withstand the force of the Federal army. He, however, did not live to see the fulfill- ment of his predictions, for he died September 3, 1863, having been an active and prominent member of the Presbyterian church. His business relations were extensive and honorable, and his loss was keenly felt by all who knew him. His record as a public and private citizen are alike untarnished, and in all the affairs of life he bore himself in an upright manner, and was recognized as a man of true worth. He was liberal in his support of the church and edu- cational institutions of all kinds, and it is probable that no man was a more earnest advocate of right principles than he. Although the property was left in rather a bad condition by the war, Mrs. Hunt immediately took the helm, and in time, by exceptionally fine business ability, steered her affairs into a safe port, being now in excellent circumstances. Her beautiful home is situated midway between Fayette and Rodney, and here she endeavors to make her life a useful one and to follow the teachings of the golden rule. Mrs. Hunt reared four of her children to maturity: David Hunt, who died September 10, 1878, was the deceased husband of Anna Baldwin, and left three children; Mattie Hunt, who died January 16, 1888, married first Edward B. Moore, of Claiborne county, Miss., and afterward Emmett Newton, and left three children; Abijah Hunt is a planter of Sharkey county, Miss.; James Hunt, who died November 20, 1880, was twenty-two years of age, and was a graduate of the University of Michigan, of Ann Arbor, was a bright and promising young man. Four chil- dren died in early childhood.

Dunbar Hunt. For many years, or since being connected with the affairs of Jefferson county, Miss., Mr. Hunt has enjoyed the reputation of being not only an able financier and a talented and highly educated gentleman, but one noted for honorable, upright dealing and seems to have been admirably fitted by nature for the calling of a planter. He has kept the name he bears, which has descended to him from a long line of illustrious and honored ancestry, pure in the sight of God and man. The first of the family of whom he has any knowledge was Ralph Hunt, who came with a party of seven from England. He settled at Newtown, Long Island, N. Y., about the year 1650, and became a man of some historic renown. He succeeded in accumulating considerable means, and of this donated a consid- erable portion for a church site on Long Island, and in many other ways did much to make his name honored by his descendants, who have a clear genealogical record of the family back to his day. David Hunt, the father of Dunbar Hunt, was born, reared and educated near the town of Ringoes, Hunterdon county, N. J., not far from Trenton, and when a young man determined to see what Dame Fortune had in store for him in a different locality, and with this end in view came to Mississippi in 1801, locating at Natchez. With the generosity that ever characterized his career through life, he gave up his share of his father's estate to his sister, on leaving home, and therefore on his arrival in Mississippi, which was then an almost unbroken wilderness, he was absolutely without means. He soon succeeded in obtain- ing employment with an uncle, Abijah Hunt, who was a member of the firm of Hunt & Smith, one of the largest business houses in Natchez, and the salary he received for his first year's service was $300. His services were found to be so valuable at the end of this time that he was reëngaged with an increased salary of $500 per year, during which time he displayed such shrewd business views, such ability, tact and judgment that he was made manager of the entire establishment, which at that time had several branch houses in adjacent counties, and was paid a salary of $3,000 per year. He was offered a partnership in the business at that time, but declined it. After filling this position with fidelity to the interests of his uncle he, with the consciousness of having performed every duty to the best of his ability, at the expiration of several years became impressed with the belief that there were better things in store for him, and after the death of his uncle Abijah Hunt, who was killed in a duel by one Poindexter in 1812, he turned his attention to other avenues of business. He came to Jefferson county, Miss., and began opening up a large plantation on Cole's creek at Woodlawn. By the use of all his mental as well as physical faculties, he became immensely wealthy, his land amounting to several thousand acres and his slaves, and those of his family, numbering seventeen hundred, whom he used to an excellent advantage in his extensive cotton fields. In direct opposition to the saying that "the more we have the more we want," Mr. Hunt was the soul of generosity and scattered his wealth with a liberal hand wherever it was needed. By his influence and support Oakland college was established, and to this institution he donated at different times over $175,000, his last bequest amounting to $50,000. He was a warm advocate of the colonization of the negro, and one of his last gifts was $50,000 for this purpose. He also gave most generously to the church; donated the site and contributed generously to the erection of the Presbyterian church at Rodney. The poor, sick and afflicted always received generous treatment at his hands, for his sympathy for the sufferings of humanity was profound, and to the recounting of their woes he lent a ready ear, his purse being at their command. He was, in truth, the poor man's friend, and that he was one of nature's noblemen can not be denied. He was married twice, his first wife being Mary Calvit, daughter of Thomas Calvit, one of the largest planters in the county. His second union was to Miss Ann Ferguson, daughter of George and Jane (Dunbar) Ferguson, of Adams county. Both Mrs. Hunt and her mother were born in Mississippi, and her union with Mr. Hunt resulted in the birth of thirteen children, four sons and three daughters of which grew to manhood and womanhood: Abijah (who died leaving a wife and children), Mary Ann (deceased wife of James Archer, whose sketch appears in this history), George F. (deceased, a sketch of whom also appears herein), Catherine (deceased, a former wife of William S. Balfour), Charlotte (wife of George M. Marshall, of Adams county), Andrew (who died at the age of twenty-one years), Dunbar (whose name heads this biography) and Elizabeth (the deceased wife of William F. Ogden, of New Orleans). David Hunt died on the 18th of May, 1861, soon after the firing on Fort Sumter. Mr. Hunt was a strong Union man, was very much opposed to secession and, when he heard of the firing on Fort Sumter, gave it as his dying conviction that it was not possible for the South to succeed, and on his deathbed said to a friend and neighbor: "I know too well the strength of both sections. Mark the words of a dying man, they will wipe us out." By his innumerable acts of generosity and kindness he had endeared himself to the hearts of many, and it was with deep and universal lamentation that the news of his death was received, gloom being cast over the entire community. He was always prompt, industrious, efficient and conscientious, and, possessing superior business qualifications, clear head and excellent practical common sense, he was much respected by his associates and soon became one of the honored and influential residents of the county. His social and domestic attachments were very strong, his friendship sincere and true and the grasp of his hand warm and cordial. Of him it might be said:

> " His life is gentle, and the elements
> So mixed in him that Nature might stand up
> And say to all the world: This is a man."

His widow survived him several years, dying in November, 1874. Dunbar Hunt was born in Jefferson county, Miss., November 14, 1840, next to the youngest of his parents' family, and, as he possessed a naturally bright intellect, his father determined to give him good advantages and he was put to school in Oakland college, from which institution he graduated in May, 1860, delivering the valedictory address of his class. After the death of his father, in connection with James Archer, his brother-in-law, took charge of the estate, and when it was divided in 1867 Dunbar Hunt remained with his mother at the homestead (Woodlawn) and here made his home up to 1875, when he took up his abode in the city of Baltimore, Md., where he has since made his home. He owns a fine cotton plantation in the western part of Jefferson county, containing twenty-two hundred acres of bottom and hill land; a plantation of twenty-five hundred acres in Issaquena county, with about twelve hundred acres under cultivation, and also real estate in Fargo, Dak., and in Florida. He inherits his father's admirable facilities for business and, being shrewd and far-seeing, perceived that the raising and fattening of stock for the market on his broad acres would be a profitable investment, and he ships from two hundred to three hundred head annually, he being the first cotton planter to successfully prosecute this business. He was married in Baltimore on the 4th of June, 1867, to Miss Leila Lawrence Brent, a daughter of Robert J. and Matilda S. Brent, the latter's mother being a daughter of Mr. and Mrs. Hager, the first settlers of Hagerstown, Md. Mrs. Hunt was born, reared and educated in Baltimore, and there and in Mississippi their only daughter, Miss Anita Dunbar Hunt, has been principally reared, although the greater part of the last three years has been spent in Europe. Miss Anita is a talented young lady, graceful and accomplished and devotes much of her time to the study of the languages and music. The winter of 1890 Mrs. Hunt and her daughter spent in Paris, the latter perfecting herself in music and French, and this winter is devoting her time and attention to music and German in Berlin. Mrs. Hunt and her daughter are members of the Episcopal church, but Mr. Hunt is a Presbyterian. In social life he is much admired and liked for his excellent conversational powers and agreeable manners, and all are inspired with ease and confidence in his presence. Kind, generous and hospitable, he wins friends and rarely loses them. In the domestic circle he is a model husband and father; is devoted to his family and makes the happiness and comfort of his wife and child his chief aim and object in life. His own happiness and comfort have not made him selfish, and he is keenly alive to the sufferings or misfortunes of others, and no one has ever appealed to him in vain for consolation or succor.

George R. Hunt, planter, Como, Miss., is one of the pioneers of Mississippi, having made his advent into this state in 1837, and into Panola county in 1842. He was originally from Elbert county, Ga., and his father, James Hunt, was a native of the same state. The mother, Mary (Vassor) Hunt, was born in Virginia. After their marriage the parents moved to South Carolina, where the mother received her final summons, and the father afterward removed to north Alabama. He subsequently located in Monroe county, Miss., and there his death occurred in 1864, at the age of eighty years. He was a very active politician and an old line whig, but never aspired to office of any kind. He was a man of brilliant mind, whose intellectual powers were surpassed by those of only a few men of his day, and had he chosen the law and politics for his profession, his career would indeed have been a brilliant one. He would have made for himself a name and fame that the state of his adoption would have been proud to have had recorded in the annals of her history. His kindness of heart, his social and genial disposition, and his many acts of charity to the poor and friendless, the widow and the orphan, won for him a name in the community in which he lived that will shine when the records graven on monuments of marble to perpetuate the memory of the deeds of the daring soldier and the illustrious statesman shall have faded and the monuments themselves shall have crumbled into dust. He was a Mason in high standing and a man of unswerving fidelity, integrity, firmness and fixedness of purpose. He had great will power, and he was an honest man—"the noblest work of God." The five children of this worthy man were named in the order of their births as follows: Sarah A., wife of the late John E. Maddox; Mary E., single, resides at home; George R.; Emily, deceased, was the wife of William P. Fuller; and Rebecca, deceased, was the wife of William C. Banks. After the death of his wife Mr. Hunt married again, and became the father of two children: James E., died in 1865 from exposure during the war in the Confederate army, and Augusta J., wife of the late John B. Cox, of Monroe county. Early in life George R. was allowed by his father to work for himself, and as a consequence, when twenty-one years of age, he had made quite a start, which he invested in land and negroes. He settled in Panola county in 1842, on three hundred and twenty acres of land, given him by his father, and this now comprises a part of the fine plantation of eight hundred acres owned by Mr. Hunt. About one-half of this is under a good state of cultivation and yields large returns in cotton and corn. Mr. Hunt is also the owner of nineteen hundred acres of fine bottom land in Sunflower county. He has been very successful and has been one of the foremost planters of the county. About 1889 he had a severe spell of sickness, from which he has never fully recovered, and which prevents him from looking after his business with his wonted energy. However, he has but to make his wishes known, and they are faithfully carried out. Mr. Hunt has never married, but is a gallant champion and great admirer of the fair sex. He is held in high esteem by all who know him, is a liberal giver to all worthy enterprises and is active in all matters of moment. He has never had trouble nor disagreement with any one except once. He was a whig, when the whig party existed, but now he is a stanch democrat in his political principles. Socially, he is a member of the Masonic fraternity, and is probably the oldest Mason in the county. He was one of the founders and charter members of Friendship lodge No. 127, of Como, and is also a member of Walker chapter, No. 28. He has held all the offices in both these lodges, and has been a delegate several times to the grand lodge of Mississippi. He is a strict observer of the Sabbath day, and is a full believer in the Christian religion, and has always contributed liberally to the support of schools and churches.

Dr. James M. Hunt, referred to in the life of his father-in-law, Col. E. G. Cooke, was more than an ordinary man. When he graduated at Tulane medical college, New Orleans, Dr. Warren Stone was so pleased with the young physician that he employed him as assistant in his infirmary. Dr. Stone's recommendation to Judah P. Benjamin, Confederate secretary of war, secured for Dr. Hunt a position in the medical department of the army in advance of others of the same age. He was in charge of the White Sulphur Springs, Va., occupied by Confederate sick and wounded in great numbers. After the war he practiced at Vicksburg, where he had been raised. He was the leading surgeon in that city, so conceded by his professional colleagues. William Hunt (deceased) was born in Massachusetts, near Boston, in 1801, and was a son of William and Mary Hunt, both of whom died when William, Jr., was but four years of age. The latter was taken to Ohio in the family of an aunt, Mrs. Brooks, resided there until twelve years of age, and then embarked as a sailor. He went to New Orleans and thence to Natchez, reaching that city in 1817. There he was employed in the banking business and was connected with some of the early institutions of that city. About 1822 or 1823 he came to Washington county, Miss., located about seven miles below Greenville, and was one of the earliest settlers. He opened up a magnificent estate of over three thousand acres and built a fine residence. which was afterward known as La Grange. This and the Ridge place, which he also purchased, he improved and made the choicest in this section. He was the early promoter of the levee system, and was one of the most prominent men of his time. In 1836 he married Miss Prudence Blackburn, of Kentucky, and daughter of George and Julia (Flurior) Blackburn. Mr. Blackburn was a Baptist preacher. and died soon after his daughter's marriage. To Mr. and Mrs. Hunt were born twelve children, four now living: William G. (died in infancy); George B. (died in 1873) was married; William E.; Julia (died in infancy); Mary E. (died in infancy); David F.; Lizzie (was the wife of F. Chinn, a lawyer at Frankfort, Ky., and died leaving four daughters); Catherine, widow of Mr. Stone, died in 1885, leaving four daughters and a son); John, (died in infancy); Churchman (died at the age of nine years); Prudence (wife of Russell Rodman, of Frankfort, Ky.); and Alice (wife of Claude Johnson, chancery clerk, of Washington county. They have two children.) Mr. Hunt died in 1866, and in full communion with the Methodist Episcopal church. Mrs. Hunt is still living, and is a worthy member of the same church.

Capt. W. E. Hunt, president of the board of Mississippi levee commissioners, Greenville, Miss. The remote ancestors of the Hunt family were of English origin, and three brothers of this family emigrated from England to the United States at a very early period. From them, it is supposed, sprang all the Hunts now residing in the United States. Capt. W. E. Hunt was born in Washington county, Miss., in 1840, and is the third in order of birth of twelve children born to William and Prudence B. (Blackburn) Hunt, the parents natives of Massachusetts and Kentucky, respectively. The father was left an orphan when but a boy, and with an elder brother, Oliver, moved to the Blue Grass state where the latter located. William came to Mississippi, was married in Washington county, and engaged in farming on a very extensive scale. He opened up a great deal of land, was one of the pioneers of Washington county, and his home, at La Grange, was one of the finest in the county. He was a worthy member of the Methodist Episcopal church, and a liberal contributor of the same. He was also a member of the board of supervisors, was early connected with the levee board, and was likely the originator of the cotton tax. He died in 1866. He was a member of the Masonic fraternity. Capt. W. E. Hunt was reared in his native county, educated in the University of North Carolina, Chapel Hill, and was in the senior class at the breaking out of the war. He threw aside his books to enlist in company D, Twenty-eighth Mississippi regiment and was promoted step by step to the position of captain. His company participated in some of the most prominent engagements of the war: Atlanta, all the engagements of Hood's retreat, and was in General Forrest's division in Georgia at the time of the surrender. After the war Mr. Hunt returned to the parental roof and with his father went to the Blue Grass state, where he remained for a short time. From there he went to Texas, secured the services of his old hands, and then returned to Mississippi, Washington county, where he reengaged in planting. He is now the owner of about five thousand acres of land in several plantations, is constantly opening up new tracts. and has twenty-five hundred acres under cultivation. He owns a plantation known as the Mound place, and on this there are twenty-two Indian mounds which are the most extensive system of mounds in this section. They are built mainly in a circle surrounding a large central mound. In overseeing his large plantations Mr. Hunt does not lose sight of the stock industry and raises fine Jersey cattle, Norman horses and many mules. He was elected sheriff of Washington county in 1865, and so ably and well did he fill this position that he continued its incumbent for fourteen years in succession. In July, 1890, he was elected president of the levee board. By his marriage, which occurred in Mississippi, in 1868, to Miss Mariah Crittenden, of Frankfort, Ky., and daughter of John Allen Crittenden, there were born eight children: William (died at the age of three years), Mamie (died, also at the age of three years), Virginia, George, Allen, Prue, Lizzie and Sallie. The family are members of the Presbyterian church. Mr. Hunt is one of the very popular men of Washington county, as the position of trust and honor which he has held plainly proves, and he has great hopes for the future development of the Delta. His brother, George P. Hunt (deceased), organized a company for the Confederate army and this was known as the Erin guards. This company was quite noted in the battles of Shiloh, Corinth, Belmont and in many of the most important engagements of the war. He was promoted and became major. He was wounded in the battle of Perryville, but served until the end of the war. He became a prominent planter in Bolivar county and died about 1870, leaving a wife and one child.

Isaac H. Hunter, of Yazoo City, Yazoo county, Miss., was born in Gates county, N. C., August 31, 1829, and is a son of John O. and Elizabeth A. (Pugh) Hunter, natives of North Carolina and Virginia respectively. The father was a merchant in North Carolina, and in 1836 removed to Mississippi, where he followed the same business. He lost his property in the great commercial crash of 1837, after which he was employed as a salesman until the time of his death, which was in his seventy-sixth year. His wife survived him, and was seventy-eight at the time of her death. He was a man of quiet, unpretentious bearing, a lover of law and order, and a man thoroughly respected by all. He was a zealous member of the Methodist Episcopal church, and organized the first Methodist Episcopal church society and the first Sabbath-school in Yazoo City. Although he was not an ordained minister, in the absence of the pastor he often conducted the service. His father, Jacob Hunter, was a Methodist preacher in North Carolina, and was possessed of no small ability. Isaac H. Hunter was reared to man's estate in Yazoo county, receiving his education in Jackson, Miss. When he left school he entered the employ of J. M. Devlin, as salesman. He was with J. Herd & Co. and Link & Harrison for some time, and then went to New Orleans, where he remained one year, returning at the end of that time to Yazoo City. In 1861 he enlisted in Barnett's company, and was in the Confederate service until the disbanding of the Mississippi troops in 1864, at which time he was captain. Upon returning to his home in 1864 he was married to Miss Carrie Roberts, a native of Mississippi, and daughter of George Q. Roberts, of North Carolina. He then removed to Lodi plantation, where he gave his attention to agriculture. He was justice of the peace for a period of eleven years and at a time when great responsibilities rested upon the office. In 1886 he came back to Yazoo City, and became the agent for the Yazoo & Tallahatchie Transportation company, which position he still holds. He cultivates three hundred acres of land and owns six hundred acres. He has a nice residence in Yazoo City, where he has all the comforts of home, surrounded by his family of five children: Lizzie is now Mrs. Blewet; Carrie married Captain White; Henry C., George R., and Isaac H., Jr. Mr. Hunter is a Mason, belonging both to the blue lodge and chapter. He is a man of no pretentions, is industrious and upright; and is an honor to the family from which he sprang.

John Hunter, D. D., pastor of the Presbyterian church of Jackson, Miss., and one of the ablest divines of the city, was born in the Emerald isle, on the 10th of September, 1824, being the eighth child and the youngest of four sons born to Alexander and Margaret (Kelso) Hunter, also natives of Ireland, who died in 1863 and 1870, respectively. Rev. John Hunter received his early education in the land of his birth, and, after coming to

America, entered Center college, Kentucky, and later studied theology in Danville. In 1856 he was ordained a minister of the Presbyterian church, and in that year became pastor of the First Presbyterian church, of Danville, Ky., in which vineyard he labored two years. In February, 1858, he was called to his present charge in the city of Jackson, Miss., where his many admirable traits of heart and head and his earnest Christian character have won him many warm friends. He has been a faithful worker for the cause of the Master in Jackson for many years, and is much beloved by his congregation, whose respect and affection for their pastor is unbounded. Since 1881 he has been stated clerk of the synod of Mississippi, and from 1865 he was, for some years, trustee of the blind asylum, in which capacity, since 1877, he has also served up to the present time for the deaf and dumb institute, and earlier in the public schools of the city. His marriage was celebrated in the city of Philadelphia, Penn., on the 24th of August, 1858, Mrs. Rosa M. Petrie, a resident of Jackson, Miss., becoming his wife and the mother of his three sons and two daughters: Rosabel, who became the wife of Gen. G. Y. Freeman, who died in 1890, leaving one son; John F. is a physician of Jackson; George A.; Idelette, and Ernest L., the latter of whom died in 1879, at the age of twelve years.

Dr. John F. Hunter is a native of Jackson, Miss., born on the 19th of February, 1860, the eldest of five children born to Rev. John and Rosa M. (Farrar) Hunter, natives of Ireland and Virginia respectively, the mother being a daughter of Dr. S. D. Farrar, the leading physician of Jackson in his day, where he practiced for many years, and died in 1871. He was a Virginian by birth, and came to Mississippi at an early day, first locating in Brandon, becoming very prominent, socially and professionally, Rev. John Hunter has been for more than thirty-two years pastor of the Presbyterian church in Jackson, and elsewhere in this work a sketch of him is given. Dr. John F. Hunter was reared in Jackson, in the higher schools of which place he received his education. He attended medical lectures in the Bellevue Hospital Medical college of New York city and the University of Louisiana, graduating from the latter, after which, in 1888, he took a course in the New York polyclinic. In 1882 he located as a physician in Jackson, and since that time has continued to do a very large and successful practice. He is the senior member of the well-known drug firm of J. F. Hunter & Co., and is also a member of the Mississippi state board of health, and for the past six years has been treasurer of the Mississippi state medical association. He is medical examiner in chief for the Mutual Life Insurance company of New York, at Jackson, and is also examiner for the K. of P. and one of two examiners for the K. of H. fraternity. On the 13th of February, 1883, he was married to Miss Perlie Prestidge, of Memphis, Tenn., a daughter of James S. and Mollie B. Prestidge, natives of Mississippi. The Doctor is a member of the K. of H., and is a Presbyterian in religious faith, and is one of the best and brightest of the young men of Jackson, and has a very bright and promising future. He commands respect and affection from all who know him, and is in every respect a high-toned Christian gentleman.

Nowhere in Bolivar county, Miss., is there to be found a gentleman who possesses more energy, determined will or force of character than Joel L. Hurley, and no agriculturist has been more deserving of success than he. He was born in Pike county, Ala., December 15, 1839, the fourth of six children born to Joel and Emily (Williams) Hurley, natives of North Carolina and South Carolina, respectively. The father was a miller and planter by occupation, and in the early history of Alabama he moved to that state, where the remainder of his days were spent. He served in the War of 1812, and was a prominent character in the war with Mexico. He died in 1852, at the age of seventy-nine years. The maternal grandfather, David Williams, was a very wealthy planter and slaveowner of his native state of South Carolina. In 1859 J. L. Hurley removed to Louisiana, where he remained until 1862. He participated in the Civil war, enlisting in a company known as the Tiger Bayou riflemen, but after remaining with it two months was sent home. After a very short period he joined the Carroll dragoons, under Dr. Arthur J. Lott. He remained in the service until the surrender, taking part in the battle of Corinth, also a great many others of minor importance. As he belonged to a party of skirmishers, he was fighting more or less all the time, serving the most of the time under Generals Price and Van Dorn, being at one time attached to Marmaduke's command. Joel L. Hurley attended for some time the private schools of his native state, but upon starting out in life for himself, in 1854, it was with no capital, and, in fact, under very inauspicious circumstances. In 1879 he came to Mississippi and settled in Bolivar county, where he has since made his home, and where he has, by earnest and unremitting endeavor, become the owner of eight hundred and eighty-nine acres of land, seven hundred and fifty acres of which are under cultivation. He also owns two plantations in Louisiana, consisting of four hundred and forty-five acres, jointly, and eighty acres in Texas. He has an excellent mercantile establishment at his riverside plantation in Mississippi, carries a stock of goods valued at $6,000, and has a large and paying patronage. He was first married to Miss Louisa V. Sherrer, a daughter of John M. and Emily (Seymour) Sherrer, by whom he became the father of five children: Lalile G., Louisa V., Emily J., Bertha, and Joel, all of whom are deceased except Louisa V. and Emily J. His second union was to Mrs. M. Eva Nash, a daughter of Almon and Abigail (Whittredge) Baldwin, natives of Connecticut and Massachusetts, respectively, having two sons, Charles and Carroll, still living. Almon Baldwin was an artist of no little fame, and for a great many years was a resident of Cincinnati, Ohio, in which city he was superintendent of the Art Union gallery. To Mr. Hurley's last union one child has been born: Baldwin. He and his wife are members in good standing of the Baptist church, are worthy and upright citizens, and in their comfortable and pleasant home dispense unbounded hospitality to their numerous friends. Mr. Hurley is a member of the A. F. & A. M., the K. of H., and in his political views is a stanch democrat. He is a stockholder in the Bank of Rosedale, and is estimated to be worth $75,000. He has served four years on the board of supervisors, and was one of the trustees of the railroad bonds of $150,000 for the building of the railroad called the Bolivar Loup, extending through Bolivar county. Mr. Hurley's career is an example of what industry, perseverance and good management can do, for his present possessions have been gained by his own hard efforts. He has lived an upright life, and has won the esteem and confidence of the community in which he resides.

David Wiley Hurst was born in what is now Amite county, Miss., July 10, 1819. His father, Capt. Richard Hurst, removed from Norfolk, Va., while Mississippi was a territory, and settled in what was then known as Adams county and under military rule, Gen. Wilkinson having command of that portion of the territory ceded by the Spanish government. Capt. Hurst was a pioneer and began anew his life as a farmer, this being quite a change from his occupation, he having, previous to this time, been captain of a merchantman, and so wedded was he to his life as a seafaring man, that he refrained from visiting Natchez which was the trading point for that portion of Mississippi, fearing that the sight of a large portion of water would irresistibly turn him to his former occupation. David W. Hurst received at an early age the rudiments of an education at what is now termed an old fieldschool and while but a lad was noticed as having an extraordinary and retentive memory, and amused his fellow-scholars by repeating sermons and speeches which he had heard delivered in the neighborhood. While quite a youth he attended school at Liberty under the tutelage of a schoolmaster named Davenport, who at a late date boasted that he had educated all the native lawyers of Amite county. He attended one session at Hanover college, Ind., but chose Oakland college, Adams county, as his alma mater. After leaving college he entered the law office of Judge James M. Smiley, a distinguished jurist of this state, and a short time before his majority, after a brilliant examination, was admitted to the practice of the law in 1843. In 1847 he was chosen as a representative in the legislature of the state and was a useful member of the judiciary committee. He left his native county and settled at Bay Saint Louis, Hancock county, and there practiced his profession with remarkable success for the space of three years. Having formed a copartnership with John T. Lamkin, who was at that time district attorney, their practice being extensive throughout the district, he removed to his old home in Amite county, and there practiced his profession until the breaking out of the war. On the 13th day of July, 1847, he was united in marriage to Miss Sarah Tilloston and reared a family of three sons and one daughter, all of whom survive him but the youngest son, who died at an early age. His political notions were firm and steadfast. Being an old line whig, he at all times was ready with poised lance and upturned visor, declining no challenge, but always in the thickest of the contest. He was the whig elector for his district on the Clay ticket in 1848, with James A. Ventress his opponent on the democratic ticket, they canvassed the district thoroughly, and with remarkable vigor and ability. Although this district was the Gibraltar of the democracy, the usual democratic majority was very materially reduced. As the signs of the times predicted and almost foretold of a gigantic struggle between the North and South, he was looked to by all parties for advice, and was elected to represent Amite county in the convention called by the governor to pass such measures as would insure safety to our people. He was one among the ablest members of the convention and was foremost in attempting to ward off the impending danger. Although in the minority the ordinance of secession from the Union was passed, yet he to the last refused to sign the ordinance. Mr. Hurst had earnestly opposed secession up to the last moment, but finding that the people of Mississippi were determined to separate from the Union he surrendered his personal opinions and pledged himself fully and unreservedly to the cause of the Confederacy. Opposed to secession, with habits of thought and education utterly opposed to revolution, the strange vicissitudes of this stormy period soon found him ready to assist in the great contest.

He raised, in 1862, a company of volunteers, was elected its captain, and joined the Thirty-third regiment of Mississippi volunteers, of which regiment he was elected colonel. The regiment participated in all the hotly contested battles in the western army. At the battle of Corinth Colonel Hurst's horse was killed from under him, and fell upon him, and disabled him from active service as commander of the regiment. Shortly after the surrender of Vicksburg a vacancy occurred on the supreme bench of the state by the death of Hon. C. Pinckney Smith, chief justice. An election was ordered to fill the vacancy, and Judge Hurst was elected to fill the same, and he remained in that office until the surrender, at which time Mississippi was reconstructed by the Federal authorities, and other judges appointed in their place. Judge Hurst removed to Vicksburg, and formed a law copartnership with Col. Upton M. Young, remained a short time, and removed to Summit and reëstablished his old practice until his death, which took place July 10, 1882. We can not refrain from making extracts from a notice written by Judge Wiley P. Harris, and which we indorse in every particular, as follows: " So far as Judge Hurst's education proceeded was thorough, what he learned he mastered whether at school or in the law office, and his memory, with singular accuracy and tenacity, retained his acquisitions. His legal education began before he had attained ·his majority, and as usual then in the offices of practicing lawyers, that course led to a speedy admission to the bar. Judge Hurst attained to the highest rank and honors of his profession, and these were due to real merit. No man was more entirely free from false pretensions, from all shams and indirect methods. Straightforward manliness and certain nobleness and elevation of character distinguished David W. Hurst, and the recollections of these qualities, however much we may exalt the fine qualities of his mind, will be more cherished by his cotemporaries." At a meeting of the bar in August, 1882, we make a few extracts from a speech delivered by H. Q. Bridges, Esq., on that occasion: "As a citizen and a son of Mississippi he grew with her growth, and strengthened with her strength, and as a lawyer and a judge added fresh laurels to her civic crown. His name is associated with many public events that have made Mississippi historic since he entered public life, in all of which he had an eye single to her glory and advancements. Under the tutelage of the lamented Smiley he received his early training in his chosen profession, and, as his life history so admirably proves, the seeds then planted in his fertile brain germinated and grew and ripened into luxuriant foliage and luscious fruit." There was usually no half-way ground with him, whether in cleaving to a friend or separating from a foe, so that it may be truthfully affirmed of him, whether he spoke or acted upon men or measures, his position was always well defined. His great desire, as once expressed to a friend, was that he might not go down behind a cloud, and that wish was in a measure gratified. His declining days, though made painful by physical suffering, were like the quiet repose of evening after the day's work is done, when the setting sun casts its lengthened shadows upon the fading landscape. His mental vigor lingered about him radiant with clear comprehension and flashing occasional scintillations of original thought, until the period of dissolution drew apace.

Dr. J. D. Hutchinson is a well-to-do and successful planter residing at Columbus, Miss., but was born in Laurens district, S. C., September 8, 1845, a son of Dr. James P. and Rachel B. (Park) Hutchinson, both of whom were born in the Palmetto state. They removed to Mississippi in 1846 and located at Cotton Gin, Monroe county, but became residents of Old Hamilton in December of the following year. The father graduated from a medical college at Lexington, Ky., and became a noted and very successful physician. He was given good advantages in his youth, was a scholarly and well-posted man, and one who was public spirited and enterprising, thoroughly identifying himself with the interests of his adopted county and state. He died on the 20th of March, 1870, in Monroe county, Miss., his widow still surviving him, being now in her sixty-fifth year. Their union resulted in the birth of seven children, only three of whom are living: Dr. J. D., Mary (Walton), and Janie (Chastaine). Dr. J. D. Hutchinson was reared in Monroe county, Miss., and received his education in the public schools. In 1869 he graduated in medicine from the University of Louisiana, at New Orleans, but prior to this, at the age of sixteen years, he left school to enlist in company G, Forty-third Mississippi regiment, of which he was made orderly-sergeant, and served in the army of the Tennessee. He was in the engagements at Resaca, the Georgia campaign, besides nearly all the important engagements of the western army. Prior to crossing the Tennessee river Dr. Hutchinson was detached and detailed on the wagon train to obtain mules to proceed on the journey. After his return home after the close of the war he pursued his medical studies as above stated and at once began practicing in Monroe county, where he followed his profession until 1875, when he was married and gave up his profession to engage in planting, thinking this calling would benefit his health, which was very delicate. At this time his weight was one hundred and thirty pounds, but he now weighs two hundred and ten pounds, and being six feet tall he is finely proportioned. He has been a resident of Lowndes county since 1873, and although engaged in planting he has made his home in Columbus since 1885. He is the owner of about seven thousand acres of land, of which some three thousand acres are under cultivation. He raises all kinds of grain and gives considerable attention to the propagation of stock, all his operations being conducted on progressive and upright principles. He is always ready to help in the advancement of the county, and is wideawake and progressive. He was married in 1873 to Miss Elonia, only child of William C. Nelson and Sarah S. (Verner) Nelson, of this county, and by her is the father of five children (one of whom is dead, little Rachel Belle): S. Irene, Jennie May, William Nelson and James Dudley, Jr. The Doctor is a member of the I. O. O. F., in which he is noble grand. He is an elder in the Presbyterian church. Mr. Nelson is one of the most liberal and one of the most charitable men to the poor, the orphans and widows that the county ever knew. No better man lived anywhere. No one ever went away from his house wanting. He was a large slaveowner. He served in the late war and was a true and brave soldier. He died December 23, 1877, his widow now surviving him being in her sixtieth year.

Anderson Hutchinson was born in Greenbrier county, Va., and was there educated. At twenty-one he removed to Knoxville, Tenn., and was there admitted to the bar. Thence he removed to Huntsville, Ala.; thence to Mississippi, taking up his residence in Hinds county in 1835. In 1840, in connection with Volney E. Howard, he published a digest of laws of Mississippi. In 1848 he published his Mississippi code. In 1850 he removed to Texas and was made one of the judges of the supreme court of that state. Soon after he was captured while on the bench, with other court officers, by a band of armed Mexicans, and kept closely confined as a prisoner in the castle of Perote. Through government interposition he was released, and Mexico was compelled to make a satisfactory explanation of the outrage. He then returned to Mississippi, where he died in 1853.

C. J. Hyatt, a banker of Iuka, Tishomingo county, Miss., was born in Lauderdale county, Miss., in 1833, a son of Thomas and Angeline (Millburn) Hyatt. His father was born in North Carolina about 1795, a son of Elisha Hyatt. He passed his youth as a farmer's boy, and also learned the cabinetmaker's trade. About 1817 he married. His wife bore him seven children, of whom the four named lived to maturity: Martha, J. B., Sarah and Suby. Martha died in 1852. Previous to his marriage Mr. Hyatt had removed to northern Alabama, where he died in 1835, and the mother, who was born in North Carolina, also came to northern Alabama with her parents, who were early settlers in that section. His mother died in Franklin county, Ala., in 1852. C. J. Hyatt began an active career as a farmer's boy, and received a common-school education, and in 1855 became a clerk on a steamboat, in which capacity he served until 1861. Soon after the beginning of the war he enlisted at Iuka as a lieutenant in the Second Mississippi regiment, company K, which was an infantry regiment. The captain of his company has since come to be known as Governor Stone, and his regiment was commanded by Colonel Fannin. He was in the battles of Bull Run and Williamsburg, the seven days' fight around Richmond, the battle of Petersburg, the second battle of Bull Run, the battle of Antietam, in the army of General Lee. He was twice slightly wounded. He surrendered in Alabama, and afterward returned to Iuka. For the nine years following he was bookkeeper for Hammersley & Price. He then went into the mercantile business on his own account, and followed it with profit till 1889, when he turned his attention to banking. He has also been interested in planting to some extent, and is the owner of about a thousand acres of land in this county. In 1863 he married Miss Mary Price, a daughter of Thomas and Mary A. (Berry) Price, of Somerville, Morgan county, Ala. The mother of the wife of our subject was a native of Augusta, Ga. Mrs. Hyatt was born in 1840, and died in 1883 at Iuka, having been for many years a consistent member of the Methodist Episcopal church. She had seven children: Anna L., Thomas B., Virginia A., Mary C., Martha J., James and Elizabeth. Her father died in Alabama, and her mother is a resident of Iuka. In 1885 Mr. Hyatt married Miss Ida S. White, a daughter of F. O. H. and Henrietta Lavonia White, of Texas. This lady, who was born at Rushville, Ala., in 1851, has borne her husband one child, named Dean. Mr. and Mrs. Hyatt are members of the Methodist Episcopal church South. He is a master Mason and a member of the Knights of Honor. He is a democrat politically, and has much local influence. From 1882 to 1886 he served as a member of the board of supervisors of Tishomongo county. He has been several times elected a member of the common council at Iuka. He is public spirited in the highest degree, and takes a deep interest in national, state and county politics, and every effort tending to the enhancement of the public welfare has his unqualified support.

Dr. W. F. Hyer, of the firm of Thompson, Hyer & Partin, physicians and surgeons of Meridian, Miss., was born in Summerville, Tenn., March 24, 1839, son of Rev. William and Jane (Tobey) Hyer. His father was a native of Pennsylvania and his mother a native of Connecticut. The former was of German and the latter of English descent. William Hyer was a schoolteacher during his early life, and was subsequently ordained as a minister of the Methodist Episcopal church. He came to Tennessee about 1837 and in 1840 went to Memphis to open a large school for girls. This was the first boardingschool in the state. He joined the Memphis conference and was stationed at Aberdeen, Miss. In 1854 he was transferred to the Mississippi conference that he might take charge of the Vicksburg congregation. He died in 1855 of yellow fever. Dr. W. F. Hyer is the only one of his sons who grew to maturity. He was reared in Memphis, Aberdeen and Vicksburg, and obtained his education in private schools. In 1854 and 1855 he studied at Cumberland institute at Mechanicsburg, Penn., but his father dying in the latter year, he returned home and took up the study of medicine, and graduated from Shelby medical college at Nashville, Tenn., in 1859, and at the University of Nashville, Tenn., in 1882. He took also a post-graduate course at the Polyclinic, New York, in 1886. He settled in Marshall county, Miss., in January, 1860, and married Miss Eliza Bowen in April, 1861. May 18, 1861, he enlisted in the Nineteenth Mississippi regiment as assistant surgeon, and was transferred for service in Virginia, and at once attached to Gen. Joseph E. Johnston's army at Winchester. He was transferred to Kirby Smith's brigade, June 5, 1861. He resigned in August following, and was appointed surgeon, in charge of one of the Mississippi state hospitals at Warrenton, Va. In November, 1861, he returned to Mississippi, and was appointed surgeon of the Second Mississippi state regiment, under General Alcorn, at Columbus, Miss., in December of that year. Upon the discharge of these troops, he was appointed surgeon in the Confederate army and was assigned to hospital duty and served at Corinth, Jackson and Holly Springs until he was appointed consulting surgeon and stationed at Oxford (Miss.) hospital. Later he was assigned to field duty with the Second Arkansas cavalry, and by virtue of his rank, acted as brigade surgeon. After the close of the war he returned home and soon became prominent in that county. In the session of 1872 and 1873 he represented Marshall county in the state legislature, and in the session of 1882 to 1884 represented his district as a member of the senate. He was elected a member of the state board of health in 1881 to represent the second congressional district, and served as president of the board in 1888 and 1889. He resigned on account of removal from the district in 1889 and was reappointed a member to fill a vacancy representing the state at large in 1890, and elected to succeed himself for a full term of six years in 1891. He moved to Holly Springs in 1883, and has been a resident of Meridian, Miss., since 1888. He is a member of the Masonic fraternity, and is past chancellor of the Knights of Pythias lodge, is high private in the Knights of Honor and is a member of the Knights of the Golden Rule. Doctor and Mrs. Hyer have become the parents of eight children, six of whom are living: Jane is the wife of Professor Moore of Magnolia, Miss.; the others are Emma, Trudchen, Grace, Thomas and Eric. The family are members of the Methodist Episcopal church.

CHAPTER XXI.

BIOGRAPHY, I.

SOUTH CAROLINA has given to Grenada county, Miss., many estimable citizens, but she has contributed none more highly respected or, for conscientious discharge of duty in every relation of life, more worthy of respect and esteem than Capt. G. F. Ingram, planter, Graysport, Miss. He was born in Kershaw district in 1829, and is a son of John U. and Margaret P. (Ingram) Ingram, the former a native of Kershaw district, born in 1804, and the latter in Lancaster district, S. C., in 1809. Both died in the former district in 1858 and 1838 respectively, he a member of the Presbyterian and she a member of the Methodist church. The father was a man of fair education, and amassed a considerable fortune by his planting operations. His name was originally Ingrem, but after his marriage he changed the spelling of the name to Ingram, which has since been retained in the family. The paternal grandfather, John Ingrem, was a native of Virginia, of Scotch-Irish descent, but prior to the Revolutionary war he went to Kershaw district, S. C., and there his death occurred in 1829. He followed the occupation of a planter all his life. During the Revolutionary war he served as a soldier under Colonel Washington. The maternal grandfather, Frank Ingram, was a native of Lancaster district, S. C., and spent all his life in that state, dying in Chester district about 1857. He followed the occupation of a planter also. His father, Arthur Ingram, was a native of the Emerald isle, and was a soldier in the Revolutionary war. He died in South Carolina. Of the four children born to his parents Capt. G. F. Ingram is the eldest in order of birth. The others are named as follows: Sarah T., the wife of J. B. Hughes, died in 1857, leaving two children; Zadock P., died in 1860; and Mary, who was the wife of J. C. Dunlap, died in 1864, leaving three children. Capt. G. F. Ingram was reared on the farm with an academic education, and began for himself when twenty-one years of age as a farmer. In 1851 he married Miss Rebecca D. Perry, a native of South Carolina, and a daughter of Zadock Perry, also a native of the Palmetto state, who came to what is now Grenada county in 1848, and there followed planting. His death occurred in 1852 or 1853. Mrs. Ingram died in South Carolina in 1864. The two children born to this union are also deceased. The Captain's second marriage occurred in 1866 to Mrs. Sarah Raiford, who was born in Spartanburg district, S. C., and was the daughter of William Clayton, who was also a native of that state. A number of years before the war Mr. Clayton removed to Mississippi, followed planting for a short time, and died in Marshall county, just previous to the late struggle. To Mr. and Mrs. Ingram have been born eight children, three of whom are living. In 1854 Mr. Ingram came to what is now Grenada county, and has since lived in the vicinity of Graysport, where he now resides. In 1862 he joined company H, Forty-second Mississippi infantry as first lieutenant in the Virginia army and served at Gettysburg and a number of places until 1864. He was a member of Graysport lodge, A. F. & A. M., No. 289, during its existence. He and Mrs. Ingram are members of the Presbyterian church. Captain Ingram, as he is called, stands high in the estimation of his neighbors, and comes of an old and prominent family.

Benajah R. Inman, a prominent citizen, was born in Wilkinson county, where he now resides, in 1820, and is the son of Richard Inman, a native of Virginia, who died in 1848, aged sixty-five years. The father came to Mississippi soon after 1809, where he married Margaret Rollins, a native of Georgia, whose mother was killed by the Indians when Margaret was an infant, and she was reared by her aunt, Miss Terril. The latter, with her family and Margaret, then about eight years of age, came to Mississippi and settled in what is now Wilkinson county, near the present location of Woodville. Margaret was the only daughter of her father's family, but there were several sons, only one of whom lived to be well advanced in years. Benjamin Rollins settled on Buffalo river, where he died at an advanced age. The family is supposed to have come to this territory in about the year 1792. The mother of B. R. Inman died in 1845, at the age of fifty-five years. She was a member of the Methodist Episcopal church, in which she took much interest. Mr. Inman, her husband and the father of B. R. Inman, served in the War of 1812 as a private and was one of the few men who escaped from Fort Mims during the awful massacre there by the Indians. He was not an educated man, owing to his defective eyesight, which prevented him from hard study, but he was a man well respected and was greatly devoted to his family and beloved by them. By his marriage were born nine children, all of whom are deceased but the subject of this sketch, yet several grew to maturity, married, and reared families: Louise died single; Lucinda became the wife of Fred Keller, of Ohio; Letitia married James Ward, of London, England; Sarah married Joseph Rider, also from England; Catharine became the wife of Alex. Johnson; Zillah wedded William Richardson, of Dayton, Ohio; Joseph and Lenora died in childhood; Alexander married Miss Susan Johnson, by whom was born one child, Mary. He died in 1862, during the war, at Columbia, Miss., of measles, while serving as a soldier in the Confederate army. Benajah R. was the fourth child born to this union, and first came to his present place at the age of eighteen years, and here he has since lived. The present place was formerly the property of Mrs. Nancy Quinn, his aunt, who was before marriage a Miss Terril, and at her death bequeathed her estate to Benajah R. He had been her manager and had been very successful and economical. The husband of Mrs. Quinn was, unfortunately, drowned soon after their marriage. She followed him to the grave in 1863, leaving no children, and was seventy-five years of age at the time of her death and a consistent member of the Baptist church and a woman of more than usual worth and character. The subject was married first to Miss Lucinda Ginn, daughter of Colonel Ginn, a native of Tennessee. She was the youngest child of her father's family and was born and reared in this county. She died in 1874, and by her marriage were born

63

six children, five of whom are yet living: Richard M.; Julia, who died at eight years of age; Susie, the widow of B. Stuart; Dr. Benajah W., who was educated at Randolph, Macon college, of Virginia, and at the medical university of New Orleans, and resides in this county, where he practices his profession; Williard L., who was educated near Woodville and at Baton Rouge, La., in Professor McGruder's college, and lives near the home place, and Lillie, who is single and at home. His first wife having died, he married Lydia Adell Bryan, a native of this county and the daughter of L. H. Bryan, also a native of this county. By this union was born one child, Inez, now aged eleven years. Mr. Inman is a member of the Methodist Episcopal church, and his wife of the Episcopal church. He owns several plantations and is a man who gives close attention to his home and family. He stands very high in the community as an upright citizen, a just man and a progressive planter. He is well to do, as is also his most excellent wife, she owning in her own name a large landed and personal estate.

John B. Ioor, real estate agent, assessor and city tax collector of Bay St. Louis, Miss., was born in Wilkinson county, Miss., and is a son of Charlotte Withers Herron and Peter Harry Ioor, natives of South Carolina. His father was a prominent citizen of Wilkinson and Hancock counties, a graduate of Columbia (S. C.) college, and a planter by vocation. His grandfather, Gen. John Ioor, was an early settler of Wilkinson county, Miss., moving there in 1810; was a cultured gentleman of large wealth, an officer of the War of 1812, and a member of the constitutional convention of Mississippi in 1817. The family are of Huguenot extraction, their ancestors having sought refuge in South Carolina from the religious persecutions of Louis XIV. John B. Ioor, at the breaking out of the Civil war, went into the army, and served until hostilities ceased; was a member of company B, Third Louisiana cavalry. After serving in various engagements was paroled in May, 1865; has since resided in Wilkinson and Hancock counties, and has carried on the real estate business.

Henry T. Ireys, cotton factor, Greenville, Miss. The ancestors of the Ireys family came to America prior to 1634 and were members of the Plymouth colony. They were from Dorsetshire, England, where they were located before the Norman conquest; had their coat of arms, and were a titled family, even barons. Among the early members in colonial times were many who achieved distinction and renown in affairs of local government and in the Indian wars. The paternal great-grandfather was a colonel of the militia of the First Rhode Island regiment and served during the Revolutionary war. The father of Mr. Ireys came to Mississippi at an early date, settled at Port Gibson in the year 1821, and entered land there. He also entered large tracts in Washington county of that state. He was married in Rhode Island in 1834 to Miss Mary Bailey, and later in life made his home in Washington county, where he was engaged in clearing up the land he had secured. His death occurred in New Orleans on the 9th of July, 1846. To his marriage were born six children, Henry T. Ireys, the subject of this sketch, being the eldest. The latter was born in Newport, R. I., 1837. He came to Mississippi to take charge of the family estate at the close of the war. He planted for a number of years successfully and then became associated with Charles P. Huntington in building the first railroad in Washington county in 1878, and moved from his plantation on Williams' bayou to Greenville in the spring of that year. He was secretary and treasurer and general manager for four years of the Greenville, Columbus & Birmingham railroad, which sold out to the Richmond & Danville (now the Georgia Pacific) railroad. After this he was associated with Maj. James E. Negus and formed the banking house of Negus, Ireys & Co. After the erection of the first cotton compress, and in the year 1866, he began as the first cotton factor in Greenville. Mr. Ireys has an interest in large tracts of land, including Mound Pleasant plantation at Winterville, which is very productive, and one of the best plantations in Washington county. He is also the owner of considerable town property. Mr. Ireys is interested in almost every enterprise of a laudable nature. He is president of the Delta Insurance company, vice president of the Greenville Cotton Exchange, a charter member of many organizations, and a director in many stock companies. He was married to Miss Elizabeth Taylor, daughter of Dr. L. L. Taylor (see sketch), May 20, 1869, at Loughboro, and the result of this union was the birth of six children: Henry T., Jr., Mary Bailey, Junius Taylor, Kate Bailey, Susan Mosby and Bettie Taylor. Mr. and Mrs. Ireys are members of the Presbyterian church, in which he is an elder. Both are actively engaged in religious work.

George S. Irving is a Scotchman by birth, born in 1836, and came to the United States with his parents in 1838, their landing being made at Mobile, Ala. The father was a brewer by occupation and came to this country to engage in that occupation, but died in 1840, while on a trip to London to purchase a plant for his business. His widow survived him until 1858, when her death occurred. Their union resulted in the birth of three sons, George S. and a brother who resides in Indiana being the only ones living. George S. Irving was educated in the public schools and an academy, but his advantages were only for a short time. At the age of twelve years he began clerking, but soon afterward began learning the trade of a blacksmith. In 1853 he came to Vicksburg and here he was engaged in the timber business for twenty years, rafting from all the streams above. In 1861 he entered the Confederate army, enlisting in the company of Julius M. Klein, was attached to Wirt Adams' regiment and was in the battle of Shiloh. He, with about one hundred other men, was detailed to join General Morgan in a raid in Kentucky, but he afterward returned with his company to Chattanooga and later took part in the engagements at Perryville, Murfreesboro and many minor battles in Tennessee. He was on the Georgia campaign with General Johnston, returned to Tennessee with Hood, and then went to North Carolina where he surrendered with Johnston, at Greensboro. During his entire service he was neither wounded nor captured. Upon his return to Vicksburg after the war was over, he once more began dealing in timber, but in 1870 opened a mercantile establishment under the firm name of Hartigan & Irving, which existed eleven months. In 1879 Mr. Irving started in the business again, and this was the beginning of his present business, which is an extensive wholesale and retail grocery concern. It is known as the George S. Irving Grocery and Provision company and is conducted on an extensive scale. Mr. Irving is also the owner of large plantations in Yazoo county, seven on Silver creek, eight in all, with about two thousand acres under cultivation. The names of the plantations are: Belle Yazoo, on Yazoo river; Valley Land, Grosvenor, Cottonwood, Waldwood, Aluvia, River Field and Niger Bend, on Silver creek. Five thousand eight hundred acres which he owns on Silver creek comprise one of the finest plantations in the South; in fact all his land is extremely fertile and valuable. He is essentially a selfmade man, and is one of the most thoroughly posted men on the timber interests and the best judge of timber in the state. He has established and built up a large commercial business and is interested in many enterprises that are advancing and building up Vicksburg. He is one of the supervisors of Warren county, and as president of that board he has advocated many public improvements, and in all has practiced economy. He was married first in 1870 to Mrs. Mary Bodine, who had two small children, Henrietta and Jeff. D. Bodine, who were educated by him, and Mrs. C. C. Reynolds, of Seattle, Wash., is the step-daughter of Mrs. Jerry S. D. Bodine, died at the age of twenty-six, a native of this state and to them one child was born, Lorenzo, who graduated in Spring Hill college with the highest honors and is now in business with his father.   His mother died in 1885 and the following year Mr. Irving wedded Miss Leda A. Sherrad, a native of Holmes county, by whom he has two children: Hazel Fisher and George G., Jr.   Mr. Irving is a member of the I. O. O. F., the K. of P., the K. of H., the L. of H., the A. F. & A. M. and the Elks. He is the oldest past commander of the L. of H. in the state and was one of the organizers of the first lodge (lodge No. 557) in Mississippi, at Vicksburg.   He has always been very enterprising and is interested in the Hill City oil mill, the First National bank, the Vicksburg Compress company, the Vicksburg Hotel company and many other worthy enterprises.   He has proved himself honorable and upright in every transaction, is a useful and progressive citizen, and his career is a worthy example to all young men.

Thomas Dudley Isom was born in Maury county, Tenn., September 5, 1816; was the second child born of James and Mary (Gale) Isom, who were natives of Virginia, and were pioneers of middle Tennesee.   The father was a farmer, and died in 1824, and the mother lived until 1851.   Dr. Isom received his education mainly under Prof. Samuel P. Black, a prominent educator of early days, at Pebble Hill academy, in Rutherford county, Tenn.   In 1835 he came to Tullahoma, Miss., and was sent by a company with a stock of goods to trade with the Indians on the ridge.   He settled his store on the present site of Oxford, and was the first white settler and merchant in the place.   He remained there until the Indians were removed, when he returned to Tennessee, and studied medicine, under Dr. John S. Spindle for one year, and then took a course of lectures at Transylvania university in 1837–8.   The years 1838 and 1839 he spent in the time-honored institution of learning, Jefferson medical college, Philadelphia, Penn., where he graduated in 1839, and came at once to Oxford to practice his profession, where he has resided ever since, except the four years of the war. In 1861 he entered the Southern army, as surgeon of the Seventeenth Mississippi volunteer infantry.   In this same year he opened the hospital at Warrenton, Va.   In March, 1862, he opened a hospital at this place, and received and treated over fifteen hundred soldiers from the battle of Shiloh, and in the fall and winter of the same year was post surgeon at Jackson and Columbus.   In 1863 he was appointed on the army medical board, and continued in this capacity until the close of the war.   He enjoys the distinction of being the oldest and most extensive practitioner in northern Mississippi in all the branches of his profession. He was the first to demonstrate in this locality the possibility of treating the febrile diseases of malarious and malignant type with large doses of quinine, and left off venesection and depletion.   He has had remarkable success in surgery, having extirpated the superior maxilliary bone in 1856, patient still living, and many successful operations in all the hernias: and his operations in extirpating tumors have been extensive.   He was the first in this locality to apply Sayres plaster jacket in Potts disease.   He was a member of the secession convention in 1860, and of the constitutional convention in 1890.   He married Sarah R. McGehee, of Abbeville district, S. C.   Nine children were born of this union, four of whom are living, Mary F., wife of C. W. Petrie; Emma G., wife of H. P. Branham; Sarah McGehee and Thomas Dudley, Jr., M. D.

H. M. Ivy is one of the oldest and best known planters of Clay county, and like many of the representative citizens of this section he is an Alabamian.   He was born in Tuscaloosa county, in 1822, to Thomas and Druscilla P. (Gartner) Ivy, the former of whom was born in Warren county, Ga., in 1783.   His boyhood was spent on a farm in his native county, and although his educational advantages were few, he was naturally intelligent and made the most of the opportunities that came in his way, and eventually became a well-posted man. He was married in 1818, his wife's birth occurring in Warren county in 1798, and soon after the celebration of their nuptuals they moved to Tuscaloosa county, Ala., where Mr. Ivy was engaged in planting for fifteen years. In 1835 they again made a change of location, removing to Pontotoc ridge, Chickasaw county, where the father died the following year. He was one of the earliest settlers of this section, and made an active and useful citizen. His widow survived him until 1884, having for many years been an active member of the Baptist church. Mr. Ivy was one of the commissioners to locate the county seat of Chickasaw county, in 1835, and as a citizen took an active interest in everything pertaining to the welfare of the community in which he resided. H. M. Ivy is the eldest of their nine children—five sons and four daughters—all of whom lived to be grown and married: H. M., Sterling, of West Point; Thomas I., who died in Texas during the war; Marion, a resident of Bowie county, Tex.; Calvin, residing near Abbott, in Clay county, Miss., Frances G., wife of Elijah Wallace, a planter of northern Alabama, for whose union the first marriage license in Chickasaw county was granted; Mary Ann, wife of J. W. Wallace, of northern Alabama; Susanna J., wife of J. W. Dawson, M. D., of Kemper county, Miss.; and Sarah, wife of J. W. Cressman, of Kemper county. H. M. Ivy was left fatherless at the age of fourteen years, and on this account and from the fact that the schools of his day did not offer attractions as they do at the present time, he received but little education, and had he been a dull boy this would have sadly interfered with his success in after life, but he was naturally bright and quick to learn, and by contact with the world and by reading, he in a great measure made amends for this early deficiency. Upon reaching the age of about eighteen years he began to make his own way in the world as a planter on Pontotoc ridge, and prior to the war succeeded in accumulating a fine property, which was swept away during that period. In 1844 he was married to Miss Mary A. Gates, who was born in Greene county, Ala., in 1826, a daughter of Thomas and Mary (Green) Gates. She removed with her parents to Chickasaw county in 1835, where she met and married Mr. Ivy. In 1846 Mr. Ivy removed to near Palo Alto, Chickasaw (now Clay) county, and purchased eight hundred acres of land on the prairie, which was then being settled up, and he now owns a good and fertile plantation, one and a half miles east of Abbott, of which he cultivates between four hundred and five hundred acres, making cotton his principal crop. He is a charter member of Palo Alto lodge of the A. F. & A. M., and is an earnest member and elder of the Christian church. To himself and wife, who died in 1882, an earnest member of the Christian church, a family of nine children was born: T. Rush (deceased), Irene (wife of W. B. Moore, of West Point), D. P., C .C., Laura, Mazie B., Henry M. (a planter), Ruby and Pearl. Mr. Ivy is a handsome gentleman, hale and hearty, and in appearance looks no older than fifty-five, although he will soon have reached the three-score-years-and-ten milestone of his life. He is respected by all, is genial and kind in disposition, and is a true type of the old time Mississippi gentleman of high birth and breeding.

J. W. Ivy, farmer, Mount Pleasant, Miss, is the youngest of a family of eight children born to Frederick and Mary (Linton) Ivy, owes his nativity to Williamson county, Tenn., his birth occurring December 23, 1821. Both father and mother were natives of the Old North state, but removed with their parents to Tennessee when but children. There they grew up, married, and there reared their family. The father was a farmer by occupation, was justice of the peace for quite a number of years in Williamson county, twenty miles from Nashville, and well known and esteemed throughout that part of the state. He served in the Cherokee war under General Jackson and was with him at the battle of the Horseshoe. He died in 1851, at the age of sixty-five years. The mother received her final summons in 1865. Both are members of the Christian church. J. W. Ivy, with two brothers and a sister, came to Mississippi, but the other children remained in Tennessee. J. W. came to Mississippi in 1847, located in Mount Pleasant, Marshall county, and has been engaged in merchandising since 1849. He was married in 1853 to Miss Margaret M. Walker, of Marshall county, and to them have been born nine children, five sons and four daughters: William W. (deceased), Mollie B. (deceased) Luella, (wife of J. W. Woody), Frederick H., Ruffie O. (wife of Rev. C. H. Owen), Albert S., John H. (deceased), Jesse W. and Maggie. Frederick graduated at Oxford university in 1881 and Jesse W. is now taking a four years course at that institution, expecting to graduate in 1892. Albert S. received his literary training at Starkville, Miss., in the state agricultural school. Mr. Ivy owns residence property in Mount Pleasant, also a steamgin, saw and gristmill in that place, and now has a general stock of merchandise, selling under the firm name of J. W. Ivy & Son. He was postmaster of the town for a number of years, and was one among the early settlers of the county. He is universally respected as a successful business man, farmer and citizen. He operates his farm with tenants. He is a member of the Masonic fraternity, Mount Pleasant lodge No. 99, and he and Mrs. Ivy are members of the Methodist church South.

ᏩHAPTEᎡ XXII.

SPECIAL RECORDS, J.

ONE of the men who have controlled circumstances in life and commanded success is Guy Jacks, general merchant, planter and miller, Scooba, Kemper county, Miss. He is descended from a family of high connection, who were leaders in all their associations. His grandfather, Patrick Jack, was a captain in the Revolutionary war, and a noted man of his time. He represented Mecklenburg county, N. C., in the congress of 1775 and 1776, wielding an unusual power. In one of his speeches before that August body he said, "Gentlemen, you may debate here about reconciliation, and memorialize your king, but bear it in mind, Mecklenburg owes no alliance to, and is separated from the crown of Great Britian forever." On the first call for troops, true to his convictions, he raised a company which he commanded through the Revolution. He was a great man, and was possessed of that true courage which resists all, in the effort to be just to one's sense of right and wrong. Abner M. Jack was born in North Carolina in 1814, and was a son of Patrick Jack. He married Sarah E. McCalebb, also a native of North Carolina, born in the year 1824, a daughter of James McCalebb. He removed to Kemper county from Greene county, Ala., about 1835, and engaged in planting. He was very prosperous, and at the time of his death was considered one of the wealthiest men in the state. He reared only two children: May, who married A. M. Rencher, died in 1878; she was the mother of four children: May J., Florence M., deceased; Henry W., and Guy Jack. Guy, the subject of this sketch, was born in Kemper county, Miss., October 11, 1853. Capt. Abner Jack enlisted in the Confederate army in 1862, but was obliged to resign on account of ill health. During the first part of the conflict, however, he saw active service. He died in 1865, and his wife had passed away the preceding year. He was a member of the Presbyterian church, and belonged to the I. O. O. F. Politically he affiliated with the democratic party, and in early times was sheriff of Kemper county. Guy Jack was educated in his native county, and at the University of Alabama. He was graduated from a commercial college at Atlanta, Ga., in 1872. Intellectually he was well equipped for business at the age of seventeen years, when he started out to meet the battle of life. He first engaged in farming, and before he was twenty-one years old, he had opened a store on his plantation, four miles from town. In 1876 he opened a general store in Scooba, Kemper county, and another at Shuqualak, Noxubee county. He was very successful in these enterprises, and conducted the business with a wisdom and sagacity that would have done credit to an older head. In 1879 he established himself in business at Wahalak, Kemper county, and was one of the most forceful factors in the building up of that place. In 1884 he was united in marriage to Miss Augusta Edwards of Kemper county, a daughter of Elisha and Jane (Neely) Edwards. Her parents belong to one of the oldest families in Mississippi. Four children were born to Mr. and Mrs. Jack: Abner M., Elisha E., Guy J., Jr., and Annie M. The father and mother are members of the Baptist church. He is a Mason in his fraternal connections. He has been a member of the city council, of which he is now clerk. In October, 1890, he began the erection of a large business block in Scooba; it is to be occupied as a store and hotel, and will be an ornament to the town and a credit to the owner. Mr. Jack owns a sawmill, and large tracts of farming land. He has acquired great wealth, and has been exceedingly liberal in his contributions to all charitable and philanthropic causes.

As a representative of the Emerald isle, Robert Jackson, florist, Sardis, Miss., stands in the front ranks, and as a man of advanced ideas and tendencies, he is well known all over Panola county, Miss. He was born in County Tyrone' on the 5th of May, 1830, to the union of George and Eliza (Fulton) Jackson, the father a native of Ireland and the mother of Scotland. The elder Jackson was a nurseryman in Armagh, Ireland, and was rather successful in that occupation. His death occurred there in 1834. His parents, Charles and Elizabeth Jackson, were natives of Scotland, and Mrs. Jackson's parents, Alexander and Mary Fulton, were natives also of that country. Of the eight children born to this union Robert Jackson was the fifth in order of birth, and he, with his four brothers, was bound out to serve an apprenticeship, he selecting the nursery business. He was reared in his native country, and on account of being bound out at an early age, received only a moderately good education. The first year of his apprenticeship he attended school half the day, the next year less than that and so on until the seven years (time allotted for serving an apprenticeship) had expired. In 1851 he came to the United States and since then has been engaged as a nurseryman, but handles flowers principally. He is an excellent judge of plants, is well read and thoroughly familiar with that subject, and not only does he supply a large demand in Panola county, but ships a great many flowers to other points. He has the finest small orchard in the state, and his flowers are noted all over Mississippi, and portions of Arkansas and Tennessee. Mr. Jackson came to Mississippi without a dollar and is now in comfortable circumstances. He has made all his property by his own exertions and deserves great credit for his perseverance and industry. He contributes liberally to all public enterprises of a laudable nature and is regarded as a most reliable citizen. He has a beautiful home and his yard is filled with the choicest plants, which, tastefully arranged, attract the eye of one and all. Mr. Jackson was married in 1858 to Miss Sarah Secor, a native of New York, and the daughter of Isaac and Mary Secor, also of New York. The Secor family is a very old and prominent one, having come to this country in colonial times. Mr. and Mrs. Jackson have eight children born to their union: Charles, Lucinda, Ephraim, David, Barham, Ruby, Lee and Ellen (deceased). Mr. Jackson is a member of the Masonic fraternity.

Col. Moses Jackson. In giving a short history of the Jackson family, it may be stated that they were among the very earliest settlers of Amite county, Miss. Willie Jackson, Colonel Jackson's father, served in both houses of the legislature, and was a very worthy and highly-honored citizen of this section of the state. In public life the influence of this family has been unbounded, for its men have possessed talent and numerous worthy characteristics. They have been found among the first ranks in every enterprise of a worthy nature, and their force of character, energy and enterprise pushed matters to a successful issue in more than one instance. Isaac Jackson, the grandfather of Col. Moses Jackson, became one of the pioneer settlers of Amite county, Miss., from the state of Georgia, this being about the year 1800, and on Bear creek, near the Liberty and Woodville road, he opened up a fine plantation and resided until death called him home. His family consisted of five sons and five daughters, of whom Capt. Willie Jackson, the father of the subject of this sketch, was a member. Captain Jackson learned many lessons of industry in his youth, while a resident of the home plantation, and these he found to be of great use to him after starting out in life for himself. When the War of 1812 opened he immediately raised a cavalry company, which he commanded, and was at the battle of New Orleans, in which he rendered effective service. From the fact that he possessed a fine mind, was very practical in his views, and a man of unblemished honor, he became a noted man in Amite county, and at different times held responsible positions of honor and trust. He served as a member of both houses of the state legislature, and his reputation as a pure and incorruptible legislator was of the very best. His many noble qualities of heart and head won him many friends, and to them he ever remained true and faithful. By his superior judgment and good management he accumulated a nice property, and became the owner of a large property in Holmes, Amite and Yazoo counties, and before the opening of the recent war owned numerous slaves. His brothers were also extensive planters and large slaveowners. Captain Jackson was married in this county to Miss Mary Robinson, a native of the county and a daughter of James Robinson, who was also one of the pioneers of the county. To their union four sons and one daughter were born, and arrived at mature years: Louisa, who became the wife of Peter Parker and died before the war, her husband dying recently; Andrew and Isaac, who were planters and are now deceased; Robert, also deceased, and Moses. After the death of the mother of these children Captain Jackson was again married, and by his second wife became the father of two children: Dr. Thomas Jackson, a prominent physician of this county, and Isadore, deceased, who was the wife of Rev. John A. Smiley, also deceased. Captain Jackson was a prominent member of the Baptist church during the latter part of his life, and died as he had lived, a worthy Christian gentleman. He was called from life in 1843, his death being universally lamented. Col. Moses Jackson was reared as all other farmers' boys, was given the advantages of the common schools near his home, but being of a naturally studious turn of mind, he improved spare moments and became an average scholar. His early life on the farm gave him a strong constitution physically, made him a practical, sensible man, and fitted him in an admirable manner for the public life he was destined to live. He made his home with his father until the latter's death, after which he took control of the home plantation. This estate was very large, and had on it one of the best farm residences in the country at that day. The lumber was all whip-sawed, for no lumber was manufactured in this or adjoining counties at that early day, and upon completion the house was considered an imposing structure. Colonel Jackson settled upon that portion of the estate where he now lives in 1845, having been married the previous year to Miss Amelia Jenkins, daughter of William Jenkins, a worthy and successful planter of this county. In 1863 he was called upon to mourn the death of his wife, she having borne him five children: Walter and Frank, planters of the county, and Eleanora, wife of John Walker, of Dardanelle, Ark. Charles died after reaching manhood, and Louisa (deceased) was the wife of D. B. Kinnebrew. Colonel Jackson's second marriage was celebrated in the year 1866, and was to Mrs. E. Rebecca Van Allen, a daughter of Robert and Elizabeth Brown. Mrs. Jackson is an accomplished and intelligent lady, and was reared and educated in this, her native county. Colonel Jackson continued to follow the occupation of a planter up to 1862, but in the early part of that year he put aside his farming implements to enter upon the career of a soldier, and with a patriotism that did not stop at the dark outlook of the future, he enlisted in the Thirty-third Mississippi regiment, being first lieutenant of company K. He was soon after promoted to the rank of captain, and in 1864 became lieutenant-colonel, in which capacity he served until the close of the war. As he was a man of indomitable will power and fine constitution, he bore the varying fortunes, the hardships and exposure of a soldier's life well, and it may be truly said of him that no braver soldier ever trod the crimson turf of a battlefield. He served under Gen. Joseph Johnston, and during the latter part of the war did not have his clothes removed from his person for over five months. He was in many bloody battles, the principal of which was the siege of Jackson, Miss., Augusta, Ga., where he received a gunshot wound in each foot and was struck in the back of the head by a piece of shell, which caused the breaking of his skull. At this time he commanded a regiment, and did valiant service for the Confederate cause. He was also in the hard fought and hotly-contested struggle from Dalton to Atlanta, the fighting being almost continuous for about five months.

At the siege of Atlanta, the Colonel, not having fully recovered from his wounds, was unfit for field duty, and was put on post duty at Augusta, where he surrendered and was paroled. With the consciousness of having performed every duty to the best of his ability, Colonel Jackson returned to his home via Florida and New Orleans, turned his sword into a plowshare, and resumed the peaceful pursuit of a planter. Although his efforts were in behalf of a losing cause, he would not allow himself to brood over this fact, but with characteristic energy devoted all his energies to restoring his plantation to its old-time fertility, and as a result is now in good circumstances. As he has always been of a very practical turn of mind, he readily adapted himself to the altered conditions of Southern life, produced by the war and the abolition of slavery, and adjusted his business habits and methods to meet the requirements of the new regime, and has met with flattering success. In politics he is an active and efficient member of the democratic party, and his qualities of leadership have never been more signally displayed than in the arena of politics. Although he has never been an officeseeker, he has been prominent in the councils of his party, and no one's opinion and advice in political matters has been considered more weighty or more sought after by those desiring preferment. In 1861 he became a member of the state legislature, and since that time has been a member of the senate, serving in that body in 1878 and 1879, and displaying sound judgment and practical ability. On various occasions he has been a delegate to county, district and state conventions, and throughout his entire public career he has shown himself to be a man of ability. Kind, generous and hospitable, he has won many warm friends, who lay at his feet unbounded respect and esteem, the result of a useful life well spent. He has long been a member of the Baptist church, and his wife, who is a member of the Presbyterian church, is ever found ready to aid him in all good works.

John C. James, planter, Williamsville, Miss., who has resided in what is now Grenada county, for the past sixty years and who was one of its first settlers was originally from Watagua county, Ala., his birth occurring in 1822, and is a son of David and Sallie (Harrell) James, natives of North Carolina where they were reared and married. From there the parents removed to Alabama, thence in 1832 to Shelby county, Tenn., and in 1833 they came to what is now Grenada county. They camped in the woods on Horsepen creek, eighteen miles east of Grenada, and in this new country, amid strange and unfamiliar scenes, Mr. James went to work to clear the forest and to provide a home for the little family growing up around him. The country at that time was almost a wilderness, bears, dear, panthers, wild cats and wolves abounded, the nearest trading post or postoffice was at Grenada and the country was full of Indians. They experienced many hardships and privations, but gradually they surmounted all difficulties and at the time of his death, in 1865, Mr. James was quite a wealthy planter. His wife, who had been a faithful helpmate to him, followed him to the grave in 1870. Both had been members of the Baptist church for many years. Their family consisted of nine children, five of whom are living: Mrs. Selina Heath, of Texas; John C.; Amanda, now the widow Pollan, of Arkansas; Emeline and Mary. John C. James was educated in the country schools of Mississippi, and, as may be supposed, his advantages were not of the best at that early day. He was married in January, 1840, to Miss Laura Davis, a native of South Carolina and the daughter of Levi and Martha (Burkitt) Davis, also natives of the Palmetto state. Mr. and Mrs. Davis moved to Mississippi at an early day, located in Grenada county and there passed the remainder of their days. Mrs. James died in 1849 leaving two children, one now living, Isaac, a planter in Grenada county. Mr. James' second marriage occurred in 1850 to Miss Lucinda J. Edmondson, a native of what is ow Montgomery county, Miss., and the daughter of Thomas Edmondson who came from Alabama to Mississippi, but who died in the former state while on a visit. Mrs. James died in 1860, leaving four children—three sons and one daughter: Allen; Charley C., assessor of Grenada county; Elizabeth, wife of Thomas A. Caffee, and William R. E. Mr. James' third marriage was in November, 1864, to Mrs. Margaret S. Ware, who was born in Lawrence district, S. C., in 1830, and was the daughter of James and Susannah Crocker, natives of the same district as their daughter. Mr. Crocker died in 1829, previous to the birth of Mrs. James, and was a planter and merchant. About 1839 Mrs. Crocker removed to Aberdeen, Miss., when that place was a mere hamlet and there she was married to William Moncrief. She spent the closing scenes of her life in Monroe county and died near Aberdeen in 1851. Mrs. James came with her mother to Mississippi when but nine years of age and was married in Pontotoc county to William Z. Ware, who died in North Carolina in 1862, while serving in the war. She had two children by her first husband: Carrie, wife of Monroe Aven, of Lee county, and Willie, wife of Hardy H. Hargrove, of Shreveport, La. By her union to Mr. James she became the mother of two children: Fannie and Byrd C. As before mentioned Mr. James has lived in this neighborhood for sixty years, is the oldest resident of this vicinity, and well remembers how the Sabbaths were spent in early days. Nearly every one went hunting, fishing, etc. People went ten miles to raise a house, roll logs, etc.; all were the best of friends, and no disturbances occurred. When a boy, Mr.

James would take turns with his brothers during the night, to keep the wolves or other wild animals from the pigpen or from carrying off the lambs. He would frequently carry a pine knot for a torch for his father to kill deer after night. The only mill was a steel one run by hand, and many days has Mr. James spent grinding the wheat and corn for family use. The country was then a vast canebrake, and stock kept fat the entire year round without any care. In about 1837 the Baptists built a log church known as Pleasant Grove church, on his father's place, and this was attended by people from over a radius of ten or twelve miles. He remembers his first trip to Grenada, how he had to hitch his horse on the east bank of Big Bogue creek (it not being fordable), and how he and his father crossed the creek on a foot log. Colonel James, as he is familiarly known, is a very interesting conversationalist, and his reminiscences of pioneer days are very interesting, indeed. He has lived on his present property over thirty-one years, and is the owner of seven hundred and forty acres, with one hundred and seventy-five acres cleared. He lost heavily during the war. He was a charter member of Graysport lodge No. 289, A. F. & A. M. He served a few months in the Mississippi militia under Col. W. N. Pass, in 1863. He has been a member of the Baptist church for about thirty-five years, and his wife is also a member of that church. His first wife held membership in the same.

Capt. Henry Jamison, of Kosciusko, Attala county, Miss., was born in Tennessee, January 23, 1823. His father was Hugh B. Jamison and his mother Susan White, both being natives of Tennessee, where the father died on December 25, 1837. He was a planter and a successful business man. Thomas Jamison was a native of this county and of Scotch-Irish descent. The great-grandfather, who was a native of Ireland, came to Pennsylvania, and was there murdered by the Indians in a terrible massacre, the only survivor being the grandfather of our subject. He was also the only one in the whole family to escape. Mr. Jamison's grandfather and great-grandfather were both farmers. His father took part in the Creek war, serving under General Coffee, of Tennessee, and taking part in the battles of Horseshoe bend and Orleans. General Jackson was in command of the whole body of forces. Mr. Jamison has his father's discharge which bears the signature of General Coffee. Hugh B. Jamison also took part in the Seminole war in Florida. He enlisted in the summer of 1836 in Captain Wilson's company and served until the summer of 1837. He was in the most of the battles which occurred during the war last mentioned, in one of which he received a wound in the neck. During both his periods of service above referred to he was a member of cavalry organizations. He was married in 1817 to Miss Susan White, who bore him nine children, of whom five are now living, but of whom Capt. Henry Jamison is the only one living in Mississippi; Elizabeth lives in Tennessee; Janes in Texas; Fannie in Stockton, Mo.; C. R. at West Panes, Mo.; Stephen fell at Resaca, Ga., while serving the Confederate cause in the late war; William died in Attala county in August, 1890; Sophia died in this county about five years ago; Charlotte died in Tennessee in the spring of 1844. Captain Jamison has always been a planter, an occupation which he chose in early life and which he has followed with much success through a long and busy career. He married Lettitia H. Jones, October 28, 1847, who died January 16, 1889, after having borne him seven children: Mary (deceased), Susan E., James H., S. W., H. B., Sophia J. (who is married) and Lettitia H. (also married). All of the above named who are living are residents of this county. Captain Jamison enlisted in 1846 as a private in Capt. L. D. Newman's company of Col. Jones E. Thomas' regiment for service in the Mexican war, and was discharged in June of the following year at the expiration of his term of enlistment. He participated in the siege of Vera Cruz, the battle of Cerro Gordo and in numerous lesser engagements. His division was commanded by Generals Patterson and Pillow, and General Scott was the commander in chief of the army in Mexico. In August, 1861, Captain Jamison enlisted for service in the late war as captain of Company K, of the Fourth Mississippi regiment. On account of ill health he was discharged after eighteen months' service, after which he was detailed for duty in the commissary department. During his active military career, however, he was in the battles of Fort Henry and Fort Donelson, Chickasaw Bayou and the siege of Vicksburg. He was made prisoner of war at Fort Donelson. His first regimental commander was Colonel Drake, who left the service in the fall of the year 1862, and he was succeeded by Colonel Layton. A younger brother of Captain Jamison was a member of Captain Love's company of Colonel George's regiment of cavalry, for some time previous to the surrender. The captain came to this state November, 1848. After living for four years in Leake county he removed to his present home in Attala county. He is a member of Trinity lodge No. 88, A. F. & A. M., of Kosciusko, in which he has been worshipful master. He is also a Royal Arch mason. He was first made a member of this grand order in Pearl River lodge No. 105, at Carthage, in the fall of 1850. In the fall of 1853 he was demitted from that lodge and joined the organization at Kosciusko. He is a member of the Farmers' Alliance, with which he identified himself in 1889, and served as its president in 1890. He is the owner of a large, well-improved plantation, and produces about fifty bales of cotton annually, and he raises besides much fine stock, both horses and cattle. He has always been known as a man of enterprise, who has devoted himself strictly to business, and his has been more than satisfactory, for he ranks now as one of the leading planters in this part of the state of Mississippi.

Hon J. H. Jamison, of Noxubee county, Miss., was born in Tennessee in 1846. In 1876 he came to Mississippi and settled in the northeastern portion of Noxubee county, where he engaged in planting. He was married in Tennessee, in 1875, to Mrs. Patty Ivy, who died in 1879. Two years later he was married to Miss Bettie Moore, of Noxubee county, Miss., a sister of his first wife. By his first marriage he was blessed with two children, Idalette and Charlie M.; by the last with two, J. H., Jr. and Bettie. Captain Jamison, as he is familiarly called, has occupied many positions of honor. While a resident of Tennessee he was a member of the state legislature from 1871 to 1876. During this time he was prominently identified with the low-tax wing of the democracy. He was in the Confederate service, a scout of General Polk. He was a student at the Military institute at Murfreesboro, Tenn., and afterward at Washington and Lee university, Virginia, where he took the degree of civil engineering. Here, as a speaker and student, he took very high rank, as was shown when, three years later, he returned, by request of his alma mater, and delivered the annual address. Chosen by his people, he went as a delegate to the state constitutional convention of 1890, which position he filled with an ability which reflected credit on the judgment of his constituency. Captain Jamison is a man of the masses, and decidedly popular. As a neighbor, he is the best; as a host, he is hospitality itself; as a friend, he is the truest of the true; as an antagonist he is worthy of the foeman's steel. In August, 1891, he was elected president of the state alliance of Mississippi. As to what other honors await him at the hands of the people, time alone can tell. Besides his public duties, he finds time to superintend a great planting enterprise, involving the cultivation of many thousand acres of land, a good portion of which is his individual interest. A model husband and father, a friend to education and to every good work for the uplifting of the race, Hon. J. H. Jamison is a genuine citizen of whom Mississippi is justly proud.

In Cooper county, Mo., on the 27th of June, 1842, there was born to the union of William E. and Margaret Howe (Wallace) Jamison a son, their eldest born, whom they named William T., now a planter of Marks. The parents were natives of Missouri, and both were descendants of old and highly respected families. During the Civil war the father enlisted in the Confederate army and was at once made captain of his company. He was captured with the entire regiment at the battle of Black Water, Mo., was retained a prisoner for two years, and was then exchanged at Camp Chase, Ohio. He returned to company A, Second Missouri cavalry, and served the remainder of the war under Captain Harper, surrendering at Memphis, Tenn. He immediately returned to Missouri and brought his family to Mississippi, locating in that part of Tunica county which is now Quitman county, where he spent the remainder of his days as an honored and respected citizen. His death occurred in 1875. His wife survives him and is now seventy-two years of age. All their children, seven in number, are now living, with the exception of one child, who died in Mississippi. William T. Jamison passed his boyhood and youth in Cooper county, received his schooling there, and when twenty-four years of age came with his parents to Mississippi, of which state he has since been a resident. He has been one of the leading citizens of Quitman county since its organization and has held many public offices, filling them in a satisfactory and very creditable manner. He has been superintent of public instruction and also chancery clerk of the county. His brother, A. H., has been treasurer of the county, and is now a member of the board of supervisors. In 1865 Mr. Jamison began for himself as a planter, and this occupation he has successfully followed ever since, accumulating a good property. During the war, or in 1863, he enlisted in company A, First regiment, Marmaduke's cavalry, and participated in the battle of Lexington, Mo. He was captured during the retreat, retained a prisoner ten months, and was paroled at Rock Island in 1864, after which he returned home to take care of his mother. In 1878 he selected as his life companion Miss Cornelia A. Mellard, of Columbus, Miss., and the daughter of Wesley and Cornelia (Burt) Mellard. Four children have been born to this union—Alfred, Alice Walton, Nealey and Mellard, all of whom are at home. Mr. Jamison is the owner of one thousand seven hundred acres of land, four hundred and fifty acres of which are under cultivation, almost all of which he has opened and improved himself. On account of educational facilities Mr. Jamison keeps his children in Memphis, Tenn. His ancestors were of Irish descent and of an old Kentucky family on the father's side, while they were Scotch on the mother's side. He is a member of the Knights of Honor and his wife is a worthy member of the Methodist church.

W. G. Jaquess, clerk of the circuit and chancery court of Tunica county, Miss., was born in Jacksonville, Ill., October 26, 1849, the only son born to the marriage of J. F. Jaquess and Sarah J. Steel, the former a native of Kentucky or Indiana, and the latter of Pennsylvania. The paternal grandfather, Jonathan Jaquess, moved from Kentucky to Indiana and in the latter state followed the occupation of farming, accumulating a large amount of worldly goods and settling his children about him. He was a worthy member of the Methodist Episcopal church. The mother's people came of good old Quaker stock. J. F. Jaquess was brought up to a knowledge of farm life, but as his father was well-to-do and a believer in education, he was given better advantages than the average farmer's boy and graduated at Asbury university, Indiana, in both law and theology, after which he preached the gospel at Springfield for two years, one year in Paris, Ill., and from 1855 to 1861 was president of the Female college at Jacksonville, and the Male and Female college at Quincy. In 1861 he entered the Federal army as chaplain of the Sixth Illinois cavalry, but in June of the following year he was made a member of the Seventy-third Illinois infantry and was elected its colonel. In 1864 he went to Richmond, Va., and had an interview with Jefferson Davis in the interests of peace. He came to Mississippi in 1866, with the intention of making this state his home, and engaged in planting in Tunica county, where he soon gathered about him many warm friends, and by them was afterward elected to the office of clerk of the courts of the county, for the benefit of a disabled Confederate friend, and gave him the benefit of all the income of the office. His generosity and kindness of heart have always been among his chief characteristics, and notwithstanding the fact that he was of Northern birth and served in the Union army during the Civil war, all this was forgotten when he came South, for he thoroughly identified himself with the interests of his adopted state and county, and showed that he was a man of excellent qualities. Although he makes this county his home, he is now in England. He gave his son, W. G. Jaquess, the advantages of a good education, and for some time the latter was a student in Quincy college, but left this institution in 1862 and entered company H, Seventy-third Illinois regiment as drummer and served until the war closed. He then returned to college and in the summer of 1866 came South and at once began planting. In 1869 he was elected to the position of county assessor, and in 1871 was chosen treasurer of the same, serving one term of two years. Recognizing his sound judgment, his practical ability and his qualities of leadership his friends showed their appreciation of the same by electing him to the office of county sheriff in 1877, and in 1880 he was appointed deputy county clerk, of which office he had charge for four years. At the end of this time he was elected to the office of clerk, and has held the position by reëlection ever since. Although this county has an excellent reputation for the superior capability of her public officials, this enviable reputation is fully sustained by Mr. Jaquess. His office is a model of neatness and order, and in every detail is manifested the most perfect arrangement, showing the workings of an intelligent, well-directed mind. He is the beau ideal of a public servant—efficient, punctual, industrious, honest and uniformly courteous to all with whom he comes in contact. His plantation comprises nine hundred acres of land, of which three hundred acres are cleared and under cultivation. In 1871, Mr. Jaquess was married to Miss Mattie A. Nelson, of this county, a daughter of Dr. J. C. Nelson, but he was left a widower in 1888, his wife having borne him four children: three sons and one daughter. Mr. Jaquess has been a member of the Masonic fraternity for the past twenty years; is a member of Tunica lodge No. 257, of which he has been master for the past ten years. He also belongs to the Knights of Pythias, Delta lodge No. 62, and was its first chancellor commander. In personal appearance Mr. Jaquess is of medium stature, rather slender and of dark complexion, his hair, eyes and beard being black. He is quite distinguished looking, and his handsome eyes beam with intelligence and kindness. He has always been interested in secret organizations and in the Masonic order is a Knight Templar.

H. L. Jarnagin, who died January 20, 1886, was a Tennesseean by birth, and in the state of his birth he was reared to mature years and received his literary education. While still a resident of Tennessee he entered upon the study of law, and while in early manhood was admitted to the bar. In 1838 he came to Macon, Miss., and at once entered upon his legal practice, and so sound was his judgment, so superior his powers of oratory, and so thorough his knowledge of law, that he in time rose to eminence. He was a member of the state legislature from 1876 to 1878, and a member of the state senate from 1880 to 1884, during which periods he made an enviable record for himself. In 1858 he was a candidate for district judge, but was defeated by Judge James S. Hamm. He was a smooth, forcible and convincing speaker, and his words at once riveted the attention, inspired respect and convinced his hearers. He thoroughly understood every intricacy of law, and his rare powers of illustration made the most complicated subjects plain and clear to the most ordinary understanding. He was first married to Miss McCaskill, of Noxubee county, Miss., by whom he became the father of three sons and four daughters: Chesley was killed in the late war; Hampton died in Macon; Dr. Calvin is a resident of Atlanta, Ga.; Mrs. Barnes is a resident of Macon, and Mrs. Bogle is a resident of Chattanooga, Tenn. These are the surviving members of the family. Mr. Jarnagan's last marriage (July 29, 1869,) was to Mrs. A. L. Perkins, who is now a resident of Macon.

Anselm H. Jayne has been an active law practitioner in the courts of Hinds and adjoining counties since May 21, 1886, at which time he was admitted to the bar by the supreme court, of the state of Mississippi, and secured his first case the next day. He is careful and painstaking in all pleadings and court proceedings, and for clearness and accuracy of all legal instruments drawn by him, ranks high in his profession. The best interests of his clients are regarded by him as of the first importance, and the matter of compensation is never regarded by him as proper reason to advise litigation. Although a comparatively young practitioner, he is known as a conservative and prudent counselor, whose advice can be safely followed and whose promise will be performed. He was born in Rankin county, Miss., September 12, 1856, the third of six children born to William McAfee and Julia (Kennon) Jayne, who were born in Mississippi and Alabama, respectively, and the grandson of Anselm Helm and Elizabeth (McAfee) Jayne. The grandfather was born at East Setauket, Long Island, N. Y., but left home at the age of thirteen, and was at sea for a year or two. In 1818 he came to Mississippi, whither he had been preceded by two elder brothers, Samuel and Brewster, who had settled in what was then Lawrence county, and were among the earliest merchants at old Brookhaven and Monticello. After clerking for his brother Samuel for a year or two, he began merchandising for himself on Bowie creek, at Jaynesville (which was named in his honor), Covington county, and became very popular and successful. He died at the untimely age of thirty-five years, but is still spoken of as one of the most highly esteemed, well known and popular of those early pioneers. His death occurred about 1835. Two of his sons reached manhood and two daughters died in early childhood. His wife was one of a large family of sons and daughters, several of whom, especially Jesse, Joseph, Morgan, Madison and John McAfee held various county and state offices, became well known and left families. Madison became state auditor, was one of the most prominent men of Mississippi and was prominently spoken of for governor. William McAfee Jayne removed to Rankin county with his mother, who had again married after the death of Mr. Jayne, at which time he was about ten years of age. He was educated in the Centenary college of Jackson, La., from which he graduated, and upon reaching his majority engaged in planting, which occupation he followed for ten years. He then followed the calling of a teacher up to the opening of the war in 1861, soon after which he enlisted in the Confederate army, becoming quartermaster of the Twenty-second Mississippi regiment, with which he remained until the close of the war. He then returned home and resumed teaching and while following this calling died very suddenly in 1867. He was a man of most exemplary habits and morals and was an active member and worker, sometimes a preacher of the Methodist Episcopal church. He was a true Christian in every sense of the word and was highly honored. His widow, who survives him, is a member of the same church and is residing at Brandon. She is a daughter of Lewis Kennon, M. D., a distinguished Methodist minister of the Alabama conference. He died about 1840 while attending conference at Columbus,

Miss. He was a native of North Carolina and a descendant of the Kennon and Lewis families of Virginia. His wife was a Miss Martha Bush, a niece of William Few, a member from Georgia of the convention of 1787 which framed the constitution of the United States. The children born to William McAfee and Julia (Kennon) Jayne are as follows: Robert Kennon, who was born September 1, 1851, is in the real estate and insurance business in Jackson, and is secretary of the State Building & Loan association, of which he was one of the organizers; William McAfee, who was born January 25, 1854, and now resides in Holmes county, engaged in merchandising and planting; Anselm, in the law at Jackson, Miss.; Madison McAfee, born December 22, 1858, has been in the office of the first comptroller of the treasury since May, 1886; Julia, born April 30, 1861, became the wife of William Walker December 22, 1887, and by him is the mother of two children: Mary Walker, born January 3, 1889, and William Jayne Walker, born October 19, 1890. Her husband, William Walker, is on the editorial staff of the New Orleans papers, but now resides at Brandon, Miss., and Joseph Lee, born May 30, 1863, who entered the United States naval academy in 1878, and after serving three years at sea in the South Atlantic squadron on the Galena and Tennessee, was detailed to Johns Hopkins university at Baltimore to continue his studies in electricity, higher mathematics and chemistry. After spending three years there he spent eighteen months in California as general agent for the Sprague Electric Motor company, of New York. He was then ordered to join the United States ship Charleston, but was soon transferred to the ship Iroquois, and for the past eighteen months has been on the Pacific ocean on that vessel, on which he is an ensign. Anselm H. Jayne, the third member of this family, was born September 12, 1856, and was educated in the University of Mississippi. He afterward entered the United States naval academy on September 20, 1873, but resigned his position March 17, 1874, at the solicitation of two of his instructors at the place, and then entered the sophomore class at Harvard university in June, 1874, graduating in 1877. After teaching two years in the high school of Columbus, Ohio, he then came to Mississippi and taught two years at Jackson. Two years he was teaching in the University of Mississippi at Oxford, and during 1883–84 he was professor of mathematics at the Agricultural and Mechanical college at Starkville. He then taught for a time in Washington county, after which, in December, 1885, he came to Jackson to complete his preliminary law reading, which he did in the office of Nugent & McWillie, and has since been an active practitioner. He is a brilliant young lawyer, and has a large and constantly growing practice. The entire family are members of the Methodist Episcopal church.

Nathaniel Jefferies (deceased). A glance at the genealogy of the Jefferies family shows that the present members are descended from English ancestry, and that the first one of the family in America of whom they have any tangible information was Nathaniel Jefferies, a son of an Episcopalian minister of the same name, who served in the colonial army throughout the entire Revolutionary war, being promoted from the ranks of a private to a colonelcy. The will of this gentleman, which was executed February 17, 1797, is now in the possession of Mrs. Benjamin Humphreys, his great-granddaughter, and is couched in beautiful and fitting language. His son, James Jefferies, was born in Virginia, the greater portion of his life followed agricultural pursuits, giving much attention to the raising of fine stock, and by the exercise of that perseverance and determination which were among his chief characteristics, he amassed a handsome fortune, but spent his wealth freely in different benevolences and for the building up and improvement of his county and state. Wealth was to him a means and not an end, and the contents of his purse was free to the poor, but not indiscriminately so, for he coupled judgment with mercy and charity, and his wealth was

STATE FEMALE INDUSTRIAL INSTITUTE, COLUMBUS.

THE GOODSPEED PUBLISHING CO., CHI.

invested where it would do the most good. His wife, whose maiden name was Priscilla Shelby, was a daughter of Col. Evan Shelby, whose brother was for some time governor of Kentucky. To Mr. and Mrs. Jefferies the following family, in time, gathered about their hearthstone: Catherine (deceased) was the wife of William Prince (also deceased), who was a planter and a resident of Lake Washington, Miss.; Sarah (deceased) was married to Berry Prince, who was a well-to-do planter but is now deceased; Nathaniel comes next in order of birth; Letitia (deceased) was the wife of Joseph Davenport, who was a planter of Claiborne county, Miss., and is now dead; Evan (deceased) was married to Sarah Terry, and was a planter of this county, and Priscilla, the last of the family, died unmarried. Nathaniel Jefferies, whose name heads this biography, was born in Clarksville, Tenn., in 1802, and his first knowledge of books was acquired in the old log cabin schoolhouse of pioneer days. He possessed a fine and susceptible mind, and being fond of his books, notwithstanding the many drawbacks with which he had to contend he became a learned man, and throughout a well spent life was a stanch friend of educational institutions of all kinds. He aided in the purchase of a female academy at Port Gibson, presented it to the Methodist society, and was one of its substantial supporters ever after. He was an earnest member of the Methodist Episcopal church, and after his death upon the reading of his will it was found that he had made a large bequest to the church, which still continues, although he has been dead a number of years. He was married in Camden, S. C., in 1825, to Miss Catherine Watson, by whom he became the father of the following children: James, a resident of Jefferson county, is unmarried: Mary Scott, is a resident of Port Gibson and is the wife of Benjamin Humphreys; Priscilla (deceased), was the wife of Job Routh, who comes of a wealthy family of Louisiana, of noble birth; Catherine (deceased) was the wife of Daniel Humphreys, also deceased; Jane, the wife of Samuel Montgomery, resides in Texas; Sarah is a resident of Port Gibson and is the widow of Dr. C. E. Buck, who was killed; Eva is the wife of Charles Kennard of Port Gibson; Ellen is also a resident of that place and is the wife of Captain Owens, a Kentuckian by birth; and Edward, who was killed during the Civil war in the second battle of Manassas. In his political views Mr. Jefferies was a democrat and he and his wife are now sleeping their last sleep in the old family cemetery, "Scroggy," in Claiborne county, Miss.

Robert T. Jennings was born in Yorkville, S. C., September 12, 1815, and is the eldest of a family of ten children. His father, Edmond Jennings, was twice married—first to Isabella Beatty, and the second time to Lucy Birchett, natives of South and North Carolina respectively. Edmond Jennings was born in North Carolina. He was a physician by profession, and was devoted to his practice. He also had some mercantile interests. He was a son of John and Elizabeth (Lanier) Jennings, natives of Virginia. His father was one of the most prominent men in Anson county, N. C., and at the time of his death had been sheriff for twenty-one years. Edmond Jennings died December 2, 1863, aged seventy-two years. The Jennings family is of English ancestry, and is descended from Charles Jennings, who, with his brother, Humphrey Jennings, emigrated to America and settled in Virginia. History says they were the brothers of William Jennings, who died in England in 1798, leaving an estate valued at $90,000,000. Robert T. was reared in his native place, and received his education in the common schools. In 1836 he came to Yazoo county, and until the breaking out of the Civil war was engaged in mercantile pursuits. He was successful and had accumulated considerable wealth; this, of course, was lost through the ravages of war. In 1869 he went to New Orleans, and became purchasing agent for a large cotton factor. He remained there twenty-three years, and through some fortunate speculations retrieved his lost property.   He then returned to his home in Yazoo county, and located in Yazoo City, where he was loaning money until 1888.   In that year he began planting, and now owns sixteen hundred acres of land, six hundred of which are under cultivation.   When he went out into the world on his own account he had a capital of $130 dollars.   The first year he worked for his board and $30 in money.   He was patient, persevering, and strictly honest from his boyhood, and thus won the confidence of all with whom he had any dealings.   He has preserved this reputation with great fidelity throughout his career.   He has never been an aspirant for public honors, and so has lived a life of quiet retirement.   He is unmarried. He is a good conversationalist, of kind and gentle address, a good neighbor and stanch friend. He is a member of the Presbyterian church.

John F. Jenkins, another extensive planter and stockbreeder of Adams county, Miss., resides on Elgin plantation, seven miles south of Natchez, and was born on the same in 1846.   His father, John C. Jenkins, owes his nativity to Churchtown, Pa., born in 1810, and was educated at Dickinson college, Carlisle, Pa., and graduated in medicine at the University of Pennsylvania at Philadelphia.   He at once came to Wilkinson county, Miss., to assume the practice of his uncle, Dr. John F. Carmichael, who had lost his eyesight.   Dr. Carmichael was a surgeon in the Revolutionary war and held a commission from General Washington, of whom he was an intimate friend.   He was a native of the Keystone state, and after the Revolutionary war was made a major in the United States army.   He came with General Wilkinson to Mississippi territory and located in what is now Wilkinson county, where he passed the closing scenes of his life.   Dr. Jenkins remained with him until his death, and in 1839 he married Miss Annis Dunbar, settling on Elgin plantation, Adams county, the following year.   There his death occurred in 1855.   He left a large estate, principally his own accumulation.   After settling in Adams county he devoted his attention largely to horticulture, principally to gratify an increasing desire for that study and for pleasure.   He raised more or less of nearly all the fruit common to this latitude, and spared no pains or expense to beautify and complete his home.   By his thorough knowledge of the subject of horticulture and from the numerous able and instructive articles penned by him for some of the leading horticultural journals of the country, Mr. Jenkins became a close friend of Charles Downing and was made a life honorary member of the Pomological society of Philadelphia. He was a man of broad and extreme views, a regular attendant and a liberal supporter of the church, but not a communicant.   His father, Hon. Robert Jenkins, was born in Chester county, Pa., and there spent all his life as an extensive iron manufacturer, and as a farmer, being largely interested in the Windsor forge.   He was at one time a member of congress and was a man of more than ordinary ability and greatness.   He was a son of John Jenkins, who was of Welsh parents, and who lived and died in Lancaster county, Pa.   Mrs. Jenkins, the mother of John F., was born on the Forest plantation, adjoining the one on which our subject was born, and died in 1855, a few weeks prior to the death of her husband, both dying of yellow fever.   She was the daughter of Dr. William Dunbar and the granddaughter of the celebrated Sir William Dunbar.   Sir William, as he was known here, was a man of great intellect and took a decided interest in subjects of a scientific nature.   While at school at Glasgow, he made the acquaintance of the celebrated astronomer, Herschel.   He made the subject of astronomy a special study, commencing it in early life and continuing it after coming to the United States.   Through his wonderful knowledge as a scientist he became an intimate friend of Thomas Jefferson, under whose instructions and authority he explored the Ouachita river to its source and made many other valuable explorations in the Southwest, which aided largely in the development of that region.   Soon after his arrival in Mississippi he was chosen by Governor Gayoso as astronomical commissioner on the part of the Spanish to locate the line between Mississippi territory and Louisiana, and was afterward made chief justice of the court of quarter session in Mississippi. To Mr. and Mrs. John C. Jenkins were born four children: . Alice was educated in New York and New Orleans; John F. (subject), Mary D., wife of Lewis M. Johnson, of New York, and William Dunbar, a distinguished engineer and now chief engineer for the New Orleans & Northwestern railroad. He finished his education at the L'Ecole centrale, or central school at Paris, France. The eldest son, John F. Jenkins, received good primary training at home, and in 1862, when but sixteen years of age, he joined the Breckinridge guards and served Gen. John C. Breckinridge in the army of Tennessee as a private. He fought at Laverne and at Murfreesboro the two leading engagements, and remained in service until in May, 1863, when he was discharged. After the war he attended Washington and Lee's university, graduating from that institution in 1868, receiving several certificates of distinction delivered in person and signed by Gen. R. E. Lee, and he has since devoted his attention to his planting interest, one of the most extensive in Adams county. He owns four large plantations, viz.: Elgin and Beverly in Adams county, and Demarkation and Tarbert in Wilkinson county, four thousand acres in all. He also runs a successful plantation store in Wilkinson county and another large one in Adams county. He makes a specialty of breeding Guernsey cattle and is perhaps the only breeder of that stock in Mississippi. Although he inherited a large portion of his property he has acquired largely himself. He was married in 1872, to Miss Louisa Winchester, who was born and educated in Natchez, and who was the daughter of Judge Josiah and Margaret (Graham) Winchester. Judge Winchester was a native of Salem, Mass., and after acquiring a thorough collegiate education, studied law in Boston, in the office of Rufus Choate. While yet a young man he came to Natchez, where he had an uncle, George Winchester, a lawyer of that city, and one of the ablest jurists that ever sat on the bench of the supreme court of Mississippi. There young Winchester married and spent the remainder of his life, dying in 1888, greatly to the loss of the Mississippi bar. He had spent probably half a century in the practice of his profession and ranked with the ablest attorneys of the state. He was at one time probate judge. He was a man of great force of character, strong and vigorous mind, and unconquerable will. He was an able debater, a man of influence before a jury, and very popular with both bench and bar. He was a stanch Union man and made a master effort in its behalf. He wrote what was known as the appeal to the "Thinking Men of the South," a remarkably able document for the Union cause. It was printed in pamphlet form and circulated widely through the South. He was elected as unionist a delegate from Adams county to the secession convention which declared Mississippi out of the Union. His wife, who is still living, is a native of Adams county, and a daughter of Howell Sprague, native of New Jersey but who came to Natchez many years ago. Mr. Sprague was cashier of the old Agricultural bank, and a man of considerable note. To Mr. and Mrs. Jenkins have been born eight children, five sons and three daughters. Mrs. Jenkins holds membership in the Presbyterian church. Mr. Jenkins is a progressive man and spares no pain for the comfort and increasing knowledge of himself and family. He has a selected library and everything that makes one cheerful in spirit and buoyant in hopes.

John D. and William A. Jewell, well known planters of Washington county, Miss., were born in Hubbard, Ohio, June 11, 1833, and September 16, 1835, respectively, being the sons of Alexander M. and Rebecca C. (Love) Jewell, who were also natives of Ohio. In the early part of his life Alexander M. Jewell was engaged in farming and stockraising, but his latter years were devoted to the banking business, which received the greater part of his attention until his death in 1886. His parents, John and Jane (Miller) Jewell, were born in Pennsylvania, the mother's parents, Robert and Rebecca (Hutchison) Love, being also natives of the same state. The gentlemen whose names head this sketch are near relatives of Marshall Jewell, who was once governor of Connecticut, and afterward postmaster-general in President Grant's cabinet. He was chairman of the national executive committee of the republican party during the Garfield campaign. James Gray Jewell, who served on a foreign mission during the administration of President Grant, was a relative of these gentlemen also. The Jewell family were originally from England, and after becoming American citizens gave to this country some of its ablest statesmen, several of the family holding honorable positions of trust under the government. The Loves were a talented people, being especially skilled in the arts, some of whom became proficient musicians. John D. and William A. Jewell were reared in the state of their birth, and received their literary education in Washington college, Pennsylvania, the former of whom graduated in 1860. After being admitted to the bar, he practiced law in Ohio until 1862, when he entered the Union army, as private, in company A, One hundred and fifth Ohio regiment, and was soon promoted sergeant of ordnance in the regular army. After the bloody battle of Stone river he was promoted to first lieutenant in the regular army and assigned to duty as judge advocate on the staff of General Schofield, and was afterward promoted captain. He was in the engagements at Perryville, Stone river, Chickamauga, and was with General Grant through the battles of the Wilderness, Petersburg, and was at Fort Fisher when it was taken by Generals Ferry and Porter. He was also at the battle of Bentonville, and at the time of Lee's surrender was at Raleigh, N. C. After the close of the war he resigned his commission in the army, and in 1866, he and his brother William A. Jewell came to Hinds county, Miss., later settled in Issaquena county, and in 1870, came to Washington county, where they have since resided, being engaged in planting at Silver lake, where they own a valuable plantation and much other property. John D. Jewell was married in 1883 to Miss Josephine H. Barnes, of New York city, a daughter of Harrison and Dorothea A. (Carpenter) Barnes, who were born in New York, of English and French ancestry, respectively. Harrison Barnes was descended from Lord Barnes, who settled at Jamestown, Va. The Jewell brothers come of a religious stock, and although they have not identified themselves with any religious denomination, they are moral men and highly respected and esteemed. The elder served for one term as judge and has since been a member of the levee board, a part of the time serving as president of the same. William A. Jewell was for several years a member of the board of supervisors, a part of which time its presiding officer. They are most excellent and estimable gentlemen, and stand high as citizens of Mississippi. They are hospitable, kind and congenial and are charitably inclined toward the world in general. They have been members of the Presbyterian church, and only for want of church privileges have they failed to connect themselves with that denomination. They are shrewd and practical men of business and have prospered in each and all of their enterprises. Although they come of an old and honored family, members of which have attained considerable note in national affairs, they are not boastful of their blue blood, and although they have every right to be proud of their family connection, they believe that worth makes the man and that no matter how humble a man's position in life may be or how poor his clothing he's a "man for a' that." They are the third and fourth of seven children born to their parents, all of whom survive save one. Their mother, who is now eighty-four years of age, is a resident of Warren, Ohio, and in the enjoyment of good health.

Col. B. F. Johns, a well-known resident of Gloster, was born in the county in which he is now residing March 9, 1830, being a son of William L. Johns, a native of Georgia, who was born in 1802. The father of the latter was a Virginian, and was one of the pioneers of Georgia, in which state he died when his son, William L., was a child. When a child of seven years the latter came with some of his relatives to Amite county, and here he was reared to manhood and married Miss Rachel Courtney, a native of Amite county, born in 1807. Her father, John Courtney, was one of the early residents here. Mr. Johns began tilling the soil on a farm on Beaver creek in the south part of the county, where he accumulated a good property. He was a leading member of the Baptist church for forty years, was a supporter of all good works, and his death, which occurred in 1882, was regretted by all. His widow survived him about one year. Col. B. F. Johns is one of a family of three sons and three daughters that grew to mature years, of which he is the eldest. One sister is now deceased. He is the only resident of Amite county, and as he was born and grew to manhood here he is well known by the citizens, and naught has ever been said derogatory to his character; in fact, many words have been said to his praise. After attending the common schools of Amite county for some time, he entered the Western military institute of Kentucky, which he attended two years, receiving a fair English education. He began life for himself as a school teacher, and after devoting two years to this occupation he began reading law, and in 1855 was licensed to practice. He opened an office at Liberty, but in 1887 located at Gloster. In 1866 he was elected to the office of probate judge, in which position he displayed sound judgment and much judicial fairness. In 1875 his numerous friends elected him to the legislature of Mississippi, and during the sitting of 1876 and 1877 displayed legislative ability of a high order. In 1880 he was reëlected to this position, and was chosen speaker of the house. Since that time he has continued his practice of law, and has served as mayor of Gloster and has also held other minor positions. He was married on the 16th of December, 1852, to Miss Mildred Luckett, a native of Kentucky, where she was reared and educated, a daughter of David Luckett, a member of an old Kentucky family, originally from Virginia. To Colonel and Mrs. Johns four children have been born: Etta, wife of Rev. A. P. Schofield, a minister of the Baptist church at Canton, Miss.; William D., a merchant of Gloster; Ellen, and Mattie, wife of B. H. Day, of Gloster. In 1861 Colonel Johns enlisted in the Confederate army as captain of company C in the Seventh Mississippi infantry, and was in time promoted to the rank of lieutenant-colonel. He served until the close of the hostilities, being in the army of Tennessee and taking an active part in the battles of Shiloh, Murfreesboro, Chickamauga, Chattanooga or Missionary Ridge, all the engagements of the Georgia campaign, Jonesboro, Franklin, Nashville and hundreds of skirmishes. He was paroled at Liberty and returned to his home once more to take up the practice of law, which he has followed with most satisfactory results up to the present time. Mrs. Johns is a worthy member of the Baptist church, and Colonel Johns has long been a member of the Masonic fraternity, in which he has attained to the Council degree, and has served as high priest and master of the Blue lodge.

The mercantile interests of Claiborne county, Miss., have been ably represented for many years past by Mr. Johnson, whose stock of goods has always been a varied, large and choice one. Mr. Johnson was born in New York July 24, 1817, to John Johnson, a native of the same state, who was born in the latter part of 1780 to Obediah Johnson, of Massachusetts. The first settlement of the family in America was made by two brothers, who came from England and settled in the vicinity of Jamestown, Va., Obediah being a descendant of one of these brothers. Upon attaining manhood he moved to western New York, where he became the owner of a large tract of land, a considerable portion of which still remains in possession of the family. He carried on farming on a large scale, and lived to be about seventy years of age. He was a man of considerable education, and in his business ventures was quite successful, accumulating a large amount of worldly goods. His wife, Lois Johnson, was born in Massachusetts also, grew to womanhood and married there, living to a ripe old age, at the time of her death being over eighty years of age. She was well educated, and she and her husband were members of the Methodist Episcopal church. To them a family of twelve children were born, all of whom lived to be grown. Several of the sons became professional men—physicians and ministers of the gospel. John Johnson was their fifth son, and was reared and educated in York state, being an attendant of the common and high schools. After his marriage in 1806 to Miss Clarrissa Palmeter, a native of Wayne county, N. Y., he removed to Genesee county, where he became an extensive farmer. He was murdered somewhere near Lockport, N. Y., on the Erie canal, about 1838, it was supposed for his money, for he was known to be possessed of considerable wealth. He started from his home for Lockport with a load of potash, and nothing was learned of him for several months, when his body was found in a field. He was an earnest member and worker in the Baptist church, was well liked and highly respected, and was not known to have an enemy. He was a democrat in politics, and took a deep interest in schools and the education of the young. His widow resided on the home place for some time after his death, when she moved to Illinois, where she made her home until her death, which occurred in Dupage county in 1866, she at that time residing with her son. She was a most faithful wife and mother, was an earnest member of the Baptist church, a true Christian and was deeply honored and loved by all her family, as well as her friends. She bore her husband ten children, most of whom lived to be grown, the subject of this sketch being the only one now living: Horace was engaged in flour milling and farming, and died in Michigan; Calvin P. became a very wealthy farmer of Illinois, and died in Dupage county a short time after his mother, who made her home with him; Charles comes next in order of birth; William C. B. S., who died in Wisconsin, held some office on board a gunboat that plied on the Mississippi river, being in the Union army during the Civil war; Orpha L. married a Mr. Adams and settled in Michigan, where she died; Caroline J. married a man by the name of Seaton, and after his death, which occurred in Michigan, she, in 1859, came to Grand Gulf, Miss., where she died the same year; Almeida married and settled in Utah, where she died in 1888; Melvina died after reaching womanhood, but was unmarried; and the other two died in their youth. At the age of sixteen years Charles Johnson began doing for himself in Wayne county, N. Y., and for one year was engaged in carrying the United States mail. He then became a wheelsman or steersman on board steamers which plied from Lake Erie to the city of Chicago. In 1835 he went to Texas and served in an independent company of scouts from New Orleans, which city he had reached by a stage route through an almost uninhabited prairie to the Illinois river and the Father of Waters from Chicago. Upon his return from Texas he went to Cincinnati, O., and engaged as a clerk for Stubbs & Andrews, but in 1837 he took charge of two flatboats from Cincinnati to New Orleans, and after several trips was made captain of the boats, which position he held for several years. While making a trip Mr. Johnson met with a thrilling experience. While going up the river on the boat McFarland and when about fifty miles above Helena, Ark., his vessel was struck in the side by the Danube, which carried away her kitchen and went almost through the boat. When the accident occurred Mr. Johnson was in his cabin, it being about one o'clock at night. He felt the shock and heard the water rushing into his room, but before he could get out the room was full.   He made his way to the door, feeling his way to the open space back of the wheelhouse, upon reaching which he could hold his breath no longer, let go his hold, and rose to the top of the water.   He was then more than twenty feet from the boat, the deck of which had broken loose and was floating.   On this he took refuge, and he and one other of his crew of sixteen were picked up by the Danube and taken to Helena. Several members of his crew lost their lives, and a large amount of sugar, molasses and boat tackle belonging to him was also lost.   From Helena Mr. Johnson returned to Cincinnati, but continued to remain on the river until the fall of 1847, when he located at Grand Gulf, Miss., where he commenced merchandising, a business which he still successfully continues.   At that time Grand Gulf was a town of about three thousand inhabitants and was in a very flourishing condition, more business being done here than in any other town in the state.   From that time until the opening of the war he continued to do a thriving business.

On the first day of May, 1862, the Federals shelled the town from the gunboats on the Mississippi river, five hundred yards distant, tearing many of the buildings in pieces while the citizens occupied them.   Two large shells (11-inch) passed through the dwelling, and several through Mr. Johnson's store.   The Federals then landed in force and carried away everything of value in the town.   Two months later they landed again and burned Mr. Johnson's house and store, as well as every other house, both large and small, and everything else that would burn, leaving no streets or bounds by which property-owners could locate their lots.   However, it was proven that there was one man among the Federals who did not wish it to be understood that the organization to which he belonged were destroyers of holy places.   He posted on the Methodist Episcopal church fence, after or during the fire, a notice, which Mr. Johnson now has, to the effect that the Fourth Wisconsin regiment did not burn the church.   In speaking of this incident Mr. Johnson says: "May God bless him in this world and in the world to come."   Even after the war Mr. Johnson's establishment was the most complete and prosperous in the place, his invoice at times reaching $100,000. He held the position of assessor from 1852 to 1866, and has, for many years, been justice of the peace.   At the present time there is only one man living in this section that was here when Mr. Johnson came—a Mr. J. W. Cox.   Mr. Johnson was married in Ohio, December 13, 1841, to Miss Elizabeth Stoddard (she spells the name Stuttard), who was born in Ohio in 1825 to Thomas and Ann Stoddard, natives of England and Ohio respectively, the latter of whom lived to be quite aged.   She bore her husband three children, Mrs. Johnson being their second child.   Mary and William, the other members of the family, reside in Ohio, and both are wealthy.   To Mr. and Mrs. Johnson five children have been born: Almedia M. (Waterous) is a resident of St. Louis, Mo.; Caroline J. (Seaton) is a widow, and lives with her parents; Charles E. is engaged in planting, and Clara is the wife of Alfred Faulk, and is a resident of Grand Gulf.   William C. was a resident of Grand Gulf, and at his death left a widow and four children.   Mr. Johnson gave his children good educational advantages, Charles E. being educated in Alabama and the rest in Port Gibson.   Mr. and Mrs. Johnson are members of the Methodist Episcopal church, and in this church Mr. Johnson is a class leader, steward, and Sunday-school superintendent.   He has taken an active part in Sunday-school work for the last thirty-five years, the most of which time he has been superintendent.   He is a member of the A. F. & A. M., and for several years was master of his lodge, while a resident of Grand Gulf.   It was one of the oldest in the state, being organized about 1819.   Besides merchandizing Mr. Johnson also manages a plantation near Grand Gulf, and during the palmy days of this place he held numerous official positions of honor and trust, being a member of the board of selectmen, with other offices. His children are nearly all earnest church workers, Charles E. being a member of the Presbyterian church, and the others Methodists.

Rev. Clayburn F. Johnson, Fort Stephens, Miss., a well-known citizen of Kemper county, Miss., was born in Iredell county, N. C., May 23, 1836, and is a son of Robert and Frances (Finch) Johnson. Robert Johnson was born in Nash county, N. C., and was reared, married and died there. He brought up a family of eleven children, ten of whom reared families. He was a son of Andrew Johnson, who was a prominent planter of his county. He died in 1850. His wife was born in Nash county, N. C., and was a daughter of Clayburn Finch, one of the wealthiest planters and largest slaveowners of his county; he died in North Carolina in 1840, and the mother of our subject passed away in 1855. Both the father and mother were members of the Missionary Baptist church. Their children were named as follows: Samuel, Caswell, Thomas, Williamson, Martha, Robert, Andrew, Simon P., William W., Noah, Clayburn F., and Frances. Clayburn F. spent his early life in North Carolina, and there received his education. In February, 1860, he emigrated to Mississippi, where he was employed in agriculture. In June, 1862, he enlisted in the cause of the South, joining company K, 43d Mississippi volunteer infantry. He was in the siege of Vicksburg, where he was captured, at Iuka, and in many lesser engagements. In July, 1863, he was honorably discharged, when he returned to his home. He was married January 1, 1862, to Sarah A. Jackson, who was born in North Carolina in 1837. Her parents, Needham and Frances (Bass) Jackson, were also natives of North Carolina, and removed to Mississippi when she was a young child. Her father died in Kemper county in 1880, and her mother is still living at the age of eighty years. Mr. and Mrs. Johnson are the parents of four children: Bunyan W., Mary E., who married I. H. Kinerd, and is the mother of two children, Anna and Spurgeon; Sidney O., and Clayburn M. Mr. Johnson entered the ministry in 1880, but was not ordained until 1882; he is now a local minister of the Freewill Baptist church, and is state organizer of Mississippi. He owns a large tract of land, comprising about eight hundred and forty acres, a large portion of which is under cultivation. In 1880 he made some investments in the mercantile trade and has been very successful. Since the war he has succeeded in accumulating some valuable property, and is one of the most enterprising of Kemper county's citizens. Politically he affiliates with the republican party. He is a man of pronounced opinions, firm in his convictions of right and wrong, and is well worthy of the esteem in which he is held.

Claude M. Johnson, chancery clerk, Greenville, Miss. Mr. Johnson's paternal grandfather, Henry Johnson, was originally from the Blue Grass state, but came to Mississippi and settled on Lake Washington, Washington county, about 1830. He entered the land and was the original settler on the lake, clearing up a large estate and becoming one of the most extensive planters of his time. His wife's maiden name was Betsey Flournoy, of Kentucky also. The good old fathers and mothers of early times were educated, not as books count perhaps, but educated in industry, educated in honesty, educated in integrity, educated in enterprise, educated in good morals, educated in all that makes noble men and noble women. Their memory is revered and their early struggles appreciated. They have given their descendants a goodly heritage, a land veritably flowing with milk and honey; and better still, sons and daughters possessed of attributes to make good noble citizens. To Mr. and Mrs. Johnson were born ten children, all of whom were born in Lexington, Ky., Robert A., C. M., Maggie, Emily, Louisa, H. J. (now resident of Washington county), Charles F., Ben, Matthew F. (now residing in Washington county), and Mary Bell (wife of A. B.

Carson of Greenville). Henry Johnson himself was one of the twelve or more children born to Robin Johnson, a native of Virginia, whose brother, Col. Richard M. Johnson, was supposed to have killed the Indian chief Tecumseh, in the battle of the Thames. The Colonel later became vice president of the United States. Henry Johnson died about 1862 on his plantation. Although very active in politics he never held any office; was an earnest supporter of Breckinridge for congress in the celebrated Ashland district of Kentucky in one campaign, and contributed $20,000 for campaign fund. His children were all mainly educated in Lexington, Ky,, and H. J. Johnson (father of subject), was a native of that state. The latter was married about 1850, to Miss Sallie Graddy, also a native of the Blue Grass state, and began life as a planter in Washington county, Miss. In 1858 he went to Arkansas, and there his wife died in 1862, leaving five children, Claude M. being among the number and second in order of birth. These children were taken to Kentucky after the death of their mother and remained with their grandparents until 1868. The year previous to this the father was married to Miss Lutie Bartlett, a native of Kentucky, who bore him four children. During the late war Mr. Johnson served as captain on a general's staff. He lost severely during the war and at one time burned four hundred bales of his cotton. Returning to Mississippi when peace was declared, he carried on agricultural pursuits and a few years later bought the Aldoma plantation, which was on the river and one of the finest places in the county. Here he has since resided, surrounded by all the comforts of life and esteemed and respected by all. Claude M. Johnson was born on the Burns' plantation at the head of Lake Washington, in Washington county, Miss., in 1853, and attended school in Kentucky from 1868 until 1871, when he came to Mississippi. He engaged in merchandising at Leota, until 1878, when he was elected chancery clerk of Washington county, being reëlected to that position in 1879, 1883 and 1887, and is now the nominee for the fifth term. He was married in 1880 to Miss Alice C. Hunt, daughter of William and Prue V. Hunt (see sketch of W. E. Hunt), and this union has been blessed by the birth of three children, Katie S., H. J. and Julia M. Mrs. Johnson · is a member of the Methodist Episcopal church. Mr. Johnson is a member of the Legion of Honor and the Elks, of Greenville. He is a pleasant and genial gentleman, most admirably fitted to perform the functions of his office, for he has ever had the interests of Washington county at heart, and is an able and efficient official. He is a member of one of the oldest and most important families in this county.

Daniel S. Johnson, planter, was born in Union district of the Palmetto state in 1835, a son of James and Elizabeth (Sartor) Johnson, they being also natives of that state. James Johnson had very limited opportunities for acquiring an education, but by persevering efforts he managed to acquire a practical English education. Throughout his entire life he followed the calling of a planter, to which he had been reared, and became possessed of a competency. His union resulted in the birth of five sons and four daughters: T. Green, E. P. and Daniel S., living, and Ann, John P., James D., Elizabeth S., wife of T. D. Hamilton, Mary D., and R. T., who was killed in a skirmish after the battle of Seven Pines, are deceased. Daniel S. Johnson was reared in the district in which he was born, and although his advantages, like his father's, were limited, he has become a well-informed man and is noted for his sound, practical and shrewd views on all matters of public interest. At the age of twenty-one years he began life for himself as a planter, but in 1856 decided that Mississippi offered better advantages to a young man than the East, and accordingly came here in that year with the intention of locating permanently. His efforts as a tiller of the soil have been attended with success, and he is now the owner of fifteen hundred acres of land, of which he cultivates about three hundred acres. His principal crops are cotton and

corn, but he also raises oats and peas.   He is interested to some extent in the raising of
stock, selling quite a large number of cattle, colts and sheep annually.   In 1860 Mr. Johnson was married to Miss Elizabeth C. Hamilton, of South Carolina, who died only a short
time after her marriage.   In 1861 Mr. Johnson enlisted in the Confederate army, becoming
a member of Captain Hill's company, but the following year was placed in the quartermaster's department, where he remained actively engaged until 1863.   From that time until
the close of the war he was in Captain Smith's company, Duff's regiment of Mississippi
cavalry.   During his service he was in the battles of Harrisburg, Selma and Plantersville,
about twenty miles from where he was taken prisoner and conveyed to Selma and kept in a
stockade, but made his escape while on the march from that place to Columbus, Ga.   While
on his way to rejoin his command the war terminated by Lee's surrender.   Mr. Johnson was
elected a member of the board of supervisors in 1875, and so admirably did he fill this position that he was reëlected for five succeeding terms.   In 1890 he was a delegate to the constitutional convention.   He is a member of Houston lodge of the A. F. & A. M., and is
a Royal Arch mason in the lodge of Houlka.   In 1869 Miss C. L. Tucker, a native of
Union district, S. C., where she was born in 1845, became his wife and the mother of his
six children: Thompson H., Bettie, John P., Daniel S., Jr., Margaret A. and George T.
The mother of these children died in 1889, a worthy and consistent member of the Methodist church at the time of her death.   Her parents were George B. and Nancy Tucker, of
South Carolina.   Mr. Johnson is a steward in the Methodist Episcopal church, is a class
leader, and is superintendent of Sunday-school at Wesley chapel.   He is a whole-souled,
genial and agreeable gentleman, and his numerous fine qualities and traits of character have
won him many warm friends.

    Henry Johnson (deceased) was born in Georgetown, Ky., in 1793, was well educated for
his time and day, and emigrated to Mississippi in 1825 with Junius R. Ward, Edward C.
Johnson (both his nephews) and Samuel G. Worthington.   They came on a keelboat,
brought their negroes, and landed at Worthington point, where they remained but a short
time.   They then moved to Lake Washington, seven miles below their place of landing, and
bought out the tomahawk improvements of Bunch, a robber and a member of Mason's bandits.
In 1827 they bought the land at the land sales at Canton and Mr. Johnson soon acquired possession of about three thousand acres.   He made many improvements, cleared about one
thousand five hundred acres and named the place Chatham, after Lord Chatham, of whom
he was a great admirer.   During the war of 1812 he was engaged as pilot and commander
of a keelboat, bringing provisions to Jackson's army at New Orleans.   This was his first
trip South.   He was the youngest of eleven sons, one of whom, Richard M. Johnson, was
colonel during the War of 1812, and commanded Kentucky volunteer cavalry.   He was
several times a member of congress as representative and senator, and was vice president
of the United States.   He was the author of the law abolishing persecution for religious
belief and made the first speech in favor of pensioning widows and soldiers of the War of
1812.   He was also the author of the Sunday mail law, and author of the bill known as the
Salary Grab.   In 1835 he made a speech before his constituents which is credited to
Henry Clay.   He bought an estate on Lake Washington, made his permanent home there
and passed the last years of his life in superintending an Indian school, secured through
congress and located at Georgetown.   He was cotemporary with Henry Clay.   His death
occurred in 1845 or '46.   Another brother of Henry Johnson settled in Arkansas, became
supreme judge, then chief justice, and his son, Robert W., was United States senator for
thirty years.   Still another brother, Joel, settled in Chicot county, and was a prominent

planter there for many years, and another one, Gen. William Johnson, was a soldier in the Indian wars, and passed his entire days in Kentucky. Henry Johnson died on his plantation in 1862 or '63. He was always active in politics, but would never accept office. His wife was formerly Betsy Flournoy, of a prominent family of that name. She died in 1880. Their family consisted of eleven children, who are named in the order of their births as follows: Robert A. owned property on the lake and was judge of the county court (his death occurred in 1887); Claud M. moved to Louisiana and owned a cotton plantation in that state (he died in 1862); Margaret A. became the wife of James Erwin, and after his death wedded Dr. C. W. Dudley (she died in 1862); Emily M. married Frank Tifford and afterward William T. Bartley (she is still living at Louisville, Ky.); Charles F. resides at Louisville, Ky.; Henry D. now resides at Allomar plantation near the river; Elizabeth died about 1858; Louisa was the wife of William R. Elly, whose father, Harry Elly, was one of the pioneers of this section, locating here about 1826 (she afterward married Dr. C. W. Dudley, the widower of her sister, and now resides at Jonestown, Pa.); Ben settled near home and died in 1870; Matthew F. (subject); and Mary Belle, now Mrs. A. B. Carson, was formerly the widow of Gen. T. Blackburn. Matthew Flournoy Johnson now resides on the old place settled by his father. He was born in Kentucky in 1839, educated at Bardstown and at St. Louis university, and in 1861, at the age of twenty-one years, he raised company A, Fourth Louisiana cavalry, and operated on the river in that state for two years. In 1863 he recruited the Fourth Louisiana or Mount Neal cavalry regiment, and became lieutenant-colonel, operating in the trans-Mississippi department under General Smith. He was in the battles of Banks' raid up Red river, then through Arkansas, and was stationed in north Louisiana at Monroe until the surrender. In 1864 he captured Judge Dent in Louisiana. Previous to the war, in 1860, he was married to Narcise Kune, a daughter of Dr. Alexander Kune, who was a native of Kentucky. Her grandfather, Judge O. J. Morgan, was the largest cotton planter in Louisiana and her father was also a very extensive planter. After the war Colonel Johnson bought his present property from the rest of the heirs, and has since resided there. He is the owner of two thousand five hundred acres, with one thousand eight hundred acres under cultivation, and this is one of the oldest and finest places on the lake. He was one of the trustees and promoters of the railroad built in 1885 and has always been a most prominent citizen. His union was blessed by the birth of five children, three now living: Harry K. in business in Greenville, was educated at Sewanee; Ben graduated at Sewanee in 1881, entered West Point in 1885, and graduated in 1889, being the sixteenth in a class of forty-nine; Matt. F., Jr. (died at the age of four years), and Willie A., a daughter, is now attending school at New Orleans, and one died unnamed. The entire family hold membership in the Episcopal church. Mr. Johnson's fine old place on Lake Washington commands a magnificent view and on the lawn are magnolia and pecan trees planted by his father. The Colonel is most gentlemanly and dignified in bearing and his estimable wife has true artistic taste and ability. The village of Chatham is on his place and the first store was started in 1875. They had a postoffice soon after and now there are four stores, all owned by Colonel Johnson, making quite a village.

George G. Johnson, a planter of the county of Washington, Miss., was born in Woodford county, Ky., June 8, 1854, being the third of six children born to Henry J. and Sally (Graddy) Johnson, both of Kentucky. The father came to Mississippi while a mere boy, and has since made it his home, with the exception of about ten years spent in Arkansas, during a part of which time he was in the Confederate army, being captain of his company (for further particulars see sketch of C. M. Johnson and Matt. F. Johnson). George G.

Johnson was reared in Mississippi, and began life for himself by hiring out to a planter, with whom he remained for one year.   At the end of this time he took the money he had saved, went to Kentucky and entered the public schools of Woodford county, where he remained for two years.   At the end of that time he returned to Mississippi and hired out to his uncle, Matt. F. Johnson, as clerk on a flatboat of Lake Washington, and this position held for eighteen months, after which he became manager of the plantation owned by Mrs. George Blackburn (now Mrs. A. B. Carson), with whom he remained for two years.   In 1876 he and his brother, C. M. Johnson, formed a copartnership, and with their gross savings entered into a mercantile enterprise at Leota, but in 1878 George G. withdrew and was soon after married to Miss Julia H. Morgan, daughter of Oliver T. and Julia (Morgan) Morgan, natives of Louisiana.   He was left a widower in 1888 with two children to care for: Narcise K. and Oliver M., both of whom reside with their father.   In 1891 his second marriage took place, Miss Mary Liddell, daughter of Gen. St. John Richardson and Mary (Roper) Liddell, of Louisiana, becoming his wife.   As the war swept away all the property belonging to Mr. Johnson's father, he and his brothers were left penniless and had to commence life on their own responsibility, with no means whatever.   After his marriage he followed planting in Louisiana for two years; then he purchased the place he now owns, Linden, on Lake Washington.   He has eighteen hundred acres of land in Louisiana, has twenty-five hundred acres in Mississippi, and has the unbounded satisfaction of knowing that his present possessions are the result of his own honest toil, persistent effort and economy.   He has one of the most beautiful homes in the Yazoo delta, and his residence, which is commodious and substantial, is situated on a terraced and well-kept lawn, and although well back from the shore, it commands a lovely view of Lake Washington on the east.   Mr. Johnson is a true gentleman in every sense of the word, is an excellent and entertaining conversationalist, and is a man who takes great pride in the beauty of his home, and is seen at his very best in his own family circle.   He fully deserves the position he now occupies, for, notwithstanding the fact that he was thrown on his own resources at an early age, he has been a loyal and attached son and brother to his father and his younger brothers and sisters, and has never willfully blotted the good old family name.   He has five brothers and three sisters living, all of whom are residents of Mississippi, with the exception of one sister, who is the wife of Peyton F. Kinkead, a son of Judge Kinkead, of Louisville, Ky., in which city she now resides.

Harvey F. Johnson (deceased) was born in Henderson county, N. C., January 7, 1831. His father, John Johnson, came of good Revolutionary stock, combining the rugged virtues of the mountaineer with the softer characteristics and refinement of lower altitudes.   Frank, honorable, positive in opinion, and of rare judgment in affairs, he was the trusted counselor of his neighborhood, a good steward and useful citizen.   His mother was one of those rare spirits who carry the sweet charities of religion and the joys of the great salvation into all the business of daily life.   To the son, who was the youngest of a large family, the characteristics of both parents descended as a rich heritage, the strong good sense of the father and the tender heart of the mother.   The early training of young Johnson may be inferred from what has been said of his parents.   At about twelve years of age he was sent to Asheville, to the academy of Erastus Rowley, a noted teacher in that day, by whom he was prepared for Emory and Henry college.   In 1848, when within a few months of graduation, he was compelled to abandon his college course by an affection of the eyes, which threatened a permanent loss of sight.   The next year, following the tide of emigration which brought from his native state to Mississippi a goodly number of our distinguished citizens, he located first at Brandon and afterward at Raleigh, where, at the age of nineteen, he was licensed to practice law. At this place, also, he was happily married to Miss Margaret Bates, who survives him. In 1854 he was a candidate for the office of district or state's attorney, and was elected by a handsome majority. In 1855 he was chosen to represent his county in the lower house of the state legislature. Under the ministry of Rev. James R. Thomas, at Westville, he was profoundly converted to God, and, while residing at Monticello and engaged in the practice of his profession, received license to preach. Admitted to the Mississippi conference in 1859, he was appointed first to Fayette circuit. The spirit and circumstances in which he entered upon this new life are indicated by the following extract from a letter written by him at this time to a brother in North Carolina: "I quit a large practice and cut off all hope of accumulating a fortune, and yet if I know my heart, I have no regret on these accounts—I have no sacrifices to make; it is all gain, eternal gain."

In 1862, while stationed at Raymond, he went out with a Mississippi regiment as chaplain, but returned the next year to the regular work, in which he remained until the close of the war, when, without solicitation, he was almost unanimously elected to the state legislature from Smith county. At the conference of 1865 he was appointed to the presiding eldership of Jackson district, and afterward to Madison college, and in April, 1867, was elected president of Whitworth college, located at Brookhaven. This institution was founded in 1859, mainly by the liberality of Rev. M. J. Whitworth, a local Methodist preacher of the neighborhood. The original frame building had seen rough usage during the war, as a soldier hospital, and was at this time not only greatly in need of repair, but incumbered with a debt of nearly $3,000. For the payment of this debt the president became personally responsible, a twenty-years' lease of the property being granted him by the board of trustees as a basis of negotiation with the creditors. The history of the school under Dr. Johnson's management has been termed phenomenal. Beginning with thirty boarders, the number increased the following year to eighty-seven, and subsequently reached two hundred and one, besides a large patronage from the town. To provide accommodations for these growing numbers, the old chapel, now called Calisthenic hall, and a building for the art and music department of the school were erected in 1868, at a personal charge to the president of over $8,000. At this point Dr. Johnson, had he been so disposed, might have retired with a competency, besides returning to the church a property largely increased by his use. But he had a higher object in view—the founding for the church of an institution of high grade for female education, and on an enduring basis. Having acquired by purchase the lots in front of the old property, he began, August, 1878, during the epidemic, the erection of the new dormitory, Margaret hall, so named by the trustees in honor of Mrs. Johnson, the wife of the president, to whose motherly care of the girls so much of her husband's large success was due. This building, worth fully $15,000, he transferred, without incumbrance, in 1879 to the Mississippi annual conference, at the same time surrendering his lease, which had yet eight years to run. Visitors to Brookhaven often remarked upon the good order of the commencement audiences. There was no whistling of small boys, no talking during exercises, and no boisterous conduct on the campus. Such order was not obtained without incessant watchfulness and occasional offense to the thoughtless, but it was maintained. On one occasion during a concert at the college some young men seated near the front began to amuse themselves by staring at the performers through an opera-glass. Having given them a warning, which had no effect, Dr. Johnson promptly stopped the exercises, walked to the edge of the rostrum, and pointing straight at the chief offender, said, "I think I can throw that man out of the window near him, and if he does not put his glass down, I will certainly proceed to do so.'' There was a moment's pause, but a glance at the determined attitude and well-knit form of the speaker showed that it might be dangerous to refuse, and the eyeglass disappeared. At another time we missed him for a few minutes from the rostrum. His absence was hardly remarked, and there was nothing unusual in his appearance when he returned, so that many present were surprised to learn upon the street a few days afterward that in that short interval he had quelled a disturbance upon the campus, in which pistols were drawn upon him, and sent several young fellows through the college gate as if driven by a catapult. Such scenes were as distasteful to him as they could be to others, but the reputation of being ready for an encounter if necessary, doubtless saved him many of the annoyances incident to the presidency of a female college. Another difficult circumstance, and one which can be fully appreciated only by those preachers who have been truly called from the itinerant field to the leadership of schools, consisted in the anomalous relation which he sustained to the conference and the local church. The relation is always more delicate when the college officer is at the same time a popular preacher. Being strictly neither minister nor layman, and yet constrained at times to act as both, he is liable in either character to be misunderstood. For a number of years Dr. Johnson acted as steward of the church, and at one time collected and disbursed all the income of the station. It need hardly be said that the pastor's salary for that period was promptly paid every month. Circumstances were such as to render his relation peculiarly delicate during the last year of his life, yet it may one day be told to the honor of himself and the Brookhaven pastor of that year, that their relations were never more kind and cordial. The prayer that he offered at the conclusion of a sermon preached by Bishop Galloway, upon his return from the general conference of 1886, was probably the tenderest ever uttered in that church.

The most cursory view of Dr. Johnson's life must regard him in the three characters of lawyer, preacher and teacher. Of the first it is sufficient to say he won high praise from those distinguished men with whom his profession brought him in contact. "His forte," says Judge Chrisman, who knew him well at that time, " was in the analysis of testimony;" he had unusual facility in extracting the truth from the fragmentary or conflicting statements of witnesses. His cases were always thoroughly studied and presented with signal force and clearness. In appeal or denunciation he often rose to eloquence. Of his success in practice enough has been said. As a preacher, he took rank from the first with the leading men of the conference. No interest of a charge ever suffered under his care. It was his ambition, he once said, "to be loyal to every enterprise of the church." In preaching and in pastoral work, his grand object was fruit. Religion in the home and in business life were frequent themes of exhortation. '' What do you propose to do, my brother?'' was a question which he pressed home with great frequency and power. "I love to hear Johnson preach," said one who often attended upon his ministry, "because he makes me ashamed of my half-hearted religion, and I want to be a better man.'' His sudden conversion from a somewhat wild and godless life, his subsequent call to preach, and the manly promptness and thoroughness with which he surrendered a lucrative law practice for the ministry, made his preaching peculiarly effective in the region in which he had spent his younger manhood. Upon the companions of his young attorneyship his preaching sometimes had a startling effect. '' Prove that, Johnson,'' said one of these excitedly in the midst of service one day. And the preacher proved the statement in the Pauline way, by giving his own experience. Though well endowed by nature for oratorical display, having a voice of unusual purity and compass, a commanding presence, perfect self-possession and a remarkable quickness of adaptation to the varying moods of an audience, he preferred to preach the gospel in simplicity with a view to its effect upon the life.   His experience as a lawyer had taught him patience with details and service in the school soon gave him the grace of reputation.   His power as a preacher may be summarized in the statement that people believe his heart was in his preaching, and that his life was behind it.   He excelled in exhortations; he could reprove without scolding, so that while persons might go away aggrieved or angry, they would come again the next time he preached.   In speech and manner Dr. Johnson was a model in the pulpit.   His English was pure, his utterance distinct and his pronunciation unusually correct.   He was a good reader of Scripture, and this arose from the fact that he never attempted to "render" the lesson or the hymn.   He read it distinctly, reverently, and as a part of the worship of the sanctuary.   He was gifted in prayer; knowing well the language of Zion, he used it freely, humbly, and with a sense of the divine presence; following in this the example of the fathers who loved God with respect, rather than with the easy familiarity which is more common now.   His singing was with melting tenderness and power.   "Dr. Johnson used to sing that" is, among those who knew him well, a remark which seldom fails to be followed by moistening eyes and a silence that speaks.   Dr. Johnson was a delegate to every general conference from 1866 to 1886.   In this high court of the church his influence was felt whenever work was to be done.   He was a good committeeman, patient, prompt and exact.   Well-read in church history, and thoroughly acquainted with the rules of deliberative bodies, he yet forebore to pester the chair with points of order, and made no needless display of learning in the subtleties of the previous questions.   He was a bad man for a vaporing orator to make a mistake before.   He heard a great deal and always accurately.   There are good judges who think that in his encounter with Bishop McTyeire, at the general conference of 1874, he rather made than lost reputation.   Dr. Johnson was better known to the church, however, as a teacher and college president.   In this capacity his life and work stand out in a broad and instructive light.   To this result nothing probably contributed more than the fact that while devoted to his profession, he never degenerated into the mere keeper of a school.   He realized that he was a citizen and minister of the gospel, as well as a teacher.

As a citizen he was recognized as the man for emergencies.   If a fire occurred in town, or an epidemic threatened, he came to the front with that common consent which is always accorded to the man who at such times knows what to do and has the courage to do it.   At one time a short crop caused much distress among the farmers of the vicinity, and engendered a spirit of discontent which threatened open violence to our merchants. At the request of prominent citizens Dr. Johnson went down to the courthouse and addressed the malcontents so wisely and candidly that better counsels prevailed and the trouble shortly subsided.   In all movements for the public good his counsel was sought and a liberal contribution in both service and money expected from him.   While therefore he was sometimes openly denounced on the streets for vigorous measures which the management of his school required, he seldom failed in the long run to command the sympathy of his fellow-citizens.   As an instructor Dr. Johnson excelled in the number of things he could do well.   He was proficient in every department of work in the college and at different times taught with marked success the entire course in English, mathematics and the classics.   He knew therefore what to expect of both teachers and pupils.   His recitation room was full of life.   He loved to bring out a slow class or a dull scholar.   Thoroughness everywhere was his own rule, and he had no patience with half work on the part of others.

That which makes Dr. Johnson's life a procession of our common Methodism is not the magnitude of his work alone, but the spirit in which it was accomplished.   "When you have been dead ten years, you will be a great man," a friend said to him on one occasion. "I care little for that," was the reply, "if only my work survives." Dr. Johnson died well. When Bishop Galloway announced that the end was near, he put his arms about the Bishop's neck and said, "I am ready, my preparations were made long ago." It was not so easy at first to believe that he died at the right time, but there is an economy of Providence which prepares work for the workman, as well as workman for the work. While that which he lived to finish will inspire other workers, its very incompleteness lays the ability of the church under obligations which are sacred. Many hands must take up the burden which he laid down, and Whitworth college must become a true seminary of schools. "I never pass the 'institute' at Whitworth college," says a writer in one of our advocates, "and see upon the cornerstone the inscription 'founded by H. F. Johnson,' that I do not want to read it, 'founded on H. F. Johnson;' for beneath that honored institution as a pledge of God's blessing and the favor of the church lies a noble, consecrated life, one which will count for more, as the years pass by, than all his other offerings for the cause of Christian education. Such a life can not but be 'fruitful of further thought and deed.' Already in our own state signs of a rich harvest appear.''

Joseph A. Johnson, sheriff and tax collector of Monroe county, Miss., was born near Amory, in this county, in 1851, a son of Col. Joseph A. and Wilmoth (Malone) Johnson. The parents were born in Maury county, Tenn., and Monroe county, Miss., respectively, and spent the most of their lives in the latter county. The father was a well-to-do planter, and mostly a selfmade man. In 1862 he joined a company as captain, which he commanded for some time, after which he was made lieutenant-colonel, and fought in all the prominent engagements in Mississippi and Tennessee. After the war he resumed farming and died in 1881, while treasurer of Monroe county, being elected to that office in 1879. He was a member of the Christian church and from a young man was always a prominent church worker. He was an active and well-known democrat and politician, and a frequent delegate to the different conventions. He had the highest regard of the community in which he lived. Grandfather Malone came from Georgia to Monroe county very early in life, and died before our subject was born, his widow surviving him until 1864. Mr. Malone was one of the first settlers of this county. He began working for himself at the age of sixteen as a clerk. He was married in 1876 to Eugenia, a daughter of Thompson and Paulina Gregory, natives of South Carolina, whence they came to Monroe county about 1857, Mr. Gregory dying there in 1869. His wife is still living and a member of the Baptist church. Joseph A. Johnson farmed until he was appointed deputy sheriff in 1883, and after serving his country in this capacity for six years he was elected to an official position, the office of sheriff in 1889. He is an Odd Fellow and a member of the Knights of Honor. Both he and his wife are members of the Christian church.

Col. J. M. Johnson, planter and merchant, Acona, Miss., owns about two thousand acres of land, with five hundred acres under cultivation, and his principal crops are cotton and corn. He is progressive and industrious and in everything connected with his farm he displays excellent judgment and thoroughness, qualities which cannot fail of success. He was born in Mississippi in December, 1829, and his father, Hon. Stephen Johnson, was a native of Tennessee, as was also his grandfather Johnson. The father was born in February, 1806, and died in the same month, in 1883. He came to Mississippi when a child, was reared and educated in that state, and was there married to Miss E. Humphrey, who died in March, 1840, leaving four children, as follows: Col. J. M., Mary, Emily and Martha. Mr. Johnson's second marriage occurred in 1840, to Miss Hampton, and eight children were the result of this union: John H. (deceased), L. L. (deceased), Laura E., Helen (deceased), Henry E. (deceased), W. T., S. A., W. C. and Elmira. The father was a planter by occupation and the last thirty years of his life he was a local minister. He was at one time state senator from Carroll county. He was a member of the Grange and took a great interest in that organization. Col. J. M. Johnson, the eldest in order of birth of the children born to his father's first union, grew to manhood and secured a liberal education in the schools of his native county. In 1854 he was wedded to Miss Louisa Lipscomb, and eight children were the fruits of this marriage: Mary A., Martha E., Emma (deceased), J. M., R. P., W. J. Annie L. and P. A. Mrs. Johnson was born in Georgia and her mother was also a native of that state; the latter died in 1872. Mr. Lipscomb was a native Virginian and died in 1852. Colonel Johnson sympathized warmly with the Southern states during the Civil war and in February, 1862, he enlisted in company A, Thirtieth regiment under the command of Colonel Neal. He participated in the battles of Perryville, Ky., Murfreesboro, Lookout Mountain, Missionary Ridge, Chickamauga, Tenn., those around Atlanta, Jonesboro, Ga., and Franklin, Tenn. At the latter place he was severely wounded and taken prisoner and sent to Fort Delaware, and was released as prisoner July, 1865. At the time of enlistment he was chosen captain and served in that capacity until the spring of 1863, when he was promoted to the office of lieutenant-colonel, serving in that position until taken prisoner. After returning home he engaged in planting and merchandising, which he has continued up to the present time. He is a Mason, having joined Mount Moriah lodge No. 86, in 1852, and has been master of the lodge at different times for several years.

Dr. Marmaduke C. Johnson (deceased). The career of this gentleman is but another example of what energy, industry and perseverance, when intelligently applied, will accomplish, for all his enterprises resulted most satisfactorily. He was born in Fairfax county, Va., about 1820, his parents, Edward and Mary Johnson, being also born there and there spending their lives on a farm. Dr. Johnson was educated in Washington, D. C., and was graduated in medicine from an institution of that city. After practicing for some time in Virginia he went to Point Coupee parish, La., this being about the year 1850, but he soon removed to Concordia parish. This parish was at that time dotted with swamps, and as Dr. Johnson's health was slowly but surely failing him he was urged by his friends in Franklin county, Miss., to locate here, which he did about the year 1853. He at once entered upon a very successful career, and as he was fitted by study and experience for a superior physician and surgeon he soon gathered around him a very large patronage. His first few thousand dollars was earned from his practice, and with this he began speculating in cotton. His undertakings resulted very fortunately for him, for he was shrewd and farseeing, and at the time of his death he was one of the wealthiest and most successful men in southwest Mississippi. Soon after his marriage, which occurred in 1855 and was to Miss Sophia Smith, he located in the southwest part of Franklin county on what was known as Turner's plantation, sixteen miles east of Natchez, and there he made his permanent home, practicing his profession for ten or twelve years prior to his death, then devoting his attention to the management of his immense estate. He died on January 23, 1887, leaving an estate worth about $125,000, his land amounting to seven thousand acres, all of which was in one tract. He was also a very active politician, and for the eminent services he rendered his party and for the sound judgment, practical ability and qualities of leadership that he displayed he was elected to the lower house of the state legislature in the session of 1882 and also in the following session. He was a prominent member of Solomon B. Stampley lodge No. 222, of the A. F. & A. M., and was one of the warm admirers and supporters of the

order. He left no issue, but his widow is a resident of the home plantation, which she manages very judiciously. She is a daughter of John and Ann (Brown) Smith, the former of
whom was born in Ireland, coming when a young man to the United States. He was married in Georgia, in which state his wife was born, and about 1819 came to Franklin county
and located near where his daughter, Mrs. Johnson, is now residing. When the latter was
a child she was left fatherless, her mother afterward marrying John Ray, and died in
Natchez in 1861. She bore her husband, Mr. Smith, three daughters: Martha, widow of
Jeremiah Mock; Sarah, wife of Silas Wells Stockwell, and Mrs. Johnson.

S. E. Johnson was born in Alabama in 1825, and emigrated from that state to Clarke
county, Miss., in the year 1857. He was united in marriage to Miss M. E. Dial, of Sumter
county, Ala., in 1846. He was a farmer by vocation all his life, and died in Mississippi in
1861, Mrs. Johnson yet surviving him in that state at the age of sixty-four. J. E. Johnson,
a son of the above, and the subject of this sketch, was born on the 18th day of September,
1847, in Sumter county, Ala., and came to Clarke county, Miss., with his parents. He
never had any but moderate advantages for his education, as he went to work on his own
account at the age of fifteen years, the family being dependent upon him at that time for
support. He enlisted in the Fourteenth Mississippi regiment in 1864, and served in various
capacities till the close of the war. After the end of the great struggle, he engaged in mercantile pursuits as a clerk, later going into merchandising on his own account, in which he
continued for four years, and then engaged in agricultural pursuits. In 1884 he gave his
whole attention to the merchant-mill business in De Soto, Clarke county, Miss. He sold out
here, and removed to Pachuta, Clarke county, Miss., in 1889. Mr. Johnson has succeeded
here also, being one of the leading men in that business in south Mississippi. He buys and
sells feed, grain, etc., and his business is extending into the adjoining counties. His gristmill has a capacity for grinding thirty bushels of grain per hour, or two hundred and fifty
bushels per day, and his gin, which is connected with it, has a capacity of fifteen bales of
cotton per day. Mr. Johnson was married in 1868 to Miss Emma E. McGowan, a daughter
of Robert McGowan, of Clarke county, Miss., who was once a native of Lowndes county,
Miss. Considering the newness of the town in which he lives, Mr. Johnson is a marked
success. He is a Mason in good and regular standing, and is a member of the Methodist
church, as is also Mrs. Johnson.

Samuel J. Johnson, Esq. Among the names of the business men of Ellisville, Miss., none
is more popular or more worthy here than that of Mr. Samuel J. Johnson. This gentleman
was born in Henry county, Ala., September 18, 1857. He is the son of William R. and Narcissus (Deason) Johnson, who settled in Mississippi in 1860. They were the parents of six
other children: Elizabeth, William R., Araminta, Butley, Lela and David B. Mr. Johnson
was obliged at a very early age to take up the hard battle of life. When he was twelve years
old he found employment in a sawmill at fifty cents per day, in which he continued for two
years. Afterward he found an opportunity to attend school for a time, and being determined to make the best of his opportunities his progress was very rapid until his money was
exhausted, and he was obliged to go to work again. He was taken into the store of his former
employers—the Winchester Mill company, the active manager of whose interests was Benjamin Meador—at a salary of $50 a year, and board. He continued in this position, faithfully
performing the duties devolving upon him, until he had obtained sufficient money to again
warrant him in entering school. His next employment was in the store of John O'Donnell,
of Waynesboro, Miss., his salary being $100 per year, in addition to his board. About one
and one-half years later he left Mr. O'Donnell and went to work in a commissary for J. R.

Hood & Co., near Winchester, at a salary of $25 a month. At the expiration of another year and a half he had saved about $400. With this money, in 1876, in partnership with Charles Smith, he engaged, on a small scale, in the manufacture of turpentine, near Winchester. In 1878 he formed a copartnership with S. T. Taylor, and opened a general merchandise store at old Ellisville, Miss. In 1880 Mr. Johnson went to Paulding, Miss., and opened another store, of which he took charge, still retaining his business at old Ellisville, which he had placed under the management of B. Du Bose. In 1881 Du Bose and Taylor purchased his interest in Ellisville store at old Ellisville, and about the same time Mr. Johnson acquired Mr. Taylor's interest in the establishment at Paulding, for which he paid $5,400. In 1883 he established a store and gristmill and cottongin at Waynesboro, which he took under his personal management, leaving his brother, David B. Johnson, in charge of his store at Paulding. In 1884 his mill and gin were burned, with no insurance, and in January, 1885, he sold his store there and removed to Ellisville, where, in the following February, he opened his present business, which he has continued with great success ever since. In 1886 he closed out his enterprise at Paulding and moved his stock of goods to this place, thus consolidating all of his business interests here. In the following year he purchased a large tract of pine timber and other land, and engaged quite extensively in the turpentine business, which, under his careful and energetic management, has become very popular. Mr. Johnson's success is an evidence of what may be accomplished by diligent labor and strict attention to business, and it has marked him as exceedingly enterprising and as a wide-awake man, and won for him the esteem and approbation of all who know him. He was married in Scott county, Miss., October 12, 1882, to Susie B., a daughter of James M. and Elizabeth (Franks) Gann. Mrs. Johnson was born in Alabama January 16, 1864. They are the parents of three children: Mabel C., born January 22, 1886; Joseph E., born March 28, 1888; James G., born April 2, 1890. Mr. Johnson is a member of the Knights of Pythias, and he and his wife are identified with the Methodist Episcopal Church South, upon the services of which his entire family are attendants. Mrs. Johnson's father was a Methodist minister. He had been preaching some forty years, and died at Poplarville, Miss., August 21, 1891, at the good old age of seventy-one years. He was well known throughout south Mississippi.

Samuel M. Johnson's father, Col. B. W. Johnson, was a native of Virginia, as was also the grandfather, who served in the Revoluntionary war. Colonel Johnson was reared to manhood in his native state and when a young man went to South Carolina, where he was married to a Miss Ottison, who was a native of that state. After his marriage the Colonel settled in Alabama, resided there a number of years, and then in 1837 moved to Mississippi, settling in Neshoba county. He there followed farming until 1842, and then moved to Leake county, where he was among the pioneers. He located near Walnut Grove, became one of the best farmers in the county and accumulated considerable property. There he reared his family and there his death occurred about 1870. His wife died about four years later. Mr. Johnson was an active member of the Methodist church. Of the eight children born to this union, four sons and four daughters, all of whom grew to mature years, only our subject, a brother and sister are now living. The brother, J. S. Johnson, is a farmer of Leake county and the sister, V. A., is the wife of R. B. Cooper, a farmer also of this county. Samuel M. Johnson became familiar with the duties of the farm at an early age and was reared in Leake county. He there met and married, first in 1852, Miss Rosalie J. Richmond, a native of Leake county and the daughter of Samuel and O. S. Richmond. Mrs. Johnson died in 1862 leaving four children, three sons and one daughter. In 1865 Mr. Johnson married

Mrs. Elizabeth Lindsay, of Carthage, a daughter of M. J. Watson. Mrs. Johnson was born in Alabama and was reared partly there and partly in Mississippi. After his first marriage Mr. Johnson settled where he now resides, opened a farm, built and improved his place, and although he had started out to fight life's battles for himself empty handed he had accumulated quite a competency up to the breaking out of the war. After that eventful period he commenced anew and is now the owner of three hundred acres of land with one hundred and twenty acres open land fenced. He has comfortable buildings, and everything about the place is in superior order. He is one of the best farmers in the county and not only that but he is held in the highest estimation as a citizen and neighbor. His word is as good as his bond. In the spring of 1862 Mr. Johnson enlisted in the Twenty-seventh Mississippi infantry as private, was promoted to sergeant and served until the close in the Tennessee army. He participated in the fights at Munfordsville, Perryville, Murfreesboro, and from Chattanooga to Atlanta, Franklin, Nashville, and afterward in Mississippi and Virginia. He surrendered, with General Lee, on April 9, 1865, and then returned to Leake county, where he resumed farming. He takes no part in politics, and is not an office seeker. His children are named as follows: R. W., a resident of Walnut Grove; Nancy R. (deceased), was married; R. C., married and engaged in farming here; Mollie, wife of Dr. J. E. Golden, and Allen, merchant at Walnut Grove. These children were born to his first union, and the following child is the result of the second marriage: Elizabeth O. Mr. and Mrs. Johnson and the family are members of the Methodist church, in which Mr. Johnson has been steward for twenty years. He is a Master mason.

Hon. William Johnson, deceased, one of the county's most worthy citizens, was born in Nashville, Tenn., June 2, 1792, and was the son of Isaac Johnson and Mary Dunham, natives of southern Virginia. The half brother of Isaac, Henry Johnson, was the father of Cave Johnson, a very prominent Tennesseean, who was postmaster-general in President Polk's cabinet. To Isaac and Mary were born a large family. Joseph, the eldest son, was the first president of the West Feliciana railroad and was a representative in the Mississippi legislature when that body drafted the first constitution of the state. He was also the clerk of the court at Woodville, and also at Pinckneyville and was very prominent in political matters, possessing a fine intellect and great personal magnetism and being unusually well informed. He was a very successful and a very extensive planter. He was married to Miss Rachel N. Dillahunty, in Nashville, and resided in this county until his death. He left a large estate, having owned several large plantations and held a large amount of stock in the railroad and in the railroad bank. He left no children. His death occurred in 1848 at the age of seventy-two years. He was buried with impressive ceremonies in the rites of the Masonic order. His wife died in 1844. Henry Johnson, the next son, was governor of Louisiana from 1824 to 1828 and helped to frame the constitution of that state. He was United States senator three terms and a member three times of the house of representatives of the United States. He first came to Mississippi but immediately moved to Louisiana, when he practiced his profession of the law in the Attakapas country. Later he practiced at Donaldsonville, La. He purchased a large tract of land and at times lived on this place but spent much of his time at his beautiful home in New Orleans. His wife was Miss Elizabeth Key, whom he married in Washington, D. C., while there as senator. She was a native of Georgetown, near Washington, D. C. Henry Johnson possessed a wonderful memory, extraordinary perception, was logical, brilliant, witty, and an extemporaneous speaker of surprising skill, readiness and power and was the peer of any lawyer he ever encountered. He gave the deciding vote that brought Texas into the Union. He was intimately connected with the political affairs of the day, state and national, and did much to perpetuate the foundational principles of the government. He died leaving no children, though two were born, a son and a daughter, but both died in youth. His wife died in July, 1861. He died in 1864, aged eighty-one years. They were members of the Episcopal church, and he was a vestryman of Bishop (afterward General) Polk's church in New Orleans, while living in that city. He was governor of Louisiana when the Marquis de la Fayette visited the United States, and entertained the nation's distinguished guest at his home. Isaac, the next son, graduated at Chapel Hill and died soon after his return home. William was educated in Lexington, Ky., Transylvania college, where he graduated in 1816. He returned to Wilkinson county and later was clerk of the court, and took a lively part in politics as a leading whig. He was with General Jackson in the Indian wars. While he was attending school there was a call for soldiers, and Dr. Gideon Blackburn with all his scholars joined the army of Jackson, and participated in two of the very prominent battles fought in 1814 with the Indians. Afterward all returned to college save two, who perished in the field. William was admitted to the bar at Woodville, Miss., where he practiced until 1829. He was intimately associated, as a law partner, with Nolnar Whitehead and Judge Child, and all of them were leading attorneys, who were located at Woodville. Going to Pinckneyville from Woodville he retired from his practice and engaged in planting until his death in 1854, at the age of sixty-two years. He was a believer of the Presbyterian faith and a supporter of that church. He was married to Miss Elizabeth Randolph, the daughter of Edward and Mary (Coleman) Randolph, who were natives of Georgia and North Carolina, respectively, and were very early settlers in the Pinckneyville neighborhood, locating there about 1790. They were the most prominent people of that place. Edward Randolph donated large sums to the Presbyterian and the Methodist Episcopal churches, and to the Pinckneyville academy, which was chartered in 1815. He also built a hotel for the accommodation of the traveling public, and in many other public enterprises stood always ready to assist, when not at the head. He entered large tracts of government land and amassed a comfortable forture. His mother was Miss Mary Bacon, of Augusta, Ga. James Coleman, father of Mary Coleman, was killed in one of the Indian battles near Natchez, Adams county, and was left on the battlefield. Elizabeth, the second child born to Isaac and Mary Johnson, was reared and educated at Nashville. Sarah, the third child, was educated in Nashville, and married William Dillahunty, a planter, by whom she had three children; she died in middle age. Rebecca, the seventh child, married Isaac Williams and both are deceased. They had one son, Daniel, who died in Texas, leaving a family of children. To William (the subject of this sketch) and wife were born eight children, six of whom lived to be grown: Mary E., the eldest daughter, became the wife of Thomas G. Stockett; she died August 1, 1884. Joseph, the next child, was educated in Georgetown college, D. C., and reared a large family; he died in 1875. Sarah J. and Anne L. live at the old home place, which is known as the Glenwood plantation, and have not married; they carry on a large farm, and are noble, self-sacrificing women. Henry died at seven years of age. William, the next son, died in 1874 soon after returning from Georgetown college, where he had been in attendance. Juliet became the wife of P. M. Stockett, a prominent planter of this county. He has a family of three sons living: William, Samuel and Thomas. A daughter was born, but died young. Isaac, the eldest son and child died at an early age. Mr. Johnson, the wife of William, died in 1883, at the age of eighty years. She was a lifelong member of the Presbyterian church, and most excellent woman. Isaac Johnson, the father of William, a soldier of the Revolution, was born in 1744, and died in 1832, at the age of eighty-eight years. Isaac Johnson with his family immigrated to Mississippi in 1801 from Nashville, Tenn. There is no more prominent family in the state than this one of the Johnsons. All have been useful, upright citizens whose high character and noble conduct have reflected upon their descendants and connections the highest renown.

Joseph Johnson (deceased), was a gentleman so well known that no special introduction need be given him to the people of this county or state. He was a native of this county, born January 8, 1823, and was the second of a family of two sons and four daughters born to William and Elizabeth (Randolph) Johnson, natives respectively of Tennessee and this county. William Johnson was a prominent attorney at Woodville at one time, and later at Pinckneyville, where he resided until his death. He was a successful planter and an excellent citizen. Henry Johnson, brother of William, was at one time governor of Louisiana. Joseph Johnson attained his majority in this county, and was educated at Georgetown, District of Columbia. He then attended the law school at New Orleans and was licensed to practice. His uncle, Joseph Johnson, one of this county's most prominent citizens, possessing great wealth and being connected with the West Feliciana railroad as president for many years, in his will chose the subject of this memoir administrator, one-third of the property being willed to him. He settled the estate satisfactorily with all concerned. On returning to this county he gave up his profession and engaged in planting, settling at the present place in 1848, at what is familiarly known as the Grove plantation, six miles south of Woodville, where he resided until his death. During the war he served as captain of the home guards, and participated in several sharp skirmishes. He did a great deal to control the lawless element. As a politician he took no special part, but was keenly intelligent and well posted on the affairs of the day. He was a member of the Masonic order, and died in middle life in the year 1874 before his powers began to wane. He was married in July, 1850, to Mary Stewart, a native of this county, born in 1830, the daughter of William Stewart and Frances M. Smith, natives of Tennessee and of this county respectively. William Stewart was born in 1793 in what is now Montgomery county, Tenn., and was one of a family of three sons and three daughters. His mother having died when the children were young, William, the eldest, came to what is now Wilkinson county and was reared by an aunt, Jane Stewart, who married a British officer, Capt. Jack Stewart. William Stewart was reared in this county and educated in Tennessee, after which he returned here and located near Woodville, and was prominently connected with the Planters' bank, of which he was president for several years before his death. He carried on several plantations and was a man full of business tact, and had the highest confidence of the community. Frances M. Smith was born in April, 1798, in what is now Wilkinson county, and was the daughter of Capt. Peter Smith, a native of South Carolina who came to this territory among the first settlers, and was here married to Miss Anna Goodby, who was also probably a native of this territory. By this union were born three sons and three daughters, all of whom lived to be grown. Augustus, one son, participated in the battle of New Orleans, and soon after that was killed in a duel fought with a Mr. Willis, who at one time was his most intimate friend. The second child was the mother of Mrs. Johnson, Matilda F. Smith. The third was Judge C. P. Smith, a noted jurist of the state and a very talented gentleman. The fourth was Eliza Smith, who was educated in Woodville and was married to Dr. Edward Farish, and resided in this county until her death. She died in middle age without issue. The fifth child, Ellen Smith, was educated in Woodville and married Henry Moore, by whom she had two children, all of whom are deceased. James, the sixth child, was killed by accident while out hunting. The members of this family were early settlers of this county and were very prominently connected with its history. Matilda M. Smith attained her majority in the county, where she was married in 1818 to Mr. Stewart, by whom was born this family: Catherine J. Stewart, who became the wife of Judge C. C. Cage, a prominent lawyer and judge of this county at one time. Catherine died in 1857 leaving a family of six children: Peter Smith Stewart (who died at eleven years of age); James D. Stewart (who is now living in Jackson, Miss.); Nolan Stewart (who was killed during the late war by Jayhawkers). he married Mary J. Reneau, of French descent, and by her had four children): Elizabeth Stewart (who became the wife of Dr. Robert L. Buck, of this county, and later moved to Jackson, Miss., where she died in 1888, aged sixty years, leaving a family of four daughters and two sons); Mrs. Mary S. Johnson (who became the wife of the subject of this sketch; Ellen (who was the wife of Hugh Connell of this county, where he was born and reared and to them were born five children; this lady died during the late war); and Caroline (who was the youngest child and was married to Jonah Hamilton, by whom she had two children; she died in 1861); the father of these children died in 1835, at the early age of forty-three years; the mother after his death married John M. Currier, M. D., of Massachusetts, who came to Mississippi to practice his profession, and throughout life was a hard student; by this union was born one son, John M., who died at the age of eleven years). Mrs. Mary Johnson is one of this county's noblest women. She was educated in Massachusetts, at Bradford, where she remained with her brother Nolan for two years and then returned to the home place. Here she was happily married and presented her husband with a fine family of eight children, who lived to be grown: William Stewart, who died June 15, 1890, aged thirty-eight; Henry, who married and lives in this county, a prominent planter; Elizabeth, who is yet single and lives on an adjoining farm, which she superintends; Nolan, who lives in Washington county, Miss.; Joseph, who is married and resides in this county; Pinckney S., who lives in Washington county; James, also residing in Washington county Mary, who resides at home, a beautiful and accomplished lady. The residence in which the family reside is one of the finest in this county. It was completed just after the war, and is a fine brick structure two and a half stories high and stands in a beautiful grove of beach, maple and magnolia. Mr. Johnson was a man of much prominence and worth and no citizen of the county or state stands higher than the members of his family. Mrs. Johnson resides on the home place and she and her accomplished daughter, Mary, successfully superintend the large plantation.

Col. William B. Johnson, planter, Courtland, Miss. Owing to the fertility of the soil in Panola county, Miss., and by energy, industry and perseverance, Colonel Johnson has become one of the wealthy farmers of this section. He was born in Dallas county, Ala., on the 19th of May, 1821, and was the younger of two children born to Littleton and Eliza (Beryman) Johnson, natives of Virginia. The father moved to Alabama and became very wealthy. Col. William B. Johnson passed his youthful days on his father's farm in Alabama, but received his education in the North, graduating in law at New Haven, Conn. He then began practicing his profession at Oxford, Miss., and later became quite prominent as a political man, serving in the legislature in 1854, and again in 1856. Farming has been his principal occupation through life, and he is now the owner of one thousand acres of excellent land with six hundred acres under cultivation. He is wideawake and thoroughgoing, and is alive to all improved methods. The Colonel was married in 1843 to Miss Laura Allen, a native of North Carolina and the daughter of Col. Henry Allen, also of the Old North state. Colonel Allen was quite prominent in the politics of his county, and was president of the police court of both Panola and Marshall counties for a number of years. Colonel and

Mrs. Johnson's union has been blessed by the birth of three children: Clarence L., H. M. and Laura. In 1861 Colonel Johnson enlisted in company I, Thirty-third Mississippi regiment of infantry, and went out as captain, which rank he held until cessation of hostilities. He was a brave and gallant officer, and served the Southern cause faithfully and well. He participated in the following engagements: Corinth, Vicksburg and Edward's depot. After the war closed he returned to the farm and has been a private citizen ever since. He was in the last whig convention held in the state, and now he affiliates with the democratic party and is a strong supporter of the same. He is social and pleasant, fond of jokes, and is not wanting in friends; is enterprising to a degree, and is ever ready to assist any scheme that has for its aim the upbuilding of the county.

Dr. Wirt Johnston, since attaining manhood, has devoted his life to the highest temporal mission among men, a combat with disease and death, and his efficiency, skill and signal success in this calling are well known. He was born at Raymond, Miss., in 1846, the younger of two children born to Amos R. and Harriet N. (Battle) Johnston, a sketch of whom appears elsewhere in this work. Dr. Johnston received his initiatory training in the common schools, but at the early age of fifteen years he dropped his books to take up arms in defense of the Confederate cause, becoming a member of company A., First Mississippi artillery. While serving in Mississippi he was in the battles of Chickasaw Bayou, Champion's Hill, Black River bridge, and the siege of Vicksburg. After being exchanged he was in the Army of Tennessee for a time, after which he was in Mississippi until the surrender. He was discharged from the service at Jackson, and immediately secured employment in a drug store, at the same time commencing the study of medicine, for which he seemed to have a decided taste and a natural aptitude. He pursued his medical studies in the Jefferson Medical college, of Philadelphia, Penn., for some time, and from this institution he was graduated as an M. D. in 1868. After spending a short time in Jackson he went to Tchula, Holmes county, Miss., where he was located, and successfully practiced his profession until 1873, when he returned to Jackson, and here has since resided. Here he immediately entered into a large and lucrative practice, and has been absorbed day and night in a profession which is perhaps the most trying on brain and body of any in the field of science. His reading in medical literature, and his practice, are abreast of the day, and he keeps in continuous touch with all forms of current thought, scientific, political and literary. He is a member and an ex-president of the State Medical association, and is secretary and executive officer of the state board of health. In 1879, when the national board of health was organized, he was an inspector. He is an ex-president of the Sanitary council of the Mississippi valley; was for years a trustee of the Lunatic asylum and Blind institute; is a local surgeon of the Illinois Central and Alabama & Vicksburg railroads, and is physician for the state penitentiary and the Deaf and Dumb institute. In 1882 he presided over the quarantine conference of the gulf states, held in New Orleans. He is an ardent friend and promoter of all worthy enterprises, and his zeal and influence in everything affecting the general weal have given him a wide and popular reputation far beyond the limits of the state in which he resides, and being a most courteous and agreeable gentleman, he has many warm personal friends, among the most distinguished in the South; and in one respect his reputation extends throughout the length and breadth of the country. Speaking in 1888 of the yellow fever epidemic and its panics, the *Medical Standard* (Chicago) called attention to the good influence which a skilled sanitarian can exert in a public panic, as shown by the rapidity with which health officers had checked the yellow fever panic, and lent their aid to suffering humanity at different points. Commenting on this article, the Chicago *Daily News* mentioned Dr.

Cochran, the state health officer of Alabama, and Dr. Thornton of Memphis, adding: "Dr. Wirt Johnston, secretary of the Mississippi state board of health, is another of these heroes. He has remained immured in Jackson in personal charge of the plague-smitten capital; and, like his brother officer in Alabama, he has instituted and enforced measures of isolation and other sanitary precautions which have insured the safety of the rest of the state. It is largely to the efforts of these two officials, Drs. Johnston and Cochran, that yellow fever has been prevented from spreading as an epidemic throughout Alabama and Mississippi." In the annual report of the Mississippi state board of health to the legislature of the state of Mississippi for the years 1878–9, the president, in his report to the governor, said: "Circulars, letters, telegrams, instructions and advice in every shape and form were forwarded to every local board in the state by Dr. Johnston, the secretary and executive officer of our board. He never tired in his arduous duties for the weal of our people. Even after the fever had attacked the city of Jackson, his mind never forgot the suffering and needs elsewhere, but wherever and whenever assistance, counsel or attention was needed, he at once gave it attention. Too much praise can not be accorded him." The press of the entire South has repeated these sentiments in one form or another. The Doctor was married in 1876 to Miss Mary M. Barrows, a daughter of D. N. Barrows, whose sketch appears in this work, but their union has not been blessed in the birth of any children. Mrs. Johnston is a member of the Presbyterian church, and the Doctor is a member of the A. F. & A. M., in which he is a Knight Templar, and the A. L. of H.

H. Johnston, president of the Tombigbee Cotton mills, at Columbus, Miss., was born in Winchester, Frederick county, Va., January 7, 1815, a son of Atwell and Rhoda (Fry) Johnston, who were also natives of the Old Dominion. Launcelot Johnston, the paternal grandfather, was also a Virginian by birth and of Scotch-Irish descent. He was a soldier in the war, with General Harrison, was a farmer by occupation, and died in the state of his birth. Atwell Johnston was also a farmer, and was called from life in Virginia, January 2, 1825, his wife having passed from life there September 10, 1818. Their union resulted in the birth of four children, two sons and two daughters, H. Johnston, the subject of this sketch, being the only surviving member of the family. Until he reached the age of thirteen years his life was spent on a plantation, but his advantages for acquiring an education up to that time were very meager, amounting to only about six months' schooling in all. In his youth he learned the tailor's trade, which he followed until 1866. In 1836 he gave up this calling for the purpose of fighting Indians, and for his three months' service in Florida, under Gen. Winfield Scott, he received $26.25. In October, 1836, he came to Columbus Miss., and began following his trade, in connection with dealing in gentlemen's furnishing goods, and these two callings were successfully carried on until 1866, when he retired from active life, and has since lived so, enjoying the fruits of his early industry. He has always been one of the foremost citizens in the county, interested in all worthy movements, many of which he has helped to bring to a successful issue. He is well posted in all the current issues of the day, and has, at all times, expressed his views freely. He was married November 11, 1838, to Miss Mary A. Ikard, a native of Tennessee, by whom he has nine children: Charles A., Harrison R., Augusta L., Eloise, Toby W., Samuel B., Juanita, Eula and William. Mrs. Johnston is a member of the Christian church.

J. C. Johnston, Friar's Point, Miss., is the elder of two children born to Oliver H. and Medora J. (Peyton) Johnston, his birth occurring in Hinds county, Miss., in 1849, and is a representative of one of the prominent families of the country. The parents were natives of Kentucky and Tennessee respectively, and the father emigrated from his native state to Hinds county, Miss., in 1847. He became quite an extensive planter of that county, and made his home there until 1851, when he moved to Copiah county, of the same state. There, in connection with planting he carried on merchandising until the breaking out of the war, when he organized a company for the Confederate army. In 1861 he was elected captain of company K, third Mississippi regiment, and led his company in every battle and skirmish in which the regiment was engaged until at New Hope church, just before reaching Atlanta, on May 31, 1864, when he was wounded. His wound did not immediately prove fatal, but he died from the effects of it on April 2, 1879, spending the intervening time in study and reading. He was a man of education and learning and was thoroughly posted on business affairs. He was rather tall and slender, hair almost blue-black and eyes also very dark. He was a member of the Presbyterian church, and the mother, who now resides with her son J. C., is a member of the same church. J. C. Johnston was reared on the farm and attended the Cumberland university of Tennessee, from which he graduated in 1872. He subsequently engaged in the newspaper business at Hazlehurst, and for six years was editor and proprietor of the *Copiahan*. In 1878 he was appointed assistant land clerk in the auditor's office at Jackson, Miss.; held that position for six months, and was then made land clerk for one year. Later he was made general bookkeeper; filled that position for one year, and was then appointed deputy auditor, which position he held for six years, when he was obliged to resign on account of ill health. After this he traveled for eighteen months and fully regained his health. In the fall of 1889 he, with others, organized the Bank of Friar's Point, which was opened on March 4, 1890, and of which he was made cashier. This position he has held since. He has always been quite active in political affairs of the county, held the position of secretary of the democratic committee, and has been a delegate to the state conventions for fifteen years. Mr. Johnston is a man of superior business capacity, and he is now holding a position to which he is eminently fitted. The Bank of Friar's Point, after one year under his management, has made a most creditable showing in the way of profits. It has a paid-up capital of $50,000, and is one of the soundest institutions in the state. Mr. Johnston was married in 1878 to Miss Emma Goodbar, a native of Lebanon, Tenn., and to them have been born two children: Oscar and Alvan. Mrs. Johnston is a member of the Methodist Episcopal church. Socially Mr. Johnston is a member of the Knights of Honor and Knights of Pythias orders.

Capt. James S. Johnston is a man of more than ordinary intelligence, energy and force of character, and for his many acts of charity, deeds of kindness and for the upright and honorable career he has led, he is held in universal respect and esteem. His life has been a rather uneventful one, but while he has continued to pursue the even tenor of his way, he has been a deep reader and thinker, and every important question of the day is given his earnest attention. He is a true Southerner in every sense of the word, his birth occurring in Richmond, Va., on January 24, 1808, but is of Scotch lineage, his grandfather, Peter Johnston, being a native of the land of the thistles and oatmeal. The latter emigrated to America while it was still subject to Great Britain, and during the Revolutionary period was a strong sympathizer with the colonists. His eldest son, Peter, father of Gen. Joseph E. Johnston, was an officer in the continental army, serving as first lieutenant in Light Horse Harry Lee's legion. Charles Johnston, his third son, and father of Capt. James S. Johnston, grew to mature years in his native state, Virginia, and during the administration of George Washington he was taken prisoner by the Indians on the Ohio river and was held a captive for several years. Being a man of intelligence and of quick perception he made the most of his opportunities while with them, learned their habits, their modes of warfare, and, after he had made his escape, the opportunity for which he was always waiting and watching, he was interviewed by President Washington, who wished to learn the disposition, strength and force of the hostile tribes. He afterward wrote and published a book of his adventures, entitled "Johnston's Indian Narratives," which was a work of considerable note. The information furnished by him led to the adoption of the plan of Crawford's and Wayne's campaigns against those tribes. After following the life of a merchant in Richmond for some time he removed to Lynchburg, where he followed the same calling, but also embarked in the banking business, and by his superiority as a financier he succeeded in accumulating a large share of this world's goods. He died at the Botetourt springs in the year 1833, leaving a very finely improved property which he had accumulated by his own exertions. He was married twice, first to a Miss Pickett, a relative of General Pickett, and afterward to Miss Elizabeth Prentiss Steptoe, a daughter of James Steptoe, a well-to-do farmer, and for forty years, continuously, clerk of Bedford county, mention of whom is made in Wirt's life of Patrick Henry. The first union was blessed in the birth of two sons and one daughter, who married Thomas M. Ambler, of Fauquier, a nephew of Chief Justice Marshall, and by his last wife, who died in 1819, he became the father of four sons and three daughters. Capt. James S. Johnston is the eldest son of the last marriage, and his brothers and sisters are as follows: Julius D. was an attorney of St. Louis, Mo., but while there he married a Catholic lady, and after her decease he became a priest, remained connected with that church in St. Louis, but died in Cincinnati, Ohio; Frederick is a lawyer at Salem, Va., was clerk of the circuit court for twenty odd years previous to being admitted to the bar, and is now in the active practice of his profession at the above-mentioned place; Francis D. died in early manhood; Frances became the wife of Dr. James T. Royal, of Lynchburg, Va., and is now deceased; Mary M. (deceased) was twice married, her first husband being Dr. John Dillon, and her second, John A. Cunningham, of Richmond, Va.; and Martha B., who died near Church Hill, Miss., while still unmarried. Capt. James S. Johnston spent his youth in his native state, principally at home, and in the New London academy, a prominent high school, famous as the alma mater of many eminent men, he obtained an excellent practical education. He soon after commenced preparing himself for the legal profession, was admitted to the bar in Virginia and for some time after locating at Clinton, in Hinds county, Miss., in 1831, he practiced his profession with success. He received the appointment from Governor Scott of district attorney, and during the time that he discharged the duties of this office he displayed ability of a high order and won encomiums from all. Finding the practice of his profession too confining for one of his active habits he concluded to abandon it, and return to Virginia for a time in search of health. He has been married twice, first in Jefferson county June 6, 1884, to Mrs. Louisa C. B. Covington, a widow and a native of Adams county, Miss. She was a daughter of John Newman, and was educated in Elizabeth Female academy. In 1834 Mr. Johnston located in the neighborhood where he at present resides, and where, as one of the leading planters, he has been engaged in the raising of cotton ever since. He now resides in what is supposed to be one of the oldest residences in Jefferson county, it being a large two-story brick structure, erected in 1813 by Colonel Wood, who came to Mississippi from Maryland about 1812, some portions of the land on which he built the house bearing evidences of having been previously tilled as far back as Spanish times. He died at this place in 1845 at the age of seventy-four years. Captain Johnston married his second wife, Ruth A. H. Wood, daughter of Col. James Gillam Wood, she being one of many descendants of Colonel Wood who are residing in this and adjoining counties. Mrs. Johnston was one of a family of ten children and died in 1861. Captain

Johnston has a family of two sons and two daughters, the eldest of the family, Charles, being a planter of Washington county, Miss.; Rev. James Steptoe is a bishop of the Protestant Episcopal church in western Texas, and is a man of exceptionally brilliant mind, possessing superior natural talent. He served in General Lee's army throughout the entire Civil war, and was that noted General's courier at the bloody battle of Sharpsburg. After Lee's surrender he returned home, began the study of law and was admitted to the bar. He began practicing, but this calling proving distasteful to him, he abandoned his profession and commenced studying for the ministry, which calling has been much more to his taste. He has been a divine since about the year 1876, and through native ability and tact has arisen to eminence. The Captain's daughters are unmarried but are content to make their home with their father. They, as well as the sons, are exceptionally well educated, and are talented, cultured and refined ladies, and in their pleasant home, where hospitality and good will abound, they are charming and graceful hostesses. While Captain Johnston is eminently fitted to fill any office within the gift of the people of the state, he has at all times peremptorily declined to enter public life, although he has been frequently and urgently asked to do so. After the death of the gallant General Quitman, he received the unanimous nomination for congress in the sixth district, when a nomination was equivalent to election, but refused to accept the honor. He has several times declined to make the race for the state legislature both upper and lower branches, and although he was petitioned and very earnestly urged to represent the county in the late constitutional convention, he remained true to his convictions and declined. He is a man of decided literary tastes and has written many strong political articles for the press, which have won attention from many prominent political leaders. His leading characteristics are extreme frankness, personal integrity, honesty of purpose, indomitable will and energy, and coupled with this, a generous and kindly disposition. Modest and retiring to a fault he does not seem to estimate himself at his true worth, but his friends know his numerous good points thoroughly, and are at all times ready to show their thorough appreciation of his merits. He has met and been personally acquainted with all the great statesmen of the country, more particularly those of the state of Mississippi, and has a large and interesting fund of reminiscences of ante-bellum days.

William B. Johnston, Yazoo City, Miss., was born in Claiborne county, Miss., December 22, 1818, and is the fifth of a family of nine children. His parents, Henry G. and Susan W. (Leake) Johnston, were natives of Virginia. The mother was a daughter of Gov. Walter Leake of Mississippi. The father was a mechanic. He was a soldier in the war of 1812, and in 1815 he was captain of a company of Mississippi troops that went out against the Creek Indians in Alabama. He was married in Virginia in 1806, and came to Claiborne county in 1810, settling on Big Black river; there he entered six hundred and forty acres of land, improving one hundred and fifty acres. In addition to his agricultural pursuits he did flatboating for his neighbors. In 1825 he removed to Hinds county, Miss., and located on the estate of Governor Leake, who had died in 1824; there he managed the cultivation of six hundred and forty acres until 1828; in that year he bought eight hundred acres of land, which is a portion of the plantation now owned by the subject of this notice. He died in Yazoo county, April 18, 1871; his wife had died ten years before, in 1861. Only four of the nine children grew to maturity: Walter L. died in 1863 from disease contracted in the Confederate service; William B.; W. L., a resident of Clinton, Miss.; Mary A., widow of James W. Terrell, who was a resident of Bentonia. Their father was an active old line whig, and represented Hinds county four or five terms in the state legislature; he was also judge of the probate court of the county for more than ten years. Both the father and mother were members of the Methodist Episcopal church. William B. Johnston was educated in the academy at Clinton, Miss., and after leaving school he managed the plantation in Hinds county for his father until 1845; he then settled on the farm where he still resides; he has six hundred and twenty acres, one hundred and fifty being under cultivation. Mr. Johnston was united in marriage in 1852 to Miss Ellen Clark, a daughter of Henry and Catherine (Brooks) Clark. Mrs. Johnston and her parents were all born in Virginia, but removed to this county in 1842; her father died in 1843, and the mother in 1846. During the war Mr. Johnston was sergeant-major of company B, Ninth Mississippi home guards, and was in active service during the entire war. All movements for the advancement of the general welfare have found in him a ready and sympathetic aid. He is a member of the Masonic fraternity. He and his wife have reared three children, two of whom are at home and one is married. Mrs. Johnston is a consistent member of the Methodist Episcopal church.

Ashberry B. Jordan was born in Pike county, Ala., July 25, 1834. His father was Peeples C. and his mother was Charlotte (Weldon) Jordan. They were natives of Georgia and were married in Alabama, and removed thence to Mississippi in 1855, locating in Jones county, where they lived until the death of the father August 5, 1867, and of the mother, April 1, 1875. They were the parents of eleven children, named Huldah, Jacob J., John H., Luvinda, Nancy S., Harriet E., William C., Ashberry B., Aaron P., Robert G. and Charlotte M. At about the age of twenty-one years Ashberry B. Jordan took up the battle of life for himself with the stern determination of winning the victory. He was married in Jones county, June 12, 1856, to Miss Mary R., daughter of Hon. Amos and Eleanor (Baskin) Deason, who bore him eight children: Susan E., William C. H., Amos, Mary R. A., Orange P., Terry C., Sarah D. and Lucinda M. In the year above mentioned Mr. Jordan located about five and one-half miles southwest of Old Ellisville, Miss., where he remained until after the beginning of the war. In April, 1862, he enlisted in company D, of the First Alabama and Mississippi battalion, under Capt. William McGill, and served until the close of the war and was mustered out at Forsyth, Ga., in May, 1865. He returned to his home and in 1868 settled on the plantation upon which he now lives. His wife died April 8, 1879, and on March 22, 1882, he married Miss Mary M., daughter of William R. and Nancy (Bua) Johnson, who bore him three children: Dennis A., John G. and Oscar M. Mr. Jordan is a member of the Masonic fraternity and has taken the Royal Arch degree. He now holds the office of treasurer of the Blue lodge, A. F. & A. M. He and his wife are members of the Methodist Episcopal Church South. He is the owner of about eight hundred acres of land and devotes considerable attention to stockraising, makes a specialty of sheepraising, generally keeping about one thousand head on hand. Hon. Amos Deason, the father of his first wife, was a prominent man of this part of the county, and represented his county (Jones) in the state legislature three times. Mr. Jordan ranks among the leading citizens of his vicinity and has done as much as any other man there to further the general welfare.

A. K. Jones, Claiborne county, Miss., the subject of this sketch, a native of Mississippi, descends on both sides from distinguished families, of which the following particulars are mentioned. His mother, Martha Augusta, was the eldest daughter of Joseph K. Green, who was the eldest son of Thomas Marston Green, a native of Virginia, who, with his family, in 1782, immigrated into the Natchez district, then a Spanish province governed by Don Estaran Miro, and obtained from the government valuable grants of land both in Jefferson and Claiborne counties, and afterward, in 1802, was elected a representative to the national congress from the Mississippi territory. Joseph K. Green married Mildred Cabell, the youngest daughter of Col. Samuel Cabell, of Lynchburg, Va., who won a most enviable reputation in the Revolutionary war. His father, Joseph Eggleston Jones, was born near Charlottesville, Va., in 1793. While a mere stripling, at the breaking out of the War of 1812, he enlisted in the volunteer troops, and was near, though not participating, in the famous battle of New Orleans. In the year 1829, Mr. and Mrs. Jones, who were married the previous year, moved to Claiborne county, and purchased "White Hall." Mr. Jones was a successful planter, and at his death, in 1852, left a valuable estate of fourteen hundred and twenty-one acres, lying on the north fork of Bayou Pierre, which estate is still in the possession of the family. To Mr. and Mrs. Jones, in this pleasant country home, were born nine sons and three daughters, in the following order, the names of those still living at this date (1891) being printed in small capitals: JOSEPH C., Thomas H., EUGENE D., Martha Augusta, Samuel Cabell, SARAH VIRGINIA, ARCHELAUS KIRKLAND, WILLIAM SYME, Merriwether Lewis, James Bailey, LUCY ANN and MERIDETH DABNEY. Those living now reside in Claiborne county, except Dr. M. D. Jones, an aurist of reputation, residing in St. Louis, Mo. A. K. Jones was born at White Hall, in Claiborne county, Miss., on the 3d of June, 1839. In his boyhood he attended the neighborhood schools, where by diligent application he made himself a good English scholar. In 1856 he entered the University of Mississippi, at Oxford, and in June, 1860, was graduated from that excellent institution, ranking eighth in a class of thirty-nine. Having decided to follow the profession of civil engineer, he entered the Glenmore school of engineers, near Troy, N. Y., in the fall of 1860, and there remained until the attack on Fort Sumter, in 1861. Then, foreseeing the approaching conflict, he promptly returned to Mississippi. Reaching Claiborne county, where the war spirit was high, young Jones, with his younger brothers, William and Merriwether, enlisted as privates in company H, Twelfth Mississippi infantry, then encamped at Corinth, Miss. This regiment was soon sent to Virginia, reaching the field of the first Manassas the morning after the engagement. The Twelfth was immediately incorporated into the army of northern Virginia, forming a part of Rhode's brigade. Upon the regimental reorganization at Yorktown (December, 1861), private Jones was elected first-lieutenant of his company, which was thenceforth known as company K, and when the captain, W. H. Hastings, fell at Seven Pines, the Twelfth's first pitched battle, he was promoted to the vacancy. This title, well earned and honorably worn, the Captain still bears. After the battle of Seven Pines, the Twelfth Mississippi regiment formed a part of Featherstone's Mississippi brigade, and its record thenceforward is a matter of history. Captain Jones received his first wound, a severe one, at Frazier's farm, June 27, 1862, the same ball first passing through his thigh and then breaking the thigh-bone of sergeant J. H. Darrah, of his company. The desperate nature of these conflicts around Richmond may be judged by the fact that out of a total of four swords and sixty-four bayonets, with which company K went into the seven days' fight, but one sword and eighteen bayonets came out fit for duty, the remainder being either killed or disabled. Among the former was his brother, Merriwether, a youth of nineteen, and Lieut. John C. Calhoun, whose only sister, five years later, became the wife of Captain Jones. Again, at Bristoe Station, October 14, 1863, while leading a strong skirmish line under the immediate eye of Gen. A. P. Hill, Captain Jones received a serious wound which disabled him for months. His third wound was received at Yellow Tavern, August 18, 1864, where he was captured, and thence sent to prison at Fort Delaware. After two months' imprisonment he was exchanged as unserviceable; when able, he rejoined his regiment, and shared its fortune to the end.   His company, now thinned to a handful of seasoned veterans, formed part of the two hundred Mississippians of the Twelfth and Sixteenth regiments who manned Fort Gregg, April 2, 1865.   For two hours they held in check the whole of Gibbon's corps, striking down twelve hundred of the enemy, and saving from capture the Confederates, protecting Petersburg when the fort was carried; on the sixth assault the battle flags of the storming regiments formed an unbroken line of bunting around the little fortress.   Captain Jones was on this occasion second in command.   He was in the old Capitol prison at Washington the night President Lincoln was assassinated, when the prisoners were in great danger from mob-violence.   Sent thence to Johnson's island (Lake Erie), he was released on the 18th of June and reached home July 4, 1865.

In 1866 he engaged in farming on a portion of the family homestead, and this occupation he followed for the next eleven years.   On the 24th of October, 1867, he married Miss Mary H. Calhoun, of Claiborne county, whose father, E. W. Calhoun, a South Carolinian, was a cousin of John C. Calhoun, the statesman.   Eight children have been born to them: John Merriwether, Cabell Calhoun, Anna Amelia, Archelaus Kirkland, William Thomas, Mary Lou, Ett Eliza and Virginia Hughes.   In 1875 he was elected a member of the board of supervisors, and upon the organization the following January he was made president. This position he filled until December, 1877, when he was elected clerk of the chancery court, an office to which he was successively reëlected in 1879, 1883, 1887 and 1891, and which he still holds.   One of his neighbors, a gentleman of Port Gibson, writes: "No citizen of Claiborne county has ever stood higher in public regard than A. K. Jones, his many sterling qualities combined with a genial disposition and cordial manners having won for him an uncommon degree of popularity.   In addition to his worth as a man, he has shown himself, during his long term of service as chancery clerk, to be a model official, diligent, systematic, accurate, faithful to his duties, and courteous to the public.   He descends from an Episcopalian family, to which faith he also adheres, himself and wife and four of their children being communicants.

Charles L. Jones, a prosperous merchant, was born in Coahoma county, Miss., April 15, 1853, and is the third of seven children born of Felix and Mary (Palmer) Jones, the former a native of Alabama and the latter of Georgia.   Felix Jones came to Mississippi when young, and in this state spent the remainder of his life, dying in 1861 at his home near Jonestown.   With the exception of that his mother was of Scotch-Irish ancestry, Charles L. knows but little of his ancestors, having lost his parents when quite young.   His youthful days were spent in Coahoma county, Miss., and in Phillips county, Arkansas; and at the age of fifteen years he began life for himself as a clerk in a drug store belonging to Jacks & Moore, of Helena, Ark., in which he remained for ten years.   He began in the capacity of stock keeper, and was gradually promoted until the last five years he was prescription clerk on a salary of $1,500 a year.   In 1878 he returned to Jonestown and opened a general mercantile store, at which he has since done a thriving business.   In connection with his mercantile establishment he operated two plantations, and is the owner of eleven hundred acres, two hundred and fifty of which are under cultivation, the most of which he has opened and improved from the forest at a cost of $5,000.   He has about $10,000 worth of property, personal and real, in Jonestown, and a $5,000 stock of goods.   He is a stockholder in the Friar's Point oil mill, and the fine property of which he is now the owner has been acquired through his own exertions, for from early childhood he has had to carve out his own career.   He is strictly self-made, and although a comparatively young man, has accumulated a valuable property.   He is safe and reliable in his business transactions, but is very progressive—a secret, no doubt of his success. He possesses agreeable manners, is entertaining and intelligent, and is full of that fire, vim and pluck so necessary to success in any calling. He was married in 1881 to Miss Cora Dixon, a native of Mississippi and a daughter of Alfonso and Ursula (Legg) Dixon, who were born in Tennessee and Georgia respectively. Mrs. Jones died in 1887, leaving three children: Ursula R., Charles F., and Mary C. Mr. Jones' second union took place in 1889, his wife being Miss Maggie Hill, a daughter of Capt. J. R. and Kittie (Townsend) Hill, natives of Tennessee. By his last wife he has one child, Pattie C. Mr. and Mrs. Jones are members of the Christian church, and he belongs to the K. of H.

Dudley W. Jones, M. D., a native of Jefferson county, Miss., was born in 1835, a son of Dr. A. P. and Olive (Watson) Jones, both natives of that state. Dr. A. P. Jones was born in 1808, a son of John Jones, who came from Charleston, S. C., in 1780, to Mississippi. He was one of the pioneers of that state. John Jones, Jr., the grandfather of our subject, was a son of John Jones, Sr., an officer in the Revolutionary war. He owned a farm on what is now a portion of the site of the city of Charleston, S. C. Upon removing to Mississippi he located in Jefferson county and engaged in farming. He married Phœbe Griffin, of South Carolina, by whom he had six children: Jonathan, John, James, Asa P., Ben F. and Sarah. Asa P. Jones, father of Dudley W. Jones, was reared in Jefferson county, Miss. He was educated at Bardstown, Ky., and at the Transylvania university, where he studied medicine. He also took a medical course at Cincinnati. He graduated at Transylvania college, Lexington, Ky., in 1833. He began the practice of his profession in Jefferson county, where he remained till 1860, when he changed his residence to Claiborne county and lived there until 1875, when he joined his son, Dr. Dudley W. Jones, in Copiah county. He was probably the best known practitioner in the southern part of Mississippi, not only on account of his very successful practice, but also from his numerous and valuable contributions to medical journals. He was a member of the Medical association and of the Kappa Lamda—a secret society in Kentucky. He and his wife were members of the Methodist Episcopal church; his wife died in 1848, the Doctor in 1889. Our subject is the eldest of a family of two children. His sister, Anna, the wife of Lieut. Eugene D. Jones, is now dead. She married her husband during the war, and only lived a short time after her marriage. Dr. Jones was reared in Jefferson county, where he remained till he was twenty-two years of age. His educational opportunities were excellent. At the age of thirteen he was sent to the Oakland college, where he remained till he graduated therefrom in 1854; he began the study of medicine with his father and Dr. J. M. Bemis in 1854, and in 1854 and 1855 he took a course of lectures at Louisville, Ky. Later he graduated at the university of Louisiana, now called Tulane university, in 1857. Returning to Clairborne county, he engaged in farming until 1861, when he enlisted in company K of the Thirty-sixth Mississippi infantry—known as the Dixie guards—and served until the close of the war. He was several times promoted, being made hospital steward, then assistant surgeon and finally brigade surgeon. He was twice wounded and twice made prisoner, being captured at Iuka Springs and at Vicksburg, and, on account of his being surgeon, he was permitted both times to return. His wounds were received at Vicksburg and Kenesaw mountain. After the war he began to practice medicine in Claiborne county, afterward removing to Copiah county, where for two years he published the *Copiah Herald*, at Hazlehurst, when, relinquishing journalism, he took up the practice of his profession, which he has continued up to the present time. He was married in 1859 to Laura Peyton, a daughter of Chief Justice Peyton, a native of Gallatin. Mrs. Jones died August 28, 1886, having borne her husband seven children, named as follows: Ernest P.,

Willie, Dudley, Ephraim, Olive, Emily and Anna; Willie having died in 1884, leaves him six living children. In February, 1887, he married Helen Jones, a native of Mississippi, and a daughter of James M. Jones, of Natchitoches parish, La. One child sprang from this union: James O. The doctor is a member of the State Medical association, and in religious affiliations he is an Episcopalian, though his family are Presbyterians. He is also a Knight of Honor. Dr. Ernest Peyton Jones, a son of Dr. Jones, graduated at Tulane university in 1887, and is now a popular practitioner at Hermanville, Claiborne county, Miss. He is having success in his profession and his practice is growing large and lucrative. Dudley is studying law in the University of Mississippi. To the remainder of the children the doctor is giving the advantages of the high school and is contemplating placing them in college when they reach a suitable age. The Doctor is a careful, successful physician, well read in his profession and well-posted on current events. His standing is high socially, professionally and politically. He is an entertaining conversationalist, and in the best sense of the word a hail fellow well met, being most popular among all classes.

Dr. E. K. Jones was born in the Palmetto state, in 1846, but was reared in Mississippi. His father, Thomas Jones, was born in South Carolina, about 1803, and throughout life followed the calling of a planter, being content to pursue the even tenor of his way, with no aspirations to public honor. About 1825 he was married to Miss Asobel Hines, of South Carolina, born in 1804, and their union resulted in the birth of nine children: Ferdinand, Francis, Arison, Sarah, Frederick, Adaline, Julia, William and E. K. The father of these children died in 1868 and the mother in 1866. Dr. E. K. Jones came to Mississippi with his parents in 1853, and was reared and educated in Scott county. After finishing his literary course he pursued a course of medical study, although he has never practiced his profession, much preferring to devote his time and attention to planting and merchandising. His plantation, which consists of eighteen hundred acres, is well improved, and the principal crops are cotton and corn. Mr. Jones has a beautiful home in the residence portion of Pelahatchee, and, in connection with his planting operations, he also conducts a retail dry goods store, at which he is doing well. His prices are reasonable, and, as he makes every effort to please his customers, and is upright in every respect, his success is not to be wondered at. He is well-known throughout the county, and wherever known is liked and respected. In 1865 Mr. Jones enlisted in the Confederate army, in the east Louisiana division, under General Scott. In 1879 he was married to Miss Jennie Span, a native of Alabama. She was born in 1846 and has borne her husband three children: Glen P., R. and E. E.

George B. Jones, sheriff and collector of Grenada county, Miss., is a native of this state, born in Yalobusha county in 1848, and the son of John E. and Harriet N. (Wells) Jones, natives of Virginia, where they were reared and married. From there the parents moved to west Tennessee and, probably about 1835, came to Yalobusha county, Miss., where Mrs. Jones died in 1854 and Mr. Jones in 1866. The father followed planting for many years, but in connection also carried on merchandising and ran a public gin and mill for many years. He was a justice of the peace for many years, and at one time was a member of the board of police. He was a public-spirited, energetic citizen, and being a promoter of all that was good, he brought into practice these great virtues, and thereby commanded the respect of all he met in a business or a social way. He had many noble qualities and died without an enemy. He was a stanch secessionist. His father, Capt. Thomas Jones, was a native Englishman, but when a boy came to America, and was a captain in the Revolutionary war. He spent his last days in Mississippi, and died before our subject was born, aged about ninety years. He followed the occupation of a farmer all his life. The maternal grand-

66

parents were natives of the Old Dominion.   George B. Jones was the sixth of eight children, six sons and two daughters, born to his parents, and they are named in the order of their birth, as follows: Rebecca (deceased), Thomas (deceased), Robert (deceased), Elizabeth, wife of A. J. Jones, of Yalobusha county; John, who enlisted in the Confederate service when but fifteen years of age, became a lieutenant, and died while at home on a furlough; William (deceased), and Richard, who died young.   George B. Jones was reared to the arduous duties of the farm, received about eight months' schooling, and began for himself as a tiller of the soil when sixteen years of age.   At the age of twenty-one he was made justice of the peace, and served four years in Grenada county.   In 1875 he was elected assessor of the same for two years.   In 1885 he was elected sheriff and collector, but still continues his planting industry, and is the owner of seven hundred and forty acres of land, principally the result of his own industry.   In September, 1869, he wedded Miss Ann Eliza, a native of what is now Grenada county, Miss., and the daughter of James M. and Martha Creekmore, natives respectively of Mississippi and Alabama.   Mr. Creekmore was captain of a company called the Dixie Boys, and was killed in front of Richmond.   His wife is now living, and makes her home with her son-in-law, G. B. Jones.   Mrs. Jones died in 1888, leaving six children, five of whom are living.   She was a member of the Baptist church, in which Mr. Jones also holds membership.   He is a prominent member of the Masonic fraternity, Grenada lodge No. 31, and was formerly a member of Graysport lodge.   He has been worthy master in both.   He is vice grand of the Grenada lodge, I. O. O. F., No. 6, a member of the Knights of Honor, Granada lodge No. 983, also the Knights and Ladies of Honor and the Farmers' Alliance.

George W. Jones, merchant, Grenada, Miss., who established a general mercantile business in Grenada in 1863, is one of the leading merchants of the city, doing an annual business of from $25,000 to $30,000, and handling several thousand bales of cotton.   He was originally from Baltimore, Md., born in 1843, and a son of Captain Washington B. and Sarah (Crawford) Jones, both natives of Dorchester county, Md.   The father followed the life a seafaring man, and served in different capacities until a number of years after his marriage, sailing between the United States and the West Indies as captain.   After he abandoned the sea he engaged in merchandising in Baltimore, and followed this with success until his death, about 1849.   He was a man of ability and good judgment, and reared an industrious family.   His father, Col. James Jones, was a native of Wales, but when a boy came to America.   During the Revolutionary war he served as a soldier, and received his final summons in Baltimore prior to the death of his son, Washington B.   The mother of our subject died in that city in 1870, a devout member of the Methodist church.   George W. Jones is one of eight children—three sons and two daughters now living: Summerfield, a merchant and trader of Christian county, Mo., served in the Confederate army all through the war.   He first served as a captain of a battery in South Carolina, and afterward was colonel of a Louisana regiment, doing special duty as a scout in General Forrest's cavalry and Armstrong's brigade.   At one time his command was surrounded by the enemy in northern Mississippi, but after a severe fight for his life the colonel was severely wounded in the arm, but continued to fight, and finally made his escape.   Rev. Louis R., a prominent and able Methodist divine of the Baltimore Methodist conference for probably forty years, was educated at Asbury college in Baltimore.   Mary A. became the wife of Abel J. Reese, a prominent and wealthy commission merchant and planter of Baltimore.   Sadie, widow of a Mr. Collins, who was of a prominent family of Baltimore, and who died soon after the war.   George W. Jones was educated in Asbury college in Baltimore, and in 1860, when seventeen years of age, he was induced by

Levin Lake, a distinguished pioneer of Grenada, who was in Baltimore on business, to come to Grenada, where he clerked in Mr. Lake's store until the war broke out. He then at once joined Stanford's battery, of Cheatham's division, and served part of the time as sergeant until cessation of hostilities. He was frequently offered an officer's commission, but preferred to serve as a private. He fought at Columbus, Ky., Shiloh, Murfreesboro, Perryville, Chickamauga, and all through the Georgia and Atlanta campaigns. He was wounded at New Hope church, but came on the field with his arm in a sling. He went back from Atlanta with General Hood, and fought at Franklin and Nashville, Tenn. From there he went to Mobile, and thence north to Cuba Station, near Meridian, Miss., where he surrendered. He then returned to Grenada and followed clerking for different individuals until 1873, when he began business in his own name. This he has continued ever since, and is a gentleman of energy, judgment, and experience, and one of the thoroughgoing business men of the city. He started business in 1873 with a capital of $400, and notwithstanding he has met with reverses, fire, etc., he is now the owner of considerable valuable real estate in the city, including one of its finest residences. He was married in 1874 to Miss Elizabeth Collins, a native of Grenada county, and the daughter of that old and highly distinguished veteran, Joseph Collins, who is well and favorably known to all in Grenada and adjoining counties. Mr. Collins was one of the early settlers of Grenada county, locating here when the country was teeming with Indians. He was an industrious and exemplary citizen; a character above reproach, and by his industry and good financiering became one of the wealthiest planters of the county. He was a large slaveowner, and was noted for his kindness to them, while they in turn had the greatest respect for him. Prior to the war he erected a fine three-story brick hotel in Grenada, and this was known over nearly the entire South as Collins' hotel, being very popular with the traveling public. He died during the war, and his estimable wife a few years later. Both were exemplary members of the Primitive Baptist church. Mr. Collins was twice married, but had no children by his first wife. He has four surviving children: Franklin P., a well-to-do planter on the old farm; Moses B., a prominent planter of Coahoma county; Mrs. McLean, and Mrs. Jones. To Mr. and Mrs. Jones have been born five children—four sons now living. They are active members and liberal supporters of the Methodist church.

James A. Jones. The mercantile interests of Hinds county have been ably represented by Mr. Jones since 1887, and the varied and choice assortment of goods which he carries cannot fail to satisfy every want of his patrons. He was born in Greene county, Ga., April 7, 1857, being the youngest of twelve children born to Thomas and Maria (Caldwell) Jones, both of whom were born in Georgia. The father was a planter and bookkeeper, and died in his native state in 1860. His father was a native of Scotland, who settled in Georgia at an early day. In the state of Georgia James A. Jones was reared to manhood and educated in the common schools, and since the early age of ten years he has made his own way in the world, and the means which he acquired in his early youth he spent in educating himself. From ten until eighteen years of age his time, or the greater part of it, was spent in a hardware store, at the end of which he engaged in business for himself at Camilla, Ga., where he continued successfully for eleven years. In 1887 he came to Mississippi, and since that time he has been one of Jackson's most enterprising and energetic merchants; in fact, his reputation is established throughout the state. He is associated with his brother, and they have three well-appointed mercantile houses in Mississippi—one at Jackson, one at Natchez and one at Yazoo City, the income from the three amounting to about $300,000 annually. They carry the most complete line of dry goods, millinery, clothing and shoes in Jackson, and their

other establishments are also well stocked and admirably conducted. James A. Jones superintends the entire business and does all the buying for the firm, his judgment and practical
knowledge of his calling being indisputable. He is one of the most intelligent, energetic
and successful of merchants, and his attention to business, and his kind, courteous and honorable conduct to his patrons have met with substantial reward. He is public spirited to a high
degree, and is in every respect a worthy and useful citizen, and a credit to the state in which
he has chosen to cast his lot. He is a purely self-made man, and the greater part of his
learning has been acquired in that thorough, but hard, school of experience. Although a
young man, he has made an independent fortune, and there are few men in the state who
have a better knowledge of business than he. On the 24th of March, 1881, he was married
to Miss Ella Jackson, a native of Georgia and a daughter of Green S. and Virginia (Peacock)
Jackson, natives of Georgia, but Mrs. Jones died in 1886, leaving two children: James A.,
Jr., and Johnnie E. In 1890 Mr. Jones was again united in marriage, Miss Annie E.
McLaughlin, a native of Quincy, Fla., and a daughter of William and Mary J. (Griffin)
McLaughlin, becoming his wife. Her parents were born of South Carolina and Georgia,
respectively.

J. C. H. Jones, M. D., is a physician and surgeon of Macon, Miss., who has become
eminent in his chosen calling, and is in command of a large practice among the finest families of Noxubee county. He was born in Pickens county, Alabama, September 11, 1835, to
Zachariah and Mary (Monett) Jones, who were natives of the state of Georgia. The father
was one of the pioneers of Pickens county, Alabama, and there followed the calling of a
planter until his demise in 1842. His widow servives him and is now in her eighty-third
year. She became the mother of four sons and two daughters, the following of whom are
living: Dr. J. C. H., William B., and Mrs. J. E. Cook. The maternal grandfather Rev.
James Monett, preached the first sermon in Pickens county, Alabama. He was a member of
the Methodist Episcopal church. Dr. J. C. H. Jones was reared in his native county and
was educated in the college of Summerfield, Ala., his knowledge of medicine being acquired
in the university of Tennessee, from which institution he graduated in 1856. He began
practicing in Pickens county, Alabama, but the interest he took in politics and his inexhaustible fund of general information led to his being chosen as a suitable man to represent
Pickens county in the general assembly of the state, of which body he was a member from
1870 to 1874, during which time he discharged his duties to the satisfaction of his constituents and with much credit to himself. He was president of the Pickens County Medical
society from 1870 to 1888, and also discharged the duties of health officer for eight years.
He was counselor of the State Medical association and postmaster and justice of the peace
for a number of years. He was the means of establishing a postoffice at Stone, Ala.,
of which he had complete charge for twenty years. In 1889 he came to Macon, Miss., and
here has since devoted his attention to his profession, and although he has only made his home
here for a short time he has been identified with the interests of the county for over thirty
years, having lived almost on its border line and practiced in the county. He still continues
to have planting and mercantile interests in Alabama, but in Mississippi devotes his attention to his profession, being associated in the practice with his son, Bolivar T., who graduated
from the Alabama Medical college at Mobile, in 1886. After twelve months' practice in the
hospital of that city he went to Birmingham, Ala., where he practiced four years, at the end
of which time he went to New York and took a post-graduate course in the Bellevue Medical college, after which he returned to Macon to enter upon the practice of his profession
with his father, the firm being now known as Jones & Jones. Dr. Jones, Jr., was married

in the fall of 1889 to Miss Jesse Shropshire, a native of Mississippi, by whom he has one child. Dr. Jones, Sr., was married in 1860 to Miss Mary Cook, a daughter of Major Cook, of Alabama, by whom he has four sons and two daughters: Dr. B. T., who was born in 1862; John C. H., of Alabama; Mrs. J. T. McClure, M. Z., George H., and Lenita L. The Doctor and his wife are members of the Methodist Episcopal church, in which he holds the position of steward, and he is also a member of the Masonic fraternity and the K. of P., having been an active member of the former order for the past thirty years. During the war he had charge of a ward in the Tishomingo hospital after the battle of Shiloh, and after the battle of Seven Pines had charge of a ward in the Third Alabama hospital at Richmond, Va.

The people of Wilkinson county, Miss., are familiar with the name of Col. J. H. Jones, for he has resided among them for many years, and has earnestly identified himself with every worthy enterprise, his brilliant mental qualities fitting him in an admirable manner to lead whenever he so desired. He was born in Autauga county, Ala., on the Alabama river, in 1838, being the eldest of seven children born to John Edmund and Mary A. (Mellard) Jones, who were born in North Carolina and South Carolina respectively, they being descendants of early Huguenot families who came to this county many years ago. When a small lad Col. J. H. Jones was taken by his parents to Mobile, where he was reared, his education being received in Barton academy, which he attended for several years. After the death of his father he removed with his mother and her father to Macon county, and while there began preparing himself for college, and so faithfully did he carry out this design that two years after entering the University of Mississippi at Oxford he was graduated (in 1858), carrying off the first honors of a class of fifty-six pupils. He was considered one of the brightest and most promising pupils that ever left the institution. Soon after leaving college he was married in this county to Miss Helen M. Davis, a daughter of William B. Davis, a native of Louisiana, but one of the early settlers of this region, and with her removed to Texas, where he engaged in the practice of law, having been admitted to the bar in Woodville, his studies being directed by Gordon & Barber, leading lawyers of this county. After following his chosen profession at Bastrop, on the Colorado river, in Texas, for two years, the clash of arms caused him to cast aside his books to don a suit of gray and take up arms in defense of the Confederate cause, three of his brothers also entering the service. John Edmund was killed in the siege of Vicksburg, Miss., at the age of nineteen years; Robert B. was killed at Harrisburg, Miss., when seventeen years of age; he was of small stature, and for this reason and on account of his youth he was twice discharged, but each time reënlisted; Elisha M. was also killed in the same battle at the age of sixteen years. Col. J. H. Jones first entered as a private in the sixty days' service under General Alcorn, but in the spring of 1862 returned to Wilkinson county, Miss., and raised a company that was incorporated in the Thirty-eighth Mississippi regiment at Jackson, and was made its captain, commanding in the following battles: Iuka, Corinth, Hayes bluff, siege of Vicksburg, and Johnsonville. After the siege of Vicksburg, the entire regiment was mounted and rejoined the army, becoming a part of Bragg's corps. The next engagement was at Harrisburg, where Captain Jones was wounded. The regiment, composed of three hundred and fifty men, made a charge on a battery, and only forty-four came out unhurt. Colonel Jones was wounded by grapeshot in both legs, and for about six months thereafter was confined to the hospital at Lauderdale, Miss. At the end of this time he rejoined his command at Macon, Miss., and was in some fierce skirmishes before the surrender of General Lee. He was commissioned colonel after the battle of Harrisburg, Colonel McKay having been killed in that engagement. He made a brave soldier and a faithful officer, and his men, like him, possessed indomitable courage, and were conspicuous for their strict adherence to duty. After the war he came to Wilkinson county once more, and began practicing law, and his success in life at the bar, and the high position he holds in social circles have been attained rather by native talent than by tact. Recognizing his sound judgment and practical ability, and the eminent services he has rendered his party, his numerous friends, in order to show their appreciation of the same, elected him in 1886 to the state legislature, his reëlection taking place in 1888, and 1890 he was elected to the state senate. He was a member at large to the constitutional convention from this state, and has ever been ardent in his support of democracy and reform, and in conjunction with Senator George, was the chief author and prime mover of the article on corporations framed in the present constitution of Mississippi. Colonel Jones ably represented Wilkinson county in the house of representatives for two successive terms, during which time he took rank with the foremost members of that body. The journals of the house show how assiduously he labored for the interests of the state, and as a pure and intelligent legislator his reputation was the very best. He was on many of the most important committees, and originated and had passed some of the principal measures found in Acts of 1886-8. As chairman of sub-committees to investigate land frauds he made full and exhaustive reports, and was an earnest advocate of reform in the jury system as well as in other institutions of the state. He was always cautious and conservative, and did much to prevent hasty legislation, and no member of the legislative body wielded a wider influence than he. In 1886 he was highly recommended by the leading journals of the state for lieutenant-governor, and as he has always showed executive ability of a high order, he eminently deserves the praise he has received, and would make a most competent lieutenant-governor, as well as an able governor. He is a member of lodge No. 63, of the A. F. & A. M., and belongs to Woodville lodge No. 10, of the I. O. O. F. He and his wife have been members of the Methodist Episcopal church for many years, and are most liberal in their contributions to worthy enterprises.

In addition to the practice of law, Colonel Jones is engaged in planting. His father, John Edmund Jones, as stated above, was born in North Carolina, his birth occurring in 1808. When a small boy he was taken to the state of Tennessee, and was reared and educated near Murfreesboro, being given the advantages of a collegiate education. He afterward moved to Alabama and was elected to the position of district attorney, and made an efficient judge of the city court of Mobile. In this capacity he discharged his duties so capably and well that he was elected to the senate, and was regarded as an able man for the position. Nothing ever caused him to swerve an inch from his loyalty to his state, and his fealty to his friends, if they deserved it, and it may with truth be said that he always subserved his own interest to that of his people and his state. He died in the month of February, 1851, when just in the prime of life, and in the zenith of his usefulness, soon after which event his widow moved with her family to Macon county, Ala., where she made her home for about five years, at the end of which time she took up her abode in east Mississippi, and at the close of the war settled in Wilkinson county, where she is still living. She is a refined and cultured lady, a noble woman in every respect, and is an active worker in the Methodist Episcopal church, of which she has been a member for many years. She was born in 1814, and bore her husband seven children, of whom are living: Emma, a resident of New York city, and widow of Henry Goodwin; Mollie, wife of C. W. Davis, a resident of Wilkinson county, Miss.; Bettie and Col. J. H. The wife of the latter is a daughter of W. B. Davis, a native of Louisiana, who came to Wilkinson county when a boy, and here attained his majority, being self-educated. He started in life with no means but a pair of willing hands and a goodly supply of determination and pluck, and in early manhood, by persistent effort, he laid the foundations of a substantial fortune. He became an extensive planter, and usually raised from twelve hundred to fifteen hundred bales of cotton per year. Although he was, at different times, compelled to pay heavy security debts, at the time of his death, in 1876, at the age of seventy-four years, he left a substantial fortune. His wife, who was formerly Miss Eliza McGraw, was born, reared, educated and married in this county, and died in 1855 at the age of thirty-four years, having become the mother of six children, that grew to mature years, five of whom are yet living: Helen, wife of Colonel Jones; Robert, Charles, John and Eugenie, the latter the wife of James D. Cage.

Hon. Lewis B. Jones, planter, Taylor, Miss., was the eldest in a family of five children born to the union of William I. and Annie (Bond) Jones, who located in Mississippi 1836, at a time when the Indians still roamed over the northern part of that state. The father was a successful planter and an unusually good business man, having by good management accumulated an immense tract of land prior to the war. This is now in the possession of his son Lewis. Mr. Jones died on his plantation in the year 1873. Lewis B. Jones was born in Madison county, Tenn., in 1831, May 22, had excellent opportunities for an education, and these he improved to the fullest extent. He matriculated at the opening of the state university, and remained in school for a term of four years. In 1851 he selected as his companion in life Miss Helen T. Jeffreys, and they are now enjoying the blessings of a prosperous and well-spent life. Unto their marriage have been born five children, only two of whom are still living—David and William. When the war between the sections began Mr. Jones enlisted and served faithfully until its close, never receiving a wound. He then, realizing fully the situation, returned to his home, and so earnestly did he apply himself, and with such determined energy, that he is to-day one of the most extensive landowners in the county, having added considerably to the estate of his father. He was chosen supervisor by the democrats in 1877, and there took place one of the most hotly contested elections in the history of the county. In 1879 he was appointed magistrate by Governor Stone, and held that position until 1881, at which time he was elected to the legislature, serving with credit and distinction for one term. Since then he has devoted his time exclusively to his plantation. He is a worthy patron to all laudable public enterprises, and he is ever ready to assist those who, through no fault of their own, are in need of help. He and his family are Methodists.

Martin Jones, planter, Sardis, Miss., is one of the oldest settlers living in the county, having emigrated here with his father as early as 1834, when everything was wild and unsettled, and when Indians and wild animals were the only inhabitants. He was born in Dallas county, Ala., on the 28th of January, 1815, and was the seventh of eleven children born to James and Sarah (Smith) Jones, natives of Georgia. The father followed planting after coming to Mississippi and he, and two or three others, were the first settlers of Panola county. On leaving his native state he first went to Alabama, thence to Tennessee, from there to Arkansas, then back to Tennessee and finally to Mississippi, locating in Panola county, where his death occurred in 1841. Martin Jones was partly reared in Alabama, Tennessee, Arkansas and Mississippi and educated in the private schools of those states. When twenty-one years of age he started out to fight life's battles for himself empty handed, and that he has been successful and is to-day one of the wealthiest men of the county is an acknowledged fact. He is the owner of twenty-one hundred and sixty acres of land and has ten hundred acres under cultivation. He was first married, in 1837, to Miss Caroline Faris, of Tennessee, and daughter of Robert and Sarah Faris, also of that state. To them were born six children: James T., Sarah J., Demarius M., William M., William F., and one died unnamed. All are now deceased.

The eldest son, James T., was in the Confederate army and was killed at the battle of Sharpsburg, Maryland. Martin Jones was married the second time on the 22d of February, 1855, to Mrs. Sarah (Harvey) Beaty, a native of North Carolina, widow of A. I. Beaty and the daughter of Alexander L. and Christian (Harrington) Harvey, also of North Carolina. Mr. Jones has the reputation of being one of the most successful planters in the county and as a citizen and neighbor is esteemed and respected. He is very strong and hearty for his age, is sociable and pleasant and delights to narrate incidents of pioneer days with which his mind is well stored. He is hospitable and wholesouled and is ever ready to assist the needy and distressed. He is a democrat but takes very little interest in politics.

Dr. Robert E. Jones, the subject of this sketch, was born at Utica, Miss., October 5, 1843, When about three months of age his mother died, leaving his grandmother, Mrs. Serene Robertson, to assist his father in the care of the children. He only received the benefits of a common-school education, the commencement of the Civil war, in his seventeenth year, having prevented further progress. Early in 1862 he enlisted in the Confederate army, company K, Thirty-sixth Mississippi regiment, as a volunteer. After a short and brilliant service as a private, he was promoted to the position of first lieutenant, in which capacity he served till the close of the war, being in command of his company most of the time. His regiment was of the army of Mississippi and Tennessee, and he participated in the battles in which that army engaged. He was slightly wounded at the battle of Altoona, Ga., on his twenty-first birthday, October 5, 1864. He was twice a prisoner of war, having been surrendered, with the forces under General Pemberton, after having undergone the fighting, starvation and other hardships incident to the siege of Vicksburg, Miss., which lasted forty-seven days, ending July 4, 1864, to Gen. U. S. Grant, commander of the United States forces. He, with the other prisoners, was placed under parole and returned, at the expiration of the parole, to the Confederate forces, an exchange of prisoners having been effected, and was again surrendered, with his entire command, to the United States forces at the battle of Blakely, Ala., in 1865. All prisoners taken at Blakely and Spanish fort, a few miles below Blakely, were carried to Ship Island, Miss., as prisoners of war, and were there kept under a strong guard of negroes about one month. He was subsequently transferred to Vicksburg, Miss. When he was released, after the close of the war, he returned to his home at Utica, Miss., and there began the study of the medical science, under his brother, Dr. Jesse R. Jones, subsequently graduating at the Eclectic college of Cincinnati, Ohio, in 1868, and at the University of Louisiana (now Tulane college), at New Orleans, in 1869. He was married, December 16, 1869, to Miss Elizabeth A. McKey, who was born in Jefferson county, Miss., February 9, 1850. Her parents, Hamden J. and Sarah A. (Hill) McKey, moved to Copiah county, Miss., in the same year. He has three living daughters, Rena, Clara and Elizabeth, and one son, Robert Hill. He has now living three brothers: Dr. Jesse R., a graduate of the Eclectic medical college of Cincinnati, Ohio, who married Miss Mary Davis; John A., who married Miss Ann Tracy; Milton R., who married Miss Emily Fulghan, and has twice represented his county in the legislature; and one sister, Mary S., who married Eugene D. Jones, of Claiborne county, Miss. His father, Dr. Robert Jones, was born in 1800, married Miss Mary Battel Robertson, of Mississippi, daughter of Nathaniel and Serene (Ragan) Robertson, who was born in Hancock county, Ga., and died February 8, 1881, at the home of the subject of this sketch, in the eighty-seventh year of her age. Mrs. Robertson was a daughter of John Ragan and Susanna (Battel) Ragan, and a granddaughter of Jonathan Ragan, who was born in Ireland. Her mother's father, Jesse Battel, came from Wales to Norfolk, Va., and married Susan Forcett, who was born in France. Dr. Jones' father left Missouri when he was nineteen years of age, to join his brother, who was then living in Louisiana. From the latter state he moved to Mississippi, and engaged in the mercantile line at Monticello and Grand Gulf; afterward moved to Utica, began the study of medicine, and graduated at the Eclectic college of Cincinnati, Ohio, and, returning to Utica, practiced his profession till his death in 1861. He was a member of the Methodist Episcopal church, an able practitioner and an honest, upright citizen. His grandfather, David Jones, was born in Virginia, married Jane Ruble, daughter of Owen Ruble and Helen (White) Ruble. The latter was born in Scotland, and her brother, Alexander White, was a member of the First congress of the United States of America. David Jones emigrated from Virginia to Kentucky, and, in 1811, to Cooper county, Mo., with his wife, two sons (Jesse Ruble and Robert) and nine daughters. Being among the first settlers of that state, he found it necessary, at times, to flee from the Indians to block houses and Fort Cooper for safety. He represented Cooper county in the legislature for two sessions, and died February 7, 1838, at the age of seventy-seven years, his wife surviving him only a few months, and dying in her seventy-fifth year. His great-grandfather, Robert Jones, was a Baptist preacher, born in Virginia, married a Miss Riley, and died at the age of one hundred and four years. His great-great-grandfather, Robert Jones, emigrated from Wales to Montgomery county, Va., when a boy, about the year 1700. He married Mary Van Metre. He was a soldier in the Revolutionary war, and was in the battle of Yorktown at the surrender of Cornwallis. The subject of this sketch, after graduating in medicine, began the practice of his profession at his home, Utica, Miss., where he acquired a large practice and many warm friends. In 1874 he moved to Crystal Springs, Miss., where he has demonstrated the verity of the adage that worth makes the man. As a citizen he has been loyal to all good causes, firm in his convictions of right, unflinching in the performance of duty, prominent in every movement for the public good; as a physician, brave, kind, conscientious, benevolent and sympathetic, his reputation so well established that the name of Dr. R. E. Jones is a synonym, where known, for skill in the art of healing; as a Christian, that highest attainment of man, he has, by an upright walk, chaste conversation and cheerful performance of duty, been above reproach. His influence for good has been felt by the community at large, and particularly by those who are daily associated with him, and the writer hereof knoweth whereof he writeth. Both he and his wife are members of the Methodist Episcopal church South. He is now president of the board of stewards of his church, and has been a member of that board most of the time since joining the church, twenty-one years ago. He is a member of the State Medical association; president of the local board of health; member of the board of school trustees; member of the United Confederate veterans, and surgeon of the local (Benjamin Humphreys) camp; past chancellor commander of the Knights of Pythias, C. S. lodge No. 21, and member of the Knights of Honor, C. S. lodge No. 1420. He is a member of the firm of Dampeer & Jones, druggists, and has some planting interests.

Robert K. Jones, M. D., was born at Wanalaw, the home of his aunt, Mrs. F. P. Eggleston, on the 25th of February, 1844, being the eldest child of H. K. and S. B. Jones, both native Virginians, the former having been born in Dinwiddie, and the latter a daughter of Dr. John R. and Fannie (Coch) Archer, in Amelia county. H. K. Jones, mentioned above, was a graduate of the medical department of the University of Pennsylvania. He was married to S. B. Archer on the 14th of February, 1843. After his marriage he removed to Mississippi, settling in Holmes county, about ten miles north of Lexington, where in connection with his practice he was engaged in farming. His death occurred at home in 1874, and his widow died in Tchula, Miss., the spring of 1881. They left six sons and one daughter.

Robt. K. Jones, the oldest of this family, commenced school when about ten years of age, his mother having taught him at home up to that time. His first teacher was Mr. L. R. Page, who is now a prominent lawyer of Richmond, Va. When he was fourteen years old he went to Virginia to school, living with his aunt, Mrs. Thomas Y. Tabb, his mother's sister, and going to school to Mr. John L. Hood. He lived with Mr. Tabb's family for a year and was treated and loved as one of their children. In the fall of 1859 he went to Lexington, Va., living with and going to school to Rev. William Pendleton, D. D., who was rector of Grace church, of Lexington, Va. He had a private boardingschool having about fifteen scholars. He remained here except during vacations, which he spent at his Virginia home, for he always felt as he would at home when going to his aunt's, until the spring of 1861, when his teacher, who was a graduate of West Point, disbanded his school, on being elected captain of the Rockbridge battery of artillery. After leaving Lexington in 1861, R. K. Jones went to his Virginia home, where he staid until the following fall, when he came to his own home, remaining until the spring of 1862. He then went back to join the Army of North Virginia, where he met his old friend and teacher, Rev. W. N. Pendleton, who was then brigadier-general and chief of artillery of Gen. R. E. Lee's army. Through the kindness and influence of General Pendleton, Mr. Jones was made sergeant-major of the Thirty-first Virginia battalion of artillery, commanded by Maj. William Nelson, who always treated Mr. Jones with great kindness. He was appointed first lieutenant and adjutant of his battalion, October, 1862, being little over eighteen years of age. He served with his battalion until the close of the war, and surrendered with General Lee's army on the 9th of April, 1865, serving temporarily at that time as aid on General Pendleton's staff. After the war he returned home and was engaged in attending to his father's business for him until 1871. He then went to Baltimore in October, 1871, to attend medical lectures at the Washington university, having read medicine for more than a year with Dr. G. C. Phillips. He graduated at the above named university in 1872, remaining at the hospital and attending lectures until the spring of 1873. After this he returned to Holmes county, Mississippi, where he has been engaged in the practice of medicine ever since, having lived in Tchula since 1881. He was married in 1884 to Miss C. A. Robertson. They have three children, Conway B., Robt. K. Jr., and Henry B. Mr. Jones was confirmed by Bishop Johns, of Virginia, in 1863 and has been a communicant of the church ever since.

R. W. Jones, Jr., cashier of the Merchants and Farmers' bank, of Macon, Miss., was born in Greenville county, near Petersburg, Va., in 1863, a son of R. W. Jones, Sr., who is professor of chemistry in the University of Mississippi. In 1876 Mr. Jones, Jr., came to Mississippi and entered the state university, from which well-known institution of learning he graduated in 1884. He then moved to Memphis, Tenn., where he was cashier of the People's Insurance company until 1888, when he came to Macon and organized the Merchants and Farmers' bank, with a capital of $25,000, since increased to $50,000, the surplus and undivided profits amounting to $15,000. Mr. Jones has been its efficient and trustworthy cashier since its organization, and as a financial manager has shown that he is shrewd, practical and capable. Although still young in years and experience, his career thus far has been one that reflects great credit upon him, and his future is bright with promise. In 1888 he was united in marriage to Miss S. V., daughter of S. V. D. Hill, a skillful and worthy physician of Macon, and by her has become the father of two sons: Van Dyke H. and Walker. Mr. Jones and his estimable wife are members of the Methodist Episcopal church, and socially he belongs to the I. O. O. F.

William Jones, M. D., of Osyka, Pike county, Miss., is a native of Amite county, where he was born April 11, 1827. Henry Jones, his father, was born in Barnwell district,

S. C., and came to Mississippi when a child with his father, William Jones, who was one of the pioneers of Amite county, who built the first house in Liberty, the county seat of that county. There he became a planter, and reared a respectable family. Henry Jones grew up in Amite county and he was educated at Liberty. He married Miss Mary Spurloch, a daughter of Allen Spurloch, a pioneer, who came from Oglethorpe county, Ga. While en route the family was besieged by the Creek Indians. Henry Jones became a successful planter and a popular citizen, and died in 1835. He was a justice of the peace in this county. While yet a young boy, he ran away and joined the United States army, at New Orleans, with which he saw service in the War of 1812. After his death, Mrs. Jones married Edward S. Brown and lived on the old homestead until 1861, and after the death of Mr. Brown the mother lived with her son, Dr. William Jones, until she died in 1888. Our subject is one of a family of four sons and four daughters, who grew to mature years. Of these, only Doctor Jones and two of his sisters are living. One of his brothers, Henry, fought for the Confederate cause, and died from the effect of a wound received in battle. Seaborn was killed in the Mexican war, at the battle of Buena Vista. Josepheus, another brother, is dead. Sarah B. married W. W. Lowry, and she and her husband are now deceased, leaving two sons. Elvira married Elijah Thompson, and they are both deceased, leaving several heirs. Elizabeth married Mr. A. J. Robinson, and lived in Rapides parish, La., where the widow still lives. Frances is the wife of Z. R. Causey, of Amite county, Miss., and moved to Ascension parish, La. Doctor Jones has had two half-brothers and three half-sisters, his mother's children by Mr. Brown. Two of these, Martha and Mary, are living. Doctor Jones is the second son in his father's family, and grew up in Amite county, Miss. He was educated at the schools of Liberty and at the Perkins Male academy. He began the study of medicine in 1852, under the tutorship of Drs. Dickson and T. J. Spurloch. In 1854–5 he attended lectures at the New Orleans school of medicine. In 1856 he returned to the medical college at New Orleans, from which he received his diploma in the spring of 1857. He began his professional practice at Osyka, locating soon in Livingston parish, La., where he practiced until the beginning of the war. In August, 1861, he enlisted in the Ninth Louisiana battalion, as an assistant surgeon, serving in that capacity until the close of the war. He assisted during the entire period, and was present at the battles of Baton Rouge, Fort Hudson, and at many minor engagements. He returned to Osyka, Miss., after his discharge, and he has ever since been actively engaged in the practice of his profession, his skill and reputation as a physician being such that he is in great demand throughout this and portions of the adjoining counties. He is president of the board of health of Pike county. He was married in Amite county to Miss M. C. Burris. His second wife was Miss Sarah Stellie, of Ponchatoula. His present wife was Mrs. M. L. Ott, of Osyka. His children by his first wife were Seburn T., who is a teacher in Texas; Emily, wife of T. C. Ott, of Osyka. His children by his second marriage were Willie, who died of yellow fever at the age of seventeen; Anna J., who is the wife of Rev. S. G. Cooper, of Hinds county, Miss., and Robert E. Lee and Harry, who are members of their father's family. By his last marriage the Doctor had a son, Octo, who is now eighteen years of age. The Doctor and his family are members of the Baptist church. The Doctor is a dimitted Mason, having taken the Royal Arch degree, and he is also identified with the Odd Fellows. Though somewhat advanced in years, the Doctor is remarkably well preserved; his form is unbent, and he walks with almost the elasticity of youth. His hair is scarcely tinged with gray. He is, without doubt, the leading physician of Osyka, and he is highly esteemed, both for his professional ability and for his social qualities.

William B. Jones, merchant and planter, Flora, Miss. When starting out for himself, Mr. Jones' capital consisted of about four hundred acres of land, and what he has made in the way of this world's goods has been accomplished by his own industry and good management. He was born in Madison county, Miss., on the 24th of September, 1847, and is the only son born to the union of Joseph M. and M. E. (Wiggins) Jones, the father a native of the Palmetto state and the mother of North Carolina. The father came to Mississippi in 1827, settled in Madison county near the town of Flora and there followed planting until his death, in 1885. The maternal grandfather, Jesse Wiggins, was a native of North Carolina. William B. Jones grew to manhood in his native state and received his education in Summerville institute, from which he graduated in 1868. He immediately afterward began planting for himself and in a small way, also engaged in merchandising. At the present time he is the owner of seven thousand acres of land, with two thousand five hundred acres under cultivation, and carries a stock of goods valued at $1,500. He was married in 1870 to Miss Flora B. Mann, a native of Mississippi, and daughter of Hon. Jackson and Penina (Atkinson) Mann, natives of North Carolina. To Mr. and Mrs. Jones have been born two children: Jesse M. and Hal G. The former is attending the Industrial institute and college at Columbus, Miss. In 1884, when the town of Flora was located (the same being named in honor of Mrs. Jones), he moved to that place and embarked in merchandising. He has been quite successful, but was burnt out in 1890, with a loss of $2,500. During that year Mr. Jones handled two thousand five hundred bales of cotton and did business to the amount of $125,-000, more than any other establishment of the kind in the county. He is trustee of the Mississippi college, Clinton, and is also a member of the investment committee of the endowment fund of the same. He is vice president of the Mississippi Fair association, and has stock in the Capital State bank, Jackson, Miss., and owns several valuable buildings in Jackson. While Mr. Jones has never aspired for any office whatever, he was urgently requested by many friends to be a candidate for state senator from his county, but he very positively refused to enter politics under any circumstances. He has, perhaps, contributed more to build churches, schools, etc., than any other man of his means in the county and takes a great pleasure in helping the poor and distressed whenever an opportunity offers. He is the largest property owner in Flora and is one of the most energetic, enterprising men in the county. He has presented several churches with lots free of charge and considers it a pleasure instead of duty to do all in his power to advance education and religion, as well as everything relating to the general welfare of the county. In 1862 Mr. Jones enlisted in company C, Thirty-ninth regiment Mississippi volunteer infantry, and was with the same one year. In 1863 he joined company M, Wirt Adams' regiment, and continued with this until 1865. He participated in the following battles: Corinth, Franklin, Grand Gulf, Port Hudson and Sypsie creek. He surrendered at Gainesville, Ala., in 1865. Mr. and Mrs. Jones are members of the Baptist church, and he is an active member of the Knights of Honor and the Knights of Pythias organizations. In politics he affiliates with the democratic party.

Hon. W. H. Jones, a lawyer and merchant of Raleigh, Smith county, Miss., was born in Rankin county, this state, in 1852, and here grew to maturity. As a student at the high school at Cato, he received a good common-school education. Much of his early life was spent upon a farm. In 1878 he became a student at the law office of Lowry & McLaurin at Brandon, under whose direction he read so diligently that he was admitted to the bar in 1879, and engaged in the practice of his profession. In 1881 he was elected to the legislature and served with credit during the session of 1881 and 1882. A reëlection was tendered him, but he declined it and has since devoted his entire attention to his profession, pleading in the courts at Rankin, Smith, Jasper, Jones, Covington and Simpson counties, with his office at Raleigh. He was married in January, 1881, to Miss Sallie A. Duckworth, who has borne him four children. His father, the Rev. Hiram Jones, was a minister of the Missionary Baptist church, to which he has devoted his entire time for the last twenty-five years, being a preacher of ability, well-known and quite popular throughout a good portion of the state. He was born in Louisiana in 1810, a son of Woody Jones, who was a veteran of the War of 1812 and served under General Jackson at the battle of New Orleans. He was a native of Georgia. The father of Woody Jones was an Irishman by birth, and came to America when he was a young man. The family have been for many years devoted to the pursuit of agriculture.

Zebulon P. Jones, whose postoffice address is Monticello, Miss., is a leading farmer and president of the board of supervisors of Lawrence county, Miss. He was born on Topisaw creek, at a point then in Lawrence county, now in Lincoln county, in the year 1846. He is the son of Andrew V. and Feraby (Hickman) Jones, natives of Lawrence county, Miss. His father was Vincent Jones, who came from South Carolina and settled in Mississippi about 1810, accompanied by several other families, among whom was the Hickman family. He located in what afterward became Lawrence county. The grandfather of our subject followed planting on the creek above-mentioned, owning a considerable quantity of land and a goodly number of slaves, and was regarded as well to do for that time. He was a man of considerable importance, and served in some of the early Indian wars. He lived to be seventy years of age and died in 1859 or 1860. He was unmarried when he came here, but later married and became the father of a large family, the father of our subject having been one of eleven out of sixteen children in this family who lived to maturity. He was reared in this county, and lived here till his death, at the age of thirty-nine years, leaving his wife and eight children, one of whom has since died. The mother, who was born in 1823, was the daughter of Aaron Hickman, a native of South Carolina, who came to Mississippi with the grandfather of our subject. She was one of a large family, and is yet living, very well and strong for one of her years. She is a member of the Baptist church. The children born to her are named as follows: Amanda, now Mrs. McGuffee; Mrs. Catherine Sauls; Zebulon P.; Mrs. Martha Maxwell; Mary, who became Mrs. Smith; William V. Jones; Aaron W. Jones, and Elizabeth, who died single, aged twenty-two years.

Our subject attained his majority in this county, which has always been his home, and in 1863 enlisted in company E, of the Fourth Mississippi regiment, with which he served until paroled at Greenville, Ala. He was in the battles at Harrisburg, Macon and a number of skirmishes. Returning home at the close of the war, he engaged in planting, locating upon his present plantation in 1885. He was married to Lusetta Smith, a daughter of Isaiah and Falitki (Carney) Smith, natives of Mississippi, but whose parents came from Georgia. Mrs. Jones is the fourth child in a family of eight born to her parents, who were reared and educated in Lawrence county. She has borne her husband one child, a son, Pleasant Zebulon Jones, now employed in the county clerk's office at Monticello, and a student at Oxford Law college. He is a young man of fine intellect, practically educated, who is deservedly popular among a wide circle of acquaintances, and whose future promises to be as brilliant as that of any other young man in this part of the county or state. Mr. and Mrs. Jones are both members of the Baptist church, and their home is one of the pleasantest and most popular in the county. For several terms Mr. Jones held the office of justice of the peace, and served the county one term as county surveyor. In 1879 he was elected a member of the board of supervisors, to which office he was again elected in 1889. He is a democrat in politics, and firmly believes in his party. He is a selfmade man, who began life with no capital, excepting a determination to succeed, and is now the owner of a fine property and commands the respect of his fellow-citizens, which respect is richly deserved by his honesty and industry.

William Joyce, a venerable and worthy man, resides near Vaiden, Miss. The position he occupies in life renders his character deserving of consideration, and it is with pleasure that his biography is recorded on these pages. He was born in Maury county, Tenn., May 25, 1822. His father, Robert Joyce, was born in Rockingham county, North Carolina, in 1779, and was of Irish descent. He was married in his native state to Nancy Jennings, who was born in North Carolina, and belonged to an old and respected family. In the year of his marriage, 1813, he removed to Tennessee from North Carolina, and became one of the prominent planters of Maury county. He accumulated a comfortable competence, and enjoyed the most pleasant business relations. He died in the year 1847. His wife passed away in 1829. William Joyce, son of the above, is one of a family of four sons and three daughters; all lived to maturity and, with the exception of one, became the heads of families. He and one brother, Harding Joyce, are the only surviving members. This brother resides in Texas, and has reached his seventy-fifth year. William Joyce spent his youth in his native county, where he received a fair English education at a private school. He came to Mississippi in the year 1843, and first located in Holmes county on a farm, where he lived for several years. He was married in Attala county, January 26, 1846, to Miss E. J. McKay, a daughter of the Rev. E. B. McKay, a minister of the Methodist Episcopal Church South. This estimable woman died in the year 1860. Mr. Joyce removed from Holmes to Leake county, and engaged in the mercantile trade, continuing in this business for a number of years. In August, 1863, he entered the Confederate army, enlisting in Colonel Armstead's cavalry brigade and serving until the close of the war. He entered as an orderly. He participated in a number of engagements of importance, and in many skirmishes and scouting parties. At the close of the war he was paroled at Gainesville, Ala., and then returned to Mississippi. He located in Durant, Holmes county, and for three years was engaged in the mercantile business. In 1871 he moved to Carroll county and purchased a plantation on which he now resides. He has about eight hundred acres of land, with a comfortable residence and many modern improvements. He is one of the most successful planters of the county, and although well advanced in years, he gives his personal attention to the management of the business. Twice a week he drives to town, where his tall straight form and long white beard make him a conspicuous figure. He was married a second time in Attala county, Miss., in November, 1866, to Miss Mollie Tribble, a daughter of Alfred Tribble, and a niece of Colonel Coffey, of Durant. She died about the year 1879. Mr. Joyce was married again in 1881, in Canton, Miss., to Miss Mary Chambers, a daughter of the Rev. Edward Chambers, of Madison county, Miss. Mrs. Joyce was reared in Madison county, but received her education at Holly Springs. By this first marriage Mr. Joyce had five children, and four by the second marriage. The children of the first marriage are: Miss N. A. Joyce, William E., unmarried; R. P. H. Joyce, married, and a planter; John F., married, and a resident of Bolivar county; E. H. Joyce, a young man of superior worth and fine character. He was beloved and respected by all who knew him. His death occurred in 1889. He was a bookkeeper by profession. In the Methodist Episcopal Church South he was an active worker and a worthy and consistent member. By his second marriage William Joyce had four children, as before stated: Fannie B.; J. R., a student at Starksville college; Valdora, a student at Grenada college, and Percy K., a lad of fourteen years, at home. Mr. Joyce is devoted to his family and is giving his children that from which the world can not rob them, a good substantial education. With the exception of the youngest child, the family are members of the Methodist Episcopal Church South. The father has for many years been a steward of the church. He is a Royal Arch Mason.

William L. Joyner, Tupelo, Lee county, was born in Pickens county, Ala., in 1853, and is a son of Thomas and Nancy (Henry) Joyner. The father was born in Lowndes county, Miss., in April, 1819, and was a son of Burrell Joyner, a Kentuckian by birth. Burrell Joyner reared a family of seven children: Isaac, Jackson, Thomas, Mrs. Mary Abrama, Mrs. Sarah Laws, William and James. Thomas Joyner was reared in Mississippi to the life of a planter, and moved to Alabama in 1847 and followed his vocation through life; he was very successful and accumulated a fortune; he was a member of the Methodist Episcopal church; his death occurred in 1887; he was a man of many sterling traits and was deeply lamented by all the citizens of his county. His wife is a daughter of William Henry and still survives; she resides on the home plantation in Alabama, which she superintends with much success. There were eight children in the family: Mary, Calvin C., Elbert S. William L. (the subject of this notice), Thomas T., Mrs. Martha A. Spruill, James B. and Ella B. William L. grew to manhood in Alabama and was trained to the occupation of a farmer. He was educated in the common schools and remained at home until he was twenty-eight years of age. In 1881 he came to Mississippi and settled near Baldwyn, Prentiss county, where he resided until 1887; in that year he purchased land one mile west of the county seat of Lee county and has since made that his home. He was married to Miss Maggie Love, a native of Alabama and a daughter of B. R. Love, a prominent planter, who was killed in the late war. Her mother's maiden name was Mary Frances Snell; she died in March, 1891. Three children were born to Mr. and Mrs. Joyner, one of whom is deceased: Ella May and Ernest; Katy Lee is dead. Mr. and Mrs. Joyner are consistent members of the Methodist Episcopal church of Tupelo. In his political opinions he sympathizes with the democratic party. He is a man of excellent business qualifications and good habits, and a citizen who has the highest regard of all who know him.

CHAPTER XXIII.

* * * ★ * * *

FAMILIES AND INDIVIDUALS, K.

A PLANTER of Clarke county, Miss., whose residence is in Enterprise, is Fred Kamper, who was born in Germany in 1845, a son of William and Wilhemina Kamper. The father of our subject came to America in 1860, settling in Alabama, residing there till he came to Enterprise, where he lived till he died in 1889; his wife only mourning his death one year—dying in 1890. These worthy people had a family of seven children: Louisa (deceased), Anna, Mary, John, Adaline, Fred., and August. The elder Mr. Kamper was a farmer by training. He was a man possessed of good business qualities and by his thrifty habits had accumulated considerable property at the time of his death. The subject of our sketch, Fred Kamper, first saw the light in the old fatherland, emigrating with his parents in 1852. He never attended school, but by self-application he has acquired a good business education, obtaining the most of it since his marriage. He went into the army when a mere boy, serving with credit in the so-called army of the Tennessee, under Captain Hardee. He was present in several battles, among them, Chattanooga, Missionary Ridge, Atlanta and in all the desperate fights that took place in the famous march to the sea. After the war he went back to Alabama and worked there till 1865, coming at the time to Enterprise. He was married in Mobile to Margaret Caster, and has a family of seven children: Anna, Addie, Fred, William, Glennie, Harmon, Henry. Mr. Kamper has a farm of over ten hundred acres of land. He is engaged in farming in a large way, making over sixty bales of cotton annually. He is a self-made man, and all he owns has been gained by his own efforts. Both he and his wife are members of the Methodist Episcopal church, while Mr. Kamper is a member of the Knights of Honor. He affiliates with the democratic party, and is very active in politics, making the most of his rights as an American citizen. He is interested in all questions pertaining to the good of his town and county, and is looked upon with respect, as is evidenced by the fact that he is one of the trustees of the Enterprise high school, to which, as to other schools and churches, he subscribes liberally.

G. T. and H. K. Kearney, merchants of Arcadia, Miss., are the sons of Col. W. G. and Susan (Owens) Kearney, natives of Tennessee and Mississippi respectively, and the grandsons of Col. Guston Kearney, of the war of 1812. The latter came to Mississippi in 1837, settled in Madison county, and there engaged in planting. He became the owner of a large tract of land and a great many slaves, and was one of the most prominent men of that county. His wife, who was a Miss Lindsey before marriage, could trace her ancestors back to the settlement of Jamestown, Va., and the Lindsey family was a very prominent one in that state

H, H, Barksdale

during the Revolution. Col. W. G. Kearney was a graduate of the Centenary college of Louisiana, and, like his father, chose planting as his occupation through life. His father gave him a handsome start and he commenced planting under very favorable circumstances. He carried on his farming operations successfully until the breaking out of hostilities during the Civil war, when he, as a matter of course, espoused the Southern cause. In 1861 he joined the Confederate army and organized the first company of his county and one of the first in the state. He was elected captain of this company, and was successively promoted from captain to major, and then to colonel of the Eighteenth Mississippi regiment. During the early part of 1863, while going into Vicksburg, he had his hand so badly crushed by a flat car that he was compelled to retire from service. At the close of the war he returned to planting and this has continued since. In 1858 he was elected to the lower house of the legislature for one term, and he was elected to the same position in 1878, serving only one term. During his younger days he intended studying law and attended for a time the same law school in which Hon. James G. Blaine was a student. To Colonel Kearney and wife were born ten children, five now surviving and named in the order of their births, as follows: Bell, lecturer for the Woman's Christian Temperance union; G. T., H. K., F. S. and W. A. Colonel and Mrs. Kearney are residing on the old home-place, in the enjoyment of excellent health, and are honored and respected by all who know them. The Colonel is a man of prominence in the county, but is of a retiring disposition. The family is noted for its intelligence. He is a leading Mason and has held membership in that organization for many years. His son, G. T. Kearney, supplemented a common school education by a term at Oxford university, and when nineteen years of age commenced for himself as clerk in a mercantile establishment. He is now the proprietor of a large store at Arcadia, where his annual sales amount to several thousand dollars in cash. The younger brother, H. K. Kearney, received his primary education in the common schools and then attended the Agricultural and Mechanical college of Mississippi for one term. Failing health caused him to go to Texas, where he taught school, but interspersed this with herding stock, as his health would not permit of his remaining in the schoolroom all the time. In 1890 he returned to Mississippi, followed different occupations for some time, but is now with his brother in the mercantile business. They are enterprising business men and have been quite successful.

One of the leading attorneys of Decatur, Miss., Thomas Keith, was born in Greene county, Ala. During his childhood his parents removed to Newton county, Miss., and there he grew to manhood. His father, M. M. Keith, M. D., was born in Virginia in 1806. He passed his boyhood and youth in his native state. In selecting a profession he chose that of medicine, and was graduated from the medical department of the University of Pennsylvania in the class of 1830. He first practiced in the county in which he was born, and then removed to Greene county, Ala., where he was among the pioneer settlers. He continued there in practice until 1850, and then came to Newton county, Miss., settling in Decatur. In 1855 he was elected to the state legislature, and served two terms. He was a member of the noted secession convention of 1861. He died in 1883, leaving a record of active usefulness. He was a deacon of the Missionary Baptist church for many years, and was known as a prominent Mason throughout eastern Mississippi. His wife, whose maiden name was Susan Gregory, was a native of Lunenburg county, Va. She died in 1863, having borne a large family of children, eight of whom grew to maturity. Thomas Keith, son of the above, was graduated in the law department of the University of Mississippi, and has been practicing his profession in Newton county. He is a member of the A. F. & A. M., and also of the K. of H. He belongs to the Delta Psi fraternity of the school at Oxford, Miss. In 1862 he enlisted in the Thirteenth Mississippi volunteer infantry, company D, under Captain Carleton. His first engagement was in the battle of Seven Pines, and he was in the seven days' fight around Richmond. He was in all the principal battles from that time until the close of the war. He was wounded at Antietam, and again at Gettysburg, where he was captured and sent to David's island, N. Y. At the end of the conflict he came back to his home and took up the profession of teaching. He was soon afterward elected probate clerk, and served two terms, being removed by Governor Ames in 1868. He was a member of the state senate during the sessions of 1882 and 1884; since that time he has devoted his time and thought to his profession. In all his connection with public office he has shown thorough uprightness of character, and won a reputation which would be a credit to any man in any station of life.

August Keller, Bay Saint Louis, Miss., has been prominently identified with the progressive element of Bay Saint Louis since 1876, at which time he began his residence here. He was born in New Orleans August 24, 1855, and is a son of Theodore A. Keller, a native of Brunswick, Germany. His mother's maiden name is Aimee Valotte, a native of France, who came to America in 1853. His father left Germany when a young man and went to Paris, where he was in the wholesale diamond business. On coming to New Orleans he engaged in the manufacture of jewelry, which he carried on for several years. In 1872 he went to Houston, Tex., and died in 1877. August was reared and educated in New Orleans, taking a commercial course after his literary education was finished; he then was employed as a book-keeper by O. H. Karstendiek, with whom he remained several years. In December, 1876, he came to Bay Saint Louis, and established himself in business, the firm name being Keller & Co. It was afterward changed to Fairchild & Keller, but in a short time Mr. Keller purchased the entire business. He carries the largest stock of goods in Bay Saint Louis, and commands an immense patronage over a large territory. He is a member of the Masonic fraternity. He is vice president of the Bay Saint Louis Ice and Manufacturing company, and is one of the originators and directors of the Gulf Coast Homestead and Building association. He organized the city government of Bay Saint Louis, and was appointed mayor of the town by Governor Lowry. He was twice elected to fill that office afterward. He is a man of untiring energy, and much of the rapid growth and improvement of the Bay is due to him. He is one of the originators of the electric movement which is to be run by the ice plant machinery. While he was mayor he widened the streets, opened new ones, put in excellent sewerage, and made so many improvements that he won the title of the Progressive Mayor of Bay Saint Louis. He has won a host of friends throughout the community, and is held in high esteem by all who know him.

William Kellis, the founder of Kellis' Store, Kemper county, Miss., is the subject of the following notice. He was born in Montgomery county, N. C., November 4, 1829, and is a son of Lewis and Margaret (McDaniel) Kellis. The father was a native of North Carolina, and a planter by occupation. He removed from his native state to Kemper county, Miss., in 1839, and engaged in planting. He is now a resident of Smith county, Tex. Politically he is identified with the democratic party. His wife was born in North Carolina in 1803, and was a daughter of Thomas McDaniel. She died in 1887, having reared a family of ten children: John died in the army; William is the subject of this sketch; Eliza, deceased, married Mr. Edwards; Elizabeth, deceased, married R. Sullins; Martha is the widow of James Bostick; Lewis P. is a resident of Houston, Tex.; N. N. resides in Smith county, Tex.; Sarah A. married N. Flake; Mary is Mrs. Wadkins; James H. died in Mississippi. Lewis Kellis is a man of great integrity of character, and is honored by all who know him. He was one of the early pioneers of this county, and resided here until four years ago, when he went to Texas. The subject of this biography received a limited education, but by the cultivation of a naturally keen observation he has acquired a fund of information that has fitted him for many vocations. He has been a practicing attorney for thirty years, and in 1853 he established Kellis' store, which he has carried on up to the present day. He has been postmaster for thirty-nine years, and is probably the oldest official in the state. He was married in 1850 to Margaret J. Dixon, a daughter of William and Eliza (Cook) Dixon. William Dixon was born in Tennessee, and was married in Alabama. He had two children: Margaret J. and A. T. He died in Alabama, and his widow removed to Kemper county, Miss. She died in 1884 at the age of fifty years. Mr. and Mrs. Kellis are members of the Presbyterian church. They are the parents of eight children: Elizabeth F., wife of J. H. Sanford, deceased; M. E., who married A. M. Van Devender; William A., M. D., a resident of Fearn's Springs, Miss.; Lewis H., a planter; John D., M. D., a resident of Kemper county; Margaret J., who died at the age of four years; Coneron D., who died at the age of twenty-three years, and Stephen D., a practicing physician at De Kalb, Kemper county, Miss. Mr. Kellis held the office of justice of the peace in 1853, and for many years was overseer of the poor. In 1870 he was superintendent of education. He has always shown a deep interest in all educational matters, and has given liberally of his means to all enterprises of an educational character. Politically he is identified with the democratic party. He has served as United States commissioner of the eastern division of northern Mississippi. He is a member of the Masonic order, belonging both to the Blue lodge and chapter. He owns six hundred and forty acres of land, which he has in a high state of cultivation.

John D. Kellis, a practicing physician of Kemper county, Miss., resides at Kellis' Store. He was born in 1858, and received his literary education in Noxubee county, Miss., and attended his first medical lectures at Mobile, Ala. He was graduated in medicine at Louisville, Ky., in the class of 1881, and immediately afterward located in Kemper county. He has met with marked success in his professional labors, and has won for himself a place in the front ranks of the fraternity of Kemper county. He was married in 1883 to Miss Cora Van Devender, a daughter of Hiram and Mary (Diggs) Van Devender. Her father was born in Virginia in 1811, and the mother in North Carolina in 1836. They removed to Mississippi at an early day, and were married in Kemper county. Mr. Van Devender died in 1890, but his widow still survives, and resides in Kemper county. Mrs. Kellis was born in Kemper county in 1860, and is one of three children: Cora, Lula and Bessie. Her mother was a member of the Methodist Episcopal church, and her father belonged to the Masonic order. Mr. and Mrs. Kellis have had born to them three children: Freddie H., Dee C. (deceased), and Patty. The father is a member of the Presbyterian church, and the mother belongs to the Cumberland Methodist church. He belongs to the Masonic order, and is an active democrat. All questions of public interest claim his attention, and those of benefit to the community find in him a zealous supporter. In addition to his professional duties he finds time to superintend the cultivation of a plantation which he owns. He is a man of industrious habits, conscientious in his dealings with his fellow-men, and a citizen of whom any community might be proud.

Dr. Stephen D. Kellis, physician and surgeon, was born in Kemper county, Miss., May 8, 1864, and is a son of William and Margaret J. (Dixon) Kellis, a full history of whom will be found in conjunction with this sketch. He was reared in this county, and received his elementary education in the common schools of this county, and at Gholson, Noxubee county, Miss. When he came to choose a profession for his life's work he selected that of medicine, and in 1884 entered the medical college at Mobile, Ala. The following year he went to Louisville, Ky., where he attended lectures until his graduation. In 1886 he came to De Kalb, Kemper county, and has since established himself in a paying practice. He is a man of ambition, and takes a just pride in the skill he has acquired through study, observation and experience. He is a student, and has not left the habit of study in the college hall, as do so many professional men. But it is needless to say that those are the men who do not stay in the profession. Politically he is identified with the democratic party, and takes an active interest in all the movements and deliberations of that body. Dr. Kellis was united in marriage in December, 1889, to Miss Lula B. Davis, a daughter of William and Sarah Davis. Mrs. Kellis was born in Mississippi, at De Kalb, Kemper county, in 1869. One child has been born of this marriage, William T. The Doctor and his wife are members of the Presbyterian church. He belongs to the Masonic fraternity, being a member of the lodge at De Kalb.

C. Clay Kelly, of Kosciusko, Miss., was born in Madison county, Ala., October 6, 1845, a son of L. A. Kelly, Sr., a native of Georgia, but who left that state at five years of age, and was reared and educated in north Alabama, afterward following the occupation of teaching. He was married to Miss Mary McAdory, and about 1880 moved with his family to Mississippi. Two years after his arrival in this state he was called from life, having been a useful, honest and progressive citizen. C. Clay Kelly was reared in his native state, and up to the time of the breaking out of the Civil war was educated by his father. In 1867 he came to Mississippi, and after a short residence in Attala county he went to West Station, Holmes county, where he was engaged in clerking from 1869 to 1871, at the end of which time he returned to Attala county, and for one year was engaged in merchandising in the country. In 1874 he moved to Kosciusko, and for ten years was successfully engaged in the general mercantile business at this point, and carried on a very extensive furnishing business. In 1884 he began keeping a private bank, and in September, 1890, organized a stock company, with himself as president, the capital stock of which was $100,000. He is now doing a general banking business, and has been remarkably successful, showing himself to be an able and experienced financier. On starting out in life for himself he had some little assistance from his parents, but the most of what he has has been earned by his own exertions. Mr. Kelly was married in Attala county, December 7, 1871, to Miss L. V. Mitchell, a daughter of Samuel Mitchell, deceased. She was born and reared in this county, although her parents were natives of North Carolina, and her education was received in Nazareth, Ky. She was a cultivated and attractive lady, and her death, which occurred on the 29th of November, 1890, was lamented by the numerous friends whom her kindly acts and many generous impulses had won. She left three children: L. N., A. S. and L. M. Mr. Kelly and his family are members of the Presbyterian church, and move in the highest social circles of Kosciusko. He is of very fair complexion, heavy built, but is active and energetic, being considered a superior business man. He has one of the handsomest residences in the town, which he erected in 1890.

Capt. John Kelly, merchant, Tchula, is a native of the Palmetto state, born in Dar-lington district on the 3d of March, 1832, and is the son of Maj. James G. and Lucretia Kelly, both natives also of South Carolina. The elder Kelly was reared in his native state and was there married in 1828, in Abbeville, to Miss Mahon, the daughter of Baily Mahon. After his marriage Major Kelly followed planting and merchandising in Darlington district for a number of years, and in 1845 came to Mississippi, locating in Yalobusha county, where he followed farming. There he resided until his death in 1882, at the age of seventy-nine years. His wife died several years previously. Captain Kelly is the eldest of eight children—seven sons and a daughter—only four of whom are now living, all sons. The Captain spent his youth in Yalobusha county, was educated at Coffeeville and Starkville, and in 1861 joined the Confederate army, Fifteenth Mississippi infantry, as a private. On the organization of the regiment he was appointed quartermaster-sergeant, and after serving in that capacity for several months he resigned. He then raised a cavalry company of young men, of which he was elected captain. Afterward this company was consolidated with others and he resigned its captaincy and joined the Henderson scouts, and served in that command until the final surrender. He participated in a number of important engagements. In the battle of Corinth he received a gunshot wound in the right arm, was disabled for about a year and did not entirely recover for several years. After the general surrender Captain Kelly returned to his home in Yalobusha county, and in January, 1866, he came to Holmes county, locating in the southwestern part. In 1869 he located near Tchula, engaged in planting, and in connection, in March, 1887, embarked in merchandising. Captain Kelly first engaged as a merchant under the firm name of Kelly & James, but Mr. James withdrew from the business in November of the same year. In February, 1888, Mr. Harris took a half interest, under the title of Kelly & Harris, and thus it has since continued. The firm has a large store, carries a complete stock of general merchandise and is doing a general furnishing business. They have a patronage established that indicates appreciation of their reliable goods and fair dealing methods, and is second to none in the city. They merit the utmost confidence and esteem and they receive it. Captain Kelly has ever been identified with the democratic party, has served as a delegate to county conventions and has held local offices in the county. He was married in Holmes county, Miss., on the 3d of September, 1854, to Miss Carrie R. Treadwell, a native of Columbia, S. C., but who was reared and educated in Yazoo City and Holly Springs, Miss. Her father, Dr. B. W. Treadwell, was a physician of Holmes county for forty years, and is now quite aged. The Captain's union resulted in the birth of three children: W. F., a planter and contractor in Indian territory; Julia G., wife of T. E. Harris, a prominent merchant of Tchula, Miss.; and Aluvia K., wife of T. W. James, a planter near Tchula lake. Captain Kelly is a member of the Masonic order, and is secretary of his lodge, and is also a member of the Knights of Honor, being dictator in that order. He and Mrs. Kelly are members of the Cumberland Presbyterian church. They have four grandchildren: Mortimer K. Harris, Furman H. Kelly and Peter and Walter James.

W. T. Kendall, M. D., of Meridian, Miss., was born in Crawfordsville, Taliaferro county, Ga., July 8, 1841, a son of W. J. and Elizabeth (Akin) Kendall, the former a native of Maryland and the latter of Georgia. His father, who was a farmer and merchant, came to Georgia at an early date, and to Mississippi in 1844, locating at Canton, where he died in 1884, in the sixty-ninth year of his age, his wife having died at the age of twenty-two years, in 1846, after having borne four interesting children, of whom the subject of this sketch is the only survivor. By his second marriage he had six children, three of whom are living at the present time. Dr. Kendall was educated partially in Baltimore, Md., where he lived from the age of five to fifteen years. Returning to Canton he studied medicine and graduated from the University of Maryland, in 1866. At the outbreak of the Civil war he was in New Orleans attending his first course of lectures. He immediately returned to Mississippi and enlisted in company I, of the Tenth Mississippi regiment, known as the Madison rifles. After one year's service with this organization he was made assistant surgeon, and detailed to hospital duty at Canton and Meridian, Miss. In 1864 he entered the cavalry service as a captain of a company of independent scouts, and served until the general surrender. After his graduation in medicine, in 1866, he began the practice of his profession at Newport, Miss., where he continued with great success until 1883, when he removed to Meridian, and has there built up a large, lucrative and increasing practice. He is a member of the Lauderdale county medical association, of the Mississippi state medical association, and of the American medical association, and state delegate to the International American medical congress. It may be said of him that he is the only physician who ever received a premature medical examination at the medical college. He is a Knight of Honor and a member of the Masonic fraternity, and is also a member of the Knights and Ladies of Honor, and in connection with his membership with the Knights of Honor he holds the position of medical examiner. Since January, 1884, it may be stated in evidence of his skill and of his trustworthiness as a medical examiner, that no candidate who has been initiated after having passed his examination has since died. He is also medical examiner for the Brotherhood of Switchmen, of Meridian. He was married September 21, 1865, to Miss Sarah B., daughter of Capt. Joseph Wyse, of Attala county, Miss. She has borne him four children named as follows: Joseph W., born July 24, 1866; Gustus C., born January 21, 1868; Myrtle A., born June 26, 1876, and Mabel B., born April 2, 1878.

John H. Kennedy was born in Lauderdale county, Miss., in May, 1858, and is the only son of William A. and Jane E. (Jemison) Kennedy, natives of the state of Alabama. The parents grew to maturity in the state of their birth and were married there. They removed to Mississippi in 1857 and located in Lauderdale county. Mr. Kennedy purchased land and at once set about the task of placing it under cultivation. He also opened a stock of dry goods at Lauderdale Station, and did a thriving business there for several years. In 1864 he returned to Alabama and opened a store at York Station, Sumter county, where he carried on both mercantile and agricultural pursuits for two years. In 1870 he came back to Mississippi and settled in Meridian, where he embarked in the livery business; he still had some land which he had cultivated under his direction. In 1876 he bought a farm four miles northwest of Meridian, on which he lived until the time of his death, in 1879. He was a consistent member of the Presbyterian church, and belonged to the I. O. O. F. several years prior to his death. While he was not actively interested in political questions, he never failed to discharge his duties as a citizen of the republic. There were only two children born to Mr. and Mrs. Kennedy, John H. and Lily, who died at the age of three years. John H. remained under the parental roof until he was twenty-one years of age, and then started out in life to meet the responsibilities of manhood. He was married to Miss Henrietta Semmes, a daughter of Maj. Frank Semmes, of Lauderdale county. Four children have been born of this union: William A., John H., deceased, Frank S. and Jane E. Mr. Kennedy owns one hundred and sixty acres of land in his own right, and superintends the cultivation of his father's place. He devotes considerable attention to the raising of livestock, and makes a decided success of this branch of farming. He has never aspired to public office, but as a private citizen has fully lived up to the standard of a loyal patriot. He affiliates with the democratic party. The Kennedy family occupy a leading position in Lauderdale county's society, and have the highest esteem of the entire community.

S. P. Kennedy, M. D. (deceased) was born in Franklin county, Ala., November 22, 1830, and died in September, 1881. He was a son of John and Harriet (Islar) Kennedy, the former's birthplace being in North Carolina, but the latter's is unknown. John Kennedy was an early settler of Alabama and reared a family of five sons and two daughters. S. P. Kennedy began the study of medicine in the state of his birth in early manhood and for two years was a student in the University of Virginia. Later he was an attendant of the University of Philadelphia, Pennsylvania, and graduated from this institution in 1852, after which he came direct to Lauderdale, Miss., where, in a very short time, he had a lucrative practice. He showed himself to be eminently worthy the confidence reposed in him by all classes and was unquestionably a physician of decided merit. He was esteemed by all who knew him, not only as a physician, but also as an honorable citizen and neighbor. In 1855 he was married in Lockhart, Miss., to Miss Kate Lockhart, a daughter of D. H. and L. E. (Brewer) Lockhart, the former of whom was a native of Scotland, and the latter of the state of New York. Of the eleven children born to them Mrs. Kennedy was the fourth in order of birth. To her union with Dr. Kennedy four sons and one daughter were born: David B. (deceased), Walter F., John B. (deceased), William L. (deceased), and the daughter that died in infancy, unnamed. Walter F., the only surviving member of the family, is the assistant agent for the Mobile & Ohio railroad, at Lauderdale. Dr. Kennedy has been quite successful in his business, accumulated considerable property and at his death was worth about $30,000. In addition to faithfully looking after his practice, he was associated with Capt. J. C. Porter in the mercantile business at Lauderdale for a number of years. He was generous, hospitable, high-minded and charitable, and the many kind acts which he did will long be remembered. His kind and cordial manners and numerous admirable qualities of heart and head made him universally loved and respected, and he was considered an acquisition, indeed, to the social circle in which he moved. Socially he was a member of the A. F. & A. M. and the K. of H. He never aspired to political preferment, much preferring to give his attention to his business. Although not a member of any church he believed in the Christian religion and gave to the support of churches with a generous hand. He was baptized by Bishop Green during the Civil war, but never attached himself to any denomination, although he was a regular attendant of church, and ministers, sooner or later, partook of his bountiful hospitality and found a home under his roof. His serivices in his professional capacity were invaluable during the war, and he not only treated his patients with Christian, but also with brotherly kindness. As an evidence of the high appreciation in which he was held by the community, many children were named for him. He was devoted to the Sabbath-school, and taught a class regularly for over three years, and for one year before his last illness held family prayers in his home night and morning. For two years he was a great sufferer. He was buried with Masonic honors, and a very large concourse of friends followed him to the grave.

Judge David Ker, a native of the Emerald isle, came to America and settled in North Carolina in 1789, and about 1798 or 1799 became a resident of Mississippi. He was given excellent educational advantages, and before leaving his native land graduated from the University of Dublin. After coming to Mississippi he located near old Greensville, in Jefferson county, where the versatility of his genius soon manifested itself. In 1802 his abilities were recognized, and he was appointed one of the three territorial judges, a position he held with marked ability until his death, in 1805. He was one of the founders of the Chapel Hill university of North Carolina, and for some time had charge of that institution. He was also a teacher in other schools of that state. His widow survived him until 1848, when her death resulted from burns which she had accidentally received. At the death of her husband Mrs. Ker was left with a family of two sons and several daughters to care for, and how well this noble woman fulfilled the trust thus imposed upon her was evident in looking upon her children who grew to honorable manhood and womanhood. She at once began teaching school, and in this manner supported herself and reared and educated her children, the names of her sons being John and David. The latter died when about twenty-three years of age, his untimely death being deeply mourned by all who knew him. He was bright and promising, and at the time of his death was filling an official position. John studied medicine in Philadelphia, and after graduating came to Natchez, Miss., where he entered at once upon his practice and became a prominent physician, his services being in demand by the leading families of this section. After a time he gave up his practice, and began giving his time and attention to planting. In 1820 he was married to Miss Mary Baker, of a well known Kentucky family, and to them were born twelve children, three of whom are living: Lewis B., in Louisiana; Mary S., and William H., who is now principal of the Natchez schools. Dr. Ker died in 1850, a member of the Presbyterian church, in which he was an elder for some time. His youngest son, William H., was given the advantages of Harvard college, which institution he was attending when the war broke out. He immediately returned to Natchez, and in 1861 enlisted in the Adams troop of cavalry, which afterward became a part of Jeff Davis' legion. He served the Confederate cause faithfully until the close of the war, being paroled with his command May 1, 1865. He then came to his home, and until 1876 followed the occupation of planting, after which he turned his attention to teaching school, a calling that has since occupied his time and attention, and for the last two years he has been principal of the schools of Natchez. In 1871 Miss Josephine Chamberlain became his wife, and by her he is the father of two children. She is a member of the Presbyterian church, and he belongs to the K. of H. and the K. and L. of H.

D. W. Kerr, Giles, Kemper county, Miss., was born in New Hanover county, N. C., September 19, 1831, and is a son of John and Mary (Bourdeaux) Kerr. The father was born in the same county, and even the same house as the son, March 16, 1797, and was a son of Daniel and Elizabeth (Myrphy) Kerr. Daniel Kerr served as a soldier in the war of the Revolution. John Kerr was married in North Carolina in 1828, and reared a family of seven children: Anthony J., Daniel W., the subject of this sketch; John F., James D., Margaret E., who married Dr. James Gage; Mary, deceased, and Laura J., wife of Maj. J. B. Robinson. The family emigrated from North Carolina to Kemper county, Miss., in 1835, the father investing in land, which he placed under cultivation. He was a successful planter, and at the breaking out of the Civil war he owned eighty-five slaves. He died December 25, 1881. He was a member of the Presbyterian church, and used his best efforts to promote the welfare of that society. Politically he was identified with the democratic party, of which he was a leader in his county. The mother of our subject was born in New Hanover county, N. C., in 1810, and was a daughter of Col. Anthony D. and Margaret E. (DeVane) Bourdeaux. Her parents were natives of Scotland, but were of French lineage; they passed their lives in North Carolina. Mrs. Kerr died in 1870. She was an honored member of the Presbyterian church. Daniel W. was but three years of age when his parents removed to Kemper county. He received a good education for that day, and in 1850 he began farming on his own account. He was married in 1879 to Peggy M. Jones, a daughter of John M. and Martha W. (Pettus) Jones. Mrs. Jones is a sister of Governor Pettus. Mrs. Kerr was born in the house on the Jones' plantation which she and her husband now occupy. Three children have been born to Mr. and Mrs. Kerr: John M. J., Anthony P. and Daniel W., Jr. In 1861 Mr. Kerr enlisted in Capt. R. O. Perrine's cavalry company, which was attached to the Jefferson Davis league; this league was organized in the army of Virginia in 1861, under Maj.-Gen. William T. Martin. Mr. Kerr was in many noted engagements of the war, and in 1864 he was made captain of company C of the Jeff Davis legion. In 1865, at Greensboro, N. C., he was paroled. He was never wounded nor taken prisoner. When the end came he cheerfully accepted the situation and returned to his home. In 1866 he went to Mexico, but after a short stay there he returned to the states and engaged in farming. He has devoted himself to general agriculture, and has raised some good livestock. He owns five hundred acres of land, which eventually will be under cultivation. He is a man of liberal views, and is interested in the growth and development of the county. Politically he is a democrat, and he is also a member of the Farmers' Alliance, of which he is the business agent for the county He and his wife are members of the Presbyterian church.

Henry Key, son of Dr. Bazil Graves Key, a native of Edgefield district, S. C., and Mrs. Martha Ann (Munday) Key, was born in Lowndes county, Ala., January 19, 1834. Their parents were married in their native district in South Carolina, and as Dr. Key was a man of superior intelligence, he met with the best of success in the practice of his profession and accumulated a handsome competency. He graduated from a school of medicine in South Carolina, but after several years devoted to attending to the wants of suffering humanity in that state, he moved to Georgia, but a few years later came to Alabama, and for a few years resided in Macon county; afterwards removed to Lowndes county in the same state, where he resided until 1835, when he moved with his family to the state of Mississippi and located in Franklin county for a time; from thence to Jefferson county and located at Fayette, the county seat. He was in the city of Natchez, Miss., during the notable hurricane or tornado in 1837 and performed yeoman services to the people disabled by that terrible cyclone. He practiced at Fayette until his death, in February, 1841, his wife surviving him a number of years and dying on the 26th day of August, 1866. Their family, numbering eight sons and three daughters, all arrived at the age of maturity, two sons and two daughters being now alive. Dr. Bazil Graves Key was a relative of Frances S. Key, the author of the "Star Spangled Banner," and a descendant of one Martin Key, who married a granddaughter of Henry the Seventh, of England, his father's family, at this late day, being able to show not only written record but English characteristics of uprightness and truth, and nearly all of them English in physique. Henry Key was a resident of his native state until he arrived at the age of twenty years, and as this time was spent on a farm, his chances for acquiring an education were not of the best. He was possessed of a determination, however, of becoming a well educated man, and with this end in view he read everything that came his way, and in this manner became well posted on the current topics of the day. In 1854 he came to Fayette and served a regular apprenticeship, learning the painter's trade, at which he has worked with good success ever since. After a few years devoted to his trade in Fayette and the adjoining country, in 1868 he removed with his then small family to Illinois, but at the end of one year decided that the congenial climate of the South was the best place for him, and accordingly returned to Fayette. He was elected clerk of the circuit court of Jefferson county in 1872, for he possessed many and warm friends, and at the expiration of his term he was honored with a reëlection to that responsible position, and discharged his onerous duties to the satisfaction of all concerned for eight years. Since retiring from office he has worked at his trade, but at the same time discharged the duties of agent for several insurance companies. He is one of the brightest and most active workers of the Masonic lodge in this part of the state, has served in various official capacities, and on several different occasions has represented his lodge in the grand lodge of the state, and for several years has been deputy grand master of his district. He is a · member of the Knights of Honor, also the Knights and Ladies of Honor, in both of which orders he now holds responsible positions. He served on important committees in the grand lodge and showed that he possessed shrewd and practical ideas and had the welfare of the order warmly at heart. He is one of the foremost and earnest members of the Methodist Episcopal church, and has several times repre-

sented his circuit in the annual conference.   At the present time the positions he is filling
are secretary of the Masonic lodge and city clerk and collector.   He has been the mayor of
Fayette and has also been a member of the city council and magistrate.   He was married in
Jefferson county, Miss., April 19, 1865, at Magnolia Grove, to Miss Martha I. Hammet, a daughter of O. D. Hammet, of Jefferson county, Miss.   She was born and reared in Jefferson county,
and obtained an excellent education, graduating in 1862 in the Fayette female college, being
now one of the most intelligent, accomplished and amiable ladies in the county.   She has
borne her husband five children: Ada H., wife of J. W. Weilenman, a planter of Washington
county, Miss.; Lucie, an accomplished young lady; Annie, who, with her sister Ada, in same
class, graduated from Port Gibson female college; Katie, eighteen years old, is one of the
successful school teachers of Fayette; Frank, fifteen years old, attending the high school of
Fayette, and Ellett, a bright lad of ten years.   Mr. Key is a man of excellent business qualifications, and in regard to principles and character he is beyond reproach.   His sterling
worth of character has won for him the respect and esteem of his fellowmen, and his desire
to live the life of a true Christian is well worthy of emulation.

   Robert D. Kilgore has been a resident and planter of Clay county, Miss., since the war,
but was born in South Carolina in 1830, a son of Dr. Benjamin and Mary D. Kilgore, the
former of whom was born in Greenville district, S. C., December 11, 1792.   He received his
literary and medical education in the state of his birth and there practiced his profession for
many years.   He was also the owner of a good plantation and was interested in the slave
trade.   His wife was a Miss Hudson, and with her and his children he removed to Oktibbeha
county, Miss., the portion in which he settled being Clay county.   After remaining there a
few years he came to the plantation which is now owned by his son, Robert D., and here, in
connection with planting, he practiced his profession.   To himself and wife the following
children were born: Keziah; Susan (Mrs. Brinker); John J., in Texas; Major Benjamin, of
Lafayette county, Miss.; Mary, who first married a Mr. Davis and afterward Rev. Foster;
Josiah, who died on his way to Mexico during that war; Robert D.; James L., of Clay county,
Miss.; Elizabeth, wife of Col. William Lylus; Pleasant M., who died in the army; Nancy,
wife of Jacob Barr, of Clay county; Margaret, the deceased wife of Capt. W. W. Robinson,
of West Point, and Harriet M., of this county.   Dr. Kilgore was a son of James and Keziah
Kilgore, and died on the 31st of December, 1864, his wife's death occurring on the 22d of
February, 1846, at the age of forty-two years.   Robert D. Kilgore, in starting out in life
for himself, went to California in search of gold in 1852, and while in that state was engaged
in mining a part of the time.   In 1862 he started home to take part in the war, and as
he came by land through Mexico, he was seven months and nine days on the way.   He
joined the Confederate forces within ten days after reaching home, becoming a member
of company E, Duff's battalion, and was in a number of engagements throughout the state
of Mississippi: Wolf River, Guice's crossroads, Harrisburg and Oxford; the war over, he
returned to Mississippi, and has since been engaged in planting, and the manner in which he
looks after his present estate denotes him to be successful and energetic.   It is but just to say
that his good name is above reproach, and that he has won the confidence and esteem of
all who know him, for this is well known by those who have the honor of his acquaintance.
He comes of an excellent and highly respected family, and is possessed of many of the
qualities which were characterstic of his people: kindness of heart, intelligence, honesty
and industry, and is of a social disposition and very hospitable.   He is unmarried.

   Bradley T. Kimbrough, Oxford, Miss., who is the chancellor of the third chancery
court district of Mississippi, including ten counties, was born in east Tennessee in 1846, and

was the youngest son born to Duke W. and Eliza (Cook) Kimbrough, natives of North and South Carolina respectively. The paternal grandfather was a pioneer settler of east Tennessee and was a noted Baptist minister, held in the highest esteem. He was an arbitrator among the people of his community, with whom his word was a just law. Duke W. Kimbrough died in 1885 at the age of eighty-four years. His wife died in 1851 or 1852. Bradley T. grew up on a farm and enjoyed only limited educational advantages. In 1863 he left the schoolroom and enlisted in the Confederate army as a private in company A, Fifty-ninth Tennessee volunteer infantry, serving in Tennessee, Virginia and North Carolina. He was wounded in a skirmish at Athens, Tenn., in the fall of 1864, and had just rejoined his command in time to be paroled at Washington, Ga., May 11, 1865. He then returned to school, attending first in Tennessee and then at Georgetown, Ky., and in the fall of 1867 he came to Mississippi. He taught school and in his leisure hours began the study of law. He finally entered the Lebanon law school and was graduated in the class of 1869. In January, 1870, he entered upon the practice of his chosen profession at Ripley, Miss., where he remained for eight months. Upon the formation of the new county of Benton he located at Ashland, the county seat, being the first lawyer in the place. He remained there until 1885, and in that year came to Oxford, where he has since resided. He has always taken an active interest in the political world, and was the first representative in the state legislature from Benton county, serving in 1872–73. He was appointed chancellor in 1884 and has held the office since that time, receiving the successive appointments. When he first came to this county he purchased his residence, which he has converted into one of the most comfortable and elegant of homes. He owns a fine plantation of twelve hundred acres, nine miles west of Oxford, five hundred of which are under cultivation. Many improvements have been made on this plantation, so that it is considered one of the most desirable in the county. He is a member of the Baptist church and is a deacon of that body. He is a Mason, and was grand master of the grand lodge in 1886. He was grand high priest of the state in 1884. In 1888 he was chairman of the law committee and made the anti-saloon report and secured its adoption by the grand lodge, that saloon-keeping is a violation of Masonic law. He is justly proud of his Masonic record. Alesville is a post-office five miles from Oxford, which was secured through the influence of Mr. Kimbrough. It is located on his land, and he has recently erected a gin and mill there and started a store. While living in Ashland Mr. Kimbrough assisted in the establishing of an academy there, being next to the largest contributor to the enterprise. He was also a liberal supporter of other measures of public interest. He is a strong temperance man, social and genial in disposition, and a reliable, upright citizen and an able judge. He has an interesting family, composed of a wife and six children. His wife, who is the charm of his home, was Miss Kate Carothers, who is a graduate of Mary Sharp college, of Tennessee, a lady of rare accomplishments, having taken several post-graduate courses, her very liberal education being finished by travel in this country and Europe.

Prof. A. A. Kincannon, Meridian, Miss., superintendent of the Meridian graded and industrial schools, is a son of Capt. James A. Kincannon, who was born in the Old Dominion in 1832, and whose parents were of Scotch descent. At an early age the Captain came to Mississippi from Tennessee as a ward of his uncle, A. A. Kincannon. He was a valiant soldier of the Mexican war, and was wounded on one of its fields. He was also a soldier of the Confederacy. Professor Kincannon's mother was Mrs. M. A. Kincannon (nee Connor), of Noxubee county, Miss. The Professor was born on the 2d of August, 1859, and attended the country schools until ten years of age, when his parents moved to Verona, Lee county,

Miss. There he attended the schools of the town, and in 1877 entered the University of Mississippi, at Oxford, where he continued, at intervals, for three years. While a student at the university he was elected anniversarian of Phi Sigma literary society, which has always been regarded as an honor of highest distinction by the authorities and students of the university. Subsequently he graduated from the Normal university of Ohio. In the autumn of 1881 he purchased property at Venora and opened a high school for boys. In 1884 he was tendered the position of principal of the preparatory department of the Agricultural and Mechanical college, at Starkville, which he accepted, and filled so satisfactorily that after one year he was promoted to the adjunct professorship of English literature of that famous institution. In 1887 he was tendered the superintendency of the city schools of Meridian, which he accepted, and has held for four years. The term for which he now stands elected does not expire until 1894. Professor Kincannon's excellent work in the schools of this enterprising city can scarcely be measured. From a position anything but creditable in the scholastic scale, Meridian now stands at the head in the state. Her few little schools in 1885, with an attendance of only two hundred and seventy pupils, have grown now (1891) into splendid schools, with ample and modern buildings, and an attendance of two thousand students. Professor Kincannon and W. G. Stevenson, who is president of the board of trustees, after making thorough personal observation and investigation in the Northwest and Northeast, gave to Meridian the fine system of methods and buildings which have now become the pride of every true citizen. He is perhaps one of the best traveled men of his age in the country. The Professor is a member of the Masonic fraternity, past chancellor of the Knights of Pythias, past dictator of the Knights of Honor and a member of the Golden Rule. In his church relationship he is a Cumberland Presbyterian. In 1890 he was made a member of the American academy of political and social science, whose membership includes many of the great scholars of Europe and America. Prof. Kincannon's management of the Meridian schools has given him great prominence, and his host of friends throughout the state urged him three years ago to become a candidate for state superintendent, but he declined. For some time he edited the Mississippi _Teacher_, a journal which took high rank and prospered so long as it continued under his management. Professor Kincannon was married in 1888 to Miss Mary George Barksdale, a daughter of Gen. William Russell Barksdale, and to them one child, Frankine, was born. The Professor is active in benevolent and charitable enterprises, strong in his friendship, and brave in the defense of the right. By his frank and kindly deportment he finds friends and admirers wherever he goes.

Benjamin F. King, Calvert, Miss., an extensive planter of Kemper county, Miss., is the subject of the following sketch: He was born in Kemper county, Miss., in 1845, and is a son of David and Elizabeth P. (Richards) King. David King was born in Georgia in 1808, and was a farmer and carpenter by occupation. He was married in Fayette county, Ala., in 1829, and removed to Kemper county in 1833. He died in Lauderdale county, Miss., in 1862. Politically he affiliated with the democratic party. He and his wife were members of the Primitive Baptist church. They reared a family of nine children: Martin D., Susan A., Francis T., Huldah H., Rufus G., Benjamin F., Miriam L., Bettie P. and Nancy P. The mother died in Lauderdale county in 1873. They were prominent people in the early history of the county and were highly respected. Martin D., Rufus G. and Benjamin F. were all soldiers in the Civil war. Martin D. was twice wounded, once at Richmond and at Gettysburg; he died in 1883 in Texas. Benjamin F. King was educated in this county, and remained with his family until he was twenty-two years of age, when he entered the lists in his own behalf. At the age of eighteen years he had fought in the cause of the South, enlisting in company C, Second Mississippi cavalry. He was in the Georgia campaign, and in a number of skirmishes. He was paroled at Gainesville, Ala., in 1865. In 1867 he was united in marriage to Miss Huldah K. Pruitt, a daughter of Thomas M. and Naomi (Windon) Pruitt, born in Kemper county, Miss., in 1845. Her grandparents were pioneers of the county, having come here in 1833. Her father died in 1862, and the mother passed away the same year. Mr. and Mrs. King had born to them six children: Rufus C., Maggie L., Kennie V., Martin D., Mamie N. and a deceased son. The mother died in 1888, July 26. Mr. King was married a second time, in 1889, to Mrs. Bettie G. Culpepper, widow of Clarence Culpepper, and daughter of Rev. J. K. Ryan, of Choctaw county, Ala. Two children have been born of this marriage: Frank H. and Alma K., twins. Frank H. is deceased. Mrs. King is a member of the Missionary Baptist church. Mr. King is a stanch adherent to the principles of the democratic party, and is an ardent supporter of home industries. He owns sixteen hundred acres of land, to the cultivation of which he devotes his time and energies. He has been postmaster of Calvert for eight years, and under his management the work has been done to the entire satisfaction of the public. Rufus C. King, son of the above, was born October 16, 1867, and was educated at the Agricultural and Mechanical college, Starkville, Miss. He was married November 20, 1890, to Miss Lockard, of Meridian, Miss. He is now secretary and treasurer of the Agricultural and Mechanical college. Mr. King has given all his children a liberal education.

Elias L. King was born in Yazoo county, Miss., in 1846, and is the younger of two sons of William L. and A. (Spell) King, of Tennessee and Mississippi, respectively. The father emigrated from his native state at the age of nineteen years, and located in Mississippi. For a few years he taught school, and then did an overseer's work until he had saved enough money to buy land. In 1849 he purchased five hundred and twenty acres of the tract on which the subject of this notice now lives. He was a successful farmer, and is an honored citizen, having attained the age of seventy-six years. His wife died August 12, 1871. Elias L. and his brother, Aaron L., served in the Confederate army during the late Civil war. They were members of company A, Wirt Adams' cavalry. Elias served one year, but his brother some time longer. After the close of the conflict our subject began to meet the world upon his own responsibility. He was married in 1866 to Miss Alma Waters, a daughter of Addison and Mary (Luse) Waters, and eight children have been born to them: William, a farmer; Lucian, also a farmer; Aaron, Kendall, Mary A., wife of Henry Smith; Amma, wife of James Cader; Ruby and May. Mr. King is the owner of a plantation consisting of twelve hundred and ninety-one acres; this is divided into three sections, and is well improved. He and his brother Aaron, who is now deceased, have always been considered the leading stockmen of the county, and have done more to promote that branch of farming than any other dealers. He raises a large amount of cotton and corn, and raises large numbers of horses, mules and cattle. He is vice-president of the Yazoo county Farmers' Alliance, and has been president of the sub-alliance since its organization. He has been wideawake on all questions pertaining to the agricultural interests of the country and has given them close attention. He and his wife have been members of the Methodist Episcopal church since their youth, and he is one of the present trustees of the church.

Capt. P. J. King, planter and merchant, Mound Landing, Miss., is the fortunate owner of a bountiful estate of over fourteen hundred acres, and of this he has nine hundred acres under cultivation. He bought an interest in Whitehall plantation in 1876, but soon bought out the interests of the others, and now controls it all. He is a model planter, and everything about his place indicates to the beholder a thorough and progressive owner. He has a good steamgin, with all the modern improvements, and by his good judgment and excellent management has accumulated a fortune. He is acknowledged to be one of the best farmers of Bolivar county. In 1886 he opened a store on his place, carries a stock of goods valued at $4,000, and does an annual business of $35,000. Aside from this, he is the owner of Lancaster place, consisting of four hundred acres, with three hundred and fifty acres under cultivation, and although this place was in a very unpromising condition, he soon made many improvements, erected a steamgin, a barn, many cabins, and cleared one hundred acres. He was born in Pennsylvania in 1842, and was the son of Joseph and Ella (McKee) King, both natives also of the Keystone state. The father followed farming all his life. His death occurred in 1852, and the mother received her final call in 1875. In youth, Captain King was apprenticed to the carpenter's trade, and worked at that in Philadelphia for several years. In 1861 he enlisted in company H, Second Pennsylvania reserve, and was attached to the army of the Potomac, serving in the seven days' fight and in nearly all the engagements of that army. He was taken prisoner at Charles City crossroads, was confined in Libby prison for three months, after which he was exchanged, and joined his command. When released, he was transferred to the United States construction department, and his trade of carpenter was of great use to him in this position. He served in that department with the rank and pay of captain until cessation of hostilities. In December, 1865, he went to Alabama, located near Montgomery, and was engaged in planting for seven years. In 1876 he came to Misissippi and bought an interest in his present plantation, as above stated.

Dr. Thomas S. King, Deasonville, Miss., one of the most popular practitioners of Yazoo county, was born in Franklin county, Miss., December 28, 1833. During his infancy his parents, Douglas and Letitia (Davis) King, removed to Yazoo county; the father opened up a farm of six hundred acres, which he cultivated with much profit; he died in 1858. The mother of Thomas S. passed away in 1840. She had born to her four children: Octavia L., the wife of B. Swayne, of this county; Thomas S.; W. P. (deceased), who was a teacher by profession, and Letitia, who was burned to death at the age of four years. The father was married a second time, in 1841, to Miss Maria E. Moore, a daughter of James Moore, of Port Gibson, Miss. Eight children were born of this union: Mary E., wife of Col. H. Luce; Frances E., wife of Solomon Swayze; Letitia; Ellen R., wife of a Mr. Hammond, of Yazoo City; John, a farmer in this county; Charles, also a farmer, and James and Florence, both of whom died in infancy. The mother of these children died in 1879. The Doctor's schooldays were passed in Sharon, Madison county, with the exception of one year spent at Dolbear's commercial college at Natchez, Miss. When he chose a profession he selected that of medicine, and entered Jefferson medical college, Philadelphia, for the purpose of fitting himself for the responsibilities of his future vocation. He was graduated in 1858, in the same class as Dr. McCann, of this county. He then returned to his home and located at Ebenezer, Holmes county, where he practiced eight months; thence he came to this county and engaged in professional labors until 1852. He was then appointed contract sergeant at Vaughn's Station, but in a few months enlisted as a private in company I, First Mississippi light artillery, commanded by Captain Bowman. He was on detached service as assistant surgeon when he was captured at Spanish Fort, Ala., in April, 1865. He was taken to Ship Island, and was held there until the final surrender, when he was paroled and returned to his home. He then took up active professional work, and has devoted his time and efforts to making a reputation second to none in the county. He has invested his surplus funds in real estate, and has a well-improved farm of two hundred and ninety acres. Dr. King was married November 25, 1858, to Miss Lenora A. Moore, a daughter of Allen and Mary (Mathisos)

Moore, pioneers and prominent settlers of Yazoo county. Two children have been born of this union: Thomas S., Jr., a farmer of the county, and Estelle D., wife of Richard Ledbetter. The Doctor is a member of Deasonville lodge, A. F. & A. M., and of the Knights of Honor. He is a member of the Methodist Episcopal church, to which he gives liberally of his means. He has witnessed many changes in the county, and has been a potent factor its growth and development.

Dr. C. T. Kirk, a prominent physician and planter, of Winston county, Miss, was originally from Alabama; his birth occurring in Autauga county, in 1835. His father, Dr. William Kirk, was born near Mount Vernon, Va., in 1803, and was educated for a professional career in New York. He was married when nineteen years of age to Miss Rebecca Billingsly, of a family of wealth and great influence, being connected with some of the best families in Virginia, Joseph E. Johnston, Mortens and Lees. He moved to Alabama, among the first settlers of Autauga county, and engaged in merchandising; his trade being principally with the Creek Indians for several years, until the farming interest of the bottom lands of the Alabama river were developed, when he moved to Mobile, Ala., and embarked in the wholesale merchandising and commission business, under the firm title of Kirk & Harris. They did a large business for several years, supplying the farmers and country merchants, until the death of the junior partner. He then attended medical lectures in New Orleans, and moved to Macon, Miss., and began the practice of medicine, continuing a few years, and then moved to Winston county, where he practiced his profession until his death, in 1887, being at the time of his death the oldest practicing physician in the state. To his marriage were born ten children, five of whom are now living and named in the order of their births as follows: Sarah, C. T. (subject of this sketch), A. S., C. D. R. and Walter M—all the sons being physicians. Dr. William Kirk was elected to represent his county in the legislature and served two years. He was a true democrat and a member of the Masonic fraternity, and devoted his entire life to the benefits of his fellow-men. Dr. C. T. Kirk was educated for his profession at St. Louis, Louisville and Cincinnati medical colleges, graduating with first honors in 1857; his thesis on medical diagnosis being considered the best ever written by any medical student, was published in all the medical journals of America. He at once began practicing in Winston county at Fern Springs, Miss. In 1858 he was married to Miss Amanda Anderson, daughter of Elijah and Margaret Anderson, a family of sterling character and wealth. The fruits of this union have been nine children, six of whom are yet living, viz.: Lula, wife of Dr. A. A. McNeel; Lona, wife of James B. McNees; Ida, Geneva, C. T., Jr. and Chalmers at home. Dr. C. T. Kirk is a member of the Masonic order and has reached the council degree. He has had considerable legislative experience, having represented his county in the legislature during the most trying times the state ever experienced. He attended four sessions; was on several of the most important committees (judiciary and finance) during the entire time. In 1861 he enlisted in company D, Thirty-fifth Mississippi volunteer infantry (Confederate states), and was at once appointed surgeon of the regiment. He served until about the close of the war, being on hospital duty most of the time. Through his efforts Dr. Kirk succeeded in getting a charter for the Meridian medical institute, and on the strength of his efforts in this matter, the legislature passed an act granting him permission to practice in any part of the state without license from the state medical board. He also started and edited the first and only medical journal of the state, *The Epitome.* He was elected by the board of trustees to the chairs of theory and practice of surgery, and also made dean of the faculty, was also elected to the chair of surgery in the Atlanta medical school. Dr. Kirk is pleasant and agreeable in manners, generous and warm hearted, a high-toned, honorable gentleman. He has a strong and vigorous mind, is progressive in his ideas, and stands in the first rank of physicians of the South. In politics, a true democrat; in religion, a Baptist; true to his friends and generous to his foes.

John M. Kirk, a prominent citizen of Bolivar county, resides at Kirkland, a plantation of one thousand two hundred acres, with seven hundred acres under cultivation, near Gunnison. In 1890 he erected an iron ginhouse, fireproof, with all the modern improvements and all in the best of shape. He was born on his father's plantation, in Bolivar county, in 1859, and is a son of John C. and Edvinia (Melchior) Kirk, natives, respectively, of South Carolina and Kentucky. The father came to Mississippi in 1845, settled on the river in Bolivar county, named his plantation Waxhaw, from the locality where he had resided in South Carolina, and became one of the most extensive planters in Bolivar county, being the owner of several plantations. He died in 1887, at the age of seventy-five years, and left his widow and four children, the latter named in the order of their births as follows: John M., Pearl (wife of Frank Scott, of Rosedale), Albert Leonidas and Anita G. John M. Kirk was reared on his father's place, secured a liberal education at Frankfort, Ky., and Sewanee, Tenn., and in 1879 graduated at the Eastman business college, at Poughkeepsie, N. Y. In 1884 he returned to this college and took the course in penmanship, after which he acted as bookkeeper for his father until 1887. In that year he was married to Miss Bessie Shattuck, a native of Wilkinson county, Miss., and the daughter of Capt. James W. Shattuck, who resides on Egypt ridge, this county, at the present time. Captain Shattuck recently moved to Bolivar county from Wilkinson county, where he was a member of the legislature, and is now an esteemed citizen of the former county. His father, Judge David O. Shattuck, resided for a time in Wilkinson county, where he was circuit judge, and before the war moved to California, where he resides at the present time. He has over one hundred descendants. To Mr. and Mrs. Kirk have been born two children: John Shattuck and Eddie May. Mrs. Kirk is a member of the Episcopal church, and Mr. Kirk is a member of the Masonic, the Knights of Honor, K. of P. and the alliance organizations. In personal appearance Mr. Kirk is about the medium hight, a good-looking blonde, and in manners is pleasant and gentlemanly.

A. H. Kirkland is the proprietor of the Mississippi Agricultural works, at Jackson, Miss. The invention and manufacture of machines and labor-saving appliances, designed to facilitate the operations of agriculture, have probably exerted a greater influence in contributing to the marvelous growth and development of this country than any other cause. Notable among the manufacturing establishments of Jackson engaged in this department of industry are the works belonging to Mr. Kirkland, which have been in operation since 1873. The implements turned out are recognized as unsurpassed in materials and workmanship, and the reputation and popularity of this house is due, not only to the acknowledged superiority of its goods, but also to the systematic correctness of its methods and the spirit of fairness by which all its transactions are characterized. Farming implements of all kinds are manufactured, which have a large sale in this state and Louisiana. He was born in Virginia in 1825, to which state his ancestors came from Scotland in colonial days. At the opening of the war he enlisted in the Confederate service, being at once placed in the arsenal at Columbus.

Dr. John R. Kirkland, of Meridian, Miss., is the son of Moses B. and Paulina (Tims) Kirkland. His parents are natives of South Carolina, but removed early to Alabama, where his father engaged in planting. They came about 1857 to Mississippi, and Mr.

Kirkland died in Scott county, leaving a large family, of whom Dr. Kirkland, who was born in Greene county, Ala., December 20, 1835, is the eldest son living. This gentleman was educated by taking a thorough course of literary training in Greene county, Ala., and in the science of medicine and surgery, in which he graduated at the University of Pennsylvania in Philadelphia, Penn., March, 1859, after more than two years of devoted study. In 1860 he hung out his professional shingle at Hillsboro, Scott county, Miss., and he had scarcely had time to establish himself in a practice when the war began. He enlisted in com F, of the Twentieth Mississippi regiment, as assistant surgeon. He was captured at Fort Donelson and taken to Mound City, Ill., and put in charge of the Confederate sick and wounded who were confined there, and to whose welfare he devoted his best professional skill for several months, until he was exchanged, and rejoined his regiment at Clinton, Miss., of which he was in charge as surgeon until the general surrender of the Confederate armies. He came to Meridian, Miss., in 1865, in September, where he has since been continuously engaged in the practice of his profession, and has built up an extensive patronage, which is also a very lucrative one. He has several times been president of the Lauderdale medical society, and is a member the state medical society. In February, 1864, he married Miss A. E. Yarborough, of Scott county, Miss., by whom he has four children living: Mrs. Annie Gray, of Atlanta, Ga., John R., Jr.; Willie F. and Nellie. He is a member of the Masonic fraternity and of the Knights of Honor, and is also a member as well as a deacon of the First Baptist church.

Dr. J. E. Knott is a Virginian by birth, in which state he was born in March, 1818, and while an infant was taken by his parents, William and Elizabeth I. (Moody) Knott, both native Virginians, to Maury county, Tenn., where his early life was passed on the plantation belonging to his father, and where he attended the common schools. He finished his literary education in a good academy and obtained his medical education in part in the medical department of the University of Kentucky at Louisville, which he attended during 1842 and 1843. The following year he entered the medical department of the University of Pennsylvania, graduating therefrom in 1845, and in 1846 began practicing his profession in Sumter county, Ala., where he continued with success for three years. In 1849 he came to Alamucha, Lauderdale county, Miss., where he practiced his profession till 1872, when he opened an office in Meridian, where he remained three years, since which he has resided at his former location, Alamucha. He has been identified with the agricultural interests for some years, and now owns a large tract of good farming land, but the most of his attention has been given to his profession. He was married in 1857 to Miss Amelia M. Knott, of Greene county, Ala., by whom he has three children: William J., Ella K. (wife of Dr. E. F. Crowther, a resident physician—specialist—of Vicksburg), and one that died in infancy. William J., the son, was married to Miss Virginia Lee Portis, of Alabama, in 1891, and is a talented young attorney of the Meridian bar. He was for four years a student of Vanderbilt university of Nashville, Tenn., where he took a collegiate as well as a law course. The mother of these children died in 1865. Dr. Knott is a member of the Missionary Baptist church, his daughter, Mrs. Crowther, being also a member of that church. His son, W. J., and his wife, are members of the Methodist Episcopal Church South. The Doctor is also a member of the A. F. & A. M. His health has been quite delicate throughout life, and at the present time he is almost retired from the practice of medicine, although his life work has been crowned with success. He is of a very benevolent, charitable and hospitable disposition, and is liberal with his means in helping those who need assistance. One of his brothers, R. F. Knott (deceased), was a resident of Mobile, Ala., and another brother, William M., is a citizen of Tennessee.

Dr. A. B. Knox, of New Albany, Union county, Miss., was born in Anderson district, S. C., in 1837. When he was one year old he removed with his parents to Franklin county, Ga. There the family remained for seven years, when they came to Tippah county, Miss., locating twelve miles south of Ripley. There Dr. Knox grew to manhood. He attended the Union university at Murfreesboro, Tenn., and after taking the prescribed course, he graduated with honor. Soon after the beginning of the war, he enlisted in the Confederate army and served for four years. In the second year of his service he was commissioned lieutenant. He was so severely wounded at Florence, Ala., as to disable him from further active participation. At the close of the war he took up the study of medicine under Dr. Hodges, graduating finally at the Kentucky school of medicine, at Louisville. Not long thereafter he married Miss Nanny J. Parks, a daughter of William Parks, who was one of the pioneers of Pontotoc county. They have one son, named Ralph. Soon after his marriage Dr. Knox engaged in the practice of his profession, with such success that he was enabled in a few years to retire. The Doctor and his family are members of the Missionary Baptist church, in which he holds the office of deacon. He has long been an active Sunday-school worker, and has all of the interests of the church closely at heart. He has at all times been helpfully identified with every movement tending to the upbuilding of public morals, and for the dissemination of education and general enlightenment. Every enterprise for the benefit of the town and county has his unqualified support. His father, William Knox, was born in Pickens district, S. C., in 1810. He located in Tippah county in 1848, where he has resided a greater part of his life, dying at Ripley in 1877. He was a popular and highly respected citizen, influential in business and in politics. In 1859 he was elected to represent his county in the legislature, and previous to that time, while a resident of Georgia, he had been a member of the legislature of the state of Georgia. He was an uncompromising democrat, but when the dissolution of the government arose he was in favor of Mississippi going out of the Union under the United States flag, instead of adopting the colors of the Southern Confederacy.

Among the very foremost of the professional men of Lauderdale county, Miss., whose skill is unquestioned and whose success has been very flattering, may be mentioned Dr. J. G. Knox, who was born in Greene county, Ala., in 1825, there also receiving the advantages of the common schools. He afterward fitted himself for college in the schools of Sumterville and Livingston, Ala., and Green Hill, Miss., entered the University of Mississippi in 1850, and graduated from that institution with the degree of A. B. in 1854, being one of the speakers of his class. After leaving college he taught school for one year, then entered the medical department of the University of Virginia, where he took his first course of lectures. He next entered Tulane university of New Orleans, where he was graduated as an M. D. in 1857, following which he entered upon his practice in Lauderdale county. After two years spent at Alamucha he removed to Rushing's store in the western part of the county, where he remained six years, the two following years being spent in Marengo county, Ala. In 1868 he located at Toomsuba, on the Alabama Great Southern railroad, twelve miles from Meridian, which place has been his home for the past twenty-three years, during which time he has enjoyed a good practice. He has also done a small mercantile business for some time. Upon the opening of the Civil war he went out as captain of a company, but upon the reorganization of the army he resumed the practice of his profession. In 1860 he was married to Miss Cornelia W. Stevens, of Lauderdale county, and by her became the father of fourteen children, nine of whom are living: Walter Eugene, Jackson Boman, Lula Cornelia, Sallie Elizabeth, Nannie Lee, Mattie Rebecca, Quintus Cincinnatus Lamar, James Gill and Rosaline

Eugenia. Dr. Knox, his wife and three daughters are members of the Missionary Baptist church, and he is a member of the A. F. & A. M. Dr. Knox is benevolent, charitable and consistent, a lover of education, and a man of exceptionally high standing, both professionally and socially. Walter Eugene, the eldest son, is married to Miss Letitia Moore, a daughter of Judge Moore, of Alabama. Dr. Knox's parents, James and Elizabeth Knox, were born in South Carolina somewhere in 1770 and 1780, respectively, and died in Alabama and Mississippi in 1827 and 1860, respectively, the former having been a farmer throughout life.

Hon. John Curtis Kyle, lawyer and planter, Sardis, Miss., is emphatically a man of the people, and the life of usefulness upon which he entered when yet in his boyhood has only acquired broader scope since he became a man. He is a native of Panola county, Miss., born on the 17th of July, 1851, and the confidence that the people have in him is therefore intelligently placed, for they have had every opportunity to judge of his character and qualifications, having known him from early boyhood. He was the third in order of birth of ten children born to the union of James M. and Susannah (Curtis) Kyle, natives of middle Tennessee. His paternal ancestors were from Scotland, and the maternal from the Emerald isle. The father immigrated from Tennessee to Panola county, Miss., in early life, and became a very successful farmer, finding his greatest delight in husbandry, and in the contentment and pleasures of the domestic circle. He was universally recognized as a man of stern integrity, fixed principles and sterling worth. No man ever enjoyed more of the confidence of the people or was more highly respected by his fellowmen than he. He reared a large family, and the prominent points in his character may be seen to-day in his children. Deprived of the benefits of a liberal education by various circumstances, Mr. Kyle nevertheless appreciated learning and determined to strain every point to afford his children the best educational advantages. In this he was successful. John Curtis Kyle, now the oldest living child of the family, worked on his father's farm, and whenever he could be spared from the arduous duties of the same he attended school. He improved every advantage offered in the common schools of the neighborhood, and his father, noticing that he was an apt and ambitious student, sent him to Bethel college, Tennessee, where he remained, employing his time industriously, until he had completed his course in the junior year. Circumstances prevented him from remaining longer, but did not prevent him from pursuing his studies at home. He neglected no opportunity to store his mind with useful knowledge, and having selected law as his vocation in life, entered Cumberland University, at Lebanon, Tenn. On the 4th of June, 1874, he graduated from that well-known institution of learning with honor, being awarded the degree of LL. D., when not yet twenty-three years of age. He immediately began practicing at Batesville, Miss., and entered upon the active duties of his profession, developing such skill, care and painstaking in the management of his business as to win and retain the confidence of his clients and of the public. From Batesville he removed to Sardis, where he continued the practice of law, part of the time in partnership with Hon. W. D. Miller and later with Hon. R. H. Taylor, continuing with that gentleman until spontaneously, without seeking or even desiring it, he was chosen mayor of the town. His administration was marked by ability, firmness and a devotion to duty such as is rarely equaled anywhere. In 1881, when politics ran high all through the state, Mr. Kyle was nominated by the democratic party to represent the county in the state senate. The strongest man in the opposition ranks was brought out against him and the county was thoroughly canvassed by both. The result was the triumphant election of Mr. Kyle over his competitor and a service of four years in the senate, where his ability was soon recognized, and where he wielded a marked influence in shaping the legislation of the period to promote the peace and welfare of the whole state. At the expiration of his term he was urgently solicited to stand for re-election, but firmly and courteously declined. Subsequently, when the board of control of the penitentiary and railroad commissioners was created by the legislature, he was, without solicitation on his part, elected a member of the board over so formidable a competitor as ex-Governor (now Governor) John M. Stone. So well did he discharge the delicate and responsible duties of the position, that upon the expiration of his first term he was elected to a second. While an incumbent of that office he devoted nearly his whole time to its important duties, and rarely spent an idle day at home with his family and friends.

In 1887 he was elected chairman of the state democratic executive committee, and conducted successfully one of the most important campaigns in the state since the political revolution of 1875 and 1876. He has never filled an appointive office, but to every one he has ever filled he was elected by the people, or their representatives in the legislature. As railroad commissioner he was vigilant, firm and always unyielding where the interests of the people were involved. As a member of the board of control of the penitentiary he visited the camps and farms where the convicts were employed and after making strict investigations, was firm and fearless in enforcing the right and the law and in laboring for the abolishment of the vicious lease system. In 1890 his friends urged him to become a candidate for congress. His competitors for the nomination were Messrs. Charles B. Howry, A. H. Whitfield, Ira D. Oglesby and the present representative, Hon. J. B. Morgan, all able and popular gentlemen, well known throughout the district. Mr. Kyle received the nomination on the three hundred and sixty-eighth ballot. The republicans nominated Capt. G. M. Buchanan, of Marshall, an ex-Confederate soldier, and the strongest, if not the ablest, man of their party in the district, and one of the shrewdest canvassers and best organizers in the state. Mr. Kyle was elected by a large majority. He was married in 1879 to Miss Sallie G. Heflin, daughter of Capt. W. D. Hefln, of Sardis, and they have one son, John Curtis, Jr., who is a bright, intelligent lad. Mr. Kyle is a member of the Methodist church South, and is steward in the same. He has been engaged in planting all this time.

A. S. Kyle, a prominent citizen and farmer of Batesville, Panola county, Miss., is a native of that county, born on February 27, 1854, and is second in order of birth of eight children born to J. M. and S. A. (Curtis) Kyle. He was early trained to the arduous duties of the farm, and on account of having considerable trouble with his eyes did not receive the collegiate education intended him by his father, whose desire was that all his children should have a college education. A. S. Kyle was thirty-one years of age at the time of his father's death, and he was made agent of the family affairs by the consent of the heirs. He settled up the estate and educated all the minor children according to the wish of the father. In 1885 he selected as his companion in life Miss Mary Heflin, daughter of W. D. and Mary (McLaurin) Heflin, and the fruits of this union were the following children: Mary Heflin, Susie Monroe and John William. After his marriage Mr. Kyle invested the money he had accumulated, $3,500, in land, three hundred and twenty acres, and upon this he has since resided. He has made many improvements, erected buildings, etc., and has added to the original tract until he is now the owner of eight hundred acres of land with three hundred acres devoted to corn, cotton and forage. He is also the owner of fifteen hundred acres of timber land in the Mississippi bottoms. Although he has not received the education desired, Mr. Kyle is a man of strong and vigorous mind, a close observer and a great student. He is well qualified to hold any position, and is one of the representative men of the county. He takes an active part in politics, frequently attending state and county conventions with the democratic party, and also takes a strong interest in the alliance movement. He is a member of the Blue lodge, A. F. & A. M., at Batesville, also the Knights of Honor, and he and Mrs. Kyle are worthy members of the Cumberland Presbyterian church, at Batesville.

CHAPTER XXIV.

PRIVATE AND BUSINESS SKETCHES, L.

AMONG the planters of Yazoo county, there is none more thoroughly wideawake and energetic than Joel H. Lacy. He is a native of Kemper county, Miss., born February 15, 1849, and is the seventh of a family of eight children. His parents, Joseph and Jennie H. (Howel) Lacy, were natives of Kentucky and Tennessee, respectively. The father came to Mississippi at an early day, and was engaged in planting until his death, in 1875. The paternal grandfather was Thomas Lacy, of Kentucky. Joel H. was brought up in Yazoo county, and passed his boyhood and youth in the private schools of the neighborhood. He remained under the parental roof until he was twenty-five years of age. He had no capital, excepting that with which nature had endowed him; but pluck and energy are faithful allies, and by their aid he has accumulated a considerable property. He owns seven hundred and sixty acres of good land, cultivating one hundred and fifty. He was married in 1872 to Miss Mary E. Kelly, of Alabama, a daughter of S. Kelly, Esq., a native of Alabama. Eight children have been born of this union: Joseph K., Ora, Annie L., Ida, Inez, Seal, John P. and Addie. Mr. Lacy was a soldier in the late Civil war, enlisting in 1863, in company C, Twentieth Mississippi cavalry, under Capt. W. D. Snead. He was taken prisoner at Liberty, Miss., in 1863, soon after his enlistment, was carried to New Orleans, and thence to Ship Island, where he was held until the close of the struggle. He is a member of the I. O. O. F., and in his political opinions he adheres to the principles of the democratic party. He is a loyal citizen, a successful planter, a good neighbor, and a true, tried friend.

Among the most enterprising and substantial merchants of Bay St. Louis, Hancock county, Miss., is Frank J. Ladner, who was born in this place in 1855, November 12th. His paternal grandfather, Frank Ladner, was the first settler in the town of Bay St. Louis. He formed a partnership with Robert Toulme, who settled there soon after, and they, too, carried on a general market business. The grandfather passed the remainder of his days here. The father, who was also named Frank, is a carpenter and contractor, and has erected a great number of buildings along the coast. He has been alderman of the Bay for several years, and is a highly esteemed citizen. He reared a family of six sons and four daughters, eight of whom are living. Frank J. is the eldest of the family. He was educated in Bay St. Louis, and when he had finished school he entered the employ of W. J. Poitevent, at Gainesville, Miss. He clerked for this gentleman several years, and then went to a town in Louisiana, where he clerked for a short time. He returned to his native place, and established himself in the transfer business, which he continued eighteen months. He was next employed as baggage master on the Louisiana & Northern railroad, and held this position for a number of years. He was promoted to the position of conductor, as he was considered too valuable a man for the work of baggage-master. He took the first passenger train into Covington, La., over the New Orleans, Northeastern & East St. Louis railroad. He has followed railroad business nearly nine years, and when he resigned his position he was presented with a fine gold-headed walking-stick. During the time he was connected with this company he did not cost them a penny through errors or carelessness. He is a thoroughly competent railroad man, and has made a record in which he takes just pride. When he left the railroad business he embarked in the mercantile trade, and in two years has built up a large and profitable business. He carries a complete stock of general merchandise, and no customer enters his store who is not well served. He is interested in the business of buying wool, and handles large quantities of it in the course of a year. He is a member of the Catholic Knights of America. He has shares in the People's building and loan association of Bay St. Louis, and has been an alderman of the place, and was chairman of the finance committee. In addition to his commercial interests he owns a large tract of land which belonged to his grandfather's estate; it is located on Jordan river, two and a quarter miles from Bay St. Louis. There are some fine pecan trees growing on this place, and there is a nice residence surrounded with many modern improvements. Mr. Ladner also owns some valuable lots in Bay St. Louis. His brother, A. E. Ladner, is the ticket agent of the Louisville & Nashville railroad at New Orleans, La., and has been for several years. Eugene Ladner, a younger brother, is a baggage master on the Louisiana & Northern railroad, and is also interested in a general store in New Orleans, La.

Capt. Gabriel P. Lake, planter, Duck Hill, Miss. Mr. Lake's parents, George and Mary (Slacum) Lake, were natives of Dorchester county, Md., and there the father passed his entire life, engaged in planting and merchandising. He had very limited educational advantages while growing up, but by his own exertions he became well posted on all subjects of moment and was a man of considerable prominence. He was a major in the War of 1812, and operated in Chesapeake bay and vicinity, and was also at one time a member of the Maryland legislature. He was very active in all public matters, and was one of the largest business men and became very wealthy. His death occurred in his native county in 1831. Mrs. Lake, who was a worthy and exemplary member of the Methodist church for many years, received her final summons in 1872. The paternal grandfather of our subject, Henry Lake, was a native of England, and came to America prior to the Revolutionary war, settling in Maryland, where his death occurred. Grandfather Slacum was also a native probably of Maryland, in which state he spent his entire life, engaged in planting. During the War of 1812 he was captured, placed in the bastile in Spain, and there remained for seven years. He then made his escape, went to Paris and there boarded a French vessel bound for the United States. He was captured by a British man-of-war and recaptured by a French vessel, returned to France and from there to his family in Maryland, who supposed him dead. In that state his death occurred. Capt. Gabriel P. Lake was the eighth of ten children, five of whom are yet living: Harriet, of Grenada, the widow of Henry McNamara, who died in Maryland, is still living and is eighty years of age; Clara, of Baltimore, widow of John S. Staplefort (deceased); Georgia Ann, wife of Dr. Joseph B. Tarpley, of Montague county, Tex.; Dr. Robert P., a planter and retired physician, of Madison county, Va., was educated at Dixon college and at Cannonsburg, Penn., and graduated in physic at Baltimore, Md. He was a surgeon in the Virginia army during the Civil war. All the children grew to mature years and became the heads of families. Captain Lake supplemented a good common school education by attending Cambridge academy and Dixon college. In 1838 he came to

Grenada, clerked for his cousin and brother-in-law for two years, and then returned to Maryland, where he followed agricultural pursuits. He was married in 1845 to Miss Henrietta, daughter of John and Nancy Crawford, her father being a successful planter of Dorchester county, Maryland, where he received his last summons. Mrs. Lake was born in that county and died there in 1850. They were the parents of two children, both deceased. In 1867 Captain Lake was married in Grenada county, Miss., to Mrs. Kate Connelly, daughter of Professor Warner and Mildred Yates, natives of Virginia, who at an early day came to Mississippi, and in 1853 located in Grenada. Mr. Yates followed the occupation of a planter, but in connection was also engaged in teaching school for some time. He died in Hernando before the war. Mrs. Yates died in Memphis. Mrs. Lake was born in Tennessee and died in 1876, leaving three children, two of whom are living: Mildred and Julia. Captain Lake's third marriage occurred in 1878 to Mrs. Nannie J. Moore, daughter of Alexander and Elizabeth Killpatrick, natives of Anderson district, South Carolina. Mr. and Mrs. Killpatrick moved from their native state to Alabama, thence in 1842 to Calhoun county, Miss., where Mr. Killpatrick died, in 1876. He was a planter and was colonel of the militia during one of the Indian wars. He was quite prominent in public affairs and held numerous minor offices. His wife, who was born in Pickens county, Ala., died in 1879. Captain Lake farmed in Maryland until 1859, and then came to what is now Montgomery county, locating near Winona, where he remained until 1869, when he moved to his present farm of five hundred and fifty acres, with two hundred and fifty acres cleared, all the result of his own exertions. While a resident of Maryland he held the position of justice of the peace a number of years, but has never aspired to public office. In 1862 he joined the Mississippi militia and served two years as captain of company A, operating in Mississippi. Afterward he joined company B, McGirke's regiment of cavalry, and after a short time the command was reorganized and he was rejected on account of age. He was detailed to recruit for reserve purposes until the close of the war. He was formerly a Mason and is a member of the Farmers' Alliance. He and Mrs. Lake are prominent members of the Methodist Church South. His cousin, William Lake, who afterward became his brother-in-law, was one of the first settlers of Grenada, where he became one of the most successful merchants and one of the most respected citizens.

Nowhere within the limits of Jefferson county, Miss., can there be found a man who takes greater interest in its agricultural affairs than George A. Lake, or who strives more continually to promote and advance these interests. Every life has a history of its own, and although in appearance it may possess little to distinguish it from others, yet the connection of Mr. Lake with the agricultural interests of this region has contributed to give him a wide and popular acquaintance with nearly every citizen of Jefferson county, if not personally, then by name. Mr. Lake was born in Claiborne county, Miss., January 16, 1846, but his father, George Lake, although born in the Palmetto state, was reared in Tennessee, and when a young man became a resident of Claiborne county, Miss., his marriage with Matilda Briggs taking place there. In that county, in which she was born, her father, Joseph Logan Briggs, was one of the early pioneers from Kentucky. Mr. Lake followed planting in Claiborne county, and by the free exercise of brain and brawn he succeeded in accumulating a comfortable fortune. While in the prime of life death called him home, his widow surviving him ten years, and dying in 1873. George A. Lake is the only survivor of two children, his sister Alice, who married F. Smith, of Claiborne county, Miss., being deceased. George A. acquired his knowledge of books in Centenary college, and although he was of a rather lively temperament, he knew the value of an education sufficiently to apply himself diligently to his studies while in college, and has never had cause to regret so doing.   Upon the opening of the late war he returned home to assist his father in the management of his plantation, continuing until 1863, when he enlisted in a cavalry company commanded by Wirt Adams, serving faithfully until Lee's surrender, participating in a number of small engagements and skirmishes, principally in Mississippi.   In the fall of 1865 he started on a trip to Europe, for the purpose of completing his education, and graduated from an excellent and superior institution of learning in Switzerland, after which he traveled through France, Germany and England.   In the spring of 1868 he returned to his native land, and from that time up to 1873 was engaged in planting in Claiborne county, but thinking to better his financial condition he went to Dallas, Tex., and after two years of merchandising in that city he sold out and went to southwestern Texas, where for one year he managed a sheep ranch.   Finding that this was not as profitable an investment as he expected, and that it was not congenial to his tastes, he sold out and returned to Mississippi, and after spending one year in Warren county and one year in Sharkey county, following the calling of an agriculturist, he in 1878 at last located permanently in Jefferson county.   Here he was married on the 14th of February of the same year to Miss Ernestine Cox, a daughter of Robert and Leminda (Green) Cox, both of whom were born in Jefferson county, Mrs. Cox being a member of one of the most prominent families of this section, her father, Filmer Green, a son of William Marston Green, having been born in this county.   About the year 1775 his father settled on the plantation on which Mr. Lake is now living, and this place has been in the hands of some of his decendants up to the present time. Mr. Cox, the father of Mrs. Lake, was a successful and very extensive planter on this place until his death, in 1882, and on this plantation Mrs. Lake was born, reared and educated, her studies being pursued under the instructions of an able and accomplished governess.   After her marriage she and her husband continued to make their home with her father, and after the death of Mr. Cox, Mr. Lake took charge of the plantation and business, and eventually bought out the heirs to the estate.   It contains about one thousand acres, with four hundred acres under cultivation, and although this land has been under cultivation for over one hundred years, it still yields abundant crops.   This is in a great measure owing to the use of fertilizers and to the judicious manner in which the place is tilled.   Although it was at one time considered worn out it is now one of the best upland plantations in Jefferson county, and his handsome, commodious and truly typical Southern residence is beautifully situated and commands a pleasing view from all sides.   To this pleasant home Mr. and Mrs. Lake welcome their friends, and the air of refinement and good taste prevading all their surroundings and the true and unbounded hospitality which they at all times display are well known and fully appreciated.   Mr. Lake usually takes an active part in local politics, and has served as a delegate to county, congressional and state conventions.   He was elected and served two years as county treasurer, and as an official was true and faithful to every interest.   Socially he is a member of the Knights of Honor, and although he is not a member of any church he is an Episcopalian in belief, his wife being a member of this church. They have two daughters, Laura and Ernestine Cox, both of whom are bright and promising.

Hon. William A. Lake, long a prominent member of the Mississippi bar, was born in Dorchester county, Md., in 1808, and was admitted to the bar at the age of twenty-one. Two years afterward he was elected to the Maryland legislature.   In 1834 he removed to Mississippi and began legal practice in Vicksburg, and rose rapidly to distinction.   He was several times elected to represent Warren county in the legislature and in the state senate.   In 1856 he was elected to congress from the fourth Mississippi district.   In 1861 he was a candidate for a seat in the Confederate congress, and was killed in a duel brought about by bad feeling engendered during the canvass, by Chambers, his opponent.

Hon. L. Q. C. Lamar was born in Milledgeville, Ga., September 25, 1825, and is the second son of L. Q. C. Lamar, a distinguished lawyer and judge, and the youngest man ever raised to the superior court of Georgia. He was educated at Emory college, and afterward studied law, being admitted to the bar about his twenty-first year. He served as adjunct professor of mathematics in the University of Mississippi from 1850 to 1852. Returning then to Georgia, he soon became prominently identified with the political history of his county, and in 1853 was elected to the state legislature. At the expiration of his term of office he formed a partnership with Robert Harper, and entered upon the practice of his profession at Macon, Ga. In 1854 he returned to Oxford, Miss., and engaged in practice there. In 1856 he was elected to congress, and was reëlected in 1858. In June, 1860, he was elected to the chair of metaphysics and ethics of the state university. One year later, at the breaking out of the Civil war, he resigned this position of honor for one of equal importance, if not of equal pleasure: he was elected lieutenant-colonel of Mott's regiment of infantry, and saw service in Virginia. His health failing, President Davis appointed him Confederate envoy to Russia. Not being received at the foreign court he returned to America, and after an adventure in running the Federal blockade landed in a skiff, losing all his effects; he arrived just in time to witness the surrender. In 1865 he formed a partnership with Senator Walthall, and located in Coffeeville for the practice of law. In 1866, however, he was re-elected to the chair of metaphysics and ethics of the state university, which he held one year, being transferred at the end of that time to the chair of governmental science and law. Upon the reorganization of the state under the new constitution of 1869, one feature of which was the reorganization of the board of trustees of the university, in 1870, he resigned his position and devoted himself exclusively to his professional work. In 1872 he was elected to congress with his political disabilities on him; the following session removed his disabilities, and in 1873 he took his seat. He served until elected to the United States senate by the legislature of 1876; he took his seat in 1877, and was re-elected without opposition. In March, 1885, he was appointed secretary of the interior by President Cleveland, and filled this office until he was appointed to the supreme bench of the United States, in 1888. Mr. Lamar was united in marriage July 15, 1847, to Virginia L. Longstreet; she died December 20, 1884, leaving four children, all of whom are living: Frances E., wife of Edward Mayes; L. Q. C.; Sarah Augusta, wife of F. Hugh Heiskell, of Memphis, and Virginia L., who married a cousin, William H. Lamar, an attorney of Washington, D. C., who was a member of the Greeley relief expedition. Mr. Lamar was married a second time, December, 1886, to Mrs. H. Holt, of Macon, Ga.

Samuel H. Lambdin, a retired planter of Edgewood plantation, which is situated seven and a half miles north of Natchez, Miss., was born in Pittsburgh, Penn., in 1811, and is a son of James and Prudence (Harrison) Lambdin. If he lives until October, 1891, he will be eighty years old. His parents were born on the east shore of Maryland, attained their growth there, married and in 1810 started for the Scioto valley in Ohio. On reaching Pittsburgh they found the water too low for navigation and accordingly they located there. Mr. Lambdin engaged in business there and died in 1812. The mother died at a son's in Philadelphia at the age of seventy-five years, a devout member of the Methodist church. Her father was a brother of the Harrison who was one of the signers of the declaration of independence, and was a man of considerable note. The ancestors of James Lambdin were among the early colonists of Maryland. He was but a little boy during the Revolutionary war and was left an orphan at an early age. He was the father of eight children, two besides Samuel H. living to be grown: Jonathan Harrison, who was a publisher and book-seller, died in Pittsburgh in 1825, and James, a portrait painter, died in Philadelphia, Penn., in 1889, at the age of eighty-three years. Samuel H., the youngest of this family, was educated in Pittsburgh, and at the age of fourteen years, began business for himself as a clerk in a commission house in Pittsburgh, continuing at this until 1829. He then engaged as clerk on a steamboat on the Ohio river for four years, and subsequently commanded the Ohioan, a steamboat operating between Louisville, St. Louis and New Orleans. After about a year, in 1835, he came to Natchez and followed clerking until 1837, when he became a partner with Mr. E. R. Bennett, under the firm title of Lambdin & Bennett, and operated a plantation supply store, which they continued until 1842. Mr. Lambdin then served one year as president of the Planters' bank of Mississippi, and later joined his father-in-law in the planting interest. In 1860 he erected his present residence, a most beautiful and attractive home, and here he and his wife have since resided, surrounded by their many warm friends, who know Mr. and Mrs. Lambdin for their generosity, benevolence, integrity and sterling worth. Mr. Lambdin is the owner of a fine plantation of one thousand five hundred acres in Concordia parish, La., and is well known as a prominent retired planter. He is a gentleman of mild temperament, good habits and is remarkably well preserved for an octogenarian. He has always taken an active part in politics and all public enterprises to advance the interests of the town and county. In 1865 he was a delegate to the reconstruction convention and for twelve years has been justice of the peace. He was married in 1842 to Miss Jane M. Bisland, a native of Adams county, Miss., and the daughter of William and Mary L. Bisland. To Mr. and Mrs. Lambdin have been born six children, five now living: Mary; Louisa, wife of Louis Winston; Elizabeth, wife of J. L. Henderson, of Fort Smith, Ark.; James Harrison, a planter of Concordia parish, La., and Samuel H., Jr., a planter of Adams county, Miss., all of whom have received good educations and stand high in the community. William Bisland, the father of Mrs. Lambdin, was born in Adams county, Miss., and spent his entire life in that county as one of its leading planters. His death occurred in 1847, and his wife followed him to the grave in 1872. His father, John Bisland, was a native of Scotland and came to America at a period ante-dating the Revolutionary war. He settled in North Carolina and at the breaking out of the war, not wishing to take up arms for or against the colonists, he returned to his native land. However, in 1778, he again returned to America, settling this time in Adams county, Miss., nine miles from Natchez, on Pine ridge, purchased a large tract of land and there spent the balance of his life as an honored and respected citizen. He died in that county in 1825, as did also his wife in 1835. Many of their descendants now reside in that county. He was one of the first permanent settlers of the county, then Spanish dominion. His wife, whose maiden name was Susannah Rucker, was the daughter of Colonel Rucker, who had been an officer in the English army, but prior to the Revolutionary war came to Virginia and settled there. When the war broke out he came to Mississippi, fifteen miles from Natchez, and settled there and spent the remainder of his days. Mrs. Lambdin's mother, whose maiden name was Witherspoon, was born in the Palmetto state, but when a child moved with her parents to the thick woods back of Baton Rouge, La., where the latter passed the balance of their lives. They left a son, Calvin, who died in that state, and two daughters, one of whom, the wife of Mr. T. R. Shields, resides in Terrebonne parish, La., and died in 1840. Many descendants of the Witherspoon family now live in Louisiana, and some of them are prominent people. Mr. and Mrs. Lambdin have been devout members of the Presbyterian church since 1846, and now hold membership at Pine Ridge church, near their home, the first established Presbyterian church in the Southwest, its history dating from 1807. Three daughters are also members of this church.

W. H. Lambeth was born in Campbell county, Va., in 1831, and is the fourth of a family of eight children. His parents, Dr. William L. and Susan H. (Davenport) Lambeth were Virginians by birth. The father was a physician by profession, and was graduated under Dr. Rush. He removed to Hinds county, Miss., in 1835, and for a few years was devoted to planting. In 1837 he lost heavily by the failure of Planters & Brandon's bank. He had forty-one negro slaves killed by the explosion of the Griffin Yateman, a steamboat on the Mississippi river, near Memphis. In 1841 he settled on the plantation now occupied by our subject. He preëmpted one hundred and sixty acres of land, to which he added by purchase one hundred and sixty. He placed all under good cultivation, being a man of untiring energy. He was a man of sterling traits of character and of excellent habits. He died in 1849, at the age of forty-nine years. His wife survived until 1853, when she died of yellow fever in New Orleans. At the same time three of her children succumbed to the dread disease. Four of the eight children lived to maturity: Mrs. Eliza D. Farrow, of Dallas, Tex.; Dr. Addison R., who died in 1851; Robert T., a planter of the neighborhood, and W. H. Mr. Lambeth passed his childhood days in the county in which he was born, receiving limited educational opportunities. He was reared amidst the scenes of farm life, but in 1852, when the opportunity presented itself for him to study law, he entered the office of Marr & Roberts, New Orleans. The following year the hand of death fell heavily upon the family, and his studies were for a time interrupted. He returned to the plantation, which he cared for until the breaking out of the Civil war, at which time he entered the Confederate army. He enlisted in Adams' cavalry, and was assigned to the Western army. The most important engagements in which his regiment participated were Shiloh, Iuka, Corinth, Port Gibson, and about fifty other battles. At Washington, Miss., he was wounded and captured. He was exchanged in August, 1864, being at Gainesville, Ala., under General Forrest at the time of the surrender. When the war was ended he resumed his agricultural pursuits in Yazoo county. During all this time of turmoil and conflict he had not abandoned his desire to enter the legal ranks of the country, so in 1866 he took up his studies again, and in the same year he was admitted to the bar of Mississippi. In 1857 Mr. Lambeth was united in marriage to Miss Sallie F. Rucker, a daughter of Col. John W. and Maria (Kibble) Rucker. Colonel Rucker was one of the well-known early settlers of Yazoo county. He died in 1870, and his wife followed him in 1883. Mr. and Mrs. Lambeth are the parents of four children: Susan and William are deceased, Maria is the wife of T. P. McMahon, of Indianola, Miss., and John R. is a student at the Capital City commercial college, Jackson, Miss. Mr. Lambeth has eleven hundred acres of land; four hundred and fifty he has placed in a high state of cultivation. He is a member of Yazoo City lodge No. 42, A. F. & A. M. Mrs. Lambeth is a member of the Episcopal church. She is a most estimable woman, and betrays in her bearing the wealth and refining influences under which she was reared. Mr. Lambeth has always taken an active part in local politics. He has held the office of commissioner in chancery since 1866, and was magistrate for six years. He was one of the prime movers in the action that was taken in 1875 to overcome the corrupt radical rule of the country, and drew up the first set of resolutions stating the grievances of the people. Among his accomplishments he numbers that of shooting. His diary shows that before the war he brought down eleven hundred deer and fifty-three bears, and his aim is still considered unerring.

Hon. John Tillman Lamkin (deceased) was one of the most prominent figures of southern Mississippi in his time, and was recognized as one of the leading jurists of the South. The following is an extract of his life, prepared at the time of his death by his intimate friend and associate, Capt. S. A. Matthews: "Hon. John Tillman Lamkin was born in the city of Augusta, Ga., July 17, 1811. Receiving from his parents an education that would properly fit him for any station in life, he chose the profession of law, and in 1831 he entered the law office of the Hon. James N. Bethune, and with industry and diligence continued there until 1833, when he was admitted to the practice of law in the state of Georgia. He continued the practice of his profession in his native state until the latter part of 1835, in November of which year he married Miss Thurza Ann Kilgore. The republic of Texas was at that time a rising star, inviting to its borders all who had the progress of liberty at heart, and to this eldorado, Mr. Lamkin, influenced by the glowing descriptions he had received, with his young bride of a few days, left his native state November 9, 1835, and located in the republic on the 25th of December following. His experience while there, and his disappointment at finding that the representations of the country had been too highly colored, led him to return to the states. He arrived in New Orleans April 26, 1836. He remained in that city under an engagement as bookkeeper in the commercial house of Hyde & Delaplaine, where he perfected himself as an accountant. This was of valuable benefit to him in afterlife in the practice of his profession, as it had trained his mind for that system and carefulness which was always a leading trait in his character. Being ambitious, and wishing to practice his profession, he left his employment among the musty ledgers and removed to Pike county, Miss., where he was admitted to the bar in November, 1838. The following month he took up his residence in Columbia, Marion county, where he began the practice of law and remained until January 20, 1840, when he removed to Holmesville, Pike county. The following year he was strongly solicited to run for the office of district attorney of his district, which extended from Amite county to the seashore, and after considerable hesitation he entered the canvass vigorously, and, notwithstanding the fact that he had for his opponent one of the leading men of south Mississippi, he was elected in November, 1841. Too much can not be said of the efficient manner in which he filled so important an office, and we may truthfully assert, without any disparagement to his predecessor or successors, that in the fullfilment of his duties, he has been seldom equaled and rarely excelled, and that he dealt out even-handed justice to all, with that purity of purpose and energetic ability which command universal admiration. When he had held this office for four years he began to realize that his largely-extended and rapidly-increasing practice demanded his undivided attention, and declining to become a candidate for a second term, he devoted himself henceforth exclusively to his practice. When the late war broke out and the people of the South were convulsed at the reality of the contest, although he had been an earnest and consistent Union man from the incipient period of the Revolution until the separation of Mississippi from the mother government, and had opposed secession in all its stages, when his adopted state took the decisive step, he felt that he owed all his allegiance to her, and with his usual energy and ability and without ostentation, he materially assisted in organizing, arming and equipping troops for the field. When the exigences of war compelled the Confederate government to call for more troops, although physically unfitted for the camp and its hardships, Mr. Lamkin responded to the call and volunteered his services, and by his influence instilled into the minds of the people of his country a relization of the necessity of prompt action, and on the 10th of April, 1862, he succeeded in raising a company known as the Holmesville guards and was at once elected their captain.

"Well do we remember his words in a letter to the writer, then in Virginia: 'The time has come when every man who has a spark of patriotism in his bosom should promptly volunteer his services.' His company was one of those which composed the Thirty-third Mississippi regiment, under the command of Col. David W. Hurst, and made a brilliant record for itself during the war. Mr. Lamkin remained with his regiment until October 5, 1863, when the people of his congressional district demanded his services in another field, and by a large vote elected him to the Confederate congress at Richmond, Va. As their representative he ably attended to the interests of his constituents at home, as well as those of others who were in the field battling for their firesides, whom he assisted materially by his wise action. While protecting their dear ones at home no member of that body had a greater reputation for honesty, industry and zeal for his country than he, and he was always regarded as one of the most active of working members. With the war closed Mr. Lamkin's congressional career, and he returned to his home and family to find that the war, with all its desolating influences, had not left him unscathed, but that the accumulations of years of toil and industry had been in a great measure swept away. With his usual energy and ability he resumed his profession, and like many other soldiers of the lost cause, began anew the battle of life. But alas for human calculation! By the inevitable decree of Providence, his usefulness was brought to a close by a long and painful illness, and for twelve months preceding his demise, he was seldom an actor in the great stage of life. He died at Holmesville, May 19, 1870. Mr. Lamkin was a man of sterling worth and merit, and was one of Mississippi's honored sons. He was of a quiet, unostentatious disposition, kind and charitable toward all people and classes. He gave liberally and quietly of his means, that his right hand should not know what his left hand doeth, and thus many of his noble deeds and kindnesses remained unknown except from the grateful recipients of his aid, whose burdens he has lightened, and into whose darkened lives he cast a golden gleam of the sunshine of kindness. Mr. Lamkin was made a Mason in Sincerity lodge No. 214, at Holmesville (now Magnolia), January 5, 1856, and at once became an active and zealous member, soon distinguishing himself in the order and taking a high position in the fraternity. Well did he deserve the many honors bestowed upon him. He was worshipful master of the lodge during many years, and was elected grand master of the grand lodge of Mississippi for 1867, and during his administration as grand master rendered many important decisions, which became a part of Masonic law. Of that quiet, unobtrusive manner so characteristic of him, he dispensed his charities where they were needed; as a friend he was true; as a citizen he scrupulously observed his country's laws and frowned down all insubordination; as an officer he was exemplary in the discharge of all his official duties, never countenancing any act which might have a tendency to subvert the peace and good order of society. As a husband and father he was kind and affectionate, ever manifesting that love for his family which adorns the home circle. Such are the lessons we find in the life example of one of those noble men, toward whom Mississippi may justly point the finger of pride and whose life and achievements are highly worthy the emulation of the youth of the rising generation. He was loved, honored and revered by all, and it was a sad day for the South when his noble, kindly heart ceased to beat. May his memory be perpetuated by the thousand whisperings of the summer zephyrs that sigh a sad requiem above his honored tomb.''

Hon. James C. Lamkin, an attorney at Summit, Miss., was born in Holmesville, Pike county, November 22, 1848. He is a son of Hon. John T. Lamkin, a sketch of whom appears elsewhere. He grew to maturity in his native town, and at the age of seventeen years he entered the Summerville institute, where he studied for three years. In 1868 he entered the University of Virginia, but was called home during the following year by the death of his father. He did not return to his studies until the fall of 1870, when he began the study of law, which he continued after his return to Holmesville, being admitted to the bar in 1873. Immediately after he located in Summit and became associated with Judge David W. Hurst, under the firm name of Hurst & Lamkin. This partnership was terminated by the death of Judge Hurst in 1882. In 1879 Mr. Lamkin was elected mayor of Summit, and in the state election of the fall of that year he was elected to the state legislature. He was reëlected in 1883. At the present time he is serving his fifth consecutive year as mayor of Summit. During the time of his representation of the county he was a member of the committee of public education and on the committee of railroads. He is a member of Summit lodge No. 93, I. O. O. F. In 1887 he was elected grand master of the jurisdiction of the state of Mississippi of that order. He is also a member of the Knights of Honor and the Knights of Pythias. His political services have been eminently satisfactory to his fellow-citizens, and he is at the present time, August 8, 1891, a nominee of his party for the state senate from his district. He is a stockholder in the Summit cotton mills, and was a promoter of and a stockholder in the Mississippi fair association. In January, 1873, he was married to Miss Kaloolah, the only daughter of Judge David W. Hurst, at one time an incumbent of the bench of the Supreme court of Mississippi, and otherwise very prominent politically. Their union has been blessed with two children: Alice A. and Gussie H. Mrs. Lamkin and her daughters are consistent members of the Methodist Episcopal church and are active in all charitable and benevolent works. Politically Mr. Lamkin has always been a democrat, and a stanch one, and he was also a member of the district congressional convention in 1886, and was chairman of the committee on credentials. He is a true type of the Southern gentlemen, and his career illustrates what may be accomplished under our free institutions by well-directed effort associated with the highest order of integrity.

The profession of the physician is one of the most important to which a man can devote his life, if followed by a conscientious and honorable man, and that Dr. William J. Lamkin is this can not be gainsaid. The skill and talent he has displayed in the practice of his profession has brought happiness to many households, but his cheerful countenance and kind encouragement has also done much to bring about the convalescence of his patients. His birth occurred in Holmesvillle, Pike county, Miss., November 24, 1843, and there his early youth was spent in the public schools, after which he spent one year in the University of Mississippi. After the firing on Fort Sumter, and at the call of the Confederacy for troops, he joined the eleventh Mississippi infantry, but was afterward transferred to the Sixteenth infantry, with which he served until the final surrender, following the varying fortunes of a private soldier, and suffering untold hardships and privations. He surrendered with General Lee at Appomattox courthouse, and returned home with the consciousness of having acquitted himself creditably in the following engagements: Manassas, where he received a flesh wound in the leg by a gunshot; Fredericksburg, Wilderness, Chancellorsville, Gettysburg, besides a great many others but of less note. After his return home he determined to follow the life of a physician, and with this end in view he began studying in Holmesville in the office of Dr. J. M. Thornhill, a physician of some local repute. He took his first course of lectures in the medical department of the University of Louisiana in 1866-7, graduating as an M. D. in March, 1868, in the class of 1867-8, the sessions beginning in November and ending in March. His first practice was done in Pike county, but he soon extended his practice to the adjoining counties of Franklin, Lincoln and Amite. In 1884 he came to Gloster, being the first physician to locate in the new town, and here he has since remained; the practice which he has succeeded in building up being exceptionally large. He was married in Holmesville on November 11, 1867, to Miss Mary A. Conerly, a daughter of Owen and Louisa (Stephens) Conerly. Mrs. Lamkin was born and reared in Pike county, Miss., and to them a family of eight children were born: J. Howard, who is now in the office of the Louisville, New Orleans & Texas railroad, at New Orleans; James O., depot agent at Coahoma, Miss.; Thurza, M. Ernie, Fannie A., Willie E., C. Boyd and Robert Lee. Mr. Lamkin and his wife are members of the Methodist Episcopal church South, and he is a prominent member of the Masonic fraternity. He is a thorough business man, enterprising, public spirited, and being very social is a most agreeable gentleman to meet. His grandfather, William Lamkin, was born in Dooley county, Ga., and was of Scotch lineage. His son, John T., was also born in Dooley county, and there spent his youth. He was married, near Augusta, to Miss Thurza Ann Kilgore, of the state of Georgia also, and some time after moved with her to Mississippi, and at Holmesville opened a law office and began practicing, continuing successfully until his death, which occurred on May 19, 1870. He was a prominent politician of Pike county, and for some time served as a member of the Confederate congress. He was in the Confederate army for about one year, being captain of a company, in which capacity he did some effective work. He was a member of the Masonic fraternity, and served as grand master of the state of Mississippi in 1867. In this order he attained to the thirty-third degree. His children were named as follows: Fannie A. (deceased) was the wife of Alfred A. Boyd, sheriff of Pike county; James C. and John A. are attorneys at Summit and Magnolia, respectively; Charles A. is a farmer in Texas, and Miss C. A. Lamkin is principal of the Peabody public school, at Summit, Miss. The Lamkin family is held in high repute throughout this section, and are among the law abiding and public-spirited citizens of Amite county.

Hugh Lammons is one of the oldest native born citizens of the state of Mississippi. He first saw the light of day in Claiborne county, March 2, 1819, and is the youngest of a family of eight children. His parents, Daniel and Margarette (McMilon) Lammons, were natives of Scotland, and emigrated to America at an early day, and were among the first settlers of Yazoo county. Daniel Lammons died in 1866. Hugh grew to maturity in his birthplace, receiving his education in the private schools, and being trained to the occupation of a planter. He was united in marriage, in 1845, to Miss Mary A. Robnett, a native of Mississippi, and a daughter of Nathan and Elizabeth Robnett, natives of Mississippi. They have had born to them twelve children: William F., Zachariah T., Hugh A. (deceased), Margarette, Ashley, Martha (deceased), Jane (deceased), Daniel, Levi C., Samuel, Malcolm and John. Mr. Lammons was a soldier in the late Civil war, serving his country faithfully and loyally. He enlisted first in 1862 in a company commanded by Capt. Walter Johnson; he was in this company but a short time, but connected himself with Capt. E. Berry, with whom he remained until the close of the conflict in 1865. He is a member of the Methodist Episcopal church, and in his political convictions adheres to the principles of the democratic party. He has lent a helping hand to all worthy efforts for the benefit of the public, and has sustained his reputation as a patriotic citizen. He has always devoted his time and attention to agriculture, and owns nine hundred and sixty acres of land, one hundred and seventy of which are under cultivation. In consideration of the fact that he began life without capital, and that it has been entirely through his own exertions that he has accumulated this property, he is justly deserving of the praise that has been accorded him. Mrs. Lammons passed from this life in 1891 mourned and lamented by a large family and a wide circle of friends. As before stated, our subject is one of the oldest native-born citizens in the state of Mississippi. He has passed all of his life of three-score years and twelve within her borders, and has made a record that is worthy of preservation. Like many another Southerner, he had the destruction of the late war to contend with, and was a heavy loser thereby. He was the owner of many slaves, whom he lost, together with other valuable property.

Benjamin Lampton, deceased, was born in Scott county, Miss., in February, 1825, and received his education in the common schools of his native place. When he started out in life on his own responsibility, he chose the mercantile trade as his vocation, and followed it all his days. He was married in 1850 to Mrs. Mary J. Lewis, a daughter of Owen Conerly, a native of North Carolina, and a young and prepossessing widow, who then lived near China Grove. About the year 1870 Mr. Lampton was appointed sheriff of Pike county to fill an unexpired term. He declined election to the office, as he considered commercial life his forte rather than politics. In the fall of 1880 he removed to Columbia, Miss., and established himself in mercantile business, in company with his two sons. He was an active, energetic, sober-minded man, well fitted in every way for the calling in life which he selected. He devoted himself indefatigably to his business, and his reward was a high degree of success. The parents of our subject were William and Lucy A. (Youngblood) Lampton. They reared a family of eight children: James A. was killed in the Civil war; Benjamin, the subject of this notice, had a family of eight children: Walter M., of Magnolia, Miss.; Lucius L., residing on the old home in Pike county; Iddo W.; W. Eddie; Mary E., wife of J. L. W. Sandifer, of Pike county; Cora E.; Thaddeus and Lelia. Iddo W. and W. Eddie are prosperous young merchants of Columbia. They are still carrying on the business established by their father, who died July 9, 1885, and have certainly inherited some of his sterling traits of character. They are both men of unquestioned reputation, and are regarded as leading merchants of the place. They belong to the Methodist Episcopal Church South.

Benjamin Lampton's parents returned to Marion county when he was about one year old; and, with the exception of a few years which he spent in Washington parish, La., he lived all of his life in Marion and Pike counties. He was raised on a farm, and knew only a farm life until about grown. In those days, less attention was given to literary attainments than at the present time, consequently, he acquired only a limited knowledge of text books. His education was obtained by practice and experience; and few students have made greater proficiency in that school than he. During his moments of leisure, he enjoyed listening to a well informed personal discourse on theological, scientific, or political subjects; but pedantry was always one of his greatest sources of amusement. His humor at the expense of such characters amounted to a species of sarcasm. When grown, the Rev. N. B. Raiford, who was then doing a large mercantile business at China Grove, Pike county, Miss., employed him to work in the store. Mr. Raiford being a man of great discernment, soon discovered that young Ben Lampton was no mediocre, but that he possessed both tact and talent in a very high degree. When he had served in the capacity of clerk some two or three years, his employer helped him with money and letters of credit to establish for himself—perhaps a partnership—a store somewhere in Topisaw. After selling goods there a few years with success, he sold out, and soon afterward was married. Mr. Lampton then located on a farm some three miles above Tylertown; where he remained only a few years. Subsequent years developed the fact that he understood the art of tilling the soil, but his inclination led him back to the store, and he bought of Mr. Cullen Conerly, his brother-in-law, an interest in both his mill and store at Tylertown, or as it was then called, Conerly's postoffice, but continued his farm interests in connection, and in a few years, purchased the entire store and perhaps mill also. Very soon came the war, at which time he was worth

H. Cassedy

a fine slave property, and his mercantile interests had attained considerable proportions. It would be unnecessary to dilate on the casualties of one resulting from the unfortunate unpleasantness; for all suffered alike the same dire calamity—the loss of all worldly accumulations. Suffice it to say that Mr. Lampton, from a handsome fortune, could command only a few thousands. His customers in ante-bellum times now owed him considerable money. But they were not in a condition to pay debts, and he had no disposition to distress them. He now had an opportunity to show himself a man with a big heart. He therefore, in effect, issued this proclamation: "Friends, you owe me; I know you have suffered a reverse of fortune, come up and let's settle the best we can; if you can not pay me a dollar, then pay me a dime and I will settle with you." It was by this means that he got together the few thousands already mentioned, with the addition of a few bales of cotton. He entered into partnership, after the war, with a man in whom and in whose ability to conduct a business he had implicit confidence, but awoke too late to a knowledge of the fact that he had made a mistake; that his capital was all squandered and a heavy debt in the city left to him for an inheritance. He had become sheriff of Pike county, and was giving no attention to his mercantile interests. What was now to be done? A family to support, and a debt, not of his own making, to be settled. It is said that this was the only gloomy period of his life; that he did feel somewhat discouraged. He then obtained the contract to build a bridge across Bogue Chitto, and realized some profit. This was the first money. During the years 1868-9 he went to the plow handles, and, in the meantime, set about to effect an amicable adjustment of his inherited debt. At the end of which time he succeeded, and again established himself in business at his old stand at Tylertown. His phenomenal success from which time to the day of his death is known to all in this part of the state. He never forgot a kindness, and invariably rewarded a benefactor substantially. He often settled a man's account with the mercantile firms in which he had an interest, thereby making the debts due to him only, rather than distress a well-meaning but diliatory customer. This country is dotted over with the monuments to his generosity, and the people of Columbia have but to look at their beautiful church edifice, to remember him who gave so cheerfully and so liberally. It is estimated that not less than five hundred persons attended his funeral, which took place from China Grove church on the day following his death. Let *Requiescat in pace* be written on his tomb, and may the sod rest lightly upon the remains of him who acted well his part of the drama of life and left the world better for his having lived.

Mrs. C. A. Lancaster, principal and proprietor of the Warren institute, of Oxford, is a native of Albemarle county, Va., where she grew to womanhood and received her education, graduating with distinction from Albemarle institute in 1860. Since that time she has been constantly engaged in school work and is rated as one of the most thorough educators in the state, her pupils being most thoroughly equipped in knowledge when leaving her school. After having taught with marked success in Virginia, Tennessee, Texas and Kentucky, in the summer of 1880, at the earnest solicitation of prominent citizens, she removed to Oxford and took charge of what was known as the Miller female school, which was reorganized and chartered under its present name. The object of the principal was to establish a school of the high grade in which the daughters of Mississippi might receive a liberal education without having to go so far to seek it. Her aim was to give thorough instruction to those under her charge, and her many patrons testify to her success. The pupils from this school invariably take a high stand on entering the University of Mississippi, either in the freshman or sophomore class. Esteeming graduation but a secondary object, the principal will not sacrifice thoroughness to gratify the desire of either parent or pupil for a diploma.

The school has always enjoyed a liberal share of local patronage, and as the buildings were enlarged a few years ago, there is room now to accommodate twenty-five boarders. Oxford, the seat of the state university and a place widely known for its healthfulness and freedom from malarial influences, seems to offer inducements to parents living in less healthy portions of the state who are seeking schools for their daughters as well as for their sons, and when combined with these advantages they find superior facilities for written examinations during the scholastic year, and quarterly reports, showing the attendance, deportment and scholarship of each pupil, are sent to the parents. The discipline of the school is firm and decided, and all pupils are expected to submit promptly and cheerfully to the rules and regulations. Distinctions are awarded to those pupils passing satisfactory examinations in the primary and intermediate grades. To those of the senior class who pass satisfactory examinations in all the studies of any one school, are awarded diplomas as graduates of that school. Graduates of all the schools of the collegiate department, except the school of languages, will receive a diploma as literary graduate, with the degree of M. E. L. Those who graduate in all the schools of that department will receive a diploma with the degree of M. A., the highest honor of the institute. Mrs. Lancaster is one of twelve children, seven of whom are teachers, born to George H. and Elizabeth (Bramhan) Crank, both natives of the Old Dominion. Mr. Crank served in the War of 1812 and died recently at the age of ninety-six years. Mrs. Lancaster is a lady of culture and refinement and is a member of the Baptist church, with which she has been identified for many years.

S. W. Langford is the efficient and successful editor and publisher of the Deer Creek *Pilot*, and is also discharging the manifold duties of the superintendent of public instruction of Sharkey county, Miss. He was born in Rankin county, Miss., in 1864, and upon obtaining a suitable age, was entered in the public schools of Brandon, where he continued to pursue the paths of knowledge until he attained his fourteenth year, at which time he started out to make his own way in the world, and began serving an apprenticeship in the office of the Brandon *Record*, with which he remained for eighteen months. He then worked a short time on the Meridian *Homestead*, but unfortunately had his hand injured in a job press, and was compelled to stop work for a short time. His next venture in journalism was on the (Jackson) *Baptist Record*, first as a compositor and afterward as foreman; but in 1881 the plant was moved to Clinton, and here Mr. Langford successfully managed for eight months, in the meantime instructing the three sons of Rev. J. B. Gambrell in the art of printing. His next move was to New Orleans, where he worked on the *Democrat* until it was consolidated with the *Times*, and continued to work on the latter until Christmas, when he returned to Jackson and acted as assistant foreman of the *Clarion* until March, 1884, when he came to Rolling Fork. Here he established the Deer Creek *Pilot*, September 6, 1884, which he has since conducted with eminent success. This paper is bright and newsy, some valuable information can always be gleaned from its columns, and it is published in the interest of Christianity, morality and progress. Mr. Langford possessed no income upon starting out in life for himself, for besides being poor in purse, his education was also limited; but he has manfully worked his way up from the most humble position and is now considered one of the able and intelligent journalists of the state, and one who is at all times an ardent advocate of worthy movements that tend toward the upbuilding of the section in which he resides. By his own efforts he has become the owner of two hundred acres of fine land, which was, when he purchased it, heavily covered with timber but is now mostly under cultivation. He has just completed an excellent two-story frame business building at a cost of $4,000, which contains two large store rooms, and operahouse and several offices, and is known as the *Pilot* building. In October, 1882, he was married in Jackson, Miss., at the youthful age of eighteen, to Miss Mary J., daughter of James and Mary McClain, the former of whom was killed in a boiler explosion in Arkansas, the latter dying in Jackson, Miss. Mrs. Langford was born in Leake county, Miss., and has borne her husband four children, three of whom are living. Mr. Langford is a member of Pioneer lodge No. 72, K. of P., and of the American Legion of Honor, being treasurer of Rolling Fork lodge No. 1097. In October, 1890, he was appointed superintendent of public instruction of Sharkey county, to fill an unexpired term, and this responsible position he has filled with ability up to the present time. He is the sixth of seven children born to his parents—two sons and five daughters. The other son, Marion Joseph, was a soldier in the Confederate army, and was captured in the siege of Fort Jackson, and was never afterward heard from, the supposition being that he died in a Northern prison. Mr. Langford's parents, George N., Jr., and Ann E. (Fisher) Langford, were born near Macon, Ga., and Jackson, Miss., in 1817 and 1825, respectively, their marriage taking place in Brandon, in 1842, where they are still living, and are now considered among the very oldest settlers of that place. Mr. Langford held the position of probate judge for some time prior to the war, and for some time after was mayor of Brandon. In 1871 he was elected to the state legislature, and made a faithful, intelligent and incorruptible legislator. In May, 1891, he was elected second vicepresident of the Mississippi state press association, at its annual session in Yazoo City. In June, 1885, he was appointed postmaster of Rolling Fork, and served until removed by President Harrison in October, 1889. He is truly a selfmade man, and for many years has taken an active interest in political questions of the day. During the Civil war he served the Confederacy in the quartermaster's department, and for many years has been a prominent member of the A. F. & A. M. He and his wife are worthy members of the Methodist Episcopal church. His father, George N. Langford, Sr., was a Georgian, and in his native state spent his entire life as a planter. Another son of the latter, Joseph H. Langford, came to Mississippi, and during the Mexican war was killed at the battle of Buena Vista. Another son, John, also came to this state, and died in Arkansas, a planter.

Dr. W. S. Langley was born in Edenton, N. C., January, 1809; graduated in medicine in Philadelphia, Penn.; came to Mississippi in 1836, and began the practice of medicine in Jackson, that state, in 1838, where he continued in active practice until the opening of the state lunatic asylum, of which he was made the first superintendent, relinquishing a practice that paid him $15,000 a year for an annual salary of $2,500. He it was who first conceived the idea of building the institution. Commencing in 1846 to work up this noble charity, he procured the services and attendance at a legislative session of the world-renowned asylum-builder and philanthropist, Miss D. L. Dix. He paid her expenses to Jackson, entertained her while there, and dined and wined the members of the legislature in meeting her. He spent his money freely, and gave his time and best energies to the cause in which he had enlisted, and never once forsook it until he was rewarded by the erection by the state of one of the best institutions of the kind to be found. Being the originator and promoter of this institution, when it was opened he was naturally looked to to take charge of it, which he was induced to do. After serving for several years, and placing the institution in a systematic and successful working order, he resigned. In 1875 Dr. Langley was elected superintendent of the institution for the blind, in which he labored faithfully for the good and advancement of those intrusted to his care until his death. His long and useful life came to a close, without a sigh or a struggle, on the night of the 17th of September, 1888. Dr. Langley was punctiliously honorable, and he scorned and abjured men who did not come up to his standard of honor.

Dr. R. E. Lanier is a well-known physician of Lowndes county, Miss., of which he has been a resident since the winter of 1844. He was born in Brunswick county, Va., November 22, 1818, and inherits French and English blood of his parents, Robert and Elizabeth P. (Sykes) Lanier, both of whom were born in Virginia. Robert Lanier was a soldier in the War of 1812, in which he served as Captain, and died about 1820, at the age of thirty-three years, having been a planter by occupation and a lawyer by profession. He left his widow with two sons and two daughters to care for, of whom Dr. R. E. Lanier is the only survivor. In the winter of 1844 Mrs. Lanier came to Mississippi, and here resided until her death, which occurred at Columbus, March 10, 1881, at the age of eighty-eight years. Dr. R. E. Lanier was a resident of Greensville county, Va., until he was fourteen years of age, after which he removed to northern Alabama, where he received the greater part of his education. When in his twentieth year he began the study of medicine, and in March, 1841, graduated from the old Medical university of Louisville, Ky. He began practicing in Moulton, Ala., but at the end of two years removed to where he had previously lived, in the vicinity of Courtland, at which place he remained one year, after which he came to Columbus. He did not practice largely here until 1847, when he located on the prairie fourteen miles from Columbus, where he successfully practiced the healing art for four and a half years. Since 1851 he has been one of the leading medical practitioners of Columbus, and is one of the oldest physicians of the county. He has built up a good practice, is experienced and possesses undoubted ability. He is a member of the A. F. & A. M., and in 1843 was united in marriage to Miss Angeline Miller, a native of Alabama, by whom he has six sons: Dr. E. S., a druggist of Columbus, Miss., and a graduate of Tulane university in 1871; Dr. H. M., city marshal of Columbus and a graduate of Tulane university in 1870; A. C., Robert E., J. W. and John S. Dr. E. S. Lanier, after graduating in medicine, entered upon his practice in Lowndes county, and at the death of his wife, in March, 1881, he removed to Columbus and was employed in the prescription department of the drug firm of Ervin & Billups, continuing in the same store for eight years, although the style of the firm was changed three different times. In 1890 he associated himself as a partner with Mr. E. C. Chapman in the drug business, and the firm has since successfully continued as Chapman & Lanier. These gentlemen carry a full line of drugs, and their establishment is well appointed and largely patronized. Dr. E. S. Lanier was married in 1874 to Miss Sue, daughter of Judge John B. Sale, of Aberdeen, Miss., by whom he became the father of four children: Callie M., Anna M., Bessie P. and James W.; but was called upon to mourn the death of his wife March 14, 1881. He is a member of the Methodist Episcopal church, is a member of the A. F. & A. M. and the I. O. O. F.; in the last named order holding the position of left-hand supporter to noble grand. In 1862 he enlisted in company B, Forty-third Mississippi regiment, under Capt. John M. Billups, and served in the cavalry until the final surrender, being orderly sergeant for two years in company F, Sixteenth Confederate cavalry. The Lanier family is an old and well-known one throughout this section, and have largely assisted in the growth and prosperity of the city of Columbus.

Abner D. Lauderdale is a man of varied talents and unusual accomplishments. He is a native of Limestone county, Ala., born February 10, 1825, and is the oldest of a family of eleven children of John G. and Penelope (Nichols) Lauderdale, natives of South Carolina and Tennessee, respectively. The father was a planter and mechanic, and was quite a genius in the science of mechanics. He died in 1872 at the age of seventy-four years. The paternal grandparents were John and Millie (Maudlin) Lauderdale, natives of South Carolina. The family has been noted for the bravery and courage of its members who have fought in the different wars of this country; many of them have occupied high official positions, and have won great distinction. The maternal grandparents were John and Martha Nichols, natives of Tennessee. Abner D. was reared in Alabama, and attended both the public and private schools. At the age of nineteen years he bade adieu to the paternal roof, and started out in the world upon his own responsibility. He is a merchant, planter and physician, and as a mechanic the mantle of his father seems to have fallen upon his shoulders. He owns four hundred and twenty acres of land, two hundred and eighty of which are under cultivation. He carries in his store a stock of $2,000, and does a profitable business. He practices the medical profession with rare intelligence and success. In the medical line he is able to manufacture any article from a hand bellows to razor, or a bowie-knife to a gun. He takes an especial pride in this ability. Mr. Lauderdale was first married in 1848, when he was united to Sarah Linard, a native of Alabama, and a daughter of John Linard, a Tennesseean by birth. Of this union three children were born: Mary, John R. and James. The father was married a second time, in 1858, to Miss Margarette E. Tillman. a native of Tennessee, and a daughter of Ivy and Catherine Tillman, of Tennessee. Five children were the result of this marriage: Sallie B., Martha, Abner L., Lizzie and Captain Jack. Mr. Lauderdale was a soldier in the late war. He enlisted in an independent company in 1861, but after a short time he joined Blythe's battalion with which he remained until 1863, returning to his home at that time to practice medicine. He and his family are members of the Christian church. He has been a sympathetic and liberal supporter of all efforts to advance the community, and is deeply interested in the welfare of his country The family is of Scotch origin, and has an unquestionable reputation for veracity and honorable dealing.

Dr. S. H. Lawrence, of Benela, Calhoun county, Miss., received a good practical education in the common schools of North Carolina, his native state, and when grown, or in 1873, he came to Mississippi, settled in Benela, where he began the study of medicine under Dr. S. T. Buchanan. He subsequently attended lectures at Louisville, Ky., and then began practicing at Benela, where he has since remained. He is a popular physician of Calhoun county, has a paying practice and is a credit to the profession. He owes his nativity to Chatham county, where his birth occurred in 1844, and is the fourth of eight children born to Thompson and Marion (Buchanan) Lawrence, both natives of North Carolina. The father was a prominent agriculturist, and passed his entire life in his native state, his death occurring in 1887, at the age of eighty-two years. In politics he adhered to the democratic party. He was well known throughout the county and was held in high esteem by all. The mother is still living, resides on the old homestead in North Carolina, and is now seventy years of age. She is a member of the Methodist Episcopal church, in which her husband also held membership. Of the eight children born to their union six are now living and named in the order of their births, as follows: John W., Mrs. Catherine Thomas. Mrs. Anga Yarber, S. H., Mrs. Sarah Jane Clock and Mrs. Frances Knight. The two deceased were: Bennett, killed at the battle of Gettysburg, during the war, and Neill, whose death occurred at home. Dr. S. H. Lawrence was married on the 7th of February, 1877, to Miss Addie Buchanan, daughter of Dr. S. T. Buchanan, one of the old and highly respected citizens of Calhoun county. To this union were born seven children: Viola Edna, Leon Oscar, Clara Frances, Cora, Walter and Sallie Ella, who died at the age of two years. Dr. and

Mrs. Lawrence are members of the Methodist Episcopal church at Benela. He is a master Mason, and in politics is a stanch supporter of the democratic party. He devotes the prin cipal part of his time and attention to his profession, but is also engaged in agricultural pur suits. Although a young man, the Doctor is recognized not only as one of the prominent physicians of the place, but a man who takes a leading part in all matters pertaining to the welfare of the county. During the late unpleasantness between the North and South he served as a soldier in a reserved corps for North Carolina.

Samuel Lawson, merchant and planter, Leota Landing, Miss., is a Mississippian by birth and bringing up, and was born in Washington county October 1, 1849. He was the eldest in a family of four children born to William H. and Frances Ann (Clark) Lawson, and inherited Virginia blood from the father and Kentucky blood from the mother. William H. Lawson came to Mississippi about 1844 or 1845, and settled on a plantation six miles east of Greenville, on what is now known as the Mound place, which is now owned by Captain Hunt. Here Mr. Lawson began clearing the land, and erected his first house in that section. He was married in 1848, and died in 1855. His wife was of an old and prominent family. Her father, William Clark, was the son of the first governor of Missouri, and her grand-uncle was Gen. George Rogers Clark. The family are connected to Gen. Albert Sidney Johnston, through his second marriage to Miss Preston. Mrs. Lawson was married the second time, to John A. Biddle, of Delaware, nephew of Commodore Biddle, of the United States navy, and who had come to Mississippi prior to his marriage to Mrs. Lawson. Here he engaged in planting, first settling near Old Greenville, and later at Princeton, where he was engaged in merchandising until the fall of 1862. In connection he also carried on planting and continued both pursuits until his death, in Chicago, in 1875. The mother is still living, and resides in Leota. Samuel Lawson was educated in the Blue Grass state, Mississippi and St. Louis, Mo. After the war, or in 1868, he embarked in merchandising for himself in Princeton, and there continued until 1870. He was married that year to Miss Katie Hamel, who was the third of four children born to the marriage of Patrick Hamel, who was a native of Mississippi. Her father was a native of the Emerald isle, and a planter by occupation, and resided on his Walnut Ridge plantation for many years, and afterward until during the war, when he died in Delaware, in the service of the Confederate states. After marriage, Mr. Lawson followed planting for two years, after which he clerked in Leota, for Charles T. Warthington. In 1877 he began business for himself, erected his store, filled it with a stock of goods valued at $5,000, and does an annual business of $12,000. While thus engaged, he does not lose sight of his planting interests, and is considered one of the most prominent planters and successful business men of his section. To his marriage were born the follow ing interesting children: William H., Mamie, Florence, Annie and Charles J. Mr. Lawson is a member of the Knights of Pythias and the Masonic fraternity. He and his sister sold the remainder of the town of Princeton, for a long time the county seat of Washington county, and which for a time comprised what is now the territory of many adjoining counties. The old town, the busy seat of trade and the site of law-making and executions of other times, is now washed away, deserted and destroyed.

Capt. James T. Lay, brick manufacturer, Winona, Miss., was originally from Alabama, born in Greene county on the 12th of June, 1834, and is the son of Vincent Lay, also a native of that state. There the elder Lay grew to manhood and married Miss Polly Flow ers, who died when our subject was but an infant. Afterward, or in 1838, the father moved to Mississippi, settled in the northern part of the state, opened a large plantation in Yalobusha county. He was married three times, but Capt. James T. Lay was the only child born to the first union. The grandfather, Amos Lay, was a native of the Palmetto state, and grandfather Eatman Flowers was also a native of that state. Both families were prominent ones of South Carolina. Captain Lay grew to manhood in Yalobusha county and was educated by private tutors. When nineteen years of age he left home and clerked at Grenada for Col. George Lake, with whom he continued for several years, becoming a thorough and practical business man. He subsequently engaged in merchandising for himself, and this continued until the Civil war, when he enlisted in the Confederate army, Fifteenth Mississippi infantry regiment, as a private. He served in the ranks about a year, and on the reorganization of the regiment at the close of the first year he was appointed commissary, with the rank of captain, holding that position until the department was abolished. He participated in the two-days' fight around Shiloh, and on the second day received a flesh wound in the leg, which disabled him for about one month. After this he was on post duty, and served in that capacity until cessation of hostilities. Afterward Captain Lay settled at Winona and again engaged in merchandising, but clerked for about six months; he was one of the most extensive merchants in Winona and had a successful and extensive business. He commenced manufacturing bricks in 1888, first as an experiment and in a small way. Last year he enlarged the business and the capacity of his works and manufactured about three million bricks of a superior quality. This year (1891) he has added to his works and the capacity and will manufacture one-half million more. He makes a pressed brick, and this year he has the machinery and will make a repressed brick. His works are now very complete, and for the superior bricks that he makes he finds a ready sale. Captain Lay was married in Winona in January, 1862, to Miss Ella Moore, daughter of Col. O. J. Moore (see sketch), and this union resulted in the birth of one son, B. W. Lay. The latter was a student at the Kentucky military institute, and was nearly through the course when he was taken sick and died in 1883, at the age of twenty years, leaving his heart-broken parents almost inconsolable. Captain Lay is enterprising and public spirited, and is one of Montgomery county's best citizens. He is a Knight Templar in the Masonic fraternity.

Virginia has given to Coahoma county, Miss., many estimable citizens, but she has contributed none more highly respected, or for conscientious discharge of duty in every relation of life, more worthy of respect and esteem, than Capt. Nathaniel W. Lea. He was born at Danville, Va., June 30, 1835, the eldest of eight children born to Willis M. and Sarah P. (Wilson) Lea, the former a native of North Carolina and the latter of Virginia. Willis M. Lea was a physician by calling, having graduated from the University of North Carolina and the old medical college of Philadelphia, Penn. His first work in the practice of medicine was done in Caswell county, N. C., but in 1837 he came to Marshall county, Miss., where he followed his calling until 1860, when, having been injured by being thrown from a horse, he retired from practice. He acquired a very large practice, rose to eminence in his profession, and it was said of him by other successful practitioners that he had acquired the first and most successful treatment of typhoid fever of any physician in the South. Although he did not aspire to office, he was unanimously chosen a member of the secession convention, which voted that Mississippi should withdraw from the Union; and while he was a strong adherent of the Jefferson Davis school of state rights; he, with many others, did not vote for secession until the final vote. He died in 1878, his widow still surviving him at the advanced age of seventy-nine years. The paternal grandfather was William Lea, a native of the old North State. The maternal grandparents, Nathaniel and Winnifred (Tunstal) Wilson, were Virginians by birth and were of English and of Scotch descent respectively, both families being wealthy and influential. Nathaniel W. Lea was reared in Mississippi, and was educated in the old La Grange college of northern Alabama, graduating in 1856. Succeeding this, he took an academic course in the University of Virginia, in which institution he remained, pursuing his studies faithfully for three years and graduating in several schools. Upon leaving school he began the study of law in the office of Judge Clapp, but the coming clash of arms caused him to put aside his books and join his comrades in defense of the South. He was one of the original members of Kit Mott's company D, Ninth Mississippi regiment, Jefferson Davis rifles, which was among the first companies organized in the state of Mississippi. Mr. Lea was promoted to the rank of sergeant of his company, and afterward to first lieutenant of company F, Second Kentucky regiment, under Morgan, which is accorded the honor of being among the bravest in Morgan's division. He was a Southern soldier, tried and true, and being a man of indomitable will power and fine physique, he bore the hardships and privations of war well, and no braver soldier or officer ever trod the crimson turf of a battlefield. His men, like him, were brave soldiers and were conspicious for their strict adherence to duty. He was in the engagement of Iala Rosa Island and Cumberland Gap with the old Ninth Mississippi, and in every engagement of Morgan's command, from Tomkinsville to Buffington Island, and from Greenville to Wythe and Marion, except when recruiting. He commanded his company before and after the promotion of T. B. Webber, the first captain to the position of major in nearly every action. His record as a soldier is one of which any man might well feel proud, for besides being noted for intrepidity and courage, he was faithful in the performance of every duty and loyalty itself, to the cause he espoused. Three of his brothers were also Southern soldiers. His eldest brother, William, from loss of an arm, not a regular soldier, could not be kept out of the service of his country, and was marked for unflinching courage and always being at the post of duty; both under Morgan and Forrest. No one ever had to prepare his horse or his arms for action. His second brother, Willis M., was in a company known as the University Grays, which distinguished itself for bravery, and he was among the leaders of this courageous and determined band, being promoted to the lieutenantcy, which position he held three years. He became noted for his coolness and courage in hours of peril, and made a record for himself in many hard-fought battles. He was severely wounded three times and was finally killed in the last battles around Richmond. Another brother, John C., was also a Southern soldier of undoubted courage and was considered by his comrades as one of the bravest men of his company. He was killed at Jonesboro, Ga., in 1864. At the close of the war, Nathaniel W. Lea returned to his home in Mississippi, and began taking charge of his father's plantation, which had greatly deteriorated in fertility and value during the war, and is now operating a fine plantation of five hundred acres upon which he erected in 1872 a substantial and commodious residence. In 1866 Miss Emma L. Hopson became his wife. She was born in Mississippi, a daughter of William H. and Elvira T. (Badget) Hopson, the former a native of Kentucky, and the latter of Tennessee, both families being prominent and highly esteemed in the localities in which they reside. Mrs. Lea is a lady of refinement and culture and is, intellectually, a superior woman, admirably fitted to become the mother of eminent men and women. Her union with Mr. Lea has resulted in the birth of three children: Willis M., who is now making an excellent record as a student in the University of Virginia, Tenn., who has developed considerable artistic talent, is attending school in Winchester; Tennessee, and Winnie Powell, who is studying under a teacher at home. Although quite young, she has made rapid progress in music and gives promise of becoming an artist in this science. After his marriage, Mr. Lea, at the earnest solicitation of the first citizens of Coahoma county, began teaching school, and for seven or eight years his brilliant mind and powers of elucidation were devoted to the improvement and advancement of the young of both sexes. His fine literary attainments and his proficiency as a teacher soon won for him public acknowledgment, and for the past twelve years he has held the position of superintendent of public education of Coahoma county, in which capacity he has done much for the cause of education, and has greatly benefited and improved the condition of the schools of the county. He possesses a brilliant and original mind, his ideas on the general topics of the day being clear and well defined, in fact, he is a scholarly, refined and Christian gentleman. He is very social in his instincts, and takes great interest in the beautifying and adornment of his home. He has one of the finest orchards in the delta, his fruits being of extra quality and of great variety.

Walter P. Leak, merchant and farmer, of Ashland, Benton county, Miss., is a native of Little Rock, Ark., his birth having occurred there during a short residence of his parents in that state. He married Miss Fannie Dupuy McDonald, March 4, 1885, and had two children, born as follows: W. Arnold Leak, February 8, 1887, and Kinneth Leak, February 4, 1890. His father, W. John Leak, was born in Rockingham, N. C., in 1834, but came with his parents to Tippah county, Miss., at an early date. He subsequently returned to his native state, however, and graduated at Chapel Hill. He then selected planting as his occupation in life, and before the war was the owner of a great deal of land and many slaves. He also dealt largely in real estate. He was kindhearted and liberal, a loving husband and father, and a conscientious Christian. He was an invalid for many years prior to his death. His father, Francis T. Leak, was also a native of the Old North state, but came to northern Mississippi soon after its settlement by the whites, and became one of the most extensive planters and slaveowners there. He supported the cause of the South during the Civil war, and spent thousands of dollars while upholding what he considered its best interests. He was highly educated, and was a man of strong force of character. He was an ardent member of the Methodist Episcopal church, and his hands were ever ready and open for the relief of suffering humanity. He died in the year 1863.

Hon. Walter Leake was born in Virginia, came early to Mississippi territory and in 1817, was chosen one of the first members of congress from the new state, serving until 1820. Soon after that date he was appointed judge of the circuit court. In 1822 he was elected governor. Upon the expiration of his term he resumed the practice of his profession.

John Lear, a son of John and Eliza (Hamilton) Lear, was born in Yazoo county, Miss., October 14, 1853, and is the eldest of a family of four children. His father was a native of Germany, and the mother was born in County Antrim, Ireland. John Lear, Sr., was born in the province of Hanover, Germany, and immigrated to America in 1834, landing in New Orleans; he proceeded at once to Yazoo county, Miss., where he passed the remainder of his days. He was a merchant and planter, and was a large property owner at the time of his death. He was born in 1804, and died in 1886. He had the honor of an acquaintance with Napoleon. John Lear, Jr., was reared and educated in Yazoo county. At the age of seventeen years he set out to make his own fortune with brightest hopes and anticipations. He embarked in the livery business, forming a partnership with J. E. Redding; they have one of the best equipped stables in the county, and do a large and successful business. Mr. Lear is also interested in planting, owning about seven hundred acres, and having under his control two thousand acres; he has made a study of agriculture, and is one of the most prosperous planters. He was married in 1890, in Cincinnati, Ohio, to Miss Mary Stigler, a native of Mississippi and a daughter of J. M. Stigler. One child has been born to them, a daughter named Marguerite.   Our subject takes an active interest in the affairs of the town, and has been a member of the council for seven years.   He is chief of the fire department of Yazoo City, a position of responsibility and one in which he takes considerable pride.   He is a member of the Knights of Pythias, and belongs to the I. O. O. F.   Mrs. Lear is a devoted member of the Episcopal church.

Rufus F. Learned, manufacturer of lumber and president of the Natchez cotton mills, also a planter of Adams county, was born in Jackson, Miss., in 1834, and is the only one now living of seven children born to the union of Edward D. and Laura (Woodward) Learned, both natives of the Pine Tree state, the father born in the town of Livermore, and the mother in Gardiner.   The parents were married in their native state, and in about 1826 came to Mississippi, first residing at Perlington, then Monticello, afterward Gallatin, and finally at Jackson, where Mr. Learned's death occurred, in 1837.   He was a graduate of Bowdoin college, Me., was a lawyer of ability, and practiced his profession with marked success the principal part of his days.   His wife received her final summons in Natchez in 1870.   The paternal grandfather, Haynes Learned, was a native of Massachusetts, and his father, Gen. Ebenezer Learned, was also a native of that state.   The latter was awarded a large tract of land in Maine for services rendered in the Revolutionary war, in which he was a prominent officer, and he sent his son, Haynes Learned, to settle this tract.   The latter was afterward in the government employ as an engineer, erecting forts in Florida for a number of years, and finally died in that state while engaged in that work.   Gen. Ebenezer Learned was of the first generation born in America, and was of French origin, although his parents were natives of England.   Rufus F. Learned attended private school in Jackson, Miss., until thirteen years of age, and then entered Maine college at Waterville, where he remained for two years.   In 1850 he was seized with the gold fever and went to California, where he spent about eighteen months engaged in mining.   After that he went to New Zealand and other Pacific islands, and finally went on a prospecting tour to Australia, being one of about four hundred persons who owned a vessel for that purpose.   He spent nearly six years cruising in different parts of the world, and then returned to his home, where he served an apprenticeship in the lumber business with his stepfather, Andrew Brown.   Soon after he engaged in the business on his own responsibility in Franklin county, and continued until the war, when he joined the Natchez Southern, company B, Tenth Mississippi, and fought at Shiloh, Munfordsville, Perryville, Murfreesboro, Chickamauga, and also in the Georgia and Atlanta campaigns.   After the fall of Atlanta he served as purchasing commissary through Tennessee and North Carolina, and surrendered with General Johnston.   He was neither captured nor wounded during his term of service.   After the war he formed a partnership with Mr. Brown in the lumber business, and after the latter's death he purchased his interest and has since continued the business with success.   He is one of the leading stockholders and founders of Natchez cottonmills, and has been president of the same since its organization in 1878.   This enterprise started with a capital stock of $75,000, but this has been increased to $225,000.   There are three hundred and thirty-six looms, eleven thousand spindles, and the daily production is five thousand pounds of fine goods.   There are about two hundred and twenty-five employes, and the monthly pay roll is about $5,000.   This is the largest exclusive cottonmill in Mississippi.   Mr. Learned started out for himself after the war with no capital, and is now one of the wealthiest men of Adams county, all the result of his own energy, good management and excellent business ability.   He was married in 1868 to Miss Lizzie C. Brown, daughter of Andrew and Elizabeth (Key) Brown, natives of Scotland, in which country they were married about 1817.   The parents then came to the United States, resided at Pittsburgh, Penn., a short time, and then made their home at various places on the Ohio river, where the father followed the occupation of an architect and builder. In 1830 he went on a flatboat to Natchez and there made his home until his death in 1871. After the death of his first wife he married the mother of Mr. Learned. He erected many of the best buildings in that city, and afterward engaged in the lumber business, which he followed successfully until his death, when he was probably worth $60,000. He was a prominent Mason, having taken the thirty-third degree, and, although a selfmade man, he had a fine intellect and was the author of a good work on geology. At the time of his death he was engaged on another work which was left uncompleted. He was a leader in matters of general advancement, and especially of a scientific nature, this being evinced by a rare collection of specimens now in the possession of Mrs. Learned. He was noble, generous, and held in the highest regard by all. He was a great lover of flowers and plants, and what has long been known as Brown's garden is a lasting testimonial to his name. Mr. Learned has never been in public life, but he is well known, and too much can not be said as to his ability as a business man. He is a member of the Masonic lodge, Harmony No. 1, Natchez, and of Rosalee commandery No. 1. Mrs. Learned, who was born in Natchez, Miss., is a member of the Presbyterian church. To Mr. and Mrs. Learned were born three children, one son and one daughter now living.

N. L. Leavell, who resides on his fine farm of one thousand and twenty-three acres, situated one and one-half miles south of Clarksdale, Coahoma county, Miss., is the son of Napoleon K. and Eliza Jane (Hopson) Leavell, the former born in the blue grass regions of Kentucky, and the latter in the state of Tennessee. Their family consisted of five children— two sons and three daughters—N. L. Leavell being the elder son. The father removed from Kentucky to Mississippi in 1832, and bought the farm where N. L. now resides, which then consisted of twelve hundred and sixty acres. He was one of the pioneers of the county, which was then in a very unsettled condition. The land bought by Mr. Leavell was covered with wood, and he immediately began clearing and making improvements. His wife died in Clarksville, Tenn., in 1867, and the father was married at that place, in 1870, to Mrs. Christina Diffenduffer, who was of Scotch parentage. To the second union was born one child, Anna K. The father died in March, 1872, on the plantation now owned by his son, N. L., who, with one sister and his half sister, Anna K., are the only ones of the family now living. N. L. Leavell was born in Clarksville, Tenn., on August 10, 1842, and was educated at Stuart college. On December 27, 1865, he was married in Clarksville, Tenn., to Miss Milbrey E. Williams, who received her education at Mary Sharp college, and who was the daughter of Joseph P. Williams, wholesale commission merchant at Clarksville, Tenn. To Mr. and Mrs. Leavell have been born three children—two sons and one daughter: Jane M. (wife of A. B. Carruthers, of Memphis, Tenn., and the mother of four children, three sons an done daughter: Mr. Carruthers is a member of the firm of the Carington Shoe company, of Memphis, which firm does a wholesale business; Joseph P., the eldest son is attending school at Ridgeway institute, Howel, Ky., and the younger son, N. Kertly, is nine years of age. Mr. Leavell and wife are members of the Methodist church South, and are esteemed and respected by all who know them. They both came of representative families. At the breaking out of the Civil war Mr. Leavell enlisted in the Confederate army, company H, Fourteenth Tennessee infantry, and served through the war in the Army of Virginia. He was in all the important battles of that state, and served the Confederacy faithfully and well. He was wounded at the second battle of Manassas, shot through both legs, was captured at the battle of the Wilderness and taken to Point Lookout, Md., where he remained three months. He then escaped and went to Canada, remained there one month, after which he returned and entered the army again. He was wounded and captured the second time at Scottsboro, Ala.; was taken to Bridgeport of that state, and there his left leg was amputated just below the knee. He came very near having his right leg amputated also. After recovering from his wounds he again entered the service, and there remained until the close of the war, when he returned to the old homestead, where he resides at the present time. He is a member of the association known as Fab Bivouac, of Clarksville, Tenn. Since the war Mr. Leavell has been actively engaged in farming, and his operations are conducted in a manner indicative of a progressive, thorough agriculturist. His land, six hundred acres under cultivation, being well adapted to the growth of cotton, he has made that his principal industry. He was elected a member of the board of supervisors of Coahoma county in 1878, and served in that capacity for two years. Mr. Leavell is about six feet two inches in hight, rather heavy set, with light hair and blue eyes, and is a good-looking man. He is wideawake and enterprising, and is one of Coahoma county's most highly respected citizens.

There is no man in the state of Mississippi who takes higher rank in theological and educational affairs than does Prof. Z. T. Leavell, Carrollton, Miss. These two subjects lie very near his heart, and to them he is devoting the best years and strongest energies of his life. He was born in Pontotoc county, Miss., August 30, 1847, and is a son of Capt. James and Emily (Worthington) Leavell. The father was a native of South Carolina, and served as a captain of the militia of his state. He removed to Mississippi about the year 1840, and located in the northern part of the state; there he resided until his death, which occurred in 1870. His wife had been called to her eternal rest two years previous, in 1868. The subject of this notice grew to manhood in his native state; he acquired a thorough education at the University of Oxford, Miss., and was graduated from this institution in 1871. Desiring to enter the ministry he entered upon a three years' theological course at Greenville, S. C., in the Southern Baptist theological institute. This college has since been removed to Louisville, Ky. Professor Leavell here pursued his studies with that ardor which is only born of a sincere desire to succeed, and to succeed in the highest sense of the word. When a lad of thirteen years he had united with the church, and all his hopes and aspirations from boyhood had lain in this path. Soon after his graduation in 1871 he was licensed to preach, and he took his first pastorate at Dalton, Ga. He was afterward stationed at Murfreesboro, Tenn., and then at Oxford, Miss.; there he presided over the Baptist church for six years. He then resigned his position, and for two years was financial manager of the Mississippi college. In 1882 he accepted a call to Natchez, Miss., and served as pastor of the Baptist church there for five years. The cause of education, which is a twin sister to the work of the church, is a subject in which the Professor has taken a deep interest. In 1890 he resigned his pastorate in Natchez and came to Carrollton to take charge of the Carrollton Female college, which he had purchased with the hope of giving it new impetus and life. This institution at that time was at a low ebb, the attendance being quite small. The experience, energy and will that have been brought to bear have been telling in their influence. The standard has been elevated, the attendance has been increased to one hundred and twenty and the future is most promising. Professor Leavell is assisted in this work by a corps of seven superior teachers. The school has already established a reputation for thoroughness that will go far toward attracting a fine class of students. The buildings are ample, the location is healthy and the accommodations are excellent for young ladies who desire a good, substantial education. Professor Leavell was married at Rome,

Ga., July 22, 1874, to Miss Julia Bass, a daughter of Col. Nathan Bass, of Macon, Ga., a man well known throughout the state as a representative of his district in congress. Mrs. Leavell was reared in Macon, where she acquired a good education and attained many accomplishments. She is the mother of two children: Carrie and Anna May. The Professor is of that genial, social disposition calculated to win the heart of the young. He is a highly esteemed member of the Masonic order, being a Knight Templar; he also belongs to the Knights of Honor.

Fred J. V. Le Cand, secretary and treasurer of Rosalie mills company, Natchez, Miss., is the elder of two children, a son and daughter, born to Benjamin and Sarah (Cousins) Le Cand, natives of London, England. In 1837 the parents left their native country and came direct to Natchez, Miss., where they made their permanent home. The father, who was engaged in merchandising, died there in 1845, but the mother is still living there, and is eighty-five years of age. She is a worthy and consistent member of the Presbyterian church. Their daughter, Josephine, married Altheron Wheelock, who was reared in Vermont, but who moved to Natchez at an early day, and became not only one of the leading drygoods merchants, but also one of the prominent citizens. He is now deceased. Fred J. V. Le Cand was born in Natchez in 1841, educated in that city, and in 1861 he joined the Natchez Fencibles, a military command which was organized in 1824 by Gen. John A. Quitman, and which is still in existence, and which for eight years has been under the command of Mr. Le Cand. In this command he served in the Virginia army the last year of the war, as adjutant of his regiment, the Twelfth Mississippi, participating in nearly all the leading engagements of that department. He was wounded at Seven Pines and at Chancellorsville, and was twice captured, the last time at Fort Gregg, near Petersburg, April 2, 1865, from which place he was sent as a prisoner to Johnson's Island, Ohio, where he remained until July, or for about three months after the general surrender. He is now commander of the veteran association at Natchez, and also aid-de-camp to Gen. W. S. Featherston, who is commander-in-chief of the state veteran association. Mr. Le Cand is past dictator of the Bluff City lodge of Knights of Honor No. 1145, and has been representative to the grand lodge. He has been twice married, first in 1865 to Miss Mary E., daughter of James and Lucinda (Hutchinson) Brown, the father a native of Liverpool, England, the mother born near St. Louis, Mo. They settled in Natchez about the year 1838 or 1839, the father following the occupation of builder until the close of the war. His death occurred in 1875. His widow is still living, and resides in New Orleans. Mrs. Le Cand was born in Natchez, and died in 1876, leaving a son. She was an Episcopalian. Mr. Le Cand's second marriage occurred in 1887, to Miss Rosalie Mason, daughter of Thomas and Caroline (Bennett) Mason, natives respectively of Philadelphia and Natchez, Miss. The parents were married in the last named city, and there they spent the balance of their lives, he engaged in merchandising. Mrs. Le Cand was born in Natchez. Two children were born to the union of Mr. and Mrs. Le Cand. After the war Mr. Le Cand engaged in merchandising, and this continued until 1887, when he became secretary and treasurer of the Rosalie mills company, which was first established in 1881. The present capital stock is $138,000. There are one hundred and sixty looms, sixty-three hundred spindles, and the daily productions are twenty-five hundred pounds of cotton goods. They have one hundred and thirty-five employes, and have a monthly pay roll of $2,000. Mr. Le Cand is a public-spirited, energetic man, and is a leader in all matters of public interest. He and wife are members of the Presbyterian church, and he has been an elder in the same for eighteen years.

R. R. Ledbetter is a druggist of Jackson, Miss., who has a well-appointed and stocked establishment in the business portion of the city, and is doing a prosperous and continually increasing trade. He was born in Jackson in 1841, being the only child born to J. H. and Susan (Ellis) Ledbetter, who were natives of Virginia and Kentucky, respectively. The father came to Jackson some time in the thirties, soon after associated himself in business with a Mr. Ellis, and for some time they formed the leading mercantile house of Jackson, the style of the firm being Ellis & Ledbetter. He died of the dreaded yellow fever during the scourge of 1878, the mother's death occurring on November 6, 1885. Both were worthy members of the Methodist Episcopal church, and he was Sunday-school superintendent for many years. The Ledbetters are of English descent and during colonial times came to the new world. The mother on one side, descended from the Morehead family of Kentucky, and two of her brothers were early settlers of Jackson. R. R. Ledbetter was educated in the city of his birth, and in 1860 became a business partner of his father. The next year, at the age of nineteen years, he entered the Confederate army, leaving Jackson in the Burt rifles, for Virginia, in which state he was a participant in the principal battles: First Manassas, Leesburg, the seven days' fight in front of Richmond, the principal battle of which was Malvern Hill, Gettysburg, Cedar Creek, Richmond and Petersburg. He was captured on the 6th of April, 1865, near High bridge, and was discharged the 1st of June. After a short time spent in Richmond he came back to Jackson via St. Louis, and followed clerking for a year or two. In 1867 he began the study of pharmacy, and in 1878 engaged in business for himself, buying out the business of Gus Asher, with whom he had long been connected. His business is firmly established in public favor, and he is considered one of the safest and most accurate pharmacists of the city. He keeps a full line of all articles pertaining to his line of business, and his establishment is largely patronized. His marriage, which occurred in 1883, was to Miss Antonia Hilzim, a native of the city and a daughter of Philip Hilzim, one of the first merchants of Jackson. He married Antoinette Monlin in Charleston, S. C., who was a native of that place and came to Jackson, Miss., in 1838, and entered the mercantile business, which he continued in successfully for many years; died in 1859, leaving a family of four sons and four daughters. Mr. Ledbetter and his wife are members of the Episcopal church, and socially he belongs to the A. F. & A. M. and the K. of H. fraternities. He has a pleasant home on State street, and he and his amiable wife have a large circle of friends.

Capt. James W. Lee, postmaster at Aberdeen, Miss., was born in Cherokee county, Ala., November 30, 1838, a son of Isome and Lucy (Smith) Lee, natives of South Carolina and Georgia respectively. The father was a farmer by vocation; in 1840 he moved to Texas, where, as was the rule, under the republic of Texas, in those times, he obtained his six hundred and forty acres of land as the head of a family. He lived there till his death, in 1870, at Lafayette, in Upshur county, near where his wife died, in 1855. Six children were born to them: Capt. James W., Mrs. George C. Hopkins, of Pittsburg, Tex.; Mrs. Mattie E. Stell, of Cooper, Tex.; and Mrs. M. E. Proctor, of Sulphur Springs, Tex.; William E. and John N., brothers, both died in the Confederate service. Our subject was educated in Pittsburg, Tex., while living on his father's farm, near that place. In 1861 he enlisted in company H, Third Texas regiment, which was the first company raised in his county, and the first to leave for the East. He entered the service as a lieutenant, and after twelve months of service he was made captain; he served as senior captain during 1863-4. After the promotion of Col. H. P. Mabry, and the reorganization and consolidation of the regiment, in the early part of 1865, he became lieutenant-colonel, and continued with the regiment until the surrender, in May, 1865. He had many narrow escapes in the war; in 1861 his horse was shot down by his side, at the battle of Wilson creek, near Springfield, Mo. ; a little later, in September, 1862, he was. shot down in front of a battery at Iuka, Miss., while in command of his company. The Third Texas then belonged to Hebert's brigade, Little's division. He was captured and taken to Camp Douglas, Chicago, but after two months' confinement, he was exchanged at Vicksburg, Miss., and again took command of his company, remaining with it till General Hood relieved Gen. J. E. Johnston of his command in July, 1864, when Captain Lee was again wounded, on the Chattahootchie river, in front of Atlanta, Ga., which disabled him, until Hood took up the line of march for Nashville, in December, in which campaign he took an active part. While Hood, with his army, occupied a position in front of Nashville, Captain Lee was sent with a portion of his regiment to Murfreesboro, where, in a sharp engagement, his horse was shot under him. Although so young, he was a most brave and gallant officer; no danger could deter him from going where he thought his duty called him, or where he was ordered. At the time of the surrender he was commanding the outpost from Grand Gulf, on the Mississippi, to Bushe's Ferry, on the Big Black. After the surrender he located in Aberdeen, Miss., where he engaged in the mercantile business till 1872, when he took to farming, and at the same time filled several official positions; he was mayor of Aberdeen from 1871 to 1873; was sheriff of Monroe county, part of 1873, 1874 and 1875; was postmaster of Aberdeen from 1880 to 1886, when he resigned and engaged in farming. In 1890 he was again appointed pastmaster, which position he now occupies. He was married in 1863 to Miss Morgia Reynolds Word, of Monroe county, Miss., by whom he has one son, Sidney Word, who is a wholesale grocer in Birmingham, Ala. Mrs. Captain Lee was recommended and appointed one of the lady managers of the World's Columbian exposition at Chicago. Captain Lee is a member of the Knights of Honor, and is one of the most upright, honorable men of his county or state, and one whom his fellow-citizens delight to honor. He and his wife and son are members of the Presbyterian church, of which he is an elder.

Hon. Robert Charles Lee is the owner of large planting interests in Mississippi and Arkansas, about seventeen thousand acres, and in 1888 he erected a handsome residence with all the modern conveniences at Madison station, in Madison county, Miss., at a cost of $7,000. He was born at Gray's Port, in Grenada county, Miss., on the 17th of July, 1861, and was the third of five children born to Dr. L. C. and Laura (Hunter) Lee, natives respectively of Tennessee and Maryland. His father came to Mississippi when about twenty-one years of age, and located in Yalobusha, afterward Grenada county, and there practiced his profession successfully until his death at Grenada, Miss., on the 8th of October, 1883, in the fifty-ninth year of his age. He was educated at Chapel Hill college, North Carolina, and graduated in medicine from Jefferson medical college, Philadelphia. He was major of the Forty-eighth Mississippi regiment in the Confederate army, and was wounded five times during the war. He was shot through the lungs at the battle of Seven Pines, and at the battle of Fredericksburg he received a severe wound in the thigh. He never fully recovered from the wound in the lungs. He was appointed surgeon when he first enlisted, but resigned to enter active service. He was a man of modest bearing, and was highly esteemed by all with whom he came in contact. He was a brave, patriotic citizen, and his professional life was one of success and honor. His mother was a Miss Sutton before marriage, and his father was a native of North Carolina. Our subject's maternal grandparents, John L. and Sophia (Green) Hunter, were both of prominent families, and Greenleaf Point, D. C., was named in honor of the Green family, one of the most prominent of the Old Dominion. Hon. Robert Charles Lee was reared in Grenada county, and educated at Oxford and Vanderbilt university, graduating in law at the former, and in literature at the latter, in 1881 and 1882, respectively. In the last-named year he was united in marriage to Miss Ella Bass, a native of Madison county, and the daughter of Rev. Isaac R. and Martha J. (Jones) Bass, natives of the Old North state. Soon after his marriage Mr. Lee commenced practicing his profession in Canton in partnership with John Handy, with whom he remained until 1888, when he retired from active practice, and has since devoted his time and energies to his large. planting interests in Mississippi and Arkansas. To his marriage have been born three interesting children, Laura E., Robert C., Jr., and Walthall Bass, all at home. In addition to his extensive cotton plantation, he is considerably interested in the raising of strawberries and vegetables. From 1886 he was for two years a member of the legislature, and declined a second term. He was the youngest member of the constitutional convention in 1890. He now lives quietly on his plantation, happy in the companionship of his wife and children. He and Mrs. Lee are members of the Episcopal church. He is a Knight Templar in the Masonic fraternity, is a Knight of Pythias and a Knight of Honor.

William D. Lee, was born in Barber county, Ala., October 7, 1836, the eldest of five children born to B. F. and Martha (Tate) Lee, the former of whom was born in Florida, and the latter in Georgia. In 1848 B. F. Lee came with his family to Mississippi, and for thirty-seven years thereafter was a resident of Hinds county, at the end of which time, 1885, he removed to Texas where he died the following year. He was in the Indian war of 1836, in which he commanded his company; was in the battle of Roanoke, and made a brave, faithful and intrepid soldier. He was a mechanic and worked at his trade the greater part of his life. His father, Durham Lee, came from Ireland, and settled in Florida in the pioneer days of that state. William D. Lee was reared in Hinds county, Miss., and although his advantages were not of the best in his youth, he is a well-informed and intelligent man and keeps his own books with as much accuracy as any trained bookkeeper. Since a boy he has made his own way in the world through many adverse circumstances, and by his own efforts has achieved considerable success in life, the property of which he is now the owner being the result of earnest and persistent effort. He is the owner of about one thousand and fifteen acres of land, about six hundred of which are under cultivation, and his home in Raymond is a comfortable, commodious and pleasant one. He has an excellent mercantile establishment at this place, and does a business of about $40,000 and a business of $10,000 at Bolton, where he also has a store. He has been a resident of Raymond since 1884, and his efforts, both as a farmer and merchant, have been crowned with success, principally because his personal supervision has been given to the enterprises in which he has engaged. He enlisted in the Confederate army in 1861, attaching himself to company H, Eighteenth Mississippi regiment and participated in the first battle of Manassas, the engagement at Leesburg, and the seven days' fight around Richmond. He was captured at the battle of Fredericksburg and taken to Fort Delaware, but was exchanged at the end of three weeks and rejoined his command in the valley of Virginia, after which he participated in the battles of Gettysburg, the second engagement at Manassas, Chickamauga, Knoxville and the Wilderness, where he was quite severely wounded and disabled for about ninety days. He was also wounded in the battle of Gettysburg. Upon recovering he rejoined his command and was in the battle of Cedar Creek where he was again captured and taken to Point Lookout, where he was retained until about six weeks before the final surrender, when he was paroled and returned home, which place he reached about three weeks later. At the close of the war he had fifty cents with which to begin the battle of life, and like a true son of the South, he at once engaged in planting, which calling he continued to follow with success until 1884.

In 1866 he was united in marriage to Miss Amanda Williams, a native of Mississippi and a daughter of Benjamin and Molsey (Barnes) Williams, natives of North Carolina. To Mr. and Mrs. Lee four children have been born: Benjamin F., Molsey B., William D., and Mattie T. The family are members of the Baptist church and Mr. Lee is an earnest Christian gentleman, honorable and industrious, seeking to do right by everybody. He is devoted to his family, has given his children liberal education, and his daughters have developed much artistic talent.

Dr. Louis D. Leger, was born near Mississippi City, Miss., in 1859, and is a son of Benoit and Rosa (Cuendet) Leger, natives of France and Switzerland respectively. The father emigrated to America about the year 1848, and traveled throughout the United States going to California where he remained but a short time. He finally settled in Mississippi, and is the present postmaster of Handsboro, Miss. He served through the Civil war on the Confederate side, and since the close of the conflict has been engaged in contracting and building. He has four sons: Joseph, a contractor and engineer; Dr. L. J. Eugene, a clerk in the war department at Washington; and John who is principal of the public schools of Pass Christian. Dr. Leger received a good practical education at Trinity high school and began his professional studies early in life. In 1882 he was graduated from the medical department, university of Louisville, Ky. He immediately began practicing, selecting Biloxi, Miss., as his home. In 1883 he went to Jacksonville, Fla., and was in the marine hospital service until March, 1885, when he made a trip to Central America. There was war being waged on the Isthmus of Panama, and he was offered a large salary to remain and take charge of the hospital at Colon. He was especially fitted for this position, as he speaks French, English and Spanish, but he declined it on account of the insurrection, and returned to Mississippi City. He resided here until 1890, when he moved to Pass Christian. He is one of the leading physicians on the coast, and is an accomplished scholar. He is fully abreast of the times on all medical topics, and is still a diligent student. He has built up a large patronage, and numbers his friends by the host. He was married in 1891 to Miss Josie Gause, of New Orleans. He is a member of the Baptist church.

Pleasant C. Legg is one of the oldest, if not the oldest, residents of Coahoma county, having made his home here for forty-five years, and there are now only six citizens residing in the county who were here at that time. The country was then wild and unsettled, and Mr. Legg experienced all the hardships incident to pioneer times. He was born in Jackson county, Ga., on the 3d of September, 1814, and, although past the age usually allotted to man, three-score years and ten, he is remarkably strong and active, bidding fair to live many years yet. He was the third of ten children born to Nathaniel and Lucy (Hampton) Legg, natives of Virginia and descendants of old and honored families of that state. The father followed the occupation of a planter, and died in 1833, at the age of forty-three years. The paternal grandfather, James Legg, was a native of Virginia, and the maternal grandparents, John and Mary (Malone) Hampton, were natives of the Old Dominion also. Pleasant C. Legg attained his growth and secured a limited education in his native state, after which, when but twenty-one years of age, he started out to fight his way in life. His means were limited, but he persevered, and is now an extensive planter of Coahoma county, being the owner of eleven hundred and twenty acres of land, with three hundred and fifty acres under cultivation. Mr. Legg has been twice married, the first time in 1841 to Miss Elvira L. Brooks, a native of Georgia, and the daughter of Thomas and Mary (Story) Brooks, natives also of that state. Eight children were born to this union: Helen, Louisa M., Richard E., Mary, Nathaniel, Crawford, Robert E. and Elvira, all of whom are deceased but Helen and

70

Mary. Mr. Legg's second marriage occurred in 1863, to Mrs. Anna E. (Hibbler) Jones, a native of Georgia, of which state her parents, Eldred M. and Nancy Hibbler, were also natives. The second union resulted in the birth of two children, Bettie L. and Nannie C., now deceased. Mr. Legg is a member of the Presbyterian church and contributes very liberally to all churches, schools and all enterprises that have for their object the welfare of the county. He was a member of the board of supervisors for twenty-one years, from 1848 to 1869, and is a gentleman held in the highest esteem by all. He came to Noxubee county, Miss., in 1836, remained there ten years, and then, after a residence of one year in Arkansas, moved to Coahoma county, Miss., where he has resided since. He has a fine farm on the Clarksdale & Tallahatchie railroad, seven miles southeast of Clarksdale, which is very productive, producing a bale of cotton to the acre. He has a nice dwelling, and is as pleasant a gentleman as one would care to meet. Although formerly a whig in politics, he is now a democrat, but is very conservative, taking very little interest in the political issues of the day. He has very little affectation about him, and is one of the honest and reliable citizens of the county. His maternal grandfather, John Hampton, was in the Revolutionary war and played a very important part in that struggle.

Hon. John G. Leggett is a native of Pike county, having been born on the farm on which he now resides, four miles south of Holmesville, September 25, 1831, a son of Hon. B. W. Leggett, a native of Georgia, who, at the age of fourteen years, came with his father, Col. William Leggett, also a native of Georgia, to Mississippi. Colonel Leggett served the cause of the colonies in the Revolutionary war, and was wounded at the battle of Cowpens. He was reared in Georgia, but moved to Mississippi in 1819, and located in Pike county, near the state line of Louisiana. There he reared his two sons: William P. and B. W. Leggett. The former was a prominent planter during his entire life. Hon. B. W. Leggett had limited educational advantages, but had a strong intellect, and was naturally studious, so that by observation and reading he acquired a vast fund of useful information. He was married in Amite county to Elizabeth K. McGehee, a daughter of William McGehee, a representative of one of the prominent families in the state of Mississippi. The husband and wife a little later settled on Love's creek, on the place upon which our subject now resides. He became prominent in the county affairs; was a member of the police jury, and in 1843 and 1846 represented Pike county in the state legislature, and was a number of times the chairman of the democratic executive committee. He died in 1857, his wife having preceded him in 1851. Our subject and his two sisters constituted his entire family. Jane is the wife of Daniel M. Pound; Anna V. is married to D. C. Walker, while our subject forms the third of this trio. Mr. Leggett's educational advantages were somewhat limited, but he is thoroughly an educated man. He was married in 1857 in this county to Mary Simmons, a daughter of George Simmons. Mrs. Leggett was born, reared and educated in Pike county. After his marriage he entered vigorously upon the work of planting on the old homestead, so often mentioned in this sketch. After the war he again took up the life of a planter. He is a democrat in politics, and has always been quite influential in public affairs. In 1875 he was elected a member of the board of supervisors, and, after serving one term, declined a reëlection. Later he was for one term school surpervisor. In 1889 he was elected to the legislature, and during the session served on the committee on public roads and ferries, and on the committee on public lands, acquitting himself with great credit. Mr. and Mrs. Leggett have seven children: William W., a planter, who lives near her father, and is married and has four children, Dixie L., who married G. W. Sauls, by whom she has five children, and is living in Osyka; Julia A., a successful schoolteacher; Mattie L., wife of E. W. Ott, of Mount Herman, La.; Theresa R., a young lady at school at Blue Mountain seminary; Dulcie M., and John G., Jr. Mr. and Mrs. Leggett are members of the Baptist church, of which Mr. Leggett is a deacon, holding also the office of moderator of the Baptist association, with which his church is connected. He is a member of the Silver Springs lodge No. 310, A. F. & A. M., and is a Royal Arch Mason of Summit lodge, and has served as presiding officer of his lodge. Judge Leggett is one of the purest and best of men, and is held in high esteem by the people of Pike county. He is a lover of his home and family, and is very domestic in his tastes. He cherishes the associations of his youth, and loves to dwell on the scenes and incidents of his childhood and early life, every place about the old homestead being dear to him. His worldly success has been all that heart could ask, and he has no further desire for political preferments, wishing rather to spend his declining years in the ease and quiet of his loving household.

Prominent among the prosperous farmers and successful stockmen of Panola county stands the name of the two brothers, E. T. and A. H. Leigh, who are proprietors of Long Branch stock farm, two miles east of Courtland in Panola county, Miss. This farm contains five hundred and fifty acres, devoted to stock, and the brothers have been engaged in this business for twelve years. They first began by raising mules, and sold from twenty-five to thirty of a high grade per year. They then turned the farm into a standard-bred horse farm, purchasing as the head of their stud, King Hal, a pacing stallion, four years old, gray in color, and sixteen hands high, sired by Gibson's Tom Hal, the sire of Hal Pointer, time 2:09¾; Brown Hal, time, 2:12⅛; Little Brown Jug, time, 2:11¾, etc. They also own a trotting stallion, Glendale, No. 2705, that was foaled in 1882. He was sired by Glenview, No. 1107, sire of Euclid, time, 2:28½. By these two stallions they have of pacers Count Hal, No. 13, time 2:27, at four years old; Emily Hal, 2:30, at two years old; Famous, time, 2:37, at four years; Sailaway, 2:46, at four years old; Panola Hal, time, 2:46, at three years. All these records were made in races. Count Hal won eight out of nine races and Famous won four out of six races. About forty acres of their farm are in clover, and herd grass or hay, and about the same number of acres are kept for grazing. The farm is well watered by two creeks and is well improved with fences and outbuildings for the convenience and comfort of the stock. There is a good half-mile race track on which their horses are daily exercised by a skillful trainer. The family residence is a handsome dwelling and everything about the place bespeaks the owners to be men of energy and determination. The Leigh brothers are natives of Yalobusha county, Miss., sons of John and Martha (Townes) Leigh, both natives of the Old Dominion. They grew to manhood in their native county, became familiar with the duties of farm life at an early age, and came to Panola county in 1875. A. H. Leigh was a member of company K, Thirty-first Mississippi cavalry, and served the last two years of the war. He was in the Atlanta fight, where nearly one-half of his brigade was lost. E. T. Leigh was a member of the First Mississippi infantry, Featherstone's brigade, and was in all the engagements of his command. He was subsequently transferred to the Twenty-ninth regiment, and was in the battle of Franklin, Tenn., where he received two wounds, one in the right arm and the other in the left thigh. After recovering from this he joined the Third Mississippi cavalry and remained with this until the surrender. A. H. Leigh was married in 1883 to Miss Rosa Ruffin (of a prominent and early family of Mississippi) and the daughter of Maj. William and Sallie (White) Ruffin. The fruits of this union were four children: Willie, Sidney, Ernest and Katie. Mr. and Mrs. Leigh and E. T. Leigh are members of the Courtland Baptist church. Aside from their stock farm Messrs. Leigh have a cotton and corn plantation of four hundred acres, which is very productive, yielding large crops yearly. They are energetic, progressive farmers, just in the prime of life, and with the knowledge they have gained by experience and observation, and with the means already in their hands, they are certain to share largely of the honors of the progressive movement now being put forth in the new South.

Max Lemler, real estate agent of Greenville, is a native of Austria, born in 1856, and was third in a family of four children born to Lemel and Hinda (Munk) Lemler, both natives also of that country. The father was a commission merchant and followed this occupation in his mother country until his death in 1868. The mother came to the United States in 1887 and now resides with her daughter in Boston, Mass. Max Lemler was reared in Austria and remained there until fifteen years of age, attending the best schools of that section until the day before he left. On account of his father's death he came to America in 1872, landed in New York, and after a short time came to Greenville, Miss., where he located in the fall of 1873. He first engaged as clerk for the firm of Landau & Pingarm, early merchants of this place, soon became bookkeeper, and continued with them until 1877, when he started in business for himself at Stoneville, Washington county, being the second merchant at that place. Mr. Lemler's brother, Henry, who had crossed the ocean about the same time with our subject, was in business with him at Stoneville and a cousin, Henry Munk, was also a partner. The firm name was Munk, Lemler & Co. The brother and cousin both died of yellow fever in 1878 at Stoneville and their bodies were removed to Greenville the following year. Mr. Lemler remained in Stoneville until the spring of 1879 when he returned to Greenville, and in the fall engaged as clerk and buyer for Weiss & Goldstein of that city, remaining with the firm for nearly eight years. In 1886 he started a general merchandising business in Greenville, continued this for about a year and then sold out to new arrivals from Bolton, Miss. After this he embarked in the real estate business and began buying city property which he improved. He has built three store buildings valued at $16,000, eight dwellings valued at $11,000, and in addition to this has a number of valuable town lots. He also owns two hundred and sixty acres in three tracts in this county and rents the cultivated portion at $8.00 per acre. He also owns a small tract in Calhoun county, five hundred acres in Sunflower county and a small portion in Le Flore county. When Mr. Lemler came to Greenville in 1873 he had nothing and what he has since obtained is the result of industry and good business ability. He is a wideawake, thoroughgoing business man, and as such merits the esteem of all. In politics he is a democrat, and for years has been an inspector of elections. Mr. Lemler was married on the 23d of June, 1883, to Miss Bertha Landau, a native of Germany, who came with her mother to Greenville in 1869, and who was educated at the Convent of St. Agnes, Memphis, Tenn. Her father died in Greenville on the 19th of June, 1887. He was an early merchant at that place, was a prominent citizen and was active in politics, running as a candidate for county treasurer in 1876. The mother is still living. She has three brothers, all in business in Greenville. Mr. and Mrs. Lemler are the parents of one child, Julius. Mr. Lemler is an active member of secret societies, being a member of the Masonic fraternity, Greenville lodge No. 206, the Knights of Pythias, Stonewall Jackson lodge, Legion of Honor, the C. B. Huntington council, and a member of the Free Sons of Israel Keshar.

Among the early settlers of Smith county, Miss., was Col. Samuel Lemly, grandfather of William S. Lemly. He was born at Salisbury, N. C., March 1, 1791, a son of Jacob and Katherine (Creson) Lemly, and was of Scotch-German ancestry. In 1811 he married

Elizabeth Furr, and in 1841 emigrated with his family to Mississippi. Settling in Smith county he invested in land, and devoted his attention to planting, The country of that section was then in a primitive condition, and the educational and religious facilities were necessarily limited. In order to secure better advantages in this direction he, after a few years, removed to Jackson with his family of thirteen children. He continued to reside there until his death in 1848, having been for years a member in the Presbyterian church, in which he also officiated as an elder. Among his children was a son, Samuel, who was born in Salisbury, N. C., in 1819. He grew to maturity in his native state, and as his father was a prominent and well-to do citizen there, he was given the advantages of a thorough educational training. At the age of twenty years he married Miss Emeline Steele, a native of York district, S. C., and a daughter of Jonathan and Martha Steele. She was left an orphan at an early age, and was reared in the family of a maternal aunt. In 1841 the young couple were among the party who, leaving behind the tender associations of kindred and home, came to Mississippi, here to take advantage of her natural resources and build up for themselves and family a competence. The journey was made overland in wagons, and lasted a number of weeks. Until 1843 Samuel Lemly was a planter in Smith county. In the year last mentioned he removed with his family to Jackson, where he became engaged in mercantile pursuits, becoming ere his death one of that city's most prominent and successful business men. His death occurred in Jackson in 1884. He was a consistent member of the Presbytsrian church, a quiet, unassuming man, giving liberally of his means without ostentation, in support of all charitable and benevolent enterprises. His worthy wife still survives him, and though now in her sixty-eighth year is well and active. To them were born thirteen children; those still surviving are: William S. Lemly, of Jackson, Miss.; Byron, a druggist at Jackson; Samuel C. is a druggist and leading citizen of Texarkana, Ark.; Amanda C., now Mrs. George W. Terrell, resides at Loving Creek, Va.; Rosa P., of Jackson, Miss.; Charles C. resides at Hot Springs, Ark., a druggist and ex-treasurer of Garland county, and Perry resides at Jackson. William Steele Lemly, the eldest of the five living children, was born in Salisbury, N. C., September 23, 1840, and is the third generation of his family born there. He came with his parents to Mississippi, being at that time but an infant. As before stated, his parents removed to Jackson in 1843, and there he spent his boyhood days, receiving his educational training in a private school, and in the meantime assisting his father in the store. Desiring to fully equip himself for a business life, he entered Crittenden's commercial college at Philadelphia, in 1858, and after a thorough course there he became a graduate from that institution. Returning to his home he resumed his duties in the store, which he continued to follow until the opening of the Civil war. In 1862 he enlisted in company A, of the First Mississippi light artillery, under the command of Colonel Withers, but after a short time was appointed assistant on the staff of Adjt. J. L. Power. The company was at once sent to Vicksburg, and in that city Mr. Lemly remained until its fall, doing, during the memorable siege, clerical and orderly duty for his adjutant. After surrendering at that place he was exchanged and sent to Mobile, where, for a period, he acted as adjutant of the regiment, Adjutant Power having in the meantime been appointed colonel. He remained at Mobile until the close of the war.

Returning at once to Jackson he became a partner with his father in a mercantile business, the firm name being S. Lemly & Son, and so continued until his father's death. After a year or so he was joined by his brother Percy, the firm name becoming W. S. Lemly & Brother. That they have been successful is shown by the large and constantly increasing business that is being carried on. They are both honorable and successful men of business, inheriting the sterling traits and methods of integrity by which their worthy father built up the house. In 1866 Mr. Lemly was united in marriage with Miss Sue J. Smith, of Marion, Ala., and their union resulted in the birth of five children: Bessie C., William S., Jr.; Frank B., Jennie B., and Thomas Mitchell. In 1880 the death angel entered the happy home, and on July 12, the faithful wife and affectionate mother was called to a higher and better reward. Mr. Lemly is a member of the Presbyterian church of Jackson, in which he has been for a number of years an elder. He is particularly interested and active in Sabbath-school work, having been for the past number of years superintendent of this department of his church, and under his efficient guidance and watchful care the growth of his school has been such as to excite admiration, and reflect upon him great credit. Socially he is member of the K. of P. and the K. of H. fraternities, and is of a pleasant, genial disposition. Percy Lemly, the junior member of the firm of W. S. Lemly & Brother, was born in Jackson, Miss., on April 3, 1860. Like his brother he received his educational training in a private school, and after becoming of sufficient age, assisted his father in the store, becoming after his father's death a half owner in the establishment. He has lived in Jackson all his life, and his reputation as a man of business, as well as his private life, has been above reproach. In October, 1880, he married Miss Ida Stewart, an accomplished daughter of Col. James D. Stewart, whose sketch appears in this volume. This union has been blessed by three bright little daughters: Eilene Alice, Amanda and Edna Hough. Mr. Lemly and his estimable wife are both consistent and respected members of the Presbyterian church, in which he is a deacon. He is a member of the American Legion of Honor, and is treasurer of Jackson lodge No. 798 of that order. The Messrs. Lemly are Christians in every sense the word implies, and enjoy the respect and esteem of all. Two other members of the family also served in the Civil war. Byron enlisted in the Burt rifles, and later was placed in charge of the medical department of the hospital at Richmond, remaining there until the close of the war. Burton enlisted in the same company when but a lad of about fifteen years. He participated in the severe campaigns of his regiment, and from the result of overmarching contracted the fever from which he died in Richmond.

William S. Lenoir, a planter of Monroe county, was born in Mississippi in 1842, a son of William T. and Mary E. (Blanchard) Lenoir. His parents were natives of South Carolina, who moved in early life to Mississippi, where they married, removing to Monroe county in 1845, and locating on the edge of the Monroe prairie, where their son, William S., now lives, the mother being a member of his family. The father died in 1860 at the old home of his father in south Mississippi, where he had gone to attend a family reunion. He was an extensive planter, having plantations in both Mississippi and Texas. He and his wife were, for many years, devoted members of the Methodist Episcopal church South. He was a whig politically, and an active worker for any cause that he espoused. He was a man of thorough education, and of admirable business qualifications. His father was Hope Hull Lenoir, a planter of southern Mississippi, who reared a family of seven sons and three daughters. Absalom Blanchard, the grandfather of our subject, was a native of South Carolina, but came to Mississippi at an early day, afterward going back to South Carolina. He came back a second time to Mississippi, where he lived out the balance of his life, and died before the war. He was a self-educated man who started in life as a blacksmith, and later became a well-to-do planter. Mr. Lenoir's mother was twice married; first to Mr. Benson, who died while still a young man. Our subject was the second of four sons: Blanchard Gwyn died June, 1860; William S.; James L., planter of Monroe county, who served through the entire war in company B, of the Twentieth Mississippi regiment, and who was captured at Fort Donelson, kept a prisoner at Camp Douglas, Chicago, for about one year, return-ing home in time to serve in the Georgia and Atlanta campaign; Winfield H. died in infancy. Mr. Lenoir was educated in the Tutwiler high school, in Greene county, Ala., but left before his course was completed to join the army, but soon became disabled to such an extent that his services were no longer accepted, though he afterward volunteered and fought at Tupelo. After the establishment of peace he turned his attention to planting, in which he has been more than successful, owning at this time over one thousand two hundred acres of land, all productive and yielding him each year from one hundred and fifty to two hundred bales of cotton, besides a large quantity of corn and hay, and it is worthy of note that he has lived on his home plantation since he was about three years of age. Besides his property here, he is a large landed proprietor in Texas. In August, 1868, he married Julia, a daughter of Sterling L. and Maria L. (Oliver) Paine, who were both consistent members of the Methodist Episcopal church South. Her father was a half brother of Bishop Robert Paine, and was born in Giles county, Tenn., educated at La Grange, and graduating in medicine at Phil-adelphia. He practiced successfully at Aberdeen, Corinth and Muldon, dying at the latter place in 1890, his wife having died in 1879. Mrs. Lenoir was born at Aberdeen, and she and her husband have five children living : Mamie B., William S., Julia P., Ruth and Ster-ling Paine Lenoir. They are both members of the Methodist Episcopal church South, with which four of the children are also identified. Mr. Lenoir has long been known as a suc-cessful planter, and his plantation is one of the finest in the county. He has always been noted for his industry and enterprise and is widely known as a man of more than average intelligence. He has always been a stanch democrat. His wife is popular, socially, and his children are bright and well educated.

Truman W. Leonard, planter, Yeagers, Miss., the second in order of birth of four children, to Daniel and Merron (Kellogg) Leonard, owns his nativity to Herkimer county, N. Y., his birth occurring in 1816, and is now owner of a fine river plantation in Adams county. It is called Briers plantation, and is situated twenty-five miles below Natchez. Mr. Leonard is another of the many successful planters who is selfmade and who has accumulated his property by industry and economy, not by speculation. He started out for himself as a farm hand, and is now well known all over the county as a man of strict integrity, uprightness, and one whose character is above reproach. His father, Daniel L., was born in Taunton, Mass., 1791, and his mother in New York in 1795. They were married in the Empire state, and there resided until in the forties, when they removed to Ohio, where Mr. Leonard died on November 10, 1865, in Maumee city. His wife died in Homer, Ill., on January 26, 1878. Both were Presbyterians. Mr. Leonard was a carpenter in good circumstances, and was one of several sons, one of whom, Elijah, afterward removed to Canada, and his son Elijah was a member of the Canadian parliament. The other children were: Betsey R., Solomon, Samuel, Thomas, Joshua, Benona, Nathaniel, Daniel and Sallie. The father of the above named children, Samuel Leonard, was probably born in Massachusetts where he reared his family, and where he was a wealthy iron manufacturer. He made the first spade in America. His last years were spent in Herkimer county, N. Y., where his death occurred, in 1824. His father was an Englishman. The maternal grandfather of Truman W. Leonard was Martin Kellogg, born in Hartford, Conn., married there Miss Lucy Seymour, and moved from there to Herkimer county, N. Y., at an early day. There both received their final summons. Both were members of the Presbyterian church. He was a rich farmer and was a soldier in the Revolutionary war, being present at the capture of General Burgoyne. He reared a large family of children and died in 1840. Truman W. Leonard, subject of this sketch, was the second of four children—two sons and two daughters. The son died before Truman was born and one sister, Harriet E., is the widow of Hartley Holmes, and resides in Homer, Ill. The other sister, Amanda O., resides in Louisville, Ky., and is the widow of Stephenson Waters. Truman W. Leonard was educated at Winfield, N. Y., and in 1839 came to Adams county, Miss., with an uncle, George W. Kellogg, who had previously settled near Palestine. There the latter received his final summons, in 1840. He was a planter. Truman W. remained in Adams county until 1848, then resided in Louisiana until 1851 engaged in overseeing, and then in Arkansas, where he followed the same business for some time. He again returned to Louisiana, resided in Concordia parish until 1855, and then returned to Adams county, where he was overseer for two years. Subsequently he was agent for D. D. Withers one year in Wilkinson county, and then returned to Louisiana, where he was overseer for the same length of time. From there he went to Maumee City, Ohio, and engaged with a cousin in the flourmill business, continuing at this until December, 1865, when he once more returned to Adams county. He there purchased his present plantation, consisting of fourteen hundred acres with about seven hundred acres under cultivation, and he some years raises six hundred bales of cotton. He was married in 1882, to Mrs. Jennie, daughter of William and Sallie Stevenson, both natives of York state, the father born in Saratoga county, in 1808, and the mother in Onondaga county, in 1814. Mr. Stevenson died in Cortland, N. Y., in 1890. His widow is still living and is a member of the Methodist church. Mr. Stevenson was a farmer. His father, Peter Stevenson, was born in Glasgow, Scotland, and when nineteen years of age joined the English army, serving under General Burgoyne until his surrender, when he joined the colonial army. After the war he married and spent the rest of his life in Saratoga county, N. Y., engaged in farming. Mrs. Leonard's maternal grandfather, was Joshua Leonard, a son of the Samuel Leonard mentioned above. Mrs. Leonard was first married to Cory Briggs who was born and received his last summons in Chenango county, N. Y., where he had tilled soil. Mr. Leonard is a member of Harmony lodge No. 1, A. F. & A. M., and of the chapter, Natchez No. 1. Mrs. Leonard is a Methodist, and an interesting and accomplished lady.

Dr. Robert Thompson Lessley, of Wilkinson county, is a native of Abbeville district, on the waters of Long Cane creek, S. C., born in 1810, and was the youngest of a family of four children born to James and Jane (Thompson) Lessley, natives of South Carolina and Ireland, respectively. Jane, the mother came from Ireland, when she was but a child, with an older sister, who had married William Norris, and settled in South Carolina. Here the mother attended the university and was married to Mr. Lessley. She died in the year 1847, a worthy member of the Presbyterian church. The father was the son of Hugh Lessley, a native of Scotland, who came to South Carolina, where he was married and reared a family of four sons, of whom the father of Dr. Lessley was the second. Hugh, the eldest of the sons, moved to Illinois, where he reared his family, and has two sons living near Sparta, of that state. William, the third son, settled in South Carolina, where he reared his family and was a useful and respected citizen. Alexander died at middle age. James, the father of the Doctor, was a wealthy and successful planter, and died a few years after his wife. By this union were born four sons and two daughters, all of whom lived to be grown. Matthew settled near Natchez, Adams county, Miss., in about 1815, and died in 1854; he had two children, both of whom are deceased. James was reared in South Carolina, and came to Mississippi, and settted for a time in Woodville. Later he moved to the Homochitto river, in this county, where he died of malarial fever in 1842. Samuel was a graduate of the Cincinnati medical college of Cincinnati, Ohio. After his graduation he came to Wilkinson county, where he practiced his profession, until his death in about 1838. He left a wife and one son, Samuel, who was killed in battle during the late war, while serving the Confederacy. Anna E. married William Weid, in South Carolina, and came to this state and resided in Wilkinson county, where she died in 1873, leaving several children. Jane married Peter Keller, in Woodville, and they settled in Pennsylvania, on Red river, but soon after moving there she died, leaving two children. Dr. Robert T., the subject, was educated in the common schools, and at the age of eight years, after his father's death, was bound out until fifteen years of age, and attended school about one-half of the time. At the close of this term he lived with his older brother, James, and continued to go to school. In 1829 he came to Mississippi and lived with his brother, and continued to go to school for a few years, at what was known as the Kingston school. In 1831 he came to Wilkinson county and read medicine with his brother Samuel, two years, when he went to Cincinnati, Ohio, where he graduated at the Cincinnati medical college in 1834. Returning to Wilkinson county, he began the practice of his profession, and has continued until the present time. He first located near Percy's creek, but came to this location in 1850, where he had purchased a section of land upon which small improvements had been made by a Mr. Foster, who, many years before, had taken the claim from the Spanish government. The Doctor since that time has purchased several other tracts, one of which was entered by Capt. Peter Smith from the Spanish government. At one time the Doctor had about six thousand acres, with one thousand five hundred acres under cultivation. He was married to Maria L. Davis, daughter of Micajah Davis, one of this county's early settlers, a native of Virginia, who came to Mississippi and settled near Pinckneyville, and had a family of five children. His wife was Lucy Bell, who was one of the early settlers of Pinckneyville, and was reared and married in this county. Their children are as follows: William B. Davis, Elizabeth (who married James Wing), James M., Mariah (wife of Dr. Lessley) and Robert. All of these children are deceased. Mrs. Lessley was reared and educated in Wilkinson county, and by her marriage with Dr. Lessley were born two sons: James M. and Robert E. The latter died in 1863, during the late war. He had been attending school in New Orleans at the medical college, but when the war broke out, came home and joined Nuterville cavalry, going with the company to Baton Rouge, La., where he took sick and was sent home, where he soon afterward died at the age of eighteen years. He was educated at Centenary college, Jackson, La., and was a bright and diligent student and a young man of high promise, well up in his classes and had just entered the medical college when the clash of war resounded. James M., the eldest of the sons, was born in 1842, and educated at Centenary college, where he was when when the war broke out. He at once came home and enlisted in the Confederate service, in Capt. J. H. Jones' company, One hundred and thirty-eighth regiment, and served about one year when he was furnished with a substitute, owing to failing health, and was compelled to quit the service. He took the measles and when he was able to get around, forty-eight of his company had died of the same disease. He was united in marriage in 1863, to Mary L. Inman, who died in 1884. She was the daughter of Alexander Inman of this county. By this union were born seven children: Susie, Julia, Robert, Eva Belle, Charles, Mary and Eliza J. His wife dying, he married Iola Row, daughter of Benjamin Row, of this county. They live near the home place, where he is engaged in planting. He is a member of the Methodist Episcopal church. The Doctor was married the second time to Harriet Barnhart, a native of Pennsylvania, near Reading, the daughter of Adam Barnhart, a native of Pennsylvania. By this union the following children were born: Harriet L., Anna E., Eliza J.

and Catharine E. Harriet is the wife of P. D. Dooly, and resides in Adams county. Anna is the wife of P. J. Stricker, and lives in Louisiana. Eliza J. is the wife of C. M. Stricker, and lives in Fort Adams. Catharine E. is the wife of G. B. Row, and lives in this county. The Doctor and wife are members of the Methodist Episcopal church, of which he has been steward for over thirty years, and many times superintendant of the Sunday school. He is very active in church work. The Doctor in early life was a stanch whig, and when that party was dissolved he became a democrat. The county has no better citizen.

A progressive and prominent attorney of Yalobusha county was Capt. George H. Lester, Coffeeville, Miss., born in Newberry county, S. C., September 16, 1834. His parents, James D. and Catherine (Jones) Lester, were natives of South Carolina and Liverpool, Eng., respectively. The mother was of Welsh descent, and was brought to America in her childhood. In 1836 they came to Mississippi and settled near Oakland, Yalobusha county. Mr. Lester purchased a small tract of land there, and by wise management and judicious investment of his means he accumulated considerable property. He served in one of the Indian wars and participated in the battle of the Horseshoe. He took no special interest in the political movements of his time, excepting to cast his vote, which right he esteemed a duty. He was a worthy member of the Baptist church, and a man of high standing in the community. He died in October, 1864. His wife died some years after; she was a member of the same church. To them were born nine children, two of whom survive: George H., is the elder, and Wesley J., the younger of those living; those deceased are Jane, James D., Ann, William B., Samson L. and Reuben. In 1854 Captain Lester entered the University of Mississippi, and was graduated from this institution in 1856. He taught one term of school of five months near his home, and then entered the law department of the University of Mississippi, and was graduated in 1860. In 1861, when there was a call for men to go to the defense of the country, he enlisted in the Twenty-second Mississippi volunteer infantry, company K. In 1863 he was made captain of his company, and served until the close of the war. This company was organized by his brother, and did gallant and faithful service in the conflict. After the close of the war Captain Lester entered upon the practice of his profession in Coffeeville. In 1866 he was elected to the legislature of the state of Mississippi, and in 1890 he was a delegate to the constitutional convention. He takes an active interest in the political world, and is fully abreast of the times on all questions of national importance. Captain Lester was united in marriage to Miss Victoria C. Baker, a daughter of James and Lavinia (Donnell) Baker, natives of Tennessee, and early settlers of this county. Mrs. Lester was born in Yalobusha county, Miss. To her have been born four children: Mary Belle, Katie L., George, H., Jr., and William B. The mother is a member of the Presbyterian church. The Captain belongs to Knights of Honor, Stonewall lodge No. 1366.

George R. Lester, of the firm of Lester Brothers of Lula, Miss., was born in Panola county, Miss., September 18, 1851, his brother, P. V. Lester, the senior member of the firm being also born there on the 4th of November, 1841. They are the sons of Simpson and Mary M. (Bedenbaugh) Lester, natives of South Carolina, and came to Mississippi in 1840 the father's death occurring in this state in 1888. In Panola county George R. and P. V. Lester were reared and educated, finishing their education at Lexington, Ky. In 1861 P. V. Lester enlisted in the Confederate army, serving in Col. K. Balentine's regiment, and took part in the battles of Franklin, Atlanta and several engagements in Mississippi. He was wounded at the battle of Manassas and was discharged from the infantry, only to join the cavalry upon his recovery. He was captured at Selma, Ala., and at the time of the surrender was a prisoner there. He has been a merchant the greater part of his life, and during 1884–5 was sheriff of Panola county. The firm of Lester Brothers was organized in 1886, but in addition to this business they have been engaged in planting for the last three years and are now the owners of eleven hundred acres of land, three hundred and fifty acres being under cultivation. They are equal partners in all their enterprises and in their mercantile establishment carry a stock of goods worth $11,000, and do an annual buisness of $25,000. Each began to make his own way in the world upon attaining his majority and their entire present possessions have been self acquired. George R. was married in 1874 to Miss Wrennie Wilson, a native of Mississippi and a daughter of James R. Wilson, a native of Georgia. Four years after their marriage his wife died, leaving him with one child: Daisy Clyde, who resides with her father. Owing to the war the school days of P. V. Lester were cut short, but he has since acquired a practical knowledge of affairs by contact with the business affairs of life, and he and his brother are thoroughgoing, practical and experienced business men. They have spent their lives in Mississippi, are deeply attached to the state of their nativity and contribute liberally of their means in the support of worthy causes and are looked up to and esteemed by the public at large. George R. Lester is a member of the K. of H., and for five years served in the capacity of deputy sheriff of Panola county.

F. E. Lewellen, M. D., Corrona, occupies an important position in professional circles of Lee county, and is also a leading planter and merchant. He is a native of Tippah county, Miss., born in 1850, and is a son of William and Sarah (Fryar) Lewellen, natives of Tennessee, and early settlers of Tippah county. Three brothers, descendants of the Prince Llewellyn, emigrated from Wales to the United States. One of them settled in North Carolina (the grandfather of Dr. Lewellen), the other one located in Pennsylvania, and the third in Virginia. All of them reared large families. On coming to Mississippi William Lewellen engaged in farming. In 1855 he met with a violent death, being killed by a log falling upon him at a house-raising, He was a man of good education, and was a member of the Presbyterian church. In his earlier days he taught school, but his latter years were devoted to agriculture. His wife died in 1876. She was also a member of the Presbyterian church. She was of Irish ancestry. They were the parents of eleven children, nine of whom lived to maturity, and eight of whom still survive. The Doctor is next to the youngest. He was reared in Tippah county, acquiring his literary education in the common schools. In 1875 he began the study of medicine in Prentiss county, Miss. When he was ready to attend lectures he went to Louisville, Ky., and attended the course provided by the medical college at that place. He afterward located at Baldwyn, Lee county, and there began the practice of his profession. He remained there four years, and at the end of that period he came to Corrona, where he has since resided. He has been more than ordinarily successful in his professional labors, and has won a good patronage. In 1887 he determined to invest some of his means in mercantile business, and opened a stock of dry goods at Corrona. Soon after he was appointed postmaster at this place, and has discharged the duties of the office with a promptness that has won him high favor among the patrons of the office. He is doing a thriving business in general merchandising, and superintends one of the most extensive plantations in the county. He has a gin and sawmill on this place, which he operates. Dr. Lewellen was married to Miss Sally C. McGee, a Mississippian by birth, and a daughter of Jesse McGee, deceased. Mrs. Lewellen's father was a native of Anderson district, S. C., and was a prominent planter there. He came to Prentiss county, where he had some planting interests, and also carried on an extensive mercantile business. He died in 1889, and his wife passed away in 1863. Mrs. Lewellen is the youngest of a family of six children, four of whom are living. Dr. Lewellen and wife have had born to them four children: Howard McGee and Vera Ethel (Jesse and Birdie are deceased.) Politically our subject adheres to the principles of the democratic party, although he takes no part in the movements of the party, beyond the exercise of his right of suffrage. He is well posted on all the leading topics of the day, and is deeply interested in the progress and growth of his county. He occupies a beautiful home, which is presided over by his accomplished wife, where he is surrounded with all the comforts of life, and enjoys the associations of a happy, well-ordered household.

A. J. Lewis is a progressive merchant, who has, by forethought, prudence and energy built up a large patronage and acquired a handsome fortune. He was born in Hinds county, Miss., March 14, 1842, the eldest child born to James J. and Eliza (Bowen) Lewis, the former of whom came from near Hickman, Ky., the latter being a native of Mississippi. James J. Lewis was also a merchant, and came to this state about 1830, settling at Auburn, where he died in 1852. The advantages which A. J. Lewis received in his youth were not of the best, for he only attended the common schools until he was about fifteen years of age. He then went to Bloomfield, Mo., where he secured a clerkship with an uncle, who was holding the position of county clerk, and with him remained for three years. He then came south and enlisted as a private in the Confederate army, being a member of Captain Mellon's company of the Third Mississippi regiment. At the close of hostilities he returned home and settled at Edwards, where he soon engaged in general merchandising. His brother-in-law, Mr. Harrison, was with him in the capacity of clerk for about four years, then became a partner in the business. Their connection lasted harmoniously, and was attended with good success until the death of Mr. Harrison in 1878, after which Mr. Lewis was associated with his sister until her demise in 1889. Mr. Lewis then bought out the heirs and has conducted affairs on his own responsibility ever since, and it can with truth be said that there is not a more successful business man, or one that more thoroughly understands every detail of his work than does Mr. Lewis. He started on his mercantile career with a very limited capital, but has succeeded far beyond his most sanguine expectations, and is now worth about $300,000, all of which he has the satisfaction of knowing is the result of honest and persistent endeavor. As he was not the owner of $5 at the close of the war, this is an excellent illustration of what can be accomplished when one is determined to make the most of the talents and opportunities given him. In the acquirement of his handsome fortune Mr. Lewis is conscious of never having wronged a soul, and for this reason he thoroughly enjoys his wealth and the good that can be accomplished with it. He carries a stock of goods worth $20,000, and his annual sales reach up into the hundreds of thousands. He owns between five and six thousand acres of land, about one-third of which is tillable, and in addition to looking after this and his mercantile establishment, he also conducts a general banking business in the same building in which his store is located. He is very free and generous in the use of his wealth, and gives liberally to all deserving enterprises. He is of a rather retiring disposition, and in the transaction of his extensive enterprises he is quiet and unassuming. He is a member of the A. F. & A. M., the K. of H., and the K. of P. He was married in September, 1871, to Miss Freeze, a daughter of John Freeze, of Jackson, and by her is the father of five children: Olive E., Minnie G., Paulina, A. J., Jr., and Marie. The family are members of the Presbyterian church.

Clarke Lewis, of Cliftonville, Miss., was born in Madison county, Ala., November 8, 1840, and three years later was brought by his widowed mother to Noxubee county, Miss., where he has since resided. He was early initiated into the duties of farm life and attended the country school until sixteen years of age, when he entered Somerville institute and took a partial course. He subsequently taught school and early in the year 1861 entered the Confederate army and served as a private until the cessation of hostilities. In May, 1865, he resumed teaching, continuing this work one year, and then clerked in a store during the year 1866, after which he engaged in merchandising and farming on his own account. He followed these occupations for thirteen years, and since 1879 he has been exclusively engaged in farming. In 1877 he was elected to the state legislature, and served one term; in 1884 he was a candidate for the democratic nomination for congress, but was defeated by the fraction of a vote; later he was elected to the Fifty-first congress as a democrat, receiving twelve thousand eight hundred and fifty-five, against two thousand three hundred and ninety-six votes for M. K. Mister, the republican candidate. He is essentially a man of the people, and is thoroughly in sympathy with all that relates to the farmer and his interests.

B. B. Lewis, Waterhole, Marion county, Miss. Lemuel Lewis, deceased, was born in the year 1804, and was reared in Robinson county, N. C. At the age of fourteen years he came to Marion county, Miss., accompanied by his brothers, Martin, Quinnea and James. They were the sons of Benjamin and Celia (Martin) Lewis. The father was left an orphan at an early age, and during his youth met with many hardships and trials. He was a soldier in the Revolutionary war under General Greene, and did gallant service. After his marriage he lived in North Carolina, where he was residing at the time of his death. Lemuel Lewis was one of a family of six children: Martin, Quinnea, James, Lemuel, Bryant and Rarety, who married Needham Barfield, and after his death became the wife of Cessum Dunn. James Lewis left one son and one daughter; Quinnea died in 1878, leaving a posterity of one hundred and fifty souls; two of his sons and four grandsons are ministers in the Methodist Episcopal church, and belong to the Mississippi conference. Martin also left a large family. The first occupation in which Lemuel Lewis engaged was teaching school, and was one of the first educators on the west side of the Pearl river, in Marion county. He afterward engaged in farming, and became prominent in local politics. He was a member of the board of police eight years, and in 1843 he was elected probate judge, holding this office without interruption for twenty-two years. He was married in 1826 to Miss Pollie Williams, a daughter of Giles Williams, of Robinson county, N. C. In 1832 he returned to Mississippi, and here passed the remainder of his days. He was an active, earnest Christian, and a worthy member of the Methodist Episcopal church South. He and his wife reared a family of thirteen children: Celia married Joseph Smith, and after his death she was married a second time, being united to Hugh McLeod, of Covington county; Sarah, Martha, Giles W., Christian B., Susan, Margaret, Benjamin B., Alexander B., John T., Rosa, Joseph W. and Malinda. All of the children grew to mature years, and ten of them are still living. Benjamin B. and Alexander B. served in the late Civil war. Benjamin B. enlisted in September, 1861, in company F, Seventh Mississippi volunteer infantry, and served faithfully and gallantly until the close of the conflict; he received a wound at Chickamauga, but was not disabled by it. When the war was over he came home, and married Miss Margaret Sumrall, and of the union six children have been born.

Frank H. Lewis, sheriff and tax-collector of Jackson county, Miss., is a native of the county, having been born March 11, 1865. He is a son of Alfred E. and Ann R. (Farrington) Lewis, natives of Mississippi. The paternal grandfather removed from Virginia to Jackson county, Miss., at an early day, and was among the first settlers, while the maternal grandfather was a citizen of Massachusetts, from which state he removed to Mississippi in

1818, and was sheriff of Simpson county several years.   Alfred E. Lewis was a farmer and stockraiser by occupation.   For fourteen years he was sheriff of Jackson county, and was a prominent man, both in agricultural and political circles.   He died in 1885, but his widow still survives.   They have four children living: Mrs. P. H. Orrell, Mrs. Kate Staples, Frank H., the subject of this notice, and Alfred E.   Frank H. received his literary education in the common schools of Bay St. Louis, Miss., and took a course in the law department of the University of Mississippi.   He did not take up the practice of law, however, but entered the office of Emile De Smet, a large lumber dealer, as assistant cashier and general clerk.   He remained in this position for three years, and was then appointed deputy clerk of Jackson county.   He was elected to the office of sheriff in 1887, and reëlected in 1889 and 1891.   He is a young official, but has displayed an aptitude for this work which has been recognized by the people of the county, and they have shown their appreciation and served their own best interests by keeping Mr. Lewis in the sheriff's office.   He was but twenty-two years of age when this honor was first conferred upon him, and he is probably the youngest man in the state holding a like official position.   He was married in 1887 to Miss Gertrude Bragg, and two children have been born to them, Lucile and Walter W.   He is a member of the Catholic church, while Mrs. Lewis belongs to the Presbyterian church. Mr. Lewis owns a fine fruit farm, the principal crop being peaches and pears; also, a pecan grove of thirty-five acres, which is a valuable investment.   He is owner and proprietor of the Scranton waterworks, and owns a considerable amount of real estate in Scranton.   He is a man of great enterprise, and a citizen whose influence is felt in all movements that are calculated to benefit the public.

Col. John S. Lewis (deceased) one of Wilkinson county's most worthy citizens, as well as one of its earliest settlers, is worthy of extended notice in this work.   He was so well and favorably known, and his high character was so strongly appreciated, that his name should be written high on the roll of fame.   He was a native of Virginia, born February 25, 1780, and died February 29, 1848, and was of a family of nine sons and three daughters.   When but a child his parents emigrated to Kentucky and located in what is now Hardin county, where they engaged in the growing of tobacco, which special occupation they had successfully followed in Virginia.   John S. was principally educated at home by his father, who was a highly-cultured gentleman of the old school, and had followed teaching to some extent. The father took special pains in educating his children and preparing them for active and useful lives.   He was himself one of a large family, having been the eldest of nine sons and one daughter, and was a native of Virginia, but came finally to Kentucky, where he lived until his death, well advanced in years and honors.   He was very highly respected, and of a noble and generous character.   He married a Miss South, also of Virginia, who was a lady of unusual refinement and education.   She lived the allotted time, three-score years and ten, and was a noble woman, full of good deeds and purposes.   John S., at the age of fourteen years, commenced flatboating down the river to New Orleans for his father, carrying tobacco, provisions, etc., and each time having to make his way back overland, following the Indian and Natchez trails to his home in Kentucky.   Thus he must have traversed what is now Wilkinson county before 1800.   He was quite prominently connected with the early history of this county and with the Indian troubles.   He distinguished himself to such a degree as to receive the title of colonel by general consent.   Some few years after 1800 he came to Woodville, and is credited in Claiborne's history as having built the second house in the place.   Here he engaged in merchandising for a great many years, and became quite well to do.   He invested quite heavily in the West Feliciana railroad and the Planters' bank, of

Woodville. After retiring from his mercantile pursuits he devoted his time to his planta-tion near Woodville, and there he spent the remainder of his days. He was an ardent sup-porter of the whig party, and kept himself thoroughly posted on the topics of the day. He was first married to a widow Bruce (nee Thomas). To Mr. and Mrs. Lewis was born one daughter, Sarah Ann, who died at the age of twelve years. Some years after the death of Mrs. Lewis the Colonel married Eunice W. Higgins, who still survives him. She was born in Maine, November 11, 1812, and was the daughter of Theopilus and Sarah (Hodg-kins) Higgins, both of whom were natives of Maine. Mrs. Lewis was the fifth child of a family of nine, all of whom lived to be grown. When a girl of thirteen sum-mers she went to New Hampshire and lived with her uncle for three years. She then entered the Wilbraham academy, near Boston, Mass., where she graduated in 1834, stand-ing high in her classes. Soon after her graduation she came South with friends, and lived near Jackson, La., with the family of Mr. Thomas, where she was married to Mr. Lewis, in 1836. By this union were born seven children—four sons and three daughters —five of whom lived to be grown, and three of whom are yet living: John S., Anna S., William H. H., Fletcher D. and Edward H., all of whom live in this county. The other two died in infancy. Anna S. was educated at Dr. McCallay's academy in New Orleans, from which institution she graduated. She was a highly accomplished lady, and was married to John H. Lewis, by whom two children were born, one of whom died in childhood, and the other, Anna S., survives her mother, who died in New Orleans. William H. H. was born June 28, 1842, and while being educated at Centenary college, Mississippi, and in the sophomore class, he entered the Confederate army, joining the Sixteenth Mississippi regiment as orderly sergeant, and soon after was promoted to first lieutenant for daring and brilliant service, and was finally killed in 1864 at Gaines' farm. In the army he was conspicuous for his daring and his military genius, and as a stu-dent, before the war, stood at the head of his classes. He would unquestionably have grad-uated with first honors had he remained at school. He was very highly respected by the faculty and the students. John S. is the editor and publisher of the *Republican*, a newsy and able local journal.

Mr. Lewis was a member of the Methodist Episcopal church, in which he took a very active part, was class leader and steward, and was also a very liberal supporter of the church. Mrs. Lewis was a teacher in the first Sabbath-school ever organized in Woodville, in which she took very active part for many years. She is a highly cultured and respected lady, and, notwithstanding her age, is well preserved and in full possession of her faculties. She is still a teacher of the Sunday-school. Fletcher D. was born in Woodville, Miss., where he was reared, and while being educated at Centenary college, La., and in the fresh-man class, the first company for the war was organized at Woodville, known as the Wilkin-son rifles. He had his brother, William H. H., come home at once and join them, and went into the company a short time afterward at Corinth, Miss., and four weeks later was ordered to Virginia, where they arrived several days after the first battle of Manassas. They belonged to Trimble's brigade under Jackson, and after the fight around Richmond were consolidated into the Mississippi brigade under General Featherston. Their company was first in Trimble's brigade, then Posey's, then Featherston's, and then N. Harris'. Fletcher D. remained with the regiment and participated in all the battles fought by it until the siege of Petersburg, Va., when he was wounded in the leg by a minieball near the last of October, 1864, from which he suffered greatly until after the surrender. He was a brave soldier, always at his post in front and ready for fight. After the war he returned to Wilkinson county, and was married to Mary E. Harris, daughter of Rev. H. J. and Nancy Harris, natives of Mississippi. Mr. Harris is now located at Hattiesburg, Miss., and is a local minister of the Methodist Episcopal church and editor of a newspaper published at that place. To him and wife were born a family of nine children. Mrs. Lewis, the fourth child, was born and reared in this state. To Mr. and Mrs. Lewis were born five children, one of whom is deceased: William H. H. (a graduate of medicine from Tulane university), Fletcher D. (a bright little boy, loved by everybody, died, aged eleven years), J. South (deputy sheriff of Wilkinson county), Nannie E. (at home, an estimable and beautiful young lady, a graduate of the Wesleyan institute of Virginia), Littleton (now at the West Point military academy, N. Y., where he is the youngest student in the academy), Sidney M. (the youngest child at home). Mr. Lewis was elected sheriff of Wilkinson county in 1885, which office he still holds to the entire satisfaction of the people. He takes no special part in politics more than to express the right of suffrage and to keep himself posted. Mr. and Mrs. Lewis are members of the Methodist Episcopal church, and are very highly respected. Mr. Lewis is engaged in planting, ginning, etc. He has a large steamgin in Woodville, and has a fine home three miles in the country on his plantation.

The J. T. Liddle Lumber company is one of the principal enterprises of Harrison county, Miss. J. T. Liddle, the senior member, has been identified with the commercial interests of Handsboro since 1848. He was born in Onondaga county, N. Y., in 1820, and received a common school education. In connection with the agricultural pursuits which he followed he engaged in teaching district school winters until 1845. He was then employed as a clerk in a flouring mill in Lockport, N. Y., where he remained three years, familiarizing himself with many of the details of that business. In 1846 he married Miss H. A. McNeal, a native of Niagara county, N. Y. In 1848, by the advice of M. B. Hand, who had preceded him one year, he came South, thinking it would improve his wife's health. On arriving in Harrison county he secured employment in a sawmill, and in 1850 established himself in an independent mill business. In 1853, retiring from the mill business, he was elected sheriff of Harrison county. He held the office two years, and in 1857 was elected treasurer of the county, holding this position until 1864. He was at the same time in the employ of L. J. Burr, a merchant of the place, whose death occurred in 1861. At the same time Mr. Liddle and Mr. Seaman purchased the business and became Mr. Burr's successors. The firm was known as Liddle & Seaman, and existed until the beginning of the Civil war. During the war Mr. Liddle was engaged in the manufacture of salt from the gulf water, which was then a profitable industry. After the war was ended he again, with Mr. Seaman, under the firm name of Liddle & Seaman, opened a mercantile house, and erected a sawmill, which they conducted in connection with the store. This firm name and business were continued until 1875. Mr. Seaman then retiring, the business was continued by Mr. Liddle until 1889, when the J. T. Liddle Lumber company was formed. A large and profitable business is transacted by this concern. The company owns about three thousand acres of pine lands. Mr. Liddle has a family of five children. Of these, his sons, C. M. and W. R., are associated with him in business; Mrs. H. E. Flournoy is a resident of Meridian, Miss.; and two other daughters are Mrs. E. Everitt and Mrs. R. Salmen, respectively. Mr. Liddle's parents both died in Orleans county, N. Y. His father was Adam Liddle, and he married Malinda Crapsey; they reared a family of seven children, five of whom survive: J. T., the subject of this sketch; Mrs. Adaline Hartridge, of Saratoga county, N. Y.; Adam P., Moses G., and Mrs. Alzira Richtmeyer. The father was a soldier in the War of 1812. The great-grandfather, John Liddle, was a native of Scotland, and he married a Dutch woman. He was a soldier

D Bunch

in the Revolutionary war. The maternal grandfather, Jacob Crapsey, was a German and a Baptist minister ; the grandmother was a native of Wales.

Henry Lienhard has been a conspicuous character in the history of Harrison county, Miss., since 1858, at which time his residence there began. He was born in Switzerland, August 3, 1833. He received but a limited education as his parents were poor. He remained at home, aiding in the support of the family, until he was twenty-one years of age, and then sailed away to America. He landed at New Orleans, and then proceeded to Biloxi, Miss., where he had a brother living. He lived there, employed as a laborer, until 1858, and in that year came to Harrison county. At the breaking out of the Civil war he was operating a gristmill, and so was exempt from military duty. He has been more than ordinarily successful in his undertakings, and has accumulated a considerable amount of money. He now owns a large planing and sawmill and a steam brick-machine, with both a lumber and brick steam dryer. He also owns three schooners which are used in shipping his lumber across the Gulf, his market being in Cuba, Mexico and Key West. He began life with no capital, and it has been through perseverance and the closest application to duty that he has built up so thriving a business. He has met with some adversities, the greatest being the loss of two vessels on the Gulf with the entire crews; not a man being left to tell the story. He employs over a hundred men. The mills are located on the Bayou Bernard so that vessels run up to the mills, and loading is easily accomplished. He is also engaged in merchandising. In April, 1889, his mill was burned and he had no insurance on it. They have both been rebuilt and are now in full operation. Mr. Lienhard was married in 1857 to Miss Henrietta Islieb, a native of Nordhausen, Prussia. They have two children living—Mollie and Emma. They are members of the Presbyterian church, of which he is an elder. In addition to his milling interests Mr. Lienhard owns four miles of logging railroad with an engine and cars. The Gulf Coast college, Handsboro, Miss., is also indebted to Mr. Lienhard for its present existence. The institution was first owned by a few citizens who finally considered it dead stock and offered to sell it. Mr. Lienhard purchased the entire property, which has a fine location and excellent improvements.

B. T. Ligon was born in Pike county, Miss., on December 9, 1839, being the sixth of ten children born to the marriage of W. B. Ligon and Eliza Lawn, the former of whom was born in the Old Dominion. He was a captain in the War of 1812, but afterward followed the callings of a merchant and farmer, and came to Mississippi in 1818, with a commission from President Madison as a surveyor, and went to Natchez. Here he threw up his commission and began merchandising at Covington, La., which he continued until 1821, when he returned to Mississippi, and for a short time resided in the southern part of the state. In 1824 he went to the Lone Star state to settle a colony at Galveston, and he and seven or eight others issued a manifesto declaring Texas independent, but were driven out by Santa Anna. He came back to Mississippi in 1825, and began merchandising at China Grove, in Pike county, continuing until 1839, when he farmed until his death, July 4, 1863. Don Carlos Barrett, one of Texas greatest men, was the grandfather of Mr. Ligon's wife. B. T. Ligon attended the common schools up to seventeen years of age, then went to clerking for Allen & Ligon, and E. & S. Virden, at which calling he successfully continued until the opening of the war. In February, 1861, he joined company A, Tenth Mississippi infantry, and during the first year he saw service at Pensacola. At the end of this time he entered the First Mississippi light artillery, company A, under Captain Ridley, and was an active participant in many battles until the capture of Vicksburg. He was paroled at this place and afterward served in the Mississippi department, being mustered out of the service at the

71

close of the war as sergeant. After clerking in Jackson, Miss., until 1869, he farmed for one year, and in 1871 opened a mercantile establishment in Jackson, in partnership with William Allen, the style of the firm being William H. Allen & Co., afterward B. T. and C. A. Ligon, and until they closed out they did the largest business in the city. After retiring from merchandising in 1876, B. T. Ligon moved to his plantation of nine hundred acres in Hinds county, where he has since made his home. He has one hundred and twenty-five acres under cultivation, and two hundred acres in meadow land, but for some time has given up the cultivation of cotton, his attention being devoted to the raising of other products. He is energetic, and has a beautiful and comfortable home, in which he and his estimable wife dispense hospitality with liberal hands. He was married in 1869 to Miss S. Cornelia Barrett, a native of Hinds county, by whom he has five daughters and three sons: Mary, Eugenie C., Allen, Buxton, Kate, Sallie Cornelia, Minnie Lucile, and Pinckney. Mrs. Ligon is a graduate of the Central Female institute, and her daughter Eugenie graduated from the same on June 24, 1891. Mr. Ligon has always been interested in the cause of education, and is giving his children every advantage.

Nelson T. Liles was born in Madison county, Miss., in 1838 and remained there until he was sixteen years of age. He received his primary education in the public schools of Madison county until 1844, when he removed with his father to Rankin county, Miss. The old Mr. Liles died here in the following year, having followed the vocation of planting all his life. At the age of twenty our subject was married to Miss Elizabeth Eubanks and from this marriage there were born eight children, four boys and four girls, two of whom died after reaching the age of maturity. The mother died in March 1890, having lived a consistent Christian life from her childhood up. In the year 1858 Mr. Liles moved to Scott county, where he located on a farm. In 1861 at the outbreak of hostilities between the states of the Union, our subject enlisted in company C, of the Thirty-ninth Mississippi regiment, holding the rank of lieutenant. His whole heart was in the Southern cause and his record shows that he served that cause faithfully and well. He took part in the battle of Corinth, and was captured at Port Hudson in July, 1863. He was sent as a prisoner of war to Johnson's island in Ohio, where he was kept in close confinement until the end came to this dreadful struggle. He then returned home and again took up the peaceful occupation of farming, to which he continued to apply himself till 1881, when he was elected sheriff and held that office till 1887. In this year he was elected to the office of chancery clerk, which he has filled most creditably to himself and most acceptably to the people at large. Mr. Liles has been honored with various positions of trust in the last twenty years, and has filled them all in such a manner as to gain for him the entire confidence of the people of the county in which he has lived so long. Socially, he is one of the most active of any who claim allegiance to the Masonic order, and he is also a member in good standing of the Knights of Honor of Forest.

Joel Lilly, a well known planter of Copiah county, was born in Stanly county, N. C., in 1837, a son of Benjamin and Sarah (Kendall) Lilly, natives of North Carolina. Benjamin Lilly was born in Stanly county in 1777, and was a son of John and Ellen Lilly. John Lilly was one of the noble heroes who fought in the Revolutionary war. He was twice captured by the tories and each time received severe punishment at their hands for his disloyalty to the king. As the result of an accident he suffered the amputation of one of his legs. Benjamin Lilly was a gunsmith by trade and a mechanic of much ability, but the most of his life was devoted to planting. He was first married to Sarah Floyd, who bore him three children: Vernon (deceased); Franklin, of North Carolina, who lives in the same house built by his grandfather before the Revolutionary war, and Ellen, wife of John Dickson. After the decease of his first wife he married Sarah E. Kendall, and to them were born six children, five of whom are living: Albert, a resident of Hazlehurst; Edmund, residing in North Carolina; Frances, wife of E. D. Huntley living in North Carolina; Joel, our subject, and Robert, whose home is in Florida. Joel began the life of a planter at about the age of twenty-one. In 1858 he bought land in Kemper county, Miss., locating in Mississippi at that time. In 1860, he married Nanie A. Garrett, of Copiah county, and in 1861 he purchased land in Copiah county, upon which he removed and has since resided. February, 1862, he entered the Confederate service as a member of company E, of the Thirty-sixth Mississippi regiment. He was in some of the hardest fought battles of the war, among them Corinth, Iuka, Vicksburg, Atlanta, Nashville, Blakely and Franklin. After the war he returned to his agricultural duties, only to find that the war had stripped him of all he possessed except his land, and that the conditions of the time necessitated his beginning business anew and planting upon an entirely different plan from that which he had hitherto pursued, but in spite of these disadvantages he went to work with a will, and his success ever since the war has been uniformly progressive. He is to-day counted as one of the leading planters of the county. He and his wife have had nine children, only two of whom are now living: Huntley B., and Joel E., both of whom live at home. Ella F. grew to womanhood, and became the wife of K. H. Lonax, of Copiah county, and is now deceased. After the death of this daughter, Mr. and Mrs. Lilly opened their home to her only child, a son named Robert G., who has since been a member of their household. Mr. Lilly is a member of the Masonic order and of the Farmers' Alliance. In 1883 he was elected a member of the board of supervisors of this county, and has been reëlected at each succeeding election except one, and has served as president of the board for five years. When he entered upon the business of this office, there was an indebtedness of $20,000 upon the county, but, largely through his good management, it has been entirely wiped out, and the county is now in a flourishing financial condition. Mr. Lilly is without doubt the most extensive landowner in Copiah county, highly respected both as a business man and as a citizen.

John A. Limerick, druggist, Rodney, Miss., was born in Tuscumbia, Ala., December 15, 1833. His father was Thomas Limerick, of Colerain, Ireland, and afterward a commission merchant in New Orleans, La. His mother was Miss Elizabeth Williams, of Virginia. He married, in 1861, Miss Irene, second daughter of Morean Stuart, a planter of Jefferson county, Miss. His family consists of Nita, now Mrs. F. M. McRae, of Vicksburg, Miss.; George Stuart, a student at Bellevue medical college, New York; John A., married in 1890 to Miss Jeannie Conner, of Natchez, Miss.; Oliver Victor, a pharmaceutical chemist in Vicksburg, Miss.; and two young daughters, Misses Irene and Annette. Mr. Limerick is a democrat in politics, a Mason and a member of the Knights of Honor. Mr. and Mrs. Limerick, two daughters and one son are members of the Presbyterian church.

Col. C. L. Lincoln, sheriff of Lowndes county, Miss. The public services of Colonel Lincoln have been characterized by a noticeable devotion to the welfare of this county, and his ability and fidelity in his present position have made a lasting impression upon this sphere of public duty. His name has been connected with the history of this county from his birth, which occurred at Columbus, October 14, 1845, his parents, Barney B. and Rebecca S. (Norman) Lincoln, having been born in North Carolina and Alabama, respectively. They removed to Mississippi about 1835, and after residing in Noxubee county until about 1842, they removed to Columbus, where the father followed the occupations of contracting and building. In 1849, having contracted the gold fever, he went to California, but shortly afterward returned to his home in Columbus, only to again make the perilous and tedious journey to California in 1854, in which state his death occurred. His widow, who survives him, is a resident of Columbus. Their union was blessed in the birth of six children: James F., Armstead T., Barney B., Sue R., (Mrs. Turnbow), C. L., and Henrietta N. (Mrs. Williams). Col. C. L. Lincoln was brought up and educated in Columbus and while yet in his early youth, when the war came on, he enlisted in company K, Fourteenth Mississippi, Columbus riflemen, enlisting as a private and serving as such until the war closed. He was a participant in all the engagements of his regiment, and made a brave, faithful and useful soldier. Upon returning home from the war he was employed in the circuit court clerk's office, which position he filled for some time, and next acted in the capacity of deputy sheriff. At the expiration of his term he was employed in the Columbus Insurance Banking company, for about four years, after which he again accepted the position of deputy sheriff. So ably did he discharge his duties that in 1885 he was elected sheriff by his numerous admirers and friends, and has since successfully filled the position. He is a social, courteous and genial gentleman and is a man who attracts the regard and respect of all who approach him. No more capable man for the position of sheriff could be found, for he not only possesses undoubted courage, but is punctual, faithful and honorable. He is a member of the A. F. & A. M., the I. O. O. F., and is a colonel in the Mississippi national guards. In 1869 he was united in marriage to Miss Tessie Alexander, by whom he has six children: Norman L., Atwell T., Barton A., Sue M., C. L. and Lonnie W. Mrs. Lincoln is a member of the Baptist church.

Capt. Eugene A. Lindsley is a successful merchant of Coahoma county, his place of business being at Lula. He was born in Steuben county, N. Y., January 14, 1840, the youngest of ten children born to William A. and Catherine (Perkett) Lindsley, who were also born in New York and Rhode Island respectively. The father was an extensive farmer of his native state and there spent all his life as an honest and industrious citizen, dying in 1844. His widow survived him until 1876, when she too passed away, being in her eighty-fourth year. The paternal grandfather, William A. Lindsley, was born in New York and was a soldier in the Revolutionary war. He was of Scotch descent, for at an early date several brothers came from Scotland to the colonies, his ancestor settling in York state. Nearly all the male members of the family have been agriculturists by calling. Eugene A. Lindsley received his early education in the state of his birth and afterward began clerking in a mercantile store in Lawrenceville, Pa. In December, 1866, he came to Coahoma county, Miss., and here has followed the occupations of planting and merchandising ever since. He is the owner of four hundred and thirty acres of land, two hundred and twenty-five being under cultivation, and also has a half interest in the mercantile establishment of Lindsley & Arnold, their stock of general merchandise being valued at about $5,000. Mr. Lindsley is now president of the board of supervisors of Coahoma county, and is an agreeable and courteous gentleman. During the thirty years that he has resided in this section he has identified himself with its progress and development, and as he is a thoroughgoing and practical business man, he has won respect and esteem from all who knew him. He has always taken a great interest in religion and the improvement of morals in his community, and is an earnest member of and steward in the Methodist Episcopal church. He is in every sense of the word a self-made man, and his earnest and sincere endeavor to live the life of a Christian and do as he would be done by, is well worthy of emulation. He is decidedly prepossessing in personal appearance and his manners are agreeable and courteous. He was first married in 1872 to Miss Lucy W. Brown, a native of Mississippi and a daughter of William M. Brown, a native of Kentucky, whose brother, Commodore Isaac N. Brown, built the gunboat, Arkansas Ram, and operated it on the Mississippi river. To his marriage one child was born: Lucy B., who has shown a decided talent for music and painting, every advantage being given her by her father to perfect herself in these arts. She was left motherless in 1874 and in 1877 her father married Miss Blandie Dinkins, a Mississippian by birth and a daughter ol Hamilton Dinkins, a native of North Carolina and a very extensive and successful planter of Madison county, Miss. Mr. Lindsley's second union was not blessed by any offspring, his wife dying in 1880. He is a member of the Masonic fraternity, is chancellor commander in the Knights of Pythias and is also a member of the Knights of Honor. The thriving little town of Lula is located on his land and was laid out by him and was named in honor of his daughter. Before the founding of this town the postoffice was called Magnolia, after his plantation. All of his brothers and sisters reached mature years, five of whom are yet living in New York and Pennsylvania.

H. F. Lipford, planter, Ashland, Miss., was one of three children born to H. F. M. M. and Frances A. (Tait) Lipford, and his birth occurred in central Georgia in 1823. His father came to Marshall county, Miss., in the early history of that county, and was a prominent educator in the northern part of that state for many years. He died at Holly Springs, at the age of sixty-three years, and was a successful teacher up to the time of his death. Mrs. Lipford was a daughter of Hudson Tait, who was an extensive planter and a prominent man in his day. H. F. Lipford, Jr., was educated at Mercer university, Penfield, Ga., but this institution has since been located at Macon. He began teaching school when sixteen years of age, and in this way earned the money to prosecute his studies. At the conclusion of his school days he engaged in teaching, and followed this until recent years. At the solicitation of prominent friends he took a theological course, and he has devoted considerable time to ministerial work, although, of late years, he has entirely withdrawn from active work in both his former callings, and is devoting his attention to his planting interests. He was married in 1841 to Miss Rhoda Casey, and they have an interesting family of six children, five daughters and one son, L. E. Lipford, who is also a leading educator, having commenced teaching at an early age, and is now serving his tenth year as county school superintendent, the duties of which office he has discharged with great satisfaction to his constituency and much credit to himself, as is shown by his unanimous nomination for another term of four years at the recent democratic primary election; he is also superintendent of a live Sunday-school at Ashland, Miss., having served in that capacity for three years, and is an earnest, faithful Christian. Mr. Lipford located in Benton county, Miss., in 1870, and was engaged in merchandising in Ashland when the town was incorporated, and has been intimately connected with all its educational and financial interests. He remained on his plantation, however, until 1884, at which time he came to Ashland, and was immediately selected as mayor of the town, a position he has since held. He makes an able and efficient officer, has the interests of the town and county at heart, and encourages all worthy movements. He has been a member of the Missionary Baptist church for many years, and has lived the life of an earnest, conscientious Christian. He has a beautiful home in Ashland, and is surrounded by all the comforts of life.

John Newland Lipscomb, merchant and planter, Canton, Miss., was born in Madison county, Miss., on January 24, 1862, and is the son of Thomas A. and Mary (Newland) Lipscomb, and grandson of John and Emeline C. (Andrews) Lipscomb, the grandparents natives of Virginia and Mississippi respectively. The grandfather, John Lipscomb, came to

Mississippi when that state was a territory, and inhabited by hundreds of Indians. His death occurred in 1874. His mother was Dicey (Scott) Lipscomb, a native of the Old Dominion, and cousin of Gen. Winfield Scott. Thomas A. Lipscomb, father of the subject of this sketch, was a native of Mississippi, and was reared and educated in his native state, graduating from Oakland college in 1851. He has been a planter the principal part of his life, and has been fairly successful. He has been married twice, first in 1852, to Miss Telula Montgomery, a native of Mississippi, who bore him one child, William M., now deceased, and the second time in 1856, to Miss Mary Newland, a native of Misisippi also and the daughter of Rev. John H. Newland, of the Blue Grass state, who founded the first Christian church in Mississippi. The fruits of this union were six children, viz.: John Newland, William M., Maggie L., Frank A., and two not named. Mr. Lipscomb was in the Confederate army for a short time, but was not in active service. He was detailed to remain home and raise supplies for the soldiers. Mr. Lipscomb is one of Madison county's much-esteemed citizens, and is a liberal contributor to all worthy movements. He and his wife are members of the Christian church, and he is democratic in his political principles. His eldest son, John N., attained his growth and received his education in his native state, and began for himself at the age of sixteen with no capital. He first clerked in a general mercantile establishment owned by J. E. Cooke, who had his business located at Cumberland, Miss., and Stafford Mills, Ala., and remained with him eighteen months. He was subsequently on the railroad for eight years, and filled various positions on the same. In 1888, he married Miss Mary L. Lipscomb, a native of Mississippi, and the daughter of Joseph F., and Lottie (White) Lipscomb, also of Mississippi. They have one child, John N., Jr. The same year of his marriage Mr. Lipscomb retired to the farm, and is the owner of nine hundred acres of land, nearly all of which are under cultivation. His principal production is cotton. In connection with this he is engaged in merchandising, carries a stock of goods valued at $2,500, and does an aunual business of $10,000. He is a young man of excellent habits, and is very energetic and enterprising. In politics he is with the democratic party. He is a member of the Farmers' Alliance. The Lipscomb family came to Mississippi in colonial times, and is among the oldest in the state. Our subject's great-grandfather was the owner of the Lipscomb estate, in Madison county, near Flora, a small town on the Yazoo, branch of the Illinois Central railroad. The estate was at that time very valuable, and has belonged to the family, with a few exceptions, since it was first settled. It is the oldest place in the county, as far as can be learned.

James W. Little was born in Marshall county, Tenn., on May 25, 1859, and in his native state was reared to manhood, on his father's plantation, receiving his education in the public schools. In 1880, at the age of twenty years, he began to make his own way in the world, and although his capital at that time was very small indeed, he has, by shrewd business methods, push and energy, become a very wealthy young man. He is very extensive in his planting operations, and is the owner of four thousand four hundred and sixty-seven acres of land, of which one thousand eight hundred acres are under cultivation, besides which he has property in Arkansas valued at $2,500. Planting has always been his principal business, and the energetic manner in which he has ever taken advantage of all methods and ideas tending to advance the value of his property has had a great deal to do with obtaining the competence he now enjoys. He came to Mississippi in 1885 and was here married in 1886, his estimable wife being formerly Miss Lucy A. Sessions, a native of this state, by whom he has two interesting children: James W. and Margarette. His wife was the widow of Daniel H. Sessions, by whom she became the mother of two children: Cornelia B. and Julia J. In the use of his means Mr. Little has been free and generous and to schools, churches, and other enterprises tending to promote the welfare and improvement of the county he has been a very generous contributor. Although he has only seen thirty summers, the admirable way in which he manages his property, and his shrewd and practical ideas on all subjects, would lead one to suppose that he was much older. He is a most agreeable gentleman to meet, for he is intelligent in conversation, courteous and cordial in manners and kind and thoughtful of the feelings and wishes of others. He inherits Scotch and Irish blood of his ancestors, and was the second of six children born to his parents, Jason D. and Mary E. (Menton) Little, who were born in the state of Tennessee. The father was a successful planter of his native state and was there called from life in 1869.

Richmond J. Little, Trenton, Smith county, Miss. This gentleman came with his parents to Smith county in the year 1844 and has since resided here. Nothing in fact is recorded of his ever having lived anywhere else, as he was born in Noxubee county in 1842, and was consequently but two years of age when his family settled here. He was the third in a family of five children born to Capt. A. J. and Catherine (McLaurin) Little, both Scotch. His father was a native of North Carolina and his mother was born in South Carolina. The birth of A. J. Little, occurred in 1811 and he came with his parents in 1823 to Mississippi, locating in Simpson county, where he grew to maturity and engaged in planting with much success, continuing in that avocation until his death in Smith county in December, 1889. He was the son of Duncan Little, who was born in North Carolina and was also a planter. His family consisted of three sons: Neil, John and Alexander J., all of whom became heads of families. Mr. Little was warmly devoted to the interests of Smith county and in 1862 he became one of its representatives in the Confederate army, enlisting in Capt. C. P. Partan's company, which was organized in Lauderdale county and with which he served until the close of the war, participating in the battles of Farmington, Iuka, Corinth, siege of Vicksburg and other engagements of greater or less importance. At the close of the war he returned to Trenton, where he has done a successful business until the present time. He was married in June, 1870, to Miss Sallie Lofton, of South Carolina. He and family are members of the Methodist Episcopal Church South. Mr. Little is connected with the Masonic fraternity.

G. T. Lockard, the subject of this biography, is identified with the leading planters of Lauderdale county, and is one of the most highly respected citizens of that section. He was born in Sumter county, Ala., February 8, 1861, and is the eldest of a family of twelve children. His parents, Edward and Amanda (Chandler) Lockard, were natives of South Carolina and Alabama respectively. The father removed to Alabama with his parents when a mere lad. There he grew to manhood and was married. He removed from Sumter county to Lauderdale county, Miss., in 1866, and remained there two years. The first year he was engaged in farming, and the next year he embarked in the mercantile business. At the end of the two years he returned to Alabama and established himself in business in Livingston, where he sold goods for nine years. He also had some agricultural interests which he conducted in connection with his store. In 1875 he came back to Mississippi and located at Meridian, where he now resides. He owns seven hundred and sixty acres of land, seven miles north of the place, which is under the management of G. T. Lockard. The father is not actively engaged in business at the present time. He has reached his seventy-third year, and has certainly earned a rest from his labors. Although not a member of any church, he has contributed of his means in sustaining all those enterprises which have had for their object the uplifting of humanity. The twelve children of the family are all living, and reside in Meridian, with the exception of Letitia, wife of R. C. King, treasurer of the Agricultural and Mechanical college at Starkville, Miss., and the subject of this notice. G. T. Lockard is the only one of the sons who is married.   February 25, 1891, he was united to Miss Bettie Halsell, a daughter of M. V. B. and Sallie (Head) Halsell.   As before stated, Mr. Lockard lives on his father's estate, but he also owns five hundred and sixty acres of land.   He has placed eighty acres of this place under good cultivation, and has made many improvements.   His principal crop is corn and cotton, and he is considered one of the most progressive and successful planters of the county.   Although deeply interested in the welfare of the community, he has never had any aspirations to conduct the affairs of state, and has taken no further interest in politics than to exercise the right of suffrage.   He and his wife are members of the best circle of society, and there is no family in the county that has a higher standing both in the social and business world.   Mrs. Lockard is a member of the Primitive Baptist church.

Dr. Theodore Prentiss Lockwood, a practicing physician and surgeon of Crystal Springs, was born one mile north of that town in 1839, a son of Ephraim T. and Nancy M. Lockwood. His father was born in Belmont county, Ohio, in 1810, and removed to Savannah, Ga., in 1814. After attending the common schools for a time he entered the high school at Cannonsburg, Penn., where he was a student for some time.   Later he studied medicine at Wheeling, W. Va., with the celebrated Dr. Clements.   Receiving a certificate which stated his abilities, he came South and passed a good examination before the examining board at Mobile, and, obtaining a certificate of proficiency, he moved to Tallahatchie, where he practiced medicine for a short while, and soon after went to Selma, Ala., whence he removed to Hinds county, Miss., in 1836.   In that year he was married to Miss Nancy M. Cottingham, then living at the place known as Shady Grove, an election precinct with one or two stores and notorious throughout the country as a neighborhood center, being one mile north of the present site of the town of Crystal Springs, which he purchased, and there passed the intervening years to 1888, dying August 5.   He had a very successful professional career, having become one of the most noted physicians in the county and practicing almost to the day of his death.   Although he was well posted in all public matters and took a deep interest in all things pertaining to the public good, he was too much engrossed in his own business affairs, and especially his professional duties, to entertain any political aspirations.   He accumulated a good property. His wife died September 7, 1886, having been for sixty years a member of the Methodist Episcopal church, with which her husband was also identified.   Dr. Ephraim T. Lockwood was one of a large family born to Judge David Lockwood, a prominent citizen of Ohio, who held various honorable positions in that state and died in Belmont county, Ohio.   His father was a descendant of one of two brothers who came from England on the Mayflower, one settling in New York state, and the other, the progenitor of Dr. Lockwood, in Philadelphia. Thomas Cottingham, the maternal grandfather of Dr. Lockwood, was a native of Georgia and came to Mississippi soon after its admission as one of the states of the Union, and lived for a time in Harrison county, but sometime in the early thirties he removed to Copiah county and located in the woods east of Crystal Springs, removing later to a point north of the town. After the marriage of his daughter to Dr. Lockwood he sold his place to him and moved to Attala county, where he died while the present Dr. Lockwood was a mere boy.   He was an industrious, thrifty, quiet and unassuming citizen, a lover of life on the frontier, and one of the most worthy pioneers of the county.   He reared a family of fourteen children.   The subject of our sketch was the second of five children, four sons and one daughter, born to his parents.   Of these Dr. Benson M. Lockwood died in 1858, soon after graduating from the university of Louisiana at New Orleans; John M. served in the Confederate army under Gen. Stonewall Jackson in the Sixteenth Mississippi infantry, and was killed at Manassas Junction, that second Bull Run of the war; and two others died young.   Dr. Theodore Prentiss

Lockwood was reared to a plantation life and while a boy attended the public schools near his home. He acquired a good English and Latin education, and was later, until 1861, a student at the university of Louisiana at New Orleans.

In the year last mentioned he joined company F, of the Sixth Mississippi infantry, in which he served one year as lieutenant. He was wounded at Shiloh, and afterward served as assistant surgeon, doing hospital work till the close of the war, surrendering at Forsyth, Ga. He was in battles also at Farmington, Corinth, Kenesaw, Ky., and other points. Upon his return from the war he engaged in planting and made a crop in 1865. In 1866 he graduated from the New Orleans School of Medicine, at New Orleans, as the valedictorian of the class, and has since practiced at Crystal Springs, being one of the oldest physicians of the county. He was once vice president of the State Medical association; is a member of the Copiah County Medical association, and was a delegate to the American Medical association, held at Chicago in 1877. He has contributed several articles of much merit to the *Southern Medical Record*, of which he was, at one time, associate editor. In 1867 he was editor of the *Copiahan*, a prominent paper and organ of the county. He was married November 22, 1869, to Emma, daughter of William Y. and Carease Patton, at the residence of Dr. E. P. Lockwood, in Copiah county. Her father, who was a planter, was also an able and successful lawyer, who died when comparatively young at his home in Claiborne county. Mrs. Lockwood was born in Claiborne county, and has had three children: Dr. Benson M. Lockwood, a graduate from Beaumont college, a medical institution at St. Louis, and who is a practicing physician; William Byron, a law student; while their daughter, Olivia Genevieve, is a bright little girl, nine years old. For many years Dr. Lockwood has been active and influential in state politics; he has been a delegate to the state conventions several times, and was a candidate in 1872 for the legislature on the Greeley ticket, and was defeated by only thirty votes, but his devotion to his professional duties has been so great and his political aspirations have been so small, that he never sought or accepted any other nomination. He is a Master Mason and is medical examiner for the Crystal Springs lodge, Knights of Honor No. 1,420, and for the New York Life Insurance company, and the Penn Mutual Life Insurance company of Philadelphia. He is also the local surgeon for the Illinois Central Railroad company. The Lockwood family, the immediate progenitors of which were among the most honored of the pioneers of this county, has always stood high socially, commercially and politically. The Doctor is a representative of that class known as the true Southern gentlemen. He has a splendid reputation as a physician, and his practice extends far into the adjoining country.

Simon Loeb & Brother are successful merchants of Columbus, Miss., their residence in this state dating from 1867. The senior member, Simon Loeb, was first associated in business with S. Mauss and continued thus associated until 1874, at which time Mr. Mauss died. The firm then became Simon Loeb & Brother, Mr. Julius Loeb having been associated with Simon Loeb and has continued such up to the present time; A. Strauss being also connected with the firm. They occupy the well known Hudson & Humphreys building at the corner of Market and Main streets, it being a three-story brick building, well stocked with goods valued at from $40,000 to $50,000. They are doing a general business, and for the purpose of carrying a stock of groceries, occupy a store near the main building above mentioned, which also serves them as a warehouse. Simon Loeb, the senior member of this firm, is a native of Rhine, Bavaria, where he received a good collegiate and commercial education and served an apprenticeship at the wine business. Upon attaining the age of eighteen years he came to the United States, taking passage at Havre, France, landing at New York. He soon came South and located at Columbus, where he has since resided and became well known as a merchant and prosperous business man. His brother Julius, who is in partnership with him, has been a resident of America since 1870, taking passage at Bremen and also landing at New York, from which city he came to Columbus. He was educated much like his brother, but was apprenticed to the wholesale and retail hardware and crockery business. Both these gentlemen possess the sterling characteristics of the German race, being thrifty, industrious and honorable, and as their financial resources were very limited on coming to this country they set to work at once to obtain a livelihood and are now wealthy. Simon was married in 1874 to Miss Lena Herzfelder, in Memphis, Tenn., her birth having occurred in Bavaria, and their union has resulted in the birth of three children: Helen, Albert and Maud. Julius Loeb married Miss Fannie Kauffman in 1888, a resident of Columbus. They have two children: Sidney and Anita. A. Strauss was born in Bavaria and came to the United States, via Bremen, when about twelve years of age, landing in New York. He remained there long enough to receive some schooling and in 1866 arrived in Columbus, where he has resided ever since. He was married in Columbus to a sister of Loeb Brothers, and by her is the father of three children: Josie, Alma and Willie. Simon Loeb is a member of the B'nai B'rith, the A. F. & A. M., the K. of P., the A. L. of H. fraternities, and is vice president of the board of trade.

Of the many prominent citizens of Marshall county, Miss., who owe their nativity to Tennessee stands W. H. Loftin, who is one of the successful planters of the county. He was born in Haywood county in May, 1841, and his parents, Arthur W. and Julia E. (Bass) Loftin, were natives respectively of Tennessee and North Carolina. The parents were married in Columbia, Tenn., and shortly after their marriage removed to Holly Springs, Miss., where they resided about two years. From there they moved to Tennessee, resided there four or five years, and then returning to Mississippi again settled in Marshall county, where the father followed farming. They were among the pioneers of the county, there being still plenty of Indians in the country when they came to it. They were also among the first families in society, and were esteemed and respected by all. The father died in 1873 and the mother in 1884, both consistent members of the Methodist church, the father being steward in the same for a number of years. Their family consisted of nine children, only two besides our subject now living: John L., a farmer of Marshall county, Miss., and Susan J. The paternal grandfather, Col. A. W. Loftin, was a very extensive planter residing near Jackson, Tenn., and was a native of that state. The maternal grandfather was born in North Carolina and was of English descent. W. H. Loftin, the fourth in order of birth of the above mentioned children, was educated in the common schools of the county, and in 1861 enlisted in company F, Seventeenth Mississippi infantry, under Col. W. S. Featherstone, of Holly Springs, Miss. He went direct to the front and was in the battle of Gettysburg, seven days' fight around Richmond, the second battle of Fredericksbug, Leesburg, Sharpsburg, Cedar creek, Harper's Ferry, Wilderness, Petersburg and others. He was wounded in the ankle by a minieball in the battle of Chickamauga and a few days later received a furlough to go home. After his wound had healed he again joined his command near Knoxville, Tenn., and was captured in the fall of 1864 near Harper's Ferry. He was sent to Camp Chase, Ohio, and kept in prison at that place for four months. He was then sent to Point Lookout, Md., and was there when Lee surrendered. He was discharged there, returned home, and resumed his occupation of farming. He was married in 1879 to Mrs. Maggie R. Pipkin, widow of H. H. Pipkin, and daughter of Robert A. Raiford, who was one of the earliest settlers of Marshall county, and who located on the place where Mr. Loftin now lives. By her union with Mr. Pipkin, Mrs. Loftin became the mother of one daughter, Mary M., who is now the wife of Dan L. Heath. The last union resulted in the birth of five children: Julia, Elizabeth (deceased), Helen (deceased), Heath, Maggie and Catherine. Mr. Loftin owns two thousand acres of land, five hundred acres under cultivation, and also has an interest in the mercantile business at Red Bank, under the firm title of Loftin & Harris. He is a wideawake, energetic business man, a successful farmer, and an honored, esteemed citizen. He is a member of the Knights of Honor, and he and wife are members of the Methodist church. Previous to her marriage to Mr. Pipkin, Mrs. Loftin was married to Fred Thomas, and had one daughter by him, Miss Freddie, who is quite an accomplished young lady, having become somewhat distinguished as an artist. She attended school at Nashville, Tenn., and Huntsville, Ala., and took a course in an art school in New York city in 1887.

George A. Logan, a most substantial and reliable citizen, was born at Abbeville, Lafayette county, Miss., August 27, 1842, and is the youngest of a family born to Tyler and Nancy (Davis) Logan. The parents were natives of South Carolina, where they grew to maturity and were married. In 1837 they removed to Mississippi and bought land where the present town of Abbeville now stands. The father was a farmer by occupation, and was very successful in his business. He did not aspire to any public position, but was highly esteemed as a citizen. He was one of the earliest settlers of the county, coming there before the removal of the Indians. There are only four of the family living. John L., a brother of the subject of this notice, was brigadier-general in the Confederate army; he died at New Orleans in 1873 of yellow fever. The mother died in 1859, near Abbeville. The father was married a second time, to Flora McEachin, and two children were born of this union, a son and a daughter. The father died in 1886; he was a consistent member of the Baptist church, a man of the highest motives, a loyal citizen, and a trusted friend. George A. Logan began life in the service of his country; he enlisted in 1861 in Captain Robertson's company of sixty-day troops, and in 1862 he enlisted in company C, Thirty-fourth Mississippi infantry, in the army of the Tennessee. He participated in the engagements at Perryville, Murfreesboro, Chickamauga, and was captured at Missionary Ridge. He was kept a prisoner at Rock Island, Ill., for eighteen months, being paroled at the end of that time, as General Lee had surrendered. After the war he resumed the more peaceful occupation of farming, and also engaged in the mercantile trade at Abbeville. He sold goods there for six years, and then disposed of the business, since which time he has devoted himself exclusively to agriculture. He was married in 1867 to Miss Mary L. Burt, of Decatur, Ala. They have had born to them a son and a daughter: John L. and Bessie (deceased). Mr. Logan is the owner of seven hundred acres of land, two hundred and fifty of which are under cultivation; it is well improved and a finer body of land can not be found in the borders of Lafayette county. His long residence here has brought him a wide acquaintance, and his honorable and upright dealings have won him a fine reputation. He and his wife are members of the Baptist church, and he also belongs to the Masonic fraternity, of which he is a member in high standing. John Lockheart, the only living child of Mr. Logan, was born in 1868. He was educated at Mississippi college, graduating there in 1889 as the third member of his class. He chose teaching as his profession and immediately after graduating was elected as an assistant in his alma mater. He has since spent a year at the University of Michigan, has received a master's degree and is now principal of the preparatory department of Mississippi college.

The Rev. Nowell Logan is a native of Charleston, S. C., and of Scotch-Irish origin. The Logans of Restalrig, through whom he traced his paternal descent, are an ancient Scottish clan, still proud of their tartan and of the heart of Bruce quartered on their coat of arms after Sir Robert Logan had accompanied the Douglas upon his ill-fated expedition. On his maternal side Mr. Logan is descended from the McNeils, who left Scotland to settle in Ireland some centuries ago. In the year 1690 Col. George Logan, a lineal descendant of Sir Robert Logan, of Restalrig (whose bones, according to Sir Walter Scott, were falsely attainted of high treason by James I. of England for alleged complicity in the Gowrie conspiracy), came from Aberdeen, Scotland, to South Carolina and was one of the founders of what is now the city of Charleston. In 1699 James Logan, of the same family, accompanied William Penn to Pennsylvania as secretary of the province. He held also other offices, such as chief justice, president of the council and provisional governor, etc., being at one time acting governor of the colony. He was a man of literary tastes and pursuits and founded the Loganian library of Philadelphia where, or in Germantown, we believe his descendants still reside. Col. George Logan, of Charleston, married, in 1719, the widow of Robert Daniel, the last proprietary governor of South Carolina. George Logan, his son by a former marriage, married Martha Daniel, daughter of the governor, and died in July, 1764, aged seventy years. His grandson, also named George, was married in Leith, Scotland, to Honoria, daughter of Christian Muldrup, a native of Christiansand, Norway, residing there as consul for Denmark. The old Norse patronymic has been perpetuated by the late Dr. Thomas Muldrup Logan, of Sacramento, Cal., and Gen. T. Muldrup Logan, Confederate states army, now living in Richmond, Va. Dr. George Logan, son of the above, and father of the subject of our sketch, was born in Charleston, S. C., January, 1778. He was graduated at the medical school in Philadelphia, and served as surgeon in the United States navy during the War of 1812. This position he resigned to accept that of physician to the city hospital and the Charleston orphan asylum. These offices he held for forty years, in addition to a large practice among private patients. Doctor Logan's first wife, Margaret Polk, died, leaving six sons. Most of these sons had reached manhood, some had become fathers themselves, when he married the second time, Ann Catharine, daughter of Capt. George Turner, and granddaughter of Commodore Daniel McNeil, both of the United States navy. Their first child, a daughter, died in infancy; the second, John Lascelles Nowell, was so named in honor of a tried and valued friend and relative; the Nowell family, of South Carolina, being also descended from Governor Daniels. The mother, a sweet, saintly soul of blessed memory, was soon taken, leaving three young children, one almost an infant. But the father's heart held all a woman's tenderness, and to his careful mental and spiritual training during those early years, all that is worthy in their after lives must eventually be traced. Not long before the war between the states, Doctor Logan, then nearing his eightieth year, removed to New Orleans, and there he entered into rest, from the home of his devoted son, Daniel Polk Logan, to whose guardianship the orphan children were entrusted, who became to them, indeed, a second father. Nowell Logan had just attained to manhood when his native state seceded from the Union. He received from Governor Moore an appointment as captain in the Fourth regiment of State troops, so called, but, being impatient at the slow development of that branch of the service, he resigned his commission in order to leave in the First battalion of Louisiana volunteers (known afterward as Drew's battalion), for Pensacola, in April, 1861. At the end of the first year this command was disbanded and reformed as an artillery company, known as Fenner's battery, with which he continued until the end of the war. At the close of the first year he was elected captain of a Mississippi command, organized on the Gulf coast, where he was then on sick furlough, but the conscript law going into effect at that time, and he being disabled by typhoid fever, this company fell a prey to the provost-marshals. Twice afterward was Mr. Logan commissioned, but by some fatality no commission ever reached him, and he remained a high private to the end. He was distinguished for undaunted bravery in a command where all were brave, and, upon his discharge at the final surrender, the lieutenant in command has written these words: "He knew naught but duty." His army career ended, Mr. Logan now entered upon a mercantile life. He had wished to study medicine, like his father and grandfather before him, but there was no time for that now. His family, in common with most Southerners, had suffered heavy losses, and found themselves reduced from wealth to indigence, from luxury to many self-denials. The commission house in which he had become a partner having failed, he was offered, by his friend, the Hon. J. B. McGehee, of Woodville, Miss., the agency at that terminus of the West Feliciana railroad. This he accepted, little dreaming what a change in plans and prospects Providence was thus preparing for him. St. Paul's church, Woodville, had been, for some time, without a rector, and a few earnest women, who were struggling to keep the parish alive, soon urged this comparative stranger to become superintendent of their Sunday-school. He had been confirmed in early youth, had always loved the church and her ways, yet had never even taught in any Sunday-school. Still he consented to try, and that trial decided his future career, for, in a few months, he was not only the superintendent of a flourishing Sunday-school, but licensed lay-reader, holding regular services, which were well attended by men, as well as women. He had now become cashier of the West Feliciana Railroad and Banking company, with promise of ample and increasing income. Were it not better to give liberally of this income and devote all spare moments to the service of the church than to add to the number of impecunious, and, perhaps, inefficient clergymen? Thus he argued with the friends who now urged him to study for the ministry. Among these were Bishop Wilmer, of Louisiana; Bishop Green, of Mississippi, and the late Rev. Alexander Marks, of Natchez. They knew that true men were most needed, and believed him to be true. So, through the guiding of Providence and the influence of these good friends, his final choice was made. In November, 1879, Mr. Logan resigned his position in the West Feliciana company, and on February 15, 1880, was ordained to the deaconate. After studying a year in Natchez, under the Rev. Alexander Marks, during which time he held occasional services at Port Gibson, he was ordered priest in Holy Trinity, Vicksburg, May 10, 1881, by the Rt.-Rev. William M. Green, bishop of the diocease. The Rev. Alexander Marks presented the candidate and delivered a very able and touching address. The Rev. Nowell Logan was immediately called to be rector of St. James church, Port Gibson. This parish, founded in 1826, had been for years in a languishing condition, having no rector and no place of worship. Strange that one of the oldest parishes in the diocease should have been so long without a church building ! The Ladies' Aid society had, however, secured and paid for a very suitable lot, on which was a cottage, which might serve as a village rectory, and they had still $35 in their treasury. Thirty-five dollars seemed a very small beginning, but, animated by the presence of a rector with whom they were in sympathy, society, vestry and Sunday-school, all went cheerfully to work. Mr. Logan, being elected deputy to the general convention, which met in Philadelphia in 1883, he, on that occasion, solicited and obtained liberal donations from kind Northern friends. With this assistance funds were raised and the cornerstone laid, October 30, 1884. On Maundy Thursday, April 2, 1885, Bishop Thompson preached and confirmed a class of six in the beautiful little church, then first opened for divine service. Mr. Logan remained nearly seven years in Port Gibson, having, also, charge of the parish of Epiphany, St. Elmo, and various missions throughout Claiborne county. With reluctance, he left this, his first and dearly-loved parish, at the call of Holy Trinity, Vicksburg, then mourning the loss of its rector, who had been elected to the episcopate of Easton. In January, 1888, he assumed charge of the church in which he had been ordained to the priesthood. Since he became its rector, little more than three years ago, Holy Trinity parish has paid off its remaining debt of $1,500, and placed a beautiful and new ceiling in its yet unfinished interior. The Sunday-school has nearly trebled its number of pupils and teachers, and the parish generally is in a flourishing condition. Mr. Logan has never married, but his sisters make their home with him in Vicksburg. He has represented Mississippi in the general convention since 1883, having been elected a deputy to this supreme council of the church the year after his ordination to the priesthood. He is a member of the standing committee, secretary of the diocesan council, dean of the Natchez convocation and register of the diocese.

Augustus Baldwin Longstreet, a son of William Longstreet, was born in Augusta, Ga., September 22, 1790. He was sent to school, but made little progress in his studies; his mother, however, resolutely kept him at his tasks until he finally became interested in his books. He was graduated at Yale college in 1813, and began the study of law at Litchfield, Conn.; he was admitted to the bar of Georgia in 1815. It was about this time that he was married to Miss Frances Eliza Parke, of North Carolina, with whom he lived happily until her decease in the year 1868. In 1821 he represented Greene county in the legislature, and the following year he was made judge of the superior court; in 1824 he was a candidate for congress and had every prospect of success, when he withdrew on account of the death of a child; this event deeply impressed him with religious feeling, and he was accustomed from that time to open his court with prayer. He declined reëlection to the bench, and returned to the bar, where he became especially distinguished for his successes in criminal cases. In 1838 he entered upon the ministry of the Methodist Episcopal church, and in 1839 he was stationed at Augusta, which was at that time visited with yellow fever in a very malignant form. In that year he was elected to the presidency of Emory college, which office he held until 1848. He was then invited to the presidency of Centenary college, Louisiana. At the end of one year he was made president of the University of Mississippi, resigning the position in 1856, with the intention of retiring to private life, but in the following year he accepted the presidency of South Carolina college, remaining there until the breaking out of the Civil war. With the end of his connection with the South Carolina college his public career closed. On the cessation of hostilities he returned to Oxford, Miss., where he resided until his death, which occurred July 9, 1869. His last illness was not painful or long, and he passed away in the full possession of his mental faculties. He died in the fullest assurance of a Christian faith. From an early period of his life Judge Longstreet was accustomed to write for the press and magazines, and many of his speeches, charges to juries and sermons have been published. His miscellaneous writings include many of a humorous character, and a novel from his pen, entitled "Master William Mitten, or the Youth of Brilliant Talent Who was Ruined by Bad Luck," was published in the *Field and Fireside*, a literary journal of Georgia; it was afterward reproduced in a volume. Upon the occasion of the quarter-century celebration of the university in 1873, Chancellor Waddel paid a most eloquent tribute to his memory; in closing he says: "As a preacher he was solemn, earnest and instructive. As a writer his style was chaste and beautiful: As man, then, take him all in all, his character will bear the closest scrutiny, both in his public and in his private life. He was a kind husband and an affectionate father, a humane master, a considerate neighbor, a genial companion, an affable teacher, a wise counselor, a man of faith and trust in God, enjoying to a degree that was remarkable the assurance of his acceptance with his Heavenly

Father. He left, as a legacy to his descendants, a spotless reputation and the example of a transcendently noble life."

Capt. Francis Loper was born in Jones county, Miss., in 1827, and since his early manhood has lead a life of useful activity. When a child of six years, he was brought by his parents to what is now known as Jasper county, Miss. There he grew to maturity, surrounded by many of the hardships that attend pioneer life. His father's plantation was located near Garlandville, or rather the present site of that place. He was a pupil in the common schools, and although his advantages were comparatively meager, he secured the foundation of a good, practical education. At the age of twenty-two years he had the pleasure of one year in the Pleasant Hill academy, after which he taught school. In 1855, however, he abandoned this work, to enter commercial life, to which he devoted his energies until the breaking out of the Civil war. He responded at once to the call for men, and enlisted in the fall of 1861. At the end of sixty days he came home, and raised a company, of which he was chosen captain. He served in this capacity until the end of the conflict. He participated in the battles of Iuka and Corinth, and at the latter place was severely wounded by two minieballs and a shell. Holland's Thirty-seventh regiment opened the fight at Resaca, Ga., and Captain Loper's company suffered great loss of life at this place. He was in all the battles following until at Atlanta, Ga., where he was again wounded and disabled from duty. The Captain had been married in 1856 to Miss Eliza J. Bridges, a daughter of William Bridges, one of the pioneers of Jasper county, Miss. Of this union six children were born, three of whom are yet living. Mrs. Loper died in 1872, and the Captain was married a second time to Mrs. S. A. Dantzler, a daughter of Judge Uriah Milsaps, of Jasper county. When Captain Loper returned from the war, he again entered commercial life, and also gave some attention to planting, until the autumn of 1883, when he was elected treasurer of Newton county. He has since held this office, and has discharged his duties with a rare fidelity and an ability that has challenged the admiration both of his constituency and his opponents. He has been identified with the Masonic fraternity since 1852, and has been worshipful master a greater portion of that time. He also belongs to the Knights of Honor. He is a zealous worker in the interests of the Methodist Episcopal church, of which he is steward. He is a conscientious, Christian gentlemen, and enjoys the esteem of the entire community. J. B. Loper, the father of our subject, was born in South Carolina, in 1804. He was a planter by occupation, and before the war owned a considerable number of slaves. He passed from this life in June, 1878, leaving behind him a record of the highest honor. His wife, Sarah (McCormick) Loper, was born in South Carolina in 1807, and was a daughter of John and Nancy (Fontaine) McCormick, who were also natives of South Carolina. They came of good old Revolutionary stock, than which there is none better in this land.

L. Lopez, of the firm of Lopez & Co., Biloxi, Miss., is a native of Spain. He received the greater part of his education in Havana, and after he left school he was employed in the store of an uncle for some years. In 1867 he came to Mississippi and located in Biloxi, where he established himself in business. His capital being limited he began with a small stock of groceries, but by economy, industry and close attention to his interests, he has risen to a leading position in the commercial circles of Harrison county. He owns a fine residence in Biloxi, and the business building in which his store is. He is a stockholder in Lopez, Dunbar, Sons & Co.'s canning factory, one of the most thriving institutions in the southern part of the state. They pack shrimps, oysters and figs, and give employment to one hundred and fifty persons during the winter months. The concern is under the management of Mr. Lopez, and its prosperity is due in a great measure to his wisdom and executive ability. He is one of the most enterprising men of Harrison county, and a citizen who would be an acquisition to any community. He married Miss Julia Dulion, and seven children were born of the union: Josephine E., Thresa, Clara, Lazarus, Arnaud, Erena and Julius. Mr. Lopez is a member of the masonic fraternity. T. B. Dulion, of the firm of Lopez & Co., Biloxi, Miss., was born in this place in 1861, and is a son of Arnold M. Dulion, a native of France. The father immigrated to the United States, and settled in Biloxi about the year 1848; he carried on a mercantile business until his death. The son was reared and educated at Biloxi, and was trained to mercantile pursuits. He was employed as a clerk for L. Lopez, and had charge of his business for several years. In January, 1889, he became a partner in the firm of Lopez & Co., with whom he is still associated. They carry on a general mercantile business, and carry the largest stock in Biloxi. Mr. Dulion was married March 20, 1886, to Miss Amy H. Park, and they have had three children born to them: Ura, Roy and an infant. Mrs. Dulion was born in the state of Nebraska. They are members of the Catholic church.

Capt. Benjamin Loughridge was born in Franklin county, Ga., April 29, 1815, and is a son of William and Jerusha (Pulliam) Loughridge, natives of South Carolina and Georgia, respectively. The father came to Georgia with his parents when a mere lad, grew to manhood and was married there. The paternal grandfather was a native of Scotland, and immigrated to America and settled in Virginia before the Revolutionary war. He was a soldier under General Washington, and served seven years. William Loughridge was a farmer and blacksmith by occupation. He died in Cass county, Ga., in 1844. Captain Loughridge passed his youth in his native state, and was married at Cedar Bluff, Ala., in 1841, to Ann E. Bogan. They had born to them six children: Eliza E. (deceased), Mary A. (wife of J. M. Eckford, of San Antonio, Tex.), Mattie P. (wife of G. S. Henderson), Margaret (wife of James M. Dillard), William J., Fanny A. The last named and Mary A. were educated at Chickasaw Female college. William J. was graduated from the literary, law and commercial department of the college at Lexington, Ky., and is now president of the Third National bank of that city. He also owns the belt railroad and street-car line of Lexington, and has other commercial interests there; he is one of the most enterprising men of the place. He was married to Fanny C. Bruce, daughter of W. W. Bruce, of Lexington, Ky. Captain Loughridge remained at home until he was seventeen years of age, and then started out to develop his own resources. He was first employed as a clerk in a store, holding the position two years. He then went to Long's Ferry (now Centerville), Ga., and opened a general stock of goods in his own name. He continued in business there for three years. At the end of that time he enlisted in the service of the United States to subdue the Creek and Seminole Indians, and saw eleven months of active duty. He was elected tax collector for Cass county, Ga., for two terms, and was appointed census taker in 1840. In January, 1848, he removed to Mississippi, and located in the territory which was then known as Pontotoc county, but which is now within the borders of Lee county. He settled on the plantation which is still his home. In the fall of 1849 he opened a store with a well-selected stock of dry goods, and succeeded in getting a postoffice established at the store; the place was named Birmingham, and he was postmaster until the breaking out of the Civil war. At the time he owned fourteen slaves, and was a zealous supporter of the Southern cause. In 1862 he enlisted in company F, Thirty-first Mississippi volunteer infantry, and was elected captain of his company. He participated in the engagements at Vicksburg, Baton Rouge, Corinth, and some of less note. In 1863 he enlisted in a cavalry company, and served until the cessation of hostilities. He was paroled at Columbus, Miss., May 17, 1865, after which he returned to his home. He again embarked

The Goodspeed Pub.Co.Chicago.

B. S. Ricks

in the mercantile trade at his old stand, and continued the business there until 1889, when he sold out, and has since lived a retired life. He owns eleven hundred acres of land, six hundred of which are in a high state of cultivation. Although Captain Loughridge has never aspired to public office, he is an enthusiastic democrat, and has labored zealously for the success of his party. Mrs. Loughridge is a member of the Methodist Episcopal church, while the other members of the family belong to the Presbyterian church. The mother of the Captain died in 1881 at the age of eighty-seven years. He is now seventy-seven years old, and is one of the oldest citizens of the county, none of whom are more highly esteemed. He has given liberally of his means in support of public enterprises, and is a typical Southerner.

Dr. Samuel Gray Loughridge, a prominent physician of Jasper county, Miss., was born in Alabama in 1824, is a son of James and Deborah Ann (McGill) Loughridge. His father was born in the north of Ireland in the year 1775, and immigrated to the United States in 1794; settled in South Carolina and remained there following his occupation, tailoring, until 1823, when he moved to Alabama and engaged in agriculture. He died in 1838, while on a business trip to Texas, and his wife survived him until 1878. They were the parents of twelve children, of whom the Doctor was the tenth born. He remained with his mother in Alabama, until 1843, when she removed to Attala county, Miss., where he finished his academic course under Rev. James Martin. In selecting a profession he chose that of medicine, and read under Dr. L. D. Read, a prominent physician of Attala county, and attended lectures in Louisville, Ky. In 1848 he located in the neighborhood of Garlandsville, Miss., where he has remained ever since. In the year 1845 he united with the Presbyterian church at Bethsalem, Winston county, whence his membership was transferred to Mount Moriah church in Newton county, where he was elected and ordained an elder. About the year 1867 a Presbyterian church was organized in Garlandsville, Miss., of which he was one of the original members; he was also elected elder, which office he has filled until the present time. In 1852 he was married to Miss Martha Taylor, of Noxubee county, by whom he had two children, the mother passing away in 1857. He was married a second time in 1862 to Miss Mary Catherine McCallum, daughter of Judge A. McCallum, of Jasper county, by whom he had ten children, eight of whom are still living. In 1847 the Doctor joined the Masonic fraternity and was made a Master Mason. In 1850 he was made a Royal Arch Mason and has been in good standing ever since. Up to the Civil war he had an extensive practice, in which he had been eminently successful, both in the practice of medicine and surgery. By close attention to his business he had made a considerable competency. He owns a valuable plantation, and during the war raised all the supplies he could for the Confederate army; also practiced free of charge in the soldiers' families. He was a whig in politics before the war, but since then has voted with the democratic party; has never been an aspirant for office. Soon after the Civil war a company of negroes living near Hickory, in Newton county, had banded themselves together for the avowed purpose of stealing and plundering from the whites. A man named Dennis, who had lost some hogs, had taken out a writ to arrest the leader of the gang (John Dias), but on going to his house found he was not at home. He with the other men who accompanied him, started home, when to their surprise they were fired upon by the negroes, who were in ambush. Two men named Dennis were killed and two or three wounded. Dr. Bragg was sent for to attend the wounded men, but as he, with several others who went out with him as a kind of guard, was riding up to the house, they were fired upon by the negroes and several wounded. This occurred on Sunday morning, and during the day there were several fights between different squads of whites and negroes; several of the latter were killed, and there were about one hundred in arms. By

72

Monday morning the whole county was aroused, and nearly every man was ordered out by the sheriff to quell the riot. The Doctor went out with others under a deputy sheriff. They arrested two negroes, who were put in jail. There were no negroes killed on Monday. After every thing had quieted down General Gillem, who commanded this department, sent out his cavalry, and in the dead hour of night arrested the Doctor and several others. They were carried to Hickory on a cold, rainy night in March, confined in a wet, muddy house without a floor, without fire or food, kept there twenty-four hours, then carried to Vicksburg and put in prison. Here the Doctor was kept fifty-eight days, tried by a military commission and honorably acquitted, some of the best men in the state voluntarily going before the commission to testify to his character. In his early days game was abundant in Mississippi. He was very fond of hunting, kept a pack of hounds and was considered one of the best shots in the county. He still lives on his farm, practicing medicine and farming.

Daniel A. Love is a man who has attained his present substantial position in life by his own indomitable perseverance and energy. His birth occurred in Virginia on March 30, 1835, to William and Elizabeth (Hannah) Love, natives of Virginia and Kentucky respectively. William Love was commissioned to raise a company for the War of 1812, which he readily did, and was on his way to Yorktown, Va., having reached Staunton, when peace was declared. He had one brother, Daniel Love, who served throughout that war and made a gallant soldier. The paternal grandparents, Allen and Susan (Creath) Love, were Virginians, the former serving throughout the Revolutionary war and dying in his native state at the age of eighty-six years, having been an honorable man and a useful member of society. Harvey Love, the paternal great-grandfather, was a native of Scotland and was one of the first settlers of Jamestown. He was at one time captured by the Indians, but at the end of six months managed to make his escape at great risk. He and his descendants were among the honored and respected residents of Virginia, as also were the Creaths, many of the male members of the latter family being ministers of the gospel, mainly of the Baptist denomination. Jacob Creath was one of the leaders of the reformation known as the Christian church, was a second cousin to the subject of this sketch, his death occurring in Blanchard Springs, Mo., at a ripe old age. The celebrated Rolfe family were lineal ancestors of Mr. Love. The latter was brought up and received his education in Virginia, but in 1859 came to Mississippi and located in Washington county, after having spent about four years traveling in the Western states. Ever since that time he has been engaged in planting. Upon the opening of the war he dropped his farming implements and in 1861 enlisted in the Confederate army, being in company D. of the twenty-eighth Mississippi regiment of cavalry. The company was organized in Washington county by Capt. George Blackburn, who was at once made captain and continued in command until taken prisoner, at which time Capt. W. E. Hunt was chosen to command and continued so to do until the war ended. Mr. Love was in the campaign of Georgia, Tennessee and Mississippi and fired the first gun in the siege of Vicksburg. Although a private throughout the war he was an unflinching defender of the Southern cause and at the time of Lee's surrender was at Gainesville, Ala. At the close of the war he found that the property which he had formerly accumulated had been swept away and he had once more to commence anew. He wasted no time in useless repining but at once set himself to the task of building up his fallen fortunes and by unswering perseverance has become the owner of fifteen hundred acres of land, one thousand of which are under cultivation, he, himself, opening three hundred acres. On this place he put about $10,000 worth of improvements. In 1890, he erected him an elegant home in Greenville at a cost of $7,000, has it elegantly furnished, and in this ideal home dispenses hospitality with a liberality unsurpassed.

He was married in 1876 to Mrs. Stella Handy, a native of Washington county and a daughter of W. R. and Margaret (Tiedaman) Campbell, the birth of the father occurring on Blue Grass soil and that of the mother in Pennsylvania. Mr. Campbell was one of the first merchants of Vicksburg, was a pioneer settler of Washington county and was one of the largest landowners in the county. Their daughter (now Mrs. Love), became the wife of Dr. John Handy, by whom she became the mother of one son, J. R. To her and Mr. Love two children have been born, Margaret C. and Garnett Reed. Mr. Love, his wife and children are members of the Episcopal church and in politics is is a Democrat. He deserves a great deal of credit for the admirable way in which he has surmounted the many difficulties that have strewn his pathway, for at the close of the war he had nothing save an untarnished record as a brave and faithful soldier. Believing that honest toil does not go unrewarded he entered life's arena with a determination to make a success of his life, and time has proved the wisdom of his views. He has always been the soul of honor in his business transactions, and he has the satisfaction of knowing that the fine property of which he is now the owner has not yet been acquired at the expense of, or by defrauding others. While his youthful education was not of the best, he is by no means void of those finer qualities that go to make up a true gentleman, and is a well posted and intelligent man of business and a favorite in social circles. He has an ideal home, is devoted to his family and in the home circle is seen at his best.

DeWitt C. Love was born in Pike county, Miss., August, 7, 1835, and is a son of Jefferson and Catherine (McLaurin) Love, natives of South Carolina and Mississippi, respectively. They had born to them eight children, of whom our subject is the fifth. The father was reared to the occupation of a farmer, and received his education in the common schools of Mississippi. In about the year 1812, he came with his father, William Love, to Mississippi, and located in Adams county, where he spent a few years; his next place of residence was Pike county, and at the age of thirty-five years, he removed to Madison county, where he lived the rest of his life; he died in 1868. His career was one of honest industry and devotion to his family. He gave a liberal education to all of his children, a legacy to which there is none of equal value. The Love family is of Irish origin, and the McLaurins are of Scotch ancestry. DeWitt was reared in Madison county, Miss., to which he was taken in early childhood. He received his education at Centenary college, Louisiana, and Wesleyan university, Florence, Ala., being graduated from the latter institution in 1856. He then returned to his home, and has since been very successfully engaged in agriculture. He recognizes that there is a best way to do everything, and the employment of this law has been of great value to him. In 1862, he enlisted in the Confederate service, joining company H., Ninth Mississippi volunteer infantry, and serving until the declaration of peace. He participated in the engagements of Munfordville, Murfreesboro, Chickamauga, Missionary Ridge and all the latter engagements of the Western army. He was slightly wounded at Murfreesboro, and was at Goldsboro, N. C., at the time of the surrender. Upon his return to his home, he set bravely to work to rebuild his shattered fortunes. The truly courageous spirit exhibited by the sons of the South at this trying time is worthy of all praise. In 1887, Mr. Love was solicited by his friends to become a candidate for the office of sheriff of the county, which he consented to do; he was elected, and carried on the business of the office with such universal satisfaction that he was re-elected to the office, of which he is the present incumbent. He owns twenty-four hundred acres of land on Silver creek, in the northern part of the county, six hundred acres being under cultivation. He was married in 1859 to Miss Mary Brown, a Mississippian, and a daughter of James and Mary (Montgomery) Brown, also of Mississippi. Mrs. Love died in 1862, leaving one child, Katie, the deceased wife of Dr. C. S. Hudson. Mr.

Love was married a second time in 1865 to Kate L. Alexander, of Madison county, Miss., a daughter of A. and Emma (Lyon) Alexander. Her father was a native of Mississippi, and her mother was born in Liverpool, England. Five children have been born to Mr. and Mrs. Love: Emma L., Hugh M., Ada, Franklin J. and De Witt. The daughters are attending school at Staunton, Va., and all the children will be given a thorough education. The parents are members of the Presbyterian church, of which Mr. Love is an elder. He is one of Yazoo county's best citizens, is thoroughly refined, public-spirited and charitable, and an ornament to any community.

Among the enterprising and substantial citizens of Oktibbeha county stands the name of Capt. J. E. Love, who owes his nativity to the Palmetto state, his birth occurring in 1834. His parents, James H. and Sarah (Bowen) Love, are both natives of that state, the father born in 1803. The latter was early taught the duties of the farm and agricultural pursuits was his chosen occupation through life. He received a common English education and when twenty-one years of age began the struggle of life for himself. When twenty-five years of age he married Miss Sarah Bowen, a native of York county, born in 1808. In 1842 they removed to Choctaw county, Miss., and reached their destination in 1843, the trip occupying about four weeks. They made the journey in carryalls and wagons and camped each night. There were two families in the company, James H. Love and a brother William, and including the slaves they brought with them there were about fifty individuals in all. James H. purchased about four hundred acres of land, seventy-five acres under cultivation and the remainder in timber land. He and wife became the parents of six children, who are named in the order of their births as follows: Joseph E., Nancy E., widow of J. K. Thompson, of Oktibbeha county, Miss.; William, farmer of Reno county, Kan.; Mary, wife of E. K. Hillyer, of Montcalm, Tex., a hardware merchant; Sarah, wife of E. S. Drain, a farmer of Ware, Choctaw county, Miss., and Frances, widow of A. S. Robinson, of Oktibbeha county. James H. Love died in 1884, but his wife had died previously, in 1862. Both had been members of the Presbyterian church from youth, and Mr. Love was a ruling elder for over fifty years. He became quite wealthy, but the emancipation proclamation destroyed his wealth. He died at the age of eighty-three years. His father, Richard Love, was born in Chester county, S. C., in 1768 and was of Irish descent. He was a prosperous farmer and accumulated considerable wealth, being the owner of a great many slaves at the time of his death. His father (great grandfather of subject) was a shoemaker, and represented Chester district in the legislature. While a member of that body he wore a jeans overcoat and the buttons on the same he had but from leather. Richard Love died in Chester county in 1842. He married a Miss Love not a relative, however,) and the fruits of this union were eight children: Benjamin, James, William, John, Marion, Amaziah, and two others whose names are forgotten. Captain Love's maternal grandparents, Joseph and Nancy (Roberts) Bowen, were both of York district, S. C., and the grandfather was of Welsh descent. They were the parents of eight children: Sarah, James, Edie, Eunice, William, Seth and John (twins) and Nancy. Joseph Bowen was quite a well-to-do farmer and died in 1850 when about seventy-two or three years of age. His widow followed him to the grave about six years later when about the same age. Joseph was the son of Samuel Bowen, a soldier of the Revolution, as were also his seven brothers. The boyhood of Capt. J. E. Love was spent in Choctaw county and there he received a fair English education, principally in boarding schools. When twenty-one years of age he began for himself as an agriculturist, farming on land he had just purchased in Choctaw county, and on the 27th of July, 1865, Miss Mattie W. Robinson, a native of Fairfield county, S. C., born in 1849, and the daughter of Alexander and Permelia (Estes) Robinson, became his wife. Her parents were natives also of Fairfield district, the father born in 1819 and the mother in 1827. They were married on the 30th of August, 1842. Alexander was the son of John and Lucretia (Mobly) Robinson and one of eight children, who are named as follows: Mary, Nancy, Eliza, John A., Sivilla, Margaret, Alexander and Samuel. Alexander and Permelia (Estes) Robinson were the parents of fifteen children, of whom the following are still living: Sarah, wife of Amos Estes; Mattie W., wife of subject; Pernecy, wife of William Love; W. Clyde, a merchant of Waco, Tex., and Walter F., a farmer of Kansas. Capt. J. E. Love's marriage was blessed by the birth of ten children: Eloise, wife of James E. Gladney, of Osborne, Miss., a stockdealer; Sarah, wife of E. C. Nance, of Lowndes county; James A., a farmer of Osborne, Miss.; Joseph E.; William C., Robert S., Edwin, John, and Ida and Ada (twins). Captain Love removed from Choctaw to Oktibbeha county in 1878, purchased five hundred acres of land where he now resides, and a half interest in a section of land in Kansas. His principal productions are corn, cotton and sweet potatoes. He raises cattle, horses and mules for market, besides a considerable number of sheep. His cattle are principally thoroughbred and grade Jerseys. Captain Love is a Mason, a member of the Farmers' Alliance, of which he is lecturer, and he and Mrs. Love are members of the Presbyterian church. The captain was elected a member of the board of supervisors in 1885, and held the office for four years, being re-elected in 1887. During the last term he was president of the board, but declined to run for re-election. On the 5th of May, 1861, Captain Love enlisted in company I, Fifteenth Mississippi infantry as a private, served in that capacity about twelve months, when he had his right arm shattered by a minieball at Fishing Creek. He was discharged as disabled, but after remaining at home eight months he enlisted as a private in Ford's company, Perrin's regiment and Ferguson's brigade. He was elected lieutenant soon after the company went out and was soon after promoted to captain of the same, filling that position until the close of the war. He was engaged in the battle of Fishing Creek, then in all the engagements from Dalton to Atlanta, when General Sherman started on his march to the sea. His brigade was thrown against Sherman's rear and there was some sharp fighting done. Afterward he was in the Savannah engagement. He was paroled near Washington, Ga., after which he immediatly returned home and began anew as an agriculturist. His daughter, Eloise, who married James E. Gladney, became the mother of three children by this union; Frank and Walter (twins) and Eunice. Thus for three generations twins have been born in the family, never more than one pair and never a pair of both sexes. Captain Love remembers very distinctly the trip his parents made from South Carolina to Choctaw county, Miss., and how he thoroughly enjoyed it. He also remembers that the night they camped below Starkville, a slight earthquake occurred, sufficiently severe to crack a brick church in that town.

Richard Love was born in Nashville, Tenn., April 11, 1844, the third in a family of ten children of Charles I. and Julia (Shrewsbury) Love. His father was a native of Virginia, his mother of Kentucky. His paternal grandfather moved from Virginia to middle Tennessee at an early date and was one of the pioneers in that part of the country, living in a tent until he could build houses for himself and workmen. His maternal grandparents were among the early settlers in Kentucky. His parents were married, and lived and ended their days in Dyer county, Tenn. His father was a turfman, owning some of the best blooded horses in that part of the country so noted for swift racers. He took great pride in the breeding of that class of stock as well as in its improvement. He was an expert rider and driver, and was a practical farmer and stockman. He died in Dyer county, Tenn., in 1890, and his wife in same county in 1879. He was a member of the Masonic fraternity,

and a liberal contributor to all worthy purposes.   In business he was honorable and enterprising, and in his social relations he was noted for his hospitality, while his generosity was
proverbial among all classes of men.   Richard Love, our subject, enlisted in 1861 in
company C, of the Twenty-seventh Tennessee infantry, under the command of Col. Kit
Williams of Memphis.   This regiment formed part of Cheatham's division of the army of
Tennessee.   Mr. Love participated in the battles of Shiloh, Murfreesboro, Prairieville
and Richmond.   He was wounded at Prairieville, receiving a gunshot in the thigh which
confined him to the hospital for about four months.   After his exchange at Vicksburg (for
he also had an experience as prisoner of war), he enlisted in company D, of the Eighteenth
Mississippi cavalry battalion, under Colonel Chalmers.   He was in the fight at Memphis
under General Forrest, and in various other skirmishes, serving till the close of the war, when
he was paroled at Gainesville, Ala.   During the period of the war he had found time and
opportunity to get married, taking for his wife Anna E. McKinzie, daughter of Capt. L. T.
McKinzie, with whom he became acquainted while being cared for at her father's house as a
wounded soldier.   After peace was declared he returned home, where he bought land and
engaged in planting and stockraising, which he has continued successfully to the present
time.   Mr. and Mrs. Love have had seven children, all of whom are dead with the single
exception of one son—Richard, the youngest.   Mr. Love owns twelve hundred acres of
land, about one-fourth of which is under cultivation.   He pays considerable attention to
stockraising, breeding and placing on the market a large number of horses and mules.

Col. William S. Lovell traces his ancestry back through five generations to John Lovell,
of Scotland, who was born in the year 1683.   His son, who also bore the name of John, was
born in 1710, and was married to Abigail Green, whose son, James S. Lovell, born in 1737,
married Mary Middleton.   Their son, James S. Lovell, was born in 1762, and upon reaching
manhood was married to Miss Deborah Gorham, who bore him a son they named Joseph.
The latter was born in 1788, and upon attaining mature years was united in marriage to
Miss Margaret Mansfield.   He was a physician by calling, and was surgeon-general of the
United States army, which office was created for him.   Between the 6th of September and
the 17th of October, 1836, he and his wife both died, leaving a family of eleven children to
fight the battle of life for themselves.   The mother traced her ancestry back through six
generations to Richard Mansfield, of Exeter, England, who settled in Boston in 1639.
William S. Lovell, son of Dr. Joseph and Margaret (Mansfield) Lovell, was born in Washington, D. C., in November, 1829, and after the death of his parents removed to Hudson, N.
Y., with an aunt, he having no living male relatives, to his knowledge.   He attended various
schools until fitted for college, and in 1845 entered Williamstown college, of Williamstown,
Mass.   Being possessed with a great desire to enter the navy, he, in 1846, left college and
went to New York city to work for his appointment, and although vacancies were few and
applicants numerous (there being only eight of the former and two thousand of the latter) he
was not discouraged, for at that time appointments were made upon the strength of the
endorsements.   It took him about one year to make his influence sufficiently felt to secure
his appointment, and in the meantime he did not idle away his time, but was in the employ
of a wholesale drug house, where his personal worth made itself so conspicuous that he
was promoted over older clerks to a responsible position.   In November, 1847, he was
appointed a midshipman in the United States army, and ordered to report at the naval
academy, and in December of that year he was ordered to the storeship, Fredonia, at New
York city.   He was soon afterward detached and ordered to the sloop-of-war, Decatur, at
Boston, on which vessel he sailed to the coast of Africa, in February, 1848, during which

cruise he touched at Liberia, Madeira, the Cape Verd islands, Santa Cruz and other ports, and returned to the United States in 1849, landing at Portsmouth, N. H. Here he was detached on leave of absence, and in May, 1850, volunteered as an officer in the expedition in which Henry Grinnell, of New York, was fitting out to search for Sir John Franklin. Under command of Lieutenant De Haven, he sailed as second officer of the brig, Advance, from New York, May 23. In September, 1850, his vessel was frozen in the ice, and during the two hundred and sixty-six days that they were in this difficulty, they drifted eleven hundred miles, at the end of which time they were released. Mr. Lovell's next cruise was to South America in the storeship, Relict. In June, 1853, he passed his examination at Annapolis as midshipman, taking an even hundred in seamanship, and ranking fifth in his class. The following letter explains itself:

NAVY DEPARTMENT, June 6, 1857.

I certify that it appears from the rolls forwarded to this department from the naval academy, under date of June 10, 1853, that William S. Lovell, United States navy, at his final examination for promotion, stood No. 1 in seamanship, having received the maximum that could be reached in that branch.

CHARLES WELCH, Chief Clerk.

After this Mr. Lovell took a short cruise on the Princeton, of the eastern squadron; in the latter part of 1853 was detached from the Princeton and ordered to the brig Bainbridge, on which he sailed for South America, returning January, 1855. Dr. Kane had returned to the Arctic regions and when Mr. Lovell arrived home from South America an expedition was being equipped for his search and Mr. Lovell volunteered as one of the officers of the expedition; he was selected by the secretary of the navy as one of a board of three to purchase vessels for said expedition, which was commanded by Lieutenant Hartstene, United States navy, Mr. Lovell going as master and executive officer. They sailed from New York with the Release and the consort Arctic, and went as far north as seventy-eight degrees and thirty-two minutes. They were successful in their search and returned with the Doctor amid the rejoicings of the people. In recognition of his services in the two expeditions he made, he received from Queen Victoria, through Lord Napier, two medals and one from the English residents of New York city. September 15, 1855, Mr. Lovell was commissioned a master and next day was commissioned lieutenant, receiving the commissions from passed midshipman to lieutenant in one envelope. In June, 1858, he married Miss Antonia Quitman, the accomplished daughter of Gen. John A. Quitman of Natchez, Miss. He did not remain long in the navy after his marriage. His last cruise was made to Pensacola, Fla.; on his return to Washington leave of absence was granted him; he resigned from the navy in May, 1859, and retired to private life and commenced planting in Mississippi. Mr. Lovell has in his possession letters and indorsements from many of his old commanders and other prominent men of the highest character. His experience in the way of planting was begun with his brother Joseph and resulted very successfully. At the opening of the recent war Mr. Lovell raised a company at Natchez (Quitman's light artillery), of which he was chosen captain. He was ordered to Pensacola under Bragg; he was soon detached from his command and was made chief of harbor police with four vessels under his command. He was soon after promoted to the rank of major and was subsequently ordered to New Orleans, where he was made lieutenant-colonel of the Twenty-second Louisiana regiment, serving on the staff of General Lovell, his brother, as ordnance officer. He had charge of fitting up the river defense vessels, constructed rafts, etc., and carried on extensively all branches in the ordnance department at and near that port, which required no little judgment and skill. After the fall of New Orleans Colonel Lovell was made inspector-general on General Pemberton's staff, with headquarters at

Vicksburg, but after the capture of that city he did duty under General Johnston for a short while. Colonel Lovell was urged by Mr. Mallory, secretary of the Confederate states navy, to take command of a vessel, which he declined; his love for his old calling returned to him and he went out of the harbor of Wilmington, N. C., in 1864, through a fleet of United States vessels—a daring thing to do—to take command of a blockade runner. He went to Bermuda and Halifax, but found no vessel at either place for him, so he went to England. He was there examined and was commissioned by the London board of trade as master. He was six months endeavoring to get a vessel ready for blockade running, but before he succeeded in accomplishing his purpose the fortunes of the Confederacy waned and her flag went down at Appomattox. He returned to the United States.

Gathering up his family at Columbia, S. C., on his way home, he returned to Natchez, Miss., and with his brother began gathering up the remnants of the wreck which the war had made of their magnificent property. After the death of his brother in 1869, the management of this plantation was left entirely in the hands of Colonel Lovell. In 1874 he extended his interests, and for six years held the second place as the largest cotton planter in the United States. He is quite an extensive raiser of corn, as well as cotton, and his plantations are probably the finest in Warren county, very little of which is overflowed during the extremely high water period. He has control of three thousand acres of open land, and pays taxes on fifty-five hundred acres. His family consists of three sons and two daughters. His eldest son, John Q., is paymaster in the United States navy; William S. is in the grain business in Birmingham, Ala.; Antonia Q. and Rosalie D. spent the most of their time with their mother in their mountain home in Tennessee, and Joseph M. is a medical student in Tulane university, New Orleans. Colonel Lovell has never interested himself in politics, has never voted but three times in his life, and the only political office he ever held was postmaster of Palmyra, and that was in connection with his store. He is justly proud of his record as a naval officer. He commanded three United States steamers before he was twenty-nine years old. He was not quite twenty-six when he received orders to command the United States steamer Engineer. On several occasions his vessels were called upon to make ready for the president and his cabinet when they wished to make some little excursion. He possesses a wide acquaintance and counts his friends by the score, many of whom are eminent statesmen of this country. Since the year 1847, with the exception of the five years during the war, he has kept a diary of his everyday doings which, owing to the eventful life he has led, is a very interesting and instructive one. Colonel Lovell is five feet ten and one-half inches in hight, weighs about one hundred and seventy-five pounds, and is of florid complexion. He possesses very decided views on all important questions of the day, and is a very superior man intellectually. His success in life, in the different callings which he has followed, and the high position he has attained as a civilian, have been attained rather by the force of native talent and culture than by tact.

Ezekiel Lovett, merchant, Walthall, Miss., is a descendant of one of the first settlers of Webster county, Miss., his grandfather, David Lovett, having located there at a very early date, when bear, deer, panthers and wolves were plentiful. The grandfather came originally from Lincoln county, Tenn., located at Jackson, Miss., before the erection of that city, but only remained there a short time, when he went to Alabama. He afterward returned to Mississippi about 1832, and died in what is now Webster county. He was a farmer, and had followed that occupation all his life. His son, John Lovett, was born in Tennessee in 1808, went with his parents to Alabama, and was married in that state, when eighteen years of age, to Miss Margaret Bryant, a native of Alabama, born in 1810. In 1833 Mr. Lovett went to Choctaw county (now Webster), settled in the woods on Shootesuppeau creek, and improved a good farm, following the occupation of a farmer, like his father before him. His death occurred in that county in 1867, and his wife only survived him until 1877. Both were members of the Primitive Baptist church. He was a member of the Masonic fraternity. To their marriage were born eleven children, eight of whom were reared to maturity and six now living, all daughters but Ezekiel. The latter's only brother, David, enlisted in the Thirty-first Mississippi regiment during the Civil war, and died while in service. Our subject's maternal grandfather, John Bryant, was a native of Ireland, where he learned the blacksmith trade when quite young. He was persecuted for supposed participation in the wars there, and about 1795 he came to the United States. He was married in Alabama and lived there until 1859, when he came to Mississippi, and died in Choctaw (now Webster) county. Ezekiel Lovett was born in Choctaw (now Webster) county in 1848, and was reared on the farm and attended the common schools at leisure times, where he received a very limited education. In 1873 Miss Louisa Kimzey, daughter of John Kimzey, of North Carolina, became his wife. Her father moved from the Old North state to what is now Lee county, Miss., followed planting, and received his last summons in Lafayette county. Mrs. Lovett was a member of the Baptist church, and died in 1883, leaving one child: John L. Mr. Lovett's second marriage was in 1884, to Miss Martha Susan Taylor, a native of Montgomery county, Miss., and daughter of William Taylor, who was a farmer, and who died in Montgomery county in 1882. To Mr. and Mrs. Lovett has been born one daughter: Alice L. Mr. Lovett resided on the old farm until 1884, and then removed to Walthall, where, in connection with merchandising, he carried on a small farm. He is the owner of three hundred and sixty-seven acres of land, all the fruits of his own exertions, and as a citizen and neighbor is esteemed and respected. He is a member of the Adelphian lodge No. 174, at Walthall, and was mayor of that city for some time; also a member of the Missionary Baptist church.

Dr. Edmund F. Lowe, a well-known physician and cotton planter of Hinds and Copiah counties, Miss., was born in Copiah county in 1827, a son of Daniel and Tabitha B. Lowe, the former of whom was a son of Daniel, Sr., and Mary (Lowe) Lowe, who were cousins. They were of an early family of South Carolina, and moved to Georgia about the year 1800 and thence to the state of Mississippi in 1812, where the rest of their days were spent. They were of English descent. Daniel Lowe, Jr., was born in the state of Georgia in 1802, was exceptionally well educated for his day and for many years was engaged in teaching school, in which he met with remarkable success. He came to Mississippi with his parents in 1812 and located in Covington county, where he was married in 1822, to Miss Tabitha B. Noble, a daughter of Stephen F. and Sarah Noble, who belonged to a very old and prominent family of this state. In 1825 Mr. Lowe moved to that portion of the state which is now Copiah county, where he became a successful cotton planter. He died in 1846 a worthy member of the Baptist church, of which his wife was also a member. To his union the following children were born, Aaron B. (deceased); John C., who was a graduate of Jefferson Medical college of Philadelphia; Daniel B. L., who was killed at the battle of Wilderness, Va.; Anna L., wife of J. W. W. Spencer (deceased); Sarah E., wife of Pheling McCalif (deceased); Margaret E., wife of E. Massey; Malora J., wife of W. M. Robertson; Mary, the deceased wife of William Cullage, and Dr. Edmund F. The latter received his education in Louisville, Ky., and in 1848 graduated from a medical institution of that place. The following winter he attended lectures in New Orleans, and has since often attended lectures there in order to keep posted in his profession. As soon as he graduated he commenced practicing in his profession in Copiah county, a calling he has since actively followed, but is at present doing but little riding, his local practice fully occupying his time. He was married in 1849, to Miss Margaret C. McNeil, a daughter of Hector and Elizabeth McNeil, who originally came from South Carolina, and their union resulted in the birth of three children, all now deceased. After the death of his first wife, Dr. Lowe was again married, in 1858, to Miss Emily M. Peyton, eldest daughter of ex-Chief Justice E. G. and Arta M. G. (Patton) Peyton, by whom he is the father of the following children: Edmund P., a practicing physician in Colorado, graduated from the literary department at the University of Mississippi at Oxford and in medicine at New Orleans in 1885, and received a government appointment under President Cleveland as surgeon of the Ute reservation in Colorado, in February, 1886; Ephraim N., a practicing physician, also in Colorado, graduated from the Mississippi university and from the New Orleans Medical college in 1887; Emily P., is the wife of M. L. Ford, of Hinds county, Miss.; Arta M. G. is the wife of Frank Dains, of Colorado, and Anna L., wife of Charles Farrer, of Colorado. Dr. Lowe comes of a fine family, is a well educated gentleman on all subjects, but is especially well posted and competent in his profession, his success as a practitioner of the healing art being truly wonderful. He is deservedly proud of the career of his sons, who are becoming eminent in their professions, and are thoroughly posted and up with the times in every respect.

James M. Lowe is the proprietor of the popular and admirably kept hostelry, the Pioneer hotel of Harriston, Miss. His native state is the Old Dominion, his birth occurring in Westmoreland county on the 17th of June, 1837. His father was also a Virginian by birth and there was united in marriage to Elizabeth W. Straughan, daughter of the Rev. Samuel Straughan, who was an eminent divine of the Baptist church. Mrs. Lowe was born and reared in Virginia and after her marriage to Mr. Lowe they resided in Westmoreland county until the death of the latter, which occurred in the month of August, 1837, the subject of this sketch being an infant at that time. Mr. Lowe, Sr., was a shipcarpenter by trade and followed that calling with fair success until his demise. He was a man strictly honorable in every respect and was one of the substantial citizens of the locality in which he resided. Upon being left a widow Mrs. Lowe removed to Northumberland county, where she reared her family, which consisted of two sons, the elder (A. J. Lowe) being a minister of the Baptist church until his death in 1865. In Northumberland county James M. Lowe grew to mature years, receiving a fair academic education. In 1857, with a view to bettering his financial prospects, he came west to Mississippi and for a few years followed the occupation of teaching school in Jefferson county, but upon the opening of the war he dropped the ferrule to take up arms in defense of the Confederate cause, becoming a member of the army in August, 1861. He first joined the Seventh Mississippi infantry, but was soon after transferred to the Jefferson light artillery, in which command he remained until the fall of 1862, when he was discharged for disability and returned to the state of his adoption. After regaining his health he re-enlisted in the Fourteenth Confederate cavalry and was appointed to the position of sergeant-major, in which capacity he served until taken prisoner on the 1st of April, 1864. He was kept in captivity until after the close of the war, during which time he was in seven different Northern prisons. He took an active part in many important engagements and at all times displayed great faithfulness to the cause he espoused, and undaunted courage. After the termination of the war he returned to Jefferson county to once more resume the duties of a civilian's life and as a means of livelihood took up the occupation of farming, a calling he followed for a number of years. He spent the year of 1867 in Bolivar county, but in 1878 he moved to Natchez, where he clerked for several years. From that city he removed to Harriston in 1883, locating on land where the town is situated, he being one of the very first settlers of the region. He erected the first storehouse in the place. In 1885 he unfortunately lost his buildings by fire, but he soon after erected his present hotel building and has since given his time and attention to the livery business and to keeping a first-class hotel, the latter being situated near the depot and commanding a large patronage from the traveling public. When the town was incorporated in 1885 Mr. Lowe was elected the first mayor, and while serving in this capacity showed that he had the interests of the town deeply at heart. When in his twenty-first year he was married in this county to Miss Jane Pearcefield, who was then in her sixteenth year, a daughter of James B. Pearcefield, who was a native of the state of Kentucky. Mrs. Lowe was born and reared in Jefferson county and has borne her husband one son: James M., Jr., who is now a young man of eighteen years. Mr. Lowe is a Royal Arch mason, a member of the Knights of Honor and approves of the majority of secret organizations. As a business man he possesses ability of a high order, and as a landlord is hospitable, courteous and obliging, his guests receiving the kindest attention at his hands.

Lowrey and Berry. Gen. M. P. Lowrey was born in McNairy county, Tenn., December 29, 1828. His father died when he was a child. As the son of a poor widow he worked very hard in his boyhood and had no school advantages. At nineteen he went with a company of Mississippi volunteers to the Mexican war, but reached Mexico only a short time before the war closed. On his return from Mexico he learned the trade of a brickmason. At twenty-one he was married to Sarah R. Holmes, of Tishomingo county, Miss. Having made a profession of religion at seventeen, at twenty-four he entered the Baptist ministry. He gave himself earnestly to private study and soon became known as a young preacher of unusual promise. When the war of the secession came on he was pastor of the Baptist church at Kossuth, Miss. Early in the contest a company of volunteers was made up from his neighbors and church members and he was elected captain. He then enlisted in the Confederate service and was soon afterward made colonel of the Thirty-second Mississippi regiment. He was noted for his bravery on the field and for his good judgment everywhere. His soldiers loved him devotedly and would follow him anywhere. At the battle of Perryville, Ky., he commanded Wood's brigade, and attracted special attention by his gallant leadership. Here he received a severe flesh wound in his left arm which disabled him for some weeks, but which was the only wound he ever received. At the battle of Chickamauga he again commanded Wood's brigade, and after this battle General Cleburne pronounced him "the bravest man in the Confederate army." After this battle he was made a brigadier-general, and Lowrey's brigade could always be depended on. He frequently commanded a division and always acquitted himself with credit. Notwithstanding the fact that he was a military officer he did a great deal of preaching. After the war he was heard to say that he thought he did as much good preaching during the years of his soldier life as during any other equal number of years. When he returned from the war he was honored throughout the South, and especially throughout Mississippi. He returned to his work as a preacher. He had a family of nine children and nothing on which to support or educate them. He bought a small farm on credit and by wise management soon paid it out. He was made state evangelist, and held meetings in many parts of the state, reorganizing the churches and encouraging the people. During his absence from home the affairs of the farm and family were managed by his wise and noble wife. He was frequently urged to enter the arena of politics, but he always refused. At one time he was urged to run for governor, at another for congress, and at another for the United States senate, but he was steadfast in his purpose and continued his work as a preacher. For seven years he was editor of the Mississippi

department of *The Baptist*, published by the Rev. J. R. Graves, D. D., of Memphis, Tenn.
He stood very high as a writer on religious subjects, and his services were sought by a number of religious papers.   In 1873 he founded the Blue Mountain Female institute, which
was chartered in 1877 as Blue Mountain Female college, and which is now one of the most
prosperous female schools in the South.   He was president of this institution for twelve
years.   He was also for ten years in succession elected president of the Mississippi Baptist
state convention.   On February 27, 1885, he dropped dead in the depot at Middleton, Tenn.
His last will and testament, written shortly before his death, closed with the following
words: "I subscribe myself the friend of all humanity and the humble servant of the Lord
Jesus Christ."   Mrs. Sarah Holmes Lowrey was born in McNairy county, Tenn., in 1828.
Her educational advantages were limited, but she was a young woman of great good sense. At
twenty-one years of age she was married to M. P. Lowrey.   General Lowrey was often heard
to say that half his success in life was due to his wife.   She has reared six sons and five
daughters, all of whom are still living, well educated, prosperous and influential.   She has
always been noted for wisdom, patience, industry, strong Christian character.   At sixty-five
years of age she is still healthy and full of energy.   Her distinguished husband had great
confidence in her judgment.   He was heard to say late in his life that he had never departed
from her advice without afterward coming to see that she was right.   Upon his death he
left his property all to her, subject to her disposal.   During the war she was as brave at
home as he was on the battlefield, and as much respected by her children as he was by his
soldiers.   Mrs. Modena Lowrey Berry, eldest daughter of Gen. M. P. Lowrey, graduated at
sixteen from Stonewall college, Ripley, Miss.; taught several years at the Baptist Female
seminary, Pontotoc, Miss.; for the last eighteen years she has been lady principal of Blue
Mountain Female college; married, 1877, to Rev. W. E. Berry, A. M.   Mrs. Maggie Lowrey
Anderson, second daughter of Gen. M. P. Lowrey, graduated from the Baptist Female seminary, Pontotoc, Miss., in 1873; married in 1875 to Rev. J. D. Anderson, A. M.   Mrs. Janie
Lowrey Graves, third daughter of Gen. M. P. Lowrey, graduated from Blue Mountain
Female college in 1875; married 1876 to Rev. John W. Sanford, A. B., who died one year later;
teacher in Blue Mountain Female college 1877 to 1881.   In 1881 went to San Francisco as a
missionary to the Chinese; in 1887 went as a missionary to Canton, China; in 1890 married to
Rev. R. H. Graves, D. D., of Canton, China.   Mrs. Linnie Lowrey Ray, fourth daughter of Gen.
M. P. Lowrey, graduated from Blue Mountain Female college in 1878; married to Rev. L. T.
Ray, 1881, who died in 1885; teacher of music for the past six years in Blue Mountain Female
college.   Rev. W. T. Lowrey, A. M., D. D., educator and Baptist minister, eldest son of Gen. M.
P. Lowrey, born 1858; worked on farm until sixteen; attended Blue Mountain Male academy
two years; graduated from Mississippi college, Clinton, Miss., in 1881; attended Southern
Baptist Theological seminary, Louisville, Ky., from 1881 to 1885; accepted presidency of
Blue Mountain Female college in 1885, Blue Mountain, Tippah county, Miss., where his
labors for six years past have been attended with great success; married in 1886 to Miss Theodosia Searcy, daughter of Rev. J. B. Searcy, D. D., of Arkansas.   Mark Booth Lowrey, son
of Gen. M. P. Lowrey; born 1860; educated at Blue Mountain Male academy and Mississippi college; studied law, but did not like the practice; traveling salesman for F. M. Swift
& Co., tobacconists, Memphis, Tenn.; married, 1885, to Miss Pattie Lowry, Forest, Miss.
Perrin Holmes Lowrey, lawyer at Batesville, Miss., son of Gen. M. P. Lowrey; born 1860; graduated from Mississippi college, 1882; has been editor of Batesville *Panolian*; chairman of
democratic executive committee of Panola county; married, 1886, to Miss Lee Stokes, Canton,
Miss.   B. G. Lowrey, A. M., professor of English in Blue Mountain Female college; son of

Gen. M. P. Lowrey; born 1862; graduated from Mississippi college, 1886; taught one year at Pittsboro, Miss.; took special course in English language and literature in Tulane university, New Orleans; married, 1888, to Miss Marylee Booth, Montgomery county, Miss. T. C. Lowrey, B. S., secretary and treasurer of Atlantic Germateur Co., Atlanta, Ga., son of Gen. M. P. Lowrey; born in 1862; graduated from Mississippi college in 1887; unmarried. Joe Johnson Lowrey, cotton buyer, with Carter & Co., Meridian, Miss., son of Gen. M. P. Lowrey; born, 1867; educated at Blue Mountain Male academy and Lexington Commercial college, Kentucky; unmarried. Sallie Leavell Lowrey, youngest daughter of Gen. M. P. Lowrey; born, 1874; student in Blue Mountain Female college.

That eminent Baptist deacon, Joel H. Berry, was born in South Carolina in February, 1807, and died at Baldwyn, Miss., March 15, 1875. In consequence of poverty in his early life his educational advantages were very poor. He had a thirst for knowledge while quite young, and availed himself of every opportunity for study. By the brilliant light of pine knots, gathered during the day, he would study until late at night. When shut in by bad weather, or otherwise hindered from outdoor work, his book was his companion. He studied English grammar without a teacher. Frequently while plowing he would carry his book to the field and parse some sentence or master some principle of grammar while holding the handles of the plow. By this means he acquired a fair English education, without the advantages of even an academic course. He served two terms in the legislature of his native state, and at once took high rank as a young politician in the palmy days of South Carolina. In his boyhood he professed faith in Christ and joined the Baptist church. He began an active Christian life that lasted over a period of fifty years. In his church he was looked upon as a leader. Wise, prudent and aggressive, he won the esteem of others, who delighted to follow his leadership. He moved to Tippah county, Miss., in 1843 and opened up a farm, surrounded by the conveniences of a farm life. When agriculture was at the highest stage in this country he took the $25 premium offered by the agricultural society of Tippah county for the best managed farm. As a politician he was prominent. He spent four years as legis- lator, and eight years as senator, in the general assembly of the state of Mississippi. He was a member of the convention when his state seceded from the Union in January, 1861. As a Baptist he was recognized as a leader in all denominational and church work. For twenty-five years he was chairman of the executive board of the Chickasaw Baptist associa- tion, which is considered the mother of associations in northern Mississippi. Although almost completely broken up by the war, he was able to give his children a liberal education, all of whom are active Christians and doing good work for the cause of Christ. His eldest daughter, Mrs. M. L. Leavell, has been for years the corresponding secretary of woman's work of Mississippi. She is the wife of Prof. R. M. Leavell, late professor of English in Mississippi college, now a member of the faculty of the state university at Oxford, Miss. His second daughter is the wife of Dr. J. E. Buchanan, a prominent Baptist preacher in Texas. His youngest daughter was for a number of years principal of the art department of Blue Mountain female college, now the accomplished wife of a prosperous farmer near Baldwyn, Miss. His youngest son died in early manhood. The two surviving sons are Baptist ministers with hands and hearts full of the work. Rev. J. S. Berry, the eldest son of J. H. Berry, was born December, 1844. He united with the Baptist church at Fellowship, Tippah county, Miss., when a boy, and was then active in all the church work. He moved from Tippah county to Baldwyn, Miss., where he married Miss Maggie Walker, and entered business as a merchant. In 1874 he gave up his business and entered the gospel ministry. He spent one term at the Southern Baptist theological seminary at Greenville, S. C., was ordained in 1875 and took the pastoral care of churches. He soon developed into an earnest, practical preacher of the gospel, and popular pastor of churches. He is now connected with Prof. W. I. Gibson in the high school at Booneville, Miss. Rev. W. E. Berry is the second son of J. H. Berry. He was born January, 1847. When but a boy he professed faith in Christ, and united with the Baptist church at Fellowship, Tippah county, Miss. By this church he was liberated to preach in 1871. He soon afterward entered Mississippi college, and graduated from that institution in 1875. He spent the session of 1875–6 at the Southern Baptist theological seminary at Greenville, S. C. He was ordained to the full work of the ministry in July, 1875. In the summer of 1876 he was married to Miss Modena Lowrey, the eldest daughter of Gen. M. P. Lowrey. He bought an interest in Blue Mountain female college in Tippah county, Miss., the institution founded by Gen. M. P. Lowrey, and became associated with him in its management. In addition to his school work he has served as pastor of a few country churches. Among these is Fellowship, the church into which he was baptized when a boy. He has served this church for more than ten years, and is still its pastor. Since 1881 he has been chairman of the executive board of Tippah Baptist association, which position he still holds. He is now the business manager of Blue Mountain female college, one of the leading female colleges of the state of Mississippi. This sterling educational institution receives due attention in the historical department of this work.

Dr. M. J. Lowry has been absorbed in the anxieties and duties of the medical profession since 1879; his reputation as a skilled and experienced physician has gone abroad, and he is now in command of a lucrative practice. He was born in Yorkville, York district, S. C., January 9, 1857, a son of John T. and Martha (Bratton) Lowry, the latter being the granddaughter of Gen. William Bratton, of Revolutionary fame. The Lowrys are of Scotch-Irish descent, and the paternal grandfather, Thomas, was a successful planter. Dr. John S. Bratton, the maternal grandfather, was a graduate of the South Carolina Medical college, and afterward practiced his profession in York county, of that state. He was a large slave and land holder, and as a medical practitioner was skillful and successful. John T. Lowry also follows the peaceful pursuit of agriculture, and is still a resident of Yorkville, S. C. He was a member of the legislature of that state before the war, and during the struggle between the North and South he was a captain in the Confederate army. He is the owner of a large amount of real estate, and is now living at his ease, enjoying the fruits of a well-spent life. To himself and wife seven sons and two daughters were born, the following of whom are living: Robert B., a merchant of Yorkville, S. C.; Rev. Thomas M., of Augusta, Ga.; Dr. M. J., of Meridian; R. K., a planter of South Carolina; Eugene, of Macon, Ga., and Hattie B., who still resides with her parents in South Carolina. Dr. M. J. Lowry was educated in military institute of his native state, which, under the bent of his ambition, yielded him a fair knowledge of the classics and mathematics. In order to lay the foundation for a medical career, he began the study of that science at an early day, for his kindly nature instinctively turned to that broad field of human suffering for his life work—a profession whose noiseless, yet marvelous, triumphs are often unknown to the multitude. He entered the Hospital Medical college, of Louisville, Ky., from which institution he graduated in the spring of 1879, the same year coming to Meridian, Miss., where he entered upon the practice of his profession, and has become well known throughout the state, as well as the county in which he practices. He is a member of the state medical association, the state board of health, is one of the state sanitary commissioners for the fourth district, is a member and ex-president of the county medical association, and is ex-president of the city board of health.

Socially he is a member of the American Legion of Honor, and in his political views is a stanch democrat. He was married in November, 1885, to Miss Mary Harris, of Meridian, Miss., by whom he has one child: Hattie H. He and his wife are members of the Presbyterian church.

The great state of Mississippi, from her first advent into the Union, has had few abler men to preside in her executive chair than ex-Governor Robert Lowry, now of Jackson, Miss. He was born in Chesterfield district, S. C., March 10, 1831. His father, Robert Lowry, was born in South Carolina in 1806, and was from an old and prominent family of that state of Irish-Scotch ancestry. His grandfather, John Lowry, was at one time a member of the state senate. The elder Robert Lowry, who was a merchant by occupation, married Jemima Rushing, a native of North Carolina, and two of their six children are living: John A. and Robert. About the year 1833 they left South Carolina and settled in the western district of Tennessee, where for two years they were engaged in teaching school. In 1840 Mr. Lowry moved to Tishomingo county, Miss., and there engaged in mercantile pursuits and farming. His wife died in 1840, and he was married the second time to Sarah E. Llewellyn, and by her had six children, only one of whom is now living, being now the wife of James M. Arnold, ex-chief justice of Mississippi. Mr. Lowry died in 1880. Robert Lowry remained under the parental roof until he was about thirteen years of age, receiving his primary education at the old fieldschools. At this period he went to live with his uncle, Judge James Lowry, of Smith county, Miss. He was a merchant and served at one time as probate judge of Smith county. Young Robert entered the store of his uncle as clerk and barkeeper, remaining about four years, when he opened business on his own account at Raleigh. He carried on his mercantile business until 1851, when he removed to Brandon, Miss., and formed a partnership with his uncle James. This partnership continued for three years, when Mr. Lowry removed to Arkansas. While in that state, believing that there was a larger and higher field of usefulness than that which had heretofore engaged his attention, he began the study of law, and was subsequently admitted to the bar. He remained in Arkansas five years, when he returned to Mississippi and formed a law partnership with Judge A. G. Mayers (at present on the circuit bench) at Brandon. This partnership continued until the outbreak of the war, when Mr. Lowry enlisted to fight for the establishment of the Confederacy. He was placed in company B, sixth Mississippi, and upon the organization of that regiment at Grenada he was chosen major. The regiment was ordered to Bowling Green, Ky., so he subsequently moved back under Gen. Albert Sidney Johnston to take part in the battle of Shiloh, April 6 and 7, 1862, in Col. Pat Cleburne's brigade. In this fight Major Lowry acted as lieutenant-colonel and was wounded twice—once in the breast and once in the arm. He rejoined his regiment at Corinth, and upon its reorganization, Colonel Thornton having resigned, was elected colonel. He commanded the sixth division at the siege of Corinth, and distinguished himself for his gallantry and bravery. He was next engaged at Baker's creek, and then at Bayou Pierre. His regiment was with General Johnston in his Georgia campaign, and subsequently under General Hood in Tennessee, participating in nearly all the engagements of those commands. He rejoined General Johnston in North Carolina, and was with him at his capitulation at Greensboro, April 26, 1865. General Lowry possesses many qualities that make good soldiers and commanders. One of his striking characteristics is his perfect devotion to what he undertakes and his desire to discharge his whole duty. From a private he became, through the various gradations of military rank, a brigadier-general. Only true merit and that courage he so signally instanced in all the battles he was engaged in could have raised him to such high honors. He was prized by the officers of the army, and beloved by the soldiers, for whose comfort and protection he was ever careful.

Returning to his home with the lost cause for which he had so gallantly fought, the property he had accumulated by his industry before the war dissipated, he again took up his profession, and forming a partnership with his old friend, Judge Mayers, he resumed the practice of law. In the fall of 1865 he was placed in nomination by the democrat party for the state senate, and was elected. After serving one session he resigned and returned to his law practice, but was subsequently elected to the lower house, serving one term. During the radical regime, he canvassed the state several times in the interest of the democrat party, and was received with enthusiasm wherever he spoke. In 1878 he was before the democratic state convention as a candidate for the nomination of governor. There was a very exciting contest, and on the tenth ballot he was defeated by Governor Stone. In 1881 he again became a candidate for the nomination, which he received and was duly elected. In 1885 he was renominated, and practically unanimously elected. After serving eight years in the executive chair of the state he retired from official life and again resumed his law practice. Governor Lowry's administration was very popular with the people and justly so, for it was economical, able, effective and honest. He entered upon his duties with his wonted zeal and conscientious desire to do his duty. His administration was eminently successful and satisfactory during his long years of service, and he did much toward the advancement and prosperity of the people. He assisted by Colonel McCargle, has been engaged for some time on a work to be entitled the "History of Mississippi," the manuscript of which is about ready for the press. This work begins with the earliest settlement of the territory now embraced by the state of Mississippi, and comes down to the present time. The Governor, by his long residence in the state, by his thorough acquaintance with its political history and its leading men, by his habits of study and close observation, is well very qualified for a work of this nature. His co-worker, Colonel McCargle, is also an able writer. It can be justly said in anticipation of this forthcoming book, that it will be a valuable acquisition to the literature of Mississippi. In person, Governor Lowry is of medium stature, solid and well-proportioned, with an elastic and easy carriage. He has a well-developed head, covered with a liberal growth of light brown hair, beneath which is a broad, intellectual brow. His eyes are blue, clear, full and expressive, his nose is aquiline, and his mouth and chin denote firmness and decision of character. Except a mustache, his face is cleanly shaven. His bearing is dignified, yet cordial, and in disposition he is generous and charitable. This, with a neat attire, makes the tout-ensemble of one of the most popular men of the state. Governor Lowry was united in marriage in 1851 to Maria M., daughter of B. V. Gammage, a prominent citizen of Jasper county, Miss. The issue of his marriage was eleven children: Eudora, wife of William Henry, present mayor of Jackson; Mary G., wife of H. H. Batti; Ela M., wife of George A· Lamb; Ada M., wife of Dr. J. W. Ellis; Rose, wife of Robert E. Wilson, of Jackson; Lela B., wife of J. M. Jayne, a member of the state senate from Greenville; Robert, a physician residing in Washington; Patrick H.; Belle M., wife of J. L. Harris, an attorney of Texas; John W. and Maria. Governor Lowry is a member of the Masonic fraternity. Shortly after the war he was commissioned by the governor of the state of Mississippi to visit President Johnson for the purpose of securing the release of Jefferson Davis, but he was unsuccessful in his mission.

The prominent dry goods establishment of Lusk & Buckley was founded on the 1st of September, 1888, by Messrs. Lusk, Buckley and Boyd, and the style of the firm continued to be Lusk, Buckley & Boyd until July, 1890, when Mr. Boyd retired from the firm, and it has since been Lusk & Buckley. They occupy spacious quarters, fitted up with every convenience calculated to facilitate the operations of the business, and carry a stock of goods valued at about $40,000, which includes the better class of staple dry goods, notions and millinery.

John Powell

Throughout, the business history of the house has been conducted upon reliable and liberal methods, which, combined with the superior quality of the stock, have secured for the firm the confidence and patronage of a large and constantly increasing circle of customers. Although the gentlemen composing the firm are men young in years, yet they are experienced and competent, and are recognized as among the most successful merchants of Jackson, which fact has been the means of inducing other young and ambitious men to enter the business arena in Jackson. James Lusk has been a resident of Jackson since his birth, in 1862, being the ninth in a family of ten children born to Pickett W. and Frances (Anderson) Lusk, who were born in Louisiana and Kentucky respectively. In youth, Pickett W. Lusk removed to Mississippi, located in Hinds county, where he devoted the most of his life to the calling of a planter, being, at the same time, a builder in Jackson and other places throughout the county. He died in 1880 at the age of seventy-three years. His widow survives him, being a worthy member of the Methodist Episcopal church. Her father was a well-to-do planter in the southwestern part of the state of Kentucky. Her union with Mr. Lusk resulted in the birth of the following children: Conrad A., a resident of Jackson; Allan P., hotel inspector for the Santa Fe railroad, with headquarters at Kansas City; Pickett W., who is in the railroad service, and is a conductor on the Mobile & Ohio railroad; James, Cornelia, Celeste, Fannie and Alice, living; and Hugh, who served in the Confederate army with the army of Virginia, and died at the age of twenty-one years, at the close of the war, and Henry Clay, who also served in the Confederate army, and died soon after, are the deceased members of the family. James Lusk was educated in Jackson by his own efforts. At the age of fifteen years he began life as a clerk in Jackson, and for eight years, or until he started in business for himself, he was with Robinson & Stevens.

James M. Buckley, of the above-mentioned firm, was born in Lawrence county, Miss., in 1866, the fourth in a family of six children born to the marriage of James M. Buckley and Bethany Craft, both of whom were native Mississippians. The paternal grandfather, who also bore the name of James M., was a Tennesseean by birth, but was among the pioneers of Lawrence county, Miss., and became one of the successful planters of his time. He died in Lawrence county. The maternal grandfather, James Craft, was born in Tennessee, but afterward became a successful planter of Pike county, Miss., perhaps the richest one in that county, both before and after the war. He was also engaged in merchandising on his plantation, and there he quietly breathed his last in 1882. James M. Buckley, the father of the subject of this sketch, was reared on a plantation, and after becoming sufficiently posted, began teaching school. For a number of years he was chancery clerk of Lincoln and Lawrence counties, and from 1879 to 1883 he was deputy auditor of the state. He was called from life in January, 1884, at which time he was a member of the A. F. & A. M. and the K. of H. fraternities. His widow, who survives him, bore him the following children: Marion, wife of A. H. Longino, a lawyer of Greenwood; Benjamin; Elizabeth, wife of Edgar Wilson, editor of *The Mississippian*; James M., and Annie and Gay, intelligent and accomplished young ladies. James M. Buckley was educated in Jackson, mainly by his own efforts, and in 1884 began the battle of life for himself as a clerk. In 1888 he assisted in founding the above-mentioned mercantile house, of which he is an active and useful member.

The mercantile house of which Thomas C. Lyle is the proprietor in Lauderdale, Miss., was established in 1866, and since that time has established itself firmly in the estimation of the public. Mr. Lyle was born in Jefferson county, Tenn., in February, 1842, the sixth of eleven children born to Caiborn and Mary (Cannon) Lyle, the former a South Carolinian and the latter a native of Tennessee. Mr. Lyle removed to Tennessee with his parents when a

73

small boy, and there grew to manhood and married. He was a farmer and stockraiser by calling and lived in the home of his adoption until his death in 1865, his widow surviving him until 1890. She was a member of the Methodist Episcopal church. The following are their children who are living: Jennie, wife of Thomas Lockhart; Nannie, wife of E. L. Moore; Mary, wife of W. P. Bradshaw; Fannie, wife of J. T. Johnson; John M., William A. and Thomas C. The latter began to make his own way in the world at the age of seventeen years and enlisted in company C of the Thirty-first Tennessee infantry, and was in the battles of Tazewell, Tenn, Harrodsburg, Ky., and Vicksburg, where he was captured, exchanged and went back to Tennessee. He was in the fight at Staunton, Va., Martinsburg, Hagerstown, Harrisonburg and various other engagements of minor importance. He was third lieutenant of his company from 1863 until the close of the war, surrendered at Abbeville, S. C., and was paroled at Macon, Miss. He remained at this place engaged in buying cotton until April, 1866, when he engaged in his present business in Lauderdale. In connection with his mercantile operations he has been engaged in buying and shipping cotton, handling fifteen hundred bales annually. He is a thorough and competent business man, and is now the owner of some fine and valuable property in Lauderdale, among which is a handsome residence and good business property. He is of the stuff of which honorable citizens are made, and socially is a member of the K. of H., the K. and L. of H., and since 1873 has been a member of the A. F. & A. M. Although he has been interested in local politics he has never aspired to office. He was married in 1868 to Miss Josephine Hitt, a daughter of J. M. Hitt, of Gainesville, Ala. To their union one son and three daughters have been born: Katie, Lizzie (who died at the age of thirteen years), Louise and T. C.

James D. Lynch is a well-known author, residing at West Point. He was born in Mecklenburg county, Va., January 6, 1836, and received his education at the University of North Carolina. Upon completing his education he began teaching school in Columbus and West Point, Miss., a calling he successfully followed from 1859 to 1862. He then enlisted in the Confederate army and raised a company of cavalry, which was placed under General Polk, and of which he was chosen captain. He was wounded at Lafayette, Ga., and was subsequenty captured while making a charge near Rome, but made his escape at Resaca and rejoined his command. At the time of the surrender he was in charge of the stores of the nitre and mining department of General Johnston's army. After the war was over he began the practice of law at West Point, Miss, but abandoned this calling to follow the more congenial pursuit of literature. He is gifted with much poetic talent and some of the most meritorious of his poems are: "The Siege of the Alamo," "The Clock of Destiny," "The Divided Pension" and "The Star of Texas." His best known works in prose are: "Kemper County Vindicated," which was published in New York in 1878; "Bench and Bar of Mississippi," published in 1881; "Bench and Bar of Texas," published in 1885; and he now has in progress an "Industrial History of Texas." He had been a life-long democrat of the most pronounced kind, but finally took strong grounds for the free exercise of all rights conferred by the constitution; in consequence of which he was without solicitation nominated for lieutenant-governor of Mississippi on the republican ticket in 1889, and is well known throughout the state. In June, 1891, he was appointed a member of the national executive committee of the people's party, a position he now holds. He possesses intelligence of a high order, and his brilliant and well poised mind has been broadened and strengthened by the highest culture. He is of a genial and affable disposition, and is courteous, generous and hospitable. His beautiful and attractive home at West Point is the abode of culture and refinement, and the hospitality that is displayed there is truehearted, yet unostentatious.

GHAPTER XXV.

≑≈⊗≈≑

PERSONAL HISTORY, Mc.

POSSESSED of a roving spirit, at the age of eleven years, Duncan P. McAllum, attorney-at-law, De Kalb, Miss., ran away from home, and came to Mississippi. He was born in the state of North Carolina in 1815, and died in Kemper county, Miss., July 10, 1864. He received his education in Sumter county, Ala., and taught school for a time. It was not until he was twenty-four years of age that he entered the practice of law. He was married in Kemper county, Miss., to Martha Porter, a daughter of Jesse Porter. She was born in North Carolina in 1828, and removed to this county with her parents in 1835. Her father was a wealthy planter, and at the time of his death owned the largest plantation in the county. She is still living and makes her home with two sons in De Kalb. Five children were born to Mr. and Mrs. McAllum; Frances M., now Mrs. Ellis; Edward M., a planter, living in De Kalb; William S., a traveling salesman; Carrie, who married D. P. McClain, and Calvin D. The last named is a general merchant of De Kalb, and has been established there since 1881. He is a democrat in his politics, and has served as postmaster of De Kalb. He owns about eight hundred acres of land in Kemper county, the cultivation of which he superintends. The family are members of the Baptist church. During the war Duncan P. McAllum was quartermaster, and was an able, conscientious official. He filled this office acceptably until he was taken ill in 1864. He then abandoned the service, returned to his home in hope of regaining his strength. But this was not to be. He passed away to the other life, mourned by his family and a wide circle of acquaintances.

Among the representative and esteemed citizens of Jefferson county, Miss., there is probably no man more deserving of honorable mention than John D. McArn, a man whose residence within the borders of the county has extended over the entire period of his life. for here he was born in the month of April, 1852. His father, Duncan McArn, was a North Carolinian, and grew to mature years in his native state, but when a young man, or about 1840, he emigrated to Mississippi and engaged in teaching school in Franklin county, a calling he followed with success for several years. About five years later he settled on the farm on which John D. McArn is now residing, which place he opened up and improved by erecting good buildings thereon, and here reared his family. He was married in this county to Miss Catherine Torrey, a sister of John Torrey, a sketch of whom appears in this work. His relations with his fellow citizens were always honorable, and as he was one of the foremost pioneers of the county. His death, which occurred in February, 1875, was keenly felt. His record as a private citizen was untarnished, and in all the affairs of life he bore himself in an upright manner and was recognized as a man of true worth. He was an elder in the

Presbyterian church, was interested in all church work, and was liberal in his contributions to that, as well as to all worthy enterprises. His wife died in 1885, having been a worthy, intelligent and kindly lady. J. D. McArn is the second son of a family of three children, the other members of the family being Dr. William T. McArn, who was educated in the city of New Orleans, and practiced his profession in Jefferson county until his death, which occurred in 1874, and Anna, who is the wife of John A. Dicks, of Natchez, Miss. John D. McArn remained with his parents on the farm until he entered Oakland and Oxford colleges, but before he had completed his course he was obliged to leave school on account of ill health, a fact he regretted very much, for he was fully aware of the value of a good education. He once more resumed farming with his father, and on the home plantation he is still residing. He has added to its former broad acres, and now has land to the amount of thirteen hundred acres, the home place consisting of ten hundred, of which about two hundred acres are cleared land. His residence is a commodious and substantial one, his buildings are all in good repair, and his cottongin is an excellent one and nets him a handsome annual income. He is one of the thrifty agriculturists of Jefferson county, and this assertion is fully testified in looking over his possessions, for every end of his work is kept up, and nothing is uselessly wasted. His marriage, which occurred in February, 1877, was to Miss Lizzie Wilkinson, a daughter of Daniel M. Wilkinson. Mrs. McArn was born and reared at Jackson, and was educated at Oxford, Miss., being an exceptionally talented and accomplished lady. She has borne her husband one son and nine daughters: Mary, Emma and Anna (twins), Willie Sue, Lizzie, Margaret, Duncan, Effie and Aline (twins) and an infant daughter. Mr. McArn and his estimable wife are members of the Presbyterian church, and are classed among the public-spirited citizens of the county. M. McArn is a representative man in every sense of the word, is energetic and enterprising, and his reputation for honesty and integrity have been tried and not found wanting, his social qualities are well known and appreciated, and he has hosts of warm friends. His residence is located near the Fayette and Union church road and here he and Mrs. McArn dispense hospitality with true Southern grace.

In connection with his planting industry, Hon. John C. McBeath is also engaged in milling and is the owner of a first-class saw, gin and grist mill near his residence. He was born in Macon county, Ala., in 1832 and came to Mississippi with his parents when twenty years of age. He there followed planting until the breaking out of the war and in July, 1861, he enlisted in the Confederate army. He was captured at Franklin, Tenn., and sent to Johnson's island, where he was detained until cessation of the hostilities. He was in the battle of Chickamauga and many of the severest engagements of the war and at its close he returned home. In 1866 he was wedded to Miss Nancy E. Brantley, daughter of Harris Brantley, who came here at an early day from Georgia, and immediately after his marriage Mr. McBeath began planting. In 1878 he bought the plantation where he now lives, consisting of one thousand acres, and in connection with this he is actively engaged in milling, operating a fine saw, gin and grist mill. In politics he was formerly an old line whig, but since the war he has been an active member of the democratic party. He served a number of years as a member of the police board and in 1881 he was elected to represent the county in the legislature, a position he held but one term, refusing reëlection. He is a leading citizen and business man, and he and wife are both well known and respected for their many estimable qualities. He is wholesouled and liberal, his hospitality amounting almost to prodigality. He is connected with the Masonic fraternity, and is a member of the Missionary Baptist church. His father, John C. McBeath, Sr., was born in North Carolina about 1790 and served in the Black Hawk war. He grew to manhood is his native state and was married there to our subject's mother, Miss Jannie Wadsworth. They afterward moved to Mississippi and located on the line of Leake and Neshoba, where he received his final summons after living an active and useful life.

Prof. Thomas F. McBeath. This well-known educator and president of the Cooper Normal college, was born on the 9th of December, 1852, the eldest child born to Robert C. and Sarepta C. (Fleming) McBeath, both of whom were born on Blue Grass soil. The father was engaged in teaching school for a livelihood the greater part of his life, and was a well-informed, intelligent and upright gentleman in every worthy particular. He died at Daleville, Miss., in 1891, his wife, who was a worthy member of the Christian church, having passed from life in Kentucky in 1870. Four of their children are living at the present time: Thomas F.; John T., a merchant at Guthrie, was for a number of years superintendent of the schools of Casey county, Ky.; Theodore J. is the principal of the Plattsburg Normal school, of Mississippi; and J. Mark, superintendent of the schools of Lauderdale county, Miss. Prof. Thomas F. McBeath was educated in the Southern Normal school, of Glasgow, Ky., from which well-conducted institution he graduated in 1882. Upon finishing his education he chose the life calling of a teacher and took charge of the English Sermon school, of Cuero, Tex., where he remained until elected to the chair of natural science in the school at Glasgow, Ky. (his former alma mater), which position he capably filled for four years. He was then called to Water Valley, Miss., at which place he was superintendent of the city schools for one year. He then resigned this position and accepted the principalship of the Cooper Normal college, at Daleville, Miss., where he is at present engaged in conducting one of the most prosperous institutions of the kind in the South, which bids fair to attain a wide-spread reputation. Under the able and well-directed efforts of Professor McBeath the school has attained an enrollment of two hundred pupils—forty young ladies, necessitating the erection of a handsome $2,000 structure for their accommodation. A full corps of trained and experienced teachers are employed, superior boarding accommodations can be had at the lowest rates; there is a normal department for the training of teachers in the science and art of teaching. The buildings are all new, well equipped and tastefully furnished and finished throughout, and a well-selected library of five thousand is at the disposal of the pupils. Every endeavor has been made to make the school a strictly first-class one, and a gentle but firm and strict discipline is maintained, appealing ever to the higher motives, the cultivation of which makes a strong and noble man and womanhood. The school was established in 1865 for the coeducation of young men and women, and comprises full literary, pedagogic, music and art courses. The location of the college is both healthful and beautiful, and the board of trustees competent and trustworthy. They are as follows: Rev. J. G. Boydstun, Judge M. H. Whitaker and S. A. Witherspoon, of Meridian; C. W. Cochran and J. L. McWilliams, of Daleville; Hon. Andrew Cooper, of Cushtusha, and Capt. W. A. Herring, of Water Valley. Professor McBeath was married in Gainesville, Ala., in March, 1890, to Miss Omeree Thomas, daughter of Dr. G. P. Thomas. He is a member of the Christian church, and his wife is a member of the Methodist Episcopal church. As an educator and disciplinarian the Professor ranks among the first of the state, and his work in the past speaks for his success in the future.

The profession of medicine has attracted to its center many good and noble men, and among them appears the name of John A. McBride, who has been prominently identified with the history of Carroll county since he entered upon his professional career. He was born in the county September 29, 1856, and is a son of J. A. McBride, a native of South Carolina. The father received a liberal education and was married to Mary Jane Haslett, a native also of South Carolina, and a daughter of George Haslett. He removed to Mississippi in 1830 and spent the first year in Tippah county, and in the following year he came to Carroll county. He engaged in planting, and accumulated considerable property which was swept away by the war. Before his death, however, he succeeded in amassing a comfortable fortune. He died in 1885. Mrs. McBride passed away in 1861. Mr. McBride was a soldier in the late war, and served until the surrender. John A. McBride is one of a family of three sons and two daughters: Andrew N. was wounded in the battle of Shiloh, and died from the effects of the wound; William W. resides on the old homestead. The Doctor grew to man's estate in Carroll county; he received his education in Roanoke college, Va., completing the course in 1875. He then began the study of medicine, taking his first course of lectures in the University of Virginia; his second course was taken at the University of Louisiana, from which institution he was graduated in March, 1878. He entered upon the practice of his profession near the old homestead, and remained there about eleven years; he then came to Carrollton, in December, 1888. At the time he purchased an established drug business, which he continues in connection with his professional work. He has won a large patronage in both lines, and has endeared himself to great numbers of suffering humanity.

Dr. McBride was united in marriage in Carroll county, January 29, 1879, to Miss Minnie Hamilton, a native of the same county, and a daughter of John Hamilton. Two daughters have been born of this union: Irene and Rosa. The Doctor and his wife are members of the Presbyterian church, where their labors are much appreciated. Dr. McBride is a member of the county board of health, and for a number of years was on the town board. He is a man interested in the public welfare, and while he pays strict attention to his private affairs, he shirks no duties as a loyal citizen.

Charles McCafferty, one of the most prominent farmers of Choctaw county, owes his nativity to Union district, S. C., his birth occurring in 1833. As his father died when Charles was but a small boy, the latter had no recollection of him, but his mother, Ellen McCafferty, removed to Pickens county, Ala., when he was yet very small, and there married Robert Huddleston. In 1848 the family moved to Choctaw county, and the next year settled in the woods on the property now owned by our subject, where the mother died in 1871. Mr. Huddleston afterward removed to Arkansas and there his life terminated. Charles McCafferty had but one brother, Ewing, who also became a wealthy planter of Choctaw county. He died in 1882, leaving a family of children. He was all through the war in the Fourth Mississippi infantry, until after the capture of Fort Donelson, when he served about a year in a Tennessee command, after which he was transferred to the First Mississippi cavalry, serving with General Forrest until his surrender at Selma, Ala. Charles McCafferty was reared on a farm, and for some years, when but a boy, was the main support of his mother. He received a fair English education, principally in Alabama, and spent two years in school after coming to Mississippi. He soon became very familiar with that part of Mississippi, and spent three years engaged in teaming to Yazoo City, Canton, Columbus, and other distant points, and became inured to the hardships of pioneer life, although he there laid the foundation for his subsequent prosperous career. Miss Mary Johnson, who became his wife in 1853, was born in Choctaw county, and was the daughter of J. T. Johnson, who removed from South Carolina to Pickens county, Ala., at a very early day. Later he came to Choctaw county, remained there a number of years, and then removed to Arkansas, where his death occurred. Mrs. McCafferty died in 1855, leaving one son, who is also deceased. In 1858 Mr. McCafferty married Miss Nancy L. Stacy, a native of Bibb county, Ala., and the daughter of Isom and Catherine Stacy, natives of South

Carolina. From there her parents removed to Bibb county, Ala., and about 1856 they came to Choctaw county, where they both died. Both were members of the Baptist church, and he was a planter by occupation. By the second union Mr. McCafferty became the father of eleven children, seven now living, viz.: Arie E., wife of Samuel C. Riddle; Lucretia E., wife of H. E. Reed; Charles C., Boyd, Vera, Lillie May and Alice. In 1862 Mr. McCafferty joined company A, First Mississippi cavalry and served as corporal in the Tennessee army, the first year on detached service around Vicksburg. He was all through the Georgia and Atlanta campaigns on detached service, and was then at Franklin and Nashville. He was in Armstrong's brigade of General Forrest's division, and surrendered at Selma, Ala. Mr. McCafferty has been frequently urged to accept office while in the army, but preferred to remain a private. After the war he returned to his family, and has continued to reside on the old home place, being the owner of six hundred and sixty acres in different tracts, besides considerable property in Birmingham, Ala., all the fruits of his own energy and industry. He has always followed trading in stock, etc., and is considered a good business man in a general way. He has his farm in fine shape, and one glance over it, by the most careless observer shows that the owner is a progressive and thoroughgoing man. He raises stock and grain, and does not depend on cotton altogether. Although he started out with a limited education, he has excellent natural abilities, is a close observer, and reads a great deal of a local nature. He is quite an interesting conversationalist, and although small of stature he is capable of great endurance, and relates many interesting experiences during his teaming in early days. His family are all Methodists. He has been a Mason since twenty-one years of age, now of Snowsville lodge No. 119, at Ackerman, and once filled the office of secretary and also treasurer for some time.

Dr. John S. McCain, Lexington, is the son of Joseph McCain, who was born in Scotland and who came to the United States with his parents when a child, and with them settled in North Carolina. There he attained his growth, received his education, and was married to Miss Mary Scales, of English descent, and a daughter of Nathaniel Scales, who was born in the Old North state. Mr. McCain was a planter and merchant, and quite a trader and speculator. He died about 1830, and his widow afterward, or in 1845, moved with the family to Mississippi, locating in Tallahatchie county near Charleston. There she received her final summons in 1849. She was the mother of ten children, nine of whom grew to mature years—four sons and five daughters. Only our subject and one sister now survive. One brother, N. H., was a lawyer and resided in Columbus, where he practiced for some time; he died in Carroll county, Miss. Another brother, J. N., was educated for a physician, practiced in North Carolina, and there his death occurred. W. A. was a planter, and a resident of Carroll county. One sister, Ann, was the wife of Constantine Payne, a brother of Bishop Payne; she died in Tennessee. Mary became the wife of James W. Watts, of Alabama, and is deceased. Sallie N. became the wife of W. P. Gunn, of North Carolina, and died in Greenwood, Miss. C. E. married W. P. Gunn after the death of her sister, and is now a widow; Elizabeth was the wife of J. D. Moore, but is now deceased. Dr. McCain was born in Rockingham county, N. C., January 6, 1829, received a good education at Colwell institute and La Grange college, Alabama, and when eight years of age began the study of medicine in North Carolina. He took his first course at Philadelphia university in 1849 and '50, and then returned and graduated the following year. After that he came West to Mississippi, locating at Greenwood, and practiced his profession there for five years. He was through two sieges of yellow fever (1853 and '55), and in 1856 he moved to Lexington, where he has since continued his practice, a period of thirty-five years, except the time spent in the army.   In 1862 he enlisted in the Confederate service, was on hospital duty until the latter part of 1863, when he went to the field with the Sixty-sixth Georgia regiment as regimental physician, continuing as such until the close of the war.   He was paroled at Greensboro, N. C., in sight of the old college that he had formerly attended.   He then returned to Lexington, resumed his practice, but of late years has given up the practice to some extent.   The Doctor is a member of the state medical association.   He was married at Greenwood, on the 14th of December, 1852, to Miss S. F. Wheeless, a native of Tennessee and the daughter of Esquire Wheeless, a native also of that state.   She was educated at the Columbia institute, Tennessee, and is a lady of culture and learning.   Dr. and Mrs. McCain have two children, both sons: Walt married Miss Sallie B. Cole, of Lexington, and they have two children, viz.: Fannie C. and Harry.   The other son, Harry, is single, and is engaged in the drug business in Memphis, Tenn.   Dr. McCain joined the Masonic fraternity in 1852, and is a Master Mason.   He and family are members of the Presbyterian church, of which the Doctor is elder.

The following space will be devoted to John S. McCain, Carrollton, Miss., who is prominently identified with the present history of the county.   July 27, 1851, he was born in Carroll county, Miss., and is a son of William A. McCain, a native of North Carolina.   The father removed to Mississippi in 1848 and located in Tallahatchie county, and two years later he came to Carroll county, where he engaged in agricultural pursuits.   In 1863 he abandoned the plow and all that was dear to him and went to the defense of his country.   He enlisted in Captain Prince's company, but before he was introduced to active service he sickened and died.   He was a man of highest motives and, although occupying a modest position in life, he was highly esteemed by all with whom he came in contact.   He was an active worker in the Presbyterian church and belonged to the Masonic fraternity.   John S. (son of the above) received a good education, the last two years of his school life being spent in an academy in North Carolina.   At the end of his career as a student he came back to Carroll county and for several years was occupied with planting.   The capital which he had to invest when he started in business was not of the sort that is counted in gold and silver, but was that of nature's own giving.   But clear grit is bound to win and Mr. McCain has the satisfaction of knowing that whatever he has accomplished has been justly won through honest endeavor.   In his political views he has been allied with the democratic party and has taken active interest in local politics.   He has served as a member of the county board of supervisors for four years, and was president of that body for two years.   In 1889 the people of Carroll county attested their appreciation of his ability by calling him to the office of sheriff, and January 1, 1890, he began the discharge of his duties in this capacity.   He has made one of the best officials the county has ever had and has reflected great credit not only upon himself but also upon his constituency.   Mr. McCain was united in marriage, January 31, 1877, to Miss Lizzie Young, a daughter of Samuel Young.   Mrs. McCain was born, reared and educated in Carroll county.   By this union five children have been born: William A., Katie Lou, John Sidney, Mary and Jimmie.   The parents are both worthy members of the Presbyterian church and stand high in the community as intelligent, progressive citizens.

Dr. William C. McCaleb, physician and surgeon, residing on Oakley Grove plantation, nine miles northeast of Natchez, was born on Pine ridge, in Adams county, in 1833, and is the son of James F., and Sophia (Moore) McCaleb, the father a native of Adams county, Miss., born in 1812, and the mother born in Danville, Ky., in 1813.   James F. was attending school at Danville, Ky., when he met Miss Moore, whom he married about 1829.   They afterward settled in the Pine Ridge neighborhood, Adams county, Miss., and there Mrs. McCaleb died about 1845. Subsequently Mr. McCaleb married Miss Martha Bisland, a native of Adams county, who is still living on the old farm on Pine ridge. Mr. McCaleb was a well-to-do planter, raiser of mules and a thoroughgoing, enterprising citizen. He was an elder in the Pine Ridge Presbyterian church. He was one of four sons and three daughters, all now deceased. His father, John McCaleb, was born in Claiborne county, Miss., where he lived until about 1800, when he moved to Adams county, of that state. He first engaged in merchandising for some time, and afterward followed planting exclusively, becoming one of the leading planters of that county. He was educated as an engineer. His death occurred about 1826. His wife, whose maiden name was Mary Collins, was born in Adams county, and died in Kentucky while there for her health. Her father, William Collins, came from Ireland to North Carolina, and the latter part of the last century came to Adams county, settling in the Pine Ridge country, where he became a prominent planter. He left all his property to two daughters. Capt. William McCaleb, the great-grandfather of Dr. McCaleb, was a native of Maryland, where he married Caroline Calvert, who was also a native of Maryland. Mr. McCaleb was a captain in the Revolutionary war, and soon after that, about 1790, came to Claiborne county, Miss., where he was granted large tracts of land from the Spanish government. There he passed the closing scenes of his career. Lawson Moore, the Doctor's maternal grandfather, was born in the Old Dominion, but moved from there to Kentucky, settling in the woods where Danville now stands, and there he followed planting until his death. He was the father of sixteen children. Of the seven children born to his father's first marriage, Dr. McCaleb is the second in order of birth. The others are named as follows: Mary, wife of Dunbar McCaleb, of Fayette; James F. (deceased) was a member of Natchez Fencibles, and died at Bowling Green, Ky.; John M., of Vicksburg; Helen, wife of Dr. P. K. Whitney, of Fayette; Caroline (deceased) was the wife of P. Darden; and Jonathan. There were also these children by the last wife: Louisa W., deceased, was the wife of Thomas G. Dicks; Bisland; Sue, wife of Joseph Hatton; Lillie, wife of James Archer, of Jefferson county; Douglas L. and Samuel L. The Doctor was educated at Oakland college, and in 1856 graduated from the medical department of the university of Louisville, Ky., immediately afterward beginning to practice in Claiborne county. There he continued successfully until the breaking out of hostilities between the two sections, when he joined as a surgeon and served in different commands, principally with General Forrest, with whom he surrendered. He continued to practice in Claiborne county until 1878, and then removed to his present farm, consisting of three hundred acres. On the 1st of March, 1870, his nuptials with Miss Martha A. Harris, daughter of Levi C. and Lucy Harris, were celebrated. Mrs. McCaleb was born at Clinton, Miss., where her parents died, and she received her final summons in 1872. She left one daughter, Lucy A. The Doctor's second marriage was in 1875, to Miss Elizabeth, daughter of Aylette and Charlotte Buckner. Mr. Buckner was born in Virginia, went with his parents from there to Kentucky, and then, in 1832, came to Natchez, where he was a prominent attorney for a long time, returning just prior to the war. His death occurred about 1888. His wife was born where the Doctor now lives, and died about 1886. Mr. Buckner was the United States attorney for closing up the Mississippi state bonds of the Planters' bank. Mrs. McCaleb was born in Natchez, and is a granddaughter of Robert Dunbar, who came from Scotland to Maryland at an early date. He soon moved to Florida and other Southern states, and about 1789 he came to Natchez, where he lived for some time. After that he resided in Fort Rosalie, and about 1791 settled the Oakley Grove plantation, soon after building the house in which the Doctor now lives. He and wife both died on this farm, the former in 1823 and the latter the following year. Both were Episcopalians, and their remains were interred in the family buryingground. This farm has been in the possession of some of the family ever since. Dr. McCaleb has an extensive practice, and ranks high as a physician. He is genial, sociable, and has many friends. He is a prominent Mason, being a member of Pattona lodge No. 232, also of the council No. 7 at Port Gibson, and in 1868 he represented his lodge in the grand lodge held at Natchez. He and family are leading members of Pine Ridge Presbyterian church.

Patrick McCalebb, general merchant and proprietor of the McCalebb hotel of Scooba, Miss., was born in 1828 in North Carolina, son of James and Mary (Carbett) McCalebb. His father was also a native of North Carolina, where he was born in 1800, and reared in that state, coming to Mississippi in 1832. He located in this county and engaged in farming, dying in 1848. His wife was also a native of North Carolina, born there in 1805, and died in this county about 1878. Both Mr. McCalebb's parents were members of the Presbyterian church. The father was an Odd Fellow, and was a democrat in politics. They reared a family of seven children: Sarah, Toomar, Patrick, Lycurgus, Margaret, Calvin and Mary. Mr. McCalebb passed his boyhood and school days in this county. At the age of twenty he engaged in the mercantile business, which he has continued until this time. He was married in 1860 to Mrs. Isabella Stewart, widow of Joseph Stewart, formerly Miss Isabella Adams, a daughter of Archibald Adams and his wife, who was Winifred Avery. Mrs. McCalebb's parents were natives of North Carolina, and came to this county at an early date. To Mr. and Mrs. McCalebb have been born two children: Anna B. and Mary W.; the former is the wife of J. C. Carothers, while Mary married J. F. Howell. Mr. McCalebb is a democrat in politics, and has been justice of the peace for four years. He is interested in all things having a tendency to the general improvement of the county, especially in churches and schools. In 1862 he enlisted at Scooba in a company commanded by Captain Jack, and served until discharged in 1865. Both he and his wife are members of the Presbyterian church.

Nowhere within the limits of Jefferson county, Miss., can there be found a man who takes greater interest in its agricultural and stock affairs than Andrew M. McCallum, or who strives more continually to promote and advance these interests. Like so many native-born residents of Mississippi, he is energetic and enterprising, and by his own good management and industry has become the owner of a fine plantation of four hundred and forty acres, of which one hundred and sixty acres are under cultivation. He was born in Marshall county on the 31st of August, 1843, his father, Rev. Angus McCallum, being of Scotch ancestry, a native of North Carolina, his birth occurring on the 7th of October, 1801. He was a man of brilliant mind, was highly cultured, being a graduate of Hampden Sidney college. He early united with the Presbyterian church, was licensed to preach about the year 1830, and for a period of about ten years was a pioneer minister of Marshall and Neshoba counties, Miss. He was married in the Old Dominion on the 19th of December, 1831, to Miss Frances Ann Bishop, a daughter of Squire Bishop, who belonged to one of the F. F. V's. Rev. McCallum first became a resident of the state of Mississippi in the year 1839, but in 1849 settled in Jefferson county in the Church Hill neighborhood, at which place he was the faithful pastor of the Presbyterian church until within a few years of his death, when his extreme age prevented him from longer filling his pastoral duties. At the advanced age of eighty-four years he was called from life, his death occurring on the 27th of October, 1885. He was an earnest Christian, a most charitable gentleman. His efforts to relieve the wants of the poor will long be remembered, and his strict integrity and methodical habits may well be emulated by the rising generation. His wife died on the 28th of March, 1858, having borne her husband six sons and four daughters that grew to mature years. Two are deceased: Henry S., who died May 4, 1868, leaving a wife and children; and Mary E., wife of Dr. Baker, of Copiah county, died August 14, 1881; Jonathan E., is a planter of Copiah county; Samuel D. follows the same occupation in Jefferson county, is an elder in the Presbyterian church and superintendent of the Sunday-school; Margaret is the wife of Henry McCallum, and resides in North Carolina; Sarah E. is the wife of George N. Cato, of Memphis; Robert A. is a physician of Copiah county; Josephine is the wife of Joe Smiley, of Wesson, Copiah county; Angus, a resident of Memphis, Tenn., and Andrew M. The latter was educated in the common schools and Oakland college, and in his youth became familiar with the details of farming and was giving this calling his time and atten tion when the war broke out. The coming clash of arms caused him to drop his farming implements, and in the month of March, 1862, he joined the First Mississippi artillery and was on active duty until the war closed. The most of the time he was in Mississippi, and was near Vicksburg when his command was captured. He and four brothers served in the Confederate army, two being in the Twelfth Mississippi, one in the Thirty-sixth Mississippi, one as a scout, and Andrew M. in the above mentioned regiment. All escaped without receiving serious wounds. After the termination of the war Andrew M. returned to Mississippi and spent about one year in Copiah county, but in 1866 returned to his home to take charge of the old plantation, of which he is now the owner. Since it has come into his possession he has greatly improved it in many ways, and everything about it now indicates that a man of thrift, industry and enterprise is at the helm. His home is located about one mile from Church Hill and his residence, which is pleasantly located, is commodious, substantial and pleasant. He was married in this county on the 20th of November, 1867, to Miss Martha L. Tucker, of Madison county, a daughter of John Tucker, of Adams county, but a former resident of Madison county. To Mr. and Mrs. McCallum a family of six children have been born: Scott is a bookkeeper in Memphis, Tenn.; John is a farmer of Jefferson county; Mary Lou; Lavenia; Samuel T. and Thomas, a lad of eleven years. Mr. Tucker is a prominent member of the Presbyterian church and ranks as a noticeable illustration of that indomitable push and energy which characterize men of determination and will. His success is due largely to his excellent judgment and strict honesty and fair dealing.

Dr. D. McCallum, physician, Westville, Miss., inherits sturdy Scotch blood from his ancestors, both his paternal and maternal grandparents having been natives of Jura, that country. They came to the United States prior to the Revolutionary war, and located in the Old North state. Grandfather McCallum was on the whig side and participated in one battle of the war. Dr. McCallum's father, John McCallum, was a native of Robeson county, N. C., and was a very successful farmer. He married Miss Lovdy Brown, also of the Old North state, and reared twelve children, eight daughters and four sons, of whom the Doctor is the tenth in order of birth. The latter was born in the same county as his father, in 1835, and received a thorough academic education at Ashland high school, taking a classical course. After leaving school he was engaged in teaching for two years in North Carolina, and in 1858 he removed to Jefferson county, Miss., where he remained two years, a part of which time he taught school. In 1859 he went to the Lone Star state, but the same year returned to North Carolina, where he began the study of medicine under his brother, Dr. W. D. McCallum, with whom he remained until the breaking out of the war. Immediately after the first battle of Manassas he enlisted in the Fortieth North Carolina regiment, company D, heavy artillery, and was captured at the last fight of Fort Fisher. He was held a prisoner at Point Lookout for six months, and after cessation of hostilities he returned to North Carolina and resumed the study of medicine. He took a course of medical lectures at the University of Michigan, Ann Arbor, in 1865 and 1866, and graduated from the medical department of the University of South Carolina, at Charleston, in the class of 1866 and 1867. After graduating he began practicing at Bladenboro, Bladen county, N. C., and there continued until in March, 1870, when he removed directly to Westville, Miss., where he has been successfully engaged in his practice since. He has an extensive practice and stands high in his profession, keeping well posted in the advance of medical science. He is an honored member of the Mississippi state medical association, of which he has been vice president and to which he has contributed numerous articles of merit. In 1875 the Doctor celebrated his nuptials with Miss Kate McLaurin, daughter of D. A. and C. McLaurin, and to them have been born four interesting children, two sons and two daughters. He is a member of Westville lodge, A. F. & A. M., and he and family hold membership in the Presbyterian church.

Dr. R. C. McCann, one of the leading members of the medical profession of Yazoo county, is the subject of the following biographical sketch. He was born in Greene county, Ala., January 21, 1831, and is the son of Dr. Hugh and Rachael N. (Norris) McCann. The paternal ancestors were of Scotch-Irish descent, and those on the mother's side were of English extraction. Dr. Hugh McCann was a celebrated physician of Alabama, although a native of the state of South Carolina. Mrs. McCann was a daughter of Col. Patrick Norris, who for seven years served in the war of the Revolution. Dr. McCann was a graduate of the University of Maryland, a member of the class of 1822; he died in 1840, but his wife survived until 1871; she died in this county at the residence of her son, Dr. McCann, Jr. They reared a family of eight children: Patrick N. died in 1864 from diseases contracted in the Confederate service; Martha J.; Susan L., deceased wife of Clayborn Bowman; James H., lieutenant of the Eighteenth Mississippi, who died of disease contracted in the service; Mary C.; William, deceased; Emma C., who married Dr. L. Reid, and is dead; and Dr. R. C. McCann. The latter was fifteen years of age when he came with his family to Yazoo county. He was educated at Greensboro, Ala., and was a member of the junior class at Center college, Danville, Ky., when his health failed. When he took up the study of medicine he entered Jefferson medical college, Philadelphia, which had the most renowned faculty of that time. He was graduated in 1858, when he began his practice in Yazoo county. He has been continuously occupied with professional duties, with the exception of three years, when he was commissioned as surgeon of the Twelfth Mississippi cavalry, Ferguson's brigade. He was in all the engagements of the army of the Tennessee, from Dallas down to Atlanta, Ga., and was in the rear of Sherman's army on to Savannah. He was surgeon of the Twelfth Mississippi cavalry, which composed a portion of the bodyguard of President Davis when he was fleeing from the representatives of the Federal government. The Twelfth escorted him on the retreat from Anderson, S. C., to Washington, Ga. He was taken prisoner by Sherman's army, and was paroled. He was at the siege and surrender of Vicksburg. At the time of the surrender he was at Macon, Ga., and his was the last regiment of the army of the Tennessee to surrender. He was then an officer of the fourth rank in his command. Each soldier was presented with $25 in silver. They filed past a window of a loghouse, receiving the money in their hats. Dr. McCann had the $25 made into silver spoons in New York city after his marriage. Upon returning to Yazoo county he resumed the practice of his profession, and has also given some attention to the cultivation of his plantation on Cypress creek. It consists of five hundred and thirty-eight acres. He also has a small farm of one hundred and twenty-seven acres, on which he resides. Dr. McCann was married to Miss Kate O'Reilly, a daughter of Edmond and Sallie R. (Bowman) O'Reilly. Mrs. McCann's father was a native of Ireland, and her mother was of a prominent family of Yazoo county. They have no children. The Doctor is a member of the Presbyterian church of Yazoo City, and his wife belongs to Bowman's chapel of the Methodist Episcopal church. He takes an active interest in the political movements in his county, and is well informed on all the leading issues of the day. His early years of mental discipline fitted him well for the more severe scientific training which he took in his professional studies, and he has always kept fully abreast of the times in all the discoveries and improved methods of treatment. His efforts have been rewarded with merited success.

Edward McCarty, father of Michael McCarty of Shubuta, Clarke county, Miss., was born in Edgefield district, S. C., in the latter part of the last century. He was married to Sarah Lorrimore before the year 1800 in South Carolina, and came to Mississippi in 1820 and settled in Wayne county, where he died. Michael McCarty, the fifth son in a family of twelve children, was born in Edgefield district, S. C., November 4, 1806, and came to Mississippi with his parents. His early educational advantages were poor, but by dint of energy he acquired a knowledge of business which has served him satisfactorily. He remained with his parents until he was twenty-two years old, when he began life on his own account. In 1828 he was married to Miss Maria Hailes, of Wayne county, Miss., a daughter of Judge Henry Hailes, probate judge of Clarke county for many years. He has had three children: Cynthia, Miranda and Visa. The first and last survive. Cynthia is married to Burrell Rington of Wayne county, Miss., and the latter, Visa, to Britton Rogers. Mr. McCarty has been engaged in farming all his life. He owns about seven hundred acres of the average land of Clarke county, located two miles north of Shubuta. The soil is sandy and his chief crops are corn, oats, potatoes, etc. He plants some cotton but restricts himself to a few acres, farming on the intensive scale and using some fertilizer. He raises some stock and has some pine land. He is a member of the Baptist church of forty-six years' standing. Mrs. McCarty, who died in May, 1890, was also a Baptist. Mr. McCarty was a member of the board of supervisors for four years, and a justice of the peace for many years. Favoring education and other interests tending to develop the country, he is in every sense a useful citizen. Mr. McCarty has never had a suit in court and only one difference in which he was concerned was ever settled by arbitration, and that was decided in his favor, which speaks volumes for the honor and fairness which have ever characterized his commercial relations.

B. McClanahan, of the firm of McClanahan, Wood, Moore, Cottongim & Kennedy, known as the Estabutchie Lumber Manufacturing company, of Estabutchie, Miss., was born in Nicholas county, Ky., October 18, 1846, one of the eight children of Charles and Elizabeth (Martin) McClanahan. He engaged in active business at the age of twenty, and two years later, in 1868, formed a partnership with J. M. Collier, of Millersburg, Ky. They purchased a portable sawmill and were engaged in the manufacture of lumber principally, until the spring of 1877, when Mr. McClanahan came to Mississippi and went into the lumber business at Bogue Chitto, his firm being known as the Keystone Lumber & Improvement company. In December, 1889, he sold out his business there, and in the spring of 1890 came to Estabutchie and purchased an interest in the Estabutchie Lumber Manufacturing company. The mill of this company is one of the most extensive in southern Mississippi, having a capacity to saw thirty thousand feet of lumber per day, and connected with it are a planingmill and adequate drying kilns. Connection is made between the mill and Leaf river, a mile distant, by a railway of the standard gauge and supplied with steel rails. On this track the company runs a train of five logging cars and a locomotive. A tract of about fifteen thousand acres of fine land covered with timber is used as the source of supply for this establishment. The company employs a large number of hands, and is one of the leading industrial institutions in southern Mississippi.

James McClure, the popular and most efficient treasurer of Jefferson county, Miss., although born in Scotland, May 23, 1822, has been a resident of the state of Mississippi since 1854, and the confidence the people have in him is therefore intelligently placed, for during the long years that he has been in business at this point, they have had every opportunity to judge of his character and qualifications. His opportunities for acquiring an education in early life were quite limited, for at the age of fourteen years he was apprenticed to a coach builder in Manchester, Eng., and there remained until he had attained his majority. He then, as is the usual custom in that country, traveled through England working at his trade as a journeyman, and this continued for seven years. At the age of twenty-eight years he determined to seek his fortune across the water and in August, 1849, arrived in the city of New York, at which place he began working for John Stevens, who was one of the largest manufacturers of carriages at that time in New York. Such was the proficiency of Mr. McClure that for his services he received $5 per day, which was excellent wages for that time and could be commanded by only first-class workmen. He continued to fill this position about three years, during which time he was united in marriage to Miss Jane Hayes. From the city of New York he went to Cincinnati, Ohio, from which place he came to the state of Mississippi. He immediately began working in a carriage manufactory but at the end of twelve months he began work on his own account, having bought out his employers. Being a skillful workman, his goods soon became widely known and orders for work began to pour in rapidly, and a period of decided prosperity set in. By excellent management he was enabled to accumulate a fine property. While he has at times been engaged in other branches of business, he has never given up the carriage building, and is still the owner of an excellent shop at Fayette, where, when he feels the need of recreation, he often lays aside his coat, dons his work apron, and taking his tools in hand can form as good a joint as in days of yore when a journeyman in England, and thoroughly enjoys the work. It has often been said of him: "He is wedded to his trade." In 1850 he sent for his widowed mother and her family to join him in America, but she died soon after her arrival and was buried at New York city. Mr. McClure has one brother, who is a prosperous planter of Jefferson county, and his only sister is the wife of Joseph E. McBride, also a planter of this county. Their parents were William and Jane (Baxter) McClure.

At the breaking out of the Civil war James McClure was among the first to respond to the call for troops, and in April, 1861, enlisted in company D of the Nineteenth Mississippi infantry, with the rank of sergeant, and was in many severe engagements under General Lee. He made as brave a soldier and officer as ever trod the crimson turf of a battlefield, and he was conspicuous for his strict adherence to duty. Being a man of decided will power and possessing a splendid physique, he bore the hardships and privations of war well, and during his entire service was never sick and never missed a roll-call. Neither was he wounded during his service, and, in fact, could be relied upon at all times by his superior officers. Since antebellum days he has taken a deep interest in political questions of the day, has been president of the democratic clubs of the county, and since 1873 has held the office of county treasurer. Notwithstanding the fact that the county has long been well and justly noted for the sterling, honest and superior capabilities of her public officials, this enviable reputation has been fully sustained by Mr. McClure, who is eminently capable of filling any position within the gift of the people. His work shows the most perfect arrangement, and the workings of an intelligent and well-directed mind. He connected himself with the I. O. O. F. society in early manhood, and is the oldest member of that order in the county, holding official positions in both the lodge and encampment. For the past fifteen years he has been treasurer of his lodge, and is also filling the same position in the Masonic lodge, of which he has been a member for many years. He and his family are members in good standing of the Methodist Episcopal church, and are well known for their charity and liberality and for their support of worthy enterprises. Personally and in every private relation and duty of life Mr. McClure may be taken for a model, for he has ever been the soul of true honor, and has the instincts and training of a true gentleman, which he manifests in his daily walk through life. He has one son, James, Jr., who was born in the city of Cincinnati, Ohio, November 19, 1854, and since the age of nine months has been a resident of the state of Mississippi. His first knowledge of the world of books was received in the Phœnix high school of Fayette, but later he entered Jefferson college, where he became thoroughly fitted to enter Washington and Lee university of Lexington, Va. Upon the recommendation of Gen. Custis Lee, son of R. E. Lee, and of the faculty, he was made first assistant teacher in Jefferson college, and this position he filled with ability for ten years. Three years prior to the abandonment of this position he had formed a copartnership with M. C. Harper in the general mercantile business in Fayette, and resigned his position as teacher to give more attention to this business, much to the regret of the trustees of the college, who thoroughly approved and appreciated his methods as a teacher. They are extensive cotton factors and are wideawake and pushing business men. He is a member of the Methodist Episcopal church, and socially belongs to the American Legion of Honor, the Knights of Pythias, the A. F. & A. M. and the I. O. O. F. On October 9, 1884, he was married to Miss Etta Girault Campbell, daughter of Robert W. and Cordelia (Girault) Campbell, of Fayette, descendants of the earliest settlers of Natchez. Mr. and Mrs. McClure have two little daughters, Etta and Coralie, and one son, James Percy.

Hon. Monroe McClurg, Vaiden, Carroll county, Miss. Many men attain distinction after reaching the meridian of life, but to few is it given to be crowned with success before they have passed the second score of the threescore years and ten allotted to man. The subject of this brief biography forms one of these rare exceptions, and therefore is worthy of consideration in this connection. He is a native of Carroll county, Miss., born March 19, 1857, on his father's farm near Vaiden. His great-grandfather, a Scotchman, come to this country before the Revolutionary war, settled in South Carolina, and raised a family. William McClurg, Monroe's grandfather, was born in Abbeville district, S. C., on December 1, 1800. Some of the older ones of the family went to Pennsylvania; one, James McClurg, was a member of the convention that framed the constitution of the United States; he was admitted May 25, 1787, as a delegate from Virginia, in the room (place) of Patrick Henry, who declined, and with Edmund Randolph, George Mason and George Wythe of that state he declined to sign the constitution, while their colleagues, the immortal George Washington, John Blair and James Madison, Jr., appended their names. William came to Mississippi in 1820 and settled in the county of Hinds; he afterward moved to Kemper county and from there to Carroll county in 1839, where he died September 29, 1863. Yancy Crawford McClurg, the father of Monroe, the youngest son of William McClurg, was born in Hinds, October 15, 1828, and came to Carroll county with his father at the age of ten years and has lived there to this date. He was a Confederate soldier in the Twenty-eighth Mississippi volunteer cavalry, and served through the war, acting as captain of company A during the last year of the conflict. After the surrender he returned to his farming pursuits and is one of the most successful farmers of Carroll county. Capt. Y. C. McClurg was married to Susan Malissa Cain, the youngest daughter of Patrick Cain, another pioneer settler from South Carolina, December 15, 1853. She died August 14, 1874, and August 25, 1875, Captain McClurg married Miss Artimisha Bagley, daughter of Josiah Bagley, also one of the oldest landmarks of Carroll county, having settled near Shongalo, now Vaiden, about 1836. Hon. Monroe McClurg received his education in the common schools of the country, taking an academic course at Louisville. He then entered the law department of the University of Mississippi, at Oxford, and was graduated in June, 1878. He paid all the expenses of his education by working on the farm and as deputy in the sheriff's and clerk's offices of his county. He opened a law office at Vaiden in November, 1879, and at once began to build up a practice. He founded the *Nucleus*, a weekly paper, at Vaiden, and was its editor for a year, when he had to dispose of it to devote his entire energies to the discharge of professional engagements, which had now grown into a lucrative practice. The *Nucleus* was a great success under his management and its sprightly columns gave splendid testimony every issue to the superior intelligence and extraordinarily sound judgment of the brilliant young editor. In 1880 he formed a copartnership with the Hon. Thomas H. Somerville, who was a lawyer of the first rank and a genuine type of a true Christian Southern gentleman. Mr. McClurg has often declared that, next to his marriage, this partnership with Mr. Somerville was the most fortunate step of his life, and the public records of Carroll and adjoining counties, as well as those of the Federal and supreme courts of the state, show that this firm has enjoyed the confidence of the people, and that its members have not been idlers. In addition to a large general practice the firm is counsel for two important railroad companies, a bank and a money syndicate. Mr. McClurg springs from an ancestry of honest, plain agriculturists, none of whom were office-seekers or politicians. Since he became a voter he has taken a lively interest in local and state affairs from the standpoint of a good citizen, advocating the doctrines of the democratic party, and attended, as a delegate from Carroll county, every state convention held, but was never a candidate for office until 1890. He was one of the delegates from Carroll county in the constitutional convention of Mississippi which framed the new constitution securing legal white supremacy to the people of his state. Although one of the youngest members of that body, Mr. McClurg at once displayed such talent and ability as to win the respect and admiration of his senior fellow-members. He was placed on the committee on apportionment, franchise and elections, the most important subdivision of the convention, and on the committee on printing. His speech in opposition to the Campbell plan, or plural voting, based upon a property qualification, was pronounced one of the most forcible, logical and conclusive arguments made during the session. It killed the plan. He secured the adoption into the constitution of those provisions providing for the election of presidential electors by the legislature and requiring the legislature to limit or prevent the ownership of lands in the state by non-resident aliens and corporations, and providing for the change of county and district lines and the removal of courthouses. He introduced a proposition to abolish capital punishment in the state, but it failed to pass. Mr. McClurg greatly preferred the quiet pursuit of his profession and the unmolested enjoyment of the association of his little family to political life. He said that "when a man went into politics he ought to make provision for his family, give his wife a divorce and devote his entire time to his worthless trade." In the spring of 1891 he opened the famous subtreasury campaign in Mississippi. The advocates of that measure were determined to defeat the reëlection of Senator George to the United States senate, for the reason that he declared their scheme undemocratic, impracticable and unconstitutional, and therefore unworthy of

support. They concentrated their efforts in Carroll county, the home of the senator, and it was evident from the first that a hard struggle had begun. Mr. McClurg finally gave a reluctant consent to the urgent requests of the friends of the senator to use his name as a legislative candidate on their ticket. He heartily endorsed the views of senator George, but he considered the fight hopeless in his county, and preferred not to abandon his purpose to keep out of politics. He made no canvass, but, while his ticket was defeated, he stood in the lead on that side for representative. While at the university he represented his fraternity, the Phi Delta Theta, in a national convention at Wooster, Ohio, in May, 1878. He is a zealous Odd Fellow, having filled all of the offices of that order up to grand master of the grand jurisdiction of Mississippi. He was a delegate from his state to the Sunday-school convention which met in international session in Chicago in June, 1888. He was married in Vaiden, December 5, 1881, to Miss Ida Blanche Williams, second daughter of Andy B. and Mary E. Williams, of Vaiden. Mrs. McClurg is a cultured, refined lady of plain, practical habits. The appointments about her household are exquisitely arranged, yet on the common-sense order. Her father was accidentally killed by a friend whom he was endeavoring to keep out of a difficulty, in 1867. Her mother is latterly the widow of the Rev. J. Neely Carothers, of Houston, Miss. Three children were the offspring of this happy union: Susie May, Ada Maud and an infant, Monroe, Jr. His family are Presbyterians. His two younger twin brothers, Hubbard E. and John E., live in Vaiden, the former a salesman, the latter a druggist and mayor of that town. He has three sisters: Mrs. J. S. Tillman; Mrs. T. A. Winborn, of Carroll county, and Mrs. J. B. Harrell, of Gainesville, Tex., and a half-sister, Miss Katie Belle, still with her father. In the Hon. Monroe McClurg Mississippi has a splendid type of the noble young manhood of which she is justly proud.

John W. McCormick was born in Jasper county, Miss., in 1835, a son of James J. McCormick and Mildred G. (Risher) McCormick, both natives of Carleton district, S. C., of whose six children four are living. James J. McCormick was born in 1805, a son of John and Martha (Fontaine) McCormick. John McCormick came to Mississippi in 1822, locating in Perry county. He removed to Jasper county in 1833 and died there in 1840. In the early history of the county he established the Hopewell Methodist Episcopal church. His son, James J., grew to manhood in the county and became a successful business man, owning at the time of his death, which occurred in 1854, considerable property. The subject of this sketch was the oldest member of his family and was married in 1860 to Miss Caldona B. Owens, a native of Pickens county, Ala., who has borne him seven children. In 1862 he enlisted in company H, of the Thirty-seventh Mississippi regiment, which was commanded by Capt. F. B. Loper, with which he served until the close of the war. He was at the siege of Vicksburg, Resaca, Atlanta, Franklin, Nashville, and took part in the engagements at those places, besides numerous others not so important. Although his clothes were several times perforated by bullets, he escaped without a wound. After the close of the war, he returned home, and engaged in planting, which he has continued so successfully that he has accumulated considerable property, including seven hundred and fifty acres of fine land. Politically, he was a whig until a short time before the war, when he endorsed the democratic principles and has voted for the nominee of that party ever since. He was a member of the board of supervisors for two terms, from 1875 to 1879, and was later a member for the two terms, 1883 to 1887, and during that period was the president of the board. He has long been a member of the Masonic fraternity, and, until the disruption of the Knights of Pythias lodge at Enterprise, Miss., was a member of that organization also. He and his wife are communicants of the Methodist Episcopal church. He is a progressive man, who is interested in the upbuilding of his town and the advancement of his county and state.

James McCutchen (deceased) was born in Ohio, but was reared in the Blue Grass regions of Kentucky. After remaining there for some time, he went to Vicksburg, Miss., with Thomas B. Warfield, and engaged in the commission business. About 1834 he came to Washington county, Miss., where he purchased ten hundred acres of land three miles below the present site of Greenville. He cleared the greater part of this plantation, Lucern, and resided on it until his death, in November, 1843. He was married on the 22d of December, 1835, to Miss Susan P. Moseby, a native of Virginia, and daughter of Dr. Littleberry H. Moseby. The Moseby family left the Old Dominion about 1828, and settled in Kentucky, locating in Louisville in 1835. In 1841 Mr. Moseby was appointed postmaster at Louisville by President Harrison. He died about 1849, while spending the winter with his daughter, Mrs. McCutchen, of Mississippi. By his marriage Mr. McCutchen became the father of three children, a son and two daughters, all deceased: Louisa Jane (born in 1837 and died in 1850), Maria Warfield (born on the 2d of April, 1839 and died in 1861), and John Moseby (born in 1841, and in 1867 was married to Miss Maggie Proctor. He died in 1884 or 1885, leaving a widow and seven children, four sons and three daughters, all residing in Greenville). Mrs. McCutchen's second marriage was with Dr. Littleton L. Taylor, a native of Virginia, who, after studying medicine in Philadelphia, began life as a physician in Florida. He came to Mississippi about 1844, settled at old Greenville, and in 1849 was married to Mrs. McCutchen. In 1855 he moved from the river to Deer creek, opened up a new plantation, and about three years later moved farther up the creek to Panola plantation. He retired from practice and applied himself to planting, which occupation he carried on until his death, in 1867. To his marriage were born three children, as follows: Susan Elizabeth, wife of Henry T. Ireys (see sketch); Robert Walter, and Junius Littleton (died in 1865). Mrs. Taylor now resides in Greenville with her daughter, Mrs. Ireys. She has seen many changes since first settling in Washington county, and recalls many pleasant incidents of the past. She has seen Greenville grow from one house to the flourishing city of to-day.

Dr. James H. McDaniel is a well-known gentleman of the county, and is actively engaged in planting and sawmilling, his residence being near Veto postoffice. He was born on the 25th of April, 1814, to John and Elizabeth (Hutchins) McDaniel, the former of whom first saw the light of day in the Old North state. His father died there when he was a small boy, and with his widowed mother and her family he removed to Georgia, but Mrs. McDaniel soon became dissatisfied and returned to her native state. John continued to make his home in Georgia, and was there married, coming, in 1810, with his wife's people to what is now Lawrence county, Miss., and the next year to Franklin county, settling on a woodland plantation on the Homochitto river. He was one of the first residents of the county, and, notwithstanding the fact that his land was heavily timbered, he set energetically to work to clear it, and succeeded in making it one of the most valuable plantations in the county. He was an honest and industrious man, and made a valuable acquisition to the county of Franklin, for, besides possessing the above mentioned characteristics, he was pushing, enterprising, and possessed shrewd and farseeing views on all subjects. He died on the 28th of January, 1885, at the age of one hundred years, ten months and two days. He superintended the opening of the upper Monticello & Natchez road in an early day, and during the War of 1812 furnished a substitute. He and his wife were members of the Methodist church for a great many years, and were worthy and upright Christians in every respect, being charitable and kind to those in less fortunate circumstances than themselves.

Mr. McDaniel never saw any of his people after leaving Georgia, but contented himself in the affection of his wife's people and in his own immediate family. His wife died on the 2d of September, 1885, at the age of ninety-two years, ten months and three days. She was a daughter of John Hutchins, who came here in 1811, removing a few years later to the east side of the Pearl river, where he and his wife passed from life. Dr. James H. McDaniel was the second of ten children, two sons and eight daughters, born to his parents, and he is the only one of the family that is living at the present time. Owing to the wildness of the region during his youth, James H. received a very meager education. He was married in 1841 to Miss Mary Ann, daughter of Lieutenant Daniel and Mary Higdon, the father receiving his title while serving in the War of 1812 at New Orleans. When a young man he came to Mississippi, married here, and became a resident of what was known as the Higdon settlement. In 1840 he was a member of the board of police in Franklin county, Tenn. He followed the life of a planter and died in this county prior to the late war, his widow surviving him until 1878, at which time she, too, passed away, being at that time sixty-three years of age. To Mr. and Mrs. McDaniel the following children were born: Fluvia J., widow of David Herring; John W.; Ione, wife of E. M. Coleman; Mary R., wife of J. F. Galbreath; Martha R., wife of Wm. L. Cato; Olivia, wife of W. L. Cato; Quitman, living, and Daniel J., James H., Cynthia and an infant son deceased.* During the Civil war John W. served in company E, of the Seventh Mississippi infantry, and at Shiloh was wounded by a falling limb and was disabled for some time. He later joined Powers' cavalry company, and until the close of the war served in southern Mississippi. Dr. James H. McDaniel remained with his father until 1846, at which time he settled on another part of the old homestead in a house of his own, and is now the owner of twelve hundred acres of land on which is a good sawmill. When a young man he took up the study of medicine and in 1852 began practicing, but at the end of four years turned his attention to planting. When the war came up he was persuaded to resume his practice, which he continued until a few years since, when advancing years caused him to retire to a less active life. In 1838–40 he was taxcollector of Franklin county, and in the last-named year acted as census enumerator for the same. Two years later he was elected to the lower house of the state legislature, and during his term was a member of the committee on propositions and grievances. He held the position of justice of the peace for many years before and after the war, and about 1841 was instrumental in establishing Veto postoffice. Just before the war he was elected and served out the unexpired term of county treasurer, and in every official capacity in which he served he was faithful, zealous and successful. He is a man of superior natural mental endowments, and is eminently capable of filling any position within the gift of the people. Many years ago he was a member of Franklin lodge No. 11, of the A. F. & A. M., afterward becoming a charter member of S. B. Stampley lodge.

E. C. McDaniel was born in Tishomingo county, Miss., November 10, 1843. His father was Charles McDaniel, who was born in Alabama in 1810. His mother was Miss Jane Blakely, and was born in Alabama in 1814. They were married in 1838, and lived in Alabama, where Mr. McDaniel was a planter until 1841, when he came to Mississippi in 1856, having lived in Tennessee a short time before coming here. By his wife above mentioned he had four children, and by his second wife, who was Miss Liddie Horn, he had three children. He married Miss Horn in 1846. Of the seven children born to these two marriages four are

*Mrs McDaniel died March, 1861, aged thirty-six years. He was married in 1863 to Miss Sallie Fortenbury, who was probably born and reared in Lawrence county, where her parents died when she was a little girl. She died in 1865, leaving a daughter, Dozzie. Quitman was educated in the neighboring schools and at Oxford, the daughters receiving their education at Brookhaven.

still living.   Mr. McDaniel and his wife were members of the Methodist Episcopal church. He was a successful business man and planter.   A not uninteresting part of the local history of Pontotoc county is the sad chapter which relates to the death of Mr. and Mrs. McDaniel, who were killed by the explosion of a water-tank at twelve o'clock July 22, 1865.   In June, 1862, E. C. McDaniel enlisted in the Confederate army, and for a time served in Colonel Julien's battalion, in General Roddy's command in northern Alabama as a private, but was later transferred to Forrest's command in north Mississippi.   He was in the battles at Jackson, Tenn., Franklin, Shiloh, Cross Roads and Harrisburg.   He received a serious wound at the last named place in July, 1863, which unfitted him from further service for three months. He joined his command about October, 1863, and was present at the shocking affair at Fort Pillow, taking part, later, in the battle of Okolona, where his colonel, Jeff Forrest, was killed. He returned to Mississippi in 1865.   Here he married Miss Lucinda Bolen, daughter of Brantley Bolen.   They have had nine children: Charles J., who is married; William B.; Thomas E.; John R. and Samuel are single; Robert L., who is deceased; Lucinda J.; and May Belle and an infant who is deceased.   Beginning with little in the way of worldly capital, Mr. McDaniel, by strict attention to business, and by the exercise of frugality, has come to be one of the most prominent planters in this part of the county, owning seven hundred and twenty acres of land, about two hundred and fifty acres of which have been cleared.   For the past twelve years he has been engaged quite extensively in cottonginning.   He and his wife are members of the Baptist church.   He enjoys the respect of all who know him, and ranks among the substantial and entirely trustworthy citizens of this section of the state.

Hon. W. A. McDonald, state senator and attorney at law, Ashland, Benton county, Miss., was born on a farm in the suburbs of Ashland, on which he now lives.   He was the third in a family of six children of Arnold and Mary A. (Ayers) McDonald.   His father was a native of Giles county, Tenn.; his mother, of Jefferson county, Ala.   Their parents moved from their respective states to Mississippi when both Mr. and Mrs. McDonald were small children, and the latter grew to maturity and were married in this state.   They had three sons and three daughters, named as follows in the order of their birth: Fannie J., who became the wife of R. F. Robison, and is now deceased; John R., William A., Mary (deceased), Martha A. and Charles E.   Mr. McDonald's paternal grandfather moved from Tennessee to Mississippi in 1836, and was one of the pioneers of this part of the country.   His maternal grandparents removed from Alabama to Mississippi in 1837.   The father of our subject was reared on his father's plantation, and accumulated considerable landed property and slaves prior to the war.   Mr. Ayers, his father-in-law, was the sheriff of Jefferson county, Ala., many years, and also during several sessions represented his county in the legislature.   Mr. McDonald's father enlisted in the Confederate service in 1861 as a lieutenant of one of the companies composing an infantry regiment, and was afterward promoted to the captaincy of his company, and was killed October 8, 1862, while bravely leading his command in the battle of Perryville, Ky.   His widow survived him, having reared her family on the old homestead so successfully as to fit them for the best society, and cause them to be honored and respected by all who know them.   She is now in her sixty-third year.   W. A. McDonald began life for himself at the age of twenty-one, as a newspaper publisher at Ashland, Miss., where he was partner and coeditor with William A. Ayers in the *Rising Sun*.   This enterprise was sold out in 1878, and in 1879 he entered the law school at Oxford, and in 1880 began the practice of his profession in Michigan city, where he was the resident practitioner for three years.   In 1883 he removed to Ashland, where he has since been engaged in the practice of law, and in planting.   He is the senior member of the firm of McDonald & McDonald, a partnership well and favorably known throughout this and adjoining counties. In 1883, soon after he took up his residence in Ashland, he was elected to the legislature; he was elected again in 1886, and in 1888 was elected to the state senate, of which he is now a member. At the bar of this county and state his standing is deservedly high, and he is regarded as a legal practitioner of more than ordinary ability. He is a member of the Masonic order, and is a liberal contributor to schools, churches and all worthy enterprises. He was married in 1886 to Sallie J. Hamer, a daughter of W. T. Hamer, of Benton county, and he and his wife are members of the Methodist Episcopal church.

Frederick J. McDonnell, a planter of Monroe county, Miss. (P. O. Kolona, Chickasaw county, Miss.), was born five miles southwest of Huntsville in Madison county, north Alabama. His great-grandfather, Andy McDonnell, married a Miss Rankin. He lived at Enisgilling, Ireland. He had three sons: William, Archie, James; and five daughters: Sallie, Jennie, Katie, Elizabeth, Mary. Archie, grandfather of the subject of the present sketch, being frail, received a better education than the others. He was sent over to the United States before the death of his father. Upon the death of his father, his mother, with her two sons and five daughters, came to this country and settled in Buncombe county, N. C. James married a Miss Hemphill of Burke county, N. C. He had two sons. William, who courted until he was fifty, married and separated from his wife in two years, had no issue. The grandfather, the subject of this sketch, Archie, married Miss Elizabeth Jackson Dinsmore, who died and is buried in Madison county, north Alabama. F. J. McDonnell's grandaunt, Sallie, ran off and married a man named Gallespie, and her people heard no more of her. Jennie married a Mr. Patton; Katie married a Mr. Hemphill; Elizabeth never married. All of these grandaunts remained in Buncombe county, N. C. Archibald McDonnell, grandfather of the subject of the present sketch, moved to north Alabama early in this century and settled in Madison county, where he lived and died. His vocation was farming. He departed this life December 15, 1829, aged sixty years. To him were born seven children. His family Bible left, shows, in his own handwriting, the following record: "(1). Martha McDonnell was born August 13, 1799, at eight o'clock in the morning. She departed this life July 17, 1826. (2). Margaret McDonnell was born March 20, 1800, at ten o'clock at night. (3). Jane McDonnell was born February 21, 1802, at twelve o'clock at night. (4). Catherine McDonnell was born April 29, 1804, at two o'clock in the morning. (5). Elizabeth J. McDonnell was born April 29, 1810, at one o'clock in the evening. (6). Archibald McDonnell was born February 24, 1815, at three o'clock in the morning. (7). Sydney, born ——, died when six months old." Martha never married; Margaret married William Matkin; Jane married Edmond Ellet; Catherine married James Smith; Elizabeth married George Stovall; Archibald McDonnell, father of the subject of the present sketch, was educated at La Grange college, married Mary Sophia, daughter of Dr. Frederick and Phillippa Jones, March 25, 1846. Living near each other (only three-quarters of a mile) and ofttimes thrown in each other's company, their marriage was but a natural sequence. To them were born twelve children: Sydney, January 15, 1847 (died in infancy); Henry, May 18, 1848; Archie, February 22, 1850; Fred J., March 4, 1852; Infant D., May 12, 1853 (died May 19, aged seven days); Mary Elizabeth, August 25, 1854; Louisa, August 6, 1855; Catherine, February 10, 1857; James S., May 20, 1859; Thomas, March 21, 1862 (died August 7); an infant daughter, June 8, 1864 (died June 18, 1864; aged ten days); and Phillippa, June 4, 1866 (died September 28, 1887, aged twenty-one years, three months and twenty-four days). Mary Sophia McDonnell died May 6, 1888, aged sixty-three years, ten months and thirteen days. Of these children, it will be noticed, seven are still living. He gave his children a good education, most of them having graduated at college. He and his wife both united with the Methodist Episcopal Church South. F. J. McDonnell, the subject of this sketch, was educated principally at Dr. Carlos G. Smith's high school, in Huntsville, Madison county, north Alabama; also attended University of Virginia (Charlottesville) a session of nine months. In 1876, September 7, he married Miss Corra M. Gaillard of Tippah county, north Mississippi, and in 1877 located at Ripley, Miss., Tippah county, and was elected principal of Ripley institute, a high grade school for boys. In the beginning of the year 1878 he moved to the prairies of Monroe county, Miss., where he has since made his home. In 1890 he was elected as one of the three delegates which Monroe county was entitled to, to a seat in the constitutional convention, which convened in the city of Jackson, August 12, 1890. He served on the committee on education. Politically he is, first, last, and all the time, a democrat. He thinks if there are wrongs, grievances, to be redressed, the work must be done through the democratic party. If relief from burdensome taxation and oppression can not thus be obtained, ours then is a hopeless and helpless case. While a member of the Alliance he is against any third party; thinks the farmers should use the organization as a means of bettering their condition, socially, morally, intellectually, financially, but should not convert the organization into a secret political organization. He is opposed violently to secret political organizations; thinks they are not in keeping with the free and open spirit of our government. Our political organizations should be free and open. He and his wife are both identified with the Methodist Episcopal Church South, of which they have been members for some time. Up to the time of their marriage, his wife was a member of the Old School Presbyterian church; of her own accord, she united with the church of her husband's choice, believing that it was more appropriate for man and wife to worship at the same church and lead their children to the same Sunday-school. To them have been born eight children, named as follows, in the order of their birth: Catherine, Corra G., Mary Lou, Jennie, Archie, Fred J., Jr., Augustus Henry, Sophie. Mrs. McDonnell, (nee Miss Corra M. Gaillard) is a graduate of the Huntsville female college, Huntsville, Madison county, north Ala. She is a daughter of Augustus McClellan Gaillard and Marthana (Thomas) Gaillard. Her father was born in South Carolina in 1835; her mother in 1845. Their parents settled in Tippah county. Mr. A. M. Gaillard and Miss Marthana Thomas, were married in 1857. Mrs. Gaillard died in January, 1884. F. J. McDonnell has devoted most of his time and attention, since coming to Monroe county, to farming. He claims to have been moderately successful, considering the uncertainty of the crops, and the uncertainty of the prices, and furthermore, the uncertainty of the negro labor. No great modicum of succes has attended the efforts of the farmers in this country.

LeRoy D. McDowell is the senior member of the well known firm of McDowell & Weir, leading druggists at Starkville, Miss. This business was established in 1875 under the firm title of Deavenport & McDowell, and thus continued until 1890, when the present firm was established. McDowell & Weir are wideawake, thoroughgoing business men, do an annual business of $30,000 and carry a stock of drugs, medicines, books, etc., that would do credit to any city in the state. Mr. McDowell is also vice president of the First National bank. Nothing of a public nature that has a forward tendency escapes his liberal support. He was active in obtaining subscriptions and otherwise materially aided in the location of the Agricultural and Mechanical college at Starkville. Mr. McDowell also has a fine farm of several hundred acres and is engaged in the breeding of fine horses, the best that the country affords. He also raises thoroughbred Jersey cattle, Devons and Red Poled, and spares no pains to perfect the breed. Mr. McDowell was born in Chester district, S.

C., in 1838, and is the son of Henry and Eleanor (Marion) McDowell, natives of Ireland, born in 1812 and 1818 respectively. They came to the United States with their parents when quite young, and the father was reared in Charleston and the mother in Fairfield district, S. C. They were married in Chester district of that state, and in 1847 removed to Chickasaw county, Miss., settling near Houston, where the father farmed for a few years. He then removed to Houston, and there the mother died. He received his final summons in Sunflower county, Miss., in 1857, while there prospecting. He ran a hotel in Houston for a number of years, but the latter part of his life he practiced law. He had a good English education, was full of business and energy, and accumulated several good fortunes in his day. He was active in political matters and was an uncompromising democrat. He was a member of the Masonic fraternity and his own as well as his wife's ancestors for several generations back were members of the Presbyterian church, and prosperous and industrious citizens. The paternal grandfather, Henry McDowell, Sr., after residing in South Carolina for some time, removed to Grenada county, Miss., where he had some children living, and there his death occurred. He was a planter by occupation. The maternal grandfather, Patrick Marion, was a rich planter of the Palmetto state and there he and wife passed the closing scenes of their lives. They were the parents of seven children. LeRoy D. McDowell, the fourth in order of birth of five sons and four daughters, received a liberal education and when about twenty-one years of age engaged in merchandising at Okolona, where he remained until the opening of the conflict between the two sections. He then joined company B, Eleventh Mississippi infantry and was all through the Virginia army as a private, fighting at Seven Pines, through the Peninsular campaign, seven days at Antietam, all through the campaign of 1864, and at the time of General Lee's surrender his division was near Petersburg, when they were surrounded and butchered, only about fifteen of the entire brigade escaping with their lives. This was the only time he was captured and he never received a wound during his four years' hard service. After the war he engaged in business at Okolona and there continued until 1874, when he came to Starkville. Since then he has been engaged in the business above mentioned. On November 14, 1868, he was married to Miss Mary M. Deavenport, a native of Pulaski, Tenn., and the daughter of Dr. Matthew Deavenport, of Virginia. When young the Doctor went to Tennessee, thence to Mississippi and was married at Clinton, of that state. He afterward returned to Pulaski, Tenn., but since then has resided in Corinth, Aberdeen, Okolona and other cities of Mississippi. He spent a few years in California after the war and then resided at Starkville, where his wife died about 1879. He died in the Lone Star state a few years later. He was a man of brilliant intellect, a successful physician and an able writer. He at one time edited a paper in Aberdeen, one also in Corinth, a daily in Griffin, Ga., and one in Starkville. He was a man of varied resources and of great information. To Mr. and Mrs. McDowell were born three children, all now deceased. Mr. McDowell stands high as a Mason, having been worthy master of Albert lodge No. 89, at Starkville. He is also a prominent member of Starkville lodge 783, Knights of Honor, and the Knights and Ladies of Honor. He and wife hold membership in the Presbyterian church. Mr. McDowell is popular with every one, has a wide circle of acquaintances, and his character is above reproach. His brothers and sisters were named as follows: R. Alexander (deceased) was captain of company H, Eleventh Mississippi regiment and served in the Virginia army all through the war; Henry M. (deceased) was in the Eighteenth Mississippi, known as the Beauregard rifles, and was killed the last day of the seven days' fight around Richmond; Hazleton died when young; William B., of Okolona, was in company H, eleventh Mississippi, and was so severely wounded at Gettysburg that he was disabled from further field

duty. He was then in the quartermaster department; James T. enlisted in the cavalry when
but a boy. His death occured at Okolona; Mary (deceased) was the wife of R. P. Black;
Carrie A. (deceased) was the wife of M. Houseman, and Eleanor A. (deceased) was the wife
of E. A. Mosley.

Dr. J. C. McElroy, physician and surgeon, Newton county, Miss., was born in Lincoln
county, Tenn., in 1825, and is a son of Archibald and Elizabeth (Herley) McElroy, natives of
North Carolina. The father was a planter by occupation and followed this calling all his
life. He died in 1835 at the age of fifty-five years. He served in the War of 1812 and was
an ardent admirer of General Jackson. His father, Micajah McElroy, was a native of North
Carolina and was a soldier in the war of the Revolution. Dr. McElroy was reared and educated in the place where he was born. In 1842 he came to Mississippi and settled in Lauderdale, where he resided seven years. There he began the study of medicine, reading under
the preceptorship of Dr. L. A. Ragland. In 1846–8 he attended medical lectures at Lexington, Ky., being graduated in the spring of 1848. He then came to Decatur, Newton county,
Miss., and entered upon the practice of medicine. This he continued in this place until the
year 1871, when he removed to Newton; here he has built up an extensive practice. He is one
of the oldest physicians in eastern Mississippi, and is widely known throughout the surrounding counties; he is conscientious and skillful and is perfectly fitted for the numerous
demands made upon the family physician. He served in the war with Mexico in 1846, being
lieutenant of a company from Tennessee; he was first a private, then physician and surgeon
and was afterward promoted to a lieutenantcy; his term of service was from early in 1846
until the treaty of peace was issued. He was married in the fall of 1848 to Miss Cynthia A.,
daughter of Mijamin Smith, of Lincoln county, Tenn. Mrs. McElroy died in July, 1869,
leaving a family of nine children, seven of whom are still living. The Doctor married a
second time Mrs. Ridgeway, a daughter of Joshua Sheptrine, of Decatur, Miss. When
the late war broke out the Doctor enlisted in 1863, and was captain of a company. He was
discharged in seven months on account of disability, and returned to his home. He and his
family are members of the Methodist Episcopal Church South, and are active workers for
the upbuilding of the cause of Christianity. He is a member of the A. F. & A. M., belonging to the Blue lodge and chapter. In 1861 the people of his county testified to the confidence which they reposed in the Doctor by electing him to represent them in the legislature
of the state; this honor was three times conferred upon him. He is an excellent gentleman,
of untarnished reputation; he has high rank in his profession and is a loyal, patriotic citizen.

Dr. J. B. McEwen, a well-known physician in Oxford, was born near Franklin, Tenn., in
1836, in the month of November. He is the second of a family of eleven children of Cyrus
and Eliza Ann (Bell) McEwen. The mother was the youngest sister of the Hon. John Bell, one
of the presidential candidates in 1860. The parents were natives of Tennessee, and father
being a planter. In 1836 he came to Lafayette county, Miss., and settled five miles west of
Oxford. He purchased six hundred and forty acres of wild land, which he cleared and placed
under cultivation; as his means increased he added to this first purchase, and at the
breaking out of the Civil war he owned fifteen hundred acres of good land, well improved.
He had been very successful in his agricultural pursuits, and had a handsome fortune, which
was swept away by the war. He died in 1882 at the age of eighty-one years, leaving a clean
record and a stainless name; his wife had passed away a short time before. They were worthy
members of the Cumberland Presbyterian church. Cyrus McEwen was a man of wide information and culture and while fully aroused to his country's welfare he never entered actively
into politics. He was what was known in his day as a Henry Clay whig, fully endorsing the

grand compromises urged by that famous statesmen. Though a slaveholder he was a kind and generous one, opposed to secession. His love for the Union made him regret the policy of separation, though, when the storm of war began he was everything he should have been to his neighbors and friends, his kindred and his country; his roof received the soldier with true and genuine hospitality, and though his fields were plundered, his barns and granaries stripped of their contents and everything he had paid tribute to the armies of both sides, yet he never failed to do his whole duty in all those times. While the Confederate soldier was warmly welcomed, the Federal soldier when kindly disposed was generously treated as well. Dr. McEwen was reared on his father's farm in this county, where he passed an uneventful youth. He received an excellent education, being graduated from the State university at Oxford, in 1858. He at once began the study of medicine and was graduated from the University at Nashville, in 1861. Just as he was ready to enter upon his work of saving men from death, he was called to that opposite science which we call war; he enlisted in the Confederate army in company K, Miller's battalion; he participated in the battles of Belmont and Shiloh, and had been promoted to the position of second lieutenant when he was obliged to resign on account of ill health. Upon recovering his strength he rejoined the service, enlisting as a private in the company of C. C. Wilburn; he was soon made first lieutenant, and was afterward made captain of company K, Fourth Mississippi cavalry; he was in several important battles, and was taken prisoner at Harrisburg, Miss.; he was taken thence to Johnson's island, where he was held for seven months; he was exchanged February 14, 1865. He then took up the practice of his profession, and also gave some attention to agriculture. In 1876 he removed to Oxford, where he has gained a large patronage. He was married October 7, 1862, to Miss S. S. Handly, of Pontotoc county. Two children have been born to this union: Courtenay Estelle and William Barron, a druggist of Oxford. Dr. McEwin takes an active interest in political matters, and has served as treasurer of his county, making an honest, capable official. Dr. McEwen is known among the people of his home as one of the kindest-hearted of men. He is also noted for his uniform courtesy and pleasant manners and for that love of his kind that makes the popular physician. No patient is too poor to command his professional services. These are for the humble and the lowly as well as for those more favored, and whether compensated or not Dr. McEwen is ever ready to obey the call of suffering humanity. Such men are blessings to any community.

B. B. McFaddin is a well-known planter, whose postoffice address is Tilden, Itawamba county, Miss. He was born in Alabama, August 22, 1819, a son of William H. and Catherine (Holloway) McFaddin, natives of Virginia. He was educated in Alabama and Mississippi, and was married, July 23, 1840, to Miss Almena Medley, who was born in Alabama in 1824, a daughter of William and Elizabeth (McWilliams) Medley. Her father was a native of Tennessee, and her mother was born in Alabama. To Mr. and Mrs. McFadden have been born fifteen children, nine sons and six daughters, twelve of these grown to maturity: Oliver P., Samantha K., Dora, Richard B. K., Martha M., Covella T., William G. (killed in battle of Resaca, Ga.) and the following, who are also deceased: Albert M., James M., Ethelbert N., Mary J., Zenobia A., Commodore, Desdemona A. and Peter F. Mr. McFaddin is a stanch democrat politically. His first official position was that of justice of the peace, which he held with much credit for two years, the fairness and wisdom of his rulings and decisions being frequently commented upon. Later he served for three terms as a member of the board of supervisors of Itawamba county, two terms by election and one by appointment, and he was appointed and served one term as registrar of the county. He is a Master Mason and a member of the Farmers' Alliance. His ruling characteristic is a great love of sport. In

his religious belief he is a Universalist.   He is liberal in his views, and has ever been generous in his support of all worthy measures.   His wife is a member of the Baptist church.   He
has lived upon his present homestead since 1840, and has one of the most beautiful and comfortable homes in Itawamba county.   It is one of the most sightly objects on the Fulton and
Detroit road.   He is the owner of more than twelve hundred acres of land, and is otherwise
well to do.   He is the oldest citizen of the county living in his immediate vicinity.

Baxter McFarland, judge of the court of chancery of the first judicial district, was born
in Lafayette county, Miss., and is the son of George W. and Ann (Clark) McFarland, both
natives of North Carolina, who emigrated to Mississippi about 1835 and located in Lafayette
county, later moving to Chickasaw county, where they both died.   George W. McFarland
was a farmer, though his county honored him by conferring upon him several offices, the
duties of which he faithfully discharged.   They had six children, three of whom are living,
viz.: Kate, Laura and Baxter.   The family seems to have been imbued with a military spirit,
the grandfather having been a Revolutionary soldier, and received a wound at Guilford courthouse.   The grandson, Baxter McFarland, was educated in private schools in Chickasaw
county, Miss., leading a farmer boy's life until he was eighteen years of age, when he left
home to attend law school at the University of Mississippi.   He began to practice his profession at Houston, Miss., but the war breaking out shortly afterward he enlisted in the
Chickasaw guards, commanded by Capt. W. F. Tucker, which belonged to the Eleventh
Mississippi regiment volunteers, which was in General Bee's and General Whiting's brigade.
He served in this company till 1863 as orderly sergeant and lieutenant, participating in all
the battles of the army of northern Virginia till that time, and was dangerously wounded
in the fights around Richmond, at Gaines' mill.   He took part in all the bitter engagements
from Chickamauga on to the close of the war, participating in such battles as Chickamauga,
Missionary Ridge, Atlanta and Hood's Tennessee campaign, Franklin, Nashville, etc.   The
wound at Gaines' mill in 1862 disabled him for months.   As soon as possible he rejoined his
regiment, but in 1863 joined the Western army and became adjutant of the Forty-first
Mississippi regiment, and afterward adjutant-general, with the rank of major.   Still later he
joined Lee's army, but the struggle coming to a close he returned to Houston, where he
became associated in the practice of law with Judge J. A. Orr and Col. J. R. McIntosh, the
firm being Orr, McFarland & McIntosh.   In 1870 he removed to Aberdeen, Miss., forming a
partnership with Gen. Reuben Davis, one of the best known criminal lawyers of the state.
Later he formed a third partnership with his brother-in-law, John W. Holliday, a young man
of a high order of mind, who died shortly after, and the firm was changed to Davis, McFarland & Paine.   In 1883 Major McFarland was appointed judge of the chancery court, and
is now serving his second term, and is highly endorsed by all classes for a third term.   He
has faithfully served his state for eight years.   He has been connected with some of the most
noted criminal cases within its boundaries, and many very important civil cases, and he has
won for himself a high reputation as a lawyer and a fluent and able speaker.   Politically he
is a democrat, and he has been a delegate frequently to the democratic state conventions, as
well as those of the county.   He was married in 1870 to Miss Mary Holliday, and has four
children: John B., Thomas H., Anne and Ben.   His wife is of illustrious descent, being a
daughter of Col. John Holliday and a granddaughter of Gen. Jesse Speight, who was a
member of the North Carolina congress for many years and was United States senator at the
time of his death.   He was also president of the state senate of Mississippi.   At the time
of his death he was not fifty years old.   He was succeeded in the United States senate by
Hon. Jefferson Davis, who filled General Speight's unexpired term.

John McFarland, deceased, was prominently identified with the early settlement of Yalobusha county, and is entitled to mention in this history of the leading citizens of the state of Mississippi. He was born in Smith county, Tenn., in 1808, and was there married to Miss Harriet Sheppard, who was born in Haywood county, Tenn. In 1840 they removed to Mississippi and settled near Water Valley, where he engaged in tilling the soil; he soon became one of the most prosperous farmers of the neighborhood. At the beginning of the Civil war he owned about seventy-five slaves, and cultivated one thousand acres of land. He lost heavily by the war, however, and had to begin at the bottom of the ladder again. But a man of his ability and energy could not stay down in the business world, and by close attention he soon gained a foothold and succeeded in acquiring a large estate. He took but little interest in politics, merely exercising his right of suffrage; for several years he served as supervisor of the county, and was a member of the Yalobusha county militia. He was a man greatly respected for his deep integrity of character and genuine worth. He was a member of the Methodist Episcopal church, taking an active part in the service of his Master. He belonged to the Water Valley lodge No. 132, A. F. & A. M. He was a strong advocate of practical education, and took delight in giving his children the best opportunities in this direction. He affiliated with the democratic party after the war. His death occurred in 1870. Mr. McFarland was twice married; by the first union there were born six children: Thomas J. McFarland, editor and proprietor of the *North Mississippi Herald* of Water Valley; Dr. J. M., a resident of California; the other four are deceased, and the mother passed out of this life in 1854; she was an earnest Christian, and a member of the Methodist Episcopal church. Mr. McFarland was married a second time to Adaline Sugg, a native of Marshall county, Miss. By this union there were born five children, one of whom is yet living, Lewis B. McFarland, who resides on the old home place. The mother, with her two daughters, died within a month; Beulah died September 15, 1883, the mother, October 2, 1883, and Ella, October 10, 1883; Sallie died October 10, 1867, and Lillie, in August, 1870. The mother was an active worker in the Methodist Episcopal church. Thomas J. McFarland was reared in Mississippi and was educated at the University of Oxford, Miss., from which he was graduated in 1871. He then returned to Yalobusha county and practiced his profession, that of the law, until 1888, when he founded the *North Mississippi Herald*. He was married to Miss W. R. Byers, of Panolo county, Miss., the daughter of A. W. Byers, a prominent planter of the county; she was educated at the Monticello (Ill.) Female seminary; one child, a son, was born of this marriage; he died at the age of one year. Thomas J. entered the Confederate army, and enlisting in the Fifteenth Mississippi regiment, company F, he served from 1861 to 1863, a period of two and a half years; he was but fifteen years of age when he enlisted; he was in many important engagements, and served both in the infantry and cavalry. In his political opinions he agreed with the democratic party. Lewis B. McFarland, the only living child of the second marriage of John McFarland, was born August 27, 1857, in Marshall county, Miss., at the home of his grandfather, where his mother was spending some time; he was reared in Yalobusha county and received his education in the common schools of Water Valley. He started out in life upon his own responsibility at the age of fifteen years, and was first employed as a clerk by T. J. West & Co. for a period of two years; at the end of that time he purchased an interest in the stock, and continued in the business for eight years; he disposed of his share of the business and returned to his home, engaging in agriculture. He was united in marriage February 24, 1887, to Miss Tommie Smith, the only child of Thomas Smith; she was born and raised in Yalobusha county, and is the mother of two children: Eliza and Ella Clyde. Mr. McFarland's plantation contains ten hundred and forty acres, three hundred of which are under cultivation. He is a young man of energy and enterprise, and has the highest respect of the community in which he lives. He and his wife are consistent members of the Methodist Episcopal church. In his political convictions he is found in the ranks of the democratic party. He is a member of Valley City lodge No. 402, A. F. & A. M.

H. B. McGee, planter, Tchula, Miss., was born in Georgia, within thirteen miles of Millegeville, on the 20th of December, 1817, and his father, Joseph McGee, was a native of Maryland, born on the 25th of March, 1786. The elder McGee was a planter by occupation and moved to Mississippi in 1834, locating in Noxubee county, and settled in Holmes county in 1843, where his death occurred in 1855. He was a whig in politics. He was twice married, first, to Miss Matilda Brantley, by whom he had two sons, Irwin G. and Thomas G., and after her death he married Miss Susan Bonner, a native of Virginia, who died in Holmes county in 1849, when in her fifty-ninth year. The children born to the second union were, named in the order of their births, as follows: H. B., Benjamin, Joe, Matilda, Levi, Mary, Susan, William and Sallie. The parents of these children were both members of the Methodist church. The paternal grandfather, Davis McGee, was a native of Maryland, and the maternal grandfather, Joseph Bonner, was a native of Virginia. The latter moved to Georgia and there received his final summons. Of the nine children born to Joseph McGee's second marriage, H. B. McGee was the eldest in order of birth. He came with his parents to Mississippi in 1834, first to Noxubee county and later to Holmes county, where he has ever since been engaged in planting. He is now the owner of two thousand five hundred acres of land, eight hundred acres of which are under the plow, and his principal crops are cotton, corn and vegetables. Mr. McGee gained his education by self-application, studying diligently evenings by the light of a pine knot. He was married first on the 25th of November, 1851, to Mrs. Sarah Red, by whom he had two children, Anna and John, both deceased. His second marriage occurred on the 30th of October, 1856, to Miss Emma Crawford, and resulted in the birth of one son, Levi, who is now at home. On the 30th of March, 1862, Mr. McGee wedded Miss Sarah Cowsert, and by her became the father of a daughter, Sallie, who is now the wife of W. H. McCarty, who is engaged in planting in Carroll county, but who was formerly a merchant and the owner of a steammill. Mr. McGee is a member of the Methodist church. He is a Mason in good standing, but at the present time is not a member of any lodge. He was first initiated in Eureka lodge, in 1845, and has taken all the degrees except the commandery He is also a member of the Grange, of which he has been master. He is a greenbacker in politics.

B. H. McGee, planter, Acona, Mississippi. Mr. McGee's father, Joseph McGee, was a native of Maryland, where he was reared and received his early education. He was one of the pioneers of Mississippi, moving there as early as 1834 and settling in Noxubee county, where he remained until 1842. From there he moved to Holmes county of that state, where he followed his former occupation, that of planting. He was a whig in politics. He was twice married, his first wife being Miss Matilda Brantler, who bore him two sons, Erwin G. and Thomas G. After the death of his first wife Mr. McGee married Miss Susan Bonner, and the fruits of this union were nine children: Henry, Benjamin, Joe, Matilda, Mary, Levi, Susan, William and Sallie. B. H. McGee, the second in order of birth of the children born to the second marriage, owes his nativity to Jones county, Ga., his birth occurring on June 24, 1819. On December 10, 1842, he was married to Miss Martha E. Ball, a native of Mississippi, and the children resulting from this union are as follows: A son (unnamed), was born on September 27, 1843, and died on July 10, 1844; Martha S., was born on March 31,

1846; Mary J., born April 7, 1848; Sarah C., born March 31, 1850; Adam M., born May 10, 1854; Joseph H., born August 24, 1856, and died at six years of age; Hester A., born March 20, 1858; William L. was born March 22, 1862. He graduated at the Experiment school near Storksville in 1885, and is now assistant director of that college, and Charles, who was born on March 16, 1866, graduated in 1886 when twenty years of age, and died in 1888. Mr. McGee has always followed the occupation of a planter, and has been quite successful in that pursuit. He has taken quite an active part in politics and was a whig prior to the war. He was a member of the board of supervisors for nine years, and has held the office of justice of the peace for four terms and is the present incumbent. He is a member of the Masonic fraternity, having joined lodge No. 119 in 1851, and is now a member of lodge No. 86. He has taken thirteen regular degrees. He was a member of the Grange and at the present time is a member of the Alliance organization. He is active in all temperance matters, and has been a member of the Methodist church for about fifty years. He is an active planter, owns five hundred acres and has three hundred acres under cultivation.

Samuel M. McGee is one of the most reliable planters of Lee county, Miss., and is cheerfully accorded the following space in this record. He was born in the state, in Tippah county, in 1846, and is a son of Jesse and Lucinda (Acker) McGee, natives of South Carolina. The paternal grandfather, John McGee, was married four times, and the father of our subject was born of the first marriage. He removed to Mississippi with his family in 1845, and settled in Tippah county, where he engaged in farming. He also understood the black-smith's trade, which he carried on in connection with his agricultural pursuits. He died at the age of forty-two years, in 1851. His wife was born in 1810, and died in 1875. They were both members of the Baptist church. They had a family of eight children: Elizabeth, wife of Thomas A. Byars; John; Frances, who first married a Mr. Phillips, and after his death, a Mr. Burroughs; William, who was killed at Gettysburg; Susan, Samuel M., James (deceased), Mary, wife of Prof. W. R. Brook, but first married to John B. Galloway. Samuel M. was reared in what is now Lee county, whither his people had removed when he was four years of age. He attended the common schools, and at the age of seventeen years enlisted in the Confederate service. He joined company B, Thirty-second Mississippi regiment, under M. P. Lowery. Afterward he was under Col. W. H. H. Tison, a full sketch of whom is found elsewhere in this volume. He was in the battles of Murfreesboro and Chickamauga, and the siege of Atlanta. He was taken prisoner near the latter place, but was soon exchanged. After the surrender he returned to his home, and assumed the duty of supporting his mother, who was a widow, a widowed sister and two unmarried sisters. He engaged in farming, and for two years he was in Texas, following the same vocation. He returned to Mississippi, however, and has placed his land in a high state of cultivation. Mr. McGee was united in marriage to Miss Nannie S. Bond, a native of Mississippi, and a daughter of John C. and Frances Bond, natives of South Carolina. Her father died in 1877, but her mother still survives. They had five children born to them: Mrs. Fannie Agnew, Mrs. May Byars (deceased), Mrs. K. Dulery, Carrie, the wife of W. D. Mayfield, and Mrs. McGee. Mr. and Mrs. McGee have no children. They are worthy members of the Baptist church. He belongs to Baldwyn lodge No. 108, A. F. & A. M. Politically he affiliates with the democratic party.

Judge Edward McGehee (deceased), one of the county's early and prominent settlers and royal-hearted citizens, is the subject of this memoir. He was so well known in this county and throughout this portion of the state, that no special introduction is necessary to call to mind his familiar face and useful life, for here he resided for more than seventy years.

He was a native of Oglethorpe county, Ga., born November 8, 1786, and was the seventh son of Micajah McGehee and Ann Scott, daughter of James Scott, a native of Prince Edward county, Va. Micajah McGehee was the second of a family of seven sons and two daughters, born to Edward and De Journet McGehee, both of whom were natives of Prince Edward county, she being a descendant of an old Huguenot family, and he the son of Thomas Mack Gehee (or McGehee, as it is now written). The latter was originally from St. John parish, King William county, where he made his will, July 27, 1724, in which the following children were mentioned: William, Ann Bultlas, Dennah, Abner, Abraham, Samuel, Jasdo, Sarah, Edward and Mary Dickson. The children born to Edward and De Journet McGehee were: John (who settled in Prince Edward county, Va., and reared two sons), Micajah (father of Judge Edward), Daniel (who settled near Augusta, Ga., and had three sons and three daughters), Mumford (who settled in Pearson county, N. C., and had four sons), William (who settled in Milledgeville, Ga.), Samuel (who settled in Amite county, Miss., and had six sons and two daughters), and Jacob (who settled in Georgia and had fourteen children). The daughters were Mrs. Charles Wommack (of Prince Edward county, Va.), and Mrs. Wright (who settled in Tennessee and had twenty-one children). The children born to James Scott were: Ann (who married Micajah McGehee), Mrs. Coleman (of Augusta, Ga.), Mrs Spencer (of Augusta, Ga.), Mrs. Stubbs (of Milledgeville, Ga.), Mrs. Fannie Gray (of Elbert county, Ga.), Mrs. Key (of Edgefield, S. C.), Thomas Scott (who married Miss Jarrett, of Virginia, and settled in Elbert county, Ga.), James Scott (of Augusta), and General John Scott (who married Miss Coleman, of Alabama, and had three children). The children born to Micajah were fourteen, of whom thirteen lived to be grown as follows: James (the eldest, who married a Miss Johns, located in Georgia and reared a family of five children), Thomas (who married Betsey Gilmore and had seven children, and settled in Texas), Elizabeth (wife of Abram Hill, by whom were born one son and one daughter), Charles (fourth son of Micajah, accidentally killed himself while getting his gun to shoot a deer that was crossing the yard), Frank (who died single), Abner (who married Charlotte Spencer, by whom he had eleven children), the seventh, a daughter, died an infant, William (who married Martha Taliaferro, by whom he had two sons, and by a second marriage to Miss Watkins, five children), Sarah (who married Thomas Hill, and had six children), Edward (the subject of this memoir), Jack (who married Malinde Hill and had eleven children), Abram (who married Harriet Hill, had two children, and by a second marriage, with a Miss Peniston, had also two children), Hugh (who married Mrs. White, by whom he had five children), and Lucinda (who married D. Oliver and had five children). Edward McGehee, the subject of this sketch, was reared on the plantation of his father, where his time and attention were required in supervising and managing the place. His technical turn of mind and exact business methods eminently fitted him for this responsible position, but these duties limited his advantages for securing a scholastic education, though his activity and inquiring mind largely overcame this in later years.

In about 1808 he left the parental roof in search of a location, came to Mississippi on a flatboat from Wheeling, Va., landed at Fort Adams July 12 of that year, and soon after returned to the old home place on horseback, called there by the death of his father, whose property had been left to the sons, after the old English custom. He at once gave his portion to his sisters, borrowing money at twenty-five per cent., and went to Virginia and bought a number of slaves, among them "Daddy," Charles, David and Eve, and with their assistance returned to a place on Thompson creek, in the southeast portion of Wilkinson county, where he entered land and built a house of logs in what is now known as the Bethel neighborhood. Returning again to the old home place on horseback, he was married, June 6, 1811, to Margaret L. Cosby, a native of Wilkes county, Ga., and returned on horseback with his bride to his home in this county, landing on his twenty-fifth birthday at the little log cabin which was to be his future home. Here he resided until about 1825, when he moved to the Bowling Green plantation, one of the most beautifully situated places in the county. The Bowling Green residence was completed in 1833, and was a stately brick of two and a half stories, with large rooms, spacious halls and veranda supported by immense columns. While building he was asked why he erected so expensive a structure. He replied that he was building a structure to stand for a hundred years. It was located in a beautiful grove of native timber, oak, beech, holly and magnolia, with charming drives, making one of the most artistic places in the entire South. Mr. McGehee, with characteristic spirit and intelligence, soon after locating on this place took upon himself the responsibility of pushing to completion the West Feliciana railroad, which was incorporated in 1830 in Louisiana, and in 1831 in Mississippi, and at that time was one of the first projected railroads in existence. For a few years the road was operated only in Louisiana, owing to trouble in getting the right of way. The enterprise was very expensive, the road costing about $35,000 per mile. Woodville was reached in about 1837. Mr. McGehee was the originator of the present system of cattleguards at crossings. He traveled on all the roads in operation, familiarizing himself with the work so that he could put his road in successful operation. He was also the principal mover and founder of the bank at Woodville that was chartered with the road. He was the founder of one of the first cotton factories in the state, it having been established in 1849 or 1850 with ninety looms and thirty-five hundred spindles. He went to Lowell, Mass., to familiarize himself with the work and also secure a number of hands from the Dog river mills in Alabama. In 1855 he purchased the entire plant, and operated it successfully until burned by the Federals in 1863. Soon after the war the West Feliciana railroad became involved, and he loaned it $100,000, taking first mortgage, which resulted in his securing final ownership of the road. Himself, and later his sons, continued to operate it until 1887, when they sold out to the present company. Mr. McGehee was the builder and founder of the Bethel church, first constructed in 1811. He later gave $2,000 toward the present building that stands as a monument to his memory. He was also the founder of the Woodville female academy that was burned in 1849, and of the present college for girls. He was administrator for President Zachary Taylor, and throughout his life occupied many positions of trust with scrupulous fidelity. As a cotton planter he was wonderfully prosperous. His judgment was unerring at all times, and success seemed to come at his bidding. He secured the best prices for his crops, cultivating his fields on American principles; had abiding faith in God, but this did not prevent him from plowing deep, planting early and keeping down the grass. He prayed to God for everything, but did not expect to secure desired ends without the use of means when means were at hand. His possessions increased until his fields stretched out as wide as a feudal estate, and his servants exceeded a thousand in number. His public spirit and liberality kept pace with his temporal prosperity. His strong and friendly hand touched the springs of enterprise and benevolence all around him. The state of Mississippi was indebted to him for its first railroad, which was the fifth built in the United States. He was the munificent benefactor of his own church. Centenary college was the child of his love. He originally purchased its buildings from the state of Louisiana, and his gifts to it were not less than $70,000. He was also chief patron of the Woodville female seminary. The Carondelet Street Methodist Episcopal church in New Orleans is a double monument of his beneficence. He gave a princely sum to this building, which, when finished, owed him $40,000. This debt he offered to cancel if the church would pay him $16,000 in cash, and when payment was tendered he declined to take anything at first, but finally accepted $2,000, which he applied toward building the Bethel church of this county. The life of Mr. McGehee was filled with such noble acts as these. "There was," says Bishop Keener, who was present, "a tremulous emotion and modesty in the manner of his making this gift that surpassed the beneficence of the gift itself, for he seemed to be the obliged party in the transaction." His love for the church and his princely way were pleasantly illustrated on one occasion when the Mississippi annual conference met at Woodville, by his giving horses to several of the ministers and blankets to every member of the body. No full earthly record could be made of what he did to equip, send forth and sustain the ministers of God, and for the support of the institution of the church in the Southwest; but it is written with his name in the Book of Life. He took time to give attention and service to all the interests of the church. While cultivating six or seven large plantations at once and taking a prominent part in all matters affecting the material interests of society, he was always punctual in the discharge of his duties as a disciple of the Lord Jesus Christ. He was spiritually minded, "a man of much devotion and private meditation." A beautiful picture of him is presented at eventide walking alone and communing with God, in the grand forest of oaks, beeches and magnolias which were the most attractive feature of Bowling Green, his family residence. He loved the songs of Zion, and to the last the old melodies of early Methodism fired his heart. He delighted in the worship of God and communion of saints. He loved the class-meeting. With rare good sense and loving fervor he bore testimony for his Lord and instructed and comforted his fellow-disciples. He wished to be honest with God as well as man. This sentiment of honor was thus exalted into a Christian grace by the transforming touch of the Holy Spirit. "Had he been charged by his Lord with special care of the poor and of the widows and orphans," said one who knew him intimately, "he could scarcely have been more attentive to their interests. He accepted the care of elders and watched over the education of youth with fatherly sympathy." In him the grace of hospitality was personified; his manner was the perfection of delicacy and refinement and of engaging sincerity that at once put the visitor at ease. "Toward his guests, or the workingmen at his table, or to his servants at a lograising, his courtesy was uniform; no matter how busy he might be, if a child entered the room it was always received with a smile and an extended hand." On the occasion of introducing Gen. Zachary Taylor, then president-elect of the United States, at a reception given him at Woodville, this noble, self-obliviousness was conspicuous. On the return home one of the servants exclaimed: "Others may have seen General Taylor but I saw only master. He was so polite and grand!" He was a thoughtful and prayerful owner of slaves. At one time he thought seriously of going to Africa to superintend a colony of his own servants planted by himself. He was an early and generous supporter of the schemes of African colonization. Good and wise men are still looking in that direction, and what was an unfulfilled aspiration to him may find its realization hereafter. All possible efforts were made by him for the promotion of the religious and social welfare of his servants. At family prayer, which was maintained by him all of his life, the servants were called in, and it was no uncommon thing for one or more to be called upon by him to lead in the prayer after he had read the morning or evening lesson from the Bible. When the slaves were freed, at the close of the Civil war, he felt that a heavy responsibility was lifted from his shoulders; but his interests in the well being of the negro race did not abate. No unmanly whinings or unchristian murmurings were indulged in by him. His pecuniary loss was enormous, but he never cared for property for its own sake; he was one of the few who could make it rapidly and use it wisely without harm to himself. He bore himself with characteristic magnanimity amid the political convulsions of the time, and his noble qualities as a Christian never shone more brightly than then. His beautiful mansion, Bowling Green, was one of the finest in the county, built with a view of home comforts, costing many thousands of dollars and supplied with several thousand volumes of the best books selected among the various authors, and many rare and valuable works, and its entire contents were burned by a regiment of negro troops just at the close of the war. Yet he never complained. Leaving the ruins of the former house undisturbed he built a second house, close by its four blackened walls and pillars, which remains as a monument of the terrible times now safely past. Exalted goodness gives no exemption from temporal calamity when the red devil of war is unchained. He had no relish for public life. He demonstrated that an American citizen may be public-spirited and patriotic without seeking official positions. He served several terms in the Mississippi legislature at the earnest demand of his fellow-citizens, who knew that he possessed in an eminent degree the qualities that make a good lawmaker. His legislative career was most honorable and useful; but as soon as he could follow his own wishes, without disregarding the obligations of citizenship, he returned to private life. President Taylor offered him the secretaryship of the United States treasury, but he declined, preferring the independence of a private gentleman, and shrinking from the glare of high official station. The fires of political ambition that have burned so fiercely in so many men, and burned out what was truest and best in them, had no place in his soul.

A holier flame had been kindled then by the touch of a heavenly spark. General Taylor voiced what everybody thought when he said "that he was the best man he ever knew." "I have known him," said the General, "to lift a drunkard from the road into the buggy and take him home." Sweet-souled disciple! He had learned his lesson at the feet of Jesus, who was the life of this good and noble-hearted man. Name after name might be mentioned, among which are the celebrated Pierces of Georgia, Dr. William Winans, Benjamin Drake, John Lane, Thomas Clinton, and many others, who have enjoyed his hospitality and entertained the sincerest admiration and affection for their princely host. He died at his home October 1, 1880, in the ninety-fourth year of his age, and the white, kingly soul was caught up to the presence of the King of Kings and to the company of the just. He stood above six feet high, was large-framed, erect, with calm, dark eyes, whose kindly magnetism none could resist; straight black hair, a nobility of countenance and dignity of mien that led many persons after meeting him to say that he reminded them of General Washington as portrayed in history; a voice singularly gentle and yet grandly brave; a brain of immense power, and a heart tuned to the finest emotions; a prince in all the elements of leadership among his fellows; a patriarch in the fatherliness of his great, affectionate nature; the strongest pillar of the church; the perfect model of a citizen; the friend of the widow and orphan; the builder of churches and colleges; the white man's exemplar and the black man's protector; the benefactor of all accessible humanity, and the humble, adoring disciple of the Lord Jesus Christ. Edward McGehee may be taken as a type of one side of the civilization of the old South in the midst of which good men and women, while, as God's instrument, they were training the lowly for whatever better things he has in store for them hereafter, bloomed into a peculiar grace and dignity and reached hights attained only by those who, being tried in the fires, come forth as gold. Mr. McGehee was married three times; by the first marriage to Miss Cosby was born the following children: Cynthia Ann, who married John S. Walton, of New Orleans, and died within one year; James Jack, who died, an infant; Sarah Houston, who married John W. Burness, and had seven children, of whom two died infants (Ann McG.,

75

Catherine F., Edward McG., Mary E. and Sally L.); James Hays, who died an infant, and Edward J., who married Ann B. Carter, and they have three sons. The mother of these children died January 9, 1821, a noble, Christian woman, loved and respected by all. On December 23, 1823, Judge McGehee married Harriet Ann Goodrich, a native of New Orleans, by whom were born three children: Charles, Micajah and Harriet Ann, who died in infancy. The mother of these children died October 15, 1827, while in Alabama, and is buried with her infant child in Abner McGehee's cemetery in that state. Judge Edward McGehee was again married February 15, 1829, to Mary H. Burruss, and by her had eleven children. She died October 30, 1873, in the sixty-second year of her age, and was the daughter of Rev. J. C. Burruss, one of this county's most honored and devoted Christian gentlemen. Mrs. McGehee was loved and esteemed for her many admirable qualities. She was a gentle and cultivated woman and a most intelligent and devoted Christian. She was from her youth a member of the Methodist Episcopal church, and to the last a considerate and generous supporter of its institutions, and among her many excellencies was her unexcelled hospitality.

Mr. J. H. Muse writes as follows: "I first became acquainted with Judge McGehee soon after 1830, being at that time a member of the legislature of Louisiana. I was called from my my seat early one morning in the lobby and introduced to him; he promptly explained to me the object of the interview. There was impending before the legislature a bill for the relief of the Woodville & West Feliciana railroad company, in which he was one of the stockholders, and on which he desired my favorable consideration. Never has that interview faded in the least degree from my memory. I never was so favorably and deeply impressed on first acquaintance with any one as I was with Judge McGehee. In his conversation, his demeanor and general bearing, combined with the simplicity and gentleness of a child, the seriousness of a sage and the dignity of a prince. Such was his character. He was then in the prime and vigor of middle age. Of course he obtained what he desired at the hands of the legislature. It was but a short time after this first acquaintance that I became professionally acquainted with him. He, together with Gen. Zachary Taylor, had signed their names as sureties to a tutor's bond who died without having filed an account of his tutorship. The sureties had to respond, but there was no appeal to the courts to delay or evade their liabilities. Competent accountants, to ascertain the amount of their liabilities, were secured, and this being done there was an end of the matter, as their liabilities were promptly met. No man placed a higher estimate upon good faith in contracts than Jndge McGehee. A few years after the railroad above alluded to had been partly constructed, a rupture occurred, under the leadership of Isaac McCord, between the railroad contractors and the railroad company, who were then locating a bank at Woodville, Miss. A very considerable amount of work had been done upon the railroad; the contractors had also dealt very liberally with the hands. They finally abandoned their contract, for alleged violation on the part of the railroad company, laying their claims for damages, loss of profits and arrearages of payments for work done at $350,000. The case was some years in court before it was tried. A special term of the district court for the parish of West Feliciana was convened to try it. On March 3, 1845, the case was called, with the railroad and banking company represented by Maj. Joseph Johnson and Judge Edward McGehee. The trial lasted some four months and the testimony formed about one thousand pages. At the conclusion of the trial the jury returned a verdict reducing the plaintiff's demand from $350,000 to six and one-fourth cents."

Edward J. McGehee (deceased) was the fifth child of Judge Edward and Margaret L. (Cosby) McGehee, and was born January 29, 1820, on Thompson's creek, the home place and original settlement of Judge McGehee. At the age of nine years he was sent to Dr.

Webb's school, in Connecticut, at Middletown, where he remained for some years, or until compelled to relinquish his studies and return home on account of failing eyesight, just before graduation; but owing to his faithfulness at school, his high standing and the respect held for him by the faculty, he was given a diploma in lieu of a graduating certificate. On returning home he first settled at what is now Westwood, the home place of Charles Mc-Gehee, and remained there for a few years. He was married December 22, 1841, to Anna B. Carter, a native of Mississippi, born and reared on the adjoining place to Westwood. She was a daughter of George Washington Carter (a native of Virginia) and Mary B. Wormley, also of Virginia. The latter was a daughter of Major Wormley, of the British army, and was a noble woman. Charles Carter, the father of George W. Carter, married Betty Lewis, a niece of Gen. George Washington. Edward J. McGehee, the subject of this biography, moved to Cold Spring plantation, at Pinckneyville, in February, 1845, where he resided until his death. He was one of the leading planters of the county, but possessed a fine mind, and devoted a great deal of his time to study and meditation. He had a fine library, containing many rare and valuable books. He was endowed in an eminent degree with a high sense of honor, and was a noble man in every sense of the term. He was strictly honest in all his dealings, charitable, generous, hospitable and kind-hearted, and was a leading member of the Methodist Episcopal church of Pinckneyville, in which he took special pride, and manifested the greatest interest in humanizing and caring for the unfortunate and poor. He possessed many noble and remarkable characteristics, and was honored and loved by all. Like his honored and respected father, he took no active or special part in politics, other than to exercise his right of suffrage. His death occurred June 20, 1860, at the early age of forty years. His widow died January 28, 1879. She was born January 26, 1825, and and was educated by Mr. Halsey, Mr. Foster and others, and was very highly accomplished. During the life of her devoted husband she was a leading member of the Methodist Episcopal church, and one of the purest of Christian women. Some time after his death she united with the Episcopal church. To her union with Mr. McGehee were born three sons: Edward J., Harry T. and A. Merwin, all of whom live in the vicinity of the old homestead. Edward J., the eldest son, now a citizen of Louisiana, was born and reared in Mississippi, and was first sent to Mr. Pride's school and placed under private tutors until going to Virginia. There he attended Dinwiddie school, at Greenwood depot, and then at Dr. Charles Minor's school near Charlottesville, Va. In April, 1861, he returned home, but soon after returned to Virginia and entered the Confederate army, first in a Mississippi battalion, and later the Twenty-first Mississippi regiment. He served bravely as a private in the following battles: Savage Station, Malvern Hill, first battle of Fredericksburg, Chickamauga, Cedar Creek, the first battle of Petersburg, Cold Harbor, etc., besides numerous skirmishes. He was not taken prisoner, but was wounded at Cedar Creek through the left side, and was disabled for some time. At the close of the war he was paroled at Fort Adams, on a gunboat. He returned and settled in the old home place in 1866, and engaged in planting. He built his present house in 1866, and there he has since lived.

In 1865 he was married to Corinne A. Evans, daughter of John N. Evans, who was a son of Nathanial Evans, one of the county's early settlers and during the war a quartermaster in General Williams' army. To their union were born six children, all living: Edward Evans, Mary Cornelia, Arthur Harry, Anna Beverly, Frances Eugenia and John Nathaniel. Harry T. McGehee, the second son of Edward J., was educated by private tutors and in the same schools as his brothers. He entered the Confederate service just after the first battle of Fredericksburg, as a member of the Twenty-first Mississippi regiment, company D, with his elder brother, under Col. B. G. Humphreys, afterward brigadier-general. He was in the second battle of Fredericksburg, Gettysburg, Cold Harbor, Chickamauga, Cedar creek and several skirmishes and the movements around Richmond. On returning home at the close of the war he settled in East Feliciana parish, La., where he remained for several years. In 1876 he moved to the old home place, where he remained a short time, and to his present place the same year, where he has since lived. He was married in 1870 to Margaret J. Percy, daughter of Dr. Thomas Percy, one of the early settlers and prominent citizens. To Mr. and Mrs. McGehee were born three children: Harry Percy, Elizabeth Rowena and Percy Carter. The mother, Mrs. McGehee, is a member of the Episcopal church. Mr. McGehee is a stanch democrat and keeps himself well posted in the political situation. The third son born was A. Merwin McGehee, who was reared in Wilkinson county and educated by private tutors, and when but sixteen years of age entered the service of the Confederate army and was detached on special duty in Mississippi and Louisiana until the close. After the war he settled on the old home place of his parents, where he has since resided. He was married in 1869 to Kate S. Towles, who was born and reared in Louisiana, being the daughter of John T. Towles, an early settler of Louisiana and one of the representative citizens. They have six children: Beverly Merwin, Arthur Merwin, Fannie Towles, Catherine Sarah, Edna and Mary Cornelia. Mr. and Mrs. McGehee are members of the Episcopal church, and in politics he is a democrat.

Charles G. McGehee is a son of Judge Edward McGehee and Harriet Ann Goodrich, and was reared on Bowling Green plantation, and educated in Lexington, Ky. He was united in marriage to Stella McNair, daughter of Robert H. McNair, of New Orleans, where she was reared and educated. This worthy lady died December 9, 1859. She was a lifelong member of the Presbyterian church, a noble Christian and a devoted mother. By this union were born six children: Robert M., a successful planter of this county, a leader in society, prominent in business circles and very popular; Edward L., one of the prominent and leading physicians of Woodville; Laura, the wife of Hugh L. Davis, by whom she bore one son, Hugh J.; Charles G. (deceased), Howard B. and Stella, wife of George J. Adams, druggist, of Woodville. Charles G. McGehee was subsequently married to Anna G. McNair, sister of his former wife, her birth occurring December 19, 1831. She was reared and educated in New Orleans, and was married August 21, 1866. She died December 12, 1884, a noble and highly respected lady, a devoted mother and faithful Christian. During the latter part of her life she suffered poor health, but bore all uncomplainingly. Mr. McGehee settled where he now resides, in 1848, on what is now known as the Westwood plantation, a beautiful place, surrounded with all the comforts of a fine Southern home. Mr. McGehee is a very extensive planter and respected citizen. He is a member of the Methodist church, and a very liberal supporter of church interests and advancement. He takes no special part in political matters. Micajah McGehee, second son of Judge Edward McGehee and Harriet Ann Goodrich, died August 21, 1880, aged fifty-four years. He was educated at Transylvania university, graduating in 1846, and in 1848, when Colonel Fremont, on his fourth exploring expedition, crossed the plains he joined the party. In this expedition he suffered untold hardships, the effects of which remained with him until death. He kept a diary of his experiences, and the same was published in the *Century* illustrated monthly magazine of March, 1891, from which the following extract is taken: " The farther we went the more obstacles we had to encounter; difficulties beset us so thickly on every hand as we advanced that they threatened to thwart our expedition. The snow became deeper daily, and to advance was but adding danger to difficulties. About one-third of the men were already more or less frost bitten; every night some of the mules would freeze to death, and every day as many more would give out from exhaustion and be left on the trail. It seemed like fighting fate to attempt to proceed, but we were bent on our course, and continued to advance. At one time men were sent ahead to report the prospect, and returned stating that grass appeared in the distance before them; they supposed that the snow was abating, but on coming up what they saw proved to be the tops of bushes six feet high projecting above the snow; nor did anything appear upon which the animals could subsist. The corn we had packed along for them was already consumed. Sometimes we would attempt to move on, and the severity of the weafher would force us back into camp. In one of these attempts before we could beat our way half a mile against the tempest, our guide, Old Bill Williams, was nearly frozen; he dropped down upon his mule in a stupor, and was nearly senseless when we got into camp. A number of men came in with their noses, ears, faces, fingers and feet partly frozen, and one or two of the mules dropped down and froze to death under their packs. Poor mules, it was pitiable to see them! They would roam about all night, generally on account of their extreme weakness, following back the path of the previous day, pawing in the snow three or four feet for some sign of vegetation to keep them alive. They would fall down every fifty yards under their packs, and we would have to unpack them and lift them up, and that with fingers frozen and lacerated by the cold. Finally they began eating the rope and rawhide lariats with which they were tied, until there were no more left in camp to tie them with; then they ate the blankets which we tied over them at night; then they came into camp and ate the pads and rigging off the pack-saddles, and ate one another's manes and tails entirely bare, even into the flesh, and would come to us while sleeping and begin to eat the blankets off us; they would even tumble into our fires over the cooking utensils. But, poor things, little relief could we afford them, for, although they suffered much, we were in no better condition. Our provisions were nearly exhausted, and we were more or less frozen.

"Finally, on the 17th of December, after frequent ineffectual attempts, we found that we could force our way no farther. By our utmost endeavors with mauls and spades we could make but half a mile or a mile per day. The cold became more severe, and storms constant, so that nothing was visible at times through the thick, driving snow. For days in succession we would labor to beat a trail a few hundred yards in length, but the next day the storm would leave no trace of the previous day's work. We were on the St. John mountain, a section of the Sierra Madre and the main range of the Rocky mountains proper. At an elevation of eleven thousand feet the cold was so intense and the atmosphere so rare that respiration became difficult, the least exertion became laborious and fatiguing, and would sometimes cause the blood to start from lips and nose. The mercury in the thermometer stood twenty degrees below zero, and snow was here from four to thirty feet deep. When we built our camp-fires deep pits were formed by the melting of the snow, completely concealing the different messes from each other. Down in these holes we slept, spreading our blankets upon the snow, every morning crawling out from under a deep covering of snow which had fallen upon us during the night. The strong pine-smoke—for here there was no timber but pine—together with the reflection from the snow, so affected our sight that at times we could scarcely see. The snow drifted over us continually, driven about by the violence of the chill blasts which swept over the mountains." After several days of awful suffering, the narrative continues as follows: " Now commenced a train of horrors which it is painful to force the mind to dwell upon, and which memory shrinks from. Before we had proceeded far Manuel, a California Indian, of the Consumne tribe, who had his feet badly frozen, stopped and begged Mr. Vincent Haler to shoot him and failing to meet death in this way turned back to the lodge at the camp we had left, there to await his fate. The same day Wise lay down on the ice and died, and the Indian boys, Joaquin and Gregorio, who came afterward, having stopped back to get some wood for Manuel, seeing his body, covered it with brush and snow. That night Carver, crazed with hunger, raved terribly all night, so that some in the camp with him became alarmed for their safety. He told them if they would follow him back he had a plan by which they might live. The next day he wandered off and we never saw him again. The next night Sorel, his system wrought upon by hunger, cold and exhaustion, took a violent fit, which lasted some time, and to which succeeded an entire prostration of all his faculties. At the same time he was almost totally snow-blind. Speaking to E. Kern of our situation, he said, 'O, Kern, this is a *misse Dieu* (a visitation from God) and we can't avoid it.' Poor fellow, the next day he traveled as long as his strength would allow, and then, telling us we would have to leave him, that he could go no farther, blind with snow, he lay down on the river bank to die. Moran soon joined him, and they never came up again. Late at night, arriving one by one, we all came into camp together on the river bank. Gloom and despondency were depicted on every face. Our condition had become perfectly desperate. We knew not what to do. The candles and parfleche had kept us alive thus far, but these were gone. Our appearance was most desolate as we sat in silence around the fires, in view of a fast approaching death by starvation, while hunger gnawed upon our vitals. Then Vincent Haler, to whom the Colonel had left the charge of the camp, and whom for that reason we had allowed to have the chief direction, spoke up and told us that he then and there threw up all authority; that he could do nothing, and knew not what to advise; that he looked upon our condition as hopeless; but he would suggest, as the best advice he could give, that we break up into small parties, and, hunting along, make the best of our way separately, each party making use of the advantages that might fall in its way, so that if they should chance to get through to a settlement they could forward relief to the others. Accordingly the next morning he joined himself with Scott, Martin, Hibbard, Bacon, Ducatel, Rohrer, and the two Indians, Joaquin and Gregorio. Ferguson and Beedle went in company, and the rest of us, the three Kerns, Captain Cathcart, Captain Taplin, Stepperfeldt, Andrews and myself went together. We agreed not to leave one another while life lasted. Again we resumed our unsteady course down the river. We traveled hard all day, and late in the evening, weak and worn out, staggered into a camp near the riverside, some coming in far behind the rest. Dr. Kern came up so exhausted that he fell down almost senseless, and remained in this torpid state a whole day. After awhile Andrews came up, and arriving within several hundred yards of camp raised a faint call and fell down completely exhausted and senseless. Two or three of us had to go and pack him in. He never recovered from this exhaustion. Soon Rohrer came up. Vincent Haler's party, to which he belonged, was ahead of us, and being too weak to proceed farther he stopped with us. Here we remained, determined, as we had promised, not to leave any while they lived. So we commenced hunting, all that had strength and sight sufficient to do so, for the rest of us were so completely snow-blind that we could not see to shoot. After long and frequent hunts, two prairie chickens, or grouse, were killed. These we divided with scrupulous exactness among nine of us, dividing the entrails and all that appertained to them, even to the pin-feathers. Taplin found part of a dead wolf upon the river, and brought it in. One side of it and the entrails had been eaten away, but we divided the skin and roasted it, hair and all, for one meal; for another we drank meager broth, and then we ate the meat and even devoured the bones. This was the last we got.

"Day after day we staid here, but no game came near. Occasionally we could hear the distant, dismal howl of a wolf, as if weary of waiting for its prey, but none came near; at distant intervals a raven would go screaming by, beyond our reach. We found a handful or two of rosebuds along the river which we divided and ate, and Dr. Kern found a few small bugs upon the water where the ice was broken, and ate them. We had already devoured our moccasin soles, and a small sack made of smoked lodge skin. We dug in the ground beneath the snow with our knives for roots, but it proved useless labor. We became weaker daily, and to walk thirty steps once a day to get some dry cottonwood sticks to keep up our fire fatigued us greatly. Our strength was rapidly failing. Andrews, after lingering several days, died in the night as he lay by our side, and the next day Rohrer was nearly gone; he was talking wildly, a fearful expression of despair resting upon his countenance. The mention of his family at home had served to rouse him and keep him going longer than his strength would otherwise have borne him up; but now it was too late. Taking from Andrew's pocket a small gilt-embossed Bible, carefully preserved, which we intended, in case any of us lived to get through, to hand over as a memento to his friends, we laid his body to one side, covered it with a blanket, and sat down, waiting till Rohrer should die, intending as soon as the breath left his body, to commence another move down the river. As we sat waiting, ———— ———— came over to the fire where Taplin, Stepperfeldt and I were sitting, and in a sad tone said: 'Men, I have come to make a proposition. I don't know how you will take it. It is a horrid one. We are starving; in two or three days more, unless something is done, we shall all be dead. As soon as we leave this body it will become the prey of wild beasts. Now, I propose instead that we make use of it to save life. It is horrible I know, but I will undertake to do the butchery, as you may call it, and you need have nothing to do with that part; you need not even see it done. Do you agree to my proposition?' All sat in silence; then several of us objected. I spoke up and said that, for my part, I had no conscientious scruples against such a procedure. I knew that early prejudice and conventional opinion founded on prejudice were at the bottom of our objections to it; but these existed; and it was a horrible proposition to entertain. I fully appreciated our situation, but I thought that, by making up our minds to it and remaining quiet, we could hold out three days longer, by which time, after finding that we could not possibly bear up longer, it would be soon enough to think of adopting so horrible alternative, and then if I did not approve, I would not censure it. ' But by that time,' he said, 'we will be too weak and too far gone ever to recover. You see what they have come to, and you see what you will come to.' 'I can't help it,' I said, 'I am determined to risk it at the peril of my life;' and so saying I walked over to the other fire. They talked about it for a few minutes, but were unwilling to follow such a course unless all united in it, and so we all waited together. We remained around the fire stirring as little as possible, and firing signal guns at frequent intervals during the day. Rohrer died. Two days passed by, and no relief came. Several times we imagined we heard an answer to our signal and would raise ourselves up to listen; but being so often disappointed, we ceased to notice. The morning of the third day arrived and was far advanced toward midday; we all sat in the deepest gloom. Suddenly, ' Hush,' said one. We all listened intently. A call was heard. ' Relief, by heaven!' exclaimed one of the men, and we all started to our feet, and relief it was, sure enough; for soon we spied Godey riding toward us followed by a Mexican. We were all so snow-blind that we took him to be the Colonel until he came up, and even then some saluted him as the Colonel. Dismounting, he quickly distributed several loaves among us, and with commendable forethought giving us but a small piece at first and making us wait until the Mexican could prepare some tole (boiled cornmeal), which he quickly made and we more quickly devoured. It required considerable persuasion to prevent us from killing the Mexican's old horse in order to eat it; but Godey informed us that there were two colts in the camp below, which, if we would wait, we might have. This was on January 25." And after the rescue he continues: "We sent for animals to take us down, for we were wholly unable to walk. They came the next day. Our blankets were tied on for saddles and rope stirrups were rigged, and we were lifted (for we could not lift even our skeleton frames) upon these miserable animals, and after two days' journey reached the camp twenty miles below. We were now lank and thin-visaged, our eyes sunken and our hair and beard long, tangled and knotty, while our faces were black with pine smoke, which had not been washed for two months. Here we fell to eating enormously, and it required the exercise of our self-restraint to prevent plenty now from being hurtful to us, as want had been before. The abundance of food where there had just been such a lack, made us all sick and kept us sick for some days, but that could not stop us. Our appetites were unbounded and we were eating constantly at all hours of the day and throughout the night. We had such a craving for meat of some kind that we killed two well-grown colts and ate them. We were even more ravenous than the ravens themselves which, now that we did not need them, came crowding around with hawks and wolves. Some of all these we killed and devoured." Mr. McGehee spent a number of years in California and then returned to Mississippi. He was a gentleman of fine attainments, well educated and exceptionally informed, amiable, benevolent, refined, loved by his kindred and friends and respected by all. He was elected to the legislature of California for several terms and was judge of his circuit also for many terms.

Capt. George T. McGehee is the third son of Hon. Edward McGehee and Mary Burruss. He was born on the Bowling Green plantation in 1833, where he was reared and educated by private tutors. His mother was born March 21, 1812, in Caroline county, Va., and was the daughter of Rev. John C. and Elizabeth (Brame) Burruss. Rev. John C. Burruss was one of the most distinguished divines of his age, and his wife, Miss Elizabeth Brame, was the daughter of Walter and Jemima Brame, of Caroline county, Va., who were prominent and highly esteemed. Mrs. McGehee's early days were spent amid the ceaseless wanderings incident to itineracy, in the early days of Methodism. In her childhood she gave promise of those qualities, which in riper years distinguished her as a living exemplification of womanly virtues. Every available means was employed to furnish her the advantages of an education, literary and scientific, and her mental activity was such that her superiority in every department of learning was readily conceded. At eleven years of age she consecrated her life to the services of her God. In 1829 she married Edward McGehee, by whom she had eleven children: William (deceased), Frances (deceased), George T., John B. (planter of Louisiana, and for fifteen years president of the West Feliciana railroad), Caroline E. (wife of Duncan Stewart, living at Laurel Hill, La.), Wilbur Fisk (born September 25, 1839, and died August 1, 1859; he had just returned from the University of Virginia, where he was a bright student; he was a cherished and loving son, and was never neglectful of the smallest courtesies of a Christian gentleman, and was the pride of his friends), Mary L. (who married Samuel Snowden, both of whom are deceased, leaving a son, now in his sixteenth year, and an attendant of the Agricultural and Mechanical college), Scott (now living in New Orleans, secretary of the Southern insurance company, and married to Louisa Schaumberg), Harriet L. (who died a child), Abner E. (died, aged six months), and Eugenia A. (who died in New York, December 16, 1882, at the age of twenty-five years). Mr. McGehee lives near Woodville, on the site of the old cotton factory. He is a well-known and prominent planter in this county. In 1851 he entered Yale college, from which he graduated in 1855, with a class of ninety-three. He then returned to Wilkinson county and engaged in planting until he entered the Confederate service, in

General Brandon's company, which later was merged into the Twenty-first Mississippi regiment of the army of northern Virginia. At first he was third sergeant, then was promoted captain, and appointed assistant quartermaster of the regiment. During the last years of the war he was on Major-General Kershaw's staff. After the surrender of General Lee, he was captured by General Palmer, at Athens, Ga., where he was paroled. He served all through the war without receiving a wound. Before the war, after finishing his education, he first settled on the banks of the Homochitto river, where he engaged in cotton planting, and to this place he returned after the war, where he continued planting until 1870, when he went to the home place to assist his aged father in looking after his many interests. There he resided until his marriage in 1874, when he came to his present place, one-half mile from Woodville. It is a beautiful home. He was married to Miss Elizabeth B. McNair, of New Orleans. She was born, reared and educated in that city, and is an accomplished lady. She is the daughter of Robert McNair, a native of Kentucky and a next-door neighbor of Henry Clay for many years, but later he moved to New Orleans, where he reared his family. Mr. and Mrs. McGehee have no children of their own, but in 1880 adopted the twin children of General Hood—Odile and Ida—two beautiful young girls. Captain McGehee is an active worker in the Methodist Episcopal church, while his estimable wife is a member of the Presbyterian church. They are liberal contributors to all worthy and charitable institutions, and very highly respected. Mr. McGehee served in the state legislature in 1878, and was reëlected in 1880, and was also a member of the constitutional convention in 1890. He is democratic in politics. He is a member of the board of trustees of the McGehee college for girls, of Woodville, of which he is secretary.

Hon. J. Burruss McGehee, one of the leading stock farmers of Louisiana, and son of Judge Edward and Mary (Burruss) McGehee, attended the University of Virginia. Coming home from school he assisted on the home place, and in his twentieth year engaged in planting in Yazoo county. In 1858 he came to his present place, where he has since resided, engaged in extensive stockraising, and was the first planter to engage in growing grass and mules in the state of Louisiana, exclusive of corn and cotton. He served in the Confederate army during the latter part of the war, and during the former part was engaged in the cotton factory of his father, near Woodville. Mr. McGehee was married in June, 1859, to Miss Catherine Eliza Stewart, and by this union was born one son, J. Stewart McGehee, who married Miss L. C. Johnson, and was for some years a resident of Wilkinson county, but now resides in St. Louis, Mo. Mr. and Mrs. McGehee are members of the Episcopal church and enjoy a very high social position. Mr. McGehee is a member of the Masonic lodge No. 63, of Woodville, Miss., and owns one of the largest stock farms in Louisiana, besides several large farms in Louisiana and Mississippi, including the home place of his father, Bowling Green, and the first settled place in the southeast portion of this county. He was president of the West Feliciana railroad from June, 1869, until the sale of the road to the present company in January, 1888. He also published a paper in Louisiana, for some time known as the *Churchman*, and later as the *Churchman and Industrial News*, separate papers, but printed in the same office. He was a member of the "Nicholls" legislature, lower house, session of 1877 and 1878.

Thomas W. McGehee, M. D., is among the very foremost of the professional men of Amite county, Miss., and as a practitioner of the healing art he has won for himself golden opinions. His cheerful countenance, encouraging words and advice, and his thorough knowledge of his profession, which only long and continuous practice can give, has placed him upon the highest pinnacle of success, and his services are sought over a large scope of territory. He received a fair education at Zion Hill. He then studied medicine under his father for a few years, and took his first course of lectures in the Cincinnati Eclectic School of Medicine in the winter of 1859–60. In the early part of the latter year he continued his studies with his father, and during the summer also practiced some. In the winter of 1860–61 he went to New Orleans, and after taking a course of lectures, left that institution to enter the army, becoming a member of the Seventh Mississippi infantry, in which he was elected regimental surgeon, in which capacity he served during his service. He, however, entered the ranks, and participated in the battle of Shiloh, where, during the second day's fight, he received seven gunshot wounds, one leg being badly broken, and resulted in his permanent disability from further service. He returned home, put himself under his father's treatment, and owing to the unwearied devotion and care of the latter, the leg was saved. After sufficiently recovering, he returned to New Orleans, to resume his medical studies, and March 6, 1866, graduated in a class of twenty-nine. He returned at once to Zion Hill, opened an office, and practiced for three years, at the end of which time he moved to Osyka, where he was associated with his father for one year. After one year's practice in Summit county, he returned to Zion Hill, but in 1882 became a resident of Liberty. Since February, 1885, he has been a resident of Gloster, of which place he has been an active practitioner ever since. During his practice in Amite county, of about a quarter of a century, he has become very favorably known, for his reputation as a student, no less than his many worthy personal characteristics, has won for him an enviable reputation. He was married in this county June 14, 1861, to Miss Margaret J., the daughter of Alexander Hughey. She was born in this county, and has borne her husband four children: Marietta, Pollard Lee, Pattie Lloyd and Nita Ellwin. The Doctor is a member of the Masonic fraternity, and he and his wife belong to the Baptist church. His father, Dr. William McGehee, was a Georgian, but was one of the early settlers of Amite county, his home, after coming to this section, being near Zion Hill. He was a soldier in the War of 1812, and by occupation was an honest tiller of the soil. His son, Dr. William C. McGehee, the father of Dr. Thomas W., was born on his father's plantation in this county in 1813. He was a well informed and intelligent man, and being somewhat interested in politics, he served as deputy-sheriff for about three years in his younger days. He was married here to Mrs. Mourning Garrett Knox, a widow, and a daughter of Aaron Butler, who was also one of the early pioneers and a soldier in the War of 1812. After his marriage, Dr. McGehee settled on a plantation near Liberty, and as he had devoted much attention to the study of medicine, he became known throughout this region as an exceptionally skillful physician. In 1868 he moved to Osyka, and was actively engaged in practicing at the time of his death in 1874, his wife having been called from life the previous year. He was a Royal Arch mason, and a worthy and estimable man. He and wife had two sons and five daughters, the younger son being a prosperous merchant of Gloster. The daughters are deceased.

John McGill, an old and prominent citizen of Jackson, Miss., was born in New Albany, Ind., in 1838, a son of Daniel and Margaret (Tearnan) McGill, who were born and reared in County Louth, Ireland, being also married there. After they had become the parents of one child, they, in 1833 or 1834, came to America, further history of whom may be found in the sketch of Richard F. McGill. John McGill came to Jackson with his parents in 1846, served an apprenticeship as a printer and worked at that calling until 1874, with the exception of from 1861 to 1865. He was mustered into the Confederate service March 27, 1861, becoming a member of company K, Tenth Mississippi regiment, which was organized at Pensacola, and became part of the Army of the Tennessee. After twelve months he re-enlisted in Capt. J.

F. Kerr's battery of heavy artillery and was ordered to Vicksburg. After the siege of Vicksburg he was detailed to work in a newspaper office at Selma, Ala., and Jackson, Miss. In 1874 he was elected to the position of mayor of Jackson, which position he filled by re-election until 1888. At the time of his first election he found city affairs in a very bad condition, but during his regime he reduced the tax from twenty-one and three-fourths mills to eight and three-fourths mills, also paid off a large bonded and floating debt, made many valuable improvements, and although warrants were very low at first, when he retired they were at par. He has been one of the firemen of Jackson since he was eighteen years of age, and has been foreman of his company, Gem No. 2, since 1876, their fine steam engine being named John McGill. He served one year as alderman before being elected to the position of mayor. He became a republican in politics in 1868, and for ten years was chairman of the Hinds county republican executive committee, and was frequently a delegate to state and county conventions, and in 1888 was a delegate from the state at large to the national republican convention at Chicago, and was chairman of the Mississippi delegation. During the fourteen years that he was mayor he never missed a meeting of the board of mayor and aldermen, and while filling this position tried over seven thousand cases, only one of which was appealed, and that was affirmed by the board. He is a member of Pearl lodge No. 23, of the A. F. & A. M., of which he is past master, and is also a member of the chapter and commandery, in which he has officiated in all the offices. In addition to being an active member of this order he belongs to the I. O. O. F. and K. of P., and the K. of H., of which he helped to organize the Grand lodge in 1877, was elected grand chaplain and was an official member until 1890. He was married in 1864 to Miss Mary Eliza Kerr, a native of Jackson and a daughter of James H. and Henrietta C. Kerr. Her brother, Capt. R. C. Kerr, who died on May 28, 1891, was for years a leading citizen of Jackson, was registrar of land office for fourteen years, was at one time state librarian and was twice elected mayor of Jackson, but resigned the position in 1861 to enter the Confederate army. Mr. McGill lost his wife in 1866, since which time he has remained a widower. During the yellow-fever epidemic of 1878 he was one of the committee of the Howard society and helped nurse the sick, bury the dead and, in fact, did not hesitate to put his hand to any work, his services during that time being invaluable. During the three months the epidemics lasted he had entire control of the affairs of the city, the board of mayor and aldermen not having had a meeting during that time.

Richard F. McGill, steward of the Mississippi state lunatic asylum, at Jackson, Miss., came from Alabama to Jackson with his parents in 1846, where he has resided continuously since. He secured his education in Alabama by walking four miles to school. He afterward learned the carriagemaker's trade, at which he worked for about eight years. In November, 1859, he was elected to the board of trustees of the state lunatic asylum as steward, which position he filled for nearly two years, or until the opening of the Civil war, when he abandoned it to join the Confederate army, enlisting May 1, 1861, in company K of the Eighteenth Mississippi infantry, with which he was ordered to Virginia; arriving at Manassas on June 16, he was in the first battle of Manassas and in the battle of Leesburg, after which he was detached from the regular service and placed in the hospital at Leesburg as steward. He was soon after sent to Richmond, where he was regularly commissioned in May, 1862, as hospital steward, being the most of the time on duty at Winder hospital until the war closed. After his return from the war he was immediately placed in his former position as steward of the state lunatic asylum, and has been successively reëlected ever since. He is a kind-hearted, generous and social gentleman, ably fills his present position, as his long term of office would indicate, and is a useful and worthy citizen. He was married in December, 1879, to Miss

Mary E. Boyd, a native of Jackson, and a daughter of James H. Boyd, a pioneer and one of the old landmarks of Jackson, of which city he was mayor and justice for some time. He was a native of Kentucky, and for many years was a member of and an elder in the Presbyterian church. His excellent wife survives him, and is making her home with her daughter, Mrs. McGill. She is also an earnest Presbyterian. Their son, John H. Boyd, is a prominent and active minister of the Presbyterian church of Memphis. Mr. Boyd died July 4, 1877. Mr. and Mrs. McGill have two children: Richard F., Jr., and Mary E., Jr. Although Mr. McGill is a member of the Methodist Episcopal church, his wife adheres to the faith of the Presbyterians. Socially he is a member of the A. F. & A. M., in which he is a Knight Templar, and he also belongs to the I. O. O. F., the K. of P., the K. of H., the K. & L. of H. and the K. of the G. R.

Oscar H. McGinty, clerk of the chancery court of Jefferson county, Miss. The public services of Mr. McGinty since November, 1878, have been characterized by a noticeable devotion to the welfare of this county, and his ability and fidelity in his present position have made a lasting impression upon this sphere of public duty. It is but saying the truth when the statement is made that no more capable man for the position could be found, and that the people are aware of this fact is shown by his long continuance in office. His paternal grandparents were residents of Warren county, Miss., and his maternal grandparents, Felix and Margaret (Miller) Hughes, were born in County Armagh, Ireland, and Pickens county, S. C., respectively. Mr. Hughes came to America in the latter part of the eighteenth century, and in South Carolina was married to Miss Miller, immigrating soon afterward to Mississippi, and settling about three miles southwest of Fayette, where he became the owner of a large plantation, on which he reared a large family of children. Felix Hughes and Margaret Miller were married July 1, 1791, and the descendants propose to have a family reunion on the one hundredth anniversary of this event, at Austin, Tex.; they had four sons and eight daughters: Jane Pickens, Mary Ann, Robert Miller, Ardle, Philip Oscar, Sally Caroline, Felicia, Jefferson Joseph, Martha Green, Zilpah C., Hibernia Mary and Octavia A. Bertram G. McGinty, the father of Oscar H., was ushered into life in Warren county, Canada, but in his youth was brought to Jefferson county, Miss., where he attained manhood and was married, Miss Zilpah C. Hughes becoming his wife, and in time the mother of his six children, of whom two sons and one daughter are now living. Oscar H. McGinty is the younger of the two sons, his birth occurring in this county, near Fayette, on November 21, 1836. At the age of fifteen years he began doing for himself, and for some time was employed in carrying the United States mail from Fayette to Malcolm, the trips being made on horseback across country, this being before the period of railroads in this part of the state. He was reared to a knowledge of farm life, and his opportunities for obtaining an education were better than the average, notwithstanding the fact that when he was quite young his father died. At the age of eighteen years he entered Jefferson college, also attending the military institute of Mississippi for some time, and upon leaving school he was an intelligent and well-informed young man, for the opportunities he had received were not thrown away. Soon after he entered the sheriff's office as deputy, his brother being sheriff of the county at that time, and after serving in this capacity for three years, he entered a mercantile establishment at Rodney as a clerk. At a still later period he became the manager of a wharfboat, and was following this calling when the war opened. He enlisted in the service at two different times, but on account of ill-health was rejected each time. He then began devoting his attention to farming, and during the remainder of the war had charge of a plantation. In November, 1878, he was appointed to the office of chancery clerk to fill an unexpired term, at the expiration of which he was elected to the position, and by re-election has held the position up to the present time. As an official he is popular with all, kind and courteous in his intercourse with his fellowmen (a secret doubtless of his great popularity), and is always found willing to aid any enterprise which tends to the interests of his county. The lessons of industry, frugality and economy which he learned in his yonth have never been forgotten, and in his subsequent career found these qualities of much benefit to him. In 1860 he was united in marriage to Miss Amanda Hammett, of this county, the daughter of O. D. Hammett, and their union has resulted in the birth of three sons: Clifford, who was educated at Jefferson college, and is now in the mercantile business in Louisiana; Horace, who was educated at Galesburg, Ill., and is now deputy chancery clerk in the office with his father, and Oren, who determined to make the profession of law his lifework, and for that purpose entered the law department of the Vanderbilt university, of Nashville, Tenn. He was very bright and promising, and made rapid progress in his studies, but before he had completed his course he was stricken down by a disease which finally proved fatal, and his friends were soon called upon to mourn his death. He was a young man of exemplary habits, and was respected and admired by all who came within his influence. His remains now repose in the family burying ground at Fayette, and the care which his grave receives shows to the passerby the love that is still cherished for him in the hearts of his mourning friends. Mrs. McGinty is a lady of excellent natural abilities and is well educated, being a graduate of the Methodist Episcopal female college, located at Port Gibson. He father, O. D. Hammett, was born in Warren county, Ky., on October 27, 1805, is now residing near Fayette, and notwithstanding the fact that he has always led a remarkably active life, he is well preserved both bodily and mentally, showing but little the ravages of time. In 1835 he was married to Miss Mary Ann Borland, who departed this life March 2, 1882. The result of this union was fourteen children, ten of whom attained mature years. Of three daughter Mrs. McGinty is the eldest. Martha Irene, the second, is the wife of Henry Key, and resides at Fayette. She is a woman of sterling worth, and has a very interesting family of two sons and three daughters, to whom she is a most devoted mother. Olive, the youngest sister, is the widow of Robert Smith, and is a resident of Natchez. The seven brothers that are living all reside near Fayette. Mr. McGinty and his family are members of the Methodist Episcopal church, and he has been a member of the A. F. & A. M. since 1856, and is also a member of the K. of H.

In connection with his practice as a physician and surgeon Dr. James McGovern is also engaged in merchandising and farming, and is one of the honest, industrious citizens of Choctaw county. He was born in County Antrim, Ireland, in 1840, and is a son of James and Mary (Cullen) McGovern, natives also of the Emerald isle. They came to New York city when the Doctor was an infant, and there both passed the closing scenes of their lives. Of their six children—three sons and three daughters—only the sons are living: Bernard, a planter of Neshoba county, came to this state in 1852, and has been justice of the peace nearly ever since the war. John came here a year later, and now resides in Navarro county, Tex., where he is engaged in planting. Dr. James McGovern came to Choctaw county, Miss., with his eldest brother when eleven years of age, and received a common-school education. When seventeen years of age he began working for himself on a farm, and after obtaining sufficient means he attended school until the war. He then joined company I, Fifteenth Mississippi infantry, as a private in the Tennessee army, and fought at Rock Castle, Fishing Creek, Shiloh, Murfreesboro, from Resaca to Jonesboro, back to Franklin and Nashville, and then to Mississippi, and was at home at the time of the surrender. He was never

captured nor wounded. After the war he taught school sixteen months, or until he accumulated sufficient means to attend college, and then entered the University of Louisiana, now
Tulane university, and in 1868 he graduated from the University of Louisville, Ky.   Since
that time he has practiced in Choctaw county, and for five years at Kenaga. He is the
owner of two thousand acres of land, twelve hundred acres near Kenaga, and a saw, gin
and gristmill; also a store which does an annual business of $8,000.   This is all the result
of his own industry, honesty and excellent management, and he deserves great credit for his
perseverance and the success he has made of different occupations. He is a Mason, Snowsville lodge No. 119, now at Ackerman, and was worshipful master ten years, when the lodge
was at Chester.   He is also a member of the Knights of Honor at Kosciusko, and the
Knights and Ladies of Honor, at French Camp.   Miss Kate Love, who became his wife in
February, 1871, was the daughter of William G. and Eunice Love, natives of the Palmetto
state. Mrs. Love came to Choctaw county, Miss., with her parents and there married. Her
death occurred when Mrs. McGovern was but four years of age, and her father died in 1871.
To Mr. and Mrs. McGovern have been born ten children, four now living, and these have
had the best advantages for an education. Dr. and Mrs. McGovern are members of t'
Presbyterian church. He has always attended strictly to his domestic affairs, and does n
meddle very much in politics.

James P. McGraw, planter and merchant, Fearn Springs, was born in Autauga county,
Ala., in 1834, and early became familiar with farm life, much to the detriment of his education.   When about nineteen years of age he started out for himself as a farm hand, but
shortly afterward entered a store as clerk, and there remained until the breaking out of the
war.   He joined company E, Fifth Mississippi infantry, and served about eleven months,
when he was discharged on account of ill health. A few months later he engaged as a citizen
clerk in the commissary department, principally at Meridian, where he was paroled after the
general surrender.   In 1865 he was married to Miss Callie A. J., daughter of Capt. John C.
and Martha Holmes (see sketch). Mrs. McGraw was born in Winston county.   The result
of this union was nine children, who are named in the order of their births as follows:
Minnie, a teacher, received her education at Macon; Mary E., Martha R., Thomas L., James
D., Alice, Robert H., John H. and Nellie. Since his marriage Mr. McGraw has lived in this
neighborhood, and is one of the most prominent and extensive planters in the county. He
owns nearly four thousand acres of land, and about half of the time since the war he has been
engaged in merchandising also. He has purchased his land at different times as he was
able, and all he has accumulated is the result of his own exertions. In 1879 he and neighbors established Handle postoffice, of which he was postmaster for some time. He is a
Mason, and a member of Winstonville lodge No. 277, which was established during the war.
He and Mrs. McGraw are members of the Missionary Baptist church, and are prominent
and popular members of society. Mr. McGraw's success has been almost phenomenal, and
he has one of the best, if not the best, farms in the county. He has a beautiful home, and is
surrounded by every comfort and convenience. He was the eldest of thirteen children, nine
of whom are living, born to Sanford H. and Sinah (Edmondson) McGraw, the father a native
of Fairfield district, S. C., born in 1810, and the mother born in Warren county, Ga., in
1814.   Three of their sons were in the Civil war. Thomas, who enlisted in the Fifth Mississippi infantry, and died at Mobile in 1862, and Dewitt W., who is now a merchant and
planter of Noxubee county, Miss., was in the militia, being too young to enter the army.
The father was reared on a farm, received a liberal education, and when a young man went
to Alabama, where he was married in Autauga county in 1833 to Miss Edmondson, who was

a noble and devout Christian and a lady universally beloved. They resided in that county until 1845, and then moved to Winston county, Miss., settling on an improved place in the eastern part of the county. He resided in different places until his death in 1887. Mrs. McGraw had died in 1880. Both were members of the Baptist church for many years, and active workers in the same. He was not a politician, but was interested in the welfare of his party. He was one of a large family of children born to James McGraw, who was of Scotch origin, and probably a native of South Carolina. The grandfather spent his last years in Alabama, where he was engaged in planting, and died there when his grandson, James P., was but a small boy. He was a good citizen and an honest and industrious man. The maternal grandfather, Thomas Edmondson, was a native of Georgia, but moved from there to Alabama and thence to Carroll county, Miss., at an early day. He died in Alabama in 1861, while there on a visit. He was a planter, and reared a large family.

T. R. McGuire, chancery clerk, Rosedale, is a native of Mississippi soil, his birth occurring in Bolivar county on the 15th of April, 1843, and is the oldest living child born to the union of Joseph and Rosina (Cupp) McGuire, the father a native of Pennsylvania, and the mother of Tennessee. The father came to Mississippi as early as 1819, settled in Bolivar county at a place known as Indian Point, opposite the mouth of the Arkansas river, and bought land of an Indian, William Foster. He opened up large tracts, became very wealthy and was one of the representative men of the county. He was quite prominent in political affairs, was elected to the legislature in 1842 and judge of the probate court for several terms. He was a soldier in the War of 1812, was at the battle of New Orleans with General Jackson, but did not participate in that engagement, as he was sick at the time. During the Civil war he was provost marshal of this district. He lost a great deal of his wealth during this trying period, a sum amounting to $360,000 in property and buildings. His death occurred on March 8, 1868, but his wife died previous to this, February, 1863. T. R. McGuire passed the days of his youth on his father's plantation, attended the Cumberland university, and left that school when sixteen years of age, or in 1861, to enter the Confederate army. He enlisted in company H, First Mississippi cavalry (commonly known as Bolivar troops), under Colonel Montgomery, and was in the battles of Belmont, Shiloh, around Corinth and Vicksburg, and in nearly all the battles of the Army of Tennessee. After the first year he was promoted to the office of orderly sergeant. He was never wounded, but was captured while at home in 1865, and while on the way to Alton prison he succeeded in making his escape. At the battle of Selma, on April 1, he was again captured, but made his escape on the 8th of that month. He surrendered to Captain Hill at the mouth of White river. He was a brave and valiant soldier, and served the Confederacy faithfully and well. After returning to Bolivar county, Mr. McGuire began farming, and continued that occupation until 1877, when he removed to Rosedale, and was in the sheriff's office for some time. In 1878 he was elected chancery clerk, and has been re-elected at the expiration of each term since. He is the owner of considerable town property. He has been twice married, first on March 18, 1868, to Miss P. A. Scruggs, a native of Kentucky, who died in March, 1881, leaving three children: Robert J. (deputy clerk in his father's office), Rosa Belle and Nellie. They had lost two children previously. The second marriage occurred, November 7, 1883, to Mrs. M. Y. Thomas nee Yerger, daughter of Col. Alex. Yerger of this county. She was the mother of two children by her former marriage: Bessie (wife of N. B. Scott) and Oscar D. Thomas (professor of bookkeeping and penmanship in the male and female college, East Fork, Miss). Mr. and Mrs. McGuire are members of the Episcopal church. He is a member of the Masonic fraternity, the Knights of Honor and the Knights of Pythias, being chancellor commander of the last-named lodge. He is president of the county alliance of this county. He was appointed postmaster of Rosedale in 1878, served until January 23, 1891, and then resigned, as the new constitution forbade holding two offices at the same time.

Oscar G. McGuire, lawyer, Rosedale, was born in Bolivar county in 1850, and is a Mississippian by birth and bringing up. His parents, Joseph and Rosina (Cupp) McGuire, were both descendants of old and honored families. The father was born in the Keystone state, and was a soldier in the War of 1812. He came to Mississippi at an early day, settled on Mississippi river at the mouth of Arkansas river, and opened up a large plantation, which has since been washed away. He was one of the representative citizens, and held the office of probate judge for some time. His wife died in 1863, and he joined the great majority five years later. Oscar G. McGuire was educated at the Christian Brothers' academy, at St. Louis, began the study of law in 1876, and was admitted to the bar in 1877. One year later he opened a drug store in Rosedale, carried this on until 1882, and then sold out and began practicing his profession. Although among the younger members of the bar, he has been very successful, and is destined to become one of the leading lawyers of Bolivar county. Aside from his legal duties he is also engaged in planting, and is the owner of about twelve hundred acres of land, with six hundred under cultivation. This is a fine place and is near Rosedale. Mr. McGuire selected his life's companion in the person of Miss Sallie Hume, daughter of Colonel Hume, an old settler of the county, and their nuptuals were celebrated in 1873. Her death occurred on December 25 of the following year. His second marriage was in 1880, to Miss Virginia Gerhart, of Tennessee, an active member of the Episcopal church. In 1881 Mr. McGuire erected a cozy residence in Rosedale, and here he expects to permanently reside. He is a member of the Masonic fraternity and the Knights of Honor, is active in the affairs of the county, and is a member of the board of aldermen of Rosedale.

Daniel McInnis, a successful planter and a prominent and efficient public officer, was originally from Covington county, Miss., where his birth occurred in 1857, and his parents, Daniel and Nancy McInnis, were natives also of that state. The father is a prosperous farmer and prominent citizen. He represented Simpson county in the lower house of the legislature in 1880, and has held other positions of importance. Daniel C. McInnis received a good business education in the schools of Simpson county, whither his father had removed when a boy, and started out for himself as a farmer, which occupation he has since continued. He is essentially a model man, full of energy, enterprise and push, and is one of Simpson county's most thoroughgoing and successful planters. He has always taken an active part in local affairs, and at the earnest solicitation of friends, in 1889, became a candidate for sheriff, and was elected by a handsome majority over a popular opponent. The gentlemanly and courteous manner with which he treats those with whom he has business or other dealings, and the vigilance with which he guards the public trust, have won for him a host of stanch friends. Mr. McInnis was married, in January, 1881, to Miss Sabra A. Griffith, of Covington county, Miss., and the result of this union has been three children, one son and two daughters. Socially Mr. McInnis is a member of the Farmers' Alliance.

The family of which Hon. L. J. McInnis is a member, is of Scotch descent, his father, John McInnis, who was born in 1797, having been born in the land of thistles and oatmeal. He was married to Miss Jennie McDuffey, of Mississippi, and both are now deceased. L. J. McInnis was born in Greene county, Miss., but about 1834 removed to Lauderdale county, Miss., settling in the central portion. He was given the advantages of the country schools, and was brought up to a knowledge of farm life by his father, who was a reasonably successful tiller of the soil. In 1852 he was married to Miss Mary E. Linton, of the same county, but was called upon to mourn her death after she had borne him two children: John A. and Elizabeth J. In 1857 Mr. McInnis took, for his second wife, Mrs. Mary Smith, who died in 1883, their daughter Leona dying in 1864. In 1862 L. J. McInnis enlisted in the Thirty-seventh Mississippi infantry, under Colonels McLain and Holland. He was with General Price at Iuka, was later in the engagement at Corinth, and at a still later period was in the engagement at Vicksburg. After being captured at this place, paroled and exchanged he went to Pensacola, thence to Dalton, and was in the campaign with Johnston before Atlanta. He was wounded at Vicksburg and also at Atlanta by bursting shells. He was afterward with Hood in his Tennessee campaign, and still later with Johnston at Montgomery, going with him to Danville, Va. After surrendering at Greensboro, he returned to Mississippi, where he resumed farming on the old place, and from twenty-five to thirty bales, his crop of cotton has increased to eighty-five or ninety bales. He owns and controls about one thousand five hundred acres of fair farming land, and besides cotton, raises an abundance of corn, oats and potatoes. In June, 1889, he started in the dairy business, and now has about $1,500 worth of full-blood and good grade Jersey cattle. The present yield of butter is about ninety pounds per week, but this he soon expects to increase to two hundred and fifty pounds per week. He is a thoroughgoing, enterprising gentleman, and in addition to the above mentioned enterprises in which he is engaged, he is a member of the firm of Smith & McInnis, of Meridian, dealers in general supplies. In 1871 he was a member of the state legislature from Lauderdale county, was treasurer of the county in 1875, and in each of these capacities he proved himself faithful, efficient and capable. He is a member of the A. F. & A. M., the Farmers' Alliance, and for over forty years he has been a worthy member of the Methodist Episcopal church. He is benevolent, charitable, and kind hearted, and is of the stuff of which useful and worthy citizens are made.

J. R. McIntosh was born, November 30, 1837, in Marengo county, Ala. His parents moved to Chickasaw county, Miss., about the year 1840, and his father was regarded as one of the most successful planters in northern Mississippi, raising for many years prior to the war five hundred bales of cotton and enough of meat, breadstuff, cattle, mules, horses and sheep to sustain his large plantation. Mr. J. R. McIntosh was educated at the University of Mississippi, at Oxford, Miss. In 1860 he was placed upon the military ticket and in November, 1860, he was elected lieutenant-colonel. He married the daughter of one of the wealthiest planters in Chickasaw county, Miss., Miss Kittie M. Buchanan, daughter of Thomas J. Buchanan, on the 20th day of December, 1860, and moved upon his plantation. In the summer of 1861 he joined company H, of the Twenty-fourth Mississippi regiment, and was elected lieutenant. Afterward, in 1863, he was made adjutant of that regiment, in which capacity he served until shot down upon the breastworks in the battle of Franklin, when he was captured and sent a prisoner to Fort Delaware. From this place he was exchanged in March, 1865, and at Richmond, whither he had gone, received a sixty days' furlough, and returned home upon his crutches. Before the expiration of his furlough, the surrender of the armies of the Confederacy took place. He then at once called up his slaves and informed them that they were free, but advised them to remain on the plantation under wages, which he would pay them from that day. They all did remain with the exception of one man, and made an excellent crop. Mr. McIntosh saw and appreciated the changed condition of affairs at once, and determined to resume the reading of law, which he had commenced when he left the university, but which had before that been read by him simply as an accomplishment and as a part of a polite education, but with no view of practicing it, but, being then poor, he moved to

76

Houston, the county seat, and resumed his legal studies in the law office of Gen. W. F. Tucker, a distinguished soldier and lawyer, until April, 1866, when he was licensed to prac tice and formed a law partnership with Baxter McFarland, now chancellor of the first chancellor district of Mississippi. Their practice was large and lucrative from the beginning. He continued to practice his profession in Chickasaw county until the fall of 1883, when he was invited by Capt. Thomas H. Woods to come to Meridian and enter into a partnership with him, which Mr. McIntosh accepted. His firm probably enjoyed the largest practice of any law firm in the state. In December, 1887, he moved to Birmingham, Ala., according to previous arrange- ments with Hon. J. J. Altman, and entered upon a law partnership with him, where he remained enjoying an excellent practice, until his old law partner, Captain Woods, was appointed chief justice of the state, in the fall of 1889, when Mr. McIntosh returned to Merid- ian as the senior of the present law firm of McIntosh, Williams & Russell. Mr. McIntosh has never occupied but one official position. In 1871, during the reconstruction period of Mississippi, he was elected by the democrats of Chickasaw county, to the legislature and served for two years, with a gallant band of democrats, who, although largely in the minority, have done great good to the state in preventing many ruinous measures from becoming law. In 1886 he was a candidate for congress in his district—the first congressional district of Mis- sissippi, when a few days before the convention assembled, his aged father was thrown from his buggy on his way to church, producing concussion of the brain, from the effects of which he died in a few days; thereupon, Mr. McIntosh, feeling the obligations of the duty he owed to his widowed mother and two widowed sisters, published a card withdrawing from the con- gressional race, when it was conceded by all that he would have been nominated on the first ballot and his election would have been assured. He has never since then become a candi- date for any office, although he participates in every canvass for the democratic party, saying that he is no politician but a partisan. He is a very active, energetic man, a hard student, and is regarded as one of the readiest speakers in the state. He was selected by a commit- tee composed of the governor and other state officers and Confederate veterans, on June 2, 1891, the day before the unveiling of the Confederate statue at Jackson, Miss., to represent the state and Confederate veteran association in receiving the statue on that great occasion, where were assembled at least twenty-five thousand men, women and children.

The second of four children, William J. McIntyre, chancery clerk, Ripley, was born in Cumberland county, N. C., in 1826. His parents were William J. and Jane (McIntyre) McIntyre, the father probably a native of North Carolina and the mother of Scotland. She was the daughter of John and — (Stewart) McIntyre, the latter descended from the Stuarts of Scotland. The parents of our subject emigrated to east Tennessee in 1831, and there the father received his final summons. In 1838 the family removed to Tippah county, Miss., where the children grew to maturity and received their education. William J. McIntyre, Jr., received liberal scholastic advantages, and afterward followed schoolteaching until the break- ing out of the war. In 1863 he enlisted in Gholson's cavalry, served until the surrender, and then returned to Tippah county, where he served as tax assessor for a period of twelve years. His ability as a public official became recognized, and in the fall of 1887 he was elected chancery clerk, which position he has filled with energy, efficiency and ability sur- passed by few, if any, public officials. In 1859 he was married to Miss Sarah E. McCoy, and the results of this alliance has been the birth of nine children, one of whom died in infancy. Mr. McIntyre and family are members of the Missionary Baptist church, and contribute lib- erally to the upbuilding of all charitable and praiseworthy enterprises. He has, for many years, been a member of the A. F. & A. M. fraternity, and is a Mason in principle and precept. In personal appearance he is tall and well proportioned, white hair and beard, blue eyes, and a very intellectual looking head.

Among the many successful planters of Amite county, Miss., none, perhaps, is more extensively engaged in his calling than J. Gip McKee, for he cultivates about three thousand acres of land and raises on an average of from eight hundred to nine hundred bales of cotton each year, besides several hundred bushels of oats and other grain in large quantities. He owns very nearly five thousand acres of land in Amite and Wilkinson counties, and as he is a superior manager and possesses fine business talents he has become wealthy. Although he was born in Anderson county, Ky., August 10, 1850, and resided in his native state until 1879, he has since been a resident of Amite county, Miss., the first three or four years of his residence here being devoted to mercantile interests alone. Since 1885 he has been engaged in planting, but still conducts a mercantile establishment on his place, in which he carries an extensive stock of plantation supplies. In his youth he obtained a good education and until eighteen years of age made his father's house his home. He commenced buying and dealing in stock in his youth, and until his location in this county was engaged in shipping mules South. He became an expert in buying and selling stock, but for some time he has devoted his attention to other avenues of business. He was married in this county on the 15th of August, 1881, to Miss Emma P. Dickson, daughter of William P. Dickson, she having been born, reared and educated in Centerville, Miss. To them two bright and interesting children have been born: Narcissus Beatrice and Margaret Winnie. Mr. McKee and his wife belong to Centerville Methodist Episcopal church, and socially he is a Mason, a member of the I. O. O. F. and the K. of H. Mr. McKee uses the wealth he has obtained wisely and well, for besides using it freely for the comfort and happiness of himself and family, much is given away in charity and in the support of enterprises that are calculated to improve and benefit the county. He has interested himself in the progress and development of this section, for here he expects to make his future abiding place, and may justly be considered one of the leading citizens of this section. His father, John A. McKee, was born in Anderson county, Ky., in 1817, but the father of the latter, Henry McKee, was born in Virginia. He was one of the early settlers of Anderson county, Ky., became a very extensive planter and stockraiser and was very active in all public affairs. He was a soldier in the War of 1812, and in various other ways showed his love for his country and his earnest desire to serve it. John A. McKee grew to mature years in Kentucky and was married there, after reaching manhood, to Miss Narcissa, daughter of Joel Coston. Mrs. McKee was also born on blue grass soil, and after her marriage she and her husband settled on a plantation near where the latter was born, and engaged in planting and stockraising. Previous, however, to making a permanent location Mr. McKee moved to Texas, where he resided from 1854 to 1864. He then permanently settled in Anderson county, Ky.

J. K. McKenzie was born in Scotland, May 24, 1848. He is the eldest child born to John H. and Mary (Thompson) McKenzie, both natives of Scotland. His father was a farmer in his native country, and was drowned in 1855 in the river Tay, of Scotland. The grandmother of our subject was Emily (Henderson) McKenzie. His paternal grandparents were Daniel and Elizabeth (Jeffry) Thompson, also of Scotland. Mr. McKenzie was reared and educated in his native land, having been a student in several first-class private schools. He came to America in 1866. Locating in Summit, Pike county, Miss., he engaged in the grocery trade, which he continued for twelve years. At the end of that time he turned his attention to the livery and stock business, in which he has continued until the present time with much success, having a well-stocked stable and doing a good livery business, besides

buying and selling horses and mules.   He has gained the reputation of being a shrewd business man.   He was married in 1876 to Miss Tillie Boyd, a native of Virginia, who has borne
her husband four children, whose names are Boyd, Henry H., John H. and Ellie E.   Mr.
McKenzie is a Mason, an Odd Fellow and a Knight of Honor, and holds the responsible
position of treasurer of the state lodge of I. O. O. F.   He has ever been a liberal contributor
to the forwarding of all public enterprises, and has at heart the welfare of his town, county
and state.   He and his wife are members of the Methodist Episcopal church.

John W. McKenzie is a native of this county, his birth having occurred in Tippah (now
Benton) county, Miss., in March, 1843, and was one of the four children who grew to maturity,
born to the union of Larkin T. and Lucy A. (Wofford) McKenzie.   The father was originally
from Kentucky, born in 1812, and died in Benton county, of that state, in 1888.   He came
to northern Mississippi with his parents long before the Indians left, and before the land
was open for settlement, and was among the pioneer settlers.   He was the first assessor and
collector of Tippah county, and when he delivered the money collected at Jackson, Miss.,
had to make the journey on horseback and through canebrakes, etc.   He became interested
in selling slaves, and took them to the nation, where he sold them to the Indians.   Later
he devoted his attention exclusively to farming and followed that until his death.   During
the Civil war he was captain of company H, Nineteenth infantry volunteers for a time, but
later returned and raised a cavalry company.   He was in the fight at Williamsburg, Va., and
there received a severe wound.   Returning to Benton county, Miss., after peace was declared,
he served as magistrate for four years, after which he retired from the duties of that office,
and devoted his attention to stockraising, at which he was unusually successful.   He was the
son of Daniel and Winneford (Taurant) McKenzie, the father born in Virginia soon after the
location of his parents, who came from Scotland to this country.   The latter grew to manhood in his native state, and soon after his marriage came to Kentucky, where he continued
to reside for many years.   He then came to Tennessee and thence to Mississippi, where he
received his final summons.   His wife was either born in London, England, or in Virginia,
as her parents came from that city to America about the time of her birth.   John W. McKenzie was reared in Benton county, Miss., and was liberally educated, attending school at
Oxford until the breaking out of the war.   He then left school, enlisted in company H,
Nineteenth Mississippi volunteers, under his father, and went direct to Virginia.   He served
in the battle of Williamsburg, and was with General Lee in all his campaigns.   He was
made lieutenant of the company, and held that position until cessation of hostilities.   He
then returned to his home, and in 1866 was wedded to Miss Mary R. Harris, a lady of culture and a true Christian.   Mr. McKenzie has figured conspicuously in the history of the
county, having held the office of circuit clerk from 1879 until the fall of 1883.   He is an
extensive land owner, having a fine tract of over fifteen hundred acres.

R. T. McKenzie was born in Benton county, Miss., 1866, the only son of D. B. and
Nannie E. (Littleton) McKenzie, both of whom were natives of Mississippi.   The father was
a practical farmer, was quite successful in his vocation, and was a man noted for his generous
contributions to all public enterprises.   He was a member of the Baptist church, and died
in August, 1883, on the farm where the subject now lives.   The mother is still living.   The
subject of our sketch received his primary education in the public schools, afterward attending the famous institution of Cecilian college in Kentucky for ten months; from there he went
to the Starkville college, where he became a student for ten months more.   He was married
in 1890 to Miss Nannie A. Cox, a daughter of Dr. G. W. Cox, of west Tennessee, a well-
known physician there.   The subject of this sketch owns nine hundred and fifty acres of land

and has three hundred acres of it in a high state of cultivation, a fact which speaks volumes for the industry and energetic habits of its owner. Mr. McKenzie has no other vocation than that of a planter, and he seems to have no desire to engage in other work than that of tilling the soil, and his present course certainly justifies the prophecy of his friends that a few years will see him placed in an enviable position—that of a successful, wealthy planter. He is a devout member of the Catholic church, while his wife is a communicant of the Presbyterian church. They move in the very best circles of society in which they are gladly welcomed, and to which they are an ornament.

John B. McKinney, a general merchant of Iuka, Tishomingo county, Miss., was born in the above-named county October 16, 1838, the eldest son of ten children belonging to Walton H. and Sarah W. (Clayton) McKinney. His father, who was a son of John and Ellen (Baker) McKinney, was born in Madison county, Ala., in 1812. His mother's brother, R. A. Baker, was a well-known merchant of Mobile, who was noted for his benefactions to the Methodist Episcopal church in Alabama. Mr. and Mrs. McKinney were married in Alabama in 1835, and soon after removed to old Farmington, Tishomingo county, Miss., where they were among the early settlers, Mr. McKinney engaging in planting. Later he moved back to Alabama and thence to southern Mississippi, and, after the building of the railroad through Iuka, he returned to that town and opened a livery stable; later turning his attention again to planting. The mother of our subject was born in North Carolina in 1816, a daughter of Benjamin Clayton. While quite young she removed with her parents to east Tennessee and about the year 1830 the family removed to Franklin county, Ala., and there she and Mr. McKinney were married. Mr. McKinney's paternal grandfather and grandmother died in Alabama, the former having met his death by a fall from a wagon. The children of Walton H. and Sarah W. McKinney are named as follows: John B., Olivia, William G., James P., Josephine, Robert B., Joseph T., Teresa A., George and Walter D. William G. was an ensign in Williams' battalion of cavalry and was badly wounded at Moulton, Ala. As a soldier he was brave and true, though he was at the time of his death, which resulted from this wound, only twenty-one years seven months and seven days old. Olivia married C. J. Rogers and had one child, dying afterward at Corinth, Miss. Josephine died at the age of three years. Robert is a merchant at Memphis, Tenn. Joseph T., who was a railroad employe, and a young man of great promise, died at Iuka in 1886. George died young in 1859. Mr. McKinney's mother, who was for many years a member of the Methodist Episcopal church South, died at Iuka January 28, 1890. The father is still living and attained to his seventy-ninth birthday in August, 1891.

The subject of this memoir was reared on a plantation, and was educated in the common schools. At the age of nineteen he became a salesman in the store of W. P. Tanner & Co., of Athens, Ala., with whom he remained until soon after the commencement of the war, when he enlisted in company I, of the Eleventh Alabama cavalry, under the command of Capt. P. D. Roddy, afterward a general in the Confederate army. He was mustered into the service with a rank of corporal, but was soon after promoted to be first sergeant. Some of the engagements in which he participated were the following: Tishomingo creek, Shiloh, Harrisburg, Day's Gap, Ala., besides a number of skirmishes of lesser importance. One memorable affair in which he had a part was the capture of General Campbell and forces at Athens, Ala. He was paroled in May, 1865, after three and one-half years of almost constant service. After the war he located at Paducah, Ky., accepting a position with J. W. Shearer & Co., wholesale grocers. He retained this position for two and one-half years, then he came to Tishomingo county, and was for the next four years engaged in planting. In 1870 he began merchandising at his present stand at Iuka. This business he has since carried on very successfully, and has a well-appointed store, with a varied stock of merchandise suited to the needs of his fellow-townsmen of all classes. His mode of doing business is such that when he gains a customer he generally retains him, and his personal popularity is so great that gaining a customer with him is no hard matter. In October, 1867, he married Linda J. McKnight, a daughter of William and Elvira (Parks) McKnight. Her father was born in North Carolina, May 3, 1806. Her mother was born in Tennessee, July 17, 1815. Mrs. McKinney was born in Lawrenceburg, Tenn., October 25, 1843, one of seven children. Her parents both died at Iuka. Her father became an early settler in this part of the state, and was for many years a merchant at the place where he died. Mr. and Mrs. McKinney have had nine children, all of whom are now living: Ellie, now the wife of J. J. Hendricks, of Columbia, Tenn.; John Ed. is connected with his father's mercantile business; William W. is employed in the store of C. W. McKnight; Carrie L. is unmarried, and is remarkable for her talent for painting; Sallie, James B., Lizzie and Joseph T. are in school; Charles W. is at home. Mr. McKinney is prominent in local politics, and is a stanch democrat. He is greatly interested in all educational affairs, and has been for several years a trustee of the Iuka normal institute and of the Iuka free schools. He is a selfmade man, who, while devoting his attention closely to his own interests, is ever cognizant of the fact that the man who would most surely build himself up is the one who must exert his influence toward the upbuilding of the community of which he forms a part.

By excellent business ability, foresight and push, William C. H. McKinney has become one of the leading merchants in the county, and has built up a very large and prosperous trade. His success as a business man has been remarkable, and the confidence which the people have in him is fully merited. Besides successfully conducting his mercantile establishment he discharges, in a very efficient and praiseworthy manner, the duties of postmaster of Anguilla and treasurer of Sharkey county. He was born in Monroe county, Miss., in 1842, to John Madison and Mary A. (Bowen) McKinney, the former of whom was born in Tennessee, and the latter in South Carolina. In 1830 John M. McKinney left his native state to settle in Monroe county, Miss., where he married and resided until 1859, when he moved to Pontotoc county, Miss., and engaged in planting, a calling that received much of his attention until his death, in 1888, at the age of sixty-eight years. His wife was the second in a family of seven children, and is yet a resident of Pontotoc county, being sixty years of age. She is, as was Mr. McKinney, an earnest member of the Methodist Episcopal church. To them a family of eight children was born, all of whom lived to be grown, six being now alive: William C. H., who is the eldest of the family; Eugenie, a resident of Washington county, is engaged in planting; John C. H. is a planter of Sharkey county; Verona is the wife of J. W. Wisinger, resides in Bolivar county, Miss.; Lucinda resides with her sister Verona. Those deceased are: Francilla, who was a member of company H, Second Mississippi regiment of infantry, and was killed at the battle of Seven Pines, Va., and Elizabeth (Mrs. Wilkinson), who died in Texas, leaving two children. William C. H. McKinney attained his majority in Monroe and Pontotoc counties, in each of which he was given the advantages of the common schools. The coming clash of arms caused him to drop his books and join the Second Mississippi infantry, company H, and serve until the close of the war, participating in the second battle of Manassas, Sharpsburg, Md.; Gettysburg, Penn., being taken prisoner in the last-named engagement and carried to Fort Delaware, where he was held until some time after the surrender of Lee. He received quite a severe wound at Sharpsburg, and was disabled for some weeks. Upon being released from prison he returned to his home in Pontotoc county, Miss., where he entered school for one season, after which he engaged in teaching for a short time. At the end of this time he went to Coahoma county, Miss., and settled on Moon lake, where he remained for three years engaged in merchandising, at the end of which time, in 1869, he came to his present place of residence, where he has since successfully conducted a general mercantile establishment. He was for some time the only merchant of the place, and was the founder of what is now known as Anguilla, but was then known as McKinneyville. It has been known by its present name since the completion of the Louisville, New Orleans & Texas railroad, in 1884. Mr. McKinney may truly be said to be a selfmade man, for he began to make his own way in the world with no capital, and by close attention to business and by honorable business methods he has become the owner of a fine general establishment, while just across the way he is the owner of a well-kept and complete drug store. Since January 6, 1891, he has been associated in business with Paul Dinkins, in the mercantile business, the firm being styled McKinney & Dinkins. Besides these two paying business houses Mr. McKinney owns a fine plantation on Deer creek, the income derived from the products of which are ample. He is a most substantial citizen, and is able and earnest in his advocacy of what he thinks best calculated to promote the best interests of his county. He is a stanch democrat in politics, and in 1879 was elected to the position of county treasurer by his numerous friends, the duties of which he has discharged in a manner that shows him to be a man of intelligent and well-directed mind. He is efficient, industrious and honest, and on all occasions displays the characteristics of a true gentleman. He is also a patron of education, and held the office of school trustee, and has been postmaster of Anguilla since 1875. He was married to Miss Mary Halbert, of Mississippi, a daughter of J. J. Halbert, of Terry, Miss., but was called upon to mourn the death of his wife in 1887, she leaving him with one child to care for: Halbert. His present wife was Miss Belle Baggett, of Vicksburg, an intelligent, highly cultured and refined lady, who received her education at Forest, N. Y. This union has resulted in the birth of a son, William C. H.

Enoch B. McLain. Among the pioneer families who founded homes for themselves in the wilderness of Mississippi may be mentioned the McLains, whose residence here dates from the year 1812. This family is of Scotch descent and the first one of the family to seek a home for himself in the then wilds of the new world was Daniel McLean, who became a resident of Georgia prior to the Revolutionary war, and was killed in one of the old Indian wars. His son Allen was born in Scotland in 1775, and when a small child was brought to this country. After reaching manhood he drifted to the state of Tennessee and was there married to Miss Naomi Bateman, a native of that state, born near the town of Franklin. After farming for a few years in Tennessee Mr. and Mrs. McLain came to Mississippi and settled in what is now Amite county, almost the entire country at that time being in a wild state, wild game of all kinds being plentiful and affording an abundance of meat to the settlers. Mr. McLain began at once to clear his land from timber but afterward turned much of his attention to speculating and dealing in land, in which occupation he showed sagacity and business capacity of a high order. He died in this county about the year 1855, his wife having passed from life July 6, 1845. Enoch B. McLain is the youngest of their seven sons and four daughters that grew to mature years, but only three members are living at the present time: Isaac, a planter in Wilkinson county; Daniel, a resident of Gloster, and Enoch B. The latter spent his youth on a farm, but received little schooling. At the age of eighteen years he engaged in planting for himself on a plantation near Gloster, and although he commenced with very limited means he has, by his own industry and good management, acquired a handsome property. Soon after reaching man's estate he saw and felt the need of a better education than he had, and began reading and studying such books as he thought to be of practical use to him, and displayed such judgment in his selections that he is now an exceptionlly well-informed man. Possessing a keen mind and business talents of a high order he has succeeded where many would have failed, and that he is a financier of more than ordinary ability it is but necessary to state that he is the owner of six thousand acres of land, five thousand of which are in his home plantation, and of this twenty-five hundred acres are under cultivation. The average amount of cotton raised on this land is between five hundred and seven hundred bales, but he also raises considerable corn and other grains. In the year 1878 he opened a mercantile establishment on his farm, but after the town of Gloster was laid off he erected a good business house, in which he placed his stock of goods. Since that time he has erected a large, double two-story brick building in which he has since done business. He carries a stock of goods very complete and well selected, and as he at all times closely studies the wants of his customers, he has never failed to please them. This will be conceded when it is known that his annual sales amount to from $75,000 to $80,000 per year. Mr. McLain is one of the most successful merchants of Gloster, and as his present prosperity is the result of his own business acumen, he deserves much credit therefor. In 1862 Mr. McLain offered his services to the Confederate cause and became a member of the Fourth Mississippi cavalry. He took part in the engagement at Port Hudson, besides a great number of lesser engagements, and at the close of the war was paroled at Clinton, La., and returned to his home, having, while in the field, proved faithful to every trust. He was first married in 1851 to Miss Nancy Berryhill, a daughter of Alexander Berryhill, one of the first settlers of this county from North Carolina. To them three children were born: F. A., whose sketch immediately follows this; Mary E., wife of J. W. Haff, a planter of Amite county, and Nannie J., wife of W. J. Toler, also a planter here. Mr. McLain married his present wife about 1857, she being Miss Matilda P. Longmire, a native of the county and a daughter of Robert Longmire, a member of one of the first families of this region. Major Longmire, his father, was a soldier and held commission in the Revolutionary war. To Mr. McLain's last marriage the following children have been born; Albert A., who is married and is the manager of the home farm; William G. McLain, manager of store; Hattie, wife of W. I. Casey; Julia V.; Mattie N., wife of E. R. Harrett; Lena, wife of Benjamin Jacobs; Allen, Robert E. Lee, Fannie, Ama and Clarence E., the three last being in college. Mr. McLain is a deacon in the Baptist church, of which he has been a member for many years, and of this church his family are also members.

Hon. Frank A. McLain, who has early become distinguished in the political affairs of Amite county, Miss., is now acting in the capacity of district attorney, and in the discharge of his duties has shown himself to be endowed with superior ability. He was born in this county, near Gloster, on the 29th of January, 1852, and was brought up on the home plantation, and by his father, who determined that his son should have better advantages than he had in his youth, he was given the benefit of the schools in the vicinity of his home, and completed his education in that most admirable institution of learning, the University of Mississippi, from which he was graduated in the month of June, 1874. The year following his graduation he devoted to teaching school in Amite county, the two subsequent years being spent in the same manner in the state of Texas. At the end of this time he returned to the state of his birth, and as he for some time had been desirous of making law his profession he entered at once upon his legal studies, and in the year 1879 was licensed to practice at Liberty. The enviable reputation he has acquired has been obtained largely through his own efforts and at the expense of diligent study and hard practical experience. In the management of the cases that have come up before him he has displayed much ability and sagacity, and the sound views he held on all questions soon became known, and his talents were rewarded by his election to the state legislature in 1882, his election to his present office taking place the following year. This he has since held by re-election, and has shown himself eminently worthy the confidence of the people. He has won considerable renown as a criminal lawyer, and in the capacity of district attorney he has had excellent opportunities of displaying his varied talents, for as an orator he is logical and ornate, and his manner of presenting facts is forcible, smooth and convincing. He always thoroughly prepares his cases, is seldom taken by surprise, and he almost invariably has the implicit confidence of his clients. He served as a delegate to the last constitutional convention, being the representative of Amite and Pike counties. He has ever been faithful to the principles of democracy, has always been interested in the political affairs of the county, and has at all times endeavored to support worthy and honorable men. He was married in Magnolia, Miss., in March, 1879, to Miss Fannie A. Tyler, daughter of W. G. Tyler, a planter and merchant of Pike county, Miss., and by her is the father of three children: Mary L., Enoch B. and William Tyler. Mrs. McLain received a good education in her youth, is a lady of remarkable intelligence, and has displayed business talents far above mediocre. She is the proprietress of a mercantile, millinery and dressmaking establishment, and is doing exceptionally well. In addition to this she is the proprietress of the Commercial hotel, which is one of the best kept hostelries in the town, and is largely patronized by traveling men, which fact alone speaks for the reputation of the house.

Col. Robert McLain was born in Virginia May 5, 1814, and died at Corinth, Miss., October 5, 1862, aged forty-eight years and six months. At an early age his father moved with his family to Knoxville, east Tenn. His father died soon after settling in Tennessee, leaving two sons, Robert and John, to support their mother. Robert was the elder, and being very sprightly and very much in earnest, managed with one horse and a cart to make a living for his mother and brother. His industrious habits, upright conduct and intelligence soon attracted the attention of the citizens of the town, and he was, by the influence of a friend of his mother, put to work in a tailor's shop to learn the trade. His promptness, honesty and other admirable characteristics he carried into his new occupation. He learned the art of cutting and sewing very rapidly, and was soon considered by his master an indispensable adjunct to the little shop. It was here that he began to lay the foundation of a life which distinguished him as a citizen, preacher, politician, and lastly as a brave officer in the army of the Confederacy. Books were his constant companions. At nights and during idle moments he read with avidity every good book that came into his hands. At this time the Presbyterians were the most numerous and prosperous denomination in and about Knoxville. An old elder, whose name can not now be recalled, proposed to educate him for a minister, and with his mother's consent he was put into a good training school in Knoxville and there prepared to enter a seminary, under the auspices of Dr. Anderson who was its president. He progressed rapidly and soon became noted as an eloquent speaker and an able debater. He had now reached his manhood and he graduated from the institution. His mother had died in the meantime and his younger brother had grown up and was profitably employed on a farm. The cost of his education had been defrayed by the elder of the Presbyterian church at Knoxville, already mentioned, and the young man felt that it was his duty to refund him the amount he had expended, with the interest. This he did to the last cent from money earned in teaching and preaching. He removed to the town of Grenada, Miss., and there received a call from the Presbyterian church of that place. Afterward he went to Clinton, Miss., and became a member of the faculty of the Presbyterian school at that place, preaching at the same time to one or two churches on Sunday. Here he married Miss Elizabeth Hooker, daughter of Nathan Hooker, an old and highly respected citizen of the town, by whom he had one daughter, Annie, who afterward became the wife of Col. Charles T. O'Ferrell, now a distinguished member of congress from Virginia, who died when her daughter Annie was quite young. Growing anxious to devote his entire time to the ministry he severed his connection with the school at Clinton and entered regularly into the work. It was about this time, in the fall of 1845, that he visited east Mississippi as a member of the presbytery, which convened at old Marion, then the seat of justice of Lauderdale county. There he met for the first time Miss Laura Ann Brown, who in the following year became his second wife. She was the daughter of L. B. Brown, Sr., a most worthy and influential gentleman, who resided in what is now known as Toomsuba, and was born in Wayne county, March 1, 1828, and died at Meridian, Miss., July 26, 1886, in her fifty-ninth year.

Her father, who was a man of considerable wealth, did not survive long after her marriage, and died in the fall of 1851, when it became necessary for Mr. McLain to remove to east Mississippi, and take charge of his father-in-law's estate. About this time the state was convulsed over the grave question of the Union. Mr. McLain was an ardent democrat and had devoted much time to the study of the constitution and to the history of his party, and being a man of decided ability and an eloquent speaker, he was soon forced into the political arena as the champion of states' rights. He was nominated by his party and elected to the state senate to represent the counties of Clarke, Jasper, Jones and Wayne, over an opposition. There he sustained his high reputation as a speaker and a defendant of states' rights. Immediately after the secession of the state he began to raise troops and to exhort the people to defend the principles for which they had voted. He was appointed chaplain of the Fourteenth Mississippi regiment, of which he was made colonel. He soon became a skillful and popular commander. In the battle of Corinth, on the last day of the fight, he fell, mortally wounded, at the head of what was known as Little's brigade, Generals Little and Martin having both been killed the day previous. He was recommended by Gen. Sterling Price and others as worthy of a brigadier's commission, and would have soon been promoted had he lived. Soon after receiving his wound, which was nothing less than the destruction of his right leg below the knee by a cannon ball, the army of the Confederates fell back, leaving him and a large number of the wounded in the hands of the enemy. He was taken to a hospital, attended by his faithful and devoted chaplain, Rev. T. C. Wier, who was with him when he closed his honorable and distinguished life. After waiting sufficiently long for reaction to set in, his leg was amputated. Just as the surgeons were preparing to administer chloroform, his chaplain informed him of the danger which would attend the operation, and advised him to give him such messages as he thought proper to convey to his family. His reply was: "Tell them I died in a just cause."

Dr. Albert G. McLaurin, of Burns, Smith county, Miss., who has an extensive medical practice in the country thereabouts, was born in Trenton in the same county, in 1850, the second in a family of eight brothers: Hon. A. J. McLaurin, of Brandon; Dr. Albert G., Horace J., a lawyer at Rolling Forks, Sharkey county; Robert S., who is the district attorney of the eighth district, and resides at Brandon; William K. and Walter, lawyers at Vicksburg; Wallace, of Brandon, and Sydney L., also residing at Brandon, and who practices law there.

It is a remarkable fact that this large family of boys, who were all reared to humble life upon a farm and accustomed to hard labor from youth, rank to-day among the noted and influential men in this part of the state. Dr. McLaurin received a liberal education at Summerville institute in Noxbubee county, and took up the study of medicine in 1871. He graduated from the university at Nashville, Tenn., with the degree of M. D., in the spring of 1873. During all of his life he has lived on the old McLaurin homestead, where his father died in 1890, having been a resident of that county for at least fifty-five years. The Doctor is a Simon-pure democrat of the old Jacksonian stamp, and affiliates with that party at all times. In the summer of 1890 he was elected a member of the constitutional convention which met at Jackson, August 12, of that year, in which body he represented his county with distinguished ability. Some account of the ancestry of Dr. McLaurin can be found in the sketch of A. J. McLaurin, which is published below.

Anselm Joseph McLaurin, of Brandon, Miss., is one of the foremost attorneys of the state, and is especially noted as a successful criminal lawyer. He was born in the town in which he is now living March 26, 1848, being the eldest of a family of eight sons born to Lauchlin and Ellen E. (Tullus) McLaurin, the former of whom was born in South Carolina and the latter in Mississippi. When a young man Lauchlin McLaurin removed to Smith county, Miss., and there became a wealthy and well-known planter, and represented that county in the state legislature several terms. Anselm McLaurin received his rudimentary education in the best schools of his section, and at an early age entered Summerville institute, which was at that time one of the finest educational institutions of the state, from which he graduated in 1867. During the latter portion of his collegiate career he pursued a private course of law study under the tutorage of Professor Puttick, and after completing his literary education he continued his law studies and was admitted to the bar of Raleigh, Miss., in 1868. He soon after opened an office at that place and entered upon his probationary period, which, however, was not destined to be of an extended duration, as is experienced by the majority of young aspirants entering the legal profession. He at once evinced a peculiar adaptability to his chosen calling, and by an energetic application of his talent, he was not long in acquiring a local reputation and a lucrative practice. In 1872 he was elected attorney for the fifth judicial district, in which capacity he served until 1876, when he removed to Brandon, which he believed to be a more favorable location, and here has since practiced with much success. He has gained a state reputation as a criminal lawyer, and is wise in counsel, cool in judgment, skillful in planning and his sound judgment and practical ability are recognized by the members of the bar throughout the state. He is a fluent and forcible speaker, and one is at once impressed with the fact that he is a man of great strength, depth and grasp of mind. He handles the most abstruse and complicated subjects with ease and grace, and by his logical reasoning they are made perceptible and plain to the most ordinary understanding. His numerous friends, desiring to show their appreciation of his ability, elected him to the legislature of Mississippi in 1879, a position he filled during that year and in 1880 with marked ability. He and his two brothers, Dr. A. G., of Smith county, and Hon. H. J., of Sharkey county, were prominent members of the constitutional convention in 1890. Mr. McLaurin is author of the provision making it unlawful for an alien to hold land in the state, and also of the measure (though it was not accepted) to disfranchise a man who should be proven guilty of wife-beating. He was married February 22, 1870, to Miss Laura Rauch, of Smith county.

There are few men of the present day whom the world acknowledges as successful, more worthy of honorable mention, or whose history affords a better example of what may be accomplished by a determined will and perseverance than Dr. John J. McLean, whose name is familiar throughout Jefferson, as well as the surrounding counties, for during his career here he has entered many homes in his professional capacity and has brought happiness to the hearts of many. The McLean family was among the first to take up its abode in Jefferson county, Miss., Charles and Daniel McLean, uncles of Dr. McLean, taking up their residence near Union Church in the early part of the present century, another uncle, Allen, locating near Gallatin. Daniel McLean was said to have been the first merchant of Union Church, and all became well known throughout this region. Dr. McLean was born in the Old North state, in Robinson county, April 25, 1828, his father, Neal McLean, having been born in Scotland. The latter, when an infant, was brought by his father, John McLean, to Robinson county, N. C., this being about the year 1785. He was a man of superior education, and for a number of years was engaged in teaching school, became prominent in that county, and was an elder in the Presbyterian church. He served as a soldier in the War of 1812, doing good service for his country, for he was faithful in the discharge of every duty and was brave and fearless. Neal McLean was reared in Robinson county, N. C., and under the able instructions of his father obtained a good education. He was married in Robinson county to Miss Catherine McLean, daughter of John McLean, who was also a native of Scotland, but the families were not related in any way. Neal McLean moved with his family to Georgia about the year 1838, and on a farm in Telfair county he resided until his death, which occurred about 1870, his widow surviving him one year. To them four sons and three daughters were born, all of whom grew to mature years and became the heads of families. The sons were: Wesley, who was a soldier in the Confederate army, and was killed at the battle of Fredericksburg; Thomas L., who was a lieutenant in the Twenty-fifth Louisiana infantry, and was killed at the battle of Murfreesboro; William, who resided at Union Church, in Jefferson county, and there died leaving a family, and Dr. John J. A daughter died in Georgia. Dr. J. J. McLean was born in Robinson county, N. C., on April 25, 1828, and his early youth was spent in that county. He was apprenticed to Dr. Reynolds, of Camden, S. C., an eminent physician, and for seven years studied medicine under him. He took his first course of lectures in the winter of 1849-50, at the Cincinnati College of Medicine, and in the spring of the latter year located in Telfair county, Ga., where he was engaged in the practice of his profession for two years. In the winter of 1853-4 he returned to Cincinnati, and completed his course of studies, graduating from that institution in the spring of the latter year. Dr. McLean then came to Mississippi, and settled at Union Church, and was one of the active and successful practitioners of this region, until the opening of the late war, at which time he entered the Confederate army, and was elected captain of company A, Twelfth Mississippi infantry, serving one year in General Ewell's command. He then resigned to return to his home and his practice by the urgent request of his friends at Union Church. In connection with his practice he was also engaged in merchandising up to the opening of the war. He has been carrying on a farm since locating here, and it may with truth be said that in every enterprise to which he has given his attention his efforts have been followed with good results, and he has every reason to be satisfied with his career. He was married in this county, in 1855, to Miss Sarah Jane McLaurin, who was born and reared here, her father, Duncan McLaurin, being one of the pioneers of the county, now deceased. Dr. and Mrs. McLean have reared a family of three sons and four daughters, the eldest, Duncan, who died after reaching mature years, leaving a wife and child; Charles died after reaching manhood; Hugh is married and is a resident of Ellisville, Jones county, Miss.; Sallie is the wife of J. A. Newman, of Union Church; Carrie, Gertie, and Ivy, who is the deceased wife of Dr. Davis, of Rozie, Franklin county, Miss., her death occuring in 1890. She left one child whom Dr. McLean and his wife are raising, a bright little infant of eight months. Dr. McLean, his wife and eldest daughter are members of the Presbyterian church, and the former is a Royal Arch mason, but has not been an active member for several years. He has been active in all good works since his location at Union Church, and his practice, which is fully merited, is very large. He has won his present enviable position in the estimation of the people of Jefferson county solely by his own merits, and his kindness and generosity has won him many warm friends. He is liberal in contributing his means to worthy causes, his purse is ever open to the wants of the poor, and in the practice of his profession he has many opportunities of manifesting his charity and good will to all.

Hon. W. C. McLean, lawyer, Grenada, was born in Grenada, Miss., on June 10, 1854, where the courthouse now stands, and is the son of Judge Robert D. McLean, a native of the Blue Grass state, born at Greenville, in November, 1811. The father graduated from Transylvania college, Lexington, Ky., where he was licensed to practice law, and after residing at New Orleans, La., and Natchez, Miss., for some time, came in 1836 to Grenada. He soon became one of the leading lawyers of the county and practiced until his death, on June 21, 1874. He was mayor of Grenada for about twenty-five years, and was appointed by Gov. B. G. Humphreys as judge of a special court, just after the war, to try the cotton claims. On coming to Grenada he was associated with the firm of McLean & Barnes, the latter being a noted politician and a leading lawyer. Mr. McLean was a member of the Presbyterian church, in which he was an elder and one of its leading members and liberal supporters. He was married to Miss Mary Whitaker, a native of Alabama and a daughter of William H. and Mary Ann (White) Whitaker, also natives of that state. Mrs. Whitaker was the daughter of Judge White, of Tennessee. Mrs. McLean was but a child when she came with her parents to Mississippi, and in this state she passed her youth and womanhood. She died in 1870, at the age of forty-seven years, a faithful member and worker in the Presbyterian church. The fruits of this union were seven children—one son and six daughters—three of whom are now living: Mrs. Lou Bedford, of Tennessee, Miss Bertie, who is single and who resides in Grenada, Miss., and W. C. McLean, the fifth child, who was reared and educated in Grenada until sixteen years of age, when he entered the University of Kentucky, at Lexington, graduating from that well-known institution of learning on June 10, 1874. He then entered the law office of William R. Barksdale, of Grenada, one of the most brilliant lawyers of northern Mississippi, and in June, 1875, was admitted to the bar, afterward forming a partnership with Mr. Barksdale, with whom he practiced until the death of that gentleman, in January, 1877. Since that time Mr. McLean has continued the practice, and has been unusually successful. He was married to Miss Susie Collins, of Grenada county, the youngest of five children born to the marriage of Joseph and Elizabeth Collins, the father dying in 1859 and the mother in 1880. Mr. Collins was one of the old settlers of the vicinity and a prominent man there before the war. Mrs. McLean received her primary education in Grenada, and finished at the female college at Memphis, Tenn., graduating from the same in 1878. The result of Mr. McLean's marriage was the birth of four children—three sons and a daughter—the latter deceased. Those living are Robert D., Alney C. and William C., Jr. As a politician Mr. McLean ranks among the best in the state. In 1888 his name was frequently mentioned for congress from this district, but he would not allow his name to go before the convention. He was elected to the constitutional convention of the state of Mississippi, and was one of the leading movers in opposing section five of the franchise clause, of which committee he was a member.   Mr. McLean has been a member of every democratic convention since 1877, was a member of the state democratic executive committee from 1885 to 1889, and seconded the nomination of Hon. John R. Cameron, of Canton, Miss., for governor in 1889.   His speech on that occasion is given below:

MR. CHAIRMAN: I have the honor to belong to that class of individuals who believe that political parties are formed and organized not for the purpose of perpetuating in office the favored few, but for the purpose of advocating and carrying out in the administration of public affairs those measures which reflect and represent the sentiments of those individuals who are the constituent element of their political party.   I am also a member of that class of individuals who believe that the success of the democratic party is superior to all things else, and that the triumph, ascendancy and the perpetuation of its principles should not be jeopardized by nor subordinated to the gratification of the ambition of any particular man or set of men.   I am also a member of the class of individuals who believe that the honor and the glory, the success and the prosperity, the advancement and the development of the state of Mississippi are not dependent upon the elevation of any particular individual to the executive chair.   The roll of the democratic party in Mississippi abounds in names that will do honor to any state.   In the democratic firmament are many stars.   You may strike out a few and yet not leave us in total darkness.   We are like the fair lady who looks into her casket of jewels and is sorely puzzled which brilliant stone or diamond shall adorn her lovely brow, and yet if we are to accept as true some of the claims which have been urged during the campaign, we have in the democratic party in the state of Mississippi but one man whose head is sufficiently clear, and whose nerves are sufficiently steady, to direct and control the management of public affairs.   Now, sir, believing that party success should be paramount to personal and individual preferment; that individual sacrifice is universal strength; that no man has a patent on the governor's office, and that the democratic party of Mississippi has, within her casket of jewels, more than one gem that will adorn and dignify the brow of our state, we ask the privilege of seconding the nomination of Hon. John R. Cameron, of Madison county.   His friends, in making their presentation, do so with a full conception of the kind of man that is needed at this particular hour, and they assure the members of this convention that he possesses all of those elements and characteristics so essentially necessary for a chief executive.   Having no friends to reward and no enemies to punish, his administration and distribution of public patronage will not be personal, but for the good of the people.   He is a frank, fearless and practical statesman, who knows by experience that wealth is won by toil, and by rigid economy, and not by wasteful extravagance.   Born in Mississippi, reared within her borders, educated at her institutions of learning, thoroughly identified with her agricultural interests, every throb and pulsation of his heart beats in sympathy and in unison with her development and prosperity.   As a friend to the people, he is an uncompromising foe to the great corporations and iniquitous trusts that are wringing unwilling tribute from the toiling masses.   His pure and unsullied record as soldier, citizen, democrat and legislator commends for him the highest praise.   As incorruptible as Cato, as brave as Leonidas, as dashing as Murat, as firm and invincible as McDonald on the field of Wagram, he is not only a fit representative of the young democracy of Mississippi, but, as her chief executive, will adorn the state and add new and additional luster to her long line of democratic governors.   He has a strong mind, a great head, true faith and ready hands.   He is one whom the lust of office can not kill, whom the spoils of office can not buy, and he will, at all times and at all places, stand four square to all the winds that blow, and will never sell the truth to serve the hour.   With a character as pure as the dewdrop that slakes the thirst of the morning sunbeams that kiss his own native hills, he will never traffic with his principles nor gamble with his conscience.   Strong in mind, firm in conviction, fertile in resources, progressive in spirit, bold in action, conservative in policy, he will administer the law, not only in accordance with the spirit of democratic principles and usages, but, under his leadership, the state of Mississippi will take greater strides in the development of her resources and the grand achievements in the art of peace than ever before in her memorable history.   With the Hon. John R. Cameron as our leader, we can confidently challenge the republican party to send forth their Achilles, and see if he can drag our Hector around the Trojan wall.

Mr. McLean is a member of the Knights of Pythias, Ivanhoe lodge No. 8, and he was grand chancellor of that lodge from May, 1888, to May, 1889.   In 1888 he was elected and served four years as supreme representative of the lodge, attending at St. Louis, Detroit, New Orleans and Montreal.   He is a leading member of the Presbyterian church, of which he is an elder, and was appointed moderator of the Northern Mississippi Presbytery in 1888, being the first instance in the history of that presbytery that a ruling elder was ever made moderator; and was a member of the general arsembly which convened in St. Louis, Mo., in May, 1887. Mrs. McLean is also an active member of the church.

Elias C. McLelland was born in North Carolina in 1810, and is a son of John and Elizabeth (Lackey) McLelland. His father was a native of Ireland, and immigrated to America when a young man, believing the opportunities were better than in the old world. He settled in Iredell county, N. C., at an early day. He and his wife passed their last days in that state. They were consistent members of the Presbyterian church. Elias C. was married in Kemper county, in 1837, to Mary S. Wooden, and they reared a large family, as follows: Calvin (died in the late war), James F. (is a resident of this county), Joseph (died in 1883), Able A. (died in 1884), one child died in 1883, Elizabeth (is the wife of J. H. Wheeler), George F. (is a resident of Kemper county), Mary S. (is Mrs. Latham, a resident of Kemper county), and William W. The mother of these children died August 29, 1890. Mr. McLelland is now eighty-two years of age, and is not actively engaged in business. In his prime he was a man of excellent business qualifications, and was very successful in all his undertakings. He was at one time interested in mercantile pursuits, and he now owns a large tract of land in Kemper county. Politically he affiliates with the democratic party. William W. McLelland, son of the above, was born in Kemper county, Miss., in 1865, and was educated at Meridian. At the age of eighteen years he started out in life for himself; he first clerked in a dry goods store in Meridian, and six years ago returned to Kemper county and engaged in planting. He was married to Miss Ella M. Jones, a native of Mississippi, born in 1867, and a daughter of O. H. and L. (Nethery) Jones, natives of Mississippi. Three children have been born of this union: Mary A., Lena G. and Susan L. The parents are members of the Baptist church. Mr. McLelland is a stanch adherent to the principles of the democratic party. He is giving his attention exclusively to planting, having the management of his father's land. George F. McLelland, son of Elias C. McLelland, is one of the progressive farmers of Kemper county. He was born in the county in 1854, and is one of a family of nine children. He was educated in the common schools, and in 1874 he was married at Meridian, Miss., to Ida Rust, a daughter of B. T. Rust. She was born in De Kalb, Kemper county, in 1861, and died July 25, 1887, leaving a family of six children: Sidney P., Lula, George, Pearl, Lettie and Thomas. She was a worthy member of the Baptist church. Mr. McLelland was married again in 1888 to Mattie McWilliams, a daughter of Manoah McWilliams, born in Kemper county in 1865. One child has been born of this union, Bert. The parents are members of the Baptist church. Mr. McLelland was but eighteen years of age when he started out in life for himself, and he has met with marked success; he now owns three hundred and twenty acres of land which he has under good cultivation. Politically he is identified with the democratic party. From 1888 to 1889 he was postmaster of Jacksonville, and made a faithful and efficient officer. He is a man of public spirit, and has lent his influence to all movements having for their object the growth and improvement of the county.

Amos McLemore is a well-to-do planter of Lauderdale county, Miss., born in Chickasaw county, of this state, December 3, 1829. His parents, William and Martha (Joiners) McLemore, were born in North Carolina and Tennessee in 1800, respectively, moved to Covington county when he was but a child, and in 1838 they moved to Lauderdale county and settled near where Meridian is now situated. Amos was married in 1855 to Miss Mary Jane McShan, of Lauderdale county, by whom he had nine children: William, Andrew, Virginia, Victoria, Fannie, Acquila, Laura, Kirkland and a son who lived only a month. Seven of these children are living at the present time, four being married. At the opening of the Civil war Mr. McLemore enlisted in the Confederate army under Colonel McClain, of the Thirty-seventh Mississippi. He entered into camp at Columbus, Miss., was ordered from there to Saltillo, from the latter place he marched to Iuka, where he obtained his first experience of war. He was captured at Iuka, afterward ordered to parole camp at Jackson, Miss. His next experience of war being at Vicksburg, he was again captured and paroled, and finally exchanged. He was afterward at Polard, Fla.; Rome, Ga., and Resaca, being with Johnston before Atlanta. He was compelled to enter the hospital at Macon, Ga., where he began working as a nurse, after recoving his health, but was afterward with Hood on his Tennessee campaign, being a participant in the battles of Franklin and Nashville. After the return of peace he turned his attention to planting, notwithstanding the fact that his plantation had been rifled of all valuables, and had grown up to weeds. He turned his attention to the culture of cotton, in which he was quite successful and made money. He now owns and controls one thousand acres of land, three miles northeast of Meridian, Miss. His cotton averages seventy-five bales each year. He also raises oats, potatoes, etc. His wife is a member of the Methodist Episcopal church, and he belongs to the Primitive Baptist church, and socially is a member of the K. of H. He is a self-made man, well posted on general topics of the day, is benevolent, charitable and generous, but is not an active politician.

Capt. C. H. McLemore was born in Covington county, Miss., in January, 1829, and is the fourth of a family of nine children. His father, Richard McLemore, was a native of North Carolina, and removed from that state to Tennessee with his parents when but a boy. He remained at home, assisting in the care of his family until he was twenty-one years of age. He then came to Mississippi, and was married in Covington county, in August, 1821, to Nancy P. Hill. They had born to them two sons and seven daughters, five of whom are living: The Captain is the eldest of the living children; Levina is the widow of J. C. Brown; Juriah is the widow of W. H. Jackson; Joshua is a farmer living near Meridian; Charity is the widow of J. W. Wiggins. The mother died in September, 1859, at her home near Meridian, the family having removed from Covington county to Lauderdale county in 1836. At that time there were few white people in the country, and the privations and trials they encountered were numerous and often severe. The father was very successful in accumulating property, and before the war owned sixteen hundred acres of land and sixty slaves. He stood very high in the community, and was a citizen of honor and integrity. Capt. McLemore was twenty-one years of age when he began to till the soil and raise livestock. He located in Lauderdale county, and there are few older residents than he. He was married in his twenty-fourth year to Mrs. L. C. Brown, widow of John Brown, of Clarke county, Miss. Seven children were born of this union: Mary V., wife of E. J. Martin; Louis R., deceased; Theodore J.; Inez G., wife of S. A. Park; Caleb O., Mittie S. and Virgil E. Captain McLemore owns four hundred acres of land, and has about one hundred and fifty improved and under excellent cultivation; his plantation lies three and a half miles northeast of Meridian, and he has a nice residence and all the comforts and many of the luxuries of life. In 1862 he enlisted in company I, Thirty-seventh Mississippi volunteer infantry, and was in the army of the Tennessee. When his captain was killed he was promoted to the position, which he held during the remainder of the war. He participated in the siege of Vicksburg, and was afterward transferred to Johnston's army and was in the Georgia campaign. He was captured at Nashville and was sent to Johnson's island, where he was held until the surrender. After the declaration of peace he returned to his home in Lauderdale county and resumed the pursuit of agriculture on the place where he now lives. In 1867 he was elected a member of the county board of supervisors and held that office six years. He and his family are members of the Baptist church. He has given his children a good education; Inez is a graduate of the Meridian Female college, Theodore of the Business college of Louisville, Ky.; he and Caleb Oscar are both clerks in Meridian. The family have always held a position in the highest circles of society and would be an ornament to the social life of any community. Captain McLemore has been a member of the Masonic fraternity for nearly thirty years, and is a Knight of Honor. He also belongs to the Farmers' Alliance.

Joshua McLemore, of Meridian, Lauderdale county, Miss., is a son of Richard McLemore, who was born in North Carolina about 1799, and was married to Miss Nancy P. Hill, of North Carolina. They removed to Tennessee and later came to Covington county, Miss., and thence to the part of the state now called Lauderdale county. Joshua McLemore, one of a family of nine, was born in Lauderdale county, Miss., in 1839. He attended the common schools and lived on the farm, later, in 1856, attending Gathright's school at Summerville, Miss. He taught some in 1858–60. He was married in February, 1860, to Miss M. E. Semmes, a daughter of F. C. Semmes, a relative of Admiral Raphael Semmes of Alabama fame. He has had eleven children: F. R., Nannie, Kate H., C. S., J. E., S. J., W. I., Sallie, Mittie B., John and Julia. In November, 1861, he enlisted for sixty days under Colonel Patton; was discharged at the expiration of his term of service and went out again in April, 1862, under Colonel McLain, in company I, of the Thirty-seventh Mississippi regiment; was with General Price at Iuka; was at Resaca and with Johnston before Atlanta; was discharged at Atlanta and came home and remained here. Peace being established, he engaged in farming, teaching also in 1866 and 1867. He settled four miles northeast of Meridian, and later removed to a point eighteen miles northwest of Meridian, thence to a place two miles east of Meridian, where he yet resides. He owns two hundred and twenty acres of rich land in the bottoms, valued at from $40 to $50 per acre, and raises corn and cotton, using commercial fertilizer to a limited extent, favoring it after the home compost is exhausted. He also raises stock, including cattle, horses and mules, making a specialty of the latter. Holstein and Jersey grades constitute his cattle. His son, J. E. McLemore, took a commercial course at the State Business college. Mr. McLemore is a member of the democratic executive committee of Lauderdale county, Miss. He is justly considered one of this county's very best citizens, and for honor, enterprise and all the other qualities that go to constitute the model citizen, he stands second to none.

Angus McLeod, father of John W. McLeod, cashier of the Merchants' bank, Grenada, Miss., was a native of North Carolina, and came to Mississippi before marriage, settling in Oxford, the Athens of Mississippi. There he followed merchandising quite extensively, became wealthy, but was a heavy loser during the war. His death occurred in March, 1870, at the age of fifty-six years. He was married in Oxford to a widow, whose maiden name was Miss E. M. Redding, a native of Tennessee, who bore him three children, two of whom died in infancy, John W., being the only survivor. Mrs. McLeod is a faithful member of the Cumberland Presbyterian church, and is a resident of Oxford, Miss., at the present time. John W. McLeod was born in Oxford, Miss., on the 7th of November, 1846, attained his growth there, and received his scholastic advantages in Oxford college. He served during the war in Captain Webb's company, McQuirk's regiment, Third Mississippi cavalry, and participated in the following battles: Harrisburg, Atlanta, Jonesboro, and was paroled at Columbus, Miss. In 1866 Mr. McLeod began clerking in a mercantile establishment, with which he remained for some time, and in 1873 was elected to the position of sheriff of Fayette county,

77

holding that office ten successive years, this proving the efficient and capable manner in which he discharged the duties of the same. He came to Grenada in 1886, and soon after was elected cashier of the Merchants' bank. This bank was organized the same year, with Samuel Lawrence as president, and Albert Bebee, of New York, as vice president. The directors were B. F. Thomas, John Powell, W. N. Pass, W. C. McLeod, of Grenada, and Ben Price, and the bank had a paid-up capital of $40,000. In 1887 a large two-story building of brick was erected and the capital increased to $60,000. At the present time John Powell is president, W. N. Pass, vice president, and John W. McLeod, cashier. The directors are John Powell, A. V. B. Thomas, Max Ginsburger, W. C. McLean, Robert Doak, W. F. Pass and Ben Price.   Mr. McLeod selected for his companion in life Miss Anna Buffalo, a native of Raleigh, N. C., and daughter of B. B. and A. A. Buffalo, who were also natives of that state. The parents came to Mississippi when Anna was but an infant, and she was reared and educated in Holly Springs, of this state. The nine children born to this union were named as follows: Anna M., William A., Charles H., Mary Pearle, Ruby, Bessie, Dodie, Thomas Dudley and a girl baby, Mattie Florence. Mr. and Mrs. McLeod are members of the Presbyterian church, and he has been deacon in the same for some time. In politics he is democratic. He is one of the representative citizens of the county, and his high position is a just tribute to his worth. He is in partnership with J. B. Snider in the fire insurance business, and they represent thirteen of the best companies.

Hon. John Nelson McLeod, state senator from the Thirty-sixth district of Mississippi and planter at Harrison, Tallahatchie county, was born in Greene county, Ala., in 1836. His parents, John and Margaret (Henderson) McLeod, were natives of Robinson county, N. C., where they were reared and married, and whence they moved to Greene county, Ala., and from there about 1837 to Panola county, Miss., where Mr. McLeod died, Mrs. McLeod surviving him till 1881; she died in Tallahatchie county. Mr. and Mrs. McLeod were both Presbyterians, but some time after his death she connected herself with the Baptist church. Norman McLeod, father of John McLeod and grandfather of our subject, was a Scotsman, but came to America when a young man and became a North Carolina planter, dying in that state. His wife was also a native of that sturdy country, Scotland. Senator McLeod's grandparents, Archibald Henderson and wife, were also natives of Scotland and came to the United States when comparatively young. After living for many years in North Carolina Mr. Henderson removed to Texas in his old age, and died there. Senator McLeod's mother was married three times, Mr. McLeod being her first husband. Our subject was the youngest of two sons and three daughters, of whom he and his brother are the only ones now living. Norman, the brother just mentioned, is a planter in Panola county, who served through the Civil war as a private in Princeton's cavalry regiment. Christiana became the wife of John Keith; Julia died young. Senator McLeod was reared on a farm and received only a limited common-school education, but he was naturally a student and great reader, and has secured a wide range of practical and general information. At the age of eighteen years he became a clerk in the store of his brother-in-law, J. H. Keith, and for a time before the war he worked on a farm for which he received $10 a month. In 1860 he was elected clerk of the probate court in Panola county, in which office he served with satisfaction for two years. He then joined Floyd's company, which was attached to Chalmers' brigade, but was soon taken sick; after his recovery he served in the commissary department until the close of the war. In 1863 he was captured in west Tennessee and, after being kept in Memphis a prisoner of war for one month, effected his escape and rejoined his command at Senatobia, Miss. He was married in 1862 to Sallie, a daughter of Jacob Harmon. She was a native of Fayette county, and died in Panola county in 1866. In 1869 Mr. McLeod married for his second wife Alice, a daughter of John and Martha (Townes) Leigh, natives of Virginia, who joined their fortunes in Alabama. Mrs. McLeod was born in Yalobusha county, Miss., and died there at the close of the war, Mr. Leigh dying some years after, a well-to-do planter and prominent citizen. He had three sons in the Confederate service during the war. Senator and Mrs. McLeod have one son, Norman, and one daughter, Ouida. Mr. McLeod lived in Panola county till 1867, then came to Harrison, which has just been made a station on the Mississippi & Tennessee railroad, where he has since resided and been a planter and merchant as well, until some few years ago, when he gave up the mercantile business, and devoted his attention exclusively to farming. He owns about three thousand acres of land, seven hundred acres of which are cleared. In 1887 he was elected to the state senate from the Thirty-sixth district, composed of Quitman, Tallahatchie and Grenada, for four years, and served on several important committees. He has always been noted for his stanch defense of all questions pertaining to the temperance cause, and has always carried out in his daily life the example he holds up for his fellowmen to follow, being strictly temperate in thought and deed. He and his family are earnest workers in the Baptist church. He is justly proud of his family, his daughter especially being a highly educated young lady, while his son is just about to graduate from a college in Tennessee. Mr. McLeod is an upright citizen and one whom his fellowmen may well honor, as he does to the extent of his power the good that he may in elevating the down-trodden, striving earnestly always to lift them up to a higher plane of manhood.

Judge Garfield S. McMillan, a prominent lawyer of Brookhaven, Miss., was born in Springville, Erie county, N. Y., in 1829. His father, Joseph McMillan, a prominent farmer of western New York, was a native of Rhode Island, and his father, also named Joseph Mc-Millan, was a native of Scotland. The mother of our subject was Miss Rachael Jones, a native of Great Barrington, Mass. Her father, Capt. Silas Jones, served in the Revolutionary war under General Washington. Mr. McMillan had been previously married in Onondaga county, N. Y., in the year 1805, to Miss Mary Haskins, one of five children. She died in 1820, a member of the Presbyterian church. His second marriage occurred in 1822. His children by his first wife were named Helen, Julia, Marcus, John and William, all deceased The children by the second marriage were as follows: Bessie, who died single, at the age of twenty; Eugenia, who died at the age of twelve; and the subject of our sketch, Garfield S. McMillan was the second of the family in order of birth, who, after attending the common schools near his home, became a student at the Springville academy, at Springville, Erie county, N. Y., of which his father was a trustee. He taught two winter terms of school in his native county and in 1847 came to Mississippi and settled in Monticello, Lawrence county. For a short time he kept books for John H. Tennisson, and later was a teacher for about one year in the Monticello academy, and at the same time was a student at law under the direction of Hon. W. P. Harris, then circuit judge in this district. He was licensed to practice law May, 1850, and during the next five years he was located in Smith county, where he became known as a successful practitioner and a representative in the legislature. He then moved to Monticello, where he was actively engaged in the practice of his profession until 1858. During this time he was a delegate to the democratic national convention held at Cincinnati in 1856, but previously, in 1850, he had been journal clerk of the state legislature of Jackson, and in 1851 he had represented his county in the state legislature, after which, in 1852, he had received the appointment of private secretary to Governor McRae. In 1858 he was elected district attorney of the second judicial district of the state and served in that

capacity for ten years.   In 1870 he was appointed chancellor of the second district by
Governor Alcorn and held that position by reappointment for six years.   In 1885 he was
elected justice of the peace and still holds that office.   He was supervisor of the census of
the fourth district of Mississippi in 1890 under the appointment of President Harrison.   In
1865 Judge McMillan married Miss Annette Darden, a native of Jefferson county, Miss., the
second daughter and third child of Buckner and Sarah (Torrey) Darden.   Mr. and Mrs.
McMillan have had five children: Lillian R. (who died at the age of five years), Stewart
(born in 1869 and died in 1871), Archibald M. (born in 1872), Viola (born in 1875) and
Beatrice (born in 1877), the three last mentioned all being members of their father's household.   Previous to the war Judge McMillan was a democrat.   He took no active part in the
Confederate cause except in the clothing of the soldiers who had enlisted in his immediate
vicinity.   Since the war he has been a republican.   His first presidential vote was cast for
Lewis Cass.   He is a master Mason and a member of the Knights of Honor, and a member
of the Presbyterian church.   He is a generous supporter of the causes of religion and education, and has always labored and given of his means to elevate the people to a higher and
better condition and to assist in the dissemination of education and general enlightenment.

John T. McMurran (deceased) made a name for himself in the legal circles of the state
of Mississippi, but was especially well known throughout Adams and adjoining counties.
He achieved a reputation for legal ability and acumen which might well be envied by any
man and fully gained the confidence of the people.   He was born in Pennsylvania in 1801,
but in the city of Chillicothe, Ohio, he was educated by an uncle, who gave him good advantages, and, unlike the majority of boys, he improved his opportunities to the utmost.   In the
year 1820 he graduated in law, and the following year came to Natchez and entered the
office of Griffith & Quitman, remaining with them three years.   In 1827, at the death of Mr.
Griffith, Mr. McMurran formed a partnership with Mr. Quitman, the firm being Quitman &
McMurran, but at the opening of the Texan war Mr. Quitman entered the service, and the
business was carried on alone by Mr. McMurran, until the former's return.   They dissolved
partnership in 1846, after which Mr. McMurran practiced his profession alone until 1861.
In 1866, while a passenger on the steamer Fashion, it was burned and he was so severely
injured that he was taken to a hospital at New Orleans and there died of his injuries on the
30th of December, 1866.   He had been married on the 6th of January, 1831, to Miss Mary
Louisa Turner, a daughter of Judge Turner (see sketch), her birth occurring on the 7th of
January, 1814.   She still survives him, and although seventy-seven years of age, shows but
little the ravages of time, either mentally or physically.   She bore her husband three children: Mary Louisa, born October 16, 1831, and died July 31, 1833; John Thompson, who
was born October 1, 1833, and is now residing in New York, and Mary Louisa, born December 28, 18—, married Farar B. Connor, but died on the 31st of March, 1864, leaving three
children, only one of whom is now living.   The family are members of the Episcopal church,
and have, during their long residence in this county, been highly respected and exceptionally
prominent people.   Mr. McMurran was a prominent lawyer in his day, was thoroughly conversant with the common law, and impressed all with whom he came in contact as a man of
great strength, depth and grasp of mind.   His words and writings inspired respect, and for
over forty years he was a leading character of Natchez.   He was the soul of honor in his
practice and in fact in every walk in life, and at the time of his death he left an unblemished
reputation and an honored name as a heritage to his children.

Angus K. McNair, M. D., has been a resident of Mississippi since early manhood and
during this time he has enjoyed the reputation of being an honest, upright man, and a solid,

substantial and thoroughly reliable citizen. The history of his life has not been unlike that of other professional men, and yet there has been that individuality about him that shows him to be a man of superior intelligence. His energy and ability have not been without the substantial rewards of success, as will be seen from a glance at his present possessions, and as a citizen he is thoroughly public spirited and law abiding. He was born in Richmond county, of the Old North state, July 28, 1838, his father, Japeth McNair, being a native of the same state and county as himself, his birth occurring in 1799. The latter was married in his native state to Miss Mary Kelly, and in 1839 they moved to Coosa county, Ala., where Mr. McNair became an extensive planter and the owner of numerous slaves. He made his home in Coosa county until his death in 1872, his wife having preceded him to the grave four years. Of their family, six sons and three daughters grew to mature years. Two of the sons entered the army, fighting for the Confederate cause, and died while in the service. Another son, Dr. William McNair, was a prominent physician and died in Arkansas; and two more sons are successful farmers of Alabama. Dr. A. K. McNair attained to man's estate in Alabama, and received a fair common-school education, but is, however, mostly self-educated. He began the study of medicine when a young man of twenty, his preceptor being his cousin, Dr. N. H. Baker, a well-known and successful physician of Coosa county. In the winter of 1859–60 Dr. McNair took his first course of lectures, and the following winter was a student in the medical department of the New Orleans university, graduating in the spring of 1861. Upon finishing his studies in that institution he came to Fayette Miss., for the purpose of entering upon the practice of his profession, but being an enthusiastic Southerner, he gave this up to enlist as a private in the Confederate army, becoming a member of the First Mississippi light artillery. He was soon promoted to assistant surgeon, with the rank of captain, and served in that capacity until the close of the war, participating in all the engagements of his battery. He received a gunshot wound in the hip at the battle of Baker's creek, and in the siege of Vicksburg he was taken prisoner. He was paroled, and after his exchange returned to active service at the front, but at the time of the final surrender was in Hinds county, Miss., where he was paroled. Shortly after this he returned to Jefferson county, and for a number of years was engaged in practicing medicine about six miles east of Fayette. Since 1879 he has been a resident of the town, and has acquired a large and profitable practice. In his journeys to alleviate the sufferings of the sick, the sunshine of his disposition as well as his medical skill is brought to bear upon his patients, and the result is very satisfactory. He is a member of the State Medical association, and was appointed one of the health officers of Jefferson county. Dr. McNair was married here in March, 1873, to Miss Frances Marion Warren, a daughter of J. J. Warren. Mrs. McNair is a native of the county, and was reared and educated in the Fayette Female college, of which institution she is a graduate. She has borne the Doctor five children: Mary, a young lady now attending college at Columbus, Miss., William, Angus K., Jr., J. Warren and Annie, the latter being ten years of age. The family are prominent members of the Presbyterian church, and the Doctor is a Royal Arch Mason, a member of the K. of H. and also of the I. O. O. F.

R. W. McNair, sheriff of Lincoln county, and a prominent resident of Brookhaven, Miss., was born in this state in 1849. He is a son of John E. and Adeline (Watts) McNair. His father was born in Richmond, N. C., August 8, 1808, and his mother was a native of Lexington, Holmes county, Miss., and was born in 1833. She was a daughter of Reuben Watts, a native of Georgia, who came to Mississippi about 1830, and settled in Holmes county, where he lived for some years, removing thence to Covington county, Miss., where he held the office of sheriff. He took a very prominent part in the political affairs; his business operations being so successful that he acquired a considerable property. He died very suddenly in this county, aged sixty-eight years. He was twice married, and by his first marriage he had six children, of whom the mother of the subject of this sketch was the second in order of birth. She accompanied her parents from Holmes county to Covington county, where she was married. Thomas Watts, the eldest child, died in Covington county, leaving a wife and two children, who reside at Williamsburg. Adeline Watts became the wife of J. E. McNair. William Watts died during the war, leaving a wife and one child. George Watts, who never married, died in Texas. Dr. V. B. Watts is a resident of Brookhaven. Jane Watts married Mr. Davis, who was killed in the battle of Harrisburg, Miss., and by whom she had one child. She married, for the second time, D. O. Summers, and lived in Marion county, Miss. The father, Reuben Watts, was afterward married to Mrs. Nancy Parish, his first wife having died about 1855, having been for many years a member of the Presbyterian church. The father of our subject's father, Alexander McNair, was a native of Scotland, and came with his parents to North Carolina when he was three years old. The family located in that state, where Alexander was reared, and followed planting until his removal to Mississippi. He settled in Simpson county, where he died at the age of eighty-four years. He was a man of considerable prominence and took some part in politics. His wife was Miss Effie Little. She died in Simpson county, considerably advanced in life, some years after her husband. To them were born eleven children, seven of whom married and had families, and two of whom are yet living. The latter are Mrs. Jane Graves and Mrs. Isabelle Stubbs, the first mentioned of whom lived in San Antonio, Tex., and the latter in Louisiana. Those deceased are as follows: Mrs. Katy Leonard, who died in Covington county, Miss.; Rodrick, who married in Mississippi and removed to Texas, and there died, leaving a large family; Cornelius died in South Carolina, unmarried; Diana, who died unmarried, in Covington county, Miss.; Rachel, who died in Covington county; Mary, who died unmarried in Simpson county, Miss.; Mrs. Betsey McDonald died in Covington county, leaving a large family; and Mrs. Belinda Fullenweider, who died in Texas, also leaving a large family. John E. McNair came to Mississippi when a young man. After his arrival he taught school for a time, studying law during his leisure hours, and in due time was admitted to the bar. He was several times elected to the office of district attorney of his county, and afterward was elected circuit judge, a position which he filled with much credit until about the close of the war. He came to Brookhaven, Miss., in 1870, and for some years taught the Peabody school. He was elected mayor and held that office until his death, which occurred in January, 1874, he being in his sixty-sixth year. He led a very active life and was quite successful as an attorney, and was regarded as one of the most able judges in the state. In his earlier life he was the founder of the Monticello academy, of Monticello, Miss. As a politician he took a very active part and was always so outspoken in his political convictions, that he was widely known as a stanch democrat of the old ante-bellum days. He was a member of the Presbyterian church, and was for many years an elder and took an active and helpful interest in everything pertaining to its welfare, being a leader in all church and Sunday-school affairs. To John and Adeline (Watts) McNair were born eight children who are yet living, another son, John E., having died at the age of four years. Of the others, Alexander C. is an attorney living at Brookhaven, and is chairman of the democratic executive committee of Sinclair county; Rachel is the wife of Walter McGee and a resident of Covington county, Miss.; Thomas McNair is a dentist of Brookhaven; Stephen D. is a telegraph operator and express agent at Harriston, lately elected chancery clerk of Jefferson county, Miss; Charles is deputy circuit clerk of Lincoln county, Miss., and received the nomination for circuit clerk of said county at recent election; Willie G. is a train dispatcher in the employ of the Natchez, Jackson & Columbus railroad company of Natchez; Mattie, the wife of Dr. C. B. Dunning, lives at Crystal Springs, Miss. Our subject was born in Simpson county, Miss., but was reared in Covington county, where he was educated in what is now Centenary college and other schools. At the age of twenty he married and settled in Covington county on a farm. In December, 1870, he came to Lincoln county and settled near Brookhaven, where he has since resided, engaged in farming. He was elected assessor of Lincoln county in 1879, for two years. He was also elected a member of the board of supervisors for two years. In the fall of 1883 he was elected sheriff, and holds that office until the present time, being reëlected at every consecutive election. Politically he is a democrat and he takes a great interest in all public affairs. He keeps himself exceptionally well posted on all current topics, and is one of the most intelligent, best informed and most companionable men in the county. He married Miss Emma Pearce, a native of Greene county, Miss., and daughter of Levi and Katy (Fairly) Pearce When quite young Mrs. McNair came with her parents to Covington county, Miss., and here she was reared and educated. To Mr. and Mrs. McNair have been born five children, Addie, Katy, Bertram, Mary and Ruby, who died at the age of six years. The family are members of the Presbyterian church, in which Mr. McNair is an elder. He is also a member of the Knights of Honor.

Stephen D. McNair is accounted among the energetic and enterprising men of Harriston, and although only in his thirty-third year he has business qualifications of a high order, and has become widely and favorably known for prudent foresight, sound judgment and an active and intelligent mind. He was born in Simpson county of this state September 22, 1858, but his father, Judge John E. McNair, was born in Robinson county of the Palmetto state, and when a young man, or about the year 1826, he came to Mississippi and took up his abode in Lawrence county, where he soon became widely known, for he was a man of superior education. After devoting his attention to teaching for some time he began reading law, with the intention of preparing himself for an active business life, and was soon admitted to the bar. After practicing a short time in the midst of able and experienced competition, his ability as an attorney began to manifest itself, and his close application and attention to his profession was rewarded by his election to the position of district attorney, in which capacity he served one or more terms. He was next elected to the office of circuit judge of this district, and while discharging the duties of this position he distinguished himself as a man of sound judgment, broad intelligence and liberal, progressive ideas. In the year 1870 he removed to Brookhaven, where he lived retired from the active duties of his life until his death in 1874. He was a very able and talented lawyer, and filled every position of honor and trust with credit to himself and honor to his profession. He was married in Covington county, Miss., to Miss Adaline Watts, a daughter of Reuben Watts. Mrs. McNair was born and reared in Covington county, Miss., and in 1870, at the early age of thirty-eight years, was called from life, her death being deeply lamented by a large circle of friends, as well as by her immediate family. Besides Mr. McNair she left a family of six sons and two daughters that grew to mature years, all of whom are living at the present time and are the heads of families, with the exception of the youngest son. She was a model mother and wife, was a kind, sincere and obliging friend, and her piety and true Christianity were undoubted. Until eighteen years of age Stephen D. McNair made his home in the town of Brookhaven, receiving the advantages of the common schools. In his youth he began learning telegrahy and was given a position as night operator at Osyka, but only remained at that point a short time. He has followed like business at different places since the age of eighteen years, and in the month of June, 1890, received the appointment of superintendent of the Natchez railroad, but this position he resigned shortly after. Since January, 1886, he has been a resident of Harriston, and has had charge of the Natchez, Jackson & Columbus railroad at this point. In 1887 he was made agent for the Louisville, New Orleans & Texas railroad, and has since been the efficient, accommodating and gentlemanly agent for both these railroads. It is conceded by all that he has done more to advance the interests of the town of Harriston than all its other citizens combined, for all things of a public nature which pointed to the material benefit of the county or town received his hearty support. He purchased the north addition to Harriston, and on this property has erected several substantial residences. He has also erected one good business house, and is president of the building association of the place. He was married in Jackson, Miss., March 2, 1882, to Miss Belle E. Patton, a daughter of John W. Patton, now deceased, a former well-known editor and a prominent man of that city. Mrs. McNair was born, reared, educated and married in Jackson, and by Mr. McNair is the mother of one child, a daughter, named Sallie Virginia. Mr. McNair has shown his approval of secret organizations by becoming a member of the K. of P., and is filling the position of chancellor commander of his lodge. He is a thoroughly well-informed business man, and as he is an intelligent and entertaining conversationalist, he is a most agreeable gentleman to meet.

Dr. William J. McNair, a physician and surgeon of Quitman, Clarke county, Miss., was born in Montgomery county, Ala., in 1846. He was the fourth in a family of five children born to and reared by John and Sarah (Jones) McNair. His father, a native of Scotland, came early to this country and settled in Alabama, where he married and lived out the balance of his life, dying about 1850. After his death the family removed to Mississippi and settled at Marion, then the county seat of Lauderdale county, where the mother of our subject soon after died. The children born to Mr. and Mrs. McNair were Martha, who died when a young lady; James, who died in Alabama before the removal of the family to this state; Benjamin, who also died in Alabama about 1850; William J. was the next in order of birth; Henry L., is a mechanic living in Lauderdale county. The parents of our subject were Christian people the father having been a Presbyterian and the mother a member of the Methodist Episcopal church. In his early life Dr. McNair was a resident of Meridian, where he received a good English education. He studied medicine with Dr. M. J. Thompson and began the practice of his profession at Meridian about 1878, and since that time he has had an extensive practice throughout Lauderdale county. He removed to Quitman in 1855, where he has established a fine practice, and in March, 1891, he opened a drug store which he manages in connection with his practice. He was married in 1883 to Mrs. Lott, formerly Mary E. Howell, of Meridian, daughter of B. W. and Mary (Pope) Howell, who was a native of Mississippi. Dr. and Mrs. McNair are members of the Baptist church, in which the Doctor holds the office of deacon. The Doctor did service during the late war, enlisting in 1863 in company G, of the Sixth regiment of Mississippi cavalry. Among other engagements in which he participated were those of Yazoo City, Miss., the fight in Yazoo county, in Harrisburg, Miss., Johnsonville, Tenn., and at Perryville and Okolahona. He was discharged at the end of the war and engaged in farming, school teaching and other vocations, devoting all of his spare time to self-education. He is a member of the Masonic order and takes great interest in schools and churches. He has been a member of the State Medical association for some time and he is also identified with the Clarke County Medical association, of which he is vice president. The parents of Mrs. McNair were born, her father in North Carolina and her mother in middle Tennessee. She was one of seven children born to her parents, whose names are as follows: John H., George W., Frank, Pope, Allen K., Mary E. and Mattie. Her parents died in Mississippi, her mother in 1852 and her father in 1875. Her father was a merchant and a prominent resident of Meridian, Miss., and with his wife were members of the Christian church. The Doctor's professional success has been great, and his standing among the medical practitioners of this and adjoining counties is high.

One of the rising young professional men of Newton county is Dr. G. H. McNeill, a native of Mississippi. His parents removed from North Carolina to this state in the early days; the father was a planter and a minister of the Methodist Episcopal Church South. He died in Clarke county, Miss., in 1867. Dr. McNeill passed his boyhood and youth in Clarke county, attending the common school until 1876; in that year he entered the Louisville Medical college, from which institution he was graduated with honors. He located at Garlandville, Miss., where he entered upon the practice of his profession. He remained there until February, 1885, removing at that time to Newton, where he has since resided. In the spring of 1891 he went to the city of New York, where he took a special course in the Polyclinic Medical college. He is a man especially adapted to the professions of medicine and surgery, and has a prospect of a brilliant career. He is energetic, and is ambitions to be fully abreast of the times and keep well posted in all discoveries pertaining to the science of medicine. Dr. McNeill was united in marriage in 1879 to Miss Annie Dent, of Garlandville, Miss. He is a member of the Knights of Pythias, belonging to the lodge at Newton.

John S. McNeily, editor and proprietor of the Greenville *Times*, Greenville, Miss., was born in Wilkinson county, Miss., November 20, 1841. The McNeilys were among the early settlers of Mississippi, having located here during the Spanish rule. Mr. McNeily's maternal ancestors (the Shelbys and Seymours) were also pioneers in Wilkinson county and in the state. Both families were prominent, and were leaders in society and in public affairs. The parents of the subject of this sketch were William and Mary (Seymour) McNeily, both natives of Wilkinson county, where they were also reared and married. There were born to them four children, only one of whom is now living, and the parents died when the children were young, and the latter were reared by relatives. The childhood of John S. McNeily was spent in Hinds county, Miss., and he was attending school at Jackson, La., when the war broke out. He felt called to contribute his part, whatever it might be, to the Confederate cause, and, enlisting, went with a company from Natchez to Pensacola, Fla., and after about a year went to Virginia and joined his brother, who was an officer in the Second Mississippi regiment, of Longstreet's command, commonly known in Mississippi as the Griffith, Barksdale, Humphrey's brigade, with which he served during the balance of the war, and participated in much active service. He escaped unscathed, and at the close of the struggle was sergeant-major of his regiment, with his brother in command. Returning to Mississippi, he located at Woodville, where he embarked in journalism. In 1869 he came to Greenville and purchased the Greenville *Times*, which he has since published. This paper is one of the ablest local journals in this part of the state, ably edited and attractively printed, and exerts a wide influence. Mr. McNeily married Miss May Perry, a niece of Colonel Perry, of Greenville, who died a few years afterward. His present wife was Mary, daughter of Col. Edmund Berkeley, of Prince William county, Va. He has three children: Mary B., Fannie P., and Margaret P. Mr. McNeily is a man of more than local reputation, who gives his unqualified support to every measure calculated to aid the development and advancement of his county and state. In 1890 he was a member of the constitutional convention of Mississippi from the state at large.

Alexander G. McNutt, ex-governor of the state of Mississippi, was born in the Old Dominion, in which state he was reared to manhood, where he received good educational advantages. After preparing himself for the practice of law he came to Mississippi and opened an office at Vicksburg in 1826, and being a very talented and brilliant young man, he soon made an enviable reputation for himself throughout the state. His ability as a lawyer soon became appreciated by the people and he was first elected a member of the state legislature, and in this body his comprehensive knowledge of law and the soundness of his views won him immediate recognition. After serving one term with fidelity, faithfulness and ability, he resumed the practice of his profession, and the business of Mrs. Elizabeth Cameron was placed in his charge, her estate being very extensive and valuable, and in the meantime their marriage was consummated, at which time she was said to have been one of the most beautiful women in the South. Not many years after their marriage Mr. McNutt was elected governor of the state, in which capacity he discharged his duties with the same faithfulness that marked his career as a legislator. Being a man of very decided character, he was very discreet in every step of his public career, and so determined was he to do whatever he considered to be right, regardless of consequences, that he often, in carrying out his principles, incurred the displeasure of his friends. While serving in this capacity he was called from life, and although his career had been a comparatively short one it was one of usefulness and full of honors. In personal appearance he was rather tall, with black hair and eyes, a high, square forehead and a prominent nose, all his features being remarkably clear cut and well defined, expressing power and determination in every lineament. After his death his widow was married to Col. George R. Fall, a native of England. He was a man of rare ability, intelligence and usefulness and an honored member of the Mississippi legislature for a number of years. He was an editor of one of the leading newspapers of the state for many years, and was a man whose intelligence manifested itself in every walk in life. Since his death, which occurred about 1874, his widow has resided on her old homestead on Deer creek in the southern part of Washington county. She is now in her seventy-seventh year, and is in the enjoyment of good health. As she is very retiring she does not seek or allow publicity, but is perfectly content with her present quiet, uneventful and peaceful life. Before her marriage she was a Miss Elizabeth Lewis, a native Mississippian. In personal appearance Colonel Fall was decidedly prepossessing, for, while not so tall as Governor McNutt, he was yet commanding in presence and his brilliant dark gray eyes were full of intelligence and expression. His hair was dark and his high forehead was indicative of a mind well balanced and far above the ordinary.

Samuel J. McPeak has been familiar with planting in Tunica county, since boyhood, and that he has profited by his experience is shown by the fact that he owns a fine plantation of four hundred and eighty acres, one mile southwest of Hollywood, of which three hundred and fifty acres are under cultivation. This plantation is his birthplace, and here he first saw the light of day, September 2, 1860. His parents, Isaac Shelby and Mary Jane (White) McPeak, were Tennesseeans by birth, but were married in Mississippi, where to their union twelve children were born—six sons and six daughters—Samuel J. being their third child. Isaac McPeak was one of the pioneers of Tunica county, for in 1836 he became a resident of old Commerce, and throughout his life he followed the occupation of planting, being also very fond of hunting and exceedingly skillful in the use of the rifle. He is now in his seventy-first year and is a resident of old Commerce, where his wife was called from life on the 19th of June, 1891. He was a member of the board of supervisors before the war, and has filled the same position since, making it between fifteen and twenty years. He has been a very useful and progressive citizen, and has rendered valuable aid in improving and building up the county, and has won an enviable reputation as a sterling citizen in this and the surrounding counties. Nine of his children are living at the present time, and are all substantial residents of this section, with the exception of two daughters who reside in Arkansas. Henry, a son, is a member of the board of supervisors, is a resident of Tunica, and is engaged in contracting for the railroad company. The other sons are planters. Samuel J. McPeak was brought up on the plantation on which he is now residing, but devoted one year to the mercantile business in Pendleton, Ark., and was then bookkeeper for the Sunnyside company, of Sunnyside, Ark., for six months, after which he returned to his old home in Mississippi, and has since been a resident on the old plantation. He expects to devote five hundred acres to the culture of cotton this year, and two hundred acres to corn, and being a very energetic and pushing young gentleman and a thorough and practical business man, he will, without doubt, do well. In connection with the admirable way in which he looks after his planting interests, he is also conducting a good general mercantile establishment at Hollywood, Miss., his stock of goods being valued at $5,000, and owing to his upright methods of conducting affairs and his efforts to please his patrons, he has built up a prosperous business. He was married November 28, 1889, to Miss Margaret K. Poage, a daughter of Robert G. Poage, of Arkansas, she being an earnest and faithful member of the Catholic church. Mr. McPeak has followed in his worthy father's footsteps, has always been interested in county affairs, and is one of the most successful, prosperous and wideawake young business men of which Tunica county can boast. He has shown his approval of secret organizations by becoming a member of the Masonic fraternity and the Knights of Honor, of which orders he is a prominent member. He has easy and engaging manners, is five feet eight inches in hight, weighs one hundred and fifty pounds and is of fair complexion, his hair being light and his eyes, which denote him to be a man of intelligence and kindly disposition, a bright blue.

William A. McPheeters, M. D., is a physician whose labors in behalf of suffering humanity have been highly appreciated, for in the practice of his noble and highly necessary calling he has won the gratitude of hundreds by the skill and talent he has displayed. He was born in Jefferson county, Miss., in the year 1833, and was the third of four children born to Dr. James A. and Maria (Dunbar) McPheeters, the father being a Kentuckian, but the latter a native of Mississippi. Mrs. McPheeter's father, William Dunbar, was born in Adams county, but his father, Robert Dunbar, came here during the Spanish reign in 1760 and was engaged in planting near Washington, where he died. He was the father of quite a large family, and his son William also followed in his footsteps, becoming a planter. The latter was married in 1804, and died in this county about 1829. Dr. James A. McPheeters began the study of medicine in his native state, Kentucky, and after locating in Natchez, Miss., in 1823 he began practicing his profession. After his marriage in 1828 he moved to Jefferson county, where he lived until his wife's death in 1835, when he came back to Natchez and here resided until his death in 1848. His father, James McPheeters, was also a physician and was a practitioner in Kentucky. In the College of South Carolina Dr. William A. McPheeters received his literary education, and in 1853 began his medical studies in New Orleans, but in 1855 graduated from the University of Pennsylvania, Philadelphia, after which two and a half years were spent in studying in Europe. In 1859 he began practicing in Natchez, and four years during the war were spent as a surgeon in the Confederate army, being promoted after he had entered the field as a private. After his return from the war he entered at once upon a successful career, which has from the first been one of gratifying results. He is thoroughly fitted by study and experience for a superior physician and surgeon, and has built up a reputation for professional skill and ability that is not merely local, but extends over a large extent of territory.   He was married in 1867 to Miss Laura Walworth, and to them nine children have been born, seven of whom are living. Mrs. McPheeters died May 11, 1891.   She was an intelligent and accomplished lady and an earnest member of the Presbyterian church.   Socially, the Doctor is a member of the Masonic order, the Knights of Pythias and the Knights of Honor.

Among the successful and enterprising planters of Carroll county is Alfred A. McPherson of Vaiden.   He is a native of Mississippi, born in Carroll county, May 8, 1836.   His father, Daniel McPherson, was a native of the state of Georgia.   He was married there to Martha Robinson, a native of Georgia, and a sister of the Rev. Norval Robinson, a prominent minister in the Baptist church, and a member of a well-known family; he was for nearly a half century the minister of the Pearl River Baptist church, near Jackson, Miss.; his father was also a Baptist minister, and a native of Georgia.   Mrs. McPherson's brothers were all self-made men, and held positions of trust and honor.   The McPherson family removed to Mississippi about the year 1827, and settled in Hinds county, near Jackson.   Daniel McPherson removed from Hinds county to Carroll county about 1834, and was one of the pioneers of that county.   He located near Carrollton, and resided there until his death in 1846.   His wife survives him, and is now ninety years old.   Alfred A. McPherson is one of a family of five sons and two daughters: James was a soldier in the Confederate army, and was wounded in Virginia, where he died; Matthew was also a soldier, and served through the war; he is now a planter in Texas; Pinckey served in the war, receiving a wound at Fort Donelson, from which he died; George is a planter in Hinds county; the sisters are Mary Permelia, wife of B. B. Byrd, a planter at Oakland, and Dillie, deceased.   Alfred grew to manhood in Carroll county, acquiring a fair English education at Carrollton.   He learned the carpenter's trade, which he followed several years.   He was a contractor and builder before the war, and accumulated a nice property.   In 1862 he enlisted in the Thirtieth Mississippi volunteer infantry, and joined Bragg's army, following that brave leader through all the varied fortunes of a soldier until taken prisoner.   He participated in the battles of Murfreesboro and Chickamauga, and a great many battles and skirmishes of less importance.   He was taken prisoner at Chickamauga and was sent to Camp Douglas, Chicago, where he was held for two years, at the end of which time peace was declared, and he was released.   He then returned to his home in Carrollton, and set about retrieving his fortunes.   Everything had been swept away by the ravages of war, and although much was due him, nothing could be collected.   His liabilities amounted to $10,000, and he has since succeeded in paying this out dollar for dollar.   On his return to Carroll county Mr. McPherson settled on a plantation, and he has proven a successful agriculturist.   He has acquired about four thousand acres of land, a large portion of which is under excellent cultivation.   He resided near Carrollton until 1879, and then removed to the vicinity of Vaiden.   In 1890 he bought residence property in the town, and now makes his home there.   In 1880 he engaged in merchandising, and for the past ten years he has carried on this business in connection with his extensive planting.   He is a man of wise judgment and sound business principles, and has succeeded in attaining a position of influence and financial independence.   Mr. McPherson was united in marriage in Carroll county, Miss., in 1858, to Miss Martha Holman; she died in 1877, leaving three children: Thaddeus is married and lives on one of his father's plantations; he also has charge of the store belonging to his father; he has three children; the second in the family, Ada, is the wife of Dr. Rogers, of West Station, Holmes county; she is the mother of one child; the youngest of the family is Thomas, who resides at home.   In 1888 Mr. McPherson was married in Holmes county to Miss Ella Downer, who is a daughter of John H. Downer, and was born in Georgia and reared near Vaiden. Our subject is a prominent member of the Baptist church, of which he is a deacon; he has served in that capacity for about twenty-five years. Mrs. McPherson is also a member of the Baptist church.

T. J. McQuiston, a prominent planter and stockbreeder of Egypt, was born in the house in which he now lives, three miles south of Egypt, in 1847, the son of Col. William and S. S. (Holder) McQuiston. His father was a native of Christian county, Ky., and his mother was born near Lexington, in the same state. Mr. McQuiston was reared on a farm, and acquired a fair English education. While yet a single man he came to Mississippi and was married in Pontiac to a Miss Clark, and had two children, both of whom are dead. After her death he married the mother of the subject of our sketch, and settled on the place now known as the McQuiston plantation, where he died in 1857. He was for some years United States tobacco inspector at New Orleans, and for four years United States marshal for the northern district of Mississippi. He was a selfmade man who accumulated a good property, a portion of which was a large plantation, in the management of which he took great pride, as well as in the breeding of fine stock. He was possessed of a strong will, much energy and liberal views. He also had great force of character, and was an amiable man and truly hospitable. He was possessed of a wide acquaintance, whom he frequently and generously entertained. He was of Scotch and Irish descent. His church affiliations were with the Methodists. Mrs. McQuiston was also twice married, her first husband having been Osmand Herndon, by whom she had one son. Her father, Richard Holder, was a descendant of Daniel Boone, and fought in the early Indian wars, dying in Tennessee. T. J. McQuiston is the eldest of two sons and three daughters, born to his parents, all of whom are living. They are as follows: Fannie G. (wife of L. S. Sykes, a prominent citizen of Aberdeen), Hattie J. (wife of Mr. F. J. Shields, a lawyer of Le Maire, Ala.), Dunbar H. (of Aberdeen), Maggie S. (wife of Q. O. Eckfort), and our subject. He was educated in the common schools and at an educational institution located at Pontotoc. In 1862 he joined Lander's battalion of cavalry which was attached to Johnston's army, and took part in the military operations from Resaca to Atlanta, and on to the sea, surrendering at the close of the war. After peace was declared, he spent one year as a merchant in New Orleans, and then returned to the old homestead upon which he was born, where he has lived the most of the time since. He owns eight hundred acres of fine land, six hundred acres of which are under cultivation, constituting one of the most productive farms in Monroe county. Mr. McQuiston takes considerable interest in politics, all affairs of local import claiming his attention. He was for some years a member of the Monroe county democratic executive committee, and also congressional committee. From 1882 to 1886 he was superintendent of the penitentiary. In 1887 he was married to Miss Lottie B. Holliday, a native of Aberdeen. (See sketch of B. P. Holliday, her brother.) Mrs. McQuiston was a lady of much culture and many admirable qualities, who died in 1889. She was a consistent member of the Methodist Episcopal church, and Mr. McQuiston was also a member of the same faith. Our subject is genial and hospitable, and stands high as a citizen. His business capacity is first-class, and his integrity is unblemished.

B. F. McRae, general merchant at Iuka, Miss., was one of eight children of Kenneth and Fatima (Thomas) McRae. His father was born in North Carolina in 1820. In early life he was a farmer, and later became a merchant. He continued in trade until his death, which occurred in 1861. He was a prominent business man, and at an early date entered a large quantity of land in this state. In all his enterprises he was successful. His wife died about 1857 or 1858. His second wife was Mrs. Isabella Wiley. By his first marriage he had children named as follows: Mary, Margaret, William, John, James, Thomas, Benjamin F. and Francis M. By his second marriage he had two children, named Daniel and Sarah. Mr. McRae was a very public-spirited man, interested in everything that promised to aid in the development and improvement of the county. In politics he was an old-line whig. B. F. McRae was born in Tishomingo county, in 1851. His boyhood days were spent on his father's plantation, and he was unable to obtain much education until after the war. He attended school at Pleasant Site, Ala. At the age of twenty-three, he married and engaged in the mercantile business. Miss Emma Doan, daughter of J. H. Doan, became his wife. Mr. and Mrs. Doan were married at Eastport, and locating there, reared a family of ten children, of whom Mrs. McRae was the eldest. She was born in Eastport in 1855. Her father died in 1885, and her mother is still living in Memphis. Mr. McRae continued in the general mercantile business with no small degree of success until 1883. In 1882 he invested largely in the tannery business, which was not a financial success, and entailed upon him the loss of $30,000. After closing out his store in 1883, he removed to Newburn, Tenn., and engaged in merchandising there. A year later, he removed to Byhalia. Miss., and at the end of another year, he returned to Iuka. He is known as an enterprising, energetic and useful citizen, helpfully interested in everything which contains the promise of benefit to the community. He is a member of the educational board of the town. He is also a member of the Knights of Honor, and of the Knights and Ladies of Honor. He and his wife are members of the Methodist Episcopal church. They have six children, and have lost one by death. Their names are James D., Benjamin F., Ernest, Ottie, Thomas and Eugene. Margaret I. is deceased.

Samuel P. McRee is a farmer and merchant of Caseyville, Miss., fifteen miles west of Brookhaven. He was born in that part of Copiah county which is now included in Lincoln county, April 13, 1843, a son of David and Epsey M. (Leech) McRee. His father was a native of North Carolina and a son of William McRee and his wife, who was Mary Savage. He was the fifth child and fourth son of their family of eight children. His mother was born in March, 1822, and died in Copiah county. Her husband was married twice after her death and removed to Louisiana in 1847, and there ended his days. David McRee came with his parents to Mississippi in 1824 and was there reared and educated. He was married in 1839 to Miss Epsey N. Leech, a native of Mississippi, and a daughter of Reuben and Sarah (Stevens) Leech, of whose six children she was the youngest. She also had two half sisters and one half brother named Watkins, who were her mother's children. Mr. and Mrs. David McRee are still living on their place at Caseyville after having traveled fifty years together in the journey of life. They are very hospitable and their home is open to all comers, a helpful hand being outstretched to all who may be in need of assistance. Mr. McRee is an influential and highly respected man and his wife is one of the noblest' women in the county. Both are members of the Methodist Episcopal church. Mr. McRee is a stanch democrat. They have had children as follows: William J. married Samantha Godbold and has nine children—four sons and five daughters—and is a planter in Lincoln county; Francis married Bettie A. Beacham and lives on a plantation in Copiah county, having two children—David D. and Versie F; Emma M. is the wife of Prentiss Buie, and lives on a plantation in Lincoln county, and has had eight children, two sons and five daughters of whom are living; Annie E. married Dr. J. W. McGee and lives on a plantation in Lincoln county with four children; Sarah H. married Robert A. Cessna and died in 1863, leaving three children, and Samuel P., the subject of this sketch, received a practical English education in the common schools of Lincoln county and assisted his father in the planting operations until 1861, when he enlisted under Capt. H. G. D. Brown in the Seven Stars artillery. The company went to Hazlehurst and thence to New Orleans, to the bay of St. Louis, and then to Camp Moore. At Camp Moore he took the fever and was obliged to return home. In 1863 he rejoined the army at Port Hudson, La., and went thence to Jackson, La. The battle at that point was the first engagement of importance in which he participated. He then went to Georgetown and then to Canton and thence back to Crystal Springs. He participated in the engagements of Coleman's lane, and also went to Yazoo county and there took part in several skirmishes. In the fall of 1863 he was promoted to be lieutenant of cavalry. He was present at the skirmish at Robertson's mills, Miss., and operated at other points in the state till the close of the war. After the war closed he again took sick and returned home, where he was at the time of the general surrender. He was paroled at Jackson, Miss., in the spring of 1865. In 1867 he entered Soule's Commercial college at New Orleans and took a course in bookkeeping and telegraphy. Previous to this, however, he had purchased a retail store of James and John C. Casey and began merchandising, which he still continues at the present time in connection with other business operations and has been so successful that he has acquired considerable property, ranking at this time as one of the very well-to-do men of the county. He is a citizen of influence and high standing. That which he owns he has accumulated by his own unaided efforts, helped by his good judgment and business ability, and it is to these facts and to his admirable personal qualities that he is recognized as one of the leading men of the community. He was married January 12, 1870, to Laura T. Easterling, who was born in Mississippi in 1848, a daughter of William K. and Anna Easterling. She is one of four sons and five daughters, of whom she was the third in order of birth. To Mr. and Mrs. McRee, three sons and three daughters have been born: William D., Mary, Ina and David M., are all members of their parents' household; Ida died at the age of two years; Samuel P. McRee, Jr., met his death at the hands of William Blue while defending his cousin, David McRee, who was in a difficulty which occurred at a sociable at Robert McCormick's house, about seventeen miles northeast of Fayette, Jefferson county, Miss. He was an industrious, promising young man. He was born May 22, 1871, and died on the night of October 11, 1890, in his twentieth year. He was buried from Bethel church, Caseyville. Politically he is a democrat. S. P. McRee is a member of the Knights of Honor, of the Knights and Ladies of Honor and of the Knights of Pythias. He and his wife are members of the Methodist Episcopal church, and are earnest and helpful advocates and supporters of all church and Sunday-school work, having at heart the cause of their Redeemer in their community.

Dr. William McSwine, planter and representative of Grenada county, Miss., is the son of John McSwine, who was a native of the Old Dominion. When but a boy the latter moved with his parents to Tennessee, located with them in Humphreys county and there attained his majority. He was the youngest of a large family of children, two of whom served in the Mexican war under Jackson and one never returned, having been killed at the battle of New Orleans. John McSwine was married to Miss Annie Ross, of Texas, and in 1835 he and family moved to Mississippi, settling on the place where our subject now resides, which at that time was unimproved. Here Mr. McSwine opened up and put under cultivation a large tract of land and became one of the substantial and leading citizens of what was then Yalobusha county. He led a quiet, unpretentious life and took no part in politics more than to exercise his right to vote. He was not connected with any church, but was a man of good morals and upright character. He died in 1855 at the age of fifty-five years. His wife had passed away a few years before at the age of thirty-five years. Of the eleven children born to this union all lived to be grown, but only two besides our subject now survive: Mrs. Keziah Ferrill, of Love Station, Miss., and Mrs. Hester Slack, wife of J. J. Slack, district attorney of this district who resides at Grenada. Those deceased were: John, Stephen, Lucretia (Mrs. Crenshaw), Margaret (Mrs. Burt), Thomas, Hugh, Griffith and Robert. The six sons last mentioned served in the war and John was killed at the battle of Fisher's Creek, while Stephen fell at the bloody battle of Shiloh. Both Mrs. Crenshaw and Mrs. Burt died in Mississippi, leaving families. Dr. William McSwine, the seventh in order of birth of the above named family, was born in Humphreys county, Tenn., in 1837, and was reared on the plantation where he now resides. As his parents bent all their energies to obtain for their children the best educational advantages, he entered the University of Mississippi at Oxford and graduated from that celebrated institution of learning in 1855. He then returned to the home place, where he resided, until after the war, engaged in the practice of his profession and in planting. He did not serve in the war, owing to injury received from falling from a horse, and after that eventful period he took up the study of medicine under Dr. W. F. Barksdale, of Hardy Station, and graduated from the medical department of the University of Louisiana in 1866. After that he returned to the home place and there practiced his profession until 1878. Since then he has been very extensively engaged in planting, etc., and has about one thousand two hundred acres under cultivation. Dr. McSwine has always been a democrat and devoted to the principles of that party. He has not sought office, but the office has sought him, and although he would rather not accept any official position he was elected by his party to the legislature in 1878, 1882, and 1890. He is now serving his third term, thus proving to the satisfaction of all, and especially his constituents, his fitness for that position. He keeps himself well posted on all the leading topics of the day, and that he is a man of strong sense and acute judgement is patent to every one. His clear views on every subject and his trenchant but pleasant wit make him a favorite with all into whose society he is thrown. Although not connected with any church, he is a man who merits respect and esteem. Socially he is a member of Grenada lodge No. 31. He is very fond of hunting and fishing and all outdoor sports.

Dr. Andrew J. McWilliams, of Tupelo, is one of the most skillful physicians of Lee county, and is well known throughout the state as an able member of the profession. He is a native of Alabama, and a son of Andrew McWilliams. His paternal grandfather was William McWilliams, who was of Irish descent. His father was a native of Kentucky, and removed to Alabama about the year 1818. He was married to Miss Elizabeth Robertson, and by frugality and wise management they soon laid the foundation of a comfortable fortune. Before the war they owned forty slaves, and valuable real estate. They were members of the Cumberland Presbyterian church, and liberal contributors to its support. They reared a family of ten children, only two of whom are living—the subject of this notice and Martha, wife of John Hayes. Andrew J. was the seventh-born. He attained his majority in Limestone county, Ala., where he began the study of medicine under the preceptorship of Dr. W. K. Adams, a leading physician of the county. At the age of twenty-one years he came to Mississippi and located at Fulton. For thirty years he practiced in that neighborhood, and then came to Tupelo, where he has since devoted himself to professional work. He was united in marriage to Miss Emily Pryor, a daughter of Luke Pryor, Sr., and a sister to Hon. Luke Pryor, Jr., of Athens, Ala., a leading attorney of his state, a congressman and a United States senator. This lady was born in Limestone county, Ala., September 15, 1829. Early in life she made a profession of religion and united with the Cumberland Presbyterian church. In her death the community was deprived of a most excellent woman, and her family, of a devoted wife and mother. Her Christian faith was beautifully exemplified in deeds of kindness and charity, and she left the assurance that she would pass into the highest state of existence beyond this life. Her death occurred the 8th day of March, 1884. She was the mother of three children: Prior McWilliams, who entered the war at the age of fifteen years, and made a most brilliant record. Just before he received the fatal shot he shouted to his men: "For God Almighty's sake, remember you are Mississippians, and come on!" Alice, wife of R. D. Porter, and Hattie, wife of I. W. Lindsley, are the daughters. Dr. McWilliams was married, a second time, to Mrs. M. B. Edwards, widow of E. A. Edwards. They are members of the Cumberland Presbyterian church, of which the Doctor has been a member forty-seven years. Politically he adheres to the principles of the democratic party. He represented Itawamba county in the state legislature of 1847, and was treasurer of that county two terms. During the war he was tendered the office of surgeon of the Tenth Mississippi regiment, but his friends would not agree to his accepting. He is a member of the Masonic fraternity, belonging to the Blue lodge, chapter and commandery. He is a member of the Lee County Medical association.

The Mississippi family of McWillies are descendants of John McWillie, a Scotch gentleman who, although then quite young, took part, to the ruin of his fortune and the great hazard of his life, in the attempt to place Prince Charles Edward upon the English throne in 1745. After his capture at the disastrous battle of Culloden he was for some time held in a prison ship at Plymouth, expecting daily to be executed, but was at length pardoned through the intercession of an English friend of his family, who interested himself in his behalf on certain conditions, one of them being his taking service in the British army, and another his refraining from any return to his home in the Highlands. Both obligations were observed, his subsequent military service extending to nearly every quarter of the globe. His descendants in Mississippi preserve with much pride his sword and several of his commissions. Several years after his release from prison he married at Stirling, Scotland, Margaret Churchill, a lady of high English connection, who bore to him a son, Adam McWillie. The son inherited something of the rebellious spirit of his father; on reaching manhood, married, against the paternal will, Anne Agnew, and emigrated to America, without waiting for a blessing. Adam McWillie, on reaching the new world, made his home in Kershaw district, in the state of South Carolina, and although beginning with no other resources than a fine mind and vigorous body, soon acquired an ample estate. He became thoroughly identified with his adopted country, and in the War of 1812 was colonel of a regiment of South Carolina troops, which he commanded with great credit till the close of the struggle. The faithful wife, whose attractions had prevailed against the opposing influences of his family, showed amid the hardships of the transition period through which the country was then making its way that she was well worthy of whatever sacrifice he had made. She greatly aided him in the accumulation of his fortune, and bore him a number of children, who, under his training, grew up to honor and usefulness in their generation. Among these was William McWillie, who alone has left descendants of the family name.

William McWillie was born in the home of his parents in South Carolina, on November 17, 1795. He was preparing for college when the regiment commanded by his father was ordered to Haddrell's Point during the War of 1812. He became adjutant and served until the close of the campaign, when he entered the South Carolina college at Columbia and was graduated there with high honor in 1817. After the usual course of reading he was admitted to the bar in 1818 and established himself in the historic town of Camden, practicing with great success in Kershaw and the adjoining districts. His rank in the profession can be

78

inferred from the fact that along with the famous Grimkë he was selected by the friends of the Union to argue the Test Oath case before the supreme court of South Carolina, at the time of the nullification excitement. In 1836, having acquired a considerable fortune, he was elected president of the Bank of Camden, and relinquished the practice of his profession. From 1836 to 1840 he served successively in each branch of the South Carolina legislature, and in 1845 removed to Mississippi, although at the time of his removal the prospects of preferment held out by his political friends were of the most tempting description. He had established several plantations in Mississippi, which were beginning to demand attention, and he determined to devote himself to the pursuit of agriculture. In a short time, however, he was called to the public service in Mississippi. He was elected to congress as a democrat in 1849, being the first candidate in that party who ever carried the congressional district in which he resided, and served from December 3, 1849, until March 3, 1851. In 1858 he became governor of Mississippi, which office he held until the close of his term in 1860. Although he greatly loved the Union, he was a devout believer in the right of secession, and when that step was taken by his state he was in full sympathy with the movement and had no reservations in case of failure. Sketches of this gentleman's life are to be found in Appleton's Cyclopedia of American Biograpy, and O'Neal's Bench and Bar of South Carolina, the author of the latter work (Judge John Belton O'Neal) being evidently inspired with an affectionate remembrance of his old friend that made him loth to part with the subject. On his removal to Mississippi, Governor McWillie established himself in Madison county, and his beautiful home, called Kirkwood, was long the seat of the most elegant and generous hospitality. He was twice married, his first wife being Miss Cunningham, of a well-known South Carolina family of that name, and his second wife, who bore him company to Mississippi, being Catherine Anderson, the daughter of Dr. Edward H. Anderson, formerly of Camden, S. C. This lovely lady, so well known to the elderly citizens of Mississippi, occupied in the social life of her day and in the good works of charity and religion, a part fully commensurate with the public and professional career of her husband. Both were devout members of the Episcopal church. The children of Governor McWillie, who remained in South Carolina, were married daughters, and, with their descendants, are now represented by the names of Shannon, Richardson, Kershaw, Boykin, Burnet, Withers and others. One daughter, Mrs. Burrell Salmon, removed to Pickens county, Ala., where she still resides. Those who removed to or were born in Mississippi, and are more properly within the object of this work, with their descendants also make a large connection.

Adam McWillie, eldest son of William, was born in Camden, S. C., on November 7, 1821. While pursuing his studies in the South Carolina college, he became impressed with the struggle for independence, and leave to take part in it having been refused him, like the old Adam he rebelled, and ran away. Happily, however, the war had been brought to a conclusion when he reached the scene of it, and a natural disinclination to return home under the circumstances led to his being altogether emancipated, and set up on a plantation in Madison county. In a short time he was again drawn westward by the Mexican war in which he engaged first as an independent private, attached to Col. Jefferson Davis' first Mississippi regiment. After praticipating in several of the heaviest battles in which that command took part, he was forced to return home by ill health, but soon returned as captain of one of the companies in Col. Reuben Davis' second Mississippi regiment, and served in that capacity until the close of the war. Again resuming his planting operations in which he was markedly successful, he was shortly afterward married to Miss Lucy Anderson, who bore him three daughters; the eldest, Lily, now Mrs. Horace Fluker, of East Feliciana parish, La., the second, Catherine, now Mrs. W. L. Dinkins, of Canton, Miss., and the third, Lula, who is unmarried and resides with her mother in Madison county. In 1861 Captain McWillie was elected captain of the Camden rifles, Eighteenth Mississippi regiment, Confederate states army, and at the battle of Manassas, on July 21, of that year, while charging a Federal battery at the head of his company, gave his noble life as a sacrifice to his country. His many fine qualities gave him great popularity with those who knew him well, and his natural taste and adaptation for military life presaged no little distinction in the service. His old commanders in Mexico had great confidence in and affection for him, and united in deploring his early death. Jefferson Davis sent from the battlefield the telegram that first announced it to his family. Reuben Davis in his charming work entitled "Recollections of Mississippi and Mississippians" has this to say of him: "Captain McWillie was from Madison county. What can I say of him, but that he seemed to live in the highest regions of honor and devotion. His heart was soft and pure. It seemed almost impossible for him to comprehend meanness or villainy, and he so naturally expected everything good in persons he was thrown with, that bad men seemed shamed to better feelings by his mere presence. There was a wonderful atmosphere of honor and virtue about the whole man. He had seen much service, but never lost his tenderness of nature. At the battle af Monterey he shot at a Mexican and saw him fall dead in the street. The man was slain in full tide of battle, and it was the duty of McWillie to shoot him when he did. It was also possible that other Mexicans had fallen by his hand, but there was the relief of uncertainty in all cases except this one. Often afterward McWillle confided to me that the recollection of this man was a torture to him, and that with no sense of quiet or responsibility, the picture of that poor wretch rolling in the dust would remain with him as long as he lived. At the beginning of the Civil war he went into the Confederate army as captain. In the battle of Manassas, when the Seventeenth and Eighteenth regiments were forced to retreat, McWillie kept his ground until he fell, by a bullet. He died knight-like, with his sword in hand."

William McWillie, next son, is also a native of Camden, S. C. He was born in 1842, and was only about three years old when brought to Mississippi by his parents. His early life was spent at the family home in Madison county. In May, 1861, he was married to Miss Sallie Tucker, daughter of the late Tighlman Tucker, a former governor of Mississippi, and three days later left for the seat of war in Virginia. He served throughout the entire war, first as a private in his brother's company, and afterward as captain on the staff of Gen. R. H. Anderson, a relative on the maternal side, and was present at the final disaster at Appomattox. He was several times commended by his commander for special acts of gallantry. For several years after the war he followed the pursuit of agriculture, to which he subsequently added that of merchandising. In 1884 he was appointed one of the three railroad commissioners of Mississippi, and in 1886 was continued in that position by election of the legislature, the manner of filling the office having been changed during his first term. In 1888 he went into the mercantile business in Canton, Miss., and is still so engaged. He has three daughters: Sallie, now Mrs. J. Bowmar Harris, of Jackson, Miss.; Kate and Lucy, who are unmarried, and a son, Tighlman Tucker, a youth of eighteen years.

James McWillie, the next succeeding son, was born at Kirkwood, in Madison county, on the 21st of December, 1847. His education was interrupted by the Civil war, in which he took part for some time as a private in Gen. Wirt Adams' cavalry command, although quite young and already a great sufferer from the asthmatic trouble, of which he has since died. He studied medicine after the war and graduated at the medical college at Baltimore, Md. He was for a number of years assistant physician of the state lunatic asylum at Jackson, Miss., and was greatly beloved by the inmates and employes of that institution, and respected by the public for his devotion to the duties of his position. He resigned on account of ill health in 1889, and died at his residence in Jackson on March 1, 1890. He married Nannie, the eldest daughter of Dr. William M. Compton, who with five children survive him, three daughters: Beatrice, Kate and Margaret, and two sons: William Compton and James.

Thomas Anderson McWillie, the next son, was born at Kirkwood on July 18, 1849. He received his higher education at the University of Mississippi and was admitted at the bar in 1874, and began the practice of his profession in Jackson. In January, 1875, he was invited to form a partnership with Col. W. L. Nugent of that city, then enjoying a large and lucrative practice and widely known for professional ability. The connection thus formed still exists, and the firm of Nugent & McWillie has taken part in much of the important litigation that has risen in Mississippi since its formation. Mr. McWillie has served one term in the state legislature (1880), but while occasionally appearing before the public, has never been solicitous of its favors. In April, 1875, he married Miss Elizabeth Clayton Webb, formerly of Alabama, who still shares and brightens his lot in life. As estimated by one long and intimately acquainted with him, McWillie is remarkable for cool, clear judgment and perspicuousness and elegance of diction with tongue or pen. He is thoroughly grounded in the elementary principles of his profession and his great power consists in reasoning from them. His range of general reading is quite extended and he is thorougly versed in the classics, ancient and modern, and they have given him a charming style of composition. He is quite popular and a most delightful conversationalist.

Richard Laurence McWillie, the last of the sons, was born at Kirkwood, on August 22, 1853. He is a civil engineer by profession, and although in a large measure self-taught, has won no little reputation for skill in his calling. He has lived for a number of years in Texas, and now resides in Denison, in that state, where, in 1888, he married Miss Ada Collins. He is at present superintending the construction of a railway that runs into Denison.

Miss Jane McWillie was born in 1829, in Camden, S. C., and in 1845 married Dr. R. B. Johnson, of that place. They have two sons: William E. Johnson, a civil engineer, who resides at Carrollton, Miss., and McWillie Johnson, who is still quite young, and resides with his parents; and two daughters. Nannie, the wife of Hon. C. L. Anderson, late member of congress from the fourth district of Mississippi; and Mary, the wife of Rev. W. P. Browne, an Episcopal clergyman of the diocese of Texas. In 1867 Dr. Johnson removed with his family from Carolina, and has since resided at Kirkwood, Miss.

Miss Kate McWillie was born in 1832, at Camden, S. C., and in her twentieth year married Avery Noland, of Louisiana. They resided in Louisiana prior to the late war, but since then in Mississippi. Of this marriage two sons and three daughters survive: Pearce and William McWillie Noland, the former a merchant in Louisville, Ky., and the latter quite a young man, who has not yet selected his vocation. The daughters are Mrs. Lawson Ballon and Misses Ida and Victoria Noland. This lady was noted in her youth for her great beauty and charm of manner, and was much admired throughout the South.

Miss Annie McWillie was born in Camden, S. C., in 1834, and was married to Dr. T. J. Mitchell, of Jackson, Miss., in 1858. She died in 1878. Of her children five survive: two young sons, Thomas J. and Cullen C., and three daughters, Mrs. C. C. Johnston, of New Orleans, Mrs. John William Robinson, of Jackson, and Miss Etta Mitchell. Dr. Mitchell has been for many years the superintendent of the State Lunatic asylum.

Miss Ida McWillie was born in Camden, S. C., in 1836, and in 1865 married Capt. J. R. Chambers of East Feliciana parish, La. They have since resided on his plantation and have two sons: Joseph N. and McWillie, and two daughters: Mrs. Howell of Laurel Hill, La., and Miss Margaret Chambers. Miss Lucy McWillie, the next daughter, has never married, and resides in Jackson, Miss. Miss Margaret McWillie, the youngest daughter, is the wife of Hon. S. S. Calhoon, of whom a sketch elsewhere appears in this volume. They reside in Jackson.

Addenda, errors and omissions:

Elsewhere in this work appears a sketch of Dr. Henry Alexander, in which the age at which he was married and other data concerning his marriage were incorrectly given to the compilers. Doctor Alexander was married at the age of thirty-five years to Mary Imogene Roberts, the daughter of Griffin and Mary Rodolphia Roberts.

Griffin Roberts was a merchant at Hamilton, Miss., at the time Doctor Alexander's father was a merchant at the same place. Griffin Roberts and Parker Alexander bought the lands on which the town of Hamilton was situated, also the surrounding lands, and lived on adjoining places during their entire lives. The place on which they now live was owned by William Martin, the father of Mary Rodolphia Roberts, which she inherited from her parents. Griffin Roberts and his wife lived and died on this place. Mary Imogene bought the interests of her brothers, Addison, Griffin and John, and her sister, M. Antoinette Roberts. Her sister, Antoinette Roberts, married James Alexander, the brother of her husband. They left three children; Parker Alexander, Mary Sidney Alexander, and Imogene Norma Alexander. Addison Roberts married Julia C. Booth. They reside at Tampa, Fla. Griffin Roberts married Julia Shaw and lived in Columbus, Miss., to the time of his death. His wife and children still reside at that place. John Roberts married Mattie Booth. He now resides in Dallas, Tex. Parker Alexander, grandson of Parker Alexander and Griffin Roberts, married Ida May Lowe and resides at Hamilton, Miss. Mary Sidney Alexander married William B. Lowe and resides at New Orleans, La. Imogene Norma Alexander married William Taylor and resides in Dallas, Tex. Sidney Alexander, eldest son of Parker Alexander, a bachelor, resides at Hamilton, Miss.

The following sketch was received after the one on page 298 of this volume, and contains so many changes that it is given here entire:

The W. T. Adams Machine company, of Corinth, Miss. The invention and manufacture of machines and labor-saving appliances designed to facilitate the operation of many branches of human industry, have probably exerted a greater influence in contributing to the marvelous growth and development of our country than any other cause. Notable among these great manufacturing establishments engaged in this most useful department of industry is the W. T. Adams Machine company, which is engaged in the manufacture of steam engines, boilers, sawmills, planers, re-saws, gang edgers, lathmills, gristmills, cottongins and presses, and steamfitting goods, etc. This business was established by Mr. W. T. Adams in 1879, who at that time had but a small capital, but by indefatigable labors, persistent endeavor and meritorious work his establishment soon began to gain renown, and a large trade was built up in a few years. The business was incorporated in 1887. W. T. Adams was born at Jacinto, Tishomingo county, Miss., in 1853, a son of Barnett and Lucinda A. (Sutherland) Adams, the former of whom was also born in this state, a son of Vincent Adams, who was an early immigrant to this section. Barnett and Lucinda Adams reared a family of seven children: W. T., Barnett V., Lucinda Ann, Richard, Joseph, who died at the age of twenty years, Mattie P. and Robert T. Barnett Adams was a wagonmaker by trade and followed this calling in Jacinto for a number of years, moving to Rienzi in 1858, where he died in 1864. In connection with his trade he also followed the occupation of planting. He was a member of the Baptist church and was a Master mason. His wife was a Virginian, born in 1830, a daughter of James M. Sutherland, who was a native of Danville, Va. He was one of the pioneers of Mississippi, and having learned the trade of wagonmaking in Virginia he followed this calling after coming to Tishomingo county.   For many years in later days he followed farming.   Mrs. Lucinda A. Adams died in 1857, at which time she was an earnest member of the Baptist church, having lived a devoted Christian life.   W. T. Adams received a good practical education in the schools of Rienzi, and at the age of twenty-one years embarked in business for himself.   After tilling the soil and clerking in a store he became agent for the Southern Exchange company, at Rienzi, but later purchased an interest in a small foundry at that place, where he engaged in the manufacture of agricultural implements, continuing until 1879.   He then came to Corinth·and established a small business, which was the foundation of the magnificent establishment of which he is now the president and general manager.   Since that time his business has increased so steadily and rapidly that it has grown into vast proportions, and now constitutes one of the largest businesses in its line throughout the entire South.   The goods are standard and are recognized as unsurpassed in materials and workmanship, and the great popularity and high reputation of the factory is due, not only to the acknowledged superiority of the goods, but also to the systematic correctness of its methods, and by the spirit of fairness by which all its transactions are characterized.   This establishment gives employment to about one hundred and thirty-five men. Mr. Adams is a man of marked administrative ability, endowed with the necessary qualifications for the judicious management of this great enterprise.   His energy and attention to his business is the secret of his success, and he deserves great credit for the way in which he has climbed the ladder of success.

In addition to building up the machine business of the W. T. Adams Machine company, he has also aided in establishing other enterprises which have marked the progress of the new South.   He was married in 1875 to Miss Virgia Johnston, a daughter of J. C. Johnston, of Rienzi, who moved from middle Tennessee to that place in 1867.   Mrs. Adams was born in middle Tennessee in 1855, and is related to some of the first families of that state.   She is a devoted Christian member of the Cumberland Presbyterian church.   To them have been born five children: Bertha, Anna Orville, Estelle, William T. and Winfred.   Mr. Adams is a self-made man in every sense of the word; is honest in his business methods and is a genial companion and a wholesouled gentleman.   He is a worthy member of the Baptist church, a strong supporter of the temperance cause, a democrat in politics, and a member of the Knights of Pythias fraternity.

John M. Allen, of Tupelo, was born in Tishomingo county, Miss., July 8, 1847; received a common school education up to his enlistment as a private in the Confederate army, in which he served through the war; after the cessation of hostilities attended the law school at the Cumberland university in Lebanon, Tenn., and graduated in law in the year 1870 at the University of Mississippi; commenced the practice of his profession at Tupelo, Lee county, Miss., in 1870; in 1875 was elected district attorney for the first judicial district of Mississippi; served a term of four years and retired from that office; was elected to the XLIXth and Lth congresses, and was re-elected to the LIst congress as a democrat, receiving eleven thousand three hundred and fifty-three votes, against one thousand seven hundred and thirty-two votes for J. M. Bynum, republican.

Page 297, sketch of C. R. Ales.   It should read that the father removed with his wife and two children, instead of with his parents, to Henry county, Tenn.   C. R. Ales was the third son.   He was wounded once, instead of receiving no wound.   He married Sallie Wallar, instead of Wallie.

On page 88, Captain Milling should read Captain Willing.

Chapter XIV was wrongly printed XVI.

INDEX.

SUPPLEMENTARY INDEX FOR VOLUME I.

The matter indicated below for Volume I, was, much of it, received or returned revised too late to be indexed in its due order; hence this supplementary index.